CW00402190

SOCIAL SECURITY LEGISLATION 2009/10

VOLUME I:
NON MEANS TESTED BENEFITS AND EMPLOYMENT AND SUPPORT ALLOWANCE

SOCIAL SECURITY LEGISLATION 2009/10

General Editor
David Bonner, LL.B., LL.M.

VOLUME I:
NON MEANS TESTED BENEFITS AND EMPLOYMENT AND SUPPORT ALLOWANCE

Commentary By

David Bonner, LL.B., LL.M.
Professor of Law, University of Leicester,
Formerly Member, Social Security Appeal Tribunals

Ian Hooker, LL.B.
Formerly Lecturer in Law, University of Nottingham,
Formerly Chairman, Social Security Tribunals

Richard Poynter, B.C.L., M.A.(Oxon.)
District Tribunal Judge,
Deputy Judge of the Upper Tribunal

Robin White, M.A., LL.M.
Professor of Law, University of Leicester,
Deputy Judge of the Upper Tribunal

Nick Wikeley, M.A.
Emeritus Professor of Law, University of Southampton,
Judge of the Upper Tribunal

Penny Wood, LL.B., M.Sc.
District Tribunal Judge

Consultant Editor
Child Poverty Action Group

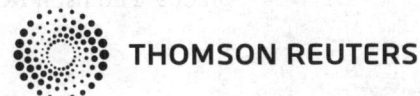

SWEET & MAXWELL   THOMSON REUTERS

Published in 2009 by
Thomson Reuters (Legal) Limited (Registered in England and Wales,
Company No 1679046. Registered office and address for service:
100 Avenue Road, Swiss Cottage,
London NW3 3PF, trading as Sweet & Maxwell)

For further information on our products and services, visit
http://www.sweetandmaxwell.co.uk

Typeset by Servis Filmsetting Ltd, Stockport, Cheshire
Printed and bound in Great Britain
by Ashford Colour Press, Gosport, Hants

ISBN 978-0-414-04116-5

No natural forests were destroyed to make this product;
only farmed timber was used and replanted.

A CIP catalogue record for this book is available
from the British Library

All rights reserved. Crown Copyright Legislation is reproduced under the
terms of Crown Copyright Policy Guidance issued by HMSO.

No part of this publication may be reproduced or transmitted, in any
form or by any means, or stored in any retrieval system of any nature
without prior written permission, except for permitted fair dealing under
the Copyright, Designs and Patents Act 1988, or in accordance with the
terms of a licence issued by the Copyright Licensing Agency in respect of
photocopying and/or reprographic reproduction.
Application for permission for other use of copyright material including
permission to reproduce extracts in other published works shall be made
to the publishers. Full acknowledgement of author, publisher and source
must be given.
Application for permission for other use of copyright material controlled
by the publisher shall be made to the publishers.
Material is contained in this publication for which publishing permission
has been sought, and for which copyright is acknowledged. Permission
to reproduce such material cannot be granted by the publishers and
application must be made to the copyright holder.

Thomson Reuters and the Thomson Reuters logo are trademarks of
Thomson Reuters. Sweet & Maxwell® is a registered trademark of
Thomson Reuters (Legal) Limited.

Commentators have asserted their moral rights under the Copyright,
Designs and Patents Act 1988 to be identified as the authors of the
commentary in this Volume.

© 2009 Thomson Reuters (Legal) Limited

FOREWORD

I am especially pleased to be invited to write a Foreword to this work, because I am in a position to offer my personal endorsement of its immense worth, having been an appreciative reader since John Mesher's first edition in 1984.

The statute-derived law of social security is extensive, dynamic and notoriously complex. The case-law is profuse. The European dimension adds a further layer of difficulty. A practitioner's guide which not only assembles the diverse law but also supplies a detailed, lucid and balanced commentary from a widely-respected team of authors is indispensable.

This work is a staple resource for our tribunals. I commend it to all who need a serious understanding of the law of social security.

HHJ Robert Martin
President of the Social Entitlement Chamber
First-tier Tribunal

PREFACE

Non Means Tested Benefits and Employment and Support Allowance is Volume I of what is now a four volume series: *Social Security Legislation 2009/10*. The companion volumes are: Wood, Poynter, Wikeley and Bonner, *Vol. II: Income Support, Jobseeker's Allowance, State Pension Credit and the Social Fund*; Rowland and White, *Vol.III: Administration, Adjudication and the European Dimension*, and Wikeley, Williams and Hooker, *Vol.IV: Tax Credits and HMRC-administered Social Security Benefits*. As with the last edition of this series, the "year" in the title of the works covers a tax/contribution year, the better to convey the period the books (plus between editions, the *Supplement*) are designed to cover.

Each of the volumes in the series provides a legislative text, clearly showing the form and date of amendments, and commentary up to date to April 13, 2009.

This volume is much changed from its predecessors. The period since October 2008 has seen major change with respect to adjudication in social security and to benefits for those with no or limited capacity for work. The adjudication changes—the introduction of the First-tier Tribunal (Social Entitlement Chamber) and the Upper Tribunal (Administrative Appeals Chamber), and the designation of their legally qualified members as "judge"—are principally covered in Vol.III, but have necessitated numerous amendments to the text of legislation in all volumes. They have also produced a neutral form of citation for Upper Tribunal decisions operating, for the time being at least alongside the standard form of citation of Commissioners' decisions (see further "Using this Book"). The introduction of Employment and Support Allowance (ESA) for persons with limited capability for work has similarly affected the text of legislation across all volumes. Operating alongside incapacity benefit and income support for those incapable of work which are retained for existing claimants for the time being, ESA, in both its contributory (CESA) and income-related (IRESA) forms, is contained in this volume. This accounts in great part for the increased length of the volume and the welcome addition of Richard Poynter and Penny Wood to the list of commentators. It also accounts for the change of title to *Non Means Tested Benefits and Employment and Support Allowance*. Principally because they are benefits now administered by HMRC, we have transferred to Vol.IV material formerly in this volume on Child Benefit and Guardian's Allowance, adding Ian Hooker as a commentator to that volume. We have in so doing used the space not only for ESA, but have taken the opportunity to add another specialist jurisdiction on mesothelioma payments, in respect of which Nick Wikeley provides commentary. As always, case law on disability and incapacity benefits continues to grow (note particularly the Court of Appeal decision in *Charlton* on the "exceptional circumstances" provision in Incapacity for Work (General) Regulations 1995, reg.27 and its ESA equivalent). There have been some important changes to regulations in industrial injuries as regards prescribed disease D12 (chronic bronchitis and/or emphysema) and developments in case law in respect of previous changes to prescribed disease A11 (vibration white finger).

As always, revising and updating the legislative text and commentary has required considerable flexibility on the part of the publisher and a great deal of help from a number of sources, including CPAG as advisory editor to the series, for which we express sincere thanks. Particular mention must be made here of the debt owed by all of us to John Mesher, who began the provision of annotated legislation for Tribunals, has given wise advice on the development of this series, and who happily remains on call as consultant in respect of Vol.II.

To maximise space for explanatory commentary we have provided lists of definitions only where the commentary to the provision is substantial, or where reference to definitions is essential for a proper understanding. Users of this book should always check whether particular words or phrases they are called on to apply have a particular meaning ascribed to them in legislation. Generally the first or second regulation in each set of regulations contains definitions of key terms (check the "Arrangement of Regulations" at the beginning of each set for an indication of the subject matter covered by each regulation or Schedule). There are also "definition" or "interpretation" sections in each of the Acts (check the "Arrangement of Sections" at the beginning of each Act for an indication of the subject matter covered by each section or Schedule).

Users of the series, and its predecessor works, have over the years provided valuable comments which have invariably been helpful to the editors in ensuring that the selection of legislative material for inclusion and the commentary upon it reflect the sorts of difficulties encountered in practice. In doing so, readers have thus helped to shape the content of each of the volumes in the current series. We hope that readers will maintain that tradition. Please write to the General Editor of the series, David Bonner, School of Law, University of Leicester, University Road, Leicester, LE1 7RH, who will pass on any comments received to the appropriate commentator.

Our gratitude must also go to the Chamber President HH Judge Robert Martin and his staff for continuing the tradition of help and encouragement.

July 18, 2009

David Bonner
Ian Hooker
Richard Poynter
Robin White
Nick Wikeley
Penny Wood

CONTENTS

PART I
STATUTES

REGULATIONS

PART II
CONTRIBUTION CREDITS AND HOME RESPONSIBILITIES
PROTECTION

Contents

PART III
REGULATIONS COMMON TO SEVERAL BENEFITS

PART IV
DISABILITY BENEFITS

PART V
MATERNITY BENEFITS

PART VI
WIDOW'S BENEFIT, RETIREMENT PENSIONS AND GRADUATED RETIREMENT BENEFIT

Contents

PART VII
UNEMPLOYMENT, SICKNESS AND INVALIDITY BENEFIT

PART VIII
INCAPACITY BENEFIT AND INCAPACITY FOR WORK

PART IX
CHILDREN AND GUARDIANS

PART X
INDUSTRIAL INJURIES AND PRESCRIBED DISEASES

PART XI
VACCINE DAMAGE PAYMENTS

Contents

PART XII
MESOTHELIOMA LUMP SUM PAYMENTS

USING THIS BOOK: AN INTRODUCTION TO LEGISLATION AND CASE LAW

Introduction

This book is not a general introduction to, or general textbook on, the law relating to social security but it is nonetheless concerned with both of the principal sources of social security law—*legislation* (both primary and secondary) and *case law*. It sets out the text of the most important legislation, as currently in force, and then there is added commentary that refers to the relevant case law. Lawyers will be familiar with this style of publication, which inevitably follows the structure of the legislation.

This note is designed primarily to assist readers who are not lawyers to find their way around the legislation and to understand the references to case law, but information it contains about how to find social security case law is intended to be of assistance to lawyers too.

Primary legislation

Primary legislation of the United Kingdom Parliament consists of *Acts of Parliament* (also known as *Statutes*). They will have been introduced to Parliament as *Bills*. There are opportunities for Members of Parliament and peers to debate individual clauses and to vote on amendments before a Bill is passed and becomes an Act (at which point the clauses become sections). No tribunal or court has the power to disapply, or hold to be invalid, an Act of Parliament unless it is inconsistent with European Community law.

An Act is known by its "short title", which incorporates the year in which it was passed (e.g. the Social Security Contributions and Benefits Act 1992), and is given a chapter number (abbreviated as, for instance, "c.4" indicating that the Act was the fourth passed in that year). It is seldom necessary to refer to the chapter number but it appears in the running heads in this book.

Each *section* (abbreviated as "s." or, in the plural, "ss.") of an Act is numbered and may be divided into *subsections* (abbreviated as "subs." and represented by a number in brackets), which in turn may be divided into *paragraphs* (abbreviated as "para." and represented by a lower case letter in brackets) and *subparagraphs* (abbreviated as "subpara." and represented by a small roman numeral in brackets). Subparagraph (ii) of para.(a) of subs.(1) of s.72 will usually be referred to simply as "s.72(1)(a)(ii)". Upper case letters may be used where additional sections or subsections are inserted by amendment and additional lower case letters may be used where new paragraphs and subparagraphs are inserted. This accounts for the rather ungainly s.171ZS of the Social Security Contributions and Benefits Act 1992 (in Vol.IV)

Sections of a large Act may be grouped into a numbered *Part*, which may even be divided into *Chapters*. It is not usual to refer to a Part or a Chapter unless referring to the whole Part or Chapter.

Where a section would otherwise become unwieldy because it is necessary to include a list or complicated technical provisions, the section may simply refer to a *Schedule* at the end of the Act. A Schedule (abbreviated as "Sch.") may be divided into paragraphs and subparagraphs and further divided into heads and subheads. Again, it is usual to refer simply to, say, "para.23(3)(b)(ii) of Schedule 3". Whereas it is conventional to speak of a section *of* an Act, it is usual to speak of a Schedule *to* an Act.

When Parliament wishes to change the law, it may do so by passing a new Act that amends a previous Act or it may do so by passing a freestanding Act, although even then consequential amendments to other legislation are usually required. Thus, for instance, when incapacity benefit was introduced by the Social Security (Incapacity for Work) Act 1994, the changes were largely made by inserting sections 30A to 30E and Part XIIA into the Social Security Contributions and Benefits Act 1992 and repealing the provisions in that Act dealing with sickness and invalidity benefit. In contrast, when jobseeker's allowance was introduced by the Jobseekers Act 1995, it was decided that the main provisions relating to the new benefit would be found in the 1995 Act itself and the 1992 Act was amended only so as to repeal, or amend, the provisions dealing with, or referring to, unemployment benefit.

When there has been a proliferation of Acts or Acts have been very substantially amended, the legislation may be consolidated in a new Act, for which there is a fast track procedure in Parliament. Only limited amendments may be made by a consolidation Act but such an Act reorganises and tidies up the legislation. Because social security law is so frequently amended, it tends to be consolidated every decade or two. The last consolidation Acts relevant to this book were the Social Security Contributions and Benefits Act 1992 (in Vols I and II) and the Social Security Administration Act 1992 (in Vol.III).

Secondary legislation

Secondary legislation (also known as *subordinate legislation* or *delegated legislation*) is made by *statutory instrument* in the form of a set of *Regulations* or a set of *Rules* or an *Order*. The power to make such legislation is conferred on ministers and other persons or bodies by Acts of Parliament. To the extent that a statutory instrument is made beyond the powers (in Latin, *ultra vires*) conferred by primary legislation, it may be held by a tribunal or court to be invalid and ineffective. Secondary legislation must be laid before Parliament. However, most secondary legislation is not debated in Parliament and, even when it is, it cannot be amended although an entire statutory instrument may be rejected.

A set of Regulations or Rules or an Order has a name indicating its scope and the year it was made and also a number, as in the Social Security (Disability Living Allowance) Regulations 1991 (SI 1991/2890) (the 2890th statutory instrument issued in 1991). Because there are over 3,000 statutory instruments each year, the number of a particular statutory instrument is important as a means of identification and it should usually be cited the first time reference is made to that statutory instrument.

Sets of Regulations or Rules are made up of individual *regulations* (abbreviated as "reg.") or *rules* (abbreviated as "r." or, in the plural, "rr."). An Order is made up of *articles* (abbreviated as "art."). Regulations, rules and articles may be divided into paragraphs, subparagraphs and heads. As in Acts, a set of Regulations or Rules or an Order may have one or more Schedules attached to it. The style of numbering used in statutory instruments is the same as in sections of, and Schedules to, Acts of Parliament. As in Acts, a large statutory instrument may have regulations or rules grouped into Parts and, occasionally, Chapters. Statutory instruments may be amended in the same sort of way as Acts.

Northern Ireland legislation

Most of the legislation set out in this book applies only in Great Britain, social security not generally being an excepted or reserved matter in relation to Northern Ireland. However, Orders in Council, which are statutory instruments but have the effect of primary legislation in Northern Ireland, largely replicate the primary legislation in Great Britain and enable subordinate legislation to be made that, again, largely replicates the subordinate legislation in Great Britain. Much of the commentary in this book will therefore be relevant to the equivalent provision in Northern Ireland legislation.

European Community legislation

The United Kingdom being a Member State of the European Union, European Community legislation has effect within the United Kingdom. The primary legislation is in the form of the *Treaties* agreed by the Member States. Relevant subordinate legislation is in the form of *Regulations*, adopted to give effect to provisions of the Treaties, and *Directives*, addressed to Member States and requiring them to incorporate certain provisions into their domestic laws. Directives are relevant because, where a citizen brings proceedings against an organ of the state, as is invariably the case where social security is concerned, the citizen may rely on the Directive as having direct effect if the Member State has failed to comply with it. European Community Treaties, Regulations and Directives are divided into *Articles* (abbreviated as "Art."). United Kingdom legislation that is inconsistent with European Community legislation may be disapplied. The most relevant provisions of European Community legislation are set out in Part III of *Vol.III: Administration, Appeals and the European Dimension*.

Finding legislation in this book

If you know the name of the piece of legislation for which you are looking, use the list of contents at the beginning of each volume of this book which lists the pieces of legislation contained in the volume. That will give you the paragraph reference to enable you to find the beginning of the piece of legislation. Then, it is easy to find the relevant section, regulation, rule, article or Schedule by using the running heads on the right hand pages. If you do not know the name of the piece of legislation, you will probably need to use the index at the end of the volume in order to find the relevant paragraph number but will then be taken straight to a particular provision.

The legislation is set out as amended, the amendments being indicated by numbered sets of square brackets. The numbers refer to the numbered entries under the heading "AMENDMENTS" at the end of the relevant section, regulation, rule, article or Schedule, which identify the amending statute or statutory instrument. Where an Act has been consolidated, there is a list of "DERIVATIONS" identifying the provisions of earlier legislation from which the section or Schedule has been derived.

Finding other legislation

Legislation in its unamended form may be found on *http://www.opsi.gov.uk/ legislation/*. Obscure provisions of Great Britain social security legislation not included in this book may be found, as amended, but without a commentary, at *http://www.dwp.gov.uk/publications/specialist-guides/law-volumes/*. Northern Ireland social security legislation may be found at *http://www. dsdni.gov.uk/law_relating_to_social_security*. European Community legislation may be found at *http://eur-lex.europa.eu/en/index.htm*.

Interpreting legislation

Legislation is written in English and generally means what it says. However, more than one interpretation is often possible. Most legislation itself contains definitions. Sometimes these are in the particular provision in which a word occurs but, where a word is used in more than one place, any definition will appear with others. In an Act, an interpretation section is usually to be found towards the end of the Act or of the relevant Part of the Act. In a statutory instrument, an interpretation provision usually appears near the beginning of the statutory instrument or the relevant Part of it. In the more important pieces of legislation in this book, there is included after every section, regulation, rule, article or Schedule a list of "DEFINITIONS", showing where definitions of words used in the provision are to be found.

However, not all words are statutorily defined and there is in any event more to interpreting legislation than merely defining its terms. Decision-makers and tribunals need to know how to apply the law in different types of situations. That is where case law comes in.

Case law and the commentary in this book

In deciding individual cases, courts and tribunals interpret the relevant law and incidentally establish legal principles. Decisions on questions of legal principle of the superior courts and appellate tribunals are said to be binding on decision-makers and the First-tier Tribunal, which means that decision-makers and the First-tier Tribunal must apply those principles. Thus the judicial decisions of the superior courts and appellate tribunals form part of the law. The commentary to the legislation in this book, under the heading "GENERAL NOTE" after a section, regulation, rule, article or Schedule, refers to this *case law*.

The commentary itself in this book is not binding on any decision-maker or tribunal because it is merely the opinion of the author. It is what is actually said in the legislation or in the judicial decision that is important. The legislation is set out in this book, but it will generally be necessary to look elsewhere for the precise words used in judicial decisions. The commentary refers to decisions in a way that enables that to be done.

The largest part of the case law regarding social security benefits is still in the form of decisions of the former Social Security Commissioners and former Child Support Commissioners, who heard appeals from decisions of appeal tribunals. However, on November 3, 2008, when the functions of appeal tribunals were transferred to the First-tier Tribunal, the functions of the Social Security Commissioners and Child Support Commissioners in Great Britain were transferred to the Upper Tribunal and allocated to the Administrative Appeals Chamber of that tribunal. In Northern Ireland, which has a largely separate judiciary and tribunal system, there continue to be Commissioners.

The reporting of decisions of the Upper Tribunal and Commissioners

About 50 of the most important social entitlement decisions of the Administrative Appeals Chamber of the Upper Tribunal are selected to be "reported" each year, using the same criteria as were formerly used for reporting Commissioners' decisions in Great Britain. The selection is made by an editorial board of judges and decisions are selected for reporting only if they are of general importance and command the assent of at least a majority of the relevant judges (i.e. currently, the former Commissioners). The term "reported" simply means that they are published in printed form and on the Internet (see *Finding case law*, below) with headnotes (i.e. summaries) and an index, but there are two other important consequences of a decision being reported. Reported decisions are available in all tribunal venues and can be consulted in local social security offices and some main libraries. They also have a greater precedential status than ordinary decisions (see *Judicial precedent* below).

A handful of Northern Ireland Commissioners' decisions are also selected for reporting each year, the selection being made by the Chief Social Security Commissioner in Northern Ireland.

Citing case law

Unreported decisions of the Commissioners in Great Britain were known simply by their file number, which began with a "C", as in *CIS/2287/2008*. The letters following the "C" indicated the type of benefit in issue in the case (e.g. "IS" is income support, "P" is retirement pension, and so on). Scottish and, at one time, Welsh cases were indicated by a "S" or "W" immediately after the "C", as in *CSIS/467/2007*. The last four digits indicated the calendar year in which the case was registered, rather than the year it was decided. A similar system still operates in Northern Ireland, save that the letters indicating the type of benefit appear in brackets after the numbers and, in recent years, the financial year, rather the calendar year, has been identified, as in *C 10/06-07 (IS)*.

Reported decisions of Commissioners were then given a different number, beginning with an "R". The type of benefit in issue was indicated by letters in brackets and the year in which the decision was selected for reporting or, since 2000, the year in which it was published as a reported decision, was indicated just by two digits, as in *R(IS) 2/08*. Scottish and Welsh reported decisions were not distinguished in any way. Again, in Northern Ireland there is a similar system, save that the type of benefit is identified by letters in brackets after the number, as in *R 1/07 (DLA)*.

When they are first registered, Upper Tribunal social security cases are given the same sort of file number as Commissioners' cases were but, once a case is decided, it ceases to be known by that number. Instead, the case is known by the names of the appellant and respondent (or one of each if there was more than one), with the names of individuals anonymised through the use of letters, and it is given a *neutral citation number*, indicating the year and the tribunal that made the decision. "UKUT" stands for the Upper Tribunal and "(AAC)" stands for the Administrative Appeals Chamber. In this book, the names of official bodies are also abbreviated (e.g. SSWP (for Secretary of State for Work and Pensions), HMRC (for Her Majesty's Revenue and Customs) and CMEC (for the Child Maintenance and Enforcement Commission). Thus, one case is *SSWP v JJ* [2009] UKUT 2 (AAC). For the 2009 volume of reported decisions, the same style of number is used for Upper Tribunal decisions as was used for Commissioners' decisions and, when a reported decision is being cited, this should be added after the neutral citation number. *NT v SSWP* [2009] UKUT 37 (AAC); R(DLA) 1/09 is one example.

Decisions of courts are also known by the parties' names (not usually anonymised) and, since 2001, a neutral citation number ("EWCA Civ" for the Civil Division of the Court of Appeal in England and Wales, "NICA" for the Court of Appeal in Northern Ireland, "CSIH" for the Inner House of the Court of Session (in Scotland), "UKHL" for the House of Lords, and so on). If the case is reported, a reference to the relevant set of law reports usually follows. Conventionally, this includes either the year the case was decided (in round brackets) or the year in which it was reported (in square brackets), followed by the volume number (if any), the name of the series of reports (in abbreviated form, so see the Table of Abbreviations at the beginning of each volume of this book) and the page number. *Abdirahman v Secretary of State for Work and Pensions* [2007] EWCA Civ 657; [2008] 1 W.L.R. 254 (also reported as *R(IS) 8/07*) was a Court of Appeal decision, decided in 2007 but reported in 2008 in volume 1 of the Weekly Law Reports at page 254 (and also in the 2007 volume of reported Commissioners' decisions).

It is only necessary to include the neutral citation number or a reference to a series of reports the first time a decision is cited. After that, the name of the case is usually sufficient.

All decisions on the Tribunals Service website have neutral citation numbers. If you wish to refer a tribunal or decision-maker to a decision of the Upper Tribunal that does not have a neutral citation number, contact the office of the Administrative Appeals Chamber (*adminappeals@tribunals. gsi.gov.uk*) who will provide a number and add the decision to the website.

Decision-makers and claimants are entitled to assume that judges and other members of both the First-tier Tribunal and the Upper Tribunal have immediate access to reported decisions of Commissioners or the Upper Tribunal and they need not provide copies, although it may sometimes be helpful to do so. However, where either a decision-maker or a claimant intends to rely on an unreported decision, it will be necessary to provide a copy of the decision to the judge and any other members of the tribunal. A copy of the decision should also be provided to the other party before the hearing because otherwise it may be necessary for there to be an adjournment to enable that party to take advice on the significance of the decision.

Finding case law

The extensive references described above are used so as to enable people easily to find the full text of a decision. Most decisions of any significance since the late 1990s can be found on the internet.

Decisions of the Commissioners in Great Britain and of the Upper Tribunal may be found on the Tribunals Service website at *http://www. administrativeappeals.tribunals.gov.uk/Decisions/decisions.htm.* This includes reported decisions since 1991 and other decisions considered likely to be of interest to tribunals and tribunal users since about 2000. Decisions of Commissioners in Northern Ireland may be found on *http://www.dsdni.gov. uk/index/law_and_legislation.htm.*

In addition, reported decisions of Commissioners in Great Britain were published in bound volumes by The Stationery Office and in looseleaf form by Corporate Document Services, 7 Eastgate, Leeds LS2 7LY (CDS Orderline: tel 0113 3994040) on behalf of the Department for Work and Pensions. The Department reproduce the looseleaf version on the internet *(http://www.dwp.gov.uk/publications/specialist-guides/decisions-of-the-commissioners/),* so reported decisions may be found both there and on the Tribunals Service website. Decisions of the Upper Tribunal are being included in the 2009 bound and looseleaf volumes.

Reported decisions of the Northern Ireland Commissioners are published by The Stationery Office, in the same bound volumes as Great Britain decisions since 2000 and in separate volumes before then. The Stationery Office also publishes individual Northern Ireland decisions in looseleaf form.

Copies of decisions of Commissioners or of the Administrative Appeals Chamber of the Upper Tribunal that are otherwise unavailable may be obtained from the offices of the Upper Tribunal (Administrative Appeals Chamber) or, in Northern Ireland, from the Office of the Social Security and Child Support Commissioners.

Decisions of courts in the United Kingdom may be found on, or through links from, the free website of the British and Irish Legal Information Institute, *http://www.bailii.org/,* which also carries several Northern Ireland Commissioners' decisions. It provides fairly comprehensive coverage of decisions of the House of Lords (through a link to *http://www.publications. parliament.uk/pa/ld/ldjudgmt.htm*) and most of the higher courts in England and Wales since about 1996, decisions of the Court of Session since 1998 and decisions of the Court of Appeal in Northern Ireland since 2000 (although some earlier decisions have been included, so it is always worth looking).

Decisions of the European Court of Justice (concerned with the law of the European Community) are all to be found on *http://www.curia.europa. eu.*

Decisions of the European Court of Human Rights are available at *http:// www.echr.coe.int,* using the HUDOC database.

Most decisions of the courts in social security cases, including decisions of the European Court of Justice on cases referred by United Kingdom courts and tribunals, are reported with the decisions of the Commissioners and Upper Tribunal and may therefore be found on the same websites and in the same printed series of reported decisions. So, for example, *R(I)1/00* contains Commissioner's decisions *CSI/12/1998,* the decision of the Court of Session upholding the Commissioner's decision and the decision of the House of Lords in *Chief Adjudication Officer v Faulds* reversing the decision of the Court of Session. The most important decisions of the courts can also be found in the various series of law reports familiar to lawyers (in particular, in the *Law Reports,* the *Weekly Law Reports,* the *All England Law*

Reports, the *Public and Third Sector Law Reports*, the *Industrial Cases Reports* and the *Family Law Reports*) but these are not widely available outside academic or other law libraries, although the *All England Law Reports* are occasionally to be found in the larger public libraries. See the Table of Cases at the beginning of each volume of this book for all the places where a decision mentioned in that volume is reported.

If you know the name or number of a decision and wish to know where in a volume of this book there is a reference to it, use the Table of Cases, the Table of Upper Tribunal Decisions or the Table of Social Security Commissioners' Decisions at the beginning of the relevant volume to find the paragraph(s) where the decision is mentioned.

Judicial precedent

As already mentioned, decisions of the Upper Tribunal, the Commissioners and the higher courts in Great Britain become *case law* because they set binding precedents and which must be followed by decision-makers and the First-tier Tribunal in Great Britain. This means that, where the Upper Tribunal, Commissioner or court has decided a point of legal principle, decision-makers and appeal tribunals must make their decisions in conformity with the decision of the Upper Tribunal, Commissioner or court, applying the same principle and accepting the interpretation of the law contained in the decision. So a decision of the Upper Tribunal, a Commissioner or a superior court explaining what a term in a particular regulation means, lays down the definition of that term in much the same way as if the term had been defined in the regulations themselves. The decision may also help in deciding what the same term means when it is used in a different set of regulations, provided that the term appears to have been used in a similar context.

Only decisions on points of law set precedents that are binding and, strictly speaking, only decisions on points of law that were necessary to the overall conclusion reached by the Upper Tribunal, Commissioner or court are binding. Other parts of a decision (which used to be known as *obiter dicta*) may be regarded as helpful guidance but need not be followed if a decision-maker or the First-tier Tribunal is persuaded that there is a better approach. It is particularly important to bear this in mind in relation to older decisions of Social Security Commissioners because, until 1987, the right of appeal to a Commissioner was not confined to points of law.

Where there is a conflict between precedents, a decision-maker or the First-tier Tribunal is generally free to choose between decisions of equal status. For these purposes, most decisions of the Upper Tribunal and decisions of Commissioners are of equal status. However, a decision-maker or First-tier Tribunal should generally prefer a reported decision to an unreported one unless the unreported decision was the later decision and the Commissioner or Upper Tribunal expressly decided not to follow the earlier reported decision. This is simply because the fact that a decision has been reported shows that at least half of the relevant judges of the Upper Tribunal or the Commissioners agreed with it at the time. A decision of a Tribunal of Commissioners (i.e. three Commissioners sitting together) or a decision of a three-judge panel of the Upper Tribunal must be preferred to a decision of a single Commissioner or a single judge of the Upper Tribunal.

A single judge of the Upper Tribunal will normally follow a decision of a single Commissioner or another judge of the Upper Tribunal, but is not bound to do so. A three-judge panel of the Upper Tribunal will generally follow a decision of another such panel or of a Tribunal of Commissioners, but similarly is not bound to do so, whereas a single judge of the Upper Tribunal will always follow such a decision.

Strictly speaking, the Northern Ireland Commissioners do not set binding precedent that must be followed in Great Britain but their decisions are relevant, due to the similarity of the legislation in Northern Ireland, and are usually regarded as highly persuasive with the result that, in practice, they are generally given as much weight as decisions of the Great Britain Commissioners. The same approach is taken in Northern Ireland to decisions of the Upper Tribunal on social security matters and to decisions of the Great Britain Commissioners.

Decisions of the superior courts in Great Britain and Northern Ireland on questions of legal principle are almost invariably followed by decision-makers, tribunals and the Upper Tribunal, even when they are not strictly binding because the relevant court was in a different part of the United Kingdom or exercised a parallel—but not superior jurisdiction.

Decisions of the European Court of Justice come in two parts: the Opinion of the Advocate General and the decision of the Court. It is the decision of the Court which is binding. The Court is assisted by hearing the Opinion of the Advocate General before itself coming to a conclusion on the issue before it. The Court does not always follow its Advocate General. Where it does, the Opinion of the Advocate General often elaborates the arguments in greater detail than the single collegiate judgment of the Court. Decision-makers, tribunals and Commissioners must apply decisions of the European Court of Justice, where relevant to cases before them, in preference to other authorities binding on them.

The European Court of Human Rights in Strasbourg is quite separate from the European Court of Justice in Luxembourg and serves a different purpose: interpreting and applying the European Convention on Human Rights, which is incorporated into United Kingdom law by the Human Rights Act 1998. Since October 2, 2000, public authorities in the United Kingdom, including courts, Commissioners, tribunals and decision-makers have been required to act in accordance with the incorporated provisions of the Convention, unless statute prevents this. They must take into account the Strasbourg case law and are required to interpret domestic legislation, so far as it is possible to do so, to give effect to the incorporated Convention rights. Any court or tribunal may declare secondary legislation incompatible with those rights and, in certain circumstances, invalidate it. Only the higher courts can declare a provision of primary legislation to be incompatible with those rights, but no court, tribunal or Upper Tribunal can invalidate primary legislation. The work of the Strasbourg Court and the impact of the Human Rights Act 1998 on social security are discussed in the commentary in Part IV of *Vol.III: Administration, Appeals and the European Dimension*.

See the note to s.3(2) of the Tribunals, Courts and Enforcement Act 2007 in Part V of *Vol.III: Administration, Appeals and the European Dimension*) for a more detailed and technical consideration of the rules of precedent.

Other sources of information and commentary on social security law

For a comprehensive overview of the social security system in Great Britain, CPAG's *Welfare Benefits and Tax Credits Handbook*, published annually each spring, is unrivalled as a practical introduction from the claimant's viewpoint.

From a different perspective, the Department for Work and Pensions publishes a number of guides to the law and to the way it applies the law, available at *http://www.dwp.gov.uk/publications/specialist-guides/*, the most important of which is the fourteen-volume *Decision Makers' Guide*. Similarly, Her Majesty's Revenue and Customs publish manuals relating to tax credits, child benefit and guardian's allowance, which they administer, see *http://www.hmrc.gov.uk/thelibrary/manuals-subjectarea.htm*. (Note that the *Child Benefit Technical Manual* (also dealing with guardian's allowance) is found under the heading "personal taxation".) These guides and manuals are extremely useful but their interpretation of the law is not binding on tribunals and the courts, being merely internal guidance for the use of decision-makers.

There are a number of other sources of valuable information or commentary on social security case law: see in particular publications such as the *Journal of Social Security Law*, CPAG's *Welfare Rights Bulletin*, *Legal Action* and the *Adviser*. As far as online resources go there is little to beat *Rightsnet* (*http://www.rightsnet.org.uk*). This site contains a wealth of resources for people working in the welfare benefits field but of special relevance in this context are Commissioners'/Upper Tribunal Decisions section of the "Toolkit" area and also the "Briefcase" area which contains summaries of the decisions (with links to the full decisions). Sweet and Maxwell's online subscription service *Westlaw* is another valuable source (*http://www.westlaw. co.uk*), as is the Merrill Corporation's *Casetrack* (*http://www.casetrack.com/ ct/casetrack.nsf/index?openframeset*) and LexisNexis *Lexis* (*http://www.lexis. com*).

Conclusion

The internet provides a vast resource but a search needs to be focused. Social security schemes are essentially statutory and so in Great Britain the legislation which is set out in this book forms the basic structure of social security law. However, the case law shows how the legislation should be interpreted and applied. The commentary in this book should point the way to the case law relevant to each provision and the Internet can then be used to find it where that is necessary.

CHANGE OF NAME FROM DEPARTMENT OF SOCIAL SECURITY TO DEPARTMENT FOR WORK AND PENSIONS

The Secretaries of State for Education and Skills and for Work and Pensions Order 2002 (SI 2002/1397) makes provision for the change of name from the Department of Social Security to Department for Work and Pensions. Article 9(5) provides:

"(5) Subject to article 12 [which makes specific amendments], any enactment or instrument passed or made before the coming into force of this Order shall have effect, so far as may be necessary for the purposes of or in consequence of the entrusting to the Secretary of State for Work and Pensions of the social security functions, as if any reference to the Secretary of State for Social Security, to the Department of Social Security or to an officer of the Secretary of State for Social Security (including any reference which is to be construed as such as reference) were a reference to the Secretary of State for Work and Pensions, to the Department for Work and Pensions or, as the case may be, to an officer of the Secretary of State for Work and Pensions."

TABLE OF CASES

Table of Cases

TABLE OF UPPER TRIBUNAL DECISIONS

TABLE OF SOCIAL SECURITY COMMISSIONERS' DECISIONS

TABLE OF ABBREVIATIONS USED IN THIS SERIES

(No.2) Regulations	Statutory Paternity Pay (Adoption) and Statutory Adoption Pay (Adoptions from Overseas) (No.2) Regulations 2003
1978 Act	Employment Protection (Consolidation) Act 1978
1998 Act	Social Security Act 1998
2002 Act	Tax Credits Act 2002
2004 Act	Child Trust Funds Act 2004
AA	Attendance Allowance
AAC	Administrative Appeal Chamber
AA 1992	Attendance Allowance Act 1992
AA Regulations	Social Security (Attendance Allowance) Regulations 1991
A.C.	Law Reports Appeal Cases
A.C.D.	Administrative Court Digest
ADHD	Attention Deficit Hyperactivity Disorder
Adjudication Regs	Social Security (Adjudication) Regulations 1986
Admin L.R.	Administrative Law Reports
Administration Act	Social Security Administration Act 1992
AIDS	Acquired Immune Deficiency Syndrome
All E.R.	All England Reports
All E.R. (E.C.)	All England Reports (European Cases)
AMA	Adjudicating Medical Authority
AO	Adjudication Officer
AOG	*Adjudication Officers' Guide*
ASPP	Additional Statutory Paternity Pay
A.T.C.	Annotated Tax Cases
Attendance Allowance Regulations	Social Security (Attendance Allowance) Regulations 1991
BAMS	Benefits Agency Medical Service
Benefits Act	Social Security Contributions and Benefits Act 1992
B.H.R.C.	Butterworths Human Rights Cases
B.L.G.R.	Butterworths Local Government Reports
Blue Books	*The Law Relating to Social Security*, Vols 1–11
B.M.L.R.	Butterworths Medico Legal Reports
B.P.I.R.	Bankruptcy and Personal Insolvency Reports

B.T.C.	British Tax Cases
B.W.C.C.	Butterworths Workmen's Compensation Cases
C	Commissioner's decision
C&BA 1992	Social Security Contributions and Benefits Act 1992
CAA 2001	Capital Allowance Act 2001
CAB	Citizens Advice Bureau
CAO	Chief Adjudication Officer
CBJSA	Contribution-Based Jobseeker's Allowance
C.C.L. Rep.	Community Care Law Reports
CCM	Claimant Compliance Manual
CCN	New Tax Credits Claimant Compliance Manual
C.E.C.	European Community Cases
CERA	Cortical Evoked Response Audiogram
CESA	Contributory Employment and Support Allowance
Ch.	Chancery Division Law Reports
Child Benefit Regulations	Child Benefit (General) Regulations 2006
Claims and Payments Regulations	Social Security (Claims and Payments) Regulations 1987
Claims and Payments Regulations 1979	Social Security (Claims and Payments) Regulations 1979
C.M.L.R.	Common Market Law Reports
C.O.D.	Crown Office Digest
Com. L.R.	Commercial Law Reports
Commissioners Procedure Regulations	Social Security Commissioners (Procedure) Regulations 1999
Computation of Earnings Regulations	Social Security Benefit (Computation of Earnings) Regulations 1978
Computation of Earnings Regulations 1999	Social Security Benefit (Computation of Earnings) Regulations 1996
Const. L.J.	Construction Law Journal
Contributions and Benefits Act	Social Security Contributions and Benefits Act 1992
Convention	Human Rights Convention
Council Tax Benefit Regulations	Council Tax Benefit (General) Regulations 1992 (SI 1992/1814)
CP	Carer Premium
CP	Chamber President
CPAG	Child Poverty Action Group
C.P.L.R.	Civil Practice Law Reports
CPR	Civil Procedure Rules
C.P. Rep.	Civil Procedure Reports
Cr. App. R.	Criminal Appeal Reports
Cr. App. R. (S.)	Criminal Appeal Reports (Sentencing)

CRCA 2005	Commissioners for Revenue and Customs Act 2005
Credits Regulations 1974	Social Security (Credits) Regulations 1974
Credits Regulations 1975	Social Security (Credits) Regulations 1975
Crim. L.R.	Criminal Law Review
CRU	Compensation Recovery Unit
CSA 1995	Child Support Act 1995
CS(NI)O	Child Support (Northern Ireland) Order 1995
CSO	Child Support Officer Act 2000
CSPSSA 2000	Child Support, Pensions and Social Security Act 2000
CTC	Child Tax Credit
DAT	Disability Appeal Tribunal
DCP	Disabled Child Premium
Decisions and Appeals Regulations 1999	Social Security Contributions (Decisions and Appeals) Regulations 1999
Dependency Regulations	Social Security Benefit (Dependency) Regulations 1977
DLA	Disability Living Allowance
DLA Regulations	Social Security (Disability Living Allowance) Regulations 1991
DLAAB	Disability Living Allowance Advisory Board
DLAAB Regs	Disability Living Allowance Advisory Board Regulations (SI 1991/1746)
DLADWAA 1991	Disability Living Allowance and Disability Working Allowance Act 1991
DM	Decision Maker
DMA	Decision-making and Appeals
DMG	Decision Makers Guide
DMP	Delegated Medical Practitioner
DPTC	Disabled Person's Tax Credit
DSDNI	Department for Social Development, Northern Ireland
DSS	Department of Social Security
DTI	Department of Trade and Industry
DWA	Disability Working Allowance
DWP	Department of Work and Pensions
DWPMS	Department of Work and Pensions Medical Services
EAA	Extrinsic Allergic Alveolitis
EAT	Employment Appeal Tribunal
ECHR	European Convention on Human Rights
ECHR rights	European Convention on Human Rights rights
EctHR	European Court of Human Rights
ECJ	European Court of Justice
E.C.R.	European Court Report

ECSMA Agreement	European Convention on Social and Medical Assistance
EC Treaty	European Community Treaty
EEA	European Economic Area
E.H.R.R.	European Human Rights Reports
E.L.R.	Education Law Reports
EMA	Education Maintenance Allowance
EMO	Examining Medical Officer
EMP	Examining Medical Practitioner
ERA	Evoked Response Audiometry
ERA 1996	Employment Rights Act 1996
ER(NI)O	Employers Rights (Northern Ireland) Order 1996
ESA	Employment and Support Allowance
ESA Regulations	Employment and Support Allowance Regulations 2008
ESA WCAt	Employment and Support Allowance Work Capability Assessment
Eu.L.R.	European Law Reports
FA 1990	Finance Act 1990
FA 1996	Finance Act 1996
FA 2000	Finance Act 2000
FA 2004	Finance Act 2004
F(No.2) A 2005	Finance (No.2) Act 2005
Family Credit Regulations	Family Credit (General) Regulations 1987
Fam. Law	Family Law
F.C.R.	Family Court Reporter
FIS	Family Income Supplement
Fixing and Adjustment of Rates Regulations 1976	Child Benefit and Social Security (Fixing and Adjustment of Rates) Regulations 1976
F.L.R.	Family Law Report
FTT	First-tier Tribunal
GA	Guardians Allowance
GA Regulations	Social Security (Guardian's Allowance) Regulations 1975
General Benefit Regulations 1982	Social Security (General Benefit) Regulations 1982
General Regulations	Statutory Maternity Pay (General) Regulations 1986
GMP	Guaranteed Minimum Pension
G.P.	General Practitioner
GRA	Gender Recognition Act
GRB	Graduated Retirement Benefit
GRP	Graduated Retirement Pension
G.W.D.	Greens Weekly Digest

HASSASSA	Health and Social Services and Social Security Adjudication Act 1983
HCD	House of Commons Debates
HCV	Hepatitis C Virus
HCWA	House of Commons Written Answer
HESC	Health, Education and Social Care
H.L.R.	Housing Law Reports
HMIT	Her Majesty's Inspector of Taxes
HMRC	Her Majesty's Revenue & Customs
HNCIP	(Housewives') Non-Contributory Invalidity Pension
Hospital In-Patients Regulations 1975	Social Security (Hospital In-Patients) Regulations 1975
Housing Benefit Regulations	Housing Benefit (General) Regulations 1987 (SI 1987/1971)
HPP	Higher Pensioner Premium
HRA 1998	Human Rights Act 1998
H.R.L.R.	Human Rights Law Reports–UK Cases
HSE	Health and Safety Executive
IB	Incapacity Benefit
IB/IS/SDA	Incapacity Benefits' Regime
IBJSA	Income based Jobseekers Allowance
IB PCA	Incapacity Benefit Person Capability Assessment
IB Regs	Social Security (Incapacity Benefit) Regulations 1994
IB Regulations	Social Security (Incapacity Benefit) Regulations 1994
IBS	Irritable Bowel Syndrome
ICA	Invalid Care Allowance
ICA Regulations	Social Security (Invalid Care Allowance) Regulations 1976
ICA Unit	Invalid Care Allowance Unit
I.C.R.	Industrial Cases Reports
ICTA 1988	Income and Corporation Taxes Act 1988
IFW Regs	Incapacity for Work (General) Regulations 1995
IIAC	Industrial Injuries Advisory Council
Imm. A.R.	Immigration Appeal Reports
Incapacity for Work Regulations	Social Security (Incapacity for Work) (General) Regulations 1995
Income Support General Regulations	Income Support (General) Regulations 1987
Increases for Dependants Regulations	Social Security Benefit (Dependency) Regulations 1977
IND	Immigration and Nationality Directorate of the Home Office
I.N.L.R.	Immigration and Nationality Law Reports

IO	Information Officer
I.O.	Insurance Officer
IPPR	Institute of Public Policy Research
IRESA	Income Related Employment and Support Allowance
I.R.L.R.	Industrial Relations Law Reports
IS	Income Support
ISAs	Individual Savings Accounts
IS Regs	Income Support Regulations
ITA 2007	Income Tax Act 2007
ITEPA	Income Tax (Earnings and Pensions) Act
ITEPA 2003	Income Tax (Earnings and Pensions) Act 2003
I.T.L. Rep.	International Tax Law Reports
ITS	Independent Tribunal Service
ITTOIA	Income Tax (Trading and Other Income) Act 2005
IVB	Invalidity Benefit
IWA 1994	Social Security (Incapacity for Work) Act 1994
IW (Dependants) Regs	Social Security (Incapacity for Work) (Dependants) Regulations
IW (General) Regs	Social Security (Incapacity for Work) (General) Regulations 1995
IW (Transitional) Regs	Incapacity for Work (Transitional) Regulations
JHRC	Joint Human Rights Committee
Jobseeker's Regulations 1996	Jobseekers Allowance Regulations 1996
J.P.	Justice of the Peace Reports
JSA	Jobseekers Allowance
JSA 1995	Jobseekers Allowance Act 1995
JSA Regs 1996	Jobseekers Allowance Regulations 1996
JSA Regulations	Jobseekers Allowance Regulations
JSA (Transitional) Regulations	Jobseeker's Allowance (Transitional) Regulations 1996
JS(NI)O 1995	Jobseekers (Northern Ireland) Order 1995
J.S.S.L.	Journal of Social Security Law
J.S.W.F.L.	Journal of Social Welfare and Family Law
J.S.W.L.	Journal of Social Welfare Law
K.I.R.	Knight's Industrial Law Reports
L. & T.R.	Landlord and Tenant Reports
LCWA	Limited Capability for Work Assessment
LEL	Lower Earnings Limit
Lewis	R. Lewis, *Compensation for Industrial Injury* (1987)
L.G.R.	Local Government Law Reports
Ll.L.Rep	Lloyd's List Law Report

Lloyd's Rep.	Lloyd's Law Reports
L.S.G.	Law Society Gazette
LTAHAW	Living Together as Husband and Wife
Luxembourg Court	Court of Justice of the European Communities (also referred to as ECJ)
MA	Maternity Allowance
MAF	Medical Assessment Framework
MAT	Medical Appeal Tribunal
Maternity Allowance Regulations	Social Security (Maternity Allowance) Regulations 1987
Maternity Benefit Regulations	Social Security (Maternity Benefit) Regulations 1975
Medical Evidence Regulations	Social Security (Medical Evidence) Regulations 1976
MS	Medical Services
NCIP	Non-Contributory Invalidity Pension
NDPD	Notes on the Diagnosis of Prescribed Diseases
NI	National Insurance
N.I..	Northern Ireland Law Reports
NICs	National Insurance Contributions
NIRS 2	National Insurance Recording System
N.L.J.	New Law Journal
N.P.C.	New Property Cases
OCD	Obsessive compulsive disorder
Ogus, Barendt and Wikeley	A. Ogus, E. Barendt and N. Wikeley, *The Law of Social Security* (4th ed., Butterworths, 1995)
OPA	Overseas Pensions Act 1973
OPB	One Parent Benefit
OPSSAT	Office of the President of Social Security Appeal Tribunals
Overlapping Benefits Regulations	Social Security (Overlapping Benefits) Regulations 1979
Overpayments Regulations	Social Security (Payments on account, Overpayments and Recovery) Regulations
P.	Probate, Divorce and Admiralty Law Reports
P. & C.R.	Property and Compensation Reports
PAYE	Pay As You Earn
PCA	Personal Capability Assessment
PD	Prescribed Diseases
P.D.	Practice Direction
Pens. L.R.	Pensions Law Reports
Persons Abroad Regulations	Social Security Benefit (Persons Abroad) Regulations 1975
Persons Residing Together Regulations	Social Security Benefit (Persons Residing Together) Regulations 1977
PIE	Period of Interruption of Employment

PILON	Pay In Lieu of Notice
PIW	Period of Incapacity for Work
P.I.W.R.	Personal Injury and Quantum Reports
P.L.R.	Estates Gazette Planning Law Reports
Polygamous Marriages Regulations	Social Security and Family Allowances (Polygamous Marriages) Regulations 1975
PPF	Pension Protection Fund
Prescribed Diseases Regulations	Social Security (Industrial Injuries) (Prescribed Diseases) Regulations 1985
PSCS	DWP's Pension Service Computer System
PTA	Pure Tone Audiometry
PTSR	Public and Third Sector Law Reports
PVS	Private of Voluntary Sectors
Q.B.	Queens Bench Law Reports
R	Reported Decision
RC	Rules of the Court of Session
REA	Reduced Earnings Allowance
Recoupment Regulations	Social Security (Recoupment) Regulations 1990
RIPA	Regulation of Investigatory Powers Act 2000
RMO	Regional Medical Officer
RSI	Repetitive Strain Injury
R.T.R.	Road Traffic Reports
S	Scottish Decision
SAP	Statutory Adoption Pay
SAYE	Save As You Earn
SB	Supplementary Benefit
SBC	Supplementary Benefits Commission
S.C.	Session Cases
S.C. (H.L.)	Session Cases (House of Lords)
S.C. (P.C.)	Session Cases (Privy Council)
S.C.C.R.	Scottish Criminal Case Reports
S.C.L.R.	Scottish Civil Law Reports
SDA	Severe Disablement Allowance
SDP	Severe Disability Premium
SEC	Social Entitlement Chamber
SERPS	State Earnings Related Pension Scheme
Severe Disablement Allowance Regulations	Social Security (Severe Disablement Regulations Allowance) Regulations 1984
S.J.	Solicitors Journal
S.J.L.B.	Solicitors Journal Law Brief
S.L.T.	Scots Law Times
SMP	Statutory Maternity Pay
SMP (General) Regulations	Statutory Maternity Pay (General) Regulations

Table of Abbreviations used in this Series

SMP (General) Regulations 1986	Statutory Maternity Pay (General) Regulations 1986
SP	Senior President
SPC	State Pension Credit
SPCA	State Pension Credit Act 2002
SPCA(NI)	State Pension Credit Act (Northern Ireland) 2002
SPP	Statutory Paternity Pay
SPP and SAP (Administration) Regs 2002	Statutory Paternity Pay and Statutory Adoption Pay (Administration) Regulations 2002
SPP and SAP (General) Regulations 2002	Statutory Paternity Pay and Statutory Adoption Pay (General) Regulations 2002
SPP and SAP (National Health Service)	Statutory Paternity Pay and Statutory Adoption Pay (National Health Service Employees) Regulations 2002
SPP and SAP (Weekly Rates) Regulations	Statutory Paternity Pay and Statutory Adoption Pay (Weekly Rates) Regulations 2002
SSA	Social Security Agency
SSA 1975	Social Security Act 1975
SSA 1978	Social Security Act 1978
SSA 1979	Social Security Act 1979
SSA 1981	Social Security Act 1981
SSA 1986	Social Security Act 1986
SSA 1989	Social Security Act 1989
SSA 1990	Social Security Act 1990
SSA 1992	Social Security Act 1992
SSA 1998	Social Security Act 1998
SSAA 1992	Social Security Administration Act 1992*
SSAC	Social Security Advisory Committee
SSAT	Social Security Appeal Tribunal
SSCBA 1992	Social Security Contributions and Benefits Act 1992*
SSCB(NI) Act 1992	Social Security Contributions (Northern Ireland) Act 1992
SS(CP)A	Social Security (Consequential Provisions) Act 1992
SSHBA 1982	Social Security and Housing Benefits Act 1982
SS(MP) A 1977	Social Security (Miscellaneous Provisions) Act 1977
SS (No.2) A 1980	Social Security (No.2) Act 1980
SSP	Statutory Sick Pay
SSPA 1975	Social Security Pensions Act 1975
SSP (Gen.) Regulations	Statutory Sick Pay (General) Regulations 1982
SSP (General) Regulations 1982	Statutory Sick Pay (General) Regulations 1982

* Where the context makes it seem more appropriate, these could also be referred to as Contributions and Benefits Act 1992, Administration Act 1992.

SSPA 1975	Social Security Pensions Act 1975
SSWP	Secretary of State for Work and Pensions
State Pension Credit Regulations	State Pension Credit Regulations 2002
S.T.C.	Simon's Tax Cases
S.T.C. (S.C.D.)	Simon's Tax Cases: Special Commissioners Decisions
S.T.I.	Simon's Tax Intelligence
STIB	Short-Term Incapacity Benefit
Strasbourg Court	European Court of Human Rights
T	Tribunal of Commissioners' Decision
Taxes Act	Income and Corporation Taxes Act 1988
T.C.	Tax Cases
TCA 1999	Tax Credits Act 1999
TCA 2002	Tax Credits Act 2002
TC (Claims and Notifications) Regs 2002	Tax Credits (Claims and Notifications) Regulations 2002
TCGA	Taxation of Chargeable Gains Act 1992
TCTM	Tax Credits Technical Manual
TEU	Treaty on European Union
TMA 1970	Taxes Management Act 1970
T.R.	Taxation Reports
Transfer of Functions Act	Social Security Contributions (Transfer of Functions etc.) Act 1999
Treaty	Rome Treaty
U	Unemployment Benefit
U.K.H.R.R.	United Kingdom Human Rights Reports
UKUT	United Kingdom Upper Tribunal
Unemployment, Sickness and Invalidity Benefit Regs	Social Security (Unemployment, Sickness and Invalidity Benefit) Regulations 1983
USI Regs	Social Security (Unemployment, Sickness and Invalidity Benefit) Regulations 1983
UT	Upper Tribunal
VAMS	Veterans Agency Medical Service
VCM	Vinyl Chloride Monomer-Related
VERA 1992	Vehicle Excise and Registration Act 1992
VWF	Vibration White Finger
W	Welsh Decision
WCA	Work Capability Assessment
WCAt	First Element of Limited Work Capability Assessment
WFHRAt	Work Focused Health Related Assessment
WFTC	Working Families Tax Credit
Widow's Benefit and Retirement Pensions Regs	Social Security (Widow's Benefit and Retirement Pensions) Regulations 1979
Wikeley, Annotations	N. Wikeley, "Annotations to Jobseekers Act 1995 (c.18)" in *Current Law Statutes Annotated* (1995)

Table of Abbreviations used in this Series

Wikeley, Ogus and Barendt	Wikeley, Ogus and Barendt, *The Law of Social Security* (5th ed., Butterworths, 2002)
W.L.R.	Weekly Law Reports
Workmen's Compensation Acts	Workmen's Compensation Acts 1925 to 1945
WRA 2007	Welfare Reform Act
WRAAt	Work Related Activity Assessment
WRPA 1999	Welfare Reform and Pensions Act 1999
WRP(NI)O 1999	Welfare Reform and Pensions (Northern Ireland) Order
WTC	Working Tax Credit
WTC (Entitlement and Maximum Rate) Regulations 2002	Working Tax Credit (Entitlement and Maximum Rate) Regulations 2002
W.T.L.R.	Wills & Trusts Law Reports

PART I

STATUTES

Vaccine Damage Payments Act 1979

(1979 c.17)

An Act to provide for payments to be made out of public funds in cases where severe disablement occurs as a result of vaccination against certain diseases or of contact with a person who has been vaccinated against any of those diseases; to make provision in connection with similar payments made before the passing of this Act; and for purposes connected therewith.

[22nd March 1979]

Payments to persons severely disabled by vaccination

1.—(1) If, on consideration of a claim, the Secretary of State is satisfied—

    (a) that a person is, or was immediately before his death, severely disabled as a result of vaccination against any of the diseases to which this Act applies; and

    (b) that the conditions of entitlement which are applicable in accordance with section 2 below are fulfilled,

he shall in accordance with this Act make a payment of [¹the relevant statutory sum] to or for the benefit of that person or to his personal representatives.

[¹(1A) In subsection (1) above "statutory sum" means £10,000 or such other sum as is specified by the Secretary of State for the purposes of this Act by order made by statutory instrument with the consent of the Treasury; and the relevant statutory sum for the purposes of that subsection is the statutory sum at the time when a claim for payment is first made.]

(2) The diseases to which this Act applies are—

    (a) diphtheria,

    (b) tetanus,

    (c) whooping cough,

    (d) poliomyelitis,

    (e) measles,

(f) rubella,

(g) tuberculosis,

(h) smallpox, and

(i) any other disease which is specified by the Secretary of State for the purposes of this Act by order made by statutory instrument.

(3) Subject to section 2(3) below, this Act has effect with respect to a person who is severely disabled as a result of a vaccination given to his mother before he was born as if the vaccination had been given directly to him and, in such circumstances as may be prescribed by regulations under this Act, this Act has effect with respect to a person who is severely disabled as a result of contracting a disease through contact with a third person who was vaccinated against it as if the vaccination had been given to him and the disablement resulted from it.

(4) For the purposes of this Act, a person is severely disabled if he suffers disablement to the extent of [2 60] per cent. or more, assessed as for the purposes of section 57 of the Social Security Act 1975 or the Social Security (Northern Ireland) Act 1975 (disablement gratuity and pension).

[1 (4A) No order shall be made by virtue of subsection (1A) above unless a draft of the order has been laid before Parliament and been approved by a resolution of each House.]

(5) A statutory instrument under subsection (2)(i) above shall be subject to annulment in pursuance of a resolution of either House of Parliament.

AMENDMENTS

1. Social Security Act 1985, s.23.
2. Regulatory Reform (Vaccine Damage Payments Act 1979) Order 2002 (SI 2002/1592), art.2 (June 16, 2002).

GENERAL NOTE

Subs.(1A)

1.3   The statutory sum was increased to £120,000 by the Vaccine Damage Payments Act 1979 Statutory Sum Order 2007 (SI 2007/1931) with effect from July 12, 2007.

Subs.(2)

1.4   Mumps is added to the lists of diseases by the Vaccine Damage Payments (Specified Disease) Order 1990 (SI 1990/623) and haemophilus influenza type b infection was added by the Vaccine Damage Payments (Specified Disease) Order 1995 (SI 1995/1164).

Meningococcal Group C was added to the list by the Vaccine Damage Payments (Specified Disease) Order 2001 (SI 2001/1652).

With effect from September 4, 2006, pneumococcal infection was added to the list of diseases by the Vaccine Damage Payments (Specified Disease) Order 2006 (SI 2006/2066).

With effect from September 1, 2008, human papillomavirus was added to the list of diseases by the Vaccine Damage Payments (Specified Disease) Order 2008 (SI 2008/2103).

Subs.(4)

The substitution of 60 per cent for 80 per cent applies to claims made on or after June 16, 2002 (the specified date). There is transitional provision in Art.4 and the Schedule to the Order. Art.4 provides:

"Transitional claims

4. The provisions in the Schedule to this Order shall have effect and are designäted as subordinate provisions for the purposes of section 4(3) of the Regulatory Reform Act 2001."

The Schedule to the Order deals with Transitional Claims (defined in paragraph 3(1) of the Schedule) and provides as follows:

Article 4   SCHEDULE

TRANSITIONAL CLAIMS

1.—A transitional claim may be made in the cases specified in paragraph 3(1).   1.5
2. In this Schedule—
- (a) references to sections are to sections of the Act;
- (b) "advised" means—
    - (i) informed in written form; or
    - (ii) informed orally where there is a record in written form created by the adviser at the time when, or shortly after the time when, that advice was given;
- (c) "in written form" means in a manner which is in, or which is capable of being reproduced in, legible form;
- (d) "the amended section 1(4)" means section 1(4) as it is in force on or after the specified date;
- (e) "the amended section 3(1)(c)" means section 3(1)(c) as it is in force on or after the specified date;
- (f) "the extra-statutory scheme" means the non-statutory scheme of payments referred to in section 7;
- (g) "the previous section 1(4)" means section 1(4) as it was in force prior to the specified date;
- (h) "the previous section 3(1)(c)" means section 3(1)(c) as it was in force prior to the specified date;
- (i) "the specified date" means the date this Order comes into force; and
- (j) "transitional claim" has the meaning given in paragraph 4.

3.—(1) Subject to sub-paragraph (2), the specified cases are those where—
- (a) a claim for a payment under section 1(1) was made prior to the specified date and—
    - (i) the Secretary of State refused to consider the application for a claim on the ground that the previous section 3(1)(c) was not satisfied but the amended section 3(1)(c) would have been satisfied had it been in force at the time of that refusal; or
    - (ii) it was determined that no payment was due under section 1(1) on the basis that the previous section 1(4) was not satisfied;
- (b) a claim for a payment was made under the extra-statutory scheme and it was determined that no payment was due on the basis that the disabled person did not suffer disablement to the extent of 80 per cent. or more;
- (c) no claim for a payment under section 1(1) was made prior to the specified date and the Secretary of State is satisfied that—
    - (i) the reason such a claim was not made was that the disabled person, those acting on his behalf or, as the case may be, his personal representatives had been advised prior to the specified date that either the previous section 1(4) or the previous section 3(1)(c) would not be satisfied if such a claim were made; and
    - (ii) the amended section 3(1)(c) would have been satisfied had it been in force at the date the advice referred to in paragraph (i) was given; or
- (d) no claim for a payment under the extra-statutory scheme was made whilst it was in force and the Secretary of State is satisfied that the reason such a claim was not made was that the disabled person, those acting on his behalf or, as the case may be, his personal representatives had been advised whilst the extra-statutory scheme was in force that the requirement in the extra-statutory scheme that the disabled person suffers disablement to the extent of 80 per cent. or more would not be satisfied if such a claim were made.

(2) The Secretary of State shall not be satisfied for the purposes of sub-paragraph (1)(c) or (d) unless there has been produced to him the written form of the advice referred to in those paragraphs or a copy of it.

4.—A "transitional claim" is a claim for a payment under section 1 (1) which is made—
- (a) by or on behalf of the disabled person concerned or, as the case may be, by his personal representatives;

(b) in the manner prescribed by regulations under the Act for a claim under section 3; and

(c) within 3 years after the date on which this Order came into force.

5.—(1) Where sub-paragraph (2) or (3) applies, a transitional claim shall be determined on the basis that the disabled person is, or was immediately before his death, disabled as a result of vaccination against any of the diseases to which the Act applies and whether he is, or was, severely disabled shall be determined in accordance with the amended section 1(4).

(2) This sub-paragraph applies where—

(a) a case is a specified case by virtue of paragraph 3(1)(a)(ii); and

(b) at the time of the claim referred to in paragraph 3(1)(a) it was determined that the condition that the person was disabled as a result of vaccination against any of the diseases to which the Act applies was satisfied but the condition that he was severely disabled in accordance with the previous section 1(4) was not satisfied.

(3) This sub-paragraph applies where—

(a) a case is a specified case by virtue of paragraph 3(1)(b); and

(b) at the time of the claim referred to in paragraph 3(1)(b) it was determined that the condition that the person was disabled as a result of vaccination against any of the diseases to which the extra-statutory scheme applied was satisfied but the condition that he suffered disablement to the extent of 80 per cent. or more was not satisfied.

6.—Subject to paragraph 5, a transitional claim shall be treated for the purposes of the Act as a claim which satisfies the conditions in section 3(1).

GENERAL NOTE

1.6   Note that the method of assessing the percentage degree of disablement is the same as that for industrial injuries disablement pension: see further SSCBA 1992, s.103 and commentary thereto.

Conditions of entitlement

1.7   **2.**—(1) Subject to the provisions of this section, the conditions of entitlement referred to in section 1(1)(b) above are—

(a) that the vaccination in question was carried out—
   (i) in the United Kingdom or the Isle of Man, and
   (ii) on or after 5th July 1948, and
   (iii) in the case of vaccination against smallpox, before 1st August 1971;

(b) except in the case of vaccination against poliomyelitis or rubella, that the vaccination was carried out either at a time when the person to whom it was given was under the age of eighteen or at the time of an outbreak within the United Kingdom or the Isle of Man of the disease against which the vaccination was given; and

(c) that the disabled person was over the age of two on the date when the claim was made or, if he died before that date, that he died after 9th May 1978 and was over the age of two when he died.

(2) An order under section 1(2)(i) above specifying a disease for the purposes of this Act may provide that, in relation to vaccination against that disease, the conditions of entitlement specified in subsection (1) above shall have effect subject to such modifications as may be specified in the order.

(3) In a case where this Act has effect by virtue of section 1(3) above, the reference in subsection (1)(b) above to the person to whom a vaccination was given is a reference to the person to whom it was actually given and not to the disabled person.

(4) With respect to claims made after such date as may be specified in the order and relating to vaccination against such disease as may be so specified, the Secretary of State may by order made by statutory instrument—

6

(a) provide that, in such circumstances as may be specified in the order, one or more of the conditions of entitlement appropriate to vaccination against that disease need not be fulfilled; or

(b) add to the conditions of entitlement which are appropriate to vaccination against that disease, either generally or in such circumstances as may be specified in the order.

(5) Regulations under this Act shall specify the cases in which vaccinations given outside the United Kingdom and the Isle of Man to persons defined in the regulations as serving members of Her Majesty's forces or members of their families are to be treated for the purposes of this Act as carried out in England.

(6) The Secretary of State shall not make an order containing any provision made by virtue of paragraph (b) of subsection (4) above unless a draft of the order has been laid before Parliament and approved by a resolution of each House; and a statutory instrument by which any other order is made under that subsection shall be subject to annulment in pursuance of a resolution of either House of Parliament.

GENERAL NOTE

Subs. (1)(b), (2)
The condition in subs. (1)(b) (age or time at which vaccination was carried out) does not apply to vaccination against Meningococcal Group C. See the Vaccine Damage Payments (Specified Disease) Order 2001 (SI 2001/1652), art.3.

1.8

Determination of claims

3.—(1) Any reference in this Act, other than section 7, to a claim is a reference to a claim for a payment under section 1(1) above which is made—

1.9

(a) by or on behalf of the disabled person concerned or, as the case may be, by his personal representatives; and

(b) in the manner prescribed by regulations under this Act; and [²(c) on or before whichever is the later of—

   (i) the date on which the disabled person attains the age of 21, or where he has died, the date on which he would have attained the age of 21; and

   (ii) the end of the period of six years beginning with the date of the vaccination to which the claim relates;]

and, in relation to a claim, any reference to the claimant is a reference to the person by whom the claim was made and any reference to the disabled person is a reference to the person in respect of whose disablement a payment under subsection (1) above is claimed to be payable.

(2) As soon as practicable after he has received a claim, the Secretary of State shall give notice in writing to the claimant of his determination whether he is satisfied that a payment is due under section 1(1) above to or for the benefit of the disabled person or to his personal representatives.

(3) If the Secretary of State is not satisfied that a payment is due as mentioned in subsection (2) above, the notice in writing under that subsection shall state the grounds on which he is not so satisfied.

(4) If, in the case of any claim, the Secretary of State—

(a) is satisfied that the conditions of entitlement which are applicable in accordance with section 2 above are fulfilled, but

(b) is not satisfied that the disabled person is or, where he has died, was

immediately before his death severely disabled as a result of vaccination against any of the diseases to which this Act applies,
the notice in writing under subsection (2) above shall inform the claimant
[¹of the right of appeal conferred by section 4 below.]

(5) If in any case a person is severely disabled, the question whether his
severe disablement results from vaccination against any of the diseases to
which this Act applies shall be determined for the purposes of this Act on
the balance of probability.

AMENDMENTS

1. Social Security Act 1998, Sch.7, para.5 (October 18, 1999).
2. Regulatory Reform (Vaccine Damage Payments Act 1979) Order 2002
(SI 2002/1592), art.2 (June 16, 2002).

[¹ Decisions reversing earlier decisions

1.10   **3A.**—(1) Subject to subsection (2) below, any decision of the Secretary
of State under section 3 above or this section, and any decision of [² a tri-
bunal] under section 4 below, may be reversed by a decision made by the
Secretary of State—

(a) either within the prescribed period or in prescribed cases or circumstances; and

(b) either on an application made for the purpose or on his own initiative.

(2) In making a decision under subsection (1) above, the Secretary of
State need not consider any issue that is not raised by the application or, as
the case may be, did not cause him to act on his own initiative.

(3) Regulations may prescribe the procedure by which a decision may be
made under this section.

(4) Such notice as may be prescribed by regulations shall be given of a
decision under this section.

(5) Except as provided by section 5(4) below, no payment under section
1(1) above shall be recoverable by virtue of a decision under this section.

(6) In this section and sections 4 and 8 below "appeal tribunal" means an
appeal tribunal constituted under Chapter I of Part I of the Social Security
Act 1998.]

AMENDMENTS

1. Social Security Act 1998 s.45 (October 18, 1999).
2. Transfer of Tribunal Functions Order 2008 (SI 2008/2833), art.6 and Sch.3,
para.31 (November 3, 2008).

[¹ Appeals to appeal tribunals

1.11   **4.**—(1) The claimant may appeal to [²the First-tier Tribunal] against any
decision of the Secretary of State under section 3 or 3A above.

(2) Regulations may make—

(a) provision as to the manner in which, and the time within which,
appeals are to be brought; [² ...].

(3) The regulations may in particular make any provision of a kind mentioned in Schedule 5 to the Social Security Act 1998.

(4) In deciding an appeal under this section, [² the First-tier Tribunal]
shall consider all the circumstances of the case (including any not obtaining
at the time when the decision appealed against was made.]

AMENDMENTS

1. This version of s.4 (October 18, 1999) was substituted by Social Security Act 1998 s.46.
2. Transfer of Tribunal Functions Order 2008 (SI 2008/2833), art.6 and Sch.3, para.32 (November 3, 2008).

Reconsideration of determinations and recovery of payments in certain cases

5.—[¹ *Subss. (1)–(3) Repealed.*]   1.12

(4) If, whether fraudulently or otherwise, any person misrepresents or fails to disclose any material fact and in consequence of the misrepresentation or failure a payment is made under section 1(1) above, the person to whom the payment was made shall be liable to repay the amount of that payment to the Secretary of State unless he can show that the misrepresentation or failure occurred without his connivance or consent.

(5) [¹ *Repealed*]

AMENDMENT

1. Social Security Act 1998, Sch.7, para.6 (October 18, 1999).

Payments to or for the benefit of disabled persons

6.—(1) Where a payment under section 1(1) above falls to be made in   1.13
respect of a disabled person who is over eighteen and capable of managing his own affairs, the payment shall be made to him.

(2) Where such a payment falls to be made in respect of a disabled person who has died, the payment shall be made to his personal representatives.

(3) Where such a payment falls to be made in respect of any other disabled person, the payment shall be made for his benefit by paying it to such trustees as the Secretary of State may appoint to be held by them upon such trusts or, in Scotland, for such purposes and upon such conditions as may be declared by the Secretary of State.

(4) The making of a claim for, or the receipt of, a payment under section 1(1) above does not prejudice the right of any person to institute or carry on proceedings in respect of disablement suffered as a result of vaccination against any disease to which this Act applies; but in any civil proceedings brought in respect of disablement resulting from vaccination against such a disease, the court shall treat a payment made to or in respect of the disabled person concerned under section 1(1) above as paid on account of any damages which the court awards in respect of such disablement.

Payments, claims etc. made prior to the Act

7.—(1) Any reference in this section to an extra-statutory payment is a   1.14
reference to a payment of £10,000 made by the Secretary of State to or in respect of a disabled person after 9th May 1978 and before the passing of this Act pursuant to a non-statutory scheme of payments for severe vaccine damage.

(2) No such claim as is referred to in section 3(1) above shall be entertained if an extra-statutory payment has been made to or for the benefit of the disabled person or his personal representatives.

(3) For the purposes of [¹section 3A above], a determination that an extra-statutory payment should be made shall be treated as a determination that a payment should be made under section 1(1) above [¹ . . .].

(4) [¹ Section 5(4) above] and section 6(4) above shall apply in relation to an extra-statutory payment as they apply in relation to a payment made under section 1(1) above.

(5) For the purposes of this Act (other than this section) regulations under this Act may—

(a) treat claims which were made in connection with the scheme referred to in subsection (1) above and which have not been disposed of at the commencement of this Act as claims falling within section 3(1) above; and

(b) treat information and other evidence furnished and other things done before the commencement of this Act in connection with any such claim as is referred to in paragraph (a) above as furnished or done in connection with a claim falling within section 3(1) above.

AMENDMENT

1. Social Security Act 1998, Sch.7, para.7 (October 18, 1999).

[¹ Correction of errors and setting aside of decisions

1.15   **7A.**—(1) Regulations may make provision with respect to—

(a) the correction of accidental errors in any decision or record of a decision under section [² 3 or 3A] of this Act; [² . . .].

(2) Nothing in subsection (1) shall be construed as derogating from any power to correct errors [² . . .] which is exercisable apart from regulations made by virtue of that subsection.]

AMENDMENTS

1. Inserted by Social Security Act 1998 s.47 (October 18, 1999).
2. Transfer of Tribunal Functions Order 2008 (SI 2008/2833), art.6 and Sch.3, para.34 (November 3, 2008).

[¹Finality of decisions

1.16   **7B.**—(1) Subject to the provisions of this Act [² and article 4 of, and the Schedule to, the Regulatory Reform (Vaccine Damage Payments Act 1979) Order 2002 (modifications of this Act in relation to transitional claims)], any decision made in accordance with the foregoing provisions of this Act shall be final.

(2) If and to the extent that regulations so provide, any finding of fact or other determination embodied in or necessary to such a decision, or on which such a decision is based, shall be conclusive for the purposes of—

(a) further such decisions;

(b) decisions made in accordance with sections 8 to 16 of the Social Security Act 1998, or with regulations under section 11 of that Act; and

(c) decisions made under the Child Support Act 1991.]

AMENDMENTS

1. Inserted by Social Security Act 1998, Sch.7, para.8 (October 18, 1999).
2. Regulatory Reform (Vaccine Damage Payments Act 1979) Order 2002 (SI 2002/1592), art.5 (June 16, 2002).

GENERAL NOTE

Subs. (1)
   Article 4 of and the Schedule to the Order are reproduced in the annotation to s.1(4), above.

Regulations

8.—(1) Any reference in the preceding provisions of this Act to regula-   1.17
tions under this Act is a reference to regulations made by the Secretary of
State.
   (2) Any power of the Secretary of State under this Act to make
regulations—
   (a) shall be exercisable by statutory instrument which shall be subject
       to annulment in pursuance of a resolution of either House of
       Parliament; and
   (b) includes power to make such incidental or supplementary provision
       as appears to the Secretary of State to be appropriate.
   (3) Regulations made by the Secretary of State may contain provision—
   (a) with respect to the information and other evidence to be furnished in
       connection with a claim;
   (b) requiring disabled persons to undergo medical examination before
       their claims are determined or for the purposes of [¹ a decision under
       section 3A above];
   (c) restricting the disclosure of medical evidence and advice tendered in
       connection with a claim or [¹ a decision under section 3A above]; and
   (d) conferring functions on [¹ appeal tribunals] with respect to the
       matters referred to in paragraphs (a) to (c) above.

AMENDMENT

   1. Social Security Act 1998, Sch.7, para.9.

Fraudulent statements etc.

9.—(1) Any person who, for the purpose of obtaining any payment under   1.18
this Act, whether for himself or some other person,—
   (a) knowingly makes any false statement or representation, or
   (b) produces or furnishes or causes or knowingly allows to be produced
       or furnished any document or information which he knows to be
       false in a material particular,
shall be liable on summary conviction to a fine not exceeding [¹ level 5 on
the standard scale]
   (2) In the application of subsection (1) above to the Isle of Man, for
the words following "liable" there shall be substituted the words "on
summary conviction, within the meaning of the Interpretation Act 1976
(an Act of Tynwald), to a fine of £400 and on conviction on information
to a fine".

AMENDMENT

   1. Words substituted by virtue of Criminal Justice Act 1982 (c.48), s.46, Criminal
Procedure (Scotland) Act 1975 (c.21) s.289G, and for Northern Ireland by SI
1984/703 (NI3), arts 5, 6.

1.19   *Sections 9A, 10 and 11 omitted.*

Financial provisions

1.20   **12.**—(1) [² *Repealed*].

(2) The Secretary of State shall pay such fees as he considers appropriate to medical practitioners, as defined in [¹ section 191 of the Social Security Administration Act 1992] who provide information or other evidence in connection with claims.

(3) The Secretary of State shall pay such travelling and other allowances as he may determine—

   (a) to persons required under this Act to undergo medical examinations; [³ . . .] and

   (c) in circumstances where he considers it appropriate, to any person who accompanies a disabled person to such a medical examination [³ . . .].

(4) There shall be paid out of moneys provided by Parliament—

   (a) any expenditure incurred by the Secretary of State in making payments under section 1(1) above;

   (b) any expenditure incurred by the Secretary of State by virtue of subsections (1) to (3) above; and

   (c) any increase in the administrative expenses of the Secretary of State attributable to this Act.

(5) Any sums repaid to the Secretary of State by virtue of section 5(4) above shall be paid into the Consolidated Fund.

AMENDMENTS

1. Social Security (Consequential Provisions) Act 1992, Sch.2, para.54 (July 1, 1992).

2. Social Security Act 1998, Sch.7, para.10 (October 18, 1999).

3. Transfer of Tribunal Functions Order 2008 (SI 2008/2833), art.6 and Sch.3, para.36 (November 3, 2008).

Short title and extent

1.21   **13.**—(1) This Act may be cited as the Vaccine Damage Payments Act 1979.

(2) This Act extends to Northern Ireland and the Isle of Man.

Pneumoconiosis etc. (Workers' Compensation) Act 1979

(1979 c.41)

ARRANGEMENT OF SECTIONS

An Act to make provision for lump sum payments to or in respect of certain persons who are, or were immediately before they died, disabled by pneumoconiosis, byssinosis or diffuse mesothelioma; and for connected purposes.

[4th April 1979]

Dependants

3. — (1) In this Act "dependant", in relation to a person who, immediately before he died, was disabled by a disease to which this Act applies, means—

(a) if he left a spouse [¹ or civil partner] who was residing with him or was receiving or entitled to receive from him periodical payments for her maintenance, that spouse [¹ or civil partner];

(b) if paragraph (a) above does not apply but he left a child or children who fall within subsection (2) below, that child or those children;

[¹ (c) if neither of the preceding paragraphs applies but he left a person who was residing with him and with whom he was in a qualifying relationship, that person;]

(d) if none of the preceding paragraphs applies, any relative or relatives of his who fall within subsection (2) below and who were, in the opinion of the Secretary of State, wholly or mainly dependent on him at the date of his death.

(2) A person falls within this subsection if, at the relevant date, he was—

(a) under the age of 16;

(b) under the age of 21 and not gainfully employed full-time; or

(c) permanently incapable of self-support;

and in this subsection "relevant date" means the date of the deceased's death or the date of the coming into force of this Act, whichever is the later.

[¹ (2A) For the purposes of subsection (1)(c)—

(a) two persons of the opposite sex are in a qualifying relationship if they are living together as husband and wife;

(b) two persons of the same sex are in a qualifying relationship if they are living together as if they were civil partners.

(2B) For the purposes of subsection (2A)(b), two persons of the same sex are to be regarded as living together as if they were civil partners if, but only if, they would be regarded as living together as husband and wife were they instead two people of the opposite sex.]

(3) Where any payment under this Act falls to be made to two or more persons, the payment shall be made to one of them or divided between some or all of them as the Secretary of State thinks fit.

(4) In this section—

"child" includes posthumous child;

"relative" means brother, sister, lineal ancestor or lineal descendant;

and for the purposes of this section a relationship shall be established as if any illegitimate child or step child of a person had been a child born to him in wedlock.

(5) [¹ . . .]

AMENDMENT

1. Welfare Reform Act 2007 s.59 (July 3, 2007).

1.23

13

Short title, construction, commencement and extent

1.24   **10.** — (1) This Act may be cited as the Pneumoconiosis etc (Workers' Compensation) Act 1979.

(2) Except where the context otherwise requires, any expression to which a meaning is assigned by [¹ the Social Security Contributions and Benefits Act 1992 or the Social Security Administration Act 1992], or by any regulations made under [¹ either of those Acts], has that meaning also for the purposes of this Act.

(3) This Act shall come into force on the expiration of a period of three months beginning with the day on which it is passed.

(4) This Act does not extend to Northern Ireland.

AMENDMENT

1. Social Security (Consequential Provisions) Act 1992 s.4, Sch.2, para.57 (July 1, 1992).

GENERAL NOTE

1.25   Sections 3 and 10 of the Pneumoconiosis etc (Workers' Compensation) Act 1979 have been included in this volume as the definitions therein have been incorporated by reference into the 2008 Diffuse Mesothelioma Scheme.

Social Security Contributions and Benefits Act 1992

(1992 c.4)

ARRANGEMENT OF SECTIONS

PART I

CONTRIBUTIONS

Preliminary

PART II

CONTRIBUTORY BENEFITS

Preliminary

PART III

NON-CONTRIBUTORY BENEFITS

PART V

BENEFIT FOR INDUSTRIAL INJURIES

General provisions

Sickness benefit

Disablement pension

Other benefits and increases

PART VII

INCOME-RELATED BENEFITS

Omitted.

See *Vol.II: Income Support, Jobseeker's Allowance, State Pension Credit and the Social Fund.*

PART VIII

THE SOCIAL FUND

Omitted.

See *Vol.II: Income Support, Jobseeker's Allowance, State Pension Credit and the Social Fund.*

PART IX

CHILD BENEFIT

141.–147. *Omitted.* See *Vol.IV Tax Credits and HMRC–administered Social Security Benefits.*

PART X

CHRISTMAS BONUS FOR PENSIONERS

148.   Entitlement of pensioners to Christmas bonus.
149.   Provisions supplementary to section 148.
150.   Interpretation of Part X.
150A.   Annual up-rating of basic pension etc. and standard minimum guarantee.

PART XI

STATUTORY SICK PAY

151.–163.   *Omitted.*
See *Vol.IV: Tax Credits and HMRC-administered Social Security Benefits.*

PART XII

STATUTORY MATERNITY PAY

164.–171.   *Omitted.*
See Vol.IV: Tax Credits and HMRC-administered Social Security Benefits.

PART XIIZA

STATUTORY PATERNITY PAY

171ZA.–171ZK.   *Omitted.*
See Vol.IV: Tax Credits and HMRC-administered Social Security Benefits.

PART XIIZB

STATUTORY ADOPTION PAY

171ZL.–171ZT.   *Omitted.*
See Vol.IV: Tax Credits and HMRC-administered Social Security Benefits.

PART XIIA

INCAPACITY FOR WORK

PART XIII

GENERAL

Interpretation

An Act to consolidate certain enactments relating to social security contributions and benefits with amendments to give effect to recommendations of the Law Commission and the Scottish Law Commission.

[13TH FEBRUARY 1992]

PART I

CONTRIBUTIONS

Preliminary

Outline of contributory system.

1.—(1) The funds required—   1.27
  (a) for paying such benefits under this Act as are payable out of the
      National Insurance Fund and not out of other public money; and
  (b) for the making of payments under section 162 of the Administration
      Act towards the cost of the National Health Service,
shall be provided by means of contributions payable to the [¹ Inland
Revenue] by earners, employers and others, together with the additions
under subsection (5) below [² and amounts payable under section 2 of the
Social Security Act 1993].

  (2) Contributions under this Part of this Act shall be of the following [³
six] classes—
  (a) Class 1, earnings-related, payable under section 6 below, being—
        (i) primary Class 1 contributions from employed earners; and
       (ii) secondary Class 1 contributions from employers and other
            persons paying earnings;
  (b) Class 1A, payable under section 10 below [⁴. . .] by persons liable to
      pay secondary Class 1 contributions and certain other persons;
[⁵(bb) Class 1B, payable under section 10A below by persons who are
      accountable to the Inland Revenue in respect of income tax on [⁶
      general earnings] in accordance with a PAYE settlement agree-
      ment;]
  (c) Class 2, flat-rate, payable weekly under section 11 below by self-
      employed earners;
  (d) Class 3, payable under section 13 below by earners and others volun-
      tarily with a view to providing entitlement to benefit, or making up
      entitlement; and
  (e) Class 4, payable under section 15 below in respect of the profits or
      gains of a trade, profession or vocation, or under section 18 below in
      respect of equivalent earnings.

  (3) The amounts and rates of contributions in this Part of this Act and
the other figures in it which affect the liability of contributions shall—
  (a) be subject to regulations under sections 19(4) and 116 to 120 below;
      and
  (b) to the extent provided for by Part IX of the Administration Act be
      subject to alteration by orders made by the [⁷ Treasury] from year to
      year under that Part,
and the provisions of this Part of this Act are subject to the provisions
of [⁸ Chapter II of Part III of the Pensions Act (reduction in state scheme
contributions and benefits for members of certified schemes)].

  (4) Schedule 1 to this Act—

23

(a) shall have effect with respect to the computation, collection and recovery of contributions of Classes 1, 1A, [⁹ 1B,] 2 and 3, and otherwise with respect to contributions of those classes; and

(b) shall also, to the extent provided by regulations made under section 18 below, have effect with respect to the computation, collection and recovery of Class 4 contributions, and otherwise with respect to such contributions [¹⁰ . . .].

(5) For each financial year there shall, by way of addition to contributions, be paid out of money provided by Parliament, in such manner and at such times as the Treasury may determine, amounts the total of which for any such year is equal to the aggregate of all statutory sick pay [¹¹ , statutory maternity pay, statutory paternity pay and statutory adoption pay] recovered by employers and others in that year, as estimated by the Government Actuary or the Deputy Government Actuary.

(6) No person shall—

(a) be liable to pay Class 1, Class 1A [¹² , Class 1B] or Class 2 contributions unless he fulfils prescribed conditions as to residence or presence in Great Britain;

(b) be entitled to pay Class 3 contributions unless he fulfils such conditions; or

(c) be entitled to pay Class 1, Class 1A [¹² , Class 1B] or Class 2 contributions other than those which he is liable to pay, except so far as he is permitted by regulations to pay them.

[¹³ (7) Regulations under subsection (6) above shall be made by the Treasury.]

AMENDMENTS

1. Social Security Contributions (Transfer of Functions, etc.) Act 1999, Sch.1, para.5(2) (February 25, 1999 for the purpose of enabling the Secretary of State to make subordinate legislation conferring functions on the Commissioners of Inland Revenue; April 1, 1999 otherwise).

2. Social Security Act 1993 s.2(9) (January 29, 1993).

3. Social Security Act 1998, Sch.7, para.56(1) (September 8, 1998 for the purpose of authorising the making of regulations or orders; April 6, 1999 otherwise).

4. Child Support, Pensions and Social Security Act 2000, Sch.9(VIII), para.1 (April 6, 2000: repeal has effect in relation to the tax year beginning April 6, 2000 and subsequent tax years).

5. Social Security Act 1998, Sch.7, para.56(1) (September 8, 1998 for the purpose of authorising the making of regulations or orders; April 6, 1999 otherwise).

6. Income Tax (Earnings and Pensions) Act 2003, Sch.6(2), para.170 (April 6, 2003 subject to transitional provisions and savings specified in 2003 c.1 Sch.7).

7. Social Security Contributions (Transfer of Functions, etc.) Act 1999, Sch.3, para.1(2) (April 1, 1999).

8. Pension Schemes Act 1993, Sch.8, para.32 (February 7, 1994).

9. Social Security Act 1998, Sch.7, para.56(2) (September 8, 1998 for the purpose of authorising the making of regulations or orders; April 6, 1999 otherwise).

10. Social Security Contributions (Transfer of Functions, etc.) Act 1999, Sch.1, para.5(3) (February 25, 1999 for the purpose of enabling the Secretary of State to make subordinate legislation conferring functions on the Commissioners of Inland Revenue; April 1, 1999 otherwise).

11. Employment Act 2002, Pt 1, s.6(3) (December 8, 2002 subject to transitional provisions specified in SI 2002/2866 Sch.3; not yet in force otherwise).

12. Social Security Act 1998, Sch.7, para.56(3) (September 8, 1998 for the

purpose of authorising the making of regulations or orders; April 6, 1999 otherwise).

13. Social Security Contributions (Transfer of Functions, etc.) Act 1999, Sch.3, para.1(3) (April 1, 1999).

Categories of earners

2.—(1) In this Part of this Act and Parts II to V below—   1.28
   (a) "employed earner" means a person who is gainfully employed in Great Britain either under a contract of service, or in an office (including elective office) with [² general earnings]; and
   (b) "self-employed earner" means a person who is gainfully employed in Great Britain otherwise than in employed earner's employment (whether or not he is also employed in such employment).
(2) Regulations may provide—
   (a) for employment of any prescribed description to be disregarded in relation to liability for contributions otherwise arising from employment of that description;
   (b) for a person in employment of any prescribed description to be treated, for the purposes of this Act, as falling within one or other of the categories of earner defined in subsection (1) above, notwithstanding that he would not fall within that category apart from the regulations.
[¹ (2A) Regulations under subsection (2) above shall be made by the Treasury and, in the case of regulations under paragraph (b) of that subsection, with the concurrence of the Secretary of State.]
(3) Where a person is to be treated by reference to any employment of his as an employed earner, then he is to be so treated for all purposes of this Act; and references throughout this Act to employed earner's employment shall be construed accordingly.
(4) Subsections (1) to (3) above are subject to the provision made by section 95 below as to the employments which are to be treated, for the purposes of industrial injuries benefit, as employed earner's employments.
(5) For the purposes of this Act, a person shall be treated as a self-employed earner as respects any week during any part of which he is such an earner (without prejudice to his being also treated as an employed earner as respects that week by reference to any other employment of his).

AMENDMENTS

1. Welfare Reform and Pensions Act 1999, Sch.11, para.2 (April 6, 2000), replacing an earlier amendment made by the Transfer of Functions Act 1999, Sch.3, para.2 (April 1, 1999).
2. Income Tax (Earnings and Pensions) Act 2003, s.722, Sch.6, paras 169 and 171 (April 6, 2003).

DERIVATION

   SSA 1975, s.2.   1.29

DEFINITIONS

   "contract of service"—s.122.
   "employment"—s.122.
   "prescribed"—s.122.

GENERAL NOTE

1.30   The definitions in this section are primarily of importance in determining liability to pay contributions of a particular class, which is a matter for Her Majesty's Revenue and Customs. Their importance for tribunals is that the definition of "earnings" in s.3 refers back to this section.

The definition of employed earners refers to a person being "gainfully employed". This notion has caused some difficulty but it appears that it refers to cases where there is an obligation by an employer to pay remuneration to an employee for those tasks the employee is bound to perform for the employer under the contract of employment: see Slade J. in *Vandyk v Minister of Pensions and National Insurance* [1955] 1 Q.B. 29 at 38.

"Contract of service"

1.31   This is broadly defined by the Act to include any contract of service or apprenticeship, whether written or oral and whether express or implied. The existence of an employer/employee relationship may not always be obvious. The trend of a complex general case law on the issue is that in determining whether a person is self-employed or employed, particular regard will be had to whether the person has risked his or her own capital in the enterprise: *Young and Woods v West* [1980] I.R.L.R. 201 at 209. For a detailed, discussion of the question see *Wikeley Ogus & Barendt*, pp.96–109.

"Earnings" and "earner"

1.32   **3.**—(1) In this Part of this Act and Parts II to V below—
   (a) "earnings" includes any remuneration or profit derived from an employment; and
   (b) "earner" shall be construed accordingly.
   (2) For the purposes of this Part of this Act and of Parts II to V below other than those of Schedule 8—
   (a) the amount of a person's earnings for any period; or
   (b) the amount of his earnings to be treated as comprised in any payment made to him or for his benefit,
shall be calculated or estimated in such manner and on such basis as may be prescribed [1 by regulations made by the Treasury with the concurrence of the Secretary of State.]
   [2 (2A) Regulations made for the purposes of subsection (2) above may provide that, where a payment is made or a benefit provided to or for the benefit of two or more earners, a proportion (determined in such manner as may be prescribed) of the amount or value of the payment or benefit shall be attributed to each earner.]
   (3) Regulations made for the purposes of subsection (2) above may prescribe that payments of a particular class or description made or falling to be made to or by a person shall, to such extent as may be prescribed, be disregarded or, as the case may be, be deducted from the amount of that person's earnings.
   [3 (4) Subsection (5) below applies to regulations made for the purposes of subsection (2) above which make special provision with respect to the earnings periods of directors and former directors of companies.
   (5) Regulations to which this subsection applies may make provisions—
   (a) for enabling companies, and directors and former directors of companies, to pay on account of any earnings-related contributions that may become payable by them such amounts as would be payable

26

by way of such contributions if the special provision had not been made; and

(b) for requiring any payments made in accordance with the regulations to be treated, for prescribed purposes, as if they were the contributions on account of which they were made.]

AMENDMENTS

1. Transfer of Functions Act 1999, Sch.3, para.3 (April 1, 1999).
2. Social Security Act 1998, s.48 (September 8, 1998).
3. Social Security Act 1998, s.49(1) (September 8, 1998).

DERIVATION

SSA 1975, s.3(1)–(3).   1.33

DEFINITIONS

"employment"—s.122.
"prescribed"—s.122.

GENERAL NOTE

The computation of earnings is required in connection with a number of   1.34
benefits:

(1) to calculate reduced earnings allowance;

(2) in disregarding casual or subsidiary work producing small sums in relation to entitlement to benefits based on incapacity for work, unemployment or retirement, and allowance;

(3) to determine entitlement to increases of benefit for children and dependants; and

(4) to determine any reduction of retirement pensions by reason of earnings.

The rules on computation are to be found in the Computation of Earnings Regulations and in Commissioners' decisions. The Computation of Earnings Regulations 1996 take an approach to the calculation of earnings in relation to non-means tested benefits which closely parallels that which has applied for some time to the calculation of earnings for income-related benefits.

Payments treated as remuneration, and earnings

4.—(1) For the purposes of section 3 above there shall be treated as   1.35
remuneration derived from employed earner's employment—

(a) any sum paid to or for the benefit of a person in satisfaction (whether in whole or in part) of any entitlement of that person to—
  (i) statutory sick pay; or
  (ii) statutory maternity pay;
  [⁵ (iii) statutory paternity pay; or
  (iv) statutory adoption pay;] and

(b) any sickness payment made—
  (i) to or for the benefit of the employed earner; and
  (ii) in accordance with arrangements under which the person who is the secondary contributor in relation to the employment concerned has made, or remains liable to make, payments towards the provision of that sickness payment.

27

(2) Where the funds for making sickness payments under arrangements of the kind mentioned in paragraph (b) of subsection (1) above are attributable in part to contributions to those funds made by the employed earner, regulations may make provision for disregarding, for the purposes of that subsection, the prescribed part of any sum paid as a result of the arrangements.

(3) For the purposes of subsections (1) and (2) above "sickness payment" means any payment made in respect of absence from work due to incapacity for work, [¹ . . .].

[² (4) For the purposes of section 3 above there shall be treated as remuneration derived from an employed earner's employment—

[⁷ (a) the amount of any gain calculated under section 479 or 480 of ITEPA 2003 in respect of which an amount counts as employment income of the earner under section 476 or 477 of that Act (charge on exercise, assignment or release of share option);]

(b) any sum paid (or treated as paid) to or for the benefit of the earner which is chargeable to tax by virtue of [section 225 or 226 of ITEPA 2003] (taxation of consideration for certain restrictive undertakings).]

(5) For the purposes of section 3 above regulations may make provision for treating as remuneration derived from an employed earner's employment any payment made by a body corporate to or for the benefit of any of its directors where that payment would, when made, not be earnings for the purposes of this Act.

[³ (6) Regulations may make provision for the purposes of this Part—

(a) for treating any amount on which an employed earner is chargeable to income tax under [⁶ [⁷ the employment income Parts of ITEPA 2003] as remuneration derived from the earner's employment; and

(b) for treating any amount which in accordance with regulations under paragraph (a) above constitutes remuneration as an amount of remuneration paid, at such time as may be determined in accordance with the regulations, to or for the benefit of the earner in respect of his employment.]

[⁴ (7) Regulations under this section shall be made by the Treasury with the concurrence of the Secretary of State.]

AMENDMENTS

1. Incapacity for Work Act 1994, Sch.1, para.1 (April 13, 1995).
2. Social Security Act 1998, s.50(1) (September 8, 1998).
3. Social Security Act 1998, s.50(2) (September 9, 1998).
4. Transfer of Functions Act 1999, Sch.3, para.5 (April, 1999).
5. Employment Act 2002, s.53 and Sch.7, paras 2 and 3 (December 8, 2002).
6. Child Support, Pensions and Social Security Act 2000, s.74(3) (April 6, 2000).
7. Income Tax (Earnings and Pensions) Act 2003, s.722, Sch.6, paras 169 and 172 (April 5, 2003).

DERIVATION

1.36   SSA 1975, s.3(1A)–(1D) and (4).

1.37   *Sections 5–19 omitted.*

PART II

CONTRIBUTORY BENEFITS

Preliminary

Descriptions of contributory benefits

20.—(1) Contributory benefits under this Part of this Act are of the fol-   1.38
lowing descriptions, namely—
(a) *Repealed.*
(b) incapacity benefit, comprising—
    (i) short-term incapacity benefit, and
    (ii) long-term incapacity benefit;
(c) *Repealed.*
(d) maternity allowance (with increase for adult dependants);
(e) widow's benefit, comprising—
    (i) [^{1} . . .]
    (ii) widowed mother's allowance [^{2} . . .]
    (iii) widow's pension;
[^{1}(ee) bereavement benefits, comprising—
    (i) bereavement payment;
    (ii) widowed parent's allowance [^{2} . . .]
    (iii) bereavement allowance.]
(f) retirement pensions of the following categories—
    (i) Category A, payable to a person by virtue of his own contribu-
    tions (with increase for adult [^{2} . . .] dependants); and
    [^{4}(ii) Category B, payable to a person by virtue of the contributions
    of a spouse [^{2} . . .] [^{5}or civil partner];]
    [^{3} (fa)   shared additional pensions]
(g) for existing beneficiaries only, child's special allowance.
(2) In this Act—
"long-term benefit" means—
    (a) long-term incapacity benefit;
    (b) a widowed mother's allowance;
[^{1}(ba) a widowed parent's allowance;
    (bb) a bereavement allowance;]
    (c) a widow's pension; and
    (d) a Category A or Category B retirement pension; and
    [^{3}(e) a shared additional pension under section 55A below].
"short-term benefit" means—
    (a) *Repealed.*
    (b) short-term incapacity benefit; and
    (c) maternity allowance.
(3) The provisions of this Part of this Act are subject to the provisions of
Part III of the Pensions Act (contracting-out—reduced rates of benefit).

AMENDMENTS
1. Welfare Reform and Pensions Act 1999, Sch.8, para.3 (April 9, 2001).

2. Tax Credits Act 2002, Sch.6 (April 6, 2003).
3. Welfare Reform and Pensions Act 1999, Sch.12, para.15 (April 9, 2001).
4. Pensions Act 1995, Sch.4, para.21(1) (July 19, 1995).
5. Civil Partnership Act 2004, s.254 and Sch.24, Pt 3, para.13 (December 5, 2005).

Contribution conditions

1.39   **21.**—(1) Entitlement to any of the benefits specified in section 20(1) above, [¹ other than [² short-term incapacity benefit under subsection (1) (b) of section 30A below] long-term incapacity benefit under [² subsection (5) of that section] [³ maternity allowance under section 35 below] or short-term or long-term incapacity benefit under 40 or 41 below], [⁴ or a shared additional pension under section 55A below] depends on contribution conditions being satisfied (either by the claimant or by some other person, according to the particular benefit).

(2) The class or classes of contribution which, for the purposes of sub-section (1) above, are relevant in relation to each of those benefits are as follows—

Short-term benefit

[⁵ . . .]
[¹ short-term incapacity benefit under section [⁶ 30A(1)(a)] below. Class 1 or 2
[⁷ . . .]

Other benefits

[⁸ Bereavement payment] Class 1, 2 or 3
Widowed mother's allowance Class 1, 2 or 3
[⁸ Widowed parent's allowance Class 1, 2 or 3
Bereavement allowance Class 1, 2 or 3]
Widow's pension Class 1, 2 or 3
Category A retirement pension Class 1, 2 or 3
Category B retirement pension Class 1, 2 or 3
Child's special allowance Class 1, 2 or 3

(3) The relevant contribution conditions in relation to the benefits specified in subsection (2) above are those specified in Part I of Schedule 3 to this Act.

(4) Part II of Schedule 3 to this Act shall have effect as to the satisfaction of contribution conditions for benefit, [⁷ . . .] in certain cases where a claim for a short-term benefit or a [⁸ bereavement payment] is, or has on a previous occasion been, made in the first or second year after that in which the contributor concerned first became liable for primary Class 1 or Class 2 contributions.

(5) In subsection (4) above and Schedule 3 to this Act—
(a) "the contributor concerned" for the purposes of any contribution condition, means the person by whom the condition is to be satisfied.
(b) "a relevant class", in relation to any benefit, means a class of contributions specified in relation to that benefit in subsection (2) above;
(c) "the earnings factor"—

(i) where the year in question is 1987–88 or any subsequent tax year, means, in relation to a person, the aggregate of his earnings factors derived from [^{12} so much of his earnings as did not exceed the upper earnings limit] upon which primary Class 1 contributions have been paid or treated as paid and from his Class 2 and Class 3 contributions; and

(ii) where the year in question is any earlier tax year, means, in relation to a person's contributions of any class or classes, the aggregate of his earnings factors derived from all those contributions;

(d) except in the expression "benefit year", "year" means a tax year.

[^{9} (5A) Where primary Class 1 contributions have been paid or treated as paid on any part of a person's earnings, the following provisions, namely—

(a) subsection (5)(c) above;

(b) sections 22(1)(a) [^{10} (2A)] and (3)(a), 23(3)(a), 24(2)(a), [^{10} 44(6) (za) and (a)] [^{11} . . .] below; and

(c) paragraphs 2(4)(a) and (5)(a), 4(2)(a), 5(2)(b) and 4(a) and 7(a) of Schedule 3 to this Act,

shall have effect as if such contributions had been paid or treated as paid on so much of the earnings as did not exceed the upper earnings limit.]

(6) In this Part of this Act "benefit year", means a period—

(a) beginning with the first Sunday in January in any calendar year, and

(b) ending with the Saturday immediately preceding the first Sunday in January in the following calendar year;

but for any prescribed purposes of this Part of this Act "benefit year" may by regulations be made to mean such other period (whether or not a period of 12 months) as may be specified in the regulations.

AMENDMENTS

1. Social Security (Incapacity for Work) Act 1994, Sch.1, para.3 (April 13, 1995).
2. Welfare Reform and Pensions Act 1999, s.70 (April 6, 2001).
3. Welfare Reform and Pensions Act 1999, Sch.8, para.31(2) (April 2, 2000).
4. Welfare Reform & Pensions Act 1999, Sch.12, para.15(16) (December 1, 2000).
5. Jobseekers Act 1995, Sch.3 (October 10, 1996).
6. Welfare Reform and Pensions Act 1999, s.88 (April 6, 2001).
7. Welfare Reform and Pensions Act 1999, Sch.8, para.31(3) & (4) (April 2, 2000).
8. Welfare Reform and Pensions Act 1999, s.70 (April 8, 2001).
9. Social Security Act 1998, Sch.7, para.61 (April 6, 1999).
10. Child Support, Pensions and Social Security Act 2000, s.35(2) (April 6, 2002).
11. Tax Credits Act 2002, Sch.6 (April 6, 2003).
12. National Insurance Contributions Act 2002, Sch.1, para.6 (April 6, 2003).

Earnings factors

22.—(1) A person shall, for the purposes specified in subsection (2) below, be treated as having annual earnings factors derived— 1.40

(a) in the case of 1987–88 or any subsequent tax year, from [^{3} so much of his earnings as did not exceed the upper earnings limit] upon which primary Class 1 contributions have been paid or treated as paid and from Class 2 and Class 3 contributions; and

   (b) in the case of any earlier tax year, from his contributions of any of
      Classes 1, 2 and 3;
but subject to the following provisions of this section and those of section
23 below.
   (2) The purposes referred to in subsection (1) above are those of—
   (a) establishing, by reference to the satisfaction of contribution condi-
      tions, entitlement to [¹ a contribution-based jobseeker's allowance or
      to] any benefit specified in section 20(1) above, other than maternity
      allowance; and
   (b) calculating the additional pension in the rate of a long-term benefit.
   [² (2A) For the purposes specified in subsection (2)(b) above, in the case
of the first appointed year or any subsequent tax year a person's earnings
factor shall be treated as derived only from [³ so much of his earnings as did
not exceed [⁴the applicable limit]] on which primary Class 1 contributions
have been paid or treated as paid.][⁵This subsection does not affect the
operation of sections 44A and 44B (deemed earnings factors).]
   [⁵ (2B) "The applicable limit" means—
   (a) in relation to a tax year before the flat rate introduction year, the
      upper earnings limit;
   (b) in relation to the flat rate introduction year or any subsequent tax
      year, the upper accrual point.]
   (3) Separate earnings factors may be derived for 1987–88 and subsequent tax years—
   (a) from earnings upon which primary Class 1 contributions have been
      paid or treated as paid.
   (b) from earnings which have been credited;
   (c) from contributions of different classes paid or credited in the same
      tax year;
   (d) by any combination of the methods mentioned in paragraphs (a) to
      (c) above,
and may be derived for any earlier tax year from contributions of different
classes paid or credited in the same tax year, and from contributions which
have actually been paid, as opposed to those not paid but credited.
   (4) Subject to regulations under section 19(4) to (6) above, no earnings
factor shall be derived—
   (a) for 1987–88 or any subsequent tax year, from earnings upon which
      primary Class 1 contributions are paid at the reduced rate, or
   (b) for any earlier tax year, from primary Class 1 contributions paid at
      the reduced rate or from secondary Class 1 contributions.
   (5) Regulations may provide for crediting—
   (a) for 1987–88 or any subsequent tax year, earnings or Class 2 or Class
      3 contributions, or
   (b) for any earlier tax year, contributions of any class,
for the purpose of bringing a person's earnings factor for that tax year to
a figure which will enable him to satisfy contribution conditions of entitlement to [¹ a contribution-based jobseeker's allowance or to] any prescribed
description of benefit (whether his own entitlement or another person's).
   [⁶ (5A) Section 23A makes provision for the crediting of Class 3 contributions for the purpose of determining entitlement to the benefits to which
that section applies.]
   (6) Regulations may impose limits with respect to the earnings factors which
a person may have or be treated as having in respect of any one tax year.

(7) The power to amend regulations made before 30th March 1977 (the passing of the Social Security (Miscellaneous Provisions) Act 1977) under subsection (5) above may be so exercised as to restrict the circumstances in which and the purposes for which a person is entitled to credits in respect of weeks before the coming into force of the amending regulations; but not so as to affect any benefit for a period before the coming into force of the amending regulations if it was claimed before 18th March 1977.

AMENDMENTS

1. Jobseekers Act 1995, Sch.2, para.22 (October 7, 1996).
2. Child Support, Pensions and Social Security Act 2000, s.30(1) (April 6, 2002).
3. National Insurance Contributions Act 2002, Sch.1, para.7 (April 6, 2002).
4. Pensions Act 2007, s.12 (September 26, 2007).
5. Pensions Act 2007, Sch.1, para.33 (September 26, 2007).
6. Pensions Act 2007, Sch.1, para.9 (September 26, 2007).

Sections 23 and 24. *Omitted because the province of the Board of Inland Revenue.* 1.41

Unemployment benefit

Unemployment benefit

[¹ Sections 25–30 repealed.] 1.42

REPEAL

1. Jobseekers Act 1995, Sch.3 (October 7, 1996).

[¹ Incapacity Benefit]

AMENDMENT

1. Sections 30A–30E were inserted by Social Security (Incapacity for Work) Act 1994, ss.1–3 (April 13, 1995).

GENERAL NOTE

A brief overview of incapacity benefit 1.43

Incapacity benefit, a contributory benefit for those incapable of work (replacing sickness and invalidity benefits), and new tests of incapacity for work for it and all aspects of the social security system other than statutory sick pay (hereinafter "SSP") and the industrial injuries scheme (see Pt XIIA, below), became operational on April 13, 1995 (hereinafter "commencement"). It may be helpful here to set out some of the background to their introduction and to give an overview of the nature of the benefit and some more detail on the range of contexts, beyond incapacity benefit, to which the new tests are applicable.

The new benefit and new tests were introduced by the Social Security (Incapacity for Work) Act 1994, which amended this Act. As always, much of the key detail is found in Regulations (see the Incapacity Benefit section of the Regulations part of the book). Significant changes to the scheme were effected from April 6, 2001 by ss.62–64 of the Welfare Reform and Pensions Act 1999 which, a year earlier, had given the "all work test"—the central distinguishing feature of the incapacity benefit regime—a new name: the "personal capability assessment". That change was part of the Labour Government's policy of "work for those who can and security for those who cannot", a change made to focus attention, for administrative rather than benefit entitlement purposes, on what people *can* do, rather than on what they cannot.

Incapacity benefit is a less generous benefit than those it replaced. Although there were no cash losers in terms of those who transferred in from sickness or invalidity benefits or SSP (in that no one received less in cash terms than he was receiving immediately prior to April 13, 1995) (see further the IWA 1994, ss.4, 7 and 12, and the IW (Transitional) Regs, below), new claimants in May 1995, incapable of work, received less generous treatment than if their incapacity and claim had been in May 1994. They only transferred to long-term incapacity benefit after a year, the allowances to compensate for the age of onset of incapacity were reduced from three to two, and the availability of additions for adult dependants was restricted. Further those receiving sickness benefit or SSP at the changeover date were less generously treated than if the old regime had continued in that, instead of being transferred to invalidity benefit after 28 weeks, they only moved on to short-term incapacity benefit, albeit at the higher rate (equivalent to the rate of SSP) and albeit that for those transferring from sickness benefit the more generous regime of increases of that benefit for adult dependents will still be applied to them. They could not become entitled to long-term incapacity benefit until 364 days have elapsed in their period of incapacity (see further IW (Transitional) Regs, below). Although some groups are exempt from it, the test of incapacity for most new claimants and a good number of transferees is the essentially medical and functional "all work" test (from April 2000, the "personal capability assessment"), applicable for most claimants at the latest after 28 weeks of incapacity (during which the "own occupation" test will apply), but for some applicable immediately. It was estimated that the switch to the "all work" test would mean that over the first two years after its introduction some 220,000 existing recipients would be denied benefit because capable of work under it, while some 55,000 new claimants, who would have qualified had the old invalidity benefit test applied, would be ruled out by it (*Hansard*, HC Vol. 253, cols 1233, 1242). The change of test has, however, not been as successful in that regard as had been envisaged.

Before examining the key conditions of entitlement to incapacity benefit, it is appropriate to set out the new structure into which it fits (assuming someone claiming for the first time on or after April 13, 1995 and continuously incapable), and to give some brief indication of the range of contexts (beyond incapacity benefit) in which the new tests are applicable. Given the significant changes effected from April 6, 2001, this overview also distinguishes between those whose period of incapacity commenced prior to that date and those newly claiming on or after that date.

There are two types, and three rates, of incapacity benefit. Short-term incapacity benefit is payable for up to one year, at the lower rate for the first 28 weeks, at a higher rate for the remainder of the period. Long-term incapacity benefit (the highest rate of incapacity benefit) is payable after 52 weeks of incapacity. (Note that short-term incapacity benefit is paid after 28 weeks at the same rate as long-term incapacity benefit where the claimant is terminally ill or receiving the highest rate of the care component of disability living allowance. See s.30B(4).)

Most people with an employer will, as under the former incapacity regime, look to SSP for the first 28 weeks, payable at a single rate from April 1995 (IWA 1994, s.8(1), below). There has been no change in the applicable test of incapacity. Thereafter, those with the requisite contribution record may look to incapacity benefit (to short-term incapacity benefit (the higher rate) for weeks 29–52 of incapacity, and to long-term incapacity benefit thereafter). The applicable test of incapacity, save for those in a protected group, is the "personal capability assessment" (formerly the "all work" test). Until April 6, 2001, those without a valid contribution record could look to SDA and/or income support, once any entitlement to SSP was exhausted. SDA was abolished as regards new claims from that date, but certain of those incapacitated before the age of 20 (or, sometimes, 25) can access short-term incapacity benefit at the higher rate without having a valid contribution record (see s.30A(1), (2A)).

Generally speaking, persons without an employer (and employees excluded from

SSP) can only turn to incapacity benefit if they have the requisite contribution record. The concession in respect of sickness and invalidity benefits for those incapacitated by industrial injury or prescribed industrial disease was not carried forward into incapacity benefit. From April 6, 2001, however, access to incapacity benefit is available without a contribution record where the person was incapacitated in youth (before 20, or, in some cases, 25) (s.30(1), (2A)). For weeks 1–28, short-term incapacity benefit at the lower rate is payable. The test of incapacity will be the "own occupation" test for those who have been engaged in remunerative work for more than eight weeks in the 21 weeks preceding the claim (s.171B). Otherwise (unless in a protected group) the "personal capability assessment" or "all-work" test (see s.171C and Pt III of the IW (General) Regs) applies. For weeks 29–52, short-term incapacity benefit at the higher rate is available, the "personal capability assessment", formerly the "all-work" test of incapacity, applying to those not in a protected group. Long-term incapacity benefit is payable thereafter, the "personal capability assessment" (formerly the "all-work" test) governing those not in a protected group.

Prior to April 6, 2001, those without an employer, but lacking the requisite contribution record, had to look to income support for both the short and long term. Title to income support would depend, inter alia, on meeting the tests of incapacity that would have been applicable were the claim for incapacity benefit. After 28 weeks, they could look instead or as well to SDA. Title to that would involve incapacity before 20 or, if older, incapacity for work plus an assessment of disablement of 80 per cent or more (see ss.68, 69). The "personal capability assessment" (formerly the "all work" test) was the test of incapacity applicable to those not in a protected group. Those newly claiming on or after April 6, 2001 can no longer get SDA. Instead, those incapacitated in youth (before 20, or in some cases 25) (see s.30A(1), (2A)), can access incapacity benefit without fulfilling the contribution conditions. Those new claimants not incapacitated in youth who lack the requisite contribution record will have to rely on income support.

The new tests of incapacity apply right across the social security system, except for industrial injuries and SSP (s.171G). So, for example, the change of regime means that entitlement to an income support disability premium based on the ground of incapacity for work, formerly linked to receipt of invalidity pension, is from April 13, 1995, linked to receipt of long-term incapacity benefit, and is thus payable only after one year, rather than, for incapacity prior to that date, after 28 weeks. The "all work" test (renamed "personal capability assessment" from April 2000) governed new claims for SDA on or after April 13, 1995, but not for those entitled to SDA prior to that date (see IW (Transitional) Regs, reg.31(3), (4), (5)(c)). The new tests also regulate entitlement to social security contributions credits.

Incapacity benefit, like its predecessors is a daily benefit, but one based on a seven day week (Sundays count). Essentially, to be entitled to incapacity benefit for a particular day (for which he would receive one-seventh of the appropriate weekly rate), a claimant must (1) meet the contribution conditions [unless he is someone incapacitated in youth (before 20 or in some cases 25) (see s.30A(1), (2A)]; (2) be incapable (or treated as incapable) of work on that day; (3) not fall foul of rules that treat him as capable; (4) not be disqualified for that day; and (5) establish that the day forms part of a period of incapacity for work.

Short-term incapacity benefit is not payable for the first three "waiting days" of incapacity in any period of incapacity for work, and eligibility for it ceases after 364 days of incapacity in the same period of incapacity. Long-term incapacity benefit is then available for any subsequent day of incapacity for work in the same period of incapacity for work on which the claimant is not over pensionable age and not disqualified from benefit. Short-term incapacity benefit at the lower rate is not taxable. Incapacity benefit at other rates is taxable.

One can thus at this juncture note two changes from the previous incapacity regime. First, the "long-term" is reached rather later: after 52 weeks rather than 28 weeks. The second change is that persons over pensionable age cannot be eligible for long-term incapacity benefit, whereas they were eligible for invalidity benefit.

Age allowances are also payable on top of long-term incapacity benefit. Like their predecessors, they compensate for inability through incapacity to make provision for the future through saving or use of the private pension or insurance markets. The earlier the age of onset, the more difficult it is to make such provision. In addition those whose long-term incapacity begins early in life may well have greater financial commitments (mortgage, children, not yet reached the peak of their earning capacity). There are two rates of allowance: the higher rate for those incapacitated below the age of 35 and the lower rate for those incapacitated between that age and the age of 45. No age allowance is payable where incapacity commenced after the age of 45 (s.30B(7); IB Regs, regs 10–13). The key matter is the age on the qualifying date, being generally the first day of the period of incapacity for work in which the claimant transferred to long-term incapacity benefit (but with due adaptation for those whose period started with SSP and with special provision with respect to widows and to members of the armed forces). There were, of course, three invalidity allowances payable as part of invalidity benefit, and the scheme compensated at varying rates the onset of incapacity from below 35 right up to five years before pensionable age. The reduction from three to two was effected to focus resources on those who had the least opportunity to make extra provision.

Additions to both short-term incapacity benefit and long-term incapacity benefit are payable in respect of both adult and (until April 2003) child dependants. Additions for children mirrored those available under the previous regime, and were only available in respect of short-term incapacity benefit at the higher rate or where the beneficiary was over pensionable age (s.80(2)(b) and (c)). Those for adult dependants are more restrictive than the old regime. An adult dependant addition to incapacity benefit is available if the claimant's dependant spouse is 60 or over. Otherwise adult dependency additions are limited to families (whether one parent or two adult) with one or more children.

Since the inception of the incapacity benefit regime, the amount of benefit payable has been subject to reduction for councillor's allowance (see s.30E). As regards most new claims on or after April 6, 2001, it is also subject to reduction for a variety of pension payments (see ss.30B(8), 30DD; IB Regulations, Pt V, regs 20–26).

On October 27, 2008, Employment and Support Allowance (ESA) came into being. This is a new benefit for persons with limited capability for work. For the moment, it coexists with IB and IS, dealing only with "new" claimants after its entry into force, while IB and/or IS deal with those who had claimed in respect of incapacity before that or were in receipt of one or both of those benefits. The intention, however, is that in due course existing IB and/or IS claimants will migrate to ESA. For more on ESA see the Welfare Reform Act 2007, set out later in the "Statutes" section of the book and Part IX of this book, which deals with the voluminous Regulations covering ESA and transitional cases.

Incapacity benefit; entitlement

1.44   **30A.**—(1) Subject to the following provisions of this section, a person who satisfies
    [[1](a) either of the conditions mentioned in subsection (2) below; or
    (b) if he satisfies neither of those conditions, each of the conditions mentioned in subsection (2A) below,]
is entitled to short-term incapacity benefit in respect of any day of incapacity for work [[1] "the relevant day"] which forms part of a period of incapacity for work.
    (2) The conditions [[1] mentioned in subsection (1)(a) above] are that—
    (a) he is under pensionable age on [[1] the relevant day] and satisfies the contribution conditions specified for short-term incapacity benefit in Schedule 3, Part I, paragraph 2; or

(b) on that day he is over pensionable age but not more than 5 years over that age, the period of incapacity for work began before he attained pensionable age, and—

    (i) he would be entitled to a Category A retirement pension if his entitlement had not been deferred or if he had not made an election under section 54(1) below, or

    (ii) he would be entitled to a Category B retirement pension by virtue of the contributions of his deceased spouse [2 or deceased civil partner], but for any such deferment or election.

[1 (2A) The conditions mentioned in subsection (1)(b) above are that—

(a) he is aged 16 or over on the relevant day;

(b) he is under the age of 20 or, in prescribed cases, 25 on a day which forms part of the period of incapacity for work;

(c) he was incapable of work throughout a period of 196 consecutive days immediately preceding the relevant day, or an earlier day in the period of incapacity for work on which he was aged 16 or over;

(d) on the relevant day he satisfies the prescribed conditions as to residence in Great Britain, or as to presence there; and

(e) he is not, on that day, a person who is receiving full-time education.]

(3) A person is not entitled to short-term incapacity benefit [1 under subsection (1)(a) above] for the first 3 days of any period of incapacity for work.

(4) In any period of incapacity for work a person is not entitled to short-term incapacity benefit for more than 364 days.

(5) Where a person ceases by virtue of subsection (4) above to be entitled to short-term incapacity benefit, he is entitled to long-term incapacity benefit in respect of any subsequent day of incapacity for work in the same period of incapacity for work on which he is not over pensionable age.

[1 (6) Regulations may provide that persons who have previously been entitled to incapacity benefit shall, in prescribed circumstances, be entitled to short-term incapacity benefit under subsection (1)(b) above notwithstanding that they do not satisfy the condition set out in paragraph (b) of subsection (2A) above.

(7) Regulations may prescribe the circumstances in which a person is or is not to be treated as receiving full-time education for the purposes of paragraph (e) of that subsection.]

AMENDMENTS

    1. Welfare Reform and Pensions Act 1999, s.64 (April 6, 2001).
    2. Civil Partnership Act 2004, s.254 and Sch.24, Pt 3, para.14 (December 5, 2005).

DEFINITIONS

    "day of incapacity for work"—see s.30C(1)(a), below.
    "pensionable age"—see s.122(1), below.
    "period of incapacity for work"—see s.30C(1)(b), (4); IB Regs, reg.6, below.
    "the relevant day"—see subs.(1).

GENERAL NOTE

    This section deals with entitlement to incapacity benefit, the contributory benefit which replaced sickness and invalidity benefits with effect from April 13, 1995. There are two types: short-term and long-term. Subss.(1)–(4) deal with the former, and subs.(5) with the latter. Subss.(1)(b), (2A), (6) and (7) deal with non-contributory access to incapacity benefit for persons incapacitated in youth. **1.45**

Subs. (1) (a)

1.46   This provides that a person who satisfies the appropriate contribution conditions set out in subs.(2), is entitled to short-term incapacity benefit for any day of incapacity for work forming part of a period of incapacity for work. "Day of" and "period of incapacity" are defined in s.30C(1) and are further commented on there. Entitlement is subject to the other provisions of this section which set the starting point of entitlement in terms of payment (after the three waiting days have been served) (subs.(3)) and the exhaustion point (364 days) (subs.(4)).

Care needs to be taken in applying these conditions in the case of someone who in the relevant period has changed gender, since Commissioner Jacobs in one such case (*CIB/2248/2006*) has disapplied the conditions to the extent necessary to enforce the claimant's EC right under Directive 79/7. He also thought the obstacles created violated ECHR rights but could give no remedy through interpretation under HRA 1998, s.3 and, as a Commissioner, had no power to issue a declaration of incompatibility under s.4 of that Act. It is as yet unclear whether the decision will be appealed.

Subs. (1) (b)

1.47   This provision, introduced from April 6, 2001, provides that someone who satisfies neither of the sets of contribution conditions referred to in subs.(2), can nonetheless gain entitlement to short-term incapacity benefit if he fulfills all of the conditions stipulated in subs.(2A), inserted from that same date. Read with the relevant regulations (IB Regulations, Pt IV, regs 14–19), those conditions identify him as someone elsewhere referred to in the scheme as a "person incapacitated in youth" (before 20 or, sometimes, 25).

Subs. (2)

1.48   This sets out the contribution conditions governing eligibility for short-term incapacity benefit. Unless he is a person incapacitated in youth (before 20 or, sometimes, 25) (see subss.(1)(b), (2A)), a claimant must have the requisite contribution record. The relevant contribution conditions must be met. Until April 6, 2001, these were essentially the same as those applied to sickness and invalidity benefits. As regards new claims on or after that date, however, for those under pensionable age a more recent connection with the world of work is required in terms of paid contributions. The requirement that the conditions actually be met thus marked a change from eligibility for sickness and invalidity benefits, where failure to satisfy the conditions was not fatal so long as incapacity was due to an industrial accident or to some prescribed industrial disease. That concession, made to compensate for the demise of injury benefit (the preferential incapacity benefit of the industrial injuries system) in 1982, was not continued because government saw it as anachronistic, an unnecessary complication in a new benefit. Only about one per cent of sickness benefit claimants had needed to use the concession and government saw income support, housing benefit and SDA as providing sufficient coverage. Note, however, that those transferring to incapacity benefit from sickness or invalidity benefit, whose title to that benefit depended on the concession, may still be protected (see IW (Transitional) Regs, regs 11, 14 and 21, below).

The contribution conditions to be satisfied vary according to whether the claimant is over or under pensionable age. They are such that both employed and self-employed earners can have access to the benefit; both primary Class 1 contributions (employed earners) and Class 2 contributions (self-employed earners) count (s.21). As regards those under pensionable age, the position has been rendered the more complicated by changes effected by s.62 of the Welfare Reform and Pensions Act 1999 as regards new claims on or after April 6, 2001, requiring a more recent connection with the world of work in terms of paid contributions; by the relaxation of the first condition afforded certain new claimants set out in regulations (IB Regulations, Pt IA, reg.2B); and by the fact that the change is not retrospective so that those whose continuing period of incapacity began before April 6, 2001 remain subject to the former condition one until that period of incapacity ends

(Welfare Reform and Pensions Act 1999 (Commencement No. 9 and Transitional and Savings Provisions Order) 2000 (SI 2000/2958), art.3(1)). And even when that period does terminate, some of those persons when claiming in a new period of incapacity for work after April 6, 2001—in principle ranking as "new" claimants subject to the "new" condition one—will be able to take advantage of the previously mentioned relaxations of that condition.

The "linking" and "continuity" rules on periods of incapacity for work (s.30C) are thus of crucial importance, here as elsewhere in the scheme. "Period of incapacity for work" marked a change from the sickness and invalidity benefit regimes which had instead been based on "period of interruption of employment" such that spells of unemployment and ones of incapacity could be linked to forge a single and long-running "period of interruption of employment", complicating the ascertainment of the relevant benefit and tax/contribution years for the purposes of the contribution conditions. The change to "period of incapacity for work", breaking that link to spells of unemployment, simplified administration. But, since some people have a better contribution record in some tax years than in others, doubtless there were gainers and losers from that change.

The *contribution conditions themselves* must now be more closely examined. Since the coming into force of the SSA 1998, those conditions are more directly relevant to appeal tribunals than in the past, although cases raising them are likely to be rare.

Prior to the implementation of the decision-making and appeals changes in that Act, whether the contribution conditions were satisfied or not, was a "Secretary of State's question" rather than a matter of decision for the AO. It was, accordingly, not as such appealable to an SSAT (SSAA 1992, s.17(1)(b), (2) set out with commentary in Bonner, Hooker and White, *Non Means Tested Benefits: The Legislation* (1999), pp.16–19). It was thought at one time that the terms of s.17 were, however, to be narrowly construed, so that while a tribunal could not properly deal with whether the claimant should have been credited with contributions *(R(U) 6/89)*, the "statutory authorities" (AO, SSAT and Commissioner) were the ones with jurisdiction over certain phrases in the contribution conditions: over establishing the date of claim ("the relevant time"), over identifying the pertinent benefit year (the one in which there falls the first day of the period of incapacity for work of which the day of claim forms part) and thus over identifying the appropriate past tax/contribution years to be considered with regard to the question (determinable by the Secretary of State and not appealable to an SSAT) of whether in the relevant tax years the requisite level of paid contributions (the first contribution condition) or paid and/or credited contributions (the second contribution condition) had been reached (see *R(G) 1/82(T)*). But the approach in *R(G) 1/82(T)* was rejected by the Court of Appeal in *Secretary of State v Scully* (reported as *R(S) 5/93*). The section (then SSA 1975, s.93) was to be read according to its "plain and natural meaning" and left it to the Secretary of State to make all determinations relevant to the contribution conditions.

After implementation of the SSA 1998 changes, whether the contribution conditions for entitlement to a benefit are met is a decision for the Secretary of State which would now seem to be appealable to an appeals tribunal as a decision made on a claim for a relevant benefit (SSA 1998, s.12) not excluded by Sch.2 to that Act or by the Decision and Appeals Regulations 1999, reg.27 and Sch.2. See further *Vol.III: Administration, Adjudication and the European Dimension.* Matters of the categorisation of earners, which class of contributions a person is liable or entitled to pay, and whether they have been paid in respect of any period, are under the Social Security (Transfer of Functions) Act 1999, s.81(1)(a)-(e), decisions for officers of the Board on Inland Revenue, thus impacting to some degree on the Secretary of State's (and thus an appeal tribunal's or a Commissioner's) decision on whether the contribution conditions are met. Note that under s.8(1)(m) of that Transfer of Functions Act, regulations can transfer further issues relating to contributions. So the decision-maker could change (see further *Vol.III: Administration, Adjudication and the European Dimension*).

What, then, do the contribution conditions stipulate? It is, to reiterate, necessary to distinguish between claimants over and under pensionable age, and, as regards the latter group, between those newly claiming on or after April 6, 2001 and those with a period of incapacity running immediately before and spanning that date.

A person over pensionable age cannot, of course, be entitled to long-term incapacity benefit (subs.(5)). But someone over (but not more than five years over) pensionable age may be eligible for short-term incapacity benefit, provided that the period of incapacity for work began before he attained pensionable age. Such a claimant must show that he would (but for deferment or an election to "de-retire") be entitled to Category A or B retirement pension (para.(b)).

As regards *a claimant under pensionable age*, see commentary to Sch.3, para.2, below.

Note the ability under para.2(8) of Sch.3 to 'relax' the rules in certain cases. The 'relaxation' rules are found in IB Regulations, reg.2B. The effect of those rules is that those protected by them are in effect subject to the first contribution condition as it stood before the April 6, 2001 changes (*i.e.* one could have paid the requisite level of contributions (25 times the year's lower earnings limit) in any tax year prior to the claim).

Similarly, as noted earlier, the changes effected by s.62 of the Welfare Reform and Pensions Act 1999 are not retrospective so that those whose continuing period of incapacity began before April 6, 2001 remain subject to the previous first contribution condition until that period of incapacity ends. Art.3(1) of the Welfare Reform and Pensions Act 1999 (Commencement No. 9 and Transitional and Savings Provisions Order) 2000 (SI 2000/2958) provides:

"Transitional provision in relation to incapacity benefit

1.49   **3.**—(1) Notwithstanding the commencement of section 62 (incapacity benefit: restriction to recent contributors), where a person is entitled to incapacity benefit by virtue of paragraph 2 of Schedule 3 to the Contributions and Benefits Act (contribution conditions for short-term incapacity benefit) on any day of incapacity for work in a period of incapacity for work beginning before 6th April 2001 which continues, whether or not by virtue of section 30C of the Contributions and Benefits Act or regulations made thereunder, on or after that date, that paragraph of that Schedule shall have effect in relation to him, in that period of incapacity for work, as if section 62 had not been commenced."

And even when that period does terminate, some of those persons when claiming in a new period of incapacity for work after April 6, 2001—in principle ranking as 'new' claimants subject to the 'new' first contribution condition— will be able to take advantage of the previously mentioned 'relaxations' of that condition.

In what appears to this commentator something of a rewriting of history, Government saw all this as restoring incapacity benefit to its originally intended clientele: those with a recent connection with the world of work. Opponents of the change characterised it in Parliament as a breach of the contributory principle, a regionally discriminatory attack on the rights of the longer-term unemployed whose unemployment might render them sick. It was also seen as hitting hard those who for health reasons moved into part-time work earning below the LEL (mainly women), before moving onto benefit as health declined. See further Bonner, "The Incapacity and Disability Provisions of the Welfare Reform and Pensions Act 1999: Work for those who can and security for those who cannot" (2000) 7 J.S.S.L. 208.

Various groups will have difficulty meeting the new contribution conditions:

   (a) *those who have never been employed*: the requirement in the first contribution condition for payment of contributions effectively excludes those who, whether through unemployment, incapacity or disability, have been unable to build a contribution record in terms of paid contributions;

   (b) *some of the long-term unemployed* (last employed in a tax year earlier than the first of the three on which the first contribution condition focuses);

(c) *very low-paid, probably part-time, employees*: those whose weekly or monthly earnings fall below the lower earnings limit for the whole or main part of the relevant tax years will not satisfy the contribution conditions since there is no liability or ability to pay Class 1 contributions where earnings fall below that limit, and, because they are in work, no Class 1 credits are generated from unemployment;

(d) *certain married women and widows paying reduced rate contributions*: these do not generate any earnings factor (and so do not count) for incapacity benefit purposes (s.22(4)).

Severe Disablement Allowance (SDA) was introduced in 1984 to cater for those incapacitated below 20, or, if incapacitated later, who were also assessed as 80 per cent disabled (see ss.68, 69). SDA was abolished on April 6, 2001 for new claims. Of course, some of the above, if incapacitated in youth (before 20 or sometimes 25) (s.30A(1)(b), (2A); IB Regulations, Pt IV, regs14–19), will be able to take advantage of the intended counter-balancing measure for those more likely than others to have been unable to build up a contribution record—the non-contributory route into incapacity benefit (see commentary to subs.(2A)). Those incapacitated, even through severe disability, later in life, will have to look to income support, with all its disability premiums, to underwrite their incapacity for work. While they may well be eligible for various components of disability living allowance, that is a benefit designed to provide for the extra costs that disability, as opposed to incapacity for work, brings with it. The transitional provisions protect existing recipients and those whose period of incapacity (without receipt of SDA) spans April 6, 2001. See further the prefatory commentary to ss.68 and 69, preserved in force for those individuals.

Subs. (2A)
This provision, dealing with non-contributory access to incapacity benefit for persons incapacitated in youth (below 20 or sometimes 25), is part of a package of measures introduced by the Welfare Reform and Pensions Act 1999 to "modernise" incapacity and disability benefits in order to direct greater help to those severely disabled people in most need. SDA has been abolished from April 6, 2001, save for existing recipients. Persons incapacitated on or after that date, if unable to access incapacity benefit because of failure to satisfy the contribution conditions, will generally have to look to income support to underwrite their incapacity for work. But this provision affords a much-improved position to those who become incapable before the age of 20 (or in certain cases 25). They will now have access to incapacity benefit (in the longer term a higher rate) despite not having a valid contribution record. The protection for those aged up to 25 is designed to help young disabled people who go into various forms of education or into vocational or work-based training. In the long term, some 175,000 people are expected to benefit (*Hansard.*, HL Vol. 604, col.832 (Baroness Hollis of Heigham).

    1.50

In effect, this subs. defines "person incapacitated in youth". It must be read with subs.(1)(b) and with a number of amplifying regulations: IB Regulations, Pt IV, regs14–19. The terms of those regulations are annotated at their location in this book.

To gain non-contributory access to incapacity benefits as a person incapacitated in youth (the term used elsewhere in the legislative scheme), a claimant must meet *all* of the stipulated conditions:

• he must be 16 or over on the day of incapacity for which he claims (para.(a));

• on one of the days in the period of incapacity for work that includes that day of claim, he must be aged below 20 or, in cases prescribed in regulations (see IB Regulations, Pt IV, reg.15), 25 (para.(b));

• he must have been incapable of work for a period of 196 consecutive days immediately preceding the day of claim or an earlier day in the period of incapacity for work on which he was aged 16 or over (para.(c));

● he must meet such conditions as to residence or presence in Great Britain as are stipulated in regulations (both residence and presence are generally required—see IB Regulations, Pt IV, reg.15) (para.(d));

● he must not be receiving relevant education on any day claimed as one of incapacity for work (para.(e)).

Pursuant to subs.(6), below, IB Regulations, Pt IV, reg.18 deals with the situation where someone has been entitled to incapacity benefit as a person incapacitated in youth, ceases to be entitled to it other than on the basis of being found not to be incapable of work, and claims again in a new period of incapacity for work (not being helped by the variety of linking rules in the scheme), but is over age (20 or 25 as the case may be) when he makes that new claim. It enables him to gain non-contributory access to short-term incapacity benefit in certain cases where his previous entitlement was terminated solely with a view to him taking up employment or training which proved to be very low paid, or in certain cases where his entitlement was terminated solely by reason of absence from Great Britain producing disqualification from benefit under s.113.

IB Regulations, Pt IV, reg.19(1) deals with those persons, aged under 20, immediately before April 6, 2001, who are entitled to SDA on or immediately before April 5, 2002, but do not qualify for incapacity benefit as a person incapacitated in youth under the "normal" provisions. The provision transfers them to long-term incapacity benefit for days of incapacity on or after April 6, 2002. Such persons are from then treated as persons incapacitated in youth and so will be eligible to rely on the help afforded by reg.18, should they leave benefit and claim in a new period of incapacity for work. Regulation 19(2) similarly transfers those aged under 20 immediately before April 6, 2001 and entitled to or receiving SDA whose continuing period of incapacity for work spans April 5, 2002.

Subs.(3)

1.51   There is no entitlement to short-term incapacity benefit, based on fulfilment of the contribution conditions rather than the "person incapacitated in youth" route, for the first three "waiting days" of any period of incapacity for work. In reality, where there is an extended period of incapacity (continuous in calendar terms, or formed of separate spells which link because they are less than eight weeks apart) the main effect of this provision is to preclude payment for these waiting days, since they count as ones of entitlement for purposes of calculating the point at which title to short-term incapacity benefit is exhausted (364 days of entitlement in any one period of incapacity), the point at which the higher rate of that benefit is payable or the point of time at which that benefit is payable at the long-term rate for those terminally ill or entitled to the highest rate of care component of DLA (in both situations after 196 days of entitlement in any one period of incapacity), and for purposes of construing references to short-term incapacity benefit at the higher rate (again after 196 days of entitlement in a single period of incapacity) (see s.30D(1), (2), below).

Note the modification to subs.(3) effected from May 5, 2003 by reg.2 of the Social Security Contributions and Benefits Act 1992 (Modifications for Her Majesty's Forces and Incapacity Benefit) Regulations 2003, below. This means that subs.(3) does not apply to someone discharged from Her Majesty's forces for whom days of sickness absence from duty (recorded by the Secretary of State for Defence) are included in calculating the number of days for which that person has been entitled to short-term incapacity benefit (see modification to s.30D [insertion of subs.(3A)], effective April 6, 2003).

Subs.(4)

1.52   This sets the point of time at which title to short-term incapacity benefit is exhausted: after 364 days of entitlement (constructed as dictated by s.30D, below) in any single period of incapacity for work (on the construction of which see s.30C, below, and IB Regs, regs 4–7, below).

Subs.(5)

This governs entitlement to long-term incapacity benefit. Where a claimant has   **1.53**
exhausted his entitlement to short-term incapacity benefit after 364 days (subs.(4)),
then he is entitled to long-term incapacity benefit in respect of any subsequent day
of incapacity for work in the same period of incapacity for work on which he is not
over pensionable age. On day and/or period of incapacity, see s.30C(1) and commentary there.

There are thus two points of difference from the sickness/invalidity benefits
regime. First, the point of transfer from short-term to long-term sick/disabled
comes much later; after 52 rather than 28 weeks. This statement in terms of weeks
is an example assuming continuous incapacity. If the period of incapacity was interspersed with spells of capacity none of which lasted more than eight weeks, thus
linking into one the apparently separate spells of incapacity, the calendar period to
exhaustion/transfer point would be longer. The second difference is that persons
over pensionable age cannot be entitled to long-term incapacity benefit, whereas
they could to invalidity benefit. But note that transferees from invalidity benefit to
long-term incapacity benefit (a transitional award), who are over pensionable age
before April 13, 1995 are protected (see IW (Transitional) Regs, reg.17(3)). Those
transferees from that benefit who attain pensionable age on or after that date cease
to be entitled to incapacity benefit (IW (Transitional) Regs, reg.17(4)).

Subs.(6)

See IB Regulations, reg.18.   **1.54**

Subs.(7)

See IB Regulations, reg.17.   **1.55**

Incapacity benefit: rate

30B.—(1) The amount payable by way of incapacity benefit in respect of   **1.56**
any day is 1/7th of the appropriate weekly rate.

(2) Subject to the following provisions of this section, the weekly rate
of short-term incapacity benefit is the lower or higher rate specified in
Schedule 4, Part I, paragraph 2.

The benefit is payable at the lower rate so specified for the first 196 days
of entitlement in any period of incapacity for work and at the higher rate so
specified thereafter.

(3) In the case of a person over pensionable age the weekly rate of short-
term incapacity benefit is, subject to subsection (4) below, that at which the
relevant retirement pension referred to in section 30A(2)(b) above would
have been payable.

But in determining that rate any increase of the following descriptions
shall be disregarded—

(a) any increase (for married people [³ or civil partners]) under section
53(2) below or (for deferred retirement) under Schedule 5 to this
Act;

(b) any increase (for dependants) under section [¹ . . .] 83 or 85 below;
and

(c) any increase (for Category A or Category B pensioners) under
section 150 of the Administration Act (annual up-rating) of the sums
mentioned in subsection (1)(e) of that section.

(4) In the case of a person who has been entitled to short-term incapacity
benefit for 196 days or more in any period of incapacity for work and—

(a) is terminally ill, or

(b) he is entitled to the highest rate of the care component of disability living allowance,

the weekly rate of short-term incapacity benefit payable, if greater than the rate otherwise payable to him under subsection (2) or (3) above, shall be equal to the rate at which long-term incapacity benefit under section 30A above would be payable to him if he were entitled to it.

For the purposes of this subsection a person is terminally ill if he suffers from a progressive disease and his death in consequence of that disease can reasonably be expected within 6 months.

(5) References to short-term incapacity benefit at the higher rate shall be construed as including short-term incapacity benefit payable to any person who has been entitled to that benefit for 196 days or more in a period of incapacity for work, notwithstanding that the rate of benefit is determined in accordance with subsection (3) or (4) above.

(6) Subject as follows, the weekly rate of long-term incapacity benefit under section 30A above is that specified in Schedule 4, Part I, paragraph 2A.

(7) Regulations may provide that if a person is, on the qualifying date in relation to a period of incapacity for work, under such age as may be prescribed, the rate of long-term incapacity benefit under section 30A above payable to him in respect of any day in that period shall be increased by such amount as may be prescribed.

For this purpose "the qualifying date" means the first day of the period of incapacity for work or such earlier day as may be prescribed.

[² (8) This section has effect subject to sections 30DD (reduction for pension payments) and section 30E (reduction for councillor's allowance) below).]

AMENDMENTS

1. Tax Credits Act 2002, Sch.6 (April 6, 2003).
2. Welfare Reform and Pensions Act 1999, Sch.8, para.22 (April 6, 2001).
3. Civil Partnership Act 2004, s.254 and Sch.24, Pt 3, para.15 (December 5, 2005).

DEFINITIONS

"entitled"—see s.122(1), below.
"pensionable age"—*ibid.*
"prescribed"—*ibid.*
"qualifying date"—see subs.(7).
"terminally ill"—see subs.(4).

GENERAL NOTE

Subs. (1)

1.57   Like its predecessors, incapacity benefit is a daily benefit. Unlike sickness and invalidity benefits, however, which were based on a six day week, incapacity benefit emulates SSP and income support and is based on a seven day week (Sundays now count). Hence the daily rate is one seventh of the appropriate weekly rate.

Subs. (2)

1.58   Being "subject to the following provisions of this section", including subs.(3) which deals with the rate of short-term incapacity benefit for those *over* pensionable age, this subsection sets the normally applicable (see subss.(3)–(5)) weekly rate of short-term incapacity benefit for those *under* that age. There are two rates: (i) the lower rate, which is payable for the first 196 days of entitlement in any period of incapacity for work; and (ii) the higher rate, payable for any subsequent day of entitlement in that same period of incapacity for work. The amounts are those specified in Sched.4, Pt I, para.2, below. On determining days of entitlement, see s.30D, below. On constructing periods of incapacity for work, see s.30C, IB Regs, regs 4–7, and IW (Transitional) Regs, regs 2–4, below.

Subs. (3)

This sets the rate of short-term incapacity benefit for claimants *over* pensionable age. It is normally payable (see subs.(4)) at the same rate as the retirement pension that would otherwise have been payable to the claimant. However, as with the benefits it replaced, this rate of short-term incapacity benefit does not include the increases of pension listed in paras (a)–(c) of this subsection: increases for married women, deferred retirement, dependants or guaranteed minimum pension. **1.59**

Subs. (4)

This provides for departure from the norm set by subss.(2) and (3) in the case of those who have been entitled to short-term incapacity benefit for 196 or more days in a single period of incapacity for work, and are *either* (a) terminally ill, *or* (b) entitled to the highest rate care component of DLA. For this purpose, someone is terminally ill if he is suffering from a progressive disease and his death in consequence of it can reasonably be expected within six months (the same definition as for attendance allowance and DLA purposes). In these situations the rate payable is one equivalent to that for long-term incapacity benefit (set by subs.(6)). The words "payable to him if he were entitled to it" are there to cover such persons over pensionable age, since they could not be entitled to long-term incapacity benefit (see s.30A(5), above). The words "if greater than the rate otherwise payable to him under subss.(2) or (3) above" may appear confusing, since for claimants *under* pensionable age the rate set by this subsection (one equivalent to the rate of long-term incapacity benefit normally only applicable after 364 days of entitlement: see s.30A(5), above)), will inevitably be greater than the otherwise applicable higher rate of short-term incapacity benefit set by subs.(2), since the rate for long-term incapacity benefit is the highest rate of incapacity benefit. The wording is there to enable those over pensionable age to receive the more beneficial in monetary terms of either the rate set by this subsection or that set by reference to retirement pension by subs.(3). **1.60**

On determining days of entitlement see s.30D, below. On constructing periods of incapacity for work, see s.30C, IB Regs, regs 4–7, and IW (Transitional) Regs, regs 2–4, below.

Subs. (5)

This provides that references to "short-term incapacity benefit at the higher rate" (payable after 196 days of entitlement) include the rates payable beyond that 196 days to those over pensionable age (set by subs.(2)), to the terminally ill and to those receiving the highest rate of care component of DLA (the latter two set by subs.(4)). It ensures that all claimants are eligible to benefit from the longer linking rules in respect of disability working allowance (see s.30C(5), below) and training for work (see s.30C(6), below). **1.61**

Subss. (6), (7)

The basic weekly rate of long-term incapacity benefit is set by subs.(6), being the amount specified in Sch.4, Pt I, para.2A, below. But subs.(7) enables the making of regulations to allow for age related increases to that rate to be payable to a claimant under a prescribed age on the qualifying date in a period of incapacity for work (thus creating an equivalent of invalidity allowance in the invalidity benefit system). For this purpose, "the qualifying date" is the first day of the period of incapacity for work in which the claimant transferred to long-term incapacity benefit or such *earlier* date as may be prescribed in regulations. On constructing periods of incapacity for work, see s.30C, IB Regs, regs 4–7, and IW (Transitional) Regs, regs 2–4, below. **1.62**

The regulations dealing with the matter of age-related increases are the IB Regs, regs 10–13, below. Like their predecessors, invalidity allowances, these age-related increases compensate for inability through incapacity to make provision for the future through saving or use of the private pension or insurance markets. The earlier the age of onset, the more difficult it is to make such provision. In addition those whose long-term incapacity begins early in life may well have greater financial commitments (mortgage, children, not yet reached the peak of their earning capacity). There are two rates of increase: the higher rate for those incapacitated below the age of 35 and the lower rate for those incapacitated between that age and the age of 45 (reg.10). No age-related increase is payable where incapacity commenced after the age of 45. There were, of course, three invalidity allowances payable as part of invalidity benefit, and the scheme compensated at varying rates the onset of incapacity from below the age of 35 right up to five years before pensionable age (see the former SSCBA 1992, s.34 on pp.152–153 of Bonner, Hooker and White, *Non-Means Tested Benefits: The Legislation (1994)*). The reduction from three to two was effected to focus resources on those who had the least opportunity to make extra provision. It was thought that those incapacitated later in life (after 45) would have had plenty of time to build up provision and would often have savings or income from an occupational pension, although with respect to the latter, the proportion who did was hardly encouraging in this regard.

As stated above, the qualifying date is normally the first day of the period of incapacity for work in which the claimant transferred to long-term incapacity benefit. Where part of that period is made up of entitlement to statutory sick pay (s.30D(3), IB Regs, reg.7), the qualifying date will be the first day in that relevant period of SSP entitlement (IB Regs, reg.11). IB Regs, reg.12 provides that if the qualifying date would have been earlier than that ascertained by the normal method in subs.(7) but for the fact that the person was on that earlier date a serving member of the forces, then that earlier date is the qualifying date. For the definition of "serving member of the forces", see IB Regs, reg.12(2) modifying the definition in reg.1(2) of the Social Security (Contributions) Regulations 1979. An earlier qualifying date can also apply for certain widows entitled to a widow's allowance (IB Regs, reg.13).

After the introduction of ESA, the amounts of these additions have begun gradually to be reduced, starting in April 2009. As noted earlier in the introduction to incapacity benefit, the governmental intention is that all IB claimants, and those on IS because of incapacity for work, will in due course migrate to ESA. The Government intends to move to a system where all claimants claiming incapacity benefits receive the same amount of benefit. So as to prevent the differences widening for IB claimants with an age addition, the up-rating arrangements have been modified so that the order made under s.150 of the SSAA 1992 may reduce certain amounts (see Employment and Support Allowance (Up-rating Modification) (Transitional) Regulations 2008 (SI 2008/3270), reg.2 (January 20, 2009)).

Subs. (8)

1.63   This emphasises that the rate payable under this section is subject to reduction for a variety of pension payments (see s.30DD and the IB Regs, Pt V, regs20–26) and councillor's allowance (see s.30E). See further the notes to those provisions.

Incapacity benefit: days and periods of incapacity for work

1.64   **30C.**—(1) For the purposes of any provisions of this Act relating to incapacity benefit, subject to the following provisions and save as otherwise expressly provided—

(a) a day of incapacity for work means a day on which a person is incapable of work;

(b) a period of incapacity for work means a period of 4 or more consecutive days, each of which is a day of incapacity for work; and

(c) any two such periods not separated by a period of more than 8 weeks shall be treated as one period of incapacity for work.

(2) Any day which falls within the maternity allowance period (as defined in section 35(2) below) shall be treated for the purposes of any provision of this Act relating to incapacity benefit as a day of incapacity for work unless the woman is disqualified for receiving a maternity allowance for that day by virtue of regulations under section 35(3)(a) below.

(3) Regulations may make provision (subject to the preceding provisions of this section) as to the days which are or are not to be treated as days of incapacity for work for the purposes of any provision of this Act relating to incapacity benefit.

(4) The Secretary of State may by regulations provide—

(a) that paragraph (b) of subsection (1) above shall have effect as if the reference there to 4 consecutive days were to such lesser number of days, whether consecutive or not, within such period of consecutive days as may be prescribed; and

(b) that paragraph (c) of that subsection shall have effect as if for the reference to 8 weeks there were substituted a reference to such larger number of weeks as may be prescribed.

[¹ (5) Where a person claims the higher rate of short-term incapacity benefit, or long-term incapacity benefit, under section 30A above for a period commencing after he has ceased to be in qualifying remunerative work (within the meaning of Part 1 of the Tax Credits Act 2002) and—

(a) the day following that on which he so ceased was a day of incapacity for work for him,

(b) he has been entitled to the higher rate of short-term incapacity benefit, or to long-term incapacity benefit, under section 30A above within the period of two years ending with that day of incapacity for work, and

(c) he satisfied the relevant tax credit conditions on the day before he so ceased,

every day during that period on which he satisfied those conditions is to be treated for the purposes of the claim as a day of incapacity for work for him.

(5A) A person satisfies the relevant tax credit conditions on a day if–

(a) he is entitled for the day to the disability element of working tax credit (on a claim made by him or by him jointly with another) or would be so entitled but for the fact that the relevant income (within the meaning of Part 1 of the Tax Credits Act 2002) in his or their case is such that he is not so entitled, and

(b) either working tax credit or any element of child tax credit other than the family element is paid in respect of the day on such a claim.]

(6) Where—

(a) a person becomes engaged in training for work, and

(b) he was entitled to the higher rate of short-term incapacity benefit, or to long-term incapacity benefit under section 30A above, for one or more of the 56 days immediately before he became so engaged, and

(c) the first day after he ceases to be so engaged is for him a day of incapacity for work and falls not later than the end of the period of two years beginning with the last day for which he was entitled to such benefit,

any day since that day in which he was engaged in training for work shall be treated for the purposes of any claim for such benefit for a period commencing after he ceases to be so engaged as having been a day of incapacity for work.

In this subsection "training for work" means training for work in pursuance of arrangements made under section 2(1) of the Employment and Training Act 1973 or section 2(3) of the Enterprise and New Towns (Scotland) Act 1990 or training of such other description as may be prescribed.

(7) For the purposes of this section "week" means any period of 7 days.

AMENDMENT

1. Tax Credits Act 2002, Sch.3, para.5(2) (April 6, 2003).

DEFINITIONS

"day of incapacity for work"—see subs.(1)(a).
"maternity allowance period"— see s.35(2), below.
"period of incapacity for work"—see subss.(1)(b), (c); (4); IB Regs, reg.6, below.
"training for work"—see subs.(6) and IB Regs, reg.3.
"week"—see subs.(7).

GENERAL NOTE

Subs. (1)

1.65 Short-term incapacity benefit is only payable "for any day of incapacity for work which forms part of a period of incapacity for work" (s.30A(1)). Long-term incapacity benefit is only payable after 364 days of entitlement to short-term incapacity benefit "in any period of incapacity for work" (s.30A(4)) in respect of "any subsequent day of incapacity for work" (s.30A(5)). This subsection sets out definitions of "day of incapacity for work" and "period of incapacity for work", definitions which apply for any purposes of the SSCBA 1992 relating to incapacity benefit. But this is both "subject to the following provisions" of this section and "save as otherwise expressly provided", thus enabling departures from the standard position set out in this subsection and noted here.

1.66 *Para. (a): "day of incapacity for work":* This means a day on which a person is incapable of work. "Day" is not defined, but was taken for unemployment benefit purposes (see *R(U) 4/71*) and was regarded for purposes of sickness and invalidity benefits (see annotation to SSCBA 1992, s.57(1)(a), as in force prior to April 13, 1995—see p.187 of Bonner, Hooker and White, *Non Means Tested Benefits: The Legislation* (1994)) as the period midnight to midnight. That this is still so is borne out by the carrying forward of special provision for nightworkers (IB Regs, reg.5) and the provision treating someone incapable of work for part of a day as incapable throughout that day (so long as he does no work other than permitted work) (see IW (General) Regs, regs 15–17).

Whether someone is "incapable of work" is to be determined in accordance with the provisions of Pt XIIA of the SSCBA 1992, headed "Incapacity for Work" (see s.171A(1), below, and commentary there and cross-reference to the provisions of and commentary on the IW (General) Regs). Note that those provisions apply, not just for incapacity benefit, but for the whole of the social security system other than SSP or industrial injuries benefits (s.171G(1), below).

See further subs.(2) treating days within the maternity allowance period as ones of incapacity for work.

1.67 *Para. (b): "period of incapacity for work": the "continuity" rule:* This provides that a period of incapacity for work (PIW) consists of a period of four or more consecutive days of incapacity for work. The effect of the rule is to preclude entitlement for very small spells of incapacity for work: a claimant must be able to group his spells of incapacity in the manner specified. A similar rule applies for SSP purposes (see s.152(2)) and a similar concept was deployed for purposes of sickness and invalidity benefits (see s.57(1)(d), (e) as in force prior to April 13, 1995—see p.180 of Bonner, Hooker and White, *Non Means Tested Benefits: The Legislation* (1994)). Note, however, that in contrast to sickness and invalidity benefits, Sundays now count in determining consecutive days and days of incapacity, just as they do for SSP. A modified version of the continuity rule (two days of incapacity within a period of seven consecutive days) applies for certain persons receiving certain regular treatments (e.g. chemotherapy) by virtue of subs.(4)(a) and IB Regs, reg.6, noted in the commentary to sub.(4)(a), below.

Para.(c): the "linking" rule: This requires that any two PIWs as identified by the continuity rule (whether in its standard or modified form) be "linked", that is be treated as one PIW, where they are not separated by more than eight weeks, counting the separation period from the end of the first PIW. "Week" means any period of seven days (subs.(7)). The single PIW thus formed by the operation of the linking rule must similarly be linked to any other PIW (as identified by the normal and/or modified continuity rule) not more than eight weeks from it, and thus a single PIW will continue to grow until there are no more PIWs to link with or any that exist are more than eight weeks away. So a single PIW might consist of a continuous spell of incapacity for work. Or it might be formed of several apparently separate spells, each interspersed with a spell of employment so long as the spells of employment lasted less than eight weeks. The linking rule thus gives a claimant a small incentive to try out employment knowing that he will be able to return to his previous rate of incapacity benefit should that employment not last for more than eight weeks.

1.68

Because of subs.(2), days within the maternity allowance period are treated as ones of incapacity for work unless the woman is disqualified for receiving a maternity allowance for those days, so that a spell of entitlement to maternity allowance within eight weeks of a PIW would not "break" that PIW, but would "link" with it and become part of it, so that if not more than eight weeks after the end of that spell of entitlement to maternity allowance the person again became incapacitated, the PIW then formed by the continuity rule would not be a new one, but would be part of the previous PIW.

Under the sickness and invalidity benefits regime, of course, periods of incapacity identified by the then continuity rule, formed "a period of interruption of employment" (PIE) as did certain spells of unemployment. Thus, under that regime, a period of incapacity for work forming a PIE, followed by a period of unemployment, of whatever length, forming a PIE, would "link", so that a period of incapacity immediately (or no more than eight weeks) after such a spell of unemployment would link with the earlier period of incapacity. So that, for example, someone on invalidity benefit prior to a twelve week spell of unemployment, would, when incapacitated after that spell, resume entitlement to invalidity benefit. The position is very different under the incapacity benefit regime. There is now no link with a period of interruption of employment formed of days of unemployment (something designed to simplify administration) and unemployment benefit itself disappeared in October 1996. So, someone on long-term incapacity benefit (the replacement for invalidity benefit), who becomes capable of work and is unemployed for a period of more than eight weeks before again becoming incapacitated, will not be able to link the two PIWs identified by the incapacity benefit continuity rule; they are more than eight weeks apart. He will be eligible only for short-term incapacity benefit at the lower rate. In principle, of course, the same is true of those on incapacity benefit who become employed or move into training for work (the better to enhance prospects of returning to the labour market by acquiring occupational or vocational skills) for more than the eight week permitted gap. But note subs.(5), below, which provides a more generous two year linking rule for those receiving short-term incapacity benefit at the higher rate or on long-term incapacity benefit who move into work and receive a relevant tax credit in consequence of such receipt, enabling them to return to that rate of incapacity benefit on leaving their job, without having to serve again the relevant qualifying period appropriate to that rate. Note also subs. (6) which similarly provides a two year linking rule for such persons who have moved from those rates of incapacity benefit into certain training for work, rather than into work and onto a relevant tax credit.

Aside from its impact on contributions questions, this concept of linking is important to the application of the "waiting days" rule (s.30A(3), above): they only have to be served once in a single period of incapacity for work. This is of great assistance to the claimant intermittently incapable of work for short spells satisfying the continuity and linking rules and thus forming a single PIW. Without the linking rule the impact on such a claimant of the waiting days rule would be very harsh: he would have to serve the waiting days each time, and so, if incapable of work for four days each time, would only be eligible for one day's benefit. Linking, and through it identifying whether this ostensibly separate PIW is in fact part of an earlier one, is also crucial to identifying the point of time at which a claimant moves from one rate of short-term incapacity benefit to another (after 196 days of entitlement in any PIW: s.30B(2), above) or from short-term incapacity benefit to long-term incapacity benefit (after 364 days of entitlement in a single PIW: s.30A(4)).48

In *Chief Adjudication Officer v Astle* (Court of Appeal, judgment of March 17,1999 available on LEXIS, noted in [1999] 6 J.S.S.L. 203), the Court of Appeal considered generally the concept "period of incapacity for work" and its role in the legislation governing entitlement to incapacity benefit (SSCBA 1992, ss.30A–C). It examines more specifically the concept's application where the claimant has two spells of undoubted incapacity (spells when the claimant satisfies the test of incapacity—in this case the "all work" test) separated by a spell of undoubted capacity for work (a spell when he does not satisfy that test). In short, the decision focuses on the proper construction of SSCBA 1992, s.30(C)(1)(c) (the "linking" rule). As Sir Christopher Staughton put it in his judgment:

> "The issue in this present appeal is, in broad terms, whether Mr Astle should have incapacity benefit for those days when, let it be assumed, he does not have the necessary degree of disablement to entitle him to benefit, if those days are sandwiched between periods when, let it be assumed, he does suffer that degree of disablement. . . . Mr Astle . . . asserts that for on average seven days a month he is severely handicapped; and his claim is that he should have [incapacity] benefit continuously."

The Court of Appeal's answer is that where two spells of incapacity satisfying the "continuity" rule (SSCBA 1992, s.30C(1)(b)), and being no more than eight weeks apart, are treated as one period of incapacity for work under the "linking" rule (applied to defeat the claim in *R(IB) 1/07*), no entitlement to incapacity benefit arises in respect of the days sandwiched between those two periods merely because of their location in the sandwich: the maximum eight week separation period is not thereby accorded the status of "period of incapacity for work". A "period of incapacity for work" must be composed of days of incapacity according to the applicable tests of incapacity and relevant "deemed incapacity" rules.

Subs. (2)

1.69   This takes into the new scheme a provision which also formed part of the previous regime (see s.57(2) as in force prior to April 13, 1995—see p.180 of Bonner, Hooker and White, *Non Means Tested Benefits: The Legislation* (1994)). Any day within the maternity allowance period (as defined in s.35(2), below) is to be treated for the purposes of incapacity benefit as a day of incapacity for work, unless the woman is disqualified for receiving a maternity allowance for that day by virtue of regulations made under s.35(3)(a), below (currently Maternity Allowance Regulations, reg.2, below). The effect of the subsection is noted in the commentary on subs.(1), above.

Subs.(3)

On days which are *not* to be treated as ones of incapacity, see IB Regs, reg.4, below, ruling out days of no claim, days of late claim not saved by the good cause exception, or late claims so saved but ruled out by the 12 month limit; days of disqualification for absence from Great Britain or imprisonment or detention in legal custody, if the disqualification exceeds six weeks; and days of attendance at certain training courses in respect of which the person is paid a training allowance. The "training course" exclusion does not apply for purposes of any claim for incapacity benefit for a period beginning after he has ceased attending such a course, nor in calculating a period of continuous incapacity for work for purposes of reg.2 of the Persons Abroad Regs. On days to be treated as ones of incapacity, see IB Regs, reg.4A (SSP and persons incapacitated in youth) and reg.5 (nightworkers).

1.70

Subs.(4)

Para.(a): See IB Regs, reg.6, below. This provides a modification of the general four day rule in subs.(1)(b) to assist claimants who are incapable of work for lesser spells consisting of days of incapacity which result from regular weekly treatment by way of haemodialysis for chronic renal failure or peritoneal dialysis for chronic renal failure; or from treatment by way of plasmapheresis, by way of parenteral chemotherapy with cytotoxic drugs, anti-tumour agents or immunosuppressive drugs or by way of radiotherapy; or from regular weekly treatment by way of total parenteral nutrition for gross impairment of enteric function. In such cases any two days of incapacity on such grounds within a period of seven consecutive days will constitute a period of incapacity for work. This modification in practice assists to get benefit such claimants who are capable of work on the days on which they are not receiving or on which they are recovering from such treatment, who would otherwise be precluded by the four or more consecutive days rule. Consequent receipt of benefit in such periods thus compensates to some extent for any loss of earnings or profits because of the days of treatment.

Note further in a different context IW (General) Regs, reg.13, below, providing other relief from otherwise applicable rules on incapacity for work for persons receiving such treatment, both on the day(s) of treatment and during a week in which such a day occurs.

1.71

Para.(b): This confers power to prescribe in regulations a linking period larger than eight weeks. See IB Regulations, reg.5A, below.

1.72

Subss.(5), (5A)

As indicated in the commentary on subs.(1), above, these afford a more generous (up to two years) linking rule for a claimant who was in receipt of a relevant tax credit on the basis that the higher rate of short-term incapacity benefit or long-term incapacity benefit was payable to him. It makes parallel provision to that which applied to invalidity benefit prior to April 13, 1995 (see s.33(7) as in force immediately prior to that date—see p.148 of Bonner, Hooker and White, *Non Means Tested Benefits: The Legislation* (1994)). It provides that where the first day after his ceasing to be engaged in remunerative work is one of incapacity for work, and is no more than two years away from a previous day of entitlement to incapacity benefit (whether long-term or short-term at the higher rate), then any day in that period falling within a week in which he was entitled to a relevant tax credit, is to be treated as one of incapacity for work for the purposes of a claim to incapacity benefit for the period after he ceased work. In short, it enables such a person to return to his pre-tax credit rate of incapacity benefit without having to serve the relevant qualifying period for it. It is as if he had never left it. For the purposes of incapacity benefit, nothing has been lost by trying out low-paid work supplemented by a relevant tax credit.

Note, however, that in respect of someone who claims the higher rate of

1.73

shortterm incapacity benefit, or long term incapacity benefit on or before
6th April 2005 section 30C has effect as if, after subsection (5A) there were
inserted—

"(5B) A person also satisfies the relevant tax credit conditions on any day before
7th April 2003 if that day falls within a week for which he is entitled to a disabled
person's tax credit."

See Tax Credits Act 2002 (Commencement No. 4, Transitional Provisions and
Savings) Order (SI 2003/962), Art 5(2).

In *R(S) 1/02*, Commissioner Rowland considered the meaning of subsection (5)
(a): "where a person who is engaged and normally engaged in remunerative work
ceases to be so engaged", in particular the phrase "engaged and normally engaged
in remunerative work". He noted:

"that phrase is precisely the same phrase that appears in section 129(1)(a) and
I do not consider that to be an accident. It seems plain that sections 30C(5) and
68(10) are designed to have effect when a person is no longer entitled to claim
disability working allowance and that the phrase "engaged and normally engaged
in remunerative work" is to be given much the same meaning in those sections as
it has in section 129." (para.9)

The Commissioner then set out reg.6 of the Disability Working Allowance
(General) Regulations 1991 (then covering DPTC), and continued:

"Regulation 6 of the 1991 Regulations is expressed as being made only for the
purposes of Part VII of the 1992 Act in which falls section 129. It does not,
therefore, have direct application to sections 30C(5) and 68(10) and it is drafted
on the assumption that there is a current claim for disability working allowance.
Nevertheless, it is part of the statutory context in which I must determine the
appeals before me.

Having regard to that context, I am satisfied that, for the purposes of sections
30C(5) and 68(10), a person who is incapable of work (which is, of course, a
condition of entitlement to incapacity benefit or severe disablement allowance)
and who is not actually working has ceased to be 'engaged . . . in remunerative
work'. The legislation does not require that the claimants have ceased normally
to be engaged in such work but, in any event, in the present cases, the cessation
was permanent, even though the claimants and their employees may initially have
hoped that it would not be, and so the claimants had also ceased to be 'normally
engaged in remunerative work'" (paras 11, 12).

Subs.(6)

1.74   This makes analogous provision to subs.(5) in respect of those whose route was
from incapacity benefit (long-term or short-term at the higher rate) into "training
for work" rather than into work and onto a relevant tax credit. It protects not only
those who move immediately from incapacity benefit into such training, but also
those who do so within 55 days after last being entitled to incapacity benefit. Should
such persons cease to be so engaged, and the first day after doing so is one of incapacity for work not more than two years since his last pre-training day of incapacity,
then they will be eligible to move onto their pre-training rate of incapacity benefit
without having to serve the appropriate qualifying period. Once again, it is as if
they had never left. For the purposes of incapacity benefit, nothing has been lost by
moving into such training.

Here, "training for work" means either (i) training for work in pursuance of
arrangements made under s.2(1) of the Employment and Training Act 1973 or
s.2(3) of the Enterprise and New Towns (Scotland) Act 1990, or (ii) training of
such other description as may be prescribed in regulations. As to (i), examples given
in Parliament were Employment Rehabilitation, Community Action and North
Norfolk Action (*Hansard*, HL Vol.554, col.1465). As to (ii), IB Regs, reg.3 pro-

vides that for the purposes of this subsection "training for work" also includes any training received on a course which a person attends for 16 hours or more a week, where the primary purpose of the course is the teaching of occupational or vocational skill. This brings into the ambit of the provision a range of non-government training courses.

Incapacity benefit: construction of references to days of entitlement

30D.—(1) The following provisions have effect in calculating for the purposes of— 1.75

(a) section 30A(4) above (length of entitlement to short-term incapacity benefit),

(b) section 30B(2) above (period after which short-term incapacity benefit is payable at higher rate),

(c) section 30B(4) above (period after which incapacity benefit is payable at long-term rate in case of terminal illness), and

(d) section 30B(5) above (construction of references to short-term incapacity benefit at the higher rate),

the number of days for which a person has been entitled to short-term incapacity benefit.

(2) There shall be included—

(a) the first three days of the period of incapacity for work, and

(b) in the case of a woman, any days for which she was entitled to maternity allowance.

(3) There shall also be included such days as may be prescribed in respect of which a person was entitled to statutory sick pay, and on the first of which he satisfied the contribution conditions for short-term incapacity benefit.

(4) There shall be excluded any days in respect of which a person was disqualified for receiving incapacity benefit.

GENERAL NOTE

Obviously, it goes without saying that actual days of entitlement to short-term incapacity benefit (see s.30A(1)) count for the purpose of determining the number of days someone has been entitled to short-term incapacity benefit. This section deals further with calculating, for a number of purposes, the number of days for which a person has been entitled to short-term incapacity benefit by providing that certain days which would not appear to be ones of entitlement to that benefit, in law count as such, and also providing, perhaps for the avoidance of doubt, that days that might otherwise appear to be ones of entitlement to it, do not so rank. 1.76

According to subs.(1), the other provisions of this section affect calculation for the following purposes: (1) determining the point at which title to short-term incapacity benefit is exhausted (after 364 days of entitlement in any period of incapacity for work (PIW): see s.30A(4), above); (2) determining the period after which short-term incapacity benefit is payable at the higher rate (after 196 days of entitlement in any single PIW: see s.30B(2), above); (3) determining the period after which short-term incapacity benefit is payable at a rate equivalent to the long-term rate in cases of terminal illness or entitlement to the highest rate of care component of disability living allowance (after 196 days of entitlement in any one PIW: see s.30B(4), above); and (4) construing references in the legislation to the term "short-term incapacity benefit at the higher rate" (see s.30B(5), above).

Days included by virtue of this section

1.77   For these purposes, subs.(2) provides that one includes as days of entitlement the three waiting days in any PIW (despite s.30A(3) which says one is not entitled to benefit for those days) and, for women, days of entitlement to maternity allowance.

Subs.(3) empowers the making of regulations to rank as ones of entitlement for the purposes set out in subs.(1), days in respect of which the claimant was entitled to statutory sick pay (SSP), being (a) the day of entitlement to SSP on which he satisfied the contribution conditions for short-term incapacity benefit and (b) days of entitlement to SSP subsequent to that day. IB Regs, reg.7 provides the detail here. It covers specified days of entitlement to SSP falling on or after the day on which the claimant satisfied those contribution conditions and falling within a period of entitlement to SSP as between him and his employer ending not more than 57 days before the first day of the PIW for incapacity benefit purposes to which the calculation relates (para.(1)). The specified days are each day of any week in which the employer was liable to pay the claimant SSP at the weekly rate set out in s.157(1) and, in any week in which the employer was only liable to pay SSP at a fraction of that weekly rate, each of the days of that week which would comprise the same fraction of a seven day week (para.(2)). Fractions of days produced by this part-week calculation are to be carried forward into the calculation for the following week and for any fraction of a day not so accounted for at the end of any SSP period of entitlement, one extra day is to be added (para.(2)).

Note that with effect from April 6, 2003, this section was modified by reg.3 of the Social Security Contributions and Benefits Act 1992 (Modifications for Her Majesty's Forces and Incapacity Benefit) Regulations 2003, below. The modification inserts a new subs.(3A) so that in respect of someone discharged from Her Majesty's forces after May 3, 2003, such days as are prescribed shall also be included in the calculation of days for which he has been entitled to short-term incapacity benefit. See also annotation to s.30A(3).

Days excluded by this section

1.78   Subs.(4) stipulates that days in respect of which the person was disqualified from receiving incapacity benefit are not to count, for the purposes in sub.(1), as days of entitlement to it.

[¹ Incapacity benefit: reduction for pension payments [² and PPF periodic payments]

1.79   **30DD.**— [²(1) Where—
(a) a person is entitled to incapacity benefit in respect of any period of a week or part of a week,
(b) there is—
  (i) a pension payment;
  (ii) a PPF periodic payment; or
  (iii) any combination of the payments specified in sub-paragraphs (i) and (ii) above,
  payable to him in respect of that period (or a period which forms part of that period or includes that period or part of it), and
(c) the amount of the payment or payments (or, as the case may be, the amount which in accordance with regulations is to be taken as payable to him by way of pension payments or PPF periodic payments in respect of that period), when taken together exceeds the threshold,
the amount of that benefit shall be reduced by an amount equal to 50 per cent. of that excess.]

(2) In subsection (1) above "the threshold" means—

(a) if the period in question is a week, £85 or such greater amount as may be prescribed; or

(b) if that period is not a week, such proportion of the amount mentioned in paragraph (a) as falls to be calculated in accordance with regulations on such basis as may be prescribed.

(3) Regulations may secure that a person of any prescribed description does not suffer any reduction under subsection (1) above in any amount of incapacity benefit to which he is entitled.

(4) Regulations may provide—

(a) for sums of any specified description to be disregarded for the purposes of this section;

(b) for sums of any specified description to be treated for those purposes as payable to persons as pension payments [²or PPF periodic payments] (including, in particular, sums in relation to which there is a deferred right of receipt);

(c) for the aggregation of sums of any specified description which are payable as pension payments [²or PPF periodic payments] (or treated as being so payable) in respect of the same or different periods;

(d) for such sums or aggregate sums to be apportioned between or otherwise allocated to periods in respect of which persons are entitled to incapacity benefit.

(5) In this section "pension payment" means—

(a) a periodical payment made in relation to a person under a personal pension scheme or, in connection with the coming to an end of an employment of his, under an occupational pension scheme or a public service pension scheme;

(b) a payment of any specified description, being a payment made under an insurance policy providing benefits in connection with physical or mental illness, disability, infirmity or defect; or

(c) a payment of any other specified description;

and "specified" means prescribed by or determined in accordance with regulations under this section.

(6) For the purposes of subsection (5) "occupational pension scheme", "personal pension scheme" and "public service pension scheme" each have the meaning given by section 1 of the Pension Schemes Act 1993, except that "personal pension scheme" includes a contract or trust scheme approved under Chapter III of Part XIV of the Income and Corporation Taxes Act 1988 (retirement annuities).]

AMENDMENTS

1. Inserted by Welfare Reform and Pensions Act 1999, s.63 (April 6, 2001).

2. Pensions Act 2004 (PPF Payments and FAS Payments) (Consequential Provisions) Order 2006 (SI 2006/343), art.2, Sch., para.1 (February 14, 2006).

DEFINITIONS

"occupational pension scheme"—see subs.(6).
"pension payment"—see subs.(5).
"personal pension scheme"—see subs.(6).
"PPF periodic payments"—see s.122(1).
"public service pension scheme"—see subs.(6).

"specified"—see subs.(5).
"the threshold"—see subs.(2).

GENERAL NOTE

1.80   This section provides that in respect of periods of incapacity starting on or after April 6, 2001 (see further, below), weekly incapacity benefit must be reduced by 50 per cent of the amount by which the properly calculated pension payment and/or PPF periodic payment exceeds "the threshold" (the currently weekly "threshold" is £85, alterable by regulations). The reduction applies to part-week receipt of incapacity benefit and covers also part-week receipt of pension payment and/or PPF periodic payment, with proportionate reductions (subss.(1), (2)(b)).

This partial extension of means-testing into this contributory benefit was seen by government as "a fairer partnership between the state and individuals by changing the way that occupational or personal pensions are treated for incapacity benefit" (*Hansard*, HC Vol.326, col.221 (Mr A. Darling, Secretary of State for Social Security), helping to deal with the problem of incapacity benefit as a disguised early retirement benefit. In contrast, many critics viewed the change, as with that already effected in the creation of JSA, as another erosion of the contributory principle, a further denial of Beveridge-type "universalism" in favour of enhanced "selectivity" and "means-testing".

The definition of "pension payment" is crucial. Pursuant to subs.(5) and IB Regulations, Pt V, regs20, 21, the term covers a range of schemes. It embraces:

- *a periodical payment under a personal pension scheme (subs.(5)(a))*—"personal pension scheme" is defined in subs.(6) by reference to its definition in the Pensions Scheme Act 1993, s.1:

   "any scheme or arrangement which is comprised in one or more instruments or agreements and which has, or is capable of having, effect so as to provide benefits, in the form of pensions or otherwise, payable on death or retirement to or in respect of [earners (whether employed or self-employed)] who have made arrangements with the trustees or managers of the scheme for them to become members of it".

But it also includes a contract or trust scheme approved under Ch.III of Pt XIV of the Income and Corporation Taxes Act 1988 (retirement annuities) (subs.(6)).

- *a periodical payment, in connection with the coming to an end of an employment of the claimant, under an occupational pension scheme (subs.(5)(a))*—"occupational pension scheme" scheme is defined in subs.(6) by reference to its defintion in the Pensions Scheme Act 1993, s.1:

   "any scheme or arrangement which is comprised in one or more instruments or agreements and which has, or is capable of having, effect in relation to one or more descriptions or categories of employments so as to provide benefits, in the form of pensions or otherwise, payable on termination of service, or on death or retirement, to or in respect of earners with qualifying service in an employment of any such description or category".

- *a periodical payment, in connection with the coming to an end of an employment of the claimant, under a public service pension scheme" (subs.(5)(a))*—"public service pension scheme" scheme is defined in subs.(6) by reference to its definition in the Pensions Scheme Act 1993, s.1:

   "an occupational pension scheme established by or under an enactment or the Royal prerogative or a Royal charter, being a scheme—

   (a) all the particulars of which are set out in or in a legislative instrument made under, an enactment, Royal warrant or charter, or

(b) which cannot come into force, or be amended, without the Scheme or amendment being approved by a Minister of the Crown or government department,

and includes any occupational pension scheme established, with the concurrence of the Treasury, by or with approval of any Minister of the Crown and any occupational pension scheme prescribed by regulations made by the Secretary of State and the Treasury jointly as being a scheme which ought in their opinion to be treated as a public service pension scheme for the purposes of this Act".

It will be noted that, thus far, the definitions are almost coterminous with those applying for abatement of JSA under the Jobseekers Act 1995, ss.4(1), (2), 35(1) and reg.80 of the JSA Regulations, with an exception as regards "personal pension scheme" in that the JSA scheme (but not the incapacity benefit regime) takes on board a personal pension scheme approved under Ch.IV of the Income and Corporation Taxes Act 1988 (Jobseekers Act 1995, s.35(1)). Crossreference to case law under the JSA scheme will be appropriate insofar as the definitions are identical (see further the commentary to JSA Regulations, reg.80 in *Vol.II; Income Support, Jobseeker's Allowance, State Pension Credit and the Social Fund*).

But "pension payment", for incapacity benefit reduction purposes, also embraces a number of schemes not covered by the JSA regime. The term also covers:

- *a payment of any description specified in regulations, being a payment made under an insurance policy providing benefits in connection with physical or mental illness, disability, infirmity or defect (subs. (5) (bb))*—IB Regulations, reg.20 specifies as covered any "permanent health insurance payment". This is defined there as:

  "any periodical payment arranged by an employer under an insurance policy providing benefits in connection with physical or mental illness, disability, infirmity or defect, in relation to a former employee on the termination of his employment".

  Note, however, that there is to be disregarded any such payment in respect of which the employee had contributed to the premium to the extent of more than 50 per cent (IB Regulations, reg.21(c)).

- *a payment of any other specified descriptions (subs. (5) (c))*—no such payment has yet been specified. When concern was voiced at the width of this rule-making power, the Government spokesperson indicated that it would not be used to take account of privately arranged health insurance, or of mortgage protection or income replacement policies (*Hansard* HL Vol.604, col.322 (Baroness Hollis of Heigham)).

Subsection (4)(a) enables the making of regulations providing for certain sums to be disregarded. One such has already been noted with respect to "permanent health insurance" (IB Regulations, reg.21(c)). IB Regulations, reg.21 specifies two others:

- any pension payment made to a beneficiary on the death of a member of any pension scheme must be ignored (reg.21(a));

- there must be disregarded the extent of the shortfall where a pension scheme is in deficit or has insufficient resources to meet the full payment (reg.21(b)).

From February 14, 2006, reduction must also be made for PPF periodic payments. "PPF periodic payments" are defined in s.122(1) as (a) any periodic compensation payments made in relation to a person, payable under the pension compensation provisions as specified in s.162(2) of the Pensions Act 2004 or art.146(2) of the Pensions (Northern Ireland) Order 2005 (the pension compensation provisions); or

(b) any periodic payments made in relation to a person, payable under s.166 of the Pensions Act 2004 or art.150 of the Pensions (Northern Ireland) Order 2005 (duty to pay scheme benefits unpaid at assessment date etc.). The PPF is a statutory fund run by a Board. It became operational on April 6, 2005. The PPF aims to provide compensation for members of defined benefits and the defined benefit elements of hybrid pension schemes should the employer become insolvent and the pension scheme is underfunded to a certain level.

Reduction can only come into play where a pension payment is "payable to" the person entitled to incapacity benefit. So, in *R(IB) 1/04*, Commissioner Turnbull held that, where under a court order part of the claimant's occupational pension was paid over by the pension trustees to his former spouse, that part of the pension so paid over was not "payable to" the claimant, it could not be taken into account in effecting a reduction, and the remainder which was payable to him fell below the threshold so that no reduction of incapacity benefit could be made. The Commissioner did not find helpful decisions on abatement of unemployment benefit (*R(U)4/83* and *R(U)8/83*) since the statutory wording there referred to payments which "fall to be made to him". Nor was a decision on income support (*R(IS)4/01*) in point since the issue there was whether the payments constituted part of the claimant's "income". He noted that the "earmarking" provisions in financial settlements on divorce had been operative for some four years before s.30DD was inserted by the Welfare Reform and Pensions Act 1999. He thought

> "it reasonable to infer that it would have been apparent to the framers of s.30DD that one of the common situations in which it would fall to be applied was that where an earmarking order had been made. I think that there is some argument for saying that, if it had been intended that sums which by such an order are required to be paid to W should be treated for the purposes of s.30DD(1) as nevertheless payable to H, the opportunity would have been taken expressly so to provide" (para.15).

In *R(IB)3/05*, however, deputy Commissioner Paines applied the approach in *R(U)8/83* to hold with regret that the amount of pension to be taken into account was the gross amount before tax.

A Tax Free Service Invaliding Pension (on the nature of which see *R(IS) 3/99*, para.3) comes within the abatement provisions (*CIB/3019/2004*). While part of its purpose is compensatory and partly for help with the extra costs disability brings, it was also payable in connection with, and on, the termination of his employment.

Note carefully that not all claimants in receipt of pension payments will have their incapacity benefit reduced. First, this section only applies to periods of incapacity for work commencing on or after April 6, 2001 (that is, it catches only wholly new claimants). Art.3(2) of the Welfare Reform and Pensions Act 1999 (Commencement No. 9, and Transitional and Savings Provisions) Order 2000 (SI 2000/2958) as amended by art.3 of the Welfare Reform and Pensions Act 1999 (Commencement No. 10, and Transitional and Savings Provisions) Order 2001 (SI 2001/993) provides that:

> "Notwithstanding the commencement of section 63 (incapacity benefit: reduction for pension payements) [*inserting this section*] and paragraph 22 of Schedule 8 (incapacity benefit: rate) [*inserting s.30B(8)*], where a person is entitled to incapacity benefit under [ss.30A, 40 or 41] of the Contributions and Benefits Act on any day of incapacity for work in a period of incapacity for work beginning before 6th April 2001 which continues, whether or not by virtue of section 30C of that Act or regulations made under that section, on or after that date, sections 30A to 30E of that Act shall have effect in relation to him, in that period of incapacity for work, as if section 63 and paragraph 22 of Schedule 8 had not been commenced".

It should be noted that this paragraph protects only those entitled to incapacity benefit before April 6, 2001. It does not protect those in receipt of SSP at that time even though they subsequently in the same spell of sickness progress onto incapacity benefit; while their period of entitlement began before the key date and continued later as a period of incapacity, the period of entitlement to SSP is not one of incapacity for purposes of incapacity benefit (*CIB/4381/2001*). Whether the differentiation thus effected between two people becoming incapable of work on the same day, one employed (SSP), the other self-employed (incapacity benefit), was discrimination contrary to Art.14 of the ECHR was not decided since the Commissioner has no power to make a declaration of incompatibility (HRA 1998, s.4).

The second way in which one identifies claimants not subject to reduction is through subs.(3) which enables the making of regulations specifying others not subject to reduction. IB Regulations, reg.26 is the most obvious product protecting from reduction of benefit a claimant entitled to the highest rate of disability living allowance care component. But note that reg.19 of those same regulations, transferring certain recipients of SDA to long-term incapacity benefit on April 6, 2002, stipulates in para.(2)(c) that their benefit is not subject to reduction for pension payments.

Incapacity benefit: reduction for councillor's allowance

30E.—(1) Where the net amount of councillor's allowance to which a person is entitled in respect of any week exceeds such amount as may be prescribed, an amount equal to the excess shall be deducted from the amount of any incapacity benefit to which he is entitled in respect of that week, and only the balance remaining (if any) shall be payable.

    (2) In this section "councillor's allowance" means—
    (a) in England or Wales, an allowance under or by virtue of—
       (i) section 173 or 177 of the Local Government Act 1972, or
      (ii) a scheme made by virtue of section 18 of the Local Government and Housing Act 1989,
    other than such an allowance as is mentioned in section 173(4) of the Local Government Act 1972, or
    (b) in Scotland, an allowance under or by virtue of section 49 of the Local Government (Scotland) Act 1973 or a scheme made by virtue of section 18 of the Local Government and Housing Act 1989;
and where any such allowance is paid otherwise than weekly, an amount calculated or estimated in accordance with regulations shall be regarded as the weekly amount of the allowance.

    (3) In subsection (1) above "net amount", in relation to any councillor's allowance to which a person is entitled, means the aggregate amount of the councillor's allowance or allowances to which he is entitled for the week in question, reduced by the amount of any expenses incurred by him in that week in connection with his membership of the council or councils in question.

DEFINITIONS

    "councillor's allowance"—see subs.(2).
    "net amount"—see subs.(3).

GENERAL NOTE

    Like the scheme for sickness and invalidity benefits, the incapacity benefit regime seeks to enable those who are sick and those with disabilities to undertake duties

1.81

1.82

as councillors without undue effect on their entitlement to benefit. With respect to sickness and invalidity benefits, that protection was afforded by SSCBA, s.58 as in force until April 13, 1995 (p.197 of Bonner, Hooker and White, *Non Means Tested Benefits: The Legislation* (1994)). Now protection is divided between this section (further amplified by IB Regs, regs 8, 9, below) and s.171F, below. The latter section deals with the matter of determining whether someone is capable or incapable of work; something which will apply across the whole of the social security system other than for SSP or the industrial injuries scheme. It requires that in determining that question, any work which the person has undertaken as a councillor is to be disregarded. This section, in contrast, is of narrower scope, providing for the reduction (even to nil) of incapacity benefit by the amount by which the net amount of councillor's allowance exceeds a prescribed amount.

The prescribed amount is £92.00, with effect from October 1, 2008 (£88.50 prior to that). "Councillor's allowance" is defined in subs.(2), and embraces a number of types of allowance (attendance, basic, and special responsibility). IB Regs, reg.9, below, provides the mechanism for determining a weekly amount in cases where the allowance in question is paid other than weekly. "Net amount" is defined in subs.(3) to be the aggregate amount of the councillor's allowance(s) to which the person is entitled for the week in question, reduced by the amount of any expenses incurred by him in that week in connection with his membership of the council(s) concerned. Unlike the position with computation of earnings under the Computation of Earnings Regulations, no concept of averaging across the year is to be applied. In *CS 7934/95*, Commissioner Rice decided "that the expenses incurred in any week by the claimant for the performance of her duties as a local authority councillor (whether for clothes, telephone rental, telephone calls, subscriptions, travel, or whatever it might be) shall for the purposes of calculating her entitlement to invalidity benefit [pursuant to SSCBA 1992, s.58(4), the similarly worded precursor of para.(3) of this section, defining "net amount"], be deducted from the allowance or allowances to which she is entitled in respect of that week" (para.1). It is immaterial that the benefits of expenses incurred in that week (e.g. the purchase of a dress to be worn more than once for official functions) are enjoyed in future weeks (para.9). In *CIB 2858, 2859 and 2864/2001*, Commissioner Jacobs supported as correct the approach taken by Commissioner Rice in *CS 7934/95*. He disagreed with Commissioner Williams in *R(IB) 3/01*. He accepted that s.30E should be interpreted as a whole. The phrase "in connection with" membership of the council set a limit of reasonableness on the expenditure. An expense is incurred when the liability to discharge it arises (a matter on which he agreed with Commissioner Williams), but it is not incurred in the week in which the item is used (a matter of disagreement with Commissioner Williams). In Commissioner Jacob's view the result is that s.30E has to be applied week by week, either in each week or retrospectively over a past period. An expense is incurred in the week in which the liability arises and can only be used to reduce the reduction in incapacity benefit for that week. Income tax and national insurance deductions do not rank as "expenses in connection with a claimant's membership of a council" and cannot be deducted from the gross councillor's allowances for purposes of incapacity benefit (*R(IB) 3/01*).

1.83   *Sections 31–34 omitted.*

Maternity

State maternity allowance

1.84   **35.**—[1 (1) A woman shall be entitled to a maternity allowance, at the appropriate weekly rate determined under section (35A) below if—

  (a) she has become pregnant and has reached, or been confined before reaching, the commencement of the 11th week before the expected week of confinement; and

  (b) she has been engaged in employment as an employed or self-employed earner for any part of the week in the case of at least 26 of the 66 weeks immediately preceding the expected week of confinement; and

  (c) (within the meaning of section 35A) her average weekly earnings are not less than the maternity allowance threshold; and

  (d) she is not entitled to statutory maternity pay for the same week in respect of the same pregnancy].

(2) Subject to the following provisions of this section, a maternity allowance shall be payable for the period ("the maternity allowance period") which, if she were entitled to statutory maternity pay, would be the maternity pay period under section 165 below.

(3) Regulations may provide—

  (a) for disqualifying a woman for receiving a maternity allowance if—

    [5(i) during the maternity allowance period, except in prescribed cases, she does any work in employment as an employed or self-employed earner;

    (ia) during the maternity allowance period she fails without good cause to observe any prescribed rules of behaviour; or]

    (ii) at any time before she is confined she fails without good cause to attend for, or submit herself to, any medical examination required in accordance with the regulations;

  (b) that this section and [1 Section 35A below] shall have effect subject to prescribed modifications in relation to cases in which a woman has been confined and—

    (i) has not made a claim for a maternity allowance in expectation of that confinement (other than a claim which has been disallowed); or

    (ii) has made a claim for a maternity allowance in expectation of that confinement (other than a claim which has been disallowed), but she was confined more than 11 weeks before the expected week of confinement.

  [2(c) that subsection (2) above shall have effect subject to prescribed modifications in relation to cases in which a woman fails to satisfy the conditions referred to in subsection (1)(b) [1 above or in section 35A (2) or (3) below] at the commencement of the 11th week before the expected week of confinement, but subsequently satisfies those conditions at any time before she is confined.]

(4) A woman who has become entitled to a maternity allowance shall cease to be entitled to it if she dies before the beginning of the maternity allowance period; and if she dies after the beginning, but before the end, of that period, the allowance shall not be payable for any week subsequent to that in which she dies.

(5) Where for any purpose of this Part of this Act or of regulations it is necessary to calculate the daily rate of a maternity allowance [4the amount payable by way of that allowance for any day shall be taken as one seventh of the weekly rate of that allowance.]

(6) In this section "confinement" means—

  (a) labour resulting in the issue of a living child, or

61

(b) labour after [³24 weeks] of pregnancy resulting in the issue of a child whether alive or dead,

and "confined" shall be construed accordingly; and where a woman's labour begun on one day results in the issue of a child on another day she shall be taken to be confined on the day of the issue of the child or, if labour results in the issue of twins or a greater number of children, she shall be taken to be confined on the day of the issue of the last of them.

(7) The fact that the mother of a child is being paid maternity allowance shall not be taken into consideration by any court in deciding whether to order payment of expenses incidental to the birth of the child.

AMENDMENTS

1. Welfare Reform and Pensions Act 1999, s.53 (April 2, 2000).
2. Maternity Allowance and Statutory Maternity Pay Regulations 1994 (SI 1994/1230), reg.2 (October 16, 1994).
3. Still Birth (Definition) Act 1992, s.2(1)(a) (October 1, 1992).
4. Social Security Act 1998, s.67 (October 1, 2006).
5. Work and Families Act 2006, Sch.1, para.6 (October 1, 2006).

DERIVATION

1.85   SSA 1978, s.22.

DEFINITIONS

"Confinement"—see subs.(6).
"Confined"—*ibid.*

GENERAL NOTE

1.86   State Maternity Allowance, MA, is a benefit equivalent to Statutory Maternity Pay. It is paid chiefly to women who have been self-employed. It will also cover women whose service with their current employer does not qualify them for SMP; and women who have been in employment and whose job ended more than 15 weeks before their expected date of confinement and for a reason other than their pregnancy.

From April 2000 this benefit is no longer a contributory benefit. When the claimant's expected week of confinement is on or after April 2, 2000, entitlement will depend upon her showing involvement in work as either an employee or as a self-employed person for a total of 26 weeks out of the preceding 66 weeks. As well, she will have to show a certain level of earnings depending upon which she will qualify for benefit and be paid either standard rate MA, or a lower variable rate MA.

Claimants whose expected week of confinement was prior to April 2, 2000 continue to qualify on the basis of a contribution record and are paid benefit at one of two rates, depending upon whether the claimant was working as an employee in her qualifying week.

The allowance is payable when the claimant has become pregnant and has been confined, or has reached a stage in her pregnancy, which is the beginning of the 11th week before her expected week of confinement (s.165). There is no definition of pregnancy in the legislation but sufficient proof of that condition will normally follow from the need to prove an expected confinement. Confinement is defined in subs.6 as labour resulting in a living child, or labour after 24 weeks of pregnancy resulting in the issue of a child whether alive or dead. The only dispute that is likely to arise is whether a woman has been pregnant for 24 weeks, or more, before she gives birth to a still-born child. In one case, the Commissioner fixed the date that the pregnancy would be assumed to have commenced by calculating back from the estimated date of confinement for the period of a normal pregnancy *(R(G) 4/56).*

---

(5) Regulations may, for the purposes of subsection (4) above, provide—

(a) for the amount of any payments falling within paragraph (a) or (b) of that subsection to be calculated or estimated in such manner and on such basis as may be prescribed;

(b) for a payment made outside the specified period to be treated as made during that period where it was referable to that period or any part of it;

(c) for a woman engaged in employment as a self-employed earner to be treated as having received a payment in respect of a week—

(i) equal to the lower earnings limit in force on the last day of the week, if she paid a Class 2 contribution in respect of the week, or

(ii) equal to the maternity allowance threshold in force on that day, if she was excepted (under section 11(4) above) from liability for such a contribution in respect of the week;

(d) for aggregating payment made or treated as made to or for the benefit of a woman where, either in the same week or in different weeks, she was engaged in two or more employments (whether, in each case, as an employed earner or a self-employed earner).

[² (5A) Where subsection (5B) below applies the appropriate weekly rate is the weekly rate for the time being prescribed under section 166(1)(b) below.

(5B) This subsection applies where a woman is treated by virtue of regulations under sub-paragraph (i) of paragraph (c) of subsection (5) above as having received a payment in respect of each week in the specified period equal to the amount mentioned in that sub-paragraph.]

[³ (6) In this section "the maternity allowance threshold" has the same meaning as in section 35 above and "specified" means prescribed by or determined in accordance with regulations.]

AMENDMENTS

1. Welfare Reform and Pensions Act 1999, s.53 (April 2, 2000).
2. Employment Act 2002, s.48 (April 6, 2003).
3. Employment Act 2002, Sch.7 (April 6, 2003).

GENERAL NOTE

1.91   This section will apply when the woman's expected week of confinement begins on or after August 20, 2000.

Benefits for widows and widowers

[¹ **Bereavement payment**

1.92   **36.**—(1) A person whose spouse [² or civil partner] dies on or after the appointed day shall be entitled to a bereavement payment if—

(a) either that person was under pensionable age at the time when the spouse [² or civil partner] died or the spouse [² or civil partner] was then not entitled to a category A retirement pension under section 44 below; and

(b) the spouse [² or civil partner] satisfied the contribution condition for a bereavement payment specified in Schedule 3, Part I, paragraph 4.

(2) [²A bereavement payment shall not be payable to a person if—

(i) that person and a person of the opposite sex to whom that person was not married were living together as husband and wife at the time of the spouse's or civil partner's death, or

(ii) that person and a person of the same sex who was not his or her civil partner were living together as if they were civil partners at the time of the spouse's or civil partner's death.]

(3) In this section "the appointed day" means the day appointed for the coming into force of sections 54 to 56 of the Welfare Reform and Pensions Act 1999.]

AMENDMENTS

1. Welfare Reform and Pensions Act, s.54, (April 9, 2001).
2. Civil Partnership Act 2004, Sch.24, (December 5, 2005).

DEFINITION

"pensionable age"—see s.122.

GENERAL NOTE

Bereavement payments replace Widow's payment from April 9, 2001. From that date a payment can be claimed by either spouse provided that they were under pensionable age (or the spouse was not entitled to a Category A pension) and that the deceased spouse has satisfied the requisite contribution conditions. Like Widow's payment that it replaces, no payment will be made if the claimant was living with another person of the opposite sex as husband and wife at the time of the spouse's death.   **1.93**

The Commissioner's decision in *R(G)1/06* confirms that under s.36(1), the claimant cannot succeed in a claim for a bereavement payment if they are over retirement age and entitled to a Category A Retirement Pension. This is because the benefit, like Widows Allowance that preceded it, was intended only for the loss of a breadwinner who was still in work and when the spouse would still would have been dependent on the deceased as a source of their income. The decision also holds that this section is not in breach of the claimant's Convention Rights and that, under the Human Rights Act, it could not be interpreted in any other way.

For details of Widow's payment see the 2000 edition of this work. For claims made by widowers before 2001, see the notes following s.38.

[¹ Cases in which sections 37 to 41 apply

36A.—(1) Sections 37 to 39 and section 40 below apply only in cases where a woman's husband has died before the appointed day, and section 41 below applies only in cases where a man's wife has died before that day.   **1.94**

(2) Sections 39A to 39C below apply in cases where a person's spouse [² or civil partner] dies on or after the appointed day, but section 39A also applies (in accordance with subsection (1)(b) of that section) in cases where a man's wife has died before that day.

(3) In this section, and in sections 39A and 39B below, "the appointed day" means the day appointed for the coming into force of sections 54 to 56 of the Welfare Reform and Pensions Act 1999.]

AMENDMENTS

1. Welfare Reform and Pensions Act 1999, s.55, (April 9, 2001).
2. Civil Partnership Act 2004, Sch.24, (December 5, 2005).

GENERAL NOTE

1.95   The "appointed day" for these provisions was April 9, 2001.

Widowed mother's allowance

1.96   **37.**—(1) A woman who has been widowed shall be entitled to a widowed mother's allowance at the rate determined in accordance with section 39 below if her late husband satisfied the contribution conditions for a widowed mother's allowance specified in Schedule 3, Part I, paragraph 5 and either—

  (a) the woman is entitled to child benefit in respect of a child [3 or qualifying young person] falling within subsection (2) below; or
  (b) the woman is pregnant by her late husband; or
  (c) if the woman and her late husband were residing together immediately before the time of his death, the woman is pregnant as the result of being artificially inseminated before that time with the semen of some person other than her husband, or as the result of the placing in her before that time of an embryo, of an egg in the process of fertilisation, or of sperm and eggs.

  (2) A child [3 or qualifying young person] falls within this subsection if [4 [5 . . .]] the child [3 or qualifying young person] is either—

  (a) a son or daughter of the woman and her late husband; or
  (b) a child [3 or qualifying young person] in respect of whom her late husband was immediately before his death entitled to child benefit; or
  (c) if the woman and her late husband were residing together immediately before his death, a child [3 or qualifying young person] in respect of whom she was then entitled to child benefit.

  (3) The widow shall not be entitled to the allowance for any period after she remarries [2 or forms a civil partnership], but, subject to that, she shall continue to be entitled to it for any period throughout which she satisfies the requirements of subsection (1)(a), (b) or (c) above.

  (4) A widowed mother's allowance shall not be payable—

  (a) for any period falling before the day on which the widow's entitlement is to be regarded as commencing for that purpose by virtue of section 5(1)(k) of the Administration Act;
  (b) for any period during which she and a man to whom she is not married are living together as husband and wife. [2 or
  (c) for any period during which she and a woman who is not her civil partner are living together as if they were civil partners].

AMENDMENTS

1. Tax Credits Act 2003, Sch.3 (April 6, 2003).
2. Civil Partnership Act 2004, Sch.24 (December 5, 2005).
3. Child Benefit Act 2005, Sch.1 (April 10, 2006).
4. Welfare Reform Act 2007 s.50 and art.2(3)(a) of the Welfare Reform Act 2007 (Commencement No.7, Transitional and Savings Provisions) Order 2008 (SI 2008/2101) (October 7, 2008).

5. Welfare Reform Act 2007, s.67 and art.2(b) of the Welfare Reform Act 2007 (Commencement No. 10, Transitional and Savings Provisions) Order 2009 (SI 2009/775) (March 27, 2009).

DERIVATION

SSA 1975, s.25.   1.97

DEFINITION

"late husband"—see s.122 below.

GENERAL NOTE

This benefit is payable only to a widow whose husband died before April 9, 2001.   1.98
For general points relating to widowhood see s.38 below. Widowed mother's allowance is paid to a widow whose late husband satisfied contribution conditions and
who now is entitled to child benefit in respect of certain children. These children
are defined in subs.(2). They include children of the couple, children in respect of
whom the late husband was entitled to child benefit, and, providing they were living
together at the time of his death, children for whom she was then entitled to child
benefit. In effect it covers those children for whom the late husband might have been
expected to be the source of support. Widowed mother's allowance is extended also
to a woman who is pregnant by her husband at the time of his death, or one who,
provided they were living together at the time of his death, was pregnant by artificial
insemination by a donor, or by the implantation of an egg or embryo.

There is a Commissioner's decision *R(G) 1/92* on the application of subs.(1)
(b)—entitlement of a woman who is pregnant by her late husband at the time of his
death. An addition in respect of that child had been refused in this case because,
it was alleged, at her initial interview after her husband's death, the claimant had
remarked that the child with which she was pregnant was not her husband's. The
AO had accordingly refused the additional benefit. At her subsequent appeal to a
tribunal the claimant denied that she had been so categorical, and said that she was
in doubt as to whether her husband was the father of her child. She was, at the time
of his death, still living and having sexual relations with her husband. The tribunal
found on the balance of probabilities that the child was not that of her husband,
accepting the evidence of the clerk who took the original statement from her and
who apparently gave evidence in person to the tribunal. The Commissioner allowed
the appeal because no regard had been given to the presumption of legitimacy.
There is a firmly established presumption that, as the Commissioner put it, "a child
born in wedlock to a married woman was begotten by her husband". The presumption can be rebutted by clear evidence to the contrary, but in this case the tribunal
had not approached the matter by reference to the presumption and the consequent
burden of proof thrown on the Department, and had, therefore, made an error of
law. The Commissioner went on to give his own decision on this issue. He had the
advantage of further evidence from the claimant not given to the tribunal and from
which he was satisfied that the claimant had been having intercourse with both her
husband and another man at the time the baby was conceived. In the light of that
it could not be said it was clearly more probable than not that the husband was not
the father of her child. Consequently, the presumption of legitimacy applied and the
claimant was entitled to the addition to her widowed mother's allowance.

Widowed mother's allowance is subject to the proviso that it is not payable if the
widow has remarried or is living with a man as his wife—see notes to s.38 below. For
claims made by widowers before 2001, see the notes following s.38.

From April 2001 widows' benefits have been replaced by benefits that are
available to both widows and widowers. Prior to that date several cases had been
brought by widowers on the ground that refusing a claim by them constituted
discrimination on the grounds of their sex contrary to Art.14 ECHR taken in

conjunction with Art.8 and Art.1 of Protocol 1. In *Willis v United Kingdom* (2002) 35 E.H.R.R. 21, the ECHR upheld their claims in respect of Widow's payment and of Widowed Mother's Allowance, but, effectively, made no finding in respect of Widow's Pension. Subsequently, discretionary payments equivalent to those benefits were made by the Secretary of State until the Human Rights Act came into effect, October 2, 2000. From that date payments were refused on the basis that claimants should first exhaust their rights to claim under that act in a UK court. A selection of test cases in respect of each widow's benefit duly followed. These cases have now been concluded in the House of Lords and are reported as *R. v Secretary of State for Work and Pensions Ex p. Hooper* [2005] UKHL 29. All of the claims failed. To begin with, counsel for the claimants conceded that none of ss.36–38 could be read, even in the light of the Human Rights Act, to include a claimant of the male sex (a point that had been argued unsuccessfully in the courts below). The claims depended, therefore, on the anti-discrimination provisions adopted from the ECHR.

In respect of Widow's Pension the House held that there had been no breach of Art 14. The fact that men and women were treated differently was justified by the different cultural and economic position of women in society even at the end of the twentieth century. Whereas the Court of Appeal had held that this argument was no longer sustainable in the latter part of the 1990's, Lord Hoffman, with whom other members of the House agreed, held that the matter of justification was essentially one of parliamentary judgment rather than judicial judgment, and for parliament to have delayed until 1999 in enacting the amending legislation, and until 2001 before implementing it, did not necessarily take them outside the margin of appreciation that should be allowed.

The claims to Widow's Payment and Widowed Mother's Allowance also failed, this time on the grounds that even if the different treatment were discriminatory, the Secretary of State had a defence under s.6(2) of the Human Rights Act. This subsection provides a defence where the action is taken under a statute which either compels that course of action (sub-para.(i)), or where it is taken in order to "give effect to" that statutory provision (sub-para.(ii)). Here the members of the House were divided as to which of these was appropriate, but all agreed that the claim must fail under one or other of those provisions. (Though, of course, a discretionary payment may still be appropriate in respect of the breach of a claimant's ECHR rights.)

The claimant complained also of the fact that between October 2, 2000, and April 2001 no discretionary payment was made to them as previously under the *Willis* principle. They said that this, too, amounted to discrimination. That claim also failed either because any "right" to a discretionary payment was not a matter that engaged their human rights, or because it did not demonstrate discrimination on any relevant ground between themselves and claimants prior to the year 2000.

The conclusion reached in *Hooper* (and in *Willis*) has now been upheld in the ECHR in the cases of *Runkee* and *White* (May 10, 2007). The Court accepted the reasoning that the differential treatment of widows prior to 2001 could be justified by the social and economic status of older widows before that date.

For the position regarding widows whose husbands died before April 4, 1988, see notes to earlier editions of this book.

This benefit will, in appropriate circumstances, be affected by the operation of the Gender Recognition Act 2004. Where a person in receipt of Widowed Mother's Allowance obtains a gender recognition certificate under that Act, he will be transferred to Widowed Parent's Allowance under s.39A without making a fresh claim. Where the claimant would have been entitled to Widowed Mother's Allowance, but had not claimed, he will become entitled to Widowed Parent's Allowance on making a claim for that benefit. Note, however, that a woman in receipt of Widowed Mother's Allowance, may be entitled to go on to Widow's Pension when her entitlement to the former benefit has ceased (e.g. her children have grown up), but there is no such provision in respect of Widowed Parent's Allowance. See the note to Gender Recognition Act in Volume III of this work.

Widow's pension

38.—(1) A woman who has been widowed shall be entitled to a widow's 1.99
pension at the rate determined in accordance with section 39 below if her
late husband satisfied the contribution conditions for a widow's pension
specified in Schedule 3, Part I, paragraph 5 and either—
  (a) she was, at the husband's death, over the age of 45 but under the age
      of 65; or
  (b) she ceased to be entitled to a widowed mother's allowance at a time
      when she was over the age of 45 but under the age of 65.
  (2) The widow shall not be entitled to the pension for any period after
she remarries [¹ or forms a civil partnership], but, subject to that, she shall
continue to be entitled to it until she attains [² pensionable age].
  (3) A widow's pension shall not be payable—
  (a) for any period falling before the day on which the widow's entitle-
      ment is to be regarded as commencing for that purpose by virtue of
      section 5(1)(k) of the Administration Act;
  (b) for any period for which she is entitled to a widowed mother's allow-
      ance;
  (c) for any period during which she and a man to whom she is not
      married are living together as husband and wife. [¹ or
  (d) for any period during which she and a woman who is not her civil
      partner are living together as if they were civil partners].
  (4) In the case of a widow whose late husband died before 11th April
1988 and who either—
  (a) was over the age of 40 but under the age of 55 at the time of her
      husband's death; or
  (b) is over the age of 40 but under the age of 55 at the time when she
      ceases to be entitled to a widowed mother's allowance,
subsection (1) above shall have effect as if for "45" there were substituted "40".

AMENDMENT

1. Civil Partnership Act 2004, Sch.24 (December 5, 2005).
2. Pensions Act 2007, Sch.1 para.40 (July 26, 2007).

DERIVATION

SSA 1975, s.26.   1.100

DEFINITION

"late husband"—see s.122.

GENERAL NOTE

This benefit is payable only to a widow whose husband died before April 9, 2001.   1.101
Widow's pension is payable to a woman whose husband dies while the marriage is
still continuing, and who is over the age of 45, either at the time of her husband's
death, or when she ceases to be entitled to a widowed mother's allowance (see s.37,
above). It is paid at the full rate if she was over the age of 55, at that time, and at a
reduced rate between the ages of 45 and 55. Until April 11, 1988 the threshold age
was 40 years. Subs.4 retains entitlement for widows whose husbands died before
that date. For other transitional problems arising out of that change see earlier editions of this book.

Qualification for widow's benefits depends upon proof of a valid marriage subsisting at the time of the husband's death. For details of marriage and its validity as well as the disqualification arising when a widow cohabits with a man as husband and wife, see notes following s.39C. This benefit cannot be claimed by a person who has changed from a male sex to a female sex after that person has obtained a gender recognition certificate under the Gender Recognition Act 2004 even if her marriage partner died before 2001, because that person will not be able to satisfy the wording of this section in respect of the death of her "late husband". Conversely, however, an existing female claimant who obtains a gender recognition certificate will lose entitlement to the benefit because he will no longer be a "woman who has been widowed".

Rate of widowed mother's allowance and widow's pension

1.102   **39.**—(1) The weekly rate of—
(a) a widowed mother's allowance,
(b) a widow's pension,
shall be determined in accordance with the provisions of sections [¹ 44 to [² 45B]] [³ [⁵. . .]] below as they apply in the case of a Category A retirement pension, but subject, in particular, to the following provisions of this section and section 46(2) below.

(2) In the application of sections [¹ 44 to [² 45B]] [³ [⁵. . .]] below by virtue of subsection (1) above—
(a) where the woman's husband was over pensionable age when he died, references in those sections to the pensioner shall be taken as references to the husband, and
(b) where the husband was under pensionable age when he died, references in those sections to the pensioner and the tax year in which he attained pensionable age shall be taken as references to the husband and the tax year in which he died.

[⁴ (2A) In its application by virtue of subsection (1) above, section 44(4) below is to be read as if for the first amount specified in that provision there were substituted a reference to the amount prescribed for the purposes of this subsection.]

(3) [⁶ omitted]

(4) Where a widow's pension is payable to a woman who was under the age of 55 at the time when the applicable qualifying condition was fulfilled, the weekly rate of the pension shall be reduced by 7 per cent. of what it would be apart from this subsection multiplied by the number of years by which her age at that time was less than 55 (any fraction of a year being counted as a year).

(5) For the purposes of subsection (4) above, the time when the applicable qualifying condition was fulfilled is the time when the woman's late husband died or, as the case may be, the time when she ceased to be entitled to a widowed mother's allowance.

(6) In the case of a widow whose late husband died before 11th April 1988 and who either—
(a) was over the age of 40 but under the age of 55 at the time of her husband's death; or
(b) is over the age of 40 but under the age of 55 at the time when she ceases to be entitled to a widowed mother's allowance, subsection (4) above shall have effect as if for "55" there were substituted "50" in both places where it occurs.

AMENDMENTS

   1. Pensions Act 1995, s.127(2) where ss.127(3)–(5) of that Act apply.
   2. Welfare Reform and Pensions Act 1999, Sch.12, (April 9, 2001).
   3. Child Support, Pensions and Social Security Act 2000, s.35 (April 6, 2002).
   4. Pensions Act 2007, s.6(5) (July 26, 2007).
   5. Pensions Act 2007, Sch.7, Pt.5 (September 26, 2007).
   6. Pensions Act 2007, Sch.2, Pt.3, para.3 (September 26, 2007).

DERIVATIONS

   SSA 1975, s.13 and s.26.   **1.103**
   SSA 1986, s.19 and s.36.

[¹ Widowed parent's allowance

   39A.—(1) This section applies where—   **1.104**
  (a) a person whose spouse [³ or civil partner] dies on or after the appointed day is under pensionable age at the time of the spouse's [³ or civil partner's] death, or
  (b) a man whose wife died before the appointed day
     (i) has not remarried before that day, and
    (ii) is under pensionable age on that day.
   (2) The surviving spouse [³ or civil partner] shall be entitled to a widowed parent's allowance at the rate determined in accordance with section 39C below if the deceased spouse [³ or civil partner] satisfied the contribution conditions for a widowed parent's allowance specified in Schedule 3, Part I, paragraph 5 and—
  (a) the surviving spouse [³ or civil partner] is entitled to child benefit in respect of a child [⁴ or qualifying young person] falling within subsection (3) below;
  (b) the surviving spouse is a woman who either—
     (i) is pregnant by her late husband, or
    (ii) if she and he were residing together immediately before the time of his death, is pregnant in circumstances falling within section 37(1)(c) above. [³ or
  (c) the surviving civil partner is a woman who—
     (i) was residing together with the deceased civil partner immediately before the time of the death, and
    (ii) is pregnant as the result of being artificially inseminated before that time with the semen of some person, or as a result of the placing in her before that time of an embryo, of an egg in the process of fertilisation, or of sperm and eggs].
   (3) A child [⁴ or qualifying young person] falls within this subsection if [⁵[⁶. . .]]the child [⁴ or qualifying young person] is either—
  (a) a son or daughter of the surviving spouse [³ or civil partner] and the deceased spouse [³ or civil partner]; or
  (b) a child in respect of whom the deceased spouse [³ or civil partner] was immediately before his or her death entitled to child benefit; or
  (c) if the surviving spouse and the deceased spouse were residing together immediately before his or her death, a child [⁴ or qualifying young person] in respect of whom the surviving spouse [³ or civil partner] was then entitled to child benefit.

(4) The surviving spouse [³ or civil partner] shall not be entitled to the allowance for any period after she or he remarries [³ or forms a civil partnership], but, subject to that, the surviving spouse shall continue to be entitled to it for any period throughout which she or he—

(a) satisfied the requirements for subsection (2)(a) or (b) above; and

(b) is under pensionable age.

[³ (4A) The surviving civil partner shall not be entitled to the allowance for any period after she or he forms a subsequent civil partnership or marries, but, subject to that, the surviving civil partner shall continue to be entitled to it for any period throughout which she or he—

(a) satisfies the requirements of subsection (2)(a) or (b) above; and

(b) is under pensionable age].

(5) A widowed parent's allowance shall not be payable—

(a) for any period falling before the day on which the surviving spouse's [³ or civil partner's] entitlement is to be regarded as commencing by virtue of section 5(1)(k) of the Administration Act;

(b) for any period during which the surviving spouse and a person of the opposite sex to whom she or he is not married are living together as husband and wife.[³ or

(c) for any period during which the surviving spouse or civil partner and a person of the same sex who is not his or her civil partner are living together as if they were civil partners].

AMENDMENTS

1. Welfare Reform and Pension Act 1999, s.55 (April 9, 2001).

2. Tax Credits Act 2003, Sch.3, (April 6, 2003).

3. Civil Partnership Act 2004, Sch.24 (December 5, 2005).

4. Child Benefit Act 2005, Sch.1 (April 10, 2006).

5. Welfare Reform Act 2007, s.51 and art.2(3)(b) of the Welfare Reform Act 2007 (Commencement No.7, Transitional and Savings Provisions) Order 2008 (SI 2008/2101) (October 7, 2008).

6. Welfare Reform Act 2007, s.67 and art.2(b) of the Welfare Reform Act 2007 (Commencement No. 10, Transitional and Savings Provisions) Order 2009 (SI 2009/775) (March 27, 2009).

GENERAL NOTE

1.105   For discussion of the conditions of entitlement depending upon marriage etc., see notes following s.39C.

Bereavement allowance where no dependent children

1.106   [¹ 39B.—(1) This section applies where a person whose spouse [² or civil partner] dies on or after the appointed day is over the age of 45 but under pensionable age at the spouse's [² or civil partner's] death.

(2) The surviving spouse [² or civil partner] shall be entitled to a bereavement allowance at the rate determined in accordance with section 39C below if the deceased spouse [² or civil partner] satisfied the contribution conditions for a bereavement allowance specified in Schedule 3, Part I, paragraph 5.

(3) A bereavement allowance shall be payable for not more than 52 weeks beginning with the date of the spouse's [² or civil partner's] death or (if later) the day on which the surviving spouse's [² or civil partner's] entitlement is to be regarded as commencing by virtue of section 5 (1)(k) of the Administration Act.

(4) The surviving spouse shall not be entitled to the allowance for any period after she or he remarries [² or forms a civil partnership], but, subject to that, the surviving spouse shall continue to be entitled to it until—

   (a) she or he attains pensionable age, or

   (b) the period of 52 weeks mentioned in subsection (3) above expires, whichever happens first.

[² (4A) The surviving civil partner shall not be entitled to the allowance for any period after she or he forms a subsequent civil partnership or marries, but, subject to that, the surviving civil partner shall continue to be entitled to it until

   (a) she or he attains pensionable age, or

   (b) the period of 52 weeks mentioned in subsection (3) above expires, whichever happens first].

(5) The allowance shall not be payable—

   (a) for any period which the surviving spouse [² or civil partner's] is entitled to a widowed parent's allowance;

   (b) for any period during which the surviving spouse [² or civil partner's] and a person of the opposite sex to whom she or he is not married are living together as husband and wife. [² or

   (c) for any period during which the surviving spouse or civil partner and a person of the same sex who is not his or her civil partner are living together as if they were civil partners].

AMENDMENTS

1. Welfare Reform and Pension Act 1999, s.55 (April 9, 2001).
2. Civil Partnership Act 2004, Sch.24 (December 5, 2005).

GENERAL NOTE

For discussion of the conditions of entitlement depending upon marriage etc., see notes following s.39C.

1.107

[¹ Rate of widowed parent's allowance and bereavement allowance

39C.—(1) The weekly rate of a widowed parent's allowance shall be determined in accordance with the provisions of section 44 to [³ 45] [² and Schedule 4A] below as they apply in the case of a Category A retirement pension, but subject, in particular, to the following provisions of this section 46(2) [⁶ and (4)] below.

1.108

[⁵ (1A) In its application by virtue of subsection (1) above, section 44(4) below is to be read as if for the first amount specified in that provision there were substituted a reference to the amount prescribed for the purposes of this subsection.

(2) The weekly amount of a bereavement allowance is an amount equal to the amount prescribed for the purposes of subsection (1A) above.]

(3) In the application of sections 44 to [³ 45] [² and Schedule 4A] [⁵ by virtue of subsection (1) above]

   (a) where the deceased spouse [⁴ or civil partner] was over pensionable age at his or her death, references in those [⁶ provisions] to the pensioner shall be taken as references to the deceased spouse [⁴ or civil partner], and

   (b) where the deceased spouse [⁴ or civil partner] was under pensionable age at his or her death, references in those [⁶ provisions] to the pensioner and the tax year in which he attained pensionable age shall be taken as references to the deceased spouse [⁴ or civil partner] and the tax year in which he or she died.

(4) Where a widowed parent's allowance is payable to a person whose spouse [⁴ or civil partner] dies after 5th April 2000, the additional pension falling to be calculated under sections 44 to [³ 45] [² and Schedule 4A] below by virtue of subsection (1) above shall be one half of the amount which it would be apart from this subsection.

(5) Where a bereavement allowance is payable to a person who was under the age of 55 at the time of the spouse's [⁴ or civil partner's] death, the weekly rate of the allowance shall be reduced by 7 per cent of what it would be apart from this subsection multiplied by the number of years by which that person's age at that time was less than 55 (any fraction of a year being counted as a year).]

AMENDMENTS

1. Welfare Reform and Pension Act 1999, s.55 (April 9, 2001).
2. Child Support, Pensions and Social Security Act 2000, s.35 (April 6, 2002).
3. Tax Credit Act 2002, Sch.3 (April 6, 2003).
4. Civil Partnership Act 2004, Sch.24 (December 5, 2005).
5. Pensions Act 2007, s.6(6) (July 26, 2007).
6. Pensions Act 2007, Sch.2 Pt.3 (July 26, 2007).

GENERAL NOTE

1.109   Sections 39A–39C have been inserted by the Welfare Reform and Pensions Act 1999 with effect from April 9, 2001. They replace the old widow's benefits by new ones available to both spouses on the basis of the other, deceased, spouse's contribution record. In doing so, however, they have effectively abolished Widow's Pension, as a really long-term benefit, for new claimants. Instead either spouse can claim the new Bereavement Allowance but this only lasts for up to 52 weeks (*cf.* the old Widow's Allowance that predated the old Widow's Payment).

The only long-term benefit now is the Widowed Parent's Allowance available under s.39A to either surviving spouse for so long as they have children living with them for whom they are entitled to receive Child Benefit.

Bereavement payments, like widows benefits, depend upon proof of a valid subsisting marriage at the time of the spouse's death. From December 2005 it will also be possible to qualify for bereavement benefits and widow's benefits if you are the surviving partner of a same sex civil partnership registered in accordance with the Civil Partnership Act 2004. A bereavement payment will not be made if at the time of the death the claimant was living with a person of the opposite sex as husband and wife, and neither Widowed Parent's Allowance nor Bereavement Allowance will be paid for any period in which the claimant is so living. Equivalent disqualifications will apply where the claimant lives with a partner in circumstances where they could register a civil partnership.

It will now be possible for a valid marriage to be contracted with a transsexual where that person holds a full gender recognition certificate in accordance with the Gender Recognition Act 2004. (See s.9 of that Act). A change of gender may also affect the provision for disqualification from these benefits—where e.g. a claimant is living with a person of the opposite sex as man and wife, an official change of gender by either of them would prevent that disqualification from arising, though that will cease to be the case when the Civil Partnership Act 2004 comes into effect.

The essential requirements for qualification are that there should have been a valid subsisting marriage and that the spouse has died. Without any marriage at all, or even a belief that there has been a marriage (see below), there can be no claim for bereavement benefits. See *Shackell v United Kingdom* (ECHR) April 27,

2000, unreported (Application No. 45851/99), where the court rejected a claim for widowed mother's allowance by the mother of two children whose father, her partner, had died.

In *R(G) 1/04* a claim to bereavement benefits was made by a woman following the death of her long term partner. Her claim was made firstly on the ground that there should be a marriage presumed after long term cohabitation or, alternatively, that the words of ss.36 to 38 should be construed in the light of the Human Rights Act to extend to such a common law marriage. The Commissioner rejected both arguments. There could be no room for presumption of marriage where the parties had expressly decided against marrying. Nor was it necessary to construe the Benefits Act in accordance with the Human Rights Act because the decision refusing benefit, and now under appeal, was made before that Act came into force. Even if it had been necessary to so construe the Benefits Act it would be impossible to read those words in any way other than to require there to have been a valid marriage. Finally, it would not have been open to the Commissioner to make a declaration of incompatibility and in any case the *Shackell* case showed that there was no discrimination in the different treatment of married and unmarried couples.

As to whether a marriage is valid the matter is determined by the general law including those rules of law concerning the recognition of foreign marriages and divorces. A marriage celebrated in England and Wales must satisfy the formalities of the law as to notice and ceremony, civil or religious, and is usually proved by production of a copy of the marriage certificate. If the certificate is not available, other evidence of the ceremony coupled with subsequent cohabitation will raise a presumption that there was a valid marriage. That presumption can be rebutted by evidence that the marriage was invalid, but it will probably require proof beyond reasonable doubt that it was invalid *(R(G) 2/70)*. It should be noted that in this instance the presumption of marriage is supported by the evidence of cohabitation but only when there is also evidence that the appropriate ceremony took place. In *R(G) 2/70* the parties went through what was apparently a bogus ceremony (though it was thought by the claimant to be genuine) followed by many years of cohabitation. It was held that no marriage could be presumed. This case must now be viewed as doubtful. Although it was distinguished by the Court of Appeal in *Adjudication Officer v Bath* reported as *R(G) 1/00* Lord Justice Evans, giving the leading judgment, says that the basis of the argument used in *R(G) 2/70* is not correct. The decision in *R(G) 1/00* would suggest that the presumption should have also availed the claimant in the earlier case. In *R(G) 1/00* the partners were "married" in a religious ceremony in a Sikh Temple in West London (1956). They lived together thereafter for 37 years, bringing up a family, until the "husband" died in 1994. The Sikh Temple was not at that time a registered building for marriages under the Marriage Act 1949. (It was so registered in 1983 but such registration is not retrospective.)

There was no evidence, and it was not suggested by the claimant, that there had been any other civil ceremony of marriage at a Registry Office. It appears that the claimant believed herself to have been validly married in the religious ceremony and made her claim to widow's benefits accordingly.

The AO rejected that claim on the basis that no marriage, valid in accordance with the Marriage Act 1949, had been shown. That decision was upheld by the SSAT, with an expression of sympathy for the claimant's situation. The Commissioner allowed an appeal after recourse to the presumption outlined above as stated in *Halsbury's Laws of England*, paras 992 and 993 (4th ed., Vol.22).

The second of these paragraphs is headed "Presumption from cohabitation after Ceremony" and would appear to be the more appropriate. That paragraph makes clear, however, that the presumption is only that all essentials of the ceremony will be presumed valid *unless the contrary is proved*. Here, it would seem the evidence rebutted the validity of the ceremony because the Temple was not a registered building. However, the footnotes in *Halsbury* include the case of *Re Shephard, George v Thyer* (1904) in which the presumption was applied although the only ceremony alleged was a marriage in France that was agreed to be invalid. The Commissioner took the view that he could follow this case as an earlier High Court precedent. In doing so he rejects the conclusion of the Commissioner in *R(G) 2/70* who had himself refused to follow *Re Shephard*. In any case, Commissioner Goodman suggests that *R(G) 2/70* might be distinguished on the narrow ground that the ceremony relied upon there had been in a bogus Registry Office (although believed to be genuine by the claimant), whereas the ceremony in this case had been in a genuine religious Temple.

The Commissioner also found the claim to be supportable under the first paragraph cited. This paragraph is headed "Presumption from Cohabitation without Ceremony". This presumption should apply after long cohabitation even in the absence of evidence of a marriage ceremony. The Commissioner's reasoning here seems to be that someone who has gone through what they believed to be a valid ceremony should not be worse off than someone who believed themselves to be married without any ceremony at all.

The Commissioner seems to have created a marriage very similar to the Scottish marriage "by habit and repute". There is, however, this difference. In Scotland, marriage can be presumed by long cohabitation with a willingness (and ability) to marry. In the English case it would seem to be necessary to prove a *belief* that the parties were married. That is just as well for otherwise we would have invented a true common law marriage that depended only on the parties long monogamous cohabitation.

The Court of Appeal's decision confirms the reasoning of the Commissioner, though they did also doubt whether the evidence available was sufficient to prove that the Sikh Temple was not a registered building in 1956. The sympathy of the judges was apparent for the widow of a man who had duly paid his income tax and national insurance contributions throughout his working life only for her to be told, when it was already too late, that she had never been married at all, but the key to their reasoning seems to be that nothing in the Marriage Act 1949 invalidates such a marriage unless the parties "knowingly and wilfully" intermarry without compliance with that Act. There was no evidence in this case that the parties were acting otherwise than in the honest belief that their marriage was validly celebrated, and in the absence of any statutory disqualification they were entitled to the benefit of the presumption outlined above.

In Scotland a valid marriage may be proved as well by "cohabitation with habit and repute". There must be a substantial period during which the parties have cohabited as man and wife. It is probable that most of that period must have been spent in Scotland, though in *R(G) 1/71* the Commissioner refused to hold that the shortness of time spent in Scotland was in itself a reason to refuse acceptance of the marriage. Secondly, it must be possible to infer from the cohabitation at least a tacit consent to a real marriage. In *R(G) 4/84* the Commissioner refused to find a marriage proved when the parties who had lived together for a number of years and had two children, as a matter of personal belief rejected the institution of marriage in itself. Finally the consent to marriage cannot be inferred so long as there is a legal impediment to a marriage taking place. Nor can consent to marriage be inferred so long as the parties believe that they are not free to marry (*R(G) 2/82*). Where there is an impediment to marriage throughout most of the period of cohabitation, but the parties know that they are free to marry at the time of the man's death, this may be sufficient to show the tacit consent to marriage. In *R(G) 5/83* the parties had lived together in Scotland for 12 years but it was only during the last three months that they were legally free to marry. Tacit consent to marriage was found from the whole period of cohabitation together with the steps that had been taken during those three months to arrange a marriage ceremony. A fine distinction is to be drawn between the decision in *R(G) 5/83* and a recent unreported Commissioner's decision *CSG 4/92*. In the recent case, the claimant had lived with the deceased (and children of each of them) for 15 years. For all but the last six months the deceased was not free to marry because his wife was alive, and the deceased, a devout Roman

Catholic, was not prepared to divorce her. Even after her death, the deceased wished to postpone marriage out of respect for his late wife. A marriage had been planned but the deceased died before it could take place. The Commissioner held that the deceased's unwillingness to contemplate marriage while his wife was alive together with his wish to postpone, after her death, prevented the formation of the necessary tacit consent to marriage. The application of the rule may have been extended by a recent decision in the Scots courts (*Kamperman and MacIver* [1994] S.L.T. 763) which seems to suggest that a period of cohabitation as short as six months might be substantial if the "quality" of the habit and repute is sufficient. But as well it should be noted that marriage is imputed only when the parties are generally believed to be married—habit is not enough without repute. In *CSG 7/95* the parties had lived together for 12 years, during the last eight-and-a-half of which they were free to marry, yet friends and family generally knew them to be merely cohabiting and no one took them to be married. The Commissioner upheld the SSAT decision to reject a claim for widow's benefit. Now that living together is more readily acceptable in society there may be less scope for the marriage by habit and repute. Decision *CSG 7/96* examines further the nature of marriage by habit and repute in Scotland. The parties had lived together for almost 20 years but never formally married. They had each been married previously and divorced, and that experience caused them both to be wary of remarriage. There was evidence that the couple were received in the community as a couple living in a stable relationship but none that they were taken to be married. The Commissioner holds that the repute required to be shown is not confined to a general belief that the parties are formally married—it may suffice that people generally take them to be married in the sense that they accept all the usual consequences of marriage on an irregular basis. On the facts of this case, however, he found the evidence did not support the view that the parties were generally regarded as married even on that basis, and furthermore, that if they had been, their reluctance to introduce the formal ties of marriage would negative the necessary consent to living in a married state. Modern social conditions do seem to be taking their toll on this form of marriage. In the case of *Vosilius* v *Vosilius* 2000 SCHR 679, the Lord Ordinary has prescribed seven requirements that must be satisfied. They are that:

(a) there must be cohabitation;

(b) the cohabitation must be as husband and wife;

(c) the cohabitation must be in Scotland;

(d) the cohabitation must be for a sufficient time;

(e) the parties must be reputed to be husband and wife;

(f) the repute must be sufficiently general;

(g) the parties must be free to marry each other.

Even if these requirements are satisfied the claim may yet fail if the presumption of tacit consent to marriage, which these requirements would supply, can be rebutted. The difficulties that there may be in negotiating this tricky course can be illustrated by the decision of the Scottish Commissioners in *CSG/ 648/2007*. There the couple had lived together in Scotland for many years. They were regarded by their families and by others (e.g. work colleagues) as living together as husband and wife (both of them wore wedding rings) and they spoke frequently of marrying at some time in the future. But after the male partner's death a claim for bereavement benefits failed for two reasons. First, although they were generally regarded as living in a stable relationship as if they were husband and wife, they were not reputed to *be* husband and wife, and therefore point (e) above was not satisfied. Secondly, an expressed intention to marry in the future (the claimant had frequently said that she would "one day make an honest man of him") was inconsistent with a tacit consent to being already married and must therefore rebut the presumption. Given the modern attitude of couples to the matter of whether they are in fact married it seems unlikely that many will succeed in future to show that they are married by habit and repute, but it should be noted that this case may yet be taken to appeal.

An attempt to gain the benefit of the Scots law for the female survivor of a couple who had lived together in England for 15 years failed in *CG/1259/2002*. It had been argued that to refuse her a widows benefit was to discriminate against her contrary to the Art.12 of the EC Treaty (prohibition of discrimination on grounds of nationality). The Commissioner held that in EC law (unlike UK law) there was no such concept of Scottish (or English) nationality and therefore there could be no discrimination. He held also that an argument based on the Human Rights Act 1998 must also fail, because even if a breach could be made out, a Commissioner has no jurisdiction to make a declaration of incompatibility and the words of the Social Security Act 1998 confining these benefits to widows were plain.

Foreign marriages, and divorces, raise difficult and often obscure points of law that may depend upon proof of foreign law. It is impossible to deal with these points in this note. Tribunals which require assistance on matters of foreign law are unlikely to gain assistance from s.7(4) of the Social Security Act 1998, which provides for an appeal tribunal to have the assistance of an expert on matters of fact (which proof of foreign law is). This is because subs.(5) of that section requires that the expert must be a member of the panel of tribunal members; it is thought unlikely that such members will be found. This means that tribunals who require the assistance of an expert in foreign law will have to resort to the practice suggested in *R(G) 2/71* and followed in *CG/1822/1998*. This was to identify the party raising the issue that required proof of foreign law and requiring that party to obtain suitable evidence. Note that the foreign law as found by a Commissioner is a finding of fact. When the Commissioner applies that law it does not thereby become a part of the social security law being used by the Commissioner. This means that a subsequent tribunal is not bound to accept the same conclusion as to the foreign law as has been accepted in a previous Commissioner's decision. In the absence of a contrary expert opinion a tribunal will doubtless accept the view adopted in an earlier decision when that is provided to them, but where there is conflicting expert evidence available, the tribunal must consider all of the evidence and choose that which is most persuasive to them.

This was the course adopted in *R(G) 2/00*. The issue there was the validity of a foreign marriage which itself depended upon the recognition of the previous divorce of one of the parties. The divorce was by talaq in Bangladesh in 1973. Earlier Commissioners' decisions had accepted that a talaq divorce would be recognised only when the formalities had included its notification to the Chairman of the Union Council. In the present case, new expert evidence was given to the effect that, at the time when Bangladesh was only very recently created as a state, there was no such official. In any case, further evidence suggested that more recently talaq divorces were accepted in Bangladesh as valid without notification and might therefore be recognised in English law also. In this case, the Commissioner upheld the decision of a tribunal which had accepted the validity of the divorce and subsequent marriage (and therefore awarded a widow's pension) notwithstanding the contrary conclusion in earlier cases. Other cases involving foreign law include *R(G) 4/93* (marriage celebrated in Bangladesh) and *R(G) 1/94* (talaq divorce). Note that a talaq divorce, even if valid by the law of domicile of the parties, cannot be effective if it is proclaimed in this country. This is because s.16 of the Domicile and Matrimonial Proceedings Act 1973, provides that no proceedings in this country shall be regarded as validly dissolving marriage unless those proceedings are instituted in a court of law.

Even proving the existence of a marriage that is claimed to have been celebrated in a foreign country may be difficult where there is, or was at the time, little formality in connection with the ceremony and no reliable records of marriages are maintained The difficulties associated with proof of some marriages have been demonstrated in *CP/4062/2004* and again in *CP/891/2008*. In both these cases the parties had been married in Yemen from where no formal record of the marriage was available. Both parties to the marriage made statements about the celebration of the marriage and the wife, who had remained at all times in Yemen, was interviewed there through an interpreter. Some of the information that was given about the marriage appeared to be contradictory. For that reason, and others, the claim for a Category B pension was refused. The interest in both of these cases lies in the approach taken by Commissioner Jacobs, and adopted in the later case by Deputy Commissioner Wikeley, to the absence of reliable documentary evidence of the marriage. In both cases the DM and the appeal tribunal had relied upon that absence, at least in part, as the reason for their decision that no marriage had been shown to exist. The commissioners find this to be a wrong approach. In the words of Commissioner Jacobs the absence of contemporary documentary evidence

"is a neutral factor. The decision maker and the tribunal have to decide if the claimant is genuine or dishonest. It is wrong to approach that task by taking the lack of contemporaneous evidence as a factor against the claimant. To do so would be to assume what has to be decided."

Polygamous marriages raise special problems of their own. As the law stands, a marriage which is actually polygamous will not be recognised as a valid marriage at all—even when only one wife is in this country. However, where the marriage is only potentially polygamous or was previously polygamous, but is no longer so, it will be treated as a valid marriage for any period in which it is in fact monogamous. But the marriage must be valid according to the foreign law in question, and a person domiciled in England at the time cannot contract a valid polygamous marriage. There have been several recent Commissioners' decisions on this point. All of them involve parties from the Indian subcontinent who have married there, then come to live in the UK (or at least the husband has) and then returned to India for a period during which the husband has contracted a second marriage. This second marriage is valid by the law of, say, Bangladesh, but will not be valid in English law if the husband at the time of that marriage had acquired a domicile of choice in the UK. If he was then domiciled in the UK the second marriage is void and his first marriage remains legally monogamous. In the event of his death the first wife may then claim a widow's pension whether she is resident in the UK or not (*R(G) 1/95*).

The matter of domicile is a complex question of law. In *R(G) 1/93*, the Commissioner relied upon the principle set out in the standard work, Dicey and Morris, *Conflict of Laws*. He puts it as follows:

"Under English law every person receives a domicile of origin at birth and, throughout his life, cannot ever be without a domicile and, further, at any one time, can only have one domicile. However, a person can acquire a domicile of choice by residing in a country, other than that of his domicile of origin, with the intention of staying there either permanently or indefinitely. All surrounding circumstances must be taken into account when determining whether a person has acquired a domicile of choice, including his motive for taking up residence initially and whether or not that residence was precarious. A person may abandon a domicile of choice only if he both ceases to reside and ceases to intend to reside there; it is not, for example, necessary to show a positive intention not to return, it suffices to prove an absence of intention to continue to reside. When a person abandons a domicile of choice he either acquires a new domicile of choice or his domicile of origin revives."

In the present case the Commissioner substituted his own decision for that of the tribunal. He found that the husband had a domicile of origin in what is now Bangladesh; had acquired a domicile of choice by many years of residence in the UK, but that he had abandoned that domicile of choice when he returned to Bangladesh for a period of two years and tried to set up business there. It was at that time that he married a second wife. Subsequently, he returned to England and to his first wife who had remained here all along. At the time of his death in England he may well have re-acquired his domicile of choice here but that was not important. What mattered was his domicile at the time of the second marriage. Since that was in Bangladesh the marriage was valid and since both wives survived him they were both polygamous marriages. Neither wife could therefore claim a widow's pension.

Even where no issue of domicile arises it will still be necessary for the claimant to show that her marriage was in fact monogamous at the time of her husband's death. Where the marriage has been polygamous at some earlier time that may require proof either that all other wives have predeceased their husband or that the earlier marriage has been dissolved by a valid decree of divorce as well as proof that the claimant's own marriage was valid. All of these issues arose in *CG/1822/1998*. Deputy Commissioner Gamble gave extensive instructions to the legally qualified member of the tribunal, to whom the decision was returned, which other tribunals may find of assistance.

The complications of qualifying for a widow's benefit and the difficulties that can arise in determining the validity of the claimant's foreign marriage when that in turn depends upon a foreign divorce, are graphically illustrated in *CP/3108/2004*.

The divorce and marriage had taken place in Pakistan in 1961 so this required consideration of no fewer than three recognition statutes, and two versions of the common law. Perhaps the most interesting feature of this case is, however, that the claimant was the second widow to claim a pension on the basis of marriage to the same husband; both claims have gone before a Commissioner and both have been successful! There are, therefore, conflicting decisions as to the validity of the same divorce. Commissioner Edward Jacobs points out that at the moment there is no way effectively to avoid the possibility of this happening. He suggests that there should be a power for the Secretary of State to refer decisions to be considered together by a Tribunal or by a Commissioner. An appeal to the Court of Appeal might be expected, but the decision in respect of the first widow is now probably out of time.

The effect of the Human Rights Act on the treatment of polygamous marriages has been considered by a Tribunal of Commissioners considering appeals in three cases. *(R(P)2/06)*.

In all of them both marriages had taken place in Bangladesh and all the partners had been domiciled there at the time of those marriages. Both marriages would therefore be regarded by English Law as valid marriages for most purposes. However, it was accepted that for widow's benefits the Court Appeal had decided in *(Fuljuan) Bibi v CAO* [1998] 1 F.L.R. 375 that where a man was survived by two polygamously married wives neither of them could qualify as his "widow" for the purpose of claiming benefits. The question was, therefore, whether this treatment amounted to an improper interpretation of the legislation in the light of the Human Rights Act. It was conceded, at least before the commissioners, that the claim engaged their rights under Art.8 (right to family life) and it was argued that disqualifying a polygamous wife was unlawful discrimination under Art.14. All of the tribunal held that it was not. A majority (Chief Commissioner Heginbotham and Commissioner Howell) held that to treat a person who was polygamously married at the relevant time, differently from one who was monogamously (even if potentially polygamously) married, was not discrimination within any of the grounds of Art.14. In their view it was a difference of treatment based upon a factual difference that was rational and in accordance with the accepted norms of our society, and therefore, not discrimination.

Perhaps more convincingly, Commissioner Levenson held that it was discrimination on the grounds of "status", but that it was justified and proportional for the same reasons.

A marriage lasts until it is dissolved by a decree of divorce or of annulment. In either case the marriage persists until the decree absolute is granted. Foreign divorces raise the same problems as foreign marriages. Recognition is provided for under s.46 of the Family Law Act 1986. Foreign divorces will be recognised where they are valid by the law of the country in which they are obtained and if, at that time, either party to the marriage was habitually resident in that country, or was domiciled there, or was a national of that country. Where a marriage is void, for example, because it is bigamous, it has no legal effect whatsoever, and no benefits can be claimed on the basis of it. Where, however, a marriage is annulled for a reason that makes it only voidable, for example because of non-consummation, it is now clear that the marriage is to be regarded as valid and subsisting up to the date of annulment (see Nullity of Marriage Act 1975, s.5 and *R(G) 1/85*).

The death of the claimant's spouse is usually proved by production of the death certificate. Difficulties can arise, however, where no certificate is issued because the spouse has simply disappeared. In Scotland, death may be decreed by the adjudicating authority where a person has not been known to be alive for at least seven years (Presumption of Death (Scotland) Act 1977 and *R(G) 1/80*). In England however, where it is necessary to rebut the common law presumption that life continues, the claimant may be required to show that the spouse has disappeared in circumstances that point towards death. That was the position taken in *R(G) 1/62* when 25 years' absence without any information was held not to be sufficient. But in *Chard v Chard* [1956] P.259 (a case concerning the validity of a marriage) the High Court held that after seven years' absence without anything being heard by those whom one would expect to hear, and when all due inquiries had been made, a person could be presumed to have died within that period. This case was not referred to in *R(G) 1/62* and may offer a preferable solution in these cases. Special provision is now made in ss.3 and 4 of the Administration Act for late claims to be made in respect of a death which is only recently discovered or presumed so that such spouses can claim back-payment of benefit in respect of a period of more than the usual one year. Note, however, that in the case of a widow who had only just discovered the fact of her husband's death, though that may have occurred several years earlier, the effect of s.3 is only to permit a claim for back-payment of benefit for up to 24 months at most (see *CG/75/96*).

There is one situation in which a spouse will forfeit all their rights to bereavement benefit though it is not mentioned in the legislation at all. This is where the claimant has been guilty of the homicide of the spouse (see *R. v Chief N.I. Commissioner Ex p. Connor* [1981] 1 Q.B. 758). The rule is one of public policy, based upon the principle that no one should profit by their own wrongdoing and applies generally to all interests deriving from the death of the deceased.

At common law the consequence of the forfeiture rule was that the spouse lost the pension rights entirely, but since the introduction of the Forfeiture Act 1982, it has been possible for a Commissioner to modify the effect of the rule. Under the Forfeiture Act 1982, the question whether a spouse's right to any benefit is to be forfeited must be determined at first instance by a Commissioner. The matter can no longer come before an appeal tribunal though where a Commissioner has determined that the right to benefit is not to be forfeited, any other issues as to entitlement should be determined by a decision-maker in the usual way, unless the claimant has consented to the Commissioner deciding the matter (*R(G) 3/84*).

Not all homicides will result in forfeiture. Even before 1982 the courts had developed some exceptions to the rule, e.g. in motor manslaughter cases and, later, in cases of diminished responsibility where the level of culpability was non-existent. Now, however, the Court of Appeal has suggested (in *Dunbar v Plant* [1997] 4 All E.R. 289) that the better approach is to regard the forfeiture rule as applicable to all homicides and to leave any relief against the rule to be achieved using the Forfeiture Act. In *Dunbar v Plant* the rule was applied to the property rights of the survivor of a suicide pact, though the majority of that court thought that she should then be relieved from any forfeiture at all, so that she took both the title to joint property by survivorship, and the proceeds of an insurance policy on the life of her partner. In that case also the Court of Appeal settles a point previously the subject of dispute; it is now clear that the Forfeiture Act permits the court (or Commissioner) to remove the effect of forfeiture entirely where it is appropriate to do so.

In *CFP/2688/2004* (to be reported as *R(FP) 1/05*) Commissioner Rowland confirms that the effect of *Dunbar v Plant* is that the forfeiture rule should normally apply in all cases where a commissioner is satisfied that the claimant is guilty of manslaughter. That applies even where the claimant may have been acquitted of manslaughter in the Crown Court, as in *Gray v Barr* [1971] 2 Q.B. 554.

Commissioner Rowland does leave open the possibility, however, that a commissioner could find a conviction of manslaughter on the ground of diminished responsibility to be inappropriate, and conclude that the claimant should be regarded instead, as not guilty of homicide by reason of insanity. This could happen, for example, where the claimant has pleaded guilty to manslaughter on the ground of diminished responsibility and a hospital order has been imposed, rather than to have stood trial and pleaded not guilty to murder by reason of insanity. In such a case, if a commissioner finds that a claimant should have been found not guilty by reason of insanity, the rule of forfeiture would not apply at all. It is likely, however, that it will be more usual for the forfeiture rule to be applied and the commissioner then grant full, or partial, relief against that forfeiture. In the present case no relief was allowed because the sum involved was only 47p per week and the commissioner felt its loss reflected the role of the claimant in causing the death of his wife.

The Act, however, does not permit any relief where the party claiming has committed murder. A spouse convicted of murder, therefore, must lose all bereavement benefits—see *R(G) 1/90*. In *R(FG) 1/04* the claimant had been convicted of soliciting her husband's murder (an offence under the Offences Against the Person Act, 1861). She claimed a widow's pension after her release from prison. The Commissioner held that the forfeiture rule applied to her claim because she had "unlawfully counselled" her husband's death within s.1(2) of the Forfeiture Act 1982, but that it was not caught by s.5 of that Act which proscribed any relief where the claimant was convicted of murder. This meant that it was open to the Commissioner to modify the effect of forfeiture. On the facts of this case however, he held that no modification was appropriate because she had been closely and directly involved in the murder. Where the spouse has been convicted only of manslaughter the matter will depend upon all the circumstances of the case, in particular upon the degree of culpability inherent in the act (compare *R(G) 1/83 and R(G) 3/84*) and upon whether the killing was the result of provocation—see *R(G) 1/98* where the Commissioner restored benefits from the date of his decision, some seven years after the death, and limited, to 50 per cent, the widow's future entitlement to a Category B pension. In *CFG 4622/03* the claimant had been convicted of manslaughter of his wife on his own admission (the jury having been directed to find him not guilty of murder because of his wife's provocation). The Commissioner, taking account of the comments made by the judge in passing sentence, applied the rule of forfeiture to the bereavement payment, but relieved him of forfeiture in all other respects so that he was entitled to Widowed Parent's Allowance in respect of 2 children for whom he was responsible, and for any potential pension entitlement that he might have as a result of his wife's contributions.

Note that it is not necessary that the spouse should have been convicted of the homicide; it is enough that they have committed it. Accordingly, when bereavement benefits have been paid between the death and the conviction (or more usually apprehension) there will be an overpayment that is almost certainly recoverable. Note as well, that although forfeiture is mandatory following a conviction for murder, there is no principle under which there must necessarily be relief when the claimant is convicted of manslaughter. In *R(G) 1/91* the claimant's conviction of murder was quashed, because some evidence was admitted that was technically hearsay, but a sentence of life imprisonment was imposed and the Commissioner held that there should be no relief of the forfeiture rule.

Entitlement to any of the bereavement benefits is subject to the proviso that they are not payable if the spouse has remarried, or if they are living with another as man and wife.

As to remarriage, the points above about marriage will apply again, but note that the event which terminates entitlement is a valid marriage—a Bereavement Benefit does not revive if that marriage subsequently terminates by divorce, or a decree of annulment, or by that spouse's death (it is otherwise if the second marriage is void). If the second marriage ends by that spouse's death, the widow must claim Bereavement Benefit afresh, on the basis of the second spouse's contributions, not the first. Where a person lives with another as man and wife the disqualification from benefit lasts only for so long as that relationship exists. If they separate, or the other dies, Bereavement Benefit revives. This may seem an incentive to live in sin!

The concept of a couple who "live together as husband and wife" is one that recurs throughout the social security system. In the past it was usually referred to as the "cohabitation test". Generally it is used as a device that disqualifies, or reduces the claimant's entitlement to benefit. Occasionally it may occur as a test of entitlement, for example, to increases for an adult dependant.

Appeals against a Secretary of State's decision that a couple are living as husband and wife are frequently among the most contentious and hotly disputed cases that an appeal tribunal has to consider. Direct evidence is often lacking and much may be left to inferences to be drawn by the appeal tribunal on the basis of their common sense and experience of the world. Nevertheless, an appeal tribunal must be careful that its inferences are drawn from some evidence, and are not just supposition and prejudice—the finding is a determination of a matter of law and must be reached in a judicial manner.

The early cases on this subject were decided in the context of Widow's Benefit; most of the more recent cases have involved entitlement to Income Support (or its predecessors), but in several places it has been said that the same principles should apply to this test throughout the social security system (see *R(G) 17/81* and *R(G) 3/81*). The adoption since 1984 of a single tribunal to hear appeals for most social security benefits (an appeal tribunal) should have facilitated this development. To the extent that this is an issue that must reflect current social conditions and mores, the later cases may be preferred to the earlier ones.

The philosophy behind this test must be to protect the institution of marriage as a corner-stone of our society—essentially it means that a couple in receipt of benefits will be no better off living together without marriage than they would be if married. It is not a test based upon morals to punish illicit sex, because sexual relations alone do not amount to living together, nor can it ever be applied to a homosexual relationship. It is not a test based simply on reduced living costs—the "two can live as cheaply as one" theory—because two persons can live as a common household without the test applying to them. The essential question is whether the parties' relationship approximates enough to marriage for them to be regarded as "living together as husband and wife". Guidance has been given by both the Commissioners and the courts.

The early Commissioners' decisions pointed to the need to consider the relationship from three aspects: their relationship with regard to sex; their relationship with regard to money; and their general relationship (see *R(G) 3/71*). These matters have now been subsumed within the guidelines that were subsequently issued by the DSS in their Supplementary Benefits Handbook and are now contained in the guidance issued to decision-makers (DMG). These guidelines have frequently been adopted by the Commissioners and the courts. The courts, in *Robson v Secretary of State for Social Services* (1982) 3 F.L.R. 232, and in *Butterworth v Supplementary Benefits Commission* [1982] 1 All E.R. 498, have also emphasised the importance of ensuring that more must be shown than that the parties are living in a single house, or as a single household. Sharing a roof is only the beginning of the test—it must be shown as well that their relationship within the household is in the style and manner of a married couple. These cases also introduce the difficult question of the intention of the parties. In *Robson* the parties were both disabled. They moved to share a maisonette, at their social worker's suggestion, after they had both been widowed, and in order simply to give each other mutual help and support. Webster J. held that they were not living as husband and wife. In doing so, he said that such decisions must usually be based upon objective facts

"because usually the intention of the parties is either unascertainable, or, if ascertainable, is not to be regarded as reliable. But if it is established to the satisfaction of the tribunal that the two persons concerned did not intend to live together as husband and wife, and still do not intend to do so, in my judgment it would be a very strong case indeed sufficient to justify a decision that they are, or ought to be treated as if they are, husband and wife."

It is suggested that it may be preferable to think in terms of "purpose" rather than "intention". It was the parties' purpose that they live together for mutual aid and support in relation to their disability, rather than for the purpose of a social and sexual companionship akin to marriage. This approach is consistent with *Butterworth* and also with *R(SB) 35/85* in both of which the facts were similar to *Robson*. At any rate it should be clear that it is not sufficient that the parties do not intend to live as husband and wife simply because they do not believe in marriage and do not wish to involve themselves in the social conventions and legal consequences that a marriage would entail (see *R(SB) 17/81*). Most cohabitation cases now revolve around an examination of the six criteria that are given as guidelines in the DMG, and are relied upon by the DWP in preparing each submission for an appeal tribunal. These are:

1. Membership of the same household

1.110   This is a prerequisite to any further consideration—without it, the parties can hardly be said to be living together at all. A "household test" has also been developed in relation to assessing the requirements of a claimant for Income Support. This test lays a great deal of emphasis upon the extent to which persons who share a house live in the manner of a family. It may be doubted whether all of these factors should be regarded as relevant in this context. The fact that parties never, or rarely, take their meals together, and perhaps do not even shop collectively may be highly significant in determining whether the claimant should be assessed for Income Support as maintaining a separate household, because his costs will be higher, but it should not be decisive in determining whether he is living as husband and wife, if, in every other way, that relationship is indicated. In any case there will usually be some explanation as to why the parties do not take their meals together, e.g. shift work, vegetarianism, and their practice will need to be considered as evidence of their relationship only in the light of that cause. The DMG points to the question of whether either of the parties maintains another home where they usually live—in which case, cohabitation is unlikely. In *R(SB) 8/85* the Commissioner held that a man could be a member of only one household at a time; if he was a member of his wife's household to which he returned at weekends, he could not at the same time be living in the same household as a woman with whom he lived for five days a week, in the town to which his work took him (though in that case, the issue was referred to another tribunal to determine in which household he was living). In the context of Bereavement Benefit, this would mean that a widow who is kept as a mistress is unlikely to be living with a man as his wife. The Handbook also points out that the parties may continue to live together during a period of temporary separation. In regard to Bereavement Benefit, reference might be made to reg.2(4) of the Persons Residing Together Regulations. This provides that two persons are not to be treated as having ceased to reside together by reason of any temporary absence from each other. Although the word is "reside", rather than "living", and the Regulations were designed primarily for another purpose, they do correspond to the provisions applicable to Income Support. In *R(SB) 30/83* the couple were regarded as continuing to live together though the woman was absent throughout a University term.

2. Stability

The stability of the relationship is important because if the claimant is to be deprived of benefit even temporarily, this should not be done lightly and unless there is some basis upon which the support might be expected to come from elsewhere or by a joint assessment for benefit. In any case it is of the essence of the marriage relationship that the parties are joining in union, at least at the outset, for life. A relationship does not need to have been long-lasting to be stable—a stable relationship may be formed quite quickly, but where there is doubt as to the nature of the relationship, its duration and its resilience may be relevant. Nor does it mean simply that because a relationship is stable that the parties are living as husband and wife—there may be very long-standing landlady and lodger relationships, and long-standing homecare relationships (see *R(SB) 35/85* above). In some cases it may be relevant to consider whether the parties have chosen to move house together, or to move to another town together, though, again, it is not unknown for long-standing house-sharers to move together simply because they know themselves to be compatible cotenants. It will be important to consider carefully the timetable of events and the reasons for staying together.

1.111

3. Financial support

This is seldom as helpful as might be expected. It is unusual for there to be evidence of financial support of one partner by another, beyond an equal sharing of rent and household utility costs, which is equally consistent with simply sharing a household or even just co-tenancy. Where one person has supported another, it is usually only after benefit has been withdrawn, and then may be explicable on the basis that it is the kind of action that one might expect of a person to help a friend in extremity. In any case claimants are usually at pains to borrow for support elsewhere pending the hearing of an appeal.

1.112

Where a payment is explained as board and lodging paid by a lodger to his landlady it is important to look not only at the amount of the payment but the parties' reasoning and the process by which they came to that sum. Frequently a low payment, or no payment (that might indicate a non-commercial relationship) is explained on the basis of doing a favour and because the person did not want any payment to interfere with his own receipt of benefits. Nor is it any help to rephrase the question by asking whether there should be financial support. This is to beg the question because it is only if the parties are living as husband and wife that it might be said that there should be financial support for one another. This amounts only to posing the same question another way. However, if the parties operate a joint bank account this may indicate a mutual sense of trust and a willingness to give unquestioning support, that would be common only in a marriage-like relationship. The absence of a joint bank account is not, of course, strongly probative.

4. Sexual relationship

After much criticism in the 1970s which included newspaper stories about sex snoopers, the Department has been concerned to reduce the emphasis placed upon a sexual relationship. It is of the essence of a marriage that, initially at least, its purpose is to facilitate a stable heterosexual relationship. Early editions of the DSS Handbook on SB emphasised the importance of a sexual relationship and for a time contained the sentence "However if a couple have never had such a relationship it is most unlikely that they should be regarded as living together as husband and wife". These words were dropped from later editions of the handbook, but in *R(SB) 35/85* the Commissioner said that he thought they had reflected the sense of what Woolf J. had meant in *Butterworth*. In *R(SB) 35/85* itself (another case of mutual carers) it was held that the absence of any sexual purpose precluded a finding of living together. Again in *CSB/150/85* the Commissioner held that a couple who were both Mormons were not to be regarded as living together as husband and wife. Although they were engaged to be married they had refrained from any sexual relationship as they were required to do by their religion. *CG/001/1990* upholds the finding of a

1.113

tribunal that the claimant was living with a man as husband and wife even though the tribunal had found as a fact that the parties had not had sexual intercourse until after they were married. (The claimant had informed the DSS when she married.) This was an unusual case. The couple were certainly living together and had a stable relationship—it was found that they had already agreed to marry. What seems to have convinced the Commissioner was that at about the time they agreed to marry, they each sold a property and purchased a new home together on a joint tenancy. This was described by the claimant as a "business arrangement" (it was subsequently sold at a profit), but the Commissioner observed that she was content to trust her partner in the event of her death to see that her sons inherited her substantial share of the value. This certainly suggested something other than a business relationship, but was it that of husband and wife; or only that of a couple who had agreed to become husband and wife? The Commissioner in this case refers to *R(SB) 17/81*, but not the *Robson* or *Butterworth* (1982) cases, nor *R(SB) 35/85* where the importance of a sexual relationship was reemphasised. The DMG is correct in asserting that the absence of a sexual relationship at any particular time does not prove that the parties are not cohabiting—a "common law marriage" may evolve into a state of abstinence from sexual relations just as easily as a marriage may, and the parties will not thereby cease to live together as man and wife, but that is not a justification for omitting the question of sexual relations altogether and asking only are the couple sharing costs and giving companionship. It should be repeated that the question is whether the parties' relationship sufficiently approximates to marriage, and in that the possibility of, or the history of, a sexual relationship is important.

The importance of a sexual relationship, as well as the whole approach to be adopted in deciding whether a couple are living together as man and wife, has been examined again in *CIS/4156/2006*. This was a case where the couple had admittedly lived together in the past; but had resumed the shared occupation of a house (not the same home as they had shared previously) as "friends". The house they now shared was originally rented from the council by the claimant, but at some time in the course of their renewed relationship, she purchased it with the help of a loan from her (former) partner. The claimant was, throughout the period in question, in receipt of Income Support, and this was an appeal against a claim for recovery of overpaid benefit in the sum of £24,000. Deputy Commissioner Wikeley allowed the appeal on the grounds that the tribunal had failed to explain the reasons for their decision and in particular that they failed to explain why they were rejecting the argument advanced on behalf of the appellant that there was no sexual relationship involved in their renewed relationship.

There may be a connection between the sexual relationship and stability. In marriage the sexual relationship is usually confined for the most part to one partner (though adultery is not unknown). It may be that where the parties in an unmarried couple have many other sexual liaisons, that it would be wrong to regard the relationship as sufficiently stable. This may mean that the more licentious the claimant's behaviour is, the less likely he or she is to lose benefit! In such cases, however, it will be important to consider other evidence of the stability of the relationship.

5. Children

1.114   Where the couple have had children born to them and they are living together to provide for the care of the children, that is strongly indicative of living in a marriage-like state. However, cases like that are rarely much in dispute.

6. Public acknowledgment

1.115   If a woman takes a man's name, either by repute or by deed poll, that is a strong indication that they are living as man and wife. In *R(G) 1/74* a widow had changed her name by deed poll, and for an earlier period listed herself by that name on the electoral register, and had allowed herself to be known for business and social purposes as the wife of the man with whom she was living. It was held that this was all evidence from which a sexual relationship, which was denied, might properly be inferred, and that in any case they lived together as husband and wife. The cases are usually less explicit and nowadays even married couples may not use the same name. Under this head it may also be important to consider not only how the parties present themselves publicly, but how others have regard to them—are they regarded as a "couple" in the way that a married couple would be received? It will also be important to consider somewhere the rest of the parties' social behaviour. Do they choose to spend leisure time together? Do they go on holiday together? Do they share their friends, or do they have independent social lives? All of these may be some indication, but like so many other factors, all might be as equally consistent with the behaviour of good friends, as they are of married couples. It is frequently reiterated in the reported decisions that all the circumstances of a relationship must be looked at, and that no one circumstance is conclusive (*R(G) 1/79*).

Certain relationships may give rise to more difficulty than others.

1. The lodger and landlady relationship. Several of the criteria may appear to be satisfied. The whole point of their arrangement is that one should give financial support to the other and that living costs should be reduced by being shared. The best that a tribunal can do is to try to form an impression of the veracity of the parties. As the Department will not have asked questions about a sexual relationship, it is important to note whether the claimant has volunteered information and it may be necessary to ask whether they are willing to provide such information. The claimant may not have provided any information simply because they were not asked for it earlier.

2. The group of friends house-sharing. Again several of the more visible criteria may seem to be satisfied and if the friends form a stable group of house-sharers who also share their social life it may be difficult to identify the point at which two of them can be said to have formed a couple that live as husband and wife. Much of what is said above may apply again.

3. The ex-husband and wife who move back together (though this cannot apply to a claim for bereavement benefits). This is less common. A couple may divorce and then after some time agree to share the former matrimonial home, or some other home, again. This may be on the basis of a landlady–lodger arrangement, or simply as house-sharers. Most of the criteria will be satisfied. It is suggested that in such a case it may be proper to test the re-created relationship as if they had not formerly been married (e.g. in relation to the sexual relationship). This may depend upon the length of time that they have lived apart, and their age, especially if they are both caring for a child of the family in the home.

Finally, it should be emphasised that the onus of proof in most of these cases will be on the Secretary of State. If the issue is one of disqualification (as for Bereavement Benefit) the Department must prove, on the balance of probabilities, that the couple are living as husband and wife. Nevertheless, Tribunal members may find it helpful to ask themselves, and occasionally to ask the claimant, in what way the parties' relationship would differ if they were married. This may be helpful to point up the differences between the claimant's relationship and marriage, as well as the similarities, but it should always be remembered that this is the last piece of the jig-saw puzzle and not the first.

Long-term incapacity benefit for widows

[¹ **40.**—(1) Subject to subsection (2) below, this section applies to a woman who—

    (a) on her late husband's death is not entitled to a widowed mother's allowance or subsequently ceases to be entitled to such an allowance;

1.116

Social Security Contributions and Benefits Act 1992

(b) is incapable of work at the time when he dies or when she subsequently ceases to be so entitled;

(c) either—

    (i) would have been entitled to a widow's pension if she had been over the age of 45 when her husband died or when she ceased to be entitled to a widowed mother's allowance; or

    (ii) is entitled to such a pension with a reduction under section 39(4) above; and

(d) is not entitled to incapacity benefit apart from this section.

(2) This section does not apply to a woman unless—

(a) her husband died after 5th April 1979; or

(b) she ceased to be entitled to a widowed mother's allowance after that date (whenever her husband died).

(3) A woman to whom this section applies is entitled to long-term incapacity benefit under this section for any day of incapacity for work which—

(a) falls in a period of incapacity for work that began before the time when her late husband died or she subsequently ceased to be entitled to a widowed mother's allowance; and

(b) is after that time and after the first 364 days of incapacity for work in that period.

(4) A woman to whom this section applies who is not entitled to long-term incapacity benefit under subsection (3) above, but who is terminally ill, is entitled to short-term incapacity benefit under this section for any day of incapacity for work which—

(a) falls in a period of incapacity for work that began before the time when her late husband died or she subsequently ceased to be entitled to a widowed mother's allowance, and

(b) is after that time and after the first 196 days of incapacity for work in that period

For the purposes of this subsection a woman is terminally ill if she suffers from a progressive disease and her death in consequence of that disease can reasonably be expected within 6 months.

(5) The weekly rate of incapacity benefit payable under this section is—

(a) if the woman is not entitled to a widow's pension, that which would apply if she were entitled to long-term incapacity benefit under section 30A above; and

(b) if she is entitled to a widow's pension with a reduction under section 39(4) above, the difference between the weekly rate of that pension and the weekly rate referred to in paragraph (a) above.

(6) A woman is not entitled to incapacity benefit under this section if she is over pensionable age; but if she has attained pensionable age and the period of incapacity for work mentioned in subsection (3)(a) or (4)(a) above did not terminate before she attained that age—

(a) she shall, if not otherwise entitled to a Category A retirement pension, be entitled to such a pension, and

(b) the weekly rate of the Category A retirement pension to which she is entitled (whether by virtue of paragraph (a) above or otherwise) shall be determined in the prescribed manner.

(7) Where a woman entitled to short-term incapacity benefit under subsection (4) above attains pensionable age and defers her entitlement to a Category A pension or makes an election under section 54(1) below, the

88

days of incapacity for work falling within the period of incapacity for work mentioned in that subsection shall, for the purpose of determining any subsequent entitlement to incapacity benefit under section 30A above or the rate of that benefit, be treated as if they had been days of entitlement to short-term incapacity benefit.

(8) References to short-term incapacity benefit at the higher rate shall be construed as including short-term incapacity benefit payable under subsection (4) above.]

AMENDMENT

1. Social Security (Incapacity for Work) Act 1994, Sch.1 (April 13, 1995).

DERIVATION

SSA 1975, s.15.   1.117
Substituted by Social Security (Incapacity for Work) Act 1994.

DEFINITIONS

"entitled"—see s.122,
"day of incapacity for work"—see s.57.
"period of interruption of employment"—see s.57.

GENERAL NOTE

This benefit will in appropriate circumstances, be affected by the Gender   1.118
Recognition Act 2004. A person in receipt of benefit by virtue of this section who obtains a gender recognition certificate will cease to be entitled to benefit (and will lose, as well, the right to transfer to Category A Retirement Pension in due course). This is surprising because s.41 that follows makes an equivalent provision for widowers. See the notes to the Gender Recognition Act in Vol.III of this work.

Long-term incapacity benefit for widowers

[¹ **41.**—(1) This section applies to a man whose wife has died on or after   1.119
6th April 1979 and who either—
  (a) was incapable of work at the time when she died, or
  (b) becomes incapable of work within the prescribed period after that time,
and is not entitled to incapacity benefit apart from this section.

(2) A man to whom this section applies is entitled to long-term incapacity benefit under this section for any day of incapacity for work which—
  (a) falls in a period of incapacity for work that began before the time when his wife died or within the prescribed period after that time, and
  (b) is after that time and after the first 364 days of incapacity for work in that period.

(3) A man to whom this section applies who is not entitled to longterm incapacity benefit under subsection (2) above, but who is terminally ill, is entitled to short-term incapacity benefit under this section for any day of incapacity for work which—
  (a) falls in a period of incapacity for work that began before the time when his wife died or within the prescribed period after that time, and

(b) is after that time and after the first 196 days of incapacity for work in that period.

For the purposes of this subsection a man is terminally ill if he suffers from a progressive disease and his death in consequence of that disease can reasonably be expected within 6 months.

(4) The weekly rate of incapacity benefit payable under this section is that which would apply if he were entitled to long-term incapacity benefit under section 30A above.

(5) A man is not entitled to incapacity benefit under this section if he is over pensionable age; but if he has attained pensionable age, and the period of incapacity for work mentioned in subsection (2)(a) or (3)(a) above did not terminate before he attained that age—

(a) he shall, if not otherwise entitled to a Category A retirement pension and also not entitled to a Category B retirement pension by virtue of [[2] the contributions of his wife] be entitled to Category A retirement pension; and

(b) the weekly rate of the Category A retirement pension to which he is entitled (whether by virtue of paragraph (a) above or otherwise) shall be determined in the prescribed manner.

(6) Where a man entitled to short-term incapacity benefit under subsection (3) above attains pensionable age and defers his entitlement to a Category A pension or makes an election under section 54(1) below, the days of incapacity for work falling within the period of incapacity for work mentioned in that subsection shall, for the purpose of determining any subsequent entitlement to incapacity benefit under section 30A above or the rate of that benefit, be treated as if they had been days of entitlement to short-term incapacity benefit.

(7) References to short-term incapacity benefit at the higher rate shall be construed as including short-term incapacity benefit payable under subsection (3) above.]

AMENDMENTS

1. Social Security (Incapacity for Work) Act 1994, Sch.1, para.9 (April 13, 1995).
2. Pensions Act 1995, Sch.4, para.21(4) (July 19, 1995).

DERIVATIONS

1.120   SSPA 1975, s.16.
SSA 1977, s.4.
SSA 1979, s.5.
SSA 1986, s.19.
SSA 1989, s.7.
SSA 1990, s.4.
Substituted by Social Security (Incapacity for Work) Act 1994.

GENERAL NOTE

1.121   This benefit will in appropriate circumstances, be affected by the Gender Recognition Act 2004. A person in receipt of benefit by virtue of this section who obtains a gender recognition certificate will cease to be entitled to benefit (and will lose, as well, the right to transfer to Category A Retirement Pension in due course). This is surprising because Section 40 above makes an equivalent provision for widows. See the notes to the Gender Recognition Act in Vol.III of this work.

Entitlement under s.40 or 41 after period of employment or training for work

42.—[²(1) Where a person claims incapacity benefit under section 40 or   1.122
41 above for a period commencing after he has ceased to be in qualifying
remunerative work (within the meaning of Part 1 of the Tax Credits Act
2002) and—

(a) the day following that on which he so ceased was a day of incapacity
    for work for him,

(b) he has been entitled to incapacity benefit under that section within
    the period of two years ending with that day of incapacity for work,
    and

(c) he satisfied the relevant tax credit conditions on the day before he so
    ceased,

every day during that period on which he satisfied those conditions is to be
treated for the purposes of the claim as a day of incapacity for work for him.

(1A) A person satisfies the relevant tax credit conditions on a day if—

(a) he is entitled for the day to the disability element of working tax
    credit (on a claim made by him or by him jointly with another) or
    would be so entitled but for the fact that the relevant income (within
    the meaning of Part 1 of the Tax Credits Act 2002) in his or their
    case is such that he is not so entitled, and

(b) either working tax credit or any element of child tax credit other than
    the family element is paid in respect of the day on such a claim.]

(2) Where—

(a) a person becomes engaged in training for work, and

(b) he was entitled to incapacity benefit under section 40 or 41 above
    for one or more of the 56 days immediately before he became so
    engaged, and

(c) the first day after he ceases to be so engaged is for him a day of incap-
    acity for work and falls not later than the end of the period of two
    years beginning with the last day for which he was entitled to incap-
    acity benefit under that section,

any day since that day in which he was engaged in training for work shall
be treated for the purposes of any claim for incapacity benefit under that
section for a period commencing after he ceases to be so engaged as having
been a day of incapacity for work.

In this subsection "training for work" means training for work in pursuance
of arrangements made under section 2(1) of the Employment and Training
Act 1973 or section 2(3) of the Enterprise and New Towns (Scotland) Act
1990 or training of such other description as may be prescribed.

(3) For the purposes of this section "week" means any period of 7 days.]

AMENDMENTS

1. Social Security (Incapacity for Work) Act 1994, Sch.1. para.10 (April 13,
1995).
2. Tax Credits Act 2002, Sch.3, para.30 (April 6, 2003).

DERIVATIONS

SSPA 1975, s.16A.   1.123
DLA and DWA A 1991, s.9.
Substituted by Social Security (Incapacity for Work) Act 1994.

GENERAL NOTE

1.124   Note that in respect of someone who claims incapacity benefit on or before 6th April 2005 under s.40 or 41, s.42 has effect as if, after subs.(1A) there were inserted

"(1B) A person also satisfies the relevant tax credit conditions on any day before 7th April 2003 if that day falls within a week for which he is entitled to a disabled person's tax credit."

See Tax Credits Act 2002 (Commencement No. 4, Transitional Provisions and Savings) Order SI 2003/962, Art 5(3).

Retirement pensions (Categories A and B)

Persons entitled to more than one retirement pension

1.125   **43.**—(1) A person shall not be entitled for the same period to more than one retirement pension under this Part of this Act except as provided by subsection (2) below.

(2) A person who, apart from subsection (1) above, would be entitled for the same period to both—

(a) a Category A or a Category B retirement pension under this Part; and

(b) a Category C or a Category D retirement pension under Part III below,

shall be entitled to both of those pensions for that period, subject to any adjustment of them in pursuance of regulations under section 73 of the Administration Act.

(3) A person who, apart from subsection (1) above, would be entitled—

[² (a) to both a Category A retirement pension and one or more Category B retirement pensions under this Part for the same period,

(aa) to more than one Category B retirement pension (but not a Category A retirement pension) under this Part for the same period, or]

(b) to both a Category C and a Category D retirement pension under Part III below for the same period,

may from time to time give notice in writing to the Secretary of State specifying which of the pensions referred to in [²paragraph (a), (aa) or (b) (as the case may be)] he wishes to receive.

(4) If a person gives such a notice, the pension so specified shall be the one to which he is entitled in respect of any week commencing after the date of the notice.

(5) If no such notice is given, the person shall be entitled to whichever of the pensions is from time to time the most favourable to him (whether it is the pension which he claimed or not).

[¹ (6) For the purpose of this section a provision under section 55A below is not a retirement pension.]

AMENDMENTS

1. Welfare Reform and Pensions Act 1999, Sch.12, para.18 (April 9, 2001).
2. Pensions Act 2004, s.296 (November 18, 2004).

DERIVATIONS

SSA 1975, ss.25 and 27.
SSA 1977, ss.4 and 5.

1.126

GENERAL NOTE

Retirement pensions present a complex pattern of rules of entitlement that depend upon age, and upon contributions.

1.127

Until October 1989 it was also necessary to show that the claimant had retired from regular employment. This is no longer necessary and the benefit became, in effect, simply an old age pension. Doubtless it will continue to be known as Retirement Pension since that remains the purpose of the pension. It will no longer be necessary for the claimant to give notice of retirement though it is still possible to defer the receipt of pension for a period of up to five years. During that period his pension will be enhanced at the rate of 1 per cent for every seven weeks of deferment. From April 6, 2005 this rate will increase to one per cent for each five weeks of deferment.

Retirement Pensions are paid under four categories:

Category A—paid on the basis of the claimant's own contribution record.

Category B—paid to married women on the basis of their husband's contribution record and also certain widows and widowers on the basis of their late spouse's contributions or entitlement to widowed parent's allowance or a bereavement allowance.

Category C—paid to those who were over pensionable age on July 5, 1948, or whose husband, or late husband, or in some cases former husband, was then over that age.

Category D—paid to those over 80 years of age and who do not qualify for another retirement pension.

In *Secretary of State for Work and Pensions v Nelligan* [2003] EWCA Civ. 555, [2004] 4 All E.R. 171, *R(P) 2/03*, the application of s.43(5) is explained. The claimant had retired in 1986 at the age of 60 and claimed for, and received, her Category A pension. When her husband retired some 6 years later he too received a Category A pension. The claimant could then have claimed a Category B pension, and had she done so, would have received more than her existing pension. The claimant did not realise this until a further 8 years later when she made a claim for the extra payment to be backdated for that period. The Court of Appeal's decision limits the extent of backdating to 3 months, the maximum period permitted under the Claims and Payments Regulations.

Section 43(5) operates, they explain, only to declare priority between pensions when the claimant is entitled to them both. Under s.1 of the SSA 1992 the claimant was not entitled to the Category B pension until she had made a claim for it. Therefore there was nothing for s.43(5) to act upon earlier.

While such interpretation would seem to make the bracketed words in this section almost useless, they are reinvigorated by a provision in the Claims and Payments Regulations that permits a claim for one pension to be treated as a claim for another as well. Thus a pensioner may claim only a Category A pension, but if they are at the same time entitled to a Category B, the claim can be treated as made for both, and under s.43(5) the claimant will be paid the greater amount. Unfortunately this provision could not aid the claimant in the present case because the claimant must qualify for both pensions at the time the claim for one of them is made; in this case when she claimed the Category A pension in 1986 that was the only pension to which she was entitled because her husband had then not retired.

Where entitlement to a pension depends upon proof of a valid marriage or civil partnership there may be difficulty where that relationship is claimed to have been celebrated in a foreign country where there is, or was at the time, little formality in connection with the ceremony and no reliable records are kept. For commentary regarding the correct approach to be adopted in these cases see the notes following s.39C.

Category A retirement pension

1.128   **44.**—(1) A person shall be entitled to a Category A retirement pension if—

(a) he is over pensionable age; and

[10(b) he satisfies the relevant conditions or condition.

(1A) In subsection (1)(b) above "the relevant conditions or condition" means—

(a) in a case where the person attains pensionable age before 6th April 2010, the conditions specified in Schedule 3, Part I, paragraph 5;

(b) in a case where the person attains pensionable age on or after that date, the condition specified in Schedule 3, Part I, paragraph 5A.]

(2) A Category A retirement pension shall not be payable in respect of any period falling before the day on which the pensioner's entitlement is to be regarded as commencing for that purpose by virtue of section 5(1)(k) of the Administration Act.

(3) A Category A retirement pension shall consist of—

(a) a basic pension payable at a weekly rate; and

(b) an additional pension payable where there are one or more surpluses in the pensioner's earnings factors for the relevant years.

(4) The weekly rate of the basic pension shall be [1 £95.25] except that, so far as the sum is relevant for the purpose of calculating the [2 rate of short-term incapacity benefit under section 30B(3) above] it shall be [1 £86.20]

(5) For the purposes of this section and section 45 below—

(a) there is a surplus in the pensioner's earnings factor for a relevant year if that factor exceeds the qualifying earnings factor for the final relevant year; and

(b) the amount of the surplus is the amount of that excess; and for the purposes of paragraph (a) above the pensioner's earnings factor for any relevant year shall be taken to be that factor as increased by the last order under section 148 of the Administration Act to come into force before the end of the final relevant year.

[3 (5A) For the purposes of this section and section 45 [8 and [11 Schedules 4A and 4B]] below—

(a) there is a surplus in the pensioner's earnings factor for a relevant year if that factor exceeds the qualifying earnings factor for [8that year,

(b) the amount of the surplus is the amount of that excess, and

(c) for the purposes of section 45(1) and (2)(a) and (b) below, the adjusted amount of the surplus] is the amount of that excess, as increased by the last order under section 148 of the Administration Act to come into force before the end of the final relevant year.

(6) [5Subject to subsection (7A) below] any reference in this section or section 45 [8 and 1 Schedule 4A] below to the pensioner's earnings factor for any relevant year is a reference—

(a) where the relevant year is 1987–88 or any subsequent tax year, before the first appointed year to the aggregate of—

    (i) his earnings factors derived from earnings upon which primary Class 1 contributions were paid or treated as paid in respect of that year, and

    (ii) his earnings factors derived from Class 2 and Class 3 contributions actually paid in respect of it; and

  (b) where the relevant year is an earlier tax year, to the aggregate of his earnings factors derived from contributions actually paid by him in respect of that year.]

(6) [⁴ [⁵Subject to subsection (7A) below] any reference in this section or section 45 [⁸ or [¹¹ Schedule 4A or 4B]] below to the pensioner's earnings factor for any relevant year is a reference—

[⁷ (za)] where the relevant year is the first appointed year or any subsequent year, to the aggregate of his earnings factors derived from [⁹ so much of his earnings as did not exceed [¹² the applicable limit]] upon which primary Class 1 contributions have been paid or treated as paid in respect of that year;

  (a) where the relevant year is 1987–88 or any subsequent tax year, to the aggregate of—

    (i) his earnings factors derived from earnings upon which primary Class 1 contributions were paid or treated as paid in respect of that year, and

    (ii) his earnings factors derived from Class 2 and Class 3 contributions actually paid in respect of that year, or, if less, the qualifying earnings factor for that year; and

  (b) where the relevant year is an earlier tax year, to the aggregate of—

    (i) his earnings factors derived from Class 1 contributions actually paid by him in respect of that year, and

    (ii) his earnings factors derived from Class 2 and Class 3 contributions actually paid by him in respect of that year, or, if less, the qualifying earnings factor for that year.]

(7) In this section—

  (a) "relevant year" means 1978–79 or any subsequent tax year in the period between—

    (i) (inclusive) the tax year in which the pensioner attained the age of 16, and

    (ii) (exclusive) the tax year in which he attained pensionable age;

  (b) "final relevant year" means the last tax year which is a relevant year in relation to the pensioner.

[¹⁰ (c) "the applicable limit" means—

    (i) in relation to a tax year before the flat rate introduction year, the upper earnings limit;

    (ii) in relation to the flat rate introduction year or any subsequent tax year, the upper accrual point.]

[⁵ (7A) The Secretary of State may prescribe circumstances in which pensioners' earnings factors for any relevant year may be calculated in such manner as may be prescribed.]

(8) For the purposes of this section any order under [⁶ section 21 of the Social Security Pensions Act 1975] (which made provision corresponding to section 148 of the Administration Act) shall be treated as an order under section 148 (but without prejudice to sections 16 and 17 of the Interpretation Act 1978).

AMENDMENTS

1. Social Security Benefits Up-rating Order 2009 (S1 2009/497) art.4(3) (April 6, 2009).
2. Social Security (Incapacity for Work) Act 1994, Sch.1, para.11 (April 13, 1995).
3. Pensions Act 1995, s.128(1), subs.(5A) applies in substitution for subs.(5) where ss.128(4)–(6) of that Act apply.
4. Pension Act 1995, s.128. This version of subs.(6) takes effect where the relevant person reaches pensionable age, or dies, after April 5, 2000.
5. Social Security (Consequential Provisions) Act 1992, Sch.4, para.3.
6. Pensions Schemes Act 1993, Sch. 8, para.38 (February 7, 1994).
7. Child Support, Pensions and Social Security Act 2000, s.30 (April 6, 2002).
8. Child Support, Pensions and Social Security Act 2000, s.35 (April 6, 2002).
9. National Insurance Contributions Act 2002, Sch.1, para.8 (April 6, 2002).
10. Pensions Act 2007, Sch.1, para.1 (September 26, 2007).
11. Pensions Act 2007, Sch.2, Pt.3, para.5 (September 26, 2007).
12. Pensions Act 2007, s.12 (September 26, 2007).

DERIVATION

1.129   SSA 1975, s.28; Social Security Pensions Act 1975, s.6.

DEFINITION

"pensionable age": see s.122.

GENERAL NOTE

1.130   A Category A retirement pension consists of two elements; basic pension under subs.(3)(a) and an additional pension under subs.(3)(b). Claimants who at some time had pensions based upon a contracted out provision (introduced originally under the SSPA 1975) will be entitled to a guaranteed minimum pension (GMP) under that scheme. Where a person is entitled to both a retirement pension and a GMP there is provision for offsetting, under sub.3(b), the amount of either the GMP, or the amount of the additional pension for certain years, whichever is the less. This provision is found in Pension Schemes Act 1993, s.46 and see the notes following that section.

Retirement Pension is payable to a man on attaining the age of 65, and to a woman at age 60. This difference was attacked by the claimant as being discriminatory and contrary to the laws of the European Community. The Commissioner held that discriminatory age conditions were lawful under Art.7 of Council Directive 79/7 which encompassed not merely different pension ages in different states but also different (i.e. discriminatory) pension ages within a state. See *R(P) 3/90*.

The difference in ages between a man and a woman may mean that it is necessary for the adjudicating authority to determine whether the claimant is a man or a woman. In two cases *R(P) 1/80* and *R(P) 2/80* Commissioners have held that a transsexual does not change sex for this purpose—the sex will usually be that denoted by the birth certificate, but this will now be affected, by the Gender Recognition Act 2004. Where a claimant has obtained a full certificate of gender recognition under that Act they will be regarded for the purposes of entitlement as being a person of the appropriate sex. Although they are to be regarded then as having always been of that sex, any entitlement to benefit (or disentitlement) will date only from the date of the certificate. Thus a woman of say 63 who changes her sex will lose her pension, whereas a man of that age who changes his, will become entitled to benefit. See note to Gender Recognition Act 2004 in Vol.III of this work.

Although the position should now be clear for claimants who have obtained a Gender Recognition Certificate some of the same effect has recently been confirmed either by the assertion of the claimant's human rights or by a claim based upon sex discrimination under European Law.

In the case of *Grant v United Kingdom* (32570/03) (2007) 44 E.H.R.R. 1, ECHR, it was held that a refusal to pay benefit to the claimant on the basis of the female sex to which she had changed (i.e. from age 60) was a breach of Art.8 and Art.12 of the Convention. However, the Court also held that it was effective only from the date of its decision in *Goodwin* [2002] 35 H.R.R.R. 18 (2002) by which time the claimant had attained the age of 65 and had been paid her pension. Her claim in respect of earlier years therefore failed.

In *Richards v Secretary of State for Work and Pensions R(P) 1/07*, ECJ, the Commissioner had referred to the Court the question of whether a refusal of benefit to a male to female transsexual who had claimed her pension in 2002 at age 60 (before the operation of the Gender Recognition Act) was a breach of the equal treatment directive (Directive 79/7). The ECJ held that it was, and furthermore, that they saw no reason to limit the temporal effect of the directive. This means that Ms Richards will be entitled to her pension from age 60 (even though she had not at the date of her claim obtained a Gender Recognition Certificate) but it suggests, as well, that the ECJ route would have been more fruitful for Ms Grant.

The effect of *Richards* has been considered further by a Tribunal of Commissioners in three cases; *R(P) 1/09, R(P) 2/09* and *CSP/503/2007*. In those cases it was held that a claimant who has changed their gender (in all three cases a male to female change) could take advantage of the direct effect of the Directive only from the point at which she could have satisfied the conditions of the Gender Recognition Act had that Act been in force at the time. Where that was so, the claimant was entitled to be treated in all respects equally to the way in which she would have been treated had she been, at the time, a natural woman. In the case of *R(P) 1/09* this meant, for example, that her retirement pension should have been increased by a period of deferment between the ages of 60 and 65 because she would have satisfied the conditions for gender reassignment in those years, notwithstanding art.10 of Sch.5 of the Gender Recognition Act 2004 which the Commissioners found to be in conflict with the Directive. In *R(P) 2/09* on the other hand, the claim for deferment failed because the claimant had not shown compliance with the conditions necessary for a change of gender until after she had attained the age of 65, and so would not have been entitled any earlier to her retirement pension.

The complications presented by these cases have been demonstrated again in *CP/1161/2007* where Judge Jupp (who had been one of the commissioners in the Tribunal referred to above) considered a claim brought by a male to female trans-sexual for payment to be made of her Retirement Pension from age 60. She had reached that age in 2001 and was found, after some confusion, to have made a claim for her pension that would have been effective from that time. Her claim was made, therefore, on the ground that had been accepted in *Richards*. In the three cases referred to above it had been established that the claimant would succeed only if she were able to show that she could comply in all respects with the conditions that were subsequently laid down in the Gender Recognition Act. The claimant was at all relevant times married to a wife and she said that she had no intention of dissolving that marriage. If the claimant had obtained a gender recognition certificate under the GRA its effect would have been to dissolve any existing marriage, but in the period for which the claim was made no such process existed. Before the judge the representative of the Secretary of State conceded that it would be unfair to require the claimant to have dissolved the marriage when no procedure to do so then existed. Nevertheless, Judge Jupp concluded that because the claimant was at that time still married she could not show herself to be in all respects in the position that a claimant would, or at least could, have been after GRA. In his view it was more important to adhere to the certainty that this approach produced, and that in doing so it avoided anomalies that would arise if the claim had been allowed. For example, if the claimant could receive a pension at the age of 60, while still remaining married to a wife, it would mean that the wife could also receive a Category B pension (based on her "husband's" contribution record) when she attained the age of 60. This would be an unfair discrimination when compared to a normal married couple or partnership. The judge noted that in *Richards* the early record in the case seemed to suggest the claimant there might have also remained married to his wife. But Judge Jupp observed that the decision of the court in *Richards* was on matters of principal only, and the marriage having not been referred to subsequently in the case, it could now be distinguished on that point.

The conditions necessary for a claimant to show that there has been a gender reassignment are now set out in the Gender Recognition Act, but where a claim has been made prior to that act coming into force, it will be necessary for a tribunal to determine whether the claimant has succeeded in showing that they have met the conditions of gender reassignment as required by the decision in *R(P) 1/07*. In *CP/3485/2003*, the claimant had begun the process of male-to-female gender reassignment by counselling and hormone treatment, and was on the waiting list for surgery, when she reached the age of 60 and made a claim for retirement pension. The Commissioner held that he should decide whether she had met those conditions by analogy to the conditions set out in the Gender Reassignment Act—even though the Act had not been in force at the time of her claim. As she had, at the time, already lived in the female role for over two years, he allowed her appeal subject to evidence being provided to satisfy the other conditions of the Act.

The age of the claimant will also usually be proved by production of a birth certificate, but where that is not possible other documentary evidence, and even medical evidence, may be relied upon to prove age. (See *R(P) 1/75*.) Regulations provide for the day on which entitlement is to begin. A regulation which postponed entitlement until the pay day following the claimant's requisite birthday was upheld in *R(P) 2/73*.

There are two versions of both subs. (5) and subs. (6) of this section. In the case of subs. (5) the second version is titled (5A); in the case of subs. (6) both versions appear with the same title. In each case the second version applies to someone who reaches pensionable age, or dies, after April 5, 2000, and to someone whose entitlement is derived from such a person (see s.128(4)–(6) Pensions Act 1995). The first version is retained for those reaching that age, or dying, before that date.

Deemed earnings factors

1.131   **44A.** [3 (A1) Subsections (1) to (4) below apply to the first appointed year or any subsequent tax year before 2010–11.]

(1) For the purposes of section 44(6)(za) above, if any of the conditions in subsection (2) below is satisfied for a relevant year [3 to which this subsection applies], a pensioner is deemed to have an earnings factor for that year which—

(a) is derived from [2 so much of his earnings as did not exceed the upper earnings limit and] on which primary Class 1 contributions were paid; and

(b) is equal to the amount which, when added to any other earnings factors taken into account under that provision, produces an aggregate of earnings factors equal to the low earnings threshold.

(2) The conditions referred to in subsection (1) above are that—

(a) the pensioner would, apart from this section, have an earnings factor for the year—

(i) equal to or greater than the qualifying earnings factor for the year; but

(ii) less than the low earnings threshold for the year;

(b) [1 carer's allowance]—

(i) was payable to the pensioner throughout the year; or

    (ii) would have been so payable but for the fact that under regula-
tions the amount payable to him was reduced to nil because of
his receipt of other benefits;

  (c) for the purposes of paragraph 5(7)(b) of Schedule 3, the pensioner
is taken to be precluded from regular employment by responsibilities
at home throughout the year by virtue of—

    (i) the fact that child benefit was payable to him in respect of a
child under the age of six; or

    (ii) his satisfying such other condition as may be prescribed;

  (d) the pensioner is a person satisfying the requirement in subsection (3)
below to whom long-term incapacity benefit was payable throughout
the year, or would have been so payable but for the fact that—

    (i) he did not satisfy the contribution conditions in paragraph 2 of
Schedule 3; or

    (ii) under regulations the amount payable to him was reduced to nil
because of his receipt of other benefits or of payments from an
occupational pension scheme or personal pension scheme.

(3) The requirement referred to in subsection (2)(d) above is that—

  (a) for one or more relevant years the pensioner has paid, or (apart from
this section) is treated as having paid, primary Class 1 contributions on
earnings equal to or greater than the qualifying earnings factor; and

  (b) the years for which he has such a factor constitute at least one tenth
of his working life.

(4) For the purposes of subsection (3)(b) above—

  (a) a pensioner's working life shall not include—

    (i) any tax year before 1978–79; or

    (ii) any year in which he is deemed under subsection (1) above to
have an earnings factor by virtue of fulfilling the condition in
subsection (2)(b) or (c) above; and

  (b) the figure calculated by dividing his working life by ten shall be
rounded to the nearest whole year (and any half year shall be
rounded down).

[[3] (4A) The following do not apply to a pensioner attaining pensionable
age on or after 6th April 2010—

  (a) the requirement referred to in subsection (2)(d) above, and

  (b) subsections (3) and (4) above.]

(5) The low earnings threshold for the first appointed year and subsequent tax years shall be £9,500 (but subject to section 148A of the
Administration Act).

(6) In subsection (2)(d)(ii) above, "occupational pension scheme" and
"personal pension scheme" have the meanings given by subsection (6) of
section 30DD above for the purposes of subsection (5) of that section.]

AMENDMENTS

  1. Regulatory Reform (Carer's Allowance) Order 2002 (SI 2002/1457), art.2
(April 1, 2003).

  2. National Insurance Contributions Act 2002, Sch.1 para.11 (April 6, 2003).

  3. Pensions Act 2007, Sch.1, para.34 (September 26, 2007).

GENERAL NOTE

  This section introduced what is sometimes known as the second state pension.   **1.132**
In *Jayawardhana v Secretary of State for Work and Pensions* [2006] EWCA Civ 1865,

19.12.06, it was held that the effect of this and the preceding section could apply only prospectively and not retrospectively. Where, therefore, the claimant had reached retirement age in the tax year 2002/03, (which year could not be counted under s.44(7)(a)(ii)) and the amended version of this section became effective only from April 2002, it could have no application to him.

For the tax years following the tax year 2008-09, the low earnings threshold is fixed at £13,900, in accordance with the Social Security Pensions (Low Earnings Threshold) Order 2009 (SI 2009/610), art.2 (April 6, 2009).

[¹ 44B Deemed earnings factors: 2010–11 onwards

1.133

(1) This section applies to 2010–11 and subsequent tax years.

(2) For the purposes of section 44(6)(za) above, if any of Conditions A to C in subsections (3) to (5) below is satisfied for a relevant year to which this section applies, a pensioner is deemed to have an earnings factor for that year which—

    (a) is derived from so much of his earnings as did not exceed the applicable limit and on which primary Class 1 contributions were paid; and

    (b) is equal to the amount which, when added to any other earnings factors taken into account under that provision, produces an aggregate of earnings factors equal to the low earnings threshold.

(3) Condition A is that the pensioner would, apart from this section, have an earnings factor for the year—

    (a) equal to or greater than the qualifying earnings factor ("the QEF") for the year, but

    (b) less than the low earnings threshold for the year.

(4) Condition B is that the pensioner—

    (a) would, apart from this section and section 44C below, have an earnings factor for the year less than the QEF for the year, but

    (b) is entitled to an aggregate amount of earnings factor credits for that year under section 44C below equal to the difference between the QEF for the year and the earnings factor mentioned in paragraph (a) above.

(5) Condition C is that the pensioner is entitled to 52 earnings factor credits for that year under section 44C below.

(6) This section has effect in relation to the flat rate introduction year and any subsequent tax year as if—

    (a) subsection (2)(b) referred to an aggregate of earnings factors greater than the QEF, but less than the low earnings threshold, for the year (rather than to one equal to that threshold); and

    (b) Condition A in subsection (3) (and the reference to it in subsection (2)) were omitted.

(7) In this section—

    (a) "the applicable limit" has the same meaning as in section 44 above;

    (b) "the low earnings threshold" means the low earnings threshold for the year concerned as specified in section 44A above; and

    (c) in subsections (3) and (4), any reference to the pensioner's earnings factor for a relevant year is to be construed in accordance with section 44(6)(za) above.

44C Earnings factor credits

1.134

(1) This section applies, for the purposes of Conditions B and C in section 44B(4) and (5) above, to 2010–11 and subsequent tax years.

(2) In respect of each week—

(a) which falls in a relevant year to which this section applies, and

(b) in respect of which a pensioner is eligible for earnings factor enhancement, the pensioner is entitled to an earnings factor credit equal to 1/52 of the QEF for that year.

This is subject to subsection (5) below.

(3) A pensioner is eligible for earnings factor enhancement in respect of a week if one or more of the following apply—

(a) he was a relevant carer in respect of that week for the purposes of section 23A above (see section 23A(3));

(b) carer's allowance was payable to him for any part of that week, or would have been so payable but for the fact that under regulations the amount payable to him was reduced to nil because of his receipt of other benefits;

(c) severe disablement allowance was payable to him for any part of that week;

(d) long-term incapacity benefit was payable to him for any part of that week or would have been so payable but for the fact that—

(i) he did not satisfy the contribution conditions in paragraph 2 of Schedule 3, or

(ii) under regulations the amount payable to him was reduced to nil because of his receipt of other benefits or of payments from an occupational pension scheme or personal pension scheme;

(e) he satisfies such other conditions as may be prescribed.

(4) In subsection (3)(d)(ii) above "occupational pension scheme" and "personal pension scheme" have the meanings given by subsection (6) of section 30DD above for the purposes of subsection (5) of that section.

(5) For the purposes of Condition B in section 44B(4) above a person is not entitled to an aggregate amount of earnings factor credits in respect of a year that is greater than the difference referred to in that Condition.

(6) For the purposes of this section a week that falls partly in one tax year and partly in another is to be treated as falling in the year in which it begins and not in the following year.

(7) In section 44B above and this section—

(a) "the QEF" means the qualifying earnings factor, and

(b) any reference to a person being entitled to an earnings factor credit of a particular amount (or to an aggregate amount of earnings factor credits) for a year is a reference to the person being treated as having for that year an earnings factor (within the meaning of section 44(6) (za) above) of the amount in question by virtue of subsection (2) above.]

AMENDMENT

1. Pensions Act 2007, s.9(1) (September 26, 2007).

The additional pension in a Category A retirement pension

45.—(1) The weekly rate of the additional pension in a Category A retirement pension in any case where the pensioner attained pensionable age in a tax year before 6th April 1999 shall be the weekly equivalent of 1 1/4 per cent of the [[1] adjusted amount of the surpluses mentioned in section 44(3) (b) above.

1.135

(2) The weekly rate of the additional pension in a Category A retirement pension in any case where the pensioner attained pensionable age in a tax year after 5th April 1999 shall be [² the sum of the following]

    (a) in relation to any surpluses in the pensioner's earnings factors for the tax years in the period beginning with 1978–79 and ending with 1987–88, the weekly equivalent of 25/N per cent. of the [¹ adjusted] amount of those surpluses; and

    (b) in relation to any surpluses in the pensioner's earnings factors in a tax year after 1987–88 [² but before the first appointed year], the weekly equivalent of the relevant percentage of the [¹ adjusted] amount of those surpluses.

[² (c) in relation to any tax years falling within subsection (3A) below, the weekly equivalent of the amount calculated in accordance with Schedule 4A to this Act.]

[³ and

    (d) in relation to the flat rate introduction year and subsequent tax years, the weekly equivalent of the amount calculated in accordance with Schedule 4B to this Act.]

(3) In subsection (2)(b) above, "relevant percentage" means—

    (a) 20/N per cent., where the pensioner attained pensionable age in 2009–10 or any subsequent tax year;

    (b) (20 + X)/N per cent., where the pensioner attained pensionable age in a tax year falling within the period commencing with 1999–2000 and ending with 2008–9.

[² (3A) The following tax years fall within this subsection—

    (a) the first appointed year;

    (b) subsequent tax years.]

[³ before the flat rate introduction year.]

(4) In this section—

    (a) X = 0.5 for each tax year by which the tax year in which the pensioner attained pensionable age precedes 2009–10; and

    (b) N = the number of tax years in the pensioner's working life which fall after 5th April 1978;

but paragraph (b) above is subject, in particular, to subsection (5) and, where applicable, section 46 below.

(5) Regulations may direct that in prescribed cases or classes of cases any tax year shall be disregarded for the purpose of calculating N under subsection (4)(b) above, if it is a tax year after 5th April 1978 in which the pensioner—

    (a) was credited with contributions or earnings under this Act by virtue of regulations under section 22(5) above, or

    (b) was precluded from regular employment by responsibilities at home, or

    (c) in prescribed circumstances, would have been treated as falling within paragraph (a) or (b) above,

but not so as to reduce the number of years below 20.

(6) For the purposes of subsections (1) and (2) above, the weekly equivalent of [¹ any amount] shall be calculated by dividing that amount by 52 and rounding the result to the nearest whole penny, taking any 1/2p as nearest to the next whole penny.

(7) Where the amount falling to be rounded under subsection (6) above is a sum less than 1/2p, the amount calculated under that subsection shall

be taken to be zero, notwithstanding any other provision of this Act or the Administration Act.

(8) The sums which are the weekly rate of the additional pension in a Category A retirement pension are subject to alteration by orders made by the Secretary of State under section 150 of the Administration Act.

AMENDMENTS

1. Child Support, Pensions and Social Security Act 2000, s.35 (April 6, 2002).
2. Child Support, Pensions and Social Security Act 2000, s.31 (April 6, 2002).
3. Pensions Act 2007, s.11 (September 26, 2007).

DERIVATION

SSPA 1975, s.6.   1.136

[**45A.**—[¹ *Repealed*]   1.137

REPEALS

1. Tax Credits Act 2002, Sch.6 (April 1, 2003).

[¹ Reduction of additional pension in Category A retirement pension: pension sharing

45B.—(1) The weekly rate of the additional pension in a Category A   1.138
retirement pension shall be reduced as follows in any case where—
   (a) the pensioner has become subject to a state scheme pension debit, and
   (b) the debit is to any extent referable to the additional pension.
(2) If the pensioner became subject to the debit in or after the final relevant year, the weekly rate of the additional pension shall be reduced by the appropriate weekly amount.
(3) If the pensioner became subject to the debit before the final relevant year, the weekly rate of the additional pension shall be reduced by the appropriate weekly amount multiplied by the relevant revaluation percentage.
(4) The appropriate weekly amount for the purposes of subsections (2) and (3) above is the weekly rate, expressed in terms of the valuation day, at which the cash equivalent, on that day, of the pension mentioned in subsection (5) below is equal to so much of the debit as is referable to the additional pension.
(5) The pension referred to above is a notional pension for the pensioner by virtue of section 44(3)(b) above which becomes payable on the later of—
   (a) his attaining pensionable age, and
   (b) the valuation day.
(6) For the purposes of subsection (3) above, the relevant revaluation percentage is the percentage specified, in relation to earnings factors for the tax year in which the pensioner became subject to the debit, by the last order under section 148 of the Administration Act to come into force before the end of the final relevant year.
[(7) The Secretary of State may by regulations make provision about the calculation and verification of cash equivalents for the purposes of this section.
(7A) The power conferred by subsection (7) above includes power to provide—

(a) for calculation or verification in such manner as may be approved by or on behalf of the Government Actuary, and

(b) for things done under the regulations to be required to be done in accordance with guidance from time to time prepared by a person prescribed by the regulations.]

(8) In this section—

"final relevant year" means the tax year immediately preceding that in which the pensioner attains pensionable age;

"state scheme pension debit" means a debit under section 49(1)(a) of the Welfare Reform and Pensions Act 1999 (debit for the purposes of this Part of this Act);

"valuation day" means the day on which the pensioner became subject to the state scheme pension debit.]

AMENDMENT

1. Welfare Reform and Pensions Act 1999, Sch.6, para.2 (December 1, 2001).

Modifications of section 45 for calculating the additional pension in certain benefits

1.139   **46.**—(1) *Omitted.*

(2) For the purpose of determining the additional pension falling to be calculated under section 45 above by virtue of section 39(1) [¹ or 39C(1)] above or section [² 48A(4) or 48B(2) [¹ or 48BB(5)] below in a case where the deceased spouse died under pensionable age [⁴ or by virtue of section 39C(1) above or section 48A(2) or 48BB(5) below in a case where the deceased civil partner died under pensionable age], the following definition shall be substituted for the definition of "N" in section 45(4)(b) above—

[² "N" =

(a) the number of tax years which begin after 5th April 1978 and end before the date when the entitlement to the additional pension commences, or

(b) the number of tax years in the period—

    (i) beginning with the tax year in which the deceased spouse ("S") attained the age of 16 or if later 1978–79, and

    (ii) ending immediately before the tax year in which S would have attained pensionable age if S had not died earlier,

whichever is the smaller number].

[³ (3) For the purpose of determining the additional pension falling to be calculated under section 45 above by virtue of section 48BB below in a case where the deceased spouse [4 or civil partner] died under pensionable age, the following definition shall be substituted for the definition of "N" in section 45(4)(b) above—

" 'N' =

(a) the number of tax years which begin after 5th April 1978 and end before the date when the deceased spouse [⁴ or civil partner] dies, or

(b) the number of tax years in the period—

    (i) beginning with the tax year in which the deceased spouse [⁴ or civil partner] ('S') attained the age of 16 or, if later, 1978–79, and

(ii) ending immediately before the tax year in which S would have attained pensionable age if S had not died earlier, whichever is the smaller number."]

[⁵ (4) For the purpose of determining the additional pension falling to be calculated under section 45 above by virtue of section 39C(1) above in a case where the deceased spouse or civil partner died under pensionable age, section 45 has effect subject to the following additional modifications—

(a) the omission of subsection (2)(d), and
(b) the omission in subsection (3A)(b) of the words "before the flat rate introduction year".]

AMENDMENTS

1. Welfare Reform and Pensions Act 1999, Sch.8 (April 9, 2001).
2. Pensions Act 1995, Sch.4 (July 19, 1995).
3. Child Support, Pensions and Social Security Act 2000, s.32 (April 9, 2001).
4. Civil Partnership Act 2004, Sch.24 (December 5, 2005).
5. Pensions Act 2007, Sch.2, Pt 3, para.46 (September 26, 2007).

DERIVATION

SSA 1986, s.18.   1.140

Increase of Category A retirement pension for incapacity

47.—(1) Subject to section 61 below, the weekly rate of a Category A   1.141
retirement pension shall be increased if the pensioner was entitled to an [¹ age addition to long-term incapacity benefit by virtue of regulations under section 30B(7) above] in respect of—

(a) any day falling within the period of 8 weeks ending immediately before the day on which he attains pensionable age; or
(b) the last day before the beginning of that period; and the increase shall, subject to subsection (2) below, be of an amount equal to the appropriate weekly rate of the [¹ age addition to long-term incapacity benefit by virtue of regulations under section 30B(7) above on that day.]

(2) Where for any period the weekly rate of a Category A retirement pension includes an additional pension, for that period the relevant amount shall be deducted from the amount that would otherwise be the increase under subsection (1) above and the pensioner shall be entitled to an increase under that subsection only if there is a balance remaining after that deduction and, if there is such a balance, of an amount equal to it.

(3) In subsection (2) above the "relevant amount" means an amount equal to the additional pension, reduced by the amount of any reduction in the weekly rate of the Category A retirement pension made by virtue of [² section 46] of the Pensions Act.

(4) In this section any reference to an additional pension is a reference to that pension after any increase under section 52(3) below but without any increase under paragraphs 1 and 2 of Schedule 5 to this Act.

(5) In ascertaining for the purposes of subsection (1) above the rate of a pensioner's [¹ age addition to long-term incapacity benefit by virtue of regulations under section 30B(7) above] regard shall be had to the rates in force from time to time.

(6) Regulations may provide that subsection (1) above shall have effect as if for the reference to 8 weeks there were substituted a reference to a larger number of weeks specified in the regulations.

AMENDMENTS

1. Social Security (Incapacity for Work) Act 1994, Sch.1 (April 13, 1995).
2. Pensions Schemes Act 1993, Sch.8 (February 7, 1994).

DERIVATIONS

1.142   SSA 1975, s.28.
         SSA 1975, s.9.

GENERAL NOTE

1.143   Note that under s.46 of the Pensions Schemes Act 1993, the amount of any retirement pension is reduced by the guaranteed minimum pension to which the claimant may be entitled. See notes to that section.

Use of former spouse's contributions

1.144   **48.**—(1) Where a person—
         (a) has been [¹ in a relevant relationship], and
         (b) in respect of the tax year in which the [¹ relationship] terminated or any previous tax year, does not with his own contributions satisfy the contribution conditions for a Category A retirement pension,
then, for the purpose of enabling him to satisfy those conditions (but only in respect of any claim for a Category A retirement pension), the contributions of his former spouse may to the prescribed extent be treated as if they were his own contributions.

(2) Subsection (1) above shall not apply in relation to any person who attained pensionable age before 6th April 1979 if the termination of his [¹ relevant relationship] also occurred before that date.

(3) [¹ (3) Where a person has been in a relevant relationship more than once, this section applies only to the last relevant relationship and the references to his relevant relationship and his former spouse or civil partner shall be construed accordingly.

(4) In this section, "relevant relationship" means a marriage or civil partnership].

AMENDMENT

1. Civil Partnership Act 2004, Sch.24 (December 5, 2005).

DERIVATIONS

1.145   SSPA 1975, s.20.
         SSA 1979, s.5.

GENERAL NOTE

1.146   The principle of forfeiture will apply in a case where the death of the former spouse is the result of homicide committed by the claimant. An example of its application and the exercise of discretion by the Commissioner is *CFP/4349/2004*. There the claimant had pleaded guilty to the manslaughter of her husband on the grounds of diminished responsibility and was sentenced to a term of probation. She made no claim to widows' benefits for the next 13 years, but then claimed retirement pension relying, in part, on her husband's contribution record. It was held that the forfeiture rule applied, but that relief should be granted with effect from the time of the claim for retirement pension.

Category B retirement pension for married person

[¹ **48A.**—(1) A person who—

(a) has attained pensionable age, and

(b) on attaining that age was a married person or marries after attaining that age,

shall be entitled to a Category B retirement pension by virtue of the contributions of the other party to the marriage ("the spouse") if the following requirement is met.

(2) The requirement is that the spouse—

(a) has attained pensionable age [⁶ and become entitled to a Category A retirement pension], and

[⁷(b) satisfies the relevant conditions or condition.]

[⁵ (2A) A person who—

(a) has attained pensionable age, and

(b) on attaining that age was a civil partner or forms a civil partnership after attaining that age,

shall be entitled to a Category B retirement pension by virtue of the contributions of the other party to the civil partnership ("the contributing civil partner") if the following requirement is met.

[⁷ (2ZA) In subsection (2)(b) above "the relevant conditions or condition" means—

(a) in a case where the spouse is a married man who attains pensionable age before 6th April 2010, the conditions specified in Schedule 3, Part I, paragraph 5;

(b) in a case where the spouse attains pensionable age on or after that date, the condition specified in Schedule 3, Part I, paragraph 5A.]

(2B) The requirement is that the contributing civil partner—

(a) has attained pensionable age [⁶ and become entitled to a Category A retirement pension], and

[⁷(b) satisfies the condition specified in Schedule 3, Part I, paragraph 5A.]

(3) During any period when the spouse [⁵ or civil partner] is alive, a Category B retirement pension payable by virtue of this section shall be payable at the weekly rate specified in Schedule 4, Part I, paragraph 5.

(4) During any period after the spouse [⁵ or civil partner] is dead, a Category B retirement pension payable by virtue of this section shall be payable at a weekly rate corresponding to—

(a) the weekly rate of the basic pension, plus

(b) half of the weekly rate of the additional pension,

determined in accordance with the provisions of sections 44 to [² 45B] above [³ and [⁸ Schedules 4A and 4B] below] as they apply in relation to a Category A retirement pension, but subject to section 46(2) above and the modification in section 48C(4) below.

[² (4A) Subsection (4) above shall have effect with the omission of the words from "plus" to the end if the pensioner is not the [⁵ widow, widower or surviving civil partner] of the person by virtue of whose contributions the pension is payable.]

1.147

[[6] (5) A person's Category B retirement pension payable by virtue of this section shall not be payable for any period falling before the day on which the spouse's [or contributing civil partner] entitlement is to be regarded as beginning for that purpose by virtue of section 5(1)(k) of the Administration Act.]

AMENDMENTS

1. Pensions Act 1995, Sch.4 (July 19, 1995).
2. Welfare Reform and Pensions Act 1999, Sch.12 (April 9, 2001).
3. Child Support, Pensions and Social Security Act 2000, s.35 (April 6, 2002).
4. Welfare Reform and Pensions Act 1999, Sch.8 (April 9, 2001).
5. Civil Partnership Act 2004 Sch.24 (December 5, 2005).
6. These words have been omitted by virtue of s.2 of the Pensions Act 2007, but the effect of that amendment is postponed until April 6, 2010. (Pensions Act 2007 s.2(5)).
7. Pensions Act 2007, Sch.1, para.2 (September 26, 2007).
8. Pensions Act 2007, Sch.2, Pt 3, para.7 (September 26, 2007).

GENERAL NOTE

1.148   Note that because of the reservation made in Sch.4 para.3(2) of the Pensions Act 1995 (which introduced this section) it does not apply in the case of a man whose wife was born before April 6, 1950, nor to a partner born before that date. (Civil Partnership Act 2004 Sch.24, Pt. 3, para.25(6).)

All category B retirement pensions may, in appropriate circumstances be affected by the provisions of the Gender Recognition Act 2004. This means that any question of entitlement after the claimant has obtained a certificate of gender recognition will be determined according to the criteria applicable to a person of the acquired gender. See notes to Gender Recognition Act 2004 in Vol.III of this work.

From March 17, 2008 it is not necessary for a claim to be made for a Category B retirement pension where either the claimant, or the claimant's spouse, is entitled already to a Category A retirement pension. (Social Security (Claims and Payments) Amendment Regulations 2008 (SI 2008/441).)

Category B retirement pension for widows and widowers

1.149   [[1] 48B.—(1) A person ("the pensioner") whose spouse died—
    (a) while they were married, and
    (b) after the pensioner attained pensionable age,
shall be entitled to a Category B retirement pension by virtue of the contributions of the spouse if the spouse satisfied [[6] the relevant conditions or condition].
    [[6] (1ZA) In subsection (1) above "the relevant conditions or condition" means—
    (a) in a case where the spouse—
        (i) died before 6th April 2010, or
        (ii) died on or after that date having attained pensionable age before that date, the conditions specified in Schedule 3, Part I, paragraph 5;
    (b) in a case where the spouse died on or after that date without having attained pensionable age before that date, the condition specified in Schedule 3, Part I, paragraph 5A.]
    [[5] (1A) A person ("the pensioner") who attains pensionable age on or after 6th April 2010 and whose civil partner died—
    (a) while they were civil partners of each other, and

(b) after the pensioner attained pensionable age,
shall be entitled to a Category B retirement pension by virtue of the contributions of the civil partner if the civil partner satisfied [⁶ the condition specified in Schedule 3, Part I, paragraph 5A].

(2) A Category B retirement pension payable by virtue of subsection (1) [⁵ or (1A)] above shall be payable at a weekly rate corresponding to—

(a) the weekly rate of the basic pension, plus

(b) half of the weekly rate of the additional pension,
determined in accordance with the provisions of sections 44 to [² 45B] [³ and [⁶ Schedules 4A and 4B] below] above as they apply in relation to a Category A retirement pension, but subject to section 46(2) above and the modifications in subsection (3) below and section 48C(4) below.

(3) Where the spouse [⁵ or civil partner] died under pensionable age, references in the provisions of sections 44 to [³ 45B] [² and Schedule 4A below] above as applied by subsection (2) above to the tax year in which the pensioner attained pensionable age shall be taken as references to the tax year in which the spouse [⁵ or civil partner] died.

(4) A person who has attained pensionable age ("the pensioner") whose spouse died before the pensioner attained that age shall be entitled to a Category B retirement pension by virtue of the contributions of the spouse if—

(a) where the pensioner is a woman, the following condition is satisfied, and

(b) where the pensioner is a man, the following condition would have been satisfied on the assumption mentioned in subsection (7) below.

(5) The condition is that the pensioner—

(a) is entitled (or is treated by regulations as entitled) to a widow's pension by virtue of section 38 above, and

(b) became entitled to that pension in consequence of the spouse's death.

(6) A Category B retirement pension payable by virtue of subsection (4) above shall be payable—

(a) where the pensioner is a woman, at the same weekly rate as her widow's pension, and

(b) where the pensioner is a man, at the same weekly rate as that of the pension to which he would have been entitled by virtue of section 38 above on the assumption mentioned in subsection (7) below.

(7) The assumption referred to in subsections (4) and (6) above is that a man is entitled to a pension by virtue of section 38 above on the same terms and conditions, and at the same rate, as a woman.]

[⁴ (8) Nothing in subsections (4) to (7) above applies in a case where the spouse dies on or after the appointed day (as defined by section 36A(3)).]

AMENDMENTS

1. Pensions Act 1995, Sch.4 (July 19, 1995).
2. Welfare Reform and Pensions Act 1999, Sch.12, para.00 (April 9, 2001).
3. Child Support, Pensions and Social Security Act 2000, s.35 (April 6, 2002).
4. Welfare Reform and Pensions Act 1999, Sch.8, para.00 (April 9, 2001).
5. Civil Partnership Act 2004 Sch.24 (December 5, 2005).
6. Pensions Act 2007, Sch.1 (September 26, 2007).
7. Pensions Act 2007, Sch.2, Pt 3, para.8 (September 26, 2007).

GENERAL NOTE

1.150   From March 17, 2008 it is not necessary for a claim to be made for a Category B retirement pension where either the claimant, or the claimant's spouse, is entitled already to a Category A retirement pension. (Social Security (Claims and Payments) Amendment Regulations 2008 (SI 2008/441)).

Note that because of the reservation made in Sch.4 para.3(3) of the Pensions Act 1995 (which introduced this section) it does not apply in the case of a man who attains pensionable age before April 6, 2010.

All category B retirement pensions may, in appropriate circumstances be affected by the provisions of the Gender Recognition Act 2004. This means that any question of entitlement after the claimant has obtained a certificate of gender recognition will be determined according to the criteria applicable to a person of the acquired gender.

There is, however, an exception under subs.(4) of this section. Where the claimant becomes a female and attains the age of 65 before April 6, 2010 and would not otherwise be entitled to a category B pension, she does not qualify for benefit under s.48B because the operation of this section is suspended generally for men until that date. See notes to Gender Recognition Act 2004 in Vol.III of this work.

[¹ **Category B retirement pension: entitlement by reference to benefits under section 39A or 39B**

1.151   **48BB.**—(1) Subsection (2) below applies where a person ("the pensioner") who has attained pensionable age—

(a) was, immediately before attaining that age, entitled to a widowed parent's allowance in consequence of the death of his or her spouse [⁵ or civil partner]; and

(b) has not [⁵ following the death, married or formed a civil partnership].

(2) The pensioner shall be entitled to a Category B retirement pension by virtue of the contributions of the spouse [⁵ or civil partner], which shall be payable at the same weekly rate as the widowed parent's allowance.

(3) Subsections (4) to (10) below apply where a person ("the pensioner") who has attained pensionable age—

(a) was in consequence of the death of his or her spouse [⁵ or civil partner] either—

(i) entitled to a bereavement allowance at any time prior to attaining that age, or

(ii) entitled to a widowed parent's allowance at any time when over the age of 45 (but not immediately before attaining pensionable age); and

(b) has not [⁵ following the death, married or formed a civil partnership].

(4) The pensioner shall be entitled to a Category B retirement pension by virtue of the contributions of the spouse [⁵ or civil partner].

(5) A Category B retirement pension payable by virtue of subsection (4) above shall be payable at a weekly rate corresponding to the weekly rate of the additional pension determined in accordance with the provisions of sections 44 to [⁴ 45] above [² and [⁶ Schedules 4A and 4B] below] as they apply in relation to a Category A retirement pension, but [⁶ subject to section 46(3) above and to the following provisions of this section and the modification in section 48C(4) below.]

(6) Where the spouse [⁵ or civil partner] died under pensionable age, references in the provisions of sections 44 to [⁴ 45] above [² and Schedule 4A below], as applied by subsection (5) above, to the tax year in which the

110

pensioner attained pensionable age shall be taken as references to the tax year in which the spouse [5 or civil partner] died.

(7) Where the spouse [5 or civil partner] dies after 5th April 2000, the pension payable by virtue of subsection (4) above shall (before making any reduction required by subsection (8) below) be one half of the amount which it would be apart from this subsection.

(8) Where the pensioner was under the age of 55 at the relevant time, the weekly rate of the pension shall be reduced by 7 per cent. of what it would be apart from this subsection multiplied—

(a) by the number of years by which the pensioner's age at that time was less than 55 (any fraction of a year being counted as a year), or

(b) by ten, if that number exceeds ten.

(9) In subsection (8) above "the relevant time" means—

(a) where the pensioner became entitled to a widowed parent's allowance in consequence of the death of the spouse [5 or civil partner], the time when the pensioner's entitlement to that allowance ended; and

(b) otherwise, the time of the spouse's [5 or civil partner's] death.

(10) The amount determined in accordance with subsections (5) to (9) above as the weekly rate of the pension payable to the pensioner by virtue of subsection (4) above shall be increased by such percentage as equals the overall percentage by which, had the pension been in payment as from the date of the spouse's [5 or civil partner's] death until the date when the pensioner attained pensionable age, that weekly rate would have been increased during that period by virtue of any orders under section 150 of the Administration Act (annual up-rating of benefits).]

AMENDMENTS

1. Welfare Reform and Pensions Act 1999, s.56 (April 9, 2001).
2. Child Support Pensions and Social Security Act 2000, s.35 (April 6, 2002).
3. Child Support Pensions and Social Security Act 2000, s.32(2) (April 9, 2001).
4. Tax Credit Act 2002, Sch.3 (April 6, 2003).
5. Civil Partnership Act 2004 Sch.24 (December 5, 2005).
6. Pensions Act 2007, Sch.2, Pt 3, para.9 (September 26, 2007).

Category B retirement pension: general

[1 **48C.**—(1) Subject to the provisions of this Act, a person's entitlement to a Category B retirement pension shall begin on the day on which the conditions of entitlement become satisfied and shall continue for life.

1.152

(2) In any case where—

(a) a person would, apart from section 43(1) above, be entitled both to a Category A and to a Category B retirement pension, and

(b) section 47(1) above would apply for the increase of the Category A retirement pension,

section 47(1) above shall be taken as applying also for the increase of the Category B retirement pension, subject to reduction or extinguishment of the increase by the application of section 47(2) above or section 46(5) of the Pensions Act.

(3) In the case of a pensioner whose spouse died on or before 5th April

2000, sections 48A(4)(b) and 48B(2)(b) above shall have effect with the omission of the words "half of".

(4) In the application of the provisions of sections 44 to [² 45B] [³ and [⁵ Schedules 4A and 4B] below] above by virtue of sections 48A(4) or 48B(2) [⁴ or 48BB(5) above, references in those provisions to the pensioner shall be taken as references to the spouse.]

AMENDMENTS

1. Pensions Act 1995, Sch.4 (July 19, 1995).
2. Welfare Reform and Pensions Act 1999, Sch.12, para.00 (April 9, 2001).
3. Child Support Pensions and Social Security Act 2000, s.35 (April 6, 2002).
4. Welfare Reform and Pensions Act 1999, Sch.8, para.00 (April 9, 2001).
5. Pensions Act 2007, Sch.2, Pt 3, para.10 (September 26, 2007).

GENERAL NOTE

1.153   All category B retirement pensions may, in appropriate circumstances be affected by the provisions of the Gender Recognition Act 2004. This means that any question of entitlement after the claimant has obtained a certificate of gender recognition will be determined according to the criteria applicable to a person of the acquired gender. See notes to Gender Recognition Act 2004 in Vol.III of this work.

1.154   *Sections 49 and 50 repealed.*

Category B retirement pension for widowers

1.155   **51.**—(1) A man shall be entitled to a Category B retirement pension if—
   (a) he has had a wife and she has died on or after 6th April 1979, and he was married to her when she died; and
   (b) they were both over pensionable age when she died; and
   (c) before her death she satisfied the contribution conditions for a Category A retirement pension in Schedule 3, Part I, paragraph 5.

[⁴ (1A) A civil partner shall be entitled to a Category B retirement pension if—
   (a) his or her civil partner has died and they were civil partners of each other at the time of that death,
   (b) they were both over pensionable age at a time of that death, and
   (c) before that death the deceased civil partner satisfied the contribution conditions for a Category A retirement pension in Schedule 3, Part 1, paragraph 5].

(2) The weekly rate of a [⁴ person's] Category B retirement pension under this section shall, subject to subsection (3) below, be determined in accordance with the provisions of [¹ sections 44 to [³ 45]] [² and Schedule 4A below] above as they apply in the case of a Category A retirement pension, taking references in those sections to the pensioner as references to the wife [⁴ or deceased civil partner].

(3) In the case of a widower whose wife dies after 5th April 2000 [⁴ or a surviving civil partner], the additional pension falling to be calculated under [¹ sections 44 to [³ 45]] above [² and Schedule 4A below] by virtue of subsection (2) above shall be one half of the amount which it would be apart from this subsection.

(4) Subject to the provisions of this Act, a [⁴ person] shall become entitled to a Category B retirement pension [⁴ under this section] on the day

on which the conditions of entitlement become satisfied in his case and his entitlement shall continue throughout his life.

AMENDMENTS

1. Pensions Act 1995, s.127(2) (where relevant person is pensionable or dies after April 5, 1995).
2. Child Support Pensions and Social Security Act 2000, s.35 (April 6, 2002).
3. Tax Credit Act 2002, Sch.3 (April 6, 2003).
4. Civil Partnership Act 2004 Sch.24 (December 5, 2005).

DERIVATION

SSPA 1975, s.8.   **1.156**

DEFINITION

"pensionable age"—see s.122.

GENERAL NOTE

Note that because of Sch.4 para.3(3) of the Pensions Act 1995 there is no entitle-   **1.157**
ment under this section in the case of a man who attains pensionable age on or after April 6, 2010, nor in the case of a civil partner, after that date. (Civil Partnership Act 2004, Sch.24 Pt 3, para.28(b).)

This section may be affected, in appropriate cases, by the operation of the Gender Recognition Act 2004. See notes to that Act in Vol.III of this work.

Special provision for married people

[¹ **51A.**—This section has effect where, apart from section 43(1) above, a   **1.158**
married person [² or civil partner] would be entitled both—
(a) to a Category A retirement pension, and
(b) to a Category B retirement pension by virtue of the contributions of the other party to the marriage [² or civil partnership].

(2) If by reason of a deficiency of contributions the basic pension in the Category A retirement pension falls short of the weekly rate specified in Schedule 4, Part I, paragraph 5, that basic pension shall be increased by the lesser of—
(a) the amount of the shortfall, or
(b) the amount of the weekly rate of the Category B retirement pension.

(3) This section does not apply in any case where both parties to the marriage [² or civil partnership] attained pensionable age before 6th April 1979].

AMENDMENTS

1. Pensions Act 1995, Sch.4, para.21(6) (July 19, 1995).
2. Civil Partnership Act 2004, Sch.4 (December 5, 2005).

GENERAL NOTE

The effect of *Secretary of State for Work and Pensions v Nelligan, R(P)2/03* is   **1.159**
extended to include s.51A in *CP/271/2005*. The claimant's wife had, like that in *Nelligan*, qualified for a Category A pension of her own on reaching age 60, but at a reduced rate. Subsequently, her husband qualified for his pension at the full rate at which point the claimant could have qualified for an increased pension on the basis of s.51A. Unfortunately the claimant did not discover this until some two years later

and when she then claimed, she was allowed backdating for only the usual three month period.

The claimant argued that *Nelligan* did not apply to s.51A, and that if it did, then *Nelligan* was decided per incuriam since no reference there had been made to s.51A. That section, it was argued, should be read as creating entitlement without the need for a claim to be made. It was contended, on her behalf, that her increased entitlement arose under s.51A as a result of a decision to supersede her existing award of Category A pension and without a fresh claim being made.

This argument failed, however, because, as the Commissioner points out, the supersession takes effect only from the date of a relevant change of circumstances which, for the purpose of s.51A, could only be by her becoming entitled to a Category B pension, and as *Nelligan* had held, that entitlement depended upon a claim having been made.

Special provision for surviving spouses

1.160   **52.**—(1) This section has effect where, apart from section 43(1) above, a person would be entitled both—

    (a) to a Category A retirement pension; and

[¹ (b) to a Category B retirement pension by virtue of the contributions of a spouse [² or civil partner] who has died]

    (2) If by reason of a deficiency of contributions the basic pension in the Category A retirement pension falls short of the full amount, that basic pension shall be increased by the lesser of—

    (a) the amount of the shortfall, or

    (b) the amount of the basic pension in the rate of the Category B retirement pension,

"full amount" meaning for this purpose the sum specified in section 44(4) above as the weekly rate of the basic pension in a Category A retirement pension.

    (3) If the additional pension in the Category A retirement pension falls short of the prescribed maximum, that additional pension shall be increased by the lesser of—

    (a) the amount of the shortfall, or

    (b) the amount of the additional pension in the Category B retirement pension.

    (4) This section does not apply in any case where the death of the wife or husband, as the case may be, occurred before 6th April 1979 and the surviving spouse had attained pensionable age before that date.

AMENDMENTS

    1. Pensions Act 1995, Sch.4, para.21(7) (July 19, 1995).
    2. Civil Partnership Act 2004 Sch.24 (December 5, 2005).

DERIVATION

1.161   SSPA 1975, s.9.

GENERAL NOTE

1.162   The operation of s.52(3) is examined in *R(P) 1/03*. The case concerned the calculation of the additional pension and the treatment of a guaranteed minimum pension derived from an occupational pension scheme which, under s.46 of the Pension Scheme Act, had to be deducted from that entitlement. The claimant contended that this deduction should be made from the additional pension derived only from her own earnings as an intermediate stage in calculating the pension. The Secretary of State, on the other hand, contended that the GMP deduction fell to be made only at the end of the calculation process. The difference was significant in this case (some £35 per week) because it meant that the claimant avoided the cap (the "prescribed maximum") in s.52(3). The tribunal had found in favour of the claimant—her argument had the advantage that it seems natural to attach the GMP deduction only to the additional pension element to which it related. But Commissioner Williams allowed the Secretary of State's appeal. He finds the wording of s.46 clear, it provides for a deduction to be made from the pension to which the claimant is entitled, and this could only mean the deduction is made from the rate of Category A or Category B pension as finally determined. To have decided otherwise created other anomalies in the legislation.

Section 53 repealed.   1.163

Category A and Category B retirement pensions: supplemental provisions

54.—(1) Regulations may provide that in the case of a person of any   1.164
prescribed description who—
  (a) has become entitled to a Category A or Category B retirement pension but is, in the case of a woman, under the age of 65 or, in the case of a man, under the age of 70; and
  (b) elects in such manner and in accordance with such conditions as may be prescribed that the regulations shall apply in his case,
this Part of this Act shall have effect as if that person had not become entitled to such a retirement pension. [¹ or to a shared additional pension].

(2) Regulations under subsection (1) above may make such modifications of the provisions of this Part of this Act, or of those of Part II of the Administration Act [² or Chapter II of Part I of the Social Security Act 1998] as those provisions apply in a case where a person makes an election under the regulations, as may appear to the Secretary of State necessary or expedient.

[⁴[⁵ (3) Where both parties to a marriage [⁴or civil partnership] (call them "P" and "S") have become entitled to retirement pensions and–
  (a) P's pension is Category A, and
  (b) S's pension is–
      (i) Category B by virtue of P's contributions, or
      (ii) Category A with an increase under section 51A(2) above by virtue of P's contributions,
P shall not be entitled to make an election in accordance with regulations made under subsection (1) above without S's consent, unless that consent is unreasonably withheld].

(4) *Repealed.*

AMENDMENTS

  1. Welfare Reform and Pensions Act 1999, Sch.12, para.12 (April 9, 2001).
  2. Social Security Act 1998, Sch.7, para.62 (September 6, 1999).
  3. Pensions Act 1995, Sch.4, para.21(8) (July 19, 1995).
  4. Civil Partnership Act 2004, Sch.24 (December 25, 2005).
  5. These words have been omitted by the s.2 and Sch.1 of Pensions Act 2007, but the eVect of that amendment has been postponed until April 6, 2010. (Pensions Act 2007 s.2(5)).

DERIVATION

1.165   SSA 1975, s.30.

GENERAL NOTE

1.166   An election to cancel entitlement is made under reg.2 of the Widow's Benefit and Retirement Pensions Regulations. Note that an election to cancel entitlement can be made only once. A person who retires twice and then goes back to work again does not gain increments to his pension for the second period of employment. Where a wife is entitled to a pension by virtue of her husband's contribution record the husband can elect to cancel entitlement only with his wife's consent, unless such consent has been unreasonably withheld. The only reported case is from Northern Ireland *R6/60(P)*. The Commissioner suggested that the consent might be unreasonably withheld if the only reason were pique or spite, but not where it would make a significant reduction in the wife's income.

The discriminatory effect of s.54 on women (they cannot de-retire after the age of 65) has been found to be exempted from the Equal Treatment Directive, EG 79/7, at least in so far as it impinges on a claimant's entitlement to Income Support (*R(P) 1/95*). In that case the claimant wanted to de-retire so as to be able to claim Invalidity Benefit which would in turn have given access to a Higher Pensioner Premium with her Income Support. The Commissioner held that art.3(1) did not apply to Income Support and hence the claim failed. An argument that s.54 discriminated against men, in that a woman could accrue extra benefits between the ages of 60 and 65 while a man could not, was also rejected in *CP/029/94*. The Commissioner held that the discriminatory effect was inherent in the adoption of different retirement ages for men and women and therefore covered by the derogation under art.7.

This section may be affected, in appropriate cases, by the operation of the Gender Recognition Act 2004. See notes to that Act in Vol.III of this work.

[²55.— Pension increase or lump sum where entitlement to retirement pension is deferred

1.167   (1) Where a person's entitlement to a Category A or Category B retirement pension is deferred, Schedule 5 to this Act has effect.

(2) In that Schedule—

paragraph A1 makes provision enabling an election to be made where the pensioner's entitlement is deferred

paragraphs 1 to 3 make provision about increasing pension where the pensioner's entitlement is deferred

paragraphs 3A and 3B make provision about lump sum payments where the pensioner's entitlement is deferred

paragraph 3C makes provision enabling an election to be made where the pensioner's deceased spouse has deferred entitlement

paragraphs 4 to 7 make provision about increasing pension where the pensioner's deceased spouse has deferred entitlement

paragraphs 7A and 7B make provision about lump sum payments where the pensioner's deceased spouse has deferred entitlement

paragraphs 7C to 9 make supplementary provision.

(3) For the purposes of this Act a person's entitlement to a Category A or Category B retirement pension is deferred if and so long as that person—

[³ (a) does not become entitled to that pension by reason only of not satisfying the conditions of section 1 of the Administration Act (entitlement to benefit dependent on claim), or]

(b) in consequence of an election under section 54(1), falls to be treated as not having become entitled to that pension, and, in relation to any such pension, "period of deferment" shall be construed accordingly.]

AMENDMENTS

1. Pensions Act 1995, s.134(3) (July 19, 1995).
2. Pensions Act 2004, s.297 (April 6, 2005, subs.(3) from November 18, 2004).
3. Pensions Act 2007, Sch.1, para.7 (September 26, 2007).

DERIVATIONS

SSPA 1975, s.12.   1.168
SSA 1989, s.7.

GENERAL NOTE

Note that the increase in pension does not depend upon the claimant having   1.169
decided to defer his claim. As subs.(2)(a)(i) makes clear, it applies equally to a
person making a late claim for pension where the delay is the result of ignorance
of entitlement, or otherwise. In *CP/14276/1996* the claimant had been resident in
China and made her claim five years after she reached pensionable age. Although
her claim could be backdated only one year (see SSAA 1992, s.1), it was paid at an
enhanced rate to reflect the effective period of delay—four years.

The provisions for calculating the amount of the increase are found in Sch.5 to
this Act and any increases provided for in the annual up-rating of Benefits Order.
Note that from April 2005, benefit that is deferred for a year or more may be taken
in the form of a lump sum.

This section may be affected, in appropriate cases, by the operation of the Gender
Recognition Act 2004. See notes to that Act in Vol.III of this work.

[¹ Shared additional pension

55A.—(1) A person shall be entitled to a shared additional pension if he   1.170
is—

(a) over pensionable age, and

(b) entitled to a state scheme pension credit.

(2) A person's entitlement to a shared additional pension shall continue
throughout his life.

(3) The weekly rate of a shared additional pension shall be the appropriate weekly amount, unless the pensioner's entitlement to the state scheme
pension credit arose before the final relevant year, in which case it shall be
that amount multiplied by the relevant revaluation percentage.

(4) The appropriate weekly amount for the purposes of subsection
(3) above is the weekly rate, expressed in terms of the valuation day, at
which the cash equivalent, on that day, of the pensioner's entitlement, or
prospective entitlement, to the shared additional pension is equal to the
state scheme pension credit.

(5) The relevant revaluation percentage for the purposes of that subsection is the percentage specified, in relation to earnings factors for the tax
year in which the entitlement to the state scheme pension credit arose, by
the last order under section 148 of the Administration Act to come into
force before the end of the final relevant year.

[² (6) The Secretary of State may by regulations make provision about
the calculation and verification of cash equivalents for the purposes of this
section.

(6A) The power conferred by subsection (6) above includes power to provide—

    (a) for calculation or verification in such manner as may be approved by or on behalf of the Government Actuary, and

    (b) for things done under the regulations to be required to be done in accordance with guidance from time to time prepared by a person prescribed by the regulations.]

(7) In this section—

"final relevant year" means the tax year immediately preceding that in which the pensioner attains pensionable age;

"state scheme pension credit" means a credit under section 49(1)(b) of the Welfare Reform and Pensions Act 1999 (credit for the purposes of this Part of this Act);

"valuation day" means the day on which the pensioner becomes entitled to the state scheme pension credit.]

AMENDMENTS

    1. Welfare Reform and Pensions Act 1999, Sch.6, para.3 (April 9, 2001).

    2. Child Support, Pensions and Social Security Act 2000, s.41 (September 29, 2000).

    3. Pensions Act 2007, Sch.1, para.7 (September 26, 2007).

GENERAL NOTE

1.171   Note the special provisions made for persons claiming a shared additional pension between April 6, 2005 and April 5, 2006 in reg.10 of the Shared Additional Pensions (Miscellaneous Amendments) Regulations 2005 (S1 2005/1551).

[¹ Reduction of shared additional pension: pension sharing

1.172   **55B.**—(1) The weekly rate of a shared additional pension shall be reduced as follows in any case where—

    (a) the pensioner has become subject to a state scheme pension debit, and

    (b) the debit is to any extent referable to the pension.

(2) If the pensioner became subject to the debit in or after the final relevant year, the weekly rate of the pension shall be reduced by the appropriate weekly amount.

(3) If the pensioner became subject to the debit before the final relevant year, the weekly rate of the additional pension shall be reduced by the appropriate weekly amount multiplied by the relevant revaluation percentage.

(4) The appropriate weekly amount for the purposes of subsections (2) and (3) above is the weekly rate, expressed in terms of the valuation day, at which the cash equivalent, on that day, of the pension mentioned in subsection (5) below is equal to so much of the debit as is referable to the shared additional pension.

(5) The pension referred to above is a notional pension for the pensioner by virtue of section 55A above which becomes payable on the later of—

    (a) his attaining pensionable age, and

    (b) the valuation day.

(6) For the purposes of subsection (3) above, the relevant revaluation percentage is the percentage specified, in relation to earnings factors for the tax year in which the pensioner became subject to the debit, by the last order under section 148 of the Administration Act to come into force before the end of the final relevant year.

[² (7) The Secretary of State may by regulations make provision about the calculation and verification of cash equivalents for the purposes of this section.

(7A) The power conferred by subsection (7) above includes power to provide—

(a) for calculation or verification in such manner as may be approved by or on behalf of the Government Actuary, and

(b) for things done under the regulations to be required to be done in accordance with guidance from time to time prepared by a person prescribed by the regulations.]

(8) In this section—

"final relevant year" means the tax year immediately preceding that in which the pensioner attains pensionable age;

"state scheme pension debit" means a debit under section 49(1)(a) of the Welfare Reform and Pensions Act 1999 (debit for the purposes of this Part of this Act);

"valuation day" means the day on which the pensioner became subject to the state scheme pension debit.]

AMENDMENTS

1. Welfare Reform and Pensions Act 1999, Sch.6, para.3 (April 9, 2001).
2. Child Support, Pensions and Social Security Act 2000, s.41 (September 29, 2000).

[³55C Pension increase or lump sum where entitlement to shared additional pension is deferred

(1) Where a person's entitlement to a shared additional pension is deferred, Schedule 5A to this Act has effect.

1.173

(2) In that Schedule—

paragraph 1 makes provision enabling an election to be made where the person's entitlement is deferred

paragraphs 2 and 3 make provision about increasing pension where the person's entitlement is deferred

paragraphs 4 and 5 make provision about lump sum payments where the person's entitlement is deferred.

(3) For the purposes of this Act, a person's entitlement to a shared additional pension is deferred—

(a) where he would be entitled to a Category A or Category B retirement pension but for the fact that his entitlement is deferred, if and so long as his entitlement to such a pension is deferred, and

(b) otherwise, if and so long as he does not become entitled to the shared additional pension by reason only of not satisfying the conditions of section 1 of the Administration Act (entitlement to benefit dependent on claim),

and, in relation to a shared additional pension, "period of deferment" shall be construed accordingly.]]

1. Inserted by Welfare Reform and Pensions Act 1999, Sch.6, para.3 (April 9, 2001).
2. Child Support, Pensions and Social Security Act 2000. These changes have effect for incremental periods on or after April 6, 2010.
3. Pensions Act 2004, s.297 (April 6, 2005).

Child's special allowance

Child's special allowance—existing beneficiaries

1.174 **56.**—*Omitted.*

1.175 *Sections 57 to 59 repealed.*

1.176 *Sections 60 and 61 omitted.*

Graduated retirement benefit

1.177 **62.**—(1) So long as sections 36 and 37 of the National Insurance Act 1965 (graduated retirement benefit) continue in force by virtue of regulations made under Schedule 3 to the Social Security (Consequential Provisions) Act 1975 or under Schedule 3 to the Consequential Provisions Act, regulations may make provision—

(a) for [¹ amending section 36(2) of the National Insurance Act 1965 (value of unit of graduated contributions) so that the value is the same for women as it is for men and for replacing section 36(4) of that Act] (increase of graduated retirement benefit in cases of deferred retirement) with provisions corresponding to those of paragraphs 1 to 3 of Schedule 5 to this Act;

[² (aa) for amending section 36(7) of that Act (persons to be treated as receiving nominal retirement pension) so that where a person has claimed a Category A or Category B retirement pension but—
  (i) because of an election under section 54(1) above, or
  (ii) because he has withdrawn his claim for the pension, he is not entitled to such a pension, he is not to be treated for the purposes of the preceding provisions of that section as receiving such a pension at a nominal weekly rate;]

[⁵ (ab) for extending section 37 of that Act (increase of woman's retirement pension by reference to her late husband's retirement benefit) to civil partners and for that section (except subsection (5)) so to apply as it applies to women and their late husbands;]

[⁴ (ac) for extending section 37 of that Act (increase of woman's retirement pension by reference to her late husband's graduated retirement benefit) to civil partners and their late civil partners who attain pensionable age before 6th April 2010 and for that section (except subsection (5)) so to apply as it applies to men and their late wives;]

(b) for extending section 37 of that Act (increase of woman's retirement pension by reference to her late husband's graduated retirement benefit) to men and their late wives [³ and for that section (except subsection (5)) so to apply as it applies to women and their late husbands].

(2) This section is without prejudice to any power to modify the said sections 36 and 37 conferred by Schedule 3 to the Consequential Provisions Act.

AMENDMENTS

1. Pensions Act 1995, Sch.4, para.7(a). (July 19, 1995).
2. Pensions Act 1995, s.131(1) (July 19, 1995).
3. Pensions Act 1995, Sch.4, para.7(b) (July 19, 1995).
4. Civil Partnership (Miscellaneous and Consequential Provisions) Order 2005 (S 2005/3029) Sch.1, (October 29, 2005).
5. Civil Partnership Act 2004, Sch.24 (December 5, 2005).

DERIVATION

SSPA 1975, s.24.   **1.178**

GENERAL NOTE

In *CP/3593/2006* (to be reported as *R(P) 1/08*) Commissioner Williams has dem-   **1.179**
onstrated the complexity that arises in relation to claims for GRB and to appeals
from those decisions. Unlike other contributory benefits no part of the functions of
the Secretary of State for Work and Pensions has been transferred to Her Majesty's
Revenue and Customs. Yet HMRC are still responsible for recording and providing
any information necessary in relation to a claimant's contribution record. This means
that officers of HMRC must do so as agents acting on behalf of the SSWP, and any
decision made by them becomes one for which the SSWP is legally responsible. This
means, in turn, that all such decisions are appealable to a Social Security Tribunal
and thence to the Commissioners. This decision also contains useful guidance for tribunals on the correct approach to questions that arise from the contribution record.

PART III

NON-CONTRIBUTORY BENEFITS

Descriptions of non-contributory benefits

63.—Non-contributory benefits under this Part of this Act are of the fol-   **1.180**
lowing descriptions, namely—
  (a) attendance allowance;
  (b) severe disablement allowance (with age related addition and increase
      for adult and child dependants);
  (c) [¹ carer's allowance] (with increase for adult [² . . .] dependants);
  (d) disability living allowance;
  (e) guardian's allowance;
  (f) retirement pensions of the following categories—
       (i) Category C, payable to certain persons who were over pension-
           able age on 5th July 1948 and their wives and widows (with
           increase for adult [² . . .] dependants), and
      (ii) Category D, payable to persons over the age of 80;
  (g) age addition payable, in the case of persons over the age of 80, by
      way of increase of a retirement pension of any category or of some
      other pension or allowance from the Secretary of State.

AMENDMENTS

1. Regulatory Reform (Carer's Allowance) Order 2002 (SI 2002/1457), art.2 (April 1, 2003).
2. Tax Credits Act 2002, Sch.6 (April 6, 2003).

DERIVATION

1.181   SSA 1975, s.34.

Attendance allowance

Entitlement

1.182   **64.**—(1) A person shall be entitled to an attendance allowance if he [² has attained pensionable age], he is not entitled to the care component of a disability living allowance and he satisfies either—
(a) the condition specified in subsection (2) below ("the day attendance condition"), or
(b) the condition specified in subsection (3) below ("the night attendance condition"),
and prescribed conditions as to residence and presence in Great Britain.
(2) A person satisfies the day attendance condition if he is so severely disabled physically or mentally that, by day, he requires from another person either—
(a) frequent attention throughout the day in connection with his bodily functions, or
(b) continual supervision throughout the day in order to avoid substantial danger to himself or others.
(3) A person satisfies the night attendance condition if he is so severely disabled physically or mentally that, at night,—
(a) he requires from another person prolonged or repeated attention in connection with his bodily functions, or
(b) in order to avoid substantial danger to himself or others he requires another person to be awake for a prolonged period or at frequent intervals for the purpose of watching over him.
[¹ (4) Circumstances may be prescribed in which a person is to be taken to satisfy or not to satisfy such of the conditions mentioned in subsections (2) and (3) above as may be prescribed.]

AMENDMENT

1. Welfare Reform and Pensions Act 1999, s.66 (January 12, 2000).
2. Pensions Act 2007, Sch.1, para.41 (September 26, 2007).

DERIVATION

1.183   SSA 1975, s.35(1).

GENERAL NOTE

1.184   Attendance Allowance is a weekly benefit paid to those who are disabled so as to need a sufficient level of care and attention from someone else. The benefit is usually paid to the claimant rather than to the carer. It is not necessary that the claimant is actually paying for the care (or, in theory, even that he is receiving the care). What is necessary is that he should *need* the care.

Attendance Allowance was originally introduced in 1970 and was then payable at just one rate to those who needed attention or supervision both day and night. In 1972, the lower rate was introduced for those who required attention or supervision by day or at night but not both.

The Disability Living Allowance and Disability Working Allowance Act 1991 substantially reduced the scope of attendance allowance so that now it is applicable only to those people over 65 who are not entitled under what is now s.72 of the Social Security Contributions and Benefits Act to the care component of disability living allowance. Since those who have become entitled to the care component of disability living allowance while under 65 remain entitled to it thereafter, attendance allowance is now payable only to those who become disabled after reaching that age or who, though disabled earlier, fail to claim before they are 65. Attendance allowance is less generous than the care component of disability living allowance in two respects. First, it has a six-month qualifying period (s.65(1)(b)) as opposed to the three-month period for the care component (s.72(2)(a)) although neither qualifying period applies in the case of a person who is terminally ill. Secondly, there are only two rates of attendance allowance, which are the same as the highest and middle rate of the care component. There is no equivalent to the lowest rate of the care component.

The limitations that these conditions impose are shown by the decision in *CA/2574/2007*. The claimant was a widow who was agoraphobic, anorexic and depressed, and had lived as a recluse since the death of her husband. She was visited daily by her daughter who supplied all her physical needs and remained each day for a period of several hours to stimulate and encourage her mother. A report by a consultant psychiatrist suggested that the claimant was being kept alive by the services and the visits of her daughter. This much was accepted as true by the Commissioner, but still could not qualify her for AA. The services such as shopping and housekeeping supplied by the daughter could not qualify as they were not sufficiently "personal" (see notes that follow s.72) and, although the Commissioner was prepared to accept that the time spent stimulating her mother might qualify as attention in connection with the bodily functioning of the brain, it was neither "frequent" nor "continual" throughout the day so as to satisfy the conditions of subs. (2). Had the claimant been able to claim DLA (she could not because of her age) she might have succeeded in a claim for the lowest rate of that benefit on the basis that the attention was for a "significant portion of the day".

Subs.(1)

For the circumstances in which a person over 65 is entitled to the care component of a disability living allowance, see s.75 and also reg.3 of and Sch.1 to the Disability Living Allowance Regulations. For prescribed conditions as to residence and presence, see reg.2 of the Social Security (Attendance Allowance) Regulation 1991.   **1.185**

Subss.(2) and (3)

Subs.(3) contains two alternative "day" conditions and subs.(3) contains two alternative "night" conditions. Subject to the waiting period imposed by s.65(1)(b), attendance allowance is paid at the higher rate if both a "day" and a "night" condition are satisfied and at the lower rate if the conditions are satisfied only for the day or the night (s.65(3)).   **1.186**

The attendance conditions in subss.(2) and (3) are the same as those in paras (b) and (c) of s.72(1) and reference should be made to the notes to that subsection.

Note that both conditions may be deemed to be satisfied in the case of a person who is terminally ill and can reasonably be expected to die within six months (s.66).

Note also that reg.5 of the Attendance Allowance Regulation provides that certain people undergoing renal dialysis are deemed to satisfy either the day or the night attention condition so as to qualify them for attendance allowance at the lower rate. There is no reason why they should not satisfy another condition for other reasons and so qualify for the higher rate.

Before March 15, 1988, the night condition was different. Under the earlier version it was possible for supervision to be provided by someone who was "on call", though not necessarily awake, so as to be ready to render assistance as necessary (*Moran v Secretary of State for Social Services* reported as appendix to *R(A) 1/88*). After that date it has been necessary for the carer to be awake and watching over the claimant. Determinations made under the earlier provision continue to be effective (see Social Security (Consequential Provisions) Act 1992, Sch.3, para.19). It is arguable that determinations made after that date, but in respect of entitlement before it, should also be governed by the old law, though it is now unlikely that any such issue remains extant.

Attendance Allowance will now be administered in the same way as other benefits for the disabled. Decisions will be taken by the Secretary of State with appeal to an appeal tribunal, including a medically qualified member and one with a disability qualification.

Attendance Allowance can be claimed only by persons resident in the UK It is no longer payable to a claimant who has gone to live in another Member State of the European Community. This is because the UK has (from June 1992) designated Attendance Allowance as a benefit confined to the UK. This was confirmed on a reference to the European Court of Justice in *Partridge v AO* [1998] E.C.R. I-3467 reported as *R(A) 1/99*. However, further developments in the European Court of Justice have raised some doubts as to the reasoning in *Partridge* and the question of whether this benefit (and DLA and Carers Allowance) should be exportable is the subject of proceedings issued against the UK by the European Commission in Case C-299/05.

Period and rate of allowance

1.187   **65.**—(1) Subject to the following provisions of this Act, the period for which a person is entitled to an attendance allowance shall be—

    (a) a period throughout which he has satisfied or is likely to satisfy the day or the night attendance condition or both; and

    (b) a period preceded immediately, or within such period as may be prescribed, by one of not less than six months throughout which he satisfied, or is likely to satisfy, one or both of those conditions.

(2) For the purposes of subsection (1) above a person who suffers from renal failure and is undergoing such form of treatment as may be prescribed shall, in such circumstances as may be prescribed, be deemed to satisfy or to be likely to satisfy the day or the night attendance condition or both.

(3) The weekly rate of the attendance allowance payable to a person for any period shall be the higher rate specified in Schedule 4, Part III, paragraph 1, if both as regards that period and as regards the period of six months mentioned in subsection (1)(b) above he has satisfied or is likely to satisfy both the day and the night attendance conditions, and shall be the lower rate in any other case.

(4) A person shall not be entitled to an attendance allowance for any period preceding the date on which he makes or is treated as making a claim for it.

(5) Notwithstanding anything in subsection (4) above, provision may be made by regulations for a person to be entitled to an attendance allowance for a period preceding the date on which he makes or is treated as making a claim for it if such an allowance has previously been paid to or in respect of him.

(6) Except in so far as regulations otherwise provide and subject to section 66(1) below—

(a) a claim for an attendance allowance may be made during the period of six months immediately preceding the period for which the person to whom the claim relates is entitled to the allowance; and

(b) an award may be made in pursuance of a claim so made, subject to the condition that, throughout that period of six months, that person satisfies—

    (i) both the day and the night attendance conditions, or

    (ii) if the award is at the lower rate, one of those conditions.

DERIVATION

SSA 1975, ss.35(2), (2A), (3), (4) and (4A).   **1.188**

GENERAL NOTE

Subs.(1)

Paragraph (a) has the effect that an award of attendance allowance should be for **1.189** the period for which the claimant has satisfied or is *likely* to satisfy one or both of the attendance conditions. An award may be for life or for a specified period. There is no minimum period specified but it will seldom be appropriate to make an award for less than six months which is the minimum period for an award of the care component of a disability living allowance (see s.72(2)(b)). In this case, "likely" can be read as "more likely than not" since the subsection is concerned with the continued satisfaction of the conditions of entitlement. If the prognosis is uncertain, the award should be limited in time.

It is not necessary that the conditions are likely to be satisfied in respect of every day. *R(A) 2/74* concerned a claimant who had to undergo renal dialysis for 10 hours on three nights a week, at a time before any specific provision was made for such claimants (see now reg.5 of the Social Security (Attendance Allowance) Regulations 1991). The Commissioner held that it was wrong to take a purely arithmetical approach and that the claimant was not, as a matter of law, excluded from entitlement. Variations in a claimant's condition present greater problems because they are irregular and difficult to predict. "These are matters for the good sense and judgment of the [decision-maker]."

Both attendance conditions are deemed to be satisfied for the remainder of the life of a person suffering from a progressive disease and likely to die within six months (s.66(1)(a)(i)).

Paragraph (b) provides for the six-month qualifying period. A person is not entitled to attendance allowance until he or she has satisfied an attendance condition for six months. The combined effect of this subsection and subs.(3) is that, if a person has been receiving the lower rate because he or she satisfies only, say, the day attendance condition and then his or her condition deteriorates so that he or she also satisfies the night condition, he or she does not become entitled to the higher rate until six months have elapsed. This six-month qualifying period is waived in the case of a person who is suffering from a progressive disease and likely to die within six months (s.66(1)(a)(ii)). Other claimants may make their claims during the qualifying period so that a decision can be made straightaway and payment can start as soon as the qualifying period has been completed (subs. (4)(a)).

Usually the six-month qualifying period immediately precedes the period of entitlement but it may fall within such other period as may be prescribed. Reg.3 of the Social Security (Attendance Allowance) Regulations 1991 prescribes the period of two years.

Subs.(2)

This enables regulations to be made so that a person who undergoes renal dialysis **1.190** is deemed to satisfy either or both of the day and the night attendance conditions.

Reg.5 of the Social Security (Attendance Allowance) Regulations 1991 allows a person having such treatment at least twice a week to be deemed, in some circumstances, to satisfy one, but not both, of the attendance conditions. Any question whether a person suffers renal failure is determined by an appeal tribunal which includes a medically qualified member and one with a disability qualification on appeal from the Secretary of State.

Subs. (4) and (5)

1.191   Awards of attendance allowance cannot usually be made in respect of a period before the date of claim. For details affecting the date a claim is treated as made see Reg.6 of Claims and Payments Regulations in Vol.I of this work.

Regulation 4 of the Social Security (Attendance Allowance) Regulations 1991, treated as made under subs.(5), allowed an award to be made from the end of a previous period of entitlement if the renewal claim was made within six months but that regulation was revoked from September 1, 1997.

Subs. (6)

1.192   A claim may be made in advance during the six-month waiting period. The award is, of course, conditional on the claimant continuing to satisfy the attendance conditions. In *CA/1474/97*, the Commissioner held that a tribunal who found that the attendance conditions had been satisfied for a period of less than six months could make a prospective award. However, they were not bound to do so and could decline to reach any firm conclusion as to whether the attendance conditions had been satisfied for that period although, if they took that course, they were obliged to tell the claimant that he or she could make another claim so as to have the question determined. Since the coming into force of para.3(2) of Sch.6 to the Social Security Act 1998 on May 21, 1998, it is possible to make a prospective award only if the attendance conditions were satisfied at the date of the decision-maker's decision so that the decision-maker could have made a prospective award.

Attendance allowance for the terminally ill

1.193   **66.**—(1) If a terminally ill person makes a claim expressly on the ground that he is such a person then—

(a) he shall be taken—
  (i) to satisfy, or to be likely to satisfy, both the day attendance condition and the night attendance condition [¹ for so much of the period for which he is terminally ill as does not fall before the date of claim.] and
  (ii) to have satisfied those conditions for the period of six months immediately preceding [¹ the date of the claim or, if later, the first date on which he is terminally ill.] (so however that no allowance shall be payable by virtue of this sub-paragraph for any period preceding that date); and

(b) the period for which he is entitled to attendance allowance shall be [¹ so much of the period for which he is terminally ill as does not fall before the date of the claim].

(2) For the purposes of subsection (1) above—

(a) a person is "terminally ill" at any time if at that time he suffers from a progressive disease and his death in consequence of that disease can reasonably be expected within six months; and

(b) where a person purports to make a claim for an attendance allowance by virtue of that subsection on behalf of another, that other shall be regarded as making the claim, notwithstanding that it is made without his knowledge or authority.

AMENDMENT

1. Welfare Reform and Pensions Act 1999, s.66 (January 12, 2000).

DERIVATION

SSA 1975, ss.35(2B), (2C).

1.194

GENERAL NOTE

Terminally ill patients are deemed to satisfy both attendance conditions and therefore qualify for benefit at the higher rate. Furthermore, in order to meet the criticism that such patients sometimes died before they could complete the normal six-month qualifying period, the benefit is paid under this section from the date of claim. (The claimant is deemed to satisfy the conditions for the remainder of his life and to have done so in the six months preceding his claim.) Nor is it necessary for the claimant to show that he requires attention, etc.; this is assumed to be the case for those who are terminally ill.

1.195

Subs.(2)(a) provides the definition of when a person is "terminally ill". A person is terminally ill when he suffers from a progressive disease and his death from the cause can "reasonably be expected within six months".

This phrase, though potentially of uncertain meaning, does not seem to have given rise to difficulty. It is fairly clear that someone whose death is more likely than not is "reasonably expected" to die. Equally, where the doctor says that his patient is likely to survive beyond six months it would seem true to say his death is not "expected" within that period. But what of those cases where the outcome is simply very uncertain? Could death be "reasonably expected" when it is "quite possible", though not yet "probable"? Note that some of this difficulty will be obviated by the need to show that death is expected from a "progressive disease". This will include conditions such as cancer but in most cases will not cover other common causes of death such as heart attacks.

It is important to note that the question to be considered by the decision-maker, and a tribunal on appeal, is prospective in the sense that what must be determined is whether death is reasonably to be expected within six months of the date of claim. Medical evidence in the form of the doctor's opinion must relate to that question regardless of what may have transpired since the claim was made. In *R(A) 1/94* a claim had been made for a baby born with brain damage. The award was made from a date six months after the baby's birth. The baby's mother applied for review of the award to run from the date of birth and a consultant was asked to answer the question as above. However, by the time he came to answer the baby had already survived for more than a year and he felt unable to answer, given what was now known. The AO decided that death was not to be expected, etc. The Commissioner allowed an appeal, holding that the survival of the baby was irrelevant to the question that had to be answered, *viz.* what was reasonably to be expected at the date the review was requested, and he allowed the appeal. This did not avail the mother, however, as this claim was made under the old legislation for attendance allowance. Those provisions required a claimant to have been present in Great Britain for six months. In the case of a baby the Commissioner held that this meant an award could not begin until six months after its birth. In the case of disability living allowance, for which a claim of this sort would now be made, this requirement is expressly removed (reg.2(4) of the Disability Living Allowance Regulations) and benefit would be paid from birth, or from the time the baby left an NHS hospital.

In any event, death must be expected as a result of a progressive disease, rather than some other cause. This may be a significant qualification for a few very elderly people. A question whether a person is terminally ill is decided by the Secretary of State with appeal to an appeal tribunal which includes a medically qualified member and one with a disability qualification. Although a claim must be made expressly on the ground that the claimant is terminally ill, the Secretary of State may accept any notification that a person is terminally ill as being sufficient to amount to a claim (reg.4 of the Social Security (Claims and Payments) Regulations 1987). Presumably, in the case of a claimant with an existing award of attendance allowance at the lower rate, an application for a review on this ground counts as a claim for the purposes of s.66. In any case this decision will now be made by the Secretary of State. Subs.(2)(b) allows someone else to make a claim on this basis on behalf of the claimant, which enables a claim to be made in a case where the claimant's prognosis is being kept from him or her.

Exclusions by regulation

1.196   **67.**—(1) Regulations may provide that, in such circumstances, and for such purposes as may be prescribed, a person who is, or is treated under the regulations as, undergoing treatment for renal failure in a hospital or other similar institution otherwise than as an in-patient shall be deemed not to satisfy or to be unlikely to satisfy the day attendance condition or the night attendance condition or both of them.

[³ (2) Regulations may provide that an attendance allowance shall not be payable in respect of a person for a period when he is a resident of a care home in circumstances in which any of the costs of any qualifying services provided for him are borne out of public or local funds under a specified enactment.

(3) The reference in subsection (2) to a care home is to an establishment that provides accommodation together with nursing or personal care.

(4) The following are qualifying services for the purposes of subsection (2)—

(a) accommodation,
(b) board, and
(c) personal care.

(5) The reference in subsection (2) to a specified enactment is to an enactment which is, or is of a description, specified for the purposes of that subsection by regulations.

(6) The power to specify an enactment for the purposes of subsection (2) includes power to specify it only in relation to its application for a particular purpose.

(7) In this section, "enactment" includes an enactment comprised in, or in an instrument made under, an Act of the Scottish Parliament.]

AMENDMENTS

1. Mental Health (Care and Treatment) (Scotland) Act 2003 (Consequential Provisions) Order (SI 2005/2078) Sch.1 para.4 (October 5, 2005).
2. National Health Service (Consequential Provisions) Act 2006, Sch.1, para.143 (March 1, 2007).
3. Welfare Reform Act 2007, s.60(1) (October 29, 2007).

DERIVATION

1.197   SSA 1975, ss.35(5A), (6).

GENERAL NOTE

Subs.(1)

1.198   See reg.5(3) and 5(4) of the Social Security (Attendance Allowance) Regulations 1991.

Subs.(2)

1.199   See regs 6–8 of the Social Security (Attendance Allowance) Regulations 1991.

Severe disablement allowance

[The entry into force on April 6, 2001 of s.65 of the Welfare Reform and Pensions Act means that ss.68 and 69 ceased to have effect on that date. However, certain existing entitlements continue under a transitional provision in art.4 of the Welfare Reform and Pensions Act 1999 (Commencement No. 9, and Transitional and Savings Provisions) Order 2000 (SI 2000/2958) in respect of any entitlement to SDA for a day of incapacity on or after April 6, 2001 forming part of a period of incapacity beginning before April 6, 2001. Art.4 of the Order provides:

1.200

"Saving for existing severe disablement allowance beneficiaries

4.—Notwithstanding the commencement of the provisions referred to in article 2(3)(d), (f) and (g) and (6)(b) ("severe disablement allowance provisions"), the provisions referred to in paragraphs 26 *[SSCBA 1992, s. 90]* and 27 of Schedule 8 and Part IV of Schedule 13 *[SSCBA 1992, ss. 68, 69]* shall continue to have effect, in the period of incapacity for work beginning before 6th April 2001 which would have continued, whether or not by virtue of section 30C or 68(10) or (10A) of the Contributions and Benefits Act or regulations made thereunder, on or after that date but for the commencement of the severe disablement allowance provisions, as if those provisions had not been commenced—

1.201

    (a) in relation to a person, to whom paragraph (b) does not apply, who is entitled to severe disablement allowance under section 68 or 69 of the Contributions and Benefits Act on any day of incapacity for work in that period of incapacity for work; or

    (b) until the beginning of 6th April 2002, in relation to a person who —

        (i) was under the age of 20 years on 6th April 2001, and

        (ii) is entitled to severe disablement allowance under section 68(1) of the Contributions and Benefits Act on any day of incapacity for work in that period of incapacity for work." (Provisions in italics added by commentator.)

Accordingly, ss.68 and 69 can be found in the 2005 edition of this volume for the purposes of those continued entitlements, which cover those over 20 on April 6, 2001 until SDA entitlement ceases under the preserved SDA rules. Those under 20 on April 6, 2001 who remain entitled to, or are receiving, SDA in that period of incapacity until on or immediately before April 5, 2002, will on April 6, 2002, if still incapable of work, be transferred to long-term incapacity benefit without having to satisfy the contribution conditions, and without that entitlement being subject to reduction for pension payments under s.30DD. So will those aged under 20 on April 6, 2001, then entitled to SDA, whose period of incapacity for work covers the period on or immediately after April 5, 2002. See SSCBA s.30A(1)(b), (2A), and IB Regs, Pt IV, reg.19.

Entitlement and rate

  68.—*Section 68 omitted*

  69.—*Section 69 omitted*

1.202
1.203

Invalid Care Allowance

1.204   **70.**—(1) A person shall be entitled to [² a carer's allowance] for any day on which he is engaged in caring for a severely disabled person if—

    (a) he is regularly and substantially engaged in caring for that person;

    (b) he is not gainfully employed; and

    (c) the severely disabled person is either such relative of his as may be prescribed or a person of any such other description as may be prescribed.

[³ (1A) A person who was entitled to an allowance under this section immediately before the death of the severely disabled person referred to in subsection (1) shall continue to be entitled to it, even though he is no longer engaged in caring for a severely disabled person (and the requirements of subsection (1)(a) and (c) are not satisfied), until—

    (a) the end of the week in which he ceases to satisfy any other requirement as to entitlement to the allowance; or

    (b) the expiry of the period of eight weeks beginning with the Sunday following the death (or beginning with the date of the death if the death occurred on a Sunday), whichever occurs first].

(2) In this section, "severely disabled person" means a person in respect of whom there is payable either an attendance allowance or a disability living allowance by virtue of entitlement to the care component at the highest or middle rate or such other payment out of public funds on account of his need for attendance as may be prescribed.

(3) A person shall not be entitled to an allowance under this section if he is under the age of 16 or receiving full-time education.

(4) A person shall not be entitled to an allowance under this section unless he satisfies prescribed conditions as to residence or presence in Great Britain.

(5) [³ . . .]

(6) [³ . . .]

(7) No person shall be entitled for the same day to more than one allowance under this section; and where, apart from this subsection, two or more persons would be entitled for the same day to such an allowance in respect of the same severely disabled person, one of them only shall be entitled and that shall be such one of them—

    (a) as they may jointly elect in the prescribed manner, or

    (b) as may, in default of such an election, be determined by the Secretary of State in his discretion.

(8) Regulations may prescribe the circumstances in which a person is or is not to be treated for the purposes of this section as engaged, or regularly and substantially engaged, in caring for a severely disabled person, as gainfully employed or as receiving full-time education.

(9) [² A carer's allowance] shall be payable at the weekly rate specified in Schedule 4, Part III, paragraph 4.

(10)[¹ . . .]

AMENDMENTS

1. Social Security (Severe Disablement Allowance and Invalid Care Allowance) Amendment Regulations 1994(SI 1994/2556), reg.2(3) (October 28, 1994).

2. Regulatory Reform (Carer's Allowance) Order 2002 (SI 2002/1457), art.2 (April 1, 2003).

3. Regulatory Reform (Carer's Allowance) Order 2002 (SI 2002/1457), art.3 (October 28, 2003).

DERIVATION

SSA 1975, s.37.   1.205

GENERAL NOTE

Carer's Allowance, which until April 1, 2003, was known as Invalid Care   1.206
Allowance is a weekly benefit for those who spend at least 35 hours a week caring
for another person who is in receipt of attendance allowance, disability living allowance at the higher or middle rate, or constant attendance allowance under industrial
injuries or war disablement schemes.

Where the person who is being cared for dies so that the claimant is no longer
caring, subs.(1A) now provides that the carer's entitlement will continue for a
period of 8 weeks following the death, but only so long as the claimant satisfies the
remaining conditions of entitlement. When first enacted, s.37 of the Social Security
Act 1975 excluded married or cohabiting women from entitlement. In Case 150/85
Drake v Chief Adjudication Officer [1987] Q.B. 166 that exclusion was held to be
contrary to Council Directive 79/7 so the offending words were removed from subs.
(3) retrospectively by the Social Security Act 1986

Subs.(1)(a)

Neither this section nor the Regulations define what is meant by "caring". Given   1.207
the degree of disablement that has to be shown in the patient, it is likely that the statutory authorities have accepted any period in which the claimant is present for the
purpose of company and supervision, as well as actual assistance, as qualifying.

Two unreported Commissioners' decisions throw some light on the meaning
of caring. In the first, a starred decision, *CG/012/91*, the claimant received ICA
in respect of her brother who was tetraplegic. Notwithstanding his condition he
went abroad on holiday with friends for four months. The claimant remained in
the UK and continued to draw ICA. When the absence became known to the DSS
they sought to recover the ICA paid beyond the usual four-week period of absence
(see ICA regulations). The claimant resisted recovery using two arguments: first,
that in respect of the whole period she continued to care for her brother because
she had to be ready on "stand-by" to fly immediately to his aid. His condition was
such that he could very quickly suffer major problems in the hands of inexperienced
nurses or assistants. Secondly, that in respect of at least the final month of absence
she was engaged for long hours each week (in excess of 35) in trying to arrange
sufficient nursing care for her brother upon his return. The Commissioner rejected
both arguments. He points to the connection between ICA of the claimant and AA
(or DLA) of the patient. This connection, he says, supports the view that caring
presupposes the more or less continuous presence of the person cared for. Some
degree of absence might be acceptable, for example shopping for the patient, or the
patient's absence for treatment, and dealing with the affairs of the patient might be
seen as caring. But the claimant could not be caring, he said, when the patient was
not "from day to day available to be cared for". Even the month spent in making
arrangements therefore, did not count as caring.

This contrasts, though is not necessarily inconsistent with the other decision,
CG/006/1990. This case arose through the question of whether the claimant could
satisfy the 35 hours per week which is defined by regulation as "regularly and substantially caring". The claimant's son was normally resident in a special school for
severely disabled patients. He returned to the claimant's home every other weekend,
Friday evening to Monday morning—approximately 60 hours. The claimant said
she spent at least five hours of the Friday preparing for his visit in shopping, cooking
and other matters that related solely to his visit. She also spent at least another five
hours cleaning up and washing on the Monday after his visit. When aggregated this

gave at least 35 hours of caring in each week. The Commissioner accepted that all of this time qualifies as time spent in caring.

The difference between the cases is one of degree. A month spent in preparation and making arrangements cannot be seen as caring "on a day to day basis" as required in the starred decision, while preparation (and cleaning up) on the day of presence can.

The meaning of "regularly and substantially engaged" in caring is provided for in reg.4 of the ICA Regulations.

Subs. (1) (b)

1.208   What amounts to gainful employment is defined in reg.8, ICA Regs. This fixes a limit on earnings, but higher sums may be earned in weeks while the claimant is on holiday.

Several unreported Commissioners' decisions have highlighted the problem of claimants who have been paid a "salary" usually from a firm owned by their husband or in which they are partners, with little or nothing having been required from them by way of work. In such circumstances they have claimed ICA not realising that the sum received may disqualify them on the grounds that they are "gainfully employed" and claims to recover substantial overpayments have resulted.

In such a case it is important to ascertain that the claimant is in fact employed by that employer, or working as a self-employed person. As decision *CG/068/1993* makes clear it is not enough that the claimant's name appears on the company's books as receiving a salary, if, as was claimed in this case, she does not realise that she is being paid as an employee. The claimant, whose husband was a solicitor, was, at first, paid a personal cheque each month for housekeeping. Later, when he became a partner in the firm, she was paid by a cheque drawn on the firm's account and appeared in the books as an employee, but she claimed to know nothing of her new status. The Commissioner held that she could not become an employee without her knowledge and consent, and directed that the appeal be re-heard to make further findings of fact. Earlier cases such as *R(P) 4/67* have referred to the undesirability of allowing claimants to "blow hot and cold" in their dealings with different departments of state (namely the HM Revenue and Customs). But that does not answer the question as to which of the inconsistent statements is inaccurate. In any case, the claimant here could not be treated as adopting the role of employee unless she herself had assented to it in a tax return, rather than a return made by her husband or his firm.

The difficulties presented by the definition of "gainful employment" (reg.8) are highlighted by a further unreported Commissioner's decision. In *CG/058/92*, the claimant who looked after her disabled daughter had, with her husband, purchased a seaside hotel. Annual accounts submitted to the Inland Revenue disclosed the business to be run as a partnership and in four out of the five relevant years, the claimant's share of profits had clearly exceeded the limit prescribed by reg.8. The tribunal which had heard her appeal accepted that the claimant did not work to any appreciable extent in the business and that she did not draw any share of the profits at all. Nevertheless because of the width of the definition in reg.8 the claimant was disqualified from receiving ICA and an overpayment was recoverable from her.

Regulation 8 refers to "earnings" which in turn is defined in s.3. The essence of earnings is that it is reward from employment or self-employment but not income from investment (see General Note to s.3). In this case, the Commissioner holds that the tribunal was correct to find that the claimant was a partner in the hotel business, that she was entitled to a half share of the profits, and that she was, therefore, not entitled to ICA. But what of the true "sleeping partner". Someone whose only interest is to put capital into a business and to draw on income in the form of a share of profit, if there is any, should be regarded as receiving an investment income. It would be unfortunate if entitlement to ICA, (and liability to repay an overpayment) were to turn upon the precise legal forms used by an investor as to whether he is partner or a creditor or a shareholder.

It should also be noted that Statutory Sick Pay or Statutory Maternity Pay qualify as "earnings" (see Contributions and Benefits Act, s.4) and therefore, under reg. 8 of ICA Regs, mean that a person is in gainful employment for the purposes of the section.

Subs. (1) (c)

This creates no limit on the persons who may claim because reg.6 of the ICA Regulations prescribes for this purpose, all persons who are in fact caring for a severely disabled person.　　**1.209**

Subs. (2)

The person cared for must be in receipt of attendance allowance, or of disabil- **1.210** ity living allowance care component, at the highest or the middle rate. The DLA entitlement did formerly create a trap for a claimant receiving ICA and whose patient had their DLA reduced to the lowest rate. This was because the two benefits were administered separately by the Benefits Agency and originally there was no mechanism for information to be passed between the departments. The system relied upon a disclosure by the claimant and overpayments were not uncommon. However, from December 1996 a change in DLA, or loss of AA, is notified auto matically to the ICA department. In *CG/5631/99(T)* a Tribunal of Commissioners accepted a concession made on behalf of the Secretary of State that recovery for overpayments would not be sought for payments made after that date. The Commissioners reaffirm the rule that there can be no failure to disclose that which is already known. For overpayments before that date, *CG/160/1999* on similar facts confirms that an appeal tribunal must find that the claimant for ICA either knew, or could reasonably be expected to know, of the change in the patient's benefits. For overpayments generally, see Vol.III of this work.

Subs. (3)

A claimant must be at least 16 years of age and not in full-time education. For **1.211** the meaning of full-time education in this context, see reg.5 of the Invalid Care Allowance Regulations and the notes to that regulation. The former restriction on married women, and women cohabiting with a man as his wife, no longer applies (following the decision on the European Court of Justice in Case 150/85 *Drake v Chief Adjudication Officer* [1987] Q.B. 166).

Subs. (4)

Benefit is payable only if the claimant is present and ordinarily resident in Great **1.212** Britain but regulations provide for some absences (reg.9 of the ICA Regulations).

It is no longer possible for a claimant to retain entitlement whilst abroad in a Member State of the EC. ICA is one of those benefits which the UK has chosen (from July 1992) to confine to this country. Though note, the question of whether this benefit is exportable is the subject of proceedings issued against the UK by the European Commissioners in Case C-299/05.

Subss. (5) and (6)

These subsections were repealed with effect from October 28, 2002 so that a **1.213** claim may now be made by a person over the age of 65. Previously a person over that age was not entitled to benefit unless they were already claiming at the time they reached that age. But once such a claimant reached the age of 65 they remained entitled even though they ceased to care for the invalid. This will no longer be so. A claimant over 65 whose patient dies will lose benefit after 8 weeks in the same way as any other claimant. There is however a saving for existing claimants who were over 65 on October 28, 2002 under art.4 of the Regulatory Reform (Carer's Allowance) Order 2002 (SI 2000/1457).

Prior to October 1994, ICA was not payable to a claimant over pensionable age. This meant a cut-off age for women of 60 years and for men of 65 years. That discrimination was held to be unlawful under the Equal Treatment Directive (79/7) in *Secretary of State v Thomas* [1993] Q.B. 747 and *R(G) 2/94*. The UK law should have been amended to provide equality from 1984, when the Equal Treatment Directive should have been implemented. The United Kingdom law was so amended, but not until October 1994. In the meantime many women had been refused benefit, or discouraged from making a claim for benefit, because of the continued insistence on differential ages. Art.4(1) of Directive 79/7 (which imposes the requirement of equal treatment) has been held to be sufficiently clear and precise for those rights to be directly enforceable within the Member States by those persons entitled to rely upon them. A Commissioner's decision, *CG/5425/95*, has helped to clarify a number of points that may arise in such claims.

The claimant had cared for her invalid mother for a number of years but attendance allowance and hence entitlement to ICA became payable in respect of her mother only from a time about six months after the claimant's 60th birthday. She became aware that she may have had a valid claim under European law only in 1989 (when she did make a claim), by which time she was already over 65 years. At about that time, too, her mother died, but under subs.(6) the claimant would have remained entitled to ICA for the rest of her life.

Clearly, under UK law the claimant became entitled by virtue of reg.10A of the ICA Regulations, but only from October 1994. Could she use her rights under European law to claim from some other earlier point in time?

In the case of this particular claimant, the Commissioner decided that she could not. But that was because she did not form a part of the "working population" to whom the rights under Art.4 are confined. The claimant had last worked in 1949 when she left work to commence a family. She had never re-entered the workforce or sought paid employment and she could not therefore claim under European law. However, the Commissioner did go on to consider what the position would have been had she been so qualified. The Department argued that because she did not claim until after she was 65, she could not now be entitled (as neither would a man) even under European law. The Commissioner held that her failure to claim before reaching 65 years of age was because the legislation, the department's publications and its officers all then said that she could not do so. To accept its argument would be to perpetuate their own failure to implement the Directive. In his view the claimant would have been entitled to benefit from when it was claimed (1989) and back-dated for 12 months from that date (*i.e.* 1988). Further back-dating would be prevented by the SS(A) Act, s.1. Such limitation is not a breach of Directive 79/7: *Johnson v CAO (No. 2) (R(S) 1/95)*. Before leaving the case the Commissioner made one further observation. Since the claimant had plainly been deprived of benefit since at least 1988 by the United Kingdom Government's failure to implement equal treatment, he suggested that the minister might consider an *ex gratia* payment of an equivalent amount rather than put the claimant and her legal advisers to the trouble and expense of pursuing a claim under the principle of *Francovich v Republic of Italy* [1991] E.C.R. 5357—though whether the *Francovich* claim should start at 1988 rather than 1984 is another matter.

A different approach on the question of late claims made by women past retirement age has been taken in decision *CSG/6/95*. The Commissioner there rejects the robust approach adopted, *obiter*, in *CG/5425/95*, but reaches a similar conclusion, at least on the facts of the new case, by another route. The claimant had given up work in 1979 in order to care for her husband. She reached the retirement age for women (60) in December 1982, but under Directive 79/7 (which came into force in December 1984) would have remained entitled to claim until December 1987. In the meantime (September 1985) the UK law had been changed to require a claim to be made for entitlement to benefit to begin. The claimant eventually made her claim in November 1993 well past her 65th birthday. The Commissioner rejected the argument that had found favour in *CG/5425/95*, namely that the requirement to claim before that age could be ignored because of the continued non-compliance of UK domestic law. Instead, he held that the claimant had, in 1984, become "entitled" to benefit in accordance with *I.O. v McCaffrey* [1985] 1 All E.R. 5 and that entitlement had not been removed by the introduction of the need for a claim to be made in 1985. It followed that the claimant could satisfy the conditions for entitlement in accordance with reg.10 of the ICA Regulation prior to her 65th birthday and was accordingly entitled to payment of that benefit from the time that she did claim (1993) though back-dating was limited to one year.

Subs. (7)

This makes it clear that a claimant can receive only one payment of ICA no matter how many patients he may be caring for, and that each patient can provide the basis for payment to only one carer at a time. Furthermore, reg.4 of the ICA Regulations has been amended to ensure that a claimant must qualify for the benefit by looking after a single patient for the requisite number of hours each week and cannot aggregate the hours spent looking after two or more patients. It should be noted as well that Invalid Care Allowance overlaps with several other benefits. (See reg.4 of the Overlapping Benefits Regulations.)

1.214

In *R(S)2/89* a widow who gave up work to care for her invalid daughter was refused Invalid Care Allowance because she was already in receipt of a widow's pension. She argued that this was discriminatory, contrary to Art. 4 of European Community Directive 79/7, in that a man would not be refused Invalid Care Allowance. The Commissioner rejected that argument on the ground that the difference in treatment did not arise from discrimination in relation to that benefit, but because a man could not qualify for widow's pension at all; the regulations were therefore not discriminatory in terms of the European Community Directive.

Disability living allowance

Disability living allowance

71.—(1) Disability living allowance shall consist of a care component and a mobility component.

1.215

(2) A person's entitlement to a disability living allowance may be an entitlement to either component or to both of them.

(3) A person may be awarded either component for a fixed period or [[1] for an indefinite period], but if his award of a disability living allowance consists of both components, he may not be awarded the components for different fixed periods.

(4) The weekly rate of a person's disability living allowance for a week for which he has only been awarded one component is the appropriate weekly rate for that component as determined in accordance with this Act or regulations under it.

(5) The weekly rate of a person's disability living allowance for a week for which he has been awarded both components is the aggregate of the appropriate weekly rates for the two components as so determined.

(6) A person shall not be entitled to a disability living allowance unless he satisfies prescribed conditions as to residence and presence in Great Britain.

AMENDMENT

1. Welfare Reform and Pensions Act 1999, s.67(1) (January 12, 2000).

1.216   SSA 1975, s.37ZA.

GENERAL NOTE

1.217   In general terms Disability Living Allowance (DLA) is a non-contributory benefit paid to those people who are so disabled as to need assistance in leading a normal life, or so disabled as to be unable to walk properly. It was introduced in 1992 and replaced two separate benefits—attendance allowance, and mobility allowance. Attendance Allowance remains for those first claiming for their disability when they are over the age of 65 (see ss.64–67).

DLA consists of two components. The care component (s.72) is similar to attendance allowance but includes a third lower rate of payment for those requiring a lesser degree of care. The mobility component (s.73) is paid at two rates. For both components there is a qualifying period of three months, rather than the six months for attendance allowance, and the disability must be one which is likely to continue for at least six months.

Subss. (2)–(5)

1.218   Although a person may be awarded either just one component or both, the components are not entirely separate benefits. In *R(DLA) 2/97*, it was held:

"Where a claim under appeal relates only to one component and there is no award of the other component and no evidence of substance relating to that other component, a tribunal may safely accept, record and proceed upon a restriction of the appeal to the component claimed."

Although DLA consists of two components it is paid as only a single allowance. It is not uncommon, however, for decisions on the two components to be taken separately. It should be noted that where the separate components are each awarded for a fixed period, that must be for the same period. In other words, the issue of "limping" awards can arise only where one component has been awarded for an indefinite period and the other for a fixed period.

There is now (under the Social Security Act 1998) no special protection for awards for life. (For discussion of the problems that did arise under the older system of review & revision of awards in the SSAA 1992, see earlier editions of this work.) In *CDLA/1000/2001*, the Commissioner held that an appeal under s.12 of the SSA 1998 raised anything that was covered by the substance of the information provided by the appellant and was not confined to the specific point against which he had appealed. This means that where the claimant appeals against an award of benefit at, say, the lower or middle rate on the ground that it is too low, it is open to a tribunal to find, on the contrary, that it is too high, and reduce the award accordingly. But where a tribunal is minded to do this it may do so only deliberately and consciously and, furthermore, it can do so only after giving a clear warning to the claimant that such may be the outcome of the appeal so that the claimant has a chance then to abandon the appeal. See *CDLA/2084/2007*.

If a person is awarded both components, there is one award of DLA at a rate calculated by aggregating the appropriate rates of the components and the award, if for a fixed period, must be for one common period and not different periods for the different components. It follows that, if one component has been awarded and the claimant appeals against refusal of the other, the tribunal must be informed of the period of the award (*CDLA/52/94*).

In determining whether a claimant qualifies for these benefits, a tribunal, must reach its conclusion in accordance with the restrictions imposed upon it by s.20(3) of the SSA 1998. This section prevents the tribunal from making a physical examination of the claimant and it precludes a physical test for the purposes of the mobility component of DLA. It does not, however, prevent the tribunal from reaching a conclusion based upon their observation of the claimant's physical abilities, or based upon his response to questions that test what he is capable of doing and, except in relation to mobility, it does not prevent the tribunal asking the claimant to carry out a simple physical task e.g. to pick an object up from the floor. The claimant may refuse, but in that case the tribunal may draw an inference from his refusal provided that in doing so they make due allowance for any reason he may give for that refusal. (*See R(DLA)5/03* and commentary to section 20 in *Vol.III: Administration, Adjudication and the European Dimension.*

In case *CDLA/433/99* the Commissioner holds that a tribunal which has, contrary to s.55(2)(a) of AA 1992, conducted an examination of the claimant does not make an error of law that requires the decision to be set aside unless the evidence obtained by that examination has influenced the tribunal's decision. In this case he held that it did not. The claimant had appealed against the disallowance of DLA care component in respect of eczma on her hands. The note of evidence recorded that the medical member had "examined" her hands, but the decisions, and the reasons for decision, made clear that the tribunal had not regarded the condition as viewed on the day, as being indicative of her condition generally, which was said to vary from time to time. The Commissioner also suggested that a distinction could be drawn between an "examination" and a general observation as, for example, when the claimant might show her hands to the tribunal.

Subs.(6)

See reg.2 of the DLA Regulations.   **1.219**

The European Court of Justice has now held that this and other care benefits (Attendance Allowance and Carer's Allowance) are exportable within the European Community. (The mobility component was held not to be exportable for a temporary period.) See *Commission of the European Communities v European Parliament and the Council of the European Union* (C-299/05), October 18, 2007.

The care component

72.—(1) Subject to the provisions of this Act, a person shall be entitled to   **1.220**
the care component of a disability living allowance for any period throughout which—

(a) he is so severely disabled physically or mentally that—
   (i) he requires in connection with his bodily functions attention from another person for a significant portion of the day (whether during a single period or a number of periods); or
   (ii) he cannot prepare a cooked main meal for himself if he has the ingredients; or
(b) he is so severely disabled physically or mentally that, by day, he requires from another person—
   (i) frequent attention throughout the day in connection with his bodily functions; or
   (ii) continual supervision throughout the day in order to avoid substantial danger to himself or others; or
(c) he is so severely disabled physically or mentally that, at night,—
   (i) he requires from another person prolonged or repeated attention in connection with his bodily functions; or
   (ii) in order to avoid substantial danger to himself or others he requires another person to be awake for a prolonged period or at frequent intervals for the purpose of watching over him.

[⁴ (1A) In its application to a person in relation to so much of a period as falls before the day on which he reaches the age of 16, subsection (1) has effect subject to the following modifications—

(a) the condition mentioned in subsection (1)(a)(ii) shall not apply, and
(b) none of the other conditions mentioned in subsection (1) shall be taken to be satisfied unless—
    (i) he has requirements of a description mentioned in the condition substantially in excess of the normal requirements of persons of his age, or
    (ii) he has substantial requirements of such a description which younger persons in normal physical and mental health may also have but which persons of his age and in normal physical and mental health would not have.]

(2) Subject to the following provisions of this section, a person shall not be entitled to the care component of a disability living allowance unless—
(a) throughout—
    (i) the period of three months immediately preceding the date on which the award of that component would begin; or
    (ii) such other period of three months as may be prescribed,
he has satisfied or is likely to satisfy one or other of the conditions mentioned in subsection (1)(a) to (c) above; and
(b) he is likely to continue to satisfy one or other of those conditions throughout—
    (i) the period of six months beginning with that date; or
    (ii) (if his death is expected within the period of six months beginning with that date) the period so beginning and ending with his death.

[⁴ (2A) The modifications mentioned in subsection (1A) shall have effect in relation to the application of subsection (1) for the purposes of subsection (2), but only—
(a) in the case of a person who is under the age of 16 on the date on which the award of the care component would begin, and
(b) in relation to so much of any period mentioned in subsection (2) as falls before the day on which he reaches the age of 16.]

(3) Three weekly rates of the care component shall be prescribed.
(4) The weekly rate of the care component payable to a person for each week in the period for which he is awarded that component shall be—
(a) the highest rate, if he falls within subsection (2) above by virtue of having satisfied or being likely to satisfy both the conditions mentioned in subsection (1)(b) and (c) above throughout both the period mentioned in paragraph (a) of subsection (2) above and that mentioned in paragraph (b) of that subsection;
(b) the middle rate, if he falls within that subsection by virtue of having satisfied or being likely to satisfy one or other of those conditions throughout both those periods; and
(c) the lowest rate in any other case.

(5) For the purposes of this section, a person who is terminally ill, as defined in section 66(2) above, and makes a claim expressly on the ground that he is such a person, shall [⁴ (notwithstanding subsection (1A)(b))] be taken—
(a) to have satisfied the conditions mentioned in subsection (1)(b) and (c) above for the period of three months immediately preceding the date of the claim, or, if later, the first date on which he is terminally

ill (so however that the care component shall not be payable by virtue of this paragraph for any period preceding that date); and

(b) to satisfy or to be likely to satisfy those conditions [¹ for so much of the period for which he is terminally ill as does not fall before the date of the claim.]

(6) [⁵ *repealed*]

(7) Subject to [⁴ subsection (5)] above, circumstances may be prescribed in which a person is to be taken to satisfy or not to satisfy such of the conditions mentioned in subsection (1)(a) to (c) above as may be prescribed.

[⁴ (7A) Subsection (1A) has effect subject to regulations made under subsection (7) (except as otherwise prescribed).]

[⁶ (8) Regulations may provide that no amount in respect of a disability living allowance which is attributable to entitlement to the care component shall be payable in respect of a person for a period when he is a resident of a care home in circumstances in which any of the costs of any qualifying services provided for him are borne out of public or local funds under a specified enactment.

(9) The reference in subsection (8) to a care home is to an establishment that provides accommodation together with nursing or personal care.

(10) The following are qualifying services for the purposes of subsection (8)—

(a) accommodation,

(b) board, and

(c) personal care.

(11) The reference in subsection (8) to a specified enactment is to an enactment which is, or is of a description, specified for the purposes of that subsection by regulations.

(12) The power to specify an enactment for the purposes of subsection (8) includes power to specify it only in relation to its application for a particular purpose.

(13) In this section, "enactment" includes an enactment comprised in, or in an instrument made under, an Act of the Scottish Parliament.]

AMENDMENTS

1. Welfare Reform and Pension Act 1999, s.67(2) (January 12, 2000).
2. Mental Health (Care and Treatment) (Scotland) Act 2003 (Consequential Provisions) Order 2005 (SI 2005/2078) Sch.1 para.4 (October 5, 2005).
3. National Health Service (Consequential Provisions) Act 2006, Sch.1, para.144 (March 1, 2007).
4. Welfare Reform Act 2007, s.52 (October 1, 2007).
5. Welfare Reform Act 2007, Sch.8 (October 1, 2007).
6. Welfare Reform Act 2007, s.60(2) (October 29, 2007).

DERIVATION

SSA 1975, s.37ZB.

1.221

GENERAL NOTE

This section defines the conditions for the care component of DLA. Subsection (1) provides for three levels of benefit according to different requirements for care. Para.(a) specifies two alternative conditions by which some form of attention is required; para.(b) specifies one condition of attention and one alternative condition for supervision, both during the day; and para.(c) has one condition for attention

1.222

and an alternative one for supervision, both by night. Benefit is paid at the lowest rate if the patient satisfies only para.(a); at the middle rate if they satisfy either paras (b) or (c); and at the highest rate if they satisfy both (b) and (c). There is no increase if the claimant satisfies (a) and another paragraph.

Note that reg.7 of the DLA Regulations deems certain people undergoing renal dialysis to satisfy either the day or the night attention condition and so qualify for the middle rate of the care component.

Note also that, under subs.(5), terminally ill claimants may be deemed to satisfy both the day and night conditions and so qualify for the highest rate of the care component for the rest of their lives.

Certain phrases in this section will apply to all claims:

1.223   *For any period throughout which:* These words require some consistency in the claimant's need for attendance over the whole period of an award but they do not require that the conditions should be satisfied on every day. The Attendance Allowance Board's *Handbook for Delegated Medical Practitioners* suggested that a man satisfies the night attention condition if he "invariably requires prolonged or repeated attention on more nights of the week than he does not". Although DLA is a weekly benefit, there does not seem to be any particular reason for requiring that it should *invariably* be the case that a person should satisfy the statutory criteria in the majority of the days of a week. In *R(A) 2/74*, the Commissioner said:

> "I think that the delegate should take a broad view of the matter, asking himself some such question as whether in the whole circumstances the words of the statute do or do not as a matter of the ordinary usage of the English language cover or apply to the facts. These are matters for the good sense and judgment of the delegate."

Thus, it may be appropriate in some cases to make an award covering a substantial period notwithstanding that there may be expected to be periods of remission in the claimant's condition lasting longer than a week. Both the length of the periods of remission and their frequency are likely to be relevant considerations as, perhaps, is the severity of the disablement during other periods. If the disability is one from which a substantial period of remission is quite likely, an award for a short period may be appropriate. If at the end of that period the claimant no longer satisfies the conditions for an award, or an award at the same rate, but the period of remission lasts less than two years, reg. 6 of the DLA Regulations enables the claimant to qualify again without having to wait the usual three months (or six months if the claimant is over 65).

A different problem in the application of this phrase has been considered in *CDLA/3737/2002*. The claimant was a child who was partially sighted. Her care needs at home were found by a tribunal to be insufficient to qualify for an award of the care component and they gave no account to her needs while at school. The Commissioner allowed an appeal and awarded the middle rate of care component. He accepted that she required extra attention in connection with her bodily function of seeing whilst learning at school and, applying the principles above, accepted that these needs could be said to apply "throughout the period", notwithstanding that the needs at school would not exist during vacation period. The Secretary of State appealed against this decision but the Court of Appeal *R(DLA) 1/04*, refused to consider the appeal because the way in which the appeal had been argued before the Commissioner meant that, effectively, there was now no point of law to be considered by the CA, or, at any rate, no point on which the considered views of the Commissioner had been expressed. The court stressed the importance of having such issues fully considered before they reach the court. It seems likely that this issue will be considered again. The claimant would probably do well to emphasise that the attention provided by a teacher in term time would be replaced by extra parental attention in keeping a child occupied and entertained in vacation.

So severely disabled mentally or physically: There has been a difference of opinion   1.224
between Commissioners on the significance of these words. On the one hand the
view has sometimes been taken that they act as a prerequisite by which a claimant
must show a disability in a medical sense that is recognised and labelled as such
by a doctor; on the other hand the words are regarded simply as a complement to
the need for care so that if it is shown that the claimant requires care and that it is
something to do with their mental or physical condition they succeed.

This issue has been resolved by a decision of a Tribunal of Commissioners in
R(DLA)3/06. They held that the words do not require the finding of a specific
disease or medical condition that is identifiable as the cause of the claimant's disability. All that is necessary is to identify some functional lack of ability that can
be traced to a physical or mental cause in the claimant. This means that a medical
condition will often be a relevant piece of evidence to support the claim (see e.g.
CDLA/4475/2004), but it is not an essential prerequisite. For example, where the
claimant is a child, as in the present case, behavioural difficulties may cause a need
for care, so as to satisfy the conditions necessary for the care component, and for the
mobility component too if the child may not be trusted to walk out alone. In that
case the child may need the care etc. to compensate for a functional inability, without
having to prescribe a medical condition. But this conclusion still requires two
matters to be satisfied: first, does the inability have some physical or mental cause?
This would be satisfied where the child suffers from arrested development or from a
very low I.Q., or where they do suffer from some diagnosable medical condition, but
not where their conduct is simply wilful or irresponsible misbehaviour, and cases,
like those in the past where that may have been the cause of the claimant's inability,
would still fail. (See, for example *R(A)2/92*, where the Commissioners suggest that
the correct approach would have been to ask whether the claimant could desist from
his aggressive and irresponsible behaviour.)

Apart from the element of volition, however, the Commissioners otherwise found
it difficult to envisage a situation in which a disability that expressed a need for care
etc. was not the result of some physical or mental cause. Those words, they thought,
were intended to be inclusive rather than exclusive so as to include any psychological as well as physical cause. But they do confirm the decision in *CA/137/1984*. That
was the case in which the claimant, a Muslim child who had a disabled right hand,
had claimed on the basis that he needed assistance in eating. In his religion all food
must be handled only with the right hand because the left is used for washing after
defecating. The claim failed because the Commissioner took the view that his need
arose from his culture rather than his disability. The Tribunal here confirm that
decision, though they do not explain how it is to be reconciled with the decision in
Fairey (see below) where the emphasis is on allowing the claimant to lead a normal
life which should presumably mean normal in his own culture.

The second requirement of this phrase is that the disability must be "severe".
Here the tribunal of Commissioners confirms that the test of severity does not
condition the degree of disability other than by reference to the scale of requirements that the section provides for. The words of the section, they point out, are
"so severely disabled . . . that." In other words the test of severity is satisfied by
the claimant proving the requisite level of need according to the particular claim
he has made, (adopting the approach used in *R(DLA) 10/02*). The commissioners
therefore conclude:

> "in our view, section 72 raises two issues. (i) Does the claimant have a disability,
> i.e. does he have a functional deficiency, physical or mental? (ii) If so, do the care
> needs to which the functional deficiency give rise satisfy any of paragraphs (i)
> or (ii) of section 72 (1)(a) to (c),and if so which? Section 73 (1)(d) gives rise to
> similar questions in relation to mobility".

The decision in *R(DLA)3/06* will affect the approach to be adopted in a number of
other analogous situations. In relation to alcoholism there has already been a
decision by another Tribunal of Commissioners in R(*DLA*) 6/06. There the

Tribunal apply the decision above so that the question becomes one essentially of the claimant's need for assistance etc., rather than of its cause. However, its cause is not irrelevant because the tribunal accept that voluntary intoxication cannot be said, of itself, to produce a state of disablement in the sense required for the legislation, any more than a claimant who had requested that his legs be bound would be said to be disabled so as to require care and attention. So the question of whether the claimant can be said to be disabled as a result of alcoholism will involve, at least to some extent, his ability to choose to remain (or become) sober. The test, according to the Tribunal, should be whether the claimant can be expected realistically to stop drinking. If he cannot, because of a medical condition (physical or mental), then any attention and supervision he might require should be taken into account to determine his entitlement to this benefit. (Though if the cause of his alcohol dependence is only mental, then in accordance with *R(DLA)4/06* any claim for higher rate mobility component would fail.) (See s.73 and reg.12 below.) The Tribunal suggests a number of other limiting devices that would affect a claim based upon the needs of someone suffering from alcoholism. As suggested by Commissioner Fellner in *CDLA/778/2000* the claimant should be encouraged to control his alcoholism either with or without professional assistance, and any award of benefit should be time limited to take account of such a possibility. Furthermore, the care needs of an alcoholic will vary through the day on the assumption that his day may commence with relative sobriety. This means that some levels of care component will not be appropriate, if, for example they require "continual" supervision, or attention "throughout" the day, or even for a "significant portion" of the day. Again the Tribunal confirms a point made in *CDLA/3542/2002* that assistance can only be said to be properly required if it could serve some useful purpose. Thus supervision designed to prevent the claimant drinking, or even to assist him when he has done so, would not be "required" if it were impossible or impractical to achieve that end.

In relation to the problem of bed wetting which has also caused a divergence of decisions among Commissioners it will no longer (in accordance with *R(DLA)3/06*) be necessary to find some medical reason for the incontinence. However, it will still remain necessary to establish that the claimant is suffering from a disability. This means that the incontinence must at least, be something that is not normal for a person of his age, and, in the case of a young child, that he has requirements that are substantially in excess of what is normal for a child of that age. (See subs.(6), and *R(DLA)1/05*.)

Similar reasoning will now apply to cases of chronic fatigue syndrome and psychosomatic pain. The only question should be whether the claimant suffers the fatigue or pain, genuinely and is thereby disabled so as to need the care, without any need to provide a medical diagnosis.

In many cases the claimant's disablement will be defined by the extent to which they can do things without experiencing pain or discomfort to an unacceptable extent. Detailed advice for tribunals on the matter of pain is given by Commissioner Jacobs in *CDLA/0902/2004*.

Tribunals sometimes have a difficult task in determining whether a claim of disablement involving pain or discomfort is genuine. Medical examiners sometimes remark upon inappropriate responses made by patients during examination that might tend to suggest that they are exaggerating their condition—the so-called "Waddell signs" (named after Prof. Waddell). In *CDLA/2747/2006* the tribunal had dismissed an appeal on the grounds that the claimant had displayed those signs and his claim could then be taken, for that reason, to be unjustified. The Commissioner allowed an appeal. It was an error of law he said, to reach such a conclusion on the basis of Waddell signs alone. That evidence, he says, might be indicative of exaggeration, but could equally indicate that the claimant has both physical and mental components in his disablement. The correct approach, he says, is to look at that evidence within the context of the evidence as a whole that is before the tribunal, and reach a conclusion on the whole of the evidence.

Requires: This means reasonably requires not medically requires (see *Mallinson*).   **1.225**
In *CA/96/84* it was suggested that an eight-year-old girl who suffered from enuresis would suffer no harm if left in her wet bedding for the rest of the night. The
Commissioner held that attention was reasonably required simply to make her
comfortable again and added that otherwise a person unable to dress themselves
could be said to have no need for attention because they could stay in a dressing
gown all day.

The section provides that care must be required; it does not have to be
shown that care is in fact provided. But if care, whether by attention or supervision,
is in fact provided, that may be strong evidence that the care is required. As one
Commissioner put it "mothers would be unlikely to exhaust themselves by providing
it for years" *(R(A) 1/73)*. On the other hand if the claimant chooses to do without
care, that may be a clear indication that care is not required *(CDLA/899/1994)*.
Tribunals should consider why the claimant does not use the care and whether
their life can be considered normal without it (see below). In *CA/3943/2006*, the
Deputy Commissioner held that it would be difficult ever to conclude that the
use of a bucket in the kitchen, as a substitute for a lavatory, could be regarded as
acceptable so as to render assistance that was needed to climb the stairs, no longer
"reasonably required". The question of whether the use of a commode downstairs,
if that were available, would be acceptable she decided should be left to a subsequent tribunal.

Though in *CDLA/2495/2004* the Commissioner held that the claimant, who had
mental health problems and required prompting by his mother before he would do
anything more than get out of bed, did not qualify for benefit at the middle rate—
frequent attention—because some of the tasks for which he needed to be prompted,
such as shaving, were performed only every four days, and the Commissioner
suggested that as the claimant rarely went out, even help with dressing did not
necessarily require her attention every day.

It is sometimes suggested, particularly in relation to supervision, that the claimant
could avoid the need for care by adapting their lifestyle to avoid that risk. The scope
for this suggestion now seems strictly limited.

In *R(A) 3/89* the Commissioner ridiculed the suggestion by asking whether the
claimant was expected to remain chairbound to avoid the risk of falling and in *R(A)
5/90* a Tribunal of Commissioners said that any tribunal adopting the argument that
the claimant could avoid a danger should identify the precautions to be taken and
explain how they were compatible with normal domestic arrangements. The leading
case on this point must now be *Secretary of State v Fairey* [1997] 1 W.L.R. 799
(reported as *R(A) 2/98*) in which the House of Lords held that the claimant who
was profoundly deaf was entitled to care on the basis that she needed the assistance
of an interpreter by way of sign language to assist her in travelling and carrying out
other social activities. Lord Slynn of Hadley said at 815:

"In my opinion the yardstick of a 'normal life' is important; it is a better approach
than adopting the test as to whether something is 'essential' or 'desirable.' Social
life in the sense of mixing with others, taking part in activities with others, undertaking recreation and cultural activities can be part of normal life. It is not in any
way unreasonable that the severely disabled person should wish to be involved
in them despite his disability. What is reasonable will depend on the age, sex,
interests of the applicant and other circumstances. To take part in such activities
sight and hearing are normally necessary and if they are impaired attention is
required in connection with the bodily functions of seeing and hearing to enable
the person to overcome his disability. As Swinton Thomas L.J. in the Court of
Appeal said: 'Attention given to a profoundly deaf person to enable that person
to carry on, so far as possible in the circumstances, an ordinary life is capable of
being attention that is reasonably required.'

How much attention is reasonably required and how frequently it is required
are questions of fact for the adjudication officer."

But it may not yet be possible to say that the claimant should be put in exactly the same position as if they had no disability. In *CDLA/267/94* it was suggested that a claimant who was blind and needed assistance to find anything he had lost, might reasonably be expected to wait for periods of attention by finding. This would affect the issue of whether his need was "frequent" (see below).

In *Miller v Chief Adjudication Officer* (reported as *R(A) 4/94*), the claimant and her husband were both disabled and in receipt of attendance allowance. The Court of Appeal held that the claimant's requirements arising out of her attending to the needs of her husband had been rightly ignored because otherwise there would be "double recovery" for the needs of the husband or an aggregation of his needs with those of the claimant. The court expressly reserved the question whether there might be taken into account requirements arising from a claimant attending to an infant daughter not in receipt of attendance allowance. That question has not received a uniform answer from Commissioners. In *CDLA/16996/96*, the Commissioner dismissed an appeal against a tribunal who had said:

> "The majority of the tribunal decided that there was no more fundamental a social activity than that of a mother bringing up young children. It was essential to her well-being that she did, as far as possible, as much as any other mother would do for a young family. Playing with children, supervising their behaviour, washing and dressing them, taking them out to play, reading their school work and generally performing all the functions which a sighted mother would perform for herself were all activities which required a third party's assistance, either to carry them out in safety or at all. [The claimant] needed help, not for someone to do these things for her, but with the function of seeing to do these things herself: she needed someone to act as her eyes."

But in *CSDLA/314/97*, another case of a blind mother, the Commissioner expressly disagreed with the earlier decision. He questioned whether the attention required was sufficiently closely related to the claimant's bodily function of sight. (But as to this, see below.) He also found that the evidence was not clear on whether the attention was provided as assistance for the mother to care for the children herself, or whether it was provided as a substitute for the mother's caring. This point was regarded as crucial in *CDLA/16996/96* and was adopted in the third case of a blind mother (*CDLA/16129/96*) in which the Commissioner preferred to follow the first case. It has also been found to be critical in *CDLA/5216/1998*. In this case the claimant suffered from arthritis and hearing loss in one ear. She was caring for her twin babies, themselves also disabled. The Commissioner allowed the claimant's appeal against refusal of benefit and sent the case back to be determined by a fresh tribunal but with extensive directions as to how they should proceed. The Commissioner considers all three of the previous decisions on this point. Although he accepts the conclusion reached on the facts in *CSDLA/314/97* he finds some of the statements there to be too broad. In principle he agrees with the reasoning of the other cases. First, that it is possible for a claimant to require supervision to ensure the safety of others, i.e. her children. In this case it seems unlikely that the claimant would succeed on the basis of supervision, because, by day, it was unlikely that the requirement would be "continual", and by night, she did not need "watching over", but only that someone could wake her when she could not hear the babies' crying. Secondly, that attention given to the claimant to enable her to care for her children could qualify so long as the attention was given to *her* to enable her to do the activity rather than the assitance being a substitute for the claimant's own caring. Furthermore the assistance has to be personal and intimate to the bodily functions of the claimant. Thus the Commissioner envisaged that a mother who was deaf and needs to be told always when the baby cried, or a mother whose arms were impaired and needed help to hold the baby might qualify, but a mother whose hands were arthritic and could not manage the fastenings on the babies' clothes, so that someone else had to dress the baby for her, would not. By the same reasoning taking the children to the park for their mother would not be attention to her bodily functions, but taking the mother in a wheelchair to the park to be with her children would be. Finally, the Commissioner noted that by the time the case had reached him an award of DLA had been made to each of the children for their own care needs. He directed the fresh tribunal that from the date of that award they could not include any help that the claimant needed to look after her children as being assistance required in her claim. To do so would be to allow double recovery for the children's needs (see *Miller v CAO*, reported as *R(A) 4/94*).

Attention and Supervision: The difference between these terms has been explored in   1.226
CA/6/72 (approved in R(A) 3/74). Attention was taken to involve personal service of an active nature, such as bathing or feeding, while supervision was more passive, such as being present to warn or give guidance and to intervene when necessary. This distinction was accepted by the Court of Appeal in *Moran v Secretary of State for Social Services* (reported as appendix *R(A) 1/88*) and approved in *Mallinson v Secretary of State for Social Security* [1994] 1 W.L.R. 630, also reported as appendix to *R(A) 3/94* where the point was made that the concepts were not necessarily mutually exclusive—a person might be supervising a blind person while at the same time providing attention by way of guidance.

Attention in connection with bodily functions: From the start it has been recognised   1.227
that these words hold the key to qualification for most claimants. In *R. v National Insurance Commissioner Ex. p. the Secretary of State for Social Services (Packer's case)* [1981] 1 W.L.R. 1017 Lord Denning M.R. said bodily functions:

> "include breathing, hearing, seeing, eating, drinking, walking, sitting, sleeping, getting out of bed, dressing, undressing, eliminating waste products—and the like—all of which an ordinary person—who is not suffering from any disability—does for himself. But they do not include cooking, shopping or other things which a wife or daughter does as part of her domestic duties: or generally which one member of the household normally does for the rest of the family".

Although he accepted that cooking could be said to be "connected with" the function of eating, it was, he thought, too remote. In subsequent cases (*R . v Woodling* 1984 1 W.L.R. 348; *Cockburn* (reported as *R(A) 2/98*): and *Fairey*) this distinction between activities that are close and intimate to the claimant and those which are not has been sustained. It has, however, created a complex and often conflicting path between Commissioners' decisions.

The concept of "bodily functions" has been examined by a tribunal of Commissioners in *R(DLA) 1/07*. The case concerned a child claimant whose mother described her as having behavioural problems, memory loss, difficulty concentrating and other problems, as well as being hyperactive. It was clear that at school she required special attention to motivate her and to aid in integrating with her peers, while at home her mother said she had to be with her all the time to control her behaviour and to ensure her safety. While there was no medical diagnosis of the condition a report by a paediatric neuropsychologist described her as "having significant learning difficulties with prominent language processing disorder and associated behavioural problems". The claimant's need for attention could probably be summed up as requiring help with motivation, communication and social integration. Her claim for the mobility component of DLA at the lower rate, and for care component at the middle rate, was refused and her appeal to a tribunal dismissed on the ground that the assistance she needed was not help in relation to her bodily functions.

The Tribunal of Commissioners allowed an appeal. They begin their reasons by facing the issue squarely and deciding: "Firstly, the functions of the brain are included within the term 'bodily functions'. They found authority for that proposition in a series of cases including *Packer's Case, Mallinson, Cockburn*, and *Fairey*.

In accepting that cognitive functioning (thinking) can be a bodily function they expressly overrule a line of cases (*CSDLA/867/1997, CSDLA/832/1999* and *CSDLA/860/2000)* asserting that it was not. The Commissioners also refer to *R(DLA) 3/03*, which had been relied on by the appeal tribunal, but they distinguished it as deciding only that the claimant there did not need the assistance for which he was claiming — the evidence suggested that he was able to communicate adequately without assistance — and did not decide that communication could never be a bodily function.

The Commissioners in the present case made no reference to *CDLA/2974/2004*, a decision of Mr Commissioner Rowland, in which he accepted that the defective cognitive processes of a 16-year-old autistic boy could amount to a defective bodily function.

The problem that the Commissioners then faced in their decision was to make any distinction between what has been known as activities and bodily functions. Here they break new ground by suggesting that what may be regarded as activities should be broken down into the parts that are contributed by individual organs of the body. If such organs are defective so as to need assistance then that may be help in connection with a bodily function for the purposes of a claim to DLA. The Tribunal express their reasons for this as follows:

"33. As identified by Dunn LJ in *Packer's Case*, a 'bodily function' primarily refers to the normal action of any organ of the body. For example, the function or a function of the lower jaw is to move up and down, i.e. its normal action. By way of extension, we consider it quite appropriate to extend this reference to the organ's immediate purpose: in our example, the purpose of the lower jaw moving up and down is to masticate food, and we do not consider it would be incorrect to refer to such mastication as a 'bodily function', i.e. a function of the lower jaw. It appears to us that the term is sufficiently wide to cover this extension.

34. Such functions might be voluntarily controlled (e.g. the lower jaw, as in our example), or involuntary (e.g. it is the function of the kidneys to filter waste products from the blood, which it does without any voluntary instigating action).

35. Furthermore, as Dunn LJ indicated in *Packer's Case* (see paragraph 30 above), 'bodily functions' includes not only the action of one organ of the body, but also those of any set of such organs in concert. Therefore, when the lower jaw is looked at with the mouth and various internal organs including the stomach and alimentary tract, it can properly be said of that set of organs of which the jaw is a part that the bodily function (in the sense of purpose as described above) is eating. We see no inconsistency between the proposition that it is a function of the lower jaw to move up and down and masticate food, and, as part of a set of organs, its function is also eating. Indeed, far from there being a strict dichotomy between 'microfunctions' and 'macrofunctions' — and to be fair to Mr Collins he did not submit that there was such a clear and absolute dichotomy — in terms of the organs of the body, there is complex web of functionality that requires acknowledgment.

36. However, of course, there are limits. Not every activity performed by the body is a 'bodily function', because it cannot properly be said that that activity is either a normal action or purpose of that organ or set of organs. Shopping is one example which falls clearly on the wrong side of the line: whilst no doubt involving various functions of the body, shopping could not properly be said itself to be a function (in terms of either simple actions or purpose) of any organ or set of organs of the body. Similarly, it was not suggested by any of the judges in *Packer's Case* that cooking could itself be a 'bodily function'. There may be difficult, borderline cases; but, like Lord Slynn (and with respect to Lord Denning's obiter dicta in *Packer's Case* and those of subsequent judges, to which we have referred: see paragraph 31 above), we do not consider that getting in and out of bed, or dressing and undressing, are 'bodily functions', because (in our respectful view) it cannot properly be said that it is the normal action or purpose of any organ or sets of organs to perform these exercises. These are not functions of organs of the

body, but merely things which a body can do if the relevant bodily functions (e.g. movement of the limbs) are working normally.

37. However, given that activities such as shopping, dressing and undressing, getting in and out of bed necessarily involve bodily functions of one sort or another (which can be specifically identified, if necessary), why does the relevant 'bodily function' matter in any specific case? The answer to this lies in looking at the wording of the statutory provisions as a whole, as has been urged by the House of Lords (see paragraph 16 above) and in the approach to those provisions of Lord Woolf in *Mallinson* and the tribunal of Commissioners in *R(DLA) 3/06*. As already indicated (paragraphs 8–11), the focus of these provisions is on the disablement (i.e. functional deficiency) of the claimant. Even where such a disablement is shown, the relevant attention is that *reasonably required* by virtue of that functional deficiency. On the issue of relevant attention, it may therefore be necessary to focus upon the functional deficiency with some particularity. It may not be crucial whether the bodily function impaired in someone who cannot move his legs and consequently walk is looked at as (i) movement of the legs, or (ii) walking. We consider both have equal validity for the reasons we give above. However the function is viewed, the necessary attention to address the claimant's reasonable care requirements will be the same. But in other cases it may be of importance, because it will be necessary to identify the bodily function that is impaired with some precision so that the attention reasonably required to address the impairment can be properly identified and assessed.

38. For example, Mr Mallinson was blind, and was consequently unable to walk in unfamiliar surroundings because (as Lord Woolf put it, at page 639H) he did not know where to walk or (e.g. when crossing the road) when to walk. As Lord Woolf pointed out (at page 639G), to say whether the attention he received in the form of being guided was 'in connection with his bodily functions' (i.e. reasonably necessary as the result of an impairment to those functions), it was necessary to identify the bodily function or functions to which the attention relates. We consider that in substance this is no more than ensuring that the relevant attention is reasonably necessary — because, as indicated above (paragraphs 8–9), the severity of the functional disablement is in fact defined by that attention. Therefore, although in one sense it could be said that Mr Mallinson's ability to walk was impaired (in the ways identified by Lord Woolf), in considering this question, as Mr Mallinson's legs were working normally — but his eyesight was not — of the interwoven bodily functions involved, 'it is preferable to focus on that function [i.e. his deficient ability to see]' (per Lord Woolf at page 641A). The relevant 'bodily function' that is impaired (i.e. the disablement) must therefore be identified with sufficient particularity so that the assistance reasonably required can be identified and assessed; and this is why 'bodily function' cannot be given a definition so wide as to include all human activity or indeed any particularly complex activity. This is therefore another reflection of the close relationship between functional disablement and the assistance reasonably required to cope with that disablement referred to in paragraph 9 above of identifying the relevant bodily functions given above.

39. However, even where an activity is such that it cannot itself properly be described as a bodily function, that will not be the end of the matter — because recourse will then have to be had to the discrete bodily functions which are involved in the activity and the extent to which they are impaired, and particularly as to whether the functions or any of them are so impaired that assistance to the level of any of the provisions of section 72 is required in respect of the disablement. In these circumstances, the relevant discrete bodily functions will have to be identified and 'unbundled', considered and assessed. Indeed, given the purpose 36–37), in functionally complex activities which may be borderline, we regard this 'unbundling' exercise as the correct approach in any event, and warn against the temptation of considering in very fine detail whether the complex activity can truly be described as a single bodily function or not. We consider the

potential dangers of such an arid exercise are well illustrated in this very case. As the various House of Lords opinions referred to above (but notably that of Lord Slynn in *Cockburn*) make clear, in borderline cases it cannot be incorrect to unbundle functions in this way, and it is likely to be helpful in approaching the issue of assistance reasonably required."

The Commissioners then go on to point out that just identifying a bodily function that is deficient so as to need assistance, is not a sufficient condition to qualify for DLA. It will remain necessary, as well, to show that the assistance has the requisite degree of intimacy, and also that it satisfies one of the tests as to frequency, constancy, etc.

Applying all this to the facts of the present case the Commissioners found it to be an error of law to say that communication was not a bodily function. It was necessary, they say, to "unbundle" that word and examine what the claimant's difficulty in communicating was caused by. Clearly elements such as hearing, seeing and speaking can qualify for assistance and now we can say also, in the light of their decision above, comprehending, thinking and concentrating. Cases that have held to the contrary were disapproved. Similarly, social integration needed to be unbundled so as to analyse the parts with which the claimant required assistance. Where these could be identified as requiring assistance in the form of close personal care and attention to particular mental processes the claimant may be regarded as requiring assistance with bodily functions. The case was referred to a fresh tribunal for further consideration of the evidence.

But this is unlikely to be the last word on these matters. Dyslexia has also produced a crop of disputed cases in recent years. In *CDLA/395/2005* Commissioner Williams refers to *CDLA/1420/2004* and *CDLA/2680/2001*, in both of which it was held that assistance to cope with dyslexia could qualify for DLA.

In the case of *CDLA/395/2005* itself, the Commissioner dismissed the claimant's appeal because the tribunal had found as a fact that the claimant did not need such assistance. However, as both parties had submitted arguments on whether assistance to deal with dyslexia could qualify, he went on to hold that it could, though subject to the warning that dyslexia is a label that covers a variety of conditions affecting the ability to communicate. In the language of the decision above it will be necessary to unbundle the deficiency and see what particular brain function is affected.

A contrary conclusion has, however, been reached by Commissioner May in *CSDLA/427/2006*. There, a claim was made on behalf of an eight-year-old boy on the basis of the extra attention he required when learning at school and for help at home with his homework. The claim was refused and an appeal failed. The further appeal to the Commissioner was also dismissed. The Commissioner found that the help required by the claimant was assistance with his education and, as such, could not be attention in connection with a bodily function. In particular, the Commissioner compares the claimant's inability to read, to his own inability to read Japanese. He can, he says, see the script but he cannot understand it because he has not learned that language. This is right. But the Commissioner's inability derives from a lack of knowledge, whereas the claimant's inability to read (or at least difficulty in acquiring the skill to do so), derives from a brain malfunction in being unable to remember the shapes or arrangements of letters. In other words the activity of learning needs to be unbundled to examine whether any organ of the body is dysfunctional. The decision makes no reference to *R(DLA)1/07T*, because that case was decided only a few days earlier, and so this part of the decision may require reconsideration in the light of that decision, and already it has been rejected in two decisions by other Commissioners. In *CDLA/3204/2006*, the Commissioner followed earlier cases in treating help for a dyslexic claimant as being help with the bodily function of "seeing". Seeing, in this sense, he explains, is a four stage process involving transmission of light through the eye to the brain, and its interpretation by the brain to convey a meaningful message. In his view a malfunction at the latter stage which called for assistance, was just as much help with a bodily function as if the defect occurred at the previous stage. In *CDLA/1983/2006*, on the other hand, the Commissioner adopts the reasoning suggested above, and applies *R(DLA) 1/07T* so that dyslexia is treated as displaying a malfunction of the brain which is itself the defective bodily function.

But another argument, from CSDLA/427/2006, is more problematic. It appears that the initial refusal may have included in the reason given, the argument that DLA could not be available for assistance with "educational activities" and that reason was part of the appeal tribunal's conclusion. The Commissioner agreed. As he rightly points out, such assistance, at least in a state school, would be provided from public funding and to say that it qualified, as well, for entitlement to DLA would mean that the public purse was paying for the same service twice over. That can hardly, he suggests, have been the intention of Parliament in creating this benefit. Yet the section makes no reference to the source of funding for any assistance and it must be common place for some of the assistance received by DLA claimants to come from care workers who are publicly funded. The source of funding for the provision of care is accounted for in one sense in the DLA Regulations (reg.8), but that is only where the claimant is provided for in certain defined accommodation. This issue has been raised before (in *R(DLA) 1/04*) but, as Commissioner May correctly observed, that point was not dealt with at all by the Court of Appeal in that case.

The activity of the brain as a bodily function was considered by Commissioner Mesher in *CA/2574/2007*. The claimant was an elderly widow who suffered from agoraphobia, anorexia and depression and had lived as a recluse since the death of her husband three years earlier. She was visited daily by her daughter who, in addition to taking care of all her mother's physical needs by way of shopping, housekeeping etc., also spent several hours each day providing stimulation and encouragement to her mother. The Commissioner allowed an appeal against the decision of a tribunal, who had failed to consider the latter involvement as attention in connection with the bodily function of brain activity, though he then went on to reject the claim in entering his own decision on the ground that she could not satisfy the more restricted requirements for AA. A claim for DLA at lowest rate (had she been younger) might have been successful.

After *Mallinson* and *Fairey* it is clear that a sense of physical intimacy will suffice and that physical contact is not necessary. Thus in the case of a blind man, guidance by words is sufficient and interpreting by sign language is sufficient for the deaf. In the case of *Cockburn* (reported as *R(A) 2/98*) it was accepted that some attention might even be given without the claimant being present so long as it was a continuance of attention that began in person (though this will now be limited by reg.10c of the DLA Regulations). In that case the claimant was both incontinent and arthritic. Help that was given in changing her bedclothes and wringing out wet sheets was all a part of the attention to her bodily functions, though this did not extend to doing her laundry for her the next day. Many services such as shopping, cooking and cleaning done for another would not count as attention, being too remote, but if these same activities are attempted by the claimant in person, with the carer providing assistance to them, for example reading labels to a blind claimant, or reaching items on the shelf for a physically disabled one, then they should qualify as attention in connecting with seeing and lifting respectively (*CDLA/3711/95* and *CDLA/12381/96* though there are conflicting Commissioners' decisions in *CSDLA/281/1996* and *CSDLA/314/1997*).

It needs to be borne in mind that there is still a distinction between attention in the sense of any assistance that is given to a disabled person to enable them to lead a normal life and "attention in connection with a bodily function". It is only that help which has the sufficient degree of closeness and intimacy with the claimant's person that will qualify. A useful examination of the criteria was made in *CDLA/8167/95*. There the claimant was a blind woman who was in receipt of the care component at the lowest rate. She applied for a review of her entitlement claiming the middle rate. In order to demonstrate the frequency with which she needed help from others she listed at least 17 occasions daily when she needed such assistance. These included checking that the food in her kitchen was fit to eat, that her appearance was acceptable and that her clothing was appropriate, as well as help with public transport, shopping, dealing with correspondence, domestic chores, gardening and, finally, cleaning up after her guide dog. The commissioner, allowing an appeal, rejected her claim on the basis that many of these actions were not sufficiently closely related to her bodily function of seeing. As he put it;

"If you have to tell another person they have gravy on their chin this is not an act of close personal contact or intimacy, whether they are sighted and have forgotten to look in the mirror or are blind and unable to do so. The required closeness of contact or intimacy only comes if the degree and nature of the disability means that you also have to do something like guiding their arm or standing over them to help with the applying of a wet cloth to their face, without which they could not reasonably cope with such a personal thing for themselves. Steering a blind person across the road or on to a bus or helping them to read their own correspondence all count, as these actions have been accepted by the House of Lords to involve the required degree of contact or intimacy beyond what is ordinary between adult human beings apart from the disability. So has enabling a deaf person to conduct a conversation with someone else by taking part in it for them as an interpreter. Again the help involves what would ordinarily be an intrusion into the personal space and privacy of the individual. On the other hand merely telling a blind person about their appearance, helping them choose matching clothes to put on, helping them locate things they have put down somewhere, telling them whether the carpet is hovered properly, a picture hung straight or the windows smeary, all things readily acceptable as reasonably required to help deal with their disability in the course of leading a normal life, are not things that appear to me self-evidently to have the special character of personal contact or intimacy which the House of Lords has expressly confirmed is essential for 'attention'."

The distinction is not, he says, between household duties and other tasks—even help with domestic duties may qualify—but what is important, in his words, is that the attention should be given to the blind person so as to enable them to do the housework, rather than that housework is done for them. But the importance of a close enough connection between the claimant's disability and the assistance needed has been reasserted by the Court of Appeal in Secretary of State for Work and Pensions v Batty (2005) EWCA Civ 1746 R(A) 1/06. The claimant, who was severely restricted by arthritis, could not carry a drink of any kind from a place where it was prepared to a place where it might conveniently be consumed. She therefore needed someone's assistance every time she wished to have a drink both at home and at work, where she was able to work at her desk. The Commissioner who had found in her favour did so on the basis that, short of standing at the sink every time she needed a drink, she could not live a reasonably normal life without such assistance. The Court of Appeal, however, returned to the basics of earlier decisions such as Packer and decided that while helping a claimant to drink was clearly attention in connection with a bodily function, bringing a drink to them was not. And see too *CSA/694/2007* where it was held that assistance given to a blind claimant with her correspondence could qualify whereas assistance in driving her to social and other events would not.

A more recent attempt to extend the scope of assistance to include any support that might enable the claimant to lead a normal life was rejected in *CDLA/3376/2005*, but the decision still demonstrates the breadth of activities for which assistance may be required and can qualify the claimant for the care component. It also demonstrates the correct approach to be adopted to the question by tribunals. The claimant, who was blind from birth, had been allowed mobility component at the lower rate and care component at the lowest rate. She appealed against a refusal to grant the care component at a higher rate. The appeal tribunal, who rejected that appeal, did so by approaching the list of activities for which she claimed she needed assistance as falling into a category of domestic activities for which no assistance could qualify. The decision of Commissioner Jacobs demonstrates the error in this approach. The decisions of the House of Lords in *Cockburn* (reported as *R(A) 2/98*) and the Court of Appeal in *Ramsden (R(DLA) 2/03)* make clear that the only limiting device on the range of activities to be considered is whether it is reasonable for the claimant to experience that as part of a normal family and community life. (Together with the fact that the assistance given must be sufficiently intimate and personal to qualify.) In this case the Commissioner accepted that help given to the claimant to assist her in doing her own shopping, laundry and housework could all qualify for the benefit. This decision was made before the decision in *R(DLA)1/07T*, and it may be useful to counter the impression that could be given by that decision that shopping, dressing etc could not be considered as the subject of assistance (see paras36 and 37 above). What is said there is that shopping, for example, should not itself be regarded as a bodily function for which assistance is given. Quite so, but the bodily function, in this case, would be seeing, for which assistance is given in connection with the reasonable activity of shopping.

In the case of the claimants who are mentally disabled the appropriate "bodily function" is of course, thinking; this is confirmed in *CDLA/2974/2004*.

The Court of Appeal gave further consideration to this phrase in *Ramsden v Secretary of State for Work and Pensions* [2003] EWCA Civ 32, R(DLA) 2/03. The claimant, aged twelve, was faecally incontinent as a result of spina bifida, but for psychological reasons did not wear incontinence pads. He soiled himself once or twice a day and required attention from his mother in cleaning him up in a bath and shower, and also cleaning up the clothes, towels, bedding, carpets, furniture and other surfaces that had been fouled. On a renewal claim the AO refused to renew and that decision was upheld by a tribunal. The tribunal took into account the washing of the claimant, and the rinsing of his soiled clothing, bedding, etc, but specifically excluded any time spent in laundering the clothing etc as required, in their view, by the decision in *Cockburn*. The tribunal made no overt reference to the time spent cleaning carpets, furniture, and other surfaces, though, in the proceedings that followed, it was assumed that that time, too, was excluded on the basis that it was not sufficiently closely connected with the child's bodily function. A Commissioner upheld the tribunal decision.

The Court of Appeal, in allowing the appeal, reviewed thoroughly the speeches in *Cockburn*. That case, they concluded, recognised that certain acts of attendance performed by way of cleaning-up after an incident of incontinence could qualify as acts of attendance for the purpose of this benefit. Potter L.J., giving the first judgment continued:

"Within the constraints of the requirement that such cleaning-up should take place in the presence or the vicinity of the applicant, I consider that steps taken for the **immediate** removal of soiling from clothes, towels or bed linen or adjacent surfaces are apt to qualify under this head. In a case of faecal incontinence which results in the soiling of clothes, towels or bed linen, or the dropping or smearing of faeces on carpets or furniture, it is at the very least in the interests of hygiene that such occurrences be rectified immediately as a part and parcel of the cleaning-up operation necessary following the incident of incontinence giving rise to such soiling. If that is done, then, even if the operation concerned is one of thorough washing rather than merely 'rinsing', the criteria of immediacy and intimacy are sufficiently satisfied and the time spent in cleaning-up should be taken into account when assessing whether or not the attention given amounts to a significant portion of the day".

The court returned the case to a fresh tribunal to consider whether the attention amounted to "a significant portion of the day". On that point, too, they take a flexible view of what is meant by "significant". (See below.)

1.228

Giving support and encouragement to someone who is severely disabled by phobias, depression and paranoid illnesses has now been held to be attention in connection with bodily functions. With that support the claimant was able to get up from bed, to cook, to eat properly, and generally to take care of herself so as to create a reasonable quality of life (*CDLA/1148/97*). This was a re-hearing of the case after an appeal to the Court of Appeal. The other point held by the Commissioner in this case, that such care could be provided over the telephone, has been short lived. Its effect was reversed by reg.10c of DLA regulations (and reg.8BA of the AA regulations). But see *CDLA/4333/2004* noted after that regulation. Support and encouragement has also been held to qualify as attention when it is given to a person suffering from obsessive compulsive disorder (OCD), to encourage him to desist from his behaviour. In *CDLA/618/2006* the claimant had been awarded the lowest rate of care component because his obsessive need to wash and clean himself, or his equipment, effectively prevented him from accomplishing the task of cooking a meal. But the Commissioner considered that, as well, he might qualify for care component at the middle rate, if he could show that encouragement for the purpose of dissuading him from his compulsive behaviour was necessary. On the facts of this case, however, he held that there was no evidence that such encouragement would have assisted him. Attention in soothing a person to sleep (at least in the case of a child) has been held to be attention in connection with a bodily function so long as the difficulty in sleeping is connected with a physical or mental disability (*CSDLA/567/2005*).

The question of whether Asperger's Syndrome (a form of autism) should be regarded as requiring attention in connection with bodily functions has arisen in two cases. In the first (*R(DLA) 3/03*), Commissioner Howell considered the appeal of a 34-year-old man who had obtained a degree, a diploma in court procedure and had worked in a magistrates court (though not still at the time of the claim) for a period of five years. Despite the fact that the claimant was able in many ways to function effectively in society the further evidence suggested that he had difficulty in communicating effectively, in forming normal social relationships including those in a work place and that any unusual or unexpected incidents would cause him to panic and require guidance and reassurance from someone else. The tribunal had rejected his claim and the Commissioner upheld that decision. In his view the areas in which the claimant expressed a need for attention were not in connection with any bodily function — communicating is, in his view, at best, an activity and not a bodily function.

The other case is *CSDLA/860/00* in which Commissioner May gives some guidance to the tribunal to whom the case was returned. In this case, the claimant, a 14-year-old boy, was said to suffer from dyspraxia and Asperger's Syndrome. As to the dyspraxia no difficulty arose. It was a disablement both mental and physical arising from defective communication between the brain and the claimant's hands — the tribunal had only to find the amount and frequency of attention this required. But the Asperger's Syndrome was said to cause only a lack of ability to communicate effectively with other people, difficulty in understanding emotion and in empathising. His lack of social skills had led to bullying at school and a consequent reluctance to attend. The Commissioner warned the new tribunal that they would have to make clear findings as to what bodily functions were affected by this condition. In particular he warns that "communicating" is not a bodily function (see his own decision in *CSDLA/867/97*—a deaf claimant) but only an activity, and he decides that the supervision required of the claimant, by teachers, to protect him from bullying, would not satisfy the statutory formula because that is protection of the claimant from others, whereas the section envisages protection of the claimant (and others) from himself.

There are conflicting decisions on whether the preparation of meals that involve a special diet with careful control of the ingredients for illnesses such as pheylketonuria, or even diabetes, could qualify as attention in connection with a bodily function. In *R(A) 1/87* the Commissioner held that the extra care and attention required over and above that of normal cooking made a difference, but in *CSDLA/160/95* that decision was disapproved of on the ground that it had not referred to the concept of intimacy as required in *Woodling*.

With regard to the attention that is given to a deaf person by someone using sign language when the *Fairey* case was before Commissioner Sanders (*CA/780/91*) he drew a distinction between someone communicating with a claimant who is deaf by the use of sign language when they are acting as an interpreter to a third party, and when they are not. In the former, the interpreter is clearly providing attention to the claimant in connection with the bodily function of hearing and speaking; in the latter he may be merely holding a conversation with the claimant in the language in which they are both comfortable. The Commissioner seems to have been saying that merely because the signing might be slower or involve more effort than oral communication for both of them, it could not, for that reason alone, be regarded as "attention". Thus a conversation between the claimant and his wife using sign language about ordinary domestic matters would not be "attention" but his wife communicating those matters to a visitor would be. What subsequently emerged in the Court of Appeal, and was not criticised in the House of Lords, was that this did not preclude the possibility that an attendant who had to use physical contact to make the claimant aware, or "if the person giving the attention . . . has to do extra work, or take extra time, away from the attendant's ordinary duties to help the disabled person that may, as a question of fact, qualify as attention". This much seems clear from two decision of Commissioner Sanders, himself (*CDLA/17189/96* and *CDLA/15884/96*), where he draws these conclusions from what was said in the Court of Appeal. The same formulation has been approved by another Commissioner in *CDLA/16668/96* and again, after a very full consideration, in *R(DLA) 1/02*. In a similar case (*R(DLA) 2/02*) Commissioner Levenson, after careful consideration of all the authorities, has suggested the following propositions as representing the current law:

- the operation of the senses is a bodily function and a defect in the senses leads to disability in connection with which attention might be required;

- the test is whether the attention is reasonably required to enable the severely disabled person as far as reasonably possible to live a normal life;

- the aggregate of attention that is reasonably required includes such attention as may enable the claimant to carry out a reasonable level of social activity;

- what is reasonable will depend on the age, sex, interests of the applicant and other circumstances;

- how much attention is reasonably required and how frequently it is required are questions of fact;

- attention in connection with bodily functions includes unusual efforts reasonably required to attract the attention of the deaf person in order to communicate with her. Unusual in this context means steps that are not or would not be required in respect of attracting the attention of a person in the same environment who is not deaf;

- a person is not providing attention when communicating with a deaf claimant by means of reasonably fluent signing unless communication is particularly slow and difficult;

- if communicating through an interpreter is significantly more efficient or effective than communicating through writing, or trying to converse with a person who has to shout loudly, then it might well be that the services of an interpreter are reasonably required even if initiating the communication or conducting a two-way conversation does not itself constitute attention;

- help required to undertake activities other than those "concerned with the relatively mundane everyday activities of functioning as a human being in ordinary life" does not count as attention for these purposes;

- although, in order to count as attention, any service provided must be of a close and intimate nature involving personal contact carried out in the presence of a disabled person, in the case of a deaf person this includes communication between that person and an interpreter;

- for these purposes there is no significant difference between the interpretation of the written word and the interpretation of speech.

1.229   With the possible proviso that a decision-maker must remember that "communicating with" is not the same thing as "interpreting for" (which will always be attention) these points seem unexceptionable.

Two Commissioners' decisions return to the question of the extra effort required to communicate with a deaf person, and the extra effort that may be required to initiate communication with them. In *R(DLA) 3/02*, Commissioner Fellner had to consider the case of a pre-lingually deaf person, now of middle age, who had completed City & Guilds qualifications, and worked as a foreman joiner on building sites and other places. She allowed an appeal against a decision awarding only lowest rate care component (on the grounds of inadequate facts and reasons) but substituted her own decision also at the lowest rate.

In doing so she accepted the law developed in the decisions cited above, including, generally, the points made by Commissioner Levenson, but with the *caveat* that the extra effort involved both in effecting two-person communication, and in attracting the attention of a person for that communication must be something more than *de minimis*. It must also be more than would be required to communicate with a hearing person in like circumstances. While she emphasises that these matters must always be ones for the decision-maker on the basis of the particular facts found by them, she suggests that tapping the shoulder, stamping a foot, flashing a light or throwing a paper ball, might all be regarded as so minimal as not to count on this basis. Similarly, though the claimant probably required people to go to him to communicate in the workplace, the same would be true of a hearing person doing that job because of the general level of noise on a building site. The Commissioner suggests the same may be true of many instances of initiating communication in the home — even hearing-able people may need to be contacted by going to them when they are cooking, watching television or doing DIY. The Commissioner suggested that the fact-finding stage of the decision process should begin with the claimant's need for attention in relation to his current level of activity, and then go on to explore further needs for attention based upon the "wish list" suggested by the claimant. But in doing so the decision-maker must approach the claimant's declared aspirations with a robust sense of what would be feasible, realistic and practicable as well as the established (but not very helpful) test of what is reasonable.

In this case, for example, she thought it would not be feasible for the claimant to have someone read the newspaper and magazines to him, given the time that it would take and the pattern of his existing daily life. Again, she thought it would be unrealistic to suggest that the claimant might accept the presence of an interpreter in the home, every evening, to help him watch television programmes without subtitles, and impractical to suggest that an interpreter could assist at the cinema (because of darkness) or on a building site (because of danger and unfamiliarity). She did not accept that an interpreter could attend work site meetings and that his services would be justified to replace the extra time and effort that was currently spent in communicating with the claimant. This is a useful case for decision-makers because it goes a long way to explore some of the practical application of the legal principles.

In the other case, *R(A) 1/03*, Commissioner Parker allowed an appeal against refusal of the lower rate of Attendance Allowance. (The claimant was over 65 at the date of his first claim although he was pre-lingually deaf, probably from birth.) The appeal was allowed for more than one reason, one of them being that the tribunal had discounted the assistance that the claimant already received from a centre for sensory impaired people. Commissioner Parker follows both the decision of Commissioner Levenson, *CDLA/3433/1999*, and that of Commissioner Fellner, *CDLA/1534/00*, above. In doing so she accepts the latter's constraint that the extra effort involved either in communication or attracting attention must be more than *de minimus*, but she reconciles this to some extent with Commissioner Levenson by drawing attention to his point that the extra effort in communicating, once it is significant, may justify a need for an interpreter which then will qualify as attention.

It is also clear from *Mallinson* that a claimant may receive attention in connection with a bodily function even though that bodily function is completely inoperative. A person who is totally blind, for example, receives attention in connection with the bodily function of sight when his guide provides a substitute method of seeing.

In *CDLA/2333/2005* Commissioner Mesher holds that care in the form of supervision for the purpose of walking outside (mobility component) counts also for the purpose of attention or supervision of the bodily function of walking in the care components. This is not surprising because it is simply the converse of *R(DLA) 4/01*, but is a point that deserves to be noted.

The lowest rate conditions: To qualify under para.(a)(i) the claimant must show that he requires attention in connection with his bodily functions for a *significant portion of the day*. In *CDLA/205/2005* it appeared to the Commissioner that the tribunal had before it evidence of how long it took the claimant to do things for himself, but not how long it might have taken, were assistance to be given. The Commissioner points out that it is the latter which is relevant to the question of whether attention is for a significant portion of the day. How long things took for the claimant to do for himself might, however, be relevant to the question of whether he required assistance in the first place. This phrase has now been considered by the Court of Appeal in *Ramsden v Secretary of State for Work and Pensions* [2003] EWCA Civ 32 reported as *R(DLA) 2/03*. This case determines that the meaning of the word "day" is to be consistent with the time remaining as a residue of 24 hours when the "night" has been accounted for as in *R. v National Insurance Commissioner Ex p. Secretary for Social Services* [1974] 1 W.L.R. 1290; in other words it is the period between the time when the household becomes active in the morning and when its members finally retire to bed at night. The earlier suggestion in *CDLA/1463/99* that "day" should mean the whole 24 hour period is thus overruled. While this undoubtedly is the better interpretation of the section it does seem to work unjustly in the case of a claimant who requires some, though not significant, attention, during the day and one, far more disruptive, event at night, because, unless the night time attention is prolonged or repeated, it appears that that attention cannot be accounted for at all. On the other hand, of course, by limiting the time period of day it does become easier for the claimant to show that his day time attention is significant as a proportion of that period.

The Court of Appeal also considers what should be regarded as a "significant portion" of a day and they endorse the view that the phrase should be interpreted so as to make a "broad determination" of the question. Lord Justice Potter, giving the leading judgment, accepts that the task for the tribunal is principally a mathematical exercise involving comparison of the aggregate of time spent in giving attention, with the day as a whole. But he continues,

> "However it is also likely to be affected by the total time available in the day, by the extent to which the relevant tasks become a matter of routine, and the concentration and intensity of the activity comprised in those tasks. Thus while in broad terms it seems to me that a period of one hour, made up of two half-hour periods [of] concentrated activity, would reasonably be regarded as a significant portion of a day, in different circumstances there may well be room for a different view".

This passage is followed by one in which Potter, L.J. expressly approves the reasoning in *CSDLA/29/94* in which Commissioner Walker puts forward the view that the

1.230

day, and the "significant portion" of it, must be assessed from the position of the attender. In that case the Commissioner had held that even a lesser period than an hour might be significant if it consisted of many short periods that so broke up the day of the attender that for *them* the total, represented a greater inconvenience that the arithmetic sum of time might suggest. He also suggested that the tribunal should take a broad determination to record the total portion or percentage of the normal day that was involved for this household. Combining this with the decision of the Court of Appeal it would seem now possible to argue that, for an attender with an especially long and busy day, the time spent attending does become significant when it might not be for someone who was otherwise largely idle. For the busy attender, the time spent attending is significant because without it their day might seem already full, or, again, if the tasks required are arduous and physically or mentally demanding the time spent becomes significant because the effect of those tasks may be to exhaust the attender. For him or her their "day" (in the sense of what is achievable) would be largely used up. On the other hand if the tasks become routine and can be fitted in to the attender's regular daily pattern of life they will offer less inconvenience and may become a less than significant part of their "day".

As to the "one-hour" rule of thumb used by many tribunals and referred to in the Parliamentary debates, this case makes clear that there is no such minimum period– *CDLA/58/93* must to that extent be overruled. While, no doubt, tribunals may still choose to centre their thinking around a total time period of an hour, it is now clear that they must reach their decision on the basis of their own common sense and judgment of what is significant and explain that in their reasoning.

The Cooking Test

1.231   To qualify under para.(a)(ii) the claimant has to show that he cannot prepare a cooked main meal for himself. This enables some claimants to qualify who are otherwise excluded from the care component because the provision of meals by another is not attention in connection with a bodily function (*Re Woodling*). Note that the claimant is assumed to have the ingredients to hand, which eliminates any need for help with planning and shopping. It is not sufficient for the claimant to say that he has never cooked and is unwilling to learn (see *R. v Secretary of State for Social Security Ex p. Armstrong*, (1996) 8 Admin. L.R. 626, CA) but a claimant cannot be expected to learn to cook if his mental condition is such that he is incapable of learning (*CDLA/2457/97*).

In *Moyna v Secretary of State for Work and Pensions* [2003] 4 All E.R. 162, *R(DLA) 7/03*, the House of Lords have confirmed that the cooking test is one of overall impression to be reached by tribunals by a general approach rather than by fixed rules. The case dealt with the vexed question of claimants whose ability to cook was sporadic. In that case the claimant was unable to prepare herself a main meal on at least one day every week, and in some weeks she was incapable on as many as three days. A tribunal had found that this did not mean that she was unable to cook for herself and the Commissioner, to whom she appealed, upheld that decision because he could find no error of law in it. The Court of Appeal disagreed. They thought that someone who could not prepare a meal on a regular and not infrequent basis could not be said to be capable of cooking, and to decide that they were, would be an error of law. The House of Lords restored the decision of the Commissioner; the test, they say, is a general one of overall impression and whilst others might disagree with the conclusion reached, that would not be an error of law.

But this does leave us in some difficulty, for if the tribunal had found initially that Mrs Moyna was not capable of cooking then, it would seem, that that too, would have been a decision that was properly made and could not be reviewed as an error of law. This does nothing to assist tribunals hearing appeals in the case of claimants whose abilities fluctuate within the nine month period for qualification. The House of Lords make clear that the test is not one of frequency (only the claim form for the benefit introduces the matter of the number of days on which the claimant is unable to cook a meal) and they make clear also that it never has been the case that a claimant's inability to cook must be total throughout the qualifying period, but beyond that their Lordships leave it to the good sense of tribunals to decide whether a claimant is capable of cooking, by "taking 'a broad view' of the matter and making a judgment". It is, they say "an exercise in judgment rather than in arithmetical calculation of frequency".

Past cases on the cooking test must all now be approached with some caution. The emphasis of the House of Lords reasoning makes these decisions essentially ones of fact for the tribunal. The approach to be adopted is demonstrated in *R(DLA) 2/05*. The Commissioner there upholds a decision by the tribunal in which they assessed her ability to cook, directly from what she told them of what she did do, and, indirectly from what they concluded she could not do on the basis of her evidence, and inferences drawn from her general condition. In that case the tribunal had decided that the claimant was capable of cooking a meal.

The "cooking test" was considered at length in *R(DLA) 2/95*, where the Commissioner said:

". . . In my view the 'cooking test' is a hypothetical test to be determined objectively. Factors such as the type of facilities or equipment available and a claimant's cooking skills are irrelevant.

8. The nature of the 'cooked main meal' which the claimant 'cannot prepare' is crucial. In my view it is a labour intensive reasonable main daily meal freshly cooked on a traditional cooker. What is reasonable is a question of fact to be determined by reference to what is reasonable for a member of the community to which the claimant belongs, e.g. a vegetarian meal as opposed to one which is not. The use of the phrase 'for himself' shows that the meal is intended to be just for one person, not for the whole family. The 'main meal' at issue is therefore a labour intensive, main reasonable daily meal for one person, not a celebration meal or a snack. The main meal must be cooked on a daily basis and it is irrelevant that a claimant may prepare, cook and freeze a number of main meals on the days that help is provided and then defrost and heat them in a microwave on subsequent days. The test depends on what a claimant cannot do without help on each day. Because the main meal has to be cooked, the test includes all activities auxiliary to the cooking such as reaching for a saucepan, putting water in it and lifting it on and off the cooker. All cooking utensils must of course be placed in a reasonable position.

9. The word 'prepare' emphasises a claimant's ability to make all the ingredients ready for cooking. This includes the peeling and chopping of fresh vegetable as opposed to frozen vegetables, which require no real preparation. However in my view a chop, a piece of fish or meat ready minced does not fall in the category of 'convenience foods' and are permissible as basic ingredients. I should add for completeness that because the test is objective it is irrelevant that a claimant may never wish to cook such a meal or that it is considered financially impossible."

In *CDLA/2267/95*, the same Commissioner said:

"It cannot be overstressed that the 'main meal' at issue is a main reasonable daily meal for *one* person. It follows that the use of heavy pans or dishes is not necessary for the preparation of such a meal. Nor is it necessary to use the oven. If the claimant is unable to stand for any length of time, such a meal can be prepared and cooked while sitting on a high stool or chair if necessary. It is all a question of what is reasonable in the circumstances of the case."

Two Commissioners' decisions give further consideration to the "cooking test". **1.232** The first (*CDLA/5686/1999*) is a decision of Mr Commissioner Rowland. In it he confirms that the test is abstract in the sense of being unrelated to the claimant's ability, inclination or even need to cook a meal, but that it may take account of devices and stratagems that the claimant might have available to him. This was a case where the claimant used sticks to get about the home, and was unable to bend. The Commissioner confirmed earlier decisions to the effect that it was unnecessary to be able to use the oven by bending. The adjudication officer had allowed the claim on the basis that the claimant could not manage safely in lifting pans of hot water, etc. The claimant appealed in an attempt to get the middle rate of benefit and the tribunal decided that he was not entitled to even the lowest rate because he could use a slotted spoon to remove food from a hot pan and empty the pan safely when it had cooled. The Commissioner's decision upholds this reasoning although he did allow the appeal on the facts of this case.

The other decision, *CDLA/770/2000*, is a decision of Commissioner Fellner, and makes a thorough investigation of the background and application, to date, of the cooking test. The claimant in this case was a middle-aged man who had been injured in a road accident and left with an unstable knee joint on which he had to wear a brace and walked with the support of a stick. Although he assisted his wife in the kitchen she would not leave him to prepare and cook a main meal because she thought there was a danger of him stumbling, dropping hot containers, and injuring himself.

The claimant had been refused benefit on a renewal decision and the tribunal that heard his appeal also concluded that he did not satisfy the cooking test. They said he could use the microwave and sit down while cooking. The Commissioner seems to have regarded these reasons as inadequate and the appeal was allowed and sent back for re-hearing by a fresh tribunal. The Commissioner's survey of the decisions on cooking begins by pointing to the divergence that has arisen between those Commissioners who have regarded the test as almost entirely objective (e.g. *R(DLA) 2/95* and *CDLA/2293/95* where a wheelchair user whose kitchen had been specially adapted so that she could cook her own meals, nevertheless qualified on the basis that she could not have cooked in an ordinary kitchen) and those Commissioners who have admitted subjective elements so that the use of special devices and adaptations, if available to the claimant, may deprive them of benefit by showing that the claimant is in fact able to cook a main meal.

The Commissioner accepted the invitation of the parties to look at parliamentary material in determining the "intention" of Parliament in inventing the cooking test. She accepted that this material showed that what was intended was a purely object-ive test akin to that adopted subsequently for Incapacity Benefit. Nevertheless, she rejected this interpretation because in her view the wording of s.72 was not ambigu-ous so as to require, or entitle, her to have regard to the parliamentary material.

Without it she was clear that the words of the statute, "cannot prepare a cooked main meal", meant a test that took account of what the claimant could in fact do for himself given the provision of reasonably available special devices and the adoption of special stratagems. The touchstone, she thought, was a reasonable compromise between what able cooks might do and what a disabled claimant might be expected to do. Thus, sitting to prepare food could be expected even though an able cook might prefer to stand; the use of food from tins and jars and the use of reasonable devices to open them was also acceptable (though the use of frozen vegetables and the reheating of meals previously prepared by, or with the help of, others had been rejected in earlier decisions and remains outside the range of acceptable stratagems). The disabled cook could be expected to avoid particularly dangerous procedures, such as deep fat frying; oven chips were a reasonable alternative. The kitchen should be organised so that items and utensils were readily to hand. Where the claimant suffered from achondroplasia, a condition that restricted his height and meant that he had especially short arms and legs, it was held (in *CDLA/4351/2006*) that the availability of a "Baby Belling" cooker and a microwave, on which he could cook a main meal, meant the claim should fail.

The time taken by the claimant over preparing a meal may also be relevant in deciding whether they are capable of cooking themselves a meal (*CDLA/4051/2007*). But this too must now be taken to be a matter of judgment for a tribunal to say whether a claimant can fairly be described as capable, and a strategy of resting between stages of meal preparation has been adopted as a sensible and acceptable mode of preparing a meal.

There remains some doubt about the use of special devices—the Commissioner accepted that devices designed specially for the disabled would be outside the spirit of the legislation. But at what point does an ergonomically designed tin opener become one that is intended only for those who suffer from arthritis? Only the common sense of tribunals can save us! And finally what about the microwave? Microwaves used to reheat food as described above do not count, but (assuming the claimant does in fact have one) they may be taken account of when used to cook fresh vegetables, and otherwise as an ordinary cooking appliance. The use of a microwave oven as an ordinary means of cooking food that has been prepared by the claimant, rather than as a means of reheating meals prepared by others, has been accepted in *CDLA/2367/2004*.

It is sufficient if the claimant can cook a sufficient number of dishes to provide a reasonable degree of variety to his diet (*CDLA/17329/96*). The test assumes the claimant will use the equipment available to him—devices and appliances that he does not have should be ignored (*R(DLA) 2/95*)—but where the claimant has such equipment there is no reason why the test should not assume that he will use them (*CDLA/17329/96*).

In *R(DLA) 1/97* it was held that the claimant was not entitled where he was capable of cooking a main meal (and did so) even though it involved risk to himself. The claimant could have succeeded only if that risk became unreasonable. The claimant was a haemophiliac for whom the process of preparing and cooking clearly presented extra risk. The Commissioner said:

"Clearly it takes the claimant rather longer to prepare a meal than it would for most people and clearly also he suffers some anxiety when he does so, but the fact remains that he can and does prepare traditional cooked main meals. To say that he acts unreasonably in doing so would be to imply that a person in his position acts reasonably only if he or she gives up traditional meals or cooking methods or has someone else cook such meals. It is not unreasonable for a person with a disability to try and pursue as normal a life as possible unless the risks involved in carrying out a particular task make it so. I do not think that the additional risk and associated anxiety involved in cooking, over and above the risk attending all the claimant's activities, justifies a finding that it is unreasonable to expect him to prepare a cooked main meal."

On the other hand where the claimant was prevented from cooking because heat from the cooker brought on an attack of asthma he was entitled to the benefit (*CDLA/20/94*). It was not suggested that his main meal might always be a cold meal of raw ingredients!

In *CDLA/1471/2004*, Commissioner Jacobs had to consider whether a risk of self-harming could cause the claimant to be unable to cook a main meal for himself, presumably because he could not be trusted to be in possession of sharp knives or, possibly, to have access to hot surfaces. An argument was put on behalf of the Secretary of State that, as the cooking test was of an hypothetical ability to cook, it was sufficient that the claimant could have been able to cook were he able to have the means to do so. The Commissioner rejects this argument. The test, he says, was hypothetical only in the sense that the claimant's need to cook, or his inclination to do so, were irrelevant in determining his ability to cook a main meal. In other words anything that derives from the claimant's mental or physical condition and prevents him from cooking can be a disability for this purpose and that includes the safety risk arising from a propensity for self-harm.

Where the claimant is unable to cook because of nausea brought on by the smell of cooking the claim should succeed so long as the nausea makes it unreasonable to expect the claimant to endure that experience. See *R(DLA) 1/08* in which the contrary view expressed in *CSDLA/854/2003* (discussed in earlier editions of this book) was rejected. A claimant who has lost their sense of smell, (and in this case their sense of taste also), is not for that reason to be regarded as unable to cook a main meal for themselves. In *CDLA 1984/2008* Judge Rowland thought that while such a person might have to adapt their behaviour by, for example, remaining in the kitchen to watch what was cooking rather than relying upon the smell of burning, and while they might also have to store food for less time to avoid the risk of using things that were unfit and could not be detected by their smell, he thought that such stratagems as these were a reasonable adaptation of a normal cook's behaviour so that a claimant would remain capable of cooking.

An inability to concentrate sufficiently to accomplish cooking tasks safely has been accepted, at least in principal, to be sufficient in *R(DLA) 6/05* and in *CSDLA/725/2004* Commissioner Parker has held that a lack of motivation to cook a main meal, if it derives from the claimant's physical or mental disability (and is not simply a manifestation of laziness), may be a basis upon which to award the benefit. In *CDLA/1572/2005* the claimant objected to the use, as evidence of his ability to cook, of the fact that he was capable of driving his motor car. While the Commissioner agreed that an ability to drive might not be much evidence of the claimant's grip and manual dexterity, he affirmed that it could be evidence of other relevant factors such as an ability to concentrate and to co-ordinate physical movements. Note that the cooking test route for qualification is not available to a person under 16 (subs.(6)(a)).

1.233   *The day conditions:* To satisfy the condition posed by para.(b)(i) the claimant must show that he requires *"frequent attention throughout the day"*. The meaning of "day" is resolved by the meaning of "night" for which see below, para.(c). Frequent attention has been said to be "several times—not once or twice" (*per* Lord Denning M.R., *R. v National Insurance Commissioner Ex. p. the Secretary of State for Social Services*) and in *CA/281/89* the Commissioner held that the need should be "at intervals spread over the day".

In *CA/147/84* a child who required attention on four occasions spread approximately equally across the day was held not to qualify, but in *CA/1140/85* the Chief Commissioner stressed that even a person whose main attention was required at the beginning and end of each day could qualify so long as there were other events that required some brief attention during the day. The claimant was blind, and help in making tea, eating meals, putting on his coat and outdoor shoes qualified him even though he was largely self reliant once he had been got up and dressed each morning.

Commissioner's decision *CSDLA/590/00* considers the relationship between frequency of attention and the duration of that attention. It holds (as had *CDLA/12150/1996*) that the proper approach to frequency takes no account of the duration of attention, either in aggregate, or separately—except to exclude the instance of attention that is *de minimis* in the latter respect.

In this case the claimant was a five-year-old child with talipes of one foot. This caused him to fall between 5 and 10 times each day. In addition his mother had to manipulate his foot "several times" each day. The tribunal had rejected the claim on the basis that the need for attention did not amount to frequent attention throughout the day because it would amount to only, approximately, one hour in total during the day. Both representatives and the Commissioner thought this wrong. But the representative of the Secretary of State drew on *CSDLA/24/98* to suggest that the aggregate of attention time could be considered a factor in determining frequency. This seems to be a misinterpretation of that case where it seems the Commissioner was willing to uphold the decision because the tribunal had given its attention specifically to frequency as a separate issue in holding that four or five attendances were not frequent (although other cases have held that they can be).

In the present case the Commissioner accepts that entitlement depends solely upon pattern and frequency and not the total duration. It may be that the thinking of the tribunal in this case, and in *CSDLA/24/1998*, was inspired by the thought that if attention amounting to no more than one hour per day could not qualify a claimant for the lowest rate of care component, it might seem odd that it should, nevertheless, qualify him for the middle rate if it were spread in small periods frequently throughout the day. This point is answered effectively in *CDLA/12150/1996* (and quoted again in this decision). In the first place it is the inevitable outcome of giving the different words their natural meaning and secondly it would be supported as a rational outcome if the cost of providing numerous instances of attention spread over the whole day were greater than fewer points at either end of it, as would seem likely to be the case.

But all this must now be considered in the light of *R(DLA) 5/05*. Judge G. R. Hickinbottom, the Chief Commissioner, has carried the approach to interpretation that was set by the House of Lords in *Moyna* across to the rest of the criteria for qualification for DLA care component in s.72(1). This means, he says, that decision makers and tribunals must take a broad view of the matter, reading the words of the section in their context so as to identify the correct legal test and then deciding each case as a question of fact according to whether it falls on one side of that line of the other. Thereafter, an appeal on points of law could only interfere with their decision if either they have identified the wrong legal line or if they have reached a conclusion which is "outside the bounds of reasonable judgment", *i.e.* irrational.

Judge Hickinbottom goes on to point out that the oft quoted guidance taken from the judgment of Lord Denning in *R. v National Insurance Commissioner, Ex p. Secretary of State for Social Services* [1981] 1 W.L.R. 1017, on the meaning of these phrases, was not only *obiter*, but was only a limited attempt to identify some fairly obvious characteristics of the words used, and must not be regarded as providing anything like definitions—as he suggests commentators appear to have done. He also takes to task certain Commissioners for attempting to paraphrase the sections in alternative words to explain their meaning.

The test of "frequently throughout the day", he suggests, is not to be approached in two stages—how often and over what period—but is to be treated as a single composite impression. Again, frequency is not just a question of number, but may be affected by the nature and duration of the occurrences, thus disagreeing with Commissioner Parker in *CSDLA/590/2000*. By way of example he contrasts the meaning of frequent when used in relation to an ice age with its use in relation to a train timetable; or again, a long distance train service every hour might be regarded as frequent when an hourly local service was not. As well, he points out that, although the scheme of s.72(1) is not necessarily one of gradation, in as much as the qualifying conditions in each of the three paragraphs are quite distinct and different, the context requires a recognition that Parliament can hardly have intended that a claimant should qualify for the middle-rate benefit on a lesser requirement for care than was necessary to gain the lowest rate of benefit.

All of this makes good sense. But it may make things difficult for tribunals for two reasons. First, tribunals must give reasons to support their decision. Often, an attempt to explain a decision will consist of rephrasing the statute to explain the line the tribunal is taking. If tribunals are not to rephrase the section to explain what they take to be its meaning, will it suffice for a tribunal to say, e.g. "we find this to be frequent attention because we think it is"? Secondly, decisions that are treated as findings of fact and appealable to a Commissioner only when they are grossly unreasonable may result in inequitable chaos. For example, in one of the cases that was considered in this appeal the Judge concluded, as had the tribunal, that an epileptic claimant who regularly required attention, at night, once or twice a week for up to 20 minutes on each occasion, did not satisfy the test of requiring "prolonged attention" throughout the period of his claim. Taking a broad view of the matter, and in particular the length of the fits and the pattern on an unpredictable but regular basis, he concluded that the claimant's need did not constitute prolonged attention throughout the relevant period. But what if a more generously inclined tribunal on a similar case were to conclude that it did? Would that be so unreasonable as to be appealable? (It could not be said to be out of line with the treatment of a lowest-rate claimant because the drafting of the section envisages that night-time care will be

1.234

treated differently.) But if it is not appealable, then will it not be inequitable for the first claimant?

To satisfy para.(b)(ii) the claimant must show that he requires *"continual supervision . . . in order to avoid danger to himself or others."*

Supervision may be of two kinds. It can be precautionary or anticipatory, as when a carer watches over his patient ready to intervene when necessary; or, it may be ancillary to a series of acts of attention, as when the carer accompanies a blind person on a walk and offers guidance both physical and verbal. (In either case where the intervention becomes frequent the claimant may qualify anyway under para.(b)(i).)

Supervision is more passive than attention, but even supervision of the precautionary kind must be something more than mere presence (*CDLA/42/94*). It requires a degree of monitoring by the carer so that they do more than merely respond to a call from the claimant. Even so, it has been held in *Moran v Secretary of State for Social Services* (*The Times*, March 14, 1987, CA) that a supervisor could be in another room and even may be asleep, if they are so attuned to the needs of their patient that they would respond immediately by sensing the onset of, in that case, a fit.

In order to be *substantial* the danger must be "considerable, solid or big" (*R(A) 1/73*) but it need not be life threatening. In *R(A) 11/83* a Tribunal of Commissioners felt that the risk of a claimant biting his tongue in an epileptic fit was a substantial danger to him and in *CSA/68/89* the risk of impulsive suicide was a substantial danger even though it was not determined and was unlikely to succeed.

The danger is also substantial if the risk of harm is high. Although the language used by Commissioners in a number of decisions is sometimes inconsistent it is clear that risk is a factor of both the degree of harm that is possible, and the likelihood of a harmful event occurring. Thus although the likelihood of a house catching fire might be low, the consequence to a tetraplegic who was caught within it, would be fatal and the danger to him would therefore be substantial (see *R(A) 2/89*). Likewise in *R(A) 1/81* and *R(A) 5/81* the point is made that it only takes a child to run out into traffic once to present a substantial danger to himself and others.

In *R(A) 1/73* the Commissioner said that the word "continual" was not synonymous with continuous. This means that supervision may be continual notwithstanding some short breaks. In order to "avoid" substantial danger it is not necessary to eliminate the risk altogether; it is enough to effect a real reduction in the risk. In *R(A) 3/92* the Commissioner accepted that no amount of supervision could prevent a determined suicide but it could substantially reduce the risk that it would succeed.

Many cases on supervision involve the risk of falling. In *R(A) 3/89* a Commissioner proposed that in such cases the following questions should be determined.

"(i) Are the situations in which the claimant may fall predictable or unpredictable? That is to say, does the claimant have a liability to fall anywhere at any time? Or does he fall only in certain circumstances or situations? This is, of course, a matter of medical opinion: but the opinion must be based on evidence.

(ii) If the falling is predictable, can the claimant reasonably be expected to avoid the risk of falling or to place himself at such risk only when adequately supervised? That again is a matter of medical opinion. If the claimant cannot reasonably be expected either to avoid the risk or to place himself at risk only when adequately supervised, the DMP should treat the case as one in which the falling was unpredictable.

(iii) If the falling is unpredictable, will the falling give rise to substantial danger to himself? This is again, of course, a matter of medical opinion. Nevertheless it must be borne in mind that a person, particularly a disabled person, may when falling hit his head on the corner of a cupboard or on a fire kerb or radiator; and whether or not he is injured in the course of falling, he may by reason of his disability be unable to rise or be unable to summon help. Or he may be of such an age that a fall will be likely to have serious consequences. Clearly such matters ought in an appropriate case to be taken into account.

(iv) Is the substantial danger too remote? In the present case, the DMP stated that in his medical opinion the risk of substantial danger arising from a fall 'is so remote a possibility that it ought to be reasonably disregarded.' But he has failed to give any indication why he reached that conclusion or to indicate on what evidence he relied to support that conclusion. Although, as I have said, those questions are matters of medical opinion, it is incumbent upon a DMP to consider all the evidence, including the evidence of the claimant, to make the relevant findings of fact and to give adequate reasons for the conclusions which he reaches upon those findings of fact so that the claimant 'looking at the decision should be able to discern on the face of it the reasons why' the evidence failed to satisfy the DMP: *R(A) 1/72* at paragraph 8. In my judgment the DMP has failed to do so in the present case."

In *R(A) 5/90* a Tribunal of Commissioners cautioned against treating these questions as a statutory requirement and said that it was not an error of law if the DMP failed to answer them. But they also said that his failure to do so might well reflect an insufficiency of reasons for his decision. A single instance of falling does not show a propensity to fall (*CA/233/95*) and even where there is a propensity to fall it does not follow that there is a need for continual supervision to avoid danger. In *CDLA/899/94* the Commissioner said:

"10. . . . This is not a case of a person who is so unsteady that he requires to be supported whenever he stands, which may have been the case in *R(A) 3/89*. It is always possible that a person who falls may suffer some injury. However, that is far more likely in the case of a person who falls due to a fit or loss of consciousness and therefore cannot take any steps to mitigate the effects of the fall. In the present case, the risk of falling at home is slight and the risk of serious injury when falling at home is even slighter. This is not the case of an elderly person who is particularly frail. It really cannot be said that the claimant reasonably requires someone to be so close to him the whole time as to be able to catch him should he fall.
11. It is of course theoretically possible that a person falls and the effects of the fall are made worse by the lack of immediate response. Supervision may be required in some case in order to avoid the risk of danger arising after a fall. However, one must have regard to the relative frequency of falls and the likelihood of serious injury, *of a type that might be avoided if there were supervision*, arising from them."

But it is not necessary that the supervision should be able to prevent the fall— it is enough that supervision will reduce the risk of serious harm as a consequence of falling (*R(A) 2/92*).

Where the need for supervision is based upon the claimant's mental disablement some medical evidence may be necessary (*CA/147/84*), though it is possible that a history of previous suicide attempts may suffice. In *R(A) 2/91* the Commissioner held that a view expressed by the consultant psychiatrist that "the claimant was at times significantly depressed and potentially at risk to herself" was sufficient to justify supervision.

The night conditions: In order to satisfy either part of para.(c) the claimant must show that they need care to be provided for them at *night*.   **1.235**

Night was defined in *R. v National Insurance Commissioner Ex p. Secretary of State for Social Services* [1974] 1 W.L.R. 1290, Appendix to *R(A) 4/74*, as being:

"that period of inactivity or that principal period of inactivity through which each household goes in the dark hours and to measure the beginning of the night from the time at which the household as it were, closed down for the night".

This case has probably been credited with deciding more than it did. The Court of Appeal were considering an appeal from a Commissioner who had himself allowed an appeal from an Attendance Allowance Board. Then, as now, the Commissioner was limited to allowing an appeal on a point of law. The decision of the Court was simply that in their view no error of law could be seen in the decision of the Board and that the Commissioner had therefore been wrong in allowing an appeal. Any definition that they gave was strictly speaking *obiter*, but in any case they expressly eschew any attempt to provide any general definition. Nevertheless they did adopt the formulae that had been agreed by counsel which formed the test above and which has since been adopted and applied elsewhere (see e.g. *Ramsden R(DLA) 2/03*). But that is not the end of the matter. The definition of night which the Court of Appeal commended was no different from that of the Commissioner in that case, nor so far as can be seen, from the Board. Where they differed was in the application of that test to the facts. The particular point of contention was whether assistance given to the claimant, (a paraplegic) in undressing and getting into bed, and in getting up and dressing the morning, should be regarded as assistance rendered by night. The Board had regarded both as being given by day. The Commissioner thought that at least the process of getting to bed should be part of his night attention-in his view, applying the words of the test, getting undressed and into bed is a part of the process of "closing down" for the night. All that the Court of Appeal decided was that there was no error of law in the decision of the Board that undressing etc was accomplished as a part of the day, but they make equally clear that the decision on the point, in their view, was one of fact to be decided in accordance with the common sense of the Board and, it follows, that were the Board, (or a tribunal now) to decide that going to bed was part of what one does at night, there would be, equally, nothing wrong with that decision.

For the past thirty years, however, tribunals have accepted that night begins only when the claimant has got into bed and ends when he climbs out. It may be too late for such a revolutionary change.

While this definition seems to address itself to the habits of the particular household there should be room to take account of a more objective, typical household. Thus if one (possibly the only other) member of the household remains up late to undertake what is a regular attention need that should be regarded as a night time need because otherwise the household would, as a whole, have been retired to bed. Conversely, when children have gone to bed, but their parents have not, any attention prior to the parents normal bed time will be attention by day, and any attention to the child before the parents' usual time of rising will be attention at night. The first part of this approach was confirmed in *R(A)1/78* (rejecting another part of Lord Widgery's judgment in the case above).

In *CDLA/997/2003*, the child who, because of his disabilities, had to be attended to whenever he was awake, woke regularly every morning at about 5.00 am. His mother had to rise then to give continual supervision. Had the child not woken at that time she would not have risen until 7.00 am. The Commissioner accepted the argument that the night of the household should be defined by what the household would normally do. In this case the household as a whole would not have risen before 7.00 am and therefore the period of supervision between 5.00 am and 7.00 am should count as being given at night.

Again, in *R(A)1/04*, the claimant frequently got up at 4.30 am and then went for a walk. The Commissioner held that a tribunal was wrong to fix the end of the night by reference to what that particular claimant did; the distinction should have a more objective element to reflect what ordinary households did. In this case it would probably be fair to say that the ordinary use of language would be to describe the claimant as going out for a walk in the night. The Commissioner suggests that a normal period of night, as identified in accordance with the test above, would be something like the hours between 11.00 pm and 7.00 am.

In order to satisfy para.(c)(i) the claimant must show that he requires, by night, *"prolonged or repeated attention . . ."*.

"Prolonged", seems to be accepted by decision-makers to mean 20 minutes or more. In *R. v National Insurance Commissioners Ex p. Secretary of State for Social Services*, [1981], W.L.R. 1017, CA, *R(A) 2/80*, Lord Denning said "repeated means more than once at any rate". Since the decision of the Court was that the Attendance Allowance Board had been correct in finding that the claimant satisfied only the day conditions it would seem that anything said as to the meaning of the night conditions was obiter, as a minimum, at least twice. It is therefore open to a tribunal to require more than two acts of attention during the night, but current experience suggests that generally twice per night has suffered.

It is not necessary that the care is needed every night. If the need is there on most nights the claim should succeed and in *R(A) 2/74* the Commissioner suggested that decision-makers should take a broad view of the matter and consider whether, in all of the circumstances, their good sense indicates that the words of the statute are satisfied. This might suggest care that is needed several times a week without focusing on counting nights every week.

In order to satisfy para.(c)(ii) the claimant must show that, by night, he requires someone to be *"awake for a prolonged period or at frequent intervals for the purpose of watching over him"* to avoid substantial danger.

For the meaning of "prolonged", see above under para.(c)(i). For the meaning of "frequent", see above under para.(b)(i)—though it is possible that fewer occurrences should be spread throughout the night (*cf.* the wording of para.(b)(i)).

Under this paragraph it is no longer possible for the carer to be asleep "on call". They must be awake and watching over the claimant. It is suggested that, as with supervision, the carer might be watching over, without actually looking at, the claimant at the time, e.g. they could be watching television in a room nearby. But as to the requirement of being awake there can be no compromise.

Subs. (1A)

A child (being for this purpose someone under 16) cannot qualify under the cooking test (subs.(1A)(a)), but otherwise there is no lower age limit for the care component. However, since all young children need a certain amount of attention and supervision, a disabled child qualifies for the care component only if he or she requires more attention or supervision than children of the same age who are not disabled. Note that the child is the claimant although an adult will be appointed to act on his or her behalf. In *CSDLA/567/2005* it was held that even attention given in soothing a child to sleep could be attention in connection with their bodily functions but only if the difficulty in sleeping were caused by a disability and, under this subsection, would qualify only if it were substantially in excess of that which would be normal for a child of that age.

1.236

In *CDLA/3737/2002* the Commissioner held that attention provided to a partially sighted child by her teachers at school to assist her in the bodily function of seeing and so learning could qualify her for the middle rate of care component. The amount of attention she required was considerably in excess of that which was required by a normally sighted child. There is nothing in the legislation to suggest that this sort of care should not be taken into account even if it is provided by a publicly funded institution.

An appeal against this decision was dismissed by the Court of Appeal and is now reported as *R(DLA) 1/04*. The Secretary of State argued, *inter alia*, that the time spent by a teacher at school with a pupil could not be regarded as attention for the purposes of s.72. The Court refused to enter into the merits of this argument because that ground of appeal had not been put before the Commissioner, despite his having given a provisional indication of his thinking before reaching his final decision. The Court of Appeal did suggest that the fact that this point had not been fully argued before the Commissioner might detract from the value of his decision as a precedent. We may well look forward to a further test case, or to statutory amendment. The Court of Appeal also took the opportunity to remind us (and themselves) of the need for caution when the ordinary courts enter upon a field where the process of adjudication (including two levels of appeal) has been entrusted to a specialist system.

Where a claim is made on behalf of a child, and it is based on the care and attention necessary to clean and wash as a result of the child not having developed control over their bowel or bladder, it may seem that the most obvious question is whether the child satisfies the requirement set in this subsection namely, is that attention substantially in excess of the normal requirements for a child of his age. But, as has been pointed out in *CSDLA/552/01*, and now again in *R(DLA)1/05*, there is another question that needs to be decided first—is there evidence that the child's condition is the result of any physical or mental disability? The fact that a child is late in developing control of the bowels, etc. is not, in itself, evidence of disability, and nocturnal enuresis may continue in a normal child for several years. In this case a claim for a child of six failed because the evidence did not necessarily show a disability even though she wet and sometimes fouled herself on most nights of the week. But the Commissioner did add that as she grew older a continuing failure to develop control might become some evidence of disability that might then be supported by medical evidence, though the need to find a medical condition will no longer apply since the decision in *R(DLA)2/06*.

Paragraph (a) provides that a claim for the lowest rate cannot be based on a child's inability to prepare a main meal, even if the child is 15.

Paragraph (b) defines the extra requirement that must be shown for a child claimant to succeed. This is either, under sub-para.(i) that they have care requirements of the kind defined in subs.(1) which are substantially in excess of the requirements of a normal child of that age; or, under sub-para.(ii) that they have extra such care requirements that would be common to younger children, but which children of their age would normally have grown out of. Obviously the younger a child is the more difficult it will be to show these conditions have been satisfied.

In *CA/92/92* the Deputy Commissioner made the following points:

"5. In the case of a child, it is to be noted that the attention or supervision required must be 'substantially in excess of that normally required by a child of the same age and sex.' Attention or supervision may be required 'substantially in excess of that normally required' either by virtue of the time over which it is required or by virtue of the quality or degree of attention or supervision which is required.

6. The idea of a greater quality or degree of attention can be illustrated by considering meal times. A young child may require attention in connection with eating because he or she requires the food to be cut up. A disabled child of the same age may require attention in excess of that normally required by a child of the same age because he or she not only requires the food to be cut up but also requires it to be spooned into the mouth. The fact that the child will be supervised anyway is irrelevant: there is still an additional requirement for attention. Whether such additional attention, taken with any other additional attention requirements, is 'substantial' and 'frequent . . . throughout the day' are matters of judgement to be determined in each case where the condition in section [72(1) (b)(i)] is being considered. Those may be significant limiting factors.

7. When considering the condition in section [72(1)(b)(ii)], the additional condition that the supervision required must be substantially in excess of that normally required by a child of the same age is indeed 'stringent' as it was described in *CA/21/88*. Because young children normally require continual supervision throughout the day in order to avoid substantial danger to themselves, the focus will be on the quality or degree of supervision. Thus a very young immobile baby or an older child might normally be regarded as being adequately supervised by a person who was getting on with his or her own chores in a different part of the home. On the other hand, a disabled child of the same age may need much closer supervision amounting, perhaps, to being watched over. That would be supervision in excess of that normally required. Again, it is necessary to consider whether

such additional supervision is 'substantial' and 'continual . . . throughout the day' and those may be significant limiting factors.

8. Similar considerations apply to the night conditions in section [72(1)(c)], although it may in practice be more difficult for claimants to qualify on the basis of the additional quality or degree of attention or watching over rather than on the basis of the additional frequency or length of time for which attention or watching over is required.

9. The other general question raised by this appeal is how one judges what attention of supervision is normally required by a child of the same age and sex. Children vary considerably in their requirements for attention and supervision, particularly when they are young. At any age, there is a range of requirements for attention or supervision. It is significant that the legislation does not speak of attention or supervision substantially in excess of that which would be required by the particular child being considered were he not physically or mentally disabled. So that, if it were possible to ascribe tantrums to frustration arising out of a disability, that would not be enough for the child to qualify unless the attention or supervision was substantially in excess of that normally required by a child of the same age and sex. It seems to me that the legislation contemplates a yardstick of an average child, neither particularly bright or well behaved nor particularly dull or badly behaved, and then the attention or supervision required by the child whose case is being considered must be judged to decide whether it is 'substantially' more than would normally be required by the average child. That, I think, comes to much the same thing as saying that the attention or supervision required must be substantially more than that normally required by *most* children, which is the way the delegated medical practitioner put it in paragraph 4 of his decision in this case. Attention or supervision is not to be regarded as 'substantially' in excess of that normally required unless it is outside the whole range of attention or supervision that would normally be required by the average child. However, it need not necessarily be substantially in excess of that which would be required by a particularly dull or badly behaved, but not physically or mentally disabled, child. I appreciate that all this is pitched at a fairly theoretical level and that there may be significant evidential problems and problems of judgement in individual cases, but it seems desirable to provide some sort of theoretical framework within which the present case can be considered."

An example of how this question is to be approached in the case of a very young child (there a matter of six months) is provided by *CDLA/3525/2004*. The child required a special diet and careful supervision. The majority of the tribunal found this extra care did not amount to care substantially in excess of what would be required for such a young child anyway. The Commissioner held that the tribunal had applied the right test and the conclusion they reached, essentially a finding of fact, could not be said to show any error of law.

The care needs of a very young child were considered in *CDLA/4100/2004*. The claimant was a child of 17 months who was profoundly deaf. She was provided with hearing aids which gave limited hearing ability, but it was claimed still required considerably more attention and supervision than a normal child of that age. Commissioner Rowland allowed her appeal and awarded the middle rate care component on the basis of the written evidence before him.

Further consideration of a child's claim is given by Commissioner Parker in *CDLA/829/2004* where she extends to three stages the test she suggested earlier in *CSDLA/552/01*. In these cases it is necessary, she suggests, to decide first; whether the claimant has a mental or physical disability (as now explained in *CDLA/1721/2004*), secondly whether they satisfy one or more of the care requirements, and then thirdly whether that amount of care substantially exceeds that required for a normal child of that age. For the question of what is normal, she adopts the approach of Commissioner Rowland in *R(DLA)1/05* as being a matter of quality as well as quantity, frequency, duration etc. A useful resume of these cases can be found again in *CSDLA/535/2007*, another decision of Commissioner Parker.

In *CDLA/3779/2004* the Commissioner points out that evidence from the school of supervision, or rather, lack of any extra supervision that is required for the claimant, may be misleading because the school may find it necessary to supervise all the children together, and that supervision may suffice for the claimant. But that is not to say that at other times, and away from school, that the claimant does not need supervision in circumstances (e.g. playing on his own) when a normal child would not.

A child who is terminally ill is taken to satisfy para.(b) and (c) of subs. (1) by virtue of subs.(5). Subs.(6)(b) has no application in such a case (*R(DLA)1/99*).

Subs.(2)

1.237   Paragraph (a) imposes the three-month qualifying period but this is deemed to be satisfied in the case of a person who is terminally ill (see subs.(5)). If a person's condition deteriorates so that he or she satisfies a further condition and would qualify for a higher rate of the care component, the effect of subs.(4) is that the claimant must still wait three months before qualifying for the higher rate unless terminally ill. Under s.76(1), an award cannot usually be made before the date of claim but this does not prevent the three-month qualifying period imposed by s.72(2)(a) from being satisfied as at the date of claim if the conditions were met during the three months before the date of claim. The date of claim is determined in accordance with Reg.6 of the Social Security (Claims and Payments) Regulations—see Vol.III of this work. Reg.6 of the DLA Regulations prescribes, for the purpose of para.(a)(ii), a period of three months ending on the day on which the claimant was last entitled to the component or to attendance allowance if that was not more than two years before the current period of entitlement would otherwise begin. This has the practical effect in most cases that the three-month qualifying period is deemed to be satisfied if the current claim is within two years of a previous period of entitlement at the relevant rate.

Under paras 3(2) and 7(2) of Sch.1 to the DLA Regulations, a period of six months is substituted for the period of three months in subs.(2) in the case of a person over the age of 65 who makes a renewal claim for DLA or whose entitlement is to be revised on review.

Paragraph (b) requires that a person should be expected to satisfy the conditions for the component for six months, unless he or she is expected to die sooner. In *CDLA/3461/2006*, it was held that this requirement applies equally to a renewal claim as much as to a new claim. Thus where, on the medical evidence provided, it was reasonable to expect that the claimant would be recovered within the next six months, even though he may not have recovered yet, the claim was properly refused.

Although this means that six months will normally be the minimum period for which an award will be made this section does not prevent an award for a lesser period when that is appropriate. In *R(DLA) 11/02* the claimant had applied unsuccessfully and then appealed. Before that appeal could be heard her condition had deteriorated and she made a fresh claim that was allowed. The Commissioner held that an award of less than six months could be made to fill the gap between the date when she was now regarded as qualifying and the date when the existing award commenced even though that was less than six months. This period of six months begins as the three-month (or six-month for those over 65) qualifying period ends and both conditions are intended to ensure that only the chronically disabled are entitled to DLA.

As the condition is prospective it must be judged on the basis of the information and the prognosis available at the time of claim. The claim is not precluded if, by the time a decision on it is made or an appeal is heard by a tribunal, it has transpired that the claimant's condition did not last that long. Evidence that the claimant's condition did improve within six months could be taken into account, but only if there was a real possibility, at the date of claim, that it might well do so. If, at that time, such improvement was not "on the cards", evidence that it has subsequently happened is not relevant to the question the decision-maker has to decide.

This was the conclusion reached by the Commissioner in *CDLA/2878/2000*. The claimant (who was a nurse) developed a condition of her back as a result of which she became unable to care for herself and suffered restricted mobility. She claimed both components of DLA, but less than three months later, and, according to her, quite unexpectedly she was operated on successfully and had recovered sufficiently to return to work within six months of her date of claim. The tribunal, which heard an appeal several weeks after that, held that she could not be entitled because events had proved the condition not to have lasted the requisite period. The Commissioner allowed her appeal for the reasons stated above after making a full review of authorities across a wide range of *ex post facto* situations. He drew a distinction between those cases where the subsequent event is relevant to establish a fact that might be shown to have pre-existed, and those cases, such as this (and the situation in *R(A) 1/94*), where the decision-maker must decide what was then a likely outcome.

Subss. (3) and (4)

Regulation 4(1) of the DLA Regulations provides for three rates of benefit. Despite the strange use of the words "in any other case" in subs.(4)(c) it is plain that it is intended that the lowest rate is applicable only if a claimant satisfies the condition mentioned in subs.(1)(a) without also satisfying the condition in either subs.(1)(b) or (1)(c) If he or she were to satisfy the conditions in, say, both subs.(1)(a) and (1)(c), the middle rate would be applicable. see *CDLA/2495/2004*.

1.238

Subs. (5)

Under s.66(2), a person is "terminally ill" if "he suffers from a progressive disease and his death in consequence of that disease can reasonably be expected within six months". See the notes to that section. Note also that someone may make a claim on this ground on behalf of the claimant without the claimant's knowledge or authority (s.76(3)).

The effect of this subsection is that a terminally ill person is deemed to satisfy the three-month (or six-month in the case of a person over 65) qualifying period and is entitled to an award of the highest rate of the care component for the remainder of his or her life, subject only to satisfying presence and residence conditions and the rules about people in hospital and other accommodation. Even those are relaxed. Reg.2(4) of the DLA Regulations relaxes the presence conditions for terminally ill claimants so that it is not necessary for them to have been in Great Britain before the day in respect of which the claim is made. Reg.9(3) also enables such claimants to receive the care component even though they are in accommodation where the cost could be, but is not, borne wholly or partly out of public or local funds.

1.239

Subs. (7)

Regulation 7 of the DLA Regulations deems people undergoing renal dialysis to satisfy the condition of either subs.(1)(b) or (1)(c).

1.240

Subs. (8)

See regs 8–10 of the DLA Regulations.

1.241

The mobility component

73.—(1) Subject to the provisions of this Act, a person shall be entitled to the mobility component of a disability living allowance for any period in which he is over [¹ the relevant age] and throughout which—

(a) he is suffering from physical disablement such that he is either unable to walk or virtually unable to do so; or
(b) he falls within subsection (2) below; or
(c) he falls within subsection (3) below; or
(d) he is able to walk but is so severely disabled physically or mentally that, disregarding any ability he may have to use routes which are familiar to him on his own, he cannot take advantage of the faculty

1.242

out of doors without guidance or supervision from another person most of the time.

[¹ (1A) In subsection (1) above "the relevant age" means—

(a) in relation to the conditions mentioned in paragraph (a), (b) or (c) of that subsection, the age of 3;

(b) in relation to the conditions mentioned in paragraph (d) of that subsection, the age of 5.]

(2) A person falls within this subsection if—

(a) he is both blind and deaf; and

(b) he satisfies such other conditions as may be prescribed.

(3) A person falls within this subsection if—

(a) he is severely mentally impaired; and

(b) he displays severe behavioural problems; and

(c) he satisfies both the conditions mentioned in section 72(1)(b) and (c) above.

[³ (4A) In its application to a person in relation to so much of a period as falls before the day on which he reaches the age of 16, subsection (1) has effect subject to the modification that the condition mentioned in paragraph (d) shall not be taken to be satisfied unless—

(a) he requires substantially more guidance or supervision from another person than persons of his age in normal physical and mental health would require, or

(b) persons of his age in normal physical and mental health would not require such guidance or supervision

(5) [⁴ . . .], circumstances may be prescribed in which a person is to be taken to satisfy or not to satisfy a condition mentioned in subsection (1)(a) or (d) or subsection (2)(a) above.

[³ (5A) Subsection (4A) has effect subject to regulations made under subsection (5) (except as otherwise prescribed).]

(6) Regulations shall specify the cases which fall within subsection (3)(a) and (b) above.

(7) A person who is to be taken for the purposes of section 72 above to satisfy or not to satisfy a condition mentioned in subsection (1)(b) or (c)of that section is to be taken to satisfy or not to satisfy it for the purposes of subsection (3)(c) above.

(8) A person shall not be entitled to the mobility component for a period unless during most of that period his condition will be such as permits him from time to time to benefit from enhanced facilities for locomotion.

(9) A person shall not be entitled to the mobility component of a disability living allowance unless—

(a) throughout—

(i) the period of three months immediately preceding the date on which the award of that component would begin; or

(ii) such other period of three months as may be prescribed, he has satisfied or is likely to satisfy one or other of the conditions mentioned in subsection (1) [⁵ (a) to (d)] above; and

(b) he is likely to continue to satisfy one or other of those conditions throughout—

(i) the period of six months beginning with that date; or

(ii) (if his death is expected within the period of six months beginning with that date) the period so beginning and ending with his death.

[³ (9A) The modifications mentioned in subsection (4A) shall have effect in relation to the application of subsection (1) for the purposes of subsection (9), but only—

(a) in the case of a person who is under the age of 16 on the date on which the award of the mobility component would begin, and

(b) in relation to so much of any period mentioned in subsection (9) as falls before the day on which he reaches the age of 16.]

(10) Two weekly rates of the mobility component shall be prescribed.

(11) The weekly rate of the mobility component payable to a person for each week in the period for which he is awarded that component shall be—

(a) the higher rate, if he falls within subsection (9) above by virtue of having satisfied or being likely to satisfy one or other of the conditions mentioned in subsection (1)(a), (b) and (c) above throughout both the period mentioned in paragraph (a) of subsection (9) above and that mentioned in paragraph (b) of that subsection; and

(b) the lower rate in any other case.

(12) For the purposes of this section in its application to a person who is terminally ill, as defined in section 66(2) above, and who makes a claim expressly on the ground that he is such a person—

(a) subsection (9)(a) above shall be omitted; and

(b) subsection (11)(a) above shall have effect as if for the words from "both" to "subsection", in the fourth place where it occurs, there were substituted the words "the period mentioned in subsection (9) (b) above".

(13) Regulations may prescribe cases in which a person who has the use—

(a) of an invalid carriage or other vehicle provided by [²the Welsh Ministers under paragraph 9 of Schedule 1 to the National Health Service (Wales) Act 2006, or the Secretary of State under paragraph 9 of Schedule 1 to the National Health Service Act 2006] or under section 46 of the National Health Service (Scotland) Act 1978 or provided under Article 30(1) of the Health and Personal Social Services (Northern Ireland) Order 1972; or

(b) of any prescribed description of appliance supplied under the enactments relating to the National Health Service being such an appliance as is primarily designed to afford a means of personal and independent locomotion out of doors,

is not to be paid any amount attributable to entitlement to the mobility component or is to be paid disability living allowance at a reduced rate in so far as it is attributable to that component.

(14) A payment to or in respect of any person which is attributable to his entitlement to the mobility component, and the right to receive such a payment, shall (except in prescribed circumstances and for prescribed purposes) be disregarded in applying any enactment or instrument under which regard is to be had to a person's means.

AMENDMENTS

1. Welfare Reform and Pensions Act 1999, s.67 (April 9, 2001).

2. National Health Service (Consequential Provisions) Act 2006, Sch.1, para.145 (March 1, 2007).

3. Welfare Reform Act 2007, s.53(2) (October 1, 2007).
4. Welfare Reform Act 2007, Sch.8 (October 1, 2007).
5. Welfare Reform Act 2007, Sch.7 para.2(2) (October 1, 2007).

DERIVATION

1.243   SSA 1975, s.37ZC.

GENERAL NOTE

1.244   The mobility component of DLA is a benefit paid to claimants who experience difficulty, to the requisite extent, in getting about on foot. It is paid at two levels. From April 2001 a claimant may qualify for benefit at the higher level from the age of three, but for the lower level only from the age of five. In both cases infant claimants have to satisfy an extra requirement test until they reach the age of 16. S.75 imposes an upper limit of 65, though claimants who have been entitled before reaching that age can continue to be entitled for the remainder of their life. It is no longer possible for a person to first claim for benefit over the age of 65 except in the case of someone moving from a previous entitlement under the invalid carriage scheme (DLA Regulations, Sch.2).

Note that the inability to walk or virtual inability to walk must exist throughout the period on which the claim is based. This has been interpreted, in *CDLA/496/2008*, as having the same meaning as the same words in s.72 have been given in *Secretary of State for Work and Pensions v Moyna* [2003] UKHL 44; [2003] 1 W.L.R. 1929; and *R(DLA) 7/03*. There, it was explained as being a matter of judgment, rather than arithmetical calculation, whether a person could fairly be described as being unable to cook themselves a main meal throughout the period in question, and the same will be said of their ability to walk. In this case the claimant suffered from epilepsy and sometimes had seizures when she was out walking. Commissioner Rowland held that her walking ability needed to be considered in three phases; one when she was out walking normally (for which she was entitled to mobility component at the lower rate because she needed to be supervised in case she had a seizure); another when she was unable to walk immediately after a seizure and when she could benefit from facilities for enhanced locomotion by being transported home in a car; and thirdly when she needed to sleep for a period of hours and sometimes days, to recover after the seizure. During this third period he felt she could not benefit from enhanced locomotion because she needed to remain resting and usually asleep (see subs.(8)). On this basis it was only the relatively short period during which she was travelling home that could qualify for benefit at the higher rate (unable to walk), and this, even if repeated, was insufficient to constitute an inability to walk throughout the period.

Para. (a)

1.245   This was the original basis upon which a mobility benefit was paid and still forms the basis of most claims. The circumstances in which a person can be taken to be "unable to walk or virtually unable to do so" are set out in Reg.12 of the DLA regulations made under subs.(5) of this section. For a detailed discussion of those circumstances and the meaning of "physical disablement", see the notes to that Regulation.

Para. (b)

1.246   The claimant qualifies under this paragraph if he satisfies the conditions of subs. (2)—see below.

Para. (c)

1.247   The claimant qualifies under this paragraph if he satisfies the conditions of subs. (3)—see below.

172

Para.(d)

The phrase "so severely disabled physically or mentally" is to be treated in the same way as the identical phrase in s.72. It does not require the claimant to show that they suffer from some medically prescribed condition and that it is severe, but only that they have a disability, mental or physical, that severely affects their ability in relation to walking. (See *CDLA/3831/2004* and *R(DLA) 3/06*.) **1.248**

This paragraph which qualifies a claimant for benefit at the lower rate only, is designed to help those who do not qualify under the paragraphs above, yet still need assistance to enable them to walk normally out of doors. It was passed in consequence of the decision of the House of Lords in *Lees v Secretary of State for Social Services* [1985] 1 A.C. 930, also reported as appendix to *R(M) 1/84*. In that case the claimant was blind but suffered as well from a severe impairment of her capacity for spatial orientation. This meant that she could walk outside only with someone to guide her—otherwise she had no idea in which direction to move. An argument that this meant she was virtually unable to walk was not accepted. Under this paragraph, however, she would clearly qualify on the grounds that she needed guidance from another most of the time. The paragraph applies in cases of mental disability as well as physical disability in cases where mere supervision is required in order for the claimant to take advantage of the ability to walk. Thus a mentally handicapped adult who requires supervision before he or she can safely be allowed to walk near traffic would appear to qualify. This approach is reinforced by subs.(4) which makes it an additional condition in the case of a child under 16 that he or she should require substantially more guidance or supervision than a child of the same age in normal health. That makes it clear that the sort of supervision normally required by children may well be sufficient to enable an adult to qualify. Note that ability to use familiar routes is to be ignored so that the fact that a claimant can get to and from a local shop may not be a bar to entitlement. But, although the ability to use familiar routes is to be ignored in applying this test, such ability may still be relevant in an evidential sense in determining whether the claimant has shown at least some aspects of an inability when using unfamiliar routes. That is the approach suggested by Commissioner Parker in *R (DLA) 2/08* as follows:

"11. In *CSDLA/12/03*, cited by the representative, at paragraph 28 I gave the two usual questions relevant to entitlement to lower mobility:
  '(a) First of all, [a tribunal] must determine whether, through disablement, the appellant is unable to walk on familiar routes without guidance or supervision, in which case he satisfies;
  (b) However, if the appellant does not qualify in this way, the tribunal must then ask if it is different if the routes are unfamiliar viz. is the appellant unable to walk on such routes without guidance or supervision? If he is not so able, he satisfies.'
12. If a claimant is unable to walk even on familiar routes without guidance or supervision, then it logically follows that he will also be unable to do so on unfamiliar ones; but the converse does not apply. It will depend upon the nature of the claimant's condition. If the complaint is of a bad left knee causing falls, then the difficulties are likely to be the same whether the route is familiar or unfamiliar; however if, for example, a claimant has genuine anxiety and panic, then what he is able to do on a familiar route does not necessarily govern his capacity on an unfamiliar one.
13. The present tribunal, in effect, ran together the two stage process; however, that is not a problem provided the relevant issues are in substance addressed, and the tribunal did so. It first of all explained (when rejecting entitlement to the higher rate of the mobility component) why it refused to accept the claimed physical difficulties in the present case (particularly the asserted collapses of the appellant's left knee), which were in the circumstances relevant also to an ability both on familiar and unfamiliar routes. It then turned to the assertion about

anxiety and panic attacks, which had greater significance with respect to unfamiliar routes. For reasons it fully explained, the tribunal refused to accept that any of these claims were other than exaggerated. No error is demonstrated in the way the tribunal weighed the evidence and it was entitled to rely, if it wished, on the EMP's report.

14. In consideration of the *legal* criteria for entitlement to lower mobility, there must be ignored any ability to use familiar routes, albeit not an inability. However, when considering whether the claimant is unable to walk on unfamiliar routes without guidance or supervision, it may be *evidentially* relevant to that question as a matter of fact what, if any, are his difficulties with familiar routes. When a claimant does not differentiate between problems on familiar and unfamiliar routes, and there is nothing inherent in his condition to suggest a relevant distinction, then if he is unable to satisfy a tribunal that he has the required difficulty on familiar routes, in a context where the onus of proof on all matters lies on him, a tribunal may legitimately infer that he therefore would not need guidance or supervision on unfamiliar routes either. It is not that an adjudicating authority is requiring as a matter of law that he has difficulties on familiar routes before it will accept entitlement to lower mobility but rather that, from all the evidence, when considering his capacity on unfamiliar routes, it makes deductions from the information about his ability on familiar ones. A tribunal usually has to so reason because a claimant often says that he never walks on unfamiliar routes, which is entirely understandable.

15. In the present case, the tribunal correctly considered that, if the claimant genuinely suffered from anxiety and panic, this could make a material difference to his capacity on unfamiliar routes when compared with familiar ones. This is the clear implication of its reasoning. However, the tribunal was not satisfied of the genuine nature of his alleged problems, whether physical or mental; it neither applied the wrong legal approach nor, having regard to the evidence, drew any irrational conclusions and its explanation of which evidence was accepted, and which rejected, and why, was impeccable. It is apparent from the tribunal's whole reasoning that it answered 'no' to both the sequential questions posed in my paragraph 11 above."

Evidence as to whether a claimant has need of guidance or supervision can be derived in a number of ways. In *R 1/07(DLA)* the commissioner in Northern Ireland held that evidence of the claimant's ability to drive a motor car, was properly accepted as showing the claimant's "clear headedness and competency" which could be relevant to that aspect of her ability to walk on an unfamiliar route without the need for guidance or supervision.

The meaning of "guidance" and "supervision" in this context was considered in *CDLA/42/94* in which the Commissioner summarised his conclusions as follows:

"(i) The meaning of guidance or supervision must be considered within the context of action which is aimed at enabling the claimant to take advantage of the faculty of walking despite the limits imposed by her physical or mental condition. It is not a condition that guidance or supervision should be necessary to avoid a risk of danger to the claimant or others.

(j) Guidance means the action of directing or leading. It may, for example, be constituted by physically directing or leading the claimant or by oral direction, persuasion or suggestion.

(k) Supervision, in the context of section 73(1)(d), means accompanying the claimant and at the least monitoring the claimant or the circumstances for signs of a need to intervene so as to prevent the claimant's ability to take advantage of the faculty of walking being compromised. Other, more active, measures may also amount to supervision. The monitoring does not cease to fall within the meaning of supervision by reason only that intervention by the person accompanying the claimant has not in the past actually been necessary.

(l) The fact that the claimant derives reassurance from the presence of the other person does not prevent action which would otherwise fall within point (j) or (k) from being guidance or supervision."

In *R(DLA) 3/04* Commissioner Rowland considered the case of a claimant who, because of her state of anxiety and depression, suffered severe panic attacks if she tried to walk out on her own. She could only walk for any significant distance if she was accompanied by one of her family who would provide continuous reassurance and encouragement. The Commissioner held that this level of support could constitute guidance and supervision. He went on to hold that her claim was not precluded by reg.12(7) of the Disability Living Allowance Regulations because her state of anxiety was a symptom of a mental disability provided for under reg.12(8).

In *CDLA/52/94* the claimant suffered from epilepsy and the Commissioner said:

"7. Where a person has only occasional fits, the expression 'most of the time' focuses attention on the needs of the claimant between fits, rather than during or immediately after them. Therefore, so far as epilepsy is concerned, guidance may be of little relevance. The question then arises whether a person who is accompanying the claimant is thereby exercising 'supervision'. . . .

8. It is likely that a claimant who, due to epilepsy, satisfies the condition of section 72(1)(b)(ii) and is entitled to the care component of disability living allowance on the ground that he or she 'requires from another person . . . continual supervision throughout the day in order to avoid substantial danger to himself or others' will also satisfy the condition of section 73(i)(d). What is less clear is whether a person who fails to satisfy the condition of section 72(1)(b)(ii), because he or she merely needs a person to be nearby, will also fail to satisfy the condition of section 73(1) (d), because all that can be shown is a need to be accompanied when walking. Is a person accompanying such a claimant out walking in any different position from that of a person 'who keeps himself available to be called' while the claimant is at home?

9. It is, I think, important to bear in mind that Nicholls L.J. [in *Moran*—see note to s.72(1), above] did not exclude the possibility that a person 'who keeps himself available to be called' *might* be exercising supervision. 'It will all depend on the facts of the case.' In my view, the most significant factor is that a person who is keeping himself available while the claimant is at home (or at work) is likely to be able to get on with his or her own activities, whereas having to accompany a claimant is likely to preclude that and, unless he or she wishes to go on the same journey anyway, there is inevitably an element of service involved. It is that element of service that is significant. In my view, the use of the word 'monitoring' by the Commissioner in *CDLA/42/94* reflects the facts of the case before the Commissioner and the need for there to be some element of service rather than mere presence. In a case where a claimant can give warning to a person who is accompanying him or her, I do not think that it can reasonably be said that the accompanying person is 'monitoring' the claimant. However, even though there may be an absence of monitoring, I take the view that a need to be accompanied when walking may amount to a need for supervision. In practice, where epilepsy is concerned, the focus is likely to be on the reasonableness of the claim that there is a *need* to be accompanied when walking a modest distance. Relevant issues will be the likelihood of a fit occurring when the claimant is out walking and the risk of substantial danger if one does occur then. There may well be a greater risk of danger when the claimant has a fit out in the street than when he or she is at home."

However, in *CDLA/757/94*, a Commissioner held that a person, who was in receipt **1.249** of the care component under s.72(1)(b)(ii) on the ground that continual supervision was required due to a propensity to fall, did not *ipso facto* satisfy the condition of s.73(1)(d). He said:

". . . in the present case there was nothing to prevent the claimant from walking out of doors. She might not want to, by reason of her alleged propensity to fall four or five times a day, and such a fall might occur while she was walking outside, but the choice was entirely hers. Supervision was not a prerequisite for her exercising her power of walking; it was an additional advantage rendering her walking less open to risk. But s.73(1)(d) is not concerned with supervision to avoid danger to the claimant; that type of supervision is provided for under s.72(1)(b)(ii)."

These and other cases revealed a difference of opinion between Commissioners over the question whether the supervision required for a claimant to qualify for the care component under s.73(1)(b)(ii) could, at the same time, qualify for the mobility component when the claimant chose to walk out of doors. A decision of a Tribunal of Commissioners concerning four joined appeals, *R(DLA) 4/01*, resolved this difference in favour of the claimants. The Tribunal finds nothing in the law to prevent the same type of assistance enabling the claimant to qualify for both parts of the benefit (*CDLA/757/1994*) to the contrary is expressly overruled). On the other hand the Commissioners reject the suggestion that a claimant who qualifies for the care condition should be passported automatically to the other. While they accept that many such claimants are likely to succeed to both components, they emphasise that the test applicable to each component must be considered separately and applied by the decision-maker to the facts found in respect of each claim. The Tribunal sets out its main reasons as follows:

"(a) The words 'guidance or supervision' without qualification would, as a matter of the ordinary use of language, comprehend supervision to avoid substantial danger to the claimant: there is no justification for excluding the type of supervision which is most likely to be required when a disabled individual is walking alone outside.

(b) There is nothing in the language of either section 72 or section 73 which dictates that attention or supervision requirements which are taken into account for the purposes of entitlement to the care component should not also be taken into account for the purposes of the lower rate of the mobility component.

(c) If correct, Mr. Forsdick's main submissions would mean that decision-makers acting on behalf of the Secretary of State and tribunals would, in many cases, have to embark upon the difficult task of analysing what attention or supervision requirements were, or might be, covered by an award of the care component and of deducting those requirements from the aggregate of the requirements for supervision or guidance needed by the claimant when walking out of doors on unfamiliar routes. We do not consider, in the absence of clear statutory language, that it was intended that decision-makers or tribunals should have to embark upon such a fine analysis, involving an artificial dissection of the practical realities of the lives of claimants.

(d) Mr. Forsdick's main submissions could give rise to anomalies. For example, a claimant whose requirement for supervision to avoid substantial danger to himself or others was the same both indoors and out, was not continual but yet was required most of the time would, as we understand it, not only not qualify for the care component, but would also not qualify for the lower rate of the mobility component.

(e) Taken to its natural conclusion, Mr. Forsdick's argument on behalf of the Secretary of State would mean that a blind person (such as the claimant in *Mallinson v Secretary of State for Social Security* [1994] 1 W.L.R. 630) who required frequent attention with the bodily function of seeing while walking out of doors could not rely on those attention requirements for the purposes of entitlement of the lower rate of the mobility component. This could render section 73(1)(d) of nugatory effect for the blind, the one class of person for whom it is absolutely clear it was intended should be provided some relief, following the decision of the House of Lords in *Lees.*

(f) Section 73(1)(d) does not contain the words 'cannot exercise the faculty of walking' but uses the words 'cannot take advantage of the faculty of walking'. We observed that the Commissioner in *CDLA/757/94* and Mr. Forsdick, in the re-formulation which we invited him to make, substituted the words 'cannot exercise' for 'take advantage of'. We accept Mr. Drabble's submission that these last words are of wider import than 'cannot exercise' and carry with them the connotation that the claimant is not able most of the time to walk over unfamiliar routes so as to be able to get to a desired destination whenever he wants to without the prescribed supervision or guidance.

(g) We note (from the printed cases) that a submission was made to the House of Lords both in *Mallinson* and in *Fairey* to the effect that attention which might be connected with entitlement to mobility component should be ignored when entitlement to the care component was under consideration. Such a submission was not accepted—see *per* Lord Woolf in *Mallinson* at 633 F and 635 A and, *por* Lord Slynn in *Fairey* at 813 G II. Although the converse proposition is in issue in the present appeals, 'overlap' as a concept did not influence the majority reasoning in either decision of the House of Lords."

The decision will enable many claimants who are mentally ill, or epileptic, or deaf or blind to qualify for the mobility component. Three of the cases joined in this appeal, and several of those in which Commissioners had previously disagreed dealt with deaf claimants. In this decision the Commissioners dealt specifically with the problems of pre-lingually deaf claimants. In such cases, they thought, it would be quite appropriate to find that the claimant required guidance (or possibly supervision) all of the time he was walking over unfamiliar routes because without that company he would not attempt that route for fear of becoming lost and being unable to communicate effectively with anyone. They accept that supervision must require something more than just keeping another company, but they hold that a person who is present to lend assistance whenever that may become necessary is supervising in the sense of being ancillary to an episode of attention. In any case where the claimant is unable to communicate and is undertaking unfamiliar routes such attention may be frequent enough to be guidance. The Commissioners emphasise that such cases depend upon clear findings of fact as to the claimant's ability to communicate by writing, or lip reading and to his ability to read maps and other directions.

The Tribunal in *R(DLA) 4/01* also took the opportunity of considering whether the words "cannot take advantage of " should be read as conditioned by some word such as "reasonably" so that a claimant need not show that, without assistance, he is totally unable to take advantage of outdoor walking. The Commissioners held it is unnecessary to read in any such words because the paragraph as a whole makes it apparent that some outside walking ability is assumed, for example, the claimant's inability need apply only to unfamiliar routes, and to most of the time. The Tribunal felt that it could safely be left to the good sense of decision-makers to decide when a claimant might otherwise require assistance over unfamiliar routes.

This does not however resolve the difference between Commissioners over whether it must be shown that the claimant is capable of walking out of doors when given the benefit of guidance and supervision. Commissioners have differed as to whether guidance or supervision will only be relevant if it will enable the claimant to overcome his or her inability to make use of the faculty of walking. In *CDLA/42/94* the Commissioner said that "it would be absurd if a claimant whose disablement was so severe that she was not able to take advantage of the faculty of walking on

1.250

unfamiliar routes out of doors even with guidance or supervision was excluded from s.73(1)(d). Because of the negative formulation of the provision, a claimant does not necessarily have to show an ability to take advantage of that faculty with guidance or supervision." However, in *CDLA/2364/95* (followed in *CSDLA/12/2003*), the Commissioner rejected that approach and decided that a person who suffered from claustrophobia and agoraphobia and who could not be persuaded to walk outdoors would not be entitled to the lower rate of the mobility component. These latter decisions have been upheld by the Court of Appeal in NI in *Mongan v Department of Social Development* [2005] NICA 16. That court holds that a claimant must show that the guidance or supervision will enhance the claimant's walking ability. But a person can qualify for mobility component at the lower rate under paragraph (d) even though they may never undertake to walk on unfamiliar routes. The test is hypothetical in the sense that the claimant is entitled if they could not walk that route without guidance or supervision — it matters not that they would not walk there anyway. In *R(DLA)6/03* the tribunal had found that the claimant (to whom they had already refused mobility allowance at the higher rate) would not have gone walking on unfamiliar routes (or seemingly on familar routes) because of the danger of falling. It seems that the claimant must have said that the provision of supervision would have made no difference to her because the chairman went on to remark "There is no point in making an award if its purpose is frustrated". The Commissioner allowed the appeal remarking that the element of an award being frustrated is provided for in subs.(8), but that provision requires that the claimant be *unable to* benefit from locomotion not merely that he chooses not to. Notice that in this case the claimant *could* have walked on unfamiliar routes with supervision-it was simply that she chose not to, whereas in *CDLA/2364/95* the claimant was unable to walk outside because their medical condition prevented them from doing so even with supervision.

In *CDLA/835/97*, the Commissioner directed that, in considering entitlement to the lower rate of the mobility component under s.73(1)(d), the tribunal to whom he was referring the case should exclude any supervision required to stop the claimant from "going off and getting into trouble shoplifting and the like." He held that supervision to prevent a claimant getting himself into criminal activity or moral danger was outside the scope of the subsection. This part of the decision was, however, set aside (by consent) by the Court of Appeal in *V (a child) v Secretary of State for Social Security* (February 23, 2001), and *CDLA/3781/2003* holds that this has the effect of rendering all of *CDLA/835/97* of no legal effect.

In *C19/98(DLA)*, the Northern Ireland Commissioner holds that the use of suitable aids and appliances can be taken into account when considering s.73(1)(d) even though there is no specific provision to that effect.

Subs.(2)

1.251   Regulation 12(2) of the DLA Regulations 1991, made under subs.(5), defines blindness and deafness for the purposes of para.(a). It is not necessary for the claimant to have total loss of vision and hearing (see the note to that regulation). Reg.12(3), made under para.(b), makes it a further condition of entitlement that the combined effects of the claimant's blindness and deafness should make him unable, without the assistance of another, to walk to any intended or required destination while out of doors.

Subs.(3)

1.252   This provision is intended to reduce the immense difficulties caused in mobility allowance cases by the fact that only virtual inability to walk due to *physical* disablement could be taken into account. Some of those who would qualify under this subsection would also qualify under subs.(1)(a) but adjudication in such cases is made much simpler by this new provision. The conditions imposed by this subsection are quite stringent but those who fail to qualify may be able to qualify under subs.(1)

(a) for the higher rate (if they can show physical disablement) or under subs.(1)(d) for the lower rate.

Regulations 12(5) and 12(6) of the DLA Regulations 1991, made under subs. (6), specify who falls within paras (a) and (b) as suffering from mental impairment and displaying severe behavioural problems. A person falls within para.(a) if "he suffers from a state of arrested development or incomplete physical development of the brain, which results in severe impairment of intelligence and social functioning". In *M (A child) v Chief Adjudication Officer*, reported as *R(DLA) 1/00*, the Court of Appeal held that an I.Q. test of the claimant was not conclusive of whether the claimant satisfied this test. It has been usual to look for a score of less than 55 as indicative of a severe impairment of intelligence. In this case the claimant was autistic and had an I.Q. score considerably above that level. The Court of Appeal hold that the claimant's I.Q. is only one of several factors that are relevant. It is a useful starting point, but a full evaluation of intelligence and social functioning should include other elements of social interaction, "sagacity" and "insight". A person falls within para.(b) if the disruptive behaviour "(a) is extreme, (b) regularly requires another person to intervene and physically restrain him in order to prevent him causing physical injury to himself or another, or damage to property, and (c) is so unpredicable that he requires another person to be present and watching over him whenever he is awake." In *CSDLA/202/2007*, a claim for higher rate mobility component made on behalf of a child of 3, who was autistic, was returned for consideration by a new tribunal because the first appeal tribunal had failed to consider both of the possible routes by which such a claim might succeed; *viz.* either under s.73(1)(a) (temporary paralysis as to walking resulting from the autism), or, by s.73(1)(c) (severely mentally impaired and severe behavioural problems, etc.). In doing so, Commissioner Parker adopts both *R(DLA)1/00* and *R(DLA)7/02*. She observes, as well, that neither of these routes to entitlement involves specific reference to the age of the child (*cf.* s.73(4) and s.72(6)). But, she suggests, the factor of age is inherent in each of these routes because, in the case of s.73(1)(a), the ability to walk must be the result of some physical disablement and that test would not be satisfied by any inability, such as lack of stamina, that resulted only from the claimant's immaturity; while a claim under s.73(1)(c) (in addition to needing to satisfy s.72(6) for the highest rate of the care component) will also need to show that the claimant's severe behavioural problems result from severe mental impairment, rather than just the tantrums of a normal child.

Under para.(c), it is also necessary for the claimant to satisfy the conditions for the highest rate of the care component. It is not clear why entitlement to an allowance in respect of mobility outdoors should require satisfaction of the night attendance condition for the care component, and this may be a major obstacle for some claimants. Subs.(7) has the effect that those who are deemed to satisfy one or both of the attendance conditions for the care component because they undergo renal dialysis or are terminally ill may rely on the same provisions for the purpose of satisfying para.(c)

Subs.(4)

Subsection (4) imposes the same conditions upon a claim made in respect of child as those provided for in s.72(6). A recent decision of Commissioner Parker (*CSDLA/91/2003*) applies the same reasoning to the conditions for mobility as that adopted for the care component. When guidance and supervision is required it must be substantially more than would be required for a child of that age of normal physical and mental development. In judging what is substantially more, account must be taken of both the quality and the quantity of the supervision. Thus where all children might need to be accompanied on a certain route, a disabled child who required support, or restraint, or encouragement, or even constant surveillance should qualify. **1.253**

Subss.(5) and (6)

See regs 12 to 12c of the DLA Regulations, 1991. **1.254**

Subs. (8)

1.255   This is in the same terms as s.37A(2)(b) of the Social Security Act 1975 relating to mobility allowance which was considered by a Commissioner in *R(M) 2/83*. He approved a passage in the second edition of Ogus and Barendt, *The Law of Social Security*, in which they said:

> "This obviously excludes human vegetables and those whom it is unsafe to move, but it is arguable that of the remainder there will be few who will not receive some benefit from the occasional sortie, and it is not easy to draw a line between the deserving and the undeserving except on some arbitrary basis."

The Commissioner pointed out that the word "benefit" was a wide one and that the provision contained the words "from time to time" but he added a further category of excluded persons, "that is persons so severely mentally deranged that a high degree of supervision and restraint would be required to prevent them either injuring themselves or others."

In *CDLA/2142/2005* the Commissioner agrees with the decision in *CSDLA/12/2003* that the claimant, who was agoraphobic, must be willing to make use of the assistance by walking out of doors so as to show that she would benefit from enhanced locomotion. But he returned the case to a new tribunal with the suggestion to consider whether walking within the confines of the claimant's own back garden, which was all that she could be persuaded to do, could satisfy that test if it were beneficial to the health, both mental and physical, of the claimant.

In *CDLA/1639/2006* the Commissioner held that a tribunal which allowed a claim for higher rate mobility component in respect of a claimant suffering from severe attacks of migraine had erred in law by overlooking the effects of s.73(8). As the commissioner pointed out the only time that the claimant would have had any need for attention was during the time he was suffering a migraine attack; at that same time however, on his own evidence, he was compelled to sit or to lie down, so no amount of assistance could aid his mobility. And see also: *CDLA/496/2008* discussed above in the update to s.73(1).

Subs. (9)

1.256   Paragraph (a) imposes the three-month qualifying period but this is deemed to be satisfied in the case of a person who is terminally ill (see subs.(12)). If a person is entitled to the lower rate of the mobility component by virtue of satisfying the condition in subs.(1)(d) and his or her condition deteriorates so that he or she would satisfy one or other of the conditions in subs.(1)(a), (b) or (c) the effect of subs.(11) (a) is that the claimant must still wait three months before qualifying for the higher rate unless terminally ill. Under s.76(1), an award cannot usually be made before the date of claim which is determined in accordance with reg.6(1) and (5) of the Social Security (Claims and Payments) Regulations 1987 (see Vol.III of this work) Reg.11 of the DLA Regulations prescribes, for the purpose of para.(a)(ii) a period of three months ending on the day on which the claimant was last entitled to the component or to attendance allowance if that was not more than two years before the current period of entitlement would otherwise begin. This has the practical effect in most cases that the three-month qualifying period is deemed to be satisfied if the current claim is within two years of a previous period of entitlement at the relevant rate.

Under para.4(2) of Sch.1 to the DLA Regulations, a period of six months is substituted for the period of three months in para.(a) in the case of a person over the age of 65 who makes a claim for the mobility component and is entitled to do so because he or she was formerly entitled to a car or other assistance under an invalid vehicle scheme.

Paragraph (b) requires that a person should be expected to satisfy the conditions for the component for six months, unless he or she is expected to die sooner.

Although this means that six months will normally be the minimum period for which an award will be made, this section does not prevent an award for a lesser period when that is appropriate. In *R(DLA)11/02* the claimant had applied unsuccessfully and then appealed. Before that appeal could be heard her condition had deteriorated and she made a fresh claim that was allowed. The Commissioner held that an award of less than six months could be made to fill the gap between the date when she was now regarded as qualifying and the date when the existing award commenced even though that was less than six months. This period of six months begins as the three-month (or six-month for those over 65) qualifying period ends and both conditions are intended to ensure that only the chronically disabled are entitled to DLA.

Note that since the condition is prospective the matter must be determined on the basis of the information available and the prognosis at the time of the claim. For the effect of this, see note to s.72(2)(b) above.

Subss. (10) and (11)

The higher rate is payable if one or other of the conditions in subs.(1)(a), (b) or (c) is satisfied and the lower rate is payable if the condition in subs.(1)(d) is satisfied. To be entitled at the higher rate, it is not necessary that the *same* condition should have been satisfied throughout the qualifying period and the period of the award.

1.257

Subs. (12)

Under s.66(2), a person is "terminally ill" if "he suffers from a progressive disease and his death in consequence of that disease can reasonably be expected within six months". See the notes to that section.

1.258

The effect of this subsection is that a terminally ill person is deemed to satisfy the three-month qualifying period (or the six-month period in the case of a person over 65 formerly entitled to an invalid vehicle). Note also that reg.2(4) of the DLA Regulations relaxes the presence conditions for terminally ill claimants so that it is not necessary for them to have been in Great Britain before the day in respect of which the claim is made. However, while terminally ill claimants are deemed to satisfy the conditions for the highest rate of the care component, they are not deemed to satisfy any of the conditions for the mobility component except subs.(3) (c) (see subs.(7)). This is confirmed in *R(DLA)7/06*.

Subs. (13)

Sch.2 to the DLA Regulations makes provision allowing former invalid vehicle scheme beneficiaries to be deemed to satisfy the conditions for the higher rate of the mobility component and Sch.1, para.4 permits them to claim the mobility component even if they are aged over 65.

1.259

Subs. (14)

There is specific provision in the legislation governing disability working allowance which ensures that disability living allowance is not to be treated as income (Sch.3, para.4 to the Disability Working Allowance (General) Regulations 1991). But *quaere* whether para.8(a) of Sch.4 to those Regulations (which allows arrears of disability living allowance to be disregarded as capital only for 52 weeks and so implies it should be taken into account after that) is overridden by this subsection so that the arrears may continue to be disregarded for longer. The power to make regulations under this subsection is not referred to in the preamble to those Regulations. This provision also applies to any local authority scheme applying a means test where there is a statutory power to make charges for services, e.g. charges for home helps under para.3 of Sch.8 to the National Health Service Act 1977.

1.260

Mobility component for certain persons eligible for invalid carriages

74.—(1) Regulations may provide for the issue, variation and cancellation of certificates in respect of prescribed categories of persons to whom this

1.261

section applies; and a person in respect of whom such a certificate is issued shall, during any period while the certificate is in force, be deemed for the purposes of section 73 above to satisfy the condition mentioned in sub-section (1)(a) of that section and to fall within paragraphs (a) and (b) of subsection (9) by virtue of having satisfied or being likely to satisfy that condition throughout both the periods mentioned in those paragraphs.

(2) This section applies to any person whom the Secretary of State considers—

(a) was on 1st January 1976 in possession of an invalid carriage or other vehicle provided in pursuance of section 33 of the Health Services and Public Health Act 1968 (which related to vehicles for persons suffering from physical defect or disability) or receiving payments in pursuance of subsection (3) of that section; or

(b) had at that date, or at a later date specified by the Secretary of State, made an application which the Secretary of State approved for such a carriage or vehicle or for such payments; or

(c) was, both at some time during a prescribed period before that date and at some time during a prescribed period after that date, in possession of such a carriage or vehicle or receiving such payments; or

(d) would have been, by virtue of any of the preceding paragraphs, a person to whom this section applies but for some error or delay for which in the opinion of the Secretary of State the person was not responsible and which was brought to the attention of the Secretary of State within the period of one year beginning with 30th March 1977 (the date of the passing of the Social Security (Miscellaneous Provisions) Act 1977, section 13 of which made provisions corresponding to the provision made by this section).

DERIVATION

1.262   SS(MP)A 1977, s.13.

GENERAL NOTE

1.263   For regulations, see reg.13 of, and Sch.2 to, the Social Security (Disability Living Allowance) Regulations 1991, which are treated by s.2(2) of the Social Security (Consequential Provisions) Act 1992 as having been made under this section.

Mobility allowance (which was introduced by s.22 of the Social Security Pensions Act 1975 and has now been replaced by the higher rate of the mobility component of disability living allowance) was intended to replace the provision of invalid vehicles and the alternative system of paying for vehicles. Those who were already entitled to vehicles or payments under the Health Services and Public Health Act 1968 on January 1, 1976, have retained the right to them but may at any time exchange them for the higher rate of the mobility component of disability living allowance, even if they are over the usual maximum age of 65.

[1 Persons who have attained pensionable age]

1.264   **75.**—(1) Except to the extent to which regulations provide otherwise, no person shall be entitled to either component of a disability living allowance for any period after he attains [1 pensionable age] otherwise than by virtue of an award made before he attains that age.

(2) Regulations may provide in relation to persons who are entitled to a component of a disability living allowance by virtue of subsection (1) above

that any provisions of this Act which relates to disability living allowance, other than section 74 above, so far as it so relates, and any provision of the Administration Act which is relevant to disability living allowance—

(a) shall have effect subject to modifications, additions or amendments; or

(b) shall not have effect.

AMENDMENTS

1. Pensions Act 22007, Sch.1, para.42 (September 26, 2007).

DERIVATION

SSA 1975, s.37ZD   1.265

GENERAL NOTE

The general rule established by this subsection is that a person is not entitled to   1.266
DLA for any period after reaching the age of 65 unless entitled by virtue of an award made before he or she reaches that age. Reg.3 of, Sch.1 to, the DLA Regulations are made under this section.

An attempt was made in *NT v SSWP* [2009] UKUT 37(AAC); *R(DLA) 1/09* to show that the denial of mobility component to those over pensionable age was unlawful as a denial of the claimant's human rights by reason of discriminating on the ground of age. The judge of the Upper Tribunal, Judge Levenson, found that a claim to mobility component did engage the rights of the claimant under Article 1 of the First Protocol, and her rights under Article 8. He found, as well, that a distinction based upon age was capable of being discrimination under Article 14, but even so, the judge disallowed the appeal. He accepted that the DWP had demonstrated a rational and proportionate justification for the difference in treatment because the mobility component of DLA had always been intended to benefit those of working age who found that their earning capacity, as well as their life style, was aVected adversely by their disability. When the claimant reached an age at which earning could be assumed to be replaced by entitlement to other benefits, such as retirement pension, the reason for mobility component had largely ceased.

Regulation 3 originally provided for two exceptions to the general rule. First, a person who would have qualified at the age of 65 could be awarded DLA provided a claim was made before he or she reached the age of 66. That provision was revoked from October 6, 1997. Secondly, if a claimant reaches the age of 65 during the three-month qualifiying period for either component, having claimed before reaching that age, then the claimant is not prejudiced by the fact that the award is not made, or effective, until after his or her 65th birthday. There is a further exception under para.4 of Sch.1 of the DLA Regulations allowing a former invalid vehicle scheme beneficiary to qualify for the mobility component. Sch.1 to the DLA Regulations also enables further awards to be made to those people who have established entitlement to DLA beyond the age of 65, although there are some restrictions.

Where the claimant's entitlement to DLA is revised after reaching the age of 65 and it is concluded that he is no longer entitled to the care component at the higher or middle rate, or the mobility component at the higher rate, it is not possible for him to qualify then for the lowest rate of the care component, nor for the lower rate of mobility component, if the review is based upon a change of circumstances occurring after he has reached the age of 65 (see *R(DLA) 5/02*). Where, however, the revision is based upon a change of circumstances that occurred before he reached that age (or is based upon a mistake of law or fact made at the initial award, or a subsequent renewal, before that age), the claimant may be entitled to an award at the lowest rate for care and for the lower rate of mobility where his condition would justify such an award from the appropriate date before the age of 65. See Reg.3

and Sch.1 the Disability Living Allowance Regulations 1991 and the decision of Commissioner Parker, *CSDLA/388/2000* and see too *CDLA/754/2000* where the Commissioner draws attention, for the benefit of a new tribunal, to the effect of paras 3 and 5 of Sch.1 which is that in an appropriate case a claimant whose entitlement to the DLA components ceases even when he is over the age of 65 may have those entitlements restored if his condition then deteriorates again. See also the decisions in *CDLA/301/05* noted after Sch.1, in which the Commissioner also holds that a claim for the lowest rate of DLA may succeed even if the need for that care developed after the age of 65, so long as the basis of the review was something that occurred before that age.

People over 65 who are not entitled to DLA may instead qualify for attendance allowance under s.64.

Disability living allowance—supplementary

1.267   **76.**—(1) Subject to subsection (2) below, a person shall not be entitled to a disability living allowance for any period preceding the date on which a claim for it is made or treated as made by him or on his behalf.

(2) Notwithstanding anything in subsection (1) above, provision may be made by regulations for a person to be entitled to a component of a disability living allowance for a period preceding the date on which a claim for such an allowance is made or treated as made by him or on his behalf if he has previously been entitled to that component.

(3) For the purposes of sections 72(5) and 73(12) above where—

(a) a person purports to make a claim for a disability living allowance on behalf of another; and

(b) the claim is made expressly on the ground that the person on whose behalf it purports to be made is terminally ill,

that person shall be regarded as making the claim notwithstanding that it is made without his knowledge or authority.

DERIVATION

1.268   SSA 1975, s.37ZE.

GENERAL NOTE

1.269   This section makes provision for claims to DLA.

Subss.(1) and (2)

1.270   This states the general rule that claims for DLA cannot be backdated to cover a period before the date on which a claim is made or *is treated as made*. The general rule has been criticised as unduly severe. Claims for most other social security benefits can be backdated, including benefits in respect of incapacity for work which suggests that the gathering of medical evidence in respect of past periods is not an insuperable problem. It should, however, be noted that the three-month qualifying period (six months for people over 65) is normally before the date of claim, so to that extent, claims can be regarded as being backdated over that period. There is also some further flexibility. Reg.6(1)(a) of the Claims and Payments Regulations 1987 provides that a claim shall be treated as made on the date it is received in an appropriate office of the Department of Social Security. Reg.4(1) requires a claim to be made in writing either on a claim form or in such other manner as the Secretary of State may accept as sufficient. If the Secretary of State does not accept a document as a claim, he may ask the claimant to complete a proper claim form or simply to give further information. If that is done within a reasonable period, the claim is then treated as having been made when the original document was received (regs 4(7) and 6(1)(b)). More specific provision is made in respect of DLA and attendance allowance in reg.6(8) under which a claim is treated as having been made when a request for a claim form is received by the Department, provided that the claimant duly completes and returns the claim form within six weeks or such longer period as the Secretary of State considers reasonable. Leaflets widely available to claimants include requests for claim forms rather than claim forms themselves which are bulky documents. If a claim is delayed in the post owing to industrial action, it is treated as having been made on the date it would have arrived in the ordinary course of post (reg.6(7)). Until October 6, 1997, reg.5 of the DLA Regulations, made under subs.(2), allowed a claim to be backdated to the end of a previous period of entitlement to the same component of DLA, provided that the renewal claim was made within six months of the end of that period of entitlement and the claimant satisfied the conditions of entitlement throughout the intervening period. For these purposes, a previous period of entitlement to attendance allowance was treated as a period of entitlement to the care component and a previous period of entitlement to mobility allowance was treated as a period of entitlement to the mobility component.

Subs.(3)

This is necessary to enable a person to make a claim for DLA on behalf of someone who is terminally ill in a case when the claimant is not to be told of the prognosis in his case.

1.271

Guardian's allowance

Guardian's allowance

77. *Omitted.* See *Vol.IV: Tax Credits and HMRC-administered Social Security Benefits.*

1.272

Benefits for the aged

Category C and Category D retirement pensions and other benefits for the aged

78.—(1) A person who was over pensionable age on 5th July 1948 and who satisfies such conditions as may be prescribed shall be entitled to a Category C retirement pension at the appropriate weekly rate.

1.273

(2) If a woman whose husband is entitled to a Category C retirement pension—

(a) is over pensionable age; and

(b) satisfies such other conditions as may be prescribed,

she shall be entitled to a Category C retirement pension at the appropriate weekly rate.

(3) A person who is over the age of 80 and satisfies such conditions as may be prescribed shall be entitled to a Category D retirement pension at the appropriate weekly rate if—

(a) he is not entitled to a Category A, Category B or Category C retirement pension; or

(b) he is entitled to such a pension, but it is payable at a weekly rate which, disregarding those elements specified in subsection (4) below, is less than the appropriate weekly rate.

(4) The elements referred to in subsection (3)(b) above are—
(a) any additional pension;
(b) any increase so far as attributable to—
    (i) any additional pension, or
    (ii) any increase in a guaranteed minimum pension;
(c) any graduated retirement benefit; and
(d) [² . . .]
(5) The appropriate weekly rate of a Category C retirement pension—
(a) shall be the lower rate specified in Schedule 4, Part III, paragraph 6, where—
    (i) the pensioner is a married woman, and
    (ii) she has not, at any time since she became entitled to her pension, ceased to be a married woman; and
(b) shall be the higher rate so specified in any other case.
(6) The appropriate weekly rate of a Category D retirement pension shall be that specified in Schedule 4, Part III, paragraph 7.
(7) Entitlement to a Category C or Category D retirement pension shall continue throughout the pensioner's life.
(8) A Category C or Category D retirement pension shall not be payable for any period falling before the day on which the pensioner's entitlement is to be regarded as commencing for that purpose by virtue of section 5(1)(k) of the Administration Act.
(9) Regulations may provide for the payment—
(a) to a widow whose husband was over pensionable age on 5th July 1948; or
(b) to a woman whose marriage to a husband who was over pensionable age on that date was terminated otherwise than by his death.
of a Category C retirement pension or of benefit corresponding to a widow's pension or a widowed mother's allowance; and any such retirement pension or any such benefit shall be at the prescribed rate.

AMENDMENTS

1. Tax Credits Act 2002, Sch.6 (April 6, 2003).
2. Pensions Act 2007, Sch.1, para.13 (September 26, 2007).

DERIVATION

1.274   SSA 1975, s.39.

GENERAL NOTE

1.275   This section may be affected, in appropriate cases, by the operation of the Gender Recognition Act 2004. See notes to that Act.

Age addition

1.276   **79.**—(1) A person who is over the age of 80 and entitled to a retirement pension of any category shall be entitled to an increase of the pension, to be known as "age addition".
(2) Where a person is in receipt of a pension or allowance payable by the Secretary of State by virtue of any prescribed enactment or instrument (whether passed or made before or after this Act) and—
(a) he is over the age of 80; and

(b) he fulfils such other conditions as may be prescribed, he shall be entitled to an increase of that pension or allowance, also known as age addition.

(3) Age addition shall be payable for the life of the person entitled, at the weekly rate specified in Schedule 4, Part III, paragraph 8.

DERIVATION

SSA 1975, s.40.   1.277

PART IV

INCREASES FOR DEPENDANTS

Child dependants

Beneficiary's dependent children

80. [¹ . . .]   1.278

AMENDMENT

1. Repealed by the Tax Credits Act 2002, s.60 and Sch.6 (April 6, 2003).

SAVING

Article.3 of The Tax Credits Act 2002 (Commencement No. 3 and Transitional Provisions and Savings) Order 2003 (SI 2003/938) provides:

"Saving provision

3.—(1) Notwithstanding the coming into force of the specified provisions, the   1.279
Contributions and Benefits Act and the Administration Act shall, in cases to which paragraph (2) applies, subject to paragraph (3), continue to have effect from the commencement date as if those provisions had not come into force.

(2) This paragraph applies where a person—
(a) is entitled to a relevant increase on the day before the commencement date; or
(b) claims a relevant increase on or after the commencement date and it is subsequently determined that he is entitled to a relevant increase in respect of a period which includes the day before the commencement date.

(3) The provisions saved by paragraph (1) shall continue to have effect until—
(a) subject to sub-paragraph (c), where a relevant increase ceases to be payable to a person to whom paragraph (2) applies for a period greater than 58 days beginning with the day on which it was last payable, on the day 59 days after the day on which it was last payable; or
(b) in any other case, subject to sub-paragraph (c), on the date on which entitlement to a relevant increase ceases;
(c) where regulation 6(19) or (23) of the Social Security (Claims and Payments) Regulations 1987 applies to a further claim for a relevant increase, on the date on which entitlement to that relevant increase ceases.

(4) In this article—
"the commencement date" means 6th April 2003;
"a relevant increase" means an increase under section 80 or 90 of the Contributions and Benefits Act;

"the specified provisions" means the provisions of the 2002 Act which are brought into force by article 2."

GENERAL NOTE

1.280   The operation of section 80 is preserved in the circumstances specified in this savings provision. Section 80(4) set out income limits above which no child dependency increase are payable. The figures in that subsection are uprated for those cases where the savings provision applies. From the first day of the first benefit week to start for a particular beneficiary on or after April 1, 2009, the relevant figures are earnings of £195.00 per week in respect of the first child, and in respect of a further child for each complete £26.00 by which the earnings exceed £195.00: The Social Security Benefits Uprating Order 2009/(SI 2009/497).

Restrictions on increase—child not living with beneficiary etc.

1.281   **81.** [¹ . . .]

AMENDMENT

1. Repealed by the Tax Credits Act 2002, s.60 and Sch.6 (April 6, 2003).

SAVING

Art.3 of The Tax Credits Act 2002 (Commencement No.3 and Transitional Provisions and Savings) Order 2003 (SI 2003/938) provides:

"Saving provision

1.282   **3.**—(1) Notwithstanding the coming into force of the specified provisions, the Contributions and Benefits Act and the Administration Act shall, in cases to which paragraph (2) applies, subject to paragraph (3), continue to have effect from the commencement date as if those provisions had not come into force.

(2) This paragraph applies where a person—

(a) is entitled to a relevant increase on the day before the commencement date; or

(b) claims a relevant increase on or after the commencement date and it is subsequently determined that he is entitled to a relevant increase in respect of a period which includes the day before the commencement date.

(3) The provisions saved by paragraph (1) shall continue to have effect until—

(a) subject to sub-paragraph (c), where a relevant increase ceases to be payable to a person to whom paragraph (2) applies for a period greater than 58 days beginning with the day on which it was last payable, on the day 59 days after the day on which it was last payable; or

(b) in any other case, subject to sub-paragraph (c), on the date on which entitlement to a relevant increase ceases;

(c) where regulation 6(19) or (23) of the Social Security (Claims and Payments) Regulations 1987 applies to a further claim for a relevant increase, on the date on which entitlement to that relevant increase ceases.

(4) In this article—

"the commencement date" means 6th April 2003;

"a relevant increase" means an increase under section 80 or 90 of the
Contributions and Benefits Act;
"the specified provisions" means the provisions of the 2002 Act which
are brought into force by article 2."

Adult dependants

Short-term benefit: increase for adult dependants

82.—(1) [1] . . .   1.283
[[2] (2) Subject, in particular, to subsection (5) and section 87 below,
the weekly rate of a maternity allowance shall be increased by the amount
specified in relation to that benefit in Schedule 4, Part IV, column (3) ("the
amount of the relevant increase") for any period to which this subsection
applies by virtue of subsection (3) or (4) below.]

(3) Subsection (2) above applies by virtue of this subsection to any period
during which—

(a) the beneficiary's husband [[3] or civil partner] does not have weekly
earnings which exceed the amount of the relevant increase, and
(b) either she and her husband [[3] or civil partner] are residing together
or she is contributing to [[3] her husband's or civil partner's] maintenance at a weekly rate not less than that amount.

(4) Subsection (2) above applies by virtue of this subsection to any period
during which a person—

(a) who is neither the spouse [[3] or civil partner] of the beneficiary nor a
child [[4] or qualifying young person], and
(b) in respect of whom such further conditions as may be prescribed are
fulfilled, has the care of [[4] one or more children or qualifying young
persons] in respect of whom the beneficiary is entitled to child benefit.

(5) A beneficiary shall not under subsection (2) above be entitled for the
same period to an increase of benefit in respect of more than one person.

AMENDMENTS

1. Jobseekers Act 1995, Sch.3 (October 7, 1996).
2. Jobseekers Act 1995, Sch.2, para.24 (October 7, 1996).
3. Civil Partnership Act 2004, s.254 and Sch.24, para.35 (December 5, 2005).
4. Child Benefit Act 2005 c.6, Sch.1, Part I, para.5 (April 10, 2006).

DERIVATION

SSA, 1975, s.44 as amended.   1.284

DEFINITIONS

"beneficiary"—s.122.
"benefit"—s.122.
"earnings"—s.122 and s.3.
"employment"—s.122.

GENERAL NOTE

This section relates to maternity allowance; in its earlier guises it applied to a   1.285
wider range of short-term benefits. A claimant for one of these benefits can claim an
increase for a spouse or civil partner where:

(1) either the couple are living together: subss.(1)(a)(i) and (3), or, if they are separated, the claimant is paying weekly maintenance at a level at least equal to the increase: subss.(1)(a)(ii) and (3), *and*

(2) the total weekly earnings of the spouse or civil partner do not exceed the amount of the increase: subss.(1)(b) and (3).

But the section applies to more than just couples. It extends by virtue of subs.(4) to an increase for any one adult (who need not be related to the claimant) looking after children in those cases where no increase for a spouse or civil partner is payable. In Commissioner's Decision *CS/726/49* the Commissioner defined "having the care of a child" as importing the performance of "those duties for a child, with which a child needs assistance because he or she is a child, or exercises that supervision over a child which is one of the needs of childhood" (para.11). The adult must be residing with the claimant or be maintained by the claimant at a level at least equivalent to the addition or be employed by the claimant at a cost at least equivalent to the addition and that adult must not have earnings from other sources in excess of the amount of the addition: reg.10, Dependency Regulations.

References to "earnings" include payments by way of occupational or personal pension: s.89.

Earnings will be calculated according to the Computation of Earnings Regulations 1996. Employment under Sch.20 is to include any trade, profession, office or vocation. It is suggested that there is no material difference between the two definitions of earnings.

References to periods when a person is not engaged in employment include periods when a person is not entitled to any payment of occupational pension: s.89.

On "residing together", see the Persons Residing Together Regulations.

Regulation 3 of the Dependency Regulations contains rules relating to the allocation of contributions and reg.14 with cases where the contribution conditions for the main benefit are only partially satisfied.

Regs.4A and 4B deal with deemed entitlements to child benefit. The section is also made subject to the exclusion in s.87 and reg.13 of the Dependency Regulations.

Pension increase (wife)

1.286

83.—(1) This section applies to—
(a) a Category A or Category C retirement pension;
[¹ . . .]

(2) Subject to subsection (3) below, the weekly rate of a pension to which this section applies, when payable to a man, shall be increased by the amount specified in relation to the pension in Schedule 4, Part IV, column (3)—
(a) for any period during which the pensioner is residing with his wife; or
(b) for any period during which the pensioner is contributing to the maintenance of his wife at a weekly rate not less than that amount, and his wife does not have weekly earnings which exceed that amount.

(3) Regulations may provide that for any period during which the pensioner is residing with his wife and his wife has earnings—
(a) the increase of benefit under this section shall be subject to a reduction in respect of the wife's earnings; or
(b) there shall be no increase of benefit under this section.

AMENDMENT

1. Social Security (Incapacity for Work) Act 1994, Sch.2, para.1 (April 13, 1995).

GENERAL NOTE

This section will cease to have effect on April 6, 2010 under s.4, Pensions Act 2007.

1.287

Pension increase (husband)

84.—(1) Where a Category A retirement pension is payable to a woman for any period—

1.288

[¹ (a) which began immediately on the termination of a period for which the pensioner was entitled to an increase in incapacity benefit by virtue of any provision of regulations under section 86A below prescribed for the purposes of this paragraph, and]

(b) during which the requirements of either paragraph (a) or (b) of subsection (2) below are satisfied (without interruption),

then the weekly rate of the pensioner's Category A retirement pension shall be increased by the amount specified in relation to that pension in Schedule 4, Part IV, column (3) ("the specified amount").

(2) The requirements referred to in subsection (1)(b) above are—

(a) that the pensioner is residing with her husband;

(b) that the pensioner is contributing to the maintenance of her husband at a weekly rate not less than the specified amount, and her husband does not have weekly earnings which exceed that amount.

(3) Regulations may provide that for any period during which the pensioner is residing with her husband and her husband has earnings—

(a) the increase of benefit under this section shall be subject to a reduction in respect of the husband's earnings; or

(b) there shall be no increase of benefit under this section.

AMENDMENT

1. Jobseekers Act 1995, Sch.2, para.25 (October 7, 1996).

GENERAL NOTE

This section will cease to have effect on April 6, 2010 under s.4, Pensions Act 2007.

1.289

Pension increase (person with care of children [¹ or qualifying young person])

85.—[² . . .]

1.290

[³ (1A) Subject to subsections (2A) and (4) below, the weekly rate of a Category A retirement pension shall be increased by the amount specified in relation to that pension in Schedule 4, Part 4, column (3) for any period during which a person who is neither the spouse or civil partner of the pensioner nor a child has the care of a child or children in respect of whom the pensioner is entitled to child benefit.]

(2) Subject to [³ subsections (3) and (4) below], the weekly rate of a [³ Category C retirement pension payable by virtue of section 78(1) above] shall be increased by the amount specified in relation to that pension in Schedule 4, Part IV, column (3) , for any period during which a person who is neither the spouse of the pensioner nor a child [⁴ or qualifying young person] has the care of [⁴ one or more children or qualifying young persons] in respect of whom the pensioner is entitled to child benefit.

[³ (2A) Subsection (1A) above does not apply if the pensioner is a person whose spouse or civil partner is entitled to a Category B retirement pension, or to a Category C retirement pension by virtue of section 78(2) above or in such other cases as may be prescribed.]

(3) Subsection (2) above does not apply if the pensioner is a [⁵ person whose spouse] is entitled to a Category B retirement pension, or to a Category C retirement pension by virtue of section 78(2) above or in such other cases as may be prescribed.

(4) Regulations may, in a case within subsection [³ (1A) or] (2) above in which the person there referred to is residing with the pensioner and fulfils such further conditions as may be prescribed, authorise an increase of benefit under this section, but subject, taking account of the earnings of the person residing with the pensioner, other than such of that person's earnings as may be prescribed, to provisions comparable to those that may be made by virtue of section 83(3) above.

AMENDMENTS

1. Child Benefit Act 2005, Sch.1(1), para.6(3) (March 25, 2005 for purposes of making regulations; April 10, 2006 otherwise).
2. Civil Partnership Act 2004, Sch.30, para.1 (December 5, 2005).
3. Civil Partnership Act 2004, Sch.24(3), para.37 (December 5, 2005).
4. Child Benefit Act 2005, Sch.1(1), para.6(2) (March 25, 2005 for purposes of making regulations; April 10, 2006 otherwise).
5. Pensions Act 1995, Sch.4(III), para.21(10) (July 19, 1995).

GENERAL NOTE

1.291   This section will cease to have effect on April 6, 2010 under s.4, Pensions Act 2007.

Incapacity benefit—increases for adult dependants

1.292   [¹ **86A.**—(1) The weekly rates of short-term and long-term incapacity benefit shall, in such circumstances as may be prescribed, be increased for adult dependants by the appropriate amounts specified in relation to benefit of that description in Schedule 4, Part IV, column (3).

(2) Regulations may provide that where the person in respect of whom an increase of benefit is claimed has earnings in excess of such amount as may be prescribed there shall be no increase in benefit under this section.]

AMENDMENT

1. Social Security (Incapacity for Work) Act 1994, s.2(5) (November 18, 1994 for regulation-making purposes; April 13, 1995 for other purposes).

GENERAL NOTE

1.293   See the Social Security (Incapacity Benefit—Increases for Dependants) Regulations 1994 (SI 1994/2945) reproduced later in this book.

Rate of increase where associated retirement pension is attributable to reduced contributions

1.294   87.—(1) Where a person—
[¹ (a) is entitled to a short-term incapacity benefit under section 30A(2)
         (b); and]

(b) would have been entitled only by virtue of section 60(1) above to the retirement pension by reference to which the rate of that benefit [² . . .] is determined,

the amount of any increase of the benefit attributable to sections 82 to [³ 85] above shall be determined in accordance with regulations under this section.

(2) The regulations shall not provide for any such increase in a case where the retirement pension by reference to which the rate of the said benefit [² . . .] or invalidity pension is determined—

(a) would have been payable only by virtue of section 60 above; and
(b) would, in consequence of a failure to satisfy a contribution condition, have contained no basic pension.

AMENDMENTS

1. Jobseekers Act 1995, Sch.2, para.26 (October 7, 1996).
2. Social Security (Incapacity for Work) Act 1994, Sch.1, para.24(3) and Sch.2 (April 13, 1995).
3. Welfare Reform Act 2007 s.28 and Sch.3, para.9(7) (October 27, 2008).

DERIVATION

SSA, 1975, s.47A as amended.   1.295

GENERAL NOTE

See reg.13 of the Dependency Regulations.   1.296

Increases to be in respect of only one adult dependant

[¹ 88. A person shall not [³ by virtue of [⁴ sections 83 to 85]] above be   1.297
entitled for the same period to an increase of benefit in respect of more than
one person.]

AMENDMENTS

1. Social Security (Incapacity for Work) Act 1994, Sch.1, para.25 (April 13, 1995).
2. Pensions Act 1995, Sch.4, para.18(e) The reference to s.83 is to be replaced by a reference to s.83A with effect from April 6, 2010.
3. Pensions Act 2007, Sch.1, para.14 (September 26, 2007).
4. Welfare Reform Act 2007, Sch.3, para.9(7) (October 27, 2008).

DERIVATION

SSA, 1975, s.48.   1.298

Miscellaneous

Earnings to include occupational and personal pensions [³ etc.] for purposes of provisions relating to increases of benefits in respect of [¹. . .] adult dependants

89.—(1) Except as may be prescribed, in [¹ . . .] [² [⁴ sections 82 [⁵ to 85]]   1.299
above, any reference to earnings includes a reference to payments by way of
occupational or personal pension.

[³ (1A) Except as may be prescribed, in [⁴ sections 82 [⁵ to 85]] above, and in regulations under section 86A above, any reference to earnings includes a reference to payments by way of PPF periodic payments.]

(2) For the purposes of the provisions mentioned in [³ subsections (1) and (1A) above], the Secretary of State may by regulations provide, in relation to cases where payments by way of occupational or personal pension [³ or PPF periodic payments] are made otherwise than weekly, that any necessary apportionment of the payments shall be made in such manner and on such basis as may be prescribed.

[³ (3) In this section "PPF periodic payments" means—

(a) any periodic compensation payments made in relation to a person, payable under the pension compensation provisions as specified in section 162(2) of the Pensions Act 2004 or Article 146(2) of the Pensions (Northern Ireland) order 2005 (the pension compensation provisions); OR

(b) any periodic payments made in relation to a person, payable under section 166 of the Pensions Act 2004 or Article 150 of the Pensions (Northern Ireland) Order 2005 (duty to pay scheme benefits unpaid at assessment date etc.),

other than payments made to a surviving dependant of a person entitled to such compensation.]

AMENDMENTS

1. Tax Credits Act 2002, s.60 and Sch.6 (April 6, 2003).
2. Social Security (Incapacity for Work) Act 1994, Sch.1, para.26 (April 13, 1995).
3. The Pensions Act 2004 (PPF Payments and FAS Payments) (Consequential Provisions) Order 2006 (SI 2006/343) (February 14, 2006).
4. Pensions Act 2007, Sch.1, para.15 (September 26, 2007).
5. Welfare Reform Act 2007, s.28 and Sch.3, para.9(8) (October 27, 2008).

DERIVATION

1.300   SSA, 1975, s.47B as amended.

GENERAL NOTE

1.301   In *R(U) 1/89* it was held that payments under a Civil Service pension have sufficient cognate features with payments under ordinary occupational pensions to bring them within the ambit of the term "payments by way of occupational pension" in s.5 of the SS (No. 2) A 1980. By analogy they will fall to be treated as payments by way of occupational pension under the provisions of this Part of this Act.

Beneficiaries under sections 68 and 70

1.302   **90.**—The weekly [¹ rate]—
(a) [¹. . .]
(b) of [² a carer's allowance],
shall, in such circumstances as may be prescribed, be increased for [³ . . .] adult dependants by the appropriate amount specified in relation to the allowance [¹ . . .] in Schedule 4, Part IV.

AMENDMENTS

1. Welfare Reform and Pensions Act 1999, Sch.8, para.26 (April 9, 2001).

2. The Regulatory Reform (Carer's Allowance) Order 2002 (SI 2002/1457), art.2(2) and Sch. paras 1 and 2(d) (April 1, 2003).

3. Tax Credits Act 2002, Sch 6 (April 6 2003).

DERIVATION

SSA, 1975, s.49 as amended.   1.303

GENERAL NOTE

The relevant regulations are the Social Security Benefits (Dependency)   1.304
Regulations 1977, reproduced later in this volume.

Effect of trade disputes on entitlement to increases

91.—(1) A beneficiary shall not be entitled—   1.305
  (a) to an increase in any benefit [¹ under or by virtue of sections 82 to 88 above]; or
  (b) to an increase in benefit [² . . .] by virtue of regulations under section 90 above,
if the person in respect of whom he would be entitled to the increase falls within subsection (2) below.

[³(2) A person falls within this subsection if—
  (a) he is prevented from being entitled to a jobseeker's allowance by section 14 of the Jobseekers Act 1995 (trade disputes); or
  (b) he would be so prevented if he were otherwise entitled to that benefit.]

AMENDMENTS

1. Social Security (Incapacity for Work) Act 1994, Sch.1, para.27 (April 13, 1995).

2. Tax Credits Act 2002, s.60 and Sch.6.

3. Jobseekers Act 1995, Sch.2, para.27 (October 7, 1996).

DERIVATION

SSA, 1975, s.49A as amended.   1.306

GENERAL NOTE

This section provides that no increases of benefit are payable in respect of any   1.307
person caught by the disqualification for receiving jobseeker's allowance under s.14
of the Jobseekers Act 1995 or who would be so disqualified if otherwise entitled to
that benefit.

See annotations to s.14 of the Jobseekers Act 1995 in *Vol.II: Income Support, Jobseeker's Allowance, State Pension Credit and the Social Fund.*

SAVING

In relation to the deletion of the words "for an adult dependant" in subs.(1)(b),
there is a saving provided in art.3 of The Tax Credits Act 2002 (Commencement
No. 3 and Transitional Provisions and Savings) Order 2003 (SI 2003/938) which
provides:

"Saving provision
3.—(1) Notwithstanding the coming into force of the specified provisions, the   1.308
Contributions and Benefits Act and the Administration Act shall, in cases to which
paragraph (2) applies, subject to paragraph (3), continue to have effect from the
commencement date as if those provisions had not come into force.

(2) This paragraph applies where a person—
(a) is entitled to a relevant increase on the day before the commencement date; or
(b) claims a relevant increase on or after the commencement date and it is subsequently determined that he is entitled to a relevant increase in respect of a period which includes the day before the commencement date.
(3) The provisions saved by paragraph (1) shall continue to have effect until—
(a) subject to sub-paragraph (c), where a relevant increase ceases to be payable to a person to whom paragraph (2) applies for a period greater than 58 days beginning with the day on which it was last payable, on the day 59 days after the day on which it was last payable; or
(b) in any other case, subject to sub-paragraph (c), on the date on which entitlement to a relevant increase ceases;
(c) where regulation 6(19) or (23) of the Social Security (Claims and Payments) Regulations 1987[4] applies to a further claim for a relevant increase, on the date on which entitlement to that relevant increase ceases.
(4) In this article—
"the commencement date" means 6th April 2003;
"a relevant increase" means an increase under section 80 or 90 of the Contributions and Benefits Act;
"the specified provisions" means the provisions of the 2002 Act which are brought into force by article 2."

Dependency increases: continuation of awards in cases of fluctuating earnings

1.309   **92.**—(1) Where a beneficiary—
(a) has been awarded an increase of benefit under this Part of this Act, but
(b) ceases to be entitled to the increase by reason only that the weekly earnings of some other person ("the relevant earner") exceed the amount of the increase or, as the case may be, some specified amount,
then, if and so long as the beneficiary would have continued to be entitled to the increase, disregarding any such excess of earnings, the award shall continue in force but the increase shall not be payable for any week if the earnings relevant to that week exceed the amount of the increase or, as the case may be, the specified amount.
(2) In this section the earnings which are relevant to any week are those earnings of the relevant earner which, apart from this section, would be taken into account in determining whether the beneficiary is entitled to the increase in question for that week.

DERIVATION

1.310   SSA, 1975, s.84A as amended.

GENERAL NOTE

1.311   The meaning of this section is obscure. Nor is its relationship with reg.8(3) of the Computation of Earnings Regulations entirely clear. The difficulty arises because of the use of the term "fluctuating earnings" in the title of the section and the reference to fluctuating earnings in reg.8(3). Correspondence with the Department for Work and Pensions has revealed that its operation in practice is very different from that set out in the commentary in earlier editions. The Department's view is that the notion of fluctuating earnings in s.92 is different from the notion of earnings which fluctuate in reg.8(3). The view of the Department is that s.92 is intended to cover the situation where an award of a dependency increase is made

196

where the dependent person is either not earning or is earning under the earnings limit for the award, and on a later date becomes an earner with earnings over the earnings limit. This is what is intended by the reference in the title to the section to fluctuating. In such a situation entitlement continues but payment will cease for the period in which the earnings limit is exceeded, but can be resurrected when the earnings fall below the limit (presumably without the need for a fresh claim).

The practice of the Department is described in the correspondence as follows.

"In terms of section 92 . . . we have always operated on the basis that, for dependency benefit purposes, entitlement, once established, always exists and it is only the payment which is disqualified for the weeks following any periods during which the dependant's earnings exceeds the specified amount. In this event any change in earnings which takes the earnings over the limit or reduces them to under the limit will be grounds to review (supersede) the award to either disqualify or reinstate payment. The date of change will be that determined under the [Computation of Earnings] Regulations. In cases of actual fluctuating earnings there can be no continuation of payment until a permanent change can be established. The weekly rate of earnings are established under the provisions of regulation 8 of the above Regulations and the date on which a particular payment of earnings is due determines the date on which a disqualification of payment of dependency increase is imposed or removed."

Dependency increases on termination of employment after period of entitlement to disability working allowance

93.—Where—   1.312
  (a) [¹ a person becomes entitled—
      (i) to the higher rate of short-term incapacity benefit, or to long-term incapacity benefit, by virtue of section 30C(5) or (6) or section 42 above,] [² . . .]
  (b) when he was last entitled to that [³ benefit or] allowance, it was increased in respect of a dependant by virtue of—
      (i) regulation 8(6) of the Social Security Benefit (Dependency) Regulations 1977;
      (ii) regulation 2 of the Social Security (Savings for Existing Beneficiaries) Regulations 1984;
      (iii) regulation 3 of the Social Security Benefit (Dependency) Amendment Regulations 1984; or
      (iv) regulation 4 of the Social Security Benefit (Dependency and Computation of Earnings) Amendment Regulations 1989,
for the purpose of determining whether his [³ benefit] [² . . .] should be increased by virtue of that regulation for any period beginning with the day on which he again becomes entitled to his [³ benefit] [² . . .] the increase in respect of that dependant shall be treated as having been payable to him on each day between the last day on which his [³ benefit] [² . . .] was previously payable and the day on which he again becomes entitled to it.

AMENDMENTS

1. Social Security (Incapacity for Work) Act 1994, Sch.1, para.28(a) (April 13, 1995).
2. Welfare Reform and Pensions Act 1999, Sch.13, Pt IV (April 6, 2001).
3. Social Security (Incapacity for Work) Act 1994, Sch.1, para.28(b) (April 13, 1995).

DERIVATION

1.313   DLADWAA 1991, s.9(5).

GENERAL NOTE

1.314   Disability working allowance (now disabled person's tax credit) was a benefit modelled on family credit designed to top up low pay received by people who are disabled. In order to encourage those who are disabled to engage in work, a special rule concerning requalification for a benefit connected with the disability is provided in s.42 if they leave that work within a two-year period. They become immediately qualified to receive the benefit they were receiving before becoming in receipt of disability working allowance.

The rule in this section simply allows such persons to receive any increases of the benefit in respect of dependants.

The section has not yet been amended on the introduction of disabled person's tax credit to replace disability working allowance, nor on its replacement by the disability component of working tax credit.

PART V

BENEFIT FOR INDUSTRIAL INJURIES

General provisions

Right to industrial injuries benefit

1.315   **94.**—(1) Industrial injuries benefit shall be payable where an employed earner suffers personal injury caused after 4th July 1948 by accident arising out of and in the course of his employment, being employed earner's employment.

(2) Industrial injuries benefit consists of the following benefits—

(a) disablement benefit payable in accordance with sections 103 to 105 below, paragraphs 2 and 3 of Schedule 7 below and Parts II and III of that Schedule;

(b) reduced earnings allowance payable in accordance with Part IV;

(c) retirement allowance payable in accordance with Part V; and

(d) industrial death benefit, payable in accordance with Part VI.

(3) For the purposes of industrial injuries benefit an accident arising in the course of an employed earner's employment shall be taken, in the absence of evidence to the contrary, also to have arisen out of that employment.

(4) Regulations may make provision as to the day which, in the case of night workers and other special cases, is to be treated for the purposes of industrial injuries benefit as the day of the accident.

(5) Subject to sections 117, 119 and 120 below, industrial injuries benefit shall not be payable in respect of an accident happening while the earner is outside Great Britain.

(6) In the following provisions of this Part of this Act "work" in the contexts "incapable of work" and "incapacity for work" means work which the person in question can be reasonably expected to do.

DERIVATION

SSA 1975, s.50 as amended.

DEFINITIONS

"employed earner"—see s.2(1)(a), above.
"employed earner's employment"—see s.95, below.
"work"—see subs.(6).

GENERAL NOTE

This section contains the basic elements of the industrial injuries scheme. The scheme has undergone significant change. Injury benefit was abolished in 1982; death benefit was abolished (in respect of deaths occurring on or after April 11, 1988) in April 1988; title to disablement benefit was substantially diminished by provisions in the SSA 1986 which are dealt with below.

On July 5, 1999, AOs' functions with respect to industrial injuries benefits and the making of an industrial accident declaration were transferred to the Secretary of State (SSA 1998, ss.1, 8 and Commencement Order No. 8). He may, however, refer certain issues for report to a medical practitioner who has experience of the issues. The issues so referable are:

(a) the extent of a personal injury for the purposes of s.94;

(b) whether the claimant has a prescribed industrial disease and the extent of resulting disablement; and

(c) whether, for disablement benefit purposes, the claimant has a disablement and its extent (Decisions and Appeals Regulations 1999, reg.12).

Decisions on industrial injuries benefits and on the matter of an industrial accident declaration are appealable to a "unified" appeal tribunal composed of a legally qualified member and up to two medically qualified members (SSA 1998, ss.4, 12, Schs 2 and 3; Decisions and Appeals Regulations 1999, reg.36(2)). Like the Secretary of State, that tribunal is competent to deal with both the medical and non-medical aspect of industrial injuries matters. Note, however, that whether a claimant is an employed or self-employed earner, and whether a specific employment is, or is not, employed earner's employment, is to be decided not by the Secretary of State, but by officers of the Board of Inland Revenue (Social Security Contributions (Transfer of Functions, etc.) Act 1999, s.8(1)). Accordingly, such decisions are not matters of appeal for the "unified" appeal tribunal but rather for appeal to the tax appeal Commissioners (*ibid.*, s.11). Such decisions and appeals are regulated by the Social Security Contributions (Decisions and Appeals) Regulations 1999 (SI 1999/1027).

The key point from all this for industrial injuries matters, is that the distinction between medical issues (the disablement questions) and non-medical issues—previously crucial as demarcating the respective jurisdictions of MATs and SSATs—is no longer relevant.

Both the unified tribunal and the Commissioners now have jurisdiction over medical and non-medical matters. A Commissioner, allowing an appeal on a point of law, can now take his or her own decision on the facts rather than remitting it to another tribunal. Commissioner Williams did so in *CI/1307/1999* giving a staged assessment of disablement in respect of post-traumatic stress disorder. The decision considers the medical aspects of the claimant's case found to be an industrial accident in *CI/15589/1996*, noted on pp.197–198, below. In paras 15–17, Commissioner Williams distinguished 'diagnosis' and 'disablement' decisions. The former is essentially "a question of medical expertise". A "disablement" decision in contrast is not dissimilar to the tasks performed by judges in assessing common law damages or in applying the tariff of the Criminal Injuries Compensation Authority. In assessing disablement for industrial injuries benefits, however, that Criminal Injuries tariff is not an appropriate yardstick. Instead, supplementing SSCBA 1992, s.103 and Sch.6, regard should be had also to reg.11 and Sch.2 to the General Benefit Regulations, below. Nonetheless, the import of para.37 of the decision is that exercise of the Commissioner's power to decide on the facts available, rather than remitting to another tribunal, may well be rare. Even so, the decision contrasts markedly with the traditional view of such matters as ones for medical rather than legal judgment (see, for example, Commissioner Howell in *CI/636/93*). Note that the suitability of cross-reference to Sch.2 was also advocated in *R(I) 5/95*, where Commissioner Rowland stated that "assessment of disablement should be brought into line with those prescribed in the Schedule", with assessment also reflecting any intermittent or episodic character of the disablement (para.16).

Subs. (1)

1.318   Whilst it is possible to divide this subsection conveniently for explanation, there is some overlap between the various conditions of entitlement and the temptation to categorise issues *too* rigidly should be avoided. To qualify for benefit: (i) the claimant must be an employed earner . . . [in] employed earner's employment; (ii) the claimant must suffer personal injury caused (after July 4, 1948) by accident; (iii) [the accident] must be arising out of and in the course of his [employed earner's] employment.

"Employed earner . . . employed earner's employment"

1.319   The definition of employed earner in s.2(1)(a), above, applies. Power is given to the Secretary of State to make regulations providing that certain employment shall (or shall not) be treated as employed earner's employment (see note to s.95, below). Whether a specific employment is, or is not, employed earner's employment is determined solely by officers of the Board of Inland Revenue.

The employment that the accident occurs in must be employed earner's employment.

"Suffers personal injury caused (after 4th July 1948) by accident"

1.320   *Suffers personal injury:* The injury must be to the living body of a human being. Damage to some artificial appendage of the body (spectacles, false teeth, etc.) is not enough (*R(I) 7/56, R(I) 1/82*), unless the appendage is so intimately linked with the body so as to form a part of it (*R(I) 5/81*—damage to artificial hip joint held to be personal injury). Damage to an artificial limb *may* constitute personal injury depending on the circumstances. (How should damage to a heart pacemaker be treated?) This situation is less likely to be significant given the abolition of injury benefit because of the short-term nature of damage of this kind. However, the question may arise where the damage causes incapacity for work which lasts longer than 15 weeks (is there entitlement to disablement benefit?), or where the claimant does not meet the contribution conditions for sickness benefit (is the incapacity for work the result of a personal injury?). Despite the demise of sickness benefit on April 13, 1995, the matter retains importance for those who transferred from it or from invalidity benefit to the replacement incapacity benefit, and who are covered by the IW (Transitional) Regulations, below.

The injury must be sufficiently severe to constitute a discernible physiological change for the worse so that a "strain" or an "increase of pain" will not constitute injury unless there is such a change (*R(I) 19/60, R(I) 1/76*). If incapacity is caused by increased or aggravated pain, or the gradual worsening of an existing condition it is also relevant to consider whether the claimant has suffered an accident (see *R(I) 1/76* and notes on "accident" below).

1.321   *By accident:* Leaving the question of causation to the last, the claimant must show that his injury resulted from an identifiable *accident*. Problems arise in defining "accident"; in distinguishing between accident and process; and in cases where suffering the injury is alleged to constitute the accident.

The usual definition of accident is that of Lord MacNaughten in *Fenton v Thorley* [1903] A.C. 443, ". . . an unlooked-for mishap or an untoward event which is neither expected or designed". "Designed" means planned by the claimant and does not exclude him from benefit where the accident has been planned by others (*Trim Joint District School Board v Kelly* [1914] A.C. 667). In *CI/365/89*, Commissioner Skinner, upholding the SSAT's decision that the incidents and events in that case did not constitute an "accident", stated:

"The question of the existence of the personal injury and of its cause or causes is one of fact, but the question as to whether such cause or causes amounts to an accident within the meaning of the [legislation] is a question of law; *Fenton v. Thorley* . . . so decided in relation to the Workmen's Compensation Act and in my judgment that principle is equally applicable to the question which was before the tribunal." (para.6).

One particular claimant tested the definition by alleging, in successive cases that his disability had been caused respectively by the delivery of a letter with bad news in it; the viewing of a television programme in which he was named and his confidential work exposed; and a truculent conversation with a superior at the entrance to his work place. All these contentions were rejected by the Commissioners who held that none of the incidents could constitute an accident for the purpose of the Act (*CI/066/1986*; *CI/2041986*; *CI/236/1987*). In the latter decision, Commissioner Hoolahan cited with approval *CI/7/71*.

A more meritorious claim was upheld in a Commissioner's decision which gives further attention to the meaning of accident. In *CI/387/1988*, the claimant had worked for a long period (15 years) with a substance which subsequently became identified as a carcinogen causing angiosarcoma of the liver. One of his work colleagues contracted angiosarcoma and the claimant visited him in hospital. Sometime later the colleague returned to the workplace to collect his belongings—at that time he was dying and his appearance profoundly upset the claimant. The claimant later sought a declaration, under SSA 1975, s.107 (now SSA 1998, s.29, formerly SSAA 1992, s.44) that his seeing his colleague constituted an accident.

Commissioner Skinner found in favour of the claimant, relying on *Fenton v Thorley* (above) and also held that the accident arose out of the employment, distinguishing *R(I) 22/59*. The case is interesting and merited reporting as one of the few decisions on "accident" and on "out of the employment".

The width and imprecision of the principles on "accident" in *Fenton v Thorley* (above) and *Trim Joint District Schoolboard v Kelly* (above) are apt to cause problems if not approached with a commonsense understanding of the natural everyday sense of the word "accident" (*per* Commissioner Rice in *CI/5249/95*). Hence in *CI/5249/95*, Commissioner Rice rejected the claim that someone, suffering a nervous breakdown on being suspended from work by his employer, had suffered injury through "accident". While the suspension may have been "unexpected" (from the point of view of the claimant), it would fly in the face of the ordinary use of the English language and be regarded as absurd by the man in the street to regard it as an "accident" in the sense used in s.94.

Focusing on the "untoward" aspect of *Trim* and its deployment in respect of vaccinations in *R(I)15/61*, Commissioner Mesher in *CI/732/2007* was of the opinion that a vaccination, administered in the course of employment, to which the claimant had consented, was not an "accident" for the purposes of this section (see paras 14–17). Since she could also not show a personal injury (which might have constituted the accident) flowing from the vaccination, her claim for an industrial accident declaration was rightly rejected by the appeal tribunal.

The "not expected" or "unforeseen" aspect has given some difficulties, in so far as there are some occupations where the risk of some injury might be said to be foreseeable, for example, prison officer, fireman or policeman. The matter has been considered recently in two cases: in *CI/15589/96*, a decision of Commissioner

201

Goodman; and in *CAO v Faulds*, in which the issue was pronounced on both by
the Inner House of the Scottish Court of Session and, on appeal, by the House of
Lords. Both courts emphatically rejected the notion that the nature of such employments precludes incidents being regarded as accidents. In approaching the matter
the emphasis needs to be on the perspective of the "victim"; the incident must not
have been wanted or intended by him. But the House of Lords rightly emphasised
the need for an identifiable accident, in the sense of a particular occurrence or
series of occurrences that can properly, within that perspective, be described as an
"accident".

In *CI/15589/1996* (see further *Jones* (1983) 3 J.S.S.L. 139), Commissioner
Goodman held that an SSAT had erred in law in emphasising too much the notion
of "accident" as an "unforeseen occurrence" so as to reject a claim with respect
to psychological injury or stress reaction by a prison officer as a consequence of a
particular incident in which he placated a prisoner, known to be violent, whom he
feared might throw boiling water over him. The fact that such problems could be
anticipated with that prisoner swayed the SSAT. The Commissioner took the view
that the incident did not come within the normal range of foreseeability, was "so
much out of the normal run of things" that, in the exceptional circumstances of this
case, it properly constituted an "accident". He noted that the notion of accident
does not connote something exceptional or unforeseeable, but can embrace claimants who suffer injury through heavy exertion. Hence "on the proved *and exceptional facts* of this case the claimant has shown that there was an incident *outside the
normal scope of his duties* . . . which did constitute an industrial accident, albeit that
because of the violent nature of the prisoner in question it might have been forsee-
able" (para.12) (emphasis supplied by annotator). More worrying, for those whose
profession puts them at risk of violence, the Commissioner went on to emphasise,
citing Lord Loreburn in *Trim*:

> "that cases of psychological injury or stress reaction resulting from the normal
> incidents of an occupation (and certain occupations have more than others,
> e.g. those of policemen and firemen) will not normally involve an 'accident'
> arising out of and in the course of employment. Thus a policeman who is
> assaulted by a person he is seeking to arrest would not normally have suffered an
> accident. The accepted legal meaning of 'accident', broad though it may be, does
> not extend in my view so far" (para.13).

In the Commissioner's view:

> "a prison officer or someone in a similar occupation must expect certain dan-
> gerous incidents of that employment, which if they occur, cannot properly be
> described as an 'accident' . . . So that [this decision in favour of this particular
> claimant] is no warrant for any proposition that disablement benefit can be
> claimed for 'accident arising out of and in the course of the employment', by
> those involved in occupations where the risk of injury from members of the public
> or from persons with whom they have to deal is a relative commonplace" (paras
> 15, 16).

It remains unclear whether these remarks are limited to psychological injury or
stress reaction or extend to all injury. It is hard to square with the vast array of decisions awarding benefit where one might well say that the injury was an incident of
the job (e.g. in mining or required recreational activity, or the "lifting" cases). It
also sits ill with one Beveridge's rationales for a separate system of industrial injuries
compensation: that persons must be encouraged to enter dangerous professions (see
Wikeley, Ogus and Barendt, p.717).

In *CAO v Faulds* 1998 S.L.T. 1203, 1998 S.C.L.R. 719 (judgments included
in *R(I) 1/00*), the Inner House of the Scottish Court of Session (the equivalent
of the Court of Appeal in England and Wales) affirmed Commissioner Walker's
decision in *CSI/26/96* reported as part of *R(I) 1/00*, that a fireman who suffered

post-traumatic stress disorder after having attended a series of horrific fatalities in the course of his employment had suffered "accidents". The Inner House rejected the argument that, given his special training and the nature of his job, these horrific events did not constitute "accidents". Lord McCluskey said in giving the opinion of the court:

> "we are not persuaded that there is no room for the concept of accident just because the happening or event that causes injury (and even manifests itself only in the injury) is one that may be foreseeable or (and in this regard disa-greeing with certain of the later observations made by the Commissoner in *CI/15589/1996*) one that may be expected to be encountered by a person carrying out normal, hazardous duties. In this respect we agree with Lord Coulsfield's reasoning in *Connelly v. New Hampshire Insurance Co.* A fireman who has to enter a blazing building in order to save life knows that there is some risk that he will be injured by falling debris; but if, to save life, it is decided to go in despite the risk and a fireman while inside is hit and injured by a falling beam, no user of ordinary language could cavil at its being said that the fireman was injured 'by accident'. *In this type of case it is not the foreseeability of the occurrence or the commonness of the hazard that matters so much as the absence of any intention or plan or design that such an event should occur.* Indeed it would be usual to intend to avoid the foreseeable occurrence and to plan the firefighting operation so as to minimise the chances of its occurring. But if, despite the taking of steps to avoid the risk, the unintended occurrence happened, and the fireman was injured, it would be wholly appropri-ate to say that he was injured by accident.
>
> In a case like the present just as in *R(I)22/59*, *CI/15589/1996* and *R(I)43/55*, also quoted to us, the accidental cause is found in the exposure of the employee on one or several—or even many—occasions to shocking sights or other such phenomena, resulting in his suffering a severe—and unintended—nervous reac-tion. We do not consider that the wording of that Act requires that there be found a separable 'accident' in the form of a distinct event separate from the injury and preceding it in point of time. In circumstances in which the horror of the expos-ure triggers a response which takes the form of nervous trauma, the injury and its cause may merge indistinguishably, but the injury may still be properly said to be caused by accident" (1998 S.L.T. 1203, at 1209L–1210D) (emphasis supplied by annotator).

The Secretary of State appealed to the House of Lords. In *CAO v Faulds* [2000] 2 All E.R. 961, reported as *R(I) 1/00*, their Lordships held (Lord Hutton dissenting) that the Inner House had erred in law by not identifying the precise incidents that ranked as accidents. Rather harshly perhaps, the majority considered the Inner House to have erroneously based their decision on the notion that the post-traumatic stress disorder had arisen "accidentally". In essence they referred the case back down the line for evidential findings which would enable resolution of the accident/process issue. But their Lordships all stressed that something which happens as an ordinary element in, or an incident of, an employment can still be an "accident". Lord Hope expressly approved that part of the quotation set out above from the judgment of the Inner House, in which it rejected the CAO's argument "that an injury could not be said to have been sustained 'by accident' where the event or events causing it were foreseeable . . . the sustaining of an *unexpected* personal injury by an *expected* event or incident may itself amount to an accident" ([2000] 2 All E.R. 961 at 969). Lord Clyde (with whose opinion Lords Browne-Wilkinson, Mackay and Hope con-curred), referring to Lord Macnaghten's definition and the *Trim* case, said:

> "The decision in the *Trim* case is important not only in stressing that Lord Macnaghten's formulation is to be taken as descriptive and not definitive, but also in pointing out that the question whether there has been an accident requires particular consideration to be paid to the victim. At least the accident cannot be something he intended to happen. Where his injury came about through the

operation of some external force, that operation must have been something that he did not intend to happen. Where his injury has followed on some action or activity of his own, then the consequences of his doing what he did cannot have been intended by him. The mischance or the mishap was something which was not in any way wanted or intended. It was not meant to happen. . . . Indeed even where it may be foreseen that a person may possibly suffer physical injury in the ordinary course of his work when the incident occurs and injury is sustained it is still proper to recognise that event as an accident. Lord Shaw of Dunfermline gave the examples in this context of prison warders, lunatic asylum attendants and gamekeepers, and the same may hold true of their modern equivalents" ([2000] 2 All E.R. 961 at 978–979).

Lord Hutton, supporting the decision of the Inner House, approved that House's statement cited above, on the basis that "the authorities establish that an accident may happen in the ordinary course of the employee's work" ([2000] 2 All E.R. 961 at 983).

The need for a definition and the overall requirement that the accident should be identifiable reflects the importance of the distinction between injury caused by accident and by process, and between injury happening because of work and happening at work. Title to benefit will depend upon such distinctions.

While most diseases will tend to arise by process rather than accident—and thus be covered under the scheme only if a prescribed industrial disease—this will not invariably be the case. So where a workman was burnt on the lip by a splash of hot metal and the burn became cancerous, that cancer would arise "by accident". Similarly, a stress-related illness can be an industrial accident. Distinguishing *CI/5249/95* on the facts, Commissioner Williams in *CI/2414/98* was not prepared to say that an SSAT had no basis for finding that a claimant who had suffered extreme post-traumatic stress after a particular conversation with a senior colleague had suffered an industrial accident for the purposes of the scheme. The conversation related to a situation which had brought about a period of post-traumatic stress and depression. That situation concerned an industrial dispute during which the claimant, a team leader and deputy manager at an office of the Employment Service, had been given the job of manning the office entrance from early morning to ensure the well-being of non-striking staff crossing the picket-line to come into work. She suffered a high level of abuse from those on the picket-line and was worried by their aggressive behaviour. When she returned to work after her illness she transferred to another job at another office. In the conversation found to be an "accident" she was told by the senior colleague, wrongly as it turned out, that no disciplinary action was to be taken against those abusive and aggressive former colleagues. Commissioner Williams considered the argument that words cannot be, or cause, an industrial accident, with *CI/7/71* being cited in support of the proposition that the phrase "suffers personal injury by accident" cannot cover the use of language alone. Commissioner Williams commented that:

"while that observation may apply to most situations, I do not agree with those views as applied to all forms of personal injury in all circumstances. Given that 'accident' includes deliberate actions, and that words can constitute assault or other crimes to the person, the statement in *CI/7/71* is too general. For example verbal sexual harassment at work might be such in extreme cases as to amount to an accident or series of accidents, as might misinformation designed to shock or causing shock. I note that in the recent decision of *CI/4642/97* and linked cases, the Commissioner reaches the same conclusion. Any claim that words cause an accident must also be taken in context. This conversation reopened an issue that had clearly traumatised the claimant. That is relevant in considering its effect on her. It was not just the words by themselves that must be considered, but the context of those words and what the words concerned" (para.8).

Commissioner Williams pointed out that the incident alleged to constitute an "accident" need not be the sole or main cause of all injury suffered (para.12). Nor was the stressful nature of the claimant's job a relevant factor. This was an unusual case. An appeal to the Court of Appeal by the adjudication officer was not pursued. See also *CI/554/1992*, noted later in this annotation.

In *CI/105/1998*, Commissioner Rowland considered the case of a senior member of the teaching staff of a further education college who suffered from depression following what the tribunal found to be three aggressive and bullying interviews with the principal and vice-principal over a six-month period. The Commissioner declined to find erroneous in law the tribunal's finding that the injury arose through accident rather than process. Accepting *CI/7/71* (on file as *CI/789/70*) as correctly decided on its facts, he, like Commissioner Williams in *CI/2414/98*, disagreed with its broader *obiter* propositions. Given that a physical assault during an interview would rank as personal injury caused by accident, Commissioner Rowland found:

"it very difficult to see why a person who suffers psychological injury having been caused, by words from a superior, to apprehend immediate and unlawful violence, should not be said to have suffered personal injury caused by accident. Such a person would have been the victim of an unlawful assault at common law by the superior and it seems obvious that he or she should be covered by the industrial injuries scheme just as the schoolmaster was covered by the Workmen's Compensation Acts in *Trim* . . . But coverage by the scheme does not depend on someone having done something unlawful; it is enough that the conversation was an untoward event. I agree with the view expressed in *CI/5249/95* that a perfectly proper conversation cannot itself constitute an accident because it seems to me that it may be an event but it cannot be an untoward event. However, I do not agree with the suggestion in *CI/7/71* that use of language alone can never *constitute* an accident. In my view the tribunal in the present case were quite entitled to regard the three material interviews as being sufficient to amount to accidental causes of any injury that flowed from them. On the tribunal's findings, those interviews were quite untoward" (para.17).

However, it is the conversation itself, rather than suspension, dismissal or criticism, which must cause the injury; one looks to the *manner* of dismissal rather than dismissal itself (para.18); or, in the context of a claim in respect of the effects of an unexpected interview, said to have brought on the claimant's depression and chronic anxiety, to the manner and context of the interview (*CI/142/2006*). So the less outrageous the employer's behaviour, the more difficult will be the claimant's task. Injury arising from a series of events can rank as 'accident' rather than 'process'; the tribunal's conclusion that it so ranked here was not such that no tribunal, acting judicially and properly instructed as to the law, could have reached on the material before it (paras 22, 23). As Commissioner Fellner noted in *CI/3511/2002*, on balance, stress illnesses are more likely to arise through process rather than accident (para 14). Stress illnesses are not currently listed as Prescribed Industrial Diseases, and, in a recently published paper—Position Paper no.13, *Stress at Work* [found at URL *http://www.iiac.org.uk/papers/ 13.pdf*]—the Industrial Injuries Advisory Council considered itself unable to recommend extending the schedule of prescription to include adverse health outcomes ascribed to stress at work, but is to keep the area under review (para.56). However, as Commissioner Howell made clear in *CI/4708/2001*, work related stress can arise through accident where one can identify an event which produced a pathological change for the worse in the claimant's condition. Referring the tribunal to which he remitted the case to *CI/105/1998* noted above, he further emphasised that

"in the light of present more up-to-date knowledge about the way people can suffer breakdowns and stress reactions to particular events, it should no longer be taken to be the law, if ever it was, that words alone can never give rise to an 'accident' for this purpose" (para.11).

As *CAO v Faulds* (above) makes clear, however, there must be something describable as an accident. In *CI/3696/2005*, Commissioner Levenson, summarising and applying the principles in *Faulds* (see para.11) upheld a tribunal decision that the claimant, suffering from stress as a result of allegations made against him of false expenses claims, had not suffered an accident: neither being suspended nor receiving the letter of suspension could properly be regarded as an accident in the ordinary sense of the word (paras 12, 13).

Where the injury appears to result from a general deterioration of the claimant's condition over a period of time it may not be possible to identify a precise moment when there was a discernible physiological change for the worse, nor to identify a particular incident which occasioned the deterioration. In these circumstances, the claimant may have difficulty in establishing personal injury (see above) and/or in proving that there was an accident. Describing the distinction between accident and process, Lord Porter said,

> "... two types of case have not always been sufficiently differentiated. In one type there is to be found a simple accident followed by a resultant injury ... or a series of specific and ascertainable accidents followed by an injury which may be the consequence of any or all of them ... In the other type of case there is a continuous process going on substantially from day to day though not necessarily from hour to hour, which gradually and over a period of years produces incapacity. In the first of these types of cases the resulting incapacity is held to be injury by accident; in the second it is not ... There must come a time when the indefinite number of so-called accidents and the length of time over which they occur take away the element of accident and substitute that of process." (*Roberts v Dorothea Slate Quarries Ltd* [1948] 2 All E.R. 201).

Although an accident denotes a moment at which an injury occurred, so long as such a moment can be identified, uncertainty (years after the event) as to the precise date, does not prevent a finding of accident (*CI/278/1993*). In *CI/1714/2002* Commissioner Rowland stressed that it is not necessary for the claimant to identify when the accident took place more precisely than necessary for the determination of the claim, so that there "the summer of 1978" sufficed (para.10). The key point is rather that the tribunal should be satisfied that an accident occurred, and on this aspect it is important to note that the law does not require corroboration of the claimant's evidence if the tribunal believe that evidence (para.11).

Whether the injury is caused by accident(s) or process is an important question of fact for the decision-maker or tribunal. A number of Commissioners decisions have given guidance on the principles to be applied in reaching a decision but the facts of each case will be crucial. Modern authority has directed attention away from the length of the period over which the injury developed as the most significant factor (as Lord Porter seemed to suggest) and emphasised that it is a question of fact and degree in each case (see *R(I) 11/74* and Appendix). Attention must be given to the nature of the injury, the nature of the work, and the nature of the incidents which are alleged to constitute the accident when reaching a decision. As always where fine distinctions need to be made, it is not easy to reconcile all the cases. As Commissioner Howell put it in *CI/4708/2001*, it is a difficult and invidious line for decision-makers and tribunals to have to draw (paras 6, 11).

An examination of the accident/process distinction was undertaken by Commissioner Goodman in *CI/72/1987*. In that case, an oboeist in a world famous orchestra sought a declaration that he had suffered an industrial accident in the course of playing the oboe which had caused hernia of the throat. The Commissioner observed that the question of accident or process is one of fact and laid emphasis on medical evidence which referred to a series of incidents causing the conditions. He held that there had by a specific date (the date on which the condition had been diagnosed) been an accident or accidents which would have occurred on a distinct occasion or occasions. The decision of the adjudication officer and the unanimous decision of the local tribunal was reversed. *R(I) 6/91* affirms that usually harm suffered (e.g. asthma, bronchial complaints) because of "passive smoking" (the inhalation of the smoke from other people's smoking) will not be attributable to accident but to process. However, in the particular circumstances of that case, where the claimant was able to point to six separate and isolated incidents involving her being moved into smoky environments, the Commissioner granted her six accident declarations under SSA 1975, s.107 (now SSA 1998, s.29, formerly AA 1992, s.44). In *CI/156/1993* the claimant was unsuccessful in her claim for an accident declaration in respect of harm suffered through passive smoking, thus indicating the exceptional nature of the decision in *R(I) 6/91*. Nor had her claim in respect of prescribed disease D7 (occupational asthma) been successful. In most cases, a claimant suffering mental or physical injury because of stress at work would rightly be regarded as having suffered it through process, rather than through accident, putting the matter outside s.94. Although Commissioner Goodman was careful to characterise his decision as dependent on its "highly individual facts and on the detailed nature of the medical evidence given in the High Court action [against his employer for damages]", and while he was anxious to deny that his decision constituted a precedent "for any other case where it may be asserted that stress at work has caused a claimant mental or physical injury" (para.16), nonetheless his decision in *CI/554/1992*, granting the claimant an accident declaration, is a welcome reminder that, in circumstances which may well be rare, mental injury through stress can arise through accident. Tribunals should thus take great care in any such case with the evidence, and not assume that any case of injury through stress inevitably *must* be through process. In *CI/554/1992*, Commissioner Goodman noted *R(I) 43/55* (explosions leading to psychoneurotic disorder, an identifiable series of accidents) and decided that the medical evidence showed that the claimant was "more or less all right at one moment and severely ill the next" and that the stressful situation at work in September/October 1974 was an industrial "accident" which tipped him over the edge into depression. The fact that he was abnormally sensitive to stress did not prevent this finding: the "egg shell skull" principle noted in para.11 of *R(I) 6/91* (the passive smoking case) applied. See also *CI/2414/98*, noted earlier.

CI/737/1994 and *CI/1195/1995*, two decisions of Commissioner Henty, both apply *R(I) 6/91* (the "passive smoking" case) and contain useful reviews of the major authorities on the difficult accident/process distinction. In *CI/737/1994*, the Commissioner made a declaration that on each occasion between 1973 and 1983 when the claimant suffered temporary deafness/tinnitus after a shooting practice session as part of his police firearms training, he suffered an accident. Although not as well documented as in *R(I) 6/91*, the evidence was clear that there were such occasions (para.14). Furthermore, despite the fact that the permanent condition only manifested itself some four years after the claimant fired his last shot, the Commissioner declared also that the permanent injury was caused by accident (para.15). In *CI/3600/2004*, Commissioner Fellner considered the case of a school care assistant, who had to give up work, suffering from a major depressive disorder, post-traumatic stress disorder and a number of physical or somatic manifestations. It was argued that this had arisen through process, since she had become increasingly concerned at the nature of physical restraint applied by school staff, and the tribunal had so decided. There was, indeed, that backdrop, but Commissioner Fellner, taking account of *Mullen* noted below, considered that the evidence established that the "trigger" incident was one some three weeks before she left, when she witnessed a pupil being inappropriately restrained by another teacher, and granted an industrial accident declaration (see esp. paras 14–18). In contrast, in *CI/1195/1995*, Commissioner Henty could point to no particular incidents triggering off the claimant's heart attack; it came about as a result of a cumulative process (para.9).

The following situations are only illustrative—the tribunal must decide each case upon its facts: **1.322**

(i)   The period of development may be too short to indicate process:

R(I) 18/54   (two months, but there was also an identifiable point at which the injury was first noticed)

R(I) 43/61   (less than three days' use of scissors causing digital neuritis—but compare *R(I) 19/56*)

R(I) 4/62   (about two weeks' welding causing ganglion)

(ii) There may be an identifiable series of individual accidents:

R(I) 77/51   (repeated operation of stiff levers)

R(I) 24/54   (repeated burns and pricks on hands)

R(I) 43/55   (explosions leading to psychoneurotic disorder) (see note above)

CI/71/1987   (oboe playing and rehearsal leading to laryngoceles) (see note above)

CI/737/1994   (shooting practice leading to temporary deafness/tinnitus) (see note above)

CAO v Faulds   1998 S.L.T. 1203 (remitted for further evidence by the House of Lords (see [2000] 2 All E.R. 961))

CI/3370/1999   (the case of a teacher who claimed that her injury (nodules on her bilateral vocal chords) had resulted from a series of interacting incidents, constituting "accident", at school. The decision-maker had already given an accident declaration in respect of one such incident when she was trapped in a stock cupboard by a pupil and had to shout before escaping. Commissioner remitted to tribunal for further consideration but implying support for the "accident" view')

Mullen v Secretary of State for Work and Pensions, 2002 S.L.T. 149   (the Court of Session Second Division in a Scottish case held that a former assistant care officer incapacitated by back pain brought about through lifting patients had suffered a series of accidents over a seven year period, and had thus suffered injury caused by accident, even though it was not possible to identify the date of each of the accidents or to state which of them, if not all, caused or contributed to the back condition.)

(iii) There may be a process:

CI/257/49   (development of "Raynaud's phenomenon" as a result of operating a grinding machine for five years)

CI/83/50   (doctor developing tuberculosis after two years of treating persons suffering from it)

R(I) 42/51   (strained chest muscles over two-month period)

R(I) 19/56   (osteoarthritis of the fingers was the "cumulative result" of three days of leather stitching and had come on gradually during that period)

R(I) 7/66   (prolonged exposure to nitro-glycerine resulting in death)

R(I) 11/74   (condition of left elbow developing over five months' work with heavy electrical boring machine)

CI/1195/1995   (cumulative process leading to heart attack) (see note above)

CAO v Faulds   [2000] 2 All E.R. 961, reported as *R(I) 1/00* (post-traumatic stress disorder remitted by House of Lords to Court of Session for further evidence on the issue).

CSI/371/2001   (not available on the Commissioners' website) placed on the process side of the line a case where a civil servant had suffered stress and anxiety because of excessive workload and a number of incidents of friction with his line manager, whom he saw as unreasonable. The tribunal had not there been prepared to find that the claimant's appreciation of excessive workload was the sort of triggering event that had enabled success in *CI/554/1992*, noted above, one of the rare cases where mental injury through stress resulted from accident)

CI/3511/2002   (Commissioner Fellner considered the case of an ambulance technician incapacitated because of work-related stress. The single person tribunal erred in law by holding that the claimant was entitled to an industrial accident declaration because this was a case of accident by process. Commissioner Fellner held that the case fell on the 'process' side of the line — there was no identifiable accident or series of accidents).

The claimant who develops a disease or other condition as a result of his work may be entitled to benefit notwithstanding that there is no accident so long as the disease or condition is one which is "prescribed" for his employment (see s.108, below).

The Secretary of State and the tribunal may also have to make a difficult decision where the claimant alleges that the injury suffered constitutes the accident for the purposes of the section.

The supermarket shelf stacker who strains back muscles when picking up a case of baked beans is likely to say that he has had an "accident" at work—but he is doing nothing other than he is accustomed to do and the accident is the injury. Has he had an accident within the meaning of the section? The authorities suggest that the section covers both the standard case (accident—injury— incapacity) and the case under consideration (accident/injury—incapacity) so long as, in the latter case, there is an internal physiological change for the worse which is partly caused by the work which the claimant is doing at the time.

In *Jones v Secretary of State for Social Services* [1972] A.C. 944, the claimant suffered a heart attack some days after he had been doing heavy lifting at work. A tribunal held that the heart attack had been brought on by the heavy work and the House of Lords decided that there had been an accident within the terms of the section. Lord Diplock said that he would call a perfectly ordinary part of a man's work an accident if it had the effect of causing injury. It would appear that the only injuries excluded will be those which would have happened whether the claimant was at work or not. Such injuries are not attributable to the work done but are risks of everyday activity.

The law was stated thus in *R(I)11/80* (where the claimant sustained a head injury by banging his head after an unexplained fall):

> "where (in what is sometimes called an internal accident) a physiological or pathological change for the worse occurs while a person is at work, such as a fit or a heart attack or a dislocation, that change for the worse is, if caused by the work that is being done itself, injury by accident for the purposes of the section; but that, on the other hand, where one of these happens while a person is at work but not because of his work the change is not itself injury by accident . . . But in any case if the internal accident causes the person concerned to fall and injure himself that injury may be injury by accident arising out of and in the course of employment even if the change itself was not."

This statement was approved in *R(I) 6/82* where the claimant had broken his ankle while carrying out his duties as a maintenance engineer in a bakery. In holding that the claimant had not had an accident, the Commissioner said,

> "walking, standing, sitting etc. are all part of everyday human activity and unless they represent a special danger to a claimant because of some inherent,

idiopathic, characteristic of the individual claimant, accidents happening during those activities, even in the course of employment cannot be said to arise out of the employment unless there is the additional factor of an injury by contact with the employer's premises etc. There is no distinction in my view between a heart attack suffered by a sedentary employee and an unexplained bone fracture or dislocation suffered by a walking employee. Neither will constitute an industrial accident unless some aspect of the employment caused the heart attack, the fracture or the dislocation or they were caused by the employee coming into contact with the employer's plant, premises, or machinery."

In *CAO v Faulds* 1998 S.L.T. 1203, 1998 S.C.L.R. 719, reported with *R(I) 1/00*, the Inner House of the Scottish Court of Session (the equivalent of the Court of Appeal in England and Wales) affirmed Commissioner Walker's decision in *CSI/26/96* (reported as part of *R(I) 1/00*), that a fireman who suffered post-traumatic stress disorder after having attended a series of horrific fatalities in the course of his employment had suffered "accidents" (a series of "accidents", not a "process") (see above). Lord McCluskey said in giving the opinion of the court:

"in a case like the present just as in *R(I) 22/59*, *CI/15589/1996* and *R(I) 43/55*, also quoted to us, the accidental cause is found in the exposure of the employee on one or several—or even many—occasions to shocking sights or other such phenomena, resulting in his suffering a severe—and unintended— nervous reaction. We do not consider that the wording of the Act requires that there be found a separable 'accident' in the form of a distinct event separate from the injury and preceding it in point of time. In circumstances in which the horror of the exposure triggers a response which takes the form of nervous trauma, the injury and its cause may merge indistinguishably, but the injury may still be properly said to be caused by accident" (1998 S.L.T. 1203 at 1210).

In *CAO v Faulds* [2000] 2 All E.R. 961, reported as *R(I) 1/00* the majority of the House of Lords (Lord Hutton dissenting) rather harshly read this passage as failing sufficiently to identify, as was necessary, particular incidents, constituting accidents, which produced the injury (the post-traumatic stress disorder) and as erroneously tending to suggest that it sufficed for purposes of the industrial injuries scheme that the injury had arisen "accidentally" (see Lord Hope at 969, Lord Clyde at 973). In short, their Lordships considered that there was insufficient evidence for SSAT, Commissioner and the Inner House to find "accident" rather than "process" and remitted the matter back to the Inner House (doubtless to pass on to the Commissioner and to a differently constituted appeal tribunal) for further consideration. Lord Hutton took the view that the Inner House had identified a series of incidents producing and aggravating the post-traumatic stress disorder and was entitled to find as it did. The House of Lords, while unhappy with its precise application in the particular case of psychological injury before them in *Faulds*, approved a line of cases involving physical injury held to be within the scheme in which the distinction between "accident" and "injury" becomes blurred: *Fenton v Thorley* [1903] A.C. 443 (rupture when turning an unexpectedly resistant wheel); *Welsh v Glasgow Coal* 1916 S.C. (HL) 141 (workman immersed in water developed rheumatism); *Clover, Clayton & Co. Ltd v Hughes* [1910] A.C. 242 (death from burst aneurism when tightening a nut with a spanner); *Falmouth Docks and Engineering Co. Ltd v Treloar* [1933] A.C. 481 (man suffering from heart disease dropped dead when lifting his hand, holding a hook, above his head) (see Lord Clyde [2000] 2 All E.R. 961 at 976–977). The key point is the need to identify some causative event or small series of events, remembering, in Lord Hope's words, "that the sustaining of an *unexpected* personal injury caused by an *expected* event or incident may itself amount to an accident" ([2000] 2 All E.R. 961 at 969). In the context of injury through shock or stress, there is still need to:

"identify the accident of which notice would require to be given, and the injury which was caused by it. The principle established in the cases of physical injury should in that respect be applicable to cases of psychological injury. In cases of shock and stress the activity which triggers the accident may only consist of the claimant confronting an horrific spectacle. It may involve some additional activity, such as the handling or the close examination of something particularly gruesome or distressing. But in every case, although the concepts may overlap, it should be possible to identify an accident as well as the consequent injury. But the identification of the accident and the establishment of a causal connection between the incident and the injury may well call for a very careful investigation of the circumstances of the case and the nature of the condition" ([2000] 2 All E.R. 961 at 979, *per* Lord Clyde).

Commissioner Parker, sitting as a Deputy Commissioner in Northern Ireland, in broader context, encapsulated the matter well:

"although the majority of the House of Lords recognises that there are cases where the elements of accident and injury overlap, it is nevertheless stressed that there is a distinction between the two which must be observed. A physiological or psychological change for the worse can only constitute an accident if it is, at least partly, caused by the work which the claimant is doing at the time; if there is no causal link to the relevant work and the injury would have happened whether the claimant was at work or not then the internal accident does not count as amounting to accidental injury in the sense of the statute. A claimant must identify some causative event or events which produced the physiological or pathological change for the worse, such as turning a wheel or a screw or lifting his hand, and that such trigger was *because* of his ordinary work not merely *at* his work. That in such case it is hardly possible to distinguish in time between "accident" and "injury" does not negate the distinction. The reasoning of the House of Lords stressed the essential requirement of identifying an incident which brought about the physiological injury which constitutes, in effect, the required accident/injury. It is only when there is a triggering work event for an injury that it can be accepted that the very injury suffered constitutes the necessary accident for the purposes of the section" (*C1/06-07(II)*, para.30).

Accordingly, accepting this, Commissioner Bano in *CI/2842/2006*, held that, since his cardiologist accepted that the claimant's work conditions might have contributed to his condition, it was more likely than not that the exceptional work pressures, to which he was subject immediately prior to his suffering a cardiac arrest at work, contributed to that cardiac arrest and that this was properly to be regarded as an accident, "even though it occurred in the normal course of the claimant's duties and was not preceded by any [separate] abnormal event" (paras 13, 16).

Caused (after July 4, 1948) by accident: The meaning of "accident" has been discussed above, and the significance of the date can be quickly explained. July 5, 1948 was the first day of the new industrial injuries scheme and only injuries suffered during the currency of the scheme may be compensated. (It is possible to found a claim on an industrial accident which happened a long time ago if its effects are only now becoming apparent, but the more distant the accident, the more difficult it is likely to be for the claimant to establish entitlement.)

1.323

The injury must be *caused* by the accident. Three situations should be noted: (i) where the claimant is predisposed to the injury suffered because of disease or constitutional weakness; (ii) where the injury suffered renders the claimant susceptible to other forms of injury; (iii) where the injury suffered is aggravated by a further non-industrial accident.

If the claimant is predisposed to injury it will still be proper to say that the accident caused the injury if it would not have happened but for the accident *(R(I) 12/52*—a bus conductor with abnormally fragile bones; *R(I) 14/51*—a miner with an existing heart condition; *R(I) 73/51*—a labourer suffering from Paget's disease). Note that there must still be something which can be termed an accident occurring as a result of the particular duties of the employment (see above).

Where the claimant can show that the original industrial injury was an effective cause of the eventual non-industrial injury he will also succeed in his claim. In *R(I) 3/56*, a Tribunal of Commissioners allowed a claim by a man who had been injured in a fall on the way to work as a result of a previous accident at work. The Tribunal said,

". . . if the immediate cause of his incapacity is an injury by non-industrial accident the claimant will be entitled to injury benefit if he can prove that a previous injury by industrial accident was an effective cause of the injury by non-industrial accident which was the immediate cause of his incapacity."

Similar successful claims may be found in *CI/129/49* and *R(I) 59/51*.

The same principle is relevant to determine cases where the non-industrial injury is an aggravation of the industrial injury but is not related to it. Illness following upon an injury or a completely unrelated non-industrial accident which incapacitates the claimant will not be taken into account except in so far as the industrial injury continues to be an effective cause of the claimant's incapacity.

Provision is made for taking into account a combination of industrial and non-industrial accidents in assessing the extent of disablement for the purposes of disablement benefit. See ss.103, 107, and General Benefit Regs below.

"arising out of and in the course of employment"

1.324   This phrase first appeared in the Workmen's Compensation Act 1897 to limit compensation paid under the original scheme to injuries which were suffered through work and not merely at work.

The two tests, "in the course of" and "out of", look to different things. The former embraces time, place and activity. The latter requires a causal nexus between the injury and the employment. The separateness of the two tests is affirmed by the statutory presumption in s.94(3), readily defeasible if there is any evidence to the contrary, that an accident "in the course of" also arises "out of" the employment (*Chief Adjudication Officer v Rhodes*, reported as *R(I) 1/99*). The distinct nature of the two tests is also manifest in the deeming provision in s.101 (an accident arising "in the course of" employment will be deemed to arise "out of" it in a bewildering range of situations whose only common factor consists of their being situations which courts or commissioners had ruled as not arising out of the employment applying general principles). A person may satisfy one test but not secure benefit because failing to meet the other. So, in *Rhodes*, above, in the case of the civil servant assaulted on her drive by a neighbour because of her work (she had reported him as claiming benefit whilst working), the work nexus satisfied the "out of" test, but her claim failed. While all the other requisites of s.94(1) were met, she was not "in the course of" her employment because when assaulted she was at home on sick leave, returning from a visit to her doctor, and not engaged at the material time in performing any work tasks.

1.325   *Arising out of . . . employment:* The first part of the phrase confines the industrial injuries scheme to those injuries which are work-related and seeks to exclude those which result from the ordinary risks which affect everybody. To give two examples, in *R(I) 62/53* a lorry driver suffered a corneal abrasion when something went into his eye whilst he was driving. The Commissioner held that he was not entitled to benefit because the accident did not arise out of the employment—the risk was general and not particular to his employment. By contrast, a policeman on motorbike patrol duty who was similarly injured *was* entitled to benefit because the risk of eye injury whilst riding a motor-bike on duty was greater than normal (*R(I) 67/53*).

There is a further interesting comparison between *R(I) 22/59* and unreported decision *CI/387/1988*. In the former case, a miner suffered nervous debility resulting from the shock of hearing of his son's death in an accident at the same mine; in the latter case, a worker suffered anxietal depression after seeing a colleague in the terminal stages of angiosarcoma of the liver, a disease to which his own work exposed him.

In *R(I) 22/59*, the accident (hearing of the death) was held not to have arisen out of employment; in *CI/387/1988*, the accident (sighting the colleague) was held to have arisen out of the employment. The distinction taken was that the father could have been shocked at the son's death wherever he worked; the latter claimant would not have suffered shock unless he had been working at the particular place where industrial conditions created the hazard which threatened him. *CI/387/1988* was distinguished by Commissioner Goodman in *CI/289/1994* when he upheld the decision of an SSAT (which applied *R(I) 22/59* and *R(I) 62/53*) that the post-traumatic stress disorder suffered by a lorry driver when he learned over the radio in his cab of the Zeebrugge ferry disaster did not arise out of his employment:

"In [*CI/387/1988*], the claimant himself had worked for many years with vinyl chloride monomer and therefore was at potential risk of developing cancer of the liver . . . But that is not the same as the facts of the present case. Admittedly the claimant had had to use the same ferry crossing but he had successfully made the trips. Any danger that there might have been from the ferry sailing [which had been on a different vessel] had gone as soon as the claimant had driven off the ferry. There was no continuing risk such as the continuing risk of cancer [in *CI/387/1988*] nor was there necessarily any such risk in the future, particularly as the claimant could reasonably assume that the occurrence of the disaster would cause further safety precautions to be taken" (para.10).

It is thus crucial for the "out of" employment issue properly to analyse the nature of the risk in the case. *CSI/154/89*, a decision of Commissioner Walker shows the difficulties of drawing a line between injuries resulting from the ordinary risks to which everyone is exposed, whether employed or not (not arising out of employment) and those injuries resulting from risks created by the employment (which do arise out of the employment as being work-related). The case takes a more generous approach than some other decisions (e.g. *R(I) 62/53* and *R(I) 52/54*). Indeed the case is strikingly similar on its facts to *R(I) 52/54*, but it is an approach which draws on leading authorities on the interpretation of the same phraseology in the Workmen's Compensation legislation (*White v W & T Avery*, 1916 S.C. 209, *McNeice v Singer Sewing Machine Co Ltd* 1911 S.C. 12 and the House of Lords' decision, *Dennis v AJ White & Co.* [1917] A.C. 479). In *Dennis*, Lord Finlay L.C. said:

"If a servant in the course of his master's business has to pass along the public street, whether it be on foot or on a bicycle, or on an omnibus or car, and he sustains an accident by reason of the risks incidental to the street, the accident arises out of as well as in the course of his employment. The frequency or infrequency of the occasions on which the risk is incurred has nothing to do with the question whether an accident resulting from that risk arose out of the employment . . . but as soon as it is established that the work itself involves exposure to the perils of the streets the workmen can recover for any injury so occasioned.

Where the risk is one shared by all men, whether in or out of employment, it must be established that special exposure to it is involved. But when a workman is sent into the street on his master's business, whether it be occasionally or habitually, his employment necessarily involves exposure to the risks of the streets, and injury from such a cause arises out of his employment." (cited in para.17).

Further, Commissioner Walker recalls Lord Denning's exhortation in *Vandyke v Fender* [1970] 2 Q.B. 292 that this phraseology be given the same interpretation whether used in industrial injuries legislation, road traffic legislation or employer's liability policies. One can here note that something like that approach is inherent in the way Commissioners, dealing with "travelling cases" under the industrial injuries scheme, have drawn on the tests in the House of Lords' decision in *Smith v Stages* [1989] 1 All E.R. 833, dealing with similar issues in the law of torts. Commissioner Walker then noted, looking to *Smith v Stages*, that what is incidental to the employment appears to be relevant to the issue "out of" as well as that of "in the course of" with which that case dealt. The court decisions he had cited persuaded him that the SSAT had adopted an incorrect analysis of the claimant's situation, and was thus erroneous in law:

> "The question which they should have asked themselves was whether the claimant was exposed to the risk by the job or whether the risk was one that could have affected her whether or not in the employment at that time. That raises the question as to what was the risk. In this case I conclude that it was the risk of falling, as evidenced by the finding of fact that she fell on the pavement. That is a normal risk of the streets but it was a risk to which she became exposed only because her employment put her in the relevant place at the relevant time. And so I come at last to the question whether the fact that Mrs Falconer was reacting there and then to an emergency [trying to save a child who had run into the road] yet takes her out of the scope and/or course of her employment.
>
> I approach these two questions separately. 'In the course of ' is simple. The Commissioner in *R(I) 52/54* would have taken it for granted. The claimant was where she was at the time of the accident because so required or at least permitted by her employment. She had not deviated nor gone deliberately out of her way. The employment was not interrupted. So I hold that Mrs Falconer's accident occurred in the course of her employment. As to whether it arose 'out of ' that employment I am persuaded by the language quoted above from *White v Avery, McNeice* and *Dennis v AJ White & Co.* that it is the risk that has to be considered rather than what brought it to pass. How it came to pass might affect liability in a damages claim but not for present purposes—*cf.* the potato picker's case [*R(I) 17/63*]. It was not outwith the nature and type of risk that might befall a messenger. That seems to me to be enough. I think that the word 'emergency' is misleading in, and inappropriate to this case. I have therefore to add that I am unable to agree with the decision *R(I) 52/54*. So I hold that the accident here arose 'out of ' the claimant's employment as well." (paras 19 and 20; words in brackets added by commentator).

In *CI/1654/2008* Commissioner Jacobs considered the case of an employee who slipped and was injured while showering at a hotel before attending a training session there. He held that the accident befell her when in the course of her employment; her actions in making herself presentable were reasonably incidental to her duties and she was where she was because of her work. But it did not arise "out" of the employment:

> "The risk was not created by her employment. It was inherent in the nature of a shower. It was a risk that anyone would run who took a shower. Indeed, it was not limited to the shower. There was a similar risk in the bathroom outside the shower. The claimant's employment did not expose her to any hazard that was additional to, or exceptional when compared with, the risk that anyone else would run who was taking a shower or using a hotel bathroom" (paras 36, 37).

Nor did SSCBA 1992 s.101 operate so as to treat this accident arising in the course of employment as also arising out of it; there was "no evidence that the accident was caused by someone else's misconduct, skylarking or negligence" (para.28).

Note the relationship between this concept and the question of whether an accident has occurred, in circumstances where the claimant merely suffers injury at work which might have happened anywhere, e.g. a heart attack, a fit or a dislocation. In *R(I) 6/82* (above), the Commissioner held that there was no accident, but, even if there had been, it would not have arisen out of the course of employment unless there had been an injury caused by contact with the employer's plant, premises or machinery or unless some aspect of the employment caused the injury.

The claimant is assisted by the provision in subs.(3) of this section (noted below) that an accident which occurs in the course of employment shall be deemed to have arisen out of the employment unless there is evidence to the contrary. Note also, for cases of any doubt, the role of s.101 (deemed "out of").

Arising . . . in the course of employment: This looks to matters of time, place and activity. As Lord Loreburn put it in *Moore v Manchester Liners Ltd* [1910] A.C. 498 at 500–501:

> "An accident befalls a man 'in the course of' his employment if it occurs while he is doing what a man so employed may reasonably do within a time during which he is employed, and at a place where he may reasonably be during that time to do that thing".

The test requires a focus on what the claimant is doing rather than on what was done to the claimant. In *Chief Adjudication Officer v Rhodes*, reported as *R(I) 1/99*), Schiemann L.J. (with whose judgment Roch L.J. concurred to give the majority in the case) approved Hoffman L.J.'s statement in *Faulkner v Chief Adjudication Officer* [1994] P.I.Q.R. 244 at 256; *The Times*, April 8, 1994(one citing as authority *Smith v Stages* [1989] A.C. 928) reported as *R(I) 8/94* and adapted it so as to read (adaptation in square brackets):

> "An office or employment involves a legal relationship: it entails the existence of specific duties on the part of the employee. An act or event happens 'in the course of employment' if [what the employee is doing] constitutes the discharge of one of those duties or is reasonably incidental thereto".

One must first ascertain what the employee is employed to do and then consider whether what the employee was doing at the material time constitutes the discharge of one of those duties or something reasonably incidental thereto.

This "back to basics" approach in *Rhodes* is firmly located within the structure of this statutory regime and within the mass of authority since the tests were first included in the Workmen's Compensation Act 1897 (see R. Lewis, *Compensation for Industrial Injury* (1987), p.51). So, for example, the approach meshes with the general formulation found in the headnote to an earlier Court of Appeal decision, *R. v Industrial Injuries Commissioner Ex p. A.E.U. (No. 2)* [1966] 2 Q.B. 31 (*Culverwell's* case):

> "The test whether a man is acting 'in the course of his employment' is not the strict test of whether he is at the relevant time performing a duty for his employer, for he may be 'in the course of his employment' when he acts casually, negligently or even disobediently, so long as it is something reasonably incidental to his contract of employment".

With respect to the dissenting Swinton Thomas L.J. in *Rhodes*, above, matters of time and place are important: those injured away from the employer's premises during a lunch break, unless performing tasks for their employer, are not "in the course of employment". The system has always been predicated on there being a difference between injuries suffered at work during working hours and those suffered while resting at home or when travelling to or from a fixed point of work. Were that not so, the justifications for a separate system of compensation for work injuries would be further called into question. Crucial lines drawn by a raft of previous authority (e.g. on travelling to and from a fixed place of work generally being outside the scheme [*Lewis*, pp.76, 77] and, by implication, the deeming provision in s.99 (passengers travelling in employer provided transport)) would respectively be rendered nugatory and unnecessary.

The matter of the proper approach to "in the course of employment" had been thrown into some disarray by the Court of Appeal decision in *Nancollas v Insurance Officer* [1985] 1 All E.R. 833. That case dealt with the issue of whether two claimants injured in motor accidents were injured in the course of employment. In the case, Lord Donaldson M.R. went so far as to suggest that there were no legal rules (other than the plain statutory language) for courts or tribunals to follow, merely factors pointing one way or the other. Hence the proper approach was for tribunals to look at the factual picture as a whole, rejecting any approach based on the fallacious concept that any one factor is conclusive. The Court of Appeal decision in *Rhodes*, above, is a firm affirmation of the trend (see *Smith v Stages* [1989] A.C. 928, especially Lord Lowry at 948, 955–956, and the Court of Appeal in *Faulkner v Chief Adjudication Officer* [1994] P.I.Q.R. 244 reported as *R(I) 8/94*), of effectively relegating the *Nancollas* impressionistic "factor" approach to the secondary issue of the characterisation of particular acts once the central questions have been posed: what was the claimant employed to do and was s/he doing it, or something reasonably incidental to it, when the accident occured. This is both right in principle and, by more clearly establishing parameters, enables an expert body of Commissioners more closely to scrutinise decisions of appeals tribunals, the better to ensure a degree of "horizontal equity between claimants" (see Wikeley, Ogus and Barendt, *The Law of Social Security*, p.728), since it is submitted that the "back to basics" approach in *Rhodes* offers a framework of analysis relatively more certain and consistent than the impressionist, artistic brushwork of Lord Donaldson M.R. in *Nancollas*. Whilst part of his judgment in *Nancollas* was approved by Lord Goff in *Smith v Stages*, it is clear that the House of Lords did not approve the proposition that there are no rules. Indeed, Lord Lowry set out six propositions designed to assist with the question whether a person travelling could be regarded as being in the course of employment (see annotations to s.99, below, "Introduction"). Although *Smith v Stages* was not concerned with a social security question, but rather with the matter of an employer's vicarious liability for the acts of his employee in the law of torts, the same phrase, "acting in the course of employment" was under consideration. Moreover, their Lordships reverted to older authorities for guidance, relying particularly on *St Helens Colliery Limited v Hewitson* [1924] A.C. 59, and stated that *Vandyke v Fender* [1970] 2 Q.B. 292 is still good law. Indeed in *R(I) 1/88* (see further the annotations to s.99, below, "Introduction"), the Commissioner held that *Nancollas* did not remove the well-accepted distinction betwen acts done under an obligation to an employer and acts merely done with his permission: in the former case it almost necessarily follows that the employee was acting in the course of his employment, but this does not equally necessarily follow from the fact that the employee was doing what was authorised by the employer.

Rightly, however, given the immense variety of the world of work, the post-*Nancollas* reappraisal culminating in *Rhodes* nonetheless requires the application of broad principle to the facts of individual cases rather than proceeding on the basis that a similar fact case *dictates* the result. Tribunals should not rely too heavily on previous decisions without relating them to a detailed consideration of the facts of the particular case *(R(I) 1/93; CI 110/98)*. In *R(I) 1/93*, Commissioner Johnson set aside an SSAT decision as erroneous in law because it failed to look at the factual picture as a whole:

> "the tribunal clearly relied on apparently similar cases [Commissioners' decisions] in reaching their decisions, whereas they should have given primary consideration to the particular facts of the case before them" (para.6).

In the particular case the claimant was injured when she tripped and fell during a site meeting, held on her employer's premises, but not at her usual workplace. The purpose of the meeting was to discuss the pending actions brought against the company by the claimant and others with respect to repetitive strain injury (RSI). The factor which tipped the balance for the Commissioner, who held that the accident befell her out of and in the course of her employment, was "the company's interest in her attending the site meeting" which might well save time and costs in the litigation even if it did not secure a settlement of the claims (paras 10, 11).

"In the course of employment" and the tests noted above have a good degree of elasticity. That, as held in *Rhodes* above (see further below, "(iv) Flexible working and employees on sick leave"), those incapable of work, and thus not as such "in the course of their employment", can still be protected if injured while performing one of their work tasks (the performance bringing them back within the course of their employment) amply illustrates the flexibility of application inherent in the central tests, adherence to which is essential in a compensation system for accidents suffered at or during work and because of it.

There are four statutory "extensions" in ss.98–101 bringing certain accidents, which would otherwise not arise in the course of [ss.98–100], or out of [s.101], employment, within the scope of the scheme. Travelling accidents, a continual problem, are dealt with in the note to s.99. Three other common types of claim illustrate the difficulty of determining the course of employment when applying s.94.

(i) Beginnings and endings

When does the course of employment start and finish on the normal working day? **1.327** Clocking in and out? Getting into and out of working clothes? Getting onto and off the employer's premises? The terms of employment may be part of the answer but all the facts must be considered and weighed, perhaps with a view to asking whether at the point at which the accident happened the employee was exposed to the risks of the workplace or merely those risks which he would run as a member of the general public. By way of example of successful claims:

R. v N.I. Commissioner Ex p. East [1976] I.C.R. 206 (accident suffered by claimant in works canteen prior to clocking-on)

R(I) 3/62 (employee habitually arriving very early at work to avoid rush-hour travel)

R(I) 22/56 (miner suffering accident on colliery road after visiting colliery canteen at the end of work to avoid the rush for the first bus)

R(I) 72/54 (miner suffering accident on way to collect replacement for bootlace broken whilst changing into working clothes)

CI/105/1990 (employee injured while getting into taxi to have her injury checked and, if necessary, treated, in hospital: see below).

Unsuccessful claims:

R(I) 22/53 (railwayman injured on his way from home to work—on railway land but half a mile from the depot where he worked)

R(I) 11/54 (miner visiting canteen before his shift to buy sandwiches to eat during shift—injured on canteen steps)

R(I) 14/61 (part-time clerk completing work at 1.00pm then taking lunch in the canteen and suffering injury on leaving)

CI/114/1987 (employee going in to work on day off for sole purpose of collecting pay and suffering injury outside the wages office).

(ii) Taking a break

Is the course of employment interrupted where the claimant takes a break in **1.328** the working day? Again, a matter of fact for the decision-maker or tribunal, but it may be useful to discover whether the break was imposed by the employer, permitted, condoned, provided for in the terms of employment, or proscribed. Were any particular activities required (or prohibited) during the break? Was the claimant still on duty, or on call during the break? *R. v Industrial Injuries Commissioner Ex p. A.E.U. (No. 2)* [1996] 2 Q.B. 31 (*Culverwell's* case) concerned an accident happening during a break. The claimant was only permitted to smoke in a designated booth. Throughout a permitted break the booth was occupied and the claimant was injured by a fork-lift truck as he waited outside the booth after the end of the permitted break. The Court of Appeal held that he was not in the course of employment because he had overstayed the permitted break and was doing something for his own purposes quite unconnected with his employment.

As examples of successful claims:

R(I) 21/53, R(I) 11/55, R(I) 20/61 and *R(I) 4/67* (all concern bus drivers or conductors injured during a break from duty and observing the instructions or permission of their employer about the way the break should be spent)

R(I) 7/80 (police sergeant in charge of station permitted to take meal break at home whilst remaining on call—injured on journey back to station).

Unsuccessful claims:
R(I) 6/53 and *R(I) 4/79* (bus crews)
R(I) 6/76 (interruption of work due to bomb scare)
R(I) 5/81 (fire officer travelling from office to home to begin on-call period)
R(I) 10/81 (merchant seaman going ashore for his own purposes during an official break).

(iii) Recreational activity

1.329   Some employments have recreational activity as a part of the work; some offer facilities for recreation; some offer periods of inactivity during which employees may take recreation. Whether an accident occurring during recreational activity has arisen in the course of employment must be a question of mixed fact and law, but whereas one type of claim has generally been successful, two other types have not. This may indicate the important questions to ask in such a case.

The successful claims have been in cases where the employee is required to take part in the activity:

CI/228/50 (apprentice injured during compulsory physical training as part of day class he was required to attend—see also *R(I) 4/51, R(I) 31/53*)

R(I) 13/51 (male nurse at mental hospital injured whilst playing football with patients—see also *R(I) 3/57*)

R(I) 68/51 (fireman injured playing volleyball during compulsory fitness training period—see also *R(I) 13/66*)

R(I) 3/81 (police cadet injured whilst travelling back from National Swimming Championships in which she had been detailed to take part).

The unsuccessful claims have been in cases where the recreational activity is merely encouraged (even strongly encouraged) rather than compulsory (*R . v N.I. Commissioners Ex p. Michael* [1977] 1 W.L.R. 109, Appendix to *R(I) 5/75*); or where the employee takes recreation during an off-duty period or during an enforced break in employment:

R(I) 2/69 (laboratory technician playing football during the lunch-hour)

R(I) 2/80 (fireman attending residential college injured playing football in the evening)

R(I) 4/81 (airline stewardess injured playing tennis during a stop-over between flights).

R. v N.I. Commissioners Ex p. Michael has been followed by the Court of Appeal, in preference to *Nancollas*, in *Faulkner v Chief Adjudication Officer, The Times*, April 8, 1994 reported as *R(I) 8/94*. In *Faulkner*, the claimant policeman sustained personal injury while playing football for his police football team. The SSAT held this to have arisen in the course of his employment but their decision was set aside as erroneous in law on September 30, 1990 by Commissioner Johnson. The Court of Appeal upheld the Commissioner's decision; there was no evidence before the SSAT which could justify such a conclusion. Following *Michael*, the question was whether the claimant was doing his job when injured and not whether he was doing something reasonably incidental to it. The court considered that the implication of a contractual term was not to be made because it seemed sensible or reasonable that such a term should be implied or because the chief police officer, the Police Federation representative, or the claimant regarded community policing as a good and useful policy, but in accordance with the ordinary legal principle that an obligation could be read into a contract if it was such as the nature of the contract itself implicitly required. The claimant had sought to rely on *Nancollas* to argue that *Michael* should be reconsidered in the light of changing social circumstances. The Court decided that *Nancollas* gave no basis for distinguishing *Michael*.

(iv) Flexible working and employees on sick leave

1.330   In *R(I) 1/99*, Commissioner Goodman held that "in the course of employment" embraced the employee, a Benefits Agency clerical officer at home on sick leave, incapable of work and, by rights, doing none, who was assaulted in her drive by her neighbour for reasons clearly connected with and the product of her employment (she had reported the neighbour to the appropriate Benefits Agency authorities for claiming benefits whilst working). While the injury undoubtedly arose out of the employment, it is difficult, applying factors of time, place and activity, to regard such a claimant as properly being in the course of her employment (see further D. Bonner, "Compensation for Assault: an Unusual Dimension to the Industrial Injuries System" (1998) 5 J.S.S.L. 68). The Court of Appeal, by majority (Schiemann and Roch L.JJ., Swinton Thomas L.J. dissenting), upheld the appeal against Commissioner Goodman's decision: *Chief Adjudication Officer v Rhodes*, reported as *R(I) 1/99*; see further Bonner (1999) 6 J.S.S.L. 33). Commissioner Goodman had erred in law. While Mrs Rhodes at the time of the assault was clearly still employed as an employed earner, and while the work-connected reason for the assault undoubtedly rendered this "accident" one arising "out of" of the employment, the reason for the assault could not of itself bring her within "the course of employment". "Out of" and "in the course of" are distinct conditions *both* of which must be satisifed to render the accident an industrial one. "In the course of" requires a focus on what the claimant was doing rather than on what was done to her. There was no basis for saying that at the material time Mrs Rhodes was doing something she was employed to do or something reasonably incidental thereto, that being the established test (see above). Commissioner Goodman had instead concentrated in effect (though not in form) on whether or not she was an employed earner. Undoubtedly she was, even when on sick leave. But so too would be a claimant injured when on a skiing holiday. Merely being still an employed earner does not render one in the course of employment. Roch L.J. rejected Commissioner Goodman's view that, being still employed and on sick leave, she was thus at home only with the consent and authority of her employer, in so far as that view misleadingly suggested that the employer required her to be at home. Hence, merely being on permitted sick leave does not bring a claimant within the course of employment. Roch L.J. saw the Commissioner's decision and the points made in support of Mrs Rhodes (and by implication Swinton Thomas L.J.'s dissent?) as foundering "on the ground that they elide the two requirements into a single requirement, namely has the accident arisen out of the claimant's employment". The two are separate, something affirmed as Parliament's intention by the presumption in s.94(3) that accidents in the course of also arise out of employment in the absence of any evidence to the contrary. "In the course of" requires examination of *the activity of* the claimant, not of *what is being done to* the claimant. Schiemann L.J. considered, however, (and Roch L.J. agreed with his reasoning) that someone on sick leave can still be in the course of employment if performing duties required of him (and similar propositions must apply to those working at home under flexible working arrangements). For example someone in hospital with a broken leg in traction but whose mental faculties are unimpaired could be given files to read and would be in the course of employment when doing that. Similarly if Mrs Rhodes had actually been working on material from the office. If, when off sick, she had been assaulted while using a mobile phone to report a fraudulent claimant, that, for Schiemann L.J., would be something reasonably incidental to what she was employed to do. He might also have so held, though he saw lesser force in this situation, if the assault had occurred just after she had ended the telephone conversation. But none of this could avail Mrs Rhodes whose information was given days, if not weeks, before. Although she sometimes did work at home under the Agency's flexi-time system, there was no material before the Commissioner for him to find as a fact that at the relevant time Mrs Rhodes was working at home. The matters the claimant drew to the court's attention—the fact that she was sometimes sent material to help her to keep up to date with the law and practice in the field in which she was employed:

"did not suggest that on that particular day she was actually doing anything, although she could have been required to do something . . . simply as a matter of construction of the relevant section [SSCBA, s.94(1)], the twin test is not satisfied.

One of the pillars is fulfilled, the accident did arise out of the employment, but it does not seem to me that it arose in the course of the employment. To say that something was causally linked to something which has been done in the course of employment does not seem to me to be good enough".

However, had Mrs Rhodes been assaulted on her drive while giving advice in her official capacity to her neighbour on benefit matters, one might surely agree with the dissenting Swinton Thomas L.J. that such an accident arose not only "out of" but also "in the course of" her employment.

In *CI/1098/2004*, Commissioner Howell was faced with an application for an accident declaration from a hospital staff nurse, who argued that he had suffered psychological damage because of what he was told in the course of a telephone conversation he made to his Directorate Manager when at home on sick leave, having earlier been telephoned from work and asked to call his Directorate Manager. Commissioner Howell directed the tribunal to which he remitted the application for an accident declaration that for that purpose the telephone conversation was one made in the course of and out of the applicant's employment

"but that it is for the claimant to establish to the satisfaction of the tribunal that he did in fact suffer something in the course of or as the immediate consequence of that conversation which is identifiable as an 'accident' before he can be granted the declaration he seeks. This is something the tribunal must determine for itself, the apparent departmental acceptance that he has suffered some form of personal injury being insufficient" (para.2).

It cannot be emphasised too strongly that the whole of this note on the course of employment should be read in the light of the comments in the *Nancollas* case, *Smith v Stages*, *Faulkner v Chief Adjudication Officer* and *CAO v Rhodes* (above) about the proper approach to determining the question of whether a claimant is, or is not, in the course of his employment. In starred decision *CI/105/1990*, Commissioner Goodman considered how one should approach the case in which several accidents (in this instance two on the same day) are each said to be industrial accidents:

"[I]n deciding whether or not first, second or subsequent accidents are of themselves industrial accidents, each must be looked at in isolation, though what happened in one accident may have some bearing on whether or not when a subsequent accident occurred the claimant was still within the course of employment. *But* it must still be established independently that the second accident did arise out of and in the course of employment, as that is required imperatively by section 50(1) of the Social Security Act 1975 [now s.94(1)]" (para.13).

In *CI/105/1990*, the claimant home carer (home help) slipped on an icy pavement on her way to her first visit of the day, incurring what was later established to be a hairline fracture of the fibula. She nevertheless continued work and undertook a number of tasks at and in relation to her first call. Being still in pain, she informed her supervisor that she was going to hospital to have her leg checked and, if necessary, treated. "It was either expressed or implied that if all was well she would be carrying on with her schedule of visits for the day." Unfortunately, she slipped on the icy pavement when the taxi came, suffering a "potts fracture" of the right ankle, so severe that she had not at the time of the Commissioner's hearing been able to resume work as a home carer. The SSAT upheld her appeal against the AO's refusal to grant any declaration of industrial accident, but only in relation to the first incident. On appeal by the claimant from the SSAT, Commissioner Goodman considered the proper course was to regard there as having been two separate decisions by the SSAT, so that he was only concerned with the second incident. He considered that when it occurred, the claimant was still in the course of her employment, acting as an employee would if there was continued pain in the leg, namely to obtain some medical investigation of it, in her case in the only way open to a peripatetic worker, that is, by going to hospital. In this case, dependent on this point entirely on its own facts, the line dividing the course of employment and its cessation for that day was to be drawn only when it was clear that the claimant would not be coming back to work that day, something which only became clear when investigations took place in the hospital (see paras 10 and 11).

Subs. (2)

Industrial death benefit is no longer payable except in respect of deaths occurring before April 11, 1988. On reduced earnings allowance and retirement allowance, see commentary to Sch.7, Pts IV and V.   **1.331**

Subs. (3)

This provision has been referred to in the note on subs.(1) above. The so-called presumption created by this subsection has no operation where all the facts are known—it can only help the claimant where there is some doubt about the circumstances of the accident.   **1.332**

In *R. v N.I. (Industrial Injuries) Commissioner Ex p. Richardson* [1958] 1 W.L.R. 851 (Appendix to *R(I) 21/58*), the Divisional Court considered the equivalent provision in an earlier statute:

"if . . . there is no other evidence except that [the claimant] suffered an accident in the course of his employment, then it is to be deemed, it is taken to be proved, that it arose out of the employment. But if there is evidence to the contrary by whoever it is given, that is to say, the facts which are before the Commissioner can amount to evidence to the contrary, then the presumption or the deeming disappears, and if once that deeming disappears it is then for [the claimant] to prove that the accident did arise not only in the course of but also out of his employment."

In *R(I) 16/61*, a Tribunal of Commissioners said that, ". . . as the facts are known and it is a question of applying the law to them it seems to us that there is no room for the application of [the presumption]."

In *R(I) 1/64*, the Commissioner suggested that "evidence to the contrary" in the subsection meant something more than speculative inference, but something less than proof. All the authorities were considered in *R(I) 6/82* (maintenance engineer in bakery suffering unexplained fracture to ankle whilst walking round a milling machine) where the subsection was held to be inapplicable because all the circumstances of the accident were known.

The presumption was considered again recently in *CI/207/1987*, where Commissioner Hoolahan considered the nature of the evidence required to rebut the presumption. He rejected the proposition that an inference could amount to evidence, since an inference may only be drawn from an established fact. If no clear inference can be drawn from the established facts, there is no evidence "to the contrary" for the purposes of this section.

Subs. (5)

Except for the special groups of workers referred to, industrial injuries benefit is not payable in respect of accidents happening outside Great Britain, notwithstanding that the victim may be carrying out his job abroad. This apparent anomaly was rectified by an amendment to the Persons Abroad Regulations which permits a claim for benefit in respect of accidents happening abroad to an employed earner, with effect from October 1, 1986.   **1.333**

Subs. (6)

For "incapable of work" and "incapacity for work" see the notes to s.57 (pp.180–182, and 187–194 of Bonner, Hooker and White, *Non Means Tested Benefits: The Legislation* (1994)). The new tests of incapacity in Pt XIIA do not apply for the purposes of industrial injuries benefits (s.171G(1)(a), below).   **1.334**

Relevant employments

1.335   **95.**—(1) In section 94 above, this section and sections 98 and 109 below "employed earner's employment" shall be taken to include any employment by virtue of which a person is, or is treated by regulations as being for the purposes of industrial injuries benefit, an employed earner.

(2) Regulations may provide that any prescribed employment shall not be treated for the purposes of industrial injuries benefit as employed earner's employment notwithstanding that it would be so treated apart from the regulations.

(3) For the purposes of the provisions of this Act mentioned in subsection (1) above an employment shall be an employed earner's employment in relation to an accident if (and only if) it is, or is treated by regulations as being, such an employment when the accident occurs.

(4) Any reference in the industrial injuries and diseases provisions to an "employed earner" or "employed earner's employment" is to be construed, in relation to any time before 6th April 1975, as a reference respectively to an "insured person" or "insurable employment" within the meaning of the provisions relating to industrial injuries and diseases which were in force at that time.

(5) In subsection (4) above "the industrial injuries and diseases provisions" means—

(a) this section and sections 96 to 110 below;

(b) any other provisions of this Act so far as they relate to those sections; and

(c) [¹ any provisions of the Administration Act, Chapter II of Part I of the Social Security Act 1998 or Part II of the Social Security Contributions (Transfer of Functions, etc.) Act 1999, so far as they so relate.]

AMENDMENT

1. Social Security Act 1998, Sch.7, para.64 and Social Security Contributions (Transfer of Functions, etc.) Act 1999, Sch.7, para.4 (July 5, 1999).

DERIVATION

1.336   SSA 1975, s.51 as amended; SS(MP)A 1977, s.17(3).

GENERAL NOTE

1.337   The regulations referred to in this section are the Social Security (Employed Earner's Employments for Industrial Injuries Purposes) Regulations 1975 (SI 1975/467). Decisions on whether a person is, or was, employed in employed earner's employment so as to bring him within the scheme were until April 1, 1999 solely for the Secretary of State (SSAA 1992, s.17). From April 1, 1999, such decisions are matters for officers of the Board of Revenue and Customs (see Social Security Contributions (Transfer of Functions, etc.) Act 1999, s.8(1)(b), below).

Persons treated as employers for certain purposes

1.338   **96.**—In relation to—

(a) a person who is an employed earner for the purposes of this Part of this Act otherwise than by virtue of a contract of service or apprenticeship; or

(b) any other employed earner—
    (i) who is employed for the purpose of any game or recreation and is engaged or paid through a club; or
    (ii) in whose case it appears to the Secretary of State there is special difficulty in the application of all or any of the provisions of this Part of this Act relating to employers,

regulations may provide for a prescribed person to be treated in respect of industrial injuries benefit and its administration as the earner's employer.

Accidents in course of illegal employments

97.—(1) Subsection (2) below has effect in any case where—   **1.339**
(a) a claim is made for industrial injuries benefit in respect of an accident, or of a prescribed disease or injury; or
(b) [¹ an application is made under section 29 of the Social Security Act 1998 for a declaration that an accident was an industrial accident, or for a corresponding declaration as to a prescribed disease or injury.]

(2) The Secretary of State may direct that the relevant employment shall, in relation to that accident, disease or injury, be treated as having been employed earner's employment notwithstanding that by reason of a contravention of, or non-compliance with, some provision contained in or having effect under an enactment passed for the protection of employed persons or any class of employed persons, either—
(a) the contract purporting to govern the employment was void; or
(b) the employed person was not lawfully employed in the relevant employment at the time when, or in the place where, the accident happened or the disease or injury was contracted or received.

(3) In subsection (2) above "relevant employment" means—
(a) in relation to an accident, the employment out of and in the course of which the accident arises, and
(b) in relation to a prescribed disease or injury, the employment to the nature of which the disease or injury is due.

Amendment

1. Social Security Act 1998, Sch.7, para.64 (July 5, 1999).

Earner acting in breach of regulations, etc.

98.—An accident shall be taken to arise out of and in the course of an   **1.340**
employed earner's employment, notwithstanding that he is at the time of the accident acting in contravention of any statutory or other regulations applicable to his employment, or of any orders given by or on behalf of his employer, or that he is acting without instructions from his employer, if—
(a) the accident would have been taken so to have arisen had the act not been done in contravention of any such regulations or orders, or without such instructions, as the case may be; and
(b) the act is done for the purposes of and in connection with the employer's trade or business.

Derivation

SSA 1975, s.52.   **1.341**

GENERAL NOTE

1.342   This is the first of four successive sections which extend the scheme to situations in which, on general principle, the accident would not be regarded as arising out of, or in the course of, employment. For three of the four sections it is still necessary to consider the question of whether, on a given hypothesis, the accident happened in the course of employment and reference must, therefore, be made to the general discussion in the note to s.94(1) above.

If an accident happens to an employee who is acting contrary to regulations, or without the permission of or contrary to the instructions of his employer it would not be difficult to conclude that he had taken himself out of the course of employment by virtue of his acts. This section *deems* the accident to have arisen out of and in the course of employment provided two conditions are fulfilled. In *CI/210/50*, where a miner had (contrary to the Coal Mines Act 1911) jumped on a tram to ride back to the shaft bottom and was injured when it was derailed, the Commissioner formulated the following approach to the application of the equivalent section of the National Insurance (Industrial Injuries) Act 1946:

(a) looking at the facts as a whole, including any regulations or orders affecting the claimant, was the accident one which arose out of and in the course of employment?

(b) if the answer to the first question is "no"—is that because the claimant was acting in contravention of some regulation or order?

(c) if the answer to the second question is "yes"—was the claimant's act done for the purposes of and in connection with the employer's business?

Following through the reasoning, if the answer to the first question is "yes", the claimant will have proved that part of his case without recourse to the section. The approach recommended by the Commissioner demonstrates that it is still necessary to determine whether the accident arose in the course of employment, either taking account of or ignoring the breach of regulation or instruction. That question must be answered on general principles.

Particular difficulty has been encountered in cases where the claimant has done something unauthorised which was outside his normal duties. In *R(I) 12/61*, a repairer in a colliery was injured in an explosion occurring as he illegally connected up detonators—a job reserved for shotfirers, and in *R(I) 1/66*, a dock labourer was killed when, to expedite the loading of a ship, he attempted to use a fork-lift truck which he drove off the dock—driving being a job reserved for authorised fork-lift drivers. Both claims for benefit failed because the Commissioner held that the victim had been doing something which was not part of his job and, therefore, was not in the course of his employment. The victim was not doing his job in an unauthorised way—he was not doing *his* job. This restrictive approach was relaxed somewhat in *R(I) 1/70* where a wider view was taken of what amounted to the claimant's "job".

Earner travelling in employer's transport

1.343   **99.**—(1) An accident happening while an employed earner is, with the express or implied permission of his employer, travelling as a passenger by any vehicle to or from his place of work shall, notwithstanding that he is under no obligation to his employer to travel by that vehicle, be taken to arise out of and in the course of his employment if—

(a) the accident would have been taken so to have arisen had he been under such an obligation; and

(b) at the time of the accident, the vehicle—

(i) is being operated by or on behalf of his employer or some other person by whom it is provided in pursuance of arrangements made with his employer; and

   (ii) is not being operated in the ordinary course of a public trans-
        port service.
   (2) In this section references to a vehicle include a ship, vessel, hovercraft
or aircraft.

DERIVATION

SSA 1975, s.53.   1.344

GENERAL NOTE

(1) Introduction: looking at "travelling" accidents within the general principles set out   1.345
in s.94

   Accidents occurring in the course of travel cause many problems. A person whose
work requires travel (the sales representative, the fireman, the lorry driver, etc.)
should be able to show that an accident happening during such travelling arose in
the course of his employment, although there may be the same uncertainty about
when the course of employment begins and ends as in other jobs. Equally, a person
who is merely travelling to his work is unlikely to be able to show that the course of
his employment has begun until, at least, he has reached work.
   There are a mass of decisions on travelling accidents which attempt to distinguish
significant features to place the accident inside or outside the course of employment. Some of them are considered in *Nancollas v Insurance Officer* [1985] 1 All
E.R. 833 and others in the later House of Lords decision *Smith v Stages* [1989] 1 All
E.R. 833, considered further, below. The *Nancollas* decision deals with two appeals
from the Commissioner *(R(I) 14/81* and *R(I) 7/85)* which had both been decided
against the claimant concerned. In the former, N was in a job (disablement resettlement officer) based at Worthing which required him to call in at other centres and
to make home visits throughout Sussex and Surrey. He did not work fixed hours
and determined his own itinerary. On the day in question he had to visit Aldershot
and set out to travel there direct from home without first going into the office at
Worthing. He was injured in a motor accident. In the other appeal, B was a police
finger-print expert living, and normally working, at Wakefield. He was also a sailing
instructor and, as part of his police duties, gave sailing courses to police cadets at a
reservoir 40 miles from Wakefield. He was injured in an accident whilst travelling
on his motorcycle to the reservoir to give a course. In both cases the Commissioner
held that the accident did not arise in the course of employment, but the Court of
Appeal allowed both appeals. The impressionistic, total factor, no rules, no binding
precedents approach in *Nancollas* has been considered in the annotations to "arising
in the course of employment" in s.94. Subsequent decisions seem to have relegated
it to the secondary characterisation of particular acts once the principal questions
have been posed: what was the claimant employed to do and was s/he doing it, or
something reasonably incidental to it, when the accident occurred. But in *R(I) 1/88*
(decided before this reappraisal), the Commissioner had in any event held that
Nancollas did not remove the well-accepted distinction between acts done under an
obligation to an employer and acts merely done with his permission: in the former
case it almost necessarily follows that the employee was acting in the course of his
employment, but this does not equally necessarily follow from the fact that the
employee was doing what was authorised by the employer. So that in *R(I) 1/88*, a
British Telecom employee, who usually travelled by train, was given the use of a
company vehicle to enable him to work overtime on a specific project, and was given
specific permission, subject to strict rules, to use the vehicle to return home when
the job was completed later than expected. The Commissioner held that the accident suffered on the journey home arose in the course of the man's employment.
   The House of Lords decision in *Smith v Stages* was not concerned specifically
with s.99, nor even with the industrial injuries legislation generally, but it is instructive to set out the propositions formulated by Lord Lowry since they have general

application to the interpretation of the phrase "arising in the course of employment" and specific application to travelling.

In *Smith v Stages* there had been a motor accident causing injury which had occurred whilst the employees were on their way home from a job away from their normal place of work. There were, of course, specific circumstances which led to the particular decision, but Lord Lowry attempted a more general analysis. He said (at [1989] 1 All E.R. at 851):

> "It is impossible to provide for every eventuality and foolish, without the benefit of argument, to make the attempt, but some prima facie propositions may be stated with reasonable confidence. (1) An employee travelling from his ordinary residence to his regular place of work, whatever the means of transport and even if it is provided by his employer, is not on duty and is not acting in the course of his employment, but, if he is obliged by his contract of service to use the employer's transport, he will normally, in the absence of an express condition to the contrary, be regarded as acting in the course of his employment while doing so. (2) Travelling in the employer's time between workplaces (one of which may be the regular workplace) or in the course of a peripatetic occupation whether accompanied by goods or tools or simply in order to reach a succession of workplaces (as an inspector of gas meters might do), will be in the course of employment. (3) Receipt of wages (though not receipt of a travelling allowance) will indicate that the employee is travelling in the employer's time and for his benefit and is acting in the course of his employment, and in such a case the fact that the employee may have discretion as to the mode and time of travelling will not take the journey out of the course of his employment. (4) An employee travelling *in the employer's time* from his ordinary residence to a work-place other than his regular workplace or in the course of a peripatetic occupation or to the scene of an emergency (such as a fire, an accident or a mechanical breakdown of plant) will be acting in the course of his employment. (5) A deviation from or interruption of a journey undertaken in the course of employment (unless the deviation or interruption is merely incidental to the journey) will for the time being (which may include an overnight interruption) take the employee out of the course of his employment. (6) Return journeys are to be treated on the same footing as outward journeys."

These remarks were said expressly not to refer to salaried employees and there are, of course, some observations which are not entirely appropriate to a social security context. Nonetheless, the case was quickly referred to with approval in two unreported decisions, *CI/110/1988* and *CI/163/1988*. In *R(I)1/91*, Commissioner Rice considered the above quoted statement of Lord Lowry in *Smith v Stages* in upholding the tribunal's decision that the claimant, severely injured in a motor accident 10 minutes after finishing work, was not still in the course of his employment when the accident occurred. On the facts, the Commissioner rejected the view that the claimant was being paid by the employer to travel to and from the place of work, but went on to say that, even if he had been, "it did not necessarily follow that this in itself meant that he was in the course of his employment" (para.9). Here the Commissioner cited Lord Goff in *Smith v Stages* [1989] 2 W.L.R. 529 at 534:

> ". . . the fact that a man is being paid by his employer in respect of the relevant period of time is often important, but cannot of itself be decisive. A man is usually paid nowadays during his holidays; and it often happens that an employer may allow a man to take the afternoon off, or even a whole day off, without affecting his wages. In such circumstances, he would ordinarily, not be acting in the course of his employment despite the fact that he is being paid. Indeed, any rule that payment at the relevant time is decisive would be very difficult to apply in the case of a salaried man. Let me however give an example concerned with travelling to work. Suppose that a man is applying for a job, and it turns out that he would have a pretty arduous journey between his home and his new place of work, lasting about an hour each way, which is deterring him from taking the job. His

prospective employer may want to employ him, and may entice him by offering an extra hour's pay at each end of the day—say 10 hours' pay instead of eight. In those circumstances he would not I think, be acting in the course of his employment when travelling to or from work. This is because he would not be employed to make the journey: the extra pay would simply be given to him in recognition of the fact that his journey to and from work was an arduous one."

(2) The effect of s.99

The provisions of this section extend the course of employment to include an accident occurring on transport provided by the employer for the benefit of his workers, but which is not obligatory. (If use of the transport *is* obligatory, as with building contractors taking employees to a site by lorry from an arranged pick-up point, then the course of employment is likely to begin when the employee boards the transport.)   **1.346**

Subs. (1)

The extension is limited by the conditions which are attached by the section.   **1.347**

(a) The claimant must be travelling with the express or implied permission of his employer. Implied permission is sufficient (*R(I) 8/62*—bus conductress on her way to work picked up by empty bus returning to depot, a practice condoned by the employer), but must normally be given in advance. If permission is given retrospectively it must be express (*R(I) 5/80*—no permission given by employer for bus journey to be continued in the private car of the bus driver);

(b) The accident would have been in the course of employment if the claimant had been under an obligation to use the transport.

This again involves a consideration of the general principles in the note to s.94(1) and "Introduction", above. The nature of the accident and its relationship to the claimant's employment and his presence on the transport will be relevant.

(c) The transport is operated by or on behalf of the employer, *or* is operated as a result of arrangements made by the employer. These are alternative conditions. It should not be difficult to ascertain whether the transport is provided by the employer or on his behalf—so long as there is some measure of control exercised by the employer over the transport that should be enough (*R(I) 42/56*). The meaning of "arrangements" is less clear, but a similar concept of control has been used to determine what sort of transport service should fall within the section. It is not necessary that there should be a contract between the employer and the person who provides the transport, but there must be something more than a mere request or suggestion from the employer.

In *R(I) 67/51*, the Commissioner said,

"The 'arrangements' would normally be made by contract between the employer and the provider of the vehicle but in the absence of a contract one would expect to find at least some definite ascertainable engagement between the employer and the provider of the service whereby the employer 'arranged' for it to be provided. One would expect to find also that the employer had the exclusive use of the vehicle and that members of the public travelling as ordinary fare-paying passengers would not be carried."

Acquiescence in a scheme made by another employer is sufficient (*R(I) 49/53*), but a purely private agreement under which an employee was given the use of a company car to get to work whilst his own was under repair is not, even though he was in the habit of bringing other employees to work in his own car (*R(I) 5/60*).

(d) The transport is not being operated in the ordinary course of a public transport service.

This condition may already have been taken into account in deciding whether the employer had sufficient control over the provision of the
transport for it to be said that it was provided under an arrangement with
him, but it is a separate statutory requirement. In *R(I) 15/57* it was regarded
as significant that the bus bore no destination indicator, did not stop to pick
up members of the public, did not appear on published timetables, did not
run during factory closures, and finished the journey on a private road to the
factory. It was suggested in *R(I) 3/59* that once members of the public were
permitted to ride on the bus it would lose its "private" status, but this may be
too restrictive given the words "operated in the ordinary course of . . .".

Subs. (2)

1.348   Special provision is made for mariners and airmen by SI 1975/470 and
SI 1975/469 respectively.

Accidents happening while meeting emergency

1.349   **100.**—An accident happening to an employed earner in or about any
premises at which he is for the time being employed for the purposes of his
employer's trade or business shall be taken to arise out of and in the course
of his employment if it happens while he is taking steps, on an actual or supposed emergency at those premises, to rescue, succour or protect persons
who are, or are thought to be or possibly to be, injured or imperilled, or to
avert or minimise serious damage to property.

DERIVATION

1.350   SSA 1975, s.54.

GENERAL NOTE

1.351   Prior to 1946, when the forerunner of this section first appeared in the National
Insurance (Industrial Injuries) Act, the courts had decided that accidents sustained
in responding to an "emergency" could be regarded as "arising out of and in the
course of employment" so long as the response was broadly incidental to the
employee's duties. Since 1946, the Commissioners have taken the same line and
this section need only be considered when, on general principle, the accident has
not arisen in the course of employment (*CI/280/49*).

Emergencies under general principle (i.e. within s.94)

1.352   Once the Court of Appeal had decided that a ship's baker, injured on remon-
strating with an Egyptian who had used foul language to two lady passengers,
had suffered an accident arising out of and in the course of his employment (*Culpeck
v Orient Steam Navigation Co. Ltd* (1922) B.W.C.C. 187), the way was clear for
a reasonable response to any unexpected occurrence to be within the course of
employment so long as the acts done were within the general nature of the claimant's employment. Hence, an employee assisting a fellow employee in difficulties
(*CI/280/49*); a lorry driver assisting a stranded motorist (*R(I) 11/51*); a security
guard assisting a policeman to investigate suspicious circumstances in another
building (*R(I) 62/51*); a delivery driver assisting in moving an obstructing concrete
mixer (*R(I) 11/56*); and an Admiralty policeman stopping an inhabited runaway
push-chair (*R(I) 46/60*), were all acting in the course of their employment.

There seem to have been relatively few unsuccessful claims on this ground. In
R(I) 32/54, the response of climbing through a first-floor window to enter a locked
factory rather than waiting for the key was held to be unreasonable, and in *R(I)*

52/54, a civil servant was held not to be in the course of his employment when rescuing a child on a runaway tricycle on his way to make an interview visit to a private house. For a different approach to a similar situation to *R(I) 52/54* see *CSI/54/89,* noted above in the annotation to s.94(1) ("arising out of the employment").

Emergencies under the section

The section has only been considered extensively in *R(I) 6/63.* It is clear from that decision that the section can operate where the acts done were no part of the general duties of the employee, nor done for the employer's purposes. However, some of the phrases in the section may be restrictive.   **1.353**

"in or about premises"—does not include the highway generally (*R(I) 52/54*), but does include the road adjacent to particular premises (*R(I) 46/60*).

"rescue, succour or protect"—should be wide enough to cover most circumstances where there is actual or supposed danger to the person, but note that if steps are taken to protect property the damage to be averted or minimised must be "serious".

Note that the "emergency" must be "*at* these premises".

Accident caused by another's misconduct, etc.

101.—An accident happening after 19th December 1961 shall be treated for the purposes of industrial injuries benefit, where it would not apart from this section be so treated, as arising out of an employed earner's employment if—   **1.354**

  (a) the accident arises in the course of the employment; and
  (b) the accident either is caused—
    (i) by another person's misconduct, skylarking or negligence, or
    (ii) by steps taken in consequence of any such misconduct, skylarking or negligence, or
    (iii) by the behaviour or presence of an animal (including a bird, fish or insect), or is caused by or consists in the employed earner being struck by any object or by lightning; and
  (c) the employed earner did not directly or indirectly induce or contribute to the happening of the accident by his conduct outside the employment or by any act not incidental to the employment.

DERIVATION

SSA 1975, s.55.   **1.355**

GENERAL NOTE

This deeming provision brings within the scheme some accidents which happen *at* work, rather than *through* work. It was a response to some apparent injustices in the operation of the scheme and was first introduced in 1961. For a rare case where this was considered, see *CI/1654/2008,* noted in the commentary to s.94, above ("out of . . . the employment"). It did not there assist the claimant.   **1.356**

Subs.1(a)

The accident must still arise in the course of employment (see note to s.94(1), above). The "deeming" effect of the section applies only to the "out of employment" aspect.   **1.357**

Subs.1(b)

R(I) 3/67 seems to be the only reported decision on this section and it concerned "skylarking" and its aftermath. The claimant, whilst having a permitted smoking   **1.358** break in the appointed place, was hit by a snowball thrown by a fellow-employee. He followed the snowballer towards the cloak-room to remonstrate. As he reached the cloakroom, the door was slammed on him and his hand went through it. Was he still in the course of his employment? The Commissioner held that remonstration was reasonably incidental to his employment.

Subs. 1 (c)

1.359   *R(I) 3/67* (above) also considered whether the claimant had fallen foul of this subsection, but the Commissioner held that whereas remonstration was incidental to employment, retaliation would not have been. Note also that conduct outside employment which induces or contributes to the happening of the accident may debar the claimant.

Sickness benefit

1.360   *Section 102 repealed from April 13, 1995 by the Social Security (Incapacity for Work) Act 1994, Sch. 1, para. 29.*

Disablement pension

Disablement pension

1.361   **103.**—(1) Subject to the provisions of this section, an employed earner shall be entitled to disablement pension if he suffers as the result of the relevant accident from loss of physical or mental faculty such that the assessed extent of the resulting disablement amounts to not less than 14 per cent. or, on a claim made before 1st October 1986, 20 per cent.

(2) In the determination of the extent of an employed earner's disablement for the purposes of this section there may be added to the percentage of the disablement resulting from the relevant accident the assessed percentage of any present disablement of his—

(a) which resulted from any other accident after 4th July 1948 arising out of and in the course of his employment, being employed earner's employment, and

(b) in respect of which a disablement gratuity was not paid to him after a final assessment of his disablement,

(as well as any percentage which may be so added in accordance with regulations under subsection (2) of section 109 below made by virtue of subsection (4)(b) of that section).

(3) Subject to subsection (4) below, where the assessment of disablement is a percentage between 20 and 100 which is not a multiple of 10, it shall be treated—

(a) if it is a multiple of 5, as being the next higher percentage which is a multiple of 10, and

(b) if it is not a multiple of 5, as being the nearest percentage which is a multiple of 10,

and where the assessment of disablement on a claim made on or after 1st October 1986 is less than 20 per cent., but not less than 14 per cent., it shall be treated as 20 per cent.

(4) Where subsection (2) above applies, subsection (3) above shall have effect in relation to the aggregate percentage and not in relation to any percentage forming part of the aggregate.

(5) In this Part of this Act "assessed", in relation to the extent of any disablement, means assessed in accordance with Schedule 6 to this Act; and for the purposes of that Schedule there shall be taken to be no relevant loss of faculty when the extent of the resulting disablement, if so assessed, would not amount to 1 per cent.

(6) A person shall not be entitled to a disablement pension until after the expiry of the period of 90 days (disregarding Sundays) beginning with the day of the relevant accident.

(7) Subject to subsection (8) below, where disablement pension is payable for a period, it shall be paid at the appropriate weekly rate specified in Schedule 4, Part V, paragraph 1.

(8) Where the period referred to in subsection (7) above is limited by reference to a definite date, the pension shall cease on the death of the beneficiary before that date.

DERIVATION

SSA 1975, s.57 as amended.   1.362

DEFINITIONS

"employed earner"—s.2(1)(a), above.
"relevant accident"—s.122(1).
"loss of physical faculty"—*ibid.*

GENERAL NOTE

Subs. (1)

Disablement benefit is payable in respect of disablement even if the claimant's   1.363
capacity for work is unimpaired. The practice of the Department has been to require a separate claim for disablement benefit in respect of each industrial accident. However, in *CI/6872/95*, following the approach he had taken in *CI/420/94*, the Commissioner held that, where disablement benefit had been claimed in respect of one accident but had not been finally determined, a further claim in respect of another accident was not required. If disablement benefit is already in payment in respect of one accident, a further "claim" in respect of another accident is really an application for review. Equally, if there is in existence an assessment of disablement but disablement benefit is not payable because the assessment is below 14 per cent, an application for review of the assessment must be treated as a claim for disablement benefit if benefit is to be paid.

A useful checklist of questions

In *CI/2930/2005*, Commissioner Williams applied a key statement (definitions   1.364
and cautions) of Lord Simon in *Jones v Secretary of State for Social Services* [1972]
A.C. 944 at p.1019:

"although in particular cases the concepts may overlap, the statute envisages them as separate — in order for 'disablement' benefit to be payable, the 'accident' must result in 'injury', which must result in 'loss of faculty', which must result in 'disability' . . . my understanding of the terminology is as follows: . . . 'injury' is hurt to body or mind . . . 'loss of faculty' is impairment of the proper functioning of part of the body or mind . . . 'disability' is partial or total failure of power to perform normal bodily or mental processes . . . 'disablement' is the sum of disabilities which, by contrast with the powers of a normal person, can be expressed as a percentage."

231

He then set out in para.36 a useful framework of questions to be answered and the order of the rules to be applied under s.103:

"Reading that vocabulary into the statutory issues that I must consider, the questions to be answered are:

(a) Did the claimant 'suffer personal injury ['hurt to body or mind'] caused' by the relevant accident?
Social Security Contributions and Benefits Act 1992 ('1992 Act'), section 94(1)

(b) If so, did the claimant 'suffer as a result of the relevant accident from loss ofphysical or mental faculty' ['impairment of the proper functioning of part of the body or mind'] during the period relevant to this assessment?
1996 22 Act, section 103(1)

(c) If so, what were 'the disabilities ['the partial or total failure of power to perform normal bodily or mental functions'] incurred by the claimant as a result of the relevant loss of faculty ['impairment of the proper functioning']'?
1992 Act, Schedule 6, paragraph 1. Paragraph 1(a) requires that 'the disabilities to be taken into account shall be all disabilities so incurred (whether or not involving loss of earning power or additional expense) to which the claimant may be expected, having regard to his physical and mental condition at the date of the assessment, to be subject during the period taken into account by the assessment as compared with a person of the same age and sex whose physical and mental condition is normal'

(d) Do those disabilities ['failure of power to perform . . .'] take into account 'disabilities which, though resulting from the relevant loss of faculty ['impairment of the proper functioning . . .'], also result, or without the relevant accident might be expected to result, from a cause other than the relevant accident', if there are any?
This is required by 1992 Act, Schedule 6, paragraph 1(b) and Social Security (General Benefit) Regulations 1982 (SI 1982 No 1408 as amended) ("1982 Regulations"), regulation 11.

(e) What is the total percentage of the 'assessed extent of the resulting disablement' ['the sum of disabilities', or of 'failure of power to perform . . .'] —

　(i) by reference to those disabilities ['failure of power to perform . . .'] without reference to the particular circumstances of the claimant other than age, sex and physical and mental condition, and

　(ii) adding 'to the percentage of the disablement ['the sum of disabilities . . .'] . . . the assessed percentage of any present disablement" of the claimant resulting from any other industrial accident or any prescribed disease?

1992 Act, section 103(1), (2), and Schedule 6, paragraph 1(c)

(f) If the answers to (d) and (e) include disabilities ['failure of power to perform...'] resulting from the loss of faculty ['impairment of the proper functioning...'] both from the relevant accident and from any effective cause other than the relevant accident (whether congenital defect, injury or disease) that predate the accident, then what is the extent of disablement ['the sum of disabilities'] 'to which the claimant would have been subject . . . if the relevant accident had not occurred'?
1992 Act, Schedule 6, paragraph 1(c) and 1982 Regulations, regulation 11(3). Regulation 11(5) requires that where there are two or more industrial accidents (or disease) then the disablement resulting from both or all "shall only be taken into account in assessing the extent of disablement resulting from . . . the one which occurred or developed last in point of time".

(g) If the answers to (d) and (e) include disabilities ['failure of power to perform . . .'] resulting from the loss of faculty ['impairment of the proper functioning . . .'] both from the relevant accident and from any effective cause that postdates the accident and are not directly attributable to it, then what is the extent of disablement if that other effective cause had not arisen?

1982 Regulations, regulation 11(4). That requires that if the answer to (g) is not less than 11 per cent, then the answer to (e) 'shall also take account of any disablement to which the claimant may be subject as a result of that other effective cause except to the extent to which the claimant would have been subject thereto in the relevant accident had not occurred'. See also regulation 11(5) noted to question (f)".

Employed earner: See the note to s.94.   **1.365**

Accident: See the note to s.94. S.108 has the effect that disablement benefit is also payable in respect of prescribed diseases and prescribed personal injuries not caused by accident.

Loss of physical or mental faculty: This means "an impairment of the proper function-   **1.366**
ing of part of the body or mind" (*Jones v Secretary of State for Social Services* [1972] A.C. 944 at 1009 also reported as an appendix to *R(I) 3/69*). Thus a loss of a kidney by a claimant, which necessarily results in a loss of useful function, must, as a matter of law, mean he or she has suffered a loss of faculty even if the claimant can live normally in every way (*R(I) 14/66*). It was pointed out in *R(I) 14/66* that it does not follow that there is any resulting disablement. Nevertheless, adjudicating medical authorities have been advised to assess a "loss of reserve function" which in the case of a kidney is usually put at between 5 and 10 per cent. It is doubtful whether that is correct since that seems to be an assessment of loss of faculty rather than an assessment of disablement. The Deputy Commissioner in *R(I) 14/66* expressed concern that a claimant's assessment of disablement could not be increased if he or she lost the other kidney owing to a non-industrial disease or accident. Although *R(I) 11/66*, to which he referred, was overturned in the Court of Appeal (*R. v Medical Appeal Tribunal Ex p. Cable*, appendix to *R(I) 11/66*), reg.11(4) of the Social Security (General Benefit) Regulations 1982 appears to limit the effect of *Cable* to cases where the assessment of disablement before the loss of the second kidney has been assessed at not less than 11 per cent.

The definition of "loss of physical faculty" in s.122(1) makes special provision so that it includes disfigurement whether or not accompanied by any actual loss of faculty.

Resulting disablement amounts to not less than 14 per cent: It is disablement which must   **1.367**
be assessed and not loss of faculty. In *R(I) 3/76*, it was held that:

" 'disability' means inability to do something which persons of the same age and sex and normal physical and mental powers can do; 'disablement' means a collection of disabilities, that is to say the sum total of all the relevant disabilities found present in a given case."

"14 per cent" was substituted for "one per cent" in s.57(1) of the Social Security Act 1975 from October 1, 1986 (SSA 1986, Sch.3, para.3). Before that date, disablement benefit was paid in the form of a gratuity if the assessment was less than 20 per cent and in the form of a pension if the assessment was 20 per cent or more. That remains the case where a claim was made before that date (Social Security (Industrial Injuries and Diseases) Miscellaneous Provisions Regulations 1986, reg.14). Any pension is payable under this section and any gratuity is payable under Sch.7, para.9. This remains important where, on a claim made before October 1, 1986, there have been a series of provisional assessments. If a claim is made after

October 1, 1986 in respect of a period before that date, the new legislation applies (*R(I) 1/90, R(I)/3/96*).

Disablement benefit is also payable where the assessment is less than 14 per cent, but at least one per cent, if it is due to pneumoconiosis, byssinosis or diffuse mesothelioma (Prescribed Diseases Regulations, reg.20(1)).

The provisions for aggregating assessments of disablement have been considered in *R(I) 3/00*. The claimant had received a disablement gratuity in respect of prescribed disease A11 giving rise to disablement assessed at 7 per cent from April 1, 1985 for life. In May 1992, he claimed disablement benefit in respect of prescribed disease D4 and the disablement owing to that disease was assessed at 8 per cent from January 1, 1960 for life. He then applied for a review of the assessment of disablement in respect of prescribed disease A11 on the ground of unforeseen aggravation and the consequent disablement was assessed at 8 per cent from May 3, 1995 for life.

The Commissioner considered the way in which disablement gratuities were calculated and, in particular, the way further gratuities payable following reviews had been calculated under reg.85 of the Social Security (Adjudication) Regulations 1984. He concluded that disablement in respect of which a gratuity had been awarded did not fall to be aggregated under s.103 for the first seven years of the period of the assessment but did thereafter and that, following a review on the ground of unforeseen aggravation, the whole of the new assessment fell to be aggregated and not just the difference between the old and the new assessments. Accordingly, no disablement pension was payable to the claimant in respect of the period before April 1, 1992 (because only the 8 per cent in respect of prescribed disease D4 could be taken into account) but disablement pension was payable to the claimant thereafter on the basis that his aggregated disablement was 15 per cent from April 1, 1992 and 16 per cent from May 3, 1995.

Following *R(I)4/03*, Commissioner Rowland in *CI/954/2006* agreed that aggregation is a mere alternative to a separate award of disablement pension (para.16). It can be set in motion by an application for supersession.

Subs.(5)

1.368 There is deemed to be no loss of faculty if the resulting disablement is assessed at less than 1 per cent. In *R(I) 6/61*, the Commissioner held that it was desirable that a medical appeal tribunal should indicate whether they have concluded that there is *no* loss of faculty or whether they have concluded that there *is* a loss of faculty, but that the resulting disablement does not amount to 1 per cent. Note that, under s.110(3), a person suffering from pneumoconiosis *shall* be treated as suffering from a loss of faculty such that the assessed extent of disablement amounts to not less than 1 per cent.

For notes on the assessment of disablement; see the annotations to Sch.6 to the Act and to reg.11 of the General Benefit Regulations 1982.

Both the unified tribunal and the Commissioners now have jurisdiction over medical and non-medical matters. A Commissioner, allowing an appeal on a point of law, can now take his or her own decision on the facts available rather than remitting it to another tribunal. Commissioner Williams did so in *CI/1307/1999* giving a staged assessment of disablement in respect of post-traumatic stress disorder. The decision considers the medical aspects of the claimant's case found to be an industrial accident in *CI/15589/1996*, noted in the annotation to "accident" in respect of SSCBA 1992, s.94. In paras 15–17, Commissioner Williams distinguished "diagnosis" and "disablement" decisions. The former is essentially "a question of medical expertise". A "disablement" decision in contrast is not dissimilar to the tasks performed by judges in assessing common law damages or in applying the tariff of the Criminal Injuries Compensation Authority. In assessing disablement for industrial injuries benefits, however, that Criminal Injuries tariff is not an appropriate yardstick. Instead, supplementing SSCBA 1992, s.103 and Sch.6, regard should be had also to reg.11 and Sch.2 to the General Benefit Regulations below. Nonetheless, the import of para.37 of the decision is that exercise of the Commissioner's power to decide on the facts, rather than remitting to another tribunal, may well be rare. Even so, the decision contrasts markedly with the traditional view of such matters as ones for medical rather than legal judgment (see, for example, Commissioner Howell in *CI/636/93*). Note that the suitability of cross-reference to Sch.2 was also advocated in *R(I) 5/95*, where Commissioner Rowland stated that "assessment of disablement should be brought into line with those prescribed in the Schedule", with assessment also reflecting any intermittent or episodic character of the disablement (para.16).

Subs.(6)

This does not apply where a person is awarded disablement benefit in respect of occupational deafness (reg.28 of the Prescribed Diseases Regulations) or where a claim is made in respect of diffuse mesothelioma, see *ibid.* reg.20(4).

1.369

Subs.(7)

Under Sch.4, the amount of the pension depends on whether the claimant is over 18 and on the extent of disablement. A person over 18 whose disablement is assessed at 100 per cent receives £120.10 per week. The amount paid to people with lower assessments is proportionately less.

1.370

Increase where constant attendance needed

104.—(1) Where a disablement pension is payable in respect of an assessment of 100 per cent, then, if as the result of the relevant loss of faculty the beneficiary requires constant attendance, the weekly rate of the pension shall be increased by an amount, not exceeding the appropriate amount specified in Schedule 4, Part V, paragraph 2 determined in accordance with regulations by reference to the extent and nature of the attendance required by the beneficiary.

1.371

(2) An increase of pension under this section shall be payable for such period as may be determined at the time it is granted, but may be renewed from time to time.

(3) The Secretary of State may by regulations direct that any provision of sections 64 to 67 above shall have effect, with or without modifications, in relation to increases of pension under this section.

(4) In subsection (3) above, "modifications" includes additions and omissions.

DERIVATION

SSA 1975, s.61.

1.372

DEFINITIONS

"beneficiary" and "relevant loss of faculty"—see s.122(1).
"modifications"—see subs.(4).

GENERAL NOTE

See regs 19–21 of the Social Security (General Benefit) Regulations 1982 for further provisions relating to constant attendance allowance. Note that, under para.5 of Sch.1 to the Overlapping Benefits Regulations, constant attendance allowance overlaps with attendance allowance under s.35 and the care component of disability living allowance.

1.373

The Secretary of State's decision on constant attendance allowance is not appealable (Decisions and Appeals Regulations 1999, Sch.2, para.14(a)).

Increase for exceptionally severe disablement

1.374   **105.**—(1) Where a disablement pension is payable to a person—

(a) who is or, but for having received medical or other treatment as an in patient in a hospital or similar institution, would be entitled to an increase of the weekly rate of the pension under section 104 above, and the weekly rate of the increase exceeds the amount specified in Schedule 4, Part V, paragraph 2(a); and

(b) his need for constant attendance of an extent and nature qualifying him for such an increase at a weekly rate in excess of that amount is likely to be permanent,

the weekly rate of the pension shall, in addition to any increase under section 104 above, be further increased by the amount specified in Schedule 4, Part V, paragraph 3.

(2) An increase under this section shall be payable for such period as may be determined at the time it is granted, but may be renewed from time to time.

DERIVATION

1.375   SSA 1975, s.63.

DEFINITIONS

"medical treatment"—see s.122(1).

GENERAL NOTE

1.376   The Secretary of State's decision on exceptionally severe disablement allowance is not appealable (Decisions and Appeals Regulations 1999, Sch.2, para.14(b)).

Other benefits and increases

Benefits and increases subject to qualifications as to time

1.377   **106.**—Schedule 7 to this Act shall have effect in relation—

(a) to unemployability supplement;
(b) to disablement gratuity;
(c) to increases of disablement pension during hospital treatment;
(d) to reduced earnings allowance;
(e) to retirement allowance; and
(f) to industrial death benefit,

for all of which the qualifications include special qualifications as to time.

Successive accidents

Adjustments for successive accidents

1.378   **107.**—(1) Where a person suffers two or more successive accidents arising out of and in the course of his employed earner's employment—

(a) he shall not for the same period be entitled (apart from any increase of benefit mentioned in subsection (2) below) to receive industrial injuries benefit by way of two or more disablement pensions at an aggregate weekly rate exceeding the appropriate amount specified in Schedule 4, Part V, paragraph 4; and

(b) regulations may provide for adjusting—

    (i) disablement benefit, or the conditions for the receipt of that benefit, in any case where he has received or may be entitled to a disablement gratuity;

    (ii) any increase of benefit mentioned in subsection (2) below, or the conditions for its receipt.

(2) The increases of benefit referred to in subsection (1) above are those under the following provisions of this Act—

section 104,

section 105,

paragraph 2, 4 or 6 of Schedule 7.

DERIVATION

SSA 1975, s.91.

1.379

DEFINITIONS

"employed earner"—see ss.2 and 95(4).

"employed earner's employment"—see ss.95 and 97.

"entitled", "employment" and "industrial injuries benefit"—see s.122(1).

GENERAL NOTE

In *CI/402/1994*, the Commissioner stated that the 1986 amendments to the industrial injuries scheme "stopped the making of separate awards" so from then on there could only ever be one award of disablement benefit in respect of any period. On that view, it appeared that this section was only of relevance where the last claim was made before October 1, 1986. Commissioner Howell in *R(I)4/03* makes it clear that this is not in fact so:

1.380

" . . . unfortunately the continued provision in the post-1986 legislation for a person to have two or more disablement pensions for successive accidents (section 107(1)(a) above, and its predecessor section 91 Social Security Act 1975), was not drawn to the Commissioner's attention in that case. Moreover the later decision in *CI/12311/1996* above plainly holds otherwise, and a similar line of reasoning on separate claims for reduced earnings allowance has since been overruled by the Court of Appeal, in *Hagan v. Secretary of State* [2001] EWCA Civ 1452, 30 July 2001. I do not therefore think what was said in *CI/420/1994* should be taken as a ground for depriving claimants of the benefit of the normal prescribed time for claiming a new entitlement in the way that happened here" (para.34).

Regulations 38 and 39 of the General Benefit Regulations 1982 are treated as made under this section (SSCBA 1992, s.2(2)).

Prescribed industrial diseases, etc.

Benefit in respect of prescribed industrial diseases, etc

108.—(1) Industrial injuries benefits shall, in respect of a person who has been in employed earner's employment, be payable in accordance with this section and sections 109 and 110 below in respect of—

(a) any prescribed disease, or

1.381

(b) any prescribed personal injury (other than an injury caused by accident arising out of and in the course of his employment),
which is a disease or injury due to the nature of that employment and which
developed after 4th July 1948.

(2) A disease or injury may be prescribed in relation to any employed
earners if the Secretary of State is satisfied that—

(a) it ought to be treated, having regard to its causes and incidence and
   any other relevant considerations, as a risk of their occupations and
   not as a risk common to all persons; and
(b) it is such that, in the absence of special circumstances, the attribution of particular cases to the nature of the employment can be established or presumed with reasonable certainty.

(3) Regulations prescribing any disease or injury for those purposes may
provide that a person who developed the disease or injury on or at any time
after a date specified in the regulations (being a date before the regulations
come into force but not before 5th July 1948) shall be treated, subject to any
prescribed modifications of this section or section 109 or 110 below, as if
the regulations had been in force when he developed the disease or injury.

(4) Provision may be made by regulations for determining—

(a) the time at which a person is to be treated as having developed any
   prescribed disease or injury; and
(b) the circumstances in which such a disease or injury is, where the
   person in question has previously suffered from it, to be treated as
   having recrudesced or as having been contracted or received afresh.

(5) Notwithstanding any other provision of this Act, the power conferred
by subsection (4)(a) above includes power to provide that the time at
which a person shall be treated as having developed a prescribed disease or
injury shall be the date on which he first makes a claim which results in the
payment of benefit by virtue of this section or section 110 below in respect
of that disease or injury.

(6) Nothing in this section or in section 109 or 110 below affects the right
of any person to benefit in respect of a disease which is a personal injury by
accident within the meaning of this Part of this Act, except that a person
shall not be entitled to benefit in respect of a disease as being an injury by
accident arising out of and in the course of any employment if at the time of
the accident the disease is in relation to him a prescribed disease by virtue
of the occupation in which he is engaged in that employment.

DERIVATION

1.382   SSA 1975, s.76.

DEFINITIONS

"employed earner"—see ss.2 and 95(4).
"employed earner's employment"—see ss.95 and 97.
"entitled", "employment", "industrial injuries benefit" and "prescribe"—see
   s.122(1).

GENERAL NOTE

1.383   This section makes general provision for payment of industrial injuries benefits to
employed earners who are suffering from a disease or personal injury which was
not caused by accident and so could not give rise to entitlement under s.94. S.109
makes more detailed provision. For the prescribed diseases, see col.1 of Sch.1 to the

Social Security (Industrial Injuries) (Prescribed Diseases) Regulations 1985. Each disease is prescribed in relation to a fairly narrowly defined occupation.

Subs. (3)
See reg.43 of, and Sch.4 to, the Prescribed Diseases Regulations 1985.   **1.384**

Subss. (4) and (5)
See regs 6 and 7 of the Prescribed Diseases Regulations 1985.   **1.385**

Subs. (6)
This makes it clear that a person who develops, as the result of an accident, a   **1.386**
disease which *is not* prescribed in relation to him or her remains entitled to benefit under s.94. On the other hand, if the disease *is* prescribed in relation to the claimant, he or she must rely on the provisions relating to prescribed diseases and cannot claim benefit in respect of it under s.94.

General provisions relating to benefit under section 108

109.—(1) Subject to the power to make different provision by regulations,   **1.387**
and to the following provisions of this section and section 110 below—
  (a) the benefit payable under section 108 above in respect of a prescribed disease or injury, and
  (b) the conditions for receipt of benefit,
shall be the same as in the case of personal injury by accident arising out of and in the course of employment.
  [¹ (2) In relation to prescribed diseases and injuries, regulations may provide—
  (a) for modifying any provisions contained in this Act, the Administration Act or Chapter II of Part I of the Social Security Act 1998 which relate to disablement benefit or reduced earnings allowance or their administration; and
  (b) for adapting references in this Act, that Act and that Chapter to accidents,
and for the purposes of this subsection the provisions of that Act and that Chapter which relate to the administration of disablement benefit or reduced earnings allowance, shall be taken to include section 1 of that Act and any provision which relates to the administration of both the benefit in question and other benefits.]
  (3) Without prejudice to the generality of subsection (2) above, regulations under that subsection may in particular include provision—
  (a) for presuming any prescribed disease or injury—
    (i) to be due, unless the contrary is proved, to the nature of a person's employment where he was employed in any prescribed occupation at the time when, or within a prescribed period or for a prescribed length of time (whether continuous or not) before, he developed the disease or injury,
    (ii) not to be due to the nature of person's employment unless he was employed in some prescribed occupation at the time when, or within a prescribed period or for a prescribed length of time (whether continuous or not) before, he developed the disease or injury;
  (b) for such matters as appear to the Secretary of State to be incidental to or consequential on provisions included in the regulations by virtue of subsection (2) and paragraph (a) above.

(4) Regulations under subsection (2) above may also provide—

(a) that, in the determination of the extent of an employed earner's disablement resulting from a prescribed disease or injury, the appropriate percentage may be added to the percentage of that disablement; and

(b) that, in the determination of the extent of an employed earner's disablement for the purposes of section 103 above, the appropriate percentage may be added to the percentage of disablement resulting from the relevant accident.

(5) In subsection (4)(a) above "the appropriate percentage" means the assessed percentage of any present disablement of the earner which resulted—

(a) from any accident after 4th July 1948 arising out of and in the course of his employment, being employed earner's employment, or

(b) from any other prescribed disease or injury due to the nature of that employment and developed after 4th July 1948,

and in respect of which a disablement gratuity was not paid to him after a final assessment of his disablement.

(6) In subsection (4)(b) above "the appropriate percentage" means the assessed percentage of any present disablement of the earner—

(a) which resulted from any prescribed disease or injury due to the nature of his employment and developed after 4th July 1948, and

(b) in respect of which a disablement gratuity was not paid to him after a final assessment of his disablement.

(7) Where regulations under subsection (2) above—

(a) make provision such as is mentioned in subsection (4) above, and

(b) also make provision corresponding to that in section 103(3) above,

they may also make provision to the effect that those corresponding provisions shall have effect in relation to the aggregate percentage and not in relation to any percentage forming part of the aggregate.

AMENDMENT

1. Social Security Act 1998, Sch.7, para.65 (July 5, 1999).

DERIVATION

1.388   SSA 1975, s.77.

DEFINITIONS

"employed earner"—see ss.2 and 95(4).
"employed earner's employment"—see ss.95 and 97.
"assessed"—see s.103(5).
"employment", "employed", "prescribe" and "relevant accident"—see s.122(1).

GENERAL NOTE

1.389   In general the same benefits are payable in respect of prescribed diseases as are payable in respect of injuries caused by accident. For regulations, see the Prescribed Diseases Regulations 1985. The practice of the Department has been to require a separate claim for disablement benefit in respect of each disease. However, in *CI/420/94*, it was held that, where disablement benefit was in payment in respect of one disease, a "claim" in respect of another disease was really an application for review. The concluding words of subs.(2) were added to s.77(2) of the Social

Security Act 1975 in order to reverse the effect of *McKiernon v Secretary of State for Social Security, The Times,* November 1, 1989 in which reg.25 of the 1985 Regulations had been held to be *ultra vires.* In *Chatterton v Chief Adjudication Officer, McKiernon v Chief Adjudication Officer* (reported in *R(I) 1/94),* the Court of Appeal held that the amendment did have the intended effect.

Respiratory diseases

110.—(1) As respects pneumoconiosis, regulations may further provide that, where a person is found to be suffering from pneumoconiosis accompanied by tuberculosis, the effects of the tuberculosis shall be treated for the purposes of this section and sections 108 and 109 above as if they were effects of the pneumoconiosis.

(2) Subsection (1) above shall have effect as if after "tuberculosis" (in both places) there were inserted "emphysema or chronic bronchitis", but only in relation to a person the extent of whose disablement resulting from pneumoconiosis, or from pneumoconiosis accompanied by tuberculosis, would (if his physical condition were otherwise normal) be assessed at not less than 50 per cent.

(3) A person found to be suffering from pneumoconiosis shall be treated for the purposes of this Act as suffering from a loss of faculty such that the assessed extent of the resulting disablement amounts to not less than 1 per cent.

(4) In respect of byssinosis, a person shall not (unless regulations otherwise provide) be entitled to disablement benefit unless he is found to be suffering, as the result of byssinosis, from loss of faculty which is likely to be permanent.

1.390

DERIVATION

SSA 1975, s.78.

1.391

DEFINITIONS

"assessed"—see s.103(5).
"pneumoconiosis"—see s.122(1).

GENERAL NOTE

Subss.(1) and (2)
See regs 21 and 22 of the Prescribed Diseases Regulations 1985.

1.392

Subs.(3)
This requires that a person suffering from pneumoconiosis *shall* be treated as being disabled to the extent of at least 1 per cent, even if the disablement is in fact negligible. Under reg.20(1) of the Prescribed Diseases Regulations 1985 a person suffering from pneumoconiosis is entitled to disablement benefit if the resulting disablement is at least 1 per cent.

1.393

Subs.(4)
This subsection is disapplied by reg.20(2) of the Prescribed Diseases Regulations 1985.

1.394

Section 111 omitted.

1.395

PART VI

MISCELLANEOUS PROVISIONS RELATING TO PARTS I TO V

Earnings

Certain sums to be earnings

1.396   **112.**—(1)[¹ The Treasury may by regulations made with the concurrence of the Secretary of State] provide—

(a) that any employment protection entitlement shall be deemed for the purposes of this Act and the Administration Act to be earnings payable by and to such persons as are prescribed and to be so payable in respect of such periods as are prescribed; and

(b) that those periods shall, so far as they are not periods of employment, be deemed for those purposes to be periods of employment.

(2) In subsection (1) above "employment protection entitlement" means—

(a) any sum, or a prescribed part of any sum, mentioned in subsection (3) below; and

(b) prescribed amounts which the regulations provide are to be treated as related to any of those sums.

[¹(2A) Regulations under subsection (2) above shall be made by the Treasury with the concurrence of the Secretary of State.]

(3) The sums referred to in subsection (2) above are the following—

(a) a sum payable in respect of arrears of pay in pursuance of an order for reinstatement or re-engagement under [² the Employment Rights Act 1996],

(b) a sum payable by way of pay in pursuance of an order under that Act [³ or the Trade Union and Labour Relations (Consolidation) Act 1992] for the continuation of a contract of employment,

(c) a sum payable by way of remuneration in pursuance of a protective award under [⁴ the Trade Union and Labour Relations (Consolidation) Act 1992].

AMENDMENTS

1. Transfer of Functions Act 1999, Sch.3, para.21 (April 1, 1999).
2. Employment Rights Act 1996, Sch.1, para.51(4)(a) (August 22, 1996).
3. Employment Rights Act 1996, Sch.1, para.51(4)(b) (August 22, 1996).
4. Employment Rights Act 1996, Sch.1, para.51(4)(c) (August 22, 1996).

DERIVATION

1.397   SS(MP)A 1977, s.18.

Disqualification and suspension

General provisions as to disqualification and suspension

1.398   **113.**—(1) Except where regulations otherwise provide, a person shall be disqualified for receiving any benefit under Parts II to V of this Act, and an increase of such benefit shall not be payable in respect of any person as the beneficiary's [² wife, husband or civil partner], for any period during which the person—

(a) is absent from Great Britain; or

(b) is undergoing imprisonment or detention in legal custody.

(2) Regulations may provide for suspending payment of such benefit to a person during any period in which he is undergoing medical or other treatment as an in-patient in a hospital or similar institution.

(3) Regulations may provide for a person who would be entitled to any such benefit but for the operation of any provision of this Act [¹, the Administration Act or Chapter II of Part I of the Social Security Act 1998] to be treated as if entitled to it for the purposes of any rights or obligations (whether his own or another's) which depend on his entitlement, other than the right to payment of the benefit.

AMENDMENTS

1. Social Security Act 1998, Sch.7, para.66 (July 5, 1999).
2. Civil Partnership Act 2004, s.254 and Sch.24, para.38 (December 5, 2005).

DERIVATION

SSA 1975, s.82(5)–(6) and s.83 as amended.   1.399

DEFINITION

"Great Britain"—by art.1 of the Union with Scotland Act 1706, this means England, Scotland and Wales and see s.172.

GENERAL NOTE

Subs.(1) states two general disqualifications for receiving benefit: absence from Great Britain and undergoing imprisonment or detention in legal custody.   1.400

A Tribunal of Commissioners has clarified that this provision stops the payment of benefit rather than entitlement: *CIB/3645/2002*.

Absence from Great Britain

Absence means "not physically present" in England, Scotland or Wales; it does not necessitate the presence of the person in the past in England, Scotland or Wales: *R(U) 18/60* and *R(U) 16/62*. To be absent from Great Britain, a person must be absent throughout a whole day: *R(S) 1/66*. For the impact of absence from Great Britain on particular benefits, see the Persons Abroad Regulations, which are largely concerned with displacing the disqualification either permanently or temporarily. Very broadly speaking, the disqualification is displaced where the benefit is not related to the ability to work; some temporary relief is given where the benefit arises by reason of incapacity or confinement; and no relief at all is given where the benefit arises by reason of unemployment.   1.401

Undergoing imprisonment or detention in legal custody

Although the wording of subs.(1)(b) makes no reference to imprisonment being connected with criminal proceedings, there is now authority for reading in such a requirement. The history of the controversy is well summarised by the Commissioner in *R(S) 8/79* where the Commissioner concludes,   1.402

"I am bound by these decisions to hold that a person is not disqualified under section 82(5)(b) of the Social Security Act 1975 by reason of undergoing detention in legal custody which has nothing to do with a criminal offence" (para.5). "The decisions that I am following are all based on the proposition that imprisonment in the section means imprisonment imposed by a court exercising criminal jurisdiction . . ." (para.8).

So imprisonment for non-payment of maintenance did not disqualify the claimant from receiving invalidity benefit.

See also regs 2 and 3 of the General Benefit Regulations.

In *R(P) 1/02* the Commissioner upholds a decision to disqualify the claimant while in prison from entitlement to any part of his retirement pension. In particular, he holds that the disqualification extends to additional pension under SERPS and to graduated retirement pension. The disqualification is also held to be compatible with the requirements of the Human Rights Act 1998.

For a decision of the Administrative Court on the eligibility of post-tariff life prisoners to income support on transfer from prison to a mental health hospital, see *R. (RD and PM)* v *Secretary of State for Work and Pensions* [2008] EWHC 2635 (Admin), which confirmed that there was no such entitlement.

Reciprocal agreements

1.403   When considering benefit entitlements for persons from abroad, you should first consider whether the European Union rules apply. These apply to nationals of the European Economic Area: the countries of the European Union, that is, Austria, Belgium, Denmark, Finland, France, Germany, Greece, Ireland, Italy, Luxembourg, Netherlands, Portugal, Spain, Sweden, UK, plus Iceland, Liechtenstein and Norway (and from June 1, 2002, Switzerland). Material on the European Community rules can be found in *Vol.III: Administration, Adjudication and the European Dimension*.

Note that with effect from May 1, 2004, ten new countries joined the system of co-ordination provided for under European Community Law. They are: Cyprus, Czech Republic, Estonia, Hungary, Latvia, Lithuania, Malta, Poland, Slovakia, and Slovenia. On January 1, 2007, Romania and Bulgaria became Member States.

There are also Association Agreements with certain countries which extend entitlement to social security benefits to nationals of those countries: note in particular the agreements with Algeria, Morocco and Turkey. For a decision on the EEC–Morocco agreement, see *R(S) 1/00*.

You will also need to consider whether there is a reciprocal agreement which may smooth the way to benefit entitlement for a particular claimant. There are currently reciprocal agreements with the following countries or territories: Barbados, Bermuda, Canada, Israel, Jamaica, Jersey and Guernsey, Mauritius, New Zealand, Phillipines, Turkey, USA, and Yugoslavia (which relates to the republics of the former Yugoslavia). The text of the Conventions and the Orders bringing them into effect in national law can be found on Vol.10 of the Law Volumes maintained by the Department for Work and Pensions (the so-called "Blue Books"). These are kept up to date on the Department's website: *www.dwp.gov.uk*. For a decision that explores the GB/Jamaica agreement, and the lack of appeal rights in respect of Secretary of State decisions made thereunder, see *CIB/3645/2002*.

Note too that there remain some reciprocal agreements with EEA countries, which may assist in some circumstances where the Community rules do not, though most of these agreements have been superseded by the Community rules.

In addition, there are a number of reciprocal agreements orders of more general application, including specific rules for refugees.

R(S) 1/93 illustrates the need to take care to look at the definitions contained in each set of relevant regulations requiring to be considered in determining a question arising on appeal and to distinguish between points of legal principle and distinctions of fact. In this case the tribunal had correctly concluded that a claimant who had been resident in Malta for nearly seven years, because he found relief in the warm climate for the symptoms of his multiple sclerosis, was not temporarily absent from Great Britain under reg.2 of the Persons Abroad Regulations. The tribunal nevertheless went on to hold that the claimant was "temporarily" in Malta under

Art.9A of the Order establishing reciprocal arrangements with Malta, because it felt bound by the decision in *CS/02/1976* in which the immigration status of the claimant, described in that case as being that of a "temporary visitor", was regarded as powerful evidence for consideration even though the claimant had been in Malta for two years with no foreseeable prospect of leaving unless required to do so by the immigration authorities. The fact remained that for immigration purposes the claimant's presence was "on sufferance without a right of permanent residence".

Commissioner Johnson held that *CS/02/1976* turned on a question of fact and degree and that the conclusion in *CS/02/1976* was not binding upon the tribunal. Commissioner Johnson says the facts of the two cases are "plainly distinguishable" whereas the tribunal had described them as "virtually indistinguishable". The outcome was that the expressed inclination (as distinct from the decision) of the tribunal that the claimant was not temporarily in Malta was correct.

The result is that there are now two decisions of Commissioners which place differing emphasis on the immigration status of the individual. *CS/02/1976* suggests that it is powerful evidence of status, whereas *R(S) 1/93* (paras 13–15) suggests that it is just one factor which can be displaced by other facts present in the case.

The Social Security (Reciprocal Agreements) Order 1995 (SI 1995/767) amends the reciprocal agreements listed in Sch.2 to the Order (which includes all the agreements mentioned in these annotations) by deeming references to sickness and invalidity benefits to include references to incapacity benefit. References to the calculation of benefit under the law of the UK are to be read so as to apply to short-term and long-term incapacity benefit.

The Social Security (Reciprocal Agreements) Order 1996 (SI 1996/1928) provides for certain reciprocal agreements listed in its Sch.2 to be modified to take account of changes made by the Jobseekers Act 1995.

The Social Security (Reciprocal Agreements) Order 2001 (SI 2001/407) entering into force on April 9, 2001, provides for social security legislation to be modified or adapted in the reciprocal agreements listed in the Order to accommodate changes made by the Welfare Reform and Pensions Act 1999 in introducing new bereavement benefits.

Note that the Social Security (Reciprocal Agreements) Order 2005 (SI 2005/2765) makes provision for the Social Security Contributions and Benefits Act 1992 and the Social Security Administration Act 1992 to be modified to reflect changes made to the benefit entitlement of spouses and civil partners by the Welfare Reform and Pensions Act 1999 and the Civil Partnership Act 2004 in relation to the Orders in Council referred to in Sch.2 to the Order.

A new agreement with the Netherlands has been concluded: see the Social Security (Netherlands) Order 2007 (SI 2007/631) coming into force on June 1, 2007. A new agreement with Ireland has been concluded: see the Social Security (Ireland) Order 2007 (SI 2007/2122) coming into force on October 1, 2007.

Persons maintaining dependants, etc.

Persons maintaining dependants, etc.

114.—(1) Regulations may provide for determining the circumstances in which a person is or is not to be taken, for the purposes of Parts II to V of this Act—

    (a) to be wholly or mainly, or to a substantial extent, maintaining, or to be contributing at any weekly rate to the maintenance of, another person; or

    (b) to be, or have been, contributing at any weekly rate to the cost of providing for a child [4 or qualifying young person].

1.404

(2) Regulations under this section may provide, for the purposes of the provisions relating to an increase of benefit under Parts II to V of this Act in respect of a [³ wife, civil partner] or other adult dependant, that where—

   (a) a person is partly maintained by each of two or more beneficiaries, each of whom would be entitled to such an increase in respect of that person if he were wholly or mainly maintaining that person, and

   (b) the contributions made by those two or more beneficiaries towards the maintenance of that person amount in the aggregate to sums which would, if they had been contributed by one of those beneficiaries, have been sufficient to satisfy the requirements of regulations under this section.

that person shall be taken to be wholly or mainly maintained by such of those beneficiaries as may be prescribed.

(3) Regulations may provide for any sum or sums paid by a person by way of contribution towards either or both the following, that is to say—

   (a) the maintenance of his or her spouse [³ or civil partner], and

   (b) the cost of providing for one or more children [⁴ or qualifying persons], to be treated for the purposes of any of the provisions of this Act specified in subsection (4) below as such contributions, of such respective amounts equal in the aggregate to the said sum or sums, in respect of such persons, as may be determined in accordance with the regulations so as to secure as large a payment as possible by way of benefit in respect of the dependants.

[¹ (4) The provisions in question are section 56, 82 [⁵ . . .], 86 and paragraphs 5 and 6 of Schedule 7 to this Act.].

AMENDMENTS

   1. Tax Credits Act 2002, s.47 and Sch.3, paras 24 and 34 (April 6, 2003)

   2. Pensions Act 1995, Sch.4, para.18(f); reference to s.84 to be replaced with reference to s.83A (April 6, 2010).

   3. Civil Partnership Act 2004, s.254 and Sch.24, para.39 (December 5, 2005).

   4. Child Benefit Act 2005 c.6, Sch.1, Pt I, para.7 (April 10, 2006).

   5. Pensions Act 2007, Sch.1, para.16 (September 26, 2007).

DERIVATION

1.405   SSA 1975, s.84 as amended.

Special cases

Crown employment—Parts I to VI

1.406   **115.**—(1) Subject to the provisions of this section, Parts I to V and this Part of this Act apply to persons employed by or under the Crown in like manner as if they were employed by a private person.

(2) Subsection (1) above does not apply to persons serving as members of Her Majesty's forces in their capacity as such.

(3) Employment as a member of Her Majesty's forces and any other prescribed employment under the Crown are not, and are not to be treated as, employed earner's employment for any of the purposes of Part V of this Act.

(4) The references to Parts I to V of this Act in this section and sections 116, 117, 119, 120 and 121 below do not include references to section 111 above.

DERIVATION

SSA 1975, s.127.   1.407

GENERAL NOTE

In *CI/7507/1999,* the Commissioner notes that s.115(1) is designed to reverse the   1.408
common law rule that persons serving the Crown in whatever capacity are not "in a
master and servant" relationship with the Crown (para.13). But the reversal of the
common law rule in s.115(1) is made subject to exceptions in subs.(2) and (3) in
relation to persons serving as members of Her Majesty's forces in their capacity as
such. So, during a period of service in the Royal Air Force, a person is not treated
as being employed by the Crown for the purpose of being in employed earner's
employment for industrial injuries purposes.

The preclusion covers service in the Territorial Army (see subs.(3) and Social
Security (Contribution) Regulation 2001, Sch.6, Pt I item 6). Exemptions in
the Social Security (Benefit) (Members of the Forces) Regulations, reg.2, do not
embrace industrial injuries benefits. Accordingly, in *CI/0293/2005,* Commissioner
Fellner held that a Territorial Army cook, injured through slipping when cooking,
was not entitled to those benefits.

Her Majesty's forces

116.—(1) Subject to section 115(2) and (3) above and to this section, a   1.409
person who is serving as a member of Her Majesty's forces shall, while he is
so serving, be treated as an employed earner, in respect of his membership
of those forces, for the purposes—

(a) of Parts I to V and this Part of this Act; and

(b) of any provision of the Administration Act in its application to him
as an employed earner.

(2) [¹ The Treasury may with the concurrence of the Secretary of State]
make regulations modifying Parts I to V and this Part of this Act, [² and Part
II of the Social Security Contributions (Transfer of Functions, etc.) Act
1999] and any [³ provisions of Chapter II of Part I of the Social Security Act
1998 which correspond to] provisions of Part III of the 1975 Act, in such
matter as [¹ the Treasury think] proper, in their application to persons who
are or have been members of Her Majesty's forces; and regulations under
this section may in particular provide [⁴, in the case of persons who are
employed earners in respect of their membership of those forces, for reducing the rate of the contributions payable in respect of their employment and
determining—

(a) the amounts payable on account of those contributions by the
Secretary of State and the time and manner of payment, and

(b) the deduction (if any) to be made on account of those contributions
from the pay of those persons;]

(3) For the purposes of Parts I to V and this Part of this Act, Her
Majesty's forces shall be taken to consist of such establishments and
organisation as may be prescribed, [¹ by regulations made by the Treasury
with the concurrence of the Secretary of State] being establishments and
organisations in which persons serve under the control of the Defence
Council.

AMENDMENTS

1. Transfer of Functions Act 1999, Sch.3, para.22 (April 1, 1999).
2. Transfer of Functions Act 1999, Sch.7, paras 5–6 (April 1, 1999).
3. Social Security Act 1998, Sch.7, paras 67–68 (July 5, 1999).
4. Jobseekers Act 1995, Sch.2, para.28

DERIVATION

1.410   SSA 1975, s.128.

GENERAL NOTE

1.411   In *CI/7507/1999*, the Commissioner notes that s.116 is "dealing largely with the question of the payment of contributions" (para.13) and so there is no real contradiction between the wording of ss.115 and 116.

Mariners, airmen, etc.

1.412   **117.**—[¹ (1) The Treasury may with the concurrence of the Secretary of State] make regulations modifying provisions of Parts I to V and this Part of this Act, [² and Part II of the Social Security Contributions (Transfer of Functions, etc.) Act 1999] and any [³ provisions of Chapter II of Part I of the Social Security Act 1998 which correspond to] provisions of Part III of the 1975 Act, in such manner as [¹ the Treasury think] proper, in their application to persons who are or have been, or are to be, employed on board any ship, vessel, hovercraft or aircraft.

(2) Regulations under subsection (1) above may in particular provide—

(a) for any such provision to apply to such persons, notwithstanding that it would not otherwise apply;

(b) for excepting such persons from the application of any such provision where they neither are domiciled nor have a place of residence in any part of Great Britain;

(c) for requiring the payment of secondary Class 1 contributions in respect of such persons, whether or not they are (within the meaning of Part I of this Act) employed earners;

(d) for the taking of evidence, for the purposes of any claim to benefit, in a country or territory outside Great Britain, by a British consular official or such other person as may be prescribed;

(e) for enabling persons who are or have been so employed to authorise the payment of the whole or any part of any benefit to which they are or may become entitled to such of their dependants as may be prescribed.

AMENDMENTS

1. Transfer of Functions Act 1999, Sch.3, para.23 (April 1, 1999).
2. Transfer of Functions Act 1999, Sch.7, paras 5–6 (April 1, 1999).
3. Social Security Act 1998, ss.116–17 (July 5, 1999).

DERIVATION

1.413   SSA 1975, s.129.

Married women and widows

1.414   **118.** [¹ The Treasury may with the concurrence of the Secretary of State] make regulations modifying any of the following provisions of this Act, namely—

(a) Part I;
(b) Part II (except section 60); and
(c) Parts III and IV, in such manner as [¹ the Treasury think] proper, in their application to women who are or have been married.

AMENDMENT

1. Transfer of Functions Act 1999, Sch.3, para.24 (April 1, 1999).

DERIVATION

SSA 1975, s.130.   **1.415**

Persons outside Great Britain

119.—[¹ The Treasury may with the concurrence of the Secretary of   **1.416**
State] make regulations modifying Parts I to V of this Act [² and Part II of
the Social Security Contributions (Transfer of Functions, etc.) Act 1999]
and any [³ provisions of Chapter II of Part I of the Social Security Act
1998 which corresponds to] provisions of Part III of the 1975 Act, in such
manner as [¹ the Treasury think] proper, in their application to persons
who are or have been outside Great Britain at any prescribed time or in any
prescribed circumstances.

AMENDMENTS

1. Transfer of Functions Act 1999, Sch.3, para.25 (April 1, 1999).
2. Transfer of Functions Act 1999, Sch.7, paras 7–8 (April 1, 1999).
3. Social Security Act 1998, Sch.7, paras 69–70.

DERIVATION

SSA 1975, s.131.   **1.417**

Employment at sea (continental shelf operations)

120.—(1) [¹ The Treasury may with the concurrence of the Secretary of   **1.418**
State] make regulations modifying Parts I to V and this Part of this Act [² and
Part II of the Social Security Contributions (Transfer of Functions, etc.)
Act 1999], and any [³ provisions of Chapter II of Part I of the Social
Security Act 1998 which corresponds to] provisions of Part III of the 1975
Act, in such manner as [¹ the Treasury think] proper, in their application to
persons in any prescribed employment (whether under a contract of service
or not) in connection with continental shelf operations.

(2) "Continental shelf operations" means any activities which, if paragraphs (a) and (d) of [⁴ subsection 18) of section 11 of the Petroleum Act
1998] (application of civil law to certain offshore activities) were omitted,
would nevertheless fall within subsection (2) of that section.

(3) In particular (but without prejudice to the generality of subsection (1)
above), the regulations may provide for any prescribed provision of Parts I
to V and this Part of this Act to apply to any such person notwithstanding
that he does not fall within the description of an employed or self-employed
earner, or does not fulfil the conditions prescribed under section 1(6) above
as to residence or presence in Great Britain.

AMENDMENTS

1. Transfer of Functions Act 1999, Sch.3, para.26 (April 1, 1999).

2. Transfer of Functions Act 1999, Sch.7, paras 7–8 (April 1, 1999).
3. Social Security Act 1998, Sch.7, paras 69–70.
4. Petroleum Act 1998, Sch.4, para.30 (February 15, 1999).

DERIVATION

1.419   SSA 1975, s.132 as amended.

Treatment of certain marriages

1.420   **121.**—(1) Regulations [¹ made by the Treasury with the concurrence of the Secretary of State] may provide—

(a) for a voidable marriage which has been annulled, whether before or after the date when the regulations come into force, to be treated for the purposes of the provisions to which this subsection applies as if it had been a valid marriage which was terminated by divorce at the date of annulment;

[³ (aa) for a voidable civil partnership which has been annulled, whether before or after the date when the regulations come into force, to be treated for the purposes of the provisions to which this subsection applies as if it had been a valid civil partnership which was dissolved at the date of annulment;]

(b) as to the circumstances in which, for the purposes of the enactments to which this section [² applies, a marriage during the subsistence of which a party to it is at any time married to more than one person is to be treated as having, or as not having, the same consequences as any other marriage.]

(2) Subsection (1) above applies—

(a) to any enactment contained in Parts I to V or this Part of this Act; and

(b) to regulations under any such enactment.

AMENDMENTS

1. Transfer of Functions Act 1999, Sch.3, para.27 (April 1, 1999).
2. Private International Law (Miscellaneous Provisions) Act 1995, Sch., para.4(2) (January 8, 1996).
3. Civil Partnership Act 2004, s.254 and Sch.24, para.40 (December 5, 2005).

DERIVATION

1.421   SSA 1975, s.162.

Interpretation

Interpretation of Parts I to VI and supplementary provisions

1.422   **122.**—(1) In Parts I to V above and this Part of this Act, unless the context otherwise requires—

[¹ "additional Class 4 percentage" is to be construed in accordance with section 15(3ZA)(b) above;

"additional primary percentage" is to be construed in accordance with section 8(2)(b) above;]

[¹⁹ "Bank of England base rate" means—

    (a) the rate announced from time to time by the Monetary Policy Committee of the Bank of England as the official dealing rate, being the rate at which the Bank is willing to enter into transactions for providing short term liquidity in the money markets, or

    (b) where an order under section 19 of the Bank of England Act 1998 is in force, any equivalent rate determined by the Treasury under that section;]

"beneficiary", in relation to any benefit, means the person entitled to that benefit;

"benefit" means—

    (a) benefit under Parts II to V of this Act other than Old Cases payments;

    (b) as respects any period before 1st July 1992 but not before 6th April 1975, benefit under Part II of the 1975 Act; or

    (c) as respects any period before 6th April 1975, benefit under—

      (i) the National Insurance Act 1946 or 1965; or

      (ii) The National Insurance (Industrial Injuries) Act 1946 or 1965;

[12 "the benefits code" has the meaning given by section 63(1) of ITEPA 2003;]

[15 "child" has the same meaning as in Part 9 of this Act;]

"claim" is to be construed in accordance with "claimant";

"claimant", in relation to benefit other than industrial injuries benefit, means a person who has claimed benefit;

"claimant", in relation to industrial injuries benefit, means a person who has claimed industrial injuries benefit;

"contract of service" means any contract of service or apprenticeship whether written or oral and whether express or implied;

[2 "contribution-based jobseeker's allowance" has the same meaning as in the Jobseeker's Act 1995];

"current", in relation to the lower and upper earnings limits [3 and primary and secondary thresholds] under section 5(1) above, means for the time being in force;

[4 "day of interruption of employment" has the meaning given by section 25A(1)(c) above];

"deferred" and "period of deferment" have the meanings assigned to them by section 55 above;

"earner" and "earnings" are to be construed in accordance with sections 3, 4 and 112 above;

"employed earner" has the meaning assigned to it by section 2 above;

"employment" includes any trade, business, profession, office or vocation and "employed" has a corresponding meaning;

[20 "the employment income parts of ITEPA 2003" means Parts 2 to 7 of that Act;]

"entitled", in relation to any benefit, is to be construed in accordance with—

    (a) the provisions specifically relating to that benefit;

    (b) in the case of a benefit specified in section 20(1) above, section 21 above; and

    (c) sections 1 to 3 of the Administration Act [5 and section 27 of the Social Security Act 1998];

[12 "excluded employment" has the meaning vien by section 63(4) of ITEPA 2003;]

[6 "first appointed year" means such tax year, no earlier than 2002–03, as may be appointed by order, and "second appointed year" means such subsequent tax year as may be so appointed;]

[21 "the flat rate introduction year" means such tax year as may be designated by order;]

"industrial injuries benefit" means benefit under Part V of this Act, other than under Schedule 8;

[7 . . .]

[12 "general earnings" has the meaning given by section 7 of ITEPA 2003 and accordingly sections 3 and 112 of this Act do not apply in relation to the word "earnings" when used in the expression "general earnings"]

"the Inland Revenue" means the Commissioners of Inland Revenue;

[12 "ITEPA 2003" means the Income Tax (Earnings and Pensions) Act 2003;]

"late husband", in relation to a woman who has been more than once married, means her last husband;

"long-term benefit" has the meaning assigned to it by section 20(2) above;

"loss of physical faculty" includes disfigurement whether or not accompanies by any loss of physical faculty;

[8 "lower earnings limit" and "upper earnings limit" [3 . . .] [3 "primary threshold" and "secondary threshold"] are to be construed in accordance with subsection (1) of section 5 above, and references to the lower or upper earnings limit, or to [3 . . .] [3 the primary or secondary] threshold, of a tax year are to whatever is (or was) for that year the limit or threshold in force under that subsection;]

[7 . . .]

[1 "main Class 4 percentage" is to be construed in accordance with section 15(3ZA) above;

"main primary percentage" is to be construed in accordance with section 8(2)(b) above;]

"medical examination" includes bacteriological and radiographical tests and similar investigations, and "medically examined" has a corresponding meaning;

"medical treatment" means medical, surgical or rehabilitative treatment (including any course or diet or other regimen), and references to a person receiving or submitting himself to medical treatment are to be construed accordingly;

"the Northern Ireland Department" means the Department of Health and Social Services for Northern Ireland;

"Old Cases payments" means payments under Part I or II of Schedule 8 to this Act;

[2 "PAYE settlement agreement" has the same meaning as in [12 Chapter 5 of Part 11 of ITEPA 2003];]

"payments by way of occupational or personal pension" means, in relation to a person, periodical payments which, in connection with the coming to an end of an employment of his, fall to be made to him—

    (a) out of money provided wholly or partly by the employer or under arrangements made by the employer; or

(b) out of money provided under an enactment or instrument having the force of law in any part of the United Kingdom or elsewhere; or

(c) under a personal pension scheme as defined in section 84(1) of the 1986 Act; or

[²² (d) under a pension scheme registered under section 153 of the Finance Act 2004;]

and such other payments as are prescribed.

[⁴ "pensionable age" has the meaning given by the rules in paragraph 1 to Schedule 4 to the Pensions Act 1995];

[¹⁶ "PPF periodic payments" means—

(a) any periodic compensation payments made in relation to a person, payable under the pension compensation provisions as specified in section 162(2) of the Pensions Act 2004 or Article 146(2) of the Pensions (Northern Ireland) order 2005 (the pension compensation provisions); OR

(b) any periodic payments made in relation to a person, payable under section 166 of the Pensions Act 2004 or Article 150 of the Pensions (Northern Ireland) Order 2005 (duty to pay scheme benefits unpaid at assessment date etc.);

"pneumoconiosis" means fibrosis of the lungs due to silica dust, asbestos dust, or other dust, and includes the condition of the lungs known as dust-reticulation;

"prescribe" means prescribe by regulations;

[. . .]

"qualifying earnings factor" means an earnings factor equal to the lower earnings limit for the tax year in question multiplied by 52;

[¹⁵ "qualifying young person" has the same meaning as in Part 9 of this Act;]

"relative" includes a person who is a relative by marriage [¹⁴ or civil partnership];

"relevant accident" means the accident in respect of which industrial injuries benefit is claimed or payable;

"relevant injury" means the injury in respect of which industrial injuries benefit is claimed or payable;

"relevant loss of faculty" means—

[⁹ . . .]

(b) in relation to industrial injuries benefit, the loss of faculty resulting from the relevant injury;

[¹ "secondary percentage" is to be construed in accordance with section 9(2) above;]

"self-employed earner" has the meaning assigned to it by section 2 above;

"short-term benefit" has the meaning assigned to it by section 20(2) above;

"tax week" means one of the successive periods in a tax year beginning with the first day of that year and every seventh day thereafter, the last day of a tax year (or, in the case of a tax year ending in a leap year, the last two days) to be treated accordingly as a separate tax week;

"tax year" means the 12 months beginning with 6th April in any year, the expression "1978–79" meaning the tax year beginning with 6th April 1978, and any correspondingly framed reference to a pair of successive years being construed as a reference to the tax year beginning with 6th April in the earlier of them;

[¹⁸ "the upper accrual point" is to be construed in accordance with sub-sections (7) and (8) below;]

"trade or business" includes, in relation to a public or local authority, the exercise and performance of the powers and duties of that authority;

"trade union" means an association of employed earners;

"week", [¹³ . . .], means a period of 7 days beginning with Sunday.

[² "working life" has the meaning given by paragraph 5(8) of Schedule 3 to this Act].

[¹⁴ (1A) For the purposes of Parts 1 to 5 and this Part of this Act, two people of the same sex are to be regarded as living together as if they were civil partners if, but only if, they would be regarded as living together as husband and wife were they instead two people of the opposite sex.]

(2) Regulations [¹¹ made by the Treasury with the concurrence of the Secretary of State] may make provision modifying the meaning of "employment" for the purposes of any provision of Parts I to V and this Part of this Act.

(3) Provision may be made [¹¹ by the Treasury by regulations made with the concurrence of the Secretary of State] as to the circumstances in which a person is to be treated as residing or not residing with another person for any of the purposes of Parts I to V and this Part of this Act and as to the circumstances in which persons are to be treated for any of those purposes as residing or not residing together.

(4) A person who is residing with his spouse shall be treated for the purposes of Parts I to V and this Part of this Act as entitled to any child benefit to which his spouse is entitled.

(5) Regulations may, for the purposes of any provision of those Parts under which the right to any benefit or increase of benefit depends on a person being or having been entitled to child benefit, make provision whereby a person is to be treated as if he were or had been so entitled or as if he were not or had not been so entitled.

(6) For the purposes of Parts I to V and this Part of this Act a person is "permanently incapable of self-support" if (but only if) he is incapable of supporting himself by reason of physical or mental infirmity and is likely to remain so incapable for the remainder of his life.

[²³ (6A) The Treasury may by regulations prescribe an equivalent of the upper accrual point in relation to earners paid otherwise than weekly (and references in this or any other Act to "the prescribed equivalent", in the context of the upper accrual point, are to the equivalent prescribed under this subsection in relation to such earners).

(6B) The power conferred by subsection (6A) includes power to prescribe an amount which exceeds by not more than £1 the amount which is the arithmetical equivalent of the upper accrual point.]

[²³ . . .]

AMENDMENTS

1. National Insurance Contributions Act 2002, s.6 and Sch.1, para.12 (has effect in relation to the tax year beginning April 6, 2003 and subsequent tax years: see National Insurance Contributions Act 2002, s.8(2)).
2. Jobseekers Act 1995, Sch.2, para.29 (October 7, 1996).
3. Welfare Reform and Pensions Act 1999, Sch.12, para.77 (April 6, 2000).
4. Social Security (Incapacity for Work) Act 1994, Sch.1, para.30 (April 13, 1995).
5. Social Security Act 1998, Sch.7, para.71(a) (July 5, 1999).

6. Child Support, Pensions and Social Security Act 2000, s.35 (January 8, 2001).
7. Social Security Act 1998, Sch.7, para.71(b) (July 5, 1999).
8. Social Security Act 1998, Sch.7, para.71(c) (July 5, 1999).
9. Welfare Reform and Pensions Act 1999, Sch.13, Pt IV (April 6, 2001).
10. Tax Credits Act 1999, Sch.1, para.2 (October 5, 1999).
11. Transfer of Functions Act 1999, Sch.3, para.28 (April 1, 1999).
12. Income Tax (Earnings and Pensions) Act 2003, s.722, Sch.6, Pt 2, paras 169, 178(1) and (3).
13. Tax Credits Act 2002, Sch.6 (April 6, 2003).
14. Civil Partnership Act 2004, s.254 and Sch.24, para.41 (December 5, 2005).
15. Child Benefit Act 2005 c.6, Sch.1, Part, para.8 (April 10, 2006).
16. The Pensions 2004 (PPF Payments and FAS Payments)(Consequential Provisions) Order 2006 (SI 2006/343) (February 14, 2006).
17. Pensions Act 2007, s.11 (September 26, 2007).
18. Pensions Act 2007, s.12 (September 26, 2007).
19. Pensions Act 2004, Sch.11(2), para.18(a) (November 18, 2004 for enabling the making of regulations; April 6, 2005 otherwise).
20. Income Tax (Earnings and Pensions) Act 2003, Sch.6(2), para.178(2) (April 6, 2003 subject to transitional provisions and savings specified in 2003 c.1, Sch.7).
21. Pensions Act 2007, Pt 1, s.11(4) (September 26, 2007).
22. Taxation of Pension Schemes (Consequential Amendments) Order 2006 (SI 2006/745) Pt 1, art.4(3) (April 6, 2006).
23. National Insurance Contributions Act 2008, Sch.2, para.1 (September 22, 2008 for purposes specified in 2008 c.16, s.6(1); shall come into force on the commencement of 2007 c.22, Sch.4, para.45(2) otherwise).

DERIVATION

SSA 1975, s.168(1) and Sch.20 as amended.   1.423

For Pts VI and VII see Vol.II.

PART IX

CHILD BENEFIT

Child benefit

141.—147. *Omitted.* See *Vol.IV: Tax Credits and HMRC-administered Social Security Benefits.*   1.424

PART X

CHRISTMAS BONUS FOR PENSIONERS

Entitlement of Pensioners to Christmas Bonus

148.—(1) Any person who in any year—   1.425

255

(a) is present or ordinarily resident in the United Kingdom or any other member State at any time during the relevant week; and

(b) is entitled to a payment of a qualifying benefit in respect of a period which includes a day in that week or is to be treated as entitled to a payment of a qualifying benefit in respect of such a period,

shall, subject to the following provisions of this Part of this Act and to section 1 of the Administration Act, be entitled to payment under this subsection in respect of that year.

(2) Subject to the following provisions of this Part of this Act, any person who is a member of a couple and is entitled to a payment under subsection (1) above in respect of a year shall also be entitled to payment under this subsection in respect of that year if—

(a) both members have attained pensionable age not later than the end of the relevant week; and

(b) the other member satisifies the condition mentioned in subsection (1)(a) above; and

(c) either—

(i) he is entitled or treated as entitled, in respect of the other member, to an increase in the payment of the qualifying benefit; or

(ii) the only qualifying benefit to which he is entitled is [² state pension credit].

[² (2A) In a case falling within paragraph (c)(ii) of subsection (2) above, paragraph (a) of that subsection has effect with the substitution of "qualifying age for state pension credit" for "pensionable age".]

(3) A payment under subsection (1) and (2) above—

(a) is to be made by the Secretary of State; and

(b) is to be of [³ £ 70]or such larger sum as the Secretary of State may by order specify.

[² . . .]

(4) Only one sum shall be payable in respect of any person.

AMENDMENTS

1. Pensions Act 1995, Sch.4 (July 19, 1995).
2. State Pension Credit Act 2002, Sch.2(1), para.5(2) (July 2, 2002 for the purposes of exercising powers to make regulations or orders; October 6, 2003 otherwise).
3. Christmas Bonus (Specified Sum) Order 2008 (SI 2008/3255), para.2 (December 19, 2008).

Provisions supplementary to section 148

1.426

149.— (1) For the purposes of section 148 above the Channel Islands, the Isle of Man and Gibraltar shall be treated as though they were part of the United Kingdom.

(2) A person shall be treated for the purposes of section 148(1)(b) above as entitled to a payment of a qualifying benefit if he would be so entitled—

(a) in the case of a qualifying benefit[² other than state pension credit], but for the fact that he or, if he is a member of a couple, the other member is entitled to receive some other payment out of public funds;

(b) in the case of [² state pension credit], but for the fact that his income or, if he is a member of a couple, the income of the other member was exceptionally of an amount which resulted in his having ceased to be entitled to [² state pension credit]

(3) A person shall be treated for the purpose of section 148(2)(c)(i) above as entitled in respect of the other member of the couple to an increase in a payment of a qualifying benefit if he would be so entitled—

(a) but for the fact that he or the other member is entitled to receive some other payment out of public funds;

(b) but for the operation of any provision of [¹ . . .] paragraph 6(4) of Schedule 7 to this Act or any regulations made under paragraph 6(3) of that Schedule whereby entitlement to benefit is affected by the amount of a person's earnings in a given period.

(4) For the purposes of section 148 above a person shall be taken not to be entitled to a payment of a war disablement pension unless not later than the end of the relevant week he has attained [³ the age of 65].

(5) A sum payable under section 148 above shall not be treated as benefit for the purposes of any enactment or instrument under which entitlement to the relevant qualifying benefit arises or is to be treated as arising.

(6) A payment and the right to receive a payment—

(a) under section 148 above or any enactment corresponding to it in Northern Ireland; or

(b) under regulations relating to widows which are made by the Secretary of State under any enactment relating to police and which contain a statement that the regulations provide for payments corresponding to payments under that section,

shall be disregarded for all purposes of income tax and for the purposes of any enactment or instrument under which regard is had to a person's means.

AMENDMENTS

1. Pensions Act 2007, Sch.1, para.17 (September 26, 2007).
2. State Pension Credit Act 2002, Sch.2(1), para.6(2) (July 2, 2002 for the purposes of exercising powers to make regulations or orders; October 6, 2003 otherwise).
3. Pensions Act 1995, Sch.4(II), para.8 (July 19, 1995).

Interpretation of Part X

150.—(1) In this Part of this Act "qualifying benefit" means—

1.427

(a) a retirement pension;

(b) [¹ long term incapacity benefit]

[⁷(ba) a qualifying employment and support allowance]

(c) a widowed mother's allowance [,² widowed parent's allowance] or widow's pension;

(d) [³ . . .];

(e) [⁴ a carer's allowance];

(f) industrial death benefit;

(g) an attendance allowance;

(h) an unemployability supplement or allowance;

(i) a war disablement pension;

(j) a war widow's pension;

(k) [⁸ state pension credit;]

[⁵ (l) a mobility supplement.

(2) In this Part of this Act—

"attendance allowance" means—

(a) an attendance allowance;

(b) a disability living allowance;

(c) an increase of disablement pension under section 104 or 105 above;

(d) a payment under regulations made in exercise of the powers in section 159(3)(b) of the 1975 Act or paragraph 7(2) of Schedule 8 to this Act;

(e) an increase of allowance under Article 8 of the Pneumoconiosis, Byssinosis and Miscellaneous Diseases Benefit Scheme 1983 (constant attendance allowance for certain persons to whom that Scheme applies) or under the corresponding provision of any Scheme which may replace that Scheme;

(f) an allowance in respect of constant attendance on account of disablement for which a person is in receipt of war disablement pension, including an allowance in respect of exceptionally severe disablement;

[5 "mobility supplement" means a supplement awarded in respect of disablement which affects a person's ability to walk and for which the person is in receipt of war disablement pension];

[6 "pensionable age" has the meaning given by the rules in paragraph 1 of Schedule 4 to the Pensions Act 1995];

[8 "the qualifying age for state pension credit" is (in accordance with section 1(2)(b) and (6) of the State Pension Credit Act 2002)—

(a) in the case of a woman, pensionable age; or

(b) in the case of a man, the age which is pensionable age in the case of a woman born on the same day as the man;]

[7 "qualifying employment and support allowance" means an employment and support allowance under Part 1 of the Welfare Reform Act 2007 the calculation of the amount of which includes an addition in respect of the support component or the work-related activity component;]

"retirement pension" includes graduated retirement benefit, [5 . . .];

[8 "state pension credit" means state pension credit under the State Pension Credit Act 2002;]

"unemployability supplement or allowance" means—

(a) an unemployability supplement payable under Part I of Schedule 7 to this Act; or

(b) any corresponding allowance payable—

  (i) by virtue of paragraph 6(4)(a) of Schedule 8 to this Act;

  (ii) by way of supplement to retired pay or pension exempt from income tax under section 315(1) of the Income and Corporation Taxes Act 1988;

  (iii) under the Personal Injuries (Emergency Provisions) Act 1939 [5 . . .];

  (iv) by way of supplement to retired pay or pension under the Polish Resettlement Act 1947; [or

  [9 . . .]

"war disablement pension" means—

(a) any retired pay, pension or allowance granted in respect of disablement under powers conferred by or under the Air Force (Constitution) Act 1917, the Personal Injuries (Emergency Provisions) Act

1939, the Pensions (Navy, Army, Air Force and Mercantile Marine) Act 1939, the Polish Resettlement Act 1947, or Part VII or section 151 of the Reserve Forces Act 1980;

(b) without prejudice to paragraph (a) of this definition, any retired pay or pension to which subsection (1) of section 315 of the Income and Corporation Taxes Act 1988 applies;

"war widow's pension" means any widow's [^{10} or surviving civil partner's] pension or allowance granted in respect of a death due to a service or was injury and payable by virtue of any enactment mentioned in paragraph (a) of the preceding definition or a pension or allowance for a widow [or surviving civil partner] granted under any scheme mentioned in subsection (2)(e) of the said section 315;

and each of the following expressions, namely "attendance allowance", "unemployability supplement or allowance", "war disablement pension" and "war widow's pensions", includes any payment which the Secretary of State accepts as being analogous to it.

[^{10} (3) In this Part of this Act, "couple" has the meaning given by section 137(1) above.]

(4) In this Part of this Act "the relevent week", in relation to any year, means the week beginning with the first Monday in December or such other week as may be specified in an order made by the Secretary of State.

AMENDMENTS

1. Social Securiy (Incapacity for Work Act) 1994, Sch.1 (April 13, 1995).
2. Welfare Reform and Pensions Act 1999, s.70 (April 9, 2001).
3. Welfare Reform and Pensions Act 1999, s.88 (April 6, 2001).
4. Regulatory Reform (Carer's Allowance) Order (SI 2002/1457), Sch. (April 1, 2003).
5. Pensions Act 1995, s.132 (July 19, 1995).
6. Pensions Act 1995, Sch.4 (July 19, 1995).
7. Welfare Reform Act 2007, Sch.3, para.9(11) (October 27, 2008).
8. State Pension Credit Act 2002, Sch.2(1), para.7(2) (July 2, 2002 for the purposes of exercising powers to make regulations or orders; October 6, 2003 otherwise).
9. Income Tax (Earnings and Pensions) Act 2003, Sch.8(1), para.1 (April 6, 2003: repealed subject to transitional provisions and savings specified in 2003 c.1, Sch.7, paras 15, 19, 36 and 57).
10. Civil Partnership Act 2004, Sch.24(3), para.49(2) (December 5, 2005).

[^{1}150A Annual up-rating of basic pension etc. and standard minimum guarantee

(1) The Secretary of State shall in each tax year review the following amounts in order to determine whether they have retained their value in relation to the general level of earnings obtaining in Great Britain—

(a) the amount of the basic pension;
(b) the specified amounts in the case of Category B, C or D retirement pensions;
(c) the specified amounts in the case of industrial death benefit; and
(d) the amounts of the standard minimum guarantee for the time being prescribed under section 2(4) and (5)(a) and (b) of the State Pension Credit Act 2002.

(2) Where it appears to the Secretary of State that the general level of earnings is greater at the end of the period under review than it was at the

1.428

beginning of that period, he shall lay before Parliament the draft of an order which increases each of the amounts referred to in subsection (1) above by a percentage not less than the percentage by which the general level of earnings is greater at the end of the period than it was at the beginning.

(3) Subsection (2) above does not require the Secretary of State to provide for an increase in any case if it appears to him that the amount of the increase would be inconsiderable.

(4) The Secretary of State may, in providing for an increase in pursuance of subsection (2) above, adjust the amount of the increase so as to round the sum in question up or down to such extent as he thinks appropriate.

(5) The Secretary of State shall lay with a draft order under this section a copy of a report by the Government Actuary or the Deputy Government Actuary giving that Actuary's opinion on the likely effect on the National Insurance Fund of any parts of the order relating to sums payable out of that Fund.

6) If a draft order laid before Parliament under this section is approved by a resolution of each House, the Secretary of State shall make the order in the form of the draft.

(7) An order under this section shall be framed so as to bring the increase in question into force in the week beginning with the first Monday in the tax year following that in which the order is made.

(8) For the purposes of any review under subsection (1) above the Secretary of State shall estimate the general level of earnings in such manner as he thinks fit.

(9) If a draft order under this section is combined with a draft up-rating order under section 150 above, the report required by virtue of subsection (5) above may be combined with that required by virtue of section 150(8) above.

(10) In this section—

"the amount of the basic pension" means the first amount specified in section 44(4) of the Contributions and Benefits Act (weekly rate of Category A retirement pension);

"the specified amounts in the case of Category B, C or D retirement pensions" means—

(a) the amount specified in paragraph 5 of Part 1 of Schedule 4 to the Contributions and Benefits Act, and

(b) the amounts specified in paragraphs 6 and 7 of Part 3 of that Schedule;

"the specified amounts in the case of industrial death benefit" means—

(a) the amounts specified in paragraph 10 of Part 5 of that Schedule (apart from the amount of the initial rate), and

(b) the amount specified in paragraph 11 of that Part of that Schedule.]

AMENDMENT

Section added with effect from September 27, 2007 by the Pensions Act 2007, s.5.

GENERAL NOTE

1.429   Section 5(3) to (7) of the Pensions Act 2007 provides as follows:

"(3) The section 150A inserted by subsection (1) and the amendments made by Part 5 of Schedule 1, so far as relating to the amounts referred to in section 150A(1) (a) to (c), have effect in relation to the designated tax year and subsequent tax years (with the result that the first review to be carried out under section 150A(1) in relation to those amounts is to be carried out in the designated tax year).

(4) 'The designated tax year' means such tax year as the Secretary of State may designate by an order made before 1st April 2011.

(5) The Secretary of State must exercise his power under subsection (4) in such a way as to secure that the tax year immediately following the designated tax year is one that begins before the relevant dissolution date.

(6) 'The relevant dissolution date' means the latest date on which, having regard to the maximum period for which a Parliament may exist, the Parliament in existence at the time of exercise of the power could be dissolved.

(7) The new section 150A inserted by subsection (1) and the amendments made by Part 5 of Schedule 1, so far as relating to the amounts mentioned in section 150A(1)(d), have effect in relation to the tax year in which this Act is passed and subsequent tax years."

PART XI

STATUTORY SICK PAY

Omitted as the province of the Board of Inland Revenue. See Vol.IV.   1.430

[¹ PART XIIA

INCAPACITY FOR WORK

AMENDMENT

1. Pt XIIA was inserted by Social Security (Incapacity for Work) Act 1994, ss.5 and 6 (April 13, 1995).

Test of incapacity for work

171A.—(1) For the purposes of this Act, save as otherwise expressly provided, whether a person is capable or incapable of work shall be determined in accordance with the provisions of this Part of this Act.   1.431

(2) Regulations may make provision as to—

(a) the information or evidence required for the purpose of determining whether a person is capable or incapable of work, and

(b) the manner in which that information or evidence is to be provided, and may provide that if a person without good cause fails to provide that information or evidence, or to do so in the manner required, he shall be treated as capable of work.

[¹ (2A) In subsection (2)(a) above the reference to such information or evidence as is there mentioned includes information or evidence capable of being used for assisting or encouraging the person in question to obtain work or to enhance his prospects of obtaining it.]

(3) Regulations may provide that in any case where [² it falls to be determined] whether a person is capable of work—

(a) he may be called to attend for such medical examination as may be required in accordance with regulations, and

(b) if he fails without good cause to attend for or submit himself to such examination, he shall be treated as capable of work.

(4) Regulations may prescribe for the purposes of this section—

(a) matters which are or are not to be taken into account in determining whether a person does or does not have good cause for any act or omission, or

(b) circumstances in which a person is or is not to be regarded as having or not having good cause for any act or omission.

[³ (5) All information supplied in pursuance of this section shall be taken for all purposes to be information relating to social security.]

AMENDMENTS

1. Welfare Reform and Pensions Act 1999, Sch.8, para.23(2) (December 13, 1999).
2. Welfare Reform and Pensions Act 1999, Sch.8, para.23(3) (April 3, 2000).
3. Welfare Reform and Pensions Act 1999, Sch.8, para.23(4) (December 13, 1999).

GENERAL NOTE

Subs.(1)

1.432   Generally, for any purpose of the SSCBA 1992, whether someone is capable or incapable of work must be determined in accordance with the provisions set out in this Part (Pt XIIA) of the SSCBA 1992 (ss.171A–171G). This is "save as otherwise expressly provided": s.171G, below, stipulates that the provisions of this Part of the Act do not apply for purposes of SSP or of the industrial injuries scheme, nor for such other purposes as may be prescribed in regulations. No such preclusive regulations appear as yet to have been made.

Section 31 of the SSA 1998, above, enables regulations to be made enabling an adjudication decision on incapacity to be valid across the whole social security system other than SSP or the industrial injuries scheme, and to allow matters to be decided by the Secretary of State notwithstanding that other questions fall to be determined by another authority. See further Decisions and Appeals Regulations 1999, regs 10, 11 (see *Vol.III: Administration, Adjudication and the European Dimension.* What all this means is that decisions on incapacity under this Part of the Act are determinative not just of entitlement to incapacity benefit, but also in respect of entitlement to income support on incapacity grounds and the disability premium in income support, in respect of severe disablement allowance (but note transitional protection in the IW (Transitional) Regs, below), on the matter of capacity for work for jobseeker's allowance purposes, and on the question of title to social security contributions credits on incapacity grounds. In addition, it enables the Secretary of State to determine questions of incapacity for purposes of entitlement to the disability premiums in housing benefit and council tax benefit.

Whether someone is incapable of work will be determined by reference to either the "own occupation" test (s.171B, below) or the "personal capability assessment ("all work" test) (s.171C, below) as appropriate. Note further that persons incapable of work on these tests may nonetheless not be entitled to benefit because some aspect of their conduct (e.g. working) means that they are treated by the scheme as capable of work (subs.(3); s.171D; IW (General) Regs, regs 6–9, 16–18, below) or are disqualified from benefit (s.171E; IW (General) Regs, reg.18). Equally, some people may be exempt from the tests and treated as incapable of work (s.171E; IW (General) Regs, regs 10–15, below). Moreover, where the "personal capability assessment" ("all work test") applies, provision is made for people to be treated as incapable of work until assessed (s.171C(3); IW (General) Regs, reg.28, below).

Subs.(2)

See the IW (General) Regs, regs 6, 7, below. So far, the sanction of being treated as capable of work for failing to provide information or evidence attaches only to failure to complete and/or return the personal capability assessment ("all work test") questionnaire.

1.433

Subs.(3)

See the IW (General) Regs, reg.8, below.

1.434

Subs.(4)

See the IW (General) Regs, reg.9, below. So far, the regulation only prescribes matters to be taken into account in determining good cause for failure to provide evidence and/or information and for failing to attend for or submit to a medical examination.

1.435

The own occupation test

171B.—(1) Where a person has been engaged in remunerative work for more than 8 weeks in the 21 weeks immediately preceding the day with respect to which it falls to be determined whether he is or was incapable of work, [¹ the own occupation test is applicable in his case.]

1.436

(2) The own occupation test is whether he is capable by reason of some specific disease or bodily or mental disablement of doing work which he could reasonably be expected to do in the course of the occupation in which he was so engaged.

(3) Where for any purpose of this Act it is determined in relation to a person—

(a) that the test applicable with respect to any day is the own occupation test, and

(b) that he is on that test incapable of work,

that test remains applicable in his case until the end of the spell of incapacity beginning with that day or, as the case may be, in which that day falls, or until the 197th day of incapacity for work in that spell, whichever is the earlier.

For this purpose a "spell of incapacity" means a series of 4 or more consecutive days of incapacity for work; and any two such spells not separated by a period of more than 8 weeks shall be treated as one spell of incapacity.

(4) For the purposes of subsection (3) above a day of incapacity for work means a day—

(a) with respect to which it has been determined for any purpose of this Act that the person in question was incapable of work, or

(b) in respect of which he was entitled to statutory sick pay, or

(c) in the case of a woman, which falls within the maternity allowance period, or

(d) which in accordance with regulations is to be treated for those purposes as a day of incapacity for work.

(5) Any provision of this Act apart from subsection (4) above under or by virtue of which a day is or is not to be treated for any purpose as a day of incapacity for work shall be disregarded for the purposes of this section.

(6) Provision may be made by regulations defining for the purposes of this section what is meant by "remunerative work".

The regulations may, in particular, provide—

(a) for "remunerative work" to be defined by reference to the number of hours worked per week; and

(b) for training of any prescribed description to be treated as if it were remunerative work.

(7) Provision may be made by regulations as to the application of this section in cases where a person engages in more than one occupation or in different kinds of work.

(8) The Secretary of State may by regulations provide that subsection (3) above shall have effect as if—

(a) the reference there to 4 consecutive days were to such lesser number of days, whether consecutive or not, within such period of consecutive days as may be prescribed; and

(b) for the reference to 8 weeks there were substituted a reference to such larger number of weeks as may be prescribed.

AMENDMENT

1. Welfare Reform and Pensions Act 1999, Sch.8, para.24 (April 3, 2000).

DEFINITIONS

1.437   "day of incapacity for work"—see subs.(4).
"maternity allowance period"—see s.35(2), above.
"remunerative work"—see subs.(6); IW (General) Regs, reg.4, below.
"spell of incapacity"—see subs.(3).
"week"—see s.171G(2), below.

GENERAL NOTE

The structure of the section

1.438   This section determines whether the "own occupation" test applies to a claimant (subs.(1)), defines that test (subs.(2)), and stipulates that if applicable and satisfied, it is to apply until the end of the spell of incapacity or the 197th day in that spell, whichever is the earlier (subs.(3)). The other five subsections, not so far mentioned, are interpretative provisions or rule-making powers.

Subs.(1)

1.439   This defines when the "own occupation" test is applicable. It needs to be read with IW (General) Regs, regs 4 and 5, below, made pursuant to subss.(6) and (7). Those regulations define remunerative work, both where a person has only one occupation and engages in only one kind of work and where he has more than one occupation and engages in different kinds of work.

The test can only apply where the claimant has the requisite recent connection with the world of work. It applies if the claimant has been engaged in remunerative work for more than eight of the 21 weeks immediately preceding the day with respect to which his capacity or incapacity for work has to be determined. For example, take a wholly new claim for incapacity benefit (which would be one for short-term incapacity benefit at the lower rate (ss.30A, 30B(2)). One would look back from the first day of claim to see whether these "work connection" conditions were satisfied. If so, and the claimant meets the requisites of the test set out in subs.(2), he is incapable of work and the "own occupation" test will govern the matter of his incapacity for work for a maximum of 196 days in that spell of incapacity (see subss.(3), (4)), that is, in real terms, assuming continuing incapacity, until the point of transfer to short-term incapacity benefit at the higher rate (subs.(3); s.30B(2), above). If, in contrast, looking back in our example from the first day of claim, the "work connection" conditions are not met, the "own occupation" test cannot be applicable. Thus someone unemployed for 13 or more weeks in the last 21 will, unless treated as incapable by other provisions, be immediately subject to the more stringent "personal capability assessment", formerly "all work" test (see s.171C, below) throughout his period of incapacity (although it might be some time until he was assessed and he would usually be deemed incapable pending assessment under it—see IW (General) Regs, reg.28).

"Remunerative work" here means paid work (or work done in expectation of payment) in one occupation in which the claimant was engaged for 16 or more hours per week for more than eight weeks. Someone normally so engaged is still covered in any week when on leave from that occupation, whether that leave is paid or unpaid. "One occupation" is constituted *either* by all work of the same kind, whether or not for the same employer and whether a person is employed or self-employed, *or* by all work for the same employer (IW (General) Regs, reg.4). If someone is engaged in more than one qualifying occupation, the one for the purposes of the test is generally the last one engaged in during the 21-week period; however, if in the last week of the 21-week period he was engaged in more than one qualifying occupation, the test has to be satisfied with respect to each one (IW (General) Regs, reg.5).

Unless treated as incapable of work by regulations, where the "own occupation" test applies the claimant must, as was the case with sickness benefit, supply evidence of incapacity as required by the Medical Evidence Regulations (self-certification followed by a doctor's statement) and such additional information relevant to the test as the Secretary of State may request. Claimants can be called for a medical examination. Those who, having been given proper notice, without good cause fail to attend or submit to such an examination, will be treated as capable of work. There has been no exercise of the power to prescribe what does and does not constitute "good cause" here. Regulations now stipulate, however, that in determining that issue in this context, the adjudicating authorities (decision-maker, appeal tribunal, Social Security Commissioner) must take into account the defaulter's state of health at the relevant time, any disability from which he suffers and whether at the relevant time he was outside Great Britain. Otherwise what constitutes "good cause" here remains at large for those authorities, doubtless guided by case law from the previous system of sickness and invalidity benefits (which used the device of disqualification) and the analogous context of disqualification under that and the new scheme.

Subs.(2)

1.440

This defines the "own occupation" test: whether the claimant is incapable by reason of some specific disease or bodily or mental disablement of doing work which he could reasonably be expected to do in the course of the relevant occupation(s). The test is thus much the same as that applied to SSP cases (s.152(4), see Bonner, Hooker and White, *Non Means Tested Benefits: Legislation 1999*) and to that applicable before commencement to sickness benefit cases (SSCBA 1992, s.57(1)(a) (ii) as in force prior to April 13, 1995—see pp.180 [statutory text] and 187–88, 190–94[commentary] of Bonner, Hooker and White, *Non Means Tested Benefits: Legislation 1994*). The Department's general practice (not required by law, which would have allowed in some cases the field to be widened earlier) under the sickness/invalidity benefits regime, of not looking to a wider field of work until after the transfer to invalidity benefit (28 weeks), has thus, where the test applies, been enshrined in law.

Under the "own occupation" test one thus looks to the claimant's capacity to perform his usual job. Incapacity to do so, to satisfy the test, must be "by reason of some specific disease or bodily or mental disablement". That phraseology was found in the sickness/invalidity benefits statutory test referred to above, so decisions on that part of that test will still be authoritative here. "Specific" means "of a kind identified by medical science" (*CS/57/82*, noted in [1983] J.S.W.L. 306). "Disease" has been described as "a departure from health capable of identification by its signs and symptoms, an abnormality of some sort", and sickness falls within the definition (*CS/221/49*, para.3; *CS/7/82*, noted in [1983] J.S.W.L. 306). "Disablement"—which may be bodily or mental—constitutes a state of deprivation or incapacitation of ability measured against the abilities of a normal person (*CS/7/82, ibid.*).

In most cases there will be little problem, given the medical evidence, as to whether the claimant's condition amounts to disease or disablement; disagreement will generally centre on whether it incapacitates him for work. But a number of areas can be identified where difficult lines may have to be drawn on whether or not the condition comes within the rubric "disease or . . . disablement" at all. Mere pregnancy does not, but a disease or disablement associated with, but going beyond the normal incidents of pregnancy does, as in *CS/221/49* where the certified incapacity, "sickness of pregnancy", was suffered throughout the day. See also *R(S) 4/93*. But note now that certain pregnant women are to be treated as incapable of work (see IW (General) Regs, reg.14, below). Alcoholism can come within the rubric, but in some circumstances might bring about a period of disqualification from benefit (see IW (General) Regs, reg.18(1)(a), below). Whether certain conditions constitute a disease of the mind or a mental disablement can be problematical in that the line between a recognisable mental illness or disablement, on the one hand, and states of malingering or being workshy on the other, can be fine and uncertain. The difficulty is to decide from the available evidence whether the claimant is genuinely ill or disabled and thereby incapacitated for work in the sense understood above, or whether his is a voluntary attitude of workshyness where he could but will not work. The problem will be compounded where the outward symptoms of these alternative states are the same. What will be crucial will be the terms in which the medical (psychiatric) evidence is cast, and the inevitable value judgments about whether a particular claimant's attitudes to doing work are voluntary or involuntary. Perhaps here the appellate authorities' jurisdiction to seek further medical (in this case psychiatric) reports at public expense could prove valuable. In *R(S) 6/59*, the Commissioner considered a particular case of Munchausen's syndrome, under which condition a person repeatedly presents himself for treatment to a hospital or series of hospitals recounting symptoms of a particular disease or disability from which he is not in fact suffering, which the Commissioner there described as a strange condition in the nature of malingering. The Commissioner in that case was not satisfied on the evidence that the claimant believed the symptoms actually to exist, and felt unable to regard the condition as a psychosis, which would have come within the statutory rubric. The claim for benefit failed, the Commissioner stating as an additional ground for the decision his view that the syndrome in any event did not affect that particular claimant's capacity to work since he had driven from hospital to hospital in his lorry. In effect, the condition was treated as a defect of character. In *CS/1/81* (noted in [1982] J.S.W.L. 48), the dispute initially centred on whether the claimant, suffering from what the RMO (now a BAMS doctor) and his own doctor described as an anxiety state, was as a result incapable of work. The consultant psychiatrist to whom the claimant was referred considered him an inadequate personality by reason of his total self-indulgence and extreme degree of sheltering behind psychiatric symptoms to avoid responsibility. His condition resulted from a dismal personality structure rather than illness. Accordingly the Commissioner held that he was incapable of work but not by reason of disease or disablement, so the claim failed. Mesher (now Commissioner Mesher) suggests in [1982] J.S.W.L. 48 that the Commissioner there gave inadequate consideration to whether the defect (clearly on the evidence not an illness) could nevertheless be a mental disablement. In contrast, *CS 7/82* (noted in [1983] J.S.W.L. 306) dealt with a situation in which the claimant was said to have a severe personality disorder but not to be mentally ill. "Personality disorder" is a term sometimes used as a euphemism for workshy. The Commissioner held that its use in the particular case conveyed a notion of disability of mind sufficient to bring the claimant within the statutory rubric. It is submitted that one should avoid using euphemisms which may confuse; the loser in the case is entitled to know why he has lost. If he is thought workshy, that should be stated and reasons given for that conclusion. Sheltering behind euphemisms may also cloud the steps in reasoning which go towards good adjudication and decision-making.

What has to be established, to what standard of proof, and by what evidence, is analysed well by Commissioner Jacobs in *CIB/26/2004*. There must be established, on the civil standard of balance of probabilities, that the claimant has a recognised medical condition (paras 18, 25, citing *R2/99 (IB)*, para.8; *CSDLA/552/2001*, para. 27; and *CDLA/944/2001*, paras 9 and 10). A medical diagnosis is useful evidence, but is not decisive in that an appeal tribunal, giving appropriate reasons, can refuse to accept it. The cogency of a diagnosis varies according to a number of factors: the nature of the condition (some being easier to diagnose than others); how well qualified in the relevant area of medicine the doctor is who makes the diagnosis; the range of information and material on which the diagnosis is based; and the degree of certainty with which it is made (e.g. is the diagnosis "firm", or qualified as "working", "presumptive" or "provisional") (para.22). If there is general consensus among medical authorities as to the existence of a particular condition, a tribunal (even one containing a medical member) will normally err in law if, being sceptical, it denies its existence (para.21, citing a Northern Ireland Tribunal of Commissioners in *C38/03-04 (DLA)*, para.20(3)). If a medical diagnosis is not necessarily decisive, nor is the lack of one necessarily fatal; in appropriate circumstances a tribunal can make a diagnosis without medical evidence (para.19). While agreeing to some extent with Commissioner Brown's view (*R 2/99 (IB)*, para.11) that a tribunal should be cautious of making a diagnosis of mental disease or disablement in the absence of supportive medical evidence, Commissioner Jacobs qualified that by noting that at the time of that decision there was no medical member on the tribunal — it merely then had advice from an assessor — that change in composition rendering it easier now for a tribunal to make a diagnosis on the evidence available (para.20).

Subs.(3)

This stipulates the period for which the "own occupation" test, once applicable **1.441** to and satisfied on a particular day, can remain applicable. It remains applicable to such a claimant until the end of the spell of incapacity for work beginning with or including that day or, if earlier, until the 197th day of incapacity for work in that spell. Here, "spell of incapacity" normally means a series of four or more consecutive days of incapacity for work (an analogue of the "continuity" rule for determining a period of incapacity for work (PIW) (see s.30C(1), above). Moreover, any two such spells not separated by more than eight weeks ("week" meaning any period of seven days—see s.171G(2), below) must be treated as one spell of incapacity (an analogue of the "linking" rule for determining a PIW—see s.30C(1), above). The usual four or more consecutive days rule has been modified by the IW (General) Regs, reg.13, below. This provides a modification of the general four-day rule for claimants receiving regular weekly treatment by way of haemodialysis for chronic renal failure or peritoneal dialysis for chronic renal failure; or by way of plasmapheresis, by way of parenteral chemotherapy with cytotoxic drugs, anti-tumour agents or immunosuppressive drugs or by way of radiotherapy; or regular weekly treatment by way of total parenteral nutrition for gross impairment of enteric function. In such cases, days on which the person is engaged in that treatment are treated as ones on which he is incapable of work. Further, in the case of persons receiving such treatment, any two days of incapacity within a period of seven consecutive days will constitute a spell of incapacity for work.

"Day of incapacity", for the purposes of this subsection, is defined in subs.(4), below, but in terms that are occasionally less than crystal clear.

Subss.(4), (5)

Subsection (4) defines "day of incapacity" for the purposes of constructing a "spell **1.442** of incapacity" under subs.(3), above. Subsection (5) establishes the exclusivity of subs.(4) in that regard. Sub.(4) is the sole "gateway" through which a day becomes one of incapacity for the purpose of determining for how long in an individual case the "own occupation" test is to be applied in his term of incapacity.

For those purposes, a day of incapacity means any day (i) with respect to which it has been determined for any purpose of the SSCBA 1992 that the claimant is incapable of work (subs.(4)(a)); or (ii) in respect of which he is entitled to SSP (subs.(4)(b)); or (iii) if a woman, which falls within the maternity allowance period (subs.(4)(c)); or (iv) "which in accordance with regulations is to be treated for those purposes as one of incapacity for work" (subs.(4)(d)). As regards (iii), the maternity allowance period is defined in s.35(2), above, as the equivalent of the maternity pay period for statutory maternity pay (see s.165, in Vol.IV of this series), were the person entitled to that. Category (iv) may be thought ambiguous in its use of the phrase "treated for those purposes". If this just meant "for the purposes of subsection (3)" one would be hard pressed to find any regulations referring specifically to treating a day as one of incapacity purely for that purpose. It is submitted that it means "treated [by regulations] for any purpose of this Act" linking back to the reference to that phrase in the opening words of subs.(3) and to that phrase in subs.(4)(a). In other words it encompasses all cases whereby for a purpose of the SSCBA 1992, a day is to be treated by regulations as one of incapacity for work (even where there has been no determination of "actual" incapacity in respect of that day). So that, in short, "day of incapacity" here embraces "actual" incapacity (through head(i)) and "deemed" incapacity (through head(iv)). Any other approach would seem to involve ignoring the several situations in which someone is to be treated as incapable of work rather than actually being found to be so, which cannot surely be right, especially since categories (ii) and (iii) bring in other instances of "deemed" incapacity.

That the concept "days of incapacity" here embraces both days on which the person is found incapable and days on which he is treated as such, is borne out by the inclusion of the opaque subs.(5), which, as has been said, establishes subs.(4)'s exclusive role in determining for the purposes of subs.(3) what is a day of incapacity in order to construct a spell of incapacity to determine the point at which the "own occupation" test, having been successfully applied to the case, ceases to apply (i.e. when one reaches the 197th day in that spell). Subs.(5) stipulates that other provisions of the SSCBA 1992 under or by virtue of which a day is or is not to be treated for any purpose as one of incapacity for work, must be disregarded in constructing a spell of incapacity. In short, unless the day at issue is one of incapacity as defined in subs.(4), it does not count in constructing that spell.

One effect of subs.(5) (the sole effect presented to Parliament by the Government) is to protect those persons benefiting from the longer linking rule for those who move from incapacity benefit into a relevant tax credit (e.g. the disability element of working tax credit) or training for work and within two years wish to transfer back onto their previous rate of incapacity benefit under s.30C(5) and (6), above. Those subsections treat days in that intervening period between incapacity claims (up to two years) which were ones of engagement in remunerative work or in training for work as ones of incapacity (despite them being in fact ones of "work" in a broad sense). The effect of subs.(5) is to ignore the fact that those days are regarded as ones of incapacity for one purpose, so that whether the "own occupation" test rather than the "all work" test applies is determined in those situations by reference to the actuality of those days in the light of the standard remunerative work criteria governing the operation of the "own occupation" test (Viscount Astor, government spokesman, *Hansard*, HL Vol.554, cols 322–323). That is clearly a beneficial effect, but it may not be the sole effect of subs.(5) which, it is submitted, may also, in combination with subs.(4), have a bearing on where some days of disqualification can count for the purpose of constructing a spell of incapacity and thus determining when the applicable period of operation for the own occupation test comes to an end.

At this point, one must recall that the own occupation test applies not just for the purpose of incapacity benefit, but for all purposes for which the new tests are relevant, that is, across the whole social security system apart from SSP and industrial injuries benefits. To start, however, with incapacity benefit s.30C(3) empowers the making of regulations "as to the days which are or are not to be treated as days of incapacity for work for the purposes of any provision of this Act relating to incapacity benefit." Pursuant to that, IB Regs, reg.4 stipulates that certain days (e.g. ones of no claim, attendance at certain training courses, disqualification for absence abroad if that disqualification is for more than six weeks) are not to be treated as ones of incapacity. The effect of subs.(5) would seem to be that one ignores that for determining a spell of incapacity. That does not mean such days *will* be taken into account; merely that they are not precluded from counting. Whether they do depends on whether their actuality fits the terms of subs.(4). Similarly (and here the effect goes beyond incapacity benefit), s.171E(1), below, stipulates that regulations can provide in certain situations (e.g. claimant incapable of work through his own misconduct) either for disqualifying a person from receiving any benefit, allowance or advantage for which the new incapacity tests are relevant, or for treating him as capable of work. The relevant regulation is IW (General) Regs, reg.18 which provides, in the misconduct example given, (a) that if the claimant is entitled to incapacity benefit he shall be disqualified for receiving it, and (b) in the case of any other benefit he shall be treated as capable of work (albeit that in reality he is incapable). As to (b), it is arguable that subs.(5) requires one to look past the legal effect (treated as capable, so the day cannot be one of incapacity) to the reality (incapable so the day is one of incapacity—arguably category (i) in the note to subs. (4) (paraphrasing subs.(4)(a)), and those days count for the purpose of computing the spell of incapacity. As regards (a) (disqualification from incapacity benefit), it is submitted that these days also count, not by virtue of subs.(5) but from the words of subs.(4)(a) read with reg.18 itself. That regulation provides that if any of the "heads" in para.(1) of the regulation apply (in the chosen example, incapable through misconduct), then *if that person is entitled to incapacity benefit*, he shall be disqualified for receiving it. The terms of the regulation seem to dictate that there be a determination on incapacity for some at least of the days, so that subs.(4)(a) operates to make those days ones of incapacity for purposes of constructing a spell of incapacity, unless some other provision precludes that. On that analysis, the days of disqualification nonetheless rank as ones of incapacity and as ones of entitlement to benefit. Hence the need to make specific provision in s.30C(4) that days of disqualification do not count for the purposes set out in s.30D(1) (e.g. constructing the 364-day period after which title to short-term incapacity benefit is exhausted and, if incapacity continues, one transfers to long-term incapacity benefit). There is no such preclusive rule in this section, nor in s.171E, below, which empowered the making of the regulation. IB Regs, reg.4 treats certain other days of disqualification as not being ones of incapacity, but makes no mention of days of disqualification under reg.18. That they count in computing the application period for the test would be consistent with the policy underlying the other provisions just considered of not giving an advantage to someone disqualified, so that days of disqualification in calendar terms put off the point of transfer to long-term benefit and, in the case under discussion, do not prolong, in calendar terms, the period of operation of the "own occupation" test.

It ought not to have been beyond the wit of man or woman to have made simpler this process of computing "spell of incapacity" by a more specific listing definition of what is and what is not included.

Subs. (7)
See IW (General) Regs, regs 4, 5, noted above in the commentary on subs.(1).   1.443

Subs. (8)
No use appears to have been made of the power in para.(b) to lengthen the eight-   1.444
week "linking" period. Under para.(a), see IW (General) Regs, reg.13, noted above in the commentary on subs.(3).

[¹ **Personal capability assessments**

1.445   **171C.**—(1) Where the own occupation test is not applicable, or has ceased to apply, in the case of a person, the question whether the person is capable or incapable of work shall be determined in accordance with a personal capability assessment.

(2) Provision shall be made by regulations—

(a) defining a personal capability assessment by reference to the extent to which a person who has some specific disease or bodily or mental disablement is capable or incapable of performing such activities as may be prescribed;

(b) as to the manner of assessing whether a person is, in accordance with a personal capability assessment, incapable of work.

(3) Regulations may provide that, in any prescribed circumstances, a person to whom subsection (1) above applies shall, if the prescribed conditions are met, be treated as incapable of work in accordance with a personal capability assessment until such time as—

(a) such an assessment has been carried out in his case, or

(b) he falls to be treated as capable of work in accordance with regulations under section 171A(2) or (3) above or section 171E below.

The prescribed conditions may include the condition that it has not previously been determined, within such period as may be prescribed, that the person in question is or is to be treated as capable of work.

(4) Except in prescribed circumstances, a personal capability assessment carried out in the case of a person before the time when subsection (1) above applies to him shall be as effective for the purposes of that subsection as one carried out thereafter.

(5) The Secretary of State may, in the case of a person who for any purpose of this Act has been determined to be incapable of work in accordance with a personal capability assessment (including one carried out by virtue of this subsection), require the question whether the person is capable or incapable of work to be determined afresh in accordance with a further personal capability assessment.]

AMENDMENT

1. Welfare Reform and Pensions Act 1999, s.61 (April 3, 2000).

GENERAL NOTE

Subs. (1)

1.446   Where the "own occupation" test (s.171B, above) is inapplicable to the claimant because he lacks the requisite recent connection with work, and also where, although earlier applicable in the period of incapacity the maximum period of its application (196 days of incapacity in a single spell) has been reached, the test of incapacity is the more stringent medical/functional "personal capability assessment", the new name for the "all work" test, the centrepiece of the new scheme of benefits for incapacity for work other than SSP and the industrial injuries system. Despite its being at the heart of the system, it is defined not in the Act, but in the IW (General) Regulations, Pt III, below, and is annotated there.

Although the personal capability assessment forms and medical examination will feed more information to the decision-maker in the DWP, as regards determination of incapacity for work the "all work" test has merely been re-named with effect from April 3, 2000. The assessment still involves scoring claimants by reference to the same Schedule of activities and descriptors as before.

DERIVATION

SSA 1975, ss.162, 166 and 168 as amended.   **1.464**

GENERAL NOTE

By virtue of Sch.2, Pt V, para.20 and with effect from October 5, 1999, s.175 is to   **1.465**
be construed, in relation to tax credit, as if references to the Secretary of State were
references to the Treasury or, as the case maybe, the Board of the Inland Revenue
now Her Majesty's Revenue and Customs.

Parliamentary control

176.—(1) Subject to the provisions of this section, a statutory instrument   **1.466**
containing (whether alone or with other provisions)—

    [¹ (za) regulations under section 5 specifying the lower earnings limit
for the tax year following the designated tax year (see section 5(4) of
the Pensions Act 2007) or any subsequent tax year;]

    [² (zb) regulations under section 5 specifying the upper earnings
limit;]

  (a) regulations made by virtue of—

    [³ section 4B(2);

    section 4C;]

    [⁴ section 10ZC;]

    section 11(3);

    section 18;

    section 19(4) to (6);

    section 28(3);

    [⁵ section 30DD(5)(b) or (c);]

    [⁶ . . .]

    section 104(3);

    section 117;

    section 118;

    [⁷ section 130B(4);]

    section 145;

    [⁸ section 171ZE(1);

    section 171ZN(1).]

    [⁹ . . .]

    [¹⁰ (aa) the first regulations made by virtue of section 23A(3)(c);]

  (b) regulations prescribing payments for the purposes of the definition
of "payments by way of occupational or personal pension" in section
122(1) above;

    [¹¹ (bb) regulations prescribing a percentage rate for the purposes
of–

    (i) paragraph 3B(3) or 7B(3) of Schedule 5, or

    (ii) paragraph 5(3) of Schedule 5A;]

  (c) an order under—

    [¹² section 25B(1);]

    section 28(2);

    [¹³ section 35A(7);]

    [¹⁴ . . .]

    [¹⁵ section 130D(2);]

    [⁶ . . .]

    section 148(3)(b);

section 157(2);

[16. . .]

[17 section 159A(1),]

shall not be made unless a draft of the instrument has been laid before Parliament and been approved by a resolution of each House.

(2) Subsection (1) above does not apply to a statutory instrument by reason only that it contains—

(a) regulations under section 117 which the instrument states are made for the purpose of making provision consequential on the making of an order under section 141, 143, 145, 146 or 162 of the Administration Act;

(b) regulations under powers conferred by any provision mentioned in paragraph (a) of that subsection [18 . . .] which are to be made for the purpose of consolidating regulations to be revoked in the instrument;

(c) regulations which, in so far as they are made under powers conferred by any provision mentioned in paragraph (a) of that subsection (other than [19 section 145]), only replace provisions of previous regulations with new provisions to the same effect.

[20 (2A) In the case of a statutory instrument containing (whether alone or with other provisions) regulations made by virtue of section 4B(2) to which subsection (1) above applies, the draft of the instrument must be laid before Parliament before the end of the period of 12 months beginning with the appropriate date.

(2B) For the purposes of subsection (2A), the "appropriate date" means–

(a) where the corresponding retrospective tax provision was passed or made before the day on which the National Insurance Contributions Act 2006 was passed, the date upon which that Act was passed, and

(b) in any other case, the date upon which the corresponding retrospective tax provision was passed or made.

(2C) For the purposes of subsection (2B), "the corresponding retrospective tax provision" in relation to the regulations means–

(a) the retrospective tax provision mentioned in subsection (1) of section 4B in relation to which the regulations are to be made by virtue of subsection (2) of that section, or

(b) where there is more than one such tax provision, whichever of those provisions was the first to be passed or made.]

(3) A statutory instrument—

(a) which contains (whether alone or with other provisions) any order, regulations or scheme made under this Act by the Secretary of State, [21 the Treasury or the Commissioners of Inland Revenue] other than an order under section 145(3) above; and

(b) which is not subject to any requirement that a draft of the instrument shall be laid before and approved by a resolution of each House of Parliament,

shall be subject to annulment in pursuance of a resolution of either House of Parliament.

[23 (4) Subsection (3) above does not apply to a statutory instrument by reason only that it contains an order appointing the first or second appointed year [or designating the flat rate introduction year] (within the meanings given by section 122(1) above).

AMENDMENTS

1. Pensions Act 2007, Pt 1, s.7(5) (September 26, 2007).
2. National Insurance Contributions Act 2008 s.1(2) (September 22, 2008: insertion has effect in relation to regulations specifying the upper earnings limit for 2009-10 or any subsequent tax year).
3. National Insurance Contributions Act 2006 s.1(2)(a) (March 30, 2006).
4. National Insurance Contributions Act 2006 s.3(2) (March 30, 2006).
5. Welfare Reform and Pensions Act 1999, Sch.8(II), para.25 (November 3, 2000).
6. Social Security (Incapacity for Work) Act 1994, Sch.2, para.1 (April 13, 1995).
7. Welfare Reform Act 2007, Pt 2, s.31(2)(a) (June 14, 2007 for the purpose only of the exercise of the power to make regulations; November 1, 2007 otherwise).
8. Employment Act 2002, Sch.7, para.7 (December 8, 2002).
9. Statutory Sick Pay Percentage Threshold Order 1995 (SI 1995/512), art.6(1)(a)(i) (April 6, 1995).
10. Pensions Act 2007, Sch.1(3), para.10 (September 26, 2007).
11. Pensions Act 2004, Sch.11(2), para.19 (November 18, 2004 for enabling the making of regulations; April 6, 2005 otherwise).
12. Social Security (Incapacity for Work) Act 1994, Sch.1(I), para.37(b) (April 13, 1995).
13. Welfare Reform and Pensions Act 1999, Sch.8(VI), para.32 (January 12, 2000 for the purpose of making regulations; April 2, 2000 otherwise).
14. National Insurance Contributions Act 2008, Sch.2, para.1 (September 22, 2008 for purposes specified in 2008 c.16, s.6(1); shall come into force on the commencement of 2007 c.22, Sch.4, para.45(2) otherwise).
15. Welfare Reform Act 2007, Pt 2, s.31(2)(b) (June 14, 2007 for the purpose only of the exercise of the power to make regulations; November 1, 2007 otherwise).
16. Statutory Sick Pay Percentage Threshold Order 1995 (SI 1995/512), art.6(1)(a)(ii) (April 6, 1995).
17. Statutory Sick Pay Act 1994 s.3(2) (February 10, 1994).
18. Statutory Sick Pay Percentage Threshold Order 1995 (SI 1995/512), art.6(1)(a)(iii) (April 6, 1995).
19. Statutory Sick Pay Percentage Threshold Order 1995 (SI 1995/512), art.6(1)(a)(iv) (April 6, 1995).
20. National Insurance Contributions Act 2006 s.1(2)(b) (March 30, 2006).
21. Social Security Contributions (Transfer of Functions, etc.) Act 1999, Sch.3, para.30 (April 1, 1999).
22. Child Support, Pensions and Social Security Act 2000 s.35(15) (April 6, 2002).
23. Pensions Act 2007, Sch.1(7), para.35(b) (September 26, 2007).

DERIVATION

SSA 1975, s.167 as amended.   1.467

GENERAL NOTE

By virtue of Sch.2, Pt V, para.20 and with effect from October 5, 1999, s.176(3)   1.468
is to be construed, in relation to tax credit, as if references to the Secretary of State
were references to the Treasury or, as the case may be, the Board of the Revenue
and Customs.

Short title, commencement and extent

177.—(1) This Act may be cited as the Social Security Contributions and   1.469
Benefits Act 1991.

(2) Except as provided in Schedule 4 to the Consequential Provisions Act, this Act shall come into force on 1st July 1992.

(3) The following provisions extend to Northern Ireland—
section 16 and Schedule 2;
section 116(2); and this section.

(4) Except as provided by this section, this Act does not extend to Northern Ireland.

SCHEDULES

Schedules 1 and 2 *Omitted because the province of the Board of Inland Revenue.*

SCHEDULE 3

CONTRIBUTION CONDITIONS FOR ENTITLEMENT TO BENEFIT

PART I

THE CONDITIONS

[¹ Unemployment benefit

1.470   **1.**—. . .]

[² Short-term incapacity benefit]

1.471   **2.**—(1) The contribution conditions for [² short-term incapacity benefit] are the following.

(2) The first condition is that—
[³
(a) the claimant must have actually paid contributions of a relevant class in respect of one of the last three complete years before the beginning of the relevant benefit year, and those contributions must have been paid before the relevant time; and]
(b) the earnings factor derived as mentioned in sub-paragraph (4) below must be not less than that year's lower earnings limit multiplied by 25.

(3) The second condition is that—
(a) the claimant must in respect of the last two complete years before the beginning of the relevant benefit year have either paid or been credited with contributions of a relevant class or been credited (in the case of 1987–88 or any subsequent year) with earnings; and
(b) the earnings factor derived as mentioned in sub-paragraph (5) below must be not less in each of those years than the year's lower earnings limit multiplied by 50.

(4) The earnings factor referred to in paragraph (b) of sub-paragraph (2) above is that which is derived—
(a) if the year in question is 1987–88 or any subsequent year—
(i) from [¹⁸ so much of the claimant's earnings as did not exceed the upper earnings limit and] upon which primary Class 1 contributions have been paid or treated as paid; or
(ii) from Class 2 contributions; and
(b) if the year in question is an earlier year, from the contributions paid as mentioned in paragraph (a) of that sub-paragraph.

(5) The earnings factor referred to in paragraph (b) of sub-paragraph (3) above is that which is derived—
(a) if the year in question is 1987–88 or any subsequent year—
(i) from [¹⁸ so much of the claimant's earnings as did not exceed the upper earnings limit and] upon which primary Class 1 contributions have been paid or treated as paid or from earnings credited; or
(ii) from Class 2 contributions; and
(b) if the year in question is an earlier year, from the contributions referred to in paragraph (a) of that sub-paragraph.

(6) For the purposes of these conditions—

(a) "the relevant time" is the day in respect of which benefit is claimed;
(b) "the relevant benefit year" is the benefit year in which there falls the beginning of the [⁴ period of incapacity for work] which includes the relevant time.

[⁵ (7) Where a person makes a claim for incapacity benefit and does not satisfy [⁶ the first contribution condition (specified in sub-paragraph (2) above) or, as the case may be,] the second contribution condition (specified in sub-paragraph (3) above) and, in a later benefit year in which he would satisfy that condition had no such claim been made, he makes a further claim for incapacity benefit, the previous claim shall be disregarded.]

[⁶ (8) Regulations may—
(a) provide for the first contribution condition (specified in sub-paragraph (2) above) to be taken to be satisfied in the case of persons who have been entitled to any prescribed description of benefit during any prescribed period or at any prescribed time;
(b) with a view to securing any relaxation of the requirements of that condition (as so specified) in relation to persons who have been so entitled, provide for that condition to apply in relation to them subject to prescribed modifications.

(9) In sub-paragraph (8)—
"benefit" includes (in addition to any benefit under Parts II to V of this Act)—
(a) any benefit under Parts VII to XII of this Act, and
(b) credits under regulations under section 22(5) above;
"modifications" includes additions, omissions and amendments.]

Maternity Allowance

3.—[⁷...]   **1.472**

[⁸ Bereavement payment]

4.—(1) The contribution condition for a [⁸ bereavement payment] is that—   **1.473**
(a) the contributor concerned must in respect of any one relevant year have actually paid contributions of a relevant class; and
(b) the earnings factor derived as mentioned in sub-paragraph (2) below must be not less than that year's lower earnings limit multiplied by 25.

(2) The earnings factor referred to in paragraph (b) of sub-paragraph (1) above is that which is derived—
(a) if the year in question is 1987–88 or any subsequent year, from [¹⁸ so much of the claimant's earnings as did not exceed the upper earnings limit and] upon which primary Class 1 contributions have been paid or treated as paid and from Class 2 and Class 3 contributions, or
(b) if the year in question is an earlier year, from the contributions referred to in paragraph (a) of that sub-paragraph.

(3) For the purposes of this condition a relevant year is any year ending before the date on which the contributor concerned attained pensionable age or died under that age.

Widowed mother's allowance [⁹, widowed parent's allowance, bereavement allowance,] and widow's pension; retirement pensions (Categories A and B)

5.—(1) The contribution conditions for a widowed mother's allowance, [⁹ a widowed par-   **1.474**
ent's allowance, a bereavement allowance,] a widow's pension or a Category A or Category B retirement pension [¹⁹ (other than one in relation to which paragraph 5A applies)] are the following.

(2) The first condition is that—
(a) the contributor concerned must in respect of any one relevant year have actually paid contributions of a relevant class; and
(b) the earnings factor derived—
    (i) if that year is 1987–88 or any subsequent year, from [¹⁸ so much of the claimant's earnings as did not exceed the upper earnings limit and] upon which such of those contributions as are primary Class 1 contributions were paid or treated as paid and any Class 2 or Class 3 contributions, or
    (ii) if that year is an earlier year, from the contributions referred to in paragraph (a) above,
must be not less than the qualifying earnings factor of that year.

(3) The second condition is that—
(a) the contributor concerned must, in respect of each of not less than the requisite number of years of his working life, have paid or been credited with contributions of

a relevant class [¹⁰ or been credited (in the case of 1987–88 or any subsequent year) with earnings]; and

 (b) in the case of each of those years, the earnings factor derived as mentioned in sub-paragraph (4) below must be not less than the qualifying earnings factor for that year.

(4) For the purposes of paragraph (b) of sub-paragraph (3) above, the earnings factor—

 (a) in the case of 1987–88 or any subsequent year, is that which is derived from—

  (i) any [¹⁸ so much of the claimant's earnings as did not exceed the upper earnings limit and] upon which such of the contributions mentioned in paragraph (a) of that sub-paragraph as are primary Class 1 contributions were paid or treated as paid or earnings credited; and

  (ii) any Class 2 or Class 3 contributions for the year; or

 (b) in the case of any earlier year, is that which is derived from the contributions mentioned in paragraph (a) of that sub-paragraph.

(5) For the purposes of the first condition, a relevant year is any year ending before that in which the contributor concerned attained pensionable age or died under that age; and the following table shows the requisite number of years for the purpose of the second condition, by reference to a working life of a given duration—

(6) The first condition shall be taken to be satisfied if the contributor concerned was entitled

Duration of working life	Requisite number of years
10 years or less	The number of years of the working life, minus 1.
20 years or less (but more than 10)	The number of years of the working life, minus 2.
30 years or less (but more than 20)	The number of years of the working life, minus 3.
40 years or less (but more than 30)	The number of years of the working life, minus 4.
More than 40 years	The number of years of the working life, minus 5.

to [¹¹ long-term incapacity benefit] at any time during—

 (a) the year in which he attained pensionable age or died under that age, or

 (b) the year immediately preceding that year.

(7) The second condition shall be taken to be satisfied notwithstanding that paragraphs (a) and (b) of sub-paragraph (3) above are not complied with as respects each of the requisite number of years if—

 (a) those paragraphs are complied with as respects at least half that number of years [¹² (or at least 20 of them, if that is less than half)]; and

 (b) in each of the other years the contributor concerned was, within the meaning of regulations, precluded from regular employment by responsibilities at home.

[¹³ (7A) Regulations may provide that a person is not to be taken for the purposes of sub-paragraph (7)(b) above as precluded from regular employment by responsibilities at home unless he meets the prescribed requirements as to the provision of information to the Secretary of State.]

(8) For the purposes of [¹⁴ Parts I to VI of this Act] a person's working life is the period between—

 (a) (inclusive) the tax year in which he attained the age of 16; and

 (b) (exclusive) the tax year in which he attained pensionable age or died under that age.

1.475 [¹⁹ 5A—(1) This paragraph applies to—

 (a) a Category A retirement pension in a case where the contributor concerned attains pensionable age on or after 6th April 2010;

 (b) a Category B retirement pension payable by virtue of section 48A above in a case where the contributor concerned attains pensionable age on or after that date;

 (c) a Category B retirement pension payable by virtue of section 48B above in a case where the contributor concerned dies on or after that date without having attained pensionable age before that date.

(2) The contribution condition for a Category A or Category B retirement pension in relation to which this paragraph applies is that—

 (a) the contributor concerned must, in respect of each of not less than 30 years of his working life, have paid or been credited with contributions of a relevant class or been credited (in the case of 1987–88 or any subsequent year) with earnings; and

 (b) in the case of each of those years, the earnings factor derived as mentioned in sub-paragraph (3) below must be not less than the qualifying earnings factor for that year.

(3) For the purposes of paragraph (b) of sub-paragraph (2) above, the earnings factor—
  (a) in the case of 1987–88 or any subsequent year, is that which is derived from—
    (i) so much of the contributor's earnings as did not exceed the upper earnings limit and upon which such of the contributions mentioned in paragraph (a) of that sub-paragraph as are primary Class 1 contributions were paid or treated as paid or earnings credited; and
    (ii) any Class 2 or Class 3 contributions for the year; or
  (b) in the case of any earlier year, is that which is derived from the contributions mentioned in paragraph (a) of that sub-paragraph.
(4) Regulations may modify sub-paragraphs (2) and (3) above for the purposes of their application in a case where—
  (a) the contributor concerned has paid, or been credited with, contributions, or
  (b) contributions have been deemed to be, or treated as, paid by or credited to him, under the National Insurance Act 1946 or the National Insurance Act 1965.]

Child's special allowance

6.—(1) The contribution condition for a child's special allowance is that—   **1.476**
  (a) the contributor concerned must in respect of any one relevant year have actually paid contributions of a relevant class; and
  (b) the earnings factor derived from those contributions must be not less than that year's lower earnings limit multiplied by 50.
(2) For the purposes of this condition, a relevant year is any year ending before the date on which the contributor concerned attained pensionable age or died under that age.

PART II

SATISFACTION OF CONDITIONS IN EARLY YEARS OF CONTRIBUTION

7.—(1) Sub-paragraph (3) below shall apply where a claim is made for a [15 bereavement   **1.477**
payment] and the last complete year before the beginning of the benefit year in which the relevant time falls was either—
  (a) the year in which the contributor concerned first became liable for primary Class 1 or Class 2 contributions; or
  (b) the year preceding that in which he first became so liable.
(2) The relevant time for the purposes of this paragraph is the date on which the contributor concerned attained pensionable age or died under that age.
(3) For the purposes of satisfaction by the contributor concerned of paragraph (b) of the contribution condition for a [15 bereavement payment], all earnings factors falling within sub-paragraph (4) below may be aggregated and that aggregate sum shall be treated as his earnings factor for the last complete year before the beginning of the benefit year in which the relevant time falls.
(4) The earnings factors referred to in sub-paragraph (3) above are—
  (a) the contributor's earnings factors for 1987–88 and each subsequent year derived from the aggregate of [18 so much of the claimant's earnings as did not exceed the upper earnings limit and] upon which primary Class 1 contributions were paid or treated as paid and from Class 2 contributions actually paid by him before the relevant time; and
  (b) his earnings factors for each earlier year, derived from his contributions of a relevant class actually paid by him before the relevant time.
8. Where a person claims [16 short-term incapacity benefit], he shall be taken to satisfy the first contribution condition for the benefit if on a previous claim for any short-term benefit he has satisfied the first contribution condition for that benefit, by virtue of paragraph 8 of Schedule 3 to the 1975 Act, with contributions of a class relevant to [16 shortterm incapacity benefit].
9. Where [17 a claim is made for a bereavement payment], the contributor concerned for the purposes of the claim shall be taken to satisfy the contribution condition for the payment if on a claim made in the past for any short-term benefit he has satisfied the first contribution condition for the benefit, by virtue of paragraph 8 of Schedule 3 to the 1975 Act, with contributions of a class relevant to [17 bereavement payment].

REPEALS AND AMENDMENTS

1. Repealed by Jobseekers Act 1995, Sch.3, para.1 (October 10, 1996).
2. Social Security (Incapacity for Work) Act 1994, s.1(2) (April 13, 1995).
3. Welfare Reform and Pensions Act 1999, s.62(2) (April 6, 2001).

4. Social Security (Incapacity for Work) Act 1994, Sch.1, para.38(2) (April 13, 1995).

5. Social Security (Incapacity for Work) Act 1994, s.3(2) (April 13, 1995).

6. Welfare Reform and Pensions Act 1999, ss.62(3), (4) (April 6, 2001).

7. Welfare Reform and Pensions Act 1999, Sch.13, Pt V (April 2, 2000).

8. Welfare Reform and Pensions Act 1999, Sch.8, Pt I, para.13(2) (April 9, 2001).

9. Welfare Reform and Pensions Act 1999, Sch.8, Pt I, para.13(3) (April 9, 2001).

10. Pensions Act 1995, s.129 (July 19, 1995).

11. Social Security (Incapacity for Work) Act 1994, Sch.1, para.38(3) (April 13, 1995).

12. These words are deleted as regards any person reaching pensionable age after April 5, 2010, by the Pensions Act 1995, Sch.4, para.4 and Sch.7 Pt II.

13. Child Support, Pensions and Social Security Act 2000, s.40 (January 8, 2001).

14. Pensions Act 1995, s.134(5) (July 19, 1995).

15. Welfare Reform and Pensions Act 1999, Sch.8, Pt I, para.13(4) (April 24, 2000).

16. Social Security (Incapacity for Work) Act 1994, Sch.1, para.38(4) (April 13, 1995).

17. Welfare Reform and Pensions Act 1999, Sch. 8, Pt I, para.13(5)(b) (April 24, 2000).

18. National Insurance Contributions Act 2002, Sch.1, para.4 (April 6, 2003).

19. Pensions Act 2007, s.1 (September 26, 2007).

DERIVATIONS

1.478   SSA 1975, Sch.3.
        SSPA 1975, Sch.1.

DEFINITIONS

"benefit" (in para.2(8))—see para.2(9).
"benefit"—see s.122(1).
"benefit year"—see s.21(6).
"claimant"—see s.122(1).
"contributor concerned"—see s.21(5)(a).
"earnings"—see s.122(1).
"earnings factor"—see s.21(5)(c).
"lower earnings limit"—see s.122(1).
"modifications" (in para.2(8))—see para.2(9).
"period of incapacity for work"—see s.30C(1).
"qualifying earnings factor"—see s.122(1).
"relevant benefit year"—see para.2(6)(b).
"relevant class"—see s.21(5)(a).
"relevant time"—see para.2(6)(a).
"relevant year" (in para.6)—see para.6(2).
"short-term benefit"—see ss.122(1), 20(2).
"working life"—see para.5(8).
"year"—see s.21(5)(d).

GENERAL NOTE

What the Schedule covers

1.479   By their nature, certain "contributory benefits" require, as a precondition of entitlement, that the claimant, or in certain cases, the claimant's husband or, sometimes, spouse, have a valid contribution record in terms of national insurance contributions. Pt I of this Schedule sets out the contribution conditions which must be met for entitlement to certain "contributory benefits":

- short-term incapacity benefit (s.30A);
- bereavement payment (s.36);
- widowed mothers allowance (s.37);
- widowed parent's allowance (s.39A);
- bereavement allowance (s.39B);
- widow's pension (s.38);
- categories A and B retirement pensions (ss.43–54);
- child's special allowance (s.59).

Pt II of the Schedule, deals with the matter of satisfaction of conditions in early years of contribution in respect of bereavement payment and of short-term incapacity benefit.

Contributions matters: a division of responsibility

Since the coming into force of the SSA 1998, contribution conditions are more **1.480** directly relevant to appeals tribunals and the Commissioners, although cases raising them are likely relatively to be rare. The position is also complicated because some relevant matters are ones for HM Revenue and Customs (not appealable to appeals tribunals or social security commissioners) while others are ones for the Secretary of State and are appealable to unified appeals tribunals and to the social security commissioners.

Prior to the implementation of the decision-making and appeals changes in that Act, whether the contribution conditions were satisfied or not was a "Secretary of State's question" rather than a matter of decision for the AO. It was, accordingly, not as such appealable to an SSAT (SSAA 1992, s.17(1)(b), (2), set out with commentary in Bonner, Hooker and White, *Non Means Tested Benefits: Legislation 1999*, pp.16–19). It was thought at one time that the terms of section 17 were, however, to be narrowly construed, so that while a tribunal could not properly deal with whether the claimant should have been credited with contributions (*R(U) 6/89*), the "statutory authorities" (AO, SSAT and Commissioner) were the ones with jurisdiction over certain phrases in the contribution conditions: over establishing the date of claim ("the relevant time"), over identifying the pertinent benefit year (the one in which there falls the first day of the period of incapacity for work of which the day of claim forms part) and thus over identifying the appropriate past tax/contribution years to be considered with regard to the question (determinable by the Secretary of State and not appealable to an SSAT) of whether in the relevant tax years the requisite level of paid contributions (the first contribution condition) or paid and/or credited contributions (the second contribution condition) had been reached (see *R(G) 1/82(T)*). But the approach in *R(G) 1/82(T)* was rejected by the Court of Appeal in *Secretary of State v Scully* (reported as *R(S) 5/93*). The section (then SSA 1975 s.93) was to be read according to its "plain and natural meaning" and left it to the Secretary of State to make all determinations relevant to the contribution conditions.

After the implementation of the SSA 1998 changes, as regards all contributory benefits, whether someone satisfies the contribution conditions for the benefit is a decision of the Secretary of State and now appealable to a tribunal, and onwards to the Commissioners, as a decision on a claim or award of benefit not otherwise rendered non-appealable (SSA 1998, s.12 and Sch.2; Decisions and Appeals Regs, reg.27 and Sch.2). See further *Vol.III: Administration, Adjudication and the European Dimension*.

Some contributions matters are ones, however, for officers of HM Revenue and Customs, and appealable through a different system (Social Security Contributions (Transfer of Functions) Act 1999, ss.8(1)(a)–(e), 11, 12). The matters in question are those of the categorisation of earners, which class of contributions a person is liable or entitled to pay, and whether they have been paid (or should be treated as having been paid: see *R(JSA) 8/02*) in respect of any period. Decisions on such matters will impact to some degree on the Secretary of State's (and thus an appeal tribunal's or a Commissioner's) decisions on whether the contribution conditions for a benefit are met. There is a special procedure for the Secretary of State or the appeal tribunal to refer relevant questions to HM Revenue and Customs (SSA 1998, ss.10A, 24A; Decisions and Appeals Regs, regs.11A, 38A). Note that under s.8(1)(m) of that Transfer of Functions Act, regulations can transfer further issues relating to contributions. So the decision-maker on particular issues could change (see further *Vol.III: Administration, Adjudication and the European Dimension*).

The administrative process on the matter of referring to HM Revenue and Customs [formerly Board of Inland Revenue] questions on whether contributions have been paid has been subjected to scathing criticism by two Commissioners. In *CIB/1602/2006*, Commissioner Williams, like Commissioner Rowland in interim decision *CIB/3327/2004*, criticised the process as set out in the DMG guidance (Vol.3, ch.3, paras 03230–03233). Reading it with the more accurate guidance in Vol.1, ch.1, he thought the guidance to be:

> "internally inconsistent. Compare 01055 and 01056 with 56014. And it also guides administrators to make assumptions about contribution issues rather than decide them. See 01055 and 03231. And it does not tell the administrators to make it clear that their decisions depend on assumptions about a claimant's NI record rather than decisions about it. In my view the instruction to officials to make undisclosed assumptions about contribution issues combined with the failure to make it clear that there has been no decision on a contribution question have contributed to the systems failure to which Commissioner Rowland draws attention. In particular, there is a recurring failure to make a clear appealable decision on a question of credited earnings and a system in place that enables administrators to avoid the need to make the required decisions. This may explain why, even in this case where there was a decision, it has been assumed that there was no decision." (Para.19.)

He also considered DMG, paras 56014 and 56015 to "contain errors of law" (para.16).

In *CIB/1602/2006*, the matter in dispute was whether the claimant had sufficient credited earnings in tax/contribution year 2002–2003 to meet the second contribution condition. This turned on a much neglected area: in this case the complicated provisions of the Credits Regulations 1974, regs 3 and 8A. Commissioner Williams' decision on that is noted in the commentary to those regs, below. In *R(IB)1/09*, he set out the proper procedure for determining issues in a dispute about the application of the Social Security (Earnings Factor) Regulations 1979 to a claim for incapacity benefit:

> "(a) It is for the National Insurance Contributions Office of Her Majesty's Revenue and Customs to decide any question about the contribution record of a claimant for incapacity benefit.
>
> (b) Any challenge to that decision on either an issue of fact or a question of law goes to a tax tribunal, not a social security tribunal. If an appeal involving a question about a claimant's contributions comes before a social security tribunal, then the social security tribunal must apply regulation 38A of the Social Security and Child Support (Decisions and Appeals) Regulations 1999. This requires it to adjourn the appeal and refer the matter to the Secretary of State for onward reference to Her Majesty's Revenue and Customs for decision. The tribunal may decide the appeal only after a decision has been received from Her Majesty's Revenue and Customs.
>
> (c) It is for the Secretary of State for Work and Pensions to decide any question about the interpretation and application of the Social Security (Earnings Factor) Regulations 1979 to the individual contribution record of any claimant for incapacity benefit.

(d) If a claimant disputes the decision of the Secretary of State on any issue of fact or law arising under the 1979 Regulations, then that dispute is to be decided by a social security tribunal. This includes any dispute about calculating the earnings factor attributable to a claimant under those regulations. If necessary, it is the task of the tribunal itself to check any disputed calculations" (para.7).

For further consideration of some of the difficulties arising where records have been destroyed as part of normal administrative processes and for the text of the regulations on unemployment credits covering 1977-89, see Commissioner Williams' decision in *CP/1792/2007.*

Commissioner Rowland's interim decision in *CIB/3327/2004* delineated the effect on a claimant's claim and appeals of the confusion generated by changes in jurisdiction on contributions matters (paras 2–4) and on the matter of awarding credits for spells of unemployment, a situation in which she was passed from pillar to post, a process during which Commissioner Rowland considered that there had been no actual decision on the award of credits for those spells, but only on non-entitlement to JSA (paras 19–21). This resulted in part from the changes on decision-making, appeals and jurisdictions wrought by the 1998 and 1999 legislation. But Commissioner Rowland rightly drew to attention for remedial action "some more fundamental flaws in the way in which the Department functions" in respect of these matters. Essentially, the key flaw was that no system had been put in place for informing the claimant that credits for unemployment had not been awarded. In the Commissioner's view, what was needed, "above all" was the establishment of:

"a system . . . to ensure that challenges to refusals of credits result in formal decisions that comply with regulation 28 of the [Decisions and Appeals Regs] and inform the contributor of his or her right of appeal. That is so whether credits decisions are to be made during the relevant contribution year or after it has ended" (para.29).

Commissioner Williams considered in *CIB/1602/2006* that he had to reiterate that call for action:

"That decision was made a year ago. It was an interim decision. I understand that as a result of later proceedings in the appeal the matter has now ceased to be an active appeal and that therefore the Commissioner will not be issuing a final decision. I have also seen no official response to that decision beyond the specific case. I therefore consider that I should adopt and repeat some of that analysis as it applies to this case in order to make clear why I entirely agree with him that the existing situation does not accord with the law. I depart from the approach of Commissioner Rowland in taking the view that in this case there is an appealable decision. But his criticisms of the lack of system are clearly part of the explanation for the confusion on the part of the secretary of state's representatives and the tribunal in this case" (para.14).

To that, this commentator can only add his support. This is a crucial area for contribution-based benefits and claimants and tribunals are entitled to expect at least as much decision-making clarity here as elsewhere in the benefits system. So far it is conspicuously lacking.

Some problems, of course, have arisen because of the mismatch in data on credits in the respective departments' computer and recording systems: the DWP's Pension Service Computer System (PSCS) and the National Insurance Recording System (NIRS 2) system. Work is in hand to reconcile the latter with the former. It appears that up to 30,000 people may have been underpaid and about 90,000 may have been overpaid as a result of incorrect records. Overpayments are dealt with in amendments to the Credits Regulations 1975. Underpayments are to be made good by administrative action. See further the Explanatory Memorandum to the amending regulations (SI 2007/2582) at *http://www.opsi.gov.uk/si/si200725.htm.*

Whether a person's contributions record should be *credited* with contributions/ earnings remains, however, one for the Secretary of State and is now appealable to an appeal tribunal (SSA 1998, Sch. 3, para.17; *CIB/2338/00, CG2309/2002, CIB/2161/2000*). So does the question whether a person was (within the meaning of regulations) precluded from regular employment by responsibilities at home (SSA 1998, Sch.3, para.16). On when contributions may be credited, see s.22, above, and the Social Security (Credits) Regulations 1975, below. On entitlement to home responsibilities protection, see para.5(7) of this Schedule and the Social Security Pensions (Home Responsibilities) Regulations 1994.

On difficulties arising where the periods to be considered predate the abolition of sickness benefit and unemployment benefit and the re-allocation of functions and jurisdictions, see the decision of Commissioner Williams in *CIB/3734/2002*. On the complexities split jurisdiction can produce in pensions' entitlement cases, see his decision in *CP/4205/2006*.

With that division of responsibilities in mind, it is useful to give a brief outline of the contributory system as regards payments and credits, the better to understand the contributions conditions for entitlement to a contributory benefit.

An outline of the contributory system: payments, credits and the earnings factor (the amount added to the contribution record)

1.481   The contributory system embraces five distinct classes of contribution: Class 1 (primary and secondary), Class 1A, Class 2, Class 3 and Class 4. This last category—a levy on the profits of the self-employed—is irrelevant in respect of title to benefit. So are secondary Class 1 contributions and Class 1A contributions.

1.482   *Class 1 contributions*—capable of establishing entitlement to all the contributory benefits listed in s.21(2)—are paid by employed earners (see s.2(1)(a)), that is by persons employed under a contract of service (employees) and by certain office holders (e.g. constables, MPs). They are earnings-related, and are paid on weekly/ monthly earnings between a lower and an upper earnings limit. Those limits change for each tax (contribution) year. Where earnings fall below the relevant lower limit for the tax (contribution) year, there is no liability or ability to pay— for the period in question the contribution record will be blank in terms of Class 1. Primary Class I contributions are also the only class of contribution relevant for title to contribution-based jobseeker's allowance (see Jobseekers Act 1995, s.2 and commentary in *Vol.II: Income Support, Jobseeker's Allowance, State Pension Credit and the Social Fund*). Secondary Class 1 contributions and Class IA contributions are paid by the primary contributor's employer and are not relevant to title to benefit.

Basically, each primary Class I contribution paid generates an earnings factor, that is puts into the person's contribution record for the year an amount equivalent to the weekly/monthly earnings (but only up to the relevant upper earnings limit for that year) in respect of which it is paid. So in each week in tax (contribution) year 1999/2000, a weekly paid person earning £300 per week would each week have that amount added to his record.

1.483   *Class 2 contributions*—also capable of establishing entitlement to all the contributory benefits listed in s.21(2)—are paid by self-employed earners (see s.2(1)(b)), basically those employed under a contract for services. A Class 2 contribution generates an *earnings factor*, that is puts into the person's contribution record for the year a weekly amount equivalent to the lower earnings limit for that year for Class 1 contributions' liability. Even where a person is not liable to pay them, s/he can pay voluntarily so as to maintain their contribution record.

1.484   *Class 3 contributions* cannot generate title to incapacity benefit, but can in respect of the other contributory benefits listed in s.21(2): bereavement payment; widowed mother's allowance, widowed parent's allowance, bereavement allowance, widow's pension, category A and B retirement pensions. There is no liability, only an ability, to pay—they are always voluntary, paid to remedy deficiencies in the contribution record for particular years. Each Class 3 contribution paid generates an earnings factor, that is puts into the person's contribution record for the year a weekly amount equivalent to the lower earnings limit for that year for Class 1 contributions' liability.

Certain married women and widows could before April 5, 1977 elect to pay Class 1 contributions at a *reduced rate*, or not to pay a Class 2 contribution. Non-payment of the latter means no earnings factor, no amount added to the contribution record. Payment of Class 1 at the reduced rate generates no earnings factor, produces no amount to add to the contribution record (see s.22(4)).

The scheme recognises that in certain situations, for socially valid reasons someone may not be able to pay contributions, and protects that person's contribution record by crediting a certain amount to the person's contribution account (see s.22(5), Social Security (Credits) Regulations 1975). The weekly amount generated (the earnings factor) is one equivalent to the lower earnings limit for purposes of Class 1 contributions' liability. Where someone is precluded from working because of responsibilities at home, the scheme gives protection by a different route; it provides a degree of home responsibilities protection for the contribution record by, in certain circumstances, treating the second contribution condition (the one that can be satisfied by paid and/ or credited contributions) as fulfilled in any year in which the person "was, within the meaning of regulations, precluded from regular employment by responsibilities at home" (Sch.3, para.5(7); Social Security Pensions (Home Responsibilities) Regulations 1994). This applies only in respect of bereavement payment (s.36); widowed mothers allowance (s.37); widowed parent's allowance (s.39A); bereavement allowance (s.39B); widow's pension (s.38); and categories A and B retirement pensions (ss. 43–54).

With that outline in mind, the particular contribution conditions for each of the benefits listed in s.21 can now be examined in more detail.

PART I

THE CONDITIONS

Para. 2 read with s.30A(2)(a): short-term incapacity benefit for claimants under pensionable age

Unless he is a person incapacitated in youth (before 20 or sometimes 25) (see s.30A(1)(b), (2A)) a claimant must fulfil the requirements of this paragraph. There are two contribution conditions. The first can be met only by *paid* contributions of the relevant class (primary Class 1 or Class 2) reaching the requisite level in a tax year. The second can be satisfied by *paid and/or credited* contributions in a tax year.

1.485

This aspect of title to short-term incapacity benefit has been rendered more complex in that the first condition was altered substantially from April 6, 2001 to require for those under pensionable age a more recent connection with the world of work in terms of paid contributions than had previously been the case, whether with incapacity benefit or its predecessors, sickness and invalidity benefits. However, the rigour of the new rule is relaxed in certain situations (para.2(8), (9), IB Regulations, Pt IA, reg.2B) and by the fact that the change is not retrospective so that those whose continuing period of incapacity began before April 6, 2001 remain subject to the previous contribution condition first until that period of incapacity ends.

In order to appreciate the requirements of para.2, and the terms and operation of the contribution conditions, take first, as an illustrative example, the position of someone claiming incapacity benefit for the very first time in May 2001 (that is, with no link back to any previous period of incapacity for work) and never having claimed or received any other benefit. He must meet *both of the two contribution conditions* set out in para.2. The first step is to identify the relevant benefit year, the one which includes the first day of the period of incapacity of which his claim is part (para.2(6)). This identification of the relevant benefit year is the real substantive matter for the Secretary of State or the appeal tribunal to focus on, since that determines the tax/contribution years in which the requisite record must be fulfilled. His first day of claim—the relevant time (para.2(6))—in May 2001 falls in benefit year 2001–2002 (the relevant benefit year: see s.21(6)). "Year", standing alone, means tax/contribution year (s.21(5)(d). The tax/contribution years in *one of which* the first contribution condition (sub-para.(2)) must be fulfilled are the last three tax/contribution years (April 6–April 5) complete before the start of the relevant benefit year (early January 2001). The tax/contribution years to which to have regard are thus 1999/2000, 1998/1999, and 1997/1998. The contribution record in tax/ contribution year 2000/2001 cannot be taken into account because it was not complete at the start of the relevant benefit year (early January 2001). The first contribution condition (sub-para.(2)) can only be met with paid contributions of the relevant class—Class 1 (employed earners) or Class 2 (self-employed earners)—reaching the requisite level (an earnings factor of 25 times the lower earnings limit (LEL) for Class 1 contributions purposes for the tax year in question — remember that each Class 2 contribution generates an earnings factor equal to the LEL pertinent to the tax/contribution year in question, while the amount of earnings on which Class 1 contributions are paid generates the earnings factor for an employed earner claimant. See further, s.21, and the "outline of the contributory system" earlier in this annotation.

The second contribution condition (sub-para.(3)) requires examination of the last two tax years complete before the start of the relevant benefit year (early January 2001), that is 1999/2000 and 1998/1999. The claimant's contribution record in each of those tax/contribution years must attain 50 times the lower earnings limit for the year. But the condition can be met through paid and/or credited contributions (a Class 1 credit can be received, for example, for each week of unemployment; see further Social Security (Credits) Regulations 1975). On difficulties arising where the periods to be considered predate the abolition of sickness benefit and unemployment benefit and the re-allocation of functions and jurisdictions, see the decision of Commissioner Williams in *CIB/3734/2002*.

From May 5, 2003, the definition of "relevant benefit year" is different in the case of someone discharged from Her Majesty's forces and in respect of whom days of sickness absence from duty recorded by the Secretary of State for Defence are, under s.30D, included in calculating the number of days for which he has been entitled to short-term incapacity benefit. In such a case, the "relevant benefit year" is that in which there falls the beginning of the period to which the claim for incapacity benefit relates. See reg.4 of the Social Security Contributions and Benefits Act 1992 (Modifications for Her Majesty's Forces and Incapacity Benefit) Regulations 2003, below. See also annotations to s.30A(3) and s.30D.

Note that sub-para.(8) enables regulations to relax the rules set out above which apply to all claims in a period of incapacity for work commencing on or after April 6, 2001. So a claim in principle subject to these rules, is not just the first ever claim for incapacity benefit as used in the illustrative example, above. A "new" claim subject to those rules, could, for instance, just as well come from someone on incapacity benefit during 2000 whose "period of incapacity" came to an end in December 2000. If such a person claims again in, say, August 2001, he would, in principle, be subject to those rules, because his two spells of incapacity do not "link" to form one under the "linking rule" in s.30C. Note that the relaxation afforded applies not just to benefits under Pts II–V and VII–XII of the SSCBA 1992 but also to contributions credits (sub-paras(8), (9)). The "relaxation" rules are contained in IB Regulations, Pt 1A, reg.2B, and are annotated there.

Various groups will have difficulty meeting these new contribution conditions:

(a) *those who have never been employed*: The requirement in the first contribution condition for payment of contributions effectively excludes those who, whether through unemployment, incapacity or disability, have been unable to build a contribution record in terms of paid contributions.

(b) *some of the long-term unemployed* (last employed in a tax year earlier than the first of the three on which the first contribution condition focuses).

(c) *very low-paid, probably part-time, employees*: those whose weekly or monthly earnings fall below the lower earnings limit for the whole or main part of the relevant tax years will not satisfy the contribution conditions since there is no liability or ability to pay Class 1 contributions where earnings fall below that limit, and, because they are in work, no Class 1 credits are generated from unemployment.

(d) *certain married women and widows paying reduced rate contributions*: these do not generate any earnings factor (and so do not count) for incapacity benefit purposes (s.22(4)).

Severe Disablement Allowance (SDA) was introduced in 1984 to cater for those who were incapacitated below the age of 20, or, if incapacitated later, were also assessed as 80 per cent disabled (see ss.68, 69). SDA was abolished on April 2, 2001 for new claims. Of course, some of the above, if incapacitated in youth (before 20 or sometimes 25) (s.30A(1)(b), (2A); IB Regulations, Pt IV, regs14–19), will be able to take advantage of the intended counter-balancing measure for those more likely than others to have been unable to build up a contribution record— the non-contributory route into incapacity benefit (see commentary to subs.(2A)). Those incapacitated, even through severe disability, later in life, will have to look to income support, with all its disability premiums, to underwrite their incapacity for work. While they may well be eligible for various components of disability living allowance, that is a benefit designed to provide for the extra costs that disability, as opposed to incapacity for work, brings with it. The transitional provisions protect existing recipients and those whose period of incapacity (without receipt of SDA) spans April 6, 2001. See further the prefatory commentary to ss.68 and 69, preserved in force for those individuals.

Para.3: maternity allowance

There are now no contribution conditions in respect of maternity allowance. See s.35.   **1.486**

Para.4: bereavement payment

This has only one contribution condition (sub-para(1)), satisfiable only by contributions of the relevant class—Class 1, 2 or 3, separately or combined [sub-para (2)—*paid* by the contributor concerned in respect of any one relevant tax (contribution) year to a level not less than 25 times that year's lower earnings limit. A "relevant year" is any one ending before the date on which the contributor concerned attained pensionable age or died under that age (sub-para.(3)). The "contributor concerned" is the deceased spouse (s.36). Note the assistance afforded by Pt II, para.7, below, where the claim is made in the early years of the contributor's liability for primary Class 1 or Class 2 contributions. Note also the degree of protection for some recipients of maternity allowance afforded by para.9.   **1.487**

Para.5: widowed mother's allowance, widowed parent's allowance, bereavement allowance, widow's pension, category A and B retirement pensions

These long-term benefits all require satisfaction of the same contribution conditions. Like the short-term benefits there are two conditions to be satisfied. The first requires actual payment of contributions; the second may be satisfied by payments or by credits.   **1.488**

The person whose contribution record is to be tested will depend upon the benefit claimed. For a Category A Retirement Pension it will be the claimant's own record. For a Category B Retirement Pension it will be the record of the claimant's spouse. For a Widowed Parent's Allowance and a Bereavement Allowance it is the late spouse's contribution record; and for a Widowed Mother's Allowance or Widow's Pension her late husband's record. (For the various widow's and bereavement benefits the condition may also be satisfied if the contributor has died as a result of an industrial injury or disease.)

The first condition for these benefits requires that the contributor has actually paid contributions (either Class 1, Class 2 or Class 3) in any one year to produce an earnings factor of at least 52 times the lower earnings limit for that year (the "qualifying earnings factor": see s.122(1)). The year can be any year that ends before the year in which that person retires or dies. The condition is also deemed to be satisfied if that person was in receipt of long-term incapacity benefit in the year in which they reached retirement age or died, or if they were in receipt of that benefit in the preceding year. Before 1975, Class 1 contributions were paid as a flat rate "stamp" each week. This condition will also be satisfied by 50 flat rate contributions in any year.

The second condition must be fulfilled in each of what may be a much longer period of years. The requisite period is defined by reference to the length of the person's working life (the years between that in which they reach the age of 16 and the last complete tax year before they reach retirement age or die under that age), but subject to a reduction in the total number of years according to the scale that appears in App.3, para.5, sub-para.5 above. Once the "requisite number of years" has been defined the contributor must be shown to have paid, or been credited with, payments that produce an earnings factor equal to at least 52 times the lower earnings limit for each of those years. (For years before 1975 the number of satisfied years is calculated by counting all the weekly payments made over those years and dividing by 50. The answer is rounded up to the next whole number.)

The requisite number of years may also be reduced by years of home responsibility as explained above. Such years are deducted from the working life and may reduce the requisite number of years to 20 or to half of what they would otherwise have been, whichever is the lower.

Where the second condition is satisfied the long-term benefits will be paid at their full rate. Where the condition is only partially satisfied, benefit will be paid at a percentage of that rate corresponding to the percentage of satisfied years, so long as at least 25 per cent of those years are so satisfied.

Para.6: child's special allowance

1.489   This has only one contribution condition (sub-para(1)), satisfiable only by contributions of the relevant class—(Class 1, 2 or 3, separately or combined (s.21(2))—paid by the contributor concerned in respect of any one relevant tax (contribution) year to a level not less than 50 times that year's lower earnings limit. A "relevant year" is any one ending before the date on which the contributor concerned attained pensionable age or died under that age (sub-para.(2)). The claimant for child's special allowance is a woman whose marriage has been terminated by divorce, and the "contributor concerned" is the deceased husband of that marriage who was contributing to the cost of providing for the child or from whom she was entitled to receive, under a court order, a trust or agreement, maintenance for the child (s.56).

PART II

SATISFACTION OF CONDITIONS IN EARLY YEARS OF CONTRIBUTION

Para.7

1.490   This is relevant only to a claim for *bereavement payment*. It applies only where the last complete tax year before the benefit year (Jan–Jan) in which the contributor concerned (the now deceased spouse) attained pensionable age or died under that age, is either the year in which s/he first became liable for primary Class 1 or Class 2 contributions or is the one preceding that in which s/he first became liable. This paragraph enables to bring into that one year, for the purposes of her/his record attaining the requisite level of 25 times that year' lower earnings' limit, the aggregate sum of all the earnings factors (the amount put into the contribution account) in sub-paragraph (4), that is, to bring into that crucial year, earnings factors from other years.

Para. 8

This applies only to short-term incapacity benefit, and seems to protect previous recipients of the contributory maternity allowance. It enables a claimant for short-term incapacity benefit to be treated as satisfying its first contribution condition (see para. 2(2)) if on a previous claim for any short-term benefit (defined in s.20(2) to cover short-term incapacity benefit and maternity allowance) he satisfied the first contribution condition for that shortterm benefit by virtue of SSA 1975, Sched. 3, para. 8, with contributions of the class relevant to short-term incapacity benefit (Class 1 or 2 and their predecessors). Paragraph 8 in the 1975 Act dealt with aggregation of contributions as regards early years of contribution in a similar way to para. 7 of this Schedule and bereavement payment.

1.491

Para. 9

This applies only to a claim for bereavement payment, and protects previous recipients of maternity allowance in much the same way as paragraph 8 of this Schedule, above.

1.492

[¹SCHEDULE 1

PROVISIONS OF SCHEDULE 4 TO THE CONTRIBUTIONS AND BENEFITS ACT AS AMENDED BY THIS ORDER

PART I

CONTRIBUTORY PERIODICAL BENEFITS

Description of benefit	Weekly rate	
2. Short-term incapacity benefit.	(a) lower rate (b) higher rate	£67.75 £80.15
2A. Long-term incapacity benefit.		£89.80
5. Category B retirement pension where section 48A(3) applies.		£57.05

1.493

PART II

BEREAVEMENT PAYMENT

Bereavement payment.	£2,000.00.

1.494

PART III

NON-CONTRIBUTORY PERIODICAL BENEFITS

1.495

Description of benefit	Weekly rate	
1. Attendance allowance.	(a) higher rate (b) lower rate (the appropriate rate being determined in accordance with section 65(3)).	£70.35 £47.10
2. Severe disablement allowance.		£57.45
3. Age related addition.	(a) higher rate (b) middle rate (c) lower rate (the appropriate rate being determined in accordance with section 69(1)).	£15.65 £9.10 £5.35
4. Carer's allowance.		£53.10
5. Guardian's allowance		[² £14.10]
6. Category C retirement pension.	(a) lower rate (b) higher rate (the appropriate rate being determined in accordance with section 78(5)).	£34.15 £57.05
7. Category D retirement pension.	The higher rate for Category C retirement pensions under paragraph 6 above.	
8. Age addition (to a pension of any category, and otherwise under section 79).		£0.25

PART IV

INCREASES FOR DEPENDANTS

1.496

Benefit to which increase applies (1)	Increase for qualifying child (2) £	Increase for adult dependant (3) £
1A. Short-term incapacity benefit— (a) where the beneficiary is under pensionable age; (b) where the beneficiary is over pensionable age.	11.35 11.35	41.35 51.10
2. Long-term incapacity benefit.	11.35	53.10
3. Maternity allowance.	—	41.35
4. Widowed mother's allowance.	11.35	—
4A. Widowed parent's allowance.	11.35	—

Benefit to which increase applies (1)	Increase for qualifying child (2) £	Increase for adult dependant (3) £
5. Category A or B retirement pension.	11.35	57.05
6. Category C retirement pension.	11.35	34.15
8. Severe disablement allowance.	11.35	31.90
9. Carer's allowance.	11.35	31.70

PART V

RATES OF INDUSTRIAL INJURIES BENEFIT

Description of benefit, etc.	Rate	
1. Disablement pension (weekly rates).	For the several degrees of disablement set out in column (1) of the following Table, the respective amounts in that Table, using— (a) column (2) for any period during which the beneficiary is over the age of 18 or is entitled to an increase of benefit in respect of a dependant; (b) column (3) for any period during which the beneficiary is not over the age of 18 and not so entitled; **TABLE**	1.497

Degree of Disablement		Amount	
(1) Per cent.	(2) £	(3) £	
100	143.60	88.05	
90	129.24	79.25	
80	114.88	70.44	
70	100.52	61.64	
60	86.16	52.83	
50	71.80	44.03	
40	57.44	35.22	
30	43.08	26.42	
20	28.72	17.61	

2. Maximum increase of weekly rate of disablement pension where constant attendance needed.	(a) except in cases of exceptionally severe disablement (b) in any case	£57.50; £115.00.
3. Increase of weekly rate of disablement pension (exceptionally severe disablement).		£57.50.

Description of benefit, etc.	Rate	
4. Maximum of aggregate of weekly benefit payable for successive accidents.	(a) for any period during which the beneficiary is over the age of 18 or is entitled to an increase in benefit in respect of a dependant	£143.60;
	(b) for any period during which the beneficiary is not over the age of 18 and not so entitled	£88.05.
5. Unemployability supplement under paragraph 2 of Schedule 7.		£88.75.
6. Increase under paragraph 3 of Schedule 7 of weekly rate of unemployability supplement.	(a) if on the qualifying date the beneficiary was under the age of 35 or if that date fell before 5th July 1948	£18.65;
	(b) if head (a) above does not apply and on the qualifying date the beneficiary was under the age of 40 and he had not attained pensionable age before 6th April 1979	£18.65;
	(c) if heads (a) and (b) above do not apply and on the qualifying date the beneficiary was under the age of 45	£12.00;
	(d) if heads (a), (b) and (c) above do not apply and on the qualifying date the beneficiary was under the age of 50 and had not attained pensionable age before 6th April 1979	£12.00;
	(e) in any other case	£6.00.
7. Increase under paragraph 4 of Schedule 7 of weekly rate of disablement pension.		£11.35.
8. Increase under paragraph 6 of Schedule 7 of weekly rate of disablement pension.		£53.10.
9. Maximum disablement gratuity under paragraph 9 of Schedule 7.		£9540.00.
10. Widow's pension (weekly rates).	(a) initial rate	£57.65;
	(b) higher permanent rate	£95.25;
	(c) lower permanent rate 30 per cent. of the first sum specified in section 44(4) (Category A basic retirement pension) (the appropriate rate being determined in accordance with paragraph 16 of Schedule 7).	

Description of benefit, etc.	Rate	
11. Widower's pension (weekly rate).		£95.25.
12. Weekly rate of allowance in respect of children and qualifying young persons under paragraph 18 of Schedule 7.	In respect of each child or qualifying young person	£11.35.

AMENDMENTS

1. The whole Schedule was substituted by the Social Security Benefits Up-rating Order 2009 (SI 2009/497), art.3 to take effect on dates between April 1, 2009 and April 9, 2009 (see art.6).

2. The amount in para.5 of Pt III was amended by the Guardian's Allowance Up-rating Order 2009 (SI 2009/797), art.2 (April 6, 2009). But where a question arises as to the entitlement to Guardian's Allowance by virtue of the up-rating order, or whether conditions for the receipt of benefit at that rate are satisfied, the altered rates will not apply until the question has been decided by HM Revenue and Customs, or the First-tier or Upper Tribunal (see the Guardian's Allowance Up-rating Regulations 2009 (SI 2009/810), reg.2 (April 6, 2009).

[¹ SCHEDULE 4A

[² ADDITIONAL PENSION ACCRUAL RATES FOR PURPOSES OF SECTION 45 (2)(C)]

PART I

THE AMOUNT

1.—(1) The amount referred to in section 45(2)(c) above is to be calculated as follows—   **1.498**
  (a) take for each tax year concerned the amount for the year which is found under the following provisions of this Schedule;
  (b) add the amounts together;
  (c) divide the sum of the amounts by the number of relevant years;
  (d) the resulting amount is the amount referred to in section 45(2)(c) above, except that if the resulting amount is a negative one the amount so referred to is nil.

(2) For the purpose of applying sub-paragraph (1) above in the determination of the rate of any additional pension by virtue of section [² . . .], 39C(1), 48A(4) or 48B(2) above, in a case where the deceased spouse died under pensionable age, the divisor used for the purposes of sub-paragraph (1)(c) above shall be whichever is the smaller of the alternative numbers referred to below (instead of the number of relevant years).

(3) The first alternative number is the number of tax years which begin after 5th April 1978 and end before the date when the entitlement to the additional pension commences.

(4) The second alternative number is the number of tax years in the period—
  (a) beginning with the tax year in which the deceased spouse attained the age of 16 or, if later, 1978–79; and
  (b) ending immediately before the tax year in which the deceased spouse would have attained pensionable age if he had not died earlier.

(5) For the purpose of applying sub-paragraph (1) above in the determination of the rate of any additional pension by virtue of section 48BB(5) above, in a case where the deceased spouse died under pensionable age, the divisor used for the purposes of sub-paragraph (1)(c) above shall be whichever is the smaller of the alternative numbers referred to below (instead of the number of relevant years).

(6) The first alternative number is the number of tax years which begin after 5th April 1978 and end before the date when the deceased spouse dies.

(7) The second alternative number is the number of tax years in the period—
  (a) beginning with the tax year in which the deceased spouse attained the age of 16 or, if later, 1978–79; and
  (b) ending immediately before the tax year in which the deceased spouse would have attained pensionable age if he had not died earlier.
(8) In this paragraph "relevant year" has the same meaning as in section 44 above.

PART II

SURPLUS EARNINGS FACTOR

1.499   **2.**—(1) This Part of this Schedule applies if for the tax year concerned there is a surplus in the pensioner's earnings factor.
(2) The amount for the year is to be found as follows—
  (a) calculate the part of the surplus for that year falling into each of the bands specified in the appropriate table below;
  (b) multiply the amount of each such part in accordance with the last order under section 148 of the Administration Act to come into force before the end of the final relevant year;
  (c) multiply each amount found under paragraph (6) above by the percentage specified in the appropriate table in relation to the appropriate band;
  (d) add together the amounts calculated under paragraph (c) above
(3) The appropriate table for persons attaining pensionable age after the end of the first appointed year but before 6th April 2009 is as follows—

1.500   **TABLE 1**

Amount of surplus	Percentage
Band 1. Not exceeding LET	40 + 2N
Band 2. Exceeding LET but not exceeding 3LET–2QEF	10 + N/2
Band 3. Exceeding 3LET–2QEF	20 + N

(4) The appropriate table for persons attaining pensionable age on or after April 6th 2009 [² where the tax year concerned falls before 2010–11] is as follows—

1.501   **TABLE 2**

Amount of surplus	Percentage
Band 1. Not exceeding LET	40
Band 2. Exceeding LET but not exceeding 3LET–2QEF	10
Band 3. Exceeding 3LET–2QEF	20

[² (4A) The appropriate table for persons attaining pensionable age on or after 6th April 2009 where the tax year concerned is 2010–11 or a subsequent tax year is as follows—

1.502   **TABLE 2A**

Amount of surplus	Percentage
Band 1. Not exceeding LET	40
Band 2. Exceeding LET but not exceeding AUEL	10]

(5) Regulations may provide, in relation to persons attaining pensionable age after such date as may be prescribed, that the amount found under this Part of this Schedule for the second appointed year or any subsequent tax year is to be calculated using only so much of the surplus in the pensioner's earnings factor for that year as falls into Band 1 in the table in sub-paragraph (4) above.
(6) For the purposes of the tables in this paragraph—
  (a) the value of N is 0.5 for each tax year by which the tax year in which the pensioner attained pensionable age precedes 2009–10;
  (b) "LET" means the low earnings threshold for that year as specified in section 44A above;
  (c) "QEF" means the qualifying earnings factor for the tax year concerned.
  [² (d) "AUEL" means the amount equal to the upper earnings limit for the tax year concerned multiplied by 52.]
(7) In the calculation of "2QEF" the amount produced by doubling QEF shall be rounded to the nearest whole £100 (taking any amount of £50 as nearest to the previous whole £100).
(8) In this paragraph "final relevant year" has the same meaning as in section 44 above.

PART III

Contracted-Out Employment

Introduction

3.—(1) This Part of this Schedule applies if the following condition is satisfied in relation to each tax week in the tax year concerned.

(2) The condition is that any earnings paid to or for the benefit of the pensioner in the tax week in respect of employment were in respect of employment qualifying him for a pension provided by a salary related contracted-out scheme or by a money purchase contracted-out scheme or by an appropriate personal pension scheme.

(3) If the condition is satisfied in relation to one or more tax weeks in the tax year concerned, Part II of this Schedule does not apply in relation to the year.

1.503

The amount

4.—The amount for the year is amount C where—
(a) amount C is equal to amount A minus amount B, and
(b) amounts A and B are calculated as follows.

1.504

Amount A

5.—(1) Amount A is to be calculated as follows.
(2) If there is an assumed surplus in the pensioner's earnings factor for the year
(a) calculate the part of the surplus for that year falling into each of the bands specified in the appropriate table below;
(b) multiply the amount of each such part in accordance with the last order under section 148 of the Administration Act to come into force before the end of the final relevant year;
(c) multiply each amount found under paragraph (b) above by the percentage specified in the appropriate table in relation to the appropriate band;
(d) add together the amounts calculated under paragraph (c) above
(3) The appropriate table for persons attaining pensionable age after the end of the first appointed year but before 6th April 2009 is as follows—

1.505

TABLE 3

1.506

Amount of surplus	Percentage
Band 1. Not exceeding LET	40 + 2N
Band 2. Exceeding LET but not exceeding 3LET–2QEF	10 + N/2
Band 3. Exceeding 3LET–2QEF	20 + N

(4) The appropriate table for persons attaining pensionable age on or after 6th April 2009 [2 where the tax year concerned falls before 2010–11] is as follows—

TABLE 4

1.507

Amount of surplus	Percentage
Band 1. Not exceeding LET	40
Band 2. Exceeding LET but not exceeding 3LET–2QEF	10
Band 3. Exceeding 3LET–2QEF	20

[2 (4A) The appropriate table for persons attaining pensionable age on or after 6th April 2009 where the tax year concerned is 2010–11 or a subsequent tax year is as follows—

TABLE 4A

1.508

Amount of surplus	Percentage
Band 1. Not exceeding LET	40
Band 2. Exceeding LET but not exceeding AUEL	10]

Amount B (first case)

6.—(1) Amount B is to be calculated in accordance with this paragraph if the pensioner's employment was entirely employment qualifying him for a pension provided by a salary related contracted-out scheme or by a money purchase contracted-out scheme.

(2) If there is an assumed surplus in the pensioner's earnings factor for the year—
(a) multiply the amount of the assumed surplus in accordance with the last order under section 148 of the Administration Act to come into force before the end of the final relevant year;

1.509

(b) multiply the amount found under paragraph (a) above by the percentage specified in sub-paragraph (3) below.

(3) The percentage is—
(a) 20 + N if the person attained pensionable age after the end of the first appointed year but before 6th April 2009;
(b) 20 if the person attained pensionable age on or after 6th April 2009.

Amount B (second case)

1.510 **7.**—(1) Amount B is to be calculated in accordance with this paragraph if the pensioner's employment was entirely employment qualifying him for a pension provided by an appropriate personal pension scheme.

(2) If there is an assumed surplus in the pensioner's earnings factor for the year—
(a) calculate the part of the surplus for that year falling into each of the bands specified in the appropriate table below;
(b) multiply the amount of each such part in accordance with the last order under section 148 of the Administration Act to come into force before the end of the final relevant year;
(c) multiply each amount found under paragraph (b) above by the percentage specified in the appropriate table in relation to the appropriate band;
(d) add together the amounts calculated under paragraph (c) above.

(3) The appropriate table for persons attaining pensionable age after the end of the first appointed year but before April 6th 2009 is as follows—

1.511 **TABLE 5**

Amount of surplus	Percentage
Band 1. Not exceeding LET	40 + 2N
Band 2. Exceeding LET but not exceeding 3LET–2QEF	10 + N/2
Band 3. Exceeding 3LET–2QEF	20 + N

(4) The appropriate table for persons attaining pensionable age on or after April 6th 2009 [² where the tax year concerned falls before 2010–11] is as follows—

1.512 **TABLE 6**

Amount of surplus	Percentage
Band 1. Not exceeding LET	40
Band 2. Exceeding LET but not exceeding 3LET–2QEF	10
Band 3. Exceeding 3LET–2QEF	20

[² (4A) The appropriate table for persons attaining pensionable age on or after 6th April 2009 where the tax year concerned is 2010–11 or a subsequent tax year is as follows—

1.513 **TABLE 6A**

Amount of surplus	Percentage
Band 1. Not exceeding LET	40
Band 2. Exceeding LET but not exceeding AUEL	10.]

Interpretation

1.514 **8.**—(1) In this Part of this Schedule "salary related contracted-out scheme", "money purchase contracted-out scheme" and "appropriate personal pension scheme" have the same meanings as in the Pension Schemes Act 1993.

(2) For the purposes of this Part of this Schedule the assumed surplus in the pensioner's earnings factor for the year is the surplus there would be in that factor for the year if section 48A(1) of the Pension Schemes Act 1993 (no primary Class 1 contributions deemed to be paid) did not apply in relation to any tax week falling in the year.

(3) Section 44A above shall be ignored in applying 44(6) above for the purpose of calculating amount B.

(4) For the purposes of this Part of this Schedule—
(a) the value of N is 0.5 for each tax year by which the tax year in which the pensioner attained pensionable age precedes 2009–10;
(b) "LET" means the low earnings threshold for that year as specified in section 44A above;
(c) "QEF" is the qualifying earnings factor for the tax year concerned.
[² (d) "AUEL" means the amount equal to the upper earnings limit for the tax year concerned multiplied by 52.]

(5) In the calculation of "2QEF" the amount produced by doubling QEF shall be rounded to the nearest whole £100 (taking any amount of £50 as nearest to the previous whole £100).

(6) In this Part of this Schedule "final relevant year" has the same meaning as in section 44 above.

PART IV

OTHER CASES

9.—The Secretary of State may make regulations containing provisions for finding the amount for a tax year in—

    (a) cases where the circumstances relating to the pensioner change in the course of the year;

    (b) such other cases as the Secretary of State thinks fit.]

1.515

AMENDMENTS

1. Sch.4A inserted by Child Support, Pensions and Social Security Act 2000, s.31 and Sch.4 (April 6, 2002).

2. Pensions Act 2007, s.10 and Sch.7, Pt 5 (September 26, 2007).

[1 SCHEDULE 4B

ADDITIONAL PENSION: ACCRUAL RATES FOR PURPOSES OF SECTION 45(2)(D)

PART I

AMOUNT FOR PURPOSES OF SECTION 45(2)(D)

1 (1) The amount referred to in section 45(2)(d) is to be calculated as follows—

    (a) calculate the appropriate amount for each of the relevant years within section 45(2)(d) to which Part 2 of this Schedule applies;

    (b) calculate the appropriate amount for each of the relevant years within section 45(2)(d) to which Part 3 of this Schedule applies; and

    (c) add those amounts together.

(2) But if the resulting amount is a negative one, the amount referred to in section 45(2)(d) is nil.

1.516

PART II

NORMAL RULES: EMPLOYMENT NOT CONTRACTED-OUT

Application

2 This Part applies to a relevant year if the contracted-out condition is not satisfied in respect of any tax week in the year.

1.517

Appropriate amount for year

3 The appropriate amount for the year for the purposes of paragraph 1 is either—

    (a) the flat rate amount for the year (if there is a surplus in the pensioner's earnings factor for the year which does not exceed the LET), or

    (b) the sum of the flat rate amount and the earnings-related amount for the year (if there is such a surplus which exceeds the LET).

4 The flat rate amount for the year is calculated by multiplying the FRAA in accordance with the last order under section 148AA of the Administration Act to come into force before the end of the final relevant year.

5 The earnings-related amount for the year is calculated as follows—

    (a) take the part of the surplus for the year which exceeds the LET but which does not exceed the UAP;

    (b) multiply that amount in accordance with the last order under section 148 of the Administration Act to come into force before the end of the final relevant year;

1.518

(c) multiply the amount found under paragraph (b) by 10%;
(d) divide the amount found under paragraph (c) by 44.

PART III

CONTRACTED-OUT EMPLOYMENT

Application

1.519   6 This Part applies to a relevant year if the contracted-out condition is satisfied in respect of each tax week in the year.

Appropriate amount for year

1.520   7 The appropriate amount for the year for the purposes of paragraph 1 is calculated as follows—
(a) calculate amounts A and B in accordance with paragraphs 8 to 10;
(b) subtract amount B from amount A.

Amount A: assumed surplus not exceeding LET

1.521   8 (1) Amount A is calculated in accordance with this paragraph if there is an assumed surplus in the pensioner's earnings factor for the year which does not exceed the LET.
(2) In such a case, amount A is the flat rate amount for the year.
(3) The flat rate amount for the year is calculated by multiplying the FRAA in accordance with the last order under section 148AA of the Administration Act to come into force before the end of the final relevant year.

Amount A: assumed surplus exceeding LET

1.522   9 (1) Amount A is calculated in accordance with this paragraph if there is an assumed surplus in the pensioner's earnings factor for the year which exceeds the LET.
(2) In such a case, amount A is calculated as follows—
(a) take the part of the assumed surplus for the year which exceeds the LET but which does not exceed the UAP;
(b) multiply that amount in accordance with the last order under section 148 of the Administration Act to come into force before the end of the final relevant year;
(c) multiply the amount found under paragraph (b) by 10%;
(d) divide the amount found under paragraph (c) by 44;
(e) add the amount found under paragraph (d) to the flat rate amount for the year.
(3) The flat rate amount for the year is calculated by multiplying the FRAA in accordance with the last order under section 148AA of the Administration Act to come into force before the end of the final relevant year.

Amount B

1.523   10 (1) Amount B is calculated as follows—
(a) take the part of the assumed surplus for the year which exceeds the QEF but which does not exceed the UAP;
(b) multiply that amount in accordance with the last order under section 148 of the Administration Act to come into force before the end of the final relevant year;
(c) multiply the amount found under paragraph (b) by 20%;
(d) divide the amount found under paragraph (c) by the number of relevant years in the pensioner's working life.
(2) Section 44B is to be ignored in applying section 44(6) for the purposes of this paragraph.

PART IV

OTHER CASES

1.524   11 The Secretary of State may make regulations containing provision for finding for a tax year the amount referred to in section 45(2)(d)—
(a) in cases where the circumstances relating to the pensioner change in the course of the year, and
(b) in such other cases as the Secretary of State thinks fit.

PART 5

INTERPRETATION

12 In this Schedule—   1.525
- "assumed surplus", in relation to a pensioner's earnings factor for a year, means the surplus there would be in that factor for the year if section 48A(1) of the Pension Schemes Act 1993 (no primary Class 1 contributions deemed to be paid) did not apply in relation to any tax week falling in the year;
- "the contracted-out condition", in relation to a tax week, means the condition that any earnings paid to or for the benefit of the pensioner in that week in respect of employment were in respect of employment qualifying him for a pension provided by a salary related contracted-out scheme (within the meaning of the Pension Schemes Act 1993);
- "the FRAA" has the meaning given by paragraph 13;
- "the LET", in relation to a tax year, means the low earnings threshold for the year as specified in section 44A above;
- "the QEF", in relation to a tax year, means the qualifying earnings factor for the year;
- "relevant year" and "final relevant year" have the same meanings as in section 44 above;
- "the UAP" means the upper accrual point.

13 (1) "The FRAA" means the flat rate accrual amount.

(2) That amount is £72.80 for the flat rate introduction year and subsequent tax years (but subject to section 148AA of the Administration Act).]

AMENDMENT

1. Schedule 4B was added by Sch.2 of the Pensions Act 2007 (September 26, 2007).

SCHEDULE 5

[⁵ PENSION INCREASE OR LUMP SUM WHERE ENTITLEMENT TO RETIREMENT PENSION IS DEFERRED]

[⁵ *Choice between increase of pension and lump sum where pensioner's entitlement is deferred*

A.—(1) Where a person's entitlement to a Category A or Category B retirement pension   1.526
is deferred and the period of deferment is at least 12 months, the person shall, on claiming his pension or within a prescribed period after claiming it, elect in the prescribed manner either—
  (a) that paragraph 1 (entitlement to increase of pension) is to apply in relation to the period of deferment, or
  (b) that paragraph 3A (entitlement to lump sum) is to apply in relation to the period of deferment.

(2) If no election under sub-paragraph (1) is made within the period prescribed under that sub-paragraph, the person is to be treated as having made an election under sub-paragraph (1)(b).

(3) Regulations—
  (a) may enable a person who has made an election under sub-paragraph (1) (including one that the person is treated by sub-paragraph (2) as having made) to change the election within a prescribed period and in a prescribed manner, if prescribed conditions are satisfied, and
  (b) if they enable a person to make an election under sub-paragraph (1)(b) in respect of a period of deferment after receiving any increase of pension under paragraph 1 by reference to that period, may for the purpose of avoiding duplication of payment—
    (i) enable an amount determined in accordance with the regulations to be recovered from the person in a prescribed manner and within a prescribed period, or
    (ii) provide for an amount determined in accordance with the regulations to be treated as having been paid on account of the amount to which the person is entitled under paragraph 3A.

(4) Where the Category A or Category B retirement pension includes any increase under paragraphs 5 to 6, no election under sub-paragraph (1) applies to so much of the pension as consists of that increase (an entitlement to an increase of pension in respect of such an increase after a period of deferment being conferred either by paragraphs 1 and 2 or by paragraph 2A).]

[⁵ 1.— (1) This paragraph applies where a person's entitlement to a Category A or Category B retirement pension is deferred and one of the following conditions is met—
  (a) the period of deferment is less than 12 months, or
  (b) the person has made an election under paragraph A1(1)(a) in relation to the period of deferment.

(2) The rate of the person's Category A or Category B retirement pension shall be increased by an amount equal to the aggregate of the increments to which he is entitled under paragraph 2, but only if that amount is enough to increase the rate of the pension by at least 1 per cent.]

2.—(1) Subject to paragraph 3 below, a person is entitled to an increment under this paragraph for each complete incremental period in his period of enhancement.

(2) In this Schedule—

"incremental period" means any period of six days which are treated by regulations as days of increment for the purposes of this Schedule in relation to the person and the pension in question: and
"the period of enhancement", in relation to that person and that pension, means the period which—

  (a) begins on the same day as the period of deferment in question; and
  (b) ends on the same day as that period or, if earlier, on the day before the 5th anniversary of the beginning of that period.

(3) Subject to paragraph 3 below, the amount of the increment for any such incremental period shall be 1/7 per cent. of the weekly rate of the Category A or Category B retirement pension to which that person would have been entitled for the period if his entitlement had not been deferred.

(4) Where an amount is required to be calculated in accordance with the provisions of sub-paragraph (3) above
  (a) the amount so calculated shall be rounded to the nearest penny, taking any 1/2p as nearest to the next whole penny above; and
  (b) where the amount so calculated would, apart from this sub-paragraph, be a sum less than 1/2p, that amount shall be taken to be zero, notwithstanding any other provision of this Act, the Pensions Act or the Administration Act.

(5) For the purposes of sub-paragraph (3) above the weekly rate of pension for any period shall be taken—
  (a) to include any increase under section 47(1) above and any increase under paragraph 4 , [²5, 5A or 6] below, but
  (b) not to include any increase under section [¹. . .], [⁵83A or] 85 above or any graduated retirement benefit.

(6) The reference in sub-paragraph (5) above to any increase under subsection (1) of section 47 above shall be taken as a reference to any increase that would take place under that subsection if subsection (2) of that section and [⁴section 46(5)] of the Pensions Act were disregarded.

(7) Where one or more orders have come into force under section 150 [⁷ or 150A] of the Administration Act during the period of enhancement, the rate for any incremental period shall be determined as if the order or orders had come into force before the beginning of the period of enhancement.

(8) Where a pension's rights premium is paid in respect of a person who is, or if his entitlement had not been deferred would be, entitled to a Category A or Category B retirement pension, then, in calculating any increment under this paragraph which falls to be paid to him in respect of such a pension after the date on which the premium is paid there shall be disregarded any guaranteed minimum pension to which the pensioner was entitled in connection with the employment to which the premium relates.

[⁵ 2A.—(1) This paragraph applies where—
  (a) a person's entitlement to a Category A or Category B retirement pension is deferred,
  (b) the pension includes an increase under paragraphs 5 to 6, and
  (c) the person has made (or is treated as having made) an election under paragraph A1(1)
    (b) in relation to the period of deferment.

(2) The rate of the person's Category A or Category B retirement pension shall be increased by an amount equal to the aggregate of the increments to which he is entitled under sub-paragraph (3).

(3) For each complete incremental period in the person's period of deferment, the amount of the increment shall be 1/5th per cent. of the weekly rate of the increase to which the person would have been entitled under paragraphs 5 to 6 for the period if his entitlement to the Category A or Category B retirement pension had not been deferred.]

3.—(1) Regulations may provide that sub-paragraphs (1) to (3) of paragraph 2 above shall have effect with such additions, omissions and amendments as are prescribed in relation to a person during whose period of enhancement there has been a change, other than a change made by such an order as is mentioned in sub-paragraph (7) of that paragraph, in the rate of the Category A or Category B retirement pension to which he would have been entitled if his entitlement to the pension had commenced on attaining pensionable age.

(2) Any regulations under this paragraph may make such consequential additions, omissions and amendments in paragraph 8(3) below as the Secretary of State considers are appropriate in consequence of any changes made by virtue of this paragraph in paragraph 2 above.

[⁵ Lump sum where pensioner's entitlement is deferred

3A.—(1) This paragraph applies where—
  (a) a person's entitlement to a Category A or Category B retirement pension is deferred, and
  (b) the person has made (or is treated as having made) an election under paragraph A1(1)
    (b) in relation to the period of deferment.

(2) The person is entitled to an amount calculated in accordance with paragraph 3B (a "lump sum").

1.527

Calculation of lump sum

3B.—(1) The lump sum is the accrued amount for the last accrual period beginning during the period of deferment.

(2) In this paragraph—

"accrued amount" means the amount calculated in accordance with sub-paragraph (3);
"accrual period" means any period of seven days beginning with a prescribed day of the week, where that day falls within the period of deferment.

(3) The accrued amount for an accrual period for a person is—

$$(A + P) \times {}_{52}\left(1 + \frac{R}{100}\right)$$

where—
A is the accrued amount for the previous accrual period (or, in the case of the first accrual period beginning during the period of deferment, zero);
P is the amount of the Category A or Category B retirement pension to which the person would have been entitled for the accrual period if his entitlement had not been deferred;
R is—
  (a) a percentage rate two per cent. higher than the Bank of England base rate, or
  (b) if regulations so provide, such higher rate as may be prescribed.

(4) For the purposes of sub-paragraph (3), any change in the Bank of England base rate is to be treated as taking effect—
  (a) at the beginning of the accrual period immediately following the accrual period during which the change took effect, or
  (b) if regulations so provide, at such other time as may be prescribed.

(5) For the purposes of the calculation of the lump sum, the amount of Category A or Category B retirement pension to which the person would have been entitled for an accrual period—
  (a) includes any increase under section 47(1) and any increase under paragraph 4 of this Schedule, but
  (b) does not include—

1.528

    (i) any increase under section 83A or 85 or paragraphs 5 to 6 of this Schedule,

    (ii) any graduated retirement benefit, or

    (iii) in prescribed circumstances, such other amount of Category A or Category B retirement pension as may be prescribed.

(6) The reference in sub-paragraph (5)(a) to any increase under subsection (1) of section 47 shall be taken as a reference to any increase that would take place under that subsection if sub-section (2) of that section and section 46(5) of the Pensions Act were disregarded."

Choice between increase of pension and lump sum where pensioner's deceased spouse has deferred entitlement

1.529
    3C.—(1) Subject to paragraph 8, this paragraph applies where—

    (a) a widow or widower ("W") is entitled to a Category A or Category B retirement pension,

    (b) W was married to the other party to the marriage ("S") when S died,

    (c) S's entitlement to a Category A or Category B retirement pension was deferred when S died, and

    (d) S's entitlement had been deferred throughout the period of 12 months ending with the day before S's death.

(2) We shall within the prescribed period elect in the prescribed manner either—

    (a) that paragraph 4 (entitlement to increase of pension) is to apply in relation to S's period of deferment, or

    (b) that paragraph 7A (entitlement to lump sum) is to apply in relation to S's period of deferment.

(3) If no election under sub-paragraph (2) is made within the period prescribed under that sub-paragraph, W is to be treated as having made an election under sub-paragraph (2)(b).

(4) Regulations—

    (a) may enable a person who has made an election under sub-paragraph (2) (including one that the person is treated by sub-paragraph (3) as having made) to change the election within a prescribed period and in a prescribed manner, if prescribed conditions are satisfied, and

    (b) if they enable a person to make an election under sub-paragraph (2)(b) in respect of a period of deferment after receiving any increase of pension under paragraph 4 by reference to that period, may for the purpose of avoiding duplication of payment—

        (i) enable an amount determined in accordance with the regulations to be recovered from the person in a prescribed manner and within a prescribed period, or

        (ii) provide for an amount determined in accordance with the regulations to be treated as having been paid on account of the amount to which the person is entitled under paragraph 7A.

(5) The making of an election under sub-paragraph (2)(b) does not affect the application of paragraphs 5 to 6 (which relate to an increase in pension where the pensioner's deceased spouse had deferred an entitlement to a guaranteed minimum pension).]

Increase of pension where pensioner's deceased spouse has deferred entitlement

1.530
    [5 (1) Subject to paragraph 8, this paragraph applies where a widow or widower ("W") is entitled to a Category A or Category B retirement pension and was married to the other party to the marriage ("S") when S died and one of the following conditions is met—

    (a) S was entitled to a Category A or Category B retirement pension with an increase under this Schedule,

    (b) W is a widow or widower to whom paragraph 3C applies and has made an election under paragraph 3C(2)(a), or

    (c) paragraph 3C would apply to W but for the fact that the condition in sub-paragraph (1)(d) of that paragraph is not met.

(1A) Subject to sub-paragraph (3), the rate of W's pension shall be increased—

    (a) in a case falling within sub-paragraph (1)(a), by an amount equal to the increase to which S was entitled under this Schedule, apart from paragraphs 5 to 6,

    (b) in a case falling within sub-paragraph (1)(b), by an amount equal to the increase to which S would have been entitled under this Schedule, apart from paragraphs 5 to 6, if the period of deferment had ended immediately before S's death and S had then made an election under paragraph A1(1)(a), or

    (c) in a case falling within sub-paragraph (1)(c), by an amount equal to the increase to which S would have been entitled under this Schedule, apart from paragraphs 5 to 6, if the period of deferment had ended immediately before S's death.]

(2) [² . . .]

(3) If a married person dies after 5th April 2000, the rate of the retirement pension for that person's widow or widower shall be increased by an amount equivalent to the sum of—

(a) the increase in the basic pension to which the deceased spouse was entitled; and

(b) one-half of the increase in the additional pension.

(4) In any case where—

(a) there is a period between the death of the former spouse and the date on which the surviving spouse becomes entitled to a Category A or Category B retirement pension, and

(b) One or more orders have come into force under section 150 of the Administration act during that period,

the amount of the increase to which the surviving spouse is entitled under this paragraph shall be determined as if the order or orders had come into force before the beginning of that period.

(5) This paragraph does not apply in any case where the deceased spouse died before 6th April, 1979 and the widow or widower attained pensionable age before that date.

[³ 5.—(1) Where—

(a) a widow or widower (call that person 'W') is entitled to a Category A or Category B retirement pension and was married to the other party to the marriage (call that person 'S') when S died, and

(b) S either—

(i) was entitled to a guaranteed minimum pension with an increase under section 15(1) of the Pensions Act, or

(ii) would have been so entitled if S had retired on the date of S's death, the rate of W's pension shall be increased by the following amount.

(2) The amount is—

(a) where W is a widow, an amount equal to the sum of the amount set out in paragraph 5A(2) or (3) below (as the case may be), and

(b) where W is a widower, an amount equal to the sum of the amounts set out in paragraph 6(2), (3) or (4) below (as the case may be).

5A.—(1) This paragraph applies where W (referred to in paragraph 5 above) is a widow. **1.531**

(2) Where the husband dies before April 6th, 2000, the amounts referred to in paragraph 5(2)(a) above are the following—

(a) an amount equal to one-half of the increase mentioned in paragraph 5(1)(b) above,

(b) the appropriate amount, and

(c) an amount equal to any increase to which the husband had been entitled under paragraph 5 above.

(3) Where the husband dies after 5th April, 2000, the amounts referred to in paragraph 5(2)(a) above are the following—

(a) one-half of the appropriate amount [⁸ . . .], and

(b) one-half of any increase to which the husband had been entitled under paragraph 5 above.

6.—(1) This paragraph applies where W (referred to in paragraph 5 above) is a widower.

(2) Where the wife dies before 6th April, 1989, the amounts referred to in paragraph 5(2)(b) above are the following—

(a) an amount equal to the increase mentioned in paragraph 5(1)(b) above,

(b) the appropriate amount, and

(c) an amount equal to any increase to which the wife had been entitled under paragraph 5 above.

(3) Where the wife dies after 5th April, 1989 but before 6th April, 2000, the amounts referred to in paragraph 5(2) above are the following—

(a) the increase mentioned in paragraph 5(1)(b) above, so far as attributable to employment before 6th April, 1988,

(b) one-half of that increase, so far as attributable to employment after 5th April, 1988,

(c) the appropriate amount reduced by the amount of any increases under section 109 of the Pensions Act, and

(d) any increase to which the wife had been entitled under paragraph 5 above.

(4) Where the wife dies after 5th April, 2000, the amounts referred to in paragraph 5(2)(b) above are the following—

(a) one-half of the increase mentioned in paragraph 5(1)(b) above, so far as attributable to employment before 6th April, 1988,

(b) one-half of the appropriate amount [⁸ . . .], and

(c) one-half of any increase to which the wife had been entitled under paragraph 5 above].

1.532   [^{6} **6A.**—(1) This paragraph applies where W (referred to in paragraph 5 above) is a surviving civil partner.

(2) The amounts referred to in paragraph 5(2)(c) above are the following—

    (a) one-half of the increase mentioned in paragraph 5(1)(b) above, so far as attributable to employment before 6th April 1988,

    (b) one-half of the appropriate amount [^{7} . . .] and

    (c) one-half of any increase to which the deceased civil partner had been entitled under paragraph 5 above.]

7.—(1) For the purpose of [paragraphs 5 to 6A] above, the "appropriate amount" means the greater of—

    (a) the amount by which the deceased person's Category A or Category B retirement pension had been increased [by virtue of section 150(1)(e)] of the Administration Act; or

    (b) the amount by which his Category A or Category B retirement pension would have been so increased had he died immediately before his surviving spouse [or civil partner] became entitled to a Category A or Category B retirement pension.

(2) Where an amount is required to be calculated in accordance with the provisions of [paragraphs 5, 5A, 6 or 6A] or sub-paragraph (1) above—

    (a) the amount so calculated shall be rounded to the nearest penny, taking any 1/2p as nearest to the next whole penny above; and

    (b) where the amount so calculated would, apart from this sub-paragraph, be a sum less than 1/2p, that amount shall be taken to be zero, notwithstanding any other provision of this Act, the Pensions Act or the Administration Act.

[^{5} Entitlement to lump sum where pensioner's deceased spouse has deferred entitlement

1.533   **7A.**—(1) This paragraph applies where a person to whom paragraph 3C applies ("W") has made (or is treated as having made) an election under paragraph 3C(2)(b).

(2) W is entitled to an amount calculated in accordance with paragraph 7B (a "widowed person's lump sum").

Calculation of widowed person's lump sum

1.534   **7B.**—(1) The widowed person's lump sum is the accrued amount for the last accrual period beginning during the period which—

    (a) began at the beginning of S's period of deferment, and

    (b) ended on the day before S's death.

(2) In this paragraph—

"S" means the other party to the marriage;

"accrued amount" means the amount calculated in accordance with sub-paragraph (3);

"accrual period" means any period of seven days beginning with a prescribed day of the week, where that day falls within S's period of deferment.

(3) The accrued amount for an accrual period for W is—

$$(A + P) \times {}_{52}\left(1 + \frac{R}{100}\right)$$

where—

A is the accrued amount for the previous accrual period (or, in the case of the first accrual period beginning during the period mentioned in sub-paragraph (1), zero);

P is—

    (a) the basic pension, and

    (b) half of the additional pension, to which S would have been entitled for the accrual period if his entitlement had not been deferred during the period mentioned in sub-paragraph (1);

R is—

    (a) a percentage rate two per cent. higher than the Bank of England base rate, or

    (b) if regulations so provide, such higher rate as may be prescribed.

(4) For the purposes of sub-paragraph (3), any change in the Bank of England base rate is to be treated as taking effect—

(a) at the beginning of the accrual period immediately following the accrual period during which the change took effect, or

(b) if regulations so provide, at such other time as may be prescribed.

(5) For the purposes of the calculation of the widowed person's lump sum, the amount of Category A or Category B retirement pension to which S would have been entitled for an accrual period—

(a) includes any increase under section 47(1) and any increase under paragraph 4 of this Schedule, but

(b) does not include—

  (i) any increase under section 83A or 85 or paragraphs 5 to 6 of this Schedule,

  (ii) any graduated retirement benefit, or

  (iii) in prescribed circumstances, such other amount of Category A or Category B retirement pension as may be prescribed.

(6) The reference in sub-paragraph (5)(a) to any increase under subsection (1) of section 47 shall be taken as a reference to any increase that would take place under that subsection if sub-section (2) of that section and section 46(5) of the Pensions Act were disregarded.

(7) In any case where—

(a) there is a period between the death of S and the date on which W becomes entitled to a Category A or Category B retirement pension, and

(b) one or more orders have come into force under section 150 of the Administration Act during that period,

the amount of the lump sum shall be increased in accordance with that order or those orders.]

[5 *Supplementary*]

7C.—(1) Any lump sum calculated under paragraph 3B or 7B must be rounded to the nearest penny, taking any 1/2p as nearest to the next whole penny above.   **1.535**

(2) In prescribing a percentage rate for the purposes of paragraphs 3B and 7B, the Secretary of State must have regard to—

(a) the national economic situation, and

(b) any other matters which he considers relevant.]

[5 *Married Couples*]

[2 **8.**—(1) For the purposes of paragraphs 1 to 3 above in their application to a Category B retirement pension to which a married woman is entitled by virtue of her husband's contributions, a married woman who would have become entitled to such a pension on an earlier day if her husband's entitlement to his Category A retirement pension had not been deferred shall be treated as having (in addition to any other period of enhancement) a period of enhancement which begins on that earlier day and ends on the same day as her husband's period of enhancement.   **1.536**

(2) The reference in sub-paragraph (1) above to the day on which the woman's husband's period of enhancement ends shall, where the marriage is terminated before that day, be construed as a reference to the day on which the marriage is terminated.]

[2 (3) [8 . . .]

[5(4) The conditions in paragraph 3C(1)(c) and 4(1)(a) are not satisfied by a Category B retirement pension to which S was or would have been entitled by virtue of W's contributions.

(5) Where the Category A retirement pension to which S was or would have been entitled includes an increase under section 51A(2) attributable to W's contributions, the increase or lump sum to which W is entitled under paragraph 4(1A) or 7A(2) is to be calculated as if there had been no increase under that section.

(6) In sub-paragraphs (4) and (5), "W" and "S" have the same meaning as in paragraph 3C, 4 or 7A, as the case requires.]

Uprating

9.—The sums which are the increases in the rates of retirement pension under this Schedule are subject to alteration by order made by the Secretary of State under section 150 of the Administration Act.   **1.537**

AMENDMENTS

1. Tax Credits Act 2002, Sch.6 (April 6, 2003).

2. Pensions Act 1995, Sch.4 (July 19, 1995).

3. Social Security (Incapacity for Work) Act 1994, Sch.1 para.40 (April 13, 1995).

4. Pensions Schemes Act 1993, Sch.8 (Feb. 7, 1994).

5. Pensions Act 2004, Sch.11 (April 6, 2005).

6. Civil Partnership (Pensions and Benefit Payments) (Consequential Provisions) Order 2005, (SI 2005/2053) (December 5, 2005).

7. Pensions Act 2007, Sch.1, para.19 (July 26, 2007).

8. Pensions Act 2007, Sch.7 (September 26, 2007).

GENERAL NOTE

1.538   Under para.4(1) above a man reaching pensionable age before April 6, 2010 is also required to have been over pensionable age when his wife (S) died. (See Pensions Act 1995, Sch.4 para.21 (14) and (16).)

In relation to any incremental period and accrual period beginning before April 6, 2010 references in para.2 (5)(b), 3B (5)(b) and 7B (5)(b) to section 83A of the principal Act are to be taken as references to s.83 or 84 of that Act—see Sch.11 of Pensions Act 2004. The sums payable under this Schedule are increased by 5 per cent under art.4(4) of the Social Security Benefits Up-rating Order 2009 (S1 2009/497) (April 6, 2009).

[¹ SCHEDULE 5A

PENSION INCREASE OR LUMP SUM WHERE ENTITLEMENT TO SHARED ADDITIONAL PENSION IS DEFERRED

Choice between pension increase and lump sum where entitlement to shared additional pension is deferred

1.539   **1.**—(1) Where a person's entitlement to a shared additional pension is deferred and the period of deferment is at least 12 months, the person shall, on claiming his pension or within a prescribed period after claiming it, elect in the prescribed manner either—

(a) that paragraph 2 (entitlement to increase of pension) is to apply in relation to the period of deferment, or

(b) that paragraph 4 (entitlement to lump sum) is to apply in relation to the period of deferment.

(2) If no election under sub-paragraph (1) is made within the period prescribed under that sub-paragraph, the person is to be treated as having made an election under sub-paragraph (1)(b).

(3) Regulations—

(a) may enable a person who has made an election under sub-paragraph (1) (including one that the person is treated by sub-paragraph (2) as having made) to change the election within a prescribed period and in a prescribed manner, if prescribed conditions are satisfied, and

(b) if they enable a person to make an election under sub-paragraph (1)(b) in respect of a period of deferment after receiving any increase of pension under paragraph 2 by reference to that period, may for the purpose of avoiding duplication of payment—

(i) enable an amount determined in accordance with the regulations to be recovered from the person in a prescribed manner and within a prescribed period, or

(ii) provide for an amount determined in accordance with the regulations to be treated as having been paid on account of the amount to which the person is entitled under paragraph 4.

Increase of pension where entitlement deferred

1.540   **2.**—(1) This paragraph applies where a person's entitlement to a shared additional pension is deferred and either—

(a) the period of deferment is less than 12 months, or

(b) the person has made an election under paragraph 1(1)(a) in relation to the period of deferment.

310

(2) The rate of the person's shared additional pension shall be increased by an amount equal to the aggregate of the increments to which he is entitled under paragraph 3, but only if that amount is enough to increase the rate of the pension by at least 1 per cent.

Calculation of increment

3.—(1) A person is entitled to an increment under this paragraph for each complete incremental period in his period of deferment.

1.541

(2) The amount of the increment for an incremental period shall be 1/5th per cent. of the weekly rate of the shared additional pension to which the person would have been entitled for the period if his entitlement had not been deferred.

(3) Amounts under sub-paragraph (2) shall be rounded to the nearest penny, taking any 1/2p as nearest to the next whole penny.

(4) Where an amount under sub-paragraph (2) would, apart from this sub-paragraph, be a sum less than 1/2p, the amount shall be taken to be zero, notwithstanding any other provision of this Act, the Pensions Act or the Administration Act.

(5) In this paragraph "incremental period" means any period of six days which are treated by regulations as days of increment for the purposes of this paragraph in relation to the person and pension in question.

(6) Where one or more orders have come into force under section 150 of the Administration Act during the period of deferment, the rate for any incremental period shall be determined as if the order or orders had come into force before the beginning of the period of deferment.

(7) The sums which are the increases in the rates of shared additional pension under this paragraph are subject to alteration by order made by the Secretary of State under section 150 of the Administration Act.

Lump sum where entitlement to shared additional pension is deferred

4.—(1) This paragraph applies where—
  (a) a person's entitlement to a shared additional pension is deferred, and
  (b) the person has made (or is treated as having made) an election under paragraph 1(1)
        (b) in relation to the period of deferment.

1.542

(2) The person is entitled to an amount calculated in accordance with paragraph 5 (a "lump sum").

Calculation of lump sum

5.—(1) The lump sum is the accrued amount for the last accrual period beginning during the period of deferment.

1.543

(2) In this paragraph—

'accrued amount' means the amount calculated in accordance with sub-paragraph (3);
'accrual period' means any period of seven days beginning with a prescribed day of the
    week, where that day falls within the period of deferment.

(3) The accrued amount for an accrual period for a person is—

$$(A + P) \times {}_{52}\left(1 + \frac{R}{100}\right)$$

where—
  A is the accrued amount for the previous accrual period (or, in the case of the first accrual period beginning during the period of deferment, zero);
  P is the amount of the shared additional pension to which the person would have been entitled for the accrual period if his entitlement had not been deferred;
  R is—
  (a) a percentage rate two per cent. higher than the Bank of England base rate, or
  (b) if a higher rate is prescribed for the purposes of paragraphs 3B and 7B of Schedule 5,
        that higher rate.

(4) For the purposes of sub-paragraph (3), any change in the Bank of England base rate is to be treated as taking effect—

(a) at the beginning of the accrual period immediately following the accrual period during which the change took effect, or

(b) if regulations so provide, at such other time as may be prescribed.

(5) For the purpose of the calculation of the lump sum, the amount of the shared additional pension to which the person would have been entitled for an accrual period does not include, in prescribed circumstances, such amount as may be prescribed.

(6) The lump sum must be rounded to the nearest penny, taking any 1/2p as nearest to the next whole penny.]

AMENDMENT

1. Pensions Act 2004, Sch.11 (April 6, 2005).

SCHEDULE 6

ASSESSMENT OF EXTENT OF DISABLEMENT

General provisions as to method of assessment

1.544   **1.**—For the purposes of section 68 or 103 above and Part II of Schedule 7 to this Act, the extent of disablement shall be assessed, by reference to the disabilities incurred by the claimant as a result of the relevant loss of faculty in accordance with the following general principles—

(a) except as provided in paragraphs (b) to (d) below, the disabilities to be taken into account shall be all disabilities so incurred (whether or not involving loss of earning power or additional expense) to which the claimant may be expected, having regard to his physical and mental condition at the date of the assessment, to be subject during the period taken into account by the assessment as compared with a person of the same age and sex whose physical and mental condition is normal;

(b) except in the case of an assessment for the purposes of section 68 above, regulations may make provision as to the extent (if any) to which any disabilities are to be taken into account where they are disabilities which, though resulting from the relevant loss of faculty, also result, or without the relevant accident might have been expected to result, from a cause other than the relevant accident;

(c) the assessment shall be made without reference to the particular circumstances of the claimant other than age, sex, and physical and mental condition;

(d) the disabilities resulting from such loss of faculty as may be prescribed shall be taken as amounting to 100 per cent. disablement and other disabilities shall be assessed accordingly.

2.—Provisions may be made by regulations for further defining the principles on which the extent of disablement is to be assessed and such regulations may in particular direct that a pre-scribed loss of faculty shall be treated as resulting in a prescribed degree of disablement; and, in connection with any such direction, nothing in paragraph 1(c) above prevents the making of different provision, in the case of loss of faculty in or affecting hand or arm, for right-handed and for left-handed persons.

3.—Regulations under paragraph 1(d) or 2 above may include provision—

(a) for adjusting or reviewing an assessment made before the date of the coming into force of those regulations;

(b) for any resulting alteration of that assessment to have effect as from that date; so however that no assessment shall be reduced by virtue of this paragraph.

Severe disablement allowance

1.545   **4.**—(1) In the case of an assessment of any person's disablement for the purposes of section 68 above, the period to be taken into account for any such assessment shall be the period during which that person has suffered and may be expected to continue to suffer from the relevant loss of faculty beginning not later than—

(a) the first claim day, if his entitlement to benefit falls to be determined in accordance with section 68(3)(b) above as modified by regulations under section 68(11)(b);

(b) where his disablement has previously been assessed for the purposes of section 68 above at a percentage which is not less than 80 per cent.—

(i) if the period taken into account for that assessment was or included the period of 196 days ending immediately before the first claim day, the first claim day, or

(ii) if the period so taken into account included any day falling within that period of 196 days, the day immediately following that day or, if there is more than one such day, the last such day;

(c) in any other case, 196 days before the first claim day;

and, in any case, ending not later than the day on which that person attains the age of 65 [¹ . . .].

(2) In this paragraph "the first claim day" means the first day in respect of which the person concerned has made the claim in question for a severe disablement allowance.

5.—(1) An assessment of any person's disablement for the purposes of section 68 above shall state the degree of disablement in the form of a percentage and shall specify the period taken into account by the assessment.

(2) For the purposes of any such assessment—

(a) a percentage which is not a whole number shall be rounded to the nearest whole number or, if it falls equally near two whole numbers, shall be rounded up to the higher; and

(b) a percentage between 5 and 100 which is not a multiple of 10 shall be treated, if it is a multiple of 5, as being the next higher percentage which is a multiple of 10 and, in any other case, as being the nearest percentage which is a multiple of 10.

(3) If on the assessment the person's disablement is found to be less than 5 per cent., that degree of disablement shall for the purposes of section 68 above be disregarded and, accordingly, the assessment shall state that he is not disabled.

Disablement benefit

6.—(1) Subject to sub-paragraphs (2) and (3) below, the period to be taken into account by an assessment for the purposes of section 103 above and Part II of Schedule 7 to this Act of the extent of a claimant's disablement shall be the period (beginning not earlier than the end of the period of 90 days referred to in section 103(6) above and in paragraph 9(3) of that Schedule and limited by reference either to the claimant's life or to a definite date) during which the claimant has suffered and may be expected to continue to suffer from the relevant loss of faculty.

1.546

(2) If on any assessment the condition of the claimant is not such, having regard to the possibility of changes in that condition (whether predictable or not), as to allow of a final assessment being made up to the end of the period provided by sub-paragraph (1) above, then, subject to sub-paragraph (3) below—

(a) a provisional assessment shall be made, taking into account such shorter period only as seems reasonable having regard to his condition and that possibility; and

(b) on the next assessment the period to be taken into account shall begin with the end of the period taken into account by the provisional assessment.

(3) Where the assessed extent of a claimant's disablement amounts to less than 14 per cent., then, subject to sub-paragraphs (4) and (5) below, that assessment shall be a final assessment and the period to be taken into account by it shall not end before the earliest date on which it seems likely that the extent of the disablement will be less than 1 per cent.

(4) Sub-paragraph (3) above does not apply in any case where it seems likely that—

(a) the assessed extent of the disablement will be aggregated with the assessed extent of any present disablement, and

(b) that aggregate will amount to 14 per cent. or more.

(5) Where the extent of the claimant's disablement is assessed at different percentages for different parts of the period taken into account by the assessment, then—

(a) sub-paragraph (3) above does not apply in relation to the assessment unless the percentage assessed for the latest part of that period is less than 14 per cent., and

(b) in any such case that sub-paragraph shall apply only in relation to that part of that period (and subject to sub-paragraph (4) above).

7.—An assessment for the purposes of section 103 above and Part II of Schedule 7 to this Act shall—

(a) state the degree of disablement in the form of a percentage;

(b) specify the period taken into account by the assessment; and

(c) where that period is limited by reference to a definite date, specify whether the assessment is provisional or final;

but the percentage and the period shall not be specified more particularly than is necessary for the purpose of determining in accordance with section 103 above and Parts II and IV of Schedule 7 to this Act the claimant's rights as to disablement pension or gratuity and reduced earnings allowance (whether or not a claim has been made).

1.547   **8.**—(1) For the purpose of determining whether a person is entitled—
    (a) to an increase of a disablement pension under section 104 above; or
    (b) to a corresponding increase of any other benefit by virtue of paragraph 6(4)(b) or 7(2)
    (b) of Schedule 8 to this Act,
regulations may provide for the extent of the person's disablement resulting from the relevant injury or disease to be determined in such manner as may be provided for by the regulations by reference to all disabilities to which that person is subject which result either from the relevant injury or disease or from any other injury or disease in respect of which there fall to be made to the person payments of any of the descriptions listed in sub-paragraph (2) below.
    (2) Those payments are—
    (a) payments by way of disablement pension;
    (b) payments by way of benefit under paragraph 4 or 7(1) of Schedule 8 to this Act; or
    (c) payments in such circumstances as may be prescribed by way of such other benefit as may be prescribed (being benefit in connection with any hostilities or with service as a member of Her Majesty's forces or of such other organisation as may be specified in the regulations).

AMENDMENT

1. Social Security (Severe Disablement Allowance and Invalid Care Allowance) Amendment Regulations 1994, reg.2(4) (October 28, 1994).

DERIVATION

1.548   SSA 1975, Sch.8.

GENERAL NOTE

1.549   Regulation 11 of the Social Security (General Benefit) Regulations 1982 is treated (by s.2(2) of the SSCPA 1992) as having been made under this Schedule to further define the principles on which the extent of disablement is to be assessed.
    In the case of some prescribed diseases, special provision is made by the Prescribed Diseases Regulations and this Schedule and reg.11 of the General Benefit Regulations must be read as subject to that.

Para.1
1.550   Sub-paras (a) and (c) make it plain that disablement is to be assessed by comparing the claimant with a person of the same age and sex whose physical and mental condition is normal *without* taking into account loss of earning power, additional expense or other circumstances peculiar to the claimant (e.g. the distance from home to public transport or other facilities) other than, of course, age, sex and physical and mental condition. This cannot be too strongly emphasised. As Commissioner Fellner rightly noted in a deafness case, *CI/5092/2002*

> "It must not be forgotten that the comparison under Schedule 6 is simply with another person of the same age and sex, and that individual hobbies and preferences are not to be taken into account. Thus, this claimant's complaints of loss of pleasure in particular kinds of music and in birdsong, and having to have the TV volume high, are relevant only in so far as other men of his age might be able to have, or not to be burdened with, these things. His being a radio ham, as he told the tribunal, would not be relevant" (para.17).

The one exception is allowed by sub-para.(b) which permits the taking into account of disabilities which are due not only to the relevant accident or disease but also to another cause (see reg.11(2)–(4) of the General Benefit Regulations).
    Sub-para.(d) enables regulations to prescribe disabilities amounting to 100 per cent. Other disabilities must be assessed accordingly (see reg.11(7) of, and Sch.2 to, the General Benefit Regulations). In *R(I) 30/61*, it was made clear that "a man entitled to an assessment of 100 per cent is not necessarily totally disabled, and that

any scale of values which a member of an assessing body has in the back of his mind should take account of that fact".

While there are certain prescribed degrees of disablement in respect of certain injuries in Sch.2 to the General Benefit Regulations (e.g. loss of the sight in one eye [30 per cent]), these can be departed from, whether by way of increase or decrease, as may be reasonable in the case if that prescribed degree of disablement does not provide a reasonable assessment of the extent of disablement resulting from the relevant loss of faculty (reg.11(6) of the General Benefit Regulations).

Coming to a decision, within those parameters, on the appropriate percentage assessment of disablement flowing from the relevant loss of faculty is a difficult matter of judgment, the matter of guidance on which has been considered in many Commissioners' decisions (e.g. *CI/499/2000, CI/1802/2001, CI/2553/2001, CI/3758 and 3759/2003*). It has most recently been considered by a Tribunal of Commissioners in *R(I) 2/06*. In most respects, since it found no relevant error of law in the approach and decision of the tribunals appealed from, the comments are ultimately *obiter*.

That Tribunal of Commissioners, dealt specifically with two appeal tribunal decisions awarding 7 per cent and 4 per cent respectively in respect of claimants suffering from PD A11 (Vibration White Finger) as a result of their work with percussive tools as coal miners. While making it clear that it was not possible to produce a template for assessment decisions, the Tribunal hoped that its comments would assist advisers, decision-makers, and tribunals by identifying the correct approach to such decisions and indicating matters which should be taken into account, matters which should not be taken into account, and matters which need not be taken into account (para.78). The scheme leaves considerable discretion to decision-makers and tribunals. (*ibid.*). Commissioners and courts can only interfere if the decision appealed exhibits an error of law (on which see: paras 28-31, citing *R(A)1/72* and *R. (Iran)* v *Secretary of State for the Home Department* [2005] EWCA Civ 982, paras 9–10 per Brooke L.J.; and Vol III of this series). The Tribunal of Commissioners rightly stressed that the matter of assessment of the percentage of functional disablement in any given case is essentially a factual and medical assessment for the tribunal hearing and seeing the evidence in the case to make. A disputed judgement of degree on a question of fact is not an error of law in the sense set out in those cases. It is not for an appellate body whose jurisdiction is limited to points of law to offer or impose its substituted view (para.31). That said, however,

"Commissioners have always regarded it as part of their function to give guidance where needed for the assistance of tribunals and departmental decision makers on the relevant principles of law to be applied in this specialised jurisdiction: this is an area where certainty and consistency of approach and an orderly development of the law are of particular importance given the complex nature of the legislation and the very large number of individual cases potentially involved. However it is a function to be exercised cautiously, particularly in an instance such as the present where the questions of assessment of an individual's percentage level of functional disablement are not primarily matters of legal interpretation at all, but of factual judgment - including judgment on medical matters - entrusted by the legislation to the specialist tribunals best qualified to decide them. There is a danger in misinterpreting the observations of individual Commissioners on the facts of such cases as laying down additional rules of law where only helpful guidance on the fact-finding process was intended. There was some evidence of that in the way the notices of appeal before us were formulated. What matters is not whether express reference is made to some such guidance, but whether the substance of the tribunal's decision, and its statement of the factors taken into account in reaching it, demonstrates any error of law" (para. 68).

One species of error of law, of course, is a failure of an appeal tribunal to give adequate reasons for its decision. Thus in *CI/499/2000*, Commissioner Jacobs held erroneous in law a tribunal assessment of disablement because it focused purely on impaired manual dexterity resulting from the claimant's laceration to his finger. It should also have considered any mental effect, the effect of pain preventing or hindering the performance of an activity, and disfigurement (a scar had been left). The Tribunal should have made clear why it did not believe the claimant to be as disabled as he claimed. Nor had it properly explained its assessment of 8 per cent. Such explanation is required and an assessment could be explained in several ways. A Tribunal could give a general indication of why it made an assessment at a particular level (e.g. the effects were intermittent). It might properly explain its assessment by reference to the prescribed degrees of disablement in Sch.2 to the General Benefit Regulations. It might explain the significance of its clinical findings in terms of function (e.g. findings on the movement of joints might be explained in terms of how much useful grip was retained by the claimant). On this matter of giving adequate reasons, the Tribunal of Commissioners expressly approved, in para.45 of its decision, Deputy Commissioner Warren's statements in *CI/1802/2001* on what was required of tribunals assessing the degree of disablement. The Deputy Commissioner there stated:

> "7. Vibration white finger is not one of those conditions for which there is a prescribed degree of disablement in Schedule 2 of the General Benefit Regulations. Those Regulations therefore state only that the tribunal 'may have such regard as may be appropriate to the prescribed degrees of disablement' when making its assessment. This indicates the very broad discretion which individual tribunals have in this type of case. In many cases it is simply not possible for a tribunal to give precise reasons for the conclusion which it has reached.
>
> 8. In my judgment, however, as a minimum, the claimant and the Secretary of State are entitled to know the factual basis upon which the assessment has been made; in other words what disabilities were taken into account by the tribunal in concluding that a particular percentage disablement was appropriate.
>
> 9. This can often be simply expressed. In many cases it will be enough to say that the evidence given by the claimant about the effect of a particular accident or disease on his or her daily life has been accepted. In some cases, where the claimant's evidence is for some reason found to be unreliable, it may be that the tribunal will state that it felt able to accept only those disabilities which in its expert opinion were likely to flow from problems disclosed on clinical examination. Other cases may need more detail. But if it is not possible to discern the material on which the assessment is based, then the tribunal's statement of reasons is likely to be inadequate."

1.551 Commissioners had, of course, proffered guidance for tribunals approaching the task of assessment of the degree of disablement. Both Deputy Commissioner Warren and Commissioner Jacobs in their decisions referred with caveats to the role of Sch.2 of the General Benefit Regulations (and see also approval of such cross-referral in *R(I) 5/95*). The Tribunal of Commissioners had taken on board at their oral hearing a debate on whether the degrees of disablement there prescribed for hand and finger conditions could offer assistance to tribunals dealing with disablement from vibration white finger (VWF). It considered that the assistance to be derived from them to be "relatively small" (para.72). The Schedule might well inform to an extent an appropriate percentage for a particular VWF case but was of "very limited value in assessing percentages for such conditions" (para.73).

In three decisions (*CI/2553/2001, CI/3758 and 3759/2003*), Commissioner Williams had drawn the attention of tribunals to judicial guidelines on assessing damages in civil personal injury claims in tort, but had stressed the need to approach this with caution. As the Tribunal of Commissioners saw it, Commissioner Williams has stressed that he drew nothing from the bands of damages set out in those guidelines. Rather, as the Tribunal of Commissioners put it, he "merely directed the tribunal to take into account certain specific criteria referred to in those guidelines, namely the length and severity of the claimant's attacks and symptoms, the extent and/or severity and/or rapidity of deterioration of his condition, and his age and prognosis" (para.57). To that degree, the guidelines may provide a useful list of entirely unexceptional matters for a tribunal to take into account in its assessment of functional disablement (*ibid.*). Those guidelines were drawn up for an entirely different purpose (see Diplock L.J., as he then was, in *R. v Medical Appeal Tribunal Ex p Cable* reported as an Appendix to *R(I) 11/66*, quoted in full in para.75 of the Tribunal of Commissioners' decision). His caution there against cross-referencing across schemes would extend to proposed comparison with any other system, such as the Criminal Injuries Compensation Scheme (para.75).

Both Commissioner Jacobs in *CI/499/2000* and Commissioner Williams in *CI/2553/2001* offered guidance on the proper role of Departmental guidance such as the MAF (Medical Assessment Framework) used by examining doctors for disablement benefit and severe disablement allowance. Both had counseled extreme caution in referring to this "rough guide". The Tribunal of Commissioners made no specific comment on the MAF other than noting with approval that Dr Reed, the doctor giving evidence on behalf of the Secretary of State, had stressed the emphasis given to all medical staff that nothing in MAF (the current version of which needed review) was to fetter their own individual judgment on a particular case (para.77). The Tribunal of Commissioners confirmed that it was no part of a tribunal's function to apply, or even necessarily to take into account, such internal guidance which, while properly aiming at clarity and consistency of approach, sets out merely the view of one of the parties to an appeal (the Government) on what was required by the law and by good practice. Such guidance was in no way binding on tribunals. A tribunal wanting to take such guidance into account had to bear all those caveats and cautions in mind (*ibid.*).

Para.2

Regulation 11 of the General Benefit Regulations is made under this paragraph. There is no specific provision for compensating for the loss of the "dominant hand" but, even in a case where the injury is one specified in Sch.2 to the Regulations, reg.11(6) permits "such increase or reduction in [the prescribed] degree of disablement as may be reasonable in the circumstances in the case".

1.552

Para.6

The period of the assessment should cover the whole period during which it is expected that the claimant will continue to suffer from the relevant loss of faculty resulting in disablement of at least 1 per cent. If the prognosis is uncertain and the assessment is at least 14 per cent a provisional assessment should be made so that the extent of the claimant's disability is reassessed at the end of the period of the provisional assessment. A final assessment which is for a definite period rather than "life" implies *either* that the claimant will be suffering from no loss of faculty *or* the resulting disablement will be less than 1 per cent from the end of the period of assessment *or* that any disablement from which the claimant may be expected to be suffering at the end of the period of assessment would have been present even if the relevant accident had not occurred. If the claimant is still disabled at the end of the period, he or she may apply for revision under s.9 of the SSA 1998. There is no reason why the claimant's disablement should not be assessed at different percentages for different parts of the period; nor why those parts should be lengthy. In *R(I) 30/61*, the medical appeal tribunal assessed disablement from January 11 to March 25, 1960, at 30 per cent; March 26 to June 24, 1960, at 100 per cent; June 25 to July 24, 1960, at 40 per cent; and from June 25, 1960 to January 24, 1961, at 30 per cent. That was a provisional assessment and reflected the fact that the claimant had been in hospital from March to June and was then recuperating. Although an appeal was allowed on the ground of inadequate reasons, the tribunal's general approach was not criticised and the Commissioner said,

1.553

"the disabilities resulting from the relevant loss of faculty must be related to the period covered by the assessment, and . . . the assessing body must not be misled by the fact that a very serious disability is expected not to last long. The answer to that situation is a high assessment for a short period."

Since disablement benefit is calculated on a weekly basis, it might be slightly more convenient for decision-makers if short periods were calculated in weeks rather than months if the evidence permits it.

Sub-paras (3)–(5) normally prevent a provisional assessment if the assessment, at least for the last part of the period, is less than 14 per cent. If the extent of the claimant's disablement resulting from the relevant loss of faculty is likely to become less over time, the adjudicating medical authority is then bound to determine a date from which the claimant's extent of disablement may be expected to be less than 1 per cent. If the extent of disablement is expected to become greater but the adjudicating medical authority cannot tell when and so is unable to include an assessment of at least 14 per cent within the period of assessment, a life assessment should be made and the burden rests upon the claimant to make an application for revision under s.9 of the SSA 1998 when the extent of disablement does become at least 14 per cent. An exception is made by sub-para.(4) if the assessment of the extent of disablement may be aggregated with another assessment and the aggregate may amount to 14 per cent or more. In such a case, a provisional assessment may be made if the prognosis is uncertain.

Regulation 20(3) of the Prescribed Diseases Regulations provides that the minimum period of assessment in a case of byssinosis shall be one year. Reg.29 provides that the initial assessment in a case of occupational deafness shall always be provisional and for a period of five years and that all subsequent assessments shall be for a period of at least five years.

Para.6

1.554   Where a claim is made in respect of diffuse mesothelioma, see reg.20(4) of the Prescribed Diseases Regulations.

Para.7

1.555   An assessment shall not specify the percentage or period more particularly than is necessary for the purpose of determining entitlement to industrial injuries benefits. This means that, where the assessment is under 14 per cent but not under 1 per cent, it is not necessary for the adjudicating medical authority to go into greater detail unless either the assessment may be aggregated with another and the aggregate might be more than 14 per cent or else the claimant is suffering from pneumoconiosis, byssinosis or diffuse mesothelioma in which case it matters whether the assessment is greater than 10 per cent or not for the purpose of determining the amount of disablement benefit payable (reg.20 of the Prescribed Diseases Regulations).

Para.8

1.556   See reg.20 of the General Benefit Regulations.

SCHEDULE 7

INDUSTRIAL INJURIES BENEFITS

PART I

UNEMPLOYABILITY SUPPLEMENT

Availability

1.557   **1.**—This Part of this Schedule applies only in relation to persons who were beneficiaries in receipt of unemployability supplement under section 58 of the 1975 Act immediately before 6th April 1987.

Rate and duration

2.—(1) The weekly rate of a disablement pension shall, if as the result of the relevant loss of   **1.558**
faculty the beneficiary is incapable of work and likely to remain so permanently, be increased
by the amount specified in Schedule 4, Part V, paragraph 5.

(2) An increase of pension under this paragraph is referred to in this Act as an "unemployability supplement".

(3) For the purposes of this paragraph a person may be treated as being incapable of work
and likely to remain so permanently, notwithstanding that the loss of faculty is not such as to
prevent him being capable of work, if it is likely to prevent his earnings in a year exceeding a
prescribed amount not less than £104.

(4) An unemployability supplement shall be payable for such period as may be determined
at the time it is granted, but may be renewed from time to time.

Increase of unemployability supplement

3.—(1) Subject to the following provisions of this paragraph, if on the qualifying date the   **1.559**
beneficiary was—

   (a) a man under the age of 60, or

   (b) a woman under the age of 55,

the weekly rate of unemployability supplement shall be increased by the appropriate amount
specified in Schedule 4, Part V, paragraph 6.

(2) Where for any period the beneficiary is entitled to a Category A or Category B retirement pension [¹ . . .] and the weekly rate of the pension includes an additional pension such
as is mentioned in section 44(3)(b) above, for that period the relevant amount shall be
deducted from the amount that would otherwise be the increase under this paragraph and the
beneficiary shall be entitled to an increase only if there is a balance after that deduction and, if
there is such a balance, only to an amount equal to it.

(3) In this paragraph "the relevant amount" means an amount equal to the additional
pension reduced by the amount of any reduction in the weekly rate of the retirement pension
[¹ . . .] made by virtue of [² section 46] of the Pensions Act.

(4) In this paragraph references to an additional pension are references to that pension after
any increase under section 52(3) above but without any increase under paragraphs 1 and 2 of
Schedule 5 to this Act.

(5) In this paragraph "the qualifying date" means, subject to sub-paragraphs (6) and (7)
below, the beginning of the first week for which the beneficiary qualified for unemployability
supplement.

(6) If the incapacity for work in respect of which unemployability supplement is payable forms
part of a period of interruption of employment which has continued from a date earlier than the
date fixed under sub-paragraph (5) above, the qualifying date means the first day in that period
which is a day of incapacity for work, or such earlier day as may be prescribed.

(7) Subject to sub-paragraph (6) above, if there have been two or more periods for which
the beneficiary was entitled to unemployability supplement, the qualifying date shall be, in
relation to unemployability supplement for a day in any one of those periods, the beginning of
the first week of that period.

(8) for the purposes of sub-paragraph (7) above—

   (a) a break of more than 8 weeks in entitlement to unemployability supplement means
      that the periods before and after the break are two different periods; and

   (b) a break of 8 weeks or less is to be disregarded.

(9) The Secretary of State may by regulations provide that sub-paragraph (8) above shall
have effect as if for the references to 8 weeks there were substituted references to a larger
number of weeks specified in the regulations.

(10) In this paragraph "period of interruption of employment" has the same meaning as [³ a
jobseeking period and any period linked to such a period has for the purposes of the Jobseekers
Act 1995].

(11) The provisions of this paragraph are subject to [² section 46(6) and (7) (entitlement to
guaranteed minimum pensions and increases of unemployability supplement).]

Increase for beneficiary's dependent children [⁸ and qualifying young persons]

4.—(1) Subject to the provisions of this paragraph and paragraph 5 below, the weekly rate of   **1.560**
a disablement pension where the beneficiary is entitled to an unemployability supplement shall
be increased for any period during which the beneficiary is entitled to child benefit in respect
of [⁸ one or more children or qualifying young persons].

(2) The amount of the increase shall be as specified in Schedule 4, Part V, paragraph 7.

(3) In any case where—

[7(a) a beneficiary is one of two persons who are—

   (i) spouses or civil partners residing together,

   (ii) a man and woman who are not married to each other but are living together as if they were husband and wife, or

   (iii) two people of the same sex who are not civil partners of each other but are living together as if they were civil partners, and]

(b) the other person had earnings in any week,

the beneficiary's right to payment of increases for the following week under this paragraph shall be determined in accordance with sub-paragraph (4) below.

(4) No such increase shall be payable—

(a) in respect of the first child [8 or qualifying young person] where the earnings were [4 £195] or more; and

(b) in respect of a further child [8 or qualifying young person] for each complete [4 £26] by which the earnings exceeded [4 £195].

(5) The Secretary of State may by order substitute larger amounts for the amounts for the time being specified in sub-paragraph (4) above.

(6) In this paragraph "week" means such period of 7 days as may be prescribed by regulations made for the purposes of this paragraph.

Additional provisions as to increase under paragraph 4

1.561 **5.**—(1) An increase under paragraph 4 above of any amount in respect of a particular child [8 or qualifying young person] shall for any period be payable only if during that period one or other of the following conditions is satisfied with respect to the child [8 or qualifying young person]

(a) the beneficiary would be treated for the purposes of Part IX of this Act as having the child [8 or qualifying young person] living with him; or

(b) the requisite contributions are being made to the cost of providing for the child [8 or qualifying young person].

(2) The condition specified in paragraph (b) of sub-paragraph (1) above is to be treated as satisfied if, and only if—

(a) such contributions are being made at a weekly rate not less than the amount referred to in that sub-paragraph—

   (i) by the beneficiary, or

   (ii) where the beneficiary is one of two spouses [7 or civil partners] residing together, by them together; and

(b) except in prescribed cases, the contributions are over and above those required for the purposes of satisfying section 143(1)(b) above.

Increase for adult dependants

1.562 **6.**—(1) The weekly rate of a disablement pension where the beneficiary is entitled to an unemployability supplement shall be increased under this paragraph for any period during which—

(a) the beneficiary is—

   (i) residing with his spouse [7 or civil partner], or

   (ii) contributing to the maintenance of his spouse [7 or civil partner] at the requisite rate; or

(b) a person—

   (i) who is neither the spouse [7 or civil partner] of the beneficiary nor a child [8 or qualifying young person], and

   (ii) in relation to whom such further conditions as may be prescribed are fulfilled,

has the care of [8 one or more children or qualifying young persons] in respect of whom the beneficiary is entitled to child benefit.

(2) The amount of the increase under this paragraph shall be that specified in Schedule 4, Part V, paragraph 8 and the requisite rate for the purposes of sub-paragraph (1)(a) above is a weekly rate not less than that amount.

(3) Regulations may provide that, for any period during which—

(a) the beneficiary is contributing to the maintenance of his or her spouse [7 or civil partner] at the requisite rate, and

(b) the weekly earnings of the spouse [7 or civil partner] exceed such amount as may be prescribed

there shall be no increase of benefit under this paragraph.

(4) Regulations may provide that, for any period during which the beneficiary is residing with his or her spouse [⁷ or civil partner] and the spouse [⁷ or civil partner] has earnings—

    (a) the increase of benefit under this paragraph shall be subject to a reduction in respect of the spouse's [⁷ or civil partner's] earnings; or

    (b) there shall be no increase of benefit under this paragraph.

(5) Regulations may, in a case within sub-paragraph (1)(b) above in which the person there referred to is residing with the beneficiary and fulfils such further conditions as may be prescribed, authorise an increase of benefit under this paragraph, but subject, taking account of the earnings of the person residing with the beneficiary, other than such of that person's earnings from employment by the beneficiary as may be prescribed, to provisions comparable to those that may be made by virtue of sub-paragraph (4) above.

(6) Regulations under this paragraph may, in connection with any reduction or extinguishment of an increase in benefit in respect of earnings, prescribe the method of calculating or estimating the earnings.

(7) A beneficiary shall not be entitled to an increase of benefit under this paragraph in respect of more than one person for the same period.

Earnings to include occupational and personal pensions for purposes of disablement pension

7.—(1) Except as may be prescribed, any reference to earnings in paragraph 4 or 6 above includes a reference to payments by way of occupational or personal pension.   **1.563**

(2) For the purposes of those paragraphs, the Secretary of State may by regulations provide, in relation to cases where payments by way of occupational or personal pension are made otherwise than weekly, that any necessary apportionment of the payments shall be made in such manner and on such basis as may be prescribed.

Dependency increases: continuation of awards in cases of fluctuating earnings

8.—(1) Where a beneficiary—   **1.564**

    (a) has been awarded an increase of benefit under paragraph 4 or 6 above, but

    (b) ceases to be entitled to the increase by reason only that the weekly earnings of some other person ("the relevant earner") exceed the amount of the increase or, as the case may be, some specified amount,

then, if and so long as the beneficiary would have continued to be entitled to the increase, disregarding any such excess of earnings, the award shall continue in force but the increase shall not be payable for any week if the earnings relevant to that week exceed the amount of the increase or, as the case may be, the specified amount.

(2) In this paragraph the earnings which are relevant to any week are those earnings of the relevant earner which, apart from this paragraph, would be taken into account in determining whether the beneficiary is entitled to the increase in question for that week.

PART II

DISABLEMENT GRATUITY

9.—(1) An employed earner shall be entitled to a disablement gratuity, if—   **1.565**

    (a) he made a claim for disablement benefit before 1st October, 1986;

    (b) he suffered as the result of the relevant accident from loss of physical or mental faculty such that the extent of the resulting disablement assessed in accordance with Schedule 6 to this Act amounts to not less than 1 per cent.; and

    (c) the extent of the disablement is assessed for the period taken into account as amounting to less than 20 per cent.

(2) A disablement gratuity shall be—

    (a) of an amount fixed, in accordance with the length of the period and the degree of the disablement, by a prescribed scale, but not in any case exceeding the amount specified in Schedule 4, Part V, paragraph 9; and

    (b) payable, if and in such cases as regulations so provide, by instalments.

(3) A person shall not be entitled to disablement gratuity until after the expiry of the period of 90 days (disregarding Sundays) beginning with the day of the relevant accident.

PART III

INCREASE OF DISABLEMENT PENSION DURING HOSPITAL TREATMENT

1.566   **10.**—(1) This Part of this Schedule has effect in relation to a period during which a person is receiving medical treatment as an in-patient in a hospital or similar institution and which—

(a) commenced before 6th April 1987; or

(b) commenced after that date but within a period of 28 days from the end of the period during which he last received an increase of benefit under section 62 of the 1975 Act or this paragraph in respect of such treatment for the relevant injury or loss of faculty.

(2) Where a person is awarded disablement benefit, but the extent of his disablement is assessed for the period taken into account by the assessment at less than 100 per cent., it shall be treated as assessed at 100 per cent. for any part of that period, whether before or after the making of the assessment or the award of benefit, during which he receives, as an in-patient in a hospital or similar institution, medical treatment for the relevant injury or loss of faculty.

(3) Where the extent of the disablement is assessed for that period at less than 20 per cent., sub-paragraph (2) above shall not affect the assessment; but in the case of a disablement pension payable by virtue of this paragraph to a person awarded a disablement gratuity wholly or partly in respect of the same period, the weekly rate of the pension (after allowing for any increase under Part V of this Act) shall be reduced by the amount prescribed as being the weekly value of his gratuity.

PART IV

REDUCED EARNINGS ALLOWANCE

1.567   **11.**—(1) Subject to the provisions of this paragraph, an employed earner shall be entitled to reduced earnings allowance if—

(a) he is entitled to a disablement pension or would be so entitled if that pension were payable where disablement is assessed at not less than 1 per cent.; and

(b) as a result of the relevant loss of faculty, he is either—

(i) incapable, and likely to remain permanently incapable, of following his regular occupation; and

(ii) incapable of following employment of an equivalent standard which is suitable in his case,

or is, and has at all times since the end of the period of 90 days referred to in section 103(6) above been, incapable of following that occupation or any such employment; but a person shall not be entitled to reduced earnings allowance to the extent that the relevant loss of faculty results from an accident happening on or after 1st October 1990 (the day on which section 3 of the Social Security Act 1990 came into force) [⁵ and a person shall not be entitled to reduced earnings allowance—

(i) in relation to a disease prescribed on or after 10th October 1994 under section 108(2) above; or

(ii) in relation to a disease prescribed before 10th October 1994 whose prescription is extended on or after that date under section 108(2) above but only in so far as the prescription has been so extended].

(2) A person—

(a) who immediately before that date is entitled to reduced earnings allowance in consequence of the relevant accident; but

(b) who subsequently ceases to be entitled to that allowance for one or more days,

shall not again be entitled to reduced earnings allowance in consequence of that accident; but this sub-paragraph does not prevent the making at any time of a claim for, or an award of, reduced earnings allowance in consequence of that accident for a period which commences not later than the day after that on which the claimant was last entitled to that allowance in consequence of that accident.

(3) For the purposes of sub-paragraph (2) above—

(a) a person who, apart from section 103(6) above, would have been entitled to reduced earnings allowance immediately before 1st October 1990 shall be treated as entitled to that allowance on any day (including a Sunday) on which he would have been entitled to it apart from that provision;

(b) regulations may prescribe other circumstances in which a person is to be treated as entitled, or as having been entitled, to reduced earnings allowance on any prescribed day.

(4) The Secretary of State may by regulations provide that in prescribed circumstances employed earner's employment in which a claimant was engaged when the relevant accident took place but which was not his regular occupation is to be treated as if it had been his regular occupation.

(5) In sub-paragraph (1) above—

(a) references to a person's regular occupation are to be taken as not including any subsidiary occupation, except to the extent that they fall to be treated as including such an occupation by virtue of regulations under sub-paragraph (4) above; and

(b) employment of an equivalent standard is to be taken as not including employment other than employed earner's employment;

and in assessing the standard of remuneration in any employment, including a person's regular occupation, regard is to be had to his reasonable prospect of advancement.

(6) For the purposes of this Part of this Schedule a person's regular occupation is to be treated as extending to and including employment in the capacities to which the persons in that occupation (or a class or description of them to which he belonged at the time of the relevant accident) are in the normal course advanced, and to which, if he had continued to follow that occupation without having suffered the relevant loss of faculty, he would have had at least the normal prospects of advancement; and so long as he is, as a result of the relevant loss of faculty, deprived in whole or in part of those prospects, he is to be treated as incapable of following that occupation.

(7) Regulations may for the purposes of this Part of this Schedule provide that a person is not to be treated as capable of following an occupation or employment merely because of his working thereat during a period of trial or for purposes of rehabilitation or training or in other prescribed circumstances.

(8) Reduced earnings allowance shall be awarded—

(a) for such period as may be determined at the time of the award; and

(b) if at the end of that period the beneficiary submits a fresh claim for the allowance, for such further period, commencing as mentioned in sub-paragraph (2) above, as may be determined.

(9) The award may not be for a period longer than the period to be taken into account under paragraph 4 or 6 of Schedule 6 to this Act.

(10) Reduced earnings allowance shall be payable at a rate determined by reference to the beneficiary's probable standard of remuneration during the period for which it is granted in any employed earner's employments which are suitable in his case and which he is likely to be capable of following as compared with that in the relevant occupation, but in no case at a rate higher than 40 per cent of the maximum rate of a disablement pension or at a rate such that the aggregate of disablement pension (not including increases in disablement pension under any provision of this Act) and reduced earnings allowance awarded to the beneficiary exceeds 140 per cent. of the maximum rate of a disablement pension.

(11) Sub-paragraph (10) above shall have effect in the case of a person who retired from regular employment before 6th April 1987 with the substitution for "140 per cent." of "100 per cent.".

(12) In sub-paragraph (10) above "the relevant occupation" means—

(a) in relation to a person who is entitled to reduced earnings allowance by virtue of regulations under sub-paragraph (4) above, the occupation in which he was engaged when the relevant accident took place; and

(b) in relation to any other person who is entitled to reduced earnings allowance, his regular occupation within the meaning of sub-paragraph (1) above.

[⁶ (12A) The reference in sub-paragraph (11) above to a person who has retired from regular employment includes a reference—

(a) to a person who under subsection (3) of section 27 of the 1975 Act was treated for the purposes of that Act as having retired from regular employment; and

(b) to a person who under subsection (5) of that section was deemed for those purposes to have retired from it.]

(13) On any award except the first the probable standard of his remuneration shall be determined in such manner as may be prescribed; and, without prejudice to the generality of this sub-paragraph, regulations may provide in prescribed circumstances for the probable standard of remuneration to be determined by reference—

(a) to the standard determined at the time of the last previous award of reduced earnings allowance; and

(b) to scales or indices of earnings in a particular industry or description of industries or any other data relating to such earnings.

(14) In this paragraph "maximum rate of a disablement pension" means the rate specified in the first entry in column (2) of Schedule 4, Part V, paragraph 1 and does not include increases in disablement pension under any provision of this Act.

Supplementary

1.568 **12.**—(1) A person who on 10th April 1988 or 9th April 1989 satisfies the conditions—
   (a) that he has attained pensionable age;
   (b) that he has retired from regular employment; and
   (c) that he is entitled to reduced earnings allowance,
shall be entitled to that allowance for life.

(2) In the case of any beneficiary who is entitled to reduced earnings allowance by virtue of sub-paragraph (1) above, the allowance shall be payable, subject to any enactment contained in Part V or VI of this Act or in the Administration Act and to any regulations made under any such enactment, at the weekly rate at which it was payable to the beneficiary on the relevant date or would have been payable to him on that date but for any such enactment or regulations.

(3) For the purpose of determining under sub-paragraph (2) above the weekly rate of reduced earnings allowance payable in the case of a qualifying beneficiary, it shall be assumed that the weekly rate at which the allowance was payable to him on the relevant date was—
   (a) £25.84, where that date is 10th April 1988, or
   (b) £26.96, where that date is 9th April 1989.

(4) In sub-paragraph (3) above "qualifying beneficiary" means a person entitled to reduced earnings allowance by virtue of sub-paragraph (1) above who—
   (a) did not attain pensionable age before 6th April 1987, or
   (b) did not retire from regular employment before that date,
and who, on the relevant date, was entitled to the allowance at a rate which was restricted under paragraph 11(10) above by reference to 40 per cent. of the maximum rate of disablement pension.

(5) For a beneficiary who is entitled to reduced earnings allowance by virtue of satisfying the conditions in sub-paragraph (1) above on 10th April 1988 the relevant date is that date.

(6) For a beneficiary who is entitled to it by virtue only of satisfying those conditions on 9th April 1989 the relevant date is that date.

[⁶ (7) The reference in sub-paragraph (1) above to a person who has retired from regular employment includes a reference—
   (a) to a person who under subsection (3) of section 27 of the 1975 Act was treated for the purposes of that Act as having retired from regular employment; and
   (b) to a person who under subsection (5) of that section was deemed for those purposes to have retired from it.]

PART V

RETIREMENT ALLOWANCE

1.569 **13.**—(1) Subject to the provisions of this Part of this Schedule, a person who—
   (a) has attained pensionable age; and
   (b) gives up regular employment on or after 10th April 1989; and
   (c) was entitled to reduced earnings allowance (by virtue either of one award or of a number of awards) on the day immediately before he gave up such employment,
shall cease to be entitled to reduced earnings allowance as from the day on which he gives up regular employment.

(2) If the day before a person ceases under sub-paragraph (1) above to be entitled to reduced earnings allowance he is entitled to the allowance (by virtue either of one award or of a number of awards) at a weekly rate or aggregate weekly rate of not less than £2.00, he shall be entitled to a benefit, to be known as "retirement allowance".

(3) Retirement allowance shall be payable to him (subject to any enactment contained in Part V or VI of this Act or in the Administration Act and to any regulations made under any such enactment) for life.

(4) Subject to sub-paragraph (6) below, the weekly rate of a beneficiary's retirement allowance shall be—
   (a) 25 per cent of the weekly rate at which he was last entitled to reduced earnings allowance; or
   (b) 10 per cent of the maximum rate of a disablement pension, whichever is the less.

(5) For the purpose of determining under sub-paragraph (4) above the weekly rate of retirement allowance in the case of a beneficiary who—
    (a) retires or is deemed to have retired on 10th April 1989, and
    (b) on 9th April 1989 was entitled to reduced earnings allowance at a rate which was restricted under paragraph 11(10) above by reference to 40 per cent. of the maximum rate of disablement pension,
it shall be assumed that the weekly rate of reduced earnings allowance to which he was entitled on 9th April 1989 was £26.96.

(6) If the weekly rate of the beneficiary's retirement allowance—
    (a) would not be a whole number of pence; and
    (b) would exceed the whole number of pence next below it by ½p or more,
the beneficiary shall be entitled to retirement allowance at a rate equal to the next higher whole number of pence.

(7) The sums falling to be calculated under sub-paragraph (4) above are subject to alteration by orders made by the Secretary of State under section 150 of the Administration Act.

(8) Regulations may—
    (a) make provision with respect to the meaning of "regular employment" for the purposes of this paragraph; and
    (b) prescribe circumstances in which, and periods for which, a person is or is not to be regarded for those purposes as having given up such employment.

(9) Regulations under sub-paragraph (8) above may, in particular—
    (a) provide for a person to be regarded—
        (i) as having given up regular employment, notwithstanding that he is or intends to be an earner; or
        (ii) as not having given up regular employment, notwithstanding that he has or may have one or more days of interruption of employment; and
    (b) prescribe circumstances in which a person is or is not to be regarded as having given up regular employment by reference to—
        (i) the level or frequency of his earnings during a prescribed period; or
        (ii) the number of hours for which he works during a prescribed period calculated in a prescribed manner.

[³ (10) "Day of interruption of employment" means a day which forms part of—
    (a) a jobseeking period (as defined by the Jobseekers Act 1995), or
    (b) a linked period (as defined by that Act).]

(11) In this paragraph "maximum rate of a disablement pension" means the rate specified in the first entry in column (2) of Schedule 4, Part V, paragraph 1 and does not include increases in disablement pension under any provision of this Act.

PART VI

INDUSTRIAL DEATH BENEFIT

Introductory

Paras 14.–21. *Omitted* (Only applicable to deaths before April 11, 1988).   1.570

AMENDMENTS

1. Social Security (Incapacity for Work) Act 1994, Sch.1, para.41 (April 13, 1995).

2. Pensions Schemes Act 1993, Sch.8, para.43 (February 7, 1994).

3. Jobseekers Act 1995, Sch.2, para.36 (October 14, 1994).

4. Social Security (Industrial Injuries) (Dependency) (Permitted Earnings Limits) Order 2009 (SI 2009/661), art.2 (April 8, 2009).

5. Social Security (Industrial Injuries) (Prescribed Diseases) Regulations 1985, reg.14A (October 10, 1994).

6. Social Security (Consequential Provisions) Act 1992, Sch.4, paras.10 and 11 (transitorily).

7. Civil Partnership Act 2004, s.254 and Sch.24, Pt 3, para.52 (December 5, 2005).

8. Child Benefit Act 2005, ss.1 and 2, Sch.1, para.16 (April 10, 2006).

DERIVATIONS

1.571   SSA 1975, ss.57–59B, 62, 64–64A and 84A; SS (No. 2)A, s.3(4); SSA 1986, s.39 and Sch.3; SSA 1988, s.2.

GENERAL NOTE

1.572   This Schedule preserves for certain claimants entitlement to industrial injuries benefits that have been abolished. Pt I preserves unemployability supplement, which was an increase of disablement pension for those incapable of work owing to an industrial accident or prescribed disease, but only for those who were entitled to it immediately before April 6, 1987. Pt II preserves disablement gratuities, which were lump sums paid instead of disablement pension for those whose disablement was assessed at between 1 per cent and 19 per cent. It applies where the claim was made before October 1, 1986 and still has relevance where there has been a series of provisional assessments since then. Pt III preserves hospital treatment allowance for those who have been more or less continuously entitled to it since April 6, 1987. Parts IV and V preserve reduced earnings allowance and retirement allowance for those whose earning capacity has been reduced by an industrial accident occurring before, or an industrial disease the onset of which was before, October 1, 1990 (see *CI/3178/2003*).

No entitlement to REA (and therefore also retirement allowance) can arise in respect of a disease prescribed on or after October 10, 1994, nor in respect of the extension aspect of a disease prescribed prior to that date, but extended on or after October 10, 1994. Those who were entitled to reduced earnings allowance before April 10, 1989 and had retired before that date, remain entitled to the allowance for life at a frozen rate. Otherwise, people who have reached pensionable age are no longer entitled to reduced earnings allowance and become entitled to retirement allowance instead, unless they remain in regular employment for at least 10 hours a week (see the Social Security (Industrial Injuries) (Regular Employment) Regulations 1990 (SI 1990/256) as amended and *R(I) 2/99* in which the tortuous history of this legislation is examined).

As Commissioner Howell put it in *CI/5138/2002*,

"a person must *either* have a contract of service whose terms include the minimum 10-hour average requirement in (a), *or* be actually undertaking work, e.g. on his or her own account as a self-employed person or as a casual employee, which when one looks at the amount and duration of work actually done meets the alternative 10-hour average condition in (b). If there is any break, however short, in the continuity of meeting those conditions, then the person concerned is regarded for good as having given up regular employment from the start of the first week in which the conditions are no longer met, and can never thereafter regain the right to reduced earnings allowance" (para.7).

Whether activities carried on by the claimant amount to "gainful employment" is a matter of fact and degree for the tribunal seeing and hearing the evidence to determine (*ibid*, para.12). Pt VI, which is omitted, provides for industrial death benefit in relation to deaths before April 11, 1988.

Sch. Pt IV: Reduced Earnings Allowance

1.573   *(1) Reduced Earnings Allowance: its creation and slow demise*
The precursor of this Part (SSA 1975, s.59A) was inserted by SSA 1986, Sch.3, para.5(1) with effect from October 1, 1986, and was further amended with effect from October 1, 1990, so as to provide for the gradual phasing out of the benefit, as is explained below.

Reduced Earnings Allowance (REA) replaced the misnamed Special Hardship Allowance and is a benefit in its own right, rather than a mere supplement to disablement benefit. The benefits remain linked and a claimant cannot be entitled to REA without making a claim to disablement benefit (*Whalley* v *Secretary of State for Work and Pensions* [2001] EWCA Civ 166, reported as *R(I) 2/03*, disapproving Commissioner Williams on this point in *CI 6207/1999*). The conditions of entitlement are, however, similar to those that applied to Special Hardship Allowance, so that decisions on the meaning of the same statutory phrases in the context of that allowance remain authoritative. REA can continue in payment after retirement, but only for those entitled to it at retirement, who retired on or before April 9, 1989. For those retiring after that date, and entitled to REA immediately before retirement, retirement allowance (see Pt V, below) is available as a replacement for REA during retirement, and is payable for life.

In *Chief Adjudication Officer v Maguire* (reported as *R(I) 3/99*), the Court of Appeal held that it is still possible to claim special hardship allowance which was the predecessor of reduced earnings allowance. However, the Secretary of State does not issue claim forms for special hardship allowance and so must be persuaded to accept some other document as a claim although it is arguable that the fact that he does not issue proper claim forms may limit the extent to which he can properly decide not to accept other documents as valid claims.

The October 1990 changes implemented the Government's policy of preventing arising new entitlements to reduced earnings allowance, while preserving existing entitlements until they otherwise cease, so that ensuing phased reductions in expenditure on this benefit (estimated £1m in 1990–91, £15m in 1991–82 and £40m in 1992–93—see *Hansard*, HC Vol.165, col.630, *per* the Secretary of State for Social Security) could be deployed to help finance a package of new benefits to improve the position of disabled people as a whole during the 1990s. It was considered that payment of reduced earnings allowance was in many cases unnecessarily duplicative, since many non-working recipients of it also received invalidity benefit.

Note that in general, references to the date of an accident are to be construed, in the case of prescribed diseases, as references to the date of onset of the disease (see ss.108 and 109, Prescribed Diseases Regs, regs.11 and 12; (*CI/3178/2003*).

The wording of para.11(1) ("but a person shall not be entitled . . . from an accident happening on or after the appointed day") prevents arising any new entitlement, or the enhancement through increased incapacity of an existing entitlement, in respect of a loss of faculty resulting from an accident which happens on or after October 1, 1990 (that being the date s.3 of the SSA 1990 came into force.)

The benefits remain linked and a claimant cannot be entitled to REA without making a claim for disablement benefit (*Whalley* v *Secretary of State for Work and Pensions* [2001] EWCA Civ 166, reported as *R(I) 2/03*, disapproving Commissioner Williams on this point in *CI/6207/1999*). A decision by a tribunal determining the date of onset for a PD, whether given in respect of disablement benefit or REA, as the case may be, binds a later tribunal considering the issue for either benefit. Where there was a refusal by a tribunal of a claim for disablement benefit on the ground that the claimant did not have PD A11 at the date of the decision, a later decision-maker, faced with a new claim for that benefit or for REA, cannot specify a date of onset for the disease which is prior to the refusal of the first claim. See also *CI/2531/2001*, para.15:

> "if a person makes a claim or successive claims for disablement benefit (and, by the same token, reduced earnings allowance, which depend on establishing the same loss of faculty) in respect of occupational deafness, the 'date of onset' can never be earlier than that of the *first* such claim which results in the actual payment of benefit; and the date so determined is also, by regulation 6(1), to be treated as the date of onset for the purposes of each subsequent claim" (*per* Commissioner Howell).

As amended from October 10, 1994, it also precludes entitlement to REA in respect of a disease prescribed on or after that date, and prevents entitlement to the allowance in respect of the extension aspect of a disease prescribed prior to that date, but extended on or after October 10, 1994.

Sub-paras (2) and (3) set out the circumstances in which entitlement to reduced earnings allowance is protected. In effect entitlement is here a wider than normal notion since the provisions protect both those who were beneficiaries immediately before October 1, 1990, and those whose accident or onset of a prescribed industrial disease occurred before that date and who would have been beneficiaries but for the fact that the 90-day waiting period set by s.103(6) had not expired. Moreover, regulations can extend the categories of persons entitled (sub-para.(3)(b)). A single day's gap in entitlement on or after October 1, 1990, brings the preserved entitlement to an end; to remain, preserved entitlement must exist on and be continuous after October 1, 1990. Entitlement, of course, depends on the making of a valid claim (SSAA 1992, s.1). So, no doubt to prevent loss of title for example because a renewal claim is not made on the day following the lapse of the previous award, and to cater for late claims and the consequence of revision or appeal of a decision, sub-para.(2) specifically provides, to allay any doubts, that its preclusive rule does not prevent the making at any time of a claim for, or an award of, reduced earnings allowance in consequence of an accident which occurred before October 1, 1990, for a period providing complete continuity with the previous period of entitlement in respect of that accident.

On the application of para.(2) to seasonal workers who lose entitlement to REA during their off-season because there is then no reduction in earning power, see *CI/4940/01* applying *R(I) 56/53*.

1.574   *(2) Reduced Earnings Allowance: conditions of entitlement*

For those not precluded from REA by the provisions noted above, the key conditions of entitlement are set out in para.11.

The structure of the paragraph is as follows:

Sub-para.(1) Conditions of entitlement—basic concepts of "the relevant loss of faculty", "regular occupation", "suitable employment of an equivalent standard", "incapacity".

Sub-para.(4) Regular occupation—deeming regulations.

Sub-para.(5) Regular occupation; equivalent standard; standard of remuneration—partial definitions.

Sub-para.(6) Regular occupation—effect of prospects of advancement.

Sub-para.(7) Incapacity—trial period and rehabilitative work.

Sub-para.(8) Length of award—general.

Sub-para.(9) Length of award—limitation to period of assessment.

Sub-paras (10), (11) Amount of award—method of calculation.

Sub-para.(12) Relevant occupation—definition.

In *CI/4478/1999* (reported as part of *R(I)2/02*), Commissioner Rowland held that where someone had a cumulative loss of earnings due to a number of industrial accidents *each of which made him incapable of following a different "regular occupation"*, he can have only one award of REA, subject to the statutory maximum, in respect of all the accidents. In *Hagan v Secretary of State for Social Security* (neutral citation EWCA Civ 1452—reported as part of *R(I) 2/02*), the Court of Appeal on July 30, 2001 set this aside as erroneous in law. The Court of Appeal accepted the Secretary of State's argument, summarised as follows:

"(1) there can be multiple claims for awards of REA in circumstances where there are successive industrial injuries each of which causes a change from the previous regular occupation; (2) on each claim the maximum amount of REA payable is 40 per cent of the maximum disablement pension; but (3) this 40 per cent limit applies only to each claim separately and if there are multiple claims then the maximum amount payable is not 40 per cent but the 140 per cent referred to in the last part of paragraph 11(10).

The Secretary of State put before the court the following example. In 1986 a mining foreman suffers an injury in the mine and loses his hearing such that he can no longer be a foreman and has to be 'demoted' to a miner. The assessment of disability by reason of the loss of hearing is 20 per cent and the reduction in earnings is significantly in excess of 40 per cent of the disablement pension. On a claim for REA and disablement pension immediately after this accident he would have been awarded 20 per cent of the maximum disablement pension as disablement pension, and 40 per cent of the maximum disablement pension as REA. Two years later he lost the use of an arm by reason of an explosion in the mine, as a result of which he could no longer work down the mine and had to be further 'demoted' to a 'winchman'. His assessment of disability in relation to this accident (loss of use of arm) is 30 per cent, leading to an aggregated disablement pension award under section 103(2) of 50 per cent. His loss of earnings is again substantially in excess of 40 per cent of the maximum disablement pension and so on the basis of his second accident and the second change of regular occupation, he would again be entitled to 40 per cent of REA. The cumulative effect is 80 per cent of the maximum disablement pension by way of REA and 50 per cent by way of disability pension. This is less than the maximum in the final part of para.11(10) and therefore total benefit amounting to 130 per cent of the maximum amount of disablement pension is payable by reason of the two accidents under the separate benefits.

On the analysis of the Social Security Commissioner on the same facts, the miner would be entitled to 50 per cent disablement pension because of the aggregated effect of the injuries pursuant to section 103(2) but would only be entitled to make one REA claim giving rise to a maximum entitlement of 40 per cent of REA and thus an overall total of 90 per cent of the maximum disability pension. That example illustrates why it is that I said at the beginning of this judgment that the Secretary of State is in the relatively unusual position of arguing for a more generous interpretation of the law.' (paras 28–30).

In *CI/1052/2001*, Commissioner Rowland distinguished *Hagan*, which

"was concerned with a case where the claimant claimed to have lost earnings due to becoming incapable of following one occupation as a result of one accident and then to have lost further earnings due to becoming incapable of following another regular occupation as a result of another accident. In the present case, it is the Secretary of State's case that the claimant's regular occupation at the onset of his vibration white finger was the same as his regular occupation at the time of his 1985 accident" (para.7).

In the situation before him in the present case, citing *R(I) 2/56*, the Commissioner considered that

"only one award of reduced earnings allowance, which might equally well have been made in respect of either the 1985 accident or the vibration white finger, may be made. As an award had already been made at the maximum rate in respect of the 1985 accident, the tribunal's decision in respect of the vibration white finger was not erroneous in point of law" (para. 9).

Sub-para.(1)(a): For entitlement to disablement pension see s.103 and notes, above. The allowance may be paid where the assessment of disablement is at least 1 per cent, and one of the other two conditions in sub-para.1(b), below, is satisfied. Note that the allowance is still linked with disablement pension—the claimant must actually be entitled to disablement pension, or entitled but for the level of assessment. The allowance will not, therefore, be payable until the 15-week waiting period (see s.103(6), above) has elapsed.

The benefits remain linked and a claimant cannot be entitled to REA without making a claim for disablement benefit (*Whalley* v *Secretary of State for Work and Pensions* [2001] EWCA Civ 166, reported as *R(I) 2/03*, disapproving Commissioner Williams on this point in *CI 6207/1999*). A decision by a tribunal determining the date of onset for a PD, whether given in respect of disablement benefit or REA, as the case may be, binds a later tribunal considering the issue for either benefit.

1.575

Where there was a refusal by a tribunal of a claim for disablement benefit on the ground that the claimant did not have PD A11 at the date of the decision, a later decision-maker, faced with a new claim for that benefit or for REA, cannot specify a date of onset for the disease which is prior to the refusal of the first claim. See also *CI/2531/2001*, para.15:

> "if a person makes a claim or successive claims for disablement benefit (and, by the same token, reduced earnings allowance, which depend on establishing the same loss of faculty) in respect of occupational deafness, the 'date of onset' can never be earlier than that of the *first* such claim which results in the actual payment of benefit; and the date so determined is also, by regulation 6(1), to be treated as the date of onset for the purposes of each subsequent claim" (*per* Commissioner Howell).

See further *CI/4249/2003*, another decision of Commissioner Howell. But note that two Commissioners take the view that *Whalley* is not wholly applicable in respect of decisions made under the DMA regime post SSA 1998. Commissioner Rowland in *R(I) 2/04* considered the remarks in *Whalley* to have been *obiter*. Moreover, the reasoning applied on the basis of the decision-making processes prior to the SSA 1998, so that the demise of the earlier provisions on finality of an MAT's decision, means that the binding nature of a decision on a date of onset of a PD for disablement benefit purposes flows from the terms of Prescribed Diseases Regs, reg.6(para.14), a view endorsed by Commissioner Howell in *R(I) 5/04* (paras 16–18). See further the commentary to that regulation, below.

1.576   *Sub-para. (1) (b):* The claimant must show that he is (as a result of the relevant loss of faculty) incapable of following his regular occupation or suitable employment of an equivalent standard. In addition, he must show *either* that he is likely to remain permanently incapable of following his regular occupation (the "permanent" condition), *or* that he has been incapable of following his regular occupation or employment of an equivalent standard at all times since the end of the 15 week waiting period (the "continuous" condition).

In *CI/3379/2002*, Commissioner Howell reminded us that

> "[as] was held by the Commissioner in reported decision *R(I) 7/53* . . ., the question of whether a claimant is likely to remain permanently incapable of following his regular occupation for the purposes of reduced earnings allowance is one to be assessed by the tribunal, on the probabilities of the case, and having regard to the evidence before them. As the Commissioner says in paragraph 10, the burden of proving that he is likely to remain permanently incapable rests on the claimant; or as I would for my part prefer to put it in an inquisitorial jurisdiction, the tribunal must be affirmatively satisfied on the evidence before them that he *is* so incapable, on one test or the other, before they can hold him entitled to the benefit (para.14).

While PD A11 (Vibration white finger) is degenerative and will not improve once contracted, no rule of law can be deduced from *R(I) 2/81, CI 15803/1996* or AOG, para.85738 to the effect that a tribunal must necessarily assume, regardless of the full evidence, that a claimant suffering from vibration white finger cannot continue with his regular occupation. This may be so in many cases, and be a sensible medical and administrative assumption. But a tribunal must consider the matter in the light of all the evidence. Future injury and risk are relevant factors to consider, but no more than that. Nor can the claimant rely on statements in the AOG (now DMG) as creating a legitimate expectation, since neither Guide is binding on tribunals. Commissioner Williams so held in *CI/3038/2000*.

1.577   *Regular occupation:* The claimant's regular occupation is to be determined as a matter of fact taking into account the provisions of sub-paras (4), (5) and (6) and decided cases. Sub-para.(4) gives the Secretary of State power to make "deeming" regulations (see the note to the sub-para., below).

The normal case of the claimant who has worked in one job for a number of years presents no problem nor, probably, does the case of the claimant who changes jobs very frequently for it will be easy to regard him as "acquiring" a regular occupation very quickly—and in this context, regular occupation means a *type* of job not limited by reference to a particular area or a particular employer (*R. v Deputy I.I. Commissioner Ex p. Humphreys* [1966] 2 W.L.R. 63). But what of claimants with a new job, more than one job, in training for a job, or with prospects of promotion from the job they were doing at the time of the accident?

The normal approach seems to be to consider that the job which caused the loss of earning capacity should be regarded as the regular occupation (*R(I) 5/52*) (even if it was a new job) unless there is evidence that the claimant did not so regard it, or he had been in it an exceptionally short time (*R(I) 18/60*), or he had been in a previous job for a long period (*R(I) 22/52, R(I) 65/54*).

Sub-para.(5): excludes subsidiary occupations from consideration but that does not   **1.578** prevent the decision-maker or tribunal from finding that more than one job makes up the claimant's regular occupation if neither, or none, of them can be said to be truly subsidiary to the other(s). If the claimant does more than one job for the same employer, then it is probably right to regard them together as his regular occupation unless one or more of them is abnormal and irregular (*R(I) 42/52, R(I) 24/55* and *R(I) 10/65*): but such claims are not always successful (*R(I) 58/54* and *R(I) 13/62*). Where the jobs are done for different employers the question is the same—can one (or more) of the jobs be regarded as subsidiary to the other(s)?—but the claimant may have more difficulty in establishing that his regular occupation consists of the totality of the jobs (*R(I) 33/58* and *R(I) 2/70*). There is no easy test emerging from the decisions as to what will constitute subsidiary as against regular occupation, although in settling this question of fact, the number of employers, the relative remuneration in each job, and the amount of time spent on them will be significant factors.

The difficulty of ascertaining the regular occupation of a claimant in training is eased by the provision of sub-para.(7) (below) if it is reasonably clear what job the training is directed towards. Otherwise, the decision-maker or tribunal will have to speculate about future job prospects and then use the subsection (as in *R(I) 6/75*), or categorise training as the regular occupation (as in *R(I) 4/60*) with the likely disadvantages for the claimant of a low standard of remuneration in the regular occupation when it comes to determining title to benefit and, ultimately, the amount of the award.

Sub-para.(6): extends the ambit of regular occupation to jobs to which the claim-   **1.579** ant would have been promoted but for the loss of faculty, although the wording has been interpreted to mean that promotions must be almost automatic rather than selective. In *R(I) 8/67*, the claimant contended that, as a result of contracting a prescribed disease, he had been prevented from progressing from shipwright grade B to grade A. The Commissioner formulated the appropriate questions thus:

(1) In general, are persons in the claimant's position normally promoted or advanced to a higher grade or level?

(2) Would the claimant himself have had the normal prospects of advancement if he had continued in his regular occupation without loss of faculty?

(3) Was the claimant deprived in part or in whole of those prospects by the industrial injury?

R(I) 8/73 placed the emphasis in those questions on the word "normal". The Commissioner said:

"I doubt whether (the subsection) will, as a rule, assist a claimant unless the occupation which he follows is a broad-based one in which some degree of advancement is regarded as almost automatic. Where the predominant factor in a claimant's occupation or profession is that of selectivity the claimant will rarely, I think, be able successfully to invoke [the subsection]." (See also *R(I) 8/80*.)

A sideways move to a better paid job in the same basic grade was not, in *R(I) 12/81*, evidence of prospects of advancement. In determining that the new job, which the claimant actually did before ill-health forced him to abandon it, did not constitute a job of a higher grade or level, the Commissioner found that the skill and training involved was largely the same as in the former job (the regular occupation) and that the enhanced pay was merely to compensate for other unattractive features of the new job.

1.580 *Employment of an equivalent standard . . . suitable in his case:* Reduced earnings allowance compensates the claimant for loss of earning capacity, so that it is logical to require him to show not only that he cannot do his regular job, but also that he cannot do another suitable job which will bring him just as much money.

The word "standard" appears here and in sub-para.(10), below, where it has a slightly different meaning. Here, "employment of an equivalent standard" is determined by considering the normal earnings in a job of which the claimant is capable with the normal earnings in the claimant's regular occupation. If the earnings in the alternative job are at least equal to those in the regular occupation, the alternative job is of an equivalent standard:

"[T]he comparison of the standard of remuneration afforded by the two employments, the regular employment and the prospective new employment, is one which in this subsection is unaffected by any consideration personal to the beneficiary and has to be treated objectively. The standard of remuneration in each case must, I think, be taken to be the standard of remuneration which an employee of normal efficiency and industriousness, where efficiency and industriousness are relevant considerations, will be likely to earn working in that employment for such number of hours in a week or other period which can be regarded as normal for persons employed in that employment, having regard to the conditions of the employment and the circumstances of the trade or industry in the appropriate geographical area under consideration." (*R. v N.I. Commissioner Ex p. Mellors* [1971] 2 W.L.R. 593. See also *R(I) 1/72, R(I) 1/76*.)

An element of subjectivity is introduced into the test by the requirement that employment of equivalent standard should be suitable for the claimant. Once it can be shown that jobs which the claimant can do (for the test of incapacity, see next paragraph) pay as much or more than his regular occupation, the claim will fail unless the alternative job is unsuitable. The department will normally produce a list of jobs for the tribunal which are said to be suitable (see the comments of the Commissioner in *R(S) 7/85*) and each must be examined in the light of all evidence. "Suitability refers to such matters as education, experience or training and has to be judged by reference to the claimant's past industrial history" (*R(I) 22/61*). Employments which are so exceptional that they ought not to be considered as proper comparisons must be excluded (*R(I) 6/77*, employment in sheltered work offered by Remploy Ltd—see also *R(I) 42/52, R(I) 73/52, R(I) 7/58*). In *R(I) 1/74* the Commissioner pointed up an important distinction between unsuitability and incapacity—unsuitability may result from *any* of the claimant's personal characteristics (see also *R(I) 29/52*).

1.581 *Incapable:* See also the discussion of incapacity for work in relation to sickness and invalidity benefit in the annotation to SSCBA 1992, s.57 as in force prior to April 13, 1995 (the introduction of incapacity benefit), which can be found in Bonner, Hooker and White, *Non-Means Tested Benefits: Legislation 1994*, pp.187–194. Just as with those benefits, so for reduced earnings allowance it is relevant to look beyond the claimant's state of health (important though that is) to his age, education and other personal factors.

The statutory rubric requires that the claimant demonstrates that, as a result of the relevant loss of faculty, he is incapable of following his regular occupation or suitable employment of an equivalent standard. "Regular occupation", it will be recalled, means a *type* of job not limited by reference to a particular area or a particular employer (*R. v Deputy I.I. Commissioner Ex p. Humphreys* [1966] 2 W.L.R. 63). This matter of incapacity in respect of his regular occupation or of suitable employment of an equivalent standard, is more complicated when the claimant has returned to work after the accident, and even more so if he has returned to his regular occupation. Returning to his regular occupation is, of course, good evidence that he is indeed capable of it. But such a claimant may, in some cases, be able to derive assistance from regulations which leave out of account periods of rehabilitative work (see annotation to sub-para.(7), below). Assistance in such a case may also be derived from a range of Commissioner's decisions which require that one ascertain the degree to which he is actually capable of fulfilling the normal requirements of the type of job in issue, and the basis on which he has been employed to do that job. In *CI/443/50(KL) (reported)*, a Tribunal of Commissioners laid down the relevant broad test and illustrated its application:

> "If a person cannot obtain employment in his regular field of labour because (as a result of the relevant loss of faculty) he is unable to fulfil all the ordinary requirements of employers in that field of labour, he is incapable of following his regular occupation . . .
>
> The matter may be illustrated thus. If a person obtains employment in his old job only through charity or because he has an exceptional employer, he should be regarded as incapable of following his regular occupation. On the other hand if a person is able to do his old job except that as a result of the relevant loss of faculty he cannot work overtime, he should not be regarded as incapable of following his regular occupation, unless as a result of this inability he cannot comply with the ordinary requirements of employers in his regular field of labour" (paras 11, 12).

In that particular case a tool-room fitter, temporarily unable to do overtime was held capable of following his regular occupation. But ultimately the precise application of this broad test depends on the facts of the instant case with decided cases illustrating matters constituting some of the relevant factors, rather than invariably being decisive considerations (*CI/1589/1998*, paras 14, 19). It is important also to recall that in pre-1987 cases Commissioners were able to reconsider all the issues (factual or legal) arising in the case and, since Commissioner's decisions are only binding in so far as they decide points of law, "it is necessary to disentangle statements of law from the Commissioner's analysis of the facts and the application of the law to those facts" (*ibid.*, para.12). Finally, note carefully that it is not a matter of whether the claimant is doing the same job as before, nor is the test one of what is acceptable to the claimant's employer, but rather is to be related to the normal requirements of "employers in that field of labour" (*ibid.*, para.19; and see *R(I) 10/59*, para.13). So, if the claimant has to be helped by workmates (*R(I) 29/52*, *R(I) 39/52*), or if he cannot meet the normal requirements of that type of job (*R(I) 39/55*), or if he has to pay other workers to carry out some of his duties (*R(I) 5/58*), or if the employer retains him only out of sympathy (*CI/445/50(KL)(reported)*), these will all be relevant factors in deciding in the context of the case as a whole whether he is incapable of performing his regular occupation. In the five cases just mentioned, the claimants were held incapable of their regular occupation. But it does depend on the particular circumstances and on the reference point of "the ordinary requirements of employers in his regular field of labour". So, in *CI 446/50(KL)(reported)*, while the claimant farm-worker was unable to do piecework, he did remain capable of a wide range of farm work and so was held capable of his regular occupation (see para.6).

Application of the test is particularly difficult where the claimant has returned to the same occupation as before the accident but, as a result of the loss of faculty, "follows it more slowly, or for fewer hours, or less productively, or omits some parts of the occupation he used to perform" (*CI 443/50(KL) (reported)*, para.9). If the hours he can work are substantially reduced by comparison with the period prior to the loss of faculty, this may point to his being incapable of following his regular occupation. A reduction from five days to three and a half had that effect in *CI/444/50(KL) (reported)* (although there was also some element of having to have others do some lifting and carrying, that the claimant had previously managed herself), as did a drop from 44 hours to 31 hours in *R(I) 6/66*. A reduction in output or speed must be to such a degree as to prevent the claimant satisfying the ordinary requirements of employers in his regular field of labour (*CI/447/50(KL)*, *CI/448/50(KL) (both reported)*). Jobs involving piecework pose obvious difficulties here. In *R(I) 4/77*, the Commissioner warned against applying the language of the test in *CI/443/50(KL) (reported)* as if it were a statute and of the danger of isolating statements of law from the factual context of the case in which they were laid down and applied (a point re-emphasised in *CI/1589/1998*). The Commissioner in *R(I) 4/77* saw the claimant's remuneration as an important factor. He referred to the significance of remuneration in determining whether employment was of an equivalent standard and held that in determining incapacity in the case of a pieceworker it was proper to ask whether as a result of the relevant loss of faculty the claimant can attain the same level of remuneration in his regular occupation as he did before that loss of faculty.

1.582   *As a result of the relevant loss of faculty:* The incapacity must be caused by the loss of faculty. Causation is a matter of fact for the Secretary of State or tribunal. See note to s.94(1), above, on causation.

1.583   *Sub-para. (4):* Refer to note on regular occupation above. The regulation made under this section is reg.2 of the Social Security (Industrial Injuries and Diseases) Miscellaneous Provisions Regulations 1986 (SI 1986/1561).

1.584   *Sub-para. (5):* This subsection is discussed in the notes on sub-para.(1), above.

1.585   *Sub-para. (6):* See note on "regular occupation" in sub-para.(1), above.

1.586   *Sub-para. (7):* The regulations referred to are the General Benefit Regulations, reg.17.

1.587   *Sub-para. (9):* The period referred to in the section is the period for which disablement is assessed in accordance with the provisions of the Act.

1.588   *Sub-paras (10) and (11):* The phrase "standard of remuneration" used in sub-para. (1), above, to determine entitlement to the allowance is also used in this subsection to determine the amount of the award, but it bears a different meaning. In quantifying the award, the right approach is to determine the normal earnings of the claimant in the occupation which he is capable of following without any regard to the number of hours worked, the rate paid, or the working conditions in the new job. It is a crude comparison between the money the claimant would have got in his old job, and the money he gets in his new job (see the *Mellors* case, above, and *R(I) 6/68, R(I) 1/72*).

The amount of the allowance is eventually determined by the difference between the two figures, subject to the 40 per cent maximum. It is important to note that the 140 per cent figure in this subsection is modified to 100 per cent in respect of persons who retired from regular employment before April 6, 1987 (sub-para.(11)). Note that it is possible to show entitlement to the allowance by meeting the conditions in sub-para.(1), but discover that the amount is nil on applying the test in this subsection.

The "relevant occupation" for the purposes of comparison is defined in sub-para. (12).

Sub-para.(13): The difficulties of calculating the probable standard of remuneration in individual cases, often many years after the accident, have been alleviated by the provisions of this subsection. The regulations referred to are the Social Security (Industrial Injuries) (Reduced Earnings Allowance and Transitional) Regulations 1987, below. This section and the regulations apply to any award of the allowance except the first subject to specific situations covered by the regulations. See further the notes to the regulations.

1.589

Sub-para.(14): The predecessor of this sub-paragraph was inserted by SSA 1988, s.16(1), with effect from March 15, 1988.

1.590

(3) Reduced Earnings Allowance: the rate for those retired persons entitled to it

Para.12(1) preserves entitlement to REA for those who are of pensionable age and have retired from regular employment either on April 10, 1988, or on April 9, 1989. Although entitlement is preserved for life, the rate of REA is frozen: see sub-paras (2)–(6).

1.591

Sch.7, Pt V: Retirement Allowance

It was the intention of the Government that the new benefit which replaced Special Hardship Allowance (Reduced Earnings Allowance) should only subsist during the working life of the claimant up to pensionable age. A further new benefit was introduced to compensate, in retirement, the claimant who, as a result of an industrial accident or disease, may find that an earnings-related pension has been diminished by reduced earnings during his working life. This new benefit, retirement allowance, was created by the Social Security Act 1988 and introduced by way of an insertion of a new section (s.59B) into the Social Security Act 1975.

1.592

Sub-para.(1): terminates entitlement to reduced earnings allowance on retirement on or after attainment of pensionable age. It ceases from the day on which regular employment is given up. The words *"gives up* regular employment" are not used in an unusual sense. They are to be construed in their natural and ordinary meaning, so that they did not catch the particular claimant who was dismissed from his job at a newsagents shop (*R(I) 2/93*, paras 20 and 21). This does not mean, however, that all dismissals fall outwith the phrase. Citing instances where a dismissed claimant has nevertheless been held to have voluntarily left his employment for disqualification purposes under SSCBA 1992, s.28(1)(a) (*R(U) 16/52, R(U) 2/74*) (see now Jobseekers Act, s.19), the Commissioner in *R(I) 2/93* said:

1.593

"A claimant may act in such a way as to force his employer to dismiss him and it will be a question of fact in each case whether or not the claimant had by his conduct evinced an intention to give up regular employment (para.13).

In any event, to be caught by sub-para.(1), the claimant must have given up regular employment *on or after April 10, 1989*, so that those in receipt of REA when they gave up such employment before that date, are not thereby disentitled to it by virtue of para.13 of Sch.7 (see *R(I) 3/93, CI/11015/1995* and decision *CI/209/1991*).

Note, however, that with effect from March 24, 1996, regulations dictate a broader approach to "gives up regular employment" than that taken in *R(I) 2/93*. With effect from that date, reg.3 of the Social Security (Industrial Injuries) (Regular Employment) Regulations 1990 (inserted by reg.6(3) of the Social Security (Industrial Injuries and Diseases) (Miscellaneous Amendment) Regulations 1996 (SI 1996/425) provides that a person who has attained pensionable age must be regarded as having given up regular employment at the start of the first week in which *he is not in regular employment* after the later of the week during which the regulation came into force or the week in which he attained pensionable age. But this does not apply if the person is entitled to REA for life by virtue of para.12(1), above. It is submitted that the "week during which this regulation comes into force" (reg.3(a)) must be the week including March 24, 1996, the date the amendment took effect, and not that including April 1, 1990, the date set out in reg.1(1) of the 1990 Regs, which merely sets out the date the original set of regulations, not including reg.3, came into operation. Had the intention been to make the reg.3, retrospective, one would have expected clear words to that effect.

"gives up regular employment": the effect of the new reg.3.

1.594   *R(I) 2/99* is very useful in charting the bumpy and twisting path of attempts to make entitlement to REA cease on retirement, and the decisions reported there make clear that reg.3 is *intra vires* the rule-making power in SSCBA 1992, Sch.7, para.13(8).

In *Hepple v CAO* (Case C196/98, judgment of May 23, 2000 reported as *R(I) 2/00*), the ECJ held that the discriminatory cut-off conditions introduced by the UK from 1986 onwards for REA claimants over state pension age were not invalid under the Equal Treatment Directive 79/7 as they were within the permitted exclusion in Art.7 for the determination of state pension age and "the possible consequences for other benefits". The court rejected the Advocate-General's opinion. It rejected the argument that Art.7 did not permit Member States to introduce fresh heads of discrimination in non-pension benefits by linking them to the pension age long after the Directive itself was in full effect. The court held that since "the principal aim of the legislative amendments . . . was to discontinue payment of REA . . . to persons no longer of working age by imposing conditions based on the statutory retirement age", then "maintenance of the rules at issue . . . is objectively necessary to preserve . . . coherence" between REA and the state pension. In consequence, the discrimination was held "objectively and necessarily linked to the difference between the retirement age for men and that for women". It was, therefore, permitted by Art.7.

The end result is that reg.3 has now been conclusively upheld as valid in both UK national and EU law. Decisions are now being given in the numerous REA appeals stayed pending the ECJ's judgment.

1.595   *Sub-para. (2):* transfers a claimant to retirement allowance if, on the day before he ceases to be entitled to reduced earnings allowance under subs.(1), he was entitled to reduced earnings allowance at a weekly rate of not less than £2. There is some potential difficulty in the subsection since the use of the word "entitled" might suggest that the decision-maker or tribunal could investigate entitlement even if there had been no claim. However, the qualifying words in brackets, "by virtue either of one award or of a number of awards", suggest that the benefit must actually have been awarded at the relevant time.

1.596   *Sub-para. (3)–(7):* stipulate that entitlement to retirement allowance is for life, and fix the rate at which benefit will be paid. Consistent with the freezing of reduced earnings allowance for those retired people over pensionable age in receipt of that benefit (see para.12 noted above), retirement allowance will be paid at a rate fixed by reference to the date of retirement. Note, however, that the sums falling to be calculated under sub-para.(4) are subject to alteration by up-rating orders (sub-para.(7)).

The whole of s.59B was amended and subss.(7) and (8) added by SSA 1989 to take account of the abolition of the earnings rules and the substitution of the text of "giving up regular employment" for the text of retirement or deemed retirement.

The meaning of "regular employment" for the purposes of the section is defined by the Social Security (Industrial Injuries) (Regular Employment) Regulations 1990 (SI 1990/256) which are included in the regulations on individual injuries set out at the end of the volume.

Sub-para.(10): Note the link to "jobseeking period" and "linked period" as defined in the Jobseekers Act 1995. These terms are in fact given real definition in JSA Regs1996, regs47–49. See *Vol.II: Income Support, Jobseeker's Allowance, State Pension Credit and the Social Fund.*   **1.597**

Schedule 8. *Omitted.*   **1.598**

Schedules 9–11: *Omitted.* See *Vol.IV: Tax Credits and HMRC-administered Social Security Benefits.*   **1.599**

SCHEDULE 12

RELATIONSHIP OF STATUTORY SICK PAY WITH BENEFITS AND OTHER PAYMENTS, ETC.

The general principle

1.—Any day which—   **1.600**
   (a) is a day of incapacity for work in relation to any contract of service; and
   (b) falls within a period of entitlement (whether or not it is also a qualifying day), shall not be treated for the purposes of this Act as a day of incapacity for work for the purposes of determining whether a period is [¹] [² a period of incapacity for work for the purposes of incapacity benefit.]

Contractual remuneration

2.—(1) Subject to sub-paragraphs (2) and (3) below, any entitlement to statutory sick pay shall not affect any right of any employee in relation to remuneration under any contract of service ("contractual remuneration").   **1.601**
   (2) Subject to sub-paragraph (3) below—
   (a) any contractual remuneration paid to any employee by an employer of his in respect of a day of incapacity for work shall go towards discharging any liability for that employer to pay statutory sick pay to that employee in respect of that day; and
   (b) any statutory sick pay paid by an employer to an employee of his in respect of a day of incapacity for work shall go towards discharging any liability of that employer to pay contractual remuneration to that employee in respect of that day.
   (3) Regulations may make provision as to payments which are, and those which are not, to be treated as contractual remuneration for the purposes of sub-paragraph (1) or (2) above.

[² *Incapacity benefit*

3.—(1) This paragraph and paragraph 4 below have effect to exclude, where a period of entitlement as between an employee and an employer of his comes to an end, the provisions by virtue of which short-term incapacity benefit is not paid for the first three days.   **1.602**
   (2) If the first day immediately following the day on which the period of entitlement came to an end—
   (a) is a day of incapacity for work in relation to that employee, and
   (b) is not a day in relation to which paragraph 1 above applies by reason of any entitlement as between the employee and another employer,
that day shall, except in prescribed cases, be or form part of a period of incapacity for work notwithstanding section 30C(1)(b) above (by virtue of which a period of incapacity for work must be at least 4 days long).
   (3) Where each of the first two consecutive days, or the first three consecutive days, following the day on which the period of entitlement came to an end is a day to which paragraphs (a) and (b) of sub-paragraph (2) above apply, that sub-paragraph has effect in relation to the second day or, as the case may be, in relation to the second and third days, as it has effect in relation to the first.
4.—(1) Where a period of entitlement as between an employee and an employer of his comes to an end, section 30A(3) above (exclusion of benefit for first 3 days of period) does not apply in relation to any day which—
   (a) is or forms part of a period of incapacity for work (whether by virtue of paragraph 3 above or otherwise), and

(b) falls within the period of 57 days immediately following the day on which the period of entitlement came to an end.

(2) Where sub-paragraph (1) above applies in relation to a day, section 30A(3) above does not apply in relation to any later day in the same period of incapacity for work.]

[² Incapacity benefit for widows and widowers

1.603   **5.**—Paragraph 1 above does not apply for the purpose of determining whether the conditions specified in section 40(3) or (4) or section 41(2) or (3) above are satisfied.]

Unemployability supplement

1.604   **6.**—Paragraph 1 above does not apply in relation to paragraph 3 of Schedule 7 to this Act and accordingly the references in paragraph 3 of that Schedule to a period of interruption of employment shall be construed as if the provisions re-enacted in this Part of this Act had not been enacted.

AMENDMENTS

1. Words repealed by Jobseekers Act 1995, Sch.3 para.1. (October 7, 1996).
2. Words inserted by Social Security (Incapacity for Work) Act 1994, Sch.1 para.44 (April 13, 1995).

DERIVATION

1.605   SSHBA 1982, Sch.2.

GENERAL NOTE

Para. 1

1.606   No day of incapacity (whether or not a qualifying day) within a period of entitlement can count as part of a period of interruption of employment. Thus such a day cannot give entitlement to, say, incapacity benefit.

Paras 3 and 4

1.607   These assist certain persons not caught by para.1, who have days of incapacity subsequent to the end of a period of entitlement, to qualify for State benefits by not applying the normal rules on period of interruption of employment and waiting days. See also with respect to para.3., reg.12 of the SSP (Gen.) Regulations.

SCHEDULE 13

RELATIONSHIP OF STATUTORY MATERNITY PAY WITH BENEFITS AND
OTHER PAYMENTS, ETC.

The general principle

1.608   [¹ **1.**—Except as may be prescribed, a day which falls within the maternity pay period shall not be treated as a day of incapacity for work for the purposes of determining, for this Act, whether it forms part of a period of incapacity for work for the purposes of incapacity benefit.]

[² Incapacity benefit

1.609   **2.**—(1) Regulations may provide that in prescribed circumstances a day which falls within the maternity pay period shall be treated as a day of incapacity for work for the purpose of determining entitlement to the higher rate of short-term incapacity benefit or to long-term incapacity benefit.

(2) Regulations may provide that an amount equal to a woman's statutory maternity pay for a period shall be deducted from any such benefit in respect of the same period and a woman shall be entitled to such benefit only if there is a balance after the deduction and, if there is such a balance, at a weekly rate equal to it.]

Contractual remuneration

3.—(1) Subject to sub-paragraphs (2) and (3) below, any entitlement to statutory maternity pay shall not affect any right of a woman in relation to remuneration under any contract of service ("contractual remuneration").

(2) Subject to sub-paragraph (3) below—

(a) any contractual remuneration paid to a woman by an employer of hers in respect of a week in the maternity pay period shall go towards discharging any liability of that employer to pay statutory maternity pay to her in respect of that week; and

(b) any statutory maternity pay paid by an employer to a woman who is an employee of his in respect of a week in the maternity pay period shall go towards discharging any liability of that employer to pay contractual remuneration to her in respect of that week.

(3) Regulations may make provision as to payments which are, and those which are not, to be treated as contractual remuneration for the purposes of sub-paragraphs (1) and (2) above.

AMENDMENTS

1. Substituted by Jobseekers Act 1995, Sch.2, para.37 (October 7, 1996).

2. Substituted by Social Security (Incapacity for Work) Act 1994, Sch.1, para.45 (April 13, 1995).

1.610

Social Security (Consequential Provisions) Act 1992

(1992 C.6)

ARRANGEMENT OF SECTIONS

Meaning of "the consolidating Acts"

1.—In this Act—

"the consolidating Acts" means the Social Security Contributions and Benefits Act 1992 ("the Contributions and Benefits Act"), the Social

1.612

339

Security Administration Act 1992 ("the Administration Act") and, so far as it reproduces the effect of the repealed enactments, this Act; and "the repealed enactments" means the enactments repealed by this Act.

Continuity of the law

1.613   **2.**—(1) The substitution of the consolidating Acts for the repealed enactments does not affect the continuity of the law.

(2) Anything done or having effect as if done under or for the purposes of a provision of the repealed enactments has effect, if it could have been done under or for the purposes of the corresponding provision of the consolidating Acts, as if done under or for the purposes of that provision.

(3) Any reference, whether express or implied, in the consolidating Acts or any other enactment, instrument or document to a provision of the consolidating Acts shall, so far as the context permits, be construed as including, in relation to the times, circumstances and purposes in relation to which the corresponding provision of the repealed enactments has effect, a reference to that corresponding provision.

(4) Any reference, whether express or implied, in any enactment, instrument or document to a provision of the repealed enactments shall be construed, so far as is required for continuing its effect, as including a reference to the corresponding provision of the consolidating Acts.

DEFINITIONS

"the consolidating Acts"—see s.1(1).
"the repealed enactments"—see s.1(1).

GENERAL NOTE

1.614   The process of consolidation has meant that provisions in a variety of repealed social security enactments (e.g. the SSA 1975, the CBA 1975, both as heavily amended) have been gathered together, in a more logical arrangement, in the consolidating Acts: (1) the Social Security Administration Act 1992 ("SSAA 1992"), dealing with claims and payments and general administration of benefit, decision-making by AOs and other officials, with adjudication by SSATs and Commissioners, and with rights of further appeal to the courts, which has now itself been substantially replaced by the SSA 1998; (2) the Social Security Contributions and Benefits Act 1992 ("SSCBA 1992"), which covers social security contributions and the substantive conditions of entitlement to social security benefits; (3) this Act in so far as it reproduces the effect of the repealed enactments. All three Acts entered into force on July 1, 1992. Except in so far as this Act makes modifications to the SSAA 1992 and the SSCBA 1992 (see s.5 and Sch.3 and s.6 and Sch.4, below), the process has involved no change to the law: it is rather a matter of familiar friends having moved to new locations (e.g. SSA 1975, s.17 on day of unemployment and day of incapacity for work became SSCBA 1992, s.57 repealed consequent upon the introduction of incapacity benefit). This section provides, accordingly, that the substitution of the consolidating Acts for the repealed enactments does not affect the continuity of the law (subs.(1)). Anything done or having effect as if done under or for the purposes of one of the repealed provisions has effect as if done under the corresponding provision in the appropriate consolidation Act, provided that it could have been done under or for the purposes of the latter provision (subs.(2)). Subs.(3) deals with the times, circumstances and purposes in relation to which a provision in the repealed enactments has effect. The subsection provides that any reference (express or implied) in the consolidating Acts or any other enactment, instrument or document to a provision of the consolidating Acts shall, so far as the context permits, be construed as a reference to the corresponding provision of the repealed enactments. Thus any reference to SSCBA 1992, s.57(1) would be construed as a reference to SSA 1975, s.17(1). Subs.(4) requires any reference (express or implied) in the consolidating Acts or any other enactment, instrument or document to a provision of the repealed enactments to be construed so far as is necessary for continuing its effect as including a reference to the corresponding provision of the consolidating Acts. Note, however, that para.(1) of Sch.3, below, provides that in respect of any time before July 1, 1992, any question about benefit or contributions (other than a question under the SSAA 1992, ss.1–3) is to be determined (subject to SSAA 1992, s.68) in accordance with provisions in force or deemed to be in force at that time. Otherwise, the consolidating Acts apply to matters arising before their commencement (July 1, 1992) as to matters arising after it. This would appear to mean that a decision on whether a person was incapable of work for a period before July 1, 1992, would be decided in accordance with SSA 1975, s.17(1), as would any forward disallowance made before that date, even if the period covered by it extended beyond that date, but that any references in it to s.17(1) would be construed after July 1, 1992, as references to SSCBA 1992, s.57(1).

All this is complicated for the lawyer, let alone for members of tribunals. In an attempt to assist, we have included prior to each of the annotations to the key provisions of the consolidating Acts a note on which central provision of the repealed enactments the consolidated provision comes from ("derivation"). The actual text of regulations has not been altered and there has been no consolidation of regulations: many thus refer directly to specific provisions of the repealed legislation. In order to assist here we have so far as is possible replaced those references with, in square brackets, the reference to the corresponding provision(s) of the consolidating legislation (see e.g. USI Regulations, reg.4, below). That method of altering the text of the regulations, of course, has no official status, but, hopefully, makes them more "user friendly". See further the note preceding the various sets of Regulations.

Repeals

3.—(1) The enactments mentioned in Schedule 1 to this Act are repealed to the extent specified in the third column of that Schedule.

(2) Those repeals include, in addition to repeals consequential on the consolidation of provisions in the consolidating Acts, repeals in accordance with Recommendations of the Law Commission and the Scottish Law Commission, of section 30(6)(b) of the Social Security Act 1975, paragraphs 2 to 8 of Schedule 9 to that Act, paragraph 2(1) of Schedule 10 to that Act and section 10 of the Social Security Act 1988.

(3) The repeals have effect subject to any relevant savings in Schedule 3 to this Act.

1.615

GENERAL NOTE

The effect of this section has been taken into account in selecting the statutory material for this edition.

1.616

Consequential amendments

4.—The enactments mentioned in Schedule 2 to this Act shall have effect with the amendments there specified (being amendments consequential on the consolidating Acts).

1.617

GENERAL NOTE

The effect of this section has been taken into account in selecting statutory material for this edition.

1.618

Transitional provisions and savings

1.619   **5.**—(1) The transitional provisions and savings in Schedule 3 to this Act shall have effect.

(2) Nothing in that Schedule affects the general operation of section 16 of the Interpretation Act 1978 (general savings implied on repeal) or of the previous provisions of this Act.

GENERAL NOTE

1.620   The effect of this section has been taken into account in selecting the statutory material for this edition.

Transitory modifications

1.621   **6.**—The transitory modifications in Schedule 4 to this Act shall have effect.

GENERAL NOTE

1.622   The effect of this section has been taken into account in preparing the statutory text of this edition.

Short title, commencement and extent

1.623   **7.**—(1) This Act may be cited as the Social Security (Consequential Provisions) Act 1992.

(2) This Act shall come into force on 1st July 1992.

(3) Section 2 above and this section extend to Northern Ireland.

(4) Subject to subsection (5) below, where any enactment repealed or amended by this Act extends to any part of the United Kingdom, the repeal or amendment extends to that part.

(5) The repeals—

    (a) of provisions of sections 10, 13 and 14 of the Social Security Act 1980 and Part II of Schedule 3 to that Act;

    (b) of enactments amending those provisions;

    (c) of paragraph 2 of Schedule 1 to the Capital Allowances Act 1990; and

    (d) of section 17(8) and (9) of the Social Security Act 1990, do not extend to Northern Ireland.

(6) Section 6 above and Schedule 4 to this Act extend to Northern Ireland in so far as they give effect to transitory modifications of provisions of the consolidating Acts which so extend.

(7) Except as provided by this section, this Act does not extend to Northern Ireland.

(8) Section 4 above extends to the Isle of Man so far as it relates to paragraphs 53 and 54 of Schedule 2 to this Act.

SCHEDULE 3

TRANSITIONAL PROVISIONS AND SAVINGS (INCLUDING SOME TRANSITIONAL PROVISIONS RETAINED FROM PREVIOUS ACTS)

PART I

GENERAL AND MISCELLANEOUS

Questions relating to contributions and benefits

1.—(1) A question other than a question arising under any of sections 1 to 3 of the Administration Act—

    (a) whether a person is entitled to a benefit in respect of a time before 1st July 1992;

    (b) whether a person is liable to pay contributions in respect of such a time,

and any other question not arising under any of those sections with respect to benefit or contributions in respect of such a time is to be determined, subject to section 68 of the Administration Act, in accordance with provisions in force or deemed to be in force at that time.

(2) Subject to sub-paragraph (1) above, the consolidating Acts apply to matters arising before their commencement as to matters arising after it.

General saving for old savings

2.—The repeal by this Act of an enactment previously repealed subject to savings (whether or not in the repealing enactment) does not affect the continued operation of those savings.

Documents referring to repealed enactments

3.—Any document made, served or issued after this Act comes into force which contains a reference to any of the repealed enactments shall be construed, except so far as a contrary intention appears, as referring or, as the context may require, including a reference to the corresponding provision of the consolidating Acts.

Provisions relating to the coming into force of other provisions

4.—The repeal by this Act of a provision providing for or relating to the coming into force of a provision reproduced in the consolidating Acts does not affect the operation of the first provision, in so far as it remains capable of having effect, in relation to the enactment reproducing the second provision.

Continuing powers to make transitional etc. regulations

5.—Where immediately before 1st July 1992 the Secretary of State has power under any provision of the Social Security Acts 1975 to 1991 not reproduced in the consolidating Acts by regulations to make provision or savings in preparation for or in connection with the coming into force of a provision repealed by this Act but reproduced in the consolidating Acts, the power shall be construed as having effect in relation to the provision reproducing the repealed provision.

Powers to make preparatory regulations

6.—The repeal by this Act of a power by regulations to make provision or savings in preparation for or in connection with the coming into force of a provision reproduced in the consolidating Acts does not affect the power, in so far as it remains capable of having effect, in relation to the enactment reproducing the second provision.

Provisions contained in enactments by virtue of orders or regulations

7.—(1) Without prejudice to any express provision in the consolidating Acts, where this Act repeals any provision contained in any enactment by virtue of any order or regulations and the provision is reproduced in the consolidating Acts, the Secretary of State shall have the like power to make orders or regulations repealing or amending the provision of the consolidating Acts which reproduces the effect of the repealed provision as he had in relation to that provision.

(2) Sub-paragraph (1) above applies to a repealed provision which was amended by Schedule 7 to the Social Security Act 1989 as it applies to a provision not so amended.

1.624

1.625

1.626

1.627

1.628

1.629

Amending orders made after passing of Act

1.630   **8.**—An order which is made under any of the repealed enactments after the passing of this Act and which amends any of the repealed enactments shall have the effect also of making a corresponding amendment of the consolidating Acts.

PART II

SPECIFIC TRANSITIONAL PROVISIONS AND SAVINGS (INCLUDING SOME DERIVED FROM PREVIOUS ACTS)

Interpretation

1.631   **9.**—In this Part of this Schedule—

"the 1965 Act" means the National Insurance Act 1965;
"the 1973 Act" means the Social Security Act 1973;
"the 1975 Act" means the Social Security Act 1975;
"the former Consequential Provisions Act" means the Social Security (Consequential Provisions) Act 1975; and
"the 1986 Act" means the Social Security Act 1986.

Social Security Pensions Act 1975

1.632   **10.**—The repeal by this Act of any provisions contained in the 1975 Act or any enactment amending such a provision does not affect the operation of that provision by virtue of section 66(2) of the Social Security Pensions Act 1975.

1.633   *Paragraphs 11–19 omitted.*

Attendance allowance—provision derived from section 1 of Social Security Act 1988

20.—For the purposes—
   (a) of any determination following a claim made before 15th March 1988 (the date of the passing of the Social Security Act 1988);
   (b) of any review following an application made before that date; and
   (c) of any review following a decision to conduct a review made before that date,
section 64 of the Contributions and Benefits Act shall have effect as if the following subsection were substituted for subsection (3)—
"(3) A person satisfies the night attendance condition if he is so severely disabled physically or mentally that, at night, he requires from another person either—
   (a) prolonged or repeated attention during the night in connection with his bodily functions; or
   (b) continual supervision throughout the night in order to avoid substantial danger to himself or others."

1.634   *Paragraph 21 omitted.*

Substitution of disability living allowance for attendance allowance and mobility allowance and dissolution of Attendance Allowance Board—provision derived from section 5 of Disability Living Allowance and Disability Working Allowance Act 1991

1.635   **22.**—(1) The Secretary of State may make such regulations as appear to him necessary or expedient in relation to the substitution of disability living allowance for attendance allowance and mobility allowance and the dissolution of the Attendance Allowance Board.
(2) Without prejudice to the generality of this paragraph, regulations under this paragraph—
   (a) may provide for the termination or cancellation of awards of attendance allowance and awards of mobility allowance;
   (b) may direct that a person whose award of either allowance has been terminated or cancelled by virtue of the regulations or who is a child of such a person shall by virtue of the regulations be treated as having been awarded one or more disability living allowances;
   (c) may direct that a disability living allowance so treated as having been awarded shall consist of such component as the regulations may specify or, if the regulations so specify, of both components, and as having been awarded either component at such weekly rate and for such period as the regulations may specify;

(d) may provide for the termination in specified circumstances of an award of disability living allowance;

(e) may direct that in specified circumstances a person whose award of disability living allowance has been terminated by virtue of the regulations shall by virtue of the regulations be treated as having been granted a further award of a disability living allowance consisting of such component as the regulations may specify or, if the regulations so specify, of both components, and as having been awarded on the further award either component at such weekly rate and for such period as the regulations may specify;

(f) may provide for the review of awards made by virtue of paragraph (b) or (e) above and for the treatment of claims for disability living allowance in respect of beneficiaries with such awards;

(g) may direct that for specified purposes certificates issued by the Attendance Allowance Board shall be treated as evidence of such matters as may be specified in the regulations;

(h) may direct that for specified purposes the replacement of attendance allowance and mobility allowance by disability living allowance shall be disregarded;

(i) may direct that a claim for attendance allowance or mobility allowance shall be treated in specified circumstances and for specified purposes as a claim for disability living allowance or that a claim for disability living allowance shall be treated in specified circumstances and for specified purposes as a claim for attendance allowance or mobility allowance or both;

(j) may direct that in specified circumstances and for specified purposes a claim for a disability living allowance shall be treated as having been made when no such claim was in fact made;

(k) may direct that in specified circumstances a claim for attendance allowance, mobility allowance or disability living allowance shall be treated as not having been made;

(l) may direct that in specified circumstances where a person claims attendance allowance or mobility allowance or both, and also claims disability living allowance, his claims may be treated as a single claim for such allowances for such periods as the regulations may specify;

(m) may direct that cases relating to mobility allowance shall be subject to adjudication in accordance with the provisions of Part II of the Administration Act relating to disability living allowance; and

(n) may direct that, at a time before the Attendance Allowance Board is dissolved, in specified circumstances cases relating to attendance allowance shall be subject to adjudication under the system of adjudication for such cases introduced by the Disability Living Allowance and Disability Working Allowance Act 1991.

(3) Regulations under this paragraph may provide that any provision to which this subparagraph applies—

(a) shall have effect subject to modifications, additions or amendments; or

(b) shall not have effect.

(4) Sub-paragraph (3) above applies—

(a) to any provision of the 1975 Act which relates to mobility allowance, so far as it so relates;

(b) to any provision of Part VI of the 1986 Act which is relevant to mobility allowance;

(c) to any provision of the Contributions and Benefits Act which relates to disability living allowance or attendance allowance, so far as it so relates; and

(d) to any provision of the Administration Act which is relevant to disability living allowance or attendance allowance.

Regulations and orders—supplementary

23.—(1) Regulations under this Part of this Schedule shall be made by the Secretary of State.   **1.636**

(2) Powers under this Part of this Schedule to make regulations or orders are exercisable by statutory instrument.

(3) Any power conferred by this Part of this Schedule to make regulations or orders may be exercised—

(a) either in relation to all cases to which the power extends, or in relation to those cases subject to specified exceptions, or in relation to any specified cases or classes of case;

(b) so as to make, as respects the cases in relation to which it is exercised—

(i) the full provision to which the power extends or any less provision (whether by way of exception or otherwise);

    (ii) the same provision for all cases in relation to which the power is exercised, or different provision for different cases or different classes of case or different provision as respects the same case or class of case for different purposes of this Part of this Schedule;

    (iii) any such provision either unconditionally or subject to any specified condition.

(4) The powers to make regulations or orders conferred by any provision of this Part of this Schedule other than in paragraph 22 above include powers to make thereby such incidental, supplementary, consequential or transitional provision as appears to the Secretary of State to be expedient for the purposes of the regulations.

(5) A power conferred by this Part of this Schedule to make regulations or an order includes power to provide for a person to exercise a discretion in dealing with any matter.

(6) If the Treasury so direct, regulations or orders under this Part of this Schedule shall be made only in conjunction with them.

(7) A statutory instrument—

    (a) which contains (whether alone or with other provisions) orders or regulations made under this Part of this Schedule, and

    (b) which is not subject to any requirement that a draft of the instrument be laid before and approved by a resolution of each House of Parliament,

shall be subject to annulment in pursuance of a resolution of either House of Parliament.

Pensions Schemes Act 1993

(1993 C.48)

SECTIONS REPRODUCED

PART III

CERTIFICATION OF PENSION SCHEMES AND EFFECTS ON MEMBERS' STATE SCHEME RIGHTS AND DUTIES

Preliminary

CHAPTER II

REDUCTION IN STATE SCHEME CONTRIBUTIONS AND SOCIAL SECURITY BENEFITS FOR MEMBERS OF CERTIFIED SCHEMES

Preliminary

SECTION

1.637   40.   Scope of Chapter II.

Reduced rates of state scheme Class 1 contributions

41.   Reduced rates of Class 1 contributions for earners in contracted-out employment.

42.   Review and alteration of rates of contributions applicable under section 41.

Effect of entitlement to guaranteed minimum pensions on payment of social security benefits

46.—(1) Where for any period a person is entitled both—

(a) to a Category A or Category B retirement pension, a widowed mother's allowance [¹, a widowed parent's allowance] [² or a widow's pension] under the Social Security Contributions and Benefits Act 1992; and

(b) to one or more guaranteed minimum pensions

the weekly rate of the benefit mentioned in paragraph (a) shall for that period be reduced by an amount equal—

[³ (i) to that part of its additional pension which is attributable to earnings factors for any tax years ending before the principal appointed day], or

(ii) to the weekly rate of the pension mentioned in paragraph (b) (or, if there is more than one such pension, their aggregate weekly rates),

whichever is the less.

(2) [² . . .]

[² (3) Where for any period—

(a) a person is entitled to one or more guaranteed minimum pensions; and

1.638

347

(b) he is also entitled to long-term incapacity benefit under section 30A of the Social Security Contributions and Benefits Act 1992,

for that period an amount equal to the weekly rate or aggregate weekly rates of the guaranteed minimum pension or pensions shall be deducted from any increase payable under regulations under section 30B(7) of that Act and he shall be entitled to such an increase only if there is a balance after the deduction and, if there is such a balance, at a weekly rate equal to it.]

(4) Where for any period—

(a) a person is entitled to one or more guaranteed minimum pensions;

(b) he is also entitled to a Category A retirement pension under section 44 of the Social Security Contributions and Benefits Act 1992; and

(c) the weekly rate of his pension includes an additional pension such as is mentioned in section 44(3)(b) of that Act,

for that period section 47 of that Act shall have effect as if the following subsection were substituted for subsection (3)—

"(3) In subsection (2) above 'the relevant amount' means an amount equal to the aggregate of—

(a) the additional pension; and

(b) the weekly rate or aggregate weekly rates of the guaranteed minimum pension or pensions,

reduced by the amount of any reduction in the weekly rate of the Category A retirement pension made by virtue of section 46(1) of the Pension Schemes Act 1993.".

(5) Where for any period—

(a) a person is entitled to one or more guaranteed minimum pensions;

(b) he is also entitled to a Category A retirement pension under section 44 of the Social Security Contributions and Benefits Act 1992; and

(c) the weekly rate of his Category A retirement pension does not include an additional pension such as is mentioned in subsection (3)(b) of that section,

for that period the relevant amount shall be deducted from the amount that would otherwise be the increase under section 47(1) of that Act and the pensioner shall be entitled to an increase under that section only if there is a balance remaining after that deduction and, if there is such a balance, of an amount equal to it.

(6) Where for any period—

(a) a person is entitled to one or more guaranteed minimum pensions;

(b) he is also entitled—

(i) [² . . .]

(ii) to a Category A retirement pension under section 44 of that Act; or

(iii) to a Category B retirement pension under [⁴ section 48A [¹, 48B or 48BB] of that Act; and

(c) the weekly rate of the pension includes an additional pension such as is mentioned in section 44(3)(b) of that Act,

for that period paragraph 3 of Schedule 7 to that Act shall have effect as if the following sub-paragraph were substituted for sub-paragraph (3)—

"(3) In this paragraph 'the relevant amount' means an amount equal to the aggregate of—

(a) the additional pension; and
(b) the weekly rate or aggregate weekly rates of the guaranteed minimum pension or pensions,

reduced by the amount of any reduction in the weekly rate of the pension made by virtue of section 46(1) of the Pension Schemes Act 1993.".

(7) Where for any period—
(a) a person is entitled to one or more guaranteed minimum pensions;
(b) he is also entitled to any of the pensions under the Social Security Contributions and Benefits Act 1992 mentioned in subsection (6)(b); and
(c) the weekly rate of the pension does not include an additional pension such as is mentioned in section 44(3)(b) of that Act,

for that period the relevant amount shall be deducted from the amount that would otherwise be the increase under paragraph 3 of Schedule 7 to that Act and the beneficiary shall be entitled to an increase only if there is a balance after that deduction and, if there is a balance, only to an amount equal to it.

(8) In this section "the relevant amount" means an amount equal to the weekly rate or aggregate weekly rates of the guaranteed minimum pension or pensions—
(a) [2 . . .]
(b) in the case of subsection (5), reduced by the amount of any reduction in the weekly rate of the Category A retirement pension made by virtue of subsection (1);

and references in this section to the weekly rate of a guaranteed minimum pension are references to that rate without any increase under section 15(1).
(9) [2 . . .]

AMENDMENTS AND REPEALS

1. Welfare Reform and Pensions Act 1999, s.70 (April 9, 2001).
2. Social Security (Incapacity for Work) Act 1994, Sch.1 (April 13, 1995).
3. Pensions Act 1995, Sch.5, para.44, (April 6, 1997).
4. Pensions Act 1995, Sch.4, para.22 (July 19, 1995).

GENERAL NOTE

The complexities arising from the calculations of benefit entitlement under s.46, **1.639** and of the appeal structure to be followed in connection with such entitlement, are explored and explained by Commissioner Williams in *R(P) 1/04*.

The claimant was entitled to a guaranteed minimum pension (GMP). Under s.46 his state retirement pension was reduced by the amount of his GMP, but responsibility for calculation of GMP, and any appeal consequent thereon was the responsibility of the Inland Revenue. The Commissioner explains that to decide any appeal against the determination of a claim for state retirement pension, a tribunal must first ascertain what amount has been determined to be due for the GMP. Unless that sum has been formally notified to the claimant, and any appeal that he makes to the Board has been disposed of, the Secretary of State for Work & Pensions, and hence any, tribunal hearing an appeal from his decision, cannot proceed with the calculation of his relevant pension. Although it was unnecessary to do so in this appeal, the Commissioner also decided (at the invitation of the parties) that where a claimant is entitled to more than one GMP the function of the Inland Revenue is only to calculate the amount of each individual pension and communicate those to the DWP. It remains the function of Secretary of State there, to aggregate those sums once he is satisfied that they qualify as GMP pensions, and then calculate the resulting entitlement to retirement pension. Any Tribunal faced with one of these appeals will benefit from reading this decision and the appendices attached.

The operation of the section has been further explored by Commissioner Mesher in *CP/1318/2001*. There, the claimant had argued for the offsetting of the GMP from his retirement pension to be limited to the amount of GMP earned in the years for which he had been contracted out for earnings-related pension and to exclude the effect of any offsetting on the additional pension earned when contracted in. (An inaccurate but useful shorthand for not contracted out). He said that promises made by the Government spokesman at the time of the introduction of SERPS in 1975 compelled this interpretation of the legislation. The Commissioner rejected his argument. The meaning of the legislation, he said, was clear: it required the offsetting to be against the whole of the retirement pension payable including the additional pension earned in years when the claimant was contracted in. This case (and *CP/1412/2002*, heard with it) deals also with the application of subs.(3) of this section, where the claimant is entitled also to transitional invalidity allowance surviving from the shift to incapacity benefit in 1995. The provisions in this case require that the entitlement to GMP be deducted as well from the amount of any such invalidity allowance. What at first seemed to the Commissioner to be an instance of double recovery turned out, upon tracing the history of the matter, to have been in accordance with the purpose of the legislation and, therefore the correct interpretation to be applied.

A demonstration of how a claimant's entitlement to additional pension could be swallowed entirely by the offsetting procedure is provided by *CP/281/2002*. In this case the claimant, who retired early, had asked for and received, a forecast of his pension entitlement more than three years before his claim could be made. The forecast showed a possible entitlement to additional pension of £3.34, but by the time his claim was made his GMP had increased significantly and was now more than the additional pension to which he was entitled. Although the claimant's total pension was now slightly more than the forecast, the additional pension payable was nil since a deduction of the lesser sum (his additional pension) from his additional pension left precisely nothing. The claimant had appealed because he thought he had been robbed of an amount that the forecast had said was already earned. The appeal was dismissed.

The case also demonstrates a point made by Commissioner Mesher in the case above, (having been raised originally in *R(P) 1/04*), that the GMP can never reduce the amount of basic pension because it is only the lesser of the two sums that is deducted. The maximum deduction is therefore never more than the amount of the additional pension.

All these cases have now been expressly approved by the Court of Appeal in *Pearce v Secretary of State for Work and Pensions and Board of Inland Revenue* [2005] EWCA Civ 453. This was an application for leave to appeal from a decision of the Commissioner (Deputy Commissioner White) in *CP/1023/2004* and *CP/1025/2004*. In refusing leave the court examined fully the arguments put by the claimant in a written submission of her case. The claimant had worked for a number of years for an employer with whom she was a member of a private pension scheme and with whom, for the last six years of her employment she was contracted out of the SERPS additional pension scheme. For this period she therefore earned a GMP. Thereafter she worked for more than 20 years for another employer during which time she was contracted in. For this period she therefore earned additional pension but no GMP. She had made two appeals. In the first she appears to have argued that the up-rating of her GMP should be limited to the period for which she was in contracted out employment. Her argument was that her employer's pension was not up-rated thereafter and so neither should have been her GMP. Strictly, this was an appeal against the decision of the Board of Inland Revenue as to the amount of her GMP, but was taken again before the Commissioner on the basis of how much of the GMP should be applied under s.46. The Court of Appeal held that the GMP had to be taken account of at the date the calculation was to be made and must include its full revaluation at that date. There was, they said, no statutory basis for saying that the deduction should be limited to its original value at the time of leaving the contracted out employment.

The second argument was a repeat of the argument put to Commissioner Mesher in *CP/1318/2001*, namely, that the offsetting should be limited to the amount of the additional pension that would have been earned in the period of contracted out employment—so preserving her entitlement to additional pension earned during the subsequent years when she was contracted in. This time the claimant produced a booklet issued by the Department of Work and Pensions, certain passages of which the court agreed appeared to support that contention. Nevertheless, they say the words of s.46 are too plain, it refers to "any tax years" before the appointed day, not just contracted out years.

The effect of the GMP has been considered again by Commissioner Williams at length in *CP/375/2005*. An extra complication and, what to the claimant appeared to be an injustice, arose from the fact that he had converted one of his occupational pension plans into a personal pension with no guarantee that its value would be maintained. Unfortunately for him its value had halved. But the value assumed for the purposes of this section of a notional GMP, and hence the deduction to be made from his retirement pension, remained the same. This is because the claimant, has had the advantage of reduced contributions during the period he was contracted out, and the scheme assumes that he carries that advantage with him afterwards. No extra penalty would have been exacted if the claimant's investment had prospered, but, equally, no compensation is paid when it fails.

A further illustration of the sometimes surprising effect of this section is provided by *CP/3577/2006*. The appellant was a widow who had been claiming, prior to her husband's death, her own state retirement pension on the basis of her own contributions made during a long working life. As a married woman she was entitled to a weekly state benefit of £105.11. She was understandably upset to find that after her husband's death her entitlement, as his widow, was reduced to £94.18 per week. But her appeal was dismissed. Commissioner Williams demonstrates that this is the correct conclusion to be reached by the application of the principle in s.46. This is because the additional pension to which she was entitled as a widow (combining her own and her husband's additional pensions) was subject to a cap, while the maximum GMP to be deducted from it was the full amount of her own GMP and a GMP equivalent equal to half her husband's occupational pension. Although she gained small increases to her basic state pension and to the graduated retirement benefit, these were more than offset by the increased deduction to be made for the combined GMP. This is not to say that the claimant's overall income was reduced—it was not because it increased by a sum equal to half of her husband's occupational pension, but the "household" income was certainly reduced. It was reduced by half of his occupational pension, the whole of his state pension and a sum of almost £11 of her own pension!

Yet another case, *GW v SSWP 2008* [2008] UKUT 41 (AAC) in which the Court of Appeal has granted permission to appeal has come to the Upper Tribunal on the argument that the amount of the claimant's pension should be calculated on the basis that the deduction made should be limited to the pension earned during the period that the claimant was contracted out, and should not extend to the additional pension earned when previously or subsequently contracted in. Judge Rowland considered this argument again because, although the argument had been rejected already in the several cases referred to above, in none of them had the claimant been represented, none of them were reported, and in none of them had consideration been given to an argument based upon the principal in *Inco Europe v First Choice Distribution* [2000] 1 W.L.R. 586 (HL) to the effect that the legislation in question might not have represented the true intention of Parliament. The judge identified three conditions that need to be satisfied before this argument might succeed. They were, that it was clear what Parliament's purpose had been, that the words of the legislation had inadvertently failed to achieve that purpose, and that the substance (though not necessarily the precise words) of the provision that Parliament would have chosen to achieve the correct result, is also clear. To go further than this, he agreed, would stray from the judicial role of interpretation into that of legislation. For the claimant it was observed that Lloyd L.J., in refusing leave to appeal in the *Pearce* case had described the result of a literal reading of the legislation as "illogical" and reference was made as well, by Judge Rowland, to the booklet that had been produced in one of the earlier cases and from which it appeared that the meaning attributed by the department then responsible for the benefits, had been such as to support the claimant's argument. However, after a careful consideration of the background and the history of the legislation, Judge Rowland came to the conclusion that it was not "abundantly clear" that the result was unfair so as to show that Parliament's intention must have been misrepresented by the literal interpretation of this legislation, and he dismissed the appeal.

Further provisions concerning entitlement to guaranteed minimum pensions for the purposes of section 46

1.640

47.—(1) The reference in section 46(1) to a person entitled to a guaranteed minimum pension shall be construed as including a reference to a person so entitled by virtue of being the widower of an earner [¹ . . .] only if—

(a) at the time of the earner's death she and her husband had both attained pensionable age; or

(b) he is also entitled to a Category A retirement pension by virtue of section 41(7) of the Social Security Contributions and Benefits Act 1992.

(2) For the purposes of section 46 a person shall be treated as entitled to any guaranteed minimum pension to which he would have been entitled—

(a) if its commencement had not been postponed, as mentioned in section 13(4); or

(b) if there had not been made a transfer payment or transfer under regulations made by virtue of section 20 as a result of which—

(i) he is no longer entitled to guaranteed minimum pensions under the scheme by which the transfer payment or transfer was made, and

(ii) he has not become entitled to guaranteed minimum pensions under the scheme to which the transfer payment or transfer was made.

(3) Where—

(a) guaranteed minimum pensions provided for a member or the member's widow or widower under a contracted-out scheme have been wholly or partly secured as mentioned in subsection (3) of section 19; and

(b) either—

(i) the transaction wholly or partly securing them was carried out before 1st January 1986 and discharged the trustees or managers of the scheme as mentioned in subsection (1) of that section; or

(ii) it was carried out on or after that date without any of the requirements specified in subsection (5)(a) to (c) of that section being satisfied in relation to it and the scheme has been wound up; and

(c) any company with which any relevant policy of insurance or annuity contract was taken out or entered into is unable to meet the liabilities under policies issued or securities given by it; and

(d) the combined proceeds of—
  (i) any relevant policies and annuity contracts, and
  (ii) any cash sums paid or alternative arrangements made under the Policyholders Protection Act 1975,

are inadequate to provide the whole of the amount secured, the member and the member's widow or widower shall be treated for the purposes of section 46 as only entitled to such part (if any) of the member's or, as the case may be, the member's widow's or widower's guaranteed minimum pension as is provided by the proceeds mentioned in paragraph (d).

(4) A policy or annuity is relevant for the purposes of subsection (3) if taking it out or entering into it constituted the transaction to which section 19 applies.

(5) For the purposes of section 46 a person shall be treated as entitled to any guaranteed minimum pension to which he would have been entitled—

(a) if a lump sum had not been paid instead of that pension under provisions included in a scheme by virtue of section 21(1); or

(b) if that pension had not been forfeited under provisions included in a scheme by virtue of section 21(2).

[² (6) For the purposes of section 46, a person shall be treated as entitled to any guaranteed minimum pension to which he would have been entitled but for any reduction under section 15A.]

[³ (7) For the purposes of section 46, a person shall be treated as entitled to any guaranteed minimum pension to which he would have been entitled but for any order under section 32A of the Insolvency Act 1986 (recovery of excessive pension contributions) or under section 36A of the Bankruptcy (Scotland) Act 1985.]

Reduced benefits where minimum payment or minimum contributions paid

48.—(1) Subject to subsection (3), this subsection applies where for any period—   1.641

(a) minimum payments have been made in respect of an earner to an occupational pension scheme which is a money purchase contracted-out scheme in relation to the earner's employment, or

(b) minimum contributions have been paid in respect of an earner under section 43.

(2) Where subsection (1) applies then, for the purposes of section 46—

(a) the earner shall be treated, as from the date on which he reaches pensionable age, as entitled to a guaranteed minimum pension at a prescribed weekly rate arising from that period in that employment;

(b) [⁴ . . .], and

(c) in prescribed circumstances [⁴ . . .] any widow or widower or the earner shall be treated as entitled to a guaranteed minimum pension at a prescribed weekly rate arising from that period;

and where subsection (1)(b) applies paragraphs (a) to (c) of this subsection apply also for the purposes of [¹ section] 47(2) of the Social Security

Contributions and Benefits Act 1992] and paragraph 3(2) of Schedule 7 to that Act, but with the omission from paragraph (a) of the words "in that employment".

(3) Where the earner is a married woman or widow, subsection (1) shall not have effect by virtue of paragraph (a) of that subsection in relation to any period during which there is operative an election that her liability in respect of primary Class 1 contributions shall be a liability to contribute at a reduced rate.

(4) The power to prescribe a rate conferred by subsection (2)(a) includes power to prescribe a nil rate.

AMENDMENTS AND REPEALS

1. Social Security (Incapacity for Work) Act 1994, Sch.1 (April 13, 1995).
2. Welfare Reform and Pensions Act 1999, s.32 (December 1, 2000).
3. Welfare Reform and Pensions Act 1999, s.18 (April 6, 2002).
4. Pensions Act 1995, s.140(2) (April 6, 1996).

GENERAL NOTE

1.642   Section 48 ceases to have effect for minimum payments and minimum contributions from April 6, 1997 (Pensions Act 1995, s.140(3)).

[¹ Effect of reduced contributions and rebates on social security benefits

1.643   48A.—(1) In relation to any tax week where—
(a) the amount of a Class 1 contribution in respect of the earnings paid to or for the benefit of an earner in that week is reduced under section 41 or 42A, or
(b) an amount is paid under section 45(1) in respect of the earnings paid to or for the benefit of an earner,
section 44(6) of the Social Security Contributions and Benefits Act 1992 (earnings factors for additional pension) shall have effect, except in prescribed circumstances, as if no primary Class 1 contributions had been paid or treated as paid upon those earnings for that week and section 45A of that Act did not apply (where it would, apart from this subsection, apply).

(2) Where the whole or part of a contributions equivalent premium has been paid or treated as paid in respect of the earner, the Secretary of State may make a determination reducing or eliminating the application of subsection (1).

(3) Subsection (1) is subject to regulations under paragraph 5(3A) to (3E) of Schedule 2.

(4) Regulations may, so far as is required for the purpose of providing entitlement to additional pension (such as is mentioned in section 44(3) (b) of the Social Security Contributions and Benefits Act 1992) but to the extent only that the amount of additional pension is attributable to provision made by regulations under section 45(5) of that Act, disapply subsection (1).

(5) In relation to earners where, by virtue of subsection (1), section 44(6) of the Social Security Contributions and Benefits Act 1992 has effect, in any tax year, as mentioned in that subsection in relation to some but not all of their earnings, regulations may modify the application of section 44(5) of that Act.]

AMENDMENT

1. Inserted by Pensions Act 1995, s.140(1) (April 6, 1997).

[¹ Women, married women and widows

49.—The Secretary of State may make regulations modifying, in such   **1.644**
manner as he thinks proper—
  (a) this Chapter in its application to women born on or after 6th April
      1950, and
  (b) sections 41, 42, 46(1), 47(2) and (5) and 48, in their application to
      women who are or have been married].

AMENDMENT

1. Inserted by Pensions Act 1995, Sch.4, para.16 (July 19, 1995).

Social Security (Incapacity for Work) Act 1994

(1994 c.18)

ARRANGEMENT OF SECTIONS

13.   Saving for existing enactments.
14–16. *Omitted.*

SCHEDULES

Omitted.

Incapacity Benefit

1.646   *Section 1 omitted as incorporated in SSCBA 1992.*

Incapacity benefit: rate

1.647   **2.**—(1)–(6) *Omitted.*
(7) Any order under section 150 of the Social Security Administration
Act 1992 (up-rating orders) made by the Secretary of State before the commencement of this section shall include provision—
(a) making such increase (if any) in the sum specified in the provision inserted by subsection (2) above as the amount of short-term
incapacity benefit at the higher rate as is necessary to make that sum
equal to the higher rate or, if there is only one such rate, to the rate
of statutory sick pay payable after the order comes into force; and
(b) making such increases in the other sums specified in the provisions
inserted by subsections (2) and (6) above in Schedule 4 to the Social
Security Contributions and Benefits Act 1992 as would have been
required if the provisions in question had been in force at all material
times.

GENERAL NOTE

1.648   Subssections (2) and (6) of this section effected amendments to Sch.4 of the
SSCBA 1992 to take account of the replacement of sickness and invalidity benefits
by incapacity benefit, and to set the rates of short-and long-term incapacity benefit
and the dependency additions payable with them. This subsection enables the
annual up-rating of those amounts.

1.649   *Section 3 omitted as incorporated in SSCBA 1992.*

Power to provide for the transition to incapacity benefit

1.650   **4.**—(1) The Secretary of State may by regulations make such provision
as appears to him to be necessary or expedient for the purposes of, or in
connection with, the transition to incapacity benefit from sickness benefit
and invalidity benefit.
Nothing in the following provisions of this section shall be construed as
restricting the generality of that power.
(2) In this section—
"commencement" means the commencement of sections 1 to 3 above
and the consequent repeal of the provisions of the Social Security
Contributions and Benefits Act 1992 relating to sickness benefit and
invalidity benefit; and

356

"prescribed" means prescribed by regulations under this section.

(3) Regulations under this section may provide that where a person was entitled to sickness benefit or invalidity benefit immediately before commencement any award of sickness benefit or invalidity benefit shall have effect after commencement, in accordance with the regulations and subject to such modifications as may be prescribed, as an award of incapacity benefit.

In the following provisions of this section such awards are referred to as "transitional awards" of incapacity benefit.

(4) The reference in subsection (3) above to a person who was entitled to sickness benefit or invalidity benefit includes a person who would have been so entitled but for being disqualified by virtue of regulations under section 32 or 59 of the Social Security Contributions and Benefits Act 1992; and regulations under this section may provide that any such disqualification shall have such corresponding effect as may be prescribed in relation to the transitional award.

(5) Regulations under this section may provide that a person's entitlement under a transitional award of incapacity benefit shall, except as may be prescribed, be subject to satisfying the conditions of entitlement to incapacity benefit, and may in particular provide—

    (a) for the determination in accordance with Part XIIA of the Social Security Contributions and Benefits Act 1992 of the question whether that person is incapable of work; and

    (b) for the termination of his entitlement on his attaining pensionable age.

Excepted cases may be defined, in particular, by reference to the age of the person on commencement and whether he was receiving invalidity benefit on 1st December 1993 (the date of the announcement of the new scheme).

(6) Regulations under this section may provide—

    (a) that days before commencement which were days of incapacity for work for the purposes of sickness benefit or invalidity benefit, and such other days as may be prescribed, shall be treated as having been days of incapacity for work for the purposes of incapacity benefit, and

    (b) that days of entitlement to sickness benefit or invalidity benefit, and such other days as may be prescribed, shall be treated as having been days of entitlement to incapacity benefit.

Such provision may be made for the purposes of a transitional award of incapacity benefit or of enabling a claim for incapacity benefit to be made after commencement on the basis that a day of incapacity for work after commencement forms part of a period of incapacity for work beginning before commencement; and such cases are referred to in the following provisions of this section as "transitional cases".

(7) Regulations under this section may provide—

    (a) for the rate of short-term incapacity benefit under a transitional award to be increased, in such cases as may be prescribed, as if that benefit were sickness benefit and the provisions of Part IV of the Social Security Contributions and Benefits Act 1992 (increases for dependants) continued to apply to that benefit; and

    (b) for the payment in transitional cases, in such circumstances as may be prescribed, of long-term incapacity benefit to persons over pensionable age.

(8) Regulations under this section may provide that in transitional cases the rate of short-term incapacity benefit at the higher rate or of long-term incapacity benefit shall be calculated—

(a) by reference to the rate of invalidity benefit, and of any relevant related allowance, addition or increase, paid or payable immediately before commencement, with such up-rating (if any) as may be provided for in accordance with the regulations (whether by applying the provisions of section 150 of the Social Security Administration Act 1992 or otherwise), and

(b) without any increase or addition which would otherwise be payable with incapacity benefit.

(9) If regulations make provision of the kind mentioned in subsection (8) above they may also make with respect to any additional pension element of incapacity benefit provision corresponding to any of the provisions in force before commencement with respect to the additional pension element of invalidity pension.

(10) Regulations under this section may provide, in relation to transitional cases where the rate of incapacity benefit falls to be calculated by reference to the rate of dependency allowance paid or payable before commencement, that any old saving provisions shall have effect subject to the regulations or shall cease to have effect in accordance with the regulations.

For the purposes of this subsection—

"dependency allowance" means an allowance of the kind provided for in Part IV of the Social Security Contributions and Benefits Act 1992, and

"old saving provisions" means provisions of any description, including administrative provisions, in connection with a previous change affecting entitlement to or the amount of dependency allowances, preserving a person's position in any respect.

(11) Section 175(2) to (4) of the Social Security Contributions and Benefits Act 1992 (general provisions as to regulations and orders) apply in relation to the power conferred by subsection (1) above as they apply in relation to a power conferred by that Act to make regulations.

(12) For the period of four years from Royal Assent a statutory instrument which contains (whether alone or with other provisions) any regulations under this section shall not be made unless a draft of the instrument has been laid before Parliament and approved by a resolution of each House.

(13) A statutory instrument—

(a) which contains (whether alone or with other provisions) any regulations made under this section, and

(b) which is not subject to any requirement that a draft of the instrument be laid before and approved by a resolution of each House of Parliament,

shall be subject to annulment in pursuance of a resolution of either House of Parliament.

DEFINITIONS

"commencement"—see subs.(2).
"dependency allowance"—see subs.(10).
"old savings provisions"—see subs.(10).
"prescribed"—see subs.(2).

"transitional awards"—see subs.(3).
"transitional cases"—see subs.(6).

GENERAL NOTE

This section enables the making of regulations in connection with the transition **1.651**
from sickness and invalidity benefits to incapacity benefit. Subs.(1) confers a very
broad rule-making power in this regard, and other subsections confer more specific
powers, none of which restrict the generality of the broad power in subs.(1). The
regulations made pursuant to this section are the IW (Transitional) Regs, below.
The basic underlying principle of the transitional regime is that there should be no
losers in cash terms at the point of transfer.

Subss. (2)–(4)

Awards of sickness or invalidity benefit in force immediately prior to April 13, **1.652**
1995 ("commencement") become ones of incapacity benefit. Such awards are
known as "transitional awards" to distinguish them from the standard postcom-
mencement awards of incapacity benefit, from which the transitional awards differ
in some respects. Those disqualified from sickness and invalidity benefit are treated
for this purpose as still entitled to those benefits, and their disqualification imposed
before commencement, continues to run afterwards until the period of disqualification comes to an end.

See further IW (Transitional) Regs, regs 9, 11, 17.

Subs. (5)

This enables the transitional regulations to provide that entitlement to a tran- **1.653**
sitional award of incapacity benefit is conditional on satisfying the conditions
of entitlement to incapacity benefit, including (except in prescribed cases) the
determination of incapacity according to the own occupation or all work test (now
the "personal capability assessment") as appropriate, and to provide for the termination of entitlement on the attainment of pensionable age. Note particularly
that excepted cases may be defined by reference to someone's age at commencement and whether he was receiving invalidity benefit when the new scheme was
announced on December 1, 1993.

See further, IW (Transitional) Regs, regs 11, 17, and Pt VI (regs 29–32), below;
SSCBA 1992, Pt XIIA, above. Excepted cases are dealt with by IW (Transitional)
Regs, reg.31, below.

Subs. (6)

Subs.(3) introduced the concept of transitional awards. This subsection deals **1.654**
with "transitional cases", consisting of transitional awards and of cases where a
claim after commencement for incapacity benefit is based on a period of incapacity
for work after commencement forming part of such a period before commencement. Under this subsection, regulations can provide that days of incapacity for
work for purposes of sickness and invalidity benefit (and such other days as may
be prescribed) be treated as ones of incapacity for work for purposes of incapacity
benefit, and that days of entitlement to those benefits can be treated as ones of entitlement to incapacity benefit.

See further IW (Transitional) Regs, regs 2–6, below.

Subs. (7)

This enables the long-term rate of incapacity benefit, not normally payable to **1.655**
persons over pensionable age (SSCBA 1992, s.30A(5), above), to be paid to such
persons in transitional cases (defined by subs.(6)). It also provides that regulations
can increase transitional awards of short-term incapacity benefit by dependency
additions just as if the incapacity benefit were sickness benefit.

See further IW (Transitional) Regs, regs 15, 16, below.

Subs. (8)

1.656   This provides that in transitional cases (defined in subs.(6)) regulations can provide that transitional awards of short-term incapacity benefit (higher rate) and of long-term incapacity benefit can be based on the appropriate rate of invalidity benefit (including invalidity allowance and any addition or increase) paid or payable immediately prior to April 13, 1995. Such amounts will be subject to up-rating. Duplication of payments is provided for in para.(b) so that in such cases any increase or addition that would otherwise be payable with incapacity benefit, shall not be.

See further, IW (Transitional) Regs, reg.18 (dealing only with the rate of long-term incapacity benefit in transitional cases), below.

Subs. (9)

1.657   In transitional cases (defined in subs.(6), where regulations under subs.(8) make the provision there contemplated, they can also make provision corresponding to the additional pension element of invalidity benefit. This will not be up-rated, but frozen at commencement and left to wither away with inflation.

See further, IW (Transitional) Regs, reg.18 (dealing only with the rate of long-term incapacity benefit in transitional cases), below.

Subs. (10)

1.658   Regulations after April 13, 1995 can rationalise the existing forms of transitional protection contained in "old savings provisions" in connection with previous changes to dependency allowances. Note these are not just statutory provisions, but can include administrative provisions.

See further, IW (Transitional) Regs, reg.25, below.

1.659   *Section 5 omitted as incorporated in SSCBA 1992.*

Test of incapacity for work: supplementary provisions

1.660   **6.**—(1), (2) *Omitted as incorporated in SSCBA 1992 and SSAA 1992.*

(3) For the period of four years from Royal Assent a statutory instrument which contains (whether alone or with other provisions) any regulations made under any of the following provisions shall not be made unless a draft of the instrument has been laid before Parliament and approved by a resolution of each House—

(a) in the Social Security Contributions and Benefits Act 1992—
    section 171A(2), (3), or (4),
    section 171B(4)(d), (6), (7) or (8),
    section 171C(2) or (3),
    section 171D,
    section 171E(1), (2) or (3), or
    section 171G(1)(c)

(b) in the Social Security Administration Act 1992, section 61A(2), (3) or (4).

Power to provide for the transition to the new test of incapacity for work

1.661   **7.**—(1) The Secretary of State may by regulations make such provision as appears to him to be necessary or expedient for the purposes of, or in connection with, the transition to the test of incapacity for work provided for by sections 5 and 6 above.

Nothing in the following provisions of this section shall be construed as restricting the generality of that power.

(2) In this section—

"commencement" means the commencement of those sections; and

"prescribed" means prescribed by regulations under this section.

(3) Regulations under this section may provide—

(a) that days of incapacity for work before commencement, and such other days as may be prescribed, shall be taken into account for the purposes of section 171B(3) of the Social Security Contributions and Benefits Act 1992 (period after which the all work test applies);

(b) that a person's continued enjoyment after commencement of any allowance or other advantage under any provision for the purposes of which Part XIIA of the Social Security Contributions and Benefits Act 1992 applies shall, except as may be prescribed, be subject to satisfying the test of incapacity for work under that Part; and

(c) for the determination in accordance with that Part of the question whether the person is incapable of work.

(4) Section 175(2) to (4) of the Social Security Contributions and Benefits Act 1992 (general provisions as to regulations and orders) apply in relation to the power conferred by subsection (1) above as they apply in relation to a power conferred by that Act to make regulations.

(5) For the period of four years from Royal Assent a statutory instrument which contains (whether alone or with other provisions) any regulations under this section shall not be made unless a draft of the instrument has been laid before Parliament and approved by a resolution of each House.

(6) A statutory instrument—

(a) which contains (whether alone or with other provisions) any regulations made under this section, and

(b) which is not subject to any requirement that a draft of the instrument be laid before and approved by a resolution of each House of Parliament,

shall be subject to annulment in pursuance of a resolution of either House of Parliament.

DEFINITIONS

"commencement"—see subs.(2).

"prescribed"—see subs.(2).

GENERAL NOTE

Subs.(1)

This gives the Secretary of State a very wide rule-making power to provide in regulations all necessary or expedient provision for the transition to the new tests of incapacity for work in Pt XIIA of the SSCBA 1992, above, which tests apply not just to incapacity benefit, but also for all purposes of the social security system other than SSP and industrial injuries benefits (see SSCBA 1992, s.171G, above). The more specific rule-making powers afforded by subs.(3) do not restrict the generality of that under subs.(1). Under subs.(2) regulations (a) can enable days of incapacity for work before April 13, 1995 ("commencement") to be taken into account for determining when the all work test applies (SSCBA 1992, s.171B(3), above); (b) can provide that continued enjoyment after commencement of any allowance or other advantage to which the new tests apply, shall, save in excepted cases, be subject to satisfying the appropriate test; and (c) can provide for the determination in accordance with Pt XIIA of the SSCBA 1992 of the question whether someone is incapable of work.

1.662

See further, the IW (Transitional) Regs, regs 29–32 (excepted cases being dealt with by reg.31), below.

Statutory sick pay

Rate of statutory sick pay

1.663   **8.**—(1) In section 157(1) of the Social Security Contributions and Benefits Act 1992 (statutory sick pay: rates of payment), for the words following "at the weekly rate" substitute "£52.50".

(2) Any order under section 150 of the Social Security Administration Act 1992 (up-rating orders) made by the Secretary of State before the commencement of this section shall include provision making such increase (if any) in the sum specified in the amendment made by subsection (1) above as the amount of statutory sick pay as is necessary to make that sum equal to the higher rate of statutory sick pay payable after the order comes into force.

(3) *Omitted* as province of Board of Inland Revenue.

(4) *Omitted* as province of Board of Inland Revenue.

1.664   *Sections 9 and 10 omitted as incorporated in SSCBA 1992.*

General

1.665   *Section 11 omitted as amendments incorporated elsewhere in text.*

General power to make transitional and consequential provision

1.666   **12.**—(1) The Secretary of State may by regulations make such transitional provision, and such consequential provision or savings, as appear to him to be necessary or expedient in preparation for or in connection with the coming into force of any provision of this Act or the operation of any enactment repealed or amended by any such provision during any period when the repeal or amendment is not wholly in force.

(2) The power conferred by subsection (1) above is not exercisable in respect of any matter for which provision may be made under section 4 (power to provide for transition to incapacity benefit) or section 7 (power to provide for the transition to new test of incapacity for work).

(3) Section 175(2) to (4) of the Social Security Contributions and Benefits Act 1992 (general provisions as to regulations and orders) apply in relation to the power conferred by subsection (1) above as they apply in relation to a power conferred by that Act to make regulations.

(4) A statutory instrument—

(a) which contains (whether alone or with other provisions) any regulations made under this section, and

(b) which is not subject to any requirement that a draft of the instrument be laid before and approved by a resolution of each House of Parliament, shall be subject to annulment in pursuance of a resolution of either House of Parliament.

GENERAL NOTE

1.667

This section enables the Secretary of State by regulations to deal with routine transitional and consequential provisions connected with the introduction of incapacity benefit and the new tests of incapacity, other than those already covered by the rule-making powers afforded by ss.4 and 7, above.

See further, the Social Security (Incapacity Benefit) (Consequential and Transitional Amendments and Savings) Regulations 1995 (SI 1995/829), most of which effect amendments to other regulations in this work, and which are incorporated in the text of those amended regulations in the usual way, but some of which, being of more general application, are found in the Incapacity Benefit section of the Regulations part of this book.

Saving for existing enactments

1.668

13.—(1) The amendments of the Social Security Contributions and Benefits Act 1992 made by this Act shall be treated as repealing and re-enacting with modifications the provisions of that Act relating to incapacity for work, so that, subject to any amendment, repeal or revocation—

(a) any reference in any enactment to any such provision shall be construed as a reference to the corresponding new provision or, as the case may be, to the provision as amended by this Act; and

(b) subordinate legislation made under any such provision—

(i) shall continue in force and have effect as if made under the corresponding new provision or, as the case may be, the provision as amended by this Act, and

(ii) shall be construed as if originally so made.

(2) In any enactment, subject to any amendment—

(a) any reference to sickness benefit shall be construed as a reference to short-term incapacity benefit at the lower rate, and

(b) any reference to invalidity benefit or invalidity pension shall be construed as a reference to short-term incapacity benefit at the higher rate or long-term incapacity benefit.

(3) In this section "enactment" includes an enactment contained in subordinate legislation, and "subordinate legislation" has the meaning given by section 21(1) of the Interpretation Act 1978.

DEFINITIONS

"enactment"—see subs.(3).
"subordinate legislation"—see subs.(3).

GENERAL NOTE

1.669

This Act effects many amendments to legislation, both primary (Acts) and subordinate (regulations and orders). This section provides that the amendments of the SSCBA 1992 effected by this Act (and incorporated in the text of the SSCBA 1992 in this work) are to be treated as repealing and re-enacting with modifications the provisions of the SSCBA 1992 (as in force before April 13, 1995) relating to incapacity for work, so that (subject to any amendment, revocation or repeal) references within existing legislation to provisions in the SSCBA 1992 repealed or amended by this Act are to be treated as references to the form of the SSCBA 1992 on April 13,

1995. Regulations made under the pre-April 13th SSCBA 1992 are deemed to have been made under the corresponding provision of the post-commencement SSCBA 1992 as here reproduced, and are to be construed as if originally made under those new provisions. References in existing primary or subordinate legislation to sickness benefit are to be construed as references to short-term incapacity benefit (lower rate), while references in such legislation to invalidity benefit or invalidity pension are to be interpreted as references to short-term incapacity benefit (higher rate) or long-term incapacity benefit, as appropriate.

1.670   *Sections 14–16 omitted as not relevant.*

1.671   *Schedules 1 and 2 omitted as incorporated in SSCBA 1992 and SSAA 1992.*

Pensions Act 1995

(1995 c.26)

SECTIONS REPRODUCED

PART II

STATE PENSIONS

1.672   126. Equalisation of pensionable age and of entitlement to certain benefits.
127. Enhancement of additional pension, etc. where family credit or disability working allowance paid.
128. Additional pension: calculation of surpluses.

SCHEDULES

Schedule—Equalisation.
Part I—Pensionable ages for men and women.
Part II—Entitlement to certain pension and other benefits. Part III—Consequential amendments.

PART II

STATE PENSIONS

1.673   **Equalisation of pension age and of entitlement to certain benefits**

126.—Schedule 4 to this Act, of which—
  (a) Part I has effect to equalise pensionable age for men and women progressively over a period of ten years beginning with 6th April 2010,
  (b) Part II makes provision for bringing equality for men and women to certain pension and other benefits, and

(c) Part III makes consequential amendments of enactments,
shall have effect.

Enhancement of additional pension, etc., where family credit or disability working allowance paid

127.—(1) and (2) omitted.

1.674

(3) Subject to subsections (4) and (5) below, this section applies to a
person ("the pensioner") who attains pensionable age after 5th April 1999
and, in relation to such persons, has effect for 1995–96 and subsequent tax
years.

(4) Where the pensioner is a women, this section has effect in the case of
additional pension falling to be calculated under sections 44 and 45 of the
Social Security Contributions and Benefits Act 1992 by virtue of section
39 of that Act (widowed mother's allowance and widow's pension), including Category B retirement pension payable under section 48B(4), if her
husband—

(a) dies after 5th April, 1999, and

(b) has not attained pensionable age on or before that date.

(5) This section has effect where additional pension falls to be calculated
under sections 44 and 45 of the Social Security Contributions and Benefits
Act 1992 as applied by sections 48A or 48B(2) of that Act (other Category
B retirement pension) if—

(a) the pensioner attains pensionable age after 5th April, 1999, and

(b) the pensioner's spouse has not attained pensionable age on or before
that date.

Additional Pension: calculation of surplus

128.—(1) and (2) omitted.

1.675

(3) Section 148 of the Social Security Administration Act 1992 (revaluation of earnings factors) shall have effect in relation to surpluses in a person's
earnings factors under section 44(5A) of the Social Security Contributions
and Benefits Act 1992 [¹ for the purposes of section 45(1) and (2)(a) and
(b) of that Act] as it has effect in relation to earnings factors.

(4) Subject to subsections (5) [², (5A)] and (6) below, this section has
effect in relation to a person ("the pensioner") who attains pensionable age
after 5th April, 2000.

(5) Where the pensioner is a woman, this section has effect in the case
of additional pension falling to be calculated under sections 44 and 45
of the Social Security Contributions and Benefits Act 1992 by virtue of
section 39 of that Act (widowed mother's allowance and widow's pension),
including Category B retirement pension payable under section 48B(4), if
her husband—

(a) dies after 5th April, 2000, and

(b) has not attained pensionable age on or before that date.

[² (5A) This section has effect in the case of additional pension falling to
be calculated under sections 44 and 45 of the Social Security Contributions
and Benefits Act 1992 by virtue of section 39C(1) of that Act (widowed
parent's allowance), including Category B retirement pension payable
under section 48BB(2), if the pensioner's spouse—

(a) dies after 5th April, 2000; and

(b) has not attained pensionable age on or before that date.]

(6) This section has effect where additional pension falls to be calculated under sections 44 and 45 of the Social Security Contributions and Benefits Act 1992 as applied by section 48A [², 48B(2) or 48BB(5)] or 48B(2) of that Act (other Category B retirement pension) if—

(a) the pensioner attains pensionable age after 5th April, 2000, and

(b) the pensioner's spouse has not attained pensionable age on or before that date.

AMENDMENTS

1. Child Support, Pensions and Social Security Act 2000, s.33 (January 25, 2001).

2. Welfare Reform and Pensions Act 1999 s.70 (April 9, 2001).

SCHEDULE 4

[² EQUALISATION OF AND INCREASE IN PENSIONABLE AGE FOR MEN AND WOMEN]

PART I

PENSIONABLE AGES FOR MEN AND WOMEN

1.676   **1.**—The following rules apply for the purposes of the enactments relating to social security, that is, the following Acts and the instruments made, or having effect as if made, under them: the Social Security Contributions and Benefits Act 1992, the Social Security Administration Act 1992 and the Pension Schemes Act 1993.

Rules

1.677   (1) A man [² born before 6th April 1959] attains pensionable age when he attains the age of 65 years.

(2) A woman born before 6th April 1950 attains pensionable age when she attains the age of 60.

(3) A woman born on any day in a period mentioned in column 1 of [² table 1] attains pensionable age at the commencement of the day shown against that period in column 2.

[² (4) A woman born after 5th April 1955 but before 6th April 1959 attains pensionable age when she attains the age of 65]

[² TABLE 1]

(1) *Period within which woman's birthday falls*	(2) *Day pensionable age attained*
6th April 1950 to 5th May 1950	6th May 2010
6th May 1950 to 5th June 1950	6th July 2010
6th June 1950 to 5th July 1950	6th September 2010
6th July 1950 to 5th August 1950	6th November 2010
6th August 1950 to 5th September 1950	6th January 2011
6th September 1950 to 5th October 1950	6th March 2011
6th October 1950 to 5th November 1950	6th May 2011
6th November 1950 to 5th December 1950	6th July 2011
6th December 1950 to 5th January 1951	6th September 2011
6th January 1951 to 5th February 1951	6th November 2011
6th February 1951 to 5th March 1951	6th January 2012
6th March 1951 to 5th April 1951	6th March 2012
6th April 1951 to 5th May 1951	6th May 2012
6th May 1951 to 5th June 1951	6th July 2012
6th June 1951 to 5th July 1951	6th September 2012
6th July 1951 to 5th August 1951	6th November 2012

1.678 (to the left of the table)

[² TABLE 1]

(1) Period within which woman's birthday falls	(2) Day pensionable age attained
6th August 1951 to 5th September 1951	6th January 2013
6th September 1951 to 5th October 1951	6th March 2013
6th October 1951 to 5th November 1951	6th May 2013
6th November 1951 to 5th December 1951	6th July 2013
6th December 1951 to 5th January 1952	6th September 2013
6th January 1952 to 5th February 1952	6th November 2013
6th February 1952 to 5th March 1952	6th January 2014
6th March 1952 to 5th April 1952	6th March 2014
6th April 1952 to 5th May 1952	6th May 2014
6th May 1952 to 5th June 1952	6th July 2014
6th June 1952 to 5th July 1952	6th September 2014
6th July 1952 to 5th August 1952	6th November 2014
6th August 1952 to 5th September 1952	6th January 2015
6th September 1952 to 5th October 1952	6th March 2015
6th October 1952 to 5th November 1952	6th May 2015
6th November 1952 to 5th December 1952	6th July 2015
6th December 1952 to 5th January 1953	6th September 2015
6th January 1953 to 5th February 1953	6th November 2015
6th February 1953 to 5th March 1953	6th January 2016
6th March 1953 to 5th April 1953	6th March 2016
6th April 1953 to 5th May 1953	6th May 2016
6th May 1953 to 5th June 1953	6th July 2016
6th June 1953 to 5th July 1953	6th September 2016
6th July 1953 to 5th August 1953	6th November 2016
6th August 1953 to 5th September 1953	6th January 2017
6th September 1953 to 5th October 1953	6th March 2017
6th October 1953 to 5th November 1953	6th May 2017
6th November 1953 to 5th December 1953	6th July 2017
6th December 1953 to 5th January 1954	6th September 2017
6th January 1954 to 5th February 1954	6th November 2017
6th February 1954 to 5th March 1954	6th January 2018
6th March 1954 to 5th April 1954	6th March 2018
6th April 1954 to 5th May 1954	6th May 2018
6th May 1954 to 5th June 1954	6th July 2018
6th June 1954 to 5th July 1954	6th September 2018
6th July 1954 to 5th August 1954	6th November 2018
6th August 1954 to 5th September 1954	6th January 2019
6th September 1954 to 5th October 1954	6th March 2019
6th October 1954 to 5th November 1954	6th May 2019
6th November 1954 to 5th December 1954	6th July 2019
6th December 1954 to 5th January 1955	6th September 2019
6th January 1955 to 5th February 1955	6th November 2019
6th February 1955 to 5th March 1955	6th January 2020
6th March 1955 to 5th April 1955	6th March 2020

[² (5) A person born on any day in a period mentioned in column 1 of table 2 attains pensionable age at the commencement of the day shown against that period in column 2.

1.679

TABLE 2

(1) *Period within which birthday falls*	(2) *Day pensionable age attained*
6th April 1959 to 5th May 1959	6th May 2024
6th May 1959 to 5th June 1959	6th July 2024
6th June 1959 to 5th July 1959	6th September 2024
6th July 1959 to 5th August 1959	6th November 2024
6th August 1959 to 5th September 1959	6th January 2025
6th September 1959 to 5th October 1959	6th March 2025
6th October 1959 to 5th November 1959	6th May 2025
6th November 1959 to 5th December 1959	6th July 2025
6th December 1959 to 5th January 1960	6th September 2025
6th January 1960 to 5th February 1960	6th November 2025
6th February 1960 to 5th March 1960	6th January 2026
6th March 1960 to 5th April 1960	6th March 2026

(6) A person born after 5th April 1960 but before 6th April 1968 attains pensionable age when the person attains the age of 66.

(7) A person born on any day in a period mentioned in column 1 of table 3 attains pensionable age at the commencement of the day shown against that period in column 2.

1.680

TABLE 3

(1) *Period within which birthday falls*	(2) *Day pensionable age attained*
6th April 1968 to 5th May 1968	6th May 2034
6th May 1968 to 5th June 1968	6th July 2034
6th June 1968 to 5th July 1968	6th September 2034
6th July 1968 to 5th August 1968	6th November 2034
6th August 1968 to 5th September 1968	6th January 2035
6th September 1968 to 5th October 1968	6th March 2035
6th October 1968 to 5th November 1968	6th May 2035
6th November 1968 to 5th December 1968	6th July 2035
6th December 1968 to 5th January 1969	6th September 2035
6th January 1969 to 5th February 1969	6th November 2035
6th February 1969 to 5th March 1969	6th January 2036
6th March 1969 to 5th April 1969	6th March 2036

(8) A person born after 5th April 1969 but before 6th April 1977 attains pensionable age when the person attains the age of 67.

(9) A person born on any day in a period mentioned in column 1 of table 4 attains pensionable age at the commencement of the day shown against that period in column 2.

1.681

TABLE 4

(1) *Period within which birthday falls*	(2) *Day pensionable age attained*
6th April 1977 to 5th May 1977	6th May 2044
6th May 1977 to 5th June 1977	6th July 2044
6th June 1977 to 5th July 1977	6th September 2044
6th July 1977 to 5th August 1977	6th November 2044
6th August 1977 to 5th September 1977	6th January 2045
6th September 1977 to 5th October 1977	6th March 2045

TABLE 4

(1) Period within which birthday falls	(2) Day pensionable age attained
6th October 1977 to 5th November 1977	6th May 2045
6th November 1977 to 5th December 1977	6th July 2045
6th December 1977 to 5th January 1978	6th September 2045
6th January 1978 to 5th February 1978	6th November 2045
6th February 1978 to 5th March 1978	6th January 2046
6th March 1978 to 5th April 1978	6th March 2046

(10) A person born after 5th April 1978 attains pensionable age when the person attains the age of 68.]

PART II

ENTITLEMENT TO CERTAIN PENSIONS AND OTHER BENEFITS

Pension increases for dependent spouses

2.— [³ . . .]   **1.682**

Category B retirement pensions

3.—(1) *Omitted.*   **1.683**

(2) Section 48A of that Act (as inserted by this paragraph) does not confer a right to a Category B retirement pension on a man by reason of his marriage to a woman who was born before 6th April, 1950.

(3) Section 48B of that Act (as inserted by this paragraph) does not confer a right to a Category B retirement pension on a man who attains pensionable age before 6th April, 2010; and section 51 of that Act does not confer a right to a Category B retirement pension on a man who attains pensionable age on or after that date.

Home responsibilities protection

4.—(1) In paragraph 5 of Schedule 3 to the Social Security Contributions and Benefits Act   **1.684**
1992 (contribution conditions for entitlement to retirement pension), in sub-paragraph (7)(a) (condition that contributor must have paid or been credited with contributions of the relevant class for not less than the requisite number of years modified in the case of those precluded from regular employment by responsibilities at home), "(or at least 20 of them, if that is less than half)" is omitted.

(2) This paragraph shall have effect in relation to any person attaining pensionable age on or after 6th April 2010.

5.—*Omitted.*

Increments

6.—(1) In section 54(1) of the Social Security Contributions and Benefits Act 1992 (elec-   **1.685**
tion to defer right to pension), in paragraph (a), the words from "but" to "70" are omitted.

(2) In Schedule 5 to that Act—
  (a) in paragraph 2(2), the definition of "period of enhancement" (and the preceding "and") are omitted, and
  (b) for "period of enhancement" (in every other place in paragraphs 2 and 3 where it appears) there is substituted "period of deferment".

(3) In paragraph 2(3) of that Schedule, for "1/7th per cent." there is substituted "1/5th per cent."

(4) In paragraph 8 of that Schedule, sub-paragraphs (1) and (2) are omitted.

(5) [¹(5) The preceding sub-paragraphs shall come into force as follows—
  (a) sub-paragraphs (1) and (4) shall come into force on 6th April 2005;
  (b) sub-paragraphs (2) and (3) shall have effect in relation to incremental periods (within the meaning of Schedule 5 to the Social Security Contributions and Benefits Act 1992 (c. 4)) beginning on or after that date.]

Pensions Act 1995

Graduated retirement benefit

1.686   **7.**—*Omitted.*

Christmas bonus for pensioners

1.687   **8.**—*Omitted.*

PART III

CONSEQUENTIAL AMENDMENTS

Category B retirement pensions

1.688   **21.**—(1)–(13) *Omitted.*

(14) Paragraph 4(1) of that Schedule (as inserted by sub-paragraph (13) above) shall have effect where W is a man who attains pensionable age before 6th April, 2010 as if paragraph (a) also required him to have been over pensionable age when S died.

(15) *Omitted.*

(16) Paragraph 5(1) of that Schedule (inserted by sub-paragraph (15) above) shall have effect, where W is a man who attained pensionable age before 6th April, 2010, as if paragraph (a) also required him to have been over pensionable age when S died.

(17) and (18) *Omitted.*

AMENDMENTS

1. Pensions Act 2004, s.297 (April 6, 2005).
2. Pensions Act 2007, Sch.3, para.3 (September 26, 2007).
3. Pensions Act 2007, Sch.7, Pt 2 (September 26, 2007).

GENERAL NOTE

1.689–1.695   Reference to that Schedule in para.21 above is a reference to Sch.5 of the SSCBA 1992.

Welfare Reform and Pensions Act 1999

(1999 c.30)

SECTIONS REPRODUCED

PART IV

PENSION SHARING

CHAPTER II

SHARING OF STATE SCHEME RIGHTS

1.696   47. Shareable state scheme rights.
48. Activation of benefit sharing.
49. Creation of state scheme pension debits and credits.
50. Effect of state scheme pension debits and credits.
51. Interpretation of Chapter II.

370

CHAPTER II

SHARING OF STATE SCHEME RIGHTS

Shareable State Scheme rights

47.—(1) Pension sharing is available under this Chapter in relation to a person's shareable state scheme rights.

(2) For the purposes of this Chapter, a person's shareable state scheme rights are—

   (a) his entitlement, or prospective entitlement, to a Category A retirement pension by virtue of section 44(3)(b) of the Contributions and Benefits Act (earnings-related additional pension), and

   (b) his entitlement, or prospective entitlement, to a pension under section 55A of that Act (shared additional pension).

1.697

Activation of Benefits and Sharing

48.—(1) Section 49 applies on the taking effect of any of the following relating to a person's shareable state scheme rights—

   (a) a pension sharing order under the Matrimonial Causes Act 1973,

   (b) provision which corresponds to the provision which may be made by such an order and which—

      (i) is contained in a qualifying agreement between the parties to a marriage, and

      (ii) takes effect on the dissolution of the marriage under the Family Law Act 1996,

   (c) provision which corresponds to the provision which may be made by such an order and which—

      (i) is contained in a qualifying agreement between the parties to a marriage or former marriage, and

      (ii) takes effect after the dissolution of the marriage under the Family Law Act 1996,

   (d) an order under Part III of the Matrimonial and Family Proceedings Act 1984 (financial relief in England and Wales in relation to overseas divorce etc.) corresponding to such an order as is mentioned in paragraph (a),

   (e) a pension sharing order under the Family Law (Scotland) Act 1985,

   (f) provision which corresponds to the provision which may be made by such an order and which—

      (i) is contained in a qualifying agreement between the parties to a marriage,

      (ii) is in such form as the Secretary of State may prescribe by regulations, and

      (iii) takes effect on the grant, in relation to the marriage, of decree of divorce under the Divorce (Scotland) Act 1976 or of declarator of nullity,

   (g) an order under Part IV of the Matrimonial and Family Proceedings Act 1984 (financial relief in Scotland in relation to overseas divorce etc.) corresponding to such an order as is mentioned in paragraph (e),

   (h) a pension sharing order under Northern Ireland legislation, and

      (i) an order under Part IV of the Matrimonial and Family

1.698

Proceedings (Northern Ireland) Order 1989 (financial relief in Northern Ireland in relation to overseas divorce etc.) corresponding to such an order as is mentioned in paragraph (h).

(2) For the purposes of subsection (1)(b) and (c), a qualifying agreement is one which—

(a) has been entered into in such circumstances as the Lord Chancellor may prescribe by regulations, and

(b) satisfies such requirements as the Lord Chancellor may so prescribe.

(3) For the purposes of subsection (1)(f), a qualifying agreement is one which—

(a) has been entered into in such circumstances as the Secretary of State may prescribe by regulations, and

(b) is registered in the Books of Council and Session.

(4) Subsection (1)(b) does not apply if the provision relates to rights which are the subject of a pension sharing order under the Matrimonial Causes Act 1973 in relation to the marriage.

(5) Subsection (1)(c) does not apply if—

(a) the marriage was dissolved by an order under section 3 of the Family Law Act 1996 (divorce not preceded by separation) and the satisfaction of the requirements of section 9(2) of that Act (settlement of future financial arrangements) was a precondition to the making of the order,

(b) the provision relates to rights which are the subject of a pension sharing order under the Matrimonial Causes Act 1973 in relation to the marriage, or

(c) shareable state scheme rights have already been the subject of pension sharing between the parties.

(6) For the purposes of this section, an order or provision falling within subsection (1)(e), (f) or (g) shall be deemed never to have taken effect if the Secretary of State does not receive before the end of the period of 2 months beginning with the relevant date—

(a) copies of the relevant [1 . . .] documents, and

(b) such information relating to the transferor and transferee as the Secretary of State may prescribe by regulations under section 34(1)(b)(ii).

(7) The relevant date for the purposes of subsection (6) is—

(a) in the case of an order or provision falling within subsection (1)(e) or (f), the date of the extract of the decree or declarator responsible for the divorce or annulment to which the order or provision relates, and

(b) in the cases of an order falling within subsection (1)(g), the date of disposal of the application under section 28 of the Matrimonial and Family Proceedings Act 1984.

(8) The reference in subsection (6)(a) to the relevant [1 . . .] documents is—

(a) in the case of an order falling within subsection (1)(e) or (g), to copies of the order and the order, decree or declarator responsible for the divorce or annulment to which it relates, and

(b) in the case of provision falling within subsection (1)(f), to—

(i) copies of the provision and the order, decree or declarator responsible for the divorce or annulment to which it relates, and

(ii) documentary evidence that the agreement containing the provision is one to which subsection (3)(a) applies.

(9) The sheriff may, on the application of any person having an interest, make an order—

(a) extending the period of two months referred to in subsection (6), and

(b) if that period has already expired, providing that, if the Secretary of State receives the documents and information concerned before the end of the period specified in the order, subsection (6) is to be treated as never having applied.

AMENDMENT

1. Civil Partnership Act 2004, Sch.24 (December 5, 2005).

Creation of State Scheme pension debits and credits

49.—(1) On the application of this section—   1.699

(a) the transferor becomes subject, for the purposes of Part II of the Contributions and Benefits Act (contributory benefits), to a debit of the appropriate amount, and

(b) the transferee becomes entitled, for those purposes, to a credit of that amount.

(2) Where the relevant order or provision specifies a percentage value to be transferred, the appropriate amount for the purposes of subsection (1) is the specified percentage of the cash equivalent on the transfer day of the transferor's shareable state scheme rights immediately before that day.

(3) Where the relevant order or provision specifies an amount to be transferred, the appropriate amount for the purposes of subsection (1) is the lesser of—

(a) the specified amount, and

(b) the cash equivalent on the transfer day of the transferor's relevant state scheme rights immediately before that day.

(4) Cash equivalents for the purposes of this section shall be calculated in accordance with regulations made by the Secretary of State.

(5) In determining prospective entitlement to a Category A retirement pension for the purposes of this section, only tax years before that in which the transfer day falls shall be taken into account.

(6) In this section—

"relevant order or provision" means the order or provision by virtue of which this section applies;

"transfer day" means the day on which the relevant order or provision takes effect;

"transferor" means the person to whose rights the relevant order or provision relates;

"transferee" means the person for whose benefit the relevant order or provision is made.

Effect of state scheme pension debits and credits

50.—(1) *Omitted because taken into account in amending other statutory*   1.700
text.

(2) *Omitted because relevant only to incremental periods beginning on or after April 6, 2010.*

Interpretation of Chapter II

1.701   **51.**—In this chapter—
"shareable state scheme rights" has the meaning given by section 47(2); and
"tax year" has the meaning given by section 122(1) of the Contributions and Benefits Act.

Gender Recognition Act 2004

(2004 c.7)

ARRANGEMENT OF SECTIONS

Schedule 5
An Act to make provision for and in connection with change of gender.

COMMENCEMENT

Certain formalities provisions entered into force on Royal Assent, but the whole Act entered into force on April 4, 2005: The Gender Recognition Act 2004 (Commencement) Order 2005 (SI 2005/54).

GENERAL NOTE

1.703   This Act makes provision, for the first time, for recognition of a change of gender identity for a transsexual. It follows judgments of the European Court of Human Rights against the United Kingdom finding violations of Convention rights in *Goodwin v United Kingdom* (App. 28957/95), Judgment of July 11, 2002, (2002) 35 E.H.R.R. 18, and *I v United Kingdom* (App. 25680/94), Judgment of July 11, 2002, (2003) 36 E.H.R.R. 53.

The scheme introduced by the Act is essentially a system of recognition of gender identity through the issue of a gender recognition certificate. The qualifying conditions for such a certificate are that the applicant (1) has or has had gender dysphoria; (2) has lived in the acquired gender for at least two years; and (3) intends to continue to live in the acquired gender until death. There is no requirement that an applicant has undergone gender reassignment surgery. Provision is made for recognition of a change of gender identity under the law of another country.

Provision is made for two types of certificate: an interim certificate and a full certificate. Unmarried applicants can only receive full certificates, whereas married applicants can only receive interim certificates. Matrimonial law is amended so that the issue of an interim certificate constitutes a ground for a marriage to be declared a nullity provided that proceedings are begun within six months of issue of the certificate. A court declaring a marriage a nullity under this ground must also issue a full gender recognition certificate.

The effect of the full certificate is to be found in s.9 which provides that a person's gender becomes for all purposes the acquired gender, although it does not affect things done or events occurring before the certificate is issued. This general principle is made subject to the express provisions of this Act and any other enactment. It is destined to become known as the "section 9 principle".

The Act contains a range of provisions seeking to work out the practical implications of the issue of a gender recognition certificate. Section 13 and Sch.5 concern social security benefits and pensions. These provisions are concerned only with old age and survivors benefits. The operation of the provisions of the section 9 principle will apply in relation to applications for any social security benefit not covered in this part of the Act, and that should be the starting point for any determination of an application for such benefit by the holder of a full gender recognition certificate.

Social security benefits and pensions

13. Schedule 5 (entitlement to benefits and pensions) has effect.

1.704

GENERAL NOTE

The provisions of the Schedule constitute a set of free-standing rules rather than amendments to the Contributions and Benefits Act (and its counterparts elsewhere in the United Kingdom). They apply where a person holds a full gender recognition certificate. Perhaps unsurprisingly where the change of gender identity is from female to male, the rules applicable to men apply. These are, of course, generally less favourable in the field of old age and survivors benefits because of the age discrimination still operative in this area of social security. However, where the change of identity is from male to female, the position is less straightforward. Provision is made for entitlement to a retirement pension at age 60, but generally in relation to entitlement to benefits based on a spouse's national insurance contributions, there is no automatic passport to these.

1.705

Commissioners have decided that provisions of the Gender Recognition Act 2004 are not compatible with the prohibition of discrimination in art.4(1) of Directive 79/7/EEC. Note, in particular, *CIB/2248/2006* and the decisions of a Tribunal of Commissioners in *CP/1425/2007*, *CSP/503/2007* and *CP/2862/2007*. These are discussed in more detail in the annotations to art.4 of Directive 79/7/EEC in Volume III.

Interpretation

25. In this Act—

1.706

"the acquired gender" is to be construed in accordance with s.1(2),

"approved country or territory" has the meaning given by s.2(4),

"the appointed day" means the day appointed by order under s.26,

"chartered psychologist" means a person for the time being listed in the British Psychological Society's Register of Chartered Psychologists,

"enactment" includes an enactment contained in an Act of the Scottish Parliament or in any Northern Ireland legislation,

"full gender recognition certificate" and "interim gender recognition certificate" mean the certificates issued as such under [[1] section 4, 5 or 5A] and "gender recognition certificate" means either of those sorts of certificate,

"gender dysphoria" means the disorder variously referred to as gender dysphoria, gender identity disorder and transsexualism,

"Gender Recognition Panel" (and "Panel") is to be construed in accordance with Sch.1,

"subordinate legislation" means an Order in Council, an order, rules, regulations, a scheme, a warrant, bye-laws or any other instrument made under an enactment, and

"UK birth register entry" has the meaning given by s.10(2).

AMENDMENT

1. Civil Partnership Act 2004, Pt 7, s.250(7) (December 5, 2005).

SCHEDULE 5

BENEFITS AND PENSIONS

PART I

INTRODUCTORY

1.707   1. This Schedule applies where a full gender recognition certificate is issued to a person.

PART II

STATE BENEFITS

Introductory

1.708   2.—(1) In this Part of this Schedule "the 1992 Act" means—
(a) in England and Wales and Scotland, the Social Security Contributions and Benefits Act 1992 (c. 4), and
(b) in Northern Ireland, the Social Security Contributions and Benefits (Northern Ireland) Act 1992 (c. 7).

(2) In this Part of this Schedule "the Administration Act" means—
(a) in England and Wales and Scotland, the Social Security Administration Act 1992 (c. 5), and
(b) in Northern Ireland, the Social Security Administration (Northern Ireland) Act 1992 (c. 8).

(3) Expressions used in this Part of this Schedule and in Part 2 of the 1992 Act have the same meaning in this Part of this Schedule as in Part 2 of the 1992 Act.

Widowed mother's allowance

1.709   3.—(1) If (immediately before the certificate is issued) the person is, or but for section 1 of the Administration Act would be, entitled to a widowed mother's allowance under section 37 of the 1992 Act (allowance for woman whose husband died before 9th April 2001)—
(a) the person is not entitled to that allowance afterwards, but
(b) (instead) subsections (2) to (5) of section 39A of the 1992 Act (widowed parent's allowance) apply in relation to the person.

(2) If (immediately before the certificate is issued) the person is (actually) entitled to a widowed mother's allowance, the entitlement to widowed parent's allowance conferred by sub-paragraph (1) is not subject to section 1 of the Administration Act.

GENERAL NOTE

1.710   This paragraph applies in the case of a female to male transsexual. If, immediately prior to the issue of the certificate, the person was (or would be but for having made a claim) entitled to widowed mother's allowance, entitlement to that benefit ceases on issue of the certificate, but the man becomes entitled to claim a widowed parent's allowance under the specified provisions of the Contributions and Benefits Act. If, however, widowed mother's allowance has been claimed and awarded, then the benefit converts to widowed parent's allowance without the need for a claim.

Widow's pension

1.711   4. If (immediately before the certificate is issued) the person is entitled to a widow's pension under section 38 of the 1992 Act (pension for woman whose husband died before 9th April 2001), the person is not entitled to that pension afterwards.

GENERAL NOTE

1.712   This paragraph applies in the case of a female to male transsexual. Since there is no equivalent pension under the bereavement benefits scheme (a widower's pension), the entitlement to the widow's pension ceases on issue of the certificate.

Widowed parent's allowance

5. If (immediately before the certificate is issued) the person is, or but for section 1 of the Administration Act would be, entitled to a widowed parent's allowance by virtue of subsection (1)(b) of section 39A of the 1992 Act (allowance for man whose wife died before 9th April 2001), subsections (2) to (5) of that section continue to apply in relation to the person afterwards.

1.713

GENERAL NOTE

Widowed parent's allowance is predominantly a gender neutral benefit, and the provision here is simply for entitlement to widowed parent's allowance to continue where a man has claimed in respect of a bereavement before April 2001. However, women in receipt of widowed mother's allowance have the potential right to move on to widow's pension, but no provision is made for transfer in a relevant case from widowed parent's allowance to widowed mother's allowance.

1.714

Long-term incapacity benefit etc.

6. If (immediately before the certificate is issued) the person is entitled to incapacity benefit, or a Category A retirement pension, under—

(a) section 40 of the 1992 Act (long-term incapacity benefit etc. for woman whose husband died before 9th April 2001), or

(b) section 41 of the 1992 Act (long-term incapacity benefit etc. for man whose wife died before that date),

the person is not so entitled afterwards.

1.715

GENERAL NOTE

The effect of these provisions is at first surprising. Sections 40 and 41 make provision respectively for widow and widowers which enabled a person incapable of work at the time of the bereavement to claim incapacity benefit even though the contribution conditions were not satisfied. On reaching pensionable age, the incapacity benefit would convert into a Category A retirement pension if the person was not otherwise entitled to retirement pension. For both male to female, and female to male, transsexuals, the entitlement to incapacity benefit on this basis ceases. This would appear to be because the principle adopted throughout the Schedule would seem to be to treat all those holding a gender recognition certificate as if they had been bereaved *after* April 2001. Sections 40 and 41 apply only where the person was bereaved before April 2001.

For a case exploring the position prior to the Gender Recognition Act, see *CT v SSWP* [2009] UKUT 49 (AAC).

1.716

Category A retirement pension

7.—(1) Any question—

(a) whether the person is entitled to a Category A retirement pension (under section 44 of the 1992 Act) for any period after the certificate is issued, and

(b) (if so) the rate at which the person is so entitled for the period,

is to be decided as if the person's gender had always been the acquired gender.

(2) Accordingly, if (immediately before the certificate is issued) the person—

(a) is a woman entitled to a Category A retirement pension, but

(b) has not attained the age of 65,

the person ceases to be so entitled when it is issued.

(3) And, conversely, if (immediately before the certificate is issued) the person—

(a) is a man who has attained the age at which a woman of the same age attains pensionable age, but

(b) has not attained the age of 65,

the person is to be treated for the purposes of section 44 of the 1992 Act as attaining pensionable age when it is issued.

(4) But sub-paragraph (1) does not apply if and to the extent that the decision of any question to which it refers is affected by—

1.717

    (a) the payment or crediting of contributions, or the crediting of earnings, in respect of a period ending before the certificate is issued, or

    (b) preclusion from regular employment by responsibilities at home for such a period.

(5) Paragraph 10 makes provision about deferment of Category A retirement pensions.

GENERAL NOTE

1.718   The general principle in sub-paragraph (1) is an exception to the section 9 principle, because for these purposes the person's acquired gender is treated as though it has always been the person's gender. So a female to male transsexual who changes gender between the ages of 60 and 65 ceases to be entitled to any Category A retirement pension awarded, whereas a male to female transsexual who changes gender between the ages of 60 and 65 is treated for the purposes of determining entitlement to a Category A retirement pension as though she attained pensionable age on the date of issue of the certificate, but not before. There is no retrospectivity of entitlement.

     Note that, although art.7(1) provides that any question of entitlement, and, if so, the rate of entitlement, is to be decided as if the person's acquired gender had always been their gender, this is subject to an exception in para.(4) that covers the payment and crediting of contributions, and the treatment of earnings that have been made before the change of gender. In *CP/98/2007*, the claimant was over 65 at the time she changed her gender from male to female. The decision maker decided that the contributions she had made between the ages of 60 and 65, when she was a man, should not be included in calculating her additional state pension, but the Commissioner allowed her appeal on the basis of the exception provided in para.(4).

Category B retirement pension etc.

1.719   **8.**—(1) Any question whether the person is entitled to—

    (a) a Category B retirement pension (under section 48A, 48B, 48BB or 51 of the 1992 Act), or

    (b) an increase in a Category A retirement pension under section 51A or 52 of the 1992 Act (increase in Category A retirement pension by reference to amount of Category B retirement pension),

for any period after the certificate is issued is (in accordance with section 9(1)) to be decided as if the person's gender were the acquired gender (but subject to sub-paragraph (4)).

(2) Accordingly, if (immediately before the certificate is issued) the person is a woman entitled to—

    (a) a Category B retirement pension, or

    (b) an increase in a Category A retirement pension under section 51A or 52 of the 1992 Act,

the person may cease to be so entitled when it is issued.

(3) And, conversely, if (immediately before the certificate is issued) the person—

    (a) is a man who has attained the age at which a woman of the same age attains pensionable age, but

    (b) has not attained the age of 65,

the person is to be treated for the purposes of sections 48A, 48B and 48BB of the 1992 Act as attaining pensionable age when it is issued.

(4) But a person who is a man (immediately before the certificate is issued) is not entitled to a Category B retirement pension under section 48B of the 1992 Act for any period after it is issued if the person—

    (a) attains (or has attained) the age of 65 before 6th April 2010, and

    (b) would not have been entitled to a Category B retirement pension under section 51 of the 1992 Act for that period if still a man.

(5) Paragraph 10 makes provision about deferment of Category B retirement pensions.

GENERAL NOTE

1.720   These rather complex provisions reflect the four different routes to entitlement to a Category B retirement pension coupled with the change which will come into effect in 2010 under which men will begin to acquire entitlement to Category B retirement pension. The general principle adopted in relation to acquisition of entitlement to a Category B retirement pension is that any question of entitlement after the issue of a gender recognition certificate is to be determined by applying the rules applicable to persons of the acquired gender. That means that if the acquired gender is that of a woman, the rules applicable to women are applied to the claimant, and, if the acquired gender is that of a man, the rules applicable to men are applied to the claimant. In both cases no concessions to the change of gender identity are made. The exception is sub-paragraph (4) which limits the ability of a male to female transsexual acquiring entitlement under s.48B of the Contributions and Benefits Act.

Shared additional pension

9.—(1) Any question—
  (a) whether the person is entitled to a shared additional pension (under section 55A of the 1992 Act) for any period after the certificate is issued, and
  (b) (if so) the rate at which the person is so entitled for the period,
is to be decided on the basis of the person attaining pensionable age on the same date as someone of the acquired gender (and the same age).
(2) Accordingly, if (immediately before the certificate is issued) the person—
  (a) is a woman entitled to a shared additional pension, but
  (b) has not attained the age of 65,
the person ceases to be so entitled when it is issued.
(3) And, conversely, if (immediately before the certificate is issued) the person—
  (a) is a man who has attained the age at which a woman of the same age attains pensionable age, but
  (b) has not attained the age of 65,
the person is to be treated for the purposes of section 55A of the 1992 Act as attaining pensionable age when it is issued.
(4) Paragraph 10 makes provision about deferment of shared additional pensions.

1.721

Deferment of pensions

10.—(1) The person's entitlement to—
  (a) a Category A retirement pension,
  (b) a Category B retirement pension, or
  (c) a shared additional pension,
is not to be taken to have been deferred for any period ending before the certificate is issued unless the condition in sub-paragraph (2) is satisfied.
(2) The condition is that the entitlement both—
  (a) was actually deferred during the period, and
  (b) would have been capable of being so deferred had the person's gender been the acquired gender.

1.722

GENERAL NOTE

The principle applied here is that there can be no notional deferment of pension on recognition of a change of gender identity.

1.723

Category C retirement pension for widows

11. If (immediately before the certificate is issued) the person is entitled to a Category C retirement pension under section 78(2) of the 1992 Act, the person is not entitled to that pension afterwards.

1.724

GENERAL NOTE

It would be surprising if this provision proves problematic in operation, since it relates (a) to persons who attained pensionable age before July 5, 1948, and (b) to the wives and widows of such persons. A change of gender identity from woman to man results in the loss of the entitlement.

1.725

Graduated retirement benefit: Great Britain

12.—(1) The provision that may be made by regulations under paragraph 15 of Schedule 3 to the Social Security (Consequential Provisions) Act 1992 (c. 6) (power to retain provisions repealed by Social Security Act 1973 (c. 38), with or without modification, for transitional purposes) includes provision modifying the preserved graduated retirement benefit provisions in consequence of this Act.

1.726

(2) "The preserved graduated retirement benefit provisions" are the provisions of the National Insurance Act 1965 (c. 51) relating to graduated retirement benefit continued in force, with or without modification, by regulations having effect as if made under that paragraph.

Graduated retirement benefit: Northern Ireland

1.727   **13.**—(1) The provision that may be made by regulations under paragraph 15 of Schedule 3 to the Social Security (Consequential Provisions) (Northern Ireland) Act 1992 (c. 9) (corresponding power for Northern Ireland) includes provision modifying the Northern Ireland preserved graduated retirement benefit provisions in consequence of this Act.

(2) "The Northern Ireland preserved graduated retirement benefit provisions" are the provisions of the National Insurance Act (Northern Ireland) 1966 (c. 6 (N.I.)) relating to graduated retirement benefit continued in force, with or without modification, by regulations having effect as if made under that paragraph.

PART 3

OCCUPATIONAL PENSION SCHEMES

GENERAL NOTE

1.728   The Schedule does not make any rules about occupational pension schemes, but it does have to deal with the provisions guaranteeing those in receipt of occupational pensions the guaranteed minimum pension, and preserved equivalent pension benefits.

Guaranteed minimum pensions etc.: Great Britain

1.729   **14.**—(1) In this paragraph "the 1993 Act" means the Pension Schemes Act 1993 (c. 48); and expressions used in this paragraph and in that Act have the same meaning in this paragraph as in that Act.

(2) The fact that the person's gender has become the acquired gender does not affect the operation of section 14 of the 1993 Act (guaranteed minimum) in relation to the person, except to the extent that its operation depends on section 16 of the 1993 Act (revaluation); and sub-paragraphs (3) and (5) have effect subject to that.

(3) If (immediately before the certificate is issued) the person is a woman who is entitled to a guaranteed minimum pension but has not attained the age of 65—

  (a) the person is for the purposes of section 13 of the 1993 Act and the guaranteed minimum pension provisions to be treated after it is issued as not having attained pensionable age (so that the entitlement ceases) but as attaining pensionable age on subsequently attaining the age of 65, and

  (b) in a case where the person's guaranteed minimum pension has commenced before the certificate is issued, it is to be treated for the purposes of Chapter 3 of Part 4 of the 1993 Act (anti-franking) as if it had not.

(4) But sub-paragraph (3)(a) does not—

  (a) affect any pension previously paid to the person, or

  (b) prevent section 15 of the 1993 Act (increase of guaranteed minimum where commencement of guaranteed minimum pension postponed) operating to increase the person's guaranteed minimum by reason of a postponement of the commencement of the person's guaranteed minimum pension for a period ending before the certificate is issued.

(5) If (immediately before the certificate is issued) the person is a man who—

  (a) has attained the age of 60, but

  (b) has not attained the age of 65,

the person is to be treated for the purposes of section 13 of the 1993 Act and the guaranteed minimum pension provisions as attaining pensionable age when it is issued.

(6) If at that time the person has attained the age of 65, the fact that the person's gender has become the acquired gender does not affect the person's pensionable age for those purposes.

(7) The fact that the person's gender has become the acquired gender does not affect any guaranteed minimum pension to which the person is entitled as a widow or widower immediately before the certificate is issued (except in consequence of the operation of the previous provisions of this Schedule).

(8) If a transaction to which section 19 of the 1993 Act applies which is carried out before the certificate is issued discharges a liability to provide a guaranteed minimum pension for or in respect of the person, it continues to do so afterwards.

(9) "The guaranteed minimum pension provision" means so much of the 1993 Act

(apart from section 13) and of any other enactment as relates to guaranteed minimum pensions.

Guaranteed minimum pensions etc.: Northern Ireland

15.—(1) In this paragraph "the 1993 Act" means the Pension Schemes (Northern Ireland) Act 1993 (c. 49); and expressions used in this paragraph and in that Act have the same meaning in this paragraph as in that Act.   **1.730**

(2) The fact that the person's gender has become the acquired gender does not affect the operation of section 10 of the 1993 Act (guaranteed minimum) in relation to the person, except to the extent that its operation depends on section 12 of the 1993 Act (revaluation); and sub-paragraphs (3) and (5) have effect subject to that.

(3) If (immediately before the certificate is issued) the person is a woman who is entitled to a guaranteed minimum pension but has not attained the age of 65—

    (a) the person is for the purposes of section 9 of the 1993 Act and the guaranteed minimum pension provisions to be treated after it is issued as not having attained pensionable age (so that the entitlement ceases) but as attaining pensionable age on subsequently attaining the age of 65, and

    (b) in a case where the person's guaranteed minimum pension has commenced before the certificate is issued, it is to be treated for the purposes of Chapter 3 of Part 4 of the 1993 Act (anti-franking) as if it had not.

(4) But sub-paragraph (3)(a) does not—

    (a) affect any pension previously paid to the person, or

    (b) prevent section 11 of the 1993 Act (increase of guaranteed minimum where commencement of guaranteed minimum pension postponed) operating to increase the person's guaranteed minimum by reason of a postponement of the commencement of the person's guaranteed minimum pension for a period ending before the certificate is issued.

(5) If (immediately before the certificate is issued) the person is a man who—

    (a) has attained the age of 60, but

    (b) has not attained the age of 65,

the person is to be treated for the purposes of section 9 of the 1993 Act and the guaranteed minimum pension provisions as attaining pensionable age when it is issued.

(6) If at that time the person has attained the age of 65, the fact that the person's gender has become the acquired gender does not affect the person's pensionable age for those purposes.

(7) The fact that the person's gender has become the acquired gender does not affect any guaranteed minimum pension to which the person is entitled as a widow or widower immediately before the certificate is issued (except in consequence of the operation of the previous provisions of this Schedule).

(8) If a transaction to which section 15 of the 1993 Act applies which is carried out before the certificate is issued discharges a liability to provide a guaranteed minimum pension for or in respect of the person, it continues to do so afterwards.

(9) "The guaranteed minimum pension provision" means so much of the 1993 Act (apart from section 9) and of any other enactment as relates to guaranteed minimum pensions.

Equivalent pension benefits: Great Britain

16.—(1) The provision that may be made by regulations under paragraph 15 of Schedule 3 to the Social Security (Consequential Provisions) Act 1992 (c. 6) (power to retain provisions repealed by Social Security Act 1973 (c. 38), with or without modification, for transitional purposes) includes provision modifying the preserved equivalent pension benefits provisions in consequence of this Act.   **1.731**

(2) "The preserved equivalent pension benefits provisions" are the provisions of the National Insurance Act 1965 (c. 51) relating to equivalent pension benefits continued in force, with or without modification, by regulations having effect as if made under that paragraph.

Equivalent pension benefits: Northern Ireland

17.—(1) The provision that may be made by regulations under paragraph 15 of Schedule 3 to the Social Security (Consequential Provisions) (Northern Ireland) Act 1992 (c. 9) (corresponding power for Northern Ireland) includes provision modifying the Northern Ireland preserved equivalent pension benefits provisions in consequence of this Act.   **1.732**

(2) "The Northern Ireland preserved equivalent pension benefits provisions" are the provisions of the National Insurance Act (Northern Ireland) 1966 (c. 6 (N.I.)) relating to equivalent pension benefits continued in force, with or without modification, by regulations having effect as if made under that paragraph.

Welfare Reform Act 2007

(2007 c.5)

ARRANGEMENT OF SECTIONS

PART 1

EMPLOYMENT AND SUPPORT ALLOWANCE

Entitlement

Assessments relating to entitlement

Conditionality

Miscellaneous

General

PART 5

General

SCHEDULES

An Act to make provision about social security; to amend the Vaccine Damage Payments Act 1979; and for connected purposes.

[3rd May 2007]

PART 1

EMPLOYMENT AND SUPPORT ALLOWANCE

Entitlement

Employment and support allowance

1.—(1) An allowance, to be known as an employment and support allowance, shall be payable in accordance with the provisions of this Part.

1.734

(2) Subject to the provisions of this Part, a claimant is entitled to an employment and support allowance if he satisfies the basic conditions and either—

    (a) the first and the second conditions set out in Part 1 of Schedule 1 (conditions relating to national insurance) or the third condition set out in that Part of that Schedule (condition relating to youth), or

    (b) the conditions set out in Part 2 of that Schedule (conditions relating to financial position).

(3) The basic conditions are that the claimant—

    (a) has limited capability for work,

    (b) is at least 16 years old,

    (c) has not reached pensionable age,

    (d) is in Great Britain,

    (e) is not entitled to income support, and

    (f) is not entitled to a jobseeker's allowance (and is not a member of a couple who are entitled to a joint-claim jobseeker's allowance).

(4) For the purposes of this Part, a person has limited capability for work if—

    (a) his capability for work is limited by his physical or mental condition, and

    (b) the limitation is such that it is not reasonable to require him to work.

(5) An employment and support allowance is payable in respect of a week.

(6) In subsection (3)—

"joint-claim jobseeker's allowance" means a jobseeker's allowance entitlement to which arises by virtue of section 1(2B) of the Jobseekers Act 1995 (c. 18);

"pensionable age" has the meaning given by the rules in paragraph 1 of Schedule 4 to the Pensions Act 1995 (c. 26).

(7) In this Part—

"contributory allowance" means an employment and support allowance entitlement to which is based on subsection (2)(a);

"income-related allowance" means an employment and support allowance entitlement to which is based on subsection (2)(b).

DEFINITIONS

    "contributory allowance"—see subs.(7).

    "income-related allowance"—see subs.(7).

    "joint-claim jobseeker's allowance"—see subs.(6).

    "pensionable age"—see subs.(6).

GENERAL NOTE

Subs.(1)

1.735   This establishes the new Employment and Support Allowance (ESA), which is payable in accordance with the terms set out in the remainder of Part I of the Act, a framework clothed with the detail afforded by several sets of regulations:

    • *Employment and Support Allowance Regulations 2008 (SI 2008/794) (ESA Regulations)(as amended)*
       Like the JSA and IS Regs which in many respects they emulate, these set out the key detailed rules on ESA and are set out with commentary later in this section of the Supplement.

- *Employment and Support Allowance (Transitional Provisions) Regulations 2008 (SI 2008/795) (as amended)*
  These deal with the transition to ESA (key rules for "existing customers" of the IB/IS/SDA incapacity benefits' regime). They are set out with commentary later in this section of the Supplement.

- *Employment and Support Allowance (Consequential Provisions) Regulations 2008 (SI 2008/1082)*
  These effect amendments to Housing and Council Tax benefits and are not reproduced in this Supplement.

- *Employment and Support Allowance (Consequential Provisions) (No. 2) Regulations 2008 (SI 2008/1554)*
  These effect a variety of changes to legislation covered in *Social Security Legislation*. Their impact is noted in the appropriate updating sections of this Supplement.

- *Employment and Support Allowance (Consequential Provisions) (No. 3) Regulations 2008 (SI 2008/1879)*
  These effect a variety of changes to tax credits and child benefit. Their impact is noted in the appropriate updating sections of this Supplement.

A brief overview of ESA and its purpose may be useful to place the detailed rules and commentary in context.

State support towards the income replacement needs of those incapable of work has been the province of incapacity benefit (IB), income support (IS), or a mixture of both, since the non-contributory incapacity benefit, Severe Disablement Allowance (SDA), was closed to new claimants from April 6, 2001. From October 27, 2008 (the "appointed day", "commencement") both will be closed to new claimants who claim benefit on the basis of a health condition or disability which so affects their ability to work that it is not reasonable to expect them to do so. From then, any such claim will instead be treated as one for a new benefit: Employment and Support Allowance (ESA), claimed to be less complex and easier to claim. "Existing customers" (those already in receipt of those benefits, or whose claim for a new spell of incapacity links back to a period of incapacity for work prior to commencement) will be able to retain entitlement to them after the appointed day, but will lose it once the relevant period of incapacity for work comes to an end without linking to another which started prior to commencement. All new claimants (and those "existing customers" unable to link in that way) will instead have to look for income replacement to the new ESA. Thus yet another client group has been removed from IS, leaving it very much as a residual benefit, probably one ultimately to be abolished. Over time, all existing incapacity regime claimants will be migrated to ESA.

Like JSA, ESA is a single benefit with two forms: contributory ESA (CESA) and income related ESA (IRESA). A claimant may be entitled to one or the other or, in some cases, both. ESA, payable in respect of a week, is a benefit to provide support to those clearly unable to work, through a "support component" paid in addition to their basic allowance, and to require those capable of work-related activity to engage in it in return for a "work-related activity component" on top of their basic allowance, the hope being that they will eventually return to the labour force. ESA is a benefit with similarities to JSA (even CESA can be reduced on account of certain other income), but no time limit on either its contributory or income related forms, save that entitlement ceases on reaching pensionable age (s.1(3)(c)).

ESA is accessible by persons with an employer (after SSP is exhausted) (s.20(1)), the self-employed, and those without employment.

Eligibility for CESA depends, like that for IB, on fulfilment of contribution conditions showing a recent connection with the world of work. But, as with IB after the abolition of SDA for new claimants, persons incapacitated in youth (before 20 or in some cases 25) can have access to this ostensibly contributory form without meeting the contribution conditions. Otherwise, claimants who do not meet those conditions will have to seek IRESA. Depending on their precise financial circumstances, and the intricacies of the income related "balance sheet", in terms of capital and income (including income from capital), those entitled to the CESA may also receive IRESA as a top-up.

The conditions of entitlement common to the basic allowance aspect of both forms of ESA are that the claimant is at least 16; has not reached pensionable age; is in Great Britain; is not entitled to IS; is not entitled to JSA in his own right or as part of a joint-claim couple; and has limited capability for work (see subs.(3)). The matter of capacity is either assessed by a work-related capability assessment (a functional test similar to the IB personal capability assessment or all work test), involving a medical examination, or, is deemed to exist for a much reduced set of "exempt" groups. Generally, three "waiting days" of non-entitlement have to be served (s.22, Sch.2, para.4; ESA Regs, reg.144). During the (generally 13-week) assessment period, only basic allowance ESA is payable. Additional components (support or work-related activity) depend on the claimant being assessed or treated as having limited capability for work/work-related activity respectively. The personal allowance aspect of ESA basic allowance (a lower rate for those under 25) is based on the personal allowances in JSA (single person, lone parent or couple), but those able to qualify for IRESA can also access applicable premiums. After the assessment period ends (when the claimant has been assessed or treated as having limited capacity for work), claimants become eligible for one (but not both) of two additional components: the *support* component; or the *work-related activity* component. To be eligible for the *support* component, claimants must have limited capability for work-related activity (capacity for that must be limited by their physical or mental condition to such an extent that it is not reasonable to require them to undertake such activity). If they do not have limited capacity for work-related activity (i.e. capability for work-related activity is not limited by physical or mental condition or, if it is, the limitations are not such as to render it unreasonable to undertake such activity), they will be eligible for the work-related activity component on top of the basic allowance, provided they meet prescribed conditions on work-related activity. Should they not do so, they can be sanctioned by progressive reduction (ultimately removal) of the amount of that component to which they would otherwise be entitled.

As with IB/IS, claimants entitled to ESA can be disqualified from it where their conduct conduces to their incapacity (e.g. because of misconduct in bringing it about or in refusing treatment which would alleviate it) or their failure to adhere to prescribed rules of behaviour (s.18; ESA Regs, regs 157, 159). "Persons in hardship" cannot be disqualified but receive a reduced rate of personal allowance (ESA Regs, reg.158, Sch.5, para.14). Absences from Great Britain (other than certain temporary absences) preclude entitlement to ESA (s.18(4), Sch.2, paras 5, 6, 8; ESA Regs, regs 151–155). Imprisonment or detention in legal custody each disqualify from CESA and, if longer than six weeks, results in the person being treated as not having limited capability for work, thus impacting on ability to link spells of limited capability for work (s.18(4); ESA Regs, reg.159 and Sch.5, para.3).

ESA is part of a broader governmental strategy to assist people with a health condition or disability. Government is convinced that benefit dependency, particularly strong in respect of benefits for incapacity, is a major element in hardship and deprivation, and that work is the route out of poverty. The measures set out in its 2006 Green Paper (Cm 6730) were intended to increase the numbers who are able to remain in work when they fall sick or become disabled; to raise the numbers moving from benefits into employment; and better to meet the needs of those requiring extra help and support because of a health condition. Unlike IB (rather caricatured by a Government determined like its predecessors to reduce the cost to the public purpose of supporting the once favourably-treated group—those incapable of work), ESA does not automatically assume incapacity for work merely because someone has a significant health condition or disability. It is built on experience with the pilots of the Pathways to Work project which was rolled out nationally in

April 2008. It is claimed that this initiative has significantly increased the IB claimants being helped into work, and that "these pilots have demonstrated that, with the right help and support, many people on incapacity benefits can move back into work, reinforcing the view that labelling people on incapacity benefits as 'incapable of work' is wrong and damaging". Government considered that no lesser approach than ESA would provide the necessary cultural shift, from a benefits package based on "incapacity for work" to one founded firmly on what a person can do.

Government expects that ESA will have a significant and wide-ranging positive impact on disabled people and people with health conditions who are out of work. ESA is a benefit designed to help these people overcome barriers, and where appropriate move into work and improve their lives. The Work Capability Assessment (WCA) seeks to relate more accurately to modern context than the 12-year-old IB/IS system, and to focus more on what people can do, rather on what they are unable to do. The conditionality regime for the work-related activity component seeks to engage customers placed in the work-related activity group. It affords them access to the employment and condition management programmes of Pathways to Work. But ESA recognises the needs of those in the Support Group; their entitlement to the support component is not conditional on work-related activity but they can engage, if they wish, with those programmes. ESA seeks better to reflect the aspirations of disabled people, and improve the "customer experience" of individuals on the benefit.

ESA in outline was broadly welcomed as to its purpose of, and potential for, helping disabled people fulfil their aspiration to work, by spokespersons across all parties, and as a potential route out of poverty by groups representing the disabled. But concerns (becoming stronger as more detail emerged) were nonetheless expressed about a range of aspects: conditionality (sanctions welcomed and seen as vital by some to "persuade" the reluctant to engage with help and knowledge, seen as problematic or unnecessary by others); the impact on persons with a variety of conditions (mental health problems, cancer sufferers, Asperger's syndrome), particularly fluctuating ones, and on the terminally ill; which groups would be exempt from the WCA; what would be the categories of permitted work so vital to building confidence that someone could return to work; the nature of the law-making process leaving too much to secondary legislation or ministerial fiat; adding to the complexity of the benefits system with a supposed single benefit involving six rates; the nature and inter-relationship of two capability assessments with different criteria; and, crucially, the other side of the coin—the provisions deal with the attitude of the disabled to work but leave untouched the attitude of employers to the disabled would-be worker.

The introduction of ESA will generate more appeals, in part because there are more appealable issues challenging the bona fides of claimants than with IB/IS support for the sick and disabled (membership of the work-related activity group rather than the support group; sanctions for not engaging in work-related activity) and because the WCA is expected to "fail" more people than the PCA. DWP estimates put the extra appeals load in a full year at 26,500 with 21,000 going to a hearing. This obviously has expenditure implications, but, since more people are expected to move off benefit and into the labour market or into employment, Government estimates expenditure savings of £50 million in the first full year of operation of ESA (2009/10), rising progressively to £155 million in 2013/14 and £215 million in 2017/18. The impact of the recession will inevitably diminish those savings.

Subss.(2), (7)

As with JSA, read together these envisage two ways of gaining title to ESA: the "contributory route" to the "contributory allowance" (CESA); and the "income-related" route to "income-related allowance" (IRESA). They provide that entitlement to CESA is grounded on satisfaction of the "basic conditions" in subs.(3) plus *either* (a) satisfaction of the national insurance contribution conditions (Sch.1, Pt 1) *or* (b) that the claimant is someone incapacitated in youth (Sch.1, Pt 1). It provides that entitlement to IRESA is grounded on satisfaction of the basic conditions in subs.(3) plus those relating to financial position (Sch.1, Pt 2).

1.736

Subs. (3)

1.737   This stipulates the "basic conditions" which must be satisfied whether the claimant claims CESA, IRESA or both. The claimant must

- *be at least 16*
  this is the current school-leaving age and so this lower limit is apt for a benefit that is an earnings replacement one;

- *be under pensionable age*
  "pensionable age" is here defined according to the rules in Pensions Act 2004, Sch.4, para.1 (see subs.(6)). It thus links to the sliding scale of pensionable ages found there as the pensions system moves steadily towards equal pension ages for men and women;

- *be in Great Britain*
  absences from Great Britain (other than certain temporary absences) preclude entitlement to ESA. See further s.18(4), Sch.2, paras 5, 6, 8; ESA Regs, regs 151–155. Essentially this is a presence rather than a residence test. However, note that ESA Regs, regs 69–70 and Sch.5, apply to IRESA much the same rules on residence as apply in IS and IBJSA;

- *not be entitled to IS under SSCBA 1992, s.124*
  this establishes the mutual exclusivity of ESA and IS;

- *not be entitled to JSA whether in his/her own right or as part of a joint-claim couple*
  this establishes the mutual exclusivity of ESA and JSA. Entitlement to JSA as a joint-claim couple arises under Jobseekers Act 1995, s.1(2B);

- *have limited capability for work*
  the basic test for this is set out in subs.(4): claimants will have limited capability for work where their capability for work is limited by their physical or mental condition and that limitation is such that it is not reasonable to require them to work. ESA Regs 2008, reg.19(1) elaborates that this is to be determined on the basis of a limited capability for work assessment (hereinafter WCAt), one element in the three-element Work Capability Assessment which has been developed out of a review of the Personal Capability Assessment (PCA) in the IB/IS/SDA incapacity benefits' regime. The WCAt is

  > "an assessment of the extent to which a claimant who has some specific disease or bodily or mental disablement is capable of performing the activities prescribed in Schedule 2 [to the ESA Regs] or is incapable by reason of such disease or bodily or mental disablement of performing those activities" (ESA Regs, reg.19(2)).

  This is familiar stuff to anyone who has worked with the PCA or its predecessor, the "all work" test. The claimant is to be matched, in the light of all the evidence, by the decision-maker or tribunal against a reformulated range of activities and descriptors, and an appropriate "score" awarded. The threshold "score" for entitlement remains 15 points, but as regards its computation, there are both "old" and "new" elements". See further the commentary to s.8 and to ESA Regs, Pt 5 (regs 19–33) and Sch.2.

Subs. (4)

1.738   This sets out the basic definition of "limited capability for work". See commentary to subs.(3), s.8 and to ESA Regs, Pt 5 (regs 19–33) and Sch.2.

Subs. (5)

1.739   Emulating JSA, ESA is a weekly benefit, one paid in respect of a week. For cases of part-week entitlement see s.22, Sch.2, para.3 and ESA Regs, Pt 14 (regs 165–169).

Subs. (6)

1.740   This defines, by reference to other legislation, "joint-claim jobseeker's allowance" and "pensionable age".

Subs. (7)

Another definition provision. See commentary to subss.(2), (7), above. **1.741**

Amount of contributory allowance

2.—(1) In the case of a contributory allowance, the amount payable in **1.742** respect of a claimant shall be calculated by—

(a) taking such amount as may be prescribed;

(b) if in his case the conditions of entitlement to the support component or the work-related activity component are satisfied, adding the amount of that component; and

(c) making prescribed deductions in respect of any payments to which section 3 applies.

(2) The conditions of entitlement to the support component are—

(a) that the assessment phase has ended;

(b) that the claimant has limited capability for work-related activity; and

(c) that such other conditions as may be prescribed are satisfied.

(3) The conditions of entitlement to the work-related activity component are—

(a) that the assessment phase has ended;

(b) that the claimant does not have limited capability for work-related activity; and

(c) that such other conditions as may be prescribed are satisfied.

(4) Regulations may—

(a) prescribe circumstances in which paragraph (a) of subsection (2) or (3) is not to apply;

(b) prescribe circumstances in which entitlement under subsection (2) or (3) is to be backdated;

(c) make provision about the amount of the component under subsection (2) or (3).

(5) For the purposes of this Part, a person has limited capability for work-related activity if—

(a) his capability for work-related activity is limited by his physical or mental condition; and

(b) the limitation is such that it is not reasonable to require him to undertake such activity.

DEFINITIONS

"assessment phase"—see s.24(2), (3).
"claimant"—see s.24(1).
"contributory allowance"—see s.1(6).
"limited capability for work-related activity"—see subs.(5).
"prescribed"—see s.24(1).
"regulations"—see s.24(1).
"work-related activity"—see ss.24(1), 13(7), below.

GENERAL NOTE

This section deals with the calculation of amount of contributory allowance **1.743** (CESA) (see s.1(6)) to which a particular claimant can be entitled, both during the "assessment phase" and after it has ended (subss.(1)–(3)). It provides rule-making powers to modify some of the conditions, to set amounts and to enable backdating of entitlement (subs.(4)). Finally it defines when someone has "limited capability for work-related activity" (subs.(5)).

Subs. (1)

1.744   This sets out the elements making up CESA and the basic arithmetic for determining the amount of CESA to which the claimant is entitled. The basic arithmetic during the "assessment phase" is prescribed amount (age-related) minus any s.3 deductions. After the "assessment phase", it changes to single prescribed amount plus appropriate component (support or work related activity) minus any s.3 deductions. Since entitlement varies as between the period of the "assessment phase" and after it has ended, it is useful to begin with analysis of that concept.

The "assessment phase" starts on the first day of the period for which the claimant is entitled to ESA (the day after service of the three waiting days of non-entitlement (see s.22, Sch.2, para.2, and ESA Regs, reg.144)). It ends on whichever is the later of either 13 weeks from that first day of entitlement or the date of determination of limited capability for work (either of actual limited capability or of "deemed" limited capability (treated as having limited capability) (see s.24(2), ESA Regs, reg.4). The ESA scheme deals with intermittent incapacity through "linking" rules. These impact on identification of the end of the "assessment phase". Under ESA Regs, reg.145, periods of limited capability for work "link" and are treated as one single period (to which further ones may be added if the linking rules are met). Typically periods not separated by more than 12 weeks' "link" in this way (see ESA Regs, reg.145(1)), but for "work or training beneficiaries" (see ESA Regs, reg.148), the separation period rises to a maximum 104 weeks (see ESA Regs, reg.145(2)). Where the assessment phase had not ended in the first such period, it ends at the appropriate point (the later of 13 weeks or the date of the limited capability of work determination) in the linked period(s). There can only be one assessment period in any single period of limited capability for work. So where another spell of such limited capability arises and is forged into one with an earlier period by the appropriate linking rules (12 or 104 weeks), and the "assessment phase" had ended in the earlier period, the claimant's entitlement in this second (or subsequent "spell") will be to prescribed amount plus appropriate component minus any s.3 deductions (s.2(4)(a); ESA Regs, reg.7(1)(b)). If the linking rules do not operate so as to forge the two spells into one, the second "spell" constitutes a new period of incapacity, in respect of which the three "waiting days" will again have to be served and a new "assessment phase" will begin again on the first day of entitlement after service of those waiting days and end according to the rules considered above.

Note finally that appealing against a determination that the claimant does not have limited capability for work extends the "assessment phase" until the appeal is determined by an appeal tribunal (s.24(2)(b); ESA Regs, regs 6, 7(2)).

The first element of CESA is the prescribed amount of "basic allowance". Although this is not a term used in the Act or the Regulations, its use is standard in the literature, policy and explanatory documents on ESA, and accordingly is also deployed here. It is normally the only element of CESA to which a claimant (other than one terminally ill) can be entitled during the "assessment phase". During that phase, the amount of CESA (subject to any s.3 deductions) to which the claimant can be entitled varies according to age. If under 25, a lower weekly rate is prescribed: £47.95 (see ESA Regs, reg.67(2), Sch.4, para.1(1)(c)). If 25 or over the weekly amount during the assessment phase is £60.50 (see ESA Regs, reg.67(2), Sch.4, para.1(1)(b)). The rates are thus equivalent to those in CBJSA.

During the assessment phase (whether ending after 13 weeks or a later date of determination of limited capability for work), it will have been determined whether the claimant has limited capability for work (actual limited capability) or should be treated as having it (deemed limited capability). It will also have been determined whether the claimant has limited capability for work related activity or should be treated as having it. If the claimant does have (or is treated as having) such limited capacity, this grounds entitlement to "support component", subject to other conditions set out in regulations, but generally only once the assessment phase has ended (subs.(2)) (see below for an exception in respect of the terminally ill). If the claimant does not have (or is treated as not having) such limited capacity, entitlement (subject to conditionality (see commentary to ss.11–16)) can only be to the work-related activity component (see subs.(3)). So the basic picture after the assessment period is prescribed amount plus appropriate component minus any s.3 deductions.

Once the assessment phase has ended there is a single prescribed weekly amount (£60.50), regardless of age (see ESA Regs, reg.67(2), Sch.4, para.1(1)(b)). If the claimant is then entitled to support component, the weekly amount to be added to the prescribed amount is £29.00 (see para.(b); ESA Regs, reg.67(3), Sch.4, Pt 4, para.13). If entitlement is to work-related activity component, the weekly amount to be added to the prescribed amount is £24.00 (see para.(b); ESA Regs, reg.67(3), Sch.4, Pt 4, para.12). The amount of CESA actually payable, however, is subject to reduction in accordance with s.3.

For those who are "terminally ill" (subs.(4)(a); ESA Regs, regs 2(1), 7(1)(a)), entitlement to the components (support or work-related activity) is not conditioned on the assessment phase having ended. So throughout their period of limited capability for work, entitlement will be to CESA composed of basic allowance plus appropriate component minus any s.3 deductions.

Subs.(2)

This sets out the conditions of entitlement to the support component in ESA. Entitlement can generally only arise after the assessment phase has ended. An exception to this is in the case of the terminally ill (subs.(4)(a); ESA Regs, reg.7(1)(a)). The claimant must be assessed as having, or be treated by regulations as having, limited capability for work-related activity. Entitlement also depends on other prescribed conditions (i.e. ones set out in regulations).   **1.745**

Subs.(3)

This stipulates the conditions of entitlement to the work-related activity component of ESA. Entitlement can generally only arise after the assessment phase has ended. An exception to this is in the case of the terminally ill (subs.(4)(a); ESA Regs, reg.7(1)(a)). The claimant must be assessed as not having, or be treated by regulations as not having, limited capability for work-related activity. Entitlement also depends on other prescribed conditions (i.e. ones set out in regulations).   **1.746**

Subs.(5)

This defines "limited capability for work-related activity". Whether the claimant has it or not is crucial for identifying which component of ESA (support or work related activity) is applicable in the case. A claimant has it where his capability for work-related activity is limited by his physical or mental condition such that it is not reasonable to require him to undertake such activity. "Work-related activity" is defined as activity which makes it more likely that the person whose capability is being tested will obtain or remain in work or be able to do so (ss.24(1), 13(7)).   **1.747**

Deductions from contributory allowance: supplementary

3.—(1) This section applies to payments of the following kinds which are payable to the claimant—   **1.748**
  (a) pension payments,
  (b) PPF periodic payments, and
  (c) payments of a prescribed description made to a person who is a member of, or has been appointed to, a prescribed body carrying out public or local functions.
(2) Regulations may—

(a) disapply section 2(1)(c), so far as relating to pension payments or PPF periodic payments, in relation to persons of a prescribed description;

(b) provide for pension payments or PPF periodic payments of a prescribed description to be treated for the purposes of that provision as not being payments to which this section applies;

(c) provide for sums of a prescribed description to be treated for the purposes of this section as payable to persons as pension payments or PPF periodic payments (including, in particular, sums in relation to which there is a deferred right of receipt);

(d) make provision for the method of determining how payments to which this section applies are, for the purposes of section 2, to be related to periods for which a person is entitled to a contributory allowance.

(3) In this section—

"pension payment" means—

(a) a periodical payment made in relation to a person under a personal pension scheme or, in connection with the coming to an end of an employment of his, under an occupational pension scheme or a public service pension scheme,

(b) a payment of a prescribed description made under an insurance policy providing benefits in connection with physical or mental illness or disability, and

(c) such other payments as may be prescribed;

"PPF periodic payment" means—

(a) any periodic compensation payment made in relation to a person, payable under the pension compensation provisions as specified in section 162(2) of the Pensions Act 2004 (c.35) or Article 146(2) of the Pensions (Northern Ireland) Order 2005 (S.I. 2005/255) (NI 1) (the pension compensation provisions), and

(b) any periodic payment made in relation to a person, payable under section 166 of the Pensions Act 2004 or Article 150 of the Pensions (Northern Ireland) Order 2005 (duty to pay scheme benefits unpaid at assessment date etc.).

(4) For the purposes of subsection (3), "occupational pension scheme", "personal pension scheme" and "public service pension scheme" each have the meaning given by section 1 of the Pension Schemes Act 1993 (c.48), except that "personal pension scheme" includes—

(a) an annuity contract or trust scheme approved under section 620 or 621 of the Income and Corporation Taxes Act 1988 (c. 1), and

(b) a substituted contract within the meaning of section 622(3) of that Act,

which is treated as having become a registered pension scheme by virtue of paragraph 1(1)(f) of Schedule 36 to the Finance Act 2004 (c.12).

DEFINITIONS

"claimant"—see s.24(1), below.
"occupational pension scheme"—see subs.(4).
"pension payment"—see subs.(3).
"personal pension scheme"—see subs.(4).
"PPF periodic payment"—see subs.(3).
"prescribed"—see s.24(1), below.

"public service pension scheme"—see subs.(4).
"regulations"—see s.24(1), below.

GENERAL NOTE

Under s.2, the amount of CESA to which the claimant is otherwise entitled will **1.749**
normally (see subs.(2)(a) of this section) be reduced as set out in regulations (ESA
Regs, regs 72–79) by the payments set out in this section which are payable to the
claimant. This section and ESA Regs, regs 72–79 thus bring into ESA the concept
of abatement of contributory benefit familiar from unemployment benefit (see
SSCBA 1992, s.30 and USI Regs, 23–28 in the 1995 edition of Bonner, Hooker
and White, *Non-Means Tested Benefits: the Legislation*), jobseeker's allowance (see
JSA 1995, s.21, Sch.1, para.7; JSA Regs, regs 80, 81 in Vol.II) and incapacity
benefit (see SSCBA 1992, ss.30DD [pension and PPF periodic payments] and 30E
[councillor's allowance]; IB Regs, regs 20–26 in Vol.I). While not making them
fully income-related benefits along the lines of income support, income-related
jobseeker's allowance or tax credits, such abatement of ESA nonetheless continues
the practice of bringing into a contributory benefit an element of means testing. In
interpreting this section and its associated regulations, cross-reference to case law
under those JSA and IB schemes will be appropriate insofar as the definitions are
identical or analogous.

Subs.(1)

This stipulates that this section covers pension payments (para.(a)—defined in **1.750**
subss.(3), (4)), PPF periodic payments (para.(b)—defined in subs.(3)) and "payments of a prescribed description made to a person who is a member of, or has
been appointed to, a prescribed body carrying out public or local functions" (para.
(c)). For the rules on taking pension payments and PPF payments into account,
see ESA Regs, reg.74. Currently, under para.(c), ESA Regs, reg.73 prescribes only
"councillor's allowance" in respect of those councils referred to in the definition of
"councillor in ESA Regs, reg.2(1). For the rules on taking "councillor's allowance"
into account, see ESA Regs, reg.76.

On "payable to", see *R(IB) 1/04* and *R(IB) 1/05*.

Subs.(2)

Under para.(b), see ESA Regs, reg.75. **1.751**
Under para.(d), see ESA regs 77–79.

Subs.(3)

Under para.(b) of the definition of pension payment, see ESA regs, reg.72 **1.752**
whereby "pension payment" includes a "permanent health insurance payment" as
defined in that reg.

Amount of income-related allowance

4.—(1) In the case of an income-related allowance, the amount payable **1.753**
in respect of a claimant shall be—
  (a) if he has no income, the applicable amount;
  (b) if he has an income, the amount by which the applicable amount
      exceeds his income.
(2) Subject to subsection (3), the applicable amount for the purposes of
subsection (1) shall be calculated by—
  (a) taking such amount, or the aggregate of such amounts, as may be
      prescribed, and
  (b) if in the claimant's case the conditions of entitlement to the support
      component or the work-related activity component are satisfied,
      adding the amount of that component.

(3) Regulations may provide that, in prescribed cases, the applicable amount for the purposes of subsection (1) shall be nil.

(4) The conditions of entitlement to the support component are—

(a) that the assessment phase has ended,

(b) that the claimant has limited capability for work-related activity, and

(c) that such other conditions as may be prescribed are satisfied.

(5) The conditions of entitlement to the work-related activity component are—

(a) that the assessment phase has ended,

(b) that the claimant does not have limited capability for work-related activity, and

(c) that such other conditions as may be prescribed are satisfied.

(6) Regulations may—

(a) prescribe circumstances in which paragraph (a) of subsection (4) or (5) is not to apply;

(b) prescribe circumstances in which entitlement under subsection (4) or (5) is to be backdated;

(c) make provision about the amount of the component under subsection (4) or (5).

DEFINITIONS

"assessment phase"—s.24(2)
"income-related allowance"—ss.24(1) and 1(7).
"limited capability for work-related activity"—ss.24(1) and 2(5).
"prescribed"—s.24(1).
"regulations"—*ibid*.

GENERAL NOTE

1.754   This section is similar in effect to ss.124(4) and 135(1)–(2) of the Contributions and Benefits Act and ss.3(1)(a) and (4) of the Jobseekers Act. Applicable amounts (including the work-related activity component and the support component) are prescribed by regs 67–70 of, and Schs 4 and 5 to, the ESA Regulations. Income (including tariff income from capital) is governed by s.17 and Pt 10 of, and Schs 7, 8 and 9 to, the ESA Regs.

Advance award of income-related allowance

1.755   **5.**—(1) This section applies to claims for an employment and support allowance by a person who—

(a) would be entitled to an income-related allowance, but for the fact that he does not satisfy the condition in paragraph 6(1)(a) of Schedule 1,

(b) would satisfy that condition if he were entitled to the component mentioned in section 4(4) or (5), and

(c) is not entitled to a contributory allowance.

(2) In relation to claims to which this section applies, section 5(1) of the Administration Act (regulations about claims for benefit) shall have effect as if—

(a) in paragraph (d) (power to permit an award on a claim for benefit for a future period to be made subject to the condition that the claimant satisfies the requirements for entitlement when the benefit becomes payable under the award), there were inserted at the end "and to such other conditions as may be prescribed", and

(b) in paragraph (e) (power to provide for such an award to be revised or superseded under the Social Security Act 1998 (c. 14) if any of those requirements are found not to have been satisfied), for "any of those requirements" there were substituted "any of the conditions to which the award is made subject".

(3) Regulations may, in relation to claims to which this section applies, make provision enabling an award to be made on terms such that the time at which benefit becomes payable under the award is later than the start of the period for which the award is made.

DEFINITIONS

"Administration Act"—s.65.
"contributory allowance"—ss.24(1) and 1(7).
"income-related allowance"—*ibid*.

GENERAL NOTE

The support component and work-related activity component (see s.4(4) and (5) above) are normally only paid after the end of the assessment phase. During that phase, there will be some claimants who are not entitled to income-related ESA because their income exceeds their applicable amount, who would be so entitled if their applicable amount included the support component or work-related activity component. This section allows an advance award to be made where such a person makes a claim during the assessment phase. See also reg.146 of the ESA Regulations.   1.756

Amount payable where claimant entitled to both forms of allowance

6.—(1) This section applies where a claimant is entitled to both a contributory allowance and an income-related allowance.   1.757

(2) If the claimant has no income, the amount payable by way of an employment and support allowance shall be the greater of—

(a) his personal rate, and

(b) the applicable amount.

(3) If the claimant has an income, the amount payable by way of an employment and support allowance shall be the greater of—

(a) his personal rate, and

(b) the amount by which the applicable amount exceeds his income.

(4) Where the amount payable to the claimant by way of an employment and support allowance does not exceed his personal rate, the allowance shall be treated as attributable to the claimant's entitlement to a contributory allowance.

(5) Where the amount payable to the claimant by way of an employment and support allowance exceeds his personal rate, the allowance shall be taken to consist of two elements, namely—

(a) an amount equal to his personal rate, and

(b) an amount equal to the excess.

(6) The element mentioned in subsection (5)(a) shall be treated as attributable to the claimant's entitlement to a contributory allowance.

(7) The element mentioned in subsection (5)(b) shall be treated as attributable to the claimant's entitlement to an income-related allowance.

(8) In this section—

"applicable amount" means the amount which, in the claimant's case, is the applicable amount for the purposes of section 4(1);

"personal rate" means the amount calculated in accordance with section 2(1).

DEFINITIONS

"applicable amount"—see subs.(8), s.4(1).
"claimant"—see s.24(1).
"contributory allowance"—see s.1(7).
"income-related allowance"—see s.1(7).
"personal rate"—see subs.(8), s.2(1).

GENERAL NOTE

1.758　　This is similar to Jobseekers Act 1995, s.4(6)–(12), where, as with ESA, JSA has both a contributory element and an income related element. Like those provisions, this section deals with situations where a claimant is entitled to both a contributory allowance (CESA) and an income-related allowance (IRESA). Here, the amount calculated under s.2(1) (amount of CESA) is referred to as the "personal rate". The applicable amount for IRESA is made up of an amount in respect of the claimant and any partner, plus applicable premiums plus eligible housing costs (see s.4(1); ESA Regs, reg.67(1)). If the claimant has no income and the personal rate is higher than the applicable amount (the amount for the purposes of IRESA), the claimant receives the personal rate (the CESA amount). If the claimant has no income and the applicable amount exceeds the personal rate, he will receive the personal rate, topped up with an additional amount of IRESA equal to the excess. If the person has an income, the amount payable will be the greater of the personal allowance and the amount by which his applicable amount exceeds his income.

Exclusion of payments below prescribed minimum

1.759　　**7.**—Except in such circumstances as regulations may provide, an employment and support allowance shall not be payable where the amount otherwise payable would be less than a prescribed minimum.

DEFINITIONS

"prescribed"—see s.24(1).
"regulations"—see s.24(1).

GENERAL NOTE

1.760　　ESA is not payable where it falls below the minimum amount prescribed in regulations. This amount is set at 10p in the Claims and Payments Regs 1987, reg.26C(6), inserted with effect from October 27, 2008 by reg.21 of the ESA (Consequential Provisions) (No. 2) Regs 2008 (SI 2008/1554). Compare JSA Regs, reg.87A.

Assessments relating to entitlement

Limited capability for work

1.761　　**8.**—(1) For the purposes of this Part, whether a person's capability for work is limited by his physical or mental condition and, if it is, whether the limitation is such that it is not reasonable to require him to work shall be determined in accordance with regulations.

(2) Regulations under subsection (1) shall—

(a) provide for determination on the basis of an assessment of the person concerned;

(b) define the assessment by reference to the extent to which a person who has some specific disease or bodily or mental disablement is capable or incapable of performing such activities as may be prescribed;

(c) make provision as to the manner of carrying out the assessment.

(3) Regulations under subsection (1) may, in particular, make provision—

(a) as to the information or evidence required for the purpose of determining the matters mentioned in that subsection;

(b) as to the manner in which that information or evidence is to be provided;

(c) for a person in relation to whom it falls to be determined whether he has limited capability for work to be called to attend for such medical examination as the regulations may require.

(4) Regulations under subsection (1) may include provision—

(a) for a person to be treated as not having limited capability for work if he fails without good cause—

(i) to provide information or evidence which he is required under such regulations to provide,

(ii) to provide information or evidence in the manner in which he is required under such regulations to provide it, or

(iii) to attend for, or submit himself to, a medical examination for which he is called under such regulations to attend;

(b) as to matters which are, or are not, to be taken into account in determining for the purposes of any provision made by virtue of paragraph (a) whether a person has good cause for any act or omission;

(c) as to circumstances in which a person is, or is not, to be regarded for the purposes of any such provision as having good cause for any act or omission.

(5) Regulations may provide that, in prescribed circumstances, a person in relation to whom it falls to be determined whether he has limited capability for work, shall, if prescribed conditions are met, be treated as having limited capability for work until such time as—

(a) it has been determined whether he has limited capability for work, or

(b) he falls in accordance with regulations under this section to be treated as not having limited capability for work.

(6) The prescribed conditions referred to in subsection (5) may include the condition that it has not previously been determined, within such period as may be prescribed, that the person in question does not have, or is to be treated as not having, limited capability for work.

DEFINITIONS

"limited capability for work"—see s.1(4).
"medical examination"—
"prescribed"—see s.24(1).
"regulations"—see s.24(1).

GENERAL NOTE

Subss.(1), (2)

A key condition of entitlement to ESA is that the claimant has limited capability for work, namely that his capability for work is limited by his physical or mental

1.762

condition such that it is not reasonable to require him to work (s.1(3)(c), (4)). This section provides that whether this is so is to be determined in accordance with regulations made under subss.(2)–(6) of this section. The regulations are Pt 5 of the ESA Regs, regs 19–33. These embody the first element in the new three-part Work Capability Assessment, governing entitlement to ESA, an analogue of the Personal Capability Assessment (PCA) in the previous incapacity benefits' regime (Incapacity Benefit/Income Support/Severe Disablement Allowance). But while there are many similarities with the PCA there are some significant differences as regards activities/descriptors, those exempt from the test and the system of scoring. The approach taken here, however, is that where terminology and basic issues are the same as with the PCA, the extensive case law interpreting and applying the PCA will carry over into the interpretation and application of comparable provisions and the resolution of comparable issues with this first element of the WCA, referred to for convenience as the WCAt to distinguish it from the other two elements of the WCA which only come into play if, applying the WCAt, the claimant is found not to have limited capability for work. These other two elements are the work-related activity assessment (WRAAt) (more stringent than the WCAt) (see s.9) and the work-focused health related assessment (WFHRAt) (see s.11). The former determines whether or not a claimant has limited capability for work-related activity. If he does, he will be placed in the support group as eligible for the support component and will not have to undergo the WFHRAt. If he does not have limited capability for work-related activity, he will be placed in the work-related activity group, eligible for work-related activity component, subject to the conditionality regime (see ss.11–16), including having normally to undergo the WFHRAt (see s.11), participate in work-related interviews (see s.12) and (eventually) work-related activity (see s.13).

Subss.(3), (4)

1.763   Note that whether the claimant has good cause for failure to comply with the information-gathering and examination aspects of that assessment is to some extent structured by regulations in that ESA Regs, reg.24 provides an non-exhaustive list of matters to be taken into account in determining that good cause issue. No regulations have yet been made under para.(4)(c) to determine what does, or does not, rank as good cause.

Limited capability for work-related activity

1.764   **9.**—(1) For the purposes of this Part, whether a person's capability for work-related activity is limited by his physical or mental condition and, if it is, whether the limitation is such that it is not reasonable to require him to undertake such activity shall be determined in accordance with regulations.

(2) Regulations under subsection (1) shall—
(a) provide for determination on the basis of an assessment of the person concerned;
(b) define the assessment by reference to such matters as the regulations may provide;
(c) make provision as to the manner of carrying out the assessment.

(3) Regulations under subsection (1) may, in particular, make provision—
(a) as to the information or evidence required for the purpose of determining the matters mentioned in that subsection;
(b) as to the manner in which that information or evidence is to be provided;
(c) for a person in relation to whom it falls to be determined whether he has limited capability for work-related activity to be called to attend for such medical examination as the regulations may require.

(4) Regulations under subsection (1) may include provision—

(a) for a person to be treated as not having limited capability for work-related activity if he fails without good cause—

   (i) to provide information or evidence which he is required under such regulations to provide,

   (ii) to provide information or evidence in the manner in which he is required under such regulations to provide it, or

   (iii) to attend for, or submit himself to, a medical examination for which he is called under such regulations to attend;

(b) as to matters which are, or are not, to be taken into account in determining for the purposes of any provision made by virtue of paragraph (a) whether a person has good cause for any act or omission;

(c) as to circumstances in which a person is, or is not, to be regarded for the purposes of any such provision as having good cause for any act or omission.

DEFINITIONS

"regulations"—see s.24(1).
"work-related activity"—see ss.24(1), 13(7).

GENERAL NOTE

Subss.(1), (2)

Whether an ESA claimant is entitled to the more generous support component (£29 per week) or the less generous work-related activity component (£24 per week) in addition to his basic allowance turns on whether he does (support component)) or does not (work-related activity component) have limited capability for work-related activity (s.2(2), (3)). He has "limited capability for work-related activity" where his capability for such activity is limited by his physical or mental condition such that it is not reasonable to require him to undertake it (s.2(5)). "Work-related activity" is activity which makes it more likely that he will obtain or remain in work or be able to do so (ss.24(1), 13(7)). This section provides that whether or not he has such limited capability is to be determined in accordance with regulations under subss.(2), (4) of this section. The regulations in question are ESA Regs, Pt 6, regs 34–39. These flesh out the second element in the new three element Work Capability Assessment: the work related activity assessment (WRAAt). 1.765

Subss.(3), (4)

Note that whether the claimant has good cause for failure to comply with the information-gathering and examination aspects of that assessment is to some extent structured by regulations in that ESA Regs, reg.39 provides an non-exhaustive list of matters to be taken into account in determining that good cause issue. No regulations have yet been made under para.(4)(c) to determine what does, or does not, rank as good cause. 1.766

Report

10.—The Secretary of State shall lay before Parliament an independent report on the operation of the assessments under sections 8 and 9 annually for the first five years after those sections come into force. 1.767

GENERAL NOTE

The new capability assessments in respect of work and work related activity were controversial. So this section provides—but only for the first five years after 1.768

commencement—for independent annual review of their operation, a report on which must be laid before Parliament by the Secretary of State.

Conditionality

Work-focused health-related assessments

1.769   **11.**—(1) Regulations may make provision for or in connection with imposing on a person who is—

(a) entitled to an employment and support allowance, and

(b) not a member of the support group,

a requirement to take part in one or more work-focused health-related assessments as a condition of continuing to be entitled to the full amount payable to him in respect of the allowance apart from the regulations.

(2) Regulations under this section may, in particular, make provision—

(a) prescribing circumstances in which such a person is subject to a requirement to take part in one or more work-focused health-related assessments;

(b) for notifying such a person of any such requirement;

(c) prescribing the work-focused health-related assessments in which a person who is subject to such a requirement is required to take part;

(d) for the determination, and notification, of the time and place of any such assessment;

(e) prescribing circumstances in which a person attending such an assessment is to be regarded as having, or not having, taken part in it;

(f) for securing that the appropriate consequence follows if a person who is required under the regulations to take part in a work-focused health-related assessment—

(i) fails to take part in the assessment, and

(ii) does not, within a prescribed period, show that he had good cause for that failure;

(g) prescribing matters which are, or are not, to be taken into account in determining whether a person had good cause for any failure to comply with the regulations;

(h) prescribing circumstances in which a person is, or is not, to be regarded as having good cause for any such failure.

(3) For the purposes of subsection (2)(f), the appropriate consequence of a failure falling within that provision is that the amount payable to the person in question in respect of an employment and support allowance is reduced in accordance with regulations.

(4) Regulations under subsection (3) may, in particular, make provision for determining—

(a) the amount by which an allowance is to be reduced,

(b) when the reduction is to start, and

(c) how long it is to continue,

and may include provision prescribing circumstances in which the amount of the reduction is to be nil.

(5) Regulations under this section shall include provision for a requirement to take part in one or more work-focused health-related assessments to cease to have effect if the person subject to the requirement becomes a member of the support group.

(6) Regulations under this section may include provision—

(a) that in such circumstances as the regulations may prescribe a requirement to take part in a work-focused health-related assessment that would otherwise apply to a person by virtue of such regulations is not to apply, or is to be treated as not having applied;

(b) that in such circumstances as the regulations may prescribe such a requirement is not to apply until a prescribed time;

(c) that in such circumstances as the regulations may prescribe the time and place of a work-focused health-related assessment in which a person is required by regulations under this section to take part may be redetermined.

(7) In this section, "work-focused health-related assessment" means an assessment by a health care professional approved by the Secretary of State which is carried out for the purpose of assessing—

(a) the extent to which a person still has capability for work,

(b) the extent to which his capability for work may be improved by the taking of steps in relation to his physical or mental condition, and

(c) such other matters relating to his physical or mental condition and the likelihood of his obtaining or remaining in work or being able to do so, as may be prescribed.

(8) In subsection (7), "health care professional" means—

(a) a registered medical practitioner,

(b) a registered nurse,

(c) an occupational therapist or physiotherapist registered with a regulatory body established by an Order in Council under section 60 of the Health Act 1999, or

(d) a member of such other profession regulated by a body mentioned in section 25(3) of the National Health Service Reform and Health Care Professions Act 2002 as may be prescribed.

DEFINITIONS

"appropriate consequence"—see subs.(3).
"entitled"—see s.24(1).
"health care professional" (in subs.(7))—see subs.(8).
"prescribed"—see s.24(1).
"regulations"—see s.24(1).
"support group"—see s.24(4).
"work-focused health-related assessment"—see subs.(7)

GENERAL NOTE

This section covers those claimants who do not have limited capability for work-related activity and who are thus entitled not to the support component but instead to the work-related activity component (they are not part of the "support group" (see s.24(4))). Those entitled to the work-related activity component must comply with certain conditions—the regime is one of "conditionality" (stipulating required behaviour and using sanctions to regulate and change behaviour). One of these conditions is participation in work-focused health-related assessments. These assessments are defined in subs.(7). They are carried out by an approved "health care professional" as defined in subs.(8), covering a wider range of personnel than a doctor or nurse (so as to embrace, for example, a registered occupational therapist or physiotherapist), as indeed is appropriate given the aim of such assessments. They are carried out for the purpose of assessing the extent to which the claimant still has capability for work; the extent to which that might be improved by taking

1.770

steps in relation to his physical or mental condition; and other matters (to be set out in regulations) relating to that condition and the likelihood of obtaining work, remaining in work or being able to do so (subs.(7)).

This section enables the making of regulations to impose that requirement of participation in such an assessment and to exempt persons from it (subss.(1), (5), (6)); to deal with the process of carrying out such an assessment, and with the consequences of not participating in one without good cause (sub.(2)). Subsection (3) stipulates that a reduction in the amount of ESA otherwise payable is the appropriate consequence, and that subsection and subs.(4) enable the making of regulations determining the amount and period of the reduction and the circumstances in which the reduction is to be nil. Subsection (5) enables regulations to provide that the requirement shall cease to have effect if the person becomes a member of the support group, that is, if it is determined that he has, or is to be treated as having, limited capability for work-related activity.

The relevant regulations are the ESA Regs, Pt 8 (Conditionality) Ch.1 (work-focused health related assessment), regs 47–53. Despite the width of the rule-making power (which would appear to authorise reduction in the amount of ESA payable) the sanction operates only by reduction of the work-related activity component of ESA, rather than on the whole allowance. It would appear that this has always been the policy intention, but, if so, it would have been better so to confine the rule-making power (see JHRC, *Second Report of Session 2006–07*, HL 34/HC 263 (2006–07), para.3.18).

Note that whether the claimant has good cause for failure to participate in a work-focused health-related assessment is to some extent structured by regulations in that ESA Regs, reg.53(3) provides an non-exhaustive list of matters to be taken into account in determining that good cause issue. No regulations have yet been made under para.(2)(h) to determine what does, or does not, rank as good cause.

Work-focused interviews

1.771   **12.**—(1) Regulations may make provision for or in connection with imposing on a person who is—

(a) entitled to an employment and support allowance, and

(b) not a member of the support group,

a requirement to take part in one or more work-focused interviews as a condition of continuing to be entitled to the full amount payable to him in respect of the allowance apart from the regulations.

(2) Regulations under this section may, in particular, make provision—

(a) prescribing circumstances in which such a person is subject to a requirement to take part in one or more work-focused interviews;

(b) for notifying such a person of any such requirement;

(c) prescribing the work-focused interviews in which a person who is subject to such a requirement is required to take part;

(d) for determining, in relation to work-focused interviews under the regulations, when and how the interview is to be conducted and, if it is to be conducted face to face, where it is to take place;

(e) for notifying persons who are required under the regulations to take part in a work-focused interview of what is determined in respect of the matters mentioned in paragraph (d);

(f) prescribing circumstances in which a person who is a party to a work-focused interview under the regulations is to be regarded as having, or not having, taken part in it;

(g) for securing that the appropriate consequence follows if a person who is required under the regulations to take part in a work-focused interview—

      (i) fails to take part in the interview, and

      (ii) does not, within a prescribed period, show that he had good cause for that failure;

  (h) prescribing matters which are, or are not, to be taken into account in determining whether a person had good cause for any failure to comply with the regulations;

  (i) prescribing circumstances in which a person is, or is not, to be regarded as having good cause for any such failure.

(3) For the purposes of subsection (2)(g), the appropriate consequence of a failure falling within that provision is that the amount payable to the person in question in respect of an employment and support allowance is reduced in accordance with regulations.

(4) Regulations under subsection (3) may, in particular, make provision for determining—

  (a) the amount by which an allowance is to be reduced,

  (b) when the reduction is to start, and

  (c) how long it is to continue,

and may include provision prescribing circumstances in which the amount of the reduction is to be nil.

(5) Regulations under this section shall include provision for a requirement to take part in one or more work-focused interviews to cease to have effect if the person subject to the requirement becomes a member of the support group.

(6) Regulations under this section may include provision—

  (a) that in such circumstances as the regulations may prescribe a requirement to take part in a work-focused interview that would otherwise apply to a person by virtue of such regulations is not to apply, or is to be treated as not having applied;

  (b) that in such circumstances as the regulations may prescribe such a requirement is not to apply until a prescribed time;

  (c) that in such circumstances as the regulations may prescribe matters mentioned in subsection (2)(d) may be redetermined.

(7) In this section, "work-focused interview" means an interview by the Secretary of State conducted for such purposes connected with getting the person interviewed into work, or keeping him in work, as may be prescribed.

DEFINITIONS

  "appropriate consequence"—see subs.(3).
  "entitled"—see s.24(1).
  "prescribed"—see s.24(1).
  "regulations"—see s.24(1).
  "support group"—see s.24(4).
  "work-focused interview"—see subs.(7).

GENERAL NOTE

This section covers those claimants, entitled to ESA, who do not have limited capability for work-related activity and who are thus entitled not to the support component but instead to the work-related activity component (they are not part of the "support group" (see s.24(4)). Those entitled to the work-related activity component must comply with certain conditions—the regime is one of "conditionality" (stipulating required behaviour and using sanctions to regulate and change behaviour). One of these conditions is participation in one or more work-focused

1.772

403

interviews conducted either by Jobcentre Plus or (as envisaged by s.16) one of the contractors in the private or voluntary sectors (PVS).

A "work-focused interview" is one conducted for such purposes connected with keeping the interviewee in work or getting him into work, as may be set out in regulations (subs.(7)).

This section enables the making of regulations to impose the requirement of participation in such an interview and to exempt persons from it, whether totally or delaying its application for a particular period (subss.(1), (5), (6)); to deal with the process of carrying out such an interview, and with the consequences of not participating in one without good cause (subs.(2)). Subsection (3) stipulates that a reduction in the amount of ESA otherwise payable is the appropriate consequence, and that subsection and subs.(4) enable the making of regulations determining the amount and period of the reduction and the circumstances in which the reduction is to be nil. Subsection (5) enables regulations to provide that the requirement shall cease to have effect if the person becomes a member of the support group, that is, if it is determined that he has, or is to be treated as having, limited capability for work-related activity.

The relevant regulations are the ESA Regs, Pt 8 (Conditionality) Ch.2 (work-focused interviews), regs 54–62. Despite the width of the rule-making power (which would appear to authorise reduction in the amount of ESA payable) the sanction operates only by reduction of the work-related activity component of ESA, rather than on the whole allowance. It would appear that this has always been the policy intention, but, if so, it would have been better in terms of compliance with Convention Rights so to confine the rule-making power (see JHRC, *Second Report of Session 2006–07*, HL 34/HC 263 (2006–07), para.3.18).

Note that whether the claimant has good cause for failure to participate in a work-focused health-related interview is to some extent structured by regulations in that ESA Regs, reg.61(3) provides a non-exhaustive list of matters which may be taken into account by decision-maker or appeal tribunal in determining that good cause issue. No regulations have yet been made under para.(2)(i) to determine what does, or does not, rank as good cause.

Work-related activity

1.773   **13.**—(1) Regulations may make provision for or in connection with imposing on a person who is subject to a requirement imposed under section 12(1) a requirement to undertake work-related activity in accordance with regulations as a condition of continuing to be entitled to the full amount payable to him in respect of an employment and support allowance apart from the regulations.

(2) Regulations under this section may, in particular, make provision—

(a) prescribing circumstances in which such a person is subject to a requirement to undertake work-related activity in accordance with regulations;

(b) for notifying such a person of any such requirement;

(c) prescribing the time or times at which a person who is subject to such a requirement is required to undertake work-related activity and the amount of work-related activity he is required at any time to undertake;

(d) prescribing circumstances in which a person who is subject to such a requirement is, or is not, to be regarded as undertaking work-related activity;

(e) for securing that the appropriate consequence follows if a person who is subject to such a requirement—

(i) fails to comply with the regulations, and

(ii) does not, within a prescribed period, show that he had good cause for that failure;

(f) prescribing the evidence which a person who is subject to such a requirement needs to provide in order to show that he has complied with the regulations;

(g) prescribing matters which are, or are not, to be taken into account in determining whether a person has complied with the regulations;

(h) prescribing matters which are, or are not, to be taken into account in determining whether a person had good cause for any failure to comply with the regulations;

(i) prescribing circumstances in which a person is, or is not, to be regarded as having good cause for any such failure.

(3) For the purposes of subsection (2)(e), the appropriate consequence of a failure falling within that provision is that the amount payable to the person in question in respect of an employment and support allowance is to be reduced in accordance with regulations.

(4) Regulations under subsection (3) may, in particular, make provision for determining—

(a) the amount by which an allowance is to be reduced,

(b) when the reduction is to start, and

(c) how long it is to continue,

and may include provision prescribing circumstances in which the amount of the reduction is to be nil.

(5) Regulations under this section shall include provision for a requirement to undertake work-related activity in accordance with regulations to cease to have effect if the person subject to the requirement becomes a member of the support group.

(6) Regulations under this section may include provision that in such circumstances as the regulations may provide a person's obligation under the regulations to undertake work-related activity at a particular time is not to apply, or is to be treated as not having applied.

(7) In this Part, "work-related activity", in relation to a person, means activity which makes it more likely that the person will obtain or remain in work or be able to do so.

DEFINITIONS

"appropriate consequence"—see subs.(3).
"regulations"—see s.24(1).
"support group"—see s.24(4).
"work-related activity"—see subs.(7).

GENERAL NOTE

This section applies only to those subject to a requirement to participate in a work-focused interview ("a requirement imposed under s.12(1)"). It thus covers those claimants, entitled to ESA, who do not have limited capability for work-related activity and who are thus entitled not to the support component but instead to the work-related activity component (they are not part of the "support group" (see s.24(4)), who have not been exempted from the requirement or had it delayed. Those entitled to the work-related activity component must comply with certain conditions in order to retain entitlement—the regime is one of "conditionality" (stipulating required behaviour and using sanctions to regulate and change behaviour). The first envisaged condition is participation in a work-focused health related assessment" (s.11). The second is participation in

1.774

a work-focused interview (s.12). This section enables the imposition on those subject to the second of a third condition: a requirement to undertake work-related activity. That is to undertake activity which makes it more likely that the person to be subjected to the condition will obtain or remain in work or be able to do so (ss.24(1), 13(7)).

This section enables the making of regulations to impose the requirement to undertake such activity and to exempt persons from it, whether totally or delaying its application for a particular period (subss.(1), (5), (6)); to deal with the process of imposition of the requirement, and with the consequences of not undertaking it without good cause (subs.(2)). Subsection (3) stipulates that a reduction in the amount of ESA otherwise payable is the appropriate consequence, and that subsection and subs.(4) enable the making of regulations determining the amount and period of the reduction and the circumstances in which the reduction is to be nil. Subsection (5) enables regulations to provide that the requirement shall cease to have effect if the person becomes a member of the support group, that is, if it is determined that he has, or is to be treated as having, limited capability for work-related activity.

As yet, no regulations have been made. It is envisaged that this aspect of "conditionality" will only come in when resources permit, probably not before late 2010 with a series of "Progression to Work" pilots for some ESA claimants. Activities envisaged are work tasters; programmes to manage health in work; job search assistance; and programmes to assist in stabilising the individual's life (*Explanatory Notes to the Welfare Reform Act 2007*, paras 86–91). Information presented to the Commons by the DWP when the Welfare Reform Bill was being considered there indicated that claimants would be asked to participate in a minimum amount of work-related activity (e.g. one activity) in a given time period (e.g. four weeks), and in between each period they would in their work-focused interview review what they had done and discuss what they would like to do in the next period (DWP, *Welfare Reform Bill: Draft Regulations and Supporting Material*, January 2007). That same material stressed that no-one would be forced to undertake a particular activity; the requirement is to participate in some work-related activity. Perhaps an appropriate analogy may be with the proper approach to the question in JSA of whether a claimant is actively seeking work (see commentary to Jobseekers Act 1995, ss.7, 9; and to JSA Regs, regs 18. Note also the power to direct that specific activity will not count a work-related activity for a particular person (s.15).

Despite the width of the rule-making power (which would appear to authorise reduction in the amount of ESA payable) it is envisaged that, as with that applicable to the other elements in respect of work-related activity "conditionality" (see ss.11, 12, above), the sanction will operate only by reduction of the work-related activity component of ESA, rather than on the whole allowance. It would appear that this has always been the policy intention, but, if so, it would have been better so to confine the rule-making power (see JHRC, *Second Report of Session 2006–07*, HL 34/HC 263 (2006–07), para.3.18).

Action plans in connection with work-focused interviews

1.775   **14.**—(1) The Secretary of State shall in prescribed circumstances provide a person subject to a requirement imposed under section 12(1) with a document prepared for such purposes as may be prescribed (in this section referred to as an action plan).

(2) Regulations may make provision about—

(a) the form of action plans;

(b) the content of action plans;

(c) the review and updating of action plans.

(3) Regulations under this section may, in particular, make provision for action plans which are provided to a person who is subject under section

13 to a requirement to undertake work-related activity to contain particulars of activity which, if undertaken, would enable the requirement to be met.

(4) Regulations may make provision for reconsideration of an action plan at the request of the person to whom the plan is provided and may, in particular, make provision about—

(a) the circumstances in which reconsideration may be requested;
(b) the period within which any reconsideration must take place;
(c) the matters to which regard must be had when deciding on reconsideration whether the plan should be changed;
(d) notification of the decision on reconsideration;
(e) the giving of directions for the purpose of giving effect to the decision on reconsideration.

DEFINITIONS

"action plan"—see subs.(1).
"prescribed"—see s.24(1).
"regulations"—see s.24(1).
"work-related activity"—see ss.24(1), 13(7).

GENERAL NOTE

Part of the "work-related activity" process requires the drawing up of written "action plans" as part of the work-related interview process, envisaging that these will be reviewed and amended as conditions change. This section imposes that requirement and authorises regulations to give it effect. The regulation is the ESA Regs, reg.58. An action plan records the interview; any work-related activity the claimant is willing to undertake; and any other information considered appropriate by the Secretary of State. The plan will doubtless influence the shape of future interviews and be relevant to the question of whether the claimant is undertaking work-related activity and whether he should be sanctioned by reduction or eventually removal of work-related activity component in accordance with ESA Regs, regs 63, 64. It may be tempting to draw analogies with the jobseeker's agreement in JSA, but the plan is just that: a plan drawn up by officialdom and agreement to it is not directly a condition of entitlement to ESA.

1.776

Directions about work-related activity

15.—(1) In prescribed circumstances, the Secretary of State may by direction given to a person subject to a requirement imposed under section 13(1) provide that the undertaking of activity specified in the direction is, in his case, to be treated as not being the undertaking of work-related activity.

1.777

(2) The power under subsection (1) to give directions—

(a) is exercisable by instrument in writing, and
(b) includes power to vary or revoke a direction given in previous exercise of the power.

(3) Where a direction under subsection (1) varies or revokes a previous direction, it may provide for the variation or revocation to have effect from a time before the giving of the direction.

DEFINITIONS

"prescribed"—see s.24(1).
"work-related activity"—see ss.24(1), 13(7).

1.778   Engagement in work-related activity is a condition of entitlement to work-related activity component for most of the claimants who are not in the support group. Failure to engage in such activity can be sanctioned by reduction or removal of work-related activity component, leaving such a claimant reliant solely on basic allowance ESA. This section enables a written direction to be given to a claimant with the effect that the activity specified in the direction will in his case be treated as not being work-related activity. The DWP envisages that this power will only be used in limited circumstances "where a given activity was wholly inappropriate for the claimant" (DWP, *Welfare Reform Bill: Draft Regulations and Supporting Material*, January 2007). Since engagement in work-related activity will not be an operative part of "conditionality" until resources permit (probably not before 2011 (see commentary to s.13), the regulations envisaged by subs.(1), setting out the circumstances, in which a direction can be given, have not yet been made

Contracting out

1.779   **16.**—(1) The following functions of the Secretary of State may be exercised by, or by employees of, such person (if any) as the Secretary of State may authorise for the purpose, namely—

(a) conducting interviews under section 12;

(b) providing documents under section 14;

(c) giving, varying or revoking directions under section 15.

(2) Regulations may provide for any of the following functions of the Secretary of State to be exercisable by, or by employees of, such person (if any) as the Secretary of State may authorise for the purpose—

(a) any function under regulations under any of sections 11 to 15, except the making of a decision to which subsection (3) applies (an "excluded decision");

(b) the function under section 9(1) of the Social Security Act 1998 (c. 14) (revision of decisions), so far as relating to decisions, except excluded decisions, that relate to any matter arising under such regulations;

(c) the function under section 10(1) of that Act (superseding of decisions), so far as relating to decisions, except excluded decisions, of the Secretary of State that relate to any matter arising under such regulations;

(d) any function under Chapter 2 of Part 1 of that Act (social security decisions), except section 25(2) and (3) (decisions involving issues that arise on appeal in other cases), which relates to the exercise of any of the functions falling within paragraphs (a) to (c).

(3) This subsection applies to the following decisions—

(a) a decision about whether a person has failed to comply with a requirement imposed by regulations under section 11, 12 or 13;

(b) a decision about whether a person had good cause for failure to comply with such a requirement;

(c) a decision about reduction of an employment and support allowance in consequence of failure to comply with such a requirement.

(4) Regulations under subsection (2) may provide that a function to which that subsection applies may be exercised—

(a) either wholly or to such extent as the regulations may provide,

(b) either generally or in such cases or areas as the regulations may provide, and

(c) either unconditionally or subject to the fulfilment of such conditions as the regulations may provide.

(5) An authorisation given by virtue of subsection (1), or by virtue of regulations under subsection (2), may authorise the exercise of the function concerned—

(a) either wholly or to such extent as may be specified in the authorisation,

(b) either generally or in such cases or areas as may be so specified, and

(c) either unconditionally or subject to the fulfilment of such conditions as may be so specified.

(6) In the case of an authorisation given by virtue of regulations under subsection (2), subsection (5) is subject to the provisions of the regulations.

(7) An authorisation given by virtue of subsection (1), or by virtue of regulations under subsection (2)—

(a) may specify its duration,

(b) may be revoked at any time by the Secretary of State, and

(c) shall not prevent the Secretary of State or any other person from exercising the function to which the authorisation relates.

(8) Where a person is authorised to exercise any function by virtue of subsection (1), or by virtue of regulations under subsection (2), anything done or omitted to be done by or in relation to him (or an employee of his) in, or in connection with, the exercise or purported exercise of the function shall be treated for all purposes as done or omitted to be done by or in relation to the Secretary of State.

(9) Subsection (8) shall not apply—

(a) for the purposes of so much of any contract made between the authorised person and the Secretary of State as relates to the exercise of the function, or

(b) for the purposes of any criminal proceedings brought in respect of anything done or omitted to be done by the authorised person (or an employee of his).

(10) Any decision which a person authorised to exercise any function by virtue of subsection (1), or by virtue of regulations under subsection (2), makes in exercise of the function shall have effect as a decision of the Secretary of State under section 8 of the Social Security Act1998.

(11) Where—

(a) a person is authorised to exercise any function by virtue of subsection (1), or by virtue of regulations under subsection (2), and

(b) the authorisation is revoked at a time when a relevant contract is subsisting,

the authorised person shall be entitled to treat the relevant contract as repudiated by the Secretary of State (and not as frustrated by reason of the revocation).

(12) In subsection (11), the reference to a relevant contract is to so much of any contract made between the authorised person and the Secretary of State as relates to the exercise of the function.

(13) In this section, references to functions of the Secretary of State under—

(a) an enactment contained in, or in regulations under, this Part, or

(b) an enactment contained in Chapter 2 of Part 1 of the Social Security Act 1998, include a reference to any function which the Secretary of State has by virtue of the application in relation to that enactment of section 8(1)(c) of that Act (decisions under certain enactments to be made by the Secretary of State).

DEFINITIONS

"regulations"—see s.24(1).

GENERAL NOTE

1.780   This section authorises, to such a degree as is specified in regulations and/or an authorisation (subss.(5), (6)), the contracting out of certain functions vested in the Secretary of State (DWP/JobCentre Plus decision-makers and Personal Advisers) in respect of the conditionality aspect of entitlement to the work-related activity component, and of a wide (but not unlimited) range of decisions related to the exercise of those functions.

Those functions are conducting work-focused interviews under s.12; providing documents under s.14 (action plans in connection with work-focused interviews); and giving, varying or revoking directions under s.15 (subs.(1)). The functions can be exercised by the contractor ("such person as the Secretary of State may authorise for the purpose") or by employees of the contractor (subs.(1)). Anything done (or omitted to be done) by them must be treated as if done (or omitted to be done) by the Secretary of State (subss.(8), (9)). Their decisions in respect of the authorised functions are to be given effect as ones of the Secretary of State under s.8 SSA 1998 (subs.(10). Revocation of the authorisation may be treated as a repudiation of the contract by the Secretary of State and not as a matter of frustration of the contract (subss.(11, (12)).

In addition, subs.(2) enables the making of regulations authorising a number of other functions to be so exercisable by the contractor or the contractor's employees. The regulations can authorise the exercise of any functions under ss.11–15, above (subs.(2)(a)), other than "excluded decisions" which are enumerated in subs.(3). Put shortly, this prevents authorising contractors or their employees to make decisions in respect of the sanctioning aspect of "conditionality" as regards entitlement to the work-related activity component, although information and material from them will perforce feed into and inform decisions on these matters made by DWP/JobCentre Plus decision-makers. Thus subs.(3) provides that regulations cannot enable the making by contractors or their employees of decisions on whether the claimant has failed to comply with requirements, set out in regulations, on work-focused health-related assessments (s.11), work-focused interviews (s.12) or work-related activity (s.13) (para.(a)). Regulations cannot authorise them to make decisions on whether the claimant had good cause for any failure to comply with such a requirement (para.(b)), or on whether failure to comply must be sanctioned by reduction or removal of the amount of work-related activity component to which the claimant would otherwise be entitled (para.(c)). But, save so far as they relate to excluded decisions, regulations can authorise contractors or their employees to exercise powers of revision and supersession under ss.9 and 10, respectively, of the Social Security Act 1998, in respect of any functions under ss.11–15 (subs.(2)(b), (c)). Subsection (2)(d) enables regulations to authorise them also to exercise, in respect of those functions, any function under Ch.2 of Pt I of that 1998 Act, other than ones under ss.25(2) and (3) of it (decisions involving issues that arise on appeal in other cases).

The ESA regime envisages that helping claimants return to work or to the labour market need not solely be the task of the DWP or Jobcentre Plus, important as their role is. Contractors in the private and voluntary sector (PVS) have specialist knowledge and innovative approaches which, properly harnessed and deployed, may well ensure the best possible support for claimants in the work-related activity group. As with the Provider Led Pathways aspect of the Pathways to Work project on which the ESA approach is built, JobCentre Plus will conduct the first work-focused interview. It will be recalled that a "work-focused interview" is one conducted for such purposes connected with keeping the interviewee in work or getting him into work, as may be set out in regulations (s.12(7)). A secondary purpose will be to provide information on benefit and service entitlement. This renders it appropriate that it be done by JobCentre Plus. But a principal reason for its staff doing so is that at that stage, very early in a claim, eligibility for ESA will not have been determined by the medical test. Although interviews after the claimant's first work-focused interview may well be carried out by PVS providers, JobCentre Plus will during the lifetime of the claim exercise functions relating to entitlement to benefit, sanctioning decisions and processing of benefit payments.

Miscellaneous

Income and capital: general

17.—(1) In relation to a claim for an employment and support allowance, the income and capital of a person shall be calculated or estimated in such manner as may be prescribed.   1.781

(2) A person's income in respect of a week shall be calculated in accordance with prescribed rules, which may provide for the calculation to be made by reference to an average over a period (which need not include the week concerned).

(3) Circumstances may be prescribed in which—
(a) a person is to be treated as possessing capital or income which he does not possess;
(b) capital or income which a person does possess is to be disregarded;
(c) income is to be treated as capital;
(d) capital is to be treated as income.

(4) Regulations may provide that a person's capital shall be deemed for the purposes of this Part to yield him an income at a prescribed rate.

DEFINITIONS
"prescribed"—see s.24(1).
"regulations"—*ibid.*
"week"—*ibid.*

GENERAL NOTE

This section is very similar to s.136(3)–(5) of the Contributions and Benefits Act and s.12 of the Jobseekers Act (see *Vol.II: Income Support, Jobseekers Allowance, State Pension Credit and the Social Fund*).   1.782

It enables the Secretary of State to introduce detailed regulations governing the treatment of income and capital for the purposes of ESA. See Pt 10 of and Schs 7, 8 and 9 to the ESA Regulations.

See also para.6(2) of Sch.1 which contains the "aggregation rule" for the purposes of income-related ESA, i.e., that where the claimant is a member of a couple, his partner's income and capital counts as that of the claimant (except in prescribed circumstances).

Disqualification

18.—(1) Regulations may provide for a person to be disqualified for receiving an employment and support allowance, or treated for such purposes as the regulations may provide as not having limited capability for work, if—   1.783

411

(a) he has become someone who has limited capability for work through his own misconduct,

(b) he remains someone who has limited capability for work through his failure without good cause to follow medical advice, or

(c) he fails without good cause to observe any prescribed rules of behaviour.

(2) Regulations under subsection (1) shall provide for any such disqualification, or treatment, to be for such period not exceeding 6 weeks as may be determined in accordance with Chapter 2 of Part 1 of the Social Security Act 1998 (c. 14).

(3) Regulations may prescribe for the purposes of subsection (1)—

(a) matters which are, or are not, to be taken into account in determining whether a person has good cause for any act or omission;

(b) circumstances in which a person is, or is not, to be regarded as having good cause for any act or omission.

(4) Except where regulations otherwise provide, a person shall be disqualified for receiving a contributory allowance for any period during which he is—

(a) absent from Great Britain, or

(b) undergoing imprisonment or detention in legal custody.

DEFINITIONS

"contributory allowance"—see s.1(7).
"limited capability for work"—see s.1(4).
"prescribed"—see s.24(1).
"regulations"—see s.24(1).
"week"—see s.24(1).

GENERAL NOTE

Subss. (1)–(3)

1.784
Like previous incapacity benefits' regimes (compare SSCBA 1992, s.171E and IW (General) Regs, reg.18), ESA embodies disqualification from benefit, or treating someone as not having limited capability for work, for a period not exceeding six weeks as sanctions in respect of conduct which conduces to a person's limited capability for work either by bringing it about through misconduct (subs.(1)(a)) or by remaining someone with limited capacity by failing without good cause to follow medical advice (subs.(1)(b)) or by failing without good cause to adhere to prescribed rules of behaviour (subs.(1)(c)). These subsections provide rule-making power for the regime of disqualification. The relevant regulations are the ESA Regs, regs 157–158. Note the protection from disqualification for a "person in hardship" (regs 157(3)(a), 158) and someone disqualified from receiving ESA because of regulations made pursuant to s.7 of the Social Security Fraud Act 2001 (reg.157(3)(b); for that section and the consequent Social Security (Loss of Benefit) Regs 2001, see Vol.III).

Although subs.(3) enables regs to be made dealing with aspects of the "good cause" issue (matters to take into or leave out of account; things which do or do not rank as "good cause"), no such regs have yet been made. "Good cause" thus remains a matter for the decision-maker or tribunal, circumscribed by case law on analogous provisions.

Subs. (4)

1.785
This mandates for the ESA regime disqualification from CESA in respect of periods of absence from GB or of imprisonment or detention in legal custody. Exceptions from disqualification can be afforded by regs : see ESA Regs, regs

151–155 (temporary absence from GB), 160, 161 (imprisonment or detention in legal custody). Compare, with respect to incapacity benefit, SSCBA 1992, s.113.

Pilot schemes

19.—(1) Any regulations to which this subsection applies may be made so as to have effect for a specified period not exceeding 24 months.   1.786

(2) Subject to subsection (3), subsection (1) applies to—

(a) regulations which are made under any provision of this Part, other than sections 3, 8 and 9;

(b) regulations which are made under the Administration Act, so far as they relate to an employment and support allowance.

(3) Subsection (1) only applies to regulations if they are made with a view to ascertaining whether their provisions will or will be likely to—

(a) encourage persons to obtain or remain in work, or

(b) make it more likely that persons will obtain or remain in work or be able to do so.

(4) Regulations which, by virtue of subsection (1), are to have effect for a limited period are referred to in this section as a "pilot scheme".

(5) A pilot scheme may provide that its provisions are to apply only in relation to—

(a) one or more specified areas;

(b) one or more specified classes of person;

(c) persons selected—

   (i) by reference to prescribed criteria, or

   (ii) on a sampling basis.

(6) A pilot scheme may make consequential or transitional provision with respect to the cessation of the scheme on the expiry of the specified period.

(7) A pilot scheme may be replaced by a further pilot scheme making the same or similar provision.

DEFINITIONS

"Administration Act"—see. s.65.
"prescribed"—see. s.24(1).
"regulations"—*ibid.*

GENERAL NOTE

This is modelled on s.29 of the Jobseekers Act (see Vol.II in this series), except that under subs.(1) pilot schemes are limited to 24, rather than 12, months; as in the case of JSA pilot schemes, they may be repeated (see subs.(7)). Any regulations under Pt 1 of the Act or associated rules under the SSAA 1992 may be piloted, other than regulations concerning deductions from contributory ESA (s.3), limited capability for work (s.8) and limited capability for work-related activity (s.9). Regulations made under this section are subject to the affirmative resolution procedure (s.26(1)(c)).   1.787

The power under s.29 of the Jobseekers Act has been used on a fairly regular basis to test in particular changes to "conditionality" and it seems likely that this will also be the case for ESA.

Relationship with statutory payments

20.—(1) A person is not entitled to an employment and support allowance in respect of a day if, for the purposes of statutory sick pay, that day—   1.788

(a) is a day of incapacity for work in relation to a contract of service, and

(b) falls within a period of entitlement (whether or not it is a qualifying day).

(2) Except as regulations may provide, a woman who is entitled to statutory maternity pay is not entitled to a contributory allowance in respect of a day that falls within the maternity pay period.

(3) Regulations may provide that—

(a) an amount equal to a woman's statutory maternity pay for a period shall be deducted from a contributory allowance in respect of the same period,

(b) a woman shall only be entitled to a contributory allowance if there is a balance after the deduction, and

(c) if there is such a balance, a woman shall be entitled to a contributory allowance at a weekly rate equal to it.

(4) Except as regulations may provide, a person who is entitled to statutory adoption pay is not entitled to a contributory allowance in respect of a day that falls within the adoption pay period.

(5) Regulations may provide that—

(a) an amount equal to a person's statutory adoption pay for a period shall be deducted from a contributory allowance in respect of the same period,

(b) a person shall only be entitled to a contributory allowance if there is a balance after the deduction, and

(c) if there is such a balance, a person shall be entitled to a contributory allowance at a weekly rate equal to it.

(6) Except as regulations may provide, a person who is entitled to additional statutory paternity pay is not entitled to a contributory allowance in respect of a day that falls within the additional paternity pay period.

(7) Regulations may provide that—

(a) an amount equal to a person's additional statutory paternity pay for a period shall be deducted from a contributory allowance in respect of the same period,

(b) a person shall only be entitled to a contributory allowance if there is a balance after the deduction, and

(c) if there is such a balance, a person shall be entitled to a contributory allowance at a weekly rate equal to it.

(8) In this section—

"the additional paternity pay period" has the meaning given in section 171ZEE(2) of the Contributions and Benefits Act;

"the adoption pay period" has the meaning given in section 171ZN(2) of that Act;

"the maternity pay period" has the meaning given in section 165(1) of that Act.

DEFINITIONS

"the additional paternity pay period"—see subs.(8).
"the adoption pay period"—see subs.(8).
"Contributions and Benefits Act"—see s.65.
"contributory allowance"—see s.1(7).
"entitled"—see s.24(1).
"the maternity pay period"—see subs.(8).

GENERAL NOTE

This deals with the relationship between ESA and certain other "employer paid" statutory payments, the overall responsibility for them lying with HMRC. The payments covered by this section are statutory sick pay (SSP), statutory maternity pay (SMP), statutory adoption pay (SAP) and additional statutory paternity pay (ASPP). They are dealt with in Vol.IV. The relationships are not all of a piece. ESA cannot be paid in respect of days for which there is SSP entitlement (subs. (1)). As regards SMP, SAP and ASPP, the interrelationship only concerns CESA. The general rule is that CESA cannot be payable at the same time as any of these other payments, but exceptions can be made by regulations (subss.(2)–(7)). The relevant regs are the ESA Regs, regs 80 (SMP), 81 (SAP) and 82 (ASPP). Where they operate to enable ESA to be paid, however, the amount of CESA payable is reduced by the amount of the relevant statutory payment, and only any balance of CESA remaining is payable.

1.789

Deemed entitlement for other purposes

21.—Regulations may provide for a person who would be entitled to an employment and support allowance but for the operation of any provision of, or made under, this Part, the Administration Act or Chapter 2 of Part 1 of the Social Security Act 1998 (c. 14) (social security decisions and appeals) to be treated as if entitled to the allowance for the purposes of any rights or obligations (whether his own or another's) which depend on his entitlement, other than the right to payment of it.

1.790

DEFINITIONS

"Administration Act"—see s.65.
"regulations"—see s.24(1).

GENERAL NOTE

This section is identical to SSCBA 1992, s.113(3). It enables regs to be made enabling someone to be treated as still entitled to ESA, though not to payment of it, even though provisions of or made under this Part of the WRA, the AA 1992 or SSA 1998, Pt I Ch.2 operate to disentitle him. The person will only be treated as entitled in this way to enable him or someone else to retain rights and obligations under social security law more generally.

1.791

Supplementary provisions

22.—Schedule 2 (which contains further provisions in relation to an employment and support allowance) has effect.

1.792

GENERAL NOTE

This provides the basis for giving effect to the detailed provisions on ESA set out in Sch.2. These concern rule making in respect of: treating someone as having or not having limited capability for work/work-related activity (as the case may be), waiting days, linking periods, payments of benefit for less than a week, presence in GB, entitlement to CESA by persons not in GB, retained entitlement to IRESA after someone has left GB, modifying entitlement to CESA in respect of employment on ships, vessels, aircraft or hovercraft, the effect of work, treating ESA as "benefit", attribution of reductions where someone is entitled both to CESA and IRESA, ESA information to be treated as social security information, the making of advance claims, and modifying provisions in respect of ESA as regards Members of Her majesty's forces.

1.793

Recovery of sums in respect of maintenance

1.794   **23.**—(1) Regulations may make provision for the court to have power to make a recovery order against any person where an award of income-related allowance has been made to that person's spouse or civil partner.

(2) The reference in subsection (1) to a recovery order is to an order requiring the person against whom it is made to make payments to the Secretary of State or to such other person or persons as the court may determine.

(3) Regulations under subsection (1) may include—

(a) provision as to the matters to which the court is, or is not, to have regard in determining any application under the regulations;

(b) provision as to the enforcement of orders under the regulations;

(c) provision for the transfer by the Secretary of State of the right to receive payments under, and to exercise rights in relation to, orders under the regulations.

(4) In this section, "the court" means—

(a) in relation to England and Wales, a magistrates' court;

(b) in relation to Scotland, the sheriff.

DEFINITIONS

"income-related allowance"— see s.1(7).
"regulations"— see s.24(1).

GENERAL NOTE

1.795   This is similar to the powers in relation to income-based JSA in s.23 of the Jobseekers Act (see Vol.II in this series). For the powers in relation to income support, see s.106 of the Administration Act (to be found in Vol.III in this series).

General

Interpretation of Part 1

1.796   **24.**—(1) In this Part—
"claimant" means a person who has claimed an employment and support allowance;
"contributory allowance" has the meaning given by section 1(7);
"employment" and "employed" have the meanings prescribed for the purposes of this Part;
"entitled", in relation to an employment and support allowance, is to be construed in accordance with—

(a) the provisions of this Act,

(b) section 1 of the Administration Act (entitlement dependent on making of claim), and

(c) section 27 of the Social Security Act 1998 (c. 14) (restrictions on entitlement in certain cases of error);

"income-related allowance" has the meaning given by section 1(7);
"income support" means income support under section 124 of the Contributions and Benefits Act;
"limited capability for work" shall be construed in accordance with section 1(4);

"limited capability for work-related activity" shall be construed in accordance with section 2(5);

"period of limited capability for work" has the meaning prescribed for the purposes of this Part;

"prescribed" means specified in, or determined in accordance with, regulations;

"regulations" means regulations made by the Secretary of State;

"week" means a period of 7 days beginning with a Sunday or such other period of 7 days as may be prescribed;

"work-related activity" has the meaning given by section 13(7).

(2) For the purposes of this Part, the assessment phase, in relation to a claimant, is the period—

(a) beginning, subject to subsection (3), with the first day of the period for which he is entitled to an employment and support allowance, and

(b) ending with such day as may be prescribed.

(3) Regulations may prescribe circumstances in which the assessment phase is to begin with such day as may be prescribed.

(4) For the purposes of this Part, a person is a member of the support group if he is a person in respect of whom it is determined that he has, or is to be treated as having, limited capability for work-related activity.

DEFINITIONS

"Administration Act"—see s.65.
"Contributions and Benefits Act"—see s.65.

GENERAL NOTE

This defines, sometimes by referring the reader to other provisions or leaving the meaning to be set out in regulations, a number of key terms in respect of ESA. Note in particular that the "assessment phase", during which there can generally only be entitlement to basic allowance ESA, is generally to begin on the first such day of entitlement and to end in accordance with regulations (subss.(2), (3)). See on this ESA Regs, regs (4)–(7). Note also that membership of the support group, and thus eligibility for the more generous "support component" in addition to basic allowance ESA, is dependent on a determination that the person has, or is to be treated as having, limited capability for work-related activity (subs.(4)).

1.797

General

Regulations

25.—(1) Any power under this Part to make regulations shall be exercisable by statutory instrument.

1.798

(2) Any such power may be exercised—

(a) in relation to all cases to which it extends,

(b) in relation to those cases subject to specified exceptions, or

(c) in relation to any specified cases or classes of case.

(3) Any such power may be exercised so as to make, as respects the cases in relation to which it is exercised—

(a) the full provision to which the power extends or any less provision (whether by way of exception or otherwise);

(b) the same provision for all cases in relation to which it is exercised, or different provision for different cases or different classes of case or different provision as respects the same case or class of case for different purposes of this Part;

(c) any such provision either unconditionally or subject to any specified condition.

(4) Where any such power is expressed to be exercisable for alternative purposes, it may be exercised in relation to the same case for all or any of those purposes.

(5) Any such power includes power—

(a) to make such incidental, supplementary, consequential or transitional provision or savings as appear to the Secretary of State to be expedient;

(b) to provide for a person to exercise a discretion in dealing with any matter.

(6) Without prejudice to the generality of the provisions of this section, regulations under any of sections 11 to 15 may make provision which applies only in relation to an area or areas specified in the regulations.

(7) The fact that a power to make regulations is conferred by this Part is not to be taken to prejudice the extent of any other power to make regulations so conferred.

GENERAL NOTE

1.799   This section is similar to s.175 of the Contributions and Benefits Act and s.36 of the Jobseekers Act.

Parliamentary control

1.800   **26.**—(1) None of the following regulations shall be made unless a draft of the statutory instrument containing them has been laid before, and approved by a resolution of, each House of Parliament—

(a) regulations under section 2(2)(c) or (3)(c) or 4(4)(c) or (5)(c);

(b) the first regulations under section 13;

(c) regulations which by virtue of section 19(1) are to have effect for a limited period.

(2) A statutory instrument that—

(a) contains regulations made under this Part, and

(b) is not subject to a requirement that a draft of the instrument be laid before, and approved by a resolution of, each House of Parliament, shall be subject to annulment in pursuance of a resolution of either House of Parliament.

GENERAL NOTE

1.801   This section is similar to s.176 of the Contributions and Benefits Act and s.37 of the Jobseekers Act.

Financial provisions relating to Part 1

1.802   **27.**—(1) There shall be paid out of the National Insurance Fund so much of any sums payable by way of employment and support allowance as is attributable to entitlement to a contributory allowance.

(2) There shall be paid out of money provided by Parliament—

(a) so much of any sums payable by way of employment and support allowance as is attributable to entitlement to an income-related allowance, and

(b) any administrative expenses of the Secretary of State or the Commissioners for Her Majesty's Revenue and Customs in carrying this Part into effect.

(3) The Secretary of State shall pay into the National Insurance Fund sums estimated by him to be equivalent in amount to sums recovered by him in connection with payments of contributory allowance.

(4) The Secretary of State shall pay into the Consolidated Fund sums estimated by him to be equivalent in amount to sums recovered by him in connection with payments made by way of income-related allowance.

DEFINITIONS

"contributory allowance"—ss.24(1) and 1(7).
"income-related allowance"—*ibid.*

GENERAL NOTE

This section is similar to s.163 of the Administration Act, s.38 of the Jobseekers Act and s.20 of the State Pension Credit Act.　　　　**1.803**

Consequential amendments relating to Part 1

28.—(1) Schedule 3 (which makes amendments consequential on this Part) has effect.　　　　**1.804**

(2) Regulations may make provision consequential on this Part amending, repealing or revoking any provision of—

(a) an Act passed on or before the last day of the Session in which this Act is passed, or

(b) an instrument made under an Act before the passing of this Act.

(3) In subsection (2), "Act" includes an Act of the Scottish Parliament.

DEFINITIONS

"Act"—see subs.(3).
"regulations"—see s.24(1).

GENERAL NOTE

Subs.(1)
This gives effect to a range of consequential amendments of other Acts of Parliament set out in Sch.3. Where the provisions to be amended are contained in the main volumes of *Social Security Legislation 2008/09*, the amendments are noted at the appropriate point(s) in the updating Parts of this Supplement.　　**1.805**

Subs.(2)
This enables the making of consequential regulations amending Acts (including ones of the Scottish Parliament) passed on or before the last day of the 2006–07 Westminster parliamentary session (the one in which the WRA 2007 was passed) (para.(a), subs.(3)). It also enables consequential regulations to amend subordinate legislation, already made before the passing of the WRA 2007, under Acts (including those of the Scottish Parliament) (para.(b), subs.(3)).　　**1.806**

Transition relating to Part 1

29.—Schedule 4 (which makes provision with respect to transition in relation to this Part) has effect.　　　　**1.807**

1.808   This gives effect to Sch.4, reproduced in full with provisions not yet in force set out in italics. That Schedule embodies rule-making powers for pre- and post-commencement claims, awarding ESA in respect of a pre-commencement period , converting existing awards of IB/IS/SDA to ESA, the post-commencement up-rating of IB/SDA, and a general power to provide for transitional matters with respect to ESA. The regulations so made are the Employment and Support Allowance (Transitional Provisions) Regulations 2008 (SI 2008/795).

Sections 30–63 Omitted

PART 5

GENERAL

Northern Ireland

1.809   **64.**—(1) This section applies to an Order in Council under paragraph 1(1) of the Schedule to the Northern Ireland Act 2000 (c. 1) (legislation for Northern Ireland during suspension of devolved government) which contains a statement that it is made only for purposes corresponding to those of this Act.

(2) Such an Order—

(a) is not subject to paragraph 2 of that Schedule (affirmative resolution of both Houses of Parliament), but

(b) is subject to annulment in pursuance of a resolution of either House of Parliament.

GENERAL NOTE

1.810   Part I of the WRA 2007 dealing with ESA applies only to Great Britain (England, Wales and Scotland). This is true of the social security system generally. But comparable provision in respect of social security for Northern Ireland is always made by Order in Council under its devolution Act. This section deals with parliamentary scrutiny and control over such an Order. It provides that any such Order, stated to be made only for purposes corresponding to those of the WRA 2007, is to be subject to annulment by either House of Parliament rather than to the affirmative resolution procedure that would otherwise be applicable.

General interpretation

1.811   **65.**—In this Act—

"Administration Act" means the Social Security Administration Act 1992 (c. 5);

"Contributions and Benefits Act" means the Social Security Contributions and Benefits Act 1992 (c. 4).

Financial provisions: general

1.812   **66.**—(1) There shall be paid out of money provided by Parliament—

(a) any expenditure incurred by the Secretary of State in consequence of Parts 2 to 4 of this Act, and

(b) any increase attributable to this Act in the sums payable out of money so provided under any other enactment.

(2) There shall be paid into the Consolidated Fund any increase attributable to this Act in the sums payable into that Fund under any other enactment.

Repeals

67.—The enactments specified in Schedule 8 are hereby repealed to the extent specified.

1.813

GENERAL NOTE

Insofar as this affects legislation in the main volumes, the changes are noted in the relevant updating Parts of this Supplement (II–V, as appropriate).

1.814

Section 68 omitted

Extent

69.—(1) Subject to the following provisions, this Act extends to England and Wales and Scotland only.

1.815

(2) The following provisions extend to England and Wales only—

(a) sections 42(1) to (10) and 43, and

(b) paragraphs 6, 11(2) and 16 of Schedule 3.

(3) Paragraphs 1, 2, 4, 11(3), 14 and 22 of Schedule 3 extend to Scotland only.

(4) The following provisions also extend to Northern Ireland—

(a) sections 33(7), 49, 56, 57, 61, 64, 65, 68, this section and sections 70 and 71,

(b) paragraph 15 of Schedule 2, and sections 22 and 24 to 26 so far as relating thereto,

(c) paragraphs 5, 10(1) and (28), 17(1) and (2), 19, 23(1) to (3) and (6) to (8) and 24 of Schedule 3, and section 28 so far as relating thereto,

(d) paragraph 1 of Schedule 7, and section 63 so far as relating thereto, and

(e) Schedule 8, so far as relating to the Vaccine Damage Payments Act 1979 (c. 17), the Income and Corporation Taxes Act 1988 (c. 1), the Disability (Grants) Act 1993 (c. 14), section 2 of the Social Security Act 1998 (c. 14) and the Income Tax (Earnings and Pensions) Act 2003 (c. 1), and section 67 so far as relating thereto.

(5) The following provisions extend to Northern Ireland only—

(a) section 45, and

(b) Schedule 8, so far as relating to the Social Security Administration (Northern Ireland) Act 1992 (c. 8), and section 67 so far as relating thereto.

(6) The following provisions also extend to the Isle of Man—

(a) sections 56 and 57, section 68, this section and sections 70 and 71,

(b) paragraph 1 of Schedule 7, and section 63 so far as relating thereto, and

(c) Schedule 8, so far as relating to the Vaccine Damage Payments Act 1979, and section 67 so far as relating thereto.

1.816   Only subs.(1) concerns ESA. It means that the ESA scheme under Pt I of the Act applies only to England, Wales and Scotland. Comparable provision can be made for Northern Ireland through Order in Council under the devolution legislation (s.64). The devolution arrangements and the complicated political background in Northern Ireland may, however, mean that relevant legislation may have to be enacted by the Northern Ireland Assembly.

Commencement

1.817   **70.**—(1) The following provisions shall come into force at the end of the period of 2 months beginning with the day on which this Act is passed—

(a) sections 41(2) and (3), 44, 45, 54, 55, 59, 61(1)(b) and (2) to (6) and 62,

(b) paragraphs 1 to 4, 10, 11 and 14 of Schedule 5, and section 40 so far as relating thereto,

(c) paragraphs 2(1) and (3), 3 and 4 of Schedule 7, and section 63 so far as relating thereto, and

(d) Schedule 8, so far as relating to—

(i) section 3(5) of the Pneumoconiosis etc. (Workers' Compensation) Act 1979 (c. 41),

(ii) section 140(1A) of the Contributions and Benefits Act,

(iii) sections 71(5), 71ZA(2), 134(8)(a) and 168(3)(d) of the Administration Act,

(iv) section 69(5) of the Social Security Administration (Northern Ireland) Act 1992,

(v) Schedule 13 to the Local Government etc. (Scotland) Act 1994 (c. 39), (vi) section 38(7)(a) of, and paragraph 81(2) of Schedule 7 to, the Social Security Act 1998 (c. 14), and

(vii) paragraph 65 of Schedule 24 to the Civil Partnership Act 2004 (c. 33), and section 67 so far as relating thereto.

(2) The remaining provisions of this Act, except—

(a) this section,

(b) sections 64, 65, 66, 68, 69 and 71, and

(c) paragraph 8 of Schedule 5, and section 40 so far as relating thereto,

shall come into force on such day as the Secretary of State may by order made by statutory instrument appoint, and different days may be so appointed for different purposes.

1.818   The key operative date for the ESA regime is October 27, 2008.

Short title

1.819   **71.**—This Act may be cited as the Welfare Reform Act 2007.

SCHEDULES

SCHEDULE 1

EMPLOYMENT AND SUPPORT ALLOWANCE: ADDITIONAL CONDITIONS

PART 1

CONTRIBUTORY ALLOWANCE

Conditions relating to national insurance

1.—(1) The first condition is that—

(a) the claimant has actually paid Class 1 or Class 2 contributions in respect of one of the last three complete tax years ("the base tax year") before the beginning of the relevant benefit year,

(b) those contributions must have been paid before the relevant benefit week, and

(c) the earnings factor derived as mentioned in sub-paragraph (2) must be not less than the base tax year's lower earnings limit multiplied by 25.

(2) The earnings factor referred to in sub-paragraph (1)(c) is the aggregate of the claimant's earnings factors derived—

(a) from so much of his earnings as did not exceed the base tax year's upper earnings limit and upon which primary Class 1 contributions have been paid or treated as paid, and

(b) from Class 2 contributions.

(3) Where primary Class 1 contributions have been paid or treated as paid on any part of a person's earnings, sub-paragraph (2)(a) shall have effect as if such contributions had been paid or treated as paid on so much of the earnings as did not exceed the base tax year's upper earnings limit.

(4) Regulations may—

(a) provide for the condition set out in sub-paragraph (1) to be taken to be satisfied in the case of persons who have been entitled to any prescribed description of benefit during any prescribed period or at any prescribed time;

(b) with a view to securing any relaxation of the requirements of that condition in relation to persons who have been so entitled, provide for that condition to apply in relation to them subject to prescribed modifications.

(5) In sub-paragraph (4), "benefit" means—

(a) any benefit within the meaning of section 122(1) of the Contributions and Benefits Act,

(b) any benefit under Parts 7 to 12 of that Act,

(c) credits under regulations under section 22(5) of that Act,

(d) a contributory allowance, and

(e) working tax credit.

2.—(1) The second condition is that—

(a) the claimant has in respect of the last two complete tax years before the beginning of the relevant benefit year either paid or been credited with Class 1 or Class 2 contributions or been credited with earnings, and

(b) the earnings factor derived as mentioned in sub-paragraph (2) must be not less in each of those years than the year's lower earnings limit multiplied by 50.

(2) The earnings factor referred to in sub-paragraph (1)(b) is the aggregate of the claimant's earnings factors derived—

(a) from so much of his earnings as did not exceed the upper earnings limit for the year and upon which primary Class 1 contributions have been paid or treated as paid or from earnings credited, and

(b) from Class 2 contributions.

(3) Where primary Class 1 contributions have been paid or treated as paid on any part of a person's earnings, sub-paragraph (2)(a) shall have effect as if such contributions had been paid or treated as paid on so much of the earnings as did not exceed the upper earnings limit for the year.

3.—(1) For the purposes of paragraphs 1 and 2—

(a) "benefit year" means a period which is a benefit year for the purposes of Part 2 of the Contributions and Benefits Act or such other period as may be prescribed for the purposes of this Part of this Schedule;

(b) "Class 1 contributions", "Class 2 contributions" and "primary Class 1 contributions" have the same meaning as in the Contributions and Benefits Act (see section 1 of that Act);

(c) "earnings" shall be construed in accordance with sections 3, 4 and 112 of that Act;

(d) "earnings factor" shall be construed in accordance with sections 22 and 23 of that Act;

(e) "lower earnings limit" and "upper earnings limit" shall be construed in accordance with section 5 of that Act and references to the lower or upper earnings limit of a tax year are to whatever is (or was) the limit in force for that year under that section;

(f) "relevant benefit year" is the benefit year which includes the beginning of the period of limited capability for work which includes the relevant benefit week;

(g) "tax year" means the 12 months beginning with 6th April in any year.

(2) Regulations may provide for sub-paragraph (1)(f) to have effect in prescribed circumstances with prescribed modifications in the case of—

(a) a person who has previously ceased to be entitled to a contributory allowance;

(b) a person who has made a claim for an employment and support allowance in connection with which he failed to satisfy one or both of the conditions in paragraphs 1 and 2.

Condition relating to youth

1.821 **4.**—(1) The third condition is that—

(a) the claimant was under 20 or, in prescribed cases, 25 when the relevant period of limited capability for work began,

(b) he is not receiving full-time education,

(c) he satisfies such conditions as may be prescribed with respect to residence or presence in Great Britain (or both), and

(d) there has been a day in the relevant period of limited capability for work—

(i) which was a day on which he was aged at least 16, and

(ii) which was preceded by a period of 196 consecutive days throughout which he had limited capability for work.

(2) In sub-paragraph (1), "relevant period of limited capability for work" means the period of limited capability for work which includes the relevant benefit week.

(3) Regulations may prescribe circumstances in which sub-paragraph (1)(a) does not apply in the case of a person who has previously ceased to be entitled to an employment and support allowance to which he was entitled by virtue of satisfying the condition set out in sub-paragraph (1).

(4) Regulations may make provision about when, for the purposes of sub-paragraph (1)(b), a person is, or is not, to be treated as receiving full-time education.

"Relevant benefit week"

1.822 **5.**—In this Part of this Schedule, "relevant benefit week" means the week in relation to which the question of entitlement to an employment and support allowance is being considered.

DEFINITIONS

"the base tax year"—see para.1(1)(a).

"benefit"—see para.1(5).

"benefit year"—see para.3(1)(a).

"Class 1 contributions"—see para.3(1)(b).

"Class 2 contributions"—see para.3(1)(b).

"Contributions and Benefits Act"—see s.65.

"earnings"—see para.3(1)(c).

"earnings factor"—see para.3(1)(d).

"entitled"—see s.24(1).

"limited capability for work"—see s.1(4).

"lower earnings limit"—see para.3(1)(e).

"primary Class 1 contributions"—see para.3(1)(b).

"regulations"—see s.24(1).
"relevant benefit week"—see para.5.
"relevant benefit year"—see para.3(1)(f).
"relevant period of limited capability for work"—see para.4(2).
"tax year"—see para.3(1)(g).
"upper earnings limit"—see para.3(1)(e).
"week"—see s.24(1).

GENERAL NOTE

Paras (1)–(3)
CESA is principally a contributory or national insurance benefit. Entitlement **1.823**
to it generally requires the claimant to have an adequate contribution record.
He must satisfy the first and second conditions set out in paras 1 and 2 (s.1(2)
(a)), with respect to which paras 3 and 5 provide key definitions. Paragraph 3 also
enables modifications to be effected by regs The contribution conditions, their
application and modification essentially emulate those applicable to IB after April
2001. Compare SSCBA 1992, Sch.3, para.3. This annotation should be read in
the light of those parts of the commentary to SSCBA 1992, Sch.3 dealing with
"Contributions matters: a division of responsibility" and "an outline of the contributory system· payments, credits and the earnings factor (the amount added to
the contribution record)".

The national insurance conditions: Unless he is a person incapacitated in youth **1.824**
(before 20 or sometimes 25) (see s.30A(1)(b), (2A)) a claimant must satisfy both
of the contribution conditions elaborated in paras 1 and 2. The first (para.1) can
be met only by *paid* contributions of the relevant class (primary Class 1 or Class 2)
reaching the requisite level in a specific tax year. The second can be satisfied by *paid
and/or credited* contributions in both of two specific tax years. Like those applicable
to IB since April 2001, the conditions thus require a more recent connection with
the world of work in terms of paid contributions than had previously been the case,
whether with incapacity benefit or its predecessors, sickness and invalidity benefits.
However, the rigour of the first condition is relaxed in certain situations (paras 1(4),
3(2), ESA Regs, Pt IA, reg.8).

In order to appreciate the requirements of paras 1 and 2, and the terms and
operation of the contribution conditions, take first, as an illustrative example, the
position of someone claiming CESA for the very first time in November 2008 (that
is, with no link back to any previous period of incapacity for work) and never having
claimed or received any other benefit. He must meet *both of the two contribution conditions* set out in paras 1 and 2. The first step is to identify the relevant benefit year,
the one which includes the first day of the period of limited capability for work of
which his claim is part (para.3(1(f))). This identification of the relevant benefit year
is the real substantive matter for the Secretary of State or the tribunal to focus on,
since that determines the tax years in which the requisite record must be fulfilled.
His first day of claim in the relevant benefit week (para.5, in November 2008 falls
in benefit year 2008–2009 (the relevant benefit year: defined to refer to SSCBA
1992, s.21(6) and any modifying regulations made for the purposes of this Part of
this Schedule (see para.3(1)(a))). The tax years in *one of which* the first contribution
condition (sub-para.(2)) must be fulfilled are the last three tax years (April 6–April
5)(para.3(1)(g)) complete before the start of the relevant benefit year (early January
2008). The tax years to which to have regard are thus 2004/2005, 2005/2006,
and 2006/2007. The contribution record in tax year 2007/2008 cannot be taken
into account because it was not complete at the start of the relevant benefit year
(early January 2008). The first contribution condition (para.1(1)) can only be met
with paid contributions of the relevant class—Class 1 (employed earners) or Class
2 (self-employed earners)—reaching the requisite level (an earnings factor of 25
times the lower earnings limit (LEL) for Class 1 contributions purposes for the tax
year in question—remember that each Class 2 contribution generates an earnings

factor equal to the LEL pertinent to the tax/contribution year in question, while the amount of earnings on which Class 1 contributions are paid generates the earnings factor for an employed earner claimant. See further, the "outline of the contributory system" in the commentary to SSCBA 1992, Sch.3.

The second contribution condition (para.1(2)) requires examination of the last two tax years complete before the start of the relevant benefit year (early January 2008), that is 2005/2006 and 2006/2007. The claimant's contribution record in each of those tax/contribution years must attain 50 times the lower earnings limit for the year. But the condition can be met through paid and/or credited contributions (a Class 1 credit can be received, for example, for each week of unemployment; see further Social Security (Credits) Regulations 1975).

Note that para.1(4) enables regulations to provide for the first condition to be taken to be satisfied by certain benefit recipients and provide for it to apply in modified form. The relevant "relaxation" regulation is ESA Regs, reg.8 and is the subject of commentary there. Note also that para.3(2) enables regulations to relax the rules on relevant benefit year. The product is ESA Regs, reg.13.

Various groups will have difficulty meeting the contribution conditions:

(a) *those who have never been employed:* The requirement in the first contribution condition for payment of contributions effectively excludes those who, whether through unemployment, incapacity or disability, have been unable to build a contribution record in terms of paid contributions.

(b) *some of the long-term unemployed:* (last employed in a tax year earlier than the first of the three on which the first contribution condition focuses).

(c) *very low-paid, probably part-time, employees:* those whose weekly or monthly earnings fall below the lower earnings limit for the whole or main part of the relevant tax years will not satisfy the contribution conditions since there is no liability or ability to pay Class 1 contributions where earnings fall below that limit, and, because they are in work, no Class 1 credits are generated from unemployment.

(d) *certain married women and widows paying reduced rate contributions:* these do not generate any earnings factor (and so do not count) for ESA purposes (para.3(d); SSCBA 1992, s.22(4)).

Para.4

1.825 Severe Disablement Allowance (SDA) was introduced in 1984 to cater for those who were incapacitated below the age of 20, or, if incapacitated later, were also assessed as 80 per cent disabled (see SSCBA 1992, ss.68, 69). SDA was abolished on April 6, 2001 for new claims, but non-contributory access was afforded to IB for persons incapacitated in youth (before 20 or sometimes 25). This paragraph affords the same facility in respect of CESA. Those incapacitated, even through severe disability, later in life, will have to look to IRESA, with its disability premiums, to underwrite their incapacity for work. They may well also be eligible for various components of disability living allowance. That is not an income replacement benefit, but is rather one designed to provide for the extra costs that disability, as opposed to incapacity for work, brings with it.

1.826 *Non-contributory access to CESA: Condition relating to youth:* This is the third condition referred to in s.1(2)(a). The provisions are similar to those brought into IB (SSCBA 1992, 30A(1)(b), (2A); IB Regulations 14–19) when the non-contributory incapacity benefit SDA was closed to new claimants from April 6, 2001. There is an immediate key difference, however, in that under the IB scheme the "person incapacitated in youth" route only opened if the person did not satisfy the contribution conditions (SSCBA 1992, s.30A(1)(b)), whereas with CESA there is no such pre-condition (WRA 2007, s.1(2)(a)).

To succeed by this "youth" route, all of a number of conditions must be fulfilled: (1) the claimant must be under 20 (or in some cases defined in regs, under 25) when the period of limited capability for work began (sub-para.(1)(a)); (2) he must not be receiving full-time education (sub-para.(1)(b)); (3) he must meet prescribed conditions with respect to residence and/or presence in GB (sub-para.(1)(c); ESA Regs, reg.11); and (4) in his period of limited capacity for work there must be a day on which he was at least 16 which was preceded by a period of 196 days throughout which he had limited capability for work (sub-para.(1)(d)).

The age condition in sub-para.(1)(a) is disapplied by ESA Regs, reg.10 in respect of certain claimants previously entitled to ESA as a person incapacitated in youth whose previous entitlement ended solely with a view to him taking up employment or training.

Note that regs can specify when someone is or is not to be treated as receiving full-time education (sub-para.(4)). The regulation in question is ESA Regs, reg.12.

PART 2

INCOME RELATED ALLOWANCE

6.—(1) The conditions are that the claimant–   1.827
  (a) has an income which does not exceed the applicable amount or has no income;
  (b) does not have capital which, or a prescribed part of which, exceeds the prescribed amount;
  (c) is not entitled to state pension credit;
  (d) is not a member of a couple the other member of which is entitled to an income-related allowance, state pension credit, income support or an income-based job-seeker's allowance;
  (e) is not engaged in remunerative work;
  (f) is not a member of a couple the other member of which is engaged in remunerative work;
  (g) is not receiving education.
(2) Where the claimant is a member of a couple, the income and capital of the other member of the couple shall, except in prescribed circumstances, be treated for the purpose of this paragraph as income and capital of the claimant.
(3) Regulations may prescribe circumstances in which, for the purposes of sub-paragraph (1)(e) and (f)—
  (a) a person who is not engaged in remunerative work is to be treated as engaged in remunerative work; or
  (b) a person who is engaged in remunerative work is to be treated as not engaged in remunerative work
(4) Regulations may—
  (a) make provision about when, for the purposes of sub-paragraph (1)(g), a person is, or is not, to be treated as receiving education;
  (b) prescribe circumstances in which sub-paragraph (1)(g) does not apply.
(5) In this paragraph—
  "applicable amount" means the amount which, in the claimant's case, is the applicable amount for the purposes of section 4(1);
  "couple" means—
  (a) a man and woman who are married to each other and are members of the same household;
  (b) a man and woman who are not married to each other, but are living together as husband and wife otherwise than in prescribed circumstances;
  (c) two people of the same sex who are civil partners of each other and are members of the same household; or
  (d) two people of the same sex who are not civil partners of each other, but are living together as if they were civil partners otherwise than in prescribed circumstances;
  "education" has such meaning as may be prescribed;
  "income-based jobseeker's allowance" has the same meaning as in the Jobseekers Act 1995(c.18);
  "remunerative work" has such meaning as may be prescribed.
(6) For the purposes of this paragraph, two people of the same sex are to be regarded as living together as if they were civil partners if, but only if, they would be regarded as living together as husband and wife were they instead two people of the opposite sex.
(7) Regulations may make provision for the preceding provisions of this paragraph to have effect with prescribed modifications in a case where—

(a) the claimant is a husband or wife by virtue of a marriage entered into under a law which permits polygamy,
(b) either party to the marriage has for the time being any spouse additional to the other party, and
(c) the claimant, the other party to the marriage and the additional spouse are members of the same household.

(8) Regulations may make provision for the purposes of this paragraph as to circumstances in which people are to be treated as being or not being members of the same household.

DEFINITIONS

"education"—see ESA Regs, reg.14.
"prescribed"—see s.24(1).
"regulations"—*ibid.*
"remunerative work"—see ESA Regulations, regs 2(1), 41 and 42.

GENERAL NOTE

Sub-para.(1)

1.828
This sets out the extra conditions for entitlement to income-related ESA that are additional to the basic conditions of entitlement for ESA in s.1(3). All of the conditions in sub-para.(1) must be satisfied for there to be entitlement to income-related ESA.

Under head (a) the claimant's income (which includes the income of any partner (sub-para.(2)) must be less than the applicable amount (effectively the figure set for the claimant's, or if he has a partner, the claimant's and his partner's, requirements under s.4).

Head (b) contains the capital test. The capital limit for income-related ESA is the same as for income support and income-based JSA, i.e., £16,000 (see reg.110 of the ESA Regulations). See further the note to s.134(1) SSCBA in Volume II in this series. For capital that is disregarded for the purposes of income-related ESA see Sch.9 to the ESA Regulations.

Entitlement to state pension credit excludes entitlement to income-related ESA (head (c)). If a claimant has reached the qualifying age for state pension credit (currently 60 for both men and women, although from April 2010 it will increase by stages to 65 in line with the increase in pensionable age for a woman from April 2010) but has not reached pensionable age (currently 60 for a woman and 65 for a man), it will normally be advantageous to claim state pension credit rather than income-related ESA.

If the claimant is a member of a couple (defined in sub-para.(5); see also sub-para.(6)), he will also not qualify for income-related ESA if his partner is entitled to state pension credit, income support, income-based JSA or income-related ESA (head (d)).

Under heads (e) and (f) if either the claimant or his partner is in remunerative work there is no entitlement to income-related ESA. However note that the meaning of "remunerative work" is not the same for the claimant as it is for his partner. Regulation 41 of the ESA Regulations sets out the test for the claimant; the test for the partner is in reg.42 of those Regulations. See the notes to regs 41 and 42, and note also regs 40 and 43–45.

In addition the claimant will be excluded from entitlement to income-related ESA if he is receiving education (head (g)). See regs 14–18 of the ESA Regulations (made under sub-para.(4)) and the notes to those regulations.

Sub-para.(2)

1.829
This provides that the general rule for income-related ESA is that where the claimant is a member of a couple (defined in sub-para.(5); see also sub-para.(6)) both the claimant's and his partner's income and capital are aggregated together and treated as the claimant's.

SCHEDULE 2

EMPLOYMENT AND SUPPORT ALLOWANCE: SUPPLEMENTARY PROVISIONS

Limited capability for work

1.—Regulations may make provision—

   (a) for a person to be treated in prescribed circumstances as having, or as not having, limited capability for work;

   (b) for the question of whether a person has limited capability for work to be determined notwithstanding that he is for the time being treated by virtue of regulations under sub-paragraph (a) as having limited capability for work;

   (c) for the question of whether a person has limited capability for work to be determined afresh in prescribed circumstances.

1.830

Waiting days

2.—Except in prescribed circumstances, a person is not entitled to an employment and support allowance in respect of a prescribed number of days at the beginning of a period of limited capability for work.

1.831

Periods of less than a week

3.—Regulations may make provision in relation to—

   (a) entitlement to an employment and support allowance, or

   (b) the amount payable by way of such an allowance,

in respect of any period of less than a week.

1.832

Linking periods

4.—(1) Regulations may provide for circumstances in which a period of limited capability for work which is separated from another period of limited capability for work by not more than a prescribed length of time is to be treated for the purposes of this Part as a continuation of the earlier period.

(2) Regulations may provide, in relation to periods which are linked by virtue of regulations under sub-paragraph (1), that a condition which was satisfied in relation to the earlier period is to be treated for the purposes of this Part as satisfied in relation to the later period.

1.833

Presence in Great Britain

5.—Regulations may make provision for the purposes of this Part as to the circumstances in which a person is to be treated as being, or not being, in Great Britain.

1.834

Contributory allowance: entitlement in case of absence from Great Britain

6.—Regulations may provide that in prescribed circumstances a claimant who is not in Great Britain may nevertheless be entitled to a contributory allowance.

1.835

Contributory allowance: modification in relation to employment on ships etc.

7.—(1) Regulations may modify any provision of this Part, so far as relating to a contributory allowance, in its application to any person who is, has been, or is to be—

   (a) employed on board any ship, vessel, hovercraft or aircraft,

   (b) outside Great Britain at any prescribed time or in any prescribed circumstances, or

   (c) in prescribed employment in connection with continental shelf operations.

(2) Regulations under this paragraph may, in particular, provide—

   (a) for any provision of this Part to apply even though it would not otherwise apply;

   (b) for any such provision not to apply even though it would otherwise apply;

   (c) for the taking of evidence, in a country or territory outside Great Britain, by a consular official or other prescribed person;

   (d) for enabling the whole, or any part, of a contributory allowance to be paid to such of the claimant's dependants as may be prescribed.

(3) In this paragraph, "continental shelf operations" has the same meaning as in section 120 of the Contributions and Benefits Act.

1.836

Income-related allowance: entitlement in case of absence from Great Britain

1.837   **8.**—(1) Regulations may provide that in prescribed circumstances a claimant who is entitled to an income-related allowance immediately before ceasing to be in Great Britain continues to be entitled to such an allowance after ceasing to be in Great Britain.

(2) Regulations may modify any provision of this Part, so far as relating to an income-related allowance, in its application to a person who is entitled to such an allowance by virtue of regulations under sub-paragraph (1).

(3) Regulations under sub-paragraph (2) may, in particular, provide—
  (a) for any provision of this Part to apply even though it would not otherwise apply;
  (b) for any such provision not to apply even though it would otherwise apply.

Limited capability for work-related activity

1.838   **9.**—Regulations may make provision—
  (a) for a person to be treated in prescribed circumstances as having, or as not having, limited capability for work-related activity;
  (b) for the question of whether a person has limited capability for work-related activity to be determined notwithstanding that he is for the time being treated by virtue of regulations under sub-paragraph (a) as having limited capability for work-related activity;
  (c) for the question of whether a person has limited capability for work-related activity to be determined afresh in prescribed circumstances.

Effect of work

1.839   **10.**—Regulations may prescribe circumstances in which a person is to be treated as not entitled to an employment and support allowance because of his doing work.

Treatment of allowance as "benefit"

1.840   **11.**—Regulations may provide for—
  (a) an employment and support allowance,
  (b) a contributory allowance, or
  (c) an income-related allowance,
to be treated, for prescribed purposes of the Contributions and Benefits Act, as a benefit, or a benefit of a prescribed description.

Attribution of reductions in cases where allowance taken to consist of two elements

1.841   **12.**—Where an employment and support allowance is taken by virtue of section 6(5) to consist of two elements, any reduction in the amount payable in respect of the allowance which falls to be made by virtue of—
  (a) section 11,
  (b) section 12,
  (c) section 13, or
  (d) section 2AA of the Administration Act (full entitlement to certain benefits conditional on work-focused interview for partner),
shall be treated as reducing such of those elements by such amount as may be prescribed.

Treatment of information supplied as information relating to social security

1.842   **13.**—Information supplied in pursuance of regulations under any of sections 8, 9 and 11 to 13 shall be taken for all purposes to be information relating to social security.

Advance claims

1.843   **14.**—This Part shall have effect with prescribed modifications in relation to cases where a claim to an employment and support allowance is by virtue of regulations under section 5(1)(c) of the Administration Act (advance claims) made, or treated as if made, for a period wholly or partly after the date on which it is made.

Members of the forces

1.844   **15.**—(1) Regulations may modify—
  (a) any provision of this Part, or
  (b) any corresponding provision made for Northern Ireland,
in its application to persons who are or have been members of Her Majesty's forces.

(2) For the purposes of this paragraph, Her Majesty's forces shall be taken to consist of prescribed establishments and organisations in which persons serve under the control of the Defence Council.

DEFINITIONS

"Administration Act"—see s.65.
"continental shelf operations"—see para.7(3).
"Contributions and Benefits Act"—see s.65.
"contributory allowance"—see s.1(7).
"employed"—see s.24(1).
"employment"—see s.24(1).
"entitled"—see s.24(1).
"Her Majesty's forces"—see para.15(2).
"income-related allowance"—see s.1(7).
"limited capability for work-related activity"—see s.2(5).
"period of limited capability for work"—see s.24(1).
"prescribed"—see s.24(1).
"regulations"—see s.24(1).
"week"—see s.24(1).
"work-related activity"—see ss.24(1), 13(7).

GENERAL NOTE

Para.2 (waiting days)

See ESA Regs, reg.144. The general rule, as with previous contributory inca-   **1.845**
pacity benefit regimes, is that there is no entitlement to ESA in respect of the first
three "waiting days" at the beginning of a period of limited capability for work. The
general rule has a number of exceptions set out in reg.144(2): terminally ill claimants; discharge from Her Majesty's forces where three or more days of recorded
sickness absence from duty preceded it; and where entitlement to ESA begins
within 12 weeks of entitlement to IS, SPC, JSA, carer's allowance or SSP coming to
an end. In addition, the general rule is, of course, affected by the "linking rules" (on
which see reg.145) in a case of intermittent incapacity where those rules fuse into
one ostensibly separate spells of limited capability for work: the "waiting days" only
have to be served once in a period of limited capability for work.

Para.3 (periods of less than a week)

Like JSA, ESA is a weekly benefit, paid in respect of a week of limited capability   **1.846**
for work. It is paid fortnightly in arrears, and the day of the week on which payment
is to be made is determined by reference to the last two digits of the claimant's
national insurance number (Claims and Payments Regs, reg.26C (see updating
material with respect to Vol.III). This para of Sch.2 enables regs to make provision
for payment in respect of periods of less than a week: see ESA Regs, regs 165–169.

Para.4 (linking periods)

See ESA Regs, reg.145. The linking rules are crucial for those suffering from   **1.847**
intermittent incapacity. They impact, to the claimant's benefit, as regards "waiting
days"; those days of non-entitlement (see para.(2) and ESA Regs, reg.144) only
have to be served once in any period of limited capability for work. They are also
relevant to determining the relevant benefit year and hence the appropriate tax years
to which to have regard with respect to the application of the national insurance
contribution conditions (see further the commentary to Sch.1, Pt 1, paras 1–3).

Generally, the linking rule works on the basis that two ostensibly separate spells
of limited capability for work will be fused into one where the separation period
between the spells is not more than 12 weeks. This fusing does not, however, mean
that days in the separation period thereby become ones of limited capability for
work (*Chief Adjudication Officer v Astle* (Court of Appeal, judgment of March 17,

1999, available on LEXIS and noted in [1999] 6 J.S.S.L. 203). See further for more detail the commentary to SSCBA 1992, s.30C(1)(c) (the "linking" rule)). A period of limited capability for work can only be formed of days of actual limited capability for work and/or ones which the legislative scheme treats as ones of limited capability for work.

However, where a claimant is a "work or training beneficiary", the "linking period" is 104 weeks (See ESA Regs, reg.145(2)). It is also 104 weeks between spells of limited capability for work where a claimant, entitled to ESA, then went into qualifying remunerative work supported or (but for income) supportable by tax credits ("satisfies the relevant tax credit conditions"), and the period of limited capability for work in respect of which the claimant is now seeking ESA began on the day after he ceased that work (see ESA Regs, reg.145(3), (4)).

Para.5 (presence in Great Britain)

1.848   Entitlement to ESA generally requires presence in Great Britain (s.1(3)(d)). This paragraph enables regulations to treat someone, whatever the actual reality in terms of presence or absence, as being or not being in Great Britain. See ESA Regs, reg.11 (condition relating to youth—residence or presence).

Para.6 (entitlement to CESA when absent from Great Britain)

1.849   Entitlement to CESA generally requires presence in Great Britain (s.1(3)(d)). This para. enables regulations to give entitlement where the claimant is not in Great Britain. See ESA Regs, regs 151–155, dealing with periods of temporary absence. Note also that CESA is an exportable benefit for purposes of EC law.

Para.7 (Modification of CESA for those employed on ships etc)

1.850   This enables regulations to modify the rules on entitlement to CESA as regards those who are, have been or are to be, employed on any ship, vessel, hovercraft or aircraft; outside Great Britain; or in prescribed employment in connection with continental shelf operations. See the various amendments made with effect from October 27, 2008 by the Employment and Support Allowance (Consequential Provisions) (No.2) Regulations 2008 (SI 2008/1554), regs 65 and 67, respectively to the Social Security (Airmen's Benefits) Regulations 1975 (SI 1975/494), Social Security (Mariners' Benefits) Regulations 1975 (SI 1975/529).

Para.(8) (retaining entitlement to IRESA when absent from Great Britain)

1.851   See ESA Regs, regs 151–155.

Para.10 (effect of work)

1.852   Unsurprisingly, in a benefits regime founded on limited capability for work, the general rule in respect of ESA is that the doing of any work negatives limited capability: see ESA Regs, reg.40, precluding entitlement to ESA in any week in which a claimant does work. But like the previous incapacity benefit regime, the general preclusive rule is modified to permit engagement in a range of work without loss of benefit. This recognizes that work can assist recovery or help the claimant into thinking about work and a possibility to return to work, or merely not wanting to exclude the sick and disabled from participation in civic office or a range of voluntary or charitable work. Under ESA, unlike its predecessor regime, the rules more fully protect through more generous earnings disregards those only in receipt of the income related form of the benefit as well as those receiving its contributory form. See ESA Regs, regs 41–46.

Para.12 (attribution of deductions from ESA)

1.853   A claimant may be entitled to CESA to IRESA or to both. Where someone is entitled to both IRESA and CESA, this para enables the making of regulations to provide for which component or components is or are to be reduced because of provisions enabling reduction set out in the specified provisions dealing with ESA conditionality (ss.11–13) or where, under SSAA 1992, s.2AA, entitlement depends on the claimant's partner complying with conditions in respect of work-focused interviews. See ESA Regs, reg.63. See also, in Vol.III, with respect to SSAA 1992, s.2AA, the Social Security (Jobcentre Plus Interviews for Partners) Regs 2003 (SI 2003/1886), reg.11, as amended with effect from October 27, 2008, by reg.71 of the Employment and Support Allowance (Consequential Provisions) (No.2) Regs 2008 (SI 2008/1554).

Para.14 (Advance claims)
See ESA Regs, reg.66.   1.854

Para.15 (members of Her Majesty's forces)
This enables regulations to modify the rules on entitlement to ESA in respect of   1.855
persons who are or have been members of those forces. See ESA Regs, regs 155 and Sch.1. See also the Social Security (Benefit) (Members of the Forces) Regs 1975 (S I 1975/493) as amended with effect from October 27, 2008 by reg.66 of the Employment and Support Allowance (Consequential Provisions) (No.2) Regs 2008 (SI 2008/1554).

SCHEDULE 3   **Section 28**

Consequential Amendments relating to Part 1

Insofar as the provisions in this Schedule amend legislation contained   1.856
in the main volumes, these amendments are incorporated in the Updating Sections to the relevant volume (Parts II–V) of this Supplement

SCHEDULE 4   **Section 29**

Transition relating to Part 1

General power to provide for transition relating to Part 1

1.—(1) Regulations may make such provision as the Secretary of State considers necessary   1.857
or expedient—
  (a) in connection with the coming into force of any provision of, or repeal relating to, this Part, or
  (b) otherwise for the purposes of, or in connection with, the transition to employment and support allowance.
(2) The following provisions of this Schedule are not to be taken as prejudicing the generality of sub-paragraph (1).

Pre-commencement claims

2.—Regulations may—   1.858
  (a) make provision for a claim for incapacity benefit, income support or severe disablement allowance which is made before the appointed day to be treated wholly or partly as a claim for an employment and support allowance;
  (b) make provision for the purpose of enabling claims for an employment and support allowance to be made before the appointed day for a period beginning on or after that day.

Post-commencement claims

3.—Regulations may—   1.859
  (a) *make provision excluding the making of a claim for incapacity benefit or severe disablement allowance on or after the appointed day;*
  (b) make provision for a claim for incapacity benefit, income support or severe disablement allowance which is made on or after the appointed day to be treated in prescribed circumstances as a claim for an employment and support allowance;

(c) make provision for a claim for an employment and support allowance to be treated wholly or partly as a claim for incapacity benefit, income support or severe disablement allowance;

(d) make provision excluding the making of a claim for an employment and support allowance by a person who is entitled to an existing award.

Award of employment and support allowance for pre-commencement period

1.860   **4.**—*Regulations may—*

(a) *make provision for an employment and support allowance of such a kind as the regulations may provide to be awarded in prescribed circumstances for a period before the appointed day;*

(b) *make provision with respect to conditions of entitlement in relation to an award under sub-paragraph (a) and the amount payable by way of an allowance under such an award.*

Matching of awards of employment and support allowance

1.861   **5.**—*(1) For the purposes of this paragraph, an award of an employment and support allowance is one that falls to be made on matching terms if—*

(a) *it is made in pursuance of a claim by a person who was previously entitled to an existing award, and*

(b) *had it continued to be possible to make an award of incapacity benefit, income support on grounds of incapacity for work, or severe disablement allowance, the award which would have been made to him ("the hypothetical award") would have been made on the basis of the linking of periods of incapacity for work.*

(2) Regulations may—

(a) *make provision for the purpose of securing that an award of an employment and support allowance that falls to be made on matching terms is made on terms which match in whole or part the hypothetical award;*

(b) *make provision for the modification of matched awards for the purpose of securing that the person with the award is put in the position he would have been had he been made the hypothetical award which was then the subject of conversion under paragraph 7.*

(3) In sub-paragraph (2)(b), the reference to matched awards is to awards of an employment and support allowance that have been the subject of matching in pursuance of regulations under sub-paragraph (2)(a).

1.862   **6.**—*(1) For the purposes of this paragraph an award of an employment and support allowance is one which falls to be made on matching terms if—*

(a) *it is made in pursuance of a claim by a person who was previously entitled to an existing award,*

(b) *had he continued to be entitled to that award, it would have been the subject of conversion under paragraph 7 before the date of his claim for an employment and support allowance, and*

(c) *had it continued to be possible to make an award of incapacity benefit, income support on grounds of incapacity for work, or severe disablement allowance, the award which would have been made to him would have been made on the basis of the linking of periods of incapacity for work.*

(2) Regulations may make provision for the purpose of securing that an award of an employment and support allowance that falls to be made on matching terms is made on terms which match in whole or part the award that would have resulted from conversion under paragraph 7 had entitlement to the existing award continued.

Treatment of existing awards

1.863   **7.**—*(1) Regulations may—*

(a) *make provision for converting existing awards into awards of an employment and support allowance, and with respect to the terms of conversion;*

(b) *make provision for the termination of existing awards in prescribed circumstances.*

(2) Regulations under sub-paragraph (1)(a) may, in particular—

(a) *make provision for conversion of an existing award—*

(i) *on application, in accordance with the regulations, by the person entitled to the award, or*

(ii) *without application;*

(b) *make provision about the conditions to be satisfied in relation to an application for conversion;*

I make provision about the timing of conversion;
   (d) provide for an existing award to have effect after conversion as an award of an employment and support allowance—
      (i) of such a kind,
      (ii) for such period,
      (iii) of such an amount, and
      (iv) subject to such conditions,
         as the regulations may provide;
   (e) make provision for determining in connection with conversion of an existing award whether a person has limited capability for work-related activity.

(3) Regulations under sub-paragraph (1)(a) may, in relation to existing awards which have been the subject of conversion under this paragraph, include provision about revision under section 9 of the Social Security Act 1998 (c. 14), or supersession under section 10 of that Act in respect of the period before conversion.

Transitional allowances

8.—(1) Regulations may—
   (a) make provision for a person's continuing entitlement to an employment and support allowance awarded by virtue of regulations under paragraph 7 (a "transitional allowance") to be determined by reference to such provision as may be made by the regulations;
   (b) make provision for the review of an award of a transitional allowance;
   (c) make provision for the termination of an award of a transitional allowance;
   (d) make provision for this Part, or any other enactment relating to social security, to have effect with prescribed modifications in relation to a person with a transitional allowance;
   (e) make provision for the purpose of enabling a transitional allowance to be revised under section 9 of the Social Security Act 1998 (c. 14) or superseded under section 10 of that Act.

(2) In this paragraph "enactment" includes an enactment contained in subordinate legislation (within the meaning of the Interpretation Act 1978 (c. 30)).

9.—(1) Regulations may prescribe circumstances in which a person who is entitled to a transitional allowance immediately before reaching pensionable age is to be treated as having satisfied the condition in paragraph 5(2) of Schedule 3 to the Contributions and Benefits Act (first contribution condition for entitlement to state pension).

(2) In this paragraph, "pensionable age" has the meaning given by the rules in paragraph 1 of Schedule 4 to the Pensions Act 1995 (c. 26).

1.864

1.865

Post-commencement up-rating of incapacity benefit and severe disablement allowance

10.—Regulations may provide for section 150 of the Administration Act (annual up-rating of benefits), so far as relating to—
   (a) incapacity benefit under section 30A of the Contributions and Benefits Act, or
   (b) severe disablement allowance,
      to have effect with prescribed modifications in relation to tax years beginning on or after the appointed day.

1.866

Interpretation

11.—In this Schedule—
"appointed day" means the day appointed for the coming into force of section 1;
"existing award" means—
   (a) an award of incapacity benefit,
   (b) an award of severe disablement allowance, and
   (c) an award of income support made to a person to whom regulation 6(4)(a) or 13(2)(b) or (bb) of, or paragraph 7(a) or (b), 10, 12 or 13 of Schedule 1B to, the Income Support (General) Regulations 1987 (S.I. 1987/1967) (persons incapable of work or disabled) applies;
"incapacity benefit" (except in paragraph 10(a)) means—
   (a) incapacity benefit under section 30A, 40 or 41 of the Contributions and Benefits Act,
   (b) long-term incapacity benefit under regulation 11(4) of the Social Security (Incapacity Benefit) (Transitional) Regulations 1995 (S.I. 1995/310) (former sickness benefit), and
   (c) invalidity benefit which has effect by virtue of regulation 17(1) of those regulations as if it were long-term incapacity benefit;

1.867

"severe disablement allowance" means severe disablement allowance under section 68 of that Act (as it has effect by virtue of article 4 of the Welfare Reform and Pensions Act 1999 (Commencement No. 9, and Transitional and Savings Provisions) Order 2000 (S.I. 2000/2958) (C. 89));

"transitional allowance" has the meaning given by paragraph 8(1)(a).

DEFINITIONS

"Administration Act"—see s.65.
"appointed day"—see para.11.
"Contributions and Benefits Act"—see s.65.
"enactment"—see para.8(2).
"existing award"—see para.11.
"the hypothetical award"—see para.5(1)(b).
"incapacity benefit" (except in paragraph 10(a))—see para.11.
"income support"—see s.24(1).
"limited capability for work-related activity"—see s.2(5).
"pensionable age"—see para.9(2).
"prescribed"—see s.24(1).
"regulations"—see s.24(1).
"severe disablement allowance"—see para.11.
"transitional allowance"—see paras 11, 8(1)(a).
"work-related activity"—see ss.24(1), 13(7).

GENERAL NOTE

1.868   Provisions in italics were not yet in force as at April 13, 2009.

Paras 1–3

1.869   See further the Employment and Support Allowance (Transitional Provisions) Regs 2008, regs 1–4 of which entered into force on July 27, 2008.

436

Child Maintenance and Other Payments Act 2008

(2008 C.6)

Arrangement of Sections

Part 4

Lump Sum Payments: Mesothelioma etc.

Mesothelioma lump sum payments

46. Lump sum payments
47. Conditions of entitlement
48. Determination of claims
49. Reconsideration
50. Appeal to appeal tribunal
51. *[repealed]*
52. Minors and people who lack capacity
53. Regulations: Part 4

1.870

Recovery of mesothelioma and other lump sum payments

54. Amendment of Social Security (Recovery of Benefits Act 1997 *[omitted]*

General Note

Part 4 of the Child Maintenance and Other Payments Act 2008 establishes a new no-fault compensation scheme for victims of mesothelioma, an asbestos-related cancer that is invariably fatal. Known as the 2008 Diffuse Mesothelioma Scheme, the new arrangements are modelled on, but also extend the scope of, the provisions of the Pneumoconiosis etc. (Workers' Compensation) Act 1979. Most mesothelioma victims are middle-aged or elderly men who were employed in industries where heavy exposure to asbestos dust was commonplace until better controls were gradually introduced from the 1970s onwards. There are currently about 2,000 mesothelioma deaths in Great Britain each year, a figure which is expected to rise to about 2,400 a year by 2013, before the total begins to fall away to an expected annual toll of 500 in 2050. Mesothelioma, unlike asbestosis and asbestos-related lung cancer, can be caused by relatively low levels of exposure and so can also occur outside the workplace (see generally N.J. Wikeley, *Compensation for Industrial Disease*, (Aldershot: Dartmouth Publishing Group, 1993)).

Before these reforms, mesothelioma sufferers had three main routes to claiming compensation: (1) a civil claim for damages against their former employer; (2) where no such potential defendant remained in existence, a claim under the Pneumoconiosis etc. (Workers' Compensation) Act 1979; and (3) a claim for industrial disablement benefit on the basis of having a prescribed disease (subject to the recovery rules under the Social Security (Recovery of Benefits) Act 1997). However, three groups of mesothelioma victims found it difficult or impossible to bring a claim under any of these arrangements (see further N.J. Wikeley, "The New

1.871

Mesothelioma Compensation Scheme" (2009) 16 J.S.S.L. 30, on the background to the 2008 Scheme).

The first group were self-employed workers, who by definition had no employer to sue for damages in tort. As they were not "employed earners", they also did not qualify for industrial disablement benefit (or under the 1979 Act). Self-employment has always been common in the construction industry, one of the occupations in which exposure levels to asbestos dust were at their highest in the four decades or so after the Second World War, leaving large numbers of victims with no effective means of redress.

The second category comprised para-occupational mesothelioma victims (or cases of "household exposure"), e.g. family members who were exposed to asbestos dust at home because of close contact with an asbestos worker's overalls, such as by shaking and washing overalls. Household victims may in theory have a claim in tort, but in many cases the difficulties of establishing the requisite date of knowledge on the employer's part for the purposes of establishing a duty of care will be fatal (see e.g. *Maguire v Harland and Wolff plc* [2005] EWCA Civ 1). Family members who contract mesothelioma indirectly through household exposure are not themselves "employed earners", and so have no claim under the industrial disablement scheme or the 1979 Act.

The third (and probably smallest) group comprises environmental cases, where victims have been exposed to asbestos dust in the vicinity of their home. In extreme cases they may be able to recover in tort (see e.g. *Margereson and Hancock v J. W. Roberts Ltd* [1996] EWCA Civ 1316) but again they have no claim under the industrial disablement scheme or 1979 Act because of the absence of a personal occupational link.

The new scheme under Part 4 is designed to provide early assistance to all such mesothelioma victims, irrespective of their previous employment status. The Government anticipates that up to 600 mesothelioma victims who previously received no state support will receive an average payment of £6,000 during the first year of the scheme s operation. The scheme is to be funded from recoveries from subsequent compensation payments made by defendants and insurers. The Government anticipates that payments will be brought up to the levels under the 1979 Act by the third year of the new scheme, as compensation recoveries begin to accrue. The Child Maintenance and Other Payments Act 2008 (Commencement) Order 2008 (SI 2008/1476 (C.67)) brought Part 4 into force with effect from October 1, 2008.

PART 4

LUMP SUM PAYMENTS: MESOTHELIOMA ETC.

Mesothelioma lump sum payments

Lump sum payments

1.872   **46.**—(1) A claim for a payment under this Part may be made by—
(a) a person with diffuse mesothelioma, or
(b) a dependant of a person who, immediately before death, had diffuse mesothelioma.

(2) The Secretary of State must make the payment to the claimant if satisfied that the conditions of entitlement in section 47 are fulfilled.

(3) Regulations—
(a) may prescribe the amount of any payment;
(b) may prescribe different amounts for different cases or classes of cases or for different circumstances.

(4) In this Part—
"dependant" has the meaning given by section 3 of the Pneumoconiosis etc. (Workers' Compensation) Act 1979 (c. 41) ("the 1979 Act");
"diffuse mesothelioma" has the same meaning as in the 1979 Act.

(5) Where, because of section 3(1)(b) or (d) of the 1979 Act (children, siblings etc.), a payment may be claimed by two or more persons, the payment is to be made to one of them or divided between some or all of them as the Secretary of State thinks fit.

DEFINITIONS

"dependant"—subs.(4)
"diffuse mesothelioma"—*ibid.*

GENERAL NOTE

This section provides for the Secretary of State to make lump sum payments to persons with diffuse mesothelioma, or to their dependants, if the person in question has died (subs.(1); if the payment is to a dependent minor, see s.52). Indeed, if the criteria set out in s.47 are satisfied the Secretary of State *must* make such a lump sum payment (subs.(2)). Regulations may prescribe the amounts in question, which may be different for different cases or classes of cases and circumstances (subs. (3); see further reg.5 and the Schedule to the Mesothelioma Lump Sum Payments (Conditions and Amounts) Regulations 2008 (SI 2008/1963). These regulations, like the Pneumoconiosis etc. (Workers' Compensation) Act 1979, set payments at different levels by age and according to whether they are made to a sufferer or a dependant. The terms "dependant" and "diffuse mesothelioma" both carry the same meaning as in the 1979 Act (subs.(4); note that the definition of "dependant" in the 1979 Act was amended and updated by s.59 of the Welfare Reform Act 2007). If there are two or more dependants eligible to claim, the payment may be apportioned (or not) according to the discretion of the Secretary of State (subs. (5)).

1.873

Conditions of entitlement

47.—(1) In the case of a person who has diffuse mesothelioma, the conditions of entitlement are—
(a) that no payment within subsection (3) has been made in consequence of the disease;
(b) that the person is not eligible for any payment in consequence of the disease that is of a description prescribed by regulations;
(c) that such requirement, if any, as may be prescribed by regulations as to the person's connection with the United Kingdom is satisfied.

(2) In the case of a dependant of a person who, immediately before death, had diffuse mesothelioma, the conditions of entitlement are—
(a) that no payment within subsection (3) has been made in consequence of the disease to that or another dependant or to the deceased or the deceased's personal representatives;
(b) that the dependant is not, and the deceased was not, eligible for any payment in consequence of the disease that is of a description prescribed by regulations;

1.874

(c) that such requirement, if any, as may be prescribed by regulations as to the deceased's connection with the United Kingdom is satisfied.

(3) The payments referred to in subsections (1)(a) and (2)(a) are—

(a) a payment under this Part or under corresponding provision made for Northern Ireland;

(b) a payment under the 1979 Act or under corresponding provision made for Northern Ireland;

(c) an extra-statutory payment;

(d) damages or a payment in settlement of a claim for damages;

(e) a payment of a description prescribed by regulations.

(4) A payment is to be disregarded for the purposes of subsection (1)(a) or (2)(a) if it has been, or is liable to be, repaid—

(a) under section 49 of this Act or under corresponding provision made for Northern Ireland;

(b) under section 5 of the 1979 Act or under corresponding provision made for Northern Ireland;

(c) under the terms of an extra-statutory payment;

(d) in circumstances prescribed for the purposes of this section by regulations.

(5) In this section "extra-statutory payment" has the meaning given by section 1A(5)(d) of the Social Security (Recovery of Benefits) Act 1997.

DEFINITIONS

"extra-statutory payment"—subs.(5)

GENERAL NOTE

1.875   This section sets out the conditions of entitlement for a lump sum payment. The relevant conditions for a mesothelioma sufferer are in subs.(1) and for a dependant of a mesothelioma sufferer in subs.(2). In both instances there are three criteria, each of which must be met.

First, there must have been no payment already in consequence of the disease, as defined by subs.(3) (and subject to the disregards in subs.(4)). Such payments include a payment of damages or settlement of a claim for damages, as well as payments under this Part, payments under the 1979 Act, extra-statutory payments and payments of a prescribed nature. The definition of "extra-statutory payment" is the same as for recoupment purposes, namely one made where a claim has been rejected under the 1979 Act (subs.(5) and see s.54, inserting a new s.1A(5) into the Social Security (Recovery of Benefits) Act 1997). The category of prescribed payments includes payments by government departments (including the Ministry of Defence) and payments by various public sector and other employers which are exempt from employers' liability compulsory insurance (see Employers' Liability (Compulsory Insurance) Regulations 1998 (SI 1998/2573), Sch.2, paras 1-13 and see the Mesothelioma Lump Sum Payments (Conditions and Amounts) Regulations 2008 (SI 2008/1963), reg.2(1)). Note that where a lump sum payment is made under s.46 and there is a later award of damages or settlement in a civil case, the Secretary of State may recoup part or all of the cost of the earlier payment from that figure (see s.54 and the new s.1A of the Social Security (Recovery of Benefits) Act 1997).

Second, there must be no eligibility for any payment of a description as prescribed by regulations. This category includes payments under the Ministry of Defence's War Pensions Scheme or Armed Forces Compensation Scheme: see the Mesothelioma Lump Sum Payments (Conditions and Amounts) Regulations 2008 (SI 2008/1963), reg.2(2).

Third, the mesothelioma victim must have satisfied the prescribed "connection with the United Kingdom" test. The Government's concern is to protect the scheme against (the probably fairly remote) risk of "benefit tourism" by persons who contracted mesothelioma while living abroad and who then travel to the United Kingdom to take advantage of the compensation arrangements. See further the Mesothelioma Lump Sum Payments (Conditions and Amounts) Regulations 2008 (SI 2008/1963), reg.4.

In this context it should be noted that there is no freestanding express statutory requirement that the victim contracted mesothelioma *as a result of* asbestos exposure. In practice, of course, asbestos is the only known cause of mesothelioma. However, a minority of victims have no known exposure to asbestos (this may be because they were in fact exposed, but there is no record of such exposure, or because there are indeed some instances of cryptogenic mesothelioma unrelated to asbestos exposure). The statute simply requires that the person has "diffuse mesothelioma", as defined by s.10(2) of the 1979 Act (see s.46(4)), which in turn refers to the social security definition for the purposes of the industrial injuries scheme. Regulation 1(2) of the Social Security (Industrial Injuries) (Prescribed Diseases) Regulations 1985 (SI 1985/967) defines "diffuse mesothelioma" as the disease numbered P.D. D3 in the Schedule to those Regulations. This refers (under the column headed "Prescribed disease or injury") to "primary neoplasm of the mesothelium of the pleura or of the pericardium or of the peritoneum". It is arguable that this is the limit of the definition, and that it does not include the occupational test in the next column of the Schedule, which refers specifically to asbestos exposure. If that is right, it is arguable that the terms of reg.4 of the Mesothelioma Lump Sum Payments (Conditions and Amounts) Regulations 2008 may be ultra vires, as that provision requires that the person concerned "was in the United Kingdom at a time when and place where" that person "*was exposed to asbestos*" (emphasis added).

Determination of claims

48.—(1) A claim under section 46 must be made in the manner and within the period prescribed by regulations.   1.876

(2) Regulations may prescribe different periods for different cases or classes of cases or for different circumstances.

(3) Regulations may in particular provide that no claim may be made in cases where the prescribed period expired before the commencement of section 46 (or would have done but for any discretion to extend it).

(4) The Secretary of State may, before determining any claim under section 46, appoint a person to inquire into any question arising on the claim, or any matters arising in connection with it, and to report on the question, or on those matters, to the Secretary of State.

GENERAL NOTE

Subss.(1) and (2)

This section deals with the determination of claims made under s.46. Claims   1.877
must be made in the prescribed manner and within time limits: see further the Mesothelioma Lump Sum Payments (Claims and Reconsiderations) Regulations 2008 (SI 2008/1595), regs 2 and 3. The general time limit for claims is 12 months from the diagnosis of mesothelioma (or, in the case of a dependant, 12 months from the death of the person with mesothelioma), as under s.4(1) of the Pneumoconiosis etc. (Workers' Compensation) Act 1979. As under the 1979 Act, this time limit is subject to extension for good cause.

Subs.(3)

There is an initial absolute time limit on backdating of 12 months prior to the   1.878
regulations coming into force, to avoid the possibility of claims by dependants going back as far as 1948: see Mesothelioma Lump Sum Payments (Claims and Reconsiderations) Regulations 2008 (SI 2008/1595), reg.3(1).

Subs. (4)

1.879   This provision is modelled on the now repealed s.17(4) of the Social Security Administration Act 1992, although that referred to an appointment to a person "to hold an inquiry" rather than merely "to inquire" (see also to similar effect s.4(2) of the Pneumoconiosis etc. (Workers' Compensation) Act 1979).

Reconsideration

1.880   **49.**—(1) Subject to subsection (2), the Secretary of State—

(a) may reconsider a determination that a payment should not be made under this Part, on the ground that there has been a material change of circumstances since the determination was made; and

(b) may reconsider a determination either that a payment should or that a payment should not be made under this Part, on the ground that the determination was made in ignorance of, or was based on a mistake as to, a material fact.

(2) Regulations must prescribe the manner in which and the period within which—

(a) an application may be made to the Secretary of State for reconsideration of a determination; or

(b) the Secretary of State may institute such a reconsideration without an application.

(3) Section 48(4) applies in relation to any reconsideration of a determination under this section as it applies in relation to the determination of a claim.

(4) Subsection (5) applies if—

(a) whether fraudulently or otherwise, any person misrepresents or fails to disclose any material fact, and

(b) in consequence of the misrepresentation or failure, a payment is made under this Part.

(5) The person to whom the payment was made is liable to repay the amount of that payment to the Secretary of State unless that person can show that the misrepresentation or failure occurred without that person's connivance or consent.

(6) Except as provided by subsection (5), no payment under this Part is recoverable by virtue of a reconsideration of a determination under this section.

(7) Any sums repaid to the Secretary of State by virtue of subsection (5) are to be paid into the Consolidated Fund.

GENERAL NOTE

1.881   This section makes provision for the Secretary of State to carry out a reconsideration of a determination made under s.48.

Subs. (1)

1.882   Reconsiderations are possible where there has been a material change in circumstances or the original determination was made in ignorance of or based on a mistake as to a material fact (subs.(1)). These grounds have been borrowed from the social security jurisdiction. This section also broadly follows the model of s.5 of the Pneumoconiosis etc. (Workers' Compensation) Act 1979.

Subss. (2) and (3)

1.883   See the Mesothelioma Lump Sum Payments (Claims and Reconsiderations) Regulations 2008 (SI 2008/1595), regs 4 and 5. The Secretary of State has the same power as when dealing with an initial determination to appoint a person to inquire into matters arising (see s.48(4)).

Subss.(4) and (5)

The Secretary of State may recover payments under the scheme where they have been caused by misrepresentation or failure to disclose; again, these concepts are borrowed from social security law – see Social Security Administration Act 1992, s.71. However the potential defence under subs.(5) that the misrepresentation or failure to disclose "occurred without that person's connivance or consent" does not appear in social security law (except in the context of s.5(4) of the Vaccine Damages Act 1979).   1.884

Appeal to [¹ First-tier Tribunal]

50.—(1) A person who has made a claim under section 46 may appeal against a determination made by the Secretary of State—   1.885
  (a) on the claim, or
  (b) on reconsideration under section 49 of a determination made on the claim.

(2) Subject to regulations under subsection (4)(c), the Secretary of State must refer any appeal to [¹ the First-tier Tribunal].

(3) On an appeal the tribunal may substitute for the determination concerned any determination which could have been made in accordance with this Part.

(4) Regulations may make provision—
  (a) as to the manner in which, and the time within which, an appeal may be made;
  (b) [¹. . .];
  (c) for the purpose of enabling an appeal under subsection (1)(a) to be treated as an application for reconsideration under section 49 of the determination made on the claim.

AMENDMENT

1. Transfer of Tribunal Functions Order 2008 (SI 2008/2833), art.6, Sch.3, para.226 (November 3, 2008).

GENERAL NOTE

A person making a claim under s.46 has a right of appeal to the First-tier Tribunal against the Secretary of State's determination on the claim under s.48 or reconsideration under s.49. There is a further right of appeal (on a point of law and with permission) from the First-tier Tribunal to the Upper Tribunal (Tribunals, Courts and Enforcement Act 2007, s.11).   1.886

Note that the right of appeal is under the 2008 Act; there is no right of appeal to a tribunal in respect of decisions made under the 1979 Act, although there is a reconsideration process under that legislation.

Appeal to Social Security Commissioner

51.—[¹. . .]   1.887

AMENDMENT

1. Transfer of Tribunal Functions Order 2008 (SI 2008/2833), art.6, Sch.3, para.227 (November 3, 2008).

1.888   As originally enacted, there was a further right of appeal from the decision of an appeal tribunal (now the First-tier Tribunal) under s.50 to the Social Security Commissioner. The jurisdiction of the Commissioner has now been assumed by the Upper Tribunal under the Tribunals, Courts and Enforcement Act 2007. The bringing into force of s.11 of that Act, which provides for a right of appeal, subject to permission being granted, from the First-tier Tribunal to the Upper Tribunal on a point of law swiftly made s.51 redundant.

Minors and people who lack capacity

1.889   **52.**—(1) This section applies where a payment under this Part falls to be made to—

(a) a person aged under 18, or

(b) a person who lacks capacity within the meaning of the Mental Capacity Act 2005 (or, in Scotland, who is incapable within the meaning of the Adults with Incapacity (Scotland) Act 2000 (asp 4)) in relation to financial matters.

(2) Subject to section 46(5) the payment is to be made for that person's benefit by paying it to such trustees as the Secretary of State may appoint.

(3) The trustees are to hold the payment on such trusts or, in Scotland, for such purposes and on such conditions as the Secretary of State may declare.

GENERAL NOTE

1.890   This section makes special provision for cases in which a payment is due to be made to a child or to a person who lacks capacity; in such cases payments are to be made to trustees. This provision is similar to s.6 of the Pneumoconiosis etc. (Workers' Compensation) Act 1979.

Regulations: Part 4

1.891   **53.**—(1) A reference in this Part to regulations is a reference to regulations made by the Secretary of State.

(2) The power to make regulations under this Part—

(a) is exercisable by statutory instrument;

(b) includes power to make such incidental, supplementary or transitional provision as the Secretary of State thinks fit;

(c) may be exercised so as to provide for a person to exercise a discretion in dealing with any matter.

(3) No regulations may be made under section 46 unless a draft of the statutory instrument containing the regulations has been laid before, and approved by a resolution of, each House of Parliament.

(4) No regulations may be made under any provision of section 47 if they are the first regulations to be made under that section, unless a draft of the statutory instrument containing the regulations has been laid before, and approved by a resolution of, each House of Parliament.

(5) A statutory instrument that—

(a) contains regulations under this Part, and

(b) is not subject to a requirement that a draft of the instrument be laid before, and approved by a resolution of, each House of Parliament,

shall be subject to annulment in pursuance of a resolution of either House of Parliament.

Regulations made under s.46 which make provision for lump sum payments in respect of mesothelioma are subject to the affirmative procedure (subs.(3)); all other regulations under this Part are subject to the negative procedure (subs.(4)). **1.892**

Recovery of mesothelioma and other lump sum payments

Amendment of Social Security (Recovery of Benefits) Act 1997

54—(*omitted:* see Vol.III). **1.893**

General note

This section inserts a new s.1A into the Social Security (Recovery of Benefits) Act 1997. The 1997 Act applies wherever a person makes a payment "to or in respect of any other person in consequence of any accident, injury or disease suffered by the other" and where as a result certain prescribed benefits have been (or are likely) to be paid to or for the other person during the relevant period. The new s.1A allows the Secretary of State to make regulations providing for the recovery of lump sum payments in analogous circumstances: see further the Social Security (Recovery of Benefits) (Lump Sum Payments) Regulations 2008 (SI 2008/1596). These regulations establish a freestanding compensation recovery scheme to recoup lump sum mesothelioma payments under Part 4 of the present Act as well as those under the Pneumoconiosis etc. (Workers' Compensation) Act 1979 and certain extra-statutory payments. The intention is to recover such payments from any civil compensation award paid to the person in respect of the same disease (or diseases) for which the lump sum payment was made. The underlying principle is that a person should not be compensated twice for the same loss. **1.894**

REGULATIONS

Preliminary Note: change of name from Department of Social Security to Department for Work and Pensions

1.895   The Secretaries of State for Education and Skills and for Work and Pensions Order 2002 (SI 2002/1397) make provision for the change of name from the Department of Social Security to Department for Work and Pensions. Article 9(5) provides:

"(5) Subject to article 12 [which makes specific amendments], any enactment or instrument passed or made before the coming into force of this Order shall have effect, so far as may be necessary for the purposes of or in consequence of the entrusting to the Secretary of State for Work and Pensions of the social security functions, as if any reference to the Secretary of State for Social Security, to the Department of Social Security or to an officer of the Secretary of State for Social Security (including any reference which is to be construed as such a reference) were a reference to the Secretary of State for Work and Pensions, to the Department for Work and Pensions or, as the case may be, to an officer of the Secretary of State for Work and Pensions."

PART II

CONTRIBUTION CREDITS AND HOME RESPONSIBILITIES PROTECTION

The Social Security (Credits) Regulations 1975

(SI 1975/556) (*as amended*)

ARRANGEMENT OF REGULATIONS

The Secretary of State for Social Services in exercise of the powers conferred upon her by section 13(4) of the Social Security Act 1975 and section 2(1) of, and paragraph 3 of Schedule 3 to, the Social Security (Consequential Provisions) Act 1975 and of all other powers enabling her in that behalf, without having referred any proposals on the matter to the National Insurance Advisory Committee since it appears to her that by reason of urgency it is inexpedient to do so, hereby makes the following regulations:

Citation and commencement

1.—These regulations may be cited as the Social Security (Credits) Regulations 1975 and shall come into operation on 6th April 1975.   2.2

Interpretation

2.—(1) In these regulations, unless the context otherwise requires,—   2.3
"the Act" means the Social Security Act 1975;
[1"benefit" includes a contribution-based jobseeker's allowance but not an income-based jobseeker's allowance [10and includes a contributory employment and support allowance but not an income-related employment and support allowance;].
[2 "bereavement allowance" means an allowance referred to in section 39B of the Contributions and Benefits Act;

"bereavement benefit" means a benefit referred to in section 20(1)(ea) of the Contributions and Benefits Act;]

[¹ . . .]

[¹ "contribution-based jobseeker's allowance" has the same meaning as in the Jobseekers Act 1995;]

[¹⁰ "contributory employment and support allowance" means a contributory allowance under Part 1 of the Welfare Reform Act (employment and support allowance);

[³ "the Contributions and Benefits Act" means the Social Security Contributions and Benefits Act 1992;]

"credits" and "a credit" shall be construed in accordance with regulation 3;

[⁴ . . .];

[¹ . . .];

[¹ "income-based jobseeker's allowance" has the same meaning as in the Jobseekers Act 1995;

"jobseeker's allowance" means an allowance payable under Part I of the Jobseekers Act 1995;]

[¹⁰ "income-related employment and support allowance" means an income-related allowance under Part 1 of the Welfare Reform Act (employment and support allowance);

[¹ . . .];

[⁹ "reckonable year" means a year for which the relevant earnings factor of the contributor concerned was sufficient to satisfy—

    (a) in relation to short-term incapacity benefit, widowed mother's allowance, [widowed parent's allowance, bereavement benefits,] widow's pension or Category A or Category B retirement pension, paragraph (b) of the second contribution condition specified in relation to that benefit in Schedule 3 to the Contributions and Benefits Act; [¹⁰ . . .]

    (b) in relation to contribution-based jobseeker's allowance, the additional condition specified in section 2(3) of the Jobseekers Act 1995;] [¹⁰ or

    (c) in relation to a contributory employment and support allowance, the condition specified in paragraph 2(1) of Schedule 1 to the Welfare Reform Act (conditions relating to national insurance);]

"relevant benefit year" [¹ has the same meaning as it has—

    (a) in relation to short-term incapacity benefit, in paragraph 2(6) (b) of Schedule 3 to the Contributions and Benefits Act; and

    (b) in relation to contribution-based jobseeker's allowance, the additional condition specified in section 2(4)(b) of the Jobseekers Act 1995;]

"relevant earnings factor" [⁵ in relation to any benefit, means—

    (a) [¹ if the benefit is a contribution-based jobseeker's allowance or if the contributions relevant to the benefit under section 21 of the Contributions and Benefits Act] are Class 1 contributions, the earnings factor derived from earnings [⁶ in respect of which] primary Class 1 contributions have been paid or treated as paid, or credited earnings;

    (b) if the contributions relevant to that benefit under that section

are Class 1 and Class 2 contributions, the earnings factor or the aggregate of the earnings factors derived from—
  (i) earnings [⁶ in respect of] which primary Class 1 contributions have been paid or treated as paid, or credited earnings, and
  (ii) Class 2 contributions;
  (c) if the contributions relevant to that benefit under [6 that section] are Class 1, Class 2 and Class 3 contributions, the earnings factor or the aggregate of the earnings factors derived from—
  (i) earnings [⁶ in respect of which] primary contributions have been paid or treated as paid, or credited earnings,
  (ii) Class 2 contributions, and
  (iii) Class 3 contributions paid or credited];
[⁷ "relevant past year" means the last complete year before the beginning of the relevant benefit year;]
[¹⁰ "the Welfare Reform Act" means the Welfare Reform Act 2007;
[² "widowed parent's allowance" means an allowance referred to in section 39A of the Contributions and Benefits Act;]
[⁴ "working tax credit" means a working tax credit under section 10 of the Tax Credits Act 2002];
[⁸ "year" means tax year;]
and other expressions have the same meanings as in the Act.

(2) The rules for the construction of Acts of Parliament contained in the Interpretation Act 1889 shall apply for the purposes of the interpretation of these regulations as they apply for the purposes of the interpretation of an Act of Parliament.

(3) Unless the context otherwise requires, any reference in these regulations—
  (a) to a numbered section is a reference to the section of the Act bearing that number;
  (b) to a numbered regulation is a reference to the regulation bearing that number in these regulations, and any reference in a regulation to a numbered paragraph is a reference to the paragraph of that regulation bearing that number;
  (c) to any provision made by or contained in any enactment or instrument shall be construed as a reference to that provision as amended or extended by any enactment or instrument and as including a reference to any provision which it re-enacts or replaces or which may re-enact or replace it with or without modification.

(4) Nothing in these regulations shall be construed as entitling any person to be credited with contributions for the purposes of any benefit for a day, period or event occurring before 6th April 1975.

AMENDMENTS

1. Social Security (Credits and Contributions) (Jobseeker's Allowance Consequential and Miscellaneous Amendments) Regulations 1996 (SI 1996/2367), reg.2(2) (October 7, 1996).
2. Social Security (Benefits for Widows and Widowers) (Consequential Amendments) Regulations 2000 (SI 2000/1483), reg.3(2).
3. Social Security (Incapacity Benefit) (Consequential and Transitional Amendments and Savings) Regulations 1995 (SI 1995/829), reg.6(2) (April 13, 1995).
4. Social Security (Working Tax Credit and Child Tax Credit) (Consequential

Amendments) Regulations 2003 (SI 2003/455), reg.6 and Sch.4, para.1 (April 7, 2003).

5. Social Security (Credits) Amendment Regulations 1987 (SI 1987/414), reg.2 (April 6, 1987).

6. Social Security (Contributions and Credits) (Miscellaneous Amendments) Regulations 1999 (SI 1999/568), reg.20(a) (April 6, 1999).

7. Social Security (Credits) Amendment (No. 4) Regulations 1988 (SI 1988/1545), reg.2(2) (October 2, 1988).

8. Social Security (Credits) Amendment (No. 2) Regulations 1988 (SI 1988/1230), reg.2(2) (October 2, 1988).

9. Social Security (Miscellaneous Amendments) (No. 3) Regulations 2007 (SI 2007/1749), reg.8(2) (July 16, 2007).

10. Employment and Support Allowance (Consequential Provisions) (No. 2) Regulations 2008 (SI 2008/1554), reg.48(2) (October 27, 2008).

General provisions relating to the crediting of contributions [¹ and earnings]

2.4   **3.**—[²(1) Any contributions or earnings credited in accordance with these Regulations shall be only for the purpose of enabling the person concerned to satisfy—

(a) in relation to short-term incapacity benefit, widowed mother's allowance, [³ widowed parent's allowance, bereavement allowance,] widow's pension or Category A or Category B retirement pension, the second contribution condition specified in relation to that benefit in Schedule 3 to the Contributions and Benefits Act; [⁴ . . .]

(b) in relation to contribution-based jobseeker's allowance, the condition specified in section 2(1)(b) of the Jobseekers Act 1995; [⁴or

(c) in relation to a contributory employment and support allowance, the condition specified in paragraph 2(1) of Schedule 1 to the Welfare Reform Act,]

and accordingly, where under any of the provisions of these Regulations a person would, but for this paragraph, be entitled to be credited with any contributions or earnings for a year, or in respect of any week in a year, he shall be so entitled for the purposes of any benefit only if and to no greater extent than that by which his relevant earnings factor for that year falls short of the level required to make that year a reckonable year.]

(2) Where under these regulations a person is entitled for the purposes of any benefit to—

(a) be credited [¹ with earnings] for a year, he is to be credited with such amount of [¹ earnings] as may be required to bring his relevant earnings factor to the level required to make that year a reckonable year

(b) [¹ . . .];

(3) Where under these regulations a person is entitled to be credited [¹ with earnings] or a contribution in respect of a week which is partly in one tax year and partly in another, he shall be entitled to [¹ be credited with those earnings or that contribution] for the tax year in which that week began and not for the following year.

AMENDMENTS

1. Social Security (Credits) Amendment Regulations 1987 (SI 1987/414), reg.3 (April 6, 1987).

2. Social Security (Credits and Contributions) (Jobseeker's Allowance

Consequential and Miscellaneous Amendments) Regulations 1996 (SI 1996/2367), reg.2(3) (October 7, 1996).

3. Social Security (Benefits for Widows and Widowers) (Consequential Amendments) Regulations 2000 (SI 2000/1483), reg.3(3).

4. Employment and Support Allowance (Consequential Provisions) (No. 2) Regulations 2008 (SI 2008/1554), reg.48(3) (October 27, 2008).

DEFINITIONS

"benefit"—see reg.2(1).
"reckonable year"—see reg.2(1).
"relevant earnings factor"—see reg.2(1).
"tax year"—see SSCBA 1992, s.122(1).
"year": see reg.2(1).

GENERAL NOTE

This provides that credits can only be awarded under these regulations to enable   **2.5** the person to satisfy the second contribution condition for particular benefits (paras (1) and (2) read with reg.2(1)):

- short-term incapacity benefit (SSCBA 1992, s.30A);
- widowed mother's allowance (SSCBA 1992, s.37);
- widowed parent's allowance (SSCBA 1992, s.39A);
- bereavement allowance (SSCBA 1992, s.39B);
- widow's pension (SSCBA 1992, s.38);
- Category A or B retirement pension (SSCBA 1992, ss.43–54);
- contribution-based jobseeker's allowance (Jobseekers Act 1995, s.2—see *Vol. II: Income Support, Jobseeker's Allowance, State Pension Credit and the Social Fund*).

Moreover, they can only be awarded to the extent necessary to make up the short-fall between the actual record in paid contributions in the relevant tax year and the level needed to satisfy the particular second condition (50 times the lower earnings limit for Class 1 contributions liability purposes in that year—52 times for retirement pension), that is, to make that year a "reckonable year" (para.(2)).

Paragraph (3) deals with the situation where the week in which someone is entitled to be credited spans two tax years, and provides that the tax year to be credited is the one in which the week began.

The role and importance of reg.3 is generally overlooked. It is, however, crucial in determining whether "credits" (crediting earnings and earnings factors to a claimant's contribution account) for which the claimant is eligible under other provisions of these regulations can actually be awarded in respect of the specified benefits. It is as if it had to be read as an integral part of each of those other regulations. It is, moreover, a provision that causes particular problems in respect on its interaction with the provision on credits for unemployment in reg.8A. Commissioner Williams sets out the law on crediting contributions in *CIB/1602/2006*:

"Provision is made to allow credited earnings under section 22(5) of the 1992 Act. This provides, as relevant to this appeal:
'Regulations may provide for crediting—
    (a) for 1987–88 or any subsequent year, earnings . . .
        for the purpose of bringing a person's earnings factor for that tax year to a figure which will enable him to satisfy contribution conditions of entitlement to . . . any prescribed description of benefit . . .'
This applies to D's claim for incapacity benefit. It makes clear that credited earnings can only apply when the individual has not paid enough actual contributions

for the year. This, equally clearly, can only be decided after the end of the tax year, which occurs in April each calendar year. (For employed earners this will be in practice after the time limit in the following May or June when all employers are required to make a return of total contributions collected for their employees during the year ending in April. See Schedule 4, paragraph 22 to the Social Security (Contributions) Regulations 2001 (SI 2001 No 1004)).

The regulations allowing credited earnings for periods of unemployment are regulations 3 (general provisions relating to the crediting of contributions and earnings) and 8A (credits for unemployment) of the Social Security (Credits) Regulations 1975 ("the Credits Regulations") (SI 1975 No 556). These are complicated and much amended regulations. Little attention has been paid for years past to the structure of the Credits Regulations and the way that they are empowered by, and link to, section 22(5) of the 1992 Act and its predecessors back to section 13 of the Social Security Act 1975. The Regulations follow the usual pattern of stating the commencement provisions in regulation 1 and definitions in regulation 2. Regulation 3 then lays down general provisions relating to the crediting of contributions and earnings. Regulations 4 to 9D follow with provisions for specific forms of credit or credited earnings in specific situations. It is abundantly clear from this that, reflecting the authority granted in section 22(5), regulation 3 is to be applied in each case along with the specific regulation. That has not happened here. As Commissioner Rowland commented in CIB 3327 2004, regulation 3 is rarely mentioned in connection with the award of credited earnings. It is not the subject, so far as I can see, of any comment in the *DMG*. Nor has it been mentioned in this appeal.

The Credits Regulations have been amended many times since first being written. The most important of the amendments—only partially executed—take account of the abolition of contribution credits on 6 04 1987. From that date (the start of the tax year 1987–88) the previous system of awarding weekly credits was abolished. It was replaced by a system of crediting earnings and earnings factors to a claimant only when necessary at the end of a tax year. Commissioner Rowland explores these concepts in CIB 3327 2004, and I do not repeat that. The difficulties in cases such as this are because the fundamental change in the nature of contribution "credits" does not appear yet to have been absorbed into the relevant administrative processes for identifying and awarding credited earnings. That failure is in part hidden because of a failure fully to amend the Credits Regulations themselves to reflect the changes made in 1987" (paras 24–26).

The problem this generates with claims for credits for unemployment were then considered by Commissioner Williams (and a solution found). The matter is considered in the update to the commentary to reg.8A, below. For further consideration of some of the difficulties arising where records have been destroyed as part of normal administrative processes and for the text of the regulations on unemployment credits covering 1977–89, see Commissioner Williams' decision in *CP/1792/2007*.

Starting credits for the purposes of a retirement pension, a widowed mother's allowance, a widowed parent's allowance, a bereavement allowance and a widow's pension

2.6   **4.**—(1) For the purposes of entitlement to a Category A or a Category B retirement pension, a widowed mother's allowance [¹, a widowed parent's allowance, a bereavement allowance] or a widow's pension [² by virtue of a person's earnings or contributions], he shall be credited with such number of Class 3 contributions as may be required to bring his relevant earnings factor in respect of the tax year in which he attained the age of 16 and for each of the two following tax years to the level required to make those years reckonable years; so however, subject to paragraph (2), no contribution shall be credited under this regulation in respect of any tax year commencing before 6th April 1975.

(2) Where a person was in Great Britain on 6th April 1975 and had attained the age of 16 but was not an insured person under the National Insurance Act 1965, he shall be credited with contributions under paragraph (1) in respect of the tax year commencing on 6th April 1974.

AMENDMENTS

1. Social Security (Benefits for Widows and Widowers) (Consequential Amendments) Regulations 2000 (SI 2000/1483), reg.3(4).
2. Social Security (Credits) Amendment (No. 4) Regulations 1988 (SI 1988/1545), reg.2(5) (October 2, 1988).

DEFINITIONS

"reckonable year"—see reg.2(1).
"relevant earnings factor"—see reg.2(1).
"tax year"—see SSCBA 1992, s.122(1).

GENERAL NOTE

As with all of the Regulations making claimants eligible for the award of credits, this must be read with reg.3 (*CIB/1602/2006; CIB/3327/2004*). One can only have them insofar as they are necessary to bring one's record up to the level required for satisfying the second contribution condition for the relevant benefit (see para.(1), reg.3 and reg.2(1) ("reckonable year")). **2.7**

This applies only for the purposes of a retirement pension, a widowed mother's allowance, a widowed parent's allowance, a bereavement allowance and a widow's pension. It awards someone sufficient Class 3 credits to bring his contribution record in a particular tax year up to the requisite level for the second contribution condition (to make the year a "reckonable year"). The tax years in question are the one in which he reached 16 and the two tax years following that year. No credits are awardable prior to April 6, 1975, save that tax year 1974–75 can be credited as respects someone 16 or over, who was in Great Britain on that date but was not an insured person under the National Insurance Act 1965.

Starting credits for the purposes of unemployment benefit, sickness benefit and maternity allowance

5.—[¹ . . .] **2.8**

REVOCATION

1. Social Security (Credits) Amendment (No. 2) Regulations 1988 (SI 1988/1230), reg.3(1).

Starting credits for the purposes of a maternity grant

6.—[¹ . . .] **2.9**

REVOCATION

1. Social Security (Credits) Amendment Regulations 1988 (SI 1988/516), reg.3(1).

Credits for approved training

7.—(1) For the purposes of entitlement to any benefit [¹ by virtue of a person's earnings or contributions] he shall, subject to paragraphs (2) and **2.10**

(3), be entitled to [² be credited with earnings equal to the lower earnings limit then in force], in respect of each week in any part of which he was undergoing (otherwise than in pursuance of his employment as an employed earner) a course of [³ . . .] training approved by the Secretary of State for the purposes of this regulation.

[³ (2) Paragraph (1) shall apply to a person only if—
(a) the course is—
    (i) a course of full-time training; or
    (ii) a course of training which he attends for not less than 15 hours in the week in question and he is a disabled person within the meaning of the Disabled Persons (Employment) Act 1944; or
    (iii) a course of training introductory to a course to which paragraph (i) or (ii) above applies; and
(b) when the course began it was not intended to continue for more than 12 months or, if he was a disabled person within the meaning of the Disabled Persons (Employment) Act 1944 and the training was provided under the Employment and Training Act 1973 [⁴ or the Enterprise and New Towns (Scotland) Act 1990], for such longer period as is reasonable in the circumstances of his case; and
(c) he had attained the age of 18 before the beginning of the tax year in which the week in question began.]

(3) Paragraph (1) shall not apply to a woman in respect of any week in any part of which she was a married woman in respect of whom an election made by her under regulations made under section 3(2) of the Social Security Pensions Act 1975 had effect.

AMENDMENTS

1. Social Security (Credits) Amendment (No. 4) Regulations 1988 (SI 1988/1545), reg.2(5) (October 2, 1988).
2. Social Security (Credits) Amendment Regulations 1987 (SI 1987/414), reg.5 (April 6, 1987).
3. Social Security (Credits) Amendment (No. 3) Regulations 1988 (SI 1988/1439), reg.2 (September 4, 1988).
4. Enterprise (Scotland) Consequential Amendments Order 1991 (SI 1991/387), art.3(a) (April 1, 1991).

DEFINITIONS

"benefit"—see reg.2(1).
"employed earner"—see SSCBA 1992, s.2(1)(a).
"lower earnings limit"—see SSCBA 1992, s.122(1).
"tax year"—see SSCBA 1992, s.122(1).

GENERAL NOTE

2.11   As with all of the Regulations making claimants eligible for the award of credits, this must be read with reg.3 (*CIB/1602/2006*; *CIB/3327/2004*). One can only have them insofar as they are necessary to bring one's record up to the level required for satisfying the second contribution condition for the relevant benefit (see para.(1), reg.3 and reg.2(1) ("reckonable year")). The relevant benefits are:

* short-term incapacity benefit (SSCBA 1992, s.30A);

* widowed mother's allowance (SSCBA 1992, s.37);

* widowed parent's allowance (SSCBA 1992, s.39A);

* bereavement allowance (SSCBA 1992, s.39B);

- widow's pension (SSCBA 1992, s.38);

- Category A or B retirement pension (SSCBA 1992, ss.43–54);

- contribution-based jobseeker's allowance (Jobseekers Act 1995, s.2—(see *Vol. II: Income Support, Jobseeker's Allowance, State Pension Credit and the Social Fund*)(para.(1)).

It enables credits to be awarded to a person for each week in which he was undergoing an approved course of training, otherwise than in pursuance of his employed earner's employment. Approved means approved by the Secretary of State for the purposes of this regulation. The conditions in para.(2) must be met. The course must be full time or, where someone is disabled within the meaning of the Disabled Persons (Employment) Act 1944, one attended for at least 15 hours in the week for which the credit is sought, or it must be a course of training introductory to such a course (para.(2)(a). In addition the person must have been 18 before the beginning of the tax year containing the week sought to be credited (para.(2)(c)). Furthermore, when commenced the course must not have been intended to last more than 12 months, or, where the person is disabled within the meaning of that 1944 Act and the training was provided under specified legislation, for such longer period as is reasonable in his case (para.(2)(b)).

Finally, note that a woman cannot gain a credit under this provision in respect of any week in any part of which as a married woman a certificate of election to pay contributions at reduced rate applied to her (para.(3)).

[¹ Credits for [² carer's allowance]

7A.—(1) For the purposes of entitlement to any benefit [³ by virtue of   2.12
a person's earnings or contributions] he shall, subject to paragraph (2), be entitled to [⁴ be credited with earnings equal to the lower earnings limit then in force], in respect of each week for any part of which [² a carer's allowance] is paid to him, [⁵ or would be paid to him but for a restriction under section 7 of the Social Security Fraud Act 2001 (loss of benefit provisions)] or in the case of [⁷ widow, widower or surviving civil partner] would have been so payable but for the provisions of the Social Security (Overlapping Benefits) Regulations 1975, as amended by the Social Security (Invalid Care Allowance) Regulations 1976, requiring adjustment of [² a carer's allowance] against widow's benefit, bereavement benefits or benefit by virtue of section 39(4) corresponding to a widowed mother's allowance or a widow's pension.

(2) Paragraph (1) shall not apply—
(a) to a person in respect of any week where he is entitled to [⁴ be credited with earnings] under [⁶ regulation 8A or 8B] in respect of the same week; or
(b) to a woman in respect of any week in any part of which she was a married woman in respect of whom an election made by her under regulations made under section 3(2) of the Social Security Pensions Act 1975 had effect.]

AMENDMENTS

1. Social Security (Invalid Care Allowance) Regulations 1976 (SI 1976/409), reg.19 (April 12, 1976).

2. Social Security Amendment (Carer's Allowance) Regulations 2002 (SI 2002/2497), reg.3 and Sch.2 (April 1, 2003).

3. Social Security (Credits) Amendment (No. 4) Regulations 1988 (SI 1988/1545), reg.2(5) (October 2, 1988).

4. Social Security (Credits) Amendment Regulations 1987 (SI 1987/414), reg.6 (April 6, 1987).

5. Social Security (Loss of Benefit) (Consequential Amendments) Regulations (SI 2002/490), reg.3(a) (April 1, 2002).

6. Social Security (Credits and Contributions) (Jobseeker's Allowance Consequential and Miscellaneous Amendments) Regulations 1996 (SI 1996/2367), reg.2 (October 7, 1996).

7. Civil Partnership (Pensions, Social Security and Child Support) (Consequential, etc. Provisions) Order 2005 (SI 2005/2877), art.2(3) and Sch.3, para.4(2) (December 5, 2005).

DEFINITIONS

"benefit"—see reg.2(1).
"lower earnings limit"—see SSCBA 1992, s.122(1).

GENERAL NOTE

2.13   As with all of the Regulations making claimants eligible for the award of credits, this must be read with reg.3 (*CIB/1602/2006*; *CIB/3327/2004*). One can only have them insofar as they are necessary to bring one's record up to the level required for satisfying the second contribution condition for the relevant benefit (see para.(1), reg.3 and reg.2(1) ("reckonable year")). The relevant benefits are:

- short-term incapacity benefit (SSCBA 1992, s.30A);

- widowed mother's allowance (SSCBA 1992, s.37);

- widowed parent's allowance (SSCBA 1992, s.39A);

- bereavement allowance (SSCBA 1992, s.39B);

- widow's pension (SSCBA 1992, s.38);

- Category A or B retirement pension (SSCBA 1992, ss.43–54);

- contribution-based jobseeker's allowance (Jobseekers Act 1995, s.2—see *Vol. II: Income Support, Jobseeker's Allowance, State Pension Credit and the Social Fund*).

It enables a credit equal to that tax year's lower earnings limit to be awarded for each week in respect of part of which someone has a carer's allowance paid to him; or where it would have been paid to him but for the loss of benefit provision in the Social Security Fraud Act 2001, s.7; or where, as a widow or widower it is not because of the adjustment provisions in the Overlapping Benefit Regulations. In *CG 2902/2003*, Deputy Commissioner Mark considered when it could be said that invalid care allowance (now care allowance) was "paid" to someone for the purposes of this regulation. He concluded that it is not "paid" in the required sense:

"where it has been decided subsequent to payment that the claimant was not entitled to such an allowance for that period. Accordingly, the secretary of state was correct not to award credits in respect of that period and the tribunal was correct to dismiss the claimant's appeal" (para.22).

He expressed no view as to the effect on an existing award of credits where the award of invalid care allowance is revised or superseded.

Note that a woman cannot gain a credit under this provision in respect of any week in any part of which as a married woman a certificate of election to pay contributions at reduced rate applied to her (para.(2)(b)). Nor can a credit be awarded under this provision if a credit entitlement for the week arises under reg.8A (unemployment) or 8B (incapacity for work) (para.(2)(a)).

[¹ Credits for [² disability element of working tax credit]

7B.—(1) For the purposes of entitlement to any benefit by virtue of a person's earnings or contributions he shall, subject to paragraphs (2) and (3), be credited with earnings equal to the lower earnings limit then in force in respect of each week for any part of which [² the disability element or the severe disability element of working tax credit as specified in regulation 20(1)(b) and (f) of the Working Tax Credit (Entitlement and Maximum Rate) Regulations 2002 is included in an award of working tax credit which] is paid to him.

2.14

(2) Paragraph (1) shall apply to a person only if he is—

(a) an employed earner; or

(b) a self-employed earner who is excepted from liability to pay Class 2 contributions by virtue of his earnings being less than or being treated by regulations as less than the amount specified in section 7(5) of the Act (exception from liability for Class 2 contributions on account of small earnings).

(3) Paragraph (1) shall not apply—

(a) to a person in respect of any week where he is entitled to be credited with earnings under [³ regulation 8A or 8B] in respect of the same week; or

(b) to a woman in respect of any week in any part of which she was a married woman in respect of whom an election made by her under regulations made under section 3(2) of the Social Security Pension Act 1975 had effect.]

AMENDMENTS

1. Social Security (Credits) Amendment Regulations 1991 (SI 1991/2772), reg.3 (April 6, 1992).

2. Social Security (Working Tax Credit and Child Tax Credit) (Consequential Amendments) Regulations 2003 (SI 2003/455), reg.6 and Sch.4, para.1 (April 7, 2003).

3. Social Security (Credits and Contributions) (Jobseeker's Allowance Consequential and Miscellaneous Amendments) Regulations 1996 (SI 1996/2367), reg.2 (October 7, 1996).

DEFINITIONS

"employed earner"—see SSCBA 1992, s.2(1)(a).
"lower earnings limit"—see SSCBA 1992, s.122(1).
"self-employed earner"—see SSCBA 1992, s.2(1)(b).
"working tax credit"—see reg.2(1).

GENERAL NOTE

As with all of the Regulations making claimants eligible for the award of credits, this must be read with reg.3 (*CIB/1602/2006*; *CIB/3327/2004*). One can only have them insofar as they are necessary to bring one's record up to the level required for satisfying the second contribution condition for the relevant benefit (see para.(1), reg.3 and reg.2(1) ("reckonable year")). The relevant benefits are:

2.15

• short-term incapacity benefit (SSCBA 1992, s.30A);

• widowed mother's allowance (SSCBA 1992, s.37);

• widowed parent's allowance (SSCBA 1992, s.39A);

• bereavement allowance (SSCBA 1992, s.39B);

- widow's pension (SSCBA 1992, s.38);

- Category A or B retirement pension (SSCBA 1992, ss.43–54);

- contribution-based jobseeker's allowance (Jobseekers Act 1995, s.2—see *Vol. II: Income Support, Jobseeker's Allowance, State Pension Credit and the Social Fund*)(para.(1)).

It enables a credit equal to that tax year's lower earnings limit to be awarded for each week in respect of part of which someone has a working tax credit inclusive of the disability or severe disability element paid to him (para.(1)). He must either be an employed earner, or a self-employed earner exempt from paying Class 2 contributions because of the "small earnings" exception (para.(2)). Note that a woman cannot gain a credit under this provision in respect of any week in any part of which as a married woman a certificate of election to pay contributions at reduced rate applied to her (para.(3)(b)). Nor can a credit be awarded under this provision if a credit entitlement for the week arises under reg.8A (unemployment) or 8B (incapacity for work) (para.(3)(a)).

[¹ Credits for [² working tax credit]

2.16   **7C.**—(1) [² Subject to regulation 7B], for the purposes of entitlement to a Category A or a Category B retirement pension, a widowed mother's allowance, a widowed parent's allowance, a bereavement allowance or a widow's pension by virtue of a person's earnings or contributions, where [² working tax credit] is paid for any week in respect of—
  (a) an employed earner; or
  (b) a self-employed earner who is excepted from liability to pay Class 2 contributions by virtue of his earnings being less than or being treated by regulations as less than the amount specified in section 11(4) of the Contributions and Benefits Act (exception from liability for Class 2 contributions on account of small earnings),
that person shall, subject to paragraphs (4) and (5), be credited with earnings equal to the lower earnings limit then in force in respect of that week.

(2) The reference in paragraph (1) to the person in respect of whom [² working tax credit] is paid—
  (a) where it is paid to one of [⁵ a couple], is a reference to the member of that couple specified in paragraph (3); and
  (b) in any other case, is a reference to the person to whom it is paid.

(3) the member of [⁵ a couple] specified for the purposes of paragraph (2)(a) is—
  (a) where only one member is assessed for the purposes of the award of [² working tax credit] as having income consisting of earnings, that member; or
  (b) [² . . .]
  (c) where the earnings of each member are assessed [² . . .], the member to whom the [² working tax credit] is paid.

(4) Paragraph (1) shall not apply—
  (a) to a person in respect of any week he is entitled to be credited with earnings under regulation 8A or 8B in respect of the same week; or
  (b) to a woman in respect of any week in any part of which she is a married woman in respect of whom an election made by her under regulations made under section 19(4) of the Contributions and Benefits Act has effect.

(5) [² . . .].

(6) In this regulation [⁵ couple has] the same meaning as in Part VII of the Contributions and Benefits Act.]

AMENDMENTS

1. Social Security (Credits) Amendment Regulations 1995 (SI 1995/2558), reg.2 (November 1, 1995).
2. Social Security (Working Tax Credit and Child Tax Credit) (Consequential Amendments) Regulations 2003 (SI 2003/455), reg.6 and Sch.4, para.1 (April 7, 2003).
3. Social Security (Credits and Contributions) (Jobseeker's Allowance Consequential and Miscellaneous Amendments) Regulations 1996 (SI 1996/2367), reg.2 (October 7, 1996).
4. Social Security (Benefits for Widows and Widowers) (Consequential Amendments) Regulations 2000 (SI 2000/1483), reg.3(6).
5. Civil Partnership (Pensions, Social Security and Child Support) (Consequential, etc. Provisions) Order 2005 (SI 2005/2877), art.2(3) and Sch.3, para.4(3) (December 5, 2005).

DEFINITIONS

"employed earner"—see SSCBA 1992, s.2(1)(a).
"married couple"—see para.(6); SSCBA 1992, s.137(1).
"pensionable age"—see SSCBA 1992, s.122(1).
"self-employed earner"—see SSCBA 1992, s.2(1)(b).
"unmarried couple"—see para.(6); SSCBA 1992, s.137(1).
"working families' tax credit"—see reg.2(1); SSCBA 1992, s.128.

GENERAL NOTE

As with all of the Regulations making claimants eligible for the award of credits, **2.17** this must be read with reg.3 (*CIB/1602/2006; CIB/3327/2004*). One can only have them insofar as they are necessary to bring one's record up to the level required for satisfying the second contribution condition for the relevant benefit (see para.(1), reg.3 and reg.2(1) ("reckonable year")). The relevant benefits are:

● widowed mother's allowance (SSCBA 1992, s.37);

● widowed parent's allowance (SSCBA 1992, s.39A);

● bereavement allowance (SSCBA 1992, s.39B);

● widow's pension (SSCBA 1992, s.38);

● Category A or B retirement pension (SSCBA 1992, ss.43–54).

It covers an employed earner, or a self-employed earner exempt from paying Class 2 contributions because of the "small earnings" exception, to whom working tax credit is paid for any week, and enables a credit equal to that tax year's lower earnings limit to be awarded for each such week. Where the person is one of a married or unmarried couple, note the rules in para.(3) stipulating who gets the award of the credit: the sole assessed earner; or, where both are assessed, the partner to whom working tax credit is paid.

The credit is only awardable to those attaining or due to attain pensionable age after April 5, 1999 and only with respect to weeks falling wholly or partly in tax year 1995–96 or subsequent tax years (para.(5)).

Note that a woman cannot gain a credit under this provision in respect of any week in any part of which as a married woman a certificate of election to pay contributions at reduced rate applied to her (para.(4)(b)). Nor can a credit be awarded under this provision if a credit entitlement for the week arises under reg.8A (unemployment) or 8B (incapacity for work) (para.(4)(a)).

Credits on termination of full-time education, training or apprenticeship

2.18

8.—[¹ (1) For the purposes of his entitlement to [² a contribution based jobseeker's allowance] [³ short-term incapacity benefit or a contributory employment and support allowance] a person shall be entitled to be credited with earnings equal to the lower earnings limit then in force for either one of the last two complete years before the beginning of the relevant benefit year if—

  (a) during any part of that year he was—
    (i) undergoing a course of full-time education; or
    (ii) undergoing—
      (a) a course of training which was full-time and which was arranged under section 2(1) of the Employment and Training Act 1973 or [⁴ section 2(3) of the Enterprise and New Towns (Scotland) Act 1990]; or
      (b) any other full-time course the sole or main purpose of which was the acquisition of occupational or vocational skills; or
      (c) if he is a disabled person within the meaning of the Disabled Persons (Employment) Act 1944 a part-time course attended for at least 15 hours a week which, if it was full-time, would fall within either of heads (a) or (b) above; or
    (iii) an apprentice; and
  (b) the other year is, in his case, a reckonable year; and
  (c) that course or, as the case may be, his apprenticeship has terminated.]

(2) Paragraph (1) shall not apply—

  (a) where the course of education or training or the apprenticeship commenced after the person had attained the age of 21;
  (b) to a woman in respect of any tax year immediately before the end of which she was a married woman and an election made by her under regulations made [⁵ under section 3(2) of the Social Security Pensions Act 1975] had effect[⁶;
  (c) to a person in respect of any tax year before that in which he attains the age of 18.]

AMENDMENTS

1. Social Security (Credits) Amendment Regulations 1989 (SI 1989/1627), reg.3 (October 1, 1989).
2. Social Security (Credits and Contributions) (Jobseeker's Allowance Consequential and Miscellaneous Amendments) Regulations 1996 (SI 1996/2367), reg.2(5).
3. Employment and Support Allowance (Consequential Provisions) (No. 2) Regulations 2008 (SI 2008/1554), reg.48(4) (October 27, 2008).
4. Enterprise (Scotland) Consequential Amendments Order 1991 (SI 1991/387), art.3 (April 1, 1991).
5. Social Security (Credits) Amendment and (Earnings Factor) Transitional Regulations 1978 (SI 1978/409), reg.2(2) (April 6, 1978).
6. Social Security (Credits) Amendment (No. 2) Regulations 1988 (SI 1988/1230), reg.2(3) (October 2, 1988).

DEFINITIONS

"lower earnings limit"—see SSCBA 1992, s.122(1).

"relevant benefit year"—see reg.2(1).
"tax year"—see SSCBA 1992, s.122(1).
"year"—see reg.2(1).

GENERAL NOTE

As with all of the Regulations making claimants eligible for the award of credits, 2.19
this must be read with reg.3 (*CIB/1602/2006*; *CIB/3327/2004*). One can only have
them insofar as they are necessary to bring one's record up to the level required for
satisfying the second contribution condition for the relevant benefit (see para.(1),
reg.3 and reg.2(1) ("reckonable year")).

This applies only for purposes of entitlement to contribution-based jobseeker's
allowance (CBJSA), short-term incapacity benefit (STIB) or a contributory
employment and support allowance (CESA). For both these benefits, the second
contribution condition requires that the contribution record in terms of paid and/
or credited contributions reaches the requisite level (50 times the tax year's lower
earnings limit) in respect of *each* of the last two tax years complete before the beginning of the relevant benefit year (the year in which there falls the first day of the
jobseeking period or linked period [CBJSA: see Jobseekers Act 1995, s.2(1)(b)] or
period of incapacity for work [STIB: see SSCBA 1992, Sch.3, para.2] or period
of limited capability for work [CESA, see WRA 2007, Sch.1, para.2] of which the
claim for benefit is part). It enables credits to be awarded, where in one of those tax
years the second condition is met (it is a "reckonable year"), in order to make the
record in the other tax year up to the requisite level (to make it also a "reckonable
year"). The provision applies where during any part of the relevant benefit year, he
was an apprentice, or was someone undergoing a course of full-time education, or a
course of full-time training under specified legislation, or a full-time course the sole
or main purpose of which was the acquisition of occupational or vocational skills
(para.(1)(a)). Where he is disabled within the meaning of the Disabled Persons
(Employment) Act 1944, it suffices that such a course was part-time (attended for at
least 15 hours a week) (para.(1)(a)(ii)(c)). The final condition for the award of the
credit is that the apprenticeship or course must have terminated (para.(1)(c)).

No award can be made where the apprenticeship or course commenced after
the person attained the age of 21 (para.(2)(a)) or in respect of any tax year prior to
that in which he became 18 (para.(2)(c)). Note finally that a woman cannot gain a
credit under this provision in respect of any tax year immediately before the end of
which she was a married woman and a certificate of election to pay contributions at
reduced rate had effect in relation to her (para.(2)(b)).

[¹ Credits for unemployment

8A.—(1) For the purposes of entitlement to any benefit by virtue of a 2.20
person's earnings or contributions, he shall be entitled to be credited with
earnings equal to the lower earnings limit then in force, in respect of each
week to which this regulation applies.

(2) Subject to paragraph (5) this regulation applies to a week which, in
relation to the person concerned, is—
  (a) a week for the whole of which he was paid a jobseeker's allowance;
      or
  (b) a week for the whole of which he satisfied or was treated as having
      satisfied the conditions set out in paragraphs (a), (c) and (e) to (h) of
      section 1(2) of the Jobseekers Act 1995 (conditions for entitlement
      to a jobseeker's allowance) and in respect of which he has satisfied
      the further condition specified in paragraph (3); or
  (c) a week which would have been a week described in sub-paragraph

(b) but for the fact that he was incapable of work [⁵ or had limited capability for work] for part of it, or

[³(d) a week in respect of which he would have been paid a jobseeker's allowance but for a restriction imposed pursuant to section 62 or 63 of the Child Support, Pensions and Social Security Act 2000 [² or section 7, 8 or 9 of the Social Security Fraud Act 2001 (loss of benefit provisions)]].

(3) The further condition referred to in paragraph (2)(b) is that the person concerned—

(a) furnished to the Secretary of State notice in writing of the grounds on which he claims to be entitled to be credited with earnings—

(i) on the first day of the period for which he claims to be so entitled in which the week in question fell; or

(ii) within such further time as may be reasonable in the circumstances of the case; and

(b) has provided any evidence required by the Secretary of State that the conditions referred to in paragraph (2)(b) are satisfied.

(4) This regulation also applies to a week for the whole of which the conditions set out in paragraphs (a), (c) and (e) to (h) of section 1(2) of the Jobseekers Act 1995 would have been satisfied but for its being a week in respect of which, in accordance with regulation 52(3) (persons treated as engaged in remunerative work) and Part VIII (income and capital) of the Jobseeker's Allowance Regulations 1996, there is taken into account any compensation payment referred to in regulation 98(1)(b) of those Regulations.

(5) This regulation shall not apply to—

(a) a week in respect of which the person concerned was not entitled to a jobseeker's allowance (or would not have been if he had claimed it) because of section 14 of the Jobseekers Act 1995 (trade disputes); or

(b) a week in respect of which, in relation to the person concerned, there was in force a direction under section 16 of that Act (which relates to persons who have reached the age of 16 but not the age of 18 and who are in severe hardship); or

(c) a week in respect of which, because of section 19 of that Act, a jobseeker's allowance was not payable to the person concerned even though he satisfied the conditions for entitlement to that allowance; or

[⁴(cc) a week in respect of which a joint-claim jobseeker's allowance was not payable or was reduced pursuant to section 20A of that Act because the person was subject to sanctions for the purposes of that section, even though the couple of which he was a member satisfied the conditions for entitlement to that allowance;]

(d) a week in respect of which a jobseeker's allowance was payable to the person concerned only by virtue of regulation 141 of the Jobseeker's Allowance Regulations 1996 (circumstances in which an income-based jobseeker's allowance is payable to a person in hardship); or

[⁴(dd) a week in respect of which a joint-claim jobseeker's allowance was payable in respect of a joint-claim couple of which the person is a member only by virtue of regulation 146C of the Jobseeker's Allowance Regulations 1996 (circumstances in which a joint-claim jobseeker's allowance is payable where a joint-claim couple is a couple in hardship);]

(e) where the person concerned is a married woman, a week in respect of any part of which an election made by her under regulations made under section 19(4) of the Contributions and Benefits Act had effect.]

AMENDMENTS

1. Social Security (Credits and Contributions) (Jobseeker's Allowance Consequential and Miscellaneous Amendments) Regulations 1996 (SI 1996/2367), reg.2(6) (October 7, 1996).
2. Social Security (Loss of Benefit) (Consequential Amendments) Regulations 2002 (SI 2002/490), reg.3 (April 1, 2002).
3. Social Security (Breach of Community Order) (Consequential Amendments) Regulations 2001 (SI 2001/1711) reg.2(5) (October 15, 2001).
4. Social Security Amendment (Joint Claims) Regulations 2001 (SI 2001/518), reg.3 (March 19, 2001).
5. Employment and Support Allowance (Consequential Provisions) (No. 2) Regulations 2008 (SI 2008/1554), reg.48(5) (October 27, 2008).

DEFINITIONS

"benefit"—see reg.2(1).
"jobseeker's allowance"—see reg.2(1).
"lower earnings limit"—see SSCBA 1992, s.122(1).

GENERAL NOTE

As with all of the Regulations making claimants eligible for the award of credits, **2.21** this must be read with reg.3 (*CIB/1602/2006; CIB/3327/2004*). One can only have them insofar as they are necessary to bring one's record up to the level required for satisfying the second contribution condition for the relevant benefit (see para.(1), reg.3 and reg.2(1) ("reckonable year")). The relevant benefits are:

- short-term incapacity benefit (SSCBA 1992, s.30A);

- widowed mother's allowance (SSCBA 1992, s.37);

- widowed parent's allowance (SSCBA 1992, s.39A);

- bereavement allowance (SSCBA 1992, s.39B);

- widow's pension (SSCBA 1992, s.38);

- Category A or B retirement pension (SSCBA 1992, ss.43–54);

- contribution-based jobseeker's allowance (Jobseekers Act 1995, s.2—see *Vol. II: Income Support, Jobseeker's Allowance, State Pension Credit and the Social Fund*);

- contributory employment and support allowance.

It enables a credit equal to that tax year's lower earnings limit to be awarded for each week in respect of which one of the following situations pertains (para.(1)):

- he was paid jobseeker's allowance (contribution or income-based) for the whole week (para.(2)(a));

- for the whole week he met the conditions of entitlement to jobseeker's allowance stipulated in para.2(b), or would have done so but for the fact that he was incapable of work for part of the week (paras 2(b), (c)). Those conditions are: availability for work; actively seeking work; not in remunerative work; capable of work; not in relevant education; and under pensionable age (see further Jobseekers Act 1995, s.1(2)(a), (c) and (e) to (h); *Vol.II: Income*

Support, Jobseeker's Allowance, State Pension Credit and the Social Fund). He must comply with the written notification and provision of evidence requirements stipulated in para.(3);

- he would have been paid jobseeker's allowance but for the effect of one of the specified "loss of benefit" provisions (para.(2)(d));

- he would in that week, as someone under pensionable age, have satisfied the conditions about availability for work, capable of and actively seeking it, not in remunerative work or relevant education, but for the fact that the jobseeker's allowance scheme treated him as if he was in remunerative work because of a compensation payment (e.g. money in lieu of notice) (see further Jobseeker's Allowance Regulations 1996, regs 52(3) and 98; *Vol.II: Income Support, Jobseeker's Allowance, State Pension Credit and the Social Fund*) (para.(4)).

The position is that it thus cannot be known whether a claimant is entitled to claim credits (credited with earnings) until some time after the end of the tax year for which the claim for them is made. The difficulties that can be caused by this complex interaction of Credits Regulations with those applicable to Jobseeker's Allowance, in a context in which there appear to be decision-making problems as a result of responsibilities divided between the DWP and HMRC, are explored in *CIB/1602/2006.*

Regulation 8A(3)(a)(i) stipulates that to be eligible for unemployment credits, in respect of a period of non-payment of JSA under para.(2)(b), a person must give notice in writing of the grounds on which he claims to be entitled to be credited with earnings

"(i) on the first day of the period for which he claims to be entitled in which the week in question fell; or (ii) within such further time as may be reasonable in the circumstances of the case".

In reality it is the second (fallback) option which will have to apply. This means that in a case such as that in *CIB/1602/2006,* where the claimant on a claim for incapacity benefit was arguing that he should have been awarded credits for a period of unemployment several years earlier in which he was not entitled to payment of JSA, that

"the Secretary of State can do no more than require that a claimant makes a claim in writing, setting out the grounds for it, within a reasonable time of becoming entitled. That is a question of fact. It will take into account the guidance given to a claimant (all of which is set out above, unless something is added orally).

Noting the guidance and correspondence put in evidence to the tribunal in this appeal, I have little difficulty in finding on the facts that D's correspondence with the Jobcentre and with the Member of Parliament and the Minister did raise the matter adequately in writing and within a reasonable time" (paras 33, 34).

The decision on whether earnings should be credited is not a HMRC decision, but one for the Secretary of State and appealable to the appeals tribunal, the Commissioner and the courts. In *CIB/1602/2006,* it was whether reg.8A(2)(b) applied in the claimant's case. The claimant needed two weeks' credited earnings to bring his record to the requisite level (50 times the lower earnings limit), having already been credited with 48 times that limit. Here, the Commissioner found from the correspondence that a decision had been made to refuse to credit the claimant with earnings for the period at issue because during the time at issue he was out of the United Kingdom. The Commissioner found that, although on holiday, he had satisfied the availability condition because he had informed the Jobcentre of his holiday with his children (and could thus have returned on request with the 48 hour notice period allowed). In terms of actively seeking work he could also take advantage of the "deemed actively seeking work" for two weeks of properly notified holiday (Jobseeker's Regulations 1996, reg.19(1)(p)). Absence from Great Britain precludes entitlement to JSA. But it does not as such preclude entitlement to unemployment credits for the period of absence, since reg.8A(2)(b) while linking back to specifically enumerated conditions in Jobseekers Act 1995, s.1(2), does not include the "present in Great Britain" condition. Accordingly, Commissioner Williams concluded that the claimant met the second contribution condition for entitlement to incapacity benefit.

No credit, however, can be awarded as regards a week in respect of which one of the following situations exists:

- there was (or would have been if claimed) no entitlement to jobseeker's allowance because of the trade disputes provision (see Jobseekers Act 1995, s.14; *Vol.II: Income Support, Jobseeker's Allowance, State Pension Credit and the Social Fund*) (para.(5)(a))

- the person is 16 or 17, and a direction was in force under Jobseekers Act 1995, s.16 (see *Vol.II: Income Support, Jobseeker's Allowance, State Pension Credit and the Social Fund*) (para.(5)(b))

- jobseeker's allowance was not payable, or as regards a joint-claim couple was reduced, because a sanction under s.19 or 20A of that 1995 Act applied (see *Vol.II: Income Support, Jobseeker's Allowance, State Pension Credit and the Social Fund*) (para.(5)(c), (cc));

- jobseeker's allowance was only payable under the hardship provisions (see Jobseeker's Allowance Regulations 1996, regs 141 and 146C (see *Vol.II: Income Support, Jobseeker's Allowance, State Pension Credit and the Social Fund*) (para.(5)(d), (dd)).

Note, finally, that a woman cannot gain a credit under this provision in respect of any week in any part of which as a married woman a certificate of election to pay contributions at reduced rate applied to her (para.(5)(e)).

[¹ Credits for incapacity for work [⁴ or limited capability for work]

8B.—(1) [² For] the purposes of entitlement to any benefit by virtue of a person's earnings or contributions, he shall be entitled to be credited with earnings equal to the lower earnings limit then in force, in respect of each week to which this regulation applies.

2.22

(2) Subject to paragraphs (3) and (4) this regulation applies to—

(a) a week in which, in relation to the person concerned, each of the days—
  (i) was a day of incapacity for work under section 30C of the Contributions and Benefits Act (incapacity benefit: days and periods of incapacity for work) [³ . . .]; or
  (ii) would have been such a day had the person concerned claimed short-term incapacity benefit or maternity allowance within the prescribed time; or
  (iii) was a day of incapacity for work for the purposes of statutory sick pay under section 151 of the Contributions Benefits Act and fell within a period of entitlement under section 153 of that Act;

[⁴ (aa) a week in which, in relation to the person concerned, each of the days—
  (i) was a day of limited capability for work for the purposes of Part 1 of the Welfare Reform Act (limited capability for work) or would have been such a day had that person been entitled to an employment and support allowance by virtue of section 1 of the Welfare Reform Act; or

    (ii) would have been such a day had the person concerned claimed an employment and support allowance or maternity allowance within the prescribed time; or]

[³(b) a week for any part of which an unemployability supplement or allowance was payable by virtue of—

    (i) Schedule 7 to the Contributions and Benefits Act;

    (ii) Article 18 of the Naval, Military and Air Forces etc. (Disablement and Death) Service Pensions Order 1983; or

    (iii) Article 18 of the Personal Injuries (Civilians) Scheme 1983.]

(3) Where the person concerned is a married woman, this regulation shall not apply to a week in respect of any part of which an election made by her under regulations made under section 19(4) of the Contributions and Benefits Act had effect.

(4) A day shall not be a day to which paragraph (2)(a) applies unless the person concerned has—

(a) before the end of the benefit year immediately following the year in which that day fell; or

(b) within such further time as may be reasonable in the circumstances of the case,

furnished to the Secretary of State notice in writing of the grounds on which he claims to be entitled to be credited with earnings.]

AMENDMENTS

1. Social Security (Credits and Contributions) (Jobseeker's Allowance Consequential and Miscellaneous Amendments) Regulations 1996 (SI 1996/2367), reg.2(6) (October 7, 1996).

2. Social Security (Incapacity Benefit) Miscellaneous Amendments Regulations 2000 (SI 2000/3120), reg.4(b) (April 6, 2001).

3. Social Security (Miscellaneous Amendments) (No. 3) Regulations 2007 (SI 2007/1749), reg.8(3) (July 16, 2007).

4. Employment and Support Allowance (Consequential Provisions) (No. 2) Regulations 2008 (SI 2008/1554), reg.48(6) (October 27, 2008).

DEFINITIONS

"benefit"—see reg.2(1).
"benefit year"—see SSCBA 1992, s.21(6).
"lower earnings limit"—see SSCBA 1992, s.122(1).
"year"—see reg.2(1).

GENERAL NOTE

2.23   As with all of the Regulations making claimants eligible for the award of credits, this must be read with reg.3 (*CIB/1602/2006; CIB/3327/2004*). One can only have them insofar as they are necessary to bring one's record up to the level required for satisfying the second contribution condition for the relevant benefit (see para.(1), reg.3 and reg.2(1) ("reckonable year")). The relevant benefits are:

- short-term incapacity benefit (SSCBA 1992, s.30A);

- widowed mother's allowance (SSCBA 1992, s.37);

- widowed parent's allowance (SSCBA 1992, s.39A);

- bereavement allowance (SSCBA 1992, s.39B);

- widow's pension (SSCBA 1992, s.38);

- Category A or B retirement pension (SSCBA 1992, ss.43–54);

- contribution-based jobseeker's allowance (Jobseekers Act 1995, s.2—see *Vol. II: Income Support, Jobseeker's Allowance, State Pension Credit and the Social Fund*);

- contributory employment and support allowance.

It enables a credit equal to that tax year's lower earnings limit to be awarded for each week in respect of which one of the following situations pertains (para.(1)):

- each of its days was one of incapacity for work under SSCBA 1992, s.30C (or would have been had s/he claimed in time for short-term incapacity benefit or maternity allowance or been entitled to incapacity benefit under s.30A)—provided that the written notification and statement of grounds conditions in para.(4) are met (para.(2)(a)(i), (ii));

- each of its days was one of incapacity for work within a period of entitlement for SSP purposes (SSCBA 1992, ss.151 and 153)—provided that the written notification and statement of grounds conditions in para.(4) are met (para.2(a)(iii));

- unemployability supplement was payable for part of it (see SSCBA 1992, Sch.7, Pt I) (para.(2)(b)).

Commissioner Mesher considered this phrase in *CIB/2445/2006* when concluding that the appeal tribunal was within its permitted area of judgment when concluding that what would have been a reasonable time for claiming credits for any of the years 1989/90 to 2000/01 had expired by the time the claimant claimed them on May 13, 2005 (para.27). As the Commissioner pointed out, the test in reg.8B(4) is not one of "good cause" for a late claim but

> "the more general test of what is a reasonable time in the circumstances for a claim to be made. Therefore . . . the length of the time after the period for which credits are claimed is a factor, along with all the other circumstances. When entitlement to credits rests on proof of incapacity for work, the assessment of the evidence and the making of a proper decision becomes more difficult the further away from the period in question one gets. As a general proposition it can be accepted that the longer the gap from the tax year in question the more compelling the other circumstances must be for it to be concluded that the time for claiming, outside the following benefit year, is reasonable" (para.29).

Even with respect to the most recent tax years in respect of which credits were claimed (2000/01), the range of communications indicating a shortfall in his contributions record were such that the tribunal was entitled to conclude that the time for claiming credits was, by May 2005, no longer reasonable.

Note, finally, that a woman cannot gain a credit under this provision in respect of any week in any part of which as a married woman a certificate of election to pay contributions at reduced rate applied to her (para.(3)).

Credits on termination of bereavement benefits

[¹ **8C.**—(1) This regulation applies for the purpose only of enabling a person who previously received a bereavement benefit ("the recipient") to satisfy, as the case may be, the condition referred to in— 2.24

- (a) paragraph 2(3)(b) of Schedule 3 to the Contributions and Benefits Act in relation to short-term incapacity benefit; [³ . . .]
- (b) section 2(1)(b) of the Jobseekers Act 1995 in relation to contribution-based jobseeker's allowance. [;³ or
- (c) paragraph 2(1) of Schedule 1 to the Welfare Reform Act in relation to a contributory employment and support allowance.]

(2) For every year up to and including that in which the recipient ceased to be entitled to a bereavement benefit otherwise than by reason of remarriage [², forming a civil partnership], or living together with a person of the opposite sex as husband and wife, the recipient shall be credited with such earnings as may be required to enable the condition referred to above to be satisfied.]

REVOCATION AND AMENDMENTS

1. Social Security (Benefits for Widows and Widowers) (Consequential Amendments) Regulations 2000 (SI 2000/1483), reg.3(7) (April 9, 2001).
2. Civil Partnership (Pensions, Social Security and Child Support) (Consequential, etc. Provisions) Order 2005 (SI 2005/2877), art.2(3) and Sch.3, para.4(4) (December 5, 2005).
3. Employment and Support Allowance (Consequential Provisions) (No. 2) Regulations 2008 (SI 2008/1554), reg.48(7) (October 27, 2008).

DEFINITIONS

"bereavement benefit"—see reg.2(1); SSCBA 1992, s.20(1)(ea).
"the recipient"—para.(1).

GENERAL NOTE

2.25   As with all of the Regulations making claimants eligible for the award of credits, this must be read with reg.3 (*CIB/1602/2006*; *CIB/3327/2004*). One can only have them insofar as they are necessary to bring one's record up to the level required for satisfying the second contribution condition for the relevant benefit (see para.(1), reg.3 and reg.2(1) ("reckonable year")).

Regulation 8C applies only in respect of awarding sufficient credits to satisfy the second contribution condition for contribution-based jobseeker's allowance [CBJSA], short-term incapacity benefit [STIB] or contributory employment and support allowance [ESA]. For these benefits, the second contribution condition requires that the contribution record in terms of paid and/or credited contributions reaches the requisite level (50 times the tax year's lower earnings limit) in respect of *each* of the last two tax years complete before the beginning of the relevant benefit year (the year in which there falls the first day of the jobseeking period or linked period [CBJSA: see Jobseekers Act 1995, s.2(1)(b); *Vol.II: Income Support, Jobseeker's Allowance, State Pension Credit and the Social Fund*], period of incapacity for work [STIB: see SSCBA 1992, Sch.3, para.2] or period of limited capability for work [CESA, see WRA 2007, Sch.1, para.2] of which the claim for benefit is part). It enables the award of sufficient credits to someone who previously received a "bereavement benefit". Those credits can be awarded for every tax year up to and including the one in which the person ceased to be entitled to the bereavement benefit, provided that entitlement was not lost by reason of remarriage or cohabitation as husband and wife with someone of the opposite sex. "Bereavement benefit" has the same meaning as in SSCBA 1992, s.20(1)(ea), above (reg.2(1)).

[¹ Credits for the purposes of entitlement to incapacity benefit following official error

2.26   **8D.**—(1) This regulation applies for the purpose only of enabling a person who was previously entitled to incapacity benefit to satisfy the condition referred to in paragraph 2(3)(a) of Schedule 3 to the Contributions and Benefits Act in respect of a subsequent claim for incapacity benefit where his period of incapacity for work is, together with a previous period of incapacity for work, to be treated as one period of incapacity for work under section 30C of that Act.

(2) Where—

(a) a person was previously entitled to incapacity benefit;

(b) the award of incapacity benefit was as a result of satisfying the condition referred to in paragraph (1) by virtue of being credited with earnings for incapacity for work or approved training in the tax years from 1993–94 to 2007–08;

(c) some or all of those credits were credited by virtue of official error derived from the failure to transpose correctly information relating to those credits from the Department for Work and Pensions' Pension Strategy Computer System to Her Majesty's Revenue and Customs' computer system (NIRS2) or from related clerical procedures;

(d) that person makes a further claim for incapacity benefit; and

(e) his period of incapacity for work is, together with the period of incapacity for work to which his previous entitlement referred to in sub-paragraph (a) related, to be treated as one period of incapacity for work under section 30C of the Contributions and Benefits Act,

that person shall be credited with such earnings as may be required to enable the condition referred to in paragraph (1) to be satisfied.

(3) In this regulation and in regulations 8E and 8F, "official error" means an error made by—

(a) an officer of the Department for Work and Pensions or an officer of Revenue and Customs acting as such which no person outside the Department or Her Majesty's Revenue and Customs caused or to which no person outside the Department for Work and Pensions or Her Majesty's Revenue and Customs materially contributed; or

(b) a person employed by a service provider and to which no person who was not so employed materially contributed,

but excludes any error of law which is shown to have been an error by virtue of a subsequent decision of a Commissioner or the court.

(4) In paragraph (3)—

"Commissioner" means the Chief Social Security Commissioner or any other Social Security Commissioner and includes a tribunal of three or more Commissioners constituted under section 16(7) of the Social Security Act 1998;

"service provider" means a person providing services to the Secretary of State for Work and Pensions or to Her Majesty's Revenue and Customs.

Credits for the purposes of entitlement to retirement pension following official error

8E. —(1) This regulation applies for the purpose only of enabling the condition referred to in paragraph 5(3)(a) of Schedule 3 to the Contributions and Benefits Act to be satisfied in respect of a claim for retirement pension made by a person ("the claimant")— 　　　　　　　　　　　　　　　　2.27

(a) who would attain pensionable age no later than 31st May 2008;

(b) not falling within sub-paragraph (a) but based on the satisfaction of that condition by another person—

(i) who would attain, or would have attained, pensionable age no later than 31st May 2008; or

(ii) in respect of whose death the claimant received a bereavement benefit.

(2) Where—

(a) a person claims retirement pension;

(b) the satisfaction of the condition referred to in paragraph (1) would be based on earnings credited for incapacity for work or approved training in the tax years from 1993–94 to 2007–08; and

(c) some or all of those credits were credited by virtue of official error derived from the failure to transpose correctly information relating to those credits from the Department for Work and Pensions' Pension Strategy Computer System to Her Majesty's Revenue and Customs' computer system (NIRS2) or from related clerical procedures,

those earnings shall be credited.

(3) In this regulation, "bereavement benefit" means a bereavement allowance, a widowed mother's allowance, a widowed parent's allowance or a widow's pension.

Credits for the purposes of entitlement to contribution-based job-seeker's allowance following official error

2.28   **8F.**—(1) This regulation applies for the purpose only of enabling a person to satisfy the condition referred to in section 2(1)(b) of the Jobseekers Act 1995.

(2) Where—

(a) a person claims a jobseeker's allowance;

(b) the satisfaction of the condition referred to in paragraph (1) would be based on earnings credited for incapacity for work or approved training in the tax years from 1993–94 to 2007–08; and

(c) some or all of those credits were credited by virtue of official error derived from the failure to transpose correctly information relating to those credits from the Department for Work and Pensions' Pension Strategy Computer System to Her Majesty's Revenue and Customs' computer system (NIRS2) or from related clerical procedures,

that person shall be credited with those earnings.]

AMENDMENT

1. Inserted by Social Security (National Insurance Credits) Amendment Regulations 2007 (SI 2007/2582), reg.2 (October 1, 2007).

Crediting of earnings for the purposes of entitlement to short-term incapacity benefit—further conditions

2.29   **9.**—[¹ . . .]

REVOCATION

1. Social Security (Incapacity Benefit) Miscellaneous Amendments Regulations 2000 (SI 2000/3120), reg.4(c) (April 16, 2001).

[¹ Credits for persons approaching pensionable age

2.30   **9A.**—(1) For the purposes of entitlement to any benefit by virtue of a person's earnings or contributions he shall, subject to the following paragraphs, be credited with such earnings as may be required to bring his relevant earnings factor in respect of a tax year to which this regulation applies to the level required to make that year a reckonable year.

(2) This regulation shall apply to the tax year in which a person attains the age of 60 and to each of the four succeeding tax years.

(3) Paragraph (1) shall apply, in the case of a self-employed earner, only if he is—

(a) liable to pay a Class 2 contribution in respect of any week in a tax year to which this regulation applies; or

(b) excepted from liability to pay Class 2 contributions in respect of any week in a tax year to which this regulation applies by virtue of his earnings being less than, or being treated by regulations as less than, the amount specified in section 11(4) of the Social Security Contributions and Benefits Act 1992 (exception from liability for Class 2 contributions on account of small earnings),

so that he shall be credited with earnings equal to the lower earnings limit then in force in respect of each week for which he is not so liable.

(4) [¹ . . .]

(5) Where in any tax year to which this regulation applies a person is absent from Great Britain for more than 182 days, he shall not by virtue of this regulation be credited with any earnings or contributions in that tax year.]

AMENDMENTS

1. Social Security (Credits) Amendment Regulations 1994 (SI 1994/1837), reg.3 (August 8, 1994).

2. Social Security (Credits and Contributions) (Jobseeker's Allowance Consequential and Miscellaneous Amendments) Regulations 1996 (SI 1996/2367), reg.2(8).

DEFINITIONS

"benefit"—see reg.2(1).
"pensionable age"—see SSCBA 1992, s.122(1).
"reckonable year"—see reg.2(1).
"relevant earnings factor"—see reg.2(1).
"self-employed earner"—see SSCBA 1992, s.2(1)(b).
"tax year"—see SSCBA 1992, s.122(1).
"year"—see reg.2(1).

GENERAL NOTE

As with all of the Regulations making claimants eligible for the award of credits, **2.31** this must be read with reg.3 (*CIB/1602/2006*; *CIB/3327/2004*). One can only have them insofar as they are necessary to bring one's record up to the level required for satisfying the second contribution condition for the relevant benefit (see para.(1), reg.3 and reg.2(1) ("reckonable year")). The relevant benefits are:

- short-term incapacity benefit (SSCBA 1992, s.30A);
- widowed mother's allowance (SSCBA 1992, s.37);
- widowed parent's allowance (SSCBA 1992, s.39A);
- bereavement allowance (SSCBA 1992, s.39B);
- widow's pension (SSCBA 1992, s.38);
- Category A or B retirement pension (SSCBA 1992, ss.43–54);
- contribution-based jobseeker's allowance (Jobseekers Act 1995, s.2—see *Vol. II: Income Support, Jobseeker's Allowance, State Pension Credit and the Social Fund*) (para.(1)).

It is applicable only to the tax year in which the person attained 60 and to each of the four succeeding tax years (para.(2)). It enables the award of sufficient credits to give the requisite record for the purposes of the second contribution condition (to make that year a "reckonable year") (para.(1)). As respects a self-employed earner, it can only do so if he is exempt from paying Class 2 contributions because of the "small earnings" exception (para.(3)). It cannot do so in respect of any tax year to which this regulation applies, if in that year the person is absent from Great Britain for more than 182 days (para.(4)).

[¹ Credits for jury service

2.32 **9B.**—(1) Subject to paragraphs (2) and (3), for the purposes of entitlement to any benefit [² by virtue of a person's earnings or contributions] he shall be entitled to be credited with earnings equal to the lower earnings limit then in force, in respect of each week for any part of which he attended at Court for jury service.

(2) A person shall be entitled to be credited with earnings in respect of a week by virtue of the provisions of this regulation only if—

    (a) his earnings in respect of that week from any employment of his as an employed earner are below the lower earnings limit then in force; and

    (b) he furnished to the Secretary of State notice in writing of his claim to be entitled to be credited with earnings and did so before the end of the benefit year immediately following the tax year in which that week or part of that week fell or within such further time as may be reasonable in the circumstances of his case.

(3) Paragraph (1) shall not apply—

    (a) to a woman in respect of any week in any part of which she was a married woman in respect of whom an election made by her under Regulations made under section 3(2) of the Social Security Pensions Act 1975 had effect; or

    (b) in respect of any week falling wholly or partly within a year commencing before 6th April 1988[³, or

    (c) to a person in respect of any week in any part of which he is a self-employed earner.]]

AMENDMENTS

1. Social Security (Credits) Amendment Regulations 1988 (SI 1988/516) reg.2(3) (April 6, 1988).
2. Social Security (Credits) Amendment (No. 4) Regulations 1988 (SI 1988/1545), reg.2(5) (October 2, 1988).
3. Social Security (Credits) Amendment Regulations 1994 (SI 1994/1837), reg.4.

DEFINITIONS

"benefit"—see reg.2(1).
"benefit year"—see SSCBA 1992, s.21(6).
"employed earner"—see SSCBA 1992, s.2(1)(a).
"lower earnings limit"—see SSCBA 1992, s.122(1).
"self-employed earner"—see SSCBA 1992, s.2(1)(b).
"tax year"—see SSCBA 1992, s.122(1).

GENERAL NOTE

2.33 As with all of the Regulations making claimants eligible for the award of credits, this must be read with reg.3 (*CIB/1602/2006*; *CIB/3327/2004*). One can only have them insofar as they are necessary to bring one's record up to the level required for satisfying the second contribution condition for the relevant benefit (see para.(1), reg.3 and reg.2(1) ("reckonable year")). The relevant benefits are:

- short-term incapacity benefit (SSCBA 1992, s.30A);

- widowed mother's allowance (SSCBA 1992, s.37);

- widowed parent's allowance (SSCBA 1992, s.39A);

- bereavement allowance (SSCBA 1992, s.39B);

- widow's pension (SSCBA 1992, s.38);

- Category A or B retirement pension (SSCBA 1992, ss.43–54);

- contribution-based jobseeker's allowance (Jobseekers Act 1995, s.2—see *Vol. II: Income Support, Jobseeker's Allowance, State Pension Credit and the Social Fund*).

It enables the award of a credit equal to the lower earnings limit for the tax year in question only to an employed earner as regards a week for any part of which he attended at Court for jury service, provided that his earnings in respect of that week from his employment fall below the then applicable lower earnings limit. He must claim in time and in writing (para.(2)(b)).

No award is possible in respect of a week falling wholly or partly in a tax year before April 6, 1988 (para.(3)(b)). Nor can one be made to someone in any week in part of which he is a self-employed earner (thus ruling out the person who in that week is both employed and self-employed, or who changes from one category to another during that week) (para.(3)(c)).

Note, finally, that a woman cannot gain a credit under this provision in respect of any week in any part of which as a married woman a certificate of election to pay contributions at reduced rate applied to her (para.(3)).

[¹ Credits for adoption pay period and maternity pay period

9C.—(1) For the purposes of entitlement to any benefit by virtue of—
  (a) in the case of a person referred to in paragraph (2)(a), that person's earnings or contributions;
  (b) in the case of a woman referred to in paragraph (2)(b), her earnings or contributions,
that person or that woman, as the case may be, shall be entitled to be credited with earnings equal to the lower earnings limit then in force in respect of each week to which this regulation applies.

(2) Subject to paragraphs (3) and (4), this regulation applies to each week during—
  (a) the adoption pay period in respect of which statutory adoption pay was paid to a person; or
  (b) the maternity pay period in respect of which statutory maternity pay was paid to a woman.

(3) A person or woman referred to above shall be entitled to be credited with earnings in respect of a week by virtue of this regulation only if he or she—
  (a) furnished to the Secretary of State notice in writing of his or her claim to be entitled to be credited with earnings; and
  (b) did so—
    (i) before the end of the benefit year immediately following the tax year in which that week began, or
    (ii) within such further time as may be reasonable in the circumstances of his or her case.

2.34

(4) This regulation shall not apply to a woman in respect of any week in any part of which she was a married woman in respect of whom an election made by her under regulations made under section 19(4) of the Contributions and Benefits Act had effect.

(5) In this regulation "adoption pay period", "maternity pay period", "statutory adoption pay" and "statutory maternity pay" have the same meaning as in the Contributions and Benefits Act.]

AMENDMENT

1. Inserted by Social Security (Credits) Amendment Regulations 2003 (SI 2003/521), reg.2(3) (April 6, 2003).

DEFINITIONS

"adoption pay period"—para.(5); SSCBA 1992, ss.171ZN(2), 171ZS(1).
"benefit"—see reg.2(1).
"benefit year"—see SSCBA 1992, s.21(6).
"lower earnings limit"—see SSCBA 1992, s.122(1).
"maternity pay period"—see para.(5); SSCBA 1992, s.165(1).
"statutory adoption pay"—see para.(5); SSCBA 1992, s.171ZL(1).
"statutory maternity pay"—see para.(5); SSCBA 1992, s.164(1).
"tax year"—see SSCBA 1992, s.122(1).

GENERAL NOTE

2.35   As with all of the Regulations making claimants eligible for the award of credits, this must be read with reg.3 (*CIB/1602/2006*; *CIB/3327/2004*). One can only have them insofar as they are necessary to bring one's record up to the level required for satisfying the second contribution condition for the relevant benefit (see para.(1), reg.3 and reg.2(1) ("reckonable year")). The relevant benefits are:

- short-term incapacity benefit (SSCBA 1992, s.30A);
- widowed mother's allowance (SSCBA 1992, s.37);
- widowed parent's allowance (SSCBA 1992, s.39A);
- bereavement allowance (SSCBA 1992, s.39B);
- widow's pension (SSCBA 1992, s.38);
- Category A or B retirement pension (SSCBA 1992, ss.43–54);
- contribution-based jobseeker's allowance (Jobseekers Act 1995, s.2—see *Vol.II: Income Support, Jobseeker's Allowance, State Pension Credit and the Social Fund*).

It enables the award, to a woman who has not elected to pay contributions at a reduced rate, of a credit equal to the lower earnings limit for the tax year in question in respect of each week in which in (for a woman) a maternity pay period or (for any person) an adoption pay period in respect of which, as the case may be, statutory maternity pay or statutory adoption pay was paid to the person.

[¹ **Credits for certain periods of imprisonment or detention in legal custody**

2.36   **9D.**—(1) Subject to paragraphs (2) and (4), for the purposes of entitlement to any benefit by virtue of a person's earnings or contributions, where—

    (a) a person is imprisoned or otherwise detained in legal custody by reason of his conviction of an offence or convictions in respect of two or more offences;

(b) that conviction or, as the case may be, each of those convictions is subsequently quashed by the Crown Court, the Court of Appeal or the High Court of Justiciary; and

(c) he is released from that imprisonment or detention, whether prior, or pursuant, to the quashing of that conviction or, as the case may be, each of those convictions,

that person shall, if he has made an application in writing to the Secretary of State for the purpose, be entitled to be credited with earnings or, in the case of any year earlier than 1987–88, contributions, in accordance with paragraph (3).

(2) Paragraph (1) shall not apply in respect of any period during which the person was also imprisoned or otherwise detained in legal custody for reasons unconnected with the conviction or convictions referred to in that paragraph.

(3) The earnings or, as the case may be, the contributions referred to in paragraph (1) are, in respect of any week in any part of which the person was—

(a) detained in legal custody—

    (i) prior to the conviction or convictions referred to in that paragraph, but,

    (ii) for the purposes of any proceedings in relation to any offence referred to in sub-paragraph (a) of that paragraph; or

(b) imprisoned or otherwise detained in legal custody by reason of that conviction or those convictions,

those necessary for the purpose of bringing his earnings factor, for the year in which such a week falls, to the level required to make that year a reckonable year.

(4) Subject to paragraph (5), paragraph (1) shall not apply to a woman in respect of any week referred to in paragraph (3) in any part of which she was a married woman in respect of whom an election made by her under regulations made under section 19(4) of the Contributions and Benefits Act had effect.

(5) Paragraph (4) shall not apply to any woman—

(a) who was imprisoned or otherwise detained in legal custody as referred to in paragraph (3) for a continuous period which included 2 complete years; and

(b) whose election ceased to have effect in accordance with regulation 101(1)(c) of the Social Security (Contributions) Regulations 1979 (which provides for an election to cease to have effect at the end of 2 consecutive years which began on or after 6th April 1978 during which the woman is not liable for primary Class 1 or Class 2 contributions).

(6) An application referred to in paragraph (1) may be transmitted by electronic means.]

AMENDMENT

1. Social Security (Credits and Incapacity Benefit) Amendment Regulations 2001 (SI 2001/573), reg.2.

DEFINITIONS

"benefit"—see reg.2(1).
"reckonable year"—see reg.2(1).
"year"—see reg.2(1).

GENERAL NOTE

2.37   As with all of the Regulations making claimants eligible for the award of credits, this must be read with reg.3 (*CIB/1602/2006; CIB/3327/2004*). One can only have them insofar as they are necessary to bring one's record up to the level required for satisfying the second contribution condition for the relevant benefit (see para.(1), reg.3 and reg.2(1) ("reckonable year")). The relevant benefits are:

- short-term incapacity benefit (SSCBA 1992, s.30A);
- widowed mother's allowance (SSCBA 1992, s.37);
- widowed parent's allowance (SSCBA 1992, s.39A);
- bereavement allowance (SSCBA 1992, s.39B);
- widow's pension (SSCBA 1992, s.38);
- Category A or B retirement pension (SSCBA 1992, ss.43–54);
- contribution-based jobseeker's allowance (Jobseekers Act 1995, s.2—see *Vol. II: Income Support, Jobseeker's Allowance, State Pension Credit and the Social Fund*).

It enables the award of a credit equal to the relevant lower earnings limit for each week for part of which the person was imprisoned or detained in legal custody because of a conviction of an offence, where the conviction that alone grounded that imprisonment or detention (whether prior to or *post* conviction) is quashed by a specified court. Credits can be so awarded to meet the amount by which the record for the tax year containing the weeks of imprisonment or detention falls short of the requisite level for the second condition for the benefit in question (paras (1)–(3)). The person must claim in time and in the proper manner, which can include e-mail (paras (1), (6)).

Note, finally, that a woman cannot gain a credit under this provision in respect of any week in any part of which as a married woman a certificate of election to pay contributions at reduced rate applied to her, unless the relevant period of imprisonment included two complete tax years so that the election ceased to have effect under Social Security (Contributions) Regulations 1979, reg.101(1)(c) (paras (4), (5)).

Transitional provisions

2.38   **10.**—[¹ . . .].

REVOCATION

1. Social Security (Credits) Amendment Regulations 1987 (SI 1987/414), reg.10 (April 6, 1987).

The Social Security Pensions (Home Responsibilities) Regulations 1994

(SI 1994/704) (*as amended*)

ARRANGEMENT OF REGULATIONS

2.39   1.   Citation, commencement and interpretation.
        2.   Preclusion from regular employment for the purpose of paragraph 5(7)(b) of Schedule 3 to the Act.

478

3.   *Omitted.*

Schedule. *Omitted.*

The Secretary of State for Social Security, in exercise of the powers conferred on him by sections 21(3) and 175(1) to (5) of, and paragraph 5(7)(b) of Schedule 3 to, the Social Security Contributions and Benefits Act 1992 and of all other powers enabling him in that behalf, after agreement by the Social Security Advisory Committee that proposals to make these Regulations should not be referred to it, hereby makes the following Regulations:

Citation, commencement and interpretation

1.—(1) These Regulations may be cited as the Social Security Pensions (Home Responsibilities) Regulations 1994, and shall come into force on 6th April 1994.

2.40

(2) In these Regulations, unless the context otherwise requires—

"the Act" means the Social Security Contributions and Benefits Act 1992;

"child benefit" means child benefit within the meaning of section 141 of the Act;

[¹ "foster parent" means a person approved as—

(a) a foster parent in accordance with the provisions of Part IV of the Fostering Services Regulations 2002 (approval of foster parents); or

(b) a foster carer in accordance with the provisions of Part II of the Fostering of Children (Scotland) Regulations 1996(approval of foster carers);]

[² "the General Regulations" means the Child Benefit (General) Regulations 2003;]

"Personal Injuries Scheme", "Pneumoconiosis and Byssinosis Benefit Scheme", "Service Pensions Instrument" and "1914–1918 War Injuries Scheme" have the same meaning as assigned to them in regulation 2 of the Social Security (Overlapping Benefits) Regulations 1979;

"year" means tax year.

AMENDMENTS

1. Social Security Pensions (Home Responsibilities) Amendment Regulations 2003 (SI 2003/1767), reg.2(2) (September 1, 2003).

2. Social Security Pensions (Home Responsibilities) (Amendment) Regulations 2005 (SI 2005/48), reg.2(2) (February 9, 2005).

DEFINITION

"tax year"—see SSCBA 1992, s.122(1).

Preclusion from regular employment for the purpose of paragraph 5(7)(b) of Schedule 3 to the Act

2.—(1) For the purpose of paragraph 5(7)(b) of Schedule 3 to the Act a person shall, subject to paragraph (5) below, be taken to be precluded from regular employment by responsibilities at home in any year—

2.41

(a) throughout which he satisfies any of the conditions specified in paragraph (2) below;

(b) throughout which he satisfies the conditions specified in paragraph (3) below; or

(c) in which he satisfies, for part of the year, any of the conditions specified in paragraph (2) below and for the remainder of the year, the condition specified in paragraph (3)(a) below.

(2) The conditions specified in this paragraph are—

(a) that child benefit awarded to him was payable in respect of a child under the age of 16;

[6 (aa) that child benefit awarded to his partner was payable in respect of a child under the age of 16;]

(b) that—

    (i) [6 he is a person to whom paragraphs 4 to 6 of Schedule 1B to the Income Support (General) Regulations 1987 apply, and]

    (ii) income support is payable to him;

[3 (c) that he was a foster parent] [6 throughout the year 2003–2004 or any subsequent year].

(3) The conditions specified in this paragraph are—

(a) that he was regularly engaged, for at least 35 hours per week, in caring for a person in respect of whom there was payable any of the benefits specified in paragraph (4) below;

(b) that those benefits were payable to that person for at least 48 weeks in that year.

(4) The benefits referred to in paragraph (3) above are an attendance allowance under section 64 of the Act, the care component of disability living allowance at the highest or middle rate prescribed in accordance with section 72 of the Act, a constant attendance allowance under any Service Pensions Instrument, Personal Injuries Scheme or 1914–1918 War Injuries Scheme, an increase of disablement pension under section 104 of the Act in respect of constant attendance and any benefit corresponding to such an increase under a Pneumoconiosis and Byssinosis Benefit Scheme or under Regulations under paragraph 7(2) of Schedule 8 to the Act.

[1 (4A) For the purposes of paragraph (2)(a) above, where—

(a) child benefit first becomes payable to a person in respect of a child on the first Monday in a year; and

(b) child benefit would, but for the provisions of section 147(2) of the Act, have been payable to that person in respect of that child for the part of that year falling before that Monday,

that person shall be treated as if he were entitled to child benefit and, accordingly, as if child benefit were payable to him for that part of that year.]

[5 (4B) For the purposes of paragraph (2)(a) above, in respect of the year 2004–2005 or any subsequent year, where—

(a) a notice is given under regulation 15(1) of the General Regulations (modification of priority between persons entitled to child benefit) by the person who is entitled to child benefit;

(b) that notice becomes effective in relation to any week falling in the first three months of a year;

(c) as a result of that notice, child benefit becomes payable to another person ("the new payee") in priority to anyone else;

(d) for each week of that year prior to that notice becoming effective, child benefit would, but for the provisions of regulation 15(2)(b) of those Regulations, have been payable to the new payee; and

(e) no other notice under regulation 15(1) of those Regulations was given in respect of the same child which became effective during any week referred to in sub-paragraph (d);

the new payee shall be treated as if he were entitled to child benefit and, accordingly, as if child benefit were payable to him for each week of the year prior to the notice becoming effective.]

[⁶ (4C) In paragraph (2)(aa), "partner" means the person with whom he was both residing and sharing responsibility for the child throughout that year.]

(5) Except where paragraph (6) below applies, paragraph (1) above shall not apply in relation to any year—

(a) if the person in question is a woman who has made or is treated as having made an election in accordance with regulations having effect under section 19(4) of the Act and that election had effect at the beginning of that year; or

[⁶ (aza) in the case of a person who satisfies the condition in paragraph (2) (aa) above—

   (i) such information is not furnished as the Secretary of State may from time to time require which is relevant to the question of whether in that year he was precluded from regular employment by responsibilities at home within the meaning of these Regulations;

  (ii) he attained pensionable age on or before 5th April 2008 or, in relation to a claim for a bereavement benefit in respect of his death, he died on or before that date; or

 (iii) the aggregate of his partner's earnings factors—

    (aa) in respect of any year preceding 2002–2003;

    (bb) in respect of the year 2002–2003 or any subsequent year, where those earnings factors are derived from so much of his earnings as do not exceed the upper earnings limit and upon which primary Class 1 contributions have been paid or treated as paid,

is less than the qualifying earnings factor for the year in question.]

[⁴(aa) in the case of a person who satisfies the condition in paragraph (2)(c) above in respect of the year 2003–04 or any subsequent year, if he does not furnish such information as the Secretary of State may from time to time require which is relevant to the question of whether in that year he was precluded from regular employment by responsibilities at home within the meaning of these Regulations; or]

[²(b) in the case of a person who satisfies the conditions in paragraph (3) above in respect of any year preceding 2002–2003, if he does not furnish such information as the Secretary of State may from time to time require which is relevant to the question of whether in that year he was precluded from regular employment by responsibilities at home within the meaning of these Regulations; or

(c) in the case of a person who satisfies the conditions in paragraph (3) above in respect of the year 2002–2003 or any subsequent year, if he does not, within the period of three years immediately following the end of that year, furnish such information as the Secretary of State may from time to time require which is relevant to the question of whether, in that year, he was precluded from regular employment by responsibilities at home within the meaning of these Regulations.]

(6) This paragraph applies to a woman who throughout the period beginning on 6th April 1975 and ending on 5th April 1980—

(a) had no earnings in respect of which primary Class 1 contributions were payable; and

(b) was not at any time a self-employed earner.

AMENDMENTS

1. Social Security Pensions (Home Responsibilities) (Amendment) Regulations 2001 (SI 2001/1265), reg.2 (April 6, 2002).
2. Additional Pension and Social Security Pensions (Home Responsibilities) (Amendment) Regulations 2001 (SI 2001/1323), reg.7 (April 6, 2002).
3. Social Security Pensions (Home Responsibilities) Amendment Regulations 2003 (SI 2003/1767), reg.2(3) (September 1, 2003).
4. Social Security Pensions (Home Responsibilities) Amendment Regulations 2003 (SI 2003/1767), reg.2(4) (September 1, 2003).
5. Social Security Pensions (Home Responsibilities) (Amendment) Regulations 2005 (SI 2005/48), reg.2(3) (February 9, 2005).
6. Social Security Pensions (Home Responsibilities) Amendment Regulations 2008 (SI 2008/498), reg.2 (April 6, 2008).

DEFINITIONS

"child benefit"—see reg.1(2); SSCBA 1992, s.141.
"the General Regulations"—see reg.1(2).
"year"—see reg.1(2).

GENERAL NOTE

2.42 This deals with home responsibilities protection, which provides help in satisfying the second contribution condition for the range of long-term benefits in SSCBA 1992, Sch.3, para.5:

- widowed mother's allowance (SSCBA 1992, s.37);

- widowed parent's allowance (SSCBA 1992, s.39A);

- bereavement allowance (SSCBA 1992, s.39B);

- widow's pension (SSCBA 1992, s.38);

- Category A or B retirement pension (SSCBA 1992, ss.43–54).

It helps by stipulating when a year is one of home responsibilities protection. Such years are then deducted from the number of years in which the person would otherwise have to satisfy the contribution conditions, but the reduction effected can only halve the requisite number of years or reduce them to 20 whichever is the lower (SSCBA 1992, Sch.3, para.5(a)).

A tax year is one of home responsibilities protection in the following situations:

- throughout it the person received child benefit for a child under 16 (paras (1)(a), (2)(a), (4A)) (see *CG/173/2002*) and note the aid afforded by para.(4B) in satisfying the "throughout" element;

- throughout it the person received income support as someone looking after a disabled person (paras (1)(a), (2)(b));

- throughout it the person was an approved foster parent (this applies in respect of the year 2003–04 and any subsequent year);

- for 48 weeks of the tax year the person spent 35 hours a week looking after someone receiving attendance allowance, constant attendance allowance under the industrial injuries or war pensions schemes, or the higher or middle rate components of disability living allowance (paras (1)(b), (3), (4));

- a tax year which is a mix of such periods (para.(1)(c)).

A person must claim in time and in the proper manner (para.5(aa)(b), (c)).

Although home responsibilities protection can be claimed by both sexes, substantially more women than men are covered by it. Although it affords less help when compared to an equivalent period of unemployment for which credits are awarded, deputy

Commissioner Gamble held in *CP/4017/2006* that this differentiation did not constitute indirect discrimination contrary to art.14 ECHR. *McAuslane v Secretary of State
for Work and Pensions*, the appeal against this decision, is pending before the Court of
Appeal, but has been removed from the list pending resolution of a costs issue.

Note finally that a woman with an election to pay reduced rate contributions,
which was in effect at the beginning of the tax year, cannot have that year treated as
one of home responsibilities protection, unless throughout the period April 6,
1975 to April 5, 1980, she is not a self-employed earner and had no earnings in
respect of which primary Class 1 contributions were payable (paras (5)(a), (6)).

REVOCATIONS

3.—*Omitted* as not relevant.
Schedule. *Omitted* as not relevant.

The Social Security (Benefit) (Married Women and Widows Special Provisions) Regulations 1974

(SI 1974/2010) (*as amended*)

REGULATION REPRODUCED

3. Modifications, in relation to widows, of provisions with respect to . . . [incap-   2.43
acity benefit], maternity allowance and Category A retirement pension

Modifications, in relation to widows, of provisions with respect to . . . [¹ short-term incapacity benefit] [², contributory employment and support allowance], maternity allowance, and Category A retirement pension

3.—(1) Subject to the following provisions of this regulation, where,   2.44
otherwise than by reason of remarriage or cohabitation with a man as his
wife, a woman ceases to be entitled either to a widow's allowance or to a
widowed mother's allowance—
  (a) she shall be deemed to have satisfied the first contribution condition
      for [¹ . . .] [¹ short-term incapacity benefit] or [¹ . . .] maternity allow-
      ance [¹ . . .] referred to in paragraph 1 [¹ or] 3 [¹ . . .], as the case may
      be, of Schedule 3 to the Act [³ or, in relation to contributory employ-
      ment and support allowance, she shall be deemed to have satisfied
      the first condition referred to in paragraph 1(1) of Schedule 1 to the
      Welfare Reform Act;
  (b) for the purpose only of enabling her to satisfy the second contri-
      bution condition for unemployment and [¹ short-term incapacity
      benefit] or maternity allowance referred to in paragraph 1 or 3, as
      the case may be, of Schedule 3 to the Act, [² or, in relation to con-
      tributory employment and support allowance, she shall be deemed
      to have satisfied the first condition referred to in paragraph 1(1) of
      Schedule 1 to the Welfare Reform Act] there shall be credited to her
      such Class 1 contributions (if any) for every year up to and including
      that in which she ceased to be entitled as aforesaid as are required to
      enable her to satisfy that condition; and

(c) [¹ . . .]

(2)–(10) *omitted* as not relevant and/or revoked.

AMENDMENTS

1. Words substituted for "sickness benefit" in heading to and in reg.3 by Social Security (Incapacity Benefit) (Consequential and Transitional Amendments and Savings) Regulations 1995 (SI 1995/829), reg.2(a) (April 13, 1995).

2. Employment and Support Allowance (Consequential Provisions) (No. 2) Regulations 2008 (SI 2008/1554), reg.64(3) (October 27, 2008).

GENERAL NOTE

2.45   Taken together with Social Security (Credits) Regulations 1975, reg.8C, above, the effect of para.(1)(a) appears effectively to waive altogether the contributions conditions for short-term incapacity benefit or contributory employment and support allowance for certain widows.

The Social Security (Crediting and Treatment of Contributions, and National Insurance Numbers) Regulations 2001

(SI 2001/769) (*as amended*)

REGULATIONS REPRODUCED

The Secretary of State for Social Security, with the concurrence of the Inland Revenue in so far as required, in exercise of powers conferred by sections 13(3), 22(5), 122(1) and 175(1) to (4) of, and paragraphs 8(1)(d) and (1A) and 10 of Schedule 1 to, the Social Security Contributions and Benefits Act 1992 and sections 182C and 189(1) and (3) to (6) of the Social Security Administration Act 1992 and of all other powers enabling him in that behalf and for the purpose only of consolidating other regulations hereby revoked, hereby makes the following Regulations:

Citation, commencement and interpretation

2.47   **1.**—(1) These Regulations may be cited as the Social Security (Crediting and Treatment of Contributions, and National Insurance Numbers) Regulations 2001 and shall come into force on 6th April 2001.

(2) In these Regulations, including this regulation—

"the Act" means the Social Security Contributions and Benefits Act 1992;

"the Contributions Regulations" means the Social Security (Contributions) Regulations 1979;

"contribution week" means a period of seven days beginning with midnight between Saturday and Sunday;

"contribution-based jobseeker's allowance" and "income-based jobseeker's allowance" have the same meaning as in the Jobseekers Act 1995;

"contributory benefit" includes a contribution-based jobseeker's allowance but not an income-based jobseeker's allowance; [³ and includes a contributory employment and support allowance but not an income-related employment and support allowance]

[³ "contributory employment and support allowance" means a contributory allowance under Part 1 of the Welfare Reform Act (employment and support allowance);]

"due date" [¹ (subject to regulation 4(11))] means, in relation to any contribution which a person is—

    (a) liable to pay, the date by which payment falls to be made in accordance with Part IV of the Contributions Regulations;

    (b) entitled, but not liable, to pay, the date 42 days after the end of the year in respect of which it is paid;

"earnings factor" has the meaning assigned to it in section 21(5)(c) of the Act;

[³ "income-related employment and support allowance" means an income-related allowance under Part 1 of the Welfare Reform Act (employment and support allowance);]

"relevant benefit year" has the meaning assigned to it in—

    (a) section 2(4)(b) of the Jobseekers Act 1995, in relation to a contribution-based jobseeker's allowance;

    (b) paragraph 2(6)(b) of Schedule 3 to the Act (contribution conditions for entitlement to short-term incapacity benefit), in relation to short-term incapacity benefit;

    [³ (c) paragraph 3(1)(f) of Schedule 1 to the Welfare Reform Act (conditions relating to national insurance), in relation to a contributory employment and support allowance.]

"relevant time", in relation to short-term incapacity benefit, has the meaning assigned to it in paragraph 2(6)(a) of Schedule 3 to the Act;

[³ "the Welfare Reform Act" means the Welfare Reform Act 2007;]

"year" means tax year.

[² (3) In these Regulations, "official error" means an error made by—

    (a) an officer of the Department for Work and Pensions or an officer of Revenue and Customs acting as such which no person outside the Department or Her Majesty's Revenue and Customs caused or to which no person outside the Department or Her Majesty's Revenue and Customs materially contributed; or

    (b) a person employed by a service provider and to which no person who was not so employed materially contributed,

but excludes any error of law which is shown to have been an error by virtue of a subsequent decision of [⁴ the Upper Tribunal] or the court.

    (4) [⁴. . .]

"service provider" means a person providing services to the Secretary of State for Work and Pensions or to Her Majesty's Revenue and Customs.]

AMENDMENTS

1. Social Security, Occupational Pension Schemes and Statutory Payments (Consequential Provisions) Regulations 2007 (SI 2007/1154), reg.2(2) (April 6, 2007).
2. Social Security (National Insurance Credits) Amendment Regulations 2007 (SI 2007/2582), reg.3 (October 1, 2007).
3. Employment and Support Allowance (Consequential Provisions) (No. 2) Regulations 2008 (SI 2008/1554), reg.49(2) (October 27, 2008).
4. Tribunals, Courts and Enforcement Act 2007 (Transitional and Consequential Provisions) Order 2008 (SI 2008/2683), art.6(1) and Sch.1, para.147 (November 3, 2008).

Appropriation of Class 3 contributions

2.48   **2.**—Any person paying Class 3 contributions in one year may appropriate such contributions to the earnings factor of another year if such contributions are payable in respect of that other year or, in the absence of any such appropriation, the Inland Revenue may, with the consent of the contributor, make such appropriation.

Crediting of Class 3 contributions

2.49   **3.**—Where, for any year, a contributor's earnings factor derived from—
   (a) earnings upon which primary Class 1 contributions have been paid or treated as paid;
   (b) credited earnings;
   (c) Class 2 or Class 3 contributions paid by or credited to him; or
   (d) any or all of such earnings and contributions,
falls short of a figure which is 52 times that year's lower earnings limit for Class 1 contributions by an amount which is equal to, or less than, half that year's lower earnings limit, that contributor shall be credited with a Class 3 contribution for that year.

Treatment for the purpose of any contributory benefit of late paid contributions

2.50   **4.**—(1) Subject to the provisions of regulations 5 [¹ to 6C] below and regulation 40 of the Contributions Regulations (voluntary Class 2 contributions not paid within permitted period), for the purpose of entitlement to any contributory benefit, paragraphs (2) to (9) below shall apply to contributions ("relevant contributions")—
   (a) paid after the due date; or
   (b) treated as paid after the due date under regulation 7(2) below.
   [² (1A) Any relevant contribution which is paid—
   (a) by virtue of an official error; and
   (b) more than six years after the end of the year in which the contributor was first advised of that error,
shall be treated as not paid.]
   (2) Subject to the provisions of paragraph (4) below, any relevant contribution other than one referred to in paragraph (3) below–
   (a) if paid—

    (i) after the end of the second year following the year in which liability for that contribution arises,

    (ii) following the due date for that contribution in the case of a contribution which a person is entitled, but not liable, to pay,

shall be treated as not paid;

  (b) if paid before the end of the said second year, shall, subject to paragraphs (7) and (8) below, be treated as paid on the date on which payment of the contribution is made.

(3) Subject to the provisions of paragraph (4) below, any relevant Class 2 contribution payable in respect of a contribution week after 5th April 1983 or any relevant Class 3 contribution payable in respect of a year after 5th April 1982—

  (a) if paid—

    (i) after the end of the sixth year following the year in which liability for that contribution arises,

    (ii) following the due date for that contribution in the case of a contribution which a person is entitled, but not liable, to pay,

shall be treated as not paid;

  (b) if paid before the end of the said sixth year, shall, subject to paragraphs (7) and (8) below, be treated as paid on the date on which payment of the contribution is made.

(4) A Class 3 contribution payable by a person to whom regulation 27(3)(b)(ii) or (iii) of the Contributions Regulations (which specify the conditions to be complied with before a person may pay a Class 3 contribution) applies in respect of a year which includes a period of education, apprenticeship, training, imprisonment or detention in legal custody such as is specified in that regulation—

  (a) if paid after the end of the sixth year specified in that regulation, shall be treated as not paid;

  (b) if paid before the end of the said sixth year shall, subject to the provisions of paragraphs (7) and (8) below, be treated as paid on the date on which payment of the contribution is made.

(5) Notwithstanding the provisions of paragraph (4) above, for the purpose of entitlement to any contributory benefit, where—

  (a) a Class 3 contribution other than one referred to in sub-paragraph (b) below which is payable in respect of a year specified in that sub-paragraph, is paid after—

    (i) the due date, and

    (ii) the end of the second year following the year preceding that in which occurred the relevant time or, as the case may be, the relevant event,

that contribution shall be treated as not paid;

  (b) in respect of a year after 5th April 1982, a Class 3 contribution which is payable in respect of a year specified in paragraph (4) above, is paid after—

    (i) the due date, and

    (ii) the end of the sixth year following the year preceding that in which occurred the relevant time or, as the case may be, the relevant event,

that contribution shall be treated as not paid.

(6) For the purposes of paragraph (5) above, "relevant event" means the

date on which the person concerned attained pensionable age or, as the case may be, died under that age.

(7) Notwithstanding the provisions of paragraphs (2), (3) and (4) above, in determining whether the relevant contribution conditions are satisfied in whole or in part for the purpose of entitlement to any contributory benefit, any relevant contribution which is paid within the time specified in paragraph (2)(b), (3)(b) or, as the case may be, (4)(b) above shall be treated—

(a) for the purpose of entitlement in respect of any period before the date on which the payment of the contribution is made, as not paid; and

(b) subject to the provisions of paragraph (8) below, for the purpose of entitlement in respect of any other period, as paid on the date on which the payment of the contribution is made.

(8) For the purpose of determining whether the second contribution condition for entitlement to a contribution-based jobseeker's allowance [4, short-term incapacity benefit or a contributory employment and support allowance] benefit is satisfied in whole or in part, any relevant contribution shall be treated—

(a) if paid before the beginning of the relevant benefit year, as paid on the due date;

(b) if paid after the end of the benefit year immediately preceding the relevant benefit year, as not paid in relation to the benefit claimed in respect of any day before the expiry of a period of 42 days (including Sundays) commencing with the date on which the payment of that contribution is made, and, subject to the provisions of paragraphs (2) (a) and (3)(a) above, as paid at the expiry of that period in relation to entitlement to such benefit in respect of any other period.

(9) For the purposes of paragraph (8) above, "second contribution condition" in relation to—

(a) a contribution-based jobseeker's allowance is a reference to the condition specified in section 2(1)(b) of the Jobseekers Act 1995;

(b) short-term incapacity benefit is a reference to the condition specified in paragraph 2(3) of Schedule 3 to the Act;

[4 (c) a contributory employment and support allowance is a reference to the condition specified in paragraph 2(1) of Schedule 1 to the Welfare Reform Act.]

(10) This regulation shall not apply to Class 4 contributions.

[3 (11) Where an amount is retrospectively treated as earnings ("retrospective earnings") by regulations made by virtue of section 4B(2) of the Act, the "due date" for earnings-related contributions in respect of those earnings is the date given by paragraph 11A of Schedule 4 to the Social Security (Contributions) Regulations 2001, for the purposes of this regulation and regulations 5 and 5A.]

AMENDMENTS

1. Social Security (Additional Class 3 National Insurance Contributions) Amendment Regulations 2009 (SI 2009/659), reg.3(2) (April 6, 2009).

2. Social Security (National Insurance Credits) Amendment Regulations 2007 (SI 2007/2582), reg.4(3)(b) (October 1, 2007).

3. Social Security, Occupational Pension Schemes and Statutory Payments (Consequential Provisions) Regulations 2007 (SI 2007/1154), reg.2(2) (April 6, 2007).

4. Employment and Support Allowance (Consequential Provisions) (No. 2) Regulations 2008 (SI 2008/1554), reg.49(3) (October 27, 2008).

Treatment for the purpose of any contributory benefit of late paid primary Class 1 contributions where there was no consent, connivance or negligence by the primary contributor

5.—(1) This regulation applies where a primary Class 1 contribution which is payable on a primary contributor's behalf by a secondary contributor—

2.51

(a) is paid after the due date; or

(b) in relation to any claim for—

    (i) a contribution-based jobseeker's allowance, is not paid before the beginning of the relevant benefit year,

    (ii) short-term incapacity benefit, is not paid before the relevant time,[² or

    (iii) a contributory employment and support allowance, is not paid before the beginning of the relevant benefit year,]

and the delay in making payment is shown to the satisfaction of [¹an officer of] the Inland Revenue not to have been with the consent or connivance of, or attributable to any negligence on the part of, the primary contributor.

(2) Where paragraph (1) above applies, the primary Class 1 contribution shall be treated—

(a) for the purpose of the first contribution condition of entitlement to a contribution-based jobseeker's allowance [², short-term incapacity benefit or a contributory employment and support allowance], as paid on the day on which payment is made of the earnings in respect of which the contribution is payable; and

(b) for any other purpose relating to entitlement to any contributory benefit, as paid on the due date.

(3) For the purposes of this regulation—

(a) "first contribution condition" in relation to—

    (i) a contribution-based jobseeker's allowance is a reference to the condition specified in section 2(1)(a) of the Jobseekers Act 1995,

    (ii) short-term incapacity benefit is a reference to the condition specified in paragraph 2(2) of Schedule 3 to the Act;

    [² "(iii) a contributory employment and support allowance is a reference to the condition specified in paragraph 1(1) of Schedule 1 to the Welfare Reform Act;]

(b) "primary contributor" means the person liable to pay a primary Class 1 contribution in accordance with section 6(4)(a) of the Act (liability for Class 1 contributions);

(c) "secondary contributor" means the person who, in respect of earnings from employed earner's employment, is liable to pay a secondary Class 1 contribution in accordance with section 6(4)(b) of the Act.

AMENDMENTS

1. Social Security, Occupational Pension Schemes and Statutory Payments (Consequential Provisions) Regulations 2007 (SI 2007/1154), reg.2(2) (April 6, 2007).

2. Employment and Support Allowance (Consequential Provisions) (No. 2) Regulations 2008 (SI 2008/1554), reg.49(4) (October 27, 2008).

[¹ Treatment for the purpose of any contributory benefit of duly paid primary Class 1 contributions in respect of retrospective earnings

2.52   **5A.**—Where a primary Class 1 contribution payable in respect of retrospective earnings is paid by the due date, it shall be treated—

    (a) for the purposes of the first contribution condition of entitlement to a contribution-based jobseeker's allowance [², short-term incapacity benefit or a contributory employment and support allowance], as paid on the day on which payment is made of the retrospective earnings in respect of which the contribution is payable; and

    (b) for any other purpose relating to entitlement to any contributory benefit, as paid on the due date.]

AMENDMENTS

1. Social Security, Occupational Pension Schemes and Statutory Payments (Consequential Provisions) Regulations 2007 (SI 2007/1154), reg.2(2) (April 6, 2007).
2. Employment and Support Allowance (Consequential Provisions) (No. 2) Regulations 2008 (SI 2008/1554), reg.49(5) (October 27, 2008).

Treatment for the purpose of any contributory benefit of contributions under the Act paid late through ignorance or error

2.53   **6.**—(1) In the case of a contribution paid by or in respect of a person after the due date, where—

    (a) the contribution is paid after the time when it would, under regulation 4 or 5 above, have been treated as paid for the purpose of entitlement to contributory benefit; and

    (b) it is shown to the satisfaction of [¹ an officer of] the Inland Revenue that the failure to pay the contribution before that time is attributable to ignorance or error on the part of that person or the person making the payment and that that ignorance or error was not due to any failure on the part of such person to exercise due care and diligence,

[¹ an officer of the Inland Revenue may direct], for the purposes of those regulations, the contribution shall be treated as paid on such earlier day as [¹ the officer considers] appropriate in the circumstances, and those regulations shall have effect subject to any such direction.

(2) This regulation shall not apply to a Class 4 contribution.

[¹ Treatment for the purposes of any contributory benefit of certain Class 3 contributions

2.54   **6A.**—(1) For the purposes of entitlement to any contributory benefit, this regulation applies in the case of a Class 3 contribution paid after the due date—

    (a) which would otherwise under regulation 4—

        (i) have been treated as paid on a day other than on the day on which it was actually paid; or

        (ii) have been treated as not paid; and

    (b) which is paid in respect of a year after 5th April 1996 but before 6th April 2002.

(2) A contribution referred to in paragraph (1), where it is paid on or before 5th April 2009 by or in respect of a person who attains pensionable age on or after 6th April 2008, shall be treated as paid on the day on which it is paid.

(3) A contribution referred to in paragraph (1), where it is paid on or before 5th April 2009 by or in respect of a person who attains pensionable age on or after 24th October 2004 but before 6th April 2008, shall be treated as paid on—

(a) the day on which it is paid; or

(b) the date on which the person attained pensionable age,

whichever is the earlier.

(4) A contribution referred to in paragraph (1), where it is paid on or before 5th April 2010 by or in respect of a person who attains pensionable age on or after 6th April 1998 but before 24th October 2004, shall be treated as paid on—

(a) 1st October 1998; or

(b) the date on which the person attained pensionable age,

whichever is the later.]

AMENDMENT

1. Social Security (Crediting and Treatment of Contributions, and National Insurance Numbers) Amendment Regulations 2004 (SI 2004/1361), reg.2(b) (May 17, 2004).

[¹ Treatment for the purpose of any contributory benefit of certain Class 2 or Class 3 contributions

6B.—For the purpose of entitlement to any contributory benefit, a Class 2 or a Class 3 contribution paid after the due date—   2.55

(a) which would otherwise under regulation 4 (apart from paragraph (1A) of that regulation)—

    (i) have been treated as paid on a day other than the day on which it was actually paid; or

    (ii) have been treated as not paid; and

(b) which was paid after the due date by virtue of an official error,

shall be treated as paid on the day on which it is paid.]

AMENDMENT

1. Social Security (National Insurance Credits) Amendment Regulations 2007 (SI 2007/2582), reg.4(4) (October 1, 2007).

[¹Treatment of Class 3 contributions paid under section 13A of the Act

6C.—(1) This regulation applies to a Class 3 contribution paid by an eligible person under section 13A (right to pay additional Class 3 contributions in certain cases) of the Act.   2.56

(2) A contribution paid after 5th April 2009 but before 6th April 2011 shall be treated as paid on—

(a) the day on which it is paid; or

(b) the date on which the person attained pensionable age,

whichever is the earlier.

(3) A contribution paid after 5th April 2011 shall be treated as paid on the day on which it is paid.]

AMENDMENT

1. Social Security (Additional Class 3 National Insurance Contributions) Amendment Regulations 2009 (SI 2009/659), reg.3(3) (April 6, 2009).

Treatment for the purpose of any contributory benefit of contributions paid under regulation 54 of the Contributions Regulations

2.57

7.—(1) Subject to the provisions of paragraph (2) below, for the purpose of entitlement to any contributory benefit, where—

(a) a person pays a Class 2 or Class 3 contribution in accordance with regulation 54 of the Contributions Regulations (method of, and time for, payment of Class 2 and Class 3 contributions etc.); and

(b) the due date for payment of that contribution is a date after the relevant day,

that contribution shall be treated as paid by the relevant day.

(2) Where, in respect of any part of a late notification period, a person pays a Class 2 contribution which he is liable to pay, that contribution shall be treated as paid after the due date, whether or not it was paid by the due date.

(3) For the purposes of this regulation—

(a) "late notification period" means the period beginning with the day a person liable to pay a Class 2 contribution was first required to notify the Inland Revenue in accordance with the provisions of regulation 53A of the Contributions Regulations (notification of commencement or cessation of payment of Class 2 or Class 3 contributions) and ending on the last day of the contribution quarter immediately before the contribution quarter in which he gives that notification;

(b) "relevant day" means the first day in respect of which a person would have been entitled to receive the contributory benefit in question if any contribution condition relevant to that benefit had already been satisfied;

(c) "contribution quarter" means one of the four periods of not less than 13 contribution weeks commencing on the first day of the first, fourteenth, twenty-seventh or fortieth contribution week, in any year.

Treatment for the purpose of any contributory benefit of contributions paid under an arrangement

2.58

8. For the purposes of regulations 4 to 7 above and regulation 40 of the Contributions Regulations (voluntary Class 2 contributions not paid within permitted period)—

(a) where a contribution is paid under an arrangement to which regulations 46A and 48 or, as the case may be, regulation 54A of the Contributions Regulations (other methods of collection and recovery of earnings-related contributions; special provisions relating to primary Class 1 contributions and arrangements approved by the Inland Revenue for method of, and time for, payment of Class 2 and Class 3 contributions respectively) apply, the date by which, but for the said regulations 4 to 7 and 40, the contribution would have fallen due to be paid shall, in relation to that contribution, be the due date;

(b) any payment made of, or as on account of, a contribution in accordance with any such arrangement shall, on and after the due date, be treated as a contribution paid on the due date.

Regs 9 to 12 and Schedule. *Omitted* as the province of the Board of Inland Revenue.

AMENDMENT

1. Social Security (Contributions) (Amendment No.3) Regulations 2002 (SI 2002/2366), reg.19 (October 8, 2002).

PART III

REGULATIONS COMMON TO SEVERAL BENEFITS

Social Security Benefit (Computation of Earnings) Regulations 1996

(SI 1996/2745) (*as amended*)

ARRANGEMENT OF REGULATIONS

PART I

GENERAL

3.1

PART II

EMPLOYED EARNERS

PART III

SELF-EMPLOYED EARNERS

PART IV

TRANSITIONAL PROVISIONS, CONSEQUENTIAL AMENDMENTS AND REVOCATIONS

SCHEDULES

Schedule 1—Sums to be disregarded in the calculation of earnings.
Schedule 2—Child care charges to be deducted in the calculation of earnings.
Schedule 3—Care charges to be deducted in the calculation of earnings for entitlement to carer's care allowance.
Schedule 4—*Omitted*.

The Secretary of State for Social Security, in exercise of the powers conferred by sections 3(2) and (3), 80(7), 89, 112, 119 and 175(1), (3) and (4) of, and paragraph 4(6) of Schedule 7 to, the Social Security Contributions and Benefits Act 1992, sections 5(1)(n) and (r), 71(7), 189(4) and (5) and 191 of the Social Security Administration Act 1992 and of all other powers enabling him in that behalf, after agreement by the Social Security Advisory Committee that the proposals to make these Regulations should not be referred to it hereby makes the following Regulations:

PART I

GENERAL

Citation and commencement

3.2   **1.**—These Regulations may be cited as the Social Security Benefit (Computation of Earnings) Regulations 1996 and shall come into force on 25th November 1996.

GENERAL NOTE

3.3   These regulations replace the Computation of Earnings Regulations 1978 (SI 1978/1698). They contain in a more detailed manner the rules for determining earnings and include provision for determining notional earnings.

Interpretation

3.4   **2.**—(1) In these Regulations, unless the context otherwise requires—
[¹ . . .]
"benefit week" means—
  (a) any period of 7 days corresponding to the week in respect of which the relevant social security benefit is due to be paid, and, where appropriate in respect of payments due to be paid before that week,
  (b) the period of 7 days ending on the day before the first day of the first such week following the date of claim or any one of the consecutive periods of seven days prior to that period;
"board and lodging accommodation" means—
  (a) accommodation provided to a person or, if he is a member of a family, to him or any other member of his family, for a charge which is inclusive of the provision of that accommodation and at least some cooked or prepared meals which both are cooked or prepared (by a person other than the person to whom the accommodation is provided or a member of his family) and are consumed in that accommodation or associated premises; or

(b) accommodation provided to a person in a hotel, guest house, lodging house or some similar establishment,

except accommodation provided by a close relative of his or of any other member of his family, or other than on a commercial basis;

"claim" means a claim for a benefit, pension or allowance under Parts II to V of the Contributions and Benefits Act;

"claimant" means a person claiming a benefit, pension or allowance under Parts II to V of the Contributions and Benefits Act and includes a claimant's spouse or partner and any adult in respect of whom a claim for an increase in benefit is made under Part IV of that Act;

"close relative" means a parent, parent-in-law, son, son-in-law, daughter, daughter-in-law, step-parent, step-son, step-daughter, brother, sister, [³ or if any of the preceding persons is one member of a couple, the other member of that couple;]

"the Contributions and Benefits Act" means the Social Security Contributions and Benefits Act 1992;

[³ "couple" means—

(a) a man and woman who are married to each other and are members of the same household;

(b) a man and woman who are not married to each other but are living together as husband and wife;

(c) two people of the same sex who are civil partners of each other and are members of the same household; or

(d) two people of the same sex who are not civil partners of each other but are living together as if they were civil partners;

and for the purposes of sub-paragraph (d), two people of the same sex are to be regarded as living together as if they were civil partners if, but only if, they would be regarded as living together as husband and wife were they instead two people of the opposite sex;]

"Crown property" means property held by Her Majesty in right of the Crown or by a government department or which is held in trust for Her Majesty for the purposes of a government department, except (in the case of an interest held by Her Majesty in right of the Crown) where the interest is under the management of the Crown Estate Commissioners;

"date of claim" means the date on which the claimant makes, or is treated as making, a claim for a benefit, pension or allowance for the purposes of regulation 6 of the Social Security (Claims and Payments) Regulations 1987;

"dwelling occupied as the home" means the dwelling together with any garage, garden and outbuildings, normally occupied by the claimant as his home including any premises not so occupied which it is impracticable or unreasonable to sell separately, in particular, in Scotland, any croft land on which the dwelling is situated;

"earnings" has the meaning prescribed in regulation 9 or, as the case may be, 12, and for the purposes only of sections 80, 82 to 86A and 89 of, and paragraphs 4, 6 and 7 of Schedule 7 to, the Contributions and Benefits Act includes payments by way of occupational or personal pension within the meaning of section 122 of the Contributions and Benefits Act (interpretation);

"employed earner" means a person who is in gainful employment in Great Britain under a contract of service, or in an office (including elective office) with emoluments chargeable to income tax under Schedule E and includes—

(a) a person in any employment which would be such employment if it were in Great Britain, and

(b) a person in any such employment which, in accordance with the provisions of the Contributions and Benefits Act and of any regulations made thereunder, is to be disregarded in relation to liability for contributions;

"employment" includes any trade, business, profession, office or vocation;

"invalid carriage or other vehicle" means a vehicle propelled by petrol engine or by electric power supplied for use on the road and to be controlled by the occupant;

"lone parent" means a person who has no partner and who is responsible for, and a member of the same household as, a child within the meaning of section 142 of the Contributions and Benefits Act (meaning of "child");

"lower rate" where it relates to rates of tax has the same meaning as in the Income and Corporation Taxes Act 1988 by virtue of section 832(1) of that Act [²...];

"net earnings" means such earnings as are calculated in accordance with regulation 10(4);

"net profit" means such profit as is calculated in accordance with regulation 13(4);

"occupational pension scheme" has the same meaning as in section 1 of the Pension Schemes Act 1993;

"partner" means where a claimant—

(a) is a member of a [³...] couple, the other member of that couple;

(b) is married polygamously to two or more members of his household, any such member;

"payment" includes a part of a payment;

"pay period" means the period in respect of which a claimant is, or expects to be, normally paid by his employer, being a week, a fortnight, four weeks, a month or other shorter or longer period as the case may be;

"personal pension scheme" has the same meaning as in section 1 of the Pension Schemes Act 1993 and, in the case of a self-employed earner, includes a scheme approved by the Inland Revenue under Chapter IV of Part XIV of the Income and Corporation Taxes Act 1988;

"polygamous marriage" means any marriage during the subsistence of which a party to it is married to more than one person and the ceremony of marriage took place under the law of a country which permits polygamy;

"relevant earnings limit" means the amount of a claimant's earnings in excess of which the benefit, supplement, allowance, pension or increase in question is not payable;

"retirement annuity contract" means a contract or trust scheme approved under Chapter III of Part XIV of the Income and Corporation Taxes Act 1988;

"self-employed earner" means a person who is in gainful employment in Great Britain otherwise than as an employed earner and includes—

(a) a person in any employment which would be such employment if it were in Great Britain, and

(b) a person in any such employment which, in accordance with the provisions of the Contributions and Benefits Act and of any regulations made thereunder, is to be disregarded in relation to liability for contributions;

"voluntary organisation" means a body, other than a public or local authority, the activities of which are carried on otherwise than for profit;

"week" means a period of 7 days and for the purposes of section 80 of, and paragraph 4(6) of Schedule 7 to, the Contributions and Benefits Act, a period of 7 days being the relevant benefit week;

"year of assessment" has the meaning prescribed in section 832(1) of the Income and Corporation Taxes Act 1988.

(2) In these Regulations, unless the context otherwise requires, a reference—

(a) to a numbered regulation or Schedule is to the regulation in or Schedule to these Regulations bearing that number;

(b) in a regulation or Schedule to a numbered paragraph is to the paragraph in that regulation or Schedule bearing that number;

(c) in a paragraph to a lettered or numbered sub-paragraph is to the sub-paragraph in that paragraph bearing that letter or number.

AMENDMENTS

1. The Social Security Act 1998 (Commencement No. 9 and Savings and Consequential and Transitional Provisions) Order 1999 (SI 1999/2422), Sch.13, para.2 (September 6, 1999).

2. The Social Security Benefit (Computation of Earnings) (Amendment) Regulations 2002 (SI 2002/2823), reg.2 (April 1, 2003).

3. The Civil Partnership Act 2004 (Tax Credits, etc.) (Consequential Amendments) Order 2005 (SI 2005/2919) (December 5, 2005).

GENERAL NOTE

With effect from December 5, 2005, art.3 of the Civil Partnership Act 2004   **3.5** (Relationships Arising Through Civil Partnership) Order 2005 (SI 2005/3137) applies the provisions of s.246 of the Civil Partnership Act 2004 to the definition of "close relative" in reg.2(1). For the text of s.246, see para.1.555 in Vol.III.

For a decision which is of significance in drawing the dividing line between employer earners and self-employed earners, which arose in the context of computing the earnings of a GCSE examiner, see *CG/4139/2006*. The Commissioner concludes his decision with the words:

"12. . . . . I also hope that the Secretary of State takes steps to ensure that the guidance given to officers dealing with carer's allowance and other benefits to which the Computation of Earnings Regulations are relevant takes account of the deeming in regulation 2(3) and paragraph 6 of Schedule 1 to the Categorisation of Earners Regulations."

Calculation of earnings

3.—(1) For the purposes of Parts II to V (other than those of Schedule   **3.6** 8) of the Contributions and Benefits Act (a) and of any regulations made thereunder which relate to benefit under those Parts of that Act or regulations, the earnings of a claimant shall be calculated by determining in accordance with these Regulations the weekly amount of his earnings.

(2) The amount of a claimant's earnings for any period shall be the whole of

those earnings (including any earnings which he is treated as possessing under regulation 4 (notional earnings)) except in so far as regulations 10 and 13 provide that certain sums shall be disregarded or deducted as appropriate.

GENERAL NOTE

3.7   The calculation of earnings is to be carried out in accordance with the rules contained in the Regulations. The whole of earnings after making the deductions and allowing the disregards provided for by the Regulations is to be taken into account. The provisions for estimating earnings are replaced by the notional earnings rules set out in reg.4. The rules apply to all benefits listed in Pts II to V of the Contributions and Benefits Act: incapacity benefit, sickness and invalidity benefits (so far as still relevant), maternity benefits, bereavement benefits, retirement pensions, child's special allowance, attendance allowance, disability living allowance, guardian's allowance, and increases for dependants, as well as benefits for industrial injuries.

Some of the broad areas of discretion previously available under the former Regulations are replaced by regulation-based rules for determining earnings.

In *Secretary of State for Work and Pensions v Doyle* [2006] EWCA Civ 466, reported as *R(IB) 1/06*, the Court of Appeal ruled that these regulations apply to the computation of earnings for the purposes of entitlement to incapacity benefit where a person is working "on the advice of a doctor". The essential grounding of entitlement of incapacity benefit in Pt II of the Act was sufficient for reg.3 to apply even though Pt XIIA lays down the detailed scheme.

Notional earnings

3.8   **4.**—(1) Where a claimant's earnings are not ascertainable at the date [1 on which a decision falls to be made by the Secretary of State under Chapter II of Part I of the Social Security Act 1998 or regulations made thereunder the claimant shall be treated] as possessing such earnings as is reasonable in the circumstances of the case having regard to the number of hours worked and the earnings paid for comparable employment in the area.

(2) Where—

(a) a claimant performs a service for another person; and

(b) that person makes no payment of earnings or pays less than that paid for a comparable employment in the area,

[2 the claimant shall be treated] as possessing such earnings (if any) as is reasonable for that employment unless the claimant satisfies [3 the Secretary of State] that the means of that person are insufficient for him to pay or to pay more for the service; [4 but this paragraph shall not apply to a claimant—

(i) who is engaged by a charitable or voluntary organisation or is a volunteer if the Secretary of State is satisfied in any of those cases that it is reasonable for him to provide his services free of charge; or

(ii) who is participating in an employment or training programme for which a training allowance is not payable or, where such an allowance is payable, it is payable for the sole purpose of reimbursement of travelling or meal expenses to the person participating in that programme; and for this purpose "employment in a training programme" has the meaning given in regulation 19(3) of the Jobseeker's Allowance Regulations 1996 and "training allowance" has the meaning given in regulation 1(3) of those Regulations.]

(3) Where a claimant is treated as possessing any earnings under paragraph (1) or (2) these Regulations shall apply for the purposes of calculating

the amount of those earnings as if a payment had actually been made and as if they were actual earnings which he does possess except that paragraph (4) of regulation 10 (calculation of net earnings of employed earners) shall not apply and his net earnings shall be calculated by taking into account the earnings which he is treated as possessing, less—

    (a) an amount in respect of income tax equivalent to an amount calculated by applying to those earnings the lower rate or, as the case may be, the lower rate and the basic rate of tax in the year of assessment less only the personal relief to which the claimant is entitled under sections 257(1), 257A(1) and 259 of the Income and Corporation Taxes Act 1988 (personal reliefs) as is appropriate to his circumstances; but, if the period over which those earnings are to be taken into account is less than a year, the earnings to which the lower rate of tax is to be applied and the amount of the personal relief deductible under this paragraph shall be calculated on a pro rata basis;

    (b) where the weekly amount of those earnings equals or exceeds the lower earnings limit, an amount representing primary Class 1 contributions under the Contributions and Benefits Act, calculated by applying to those earnings the initial and main primary percentages in accordance with section 8(1)(a) and (b) of that Act; and

    (c) one half of any sum payable by the claimant in respect of a pay period by way of a contribution towards an occupational or personal pension scheme.

AMENDMENTS

1. The Social Security Act 1998 (Commencement No. 11 and Transitional Provisions) Order 1999 (SI 1999/2860), Sch.15, para.3(a) (October 18, 1999).

2. The Social Security Act 1998 (Commencement No. 9 and Savings and Consequential and Transitional Provisions) Order 1999 (SI 1999/2422), Sch.13, para.3(b) (September 6, 1999).

3. The Social Security Act 1998 (Commencement No. 9 and Savings and Consequential and Transitional Provisions) Order 1999 (SI 1999/2422), Sch.13, para.1 (September 6, 1999).

4. The Social Security (Approved Work) Regulations 2000 (SI 2000/678), reg.8 (April 3, 2000).

GENERAL NOTE

    The provisions on notional earnings are new in relation to the benefits covered by these regulations.   **3.9**

Earnings not ascertainable (para.(1))

    The first question for the decision-maker will be to determine whether the earnings (which may be from employment or self-employment) are ascertainable. That   **3.10** is not the same as saying that they have not yet been ascertained. Whether the earnings are ascertainable will be for the judgment of the decision-maker. In these cases, the claimant is treated as possessing such earnings as he or she might reasonably be paid for comparable employment in the area. It is not clear who has the burden of proof. But the decision-maker is likely to be in a better position than the claimant to present the evidence needed to form the conclusions required by the regulation. Furthermore, in many cases the earnings will serve to disentitle the person from a benefit, and there is an argument that in those cases the burden should be on the decision-maker. In practice the burden is likely to be "neutral" in that both parties can be expected to come to the decision-maker with as much information as possible from which a conclusion can be drawn.

Though the terms used in para.(1) apply to both employment and self-employment, the remainder of the regulation requires that the calculation of notional earnings should be made on the basis that the person is a notional employed earner. This is presumably because there are no valid comparators in the case of self-employment. So a self-employed painter whose earnings are not ascertainable will be treated as possessing the earnings paid for comparable employment as a painter.

No earnings or low earnings (para.(2))

3.11 Provision is made for treating a person as possessing earnings when a claimant performs a service for another but receives no payment for it, or is paid than earnings paid for comparable employment in the area. The straightforward case of a claimant disclosing the performance of a service for which nothing is paid are not likely to be met frequently. Disclosed earnings which are lower than for comparable employment may be met more frequently, but presumably it will be the decision-maker who takes the initiative to show that such earnings are low.

There are three circumstances when the rules do not apply. First, they will not apply if the claimant shows on the balance of probabilities that the beneficiary of the service has insufficient means to pay at all or at the comparable rate for the area. Secondly, they will not apply if the beneficiary of the service is a charitable or voluntary organisation. Though charitable body is not defined, voluntary organisation is defined in reg.2. Thirdly, they will not apply if the claimant is a volunteer and the decision-maker concludes that it is reasonable for the service to be provided free of charge. This is a large area for the judgment of decision-makers, and could give rise to widely differing views.

In *R(IB) 7/03* the Commissioner concluded that reg.4(2) is not validly made under the power in s.3(2) of the Contributions and Benefits Act 1992 and so is *ultra vires*, and not to be applied in determining a claimant's earnings. The Commissioner also considers in some detail, at paras 22 to 34, the possible ramifications of the National Minimum Wage Act 1998. He ultimately concludes that "the general structure of the provisions for employed earners in the 1996 Computation of Earnings Regulations establishes a context which shows that what are to be taken into account are payments actually received, not entitlements, which have not resulted in payments." (para.32).

Para.(3)

3.12 Paragraph (3) provides the mechanism for determining notional earnings, which will need to be added to any actual earnings.

Rounding of fractions

3.13 **5.** Where any calculation under these Regulations results in a fraction of a penny that fraction shall, if it would be to the claimant's advantage, be treated as a penny, otherwise it shall be disregarded.

PART II

EMPLOYED EARNERS

GENERAL NOTE

3.14 Regulations 6 to 10 are replete with difficulty. In *DC v SSWP* [2008] UKUT 23 (AAC) under appeal in the name of *Cotton v Secretary of State for Work and Pensions*, the Judge said:

"... I have been trying to understand the operation of regulations 6 to 9 of the Social Security (Computation of Earnings) Regulations 1996. In the end, I have decided that was too ambitious a task. The way that those provisions operate is not entirely clear and they would benefit from being reconsidered, if not redrafted" (para.1).

It is perhaps trite to say that the purpose of the regulations is to identify what counts as earnings, to attribute earnings to particular weeks, and to provide a means for converting them to weekly amounts. The starting point is perhaps reg.9 which defines what constitute earnings of employed earners, and reg.10 which concerns net earnings. Regulation 6 provides the means for calculating the earnings of employed earners in terms of weeks. Regulation 7 treats earnings as paid on a particular date which means that the weeks to which they are attributable can be determined. Finally reg.8 provides the methods of converting earnings to weekly amounts. Particular difficulties seem to arise in relation to certain payments when employment comes to an end. The Commissioner in *CG/4172/2001* and the Judge in *DC v SSWP*, [2008] UKUT 23 (AAC) both accepted that such payments are attributable to a future period, since the money received is available for future expenditure. But the judge in the latter case also concluded:

"... the regulations do not necessarily produce an income that is in any way tied to the reality of the period for which payments are made or over which they are likely to be spent" (para.29).

Calculation of earnings of employed earners

6.—(1) Earnings derived from employment as an employed earner shall be calculated or estimated over a period determined in accordance with the following paragraphs and at a weekly amount determined in accordance with regulation 8 (calculation of weekly amount of earnings).

(2) Subject to paragraphs (3) and (5) to (8), the period over which a payment is to be taken into account—

(a) in a case where it is payable in respect of a period, shall be a period equal to a benefit week or such number of benefit weeks as comprise the period commencing on the date on which earnings are treated as paid under regulation 7 (date on which earnings are treated as paid) and ending on the day before the date on which earnings of the same kind (excluding earnings of the kind mentioned at regulation 9(1)(a) to (j)) and from the same source would, or would if the employment was continuing, next be treated as paid under that regulation;

(b) in any other case, shall be a period equal to such number of weeks as is equal to the number (less any fraction of a whole number) calculated in accordance with the formula—

$$\frac{P}{Q + R}$$

where—

P is the net earnings;

Q is the amount of the relevant earnings limit plus one penny; and

R is the total of the sums which would fall to be disregarded or deducted as appropriate under regulation 10(2) or (3) (calculation of net earnings of employed earners),

3.15

and that period shall begin on the date on which the payment is treated as paid under regulation 7 (date on which earnings are treated as paid).

(3) Where earnings not of the same kind are derived from the same source and the periods in respect of which those earnings would, but for this paragraph, fall to be taken into account overlap, wholly or partly, those earnings shall be taken into account over a period—

(a) equal to the aggregate length of those periods, and

(b) beginning with the earliest date on which any part of those earnings would otherwise be treated as paid under regulation 7 (date on which earnings are treated as paid).

(4) In a case to which paragraph (3) applies, earnings under regulation 9 (earnings of employed earners) shall be taken into account in the following order of priority—

(a) earnings normally derived from the employment;

(b) any payment to which paragraph (1)(b) or (c) of that regulation applies;

(c) any payment to which paragraph (1)(i) of that regulation applies;

(d) any payment to which paragraph (1)(d) of that regulation applies.

(5) Where earnings to which regulation 9(1)(b) to (d) (earnings of employed earners) applies are paid in respect of part of a day, those earnings shall be taken into account over a period equal to a week.

(6) Where earnings to which regulations 9(1)(i)(i) (earnings of employed earners) applies are paid in respect of or on the termination of any employment which is not part-time employment, the period over which they are to be taken into account shall be—

(a) a period equal to such number of weeks as is equal to the number (less any fraction of a whole number) obtained by dividing the net earnings by the maximum weekly amount which, on the date on which the payment of earnings is made, is specified in section 227(1) of the Employment Rights Act 1996; or

(b) a period equal to the length of the specified period,

whichever is the shorter, and that period shall begin on the date on which the payment is treated as paid under regulation 7 (date on which earnings are treated as paid).

(7) Any earnings to which regulation 9(1)(i)(ii) applies which are paid in respect of or on the termination of part-time employment, shall be taken into account over a period equal to one week.

(8) In this regulation—

"part-time employment" means—

(a) subject to the provisions of sub-paragraphs (b) to (d) of this definition, employment in which a person is engaged, or, where his hours of work fluctuate, he is engaged on average, for less than 16 hours a week being work for which payment is made or which is done in expectation of payment;

(b) subject to sub-paragraph (c) of this definition, the number of hours for which a person is engaged in work shall be determined—

(i) where no recognisable cycle has been established in respect of a person's work, by reference to the number of hours or, where those hours are likely to fluctuate, the average of the hours, which he is expected to work in a week;

(ii) where the number of hours for which he is engaged fluctuate, by reference to the average of hours worked over—

(aa)   if there is a recognisable cycle of work, the period of one complete cycle (including, where the cycle involves periods in which the person does not work, those periods but disregarding any other absences);

(bb)   in any other case, the period of five weeks immediately before the date of claim or the date [¹on which a revision or supersession of a decision falls to be made], or such other length of time as may, in the particular case, enable the person's average hours of work to be determined more accurately;

(c) where for the purpose of sub-paragraph (b)(ii)(aa) of this definition, a person's recognisable cycle of work at a school, other educational establishment or other place of employment is one year and includes periods of school holidays or similar vacations during which he does not work, those periods and any other periods not forming part of such holidays or vacations during which he is not required to work shall be disregarded in establishing the average hours for which he is engaged in work;

(d) for the purposes of sub paragraphs (a) and (b) of this definition, in determining the number of hours for which a person is engaged in work, that number shall include any time allowed to that person by his employer for a meal or for refreshment, but only where that person is, or expects to be, paid earnings in respect of that time;

"specified period" means a period equal to—

(a) a week or such number of weeks (less any fraction of a whole number) as comprise the period of notice which is applicable to a person, or would have been applicable if it had not been waived; less

(b) any part of that period during which the person has continued to work in the employment in question or in respect of which he has received a payment to which regulation 9(1)(c) applies,

and for the purposes of this definition "period of notice" means the period of notice of termination of employment to which a person is entitled by statute or by contract, whichever is the longer, or, if he is not entitled to such notice, the period of notice which is customary in the employment in question.

AMENDMENT

1. The Social Security Act 1998 (Commencement No. 9 and Savings and Consequental and Transitional Provisions) Order 1999 (SI 1999/2422), Sch.13, para.4 (September 6, 1999).

GENERAL NOTE

There are similarities between provisions of this regulation and reg.29 of the   **3.16** Income Support (General) Regulations 1987 and references to the annotations in *Vol.II: Income Support, Jobseeker's Allowance, Tax Credits and the Social Fund.*

Earnings are always related to a week or number of weeks. Those paid weekly or fortnightly (or other multiples of weeks) are likely to be easiest to deal with. In other cases (for example, monthly paid employees) the formula set out in the regulation will need to be applied.

Special rules apply to termination payments, which frequently causes difficulty, particularly where claimants have not fully appreciated their impact on benefit claims.

Paragraph (2)

3.17   In *CG/4172/2001*, the appellant received two final payments in respect of the termination of his employment on July 3, 2000. One was paid on June 25, 2000 representing his last full month's salary from his employment. Regulations 6(2)(a) and 7(b) could readily be applied to this payment. The second was paid on July 25, 2000 a consisted of a payment of £278.35 gross in respect of salary for the final working weeks and £1,031.13 gross representing 14 days accrued holiday pay up to his termination date in respect of holiday which had not been taken. The application of the same regulations enabled the salary payment to be taken into account: the start date was July 24, 2000 (the first day of the benefit week in which it was due to be paid) and the end date was August 20, 2000 (the day before the first day of the benefit week in which the next salary payment would have been made if the employment continued): para.9.

The holiday pay was much more problematic. Regulation 6(2)(a) only applies if the holiday pay was payable "in respect of a period". If it was not, then reg.6(2)(b) applied. The Commissioner concludes (following earlier decisions) that it was paid "in respect of a period". The Commissioner also concludes that the holiday pay was due on the termination of the employment. This should be interpreted in accordance with its ordinary meaning: the employment terminated on July 3, 2000 and so this was the start date for attributing this period. Determining the end date was considerably less straightforward. Regulation 6(2)(a) could not easily be applied to payments such as holiday pay. Regulation 6(2)(a) refers to "earnings of the same kind"; and reg.9 lists types of payments which are included within the concept of "earnings". This includes "holiday pay". The Commissioner concludes that the only sensible meaning of the words in reg.9 is that holiday pay and ordinary earnings both constitute earnings of the same kind.

That conclusion, according to the Commissioner, left a problem with the interpretation of paragraphs (3) and (4) of regulation 6: see para.14 of the decision. The Commissioner felt compelled to conclude that the words "earnings of the same kind" have a different meaning in reg.6(2)(a) from that in reg.6(3) and (4). As a result the end date for the holiday pay was July 23, 2000. But the effect of the overlapping provisions in paragraphs (3) and (4) is that holiday pay (as having a lower order of priority is deemed to run for the period of three weeks from July 24, 2000. So the final conclusion was as follows:

- First salary payment attributable to June 19 to July 23, 2000,

- Second salary payment attributable to July 24, to August 20, 2000,

- Holiday pay attributable to July 24 to August 13, 2000.

The judge in *DC v SSWP* [2008] UKUT 23 (AAC) has followed the Commissioner's decision. In doing so, the judge observes:

44. Left entirely to my own devices, I would have been tempted to decide that, within the meaning of regulation 6(2), accrued holiday pay was not paid in respect of a period. That would mean that regulation 6(2)(b) would apply.

45. I have not taken that course for three reasons. First, in *Chief Benefit Officer v Cunningham* [1985] ICR 660, Waller LJ (at page 665) said that one day accrued holiday pay was paid for a period. Second, neither party argued that regulation 6(2)(b) applied. Third, regulation 6(2)(b) operates to attribute a payment to the maximum number of weeks over which the claimant can be excluded from benefit. Mr Richards argued that the claimant had an entitlement under section 70 to a carer's allowance and that a provision that deprived him of it should be interpreted restrictively. I do not accept that argument. Section 70 does not confer an entitlement. It sets out the basic conditions and provides for more detailed provisions to be made by regulations. Regulation 6 is one of those regulations. However, given that the provision does operate harshly on claimant and the

Secretary of State has not argued that it applies, I do not consider it appropriate to apply regulation 6(2)(b).

Leave to appeal has been granted by the judge on March 2, 2009, and the appeal is under the name *Cotton* v *Secretary of State for Work and Pensions*.

Date on which earnings are treated as paid

7.—Earnings to which regulation 6 (calculation of earnings of employed earners) or 11(2) (calculation of earnings of self-employed earners) applies shall be treated as paid— 3.18

(a) (i) in the case of a payment in respect of an adult dependant of an increase of maternity allowance payable under section 82(2) of the Contributions and Benefits Act or an increase of [1 carer's allowance] payable under paragraph 7 of Schedule 2 to the Social Security Benefit (Dependency) Regulations 1977; or

(ii) in the case of a payment in respect of an adult dependant who is not residing with the claimant of an increase of Category A or Category C retirement pension payable under section 83(2)(b) or 84(1) and 84(2)(b) of the Contributions and Benefits Act or a disablement pension where the claimant is entitled to an unemployability supplement payable under paragraph 6(1)(a)(ii) of Schedule 7 to the Contributions and Benefits Act,

on the first day of the benefit week following the benefit week in which the payment is due to be paid;

(b) in any other case, on the first day of the benefit week in which the payment is due to be paid.

AMENDMENT

1. The Social Security Benefit (Computation of Earnings) (Amendment) Regulations 2002 (SI 2002/2823), reg.2 (April 1, 2003).

Calculation of weekly amount of earnings

8.—(1) For the purposes of regulation 6 (calculation of earnings of employed earners), subject to paragraphs (2) to (4), where the period in respect of which a payment is made— 3.19

(a) does not exceed a week, the weekly amount shall be the amount of that payment;

(b) exceeds a week, the weekly amount shall be determined—

(i) in a case where that period is a month, by multiplying the amount of that payment by 12 and dividing the product by 52;

(ii) in a case where that period is three months, by multiplying the amount of the payment by 4 and dividing the product by 52;

(iii) in a case where that period is a year, by dividing the amount of the payment by 52;

(iv) in any other case, by multiplying the amount of the payment by 7 and dividing the product by the number equal to the number of days in the period in respect of which it is made.

(2) Where a payment of earnings from a particular source is or has been paid regularly and that payment falls to be taken into account in the same benefit week as a payment of the same kind and from the same source, the amount of those earnings to be taken into account in any one benefit week shall not exceed the weekly amount determined under paragraph (1)(a) or

(b), as the case may be, of the payment which under regulation 7 (date on which earnings are treated as paid) is treated as paid first.

(3) Where the amount of the claimant's net earnings fluctuates and has changed more than once, or a claimant's regular pattern of work is such that he does not work every week, the application of the foregoing paragraphs may be modified so that the weekly amount of his earnings is determined by reference to his average weekly earnings—

    (a) if there is a recognisable cycle of work, over the period of one complete cycle (including, where the cycle involves periods in which the claimant does no work, those periods but disregarding any other absences);

    (b) if any other case, over a period of five weeks or such other period as may, in the particular case, enable the claimant's average weekly earnings to be determined more accurately.

(4) Where any payment of earnings is taken into account under paragraph (7) of regulation 6 (calculation of earnings of employed earners), over the period specified in that paragraph, the amount to be taken into account shall be equal to the amount of the payment.

GENERAL NOTE

3.20   *CG/4941/2003* concerned an overpayment of invalid care allowance which had arisen when fluctuations in the claimant's earnings took her out of entitlement to the benefit for certain weeks. The Commissioner provides useful guidance on the interpretation of reg.8 in the decision:

    18. Thus in simple terms, for a person both working and paid on a regular weekly basis, say on Fridays, the earnings for each benefit week starting on Monday will be the amount of the payment he or she receives on the Friday of the same week, and the normal rule is that if those earnings are over the weekly limit in force on the last day of that week, he or she will be "gainfully employed" for ICA purposes throughout the next benefit week starting on the following Monday. For a person paid on a regular monthly basis on the last working day of each calendar month, as this claimant was from 1 July 2001 onwards, the monthly earnings are treated as paid on the Monday of the benefit week that contains the actual monthly pay day, and that payment is treated as giving the claimant "earnings" for each of the (four or five) benefit weeks starting with that one and ending with the one before the week that will contain the next regular monthly pay day; the weekly amount of the earnings in each of those weeks being taken as the most recent monthly payment multiplied by 12 and divided by 52. For persons such as the claimant having fluctuating earnings (but, as is agreed, no recognisable "cycle" of work and non-work to bring into play the separate provision in regulation 8(3)(a) for such cases) the weekly or monthly payments received *may* instead be averaged under regulation 8(3)(b), so as to substitute a different weekly figure for the "earnings" attributable to the claimant, though still over the period of benefit weeks which each actual payment of earnings is treated as having to cover for the purposes of regulations 6 and 7.

    19. As the very helpful and detailed written submission of Mr Cahill on behalf of the Secretary of State points out, regulation 8(3)(b) gives the Secretary of State a discretion to be applied rationally on a case by case basis, but is limited in its purpose to the use of a five-week or other period in place of the actual weekly, monthly or other calculation under regulation 8(1) to **"enable the claimant's average weekly earnings to be determined more accurately"**; and this is less clear that it might be since strictly the *accuracy* of an average is simply a matter of doing the arithmetic correctly, irrespective of the periods you happen to select for the calculation. Regulation 8(3) must

I think be taken as intended less literally (or mathematically), to mean that the Secretary of State is to have the power of substituting an alternative averaging calculation to produce a standardised weekly figure for the week or month, etc., identified in regulation 8(1) as the one in respect of which a given payment is actually made *where he is satisfied this would more accurately reflect the true rate of the claimant's weekly earnings* current at the period for which a week by week figure for those earnings has to be identified, in order to determine some question of entitlement: such as the one here, of whether or at what point the claimant had crossed the line of having weekly earnings over the limit to make her count as "gainfully employed" for invalid care allowance purposes in each day of the following benefit week.

20. It has to be borne in mind that the overriding purpose of the exercise, in the context of a weekly benefit such as invalid care allowance which is there to provide assistance with current weekly living expenses for people without sufficient weekly earnings of their own, is the relatively short term one of producing a working week by week figure so as to know as quickly as possible whether benefit is payable or not. Mr Cahill is I think right in saying that the application of regulation 8(3) in this context may often have to be more a matter of judgment than of science, and there may be no necessarily "right" answer: it has to be a matter of dealing reasonably with the evidence of actual earnings for the current payment periods as disclosed (or as it should be disclosed) by the claimant to the Secretary of State week by week or month by month. It cannot in my judgment be said that the existence of the discretionary power in regulation 8(3)(b) requires the Secretary of State in a case such as this to "wait and see" over a very extended period, and then juggle and aggregate a whole succession of payments that were each in fact made in respect of specific weekly and monthly periods either side of a significant change in the rate of working and earning, so as to treat them as in effect equivalent to one lumped-together payment for work spread evenly throughout. There are no grounds on which it could be described as "more accurate" to ignore a step-change in the rate of working and earning such as shown here in the late summer of 2001, and pretend that the claimant's work and earnings had carried on at one uniform rate all year.

CG/0607/2008 concerned the calculation of earnings in relation to the earnings limit for entitlement to a carer's allowance. This lengthy decision contains much useful comment and guidance on such cases, which seem to be a problematic area (perhaps because there is no taper—if a person's earnings are one penny over the limit, then entitlement to the carer's allowance ceases completely). The context was one in which an informal employment contract was intended to provide the appellant with earnings at, but not above, the earnings limit for entitlement to a carer's allowance. The appeal turned on the proper calculation of the appellant's weekly earnings. The Commissioner counsels care in looking at the definition provision in the regulations, and goes on to comment:

36. The Regulations have the primary purpose of identifying the weekly amount of a claimant's earnings. They provide answers to the questions necessary for the conversion of actual earnings of an employee into weekly amounts of earnings by which to test those earnings against the earnings limit. They are the same essential questions that must be asked in any exercise of assessing earnings for the application of any social security or tax rate or limit. There must be defined periods with defined start and end dates and defined rules for attributing actual earnings to those periods. The key questions are:

(1) Are earnings included when received, or when entitlement arises, or on some other basis?

(2) When are specific earnings received or earned?

(3) How are specific earnings linked to specific periods of assessment or benefit?

The use of deeming provisions in the Regulations means that the answers provided to those questions for carer's allowance purposes are not findings of fact about what happened, but are questions of law about how the deeming provisions in the Regulations are to be applied to those facts.

Earnings of employed earners

3.21

9.—(1) Subject to paragraphs (2) and (3), "earnings", in the case of employment as an employed earner, means any remuneration or profit derived from that employment and includes—

(a) any bonus or commission;

(b) any payment in lieu of remuneration except any periodic sum paid to a claimant on account of the termination of his employment by reason of redundancy;

(c) any payment in lieu of notice;

(d) any holiday pay except any payable more than four weeks after the termination or interruption of employment;

(e) any payment by way of a retainer;

(f) any payment made by the claimant's employer in respect of expenses not wholly, exclusively and necessarily incurred in the performance of the duties of the employment, including any payment made by the claimant's employer in respect of—

    (i) travelling expenses incurred by the claimant between his home and place of employment;

    (ii) expenses incurred by the claimant under arrangements made for the care of a member of his family owing to the claimant's absence from home;

(g) any award of compensation made under section 112(4) or 117(3)(a) of the Employment Rights Act 1996 (remedies and compensation);

(h) any such sum as is referred to in section 112(3) of the Contributions and Benefits Act (certain sums to be earnings for social security purposes);

(i) where—

    (i) a payment of compensation is made in respect of employment which is not part-time employment and that payment is not less than the maximum weekly amount, the amount of the compensation less the deductible remainder, where that is applicable;

    (ii) a payment of compensation is made in respect of employment which is part-time employment, the amount of the compensation;

[1 (j) any remuneration paid by or on behalf of an employer to the claimant in respect of a period throughout which the claimant is—

    (i) on maternity leave;

    (ii) on paternity leave;

    (iii) on adoption leave; or

    (iv) absent from work because he is ill.]

(2) For the purposes of paragraph (1)(i)(i) the "deductible remainder"—

(a) applies in cases where dividing the amount of the compensation by the maximum weekly amount produces a whole number plus a fraction; and

(b) is equal to the difference between—

    (i) the amount of the compensation; and

    (ii) the product of the maximum weekly amount multiplied by the whole number.

(3) "Earnings" shall not include any payment in respect of expenses wholly, exclusively and necessarily incurred in the performance of the duties of the employment.

(4) In this regulation—

[¹ "adoption leave" means a period of absence from work on ordinary or additional adoption leave under section 75A or 75B of the Employment Rights Act 1996;]

"compensation" means any payment made in respect of or on the termination of employment in a case where a person has not received or received only part of a payment in lieu of notice due or which would have been due to him had he not waived his right to receive it, other than—

    (a) any payment specified in paragraph (1)(a) to (h);

    (b) any payment specified in paragraph (3);

    (c) any redundancy payment within the meaning of section 135 of the Employment Rights Act 1996;

    (d) any refund of contributions to which that person was entitled under an occupational pension scheme;

    (e) any compensation payable by virtue of section 173 or section 178(3) or (4) of the Education Reform Act 1988;

[¹ "maternity leave" means a period during which a woman is absent from work because she is pregnant or has given birth to a child, and at the end of which she has a right to return to work either under the terms of her contract of employment or under Part 8 of the Employment Rights Act 1996;]

"maximum weekly amount" means the maximum weekly amount which, on the date on which the payment of compensation is made, is specified in section 227(1) of the Employment Rights Act 1996;

"part-time employment" has the same meaning as in regulation 6(8) (calculation of earnings of employed earners);

[¹ "paternity leave" means a period of absence from work on leave under section 80A or 80B of the Employment Rights Act 1996.]

AMENDMENT

1. The Social Security Benefit (Computation of Earnings) (Amendment) Regulations 2002 (SI 2002/2823), reg.2 (April 1, 2003).

GENERAL NOTE

This regulation mirrors reg.35 of the Income Support (General) Regulations 1987 and reference to the annotations in *Social Security Legislation: Vol. II* is advised since a number of the provisions of reg.35 have been the subject of consideration by the Commissioners.

    The claimant in *CP/3017/2004* had made an advance claim for an increase of his retirement pension in respect of his wife. She had earnings and the decision maker had determined that these were in excess of the specified figure with the result that the claimant had no entitlement to the increase. The appeal tribunal confirmed the decision, but the Commissioner found that they had erred in law and substituted his own decision awarding the increase. The claimant's wife worked as a sales promoter of a variety of goods in supermarkets. She made the planning

3.22

arrangements for promotional visits to the supermarkets from home and attended at supermarkets in the region to ensure the successful operation of the promotion. She received expenses relating to travel (including travel from home), maintenance of her car and car parking. The Commissioner concluded that, in the particular circumstances of this case, the expenses were to be excluded from the calculation of the earnings of the claimant's wife under reg.9(3), which trumped the provisions in reg.9(1)(f)(i).

CG/0645/2008 raised, among other things, the question of the proper computation of a person's weekly earnings in relation to the earnings limit for entitlement to a carer's allowance. The tribunal made its decision without reference to the regulations, which are described as "a comprehensive code" (para.54). The facts were complex since the appellant argued that part of what she received was on behalf of a third party. The Deputy Commissioner says:

> 57. In my view there is a common thread running through the definitions in section 3 of SSCBA 1992 and the 1996 Regulations. That is, however expansively one defines "earnings", the earnings in question must still be the earnings of the individual in question. Thus "any remuneration or profit derived from employment" must mean derived from the claimant's employment, not from someone else's employment.

The Deputy Commissioner agrees that what are to be taken into account are payments actually received, not entitlement which has not resulted in payments, that is, payments actually received for service rendered under that person's own contract of employment.

Calculation of net earnings of employed earners

3.23   **10.**—(1) For the purposes of regulations 3 (calculation of earnings) and 6 (calculation of earnings of employed earners) the earnings of a claimant derived from employment as an employed earner to be taken into account shall, subject to paragraphs (2) and (3), be his net earnings.

(2) Except in a case to which paragraph (3) applies, there shall be disregarded or deducted as appropriate from a claimant's net earnings—

  (a) any sum, where applicable, specified in Schedule 1; and
  (b) any relevant child care charges to which Schedule 2 applies up to a maximum deduction in respect of any claimant of £60 per week.

(3) In the case of entitlement to [¹ carer's allowance] under section 70 of the Contributions and Benefits Act there shall be disregarded or deducted as appropriate from a claimant's net earnings—

  (a) any sum, where applicable, specified in Schedule 1; and
  (b) any care charges to which Schedule 3 applies up to a maximum deduction, in respect of such care charges incurred by any claimant, of 50% of his net earnings less those sums, if any, specified in Schedule 1 which are disregarded.

(4) For the purposes of paragraph (1) net earnings shall be calculated by taking into account the gross earnings of the claimant from that employment less—

  (a) any amount deducted from those earnings by way of—
    (i) income tax;
    (ii) primary Class 1 contributions under the Contributions and Benefits Act; and
  (b) one half of any sum paid by the claimant in respect of a pay period by way of a contribution towards an occupation or personal pension scheme.

AMENDMENT

1. The Social Security Benefit (Computation of Earnings) (Amendment) Regulations 2002 (SI 2002/2823), reg.2 (April 1, 2003).

GENERAL NOTE

This regulation follows, with modification, reg.36 of the Income Support (General) Regulations 1987. Child care costs are to be disregarded if Sch.2 applies provided they do not exceed £60 per week. Where entitlement to carer's allowance (formerly invalid care allowance) is the relevant benefit, care charges are to be disregarded if Sch.3 applies provided they do not exceed the maximum calculated in accordance with reg.10(3)(b).

3.24

Para. (3)

In *CG/4024/2001* the Commissioner had to consider whether the cost of the rental for a careline telephone link constituted a "care charge" under reg.10(3). The claimant paid a small rental for the telephone line, which allowed her daughter (who suffered from epilepsy) to press a button held on a cord around her neck. This sounded a warning with the monitoring station and established a telephone link; the claimant could then attend to provide care, or arrange for someone else to do so. Both the tribunal and the Commissioner decided that the cost of the rental was not a care charge. The Commissioner says,

3.25

"16. It is not necessary for me to define the word 'care'. It is sufficient to say that in the context it is not appropriate to cover the link. The natural interpretation of the arrangement is that the monitoring arrangement exists to allow someone to be called who can care for the claimant's daughter. It does not itself provide that care. Nor does the person who monitors alarms at the station.

17. The tribunal came to the correct conclusion and the only one that was open to it as a reasonable tribunal familiar with the use of language. I direct the tribunal at the rehearing that the cost of the line rental is not deductible."

PART III

SELF-EMPLOYED EARNERS

Calculation of earnings of self-employed earners

11.—(1) Except where paragraph (2) applies, where a claimant's earnings consist of earnings from employment as a self-employed earner the weekly amount of his earnings shall be determined by reference to his average weekly earnings from that employment—

3.26

(a) over a period of one year; or

(b) where the claimant has recently become engaged in that employment or there has been a change which is likely to affect the normal pattern of business, over such other period as may, in any particular case, enable the weekly amount of his earnings to be determined more accurately.

(2) Where the claimant's earnings consist of royalties or sums paid periodically for or in respect of any copyright those earnings shall be taken into account over a period equal to such number of weeks as is equal to the

number (less any fraction of a whole number) calculated in accordance with the formula—

$$\frac{S}{T + U}$$

where—
S is the earnings;
T is the relevant earnings limit plus one penny; and
U is the total of the sums which would fall to be disregarded or deducted as appropriate under regulation 13(2) or (3) (calculation of net profit of self-employed earners).

(3) The period mentioned in paragraph (2) shall begin on the date on which the payment is treated as paid under regulation 7 (date on which earnings are treated as paid).

Earnings of self-employed earners

3.27   **12.**—(1) [1 . . .] "Earnings", in the case of employment as a self-employed earner, means the gross receipts of the employment and shall include any allowance paid under section 2 of the Employment and Training Act 1973 or section 2 of the Enterprise and New Towns (Scotland) Act 1990 to the claimant for the purpose of assisting him in carrying on his business.
[1 . . .]

AMENDMENT

1. The Social Security Benefit (Computation of Earnings) (Amendment) Regulations 2007 (SI 2007/2613) (October 1, 2007).

Calculation of net profit of self-employed earners

3.28   **13.**—(1) For the purposes of regulations 3 (calculation of earnings) and 11 (calculation of earnings of self-employed earners), the earnings of a claimant to be taken into account shall be—

    (a) in the case of a self-employed earner who is engaged in employment on his own account, the net profit derived from that employment;

    (b) in the case of a self-employed earner whose employment is carried on in partnership or is that of a share fisherman his share of the net profit derived from that employment less—

        (i) an amount in respect of income tax and of social security contributions payable under the Contributions and Benefits Act calculated in accordance with regulation 14 (deduction of tax and contributions for self-employed earners); and

        (ii) one half of any premium paid in the period that is relevant under regulation 11 in respect of a retirement annuity contract or a personal pension scheme;

    (c) in paragraph (b) "share fisherman" means any person who—

        (i) is ordinarily employed in the fishing industry otherwise than under a contract of service, as a master or member of the crew of any fishing boat manned by more than one person, and is remunerated in respect of that employment in whole or in part by a share of profits or gross earnings of the fishing boat; or

   (ii) has ordinarily been so employed, but who by reason of age or infirmity permanently ceases to be so employed and becomes ordinarily engaged in employment ashore in Great Britain, otherwise than under a contract of service, making or mending any gear appurtenant to a fishing boat or performing other services ancillary to or in connection with that boat and is remunerated in respect of that employment in whole or in part by a share of the profits or gross earnings of that boat and has not ceased to be ordinarily engaged in such employment.

(2) Except in a case to which paragraph (3) applies, there shall be disregarded or deducted as appropriate from a claimant's net profit—

   (a) any sum, where applicable, specified in Schedule 1; and

   (b) any relevant child care charges to which Schedule 2 applies up to a maximum deduction in respect of any claimant of £60 per week.

(3) In the case of entitlement to [¹ carer's allowance] under section 70 of the Contributions and Benefits Act there shall be disregarded or deducted as appropriate from a claimant's net profit—

   (a) any sum where applicable, specified in Schedule 1; and

   (b) any care charges to which Schedule 3 applies up to a maximum deduction, in respect of such care charges incurred by any claimant, of 50% of his net profit less those sums, if any, specified in Schedule 1 which are disregarded.

(4) For the purposes of paragraph (1)(a), the net profit of the employment shall, except where paragraph (10) applies, be calculated by taking into account the earnings of the employment over the period determined under regulation 11 (calculation of earnings of self-employed earners) less—

   (a) subject to paragraphs (6) to (8), any expenses wholly and exclusively defrayed in that period for the purposes of that employment;

   (b) an amount in respect of—

      (i) income tax; and

      (ii) social security contributions payable under the Contributions and Benefits Act, calculated in accordance with regulation 14 (deduction of tax and contributions for self-employed earners); and

   (c) one half of any premium paid in the period that is relevant under regulation 11 in respect of a retirement annuity contract or a personal pension scheme.

(5) For the purposes of paragraph (1)(b), the net profit of the employment shall be calculated by taking into account the earnings of the employment over the period determined under regulation 11 less, subject to paragraphs (6) to (8), any expenses wholly and exclusively defrayed in that period for the purposes of that employment.

(6) Subject to paragraph (7), no deduction shall be made under paragraph (4)(a) or (5) in respect of—

   (a) any capital expenditure;

   (b) the depreciation of any capital asset;

   (c) any sum employed or intended to be employed in the setting up or expansion of the employment;

   (d) any loss incurred before the beginning of the period determined under regulation 11 (calculation of earnings of self-employed earners);

    (e) the repayment of capital on any loan taken out for the purposes of the employment;

    (f) any expenses incurred in providing business entertainment.

[4 (g) where the claimant provides accommodation to another person in the dwelling the claimant occupies as his home, any expenses defrayed by the claimant in providing the accommodation to that person (including any defrayed in providing board as well as lodging).]

    (7) A deduction shall be made under paragraph (4)(a) or (5) in respect of the repayment of capital on any loan used for—

    (a) the replacement in the course of business of equipment or machinery; and

    (b) the repair of an existing business asset except to the extent that any sum is payable under an insurance policy for its repair.

    (8) [2 A deduction shall not be made] in respect of any expenses under paragraph (4)(a) or (5) where [3 the Secretary of State] is not satisfied that the expense has been defrayed or, having regard to the nature of the expense and its amount, that it has been reasonably incurred.

    (9) For the avoidance of doubt—

    (a) a deduction shall not be made under paragraph (4)(a) or (5) in respect of any sum unless it has been expended for the purposes of the business;

    (b) a deduction shall be made thereunder in respect of—

        (i) the excess of any VAT paid over VAT received in the period determined under regulation 11 (calculation of earnings of self-employed earners);

       (ii) any income expended in the repair of an existing asset except to the extent that any sum is payable under an insurance policy for its repair;

      (iii) any payment of interest on a loan taken out for the purposes of the employment.

    (10) Where a claimant is engaged in employment as a child minder the net profit of the employment shall be one-third of the earnings of that employment, less—

    (a) an amount in respect of—

        (i) income tax;

       (ii) social security contributions payable under the Contributions and Benefits Act, calculated in accordance with regulation 14 (deduction of tax and contributions for self-employed earners); and

    (b) one half of any premium paid in respect of a retirement annuity contract or a personal pension scheme.

    (11) Notwithstanding regulation 11 (calculation of earnings of self-employed earners) and the foregoing paragraphs, [3 the Secretary of State] may assess any item of a claimant's earnings or expenditure over a period other than that determined under regulation 11 as may, in the particular case, enable the weekly amount of that item of earnings or expenditure to be determined more accurately.

    (12) For the avoidance of doubt where a claimant is engaged in employment as a self-employed earner and he is engaged in one or more other employments as a self-employed or employed earner any loss incurred in any one of his employments shall not be offset against his earnings in any other of his employments.

518

AMENDMENTS

1. The Social Security Benefit (Computation of Earnings) (Amendment) Regulations 2002 (SI 2002/2823), reg.2 (April 1, 2003).
2. The Social Security Act 1998 (Commencement No. 9 and Savings and Consequential and Transitional Provisions) Order 1999 (SI 1999/2422), Sch.13, para.5 (September 6, 1999).
3. The Social Security Act 1998 (Commencement No. 9 and Savings and Consequential and Transitional Provisions) Order 1999 (SI 1999/2422), Sch.13, para.1 (September 6, 1999).
4. The Social Security Benefit (Computation of Earnings) (Amendment) Regulations 2007 (SI 2007/2613) (October 1, 2007).

GENERAL NOTE

This regulation largely mirrors reg.38 of the Income Support (General) Regulations **3.29**
1987. See annotations to that provision in *Social Security: Legislation, Vol. II.*

In *Secretary of State v Doyle*, reported as *R(IB) 1/06*, the Court of Appeal ruled that the Computations of Earnings Regulations apply for the purpose of the calculation of entitlement to entitlement to incapacity benefit. *CIB/4174/2003*, decision of January 26, 2007, is the Commissioner's consideration of the application of the Computation of Earnings Regulations to the circumstances of the case on remission of the appeal for consideration by the Commissioner. The decision also includes as appendices the earlier decision and the decision of the Court of Appeal.

The Commissioner had to consider whether the deduction provided for in reg.13(2) and para.3 to Sch. 1 for a fixed-rate deduction to be made from earnings from board and lodging accommodation is in addition to the disregard provided for in reg.13(4) (a). The Commissioner concluded that the regulations did provide for both to be applied to a claimant's case (though in the particular circumstances presented by the claimant that was not necessary to bring him within the earnings limit for incapacity benefit).

Note the effect of the amendment to reg. 13(6) by the addition of a new subparagraph (f). The explanatory memorandum to the amending regulations says:

"A Social Security Commissioner recently decided that due to way the regulations were drafted, when the accommodation is provided in the customer's home, the formula disregard is to be applied twice, together with a further disregard of any other allowable business expenses. This provides for the provision of 3 separate disregards. The amended regulations will ensure that only one disregard of £20 and then 50% of the balance will be applied to any income from boarders, and restore the original policy intent."

Deduction of tax and contributions for self-employed earners

14.—(1) The amount to be deducted in respect of income tax under **3.30**
regulation 13(1)(b)(i), (4)(b)(i) or (10)(a)(i) (calculation of net profit of self-employed earners) shall be calculated on the basis of the amount of chargeable income and as if that income were assessable to income tax at the lower rate or, as the case may be, the lower rate and the basic rate of tax less only the personal relief to which the claimant is entitled under sections 257(1), 257A(1) and 259 of the Income and Corporation Taxes Act 1988 (personal reliefs) as is appropriate to his circumstances; but, if the period determined under regulation 11 (calculation of earnings of self-employed earners) is less than a year, the earnings to which the lower rate of tax is to be applied and the amount of the personal relief deductible under this paragraph shall be calculated on a pro rata basis.

(2) The amount to be deducted in respect of social security

contributions under regulation 13(1)(b)(i), (4)(b)(ii) or (10)(a)(ii) shall be the total of—

    (a) the amount of Class 2 contributions payable under section 11(1) or, as the case may be, 11(3) of the Contributions and Benefits Act at the rate applicable at the date [1 on which a decision is made by the Secretary of State under Chapter II of Part I of the Social Security Act 1998 or regulations made thereunder] except where the claimant's chargeable income is less than the amount specified in section 11(4) of that Act (small earnings exception) for the tax year in which that date falls; but if the assessment period is less than a year, the amount specified for that year shall be reduced pro rata; and

    (b) the amount of Class 4 contributions (if any) which would be payable under section 15 of that Act (Class 4 contributions recoverable under the Income Tax Acts) at the percentage rate applicable at the date [1 on which a decision is made by the Secretary of State under Chapter II of Part I of the Social Security Act 1998 or regulations made thereunder] on so much of the chargeable income as exceeds the lower limit but does not exceed the upper limit of profits and gains applicable for the tax year in which that date falls; but if the assessment period is less than a year, those limits shall be reduced pro rata.

(3) In this regulation "chargeable income" means—

    (a) except where sub-paragraph (b) applies, the earnings derived from the employment less any expenses deducted under paragraph (4)(a) or, as the case may be, (5) of regulation 13;

    (b) in the case of employment as a child minder, one-third of the earnings of that employment.

AMENDMENT

1. The Social Security Act 1998 (Commencement No. 9 and Savings and Consequential and Transitional Provisions) Order 1999 (SI 1999/2422), Sch.13, para.6 (September 6, 1999).

PART IV

TRANSITIONAL PROVISIONS, CONSEQUENTIAL AMENDMENTS AND REVOCATIONS

3.31   *Regulations 15–18 omitted.*

SCHEDULE 1   **Regulations 10(2) and 13(2)**

SUMS TO BE DISREGARDED IN THE CALCULATION OF EARNINGS

3.32   **1.**—Any payment made to the claimant by a person who normally resides with the claimant, which is a contribution towards that person's living and accommodation costs, except where that person is residing with the claimant in circumstances to which paragraph 2 or 3 refers.

    2.—Where the claimant occupies a dwelling as his home and the dwelling is also occupied by another person and there is a contractual liability to make payments to the claimant in respect of the occupation of the dwelling by that person or a member of his family—

    (a) £4 of the aggregate of any payments made in respect of any one week in respect of the occupation of the dwelling by that person or a member of his family, or by that person and a member of his family; and

(b) a further £9.25, where the aggregate of any such payments is inclusive of an amount for heating.

3.—Where the claimant occupies a dwelling as his home and he provides in that dwelling board and lodging accommodation, an amount, in respect of each person for whom such accommodation is provided for the whole or any part of a week, equal to—

(a) where the aggregate of any payments made in respect of any one week in respect of such accommodation provided to such person does not exceed £20.00, 100% of such payments; or

(b) where the aggregate of any such payments exceeds £20.00, £20.00 and 50% of the excess over £20.00.

4.—Except in the case of a claimant who is absent from Great Britain and not disqualified for receiving any benefit, pension, allowance or supplement, by virtue of the Social Security Benefit (Persons Abroad) Regulations 1975—

(a) any earnings derived from employment which are payable in a country outside the United Kingdom for such period during which there is a prohibition against the transfer to the United Kingdom of those earnings;

(b) where a payment of earnings is made in a currency other than sterling, any banking charge or commission payable in converting that payment into sterling.

5.—Any earnings which are due to be paid before the date of claim and which would otherwise fall to be taken into account in the same benefit week as a payment of the same kind and from the same source.

6.—Any payment made by a local authority to the claimant with whom a person is accommodated by virtue of arrangements made under section 23(2)(a) of the Children Act 1989 (provision of accommodation and maintenance for a child whom they are looking after) or, as the case may be, section 21 of the Social Work (Scotland) Act 1968 or by a voluntary organisation under section 59(1)(a) of the 1989 Act (provision of accommodation by voluntary organisations) or by a care authority under regulation 9 of the Boarding-out and Fostering of Children (Scotland) Regulations 1985 (provision of accommodation and maintenance for children in care).

7.—Any payment made by a health authority, local authority or voluntary organisation to the claimant in respect of a person who is not normally a member of the claimant's household but is temporarily in his care.

8.—In respect of regulation 16 of the Social Security (General Benefit) Regulations 1982 any earnings not earned during the period of the award.

9.—Any bounty paid at intervals of at least one year and derived from employments as—

(a) a part-time member of a fire brigade maintained in pursuance of the Fire Services Acts 1947 to 1959;

[¹(aa) a part-time fire-fighter employed by a fire and rescue authority;]

(b) an auxiliary coastguard in respect of coastal rescue activities;

(c) a person engaged part-time in the manning or launching of a lifeboat;

(d) a member of any territorial or reserve force prescribed in Part I of Schedule 3 to the Social Security (Contributions) Regulations 1979.

10.—Any amount by way of refund of income tax deducted from profits or emoluments chargeable to income tax under Schedule D or E.

11.—In the case of employment as an employed earner, any advance of earnings or any loan made by the claimant's employer.

[² **12.**—(1) Any earnings, other than items to which sub-paragraph (2) applies, paid or due to be paid from the claimant's employment as an employed earner which ended before the day in respect of which the claimant first satisfies the conditions for entitlement to the benefit, pension or allowance to which the claim relates.

(2) This sub-paragraph applies to—

(a) any payment by way of occupational or personal pension; and

(b) except in a case where the claimant's employment terminated by reason of retirement at a time when he had attained pensionable age (within the meaning given by rules in paragraph 1 of Schedule 4 to the Pensions Act 1995)—

(i) any payment or remuneration of the nature described in regulation 9(1)(e) or (j), and

(ii) any award or sum of the nature described in regulation 9(1)(g) or (h) (including any payment made following the settlement of a complaint to an employment tribunal or of court proceedings).

(3) Sub-paragraph (1) is subject to the following provisions.

(4) Sub-paragraph (1) does not apply in relation to a claim for, or an award of, incapacity benefit (within the meaning given by paragraph 11 of Schedule 4 to the Welfare Reform Act 2007) or severe disablement allowance (also within the meaning given by that paragraph).

(5) Sub-paragraph (1) applies in relation to a claim for an increase in benefit under Part IV of the Contributions and Benefits Act (increases in respect of dependants) only in a case where—
    (a) the spouse or partner or other adult in respect of whom that claim is made was in employment as an employed earner, but
    (b) that employment ended before the day referred to in sub-paragraph (1).]

AMENDMENTS

1. The Fire and Rescue Services Act 2004 (Consequential Amendments) (England) Order 2004 (SI 2004/3168) art.39 (December 30, 2004) (in relation to England only). The Fire and Rescue Services Act 2004 (Consequential Amendments) (Wales) Order 2005 (SI 2005/2929) (October 25, 2005) (in relation to Wales only).
2. The Social Security Benefit (Computation of Earnings) (Amendment) Regulations 2007 (SI 2007/2613) (October 1, 2007).

GENERAL NOTE

3.33   Pt I of Sch.3 to the Social Security (Contributions) Regulations 1979 (SI 1979/591, as amended) reads:

"Prescribed establishments and organisations for purposes of section 128(3) of the Act

1. Any of the regular navy, military or air forces of the Crown.
2. Retired and Emergency Lists of Officers of the Royal Navy.
3. Royal Naval Reserves (including Women's Royal Naval Reserve and Queen Alexandra's Royal Naval Nursing Service Reserve).
4. Royal Marines Reserve.
5. Army Reserves (including Regular Army Reserve of Officers, Regular Reserves, Long Term Reserve and Army Pensioners).
6. Territorial and Army Volunteer Reserve.
7. Royal Air Force Reserves (including Royal Air Force Reserve of Officers, Women's Royal Air Force Reserve of Officers, Royal Air Force Volunteer Reserve, Women's Royal Air Force Volunteer Reserve, Class E Reserve of Airmen, Princess Mary's Royal Air Force Nursing Service Reserve, Officers on the Retired List of the Royal Air Force and Royal Air Force Pensioners).
8. Royal Auxiliary Air Force (including Women's Royal Auxiliary Air Force).
9. The Royal Irish Regiment, to the extent that its members are not members of any force falling within paragraph 1 of this Part of this Schedule."

In *CG/1752/2006*, the Commissioner considered the proper interpretation of the word "temporarily" in para.7. Following *CIS/17020/1996* (which was about a paragraph in the same terms in the Income Support General Regulations), the Commissioner concluded that "an arrangement which is not permanent is not necessarily temporary." In defining the term "temporarily" as meaning "not permanent", the tribunal had erred in law.

SCHEDULE 2   **Regulations 10(2) and 13(2)**

CHILD CARE CHARGES TO BE DEDUCTED IN THE CALCULATION OF EARNINGS

3.34   **1.**—This Schedule applies where a claimant is incurring relevant child care charges and—
    (a) is a lone parent;
    (b) is a member of a couple both of whom are engaged in employment; or
    (c) is a member of a couple where one member is engaged in employment and the other member is incapacitated.
2.—In this Schedule—
"relevant child care charges" means the charges paid by the claimant for care provided for any child of the claimant's family who is under the age of 11 years, other than charges paid in respect of the child's compulsory education or charges paid by a claimant to a partner or by a partner to a claimant in respect of any child for whom either or any of them is responsible in accordance with section 143 of the Contributions and Benefits Act (circumstances in which a person is to be treated as responsible or not responsible for another), where the care is provided—

(a) by persons registered under section 71 of the Children Act 1989 (registration of child minders and persons providing day care for young children); or

(b) for children aged 8 and over but under 11, out of school hours, by a school on school premises or by a local authority; or

(c) by a child care scheme operating on Crown property where registration under section 71 of the Children Act 1989 is not required; or

(d) in schools or establishments which are exempted from registration under section 71 of the Children Act 1989 by virtue of section 71(16) of, and paragraph 3 or 4 of Schedule 9 to, that Act,

[¹ or

(e) by persons registered under Part XA of the Children Act 1989; or

(f) in schools or establishments which are exempted from registration under Part XA of the Children Act 1989 by virtue of paragraph 1 of Schedule 9A to that Act; or

(g) by

    (i) persons registered under section 7(1) of the Regulation of Care (Scotland) Act 2001; or

    (ii) local authorities registered under section 33(1) of that Act,

    where the care provided is childminding or daycare of children with the meaning of that Act,]

and shall be calculated on a weekly basis in accordance with paragraphs 4 to 7;

"school term-time" means the school term-time applicable to the child for whom care is provided.

3.—The age of a child referred to in paragraph 2 shall be determined by reference to the age of the child at the date on which the benefit week began.

4.—Subject to paragraphs 5 to 7, relevant child care charges shall be calculated in accordance with the formula—

$$\frac{X + Y}{52}$$

where—

X is the average weekly charge paid for child care in the most recent 4 complete weeks which fall in school term-time in respect of the child or children concerned, multiplied by 39; and

Y is the average weekly charge paid for child care in the most recent 2 complete weeks which fall out of school term-time in respect of that child or those children, multiplied by 13.

5.—Subject to paragraph 6, where child care charges are being incurred in respect of a child who does not yet attend school, the relevant child care charges shall mean the average weekly charge paid for care provided in respect of that child in the most recent 4 complete weeks.

6.—Where in any case the charges in respect of child care are paid monthly, the average weekly charge for the purposes of paragraph 4 shall be established—

(a) where the charges are for a fixed monthly amount, by multiplying that amount by 12 and dividing the product by 52;

(b) where the charges are for variable monthly amounts, by aggregating the charges for the previous 12 months and dividing the total by 52.

7.—In a case where there is no information or insufficient information for establishing the average weekly charge paid for child care in accordance with paragraphs 4 to 6, the average weekly charge for care shall be estimated by reference to information provided by the child minder or person providing the care or, if such information is not available, by reference to information provided by the claimant.

8.—For the purposes of paragraph 1(c) the other member of a couple is incapacitated where—

(a) either council tax benefit or housing benefit is payable under Part VII of the Contributions and Benefits Act to the other member or his partner and the applicable amount of the person entitled to the benefit includes—

    (i) a disability premium; or

[² (ii) a higher pensioner premium by virtue of the satisfaction of—

    (aa) in the case of council tax benefit, paragraph 11(2)(b) of Schedule 1 to the Council Tax Benefit Regulations;

    (bb) in the case of housing benefit, paragraph 11(2)(b) of Schedule 3 to the Housing Benefit Regulations 2006;

    On account of the other member's incapacity or either regulation 18(1)C of the Council Tax Benefit Regulations 2006 (treatment of child care charges) or, as the case may be, regulation 28(1)C of the Housing Benefit Regulations 2006 (treatment of child care charges) applies in that person's case;]

(b) there is payable in respect of him one or more of the following pensions or allowances—
  (i) long-term incapacity benefit under section 30A, 40 or 41 of the Contributions and Benefits Act;
  (ii) attendance allowance under section 64 of that Act;
  (iii) severe disablement allowance under section 68 of that Act;
  (iv) disability living allowance under section 71 of that Act;
  (v) an increase of disablement pension under section 104 of that Act;
  (vi) a pension increase under a war pension scheme or an industrial injuries scheme which is analogous to an allowance or increase of disablement pension under head (ii), (iv) or (v) above;
(c) a pension or allowance to which head (ii), (iv), (v) or (vi) of sub-paragraph (b) refers, was payable on account of his incapacity but has ceased to be payable in consequence of his becoming a patient (other than a person who is serving a sentence imposed by a court in a prison or youth custody institution) who is regarded as receiving free in-patient treatment within the meaning of the Social Security (Hospital In-Patients) Regulations 1975;
(d) sub-paragraph (b) or (c) would apply to him if the legislative provisions referred to in those sub-paragraphs were provisions under any corresponding enactment having effect in Northern Ireland; or
(e) he has an invalid carriage or other vehicle provided to him by the Secretary of State under section 5(2)(a) of, and Schedule 2 to, the National Health Service Act 1977 or under section 46 of the National Health Service (Scotland) Act 1978 or provided by the Department of Health and Social Services for Northern Ireland under article 30(1) of the Health and Personal Social Services (Northern Ireland) Order 1972.

AMENDMENTS

1. The Social Security Benefit (Computation of Earnings) (Child Care Charges) Regulations 2002 (SI 2002/842) (April 1, 2002).
2. The Housing Benefit and Council Tax Benefit (Consequential Provisions) Regulations 2006 (SI 2006/217) (March 6, 2006).

SCHEDULE 3   Regulations 10(3) and 13(3)

CARE CHARGES TO BE DEDUCTED IN THE CALCULATION OF EARNINGS FOR ENTITLEMENT TO [¹ CARER'S ALLOWANCE]

3.35   1.— This Schedule applies where a claimant is—
  (a) entitled to [¹ carer's allowance] under section 70 of the Contributions and Benefits Act; and
  (b) incurring relevant care charges.
2.—In this Schedule—
"close relative" means a parent, son, daughter, brother, sister or partner;
"relevant care charges" means the charges paid by the claimant for care which is provided by a person, who is not a close relative of either the severely disabled person or the claimant, for—
  (a) the severely disabled person; or
  (b) any child aged under 16 on the date on which the benefit week begins in respect of whom the claimant or his partner is entitled to child benefit under section 141 of the Contributions and Benefits Act because the claimant is unable to care for any of those persons because he is carrying out duties in connection with his employment;
"severely disabled person" means the severely disabled person in respect of whom entitlement to invalid care allowance arises.

AMENDMENT

1. The Social Security Benefit (Computation of Earnings) (Amendment) Regulations 2002 (SI 2002/2823), reg.2 (April 1, 2003).

3.36   *Schedule 4 omitted.*

Social Security Benefit (Dependency) Regulations 1977

(SI 1977/343) (as amended)

ARRANGEMENT OF REGULATIONS

PART I

GENERAL

PART II

CHILD DEPENDANTS

PART III

ADULT DEPENDANTS

PART IV

MISCELLANEOUS

PART V

TRANSITIONAL PROVISIONS AND REVOCATIONS

15.   Preservation of entitlement to benefit in payment before April 4, 1977 for a child dependant.

15A.   *Revoked.*

16.   *Omitted.*

SCHEDULE

Schedule 2—Prescribed Circumstances for Increase of an Invalid Care Allowance.

The Secretary of State for Social Services, in exercise of the powers conferred upon him by sections 33(2), 44, 46, 47, 49, 66 and 84 of, and Schedule 20 to, the Social Security Act 1975, as amended in the case of the said sections 44, 46 and 66 and Schedule 20 by section 21(1) of, and Schedule 4 to, the Child Benefit Act 1975 and section 20(1) of the Child Benefit Act 1975 and all other powers enabling him in that behalf, hereby makes the following regulations for the purpose only of consolidating regulations hereby revoked:

PART I

GENERAL

Citation, commencement and interpretation

3.38   **1.**—(1) These regulations may be cited as the Social Security Benefit (Dependency) Regulations 1977 and shall come into operation on April 4, 1977, immediately after the coming into operation of the Social Security (Child Benefit Consequential) Regulations 1977.

(2) In these regulations, unless the context otherwise requires—

"the Act" means the Social Security Act 1975;

"the Child Benefit Act" means the Child Benefit Act 1975;

[1 "the Contributions and Benefits Act" means the Social Security Contributions and Benefits Act 1992];

[2 "the determining authority" means, as the case may require, the Secretary of State, [7 the First-tier Tribunal or the Upper Tribunal]];

"entitled to child benefit" includes treated as so entitled;

"parent" has the meaning assigned to it by section 24(3) of the Child Benefit Act;

"the standard rate of increase" means the amount specified in Part IV or Part V of Schedule 4 to the Act as the amount of an increase for an adult dependant of the benefit in question,

and other expressions have the same meanings as in the Act.

[3 (3) Regulations 2(2) and (3), 4 and 5(1) shall, with any necessary modifications, apply to [4 carer's allowance] as they apply to retirement pension.]

[⁵ (3A) Nothing in these Regulations applies for the purposes of incapacity benefit under section 30A of the Contributions and Benefits Act.]

(4) Unless the context otherwise requires, any reference in these regulations to—

(a) a numbered section is to the section of the Act bearing that number;

(b) a numbered regulation is a reference to the regulation bearing that number in these regulations and any reference in a regulation to a numbered paragraph is a reference to the paragraph of that regulation bearing that number;

(c) any provision made by or contained in any enactment or instrument shall be construed as a reference to that provision as amended or extended by any enactment or instrument and as including a reference to any provision which may re-enact or replace it, with or without modification.

(5) The rules for the construction of Acts of Parliament contained in the Interpretation Act 1889 shall apply in relation to this instrument and in relation to any revocation effected by it as if this instrument, the regulations revoked by it and any regulations revoked by the regulations so revoked were Acts of Parliament, and as if each revocation were a repeal.

AMENDMENTS

1. The Social Security Benefit (Dependency) Amendment Regulations 1992 (SI 1992/3041), reg.2 (December 5, 1992).

2. The Social Security Act 1998 (Commencement No. 12 and Consequential and Transitional Provisions) Order 1999 (SI 1999/3178), Sch.2 (November 29, 1999).

3. The Social Security (Incapacity—Increases for Dependants) Regulations 1994 (SI 1994/2945), reg.15(2)(a) (April 13, 1995).

4. The Social Security Amendment (Carer's Allowance) Regulations 2002 (SI 2002/2497), reg.3 and Sch.2 (April 1, 2003).

5. The Social Security (Incapacity—Increases for Dependants) Regulations 1994 (SI 1994/2945), reg.15(2)(b) (April 13, 1995).

6. The Social Security Act 1998 (Commencement No. 9 and Savings and Consequential and Transitional Provisions) Order 1999 (SI 1992/2422), Sch.2, and The Social Security Act 1998 (Commencment No. 11 and Transitional Provisions) Order 1999 (SI 1999/2860), Sch.2 (October 18, 1999).

7. The Tribunals, Courts and Enforcement Act 2007 (Transitional and Consequential Provisions) Order 2008 (SI 2008/2683), reg.7 (November 3, 2008).

GENERAL NOTE

Interpretation Act 1889
By s.25(2) of the Interpretation Act 1978, this reference is to be treated as a reference to the 1978 Act.

3.39

Provisions as to maintenance for the purposes of increase of benefit in respect of dependants

2.—(1) Subject to paragraph (2), a beneficiary shall not for the purposes of the Act be deemed to be wholly or mainly maintaining another person unless the beneficiary—

(a) when [¹ . . .] incapable of work, or, as the case may be, [² entitled to a Category A or Category B retirement pension], contributes towards

3.40

the maintenance of that person an amount not less than the amount of increase of benefit received in respect of that person; and

(b) when in employment, or not incapable of work, or, as the case may be, not so [2 entitled] (except in a case where the dependency did not arise until after that time) contributed more than half of the actual cost of maintenance of that person.

(2) In a case where—

(a) a person is partly maintained by each of 2 or more other persons each of whom could be entitled to an increase of benefit under the Act in respect of that person if he were wholly or mainly maintaining that person, and

(b) the contributions made by those other persons towards the maintenance of that person amount in the aggregate to sums which, if they were contributed by one of them, would be sufficient to satisfy the foregoing requirements of this regulation,

that person shall for the purposes of the Act be deemed to be wholly or mainly maintained by that one of the said other persons who—

    (i) makes the larger or largest contributions to the maintenance of that person, or

    (ii) in a case where no person makes the larger or largest contributions as aforesaid, is the elder or eldest of the said other persons, or

    (iii) in any case, is a person designated in that behalf by a notice in writing signed by a majority of the said other persons and addressed to the Secretary of State,

so long as that one of the said other persons continues to be entitled to benefit under the Act and to satisfy the condition contained in paragraph (1)(a) of this regulation.

(3) A notice and the designation contained therein given under the foregoing paragraph may be revoked at any time by a fresh notice signed by a majority of such persons and another one of their number may be designated.

AMENDMENTS

1. The Social and Child Support (Jobseeker's Allowance) (Consequential Amendments) Regulations 1996 (SI 1996/1345), reg.12(2) (October 7, 1996).

2. The Social Security (Abolition of Earnings Rule) (Consequential) Regulations 1989 (SI 1989/1642), reg.4 (October 1, 1989).

DEFINITIONS

"the Act"—para.(1).
"beneficiary"—SSCBA 1992, s.122.

GENERAL NOTE

3.41   The primary rule in reg.2(1) requires two conditions to be satisfied:

(1) when incapable of work, the claimant must contribute to the maintenance of the other person an amount equal to or exceeding the amount of the increase of benefit, *and*

(2) when not incapable of work, the claimant must contribute towards the maintenance of the other person an amount exceeding half the *actual* cost of maintaining that other person.

The test under (1) is largely mathematical, but the test under (2) requires a judgment as to what amounts to the actual cost of maintaining a person. It is also arguable that maintenance may be in kind. There are certainly some old Commissioner's decisions which regard payment in kind of items the cost of which would normally be expenditure on day to day living as payment of maintenance: *R(I) 10/51*. Examples would be provision of food, clothes or coal. The principle may also be applicable to the transfer of property to a spouse: *R(U) 3/66*; or even to the transfer of a business share: *R(I) 37/54*.

The secondary rule in para.(2) deals with those rare cases where a dependant is being maintained by more than one person and establishes the order of priority between them in relation to entitlement to an increase of benefit. Note that the preferred beneficiary must also satisfy the condition in para.(1)(a). This is consistent with the principle that increases of benefit are not a means of benefiting the claimant, but to help meet the cost of supporting dependants.

The Family Fund Test

Where a number of people live in the same household, it will often be difficult to determine who supports whom and to what extent. An elaborate test known as the "family fund test" or "method" has been devised over many decades as a means of determining the actual cost of maintaining dependants in such cases and so of determining the amount of contribution required to qualify for an increase of benefit. The applicability of the test was re-affirmed by Tribunals of Commissioners in *R(I) 1/57*, *R(I) 20/60*, and *CS/130/1987*, a starred decision of a Tribunal of Commissioners. In *R(I) 20/60* the Tribunal of Commissioners confirmed that the family fund basis of calculation should be adopted unless it can be shown that it would produce a result which is clearly at variance with the evidence as to the family circumstances. More recently in *R(S) 12/83* the test has been approved and guidance given as to its application. The Commissioner said, "[T]he method should be applied where the maintainer and the person maintained are living in the same household unless there are wholly exceptional circumstances." (para.6). The Commissioner went on to spell out the test as it applies to a claimant. This may be summarised as follows:

3.42

(1) The members of the household are identified.

(2) The weekly income of the household (including its source) is calculated. Income here includes earnings, social security payments including supplementary benefit and family income supplement (now income support and working families' tax credit), and maintenance payments. From these will be deducted reasonable expenses, such as tax and national insurance contributions. The crucial date for determination is the period immediately prior to the incident which gives rise to the claim for an increase for a dependant (for example, immediately before the claimant became incapable of work or unemployed): *CS/130/1987*.

(3) The net weekly income is the family fund which is assumed to be the aggregate cost of maintaining the whole household. Each member of the household aged 14 or over counts as one unit and each member aged 13 or less counts as one-half a unit. The total number of units in the household enables the "unit cost" of each member of the household to be calculated by sharing the family fund in proportion to the units in the household. In *R(S) 7/89*, para.12, the Commissioners note that the time may now be ripe to reconsider the allocation of units and half units "to take account of social conditions at the end of the twentieth century." This point is repeated in *CS/299/1988*.

(4) The net earnings of each member of the household are treated as contributed to the family fund by that member of the household. Occupational pensions are treated as contributed by the member entitled to them (*CS/58/49*) and contributory benefits are regarded as provided by the person on whose national insurance contributions they are paid. Supplementary benefit (and

presumably now income support) is *not* attributed to its recipient: *R(S) 7/89(T)* approving para.21 of *R(I) 1/57(T)* and disapproving para.7 of *R(S) 2/85*. It would seem to follow that family income supplement (and now working families' tax credit) is not treated as attributed to its recipient.

(5) Child benefit is not treated as earmarked for the child or children in respect of whom it is paid (see below), though the Commissioner leaves open the question of whether it is contributed by "outsiders" or by the member of the family to whom it is actually paid. The Commissioner's preference in *R(S) 12/83* appears to be that child benefit is contributed by "outsiders". The rationale for the view that child benefit is not earmarked for the child in respect of whom it is payable is that in practice child benefit simply augments the family fund rather than provides resources solely for the child.

(6) The contributions to the family fund are then divided into three groups: (a) those derived from the claimant: (b) those derived from other members of the household; and (c) those derived from "outsiders". The claimant's contribution is first used up against his or her own unit cost. Only if the contribution exceeds the unit cost will there be any surplus available which can be used to contribute to the cost of maintaining others. The same principle is applied to other members of the household. The result is that each member of the household ends up with a surplus or a deficit.

(7) Contributions from outsiders are classified into those which are earmarked for particular members of the household and those which are not. Earmarked contributions are set on one side for the moment, but other contributions are applied rateably to reduce any deficits of members of the household.

(8) Earmarked contributions to the family fund by "outsiders" (for example, additions for dependants, payments of maintenance for children) are applied to reduce any deficit of the member of the household for whom they are earmarked.

(9) Where the amount of a claimant's surplus applied rateably towards meeting the deficits of members of the household amounts to more than one-half of the net unit cost of any member, the claimant is wholly or mainly maintaining that person. If it is less, the claimant is not.

An example based on figures as at January 1988 for the facts of *R(S) 12/83* will help unravel this complex provision. Suppose a household consists of an unmarried couple, M and W. There are four children, all aged under 11. M is the father of one of them, but not of the other three. Immediately before he becomes incapable of work M's net earnings are £65.00 per week. The family also receives child benefit of £29.00 and FIS of £35.70. The total net income per week is £129.70.

The family consists of four units. M and W are each one unit and each child is one-half unit. The unit cost of M and W is therefore £32.43 (£129.70 divided by four) and of each of the children is £16.21 (£129.70 divided by eight).

The only contributor to the family's income other than outsiders is M who contributes his net wages less his own unit costs: £32.57 (£65.00 less £32.43). M has a surplus of £32.57. By contrast W and each of the children have deficits of £32.43 and £16.21 respectively because they have no income of their own to contribute.

Child benefit and FIS, as contributions from "outsiders" to the family fund, are applied rateably to reduce the deficits of W and the children. So £21.57 is deducted from W's deficit leaving a deficit of £10.86 and £10.79 is deducted from the deficits of each child leaving each with a deficit of £5.42.

It is now the time to consider how M's surplus of £32.57 is to be distributed in order to determine whether he is wholly or mainly maintaining W and the children. In order to be wholly or mainly maintaining them M must contribute more than half of their unit costs out of his surplus. So M must contribute £16.21 to W's maintenance and £8.10 to the maintenance of each child in order to qualify as wholly or mainly maintaining them. Since the remaining deficits are less than these sums, M cannot be said to be wholly or mainly maintaining them. To put it another way M's contribution would need to be £48.61 before he would be deemed on the application of the family fund test to contribute sufficient to meet the test. His contribution is his surplus of £32.57.

In *CS/229/1988* the Commissioner held, distinguishing the treatment of constant attendance allowance in *R(I) 1/57*, that attendance allowance for a child is not to be taken as a contribution to the family fund by either the child or the child's mother as the person with legal entitlement. The Commissioner says that the attendance allowance must be "disregarded altogether".

CU/108/1993 provides a helpful example of the application of the family fund test to modern day circumstances. It clarifies one or two points. Child benefit should be treated as a contribution by the recipient, that is, the parent who receives it (para.5). Maintenance paid for a child should always be earmarked for the child in respect of whom it is paid (para.6). School fees are treated no differently than other payments for the maintenance of the child (para.7). Absence of a child at boarding school does not affect the unit costs for that child (para.8). Loans are disregarded (para.9). Gifts can be distinguished from payments in kind, such as the regular supply of coal to a miner, and should be disregarded (para.9).

Allocation of contributions for [¹ . . .] [² . . .] [¹⁰ spouse or civil partner.]

3.—(1) Subject to the provisions of this regulation, any sum or sums paid by a person by way of contribution towards either or both of the following, that is to say the maintenance of his [¹ spouse] [¹⁰ or civil partner] and the cost of providing for one or more children to which this regulation refers, shall be treated for the purposes of section 31(c)(i), [² . . .], [³ . . .], [⁴ 44(3)(a),] 45(2)(b), [⁴ 45A(2)(b), [⁵ . . .]] 65(1), 66(1)(a), or [⁶ 70(2)] (conditions as to maintenance) as such contributions of such respective amounts equal in the aggregate to the said sum or sums, in respect of such of the persons hereinafter mentioned, that is to say, his [⁷ spouse] [¹⁰ or civil partner] or any child or children to which this regulation refers, as may be determined by the determining authority so as to secure as large a payment as possible by way of benefit in respect of dependants.

3.43

(2) A sum paid by way of contribution towards the maintenance of a [⁸ spouse] [¹⁰ or civil partner] shall not be treated by virtue of this regulation as a sum paid by way of contribution towards the cost of providing for a child or children, and a sum paid by way of contribution towards the cost of providing for a child or children shall not be so treated as a sum paid by way of contribution towards the maintenance of a [⁸ spouse], [¹⁰ or civil partner] unless in either case the [⁸ spouse] [¹⁰ or civil partner] is entitled to child benefit in respect of the child or children.

(3) Except for the purposes of [section 56(1)(c) of the Social Security Contributions and Benefits Act 1992] (child's special allowance), the children to whom this regulation refers are any children in respect of whom, in the period for which the sum in question is paid by the person, that person is entitled to child benefit or could have been so entitled by virtue of regulations had he contributed to the cost of providing for the child at a sufficient weekly rate.

(4) For the purposes of [section 56(1)(c)]—

   (a) the children to whom this regulation refers are any such children to whom [section 56(1)(b)] applies;

   (b) a determination made under paragraph (1) in order to ascertain the weekly rate at which the husband had before his death been contributing to the cost of providing for a child may be [⁹ superseded] from time to time by the [⁹ Secretary of State] so often as may be necessary to secure as large a payment as possible by way of the child's special allowance, so however that no such [⁹ supersession] shall affect entitlement in respect of any period before the date of the [⁹ supersession]; and

(c) the condition in paragraph (2) shall be deemed to be satisfied if it would have been satisfied but for the fact that the child was not then in Great Britain.

[¹ (5) In the heading to this regulation and in paragraphs (1) and (2) the word "spouse" includes both husband and wife except in relation to maintenance contributions for the purposes of [sections 82(1)(b), 82(3), of the Social Security Contributions and Benefits Act 1992] where it means wife only, and in relation to maintenance contributions for the purposes of [sections 83(2)(b) and 84(2)(b) of the Social Security Contributions and Benefits Act 1992] where it means husband only].

AMENDMENTS

1. The Social Security Benefit (Dependency) Amendment Regulations 1983 (SI 1983/1001), reg.2(2) and (3) (November 21, 1983).
2. The Social Security (Working Tax Credit and Child Tax Credit) (Consequential Amendments) (No. 2) Regulations 2003 (SI 2003/937), reg.2 (April 6, 2003).
3. The Social Security and Child Support (Jobseeker's Allowance) (Consequential Amendments) Regulations 1996 (SI 1996/1345), reg.12(3)(a) (October 7, 1996).
4. The Social Security Benefit (Dependency) Amendment (No. 2) Regulations 1985 (SI 1985/1305), reg.2(2) (September 16, 1985).
5. The Social Security (Incapacity—Increases for Dependants) Regulations 1994 (SI 1994/2945), reg.15(3)(a) (April 13, 1995).
6. The Social Security Benefit (Dependency, Claims and Payments and Hospital In-Patients) Amendment Regulations 1984 (SI 1984/1699), reg.3(a) (November 28, 1984).
7. The Social Security Benefit (Dependency) Amendment (No. 2) Regulations 1985 (SI 1985/1305), reg.2(3) (September 16, 1985) and The Social Security and Child Support (Jobseeker's Allowance) (Consequential Amendments) Regulations 1996 (SI 1996/1345), reg.12(3)(b) (October 7, 1996).
8. The Social Security Benefit (Dependency) Amendment Regulations 1983 (SI 1983/1001), reg.2(3) and (4) (November 21, 1983).
9. The Social Security Act 1998 (Commencement No. 12 and Consequential and Transitional Provisions) Order 1999 (SI 1999/3178), Sch.2 (November 29, 1999).
10. Civil Partnership (Pensions, Social Security and Child Support) (Consequential, etc. Provisions) Order 2005 (SI 2005/2877) (December 5, 2005).

GENERAL NOTE

3.44   This regulation contains a principle of allocation which is designed to assist claimants. Regardless of the designation of payments by the payer, maintenance payments are to be apportioned by determining authorities in such a way as to entitle the claimant to the largest payment by way of an increase of benefit. The approach to be taken is to aggregate all maintenance payments and to allocate as the first slice the prescribed amount of maintenance for an adult dependant, as the second slice the prescribed amount for the maintenance of a child, and so on, although there can be no unapportioned residue. There is no possibility of carrying forward any surplus unless, of course, the payment is intended to cover more than one week: *R(S) 3/74.*

[¹ Deeming benefit under the Act abated under [section 74(3) of the Social Security Contributions and Benefits Act 1992] to be a contribution for the maintenance of children or adult dependants]

4.—Where for any period a person (in this regulation referred to as A) is entitled to, or to an increase in the amount of, any benefit prescribed pursuant to [section 74(3)(a) of the Social Security Contributions and Benefits Act 1992] (prevention of duplication of payments) in respect of another person (in this regulation referred to as B) and the amount of, or of the increase in, any such benefit is abated under [section 74(3) of the Social Security Contributions and Benefits Act 1992] then in determining for the purpose of the Act whether A is wholly or mainly maintaining or is contributing at any weekly rate to the maintenance of, or is or has been contributing at any weekly rate to the cost of providing for, B, the amount by which such benefit for any week has been so abated shall be deemed to be a contribution of that amount for that week made by A for the maintenance of B.]

3.45

AMENDMENT

1. The Social Security Benefit (Dependency) Amendment Regulations 1988 (SI 1988/554), reg.2 (April 11, 1988).

GENERAL NOTE

Most payments of most social security benefits, training allowances and social security benefits paid by other Member States of the European Union are prescribed under s.74 of the Administration Act. Section 74(3) provides that where a prescribed benefit, such as child benefit, can be claimed by a person (called A) on the basis of making contributions to the maintenance of another person (called B), then if income support has been paid to B because the contribution was not in fact made, the additional benefit paid to B as a consequence may be deducted from the prescribed benefit paid to A. This regulation contains a corresponding rule to the effect that such deductions count as contributions made by A to the maintenance of B if an issue arises as to whether A is wholly or mainly maintaining B.

3.46

Secretary of State for Work and Pensions v Adams [2003] EWCA Civ 796, Judgment of June 18, 2003, reported as *R(G) 1/03* concerned the question of whether the decision to resume payment of invalid care allowance following the application of reg.4 was a supersession decision under s.10 SSA 1998 or a decision under s.8 SSA 1998 either on a claim for a benefit or under or by virtue of a relevant enactment.

The claimant had for a number of years being caring for his severely disabled partner and had become entitled to an invalid care allowance. He subsequently became entitled to, and in receipt of, an incapacity benefit which overlapped with his invalid care allowance. In accordance with reg.4 the contributory benefit (incapacity benefit) was deducted from the non-contributory benefit (invalid care allowance). The result was that invalid care allowance ceased to be payable. The claimant's incapacity benefit subsequently terminated and the effect was to revive his entitlement to an invalid care allowance. The Court of Appeal concludes that the decision to resume payments is a decision under s.8. The court describes reg.4 as an "accounting provision designed to ensure that parallel payments do not result in excessive payment." (para.20). Were the decision allocated to s.10 the claimant would be deprived of the possibility of backdating the decision.

Circumstances in which a person who is not entitled to child benefit is to be treated as if he were so entitled

4A.—(1) For the purposes of [section 77 of the Social Security Contributions and Benefits Act 1992] (guardian's allowance) or [sections

3.47

[¹ . . .] 82(4), 85(2) and 90 of the Social Security Contributions and Benefits Act 1992] (increase of benefit in respect of dependent children, and [² . . .] persons having care of dependent children) a person shall be treated as if he were entitled to child benefit in respect of a child for any period throughout which—

(a) child benefit has been awarded to a parent of that child with whom that child is living and with whom that person is residing and either—

   (i) the child is being wholly or mainly maintained by that person; or

   (ii) that person is also a parent of the child; or

(b) he, or his spouse [⁶ or civil partner] with whom he is residing, would have been entitled to child benefit in respect of that child had the child been born at the end of the week immediately preceding the week in which birth occurred.

(2) [² . . .]

(3) For the purpose of determining whether a person is entitled to a guardian's allowance under [section 77], where in respect of a child that allowance is payable to a person for a continuous period of 7 days and would have been payable to that person for the immediately preceding 7 days had he been entitled to child benefit in respect of that child for an earlier week, he shall be treated as if he were entitled to child benefit in respect of that child for that earlier week.

(4) If for any period a person who is in Great Britain could have been entitled to receive payment of an amount by way of a benefit or allowance or an increase of a benefit or an allowance under the Act in respect of a child or [⁴ . . .] person who has the care of a child but for the fact that in pursuance of any agreement with the government of a country outside the United Kingdom he, or his [⁵ spouse] [⁶ or civil partner] who is residing with him, is entitled in respect of the child in question to the family benefits of that country and is not entitled to child benefit, he shall for the purposes of entitlement to the said payment be treated as if he were entitled to child benefit for the period in question.

(5) The expression "earlier week" in paragraph (3) means the week immediately preceding the first week for which the person referred to in that paragraph was entitled to child benefit in respect of the child referred to in that paragraph.

(6) For the purposes of paragraph (1) the word "week" has the meaning assigned to it by [section 147(1) of the Social Security Contributions and Benefits Act 1992]; and for the purposes of paragraphs (1) and (2) a child shall not be regarded as living with a person unless he can be so regarded for the purposes of [section 143 of the Social Security Contributions and Benefits Act 1992] (meaning of "person responsible for child") of the said Act.

AMENDMENTS

Regulation 4A was inserted by The Social Security Benefit (Dependency) Amendment Regulations 1980 (SI 1980/585), reg.2 (June 2, 1980).

1. The Social Security (Working Tax Credit and Child Tax Credit) (Consequential Amendments) (No. 2) Regulations 2003 (SI 2003/937), reg.2 (April 6, 2003).

2. The Social Security Benefit (Dependency) Amendment Regulations 1989 (SI 1989/523), reg.2 (April 11, 1989).

3. The Social Security Benefit (Dependency) Amendment Regulations 1984 (SI 1984/1698), reg.2(13) (November 26, 1984) subject to savings contained in SI 1984/1698, reg.3.

4. The Social Security Benefit (Dependency) Amendment Regulations 1984 (SI 1984/1968), reg.2(3) (November 26, 1984).

5. The Social Security Benefit (Dependency) Amendment Regulations 1984 (SI 1984/1968), reg.2(3) (November 26, 1984).

6. Civil Partnership (Pensions, Social Security and Child Support) (Consequential, etc. Provisions) Order 2005 (SI 2005/2877) (December 5, 2005).

GENERAL NOTE

This is a deeming rule. If the conditions are satisfied, a person is to be treated as if **3.48** he or she is entitled to child benefit even though not in fact entitled to the benefit.

On "residing together" see the Persons Residing Together Regulations.

The family fund test will be important in determining whether the child is being wholly or mainly maintained under para.(1)(a)(i). See *R(S) 12/83* and notes to reg.2.

[¹ Circumstances in which a person entitled to child benefit is to be treated as if he were not so entitled

4B.—(1) For the purposes of—   **3.49**
 (a) section 56 (child's special allowance);
 (b) section 77 (guardian's allowance);
 (c) [².. .];
 (d) section 82(4) (short-term benefits—increase for adult dependants);
 (e) [².. .];
 (f) section 90 (increase in benefits for beneficiaries under sections 68 and 70), of the Contributions and Benefits Act, and
 (g) paragraphs 4(1) (unemployability supplement: increase for beneficiary's dependent children) and 6(1) (unemployability supplement: increase for dependent adults) of Schedule 7 to,
that Act, a person who is entitled to child benefit in respect of a child shall be treated as if he were not so entitled for the periods referred to in paragraph (2) below.

(2) The periods referred to in paragraph (1) above are—
 (a) any period throughout which—
  (i) the person referred to in that paragraph, not being a parent of the child, does not fall to be treated as responsible for the child under section 143(1)(a) of the Contributions and Benefits Act, and
  (ii) a parent of that child falls to be treated as responsible for the child under the said section 143(1)(a); or
 (b) any period throughout which—
  (i) that person, not being a parent of that child, falls to be treated as responsible for the child under section 143(1)(a) of the Contributions and Benefits Act, and
  (ii) a parent of that child also falls to be treated as responsible for the child under the said section 143(1)(a); or
 (c) any day following that day on which that child died.

(3) Sub-paragraph (b) of paragraph (2) shall not apply in the case of a person who is wholly or mainly maintaining the child referred to in that sub-paragraph.

(4) For the purposes of—
(a) section 37(1) (entitlement to a widowed mother's allowance);
(b) section 39A(2) (entitlement to a widowed parent's allowance);
(c) section 56(1)(b);
(d) section 77(1);
(e) section 80;
(f) section 82(4);
(g) section 85(2);
(h) section 90;
of the Contributions and Benefits Act, and
(i) paragraphs 4(1), 6(1) and 18(1)(a)(ii) of Schedule 7 (industrial death benefit: child of deceased's family) to,
that Act, a person who is entitled to child benefit in respect of a child shall be treated as if he were not so entitled for any period for which that benefit is not payable by virtue of any of the provisions referred to in paragraph (5) below.

(5) The provisions referred to in paragraph (4) above are—
(a) regulation 7 (circumstances in which a person who has ceased to receive full-time education is to continue to be treated as a child);
(b) regulation 7A (exclusion from benefit of children aged 16 but under the age of 19 who are receiving advanced education);
(c) regulation 7B (child receiving training under the youth training scheme); or
(d) regulation 7C (child receiving income support),
of the Child Benefit (General) Regulations 1976 or any provision contained in regulations made under section 144(1) of the Contributions and Benefits Act in so far as those regulations provide that child benefit is not to be payable by virtue of section 142(1)(b) of that Act and regulations made thereunder.]

AMENDMENTS

1. The Social Security (Benefits for Widows and Widowers) (Consequential Amendments) Regulations 2000, reg.5 (SI 2000/1483) (April 9, 2001).
2. The Social Security (Working Tax Credit and Child Tax Credit) (Consequential Amendments) (No. 2) Regulations 2003 (SI 2003/937), reg.2 (April 6, 2003).

GENERAL NOTE

3.50   This regulation contains a corresponding deeming rule to that contained in reg.4A. It deems a person entitled to child benefit not to be so entitled if the conditions of the regulation are satisfied.

PART II

CHILD DEPENDANTS

Contributions towards cost of providing for child

3.51   **5.**—(1) Where, apart from [section 81(1) and (2) of the Social Security Contributions and Benefits Act 1992], a person is entitled to receive, in respect of a particular child, payment under the Act of an amount by way of a child's special allowance ([section 56]), or a guardian's allowance ([section 77]) or of an increase under any of the provisions of [section 80 of the Social Security Contributions and Benefits Act 1992] of any benefit, or payment of an increase or allowance of any amount under section 64 or section 70, for any period, and neither of the conditions set out in the following paragraphs is satisfied, that person shall nevertheless for the purposes of the said [section 81(1) or (2) of the Social Security Contributions and Benefits Act 1992] be deemed as respects that period to be making the contributions so required at a weekly rate not less than that required by the said section [81(1) or (2)] if—

(a) he gives an undertaking in writing to make such contributions; and
(b) on receiving the amount of the allowance or increase in question, he in fact makes such contributions.

(2) The conditions referred to in paragraph (1) are—

(a) the person would be treated for the purposes of [Part IX of the Social Security Contributions and Benefits Act 1992] as having the child living with him; or
(b) contributions are being made to the cost of providing for the child at a rate equal to the amount of the relevant increase of benefit.

(3) Where, in respect of any period, the person referred to in this regulation fails to make the contributions which he has undertaken to make in accordance with the first paragraph of this regulation, the decision awarding the increase or allowance in question for that period in respect of the child shall be revised.

(4) [1 . . .]

[2 (5) Except in a case to which regulation 15 (preservation of entitlement to benefit in payment before April 4, 1977 for a child dependant) or regulation 13A of the Social Security Benefit (Persons Abroad) Regulations 1975, as amended (modification of the Act in relation to title to benefit for beneficiary's child dependants) applies, paragraph (b) of [section 81(3) of the Social Security Contributions and Benefits Act 1992] (contributions mentioned in those paragraphs to be over and above those required for the purposes of [section 143(1)(b) of the Social Security Contributions and Benefits Act 1992]) shall not apply in a case where neither the beneficiary nor his spouse [3 or, as the case may be, his civil partner] (or if he has a spouse [3 or civil partner] and his spouse [3 or civil partner] is residing with him) is in fact entitled to child benefit in respect of the child in question.]

AMENDMENTS

1. The Social Security Benefit (Miscellaneous Amendments) Regulations 1978 (SI 1978/433), reg.7 (April 3, 1978).
2. The Social Security Benefit (Dependency) Amendment Regulations 1977 (SI 1977/620), reg.2 (April 4, 1977).
3. The Civil Partnership (Pensions, Social Security and Child Support) (Consequential, etc. Provisions) Order 2005 (SI 2005/2877) (December 5, 2005).

GENERAL NOTE

This useful regulation allows a claimant who fails to satisfy the requirements of para.(2) to give an undertaking in writing to make contributions for the maintenance of a child of an amount equal to the benefit or increase of benefit in order to qualify for one of the benefits mentioned in the regulation. Failure to make the

3.52

promised payments results in revision of entitlement (para.(3)). Care must be taken that the claimant increases the payments to the level of any benefit increases: *R(S) 3/74.* The undertaking cannot operate retrospectively for more than a week; *R(U) 3/78,* but a later undertaking may be regarded as merely confirming an earlier undertaking even though there has been a break in the payments made under the earlier undertaking: *R(U)6/79.*

3.53   *Regulation 6 revoked by The Social Security (Computation of Earnings) Regulations 1996 (SI 1996/2745), Sch.4 (November 25, 1996).*

3.54   *Regulation 7 revoked by The Social Security Benefit (Dependency) Amendment Regulations 1980 (SI 1980/585), reg.3 (June 2, 1980).*

PART III

ADULT DEPENDANTS

Earnings rules for increases for adult dependants

3.55   **8.**—(1) This paragraph applies in cases where an increase of benefit is claimed [¹ . . .] in respect of a spouse who is residing with the beneficiary and the increase is claimed under any of the following provisions of the Contributions and Benefits Act—

    (a) section 83(2) (increase of Category A or Category C retirement pension in respect of a wife); [⁴ or]

    (b) section 84(1) (increase of Category A retirement pension in respect of a husband); [⁴ . . .]

    (c) [⁴ . . .]

[⁴ (1A)This paragraph applies in cases where an increase of benefit is claimed in respect of a spouse or a civil partner who, in either case, is residing with the beneficiary and the increase is claimed under paragraph 6(1)(a)(i) of Schedule 7 to the Contributions and Benefits Act (increase of disablement pension in respect of a spouse or civil partner where beneficiary entitled to unemployability supplement).]

(2) Where paragraph (1) [⁴ or (1A)] applies, there shall be no increase of benefit for any period during which the beneficiary is residing with his spouse [⁴ or civil partner] and his spouse [⁴ or civil partner] has earnings if the earnings of the spouse [⁴ or civil partner] in the week in that period which falls immediately before the week in which the beneficiary is entitled to benefit under any provision specified in paragraph (1) exceed [² the amount for the time being specified in regulation 79(1)C of the Jobseeker's Allowance regulations 1996 (age related amount for a claimant who has attained the age of 25).]

(3) Where the person referred to in section 85(2) of the Contributions and Benefits Act ("the dependant") is residing with the pensioner, the weekly rate of a pension to which section 85 of that Act applies shall be increased by the amount specified in relation to that pension in column 3 of Part IV of Schedule 4 to that Act but there shall be no increase of pension for any period—

    (a) during which the pensioner is residing with the dependant; and

(b) the dependant has earnings,

if the earnings of the dependant in the week in that period which falls immediately before the week in which the pensioner is entitled to the pension exceed [² the amount as for the time being specified in regulation 79(1)(c) of the Jobseeker's Allowance Regulations 1996 (age related amount for a claimant who has attained the age of 25).]

(4) Where the person referred to in paragraph 6(1)(b) of Schedule 7 to the Contributions and Benefits Act ("the dependant") is residing with the beneficiary, the weekly rate of the disablement pension to which that paragraph applies shall be increased by the amount referred to in paragraph 8 of Part V of Schedule 4 to that Act but there shall be no increase of disablement pension for any period—

(a) during which the beneficiary is residing with the dependant; and

(b) the dependant has earnings,

if the earnings of the dependant in the week in that period which falls immediately before the week in which the beneficiary is entitled to a disablement pension [² exceed the amount as for the time being specified in regulation 79(1)(c) of the Jobseeker's Allowance Regulations 1996 (age related amount for a claimant who has attained the age of 25).]

(5) In determining the earnings of a dependant for the purposes of paragraphs (3) and (4), no account shall be taken of any earnings of that person from employment by the pensioner or the beneficiary as the case may be in caring for a child or children in respect of whom the pensioner or the beneficiary is entitled to child benefit.

(6) Where an increase of benefit is claimed in respect of a spouse [⁴ or civil partner] who is not residing with the beneficiary and the increase is claimed under paragraph 6(1)(a)(ii) of Schedule 7 to the Contributions and Benefits Act there shall be no increase of benefit for any period during which the beneficiary is contributing to the maintenance of the spouse at a rate less than the standard rate of the increase and the weekly earnings of the spouse [⁴ or civil partner] exceed that rate.

(7) In this regulation—

(a) "week" means—

(i) in relation to Category A or Category C retirement pension the period of 7 days beginning with the day on which in accordance with the provisions of regulation 22 of and paragraph 5 of Schedule 6 to the Social Security (Claims and Payments) Regulations 1987(a) is the day for payment of the retirement pension in question; and

(ii) in relation to any other benefit [³ any period of 7 days corresponding to the week in respect of which the relevant social security benefit is due to be paid or ending on the day before the first day of the first such week following the date of claim]; and

(b) any reference to earnings includes a reference to payments by way of occupational or personal pension.

AMENDMENTS

This regulation was substituted by the Social Security (Dependency) Amendment Regulations 1992 (SI 1992/3041), reg.3 (December 5, 1992).

1. The Social Security (Incapacity—Increases for Dependants) Regulations 1994 (SI 1992/2945), reg.15(4) (April 13, 1995).

2. The Social Security and Child Support (Jobseeker's Allowance) (Consequential Amendments) Regulations 1996 (SI 1996/1345), reg.12(4) (October 7, 1996).

3. The Social Security (Computation of Earnings) Regulations 1996 (SI 1996/2745), reg.17(a) (November 25, 1996).

4. The Civil Partnership (Pensions, Social Security and Child Support) (Consequential, etc. Provisions) Order 2005 (SI 2005/2877) (December 5, 2005).

GENERAL NOTE

3.56   On "having the care of a child" see annotations to s.82 of the C & BA 1992. The revised text of reg.8 set out above was inserted with effect from December 5, 1992, by the Social Security Benefit (Dependency) Amendment Regulations 1992 (SI 1992/3041). There is an important transitional provision in reg.4 of the Amendment Regulations preserving entitlement under the earlier text for those in receipt of an increase of benefit on December 4, 1992.

Two relevant unreported decisions on reg.8(6) as previously enacted are *CP/068/1989* (printed as Appendix to *R(P) 3/93*) and *R(P) 3/93*. The latter decision holds that increases of invalidity benefit and of retirement pension are different increases even though the amounts at the material time were the same. So a claimant moving from increase of invalidity benefit to increase of retirement pension on attaining the age of 70 lost the protection of reg.8(6).

Note that in paras (2), (3) and (4) a sum of £48.25 is substituted where reg.12(5) of the amending regulation (SI 1996/1345) applies. Regulation 12(5) of the amending regulation applies where, and only so long as, the amount for the time being specified in reg.79(1)(c) of the Jobseeker's Allowance Regulations 1996 is less than the amount of £48.25. The amount for the time being specified in reg.79(1)(c) as from October 7, 1996 was £47.90.

In *CP/3017/2004* the Commissioner said,

"6. Before going on to mention the legislative provisions that set out rules for calculating earnings for the purposes of benefits including retirement pension, there is one oddity arising from regulation 8(2) of the Dependency Regulations to be examined. Regulation 8(2) lays down a test to be applied week by week for each week of payment of retirement pension (see the definition in regulation 8(7)(a)), which test depends on the spouse's earnings in the previous week. The application of a week by week test seems to be reinforced by section 92 of the Social Security Contributions and Benefits Act 1992, which applies where an award of an increase has been made and causes the award to continue in force even though entitlement is interrupted by a week or weeks in which the spouse's earnings exceed the limit. In the present case, the first week of payment of retirement pension to the claimant would have been that beginning on Monday 31 May 2004. It might be said that at the date of the decision in question there could have been absolutely no evidence of what the wife's earnings would be in the week commencing Monday 24 May 2004 or in any subsequent week. How therefore could a decision be given disallowing an increase?

7. The main answer stems from regulation 15(1) of the Claims and Payments Regulations and the decision of the Tribunal of Commissioners in *CDLA/2751/2003* and others, about advance renewal claims for disability living allowance (DLA). It was held there that the legislative power to make an award of DLA in advance of the start date of the period of the award carried with it the power to disallow the claim in advance. The same must also apply to regulation 15(1), so that there is a power to disallow a claim for an increase of retirement pension for a wife up to four months before a claimant might become entitled to the pension. Then, in accordance with section 8(2) of the Social Security Act 1998 as explained by the Tribunal of Commissioners, in making such a decision the Secretary of State would be prohibited from taking into account any changes of circumstances anticipated to occur after the date of the decision. Equally, on appeal, an appeal

tribunal would be prohibited from taking into account any actual changes of circumstances after that date (Social Security Act 1998, section 12(8)(b)). The Tribunal of Commissioners seems to have thought that if there was change of circumstances in favour of a claimant between the date of the decision and the date from which the disallowance of the claim took effect, there could be a supersession on the ground of relevant change of circumstances (Social Security and Child Support (Decisions and Appeals) Regulations 1999, regulation 6(2)(a) (i)). However, there is a problem with that view because regulation 6(2)(a)(i), as amended with effect from 5 May 2003, allows supersession only where there has been a relevant change of circumstances since the decision to be superseded "had effect". That seems to rule out a supersession for a change occurring between the date of an advance decision and its effective date. A claimant would thus be restricted to making a fresh claim, on the basis of the changed circumstances, from some date after the effective date of the disallowing decision.

8. In paragraph 24 of *CDLA/2751/2003* and others, the Tribunal of Commissioners did suggest that, in some cases where there was likely to be a significant change of circumstances before the start date of the period covered by a claim, it might well be good practice to defer making a decision until it was known whether that change had actually materialised. It seems to me that the present case is one where that course should have been taken. It was plain from the evidence provided that the claimant's wife's earnings fluctuated a great deal from one pay period to another. And the nature of the case is different from that of a person suffering some potentially disabling or incapacitating condition, where in most cases there can be a sensible prediction about how the condition might progress in the future. It was simply unknown on 3 March 2004 what the claimant's wife's earnings might be in the week prior to 31 May 2004. Quite apart from the doubts that I explain below about the averaging process carried out by the officer, it would have been better to have waited until close to 28 May 2004 and then considered the current evidence about the wife's earnings. I do not think that there would have been any difficulty in making an advance decision on the claimant's own retirement pension entitlement, but deferring the decision on the increase. However, that did not happen. A decision disallowing the increase was made on 3 March 2004 and I must deal with the consequences."

In para.21 of his decision, the Commissioner concluded,

"21. If I adopt the same method as the officer who made the decision of 3 March 2004 and take an average of the seven payslips, counting only the taxable pay, the result is £32.59 per week. With the addition of the weekly amount of the wife's occupational pension, the total earnings are well below the limit in regulation 8(2) of the Dependency Regulations. I have doubts about the use of averaging under regulation 8(3) of the Computation of Earnings Regulations. That provision allows averaging over a recognisable cycle of work or some other period that will allow average weekly earnings to be identified more accurately. But, for the reasons given in paragraph 6 above, the Dependency Regulations may properly work on the amount of actual earnings received week by week (with payments received at other intervals spread according to the rules in regulation 8(1) and (2) of the Computation of Earnings Regulations). If so, the use of an average figure might not be appropriate at all. But I do not have to decide the issue. I have already shown that the result of averaging under regulation 8(3) is in favour of the claimant. If I do not apply regulation 8(3), the circumstances as at 3 March 2004 were that, for six of the payments in evidence, the weekly equivalent of the earnings received was below the limit, usually well below. It was only in respect of the payment received on 14 December 2003 that the weekly equivalent (£98) was over the limit. There might well have been unusual circumstances in the run-up to Christmas. Looking at that evidence, and not knowing what earnings had been received immediately before 3 March 2004, I have no difficulty in concluding that the level of the wife's earnings to be taken into account in respect of the period from 28 May 2004 onwards is below the limit in regulation 8(2) of the Dependency Regulations. Thus, on either approach, the claimant's appeal succeeds and he is to be awarded the increase of retirement pension."

There has been no reg. 9 since September 16, 1985 when the former regs 8 and 9 were replaced by a revised reg. 8.

Apportionment of payments by way of occupational [¹ or personal] pension made otherwise than weekly

3.57   **9A.**—[² For the purposes of section 89(1) of, and paragraph 7(1) of Schedule 7 to, the Contributions and Benefits Act, where payment by way of occupational or personal pension, or for the purposes of section 89(1A) of that Act by way of PPF periodic payment,] is for any period made otherwise than weekly, the amount of any such payment for any week in that period shall be determined—

(a) where payment is made for a year, by dividing the total by 52;

(b) where payment is made for three months, by dividing the total by 13;

(c) where payment is made for a month, by multiplying the total by 12 and dividing the result by 52;

(d) where payment is made for two or more months, otherwise than for a year or for three months, by dividing the total by the number of months, multiplying the result by 12 and dividing the result of that multiplication by 52; or

(e) in any other case, by dividing the amount of the payment by the number of days in the period for which it is made and multiplying the result by 7.

AMENDMENTS

Regulation 9A was inserted by The Social Security Benefit (Dependency) Amendment Regulations 1989 (SI 1989/523), reg.5 (April 11, 1989).

1. The Social Security (Miscellaneous Provisions) Amendment Regulations 1992 (SI 1992/247), reg.4(2) (March 9, 1992). This amendment is superseded by the amendment listed below.

2. The Social Security (PPF Payments and FAS Payments) (Consequential Amendments) Regulations 2006 (SI 2006/1069), reg.2 (May 5, 2006).

Increase of benefit for [¹ . . .] person having care of child [¹⁴ or qualifying young person]

3.58   **10.**—(1) Subject to the provisions of [section 82 of the Social Security Contributions and Benefits Act 1992] (increase [² . . .] of a maternity allowance), [section 85 of the Social Security Contributions and Benefits Act 1992] (increase of a Category A or Category C retirement pension [³ . . .]), or section 66 (increase [² . . .] of a disablement pension where the beneficiary is entitled to an unemployability supplement), this regulation shall apply for the purpose of determining whether a beneficiary is entitled to an increase of benefit under [section 82(3) and 85(2) of the Social Security Contributions and Benefits Act 1992] in respect of a [⁴ . . .] person who has the care of a child or children [¹⁴ or a qualifying young person or persons] in respect of whom the beneficiary is entitled to child benefit.

(2) A beneficiary shall not be entitled to an increase under the said [section 82(3) and 85(2)] unless the [⁴ . . .] person referred to in those sections—

(a) has the care of such a child [¹⁴ or qualifying young person] as is referred to in those sections [⁵ . . .]; and

(b) either—

    (i) is residing with the beneficiary, or

    (ii) is employed by him in an employment in respect of which the weekly expenses incurred by the beneficiary are not less than the standard rate of increase and was so employed by him before he became [⁶ . . .] incapable of work or [⁷ entitled to a Category A or Category B retirement pension], as the case may be, subject to the qualification that the condition of employment before that event shall not apply in a case where the necessity for [⁸ the] employment first arose thereafter; or

    (iii) is a person to whose maintenance the beneficiary is contributing at a weekly rate not less than the standard rate of increase; and

(c) subject to paragraph (3), is not absent from Great Britain; and

(d) is not undergoing imprisonment or detention in legal custody; and

[⁹ (e) either—

    (i) has no earnings or has earnings but they do not exceed the standard rate of increase (there being disregarded for this purpose any earnings derived from employment by the beneficiary in caring for a child or children [¹⁴ or a qualifying young person or persons] in respect of whom the beneficiary is entitled to child benefit), or

    (ii) is employed by the beneficiary in caring for such child or children [¹⁴ or a qualifying young person or persons] and is not residing with him;]

(f) [¹⁰ . . .]

(3) In the case of [¹¹ . . .] any pension to which this regulation applies, the condition referred to in sub-paragraph (c) of paragraph (2) shall not apply as respects any period during which the said [¹¹ . . .] person is residing with the beneficiary outside Great Britain and for which by virtue of the provisions of any regulations made under section 82(5) (disqualification) or 131 (persons outside Great Britain) the beneficiary is not disqualified for receiving that benefit.

(4) [¹² . . .].

(5) [¹³ . . .].

AMENDMENTS

1. The Social Security Benefit (Dependency) Amendment Regulations 1984 (SI 1984/1698), reg.10 (November 26, 1984).

2. The Social Security and Child Support (Jobseeker's Allowance) (Consequential Amendments) Regulations 1996 (SI 1996/1345), reg.12(7)(a) (October 7, 1996).

3. The Social Security (Incapacity—Increases for Dependants) Regulations 1994 (SI 1994/2945), reg.15(5)(a) (April 13, 1995).

4. The Social Security (Abolition of Injury Benefit) (Consequential) Regulations 1983 (SI 1983/186), reg.7(3) (April 6, 1983).

5. The Social Security Benefit (Dependency, Claims and Payments and Hospital In-Patients) Amendments Regulations 1984 (SI 1984/1699), reg.3(b) (November 26, 1984).

6. The Social Security and Child Support (Jobseeker's Allowance) (Consequential Amendments) Regulations 1996 (SI 1996/1345), reg.12(7)(b) (October 7, 1996).

7. The Social Security (Abolition of Earnings Rule) (Consequential) Regulations 1989 (SI 1989/1642), reg.4 (October 1, 1989).

8. The Social Security Benefit (Dependency) Amendment Regulations 1984 (SI 1984/1698), SI 1984/1698, reg.2(6) (November 26, 1984).

9. The Social Security Benefit (Dependency) Amendment Regulations 1989 (SI 1989/523), reg.6 (April 11, 1989).

10. The Social Security Benefit (Dependency) Amendment Regulations 1989 (SI 1989/523), reg.7 (April 11, 1989).

11. The Social Security Benefit (Dependency) Amendment Regulations 1984 (SI 1984/1698), reg.2(9) (November 26, 1984).

12. The Social Security Benefit (Dependency) Amendment Regulations 1985 (SI 1985/1190), reg.5 (September 16, 1985).

13. The Social Security Benefit (Dependency) Amendment Regulations 1984 (SI 1984/1698), reg.8 (January 1, 1979).

14. The Social Security (Provisions relating to Qualifying Young Persons) (Amendment) Regulations 2006 (SI 2006/692) (April 10, 2006).

GENERAL NOTE

3.59   On "residing together," see the Persons Residing Together Regulations.
On "having the care of a child," see annotations to s.82 of the SSCBA 1992.

Contribution to maintenance of adult dependant

3.60   **11.**—(1) Subject to paragraphs (2) and (3), for the purposes of [section 82(1) and (3), 83(2), 84 of the Social Security Contributions and Benefits Act 1992] (increase of a Category A or Category C retirement pension or benefit to which section 66 applies in respect of a spouse) or of regulation 10(2)(b)(iii) (increase of a Category A or Category C retirement pension or benefit to which section 66 applies in respect of a person having the care of a child [or qualifying young person])—

(a) a beneficiary shall not be deemed to satisfy the requirement contained in the said sections or the said regulation that he is contributing to the maintenance of the spouse or the person having the care of a child [or qualifying young person], as the case may be, at a weekly rate of not less than the standard rate of increase unless when in employment, or not incapable of work, or not entitled to a Category A or Category B retirement pension, as the case may be (except in a case where the dependency did not arise until later), he contributed to that spouse's or person's maintenance at a weekly rate of not less than the standard rate of increase;

(b) in a case where an increase of benefit is, apart from the said requirement, payable at a weekly rate less than the standard rate of increase, a beneficiary shall, subject to sub-paragraph (a) above, be deemed to satisfy the said requirement if he is contributing to the maintenance of the spouse or person having the care of a child [or qualifying young person], as the case may be, at a weekly rate of not less than that of the increase.

[(1A) Subject to paragraphs (2) and (3), for the purposes of section 82 of, and paragraph 6(1)(a)(i) of Schedule 7 to, the Contributions and Benefits Act (increase of maternity allowance and increase of disablement pension where beneficiary entitled to unemployability supplement) a beneficiary shall not be deemed to satisfy the requirement contained in those provisions (that he is contributing to the maintenance of his civil partner at a weekly rate of not less than the standard rate of increase) unless when in employment, or not incapable of work, or not entitled to a Category A or a Category B retirement pension, as the case may be (except in a case where the dependency did not arise until later), he contributed to his civil partner's maintenance at a weekly rate not less than the standard rate of increase.]

(2) Where, within one month of having been entitled to an increase of unemployment benefit under [section 82(1) of the Social Security Contributions and Benefits Act 1992] or under [section 82(3)(c) of the Social Security Contributions and Benefits Act 1992] by virtue of having satisfied the requirement in head (iii) of sub-paragraph (b) of regulation 10(2) (but no other requirement in that sub-paragraph), or of having been entitled to an increase of short-term incapacity benefit by virtue of having satisfied the requirements of regulation 9(1)(b) or (3) (b) of the Social Security (Incapacity Benefit—Increases for Dependents) Regulations 1994, a person becomes entitled to a benefit which attracts a standard rate of increase higher than that of the benefit to which he had been entitled, he shall be deemed to satisfy the condition in paragraph (1) (a) if he satisfies it in relation to the benefit to which he had been entitled; and in this paragraph "entitled" includes deemed to have been entitled.

(2A) Where, within one month of having been entitled to an increase of unemployment benefit under [section 82(3)(a) of the Social Security Contributions and Benefits Act 1992] by virtue of contributing to the maintenance of her husband at a weekly rate not less than the standard rate of the increase, or of having been entitled to an increase of shortterm incapacity benefit by virtue of having satisfied the requirements of regulation 9(1)(b) or (3)(b) of the Social Security (Incapacity Benefit—Increases for Dependents) Regulations 1994, a woman becomes entitled to a benefit which attracts a standard rate of increase higher than that of the benefit to which she had been entitled, she shall be deemed to satisfy the condition in paragraph (1)(a) if she satisfies it in relation to the benefit to which she had been entitled, and in this paragraph "entitled" includes deemed to have been entitled.

(3) For the purposes of paragraphs (2) and (2A) a person shall be deemed to have been entitled to an increase of unemployment benefit at a lower standard rate of increase if (assuming satisfaction of the relevant contribution conditions) he would have been so entitled but for the provisions of [section 82(1)(b) of the Social Security Contributions and Benefits Act 1992] or, as the case may be, regulation 10(2)(e) or the condition of [section 82(3)(a) of the Social Security Contributions and Benefits Act 1992] that her husband is not engaged in any one or more employments from which his weekly earnings exceed the standard rate of increase.

(4) Where a person is entitled to an addition to a contribution-based jobseeker's allowance under regulation 9(4) of the Jobseeker's Allowance (Transitional Provisions) Regulations 1995 by virtue of having satisfied the requirements for an increase of unemployment benefit referred to in paragraphs (2), (2A) or (3), he shall be treated for the purposes of those paragraphs as if he had been entitled to an increase of unemployment benefit.

AMENDMENTS

There have been multiple small amendments to the text of reg.11, none of which appear to be time sensitive. Accordingly the text of the regulation is printed above without multiple annotations.

Paragraph (1) has been amended by:

The Social Security Benefit (Dependency) Amendment Regulations 1983 (SI 1983/1001); The Social Security Benefit (Dependency) Amendment Regulations 1984 (SI 1984/1698);

The Social Security (Abolition of Earnings Rule) (Consequential) Regulations 1989 (SI 1989/1642);

The Social Security (Incapacity—Increases for Dependants) Regulations 1994 (SI 1994/2945); and

The Social Security and Child Support (Jobseeker's Allowance) (Consequential Amendments) Regulations 1996 (SI 1996/1345).

Paragraph (1A) was inserted by the Civil Partnership (Pensions, Social Security and Child Support) (Consequential, etc. Provisions) Order 2005 (SI 2005/2877) (December 5, 2005).

The Social Security (Provisions relating to Qualifying Young Persons) (Amendment) Regulations 2006 (SI 2006/692) (April 10, 2006).

Paragraph (2) has been amended by:

The Social Security Benefit (Amendment) Regulations 1987 (SI 1987/355);

The Social Security (Incapacity—Increases for Dependants) Regulations 1994 (SI 1994/2945).

Paragraph (2A) was inserted by The Social Security Benefit (Amendment) Regulations 1987 (SI 1987/355) and has been amended by The Social Security (Incapacity—Increases for Dependants) Regulations 1994 (SI 1994/2945).

Paragraph (3) has been amended by The Social Security (Incapacity—Increases for Dependants) Regulations 1994 (SI 1994/2945).

Paragraph (4) was added by The Social Security and Child Support (Jobseeker's Allowance) (Consequential Amendments) Regulations 1996 (SI 1996/1345).

GENERAL NOTE

3.61   On "having the care of a child," see annotations to s.82 of the SSCBA 1992.

PART IV

MISCELLANEOUS

Prescribed circumstances for the purposes of section 90 of the Social Security Contributions and Benefits Act

3.62   **12.**—(1) The provisions of Part IV of the Contributions and Benefits Act (increases for dependants) and of the Social Security (Incapacity Benefit—Increases for Dependants) Regulations 1994 shall apply in relation to increases of severe disablement allowance for child or adult dependants under section 90 of the Contributions and Benefits Act as they apply to increases of long-term incapacity benefit for child or adult dependants.

(2) For the purposes of increases of [¹ carer's allowance] for child or adult dependants under section 90 of the Contributions and Benefits Act, the prescribed circumstances in which a beneficiary is entitled to such an increase shall be as set out in Schedule 2 to these Regulations.

AMENDMENTS

Regulation12 substituted by The Social Security (Incapacity—Increases for Dependants) Regulations 1994 (SI 1994/2945), reg.15(7) (April 13, 1995).
1. The Social Security Amendment (Carer's Allowance) Regulations 2002 (SI 2002/2497), reg.3 and Sch.2 (April 1, 2003).

Regulation 13 revoked by The Social Security and Child Support (Jobseeker's Allowance) (Consequential Amendments) Regulations 1996 (SI 1996/1345) from October 7, 1996.   3.63

Regulation 14 ceased to have effect from October 5, 1986.   3.64

PART V

TRANSITIONAL PROVISION AND REVOCATIONS

Preservation of entitlement to benefit in payment before 4th April, 1977 for a child dependant

15.—Where—   3.65
  (a) immediately before 4th April, 1977 a person is absent from Great Britain other than temporarily; and
  (b) as respects a period before and including 3rd April, 1977 he satisfies the conditions then in force for, and is entitled to receive, payment of an amount by way of a benefit or allowance or an increase of a benefit or an allowance under the Act in respect of a child who is ordinarily resident in Great Britain; and
  (c) would cease, as from 4th April, 1977, to be entitled to that payment by reason of the fact that he does not satisfy one of the conditions for receiving such a payment, namely, that he is entitled to child benefit in respect of that child,
that person shall, for any period beginning not earlier than 4th April, 1977 during which he would, or could had he made an appropriate claim, be entitled to child benefit in respect of that child were he not absent from Great Britain, be treated as so entitled while he continues to satisfy all other conditions applicable to such a payment (including making contributions to the cost of providing for that child over and above those that would have been required for the purpose of satisfying subsection (1)(b) of section 3 of the Child Benefit Act) unless subsequent to 4th April, 1977 he becomes ordinarily resident in Great Britain.

Regulation 15A revoked by The Social Security Benefit (Dependency) Amendment Regulations 1984 (SI 1984/1698) as from November 26, 1984.   3.66

Regulation 16 omitted.   3.67

PRESCRIBED CIRCUMSTANCES FOR INCREASE OF [⁴ A CARER'S ALLOWANCE]

PART I

Increase of [⁴ carer's allowance] for child dependants

3.68   1.—For the purposes of increases of [⁴ carer's allowance] for child dependants under [section 90 of the Contributions and Benefits Act 1992], the prescribed circumstances in which a beneficiary is entitled to such an increase for any period shall be as set out in the following paragraphs.

     2.—The week rate of [⁴ a carer's allowance] for any period for which the beneficiary is entitled to child benefit in respect of a child or children shall be increased in respect of that child, or each respectively of those children, by the appropriate amount specified in relation to that allowance in column (2) of Part IV of Schedule 4 to the Act.

     [² **2A.**—Where—

     [⁶ (a) a beneficiary is a member of a couple; and]

        (b) the other [⁶ member of a couple] has earnings in any week,

the beneficiary's right to payment of increases for the following week under paragraph 2 above shall be determined in accordance with paragraph 2B below.

     2B.—No such increase shall be payable—

        (a) in respect of the first child where the earnings were [⁵ £195] or more; and

        (b) in respect of a further child for each complete [⁵ £26] by which the earnings exceeded [⁵ £195].

     [² **2BB.**—The provisions of paragraphs 2A and 2B above shall not apply so as to affect entitlement to an increase of [⁴ carer's allowance] in respect of a child in any case where the beneficiary—

        (a) was entitled to receive such an increase immediately before 26th November, 1984; and

        (b) throughout the period from and including that date to the date of coming into operation of this paragraph was, or but for the operation of those paragraphs would have been, continuously so entitled,

until such time as he would otherwise first cease to be so entitled.]

     [² **2C.**—In this Part of this Schedule—

     [⁶ . . .]

     [⁶ "couple" means—

        (a) a man and woman who are married to each other and are members of the same household;

        (b) a man and woman who are not married to each other but are living together as husband and wife;

        (c) two people of the same sex who are civil partners of each other and are members of the same household; or

        (d) two people of the same sex who are not civil partners of each other but are living together as if they were civil partners, and for the purposes of paragraph (d), two people of the same sex are to be regarded as living together as if they were civil partners if, but only if, they would be regarded as living together as husband and wife were they instead two people of the opposite sex;]

     [³ "week" means any period of 7 days corresponding to the week in respect of which the relevant social security benefit is due to be paid or ending on the day before the first day of the first such week following the date of claim.]]

     3.—Where a person is entitled to receive payment of an amount by way of an increase of [⁴ a carer's allowance] under paragraph 2 above, that increase shall not be payable unless one of the following conditions is satisfied—

        (a) that the beneficiary would be treated for the purposes of [Part IX of the Contributions and Benefits Act 1992] as having the child living with him; or

        (b) that the requisite contributions are being made to the cost of providing for the child.

     4.—The condition specified in paragraph 3(b) above is to be treated as satisfied if, but only if—

        (a) such contributions are being made at a weekly rate not less than the amount referred to in paragraph 2 above—

           (i) by the beneficiary, or

(ii) where the beneficiary is one of two spouses [⁶ or civil partners] residing together, by them together; and

(b) the contributions are over and above those required for the purposes of satisfying [section 143(1)(b) of the Social Security Contributions and Benefits Act 1992].

5.—Any sum or sums paid by a person by way of contribution towards the cost of providing for two or more children being children in respect of whom, in the period for which the sum in question is paid by the person, he is entitled to child benefit shall be treated as such contributions, of such respective amounts equal in the aggregate to the said sum or sums, in respect of those children so as to secure as large a payment as possible by way of [¹ carer's allowance] in respect of them.

PART II

Increase of [⁴ carer's allowance] for adult dependants

6.—For the purposes of increases of [⁴ carer's allowance] for adult dependants under [section 90 of the Social Security Contributions and Benefits Act 1992], the prescribed circumstances in which a beneficiary is entitled to such an increase for any period shall be as set out in paragraph 7 below.

3.69

7.—The weekly rate of an [⁴ carer's allowance] shall be increased by the amount specified in relation to that allowance in column (3) of Part IV of Schedule 4 to the Act for any period during which the beneficiary is residing with—

(a) a spouse [⁶ or civil partner] whose weekly earnings do not exceed that amount; or

(b) some person (not being a child [⁷ or qualifying young person]) who—

(i) has the care of a child or children [⁷ or a qualifying young person or persons] in respect of whom the beneficiary is entitled to child benefit;

(ii) is not undergoing imprisonment or detention in legal custody;

(iii) if he has earnings, does not have weekly earnings exceeding that amount and for this purpose there shall be disregarded any weekly earnings derived from employment by the beneficiary in caring for a child or children [⁷ or a qualifying young person or persons] in respect of whom the beneficiary is entitled to child benefit;

(iv) is not absent from Great Britain, except for any period during which the person is residing with the beneficiary outside Great Britain and for which the beneficiary is entitled to an [⁴ carer's allowance].

8.—A person who is entitled to an increase of [⁴ a carer's allowance] under paragraph 7(a) above shall not be entitled to an increase of that benefit under paragraph 7(b) above. [⁸ or PPF periodical payment.]

9.—(1) Subject to sub-paragraph (2) below in this Schedule any reference to earnings includes a reference to payments by way of occupational or personal pension.

(2) Sub-paragraph (1) above shall not apply so as to affect entitlement to an increase of [⁴ carer's allowance] in respect of a child or adult dependant in any case where the beneficiary—

(a) was entitled to receive such an increase immediately before this paragraph came into operation; and

(b) but for the operation of sub-paragraph (1) above would continue to be so entitled, until such time as he would first otherwise cease to be so entitled.

AMENDMENTS

1. The Social Security Benefit (Dependency, Claims and Payments and Hospital In-Patients) Amendment Regulations 1984 (SI 1984/1699), reg.3 (November 26, 1984).

2. The Social Security Benefit (Dependency) Amendment Regulations 1987 (SI 1987/355), reg.5 (April 6, 1987).

3. The Social Security Benefit (Computation of Earnings) Regulations 1996 (SI 1996/2745) reg.17 (November 26, 1996).

4. The Social Security Amendment (Carer's Allowance) Regulations 2002 (SI 2002/2497) reg.3 (April 1, 2003).

5. The Social Security Benefits Uprating Regulations 2009 (SI 2009/607) reg.4 (April 6, 2009).

6. The Civil Partnership (Pensions, Social Security and Child Support) (Consequential, etc. Provisions) Order 2005 (SI 2005/2877) (December 5, 2005).

7. The Social Security (Provisions relating to Qualifying Young Persons) (Amendment) Regulations 2006 (SI 2006/692) (April 10, 2006).

8. The Social Security (PPF Payments and FAS Payments) (Consequential Amendments) Regulations 2006 (SI 2006/1069) (May 5, 2006).

The Social Security (Hospital In-Patients) Regulations 2005

(SI 2005/3360) (*as amended*)

ARRANGEMENT OF REGULATIONS

SCHEDULE

Omitted—revocations

The Secretary of State for Work and Pensions makes the following regulations in exercise of the powers conferred upon him by sections 113(1)(b), 123(1)(a), (d) and (e), 124(5), 130(4), 131(10), 135(1), 136(3), 137(1), 138(2) and (4) and 175(1), (3) and (4) of the Social Security Contributions and Benefits Act 1992, sections 5(1)(p), 73(1)(b) and 189(1), (4) and (5) of the Social Security Administration Act 1992, sections 4(5) and 36(1), (2) and (4)(a) of the Jobseekers Act 1995 and sections 2(3), (6) and (9), 3(8), 17(1) and 19(1) of the State Pension Credit Act 2002.

The Social Security Advisory Committee has agreed that the proposals to make these Regulations should not be referred to it.

GENERAL NOTE

3.71   Very broadly, these regulations mark the end of the era of what has come to be known as "hospital downrating" under which benefits are reduced following lengthy periods in hospital. But some aspects of the abolished system are retained.

A challenge relating to the exclusion from benefits of prisoners transferred to mental hospital under these regulations as being in breach of Article 14 of the European Convention when read with Article 1 of Protocol No. 1 has failed with one exception: see *R. (on the application of M) v Secretary of State for Work and Pensions*, [2009] EWHC 454 (Admin). The excepted class is a small group (there were 45 such persons in detention when the case was decided) of what are described as "technical lifers", namely those, although sentenced to life imprisonment, are treated by the Secretary of State after transfer to hospital as though they had been made the subject of a hospital order under s.37 of the Mental Health Act 1983 and to a restriction order under s.41 of that Act. The trial judge said that:

> "The reality is that the 45 technical lifers are the unintended victims of a policy that had different objects in its sight. The technical lifer cannot be returned to prison and is treated for all other purposes as if he was subject to a section 37 order with a section 41 restriction. The arguments advanced by the Secretary of State in support of the policy barely touched this group of patient." (para.40)

Citation and commencement

1. These Regulations may be cited as the Social Security (Hospital In-Patients) Regulations 2005 and shall come into force for the purposes of—   3.72

(a) this regulation and regulations 2, 5, 7 and 8, on 10th April 2006,
(b) regulation 3—
   (i) in so far as it relates to a particular beneficiary other than a beneficiary in receipt of incapacity benefit or severe disablement allowance, on 10th April 2006 if it is his day for payment or, if not, on his day for payment next following 10th April 2006 ("day for payment" has the same meaning as in regulation 22(3) of, and Schedule 6 to, the Social Security (Claims and Payments) Regulations 1987),
   (ii) in so far as it relates to a particular beneficiary in receipt of incapacity benefit or severe disablement allowance, on 10th April 2006,
(c) regulation 4, in so far as it relates to a particular beneficiary, on the first day of the first benefit week to commence for that beneficiary on or after 10th April 2006 ("benefit week" has the same meaning as in the Income Support (General) Regulations 1987),
(d) regulation 6, in so far as it relates to a particular beneficiary, on the first day of the first benefit week to commence for that beneficiary on or after 10th April 2006 ("benefit week" has the same meaning as in the Jobseeker's Allowance Regulations 1996), and
(e) regulation 9—
   (i) in so far as it relates to a beneficiary specified in paragraphs (b) to (d), on the dates specified in those paragraphs for that beneficiary, and
   (ii) otherwise, on 10th April 2006.

Hospital in-patients entitled to an increase in benefit for a dependant

2.—(1) Paragraphs (2) and (3) apply where a beneficiary is entitled to an increase in benefit for an adult or child dependant under Part IV of the Social Security Contributions and Benefits Act 1992.   3.73

(2) Where the beneficiary has received free in-patient treatment for a period of not less than 52 weeks, the increase shall not be payable unless the beneficiary applies to the Secretary of State to pay the increase on behalf of the beneficiary to—
(a) the dependant, or
(b) some other person who is approved by the Secretary of State and

who satisfies the Secretary of State that he will apply the increase for the benefit of the dependant.

(3) Where both the beneficiary and the dependant are in-patients and each has received free inpatient treatment for a period of not less than 52 weeks, the increase shall not be payable unless the beneficiary applies to the Secretary of State to pay the increase on behalf of the beneficiary to—

(a) the dependant, or

(b) some other person who is approved by the Secretary of State and who satisfies the Secretary of State that he will apply the increase for the benefit of a child [¹ of the beneficiary.]

(4) For the purposes of this regulation, a person shall be regarded as receiving or having received free in-patient treatment for any period for which he is or has been maintained free of charge while undergoing medical or other treatment as an in-patient—

(a) in a hospital or similar institution under the National Health Service Act 1977, the National Health Service (Scotland) Act 1978 or the National Health Service and Community Care Act 1990, or

(b) in a hospital or similar institution maintained or administered by the Defence Council,

and such a person shall for the purposes of sub-paragraph (a) be regarded as being maintained free of charge in a hospital or similar institution unless his accommodation and services are provided under section 65 of the National Health Service Act 1977, section 57 of the National Health Service (Scotland) Act 1978 or paragraph 14 of Schedule 2 to the National Health Service and Community Care Act 1990.

(5) For the purposes of paragraph (4), a period during which a person is regarded as receiving or having received free in-patient treatment shall be deemed to begin on the day after the day on which he enters a hospital or similar institution referred to in that paragraph and to end on the day on which he leaves such a hospital or similar institution.

(6) For the purposes of this regulation—

(a) where an increase in a person's benefit is payable in respect of an adult or child dependant the increase shall be treated as a separate benefit, and

(b) where a beneficiary's spouse or civil partner ("dependant") is temporarily absent from Great Britain for the purpose of being treated for incapacity which commenced before he left Great Britain the absence shall be disregarded for the purpose of determining whether the beneficiary is residing with the dependant and is entitled to an increase in benefit for him.

AMENDMENT

1. The Social Security (Miscellaneous Amendments) Regulations 2006 (SI 2006/588) (March 10, 2006).

GENERAL NOTE

3.74   Provision is made for continued payment of an increase in benefit for a dependant after 52 weeks on application to the Secretary of State. This is the only remaining free-standing provision on payments in relation to hospital in-patients. All other aspects of payments are incorporated into the specific benefit rules by the amendments made by regs 3 to 8 of these Regulations. Note that there are no linking rules in relation to these provisions. The regulation is drafted such that the only reading possible is that the beneficiary must have been in hospital for a continuous period of at least 52 weeks. Separate periods in hospital cannot be linked to form the 52 week qualifying period.

The question of whether a person is in a "hospital or similar institution" is nowadays determined not so much by the inherent nature of the accommodation but by whether the person's assessed needs for care is such that the National Health Service is under a duty to fund the accommodation free of charge. In the less straightforward cases, tribunals will need to take evidence and consider who is actually funding the accommodation. *R(DLA) 2/06* is instructive of the complexities which can arise.

Revocation of the Social Security (Hospital In-Patients) Regulations 1975 and other regulations

9.—(1) The Social Security (Hospital In-Patients) Regulations 1975 shall be revoked.

(2) The provisions in the subordinate legislation set out in the Schedule shall be revoked.

3.75

Social Security (Overlapping Benefits) Regulations 1979

(SI 1979/597) *(as amended)*

ARRANGEMENT OF REGULATIONS

3.76

17.   Prevention of double adjustments.
18.   *Omitted.*

SCHEDULES

Schedule 1—Personal benefits which are required to be adjusted by reference to benefits not under Chapters I and II of Part II of the Act.
Schedule 2—*Omitted.*

The Secretary of State for Social Services, in exercise of powers conferred by sections 83(1) and 85 of the Social Security Act 1975 and of all other powers enabling him in that behalf hereby makes the following regulations which only consolidate the regulations herein revoked and which accordingly by virtue of paragraph 20 of Schedule 15 to the Social Security Act 1975, are not subject to the requirement of section 139(1) of that Act for prior reference to the National Insurance Advisory Committee:

Citation and commencement

3.77   **1.**—These regulations may be cited as the Social Security (Overlapping Benefits) Regulations 1979 and shall come into operation on 29th June, 1979.

Interpretation

3.78   **2.**—(1) In these regulations, unless the context otherwise requires—
"the Act" means the Social Security Act 1975;
[1 "the Contributions and Benefits Act" means the Social Security Contributions and Benefits Act 1992];
"the Pensions Act" means the Social Security Pensions Act 1975;
"benefit under Chapters I and II of Part II of the Act" includes benefit treated as included in Chapter I of Part II of the Act by virtue of section 66(2)(b) of the Pensions Act;
[2 "bereavement allowance" means an allowance referred to in section 39B of the Contributions and Benefits Act;]
"the Child Benefit Act" means the Child Benefit Act 1975;
"child benefit" means benefit under Part I of the Child Benefit Act;
[3 "contributory benefit" means any benefit payable under Part II of the Contributions and Benefits Act, [12 a contribution-based jobseeker's allowance and a contributory employment and support allowance];
"death benefit" means any benefit, pension or allowance which, apart from these regulations, is payable (whether under the Act or otherwise) in respect of the death of any person;
"the deceased" means, in relation to any death benefit, the person in respect of whose death that benefit, apart from these regulations, is payable;
"dependency benefit" means that benefit, pension or allowance which, apart from these regulations, is payable (whether under the Act or otherwise) to a person in respect of another person who is a child or an adult dependant, it includes child's special allowance and any personal benefit by way of pension payable to a child under any Personal Injuries Scheme, Service Pensions Instrument or 1914–1918 War Injuries Scheme but does not include benefit under section 73 of the

Act (allowances to a woman who has care of children of person who died as a result of an industrial accident)

[4 or child tax credit under the Tax Credits Act 2002];

"disablement pension" includes a disablement payment on a pension basis and retired pay or pension in respect of any disablement, wound, injury or disease;

[5 "the Jobseekers Act" means the Jobseekers Act 1995];

"personal benefit" means any benefit, pension or allowance [11 , except a shared additional pension] [6 (whether under the Act or otherwise)] which is not a dependency benefit [6 and includes [12 a contributory employment and support allowance but not an income-related employment and support allowance and includes] a contribution-based jobseeker's allowance but not an income-based jobseeker's allowance] and which [6 apart from these regulations,] is payable to any person;

"Person Injuries Scheme" means any scheme made under the Personal Injuries (Emergency Provisions) Act 1939 or under the Pensions (Navy, Army, Air Force and Mercantile Marine) Act 1939;

"Pneumoconiosis and Byssinosis Benefit Scheme" means any scheme made under section 5 of the Industrial Injuries and Diseases (Old Cases) Act 1975;

[7 "Service Pensions Instrument" means any instrument described in sub-paragraphs (a) or (b) below in so far, but only in so far, as the pensions or other benefits provided by that instrument are not calculated or determined by reference to length of service, namely:—

(a) any instrument made in exercise of powers—

    (i) referred to in section 12(1) of the Social Security (Miscellaneous Provisions) Act 1977 (pensions or other benefits for disablement or death due to service in the armed forces of the Crown); or

    (ii) under section 1 of the Polish Resettlement Act 1947 (pensions and other benefits for disablement or death due to service in certain Polish forces); or

(b) any instrument under which a pension or other benefit may be paid to a person (not being a member of the armed forces of the Crown) out of public funds in respect of death or disablement, wound, injury, or disease due to service in any nursing service or other auxiliary service of any of the armed forces of the Crown, or in any other organisation established under the control of the Defence Council or formerly established under the control of the Admiralty, the Army Council or the Air Council.]

[11 "shared additional pension" means a shared additional pension under section 55A of the Contributions and Benefits Act;]

"training allowance" means an allowance (whether by way of periodical grants or otherwise) payable out of public funds by a Government department or by or on behalf of [8 Scottish Enterprise, Highlands and Islands Enterprise [10, the Learning and Skills Council for England and Wales, the National Assembly for Wales] or the Secretary of State to a person for his maintenance, or in respect of any dependant of his, for the period, or part of the period, during which he is following a course of training or instruction provided by, or in pursuance of arrangements made with, that department or approved by that department in relation to him or so provided or approved by or on behalf of [8 Scottish

Enterprise, Highlands and Islands Enterprise [¹⁰, the National Assembly for Wales] or the Secretary of State; but it does not include—
(a) an allowance paid by any Government department to or in respect of a person by reason of the fact that he is following a course of full-time education or is in training as a teacher; or
(b) a payment made by or on behalf of [⁸ Scottish Enterprise, Highlands and Islands Enterprise or the Secretary of State] to any person by way of training premium or training bonus in consequence of that person's use of facilities for training provided in pursuance of arrangements made under section 2 of the Employment and Training Act 1973 or [⁸ section 2 of the Enterprise and New Towns (Scotland) Act 1990.]

"treatment allowance" means an allowance payable under a Personal Injuries Scheme, Service Pensions Instrument or 1914–1918 War Injuries Scheme only to a person undergoing a course of medical, surgical or rehabilitative treatment in consequence of a disablement in respect of which a pension may be or has been paid, or an allowance payable to any such person pending the determination of the question whether he is entitled to receive such a pension;

"unemployment supplement" includes an increase on account of unemployability under—
(a) any Pneumoconiosis and Byssinosis Benefit Scheme; and
(b) any Personal Injuries Scheme, Service Pensions Instrument or 1914–1918 War Injuries Scheme;

"war pension death benefit" means a death benefit by way of pension or allowance under any Personal Injuries Scheme, Service Pensions Instrument or 1914–1918 War Injuries Scheme, but does not include a rent allowance or a grant payable by reason of the beneficiary being in receipt of a pension and being a specific age which is not less than 65 or a pension or an allowance calculated by reference to the necessities of the beneficiary;

[² "widowed parent's allowance" means an allowance referred to in section 39A of the Contributions and Benefits Act;]

"1914–1918 War Injuries Scheme" means any scheme made under the Injuries in War (Compensation) Act 1914 or under the Injuries in War Compensation Act 1914 (Session 2) or any Government scheme for compensation in respect of persons injured in any merchant ship or fishing vessel as the result of hostilities during the 1914–1918 War.

[¹² "the Welfare Reform Act" means the Welfare Reform Act 2007].

(2) For the purposes of these regulations, unless otherwise specified, [⁹ additional pension] payable by virtue of the Act or the Pensions Act shall be deemed to include any increase so far as attributable to any additional pension or to any increase by virtue of section 126A of the Act or paragraph 4A of Schedule 1 to the Pensions Act or to any increase of graduated retirement benefit and shall be treated as a separate personal benefit included in Chapter I of Part II of the Act.

AMENDMENTS

1. The Social Security (Overlapping Benefits) Amendment (No. 2) Regulations 1992 (SI 1992/3194), reg.2 (January 13, 1993).
2. The Social Security (Benefits for Widows and Widowers) (Consequential Amendments) Regulations 2000 (SI 2000/1483), reg.6 (April 9, 2001).

3. The Social Security and Child Support (Jobseeker's Allowance) (Consequential Amendments) Regulations 1996 (SI 1996/1345), reg.22(2)(a) (October 7, 1996).

4. The Social Security (Working Tax Credit and Child Tax Credit) (Consequential Amendments) (No. 2) Regulations 2003 (SI 2003/937), reg.2 (April 6, 2003).

5. The Social Security and Child Support (Jobseeker's Allowance) (Consequential Amendments) Regulations 1996 (SI 1996/1345), reg.22(2)(b) (October 7, 1996).

6. The Social Security and Child Support (Jobseeker's Allowance) (Consequential Amendments) Reglations 1996 (SI 1996/1345), reg.22(2)(c) (October 7, 1996).

7. The Social Security (Overlapping Benefits) Amendments Regulations 1980 (SI 1980/1927), reg.2(b) (January 5, 1981).

8. The Enterprise (Scotland) Consequential Amendments Order 1991 (SI 1991/387), reg.2(1) (April 4, 1991).

9. Social Security Act 1986, s.18(1) (April 6, 1987).

10. The Social Security, Child Support and Tax Credits (Miscellaneous Amendments) Regulations 2005 (SI 2005/337) reg.11 (March 18, 2005).

11. The Social Security (Shared Additional Pension) (Miscellaneous Amendments) Regulations 2005 (SI 2005/1551) (July 6, 2005).

12. The Employment and Support Allowance (Consequential Provisions) (No. 2) Regulations 2008 (SI 2008/1554), reg.51 (October 27, 2008).

GENERAL NOTE

A new s.2 of the Employment and Training Act 1973 was substituted by s.25 of the Employment Act 1988. The new definition brings all payments made under the new training schemes within its ambit.　**3.79**

The Training for Work (Scottish Enterprise and Highlands and Islands Enterprise Programmes) Order 1993 (SI 1993/498) provides that for the purpose of these regulations, a person using facilities under the training programmes to which the Order refers are treated as participating in arrangements for training under s.2(3) of the Enterprise and New Towns (Scotland) Act 1990 and payments made to persons on those programmes are treated as payments in respect of training. See also, to the same effect, the Training for Work (Miscellaneous Provisions) Order 1993 (SI 1993/348).

Regulation 3 revoked by The Social Security (Incapacity Benefit) Consequential and Transitional Amendments and Savings) Regulations 1995 (SI 1995/829), reg.14(2) (April 13, 1995) subject to the savings set out below.　**3.80**

TRANSITIONAL PROTECTION

Regulation 3 is revoked with effect from April 13, 1995, but reg.14(9) of the Social Security (Incapacity Benefit)(Consequential and Transitional Amendments and Savings) Regulations 1995 (SI 1995/829) provides as follows:　**3.81**

"(9) Where before the appointed day regulation 3 of the Overlapping Benefits Regulations (special provisions for widow's benefit and invalidity pension) applied to a widow; and

(a) on or after that day she remains entitled to either a widowed mother's allowance or a widow's pension; and
(b) she is either a transitional case for the purposes of Part IV of the Social Security (Incapacity Benefit) (Transitional) Regulations 1995 or, has an award of long-term incapacity benefit by virtue of regulation 19 or 20 of the Social Security (Incapacity Benefit) (Transitional) Regulations 1995; and
(c) she is under pensionable age,

regulation 3 of the Overlapping Benefits Regulations shall continue to apply to her as if the revocation made by paragraph (2) above had not been made subject to the modification made in paragraph (10) below."

Regulation 14(10) of the Social Security (Incapacity Benefit)(Consequential and Transitional Amendments and Savings) Regulations 1995 (SI 1995/829) modifes revoked reg.3 so that it reads as follows in its application to those covered by the saving in Regulation 14(9) above.

"**3.**—(1) This regulation applies where, apart from these regulations, there is payable for the same period to a person under pensionable age both—

(a) a long-term incapacity benefit; and

(b) a widowed mother's allowance or widow's pension (hereafter referred to in this regulation as "the widow's benefit").

(2) The total amount payable in respect of these benefits under this regulation shall be—

(a) an amount equal to either the basic rate of long-term incapacity benefit referred to in regulation 18(1)(a) of the Social Security (Incapacity Benefit) (Transitional) Regulations 1995 paid in a transitional case or an award of widow's basic pension calculated by reference to section 44(1) of the Contributions and Benefits Act or an amount equal to the greater of them; and

(b) the sum of the incapacity benefit payable at the additional rate in accordance with regulation 18(1)(b) of the Social Security (Incapacity Benefit) (Transitional) Regulations 1995 and widow's pension determined in accordance with section 44(3) of the Contributions and Benefits Act.

(3) Subject to paragraph (4)—

(a) where the beneficiary has made application, before the payment is made, that the total amount should be treated as being made up of the rate of the long-term incapacity benefit, any balance being the widow's benefit, it shall be so treated;

(b) in any other case, that amount shall be treated as being made up of the rate of the widow's benefit, any balance being the long-term incapacity benefit.

(4) For the purposes of the remainder of these regulations (other than regulation 6(5)), which shall apply after adjustment has been made under this regulation, the total amount payable under this regulation shall be treated as a single long-term benefit payable on a weekly basis."

Adjustment of personal benefit under Parts II and III of the Contributions and Benefits Act where other personal benefit under those Parts or graduated retirement benefit is payable

3.82

4.—[¹ (1) Subject to paragraphs (2), (3) and (4) and regulation 12, an adjustment shall be made in accordance with paragraph (5) where either—

(a) two or more personal benefits (whether of the same or a different description) are, or but for this regulation would be, payable under Parts II and III of the Contributions and Benefits Act (which relate to benefits other than industrial injuries benefits) [⁹ Part 1 of the Welfare Reform Act] [² or under the Jobseekers Act] for any period; or

(b) graduated retirement benefit is payable under sections 36 and 37 of the National Insurance Act 1965 together with one or more personal benefits (whether of the same or a different description) which are, or but for this regulation would be, payable under Parts II and III of the Contributions and Benefits Act for any period].

(2) Paragraph (1) shall not require the adjustment of, or by reference to—

(a) a death grant;
(b) a maternity grant;
(c) any other sum paid otherwise than in respect of a period;
(d) an earnings-related supplement or earnings-related addition to any benefit (except as provided by regulation 5 and in the case of [[3 severe disablement allowance] or [[8 carer's allowance]);
(e) an attendance allowance;
(f) [[4 additional pension] or graduated retirement benefit (except as provided by paragraph (4));
(g) [[5 disability living allowance]

[[6 (2A) Paragraph (1) shall not require an adjustment of widow's pension reduced in accordance with section 39(4) of the Contributions and Benefits Act only by reference to long-term incapacity benefit in accordance with section 40(5)(b) of that Act].

(3) Paragraph (1) shall require an adjustment of age addition only by reference to another age addition.

(4) Where there are payable two or more personal benefits to which this regulation applies with which [[4 additional pension] or graduated retirement benefit is payable as part of the rate of benefit or as an increase of benefit, or, in a case where the person entitled to receive the benefits is over pensionable age and one or more of the benefits includes either additional pension or graduated retirement benefit while another of the benefits is payable at the rate referred to in [section 31(6) or 33(4) of the Social Security Contributions and Benefits Act 1992], then the following provisions shall apply—

(a) for the purposes of adjustment falling to be made under paragraph (5) that [[4 additional pension] or graduated retirement benefit shall be treated as part of the personal benefit with which it is so payable;
(b) the provisions of sub-paragraph (a) shall apply before any further adjustment under these regulations; and
(c) for the purpose of any such further adjustment, the beneficiary shall be treated as having a single long-term benefit inclusive of whichever before adjustment under sub-paragraph (a) is the highest of the following amounts—
  (i) the highest additional pension payable, or
  (ii) the highest graduated retirement benefit payable, or
  (iii) the highest total of additional pension and graduated retirement benefit payable together as part of the rate of and as an increase of any of those personal benefits.

(5) Where an adjustment falls to be made in accordance with this paragraph and—

(a) one of the benefits is a contributory benefit and one is a noncontributory benefit, the non-contributory benefit shall be adjusted by deducting from it the amount of the contributory benefit and only the balance, if any, shall be payable;
(b) sub-paragraph (a) above does not apply, if one of the benefits is payable on a weekly basis—
  (i) where the beneficiary has made application, before the payment is made, to have the benefit payable on a weekly basis adjusted, it shall be adjusted by deducting from it the amount of the other benefit and only the balance of it, if any, shall be payable,
  (ii) in any other case, the benefit not payable on a weekly basis

shall be adjusted by deducting from it the amount of the other benefit and only the balance of it, if any, shall be payable;

(c) sub-paragraphs (a) and (b) above do not apply, the amount payable in respect of the benefits in question shall be an amount equal to that which would but for this provision be payable in respect of—

    (i) one of them, if they would have been payable at the same rate, or

    (ii) the higher or highest of them, if they would have been payable at different rates,

so however that in a case where more than 2 benefits would be payable then the total amount payable shall not exceed the amount which would be ascertained under sub-paragraph (c).

[⁷ (6) For the purposes of this regulation—

"additional pension" means a pension payable with a personal benefit under Part II of the Contribution and Benefits Act or an additional rate; and

"additional rate" means an additional amount equal to the rate paid or payable as an additional pension with invalidity benefit immediately before 13 April 1995 which is payable after that date pursuant to regulation 18 of the Social Security (Incapacity Benefit) (Transitional) Regulations 1995.]

AMENDMENTS

1. The Social Security (Overlapping Benefits) Amendment (No. 2) Regulations 1992 (SI 1992/3194), reg.3(2) (January 13, 1993).
2. The Social Security and Child Support (Jobseeker's Allowance) (Consequential Amendments) Regulations 1996 (SI 1996/1345), reg.22(3) (October 7, 1996).
3. The Social Security (Severe Disablement Allowance) Reglations 1984 (SI 1984/1303), reg.11 (November 29, 1984).
4. Social Security Act 1986, s.18(1) (April 6, 1987).
5. The Disability Living Allowance and Disability Working Allowance (Consequential Provisions) Regulations 1991 (SI 1991/2742), reg.5(2) (April 6, 1992).
6. The Social Security (Incapacity Benefit) Consequential and Transitional Amendments and Savings) Regulations 1995 (SI 1995/829), reg.14(3) (April 13, 1995).
7. The Social Security (Incapacity for Work and Miscellaneous Amendments) Regulations 1996 (SI 1996/3207), reg.4 (January 6, 1997).
8. The Social Security (Carer's Allowance) Regulations 2002 (SI 2002/2497), Sch.2 (April 1, 2003).
9. The Employment and Support Allowance (Consequential Provisions) (No. 2) Regulations 2008 (SI 2008/1554), reg.51 (October 27, 2008).

DEFINITIONS

"benefit under Chapters I and II of Part II of the Act"—reg.2.
"personal benefit"—reg.2.

GENERAL NOTE

3.83   This complex regulation states in para.(5) the basic general rules on overlapping benefits (though no adjustment is needed for any of the benefits specified in para. (2)).

Unless reg.3 applies, only the highest of the following benefits is payable: invalid care allowance, invalidity pension, maternity allowance, non contributory widow's benefit, retirement pension, severe disablement allowance, sickness benefit, unemployment benefit, widowed mother's allowance, and widow's pension.

There are a number of points to note in relation to additions to benefits. An age addition only overlaps with another age addition (para.(3)). Paragraph (4) contains special rules where additional pensions under SERPS or graduated retirement pension is payable.

Special provision for earnings-related supplements and earnings-related addition to widow's allowance

5.—(1) Where two or more earnings-related supplements to any benefits under the Act would apart from this regulation be payable for the same period, for the purposes of regulation 4(1) each such supplement shall be treated as part of the benefit it supplements.

3.84

(2) Where an earnings-related addition to widow's allowance would apart from this regulation be payable for the same period as any other benefit under the Act which is calculated whether wholly or in part by reference to the contributions of a husband who has died, that other benefit shall be adjusted by deducting from it the amount of the earnings-related addition, provided that where the widow is also entitled for the same period to graduated retirement benefit or [¹ additional pension], or both of them, by virtue of her own contributions and the contributions of the husband who has died, the graduated retirement benefit or [¹ additional pension] to be adjusted shall be only that part which is payable by virtue of the contributions of the husband who has died.

(3) Paragraph (1) shall not apply where apart from this regulation a widow's allowance would be payable for the same period as 2 or more other benefits under the Act; in such a case the earnings-related supplement to any of those other benefits shall be adjusted so that only the higher or highest of them is payable.

(4) For the purposes of paragraph (2), [¹ additional pension] or graduated retirement benefit, where it is, or but for this regulation would be, payable as part of the rate of or as an increase of another personal benefit, shall be treated as part of the personal benefit with which it is so payable.

AMENDMENT

1. Social Security Act 1986, s.18(1) (April 6, 1987).

Adjustments of personal benefit under Chapters I and II of Part II of the Act by reference to industrial injuries benefits and benefits not under the Act, and adjustments of industrial injuries benefits

6.—(1) Subject to paragraph (5) and regulation 12, where a personal benefit which is specified in column (1) of Schedule 1 to these regulations ("the column (1) benefit") is, or but for this regulation would be payable to a person for the same period as a personal benefit which is specified in the corresponding paragraph of column (2) of that Schedule ("the column (2) benefit") the column (1) benefit shall be adjusted by deducting from it the amount of the column (2) benefit and, subject to any further adjustment under regulation 4, only the balance, if any, shall be payable.

3.85

(2) Any reference in paragraph (1), or in Schedule 1 to these regulations,

to a benefit, other than a training allowance, does not include an earnings-related supplement or earnings-related addition to it.

(3) Paragraph (1) and Schedule 1 to these regulations shall have effect in relation to an attendance allowance, [¹ or the care component of disability living allowance] and to any benefit [¹ by reference to which that allowance (as the case may be)] is to be adjusted, as requiring adjustment where both that allowance and the benefit are payable in respect of the same person (whether or not one or both of them are payable to him).

(4) Paragraph (1) and Schedule 1 to these regulations shall not require the adjustment of, or by reference to, [² additional pension] or graduated retirement benefit.

(5) Where—

(a) the column (2) benefit is industrial death benefit or war pension death benefit in either case payable to the beneficiary as the surviving spouse [⁵ or civil partner], and

(b) the column (1) benefit is Category A retirement pension [³ . . .] which

   (i) [⁴ . . .]

   (ii) has a [² basic pension] by virtue of the beneficiary's own contributions (but not by virtue of those of a former spouse [⁵ or civil partner]) which consists of either the rate specified in [section 44(3)(a) and (4) of the Social Security Contributions and Benefits Act 1992] or some percentage of that rate prescribed by regulations made under [section 60(1) of the Social Security Contributions and Benefits Act 1992],

the adjustment under paragraph (1) shall not reduce that Column (1) benefit to less than the appropriate rate in sub-paragraph (b)(ii), together with, if any, increments payable under paragraph 2 of [Schedule 5 of the Social Security Contributions and Benefits Act 1992] and increase under [section 47(1) of the Social Security Contributions and Benefits Act 1992].

AMENDMENTS

1. The Disability Living Allowance and Disability Working Allowance (Consequential Provisions) Regulations 1991 (SI 1991/2742), reg.5(3) (April 6, 1992).

2. Social Security Act 1986, s.18(1) (April 6, 1987).

3. The Social Security (Incapacity Benefit) (Consequential and Transitional Amendments and Savings) Regulations 1995 (SI 1995/829), reg.14(4)(a) (April 13, 1995).

4. The Social Security (Incapacity Benefit) Consequential and Transitional Amendments and Savings) Regulations 1995 (SI 1995/829), reg.14(4)(b) (April 13, 1995).

5. The Civil Partnership (Pensions, Social Security and Child Support) (Consequential, etc. Provisions) Order 2005 (SI 2005/2877) (December 5, 2005).

GENERAL NOTE

3.86 Regulation 14(4) of the Social Security (Incapacity Benefit) (Consequential and Transitional Amendments and Savings) Regulations 1995 (SI 1995/829) amends this regulation with effect from April 13, 1995 by revoking the reference to invalidity benefit in para.(5)(b) and omitting para.(5)(b)(i), but reg.14(11) contains a saving provision as follows:

"(11) Notwithstanding the amendment made by paragraph (4) above, where in a transitional case long-term incapacity benefit falls to be adjusted by reference to a benefit within column (2) of Schedule 1 to the Overlapping Benefits Regulations, that benefit shall be adjusted on or after the appointed day as if the words 'or invalidity benefit' had not been omitted from regulation 6 of those Regulations."

Adjustment of dependency benefit in respect of a child where other dependency benefit is payable for that child

7.—(1) Subject to regulation 12, where dependency benefit under the Act is payable, or but for this regulation would be payable, to any person in respect of a child and any other dependency benefit specified in paragraph (2) is payable to that or any other person in respect of that child for the same period, an adjustment shall be made in accordance with regulation 4(5) so however that where one of the dependency benefits is death benefit under [paras. 18 and 19 of Schedule 7 to the Social Security Contributions and Benefits Act 1992] by way of an allowance, or is a guardian's allowance under [section 77 of the Social Security Contributions and Benefits Act 1992] (the other dependency benefit not being benefit under either the said [section 77 or paragraphs 18 and 19 to Schedule 7 of the Social Security Contributions and Benefits Act 1992]) the adjustment shall be made in accordance with paragraph (4) of this regulation.

3.87

(2) Subject to paragraph (3), the other dependency benefit referred to in paragraph (1) is any dependency benefit under—

(a) the Act;

(b) any Personal Injuries Scheme, Service Pensions Instrument or 1914–1918 War Injuries Scheme;

(c) any Pneumoconiosis and Byssinosis Benefit Scheme;

(d) any scheme, being a benefit by way of training allowance.

(3) Sub-paragraph (b) of paragraph (2) does not include an allowance payable or the purpose of the child's education and for the purposes of that sub-paragraph—

(a) any personal benefit by way of a pension payable to a child shall be treated as a dependency benefit payable to another person in respect of that child;

(b) any dependency benefit payable as part of a disablement pension shall be disregarded unless it is payable as an increase of an unemployability supplement.

(4) Where one of the dependency benefits is death benefit under section 70 by way of an allowance or is a guardian's allowance, except in a case to which paragraph (5) applies, the other dependency benefit shall be adjusted by deducting from it the amount of that death benefit or, as the case may be, guardian's allowance, and only the balance, if any, shall be payable.

(5) Where a death benefit by way of an allowance under section 70 or a guardian's allowance is payable to a person in respect of a child and any other dependency benefit specified in sub-paragraph (b) or (d) of paragraph (2) is payable to that or any other person in respect of that child for the same period, the death benefit or, as the case may be, the guardian's allowance shall be adjusted by deducting from it the other benefit and only the balance, if any, shall be payable.

Child benefit

8.—(1) Subject to the following provisions of this regulation, where any benefit, or increase of a benefit, under the Act is payable to a beneficiary,

3.88

563

the weekly rate of that benefit or increase shall not be adjusted by reference to child benefit.

(2) Where child benefit is payable to a beneficiary at the rate for the time being specified in regulation 2(1)(a)(ii) of the Child Benefit and Social Security (Fixing and Adjustment of Rates) Regulations 1976 (in this regulation referred to as the "Child Benefit Rates Regulations") (weekly rate for only, elder or eldest child of a lone parent) and for the same period, in respect of the same child, any benefit or increase in benefit under the Contributions and Benefits Act [¹ except where that benefit is guardian's allowance payable to any person under section 77 of that Act,] the weekly rate of that benefit or increase thereof shall be reduced by—

   (a) [² . . .];

   (b) [² . . .] an amount equal to the amount, less [³ £3.65], by which the rate specified in regulation 2(1)(a)(ii) of the Child Benefit Rates Regulations exceeds the rate specified in regulation 2(1)(b) of those Regulations.

(3) Subject to paragraph (6) of this regulation, where child benefit is payable to a beneficiary at the rate for the time being specified in regulation 2(1)(a)(i) of the Child Benefit Rates Regulations (weekly rate for only, elder or eldest child) and for the same period, in respect of the same child, any benefit or increase in benefit under the Contributions and Benefits Act [¹ except where that benefit is guardian's allowance payable to any person under section 77 of that Act,] the weekly rate of that benefit or the increase thereof shall be reduced by an amount equal to the amount, less [³ £3.65], by which the rate specified in regulation 2(1)(a)(i) of the Child Benefit Rates Regulations exceeds the rate specified in regulation 2(1)(b) of those Regulations.

   (4) [¹ . . .]

   (5) [¹ . . .]

(6) Where the weekly rate of any benefit or increase of benefit under the Act or the weekly rate of child benefit or both are increased in consequence of an order under section 63(2) of the Social Security Act 1986 and as a result the amount by which the benefit being adjusted under paragraph (3) changes, the weekly rate of benefit or increase shall not be reduced by the increased amount until the date on which the change in that benefit or increase of benefit has effect.

   (7) [¹ . . .]]

AMENDMENTS

Regulation 8 was substituted by The Social Security (Overlapping Benefits) Amendment Regulations 1991 (SI 1991/547), reg.2 (April 8, 1991). Paragraphs (2) and (3) were substituted by The Child Benefit, Child Support and Social Security (Miscellaneous Amendments) Regulations 1996 (SI 1996/1803), reg.47(a) (April 7, 1997), and para.(6) was substituted by The Social Security (Overlapping Benefits) Amendment Regulations 1992 (SI 1992/589), reg.2(c) (April 6, 1992).

1. The Child Benefit, Child Support and Social Security (Miscellaneous Amendments) Regulations 1996 (SI 1996/1803), reg.47(b) (April 7, 1997).

2. The Social Security (Overlapping Benefits) Amendment Regulations 2003 (SI 2003/136), reg.2 (April 7, 2003).

3. The Social Security (Miscellaneous Amendments) Regulations 2004, SI 2004/565, reg.8, (April 12, 2004).

Adjustment of dependency benefit in respect of an adult dependant where other dependency benefit is payable

9.—(1) Subject to paragraph (3) and regulation 12, where for any period   **3.89**
any dependency benefit under the Act is, or but for this regulation would
be, payable to any person in respect of an adult dependant and any other
dependency benefit specified in paragraph (2) is payable for that period
to—

(a) that person in respect of that or any other adult dependant; or

(b) any other person in respect of that dependant,

an adjustment shall be made in accordance with regulation 4(5).

(2) The other dependency benefit referred to in paragraph (1) is any
dependency benefit under—

(a) the Act;

(b) any Personal Injuries Scheme, Service Pensions Instrument or
1914–1918 War Injuries Scheme;

(c) any Pneumoconiosis and Byssinosis Benefit Scheme;

(d) any scheme being a benefit by way of training allowance.

(3) Paragraph (1) shall not require an adjustment to be made where
one of the dependency benefits in question is an increase of benefit under
[section 82(4) or 85(2) of the Social Security Contributions and Benefits
Act 1992] in respect of a person who is employed by the beneficiary but
is not residing with him and the other such benefit is payable to a person
other than the beneficiary [¹ or to a person entitled to an increase of incapacity benefit under regulation 9(1)(d) of the Social Security (Incapacity
Benefit—Increases for Dependants) Regulations 1994 who satisfies the
requirements of paragraph (3)(a) of that regulation.]

(4) For the purposes of paragraph (2)(b) any dependency benefit which
is payable with a disablement pension shall be disregarded unless it is
payable as an increase of an unemployability supplement.

AMENDMENT

1. The Social Security (Incapacity Benefit) (Consequential and Transitional
Amendments and Savings) Regulations 1995 (SI 1995/829), reg.14(5)
(April 14, 1995).

Adjustment of dependency benefit where certain personal benefit is payable

10.—(1) Subject to the following provisions of this regulation, where a   **3.90**
dependency benefit under the Act is payable for the same period as one or
more of the following personal benefits is, or but for the provisions of these
regulations would be, payable to the dependant—

(a) a personal benefit under Chapter I or II of Part II of the Act (other
than a benefit specified in regulation 4(2)(a)(b)(c)(e) or (g));

(b) an unemployability supplement;

(c) [¹ . . .];

(d) industrial death benefit;

(e) war pension death benefit;

(f) a training allowance,

[² (g) a temporary allowance under the provisions of section 1 of the Job
Release Act 1977];

[³ (h) a weekly allowance pursuant to arrangements made by the Manpower Services Commission under section 2 of the Employment and Training Act 1973 or section 2 of the Enterprise and New Towns (Scotland) Act 1990 for the purpose of the Enterprise Allowance Scheme];

[⁴ (i) graduated retirement benefit];

[⁵ (j) a contribution-based jobseeker's allowance].

[⁸ (k) a contributory employment and support allowance;]

the dependency benefit shall be adjusted in accordance with paragraph (2).

(2) Where the weekly rate of the personal benefit (or, if more than one, the aggregate weekly rate payable after any adjustment made by virtue of regulations 4(1) or 6(1)—

(a) is equal to or exceeds the weekly rate of the dependency benefit, the dependency benefit shall not be paid;

(b) in any other case, the weekly rate of the dependency benefit payable shall be adjusted, if necessary, so that it does not exceed the difference between the weekly rate of the personal benefit and that of the unadjusted dependency benefit.

(3) Paragraph (1) does not apply to an increase of benefit under [section 82(4) or 85(2) of the Social Security Contributions and Benefits Act 1992] in respect of a person who is employed by, but is not residing with, the beneficiary [⁶ or to a person entitled to an increase of incapacity benefit under regulation 9(1)(d) of the Social Security (Incapacity Benefit—Increases for Dependants) Regulations 1994 who satisfies the requirements of paragraph (3)(a) of that regulation.]

(4) Where the personal benefit to which paragraph (1) applies is sickness benefit [⁷ but not incapacity benefit] payable to a married woman which falls to be adjusted by virtue of regulations under [section 73(1)(b) of the Social Security Administration Act 1992] (hospital in-patients) and the dependency benefit would be payable to her husband, the rate of sickness benefit to be taken into account for the purposes of paragraph (1) shall be the rate after it has been so adjusted.

AMENDMENTS

1. The Social Security (Abolition of Injury Benefit) (Consequential) Regulations 1983 (SI 1983/186), reg.10(2) (April 6, 1983).

2. The Social Security (Overlapping Benefits) Amendment Regulations 1980 (SI 1980/1927), reg.2 (January 5, 1981).

3. The Social Security (Overlapping Benefits) Amendment Regulations 1982 (SI 1982/1173), reg.2 (September 14, 1982).

4. The Social Security (Overlapping Benefits) Amendment (No. 2) Regulations 1992 (SI 1992/3194), reg.4 (January 13, 1993).

5. The Social Security and Child Support (Jobseeker's Allowance) (Consequential Amendments) Regulations 1996 (SI 1996/1345), reg.22(4) (October 7, 1996).

6. The Social Security (Incapacity Benefit) (Consequential and Transitional Amendments and Savings) Regulations 1995 (SI 1995/829), reg.14(6)(a) (April 13, 1995).

7. The Social Security (Incapacity Benefit) (Consequential and Transitional Amendments and Savings) Regulations 1995 (SI 1995/829), reg.14(6)(b) (April 13, 1995).

8. The Employment and Support Allowance (Consequential Provisions) (No. 2) Regulations 2008 (SI 2008/1554), reg.51 (October 27, 2008).

GENERAL NOTE

In *Jones v Chief Adjudication Officer* [1990] I.R.L.R. 533, *R(G) 2/91*, the Court   3.91
of Appeal held that reg.10 is not discriminatory on grounds of sex contrary to Art.4
of EEC Directive 79/7 on the Progressive Implementation of the Principle of Equal
Treatment of Men and Women in Matters of Social Security.

The facts arising in *R(S) 5/94* were that the claimant received an increase of
invalidity benefit in respect of his wife. She had retired and received a pension consisting of three components: the basic pension, an additional pension, and a graduated retirement pension. The question was the extent to which the pension benefits
received by the wife should be taken into account as overlapping with the increase of
invalidity benefit. No one doubted that reg.10 applied, nor that the basic component of the retirement pension was a personal benefit to be taken into account. The
argument concerned the graduated retirement pension and the additional pension.
The Commissioner held, first, that the graduated retirement pension was not to be
taken into account. This had been established in *Pearse v Chief Adjudication Officer
and Secretary of State for Social Security*, CA (Civ Div), Judgment of June 12, 1992,
The Times, June 18, 1992. The additional pension and the basic pension are aggregated for the purposes of the application of reg.10 and the total must be deducted
from the increase of invalidity benefit.

Dependency benefit under the Act not to be payable if a training allowance is payable

11.—Dependency benefit under the Act shall not be payable to any   3.92
person for any period in respect of which any personal benefit by way of
training allowance is payable to him so however that this regulation shall
not apply where such personal benefit has itself been adjusted by reference
to any benefit under the Act.

Special provision relating to the adjustment of [¹ severe disablement allowance] and [² carer's allowance]

12.—In any case where personal benefit or dependency benefit by   3.93
way of a severe disablement allowance or [² a carer's allowance] would,
in accordance with the provision of regulations 4, 6, 7 or 9, fall to be
adjusted by reference to any other personal benefit (other than [³ additional pension] or graduated retirement benefit) or dependency benefit,
it shall be reduced by the amount which is, or but for these regulations
would be, payable by way of that other benefit both as personal benefit
and as dependency benefit, so however that the amount payable by way
of a [¹ severe disablement allowance] or [² a carer's allowance] and that
other benefit shall in no case be less than the sum of the amounts which,
but for any adjustment, would have been payable by way of a [¹ severe
disablement allowance] or [² a carer's allowance] as personal benefit and
dependency benefit.

AMENDMENTS

1. The Social Security (Severe Disablement Allowance) Regulations 1984 (SI
1984/1303, reg.11 (November 29, 1984).
2. The Social Security Amendment (Carer's Allowance) Regulations 2002 (SI
2002/2497), reg.3 and Sch.2 (April 1, 2003).
3. Social Security Act 1986, s.18(1) (April 6, 1987).

Increases in respect of more than one dependant to be treated as separate dependency benefits

3.94   **13.**—For the purposes of these regulations, where dependency benefit by way of an increase is payable in respect of more than one person (whether a child or adult dependant), each such increase shall be treated as a separate dependency benefit.

Provisions for adjusting benefit for part of a week

3.95   [² **14.**—(1) Where an adjustment falls to be made under these regulations for part of a week, benefit (whether under the Contributions and Benefits Act or otherwise) shall be deemed to be payable at a rate equal to one-seventh of the appropriate weekly rate for each day of the week in respect of any such benefit.]

(2) [¹ . . .]

(3) In paragraph (1) "appropriate weekly rate" means the weekly rate at which the benefit in question would be payable but for these regulations.

AMENDMENTS

1. The Social Security and Child Support (Jobseeker's Allowance) (Consequential Amendments) Regulations 1996 (SI 1996/1345), reg.14(2) (October 7, 1996).
2. The Statutory Maternity Pay, Social Security (Maternity Allowance) and Social Security (Overlapping Benefits) (Amendment) Regulations 2006 (SI 2006/2379) (October 1, 2006).

Priority between persons entitled to increase of benefit

3.96   **15.**—(1) Subject to paragraphs (5) and (6), the following provisions shall apply for the purpose of determining priority as between two persons entitled to an increase of benefit under the Act in respect of a third person.

(2) Where, but for the provisions of this paragraph, a man and his wife would both be entitled to an increase of retirement pension (being an increase of Category A or Category C retirement pension in his case and a Category B or Category C retirement pension in hers) in respect of the same child or children, that man shall, and his wife shall not, be entitled to the increase; and he shall be treated as so entitled for the purposes of this paragraph during any period for which he would be entitled but for the operation of any provision of the Act, with the exception of [section 113(1)(b) of the Social Security Contributions and Benefits Act 1992] (disqualification while undergoing imprisonment or detention), disqualifying him for the receipt of benefit.

(3) Subject to paragraphs (2), (5) and (6), where, but for the provisions of this paragraph, more than one person would be entitled to an increase of benefit in respect of the same child for the same period—

   (a) in a case where one of those persons has been awarded child benefit in respect of the child for that period, that one of them shall be entitled to the said increase;

   (b) in the case where sub-paragraph (a) does not apply but where one of those persons is entitled otherwise than by virtue of regulations made under Schedule 20 to the Act to child benefit in respect of the child for that period, that one of them shall be entitled to the said increase;

(c) in a case where neither sub-paragraph (a) nor sub-paragraph (b) applies but where the child is living with one and no other of those persons for that period, that one of them with whom the child is living shall be entitled to the said increase;

(d) in a case where none of the preceding sub-paragraphs applies but where one of those persons is a parent of the child, that one of them shall be entitled to the said increase.

(4) Subject to paragraphs (5) and (6), where, but for the provisions of this paragraph, more than one person would be entitled to an increase of benefit in respect of an adult dependant for the same period—

(a) in a case where one of those persons is the spouse [1 or civil partner] of the adult dependant that one of them shall be entitled to the said increase;

(b) in a case where sub-paragraph (a) above does not apply that one of them with whom the adult dependant is residing shall be entitled to the said increase.

(5) Nothing in paragraphs (3) and (4) shall prevent a written notice signed by one or, as the case may be, a majority of the said persons designating another of them as the person to be entitled to the increase, being sent to the Secretary of State; so however that such notice shall not be effective to confer entitlement to an increase in respect of any period for which such increase has already been paid to someone other than the person so designated.

(6) Nothing in paragraphs (3) and (4) shall prevent a person who, in accordance with any of those paragraphs, is not entitled to an increase from being paid an amount equivalent to the amount, if any, by which the increase which would otherwise have been paid to such person exceeds the increase payable to the person entitled by virtue of any of the said paragraphs.

AMENDMENT

1. The Civil Partnership (Pensions, Social Security and Child Support) (Consequential, etc. Provisions) Order 2005 (SI 2005/2877) (December 5, 2005).

Persons to be treated as entitled to benefit for certain purposes

16.—Any person who would be entitled to any benefit under the Act [2, Part 1 of the Welfare Reform Act] [1 or under the Jobseekers Act] but for these regulations shall be treated as if he were entitled thereto for the purpose of any rights or obligations under the Act and the regulations made under it [2, Part 1 of the Welfare Reform Act and regulations made under it] [1 or under the Jobseekers Act and regulations made under it,] (whether of himself or some other person) which depend on his being so entitled, other than for the purposes of the right to payment of that benefit.

3.97

AMENDMENTS

1. The Social Security and Child Support (Jobseeker's Allowance) (Consequential Amendments) Regulations 1996 (SI 1996/1345), reg.22(6)(a) and (b) (October 7, 1996).
2. The Employment and Support Allowance (Consequential Provisions) (No. 2) Regulations 2008 (SI 2008/1554), reg.51 (October 27, 2008).

Prevention of double adjustments

17.—No adjustment shall be made under regulations 6 to 10 to any benefit under the Act [1 ...] [2 the Jobseekers Act or Part 1 of the Welfare

3.98

Reform Act] by reference to any other benefit, whether under the Act [¹ . . .] [² the Jobseekers Act or Part 1 of the Welfare Reform Act] or otherwise, where the latter benefit has itself been adjusted by reference to the former benefit.

AMENDMENTS

1. The Social Security and Child Support (Jobseeker's Allowance) (Consequential Amendments) Regulations 1996 (SI 1996/1345), reg.22(7) (October 7, 1996).
2. The Employment and Support Allowance (Consequential Provisions) (No. 2) Regulations 2008 (SI 2008/1554), reg.51 (October 27, 2008).

3.99   *Regulation 18 omitted.*

SCHEDULE 1   **Regulation 6**

3.100   PERSONAL BENEFITS WHICH ARE REQUIRED TO BE ADJUSTED BY REFERENCE TO BENEFITS NOT UNDER CHAPTERS I AND II OF PART II OF THE ACT

Column (1) *Personal benefit under the Act*	Column (2) *Other personal benefit by reference to which the benefit in column (1) is to be adjusted*
1. A contribution-based jobseeker's allowance or short-term incapacity benefit.	1. Unemployability supplement and training allowance.
2. Maternity allowance.	2. Training allowance.
3. Widow's benefit, [bereavement allowance, widowed parent's allowance] and benefit by virtue of [section 78() of the . . .] corresponding to widowed mother's allowance or widow's pension.	3. Unemployability supplement, industrial death benefit or war pension death benefit in either case payable to a woman as widow of the deceased and (except where the benefit in column (1) is widow's allowance) training allowance.
4. Retirement pension of any category (except any age addition) or incapacity benefit, severe disablement allowance, contributory employment support allowance or invalid care allowance.	4. Unemployability supplement, industrial death benefit or war pension death benefit in either case payable to that person as the surviving spouse or civil partner, and training allowance.
5. Attendance allowance or the care component of disability living allowance.	5. Any benefit based on need for attendance under section 61 or under any Pneumoconiosis and Byssinosis Benefit Scheme, Personal Injuries Scheme, Service Pensions Instruments or 1914–1918 War Injuries Scheme.
6. Invalidity allowance or an increase in the rate of incapacity benefit in accordance with regulation 10(1) of the Social Security (Incapacity Benefit) Regulation 1994.	6. An increase under section 59(1) of an unemployability supplement and an additional allowance payable only to a beneficiary who is entitled to an unemployability supplement under any Personal Injuries Scheme, Service Pensions Instrument or 1914–1918 War Injuries Scheme.
7. [. . .]	7. [. . .]
8. Unemployability supplement.	8. Any other unemployability supplement.
9. Increase of disablement pension during hospital treatment.	9. Treatment allowance.

AMENDMENTS

For the sake of clarity of the text of the Schedule, it is reproduced without indication of the amendments. The Schedule has been amended by:

The Social Security (Abolition of Injury Benefit) (Consequential) Regulations 1983 (SI 1983/186) (April, 1983).

The Social Security (Severe Disablement Allowance) Regulations 1984 (SI 1984/1303) (November 29, 1984).

The Disability Living Allowance and Disability Working Allowance (Consequential Provisions) Regulations 1991 (SI 1991/2742) (April 6, 1992).

The Social Security (Incapacity Benefit) (Consequential and Transitional Amendments and Savings) Regulations 1995 (SI 1995/829) (April 13, 1995).

The Social Security and Child Support (Jobseeker's Allowance) (Consequential Amendments) Regulations 1996 (SI 1996/1345) (October 7, 1996).

The Social Security (Benefits for Widows and Widowers) (Consequential Amendments) Regulations 2000 (SI 2000/1483), reg.6 (April 9, 2001).

The Civil Partnership (Pensions, Social Security and Child Support) (Consequential, etc. Provisions) Order 2005 (SI 2005/2877) (December 5, 2005).

The Employment and Support Allowance (Consequential Provisions) (No. 2) Regulations 2008 (SI 2008/1554), reg.51 (October 27, 2008).

Schedule 2 omitted.   **3.101**

Social Security Benefit (Persons Abroad) Regulations 1975

(SI 1975/563) *(as amended)*

ARRANGEMENT OF REGULATIONS

15.   *Omitted.*
Schedule. Up-rating in respect of certain awards made between 1st September 1985 and 7th August 1991.

The Secretary of State for Social Services, in exercise of powers conferred upon her by sections 21(3), 30(3), 32(5), 114(1), 131 and 132 of the Social Security Act 1975 and of all other powers enabling her in that behalf, without having referred any proposals on the matter to the National Insurance Advisory Committee or the Industrial Injuries Advisory Council since it appears to her that by reasons of urgency it is inexpedient to do so, hereby makes the following regulations:

Citation, commencement and interpretation

3.103   **1.**—(1) These regulations may be cited as the Social Security Benefit (Persons Abroad) Regulations 1975 and shall come into operation on April 6, 1975.
(2) In these regulations, unless the context otherwise requires—
"the Act" means the Social Security Act 1975;
[¹ " bereavement allowance" means an allowance referred to in section 39B of the Social Security Contributions and Benefits Act;
"bereavement benefit" means a benefit referred to in section 20(1)(ea) of the Contributions and Benefits Act;]
[² "bereavement payment" means a payment under section 36 of the Contributions and Benefits Act 1992;]
[³ "child benefit" means benefit under Part I of the Child Benefit Act;]
[⁴ "the Child Benefit Act" means the Child Benefit Act 1975];
[⁵ "the Contributions and Benefits Act" means the Social Security Contributions and Benefits Act 1992];
"the Contributions Regulations" means the Social Security (Contributions) Regulations [³ 1979];
[³ "entitled to child benefit" includes treated as so entitled;]
"the former Death Grant Regulations" means the National Insurance (Death Grant) Regulations 1973;
"the former Principal Act" means the National Insurance Act 1965;
"the former Widow's Benefit and Retirement Pensions Regulations" means the National Insurance (Widow's Benefit and Retirement Pensions) Regulations 1972;
[⁶ "guaranteed minimum pension" has the meaning given to it in section 26(2) of the Social Security Pensions Act 1975 as construed in accordance with section 9 of the Social Security Act 1986];
"her husband" in the case of a woman who has been married more than once, refers to the husband by virtue of whose contributions she is entitled to the benefit in question;
"the Industrial Injuries Employment Regulations" means the Social Security (Employed Earners' Employments for Industrial Injuries Purposes) Regulations 1975;
"the Overlapping Benefits Regulations" means the National Insurance (Overlapping Benefit) Regulations 1975;
"the former Old Persons' Pensions Regulations" means the National Insurance (Old Persons' Pensions) Regulations 1970;
"retired" means retired from regular employment;

[⁷ "serving member of the forces" has the meaning given to it in regulation 1(2) of the Contributions Regulations];"

[⁹ "shared additional pension" means a shared additional pension under section 55A or the Contributions and Benefits Act;]

"the Special Provisions Regulations" means the Social Security (Benefit) (Married Women and Widows Special Provisions) Regulations 1974;

"the Widow's Benefit and Retirement Pensions Regulations" means the Social Security (Widow's Benefit and Retirement Pensions) Regulations 1974;

"widow's benefit" and "widow's pension" include benefit under section 39(4) of the Act corresponding to a widow's pension or a widowed mother's allowance;

[¹ "widowed parent's allowance" means an allowance referred to in section 39A of the Social Security Contributions and Benefits Act 1992;]

and other expressions have the same meanings as in the Act.

(3) Any reference in these regulations to any provision made by or contained in any enactment or instrument shall, except in so far as the context otherwise requires, be construed as a reference to that provision as amended or extended by any enactment or instrument, and as including a reference to any provision which it re-enacts or replaces, or which may re-enact or replace it, with or without modification.

(4) The rules for the construction of Acts of Parliament contained in the Interpretation Act 1889 shall apply for the purposes of the interpretation of these regulations as they apply for the purposes of the interpretation of an Act of Parliament.

AMENDMENTS

1. The Welfare Reform and Pensions (Persons Abroad: Benefits for Widows and Widowers) (Consequential Amendments) Regulations 2000 (SI 2000/2876), reg.2, (April 9, 2001).

2. The Welfare Reform and Pensions (Persons Abroad: Benefits for Widows and Widowers) (Consequential Amendments) Regulations 2001 (SI 2001/2618), reg.2(2), (August 20, 2001).

3. The Social Security (Child Benefit) (Consequential) Regulations 1977 (SI 1977/342), reg.13(2) (April 4, 1977).

4. The Social Security (Child Benefit) (Consequential) Regulations 1977 (SI 1977/342), reg.13(2) (April 4, 1977).

5. The Social Security (Maternity Grant) Amendment Regulations 1981 (SI 1981/1157), reg.3(2) (April 1, 1982).

6. The Social Security Benefit (Persons Abroad) Amendment (No. 2) Regulations 1990 (SI 1990/621), reg.2(2) (April 6, 1990).

7. The Social Security Benefit (Persons Abroad) Amendment Regulations 1990 (SI 1990/40), reg.2(2) (February 8, 1990).

8. The Social Security (Miscellaneous Provisions) Amendment (No. 2) Regulations 1992 (SI 1992/2595), reg.9 (November 16, 1992).

9. The Social Security (Shared Additional pension (Miscellaneous Amendments) Regulation 2005 (SI 2005/1551) (July 6, 2005).

GENERAL NOTE

Interpretation Act 1889

By s.25(2) of the Interpretation Act 1978, the reference to the Interpretation Act 1889 is to be treated as a reference to the 1978 Act.

3.104

Regulation 1(2) refers to the definition of "serving member of the forces" in the Social Security (Contributions) Regulations 1979 (SI 1979/591). There the item is defined as follows:

"'serving member of the forces' means a person (not being a person mentioned in Part II of Schedule 3 to these regulations) who, being over the age of 16, is a member of any establishment or organisation in Part I of Schedule 3 to these regulations (being a member who gives full pay service) but does not include any such person while absent on desertion."

Part I of Sch.3 of these Regulations is reproduced in the annotations to reg.3 of the Computation of Earnings Regulations.
Part II of Sch.3 reads as follows:

"By virtue of regulation 113 of these regulations, Her Majesty's forces shall not be taken to consist of any of the establishments or organisations specified in Part I of this Schedule by virtue only of the employment in such establishment of the following persons—

(a) any person who is serving as a member of any naval force of Her Majesty's forces and who (not having been an insured person under the former principal Act or, as the case may be, the National Insurance Act (Northern Ireland) 1966 and not being a contributor under the Act) locally entered that force at an overseas base;

(b) any person who is serving as a member of any military force of Her Majesty's forces and who entered that force, or was recruited for that force outside the United Kingdom, and the depot of whose unit is situated outside the United Kingdom;

(c) any person who is serving as a member of any air force of Her Majesty's forces and who entered that force, or was recruited for that force, outside the United Kingdom, and is liable under the terms of his engagement to serve only in a specified part of the world outside the United Kingdom."

Modification of the Act in relation to [1 incapacity benefit], severe disablement allowance, unemployability supplement and maternity allowance

3.105   **2.**—(1) [2 Except as provided by paragraph (1A) or (1B) below, a] [person shall not be disqualified for receiving [2 any benefit in respect of incapacity]] by reason of being temporarily absent from Great Britain for any day [3 falling within the first 26 weeks beginning with the day following the day on which he left Great Britain] if—

[4 (a) the Secretary of State has certified that it is consistent with the proper administration of the Act that, subject to the satisfaction of one of the conditions in sub-paragraphs (b), (bb) and (c) below, the disqualification under [section 113(1)(a) of the Social Security Contributions and Benefits Act 1992] should not apply, and]

(b) the absence is for the specific purpose of being treated for incapacity which commenced before he left Great Britain, or

[5 (bb) in the case of incapacity benefit, the incapacity for work is the result of a personal injury of a kind mentioned in [section 94(1) of the Social Security Contributions and Benefits Act 1992], and the absence is for the specific purpose of receiving treatment which is appropriate to that injury, or]

[6 (c) on the day on which the absence began he was, and had for the past 6 months continuously been, incapable of work and on the day for which benefit is claimed he has remained continuously so incapable since the absence began]

(d) [7 . . .]

[8 (1A) Subject to paragraph (1B), a person who is in receipt of attendance allowance or disability living allowance shall not by reason of being temporarily absent from Great Britain be disqualified for receiving any benefit in respect of incapacity if—

(a) the absence is for the specific purpose of being treated for incapacity which commenced before he left Great Britain; or

(b) in the case of [2 incapacity benefit] the incapacity for work is the result of a personal injury of a kind mentioned in section 94(1) of the Social Security Contributions and Benefits Act 1992 and the absence is for the specific purpose of receiving treatment which is appropriate to that injury; or

(c) on the day on which the absence began he was, and had for the past 6 months continuously been, incapable of work and on the day for which benefit is claimed he has remained continuously so incapable since the absence began.

(1B) A person who is a member of the family of a serving member of the forces and temporarily absent from Great Britain by reason only of the fact that he is living with that member shall not by reason of being temporarily absent be disqualified—

(a) for receiving any benefit in respect of incapacity except severe disablement allowance if—

(i) the absence is for the specific purpose of being treated for incapacity which began before he left Great Britain, or

(ii) in the case of [1 incapacity benefit] the incapacity for work is the result of a personal injury of the kind mentioned in section 94(1) of the Social Security Contributions and Benefits Act 1992 and the absence is for the specific purpose of receiving treatment which is appropriate to that injury, or

(iii) on the day on which the absence began he was, and had for the past 6 months continuously been, incapable of work and on the day for which benefit is claimed he has remained continuously so incapable since the absence began; or

(b) for the receipt of severe disablement allowance.]

(2) [9 . . .]

(3) [10 . . .]

(4) [10 . . .]

[11 (5) In this regulation—

(a) "benefit in respect of incapacity" means [1 incapacity benefit], severe disablement allowance, an unemployability supplement or a maternity allowance;

(b) "member of the family of a serving member of the forces" means the spouse, [13 civil partner,] son, daughter, step-son, step-daughter, father, father-in-law, step-father, mother, mother-in-law or step-mother of such a member; and

(c) "week" means any period of seven days.]

AMENDMENTS

1. The Social Security (Incapacity Benefit) (Consequential and Transitional Amendments and Savings) Regulations 1995 (SI 1995/829), reg.7 (April 13, 1995).

2. The Social Security Benefit (Persons Abroad) Amendment Regulations 1994 (SI 1994/268), reg.2(2)(a) (March 8, 1994).

3. The Social Security Benefit (Persons Abroad) Amendment Regulations 1994 (SI 1994/268), reg.2(2)(c) (March 8, 1994).

4. The Social Security (Persons Abroad) Amendment Regulations 1977 (SI 1977/1679), reg.2(2) (November 14, 1977); The Social Security (Abolition of Injury Benefit) (Consequential) Regulations 1983 (SI 1983/186), reg.5(2) (April 6, 1983); The Social Security Benefit (Persons Abroad) Amendment Regulations 1990 (SI 1990/40), reg.2(3)(a)(ii) (February 8, 1990); and The Social Security Benefit (Persons Abroad) Amendment Regulations 1994 (and SI 1994/268), reg.2(2)(d) (March 8, 1994).

5. The Social Security (Abolition of Injury Benefit) (Consequential) Regulatins 1983 (SI 1983/186), reg.5(2) (April 4, 1983); The Social Security Benefit (Persons Abroad) Amendment (No. 2) Regulations 1986 (SI 1986/1545), reg.2 (October 1, 1986); and The Social Security (Incapacity Benefit) (Consequential and Transitional Amendments and Savings) Regulations 1995 (SI 1995/829), reg.7(b) (April 13, 1995).

6. The Social Security Benefit (Persons Abroad) Amendment Regulations 1990 (SI 1990/40), reg.2(3)(b) (February 8, 1990); and The Social Security Benefit (Persons Abroad) Amendment Regulations 1994 (SI 1994/268), reg.2(2) (e) (March 8, 1994).

7. The Social Security Benefit (Persons Abroad) Amendment Regulations 1994 (SI 1994/268), reg.2(2)(e) (March 8, 1994).

8. Reg. 2(1A) and (1B) inserted by The Social Security Benefit (Persons Abroad) Amendment Regulations 1994 (SI 1994/268), reg.2(3) (March 8, 1994).

9. The Social Security Benefit (Persons Abroad) Amendment Regulations 1977 (SI 1977/1679), reg.2(4) (November 14, 1977).

10. The Social Security (Incapacity Benefit) (Consequential and Transitional Amendment and Savings) Regulations 1995 (SI 1995/829), reg 7(e) (April 13, 1995).

11. The Social Security Benefit (Persons Abroad) Amendment Regulations 1994 (SI 1994/268), reg.2(4) (March 8, 1994).

12. The Social Security (Severe Disablement Allowance) Regulations 1984 (SI 1984/1303), reg.16 (November 28, 1984).

13. The Civil Partnership (Pensions, Social Security and Child Support) (Consequential, etc. Provisions) Order 2005 (SI 2005/2877) (December 5, 2005).

DEFINITIONS

"the Act"—reg.1.
"the former Principal Act"—reg.1.
"Great Britain"—by art.1 of the Union with Scotland Act 1706, this means England, Scotland and Wales.

GENERAL NOTE

3.106   This regulation applies to the specified benefits for incapacity. Three conditions must be satisfied for the disqualification in s.113 of the Contributions and Benefits Act to be avoided for the first 26 weeks:

(a) The absence from Great Britain must be temporary.
(b) The Secretary of State must certify that it is consistent with the proper administration of the Act that the disqualification should not apply.
(c) The claimant must establish that either
    (i) the absence is for the specific purpose of being treated for incapacity that existed before he or she left Great Britain; or
    (ii) in the case of incapacity benefit, the incapacity is the result of an industrial injury and the absence is for the specific purpose of receiving treatment appropriate to that injury; or
    (iii) on the day the absence began, the claimant was, and had for six months continuously been, incapable of work and the claimant has been continuously incapable of work since leaving Great Britain.

Paragraph (1A) exempts from the limitation to 26 weeks of the continuation of benefit those in receipt of attendance allowance or disability living allowance who meet the three conditions set out in that paragraph.

Paragraph (1B) makes a similar exemption for someone who is a member of the family of a serving member of the forces temporarily absent from Great Britain as a consequence of that status who meets the conditions set out in the paragraph.

Civil Partnership Act 2004

With effect from December 5, 2005, art.3 of the Civil Partnership Act 2004 (Relations Arising Through Civil Partnership) Order 2005 (SI 2005/3137) applies the provisions of s.246 of the Civil Partnership Act 2004 to the definition of "member of the family of a serving member of the forces" in reg.2(5)(b). Section 246 of the Civil Partnership Act 2004 is reproduced at para.1.620 of Vol.III.

3.107

Temporary absence

What amounts to temporary absence is not defined and so is a matter for the exercise of judgment by the adjudicating authorities, though considerable guidance is now available from Commissioners' decisions. In *R(S) 1/85*, Commissioner Edwards-Jones offered the following guidance:

3.108

"There is, in my judgment, no universal period by reference to which the issue as to an absence being, or not being, temporary falls to be determined: the particular circumstances of the case are crucial." (para.19).

"The phrase 'temporarily absent from Great Britain' . . . is to be construed as to give rise to the position that whilst demonstration that an absence is 'permanent' will preclude it counting as 'temporary,' demonstration that it is not necessarily 'permanent' does not of itself establish that it is 'temporary.' In particular, an absence may though intended as 'temporary' at its outset cease to count as such if by force of circumstances no certain time (and I do not by a 'certain time' mean necessarily a precise date or hour, but something broader) can be set as to when it will terminate. It is not a 'temporary' absence if it is indefinite." (para.20).

Relevant factors will be all the surrounding circumstances (including in the case of determination by tribunals events subsequent to the adjudication officer's decision: *R(S) 10/83*), which include the claimant's intentions though these will not be decisive: *R(S) 10/83*. As a general rule absences of more than 12 months are not temporary unless there are exceptional circumstances: *R(U) 16/62*. Serious doubts were cast in *R(S) 1/85* on the correctness of *R(S) 9/55* in which it was held that absence of three years and nine months undergoing treatment for tuberculosis in Switzerland was temporary, but the Commissioner in *R(S) 9/55* regarded the case in any event as restricted to its own rather special facts and notes that absences of more than a year will not normally be temporary.

In *CS/207/1990* the claimant suffered from multiple sclerosis and had been resident in Malta for almost seven years because the climate provided relief for his symptoms. He had, nevertheless, expressed a wish to return to Great Britain if and when his health improved sufficiently. Commissioner Johnson upheld the decision of the tribunal that the claimant could not be regarded as temporarily absent from Great Britain.

The Court of Appeal has considered the meaning of the word "temporarily" in this Regulation in *Chief Adjudication Officer v Belmer and Ahmed*, CA, March 16, 1994, *Guardian*, April 18, 1994 reported as *R(S)1/96*. Neill L.J. giving judgment said that it was wrong to construe "temporarily" as being synonymous with "not permanent". Though it would be exceptional to show that an absence lasting for some years remained temporary, the proper approach was to consider whether the absence could be considered as temporary in the light of all the circumstances. The quality of the absence could change with the passage of time. What began as a temporary absence could change to one of permanent absence. Equally the fact that there was no fixed return date could not be taken as showing that the absence was necessarily not temporary. The claimant's expressed intention would be relevant but not decisive, so there is an element of objectivity in the determination.

CDLA/2089/2004 concerned the interpretation of differently worded reg.2(2)(d) and (e) of the Disability Living Allowance Regulations on temporary absence from Great Britain, but the point the Commissioner makes may well have relevance when the provisions of this regulation are considered. The Commissioner rules that the continuation of benefit payment is based on two facts: first, that the absence from Great Britain must be for a temporary purpose, and secondly, that the absence has not lasted for more than 26 weeks. The period of 26 weeks does not define the word "temporary"; it merely limits to a maximum of 26 weeks the period during which benefit can remain in payment if the absence is temporary (provided that any other conditions set out in the regulations are satisfied).

Secretary of State's certificate

3.109   The certificate condition was introduced in 1975 to limit some of the problems inherent in the test. The regulation introducing it was held to be *ultra vires* by a Commissioner in *CS/5/76* and the regulation was replaced in 1977 in its current form. This formulation has been held to be lawful: *R(S) 8/83*.

Para.(1)(b) and (bb)

3.110   In *R(S) 2/86* a Tribunal of Commissioners reviewed the effect of para.(1)(b) in the light of a sizeable case law and in a majority decision explained that the requirements of para.(1)(b) were threefold:

(1) the claimant must show that immediately prior to the departure from Great Britain, he or she was incapacitated for work by reason of some specific disease or bodily or mental disablement (so pregnancy will not suffice: *R(S) 1/75*); and

(2) the going abroad is for the purpose of having treatment for the condition; and

(3) the condition giving rise to the incapacity abroad is capable of being identified with the condition giving rise to the incapacity subsisting at the date of departure abroad.

The majority specifically left open the question whether or not the incapacity for work arising during absence abroad must have continued unbroken between the start of the absence abroad and the day or days for which the claim is made. Their view was, however, that the period of incapacity need not be continuous. Commissioner Penny, the dissenting Commissioner, doubted the correctness of this view.

In *R(S) 2/86* a number of earlier decisions were qualified. In particular the presumption suggested in *R(S) 6/61* that the specific purpose of going abroad is for treatment where treatment for an incapacity is received abroad was rejected. Statements in *R(S) 1/75* were qualified by making it clear that it remained to be settled to what extent absence abroad could be for the specific purpose of receiving treatment where the initial absence was for some other reason, for example, where a person suffering an incapacity goes abroad for a holiday but subsequently extends the period abroad in order to receive treatment for the incapacity.

Treatment means "some activity by someone other than the claimant": *R(S) 10/51*. So trips abroad for convalescence, for a change of environment or for relaxation will not qualify: *R(S) 1/69, R. v National Insurance Commissioner Ex p. McMenemey* (Appendix to *R(S) 2/69*), *R(S) 4/80* and *R(S) 6/81*. Whether treatment involves some specific medical supervision or care is uncertain: *R(S) 2/51* and *R(S) 10/51* seem to assume that it does not, while *R(S) 16/51, R(S) 5/61, R(S) 10/62* and *R(S) 2/69* seem to assume that it does. Indeed it seems that being under a doctor's professional care may not be conclusive particularly if the incapacity is mental illness: *R(S) 5/61*, though treatment here may include non-medical treatment: *R(S) 1/65*.

Some Commissioners' decisions on absence for the specific purpose of receiving treatment under paras (1)(b) and (bb) have stressed that specific medical supervision is required to bring a claimant within the ambit of the provisions.

In *CS/061/1992* Commissioner Morcom adds to the list of such authorities by concluding that treatment by a herbalist in Sri Lanka who "derived his occupation partly by family tradition and partly by experience . . . does not represent the qualified skill or service required to justify the decision that the claimant's absence from Great Britain was for the specific purpose of being treated for his incapacity." (para.5). The more modern authorities requiring specific medical supervision now considerably outnumber the earlier authorities which seem to suggest that treatment need not involve such a regime.

So decision-makers are left with a confusing body of authority on the meaning of treatment from which it is difficult to draw any clear guidance. In such circumstances, tribunals should take great care to make findings of facts as to the precise nature of the incapacity and the treatment proposed for it, including findings as to the personnel who will administer it. Once this has been done, whether it constitutes "treatment" within para.(1)(b) is essentially a matter for the judgment of the tribunal in the light of all the circumstances of the case.

R(S) 1/90 is an important decision of a Tribunal of Commissioners. It contains a comprehensive review of the requirements of reg.2(1)(b) and (bb) on the intention of the claimant in going abroad. The nub of the decision is to be found in paras 29–30:

> "**29.** If we were required to approach the problem afresh, we would without hesitation take the view that for paragraph (b) to apply the purpose or intention to be treated (or to receive treatment under paragragh (bb)) must have been formed before the claimant's departure from Great Britain. There is great force in the observations of the Tribunal of Commissioners in *R(S) 2/86* at paragraph 12 . . . and we agree with them that 'it is a necessary and basic requirement for success in invoking regulation 2(1)(b)' that the claimant, in addition to the other requirements 'went abroad for the purpose of having treatment.'
>
> **30.** In our view, the decisions which favour the claimant in the present case— namely, that a claimant will avoid disqualification if, while abroad, he obtains or receives treatment although he had no such purpose or intention at the time of departure—are an over-liberal and erroneous interpretation of paragraph (b). The decisions to which we have referred span a period of 40 years. Overseas travelling facilities have in that period of time been radically changed and a re-appraisal of those earlier decisions is overdue. It falls to this tribunal to make that re-appraisal. We accept the strict construction adopted by the Tribunal of Commissioners in *R(S) 2/86* at paragraph 12, and have reached the decision set out in paragraph 29 above."

The effect of this decision is that the interpretation of the regulation in the following cases is no longer good law: *CS/317/1949(KL)*, *CSS/71/1949*, *R(S) 6/61*, *CS/01/1971*, *R(S) 1/75* and *R(S) 1/77*.

CIB/1956/2001 concerned a claimant who suffered from, among other ailments, eczema of both hands and feet. He had retired from work as a labourer on medical grounds. He received sickness benefit, followed by invalidity benefit which converted to incapacity benefit on its introduction. The principal point in the appeal concerned his absence in India for what was described by the claimant as a holiday but during which he consulted a hakim about his eczema. It was accepted that *R(S) 6/61* remained good authority for the proposition that the claimant's absence abroad must be for the specific purpose of being treated, but need not be for the sole purpose of being treated. The Commissioner goes further and indicates that medical treatment need not be the main purpose of the trip abroad, although an intention to secure treatment must have been in mind before the absence started. Just because a person has treatment abroad, it should not, however, be assumed that this was in mind before the trip began. In this case, there was enough evidence to meet that requirement. The Commissioner says,

"I have no doubt that the trip was also a holiday and, like the tribunal, I incline to the view that that was the main purpose of the journey. I therefore do not find it surprising that the claimant referred to it as a holiday. However, I accept that the claimant's eczema, which was one cause of his retirement and was obviously defeating Western medical science, was so irritating for the claimant that finding a cure for it added to his desire to go to India, even though he had no high hopes of success. That, in my view, is enough to make "being treated" in India a "specific purpose" of the absence." (para.8).

Para.(1)(c)

3.111   This condition is designed to assist the long-term incapacitated. For this group the absence, though temporary, need not be for the specific purpose of receiving treatment.

In *CS/143/1993* the claimant had been awarded sickness benefit followed by invalidity benefit from January 3, 1989 to September 20, 1990. There was then a break in the payment of invalidity benefit until July 8, 1991, because she had been on an employment training course and received an allowance from the Secretary of State. In August 1991 she went on an extended holiday to Australia returning to Great Britain in February 1992. A question arose as to her continued entitlement to invalidity benefit when outside Great Britain. The claimant sought to rely on the provisions of reg.2(1)(c) to sustain her claim to receive the benefit while abroad. The adjudication officer argued that she could not establish the necessary six months' incapacity for work because reg.7(1)(f) of the USI Regulations provides that a day is not to be *treated* as a day of incapacity for work if on that day a person is attending a training course provided by or on behalf of the Secretary of State.

Commissioner Heggs concludes that the adjudication officer's case is misconceived and that provisions included in one set of regulations are not, without clear indication that they are intended to be, to be incorporated into other sets of regulations. The test in reg.2(1)(c) is a *factual* test contained in regulations made for a different purpose than the USI Regulations.

The 1994 amendments

3.112   The Persons Abroad Amendment Regulations 1994 (SI 1994/268) make changes to this regulation with effect from March 8, 1994 which, subject to exceptions, restricts the availability of benefits to a 26 week period.

There is a transitional provision in reg.3 of the amending regulations preserving entitlement to those who already had it in the following terms:

"**3.**—(1) In this regulation "the former regulation 2" means regulation 2 of the principal Regulations as in force immediately before these Regulations came into force.

(2) Where immediately before the coming into force of these Regulations, a person was absent from Great Britain but by virtue of the former regulation 2 was not disqualified for receiving any benefit, allowance or supplement referred to in paragraph (1) of the former regulation 2, that person shall continue not to be disqualified in respect of any day, if he—

(a) has been continuously absent from Great Britain since these Regulations came into force; and

(b) would, had the former regulation 2 been in force on that day, have satisfied the provisions of that regulation in respect of that benefit, allowance or supplement."

Regulation 3 revoked by The Social Security Benefit (Persons Abroad)   3.113
Amendment Regulations 1990 (SI 1990/40), reg.3 (February 8, 1990).

Modification of the Act in relation to widow's benefit, [⁷ bereavement-benefit,] child's special allowance, guardian's allowance and retirement pension

4.—(1) Subject to the provisions of this regulation and of regulation   3.114
5 below, a person shall not be disqualified for receiving widow's benefit,
[¹ bereavement-benefit,] child's special allowance, a guardian's allowance
[², a retirement pension of any category [⁹, a shared additional pension]
or graduated retirement benefit] by reason of being absent from Great
Britain.

(2) In the case of a widow's allowance paragraph (1) above shall apply
only where either—

(a) the woman or her late husband was in Great Britain at the time of his
death; or

(b) the contribution conditions for widowed mother's allowance and
widow's pension set out in paragraph 5 of Schedule 3 to the Act
or in regulation [³ 6 of the Social Security (Widow's Benefit and
Retirement Pensions) Regulations 1979] are satisfied in relation to
the woman.

[³ (2A) In the case of a widow's payment, paragraph (1) above shall apply
only where—

(a) the woman or her late husband was in Great Britain at the time of his
death; or

(b) sub-paragraph (a) above does not apply but the woman returned to
Great Britain within 4 weeks of her husband's death; or

(c) the contribution conditions for widowed mother's allowance and
widow's pension set out in paragraph 5 of Schedule 3 to the Act
or in regulation 6 of the Social Security (Widow's Benefit and
Retirement Pensions) Regulations 1979 are satisfied in relation to
the woman.]

[1 (2B). In the case of a bereavement payment, paragraph (1) above shall
apply only where—

(a) the deceased spouse [¹⁰ or deceased civil partner] or the surviving
spouse [¹⁰ or surviving civil partner] was in great Britain at the time
of the deceased spouse's [¹⁰ or deceased civil partner's] death;]

(b) sub-paragraph (a) above does not apply but the surviving spouse
[¹⁰ or surviving civil partner] returned to Great Britain within 4 weeks
of the deceased spouse's [¹⁰ or deceased civil partner's] death; or

(c) the contribution conditions for widowed parent's allowance and
bereavement allowance set out in paragraph 5 of Schedule 3 to the
Act or in regulation 6 of the Social Security (Widow's benefit and
Retirement Pensions) Regulations 1979 are satisfied in relation to
the surviving spouse [¹⁰ or surviving civil partner].]

[⁵ (3) In the case of a Category A retirement pension the [⁶ basic pension]
of which falls to be increased under the provisions of [section 52(2) or
section 53(2) of the Contributions and Benefits Act] (special provisions for
surviving spouses and for married women), the amount of the increase shall
not exceed the sum which would be required to raise the [⁶ basic pension]
of that Category A retirement pension to the sum specified in [section 44(4)

of the Contributions and Benefits Act] (rate of [6 basic pension] of Category A retirement pension) or the weekly rate of Category B retirement pension specified in [paragraph 5 of Part 1 of Schedule 4 to the Contributions and Benefits Act], as the case may be, current at—

[7 (a) the date on which the person whose pension falls to be increased first became entitled to that pension; or]

(b) the date on which that person was last ordinarily resident in Great Britain; whichever is the later.

(4) Where, in the case of Category A retirement pension the [6 additional pension] of which falls to be increased under the provisions of [section 52(3) of the Contributions and Benefits Act], the surviving spouse [10 or surviving civil partner] whose pension falls to be so increased, being over pensionable age at the date of the death of the former spouse [10 or former civil partner], is not ordinarily resident in Great Britain, the amount of the increase shall not exceed the sum which would be required to raise the additional pension of that Category A retirement pension to the maximum prescribed by regulation 2 of the Social Security (Maximum [6 Additional Pension]) Regulations 1978 as amended by the Social Security (Maximum [6 Additional Pension Amendment]) Regulations 1979 which would have been appropriate had the former spouse [10 or former civil partner] died on—

(a) the date on which the surviving spouse was last ordinarily resident in Great Britain; or

(b) April 1979; whichever is the later.

AMENDMENTS

1. The Welfare Reform and Pensions (Persons Abroad: Benefits for Widows and Widowers) (Consequential Amendments) Regulations 2000 (SI 2000/2876), reg.2, (April 9, 2001).

2. The Social Security Benefit (Persons Abroad) Amendment Regulations 1992 (SI 1992/1700), reg.2 (August 5, 1992).

3. The Social Security Benefit (Persons Abroad) Amendment Regulations 1988 (SI 1988/435), reg.2 (April 11, 1988).

4. The Welfare Reform and Pensions (Persons Abroad: Benefits for Widows and Widowers) (Consequential Amendments) Regulations 2001 (SI 2001/2618), reg.2(3) (August 20, 2001).

5. Reg. 4(3) and (4) inserted by The Social Security Benefit (Persons Abroad) Amendment (No. 2) Regulations 1979 (SI 1979/1432), reg.2(b) (November 10, 1979).

6. Social Security Act 1986, s.18(1) (April 6, 1987).

7. The Social Security (Abolition of Earnings Rule) (Consequential) Regulations 1989 (SI 1989/1642), reg.4(3) (October 1, 1989).

8. The Social Security Benefit (Persons Abroad) Amendment (No. 2) Regulations 1979 (SI 1979/1432), reg.2(a) (November 10, 1979).

9. The Social Security (Shared Additional pension (Miscellaneous Amendments) Regulation 2005 (SI 2005/1551) (July 6, 2005).

10. The Civil Partnership (Pensions, Social Security and Child Support) (Consequential, etc. Provisions) Order 2005 (SI 2005/2877) (December 5, 2005).

GENERAL NOTE

3.115   The broad effect of this regulation taken together with regs 5 and 6 is that for the specified benefits, absence abroad is not a disqualifying condition. The reason is that the benefits are contributory, are not related to capacity to work and so require less supervision. Up-rating of benefit applies automatically only to those "ordinarily resident" in Great Britain (see notes to reg.5). A claimant cannot defer retirement if not ordinarily resident in Great Britain (reg.6).

In the case of widow's benefit, the woman or her late husband must additionally have been in Great Britain at the date of his death and the specified contribution conditions have to be met.

Application of disqualification in respect of up-rating of benefits

5.—(1) Where regulations made in consequence of an order under [¹ section 63 of the Social Security Act 1986 (up-rating of benefits and increments in guaranteed minimum pensions)] provide for the application of this regulation to any additional benefit becoming payable by virtue of that order, the following provisions of this regulation shall, subject to regulation 12 below and the provisions of those regulations, have effect in relation to the entitlement to that benefit of persons absent from Great Britain.

3.116

(2) In this regulation [² and in regulation 5A]—

(a) references to additional benefit of any description are to be construed as referring to additional benefit of that description which is, or but for this regulation would be, payable by virtue (either directly or indirectly) of the said order; and

(b) "the appointed date" means the date appointed for the coming into force of the said order.

(3) [³ Subject to paragraph (8) and the Schedule below,] where a person is not ordinarily resident in Great Britain immediately before the appointed date the provisions of these regulations (except this regulation) shall not, unless and until he becomes ordinarily resident in Great Britain, affect his disqualification while he is absent from Great Britain for receiving—

(a) in the case of a woman who immediately before the appointed date was a married woman and [⁴ was not entitled to a Category B retirement pension], any additional Category B retirement pension, if immediately before that date her husband [⁴ was entitled to a Category A retirement pension] and was not ordinarily resident in Great Britain;

[⁵ (aa) in the case of a married woman, any additional Category B retirement pension if immediately before the appointed day her husband was entitled to a Category A retirement pension and was not ordinarily resident in Great Britain (whether or not she was married to him immediately before that date);]

[⁶ (b) in the case of a person who immediately before the appointed date is [¹⁸ a widow, a widower or a surviving civil partner], any additional Category B retirement pensions, if the former spouse [¹⁸ or former civil partner] had died before the appointed day.]

[⁷ (c) in any other case, any additional retirement pension of any category [¹⁷, any additional shared additional pension] or any additional graduated retirement benefit, if that person had become entitled to a retirement pension [¹⁷, a shared additional pension] or to graduated retirement benefit before the appointed date;]

(d) any additional widow's benefit [⁸ or bereavement benefit if the deceased spouse] [¹⁸ or deceased civil partner] [⁹ had become entitled to a Category A retirement pension or had] die before the appointed date;

(e) any additional child's special allowance if her former husband had died before the appointed date;

[¹⁰ (f) any additional guardian's allowance in respect of a child if he were

entitled to that allowance in respect of that child before the appointed
date.]

(4) [[11] . . .]

(5) The provisions of these regulations shall not affect the disqualification while absent from Great Britain of a widow who—

(a) is not ordinarily resident in Great Britain immediately before the
appointed date, and was entitled to widow's benefit immediately
before attaining pensionable age, or would, but for any provision of
the Act disqualifying her for the receipt of such benefit, have been so
entitled; and

(b) is or becomes entitled to a Category A retirement pension the right
to which is determined by taking into account under [[12] regulation
8 of the Social Security (Widow's Benefit and Retirement Pensions)
Regulations 1979] her husband's contributions;

for receiving any additional Category A retirement pension the right to
which is so determined unless and until she becomes ordinarily resident in
Great Britain if—

(i) before the appointed date her husband [[13] was entitled to a
Category A retirement pension] and was not ordinarily resident
in Great Britain; or

(ii) he died before the appointed date.

[[14] (6) Subject to paragraph (8) and the Schedule below, the provisions
of these regulations shall not affect the disqualification while absent from
Great Britain of a person referred to in regulation 8 of the Social Security
(Widow's Benefit and Retirement Pensions) Regulations 1979, being any
such person other than a widow, who—

(a) is not ordinarily resident in Great Britain immediately before the
appointed date; and

(b) is or becomes entitled to a Category A retirement pension the right
to which is determined by taking into account under regulation 8
of the Social Security (Widow's Benefit and Retirement Pensions)
Regulations 1979 the contribution of that person's former spouse [[18]
or former civil partner];

for receiving any additional Category A retirement pension the right to
which is so determined unless and until that person becomes ordinarily
resident in Great Britain if—

(i) before the appointed date the former spouse [[18] or former civil
partner] was entitled to a Category A retirement pension and
was not ordinarily resident in Great Britain; or

(ii) the former spouse [[18] or former civil partner] died before the
appointed date.]

[[15] (7) Paragraph (3)(c) of this regulations shall not apply to a person in
relation to a Category B retirement pension if that person's spouse [[18] or
civil partner] was not entitled to a Category A retirement pension before
the appointed date and either that person and that person's spouse [[18] or
civil partner]—

(i) were husband and wife [[18] or were civil partners] immediately
before that date; or

(ii) became husband and wife [[18] or formed a civil partnership] on
or after that date.]

[[15] (8) The Schedule below shall have effect in relation to disqualifications for receiving additional benefit in the circumstances specified in that

Schedule (being certain cases in which a person was awarded a widow's benefit or a retirement pension or a higher rate of retirement pension between 1st September 1985 and 7th August 1991).]

AMENDMENTS

1. The Social Security Benefit (Persons Abroad) Amendment Regulations 1988 (SI 1988/435), reg.3 (April 11, 1988).
2. The Social Security Benefit (Persons Abroad) Amendment (No. 2) Regulations 1990 (SI 1990/621), reg.2(3) (April 6, 1990).
3. The Social Security Benefit (Persons Abroad) Amendment (No. 2) Regulations 1994 (SI 1994/1832), reg.2(2) (August 6, 1994).
4. The Social Security (Abolition of Earnings Rule) (Consequential) Regulations 1989 (SI 1989/1642), reg.8(3)(a)(i) (October 1, 1989).
5. The Social Security Benefit (Persons Abroad) Amendment (No. 2) Regulations 1994 (SI 1994/1832), reg.2(3) (August 6, 1994).
6. The Social Security Benefit (Persons Abroad) Amendment (No. 2) Regulations 1979 (SI 1979/1432), reg.3(3) (November 11, 1979).
7. The Social Security (Abolition of Earnings Rule) (Consequential) Regulations 1989 (SI 1989/1642), reg.8(3)(a)(ii) (October 1, 1989); and The Social Security Benefit (Persons Abroad) Amendment Regulations 1992 (SI 1992/1700), reg.3 (August 5, 1992).
8. The Welfare Reform and Pensions (Persons Abroad: Benefits for Widows and Widowers) (Consequential Amendments) Regulations 2000 (SI 2000/2876), reg.2 (April 9, 2001).
9. The Social Security (Abolition of Earnings Rule) (Consequential) Regulations 1989 (SI 1989/1642), reg.8(3)(a)(iii) (October 1, 1989).
10. The Social Security (Child Benefit) (Consequential) Regulations 1977 (SI 1977/342), reg.13(3) (April 4, 1977).
11. The Social Security (Child Benefit) (Consequential) Regulations 1977 (SI 1977/342), reg.13(3)(b) (April 4, 1977).
12. The Social Security Benefit (Person Abroad) Amendment (No. 2) Regulations 1979 (SI 1979/1432), reg.3(4) (November 10, 1979).
13. The Social Security (Abolition of Earnings Rule) (Consequential) Regulations 1989 (SI 1989/1642), reg.3(5) (October 1, 1989).
14. The Social Security Benefit (Person Abroad) Amendment (No. 2) Regulations 1979 (SI 1979/1432), reg.3(5) (November 10, 1979); The Social Security (Abolition of Earnings Rule) (Consequential) Regulations 1989 (SI 1989/1642), reg.8(3)(c) (October 1, 1989); and The Social Security Benefit (Persons Abroad) Amendment (No. 2) Regulations 1994 (SI 1994/1832), reg.2(2) (August 6, 1994).
15. The Social Security Benefit (Persons Abroad) Amendment (No. 2) Regulations 1979 (SI 1979/1432), reg.3(6) (November 10, 1979); and The Social Security (Abolition of Earnings Rule) (Consequential) Regulations 1989 (SI 1989/1642), reg.8(3)(d) (October 1, 1989).
16. The Social Security Benefit (Persons Abroad) Amendment (No. 2) Regulations 1994 (SI 1994/1832), reg.2(4) (August 6, 1994).
17. The Social Security (Shared Additional pension (Miscellaneous Amendments) Regulation 2005 (SI 2005/1551) (July 6, 2005).
18. The Civil Partnership (Pensions, Social Security and Child Support) (Consequential, etc. Provisions) Order 2005 (SI 2005/2877) (December 5, 2005).

GENERAL NOTE

See annotations to reg.4.   3.117

"ordinarily resident"

These words are used rather less frequently in the social security regulations than   3.118
simple "residence" and must mean something different from "resident". Guidance

as to the meaning of ordinary residence was given in *R(P) 1/78*. It imports more than residence (on which see guidance in *R(P)2/67*). In *R(P) 1/78* the Commissioner said "ordinary residence . . . connotes residence in a place with some degree of continuity and apart from accidental and temporary absences." He went on to say that the words are used with the intention of "seeking to exclude from entitlement to an increase persons . . . who live mostly abroad, and come to reside here intermittently without the intention of settling indefinitely." Such persons cannot be said to be ordinarily resident here. Such an approach is consistent with the general law. In *R. v London Borough of Barnet Ex p. Shah* [1983] 2 W.L.R. 16, the House of Lords considered the meaning of ordinary residence as used in regulations made under the Education Act 1962. In the absence of a statutory definition the words are to be given their natural and ordinary meaning. The House of Lords unanimously concluded that ordinary residence referred to a person's "abode in a particular place or country which he has adopted voluntarily and for settled purposes as part of the regular order of his life for the time being, whether of short or long duration." This could not apply to residence which was unlawful, for example because it was in breach of immigration laws. The reasoning of the House of Lords was adopted by the Commissioner in *R(M) 1/85*.

CP/3638/2006 has identified a lacuna in the provisions limiting the payment of pensions abroad to amounts which do not receive the benefit of annual up-rating. The decision will require careful examination in any cases where a similar point is taken. The claim in issue was initially by a wife, but later by a widow (the appellant). Her husband had become entitled to a Category A retirement pension in March 1976. When he emigrated to Canada that pension was frozen at the November 1975 rate. In September 2001 the appellant married him. She then became entitled to a Category B retirement pension from September 2001 based upon his contributions. That pension was fixed at the November 1975 rate (£7.90 per week) rather than the September 2001 rate (£45.20). The appellant took issue with that decision. The husband died in May 2002, and the appellant's claim was converted to one on widowhood, and the amount of the Category B retirement pension increased to £13.30 per week. A decision was also taken that she was entitled to half her husband s graduated retirement benefit; the appellant took issue with this award as well. The principal issue which arose in this appeal was whether the correct application of reg.5 following the death of the husband would be of benefit to the appellant.

The Commissioner concluded that the decision taken following the death of the husband was one which flowed from her change of status. Whereas prior to the husband's death, she came within reg.5(3)(aa), and this meant that she was not entitled to the additional benefit which would otherwise be paid under the annual up-rating orders, after his death she fell within reg.5(3)(c). The Commissioner says, in relation to the amount of the Category B retirement pension:

> 28. What then is the effect of regulation 5(3)(c) in the present case? The words are in my judgment clear and have only one possible meaning. They prevent the lifting of the disqualification by virtue of regulation 4(1) only in respect of up-rating orders coming into force after the first day of the <u>claimant's</u> entitlement to retirement pension. Accordingly, the claimant cannot from and including 27 May 2002 be disqualified for receiving any additional benefit payable by virtue of up-rating orders coming into force before that date (10 September 2001). In practice, from 27 May 2002 her Category B retirement pension is frozen at the rate set in section 44(4) of the Contributions and Benefits Act as from 9 April 2001, i.e. £72.50 per week.

In para.33 of the decision, the Commissioner addresses the appellant's entitlement to graduated retirement pension:

> 33. I concluded in my draft decision that the claimant's entitlement to GRB from 27 May 2002 should not have been half of £1.18, the amount actually in

payment to H immediately before his death, but should have been half of the amount generated by the graduated contributions he had paid and the amount specified in the preserved section 36(1) of the Social Security Act 1965 as at that date. I still consider that that is the "appropriate" rate under section 37(2). But, taking account of the Secretary of State's submission of 19 May 2008, I now think that I stopped at too early a point. Taking the rate of GRB identified above as appropriate, it is necessary to go on to look at the effect of regulation 5(3)(c) of the Persons Abroad Regulations. That is because the adoption of that appropriate rate to calculate the claimant's inherited GRB involves the identification of additional benefit that would be payable to her indirectly by virtue of the up-rating orders enacted since H became entitled to GRB. However, as I have decided above, regulation 5(3)(c) bites only on up-rating orders whose appointed date falls after the claimant became entitled to a retirement pension or GRB. For the reasons given in paragraph 30 above, although the context is the calculation of GRB, I am satisfied that the crucial date is that at which the claimant first became entitled to retirement pension of any kind, i.e. 10 September 2001. Accordingly, since no other sub-paragraph of regulation 5(3) applied to her as at 27 May 2002, she was able to take advantage of the appropriate rate for each unit of H's graduated contributions as specified in section 36(1) of the National Insurance Act 1965 down to April 2001 (9.06 pence). But she was not able to take advantage of the increase in that amount to 9.21 pence by the up-rating order whose appointed date was 6 April 2002.

The Commissioner also rules that the Persons Abroad Regulations were validly made. The decision is under appeal to the Court of Appeal as *Yates* v *Secretary of State for Work and Pensions*.

[¹ Rate of guaranteed minimum pension for the purposes of section 29 of the Pensions Act

5A.—Where a person is absent from Great Britain and disqualified for receiving additional Category A or Category B retirement pension, additional widowed mother's allowance [², bereavement allowance, widowed parent's allowance] or additional widow's pension then—

   (a) the rate of guaranteed minimum pension shall for the purposes only of section 29(1) of the Pensions Act be determined in his case as if any Order under section 37A of the Pensions Act which came into force while he was disqualified had instead come into force on the first day on which he ceased to be disqualified, and

   (b) so long as the person is disqualified, section 37A(7) shall apply to him as if the reference to section 29(1) were omitted.]

3.119

AMENDMENTS

   1. The Social Security Benefit (Persons Abroad) Amendment (No. 2) Regulations 1990 (SI 1990/621), reg.2(4) (April 6, 1990).
   2. The Welfare Reform and Pensions (Persons Abroad: Benefits for Widows and Widowers) (Consequential Amendments) Regulations 2000 (SI 2000/2876), reg.2 (April 9, 2001).

Modification of right to elect to be treated as not having retired

6.—Notwithstanding the provisions of regulation 2 of the Widow's Benefit and Retirement Pensions Regulations [¹ . . .] a person who is not ordinarily resident in Great Britain shall not be entitled to elect that that regulation shall apply in his case.

3.120

AMENDMENT

1. The Social Security (Abolition of Earnings Rule) (Consequential) Regulations 1989 (SI 1989/1642), reg.8(4) (October 1, 1989).

GENERAL NOTE

3.121   See annotations to reg.4.

3.122   *Regulation 7 revoked by The Social Security Benefit (Persons Abroad) Amendment Regulations 1990 (SI 1990/40), reg.3 (February 8, 1990).*

Modification of the Act in relation to age addition

3.123   **8.**—(1) A person shall not be disqualified for receiving age addition by reason of being absent from Great Britain if—

(a) he is ordinarily resident in Great Britain; or

(b) he was ordinarily resident in Great Britain and was entitled to age addition before he ceased to be ordinarily so resident; or

(c) in the case of a person who ceased to be ordinarily resident in Great Britain before September 20, 1971, he is entitled to a retirement pension of any category and, by virtue of an Order in Council made under section 143 of the Act or under section 105 of the former Principal Act, he is not disqualified for receiving that pension at a higher rate than was applicable in his case when he was last ordinarily resident in Great Britain; or

(d) in the case of a person who ceased to be ordinarily resident in Great Britain on or after September 20, 1971, he is entitled to a retirement pension of any category, and had he ceased to be ordinarily resident in Great Britain before that date, by virtue of an Order in Council made under section 143 of the Act or under section 105 of the former Principal Act, he would not have been disqualified for receiving that pension at a higher rate after that date than before it.

(2) Where a person is entitled to a retirement pension of any category at a rate which is calculated by reference to any period completed by that person in some territory outside Great Britain, any age addition to which he may be entitled shall be calculated as if it were an increase in that pension.

GENERAL NOTE

3.124   On the meaning of "ordinarily resident" see annotations to reg.5.

Modification of the Act in relation to title to [1 . . .] disablement benefit and industrial death benefit

3.125   **9.**—(1) [2 . . .]

(2) [3 . . .]

(3) A person shall not be disqualified for receiving [4 disablement benefit (other than any increase thereof under sections 58, 59, 61, 62, 63 or 66 of the Act)] by reason of being absent from Great Britain.

(4) A person shall not be disqualified for receiving an increase of disablement pension in respect of the need for constant attendance under section 61, or under regulations made under section 159(3), or in respect of exceptionally severe disablement under section 63, of the Act, by reason of being temporarily absent from Great Britain during the period of 6 months

from the date on which such absence commences or during such longer period as the Secretary of State may, having regard to the purpose of the absence and any other factors which appear to him to be relevant, allow.

(5) A person shall not be disqualified for receiving [⁵ reduced earnings allowance under section 59A of the Act,] by reason of being temporarily absent from Great Britain during the period of 3 months from the date on which such absence commences or during such longer period as the Secretary of State may, having regard to the purpose of the absence and any other factors which appear to him to be relevant, allow, so however that—

(a) such absence or any part thereof is not for the purpose of or in connection with any employment, trade or business;

(b) a claim as a result of which a decision is given awarding such allowance in respect of such period of absence or part thereof was made before the commencement of such absence; and

(c) the period taken into account by the award of such allowance to that person either includes the day of commencement of such absence or follows a period so taken into account which includes that day without there being a break in entitlement by that person to such increase from that day.

(6) A person shall not be disqualified for receiving industrial death benefit by reason of being absent from Great Britain.

[⁶ (7) A person shall not be disqualified for receiving retirement allowance under paragraph 13 of Schedule 7 to the Contributions and Benefits Act by reason of being absent from Great Britain.]

AMENDMENTS

1. The Social Security (Abolition of Injury Benefit) (Consequential) Regulations 1983 (SI 1983/186), reg.5(3) (April 6, 1983).
2. The Social Security (Abolition of Injury Benefit) (Consequential) Regulations 1983 (SI 1983/186), reg.5(4) (April 6, 1983).
3. The Social Security (Persons Abroad) Amendment Regulations 1977 (SI 1977/1679), reg.2(4) (November 14, 1977).
4. The Social Security (Industrial Injuries and Diseases) (Miscellaneous Provisions) Regulations 1986 (SI 1986/1561), reg.4(a) (October 1, 1986).
5. The Social Security (Industrial Injuries and Diseases) (Miscellaneous Provisions) Regulations 1986 (SI 1986/1561), reg.4(b) (October 1, 1986).
6. The Social Security (Miscellaenous Provisions) Amendment (No. 2) Regulations 1992 (SI 1992/2595), reg.10 (November 16, 1992).

Modification of the Act in relation to attendance allowance

10.—A person shall not be disqualified for receiving attendance allowance [¹ or disability living allowance] by reason of being absent from Great Britain.   3.126

AMENDMENT

1. The Disability Living Allowance and Disability Working Allowance (Consequential Provisions) Regulations 1991 (SI 1991/2742), reg.2(2) (April 6, 1992).

Regulation 10A revoked by The disability Living Allowance and Disability Working Allowance (Consequential Provisions) Regulations 1991 (SI 1991/2742), reg.2(3) (April 6, 1992).   3.127

Modification of the Act in relation to [² carer's allowance]

3.128   [¹ **10B.**—A person shall not be disqualified for receiving [² a carer's allowance] by reason of being absent from Great Britain.]

AMENDMENTS

1. The Social Security (Invalid Care Allowance) Regulations 1976 (SI 1976/409), reg.20 (April 12, 1976).
2. The Social Security Amendment (Carer's Allowance) Regulations 2002 (SI 2002/2497), reg.3 and Sch.2 (April 1, 2003).

Modification of Parts II and III of the Act in relation to accidents happening or prescribed diseases contracted outside Great Britain

3.129   **10C.**—(1) In this regulation—
"prescribed area" means an area over which Norway or any member State (other than the United Kingdom) exercises sovereign rights for the purpose of exploring the seabed and subsoil and exploiting their natural resources, being an area outside the territorial seas of Norway or such member State;
"prescribed disease" means a disease or injury prescribed for the purposes of Chapter V of Part II of the Act; and
"prescribed employment" means employment in a prescribed area in connection with the exploration of the seabed and subsoil and the exploitation of the natural resources of that area, or prescribed employment as defined in regulation 11 of these regulations (modification of the Act in relation to the United Kingdom continental shelf).
(2) Where on or after 30th November 1964 a person sustains or has sustained an accident or contracts or has contracted a prescribed disease while outside Great Britain, for the purposes of Chapter IV or V of Part II of the Act (benefit for industrial injuries and diseases) [section 94(5) of the Social Security Contributions and Benefits Act 1992] or regulation 14 of the Social Security (Industrial Injuries) (Prescribed Diseases) Regulations 1975 shall not operate to make benefit not payable in respect of that accident or prescribed disease if that person—
    (a) in connection with prescribed employment has sustained the accident or contracted the prescribed disease in a prescribed area, or while travelling between one prescribed area and another, or while travelling between a designated area (as defined in regulation 11 of these regulations) and a prescribed area, or while travelling between Norway or a member State (including the United Kingdom) and a prescribed area; or
    (b) has sustained the accident or contracted the prescribed disease while in the territory of a member State (other than the United Kingdom).
[¹ (2A) Where a person sustains an accident or contracts a prescribed disease while outside Great Britain in circumstances to which paragraph (2)(a) applies and the employment of that person would, but for the employment being outside of Great Britain, have been employed earner's employment, that employment shall for the purposes of Chapter IV or V of Part II of the Act (benefit for industrial injuries and diseases) be treated as employed earner's employment if:—

(a) that person is ordinarily resident in Great Britain and immediately before the commencement of the employment was resident therein, and

(b) the employer of that person has a place of business in Great Britain.]

(3) Where, before the date on which this regulation comes into operation, a decision has been given disallowing a claim for industrial injuries benefit in respect of an accident sustained or a prescribed disease contracted on or after 30th November 1964, then notwithstanding the provisions of section 107(6)(b) of the Act (decision that an accident not an industrial accident not reviewable) that decision may be reviewed by an insurance officer under [section 25(1)(b) of the Social Security Administration Act 1992] (review on ground of relevant change of circumstances) if he is satisfied that had paragraphs (1) and (2) of this regulation been in force when that decision was given those paragraphs would have applied, but a decision on review under this paragraph shall not make industrial injuries benefit payable for any period before the date on which this regulation comes into operation.

(4) Paragraph (3) of this regulation shall apply to a decision refusing a declaration that an accident was an industrial accident as it applies to a decision disallowing a claim for industrial injuries benefit.

[² (5) Where on or after October 1, 1986 a person to whom this paragraph applies sustains an accident arising out of, and in the course of, his employment, or contracts a prescribed disease due to the nature of his employment, such employment shall for the purposes of Chapters IV and V of Part II of the Act (benefit for industrial injuries and diseases) be treated as employed earner's employment notwithstanding that he is employed outside Great Britain, and any benefit which would be payable under those chapters but for the provisions of [section 94(5) of the Social Security Contributions and Benefits Act 1992] and regulation 14 of the Social Security (Industrial Injuries) (Prescribed Diseases) Regulations 1985 shall be payable from the date of his return to Great Britain notwithstanding that the accident happened or the disease was contracted while he was outside it.

(6) Paragraph (5) applies to any person in respect of whom Class 1 contributions are payable by virtue of regulation 120 of the Social Security (Contributions) Regulations 1979 or who is paying Class 2 (volunteer development workers) contributions under Case G of those regulations.]

AMENDMENTS

1. The Social Security Benefit (Persons Abroad) Amendment Regulations 1979 (SI 1982/388), reg.2 (April 14, 1982).

2. Paras (5) and (6) added by the Social Security Benefit (Persons Abroad) Amendment (No. 2) Regulations 1986 (SI 1986/1545), reg.3 (October 1, 1986).

3. The Social Security Benefit (Persons Abroad) Amendment Regulations 1979 (SI 1979/463), reg.2 (April 17, 1979).

Modification of the Act in relation to employment on the Continental Shelf

11.—(1) In this regulation—   3.130

"the Continental Shelf Act" means the Continental Shelf Act 1964;

"designated area" means any area which may from time to be

designated by Order in Council under the Continental Shelf Act as an area within which the rights of the United Kingdom with respect to the seabed and subsoil and their natural resources may be exercised;

"prescribed disease" means a disease or injury prescribed for the purposes of [sections 108–110 of the Social Security Contributions and Benefits Act 1992]; and

[¹ "prescribed employment" means any employment (whether under a contract of service or not) in any designated area or prescribed area, being employment in connection with any activity mentioned in section 23(2) of the Oil and Gas (Enterprise) Act 1982 in any designated area or in any prescribed area]; and

[¹ "prescribed area" means any area over which Norway or any member State (other than the United Kingdom) exercises sovereign rights for the purpose of exploring the seabed and subsoil and exploiting their natural resources, being an area outside the territorial seas of Norway or such member State, or any other area which is from time to time specified under section 22(5) of the Oil and Gas (Enterprise) Act 1982.]

[³ (1A) Where a claimant would be entitled to a contribution-based jobseeker's allowance but for section 1(2)(i) of the Jobseekers Act 1995 (conditions of entitlement to a jobseeker's allowance: requirement to be in Great Britain), he shall be entitled to a contribution-based jobseeker's allowance notwithstanding his absence from Great Britain if—

(a) the absence from Great Britain is due to his being or having been in prescribed employment in a designated area; or

(b) subject to paragraph (2B), he is, in connection with prescribed employment—

(i) in a prescribed area; or

(ii) travelling between one prescribed area and another; or

(iii) travelling between a designated area and a prescribed area; or

(iv) travelling between Norway or a Member State (including the United Kingdom) and a prescribed area.]

(2) Where benefit under Part II of the Act would, but for the provisions of [section 113(1)(a) of the Social Security Contributions and Benefits Act 1992] (absence from Great Britain), be payable to a person in a designated area, that benefit shall be payable notwithstanding the absence of that person from Great Britain, if the absence is due to his being or having been in prescribed employment in [¹ a designated area].

[³ (2A) Subject to paragraph (2B) where benefit under Part II of the Act would be payable to a person were that person in Great Britain, that person shall not be disqualified for receiving such benefit by reason only of the fact that he is, in connection with prescribed employment:—

(a) in a prescribed area; or

(b) travelling between one prescribed area and another; or

(c) travelling between a designated area and a prescribed area; or

(d) travelling between Norway or a member State (including the United Kingdom) and a prescribed area.

(2B) Paragraphs (1A) and (2A) shall not apply where, under the legislation administered by Norway or any member State (other than the United Kingdom) benefit is payable in respect of a person for the same contingency and for the same period for which benefit is claimed under the Act.]

(3) Where benefit under Chapter IV or V of Part II of the Act would, but

for the provisions of [section 94(5) of the Social Security Contributions and Benefits Act 1992], be payable to a person in respect of an accident arising out of and in the course of, or a prescribed disease due to the nature of, any employment by virtue of which any person is treated as an employed earner under paragraph 7 of Part I of Schedule 1 to the Industrial Injuries Employments Regulations, that benefit shall be payable notwithstanding that the accident happens or the disease is contracted while such person is outside Great Britain, if at the time that the accident happens or the disease is contracted the person is either in a designated area or travelling from one designated area to another or from or to Great Britain to or from a designated area.

(4) The provisions of the Act and of the regulations and orders made thereunder[3, and the Jobseekers Act 1995 and regulations made thereunder] shall, so far as they are not inconsistent with the provisions of this regulation, apply in relation to persons in prescribed employment with this modification, that where such a person is, on account of his being outside Great Britain by reason of his employment, being prescribed employment, unable to perform any act required to be done either forthwith or on the happening of a certain event or within a specified time, he shall be deemed to have complied with that requirement if he performs the act as soon as is reasonably practicable, although after the happening of the event or the expiration of the specified time.

AMENDMENTS

1. The Social Security and Statutory Sick Pay (Oil snd Gas (Enterprise) Act 1982 (Consequential) Regulations (SI 1982/1738), reg.2 (December 31, 1982).

2. Paras (2A) and (2B) added by The Social Security and Statutory Sick Pay (Oil and Gas (Enterprise) Act 1982) (Consequential) Regulations 1982 (SI 1982/1738), reg.2 (December 31, 1982). Word added to para.(2B) by The Jobseeker's Allowance Regulations 1996 (SI 1996/207), reg.165(3) (October 7, 1996).

3. The Jobseeker's Allowance Regulations 1996 (SI 1996/207), reg.165(4) (October 7, 1996).

4. The Jobseeker's Allowance Regulations 1996 (SI 1996/207), reg 165(2) (October 7, 1996).

Modification of the Act in relation to the Channel Islands

12.—(1) Notwithstanding any provisions of the Act or of these regulations a person shall not— 　　　　　　　　　　　　　　　　　　3.131
  (a) be disqualified for receiving any benefit under the Act by reason of absence from Great Britain [1 . . .];
  (b) be disentitled to a maternity grant in respect of a confinement outside Great Britain; or
  (c) be disqualified for receiving a death grant in respect of a death occurring outside Great Britain,
if that person is, or, as the case may be, that confinement or that death occurred, in a part of the Channel Islands which is not subject to an order made under section 143 of the Act or section 105 of the former Principal Act.

(2) A person who—
  (a)
      (i) is in any part of the Channel Islands which is not the subject of an order made under section 143 of the Act or section 84 of the National Insurance (Industrial Injuries) Act 1965, or

(ii) is going from (or to) Great Britain to (or from) such a part of the Channel Islands; and who

(b) suffers an industrial accident in the course of his employment (being employed earner's employment by virtue of regulation 94 of the Contributions Regulations),

shall, subject to the provisions of [section 95 of the Social Security Contributions and Benefits Act 1992], be treated as if the employment were employed earner's employment for the purposes of industrial injuries and as if the accident occurred in Great Britain.

AMENDMENT

1. The Social Security and Child Support (Jobseeker's Allowance) (Consequential Amendments) Regulations 1996 (SI 1996/1345), reg.15(2) (October 7, 1996).

Modification of the Act in relation to a dependant

3.132   **13.**—A husband or wife [¹ or civil partner] shall not be disqualified for receiving any increase (where payable) of benefit in respect of his or her spouse [¹ or civil partner] by reason of the spouse's [¹ or civil partner's] being absent from Great Britain provided that the spouse [¹ or civil partner] is resident with [¹ the husband, wife or civil partner], as the case may be.

AMENDMENT

1. The Civil Partnership (Pensions, Social Security and Child Support) (Consequential, etc. Provisions) Order 2005 (SI 2005/2877) (December 5, 2005).

GENERAL NOTE

3.133   See annotations to reg.2 of the Persons Residing Together Regulations.

[Modification of the Act in relation to title to benefit for beneficiary's child dependants

3.134   **13A.**—(1) By reason only of the fact that he is not entitled to child benefit in respect of a child, a person shall not be disentitled from receiving a benefit or an allowance or an increase of a benefit or an allowance under the Act in respect of a child (hereafter in this regulation referred to as "child dependency benefit") in respect of that child for any period during which he and the child are, or the child is, absent from Great Britain in a country in circumstances in which he would, in pursuance of any agreement with the government of a country outside the United Kingdom, be entitled to receive child dependency benefit in respect of the child were he entitled to child benefit in respect of the child if—

(a) he would, or could, had he made an appropriate claim, have been entitled to child benefit in respect of the child had all the requirements of [section 146(2) and (3) of the Social Security Contributions and Benefits Act 1992] (requirements as to presence in Great Britain) been satisfied; and

(b) in a case where he would not be treated for the purposes of [Part IX of the Social Security Contributions and Benefits Act 1992] as having the child living with him, he is contributing to the cost of providing for the child, in addition to any contribution he may be required to make under the Act, at a weekly rate not less than that of the child benefit which would be payable to him in respect of the child were child benefit so payable to him; and

(c) no other person is entitled to child benefit in respect of the child.

(2) For any period during which a person who is absent from Great Britain would satisfy the requirements of paragraph (1) in relation to a child but for the fact that that child is present in Great Britain that child shall, for the purposes of that paragraph, be treated as being present in the country in which that person is.

(3) By reason only of the fact that he is not entitled to child benefit in respect of a child, a person shall not be disentitled from receiving child dependency benefit in respect of that child for any period during which he or the child is, or both of them are, absent from Great Britain in circumstances in which, otherwise than in pursuance of such an agreement as is referred to in paragraph (1) or of regulations made under section 142 of the Act (co-ordination with Northern Ireland) were he entitled to child benefit in respect of the child he would be entitled to receive child dependency benefit in respect of the child if—

(a) he would, or could had he made an appropriate claim, have been entitled to child benefit in respect of the child had all the requirements of [section 146(2) and (3) of the Social Security Contributions and Benefits Act 1992] (requirements as to presence in Great Britain) been satisfied; and

(b) in a case where he would not be treated for the purposes of [Part IX of the Social Security Contributions and Benefits Act 1992] as having the child living with him, he is contributing to the cost of providing for the child, in addition to any contribution he may be required to make under the Act, at a weekly rate not less than that of the child benefit which would be payable to him in respect of the child were child benefit so payable to him; and

(c) he establishes that any absence from Great Britain of himself or the child was, when it began, intended to be temporary and has throughout continued to be temporary; and

(d) no other person is entitled to child benefit in respect of the child.

(4) For the purpose of paragraph (1), such a person or child as is there referred to may be treated as being absent from Great Britain notwithstanding that he has not previously been present in Great Britain; and for the purposes of paragraph (3), a child born during the absence from Great Britain of his mother shall, if she was pregnant of that child at a time when she was present in Great Britain, be treated as having been present in Great Britain on the date on which his mother was last present in Great Britain before the child was born.

(5) Where a person—

(a) immediately before returning to Great Britain was entitled to receive child dependency benefit in respect of a child; and

(b) would on his return to Great Britain have continued to be entitled to receive child dependency benefit in respect of that child were he entitled to child benefit in respect of the child,

he shall not be disentitled from receiving child dependency benefit in respect of the child by reason only of the fact that he is not entitled to child benefit in respect of the child if—

(i) he would, or could had he made an appropriate claim, have been entitled to child benefit in respect of the child had all the requirements of [section 146(2) and (3) of the Social Security Contributions and Benefits Act 1992] (requirements as to presence in Great Britain) been satisfied; and

(ii) in a case where he would not be treated for the purposes of [Part IX of the Social Security Contributions and Benefits Act 1992] as having the child living with him, he is contributing to the cost of providing for the child, in addition to any contribution he may be required to make under the Act, at a weekly rate not less than that of the child benefit which would be payable to him in respect of the child were child benefit so payable to him; and

(iii) no other person is entitled to child benefit in respect of the child.

(6) Where a person who was absent from Great Britain immediately before April 4, 1977, (the date on which child benefit first becomes payable) or a subsequent date on which the rate or any of the rates of child benefit is or are increased—

(a) is entitled to receive child dependency benefit in respect of a child for a continuous period beginning before and continuing after that date; and

(b) no other person is entitled to child benefit in respect of that child for that period,

any provision made pursuant to section 17(1) or (4) of the Child Benefit Act whereby, having regard to the introduction of child benefit or to an increase in the rate or any of the rates of child benefit, the weekly rate of child dependency benefit payable in respect of that child would be subject to a reduction shall not have effect so as (by reason only of that reduction) to reduce the total weekly rate of benefit (including benefit (if any) which is not child dependency benefit payable in respect of that child) payable to that person below the total weekly rate of such benefit payable to him immediately before that date.]

AMENDMENT

1. The Social Security (Child Benefit) (Consequential) Regulations 1977 (SI 1977/342), reg.13(5) (April 4, 1977).

GENERAL NOTE

3.135 The effect of this regulation is that if the claimant's child dependant is abroad, the claimant remains entitled to an increase for the child if the claimant is entitled to child benefit for the child. See Child Benefit (Residence and Persons Abroad) Regulations 1976.

If the claimant is not entitled to child benefit but would be if in Great Britain, the claimant will receive the increase if there is no one else entitled to child benefit for the child.

3.136 *Regulation 13B revoked by The Social Security and Child Support (Jobseeker's Allowance) (Consequential Amendments) Regulations 1996 (SI 1996/1345), Sch. (October 7, 1996).*

Administrative arrangements about payment of benefits

3.137 **14.**—Where the right to benefit arises by virtue of these regulations the benefit shall be payable subject to the furnishing of such information and evidence as the Secretary of State may from time to time require; and the Secretary of State shall make arrangements as to the time and manner of payment which shall have effect in place of the provisions as to time and manner of payment which would have been applicable by virtue of other regulations made under the Act [1], or in connection with jobseeker's allowance,] if the person concerned had not been absent from Great Britain.

AMENDMENT

1. The Social Security and Child Support (Jobseeker's Allowance) (Consequential Amendments) Regulations 1996 (SI 1996/1345), reg.15(3) (October 7, 1996).

Regulation 15 omitted.   **3.138**

[¹ SCHEDULE   **Regulation 5(8)**

UP-RATING IN RESPECT OF CERTAIN AWARDS MADE BETWEEN 1ST SEPTEMBER 1985 AND 7TH AUGUST 1991

1.—A person referred to in a case set out in column (1) shall not be disqualified by reason   **3.139**
of being absent from Great Britain for receiving any additional widow's benefit or retirement pension which became payable by virtue of an up-rating order which came into force on or before the date referred to in column (3) if—
  (a) the award referred to in column (1) was made during the period specified in column (2); and
  (b) immediately before 6th August 1994 that person was being paid a widow's benefit or a retirement pension (as the case may be) at the rate current at the date referred to in column (3).

(1) Case	(2) Period in which award was made	(3) Date after which disqualification to take effect
1. A woman who was awarded a widow's benefit	after 30th May 1988 but not later than 19th February 1990	the date on which she became entitled to a widow's benefit
2. A woman who had been receiving a Category B retirement pension and was awarded that pension at a higher rate after her husband's death	after 13th September 1988 but not later than 6th August 1991	the date of her husband's death
3. A woman who was first awarded a Category B retirement pension on the death of her husband after she attained the age of 60	after 31st January 1990 but not later than 6th August 1991	the date on which she became entitled to a Category B retirement pension
4. A man who had been receiving a Category A retirement pension and was awarded a Category B retirement pension after his wife's death	after 16th November 1986 but not later than 6th August 1991	the date on which he became entitled to a Category B retirement pension

(1) Case	(2) Period in which award was made	(3) Date after which disqualification to take effect
5. A woman who had been receiving a Category B retirement pension and was awarded a Category A retirement pension	after 1st September 1985 but not later than 6th August 1991	the date on which she became entitled to a Category A retirement pension
6. A person who was awarded a Category A retirement pension determined by taking into account the contributions of his or her former spouse under regulation 8 of the Social Security (Widow's Benefit and Retirement Pensions) Regulations 1979	after 16th November 1986 but not later than 6th August 1991	the date on which that person first became entitled to a Category A retirement pension

2.—In paragraph 1 "up-rating order" means an order which was made under section 124 of the Act or section 63 of the Social Security Act 1986.]

AMENDMENT

1. Schedule added by The Social Security Benefit (Persons Abroad) Amendment (No. 2) Regulations 1994 (SI 1994/1832), reg.3 (August 6, 1994). (See Vol.II at para.4.352.)

Social Security Benefit (Persons Residing Together) Regulations 1977

(SI 1977/956) (*as amended*)

ARRANGEMENT OF REGULATIONS

3.140

1. Citation, commencement and interpretation.
2. Circumstances in which a person is to be treated as residing or not residing with another person or in which persons are to be treated as residing or not residing together.
3. *Omitted.*

The Secretary of State for Social Services, in exercise of the powers conferred upon him by section 22(1) of the Social Security (Miscellaneous Provisions) Act 1977 and of all other powers enabling him in that behalf hereby makes the following regulations:

Citation, commencement and interpretation

3.141

1.—(1) These regulations may be cited as the Social Security Benefit (Persons Residing Together) Regulations 1977 and shall come into operation on June 27, 1977.

(2) In these regulations "the Act" means the Social Security Act 1975 and other expressions have the same meanings as in the Act.

(3) Any reference in these regulations to any provision made or contained

in any enactment or instrument shall be construed as a reference to that provision as amended or extended by any enactment or instrument and as including a reference to any provision which may re-enact or replace it, with or without modification.

(4) The rules for the construction of Acts of Parliament contained in the Interpretation Act 1889 shall apply in relation to this instrument and in relation to any revocation effected by it as if this instrument, the regulations revoked by it and any regulations revoked by the regulations so revoked were Acts of Parliament, and as if each revocation were a repeal.

GENERAL NOTE

Interpretation Act 1889   3.142
By s.25(2) of the Interpretation Act 1978, this reference is to be treated as a reference to the 1978 Act.

Circumstances in which a person is to be treated as residing or not residing with another person or in which persons are to be treated as residing or not residing together

2.—(1) As respects any requirement of the Act, or contained in any provision made for the purposes thereof, any question as to whether—   3.143
  (a) a person is or was residing with another person; or
  (b) persons are residing together,
shall be determined in accordance with the following provisions of this regulation.
(2) In relation to—
[(a) an increase in respect of an adult dependant under [section 82 of the Social Security Contributions and Benefits Act 1992] (short-term benefits: increase for adult dependants), [section 83 of the Social Security Contributions and Benefits Act 1992] (increase of Category A or Category C retirement pension), [section 90 of the Social Security Contributions and Benefits Act 1992] (increase of severe disablement allowance or invalid care allowance) or [section 66 of the Social Security Act 1975] (increase of disablement pension where the beneficiary is entitled to unemployability supplement) or section 86A of the Social Security Contributions and Benefits Act 1992 (incapacity benefit: increases for adult dependants);] or
  (b) an adjustment of benefit under [section 73(1)(b) of the Social Security Administration Act 1992] (hospital in-patients),
two spouses [or civil partners] shall not be treated as having ceased to reside together by reason only of the fact that either of them is, or they both are, undergoing medical or other treatment as an in-patient in a hospital or similar institution, whether such absence is temporary or not.
(3) In the case of a woman who has been widowed, she shall not be treated as having ceased to reside together with a child or person under the age of 19 by reason of any absence the one from the other which is not likely to be permanent.
(4) Subject to the foregoing provisions of this regulation, two persons shall not be treated as having ceased to reside together by reason of any temporary absence the one from the other.

The Social Security (Abolition of Injury Benefit) (Consequential) Regulations 1983 (SI 1983/186), reg.8 (April 6, 1983).

The Social Security (Severe Disablement Allowance) Regulations 1984 (SI 1984/1303), reg.11 (November 29, 1984).

The Social Security (Incapacity Benefit) (Consequential and Transitional Amendments and Savings) Regulations 1995 (SI 1995/829, reg.10 (April 13, 1995).

The Social Security and Child Support (Jobseeker's Allowance) (Consequential Amendments) Regulations 1996 (SI 1996/1345), reg.2 (October 7, 1996).

The Civil Partnership (Pensions, Social Security and Child Support) (Consequential, etc. Provisions) Order 2005 (SI 2005/2877) (December 5, 2005).

DEFINITIONS

"the Act"—reg.1.
"medical treatment"—CB & A 1992, s.122.

GENERAL NOTE

3.144   Compare reg.11 of the Child Benefit (General) Regulations. As in those regulations, "residing with" does not mean the same as "living with": *R(I) 10/51*; *R(U) 11/62* and *R(F) 2/79*. It is somewhat broader requiring only an element of continuity and permanence, which is to be assessed in the light of all the relevant circumstances of particular cases.

The general rule is that only permanent separation of two people constitutes not residing together. But the regulation sets out two specific rules.

First, if it is the sole cause of the absence of a spouse, periods by one or both spouses as in-patients in a hospital or similar institution are to be treated as periods residing together whether or not the absence is likely to be permanent. This presumably covers situations such as where a spouse is admitted to hospital for terminal care. Difficulties have arisen as to when a patient is an "inpatient". The approach consistently adopted has been that the patient must be "housed overnight" at the hospital or similar institution: *CS/65/49*, *R(S) 8/51* and *R(I) 14/56*.

Secondly, a widow and her child are treated as residing together if their absence from one another can be regarded as temporary, but they are to be treated as residing apart if their absence from one another is likely to be permanent. This appears to add little to the general rule and may owe its origins to particular difficulties over widow's benefit where persons under 19 are away from home for the purposes of full-time education and training. Such persons are presumed to be residing with the widow unless the absence can be said to be permanent.

It is clear that what constitutes a permanent residing together or parting will be a matter of judgment for adjudication officers, tribunals and Commissioners in the light of all the facts of particular cases.

The facts of *CSS/18/88* illustrate the importance of determining each case on its own facts and of avoiding an *a priori* approach to cases. In that case a couple had been married for over 40 years. In April 1978 the wife went to Canada to visit relatives. During that visit her brother-in-law was seriously injured in a road traffic accident. The wife remained in Canada to provide care for him. He subsequently died, but the wife's sister was diagnosed as suffering from cancer and the wife again remained in Canada to nurse her. Meanwhile the husband had sought permission to emigrate to Canada. This was obtained, but his own ill health prevented his travelling. The couple remained in touch and the wife returned to Scotland for visits home. This situation lasted until 1987, when the issue of the husband's receipt of an increase of benefit for his wife came before a tribunal.

The tribunal concluded that the absence of the wife in Canada could not be regarded as temporary. The Commissioner disagreed, though he noted the unusual circumstances of the case. The couple had not ceased to reside together permanently. The tribunal had erred by focusing on the nature of the absence *from the United Kingdom*, rather than by focusing on whether they were temporarily absent *from one another*. Provided the husband and wife are residing together, the absence of one spouse abroad is not a disqualifying factor (see reg.13 of the Persons Abroad Regulations).

In *R(P) 1/90* Commissioner Skinner advised:

"Whether or not there is a temporary absence is a question of fact for the tribunal, but the Commissioners have evolved a series of tests over the years which assists the members in dealing with such question. In the earlier cases the purpose of the absence of the husband was considered to be of great importance, but in the later decisions more importance was attached to the duration of the absence. In *C(P)84/50* it was said that a period of absence which has lasted for more than a year, and of which there is no reasonable prospect of its coming to an end, cannot be spoken of as 'temporary.' If a man left home, and if it was ascertained after more than a year had elapsed that there was still no prospect of his return, he would not be said to be temporarily absent. In *R(P)7/53* it was held that this was the established test for deciding whether absence had ceased to be temporary. It was pointed out that it was not a hard and fast rule, for there may be cases where it can be said long before the year is up the absence is not going to be temporary. It was pointed out that the reasonable prospect [sic] of return are not limited to the prospects within any particular period. In my judgment while the duration of the absence must be part of the test to be applied by the tribunal, the purpose of the absence and the intention of the parties are also of relevance. Indeed that is recognised in *R(P)7/53* where the absence [of] more than a year was only fatal to the claimant where there was no reasonable prospect of the absence coming to an end. I do not think it is practicable to lay down any hard and fast rules by which the question can be determined, but the intention of the claimant, the purpose of the absence and its duration are all relevant." (para.8).

In *CS/202/1991*, the Deputy Commissioner adopted the conclusion in *R(P) 1/90* that reg.2(4) modifies reg.13 of the Persons Abroad Regulations, but suggests that the approach to the determination of the temporary nature of any absence in that reported decision may be too stringent in the light of the decision in *Ex p. Akbar* (see annotations to reg.2 of the Persons Abroad Regulations).

Regulation 3 omitted. 3.145

Social Security and Family Allowances (Polygamous Marriages) Regulations 1975

(SI 1975/561) *(as amended)*

1. Citation, commencement and interpretation. 3.146
2. General rule as to consequences of a polygamous marriage [for the purpose of the . . . Acts].
3. Special rules for retirement pension for women.

The Secretary of State for Social Services, in exercise of powers conferred upon her under section 162(b) of the Social Security Act 1975 and section 12(2) of the Family Allowance Act 1965, as substituted by paragraph 18 of Schedule 2 to the Social Security (Consequential Provisions) Act 1975, hereby makes the following regulations:

Citation, commencement and interpretation

3.147 **1.**—(1) These regulations may be cited as the Social Security and Family Allowances (Polygamous Marriages) Regulations 1975 and shall come into operation on 6th April 1975.

(2) In these regulations, unless the context otherwise requires—

"the Social Security Act" means the [¹ Social Security Contributions and Benefits Act 1992]

[² "the Family Allowances Act" means the Family Allowances Act 1965;]

"polygamous marriage" means a marriage celebrated under a law which, as it applies to the particular ceremony and to the parties thereto, permits polygamy;

"monogamous marriage" means a marriage celebrated under a law which does not permit polygamy, and "in fact monogamous" is to be construed in accordance with regulation 2(2) below;

and other expressions shall, as appropriate, have the same meanings as in the Social Security Act and the Family Allowances Act.

(3) Any reference in these regulations to any provision made by or contained in any enactment or instrument shall, except in so far as the context otherwise requires, be construed as a reference to that provision as amended or extended by any enactment or instrument and as including a reference to any provision which it re-enacts or replaces, or which may re-enact or replace it, with or without modification.

(4) The rules for the construction of Acts of Parliament contained in the Interpretation Act 1889 shall apply for the purposes of the interpretation of these regulations as they apply for the purposes of the interpretation of an Act of Parliament.

General rule as to the consequences of a polygamous marriage for the purpose of the Social Security Act and the Family Allowances Act

3.148 **2.**—(1) Subject to the following provisions of these regulations, a polygamous marriage shall, for the purpose of the Social Security Act [² and the Family Allowances Act] and any enactment construed as one with those Acts, be treated as having the same consequences as a monogamous marriage for any day, but only for any day, throughout which the polygamous marriage is in fact monogamous.

(2) In this and the next following regulation—

(a) a polygamous marriage is referred to as being in fact monogamous when neither party to it has any spouse additional to the other; and

(b) the day on which a polygamous marriage is contracted, or on which it terminates for any reason, shall be treated as a day throughout which that marriage was in fact monogamous if at all times on that day after it was contracted, or as the case may be, before it terminated, it was in fact monogamous.

GENERAL NOTE

3.149 In *CG/2611/2003* the Commissioner was determining an appeal in relation to a claim for widow's benefit in respect of a man who married three times. It seems that that the husband, a Bangladeshi, entered into his first marriage in Bangladesh in the early 1960s. In 1968 he married the claimant in Bangladesh in accordance with Muslim law. Some time in the 1970s the husband took a third wife in Bangladesh. At the time of the husband's death, there was some uncertainty about the status of the first marriage, but the second and third marriages were still subsisting. The second wife claimed widow's benefit. The Secretary of State's argument was that the claim to the widow's benefit must be disallowed because the husband had contracted polygamous marriages, at least two of which subsisted at his death, and the claimant was not the husband's only wife at the date he died. Under the Polygamous Marriages Regulations, the claim could only succeed if, at the material time, the marriage was, in fact, monogamous.

The tribunal had concluded that at the time of marriage to the claimant, the husband was domiciled in the United Kingdom. The Commissioner casts doubt on the correctness of that conclusion but refers the matter back to a fresh tribunal for determination. Were it to be correct, then the marriage contracted with the claimant would have been void by the law of the law of the husband's domicile.

The decision highlights the ned for the most careful (and consistent) findings of fact in these complex cases. The place of domicile of the husband at the dates of each of the marriages he contracts will be of fundamental importance in determining the validity of those marriages and consequently the application of the Polygamous Marriages Regulations to any claim for benefit.

Special rules for retirement pension for women

3.—(1) Subject to the provisions of paragraphs (2) and (3) of this regulation, where on or after the date on which she attained pensionable age a woman was a married woman by virtue of a polygamous marriage and either—   **3.150**

    (a) throughout a day, falling on or after the date on which both she and her spouse have attained pensionable age [[3] and in respect of which neither of them has an entitlement to a Category A or Category B retirement pension which is deferred,] that marriage was in fact monogamous, or

    (b) throughout the day on which her spouse died that marriage was in fact monogamous,

that marriage, whether or not it has at all times been or continues to be in fact monogamous, shall, for the purposes of determining her right to and the rate of a retirement pension of any category under the Social Security Act be treated as having the same consequences as a monogamous marriage from and including the date on which she attained pensionable age or, if the marriage was contracted after that date, from and including the date of the marriage.

(2) Paragraph (1) of this regulation shall not operate so as to entitle a woman to a retirement pension for any period before the first such day as is referred to in sub-paragraph (a) of that paragraph or, in a case where that sub-paragraph does not apply, the day referred to in sub-paragraph (b) of that paragraph.

(3) Where the marriage of a woman is a polygamous marriage which was contracted—

    (a) before she attained pensionable age and—

        (i) was not in fact monogamous when she attained that age, but

        (ii) became in fact monogamous on a date after she attained that age; or

    (b) on or after the day on which she attained pensionable age and—

        (i) was not in fact monogamous when it was contracted, but

(ii) became in fact monogamous on a date after it was contracted; that marriage shall be treated as having the same consequences as a monogamous marriage for the purposes of section 29(10) of the Social Security Act (increase of Category B retirement pension in certain circumstances) only with effect from the date referred to in sub-paragraph (a)(ii) or, as the case may be, sub-paragraph (b)(ii) of this paragraph.

(4) In a case where section 28(3) of and Schedule 7 to the Social Security Act (retirement pension for widows who were widowed before attaining pensionable age) or regulation 4 of the Social Security (Benefit) (Married Women and Widows Special Provisions) Regulations 1974 (retirement pension for women whose marriages have been dissolved) applies to a woman and the relevant marriage for the purposes of that section and Schedule or that regulation was a polygamous marriage and throughout the day on which either—

(a) her marriage was dissolved, or

(b) her spouse died,

that marriage was in fact monogamous, that polygamous marriage shall, for those purposes, notwithstanding that it has not at all times been in fact monogamous, be treated as having the same consequences as if it had been a monogamous marriage.

(5) Where a woman is a married woman by virtue of a polygamous marriage which is in fact monogamous on the date from which she becomes entitled to a Category D retirement pension under section 39(1)(c) of the Social Security Act (retirement pensions for persons over age 80), that marriage, notwithstanding that it ceases to be in fact monogamous, shall, for the purpose of determining the rate of her Category D retirement pension, be treated as having the same consequences as a monogamous marriage.

AMENDMENTS

1. Substituted by Social Security (Consequential Provisions) Act 1992, s.2(4).
2. This provision has lapsed with the repeal of the Family Allowances Act.
3. Words substituted by the Social Security (Abolition of Earnings Rule) (Consequential) Regulations 1989 (SI 1989/1642) (October 1, 1989).

PART IV

DISABILITY BENEFITS

Social Security (Attendance Allowance) Regulations 1991

(SI 1991/2740) (*as amended*)

The Secretary of State for Social Security, in exercise of the powers conferred upon him by sections 35(1), (2)(b), (2A), (4A) and (6), 85(1)(b) and 166(2) and (3) of, and Schedule 20 to, the Social Security Act 1975 and of all other powers enabling him in that behalf, by this instrument, which contains regulations which relate to matters which, in accordance with section 140 of that Act, have been referred to the Attendance Allowance Board, hereby makes the following Regulations:

Citation, commencement and interpretation

1.—(1) These Regulations may be cited as the Social Security (Attendance Allowance) Regulations 1991 and shall come into force on 6th April 1992.

4.2

(2) In these Regulations—

"the Act" means the Social Security Act 1975;

"the NHS Act of 1977" means the National Health Service Act 1977;

"the NHS Act of 1978" means the National Health Service (Scotland) Act 1978;

"the NHS Act of 1990" means the National Health Service and Community Care Act 1990;

"terminally ill" shall be construed in accordance with section 35(2C) of the Act.

(3) Unless the context otherwise requires, any reference in these Regulations to a numbered regulation is a reference to the regulation bearing that number in these Regulations and any reference in a regulation to a

numbered paragraph is a reference to the paragraph of that regulation bearing that number.

[¹ Disapplication of section 1(1A) of the Administration Act

4.3   **1A.**—Section 1(1A) of the Administration Act (requirement to state national insurance number) shall not apply to any claim for attendance allowance made or treated as made before 9th February, 1998.]

AMENDMENT

1.—Social Security (National Insurance Information: Exemption) Regulations 1997 (SI 1997/2676) (December 1, 1997).

Conditions as to residence and presence in Great Britain

4.4   **2.**—(1) Subject to the following provisions of this regulation, the pre-scribed conditions for the purposes of section 35(1) of the Act as to residence and presence in Great Britain in relation to any person on any day shall be that—

> (a) on that day—
>> (i) he is ordinarily resident in Great Britain, and
>> [¹ (ib) he is not a person subject to immigration control within the meaning of section 115(9) of the Immigration and Asylum Act 1999 or section 115 of that Act does not apply to him for the purposes of entitlement to attendance allowance by virtue of regulation 2 of the Social Security (Immigration and Asylum) Consequential Amendments Regulations 2000,
>> (ii) he is present in Great Britain, and
>> (iii) he has been present in Great Britain for a period of, or for periods amounting in the aggregate to, not less than 26 weeks in the 52 weeks immediately preceding that day;
> (b) [⁴ . . .]
> [² (1A)—[¹ *Omitted*]].

(2) For the purposes of paragraph (1)(a)(ii) and (iii), notwithstanding that on any day a person is absent from Great Britain, he shall be treated as though he were present in Great Britain if his absence is by reason only of the fact that on that day—

> (a) he is abroad in his capacity as—
>> (i) a serving member of the forces,
>> (ii) an airman or mariner within the meaning of regulations 81 and 86 respectively of the Social Security (Contributions) Regulations 1979, and for the purpose of this provision, the expression "serving members of the forces" has the same meaning as in regulation 1(2) of the Regulations of 1979; or
> (b) he is in employment prescribed for the purposes of section 132 of the Act in connection with continental shelf operations; or
> (c) he is living with a person mentioned in sub-paragraph (a)(i) and is the spouse, [³ civil partner,] son, daughter, step-son, step-daughter, father, father-in-law, step-father, mother, mother-in-law or step-mother of that person; or
> (d) his absence from Great Britain is, and when it began was, for a tem-

porary purpose and has not lasted for a continuous period exceeding 26 weeks; or

(e) his absence from Great Britain is temporary and for the specific purpose of his being treated for incapacity, or a disabling condition, which commenced before he left Great Britain, and the Secretary of State has certified that it is consistent with the proper administration of the Act that, subject to the satisfaction of the foregoing condition in this subparagraph, he should be treated as though he were present in Great Britain.

(3) Where a person is terminally ill and makes a claim for attendance allowance expressly on the ground that he is such a person, paragraph (1) shall apply to him as if head (iii) of sub-paragraph (a) was omitted.

(4) [⁴. . .]

AMENDMENTS

1. Social Security (Immigration and Asylum) Consequential Amendments Regulations 2000 (SI 2000/636), reg.10 (April 3, 2000).
2. Social Security (Persons From Abroad) Miscellaneous Amendments Regulations 1996 (SI 1996/30) reg.2 (February 5, 1996), subject to a saving under reg.12(3). See *Social Security Legislation 2001: Vol.II: Income Support, Jobseeker's Allowance, Tax Credits and the Social Fund* at para.4.352.
3. Civil Partnership Act 2004, Sch.24 (December 5, 2005).
4. Social Security (Miscellaneous Amendments) (No.4) Regulations 2006 (SI 2006/2378), reg.7 (October 1, 2006).

GENERAL NOTE

Section 35(1) of the 1975 Act has now been replaced by s.64(1) of the Social Security Contributions and Benefits Act 1992.   4.5

Extension of qualifying period

3.—The period prescribed for the purposes of section 35(2)(b) of the Act (claimant to satisfy one or both of the conditions in section 35(1) of the Act for 6 months immediately preceeding the date from which attendance allowance is to be awarded) shall be 2 years.   4.6

GENERAL NOTE

Section 35(2)(b) of the 1975 Act has now been replaced by s.65(1)(b) of the Social Security Contributions and Benefits Act 1992.   4.7

Allowance payable before the date of claim in renewal cases

4.—*Revoked by Social Security (Miscellaneous Amendments) (No. 2) Regulations 1997 (SI 1997/793), reg.19(b) with effect from September 1, 1997.*   4.8

GENERAL NOTE

This regulation had allowed a renewal claim made within six months of the date of termination of an earlier award to be backdated to that date.   4.9

Renal dialysis

5.—(1) Subject to paragraph (3), a person who suffers from renal failure and who is undergoing the treatment specified in paragraph (2) shall be deemed to satisfy the conditions—   4.10

    (a) in section 35(1)(a) of the Act (severe physical and mental disability) if he undergoes renal dialysis by day;

    (b) in section 35(1)(b) of the Act if he undergoes renal dialysis by night;

    (c) in either paragraph (a) or paragraph (b) of section 35(1) of the Act, but not both, if he undergoes renal dialysis by day and by night.

(2) The treatment referred to in paragraph (1) is the undergoing of renal dialysis—

    (a) two or more times a week; and

    (b) which either—

        (i) is of a type which normally requires the attendance of or supervision by another person during the period of dialysis, or

        (ii) which, because of the particular circumstances of his case, in fact requires another person, during the period of dialysis, to attend in connection with the bodily functions of the person undergoing renal dialysis or to supervise that person in order that he avoids substantial danger to himself.

(3) Except as provided in paragraph (4), paragraph (1) does not apply to a person undergoing the treatment specified in paragraph (2) where the treatment—

    (a) is provided under the NHS Act of 1977 or the NHS Act of 1978;

    (b) is in a hospital or similar institution;

    (c) is out-patient treatment; and

    (d) takes place with the assistance or supervision of any member of staff of the hospital or similar institution.

(4) Paragraph (3) does not apply for the purposes of determining whether a person is to be taken to satisfy either of the conditions specified in paragraph (1) during the period of 6 months referred to in section 35(2)(b) of the 1975 Act (qualifying period for attendance allowance).

GENERAL NOTE

4.11   Under this regulation, a person undergoing renal dialysis at least twice a week may be deemed to satisfy *either* the day *or* the night attendance condition, but not both. Some degree of attention or supervision must be required. This regulation is in slightly different terms from regs 5B and 5C of the Social Security (Attendance Allowance) (No. 2) Regulations 1975 which governed entitlement before April 6, 1992.

Para.(1)

4.12   The conditions previously to be found in s.35(1)(a) and (b) of the 1975 Act are now to be found in s.64(2) and (3) of the Social Security Contributions and Benefits Act 1992.

Para.(2)(b)

4.13   The dialysis must be *either* of a type which *normally* requires the attendance of or supervision by another person (in which case the actual purpose of the attention or supervision is irrelevant) *or* the dialysis must *in the particular case* require the attention or supervision of the claimant (for the purpose specified in para.(2)(b) (ii)).

Para.(3)

4.14   This excludes from the scope of the regulation claimants whose treatment satisfies all four conditions in sub-paras (a)–(d). It is not entirely clear what assistance or supervision actually falls within sub-para.(d) but presumably it is the attention or supervision falling within para.(2)(b) so that only assistance and supervision *during the period of dialysis* is relevant and not any assistance at the beginning or end of the treatment. By virtue of para.(4), para.(3) does not apply in respect of the six-month qualifying period for attendance allowance. This means that a person previously excluded under para.(3) can qualify for attendance allowance under this reg.as soon as one of the excluding conditions of para.(3) ceases to be satisfied. S.35(2)(b) of the 1975 Act has been replaced by s.65(1)(b) of the Social Security Contributions and Benefits Act 1992.

Hospitalisation

6.—[1 (1) Subject to regulation 8, it shall be a condition for the receipt of an attendance allowance for any period in respect of any person that during that period he is not maintained free of charge while undergoing medical or other treatment as an in-patient—

4.15

   (a) in a hospital or similar institution under the NHS Act of 1977, the NHS Act of 1978 or the NHS Act of 1990; or

   (b) in a hospital or similar institution maintained or administered by the Defence Council.]

(2) For the purposes of [1 paragraph (1)(a)], a person shall only be regarded as not being maintained free of charge in a hospital or similar institution for any period where his accommodation and services are provided under section 65 of the NHS Act of 1977 or section 58 of, or paragraph 14 of Schedule 7A to, the NHS Act of 1978 or paragraph 14 of Schedule 2 to the NHS Act of 1990.

[2 (2A) For the purpose of paragraph (1), a period during which a person is maintained free of charge while undergoing medical or other treatment as an in-patient shall be deemed to begin on the day after the day on which he enters a hospital or similar institution referred to in that paragraph and to end on the day [3 before the day] on which he leaves such a hospital or similar institution.]

(3)[1 . . .].

AMENDMENTS

1. Social Security (Disability Living Allowance and Attendance Allowance) (Amendment) Regulation 1992 (SI 1992/2869), reg.2 (December 15, 1992).

2. Social Security (Hospital In-Patients, Attendance Allowance and Disability Living Allowance) (Amendment) Regulations 1999 (SI 1999/1326) (June 7, 1999).

3. Social Security (Attendance Allowance and Disability Living Allowance) (Amendment) Regulations 2000, (SI 2000/1401) reg.2 (June 19, 2000).

GENERAL NOTE

By virtue of reg.8, this regulation applies only after a person has been in hospital (or in accommodation to which reg.7 applies) for 28 days although periods separated by intervals not exceeding 28 days may be linked.

4.16

If a person is receiving treatment as an in-patient in one of the hospitals or institutions specified in para.(1), he or she is deemed to be being maintained free of charge unless a private patient (in which case para.(2) will apply). Although the wording of this regulation is different from that considered in *R(S) 4/84*, the overall conclusion reached by the Commissioner appears to be relevant here. The claimant was able to attend college during the day but received treatment from the hospital at night. The Commissioner held that she was not receiving free in-patient treatment because "any period" and "period" must relate to a period of not less than one day.

In *CDLA/11099/95*, the Commissioner decided that the equivalent provision in reg.8 of the Social Security (Disability Living Allowance) Regulations 1991 applied so as to make it a condition of entitlement to benefit only for "complete calendar (i.e. midnight-to-midnight) days throughout which the claimant is not undergoing medical or other treatment as an in-patient" but that the state of affairs existing at the beginning of a day was presumed to continue until the end. However, in *CSS/617/97*, where the claimant of severe disablement allowance went home from hospital from a Friday morning to a Monday evening, the Commissioner construed reg.2(2) of the Social Security (Hospital In-Patients) Regulations 1975 so as to find the claimant entitled to the full rate of benefit for the Friday as well as the Saturday to Monday. The explanation for the different approaches may lie in the slightly different form of the statutory provisions under consideration, in which case the approach taken in *CDLA/11099/95* must be preferred in attendance allowance cases.

In *Chief Adjudication Officer v White (R(IS)18/94)*, a health authority had made arrangements for patients in a hospital to be moved to a nursing home. It was held by the Court of Appeal that they were receiving treatment in hospital or similar institution under the National Health Service Act 1977. In *CDLA/7980/95*, the claimant was discharged from hospital and the tribunal found that she had gone to live in a house where she was one of six tenants who were all cared for by health authority staff. The tribunal found that the house was not a "hospital or similar institution". The adjudication officer appealed but the Commissioner held that the tribunal had not erred in law in reaching the conclusion they did. He distinguished *White* on the basis that it had not been disputed in that case that the nursing home was an institution. He also rejected submissions that the tribunal ought to have investigated the arrangements further, observing that the adjudication officer had failed to challenge the evidence before the tribunal. The Chief Adjudication Officer was given leave to appeal by the Commissioner but he did not lodge the appeal within time and was refused an extension by the Court of Appeal.

[¹ Persons in care homes

4.17   7.—(1) Subject to regulation 8, a person shall not be paid any amount in respect of an attendance allowance for any period where throughout that period he is a resident in a care home in circumstances where any of the costs of any qualifying services provided for him are borne out of public or local funds under a specified enactment.

(2) The specified enactments for the purposes of paragraph (1) are—
  (a)
     (i) Part III of the National Assistance Act 1948
    (ii) Part IV of the Social Work (Scotland) Act 1968,
   (iii) the Mental Health (Care and Treatment) (Scotland) Act 2003,
   (iv) the Community Care and Health (Scotland) Act 2002,
    (v) the Mental Health Act 1983, or
  (b) any other enactment relating to persons under disability.

(3) In this regulation, and in regulation 8, references to the costs of any qualifying services shall not include the cost of—
  (a) domiciliary services, including personal care, provided in respect of a person in a private dwelling; or
  (b) improvements made to, or furniture or equipment provided for, a private dwelling on account of the needs of a person under disability; or
  (c) improvements made to, or furniture or equipment provided for, a care home in respect of which a grant or payment has been made

out of public or local funds except where the grant or payment is of a regular or repeated nature; or

(d) social and recreational activities provided outside the care home in respect of which grants or payments are made out of public or local funds; or

(e) the purchase or running of a motor vehicle to be used in connection with any qualifying service provided in a care home in respect of which grants or payments are made out of public or local funds; or

(f) services provided pursuant to the National Health Service Act 2006, the National Health Service (Wales) Act 2006, or the National Health Service (Scotland) Act 1978.

(4) For the purposes of paragraph (1), a period during which a person is a resident in a care home in the circumstances set out in that paragraph shall, subject to paragraphs (5) and (6), be deemed—

(a) to begin on the day after the day on which he enters a care home, and

(b) to end on the day before the day on which he leaves a care home.

(5) Where a person enters a care home from a hospital or similar institution in circumstances in which paragraph (1) of regulation 6 applies, the period during which he is a resident in the care home shall be deemed to begin on the day he enters that care home.

(6) Where a person leaves a care home and enters a hospital or similar institution in circumstances in which paragraph (1) of regulation 6 applies, the period during which he is a resident in the care home shall be deemed to end on the day he leaves that care home.]

AMENDMENT

1. Attendance Allowance and Disability Living Allowance (Amendment) Regulations 2007, (SI 2007/2875) (October 29, 2007).

GENERAL NOTE

There is a transitional and saving provision in reg.4 of the Amendment regulations to the effect that this amendment shall not prevent any day before the coming into force of the amended regulations from counting towards the first 28 day period specified in reg.8.

This is a new version of reg.7, but the commentary that follows remains relevant.

By virtue of reg.8, this regulation applies only after a person has been in the relevant accommodation or in hospital for 28 days although periods separated by intervals not exceeding 28 days may be linked.

The former paragraph (c), now repealed, also provided for disqualification where the cost of accommodation could have been met from public funds even if it was not. Now the regulation applies only where the cost is being met. A question may still arise where costs are being met temporarily while a claimant waits to release funds from which they can meet the costs themselves, by the sale of their former home. In such cases it is usual for the claimant to undertake to reimburse the local authority when their own funds become available.

The effect of the decision in *CAO v Creighton* [2000] N.I. 222 for Northern Ireland, and its adoption in England and Wales in *R(A) 1/02* is that such arrangements do not involve the local authority in meeting the cost of accommodation because the claimant does meet and always has met that cost by virtue of the agreement to reimburse any sums advanced. It follows that the claimant then does have the resources to provide his own accommodation, and the local authority has no power to provide for his accommodation under Pt III—reg.7 does not therefore apply.

4.18

The position is more doubtful in Scotland. In *CSA/469/2005* (and in *CSA/164/2004* which preceded it), the Commissioner holds that the cost of accommodation in a private nursing home that is met by a payment made to the claimant for personal care allowances under the Community Care and Health (Scotland) Act 2002 is a payment that disqualifies the claimant from entitlement to Attendance Allowance under reg.7. This is so even though the same payment made to a claimant who was living in their own home would not disqualify them. The Commissioner finds that to be the inevitable outcome of legislation that has been enacted only for Scotland and without any amendment to the legislation for Attendance Allowance.

The treatment of a claimant for whom the cost of accommodation is being met by a Local Authority on a temporary basis and subject to repayment by the claimant, was considered again in *CDLA/5106/2001*. In this case the cost of the accommodation was met initially by the Local Authority, but first a contribution was required, and then an obligation to repay in full under s.22 of the 1948 Act. By the time of the hearing, full repayment had been made. Commissioner Turnbull, nevertheless, held that she was disqualified from receiving benefit because her accommodation was provided in accordance with reg.7(1)(a) and the claimant was not exempted by reg.8(6)(b) until she ceased to be entitled to Income Support because she was not, until then, meeting the whole of the cost of accommodation from her own resources. Although the Commissioner makes no reference to *R(A) 1/02*, his decision accords with that case because there, too, the claimant was disqualified for part of the period in question because she was then in receipt of Income Support. It does not appear that in either case an argument was made that the claimant's entitlement to Income Support should be regarded as a part of her own resources.

This has all been carried a stage further by the decision in *CA/3800/2006*. There the claimant had been in receipt of benefit because she was funding the care home fees from her own resources. Eventually, it became necessary to sell her former home and the proceeds were invested to continue that funding. The investments failed and for a time the claimant became dependant upon the local authority for continued payment of fees. The claimant's daughter, acting under a power of attorney, complained to the Financial Services Ombudsman about the investment advice given to her mother and that complaint was upheld, resulting in a compensation payment to her mother. The claimant resumed payment of fees herself and the local authority required repayment of the fees which they had advanced. The question before the Commissioner was whether the claimant should now be entitled to benefit for the period covered by the local authority. The Commissioner held that she was. The decision taken to cancel her benefit when the local authority first assumed responsibility for payment, should have been a decision to suspend payment rather than a decision to supercede. That it was not, was an official error – that being so, the appeal tribunal should have substituted its own decision to suspend and that would mean the claimant would have remained "entitled" to benefit throughout the period, though not entitled to payment during the period of suspension.

Persons to whom regulations 7 and 8 apply with modifications

7A.—[¹ . . .]

REPEAL

4.19   1. Social Security Amendment (Residential Care and Nursing Homes) Regulations 2001 (SI 2001/3767), reg.3 (April 8, 2002).

Exemption from regulations 6 and 7

4.20   **8.**—[¹ (1) Regulation 6, or as the case may be, regulation 7, shall not, [² subject to the following provisions of this regulation], apply to a person in respect of the first 28 days of any period during which he—

(a) is undergoing medical or other treatment in a hospital or other institution in any of the circumstances mentioned in regulation 6; or

(b) would, but for this regulation, be prevented from receiving an attendance allowance by reason of regulation 7(1).]

(2) For the purposes of paragraph (1)—

(a) two or more distinct periods separated by an interval not exceeding 28 days, or by two or more such intervals, shall be treated as a continuous period equal in duration to the total of such distinct periods and ending on the last day of the later or last such period;

(b) any period or periods to which either regulation 6 or regulation 7 refers shall be taken into account and aggregated with any period to which the other of them refers.

(3) Where, on the day a person's entitlement to an attendance allowance commences, he is in accommodation in the circumstances mentioned in regulation 6 or regulation 7, paragraph (1) shall not apply to him for any period of consecutive days, beginning with that day, on which he remains in that accommodation.

[² (4) Regulation 6 or, as the case may be, regulation 7 shall not apply [³ [⁴ . . .] in the case of a person who is residing in a hospice and is terminally ill where the Secretary of State has been informed that he is terminally ill—

(a) on a claim for attendance allowance,

(b) on an application for a [⁵ revision under section 9 of the Social Security Act 1998 or supersession under section 10 of that Act] of an award of attendance allowance, or

(c) in writing in connection with an award of, or a claim for, or an application for a [⁵ revision under section 9 of the Social Security Act 1998 or supersession under section 10 of that Act] of an award of, attendance allowance.

(5) In paragraph (4) "hospice" means a hospital or other institution [⁴ whose primary function is to provide palliative care for persons resident there who are suffering from a progressive disease in its final stages] other than—

(a) a health service hospital (within the meaning of section 128 of the NHS Act of 1977) in England or Wales;

(b) a health service hospital (within the meaning of section 108(1) of the NHS Act of 1978) in Scotland;

(c) a hospital maintained or administered by the Defence Council; or

(d) an institution similar to a hospital mentioned in any of the preceding sub-paragraphs of this paragraph.

[⁶ (6) Regulation 7 shall not apply in any particular case for any period during which the whole costs of all of the qualifying services are met—

(a) out of the resources of the person for whom the qualifying services are provided, or partly out of his own resources and partly with assistance from another person or a charity, or

(b) on his behalf by another person or a charity.]

(7) [³ [⁴ . . .]]]

AMENDMENTS

1. Social Security (Attendance Allowance) Amendment Regulations 1992 (SI 1992/703), reg.5 (April 6, 1992).

2. Social Security Benefits (Amendments Consequential Upon the Introduction

of Community Care) Regulations 1992 (SI 1992/3147), reg.8 (April 1, 1993 with saving).

3. Social Security (Attendance Allowance and Disability Living Allowance) (Amendment) Regulations 2000, (2000/1401) reg.2(4) (June 19, 2000).

4. Social Security Benefits (Miscellaneous Amendments) Regulations 1993 (SI 1993/518), reg.2(3) (April 1, 1993).

5. Social Security Act 1998 (Commencement No. 11, and savings and consequential and Transitional Provisions) Order 1999 (SI 1999/2860), Sch.8 (October 18, 1999).

6. Attendance Allowance and Disability Living Allowance (Amendment) Regulations 2007, (SI 2007/2875) (October 29, 2007).

GENERAL NOTE

4.21   See notes above to reg.7.

[¹ Adjustment of allowance where medical expenses are paid from public funds under war pensions instruments

4.22   **8A.**—(1) In this regulation—

"article 25B" means article 25B of the Personal Injuries (Civilians) Scheme 1983 (medical expenses) and includes that article as applied by article 48B of that Scheme; "article 26" means article 26 of the Naval, Military and Air Forces etc. (Disablement and Death) Service Pensions Order 1983 (medical expenses);

and in this regulation and regulation 8B "relevant accommodation" means accommodation provided as a necessary ancillary to nursing care where the medical expenses involved are wholly borne by the Secretary of State pursuant to article 25B or article 26.

(2) This regulation applies where a person is provided with relevant accommodation.

(3) Subject to regulation 8B, where this regulation applies and there are payable in respect of a person both a payment under either article 25B or article 26 and an attendance allowance, the allowance shall be adjusted by deducting from it the amount of the payment under article 25B or article 26, as the case may be, and only the balance shall be payable.]

AMENDMENT

1. Social Security (Attendance Allowance and Disability Living Allowance) (Amendment) Regulations 1994 (SI 1994/1779), reg.2(4) (August 1, 1994).

[¹ Exemption from regulation 8A

4.23   **8B.**—(1) Regulation 8A shall not, subject to the following provisions of this regulation, apply to a person in respect of the first 28 days of any period during which the amount of any attendance allowance would be liable to be adjusted by virtue of regulation 8A(3).

(2) For the purposes of paragraph (1) two or more distinct periods separated by an interval not exceeding 28 days, or by two or more such intervals, shall be treated as a continuous period equal in duration to the aggregate of such distinct periods and ending on the last day of the later or last such period.

(3) For the purposes of this paragraph a day is a relevant day in relation to a person if it fell not earlier than 28 days before the first day on which he was provided with relevant accommodation; and either—

(a) was a day when he was undergoing medical treatment in a hospital or similar institution in any of the circumstances mentioned in regulation 6; or

(b) was a day when he was, or would but for regulation 8 have been, prevented from receiving an attendance allowance by virtue of regulation 7(1);

and where there is in relation to a person a relevant day, paragraph (1) shall have effect as if for "28 days" there were substituted such lesser number of days as is produced by subtracting from 28 the number of relevant days in his case.]

AMENDMENT

1. Social Security (Attendance Allowance and Disability Living Allowance) (Amendment) Regulations 1994 (SI 1994/1779), reg.2(4) (August 1, 1994).

[¹ Prescribed circumstances for entitlement

8BA.—For the purposes of section 64(4) of the Social Security Contributions and Benefits Act 1992 (prescribed circumstances in which a person is to be taken to satisfy or not to satisfy the conditions mentioned in section 64(2) and (3) of that Act), a person shall not be taken to satisfy (2)(a) (day attention) or (3)(a) (night attention) unless the attention the severely disabled person requires from another person is required to be given in the physical presence of the severely disabled person.]   4.24

AMENDMENT

1. Social Security (Attendance Allowance and Disability Living Allowance) (Amendment) (No. 2) Regulations 2000, (2000/1401) reg.2 (September 25, 2000).

Regulations 8C, 8D and 8E have been revoked by Social Security Act 1998 (Commencement No. 11, and Savings and Consequential and Transitional Provisions) Order 1999 (SI 1999/2860), Sch.8, with effect from October 18, 1999.   4.25

Regulation 9 omitted.   4.26

[¹ SCHEDULE   **Regulation 7A(1)**

[¹ . . .]   4.27

REPEAL

1. Social Security Amendment (Residential Care and Nursing Homes) Regulations 2001 (SI 2001/3767), reg.3 (April 8, 2002).

Social Security (Disability Living Allowance) Regulations 1991

(SI 1991/2890) (*as amended*)

ARRANGEMENT OF REGULATIONS

PART I

INTRODUCTION

PART II

GENERAL

PART III

CARE COMPONENT

PART IV

MOBILITY COMPONENT

SCHEDULES

Whereas a draft of this instrument was laid before Parliament in accordance with section 12(1) of the Disability Living Allowance and Disability Working Allowance Act 1991 and approved by resolution of each House of Parliament; now therefore the Secretary of State for Social Security, in exercise of the powers conferred by sections 37ZA(6), 37ZB(2), (3), (7) and (8), 37ZC, 37ZD, 37ZE(2), 85(1), 114(1) and 166(2) to (3A) of and Schedule 20 to the Social Security Act 1975, section 13 of the Social Security (Miscellaneous Provisions) Act 1977 and section 5(1) of the Disability Living Allowance and Disability Working Allowance Act 1991, and of all other powers enabling him in that behalf, by this instrument, which contains only regulations made consequential upon section 1 of the Disability Living Allowance and Disability Working Allowance Act 1991, hereby makes the following Regulations:

PART I

INTRODUCTION

Citation, commencement and interpretation

1.—(1) These Regulations may be cited as the Social Security (Disability Living Allowance) Regulations 1991 and shall come into force on 6th April 1992.

4.29

(2) In these Regulations—
[¹ "the Act" means the Social Security Contributions and Benefits Act 1992;
"the Administration Act" means the Social Security Administration Act 1992];
[² "the 1998 Act" means the Social Security Act 1998]
"the NHS Act of 1977" means the National Health Service Act 1977;
"the NHS Act of 1978" means the National Health Service (Scotland) Act 1978;
"the NHS Act of 1990" means the National Health Service and Community Care Act 1990;
[² "adjudicating authority" means, as the case may require, the Secretary of State, [³ the First-tier Tribunal or the Upper Tribunal];]
"care component" means the care component of a disability living allowance;
"mobility component" means the mobility component of a disability living allowance;
"terminally ill" shall be construed in accordance with [¹ section 66(2) of the Act].

(3) Unless the context otherwise requires, any reference in these Regulations to a numbered regulation or Schedule is a reference to the regulation or Schedule bearing that number in these Regulations and any reference in a regulation or Schedule to a numbered paragraph is a reference to the paragraph of that regulation or Schedule bearing that number.

AMENDMENTS

1. Social Security (Disability Living Allowance) (Amendment) Regulations 1993 (SI 1993/1939), reg.2(2) (August 26, 1993).
2. Social Security Act 1998 (Commencement No. 11 and Savings and Consequential and Transitional Provisions) Order 1999 (SI 1999/2860) (October 18, 1999).
3. Tribunals, Courts and Enforcement Act 2007, Sch.1 (November 3, 2008).

PART II

GENERAL

[¹ Disapplication of section 1(1A) of the Administration Act

4.30   **1A.**—Section 1(1A) of the Administration Act (requirement to state national insurance number) shall not apply—
(a) to a person under the age of 16;
(b) to any claim for disability living allowance made or treated as made before 9th February, 1998.]

AMENDMENT

1. Social Security (National Insurance Information: Exemption) Regulations (SI 1997/2676) (December 1, 1997).

Conditions as to residence and presence in Great Britain

4.31   **2.**—(1) Subject to the following provisions of this regulation, the prescribed conditions for the purposes of [¹ section 71](6) of the Act as to residence and presence in Great Britain in relation to any person on any day shall be that—
(a) on that day—
(i) he is ordinarily resident in Great Britain; and
[² (ib) he is not a person subject to immigration control within the meaning of section 115(9) of the Immigration and Asylum Act 1999 or section 115 of that Act does not apply to him for the purposes of entitlement to disability living allowance by virtue of regulation 2 of the Social Security (Immigration and Asylum) Consequential Amendments Regulations 2000, and]
(ii) he is present in Great Britain; and
(iii) he has been present in Great Britain for a period of, or for periods amounting in the aggregate to, not less than 26 weeks in the 52 weeks immediately preceding that day;
(b) [⁵ . . .]
(1A) [² *omitted*]]

(2) For the purposes of paragraph (1)(a)(ii) and (iii), notwithstanding that on any day a person is absent from Great Britain, he shall be treated as though he was present in Great Britain if his absence is by reason only of the fact that on that day—

(a) he is abroad in his capacity as—
  (i) a serving member of the forces,
  (ii) an airman or mariner within the meaning of regulations 81 and 86 respectively of the Social Security (Contributions) Regulations 1979, and for the purpose of this provision, the expression "serving members of the forces" has the same meaning as in regulation 1(2) of the Regulations of 1979; or

(b) he is in employment prescribed for the purposes of [¹ section 120] of the Act in connection with continental shelf operations; or

(c) he is living with a person mentioned in sub-paragraph (a)(i) and is the spouse, [⁴ civil partner] son, daughter, step-son, step-daughter, father, father-in-law, step-father, mother, mother-in-law or step-mother of that person; or

(d) his absence from Great Britain is, and when it began was, for a temporary purpose and has not lasted for a continuous period exceeding 26 weeks; or

(e) his absence from Great Britain is temporary and for the specific purpose of his being treated for incapacity, or a disabling condition, which commenced before he left Great Britain, and the Secretary of State has certified that it is consistent with the proper administration of the Act that, subject to the satisfaction of the foregoing condition in this sub-paragraph, he should be treated as though he were present in Great Britain.

(3) [⁵ . . .]

(4) Where a person is terminally ill and—

(a) makes a claim for disability allowance; or

(b) an application is made for a [³ revision under section 9 of the 1998 Act or supersession under section 10 of that Act] of his award of disability living allowance, expressly on the ground that he is such a person, paragraph (1) shall apply to him as if head (iii) of sub-paragraph (a) was omitted.

(5) Paragraph (1) shall apply in the case of a child under the age of 6 months as if in head (iii) of sub-paragraph (a) for the reference to 26 weeks there was substituted a reference to 13 weeks.

(6) Where in any particular case a child has by virtue of paragraph (5), entitlement to the care component immediately before the day he attains the age of 6 months, then until the child attains the age of 12 months, head (iii) of sub-paragraph (a) of paragraph (1) shall continue to apply in his case as if for the reference to 26 weeks there was substituted a reference to 13 weeks.

AMENDMENTS

1. Social Security (Disability Living Allowance) (Amendment) Regulations 1993 (SI 1993/1939), reg.2 (August 26, 1993).

2. Social Security (Immigration and Asylum) Consequential Amendments Regulations 2000, (SI 2000/636) reg.11 (April 3, 2000).

3. Social Security Act 1998 (Commencement No. 11, and savings and consequential and Transitional Provisions) Order 1999 (SI 1999/2860), Sch.7 (October 18, 1999).

4. Civil Partnership (Pensions, Social Security and Child Support) (Consequential, etc. Provisions) Order 2005 (SI 2005/2877) (December 5, 2005).

5. Social Security (Miscellaneous Amendments) (No.4) Regulations 2006 (SI 2006/2378), reg.8 (October 1, 2006).

GENERAL NOTE

4.32   Regulation 2 has been amended since 1996 to require the claimant to be without any restriction on their permission to be in the UK. That restriction was subject to a saving in respect of claimants already entitled to benefit at the time it came into force. A series of decisions culminating in an appeal to the House of Lords has established that the saving is effective only in respect of an award in force at February 5, 1996, and not for a renewal of that award. Where the award was for life it remains effective until reviewed. This decision has now been reported as *R(DLA) 7/01*.

The meaning of para.(2)(d) is explained in *CDLA/2089/2004*. To retain entitlement to benefit, at least for a time when abroad, the claimant must show that their absence is temporary and that it lasts for less than six months. But these are separate requirements. Absence for more than six months does not meant that the claimant's absence was not temporary. The six-month limitation operates as a separate disqualification beyond which benefit will not be paid even though the absence was at its inception, and may remain, temporary.

Age 65 or over

4.33   **3.**—(1) A person shall not be precluded from entitlement to either component of disability living allowance by reason only that he has attained the age of 65 years [¹ if he is a person to whom paragraphs (2) and (3) apply].

(2) Paragraph (3) applies to a person who—

(a) made a claim for disability living allowance before he attained the age of 65, which was not determined before he attained that age, and

(b) did not at the time he made the claim have an award of disability living allowance for a period ending on or after the day he attained the age of 65.

(3) In determining the claim of a person to whom this paragraph applies, where the person otherwise satisfies the conditions of entitlement to either or both components of disability living allowance for a period commencing before his 65th birthday (other than the requirements of [² section 72](2) (a), or, as the case may be, [² section 73](9)(a) of the Act (3 months qualifying period)), the determination shall be made without regard to the fact that he is aged 65 or over at the time the claim is determined.

(4) Schedule 1, which makes further provision for persons aged 65 or over shall have effect.

AMENDMENTS

1. Social Security (Disability Living Allowance) Amendments Regulations 1997 (SI 1997/349), reg.2 (October 6, 1997).

2. Social Security (Disability Living Allowance) (Amendment) Regulations 1993 (SI 1993/1939), reg.2 (August 26, 1993).

GENERAL NOTE

Para. (1)

4.34   Section 75(1) of the Social Security Contributions and Benefits Act 1992 has the effect that normally a person cannot be entitled to disability living allowance after he or she has attained the age of 65 unless awarded it before that age. Before its amendment, this paragraph enabled a person who would have satisfied the conditions of entitlement continuously since the age of 65 to qualify provided he or she made a claim before reaching the age of 66. The amendment means that it is now necessary for the claimant to have made a claim before reaching the age of 65. An earlier unsuccessful claim is irrelevant *(R(M) 4/86)*. Where a claim has been determined in the claimant's favour before his or her 65th birthday, para.(4) and Sch.1 apply and make provision for reviews and renewal claims. Where a claim has not been determined before the claimant's 65th birthday, paras (2) and (3) apply. Those who are too old to be entitled to disability living allowance but who would otherwise qualify for the highest or middle rate of the care component will be entitled to attendance allowance instead, subject to satisfying the longer six-month qualifying condition.

Paras (2) and (3)

Section 75(1) of the 1992 Act specifically provides that a claimant cannot be **4.35** entitled to disability living allowance unless the *award* has been made before his or her 65th birthday. These paragraphs make provision for a person whose *claim* was made before the 65th birthday and who is not making an advance claim to follow an existing award ending on or after that birthday. In such a case, provided that the conditions of entitlement are satisfied for a period commencing before the claimant's 65th birthday, entitlement is to be determined without regard to the fact that he or she is aged 65 or over at the time of the determination. Note that it is not necessary for the three-month qualifying condition to be satisfied before the claimant reaches the age of 65. Thus a person who becomes seriously disabled, say, a month before his or her birthday, can become entitled to disability living allowance two months after the birthday.

Para. 4

See the notes to Sch.1 which deals with the determination of reviews and renewal **4.36** claims after a person's 65th birthday and with the position of former beneficiaries under the invalid vehicle scheme.

Rate of benefit

4.—(1) The three weekly rates of the care component are— **4.37**
  (a) the highest rate, payable in accordance with [[1] section 72](4)(a) of the Act, [[2] £70.35];
  (b) the middle rate, payable in accordance with [[1]section 72](4)(b) of the Act, [[2] £47.10];
  (c) the lowest rate, payable in accordance with [[1] section 72](4)(c) of the Act, [[2] £18.65].

(2) The two weekly rates of the mobility component are—
  (a) the higher rate, payable in accordance with [[1] section 73] (11)(a) of the Act, [[2] £49.10]; and
  (b) the lower rate, payable in accordance with [[1] section 73] (11)(b) of the Act, [[2] £18.65].

AMENDMENTS

1. Social Security (Disability Living Allowance) (Amendment) Regulations 1993 (SI 1993/1939), reg.2 (August 26, 1993).
2. Social Security Benefits Up-rating Order 2009 (SI 2009/497) art.13 (April 6, 2009).

Late claim by a person previously entitled

5.—[[1] . . .] **4.38**
5A.—[[2] . . .]

5B.—[² . . .]
5C.—[² . . .]

REPEALS

1. Repealed by Social Security (Miscellaneous Amendments) (No. 2) Regulations 1997 (SI 1997/793), reg.19 (September 1, 1997).
2. Repealed by Social Security Act 1998, Sch.7 (October 18, 1999).

PART III

CARE COMPONENT

Qualifying period for care component after an interval

4.39   **6.**—(1) The period prescribed for the purposes of [¹ section 72] (2)(a)(ii) of the Act is a period of 3 months ending on the day on which the person was last entitled to the care component or to attendance allowance where that day falls not more than 2 years before the date on which entitlement to the care component would begin, or would have begun but for any regulations made under [¹ section 5(1)(k) of the Administration Act] (which enables regulations to provide for the day on which entitlement to benefit is to begin or end).

(2) Except in a case to which paragraph (3) applies, this regulation shall apply to a person to whom paragraph 3 or 7 of Schedule 1 refers as if for the reference to 3 months there was substituted a reference to 6 months.

(3) Paragraph (1) and not paragraph (2), shall apply to those persons referred to in paragraph (2) who, on the day before they attained the age of 65, had already completed the period of three months referred to in paragraph (1).

(4) For the purposes of paragraph (3), the modification made in Schedule 1—

(a) in paragraph 3 (2) and 7(2), to [¹ section 72] (2)(a) of the Act, and
(b) in paragraph 5 (2), to [¹ section 73] (9)(a) of the Act,

shall be treated as not having been made.

AMENDMENT

1. Social Security (Disability Living Allowance) (Amendment) Regulations 1993 (SI 1993/1939), reg.2 (August 26, 1993).

GENERAL NOTE

4.40   The general effect of this provision is that the three-month qualifying period (six months for people aged 65 or over) for the care component is deemed to be satisfied if the new claim is within two years of a previous period of entitlement to the care component (or attendance allowance) at the relevant rate.

Renal Dialysis

4.41   **7.**—(1) A person who suffers from renal failure and falls within the provisions in paragraph (2) shall be taken to satisfy—

(a) where he undergoes renal dialysis by day, the conditions in paragraph (b) of subsection (1) of [¹ section 72] of the Act (severe physical or mental disability);

(b) where he undergoes renal dialysis by night, the conditions in paragraph (c) of that subsection; or

(c) where he undergoes renal dialysis by day and by night, the conditions in either paragraph (b) or paragraph (c) of subsection (1), but not both.

(2) Subject to paragraph (3), a person falls within this paragraph—

(a) if—

(i) he undergoes renal dialysis two or more times a week; and

(ii) the renal dialysis he undergoes is of a type which normally requires the attendance or supervision of another person during the period of the dialysis; or

(iii) because of the particular circumstances of his case he in fact requires another person, during the period of the dialysis, to attend in connection with his bodily functions or to supervise him in order to avoid substantial danger to himself; and

(b) if, where he undergoes dialysis as an out patient in a hospital or similar institution, being treatment provided under the NHS Act of 1977 or the NHS Act of 1978, no member of the staff of the hospital or institution assists with or supervises the dialysis.

[¹ (3) Paragraph (2)(b) does not apply for the purpose of determining whether a person is to be taken to satisfy any of the conditions mentioned, in paragraph (1) during the periods mentioned in section 72(2)(a)(i) and (b)(i) of the Act.]

(4) Except to the extent that provision is made in paragraph (2)(b), a person who undergoes treatment by way of renal dialysis as an outpatient in a hospital or similar institution, being treatment provided under the NHS Act of 1977 or the NHS Act of 1978, shall not be taken solely by reason of the fact that he undergoes such dialysis, as satisfying any of the conditions mentioned in subsection (1)(a) to (c) of [¹ section 72] of the Act.

AMENDMENT

1. Social Security (Disability Living Allowance) (Amendment) Regulations 1993 (SI 1993/1939), reg.2 (August 26, 1993).

GENERAL NOTE

Under this regulation, a person undergoing renal dialysis at least twice a week may be deemed to satisfy *either* the "day" *or* the "night" attendance conditions of s.72(1)(b) and (c) of the Social Security Contributions and Benefits Act 1992, but not both. Some degree of attention or supervision must be required. This regulation is in slightly different terms from reg.5 of the Social Security (Attendance Allowance) Regulations 1991.   **4.42**

Para. (2) (a)

The dialysis must be *either* of a type which *normally* requires the attendance of or supervision by another person (in which case the actual purpose of the attention or supervision is irrelevant) *or* the dialysis must *in the particular case* require the attention or supervision of the claimant (for the purpose specified in para.(2)(a)(iii)).   **4.43**

Paras (2)(b), (3) and (4).

4.44   Under paras (2)(b) and (4), a person receiving treatment under the National Health Service cannot qualify for the care component under this regulation if he or she receives assistance or supervision during the dialysis from a member of staff of the hospital or other relevant institution, although there is nothing in para.(4) to prevent the need for any such assistance or supervision from being taken into account when considering whether the ordinary "day" or "night" conditions are satisfied. Para.(3) has the effect that, where a person has been undergoing dialysis falling within para.(2)(a) but para.(2)(b) was not satisfied because, say, supervision was provided in a National Health Service hospital, he or she can qualify under this regulation as soon as that supervision ceases, as long as he or she had been undergoing the dialysis for the usual three-month qualifying period. Presumably para.(3) applies equally to the six-month qualifying period substituted under para.3 of Sch.1 for claimants aged 65 or over.

Hospitalisation

4.45   **8.**—[¹ (1) Subject to regulation 10, it shall be a condition for the receipt of a disability living allowance which is attributable to entitlement to the care component for any period in respect of any person that during that period he is not maintained free of charge while undergoing medical or other treatment as an in-patient—

    (a) in a hospital or similar institution under the NHS Act of 1977, the NHS Act of 1978 or the NHS Act of 1990; or

    (b) in a hospital or other similar institution maintained or administered by the Defence Council.]

    (2) For the purposes of [¹ paragraph (1)(a)] a person shall only be regarded as not being maintained free of charge in a hospital or similar institution during any period when his accommodation and services are provided under section 65 of the NHS Act of 1977 or section 58 of, or paragraph 14 of Schedule 7A to, the NHS Act of 1978, or paragraph 14 of Schedule 2 to the NHS Act of 1990.

    [² (2A) For the purposes of paragraph (1), a period during which a person is maintained free of charge while undergoing medical or other treatment as an in-patient shall be deemed to begin on the day after the day on which he enters a hospital or similar institution referred to in that paragraph and to end on the day [³ before the day] on which he leaves such a hospital or similar institution].

    (3) [¹ . . .].

AMENDMENTS

    1. Social Security (Disability Living Allowance and Attendance Allowance) (Amendment) Regulations 1992 (SI 1992/2869), reg.4 (December 15, 1992).

    2. Social Security (Hospital In-Patients, Attendance Allowance and Disability Living Allowance) (Amendment) Regulations 1999 (SI 1999/1326) (June 7, 1999).

    3. Social Security (Attendance Allowance and Disability Living Allowance) (Amendment) Regulations 2000, (SI 2000/1401) reg.3 (June 19, 2000).

GENERAL NOTE

4.46   See the annotations to reg.6 of the Social Security (Attendance Allowance) Regulations 1991 which is in identical terms.

    Note that, by virtue of reg.10, a person may remain entitled to the care component for up to 28 days (84 days in the case of a person under the age of 16) in hospital but that separate periods in hospital or such accommodation are aggregated unless they are more than 28 days apart.

This regulation disqualifies a claimant who is being treated in a publicly financed hospital. In decision *CDLA/11099/1996* the Commissioner had to decide if it applied to a patient who spent each night in such a hospital but was at home through the day. He held that it did; because the claimant spent a part of each day in a publicly funded hospital he could not qualify for benefit on any day.

Note that a similar issue has arisen in relation to reg.2(2) of the Hospital In-Patients Regulation 1975, where there has been a conflict in Commissioners' decisions. This decision is in accordance with the more recent of those decisions.

In decision *CSDLA/1282/01* the Commissioner holds that a claimant is being maintained free of charge in hospital notwithstanding that the claimant may continue to receive care and support from their family. In this case the claimant was fed and bathed, etc. by her family because she refused to allow nursing staff to provide those services.

In *CDLA/7980/95* the Commissioner had to decide if this provision could cover the case of a claimant formerly accomodated in a hospital, but now living in a privately rented house with full-time care provided by the local Health Service Trust, under the Care in the Community policy. He held that it did not. A privately rented home which the claimant shared with six others, and in which they paid not only the rent, but also for their own food, etc. did not become either a "hospital" or a "similar institution" simply because they were cared for there at public expense. Equally, the Commissioner could have found that while they were living there they were not "maintained free of charge" because they were paying their own rent and other outgoings—presumably being maintained includes the provision of housing, food, etc. as well as care.

It should be noted that there may be some overlap between this regulation and reg.9 because in *CAO v White* (reported as *R(IS) 18/94*) (referred to in *CDLA/7980/95*) it was held that a registered nursing home (which could fall within reg.9) also fell within the description of a "hospital or similar institution" for the purposes of the Hospital In-Patients Regulations 1975 which uses the same expression.

The complex issue of whether care has been provided for in a "hospital or similar institution" so as to be disqualified from benefit under this regulation, or whether instead it was provided under arrangements made by the local authority so as to be disqualified under reg.9, has been examined by a Tribunal of Commissioners in *CDLA/3161/2003*. (To be reported as *R(DLA) 2/06*.) Put thus, it might seem to matter little to the claimant under which regulation the claim for care must fail, but for claimants entitled also to a mobility component which is covered by transitional protection, and for claimants who are able to claim Income Support, the distinction will be significant because there is no equivalent to reg.9 disqualification for those other benefits. Indeed, in this case it was also argued that neither reg.8 or reg.9 should apply, though then any resulting benefit entitlement would be paid to the local authority for them to pay to the nursing home as had been happening in these cases.

The cases involved claimants who were formerly patients in a mental hospital and who, under the changes made in the early 1990's, were moved into private nursing homes where they still continued to receive the high level of care and nursing services consistent with their condition. No formal assessment of their needs was made, but it was clear from the charges levied for each of them that the service provided was for far more than accommodation with incidental nursing care. The Commissioners concluded therefore that the nursing home fell within the description of an institution similar to a hospital and the disqualification applied. (See *CAO v White R(IS) 18/94*)

The real protagonists in this case were the local health authority and the DWP. This was because, if the claimants' needs really were those of a hospital patient, then the health authority was liable to supply those needs under the National Health Service Act 1997. But under the ill constructed and poorly evidenced arrangements that the health authority and the local authority had tried to make in this case, they purported to make the claimants into self funding residents of the care homes so that all their benefit entitlements would be available as a contribution to their fees, the balance of which was then made up by the health authority, though paid through the local authority.

The argument put forward by the DWP was that either they were still in a "hospital" and therefore caught by reg.8, or they were being accommodated by the local authority under Pt III of the National Assistance Act and then caught by reg.9. Either way the DWP should not have been paying to the extent of the care component of DLA. In deciding that the arrangements necessary for these claimants amounted to hospital care the commissioners were also saying that the claimants could not be accommodated under Pt III because that power does not extend to accommodating persons who need full hospital care—the whole of such costs, therefore, should have been met by the health authority. The net effect was that some patients (those not qualifying for IS) had been charged considerable sums for which they should not have been liable. None of this was in issue before the Commissioners and was relevant only as being a necessary step in reaching the decisions that they did, but the Commissioners conclude by referring to the ill standards of public administration that this revealed.

[¹ Persons in care homes

4.47   **9.**—(1) Except in the cases specified in paragraphs (3) to (5), and subject to regulation 10, a person shall not be paid any amount in respect of a disability living allowance which is attributable to entitlement to the care component for any period where throughout that period he is a resident in a care home in circumstances where any of the costs of any qualifying services provided for him are borne out of public or local funds under a specified enactment.

(2) The specified enactments for the purposes of paragraph (1) are—

(a)

   (i) Part III of the National Assistance Act 1948,

   (ii) Part IV of the Social Work (Scotland) Act 1968,

   (iii) the Mental Health (Care and Treatment) (Scotland) Act 2003,

   (iv) the Community Care and Health (Scotland) Act 2002,

   (v) the Mental Health Act 1983; or

(b) any other enactment relating to persons under disability or to young persons or to education or training.

(3) Paragraph (2)(b) shall not apply in circumstances where any of the costs of the qualifying services provided for him are borne wholly or partly out of public or local funds by virtue of—

(a) section 485 of the Education Act 1996, section 14 of the Education Act 2002 or section 73 of the Education (Scotland) Act 1980 (which relate to grants in aid of educational services);

(b) sections 1, 2 or 3 of the Education Act 1962 (which relate respectively to awards by local education authorities in respect of degree courses and further education and awards by the Secretary of State to persons undergoing teacher training or postgraduate courses) or sections 49 or 73 of the Education (Scotland) Act 1980 (which relate respectively to the power of education authorities to assist persons to take advantage of educational facilities and the powers of the Secretary of State to make grants to education authorities and others);

(c) section 65 of the Further and Higher Education Act 1992 or sections 4 or 11 of the Further and Higher Education (Scotland) Act 2005 (which relate respectively to the funding of further education and the administration of funds);

(d) section 1 of the Education (Student Loans) Act 1990 (which relates to student loans); or

(e) section 22 of the Teaching and Higher Education Act 1998.

(4) Subject to paragraph (5), paragraphs (1) and (2) shall not apply in the case of a child who—

(a) has not attained the age of 16 and is being looked after by a local authority; or

(b) has not attained the age of 18 and to whom—

    (i) section 17(10)(b) of the Children Act 1989 or section 93(4)(a)(ii) of the Children (Scotland) Act 1995 (impairment of health and development) applies because his health is likely to be significantly impaired, or further impaired, without the provision of services for him, or

    (ii) section 17(10)(c) of the Children Act 1989 (disability) or section 93(4)(a)(iii) of the Children (Scotland) Act 1995 (disability) applies; or

(c) who is accommodated outside the United Kingdom and the costs of any qualifying services are borne wholly or partly by a local authority pursuant to their powers under section 320 of the Education Act 1996 or section 25 of the Education (Additional Support for Learning) (Scotland) Act 2004.

(5) Sub-paragraphs (a) and (b) of paragraph (4) shall only apply during any period which the local authority looking after the child place him in a private dwelling with a family, or a relative of his, or some other suitable person.

(6) In this regulation and in regulation 10, references to the costs of any qualifying services shall not include the cost of—

(a) domiciliary services, including personal care, provided in respect of a person in a private dwelling; or

(b) improvements made to, or furniture or equipment provided for, a private dwelling on account of the needs of a person under disability; or

(c) improvements made to, or furniture or equipment provided for, a care home in respect of which a grant or payment has been made out of public or local funds except where the grant or payment is of a regular or repeated nature; or

(d) social and recreational activities provided outside the care home in respect of which grants or payments are made out of public or local funds; or

(e) the purchase or running of a motor vehicle to be used in connection with any qualifying service provided in a care home in respect of which grants or payments are made out of public or local funds; or

(f) services provided pursuant to the National Health Service Act 2006, the National Health Service (Wales) Act 2006, or the National Health Service (Scotland) Act 1978.

(7) For the purposes of paragraph (1), a period during which a person is a resident in a care home in the circumstances set out in that paragraph shall, subject to paragraphs (8) and (9), be deemed—

(a) to begin on the day after the day on which he enters a care home, and

(b) to end on the day before the day on which he leaves a care home.

(8) Where a person enters a care home from a hospital or similar institution in circumstances in which paragraph (1) of regulation 6 applies, the period during which he is a resident in the care home shall be deemed to begin on the day he enters that care home.

(9) Where a person leaves a care home and enters a hospital or similar institution in circumstances in which paragraph (1) of regulation 6 applies, the period during which he is a resident in the care home shall be deemed to end on the day he leaves that care home.]

AMENDMENT

1. Attendance Allowance and Disability Living Allowance (Amendment) Regulations 2007, (SI 2007/2875) (October 29, 2007).

GENERAL NOTE

4.48   There is a transitional and saving provision in reg.4 of the Amendment regulations to the effect that this amendment shall not prevent any day before the coming into force of the amended regulation from counting towards the 28 day and 84 day periods specified in reg.10.

Paragraphs (1) and (3)–(6) are in identical terms to reg.7(1)–(5) of the Social Security (Attendance Allowance) Regs 1991. For further annotations, see those Regulations. Whether or not a claimant is being accommodated in a "hospital or similar institution" has been examined in *R(DLA)2/06*. For comment on that decision see the notes to reg.8, above.

Note that, by virtue of reg.10, a person may remain entitled to the care component for up to 28 days in accommodation covered by reg.9 or in a hospital, but that separate periods in such accommodation or hospital are aggregated unless they are more than 28 days apart.

Paragraph (2) makes specific provision enabling certain children to qualify for the care component even though they would otherwise fall within the provisions of para.(1).

In *CDLA/1465/98*, the claimant was living in accommodation rented from a county council. The tribunal found that the accommodation was not provided under Pt III of the National Assistance Act 1948. The adjudication officer appealed on the ground that the county council had had no power to enter into the arrangements with the claimant save under Pt III of the 1948 Act. The appeal was dismissed because the Commissioner was not satisfied that the county council could not have acted as they did outside Pt III of the 1948 Act and he was not satisfied that the tribunal had erred in law in their approach, given the way the adjudication officer had argued the case before them. However, he suggested that the claimant's evidence as to the extent to which he could live without assistance called into question the award of the highest rate of the care component, although that was not a matter within the jurisdiction of the tribunal (which was a social security appeal tribunal and not a disability appeal tribunal).

In *CA/2985/97*, it was held that provisions identical to reg.9(1)(b) and (c) had ceased to have any effect in England and Wales following amendments made to the National Assistance Act 1948 by the National Health Service and Community Care Act 1990.

In *R(DLA) 6/04* the claimant was accommodated on week days in residential accommodation run by the local authority. This accommodation was provided under the Mental Health Act 1983. The Commissioner holds that the situation is covered by sub-para.(b) of reg.9(1). The Mental Health Act 1983 is not mentioned specifically in sub-para.(a), nor is it listed in the DM guidance, but s.117 of that Act requires the local authority in exercise of its social services function to provide after- care for persons who are under supervision. The question to be answered therefore was whether persons released from hospital, but still receiving after-care under supervision, are persons under a disability within the meaning of reg.9. The Commissioner had no doubt that they were.

[¹ Persons to whom regulations 9 and 10 apply with modifications

9A.—[¹. . .]   4.49

REPEAL

1. Social Security Amendment (Residential Care and Nursing Homes) Regulations 2001 (SI 2001/3767), reg.4 (April 8, 2002).

Exemption from regulation 8 and 9

10.—(1) Regulation 8, or as the case may be, regulation 9, shall not,   4.50
[¹ subject to the following provisions of this regulation], apply to a person for the first 28 days of any period throughout which he is someone to whom paragraph (4) applies.

(2) Regulation 8 shall not, subject to paragraph (3), apply to a person who has not attained the age of 16 for the first 84 days of any period throughout which he is someone to whom paragraph (4) refers.

(3) Where on the day the person's entitlement to the care component commenced, he is a person to whom paragraph (4) refers, then paragraph (1) or, as the case may be, paragraph (2) shall not apply to him for any period of consecutive days, beginning with that day, in which he continues to be a person to whom paragraph (4) refers.

(4) This paragraph refers to a person who—
(a) is undergoing medical or other treatment in a hospital or other institution in any of the circumstances mentioned in regulation 8; or
[²(b) would, but for this regulation, be prevented from receiving the care
component of a disability working allowance by reason of regulation 9.]

(5) For the purposes of paragraphs (1) and (2)—
(a) 2 or more distinct periods separated by an interval not exceeding 28
days, or by 2 or more suchintervals shall be treated as a continuous
period equal in duration to the total of such distinct periods and
ending on the last day of the later or last such period;
(b) any period or periods to which regulations 8(1) or 9(1) refers shall
be taken into account and aggregated with any period to which the
other of them refers.

[¹ (6) Regulation 8 or as the case may be regulation 9 shall not apply
[³. . .] in the case of a person who is residing in a hospice and is terminally ill
where the Secretary of State has been informed that he is terminally ill—
(a) on a claim for the care component,
(b) on an application for a [⁴revision under section 9 of the 1998 Act or
supersession under section 10 of that Act] of an award of disability
living allowance, or
(c) in writing in connection withan award of, or a claim for, or an application for a [⁴revision under section 9 of the 1998 Act or supersession
under section 10 of that Act] of an award of, disability living allowance.

(7) In paragraph (6) "hospice" means a hospital or other institution
[⁵ whose primary function is to provide palliative care for persons resident

there who are suffering from a progressive disease in its final stages] other than—

(a) a health service hospital (within the meaning of section 128 of the NHS Act of 1977) in England or Wales;

(b) a health service hospital (within the meaning of section 108(1) of the NHS Act of 1978) in Scotland;

(c) a hospital maintained or administered by the Defence Council; or

(d) an institution similar to a hospital mentioned in any of the preceding sub-paragraphs of this paragraph.

[¹⁰ (8) Regulation 9 shall not apply in any particular case for any period during which the whole costs of all of the qualifying services are met—

(a) out of the resources of the person for whom the qualifying services are provided, or partly out of his own resources and partly with the assistance from another person or a charity, or

(b) on his behalf by another person or a charity.]

[⁵ (9) ³ . . .]

AMENDMENTS

1. Social Security Benefits (Amendments Consequential Upon the Introduction of Community Care) Regulations 1992 (SI 1992/3147), reg.7 (April 1, 1993).

2. Social Security (Disability Living Allowance) Amendment Regulations 1992 (SI 1992/633) (April 6, 1992).

3. Social Security (Attendance Allowance) (Amendment) Regulations 2000 (SI 2000/1401), reg.3 (June 19, 2000).

4. Social Security Act 1998 (Commencement No. 11, and Savings and Consequential and Transitional Provisions) Order 1999 (SI 1999/2860), Sch.7 (October 18, 1999).

5. Social Security Benefits (Miscellaneous Amendments) Regulations 1993 (SI 1993/518), reg.3(3) (April 1, 1993).

6. State Pension Credit (Consequential, Transitional and Miscellaneous Provisions) Regulations 2002 (SI 2002/3019), reg.28 (April 1, 2003).

7. Social Security and Child Support (Jobseeker's Allowance) (Consequential Amendments) Regulations 1996 (SI 1996/1345), reg. 17 (October 7, 1996).

8. Social Security (Attendance Allowance and Disability Living Allowance) (Amendment) Regulations 2002, (SI 2002/208), reg.3 (March 1, 2002).

9. Social Security (Attendance Allowance and Disability Allowance) (Amendment) Regulations 2003 (SI 2003/2259) reg.3 (October 6, 2003).

10. Attendance Allowance and Disability Living Allowance (Amendment) Regulations 2007, (SI 2007/2875) (October 29, 2007).

GENERAL NOTE

4.51 A person may remain entitled to the care component for up to 28 days in a hospital covered by reg.8 or accommodation covered by reg.9. However, separate periods in such a hospital or such accommodation are aggregated unless they are more than 28 days apart. Furthermore, under para.(3), a person cannot first qualify for the care component while in hospital or the relevant accommodation.

[¹ Adjustment of allowance where medical expenses are paid from public funds under war pensions instruments

4.52 **10A.**—(1) In this regulation—

"article 25B" means article 25B of the Personal Injuries (Civilians) Scheme 1983 (medical expenses) and includes that article as applied by article 48B of that Scheme;

"article 26" means article 26 of the Naval, Military and Air Forces etc. (Disablement and Death) Service Pensions Order 1983 (medical expenses);

and in this regulation and regulation 10B "relevant accommodation" means accommodation provided as a necessary ancillary to nursing care where the medical expenses involved are wholly borne by the Secretary of State pursuant to article 25B or article 26.

(2) This regulation applies where a person is provided with relevant accommodation.

(3) Subject to regulation 10B where this regulation applies and there are payable in respect of a person both a payment under article 25B or article 26 and a disability living allowance which is attributable to the care component, the allowance, in so far as it is so attributable, shall be adjusted by deducting from it the amount of the payment under article 25B or article 26, as the case may be, and only the balance shall be payable.]

AMENDMENT

1. Social Security (Attendance Allowance and Disability Living Allowance) (Amendment) Regulations 1994 (SI 1994/1779), reg.3(4) (August 1, 1994).

[¹ Exemption from regulation 10A

10B.—(1) Regulation 10A shall not, subject to the following provisions   4.53
of this regulation, apply to a person in respect of the first 28 days of any period during which the amount of any disability living allowance attributable to the care component would be liable to be adjusted by virtue of regulation 10A(3).

(2) For the purposes of paragraph (1) two or more distinct periods separated by an interval not exceeding 28 days, or by two or more such intervals, shall be treated as a continuous period equal in duration to the aggregate of such distinct periods and ending on the last day of the later or last such period.

(3) For the purposes of this paragraph a day is a relevant day in relation to a person if it fell not earlier than 28 days before the first day on which he was provided with relevant accommodation; and either—

(a) was a day when he was undergoing medical treatment in a hospital or similar institution in any of the circumstances mentioned in regulation 8; or

(b) was a day when he was, or would but for regulation 10 have been, prevented from receiving a disability living allowance attributable to the care component by virtue of regulation 9(1);

and where there is in relation to a person a relevant day, paragraph (1) shall have effect as if for "28 days" there were substituted such lesser number of days as is produced by subtracting from 28 the number of relevant days in his case.]

AMENDMENT

1. Social Security (Attendance Allowance and Disability Living Allowance) (Amendment) Regulations 1994 (SI 1994/1779), reg.3(4) (August 1, 1994).

[¹ Prescribed circumstance for entitlement to the care component

10C.—For the purposes of section 72(7) of the Act (prescribed circum-   4.54
stances in which a person is to be taken to satisfy or not to satisfy the

conditions mentioned in section 72(1)(a) to (c) of that Act), a person shall not be taken to satisfy subsection (1)(a)(i) or (b)(i) (day attention) or (c)(i) (night attention) unless the attention the severely disabled person requires from another person is required to be given in the physical presence of the severely disabled person].

AMENDMENT

1. Social Security (Attendance Allowance and Disability Living Allowance) (Amendment) (No.2) Regulations 2000, (SI 2000/2313) reg.3 (September 25, 2000).

GENERAL NOTE

4.55   An interesting point on the effect of this regulation was made in *CDLA/4333/2004*. The claimant suffered from depression and required support and attention during the day. Some of this was provided by regular telephone calls from her mother. The mother was herself in poor health and unable to visit her daughter. Clearly the telephone calls could not themselves count as attention because of reg.10C, but it was argued that they were evidence of the claimant's need for attention, that would have been provided by a visit, were the mother able to do so. In this particular case the argument failed because the tribunal appeared to have taken account of the telephone calls as if they were "attention", presumably having overlooked reg.10C. But could this situation breathe new life into the concept that attention must be "required"? Would the claimant need to show that her needs were not sufficiently met, or not as effectively met, by the telephone calls in order to succeed? If the mother did in fact visit in person it would be a harsh decision that held such visits were not necessary and that a telephone call would do, but where, as here, the attention is given by telephone, and if it suffices, it may be reasonable to argue that attendance in person is not required.

PART IV

MOBILITY COMPONENT

Qualifying period for mobility component after an interval

4.56   **11.**—The period prescribed for the purposes of [¹ section 73](9)(a)(ii) of the Act is a period of 3 months ending on the day which the person was last entitled to the mobility component or to mobility allowance, where that day falls not more than 2 years before the date on which entitlement to the mobility component would begin or would have begun but for any regulations made under [¹ section 5(1)(k) of the Administration Act] (which enables regulations to provide for the day on which entitlement to benefit is to begin or end).

AMENDMENT

1. Social Security (Disability Living Allowance) (Amendment) Regulations 1993 (SI 1993/1939), reg.2 (August 26, 1993).

GENERAL NOTE

4.57   The general effect of this provision is that the three-month qualifying period for the mobility component is deemed to be satisfied if the new claim is within two years of a previous period of entitlement to the mobility component (or mobility allowance) at the relevant rate.

Entitlement to the mobility component

12.—(1) A person is to be taken to satisfy the conditions mentioned in [¹ section 73](1)(a) of the Act (unable or virtually unable to walk) only in the following circumstances—   4.58

- (a) his physical condition as a whole is such that, without having regard to circumstances peculiar to that person as to the place of residence or as to place of, or nature of, employment—
    - (i) he is unable to walk; or
    - (ii) his ability to walk out of doors is so limited, as regards the distance over which or the speed at which or the length of time for which or the manner in which he can make progress on foot without severe discomfort, that he is virtually unable to walk; or
    - (iii) the exertion required to walk would constitute a danger to his life or would be likely to lead to a serious deterioration in his health; or
- (b) he has both legs amputated at levels which are either through or above the ankle, or he has one leg so amputated and is without the other leg, or is without both legs to the same extent as if it, or they, had been so amputated.

(2) For the purposes of [¹ section 73](2)(a) of the Act (mobility component for the blind and deaf) a person is to be taken to satisfy—
- (a) the condition that he is blind only where the degree of disablement resulting from the loss of vision amounts to 100 per cent; and
- (b) the condition that he is deaf only where the degree of disablement resulting from loss of hearing [² when using any artificial aid which he habitually uses or which is suitable in his case] amounts to not less than 80 per cent on a scale where 100 per cent represents absolute deafness.

(3) For the purposes of [¹ section 73](2)(b) of the Act, the conditions are that by reason of the combined effects of the person's blindness and deafness, he is unable, without the assistance of another person, to walk to any intended or required destination while out of doors.

(4) Except in a case to which paragraph (1)(b) applies, a person is to be taken not to satisfy the conditions mentioned in [¹ section 73](1)(a) of the Act if he—
- (a) is not unable or virtually unable to walk with a prosthesis or artificial aid which he habitually wears or uses, or
- (b) would not be unable or virtually unable to walk if he wore or used a prosthesis or an artificial aid which is suitable in his case.

(5) A person falls within subsection (3)(a) of [¹ section 73] of the Act (severely mentally impaired) if he suffers from a state of arrested development or incomplete physical development of the brain, which results in severe impairment of intelligence and social functioning.

(6) A person falls within subsection (3)(b) of [¹ section 73] of the Act (severe behavioural problems) if he exhibits disruptive behaviour which—
- (a) is extreme,
- (b) regularly requires another person to intervene and physically restrain

him in order to prevent him causing physical injury to himself or another, or damage to property, and

(c) is so unpredictable that he requires another person to be present and watching over him whenever he is awake.

[³ (7) For the purposes of section 73(1)(d) of the Act, a person who is able to walk is to be taken not to satisfy the condition of being so severely disabled physically or mentally that he cannot take advantage of the faculty out of doors without guidance or supervision from another person most of the time if he does not take advantage of the faculty in such circumstances because of fear or anxiety.

(8) Paragraph (7) shall not apply where the fear or anxiety is:

(a) a symptom of a mental disability; and

(b) so severe as to prevent the person from taking advantage of the faculty in such circumstances.]

AMENDMENTS

1. Social Security (Disability Living Allowance) (Amendment) Regulations 1993 (SI 1993/1939), reg.2 (August 26, 1993).

2. Social Security (Attendance Allowance and Disability Living Allowance) (Amendment) Regulations 1994 (SI 1994/1779), reg.3(5)(August 1, 1994).

3. Social Security (Disability Living Allowance) (Amendment) Regulations 2002 (SI 2002/648), reg.2 (April 8, 2002).

GENERAL NOTE

Sub-para. (1)(a)

4.59   This re-enacts reg.3(1)(a) of the Mobility Allowance Regulations 1975 and some of the words and phrases used have been considered by the Commissioners.

"physical disablement" "physical condition"

4.60   It seems fairly clear that the use of the word "physical" is intended to be limiting so that the scope of s.73(1)(a) of the Social Security Contributions and Benefits Act 1992 does not extend to those suffering from purely psychiatric conditions although such people may qualify under s.73(1)(c) or (d). Whether or not a person is suffering from "physical" disablement is regarded as primarily a medical question although, in principle, the process of reasoning used by a disability appeal tribunal to reach the conclusion is challengeable on the ground that it is erroneous in point of law. In a fairly uncontroversial case, a medical appeal tribunal did not err in law in holding that, because agoraphobia was not a physical condition, the claimant could not succeed (*R(M) 1/80*). More famously, in *R(M) 2/78*, a Commissioner held that a medical appeal tribunal had not erred in law in deciding that a child (Robert) suffering from Down's syndrome was suffering from a physical condition. The tribunal had said:

"We agree that the boy is suffering from mongolism, a condition which is due to faulty genetic inheritance and can therefore be classified as a physical disorder. We accept the evidence that while he walks for some yards he is liable to run, stop, lie down and refuse to go further; this reaction which severely impairs mobility is directly due to the physical condition of mongolism".

In refusing leave to appeal, the Chairman added:

"The submission of the Secretary of State seeks to separate the claimant's mental state from the physical condition to which that mental state is directly due. This cannot be accepted because the mental state is the direct consequence of the physical malformation of a particular chromosome (No. 21)."

The Chief Commissioner said:

"I think it is plain that the medical appeal tribunal regarded Robert's physical condition as a whole as being a disabling condition, preventing him from doing the particular action of walking. The weight to be attached to physical and mental disablement in cases where both factors may be present is for the medical authorities to decide, and the answer to the question whether the one or the other is, or both are responsible for an inability or virtual inability to walk is for their decision as a medical question. I do not consider that the medical appeal tribunal misapprehended what physical disablement means, or that it can be said that they were wrong in law in concluding from their findings that it was physical disablement which was responsible for his virtual inability to walk."

He stressed that not all Down's cases would have the same result, although it is not entirely clear whether that was because he thought that different conclusions might be reached as to whether the condition was a physical one or whether it was because not all people suffering from Down's syndrome are disabled to the same extent. The Mobility Allowance Regulations 1975 were amended in 1979 following *R(M) 2/78* but, in *R(M) 1/83*, a Tribunal of Commissioners held that the amendments did not affect the reasoning of the Commissioner in *R(M) 2/78*. *R(M) 3/86* concerned a child who had suffered brain damage at birth leading to severe mental subnormality. While capable of the physical movements of walking, his behaviour while doing so was erratic and unpredictable. In setting aside the decision of a medical appeal tribunal who had disregarded the behavioural problems, the Tribunal of Commissioners held that *R(M) 2/78* is still good law despite what was said in *Lees v Secretary of State for Social Services* (see below) and that behavioural problems arising out of a physical disability were relevant. It should be noted that in *Harrison v Secretary of State for Social Services*, reported as an appendix to *R(M) 1/88*, Lloyd L.J. suggested that *R(M) 2/78* should be regarded with caution in the light of *Lees*, but it is not clear which part of the Commissioner's decision he had in mind.

Furthermore it is not sufficient that the claimant shows that he is unable to walk out of doors because of a physical condition. It is necessary to go further and show the inability to be the result of the physical act of walking. In *Hewitt v Chief Adjudication Officer,* and *Diment v Chief Adjudication Officer* reported as *R(DLA) 6/99* the Court of Appeal held that claimants who suffered from severe porphyria, a condition of the skin that meant they could spend very little time out of doors, were not entitled to mobility component. The Court said the claimants could walk physically and that their inability to walk out of doors had nothing to do with the physical process of walking. In *CDLA/1639/2006* the claimant gave evidence that he suffered from severe attacks of migraine that caused pain, dizziness, and lack of vision. At such times — at least 80 hours a week — he could do nothing more than sit down or lie down. A tribunal, by a majority allowed his appeal, but the Commissioner held that in doing so their decision demonstrated an error of law. They had failed to examine sufficiently the way in which his headaches affected his ability to walk. The loss of vision, he said, is not relevant to a claim for higher rate mobility component because that relates only to the direction of walking and not to the ability to walk itself. Pain, too, would not count as that had nothing to do with the physical process of walking though it might clearly make the claimant disinclined to walk outside. Dizziness, or loss of balance, however, was relevant because it affects the manner of walking or even the ability to walk at all. The appeal was allowed and returned to a new tribunal to consider the extent of the element of dizziness and its effect. As well, they were asked to consider whether the claimant should qualify for mobility at the lower rate, on the basis of his need for supervision in case of a sudden onset of a migraine attack.

In *R(M) 1/88*, the claimant had injured his back in an accident in 1979. He was awarded mobility allowance up to 1983 but, on a renewal claim, a medical appeal tribunal held that his inability to walk was not due to a physical cause but was hysterical in origin. In the course of his decision, the Commissioner said:

"It may be that in the last analysis all mental disablement may be ascribed to physical causes. But, if so, it is obvious that the Act on drawing the distinction between physical and mental disablement did not mean this last analysis to be resorted to."

He held that the question what was and what was not a physical inability to walk was a medical question for the tribunal to determine but he added:

"This does not mean that in every case of hysteria the medical authorities are bound to hold that a claimant's hysteria is not a manifestation of his physical condition as a whole; but it does mean that if they do so find it will be impossible to disturb their decision on the ground that they ought to have found it to be a manifestation of the claimant's physical condition."

An appeal to the Court of Appeal was dismissed (*Harrison v Secretary of State for Social Services*, reported as an appendix to *R(M) 1/88*). The Court effectively adopted the Commissioner's reasoning. Stocker L.J. said: "Hysteria is not itself a physical condition, since physical and hysterical conditions are often used in contrasting terms, and in my view correctly so." The Commissioner points out, however, that where hysteria is itself a consequence of a physical condition, it is open to a Tribunal or medical board, as a matter of medical opinion, to find that where hysteria is caused by a physical condition, for example due to pain owing to some spinal condition, the inability to walk may itself be caused by that same physical condition. He drew attention, without apparent criticism, to the fact that the claimant has since been awarded mobility allowance on a further claim.

This question has now been considered, at length, by a Tribunal of Commissioners in *R(DLA) 4/06*. Were it not for the Court of Appeal's decision in *Harrison* the Tribunal would have accepted that the phrases "physical disability" (in s.73) and "physical condition as a whole" (in reg.12) should be interpreted to include any claimant whose condition manifested an inability to walk out of doors in the form of physical symptoms of a medical condition, whether that medical condition was physical or mental. (The Tribunal refer to these physical symptoms as being those of a medical condition though they do, as well, affirm the decision reached in *R(DLA) 3/06* so that perhaps their emphasis should have been rather on whether the claimants inability to walk was manifested by physical symptoms whether the cause of those symptoms was physical or mental.) Thus, on the view the Tribunal would prefer to have taken, the agoraphobic would still fail, but a claimant whose psychosomatic condition made it difficult or painful to walk would succeed, effectively adopting the views expressed in cases such as *CDLA/3323/2003*. However, the Tribunal held that they were bound by the decision in *Harrison*. This meant that they affirmed the view that in order to succeed, the claimant must show that his inability to walk outside has some physical cause. Pain, dizziness and fatigue that are purely psychosomatic or mental, are therefore not sufficient to qualify for the higher rate of mobility component, and cases such as *CSDLA/265/97*, *CDLA/948/2000* and *CDLA/3323/2003* should, therefore, no longer be followed.

But the Tribunal goes on to consider in some detail the difficulties and problems that decision makers will face in determining what is a physical cause. It is accepted that once it is shown that a disability involving some mental element has either a physical origin (e.g. brain damage), or a physical consequence (e.g. muscle wasting from lack of use when a claimant is depressed), that this will suffice to support the claim. The test of causation they suggest, should be one of "material contribution", so that once it is shown that the claimant's inability to walk derives to an extent that is more than trivial, from some physical factor he should succeed even though his disability is caused in part by psychological factors. A majority of the Tribunal held because of the use of the present tense in both s.73 and reg.12 that it was necessary for the physical factor to be still a current operating cause of the claimant's condition. A psychosomatic condition that derived from a past physical cause that is now corrected, would not suffice.

In applying all this to the facts of the two cases that were before them the Tribunal obtained much assistance from expert evidence given on behalf of the Department of Work and Pensions Corporate Medical group. This evidence is reproduced at para.108 of the decision and again, in relation particularly to back pain, at para.145, and for dizziness, at para.162. On the basis of this evidence the Tribunal allowed both appeals and returned the cases for a new Tribunal to consider whether there was any physical element (that was more than minimal) in the cause of the claimant's disability.

In both cases the Tribunal observes "that it may well be that in the past Tribunals have been too ready to conclude that the fact that no specific and precisely identified organic cause for [the particular disability] has been found means that there is not in fact a physical cause".

Finally the Tribunal was careful to point out that the cases before them involved only back pain, and dizziness. They say that conditions such as autism, Down's Syndrome, learning disabilities, and the extent to which mental disorders such as depression may be the result of genetics or chemical changes in the brain, and therefore also a physical condition was not before them and they refrain from expressing an opinion on these matters. However, to the extent that some of these matters have already been the subject of Commissioner's decisions it is not suggested that they are anything other than still good law. In *CDLA/1525/2008* Judge May has considered the case of a claimant suffering from anorexia nervosa. In his view the claimant could qualify (though the case was returned to another tribunal) because her condition manifested clear physical disablement that affected her ability to walk. It was not necessary, in his view, to consider how those physical conditions might have been caused.

The question of whether a claimant could qualify for mobility component, at the higher rate, on the basis of being "virtually unable to walk" under reg.12(1)(a)(ii) when, because of Alzheimer's disease, she could not progress effectively on her own was considered in *CSDLA/399/2005*. The Commissioner concludes that no error of law had been shown in the decision of a tribunal that had dismissed the claimant's appeal against a refusal of benefit, but she does so on the ground that the appellant had failed at the original hearing to make out a sufficient factual basis for her claim. On the question of whether an Alzheimer's patient could be said to be suffering from a "physical disability", the Commissioner adopted the view expressed in *CDLA/156/1994* which was in favour of such a conclusion, but felt that the claimant may still need to produce evidence in the form of medical opinion to support that view – the time had not yet come, she thought, when a tribunal could take judicial notice of the aetiology of the condition. In the present case the report of the doctor had described the claimant's condition as "100% mental due to Alzheimer's disease" and while this statement could have contained some ambiguity it did mean that there was no evidence before the tribunal to suggest a physical disability.

CDLA/3420/2005 is an example of the application of this to a claimant suffering from Marfan's disease. The risk of aortic aneurysm, which that condition causes, by the exertion of walking had caused anxiety and depression in the claimant. That, combined with his physical condition, made him reluctant to walk. His case was referred to a fresh tribunal for reconsideration on the basis that the physical contribution may have been more than minimal.

Diagnoses of chronic fatigue syndrome raise difficult questions. In *CSDLA/265/97*, the Commissioner said that, if the claimant's muscle pains and other physical problems were not mental, illusory or imaginary, they could be regarded as physical disabilities.

"The need to determine anything more, such as whether they are in turn caused by a physical condition, such as a virus, a lesion or a malfunction, may matter little for the purposes of section 73 of the Act."

In *CDLA/5183/97*, another case involving chronic fatigue syndrome, the Deputy Commissioner said:

"This is a controversial and sensitive issue. Accordingly, it is important to be clear about how the Commissioner and tribunals approach this question when it arises. It is not for the Commissioner to rule on whether or not chronic fatigue syndrome has a physical cause. It is not a question of law. Nor is it for the DAT to have some kind of general rule or policy on this matter. What the DAT must do in each individual case, is to examine the evidence before it and reach a conclusion on whether the walking difficulties which an individual appellant experiences arise from 'physical disablement', in order to satisfy the statute; and the individual appellant's 'physical condition as a whole' in order to satisfy the regulation. This evaluation of the evidence is a question of fact for the DAT. See *R(M) 2/78.*"

In that case, the Deputy Commissioner found that the tribunal had not erred in law and had reached a decision they were entitled to reach on the evidence before them. "In particular, they have regarded the advice of the DLAAB not as binding on them in any way but simply as a factor to be taken into account."

Further support for the acceptance of chronic fatigue syndrome as the basis of a claim is found in *CDLA/4486/2000*. That case accepts that the condition may not have a clinical explanation but emphasises that it is the effect of the conditions on the claimant's physical ability that matters, not the cause. Note also the discussion of psychosomatic disability in the notes following s.72 above.

"without having regard to circumstances peculiar to that person as to place of residence or as to place of, or nature of, employment"

Note that it is simply the claimant's physical condition which is relevant. The distance to his or her local shops is not relevant although it is often helpful for a tribunal to know whether, and if so how, a claimant manages to get to the local shops and then, having ascertained how far that is, to consider ability to walk in the light of that evidence.

(i) "unable to walk"

4.61   In *R(M) 3/78*, the Commissioner said:

"The word 'walk' is an ordinary English word in common usage and, in the context of regulation 3 [of the Mobility Allowance Regulations 1975], means to move by means of a person's legs and feet or a combination of them."

In *R(M) 1/83*, no definition was attempted but the Tribunal of Commissioners said:

"We consider that a person who can walk at all ought not to be regarded as unable to walk, though he may well be regarded as virtually unable to walk. This does not of course preclude the medical authorities from finding that a claimant's method of moving about does not amount to walking at all."

In the course of the litigation in *Lees* (see below) O'Connor L.J., in the Court of Appeal, said:

"A person is unable to walk if he cannot use his legs for walking, so a person who is bedridden, a person who is a paraplegic and indeed a person who has a leg amputated is unable to walk. The last category can be enabled to walk by artificial aids such as a false limb or crutches and for that reason we find regulation 3(2) [now regulation 12(4)] applies" (see the appendix to *R(M) 1/84*).

In *R(M) 2/89*, it was made clear that a person with only one foot cannot "walk" in the absence of an artificial limb. Where a person uses crutches, it is necessary to consider the way in which they are used. Unless they are used so that the claimant can walk, as opposed to simply swinging through the crutches, the claimant will satisfy the condition of reg.12(1)(a)(i) even if the distance he or she can travel is such that reg.12(1)(a)(ii) would not be satisfied.

(ii) "virtually unable to walk"

In *R(M) 1/91* the Commissioner said that "the base point is total inability to walk, which is extended [by reg.12(1)(a)(ii)] to take in people who can technically walk but only to an insignificant extent". There is clearly some scope for disagreement as to what is meant by "virtually" or "insignificant".

4.62

It is to be noted that the virtual inability to walk must be a virtual inability to do so "out of doors". A medical appeal tribunal, conducting a walking test indoors, can infer from that that the claimant is not virtually unable to walk out of doors although it is desirable that they should indicate that they have addressed their minds to the different conditions pertaining out of doors (*CM/103/1984*). In *R(M) 1/91*, the Commissioner held that the test envisaged walking on the kind of pavement or road which one would normally expect to find in the course of walking out of doors, any unusual hazards peculiar to the claimant's situation being ignored. He also pointed out that some degree of incline must be contemplated but that the question is not whether the claimant is unable or virtually unable to *climb* and any inability to surmount hills or mountains is irrelevant.

In *R(DLA) 4/02* the Commissioner held that notes made after covert observation of the claimant's walking ability, and a videotape of her walking, were admissible as evidence before a tribunal. None of this evidence, all of which related to the claimant's behaviour in a public place, could be regarded as having been obtained in breach of her human rights, and all of it was admissible without breach of her right to a fair trial.

Evidence provided by the claimant, as well as that of medical advisers, will be crucial in determining the claimant's ability to walk. But even this evidence must be considered carefully by tribunals to ascertain its reliability. In *CDLA/2423/2007* the claimant was a child whose mother said that on a "good day" her daughter could walk as far as 3 miles in 30 to 40 minutes. This was accepted by the tribunal as clear evidence that she was not "virtually unable to walk". But as the Commissioner pointed out this would suggest a walking speed of between 4.5 and 6 miles per hour; a speed that even a fit adult would find difficult, if not impossible, to achieve.

The distance a person can walk is important but it should not be considered without reference to the other relevant factors of speed, length of time and manner of walking. In *R(M) 1/78*, it was held that a medical appeal tribunal had erred in law in holding that a claimant was virtually unable to walk when she could walk a mile. However, whether the distance a person can walk means that he or she is virtually unable to walk is generally regarded as a matter of judgment for a tribunal and Commissioners have shown no inclination to interfere. Thus, medical appeal tribunals have not been held to have erred *in law* in holding that claimants were not virtually unable to walk where their walking ability has been very limited. In *CM/39/84*, the claimant could manage 100 yards at 2 mph and, in *CM/47/86*, the claimant could manage only 50 yards. On the other hand, in *R(M) 5/86*, it seems to have been accepted that a claimant who could walk only 50 yards should qualify. Apart from speed, a tribunal should probably consider how long it takes a person to recover after walking a short distance. A claimant who can walk a substantial distance provided that he or she stands still for a couple of minutes every hundred yards has a greater ability to walk than a person who has to rest for an hour after walking a hundred yards. In *CDLA/805/94* the Commissioner suggested that this factor should be taken into account when considering "the length of time for which" the claimant could walk. He pointed out that, as speed is a function of time and distance, consideration of the length of time for which the claimant can walk must involve consideration of something beyond the mere time it necessarily takes the claimant to walk the distance he can manage at the speed he can manage.

In *CDLA/717/98*, the Commissioner considered *CM 145/88* in which a Commissioner said that an ability to walk 90 yards in five minutes was "arguably" tantamount to being "virtually unable to walk". In the later case, the tribunal had found that the claimant was able to cover 100 yards in five to six minutes, including stops, and concluded that the claimant was not "virtually unable to walk". The Commissioner held that

"it is not for a Commissioner to attempt to lay down a precise formula for determining whether or not a claimant is unable to walk when the legislation does not do so. The legislation allows adjudication officers and tribunals a margin of appreciation."

He declined to interfere with the tribunal's decision, although he said that a tribunal that had reached the opposite conclusion on those facts would also have been entitled to do so. Guidance was also given in *CDLA/608/94*:

"It is impossible to lay down *a priori* rules for such questions as the distance a person must be found to walk without severe discomfort before he ceases to count as 'virtually unable' to walk, since so much depends on the circumstances and physical state of each particular claimant. However, it has been said that what 'virtually unable to walk' means is a question of law (*R(M) 1/78* para.11), and some general guidance can be gleaned from the reported decisions. In the absence of any special indications from the other three factors, if a claimant is unable to cover more than 25 or 30 yards without suffering severe discomfort, his ability to walk is not 'appreciable' or 'significant'; while if the distance is more than 80 or 100 yards, he is unlikely to count as 'virtually unable to walk' as those words have generally been interpreted in section 73 and regulation 12. In the difficult ground in between, I for my part find helpful the approach of the Commissioner in case *CM 78/89* at para.13, where he said that mobility allowance (as it then was) was never designed to—and does not—embrace those who can walk 60 or 70 yards without severe discomfort. In such a case, therefore, there would have to be some other factor such as extreme slowness or difficulty because of the manner of moving forward on foot before a claimant would count as 'virtually unable'."

The importance of not considering the distance a claimant can walk in isolation from other factors was again emphasised in *CDLA/1389/97* at para.31 but the Commissioner also said, at para.35, that a tribunal did not necessarily err in not referring to all four factors mentioned in reg.12(1)(a)(ii). It depended whether the other factors arose as issues in the circumstances of the case. This issue has been considered again by the Commissioner Rowland in *CDLA/4388/1999*. There a tribunal had held that the claimant was not entitled when the evidence showed that he could walk, with a limp for 50 metres in about 4 minutes. The Commissioner emphasised that the question of whether this should be regarded as being "virtually unable to walk" was a question of fact to be determined by the tribunal and that unless it was a decision that no tribunal, properly directed on the points of law, could have reached, it was unassailable on appeal. At the same time he expressly disagreed with the statement of another Commissioner in *CSDLA/252/94*, that someone who could limp slowly for 50 yards could not "as a matter of law" be virtually unable to walk. In either case the question is one of fact for a tribunal and whichever way they decide could, *in law*, be correct. In the instant case, however, the appeal was allowed and returned for a re-hearing before a different tribunal because the tribunal had not considered what the claimant's condition and walking ability would be after going 50 metres. Would he need to rest? And if so for how long and in what way before he could go further? In *CDLA 2195/2008* Judge Williams was given evidence of the newly introduced guidelines on walking speed that will be used by DM and by medical examiners to assess walking ability. But he reiterated the importance of treating the test as one of overall impression of the claimant's walking ability:

"Before leaving this topic, I endorse the more general submission by the Secretary of State on this appeal. Whether or not someone is virtually unable to walk is essentially a question of fact that must take into account all the matters referred to in the legislation. In one sense "speed" is central to this because regard must be had to "the distance over which or the speed at which or the length of time for which..." the claimant makes progress on foot (regulation 12 of the Social Security (Disability Living Allowance) Regulations 1991). And, of course, speed is distance covered divided by time taken. But those who are virtually unable to walk often do not walk at a consistent speed. It is therefore the whole way in which progress on foot takes place before or with discomfort that must, in fact, be determined. There are no easy ways of turning that into an arithmetical calculation."

In *R(DLA) 4/03* Commissioner Parker has given further consideration to the relationship between walking ability and severe discomfort. The appellant had appealed against refusal of benefit arguing that his walking ability should be assessed only up to the point when he began to experience severe discomfort. In decision *CSDLA/678/99* a Commissioner had said that severe discomfort—

"may onset and then be relieved by rest so that a further distance can be walked before further onset. In such a case the test stops at the first onset."

Commissioner Parker rejects this view as making an unwarranted gloss upon the statutory definition. "Without severe discomfort" is not the same, she argues, as before the onset of severe discomfort. To apply the test in that way would be to devalue the test of overall walking ability contained in the distance-time-speed formula provided by the regulation. The phrase "without discomfort" means that the claimant is not to be assessed with the inclusion of any progress that he makes only while suffering that discomfort, but so long as the rest time taken to avoid or relieve discomfort is included in the overall time taken for a journey then the consequent calculation of speed will reflect the degree of disablement he suffers. A person who can progress with short, and infrequent periods of rest will probably be able to walk for this purpose; someone who requires frequent or prolonged stops probably will not. The judgment of distance, time and speed is then a matter of fact for the tribunal.

Also in *CDLA/1389/97*, the Commissioner considered the relationship between pain and discomfort and he warned, at para.41, that a tribunal failing to use the statutory term "severe discomfort" was at risk of being held to have applied the wrong test. He suggested that there might be an escalating scale of severity from pain through severe discomfort to severe pain but it was unnecessary for him to decide the point. This issue was considered in greater detail in *R(DLA) 4/98* where the Commissioner said:

"The fact that someone suffers pain as a result of walking, or walks 'in pain', does not automatically mean that he or she is walking with severe discomfort. The pain may be mild, moderate or severe, short-lived or chronic. The tribunal must decide for itself whether there is severe discomfort considering all the evidence, and perhaps taking into account other factors causing discomfort in addition to the pain."

Breathlessness could be such a factor. The possibility of reducing the level of discomfort by taking medication may be taken into account, provided the tribunal explains why taking the medication would be "a reasonable, safe and appropriate thing to do" (*CDLA/3925/97*). Severe discomfort need not be the factor limiting the extent to which the claimant can walk. In *CDLA/17489/96*, the claimant feared that walking might damage her back. The Commissioner observed that reg.12(1)(a)(iii) might not apply because "exertion" might not be the problem but that reg.12(1)(a)(ii) could be relevant because, for the purpose of that head, "one must have regard only to walking that it is reasonable to expect a claimant to perform so that a reasonable fear of causing serious injury is a material consideration." However, a claim to have such a fear will doubtless be treated sceptically unless there is medical evidence showing the fear to be justified.

Pain that is suffered after walking, as well as while walking, yet still as a result of walking, should also be taken into account in deciding whether the claimant cannot walk without severe discomfort (*CDLA/3896/2006*).

The severe discomfort must be something that is caused by the act of walking. In *Diment v Chief Adjudication Officer* and *Hewitt v Chief Adjudication Officer* reported as *R(DLA)* 6/99, the claimants suffered from porphyria, a condition that meant they could not expose their skin to the sun, but otherwise were capable of normal perambulation.

In *R(DLA)* 4/04, Commissioner Bano held that a claimant who suffered pain all of the time, and whose pain was not made worse by attempting to walk, could still qualify if it was the pain that made it impossible or difficult for the claimant to walk.

Consideration of the manner of walking involves consideration of behaviour while walking as well as the steadiness of the claimant's gait. However, a need for supervision or attendance while walking is not, of itself, relevant. In *R(M)* 1/78, it was not material that the claimant was always accompanied because she suffered from fits. Thus a person who suffers from fits only occasionally is unlikely to qualify on that ground alone but, in *CM/125/1983*, a Commissioner held that the fact that a claimant was liable to suffer from three fits in half a mile might lead to the conclusion that the quality of walking was so poor as to amount to a virtual inability to walk. Similarly, a "propensity to trip . . . would have to be extremely marked before it became relevant to the manner of a claimant's walking" (*CM/364/92*).

While in *R(M)* 1/83 it was pointed out that the need for attendance and supervision was met through the social security system by entitlement to attendance allowance (see now the care component of disability living allowance and also the lower rate of the mobility component), the Tribunal of Commissioners did consider that the need for such assistance was a facet of the manner in which a person can make progress on foot and was to be taken into account by the medical authorities in conjunction with any other matters in determining whether the person concerned was virtually unable to walk. They said:

> "The main question in each case will be whether the child is so incapable inasmuch as his ability to walk out of doors is so limited as regards the manner in which he is able to make progress on foot, since behavioural limitations on a person's walking generally affect the manner of walking. It is possible also that speed of walking from place to place may enter into it. It will clearly be relevant that tantrums or refusals to walk are of frequent occurrence or not. We accept the submission made to us that the reference in reg.3(1)(b) [now reg.12(1)(a)(ii)] to the making of progress on foot means that it is proper to take account of the fact that a major purpose of walking is to get to a designated place. It follows that if a person can be caused to move himself to a designated place only with the benefit of guidance and supervision and possibly after much cajoling *the point may be reached at which he may be found to be virtually unable to walk*. There may be other factors such as blindness and deafness . . . to be taken into account in addition."

That passage needs to be treated with some caution in the light of the decision of the House of Lords in *Lees v Secretary of State for Social Services* (reported as an appendix to *R(M)* 1/84) but it is not inconsistent with it. Christine Lees was blind and suffered from hydrocephalus with symptoms including some impairment of balance and marked impairment of capacity for spatial orientation. She needed an intelligent adult as a "pilot". Lord Scarman rejected the argument that she was virtually unable to walk because the legislation points to consideration of the physical ability to get about on foot. In effect, he said that her position was no different from that of any other blind person who would need a guide of some sort. He also said that some Commissioners' decisions cited to the House and which differ must be regarded as erroneous in law. But it is not clear from his speech which decisions he had in mind or to what extent they are erroneous.

As already noted, in *Harrison*, Lloyd L.J. suggested that *R(M)* 2/78 must be treated with caution but in *R(M)* 3/86 a Tribunal of Commissioners said that it was correctly stating the law in that a claimant's behavioural problems, including a failure on occasion to exercise his walking powers (stemming from a physical disability) were necessarily relevant. "What is relevant is whether or not they suffer from temporary paralysis (as far as walking is concerned) and, if so, to what extent." In *CM/186/1985*, the Commissioner, relying on *R(M) 3/86*, drew a distinction between, on one hand, a child who suffered from

> "temperamental refusal episodes, these episodes occurring at distances varying between 20 and several hundred yards and on occasion [made] progress impossible by sitting down"

as a result of his physical condition (autism) and, on the other hand, the hypothetical "case of a child who is open to coaxing". Thus once it is established that, due to physical disablement, a person cannot be persuaded to walk in a desired direction, that person may be regarded as virtually unable to walk and so be entitled to the higher rate of the mobility component of disability living allowance and not just to the lower rate under s.73(1)(d) of the Social Security Contributions and Benefits Act 1992.

The distinction that was drawn by the Tribunal of Commissioners in *R(M) 3/86* between a claimant (in most cases of this sort, a child) who could not walk and a claimant who would not walk was based upon the simple question of whether such a person could be made to move by coaxing or by bribery. The Commissioners' conclusion was that if the child could be persuaded to move, it followed that the disablement was a matter of volition and could not then be the result of his physical condition.

A series of subsequent cases have questioned this conclusion. They are summarised, and the counter-argument put most powerfully, in *CDLA/4565/2003* by Deputy Commissioner McGavin. There a child suffered from Williams syndrome, a rare condition that caused both learning difficulties and behavioural problems as well as some physical symptoms. But like some claimants suffering from Down's Syndrome, autism and brain damage, though she could walk in a physical sense, she might then sit or lie down, and might become aggressive if her wishes were thwarted.

The Commissioner points out that in the case of claimants such as these, to describe their behaviour as simply that of a naughty child (as the can't walk/won't walk test would seem to compel him to do) flies in the face of all the medical evidence provided and of the combined experience of the claimants' carers. As the Commissioner in *CM/98/1989* (a case concerning the claim of an 18-year-old man with brain damage) put the matter:

> "If . . . the relevant behavioural problems have nothing to do with physical damage what do they derive from? In the case of this 18-year-old are the tribunal suggesting that his behaviour was that of a naughty child who just would not walk when required? And, if they were, is not the fact that a brain damaged 18-year-old behaves like a child something to do with the brain damage?"

In the present case the Commissioner suggests that a tribunal should not conclude that a claimant who can be persuaded to move must be regarded as capable of walking, but instead should look at the medical evidence from which they might conclude that the refusal to walk was still a consequence of the malfunctioning of the brain, rather than simply wilful naughtiness. If so, then a refusal to walk that was frequent, sustained and not easily overcome could still constitute an inability to walk. The can't walk/won't walk distinction has been considered again by Commissioner Jacobs in *CDLA/3839/2007*. The Commissioner concludes that the distinction apparently drawn in *R(M) 3/86* between a deliberate election not to walk and physical disablement; is no such thing. In his view (and that of others he cites), this was simply a disposal of the facts as presented in that particular case, and did not lay down any principal of law to be applied in others. In this case, the claimant was a child suffering from autism (a physical condition) who generally required two adults holding him firmly when taken on any public route to avoid the danger that would be caused to himself and others by his running off uncontrollably. The case was returned to a tribunal for them to consider, and give clear reasons, as to whether, on the evidence presented, the claimant should be regarded as virtually unable to walk.

R(M) 2/81 concerned a blind person who could get around perfectly well with a guide dog until some scaffolding fell on his head and caused a physical injury. The medical appeal tribunal found:

> "The claimant's legs are capable of making the movements required in the activity of walking but he is blind and has a physical disablement in his balance mechanism and sense of direction which makes it impossible for him to control the direction in which he wishes to move . . . With human guidance he can be steered and can with much help progress in a straight line in a desired direction."

In *R(M) 3/86* it was held that that case did not survive *Lees* but it is interesting that the Court of Appeal in *Lees* would have distinguished it on the facts. O'Connor L.J. said:

> "I repeat it is a medical question as to whether physical disablement including a disturbance of directional mechanism, if the doctors decide that that is a physical disablement, renders a person unable to walk or virtually unable to walk."

The House of Lords suggested that they were not disagreeing with the Court of Appeal at all. The extent to which assistance can be of use would appear to be relevant but some of the sweeping *dicta* in *R(M) 2/81* clearly go.

The distance over which, the speed at which, the length of time for which and the manner in which the claimants can make progress are all relevant. However, the need to make findings on each of the factors only applies where the factors are all in issue (*CDLA/8462/95*). Whether a tribunal errs in law in failing to deal with some factors depends very much on the evidence in the particular case.

Any ability to make progress on foot must, to be relevant, be without severe discomfort. In *R(M) 1/81*, it was held that a tribunal must ignore any walking which can be managed only with severe discomfort. The most obvious form of discomfort to be suffered by a claimant is pain. The assessment of pain is a frequent and difficult issue before tribunals. Guidance on a proper approach to the issue of pain has been given by Commissioner Jacobs in *CDLA/0902/2004*.

Note that the test to be applied is of "severe discomfort" not pain, or severe pain, and the evidence relied upon must be as to that test; or, at least explain the relationship with that test. In *CDLA/3292/2007* the Commissioner allowed the appeal of a claimant whose claim had been denied by a tribunal that relied, in part, on the evidence of her GP that she could walk only 50–100 yards "without being in severe pain". While this might have been consistent with the rest of the evidence relied upon, it could not be said that it was necessarily so, and the tribunal had failed to advert to the difference stated between "severe pain" and "severe discomfort".

In *R(M) 1/83*, the claimant's representative submitted that the words "without severe discomfort" must be interpreted as meaning "without risk of severe discomfort" and that a person who could not be allowed to go out of doors unattended for fear of his being injured in a street accident could not do so without risk of severe discomfort. The Commissioners said

> "this submission involves imputing to the draftsman the rather heavy humour of describing the risk of being run over as a risk of severe discomfort and we do not think that the words used are appropriate to carry the meaning suggested. In our view the words 'severe discomfort' relate to matters like pain and breathlessness that may be brought on by walking. . . . [They do] not extend to the screaming attack of an autistic child or the refusal to walk of the child suffering from Down's syndrome. . . . These are the consequence of resistence to the idea of walking and [*sic*] rather than of the walking itself."

In *Cassinelli v Secretary of State for Social Services (R(M) 2/92)*, the Court of Appeal held that a medical appeal tribunal had erred in law when holding that a person was not virtually unable to walk because the exertion of walking did not cause "severe pain or distress". Glidewell L.J. said that that phrase seemed

> "to be drawing a distinction between the factor of pain, of which discomfort is a lesser concomitant, and the factor of distress which may arise for other reasons than pain; distress may result of course from pain or discomfort, but may also result from breathlessness, which is another matter to which the tribunal referred."

He rejected the argument put on behalf of the Secretary of State that the tribunal had, inferentially at least, applied the right test and answered the right question. It is difficult to follow the logic of the decision but it is clear that tribunals depart from the statutory language at their peril. It remains arguable that breathlessness can give rise to severe discomfort.

In *CDLA/1361/99*, the evidence was that, when walking a very short distance, the claimant suffered pain and then lost control of her bowels. The Commissioner held that the claimant was virtually unable to walk. He said:

> "The discomfort in this case comprises not only the pain but also the physical sensation of having soiled oneself in the ways described in the papers (which would certainly be discomfort in the ordinary sense of the word, though possibly not 'severe'), the embarrassment of knowing that one has soiled oneself (which would again cause discomfort), and the distress caused. Looking at all these elements together they are in my view of such a magnitude in this case that I conclude that walking to any extent causes the claimant severe discomfort after the walking, if not during it (and often both)."

In *CDLA/313/2005* the claimant, who was a teenage girl, was disabled in one leg and as a result, was likely to fall. This could be avoided with the use of a walking stick but the claimant said she was too embarrassed to use the stick. It was argued that her embarrassment was a form of discomfort under reg.12(1)(a)(ii) and that she should be regarded as unable or virtually unable to walk within the meaning prescribed. Commissioner May rejects this argument. Her discomfort, he says, must be of a kind that was part of her "physical condition as a whole" (reg.12(1)(a)), and could not, therefore, include her embarrassment. In doing so he disapproves of the reasoning adopted by the Commissioner in *CDLA/1361/1999* though there it could be suggested that the embarrassment had more to do with physical condition of the claimant than just embarrassment at the use of a device.

An attempt to extend the reasoning of *R(DLA) 1/04* to the case of a blind man suffering from depression was made in *CDLA/3898/2006*. The claimant's depression was said to derive from his blindness and that it caused the claimant to suffer anxiety to the point of severe discomfort so that he was virtually unable to walk outside. He would thus qualify for the higher rate of benefit. This claim was refused and his appeal was rejected by Commissioner Mesher. The Commissioner held that the appeal must fail because the appeal tribunal had found, as a fact, that the claimant did not suffer discomfort from anxiety so long as he had guidance and support from someone to accompany him. The claimant argued that this finding was unjustified because his anxiety would continue unless the particular person he had for company was someone with whom he had a particular relationship of trust, and in whom he could then be confident. But no evidence of this was before the appeal tribunal, and the Commissioner held, therefore, that there could be no error of law in the conclusion they had reached. But the Commissioner comments more generally upon the argument that had been put to him. It is important, he says, in a field such as this, which is so complex as to be sometimes almost unjusticiable, (in the sense that it may appear difficult to distinguish clearly and consistently between those cases which succeed and those which fail) that one should return to the basics as explained in *Lees*, and having done so he says:

"I doubt in the light of *Lees,* and of the decision of the Tribunal of Commissioners in *R (M) 3/86,* whether 'mere' mental distress, turmoil or anxiety (as opposed to physical manifestations like breathlessness, palpitations, dizziness, chest pain or nausea) can amount to severe discomfort even where a physical disorder contributes to the effect to more than a minimal extent. There would also, if such things could count, be difficulty in distinguishing a perfectly rational heightening of caution, vigilance and concentration which presumably could not be regarded as severe discomfort on any basis."

(iii) exertion

4.63   In *R(M) 3/78,* the claimant needed oxygen to be available in case of a drop attack (which might also have occurred while she was asleep). The Commissioner held that what is now reg.12(1)(a)(iii)

"does not extend to conditions or symptoms which might intervene during the course of walking without there being any connection or relationship to or with walking or being precipitated by the exertion of walking."

Although the word "exertion" might suggest the sort of condition associated with pulmonary and cardiac deficiency there are several decisions that have extended it to include any sufficient deterioration in health effected by the act of walking. Thus, in *CDLA/5494/1997,* Commissioner Levenson accepted that a claimant who had been warned that to continue walking would endanger the spine could succeed, and in *CDLA/2973/1999* Commissioner Fellner has held that a claimant whose diabetes had led to neuropathy in his legs and feet could qualify because walking was likely to lead to ulceration of the claimant's feet and a consequent risk of amputation. The meaning of this phrase has been further considered in *CDLA/3941/2005.* The Commissioner allowed an appeal by a claimant who suffered from cartilage damage and arthritis in her knee. The effect of walking for extensive distances, which she had to do in taking her children to and from school, was said to be likely to result in more frequent arthroscopies (wash-out of the knee joint) and eventually would hasten the need for a knee replacement. This, the Commissioner thought should satisfy the test in reg.(12)(1)(a)(iii). He gave his own decision that she was entitled to benefit.

The deterioration in health need not be permanent or last for any great length of time (*CM/23/1985*) but it must be serious. In *CM/158/94,* the tribunal had found that, although exertion left the claimant exhausted, "it did not result in a serious deterioration in his health since, having rested, he would improve." The Commissioner dismissed the claimant's appeal and suggested that a serious deterioration in a claimant's health would only be shown where:

"(a) there was a worsening of his condition from which he never recovered, or
(b) there was a worsening from which he only recovered after a significant period of time, e.g. 12 months, or
(c) there was a worsening from which recovery could only be effected by some form of medical intervention."

Sub-para. (1) (b)

4.64   Double amputees may qualify under this provision even if they have recovered sufficiently to have artificial limbs fitted and are no longer either unable to walk or virtually unable to walk.

Para. (2)

4.65   There is no indication given as to how the degree of disablement is to be assessed. However, Sch.2 to the Social Security (General Benefit) Regulations 1982 provides that 100 per cent disablement is appropriate for "loss of sight to such an extent as to render the claimant unable to perform any work for which eyesight is essential". Schedule 3 to the Social Security (Industrial Injuries) (Prescribed Diseases) Regulations 1985 sets out a test for establishing an assessment of 80 per cent for occupational deafness. In *R(DLA) 3/95* the Commissioner said that these tests should be used for the purposes of reg.12(2). When the 1982 Regulations are being applied in industrial accident cases, an assessment of 100 per cent for loss of vision is regarded as appropriate where the vision is found to be less than 6/60, using both eyes whilst glasses are used; or where finger counting is not possible beyond one foot. Before *R(DLA) 3/95* was decided, an assessment of 80 per cent for deafness was regarded as appropriate where the claimant was unable to hear a shout beyond one metre using both ears (with aids). This was tested by shouting an instruction or question from just beyond one metre behind the claimant. *CDLA/7090/1999* rejects the use of that test. It emphasises the need for controlled testing and suggests that this should be in an outdoor environment.

Para.(3)

Note that it is only an inability to walk in the right direction due to the *combined* effects of blindness and deafness which can be relevant.

4.66

Para.(4)

An ability to wear an artificial prosthesis or to use an artificial aid (such as a pair of crutches) must be taken into account and the claimant's ability to get about must usually be assessed on the basis that a prosthesis or aid is used. However, if the claimant does not in fact habitually wear or use such a prosthesis or aid, it is necessary to consider whether one would be suitable for him or her (*R(M) 2/89*). If a prosthesis is habitually, or could be, worn but any walking is, or would be, achieved only with severe discomfort, such ability to walk would not fall within para.(1)(a)(ii) anyway. But a prosthesis might not be suitable even if the discomfort were not severe. It is arguable that a prosthesis or aid cannot be "suitable" until it is actually available to the claimant. Reg.12(4) cannot be read as requiring a person to undergo surgery to improve his or her medical condition (*R(M) 1/95*).

4.67

Para.(5)

Only those suffering from a state of arrested development or incomplete physical development of the brain can qualify under those provisions. If someone becomes disabled as a result of an injury after the brain has reached full development, he or she will probably have to rely on para.(1)(a) instead. In *CDLA/156/94*, the Commissioner, having heard expert medical evidence, held that sufferers from Alzheimer's disease do not satisfy the condition mentioned in reg.12(5). He found that the disease resulted in a deterioration of a developed brain rather than an arrest of development, rejecting the idea that the brain develops throughout life which, he pointed out, would render otiose the restriction implied by reg.12(5). In that case, the expert evidence suggested that the brain had reached maturity by the time a person was aged 30. In *CDLA/393/94*, the claimant was in her early 20s when she became ill and it was held to be arguable that her brain had not fully developed and that she suffered from a state of arrested development or incomplete physical development. The burden of proof rested on the claimant. In *R(DLA) 3/98*, the Commissioner heard evidence in respect of a claimant suffering from schizophrenia and concluded that she suffered from arrested development of the brain but that that did not result in severe impairment of intelligence in her case.

4.68

In *CDLA/1678/97*, the Commissioner heard expert evidence in a case where the claimant suffered from autism. He concluded that autism arises out of a state of arrested or incomplete development of the brain but he was not satisfied that the claimant's intelligence was severely impaired. The expert evidence was to the effect that only those with an I.Q. of 55 or below were regarded as having *severely* impaired intelligence and that fewer than 10 per cent of those suffering from autism fell within that category. The Commissioner found, on the basis of medical reports and other evdence, that the particular claimant before him was not one of those 10 per cent.

In *M (a child) v Chief Adjudication Officer* reported as *R (DLA) 1/00*, the Court of Appeal has held that an intelligence test should not be regarded as a definitive measure of whether a child has a severe impairment of intelligence. In that case the child, who was autistic, had an intelligence quotient well above the quotient of 55 that had been suggested by the medical experts as consistent with a rating of severe impairment. The Court of Appeal held that an intelligence test result is a useful starting point but should not be conclusive. They suggest a full assessment of intelligence should include factors such as "insight and sagacity". It is worth noting, too, that the wording of subs.(5) includes the claimant's "social functioning" as well as his intelligence.

Regulation 12(5) was considered in *CDLA/5153/97* where the claimant suffered from attention deficit hyperactivity disorder. The Commissioner had detailed medical evidence before him as to the causes of the condition and he was not satisfied that, in the present state of medical knowledge, it was possible to attribute the claimant's condition to "a state of arrested development or incomplete physical development of the brain" as is required to satisfy the condition of reg.12(5). Such a finding by a Commissioner on a question of fact is not binding on tribunals and the Commissioner himself acknowledged that different evidence might become available.

"It may become possible to make such an attribution for ADHD in the future, with the advances in scanning techniques and genetic knowledge for which Professor Barkley hopes: but it is not so now."

Nonetheless, the decision provides helpful guidance and unless a claimant has technically detailed evidence in support of his or her case, tribunals are likely to adopt the Commissioner's finding.

Para.(6)

4.69   *Physical* restraint must be *regularly* required and the behaviour must be *disruptive* and *unpredictable*. Indeed, since "extreme" conditions "disruptive behaviour", it is probably right to say that the behaviour must be extremely disruptive. A person who satisfies the conditions of sub-paras (b) and (c) but who does not exhibit extremely disruptive behaviour may qualify for the mobility component at the lower rate (under s.73(1)(d) of the 1992 Act).

Regulation 12(6) was examined in *CDLA/2054/98*. The Deputy Commissioner held that in applying sub-para.(a), it was the claimant's behaviour when taking advantage of the faculty of mobility that had to be considered. The tribunal had erred in law in finding that "to get hold of the appellant's arm to stop him causing further complications" did not amount to physically restraining him for the purpose of sub-para.(b) and they had also erred in taking the view that two carers could not watch over three residents at once for the purpose of sub-para.(c). To be "watching over" a claimant, the carer had to be awake and available to intervene but did not have to be actually watching the claimant all the time.

Commissioner's decision *R(DLA) 7/02* explores further the meaning of paras (b) and (c). The claimant was a 10-year-old boy suffering from Asbergers Syndrome and autism. The appeal from the tribunal (which had refused the claim) was allowed on the basis that they had failed to explain sufficiently why they found para.(5) not to be satisfied, but the Commissioner substituted his own decision to the same effect because he was satisfied that on the evidence before the tribunal, and confirmed to himself, the claimant could not satisfy para.(6). The claimant's mother said that he had no behavioural problems at the special school he attended, but that was because of the closely structured environment and the constant attention of a teacher. At home she said he became violent when she left the room, diverted her attention, or he could not get his own way. In the view of the Commissioner this evidence satisfied neither sub-para.(b) or (c). In his view the proper interpretation of (b) requires the person in attendance to have to intervene regularly in order to restrain, etc.; the words are not satisfied by showing that because the teacher is there, there is no need to intervene. Again, under (c) he thought the paragraph, read in context, required someone to be present in order to deal with the claimant when his behaviour became unpredictable. It was not sufficient that his mother's presence and attention would prevent the unpredictable behaviour occurring at all. This conclusion has been rejected by Judge Levenson in *LM v SSWP* [2008] UKUT 24 (AAC). There the claimant required intervention and supervision from her parents when she was at home, but, like the previous claimant, was not shown to need intervention at school because of the closely structured and controlled environment. In the judge's view to require that, both the supervision (or at least presence) and the intervention, should be continuous is to confuse paragraph (b) and paragraph (c). It is sufficient, in his view, if there is a regular (which in this context seems to mean usual or not infrequent) need for intervention and for the need for presence to be continuous because of unpredictability.

The Commissioner also refers to *CDLA/2054/1998* in which the Deputy Commissioner had suggested that the intervention and watching over elements should be focused on the claimant's needs when out of doors and away from the home because this test was directed towards a mobility component. The Commissioner in this case rejects that restriction. In his view the words of the Regulation are too plain—they require "regular intervention" and "watching over whenever he is awake". In *R(DLA) 9/02* the Commissioner also held that para.(c) is not satisfied where the child could be left alone in a specially adapted room that ensured his safety, nor could the test be satisfied where the person supervising was on the other side of a closed door; in order to be "present and watching over", immediate physical presence was necessary. Though a more lenient approach was adopted by the Commissioner in *CDLA/2470/2006*.

The difficulty experienced by a claimant seeking the higher rate of mobility component under paras (5) and (6) is further demonstrated by Commissioner Williams in *CDLA/1545/2004*. This case concerned a claimant suffering from Tourettes syndrome. The claimant had originally been allowed both the higher rate of care component and the higher rate of mobility. This appeal was from a renewal decision in which he had been allowed the highest rate of care, but only the lower rate of mobility. The appeal was allowed because, in the view of the Commissioner the tribunal had failed to explain why they were deciding against him with regard to mobility on the current claim, when the claimant's condition had not been found to have changed. (See the decision of Commissioner Howell in *R(M) 1/96* as to the need for a DM to make clear why a different conclusion had been reached on the renewal claim.) The Commissioner in this case makes a useful review of the decisions on these paragraphs so far, and concludes that the appeal should be sent back to a fresh tribunal for them to consider the medical evidence as to whether the requirements of reg.12(5) were satisfied. The evidence for the decision currently under appeal was unclear—the consultant confirmed moderate learning difficulties, but said they were of "non specific cause" going on to refer to Tourettes syndrome and mental health problems. The same or similar evidence had been accepted as qualifying the claimant by a DM on the original claim. The Commissioner thought the tribunal should have at least considered the earlier evidence to explain why the current decision was different, and that, if the evidence was unclear, perhaps they should have asked for a further opinion. On para.(6) the medical evidence was equally ambivalent. The consultant firstly answered yes to the question did the claimant require regular restraint but, in expanding upon that answer, appeared to be saying no, only to be followed by further information that might have confirmed the first impression. This last information was that the claimant was responding well to a strategy of enhanced supervision by two care helpers. The Commissioner thought that the new tribunal should enquire further into that, although it is not clear whether in suggesting this approach he was disagreeing with the decision in *R(DLA) 7/02* where it was said that supervision which precluded the need for intervention or removed the element of unpredictable behaviour could not entitle the claimant to benefit because he would not then satisfy the words of sub-paras (b) or (c). In the event, though, the non compliance with para.(6) had to be returned to the new tribunal because it appeared to have been raised in the decision only by the tribunal itself, and it was not clear that it had been put to the claimant's representative for him to deal with it.

Paras (7) and (8)

4.70   These paras have been inserted despite the opposition of the Social Security Advisory Committee. Their purpose is to negative the effect of certain words used, in passing, in the decision of the Tribunal of Commissioners *R(DLA) 4/01*.

That decision was chiefly concerned with the question of whether attention or supervision which qualified the claimant for care component could equally qualify him for lower rate mobility component when it consisted of supervision of outdoor walking.

The Tribunal of Commissioners held that it could, but in doing so remarked also that when a claimant had some disability (e.g. prelingual deafness) which inhibited his ability to go out alone through fear of getting lost and being unable to seek assistance, that this "fear and anxiety" should provide the causal link between that physical disability and his inability to take advantage of outdoor mobility. In his statement to Parliament the Secretary of State explains that the purpose of this amendment is to prevent that phrase from being used too widely to extend to anyone with a disability who then expresses a fear of going out alone because of that disability. Regrettably the Secretary of State did not respond to the request of SSAC for specific examples to be given to illustrate the intended operation and limits of these new paragraphs. While it is understandable that the department might wish to stem the possible flood of claims from, say, those suffering from a heart condition who might be afraid to walk out alone, it could be argued that fear and anxiety about onset of a heart condition is no less limiting than fear and anxiety of becoming lost for the prelingually deaf; and if not the deaf then what of the blind. It is generally accepted that the lower rate of mobility component was introduced to provide some benefit to claimants such as *Mallinson* who could not undertake routes unfamiliar to them because of blindness. Yet what was Mr. Mallinson's inability to walk unfamiliar routes based upon other than a fear that, if he did so, he might injure himself? To carry the effect of this amendment so far would be absurd, and the Secretary of State's statement to Parliament says clearly that there is no dispute with the conclusion reached in *R(DLA) 4/01* which did accord entitlement to three prelingually deaf claimants.

Paragraph (8) also provides a saving for those whose fear and anxiety is a symptom of mental disability and is so severe as to prevent the person from walking alone. The statement recognises that there will be difficulty in defining a line at which fear and anxiety become a severe mental disability. It seems likely that a clear medical diagnosis will be necessary.

The operation of these paragraphs has been considered in *R(DLA) 3/04* where the claimant was unable to walk outside for any distance unless she was accompanied by a member of her family who could, by giving her reassurance and encouragement, prevent her from having panic attacks. These attacks were a symptom of a severe state of anxiety and depression from which she was suffering. Commissioner Rowland allowed her appeal, finding that although her inability to walk outside clearly arose from fear and anxiety it was equally clear that, in her case, that anxiety was a symptom of her mental illness. The wording of para.(8) did not require that the mental disability should be some illness other than the anxiety itself.

These paragraphs were also considered in *CSDLA/430/2004*. There, the claimant suffered from asthma and also a chronic anxiety state that made him reluctant to walk outside alone for fear of suffering an asthma attack. Commissioner Parker, in allowing an appeal, points out that in this case there are really two separate questions to be answered. The first, (referring to para.(8)) is whether the anxiety attack was a symptom of mental illness and whether it was so severe as to prevent him walking unaccompanied. The second, and wholly separate question, (in accordance with s.73(1)(d)) was whether real asthma attacks did occur that disabled him, so as to make it necessary for him to be accompanied for the purpose of supervision for most of the time.

[¹ Hospitalisation in mobility component cases

12A.—(1) Subject to regulation 12B (exemption), it shall be a condition for the receipt of a disability living allowance which is attributable to entitlement to the mobility component for any period in respect of any person that during that period he is not maintained free of charge while undergoing medical or other treatment as an in-patient—

(a) in a hospital or similar institution under the NHS Act of 1977, the NHS Act of 1978 or the NHS Act of 1990; or

(b) in a hospital or other similar institution maintained or administered by the Defence Council.

(2) For the purposes of paragraph (1)(a) a person shall only be regarded as not being maintained free of charge in a hospital or similar institution during any period when his accommodation and services are provided under section 65 of the NHS Act of 1977, section 58 of, or paragraph 14 of Schedule 7A to, the NHS Act of 1978 or paragraph 14 of Schedule 2 to the NHS Act of 1990.]

[² (2A) For the purposes of paragraph (1), a period during which a person is maintained free of charge while undergoing medical or other treatment as an in-patient shall be deemed to begin on the day after the day on which he enters a hospital or similar institution referred to in that paragraph and to end on the day [³ before the day] on which he leaves such a hospital or similar institution.]

4.71

AMENDMENTS

1. Social Security (Disability Living Allowance and Claims and Payments) Amendment Regulations 1996 (SI 1996/1436), reg.2 (July 31, 1996).

2. Social Security (Hospital In-Patients, Attendance Allowance and Disability Living Allowance) (Amendment) Regulations 1999 (SI 1999/1326) (June 7, 1999).

3. Social Security (Attendance Allowance and Disability Living Allowance) (Amendment) Regulations 2000, (SI 2000/1401) reg.3 (June 19, 2000).

GENERAL NOTE

Until this regulation was introduced in 1996, the mobility component of disability living allowance, like mobility allowance before it, was payable however long the claimant was in hospital. It was only if a claimant ceased to be able to benefit at all from enhanced facilities for locomotion (see s.73(8) of the Social Security Contributions and Benefits Act 1992) that he might lose entitlement. Regs 12B and 12C set out a large number of exemptions and adjustments to the basic rule.

An argument that this regulation was *ultra vires* was rejected in *R. v Secretary of State for Social Security Ex p. Perry and Ex p. McGillivray* (CA, June 30, 1998). In *CDLA/1338/02* a further attack based on the argument that the regulation was contrary to the Human Rights Act 1998 was also rejected. The Commissioner held that he would not regard the right to a non-contributory benefit as a "possession" to be protected by Art.1. Neither did he think that the withdrawal of the benefit for those in a publicly funded hospital could be regarded as discriminatory under Art.14 because decisions based upon the source of funding could not be regarded as unjustified or irrational.

4.72

[¹ Exemption from regulation 12A

4.73   **12B.**—(1) Subject to paragraph (2), regulation 12A shall not apply to a person—

(a) for the first 28 days; or

(b) where he has not attained the age of 16, for the first 84 days,

of any period throughout which he is a person to whom paragraph (10) applies.

(2) Where, on the day on which a person's entitlement to the mobility component commences, he is a person to whom paragraph (10) applies, paragraph (1) shall not apply to him for any period of consecutive days, beginning with that day, in which he continues to be a person to whom paragraph (10) applies.

(3) For the purposes of paragraphs (1) and (4), two or more distinct periods separated by an interval not exceeding 28 days, or by two or more such intervals, shall be treated as a continuous period equal in duration to the total of such distinct periods and ending on the last day of the later such period.

(4) Subject to paragraph (5) and regulation 12C, where—

(a) immediately before 31st July 1996, a person has, for a continuous period of not less than 365 days, been a person to whom paragraph (10) applies and in receipt of the mobility component and on 31st July 1996 is a person to whom that paragraph applies; or

(b) on a day not more than 28 days prior to 31st July 1996, a person has, for a continuous period of not less than 365 days, been a person to whom paragraph (10) applies and in receipt of the mobility component, and on or after 31st July 1996 and not more than 28 days after the last day of the previous distinct period during which that paragraph applies, becomes a person to whom that paragraph again applies,

regulation 12A shall not apply until such time as paragraph (10) first ceases to apply to him for more than 28 consecutive days.

(5) Paragraph (4) shall not apply where on 31st July 1996 a person is detained under Part II or III of the Mental Health Act 1983 or [⁴ Part 5, 6 or 7 or section 136 of the Mental Health (Care and Treatment) (Scotland) Act 2003 or section 52D or 52M of the Criminal Procedure (Scotland) Act 1995].

(6) Where, on a day after 31st July 1996, a person—

(a) becomes detained under Part II or III of the Mental Health Act 1983 or [⁴ Part 5, 6 or 7 or section 136 of the Mental Health (Care and Treatment) (Scotland) Act 2003 or section 52D or 52M of the Criminal Procedure (Scotland) Act 1995].; or

(b) ceases to be entitled to the mobility component,

paragraph (4) shall cease to be applicable to that person and shall not again become applicable to him.]

(7) Subject to regulation 12C, where—

(a) on 31st July 1996, a person is a person to whom paragraph (10) applies and a Motability agreement entered into by or on behalf of that person is in force; or

(b) a person becomes a person to whom paragraph (10) applies on a day after 31st July 1996 and on that day there is in force a Motability agreement entered into by or on behalf of that person, regulation 12A shall, for the period following that referred to in paragraph (1)(a) or, as the case may be, paragraph (1)(b), continue not to apply to that person for the period referred to in paragraph (8) or, as the case may be, paragraph (9).

(8) Subject to paragraph (9), the period referred to in paragraph (7) shall terminate at the end of the period specified in regulation 44(3) or, as the case may be, regulation 44(4) of the Social Security (Claims and Payments) Regulations 1987 that is relevant to that Motability agreement.

(9) Where—

(a) the Motability agreement was made under the scheme run by Motability for wheelchairs;

(b) on the day immediately following the day that agreement ceases to be in force, a subsequent agreement of the same type is entered into by or on behalf of that person; and

(c) on the day referred to in sub-paragraph (b), the person is a person to whom paragraph (10) applies,

the period referred to in paragraph (7) shall terminate at the end of the period specified in regulation 44(3) or, as the case may be regulation 44(4) of the Social Security (Claims and Payments) Regulations 1987 that is relevant to the last such Motability agreement.

[² (9A) Regulation 12A shall not apply in the case of a person who is residing in a hospice and is terminally ill where the Secretary has been informed that he is terminally ill—

(a) on a claim for disability living allowance;

(b) on an application for a [³ revision under section 9 of the 1998 Act or supersession under section 10 of that Act] of an award of disability living allowance; or

(c) in writing in connection with an award of, or a claim for, or an application for [³ revision under section 9 of the 1998 Act or supersession under section 10 of that Act] of an award of, disability living allowance.]

(10) This paragraph refers to a person who is undergoing medical or other treatment in a hospital or other institution in any of the circumstances referred to in regulation 12A.

(11) For the purposes of paragraph (4), receipt of mobility allowance prior to 6th April 1992 shall be treated as receipt of the mobility component.

(12) In this regulation—

[² (za) "hospice" has the same meaning as that given in paragraph (7) of regulation 10;]

(a) "motability agreement" means an agreement such as is referred to in regulation 44(1) of the Social Security (Claims and Payments) Regulations 1987 (payment of disability living allowance on behalf of a beneficiary in settlement of liability for payments under an agreement for the hire or hire-purchase of a vehicle);

(b) "Motability" means the company, set up under that name as a charity and originally incorporated under the Companies Act 1985 and subsequently incorporated by Royal Charter.]

AMENDMENTS

1. Social Security (Disability Living Allowance and Claims, and Payments) Amendment Regulations 1996 (SI 1996/1436), reg.2 (July 31, 1996).

2. Social Security (Disability Living Allowance) Amendment Regulations 1996 (SI 1996/1767), reg.2 (July 31, 1996).

3. Social Security Act 1998 (Commencement No. 11, and Savings and Consequential and Transitional Provisions) Order 1999 (SI 1999/2860), Sch.7 (October 18, 1999).

4. Mental Health (Care and Treatment) (Scotland) Act 2003 (Consequential Provisions) Order 2005 (SI 2005/2078), Sch.2, para.13 (October 5, 2005).

[¹ Adjustment of benefit to certain persons exempted from regulation 12A

4.74 **12C.**—(1) Subject to paragraph (3), where a person is a person to whom regulation 12B(4) applies and the mobility component would otherwise be payable at the higher rate prescribed by regulation 4(2)(a), the benefit shall be adjusted so that it is payable at the lower rate prescribed by regulation 4(2)(b).

(2) Subject to paragraph (3), where regulation 12B(7) applies, the benefit shall be adjusted so that it is payable at a rate equal to the weekly amount payable under the relevant agreement for the period referred to in that regulation.

(3) Where paragraphs (4) and (7) of regulation 12B both apply, the benefit shall be adjusted so that it is payable either at the lower rate prescribed by regulation 4(2)(b) or at a rate equal to the weekly amount payable under the relevant agreement referred to in regulation 12B(7), whichever is the greater.]

AMENDMENT

1. Social Security (Disability Living Allowance and Claims and Payments) Amendment Regulations 1996 (SI 1996/1436), reg.2 (July 31, 1996).

Invalid Vehicle Scheme

4.75 **13.**—Schedule 2, which relates to the entitlement to mobility component of certain persons eligible for invalid carriages shall have effect.

SCHEDULES

SCHEDULE 1   **Regulation 3(4)**

PERSONS AGED 65 AND OVER

[¹ Revision or Supersession] of an award made before person attained 65

4.76 **1.**—(1) This paragraph applies where—
   (a) a person is aged 65 or over;
   (b) the person has an award of disability living allowance made before he attained the age of 65;
   (c) an application [¹ is made in accordance with section 9 of the 1998 Act or section 10 of that Act for that award to be revised or superseded.]
   (d) an adjudicating authority is satisfied that the decision awarding disability living allowance ought to be [¹ revised or superseded.]

(2) Where paragraph (1) applies, the person to whom the award relates shall not, subject to paragraph (3), be precluded from entitlement to either component of disability living allowance solely by reason of the fact that he is aged 65 or over when the [¹ revision or supersession] is made.

(3) Where the adjudicating authority determining the application is satisfied that the decision ought to be [¹ superseded] on the ground that there has been a relevant change of circumstances since the decision was given, paragraph (2) shall apply only where the relevant change of circumstances occurred before the person attained the age of 65.

[¹ Revision or Superssesion of an award other than a review to which paragraph 1 refers

2.—References in the following paragraphs of this Schedule to a [¹ revision or supersession] of an award refer only to those [¹revisions or supersessions] where the awards which are being [¹ revised or superseded] were made—

    (a) on or after the date the person to whom the award relates attained the age of 65; or

    (b) before the person to whom the award relates attained the age of 65 where the award is [¹ superseded] by reference to a change in the person's circumstances which occurred on or after the day he attained the age of 65.

4.77

Age 65 and over and entitled to the care component

3.—(1) This paragraph applies where a person on or after attaining the age of 65—

    (a) is entitled to the care component and an adjudicating authority is satisfied that the decision awarding it ought to be [¹ revised under section 9 of the 1998 Act or superseded under section 10 of that Act]; or

    (b) makes a renewal claim for disability living allowance.

(2) Where a person was entitled on the previous award or on the award [¹ being revised or superseded] to the care component payable—

    (a) at the lowest rate, that person shall not be precluded, solely by reason of the fact that he is aged 65 or over, from entitlement to the care component; or

    (b) at the middle or highest rate, that person shall not be precluded, solely by reason of the fact that he has attained the age of 65, from entitlement to the care component payable at the middle or highest rate,

but in determining that person's entitlement, [² section 72] of the Act shall have effect as if in paragraph (a) of subsection (2) of that section for the reference to 3 months there was substituted a reference to 6 months and paragraph (b) of that subsection was omitted.

(3) In this paragraph, a renewal claim is a claim made for a disability living allowance where the person making the claim had—

    (a) within the period of 12 months immediately preceding the date the claim was made, been entitled under an earlier award to the care component or to attendance allowance (referred to in this paragraph as "the previous award"); and

    (b) attained the age of 65 before that entitlement ended.

4.78

Invalid Vehicle Scheme

4.—(1) Where—

    (a) a certificate issued in respect of a person under section 13(1) of the Social Security (Miscellaneous Provisions) Act 1977 is in force, or

    (b) an invalid carriage or other vehicle is or was on or after January 1, 1976 made available to a person by the Secretary of State under section 5(2)(a) of the NHS Act of 1977 or section 46(1) of the NHS Act of 1978, being a carriage or other vehicle which is—

        (i) propelled by a petrol engine or an electric motor;

        (ii) provided for use on a public road; and

        (iii) controlled by the occupant,

that person shall not be precluded from entitlement to mobility component payable at the higher rate specified in regulation 4(2)(a), or a care component payable at the highest or middle rate specified in regulation 4(1)(a) or (b) by reason only that he has attained the age of 65.

(2) In determining a person's entitlement where paragraph (1) applies, [² section 72] of the Act shall have effect as if in paragraph (a) of subsection (2) of that section for the reference to 3 months there was substituted a reference to 6 months and paragraph (b) of that subsection was omitted.

4.79

Age 65 or over and entitled to mobility component

5.—(1) This paragraph applies where a person on or after attaining the age of 65 is entitled to the mobility component payable at the higher rate specified in regulation 4(2)(a), and—

    (a) an adjudicating authority is satisfied that the decision giving effect to that entitlement ought to be [¹ revised under section 9 of the 1998 Act or superseded under section 10 of that Act], or

    (b) the person makes a renewal claim for disability living allowance.

(2) A person to whom this paragraph applies shall not be precluded, solely by reason of the fact that he has attained the age of 65, from entitlement to the mobility component by virtue of having satisfied or being likely to satisfy one or other of the conditions mentioned in subsection (1)(a), (b) or (c) of [² section 73] of the Act.

4.80

(3) In this paragraph and paragraph 6 and 7 a renewal claim is a claim made for a disability living allowance where the person making the claim had—

(a) within the period of 12 months immediately preceding the date the claim was made been entitled under an earlier award to the mobility component (referred to in these paragraphs as "the previous award"); and

(b) attained the age of 65 before that entitlement ended.

Aged 65 or over and award of lower rate mobility component

4.81   **6.**—(1) This paragraph applies where a person on or after attaining the age of 65 is entitled to the mobility component payable at the lower rate specified in regulation 4(2) and—

(a) an adjudicating authority is satisfied that the decision giving effect to that entitlement ought to be [¹ revised under section 9 of the 1998 Act or superseded under section 10 of that Act], or

(b) the person makes a renewal claim for disability living allowance.

(2) A person to whom this paragraph applies shall not be precluded, solely by reason of the fact that he has attained the age of 65, from entitlement to the mobility component, but in determining the person's entitlement to that component [² section 73](11) of the Act shall have effect in his case as if paragraph (a), and the words "in any other case" in paragraph (b), were omitted.

Award of care component where person entitled to mobility component

4.82   **7.**—(1) This paragraph applies where a person on or after attaining the age of 65 is entitled to the mobility component and—

(a) an adjudicating authority is satisfied that the decision giving effect to that entitlement ought to be [¹ revised under section 9 of the 1998 Act or superseded under section 10 of that Act], or

(b) the person makes a renewal claim for disability living allowance.

(2) A person to whom this paragraph applies shall not be precluded solely by reason of the fact that he has attained the age of 65 from entitlement under [² section 72](1) of the Act by virtue of having satisfied either the conditions mentioned in subsection (1)(b) or in subsection (1)(c), or in both those subsections, but in determining a person's entitlement, [² section 72] of the Act shall have effect as if in paragraph (a) of subsection (2) of that section, for the reference to 3 months there was substituted a reference to 6 months and paragraph (b) of that subsection were omitted.

AMENDMENTS

1. Social Security Act 1998 (Commencement No. 11, and Savings and Consequential and Transitional Provisions) Order 1999 (SI 1999/2860), Sch.7 (October 18, 1999).

2. Social Security (Disability Living Allowance) (Amendment) Regulations 1993 (SI 1993/1939), reg.2(2) (August 26, 1993).

GENERAL NOTE

Para.1

4.83   This is concerned with reviews of awards which partly cover a period before the claimant's 65th birthday and partly cover a later period. On a review, entitlement in respect of the latter period is to be determined as though the claimant was under the age of 65 unless the review is on the ground of a change of circumstances which occurred on or after the claimant's 65th birthday (in which case see *para.2*). See *CSDLA/388/2000* noted after s.75 above.

The operation of para.1 of Sch.1. Is considered in some detail in *CDLA/301/05*. The claimant had been in receipt of the middle rate of DLA since before she attained the age of 65. Nine years later, and now over that age, she responded to a routine enquiry form sent out by the Secretary of State in consequence of which it was decided that her award should be superseded on the ground that it had been made under a mistake of fact; namely that she had ever needed any care at night. The claimant appealed against this decision, but added, as well, that in the event of that appeal failing she should be entitled to, at least, the lowest rate of DLA. At her present age the claimant could not, of course, succeed on the basis of a new claim. She could succeed only if the provisions of para.1 covered her case. (The rest of that schedule being appropriate only to cases where the award that was being reviewed had been made after the age of 65.) Paragraph 1 presented two difficulties. First, the opening words of para.(1)(c), "an application is made" seem to limit the operation of the paragraph to cases where the claimant has made an application for review, and in this case the claimant had not done so. Commissioner Mesher rejected the suggestion that the enquiry form should be treated as an application. He held instead, that the words above could not be read as limiting the paragraph in the way suggested. He did this after referring to the history of the legislation, which, prior to its amendment in 1999, would not have been so limited. The amendments that were then made were expressed to be only for giving effect to the new terminology introduced by the 1998 Act, and, therefore, he reasoned, could not have been intended to make a substantive change to the claimant's rights.

The second difficulty arose because there was some doubt as to whether this claimant's need for assistance in preparing a meal (which had been accepted by the appeal tribunal) had existed before she reached the age of 65, or had developed only later.

The Secretary of State, and the appeal tribunal contended that it was only in the former case that an award could now be made under para.1. Commissioner Mesher disagreed. In his view all the elements of para.1(1) were satisfied, and para.1(3) also was satisfied, because the change of circumstances on which the review was based, was the mistake of fact made on the original application before she reached the age of 65. This left para.1(2) to operate simply as it stated i.e. that her claim should not be precluded on the ground only that she was now over the age of 65. The whole case was returned to a new tribunal for reconsideration.

Para.2

This is concerned with reviews of awards relating solely to a period no earlier than the claimant's 65th birthday or to an award beginning before that birthday but reviewed on the ground of a change of circumstances which occurred on or after that birthday. In such cases, paras 3–7 have the effect that the conditions of entitlement may be different from those applying to younger claimants and are the same as those governing certain renewal claims made at or after the age of 65.

4.84

Para.3

On a review (within para.2) or a renewal claim (within sub-para.(3)), a person of or over 65 can continue to be entitled to the care component at the same rate as before or at a higher rate. A person who was previously entitled to the highest rate but no longer satisfies both the "day" and "night" conditions can also become entitled at the middle rate. However, a person previously entitled to either the highest or the middle rate and who no longer satisfies either of the "day" or "night" conditions cannot become entitled to the component at the lowest rate and so will cease to be entitled to any care component. Furthermore, the qualifying period required of those hoping for entitlement to the component at a higher rate than before, is six months rather than three months as it would be for younger claimants. The overall effect of this paragraph is to make the conditions for entitlement to the care component the same as those for entitlement to attendance allowance under s.64 of the Social Security Contributions and Benefits Act 1992 which is the benefit which a person would be required to claim if the claim were an entirely fresh one or a repeat claim too late to be included as a renewal claim within sub-para.(3).

4.85

Para.4

Former vehicle scheme beneficiaries who have attained the age of 65 are eligible for the middle or highest rates of the care component or the higher rate of the mobility component. The three-month qualifying period is increased to six months in respect of the care component but is removed altogether in the case of the mobility

4.86

component. This effectively re-creates the position as it was before disability living allowance replaced attendance allowance and mobility allowance on April 6, 1992. Under s.74(1) of the Social Security Contributions and Benefits Act 1992, a person issued with a certificate under Sch.2 to these Regulations is deemed to satisfy the conditions for the mobility component at the higher rate.

Para. 5

4.87   On a review (within para.2) or a renewal claim (within sub-para.(3)), a person of or over 65 previously entitled to the higher rate of the mobility component can continue to be entitled to the higher rate even if the ground of entitlement is different. However, if he or she no longer satisfies one of the conditions for entitlement to the higher rate, he or she cannot qualify for the lower rate instead. See *CDLA/754/2000* noted after s.75 above.

Para. 6

4.88   On a review (within para.2) or a renewal claim (within para.5(3)), a person of or over 65 previously entitled to the lower rate of the mobility component can still be awarded the lower rate but cannot qualify for the higher rate. However, if he or she does not qualify for the lower rate on the usual ground (by satisfying the condition of s.73(1)(d) of the Social Security Contributions and Benefits Act 1992), the claimant may qualify by satisfying one of the conditions of s.73(1)(a), (b) or (c) which are usually the grounds for qualifying for the higher rate.

Para. 7

4.89   On a review (within para.2) or a renewal claim (within para.5(3)), a person of or over 65 previously entitled to the mobility component can be awarded the care component at the higher or middle rates but the qualifying period for the care component is six months rather than the usual three months for younger claimants. Effectively, the conditions are then the same as for attendance allowance which is what a claimant of that age would claim if he or she were not entitled to the mobility component.

SCHEDULE 2   **Regulation 13**

INVALID VEHICLE SCHEME

Interpretation

4.90   1.— In this Sch., unless the context otherwise requires,—
        "the 1977 Act" means the Social Security (Miscellaneous Provisions) Act 1977;
        "vehicle scheme beneficiary" means any person of a class specified in section 13(3)(a), (c) or (d) of the 1977 Act or any person of the class specified in section 13(3)(b) of the 1977 Act whose application was approved on or after 1st January 1976 and, where an invalid carriage or other vehicle was provided or as the case may be applied for, is a person of any such class in respect of whom the invalid carriage or other vehicle provided or applied for was a vehicle—
        (a) propelled by a petrol engine or by an electric motor,
        (b) supplied for use on a public road, and
        (c) to be controlled by the occupant;
        "certificate" means a certificate issued in accordance with paragraph 3.

Prescribed periods for purposes of section 13(3)(c) of the 1977 Act

4.91   2.—For the purposes of section 13(3)(c) of the 1977 Act—
        (a) the prescribed period before 1 January 1976 shall be that commencing with 31st January 1970 and ending with 31st December 1975; and
        (b) the prescribed period after 1st January 1976 shall be that commencing with 2nd January 1976 and ending with 31st March 1978.

Issue of certificates

3.—(1) The Secretary of State shall issue a certificate in the form approved by him in respect of any person—
    (a) who has made an application for a certificate in the form approved by the Secretary of State; and
    (b) whom the Secretary of State considers satisfies the conditions specified in subparagraph (2).
  (2) The conditions specified in this sub-paragraph are that—
    (a) the person is a vehicle scheme beneficiary; and
    (b) his physical condition has not improved to such an extent that he no longer satisfies the conditions which it was necessary for him to satisfy in order to become a vehicle scheme beneficiary.

4.92

Duration and cancellation of certificates

4.—(1) Subject to sub-paragraph (2) the period during which a certificate is in force shall commence on the day specified in the certificate as being the date on which it comes into force and shall continue for the life of the person concerned.
  (2) If in any case the Secretary of State determines that the condition specified in paragraph 3(2)(b) is not satisfied, the certificate shall cease to be in force from the date of such non-satisfaction as determined by the Secretary of State (or such later date as appears to the Secretary of State to be reasonable in the circumstances).

4.93

Application of these Regulations in relation to vehicle scheme beneficiaries

5.—In relation to a person in respect of whom a certificate is in force these Regulations shall have effect as though regulation 2(1)(a)(iii) were omitted.

4.94

GENERAL NOTE

These provisions replace the Mobility Allowance (Vehicle Scheme Beneficiaries) Regulations 1977 (SI 1977/1229). A person issued with a certificate under this Schedule is deemed, by s.74(1) of the Social Security Contributions and Benefits Act 1992, to satisfy the condition of s.73(1)(a) so that he or she can qualify for the mobility component at the higher rate. He or she is also deemed to have satisfied that condition during the three-month qualifying period. Paragraph 1 of Sch.1 to these Regulations entitles such a person to the mobility component notwithstanding that he or she has attained the age of 65. Note that, under reg.7 of the 1977 Regulations, a person could be entitled to mobility allowance for a period *before* the date of claim for the allowance as long as it was after the certificate came into force. No equivalent provision appears in respect of the mobility component of disability living allowance.

4.95

[1 SCHEDULE 3   **Regulation 9A(1)**

PERSONS TO WHOM REGULATIONS 9 AND 10 APPLY WITH MODIFICATIONS

4.96

[¹ . . .]

REPEAL

1. Social Security Amendment (Residential Care and Nursing Homes) Regulations 2001 (SI 2001/3767), reg.4 (April 8, 2002).

Social Security (Invalid Care Allowance) Regulations 1976

(SI 1976/409) (*as amended*)

ARRANGEMENT OF REGULATIONS

PART I

GENERAL

PART II

MISCELLANEOUS PROVISIONS RELATING TO INVALID CARE ALLOWANCE

The Secretary of State for Social Services, in exercise of the powers conferred upon her by sections 13(4), 37, 40(2), 49, 79(1), 80, 81(1), (2) and (6), 82(1),

(5) and (6), 84(1) and (2), 85(1), 86(5) and 119(3) of the Social Security Act 1975, section 36(7) of the National Insurance Act 1965, as continued in force by regulation 2(2) of the Social Security (Graduated Retirement Benefit) Regulations 1975, and of all other powers enabling her in that behalf, and after reference to the National Insurance Advisory Committee, hereby makes the following regulations:

PART I

GENERAL

Citation and commencement

1.—These regulations may be cited as the Social Security (Invalid Care Allowance) Regulations 1976 and shall come into operation on 12th April 1976.

4.98

Interpretation

2.—[¹ (1) In these Regulations, "the Contributions and Benefits Act" means the Social Security Contributions and Benefits Act 1992].

4.99

(2) Any reference in these regulations to any provision made by or contained in any enactment or instrument shall, except in so far as the context otherwise requires, be construed as a reference to that provision as amended or extended by any enactment or instrument and as including a reference to any provision whichmay re-enact or replace it, withor without modification.

(3) The rules for the construction of Acts of Parliament contained in the Interpretation Act 1889 shall apply for the purposes of the interpretation of these regulations as they apply for the purposes of the interpretation of an Act of Parliament.

AMENDMENT

1. Social Security (Invalid Care Allowance) Amendment Regulations 1996 (SI 1996/2744), reg.2 (November 25, 1996).

[¹ Disapplication of section 1(1A) of the Administration Act

2A.—Section 1(1A) of the Administration Act (requirement to state national insurance number) shall not apply—

4.100

(a) [² *omitted*];

(b) to any claim for [³ carer's allowance] made or treated as made before 9th February, 1998;

(c) to an adult dependant in respect of whom a claim for an increase of [³ carer's allowance] is made or treated as made before 5th October, 1998.]

[⁴ (d) to an adult dependant who—

    (i) is a person in respect of whom a claim for an increase of carer's allowance is made;

    (ii) is subject to immigration control within the meaning of section 115(9)(a) of the Immigration and Asylum Act 1999; and

    (iii) has not previously been allocated a national insurance number.]

AMENDMENTS

1. Social Security (National Insurance Information: Exemption) Regulations (SI 1997/2676) (December 1, 1997).

2. Social Security (Working Tax Credit and Child Tax Credit) (Consequential Amendments) (No. 2) Regulations 2003 (SI 2003/937), reg.2 (April 6, 2003).

3. Social Security Amendment (Carer's Allowance) Regulations 2002 (SI 2002/2497), reg.3 (April 1, 2003).

4. Social Security (National Insurance Number Information: Exemption) Regulations 2009, (SI 2009/471), reg.2 (April 6, 2009).

PART II

MISCELLANEOUS PROVISIONS RELATING TO INVALID CARE ALLOWANCE

Prescribed payments out of public funds which constitute the persons in respect of whom they are payable as severely disabled persons

4.101

3.—(1) For the purposes of [¹ Section 70 of the Contributions and Benefits Act] [² carer's allowance] the prescribed payments out of public funds which constitute the persons in respect of whom they are payable as severely disabled persons are—

(a) a payment under [¹ section 104 of the Contributions and Benefits Act] (increase of disablement pension where constant attendance needed);

(b) a payment suchas is referred to in section 7(3)(b) of the Industrial Injuries and Diseases (Old Cases) Act 1975 (increase of an allowance under that Act where the person in respect of whom that allowance is payable requires constant attendance as a result of his disablement);

(c) a payment under regulation 44 of the Social Security (Industrial Injuries) (Benefit) Regulations 1975 in respect of the need of constant attendance;

(d) a payment by way of an allowance in respect of constant attendance on account of disablement for which a person is in receipt of a war disablement pension,

being a payment the weekly rate of which is not less than the amount specified in [¹ paragraph 7(a) of Part V of Schedule 4 to the Contributions and Benefits Act].

(2) For the purposes of paragraph (1)(d) of this regulation "war disablement pension" means—

(a) retired pay, pension or allowance granted in respect of disablement under powers conferred by or under the Ministry of Pensions Act 1916, the Air Force (Constitution) Act 1917, the Personal Injuries (Emergency Provisions) Act 1939, the Pensions (Navy, Army, Air Force and Mercantile Marine) Act 1939, the Polish Resettlement Act 1947, the Home Guard Act 1951 or the Ulster Defence Regiment Act 1969,

(b) any retired pay or pension to which section 365(1) of the Income and Corporation Taxes Act 1970 applies, not being retired pay, pension or allowance to which sub-paragraph (a) of this paragraph applies; or

(c) any payment which the Secretary of State has certified can be accepted as being analogous to any suchretired pay, pension or allowance as is referred to in sub-paragraph (a) or (b) of this paragraph.

AMENDMENTS

1. Social Security (Invalid Care Allowance) Amendment Regulations 1996 (SI 1996/2744), reg.2 (November 25, 1996).
2. Social Security Amendment (Carer's Allowance) Regulations 2002 (SI 2002/2497), reg.3 (April 1, 2003).

Circumstances in which persons are or are not to be treated as engaged or regularly and substantially engaged in caring for severely disabled persons

4.—(1) [¹ Subject to paragraph (1A) of this regulation,] a person shall be treated as engaged and as regularly and substantially engaged in caring, for a severely disabled person on every day in a week if, and shall not be treated as engaged or regularly and substantially engaged in caring for a severely disabled person on any day in a week unless, as at that week he is, or is likely to be, engaged and regularly engaged for at least 35 hours a week in caring for that severely disabled person.

[¹ (1A) A person who is caring for two or more severely disabled persons in a week shall be treated as engaged and regularly and substantially engaged in caring for a severely disabled person only where he is engaged and regularly engaged for at least 35 hours in that week in caring for any one severely disabled person, considered without reference to any other severely disabled person for whom he is caring.]

(2) A week in respect of which a person fails to satisfy the requirements of paragraph (1) of this regulation shall be treated as a week in respect of which that person satisfies those requirements if he establishes—

(a) that he has only temporarily ceased to satisfy them; and
(b) that (disregarding the provisions of this sub-paragraph) he has satisfied them for at least 14 weeks in the period of 26 weeks ending with that week and would have satisfied them for at least 22 weeks in that period but for the fact that either he or the severely disabled person for whom he has been caring was undergoing medical or other treatment as an inpatient in a hospital or similar institution.

AMENDMENT

1. Social Security (Invalid Care Allowance) Amendment (No. 2) Regulations 1993 (SI 1993/1851), reg.2 (August 17, 1993).

GENERAL NOTE

Para. (1)

A person is entitled to benefit in respect of "any day" on which he is caring, etc. for his patient (see s.70(1) SSCBA 1992). This regulation, however, has the effect of shifting the entitlement to the basis of a week by providing that every day in the week will qualify where the 35-hour test is satisfied, and that no day in the week will qualify where it is not (except under para.(2) below). This is much more administratively convenient.

The decision in *R(G) 3/91* confirms that the hours must be counted in respect of

4.102

4.103

each week and cannot be averaged over a period of weeks to satisfy the 35 hour rule.

Note that for Carer's Allowance a week is defined in s.122 as a period from Sunday to Saturday—this may affect a claimant who cares only on alternate week-ends.

A person qualifies for benefit where "he is, or is likely to be, engaged and regularly engaged" in caring for a patient for at least 35 hours per week. There are several difficulties in this phrase but none of them seem to have caused problems. It may be easy to determine that a person "is engaged . . . in caring," but it is not clear what is meant by "is likely to be . . . engaged". The words are probably intended to be prospective so that the benefit can be awarded for a forward period, but they might extend to cover an unexpected temporary absence by the claimant. If the absence is short and no more in total than four weeks in six months the matter would be covered by para.(2) below, but if those weeks have already been consumed or allocated to a "holiday" period, there may be an argument for saying that an unexpected absence due to, say, illness, continues to satisfy para.(1) as being a week in which the claimant had been "likely to be" caring.

Nor does the definition tell us anything about what is meant by "regularly engaged". It is probably sufficient if the care arrangement is intended to be for a reasonable period. It might preclude, for example, someone who is on unpaid holiday from his job, or a student in his vacation.

The activities of the claimant that can be regarded as caring and consequently can satisfy the 35-hour test of caring are considered in two recent unreported Commissioners' decisions: *CG/012/1991* and *CG/006/1990*. See the discussion of these decisions at s.70 of the Act.

Para.(1A)

4.104   This amendment reverses (from August 1993) the effect of an unreported Commissioners' decision that permitted a claimant to aggregate the hours spent in looking after more than one patient to satisfy the total of 35 hours per week. In that case the claimant was the mother of two severely disabled sons neither of whom could stay at home for a full week, but the claimant could look after each of them separately, for part of the week—in some weeks their combined time at home amounted to more than 35 hours per week. This paragraph now precludes such an arrangement. The only scheme now possible would involve each son staying at home for 35 hours (if that were possible) in alternate weeks. A system of care every other week, if consistent, should still be regarded as "regular".

Para.(2)

4.105   A break in the provision of care is disregarded so long as the break is temporary and so long as it has lasted, or a series of breaks has totalled, no more than four weeks in the past 26 weeks (or 12 weeks in the past 26 if the patient or the claimant has spent at least eight of those weeks in hospital for treatment). In effect the claimant can enjoy a break or "holiday" from his caring of up to four weeks in every six months. Benefit will continue to be payable for the weeks of holiday, but if the claimant continues to receive the benefit himself, it cannot be paid as well to any person who provides substitute care during that period. (See s.70(7) of the Act.)

The decision in *Secretary of State for Work and Pensions v Pridding*, [2002] EWCA Civ 306, CA, reported as *R(G)1/02* limits the effect of this regulation. It does not extend entitlement where the person cared for, has entered hospital beyond the four week period for which that person will be entitled to their own benefits.

Circumstances in which persons are to be regarded as receiving full-time education

4.106   [[1] 5.—(1) For the purposes of [[2] section 70(3) of the Contributions and Benefits Act] a person shall be treated as receiving full-time education for any period during which he attends a course of education at a university, college, school or other educational establishment for twenty-one hours or more a week.

(2) In calculating the hours of attendance under paragraph (1) of this regulation—

(a) there shall be included the time spent receiving instruction or tuition, undertaking supervised study, examination or practical work or taking part in any exercise, experiment or project for which provision is made in the curriculum of the course; and

(b) there shall be excluded any time occupied by meal breaks or spent on unsupervised study, whether undertaken on or off the premises of the educational establishment.

(3) In determining the duration of a period of full-time education under paragraph (1) of this regulation, a person who has started on a course of education shall be treated as attending it for the usual number of hours per week throughout any vacation or any temporary interruption of his attendance until the end of the course or such earlier date as he abandons it or is dismissed from it.]

AMENDMENTS

1. Social Security (Invalid Care Allowance) Amendment Regulations 1992 (SI 1992/470).
2. Social Security (Invalid Care Allowance) Amendment Regulations 1996 (SI 1996/2744), reg.2 (November 25, 1996).

GENERAL NOTE

This meaning to be given to the phase "full time education" has caused difficulty. This is because a claim for this benefit is the only context in which these words have to be applied to someone who is undertaking advanced, in some cases University, education. In *CG/4343/1998*, the Commissioner took the view that work would only be supervised when it was done under the guidance of an instructor, though that guidance could be through the medium of a computer programme or by telephone. But in *CG/5519/1999*, Commissioner Jacobs took the much wider view of supervision in the University context to include all work that was done in pursuance of an instructor's requirements—thus preparation for a discussion class or research for a set essay would be supervised work. Seemingly only peripheral, voluntary reading would be unsupervised. Commissioner Jacobs' decision has been upheld in the Court of Appeal (*Flemming v Secretary of State for Work and Pensions* [2002] EWCA Civ 641, May 10, 2002, reported as *R(G) 2/02*). This wider view also accords with a decision of the Court of Appeal in Northern Ireland in *Wright-Turner v Department for Social Development* [2002] CARC 3567, January 2002.

4.107

The application of this approach and in particular its operation in respect of an atypical student who had been granted exemption from parts of the course is considered in *CG/3189/2004*. There the case was referred to a fresh tribunal for re-consideration, to start again with the information provided (perhaps more accurately for the particular claimant) by the University.

The matter has been considered again by Judge Mesher in *AD v SSWP* [2009] UKUT 46 (AAC). He accepts the approach approved in *Fleming* and *Wright-Turner* the nuance that the test is not simply a matter of what the university authorities say they expect of students on their course, but is in the end a question of what the student in question properly does in fulfilment of that expectation. A particular student may limit their actual hours of study because of the exigencies of their caring responsibilities yet manage to satisfy the requirements of their course. While the evidence provided by the university will be highly presumptive of what the course requires in a case such as this, the DM and Tribunals should have regard as well to the evidence given by the student and ultimately they must make a finding of fact as to the hours spent in study.

Severely disabled persons prescribed for the purposes of [² section 70(1)(c) of the Contributions and Benefits Act]

4.108   [¹ **6.**—For the purposes of [² section 70(1)(c) of the Contributions and Benefits Act] (condition of entitlement to [³ a carer's allowance] that the severely disabled person is either such relative of the person caring for him as may be prescribed or a person of any such other description as may be prescribed) where a severely disabled person is being cared for by another person, that disabled person shall be a prescribed person for the purposes of that section, whether he is related to the person caring for him or not.]

AMENDMENTS

1. Social Security (Invalid Care Allowance) Amendment Regulations 1981 (SI 1981/655).
2. Social Security (Invalid Care Allowance) Amendment Regulations 1996 (SI 1996/2744), reg.2 (November 25, 1996).
3. Social Security Amendment (Carer's Allowance) Regulations 2002 (SI 2002/2497), reg.3 (April 1, 2003).

Manner of electing the person entitled to [¹ a carer's allowance] in respect of a severely disabled person where, but for [² section 70(7) of the Contributions and Benefits Act], more than one person would be entitled to [¹ a carer's allowance] in respect of that severely disabled person

4.109   **7.**—(1) For the purposes of the provision in [² section 70(7) of the Contributions and Benefits Act] which provides that where, apart from that section, two or more persons would be entitled for the same day to [¹ a carer's allowance] in respect of the same severely disabled person one of them only shall be entitled, being such one of them as they may jointly elect in the prescribed manner, an election shall be made by giving the Secretary of State a notice in writing signed by the persons who but for the said provision would be entitled to [¹ a carer's allowance] in respect of the same severely disabled person specifying one of them as the person to be entitled.

(2) An election under paragraph (1) of this regulation shall not be effective to confer entitlement to [¹ a carer's allowance] either for the day on which the election is made or for any earlier day if such day is one for which [¹ a carer's allowance] has been paid in respect of the severely disabled person in question and has not been repaid or recovered.

AMENDMENTS

1. Social Security Amendment (Carer's Allowance) Regulations 2002 (SI 2002/2497), reg.3 (April 1, 2003).
2. Social Security (Invalid Care Allowance) Amendment Regulations 1996 (SI 1996/2744), reg.2 (November 25, 1996).

Circumstances in which a person is or is not to be treated as gainfully employed

8.—(1) For the purposes of [³ section 70(1)(b) of the Contributions and Benefits Act] (condition of a person being entitled to [² a carer's allowance] for any day that he is not gainfully employed) a person shall not be treated as gainfully employed on any day in a week unless his earnings in the immediately preceding week have exceeded [³ [⁴ [⁶ £95]] and, subject to paragraph (2) of this regulation, shall be treated as gainfully employed on every day in a week if his earnings in the immediately preceding week have exceeded [³ [⁴ [⁶ £95]].

(2) There shall be disregarded for the purposes of paragraph (1) above a person's earnings—

(a) for any week which under paragraph (2) of regulation 4 of these regulations is treated as a week in which that person satisfies the requirements of paragraph (1) of that regulation;

(b) [⁵ . . .]

(c) [¹ . . .]

(3) *Revoked.*

4.110

AMENDMENTS

1. Social Security (Invalid Care Allowance) Amendment Regulations 1996 (SI 1996/2744), reg.2 (November 25, 1996 withsaving under reg.3).

2. Social Security Amendment (Carer's Allowance) Regulations 2002 (SI 2002/2497), reg.3 (April 1, 2003).

3. Social Security (Invalid Care Allowance) Amendment Regulations 1993 (SI 1993/316), reg.2 (April 12, 1993).

4. Social Security (Invalid Care Allowance) Amendment Regulations 2001 (SI 2001/538), reg.2 (April 6, 2001).

5. Social Security (Invalid Care Allowance) Amendment Regulations 1995 (SI 1995/2935), reg.2 (December 12, 1995 withsaving under reg.3).

6. Social Security (Miscellaneous Amendments) (No. 5) Regulations 2007, (SI 2007/2618) (October 1, 2007).

GENERAL NOTE

Para. (1)
Earnings include remuneration or profit from either employment or self-employment. See s.3 of the Act and definition of "employment" in s.122.

For the method of calculating earnings see Computation of Earnings Regulations.

In *CG/734/2003*, and again in *CG/4018/2005* it has been confirmed that those regulations do properly apply to the calculation of earnings for the purpose of the benefit, despite the doubts that had been expressed earlier in *CG/6329/1997*, on which see the 2005 edition of this work.

Note the observations of the Commissioner in *CG/607/2008*. Whereas most social security benefits (and most taxes) provide for a taper in respect of earnings that exceed an earnings limit, there is no such thing for Carer's Allowance; earnings that are a penny over the limit result in the total loss of benefit. In this case the claimant had taken part-time work for a charity working with the disabled. She was employed for 10 hours per week at an hourly rate calculated so that her earnings would exactly match the earnings limit currently in force. Such a carefully constructed and informed work plan should not have resulted in difficulties, but a complication arose from the fact that although the wages had been expressed to be a weekly sum, for the convenience

4.111

of the employer, they were, in fact, paid monthly. Because the regulations define benefit weeks for Carer's Allowance as being each week beginning on a Monday, and because some calendar months contain five Mondays rather than four, this meant that in those months her earnings, if spread over a calendar month, exceeded the weekly earnings limit. As this was discovered only after five years it meant that the claimant was faced with a substantial claim for overpayment. The complexity of the Computation of Earnings Regulations resulted in four different decisions, and four different overpayment claims, by the DM, together with a different calculation by the appeal tribunal (which had allowed her appeal) and yet another by her representative before the commissioner. The Commissioner came to the rescue of all of them. He suggested going back to basics. This meant examining the definitions of the concepts that are used in the regulations. From this it emerged that earnings should be the sums payable under the claimant's contract of employment. Although the contract was oral, it was clear both from the parties' intentions, and from their consistent pattern of behaviour over almost all of the five years, that her wages were to be earned weekly even though they may have been paid monthly. This meant that the correct attribution of earnings was on a weekly basis, not monthly. There were a few weeks early in the arrangement when the claimant had worked extra hours and therefore had exceeded the earnings limit, but for the most part she had remained within that limit and, therefore, her overpayment was minimal.

Another example of the all-or-nothing character of Invalid Care Allowance (Carer's Allowance) is *SJ v SSWP* [2009] UKUT 37 (AAC); *R(G) 1/09* where Judge Bano had to consider the effect of PAYE income tax liability on the claimant's earnings. The claimant was not liable to pay tax on her earnings, which were just above the earnings limit for the allowance, but, had she been in receipt of the allowance, she would then have been liable for income tax and that liability, if collected through PAYE, would have reduced her earnings to below the earnings limit, and she would then have been entitled to the allowance. This looks like a classic "Catch 22". But the refusal of benefit was correct. It is clear that Invalid Care Allowance (Carer's Allowance) is a taxable benefit (see Table A of the Income Tax (Earnings and Pensions) Act 1992) and it is also clear that the tax could, and normally would, be collected through the PAYE system, but to qualify for benefit, in the first place, the claimant must have earnings below the earnings limit, and that must be determined before the benefit is paid, not afterwards.

Para. (2)

4.112   This exempts from the earnings limit any week in which the claimant is on "holiday" from his patient. Para.(b) which exempted an employee absent from work with the consent of his employer was revoked with effect from December 12, 1995. Para.(c) which exempted earnings from the week preceding the first week of claim was revoked witheffect from November 25, 1996. In bothcases there is a saving provision in respect of continuous claims commencing before those dates.

Conditions relating to residence and presence in Great Britain

4.113   **9.**—(1) Subject to the following provisions of this regulation, the prescribed conditions for the purposes of [¹ section 70(4) of the Contributions and Benefits Act] (person not to be entitled to [² a carer's allowance] unless he satisfies prescribed conditions as to residence or presence in Great Britain) in relation to any person in respect of any day shall be—

(a) that he is ordinarily resident in Great Britain; and

[³ (ia) he is not a person subject to immigration control within the meaning of section 115(9) of the Immigration and Asylum Act 1999 or section 115 of that Act does not apply to him for the purposes of entitlement to invalid care allowance by virtue of regulation 2 of the Social

Security (Immigration and Asylum) Consequential Amendments Regulations 2000, and]
(b) that he is present in Great Britain; and
(c) that he has been present in Great Britain for a period of, or periods amounting in the aggregate to, not less than 26 weeks in the 12 months immediately preceding that day.

[⁴ (1A) [³ *omitted*]]

(2) For the purposes of paragraph (1)(b) and (c) of this regulation, a person who is absent from Great Britain on any day shall be treated as being present in Great Britain—
(a) if his absence is, and when it began was, for a temporary purpose and has not lasted for a continuous period exceeding 4 weeks; or
(b) if his absence is temporary and for the specific purpose of caring for the severely disabled person who is also absent from Great Britain and where attendance allowance [⁵, or the care component of disability living allowance at the highest or middle rate prescribed in accordance with [¹ section 72(3) of the Contributions and Benefits Act]] or a payment specified in regulation 3(1) of these regulations is payable in respect of that disabled person for that day.

[⁶ (3) For the purposes of paragraph (1)(b) and (c) notwithstanding that on any day a person is absent from Great Britain he shall be treated as though he were present in Great Britain if his absence is by reason only of the fact that on that day—
(a) he is abroad in his capacity as—
    (i) a serving member of the forces within the meaning of the definition of "serving member of the forces" in regulation 1(2) of the Social Security (Contributions) Regulations 1975, as amended, or
    (ii) an airman or mariner within the meaning of regulation 72 and regulation 77 respectively of those Regulations; or
(b) he is in prescribed employment in connection with continental shelf operations within the meaning of regulation 76 of those Regulations; or
(c) he is living with a person mentioned in sub-paragraph (a)(i) and is the spouse, [⁷ civil partner] son, daughter, father, father-in-law, mother or mother-in-law of that person.]

AMENDMENTS

1. Social Security (Invalid Care Allowance) Amendment Regulations 1996 (SI 1996/2744), reg.2 (November 25, 1996).
2. Social Security Amendment (Carer's Allowance) Regulations 2002 (SI 2002/2497), reg.4 (April 1, 2003).
3. Social Security (Miscellaneous Amendments) Regulations 1998 (SI 1998/563), reg.18(1) (April 6, 1998).
4. Social Security (Persons From Abroad) Miscellaneous Amendments Regulations 1996 (SI 1996/30), reg.9 (February 5, 1996, subject to a saving under reg.12(3)). See *Vol. II: Income Support, Jobseeker's Allowance, Tax Credits and the Social Fund* at para.4.352.
5. Disability Living Allowance and Disability Working Allowance Regulations 1991 (SI 1991/2742), reg.3 (April 6, 1992).
6. Social Security (Child Benefit Consequential) Regulations 1977 (SI 1977/342), reg.18 (April 4, 1977).

7. Civil Partnership (Pensions, Social Security and Child Support) (Consequential, etc. Provisions) Order 2005 (SI 2005/2877) (December 5, 2005).

GENERAL NOTE

4.114 For the meaning of "ordinarily resident" see the notes to Persons Abroad Regulations.

Para. (2)

4.115 A person is regarded as being still present in Great Britain for up to four weeks of temporary absence, or for longer periods if he is abroad caring for his patient who continues to receive the attendance benefit. The four-week period ties in with the period for a break in caring under reg.4 above.

Para. (3)

4.116 A person is also regarded as present in Great Britain if his absence is for one of the specified reasons, though if the absence is for more than four weeks it would be necessary for the claimant to continue caring for his patient.

Circumstances in which a person over [¹ the age of 65] is to be treated as having been entitled to invalid care allowance immediately before attaining that age

4.117 **10.**—[¹ *Revoked.*]

AMENDMENT

1. Social Security Amendment (Carer's Allowance) Regulations 2002 (SI 2002/2497), reg.3 (October 28, 2002).

[¹ Women aged 65 before 28th October 1994

4.118 **10A.**—A woman shall be entitled to [² a carer's allowance] if—
(a) she attained the age of 65 before 28th October 1994;
(b) immediately before attaining the age of 65 she would have satisfied the requirements for entitlement to [² a carer's allowance], whether or not she made a claim, but for the condition, whichapplied prior to 28th October 1994, in section 70(5) of the Contributions and Benefits Act (exclusion of persons who had attained pensionable age and had not been entitled to that allowance immediately before attaining that age); and
(c) she satisfies the requirements for entitlement to [² a carer's allowance] apart from the conditions in section 70(1)(a) and (b) [³ . . .] of the Contributions and Benefits Act.]

AMENDMENTS

1. Social Security (Severe Disablement Allowance and Invalid Care Allowance) Amendment Regulations 1994 (SI 1994/2556), reg.5 (October 28, 1994).
2. Social Security Amendment (Carer's Allowance) Regulations 2002 (SI 2002/2497), reg.3 (April 1, 2003).
3. Social Security Amendment (Carer's Allowance) Regulations 2002 (SI 2002/2497), reg.3 (October 28, 2002).

Invalid care allowance for persons over [¹ the age of 65]

11.—[*Revoked.*] 4.119

AMENDMENT

1. Social Security Amendment (Carer's Allowance) Regulations 2002 (SI 2002/2497), reg.3 (October 28, 2002).

[¹ Men aged 65 before 28th October 1994

11A.—A man who— 4.120
  (a) attained the age of 65 before 28th October 1994; and
  (b) was entitled to [² a carer's allowance] immediately before he attained
      that age,
shall be entitled to that allowance notwithstanding that, after he attained
that age, he was not caring for a severely disabled person or no longer satisfied the requirements of section 70(1)(a) or (b) of the Contributions and
Benefits Act, if he satisfies the other requirements for entitlement to that
allowance.]

AMENDMENTS

1. Social Security (Severe Disablement Allowance and Invalid Care Allowance)
Amendment Regulations 1994 (SI 1994/2556), reg.5 (October 28, 1994).
2. Social Security Amendment (Carer's Allowance) Regulations 2002 (SI
2002/2497), reg.3 (April 1, 2003).

Regulations 12 and 13 revoked. 4.121

Application of the Social Security (General Benefit) Regulations 1982 to [¹ carer's allowance]

14.—The provisions of the Social Security (General Benefit) Regulations 4.122
1982, specified in column (1) of Schedule 1 to these regulations, the subject
matter of which is described in column (2) of that Sch., shall, with any
necessary modifications, apply to [¹ carer's allowance] as they apply to incapacity benefit.

AMENDMENT

1. Social Security Amendment (Carer's Allowance) Regulations 2002 (SI
2002/2497), reg.3 (April 1, 2003).

Regulations 15–20 omitted. 4.123

Regulation 21 revoked. 4.124

SCHEDULE 1 **Regulation 14**

PROVISIONS OF THE SOCIAL SECURITY (GENERAL BENEFIT) REGULATIONS 1982 APPLIED TO
[¹ CARER'S ALLOWANCE]

4.125

Regulation applied (1)	Subject matter (2)
2	Exceptions from disqualification for imprisonment, etc.
3	Suspension of payment of benefit during imprisonment, etc.
4	Interim payments by way of benefit under the Act
9	Payment of benefit and suspension of payments pending a decision on appeals or references, arrears and repayments.

AMENDMENT

1. Social Security Amendment (Carer's Allowance) Regulations 2002 (SI 2002/2497), reg.3 (April 1, 2003).

Social Security (Severe Disablement Allowance) Regulations 1984

(SI 1984/1303) *(as amended)*

4.126   For text of, and commentary on, these Regulations, see the 2005 edition of this volume.

PART V

MATERNITY BENEFITS

Social Security (Maternity Allowance) Regulations 1987

(SI 1987/416) (*as amended*)

ARRANGEMENT OF REGULATIONS

The Secretary of State for Social Services, in exercise of the powers conferred by section 22(3) of, and Schedule 20 to, the Social Security Act 1975 and sections 84(1) and 89(1) of the Social Security Act 1986, and of all other powers enabling him in that behalf, by this instrument, which is made before the end of the period of 12 months from the commencement of the enactments under which it is made, makes the following Regulations:

Citation, commencement and interpretation

1.—(1) These regulations may be cited as the Social Security (Maternity Allowance) Regulations 1987 and shall come into operation on 6th April 1987.

(2) In these regulations—

"the Act" means the Social Security Act 1975;

"the 1986 Act" means the Social Security Act 1986.

(3) Unless the context otherwise requires, any reference in any of these regulations—

   (a) to a numbered paragraph is a reference to the paragraph bearing that number in that regulation; and

   (b) in these regulations to a Schedule is to the Schedule to these regulations.

[¹ Disapplication of section 1(1A) of the Administration Act

[² **1A.** Section 1(1A) of the Social Security Administration Act 1992 (requirement to state a national insurance number) shall not apply to an adult dependant who—

   (a) is a person in respect of whom a claim for an increase of maternity allowance is made;

   (b) is subject to immigration control within the meaning of section 115(9)(a) of the Immigration and Asylum Act 1999; and

   (c) has not previously been allocated a national insurance number.]

AMENDMENTS

1. Social Security (National Insurance Information: Exemption) Regulations (SI 1997/2676) (December 1, 1997).

2. Social Security (National Insurance Number Information: Exemption) Regulations 2009, (SI 2009/471), reg.4 (April 6, 2009).

Disqualification for the receipt of a maternity allowance

2.—(1) A woman shall be disqualified for receiving a maternity allowance if—

5.2

5.3

5.4

[¹(a) during the maternity allowance period she does any work in employment as an employed or self-employed earner, for more than 10
days, whether consecutive or not, falling within that period and the
disqualification shall be for such part of the maternity allowance
period as may be reasonable in the circumstances, provided that the
disqualification shall, in any event, be for the number of days on
which she so worked in excess of 10 days.]
  (b) during the maternity allowance period she fails without good cause
to observe the following rules of behaviour, namely to take due care
of her health and to answer reasonable enquiries (not being enquiries
relating to medical examination, treatment or advice), by the Secretary
of State or his officers directed to ascertaining whether she is doing so,
and such disqualification shall be for such part of the maternity allowance period as may be reasonable in the circumstances; or
  (c) at any time before she is confined she fails without good cause to
attend for or to submit herself to any medical examination for which
she was given at least 3 days' notice in writing by or on behalf of the
Secretary of State, and such disqualification shall be for such part of
the maternity allowance period (being a part beginning not earlier
than the day on which the failure occurs) as may be reasonable in the
circumstances, except that in the event of her being confined after
such failure she shall not by reason of such failure be so disqualified
for the day on which the confinement occurs or any day thereafter.

AMENDMENT

1. Statutory Maternity Pay, Social Security (Maternity Allowance) and Social
Security (Overlapping Benefits) (Amendment) Regulations 2006 (SI 2006/2379),
reg.4(2) (October 1, 2006).

Modification of the maternity allowance period

5.5   **3.**—(1) [Section 35(2)] of the Social Security Contributions and Benefits
Act 1992] (which relates to the maternity allowance period) shall be
modified in accordance with the following provisions of this regulation.
  (2) [³omitted].
  [¹ (2A) In relation to a woman who—
  (a) is not entitled to maternity allowance at the 11th week before the
expected week of confinement; and
  (b) subsequently becomes entitled to maternity allowance before being
confined; and
  (c) has stopped work
the maternity allowance period shall be a period of [⁴39 weeks commencing
no earlier than the day she becomes entitled to maternity allowance and no
later than the day following the day on which she is confined]]
  (3)–(6) [³*omitted*].

AMENDMENTS

1. Social Security Maternity Benefits and Statutory Sick Pay (Amendment)
Regulations 1994 (SI 1994/1367), reg.3 (where the expected week of confinement
begins after October 16, 1994).
2. Social Security (Miscellaneous Amendments) (No. 2) Regulations 1997 (SI
1997/793), reg.18 (April 7, 1997).

3. Social Security, Statutory Maternity Pay and Statutory Sick Pay (Miscellaneous Amendment) Regulations 2002, (SI 2002/2690), Reg.15 (November 24, 2002).

4. Statutory Maternity Pay, Social Security (Maternity Allowance) and Social Security (Overlapping Benefits) (Amendment) Regulations 2006, (SI 2006/2379), reg.4(3)(October 1, 2006).

Social Security (Maternity Allowance) (Work Abroad) Regulations 1987

(SI 1987/417) (as amended)

ARRANGEMENT OF REGULATIONS

1.   Citation and commencement.   5.6
2.   Special provision for certain persons who have been employed abroad.

The Secretary of State for Social Services, in exercise of the powers conferred by section 131 of and Schedule 20 to the Social Security Act 1975 and of all other powers enabling him in that behalf, after agreement by the Social Security Advisory Committee that proposals to make these Regulations should not be referred to it, hereby makes the following Regulations:

Citation and commencement

1.—(1) These regulations may be cited as the Social Security (Maternity   5.7
Allowance) (Work Abroad) Regulations 1987 and shall come into force on
6th April 1987.
(2) In these regulations—
"the Act" means the Social Security Act 1975;
"the Contributions Regulations" means the Social Security (Contribu-
      tions) Regulations 1979.

Special provision for certain persons who have been employed abroad

2.—(1) This regulation applies, subject to paragraph (5), for the purpose   5.8
of determining entitlement to a maternity allowance in respect of a
woman who—
   (a) has been absent from Great Britain;
   (b) has returned to Great Britain; and
   (c) throughout the whole period of her absence was ordinarily resident
        in Great Britain.
(2) [¹ Where a woman has paid, or is treated as having actually paid,
Class 1 contributions under the Act either]
   (a) to the full extent of her liability under regulation 120 of the
        Contributions Regulations; or
   (b) in respect of the first 52 weeks of her employment abroad by virtue
        of either—
        (i) an Order in Council made under section 143 of the Act (reci-
             procity with countries outside the United Kingdom); or
        (ii) Council Regulation No. 1408/71 EEC (application of social

security schemes to employed persons and their families moving within the Community),

and the employment by reference to which the liability arose continued throughout the first 52 weeks after the commencement of that liability, she shall be treated for any week in which she was in fact engaged in gainful employment as having been engaged in employment as an employed earner [¹ and for any such week, and for any weeks following the period of that liability and before the date of her return to Great Britain so far as those weeks are relevant to her claim for a maternity allowance, as having received an amount of specified payments for the purposes of section 35A(4) of the Social Security Contributions and Benefits Act 1992 equal to the lower earnings limit in force on the last day of that week.]

(3) Where—

(a) a woman would have been liable to pay Class 1 contributions under regulation 120 of the Contributions Regulations but for the provisions of an Order in Council made under section 143 of the Act,

(b) in relation to her case the Order does not provide for periods of insurance, employment or residence in the other country to which the Order relates to be taken into account in determining title to benefit, and

(c) the employment by reference to which she would have been liable under that regulation continued throughout the first 52 weeks,

she shall be treated for any week during her absence in which she was in fact engaged in gainful employment as having been engaged in employment as an employed earner [¹ and for each week of her absence as having received an amount of specified payments for the purposes of section 35A(4) of the Social Security Contributions and Benefits Act 1992 equal to the lower earnings limit in force on the last day of the week].

(4) Where—

(a) a woman would have been liable to pay Class 1 contributions under regulation 120 of the Contributions Regulations but for the provisions of either an Order in Council made under section [143] or Council Regulation No. 1408/71/EEC;

(b) the employment by reference to which she would have been liable under regulation 120 continued throughout the first 52 weeks from the time that the liability would have commenced; and

(c) the Order of the Council Regulations, as the case may be, provides for aggregation of periods of insurance, employment or residence only if an insurance period has been completed since her return to Great Britain, and an insurance period has not been so completed,

any period of insurance, or employment in the other country to which that Order of Council Regulations, as the case may be, relates which falls in the [²66 weeks immediately preceding] the expected week of confinement shall be treated as a period in respect of which she was engaged in employment as employed earner [¹ and in eachweek of which she received an amount of specified payments for the purposes of section 35A(4) of the Social Security Contributions and Benefits Act 1992 equal to the lower earnings limit in force on the last day of that week.]

(5) Paragraphs (2) (except in a case to which paragraph (2)(a) applies), (3) and (4) shall not apply in relation to a claim for maternity allowance for any day in respect of which the woman concerned is entitled to a corre-

sponding benefit under the social security scheme of the country in which she was employed.

(6) Where a woman satisfies the requirements of paragraph (3)(a) or (4) (a) but the employment did not continue for 52 weeks, she shall be treated in respect of those weeks in which her employment did continue as having been engaged in employment as an employed earner [¹ and as having received an amount of specified payments for the purposes of section 35A(4) of the Social Security Contributions and Benefits Act 1992 equal to the lower limit in force on the last day of each of those weeks].

AMENDMENTS

1. Social Security (Maternity Allowance) (Work Abroad) (Amendment) Regulations 2000, (2000/691) reg.2 (April 2, 2000).
2. Social Security Maternity Benefits and Statutory Sick Pay (Amendment) Regulations 1994 (SI 1994/1367), reg.8 (where the expected week of confinement begins after October 16, 1994).

The Social Security (Maternity Allowance) (Earnings) Regulations 2000

(SI 2000/688)

ARRANGEMENT OF REGULATIONS

1.   Citation, commencement and interpretation.   5.9
2.   Specified payments for employed earners.
3.   Specified payments for self-employed earners.
4.   Aggregation of specified payments.
5.   The specified period.
6.   Determination of average weekly amount of specified payments.

The Secretary of State for Social Security, in exercise of powers conferred by sections 35A(4), (5) and (6)(c), 122(1) and 175(1) to (4) of the Social Security Contributions and Benefits Act 1992 and of all other powers enabling him in that behalf by this instrument, which is made before the end of the period of six months beginning with the coming into force of the enactments under which it is made, hereby makes the following Regulations:

Citation, commencement and interpretation

1.—(1) These regulations may be cited as the Social Security (Maternity   5.10
Allowance) (Earnings) Regulations 2000 and shall come into force on April 2, 2000.

(2) In these Regulations—

"certificate of small earnings exception" means a certificate issued pursuant to regulation 24(1) of the Contributions Regulations;

"the Contributions Regulations" means the [² Social Security (Contributions) Regulations 2001]

"the Contributions and Benefits Act" means the Social Security Contributions and Benefits Act 1992;

"test period" means the period of 66 weeks specified in section 35(1)(b) of the Contributions and Benefits Act.

Specified payments for employed earners

5.11   **2.**—(1) Subject to paragraph (2), for the purposes of section 35A(4)(a) of the Contributions and Benefits Act, the payments specified for a woman who is an employed earner in any week falling within the test period shall be all payments made to her or for her benefit as an employed earner including—

[2 (za) any amount retrospectively treated as earnings by regulations made by virtue of section 4B(2) of the Contributions and Benefits Act];

(a) any sum payable in respect of arrears of pay in pursuance of an order for reinstatement under section 114 or re-engagement under section 115 of the Employment Rights Act 1996 (orders for reinstatement and re-engagement);

(b) any sum payable by way of pay in pursuance of an order made under section 129 of the Employment Rights Act 1996 (procedure on hearing of application and making of order) for the continuation of a contract of employment;

(c) any sum payable by way of remuneration in pursuance of a protective award under section 189 of the Trade Union and Labour Relations (Consolidation) Act 1992 (complaint and protective award);

(d) any sum payable by way of statutory sick pay, including sums payable in accordance with regulations made under section 151(6) of the Contributions and Benefits Act (employers' liability);

(e) any sum payable by way of statutory maternity pay, including sums payable in accordance with regulations made under section 164(9) (b) of the Contributions and Benefits Act.

[1(f) any sum payable by way of statutory paternity pay, including any sums payable in accordance with regulations made under section 171ZD(3) of the Contributions and Benefits Act;

(g) any sum payable by way of statutory adoption pay, including any sums payable in accordance with regulations made under section 171ZM(3) of the Contributions and Benefits Act.]

(2) The payments specified shall not include any sum excluded from the computation of a person's earnings under regulation [225, 27 or 123 of Schedule 3 to] the Contributions Regulations (payments to be disregarded).

AMENDMENT

1. Social Security, Statutory Maternity Pay and Statutory Sick Pay (Miscellaneous Amendments) Regulations, (SI 2002/2690), Reg 16 (December 8, 2002).

2. Social Security, Occupational Pensions Schemes and Statutory Payments (Consequential Provisions) Regulations 2007 (SI 2007/1154) reg.3 (April 6, 2007).

Specified payments for self-employed earners

5.12   **3.**—For the purposes of section 35A(4)(b) of the Contributions and Benefits Act, where a woman is a self-employed earner in any week falling within the test period, the payments treated as made to her or for her benefit shall be—

(a) a payment equal to [¹ an amount 90 per cent of which is equal to the weekly rate prescribed under section 66(1)(b) of the Contributions and Benefits Act that is in force] on the last day of that week where she has paid a Class 2 contribution and she does not hold a certificate of small earnings exception in respect of that week; or

(b) a payment equal to the maternity allowance threshold in force on the last day of that week, where she holds a certificate of small earnings exception in respect of that week.

AMENDMENT

1. Social Security, Statutory Maternity Pay and Statutory Sick Pay Regulations 2002, (SI 2002/2690) reg.17 (November 24, 2002).

Aggregation of specified payments

4.—(1) In a case [¹. . .] where a woman, either in the same week or in 5.13
different weeks falling within the test period, is engaged in two or more employments (whether, in each case, as an employed earner or a self-employed earner), any payments which are made, or treated in accordance with these Regulations as made to her or for her benefit shall be aggregated for the purpose of determining the average weekly amount of specified payments applicable in her case.

(2) In a case to which regulation 5(2) applies, any payments which are made or treated in accordance with these Regulations as made, to her or for her benefit shall not be aggregated for the purpose of determining the average weekly amount of specified payments applicable in her case.

AMENDMENT

1. Social Security, Statutory Maternity Pay and Statutory Sick Pay Regulations 2002, (SI 2002/2690) reg.17 (November 24, 2002).

[¹ The specified period

5.—(1) Subject to paragraph (2) below, for the purposes of section 5.14
35A(4) and (5) of the Contributions and Benefits Act, the specified period shall be the test period.

(2) Where a woman is treated by virtue of regulation 3(a) above as having received payments for at least 13 weeks (whether consecutive or not) falling within the test period, the first 13 weeks shall be the specified period.]

AMENDMENT

1. Social Security (Maternity Allowance) (Earnings) (Amendment) Regulations 2003 (SI 2003/659) reg.2 (April 6, 2003).

Determination of average weekly amount of specified payments

6.—[¹ (1) For the purposes of section 35A(4) of the Contributions and 5.15
Benefits Act a woman's average weekly amount of specified payments shall, subject to paragraph (2), be determined by dividing by 13 the payments made, or treated in accordance with these Regulations as made, to her or for her benefit—

(a) in the case of a woman to whom paragraph (2) of regulation 5 applies, in the 13 weeks referred to in that paragraph;

(b) in any other case, in the 13 weeks (whether consecutive or not) falling within the specified period in which such payments are greatest.]

(2) In any case where a woman receives a back-dated pay increase after the end of the period specified in regulation 5 above which includes a sum in respect of any week falling within that period, her average weekly amount of specified payments shall be determined as if such sum had been paid in that week.

AMENDMENT

1. Social Security (Maternity Allowance) (Earnings) (Amendment) Regulations 2003 (SI 2003/659) reg.3 (April 6, 2003).

PART VI

WIDOW'S BENEFIT, RETIREMENT PENSIONS AND GRADUATED RETIREMENT BENEFIT

The Social Security (Deferral of Retirement Pensions) Regulations 2005

(SI 2005/453) (*as amended*)

ARRANGEMENT OF REGULATIONS

6.1

The Secretary of State for Work and Pensions, in exercise of the powers conferred upon him by sections 54(1), 122(1) and 175(3) of, and paragraphs 2(2), 3(1), 3B(2) and (5)(b)(iii) and 7B(2) and (5)(b)(iii) of Schedule 5 to, the Social Security Contributions and Benefits Act 1992, and of all other powers enabling him in that behalf, after agreement by the Social Security Advisory Committee that proposals in respect of regulation 4 should not be referred to it, the remainder of this Instrument containing only regulations made under provisions introduced by section 297 of, and Schedule 11 to, the Pensions Act 2004 and being made before the end of the period of 6 months beginning with the coming into force of those provisions, hereby makes the following Regulations:

Citation, commencement and interpretation

1.—(1) These Regulations may be cited as the Social Security (Deferral of Retirement Pensions) Regulations 2005 and shall come into force on 6th April 2005.

(2) In these Regulations—

"the Act" means the Social Security Contributions and Benefits Act 1992;

"retirement pension" means a Category A or Category B retirement pension.

[¹ "shared additional pension" means a shared pension under section 55A of the Act.]

6.2

AMENDMENT

1. Shared Additional Pensions (Miscellaneous Amendments) Regulations 2005 (SI 2005/1551) (July 6, 2005).

Beginning of accrual period

2.—For the purposes of paragraphs 3B and 7B of Schedule 5 [¹ and paragraphs 5 of Schedule 5A] to the Act (calculation of lump sum), the accrual period shall begin on the day of the week on which retirement pension [¹ or a shared additional pension] would have been payable to a person in accordance with regulation 22(3) of, and paragraph 5 [¹ or 5A] of Schedule 6 to, the Social Security (Claims and Payments) Regulations 1987, if his entitlement to a retirement pension [¹ or a shared additional pension] had not been deferred.

6.3

AMENDMENT

1. Shared Additional Pension (Miscellaneous Amendments) Regulations 2005 (SI 2005/1551) (July 6, 2005).

Amount of retirement pension not included in the calculation of the lump sum

6.4

3.—(1) For the purposes of the calculation of the lump sum under paragraphs 3B and 7B of Schedule 5 to the Act, the amount of retirement pension to which the person ("the deferrer") would have been entitled for the accrual period if his entitlement had not been deferred shall not include any such pension where, for the entire accrual period—

(a) the deferrer has received any of the following benefits—

  (i) any benefit under Parts II and III of the Act other than child's special allowance, attendance allowance, disability living allowance and guardian's allowance;

  (ii) any severe disablement allowance under sections 68 and 69 of the Act as in force before 6th April 2001;

  (iii) any unemployability supplement within the extended meaning in regulation 2(1) of the Social Security (Overlapping Benefits) Regulations 1979 and including benefit corresponding to an unemployability supplement by virtue of regulations under paragraph 7(2) of Schedule 8 to the Act;

(b) an increase of any of the benefits specified in sub-paragraph (a) is being paid to a married man in respect of his wife where the wife is a deferrer whose period of deferment began before 6th April 2005 and who would have been entitled to a Category B retirement pension or to an increase under section 51A(2) of the Act;

(c) an increase of any of the benefits specified in sub-paragraph (a) is being paid to any person in respect of a deferrer whose period of deferment began on or after 6th April 2005 except where that deferrer is neither married to [² or in a civil partnership with,], nor residing with, that person;

(d) the deferrer would have been disqualified for receiving retirement pension by reason of imprisonment or detention in legal custody.

[¹ (1A) For the purposes of the calculation of the lump sum under paragraph 5 of Schedule 5A to the Act, the amount of a shared additional pension to which a person ("the deferrer") would have been entitled for the accrual period if his entitlement had not been deferred shall not include any such pension where, for the entire accrual period, the deferrer would have been disqualified for receiving shared additional pension by reason of imprisonment or detention in legal custody.]

(2) Where any of the benefits referred to in paragraph (1)(a) or an increase referred to in paragraph (1)(b) or (c) has been received for part only of an accrual period, the amount of retirement pension not included by paragraph (1) shall be reduced by 1/7th for each day of the accrual period in respect of which the benefit or increase has not been received.

(3) Where the deferrer would have been disqualified for receiving retirement pension as specified in paragraph (1)(d) [¹ or a shared additional pension as specified in paragraph (1A)] for part only of an accrual period, the amount of retirement pension not included by paragraph (1) [¹ or a shared additional pension not included by paragraph (1A)] shall be

reduced by 1/7th for each day of the accrual period for which he would not have been so disqualified.

(4) Subject to paragraph (5), where—

(a) a person has, in respect of any day in an accrual period, received one or more of the benefits referred to in paragraph (1)(a) or increases referred to in paragraph (1)(b) and (c) or both;

(b) the determining authority has determined that in respect of that day, he was not entitled to the benefit or increase; and

(c) the whole of the benefit or increase in respect of that day has been repaid or, as the case may be, recovered on or before the relevant date,

that day shall be treated as a day in respect of which he did not receive that benefit or increase or both.

(5) Where the benefit or increase in respect of a day to which paragraph (4)(a) and (b) applies is repaid or, as the case may be, recovered on or after the relevant date, that day shall only be treated as a day in respect of which that person did not receive that benefit or increase once the benefit or increase has been repaid in respect of all the days to which those sub-paragraphs relate and which fall within the period of deferment.

(6) In paragraph (4), "the determining authority" means as the case may require, the Secretary of State, an appeal tribunal constituted under Chapter I of Part I of the Social Security Act 1998 or a Commissioner, or a tribunal consisting of three or more such Commissioners constituted in accordance with section 16(7) of that Act.

(7) In paragraphs (4) and (5), "relevant date" means—

(a) the last day of the period of deferment; or

(b) where entitlement to a lump sum arises under paragraph 7A of Schedule 5 to the Act, the date of S's death.

(8) Any amount of retirement pension [[1] or a shared additional pension] not included in the calculation of the lump sum in accordance with this regulation must be rounded to the nearest penny, taking any 1/2 p as nearest to the next whole penny above.

AMENDMENTS

1. Shared Additional Pension (Miscellaneous Amendments) Regulations 2005 (SI 2005/1551) (July 6, 2005).

2. Civil Partnership (Consequential Amendments) Regulations 2005 (SI 2005/2878) (December 6, 2005).

Amendment of the Social Security (Widow's Benefit and Retirement Pensions) Regulations 1979

4.—*Taken into account in the text of those regulations.*

6.5

The Social Security (Deferral of Retirement Pensions, Shared Additional Pension and Graduated Retirement Benefit) (Miscellaneous Provisions) Regulations 2005

(SI 2005/2677)

PART 1

GENERAL

Citation, commencement and interpretation

6.7   **1.** —(1) These Regulations may be cited as the Social Security (Deferral of Retirement Pensions, Shared Additional Pension and Graduated Retirement Benefit) (Miscellaneous Provisions) Regulations 2005 and shall come into force on 6th April 2006.

(2) In these Regulations—

"the Claims and Payments Regulations" means the Social Security (Claims and Payments) Regulations 1987;

"the Housing Benefit Regulations" means the Housing Benefit (General) Regulations 1987.

PART 2

DEFERRAL OF RETIREMENT PENSIONS AND SHARED ADDITIONAL PENSION

Interpretation

6.8   **2.**—(1) In this Part—

"elector" means the person who may make an election under paragraph A1(1) or 3C(2) of Schedule 5 or paragraph 1(1) of Schedule 5A;

"retirement pension" means a Category A or a Category B retirement pension.

(2) In this Part, references to Schedules 5 and 5A are to those Schedules to the Social Security Contributions and Benefits Act 1992.

Timing of election

3.—(1) The period for making an election under—

6.9

(a) paragraph A1(1) of Schedule 5 (choice between increase of pension and lump sum where pensioner's entitlement is deferred); and

(b) paragraph 1(1) of Schedule 5A (choice between pension increase and lump sum where entitlement to shared additional pension is deferred),

is, subject to paragraph (4), three months starting on the date shown on the notice issued by the Secretary of State following the claim for retirement pension or shared additional pension, confirming that the elector is required to make that election.

(2) The period for making an election under paragraph 3C(2) of Schedule 5 (choice between increase of pension and lump sum where pensioner's deceased spouse or civil partner has deferred entitlement) is, subject to paragraph (4), three months starting on the date shown on the notice issued by the Secretary of State following W's claim for retirement pension or, if later, the date of S's death, confirming that the elector is required to make that election.

(3) Where more than one notice has been issued by the Secretary of State in accordance with paragraph (1) or (2), the periods prescribed in those paragraphs shall only commence from the date shown on the latest such notice.

(4) The periods specified in paragraphs (1) and (2) may be extended by the Secretary of State if he considers it reasonable to do so in any particular case.

(5) Nothing in this regulation shall prevent the making of an election on or after claiming retirement pension or, as the case may be, shared additional pension but before the issue of the notice referred to in paragraph (1) or (2).

Manner of making election

4. An election under paragraph A1(1) or 3C(2) of Schedule 5 or under paragraph 1(1) of Schedule 5A may be made—

6.10

(a) in writing to an office specified by the Secretary of State for accepting such elections; or

(b) except where the Secretary of State directs in any particular case that the election must be made in accordance with paragraph (a), by telephone call to the telephone number specified by the Secretary of State.

Change of election

5.—(1) Subject to paragraphs (2) and (6), this regulation applies in the case of an election which—

6.11

(a) has been made under paragraph A1(1) or 3C(2) of Schedule 5 or under paragraph 1(1) of Schedule 5A; or

(b) has been treated as made under paragraph A1(2) or 3C(3) of Schedule 5 or under paragraph 1(2) of Schedule 5A.

(2) This regulation does not apply in the case of an election which is—

(a) made, or treated as made, by an elector who has subsequently died; or

(b) treated as having been made by virtue of regulation 30(5D) or (5F) of the Claims and Payments Regulations.

(3) An election specified in paragraph (1) may be changed by way of application made no later than the last day of the period specified in paragraph (4).

(4) The period specified for the purposes of paragraph (3) is, subject to paragraph (5), three months starting on the date shown on the written notification issued by the Secretary of State to the elector, confirming the election which the elector has made or is treated as having made.

(5) The period specified in paragraph (4) may be extended by the Secretary of State if he considers it reasonable to do so in any particular case.

(6) An election specified in paragraph (1) may not be changed where—

(a) there has been a previous change of election under this regulation in respect of the same period of deferment;

(b) the application is to change the election to one under paragraph A1(1)(a) or 3C(2)(a) of Schedule 5 or paragraph 1(1)(a) of Schedule 5A and any amount paid to him by way of, or on account of, a lump sum pursuant to Schedule 5 or 5A, has not been repaid in full to the Secretary of State within the period specified in paragraph (4) or, as the case may be, (5); or

(c) the application is to change the election to one under paragraph A1(1)(b) or 3C(2)(b) of Schedule 5 or paragraph 1(1)(b) of Schedule 5A and the amount actually paid by way of an increase of retirement pension or shared additional pension, or actually paid on account of such an increase, would exceed the amount to which the elector would be entitled by way of a lump sum.

(7) For the purposes of paragraph (6)(b), repayment in full of the amount paid by way of, or on account of, a lump sum shall only be treated as having occurred if repaid to the Secretary of State in the currency in which that amount was originally paid.

(8) Where the application is to change the election to one under paragraph A1(1)(b) or 3C(2)(b) of Schedule 5 or paragraph 1(1)(b) of Schedule 5A and paragraph (6)(c) does not apply, any amount paid by way of an increase of retirement pension or shared additional pension, or on account of such an increase, in respect of the period of deferment for which the election was originally made, shall be treated as having been paid on account of the lump sum to which the elector is entitled under paragraph 3A or 7A of Schedule 5 or, as the case may be, paragraph 4 of Schedule 5A.

(9) An application under paragraph (3) to change an election may be made—

(a) in writing to an office specified by the Secretary of State for accepting such applications; or

(b) except where the Secretary of State directs in any particular case that the application must be made in accordance with sub-paragraph (a), by telephone call to the telephone number specified by the Secretary of State.

Amendment of the Social Security (Retirement Pensions etc.) (Transitional Provisions) Regulations 2005

6. Regulation 2(6)(a) of the Social Security (Retirement Pensions etc.) (Transitional Provisions) Regulations 2005 (modification of Schedule 5) is omitted.

6.12

The Social Security (Graduated Retirement Benefit) (No. 2) Regulations 1978

(SI 1978/393) *(as amended)*

ARRANGEMENT OF REGULATIONS

6.13

The Secretary of State for Social Services, in exercise of the powers conferred on him by section 2(1) of and paragraphs 3, 7 and 9 of Schedule 3 to the Social Security (Consequential Provisions) Act 1975 and section 24(1) of the Social Security Pensions Act 1975, and of all other powers enabling him in that behalf, hereby makes the following regulations, which only make provision consequential on the passing of the last-mentioned Act and accordingly by virtue of section 61(1) (e) of that Act are exempt from the requirements of section 139(1) of the Social Security Act 1975 (duty to consult National Insurance Advisory Committee about proposed regulations):

GENERAL NOTE

Responsibility for decisions made in respect of Graduated Retirement Pension, even those relating to contributions and the record of the claimant's contributions, remains that of the Department of Work and Pensions. This is because no transfer of function in this respect was made when other aspects of the administration of contributions was transferred to Her Majesty's Revenue. The consequence is that all such decisions made in relation to GRP entitlement that depend upon contribution questions, must either be made by officers of Department of Work and Pensions, or, if made by HMRC, must be made by them as agents of that department. The result is that all such decisions are appealable only to Social Security tribunals and not to the Commissioners. See the very clearly expressed decision in *R(P) 1/08*.

6.14

Citation, commencement and interpretation

1.—(1) These regulations may be cited as the Social Security (Graduated Retirement Benefit) (No.2) Regulations 1978.

6.15

(2) This regulation and regulation 2 below shall come into operation on 6th April 1978.

(3) The remainder of these regulations shall, for the purpose only of determining, before 6th April 1979, claims for, or questions arising as to,

benefit for any period after 5th April 1979, come into operation on 6th December 1978.

(4) Except as mentioned in paragraphs (2) and (3) above, these regulations shall come into operation on 6th April 1979.

(5) In these regulations—

"the Act" means the Social Security Act 1975;

"the Pensions Act" means the Social Security Pensions Act 1975;

"the 1965 Act" means the National Insurance Act 1965;

"the 1975 regulations" means the Social Security (Graduated Retirement Benefit) Regulations 1975, as amended;

"the 1978 regulations" means the Social Security (Graduated Retirement Benefit) Regulations 1978;

and other expressions have the same meanings as in the Act.

(6) Any reference in these regulations to any provision made by or contained in any enactment or instrument shall, except in so far as the context otherwise requires, be construed as a reference to that provision as amended or extended by any enactment or instrument and as including a reference to any provision which it re-enacts or replaces, or which may re-enact or replace it, with or without modification.

(7) The rules for the construction of Acts of Parliament contained in the Interpretation Act 1889 shall apply in relation to this instrument and in relation to the revocations effected by it as if this instrument and the regulations revoked by it were Acts of Parliament and as if the revocations were repeals.

[² Application of sections 150 and 155 of the Social Security Administration Act 1992

6.16   **2.**—The provisions of sections 150 and 155 of the Social Security Administration Act 1992, (annual up-rating of benefits and effect of alteration of rates of benefit) shall apply to—

(a) the amount of graduated retirement benefit payable for each unit of graduated contributions;

(b) increases of such benefit under the provisions of Schedule 2 to these Regulations; and

(c) any addition under section 37(1) of the 1965 Act (addition to weekly rate of retirement pension for [¹ widows, widowers and surviving civil partners]) to the amount of such benefit.

as if that amount, those increases and that addition were included in the sums mentioned in section 150(1) and (3) and graduated retirement benefit were a benefit referred to in section 155(2).]

AMENDMENT

1. Social Security (Retirement Pensions and Graduated Retirement Benefit) (Widowers and Civil Partnership) Regulations 2005 (SI 2005/3078) (April 6, 2006).

Continuation in force of sections 36, 37 and 118(1) of the 1965 Act

6.17   **3.**—(1) The provisions of this regulation shall have effect for the purpose of securing continuity between the Act and the 1965 Act in the case of persons who had, immediately before 6th April 1975, rights or prospective rights to or expectations of graduated retirement benefit under sections 36 and 37 of the 1965 Act, by preserving those rights and temporarily retaining the effect of those sections for transitional purposes.

(2) Paragraph (3) below shall have effect so that notwithstanding their repeal by the Social Security Act 1973 those sections shall, for the purpose aforesaid, continue in force subject to the making in them of the modifications required—

(a) to bring them into conformity with the provisions of the Act and the Pensions Act and to enable them to have effect as if contained in the scheme of social security benefits established by those Acts;

(b) to replace section 36(4) of the 1965 Act (increase of graduated retirement benefit in cases of deferred retirement) with provisions corresponding to those of paragraphs 1 to 3 of Schedule 1 to the Pensions Act;

(c) to extend section 37 of the 1965 Act (increase of woman's retirement pension by reference to her late husband's graduated retirement benefit) to men and their late wives. [¹; and

(d) to extend section 37 of the 1965 Act (increase of women's retirement pension by reference to her late husband's graduated retirement benefit) to civil partners and surviving civil partners.]

(3) On and after 6th April 1979 those sections shall continue in force in the modified form in which they are set out in Schedule 1 to these regulations, but not so as to save the National Insurance (Graduated Retirement Benefit and Consequential Provisions) Regulations 1961, so far as deemed to have been made under those sections, from being invalidated by the repeal; and section 118(1) of the 1965 Act (short title) shall also continue in force.

AMENDMENT

1. Social Security (Retirement Pensions and Graduated Retirement Benefit) (Widowers and Civil Partnership) regulations 2005 (SI 2005/3078) (April 6, 2006).

Modification of regulations concerning graduated retirement benefit

4.—The provisions of regulations 2 and 3 of the 1978 regulations (which were made under sections 36 and 37 of the 1965 Act) shall continue in force in the modified form set out in Schedule 3 to these regulations; and paragraphs (1) (so far as it relates to citation), (2) and (3) (interpretation) of regulation 1 of the 1978 regulations shall also continue in force. 6.18

Revocations

5.—*Omitted.* 6.19

SCHEDULES

SCHEDULE 1 **Regulation 3(3)**

SECTIONS 36 AND 37 OF THE NATIONAL INSURANCE ACT 1965 AS CONTINUED IN FORCE BY THESE REGULATIONS

Graduated retirement benefit

36.—(1) Subject to the provisions of the Act, graduated retirement benefit shall be payable to any person who is over pensionable age and who [¹ is entitled to a retirement pension], and shall be an increase in the weekly rate of his retirement pension equal to [⁶ 11.53] pence 6.20

for each unit, ascertained in accordance with subsections (2) and (3) of this section, of the graduated contributions properly paid by him as an insured person, the result being rounded to the nearest whole penny, taking 1/2p as nearest to the next whole penny above.

(2) For the purpose of graduated retirement benefit the units of graduated contributions shall be £7.50 for men and £9.00 for women.

(3) Where a person's graduated contributions calculated at the said rate do not make an exact number of units any incomplete fraction of a unit shall, if it is one-half or more, be treated as a complete unit.

[7(4) Where a person's entitlement to graduated retirement benefit is deferred—

  (a) Schedule 2 to the Social Security (Graduated Retirement Benefit) (No.2) Regulations 1978; and

  (b) Schedule 1 to the 2005 Regulations,

shall have effect and both those Schedules shall be construed and have effect as if they were part of this subsection.

(4A) For the purposes of subsection (4), a person's entitlement to graduated retirement benefit is deferred—

  (a) where he would be entitled to a Category A or Category B retirement pension but for the fact that his entitlement is deferred within the meaning in section 55(3) of the Social Security Contributions and Benefits Act 1992, if and so long as his entitlement to such a pension is deferred;

  (b) where he is treated under subsection (7) as receiving a Category A or a Category B retirement pension at a nominal weekly rate, if and so long as he does not become entitled to graduated retirement benefit by reason only of not satisfying the conditions in section 1 of the Social Security Administration Act 1992 (entitlement to benefit dependent on claim),

and in relation to graduated retirement benefit, "period of deferment" shall be construed accordingly.]

(5) For the purposes of subsection (4) of this section, the Secretary of State may by regulations provide for treating all or any of the graduated contributions paid by a person in the tax year in which he attained pensionable age as having been paid before, or as having been paid after, the day on which he attained that age, whether or not the contribution in question was so paid.

(7) A person who has attained pensionable age and [1has claimed], but is not entitled to a retirement pension [2(except a person who is not so entitled because of an election under section 54(1) of the Social Security Contributions and Benefits Act 1992 or because he has withdrawn his claim)], shall be treated for the purposes of the foregoing provisions of this section as receiving a retirement pension at a nominal weekly rate:

Provided that—

  (a) this subsection shall not confer any right to graduated retirement benefit on a person who would be entitled to a retirement pension but for some provision of the Act or of regulations disqualifying him for receipt of it; and

  (b) regulations may provide that any right by virtue of this subsection to benefit at less than a specified weekly rate shall be satisfied either altogether or for a specified period by the making of a single payment of the prescribed amount.

(8) In this section and in section 37 below—

"graduated contributions" means graduated contributions under the National Insurance Act 1965 or the National Insurance Act 1959;

"insured person" means insured person under the National Insurance Act 1965 or the National Insurance Act 1946;

"retirement pension" means retirement pension of any category;

"the Act" means the Social Security Act 1975;

[7 "the 2005 Regulations" means the Social Security (Graduated Retirement Benefit) Regulations 2005;]

and any reference in section 37 below to "section 36 of this Act" or to any of its subsections is a reference to that section or subsection as it is here set out.

(9) This section and section 37 below and the Act shall be construed and have effect as if this section and section 37 below were included in Chapter I of Part II of that Act (contributory benefits); and references to that Chapter, that Part or that Act in any other enactment or in any instrument shall be construed accordingly:

Provided that nothing in this subsection shall affect the construction of any reference to section 36 or 37 of this Act or of that Act or to any of the subsections of those sections; and any increase in the weekly rate of a person's retirement pension, to the extent that it is attributable to subsection (4) of this section, shall be left out of account in determining the weekly rate of that pension for the purposes of [3section 30B(3) of the Social Security Contributions and Benefits Act 1992 regulations 11(1) and 18(7) of the Social Security (Incapacity Benefit) (Transitional Regulations 1995] and [⁴ regulation 10(6) of the Jobseeker's Allowance (Transitional Provisions) Regulations 1996] (rates of incapacity benefit and jobseeker's allowance in transitional cases for persons over pensionable age)].

(10) [⁵ ...]

37.—(1) Subject to the provisions of this section [⁷ and to Schedule 1 to the 2005 Regulations]—

(a) where a man, having paid graduated contributions as an insured person, dies leaving a widow, and she either has attained pensionable age at the time of his death or remains his widow when she attains that age; or

(b) where a woman, having paid graduated contributions as an insured person, dies after 5th April 1979 leaving a widower, and she and he have both attained pensionable age at the time of her death, [⁸; or

(c) where a person, having paid graduated contributions as an insured person, dies on or after 5th December 2005 leaving a surviving civil partner, and they have both attained pensionable age at the time of his or her death,]

then section 36 of this Act shall apply as if the increase in the weekly rate of the retirement pension of the [⁸ widow, widower or surviving civil partner], as the case may be, provided for by subsection (1) thereof were the amount there specified by reference to his or her graduated contributions with the addition of one-half of the weekly rate of the graduated retirement benefit of his or her former spouse [⁸ or civil partner] (any amount including 1/2p being rounded to the next whole penny above); and where a man, having paid graduated contributions as an insured person, dies after 5th April 1979 leaving a widow and she has attained pensionable age at the time of his death [¹ ...], section 36 shall apply as if the increase in the weekly rate of her retirement pension provided for by subsection (1) thereof were one-half of the weekly rate of the graduated retirement benefit of her former husband (any amount including 1/2p being rounded to the next whole penny above).

(2) For the purposes of subsection (1) of this section, the weekly rate of the deceased spouse's [⁸ or civil partner's] graduated retirement benefit shall (whether or not he or she was receiving or entitled to receive any such benefit) be taken to have been the weekly rate appropriate to the amount of graduated contributions paid by him or her (determined as if any orders which have come into force under section 124 of the Act (increases in rates of benefit) since the date of the deceased spouse's [⁸ or civil partner's] death had come into force before that date), excluding any addition under section 37(1) of this Act, but including any addition under section 36(4), thereof (and for the purpose of calculating the addition under section 36(4) taking into account any addition under section 37(1)); and where at his or her death he or she had attained pensionable age but had [¹not] become entitled to graduated retirement benefit, that addition shall be computed as if he or she had [¹ ...] become entitled to graduated retirement benefit immediately before his or her death.

(3) A person's right to graduated retirement benefit by virtue of this section shall be brought into account under section 36(4) of this Act in determining the graduated retirement benefit payable to him or her under the said section 36:

Provided that, if the termination of the marriage [⁸ or civil partnership] by death occurred after he or she attained pensionable age, he or she shall for the purposes of this subsection be treated as not having attained pensionable age until the date of that termination.

(4) A person's right to graduated retirement benefit by virtue of this section in respect of a spouse he or she marries [⁸ or as the case may be, a civil partner he or she forms a civil partnership with] after attaining pensionable age shall be subject to such additional conditions as may be prescribed; and except as may be provided by regulations a person more than once married [⁸ or who has formed a civil partnership more than once or who has been both married and a civil partner] shall not be entitled for the same period to any graduated retirement benefit by virtue of this section in respect of more than one of his or her spouses [⁸ or civil partners].

(5) Regulations may provide that where a woman is entitled to graduated retirement benefit and to a widowed mother's allowance the graduated retirement benefit shall be an increase in the weekly rate of that allowance; and where the benefit is such an increase, section 36(7) of this Act shall not apply.

SCHEDULE 2   **Regulation 3(3)**

PROVISIONS REPLACING SECTION 36(4) OF THE NATIOANAL INSURANCE ACT 1965

1.—Where a person [¹defers his entitlement to a Category A or Category B retirement   **6.21** pensions] after attaining pensionable age, or has made an election by virtue of section 30(3) of the Act and has not revoked it, then for the purpose of calculating the graduated retirement benefit payable to him from the date of his retirement—

(a) there shall be added to the amount of the graduated contributions properly paid by him as an insured person one-half of the aggregate graduated retirement benefit which would have been payable to him for any period before 6th April 1979 (disregarding the effect of any order made under section 124 of the Act) if he had retired from regular employment on attaining pensionable age and had received that benefit for the whole of the period without any interruption or abatement:

Provided that, in computing the addition to be made in accordance with this paragraph in the case of a person who has made an election by virtue of section 30(3) of the Act (re-entry into regular employment) or the corresponding provisions of any earlier Act, no account shall be taken of any period between 6th April 1975 and 5th April 1979 (both dates inclusive) which falls between the date of that election and the date of his previous [¹entitlement]; and

(b) the rate of his graduated retirement benefit shall be increased by an amount equal to the increments to which he is entitled under paragraph 3 below, but only if either—

   (i) that amount is enough to increase the rate of the benefit by at least 1 per cent., or

   (ii) he has attained pensionable age before 6th April 1979, and has either deferred his [¹entitlement] before that date, or made an election by virtue of section 30(3) of the Act taking effect before that date or both.

2.—Where a woman who is over pensionable age [¹ ...]is entitled by virtue of section 37(1) of the National Insurance Act 1965 to graduated retirement benefit, and she has, on or after 6th April 1979, made an election by virtue of section 30(3) of the Act and has not revoked it, then, for the purpose only of determining her right to increments under this Schedule, her election shall be treated as if it took effect from 6th April 1979, or, if later, the date of the death of her husband by virtue of whose graduated contributions she is so entitled.

3.—(1) Subject to paragraph 4 below, a person is entitled to an increment under this paragraph for each complete incremental period (beginning not earlier than 6th April 1979) in his [¹period of enhancement].

(2) In this Schedule—

(a) "incremental period" means any period of 6 days which are treated by the Social Security (Widow's Benefit and Retirement Pensions) (Amendment) Regulations 1978 as days of increment for the purposes of Schedule 1 to the social Security Pensions Act 1975 as amended by section 3 of the Social Security (Miscellaneous Provisions) Act 1977 in relation to the person and the pension in question; and

[¹(b) 'period of enhancement' in relation to any person means the period which begins on the same day as the period of deferment and ends on the same day as that period ends or, if earlier, on the day before the fifth anniversary of the beginning of that period.]

(3) Subject to paragraph 4 below, the amount of the increment for any such incremental period shall be 1/7th per cent. of the weekly rate of the graduated retirement benefit to which that person would have been entitled for the period if he [¹had not deferred his entitlement to a Category A or Category B retirement pension], the result being rounded to the nearest whole penny, taking 1/2p as nearest to the next whole penny above.

(4) Where one or more orders have come into force under section 124 of the Act (increases in rates of benefit) during the [¹period of enhancement] the rate of the benefit for any incremental period shall be determined as if the order of orders had come into force before the beginning of the [¹period of enhancement].

4.—(1) Where during a person's [¹period of enhancement] there are one or more increases (other than any made by such an order as is mentioned in paragraph 3(4) above) in the weekly rate of graduated retirement benefit which would have been payable to him during that period if he had not [¹deferred his entitlement to a Category A or Category B retirement pension] or made an election by virtue of section 30(3) of the act, the total amount of increment for [¹the period of enhancement] shall be—

(a) 1/7th per cent, for each incremental period in the [¹period of enhancement], of the weekly rate of the graduated retirement benefit to which he would have been entitled immediately [¹after attaining pensionable age if he had not deferred his entitlement to a Category A or Category B retirement pension]; plus

(b) in respect of each such increase, 1/7th per cent., of its weekly rate for each incremental period in the period beginning with the day on which that increase occurred and ending with [¹the same day the period of enhancement ends].

(2) Where one or more orders have come into force under section 124 of the Act during the [¹period of enhancement] the weekly rates mentioned in sub-paragraph (1) above shall be determined as if the order or orders had come into force before the beginning of the [¹period of enhancement].

GENERAL NOTE

The sums which are increased in Graduated Retirement benefits under this schedule will be increased by 5 per cent in accordance with art.12(2) of the Social Security Benefits Up-rating Order 2009 (SI 2009/497), (April 6, 2009).

6.22

SCHEDULE 3   **Regulation 4**

REGULATIONS 2 AND 3 OF THE 1978 REGULATIONS AS MODIFIED BY THESE REGULATIONS

Graduated retirement benefit when retirement is deferred

2.—For the purposes of paragraph 1(a) of Schedule 2 to the Social Security (Graduated Retirement Benefit) (No. 2) Regulations 1978 (provision, where a person attains pensionable age before 6th April 1979 but does not retire from regular employment until after 5th April 1979, for calculating the graduated retirement benefit payable to him from the date of his retirement) all the graduated contributions paid by a person in the income tax year in which he attained pensionable age shall be treated as having been paid before the day on which he attained that age.

6.23

Provided that where, in any case, the aggregate amount of the graduated contributions paid by him in that year exceeded the aggregate amount of graduated contributions which would have been payable by him in that part of the year which ended with the income tax week, in which he attained pensionable age if, in each income tax week beginning in that part of the year, a graduated contribution as for an employment which was not a non-participating employment had been payable by him in respect of a weekly payment of remuneration made in that week at a level equal to the upper limit on the amount of weekly pay then taken into account under section 4(1)(c) of the 1965 Act as amended, the excess shall be treated as having been paid after the day on which he attained that age.

Graduated retirement benefit for persons who have been married more than once

3.—For the purposes of section 37 of the 1965 Act (special provisions as to graduated retirement benefit for widows and widowers) a person who has been married more than once [⁸ or has formed more than one civil partnership or who has been both married and a civil partner] and who is entitled to graduated retirement benefit for any period by virtue of the provisions of that section in respect of a second or subsequent spouse [⁸ or civil partner] shall not be precluded from entitlement to graduated retirement benefit for that period by virtue of that section in respect of a former spouse [⁸ or civil partner], but shall be so entitled to the extent only that it is payable to him or her by the application of section 36(4) of the 1965 Act in respect of any period before the death of the first-mentioned spouse [⁸ or civil partner].

6.24

AMENDMENTS

1. Social Security (Abolition of Earnings Rule) regulations 1989 (SI 1989/1642), reg.5 (October 1, 1989).

2. Social Security (Graduated Retirement Benefit) Amendment Regulations 1995 (SI 1995/2606, reg.2 (November 1, 2005).

3. Social Security and Child Support (Jobseeker's Allowance) (Consequential Amendments) Regulations 1996 (SI 1996/1345), reg.18 (July 10, 1996).

4. Social Security (Miscellaneous Amendments) Regulations 1997 (SI 1997/454), reg.5 (March 21, 1997).

5. Social Security Act 1998 (Commencement No.9, and Savings and Consequential and Transitional Provisions) Order 1999 (SI 1999/2422) (September 6, 1999).

6. Social Security Benefits Up-rating Order 2009 (SI 2009/497) art.12 (April 6, 2009).

7. Social Security (Graduated Retirement Benefit) Regulations 2005 (SI 2005/454), reg.2 (April 6, 2005).

8. Social Security (Retirement Pensions and Graduated Benefit) (Widowers and Civil Partnership) Regulations 2005 (SI 2005/3098) (April 6, 2006).

GENERAL NOTE

6.25   Regulation 3 of the Graduated Retirement Benefit Regulations 2005 makes
further changes to Sch.2 of these regulations but only in respect of periods of
deferment ending after April 6, 2005. Regulation 5 of the same regulations makes
provision for transitional cases, being those cases where the period of deferment
begins before April 6, 2005 but ends after that date.
    The sums provided for under these sections are increased by 3.9 per cent under
the Social Security Benefits Up-rating Order 2008 (SI 2008/632) (April 7, 2008).

The Social Security (Graduated Retirement Benefit) Regulations 2005

(SI 2005/454)

ARRANGEMENT OF REGULATIONS

6.26   1.   Citation, commencement, effect and interpretation.
        2.   Amendment of the 1965 Act.
        3.   Amendment of Schedule 2 to the Social Security (Graduated Retirement
              Benefit) (No.2) Regulations 1978 and saving.
        4.   Schedule 1.
        5.   Modification of Schedule 1 in transitional cases.
Schedule 1: Further Provisions Replacing Section 36(4) of the National Insurance
              Act 1965: increases of graduated retirement benefit and lump sum.
Schedule 2: Modification of Schedule 1.

    The Secretary of State for Work and Pensions, in exercise of the powers conferred
upon him by sections 62(1)(a) and (c) and 175(3) and (4) of the Social Security
Contributions and Benefits Act 1992, and of all other powers enabling him in that
behalf, after agreement by the Social Security Advisory Committee that proposals
in respect of regulations 3 and 4, and paragraphs 2, 3, 7, 13, 14 and 18 of Schedule
1 in so far as they apply to regulation 4, should not be referred to it, the remainder
of this Instrument containing only regulations made under provisions introduced by
section 297 of, and Schedule 11 to, the Pensions Act 2004 and being made before
the end of the period of 6 months beginning with the coming into force of those
provisions, hereby makes the following Regulations:

Citation, commencement, effect and interpretation

6.27   **1.**—(1) These Regulations may be cited as the Social Security (Graduated
Retirement Benefit) Regulations 2005 and shall come into force on 6th
April 2005.
    (2) Regulation 4 and paragraphs [¹4(2) and (3) and 14(2) and (3)] of
Schedule 1 in so far as they apply to that regulation, shall not have effect in
relation to incremental periods beginning before 6th April 2005.
    (3) In these Regulations—
"the 1965 Act" means the National Insurance Act 1965;
"the Administration Act" means the Social Security Administration
    Act 1992;
"the Benefits Act" means the Social Security Contributions and
    Benefits Act 1992 and references to Schedule 5 are to Schedule 5 to
    that Act;
"incremental period" shall have the meaning ascribed to it in paragraph
    4(6) of Schedule 1.

Amendment of the 1965 Act

2.—*Omitted as taken into account in the text of the Act set out in the Social Security (Graduated Retirement Benefit) (No. 2) Regulations 1978.*　　6.28

Amendment of Schedule 2 to the Social Security (Graduated Retirement Benefit) (No.2) Regulations 1978 and saving

3.—(1) Subject to paragraph (2), in Schedule 2 to the Social Security　　6.29
(Graduated Retirement Benefit) (No.2) Regulations 1978—
  (a) the word "and" at the end of paragraph 1(a) and paragraph 1(b); and
  (b) paragraphs 2 to 4,
shall be omitted.

(2) Schedule 2 to those Regulations shall have effect as if the amendments made by paragraph (1) had not been made in the case of—
  (a) periods of deferment (as defined by section 36(4A) of the 1965 Act) ending before 6th April 2005; and
  (b) incremental periods beginning before that date.

Schedule 1

4.—Schedule 1 to these Regulations (which makes further provision　　6.30
replacing section 36(4) of the 1965 Act) shall have effect.

Modification of Schedule 1 in transitional cases

5.—Schedule 1 shall be modified by Schedule 2 in relation to transitional　　6.31
cases and in this regulation, a "transitional case" means a case where a person's entitlement to graduated retirement benefit is deferred and the period of deferment begins before 6th April 2005 and continues on or after that day.

SCHEDULE 1　　　　　　　　　　　　**Regulation 4**

FURTHER PROVISIONS REPLACING SECTION 36(4) OF THE NATIONAL INSURANCE ACT 1965:
INCREASES OF GRADUATED RETIREMENT BENEFIT AND LUMP SUMS

PART 1

INCREASE AND LUMP SUM WHERE ENTITLEMENT TO RETIREMENT PENSION
IS DEFERRED

Scope
1.—This Part applies only in respect of a person who is deferring entitlement to graduated　　6.32
retirement benefit by virtue of section 36(4A)(a) of the 1965 Act.

Increase or lump sum where pensioner's entitlement is deferred
2.—(1) Where a person's entitlement to a Category A or Category B retirement pension is　　6.33
deferred and that person elects, [² . . .]—
  (a) that paragraph 1 of Schedule 5 (increase of pension) is to apply in relation to the period of deferment, paragraph 3 of this Schedule shall also apply in relation to that period;
  (b) that paragraph 3A of Schedule 5 (lump sum) is to apply in relation to the period of deferment, paragraph 5 of this Schedule shall also apply in relation to that period.

(2) The reference to an election in sub-paragraph (1) includes an election a person is treated as having made under paragraph A1(2) of Schedule 5.

Increase where pensioner's entitlement is deferred

6.34   **3.**—(1) This paragraph applies where—
  (a) entitlement to a Category A or Category B retirement pension is deferred and the period of deferment is less than 12 months; or
  (b) paragraph 2(1)(a) applies.

(2) The rate of the person's graduated retirement benefit shall be increased by an amount equal to the aggregate of the increments to which he is entitled under paragraph 4 but only if that amount is enough to increase the rate of the benefit by at least 1 per cent.

Calculation of increment

6.35   **4.**—(1) A person is entitled to an increment under this paragraph for each complete incremental period in his period of deferment.

(2) The amount of the increment for an incremental period shall be 1/5th per cent. of the weekly rate of the graduated retirement benefit to which the person would have been entitled for the period if his entitlement to a Category A or Category B retirement pension had not been deferred.

(3) For the purposes of sub-paragraph (2), the weekly rate of graduated retirement benefit shall be taken to include any increase in the weekly rate of that benefit and the amount of the increment in respect of such an increase shall be 1/5th per cent. of its weekly rate for each incremental period in the period of deferment beginning on the day the increase occurred.

(4) Amounts under sub-paragraphs (2) and (3) shall be rounded to the nearest penny, taking any 1/2p as nearest to the next whole penny.

(5) Where an amount under sub-paragraph (2) or (3) would, apart from this sub-paragraph, be a sum less than 1/2p, the amount shall be taken to be zero, notwithstanding any provision of the Benefits Act, the Administration Act or the Pension Schemes Act 1993.

(6) In this paragraph, "incremental period" means any period of six days which are treated by the Social Security (Widow's Benefit and Retirement Pensions) Regulations 1979 as days of increment for the purposes of paragraph 2 of Schedule 5 in relation to the person and pension in question.

(7) Where one or more orders have come into force under section 150 of the Administration Act during the period of deferment, the rate for any incremental period shall be determined as if the order or orders had come into force before the beginning of the period of deferment.

Lump sum where pensioner's entitlement is deferred

6.36   **5.**—(1) This paragraph applies where paragraph 2(1)(b) applies.

(2) The person is entitled to an amount calculated in accordance with paragraph 6 (a "lump sum").

Calculation of lump sum

6.37   **6.**—(1) The lump sum is the accrued amount for the last accrual period beginning during the period of deferment.

(2) In this paragraph—

"accrued amount" means the amount calculated in accordance with sub-paragraph (3);
"accrual period" means any period of seven days beginning with the day of the week on which Category A or Category B retirement pension would have been payable to a person in accordance with regulation 22(3) of, and paragraph 5 of Schedule 6 to, the Social Security (Claims and Payments) Regulations 1987, if his entitlement to a retirement pension had not been deferred, where that day falls within the period of deferment.

(3) The accrued amount for an accrual period for a person is—

$$\frac{(A + P) \times {}^{52}\sqrt{(1 + R)}}{100}$$

where—
A is the accrued amount for the previous accrual period (or, in the case of the first accrual period beginning during the period of deferment, zero);
P is, subject to sub-paragraph (5), the amount of graduated retirement benefit to which the person would have been entitled for the accrual period if his entitlement to a Category A or Category B retirement pension had not been deferred;
R is—
  (a) a percentage rate two per cent. higher than the Bank of England base rate; or

(b) if a higher rate is prescribed for the purposes of paragraphs 3B and 7B of Schedule 5, that higher rate.

(4) For the purposes of sub-paragraph (3), any change in the Bank of England base rate is to be treated as taking effect—

(a) at the beginning of the accrual period immediately following the accrual period during which the change took effect; or

(b) if regulations under paragraph 3B(4) of Schedule 5 so provide, at such other time as may be prescribed in those Regulations.

(5) Regulation 3 of the Social Security (Deferral of Retirement Pensions) Regulations 2005 shall have effect for the purposes of this paragraph in like manner to graduated retirement benefit as it does to retirement pension in the calculation of the lump sum under paragraph 3B of Schedule 5.

Increase or lump sum where pensioner's deceased spouse [² or civil partner] has deferred entitlement

7.—(1) This paragraph applies where—   **6.38**

(a) a [² widow, widower or surviving civil partner] ("W") is entitled to a Category A or Category B retirement pension;

(b) W was married to [² or in a civil partnership with] the other party to the marriage [² or civil partnership] ("S") when S died;

(c) S's entitlement to a Category A or Category B retirement pension was deferred when S died; and

(d) S's entitlement had been deferred throughout the period of 12 months ending with the day before S's death.

(2) Where W elects—

(a) that paragraph 4 of Schedule 5 (increase of pension) is to apply in relation to the period of deferment, paragraph 8 of this Schedule shall also apply in relation to that period;

(b) that paragraph 7A of Schedule 5 (lump sum) is to apply in relation to the period of deferment, paragraph 9 of this Schedule shall also apply in relation to that period.

(3) The reference to an election in sub-paragraph (2) includes an election W is treated as having made under paragraph 3C(3) of Schedule 5.

Increase where pensioner's deceased spouse [² or civil partner] has deferred entitlement

8.—(1) This paragraph applies where a [² widow, widower or surviving civil partner] is   **6.39**
entitled to a Category A or Category B retirement pension, was married to [² or in a civil partnership with] the other party to the marriage [² or civil partnership] when S died and one of the following conditions is met—

(a) S was entitled to graduated retirement benefit with an increase under this Schedule;

(b) paragraph 7(2)(a) applies; or

(c) paragraph 7 would apply to W but for the fact that the condition in sub-paragraph (1) (d) of that paragraph is not met.

(2) The increase in the weekly rate of W's graduated retirement benefit shall, in a case to which sub-paragraph (1) applies, be determined in accordance with section 37 of the 1965 Act as continued in force by virtue of regulations made under Schedule 3 to the Social Security (Consequential Provisions) Act 1975 or under Schedule 3 to the Social Security (Consequential Provisions) Act 1992.

Entitlement to lump sum where pensioner's deceased spouse [² or civil partner] has deferred entitlement

9.—(1) This paragraph applies where paragraph 7(2)(b) applies.   **6.40**

(2) W is entitled to an amount calculated in accordance with paragraph 10 (a "widowed person's [² or surviving civil partner's] lump sum").

Calculation of widowed person's [² or surviving civil partner's] lump sum

10.—(1) The widowed person's [² or surviving civil partner's] lump sum is the accrued   **6.41**
amount for the last accrual period beginning during the period which—

(a) began at the beginning of S's period of deferment; and

(b) ended on the day before S's death.

(2) In this paragraph—

"S" means the other party to the marriage [² or civil partnership];

"accrued amount" means the amount calculated in accordance with sub-paragraph (3);

"accrual period" means any period of seven days beginning with the day of the week on which Category A or Category B retirement pension would have been payable to S in accordance with regulation 22(3) of, and paragraph 5 of Schedule 6 to, the Social Security (Claims and Payments) Regulations 1987, if his entitlement to a retirement pension had not been deferred, where that day falls within S's period of deferment.

(3) The accrued amount for an accrual period for W is—

$$\frac{(A + P) \times {}^{52}\sqrt{(1 + R)}}{100}$$

where—

A is the accrued amount for the previous accrual period (or, in the case of the first accrual period beginning during the period mentioned in sub-paragraph (1), zero);

P is, subject to sub-paragraph (5), one-half of the graduated retirement benefit to which S would have been entitled for the accrual period if his entitlement had not been deferred during the period mentioned in sub-paragraph (1);

R is—

    (a) a percentage rate two per cent. higher than the Bank of England base rate; or

    (b) if a higher rate is prescribed for the purposes of paragraphs 3B and 7B of Schedule 5, that higher rate.

(4) For the purposes of sub-paragraph (3), any change in the Bank of England base rate is to be treated as taking effect—

    (a) at the beginning of the accrual period immediately following the accrual period during which the change took effect; or

    (b) if regulations under paragraph 7B(4) of Schedule 5 so provide, at such other time as may be prescribed.

(5) Regulation 3 of the Social Security (Deferral of Retirement Pensions) Regulations 2005 shall have effect for the purposes of this paragraph in like manner to graduated retirement benefit as it does to retirement pension in the calculation of the lump sum under paragraph 7B of Schedule 5.

(6) In any case where—

    (a) there is a period between the death of S and the date on which W becomes entitled to a Category A or Category B retirement pension; and

    (b) one or more orders have come into force under section 150 of the Administration Act during that period,

the amount of the lump sum shall be increased in accordance with that order or those orders.

PART 2

INCREASE OR LUMP SUM WHERE PERSON IS TREATED AS RECEIVING RETIREMENT PENSION AT A NOMINAL WEEKLY RATE

Scope

6.42   11.—This Part applies only in respect of a person who is deferring entitlement to graduated retirement benefit by virtue of section 36(4A)(b) of the 1965 Act.

Choice between increase and lump sum

6.43   12.—(1) Where the period of deferment is at least 12 months, a person shall, on becoming entitled to graduated retirement benefit, elect that—

    (a) paragraph 13; or

    (b) paragraph 15, is to apply in respect of that period.

[² (2) The election referred to in sub-paragraph (1) shall be made—

    (a) on the date on which he claims graduated retirement benefit; or

    (b) within the period after claiming graduated retirement benefit prescribed in paragraph 20B,

and in the manner prescribed in paragraph 20C.]

(3) If no election under sub-paragraph (1) is made within the period referred to in sub-paragraph (2)(b), the person is to be treated as having made an election under sub-paragraph (1)(b).

(4) A person who has made an election under sub-paragraph (1) (including one that the person is treated by sub-paragraph (3) as having made) may change the election in the circumstances [², manner and within the period prescribed, in paragraph 20D].

Increase

6.44   13.—(1) This paragraph applies where—

    (a) the period of deferment is less than 12 months; or

(b) the person has made an election under paragraph 12(1)(a) in respect of the period of deferment.

(2) The rate of the person's graduated retirement benefit shall be increased by an amount equal to the aggregate of the increments to which he is entitled under paragraph 14 but only if that amount is enough to increase the rate of the benefit by at least one per cent.

Calculation of increment

14.—(1) A person is entitled to an increment under this paragraph for each complete incremental period in the period of deferment.

(2) The amount of the increment for an incremental period shall be 1/5th per cent. of the weekly rate of the graduated retirement benefit to which the person would have been entitled for the period if his entitlement to graduated retirement benefit had not been deferred.

(3) For the purposes of sub-paragraph (2), the weekly rate of graduated retirement benefit shall be taken to include any increase in the weekly rate of that benefit and the amount of the increment in respect of such an increase shall be 1/5th per cent. of its weekly rate for each incremental period in the period of deferment beginning on the day the increase occurred.

(4) Amounts under sub-paragraphs (2) and (3) shall be rounded to the nearest penny, taking any 1/2p as nearest to the next whole penny.

(5) Where an amount under sub-paragraph (2) or (3) would, apart from this sub-paragraph, be a sum less than 1/2p, the amount shall be taken to be zero, notwithstanding any provision of the Benefits Act, the Administration Act or the Pension Schemes Act 1993.

(6) Where one or more orders have come into force under section 150 of the Administration Act during the period of deferment, the rate for any incremental period shall be determined as if the order or orders had come into force before the beginning of the period of deferment.

Lump sum

15.—(1) This paragraph applies where paragraph 12(1)(b) applies.

(2) The person is entitled to an amount calculated in accordance with paragraph 16 (a "lump sum").

Calculation of lump sum

16.—(1) The lump sum is the accrued amount for the last accrual period beginning during the period of deferment.

(2) In this paragraph—

"accrued amount" means the amount calculated in accordance with sub-paragraph (3);

"accrual period" means any period of seven days beginning with the day of the week on which Category A or Category B retirement pension would have been payable to a person in accordance with regulation 22(3) of, and paragraph 5 of Schedule 6 to, the Social Security (Claims and Payments) Regulations 1987, if he had been entitled to it, where that day falls within the period of deferment.

(3) The accrued amount for an accrual period for a person is—

$$\frac{(A + P) \times {}^{52}\sqrt{(1 + R)}}{100}$$

where—

A is the accrued amount for the previous accrual period (or, in the case of the first accrual period beginning during the period of deferment, zero);

P is, subject to sub-paragraph (5), the amount of graduated retirement benefit to which the person would have been entitled for the accrual period if he had been entitled to it;

R is—

(a) a percentage rate two per cent. higher than the Bank of England base rate; or
(b) if a higher rate is prescribed for the purposes of paragraphs 3B and 7B of Schedule 5, that higher rate.

(4) For the purposes of sub-paragraph (3), any change in the Bank of England base rate is to be treated as taking effect—

(a) at the beginning of the accrual period immediately following the accrual period during which the change took effect; or
(b) if regulations under paragraph 3B(4) of Schedule 5 so provide, at such other time as may be prescribed in those Regulations.

(5) Regulation 3 of the Social Security (Deferral of Retirement Pensions) Regulations 2005 shall have effect for the purposes of this paragraph in like manner to graduated retirement benefit as it does to retirement pension in the calculation of the lump sum under paragraph 3B of Schedule 5.

Choice between increase and lump sum where person's deceased spouse [³ or civil partner] has deferred entitlement to graduated retirement benefit

6.48   17.—(1) This paragraph applies where—
   (a) a [³ widow, widower or surviving civil partner] ("W") is entitled to a Category A or Category B retirement pension;
   (b) W was married to [³ or in a civil partnership with] the other party to the marriage [³or civil partnership] ("S") when S died;
   (c) S's entitlement to graduated retirement benefit was deferred when S died; and
   (d) S's entitlement had been deferred throughout the period of 12 months ending with the day before S's death.
(2) W shall elect either that—
   (a) paragraph 18; or
   (b) paragraph 19,
is to apply in respect of S's period of deferment.
   [² (3) The election referred to in sub-paragraph (2) shall be made within the period prescribed in paragraph 20B and in the manner prescribed in paragraph 20C.]
   (4) If no election under sub-paragraph (2) is made within the period referred to in sub-paragraph [² (3)], the person is to be treated as having made an election under subparagraph (2)(b).
   [² (5) A person who has made an election under sub-paragraph (2) (including one that the person is treated by sub-paragraph (4) as having made) may change the election in the circumstances, manner and within the period prescribed in paragraph 20D.]

Increase where person's deceased spouse [³ or civil partner] has deferred entitlement to graduated retirement benefit

6.49   18.—(1) This paragraph applies where a [³ widow, widower or surviving civil partner] is entitled to graduated retirement benefit, was married to [³ or in a civil partnership with] the other party to the marriage [³or civil partnership] when S died and one of the following conditions is met—
   (a) S was entitled to graduated retirement benefit with an increase under this Schedule;
   (b) W is a widow or widower to whom paragraph 17 applies and has made an election under paragraph 17(2)(a); or
   (c) paragraph 17 would apply to W but for the fact that the condition in sub-paragraph (1)(d) of that paragraph is not met.
(2) The increase in the weekly rate of W's graduated retirement benefit shall, in a case to which sub-paragraph (1) applies, be determined in accordance with section 37 of the 1965 Act as continued in force by virtue of regulations made under Schedule 3 to the Social Security (Consequential Provisions) Act 1975 or under Schedule 3 to the Social Security (Consequential Provisions) Act 1992.

Entitlement to lump sum where person's deceased spouse [³ or civil partner] has deferred entitlement to graduated retirement benefit

6.50   19.—(1) This paragraph applies where paragraph 17(2)(b) applies.
(2) W is entitled to an amount calculated in accordance with paragraph 20 (a "widowed person's [³ or surviving civil partner's] lump sum").

Calculation of widowed person's [³ or surviving civil partner's] lump sum

6.51   20.—(1) The widowed person's lump sum is the accrued amount for last accrual period beginning during the period which—
   (a) began at the beginning of S's period of deferment; and
   (b) ended on the day before S's death.
(2) In this paragraph—

   "S" means the other party to the marriage [³ or civil partnership];
   "accrued amount" means the amount calculated in accordance with sub-paragraph (3);
   "accrual period" means any period of seven days beginning with the day of the week on which Category A or Category B retirement pension would have been payable to S in accordance with regulation 22(3) of, and paragraph 5 of Schedule 6 to, the Social Security (Claims and Payments) Regulations 1987, if he had been entitled to it, where that day falls within S's period of deferment.

(3) The accrued amount for an accrual period for W is—

$$(A + P) \times {}^{52}\sqrt{\frac{(1 + R)}{100}}$$

where—

A is the accrued amount for the previous accrual period (or, in the case of the first accrual period beginning during the period mentioned in sub-paragraph (1), zero);

P is, subject to sub-paragraph (5), one-half of the graduated retirement benefit to which S would have been entitled for the accrual period if he had been entitled to it during the period mentioned in sub-paragraph (1);

R is—

   (a)   a percentage rate two per cent. higher than the Bank of England base rate; or

   (b)   if a higher rate is prescribed for the purposes of paragraphs 3B and 7B of Schedule 5, that higher rate.

(4) For the purposes of sub-paragraph (3), any change in the Bank of England base rate is to be treated as taking effect—

   (a)   at the beginning of the accrual period immediately following the accrual period during which the change took effect; or

   (b)   if regulations under paragraph 7B(4) of Schedule 5 so provide, at such other time as may be prescribed.

(5) Regulation 3 of the Social Security (Deferral of Retirement Pensions) Regulations 2005 shall have effect for the purposes of this paragraph in like manner to graduated retirement benefit as it does to retirement pension in the calculation of the lump sum under paragraph 7B of Schedule 5.

(6) In any case where—

   (a)   there is a period between the death of S and the date on which W becomes entitled to graduated retirement benefit; and

   (b)   one or more orders have come into force under section 150 of the Administration Act during that period,

the amount of the lump sum shall be increased in accordance with that order or those orders.

[³ Transitional provision relating to widower's entitlement to increase of graduated retirement benefit or lump sum

20ZA.—In the case of a widower who attains pensionable age before 6th April 2010, paragraphs 17 to 19 shall not apply unless he was over pensionable age when his wife died. **6.52**

Transitional provision relating to civil partner's entitlement to increase of graduated retirement benefit or lump sum

20ZB.—In the case of a civil partner who attains pensionable age before 6th April 2010, paragraphs 17 to 19 shall not apply unless he or she was over pensionable age when his or her civil partner died.] **6.53**

[² PART 2A

ELECTIONS UNDER PART 2

Scope and interpretation

20A.—(1) This Part applies in respect of elections which a person makes or is treated as having made under Part 2. **6.54**

(2) In this Part, "elector" means the person who may make an election under paragraph 12(1) or 17(2).

Timing of election

20B.—(1) The period for making an election under paragraph 12(1) is, subject to sub-paragraph (4), three months starting on the date shown on the notice issued by the Secretary of State following the claim for graduated retirement benefit, confirming that the elector is required to make that election. **6.55**

(2) The period for making an election under paragraph 17(2) is, subject to sub-paragraph (4), three months starting on the date shown on the notice issued by the Secretary of State following W's claim for a Category A or Category B retirement pension or, if later, the date of S's death, confirming that the elector is required to make that election.

(3) Where more than one notice has been issued by the Secretary of State in accordance with sub-paragraph (1) or (2), the periods prescribed in those sub-paragraphs shall only commence from the date shown on the latest such notice.

(4) The periods specified in sub-paragraphs (1) and (2) may be extended by the Secretary of State if he considers it reasonable to do so in any particular case.

(5) Nothing in this paragraph shall prevent the making of an election on or after claiming graduated retirement benefit or, as the case may be, Category A or Category B retirement pension, but before the issue of the notice referred to in sub-paragraph (1) or (2).

Manner of making election

6.56   **20C.**—An election under paragraph 12(1) or 17(2) may be made—

    (a) in writing to an office specified by the Secretary of State for accepting such elections; or

    (b) except where the Secretary of State directs in any particular case that the election must be made in accordance with sub-paragraph (a), by telephone call to the telephone number specified by the Secretary of State.

Change of election

6.57   **20D.**—(1) Subject to sub-paragraphs (2) and (6), this paragraph applies in the case of an election which—

    (a) has been made under paragraph 12(1) or 17(2); or

    (b) has been treated as made under paragraph 12(3) or 17(4).

(2) This paragraph does not apply in the case of an election which is—

    (a) made, or treated as made, by an elector who has subsequently died; or

    (b) treated as having been made by virtue of regulation [4 30(5E) or (5G)] of the Social Security (Claims and Payments) Regulations 1987.

(3) An election specified in sub-paragraph (1) may be changed by way of application made no later than the last day of the period specified in sub-paragraph (4).

(4) The period specified for the purposes of sub-paragraph (3) is, subject to sub-paragraph (5), three months after the date shown on the written notification issued by the Secretary of State to the elector, confirming the election which the elector has made or is treated as having made.

(5) The period specified in sub-paragraph (4) may be extended by the Secretary of State if he considers it reasonable to do so in any particular case.

(6) An election specified in sub-paragraph (1) may not be changed where—

    (a) there has been a previous change of election under this paragraph in respect of the same period of deferment;

    (b) the application is to change the election to one under paragraph 12(1)(a) or 17(2)(a) and any amount paid to him by way of, or on account of, a lump sum pursuant to paragraph 15 or 19, has not been repaid in full to the Secretary of State within the period specified in sub-paragraph (4) or, as the case may be, (5); or

    (c) the application is to change the election to one under paragraph 12(1)(b) or 17(2)(b) and the amount actually paid by way of an increase of graduated retirement benefit, or actually paid on account of such an increase, would exceed the amount to which the elector would be entitled by way of a lump sum.

(7) For the purposes of sub-paragraph (6)(b), repayment in full of the amount paid by way of, or on account of, a lump sum shall only be treated as having occurred if repaid to the Secretary of State in the currency in which that amount was originally paid.

(8) Where the application is to change the election to one under paragraph 12(1)(b) or 17(2)(b) and sub-paragraph (6)(c) does not apply, any amount paid by way of an increase of graduated retirement benefit, or on account of such an increase, in respect of the period of deferment for which the election was originally made, shall be treated as having been paid on account of the lump sum to which the elector is entitled under paragraph 15 or 19.

(9) An application under sub-paragraph (3) to change an election may be made—

    (a) in writing to an office specified by the Secretary of State for accepting such applications; or

    (b) except where the Secretary of State directs in any particular case that the application must be made in accordance with paragraph (a), by telephone call to the telephone number specified by the Secretary of State].

PART 3

SUPPLEMENTARY

Supplementary

6.58   **21.**—Any lump sum calculated under paragraph 6, 10, 16 or 20 must be rounded to the nearest penny, taking any 1/2p as nearest to the next whole penny above.

SCHEDULE 2   **Regulation 5**

MODIFICATION OF SCHEDULE 1

1.—In paragraph 2(1), for paragraph (b) there shall be substituted the following para-   **6.59**
graph—

"(b) that paragraph 1 of Schedule 5 is to apply in relation to so much of the period of deferment which falls before the first day of the first accrual period (as defined by paragraph
3B(2) of that Schedule) beginning on or after 6th April 2005 ('the first part') and that
paragraph 3A of that Schedule is to apply in relation to the remainder of the period of deferment ('the second part'), paragraph 3 of this Schedule shall apply in relation to the first part
and paragraph 5 of this Schedule shall apply in relation to the second part.".

2.—In paragraph 3(2), for the words from "that amount" to the end of the sub-paragraph,
there shall be substituted—

"—

    (a) there are at least 7 incremental periods in the period of deferment;
    (b) there are at least 5 incremental periods in the period of deferment and the amount
        of the increment for at least one of those periods is calculated in accordance with
        paragraph 4(2); or
    (c) paragraph 2(1)(b) applies and there is at least one incremental period before the
        first day of the first accrual period.".

3.—At the end of paragraph 6(1), there shall be added the words "or, if greater, the amount
equal to the total amount of graduated retirement benefit which would have been payable to
the person during the period of 12 months ending with the last day of the period of deferment
if his entitlement had not been deferred".

4.—In paragraph 7—
    (a) at the end of sub-paragraph (1)(d), there shall be added the words "and throughout
        the period of 12 months falling after 5th April 2005";
    (b) for sub-paragraph (2)(b) there shall be substituted the following sub-paragraph—

"(b) that paragraph 4 of Schedule 5 is to apply in relation to so much of S's period of
deferment which falls before the first day of the first accrual period (as defined by paragraph
7B(2) of that Schedule) beginning on or after 6th April 2005 ('the first part') and that paragraph 7A of that Schedule is to apply in relation to the remainder of the period of deferment
('the second part'), paragraph 8 of this Schedule shall apply in relation to the first part and
paragraph 9 of this Schedule shall apply in relation to the second part.".

5.—[² *Omitted*].

6.—In paragraph 12(1)—
    (a) after the words "12 months" there shall be inserted the words "and at least 12 months
        of that period falls after 5th April 2005";
    (b) for sub-paragraph (b), there shall be substituted the following sub-paragraph—

"(b) that paragraph 13 is to apply in relation to so much of the period of deferment which
falls before the first day of the first accrual period (as defined in paragraph 16(2)) for the
purposes of paragraph 15 and that paragraph 14 is to apply in relation to the remainder of
the period of deferment.".

7.—In paragraph 13(2), for the words from "that amount" to the end of the sub-paragraph,
there shall be substituted—

"—

    (a) there are at least 7 incremental periods in the period of deferment;
    (b) there are at least 5 incremental periods in the period of deferment and the amount
        of the increment for at least one of those periods is calculated in accordance with
        paragraph 14(2); or
    (c) the person has made (or is treated as having made) an election under paragraph
        12(1)(b) and there is at least one incremental period before the first day of the first
        accrual period.".

8.—At the end of paragraph 16(1), there shall be added the words "or, if greater, the amount
equal to the total amount of graduated retirement benefit to which the person would have been
entitled for the period of 12 months ending with the last day of the period of deferment if his
entitlement had not been deferred".

9.—In paragraph 17—

    (a) at the end of sub-paragraph (1)(d), there shall be added the words "and throughout the period of 12 months falling after 5th April 2005";

    (b) for sub-paragraph (2)(b), there shall be substituted the following paragraph—

"(b) that paragraph 18 is to apply in relation to so much of S's period of deferment which falls before the first day of the first accrual period (as defined in paragraph 20(2)) for the purposes of paragraph 19 and that paragraph 19 is to apply in relation to the remainder of that period of deferment.".

10.—[² *Omitted*].

AMENDMENTS

1. Social Security (Graduated Retirement Benefit)(Amendment) Regulations 2005 (SI 2005/846), reg.2 (April 5, 2005)

2. Social Security (Deferral of Retirement Pensions, Shared Additional Pensions and Graduated Retirement Benefit) (Miscellaneous Provisions) Regulations 2005 (SI 2005/2677) (April 6, 2006).

3. Social Security (Retirement Pensions and Graduated Retirement Benefits) (Widowers and Civil Partnership) Regulations 2005 (SI 2005/3078) (April 6, 2006).

4. Social Security (Deferral of Pensions etc) Regulations 2006 (SI 2006/516) (April 6, 2006).

The Social Security (Retirement Pensions etc.) (Transitional Provisions) Regulations 2005

(SI 2005/469)

ARRANGEMENT OF REGULATIONS

6.60
1.   Citation, commencement and interpretation.
2.   Modification of Schedule 5 to the Act.
3.   Modification of Schedule 5A to the Act.

The Secretary of State for Work and Pensions, in exercise of the powers conferred upon him by paragraph 27 of Schedule 11 to the Pensions Act 2004 and of all other powers enabling him in that behalf, hereby makes the following Regulations:

Citation, commencement and interpretation

6.61
1.—(1) These Regulations may be cited as the Social Security (Retirement Pensions etc.) (Transitional Provisions) Regulations 2005 and shall come into force on 6th April 2005.

(2) In these Regulations—

"the Act" means the Social Security Contributions and Benefits Act 1992;

"period of deferment" shall be construed in accordance with section 55(3) or, as the case may be, section 55C(3), of the Act;

"transitional case" means a case where a person's entitlement to retirement pension or shared additional pension is deferred and the period of deferment begins before 6th April 2005 and continues on or after that day.

Modification of Schedule 5 to the Act

2.—(1) Schedule 5 to the Act (pension increase or lump sum where entitlement to retirement pension is deferred) shall be modified in relation to transitional cases in accordance with the following paragraphs.

6.62

(2) In paragraph A1(1) (choice between increase of pension and lump sum where pensioner's entitlement is deferred)—

    (a) after the words "12 months" there shall be inserted the words "and at least 12 months of that period fall after 5th April 2005";

    (b) for paragraph (b) there shall be substituted the following paragraph—

"(b) that paragraph 1 is to apply in relation to so much of the period of deferment as falls before the first day of the first accrual period (as defined by paragraph 3B(2)) beginning on or after 6th April 2005 and that paragraph 3A (entitlement to lump sum) is to apply in relation to the remainder of the period of deferment.".

(3) In paragraph 1(2) (increase of pension where pensioner's entitlement is deferred), for the words from "that amount" to the end of the sub-paragraph, there shall be substituted—

"(a) there are at least 7 incremental periods in the period of deferment;

    (b) there are at least 5 incremental periods in the period of deferment and the amount of the increment for at least one of those periods is calculated in accordance with paragraph 2(3) as in force in relation to incremental periods beginning on or after 6th April 2005; or

    (c) the person has made (or is treated as having made) an election under paragraph A1(1)(b) and there is at least one incremental period before the first day of the first accrual period (as defined by paragraph 3B(2)) beginning on or after 6th April 2005.".

(4) In paragraph 3B (calculation of lump sum)—

    (a) at the end of sub-paragraph (1), there shall be added the words "or, if greater, the amount equal to the total amount of Category A or Category B retirement pension [² (excluding any increase under section 83, 84 or 85)] which would have been payable to the person during the period of 12 months ending with the last day of the period of deferment if his entitlement had not been deferred";

    (b) in the definition of "accrual period" in sub-paragraph (2), for the words "a prescribed day of the week", there shall be substituted the words "the day of the week on which the person's retirement pension would have been payable had his entitlement not been deferred";

(5) In paragraph 3C (choice between increase of pension and lump sum where pensioner's deceased spouse has deferred entitlement)—

    (a) at the end of paragraph (1)(d), there shall be added the words "and throughout the period of 12 months beginning with 6th April 2005";

    (b) for paragraph (2)(b) there shall be substituted the following paragraph—

"(b) that paragraph 4 is to apply in relation to so much of S's period of deferment as falls before the first day of the first accrual period (as defined by paragraph 7B(2)) beginning on or after 6th April 2005 and that paragraph 7A (entitlement to lump sum) is to apply in relation to the remainder of that period of deferment.".

(6) In paragraph 7B (calculation of lump sum)—

(a) [¹ *omitted*];

(b) in the definition of "accrual period" in sub-paragraph (2), for the words "a prescribed day of the week", there shall be substituted the words "the day of the week on which S's retirement pension would have been payable had his entitlement not been deferred".

AMENDMENTS

1. Social Security (Deferral of Retirement Pensions, Shared Additional Pensions and Graduated Retirement Benefit) (Miscellaneous Provisions) Regulations 2005 (SI 2005/2677) (April 6, 2006).

2. Social Security (Deferral of Retirement Pensions etc.) Regulations 2006 (SI 2006/516) (April 6, 2006)

Modification of Schedule 5A to the Act

6.63   **3.**—(1) Schedule 5A to the Act (pension increase or lump sum where entitlement to shared additional pension is deferred) shall be modified in relation to transitional cases in accordance with the following paragraphs.

(2) In paragraph 1(1) (choice between increase of pension and lump sum where pensioner's entitlement is deferred)—

(a) after the words "12 months" there shall be inserted the words "and at least 12 months of that period fall after 5th April 2005";

(b) for paragraph (b) there shall be substituted the following paragraph—

"(b) that paragraph 2 is to apply in relation to so much of the period of deferment as falls before the first day of the first accrual period (as defined by paragraph 5(2)) beginning on or after 6ᵗʰ April 2005 and that paragraph 4 (entitlement to lump sum) is to apply in relation to the remainder of the period of deferment.".

(3) In paragraph 2(2) (increase of pension where pensioner's entitlement is deferred), for the words from "that amount" to the end of the sub-paragraph, there shall be substituted—

"(a) there are at least 7 incremental periods in the period of deferment;

(b) there are at least 5 incremental periods in the period of deferment and the amount of the increment for at least one of those periods is calculated in accordance with paragraph 3(2); or

(c) the person has made (or is treated as having made) an election under paragraph 1(1)(b) and there is at least one incremental period before the first day of the first accrual period (as defined by paragraph 5(2)) beginning on or after 6th April 2005."

(4) In paragraph 5 (calculation of lump sum)—

(a) at the end of sub-paragraph (1), there shall be added the words "or, if greater, the amount equal to the total amount of shared additional pension which would have been payable to the person during the period of 12 months ending with the last day of the period of deferment if his entitlement had not been deferred";

(b) in the definition of "accrual period" in sub-paragraph (2), for the words "a prescribed day of the week", there shall be substituted the words "the day of the week on which the person's shared additional pension would have been payable had his entitlement not been deferred".

Social Security (Widow's Benefit and Retirement Pensions) Regulations 1979

(SI 1979/642) *(as amended)*

ARRANGMENT OF REGULATIONS

6.64

The Secretary of State for Social Services, in exercise of the powers conferred upon him by sections 29(5), 30(3), 33, 39(1) and (4), 40(2), 85(1) and 162 of, and Schedule 20 to, the Social Security Act 1975, section 20 of, and paragraphs 2(2)(a) and 3 of Schedule 1 to, the Social Security Pensions Act 1975 and of all other powers enabling him in that behalf, hereby makes the following regulations which only consolidate the regulations herein revoked and which accordingly, by virtue of paragraph 20 of Schedule 15 to the Social Security Act 1975, are not subject to the requirement of section 139(1) of that Act for prior reference to the National Insurance Advisory Committee:

Citation, commencement and interpretation

6.65   **1.**—(1) These regulations may be cited as the Social Security (Widow's Benefit and Retirement Pensions) Regulations 1979 and shall come into operation on 10th July 1979.

(2) In these regulations, unless the context otherwise requires—

"the Act" means Social Security Act 1975

[¹ "bereavement allowance" means an allowance awarded in accordance with section 39B of the Social Security Contributions and Benefits Act 1992;]

[² "civil partner" in relation to any person who has been in a civil partnership more than once means the last civil partner;]

"home responsibilities year" means a year in which the person in question was precluded from regular employment by responsibilities at home within the meaning of the Social Security Pensions (Home Responsibilities and Miscellaneous Amendments) Regulations 1978;

"husband", "wife" or "spouse" in relation to any person who has been married more than once means the last husband, last wife or last spouse respectively;

"a period of at least 10 years" means a period of, or periods amounting in the aggregate to, at least 3,652 days;

[⁵ . . .]

"qualifying year" in relation to any person means a year for which his earnings factor is sufficient for satisfaction of paragraph (b) of the second contribution condition specified in paragraph 5 of Schedule 3 to the Act, but not including (except for the purposes of regulation 6) a year which is treated as such a year by virtue of regulation 8(4) and not including any home responsibilities year;

[³ "the determining authority" means, as the case may require, the Secretary of State, [⁸ the First tier Tribunal or the Upper Tribunal]]

"section 9(2), 9(3) or 10(2) increase" means an increase under section 9(2), 9(3) or 10(2), respectively, of the Act of a person's Category A retirement pension attributable to his spouse's contributions;

"Service Pensions Instrument" means a provision and only a provision of any Royal Warrant, Order in Council or other instrument (not being a 1914–18 War Injuries Scheme) under which a disablement pension (not including a pension calculated or determined by reference to length of service) may be paid out of public funds in respect of any disablement, wound, injury or disease due to service in the naval, military or air force of the Crown or in any nursing service or other auxiliary service of any of the said forces or in the Home Guard or in any other organisation established under the control of the Defence Council or formerly established under the control of the Admiralty, the Army Council, or the Air Council;

[⁶ "shared additional pension" means a shared additional pension under Section 55A of the Social Security Contributions and Benefit Act 1992;]

"1914–18 War Injuries Scheme" means any scheme made under the Injuries in War (Compensation) Act 1914 or under the Injuries in War Compensation Act 1914 (Session 2) or any Government scheme for compensation in respect of persons injured in any merchant ship or fishing vessel as the result of hostilities during the 1914–18 war;

"unemployability supplement" has the extended meaning assigned to it in regulation 2 of the Social Security (Overlapping Benefits) Regulations 1979 and further includes benefit corresponding to an unemployability supplement by virtue of regulations under section 159(3) (a) of the Act;

[¹ "widowed parent's allowance" means an allowance referred to in section 39A of the Social Security Contributions and Benefits Act 1992;]

"year" means tax year.

(3) For the purposes of these regulations a person who has obtained a decree absolute of presumption of death and dissolution of marriage under the Matrimonial Causes Act 1973 shall, notwithstanding that the spouse whose death has been presumed is dead, be treated as a person whose marriage has been terminated otherwise than by the death of his spouse unless the date of his death is established to the satisfaction of the determining authority, and, in relation to a person who is so treated, the marriage in question shall be treated as having been terminated on the date of the decree absolute.

[⁴ (3A) For the purposes of regulation 8 of these Regulations, where, before the coming into force of the Nullity of Marriages Act 1971 a decree of nullity was granted in relation to a person on the ground that the marriage was voidable, that person shall be treated as a person whose marriage has been terminated by divorce from the date on which that decree was made absolute.]

(4) For the purposes of regulations 11(1)(d), 12(3) and 13(2) a person shall be deemed to be, or to have been, entitled to a pension or benefit if he would have been entitled had he made a claim for it.

AMENDMENTS

1. Social Security (Benefits for Widows and Widowers) (Consequential Amendments) Regulation 2000 (SI 2000/1483) reg.8 (April 9, 2001).

2. Social Security (Abolition of Earnings Rule) (Consequential) Regulations 1989 (SI 1989/1642), reg.11 (October 1, 1989).

3. Social Security Act 1998 (Commencement No. 9, and Savings and Consequential and Transitional Provisions) Order 1999 (SI 1999/2422) (September 6, 1999).

4. Social Security (Widows' Benefit and Retirement Pensions) Amendment Regulations 1995 (SI 1995/74), reg.1 (February 10, 1995).

5. Social Security (Deferral of Retirement Pensions) Regulations 2005 (SI 2005/453) reg.4 (April 6, 2005).

6. Shared Additional Pensions (Miscellaneous Amendments) regulations 2005 (SI 2005/1551) (July 6, 2005).

7. Civil Partnership (consequential amendments) Regulations 2005 (SI 2005/2878) (December 5, 2005).

8. Tribunals, Courts and Enforcement Act 2007, Sch.1 (November 3, 2008).

[¹ Disapplication of section 1(1A) of the Administration Act for the purposes of retirement pension

1A.—Section 1(1A) of the Administration Act (requirement to state national insurance number) shall not apply— 6.66

  (a) [² *omitted*];

  (b) to an adult dependant in respect of whom a claim for an increase of retirement pension is made or treated as made before 5th October, 1998.]

[³(c) to an adult dependant who—
  (i) is a person in respect of whom a claim for an increase of retire-
       ment pension is made;
  (ii) is subject to immigration control within the meaning of section
        115(9)(a) of the Immigration and Asylum Act 1999; and
  (iii) has not previously been allocated a national insurance number.]

AMENDMENTS

1. Social Security (National Insurance Information: Exemption) Regulations (SI
1997/2676) (December 1, 1997).
2. Social Security (Working Tax Credit and Child Tax Credit) (Consequential
Amendments) (No. 2) Regulations 2003 (SI 2003/937), reg.2 (April 6, 2003).
3. Social Security (National Insurance Number Information: Exemption)
Regulations 2009, (SI 2009/471), reg.3 (April 6, 2009).

Election to be treated as not having retired

6.67   **2.**—(1) Subject to the provisions of these regulations, where any person
(other than one mentioned in paragraph (2))—
  (a) has become entitled to either a Category A or a Category B retire-
       ment pension [³ or a shared additional pension] [² . . .]; and
  (b) elects that this regulation shall apply in his case,
the Act shall have effect as if that person had not become entitled as
aforesaid.
  (2) Paragraph (1) shall not apply to:—
  (a) a person who has previously made such an election;
  (b) in relation to a Category A retirement pension, a husband whose wife
       is entitled, by virtue of his contributions, to a Category B retirement
       pension or a section 10(2) increase and who does not consent to his
       election, unless that consent is unreasonably withheld.
  [²(3) Notice of election for the purposes of this regulation may be given
by telephone call to the telephone number specified by the Secretary of
State unless the Secretary of State directs in any particular case that the
notice or consent must be given in writing.
  (4) Subject to paragraphs (5) and (6), an election shall take effect—
  (a) on the date on which it is given; or
  (b) on such other date specified by the person making the election, being
       no earlier than the date on which it is given and no later than 28 days
       after the date on which it is given.]
  (5) In the case of a man whose wife is entitled, by virtue of his contributions, to a Category B retirement pension or a section 10(2) increase—
  (a) if she consents [² . . .] to the election, the election shall not take effect
       earlier than the date of her consent; or
  (b) if she does not so consent and the determining authority decides that
       her consent has been unreasonably withheld, the election shall take
       effect in accordance with the provisions of paragraph (4) or on such
       later date (if any) as that authority, having regard to all the circum-
       stances of the case, may determine.
  (6) Where a woman entitled to a Category B retirement pension under
section 29(4) of the Act has, on or after 6th April 1979, made an election
and has not revoked it, then, for the purpose only of determining her right
to increments under paragraph 2 of Schedule 1 to the Pensions Act, her
election shall be treated as if it took effect from 6th April, 1979 or, if later,

the date of the death of her husband by virtue of whose contributions she is so entitled.

AMENDMENTS

1. Social Security Miscellaneous Provisions Regulations 1989 (SI 1989/893), reg.4 (May 28, 1989).
2. Social Security (Deferral of Retirement Pensions) Regulations 2005 (SI 2005/453; reg.4 (April 6, 2005).
3. Shared Additional Pensions (Miscellaneous Amendments) Regulations 2005 (SI 2005/1551) (July 6, 2005).

GENERAL NOTE

Para. (5)
For the circumstances in which it is suggested that a wife's consent might be unreasonably withheld, see note to s.55 of the Act.

6.68

Provisions applying after election

3.—Where an election has been made in accordance with regulation 2—
  (a) subject to the provisions of regulations made under section 82(2)(a) of the Act (adjustment to prevent payments for periods of less than a week or at different rates for different parts of a week), no Category A or B retirement pension [2 or a shared additional pension] shall be payable to a person and no Category B retirement pension or section 10(2) increase shall be payable to a man's wife by virtue of his contributions for any period on or after the date of his election and before he subsequently [1 becomes entitled to a Category A or Category B retirement pension] [2 or a shared additional pension] or dies; and
  (b) where the person who has made the election is a woman who became entitled to a Category B retirement pension in accordance with section 29(4) of the Act and she revokes her election, she shall cease to be treated as if she had not become entitled to such a retirement pension; and
  (c) where the person who has made the election is a man whose wife is entitled to a Category B retirement pension or a section 10(2) increase by virtue of his contributions and he subsequently claims a retirement pension, his claim may be treated as including a claim by his wife, by virtue of his contributions, for a Category B retirement pension or a section 10(2) increase.

6.69

AMENDMENTS

1. Social Security (Abolition of Earnings Rule) (Consequential) Regulations 1989 (SI 1989/1642), reg.3 (October 1, 1989).
2. Shared Additional Pensions (Miscellaneous Amendments) Regulations 2005 (SI 2005/1551) (July 6, 2005).

Calculating periods of incapacity for work for welfare to work beneficiaries entitled to an increase of long-term incapacity benefit

[1 **3A.**—Section 47(1) of the Social Security Contributions and Benefits Act 1992 (increase of Category A retirement pension for long-term

6.70

incapacity) shall have effect, in any case where a person is treated in accordance with regulation 13A of the Social Security (Incapacity for Work) (General) Regulations 1995 as a welfare to work beneficiary, as if for the reference to 8 weeks there were substituted a reference to [²104] weeks.]

AMENDMENTS

1. Social Security (Welfare to Work) Regulations 1998 (SI 1998/2231), reg.7 (October 5, 1998).
2. Social Security (Miscellaneous Amendment) (No.4) Regulations 2006 (SI 2006/2378), reg.2 (October 9, 2006).

Days to be treated as days of increment

6.71   **4.**—(1) For the purposes of paragraph 2 of Schedule 1 to the Pensions Act a day shall be treated as a day of increment in relation to any person if it is a day in that person's [¹ period of [⁵deferment]] other than a Sunday, in respect of which—
[¹ (a) if that person had not deferred his entitlement to a Category A or Category B retirement pension, or, in the case of a married woman and her Category B retirement pension or section 10(2) increase, if both she and her husband had not deferred their entitlement to, respectively, a Category A or a Category B retirement pension, that person would have been entitled to such a pension (and would not have been disqualified for receiving it by reason of imprisonment or detention in legal custody); and]
  (b) that person had not received any of the following benefits:—
    (i) any benefit under Chapters I and II of Part II of the Act other than child's special allowance, attendance allowance, [² disability living allowance] and guardian's allowance; or
   [⁸ (ii) graduated retirement benefit where that person's period of deferment ended on or before 5th April 2006; or
    (iii) an unemployability supplement; and]
  (c) in the case of a married woman who would have been entitled to a Category B retirement pension or a section 10(2) increase [⁵and whose period of deferment began before 6ᵗʰ April 2005], her husband had not received an increase of any of the benefits mentioned in paragraph (1)(b) in respect of her.
[⁵ and
  (d) in the case of a person who would have been entitled to a Category A or Category B retirement pension ("the deferrer") and whose period of deferment begins on or after 6th April 2005—
    (i) no other person has received an increase of any of the benefits mentioned in sub-paragraph (b) in respect of the deferrer; or
    (ii) another person has received such an increase in respect of the deferrer and the deferrer is neither married to, [⁷ or in a civil partnership with,] nor residing with, that other person.]
  (2) Subject to the following paragraph, for the purposes of this regulation, where in respect of any day—
  (a) a person has received one or more of the benefits mentioned in paragraph (1)(b) or (c), and
  (b) either—
    (i) the determining authority, has determined that in respect of that day he was not entitled to that benefit; or

    (ii) by virtue of the provisions of the Employment Protection (Recoupment of Unemployment Benefit and Supplementary Benefit) Regulations 1977 the Secretary of State has recovered from that person's employer sums on account of [⁴ a contribution-based jobseeker's allowance] received by that person in respect of that day; and

  (c) the whole of the benefit or sum on account of benefit in respect of that day has been repaid or, as the case may be, recovered before the relevant date,

that day shall be treated as a day in respect of which he did not receive that benefit; and in this paragraph "relevant date" means—

    (i) where a person's entitlement to increments under paragraph 2 of Schedule 1 to the Pensions Act is in question, the end of his [¹ period of [⁵deferment;] or

    (ii) where a person's entitlement to increments under paragraph 4 or 4A of that Schedule in relation to the [¹deferred entitlement] of a deceased spouse is in question, the date of the death of that spouse.

(3) Where the benefit or sum on account of benefit in respect of a day to which paragraph (2)(a) and (b) applies is repaid or, as the case may be, recovered on or after the said relevant date, that day shall not be treated as a day in respect of which that person did not receive that benefit until the benefit has been repaid or, as the case may be, sums on account of the benefit have been recovered in respect of all the days to which those sub-paragraphs relate and which fall within the period to which this regulation applies.

[⁶ (4) For the purpose of paragraph 3 of Schedule 5A to the Social Security Contributions and Benefits Act 1992 a day shall be treated as a day of increment in relation to any person if it is a day in that person's period of deferment, other than a Sunday, in respect of which if that person had not deferred his entitlement to a shared additional pension he would have been entitled to it (and would not have been disqualified from receiving it by reason of imprisonment or detention in legal custody).]

AMENDMENTS

1. Social Security (Abolition of Earnings Rule) (Consequential) Regulations 1989 (SI 1989/1642), reg.11 (October 1, 1989).

2. Social Security Disability Living Allowance and Disability Working Allowance (Consequential Provisions) Regulations 1991 (SI 1991/2742), reg.6 (April 6, 1992).

3. Social Security (Widows' Benefit and Retirement Pensions) (Amendment) Regulations 1992 (SI 1992/1692), reg.2 (August 5, 1992).

4. Social Security and Child Support (Jobseeker's Allowance) (Consequential Amendments) Regulations 1996 (SI 1996/1345), reg.26 (October 7, 1996).

5. Social Security (Deferral of Retirement Pensions) Regulations 2005 (SI 2005/453) reg.4 (April 6, 2005).

6. Shared Additional Pensions (Miscellaneous Amendments) Regulations 2005 (SI 2005/1551) (July 6, 2005).

7. Civil Partnership (Consequential Amendments) Regulations (SI 2005/2878) (December 5, 2005).

8. Social Security (Deferral of Retirement Pensions etc) Regulations 2006 (SI 2006/516) (April 6, 2006).

GENERAL NOTE

6.72   Regulation 4(1)(a) is difficult to follow but a recent unreported Commissioner's decision (*CP/037/1991*) confirms that the increment accrues in respect of a married woman and her Category B pension only if both that pension and her husband's Category A pension have been deferred. In this case the husband had reached retirement age and had deferred his pension for four years. He then retired some eight months before his wife reached the age of 60 and claimed her Category B pension. In such a case the husband has an increment to his Category A pension because entitlement to that has been deferred, but his wife has no increment because her entitlement was not deferred.

Sub-para. (1)

6.73   Regulation 4(1)(b)(ii) has been amended to include graduated retirement pension with effect from August 5, 1992. This amendment is the response to the case of *Chief Adjudication Officer and Sec. of State v Pearse (R(P) 2/93)*. Mr Pearse had deferred his retirement and accrued increments to his Category A retirement pension. Mrs Pearse had, however, been refused increments to her Category B pension because she had during the deferred period been in receipt of Graduated Retirement Pension. The Department argued that GRP was covered by sub-para. (i) of reg.4(1)(b). The Commissioner, and the Court of Appeal, held that it was not. (Regulations deeming GRP to be a benefit under Pt II of the Act applied only for the purpose of continuity.) Mrs Pearse was therefore entitled to receive the increments to her Category B pension. The Department has now closed the door on this argument by amending sub-para.(ii) specifically to include GRP. But the amendment applies only from August 5, 1992. Married women whose husbands deferred their retirement for a period before that date and who were refused increments for the same reasons as Mrs Pearse will be entitled to arrears of their pension. Also married women who opted not to take the GRP so as to be allowed to accrue increments should now receive a payment of arrears for the GRP.

Modification of paragraph 2(1) to (3) of Schedule 1 to the Pensions Act

6.74   **5.**—(1) This regulation applies to a person referred to in paragraph 1 of Schedule 1 to the Pensions Act during whose [²period of [³ deferment]] there has been an increase, other than an increase made by an order under [¹ section 63 of the Social Security Act 1986] in the rate of the Category A or Category B retirement pension to which he would have been entitled if his [² entitlement to the pension had commenced on the day on which he attained pensionable age.]

(2) In relation to a person to whom this regulation applies, paragraph 2(1) to (3) of the said Schedule 1 shall have effect with the additions, omissions and amendments prescribed below.

(3) In paragraph 2(1) for the words after "incremental period" there shall be substituted—

"(a) in his [² period of [³ deferment]] and

(b) in each period beginning with the day on which an increase in the weekly rate of his pension took place and ending with the day before [² his entitlement arose]".

(4) After paragraph 2(2)(b) there shall be added—

"and

(c) 'weekly rate of his pension' means the weekly rate of the Category A or Category B retirement pension to which that person would have been entitled on attaining pensionable age; and

(d) 'increase' means an increase in the weekly rate of his pension other than an increase made by such an order as is mentioned in sub-paragraph (5) below".

(5) In paragraph 2(3) for the words after "incremental period" there shall be substituted—

"(a) in the case of an incremental period specified in paragraph 2(1)(a) above, shall be [^{3} 1/5th per cent.] of the weekly rate of his pension immediately after he attained pensionable age; and

(b) in the case of an incremental period specified in paragraph 2(1)(b) above, shall be [^{3} 1/5th per cent.] of that increase".

AMENDMENTS

1. Social Security (Widow's Benefits and Retirement Pensions) Amendment Regulations 1987 (SI 1987/1854), reg.2 (April 11, 1988).
2. Social Security (Abolition of Earnings Rule) (Consequential) Regulations 1989 (SI 1989/1642), reg.11 (October 1, 1989).
3. Social Security (Deferral of Retirement Pensions) Regulations 2005 (SI 2005/453), reg.4 (April 6, 2005).

Benefit at reduced rates for those who do not satisfy the contribution conditions in full

[^{2} **6.**—(1) Subject to paragraph (2) of this regulation, where the second contribution condition specified in paragraph 5(3) of Schedule 3 to the Act is not satisfied a person shall be entitled to—   **6.75**

(a) widowed mother's allowance;
[^{1}(aa) widowed parent's allowance;
(ab) bereavement allowance;]
(b) widow's pension;
(c) Category A retirement pension; or
(d) Category B retirement pension,

provided the percentage of the number of qualifying years in the working life of that person calculated in accordance with paragraph (3B) of this regulation is 25 per cent. or more.

(2) Where a person to whom paragraph (1) alone would otherwise apply is not entitled to benefit under that paragraph because the percentage of the number of qualifying years in his working life, calculated in accordance with paragraph (3B) of this regulation, is less than 25 per cent., but there are one or more surpluses in that person's earnings factors for the relevant years, that person shall be entitled to—

(a) widowed mother's allowance;
[^{1}(aa) widowed parent's allowance;]
(b) widow's pension;
(c) Category A retirement pension; or
(d) Category B retirement pension

consisting only of the additional pension in that benefit.

(3) Where a person is entitled to benefit under paragraph (1) of this regulation, the benefit payable shall be—

(a) the basic pension in that benefit at a reduced rate calculated in accordance with paragraph (3B) of this regulation as a percentage of the higher of the sums specified in section 6(1)(a) of the Pensions Act; and
(b) any additional pension arising from one or more surpluses in the pensioner's earnings factors for the relevant years; and

(c) any increase of benefit to which he may be entitled under sections 41, 45, 45A and 46 of the Act—

    (i) in respect of an adult dependant calculated in accordance with paragraph (3B) of this regulation as a percentage of the appropriate increase specified in Part IV of Schedule 4 to the Act;

    (ii) [² *omitted*].

(3A) Where a person is entitled to benefit under paragraph (2) of this regulation, the benefit payable shall be only the additional pension in that benefit.

(3B) Subject to paragraph (4) of this regulation, the percentage referred to in paragraphs (1), (2), (3)(a) and (3)(c)(i) of this regulation shall be ascertained by taking the number of qualifying years in the working life of the contributor concerned, expressing that number as a percentage of the requisite number of years specified for that working life in paragraph 5(4) of Schedule 3 to the Act and rounding up that percentage to the next whole number.]

(4) For the purposes of [³ paragraph (3B)] of this regulation the requisite number of years shall be taken to be that number, apart from this paragraph, reduced by the number of home responsibilities years of the contributor concerned but not to below—

    (a) in relation to a Category A or a Category B retirement pension, 20 years; or

    (b) in relation to a widow's pension [¹ bereavement allowance, widowed parent's allowance] or a widowed mother's allowance, 20 years or, where the requisite number apart from this paragraph is less than 40, half that requisite number.

(5) Where a person is entitled by virtue of this regulation to a Category A retirement pension and also to a section 9(2), 9(3) or 10(2) increase, an uprating order shall have the effect of increasing—

    (a) the [⁴ basic pension] in that pension

        (i) where there is a section 10(2) increase, in proportion to the increase under that order of the [³ higher of the sums] specified in section 6(1)(a) of the Pensions Act 10(2) and

        (ii) where there is a section [53(2)] increase, in proportion to the increase under that order of the sum specified in paragraph 9 of Part I of Schedule 4 to the Act;

    (b) the [⁴ additional pension] where there is a section 9(2) increase, by the percentage specified in that order for an increase of the sums [³ which are the additional pensions in the rates of long-term benefits.]

AMENDMENTS

1. Social Security (Benefits for Widows and Widowers) (Consequential Amendments) Regulations 2000 (SI 2000/1483) reg.7 (April 9, 2001).

2. Social Security (Working Tax Credit and Child Tax Credit) (Consequential Amendments) (No. 2) Regulations 2003 (SI 2003/937), reg.2 (April 6, 2003).

3. Social Security (Widows' Benefits and Retirement Pensions) Amendment Regulations 1990 (SI 1990/2642), reg.2 (January 29, 1991).

4. Social Security Act 1986, s.18 (April 6, 1987).

Category B retirement pension for certain widows by virtue of husband's contributions

6.76   7.—For the purposes of a woman's entitlement to a Category B retirement pension under section 29(5) of the Act, she shall be treated as being entitled to a widow's pension if she would have been so entitled but for any one or more of the following circumstances:

   (a) her failure to make, or delay in making, a claim for that widow's pension;

   (b) her entitlement to a widowed mother's allowance;

   (c) the operation of section 82 of the Act (disqualification and suspension) or section 85 of the Act (overlapping benefits and hospital in-patients) or any regulations made under either of those sections, except for the operation of section 82(5)(a) of the Act (absence from Great Britain);

   (d) the operation of any provision of the Act or any regulations made under the Act disqualifying her for the receipt of that widow's pension for any period, except for the operation of the said section 82(5)(a);

   (e) her having attained the age of 65;

   (f) her remarriage after 4th April 1971,

and for the purposes of section 29(7)(c) of the Act the weekly rate of the widow's pension shall be the weekly rate to which she would have been entitled but for any one or more of the said circumstances.

[¹ Category B retirement pension for surviving spouses [² and surviving civil partners] by virtue of deceased spouse's [² or deceased civil partner's] contributions

7A.—(1) For the purposes of entitlement of any person ("the pensioner") to a Category B retirement pension under section 48BB of the Social Security Contributions and Benefits Act 1992 (Category B retirement pension: entitlement by reference to benefit under section 39A or 39B) ("the 1992 Act"), the pensioner shall be treated as being entitled to a widowed parent's allowance or a bereavement allowance as the case may be, if he would have been so entitled but for any one or more of the circumstances specified in paragraph (2) below.   **6.77**

(2) The circumstances referred to in paragraph (1) above are—

   (a) the pensioner's failure to make, or his delay in making, a claim for that widowed parent's allowance or bereavement allowance;

   (b) the operation of section 113 of the 1992 Act (disqualification and suspension) or section 73 of the Social Security Administration Act 1992 (overlapping benefits) or any regulations made under either of those sections, except for the operation of section 113(1)(a) of the 1992 Act (absence from Great Britain);

   (c) the operation of any provision of the 1992 Act or any regulations made under the 1992 Act, disqualifying the pensioner from receipt of that widowed parent's allowance or bereavement allowance for any period except for the operation of the said section 113(1)(a);

   (d) the pensioner's having attained pensionable age;

   (e) the pensioner's having remarried [² or formed a civil partnership].

(3) Where this regulation applies the weekly rate of a Category B pension shall—

   (a) in the case of a pensioner treated as being entitled to widowed parent's allowance immediately before attaining pensionable age in consequence of the death of his or her spouse [² or civil partner], be that specified in section 48BB(2) of the 1992 Act;

(b) in the case of a pensioner treated as being entitled to—
    (i) widowed parent's allowance at any time when over the age of 45 but not immediately before attaining pensionable age, or
    (ii) bereavement allowance at any time prior to obtaining pensionable age,
be that specified in section 48BB(5) and (6) of the 1992 Act as the case may be.]

AMENDMENTS

1. Social Security (Benefits for Widows and Widowers) (Consequential Amendments) Regulations 2000 (SI 2000/1483) reg.7 (April 9, 2001).
2. Civil Partnership (Pensions, Social Security and Child Support) (Consequential, etc. Provisions) Regulations 2005 (SI 2005/2877) (December 5, 2005).

Substitution of former spouse's [³ or former civil partner's] contribution record to give entitlement to a Category A retirement pension

6.78   **8.**—(1) This regulation applies to—
(a) any person whose last marriage terminated before he attained pensionable age and who did not remarry [³ or, as the case may be, form a civil partnership] before that date;
[³ (aa) any person whose last civil partnership terminated before he attained pensionable age and who did not form a subsequent civil partnership or, as the case may be, marry before that date;]
[¹ (b) any man or woman widowed on or after attaining pensionable age [³ or where civil partner died on or after the man or woman had attained that age], his or her former spouse [³ or former civil partner], as the case may be, being under pensionable age when she or he died; and]
(c) any person whose last marriage [³ or last civil partnership] terminated on or after the date on which he attained pensionable age otherwise than by the death of his spouse [³ or, as the case may be, his civil partner],
and any such person shall be referred to in this regulation as "the beneficiary".

(2) Where the beneficiary does not, in respect of the year in which his marriage [³ or civil partner] terminated or any previous year, with his own contributions satisfy the contribution conditions for a Category A retirement pension specified in paragraph 5 of Schedule 3 to the Act, then, for the purpose of enabling him to satisfy those conditions, the contributions of his former spouse [³ or former civil partner] may, if it is advantageous to him, be treated to the extent specified in paragraphs (3) to (6) as though they were his own.

(3) The beneficiary shall be treated as satisfying the first contribution condition if his former spouse [³ or civil partner] had satisfied that condition as respects any year of his working life up to (inclusive) the year in which the marriage [³ or civil partnership] terminated.

(4) The beneficiary shall be treated as satisfying the second contribution condition as respects the number of years arrived at under paragraph 2 or 3 of Schedule 1 to these regulations, whichever is the more beneficial to him.

(5) Where a person is entitled for any period to any [² basic pension] in his Category A retirement pension by virtue of this regulation and regulation 6, he shall not be entitled for that period to a section 9(2) increase.

(6) Where any of a person's home responsibilities years falls in a period in respect of which his spouse's [³ or his former civil partner's] contributions are treated as his own under this regulation, no such year shall be taken into account in the determination of his pension entitlement either for the purposes of paragraph 5(6) of Schedule 3 to the Act or for the purposes of regulation 6.

AMENDMENTS

1. Social Security (Benefits for Widows and Widowers) (Consequential Amendments) Regulations 2000 (SI 2000/1483), reg.7 (April 9, 2001).
2. Social Security Act 1986, s.18 (April 6, 1987).
3. Civil Partnership (Pensions, Social Security and Child Support) (Consequential etc. Provisions) Regulations 2005 (SI 2005/2877) (December 5, 2005).

GENERAL NOTE

For the meaning of marriage, see the notes following s.39c of the Act.   6.79
A marriage terminated by divorce or by a decree of nullity is terminated from the date of decree absolute. A marriage terminated by a decree of presumption of death and dissolution of marriage is treated as terminated otherwise than by death, and is treated as terminated from the date of the decree absolute unless the Secretary of State or the determining authority is satisfied as to the date of the death, in which case it is presumably also treated as terminated by death (see reg.1(3) above).

Conditions for entitlement to a Category C retirement pension

9.—The conditions for entitlement to a Category C retirement pension   6.80
shall be that the person concerned—
  (a) was resident in Great Britain for a period of at least 10 years between 5th July 1948 and 1st November 1970, inclusive of both dates; and
  (b) was ordinarily resident in Great Britain on 2nd November 1970 or on the date of his claim for that pension.

GENERAL NOTE

For the meaning of "resident" and "ordinarily resident", see the notes to Persons   6.81
Abroad Regulations.

Conditions for entitlement to a Category D retirement pension

10.—The conditions for entitlement to a Category D retirement pension   6.82
shall be that the person concerned—
  [¹(a) was resident in Great Britain for a period of at least 10 years in any continuous period of 20 years which included the day before that on which he attained the age of 80 or any day thereafter; and]
  (b) was ordinarily resident in Great Britain either—
    (i) on the day he attained the age of 80; or
    (ii) if he was not so ordinarily resident on that day and the date of his claim for the pension was later than that day, on the date of his claim, so however that where a person satisfies this condition under this head he shall be deemed to have satisfied it on the date that he became so ordinarily resident.

AMENDMENT

1. Social Security (Widows' Benefit and Retirement Pensions) Amendment Regulations 1984 (SI 1984/1704), reg.2 (November 26, 1984).

GENERAL NOTE

6.83   For the meaning of "resident" and "ordinarily resident", see the notes to Persons Abroad Regulations.

Category C retirement pension for widows of men over pensionable age on 5th July, 1948

6.84   **11.**—(1) Subject to the provisions of these regulations, a widow whose husband was over pensionable age on 5th July 1948 shall be entitled to a Category C retirement pension at a rate ascertained in accordance with paragraph (3) if—

(a) she is over pensionable age; and

(b) [¹ . . .]

(c) she was over the age of [² 45] either—

(i) when her husband died; or

(ii) if she was entitled under regulation 14 to benefit corresponding to a widowed mother's allowance, when she ceased to be so entitled; and either

(d) her husband was at any time entitled to a Category C retirement pension or a retirement pension under section 1(1)(a) of the National Insurance Act 1970; or

(e) her husband died before 2nd November 1970 and—

(i) she was resident in Great Britain for a period of at least 10 years between 5th July 1948 and 1st November 1970, inclusive of both dates; and

(ii) she was ordinarily resident in Great Britain on 2nd November 1970 or on the date of her claim for a Category C retirement pension; and

(iii) he was ordinarily resident in Great Britain on the date of his death.

(2) A pension payable under paragraph (1) shall commence on 6th April 1975 or the date on which the requirements of sub-paragraphs (a) to (c) and either (d) or (e) of that paragraph are satisfied in relation to the beneficiary, whichever is the later, and shall be payable for life.

(3) The pension under paragraph (1) shall be at the higher rate specified in relation to a Category C retirement pension in Part III of Schedule 4 to the Act, so however that—

(a) in the case of a widow who was under the age of [² 55] either when her husband died, or, if she was entitled under regulation 14 to benefit corresponding to a widowed mother's allowance, when she ceased to be so entitled, the rate of such pension shall be reduced as if the provisions of section 26(2) of the Act applied to it;

(b) [¹ . . .].

AMENDMENTS

1. Social Security (Abolition of Earnings Rule) (Consequential) Regulations 1989 (SI 1989/1642), reg.11 (October 1, 1989).

2. Social Security (Widows' Benefit and Retirement Pensions) Amendment Regulations 1987 (SI 1987/1854), reg.2 (April 11, 1988).

GENERAL NOTE

6.85   For the meaning of "resident" and "ordinarily resident", see the notes to Persons Abroad Regulations.

For the purpose of para.(1)(d) a person is entitled to the benefit if he would have been entitled had he made a claim for it. (See reg.1(4).)

Category C retirement pension for certain women whose marriage has been terminated otherwise than by death

12.—(1) Subject to the provisions of these regulations, a woman whose marriage to a husband who was over pensionable age on 5th July 1948 was terminated otherwise than by his death shall be entitled to a Category C retirement pension at the higher rate specified in relation to such a pension in Part III of Schedule 4 to the Act if—

    (a) she had attained pensionable age before the date of the termination of the marriage; and

    (b) [¹ . . .]

    (c) the conditions set out in paragraph (2) or (3), as the case may be, are satisfied.

(2) The conditions applicable in the case of a woman whose marriage was terminated before 2nd November 1970 shall be—

    (a) that she was resident in Great Britain for a period of at least 10 years between 5th July 1948, and 1st November 1970, inclusive of both dates; and

    (b) that she was ordinarily resident in Great Britain on 2nd November 1970, or on the date of her claim for a Category C retirement pension; and

    (c) that her husband was ordinarily resident in Great Britain on the date of the termination of the marriage; and

    (d) that she did not remarry between the date of that termination and 2nd November 1970.

(3) The conditions applicable in the case of a woman whose marriage was terminated on or after 2nd November 1970 shall be that her husband was entitled to a Category C retirement pension or a retirement pension under section 1(1)(a) of the National Insurance Act 1970.

(4) A pension payable under paragraph (1) shall commence on 6th April 1975 or the date on which the requirements of sub-paragraphs (a) to (c) of that paragraph are satisfied in relation to the beneficiary, whichever is the later, and shall be payable for life.

6.86

AMENDMENT

1. Social Security (Abolition of Earnings Rule) (Consequential) Regulations 1989 (SI 1989/1642), reg.11 (October 1, 1989).

GENERAL NOTE

For the meaning of "resident" and "ordinarily resident", see the notes to Persons Abroad Regulations.

For the purposes of para.(3) a person is entitled to the benefit if he would have been entitled had he made a claim for it. (See reg.1(4).)

6.87

Benefit corresponding to a widow's pension for widows of men over pensionable age on 5th July 1948

13.—(1) Subject to the provisions of these regulations, a widow whose husband was over pensionable age on 5th July 1948 shall be entitled to

6.88

benefit corresponding to a widow's pension at a rate ascertained in accordance with paragraph (3) if—

    (a) she was over the age of [¹ 45] but under the age of 65 either—

        (i) when her husband died; or

       (ii) if she was entitled under regulation 14 to benefit corresponding to a widowed mother's allowance, when she ceased to be so entitled; and

    (b) the requirements of sub-paragraph (d) or (e) of regulation 11(1) are satisfied in her case.

(2) The period for which benefit is payable under paragraph (1) shall be any period commencing on the date on which the requirements of sub-paragraph (d) or (e) of regulation 11(1) are first satisfied in the case of the widow, and during which she is under the age of 65 and for which she is not entitled under regulation 14 to benefit corresponding to a widowed mother's allowance; so however that the benefit shall not be payable for any period after the widow's remarriage or for any period during which she and a man to whom she is not married are living together as husband and wife.

(3) The benefit under paragraph (1) shall be at the higher rate specified in relation to a Category C retirement pension in Part III of Schedule 4 to the Act; so however that in the case of a widow who was under the age of [¹ 55] either when her husband died, or, if she was entitled under regulation 14 to benefit corresponding to a widowed mother's allowance, when she ceased to be so entitled, the rate of such benefit shall be reduced as if the provisions of section 26(2) of the Act applied to it.

AMENDMENT

1. Social Security (Widows' Benefit and Retirement Pensions) Amendment Regulations 1987 (SI 1987/1854), reg.2 (April 11, 1988).

GENERAL NOTE

6.89   For the purposes of para.(2) a person is entitled to the benefit if he would have been entitled had he made a claim for it. (See reg.1(4).)

Benefit corresponding to a widowed mother's allowance for widows of men over pensionable age on 5th July 1948

6.90   **14.**—(1) Subject to the provisions of these regulations, a widow whose husband was over pensionable age on 5th July 1948 shall be entitled to benefit corresponding to a widowed mother's allowance, which shall be at the higher rate specified in relation to a Category C retirement pension in Part III of Schedule 4 to the Act, for any period commencing on the date on which the requirements of sub-paragraph (d) or (e) of regulation 11(1) are first satisfied in her case and during which she would have been entitled to a widowed mother's allowance under section 25 of the Act had her husband satisfied the contribution conditions set out in paragraph 5 of Schedule 3 to the Act; so however that the benefit shall not be payable for any period after the widow's remarriage or for any period during which she and a man to whom she is not married are living together as husband and wife.

(2) The provisions of section 41(4) of the Act (which related to increases of widowed mother's allowance in respect of children) shall apply to benefit

payable under this regulation as they apply to an allowance payable under section 25(1)(A) of the Act.

Restriction on benefit under regulations 13 and 14 in certain cases

15.—(1) In the case of a widow of a member of a police force or of a special constable who, as such a widow, is in receipt of a pension under regulations from time to time in force made under—

(a) the Police Pensions Act 1976;

(b) section 34 of the Police Act 1964;

(c) section 26 of the Police (Scotland) Act 1967,

benefit under regulation 13 or 14 corresponding to a widow's pension or a widowed mother's allowance shall not be payable in respect of any week during which she is receiving an increase of the said pension under either—

(i) the provisions of regulation 12 or 15 of the Police Pensions Regulations 1971, or of any corresponding regulations from time to time in force and made as mentioned in sub-paragraph (a); or

(ii) those provisions as applied by regulations from time to time in force and made as mentioned in sub-paragraph (b) or (c).

(2) For the purposes of paragraph (1), any reference in that paragraph to an enactment or regulation shall include a reference to any corresponding Northern Ireland legislation, or, as the case may be, any order or regulation having effect by virtue of such legislation, being in each case passed or made for purposes similar to the purposes of the enactment or regulation specified in that paragraph.

Provision in relation to entitlement to child benefit for the purposes of a widowed mother's allowance

16.—(1) For the sole purpose of determining whether a woman who has been widowed satisfies the requirements of section 25(1)(a) of the Act (entitlement to a widowed mother's allowance)—

[¹(a) [² any person under the age of 20 residing with the widow shall be deemed to be] within section 25(2) of the Act if—

(i) the requirements of section 25(2)(a) are satisfied in his case and child benefit would have been payable in respect of him had he not been absent from Great Britain and had a claim for it been made in the manner prescribed under section 6 of the Child Benefit Act 1975, or

(ii) the requirements of section 25(2)(b) or (c) would have been satisfied, and child benefit would have been payable in respect of him continuously since the date of death of the late husband, had he not been absent from Great Britain and had a claim for child benefit been made in respect of him in the manner prescribed under section 6 of the Child Benefit Act 1975 and]

(b) a widow shall be treated as entitled to child benefit in respect of any person deemed, in accordance with sub-paragraph (a), to be [² . . .] within the said section 25(2).

(2) In determining whether a woman who has been more than once married and who was not residing with her late husband immediately before his death is entitled to a widowed mother's allowance under section

6.91

6.92

729

25 of the Act, her late husband shall, for the purposes of section 25(2)(b) of the Act, be treated as having been entitled to child benefit in respect of any child [² or qualifying young person] in respect of whom—

(a) a previous husband of that woman by a marriage which ended with that husband's death was, immediately before his death, entitled or treated as entitled to child benefit; and

(b) that woman was entitled or treated as entitled to child benefit immediately before the death of her late husband.

(3) For the purposes of paragraph (2)(a) or (b), if the death there referred to occurred before 4th April 1977 the previous husband or, as the case may be, the woman, shall be treated as entitled to child benefit in respect of the child [² or qualifying young person] in question if he or she satisfied the relevant requirement in section 25(2)(c) of the Act as originally enacted.

AMENDMENTS

1. Social Security (Widows' Benefit and Retirement Pensions) Amendment Regulations 1987 (SI 1987/1854), reg.2 (April 11 1988).

2. Social Security (Provisions Relating to Qualifying Young Persons) (Amendment) Regulations 2006 (SI 2006/692) (April 10, 2006).

GENERAL NOTE

6.93   Regulation 16(1)(a) has been amended as from April 11, 1988 to make it clear that children under 19 living with the widow will be the basis for an award of widowed mother's allowance only so long as child benefit is payable in respect of them—in other words, so long as they remain in full-time education, or are deemed so to remain. The original drafting of this regulation, under which a widow qualified by virtue of any child living with her and under the age of 19, appears to have been accidental, but nevertheless a saving provision in favour of such widows who qualify for widowed mother's allowance before April 11, 1988 was contained in the Widow's Benefit and Retirement Pension Amendment Regs 1987. For text of the earlier version of this reg., see earlier editions of this work.

[¹ Provision in relation to entitlement to child benefit for the purposes of a widowed parent's allowance

6.94   **16ZA.**—(1) For the purpose only of determining whether a man or a woman who has been widowed ("the surviving spouse") [² or where civil partner has died ("surviving civil partner")] satisfies the requirements of subsection (2)(a) of section 39A of the Social Security Contributions and Benefits Act 1992 ("the 1992 Act")—

(a) a person shall be treated for the purposes of subsection (3)(b) or (c) of that section as having been entitled to child benefit in respect of a child [³ or qualifying young person] where that person would have been so entitled had—

(i) that child [³ or qualifying young person] not been absent from Great Britain, and

(ii) a claim for child benefit been made in respect of the child [³ or qualifying young person] in the manner prescribed under section 13 of the Social Security Administration Act 1992; and

(b) the surviving spouse [² or surviving civil partner] shall be treated, for the purposes of subsection (2)(a) of section 39A, as entitled to child benefit in respect of the child [³ or qualifying young person] who, by virtue of sub-paragraph (a) above, falls within subsection (3) of that section.

(2) In determining whether a surviving spouse [² or surviving civil partner] who has been more than once married [² has formed more than one civil partnership, or who has been both married and formed a civil partnership] and who was not residing with the deceased spouse [" or, as the case may be, the deceased civil partner] immediately before his or her death is entitled to a widowed parent's allowance under section 39A of the 1992 Act, the deceased spouse [" or deceased civil partner] shall, for the purposes of subsection (3)(b) of that section, be treated as having been entitled to child benefit in respect of any child [³ or qualifying young person] in respect of whom—

   (a) a previous spouse [² or civil partner] of that surviving spouse [² or civil partner] by a marriage [² or, as the case may be, by the formation at a civil partnership] which ended with that previous spouse's [² or previous civil partner's] death was, immediately before his or her death, entitled or treated as entitled to child benefit; and

   (b) that surviving spouse [² or civil partner] was entitled or treated as entitled to child benefit immediately before the death of the deceased spouse [² or civil partner].]

AMENDMENTS

1. Social Security (Widow's Benefits and Retirement Pensions) Amendment Regulations 2001 (SI 2001/1235) (April 9, 2001).
2. Civil Partnership (Pensions Social Security and Child Support) (Consequential etc. Provisions) order 2005 (SI 2005/2877) (December 5, 2005).
3. Social Security (Provisions relating to Qualifying Young Persons) (Amendment) Regulations (SI 2006/692) (April 10, 2006).

[¹ Disapplication of section 1(1A) of the Administration Act for the purposes of widowed mother's allowance

16A.—Section 1(1A) of the Administration Act (requirement to state national insurance number) shall not apply to a child [³ or qualifying young person] in respect of whom an increase of widowed mother's allowance [² or widowed parent's allowance] is claimed.]

6.95

AMENDMENTS

1. Social Security (National Insurance Information: Exemption) Regulations (SI 1997/2676) (December 1, 1997).
2. Social Security (Widow's Benefit and Retirement Pensions) Amendment Regulations 2001 (SI 2001/1235) (April 9, 2001).
3. Social Security (Provisions relating to Qualifying Young Persons) Regulations (SI 2006/692) (April 10, 2006).

Provisions relating to age addition for persons not in receipt of a retirement pension

17.—(1) For the purposes of section 40(2) of the Act (age addition for persons over the age of 80 who are not entitled to a retirement pension but are in receipt of certain other payments) the prescribed enactments and instruments shall be—

6.96

   (a) Chapter IV or V of Part II of the Act;

   (b) any scheme made under section 5 of the Industrial Injuries and Diseases (Old Cases) Act 1975;

    (c) any Service Pensions Instrument;
    (d) any scheme made under the Personal Injuries (Emergency Provisions) Act 1939 or under the Pensions (Navy, Army, Air Force and Mercantile Marine) Act 1939;
    (e) any 1914–18 War Injuries Scheme;
    (f) section [36] of the Act (severe disablement allowance);
    (g) section [37] of the Act ([1 carer's allowance]).
[2 (h) sections 36 and 37 of the National Insurance Act 1965 as continued in force by the Social Security (Graduated Retirement Benefit) (No. 2) Regulations 1978.]

    (2) The following shall [2 subject to paragraph (3)] be additional conditions of entitlement to age addition under section 40(2) of the Act—
    (a) that the person concerned is in receipt of a payment under an enactment or instrument specified in paragraph (1), by reference to which the amount of a retirement pension would, if it were otherwise payable to him, be extinguished by virtue of any regulations made under section 85(1)(a) of the Act (overlapping benefits); and
    (b) that had he made a claim for it, he would have been entitled to a retirement pension of any category by virtue of any provision of the Act or any regulations made under it.

    [2 (3) Paragraph (2) shall not apply to a person who is in receipt of a payment under the enactment specified in paragraph (1)(h)].

AMENDMENTS

    1. Social Security Amendment (Carer's Allowance) Regulations 2002 (SI 2002/2497), reg.3 (April 1, 2003).
    2. Social Security (Widows' Benefit and Retirement Pensions)Amendment Regulations 1993 (SI 1993/1242), reg.2 (June 7, 1993).

6.97   *Regulation 18 omitted.*

SCHEDULE 1

6.98   **Method of treating former spouse's [1 or former civil partner's] contributions as those of the beneficiary so as to entitle him to a Category A retirement pension**
    1. In this Schedule—
    (a) A is the number of former souse's or [1 former civil partner's] qualifying years up to (exclusive) the year in which the marriage [1or, as the case may be the former civil partnership] terminated;
    (b) B is the number of years in the former spouse's [1 or former civil partner's] working life up to (exclusive) the year in which the marriage [1 or, as the case may be the former civil partnership] terminated.
    2. The number of years arrived at under this paragraph is that which is obtained by—
    (a) taking the number of years in the beneficiary's working life between (inclusive) the first year in that working life and (inclusive) the year in which the marriage [1 or former civil partnership] terminated, multiplying it by A/B and rounding up the result to the next whole number; and
    (b) adding to that number of years the number of the beneficiary's qualifying years falling after the year in which the marriage [1 or former civil partnership] terminated.
    3. The number of years arrived at under this paragraph is that which is obtained by—
    (a) taking the number of years in the beneficiary's working life between (inclusive) the year in which the marriage took place [1 or the civil partnership was formed] and (inclusive) the year [1 in which the marriage or civil partnership terminated], multiplying it by A/B and rounding up the result to the next whole number; and

   (b) adding to that number of years the number of the beneficiary's qualifying years falling—

      (i) before the year in which the marriage took place [¹ or the civil partnership was formed] and

     (ii) after that in which the marriage [¹ or civil partnership] terminated.

AMENDMENT

1. Civil Partnership (Pensions Social Security and Child Support) (Consequential etc. Provisions) order 2005 (SI 2005/2877) (December 5, 2005).

PART VII

UNEMPLOYMENT, SICKNESS AND INVALIDITY BENEFIT

For the text of the few remaining Unemployment, Sickness and Invalidity Benefit Regulations (SI 1983/1598, as amended) see the 2005 edition of this volume.

PART VIII

INCAPACITY BENEFIT AND INCAPACITY FOR WORK

Social Security (Incapacity Benefit) Regulations 1994

(SI 1994/2946) (*as amended*)

ARRANGEMENT OF REGULATIONS

PART I

GENERAL

PART 1A

CONTRIBUTION CONDITIONS: SUPPLEMENTARY PROVISIONS

PART II

ENTITLEMENT TO INCAPACITY BENEFIT: SUPPLEMENTARY PROVISIONS

PART III

RATE OF INCAPACITY BENEFIT

PART IV

ADDITIONAL CONDITIONS FOR PERSONS INCAPACITATED IN YOUTH

PART V

REDUCTION OR ABATEMENT OF INCAPACITY BENEFIT FOR OCCUPATIONAL OR OTHER PENSION PAYMENTS

The Secretary of State for Social Security in exercise of the powers conferred on him by sections 30B(7), 30C(3), (4)(a) and (6), 30D(3), 30E(1) and (2), 122, and 175(1) and (3) of the Social Security Contributions and Benefits Act 1992 and of all other powers enabling him in that behalf, by this instrument, which contains only regulations made by virtue of sections 2(1) and 3(1) of the Social Security (Incapacity for Work) Act 1994 and is made before the end of the period of 6 months beginning with the coming into force of that Act, hereby makes the following Regulations.

PART I

GENERAL

Citation and commencement

1.—These Regulations may be cited as the Social Security (Incapacity   8.2
Benefit) Regulations 1994 and shall come into force on 13th April 1995.

Interpretation

2.—(1) In these Regulations, unless the context otherwise requires—   8.3
"the Administration Act" means the Social Security Administration Act
    1992; and
"the Contributions and Benefits Act" means the Social Security
    Contributions and Benefits Act 1992.
(2) In these Regulations—
(a) any reference to a numbered regulation is a reference to the regula-
    tion bearing that number in these Regulations; and
(b) any reference in a regulation to a numbered paragraph is a reference
    to the paragraph bearing that number in that regulation.

[¹ Disapplication of section 1(1A) of the Administration Act

2A.—Section 1(1A) of the Administration Act (requirement to state   8.4
national insurance number) shall not apply—
(a) to a child in respect of whom an increase of incapacity benefit is
    claimed;
(b) to an adult dependant in respect of whom a claim for an increase of
    incapacity benefit is made or treated as made before October 5, 1998;]
[² (c) to an adult dependant who—
    (i) is a person in respect of whom a claim for an increase of inca-
        pacity benefit is made;
    (ii) is subject to immigration control within the meaning of section
        115(9)(a) of the Immigration and Asylum Act 1999; and
    (iii) has not previously been allocated a national insurance number.]

AMENDMENTS

1. Social Security (National Insurance Information: Exemption) Regulations
1997 (SI 1997/2676) (December 1, 1997).
2. Social Security (National Insurance Number Information: Exemption)
Regulations 2009 (SI 2009/471), reg.6 (April 6, 2009).

[¹ PART 1A

CONTRIBUTION CONDITIONS: SUPPLEMENTARY PROVISIONS

Relaxation of the first contribution condition in certain cases

2B.—(1) For the purposes of sub-paragraph (2)(a) of paragraph 2   8.5
of Schedule 3 to the Contributions and Benefits Act (first contribution

condition) a person who satisfies any of the conditions in paragraph (2) shall be taken to satisfy the first contribution condition if—

    (a) he paid contributions of a relevant class before the relevant time in respect of any one year; and

    (b) the earnings factor is derived—

        (i) from earnings, on which primary Class 1 contributions have been paid or treated as paid, which are not less than that year's lower earnings limit multiplied by 25, or

        (ii) from Class 2 contributions multiplied by 25.

(2) The conditions referred to in paragraph (1) are that—

    (a) he was a person who, in the last [2 complete tax year] [3 immediately preceding the relevant benefit year in which] the first day of incapacity for work occurred, was entitled to [4 carer's allowance] under section 70 of the Contributions and Benefits Act or would have been in receipt of the [4 carer's allowance] but for the provision of regulation 4 of the Social Security (Overlapping Benefits) Regulations 1979;

    (b) immediately before the first day of incapacity for work, he was a person—

        (i) who had been engaged in remunerative employment for a period of more than 2 years, and

        (ii) who was entitled to disability working allowance or disabled person's tax credit, as the case may be, under section 129 of the Contributions and Benefits Act throughout that period; or

    [5 (iii) who was entitled to working tax credit where the disability element or the severe disability element of working tax credit as specified in regulation 20(1)(b) and (f) of the Working Tax Credit (Entitlement and Maximum Rate) Regulations 2002 was included in the award; or]

[6 (ba) he is, in respect of any week in any tax year preceding the relevant benefit year, a person who—

        (i) is entitled to be credited with earnings or, as the case may be, contributions in accordance with regulation 9D of the Social Security (Credits) Regulations 1975 (credits for certain periods of imprisonment or detention in legal custody), or

        (ii) would be so entitled had he made an application to the Secretary of State for the purpose of that regulation;]

    (c) he is, on the first day of his incapacity for work, a person who had received incapacity benefit in the last complete tax year immediately preceding the relevant benefit year he again becomes entitled to it.]

AMENDMENTS

1. Social Security (Incapacity Benefit) Miscellaneous Amendments Regulations 2000 (SI 2000/3120), reg.2(2) (April 6, 2001).

2. Social Security (Incapacity Benefit) Amendment Regulations 2001 (SI 2001/1305), reg.2(2) (April 25, 2001).

3. Social Security (Incapacity) (Miscellaneous Amendments) Regulations 2001 (SI 2001/2979), reg.3(a) (October 1, 2001).

4. Social Security Amendment (Carer's Allowance) Regulations 2002 (SI 2002/2497), reg.3 and Sch.2 (April 1, 2003).

5. Social Security (Working Tax Credit and Child Tax Credit) (Consequential Amendments) Regulations 2003 (SI 2003/455), reg.6 and Sch.4, para.4 (April 7, 2003).

6. Social Security (Credits and Incapacity Benefit) Amendment Regulations 2001 (SI 2001/573), reg.3 (April 6, 2001).

GENERAL NOTE

SSCBA 1992, Sch.3, para.2(8) enables regulations to relax the contribution rules set out earlier in that paragraph which apply to all claims in a period of incapacity for work commencing on or after April 6, 2001. This regulation is the product. The rules are "relaxed" in the following situations: 8.6

(a) where the claimant was, in the last complete tax year immediately preceding the relevant benefit year in which occurred the first day of incapacity for work, entitled to invalid care allowance or would have been but for the provisions of reg.4 of the Overlapping Benefit Regulations (he is receiving another higher value benefit) (para.2(a));

(b) where the claimant was engaged in remunerative employment for a period of more than two years immediately before the first day of incapacity for work falling on or after April 6, 2001, and throughout that period was in receipt of (as appropriate to the period) disability working allowance, disabled person's tax credit, or working tax credit which included in the award the disability or severe disability element (para.(2)(b));

(c) certain convicted prisoners whose conviction is overturned whose contribution record is credited in respect of their period of imprisonment under Social Security (Credits) Regulations 1975, reg.9D or would be if they applied to the Secretary of State (para.(2)(ba));

(d) where the claimant is on the first day of his incapacity for work on or after April 6, 2001 someone who had been receiving incapacity benefit in the last complete tax year before the relevant benefit year in which he again becomes entitled to it (para.(2)(c)).

The question then arises as to the terms of the "relaxation" of the usual rules. "Relaxation" means that such a claimant is treated as satisfying the first contribution condition if he has paid, in respect of any one tax/contribution year (complete or not) before the day of claim, Class 1 contributions to a level of 25 times that year's lower earnings limit or 25 Class 2 contributions (para.2B(1)). In short, such claimants are in effect subject to the first contribution condition as it stood before the April 6, 2001 changes.

PART II

ENTITLEMENT TO INCAPACITY BENEFIT: SUPPLEMENTARY PROVISIONS

Definition of "training for work" for the purposes of section 30C(6) of the Contributions and Benefits Act

3.—For the purposes of section 30C(6) of the Contributions and Benefits Act which provides for days of training for work to be treated as days of incapacity for work) "training for work" also includes any training received on a course which a person attends for 16 hours or more a week, the primary purpose of which is the teaching of occupational or vocational skills.   8.7

8.8   The provisions of this regulation are noted in the commentary to SSCBA 1992, s.30C(6), above. It provides a definition of "training for work" for the purposes of that provision.

Days not to be treated as days of incapacity for work

8.9   **4.**—(1) For the purposes of incapacity benefit a day shall not be treated as a day of incapacity for work if it is—

    (a) a day in respect of which a person—
- (i) has made no claim for incapacity benefit;
- (ii) has made a claim for incapacity benefit but not within the prescribed time and good cause for the delay is not shown; or
- (iii) has made a claim for incapacity benefit but not within the prescribed time and, whether or not the person has shown good cause for the delay, he is not entitled to benefit as a result of section 1(2) of the Administration Act (which provides for a 12 month limit on claims for incapacity benefit);

[¹ (aa) a day which is, for the purposes of section 30A(2A)(c) of the Contributions and Benefits Act (period of 196 consecutive days preceding the relevant day), not part of any consecutive days of incapacity;]

    (b) a day on which a person is disqualified for receiving incapacity benefit during a period of absence from Great Britain or imprisonment or detention in legal custody, if that disqualification is for more than 6 weeks; or

    (c) subject to paragraph (2), a day on which a person attends a training course in respect of which he is paid a training allowance pursuant to arrangements made under section 2(1) of the Employment and Training Act 1973 or section 2(3) of the Enterprise and New Towns (Scotland) Act 1990.

[³; or

    (d) to any part of such a payment made—
- (i) as a consequence of the person taking part in the scheme known as the Adult Learning Option (which is provided in pursuance of arrangements made by or on behalf of the Secretary of State under section 2 of the Employment and Training Act 1973), and
- (ii) which is not intended to meet the cost of living expenses to which paragraph (3) applies.]

(2) Paragraph (1)(c) shall not apply—

    (a) for the purposes of any claim for incapacity benefit for a period commencing after a person ceased attending such a training course; or

    (b) in calculating a period of continuous incapacity for work for the purposes of regulation 2 of the Social Security Benefit (Persons Abroad) Regulations 1975;

    (c) [² where, such payment as is made, is for the sole purpose of travelling or meal expenses incurred or to be incurred under the arrangement made under section 2(1) of the Employment and Training Act 1973 or section 2(3) of the Enterprise and New Towns (Scotland) Act 1990.]

[³(3) This paragraph applies to living expenses which relate to—

    (a) food,

(b) ordinary clothing or footwear,
(c) household fuel,
(d) rent for which housing benefit is payable,
(e) any housing costs (to the extent that they are met under regulation 83(f) or 84(1)(g) of the Jobseeker's Allowance Regulations 1996 or regulation 17(1)(e) or 18(1)(f) of the Income Support (General) Regulations 1987 (housing costs)) of the claimant or, where the claimant is a member of the family, any other member of his family, or
(f) any council tax or water charges for which that claimant or member is liable.]

AMENDMENTS

1. Social Security (Incapacity Benefit) Miscellaneous Amendments Regulations 2000 (SI 2000/3120), reg.2(3) (April 6, 2001).
2. Social Security (Approved Work) Regulations 2000 (SI 2000/678), reg.5 (April 3, 2000).
3. Social Security (Adult Learning Option) Amendment Regulations 2006 (SI 2006/2144), reg.3 (September 1, 2006).

GENERAL NOTE

The effect of this regulation, which precludes certain days from counting as ones of incapacity for incapacity benefit purposes, is noted in the commentary to SSCBA 1992, s.30C(3), above.   8.10

[¹ Days to be treated as days of incapacity for work

4A.—[²(1)] For the purposes of incapacity benefit for persons incapacitated in youth under section 30A(2A) of the Contributions and Benefits Act, any day in respect of which a person is entitled to statutory sick pay immediately before the relevant day shall be treated as a day of incapacity for work.]   8.11

[²(2) Where—
(a) any day was, as a result of official error, a day of incapacity for work in a period of incapacity for work for the purposes of the previous entitlement to incapacity benefit referred to in regulation 8D(2)(a) of the Social Security (Credits) Regulations 1975 (credits for the purposes of entitlement to incapacity benefit following official error); and
(b) that official error derived from the failure to transpose correctly information relating to credits for incapacity for work or approved training in the tax years from 1993–94 to 2007–08 from the Department of Work and Pensions' Pension Strategy Computer System to Her Majesty's Revenue and Customs' Computer System (NIRS2) or from related clerical procedures,

that day shall be treated as a day of incapacity for work for the purposes of the later claim referred to in paragraph (2)(d) of that regulation.
(3) In this regulation—
[³. . .]
"credits for incapacity for work or approved training" means earnings credited pursuant to the Social Security (Credits) Regulations 1975 for incapacity for work or approved training;
"official error" means an error made by—
(a) an officer of the Department for Work and Pensions or an officer of Revenue and Customs acting as such which no person outside the

Department or Her Majesty's Revenue and Customs caused or to which no person outside the Department for Work and Pensions or Her Majesty's Revenue and Customs materially contributed, or

(b) a person employed by a service provider and to which no person who was not so employed materially contributed,

but excludes any error of law which is shown to have been an error by virtue of a subsequent decision of [³the Upper Tribunal] or the court;

"service provider" means a person providing services to the Secretary of State for Work and Pensions or to Her Majesty's Revenue and Customs.]

AMENDMENTS

1. Social Security (Incapacity Benefit) Miscellaneous Amendments Regulations 2000 (SI 2000/3120), reg.2(4) (April 6, 2001).
2. Social Security (Miscellaneous Amendments) (No. 5) Regulations 2007 (SI 2007/2618), reg.6 (October 1, 2007).
3. Tribunals, Courts and Enforcement Act 2007 (Transitional and Consequential Provisions) Order 2008 (SI 2008/2683), art.6(1) and Sch.1, para.65 (November 3, 2008).

GENERAL NOTE

8.12   The effects of this regulation, which treats certain days as ones of incapacity for work for incapacity benefit purposes, are noted in the commentary to SSCBA 1992, s.30C(3), above. The October 2007 changes protect claimants from the effect of certain official errors with regard to transposition of material from one set of records to another in respect of credits for training and incapacity for work.

Night workers

8.13   5.—(1) For the purposes of incapacity benefit, where a person works for a continuous period which extends over midnight into the following day, the day on which the lesser part of that period falls shall be treated as a day of incapacity for work if that person was incapable of work for the remainder of that day.

(2) Where, in relation to a period referred to in paragraph (1), the number of hours worked before and after midnight is equal—

(a) if the days in question fall at the beginning of a period of incapacity for work, the second day shall be treated as a day of incapacity for work; and

(b) if the days in question fall at the end of a period of incapacity for work, the first day shall be treated as a day of incapacity for work.

DEFINITIONS

"period of incapacity"—see SSCBA 1992, s.30C(1)(b), (c), above.

GENERAL NOTE

8.14   The general rule for purposes of incapacity benefit is that a day is the period midnight to midnight, and performance of work on a day will generally preclude it ranking as one of incapacity (see commentary to SSCBA 1992, s.30C(1)(a), above, and IW (General) Regs, regs 15–17, below). Its application to nightworkers whose shifts span midnight could cause hardship since they might lose a whole shift through incapacity but still have worked on a day as thus defined, by working on the preceding or subsequent shift, and thus be treated differently from their day worker counterparts whose shift lost through incapacity occupies one day only. This regulation attempts some easing of the position of nightworkers in this regard.

Paragraph (1) provides that where someone works for a continuous period beginning one day and spanning midnight into the following day, the day on which there falls the lesser part of the period worked will be treated as one of incapacity, so long as the person was incapable of work for the rest of that day.

Paragraph (2) deals with the situation in which the hours worked each side of midnight are equal. If the two days in question fall at the beginning of a period of incapacity for work, the second day is to be treated as one of incapacity. If the two days fall at the end of a period of incapacity for work, the first day is the one to be regarded as a day of incapacity for work.

[¹ Calculating periods of incapacity for work for welfare to work beneficiaries

5A.—For the purpose of incapacity benefit, in the case of a person who has been determined in accordance with regulation 13A of the Social Security (Incapacity for Work) (General) Regulations 1995 as a welfare to work beneficiary, section 30C(1)(c) of the Contributions and Benefits Act (any two periods of incapacity for work not separated by a period of more than 8 weeks shall be treated as one period of incapacity for work) shall have effect as if for the reference to 8 weeks there were substituted a reference to [²104] weeks.]

8.15

AMENDMENTS

1. Social Security (Welfare to Work) Regulations 1998 (SI 1998/2231) (October 5, 1998).
2. Social Security (Miscellaneous Amendments) (No.4) Regulations 2006 (SI 2006/2378), reg.10(2) (October 1, 2006).

GENERAL NOTE

This is part of a package of "welfare to work" measures. It modifies SSCBA 1992, s.30C(1)(c) so as to introduce a 52-week linking rule, rather than the standard eight-week one, for those incapable of work for 28 weeks who go into remunerative work, or into training followed by remunerative work, and then seek to return to their previous incapacity benefit and rate. See further IW (General) Regs, reg.13A. Note that the rule cannot apply to those who left incapacity benefit because of being found capable of work or treated as such. It is there to assist those who, while qualifying for benefit, wish to try out work or training for work, without prejudicing a return to their previous rate of benefit should things not work out.

8.16

Calculating periods of incapacity for work for persons receiving certain regular treatment

6.—(1) In the cases specified in paragraph (2), section 30C(1)(b) of the Contributions and Benefits Act (which defines a period of incapacity for work) shall have effect as if the period of 4 days mentioned there were a period of 2 days, whether consecutive or not, within a period of 7 consecutive days.

(2) The cases referred to in paragraph (1) are those where the days of incapacity for work in question result from—

(a) regular weekly treatment by way of haemodialysis for chronic renal failure or peritoneal dialysis for chronic renal failure;
(b) treatment by way of plasmapheresis, by way of parenteral chemotherapy with cytotoxic drugs, anti-tumour agents or immunosuppressive drugs or by way of radiotherapy; or
(c) regular weekly treatment by way of total parenteral nutrition for gross impairment of enteric function.

8.17

GENERAL NOTE

8.18   The terms, effect and rationale of this regulation, modifying the standard "continuity" rule, are noted in the commentary to SSCBA 1992, s.30C(1)(a) and (4)(a), above.

Days of statutory sick pay to be included in days of entitlement to incapacity benefit

8.19   **7.**—(1) For the purposes of section 30D(3) of the Contributions and Benefits Act (which provides for days of entitlement to statutory sick pay to be included in calculating the number of days for which a person has been entitled to short-term incapacity benefit) the days which are to be included are any of the days specified in paragraph (2) which—

(a) fell within a period of entitlement to statutory sick pay as between that person and his employer which ended not later than the 57th day before the first day of the period of incapacity for work to which that calculation relates; and

(b) fell on or after a day on which the person satisfied the contribution conditions for short-term incapacity benefit.

(2) The specified days are—

(a) in any week in which the employer was liable to pay that person statutory sick pay at the weekly rate specified in section 157(1) of the Contributions and Benefits Act, each day of that week; and

(b) in any week in which the employer was liable to pay that person statutory sick pay at a fraction of that weekly rate, each of the days of that week which would comprise the same fraction of a 7 day week; and any fractions of days produced by that calculation shall be included in the calculation for the following week and for any fraction of a day not accounted for at the end of that period of entitlement one additional day shall be added.

GENERAL NOTE

8.20   SSCBA 1992, s.30D(3) empowers the making of regulations to ranks as ones of entitlement for the purposes set out in s.30D(1), days in respect of which the claimant was entitled to statutory sick pay (SSP) from his employer, being (a) the day of entitlement to SSP on which he satisfied the contribution conditions for short-term incapacity benefit and (b) days of entitlement to SSP subsequent to that day. This regulation provides the detail. It covers specified days of entitlement to SSP falling on or after the day on which the claimant satisfied those contribution conditions and falling within a period of entitlement to SSP as between him and his employer ending not more than 57 days before the first day of the period of incapacity for work (PIW) for incapacity benefit purposes to which the calculation relates (para.(1)). The specified days are set out in para.(2) and envisage whole and part-week coverage.

[¹ Effect of statutory maternity pay on incapacity benefit

8.21   **7A.**—(1) For the purpose of determining a woman's entitlement to short-term incapacity benefit at the higher rate or long-term incapacity benefit under section 30A of the Contributions and Benefits Act, a day which falls within the maternity pay period shall, notwithstanding paragraph 1 of Schedule 13 to that Act, be treated as a day of incapacity for work for the purpose of determining whether it forms part of a period of incapacity for work where—

(a) on that day she was incapable of work; and
(b) that day is not treated under section 30C(3) of the Contributions and Benefits Act as a day which is not a day of incapacity for work; and
(c) the day immediately preceding the first day in the maternity pay period falls within either a period of incapacity for work or a period of entitlement to statutory sick pay for the purposes of Part 11 of the Contributions and Benefits Act; and
(d) the woman either satisfied the contribution conditions specified for short-term incapacity benefit on the first day of incapacity for work to fall within that period of incapacity for work or would have satisfied those conditions had a claim for short-term incapacity benefit been made on the first or any subsequent day of incapacity for work falling within that period of entitlement.

(2) Any day which, by virtue of paragraph (1), forms part of a period of incapacity for work shall be further treated, for the purpose of determining entitlement to short-term incapacity benefit at the higher rate or long-term incapacity benefit under section 30A of the Contributions and Benefits Act, as being a day on which the woman has been entitled to short-term incapacity benefit.

(3) For the purposes of this regulation "period of incapacity for work" has the same meaning as in section 30C(1) of the Contributions and Benefits Act.

(4) Where by virtue of paragraph (1) a woman is entitled to short-term incapacity benefit at the higher rate or long-term incapacity benefit for any week (including part of a week) the total amount of such benefit (including any increase for a dependant) payable to her for that week shall be reduced by an amount equivalent to any statutory maternity pay to which she is entitled in accordance with Part 12 of the Contributions and Benefits Act for the same week and only the balance, if any, of the short-term incapacity benefit at the higher rate or long-term incapacity benefit shall be payable to her.]

AMENDMENT

1. Social Security, Statutory Maternity Pay and Statutory Sick Pay (Miscellaneous Amendments) Regulations 2002 (SI 2002/2690), reg.10(1) (November 24, 2002).

[¹ Effect of statutory adoption pay on incapacity benefit

7B.—(1) For the purpose of determining a person's entitlement to short-term incapacity benefit at the higher rate or long-term incapacity benefit under section 30A of the Contributions and Benefits Act, a day which falls within the adoption pay period shall, notwithstanding section 171ZP(1) of the Contributions and Benefits Act, be treated as a day of incapacity for work for the purpose of determining whether it forms part of a period of incapacity for work where—

8.22

(a) on that day he was incapable of work; and
(b) that day is not treated under section 30C(3) of the Contributions and Benefits Act as a day which is not a day of incapacity for work; and
(c) the day immediately preceding the first day in the adoption pay

749

period falls within either a period of incapacity for work or a period of entitlement to statutory sick pay for the purposes of Part 11 of the Contributions and Benefits Act; and

(d) the person either satisfied the contribution conditions specified for short-term incapacity benefit on the first day of incapacity for work to fall within that period of incapacity for work or would have satisfied those conditions had a claim for short-term incapacity benefit been made on the first or any subsequent day of incapacity for work falling within that period of entitlement.

(2) Any day which, by virtue of paragraph (1), forms part of a period of incapacity for work shall be further treated, for the purpose of determining entitlement to short-term incapacity benefit at the higher rate or long-term incapacity benefit under section 30A of the Contributions and Benefits Act, as being a day on which the person has been entitled to short-term incapacity benefit.

(3) For the purposes of this regulation "period of incapacity for work" has the same meaning as in section 30C(1) of the Contributions and Benefits Act.

(4) Where by virtue of paragraph (1) a person is entitled to short-term incapacity benefit at the higher rate or long-term incapacity benefit for any week (including part of a week) the total amount of such benefit (including any increase for a dependant) payable to him for that week shall be reduced by an amount equivalent to any statutory adoption pay to which he is entitled in accordance with Part 12ZB of the Contributions and Benefits Act for the same week and only the balance, if any, of the short-term incapacity benefit at the higher rate or long-term incapacity benefit shall be payable to him.]

AMENDMENT

1. Social Security, Statutory Maternity Pay and Statutory Sick Pay (Miscellaneous Amendments) Regulations 2002 (SI 2002/2690), reg.10(2) (December 8, 2002), but only in respect of a person with whom a child is, or is expected to be, placed for adoption on or after 6th April 2003: see Employment Act 2002 (Commencement No. 3 and Transitional and Saving Provisions) Order, Sch.1(2), para.1 and Sch.3, para.2. (SI 2002/2866).

[1 Inclusion of days of sickness absence from duty before discharge from Her Majesty's forces in calculating days of entitlement to incapacity benefit

8.23   **7C.**—(1) For the purpose of section 30D(3A) of the Contributions and Benefits Act (days to be included in respect of person discharged from Her Majesty's forces after 3rd May 2003 when calculating the number of days for which the person has been entitled to short-term incapacity benefit) there is prescribed any day which falls within a period—

(a) of 4 or more consecutive days each of which is a day which is recorded by the Secretary of State for Defence as a day on which the person was on sickness absence from duty; and

(b) which ends not more than 8 weeks before the first day of the period to which the claim for incapacity benefit relates.

(2) For the purpose of paragraph (1)(a) any two such periods not separated by a period of more than 8 weeks shall be treated as one period.]

AMENDMENT

1. Social Security (Incapacity Benefit) (Her Majesty's Forces) (Amendment) Regulations 2003 (SI 2003/1068), reg. 2 (May 5, 2003).

GENERAL NOTE

The effect of this is noted in the annotations to SSCBA 1992, ss.30A(3), 30C(3) and 30D(3A), noting modifications to those sections in respect of a member of Her Majesty's Forces for whom days of sickness absence (recorded by the Secretary of State for Defence) are included in calculating the number of days for which such a person has been entitled to short-term incapacity benefit. Those modifications were effected by the Social Security Contributions and Benefits Act 1992 (Modifications for Her Majesty's Forces and Incapacity Benefit) Regulations 2003 (SI 2003/737), below. This regulation stipulates the days to be counted as ones of entitlement to short-term incapacity benefit. **8.24**

Limit of earnings from councillor's allowance

8.—For the purposes of section 30E(1) of the Contributions and Benefits Act (net amount of councillor's allowance in excess of prescribed amount to be deducted from incapacity benefit) the prescribed amount is [¹ £92.00]. **8.25**

AMENDMENT

1. Social Security (Miscellaneous Amendments) (No. 3) Regulations 2008 (SI 2008/2635), reg.3(2) (October 1, 2008).

GENERAL NOTE

This prescribes the amount after which councillors' allowance is deducted in full from incapacity benefit, abating it even to nil. See further annotations to SSCBA 1992, s.30E and reg.9, below. **8.26**

Councillor's allowance paid otherwise than weekly

9.—(1) For the purposes of section 30E(2) of the Contributions and Benefits Act, where a councillor's allowance is paid otherwise than weekly, an amount calculated in accordance with paragraphs (2) and (3) shall be regarded as the weekly amount of the allowance. **8.27**

(2) In the case of an attendance allowance, the weekly amount shall be the amount paid in respect of attendances undertaken in the week in question.

(3) In the case of a basic allowance or a special responsibility allowance, the weekly amount shall be calculated—

(a) where that allowance is paid annually, by dividing the amount paid by 52;

(b) where that allowance is paid quarterly, by dividing the amount paid by 13;

(c) where that allowance is paid monthly, by multiplying the amount by 12 and dividing by 52; and

(d) in any other case, by dividing the amount of the allowance by the number of days in the period and multiplying it by 7.

GENERAL NOTE

For the purposes of SSCBA 1992, s.30E and reg.8, above, this regulation provides the mechanism for determining a weekly amount in respect of councillor's allowance paid otherwise than weekly. **8.28**

PART III

RATE OF INCAPACITY BENEFIT

Increase in rate of incapacity benefit where beneficiary is under prescribed age on the qualifying date

8.29   **10.**—(1) The weekly rate of long-term incapacity benefit under section 30A of the Contributions and Benefits Act (incapacity benefit: entitlement) in relation to a period of incapacity for work shall be increased—

(a) by the higher amount specified in paragraph (2) if on the qualifying date the beneficiary was under the age of 35; and

(b) by the lower amount specified in that paragraph if on the qualifying date the beneficiary had attained the age of 35 but was under the age of 45.

(2) The amounts referred to in paragraph (1) are—

(a) higher amount: .... [¹ £15.65]

(b) lower amount: .... [¹ £6.55]

AMENDMENT

1. Social Security Benefits Up-rating Order 2009 (SI 2009/497), art.14 (April 9, 2009).

DEFINITIONS

"beneficiary"—see SSCBA 1992, s.122(1), above.
"period of incapacity for work"—see SSCBA 1992, s.30B(1)(b), (c), above.
"qualifying date"—see SSCBA 1992, s.30B(7), above; regs 11–13, below.

GENERAL NOTE

8.30   See further the commentary to SSCBA 1992, s.30B(7), above.

This regulation sets in para.(2) the amount for each of the two age-related increases available for some of those entitled to long-term incapacity benefit. These increases are the counterparts of the old invalidity allowances. There are two rates of increase: the higher for those who on the qualifying date were under the age of 35 and the lower rate for those whose qualifying date is between that age and the age of 45. For this purpose, the "qualifying date" is normally the first day of the period of incapacity for work in which the person transferred to long-term incapacity benefit, but regulations can set an earlier date (SSCBA 1992, s.30B(7), above). Regs 11–13 do so. Where part of that period of incapacity for work is made up of entitlement to statutory sick pay (s.30D(3), IB Regs, reg.7), the qualifying date will be the first day in that relevant period of SSP entitlement (reg.11). Reg.12 provides that if the qualifying date would have been earlier than that ascertained by the normal method in SSCBA 1992, section 30B(7) but for the fact that the person was on that earlier date a serving member of the forces, then that earlier date is the qualifying date. For the definition of "serving member of the forces", see reg.12(2) modifying the definition in reg.1(2) of the Social Security (Contributions) Regulations 1979. An earlier qualifying date can also apply for certain widows entitled to a widow's allowance (reg.13).

Note that, as part of moves towards transferring IB claimants to ESA, since January 20, 2009 the Secretary of State has an ability to use the annual up-rating order to reduce these amounts in respect of each of the tax years beginning with 2009-10 and ending with 2013-14 (see Employment and Support Allowance (Up-rating

Modification) (Transitional) Regulations 2008 (SI 2008/3270, reg.2). The first reduction was effected from April 9, 2009 and is incorporated in the text above.

Qualifying date for entitlement to increased rate of incapacity benefit—previous entitlement to statutory sick pay

11.—For the purposes of regulation 10 the qualifying date in relation to a person to whom regulation 7 applies shall be the first day in the period of entitlement mentioned in paragraph (1)(a) of that regulation.

8.31

Qualifying date for entitlement to increased rate of incapacity benefit—members of the armed forces

12.—(1) If, for the purposes of regulation 10, the qualifying date in relation to a person would have been earlier than that specified in section 30B(7) of the Contributions and Benefits Act (incapacity benefit: rate) but for the fact that on that earlier date he was a serving member of the forces, the qualifying date in relation to him shall nevertheless be that earlier date.

8.32

(2) In this regulation "serving member of the forces" has the meaning given to it by regulation 1(2) of the Social Security (Contributions) Regulations 1979, except that it does not include a person who falls within that definition by reason only of the fact that he was undergoing training or instruction for a continuous period of not more than 72 hours in any of the forces specified in paragraphs 2 to 9 of Part I of Schedule 3 to those Regulations.

Qualifying date for entitlement to increased rate of incapacity benefit—widows

13.—If, for the purposes of regulation 10, the qualifying date in relation to a person who was entitled to a widow's allowance would have been earlier than that specified in section 30B(7) of the Contributions and Benefits Act, if in respect of that earlier date she had claimed short-term incapacity benefit and had satisfied the contribution conditions for that benefit specified in paragraph 2 of Schedule 3 to the Contributions and Benefits Act, the qualifying date in relation to her shall nevertheless be that earlier date.

8.33

[¹ PART IV

ADDITIONAL CONDITIONS FOR PERSONS INCAPACITATED IN YOUTH

General

14.—This Part of these Regulations applies to persons incapacitated in youth in accordance with section 30A(1)(b) and (2A) of the Contributions and Benefits Act.

8.34

Age Exception—Persons aged 20 and under 25

15.—(1) For the purposes of subsection (2A)(b) of section 30A of the Contributions and Benefits Act (prescribed cases in relation to

8.35

persons aged under 25 and above the age 20 limit), a person falls within a prescribed case if he satisfies the conditions specified in the following paragraphs.

(2) The conditions referred to in paragraph (1) are that, he is a person who—

(a) registered on a course of—
   (i) full-time advanced or secondary education, or
   (ii) vocational or work-based training,

at least 3 months before he attained the age of 20 years; and

(b) not more than one academic term immediately after registration under sub-paragraph (a), attended one or more such courses of education or training as are mentioned in that sub-paragraph [² in respect of a period] referred to in paragraph (3).

(3) The period mentioned in paragraph (2)(b) is a period which—

(a) began on or before a day at least 3 months before the day he attained the age of 20 years, and

[²(b) ended no earlier than the beginning of the last two complete tax years before the benefit year which would have governed a claim for incapacity benefit under section 30A(1)(a) of the Contributions and Benefits Act had he been eligible for it.]

(4) For the purposes of this regulation a person is attending a course of education or training on any day on which the course or training is interrupted by an illness or domestic emergency.

(5) For the purposes of this regulation—

"advanced education" means full-time education for the purposes of—

(a) a course in preparation for a degree, a diploma of higher education, a higher national diploma, a higher national diploma of the Business and Technician Education Council or the Scottish Vocational Education Council, or a teaching qualification; or

(b) any other course which is of a standard above ordinary national diploma, a diploma of the Business and Technician Education Council or a national certificate of the Scottish Vocational Education Council, a general certificate of education (advanced level), a Scottish certificate of education (higher grade) or a Scottish certificate of Sixth Year Studies;

"course of education" means a course of advanced education or secondary education;

"full-time" includes part-time where the disability from which a person suffers prevents him from attending a full-time course;

"relevant day" has the same meaning as in section 30A(1) of the Contributions and Benefits Act, that is to say, the day—

(a) in respect of which a person is entitled to claim incapacity benefit;

(b) which falls on any day immediately after a period of 196 consecutive days of incapacity for work; and

(c) which forms part of a period of incapacity for work;

"secondary education" means a full-time course of education below a course of advanced education—

(a) by attendance at a recognised educational establishment within the meaning of section 147(1) of the Contributions and Benefits Act, or

(b) elsewhere than at a recognised educational establishment, where the Secretary of State is satisfied that the education is equivalent to that given in a recognised educational establishment;

"training" has the same meaning as vocational training or work-based training;

"vocational training" means training for work as defined for the purposes of section 30C(6) of the Contributions and Benefits Act and in regulation 3, and includes any training, instruction or tuition (of which the primary purpose is the teaching of occupational or vocational skills) received on a course provided, for persons suffering mental or physical disability, by a person recognised by the Secretary of State; and

"work-based training" means vocational training undertaken on the premises of an employer.]

AMENDMENTS

1. Social Security (Incapacity Benefit) Miscellaneous Amendments Regulations 2000 (SI 2000/3120), reg.2(5) (April 6, 2001).
2. Social Security (Incapacity Benefit) Amendment Regulations 2001 (SI 2001/1305), reg.2(3) (April 25, 2001).

DEFINITIONS

"advanced education"   see para.(5).
"course of education"—see para.(5)
"full-time"—see para.(5)
"relevant day"—see SSCBA 1992, s.30A(1); para.(5).
"secondary education"—see para.(5).
"training"—see para.(5).
"vocational training"—see para.(5); SSCBA 1992, s.30C(6); reg.3.
"work-based training"—see para.(5).

GENERAL NOTE

SSCBA 1992, s.30A(1)(b) and (2A) provide for non-contributory access to incapacity benefit for persons incapacitated in youth. To count as such, usually a person must be aged under 20. In "prescribed cases", persons 20 or over but under 25 can also be eligible. This regulation defines those circumstances.

8.36

Someone over 20 but under 25 can rank as a person incapacitated in youth where, at least three months before reaching 20, he registered on a course of full-time education or of vocational or work-based training (see below), provided that not more than one academic term immediately after his registration, he attended one or more such courses in respect of a specified period (para.(2)). Note that he is treated as attending on any day on which the course or training is interrupted by an illness or domestic emergency (para.4). The specified period is set out in para.(3): a period beginning on or before a day three months before his twentieth birthday (para.(3)(a)) and ending on a day not earlier than the beginning of the last two complete tax years before the benefit year which would have governed a claim for incapacity benefit under s.30A(1)(a) of the SSCBA 1992 had he been eligible for it.

The terms "advanced education" and "secondary education" are defined in para.(5) in an interlocking way, so that "secondary education" is a level below that of "advanced education" and it requires attendance at a recognised educational establishment for child benefit purposes (see SSCBA 1992, s.147(1)) or elsewhere so long as the Secretary of State is satisfied that the education afforded there is equivalent to that in such an establishment. Note that while both "advanced education" and "secondary education" require a "full-time" course, para.(5) stipulates that "full-time" covers also "part-time" where the claimant's disability is such as to preclude him attending a full-time course.

Whether the claimant was registered on a "full-time" course or on a course of "vocational or work-based training" was considered by Commissioner Jacobs in

CIB/1410/2005. Her course was described as part-time by the College in question (not conclusive in itself) and she was required to attend College one day a week and undertake eight to 10 hours of private study. She had also to arrange and undertake 60 hours of work experience over the period of the course. Commissioner Jacobs held that the tribunal was entitled to disregard the work experience, since it was essential to, but not part of, the course, and to regard the course as part-time. Moreover, she could not in such circumstances be regarded as registered on a course of vocational or work-based training.

[¹ Conditions relating to residence or presence

8.37   **16.**—(1) The prescribed conditions for the purposes of section 30A(2A) (d) of the Contributions and Benefits Act as to residence or presence in Great Britain in relation to any person on the relevant day shall be that on that day—

    (a) he is ordinarily resident in Great Britain;

    (b) he is not a person subject to immigration control within the meaning of section 115(9) of the Immigration and Asylum Act 1999 or he is a person to whom paragraph (5) applies;

    (c) he is present in Great Britain; and

    (d) he has been present in Great Britain for a period of, or for periods amounting in aggregate to, not less than 26 weeks in the 52 weeks immediately preceding that day.

    (2) [³ *Omitted*].

    (3) [³ *Omitted*]

    (4) In determining whether a person satisfies paragraph (1), where a person is absent from Great Britain by reason only of the fact that—

    (a) he is abroad in his capacity as a serving member of the forces, or he is the spouse, [² civil partner,] son, daughter, father, father-in-law, mother or mother-in-law of, and living with, a serving member of the forces abroad;

    (b) he is in employment prescribed for the purposes of section 120 of the Contributions and Benefits Act in connection with continental shelf operations; or

    (c) he is abroad in his capacity as an airman within the meaning of regulation 81, or mariner within the meaning of regulation 86, of the Social Security (Contributions) Regulations 1979;

any day or period of absence shall be treated as a day on which, or period during which, the person is present or resident, as the case may be, in Great Britain; and for the purposes of this paragraph "serving member of the forces" has the same meaning as in regulation 1(2) of the Social Security (Contributions) Regulations 1979.

    (5) This paragraph applies where a person is—

    (a) a member of a family of a national of a State contracting party to the Agreement on the European Economic Area signed at Oporto on 2nd May 1992 as adjusted by the Protocol signed at Brussels on 17th March1993;

    (b) a person who is lawfully working in Great Britain and is a national of a State with which the Community has concluded an agreement under Article 310 of the Treaty of Amsterdam amending the Treaty on European Union, the Treaties establishing the European Communities and certain related Acts providing, in the field of social security, for the equal treatment of workers who are nationals of the signatory State and their families;

(c) a person who is a member of a family of, and living with, a person specified in sub-paragraph (b); or

(d) a person who has been given leave to enter, or remain in, the United Kingdom by the Secretary of State upon an undertaking by another person or persons pursuant to the immigration rules within the meaning of the Immigration Act 1971 to be responsible for his maintenance and accommodation.

(6) A person shall be treated as having satisfied the residence or presence conditions on any subsequent day of incapacity for work falling within the same period of incapacity for work where the residence or presence conditions specified in paragraphs (1) to (4) are satisfied on the first relevant day.]

AMENDMENTS

1. Social Security (Incapacity Benefit) Miscellaneous Amendments Regulations 2000 (SI 2000/3120), reg.2(5) (April 6, 2001).
2. Civil Partnership (Pensions, Social Security and Child Support) (Consequential, etc. Provisions) Order 2005 (SI 2005/2877), art. 2(3) and Sch.3, para.24 (December 5, 2005).
3. Social Security (Miscellaneous Amendments) (No.4) Regulations 2006 (SI 2006/2378), reg.10(4) (October 1, 2006).

DEFINITIONS

"Great Britain"—by art.1 of the Union with Scotland Act 1706, this means England, Scotland and Wales; and see SSCBA 1992, s.172.

"relevant day"—see SSCBA 1992, s.30A(1).

"serving member of the forces"—see para.(4); Social Security (Contributions) Regulations 1979.

"tax-free emoluments"—see para.(3); Child Benefit Regulations, reg.9.

GENERAL NOTE

SSCBA 1992, s.30A(2A)(d) requires that to gain non-contributory access to incapacity benefit as a person incapacitated in youth, a claimant must on the relevant day satisfy the prescribed conditions as to residence or presence in Great Britain. This regulation sets out those prescribed conditions. They are such as to require both residence and presence. Residence is "ordinary residence" rather than simple residence (para.(1)(a)). There is no requirement of "habitual residence". "Presence" means "physically present".

8.38

The requirements are that the claimant must on the first day of claim in the period of incapacity for work be both ordinarily resident and present in Great Britain. (On "ordinarily resident", see further the commentary to Persons Abroad Regulations, reg.5, above.) He must also have been present in Great Britain for a period or aggregate periods of at least 26 weeks in the immediately preceding 52 weeks (para.(1)(d)). In addition he must not be subject to immigration control within the meaning of Immigration and Asylum Act 1999, s.115(9) (set out in *Vol. II: Income Support, Jobseeker's Allowance, Tax Credits and the Social Fund* and see the provisions noted in the commentary thereto) or (if *prima facie* he is) he must be someone protected by para.(5). That paragraph protects the same groups as are covered in Pt II of the Sch. to the Social Security (Immigration and Asylum) Consequential Amendments Regulations 2000, set out in *Vol.II: Income Support, Jobseeker's Allowance, Tax Credits and the Social Fund.* See further in that work, the commentary to the Income Support Regulations, reg.21(3).

Absence from Great Britain would negate presence. Paragraph (4) enables certain actual absences to be treated, legally speaking, as if the person was present or resident in Great Britain. It protects airmen and mariners within the meaning of regs 81 and 86, respectively, of the Social Security (Contributions) Regulations 1979. It protects also those in employment prescribed for the purposes of SSCBA 1992, s.120 in connection with continental shelf operations. It also protects someone abroad in his capacity as a "serving member of the forces" or the spouse, son, daughter, father, mother, father-in-law, mother-in-law of and living with a serving member of the forces abroad. For the definition of "serving member of the forces", see the commentary to the Persons Abroad Regulations, reg.1(2). Section 246 of the Civil Partnership Act 2004, which provides that references to "step" relationships and "in laws" are to be read as including relationships arising through civil partnership, applies to para.(4).

Conversely, even where he might qualify under the ordinary conditions, para.(4) requires rather more of a claimant who receives, or is the spouse of someone who receives, tax-free emoluments as defined in Child Benefit (General) Regulations 1976, reg.9. Such a person cannot be regarded as fulfilling the "present in Great Britain" condition during the period of receipt of such payments unless in the four-year period immediately prior to it he had been present in Great Britain for a period or aggregate period of at least 156 days.

[¹ Circumstances in which a person is or is not to be treated as receiving full-time education

8.39

17.—(1) This regulation applies for the purposes of section 30A(7) of the Contributions and Benefits Act (the circumstances in which a person is or is not to be treated as receiving full-time education for the purposes of section 30A(2A)(e) of that Act).

(2) A person shall be treated as receiving full-time education for any period during which—

(a) he is 16 years of age or over but under the age of 19 years; and

(b) he attends a course of education for 21 hours or more in a week.

(3) For the purposes of paragraph (2)(b), in calculating the number of hours a week during which a person attends a course, no account shall be taken of any instruction or tuition which is not suitable for persons of the same age and sex who do not suffer from a physical or mental disability.

(4) In determining the duration of a period of full-time education under paragraph (2), any temporary interruption of that education may be disregarded.

(5) A person who is 19 years of age or over shall not be treated for the purposes of section 30A(2A)(e) of the Contributions and Benefits Act as receiving full-time education notwithstanding he is undergoing a full-time education.]

AMENDMENT

1. Social Security (Incapacity Benefit) Miscellaneous Amendments Regulations 2000 (SI 2000/3120), reg.2(5) (April 6, 2001).

GENERAL NOTE

8.40

SSCBA 1992, s.30A(2A)(d) precludes someone from ranking as a person incapacitated in youth (thus denying non-contributory access to incapacity benefit) where on the day of claimed incapacity he is receiving full-time education. This regulation sets out what is, and what is not, to be regarded as full-time education. Someone who is 19 or over cannot be so precluded even though he is in fact under-going a full-time education (para.(5)). Preclusive "full-time education" covers a person 16–18 inclusive for any period in which he attends a course of education for 21 or more hours a week (para.(2)). In determining the length of any such pre-clusive period, a decision-maker may disregard any temporary interruption of that education (para.(4)). This, it is submitted, is ambiguous, leaving it unclear whether such periods are to be counted as part of the preclusive period or ones that are to be left out. As regards the 21 hours aspect, no account is to be taken in calculating those hours of any instruction or tuition unsuitable for a person of the same age and sex as the claimant but who is not suffering from a physical or mental disability (para.(3)). In other words, one ignores special classes for the disabled.

[¹ Circumstances in which a previous claimant who does not satisfy the age condition becomes entitled

18.—(1) This regulation applies, for the purposes of section 30A(6) of the Contributions and Benefits Act, to a person who has previously been entitled to incapacity benefit under section 30A(1)(b) of that Act (persons incapacitated in youth) and does not satisfy the condition set out in section 30A(2A)(b) of that Act (upper age condition).

(2) A person shall be entitled to the lower rate short-term incapacity benefit where—

(a) he has previously been entitled to incapacity benefit by virtue of having been a person incapacitated in youth under section 30A(1)(b) and (2A) of the Contributions and Benefits Act;

(b) his previous entitlement had not been ended by a determination (other than a determination in the circumstances applicable to a person under paragraph (3)(a) or (4)(a)) that he was, or was treated as, capable of work;

(c) section 30C(1)(c), (5) or (6) of the Contributions and Benefits Act (days and periods of incapacity for work) or any regulation made under section 30C(4)(b) (linking provisions) does not apply in his case;

(d) he is aged 20 years or over, or, where regulation 15 would otherwise apply to him, aged 25 years or over; and

(e) he is a person to whom paragraph (3) or (4) applies.

(3) This paragraph applies to a person—

(a) whose previous entitlement to incapacity benefit for a person incap-acitated in youth was terminated solely with a view to him taking up an employment or training;

(b) whose earnings [² factor] from an employment or series of employ-ments, which he pursued in the period from the termination of his previous entitlement to the beginning of his period of incapacity for work, [² was] below the lower earnings limit in accordance with section 5(1)(a) of the Contributions and Benefits Act multiplied by 25 in any of the last three complete tax years before the beginning of the relevant benefit year; and

(c) who—

(i) in respect of the last two complete tax years before the beginning of the relevant benefit year has either paid or been credited with earnings equivalent in each of those years to the year's lower earnings limit multiplied by 50, of which at least one, in the last tax year, was in respect of disabled person's tax credit; or

8.41

    (ii) within a period of 56 days after the day he ceased his last such employment as he pursued in accordance with sub-paragraph (b), makes a claim for incapacity benefit for persons incapacitated in youth.

(4) This paragraph applies to a person—

(a) whose previous entitlement to incapacity benefit for persons incapacitated in youth was terminated by reason solely of his absence from Great Britain by virtue of disqualification under section 113 of the Contributions and Benefits Act;

(b) who has been incapable of work for a period of 196 consecutive days from the day of his absence from Great Britain ceased;

(c) who, on the first day of his incapacity for work following the day his absence from Great Britain ceased, is a person who had received incapacity benefit for persons incapacitated in youth in the last complete tax year immediately preceding the relevant benefit year which would have applied in his case; and

(d) who made his claim for benefit on a day not later than the 197th day from which his absence from Great Britain ceased.

(5) For the purposes of this regulation, "training" has the same meaning as in regulation 15.]

AMENDMENTS

1. Social Security (Incapacity Benefit) Miscellaneous Amendments Regulations 2000 (SI 2000/3120), reg.2(5) (April 6, 2001).

2. Social Security (Incapacity Benefit) Amendment Regulations 2001 (SI 2001/1305), reg.2(4) (April 25, 2001).

DEFINITIONS

"employment"—see SSCBA 1992, s.122(1).
"lower earnings limit"—see SSCBA 1992, ss.122(1), 5(1).
"relevant benefit year"—see SSCBA 1992, s.25(6), Sch.3, para.(2) (see commentary to SSCBA 1992, s.30A(2)).
"tax year"—see SSCBA 1992, s.122(1).
"training"—see reg.15(5).

GENERAL NOTE

8.42   Pursuant to SSCBA 1992, s.30A(6), this regulation deals with the situation where someone has been entitled to incapacity benefit as a person incapacitated in youth, ceases to be entitled to it other than on the basis of being found not to be incapable of work, and claims again in a new period of incapacity for work (not being helped by the variety of linking rules in the scheme [SSCBA 1992, ss.30C(1)(c), (5) or (6) or regulations made under s.30C(4)(a)], but is over age (20 or 25 as the case may be) when he makes that new claim. It enables him to gain non-contributory access to short-term incapacity benefit in certain cases where his previous entitlement was terminated solely with a view to him taking up employment or training which proved to be very low paid or very intermittent, or in certain cases where his entitlement was terminated solely by reason of absence from Great Britain producing disqualification from benefit under s.113.

Paragraph (3) covers the person whose entitlement terminated solely with a view to him taking up an employment or vocational or work-based training (see "training" in reg.15(5) and its definitions of these terms) (para.(3)(a)). He can be regarded as a person incapacitated in youth (albeit over–age) if his earnings factor from the employment or series of employments pursued since the termination of his previous entitlement was below a specified level in *any* of the three complete tax years preceding the beginning of the benefit year in which there falls the first day of the current period of incapacity for work (para.(3)(b) read with SSCBA 1992, s.21 and Sch.3, para.(2), reproduced in the commentary to SSCBA 1992, s.30A(2)). The specified level is less than 25 times the lower earnings level set for Class 1 contributions purposes in the tax year in question. However, he can only be eligible if in addition, he is either

(a) claiming as a person incapacitated in youth within 56 days of his last such employment (para.(3)(c)(ii)), or

(b) in each of the last two complete tax years (identified as above) he has paid or been credited with earnings to the level of 50 times the year's lower earnings limit for Class 1 contributions purposes, and at least one of those contributions was, in the last such year, in respect of disabled person's tax credit (para. (3)(c)(i)).

Paragraph (4) deals with the person whose previous entitlement was terminated solely because of a disqualifying absence from Great Britain (SSCBA 1992, s.113 read with the Persons Abroad Regulations). He ranks as a person incapacitated in youth (despite being over-age) if he claims again no later than the 197th day after his absence ceased, and he has since it ceased been incapable of work for a period of 196 consecutive days. But to so rank he must in that period of incapacity for work be able to say that in the last complete tax year before the benefit year in which the current period of incapacity falls, he had received incapacity benefit as a person incapacitated in youth. So, to be entitled for his new claim in, say, May 2003 (benefit year 2003–2004), he must have been so entitled in tax year 2001–2002. Someone entitled in May 2001, who, following a disqualifying absence abroad, seeks to reclaim in benefit year 2002/2003, cannot rely, it would seem, on his entitlement in tax year 2001–2002 since it was not complete prior to the relevant benefit year (2002/2003). Nor, of course, can he look to an earlier tax year since there was no eligibility as a person incapacitated in youth prior to April 6, 2001.

[¹ Persons formerly entitled to severe disablement allowance

19.—(1) Where a person was below the age of 20 years [² on 6th April, 2001] and was entitled to, or receiving, severe disablement allowance by virtue of section 68(1) of the Contributions and Benefits Act on or immediately before 5th April 2002, he shall, if he continues to be incapable of work in accordance with Part XIIA of the Contributions and Benefits Act, be—

(a) entitled to the long-term incapacity benefit from 6th April 2002; and

(b) treated as having acquired entitlement under section 30A(1)(b) and (2A) of the Contributions and Benefits Act; and

(c) treated as if section 30DD of the Contributions and Benefits Act does not apply in his case.

(2) Where a person was below the age of 20 years [² on 6th April 2001] and was entitled to, or receiving, severe disablement allowance by virtue of section 68(1) of the Contributions and Benefits Act and to whom section 30C(1) to (4) or section 68(10) or (10A), or regulations made under section 30C(4)(b), of that Act applied on or immediately after 5th April 2002, he shall be—

(a) entitled to the long-term incapacity benefit from the relevant day; and

(b) treated as having acquired entitlement under section 30A(1)(b) and (2A) of the Contributions and Benefits Act; and

8.43

(c) treated as if section 30DD of the Contribution and Benefits Act does not apply in his case.]

AMENDMENTS

1. Social Security (Incapacity Benefit) Miscellaneous Amendments Regulations 2000 (SI 2000/3120), reg.2(5) (April 6, 2001).
2. Social Security (Incapacity) (Miscellaneous Amendments) Regulations 2002 (SI 2002/491), reg.4 (April 5, 2002).

DEFINITIONS

"relevant day"—see SSCBA 1992, s.30A(1).

GENERAL NOTE

8.44   Regulation 19(1) deals with those persons, aged under 20, on April 6, 2001, who are entitled to SDA on or immediately before April 5, 2002, but do not qualify for incapacity benefit as a person incapacitated in youth under the "normal" provisions. The provision transfers them to long-term incapacity benefit for days of incapacity on or after April 6, 2002. Such persons are from then treated as persons incapacitated in youth and so will be eligible to rely on the help afforded by reg.18, should they leave benefit and claim in a new period of incapacity for work. Reg.19(2) similarly transfers those aged under 20 on April 6, 2001 and entitled to or receiving SDA whose continuing period of incapacity for work spans April 5, 2002. Note that persons treated as persons incapacitated in youth pursuant to this regulation are not subject to the reduction or abatement of incapacity benefit effected by SSCBA 1992, s.30DD and related regulations (paras (1)(c), (2)(c)).

[¹ PART V

REDUCTION OR ABATEMENT OF INCAPACITY BENEFIT FOR OCCUPATIONAL OR OTHER PENSION PAYMENTS

Permanent health insurance

8.45   20.—For the purposes of section 30DD of the Contributions and Benefits Act (incapacity benefit: reduction for pension payments)—
(a) pension payment shall include permanent health insurance payment; and
(b) "permanent health insurance payment" means any periodical payment arranged by an employer under an insurance policy providing benefits in connection with physical or mental illness, disability, infirmity or defect, in relation to a former employee on the termination of his employment.]

AMENDMENT

1. Social Security (Incapacity Benefit) Miscellaneous Amendments Regulations 2000 (SI 2000/3120), reg.2(5) (April 6, 2001).

DEFINITIONS

"pension payment"—see SSCBA 1992, s.30DD(5).
"permanent health insurance"—see para.(b).

GENERAL NOTE

For purposes of SSCBA 1992, s.30DD (reduction of incapacity benefit for pension payments), this regulation, made with respect to subs.(5)(b) of that section, includes "permanent health insurance payment" within that section's conception of "pension payment". "Permanent health insurance payment" is defined in para.(b).

The terms and effect of this regulation are noted in the commentary to SSCBA 1992, s.30DD.

8.46

[¹ Disregard of certain pension payments

21.—For the purposes of section 30DD(1) of the Contributions and Benefits Act (reduction for pension payments [² and PPF periodic payments]), there shall be disregarded—

8.47

(a) any pension payment within the meaning of section 30DD(5) of the Contributions and Benefits Act made to a person as a beneficiary on the death of a member of any pension scheme;

[² (aa) any PPF periodic payment made to a person as a beneficiary on the death of a person entitled to such a payment;]

(b) where a pension scheme is in deficit or has insufficient resources to meet the full pension payment, the extent of the shortfall; or

(c) any permanent health insurance payment in respect of which the employee had contributed to the premium to the extent of more than 50 per cent.]

AMENDMENTS

1. Social Security (Incapacity Benefit) Miscellaneous Amendments Regulations 2000 (SI 2000/3120), reg.2(5) (April 6, 2001).

2. Social Security (PPF Payments and FAS Payments) (Consequential Amendments) Regulations 2006 (SI 2006/1069), reg.4 (May 5, 2006).

DEFINITIONS

"pension payment"—see SSCBA 1992, s.30DD(5).
"permanent health insurance"—see reg.20(b).
"PPF periodic payment"—see SSCBA 1992, s.122(1).

GENERAL NOTE

For purposes of SSCBA 1992, s.30DD(1) (reduction of incapacity benefit for pension payments and PPF periodic payments), this regulation provides for the pensions it lists to be disregarded for incapacity benefit abatement purposes.

The terms and effect of this regulation are noted in the commentary to SSCBA 1992, s.30DD.

8.48

[¹ Date from which pension payment is to be taken into account

22.—Where section 30DD(1) of the Contributions and Benefits Act (reduction for pension payments [² and PPF periodic payments]) applies, deductions shall have effect, calculated, where appropriate, in accordance with regulation 24 (pension payments made other than weekly), from the first day of the week, commencing on Sunday, in which the pension payment [² or PPF periodic payment] is paid to a person who is entitled to incapacity benefit in that week.]

8.49

AMENDMENTS

1. Social Security (Incapacity Benefit) Miscellaneous Amendments Regulations 2000 (SI 2000/3120), reg.2(5) (April 6, 2001).

2. Social Security (PPF Payments and FAS Payments) (Consequential Amendments) Regulations 2006 (SI 2006/1069), reg.4 (May 5, 2006).

GENERAL NOTE

8.50   Deductions from incapacity benefit in respect of pension payments and PPF periodic payments exceeding the applicable threshold have effect from the first day of the week, beginning with Sunday, in which the pension payment is paid to someone entitled to incapacity benefit in that week.

[¹ Date from which the change in the rate of pension takes effect

8.51   **23.** Where pension payments [² or PPF periodic payments] are already in payment to a person and the rate of payment changes, the deduction at the new rate shall take effect, calculated, where appropriate, in accordance with regulation 24 (pension payments made other than weekly), from the first day of the week, commencing on Sunday, in which the new rate of the pension payment [² or PPF periodic payment] is paid.]

AMENDMENTS

1. Social Security (Incapacity Benefit) Miscellaneous Amendments Regulations 2000 (SI 2000/3120), reg.2(5) (April 6, 2001).
2. Social Security (PPF Payments and FAS Payments) (Consequential Amendments) Regulations 2006 (SI 2006/1069), reg.4 (May 5, 2006).

DEFINITIONS

"pension payments"—see SSCBA 1992, s.30DD(5).
"PPF periodic payment"—see SSCBA 1992, s.122(1).

GENERAL NOTE

8.52   Where the rate of pension payment or PPF periodic payment changes, the change takes effect from the first day of the week, beginning with Sunday, in which the new rate is paid.

[¹ Pension payment made other than weekly

8.53   **24.**—(1) Where a pension payment [² or PPF periodic payment], or an aggregate of such payments, as the case may be, is paid to a person for a period other than a week, such payments shall be treated as being made to that person by way of weekly pension payments [² or weekly PPF periodic payments] and the weekly amount shall be determined—
   (a) where payment is made for a year, by dividing the total by 52;
   (b) where payment is made for 3 months, by dividing the total by 13;
   (c) where payment is made for a month, by multiplying the total by 12 and dividing the result by 52;
   (d) where payment is made for 2 or more months, otherwise than for a year or for 3 months, by dividing the total by the number of months, multiplying the result by 12 and dividing the result of that multiplication by 52; or
   (e) in any other case, by dividing the amount of the payment by the number of days in the period for which it is made and multiplying the result by 7.
   (2) In determining the weekly amount of the pension payment [² or PPF periodic payment]—

(a) there shall be disregarded the sum of less than one half of a penny; and

(b) the sum of one half of a penny or more but less than one penny shall be rounded up to one penny.

(3) In determining the weekly pension payment [² or weekly PPF periodic payment], where two or more pension payments [² or PPF periodic payments] are payable to a person, each pension payment [² or PPF periodic payment] shall be calculated separately in accordance with paragraph (1) before aggregating the sum of those payments for the purposes of the reduction of the benefit in accordance with section 30DD(1) of the Contributions and Benefits Act.]

AMENDMENTS

1. Social Security (Incapacity Benefit) Miscellaneous Amendments Regulations 2000 (SI 2000/3120), reg.2(5) (April 6, 2001).
2. Social Security (PPF Payments and FAS Payments) (Consequential Amendments) Regulations 2006 (SI 2006/1069), reg.4 (May 5, 2006).

DEFINITIONS

"pension payment"—see SSCBA 1992, s.30DD.
"PPF periodic payment"—see SSCBA 1992, s.122(1).

GENERAL NOTE

Para. (1)

This contains the provisions for treating as a weekly amount pension payments or PPF periodic payments paid otherwise than weekly, and for calculating the amount. So, for example, one paid in respect of a year is translated into a weekly payment by dividing by 52, while one paid in respect of three months is divided by 13 to produce the weekly equivalent.   **8.54**

Para. (2)

This covers rounding fractions of a penny produced in calculating the weekly amount of pension payment or PPF periodic payment. Anything less than half a penny is to be disregarded. A halfpenny or more is to be rounded up to a penny.   **8.55**

Para. (3)

Some people will receive several pension payments or PPF periodic payments. Each is first to be calculated separately according to the paragraph (1) formula, and then those separate sums are aggregated for the purposes of determining the appropriate amount of reduction of incapacity benefit in accordance with SSCBA 1992, s.30DD.   **8.56**

[¹ Priority of deductions of pension payments taken as payable for the purposes of reduction of incapacity benefit

25.—Where a reduction in the rate of incapacity benefit payable to a person falls to be made in accordance with section 30DD(1) of the Contributions and Benefits Act the reduction shall be made, so far as is necessary—   **8.57**

(a) initially against so much of the benefit as falls to be paid at the personal rate;

(b) then against any increase in the benefit payable for adult dependants; and

(c) finally against any increase in the benefit payable for dependent children.]

AMENDMENT

1. Social Security (Incapacity Benefit) Miscellaneous Amendments Regulations 2000 (SI 2000/3120), reg.2(5) (April 6, 2001).

GENERAL NOTE

8.58   SSCBA 1992, s.30DD merely provides that incapacity benefit is to be reduced by the 50 per cent of the excess of pension payment over the threshold amount (currently £85, alterable by regulation). This regulation stipulates that reduction is first to be against the claimant's personal rate, then (if any excess remains) against any increase in respect of an adult dependant, and, should there still be pension excess, against any increase in respect of a dependant child.

[¹ Person whose benefit is not to be reduced under section 30DD(1)

8.59   **26.**—Section 30DD(1) of the Contributions and Benefits Act (reduction of incapacity benefit for pension payments) shall not apply to a person who is entitled to the highest rate of the care component of disability living allowance under s.72 of the Contributions and Benefits Act.]

AMENDMENT

1. Social Security (Incapacity Benefit) Miscellaneous Amendments Regulations 2000 (SI 2000/3120), reg.2(5) (April 6, 2001).

GENERAL NOTE

8.60   For purposes of SSCBA 1992, s.30DD(1) (reduction of incapacity benefit for pension payments), this regulation provides that abatement of incapacity benefit does not operate with respect to someone in receipt of the highest rate care component of DLA under SSCBA 1992, s.72.

Social Security (Incapacity Benefit) (Consequential and Transitional Amendments and Savings) Regulations 1995

(SI 1995/829)

ARRANGEMENT OF REGULATIONS

Part I and II omitted.

PART III

TRANSITIONAL AND SAVINGS PROVISIONS

8.61   25.   Claim or question concerning sickness or invalidity benefit to be determined after "the appointed day".

26.   Recoupment of sickness or invalidity benefit.
27.   Reviews in respect of sickness and invalidity benefit.

The Secretary of State for Social Security, in exercise of powers conferred by section 86A(1) of the Social Security Contributions and Benefits Act 1992, section 12(1) of the Social Security (Incapacity for Work) Act 1994 and of all other powers enabling him in that behalf by this instrument, which is made before the end of the period of 6 months from the coming into force of those enactments and with the consent of the Treasury to regulation 22, hereby makes the following Regulations:

PART III

TRANSITIONAL AND SAVINGS PROVISIONS

Claim or question concerning sickness or invalidity benefit to be determined after "the appointed day"

25.—For the purpose of determining any claim or question concerning sickness or invalidity benefit which falls to be determined on or after the appointed day, the Contributions and Benefits Act, the Administration Act and any regulations made under them (other than the Social Security (Claims and Payments) Regulations 1987 shall be construed as if section 13(2) of the Social Security (Incapacity for Work) Act 1994 had not been enacted.

8.62

GENERAL NOTE

Normally, after April 13, 1993 ("the appointed day": reg.1(2)), references in primary or subordinate legislation to sickness or invalidity benefit are to be interpreted as ones to the appropriate type and rate of incapacity benefit (IWA 1994, s.13(2)). This regulation provides, however, that that approach is not to be taken for the purpose of determining any claim or question with respect to sickness or invalidity benefit which falls to be determined on or after April 13, 1995. Instead one reads references to those benefits in the SSCBA 1992, the AA 1992 and regulations made under them (e.g. the USI Regs) in the normal way. This regulation does not apply to the Claims and Payments Regs 1987, simply because IW (Transitional) Regs, regs 5 and 6 make similar provisions with regard to those Claims and Payments Regs.

8.63

Recoupment of sickness or invalidity benefit

26.—Where a determination is made on or after the appointed day concerning the recoupment of sickness or invalidity benefit, regulation 2 of the Recoupment Regulations shall be read as if the references to incapacity benefit in that regulation were references to sickness or invalidity benefit.

8.64

Reviews in respect of sickness and invalidity benefit

27.—Where a decision relating to sickness or invalidity benefit is reviewed on or after the appointed day, regulations 65(1)(b) and (3)(a)(ii) of the Adjudication Regulations shall be read as if the references to incapacity benefit and short-term incapacity benefit in those regulations were references to invalidity benefit or sickness benefit.

8.65

Social Security (Incapacity Benefit—Increases for Dependants) Regulations 1994

(SI 1994/2945) (*as amended*)

ARRANGEMENT OF REGULATIONS

PART I

GENERAL

PART II

CHILD DEPENDANTS

PART III

ADULT DEPENDANTS

PART IV

CONSEQUENTIAL AMENDMENTS

PART V

TRANSITIONAL PROVISION

16.   Effect of an increase of benefit under regulation 12, 13, 15, 19, 20, 24 or 25
of the Social Security (Incapacity Benefit) (Transitional) Regulations
(1995).

The Secretary of State for Social Security, in exercise of powers conferred by sections 3(2), 80(7), 86A, 87, 89, 90, 114(1) and 122(1) and (5) of the Social Security Contributions and Benefits Act 1992 and of all other powers enabling him in that behalf, by this instrument, which contains only regulations which are either made under section 86A of that Act or consequential on the other amendments made to the Act of 1992 by the Social Security (Incapacity for Work) Act 1994, and which, being in either case made within 6 months of the coming into force of the latter Act, are required to be referred to the Social Security Advisory Committee, hereby makes the following Regulations:

PART I

GENERAL

Citation, commencement and interpretation

1.—(1) These Regulations may be cited as the Social Security (Incapacity   8.67
Benefit—Increases for Dependents) Regulations 1994 and shall come into
force as follows—
except for regulation 15(6)(b)(i) and (c)(i), on 13th April 1995; regulation 15(6)(b)(i) and (c)(i), on 13th May 1995.
(2) In these Regulations—
"the Administration Act" means the Social Security Administration Act
1992;
"benefit week" means a period of seven days ending with the day on
which the benefit is due to be paid;
"the Contributions and Benefits Act" means the Social Security
Contributions and Benefits Act 1992;
"entitled to child benefit" includes treated as so entitled;
"parent" has the meaning that it bears for the purposes of Part IX of the
Contributions and Benefits Act (child benefit);
"standard rate of increase" means the amount specified in column (3) of
Part IV of Schedule 4 to the Contributions and Benefits Act which is
appropriate in the case of the beneficiary.
(3) In these Regulations, except where the context otherwise requires—
(a) a reference to a numbered section is a reference to the section of the
Contributions and Benefits Act which bears that number;
(b) a reference to a numbered regulation is a reference to the regulation
in these Regulations which bears that number; and
(c) a reference in a regulation to a numbered paragraph is a reference to
the paragraph in that regulation which bears that number.

769

Provisions as to maintenance for the purposes of increase of benefit in respect of dependants

8.68   2.—(1) Subject to paragraph (2), a beneficiary shall not, for the purposes of the Contributions and Benefits Act in so far as they relate to incapacity benefit and of these Regulations, be deemed to be wholly or mainly maintaining another person unless the beneficiary—

(a) when incapable of work, contributes towards the maintenance of that person an amount not less than the amount of increase of benefit received in respect of that person; and

(b) when in employment, or not incapable of work, (except in a case where the dependency did not arise until after that time) contributed more than half of the actual cost of maintenance of that person.

(2) In a case where—

(a) a person is partly maintained by each of 2 or more other persons each of whom could be entitled to an increase of benefit under the Contributions and Benefits Act in respect of that person if he were wholly or mainly maintaining that person, and

(b) the contributions made by those other persons towards the maintenance of that person amount in the aggregate to sums which, if they were contributed by one of them, would be sufficient to satisfy the requirements of paragraph (1),

that person shall for purposes of the Contributions and Benefits Act in so far as they related to incapacity benefit, be deemed to be wholly or mainly maintained by that one of the said other persons who—

(i) makes the larger or largest contribution to the maintenance of that person, or

(ii) in a case where no person makes the larger or largest contribution, is the elder or eldest of the said other persons, or

(iii) in any case, is a person designated in that behalf by a notice in writing signed by a majority of the said other persons and addressed to the Secretary of State,

so long as that one of the said other persons continues to be entitled to benefit under the Contributions and Benefits Act and to satisfy the condition contained in paragraph (1)(a).

(3) A notice given under paragraph (2) and the designation contained in it may be revoked at any time by a fresh notice signed by a majority of such persons and another one of their number may be designated thereby, and accordingly the provisions of that paragraph shall apply to the one so last designated.

GENERAL NOTE

8.69   This regulation lays down the basic requirement for entitlement to an increase of incapacity benefit for a dependant. The rules differ according to whether the person is incapable of work, or in work or not incapable of work.

For those incapable of work, the requirement is to contribute to the maintenance of the dependant an amount at least equal to the amount of the increase of benefit.

For those in work or capable of work, the requirement is to contribute to the maintenance of the dependant an amount at least equal to half the actual cost of maintenance of those person. The determination of this amount will require the exercise of judgment.

Where there are a number of people in the household, it may be necessary to apply the "family fund" test; there seems no reason in principle why this should not apply as much to incapacity benefit as to other benefits. The complex case law on this is explained in the annotations to reg.2 of the Dependency Regulations.

[¹ Allocation of contributions for a spouse [² or civil partner]]

3.—For the purposes of the Contributions and Benefits Act insofar as it relates to incapacity benefit, any sum paid by a person by way of contribution towards the maintenance of his spouse [² or civil partner] shall be treated for the purposes of regulations 9 and 12 as such contributions of such respective amounts equal in aggregate to the sum in respect of his spouse [² or civil partner] as would secure as large a payment as possible by way of benefit in respect of dependants.]

8.70

AMENDMENTS

1. Substituted by the Social Security (Working Tax Credit and Child Tax Credit) (Consequential Amendments) (No.2) Regulations 2003 (SI 2003/937), reg.2 (April 6, 2003).
2. The Civil Partnership (Pensions, Social Security and Child Support) (Consequential, etc. Provisions) Order 2005 (SI 2005/2877) (December 5, 2005).

Deeming abated benefit to be a contribution for the maintenance of child or adult dependants

4.—Where for any period a person (in this regulation referred to as A) is entitled to, or to an increase in the amount of, any benefit prescribed under section 74(3)(a) of the Administration Act (income support and other payments) in respect of another person (in this regulation referred to as B) and the amount of, or of the increase in, any such benefit is abated under that section, then in determining for the purpose of the Contributions and Benefits Act whether A is wholly or mainly maintaining or is contributing at any weekly rate to the maintenance of, or is or has been contributing at any weekly rate to the cost of providing for, B, the amount by which such benefit for any week has been so abated shall be deemed to be a contribution of that amount for that week made by A for the maintenance of B.

8.71

GENERAL NOTE

See, for comment, annotations to reg.4 of the Dependency Regulations.

8.72

Attribution of earnings

5.—[¹ . . .]

8.73

AMENDMENT

1. The Social Security Benefit (Computation of Earnings) Regulations 1996 (SI 1996/2745), Sch.4 (November 25, 1996).

PART II

GENERAL NOTE

Pt II revoked by the Social Security (Working Tax Credit and Child Tax Credit) (Consequential Amendments) (No. 2) Regulations 2003 (SI 2003/937), reg.2 (April 6, 2003).

8.74

PART III

ADULT DEPENDANTS

Increase of incapacity benefit for adult dependants and persons having the care of children [⁴ or qualifying young persons]

8.75   **9.**—(1) Subject to regulation 14, a beneficiary shall be entitled to an increase of incapacity benefit under section 86A(1) if—

  (a) he is residing with a spouse [³ or civil partner] of his and either—
    (i) the spouse [³ or civil partner] is aged at least 60; or
    (ii) [¹ the beneficiary is entitled to child benefit in respect of a child [⁴ or qualifying young person]; or
  (b) he has a spouse [³ or civil partner] who is aged at least 60 and is not residing with him but to whose maintenance he contributes at a weekly rate equivalent to or greater than the rate of the increase; or
  (c) there is an adult who—
    (i) is resident with him; and
    (ii) [¹ cares for a child [⁴ or qualifying young person] in respect of whom the beneficiary is entitled to child benefit; or]
  (d) Subject to paragraph (3) there is an adult who—
    (i) is not resident with him; and
    (ii) [¹ cares for a child [⁴ or qualifying young person] in respect of whom the beneficiary is entitled to child benefit,]

and in regulation 10 "dependant" means a person who satisfies the conditions set out in any of the sub-paragraphs of this paragraph.

(2) For the purpose of paragraph (1) a person shall be treated as entitled to an increase for a child under section 80 if he would be so entitled if the day in question was a day upon which he was entitled to either short-term incapacity benefit at the higher rate or to long-term incapacity benefit.

[² (2A) For the purposes of, and subject to, paragraph (1), where, on any day, an adult dependant is a person who does approved work on a trial basis within the meaning of regulation 10A of the Social Security (Incapacity for Work) (General) Regulations 1995 (certain persons participating in work trials to be treated as incapable of work), the beneficiary shall be treated as entitled to an increase under section 86A of the Contributions and Benefits Act.]

[⁵ (2B) For the purposes of paragraph (1)(c) a beneficiary shall be treated as if he were entitled to child benefit in respect of a child or qualifying young person for any period throughout which—

  (a) child benefit has been awarded to a parent of that child or qualifying young person with whom that child or qualifying young person is living and with whom the beneficiary is residing and either—
    (i) the child or qualifying young person is being wholly or mainly maintained by the beneficiary; or
    (ii) the beneficiary is also a parent of the child or qualifying young person; or
  (b)
    (i) the beneficiary;
    (ii) his spouse or civil partner with whom he is residing; or

   (iii) a parent (other than the beneficiary) to whom sub-paragraph (a) would refer if that parent were entitled to child benefit, would have been entitled to child benefit in respect of that child had the child been born at the end of the week immediately preceding the week in which the birth occurred.

(2C) Where for any period a person who is in Great Britain could have been entitled to an increase of incapacity benefit pursuant to paragraph (1) (c) but for the fact that in pursuance of any agreement with the government of a country outside the United Kingdom—

   (a) he;

   (b) his spouse or civil partner who is residing with him; or

   (c) a parent (other than the beneficiary) to whom paragraph (2B)(a) would refer if that parent were entitled to child benefit,

is entitled in respect of the child or qualifying young person in question to the family benefits of that country and is not entitled to child benefit, he shall for the purposes of entitlement to the increase be treated as if he were entitled to child benefit for the period in question.

(2D) For the purposes of paragraphs (2B) and (2C)—

   (a) "week" means a period of 7 days beginning with a Monday; and

   (b) a child or qualifying young person shall not be regarded as living with a person unless he can be so regarded for the purposes of section 143 (meaning of "person responsible for child or qualifying young person").]

(3) A beneficiary shall not be entitled to an increase of incapacity benefit under paragraph (1)(d) unless the other person—

   (a) is employed by the beneficiary in an employment in respect of which the weekly expenses incurred by the beneficiary are not less than the standard rate of increase and was so employed before the beneficiary became incapable of work, subject to the qualification that the condition of employment before that event shall not apply in a case where the necessity for the employment first arose thereafter; or

   (b) is a person to whose maintenance the beneficiary is contributing at a weekly rate not less than the standard rate of increase.

AMENDMENTS

1. The Social Security (Working Tax Credit and Child Tax Credit) (Consequential Amendments) (No. 2) Regulations 2003 (SI 2003/937), reg.2 (April 6, 2003).

2. The Social Security (Approved Work) Regulations 2000 (SI 2000/678), reg.1 (April 3, 2000).

3. The Civil Partnership (Pensions, Social Security and Child Support) (Consequential, etc. Provisions) Order 2005 (SI 2005/2877) (December 5, 2005).

4. The Social Security (Provisions relating to Qualifying Young Persons) (Amendment) Regulations 2006 (SI 2006/692) (April 10, 2006).

5. The Social Security (Miscellaneous Amendments) (No.4) Regulations 2006 (SI 2006/2378) (October 1, 2006).

Earnings rule for increases for adult dependants

10.—(1) Subject to paragraphs (2) and (3), the increase in benefit to which a beneficiary is entitled under regulation 9 shall not be payable for the benefit week immediately following any benefit week in which the dependant has earnings which exceed the amount of the standard rate of increase.

8.76

(2) Where the beneficiary is entitled to long-term incapacity benefit or to short-term incapacity benefit at a higher rate under section 30B(4), and the dependant is residing with the beneficiary, the increase of benefit shall not be payable for the benefit week immediately following any benefit week in which the dependant has earnings which exceed [¹ the amount for the time being specified in regulation 79(1)(c) of the Jobseeker's Allowance Regulations 1996 (age related amount for a claimant who has attained the age of 25)].

(3) In determining the earnings of a dependant for the purposes of this regulation no account shall be taken of any earnings of the dependant from employment by the beneficiary to care for a child such as is mentioned in regulation 9(1)(c).

(4) Where the dependant satisfies the conditions set out in regulation 9(1)(d) and is employed by the beneficiary to care for a child such as is mentioned in that subparagraph, the increase shall be payable irrespective of the dependant's earnings.

AMENDMENT

1. The Social Security and Child Support (Jobseeker's Allowance) (Consequential Amendments) Regulations 1996 (SI 1996/1345), reg.19(2) (October 7, 1996).

Apportionment of payments by way of occupational or personal pension made otherwise than weekly

8.77   **11.**—For the purpose of section 89 (earnings to include occupational or personal pension [¹ or PPF periodic payment] for certain purposes) in so far as it relates to incapacity benefit, where payment by way of occupational or personal pension [¹ or PPF periodic payment] is for any period made otherwise than weekly, the amount of any such payment for any week in that period shall be determined—

    (a) where payment is made for a year, by dividing the total by 52;

    (b) where payment is made for three months, by dividing the total by 13;

    (c) where payment is made for a month, by multiplying the total by 12 and dividing the result by 52;

    (d) where payment is made for two or more months, otherwise than for a year or for three months, by dividing the total by the number of months, multiplying the result by 12 and dividing the result of that multiplication by 52; or

    (e) in any other case, by dividing the amount of the payment by the number of days in the period for which it is made and multiplying the result by 7.

AMENDMENT

1. The Social Security (PPF Payments and FAS Payments) (Consequential Amendments) Regulations 2006 (SI 2006/1069) (May 5, 2006).

Contribution to maintenance of adult dependant

8.78   **12.**—(1) Subject to paragraph (2), for the purposes of regulation 9 (increase of incapacity benefit for adult dependants and persons having the care of children [² or qualifying young person])—

(a) a beneficiary shall not be deemed to satisfy the requirement contained in that regulation that he is contributing to the maintenance of his spouse [¹ or civil partner] or a person having the care of a child [² or qualifying young person], as the case may be, at a weekly rate of not less than the standard rate of increase unless when in employment, or not incapable of work, (except in a case where the dependency did not arise until later), he contributed to that spouse's [¹ or civil partners] or person's maintenance at a weekly rate of not less than the standard rate of increase;

(b) in a case where an increase of benefit is, apart from the said requirement, payable at a weekly rate less than the standard rate of increase, a beneficiary shall, subject to sub-paragraph (a) above, be deemed to satisfy the said requirement if he is contributing to the maintenance of the spouse [¹ or civil partner] or the person having the care of a child [² or qualifying young person]at a weekly rate of not less than that of the increase.

(2) Where, within one month of having been entitled to an increase—

(a) of unemployment benefit under section 82 by virtue of having satisfied the requirement of either—

    (i) subsection (1)(a)(ii) of that section; or

    (ii) subsection (3)(b) of that section by reason of her contributing to the maintenance of her husband; or

(b) of incapacity benefit under regulation 9 by virtue of having satisfied either the requirement in paragraph (1)(b) or the requirement in paragraph (3)(b) of that regulation,

a person becomes entitled to incapacity benefit which attracts a standard rate of increase higher than that to which he had been entitled, he shall be deemed to satisfy the condition in paragraph (1)(a) if he satisfies it in relation to the benefit to which he had been entitled; and in this paragraph "entitled" includes deemed to have been entitled.

(3) Until 13th May 1995 the reference in paragraph (2)(a) to unemployment benefit includes a reference to sickness benefit.

AMENDMENTS

1. The Civil Partnership (Pensions, Social Security and Child Support) (Consequential, etc. Provisions) Order 2005 (SI 2005/2877) (December 5, 2005).

2. The Social Security (Provisions relating to Qualifying Young Persons) (Amendment) Regulations 2006 (SI 2006/692) (April 10, 2006).

Increase of short-term incapacity benefit for persons over pensionable age

13.—(1) In relation to any increase of short-term incapacity benefit to which section 87 (rate of increase where associated retirement pension is attributable to reduced contributions) applies the amount of such increase shall be determined in accordance with the following provisions of this regulation.

(2) The amount of the increase shall be the relevant percentage of the amount specified in column 3 of paragraph 1A of Part IV of Schedule 4 to the Contributions and Benefits Act (increases for dependants).

(3) In this regulation "relevant percentage" means the percentage specified in regulation 6(3B) of the Social Security (Widow's Benefit and

8.79

Retirement Pensions) Regulations 1979 (reduced rates of benefit where contribution record is deficient).

Disqualification for receipt of increases in cases of imprisonment and absence abroad

8.80   **14.**—(1) Subject to paragraph (2), where an adult (other than the spouse [¹ or civil partner] of the beneficiary) in respect of whom a beneficiary is entitled to an increase of incapacity benefit under paragraph (1)(c) or (d) of regulation 9 is absent from Great Britain, or is undergoing imprisonment or detention in legal custody, the beneficiary shall not be entitled to that increase.

(2) Paragraph (1) shall not apply in the case of an adult who is absent from Great Britain and who is resident with the beneficiary in circumstances where the disqualification for receipt of incapacity benefit does not apply in the case of the beneficiary by virtue of regulation 2 of the Social Security Benefit (Persons Abroad) Regulations 1975.

AMENDMENT

1. The Civil Partnership (Pensions, Social Security and Child Support) (Consequential, etc. Provisions) Order 2005 (SI 2005/2877) (December 5, 2005).

PART IV

CONSEQUENTIAL AMENDMENTS

8.81   *Regulation 15 omitted.*

[¹ PART V

TRANSITIONAL PROVISION

Effect of an increase of benefit under regulation 12, 13, 15, 19, 20, 24 or 25 of the Social Security (Incapacity Benefit) (Transitional) Regulations 1995

8.82   **16.**—Where a woman is entitled to an increase of benefit for a dependant in accordance with regulation 12, 13, 15, 19, 20, 24 or 25 of the Social Security (Incapacity Benefit) (Transitional) Regulations 1995, regulation 9(1)(a) shall be treated for the purposes of the Contributions and Benefits Act as if such an increase was an increase of incapacity benefit prescribed in regulations made under section 86A of that Act.]

AMENDMENT

1. The Social Security (Incapacity Benefit) (Consequential and Transitional Amendments and Savings) Regulations 1995 (SI 1995/829), reg.23 (April 13, 1995).

Social Security (Incapacity for Work) (General) Regulations 1995

(SI 1995/311) (as amended)

ARRANGEMENT OF REGULATIONS

PART I

GENERAL

PART II

GENERAL PROVISIONS RELATING TO INCAPACITY FOR WORK

CHAPTER I

Own occupation test

CHAPTER II

Information and evidence

CHAPTER III

Persons treated as incapable

Whereas a draft of this instrument was laid before Parliament in accordance with section 6(3) of the Social Security (Incapacity for Work) Act 1994 and approved by resolution of each House of Parliament.

Now, therefore, the Secretary of State for Social Security, in exercise of the powers conferred by section 61A of the Social Security Administration Act 1992 and sections 171A, 171B, 171C, 171D, 171E, 171G(2) and 175(2) to (4) of the Social Security Contributions and Benefits Act 1992 and of all other powers enabling him in that behalf, by this instrument which contains only regulations made by virtue of section 5 and 6 of the Social Security (Incapacity for Work) Act 1994 and which is made before the end of the period of 6 months beginning with the coming into force of that Act, after consultation with the Council on Tribunals, hereby makes the following Regulations:

PART I

GENERAL

Citation and commencement

1.—These Regulations may be cited as the Social Security (Incapacity for Work) (General) Regulations 1995 and shall come into force on 13th April 1995.

8.84

Interpretation

2.—(1) In these Regulations unless the context otherwise requires—

8.85

"activity" means an activity specified in column (1) of Parts I and II of the Schedule;

[¹ . . .];

"the Administration Act" means the Social Security Administration Act 1992;

[¹ . . .]

"benefit" does not include statutory sick pay or industrial injuries benefit;

"confinement" has the meaning given to it by section 171(1) of the Contributions and Benefits Act;

"the Contributions and Benefits Act" means the Social Security Contributions and Benefits Act 1992;

"close relative" means a parent, parent-in-law, son, son-in-law, daughter, daughter-in-law, step-parent, step-son, step-daughter, brother, sister, [⁹ or if any of the preceding persons is one member of a couple, the other member of that couple];

[⁹ "couple" means—

(a) a man and woman who are married to each other and are members of the same household;

(b) a man and woman who are not married to each other but are living together as husband and wife;

(c) two people of the same sex who are civil partners of each other and are members of the same household; or

(d) two people of the same sex who are not civil partners of each other but are living together as if they were civil partners,

and for the purposes of paragraph (d), two people of the same sex are to be regarded as living together as if they were civil partners if, but only if, they would be regarded as living together as husband and wife were they instead two people of the opposite sex;]

"descriptor" means, in relation to an activity, the descriptor in column (2) of the Schedule which describes a person's ability to perform that activity;

[² . . .];

"the Disability Living Allowance Advisory Board" means the board referred to in section 175(1) of the Administration Act;

779

"doctor" means a registered medical practitioner, [³ or in the case of a medical practitioner practising outside the United Kingdom of whom the Secretary of State may request a medical opinion, a person registered or recognised as such in the country in which he pursues his medical practice];

[¹⁰ "health care professional" means—
(a) a registered medical practitioner,
(b) a registered nurse,
(c) an occupational therapist or physiotherapist registered with a regulatory body established by an Order in Council under section 60 of the Health Care Act 1999, or
(d) a member of such other profession, regulated by a body mentioned in section 25(3) of the National Health Service Reform and Health Care Professions Act 2002, prescribed by the Secretary of State in accordance with powers under section 39(1) of the Social Security Act 1998.]

[⁴ "medical evidence" means—
(a) evidence from a doctor approved by the Secretary of State, and
(b) evidence (if any) from any other doctor, or a hospital or similar institution,
or such part of such evidence as constitutes the most reliable evidence available in the circumstances];

"the own occupation test" means the test defined in section 171B of the Contributions and Benefits Act;

[⁵ "personal capability assessment" means the assessment defined in Part III of these Regulations];

[¹ . . .];

[⁶ "relative" means a close relative, [⁹ the other member of a couple,] a spouse or, in the case of an unmarried couple, the other member of that couple, grandparent, grandchild, uncle, aunt, nephew or niece;]

[¹ . . .];

"spell of incapacity" has the meaning given to it by section 171B(3) of the Contributions and Benefits Act;

[⁷ . . .]

[⁸ "volunteer" means a person who is engaged in voluntary work otherwise than for a close relative, where the only payment received by him or due to be paid to him by virtue of being so engaged is in respect of any expenses reasonably incurred by him in connection with that work;]

"week" means any period of 7 days.

(2) In these Regulations unless the context otherwise requires, any reference—
(a) to a numbered regulation is to the regulation in these Regulations bearing that number;
(b) to the Schedule is the Schedule to these Regulations.

AMENDMENTS

1. Social Security Act 1998 (Commencement No. 9 and Savings and Consequential and Transitional Provisions) Order 1999 (SI 1999/2422), Sch.10, para.1 (September 6, 1999).

2. Social Security Act 1998 (Commencement No. 11, and Savings and Consequential and Transitional Provisions) Order 1999 (SI 1999/2860), Sch.11, para.1) (October 18, 1999).

3. Social Security (Incapacity for Work and Miscellaneous Amendments) Regulations 1996 (SI 1996/3207), reg.2(2)(a) (January 6, 1997).

4. Social Security (Incapacity for Work and Miscellaneous Amendments) Regulations 1996 (SI 1996/3207), reg.2(2)(b) (January 6, 1997).

5. Social Security (Incapacity for Work) Miscellaneous Amendments Regulations 1999 (SI 1999/3109), reg.2(1) (April 3, 2000).

6. Social Security (Incapacity for Work and Miscellaneous Amendments) Regulations 1996 (SI 1996/3207), reg.2(2)(c) (January 6, 1997).

7. Social Security (Incapacity for Work and Miscellaneous Amendments) Regulations 1996 (SI 1996/3207), reg.2(2)(e) (January 6, 1997).

8. Social Security (Incapacity for Work and Miscellaneous Amendments) Regulations 1996 (SI 1996/3207), reg.2(2)(f) (January 6, 1997).

9. Civil Partnership (Pensions, Social Security and Child Support) (Consequential, etc. Provisions) Order 2005 (SI 2005/2877), art.2(3) and Sch.3, para.25 (December 5, 2005).

10. Social Security (Miscellaneous Amendments) (No. 2) Regulations 2007 (SI 2007/1626), reg.3(2) (July 3, 2007).

GENERAL NOTE

"close relative"
Section 246 of the Civil Partnership Act 2004, which provides that references to **8.86** "step" relationships and "in laws" are to be read as including relationships arising through civil partnership, applies to this definition (see Civil Partnership Act 2004 (Relationships Arising Through Civil Partnership) Order 2005 (SI 2005/3137), art.3 and Sch., para.57).

Application

3.—These Regulations do not apply for the purposes of Part V (benefit **8.87** for industrial injuries) or Part XI (statutory sick pay) of the Contributions and Benefits Act.

GENERAL NOTE

Like SSCBA 1992, s.171G(1), above, this emphasises the separateness of SSP **8.88** and the industrial injuries scheme from the new incapacity regime governing incapacity benefit and the new tests of incapacity for work for that and other aspects of the social security system apart from SSP and industrial injuries. These regulations do not apply for the purposes of Pt V (industrial injuries) or Pt XI (statutory sick pay) of the SSCBA 1992. Note, similarly, that, unless the context otherwise requires, "benefit" elsewhere in these regulations does not include statutory sick pay or industrial injuries benefit (reg.2(1)).

PART II

GENERAL PROVISIONS RELATING TO INCAPACITY FOR WORK

CHAPTER I

Own occupation test

Definition of "remunerative work"

4.—(1) For the purposes of section 171B of the Contributions and **8.89** Benefits Act (the own occupation test) "remunerative work" in relation to the period of 21 weeks referred to in that section means work—

(a) in one occupation in which a person was engaged for 16 or more hours a week for more than 8 weeks; and

(b) for which payment was made or which was done in expectation of payment.

(2) For the purposes of this regulation and regulation 5—

(a) one occupation comprises either—

    (i) all work of the same kind, whether or not it is for the same employer and whether a person is employed or self-employed; or

    (ii) all work for the same employer; and

(b) a person who was normally engaged in one occupation for 16 or more hours a week shall be treated as if he had been engaged in that occupation in relation to any week when he was on paid or unpaid leave from that occupation.

Person with more than one occupation

8.90   **5.**—Where a person was engaged in more than one occupation which qualified as remunerative work in the period of 21 weeks referred to in regulation 4, his occupation for the purposes of the own occupation test is the last such occupation in which he was engaged during that period; but if, during his last week of remunerative work in that period, he was engaged in more than one such occupation he must satisfy the own occupation test in respect of each.

CHAPTER II

Information and evidence

Information required for determining capacity for work

8.91   **6.**—(1) [¹ Subject to paragraphs (2) and (3)] the information or evidence required for the purposes of determining whether a person is capable or incapable or work [² and the information or evidence required which is capable of being used for assisting or encouraging a person to obtain work or to enhance his prospects of obtaining it,] is—

(a) where the own occupation test applies [³ or where the question of whether a person is capable or incapable of work falls to be determined in accordance with the personal capability assessment,] evidence of incapacity for work in accordance with the Social Security (Medical Evidence) Regulations 1976 (which prescribe the form of doctor's statement or other evidence required in each case);

(b) [⁴ where the question of whether a person is capable or incapable of work falls to be determined in accordance with the personal capability assessment] [⁵, such information—

    (i) relating to a person's ability to perform the activities referred to in the Sch., or

    (ii) capable of being used for assisting or encouraging a person to obtain work or to enhance his prospects of obtaining it,

as the Secretary of State may request in the form of a questionnaire;]

(c) such additional information [⁶ as is capable of being used for the purpose referred to in paragraph (b)(ii), or relating to the own occupation test or the personal capability assessment] as the Secretary of State may request.

(2) Where the Secretary of State is satisfied that he has sufficient information for a determination whether a person is capable or incapable of work without the information specified in paragraph [⁷ (1)(b)(i)], that information shall not be required for the purposes of that determination.

[⁸ (3) Paragraph (1) shall not apply in relation to a determination—

(a) whether a person is capable of work for the purposes of a claim for jobseeker's allowance; or

(b) whether a person is to be treated as incapable of work under any of [⁹ regulations 10, 11 to 14]].

(4) [¹⁰ Information requested for the purpose referred to in paragraph (1)(b)(ii) shall not be used for the purposes of determining whether a person is capable or incapable of work in accordance with Part XIIA of the Contributions and Benefits Act.]

AMENDMENTS

1. Social Security (Incapacity for Work) Miscellaneous Amendments Regulations 1995 (SI 1995/987), reg.2(2)(a) (April 13, 1995).

2. Social Security (Incapacity for Work) Miscellaneous Amendments Regulations 1999 (SI 1999/3109), reg.2(2)(a) (December 13, 1999).

3. Social Security (Incapacity for Work) Miscellaneous Amendments Regulations 1999 (SI 1999/3109), reg.2(2)(b) (April 3, 2000).

4. Social Security (Incapacity for Work) Miscellaneous Amendments Regulations 1999 (SI 1999/3109), reg.2(2)(d) (April 3, 2000).

5. Social Security (Incapacity for Work) Miscellaneous Amendments Regulations 1999 (SI 1999/3109), reg.2(2)(c) (December 13, 1999).

6. Social Security (Incapacity for Work) Miscellaneous Amendments Regulations 1999 (SI 1999/3109), reg.2(2)(e) (April 3, 2000).

7. Social Security (Incapacity for Work) Miscellaneous Amendments Regulations 1999 (SI 1999/3109), reg.2(2)(f) (April 3, 2000).

8. Social Security (Incapacity for Work) Miscellaneous Amendments Regulations 1995 (SI 1995/987), reg.2(2)(b) (April 13, 1995).

9. Social Security (Approved Work) Regulations 2000 (SI 2000/678), reg.4(2) (April 3, 2000).

10. Social Security (Incapacity for Work) Miscellaneous Amendments Regulations 1999 (SI 1999/3109), reg.2(2)(g) (April 3, 2000).

DEFINITIONS

"the all work" test—see reg.2(1) and Part III.
"the own occupation test"—see reg.2(1) and SSCBA 1992, s.171B, above.

GENERAL NOTE

This regulation deals with the information required for determining whether someone is incapable of work under the "own occupation" test or "personal capability assessment" test (formerly the "all work test") as appropriate. Unless para.(3) operates (a matter further explored below), whichever test applies the claimant will have to supply (i) evidence of his incapacity for work in accordance with the Medical Evidence Regulations (para.(1)(a)), and (ii) such additional information relating to the relevant test as the Secretary of State asks for (para.(1)(c)). Furthermore, where the "personal capability assessment" applies, he must generally complete and return that assessment's questionnaire (para.(1)(b)), unless para.(3) operates (see

8.92

below) or the Secretary of State decides that completion of the questionnaire is not necessary because without it he has sufficient information to determine whether the claimant is capable or incapable of work (para.(2)). Note that where the claimant is requested by the Secretary of State to complete and return the questionnaire, failure to do so can result in his being treated as capable of work (reg.7). But such requests from the Secretary of State must comply with reg.7(2): at least six weeks must have elapsed since the first request was sent, a further request must have been sent at least four weeks later, and a minimum of two weeks must have elapsed since that second request. Note that "week" here means any period of seven days (reg.2(1)). In *CIB/3512/1998*, Commissioner Rowland stressed that the paragraph refers to a reminder being "sent" rather than "received". Non-receipt has, however, an important bearing on "good cause". Furthermore, as regards calculating a period before the end of which something cannot be done (e.g. "at least six weeks have elapsed" in reg.7(2)(a)), ignore the day from which the period runs as well as the day on which it expires (*per* Commissioner Jacobs in *R(IB) 1/00*. Note that a finding of capacity pursuant to regs 7 or 8 will override any apparent protection afforded by reg.31(1) of the IW (Transitional) Regulations (*CSIB/611/1998*). There is an exemption if the claimant can show good cause for the failure (reg.7(1)). "Good cause" is not exhaustively defined in legislation, although reg.9 prescribes certain matters which must be taken into account in determining the issue. Some guidance may be found in authorities on the corresponding area in unemployment benefit (see USI Regs, regs 7(1)(i), (j)—see pp.720–21 of Bonner, Hooker and White, *Non Means Tested Benefits: The Legislation* (1996)), the matter of relief from disqualification from sickness and invalidity benefit under the now revoked USI Regs, reg.17 (see pp.737–740 of the 1994 edition of *Non-Means Tested Benefits, The Legislation*), and that from disqualification/being treated as incapable under reg.18, below. Some assistance may be derived from disqualification from unemployment benefit under the now repealed SSCBA 1992, s.28, but caution must be exercised because both that section itself and the now revoked USI Regs. 12E set statutory limits to the concept applicable only for the purposes of that section, since use was made there of a power to circumscribe and define good cause (see pp.133–34, 143–44, 150, and 752–56 of *Non Means Tested Benefits: The Legislation* 1996). A similar power exists in this context but has not been exercised other than as set out in reg.9.

Paragraph (3) provides that para.(1) does not apply to a determination of whether a person is to be treated as incapable of work under regs 10–14, or to one in respect of capacity for work for purposes of jobseeker's allowance. It is understood that there is some concern at CAB/CPAG about the legitimacy of ATOS, the contractor administering medical examinations, sometimes using IB50 questionnaires to establish whether claimants exempt from the PCA under these regulations remain exempt.

Although from the terms of regs 6–8 and 28, the provision of a MED 4 appears essential to support a claim, failure to supply one does not prevent the decision-maker from subjecting the claimant to a "personal capability assessment" medical examination and making a decision in the light of that, and any other evidence, on whether the claimant is/is not incapable of work under that assessment (*R(IB) 5/98*, especially paras 10–16, followed and approved in *CIB/17533/96*, App.I and in *CIB/16603/96*).

A delay between completion of Form IB50 and the medical examination of the personal capability assessment does not affect the validity of that assessment (*CIB/762/2006*, paras 6–8, followed in *CIB/4117/2006*, paras 13–15).

Failure to provide information

8.93   7.—(1) Where a person fails without good cause to comply with a request of the Secretary of State to provide the information referred to in regulation 6(1) (b) [¹ . . .] he shall, subject to paragraph (2), be treated as capable of work.

(2) A person shall not be treated as capable of work under paragraph (1) unless—

(a) at least 6 weeks have elapsed since the Secretary of State sent that person the first request for that information; and

(b) the Secretary of State has sent that person a further request at least 4 weeks after the first, and at least 2 weeks have elapsed since that further request was sent.

AMENDMENT

1. Social Security (Incapacity for Work) Miscellaneous Amendments Regulations 1999 (SI 1999/3109), reg.2(3) (April 3, 2000).

DEFINITION

"week"—see reg.2(1).

GENERAL NOTE

The terms and effect of this regulation have been noted in the commentary to reg.6.

8.94

Person may be called for a medical examination

8.—(1) Where [¹ it falls to be determined] whether a person is capable of work, he may be called by or on behalf of a [² health care professional] approved by the Secretary of State to attend for a medical examination.

8.95

(2) Subject to paragraph (3) where a person fails without good cause to attend for or submit himself to such an examination, he shall be treated as capable of work.

(3) A person shall not be treated as capable of work under paragraph (2) unless written notice of the time and place for the examination was sent to him at least 7 days beforehand, or unless he agreed to accept a shorter period of notice.

AMENDMENT

1. Social Security (Incapacity for Work) Miscellaneous Amendments Regulations 1999 (SI 1999/3109), reg.2(4) (April 3, 2000).

2. Social Security (Miscellaneous Amendments) (No. 2) Regulations 2007 (SI 2007/1626), reg.2(3) (July 3, 2007).

DEFINITIONS

"doctor"—see reg.2(1).
"medical examination"—SSCBA 1992, s.122(1), above.

GENERAL NOTE

This regulation enables the DWP to have a claimant medically examined by a DWP Medical Service (DWPMS) doctor (technically any doctor approved by the Secretary of State) when a question arises as to the claimant's capacity for work. Failure without good cause to attend for or submit to such an examination, of which he was given proper written notice (see para.(3)), will result in the claimant being treated as capable of work. Note that proper written notice means written notice of the time and place of the examination, sent to him at least seven days beforehand, unless the person agreed to accept a shorter period of notice. Interpreted by analogy with the approach to another time period issue in *R(IB)2/00*, para.(3) requires at least seven days' clear notice so that neither the day of sending nor that of receipt count in determining that period (*CIB/2576/2007*, para.6). The notice may be given

8.96

by or on behalf of the approved (generally DWPMS) doctor concerned (para.(1)). The notice must, however, be written. So, where an appointment had been made over the telephone by leaving a message with the claimant's sister, which the claimant asserted was not passed on, he could not properly be treated as capable of work for not having attended without good cause, since the regulation's clear requisite of written notice had not been satisfied (see *CIB/969/97*).

In *R(IB) 1/01*, Commissioner Rowland considered that where, when a claimant stated that he would not be able to attend a medical examination, the Department in consequence said they would cancel it, the claimant cannot be held not to have attended it. If, however, a claimant makes it clear that s/he will not be medically examined, then that arguably constitutes failure to "submit to" an examination. Going to the medical examination but refusing to be examined, constitutes attendance but also a failure to submit.

In *CIB/849/2001*, Commissioner Turnbull stated

"The purpose of the medical examination was of course to enable the adjudication officer, with the benefit of the doctor's report, to determine whether the Claimant passed the all work test. The condition which the Claimant wished to impose on his submitting to an examination—i.e. that the doctor's report should not be passed to any layman, including an adjudication officer—rendered an examination useless for the purpose for which it was required. I have no doubt that, by imposing such a condition, the Claimant was failing to submit himself to a medical examination within the meaning of Reg.8(2). A person 'fails' to submit himself to an examination not only if he absolutely refuses to be examined, but also if he seeks to impose as a condition of being examined a term which would render the examination useless for the purpose for which it is required" (para.11).

The nature and extent of the medical examination to which the claimant must submit is a matter for the examining doctor rather than the claimant, tribunal or Commissioner, "fundamentally a medical matter and for the judgment of the clinician in each individual case" (*C1/07-08(IB)*, para.12). The doctor's demands of the claimant must, however, fall within the bounds of a "medical examination" and there remains the issue of whether a claimant has good cause for refusing to submit to the examination (*C1/07-08(IB)*, para.15).

A health care professional can insist on the presence of a suitable chaperone (e.g. a DWP employee bound by confidentiality not to broadcast details to the world at large), and unreasonable refusal to allow such a chaperone to be present constitutes refusing to submit to the examination (*CIB/2645/99*; *CIB/2011/2001*, para.15). Claimants cannot expect their medical details to be kept from those who must determine their claims; those who insist on strict medical confidentiality can do so, but only at the cost of foregoing their rights to benefit or credits (*CIB/2011/2001*, para.15).

In *AF v SSWP* [2009] UKUT 56 (AAC), Judge Wikeley considered the matter of good cause where a claimant wanted to tape record the medical examination and the examining doctor declined to conduct the examination in those circumstances. Judge Wikeley considered that this was not a case where the claimant had imposed a condition that rendered the examination useless for the purpose for which it is required, so that the tribunal had erred in law in applying *CIB/849/2001* to dismiss the claimant's appeal. He noted that a claimant has no absolute right to record an examination (his interests had to be balanced against the legitimate concerns of the DWP and the interests of other claimants), that the DWP has a policy on permitting recording (the costs to be borne by the claimant) (see para.26), the requirements of which are more stringent than those applied to police interviews (the requirement that a qualified engineer be present), and that Parliament has not provided a scheme for DWP medical examinations. It was not a question of whether the DWP's policy was unreasonable but whether the Secretary of State had shown failure to submit to an examination and the claimant had shown good cause for such failure. He decided that:

"the Department should (a) set out in writing to the appellant the conditions they insist on for tape-recording a medical examination and (b) offer the appellant a fresh appointment.

If the Department and the appellant are unable to agree the terms on which such a medical examination is to take place, and the appellant declines to attend for or submit to such an examination, the Secretary of State is of course at liberty to make a fresh decision under regulation 8 of the 1995 Regulations. The appellant will, of course, then have a fresh right of appeal to the First-tier Tribunal. In such circumstances the onus will be on the appellant to show he has 'good cause' for his failure to attend for or submit to such an examination (see Commissioner's decision R(S) 9/51)." (paras 36, 37).

In *CIB/1381/2003*, Deputy Commissioner Wikeley declined, after reviewing a range of authority on analogous provisions in child support and jobseeker's allowance, to determine whether "sent" meant "despatched" or "delivered", since a failure to attend because of not receiving the notice could in any event constitute "good cause" as the tribunal had held.

The Northern Ireland decision *C11/03-04(IB)* is a useful reminder of the need to ascertain the precise facts and be careful in applying to them the concept of "good cause". The case concerned a common "defence", where the claimant alleged he had never received a particular letter sent by the Department, a typical case of conflict of evidence. Deputy Commissioner Powell thought that sometimes it is right to reject such allegations in a robust manner, for example, where the excuse extends to a number of letters, or is coupled with suspicious circumstances, or if the non-receipt of mail is selective so that only certain letters are not received. The case before him, however, concerned a rather different situation—the uncontradicted evidence of the claimant, who did not attend the appeal hearing, of the non-receipt of a single letter in plausible circumstances, namely, a communal delivery of mail to particular premises and the possibility that another went through it before the claimant had a chance to do so. The Commissioner could not see how an effective challenge could be mounted to the claim and that, in these circumstances, the claimant had established good cause.

In *CSIB/721/2004*, however, Commissioner Parker was of the view that where the claimant proved that the notification duly despatched (a matter for the Secretary of State to establish) had not in fact been received by him, in the ordinary course of post or at all, then it had not been "sent" within the meaning of para.(3), thus precluding treating the claimant as capable of work for "failure to attend or submit to examination" so that the issue of "good cause" never arose. She there took account of a Secretary of State concession on the point noted in *CIB/4512/2002* (not on the Commissioners' website), to which the Secretary of State's representative referred her.

The Secretary of State bears the burden of proof in establishing that the requirements of para.(3) have been met, a precondition for being able to find the claimant capable of work for non-attendance etc. In *CIB/4012/2004*, deputy Commissioner Mark, considering the cases noted above, found that the burden had not been discharged. Computer records showing that a letter had been issued were not sufficient evidence of it being "sent". He said helpfully

"I can see no reason why, in establishing whether the requirements of regulation 8(3) have been met, the secretary of state cannot provide a simple short written statement from the appropriate person giving the date on which the written notice was posted, the time at least to an extent sufficient to show whether or not it would have been collected that day by Royal Mail from the post box, and the address to which it was posted, and also stating whether it was sent by first or second class post. The statement should also confirm that the letter has not been returned undelivered.

It appears to me that in future there should be evidence available from the secretary of state dealing with those issues before a decision-maker comes to a decision. If it is not stated whether first or second class post was used, the decision-maker should either seek further evidence or assume that second class post was used. If there is a further issue as to whether it was posted to the correct address, as in this case where there has been a change of address, the secretary of state will normally need better evidence of the address to which it was posted than a later computer generated print out showing the address on the file at that later date" (paras 21–22).

The effect of a finding of lack of good cause precludes benefit until a new claim is submitted and a new period of incapacity for work begins (para.6). It may also prevent the claimant being treated under reg.28 as incapable of work pending a personal capability assessment (formerly an all work test assessment). However, if the claimant is found incapable of work in that assessment, benefit can be backdated to the beginning of the period covered by the new claim or application. See also on this aspect *R(IB)2/01* and para.8 of *CIB/3512/1998*. On "good cause", see the commentary to reg.6 and note the prescription in reg.9 of matters which must be taken into account in determining good cause. If it was unreasonable of the Secretary of State to arrange a medical examination, the claimant can argue that s/he had good cause for refusing to submit to it (*CIB/2645/99; CIB/2011/2001*, para.16). But since, as Commissioner Rowland stressed, "the integrity of the system depends upon their being appropriate tests in place" (*CIB/2011/2001*, para.16), establishing unreasonableness is unlikely to be easy.

Note that a finding of capacity pursuant to regs 7 or 8 will override any apparent protection afforded by reg.31(1) of the IW (Transitional) Regulations (*CSIB/611/1998*).

Matters to be taken into account in determining good cause

8.97   **9.**—The matters which are to be taken into account in determining whether a person has good cause under regulation 7 or 8 (failure to provide information or attend a medical examination) shall include—

(a) whether he was outside Great Britain at the relevant time;

(b) his state of health at the relevant time; and

(c) the nature of any disability from which he suffers.

GENERAL NOTE

8.98   This regulation, made pursuant to SSCBA 1992, s.171A(4)(a), above, stipulates that in determining whether someone had good cause for failing to provide information (under reg.7) or for failing to attend for or submit to a medical examination (under reg.8) the adjudicating authorities must take into account (i) whether the person was outside Great Britain at the relevant time, (ii) his state of health at the relevant time, and (iii) the nature of his disability. This list is not, however, exhaustive (the regulation says "shall include"). On "good cause", see further the commentary to reg.7.

CHAPTER III

Persons treated as incapable

Certain persons with a severe condition to be treated as incapable of work

8.99   **10.**—(1) [1 Where the question whether a person is capable or incapable of work falls to be determined in accordance with the personal capability assessment], a person shall be treated as incapable of work on any day in respect of which any of the circumstances set out in paragraph (2) apply to him.

(2) the circumstances are—

[² (a) that he receives, in respect of the day in question, a payment of—

    (i) the highest rate care component of disability living allowance;

    (ii) an increase of disablement pension by virtue of section 104 of the Contributions and Benefits Act and regulation 19 of the Social Security (General Benefit) Regulations 1982 (increase of disablement pension for constant attendance) at a rate greater than that specified in paragraph 2(a) or at the rate specified in paragraph 2(b) of Part V of Schedule 4 to that Act;

    (iii) a constant attendance allowance by virtue of article 14(1)(b) of the Naval, Military, and Air Forces etc. (Disablement and Death) Service Pensions Order 1983;

    (iv) an increase of constant attendance allowance at a rate payable by virtue of article 14 of, and paragraph 3(a) of Schedule 3 to, the Personal Injuries (Civilians) Scheme 1983];

[³ (aa) that he is entitled to—

    (i) a disablement pension by virtue of section 103 of the Contributions and Benefits Act by reference to a degree of disability of not less than 80 per cent.;

    (ii) a disablement pension by virtue of Part III of the Naval, Military and Air Forces etc. (Disablement and Death) Service Pensions Order 1983 or of Part III of the Personal Injuries (Civilians) Scheme 1983 by reference to a degree of disability of not less than 80 per cent.;]

(ab) that evidence in accordance with regulation 10 of the Social Security (Severe Disablement Allowance) Regulations 1984 establishes that he suffers from a loss of physical or mental faculty such that the extent of the resulting disablement amounts to not less than 80 per cent.;]

(b) that he is suffering from a progressive disease and his death in consequence of that disease can reasonably be expected within 6 months;

(c) that he is a blind person whose name is on a register compiled and maintained by a local authority under section 29 of the National Assistance Act 1948 (welfare services) or, in Scotland, has been certified as blind and in consequence is registered as blind in a register maintained by or on behalf of a regional or islands council;

(d) that he is suffering from any of the following conditions—

    (i) tetraplegia

    (ii) persistent vegetative state;

    (iii) dementia;

    (iv) paraplegia or uncontrollable involuntary movements or ataxia which effectively renders the sufferer functionally paraplegic;

[⁴ (e) that he is suffering from any of the following conditions, and there exists medical evidence that he is suffering from any of them]—

    (i) a severe learning disability (which, for the purposes of this regulation, means a condition which results from the arrested or incomplete physical development of the brain, or severe damage to the brain, and which involves severe impairment of intelligence and social functioning);

(ii) a severe and progressive neurological or [⁵ muscle wasting disease];

(iii) an active and progressive form of inflammatory polyarthritis;

(iv) a progressive impairment of cardio-respiratory function which severely and persistently limits effort tolerance;

(v) dense paralysis of the upper limb, trunk and lower limb on one side of the body;

(vi) multiple effects of impairment of function of the brain or nervous system causing severe and irreversible motor, sensory and intellectual deficits;

[⁶ (vii) manifestations of severe and progressive immune deficiency states characterised by the occurrence of severe constitutional disease or opportunistic infections or tumour formation;]

[⁷ (viii) a severe mental illness, involving the presence of mental disease, which severely and adversely affects a person's mood or behaviour, and which severely restricts his social functioning, or his awareness of his immediate environment.]

AMENDMENTS

1. Social Security (Approved Work) Regulations 2000 (SI 2000/678), reg.4(2) (April 3, 2000).

2. Social Security (Incapacity for Work) Miscellaneous Amendments Regulations (SI 1995/987), reg.2(3)(b) (April 13, 1995).

3. Social Security (Incapacity for Work and Severe Disablement Allowance) Amendment Regulations (S. 1997/1009) (April 1, 1997).

4. Social Security (Incapacity for Work and Miscellaneous Amendments) Regulations 1996 (SI 1996/3207), reg.3(a) (January 6, 1997).

5. Social Security (Incapacity for Work and Miscellaneous Amendments) Regulations 1996 (SI 1996/3207), reg.3(b) (January 6, 1997).

6. Social Security (Incapacity for Work) Miscellaneous Amendments Regulations (SI 1995/987), reg.2(3)(b)(ii) (April 13, 1995).

7. Social Security (Incapacity for Work and Miscellaneous Amendments) Regulations 1996 (SI 1996/3207), reg.3(c) (January 6, 1997).

DEFINITION

"medical evidence"—see reg.2(1).

GENERAL NOTE

8.100   Regulation 10 covers those whose medical condition is such that applying the "personal capability assessment" (formerly the all work test) to determine capacity or incapacity for work would be a pointless and distressing formality; their condition is so severe that they would be bound to satisfy it or, if not, is such that any humane system would properly regard them as incapable of work. It treats as incapable those in receipt of the highest rate care component of disability living allowance; those receiving certain constant attendance allowances under a variety of schemes; certain persons entitled to disablement pension by reference to a degree of disability of at least 80 per cent; those assessed for purposes of SDA as at least 80 per cent disabled; those suffering from a progressive disease whose death in consequence can reasonably be expected within six months; those registered blind (registration as "partially sighted" does not suffice: *CIB/2354/2001*, para.18); persons suffering from tetraplegia, persistent vegetative state, dementia, or from paraplegia or uncontrollable involuntary movements or ataxia which effectively renders them functionally paraplegic. The "severe condition" head also treats as incapable those suffering from (and supported by "medical evidence" [defined in reg.2(1)] as suffering from) any of the following conditions: a severe learning disability (a condition resulting from the arrested or incomplete physical development of the brain, or severe damage to the brain, and which involves severe impairment of intelligence and social functioning); a severe and progressive neurological or muscle-wasting disease; an active and progressive form of inflammatory polyarthritis (on which see: *CIB/2011/2001*, paras 10, 11; *CIB/4033/2000*, paras 11–17 [does not cover osteoarthritis]); a progressive impairment of cardio-respiratory function which severely and persistently limits effort tolerance; dense paralysis of the upper limb, trunk and lower limb on one side of the body; multiple effects of impairment of the function of the brain or nervous system causing severe and irreversible motor, sensory and intellectual deficits; a severe and progressive immune deficiency state characterised by the occurrence of opportunistic infections or tumour formation; or a severe mental illness, involving the presence of mental disease, which severely and adversely affects a person's mood or behaviour, and which severely restricts his social functioning, or his awareness of his immediate environment. In *CIB/3328/1998*, Deputy Commissioner White concluded:

"that the terms 'mental illness' and 'mental disease' used in paragraph [(2)(e)](viii) do not hold any specialist meaning, but are to be given their ordinary meaning. I find the commentary in the *Incapacity Benefit Handbook for Medical Services Doctors* helpful, since it indicates that the application of the mental disabilities descriptors is not appropriate where there are severe mental health problems, but is where those problems are mild to moderate. The suggested indicators for severe mental health problems seem to me to be *useful guides* in determining the proper categorisation of the mental health problems presented by a claimant" (para.26, emphasis supplied by commentator).

That commentary indicated that severe mental health problems are characterised by the presence of mental illness so adversely affecting the claimant's mood or social or environmental awareness as to render continued psychiatric care essential. Such care can be evidenced by (i) the claimant being in a sheltered residential facility or (ii) day care at least once a week or (iii) care at home with intervention at least once a week by a qualified mental health care worker, or (iv) long-term medication with antipsychotic preparations including depot neuroleptic or mood-modifying drugs. This is, however, an illustrative rather than exhaustive list of indicators. In *CIB/2619/2007*, Commissioner Mesher endorsed that approach. He cautioned, however, that

"all that the guidance does is to suggest that, subject to consideration in each particular case of the detailed manifestations of the illness, if a claimant is going to satisfy the criteria in regulation 10(2)(e)(viii) there is likely to be one or other of the forms of ongoing psychiatric care mentioned. It does not say that everyone receiving one or other of those forms of ongoing psychiatric care is likely to satisfy the criteria or to be suffering from a severe mental illness. That is a logically different proposition" (para.23).

He thought also that whether the exemption applied to a claimant had to be judged taking account of the beneficial effect of the medication and other treatments it is reasonable for the claimant to accept, but subject of course to any adverse effect (para.16). He there applied by analogy similar propositions on taking account of medication to be found in *R2/00 (IB)* and *CIB/16182/1996*.

Endorsing and applying the approach to the Handbook in *CIB/2619/2007*, Judge Lane in *SS v SSWP* [2009] UKUT 36 (AAC) held that a claimant with severe agoraphobia was not exempt under para.(2)(e)(viii). There was no indication of "mental disease" (as opposed to mental illness), she was not being treated by mental health professionals, there was no evidence that her mood or behaviour was severely affected other than going outdoors or that her social functioning was severely affected. Nor had she been prescribed medication consistent with the paragraph (para.12). Inability to leave the house did not mean that she must be incapable of work (para.15). In *DS v SSWP* [2009] UKUT 52 (AAC), recognising that the case law held that a high threshold had to be satisfied if para.(2)(e)(viii) was to apply,

Judge Wikeley held that a claimant with alcohol problems was exempt by virtue of it and thus, while losing her entitlement to IS as a lone parent (her son lived with his grandmother who received child benefit in respect of him), continued to be entitled to IS as someone incapable of work.

In *CSIB/169/2005*, Commissioner May upheld as valid the 1997 changes to reg.10(2)(e)(viii). In *CIB/2619/2007*, Commissioner Mesher approved that decision, noting that the approach Commissioner May had taken there to the terms and effect of the *Howker* decision were fully consistent with that later laid down by a tribunal of Commissioners in *R(IB) 2/07*.

The term "medical evidence" embraces (i) evidence from a doctor approved by the Secretary of State (usually a DWPMS health care professional), (ii) evidence (if any) from any other doctor, hospital or similar institution, or such part of evidence in (i) or (ii) as constitutes the most reliable evidence available in the circumstances (reg.2(1)). On "doctor", see reg.2(1).

Note that the information/evidence gathering processes under reg.6 do not apply to a determination under this regulation (see reg.6(3)).

[¹ Certain persons participating in approved work to be treated as incapable of work

8.101   **10A.**—(1) A person to whom this regulation applies shall be treated as incapable of work on any day in a period of incapacity for work on which he does any approved work in respect of which no payment in the nature of earnings is expected or made.

(2) Subject to paragraph (3), this regulation applies to a person who is—

(a) incapable of work or treated as incapable of work;

(b) receiving a prescribed benefit; and

(c) engaged in approved work on a trial basis.

(3) Where a person to whom this regulation applies is determined to be capable of work, paragraph (1) shall cease to apply in his case.

(4) In this regulation—

"approved work" means, in relation to a person, work arranged in writing [² with an employer in respect of him by an officer of, or a person providing services to, the Secretary of State who has been authorised by the Secretary of State for the purpose;]

"a prescribed benefit" means any benefit, allowance or advantage under the Contributions and Benefits Act (other than statutory sick pay, statutory maternity pay or industrial injuries benefit) or the Jobseekers Act 1995, and for which entitlement is dependent on incapacity for work;

"trial basis" means such trial period and other related matters as may be agreed [³ between—

(a) the person;

(b) an officer of, or a person providing services to, the Secretary of State who has been authorised by the Secretary of State for the purpose; and

(c) an employer,

in relation to the approved work.]

AMENDMENTS

1. Social Security (Approved Work) Regulations 2000 (SI 2000/678), reg.4(2) (April 3, 2000).

2. Social Security (Incapacity) (Miscellaneous Amendments) Regulations 2002 (SI 2002/491), reg.2(a) (April 8, 2002).

3. Social Security (Incapacity) (Miscellaneous Amendments) Regulations 2002 (SI 2002/491), reg.2(b) (April 8, 2002).

DEFINITIONS

"approved work"—see para.(4).
"a prescribed benefit"—see para.(4).
"trial basis"—see para.(4).

GENERAL NOTE

This regulation is another plank in the government's welfare to work strategy, part of encouraging sick and disabled people to return to some form of work. It permits those incapable of work to retain certain benefits, allowances or other advantages turning on incapacity for work whilst engaged on a trial basis in approved work. So long as they neither receive nor expect any payment in the way of earnings, they will be treated as incapable of work while engaged in such work. Should they be determined to be actually incapable of work, however, they will lose the protection afforded by this regulation (para.(3)). The regulation builds on experience gained with schemes (e.g. work trials or preparation, work placements) piloted in certain areas under the Social Security (Incapacity, Earnings and Work Trials) Pilot Schemes Regulations 1999 (SI 1999/1088).

    8.102

The benefits, allowances and advantages covered are those embraced by the term, "a prescribed benefit", defined in para.(4) as any benefit, allowance or other advantage under the SSCBA 1992 (excluding SSP, SMP or industrial injuries benefits) or under the Jobseekers Act 1995, entitlement to which depends on incapacity for work. So, for example, it will cover either component of JSA, incapacity benefit, severe disablement allowance, income support or national insurance credits.

"Approved work" for a particular claimant is work arranged in writing in respect of him with an employer by an authorised officer of, or authorised person providing services to, the Secretary of State. Authorised officer or person means an officer or person authorised by the Secretary of State. The protection of this regulation is dependent on the work being on a "trial basis". That means such trial period and other matters as may be agreed between the parties stipulated in para.(4). Under the pilot schemes, the trial period was 15 days.

Person with an infectious or contagious disease

[¹11. —(1) A person shall be treated as incapable of work on any day in respect of which he is—

    8.103

(a) excluded or abstains from work pursuant to a request or notice in writing lawfully made under an enactment; or

(b) otherwise prevented from working pursuant to an enactment, by reason of his being a carrier, or having been in contact with a case, of a relevant disease.

(2) For the purposes of paragraph (1)—

"enactment" means an enactment comprised in, or in an instrument made under

(a) an Act; or

(b) an Act of the Scottish Parliament; and

"relevant disease" means—

(a) in England and Wales, any disease, food poisoning, infection, infectious disease or notifiable disease—

  (i) to which section 20(1) of the Public Health (Control of Disease) Act 1984 (stopping of work to prevent spread of disease) applies; or

  (ii) to which—

(aa) regulation 3 (public health enactments applied to certain diseases) of, and Schedule 1 to,

(bb) regulation 9(1) (provisions for preventing the spread of typhus and relapsing fever) of, and Schedule 3 to, or

(cc) regulation 9(2) (provisions for preventing the spread of food poisoning and food borne infections) of, and Schedule 4 to,

the Public Health (Infectious Diseases) Regulations 1988 apply; or

(iii) to which regulations 8 and 9 (examination, etc. of the persons on aircraft and powers in respect of persons leaving aircraft) of the Public Health (Aircraft) Regulations 1979 apply; or

(iv) to which regulations 9 and 10 (examination, etc. of the persons on ships and powers in respect of certain persons on ships) of the Public Health (Ships) Regulations 1979 apply; and

(b) in Scotland, any food poisoning or infectious disease—

(i) to which section 71(1) of the Health Services and Public Health Act 1968 (compensation for stopping employment to prevent spread of disease in Scotland) applies;

(ii) to which—

(aa) regulations 8 and 9 (examination, etc. of persons on aircraft and powers in respect of persons leaving aircraft) of the Public Health (Aircraft) (Scotland) Regulations 1971; or

(bb) regulations 9 and 10 (examination, etc. of persons on ships and powers in respect of persons on ships) of the Public Health (Ships) (Scotland) Regulations 1971, apply.]

AMENDMENT

1. Social Security (Miscellaneous Amendments) (No. 4) Regulations 2006 (SI 2006/2378), reg. 12(2) (October 1, 2006).

DEFINITIONS

"enactment"—see para. (2).
"relevant disease"—see para. (2).

GENERAL NOTE

8.104   This regulation is designed to help someone who is excluded from or abstains from work pursuant to a request or notice in writing lawfully made under an enactment or who is otherwise prevented from working pursuant to an enactment, by reason of his being a carrier, or having been in contact with a case, of a relevant disease. An enactment is any Act of the Westminster Parliament or of the Scottish Parliament. A "relevant disease" is defined differently in England and Wales, on the one had, and in Scotland, on the other. As regards England and Wales it covers any disease, food poisoning, infection, infectious disease or notifiable disease to which there applies a variety of public health legislation specified in sub-paras (i)–(iv) of head (a) in the definition in para.(2). In Scotland it covers food poisoning or any infectious disease to which there applies the legislation in head (b) of the definition in para.(2). The help given is that the person covered is treated as being incapable of work.

Hospital in-patients

8.105   **12.**—A person shall be treated as incapable of work on any day on which he is undergoing medical or other treatment as an in-patient in a hospital or similar institution.

This stipulates that those undergoing medical or other treatment as an in-patient of a hospital or other institution, must be treated as incapable of work on any day on which they are undergoing that treatment. The notion of "undergoing . . . treatment" is not defined. Note, however, that a prolonged stay in hospital (more than 52 weeks) results in benefit being reduced: see Hospital In-patients Regulations, above. Reg.6(1) does not apply to a determination under this reg.(see reg.6(3)).

8.106

Person receiving certain regular treatment

13.—(1) The following provisions of this regulation apply to a person receiving—

8.107

   (a) regular weekly treatment by way of haemodialysis for chronic renal failure or peritoneal dialysis for chronic renal failure;

   (b) treatment by way of plasmapheresis, by way of parenteral chemotherapy with cytotoxic drugs, anti-tumour agents or immunosuppressive drugs or by way of radiotherapy; or

   (c) regular weekly treatment by way of total parenteral nutrition for gross impairment of enteric function.

(2) A person referred to in paragraph (1) shall be treated as incapable of work on any day on which he is engaged in that treatment.

(3) A person who works during any week in which he receives treatment referred to in paragraph (1) shall be treated as capable of work for the purposes of regulation 16 only on the actual day or days on which he works in that week.

(4) Section 171B(3) of the Contributions and Benefits Act (which defines a spell of incapacity) shall have effect in relation to a person referred to in paragraph (1) as if the period of 4 days mentioned in that section were a period of 2 days, whether consecutive or not, in a period of 7 consecutive days.

DEFINITION

   "week"—see reg.2(1).

GENERAL NOTE

Someone undergoing certain regular treatment is treated as incapable of work on any day on which engaged in that treatment (para.(2)). The treatments concerned are regular weekly treatment by way of haemodialysis for chronic renal failure or peritoneal dialysis for chronic renal failure; treatment by way of plasmapheresis, by way of parenteral chemotherapy with cytotoxic drugs, anti-tumour agents or immuno-suppressive drugs or by way of radiotherapy; or regular weekly treatment by way of total parenteral nutrition for gross impairment of enteric function (para. (1)). Furthermore, someone working during any week in which he receives such treatment is protected from the normal rule in reg.16 which stipulates that work on any day in a week results in the person being treated as capable of work for the whole of that week; instead such a person is to be treated as capable of work for the purposes of that regulation only on the day(s) of actual work in that week (para.(3)). Para.(4) modifies the notion of "spell of incapacity" in SSCBA 1992, s.171B(3) which defines that term for the purposes of determining the maximum period of application of the "own occupation" test (or in effect the point at which someone to whom that test applied becomes subject, unless exempt, to the personal capability assessment [formerly the "all work" test]). Usually, the "continuity" aspect of "spell of incapacity" demands four or more consecutive days of incapacity for work. For those receiving a regular treatment embraced by para.(1), the "continuity" element

8.108

of "spell of incapacity" is instead a period of two days, consecutive or not, in a period of seven consecutive days.

As Commissioner Levenson pointed out in *CIB/2397/2002*, only para.(3) deals with the position of those in work on days other than when they receive dialysis. Consequently, whether for benefit purposes or those of contributions credits, regulation 13 treats days of receipt of dialysis as ones of incapacity. But what of the person claiming credits who must establish under the personal capability assessment incapacity throughout the week? Commissioner Levenson applied to the claimant in that case (someone receiving dialysis on three days a week) the broad approach developed in *R(IB)2/99*, holding her incapable of work throughout the week, the evidence showing that she was more tired on the other days even though on them she was relatively well.

Regulation 6(1) does not apply to a determination under this reg.(see reg.6(3)).

[¹Welfare to work beneficiary

8.109   **13A.**—(1) Subject to paragraph (3), a person is a "welfare to work beneficiary" on any day in a linking term, where he—

(a) was incapable of work for a period of incapacity for work of more than 196 days in his immediate past period of incapacity for work;

(b) ceased to be entitled to the benefit at the end of that immediate past period of incapacity for work on a day which falls on or after 5th October 1998; [⁵and]

(c) became engaged in remunerative work within [⁵one month] of so ceasing to be entitled to that benefit at the end of that immediate past period of incapacity for work; [⁵omitted].

(2) A welfare to work beneficiary shall be treated as incapable of work on any day in a period, consisting of a cumulative number of days of incapacity for work not exceeding 91 days in total, beginning within the linking term and ending on a day not later than 13 weeks from the end of that linking term, where he—

(a) claims benefit for any day falling within that linking term;

(b) submits evidence in accordance with regulation 2 of the Social Security (Medical Evidence) Regulations 1976; and

(c) in his immediate past period of incapacity for work—

(i) had been assessed and [³ determined to be incapable of work in accordance with the personal capability assessment under Part III], or

(ii) had been treated under regulation 10 (certain persons with a severe condition to be treated as incapable of work) as incapable of work.

[⁵(3) A person is not a welfare to work beneficiary under paragraph (1) if his immediate past period of incapacity for work was ended by a determination, other than a determination in the circumstances set out in paragraph (1) or (3A), that he was, or was treated as, capable of work.

(3A) The circumstances are that the person had successfully appealed against a determination made in respect of the personal capability assessment or the own occupation test in relation to his immediate past period of incapacity for work.]

(4) For the purposes of this regulation—

"benefit" means any benefit, allowance or advantage under the Contributions and Benefits Act (other than statutory sick pay), or under the Jobseekers Act 1995, for which entitlement is dependent on incapacity for work;

"linking term" means a period of [⁵ 104] weeks (whether or not broken by days of incapacity for work) fixed on the first day immediately following the last day of incapacity in a period of incapacity for work;

"immediate past period of incapacity for work" means [⁵the most recent of]

   (i) a period of incapacity for work under section 30C(1) of the Contributions and Benefits Act,

   (ii) a period of incapacity for work under section 152 of the Contributions and Benefits Act, or

   (iii) a term composed of a period of incapacity for work under section 30C(1) and a period of incapacity for work under section 152 and includes any two such periods of incapacity for work which are separated by a period of not more than 8 weeks.

"remunerative work" means—

   (a) work (other than exempt work under regulation 17) for which payment is made or which is done in expectation of payment, or

   (b) attendance on a training course in respect of which the person receives a training allowance in pursuance of arrangements made under section 2(1) of the Employment and Training Act 1973 or section 2(3) of the Enterprise and New Towns (Scotland) Act 1990.]

AMENDMENTS

1. The Social Security (Welfare to Work) Regulations 1998 (SI 1998/2231), reg.4 (October 5, 1998).

2. Social Security (Incapacity for Work) Miscellaneous Amendments Regulations 1999 (SI 1999/3109), reg.2(6)(a) (April 3, 2000).

3. Social Security (Incapacity for Work) Miscellaneous Amendments Regulations 1999 (SI 1999/3109), reg.2(6)(b) (April 3, 2000).

4. Social Security (Incapacity for Work) Amendment Regulations 2006 (SI 2006/757), reg.2 (April 10, 2006).

5. Social Security (Miscellaneous Amendments) (No. 4) Regulations 2006 (SI 2006/2378), reg.12(3) (October 1, 2006).

DEFINITIONS

"benefit"—see para.(4).
"welfare to work beneficiary"—see paras (1), (3).
"immediate past period of incapacity for work"—see para.(4).
"linking term"—see para.(4).
"remunerative work": see para.(4).

GENERAL NOTE

This aims to encourage persons incapable of work to try work (other than exempt work under reg.17), or training for work, by (i) extending the standard eight-week linking rule to 52 weeks to mitigate the fear that if things do not work out, they will not, despite still being incapable of work, be able to return to their former rate of, for example, incapacity benefit, and by (ii) not immediately subjecting those who had in the previous period satisfied the "personal capability assessment" (formerly all work test), or been treated as incapable under reg.10 (persons with a severe condition, for example, someone registered blind), to the "personal capability assessment" (formerly the all work test) on return to benefit. Note, however, that "benefit" is widely defined to cover any benefit, allowance or advantage under the SSCBA 1992, entitlement to which is dependent on incapacity for work, but not SSP (para. (4)) (hereafter referred to as "an incapacity benefit").

8.110

This assistance is given only to "welfare to work beneficiaries" (defined by reading paras (1) and (3) as one). On any day in a "linking term" (see below), a person is a welfare to work beneficiary if having been incapable of work for more than 196 days in his immediate past period of incapacity for work (see paras (4) *et seq.*, below), he ceases at the end of that period to be entitled to an incapacity benefit (see para.(4) for the definition of "benefit") on a day falling on or after October 5, 1998 in effect by having become engaged in remunerative work (including training but not being exempt work under reg.17) within the next week (para.(1)(a)–(c)).

To qualify he must either have given the requisite notice to the Secretary of State (see further, below), or he must have successfully appealed a decision that he was not incapable of work under the "personal capability assessment", all work, or own occupation test in relation to his immediate past period of incapacity for work such that, had that decision not been made, that period would have consisted of one in which he was incapable of work for more than 196 days (para.(1)(d)). A "linking term" is a period of 52 weeks (whether or not broken by days of incapacity for work) beginning on the day after that on which he ceased to be entitled to benefit because of moving into work or training for work (para.(4)).

As to "requisite notice", the formulation of the rules changed on April 10, 2006. The previous formulation (for text see the 2005 edition of this work), required notice of having become engaged in remunerative work (including training) to be given to the Secretary of State within one month of ceasing to be entitled to an incapacity benefit. This was considered by Commissioner Jacobs in *CIB/1886/2003* and *CIB/1887/2003* (decided together). He drew on *R(U)3/85*, *R(SB)8/89* and *CI/337/1992*, to lay down the following principles of law to govern the case before him:

"The circumstances of this case are different from those in all of those decisions I have cited. But they are covered by the principles on which those decisions are based.

What are those principles? The Secretary of State has a legitimate interest in ensuring that action is taken within the time period specified in the legislation.

But that interest is less when the information is provided too soon than when it is provided too late. If information is provided too soon and the Secretary of State does not require the claimant to comply with the time limit, the information will be treated as received and held as inchoate until the time begins to run. Certainly, this will be so if the Secretary of State effectively prevents the claimant from complying within the time specified by not giving notice of the need to comply. In this case, the claimant provided the relevant information to the Secretary of State, but did so too soon. He was prevented from providing it later and in accordance with the legislation, because the Secretary of State did not notify him of the need to do so. In those circumstances, he was not in a position to exercise his right to preserve his position in accordance with the legislation because the Secretary of State had effectively prevented it" (paras 18–20).

He left open the question of how those principles apply where the claimant was never given notice by the Secretary of State and failed to provide the information until it was too late under the legislation (para.22).

The current formulation now specifies that notice must be given not later than one month after entitlement ceased that he expects to be, or (as the case may be) had been, engaged in remunerative work within one week from the end of that past period of incapacity for work (para.(1)(d)(i)). This protects those who notify a return to work in advance in the same way as people who provide notification after work is commenced.

Under the previous formulation (for text see the 2005 edition of this work), "immediate past period of incapacity for work" was determined in accordance with the usual rules in SSCBA 1992, s.30C(1). From April 10, 2006, the term has been widened to cover also a period of incapacity for work under s.152 of the Contributions and Benefits Act (statutory sick pay [SSP]), or a term composed of a period of incapacity for work under s.30C(1) and a period of incapacity for work under s.152. It also covers any two such mixed periods of incapacity for work which are separated by a period of not more than eight weeks. The idea is to ensure that people receiving SSP qualify for the linking protection after six months of incapacity in the same way as people receiving Incapacity Benefit.

Paragraph (1) is expressed to be "subject to paragraph (3)". So note carefully, however, that someone whose immediate past period of incapacity for work terminated because of a decision that he was, or was treated as, capable of work (e.g. a decision that he failed to qualify under the "personal capability assessment" or all work test, which decision is not overturned on appeal), cannot be a "welfare to work beneficiary" (para.(3)(a)). Nor can a person be a "welfare to work beneficiary" again without 28 weeks having elapsed since the end of his last "linking term" (para. (3)(b)). In other words, to be a "welfare to work beneficiary" again, you must, as it were, serve another 196-day period of incapacity for work pursuant to the usual continuity and linking rules in SSCBA 1992, s.30C(1).

Where a "welfare to work beneficiary" claims benefit for any day falling within the 52-week linking term, he must be treated as incapable of work (i.e. exempt from the otherwise appropriate test of incapacity, the personal capability assessment), for up to 91 days in a period beginning within the 52-week linking term and ending no later than 13 weeks from the end of that linking term. But he can only be so treated if in his immediate past period of incapacity for work he had actually satisfied the personal capability assessment or all work test or was treated as incapable of work under reg.10 (certain persons with a severe condition, for example, someone registered blind). Moreover, to support the current claim he must submit evidence of incapacity in accordance with reg.2 of the Medical Evidence Regulations (para. (2)).

Pregnancy

14.—A pregnant woman shall be treated as incapable of work—
    (a) on any day on which, because of her pregnancy, there is a serious risk of damage to her health or to the health of her unborn child if—
        (i) in a case where the own occupation test applies, she does not refrain from work in the occupation which is relevant for the purposes of that test; or
        (ii) in a case [¹ where the question whether a person is capable or incapable of work falls to be determined in accordance with the personal capability assessment,] she does not refrain from work in any occupation; or
    (b) in the case of a woman whose expected or actual date of confinement has been certified in accordance with the Social Security (Medical Evidence) Regulations 1976, on any day in the period—
        (i) beginning with the first day of the 6th week before the expected week of her confinement or the actual date of her confinement, whichever is earlier; and
        (ii) ending on the 14th day after the actual date of her confinement, if she would have no entitlement to a maternity allowance or statutory maternity pay were she to make a claim in respect of that period.

8.111

AMENDMENT

1. Social Security (Incapacity for Work) Miscellaneous Amendments Regulations 1999 (SI 1999/3109), reg.2(7) (April 3, 2000).

DEFINITIONS

"confinement"—see reg.2(1); SSCBA 1992, s.171(1), above.
"the own occupation test"—see reg.2(1); SSCBA 1992, s.171B, above.
"personal capability assessment"—see reg.2(1), and Pt III.

GENERAL NOTE

8.112   This regulation, without a counterpart in the sickness and invalidity benefits regime, protects certain pregnant women, by treating them as incapable of work in two distinct situations. Pregnancy per se is not, of course a specific disease or bodily or mental disablement, but a disease associated with, but going beyond the normal incidents of pregnancy, is such, and can ground title to benefit (see further commentary to SSCBA 1992, s.171B(2), "by reason of some specific disease or bodily or mental disablement", above). Moreover, payment of an incapacity benefit is not normally possible during the maternity pay or maternity allowance period.

Accordingly, from April 13, 1995, a pregnant woman is first to be treated as incapable of work on any day on which, because of her pregnancy, there is a serious risk of damage to her health or that of her unborn child if (i) where the own occupation test is applicable, she does not refrain from work in the relevant occupation, or (ii) where the "personal capability assessment" (formerly the all work test) applies, she does not refrain from work in any occupation. On "the occupation . . . relevant for the purpose of that test", see the commentary to SSCBA 1992, s.171B(1), (2) and regs 4 and 5, above. Furthermore, secondly, where a woman's expected or actual day of confinement has been properly certified, she must be treated as incapable of work on any day in the period beginning with the first day of the sixth week preceding the earlier of the expected or actual date of confinement and ending on the fourteenth day after the actual date of confinement, provided that she would not be entitled to maternity allowance or statutory maternity pay were she to make a claim in respect of that period. "Properly certified" here refers to certification in accordance with the Medical Evidence Regulations.

Regulation 6(1) does not apply to a regulation under this reg.(see reg.6(3)).

Person to be treated as incapable of work throughout a day

8.113   **15.**—A person who at the commencement of any day is, or thereafter becomes, incapable of work by reason of some specific disease or bodily or mental disablement shall be treated as incapable of work throughout that day.

GENERAL NOTE

8.114   The situation encompassed here in which someone is to be treated as incapable, confers no exemption from the information gathering processes for the own occupation test or the personal capability assessment (reg.6(3)). Reg.15 merely provides, as did the previous system (USI Regs, reg.3(2); see pp.688, 690 of Bonner, Hooker and White, *Non Means Tested Benefits: The Legislation* 1994), that those incapable of work by reason of some specific disease or bodily or mental disablement for part of a day are to be treated as incapable of work throughout that day. In *CIB/6244/1997*, Commissioner Jacobs considered the application of the regulation to intermittent and variable conditions. He considered that this provision must be read in the light that, under the all work test and its descriptors, one cannot confine consideration merely to a particular time on a particular day—otherwise a claimant could always satisfy the "cannot" descriptors and the "sometimes" ones would never apply. The "cannot" and "sometimes" descriptors inevitably require a focus over a period and not at a specific moment in time. Thus reg.15

"does not operate to ensure that a claimant with a variable condition that incapacitates him for a part of each day must be considered as incapable throughout the whole of every day" (para.23).

However, it will

> "apply where there is a sudden onset of or recovery from an incapacitating condition, including an intermittent incapacitating condition or the incapacitating intermittent features of a condition" (*ibid.* and see also *CIB/15482/1996*, paras 7–9).

In *CIB/243/1998*. Deputy Commissioner Mark considered that a claimant who suffered an asthma attack for part of a day had to be treated as incapable of work throughout that day under this regulation, provided that the effect of the attack when ongoing was such that he would score at least 15 points for more than a minimal period on that day. In *CIB/399/2003*, Commissioner Mesher very firmly rejects the approach of Deputy Commissioner Mark in *CIB/243/1998* and prefers the approach of Commissioner Jacobs in *CIB/6244/1997* and Deputy Commissioner Ramsay in *CIB/15482/1996*, thus establishing a strong line of authority against Deputy Commissioner Mark's view of the application of reg.15. Commissioner Mesher thought the rejected approach to be inconsistent with the concept of "reasonable regularity" applicable to the "cannot" descriptors and out of tune with the tenor of *R(IB)2/99(T)*. As he noted, endorsing the reasoning of Commissioner Jacobs,

> "it is not possible to conclude that points are scored for descriptors other than the 'sometimes' descriptors merely because the condition in the descriptor is met for some time during the day. At least in cases where the particular effect of the claimant's physical disablement fluctuate, a longer period must be looked at before it can be said that a person cannot carry out some activity. Only then can the points be scored. Regulation 15 does not bite until it can be said that a person is incapable of work. It does not bite on the individual questions to be answered in reaching an overall conclusion on incapacity for work" (para.13).

Unlike its predecessor, the regulation contains no *caveat* removing protection where the person worked on the day; instead the effect of work done on a day is covered by reg.16, which applies despite the fact that a person is to be treated as incapable of work under this regulation. So, a person protected by this regulation in respect of a particular day, could find that reg.16 deprives him of that protection, either because of some work done on that day (e.g. before he became ill) or because of work done on another day in that week. There, "week" does not bear its usual meaning of any period of seven days (reg.2(1)), but instead refers to such a period commencing with Sunday (reg.16(1)). But muchwould turn on the nature of the work (was it exempt work under reg.17, or protected work as a councillor or within reg.16(4)?), and whether it was done in the middle of one's spell of incapacity or in the first or last week of any spell of incapacity (reg.16(3), in which context "week" would seem to mean any period of seven days, its meaning with respect to SSCBA 1992, s.171B(3): see SSCBA 1992, s.171G(2) and reg.2(1)).

On "by reason of some specific disease or bodily or mental disablement", see the commentary to SSCBA 1992, s.171B(2), above.

CHAPTER IV

Treating as capable, disqualification, etc.

Person who works to be treated as capable of work

[¹ **16.** —(1) A person shall be treated as capable of work on each day of   8.115
any week during which he does work.

(2) Paragraph (1) applies even if—

(a) it has been determined that he is, or is to be treated under any of regulations 10 to 15 or regulation 27 as, incapable of work, or

(b) he meets the conditions set out in regulation 28(2) for treating a person as incapable of work in accordance with the personal capability assessment until a determination has been made in accordance with that assessment.

(3) Paragraph (1) does not apply to—

(a) work as a councillor disregarded under section 171F of the Contributions and Benefits Act,

(b) approved work under regulation 10A,

(c) care of a relative or domestic tasks carried out in his own home,

(d) any activity he undertakes during an emergency solely to protect another person or to prevent serious damage to property or livestock, or

(e) any of the categories of work set out in regulation 17 (exempt work).

(4) This regulation is subject to regulation 13(3) (person receiving certain regular treatment).

(5) A person who does work to which this regulation applies in a week which is—

(a) the week in which he first becomes entitled to a benefit, allowance or advantage on account of his incapacity for work in any period, or

(b) the last week in any period in which he is incapable of work,

shall be treated as capable of work by virtue of paragraph (1) only on the actual day or days in that week on which he does that work.

(6) In this regulation—

"week" means a period of 7 days beginning with Sunday,

"work" means any work which a person does, whether or not he undertakes it in expectation of payment.".]

AMENDMENT

1. Social Security (Incapacity for Work) Amendment Regulations 2006 (SI 2006/757), reg.3 (April 10, 2006).

DEFINITIONS

"benefit"—see reg.2(1).
"personal capability assessment"—see reg.2(1) and Pt III.
"relative"—see reg.2(1).
"week"—see reg.2(1)

GENERAL NOTE

8.116   This regulation deploys the preclusive device of treating someone as capable of work in order to penalise those who work inappropriately while claiming. The current text was substituted in its entirety from April 10, 2006. However, in substance it remains the same as the previous version (for text see 2005 edition of this work), merely proving an easier read.

The regulation can operate despite the fact that, applying the appropriate incapacity test, the person is in fact incapable of work, and it can also rule out someone who is treated as incapable of work under regs 10–15, 27 or 28(2) (see para.(2) and, on the previous text, *CIB/297/2005*). Paragraph (1) sets out the general preclusive rule: a person must be treated as capable of work on each day of any week during which he does work. "Work" for the purposes of the regulation is defined in para.(6) as any work done whether or not undertaken in expectation of payment. "Week" is a period of seven days beginning with Sunday (para.(6)).

Note, however, that this ostensibly very wide general preclusive rule is subject to the partial relief afforded by para.(5) and by reg.13(3) [see para.(4)] and the complete relief afforded by para.(3).

Partial relief

Para. (5): This affords some relief from the general preclusive rule set out in para. 8.117
(1). An obviously necessary one, it covers the worker who initially falls sick part
way through his working week and/or the period in which he is incapable of work
finishes part way through a week in the course of which he returns to work. Here,
the preclusive effect of the regulation is confined to ruling out only the days actually
worked in that or those weeks.

In *R(IB)1/07*, dealing with the identically worded predecessor of this provision
(then in reg.16(3)), Deputy Commissioner Mark considered the case of a claimant
suffering from chronic fatigue syndrome who had five days of no work between his
two days of work as a lecturer each week. He rejected the claimant's argument that
this provision entitled him to make weekly claims so that the days were not caught
by the general rule in reg.16(1) because for each new claim this relieving provision
applied. The Commissioner did so because on proper construction the provisions
twofold reference to "in any period" could only be referring to "period of incapacity for work", so that the provision could apply only at the beginning and end of a
single period of incapacity for work. The "spells" of no work were not each separate
periods of incapacity for work. Rather, each of the "spells" of no work for which the
claimant claimed incapacity benefit were forged by the "continuity" and "linking"
rules into a single period of incapacity for work (see SSCBA 1992, s.30C and commentary). The Commissioner further stated:

"The claimant has contended that this would leave regulation 16(3) empty of
effect. I do not consider that to be the case. Any claimant who becomes sick will
inevitably have a first week in which he becomes entitled to benefit, and in that
week, regulation 16(3)(a) will apply. If he recovers, there will come a week in the
course of which he goes back to work. In that week regulation 16(3)(b) will, on
the face of it, apply.

There is a problem if the claimant becomes sick again within the 8 weeks period,
so that the linking provisions apply, because although it may have appeared at the
time that the week the claimant went back to work was the last week in any period
in which he was incapable of work, subsequent events will have shown that not to
be so. In my judgment, that is an evidential issue. A decision maker could defer
making a decision on the last few days of benefit until it can be seen whether the
claimant falls ill again within the linking period, or whether the period of incapacity has indeed come to an end" (paras14, 15).

Para. (4): This reg. is "subject to regulation 13(3)", which provides that those treated
as incapable on days of engagement in receiving certain regular treatments (e.g. chemotherapy), who work on other days of the week in which they receive such treatment,
are ruled out by this work provision only on the days actually worked in that week.

Complete relief

Para.(3) prevents the general preclusive rule in para.(1) applying to: 8.118

(i) any of the categories of work is in reg.17;

(ii) "approved work" under reg.10A, above

(iii) work as a councillor that falls to be disregarded under SSCBA 1992, s.171F,
above; the scheme, as before, seeks to encourage sick and disabled people so
to participate in civic office by enabling them to receive benefit reduced or
abated by the amount by which their councillor's allowance applicable to that
week exceeds a specified amount (ss.30E, 171F);

(iv) care of a relative or domestic tasks carried out in his own home; or

(v) any activity undertaken during an emergency solely to protect another person
or to prevent serious damage to property or livestock.

This exemption is essential to protect the benefit position of the rescuer; of the good neighbour who looks after his/her neighbour's children when she is rushed to hospital; of the person who helps round up livestock which have strayed into a busy road; or of the good neighbour who helps fight a fire until the emergency services arrive; or the husband on incapacity benefit who is compelled to drive to rush his pregnant wife in labour to hospital because the ambulance has not arrived. These can be but speculative examples. "Emergency" is not defined. But note it is not qualified by terms such as "severe" or "serious" or "great", so it ought not to be construed too narrowly. By way of comparison, in the industrial injuries context, case law dealing with "in the course of employment" has brought within that phrase persons responding to emergency. There "emergency" was construed broadly to encompass a wide range of unexpected occurrences (see commentary to SSCBA 1992, s.100, above). A broad approach ought to be taken, similarly, to the notion of "any activity to protect another person".

Applying the de minimis principle to ignore trivial or negligible amounts of work

8.119   *CIB/5298/1997* supports the view in AOG, paras 18782 and 18783 that the *de minimis* principle applies to enable trivial or negligible amounts of work to be ignored (paras 5–12), recognising as a practical proposition something seen as a theoretical one in *CIB/14656/96*.

Deputy Commissioner Wikeley's decision in *CIB/6777/1999* contains a thorough review of the authorities on this matter. He notes that the rule here can apply irrespective of whether the work might in any event be treated as exempt under reg.17. Whether work done is trivial or negligible is a matter of fact and degree. Like Commissioner Williams in *CIB/5298/1997*, who had approved guidance in the AOG, the Deputy Commissioner supported as illustrative but not exhaustive, relevant factors, those set out in DMG para.13867:

> "whether work on a day is negligible depends on its proportion to the normal working hours, the type of work and the effort required in relation to normal working duties."

Stressing the role of incapacity benefit as "an earnings replacement . . . benefit for those with the appropriate contributions record who cannot work in the labour market" he (rightly in the opinion of this commentator) disagreed with Commissioner Williams in *CIB/5298/1997* who took the view that the amount of remuneration earned was always wholly irrelevant since para.(2) states that work is "work" whether or not undertaken in expectation of payment. That means, of course, that the lack of remuneration or of the expectation of it is irrelevant. The key question is really what the tasks performed tell one about the person's capacity for work. But, in contrast to the irrelevance of lack of remuneration, this author, like the Deputy Commissioner, believes that the amount of remuneration received for a relatively small degree of work-like activity, when contrasted with the weekly rate of incapacity benefit, surely *is* a relevant factor in deciding whether work done should be disregarded as trivial or negligible—it brings into play the "anti-abuse" element of the rules here, which arguably takes one into the realm of when the public (including other recipients of benefit) might view as inappropriate receipt of incapacity benefit by someone with what looks like a source of income from "employment", albeit only in that one week. Is that not one purpose behind the earnings limits on exempt work in reg.17? However, that reg. 16 stipulates particular worthy tasks as ones to be disregarded seems to cast doubt on the Deputy Commissioner's view that the identity of the person for whom the task is performed may be a material factor in applying the *de minimis* rule.

CIB/3507/2003 affords another illustration of work being disregarded as *de minimis*. The work in question was described by the Commissioner as follows:

> "On 28th November 2001, DW Windows wrote a letter in which they said:

'In July of this year we approached [the claimant] to see if he would like to do a couple of hours each week at [DW Windows] doing various light duties. i.e. Making coffees, emptying bins etc and occasionally driving a vehicle to transport [Mr S. E.] the Manager who holds no driving license.

There is no dispute about what DW Windows say. Nor is there any dispute about the fact that the claimant was paid £3.85 per hour and that he worked between one and three hours per week. A schedule of his weekly hours and earnings between the beginning of July and the first week of October 2001 has been produced by DW Windows. He never worked for more than three hours and consequently never earned more than £11.55, in any one week. The period covered is one of 14 weeks. During three of those weeks he worked for 1 hour only. He worked for two hours for five of those weeks and for three hours for the remaining six weeks. The average is a little above two hours per week'" (paras 6, 7).

In marked contrast, in *CIB/4684/2003*, Commissioner Jacobs found the work done by the claimant was not so minimal that it could be disregarded. He did so, however, for a different reason to the tribunal which had so found on the basis that the claimant's contribution to the earnings from the post office was significant when compared to his wife's. Instead Commissioner Jacobs approached the matter thus:

"For 8 hours a week, spread over 2 mornings, the claimant manned the post office. He was not there merely to summon his wife if a customer arrived. He was there to serve any customer who wanted any of the services offered by the office. Covering the office in those circumstances amounted to work, even if there were no customers at all. He was in exactly the same position as a stallholder on a market who had no customers. Surely that stallholder would be working, even if no one bought from, or even visited, the stall?

How the claimant spent his time when he was not actually serving customers is irrelevant. It would be just as irrelevant whether a market stallholder at a market spent the time trying to entice customers to the stall or merely sat reading a book" (paras 10, 11).

Exempt work

[¹17. —(1) The categories of work referred to in regulation 16(3)(e) are set out in the following paragraphs.

(2) Work for which the earnings in any week do not exceed £20.00.

(3) Work for which the earnings in any week do not exceed [²£92.00] and which—

(a) is part of a treatment programme and is done under medical supervision while the person doing it is an in-patient, or is regularly attending as an out-patient, of a hospital or similar institution, or

(b) is supervised by a person employed by a public or local authority or voluntary organisation engaged in the provision or procurement of work for persons who have disabilities.

(4) Work which is done for less than 16 hours a week, for which earnings in any week do not exceed [²£92.00] and which—

(a) is done during a 52 week period beginning on the first day on which the work is done, provided that—

(i) the person has not previously done specified work,

(ii) since the beginning of the last period of specified work, he has ceased to be entitled to a relevant benefit for a continuous period exceeding 8 weeks, or

(iii) not less than 52 weeks have elapsed since he previously did specified work; or

8.120

(b) is done by a person who is treated as incapable of work under—
  (i) regulation 10 (persons with a severe condition treated as incapable of work), or
  (ii) regulation 31(3) and (5)(c) to (k) of the Social Security (Incapacity Benefit) (Transitional) Regulations 1995 (persons treated as incapable of work).

(5) Work done in the course of receiving assistance in pursuing self-employed earner's employment whilst participating in a programme provided or other arrangements made under section 2 of the Employment and Training Act 1973 (functions of the Secretary of State) or section 2 of the Enterprise and New Towns (Scotland) Act 1990 (functions in relation to training for employment etc.).

(6) Work done as a volunteer.

(7) [² Duties undertaken on either one full day or two half days a week] as —
  (a) a member of the Disability Living Allowance Advisory Board, or
[³ (b) a member of the First-tier Tribunal where the member is eligible for appointment to be such a member in accordance with article 2(3) of the Qualifications for Appointment of Members to the First-tier Tribunal and Upper Tribunal Order 2008.]

(8) In this regulation—
"less than 16 hours a week" means—
  (a) subject to paragraph (b) or (c), a combined total of less than 16 hours a week,
  (b) subject to paragraph (c), an average of less than 16 hours a week in the period which comprises that week and the 4 weeks preceding it, or
  (c) an average of less than 16 hours a week in the period of the cycle in which that week falls, where it is established that the work falls into a recognised cycle;
"relevant benefit" means—
  (a) incapacity benefit, severe disablement allowance, income support, housing benefit or council tax benefit under the Contributions and Benefits Act, or
  (b) credits under regulations under section 22(5) of that Act,
in connection with the entitlement to which the question of the person's capacity or incapacity for work arises under that Act;
"specified work" means—
  (a) work done in accordance with paragraph (4)(a), or
  (b) work done in accordance with regulation 17(1A) as then in force;
"voluntary organisation" means a body, other than a public or local authority, the activities of which are carried on otherwise than for profit.]

AMENDMENTS

1. Social Security (Incapacity for Work) Amendment Regulations 2006 (SI 2006/757), reg.4 (April 10, 2006).
2. Social Security (Miscellaneous Amendments) (No. 3) Regulations 2008 (SI 2008/2635), reg.4 (October 1, 2008).
3. Tribunals, Courts and Enforcement Act 2007 (Transitional and Consequential Provisions) Order 2008 (SI 2008/2683), art.6(1), Sch.1, para.66 (November 3, 2008).

DEFINITIONS

"the Disability Living Allowance Advisory Board"—see reg.2(1).
"less than 16 hours a week"—see para.(8).
"relevant benefit"—see para.(8).
"specified work"—see para.(8).
"voluntary organisation"—see para.(8).
"volunteer"—see reg.2(1).
"week": see reg.2(1).

GENERAL NOTE

This regulation sets out categories of 'exempt work'; that is, work which can be   8.121
done without affecting actual or deemed incapacity for work. In respect of them,
reg.16 cannot be used to find capable of work the person doing the work protected
by this regulation. The current text was substituted from April 10, 2006. For text of,
and commentary on, the previous regulation, see the 2005 edition of this book.

The changes made from April 2006 are designed extend the categories of work
people receiving incapacity benefits are able to do without losing benefit and simplify existing rules. They also make it easier for people receiving Incapacity Benefit
to attempt self employment. Unlike its predecessor, the new regulation does not
stipulate notice requirements for people doing permitted work. The need to inform
the Secretary of State now rests instead on the general obligation to report relevant
changes in circumstances in the Claims and Payments Regs.

The regulation is part of the welfare through work strategy, of encouraging people
to try out work, the better to enable a return to work.

The current categories of exempt work
Some embody an earnings limit, others both an earnings and hours limit. The   8.122
matter of assessing earnings and whether, where work patterns fluctuate, determining the hours limit are examined further below:

(1) *Work for which the earnings in any week do not exceed £20 (para.(2))*: there is
no hours limit as such here, but it is anticipated that in practice the effect of
the minimum wage laws will mean that Department of Work and Pensions'
staff will expect a claimant in this category to be working less than 5 hours a
week. Its prime role is the encouragement of social contact.

(2) *Work done as a volunteer (para.(6))*: Voluntary work is thus protected.
"Volunteer" is defined in reg.2(1) to embrace a person who is engaged in
voluntary work otherwise than for a close relative, where the only payment
received by him or due to be paid to him by virtue of being so engaged is in
respect of any expenses reasonably incurred by him in connection with that
work. "Close relative" is widely defined: it means a parent, parent-in-law, son,
son-in-law, daughter, daughter-in-law, step-parent, step-son, step-daughter,
brother, sister, or the spouse of any of these persons, or if that person is one
of an unmarried couple, the other member of that couple (reg.2(1)). There
are no hours or earnings limits.

(3) *Supported Permitted Work (para.(3))*: there are two categories here. First,
work done with the supervision of bodies providing or finding work for
disabled people. The bodies in question are a public or local authority or a
voluntary organisation (that is, a body, other than a public or local authority, whose activities are carried on otherwise than for profit (para.(8)). The
second category covers work while a patient of a hospital or similar institution
under medical supervision as part of a treatment programme. The patient
must be an in-patient or a regularly attending out-patient. The earnings from
the work must not exceed £92.00 a week (see further below). On "hospital
or similar institution", some guidance is given in DMG, paras 18031–18033,

24018–24023. But this is not binding on tribunals, commissioners or courts.

(4) *Tribunal and DLAB work (para. (7))*: So long as undertaken for no more than one full day or two half days in the week in question, duties undertaken as a member of the Disability Living Allowance Advisory Board or as a member of First-tier Tribunal with a disability qualification will not invoke the preclusive effect of reg.16 (para.(7)). Such a tribunal member is someone other than a registered medical practitioner, who is experienced in dealing with the physical or mental needs of disabled persons because they work with disabled persons in a professional or voluntary capacity, or are themselves disabled (see art.2(3) of the Qualifications for Appointment of Members to the First-tier Tribunal and Upper Tribunal Order 2008 (SI 2008/2692)).

(5) *Work done in the course of receiving assistance in pursuing self-employed earner's employment whilst participating in certain programmes or arrangements (para. (5))*: this makes it easier for people receiving an incapacity benefit to attempt self employment. Test Trading allows people to try out 'self employment' for a period of up to 26 weeks. Its introduction prevents participants being regarded as in work with the possibility of a loss of benefit should earnings exceed the permitted work limits.

(6) *Work done by those treated as incapable of work under reg.10 (or the comparable provision in the Transitional Regs) (para.(4)(b))*: those with the most limiting conditions and in consequence exempt from the Personal Capability Assessment, can work for an unlimited period providing it is for less than 16 hours a week (see further, below) and the earnings do not exceed £92.00 a week (see further below). This provides create a new category of permitted work for people who face the greatest barriers to full-time employment.

(7) *Permitted work for an initial period of up to 52 weeks (para.(4)(a))*: this simplifies matters considerably compared to the previous reg.17(4)(A) (see 2005 edition of this book). The work done must be for less than 16 hours a week (see further, below) and the earnings in any week must not exceed £92.00 (see further, below). To qualify for this permitted work period, the person must either (i) have not previously done specified work; (ii) since the beginning of the last period of specified work, he must have ceased to be entitled to a "relevant" benefit (see para.(6)) for a continuous period of more than eight weeks; or (iii) at least 52 weeks have elapsed since he last did specified work. "Specified work" is that under para.(4)(a) of this reg or under its predecessor provision reg.17(1A) (on which see the 2005 edition of this book). Since a period of specified work may have been running under that predecessor provision immediately before the current regulation came into force, a transitional provision in reg.5 of the amending regulations (see Amendments note, above) specifies when the 52 week period for purposes of para.(4A) is regarded as beginning (the first day of the relevant period in reg.17(1B), (1C) or (1D)).

The hours limit; "less than 16 hours a week"

8.123   This is defined in para.(8) to mean: a combined total of less than 16 hours a week, or, where the work falls into a recognised cycle, an average of less than 16 hours a week in the period of the cycle in which the week at issue falls; or an average of less than 16 hours a week in the period made up of the week at issue and the four preceding weeks. One looks to the hours worked rather than those contracted for (*CIB/1723/2000* on the similarly worded predecessor provisions) and must be careful to ascertain the hours of *work*. So, in *CIB/589/2002*, Deputy Commissioner Mark considered that the time the claimant (an escort on school buses) spent on the bus after dropping children at school was not to be counted as hours of work. Applying *R(IS) 3/99,* by analogy, he said that the only purpose for which the claimant remained on the coach was to reach the bus station to get another bus to return home, not because there was anything remaining to do by way of work (para.16).

The earnings limit—Computation of Earnings Regs applicable

The question arises: how to calculate earnings for the purpose of the earnings limit? The answer is: do so in accordance with the Computation of Earnings Regs 1996. The Court of Appeal so held in *Secretary of State v Doyle* [2006] EWCA Civ 466 reported as *R(IB) 1/06,* the appeal from Commissioner Angus's decision in *CIB/4174/2003,* noted below. In *CIB/4090/1999,* Commissioner Levenson held that earnings had to be dealt with on a week-by-week basis; there was no room for an averaging approach (paras 8, 9). In *CIB/4174/2003,* Commissioner Angus held that the Computation of Earnings Regs 1996 did not apply; their sphere covers Pts II to V of the SSCBA 1992 and regulations made under them, and incapacity for work is governed by Pt XIIA of that Act and regulations made under that Part. Moreover, the concept of averaging embodied in those Regs was inconsistent with the purpose of reg.17(2) which focuses on the amount earned in each week in question, as is explained in *CIB/4090/1999.* The Court of Appeal held that the Computation of Earnings Regs 1996 applied because, while Pt XIIA deals with the tests of incapacity, actual entitlement to incapacity benefit is governed by ss.30A–30E inserted into Pt II of the Act. Accordingly the case was remitted to the Commissioner to be determined in accordance with the judgment of the Court.

Commissioner Angus's re-determination, finding the claimant to be earning below the weekly earnings limit and thus within the protection of the exempt work category, is reported as *R(IB)3/07.*

8.124

[¹ **Person who claims unemployment benefit to be treated as capable of work**

17A.—[² Where the question of whether a person is capable or incapable of work falls to be determined in accordance with the personal capability assessment], a person shall be treated as capable of work throughout any period in respect of which he claims a jobseeker's allowance notwithstanding that it has been determined that he is [² incapable of work in accordance with that assessment] or that he is, or is to be treated as, incapable of work under regulation 10 or 27, if throughout that period—

  (a) the following conditions are satisfied, namely—
    (i) that he has done some work or undertaken a course of education or training or similar activity in preparation for work while suffering from the specific disease or bodily or mental disablement which led to that determination; and
    (ii) that since he did so, that disease or disablement has not worsened, nor is he suffering from any further disease or bodily or mental disablement which might affect his capacity for work; or
  (b) he is able to show that he has a reasonable prospect of obtaining employment.]

8.125

AMENDMENTS

1. Social Security (Incapacity for Work) Miscellaneous Amendments Regulations 2000 (SI 2000/590), reg.4 (April 3, 2000).
2. Social Security (Incapacity for Work) Miscellaneous Amendments Regulations 1995 (SI 1995/987), reg.2 (April 3, 1995).

GENERAL NOTE

8.126   Even where someone is found incapable of work in accordance with the personal capability assessment (formerly the all work test), or is treated as incapable of work under regs 10 or 27, he must nonetheless be treated as capable of work throughout any period in respect of which he claims a jobseeker's allowance if either the conditions in para.(a) or those in (b) are met throughout that period.

Disqualification for misconduct etc.

8.127   **18.**—(1) Paragraph (2) applies where a person—

(a) has become incapable of work through his own misconduct, except [¹ . . .] in a case where the incapacity is due to pregnancy or a sexually transmitted disease; or

(b) fails without good cause to attend for or submit himself to medical or other treatment (excluding vaccination, inoculation or major surgery) [² recommended by a doctor with whom, or a hospital or similar institution with which, he is undergoing medical treatment and,] which would be likely to render him capable of work; or

(c) fails without good cause to observe any of the following rules of behaviour, namely—

(i) to refrain from behaviour calculated to retard his recovery; or

(ii) not to be absent from his place of residence without leaving word where he may be found.

(2) A person referred to in paragraph (1) shall—

(a) if he is entitled to incapacity benefit or severe disablement allowance, be disqualified for receiving that benefit or allowance; or

(b) in the case of any other benefit, allowance or advantage, be treated as capable of work,

for such period not exceeding 6 weeks as [³ the Secretary of State may determine].

AMENDMENTS

1. Social Security (Incapacity for Work) Miscellaneous Amendments Regulations 1995 (SI 1995/987), reg.2(7) (April 13, 1995).

2. Social Security (Incapacity for Work and Miscellaneous Amendments) Regulations 1996 (SI 1996/3207), reg.6 (January 6, 1997).

3. Social Security Act 1998 (Commencement No.9, and Savings and Consequential and Transitional Provisions) Order 1999 (SI 1999/2422), Sch.10, para.2 (September 6, 1999).

DEFINITIONS

"benefit"—see reg.2(1).
"doctor"—see reg.2(1).
"week"—see reg.2(1).

GENERAL NOTE

8.128   Disqualification here represents an attempt to deny incapacity benefit to those whose behaviour has in some way brought about their incapacity, or has worsened it, or where the claimant has behaved inappropriately in some other way.

This regulation provides that, for the purposes of entitlement to incapacity benefit or to SDA, someone who falls within one of the several "heads" of disqualification examined below must be disqualified for receiving that benefit or allowance. As under the sickness and invalidity benefits regime (on which see USI Regs, reg.17, revoked from April 13, 1993—pp.737–40 of Bonner, Hooker and White, *Non-Means Tested Benefit: The Legislation* (1994)), the maximum period imposable is six weeks. The minimum must be one day (the minimum unit for benefit purposes). Where one or more of the "heads" applies (they can overlap), then for the purpose of any other benefit, allowance or advantage (thus covering social security credits entitlement as well as other benefits), the person caught is to be treated as capable of work for that selfsame period. Nor do days of disqualification count as days of entitlement for purposes of calculating the point of transfer from short-term incapacity benefit to long-term incapacity benefit, or from the lower to the higher rate of short-term incapacity benefit (s.30D(4)).

While there have been some changes of wording from that in USI Regs, reg.17, governing sickness and invalidity benefits disqualifications, in so far as the wording remains the same, case authorities on that regime and its predecessors remain authoritative. Some of the "heads" are subject to a "good cause" saving. The rule-making power to further define or restrict "good cause" has not been exercised in this context (s.171E(3)).

If one or more of the "heads" apply, there must be some disqualification (or treating as capable): the discretion afforded by the regulation goes only to the period.

As with exercising the equivalent discretion for jobseeker's allowance purposes, the authorities must act judicially and consider each case in the light of its circumstances and give reasons for their choice of period (see *R(U) 8/74(T); R(S) 1/87; CS/002/1990*, para.6). The same rules on considering and recording decisions on the matter would apply (*R(U) 4/87*). Some of the factors relevant in exercising the discretion in that context may equally be relevant here. The burden lies on the decision maker to show that the claimant falls clearly and squarely within the head of disqualification (*R(S) 7/83*). Where "good cause" is the issue, it falls to the claimant to establish that he had it (*R(S) 9/51*). *R(S) 1/87* made it abundantly clear that in the same case the same facts could put in issue more than one of the heads of disqualification in USI Regs, reg.17(1). There the heads at issue were paras 17(1) (b) and (1)(d)(ii). The poorly completed record of the SSAT's decision did not make clear on which head they rested disqualification. This was an error of law, a breach of the duty to record reasons for the decision and the material facts on which it is based (see now Adjudication Regs, reg.25(2)(b)). Presumably as well as complying with this duty, a tribunal should also comply with *R(U) 2/71* where the case involves the Secretary of State relying on a head of disqualification not set out in the appeal papers or the tribunal relying on a different ground to that relied on by the Secretary of State.

It is submitted that this regulation can only come into play where the claimant is found incapable of work (*CS/229/1991*, para 8, accepting an AO's submission to that effect); those found capable of work will be denied benefit for failure to establish incapacity for work. See, to the same effect, two Northern Ireland decisions: *R1/92(IVB), R3/84(IVB)*.

Para.(1)(a)

This penalises certain behaviour by the claimant. Disqualification must be imposed if his incapacity is due to his own misconduct, but two instances where incapacity may have arisen in consequence of what might otherwise be treated as sexual misconduct are expressly stated not to ground disqualification: (a) where the incapacity is due to a sexually transmitted disease; and (b) the case of pregnancy. Misconduct has not been exhaustively defined. Presumably, by analogy with its use in the unemployment benefit and jobseeker's allowance contexts, it denotes conduct which is blameworthy, reprehensible and wrong. It is unclear in this context, whether merely reckless or negligent conduct will suffice. *R(S)2/53* has been thought to import a requirement of wilfulness, but this may be to read too much into a particular example of misconduct. In that case the Commissioner considered alcoholism, and upheld disqualification. Drinking to such an extent to endanger health raises a prima facie inference of misconduct which can only be rebutted if

8.129

the claimant proves that the alcoholism was involuntary, the result of disease or disablement which destroyed his willpower, so that he was *unable* to refrain from excessive drinking. The particular evidence in that case of an anxiety state was insufficient to rebut the presumption. Whether in the current medical and social climate the provision could apply to incapacity through heavy smoking remains to be seen. The paragraph could have unfortunate implications for some AIDS victims such as intravenous drug users who become infected non-sexually.

Para. (1) (b)

8.130   This seems designed to deal with a specific aspect of behaviour which may contribute to further incapacity or hinder recovery. Disqualification must be imposed where the claimant fails to attend for or submit to medical or other treatment. The medical or other treatment must be recommended by a doctor with whom, or a hospital or similar institution with which, he is undergoing medical treatment and be such as would be likely to render him capable of work. This formulation thus reverses *R(S) 3/57*. There the blind claimant gave up a vocational training course when she became pregnant and refused to resume it thereafter; under USI Regs, reg.17(1)(c) she had not refused treatment for her disablement since the course could have no effect on her blindness (para.6; *cf. R2/60SB*). Failure to attend for or submit to certain medical or other treatment is explicitly exempt from the sanction, namely, failure to attend for or submit to vaccination or inoculation of any kind or to major surgery.

Establishing "good cause" for non-compliance precludes disqualification. In *R(S) 9/51* the claimant did so. Her non-attendance was founded on her own firm conviction that her religious beliefs (Christian Scientist) required her not to. It would not have been enough merely to establish membership of a sect whose religious rules forbade submission to treatment or examination.

Para. (1) (c)

8.131   Disqualification here penalises a claimant who fails to observe any of two specific rules of behaviour. Establishing good cause for the failure precludes disqualification. Mere ignorance of the rules of behaviour is not good cause (*R(S) 21/52*).

The first rule of behaviour (head (1)(c)(i)) requires the claimant to refrain from behaviour calculated to retard his recovery. "Calculated to retard his recovery" does not import an intention on his part to do so; the test is an objective one: was his behaviour likely to do so. Thus in *R(S) 21/52* the Commissioner upheld disqualification of the claimant, suffering from influenzal bronchitis who was taken ill after undertaking a 60-mile drive when so suffering. However in *R(S) 3/57* (above para. (1)(b)) the course was irrelevant to recovery from blindness, so leaving and refusing to resume the course could not ground disqualification.

The second rule of behaviour requires the claimant not to be absent from his place of residence without leaving word as to where he can be found. It is designed to penalise those who deliberately seek to avoid the Department's visiting officers who may call as part of the Department's claims control mechanisms. It will only be invoked where visits have already proved ineffective, and as a matter of law the absence must have occurred during the currency of a claim. The rule cannot apply unless the claimant has a residence; it is not to be interpreted as imposing a requirement to have one (*R(S) 7/83*), so claimants of no fixed abode cannot be caught by it. *R(S) 1/87* requires findings be made as to place of residence, any absence in the relevant period, and on whether the claimant had failed to leave word where he could be found. If those findings showed the claimant's absence from his residence without leaving word as to his whereabouts, it would then fall to the claimant to establish good cause for so acting (see para.12). A claimant's genuine difficulty in leaving word where he might be found was held to constitute good cause in *R(S) 6/55*. There the claimant lived with relatives who were out at work on the three occasions that the visiting officer called. The claimant was out in the park or at the cinema on those occasions, and there was no one with whom he could leave a message. His doctor had advised him to get out as much as possible.

CHAPTER V

Adjudication

This Chapter (regs 19–22) was revoked with effect from September 6, 1999 by Social Security Act 1998 (Commencement No. 9, and Savings and Consequential and Transitional Provisions) Order 1999 (SI 1999/2422), Sch. 10, para. 3. For the previous text see Bonner, Hooker and White, Non-Means Tested Benefits: The Legislation (1999). **8.132**

PART III

[¹ PERSONAL CAPABILITY ASSESSMENT]

AMENDMENT

1. Social Security (Incapacity for Work) Miscellaneous Amendments Regulations (SI 1999/3190), reg.3(1) (April 3, 2000).

Interpretation of Part III and the Schedule

23.—In this Part and the Sch., unless the context otherwise requires, any reference to a numbered part is to the part in the Schedule bearing that number. **8.133**

[¹ The personal capability assessment

24.—For the purposes of section 171C(2)(a) of the Contributions and Benefits Act the personal capability assessment is an assessment of the extent to which a person who has some specific disease or bodily or mental disablement is capable of performing the activities prescribed in the Schedule, or is incapable by reason of such disease or bodily or mental disablement of performing those activities.] **8.134**

AMENDMENT

1. Social Security (Incapacity for Work) Miscellaneous Amendments Regulations 1999 (SI 1999/3109), reg.3(2) (April 3, 2000).

DEFINITIONS

"activity"—see reg.2(1).
"personal capability assessment"—see reg.2(1).
"the Schedule"—see reg.2(2)(b)

GENERAL NOTE

This regulation defines "the personal capability assessment" (the new name for the "all work test"). Where the "own occupation" test is inapplicable to the claimant and also where, although earlier applicable in the period of incapacity, the maximum **8.135** period of its application (196 days) has been reached, the test of incapacity for work (for those not treated as incapable) is the "personal capability assessment" test.

This, like the "all work" test, lies at the heart of the reform effected by the Social Security (Incapacity for Work) Act 1994. According to Government, the results of two large scale evaluation studies to assess the validity and reliability of this essentially medical and functional test "indicate that [it provides] a more effective means of assessing incapacity, which will help ensure that benefit is targeted on those people who are incapable of work, because of their medical condition" (DSS/ Benefits Agency, *The medical assessment for incapacity benefit* (HMSO, 1994), p.35). The "personal capability assessment" is one which ignores the other personal/environmental factors governing access to employment by people with disabilities (R. Berthoud, "The 'medical' assessment of incapacity: a case study of the (lack of) influence of research on policy" [1995] 2 J.S.S.L. 61, at pp.70, 75). It does not measure people against the requirements of specific jobs (the "personal capability assessment" contains no definition of work for none is required given its nature). Its exclusionary effect will largely deny benefit to persons who probably are capable of work (*ibid.* at p. 82). However, it is possible that some who would have failed the previously applicable test, might qualify as incapable on this one, while some who fail this one, may well in fact be incapable of work.

The "personal capability assessment" is an assessment of the extent of the claimant's incapacity, by reason of some specific disease or bodily or mental disablement which he has, to perform the activities prescribed in the Schedule to these regulations, entitled "disabilities which may make a person incapable of work" (reg.24). On "some specific disease or bodily or mental disablement", see commentary to SSCBA 1992, s.171B(2), above, and the useful analysis there from Commissioner Jacobs in *CIB/26/2004* on what must be proved, to what standard and by what evidence.

The Schedule to these regulations lists a number of activities or functional areas of body or mind thought relevant to incapacity for work, e.g. walking (on level ground and up and down stairs), sitting, standing, manual dexterity, completion of tasks, coping with pressure, interacting with people. The first (and longer) Part of the Schedule deals with physical disabilities, the second Part with mental disabilities. Whether one (or both) applies (apply) to a particular case presumably turns on the nature of the medical diagnosis with respect to the particular claimant and the types of effect it has. This has been even clearer since reg.25(3) was inserted, with effect from January 6, 1997, by reg.2(7)(b) of the Social Security (Incapacity for Work and Miscellaneous Amendments) Regulations 1996 (SI 1996/3207). Reg.25(3) stipulates that one can determine the extent of a person's incapacity to perform an activity listed in Pt I of the Schedule (physical disabilities) only where his incapacity arises from a specific *bodily* disease or disablement. Similarly, the extent of his incapacity to perform any activity listed in Pt II of the Schedule (mental disabilities) can only be determined if that incapacity arises from some specific *mental* illness or disablement. So that the proposition—that issues under Pt II of the Schedule are raised by a diagnosis in which a physical disease or disability produces related psychological problems which are more than *de minimis*—can now only hold good if those psychological problems can themselves be characterised as a specific mental illness or disablement, a matter in practical terms turning on medical evidence and diagnosis. In respect of each activity or functional area (set out in column (1) of the Schedule), the Schedule lists in col.(2) a number of descriptors (said to be "clearly worded statements of disability ranked according to their incapacitating effect in each functional area"—DSS/Benefits Agency, *The medical assessment for incapacity benefit* (HMSO, 1994), p.4) to each of which is attached (in col.(3)) a score in terms of a number of points, ranging from 0 to 15. Essentially someone is incapable of work under the personal capability assessment when one or more of the descriptors applies to him and adding up the points attached to them (with some limitations on counting set by reg.26) he achieves a total score of at least 15 points if only physical disability descriptors apply, of 10 points if mental disability descriptors alone are relevant, or of 15 points if descriptors of both types are applicable (reg.25). These total scores are the threshold for benefit, set, it is said by government, not at the point at which a person is unable to work at all but rather at the point at which a person should not be expected to work.

So, in an appeal before it (which will not necessarily be an incapacity benefit appeal: see Decisions and Appeals Regulations 1999, regs 10, 11), the first task of the Appeal Tribunal is to decide from all the evidence which descriptors apply, the second to calculate the scores. Note that the Appeal Tribunal here as elsewhere has an inquisitorial role (*CIB/14442/96*), which it should be cautious in exercising when considering mental disablement (*R(IB) 2/98*, noted in annotations to the proper approach to Pt II of the Schedule: mental disabilities, below). See further the annotation to Social Security Act 1998, Sch.6, para.3, in *Vol.III: Administration, Adjudication and the European Dimension*, which requires Appeal Tribunals to consider matters as at the date of the Secretary of State's decision but only as regards appeals brought on or after May 21, 1998.

Task One: which descriptors apply?

The evidence before the Appeal Tribunal is likely to be oral evidence from the claim- **8.136** ant, his completed "personal capability assessment" questionnaire, the "expanded" medical certificate from his doctor under the Medical Evidence Regulations, the report and advice of the DWPMS health care professional and of any clinical exam- ination conducted by him (see "the assessment process", below). The questionnaire for the personal capability assessment is broader than that for its predecessor, the all work test, in that it covers not only information relating to the claimant's ability to perform the tasks set out in the Schedule (see reg.6(1)(b)(i), above), but also information which is capable of being used for assisting or encouraging a person to obtain work or to enhance his prospects of obtaining it (see reg.6(1)(b)(ii), above). Information requested for that broader purpose must not be used for purposes of determining capacity or incapacity for work. There may be further more detailed medical reports submitted by the claimant. His own doctor is under no obligation under this system to provide one. If he agrees to do so as part of the doctor/patient relationship, he can make a charge. Consultants' reports may prove too expensive. As in the past, Appeal Tribunals may have to make do with minimal medical evi- dence from the claimant. Their tasks under the personal capability assessment are very different from that in the commonly occurring "fit within limits" cases under the sickness and invalidity benefits test, where, although some functional elements were present in the DWPMS doctors' report(s), the task was more one of relating the effect of the claimant's medical condition to other personal factors like age, educa- tion and experience, and to decide in the light of evidence (including member's own knowledge) about the tasks involved in identified types of job, whether the claimant could reasonably be expected to do any of them (see further pp.187–94 of Bonner, Hooker and White, *Non-Means Tested Benefits: The Legislation* 1994). Here, to reiter- ate, the job of the Appeal Tribunal is to determine the extent of a person's incapacity, by reasons of some specific disease or bodily or mental disablement, to perform the activities prescribed in the Schedule to these regulations (reg.24).

The extent of a person's incapacity to perform any activity listed in col.(1) of the first Part of the Schedule (physical disabilities) is to be determined as if he were wearing any prosthesis with which he is fitted or, as the case may be, any aid or appliance which he normally wears or uses (reg.25(3)). Moreover, a number of those descriptors require assessment to take account of a range of aids normally used or worn. A number of examples may be useful: (i) walking on level ground: walking stick or other aid if such aid is normally used (Sch., para.(1), col.(1)); (ii) hearing: with a hearing aid or other aid if normally worn (Sch., para.11, col.(1)); (iii) vision: in normal daylight or bright electric light with glasses or other aid to vision if such aid is normally worn (Sch., para.12, col.(1)).

It is important properly to identify the relevant physical or mental condition and to consider the full range of activities which may be impaired by the condition. So, for example, with migraine, it is important not to confine consideration to Activity 14 (lost or altered consciousness): see Deputy Commissioner White *CIB/5757/1997* (para.25) and also *CIB/3589/2004* in which Commissioner Jacobs said:

"In the case of a migraine, the chain works like this. A migraine is a bodily *disease*. It involves *symptoms*—pain and disruption of vision. Those symptoms restrict the claimant's ability to function in various way (*disabilities*). The personal capability assessment allows those symptoms and their effects to be taken into account in respect of any *activity* which they affect. For example, flashing lights or blindness during a migraine may affect the activity of negotiating stairs without holding on and the activity of vision.

Migraines are not continuous. Their effects are intermittent. That does not mean that they are irrelevant to the personal capability assessment. They may be relevant in one of two ways. First, they may be relevant to the 'sometimes' descriptors in the activities of rising from sitting and bending and kneeling. Second, they may be relevant to the frequency and regularity with which a claimant can undertake activities.

The tribunal limited the potential relevance of the symptoms of migraine to activity 14. There is no justification in the legislation for doing so. Nor is there any justification in the nature of migraine or the effects of its symptoms. The tribunal limited the relevance of the claimant's evidence of migraines to one activity without justification" (paras 12–14).

Looking to the facts as found by the tribunal about the claimant's condition, he found that

"The claimant's migraines are sufficiently severe that they affect her ability to rise from sitting and to bend or kneel to the floor. She would not be able to do either of those activities without some support. In those circumstances, the 'sometimes' descriptors for those activities apply. Each scores 3 points, making a total of 6. The claimant already has a score of 10. The additional 6 bring the total to 16, which is sufficient to satisfy the assessment" (para.17).

Task Two: computing the scores

8.137   To reiterate, essentially someone is incapable of work under the personal capability assessment when one or more of the descriptors applies to him and, adding up the points attached to them (with some limitations on counting noted below), he achieves a total score of at least 15 points if only physical disability descriptors apply, of 10 points if mental disability descriptors alone are relevant, or of 15 points if descriptors of both types are applicable (reg.25).

The limitations set by reg.26, mean that calculation of the appropriate score is not a simple matter of totalling up all the scores identified for each descriptor found to apply in the exercise of task one. Granted, with respect to mental disabilities alone, one does count the score in respect of each descriptor which applies to the claimant. However, where these have to be added to the appropriate score in respect of applicable physical disabilities, an aggregate score of less than six points in respect of the mental health descriptors must be disregarded, but a score of between six and nine points in respect of mental health disabilities is to be treated as one of nine points (reg.26(1)). With respect to someone's score in terms of physical disabilities, where more than one descriptor specified for any activity applies to him, only the descriptor with the highest score is counted, and for this purpose where a descriptor from each of the two separate "walking" activities (walking on level ground; walking up and down stairs) applies to him, the two activities are treated as if they were one and only one descriptor (the highest scoring "walking" descriptor) counts (reg.26(2), (3)).

The assessment process

8.138   It may be useful for Appeal Tribunals, and those appearing before them, to have some idea of how the assessment process is meant to work where the "personal capability assessment" rather than the "own occupation" test is applicable to the case. For example, it helps to clarify where some of the evidence before the Appeal Tribunal (see above) comes from.

The assessment process for the "personal capability assessment" is more complicated than for the "own occupation" test. The description which follows attempts to meld the rules set out in the General Regulations and the Medical Evidence Regulations, with details provided by Ministers in the parliamentary debates on the Act and the Regulations, the analysis set out in DSS/Benefits Agency, *The medical assessment for incapacity benefit* (HMSO, 1994), pp.12–15, and practical experience. Benefit will continue to be paid until completion of the assessment process or until the person is treated as capable of work for failing to provide the information required for claims purposes or for failing to attend and/or submit to the required medical examination. But it will be paid only while he continues to provide a doctor's statement in accordance with the Medical Evidence Regulations (see below), and only if there has been no determination in the last six months that he is capable of work or that he is to be treated as capable of work for such failures to comply with those aspects of the process. If there has been such a determination, however, benefit can still be paid pending assessment if the specific disease or bodily or mental disablement from which he suffered at the time of that earlier determination has significantly worsened or the one(s) he is now suffering from is (are) different; or, if treated as capable because of failure to supply claims information, he has since complied with those requests (reg.28). The supply of medical certificates will thus continue to be required to support a claim but the form of them differs from those used to support claims subject to the "own occupation" test.

Department staff will identify those claimants exempt from the information gathering process, and send such cases direct to a decision-maker for immediate decision on whether they are incapable of work. These exempt groups are those to be treated as incapable of work under regs 10–14, above (reg.6(3)): those with a specified severe condition (e.g. those receiving the highest rate care component of disability living allowance; tetraplegics; those suffering from severe mental illness); persons excluded from work on the certificate of a Medical Officer of Environmental Health because of being a carrier of or in contact with a case of infectious or contagious disease; in-patients of a hospital or similar institution; persons receiving certain regular treatments such as haemodialysis for chronic renal failure, or chemotherapy; and certain pregnant women. Clearly some of these will always be so exempt from the process, others only for particular periods, after which they become subject to it (e.g. when no longer pregnant or after discharge from hospital or on the lifting of the certificate from the Medical Officer of Environmental Health). Note, in addition, that certain transferees from invalidity benefit are also exempt as are existing recipients of SDA at commencement (see further the IW (Transitional) Regs, reg.31(5), below).

Most of those subject to the test will have to complete an expanded questionnaire. The questionnaire gives plenty of room for a claimant to give information on all the effects of his condition, including pain, stress and variability. It seeks his views on the effects of the medical condition in each of the functional areas in the test, enabling the claimant to identify by a tick-box method the descriptor in each affected area which he thinks best describes those effects and to give such further information he thinks should also be taken into account. At the end it asks whether he wishes to say anything about pain and stress (DSS/Benefits Agency, *The medical assessment for incapacity benefit* (HMSO, 1994), p.12). But it is muchless clear and specific on mental disease or disablement. The questionnaire for the personal capability assessment is broader than that for its predecessor, the all work test, in that it covers not only information relating to the claimant's ability to perform the tasks set out in the Schedule (see reg.6(1)(b)(i), above), but also information which is capable of being used for assisting or encouraging a person to obtain work or to enhance his prospects of obtaining it (see reg.6(1)(b)(ii), above). Information requested for that broader purpose must not be used for purposes of determining capacity or incapacity for work.

The "personal capability" certificate provided by the claimant's doctor (MED 4) differs from those previously used, enabling fuller information on the diagnosis of the disorder in respect of which the doctor is advising the claimant to refrain from work or which is causing his absence from work and any other condition which could affect his capacity for work: see Medical Evidence Regulations, Sch.1B. The diagnosis should be specified as precisely as possible, unless the doctor is of opinion that a disclosure to the claimant of the precise disorder would be prejudicial to the patient's well being, in which case it can be less precise. There is also space for the doctor's remarks on the disabling effects of the condition, treatment and progress, and doctors are advised on the form that accurate and detailed completion will avoid requests for completion of a medical report. A doctor could thus, e.g. if dealing with a condition which has variable effects, describe how it varies and affects his patient. There is also a section (which will not form part of the assessment) in which the doctor is asked to state whether or not the patient should refrain from his usual occupation. This will be the requisite evidence for maintenance of his claim pending completion of the "personal capability" assessment. Doctors can include additional information, but will not be obliged to read, or to comment on, the claimant's information in the questionnaire. Nor will they be asked to provide an opinion on capacity for work. Although from the terms of regs 6–8 and 28, the provision of a MED 4 appears essential to support a claim, failure to supply one does not prevent the Secretary of State from subjecting the claimant to a "personal capability" test medical examination and making a decision in the light of that, and any other evidence, on whether the claimant is, or is not, incapable of work (*R(IB) 5/98* especially paras 10–16, followed and approved in *CIB/17533/96*, App.I and in *CIB/16603/96*).

A delay between completion of Form IB50 and the medical examination of the personal capability assessment does not affect the validity of that assessment (*CIB/762/2006*, paras 6–8, followed in *CIB/4117/2006*, paras. 13–15).

The Secretary of State could decide on the basis of the doctor's statement and the questionnaire that the claimant is or is not incapable of work. More commonly, because the effects of medical conditions vary widely as between individuals, the case will be referred for a medical opinion from a Department of Work and Pensions Medical Service health care professional (usually a doctor). This health care professional will consider and appraise the evidence so far available. He may possibly give advice to the decision-maker on that alone, but may well consider that a medical report is needed from the claimant's GP and/or that the claimant should be medically examined by a DWPMS doctor. It has been stressed that no one will be refused benefit because of not satisfying the personal capability assessment, without having been offered such an examination.

This DWP examination was intended to be both more intensive and sensitive than under the previous system which had been criticised as cursory. The DWP doctor will interview the claimant about his everyday activities and can test his ability to perform certain tasks. The test is not designed to be a snapshot at a given point in time but an assessment of variable conditions over a period. Assessment will not simply be a matter of asking the claimant to perform the activities set out in the questionnaire. The doctor will take full account of the history and evolution of the medical condition, the effect it has on daily life and normal tasks over a period of time and the limitations it places on the claimant. Training is to emphasise that the doctor, who ultimately offers advice to the decision-maker by identifying the appropriate descriptor in each relevant functional area, must justify his choice of descriptors in terms of any variability or fluctuation of these effects as well as the effects of pain and fatigue. The doctor must give a full explanation of his choice of descriptors, particularly so in any area where his opinion differs from the claimant's own perception of his functional limitations. He will also, presumably, be especially full in terms of explanation if his own views go against any that the claimant's GP has offered. Despite this, Appeal Tribunal chairmen and members will have noticed that dissatisfaction with the examination process continues to be expressed by claimants and/or their representatives. In *CSIB/12/96* (considered in the notes to the Schedule, below), Commissioner Walker (perhaps setting standards of exactitude difficult to attain) criticised the approach of one BAMS doctor to the evidence about sitting, but the doctor's approach will be one familiar to many Appeal Tribunals. The process has also been criticised by the House of Commons Select Committee on Social Security, (*Third Report of 1999–2000*, HC183 (April 2000)).

The evaluation studies which helped create the test indicated that a number of those who would fail to be regarded as incapable on this new functional test might do so because theirs was one of a minority of conditions

> "that do not lend themselves to a functional assessment . . . [so that] . . . the individual could carry out all of the functions in the test, but still be incapable of work." DSS/Benefits Agency, *The medical assessment for incapacity benefit* (HMSO, 1994), p.12).

Accordingly, reg.27 requires that someone who has been found not to be incapable of work under the "personal capability" assessment be nonetheless treated as incapable of work where any of the circumstances listed in para.(2) of that reg. apply to him. The first such circumstance is where the person is suffering from a severe life threatening disease in relation to which there is "medical evidence" (see below) that the disease is uncontrollable, or uncontrolled, by a recognised therapeutic procedure, provided that as regards the uncontrolled disease there is a reasonable cause for it not being controlled by such a procedure (reg.27(2)(a)). The second such circumstance is that the person suffers from a previously undiagnosed potentially life-threatening condition *discovered during the course of a medical examination carried out for the purposes of the "personal capability" assessment by a BAMS doctor* (reg.27(2) (b)). The third circumstance in which the person found not incapable under the personal capability assessment is to be treated despite that failure as incapable of work arises where there is "medical evidence" that he requires a major surgical operation or other major therapeutic procedure likely to be carried out within three months of the DWP medical examination (reg.27(2)(c)).

The term "medical evidence" embraces (i) evidence from a doctor approved by the Secretary of State (usually a DWPMS doctor), (ii) evidence (if any) from any other doctor, hospital or similar institution, or such part of evidence in (i) or (ii) as constitutes the most reliable evidence available in the circumstances (reg.2(1)).

Hence the DWPMS doctor will consider whether any of these criteria apply and advise the Secretary of State which and why. He will also advise on an appropriate date for reviewing the case in line with the prognosis. But as regards reg.27, the DWPMS doctor's opinion is no longer conclusive and binding on the Secretary of State. Instead the Secretary of State will have to look at the regulation in the light of all the "medical evidence", including that from the DWPMS doctor. See further the notes to reg.27, below.

The decision on incapacity is one for the Secretary of State in the light of careful consideration of all the evidence, including the questionnaire, information from the claimant's doctor and the advice from the DWPMS doctor. Given the nature of the process, one may probably expect the latter to be given the most significant weight. The Secretary of State will have to do the scoring. If the appropriate threshold of any of the functional criteria is reached or exceeded, the decision will be that the claimant is incapable of work under the functional personal capability assessment. The claimant will be so informed, and his doctor advised that he need not issue any further medical certificates. The decision-maker will also decide in the light of advice from the DWPMS doctor when, if at all, the matter of the claimant's incapacity ought to be reviewed (the prognosis might be that he is likely to improve). If the claimant fails to attain the appropriate threshold score, a decision that the claimant is capable of work under the functional personal capability assessment will be made. But if "medical evidence" shows that one of the non-functional incapacity conditions in reg.27 applies, the decision-maker must treat the claimant as incapable of work. If there is no such evidence showing that the claimant, having failed the functional personal capability assessment, is capable of work, payment of incapacity benefit will stop, and advice will be given about claiming other benefits which underwrite unemployment and on registering for work. The claimant will also be told about his right of appeal to an Appeal Tribunal.

Dealing with the evidence, in particular with differing medical opinions and reports

8.139
To reiterate: the personal capability assessment is one of the extent to which a person who has some specific disease or bodily or mental disablement is capable of performing the activities prescribed in the Schedule, or is incapable by reason of such a disease or bodily or mental disablement of performing them. The claimant must have a recognised medical condition. On "some specific disease or bodily or mental disablement", see commentary to SSCBA 1992, s.171B(2), above, and the useful analysis there from Commissioner Jacobs in *CIB/26/2004* on what must be proved, to what standard and by what evidence. In most cases, however, dispute will centre not on the diagnosis of the disease or disablement, as such, but rather on the effect it has on the claimant's ability to perform the scheduled tasks with reasonable regularity.

In paras 7–11 of *CIB/13038/1996*, Commissioner Goodman deals with the matter of different opinions expressed by the DWPMS doctor and the claimant's GP. The decision shows that Appeal Tribunals need to approach carefully the task of deciding which to prefer. In this case, the SSAT, in its majority decision turning down the claimant's appeal, had preferred the evidence of the DWPMS doctor to that of the claimant's GP simply because the GP had only known the claimant for six months (his former GP having retired) and was heavily reliant on what the claimant had told her. In fact, Commissioner Goodman found her letter (reproduced in para.9 of the decision) "a quite detailed genuine attempt to assist" and accepted that there was force in the submission of the claimant's representative that the GP would also have based her answer on her own medical opinion in the light of not only the information provided by the claimant but also on the claimant's medical record to hand at the time of her consultation with the patient. The Commissioner held that the majority of the SSAT erred in law in rejecting the GP's evidence on the basis that they did, and remitted the matter afresh to a differently constituted SSAT. He also thought (without attempting to indicate what the ultimate result should be) that the new SSAT should give appropriate weight to a medical report obtained from a consultant orthopaedic surgeon *after the original SSAT hearing* since that report "cast considerable light on the problem [of manual dexterity at issue] and does constitute strong support for the claimant's appeal" (para.12). In *CIB/17257/96*, Commissioner Rice considering the matter of conflict between the evidence of the claimant and that of the DWPMS doctor, took a view that may raise some eyebrows in that the latter, in the eyes of many, is in reality, whatever the complex legalities, "employed by" one of the parties to the appeal. He stated that:

"the evidence of an EMO is both disinterested and informed, whereas that of the claimant is neither. The tribunal will normally follow the view of the EMO unless there are grounds for supposing that the usual practice should in a particular instance not be followed. There was nothing to suggest in the present case that the normal practice should be departed from" (para.4).

A tribunal must address, and give reasons for accepting or rejecting, any argument that it ought not to rely on a DWPMS doctor's report because the examination was not conducted properly. A short examination is not necessarily improper; it may, in the circumstances, be all that was warranted (*CIB/908/2003*). But in *CSIB/69/03*, a case raising mental health descriptors, Commissioner Parker was critical of the duration of the examination, the failure to put relevant questions to the claimant's mother who attended the examination, and of the nature of the medical report. The Commissioner was unable to accept the report as sufficiently reliable to demonstrate that the Secretary of State had discharged the onus of proof to show that reg.28 (deeming incapable pending a personal capability assessment) no longer applies (para.36).

An appellant's evidence does not require corroboration unless it is self-contradictory or improbable *(R(I) 2/51)*. A tribunal must look to all the evidence *(CIB/15663/1996)*. A tribunal is not *bound to* decide in the same way as any particular doctor certifies; when faced with a conflict of medical opinion, they are at liberty to prefer, giving reasons, one view rather than another *(R(S) 1/53; CSIB/684/1997; CSIB/848/1997; CIB/309/1997; R. v Social Security Commissioner Ex p. Dobie* (QBD, October 26, 1999)—but *cf. CIB/17257/1996)*. But that does not warrant underestimating a DWPMS personal capability assessment report which is based on a more intensive and detailed clinical examination and history-taking than the invalidity benefit system *(CIB/15663/1996)*. To prefer a DWPMS doctor's report on the grounds that it is more detailed is not, as such, irrational *(R. v Social Security Commissioner Ex p. Dobie*, QBD (October 26, 1999). A tribunal should not reject a claimant's appeal on the basis that he was "not a reliable or credible witness" without giving reasons for that finding *(CSIB/459/1997)*. It should be made clear that the claimant's evidence has been considered, what account has been taken of it, and, if rejected, why it has been rejected *(CIB/309/1997)*. Nor should a tribunal simply record acceptance of the DWPMS doctor's findings; rather it should make and record its own findings on the descriptors *(CSIB/459/ 1997)*.

In *CIB/4232/2007*, Deputy Commissioner Ovey found erroneous in law a tribunal decision partly because of its too "mantra like" acceptance of the examining doctor's opinion and, mistakenly, treating him as an expert on the claimant's condition, when no full examination had been carried out. They also attributed to him the opinion of the previous examining doctor.

In *CIB/1006/2008*, Commissioner Williams in referring the case to another tribunal, noted the tribunal's failure, when preferring the examining doctor's opinion, to consider evidence about the quality of the medical examination undertaken and to take due account of errors in the IB85 report about the timing of the examination, suggesting that there might well be other errors in the report itself, and casting doubt on the weight to be given to the report. The correct approach is to weigh all the evidence in the context of the case *(CIB/3620/1998)*. In *CIB/3074/2003* Commissioner Bano allowed the claimant's appeal because the tribunal had dismissed the appeal "on the basis of a formulaic endorsement of the examining medical practitioner's report", rather than looking at it in the light of its nature and the evidence as a whole. He noted that in *CIB/15663/1996*, deputy Commissioner Fellner (as she then was)

> "stated that a tribunal was entitled to give full weight to an examining medical practitioner's findings. A tribunal should of course give full weight to all the evidence, but may often be justified in regarding the clinical findings of an examining medical officer as reliable, although even clinical findings should not be regarded as conclusive and may in some cases be displaced by other evidence. However, the impact of any given degree of loss of function will vary from claimant to claimant. In some cases (such as incontinence) a clinical examination will often give very little indication of the extent of impairment of the activities which need to be considered in carrying out the personal capability assessment, although in such cases the examining medical practitioner will often be able to make an informed assessment of the degree of impairment on the basis of the claimant's medical history and other evidence of functional ability. The examining medical officer's choice of a descriptor will therefore generally require the exercise of judgment to a greater or lesser degree, and a tribunal may therefore not necessarily give the same weight to an examining medical officer's choice of descriptors as it does to clinical findings on examination." (para.13)

Commissioner Bano considered the EMP's report as perfunctory and as failing to address the crucial issues of impairment of physical activities caused by bowel

8.140

incontinence and by backache (para.16). He awarded the claimant nine points for bowel incontinence under descriptor 13(e) (loses bowel control occasionally), with the result that the claimant with that additional score satisfied the personal capability assessment with a score of 16 points. Commissioner Rice's statement quoted above is not authority for a proposition that more weight is to be given to evidence from a DWPMS doctor than from another doctor (*CIB/407/1998; CIB/1149/1998*). Indeed, current GP medical evidence may be valuable (*CIB/21/2002*). See further a useful article "Weighing it up: medical evidence in the balance" in CPAG, *Welfare Rights Bulletin No. 152* (October 1999), pp. 5–6.'

Where a claimant attends the tribunal hearing, a tribunal should not prefer the DWPMS doctor's evidence which disputed the appellant's account of his disabilities in his questionnaire, without first listening in some detail to the appellant's oral evidence about the effect of his condition. To do so was held by Deputy Commissioner Warren in *CIB/5586/99* to be a breach of natural justice ("fair play in action") and thus an error of law (para.7).

In *CIB/3868/2001*, Commissioner Levenson criticised a tribunal's rejection of evidence from the claimant's GP:

"The tribunal allocated 8 points in respect of hearing difficulties and 3 points in respect of walking difficulties. Although on these matters it did not accept the evidence from Dr Hunt [the DWPMS doctor] it nevertheless recorded that in other respects it preferred his clinical findings, opinion and report because he had examined the claimant thoroughly and his opinion:

' . . . was very likely to be the more objective, being based on the clinical findings of a doctor who was disinterest[ed] in the outcome of the claim.'

It was irrational and prejudiced of the tribunal to make this statement about Dr Hunt and to disregard the evidence of the GP. This is particularly the case because the GP was very specific about the question of climbing stairs and Dr Hunt said nothing more in this regard than ticking the box on the report form. In this respect the decision of the tribunal was made in error and must be set aside.

It is expedient that I substitute my own decision. The evidence of the GP in relation to the stairs is specific and is consistent with the medical history and diagnosis. There is no reason to disbelieve it. Accordingly I find that in addition to the hearing descriptor carrying points which the tribunal accepted, descriptor 2(c) also applies. This carries 7 points and replaces the score of 3 points in respect of walking. When added to the 8 points for hearing, this brings the total to the threshold score of 15 points" (paras 10–12).

so that the claimant was incapable of work.

On the need to take into account previous assessments, see *CIB/516/2008* and *CIB/103/2001*.

In a Northern Ireland decision, reported as *R4/99(IB)*, Commissioner Brown stated that in dealing with evidence before it and in considering whether the personal capability assessment (formerly the all work test) is satisfied, a tribunal may use all its senses, including ocular observation of the claimant during the hearing. In *CSIB/547/02*, Commissioner Parker accepted this, but she made the important point that natural justice requires that these observations be put to the claimant and his representative for their comment during the hearing. Note also that "examining" the claimant in the sense of asking questions about the effects of the claimant's condition on daily life and ability to cope, and discussing his/her evidence on these matters with the claimant is perfectly proper (*CIB/2061/01*).

In *R1/01(IB)(T)*, a Northern Ireland Tribunal of Commissioners followed *R4/99(IB)* and gave further guidance on the line to be drawn between, on the one hand, the permitted area of merely examining and observing the claimant, and, on the other hand, the impermissible area of carrying out a physical examination. The latter is prohibited even if the claimant requests it (SSA 1998, s.20(3)). But where a claimant requested a tribunal merely to look at his knee, that fell on the permissible side of the line. But the Tribunal of Commissioners stressed:

"that there is a considerable and significant difference between a claimant requesting a Tribunal to look at some part of his body and the Tribunal itself making the request. In our view it is perfectly legitimate for a Tribunal to observe and take account of what is obvious to every one. If it were clear to everyone that a man lacks three fingers on one hand, it would be wrong for a Tribunal to ignore that fact if it is relevant to what the Tribunal has to decide. We also see nothing wrong, in a simple case, in a Tribunal asking for a better look, particularly where the disability has been referred to and such a look is likely to assist the claimant's case. Why should the man with the missing fingers not be asked to hold up his hand particularly if he is placing emphasis on the loss of some of his fingers? However, if the man wore a prosthesis which concealed the extent of his disability, or wore a glove, could a Tribunal ask him to remove the prosthesis or glove so that they could have a good look at his disability? In our view it would not be appropriate for such a request to come from the Tribunal. If such a request does not actually fall within the regulatory prohibition, it comes close to doing so. There is also the practical difficulty that a prosthesis may be difficult to remove or claimant may be embarrassed by its removal. In practice, the simple removal of a glove or the turning up of a sleeve may not cause many problems. Most claimants want their appeals to succeed and will probably offer to remove the glove, or whatever, once it becomes apparent that it is in their interest to do so. Most of those who do not offer are likely to resist a request in whatever form it is put to them.

What we think is not permissible is for a Tribunal to ask a claimant to expose some part of the body which is covered by clothing. A direct request is not permissible and nor is an indirect one which puts a claimant in the position of having to say 'yes' or 'no'. If a Tribunal considers that it does not have enough evidence to decide some issue, it should adjourn so that the claimant can undergo a proper examination by a doctor.

We also consider that a Tribunal can observe, including comparing one limb with another if the claimant suggests this, but may not go further. One of Mr Toner's arguments against the view that we take is that the members of a Tribunal—and particularly a medical member—may be tempted to go further. Indeed a claimant may ask them to do so. They may be asked to take a closer look and then to feel a lump of swelling or to manipulate a limb. He submitted that it would be particularly hard for a medical member to resist the temptation. We see the point but do not feel that resisting such temptation is beyond the powers of, even medical, Tribunal members" (paras 19–21).

In *R(IB) 2/06* Commissioner Rowland held that a tribunal medical member is not precluded by virtue of the SSA 1998, s.20(3)(a) from looking at x-rays put in evidence. That provision only precludes "physical examination" of the claimant. But a tribunal is not bound to look at such x-rays:

"In this case, both members of the tribunal have referred to the medically qualified panel member's lack of expertise in analysing X-rays. If a tribunal is presented with X-rays that it cannot analyse, there must arise the question whether it should adjourn the proceedings so as to enable the parties to obtain a report from the relevant expert from among those treating the claimant. A failure to adjourn where a claimant has brought evidence that he not unreasonably thought the tribunal would be able to understand may amount to a breach of the rules of natural justice because the claimant is effectively being denied the opportunity to put his or her case properly. Deciding whether or not to adjourn will involve consideration of the relevance of the X-rays and the likelihood of them being helpful in relation to a live issue in the case. Where a person complains of back pain, it is usually accepted that he or she suffers from some such pain. The question are usually: how much and how disabling is it? If an X-ray is unlikely to give much indication as to how disabling the condition is, except in the most serious cases, there may well be little to gain from adjourning, and a tribunal may properly refuse to do so. However, if asked for a statement of reasons, it should explain what its approach was. Whenever a tribunal declines to consider evidence, that should ideally be recorded in the record of proceedings, together with a note of the reason that will usually have been given orally to the parties. Whether or not that is done, a reference to the refusal to consider the evidence is usually to be expected in the statement of reasons particularly where, as in this case, the claimant's application for a statement of reasons specifically stated that he wanted to know why his X-rays were not looked at (para. 10)."

Dealing with the evidence: the need carefully to appraise the computerised medical examination report IB 85

8.141   The computerised medical examination report IB85 is the end product of a system in which statements or phrases can be produced mechanically by the software, which produces relevant phrases from its memory bank, and, unless the examining doctor using it is very careful, may not necessarily represent actual wording chosen and typed in by him. This generates an increased risk of accidental mistakes or discrepancies being left undetected in the final product of the process. The need for careful appraisal of the computerised IB85 has been stressed by Commissioners Howell and Williams (*CIB/511/2005; CIB/476/2005; CIB/1522/2005; CIB/0664/2005; CIB/3950/2007*). Tribunals must "take particular care to satisfy themselves that reports presented to them in this form really do represent considered clinical findings and opinions by the individual doctor whose name they bear, based on what actually appeared on examination of the particular claimant" (*CIB/511/2005,* para.3). They must identify and deal with apparent discrepancies and avoid such standard phrases as "The tribunal preferred the evidence of the medical advisor which was based on clinical examination and findings." The electronic IB85 does not distinguish the original insertion of a phrase in a report from its repetition elsewhere in the report. Moreover, the system can also produce repeated omissions, such that a tribunal not proceeding carefully may miss an issue (*CIB/476/2005*). The default phrase—"claimant states no other problems"— which automatically comes in unless the doctor stops it, is ambiguous, and the tribunal is wrong to draw any significant conclusions from something that was merely an electronic default. The system can also repeat, unless the doctor overrides it, standard phrases from its software memory bank which may be at odds with the evidence. It is vital for the tribunal carefully to execute the judgmental and never simple task of weighing all available evidence about the claimant's condition at the date of the decision under appeal (*CIB/0664/2005*). Where the computer program generates, or by an override the examining doctor chooses, the phrase "inconsistent with other available evidence", the evidence in question must be identified and made available to the tribunal if challenged (*CIB/3950/2007,* para.16). The technical manual supplied to doctors to operate the computer programme for the IB85, must be read alongside *The Incapacity Benefit Handbook for Approved Doctors* ("the Handbook") most recently issued in 2004 (see *www.dwp.gov.uk/medical/guides_detailed.asp*). "Equality of arms" demands that a copy of the technical manual be available at all tribunals (paras 18–20).

In *CIB/1006/2008*, Commissioner Williams in referring the case to another tribunal, noted the tribunal's failure, when preferring the examining doctor's opinion, to consider evidence about the quality of the medical examination undertaken and to take due account of errors in the IB85 report about the timing of the examination, suggesting that there might well be other errors in the report itself, and casting doubt on the weight to be given to the report. In *CIB/1381/2008*, he expressed concern that the wording of the IB85 report does not deal accurately with the current reg.27(2)(c) but reflects the pre-1997 wording. There is a key difference in terms of the timescale concerning the operation envisaged by that provision. The current text of reg.27 refers to "likely to be carried out within three months" of the PCA medical examination, the IB85 formulation in contrast is that it is to occur within the three month period. The tribunal had also failed to exercise its inquisitorial and enabling function by ignoring reg.27.

In *R(IB)7/05*, Commissioner Bano doubted whether s.7 of the Electronic Communications Act 2000 has any application to the electronic form IB85, since there is nothing in the form which purports to establish the authenticity of the data in the document, as required by subs.(2)(b) of that Act. The IB85 contains no signature. Moreover, s.7 does not apply to tribunals constituted under the Social Security Act 1998, because strict rules of evidence do not apply to proceedings before them (see also *R(U) 5/77* and other cases referred to in *CDLA/2014/2004*). Accordingly he held that *CIB/3984/2004* was wrongly decided.

Dealing with the evidence: the issue of adviser/representative revision to the picture painted by the claimant's questionnaire answers and the EMP's report

In *CIB/2913/2001*, Commissioner Henty commented: **8.142**

"Rightly or wrongly there has, I have noted, been an apparent trend that when a case is later considered by some semi-professional body, it is very often put on a stronger basis. A mere statement by the representative concerning the claimant's capabilities or disabilities which is significantly different from the claimant's original own assessment of his or her condition, requires some supporting evidence. The original questionnaire is expressed in pretty plain and simple language, and, doubtless, it has been drafted with that in mind. It makes the gist, although not necessarily the detail, of the questions to be answered fairly clear. In those circumstances, I think that a decision-maker is normally entitled to accept the answers as prima facie truthful, subject to the result of the medical examination. I would note that in this case there is, in fact, a large measure of agreement between the claimant's own assessment of her condition and that made by the EMP. The only differences were that the EMP awarded 3 points for bending and kneeling, and refused any points for incontinence. The fact that he awarded 3 points rather than 7 for stairs is, for practical purposes, insignificant. When faced, as in this case, with a very significant amendment of the claimant's alleged capabilities it seems to me that some further corroborative evidence is required. In *R. v Kilbourne* [1973] A.C. 729, Lord Reid helpfully addressed the question of corroboration generally at p.750 thus:—

'There is nothing technical in the idea of corroboration. When in the ordinary course of affairs of life one is doubtful whether or not to believe a particular statement one naturally looks to see whether it fits in with the other statements or circumstances relating to the particular matter; the better it fits in, the more one is inclined to believe it. The doubted statement is corroborated to a greater or lesser extent by the other statements or circumstances with which it fits in.'

That dictum is, I think, in point in the present case.

8. It, therefore, seems to me to be altogether expected that the tribunal were somewhat sceptical of the representative's submissions. What they said was:—

'The main issue was whether the appellant's account in the IB50s and the Examining Medical Practitioner was more accurate than that given to the tribunal. The tribunal considered that the evidence given to it by the appellant was less likely to be reliable because she would have had the benefit of discussing the descriptors with her representative whereas in the IB50s and before the examining medical practitioner she gave her own account. It is true that the examining medical practitioner allowed a limitation on bending and kneeling which was not in the IB50s but that was based on observed difficulty during the examination.'

Accordingly they regarded the submissions of the representative and the evidence at the tribunal as exaggerated. I see no reason to interfere with that finding."

[¹ Incapacity under the personal capability assessment

8.143   **25.**—(1) For the purposes of section 171C(2)(b) of the Contributions and Benefits Act a person is incapable of work in accordance with the personal capability assessment when one or more of the descriptors in Part I or Part II apply to him if, by adding the points listed in column
(3) of the Schedule against the descriptor, he obtains a total score of at least—
  (a) 15 points in respect of descriptors specified in Part I; or
  (b) 10 points in respect of descriptors specified in Part II; or
  (c) 15 points in respect of descriptors specified in Parts I and II.]
(2) In determining the extent of a person's incapacity to perform any activity listed in Part I he shall be assessed as if he were wearing any prosthesis with which he is fitted [² or, as the case may be, any aid or appliance which he normally wears or uses.
(3) In determining the extent of a person's incapacity to perform any activity listed in Part I or Part II, it shall be a condition that the person's incapacity arises—
  (a) in respect of a disability listed in Part I, from a specific bodily disease or disablement; or
  (b) in respect of a disability listed in Part II, from some specific mental illness or disablement.]

AMENDMENTS

1. Social Security (Incapacity for Work) Miscellaneous Amendments Regulations 1999 (SI 1999/3109), reg.3(3) (April 3, 2000).
2. Social Security (Incapacity for Work and Miscellaneous Amendments) Regulations 1996 (SI 1996/3207), reg.2(7) (January 6, 1997).

DEFINITIONS

   "activity"—see reg.2(1).
   "descriptor"—see reg.2(1).
   "personal capability assessment"—see regs 2(1) and 24.
   "the Schedule"—see reg.2(2).

GENERAL NOTE

Para.(1)
8.144   This sets the threshold scores for incapacity under the "personal capability assessment" (defined in reg.24). The Schedule to these regulations lists in col.(1) a number of activities or functional areas of body or mind thought relevant to incapacity for work, for example, walking (on level ground and up and down stairs), sitting, standing, manual dexterity, completion of tasks, coping with pressure, interacting with people. The first (and longer) Part of the Schedule deals with physical disabilities, the second Part with mental disabilities. In respect of each activity or functional area, the Schedule lists in col.(2) a number of descriptors ("clearly worded statements of disability ranked according to their incapacitating effect in each functional area" (DSS/Benefits Agency, *The medical assessment for incapacity benefit* (HMSO, 1994), p.4) to each of which is attached in col.(3) a score in terms of a number of points, ranging from zero to fifteen. Essentially reg.25(1) stipulates that someone is incapable of work under the personal capability assessment when

one or more of the descriptors applies to him and, adding up the points attached to them (with some limitations on counting, set by reg.26), he achieves a total score of at least 15 points if only physical disability descriptors apply, of 10 points if mental disability descriptors alone are relevant, or of 15 points if descriptors of both types are applicable. These total scores are the threshold for benefit, set, it is said by government, not at the point at which a person is unable to work at all but rather at the point at which a person should not be expected to work.

Para. (2)

The extent of a person's incapacity to perform any activity listed in the first part   **8.145** of the Schedule (physical disabilities) is to be determined as if he were wearing any prosthesis with which he is fitted or, as the case may be, any aid or appliance which he normally wears or uses. See further the cases noted in the annotations to the Sch., specific descriptors 12 and 13, dealing respectively with urinary and bowel incontinence.

This provision cannot be used in a manner which essentially alters the nature of the activity under assessment (*CIB/5654/97*, para.3; *CIB/614/98*, para.15). So in *CIB/5654/97* Commissioner Lloyd-Davies directed the tribunal to which he remitted the case to ignore the use made by the claimant of a special cushion to relieve alleged discomfort:

"the test concerns sitting in an armless upright chair: if the use of a cushion or cushions were not to be disregarded, the test would not be equivalent to sitting in a typical office, waiting-room or dining-room chair but would be more akin to sitting in an easy chair, which is not what the regulations provide . . . sitting in an upright chair without arms is not the same activity as sitting in a cushioned chair" (para.3).

Similarly in *CIB/614/98*, where Commissioner Howell was concerned with Activity 5 (rising from sitting), he disregarded the use the claimant made of crutches to rise from sitting, since the wording of the activity and its descriptors make clear that what is being tested is the ability to rise to an upright position without the use of arms and shoulders (para.16). What are being tested are principally disabilities to do with the functioning of legs, spine, general muscular co-ordination and balance. This approach did not render reg.25(2) of useful effect, since,

"for example a person who has to wear a calliper or a body support must now be clearly assumed to be wearing it, and its effect taken into account, in determining whether they can get themselves upright from a chair without having to use their arms to hold on to something as well" (*ibid.*).

Para. (3)

This paragraph makes it clear that one can determine the extent of a person's   **8.146** incapacity to perform an activity listed in Pt I of the Schedule (physical disabilities) only where his incapacity arises from a specific *bodily* disease or disablement. Similarly, the extent of his incapacity to perform any activity listed in Pt II of the Schedule (mental disabilities) can only be determined if that incapacity arises from some specific *mental* illness or disablement. So that the proposition—that issues under Pt II of the Schedule are raised by a diagnosis in which a physical disease or disability produces related psychological problems which are more than *de minimis*—can now only hold good if those psychological problems can themselves be characterised as a specific mental illness or disablement, a matter in practical terms turning on medical evidence and diagnosis.

It is important properly to identify the relevant physical or mental condition and to consider the full range of activities which may be impaired by the condition. So, for example, with migraine, it is important not to confine consideration to Activity 14 (lost or altered consciousness): see Deputy Commissioner White *CIB/5757/1997* (para.25) and also *CIB/3589/2004* in which Commissioner Jacobs said:

"In the case of a migraine, the chain works like this. A migraine is a bodily *disease*. It involves *symptoms*—pain and disruption of vision. Those symptoms restrict the claimant's ability to function in various way (*disabilities*). The personal capability assessment allows those symptoms and their effects to be taken into account in respect of any *activity* which they affect. For example, flashing lights or blindness during a migraine may affect the activity of negotiating stairs without holding on and the activity of vision.

Migraines are not continuous. Their effects are intermittent. That does not mean that they are irrelevant to the personal capability assessment. They may be relevant in one of two ways. First, they may be relevant to the 'sometimes' descriptors in the activities of rising from sitting and bending and kneeling. Second, they may be relevant to the frequency and regularity with which a claimant can undertake activities.

The tribunal limited the potential relevance of the symptoms of migraine to activity 14. There is no justification in the legislation for doing so. Nor is there any justification in the nature of migraine or the effects of its symptoms. The tribunal limited the relevance of the claimant's evidence of migraines to one activity without justification" (paras 12–14).

Looking to the facts as found by the tribunal about the claimant's condition, he found that

"The claimant's migraines are sufficiently severe that they affect her ability to rise from sitting and to bend or kneel to the floor. She would not be able to do either of those activities without some support. In those circumstances, the 'sometimes' descriptors for those activities apply. Each scores 3 points, making a total of 6. The claimant already has a score of 10. The additional 6 bring the total to 16, which is sufficient to satisfy the assessment" (para.17).

Applying these statements of Deputy Commissioner White and Commissioner Jacobs, in *CIB/3671/2006* Deputy Commissioner Mark considered that "if a person's mental disablement causes a migraine which prevents a person from performing such an activity, then the disability does arise from the mental disablement" (para.11). He remitted the matter to the tribunal to consider the evidence and determine as best it can the extent to which the claimant's migraine attacks are triggered by her mental disabilities, and then to consider how those migraines affect her ability to perform the mental descriptors. He thought that regular migraine attacks might well be said to impair the claimant's ability to communicate with other people, and she might fear that pressures if she returned to work might trigger further migraine attacks brought on by anxiety.

The provision requires decision-makers to characterise a particular condition so as to be able properly to apply the personal capability assessment. In *CIB/6244/1997*, Commissioner Jacobs dealt with a case of chronic fatigue syndrome. In referring the case back to a differently constituted tribunal, he stated that:

"the evidence before me contains no reference to any mental features of the case. Some claimants who have chronic fatigue syndrome are resistant to the idea that their condition is wholly or partly mental in origin. Nevertheless the tribunal that rehears this case must determine whether the claimant's condition is entirely physical, entirely mental, or partly physical and partly mental in origin. It must then apply the all work test accordingly . . .

In determining the proper classification of the claimant's condition, the tribunal must have regard to any evidence put before it. It will find the advice and assistance of its medical assessor invaluable" (paras 25, 28).

In *CIB/2357/2006*, Commissioner Rowland held that a tribunal erred by ignoring physical descriptors in any detail in a case of chronic fatigue syndrome simply because the claimant had not identified any problems with the physical activities on her IB50 form. She had characterised herself as "ill" rather than disabled, but had also stated that she was often so exhausted that she was unable to do anything except retire to bed. The tribunal itself had also noted her claim that after getting up there was only a "five-hour window" in which she could function relatively normally. Commissioner Rowland held that this put the tribunal on notice that the claimant's condition manifested itself both in physical signs and symptoms. It seemed to Commissioner Rowland that "she was therefore in fact claiming to be physically disabled during much of the day" (para.3), thus putting in issue matters of whether she could "normally" perform certain activities as and when called upon to do so and whether it could be done on a repeated basis (ibid).

In a Northern Ireland decision *C10/00–01(IB)*, Commissioner Brown considered whether, and if so, when, the side effects of medication for a physical condition could score points under the mental health descriptors, given the wording of para. (3). She stated:

"More fundamentally however it is necessary to consider whether the side effects of the medication can be classed as a mental disablement. It appears from the Regulations mentioned above that the specific mental disablement must be something other than the functional impairments in activities listed in the All Work Test. In other words there must be some underlying condition separate from those impairments and disablement and disabilities are to be differently interpreted. If that were not so there would be no need for Regulation 25(3) as it would be meaningless. The claimant's underlying mental ability had to be impaired. The side effects of medication do not mean that a person is suffering from a mental disablement. Mentally, he is quite normal, but because of the physical effects of the drugs he simply cannot perform certain activities (if his evidence is accepted). His mental powers may be affected by drugs but they are not impaired of themselves. It is straining language artificially to say that the side effects of medication for a physical condition constitute a specific mental disablement unless they do impair these underlying mental powers. I find it impossible, and it is obvious that the Tribunal found it impossible to ascertain what if any specific mental disablement the claimant suffers. The medication is not itself a condition it is simply a compound of ingredients. The descriptors in the All Work Test are not themselves a specific mental disablement or there would be no need for a specific mental disablement to be referred to separately in the Regulations. They are impairments in the activities on the test not specific physical or mental disablement. I consider that the Tribunal was quite entitled to its view that there was no mental disablement or mental illness in this case.

I would refer further to the decision of Mr Commissioner Goodman in Great Britain in *CIB/14202/96* approved by me in decision *C53/98(IB)* both of which establish the need for a mental disablement in the nature of an illness before points can be awarded under Part II of the All Work Test." (paras 29, 30).

Some conditions from which a claimant is suffering may properly be treated as both a physical and a mental illness or disablement, and its effects considered under both physical and mental descriptors. Alcoholism is one example (*CSIB/287/2003*, para.17; *C10/07–08(IB)*).

In *CIB/4828/99*, Commissioner Jacobs held that the tribunal had misinterpreted regulation 25(3):

"The wording of the full statement of the tribunal's decision suggests that the tribunal applied the wrong legal test. It repeatedly states that the claimant's hypertension did not give rise to 'any physical manifestations' or that the dizziness was 'not a manifestation of a specific bodily disease or disablement'. That is not the legal test for the physical disabilities section. The legal test is whether the claimant's 'incapacity arises in respect of' one of the descriptors 'from a specific bodily disease or disablement'. That is slightly different from the terms used in the chairman's statement of tribunal's reasons. However, I do not take that difference in expression as showing that the tribunal did not have regard to the correct wording. The statement bespeaks the chairman's care and attention to detail. I treat the differences in language as merely differences of expression rather than substance.

15. However, the tribunal did misinterpret regulation 25(3).

16. I begin by accepting the tribunal's analysis of the chain of causation. Hypertension is a specific bodily disease. I[f] that disease gave rise directly to dizziness, the resulting incapacities would arise from it. I see no reason why the incapacity has to arise directly. The Secretary of State argues otherwise; I disagree. If there was a causal link in which the hypertension caused anxiety and depression which in turn caused the dizziness, a tribunal might be entitled to find that the incapacities resulting from the dizziness arose from the hypertension.

17. Next, I assume that the tribunal's analysis was wrong and the hypertension was neither by cause nor contribution related to the hypertension. On this assumption, the dizziness arose from, and only from, the anxiety and depression. The dizziness would not of itself [be] a specific bodily disease, but it might be a bodily disablement. If it was a bodily disablement, any incapacity that arose from it would fall within the physical disabilities section of the all work test.

18. I have worded paragraphs 16 and 17 in terms of possibilities. I am not saying that any link, however tenuous, is sufficient to allow or require a tribunal to find that an incapacity arises from a bodily disease somewhere earlier in the chain of causation. Nor am I saying that any physical symptom of a mental illness or disablement will constitute a bodily disablement. All I am saying is that, depending on the circumstances, either of these is possible.

19. So, regulation 25(3)(a) and (b) do not create rigid categories. A physical symptom that arises from a mental illness or disablement may be a bodily disablement. Or it may arise from a bodily disease that itself gave rise to the mental illness [or] disablement. In either case, the symptom may give rise to incapacity in respect of a disability under the physical disabilities section of the all work test. It would be surprising if it were otherwise, as a person's condition is often the result of the complex interaction of physical and mental factors."

8.147 In *CIB/5435/2002*, Commissioner Jacobs considered the meaning of "bodily disablement" in para.(3) in the context of a claimant diagnosed with "chronic pain syndrome". It and "illness behaviour" are recognised by a respectable body of medical opinion as medical conditions. They are

> "terms used to describe symptoms that are caused by the influence of psychological makeup and social environment on the perception of the disabling effects of a medical condition. The recognition of this phenomenon is reflected in more modern approaches to treatment, which address the psychosocial as well as the medical factors. The symptoms are subjective in the sense that they depend on an experience of pain or fatigue. This does not, though, mean that they are not genuinely experienced, nor that they do not prevent or restrict function" (para.12).

But where do they fit in para.(3), since classification is crucial in determining which set of activities and descriptors can be applied? Neither is a disease. Commissioner Jacobs decided that "bodily" refers to the function that is affected rather than to the source of the condition, so that "chronic pain syndrome and related conditions bring the clamant within the scope of the physical disabilities section of the personal capability assessment" (para.16).

In *CIB/4841/2002*, Commissioner Jacobs gave the following description of "illness behaviour":

> "Abnormal illness behaviour is one of a number of terms used to describe symptoms which are caused by the influence of psychological makeup and social environment on the perception of the disabling effects of a medical condition. This phenomenon is reflected by more modern approaches to treatment, which address the psychosocial as well as the medical factors. The symptoms are subjective in the sense that they depend on an experience of pain or fatigue. In order

to distinguish between claimants who genuinely experience a particular disability from those who merely claim to do so, it is helpful to consider the history of their daily activity and unobtrusive observations. This can identify consistency or inconsistency" (para.10).

In *CIB/4718/2003*, Commissioner Jacobs held that a tribunal erred in law in saying that stress cannot be a mental illness or disablement: he was

"surprised that the tribunal did not consider that stress was a relevant disablement for this purpose. Stress is referred to in both of the standard classifications of mental disorders.

- The Diagnostic and Statistical Manual IV includes post traumatic stress disorder and acute stress disorder. Neither of the definitions are appropriate to the claimant's circumstances in so far as they appear from the evidence. However, the claimant's symptoms might fall within one of the more general anxiety disorders.
- The World Health Organisation's classification ICD-10 includes acute stress reaction which might be appropriate.

The chairman did not explain why the tribunal came to the conclusion that I have quoted. It cannot have had regard to the extensive and expert body of opinion that is reflected in the standard classification systems. Given the contents of those systems, the tribunal's conclusion was not self-evident and required an explanation.

It is also possible that the tribunal may have reached its conclusion by an over-emphasis on the words used by the claimant's GP. It may be that the medically qualified panel member on the tribunal did not accept that stress of itself was a mental disablement. However, it was necessary to go beyond the GP's choice of word to the substance of the matter. Stress is a cause. What matters is not the cause, but the consequence. And the consequence may be a recognised form of mental disablement, such as anxiety" (paras 8–10).

Calculation of scores

26.—(1) In determining a person's score for the purposes of regulation 25(1)(c)—

    (a) [¹ an aggregate score] of between 6 and 9 points in respect of those descriptors specified in Part II shall be treated as a score of 9 points when added to the score in respect of descriptors specified in Part I:

    (b) [¹ an aggregate score] of less than 6 points in respect of [¹ the descriptors] specified in Part II shall be disregarded.

(2) In determining a person's score where descriptors specified for the activities 1 and 2 in Part I apply to him, only one descriptor shall be counted and that shall be the descriptor with the highest score in respect of either activity which applies to him.

(3) In determining a person's score in respect of descriptors specified in Part I where more than one descriptor specified for any activity applies to him, only one descriptor shall be counted and that shall be the descriptor with the highest score in respect of each activity which applies to him.

(4) In determining a person's score in respect of descriptors specified in Part II the score in respect of each descriptor which applies to him shall be counted.

8.148

AMENDMENT

1. Social Security (Incapacity for Work and Miscellaneous Amendments) Regulations 1996 (SI 1996/3207), reg.2(8). (January 6, 1997).

DEFINITIONS

"activity"—see reg.2(1).
"descriptor"—see reg.2(1).

GENERAL NOTE

8.149   This sets some limits on totalling scores in terms of points for the "personal capability" assessment (regs 24, 25). Essentially someone is incapable of work under the personal capability assessment when one or more of the descriptors in the Schedule to these regulations applies to him and adding up the points attached to them (within the limitations on counting set by this regulation) he achieves a total score of at least 15 points if only physical disability descriptors apply (Pt I of the Schedule), of 10 points if mental disability descriptors alone are relevant (Pt II of the Schedule), or of 15 points if descriptors of both types are applicable (reg.25). These total scores are the threshold for benefit.

So, the first task is to decide from the evidence which descriptors apply, the second to calculate the scores. Calculation of the appropriate score is not, however, a simple matter of totalling up all the numbers thus identified. Granted with respect to mental disabilities alone one does count the score in respect of each descriptor which applies to the claimant (para.(4)). However, where these have to be added to the appropriate score in respect of applicable physical disabilities, scores of less than six points in respect of the mental health descriptors must be disregarded, but a score of between six and nine points in respect of mental health disabilities is to be treated as one of nine points (para.(1)). With respect to someone's score in terms of physical disabilities, where more than one descriptor specified for any activity applies to him, only the descriptor with the highest score is counted, and for this purpose where a descriptor from each of the two separate "walking" activities (walking on level ground; walking up and down stairs: see Sch., Pt I, paras 1 and 2) applies to him, the two activities are treated as if they were one and only one descriptor (the highest scoring "walking" descriptor) counts (paras (2), (3)). In *CIB/5361/97*, Commissioner Howell was faced with the alarming revelation that the DWPMS doctor in the case, on whose evidence the SSAT had relied, had taken a "bottom-up" approach to scoring with respect to the descriptors connected with each activity, that is, he had started at the bottom (no points) and worked up until he found a descriptor which fitted the claimant. Even more worryingly, he claimed that the training sessions he had attended had given him the impression that this was the proper approach. Commissioner Howell, applying para.(3), rejected this approach as invalid:

"Since the decriptors with the highest score are the ones which appear the furthest up each section of the table [activities and descriptors in the Schedule], the only valid way to conduct an assessment of a person's physical descriptor score in accordance with this mandatory requirement of the regulations must therefore be to work down from the top of each section of the table and stop as soon as one comes to a descriptor that applies to him" (para.7).

Are there in the regs and Schedule any implied limits on counting? In *R(IB) 3/98*, Commissioner Mitchell considered

"whether ascribing points for the claimant's inability to walk up and down a flight of stairs without holding on involves an impermissible double counting, where the cause of the claimant's inability to do so is his defective vision and he also scores under a descriptor specifically related to vision in paragraph 12" (para.11).

He saw no compelling reason "for implying a scoring limitation which could have been but has not been made explicit" (para.16). Accordingly, the only limits on "double counting" are those expressly found in paras (2) and (3) of this regulation or in the wording of the Schedule. In this regard note the revised wording of activity 8: "lifting and carrying by the use of the upper body and arms (excluding all other activities specified in Part I of this Schedule". It is submitted that this does not mean that scoring under one of the "lifting and carrying" descriptors precludes scoring under any other activity in Pt I. Rather, it follows the sort of line in the DWP Medical Advisers Guide to incapacity benefit, reproduced as Appendix Two in CPAG's *Rights Guide to Non-Means-Tested Benefits* (1997). It means that one asks essentially whether the claimant can lift, in the sense of pick up, the object from a convenient place (without bending or reaching) and hold it; and, if so, would the claimant be able to carry that object considering only the ability to lift and carry and not walking or climbing stairs.

That there is no other bar on "double counting" is of particular importance with respect to the mental health descriptors, several of which may be applicable to the same factual context. In *CSIB/1521/01* and *CSIB/451/01*, Commissioner Parker applied *CSIB/13/96*, now reported as *R(IB) 3/98*. In *CSIB/1521/01*, she noted the overlap between descriptors 18(b) and 18(d), and with 16(c). In *CSIB/451/01*, she noted the overlapping terms of 16(a) and 18(a), and of 16(a) and 16(d).

[¹ Exceptional circumstances

27.—(1) A person who [² is not incapable of work in accordance with the personal capability assessment] shall be treated as incapable of work if any of the circumstances set out in paragraph (2) apply to him.

(2) The circumstances are that—

  (a) he is suffering from a severe life threatening disease in relation to which—

    (i) there is medical evidence that the disease is uncontrollable, or uncontrolled, by a recognised therapeutic procedure, and

    (ii) in the case of a disease which is uncontrolled, there is a reasonable cause for it not to be controlled by a recognised therapeutic procedure;

  (b) he suffers from a previously undiagnosed potentially life threatening condition which has been discovered during the course of a medical examination carried out for the purposes of the [³ personal capability assessment] by a doctor approved by the Secretary of State;

  (c) there exists medical evidence that he requires a major surgical operation or other major therapeutic procedure and it is likely that that operation or procedure will be carried out within three months of the date of a medical examination carried out for the purposes of the [³ personal capability assessment].]

8.150

AMENDMENTS

1. Social Security (Incapacity for Work and Miscellaneous Amendments) Regulations 1996 (SI 1996/3207), reg.2(9) (January 6, 1997).

2. Social Security (Incapacity for Work) Miscellaneous Amendments Regulations 1999 (SI 1999/3109), reg.3(5) (April 3, 2000).

3. Social Security (Incapacity) Miscellaneous Amendments Regulations 2000 (SI 2000/590) (April 3, 2000).

DEFINITIONS

  "doctor"—see reg.2(1).
  "medical evidence"—see reg.2(1).
  "personal capability assessment"—see regs 2(1) and 24.

GENERAL NOTE

The evaluation studies which helped create the all work test (now the "personal capability assessment") (see further regs 24–26 and commentary) indicated that a

8.151

number of those who would fail to be regarded as incapable on this new functional test might do so because theirs was one of a minority of conditions "that do not lend themselves to a functional assessment . . . [so that] . . . the individual could carry out all of the functions in the test, but still be incapable of work." (DSS/Benefits Agency, *The medical assessment for incapacity benefit* (HMSO, 1994), pp.7–8, 62).

This regulation, headed "exceptional circumstances", is designed to deal with such cases and sets out a range of circumstances in which someone who is found not incapable of work under the assessment test (a finding on that is an essential precondition to the application of this regulation) must nonetheless be treated as incapable of work.

Non satisfaction of the appropriate incapacity test (own occupation or personal capability assessment) is a pre-condition of the operation of this regulation (*Charlton v Secretary of State for Work and Pensions* [2009] EWCA Civ 42, para.29). The degree to which a tribunal needs to explore that matter of non-satisfaction of the appropriate test has been the subject of disagreement between Commissioners (contrast *CIB/248/1997* and *CIB/601/1997* with *CSIB/146/2004*). Clearly the extent of the requisite inquiry will vary from case to case. Is the issue of non-satisfaction contested? Does the claimant argue that he does satisfy the test? As Commissioner Williams has put it

"The current wording [of reg.27] is in my view unambiguous. An official must decide that the assessment is not satisfied before moving on to consider regulation 27.

CSIB 146 2004 was an unusual case because the tribunal rejected the official evidence about the claimant's personal capability assessment before deciding that regulation 27 applied to the claimant. As Commissioner May commented at paragraph 11, that removed the evidential basis for the official decision that the claimant failed the personal capability assessment. On the facts the tribunal therefore left the assessment undecided. But I disagree with his generalisation from those unusual facts to the proposition that all tribunals must look at the personal capability assessment before examining regulation 27. An official must do that. A tribunal need not. It has the benefit of section 12(8)(a) of the Social Security Act 1998. It need not consider any issue that is not raised in the appeal. If there is no dispute about the application of the assessment in a particular appeal, then it need not be in issue" (*CIB/143/2007*, paras 20–21).

The substance of the current version of this regulation was inserted, with effect from January 6, 1997, by reg.2(9) of the Social Security (Incapacity for Work and Miscellaneous Amendments) Regulations 1996 (SI 1996/3207). Its predecessor had successfully been challenged in *R. v Secretary of State for Social Security Ex p. Moule* (noted at p.23 of *Legal Action*, October 1996). On September 12, 1996, Collins J., sitting in the Divisional Court, granted, on an application for judicial review, a declaration that reg.27 as then worded was *ultra vires* in so far as it purported to make satisfaction of its conditions conditional on the binding and nonappealable opinion of a doctor approved by the Secretary of State (usually a DWPMS doctor). He quashed the AO's decision withdrawing disability premium in income support from Mr Moule who suffered from widespread psoriasis. The premium had been withdrawn because Mr Moule scored no points on the all work test and the DWPMS doctor did not regard reg.27 as covering his case.

The position after *Moule* would seem to be that the version of reg.27 extant until January 6, 1997 (see p.808 of Bonner, Hooker and White, *Non Means Tested Benefits: The Legislation* (1996)) operated as if the words "in the opinion of a doctor approved by the Secretary of State" in its first line were not there. So that it fell to the AO to decide from all the evidence in the case, including the DWPMS doctor's opinion, whether the conditions in reg.27 were met so that a claimant, who had failed the all work test, was nevertheless to be treated as incapable of work. Appeal against an adverse AO decision on that would lie to the SSAT which had then to decide, in the light of all the evidence including the DWPMS doctor's opinion, whether it regarded the reg.27 conditions as met so as to treat the claimant as incapable of work. See further *CIB/1748/97*.

In *Howker v Secretary of State* ([2002] EWCA Civ 1623, November 8, 2002; reported as *R(IB) 3/03*), the Court of Appeal allowed Mr Howker's appeal from Commissioner Howell's decision in *CIB/4563/98*. The SSAC had been misled by information that those covered by para.(b) of the version of reg.27 the subject of the decision in *Moule* (the "head" deleted by the 1996 amending regulations) would be covered by one or other of the replacement "heads". In consequence they accepted that formal reference to them of the amending regulation need not be made. Thus, by the misstatement Parliament was deprived of a report from the SSAC. Since the procedure envisaged by Parliament had not been followed, in this case the Court of Appeal granted a declaration that the amending regulation was invalid in so far as head (b) had wrongly been deleted. Mr Howker's case was thus subject to the old head 27(b) as modified by *Moule* and he would continue to be assessed under that old regime. In short, this means that the test to be applied to him (someone who does not satisfy the all work test (now personal capability assessment)) is whether in the light of all the evidence including any opinion from a DWPMS doctor,

"he suffers from some specific disease or bodily or mental disablement and, by reasons of such disease or disablement, there would be a substantial risk to the mental or physical health of any person if he were found capable of work".

This would appear to mean that the "old" head (b) as modified by *Moule* continues in existence alongside the current version of reg.27 so that claimants who satisfy it, whether or not on benefit in 1997, can take advantage of it from November 8, 2002 if their cases meet its more generous conditions. The antitest case rule, however, will probably prevent claimants already on benefit from benefiting from the ruling before November 8, 2002.

The meaning of the phrase "there would be a substantial risk to the mental or physical health of any person if he were found capable of work" was considered in a number of conflicting Commissioners' decisions, but its meaning and the approach to take to its application has now been resolved by the Court of Appeal in *Charlton v Secretary of State for Work and Pensions* [2009] EWCA Civ 42. Regulation 27(b) requires a decision firstly that a person suffers as a consequence of some specific disease or bodily or mental disablement which does not of itself cause such functional limitation as to justify a total score warranting a finding of incapacity for work under the PCA. It requires, secondly, a decision on whether because of the disease or disablement there would be a substantial risk to the mental or physical health of any person if the claimant were found capable of work (*Charlton*, para.30). The risk to be assessed must arise as a consequence of work the claimant would be found capable of undertaking, but for reg.27 (*Charlton*, para.33). Regulation 27(b) might be satisfied

"where the very finding of capability might create a substantial risk to a claimant's health or that of others, for example when a claimant suffering from anxiety or depression might suffer a significant deterioration on being told that the benefit claimed was being refused. Apart from that, probably rare, situation, the determination must be made in the context of the journey to or from work or in the workplace itself" (*Charlton*, para.34).

The Court held that the correct approach to identifying the nature of the relevant work and workplace for the claimant was that identified in paragraphs 17-18 of Deputy Commissioner Paines' decision in *CIB/360/2007*. It rejected the view that decision-makers and tribunals had to speculate as to the type of job which would have been set out for purposes of a JSA claim in a hypothetical Jobseeker's Agreement. Rather:

"The decision-maker must assess the range or type of work which a claimant is capable of performing sufficiently to assess the risk to health either to himself or to others.

Sufficient information may be elicited by reference to the claimant's completion of the initial questionnaire, questioning during his medical examination, or by any evidence he may choose to give on an appeal to the Tribunal. The process to be adopted by the decision-maker or Tribunal is to be regarded as inquisitorial and not adversarial. It is a process described by Diplock J in *R v Medical Appeal Tribunal (North Midland Region ex-parte Hubble)* 1958 2 QB 228 at 240 as a fact-gathering exercise in which there is no formal burden of proof on either side. There should be no difficulty provided the decision-maker or Tribunal recall that the essential question is whether there is an adequate range of work which the claimant could undertake without creating a substantial risk to himself or to others.

This conclusion is consistent with the practical application of these regulations. Any interpretation must bear in mind that the regulations are designed to provide a fair and effective system for assessing entitlement to incapacity benefit and to allied benefits when a claimant has passed the Personal Capability Assessment. It would not be possible to achieve the aim of those regulations were the decision-maker to be required to make findings of the particularity for which the claimant contends. The decision-maker, it must be recalled, will be provided only with the report of the doctor based upon the doctor's interview with the claimant and the claimant's completion of the questionnaire. It is quite impossible for the decision-maker to identify actual positions of employment or the nature of the duties and location of any job which the claimant might undertake, not least because the decision-maker may often be based in Belfast, or elsewhere, and can have no possible means of discovering employment circumstances throughout the country. The conclusion which requires no more than that the decision-maker or Tribunal assess the range of work of which the claimant is capable for the purposes of assessing risk to health has the merit of achieving the objective of the regulations" (*Charlton*, paras 45-47).

In *PC v SSWP* [2009] UKUT 101 (AAC) Deputy Judge Paines applied *Charlton* to hold that the claimant, who had his alcohol dependence under control, would not by reason of that dependence pose a risk to himself or others in respect of undertaking manual work such as building work. That work, and not clerical work of which he had no experience and to which he would not be suited, constituted the range of work reasonably to have in contemplation. Nor, given a recent absence of falls, was his knee injury serious enough to pose the necessary risk.

In *CIB/3519/2002*, Commissioner Rowland considered that "substantial" in the "old" head (b) as modified did not only refer to the likelihood of the risk occurring:

"a risk may be 'substantial' if the harm would be serious, even though it was unlikely to occur and, conversely, may not be 'substantial' if the harm would be insignificant, even though the likelihood of some such harm is great. Paragraph (b) must be viewed in the light of the other paragraphs of regulation 27 and the general scheme of the Regulations" (para.7).

Commissioner Fellner accepted this as "probably right" in *CIB/2767/2004*, but added that

"his invocation of the other paragraphs of regulation 27 as guides to interpretation suggests that the interpretation should be rather narrow. Under the original as well as the amended form, the other paragraphs refer to more or less factual medical questions—presence of life-threatening or severe uncontrolled or uncontrollable disease, need for an identified major medical procedure within a short time" (para.6).

In *CIB/1064/2006*, Deputy Commissioner Ovey, having considered the authorities noted above, encapsulated her task thus:

"I must consider whether there is evidence that a job of the kind which it is likely the claimant would be required to be available for would result in consequences for his health which, although not necessarily life-threatening, would be substantial having regard to both likelihood of occurrence and degree of harm" (para.20).

Here the claimant had been a chauffeur, a job he had lost because of his dermatitis. The Deputy Commissioner concluded that the evidence before the tribunal was capable of putting the provision in issue. The claimant, to a degree supported by his doctor, stated that his removal from that working environment, in which friction and repeated activities would cause his dermatitis to flare up, had improved matters. Where the Deputy Commissioner parted company with the tribunal was in its failure adequately to explain its confinement of the work the claimant should be measured against to driving (his previous job) and why it thought the risk to the claimant to be "substantial". The tribunal in this way had erred in law and the Deputy Commissioner remitted to matter to another tribunal.

As Commissioner Parker stated in *CSIB/33/2004* (para.40) and reiterated in *CSIB/719/2006* (para. 11).

"the risk must arise from the broad results of a claimant being found capable of work and is not confined to the risks arising directly from the tasks within a claimant's job description. Thus, for example, if a claimant sustains the relevant risk because she has to get up quickly in the morning to go to work, rather than pace herself as would be the situation if no such necessity arose, this is a pertinent factor for consideration. Likewise, [the Secretary of State's representative] accepted that any apprehension sustained by a claimant with mental disablement at the prospect of having to look for work, is pertinent. But there must be a causal link between being 'found capable of work' and an ensuing 'substantial risk to the mental or physical health of any person if [the claimant] were found capable of work'".

Paras (2)(a) and (c): "medical evidence"
The term "medical evidence" embraces (i) evidence from a doctor approved by the Secretary of State (usually a DWPMS doctor), (ii) evidence (if any) from any other doctor, hospital or similar institution, or such part of evidence in (i) or (ii) as constitutes the most reliable evidence available in the circumstances (reg.2(1)). In a Northern Ireland decision *C5/00–01(IB)* Commissioner Brown stated that the evidence "must relate to the claimant himself, it is not constituted by extracts from medical textbooks unless the doctor relates them to the claimant" (para.16).

8.152

Para.(2)(a)(i): "the disease is uncontrollable, or uncontrolled, by a recognised therapeutic procedure"
In *CIB/4506/01*, Commissioner Howell stated that here

"the question is only whether the nature of [the claimant's] condition is such that it is capable of being controlled by medical science, or not. Consequently the tribunal were right in taking account not only of the inhalers and adrenaline injector she is able to use for herself, but also the hospital treatment which unhappily she finds also has to be used on occasions as a means of bringing the condition under control. On the tribunal's findings the claimant's condition is thus controllable in the relevant sense, and their reasons are clearly and adequately given" (para.10).

8.153

The tribunal had not erred in law.

In *CIB/155/2004*, Commissioner Jacobs thought it inappropriate to deploy as a test whether the level of control would suffice to allow the claimant to work; since that test would always be satisfied. Rather, he thought that reg.27 comes into play where a claimant is capable of work but has a condition that makes it inappropriate that he be expected to work. Since, as regards para.(2)(a) what makes that inappropriate is the fact that the condition is a threat to the claimant's life, the threshold for control should be whether the control is sufficient to remove the threat to the claimant's life. In the case at hand, while the evidence disclosed that the claimant's diabetes was poorly controlled, it was nonetheless sufficiently controlled that para.

(2)(a) was inapplicable. While there were longer-term complications to which the Consultant referred, they were not yet present, and not currently threatening the claimant's life.

Para. (2)(b) Meaning of "previously undiagnosed"

8.154   In *R1/04(IB)*, a decision by a Northern Ireland tribunal of Commissioners, it was held that "previously undiagnosed" refers to the diagnosis of a medical practitioner, so that once a condition is diagnosed by such a practitioner, it can no longer be argued that the condition was previously undiagnosed.

Para. (2)(c): "major surgical operation"

8.155   In *CIB/14667/1996*, Commissioner Williams considered the meaning of "major surgical operation". The term is to be given its ordinary meaning rather than a purposive meaning. Subject to two comments, the Commissioner in para.16 accepted as an accurate summary of the position the guidance given in paras 22 and 23 of the *Incapacity Benefit Handbook for Medical Services Doctors* (cited in para.11):

> "22. There is no legal definition of 'major surgical operation' or 'major therapeutic procedure'. Your opinion has to be reasonable and based on the facts of the individual case.
> 23. It is not possible to give a definitive list of 'operations' and 'procedures' which would medically be thought of as major since other circumstances such as the diagnosis, the form of operation and presence of any other related treatments would reasonably need to be considered".

Commissioner Williams commented that, of course, the decision whether a particular procedure or operation qualified was one for the AO (now the Secretary of State) and not the DWPMS doctor, and, moreover that the decision should take into account all the circumstances, including, for example, any other disabilities. In the case before him, the Commissioner held that the arthrolysis performed on a 33-year-old's non-dominant left elbow was not a major surgical operation. In *C22/01–02(IB)*, Commissioner Brown endorsed this approach to the phrase "major surgical operation or other major therapeutic procedure".

Para. (2)(c): the time scale "Within three months"

8.156   In *CIB/1381/2008*, Commissioner Williams expressed concern that the wording of the IB85 report does not deal accurately with the current reg.27(2)(c) but reflects the pre-1997 wording. There is a key difference in terms of the timescale concerning the operation envisaged by that provision. The current text of reg.27 refers to "likely to be carried out within three months" of the PCA medical examination, the IB85 formulation in contrast is that it is to occur within the three month period. The tribunal had also failed to exercise its inquisitorial and enabling function by ignoring reg.27.

[¹ Conditions for treating a person as incapable of work until the personal capability assessment is carried out

8.157   **28.**—(1) Where the question of whether a person is capable or incapable of work falls to be determined in accordance with the personal capability assessment that person shall, if the conditions set out in paragraph (2) are met, be treated as incapable of work in accordance with the personal capability assessment until such time as he has been assessed or he falls to be treated as capable of work in accordance with regulation 7 or 8.]

(2) The conditions are—

(a) that the person provides evidence of his incapacity for work in accordance with the Social Security (Medical Evidence) Regulations 1976 (which prescribe the form of doctor's statement or other evidence required in each case); and

(b) that it has not within the preceding 6 months been determined, in relation to his entitlement to any benefit, allowance or advantage [² which is dependent on him being incapable of work,] that the person is capable of work, or is to be treated as capable of work under regulation 7 or 8, unless—

   (i) he is suffering from some specific disease or bodily or mental disablement which he was not suffering from at the time of that determination; or

  (ii) a disease or bodily or mental disablement which he was suffering from at the time of that determination has significantly worsened; or

 (iii) in the case of a person who was treated as capable of work under regulation 7 (failure to provide information), he has since [³ provided the information requested by the Secretary of State under that regulation.]

AMENDMENTS

1. Social Security (Incapacity for Work) Miscellaneous Amendments Regulations 1999 (SI 1999/3109), reg.3(5) (April 3, 2000).
2. Social Security (Incapacity for Work and Miscellaneous Amendments) Regulations 1996 (SI 1996/3207), reg.2(10) (January 6, 1997).
3. Social Security (Incapacity for Work) Miscellaneous Amendment Regulations 1995 (SI 1995/987), reg.2(10) (April 13, 1995).

DEFINITIONS

"benefit"—see reg.2(1).
"doctor"—see reg.2(1).
"the personal capability assessment"—see regs 2(1) and 24.

GENERAL NOTE

Where the personal capability assessment (formerly the all work test) rather than the own occupation test applies (on which see commentary to SSCBA 1992, ss.171B, 171C(1), above), the test is to be treated as satisfied, enabling benefit to be paid, until completion of the assessment process or until the claimant is treated as capable of work for failing to provide the information required (the questionnaire) for claims purposes (reg.7) or for failing to attend and/or submit to the required medical examination (reg.8) (para.(1)). But the test will be treated as satisfied only where the conditions in para.(2) are met. So it will be treated as satisfied only while the person continues to provide a doctor's statement in accordance with the Medical Evidence Regulations (see below and see further those regulations and the commentary to them), and only if there has been no determination in the last six months that he is capable of work or that he is to be treated as capable of work for such failures to comply with those aspects of the process. If there has been such a determination, however, benefit can still be paid pending assessment if the specific disease or bodily or mental disablement from which he suffered at the time of that earlier determination has significantly worsened or the one(s) he is now suffering from is (are) different; or, if treated as capable because of failure to supply claims information, he has since complied with the Secretary of State's requests. The supply of medical certificates will thus continue to be required to support a claim but the form of them differs from those used to support claims subject to the "own occupation" test.

Useful clarification of the operation of this regulation has been given by Commissioner Rowland in *CIB/3106/2003* and by Commissioner Howells in *R(IB) 8/04*. Where the six month period mentioned has expired, there is no need to make

8.158

a new claim to take advantage of the protection of the regulation. It should be considered by the decision-maker as a change of circumstances (*CIB/3106/2003*, para.5). Moroever, where on a claim for incapacity the decision-maker decides that the claimant cannot be treated as incapable under reg.28 pending assessment, the decision-maker must still arrange a personal capability assessment to determine *actual* incapacity. If the result of that assessment was incapacity for work arrears of benefit will be payable from the date of claim. As explained in *R(IB) 1/01* and *R(IB) 2/01*, the purpose of reg.28 is simply to enable payment of benefit pending assessment and irrespective of the results of that assessment (*ibid.*, para.6). In contrast, where the period of six months since a previous determination has not expired, reg.28 can only come into play where one of the conditions in para.(2)(b)(i)–(iii) are met, for example, that the claimant is suffering from some fresh disease or disablement, or a significant worsening of an existing disease or disablement, since the date of that determination (the determination by the Secretary of State, not the date of a tribunal decision confirming it on appeal) (*R(IB) 8/04*). The opening words of reg.28(1) refer to the necessity to make a determination in respect of each day of claimed incapacity, and so the six month period must thus be run back from each day of the current claim to see if on that day the claimant can benefit from the protection of the regulation. Where such days are not covered by that protection, the decision-maker must nonetheless consider actual incapacity in respect of those days, to be determined by carrying out a personal capability assessment and drawing the appropriate conclusions from it. Where a claim is made for a period that started within six months of a previous adverse determination, but is not decided until after the expiry of that six months period, the further determination must take account of that expiry of the six months period as a change of circumstances

> "so that days of claimed incapacity within the period of the new claim supported by prescribed medical evidence and falling outside the six months are entitled to the protection of regulation 28(1) (even though earlier days were not) until such time as a personal capability assessment has actually been carried out or for some other reason that protection ceases to apply" (*ibid.*, para.8).

Since the regulation only applies until the claimant has been "assessed", it cannot apply where the claimant is immediately assessed (*CIB/1959/1997 and CIB/2198/1997*, paras 28, 29). The words "significantly worsened", as regards the claimant's condition, must be related to the all work test (now the personal capability assessment), so that it will only have significantly worsened if it has done so to an extent that the claimant would satisfy that test of incapacity if he were subjected to it. If there is actual evidence that he would fail to satisfy that test, the Secretary of State can proceed on the basis that the condition has not significantly worsened (*CIB/1959/1997 and CIB/2198/1997*, para.30).

Where a tribunal finds that a case does not come within reg.28, rejecting the claimant's argument that his condition has significantly worsened, it should nonetheless go on to consider whether the claimant satisfied the personal capability assessment (all work test). See *CIB/1031/2000*, paras 12–17.

The "personal capability" certificate (MED 4) provided by the claimant's doctor differs from those previously used, enabling fuller information on the diagnosis of the disorder in respect of which the doctor is advising the claimant to refrain from work or which is causing his absence from work and any other condition which could affect his capacity for work (see further Medical Evidence Regulations, Sch.1B). The diagnosis should be specified as precisely as possible, unless the doctor is of opinion that a disclosure to the claimant of the precise disorder would be prejudicial to the patient's well being, in which case it can be less precise. There is also space for the doctor's remarks on the disabling effects of the condition, treatment and progress, and doctors are advised on the form that accurate and detailed completion will avoid requests for completion of a medical report. A doctor could thus, for example, if dealing with a condition which has variable effects, describe how it varies and affects his patient. There is also a section (which will not form part of the personal capability assessment) in which the doctor is asked to state whether or not the patient should refrain from his usual occupation. This will be the requisite evidence for maintenance of his claim pending completion of the personal capability assessment. Doctors can include additional information, but will not be obliged to read, or to comment on, the claimant's information in the questionnaire. Nor will they be asked to provide an opinion on capacity for work. Although from the terms of regs 6–8 and this regulation, the provision of a MED 4 appears essential to support a claim, failure to supply one does not prevent the Secretary of State from subjecting the claimant to a personal capability assessment medical examination and making a decision in the light of that, and any other evidence, on whether the claimant is, or is not, incapable of work (*R(IB) 5/98*, especially paras 10–16, followed and approved in *CIB/17533/96*, App.I and in *CIB/16603/96*).

On "specific disease or bodily or mental disablement", see commentary to SSCBA 1992, s.171B(2), above.

Although this regulation is generally forward looking, medical evidence looking to a past period, can be taken into account, provided that it was available at the date of the decision which is under appeal to the appeal tribunal: see Commissioner Mesher in *CIS/2699/2001*.

A tribunal must address, and give reasons for accepting or rejecting, any argument that it ought not to rely on a DWPMS doctor's report because the examination was not conducted properly. A short examination is not necessarily improper, it may, in the circumstances, be all that was warranted (*CIB/908/2003*). But in *CSIB/69/03*, a case raising mental health descriptors, Commissioner Parker was critical of the duration of the examination, the failure to put relevant questions to the claimant's mother who attended the examination, and of the nature of the medical report. The Commissioner was unable to accept the report as sufficiently reliable to demonstrate that the Secretary of State had discharged the onus of proof to show that reg.28 (deeming incapable pending a personal capability assessment) no longer applied (para.36).

SCHEDULE   Regulations 6(1) (b), 24

DISABILITIES WHICH MAY MAKE A PERSON INCAPABLE OF WORK

PART I

PHYSICAL DISABILITIES

8.159

(1) *Activity*		(2) *Descriptor*	(3) *Points*
1. Walking on level ground with a walking stick or other aid if such aid is normally used.	1(a)	Cannot walk at all.	15
	(b)	Cannot walk more than a few steps without stopping or severe discomfort.	15
	(c)	Cannot walk more than 50 metres without stopping or severe discomfort.	15
	(d)	Cannot walk more than 200 metres without stopping or severe discomfort.	7
	(e)	Cannot walk more than 400 metres without stopping or severe discomfort.	3
	(f)	Cannot walk more than 800 metres without stopping or severe discomfort.	0
	(g)	No walking problem.	0
2. Walking up and down stairs.	2(a)	Cannot walk up and down one stair.	15
	(b)	Cannot walk up and down a flight of 12 stairs.	15

PHYSICAL DISABILITIES

(1) *Activity*		(2) *Descriptor*	(3) *Points*
	(c)	Cannot walk up and down a flight of 12 stairs without holding on and taking a rest.	7
	(d)	Cannot walk up and down a flight of 12 stairs without holding on.	3
	(e)	Can only walk up and down a flight of 12 stairs if he goes sideways or one step at a time.	3
	(f)	No problem in walking up and down stairs.	0
3. Sitting in an upright chair with a back, but no arms.	3(a)	Cannot sit comfortably.	15
	(b)	Cannot sit comfortably for more than 10 minutes without having to move from the chair [1 because the degree of discomfort makes it impossible to continue sitting.]	15
	(c)	Cannot sit comfortably for more than 30 minutes without having to move from the chair [1 because the degree of discomfort makes it impossible to continue sitting.]	7
	(d)	Cannot sit comfortably for more than 1 hour without having to move from the chair [1 because the degree of discomfort makes it impossible to continue sitting.]	3
	(e)	Cannot sit comfortably for more than 2 hours without having to move from the chair [1 because the degree of discomfort makes it impossible to continue sitting.	0
	(f)	No problem with sitting.	0
4. Standing without the support of another person or the use of an aid except a walking stick.	4(a)	Cannot stand unassisted.	15
	(b)	Cannot stand for more than a minute before needing to sit down	15
	(c)	Cannot stand for more than 10 minutes before needing to sit down.	15
	(d)	Cannot stand for more than 30 minutes before needing to sit down.	7
	(e)	Cannot stand for more than 10 minutes before needing to move around.	7
	(f)	Cannot stand for more than 30 minutes before needing to move around.	3
	(g)	No problem standing.	0
5. Rising from sitting in an upright chair with a back but no arms without the help of another person.	5(a)	Cannot rise from sitting to standing.	15
	(b)	Cannot rise from sitting to standing without holding on to something.	7
	(c)	Sometimes cannot rise from sitting to standing without holding on to something.	3
	(d)	No problem with rising from sitting to standing.	0
6. Bending and kneeling.	6(a)	Cannot bend to touch his knees and straighten up again.	15
	(b)	Cannot [2 either, bend or kneel, or bend and kneel] as if to pick up a	15

PHYSICAL DISABILITIES

(1) Activity		(2) Descriptor	(3) Points
		piece of paper from the floor and straighten up again.	
	(c)	Sometimes cannot [² either, bend or kneel, or bend and kneel] as if to pick up a piece of paper from the floor and straighten up again.	3
	(d)	No problem with bending or kneeling.	0
7. Manual dexterity.	7(a)	Cannot turn the pages of a book with either hand.	15
	(b)	[³ Cannot turn a sink tap or the control knobs on a cooker with either hand.]	15
	(c)	Cannot pick up a coin which is 2.5 centimetres or less in diameter with either hand.	15
	(d)	Cannot use a pen or pencil.	15
	(e)	Cannot tie a bow in laces or string	10
	(f)	[³ Cannot turn a sink tap or the control knobs on a cooker with one hand, but can with the other.]	6
	(g)	Cannot pick up a coin which is 2.5 centimetres or less in diameter with one hand, [³ but can with the other.]	6
	(h)	No problem with manual dexterity	0
8. Lifting and [⁴ carrying by the use of the upper body and arms (excluding all other activities specified in Part I of this schedule).]	8(a)	Cannot pick up a paper-back book with either hand.	15
	(b)	Cannot pick up and carry a 0.5 litre carton of milk with either hand.	15
	(c)	Cannot pick up and pour from a full saucepan or kettle of 1.7 litre capacity with either hand.	15
	(d)	Cannot pick up and carry a 2.5 kilogramme bag of potatoes with either hand.	8
	(e)	Cannot pick up and carry a 0.5 litre carton of milk with one hand, [⁵ but can with the other.]	6
	(f)	Cannot pick up and carry a 2.5 kilo-gramme bag of potatoes with one hand, [⁵ but can with the other.]	0
	(g)	No problem with lifting and carrying	0
9. Reaching.	(a)	Cannot raise either arm [⁶ as if] to put something in the top pocket of a coat or jacket.	15
	(b)	Cannot raise either arm to his head [⁶ as if] to put on a hat.	15
	(c)	Cannot put either arm behind back [⁶ as if] to put on a coat or jacket.	15
	(d)	Cannot raise either arm above his head [⁶ as if] to reach for something.	15
	(e)	Cannot raise one arm to his head [⁶ as if] to put on a hat, but can with the other.	6
	(f)	Cannot raise one arm above his head [⁶ as if] to reach for something, but can with the other.	0
	(g)	No problem with reaching.	0

Social Security (Incapacity for Work) (General) Regulations 1995

PHYSICAL DISABILITIES

(1) Activity		(2) Descriptor	(3) Points
10. Speech.	10(a)	Cannot speak.	15
	(b)	Speech cannot be understood by family or friends.	15
	(c)	Speech cannot be understood by strangers.	15
	(d)	Strangers have great difficulty understanding speech.	10
	(e)	Strangers have some difficulty understanding speech.	8
	(f)	No problems with speech.	0
11. Hearing with a hearing aid or other aid if normally worn.	11(a)	Cannot hear sounds at all.	15
	(b)	Cannot hear well enough to follow a television programme with the volume turned up.	15
	(c)	Cannot hear well enough to understand someone talking in a loud voice in a quiet room.	15
	(d)	Cannot hear well enough to understand someone talking in a normal voice in a quiet room.	10
	(e)	Cannot hear well enough to understand someone talking in a normal voice on a busy street.	8
	(f)	No problem with hearing.	0
12. Vision in normal daylight or bright electric light with glasses or other aid to vision if such aid is normally worn.	12(a)	Cannot tell light from dark.	15
	(b)	Cannot see the shape of furniture in the room.	15
	(c)	Cannot see well enough to read 16 point print at a distance greater than 20 centimetres.	15
	(d)	Cannot see well enough to recognise a friend across the room [7 at a distance of at least 5 metres.]	12
	(e)	Cannot see well enough to recognise a friend across the road [7 at a distance of at least 15 metres.]	8
	(f)	No problem with vision.	0
13. Continence [8 (other than enuresis (bed wetting)).]	13(a)	No voluntary control over bowels.	15
	(b)	No voluntary control over bladder.	15
	(c)	Loses control of bowels at least once a week.	15
	(d)	Loses control of bowels at least once a month.	15
	(e)	Loses control of bowels occasionally.	9
	(f)	Loses control of bladder at least once a month.	3
	(g)	Loses control of bladder occasionally.	0
	(h)	No problem with continence.	0
14. Remaining conscious [9 without having epileptic or similar seizures during waking moments.]	14(a)	Has an involuntary episode of lost or altered consciousness at least once a day.	15
	(b)	Has an involuntary episode of lost or altered consciousness at least once a week.	15
	(c)	Has an involuntary episode of lost or altered consciousness at least once a month.	15
	(d)	Has had an involuntary episode of lost or altered consciousness at least	12

twice in the 6 months before the day
in respect to which it falls to be
determined whether he is incapable of
work for the purposes of entitlement
to any benefit, allowance or advantage.

(e)	Has had an involuntary episode of lost or altered consciousness once in the 6 months before the day in respect to which it falls to be determined whether he is incapable of work for the purposes of entitlement to any benefit, allowance or advantage.	8
(f)	Has had an involuntary episode of lost or altered consciousness once in the 3 years before the day in respect to which it falls to be determined whether he is incapable of work for the purposes of entitlement to any benefit, allowance or advantage.	0
(g)	Has no problems with consciousness.	0

PART II

MENTAL DISABILITIES

(1) Activity		*(2)* Descriptor	*(3)* Points
15. Completion of tasks.	15(a)	Cannot answer the telephone and reliably take a message.	2
	(b)	Often sits for hours doing nothing.	2
	(c)	Cannot concentrate to read a magazine article or follow a radio [¹⁰ or television] programme.	1
	(d)	Cannot use a telephone book or other directory to find a number.	1
	(e)	Mental condition prevents him from undertaking leisure activities previously enjoyed.	1
	(f)	Overlooks or forgets the risk posed by domestic appliances or other common hazards due to poor concentration.	1
	(g)	Agitation, confusion or forgetfulness has resulted in [¹¹ potentially dangerous] accidents in the 3 months before the day in respect to which it falls to be determined whether he is in incapable of work for the purposes of entitlement to any benefit, allowance or advantage.	1
	(h)	Concentration can only be sustained by prompting.	1
16. Daily living.	16(a)	Needs encouragement to get up and dress.	2
	(b)	Needs alcohol before midday.	2
	(c)	Is frequently distressed at some time of the day due to fluctuation of mood.	1
	(d)	Does not care about his appearance and living conditions.	1
	(e)	Sleep problems interfere with his daytime activities.	1

MENTAL DISABILITIES

(1) Activity		(2) Descriptor	(3) Points
17. Coping with pressure.	17(a)	Mental stress was a factor in making him stop work.	2
	(b)	Frequently feels scared or panicky for no obvious reason.	2
	(c)	Avoids carrying out routine activities because he is convinced they will prove too tiring or stressful.	1
	(d)	Is unable to cope with changes in daily routine.	1
	(e)	Frequently finds there are so many things to do that he gives up because of fatigue, apathy or disinterest.	1
	(f)	Is scared or anxious that work would bring back or worsen his illness.	1
18. Interaction with other people.	18(a)	Cannot look after himself without help from others.	2
	(b)	Gets upset by ordinary events and it results in disruptive behavioural problems.	2
	(c)	Mental problems impair ability to communicate with other people.	2
	(d)	Gets irritated by things that would not have bothered him before he became ill.	1
	(e)	Prefers to be left alone for 6 hours or more each day.	1
	(f)	Is too frightened to go out alone.	1

AMENDMENTS

1. Social Security (Incapacity for Work and Miscellaneous Amendments) Regulations 1996 (SI 1996/3207), reg.2(11)(b)(i) (January 6, 1997).

2. Social Security (Incapacity for Work and Miscellaneous Amendments) Regulations 1996 (SI 1996/3207), reg.2(11)(b)(ii) (January 6, 1997).

3. Social Security (Incapacity for Work and Miscellaneous Amendments) Regulations 1996 (SI 1996/3207), reg.2(11)(b)(iii) (January 6, 1997).

4. Social Security (Incapacity for Work and Miscellaneous Amendments) Regulations 1996 (SI 1996/3207), reg.2(11)(a)(i) (January 6, 1997).

5. Social Security (Incapacity for Work and Miscellaneous Amendments) Regulations 1996 (SI 1996/3207), reg.2(11)(b)(iv) (January 6, 1997).

6. Social Security (Incapacity for Work and Miscellaneous Amendments) Regulations 1996 (SI 1996/3207), reg.2(11)(b)(v) (January 6, 1997).

7. Social Security (Incapacity for Work and Miscellaneous Amendments) Regulations 1996 (SI 1996/3207), reg.2(11)(b)(vi) (January 6, 1997).

8. Social Security (Incapacity for Work and Miscellaneous Amendments) Regulations 1996 (SI 1996/3207), reg.2(11)(a)(ii) (January 6, 1997).

9. Social Security (Incapacity for Work and Miscellaneous Amendments) Regulations 1996 (SI 1996/3207), reg.2(11)(a)(iii) (January 6, 1997).

10. Social Security (Incapacity for Work and Miscellaneous Amendments) Regulations 1996 (SI 1996/3207), reg.2(11)(c)(i) (January 6, 1997).

11. Social Security (Incapacity for Work and Miscellaneous Amendments) Regulations 1996 (SI 1996/3207), reg.2(11)(c)(ii) (January 6, 1997).

GENERAL NOTE

I. The "personal capability assessment"

The "personal capability assessment" (the new name for the "all work" test) **8.160**
is a test of the extent of the claimant's incapacity, because he has some specific
disease or bodily or mental disablement, to perform the activities prescribed in
this Sch., entitled "disabilities which may make a person incapable of work"
(reg.24). The first (and longer) Part of this Schedule deals with physical disabilities, the second Part with mental disabilities. Whether one (or both) applies
(apply) to a particular case turns on the nature of the medical diagnosis with
respect to the particular claimant and the types of effect it has. This has been
abundantly clear since reg.25(3) was inserted, with effect from January 6, 1997,
by reg.2(7)(b) of the Social Security (Incapacity for Work and Miscellaneous
Amendments) Regulations 1996 (SI 1996/3207). Reg.25(3) stipulates that one
can determine the extent of a person's incapacity to perform an activity listed in
Pt I of the Schedule (physical disabilities) only where his incapacity arises from
a specific *bodily* disease or disablement. Similarly, the extent of his incapacity
to perform any activity listed in Pt II of the Schedule (mental disabilities) can
only be determined if that incapacity arises from some specific *mental* illness or
disablement. So that the proposition that issues under Pt II of the Schedule are
raised by a diagnosis in which a physical disease or disability produces related
psychological problems which are more than *de minimis*, can now only hold good
if those psychological problems can themselves be characterised as a specific
mental illness or disablement, a matter in practical terms turning on medical evidence and diagnosis. This Schedule lists in col.(1) a number of activities or functional areas of body or mind thought relevant to incapacity for work, for example,
walking (on level ground and up and down stairs) (Pt I, paras 1, 2), sitting (Pt
I, para.3), standing (Pt I, para.4), manual dexterity (Pt I, para.7), completion
of tasks (Pt II, para.15), coping with pressure (Pt II, para.17), interacting with
people (Pt II, para.18). In respect of each activity or functional area, the Schedule
lists in col.(2) a number of descriptors (said to be "clearly worded statements
of disability ranked according to their incapacitating effect in each functional
area"—DSS/Benefits Agency, *The medical assessment for incapacity benefit* (HMSO,
1994), p.4) to each of which is attached a score in terms of a number of points,
ranging from zero to fifteen. Essentially someone satisfies the "personal capability
assessment" (all work test) when one or more of the descriptors applies to him
and, adding up the points attached to them (with some limitations on counting
set by reg.26), he achieves a total score of at least 15 points if only physical disability descriptors apply, of 10 points if mental disability descriptors alone are
relevant, or of 15 points if descriptors of both types are applicable (reg.25). These
total scores are the threshold for incapacity for work under the functional "personal capability assessment" (all work test).

So, the first task is to decide from all the evidence (see further commentary to
reg.24, above) which descriptors apply, the second to calculate the scores. These
matters are fully explored in the commentary to regs 24–26, above.

Generally, the descriptors are clear. Some are very specific (e.g. the diameter of
the coin for purposes of manual dexterity descriptor 7(c); the weight of the bag of
potatoes for purposes of lifting and carrying descriptor 8(f)). Others are more vague.
For example, one might ask how big is the paperback book for purposes of lifting
and carrying descriptor 8(a). Presumably the answer is the average paperback, rather
than this physically weighty tome or the complete works of Shakespeare. Yet others
import measures of judgment. For example, "comfortably" in sitting descriptors
3(a)–(e), or "severe discomfort" in walking on level ground descriptor 1(b)–(f).
Some of the speech ones are such as to enable an Appeal Tribunal to appraise the
claimant who appears before them merely from part of the usual activities or course
of proceedings at a tribunal hearing (e.g. descriptor 10(e), "strangers have some difficulty understanding speech").

8.161   *An Important Note on Amendments and Possible Invalidity*: Some activities and some descriptors have undergone important changes in wording—reg.2(11) of the Social Security (Incapacity for Work and Miscellaneous Amendments) Regulations 1996 (SI 1996/3207) effected a variety of changes with effect from January 6, 1997 (which changes have been incorporated in the text above). However, in *Howker* v *Secretary of State* ([2002] EWCA Civ 1623, reported as *R(IB) 3/03*), noted more fully in the commentary to reg.27, above, the Court of Appeal invalidated, for failure to follow the correct procedure, the deletion of "old" head (b) from that regulation, which that set of amending regulations had purported to effect, because the Department had misled the SSAC on the effect of the change, wrongly describing it as "neutral" whereas its potential effect was "adverse" to claimants. The Court of Appeal held that the 'old' head (b) remained in existence alongside the replacement provision. Whether that ruling could extend to other changes effected by those amending regulations in circumstances where the SSAC had been misled as to the effect of the change, generated a variety of responses and disagreement between Commissioners—particularly Commissioners Jacobs and May—on the proper approach. The conflict of authorities has now been resolved by a Tribunal of Commissioners (*R(IB)2/07*) endorsing that of Commissioner May in *CSIB/0148/2005* and *CSIB/196/2005* and rejecting that taken by Commissioner Jacobs in *R(IB)3/04*.

In *R(IB)3/04*, Commissioner Jacobs held, and the Secretary of State's representative accepted, that while in terms the decision in *Howker* was limited to reg.27(b), the court's reasoning could apply to other amendments (para.6). He decided that improper procedure in securing the amendment to Activity 14 rendered it "of no force or effect", so that the claimant's capacity for work had to be determined under the terms of Activity 14 as originally enacted (para.12). Other amendments were not in issue in the case, but Commissioner Jacobs stated that tribunals dealing with cases involving them

> "will have to decide whether they are covered by the reasoning in *Howker*, which I have applied in this decision. Mr Lewis [the Secretary of State's representative] told me that all those amendments were described to the Social Security Advisory Committee as 'neutral' in their potential effect on claimants. The issue for tribunals will be whether that was an accurate description. It would, no doubt, be helpful to claimants and tribunals if the Secretary of State were to take a realistic view on the other amendments in the guidance issued to decision-makers and in the submissions made to appeal tribunals and Commissioners. But that is not a matter for me" (paras 12, 13).

Applying *Howker* in respect of the changes made by the 1996 Regulations has not proved an easy task, and has evoked a variety of responses. In *CIB/1239/2004*, Commissioner Henty followed *Howker* and Commissioner Jacobs in *CIB/884/2003* (now reported as *R(IB) 3/04*) to hold invalid the 1996 amendments to Activity 3 (sitting in an upright chair with a back but no arms). However, in *CIB/3397/2004*, Commissioner Jupp expressly disagreed with Commissioner Henty and held that the 1996 amendments to Activity 3 were not *ultra vires*—the amendment was correctly advised to the SSAC as neutral, adding only clarification—so that the tribunal to which she remitted the case would not need to disregard the wording added by the 1996 Regulations (see paras 25 and 26). In *CIB/2821/2004*, Deputy Commissioner Gamble held that the 1996 amendment to descriptor 15(c) was invalid, applying the *Howker* principle, so that the new tribunal should apply the unamended text of that descriptor (para.9). Both Commissioner Gamble in that case (para.8) and Commissioner Jupp in *CIB/3397/2004*, paras 11–20, held that the changes effected to Activity 8 (lifting and carrying) were neutral and accordingly valid.

In *R(IB) 5/05*, Commissioner Parker held that where the Secretary of State wrongly applied the personal capability assessment by reference to the form of words as amended by the regulations considered in *Howker*, this does not invalidate the whole process and can be corrected by a tribunal applying the original version of the Schedule:

"What the tribunal quintessentially did in the present appeal was to determine questions fully within 'the scope of that which the officer below could have done on the proper legal view of the issues before him'.

In particular, I am unable to accept Mr Orr's submission that, because the PCA assessment is a creature of statute, any deviation from that statutory basis means that there is no connection whatsoever to legal powers: with the result that no decision, whether under s.10 of the Social Security Act 1998 or otherwise, arises. Howker did not strike down either the whole PCA assessment as set out in the amended 1995 regulations nor even all of the purported changes made by the 1996 regulations. In effect, the Court of Appeal left the question of when the original text remained the valid version to be decided on a case by case basis. I therefore agree with the Secretary of State that there is no error of law in the tribunal's approach to the effect of Howker. On the contrary, I commend the tribunal for its analysis" (paras 31, 32).

In *CIB/3649/2004*, Commissioner Jupp held that the tribunal had erred in law in not considering the issue of invalidity of the 1997 changes, but that the outcome to the case could not have been affected since the changes to the relevant Activity 7 descriptors were not invalid, having correctly been described to the SSAC as neutral in effect. **8.162**

In *CSID/0148/2005*, however, Commissioner May disagreed with the approach adopted by Commissioner Jacobs in paras 8 and 11 of his decision in *R(IB) 3/04*, Commissioner May thought, therefore, that the approaches by the other Commissioners noted in the annotation were flawed and in error. He considered Commissioner Jacob's paraphrase of the Court of Appeal in *Howker* to be incorrect. Commissioner May saw *Howker* as limited to reg.27 and that the defective procedure in that case went beyond a statement that the impact of the changes was neutral. Accordingly, Commissioner May sought to apply this view of the Court of Appeal's reasoning to the 1997 changes to Activity 14.

Commissioner May reiterated and applied his approach in *CSIB/196/2005*, upholding as valid amendments to reg.10(2)(e)(viii), Activity 13, and descriptors 3(b), 6(b), and 8(b) and (c). His approach has also been endorsed by Commissioner Rowland in *CIB/1205/2005*. He was not prepared, however, to hold that *R(IB) 3/04* was wrongly decided (para.12).

In their decision on two appeals heard jointly, a Tribunal of Commissioners (Commissioner Rowland, Commissioner Parker and Deputy Commissioner Sir Crispin Agnew of Lochnaw BT Q.C.) has in *R(IB) 2/07* resolved the conflict of authorities. To hold invalid on *Howker* procedural impropriety grounds any of the January 1997 changes to the Incapacity for Work regulations, it must be established both that the Department's presentation to the SSAC of the change in question as neutral was inaccurate and that the SSAC was misled by that characterisation into not requiring the change to be the subject of a formal reference to it.

"In practice, we suggest, a party seeking to show that a regulation is invalid on the grounds that the Committee was given misleading information must show both that there is a real possibility that the information might have misled the Committee as to the effect that the proposed regulation would have and that there is a real possibility that, had the Committee been aware of its true effect, it would have wished to have the proposed regulation formally referred to it" (para.37).

This will require examination of all of the material placed before the SSAC to consider whether the overall effect was misleading since only then will the Secretary of State be in breach of his duty under section 170(4) of the Social Security Administration Act 1992 to provide information to enable the Committee properly to carry out its functions so that there was [as in *Howker*] no "informed agreement" by the SSAC not to require a formal reference of the proposed change (para.35). It is not enough merely to consider whether applying the label "neutral" to the change was correct, since sometimes an incorrect application may have negligible impact because the further description of the change in explanatory material makes its effect sufficiently clear (para.35).

The matters of validity and the proper construction of the proposed change are intertwined, since something that might be invalid on one construction might on another albeit strained construction be found valid, and wherever possible "a provision should be construed so that it is valid" (para.38).

With respect to the change in wording to Activity 14, the Tribunal of Commissioners found that the SSAC was not misled. The Commissioners stressed that although an omission to mention other possible cases that might be affected may have a misleading effect, care had to be taken before finding that the SSAC was misled. Members of the Committee have considerable expertise. They are neither naive nor passive. They will probably have done preparatory work before a meeting and so have a broad understanding of the context in which new regulations are proposed, and are likely to understand the significance of most proposed regulations notwithstanding minor inaccuracies or omissions in the information provided (para.51). If in doubt they can and are likely to ask questions (ibid.).

Applying this to the changes to Activity 14, the Tribunal of Commissioners considered the situation clearly distinguishable from that in *Howker*. There was in that case a clear misrepresentation of the difference between the old regulation and the proposed new one, only discoverable by careful study of them side by side, something which the commentary accompanying the proposed text implied was not necessary. The case before the Tribunal of Commissioners was different:

> "What is important in this instance is that, from the terms of the draft amendment itself and from the commentary, the Committee could see for themselves that only those who suffered from seizures would be within the scope of Activity 14 when the amendment came into force. The commentary was plainly not intended to be a detailed policy document dealing with all possible issues and it had to be read with the draft regulation. When the two documents are read together, it is impossible to say that the Secretary of State misled the Committee or was in breach of his duty to furnish the Committee with such information as it might reasonably require, provided that the word "seizures" was not intended to be understood only in its technical sense. The point that there might be some people who would suffer from a condition causing them to lose consciousness without experiencing a seizure and that those people would be excluded from the scope of Activity 14 was implicit in the material before the Committee and members could have asked about it had they wished. If they overlooked the point, that was not, in our judgment, because they were misled by the information in the commentary.
>
> . . . Here, the fact that people who did not suffer seizures were to be omitted from the scope of the amended Activity 14 was abundantly clear from the material provided to the Committee as was the fact that there were at least different views as to whether such people were anyway outside the scope of the original version" (paras.52, 53).

8.163   *Howker inapplicable to Northern Ireland:* In *C13/03–04(IB)(T)* a Tribunal of Northern Ireland Commissioners considered whether *Howker* applied in Northern Ireland. It was common ground between the parties that decisions of the Court of Appeal in England and Wales do not bind courts and tribunals in Northern Ireland. Moreover, nor could the reasoning of the Court of Appeal in the *Howker* case be directly applicable in Northern Ireland, since the statutory procedure for amending the 1995 Northern Ireland regulations was different from that required to amend the Great Britain Regulations. The idea of the legislative scheme was that the Northern Ireland Regulations should match those in Great Britain. The time to judge whether they did so was at the time the Northern Ireland Regulations were made and correspondence then could not be altered by any subsequent finding of invalidity of the Great Britain Regulations. The relevant statutory provisions in Northern Ireland (s.149 and para.10 of Sch.5 to the Social Security Administration (Northern Ireland) Act 1992) did not

"require those responsible in Northern Ireland to carry out an investigation as to whether the statutory machinery in Great Britain has been complied with. Indeed, neither the subsection nor the paragraph say anything at all about such machinery. Paragraph 10 simply refers to 'regulations made by the Secretary of State or the Lord Chancellor in relation to Great Britain'. Nor do we think that an investigation must be undertaken into a possibility of legal challenge to the Great Britain regulations. It would, we consider, be both unrealistic and pointless to do so. All the more so given that any challenge would be a matter for either the courts of England and Wales or the courts in Scotland but not those in Northern Ireland" (para.34).

The Northern Ireland Department of Social Development could not become party in any such challenges.

A Note on Attention to Detail: As is clear from *CSIB/12/96*, decision-makers must pay very close attention to the precise wording of the activities and descriptors and to the matter of appropriate evidence to ground their findings.   **8.164**

II. Order of treatment in this annotation
In the nature of things, this is a lengthy annotation to a Schedule which lies at the heart of determining the key question whether a claimant for a variety of social security benefits (other than SSP and industrial injuries benefits) is capable or incapable of work where the appropriate test for his claim is the "personal capability assessment" (the new name for the "all work" test). Treatment of the issues and the pertinent and burgeoning case law is sub-divided as follows: **8.165**

[A] Approaching interpretation of the Schedule as a whole: some general points of concern

[B] Some specific matters on dealing with Pt II of the Schedule: mental disabilities

[C] Making and recording decisions

[D] Case law on specific activities/descriptors: Pt I: physical disabilities

[E] Case law on specific activities/descriptors: Pt II: mental disabilities.

[A] Approaching interpretation of the Schedule as a whole: some general points of concern

This part examines a range of general issues:

(i)   the concept "reasonable regularity";

(ii) the (lack of) relevance of the "working situation";

(iii) the effect of pain and discomfort, and of fears for the claimant's health;

(iv) the relevance of medical advice to refrain from activities; and

(v)   the vexed issue of applying the test of incapacity to those suffering from variable, sporadic and intermittent conditions with consequent loss of earning capacity.

When applying the principles to a particular case, it should be remembered that an Appeal Tribunal has an inquisitorial role (*CIB/14442/96*). It should be cautious about exercising that role when considering mental disablement (*CIB/14202/1996*, see head [B] below). Where the claimant is represented by a competent adviser (e.g. a Welfare Rights officer employed by a "responsible" local authority), a tribunal is entitled to proceed on the basis that the representative will put forward all relevant points on his client's behalf and to know the case that is being made for the client. The tribunal in such a case should not be expected to inquire further into the claimant's case; to require that would be to place an impossible administrative burden on tribunals (*CSIB/389/1998*).

Overall, the tribunal's task is rendered easier now in that, in most circumstances, because of the SSA 1998, the focus is on matters as at the date of the Secretary of State's decision rather than covering matters in the often lengthy period down to the date of the hearing (see further *Vol. III: Administration, Appeals and the European Dimension*).

In *CIB/4406/00*, Commissioner Fellner considered the case of

"a claimant who although, except when having an allergy attack, had no or few physical difficulties which would score points on the All Work Test, nonetheless claimed that this was because she carefully monitored the environments into which she ventured, something she would be unable to do if required to return to work" (para.2).

Commissioner Fellner directed the tribunal to have regard to points A(i)–(v), above, "particularly the effects of pain and discomfort (with which *CIB/14722/96(T)* equates dizziness and nausea), a claimant's fear of, or medical advice to refrain from, doing particular activities, and variable or intermittent conditions" (para.19). But she added the following cautionary riders—about proper evidence of points—to this part of the commentary:

"I have no difficulty in accepting that, to paraphrase the authorities there set out, the effects of pain or fatigue or dizziness or nausea on the performance of the All Work Test activities must be taken into account. So must the effect of a claimant's fear of performing them, though I think a tribunal is entitled to require fairly stringent proof of what it is a claimant fears and that this fear is reasonably-founded. If it is not, we may be in the realm of mental health. Medical or other therapeutic advice not to do certain things such as lifting must be considered, though again I think something more than a claimant's unsupported assertion would be desirable. Variable or intermittent conditions require an overall view to be taken, unless there are reasonably clearly definable periods of illness and remission—e.g. where a claimant has regular steroid injections which help for part of the time in between but wear off before the next one is due. Activities must be capable of being performed with reasonable regularity—"most of the time" and "normally" are expressions that have been used, and the activity must be capable of repetition within a reasonable time. *CIB/14587/96* suggested that the Test would not be satisfied if a person, having once done something, could not repeat it for hours or days thereafter. I would agree with this, as it takes into account the fact that in ordinary life one does not repeatedly walk up and down the stairs or write shopping lists or lift and carry bags of potatoes or hang out the washing. (But common sense must always prevail, and lifting a kettle to fill it and then again to pour from it, or taking a carton of milk from the refrigerator and replacing it will in the nature of things require repetition within a short space of time.)

28. But most of these authorities, not surprisingly, refer to and concentrate on *activities*, as Miss Rayner pointed out, and not on the environment in which those activities are to be performed. *CIB/4381/99* held that the All Work Test depends wholly on the fulfilment or otherwise of the prescribed descriptors, and that a person who had lost the sight in one eye and was afraid that working would risk losing it in the other could not, even if there had been medical evidence supporting such risk, pass the Test so long as he still had unimpaired vision in one eye. It could be argued that since the present appellant said she was having fewer attacks than previously because she had learnt what environments to avoid, her correct course of action was to make herself available for work but insist on a jobseeker's

agreement tailored to ensure that she was not exposed to the trigger factors she had identified—e.g. a no-smoking workplace and one where she would not be exposed to chemicals or anything else which might place her at risk. She would then have to take her chance with jobseekers allowance, and if she became ill again, reapply for benefit on grounds of incapacity. One cannot overlook that the original regulation 27(b) was doubtless revoked because it was considered that decision makers were applying it too generously.

29. However, I narrowly persuade myself that the logic of Miss Rayner's acceptance (as I understand it and I hope I have not traduced her) of the permissibility of postulating a normal everyday environment not adapted to a particular claimant but then looking at what reasonable precautions a particular claimant would have to take in such an environment leads to the conclusion that, *subject always to satisfactory evidence*, the type of condition the present appellant claims would be capable in principle of satisfying the All Work Test. I think this situation can be distinguished from *CIB/4381/99*, where the claimant's sight would have been no more at risk in a working environment than in any other. I stress that this is the type of situation where convincing and specific medical evidence would be required, in addition to what a claimant says, and that such evidence should be produced at the outset. If a fear of triggering allergies is asserted, medical evidence should support its reasonableness."

(i) "Reasonable regularity": Some descriptors use the words "can" or "cannot". An **8.166** inappropriate approach, taken by some presenting officers, is almost to construe this literally, so that if someone "can" do something on one occasion (e.g. walk up and down a flight of stairs without holding on—para.2(d)), any descriptor phrased "cannot" is inapplicable. That approach is inappropriate, in the first place because the "all work" test (now re-named "personal capability assessment") was never designed to be a simple "snapshot" but an assessment of the claimant's condition and its variations over a period, taking due account of pain and fatigue. Hence the questionnaire asks about variability, the claimant's own doctor can include material on this in the MED 4 and DWPMS doctors were to be trained with these issues in mind. In the Northern Ireland decision *C1/95(IB)* (noted in (1966) 3 J.S.S.L. D176–177), Chief Commissioner Chambers endorsed using a concept of "reasonable regularity". While the case is only of persuasive authority in the British system, Commissioners on this side of the water have approved and developed it. Chief Commissioner Chambers stated:

"I agree that, apart from those few descriptors in which the word 'sometimes' appears there is no specific requirement that a claimant must be able to perform the activity in question 'with reasonable regularity'. Nevertheless, a SSAT must in my opinion have regard to some such concept in reaching their decision. The real issue is whether, taking an overall view of the individual's capacity to perform the activity in question, he should reasonably be considered to be incapable of performing it. The fact that he might occasionally accomplish it, would be of no consequence if, for most of the time, and in most circumstances, he could not do so. I consider, moreover, that this approach is broadly supported by the inclusion in a small number of the descriptors of the word 'sometimes'. The effect of the inclusion of this word is that, whereas in most cases a claimant who could perform the activity 'most of the time' but who sometimes was unable to do so, would normally not score any points, where these few descriptors are concerned he qualifies for a modest score. Accordingly, as I see it, there must be a 'reasonableness' in the approach of the SSAT to the question of what a person is or is not capable of doing, and this may include consideration of his ability to perform the various specified activities most of the time. To that extent 'reasonable regularity' may properly be considered."

This approach was supported by Commissioner Walker in *CSIB/17/96*; dealing with ability to use a pen or pencil, he stated:

"On the question of the use of a pen I regard the tribunal's approach as faulty. That an individual managed to complete a form does not necessarily and simply mean, as the tribunal seemed to have concluded, that a pen or pencil could be used. Applying the Northern Ireland Chief Commissioner's approach, that has to be determined in the light of reasonableness and some regularity. The evidence before the tribunal was that the claimant did complete the form using a pen—'but it took a while'. That qualification should have been explored. It may be that even so the claimant was in a general way able to use a pen or a pencil. But if the 'while' was sufficiently long or if there were breaks or rests it may be that the answer should be otherwise. The tribunal decision is further defective in law because they have not dealt as fully as they should with these matters" (para.10).

Similarly, in *CIB/14587/1996*, Commissioner Rice, faced with activity 6 (bending and kneeling) and a claimant who could bend and kneel "but not repeatedly", imposed a requirement of being able to do so "with reasonable frequency":

"There would seem to be no doubt that the claimant is capable of bending and kneeling. However, can he do so without discomfort, and can he do so with reasonable frequency? For I do not think it is enough to treat him as capable of bending and kneeling if he can only do so subject to excruciating agony or, if having bent or knelt once, he is unable to repeat the exercise for hours or days thereafter. It is all a matter of degree. Can he bend or kneel without, at least too much discomfort, and can he repeat the exercise within a reasonable time. In other words, can he in the general sense of the word, in the course of his normal everyday activities, be said to be capable of bending and kneeling? It will be a matter for the tribunal to determine" (para.7).

Commissioner Howell, considering matters of repetition and the effect of pain in decisions *CIB/13161/96* and *CIB/13508/96*, took as his starting point a concept of normality and adopted the approach of the Chief Commissioner for Northern Ireland on reasonable regularity:

"In my judgment, the context in which this new benefit test was introduced and the use of a very basic set of mundane everyday activities intended to test whether a person can really be said to be incapable of any work at all, mean that by necessary implication the simple language used must be read in a reasonably broad and not a restricted literal sense. I do not think it is reading anything into reg.24 to say that the test is one of the extent to which the disease or disability from which the claimant suffers impairs his normal capacity to perform the stated activities as compared with a person of normal capabilities in full working order.

The word 'normal' appears twice in that last sentence, and is in my view the key to applying the various descriptors in accordance with the legislative intention. Thus in my judgment the score of 15 points for 'Cannot walk up and down a flight of 12 stairs' is applicable to a person who cannot normally do this as and when called upon to do so. It is not necessary to find that he is so incapacitated that he simply could not manage ever to get up a dozen stairs, even with the most supreme effort on one isolated occasion to avoid some terrible danger. For that matter there is no definition of what is meant by 'stairs' in the schedule: but no reasonable person could have any difficulty in reading by implication that these are assumed to be stairs of normal size, breadth and grip, not some imaginary set of steep awkward metal stairs in something like a ship's engine room. Similarly the descriptor 'cannot use a pen or pencil' in activity 7 ('Manual dexterity') must mean by necessary commonsense implication that the claimant scores the points if he is physically unable to use a pen or pencil to write in a normal manner. A fair reading does not need the schedule itself to spell out that this is what is meant, rather than a total inability to wield a pen or pencil for any purpose at all, even punching a hole in a sheet of paper.

The question of how far the descriptors are to be intended to measure a claimant's ability to perform the stated tasks on a repeated basis and without pain must in my judgment be answered in the same empirical way" (paras 37–39).

The Commissioner then cited with approval the passage from *C1/95(IB)* quoted above, but was of the opinion that the reference in it:

"to a claimant being able to accomplish a task 'most of the time' is . . . to be read in its context as meaning that the claimant would normally be able to perform the stated activity if and when called upon to do so. Consistently with this, the possibility of pain and fatigue and the increasing difficulty of performing an activity on a repeated basis must in my judgment be taken into account by considering how far the claimant's normal capabilities are impaired by comparison with those of a healthy person in normal working order. Even a fit man will suffer fatigue and his knees will start to ache if you make him walk up and down stairs many times in succession. The choice of descriptor should take into account whatever effects pain and fatigue may have on the claimant's ability to perform the task so far as they are beyond the normal by reason of his specific disability. The words 'most of the time' are not to be taken as giving rise to some need to try and calculate the percentage of successful or failed attempts over any real or imagined period" (para.41).

(ii) The (lack of) relevance of the "working situation": The second justificatory reason   **8.167** for rejecting the literal snapshot approach is, quite simply, that this is, ultimately, a test of capacity for work. Granted, under this scheme, unlike the previous Invalidity Benefit scheme, no definition of work is required: the test is one of ability to perform the activities in the Schedule. But in fashioning a general approach to interpretation of the key terms in which the activities and descriptors are cast, it is submitted that one cannot wholly ignore the general requirements of employers and the typical realities of the workplace. Indeed an element of this underlies the "reasonable regularity", "with reasonable frequency" and "repetition of performance" approaches noted above. But on this matter, Chief Commissioner Chambers in the unreported Northern Ireland Decision *C1/95(IB)* (noted in (1996) 3 J.S.S.L. D176–177) appears to take a different view. There the SSAT noted that some descriptors relate to a "working situation" to support their view on the requirement of "reasonably frequent repetition". Chief Commissioner Chambers opined:

"On the further subject of a 'working situation', I agree that the SSAT should not have regard to this factor; but should confine their considerations to the claimant's ability to perform the everyday activities specified in the descriptors".

This passage was considered by Commissioner Howell in decisions *CIB/13161/96* and *CIB/13508/96*. Commissioner Howell supported the "everyday activities" approach, rejecting the working environment aspect in so far as creating a separate and additional test over and above the statutory wording, but not, it is submitted, in so far as a reference to the work context might import a particular commonsense approach to the interpretation of words used therein (e.g. "can/ cannot"). In passages which point up graphically the differences between the "all work" test ["personal capability assessment"] and the IVB regime, he stated:

"While the heading to the schedule and its legislative context identify its sole reason for existing as being to test for disablement (*sic*) from work, the fourteen activities themselves are specified in entirely general terms. They consist of things like walking, sitting, standing, bending, lifting, reaching and so forth that are in no way restricted to a work situation. The descriptors too refer only to commonplace situations in daily life such as turning a knob on a cooker, using a pen or carrying a carton of milk or a bag of potatoes, and are obviously intended to reflect a measurement of only the most basic physical and manual skills. *There is no indication or apparent scope for any separate or more substantive inquiry into how far a claimant's condition has really depleted his working skills, or whether those he has left are saleable in any real sense to an employer* . . .

40. As the Chief Commissioner [for Northern Ireland] points out there is no warrant in the regulations for a separate consideration of whether the claimant could or could not perform the listed activities in some imaginary working context such as a factory, if this means that some additional test is to be imported over and above that of whether the claimant can normally perform these activities in the sense that I have indicated. *I am not sure however that the tribunal in that case was really doing more than using their reference to a working context as a common sense reason to justify importing the concept of reasonable regularity approved in the passage* [from *C1/95(IB)*] quoted above. A mere reference to work in that sense would not amount to using it as a separate factor.

42. *Nor in my judgment is there any ground for attempting any kind of quantitative assessment of the number of different working situations a claimant might be able to cope with. That would be going beyond the plain intention to focus only on the ability to perform the list of everyday tasks,* as the yardstick for a common sense assumption that if a person is not seriously handicapped in these, there must be at least some kind of work he could do. *Consideration of the requirements for specific jobs, and the kind of evidence that occupied so much time before tribunals under the old law, (with adjudication officers coming up with specimen job descriptions of very simple jobs that could be performed by anyone, and claimants coming up with detailed reasons why they thought them unsuitable) are now irrelevant"* (paras 3, 40, 42, emphasis and square bracket references added by commentator).

In *CSIB/17/96*, the matter arose of the claimant's ability to use a kettle. It was common ground between the parties that his specially adapted kettle was not the one to focus on; the focus should (at the very least) be on a normal one. The claimant's representative, however, argued that:

"the proper context within which to determine the descriptors was that of a working situation. Thus, he submitted that kettle pouring or saucepan pouring should be considered in the context of a commercial kitchen".

Commissioner Walker, applying the above quoted statement of the Chief Commissioner for Northern Ireland rejected this:

"[A]lthough this is described as the 'all work test', I have no doubt that the Chief Commissioner in Northern Ireland was correct when he determined in the case cited that an appeal tribunal should not have regard to such a factor but should confine their considerations to ability to perform the everyday activities specified in the descriptor. That, as it seems to me, is so because the range of descriptors taken as a whole [is] designed to give an overall picture of an individual's general ability or inability to undertake activities which may bear upon a general working situation. It seems to me that the purpose of the scheme is sufficiently obvious, namely that if sufficient descriptors are satisfied there is probably little useful work or employment which an individual could either do or obtain. I therefore direct the new tribunal to apply the descriptors generally in line with the foregoing guidance, but not in a working situation" (para.13).

In *CIB/14587/1996* in which "bending and kneeling" was at issue, the claimant's representative had sought to persuade Commissioner Rice to go further than taking accounts of the effects of pain (see further below) and the "reasonable frequency" approach (examined above), arguing that ability to bend and kneel should be judged in a "work context" or a "work environment". His argument drew support from this being a test of capacity for work and from the following statement in para.17 of the *Medical Services Incapacity Benefit Handbook for Medical Services Doctors*:

"There will be instances where the claimant can carry out an activity, but the activity promotes moderate pain. Consider whether the client could carry out such an action reliably, safely and repeatedly in the workplace. Reasonable risk cannot be ignored, and if, for example, the client would be at risk of falls when climbing stairs, this should be taken into account".

Commissioner Rice rejected the argument made by the claimant's representative. Drawing support from Chief Commissioner Chambers in *C1/95(IB)*, the Commissioner instead ruled that:

"The 'All Work Test' consists of a variety of tests as to a claimant's physical capacity under various heads. Shortcomings will result in the award of points, and if the claimant obtains 15 points or more, he will have satisfied the 'All Work Test' and will be deemed to have demonstrated his incapacity for all forms of work. *But these individual tests relate to the claimant's capacity to carry out ordinary functions in every-day life.* They are a convenient means of assessing the claimant's physical condition, on the basis of which he can, depending on the results, be treated as either capable or incapable of work. The individual tests are not themselves to be evaluated on the basis that, at the time they are applied, the claimant is deemed to be at work, and subject to the normal demands of his employment. Thus, his ability to bend or kneel will not be subject to the requirements and pressure incidental to employment; *it will be adjudged by reference to the nominal needs of every-day living at home.*

12. It should also be mentioned that if a claimant's capacity to carry out the activities appearing in the Schedule were to be evaluated in a 'work context', difficulty would arise in determining which was the particular work context applicable to the claimant in question. What form of employment was he expected to undertake, on the basis of which the tests were to be judged? In my view this kind of difficulty has been deliberately side-stepped by *requiring the tests to be evaluated from the standpoint of general every-day living*" (paras 9, 12, emphasis added by commentator).

Note, however, on this matter of the relevance of a "work environment", that Commissioner Goodman, while declining to comment in detail on those cases rejecting testing in the "work environment", has nonetheless stated that he "would wish to consider the matter carefully if it became critical, bearing in mind that the Schedule is headed 'Disabilities which may make a person incapable of work' " (*CIB/14332/1996*, para.12). Commissioner Goodman's by-the-way comment runs counter to a clear line of authority in Commissioners' decisions, as was pointed out by Commissioner Jacobs in *CIB/16681/1996* (para.20). There Commissioner Jacobs considered the legislative structure of and background to incapacity benefit as a replacement for sickness and invalidity benefits, which had, of course, made reference to a work context (work the claimant could reasonably be expected to do). While a work context is retained under the "own occupation" test, reg.24 is silent on whether or not the activities are to be applied in the context of employment. Nor does any other provision provide for reference to a work context. Commissioner Jacobs concluded that:

"the structure and wording of the legislation is clear. The activities of the all work test have to be applied as they stand and not in any particular context. There is no basis for spelling out from the legislation a requirement that the activities be applied in the context of work. Any attempt to define such a context is fraught with difficulty and liable to produce irrational results" (para.20).

In most "personal capability assessment" "all work test" cases, the claimant will not be working. The only evidence of disability will tend to be evidence related to activities carried out in a domestic or social context. One cannot look to the claimant's former or usual occupation. He may not have one and that is the province of the "own occupation" test, and the "all work test" ["personal capability assessment"] applies only where the "own occupation" test does not. Since incapacity benefit was designed to replace the approach taken in sickness and invalidity benefits, it cannot be by reference to some specific type of work of which it is alleged the claimant is capable.

"Once outside the context of the claimant's own employment record and of other specific types of employment, there is no basis for identifying any particular working context in which to apply the all work test. Accordingly, the only possibility is some hypothetical working context. There are no criteria that can be extracted from the legislation for defining such a context and no principles from which such criteria could be developed.

As soon as touch is lost with any particular type of work, any attempt to consider the application of the activities in the context of work becomes an abstract exercise. Such an exercise is no more rational as a policy than a test of disability that determines the claimant's capacity for work by reference to disability displayed in a domestic or social context. Indeed the latter is arguably more rational as being founded in fact rather than speculation" (paras 16, 17).

8.168   *(iii) The effects of pain and the claimant's fears for his health:* Another problem concerns the claimant who can perform certain tasks (e.g. bending as if to pick up a piece of paper from the floor and straighten up again—paras 6(b) or (c)) but suffers pain on doing so. Under the previous sickness and invalidity benefit regime, there was some authority (*CS/ 46/92*, interpreting *R1/62SB*, a Northern Ireland decision of persuasive authority with respect to the system in Great Britain) to suggest that functions which could be performed only with *substantial* pain were not properly to be regarded as within a claimant's capacity. In *CIB/14587/1996* in which "bending and kneeling" was at issue, the claimant had told the SSAT that he could bend and kneel "but not repeatedly". It was unclear from the tribunal's decision why they had rejected that and accordingly the Commissioner set the decision aside as erroneous in law. He then proceeded to give guidance on how a differently constituted SSAT should approach the appeal:

"There would seem to be no doubt that the claimant is capable of bending and kneeling. However, can he do so without discomfort, and can he do so with reasonable frequency? For I do not think it is enough to treat him as capable of bending and kneeling if he can only do so subject to excruciating agony or, if having bent or knelt once, he is unable to repeat the exercise for hours or days thereafter. It is all a matter of degree. Can he bend or kneel without, at least too much discomfort, and can he repeat the exercise within a reasonable time. In other words, can he in the general sense of the word, in the course of his normal everyday activities, be said to be capable of bending and kneeling? It will be a matter for the tribunal to determine" (para.7).

Commissioner Rice thus not only endorses the "reasonable regularity" approach examined above. He also in effect supports the proposition that functions that can only be performed with more than an acceptable pain or discomfort are not to be regarded as within a claimant's capacity. The difficulty then becomes the twofold one of assessing from all the evidence the degree of pain (if any) and determining what is an acceptable level of pain or discomfort (is it "without discomfort", "moderate pain", "at least not too much discomfort" or "substantial pain"—it would, it is submitted, be unreasonable to ignore a function only if it could be performed with "excruciating agony"). As Commissioner Howell noted in decisions *CIB/13161/96* and *CIB/13508/96*, citing with approval the passage from *C1/95(IB)* quoted above:

"the possibility of pain and fatigue and the increasing difficulty of performing an activity on a repeated basis must in my judgment be taken into account by considering how far the claimant's normal capabilities are impaired by comparison with those of a healthy person in normal working order. Even a fit man will suffer fatigue and his knees will start to ache if you make him walk up and down stairs many times in succession. The choice of descriptor should take into account whatever effects pain and fatigue may have on the claimant's ability to perform the task so far as they are beyond the normal by reason of his specific disability" (para.41).

Commissioner Jacobs, in a case on disability living allowance *CDLA/0902/2004*, has given useful guidance on the matter of assessing from all the evidence the degree of pain, if any, suffered by a claimant, whether for DLA or incapacity for work purposes. He noted that pain is one of the most common and difficult issues that tribunals have to deal with. It raises factual issues of what pain the claimant experiences and how it affects his/her activities. It raises legal issues such as whether it arises (for incapacity for work purposes) from a specific bodily disease or disablement. "Pain" has been defined by the International Association for the Study of Pain as "an unpleasant sensory and emotional experience associated with actual or potential tissue damage, or described in terms of such damage" (cited in para.14). It now seems accepted by medical experts that there is no direct and proportionate relationship between the disease or injury at issue and the nature and level of the pain experienced by the sufferer, so that

"it is no longer rational for tribunals to reason simply from the clinical findings on examination to the level of pain that a claimant experiences. Tribunals must investigate the evidence of the claimant's pain and explain how they have dealt with it. As there is no direct causal link between disease or injury and pain, the only direct evidence of pain can come from the claimant" (para.15).

This raises difficulties of language. The language of pain is threefold. *Sensory*, describes the sensation itself (e.g. shooting or stabbing). The effect of the pain on the patient (e.g. sickening or blinding) is *affective* language, while *evaluative* language (e.g. distressing or unbearable) describes the extent to which the sufferer is suffering. The McGill pain questionnaire embodies 66 different words to cover these three aspects. The problem is, of course, that such a range of words is not likely to be matched in most claimants' vocabularies, so that it becomes a matter for representatives and tribunal members so to question the claimant and the evidence in a way that gets beyond the language itself to what that language conveys. Importantly, Commissioner Jacobs stated that

"this does not mean that the tribunal has to accept the claimant's evidence. Even when analysed as I have suggested, it may still be unreliable or incredible. It may even be dishonest. What I am saying is this. If pain is an issue, the tribunal must obtain the best evidence it can of that pain and its effect on the claimant and it must then interpret that evidence realistically. Only then, is the tribunal in a position to decide whether or not to accept it" (para.19).

A decision on whether to accept the claimant's evidence of pain must take on board the entirety of the evidence relative to his/her disablement, something likely to include

- evidence of the activities undertaken by the claimant

- his/her medication

- other treatment or referrals, whether actual or considered

- informal observations of the claimant's functional ability and activities whether made and recorded by the examining medical practitioner or the tribunal itself, so long, of course, as they can be related to the time of the decision under appeal

- opinions of examining medical practitioners

This advice from Commissioner Jacobs relates to oral hearings at which the claimant is present. Where the hearing is a paper one, a tribunal must consider whether it should adjourn to allow the claimant to attend or, if that is inappropriate, endeavour to do the best it can on such evidence as is before it (para.31).

In *CIB/243/1998*, dealing with a case of intermittent asthma, Deputy Commissioner Mark considered that a claimant would be unable to perform a particular activity/ descriptor if he would not do so because of a real fear of the consequences to his health. Assessing whether a fear is genuine, is, of course, difficult, but will turn not only on the credibility of the claimant's account, but also on its consistency with the medical evidence. It remains unclear whether a genuine but wholly unreasonable fear can be regarded as having this disabling effect.

8.169   *(iv) The relevance of medical advice to refrain from activities:* A related problem concerns the claimant who has received medical advice to refrain from certain activities. In *CSIB/12/96*, Commissioner Walker considered the case of a woman whose physiotherapist advised her not to bend over to pick things up but rather to bend her knees and crouch, and who had also been advised not to lift anything heavy. He rejected the view that such advice had to be ignored for the purposes of applying the descriptors, and said:

> "any risk consequent on bending has to be borne in mind and if it be a real risk which would deter a reasonable person from bending then it may be legitimate to say that they are unable to bend for the purpose of the descriptor. That I think . . . is a legitimate approach bearing in mind that the whole object of the descriptors is to try to present a picture of the extent to which an individual can perform various activities with a view to determining whether he can work. I doubt if an activity which could only be undertaken with some risk to the individual's health was intended to be discounted for that purpose." (para.8).

8.170   *(v) Variable, intermittent and sporadic conditions and consequent effect on earning capacity:* Difficult questions of judgment in assessing incapacity for work arise where the claimant can sometimes do things but at other times not. Neither the all work test nor the personal capability assessment were designed to be a simple "snapshot". The system aims to assess the claimant's condition over a particular period, taking account of pain and fatigue, fears for health and the medical advice received by the claimant. The questionnaire asks about variability—the claimant's own doctor can include material on this in the MED 4, and DWPMS doctors have been trained to conduct examinations with these issues in mind.

The structure of the legislative scheme, however, produces a problem. It embodies a test based on an examination on a particular day designed to provide information on, and assessment of, a claimant over a period of time. But the legislation created a daily benefit, and deals with single days of incapacity requiring them to be grouped in a certain way as to form a period of incapacity. This suggests that one cannot altogether proceed on the basis that the picture that applies for a preponderance of days in a period always determines the claim. The "normality" approach noted above in the context "reasonable regularity" deals with one aspect of the problem: the reference in *C1/95(IB)* to a claimant being able to accomplish a task most of the time is to be read as meaning "as and when called upon to do so". On this basis, one looks at the position which normally prevails in the period (see *CSIB/459/1997*, para.13; *CIB/911/1997*, paras 12, 13). The more difficult situation is where it is accepted that the claimant's condition is such that for certain periods he is able to cope satisfactorily with normal activities; the problem of the sporadic or intermittent condition. The problem generated significant disagreement among Commissioners on approach. Some (e.g. Commissioner Howell in *CIB/13161/1996* and *CIB/13508/1996*) took a strict daily approach, one logical in the context of the legislative structure, but one liable to create evidentiary difficulties for claimants, since few would keep a detailed daily "log" or "diary". It also imposed tremendous burdens on Appeal Tribunals especially when required to look at the lengthy period down to the date of their decision. Others (see, for example, *CSIB/684/1997*; *CSIB/597/1997*; *CIB/15231/1996*; and *CIB/6244/1997*) took a broader approach, requiring decision-makers to look to such period as would give a true and fair picture of the claimant's capacity. Commissioner Jacobs in *CIB/6244/1997* drew a distinction between variable and intermittent conditions. With variable ones (conditions where the symptoms vary in intensity), one looked to the claimant's condition overall across a representative period of time, having regard to his condition, reasonableness and the concept of reasonable regularity. With intermittent conditions (ones which give rise to discrete attacks followed by periods of complete remission), one had to identify the particular days on which the claimant was incapable of work under the all work test by reference to his condition. One would then determine whether the claimant satisfied the continuity and linking rules in SSCBA 1992, s.30C(1) and award or not award benefit accordingly.

On June 15, 1999, a Tribunal of Commissioners (Chief Commissioner Machin, Commissioner Sanders and Commissioner Rowland) issued its authoritative decision *R(IB) 2/99(T)* dealing with the situation where a claimant suffers from a condition causing greater disability on some days than on others. The key question is whether the claimant is incapable of work under that test on days on which, if the days were viewed in isolation, he or she might not satisfy that test (para.2). While the Tribunal decision does not prescribe any one approach as *universally* applicable, the central thrust of the decision is to see as justified for the majority of cases, the "broad approach" typified by *CIB/6244/97* rather than the stricter "daily approach" exemplified by *CIB/13161/96* and *CIB/13508/96*. The Tribunal did not, however, find helpful the distinction drawn between "variable" and "intermittent" conditions in *CIB/6244/97*. Moreover, the Tribunal recognised that in some cases at least—generally when looking backwards over a prolonged period in the course of which the claimant has only had "short episodes of disablement" (for example, in the dwindling number of cases where the Appeal Tribunal has to consider matters "down to the date of the hearing", or in "review or overpayment cases")—something akin to the meticulous approach in *CIB/13161/96* and *CIB/13508/96* along the lines of Commissioner Jacobs' approach to intermittent conditions in *CIB/6244/1997* would be appropriate (para.17).

The practical reality is that most cases which fall to be decided by the decision-maker in the Department do not concern entitlement to benefit for a past period. Generally, a decision on the award of benefit is "forward looking" and usually made for an indefinite period. Although the decision-maker must of course consider the period from the medical examination up to the date of his decision, that decision will rarely be concerned with entitlement to benefit for a substantial period in the past. While both the "broad" and the "daily basis" approaches are each consistent with the wording of the legislation, and, in particular, the Schedule to the IW (General) Regs, the "broad approach" is "the only approach that can sensibly be applied by a decision-maker, making what is in effect a prospective determination for an extended period" (para.11). The Tribunal considered the broader-based approach adopted in *R(A) 2/74* to the attendance allowance issue—was there a period *throughout* which the claimant could be said to be so severely disabled as to require at night prolonged or repeated attention in connection with bodily functions? The Tribunal decided that such an approach applies equally to incapacity benefit despite its daily basis. It noted (without using those statements to support its construction of the legislation) that such an approach accorded with ministerial statements in Parliament on the introduction of the all work test (for example, that the "all work test" [now the "personal capability assessment"] is not a "snapshot"). Nonetheless, the Tribunal stressed that:

> "the words of the legislation cannot be ignored . . . [I]n those cases where relevant descriptors are expressed in terms that the claimant 'cannot', rather than 'sometimes cannot', perform the activity, one should not stray too far from an arithmetical approach that considers what the claimant's abilities are 'most of the time'—the phrase used in *C1/95(IB)*. Nevertheless, we agree that all the factors mentioned by counsel [neither of whom argued for a 'daily basis' approach]—the frequency of 'bad' days, the lengths of periods of 'bad' days and of intervening periods, the severity of the claimant's disablement on both 'good' and 'bad' days

and the unpredictability of 'bad' days—are relevant when applying the broad approach. Thus a person whose condition varies from day to day and who would easily satisfy the 'all work test' on three days a week and would nearly satisfy it on the other four days might well be considered to be incapable of work for the whole week. But a person who has long periods of illness separated by periods of remission lasting some weeks during which he or she suffers no significant disablement, might well be considered to be incapable of work during the periods of illness but not to be incapable of work during the periods of remission, even if the periods of illness are longer than the periods of remission. Each case must be judged on its merits and . . . there are some cases where a claimant can properly be regarded as incapable of work both on days when the 'all work test' is clearly satisfied and on other days in between those days and that there are other cases where the claimant can be regarded as incapable of work only on 'bad days' . . ." (para.15).

Hence, as regards forward-looking decisions, claimants whose condition is such as only to satisfy the test on four or five days a month (albeit days of severe disablement) cannot, however unpredictable those days may be, properly be regarded as satisfying the test for the whole month. It thus may be that some claimants who are unemployable nonetheless are seen as "capable of work" under the "all work test". That effect of the legislation can only be remedied by modifying it (e.g. by expanding the scope of reg.27 or using more frequently in other areas the type of terminology used in descriptor 14(c) [has an involuntary episode of lost or altered consciousness at least once a month]). Where, however, a decision-maker is looking backwards over a prolonged period at such a scenario (and such cases will gradually become rarer), an isolated day of incapacity can be ignored. One will be looking, generally, for spells of at least four consecutive days of incapacity, since the scheme only provides for entitlement where the day can be grouped with others in a period of incapacity (generally a chain of ostensibly separated "spells" of four or more consecutive days of incapacity "forged" together into one if no more than eight weeks apart).

In a Northern Ireland decision, *R1/02(IB)(T)*, a tribunal of Commissioners endorsed the "broad brush" approach to variable conditions in *R(IB)2/99(T)*, but also laid emphasis on para.15 of it, set out above, with one reservation. They were unhappy with the phrase "the unpredictability of 'bad' days", commenting that those who decide cases

"will simply have to try to determine the likely patterns of functional limitation. Uncertainty as to the possibility of a future recurrence would not of itself usually be enough to satisfy the test which must be satisfied on the balance of probability at the time of the decision maker's decision" (para.26).

Applying para.15 of *R(IB)2/99* in *CIB/2620/2000*, Commissioner Bano held that the case before him (a sufferer from dysmenorrhoea) was one of the minority of cases in which the broad approach could not be applied, one where the claimant could only be considered incapable of work on "bad days".

8.171 *[B] Some specific matters on approaching Pt II of the Schedule: mental disabilities* As Commissioner Goodman stressed in *R(IB) 2/98*, it must be remembered that the "all work" test ["personal capability assessment"] is one of a person's incapacity, by reason of some specific disease or bodily or mental disablement which he has, to perform the activities specified in the Schedule:

"In this context, therefore, the matters specified in Part II . . . can qualify for 'points' only if they result from 'mental disablement' (reg.24). In other words, they must not be mere matters of mood but must relate to a recognisable mental disablement, in the nature of an illness and not shared by healthy members of the population. The generality of such a phrase as 'often sits for hours doing nothing' (para.15(b)), for example, must be restricted to such a state resulting from a definite mental disability" (*ibid.*, para.8).

Accordingly, while Appeal Tribunals have an inquisitorial function requiring them to investigate all relevant matters (see also *CIB/14442/96*), they should be cautious in exercising it in the sphere of mental disablement. In the case before Commissioner Goodman, the tribunal had done so of its own accord and without being presented with any preceding evidence, medical or otherwise on the matter, relying merely on what the claimant said to them although it was not clear whether the claimant's statements came in answer to questions put by the tribunal or not. Commissioner Goodman was of the opinion that tribunals:

"should be hesitant in going into the question of possible mental disabilities unless they have been raised beforehand and in addition there is some medical or similar evidence on the point . . .

6. When looking in isolation at the list of 'mental disabilities' in the Schedule . . . it would be easy, without I hope being cynical to say of almost anyone that they could acquire some points under the various descriptors. For example the descriptor 'Avoids carrying out routine activities because he is convinced they will prove too tiring or stressful', could . . . describe anyone at a given point in time. The same is true of the descriptor, 'Is scared or anxious that work would bring back or worsen his illness'. In view of the general nature of some of these descriptors, I consider that tribunals ought to be sure that they do have some corroborative evidence preferably medical evidence, on these points. They should be careful not to elevate to 'mental disabilities', for example a mere disinclination to do certain tasks or to go to work on a certain day or a disinclination for the society of one's fellow human beings on certain occasions" (paras 5, 6).

Hence the Commissioner's stress, noted above, that application of a "mental disability" descriptor must be restricted to a state resulting from a definite mental disability, a matter now put beyond any doubt by reg.25(3)(b) as amended from January 6, 1997, which states categorically

"in determining the extent of a person's incapacity to perform any activity listed in . . . Part II, it shall be a condition that the person's incapacity arises . . . in respect of a disability listed in Part II, from some specific mental illness or disablement".

In a Northern Ireland decision *R2/99(IB)*, Commissioner Brown supported Commissioner Goodman's observations in para.8 of *R(IB) 2/98*. She also supported his cautious approach to tribunals examining the issue of mental disease or disablement without supporting medical evidence. She thought, however, that for a tribunal to do so did not necessarily amount to an error of law (paras 11, 12). While agreeing to some extent with Commissioner Brown's view, however, Commissioner Jacobs in *CIB/26/2004* qualified that by noting that at the time of that decision there was no medical member on the tribunal—it merely then had advice from an assessor—that change in composition rendering it easier now for a tribunal to make a diagnosis on the evidence available (para.20). Authorities prior to that change may thus not have as much force as once they had.

Where mental descriptors are in issue, a tribunal must at least ask if the claimant accepts the DWPMS score and, if not, go through the descriptors in so far as there is evidence enabling it to do so (*CIB/15693/96*). In *CSIB/160/2000*, Commissioner May thought *CIB/15693/96* confined to its own facts, and in any event disagreed with its approach in so far as it purported to lay down any general rule that appeal tribunals satisfy themselves that none of the mental health descriptors applied. There was certainly no need, where a claimant was represented at an oral hearing to go beyond the descriptors put in issue by the claimant and his representative. In *C12/01–02(IB)*, Commissioner Brown expressed agreement with Commissioner May's point in *CSIB/160/00* that *CIB/15693/1996* lays down no rule of general application. In the case before her, the claimant through a representative not legally qualified, conceded that the mental health descriptors were not in issue. While in such circumstances tribunals should be wary of accepting without exploration a concession on a legal issue, they were able here to accept the factual concession that the claimant did not suffer from any of the functional limitations set out in the mental health test. But there is no pre-requisite that the DWPMS doctor has dealt with the matter; if there is sufficient evidence to warrant it, the tribunal should consider the mental health descriptors (*CIB/14908/96*). A diagnosis of hypertension does not require consideration of the mental descriptors (*CIB/14516/96*).

Throughout, it must be remembered, as Commissioner Jacobs noted in *CIB/3785/2007*, that a mental health assessment is not based on clinical findings in the same way as is a physical assessment. The processes involved are different. A mental health assessment is essentially an exercise in credibility against a background of clinical diagnosis, rather than an exercise in clinical examination. There must be medical evidence that the claimant has a specific mental illness or disablement (a clinical opinion by a doctor). Whether the claimant's evidence reports particular manifestations matching the mental health descriptors is, however, not a clinical opinion but a matter of judgment open to the tribunal. Similarly, whether the doctor or tribunal accepts the claimant's evidence is again a matter of judgment. Clinical opinion is in contrast part of the causation question: do the manifestations result from the accepted mental illness or disablement. For example, if a claimant does not care about their living conditions or appearance, this may stem from their nature (s/he is a slovenly and untidy person) or because of depression or mental illness. Thus

"the application of the mental disabilities section of the personal capability assessment essentially involves issues of credibility and consistency. Are the symptoms described by the claimant a reliable account of the effects of the claimant's mental disablement? As part of that question, the medical adviser and the tribunal have to take account of whether the symptoms described are consistent with the diagnosed mental conditions" (para.7).

The nature of the IB50 questionnaire is such as to require tribunals to be "particularly careful" in exploring the application of the mental health descriptors. It contains no specific descriptors and, although it provides space for claimants to give information about their mental health, no guidance is given about the functional difficulties relevant to the personal capability assessment. This means that those new to the system may not know what to include until after the medical examination, so that when, realising what is required, on appeal they produce further evidence with respect to particular activities/descriptors , that can appear, not necessarily deservedly, as mere *ex post facto* justification (*NS v SSWP* [2009] UKUT 21 (AAC), para.5). Tribunals must be wary of too readily finding on that basis alone that the new material is exaggerated or lacks credibility, but must weigh all the evidence (*ibid.*, paras 9, 10).

8.172   *[C] Making and recording decisions*
Setting rigorous standards for Appeal Tribunals (*cf.* his approach to activity 3 in *CSIB/12/96*), Commissioner Walker in *CSIB 324/97* stipulated the following approach to making and recording decisions under the "all work" test ["personal capability assessment"]:

"the best and safest practice is for a tribunal to consider and make findings of fact about, first, the disability or disabilities, be they disease or bodily or mental problems, from which an individual has been proved on the evidence to suffer. Second, they should consider and make findings of fact about which, if any of the activities set out in the Sch., are established to be adversely affected by any of those disabilities. Thirdly, and based upon appropriate findings of fact, in the case of each and every activity the tribunal should determine which descriptor best fits the case having regard to the evidence, in their view. Finally, in the reasons, they should explain why a particular activity has been held not to be adversely affected where there was a contention that it was so affected, and why a particular descriptor has been preferred to any other contended for" (para.11).

But that best and safest practice need not necessarily always be followed. For example where the issue is whether or not the tribunal believes the claimant on a matter fundamental and relevant, if on reasonable grounds the tribunal did not believe the claimant when he alleged that his responses in the questionnaire were not accurate, then the finding that the tribunal did not believe that he had been mistaken when providing those responses covered in reality all the disputed areas raised at the hearing, and it was not necessary to record specific findings of fact on each of the activity questions brought up by the claimant (*per* Northern Ireland Chief Commissioner Martin in *C46/97(IB)*, drawing with approval on Deputy Commissioner Ramsay's decision in *CIB/16572/96*). In para.5 of *CIB/4497/1998*, Commissioner Rowland sets out useful guidance on the minimum requirements of giving reasons. He noted that:

"a statement of reasons may be adequate even though it could be improved on and, in particular, a failure to observe the 'best and safest practice' recommended in *CSIB 324/97* . . . is not necessarily an error of law . . . What is required by way of reasoning depends very much on the circumstances of the case before the tribunal. Those challenging reasoning must explain its inadequacy and show the significance of the inadequacy."

[D] Case law on specific activities/descriptors: Pt I: physical disabilities   8.173
The proper approach to scoring under Pt I of the Schedule is set out in *CIB/5361/97*. There Commissioner Howell was faced with the alarming revelation that the DWPMS doctor in the case, on whose evidence the tribunal had relied, had taken a "bottom-up" approach to scoring with respect to the descriptors connected with each activity, that is, he had started at the bottom (no points) and worked up until he found a descriptor which fitted the claimant. Even more worryingly, he claimed that the training sessions he had attended had given him the impression that this was the proper approach. Commissioner Howell, applying reg.26(3), rejected this approach as invalid:

"Since the descriptors with the highest score are the ones which appear the furthest up each section of the table [activities and descriptors in the Schedule], the only valid way to conduct an assessment of a person's physical descriptor score in accordance with this mandatory requirement of the regulations must therefore be to work down from the top of each section of the table and stop as soon as one comes to a descriptor that applies to him" (para.7).

It is important properly to identify the relevant physical condition and to consider the full range of activities which may be impaired by it. So, for example, with migraine, it is important not to confine consideration to Activity 14 (lost or altered consciousness): see Deputy Commissioner White *CIB/5757/1997* (para.25) and also *CIB/3589/2004* in which Commissioner Jacobs said:

"In the case of a migraine, the chain works like this. A migraine is a bodily *disease*. It involves *symptoms*—pain and disruption of vision. Those symptoms restrict the claimant's ability to function in various way (*disabilities*). The personal capability assessment allows those symptoms and their effects to be taken into account in respect of any *activity* which they affect. For example, flashing lights or blindness during a migraine may affect the activity of negotiating stairs without holding on and the activity of vision.

Migraines are not continuous. Their effects are intermittent. That does not mean that they are irrelevant to the personal capability assessment. They may be relevant in one of two ways. First, they may be relevant to the 'sometimes' descriptors in the activities of rising from sitting and bending and kneeling.

Second, they may be relevant to the frequency and regularity with which a claimant can undertake activities.

The tribunal limited the potential relevance of the symptoms of migraine to activity 14. There is no justification in the legislation for doing so. Nor is there any justification in the nature of migraine or the effects of its symptoms. The tribunal limited the relevance of the claimant's evidence of migraines to one activity without justification" (paras 12–14).

Looking to the facts as found by the tribunal about the claimant's condition, he found that

"The claimant's migraines are sufficiently severe that they affect her ability to rise from sitting and to bend or kneel to the floor. She would not be able to do either of those activities without some support. In those circumstances, the 'sometimes' descriptors for those activities apply. Each scores 3 points, making a total of 6. The claimant already has a score of 10. The additional 6 bring the total to 16, which is sufficient to satisfy the assessment" (para.17).

8.174   *Activity 1: walking on level ground: descriptors (b)–(f) "without . . . severe discomfort":* In *CSIB/60/96* Commissioner May took the view that tribunals should not here have regard to the case law on the same words in the context of the statutory definition of virtually unable to walk as respects the mobility component of disability living allowance. He did so not just because of the different statutory context but because the tribunal issue is essentially one of degree (para.18). A tribunal must not only consider the point in distance when a claimant stops walking because of severe discomfort but also the point of onset of that discomfort (descriptors 1(b)-(d) read "without stopping *or* severe discomfort") (*CIB/3013/97*).

8.175   *Activities 1 and 2: walking on level ground; walking up and down stairs: the problem of double counting:* It cannot be emphasised too much that with respect to someone's score in terms of physical disabilities, where more than one descriptor specified for any activity applies to him, only the descriptor with the highest score is counted, and for this purpose where a descriptor from each of the two separate "walking" activities (walking on level ground; walking up and down stairs) applies to him, the two activities are treated as if they were one, and only one descriptor (the highest scoring "walking" descriptor) counts (reg.26(2), (3); *CIB/14516/1996*).

The phrase "if such aid is normally used" means if it is normally used by people acting reasonably (by analogy with the interpretation given "if such aid is normally worn" in *CIB/14499/1996*, below, activity 12).

8.176   *Activity 2: walking up and down stairs:* In *R(IB) 3/98*, Commissioner Mitchell considered

"whether ascribing points for the claimant's inability to walk up and down a flight of stairs without holding on involves an impermissible double counting, where the cause of the claimant's inability to do so is his defective vision and he also scores under a descriptor specifically related to vision in paragraph 12" (para.11).

He saw no compelling reason "for implying a scoring limitation which could have been but has not been made explicit" (para.16). Accordingly, the only limits on "double counting" are those expressly found in paras (2) and (3) of reg.26 or in the wording of the Schedule.

In *CIB/13161/96* and *CIB/13508/96*, Commissioner Howell commented:

"there is no definition of what is meant by 'stairs' in the schedule: but no reasonable person could have any difficulty in reading by implication that these are assumed to be stairs of normal size, breadth and grip, not some imaginary set of steep awkward metal stairs in something like a ship's engine room" (para.38).

In *R(IB) 1/99*, Commissioner Rice considered descriptor 2(e): "can only walk up and down a flight of 12 stairs if he goes . . . one step at a time". There is, of course, no difficulty here if that mode is the claimant's continuous mode of progression throughout his journey up and down that flight of stairs. But what if such a mode of progress is only required for part of that journey, for example, as with the claimant in the case, he only needed to move one step at a time when going *down* the flight of stairs? Commissioner Rice considered that:

"the language of the provision is clearly unsatisfactory, as it does not contemplate the possibility that a claimant suffering from the relevant disability might not at all times need to progress one step at a time. But doing the best I can with the language used, I take the view that the condition that the draftsman really had in contemplation was an inability to go up and down a flight of stairs without the necessity *at some stage at least* to restrict one's movements to one step at a time. And on this basis, as the claimant was clearly unable to walk downstairs without recourse to proceeding one step at a time, he satisfies the test, and as a result is entitled to the 3 points" (para.6).

The descriptors must be interpreted in a common-sense manner. One must not treat "up and down" as one continuous process. Both tasks have to be managed in the context of normal everyday living, a context in which people typically do not go upstairs, turn round immediately and then come straight back down. So a claimant who could walk up stairs but had to take a rest at the top could not score under descriptor 2(c) (*CIB/88/1997*).

Activity 3: "sitting in an upright chair with a back, but no arms": In *CSIB/12/96*, Commissioner Walker stressed the need for precision with respect to relating evidence about the claimant's ability to sit (e.g. "reads a lot", "watches TV", "plays bingo at the local club") to ability to sit in the type of chair prescribed: "an upright chair with a back, but no arms". He opined that

8.177

"the examining doctor should make clear how he has reached his conclusion in respect of the prescribed chair. Thus the chair in which somebody may be comfortable to read or to watch television, or even to sit and play bingo for an hour, may be very different from that prescribed" (para.5).

The SSAT had recorded that:

"we prefer the opinion of the Benefits Agency Medical Doctor who examined [the claimant] and also rely in part, on [her] own evidence to the effect that she is able to sit for reasonably long periods. Although she described the chair which she uses within her own home, where she gets some support from additional pillows, she does not require to use an orthopaedic chair and she appeared to sit during the tribunal hearing which lasted in excess of half an hour without indicating any discomfort." (cited *ibid*).

Commissioner Walker criticised this reasoning:

"In the first place that reasoning does not record any consideration of the designated type of chair nor does it show how, from the evidence about the amount of sitting the claimant could do in the chairs that she described, an appropriate deduction could be or was made or, for example, that the tribunal chair was of the prescribed kind. That failure was an error in law." (para.5).

Such concern for exactitude places a heavy burden on the relevant decisionmakers. It is, of course, important that the proper test is applied in all cases. In *CIB/177/1997*, Deputy Commissioner White suggests that:

"Where conclusions are drawn about a person's capacity for sitting, care should be taken that minds are addressed to sitting in the type of chair described in the regulations. But in the normal course of events, . . . it can be presumed (unless the tribunal record suggests the contrary) that it has considered both sitting and rising from sitting in an upright chair with a back but no arms" (para.7).

Similarly in *CSIB/457/02*, Commissioner Parker again stressed the need for the tribunal to make clear when making observations of the claimant at the hearing, that they had the statutorily stipulated type of chair in mind.

Hence, following *CSIB/12/96* an Appeal tribunal will err in law where its record shows that they may have drawn too sweeping a conclusion from the claimant's capacity to sit in, or rise from, a different type of chair. In *CIB/15663/1996*, Deputy Commissioner Fellner considered that if a DWPMS doctor with knowledge of the requirements of the sitting test, stated that he observed a claimant sitting with no apparent problems during the interview and selected in consequence a particular descriptor, a tribunal is entitled to have regard to that view, even where the chair in which the claimant sat may not have been the prescribed chair. In *CIB/2404/2001*, Commissioner Rowland commented that capacity to sit in another type of chair could have some relevance and be taken into account, provided always that "the tribunal makes it clear that their ultimate conclusion relates to the claimant's capacity to sit in the [statutorily stipulated chair]" (para.5). But see also *CSIB/324/97*, para.14, where Commissioner Walker reiterated his rigorous approach.

In *CIB/5654/97* Commissioner Lloyd-Davies remitted to a differently constituted tribunal, the case of a woman who made use of a special cushion to alleviate the discomfort she claimed she had while sitting. Despite the wording of reg.25(2) on aids and appliances normally worn or used, the Commissioner directed that:

> "the tribunal should ignore any use that the claimant may make of a special cushion to alleviate any discomfort she alleges she feels. The test concerns sitting in an armless upright chair: if the use of a cushion or cushions were not to be disregarded, the test would not be equivalent to sitting in a typical office, waiting-room or dining-room chair but would be more akin to sitting in an easy chair, which is not what the regulations provide. In so holding I recognise that regulation 25(2) of the Social Security (Incapacity for Work) General Regulations 1995, as amended with effect from 6 January 1997, provides:—
>
> > 'In determining the extent of a person's incapacity to perform any activity listed in Part I he should be assessed as if he was wearing any prosthesis with which he is fitted or, as the case may be, any aid or appliance which he normally wears or uses.'
>
> Apart from the fact that the grammar, notwithstanding the final 6 words, nonetheless seemingly requires the aid or appliance to be worn, I do not consider that this provision can be used in a manner which essentially alters the nature of the activity which is under assessment: sitting in an upright chair without arms is not the same activity as sitting in a cushioned chair." (para.3).

That general limitation on the scope of reg.25(2) was accepted and applied by Commissioner Howell in *CIB/614/98* with respect to Activity 5, below.

8.178   *Activity 3: "sitting in an upright chair with a back, but no arms": Descriptors 3(a)–(e):*
In *CSIB/12/96*, Commissioner Walker, considering the text of these descriptors prior to the changes effected in January 1997 by SI 1996/3207, stated:

> "What the descriptors, other than the first, require for satisfaction, in my judgement is first whether the individual is suffering discomfort from sitting which, after a time becomes so uncomfortable that the chair has to be left. Whether or not an activity can be carried on, as the tribunal sought to consider, is strictly irrelevant. That they did so is a further error in law. The time concerned then simply determines which of descriptors 3(b) to (c) is satisfied in the particular case." (para.6).

His approach is thus the same as the one effected by those textual changes, which were subsequently held invalid in *CIB/1239/2004* but valid in *CIB/3984/2004*, both noted at the end of the commentary on these descriptors.

In *CSIB/12/96*, the Commissioner, however, doubted the argument put by the claimant's representative, Mr Orr, "that comfort involved a positive state and was not just a lack of discomfort" (para.6). The Commissioner thought that:

" 'Discomfort' connotes only the state of being uncomfortable and the prefix 'un' is simply a negative. Accordingly, in sitting, a person who is not actually or positively comfortable falls to be described as uncomfortable or in discomfort—to however minor a degree. I doubt whether a possible semantic position of neutrality in this test is relevant to or practicable in such an exercise as the 'all work' test" (para.6).

Otherwise the Commissioner does not address descriptor 3(a). Since it neither refers to a requisite degree of discomfort nor specifically to any necessity to move from the chair because of the degree of discomfort, it might be thought arguable, with respect to descriptor 3(a), that someone who is always in discomfort (whether sitting or standing or lying down?), might qualify under it, even though the discomfort does not specifically arise as a result of sitting. But in *CSIB/38/96*, Commissioner Walker opined that "it is only if the sitting itself causes the lack of comfort which requires the individual to move about that activity 3, sitting, comes into play" (para.12) (followed in *CIB/4498/97*).

In *CIB/4553/1999*, Commissioner Rowland applied *CSIB/13/1996* and *CSIB/38/96*. He stated:

"I do not consider that, as a matter of law, only discomfort due to loss of spinal function can be relevant to the 'activity' of sitting, although loss of spinal function may be the most likely cause of relevant discomfort. However, the significance of the description of the neuritis, which was accepted as the cause of the present claimant's pain, is that it contains nothing to suggest that rising from a chair would alleviate discomfort caused by the neuritis while the claimant was sitting. In that sense, it was not shown that the 'activity' of sitting aggravated the condition causing the pain" (para.8).

Whether on the pre-1997 wording or the current wording, discomfort was relevant only if it required movement from the chair to alleviate it. Otherwise, the words "without having to move from the chair" would have had no purpose. Discomfort that could be alleviated by moving the upper body without rising from the chair was not material. The point had been made clearer by the 1997 amendment, which added the words "because the degree of discomfort makes it impossible to continue sitting" and possibly requires the discomfort to be more severe than was previously the case. Descriptor 3(b) gives rise to a score of 15 points. Descriptors 3(c) to 3(e) are in similar terms but refer to periods of 30 minutes, 1 hour and 2 hours, giving rise to scores of 7, 3 and 0 points respectively. Descriptor 3(a) is simply: "Cannot sit comfortably" but that gives rise to a score of 15 points (the maximum) and so the word "comfortably" must be construed in the same sense as it is used in the later descriptors to avoid the anomaly that would arise if the descriptor applied where discomfort was less disabling than that required for descriptor 3(c)" (para.7).

In *CIB/1239/2004*, Commissioner Henty followed *Howker* and Commissioner Jacobs in *CIB/884/2003* to hold invalid the 1996 amendments to Activity 3, thus striking out the added words "[because the degree of discomfort makes it impossible to continue sitting]". This made a difference because in his view those words had tangibly altered the meaning of the descriptor in question. The words struck out

"connote a high degree of discomfort which means that, albeit maybe only temporarily, the claimant *cannot* continue to sit. The words of the descriptor, without the offending words, in my view, connotes some lesser degree of discomfort which, while not making continued sitting actually impossible, necessarily means that the act of moving from the chair affords some relief. There is a difference between not being able to continue sitting comfortably and not being able to continue sitting because the discomfort makes it impossible.

The tribunal should therefore have considered the descriptor without the offending words in brackets. That must have some effect on how long it takes a claimant to satisfy any relevant condition" (paras 6, 7, emphasis in original).

Looking at the evidence before the tribunal, he held that the claimant could sit for 1–2 hours, thus adding to his total a score of three points from descriptor 3(d), and bringing his score to 15 points so that he satisfied the personal capability assessment.

In marked contrast, however, in *CIB/3397/2004*, Commissioner Jupp expressly disagreed with Commissioner Henty and held that the 1996 amendments to Activity 3 were not *ultra vires*—the amendment was correctly advised to the SSAC as neutral, adding only clarification—so that the tribunal to which she remitted the case would not need to disregard the wording added by the 1996 Regulations (see paras 25 and 26).

In *CSIB/169/2005* and *CIB/1205/2004*, Commissioners May and Rowland respectively, taking a different approach to the test for invalidity from Commissioner Jacobs in *R(IB) 3/04*, held valid the changes to Activity 3 descriptors. Commissioner Rowland expressly preferred Commissioner Jupp's approach to that of Commissioner Henty, pointing out that the latter's decision was made without him being referred to *CSIB/12/1996*.

8.179 *Activity 4: "Standing without the support of another person"*: In *CIB/4533/1999*, noted in the commentary to "sitting in an upright chair with a back but no arms", Commissioner Rowland stated that the reasoning applied there to "sitting" applied equally to "standing" (see para.9). "Standing" does not mean standing stock-still. The normal person (the yardstick for applying the descriptors) does not do so for any length of time. As Commissioner Lloyd-Davies stated in *R(IB) 6/04*:

> "The quasi-involuntary movements that most people make in standing for prolonged periods do not . . . count. Instead the tribunal should concentrate on how long a claimant can stand before needing or having to move around or sit down (usually because of pain in the back or legs)" (para.5).

8.180 *Activity 5: "rising from sitting in an upright chair with a back but no arms . . ."*: Decision-makers must apply the correct test in terms of the type of chair prescribed. Comments on that in *CSIB/12/96*, *CSIB/457/02* and *CIB/171/1997* (noted under *"Activity 3: sitting in an upright chair with a back but no arms"*, above) are equally applicable here. That need was again emphasised by Judge Ward in *GB v SSWP* [2009] UKUT 26 (AAC) in the context of whether a claimant could rise from such a chair without having to hold on to something.

In *CIB/614/98*, Commissioner Howell endorsed the principle in *CIB/5654/97* (see *Activity 3*, above) that reg.25(2), which requires assessment to take account of aids or appliances normally worn or used, cannot be used in a manner which essentially alters the nature of the activity under assessment. Accordingly, Commissioner Howell disregarded the claimant's use of crutches to rise from sitting, since the wording of the activity and its descriptors make clear that what is being tested is the ability to rise to an upright position without the use of arms and shoulders (para.16). What are being tested are principally disabilities to do with the functioning of legs, spine, general muscular co-ordination and balance. This approach did not render reg.25(2) of no useful effect, since,

> "for example a person who has to wear a calliper or a body support must now be clearly assumed to be wearing it, and its effect taken into account, in determining whether they can get themselves upright from a chair without having to use their arms to hold on to something as well" (*ibid.*)

Activity 5: "rising from sitting in an upright chair with a back but no arms": descriptors   **8.181**
(b) and (c) "without holding onto something": In *R(IB) 2/03*, Commissioner Jacobs
reviewed a number of authorities in coming to his conclusion, based on a linguistic
and functional analysis,

> "that a claimant who has to rely on some other part of the chair (the seat or
> the back) in order to deliver the force necessary to rise or to provide stability
> while rising is 'holding onto something' and scores points. This is subject to two
> qualifications. First, the points are only scored if the claimant 'cannot' rise from
> sitting without using his arms to provide power or stability. Second, the disability
> must arise from a specific bodily disease or disablement under regulation 25(3)
> (a) of the Social Security (Incapacity for Work) (General) Regulations 1995
> (para.21)".

The authorities analysed in support of his proposition were *CSIB/1124/2000*
(applying by analogy *CIB/614/1998*) and *CIB/16310/1996*. He rejected an opposing
authority—Commissioner Levenson in *CIB/15456/1996* which took no account of
the functional analysis.

In *CIB/5083/2001*, Deputy Commissioner Mark was of the view that "without
holding onto something" did not cover the claimant holding onto his own knees to
assist him rising so the tribunal's conclusion that he scored no points on the descriptor was correct (para.8).

Activity 6: bending and kneeling: In *R(IB) 2/02*, Commissioner Lloyd-Davies con-   **8.182**
sidered a case where the:

> "issue between the majority and the dissenting minority was whether 'squatting'
> constituted 'bending or kneeling'. The claimant submitted that squatting was
> neither (i) bending, that is to say, bending at the waist nor (ii) kneeling, that is to
> say placing one or both knees to the floor. On behalf of the Secretary of State it
> was submitted, by reference to various dictionary definitions, that 'bend' could
> refer not only to vertebral movement but also to bending of the knees.
> In my judgment 'bending or kneeling' does encompass squatting. I reached
> this conclusion not so much on the dictionary definitions recited to me on behalf
> of the Secretary of State, but rather in the context of the descriptors taken as a
> whole. The descriptors refer to bending or kneeling 'as if to pick up a piece of
> paper from the floor'. In my judgment these words colour the words 'bend or
> kneel' and require one to consider how people normally pick up a piece of paper
> from the floor. This is normally done by a combination of bending at the waist
> and bending at the knee, with an inclination of the head in order the better to be
> able to see: the number of people who actually *kneel*, in the sense of placing one
> or both knees to the floor, in order to pick up a piece of paper, are relatively few,
> as are the number of people who *bend only at the waist* without flexing at the knee
> at all. The descriptors thus must encompass bending the knees. On this analysis
> a person who *only* bends the knees, or squats, *can* bend or kneel as if to pick up
> a piece of paper from the floor and therefore does not satisfy the descriptors. As
> mentioned above the majority of the tribunal, however, found that the claimant
> was sometimes disabled from picking up a piece of paper from the floor even by
> squatting and for this reason correctly awarded the claimant 3 points". (paras 4,
> 5).

When the claimant sought from the Court of Appeal leave to appeal the descion
to that court, leave was refused. Aldous L.J. stated in *Purdy v Secretary of State for
Social Security* (October 6, 2000 reported with *R(IB) 2/02*):

> "The way Mr Purdy argues the case is this: because he cannot bend his back,
> in the sense of curving his back so as to enable him to pick up a piece of paper,
> he is entitled to the 15 points. In my view he has misunderstood the descriptor.
> As the Commissioner pointed out, it contains not just the statement 'cannot

bend', it goes on 'as if to pick up a piece of paper from the floor and straighten up again'. It is concerned with the disability of a person who is unable to get down to the floor and pick up a piece of paper without assistance. Mr Purdy has demonstrated to me when going down to pick up a piece of paper that he bends his knees, he bends at the hips and he bends his head. All that he does not do, or cannot do, is to curve his spine.

In my view, there is no way that this court would construe the descriptor in any way other than the way the Commissioner did. I therefore believe he stands no real chance of success in this court on his appeal. I therefore refuse the application for permission to appeal."

In *R(IB) 3/02*, Commissioner Howell applied *Purdy* as one reason for rejecting the view of the Commissioner who had granted leave to appeal.

The simple issue in the case:

"on which the Commissioner who granted leave in this case is I think in a minority of one, is whether a claimant who sometimes has a problem with bending but remains able to kneel, or sometimes has a problem with kneeling but remains able to bend, or can manage both but only partially, in each case so as to be able to get within sufficient reach of the floor to pick up a piece of paper, qualifies for the score of three points under descriptor 6(c) or not" (para.19).

In Commissioner Howell's view, someone who can bend but not kneel, or kneel but not bend, cannot score under descriptors 6(b) or (c). This approach was to be preferred for three reasons:

"First, the actual words used. To say that a person cannot do A or B means, if I may be forgiven a statement of the obvious, that he cannot do either of those things: in other words he can do neither. To convey in normal English the meaning that either he cannot do A or he cannot do B, a different sentence construction is needed, or the use of a word such as 'each' or 'both' after the negative. I agree with what is said in decision *CIB/3809/97* para. 14 that the scoring descriptors (b) and (c) are not satisfied if the claimant can reach the floor by bending but not by kneeling or vice versa, and the language used excludes the contrary view.
24. Second, the additional words inserted into these two descriptors in the form in which they now stand place beyond argument that they are intended to be read in the majority sense. It is simply inconsistent with any conceivable rational intent that a person not able either to bend or to kneel fully, but still able to struggle and reach the floor by a partial combination of the two should be given no score, when a person who has no problem at all doing it by one means alone should still get the points.
25. Third, the minority view is in my judgment necessarily inconsistent with the approach of Aldous L.J. in the Court of Appeal in *Purdy v Secretary of State*, October 6, 2000, rejecting as unarguable the claimant's application for leave to appeal against the Commissioner's decision in case *CIB/228/99*. There the claimant was able to reach the floor mainly by bending at his knees and squatting or crouching though he had to keep his back straight, and the refusal of a scoring descriptor was held correct, Aldous L.J. observing in particular that the descriptor was

'concerned with the disability of a person who is unable to get down to the floor and pick up a piece of paper without assistance.'

Subject to the qualification that the manual dexterity needed for the operation of actually picking up the paper is separately tested under the next activity, and is not part of this one, that decision seems to me to confirm that the scoring descriptors do not apply to a person who is able to get down and up again by one means or another, even if he cannot do both. Although given on an ex parte application for leave to appeal, it was a reasoned decision given in the Court of Appeal and thus in my view to be taken as authoritative so far as Commissioners are concerned" (paras 23–25).

Purdy was followed by the Deputy Commissioner in *CIB/459/00*, but that decision is now under appeal to the Court of Appeal as *Housam v DWP*.

Activity 6: bending and kneeling: descriptors 6(a)–(c): Note that, even after the January 1997 textual changes, these descriptors all contain the words "and straighten up again". Hence a tribunal's failure to consider that aspect of the case was held to be a further error in law in *CSIB/12/96* (considering the test as it was before the January 1997 changes) (see para.7). In that case, Commissioner Walker also held that if the person required assistance in order to straighten up, descriptor 6(a) is satisfied (para.9). That decision was rendered in respect of regulations not then containing the italicised words in reg.25(2) as currently worded:

> "In determining the extent of a person's incapacity to perform any activity listed in Part I he shall be assessed as if he were wearing any prosthesis with which he is fitted, *or, as the case may be, any aid or appliance which he normally wears or uses.*"

It is submitted that the addition of the italicised phrase does not on its current wording cover assistance from another person: the phrase seems to refer to things, rather than assistance from people. Note also in support of this view that some activities/descriptors distinguish between aids and assistance or support (or lack of it) from another person (see Activities 4, 5). In *CIB/4300/2003*, Commissioner Rowland held erroneous a tribunal decision that found a claimant had "no problem with bending and kneeling" when the evidence before it showed that to do so she needed to hold onto the couch with one hand. They erred by thus regarding that support as irrelevant whereas the "approach that an ability to carry out the function only with support is to be disregarded was taken in *CIB 2945 00* as well as *CSIB 12 96*" (para.7).

Descriptor (a) reads "cannot bend to touch his knees and straighten up again". In *CIB/15262/1996*, Commissioner Williams pointed out that:

> "the test is 'bend to touch the knees', not 'bend the knees to touch them', which is the only other normal physical way of being able to touch the knees when in an upright position. It is also a test of touching 'the knees' not one of them, so the actions of lifting a leg or bending sideways to touch one knee are not included. This is confirmed by the full test, which is to bend to touch the knees 'and straighten up again'. If the claimant has not bent to touch his knees he does not need to 'straighten up again' " (para.11).

There was evidence in the case that this claimant could not bend forward without severe pain although he could, keeping his back straight, bend his knees to pick up light objects from the floor. The tribunal erred in law by failing specifically to consider descriptor (a).

Activity 6: bending and kneeling: descriptors (b) and (c): "as if to pick up a piece of paper from the floor": In *CIB/1265/2002*, Commissioner Williams held that this language could not assist a claimant who suffered severe allergic reactions to paper. The words are "as if to". No actual ability to pick up paper is involved. In *CSIB/169/2005*, Commissioner May upheld as valid the 1997 changes to descriptor (b).

Activity 6: bending and kneeling: descriptor (d) "no problem with bending and kneeling": In its context this has to mean, "no problem with bending or kneeling such as would cause the claimant to satisfy one of the other descriptors" with respect to Activity 6 (*CIB/4300/2003*, para.8).

8.183

8.184

8.185

8.186 *Activity 7 descriptors: validity of 1997 amendments:* In *CIB/3649/2004*, Commissioner Jupp held that the changes to the relevant Activity 7 descriptors were not invalid, having correctly been described to the SSAC as neutral in effect.

8.187 *Activity 7: manual dexterity: descriptor (d) "cannot use a pen or pencil":* In *R(IB) 1/98*, Commissioner Rice noted that the rubric, unlike those in paras (a)–(c) of activity 7 descriptors, does not include the words "with either hand". Despite that he did not consider that this meant:

> "that a person is entitled under descriptor 7(d) to 15 points if he cannot use a *pencil in each hand*. As most people can only use a pen or pencil in one hand, such a construction would make nonsense of the descriptor. Accordingly, I am satisfied that the test is whether or not a person cannot use a pen or pencil *with either hand*.
>
> 7. Accordingly, if a person cannot use a pen or pencil for the purposes for which a pen or pencil is normally used with either the right or the left hand, depending on which is dominant, he will prima facie be entitled to 15 points. Of course, it may be that in unusual circumstances a person who is, for example right-handed and has lost the use of that hand for writing, has acquired a compensating skill in his left hand. If that is the case, then he will not satisfy the descriptor. It may be that his skill in the left hand is not as good as it was originally in the right hand, but provided he still attains a reasonable standard so that he could be said in everyday language to be able to use a pen or pencil to write reasonably clearly and at reasonable speed, as well as to accomplish other things such as ticking forms and signing his name, he will not be entitled to the 15 points. Seemingly in the case of an ambidextrous person, he will not satisfy the test, so long as he has sufficient use of *one* hand" (paras 6, 7, emphasis in the original).

In the case before the Commissioner, the claimant succeeded; he was righthanded, unable to hold a pen or pencil in that hand, and unable to use the same in his left hand to produce anything more than a scrawl, nothing legible (para.8). In *CIB/13161/96* and *CIB/13508/96*, Commissioner Howell commented

> "the descriptor 'cannot use a pen or pencil' . . . must mean by necessary common sense implication that the claimant scores the points if he is phyically unable to use a pen or pencil to write in a normal manner. A fair reading does not need the schedule itself to spell out that this is what is meant, rather than a total inability to wield a pen or pencil for any purpose at all, even punching a hole in a sheet of paper" (para.38).

8.188 *Activity 7: Manual dexterity:* In *CSIB/20/1996*, the Commissioner refused to read the words "safely or in safety" into the descriptors. Commissioner Levenson disagreed with that in *CIB/4315/1997*, upholding as legitimate a tribunal award of a score on manual dexterity to a claimant allergic to, amongst other things, nickel in silver coins and taps, so that wearing gloves did not help. It was legitimate bearing in mind the "reasonable regularity" approach and that a claimant should be able to perform activities without an unreasonable degree of pain and discomfort.

8.189 *Activity 7 (manual dexterity): descriptors (b) and (f) [knobs on sink tap or cooker: the meaning of "or"]* In a Northern Ireland decision, *R1/03(IB)*, Chief Commissioner Martin held the "or" was here to be read disjunctively so that the adjudicating authorities are concerned with the capacity, or lack thereof, of a claimant to turn a sink tap *or* control knobs of a cooker. The movements required to turn a sink tap rather than a cooker knob are not necessarily the same or similar, so that a claimant can have real difficulty with one rather than the other. Hence, if a claimant is not able to carry out either one or the other function he will satisfy the appropriate test and score the relevant score.

8.190 *Activity 7 (manual dexterity): descriptors (b) and (f) [knobs on sink tap: the type of sink tap contemplated]* The sink tap contemplated by descriptors 7(b) and (f) is "a tap requiring an ordinary amount of force to turn it, when it is closed so as to prevent water dripping through it" (*CIB/2404/2001*, para.10). So a tribunal there did not err by finding that the claimant could turn a tap "if it is not too tight", since anyone can have difficulty with a tap that is jammed or overtightened (*ibid.*).

Activity 7 (manual dexterity): descriptor (e): cannot tie a bow in laces or string: tying a bow in laces or string requires more than finger movements; the need to pull the bow tight involves a gripping action of the respective loops by the fingers of the respective hand and a pulling action by both wrists (*CIB/1690/2007*, para.6).

8.191

Activity 8: lifting and carrying: In *CIB/483/2001*, Commissioner Rowland held that a tribunal which asked the claimant whether he could lift 2.5 kilos from table top height and hand it to another person, erred in law by applying the wrong test:

8.192

> " 'carry' connotes a degree of movement from one place to another. Merely handing something to someone is not carrying it. The claimant's case is that he could lift a 2.5 kilogramme bag but that he could not carry it and it is therefore plain that his case must be considered by another tribunal" (para.3).

In *CIB/5027/2001* [now *R(IB) 5/03*], Commissioner Turnbull considered him wrong so to hold, because that approach ignores the wording of the activity, which has since January 6, 1997 required one to look to the ability to lift and carry "by the use of the upper body and arms (excluding all other activities specified in Pt I of the Schedule)". He thought that abilities to "pick up and carry" an object thus "do not require [the claimant] to be able to do more than move the object by means of his upper body and arms, and in particular do not require him to be able to walk with it" (para.8). In *CIB/727/1998* (now reported as *R(IB) 4/03*), Deputy Commissioner Parker (as she then was) thought that the purpose of the 1997 amendments was to compartmentalise from "lifting and carrying" activities such as walking, climbing stairs, etc. to prevent them assisting the claimant under Activity 8 merely because they were sometimes associated with lifting and carrying. Although read literally the revised rubric of the activity might be thought to preclude taking account of an impairment of the hands (something also covered by "manual dexterity"—activity 7 in Pt I of the Schedule), common sense, context (all the Activity 8 descriptors refer to use of hands) and a purposive construction combined so that the limiting phrase "excluding all other activities specified in Part I of this Schedule" by necessary implication exempts from the exclusion the activity of manual dexterity" (paras 15, 16).

In *Capello v Secretary of State for Work and Pensions*, 2004 S.L.T. 115, in the Outer House of the Court of Session, Lady Paton, refusing the applicant's application for judicial review of a refusal of a Commissioner to grant leave to appeal a tribunal decision to Commissioner level, expressed agreement with Commissioners Turner and Parker and disagreement with Commissioner Rowland (see paras 73–78). That, and the fact that both the decisions of Commissioners Parker and Turnbull are reported establishes their view as fully authoritative on the point.

In *CIB/2916/2004*, taking due account of *R(IB) 5/03*, Commissioner Rowland held that a tribunal erred in law in not considering the impact on Activity 8 (lifting and carrying) of the claimant's pulmonary problems, his breathlessness; "[t]he personal capability assessment is intended to be a practical test and I can see no reason why the impact that loss of pulmonary function has on a claimant's ability to make use of his upper limbs should be ignored" (para.6). Both Commissioner Gamble in *CIB/2821/2004* (para.8) and Commissioner Jupp in *CIB/3397/2004* (paras 11–20), applying the *Howker* principle, held that the changes effected by the 1996 amending Regulations to Activity 8 (lifting and carrying) were neutral and accordingly valid. Agreeing with the result, but not their approach, so did Commissioner May in *CSIB/169/2005*, applying his own decision and reasoning in *CSIB/148/2005*. See further the discussion at the beginning of the commentary to this Sch. (*An Important Note on Amendments and Possible Invalidity*).

Since the wording of the descriptor stipulates "by the use of the upper body and arms", that legal test "permits a tribunal to take account of a claimant's back pain", and a tribunal which refuses to do so misdirects itself in law. Commissioner Jacobs so held in *CIB/0960/2006* (para.15). However, a mere misdirection which did not affect the outcome is not an error of law (*R. (Iran) v Secretary of State for the Home Department* [2005] EWCA Civ 982). Accordingly, since the claimant could only have scored eight points, the mistake did not affect the outcome of the appeal to the tribunal and its decision was thus not erroneous in law.

8.193   *Activity 9: Reaching:* In *CIB/2811/2005*, Deputy Commissioner Mark considered that while descriptor (b) (cannot raise either arm to his head as if to put on a hat) did not involve raising the upper arm above head level, descriptor (d) (cannot raise either arms above his head as if to reach for something) "means that more than a minimal amount of the arm must be above head level. Reaching involves a degree of stretching, and involves being able to raise the upper arm above shoulder level and to go at least some way towards straightening the arm in moving it towards a notional object" (para.7) So that a claimant with full elbow flexion could probably achieve the task in (b) but not (d).

8.194   *Activity 10: Speech:* In *CSIB/413/1998*, Commissioner May appeared to cast doubt on the proposition that pain was relevant to the activity of speaking. In contrast, in *CIB 4306/1999* Deputy Commissioner White considered the speech descriptors. In his view:

> "descriptor (a) covers someone who has no power of speech, and could also cover someone whose condition was such that either they had been advised not to speak or whom speaking caused such pain that they could not reasonably be said to be able to speak. I can conceive of situations in which the act of talking causes such pain that it would be right to conclude that a claimant was unable to speak. . . . What the threshold of pain is in any particular case is an issue of fact for the tribunal in the light of all the evidence." (para.17)

Whether a claimant cannot be understood or cannot easily be understood so as to satisfy descriptors (b) to (e) is similarly a matter of fact for the tribunal to resolve in the light of all the evidence in the case.

8.195   *Activities 11 (hearing) and 12 (vision): "if such aid is normally worn":* In *CIB/14499/1996*, Commissioner Levenson interpreted this to mean if the aid in question is normally worn by people in the claimant's situation acting reasonably in all the circumstances. So if someone would be able to see perfectly well if wearing prescription sunglasses, but unreasonably refused to wear them and could not see without them, that person cannot score points under Activity 12.

8.196   *Activity 11 (hearing):* ability to understand what is being said by lip-reading is irrelevant to assessment under the descriptors attached to this activity; understanding through hearing is what is being tested (*SM v SSWP* [2008] UKUT 39 (AAC), paras 5, 6).

8.197   *Activity 11: hearing: descriptor (e) "cannot hear well enough to understand someone talking in a normal voice on a busy street":* In *CIB/590/1998*, Commissioner Angus accepted to some degree that the descriptors

> "had to be considered in the light of what is reasonable. It is not reasonable to say that a claimant can understand someone talking in a normal voice in a busy street if he can gain that understanding only by making frequent requests for repetition of what has been said" (paras 9, 12),

so that descriptor 11(e) applied to the claimant.
Agreeing with this in *CIB/3123/2002*, Commissioner Bano added that the descrip-

tor should be considered by reference to a claimant's ability to understand someone with whom s/he is not familiar, so that the tribunal erred in law in considering the claimant's ability to understand his wife (who always accompanied him outdoors) when on busy streets (para.8).

Activity 12: vision: descriptor (c) cannot see well enough to read 16 point print at a distance greater than 20 centimetres: In a Northern Ireland decision *C12/00–01(IB)*, Commissioner Brown stated

8.198

"14. In my view the descriptor in this case relates to the visual ability to distinguish 16 point print characters so as to be able to decipher and distinguish individual words. It does not import any sustained reading ability. One reads whether one reads a word or a paragraph. It is the visual ability which is the salient factor. The ability to read is not being tested just whether or not the vision is good enough to read 16 point print characters at the relevant distance.

15. In light of my decision on the interpretation of the descriptor the other arguments relating to reasonableness and reasonable regularity are not relevant. The descriptor does not require the claimant to read for any particular length of time so the recurrence of floaters after ten seconds of reading is not relevant. It is vision which is tested not any sustained reading ability.

16. I am strengthened in this view by the fact that in another descriptor within the All Work Test i.e. descriptor 15(c) the ability to concentrate to read a magazine article is referred to. Had the legislature in this particular descriptor wished to provide for sustained reading ability it could quite easily have done so. The absence of such provision indicates to me that it was only the visual ability mentioned above which was being referred to."

The Commissioner here followed Deputy Commissioner Warren in *CIB/4998/1998*. A similar approach was taken by Deputy Commissioner Street in *CIB/333/1998*. Limiting her comments on reasonableness and reasonable regularity to the context of her case, Commissioner Brown's interpretation was endorsed by Commissioner Williams in *CIB/2354/2001* in which he considered descriptor 12(c) to be

"a specific application of the approach of the standard medical test for vision by use of a test card with letters of different sizes on it (the Snellen eye chart used by doctors and opticians). That requires ability to identify individual letters of different sizes rather than to read any meaning into them" (para.11).

So that "the question for [this descriptor] is whether the claimant . . . has the visual ability to distinguish letters *under the required conditions* on a reasonably regular basis" (para.12, emphasis added by commentator). The conditions are set by Activity 12, which requires assessing "vision in normal daylight or bright electric light with glasses or other aid to vision if such aid is normally worn". On the "normally worn" aspect see *CIB/14499/1996*. The rubric is "daylight *or* bright electric light". In *CIB/2584/2002* Commissioner Williams saw this as meaning that an inability to meet the visual descriptors in one of those contexts, while being able to meet them in the other, would suffice (para.8). Dealing with a claimant adversely affected in the proximity of intense bright light, and taking account of concepts of reasonable regularity and the relevance of pain and discomfort, he was of the view (again endorsing the interpretation in *C12/00–01 (IB)*) that the

"claimant does not need a sustained ability to read in bright artificial light to have adequate vision for these purposes, but if the exposure to bright artificial light for any significant time causes pain and/or stops her focussing and/or makes her shut her eyes to avoid the effects of the light at some point, then from that point she presumably cannot meet that descriptor even for the shortest period. The question is whether, taking those limits into account, she does or does not have the relevant level of vision" (para.18).

He remitted this matter to another tribunal because further findings needed to be made in respect of the key issues.

In *CIB/2952/2004*, Commissioner Bano considered the meaning of "bright electric light" in the statutory wording of the Activity:

"The tribunal held that fluorescent light was not 'bright electric light', but I agree with the claimant and the Secretary of State's representative that that was wrong in law. In *CIB/2584/2002* the Commissioner held that the term 'bright electric light' was intended to encompass the sort of lighting which complies with health and safety standards. Fluorescent light is the form of light now generally provided in workplaces, and I agree with the Secretary of State's representative that the term 'electric light' in its ordinary and natural meaning extends to fluorescent light. In *Tilling-Stevens Motors Limited v Kent County Council* [1929] AC 354 it was held that the term 'electrically-propelled vehicle' covered a vehicle driven by electricity generated by an internal combustion engine, and in my judgement the term 'electric light' must be taken to encompass fluorescent lighting, as well as lighting produced by the electrical heating of a filament" (para.6).

8.199 *Activity 12: vision: descriptors (d) and (e): cannot see well enough to recognise a friend across the room (road):* In Commissioner Turnbull's judgment, this test only requires the claimant to be able to identify a friend who is alone the requisite distance across the room or road. It does not stipulate that he be able to pick the friend out from a number of people. The time it may take to "recognise" the friend is material in that it may take so long a time that it is proper to regard that time lapse as amounting to "cannot" recognise the friend (*CIB/1323/2007*).

8.200 *Activity 13: Continence (other than enuresis (bed wetting):* Applying the descriptors in the "all work test" ["personal capability assessment"] involves intrusive scrutiny of the lives of claimants, those in respect of Activity 13 particularly so, embracing intimate and embarrassing areas affecting a claimant's dignity. It is necessary to appreciate the nature of the problems of sufferers, the role of diet, colostomy, ileostomy and urostomy bags, and the effect of medication. It is also necessary to define carefully the terms used in the descriptors and apply them carefully.

8.201 *Activity 13: Continence (bowel or bladder) other than enuresis (bed wetting): the meaning of continence:* In *R(IB) 4/04*, a Tribunal of Commissioners rejected as too broad the definition advanced on behalf of the Secretary of State that "continence" relates to whether a person is able, by his actions, simply to contain his emissions of urine and excrement (para.34). Instead it made use of the relevant definition in Blakiston's Gould Medical Dictionary (4th ed.):

"The proper functioning of any sphincter or other structure of the gastro intestinal tract so as to prevent regurgitation or premature emptying".

Commissioner May in *CSIB/169/2005*, applying his own decision, reasoning and approach to the invalidity question and test in *CSIB/148/2005*, upheld as valid the 1997 revision of the terms of Activity 13. See further the discussion at the beginning of the commentary to this Sch. (*An Important Note on Amendments and Possible Invalidity*).

8.202 *Activity 13: bowel incontinence:* Apparently some 20 per cent of the population suffers from irritable bowel syndrome (IBS), a condition which may have a disruptive and distressing effect on their personal lives and their ability to undertake work. A medical report from a consultant physician with considerable expertise cited in *CIB/14332/96* is very telling:

"Urgency of defecation is a well recognised symptom of Irritable Bowel Syndrome, but not one suffered by all patients with IBS. It is sometimes so severe that patients are restricted in their activities and afraid to go out. This urgency is disabling and perhaps 10–15 per cent of patients with IBS and a similar proportion are unable to work. You are of course right in saying that there is a wide range of severity and in the type of symptoms suffered by patients with IBS, ranging from mild discomfort to excruciating pain and mild bowel irregularity to severe irregularity suffered by [the claimant]. The urgency suffered by patients with IBS does occasionally lead to incontinence of faeces. You ask if there is a medical definition of losing control of the bowels. The term used by doctors is faecal incontinence and this covers everything from minor stain on the under-pants when evacuating wind to liquid running down the legs. Obviously the distress caused by incontinence varies with its severity. However fear of incon-tinence is very severe in some people and has even made IBS patients suicidal. You ask if there is a medical definition of the bowel and does this include the external anal sphincter. The term bowel is not a precisely definable one and it is better to talk about the specific part of the intestines such as the small intestine, large intestine, rectum and anus. Obviously 'bowel function' in the ordinary sense of the word is greatly determined by the efficiency and function of the anal sphincters (internal as well as external). Finally you ask if treatment of IBS with antidiarrhoeal drugs can lead to an increase in abdominal pain. The answer is yes it certainly can and this causes considerable problems in management."

In *R(IB) 4/04*, a tribunal of Commissioners considered the function of intestines (bowels) and the nature and role of a colostomy bag or an ileostomy bag, stating that

"The intestines (or bowels) comprise that portion of the alimentary canal from the stomach to the anus, comprising a convoluted part extending from the stomach to the cecum (the small intestine) and a sacculated part overarching the small intestine and extending from the ileum to the anus (the large intestine). Crohn's disease is a chronic, recurrent regional inflammation of the intestines, characterised by abdominal pain and diarrhoea. It can be treated by an operation establishing an opening or stoma from the intestines through the abdomen, to divert the faecal flow from the diseased area into a fitted bag, which is external to the body. The starting point for the by-pass depends upon the location of the diseased area. Where the starting point is the ileum, the operation is known as an "ileostomy"; and where it runs from the colon, as a "colostomy" - but the effect of these two operations is identical. The person who has had the benefit of the operation in either case has no control over what flows from his body into the bag (in the sense that he cannot by any act of will stop or otherwise affect the flow), but, of course, he has complete control over emptying the bag so that, if the bag is efficient, he can lead a virtually normal functional life" (para.10).

In *CIB 3074/2003*, Commissioner Bano emphasised the need to look at the EMP's evidence in the light of all the evidence in the case and to examine the claimant's questionnaire as a whole (including statements in the "additional information" section of the form), rather than relying exclusively on the boxes ticked or not ticked by the claimant. He applied this to the difficult area of bowel incontinence attribut-able to "irritable bowel syndrome". He stated that such claims

"need to be treated with caution, and I must bear in mind that the claimant did not tick the boxes indicating problems controlling his bowels on either of the two incapacity benefit questionnaires which he completed. On the other hand, the claimant did give a detailed account in both questionnaires of 'accidents', and other circumstantial details indicating genuine loss of control of bowel function, rather than mere urgency of defecation. Since the claimant did tick the box indi-cating no problems controlling his bladder, I think it likely that the claimant did not tick the boxes relating to bowel control because he considered that he had given all the information which was needed in relation to control of his bowels in the 'additional information' section of the form. The diagnosis of irritable bowel syndrome has been corroborated by the claimant's general practitioner and the symptoms described by the claimant are entirely consistent with those which were described by the consultant physician who provided an expert report on the condition in *CIB/14322/1996*. I can find no reason to doubt the claimant's account and, on that basis, I am satisfied that the claimant does lose bowel control at least occasionally, attracting an award of 9 points in respect of descriptor 13(e)." (para.18).

8.203   *Activity 13: bowel incontinence; effect of diet:* In *CSIB/889/1999*, Commissioner May thought it

> "obvious that it would be absurd that if satisfaction of points scoring descriptors could on a reasonable and practical basis be avoided by the claimant controlling his diet then if the claimant fails or neglects to take these steps he could obtain the benefit of scoring points" (para.9).

To hold otherwise would run contrary to a scheme aimed at measuring by points whether someone is capable or incapable of work. He declined, however, to attempt to resolve the conflict over the effect of medication and the issue of "voluntary" control found in decisions *CSIB/38/1996* and the Northern Ireland decision *R2/00(IB)*, noted below.

8.204   *Activity 13: Continence: "loses control of bowels":* In *CIB/14332/96*, a decision which will give aid and comfort to severe IBS sufferers like the claimant in that case, Commissioner Goodman held that the term

> " 'loses control of bowels' does not require a claimant to suffer a wet discharge, but 'can comprehend a situation where a claimant does not in fact 'mess himself', provided he is able immediately to rush to a nearby lavatory" (para.16),

and the decision is a precedent for that proposition (*ibid.*). In thus supporting the decision of the majority of the SSAT in favour of the claimant, Commissioner Goodman drew on the distinction in the Activity 13 descriptors (a) and (d) between "no voluntary control of the bowels" and "loses control of bowels". He also used as an aid to interpretation of the term the statement in para.7 of the Benefit Agency's *Medical Services Incapacity Benefit Handbook for Medical Services Doctors*:

> "Clients with gastro-intestinal problems or frequency of micturition should be considered as having no voluntary control when their problem is such that they would become incontinent if they did not leave their work place immediately or within a very short space of time."

The Commissioner did not consider that decisions on disregarding the working situation precluded drawing on the statement as an interpretative aid (para.13) and indeed gave some indication that he did not necessarily endorse the approach taken in those cases (para.12), although such a view is very much out of line with the prevailing authorities in the area. He considered that

> "the expression loses 'control of bowels' is apt (as indeed the Handbook indicates) to include a situation like this where the claimant suffers from severe Irritable Bowel Syndrome. He loses control of his bowels at least once a month (indeed it appears once a week probably) in the sense that he is not able to 'hold himself', as the normal person can do even when faced with a considerable urge to defaecate. If the claimant did not immediately rush to the lavatory, he would indeed 'mess himself' " (para.14).

The decision turns to a great extent on the facts of that particular case "and is not to be regarded as a precedent for a view that every sufferer from Irritable Bowel Syndrome (which is widespread) could be said to fulfill any of the descriptors specified in para.13. The likelihood is that the majority of such sufferers could not comply with any of those descriptors" (para.16). The case seems to be the first such brought before the Commissioners (para.15). Other diseases like Crohn's Disease give rise to similar problems but "must await decision when cases involving them arise" (para.16). The principle laid down by Commissioner Goodman was accepted by Northern Ireland's Chief Commissioner in *C18/97(IB)* and in *C70/98(IB)*.

Activity 13: Continence: descriptor (a) "no voluntary control over bowels": The meaning of "voluntary control" and how this relates to claimants able to operate a colostomy or an ileostomy bag has caused problems for decision-makers, tribunals, Commissioners and Courts (see *C11/96 (IB), C2/98 (IB),* decisions of Northern Ireland Commissioners of persuasive authority in the British system, and, by analogy on bladder incontinence, *CIB/14210/96; Perry v Adjudication Officer,* a decision of the Northern Ireland Court of Appeal, reported as an appendix to *R 8/99 (IB)).* These decisions examined the notion of "voluntary control", whether such a bag could be regarded as a substitute for final part of the anus, and therefore whether it constituted a prosthesis, or whether it could properly be regarded as an aid or appliance which the claimant normally wears or uses. As regards Northern Ireland, in *Perry v Adjudication Officer,* the appeal from *C2/98(IB),* the Northern Ireland Court of Appeal held that a colostomy bag was no more a prosthesis (an artificial substitute for a body part) than the incontinence pad rejected as such in *CSIB/74/1996* or than a wheelchair, zimmer frame or dialysis machine. It would, however, rank on the amended version of reg.25(2) as an aid or appliance normally worn or used. Nonetheless, the claimant who can successfully use a colostomy bag so that he avoids accidents by wearing the bag and emptying it at appropriate intervals, can still satisfy the all work test (or now be held incapable under the personal capability assessment) by means of satisfying the descriptor 13(a): no voluntary control over bowels. Carswell L.C.J. stated that the court was conscious that, even after the changes to reg.25(2), such a claimant would be entitled to incapacity benefit although his working ability is substantially intact. The court doubted that this was Parliament's intention.

8.205

"Nevertheless, we do not see any escape from such a conclusion. Even if we adopt a purposive construction of the regulations, we do not find it possible to hold that the wearer of a colostomy bag has voluntary control over his bowels. It is true that he can prevent 'bowel accidents', the uncontrolled escape of faeces, by keeping in place the bag, which acts as a secure receptacle, and emptying it at convenient intervals. But on the ordinary use of language that is not voluntary control of the bowels themselves, which is the way in which paragraph 13(a) is worded. The Commissioner held that the appellant had 'no problems with his bowels', which in one sense may be true. In the context of paragraph 13, however, that has to be contrasted with lack of voluntary control over his bowels and must in our view mean that the claimant has normal voluntary control. The appellant patently has not such control, as the Commissioners who gave decisions numbers *C11/96(IB)* and *CSIB/74/96* indicated. We accordingly are unable to agree with the conclusion of the Commissioner in the present case that the 'appellant has no problem with his bowels'."

The court allowed the appeal.

As regards Great Britain, in *R(IB) 4/04,* following *R(SB) 1/90,* a Tribunal of Commissioners held that decisions of the Northern Ireland Court of Appeal are binding on Commissioners across the United Kingdom as regards the *ratio decidendi* of its judgments. As regards obiter statements like those in *Perry,* the Tribunal of Commissioners held that

"The extent to which *obiter dicta* of those courts should be followed depends upon the circumstances in which the judicial comment was made. Where such comments are made without full argument, and, having heard full argument, Commissioners consider the view expressed to be erroneous, then it is open to them to depart from the statement of law expressed. However, where, as in this case, the Lord Chief Justice of Northern Ireland expresses the view of a unanimous Court of Appeal, after full argument by Leading Counsel (including Leading Counsel acting as *amicus curiae*), on a regulatory provision identically worded in Northern Ireland as in Great Britain, expressly for the purpose of giving guidance to Commissioners, then it seems to us that such comments are hardly less persuasive upon Commissioners than the *ratio* of a Northern Ireland Court of Appeal decision. Where an appellate court makes it clear that it is giving guidance on a potentially controversial point to prevent further unnecessary adjudications, such *dicta* are of the highest possible persuasive authority. A Commissioner (or a Tribunal of Commissioners) could only not follow such *dicta* in quite exceptional circumstances, circumstances which are certainly not present in the case before us" (para.30).

Even had they not been constrained to do so by *Perry*, the Tribunal of Commissioners would have held that for the reasons advanced by Caswell L.C.J., stated above, that a person wearing an ileostomy or colostomy bag falls with descriptor 13(a) as having no "voluntary control" over his bowels (para.31 read with para.37):

"Descriptor 13(a) is 'No voluntary control over bowels'. As indicated above (Paragraph 10), the term 'bowel' is usually used to describe the alimentary canal from the stomach to the anus. Mr Keeny indicated that there was a medical debate as to whether the term should properly be used to include the anal sphincter. However, this tract works by peristaltic reflex action, and the only voluntary control a person in normal health exercises over it derives from muscular control exerted by the anal sphincter. In this specific context, the reference to 'voluntary control' can therefore only refer to control of the urge to expel waste from the body by the anal sphincter muscle. This is consistent with the definition of 'Continence' within the activity title (Paragraph 34 above).

An ileostomy bag plays no part whatsoever in assisting a person's control over the one part of bowel activity in which a healthy person can actively participate, *viz* the urge to expel waste from the body. Such a bag does not make a person continent. As the Medical Services Handbook indicates (see Paragraph 31 above), what it does is to mitigate the consequences of incontinence by, in common terms, preventing a mess occurring. An incontinence pad performs the same function. As their name suggests, incontinence pads do not render a person continent but, again, simply mitigate the results of incontinence. Therefore, in our judgment, neither ileostomy nor colostomy bags, nor incontinence pads, affect a person's capacity to perform the activity in issue, *i.e.* continence. This can be compared with, say, a pair of spectacles which is an external aid which does affect the wearer's ability to perform the activity in issue, in that case vision." (paras 35, 36).

8.206 *Activity 13: continence: descriptor (b) "no voluntary control over bladder":* In *CSIB/38/96*, Commissioner Walker set aside as erroneous in law, because not supported by the evidence, a tribunal finding that this descriptor applied to the claimant. Remitting the matter to another tribunal, he said of the descriptor:

"the proper starting point is to determine whether the frequency of visits [to the toilet] are (*sic*) simply anticipatory or as a matter of precaution, or whether they proceed upon some indication of urgency which the exercise of will cannot postpone, otherwise than perhaps *de minimis*, that the new tribunal will be entitled to conclude that this claimant has no 'voluntary control' over his bladder" (para.8).

Since "voluntary", in his view, referred to that part of control requiring effort of will (para.7), however, the matter would have to be assessed ignoring the medication which helped the claimant to control his bladder since the Commissioner did not regard "any control assisted by medication as fairly voluntary"(para.9). In *CSIB/889/1999*, noted earlier on the effect of diet, Commissioner May declined to attempt to resolve the conflict over the effect of medication and the issue of "voluntary" control found in decisions *CSIB/38/1996* and the Northern Ireland decision *R2/00(IB)*. His decisions on the effect of diet as a means of avoiding and controlling incontinence, is, it is submitted, more consistent with the line taken in the Northern Ireland decision. In *R2/00(IB)*, Commissioner Brown stated that she agreed:

"with Ms Slevin that close attention to the wording of the descriptors must be given. The descriptor in question is 'no voluntary control'. The word 'voluntary' describes the control. It delineates the nature of the control. It does not limit how voluntary control is to be brought about. The phrase 'no voluntary control' appears to me to contemplate, though not necessarily exclusively, situations where a person either has no mental awareness of a need to empty bladder or bowel and thus no control over it by will or choice or has such awareness but has no ability to control that need by exercise of the will. Medication may work in several ways. It may give the person the relevant mental awareness and enable that person to exercise control by will. It may remedy a defect in the relevant organ or in the central nervous system and enable the person to exercise control by will. It may work in other ways, the above is not an exhaustive list. What the medication may do is not per se provide voluntary control (that is done by the person himself), rather it may enable the person to exercise such control. If the person acquires control by will over the emptying of bladder or bowel then it seems to me that that person cannot be said to have no voluntary control. For example a child in normal health becomes continent because training gives the child the ability to exercise voluntary control over the emptying of bladder and bowel. Either an organ or the child's nervous system may become defective and control by will or choice may be lost. Medication may remedy the defect in the organ or nervous system and enable that control to be restored. The control is by choice or will. The medication has remedied the defect in the organ or central nervous system and enabled the control to be regained or acquired for the first time. The control itself is still voluntary. Its nature has not altered. The person is aware of a need to go to the toilet but by exercise of will can refrain from doing so. Reflex emptying does not take place.

As regards Commissioner Walker's decision in *CSIB/38/96*, if he meant that all medication must be disregarded in determining whether or not a claimant has voluntary control, I do not share his views. Medication can enable a person to exercise control by will where previously he could not have done so. If a person acquires or regains control by will over the emptying of bladder or bowel, however the ability to exercise that control was brought about, he cannot, in my view be said to have 'no voluntary control'. Even, therefore, adopting Ms Slevin's contention of 'voluntary' as meaning 'having the action controlled by will' the use of medication need not be excluded. I do not therefore consider that the Tribunal erred in taking account of medication in this case" (para.15).

In *CIB/3519/2002*, Commissioner Rowland endorsed the views of Commissioner Brown on the need to take account of medication. A tribunal must still, however, address the question whether in all the circumstances, including the effect of the medication, the claimant could properly be said to have voluntary control over his bladder.

It is submitted that Commissioner Walker's remarks on ignoring the effects of medication, if not wholly mistaken, must at least be confined to the specific context of this descriptor, it being common and appropriate practice generally to assess what a claimant can and cannot do in the light of appropriately prescribed medication (see Wikeley, (1997) 4 J.S.S.L. D.133–134). After all, medication, if not able to effect a cure, is surely there to control symptoms so as to assist a claimant to enjoy a reasonable life, including helping render him capable of work.

In *CIB/2873/2003*, a Tribunal of Commissioners considered *CIB/14210/96* (a decision of Deputy Commissioner Jacobs, as he then was) to have been wrongly decided (para.40). In *CIB/14210/96*, Deputy Commissioner Jacobs considered the case of a claimant whose bladder had been removed and who had a urostomy bag. Disagreeing with the approach in *C11/96(IB)*, noted immediately above with respect to bowel incontinence and an ileostomy bag, he thought it incorrect to regard the claimant as having no voluntary control over the bladder; with the object removed no question of control can arise, and the claimant must be assessed as having no problems with their bladder (i.e. no score). Nor was it right to consider how well the claimant controlled the bag; "bladder" could not be translated as "disposal of water/urine", and control by artificial means cannot be voluntary in the sense of control of impulses from the motor area of the cerebral cortex. Regulation 25(2) on aids and appliances was not relevant. There can be no assessable capacity in respect of an organ the claimant does not have. Nor did the aid relate to voluntary control. The tribunal of Commissioners stated:

> "The activities and descriptors in the Schedule to the 1995 Regulations need to be given a purposive construction, bearing in mind that the PCA is an assessment of functionality. For example, if a claimant has only one arm, and that arm is paralysed, then he would still fall within the descriptor 'Cannot raise either arm to his head as if to put on a coat or jacket' (Descriptor 8(b)), although the claimant himself would more likely say, for example, 'I cannot reach my head with my only arm'. That is because the descriptor relates to 'Reaching' and, as a matter of functionality, he cannot reach his head with an arm. Similarly, the claimant in *CIB/14210/1996* could not restrain or advance the process of urination at will and, in a functional sense, he was as incontinent as a person with a malfunctioning bladder that had been by-passed so that his urine passed into a bag. Mr Jacobs described the submission to him, that a claimant who has no bladder can have no control over it, as 'an attractive argument'. For the reasons we have given, we consider it to have been not only attractive but also correct" (para.40).

There is a difference between "no voluntary control of the bladder" and "loses control of the bladder"; dribbling and leaking do not constitute "no voluntary control" (*CSIB/625/1997*, para.12; *C70/98(IB)*, para.18), but might raise issues under the "loses control" descriptors, depending on the degree, extent and frequency of the problem (*CSIB/880/2003*). In *CIB/1005/2004*, Commissioner Mesher agreed with Commissioner May on there being a difference between "no voluntary control" and "loses control": the former imports no voluntary control at all, the latter imports some control that is lost. Commenting on Commissioner Walker's starting point in *CSIB/38/1996* and giving valuable guidance on pertinent questions, Commissioner Mesher thought that there is

> "room in the concept of 'no voluntary control' for a person only to be able to resist, by the exercise of the will, the muscular reflex to empty the bladder for a very short time indeed. I consider that Mr Commissioner Walker's reference to de minimis was intended to cover time as well as the degree of leakage. But the time must be very short indeed, in the context of 'no voluntary control', and it must be remembered that cases like *CIB/14332/1996*, *CIB/1995/2002* and *CIB/2200/2003* were about when a person loses control of bowels or bladder. Moreover, too much must not be read into Mr Commissioner Walker's statement. He had set aside an appeal tribunal's decision that a claimant had no voluntary control over the bladder because there was not evidence to support that conclusion, merely evidence of frequency. Then in paragraph 8 he was merely setting out, for the guidance of a new appeal tribunal, a starting point in the proper consideration of the descriptor, not an exhaustive set of conditions. There would not only have to be evidence of an inability to postpone by exercise of the will the operation of the muscular reflex, but that inability would have to exist at all times and on all occasions, subject to trivial exceptions, before it could be concluded that a person had 'no' voluntary control.

It follows from the above that the fact that a claimant, or even an EMP, ticks a box labelled 'occasionally loses control' is not inconsistent with the true situation being 'no voluntary control'. Such answers may be given on an assumption that only actual wetting or soiling counts for that purpose, whereas that is not the case. And if a person can only postpone the muscular reflex for a very short time, with occasional failures, that can be consistent with 'no voluntary control'. In the present case, the claimant's evidence to the effect that, if he needed a toilet, he had to go because he could not hold his water at all (if accepted) would go part of the way to establishing his case. But questions needed to be asked about just how quickly he needed to get to a toilet and about how often and in what circumstances he was able to do so without an accident. Those questions needed to include what happened during the night when the claimant woke needing to empty his bladder. Possibly questions should also have been asked about the claimant's ability to terminate the stream of urine by the exercise of will (another element of voluntary control), but there was evidence from the GP of a failure of voluntary control to that extent. And express consideration needed to be given to the consistency of the claimant's evidence as above with the normal effects of prostate problems and of hesitancy (see the GP's evidence that the claimant has to stand at the toilet for quite some time before urine started to flow), but that is a matter where medical expertise and experience would be needed for a proper evaluation to be made. Finally, the consistency with measures taken to mitigate the effects of the claimed absence of voluntary control was a relevant factor" (paras 13, 14).

In *CSIB/880/2003* Commissioner Parker considered incontinence pads irrelevant to the issue of "voluntary control":

"That [the claimant] can take reasonable precautions by using incontinence pads does not affect the matter. Regulation 25(2) of the Social Security (Incapacity for Work) (General) Regulations 1995 provides that the extent of a person's incapacity to perform any activity shall be assessed having regard to any aid or appliance which he normally wears or uses. However, it has been held in several cases that this provision cannot be used in a manner which essentially alters the nature of the activity under assessment.

'Continence' means having the ability to control evacuation of the bowels or bladder. That is why 'voluntary control' refers to what a claimant can do by exercise of the will to assert control. Regulation 25(2) encompasses an aid or appliance which affects the extent of a person's capacity to perform the activity in issue, for example, the use of a calliper in walking. An incontinence pad assists the claimant in coping with or mitigating the *effect of* a loss of control but it does not assist the normal control of the bladder's evacuation, which is what is being tested" (paras 4, 5).

In *R(IB) 4/04*, a Tribunal of Commissioners held that, incontinence pads, just like the ileostomy bag in direct issue in that case, were not relevant to the matter of "voluntary control"; "they do not affect the person's capacity to perform the activity at issue, i.e. continence" (para.36). See, to the same effect, *CSIB/74/1996*.

Activity 13: descriptor (e): "loses control of bowels occasionally": In *CIB/3339/2006*, Commissioner Rowland stated: "if a claimant merely feels an urgent desire to go to the toilet and is able to control his bowels for long enough to get there, he is not entitled to any points under activity 13 in the Schedule. . . . Applying a purposive construction to this legislation, as one must, it is clear that an occasional partial loss of control is sufficient to meet the terms of descriptor 13(e) unless the extent of the loss of control can be said to be *de minimis* in its effects" (para.5). **8.207**

Activity 13: descriptors (f) and (g): "loses control over bladder": As noted above, dribbling and leaking do not constitute "no voluntary control" (*CSIB/625/1997*, para.12; *C70/98(IB)*, para.18), but might raise issues under the "loses control" descriptors, depending on the degree, extent and frequency of the problem. As Commissioner Parker put it in *CSIB/880/2003*, **8.208**

"Dribbling and leaking, unless completely trivial, can satisfy descriptor 13(f) provided there is such an episode 'at least once a month' " (para.3).

Stress incontinence resulting in leakages can raise issues under these descriptors, but, if very minor, ought properly not be regarded as incontinence of the bladder

(C70/ 98(IB), para.17). Stress incontinence resulting in leakage or dribbling must be distinguished from the situation where a person has an urgent need to urinate requiring an immediate rush to the lavatory if there was not to be a loss of control. In that latter situation, Commissioner Goodman's principle as regards faecal incontinence would properly bring that situation within the realms of incontinence of the bladder.

8.209   *Activity 14: "remaining conscious without having epileptic or similar seizures during waking moments": meaning of "epileptic or similar seizures":* The wording of this activity was narrowed to its current formulation with effect from January 6, 1997. Prior to that it read: "remaining conscious other than for normal periods of sleep". The change was effected by the same set of amending regulations as those in issue in *Howker* v *Secretary of State* ([2002] EWCA Civ 1623, reported as *R(IB) 3/03)*, noted more fully in the commentary to reg.27, above. There the Court of Appeal invalidated, for failure to follow the correct procedure, the deletion of "old" head (b) from that regulation, which that set of amending regulations had purported to effect, because the Department had misled the SSAC on the effect of the change, wrongly describing it as "neutral" whereas its potential effect was "adverse" to claimants. The Court of Appeal held that the "old" head (b) remained in existence alongside the replacement provision. As noted in discussion at the beginning of the commentary to this schedule *(An Important Note on Amendments and Possible Invalidity)*, a Tribunal of Commissioners has in *R(IB) 2/07* resolved the conflict of authorities on the approach to invalidity on *Howker* procedural impropriety grounds. It has upheld the validity of the January 1997 change of wording. It has also considered the meaning of that wording, and the interpretations proffered in the cases noted in the annotation need to be considered in the light of what the Tribunal of Commissioners said:

". . . the word 'seizures' is to be construed as meaning episodes that are involuntary, overwhelming and sudden and the phrase 'similar seizures' is to be construed by reference to the similarity of the *effects* of the seizures to epileptic seizures, including the degree of suddenness of the loss or alteration of consciousness but without consideration of whether the seizures are characterised by the discharge of cerebral neurones, the amendment to Activity 14 is not invalid on procedural grounds. . . .. [D]rawing a distinction between events characterised by electrical activity in the brain and other sudden losses or alterations of consciousness makes little sense" (para.56).

The meaning of "epileptic or similar seizures" was considered by Northern Ireland Commissioner Brown in *C30/98(IB)*. In para.14 of the decision, she stated that, given the phrase, and that whether or not someone suffers from epileptic seizures is essentially a matter of medical diagnosis, then "similar seizures" means ones resembling epileptic seizures. The change in wording to the Activity, effected by the square bracketed words in the statutory text, was made to narrow down the range of attacks which could qualify to those coming from epileptic seizures or ones from similar seizures, rather than covering any attack of lost or altered consciousness. The characteristics of an epileptic seizure are threefold: (a) its origin as a result of excessive neuronal discharge; (b) its manifestation as an episode of motor, sensory or psychic dysfunction, etc; and (c) its concomitants in terms of marked changes in recorded electrical brain activity. In deciding whether an alleged seizure is similar to an epileptic one, all three must be borne in mind, but particularly (a) and (b). Usually the burden of proof will rest on the claimant (para.16). Medically, the cause of an epileptic fit is the abnormal activity of cerebral neurones Its effect is lost or altered consciousness. Migraine does not arise from that abnormal activity, and so, as Commissioner Jacobs recognised in *CIB/4598/2002*, if the medical cause is the relevant one for purposes of Activity 14, the claimant migraine sufferer in that case does not suffer from seizures similar to epileptic ones. He did, however, have sympathy with a different approach suggested in the directions on the appeal given by Commissioner Levenson (who had given leave and transferred the appeal to Commissioner Jacobs). He had suggested that since capacity to work is the central issue, rather than diagnosis, it was arguable that whether a seizure was similar to an epileptic one should be determined by effect rather than cause. Commissioner Jacobs saw this as having two advantages:

"First, it emphasises the impact of a claimant's symptoms on capacity for work rather than their medical causation. Second, his approach is the easier to apply for decision-makers and appeal tribunals. If the claimant has a firm diagnosis, medical science will probably be able to provide the evidence necessary to apply the medical adviser's approach. But suppose the claimant's condition has not yet been diagnosed. How in those circumstances is it possible for the practical purposes of a decision-maker or an appeal tribunal to prove what is causing the claimant's symptoms?" (para.19).

Since this claimant had not suffered lost or altered consciousness, however, Commissioner Jacobs did not have to decide whether the medical approach, Commissioner Levenson's approach, or some other approach, was the correct one. If such a claimant had lost consciousness, then, if Commissioner Jacobs' view that the original wording of the Activity still stands is correct ("remaining conscious other than for normal periods of sleep"), there is no need to consider whether medically either in terms of cause or effect, the seizure is similar to an epileptic one; the issue simply does not arise.

Activity 14 descriptors: "altered consciousness": The wording of this activity was sought to be narrowed to its current formulation with effect from January 6, 1997. Prior to that it read: "remaining conscious other than for normal periods of sleep". As noted above, a Tribunal of Commissioners has in *R(IB) 2/07*, resolved the conflict of authorities on the approach to invalidity on *Howker* procedural impropriety grounds. It has upheld the validity of the January 1997 change of wording. However, throughout the period since original enactment, each of its associated descriptors 14(a)–(f) has used the words "an involuntary episode of lost or altered consciousness", and so cases throughout the period are pertinent. In the Tribunal of Commissioners decision in *R(IB) 2/07*, the Commissioners in para.69 noted that mere sleepiness or doziness is not "altered consciousness". But a person who regularly feels sleepy during the day due to his medication will, during periods when he actually falls asleep, suffer episodes of "lost consciousness".

In *CSIB/14/96*, Commissioner Walker considered the meaning of and the proper approach to "altered consciousness" in a case involving the pre-January 1997 wording of Activity 14. The case turned on descriptors (a) and (b) (worded then as now), satisfaction of either of which would have given the claimant the necessary 15 points to satisfy the "all work" test. The relevant disabling condition was argued to be a series of severe and frequent headaches which necessitated the claimant lying down for periods of between half an hour and two hours, during which periods the claimant was unable to conduct his normal activities but did not lose consciousness. The question was whether, during these periods, the claimant could be said to have suffered "altered consciousness".

In *CSIB/14/1996* Commissioner Walker considered the meaning of the term. He saw it as different from "lost consciousness" and as not coloured by that term:

"The discussion satisfied me that it is not possible to lay down guidelines as to what, in law, is meant by 'altered consciousness'. It is, I am equally satisfied, essentially a practical matter for a tribunal to determine in the light of medical guidance from their assessor [now medical member] and the application of commonsense. But where, as here, episodes of pain are the disabling condition it will be necessary for the tribunal to explore, and for the claimant to present appropriate evidence to allow such exploration, in some detail how the pain affects the individual during an episode. It is not, in my view, sufficient to find as a fact that during the period 'the appellant is disabled'. Nor that 'he is unable to conduct his normal daily activities'. *It is for determination first how pain forecloses these and the way in which and the extent to which it does so. Thus ... if an individual is so distracted by the pain that he requires to lie down and otherwise retire from what he is doing then it may be possible to conclude that his consciousness has become altered by the degree of pain and he is incapable of doing anything effective other than coping with it.* But that would be a secondary finding which would require proper primary findings to justify it. Above all, I am persuaded that the concept of 'altered consciousness', which may have some medical significance, is impossible of legal definition and is a concept of difficulty for application by lay tribunals. For these reasons I do not think that it is appropriate that I should give any further guidance to the new tribunal in this case" (para.9, emphasis supplied by commentator).

The Tribunal of Commissioners in *R(IB) 2/07(T)* held *CSIB/14/1996* to be wrongly decided (para.47). It instead preferred the approach taken by Chief Commissioner Chambers in Northern Ireland in *C13/96(IB)*, which he saw as embracing epilepsy, diabetes and possibly severe vertigo:

"a person has an involuntary episode of altered consciousness when he has reached a state of mental confusion such that he is no longer properly aware of his surroundings or his condition".

What was there envisaged was alteration of consciousness such that the sufferer was not capable of any deliberate act; merely losing *some* control of one's actions due to vertigo would not suffice. The Tribunal of Commissioners in para.47 approved that strict approach to the pre-1997 wording. Commissioner Walker's highlighted comments about the effects and implications of severe pain in this context opened up possibilities under Activity 14 for, for example, those suffering frequent disabling migraines (a point supported by *C7/96(IB)* if severe) or very severe back pain. The strict approach supported in *R(IB) 2/07(T)* limits those possibilities. The change to the current formulation of Activity 14 severely limits those possibilities for any period from January 6, 1997. The new formulation does not cover distraction arising from severe pain (*CIB/12668/1996*), in that case from endometriosis. But those highlighted comments will be highly relevant in cases involving any period prior to that date, based on the then wider wording of the activity. All such cases will require a careful approach to the evidence, to fact-finding, and to the appropriate conclusions to draw from the primary facts. As regards that earlier period, "altered consciousness" could include severe vertigo (*C8/96(IB)*; *C13/96(IB)*; *CIB/15231/1996*). "Lost consciousness" could embrace irresistible periods of sleep due to disease or medication (*CSIB/44/1997*).

In *CIB/5757/1997*, Deputy Commissioner White considered the new wording of Activity 14 and its application to cases involving difficulties the product of severe migraine attacks. He noted that the *Incapacity Benefit Handbook for Medical Services Doctors* states at p.139 that "migraine, even when headache is preceded by an aura, does not result in altered consciousness". That is, of course, guidance for doctors rather than an authoritative statement of the law, and does not bind tribunals. The Deputy Commissioner suggests the following approach:

"First, it will be for the tribunal to determine what weight can be given to the medical guidance quoted above. . . . The new tribunal must first make detailed findings of fact on how the claimant's migraine attacks affect him, and about what the claimant can and cannot do for the duration of those attacks; the duration of the attacks should also be clearly specified. Applying their common-sense in the light of the advice they receive from the medical adviser and of their own findings of fact, they must decide whether the claimant experiences what can properly be described as 'altered consciousness' resulting from a 'seizure' similar to an epileptic seizure. I will simply observe that the new wording would, on the face of it, make it more difficult to bring the effects of a migraine attack within the term 'altered consciousness' since under the previous wording there was no reference in Column 1 to 'epileptic or similar seizures'. The nature of 'altered consciousness' has been narrowed by the revised wording. However, the new wording does not transfer the decision to doctors; it remains for tribunals to decide for themselves whether a person comes within the terms of any of these descriptors" (para.22).

But the tribunal must also look beyond Activity 14 and consider the effect the migraine attacks have on ability to perform the other physical activities in the Schedule;

"it is now accepted in the context of the application of the all work test that a person cannot do things which are accompanied by an unacceptable level of pain or discomfort, which is to be determined by the tribunal in the light of all the circumstances of each case" (*ibid.*, para.25).

Thus, to ascertain the incapacitating effects of a migraine, the tribunal must consider the application of each of the physical descriptors when the claimant is experiencing a migraine

"and decide which of them the claimant cannot do. This will inform them as to the capacity of the claimant to meet the functional tests in the physical descriptors during the times at which he is experiencing migraine attacks" (*ibid.*, para.26).

If that took the claimant over the 15 points threshold, and, say, the claimant suffered attacks on four days each week, the tribunal would have to consider whether the claimant is properly to be regarded as achieving that score on a day to day basis, applying the broader "reasonable period" approach to intermittent conditions examined earlier (see above, "variable, sporadic and intermittent conditions and loss of earning capacity"). The need to look wider, to all the activities which might be impaired by migraine attacks was stressed and applied to the claimant's benefit by Commissioner Jacobs in *CIB/3589/2004* (paras 12–17).

Descriptors (d), (e) and (f) look to particular periods (six months or a year, as the case may be) "before the day in respect of which it falls to be determined whether he is incapable of work". Normally that will be the date of the Secretary of State's decision. But it can also be the day on which a relevant rule change came into effect (specifically the amendment to Activity 14) and, where matters have to be examined down to the date of the tribunal hearing, that date (see *CSIB/597/97*, paras 11, 12).

[E] Case law on specific activities/descriptors: Pt II: mental disabilities

Activity 15: completion of tasks: descriptor (a) "cannot answer a telephone and reliably take a message": In *CIB/0215/2002*, Commissioner Turnbull was of the opinion that this   **8.211**

"is concerned with whether the claimant has the mental ability to answer the telephone and take a message reliably. It is not in my judgment satisfied if the disability arises from fear that it may be a particular person calling, because it seems to me that fear could in practice be allayed by a change of telephone number to an ex-directory number not known by the father. The Claimant would then in practice have the ability to answer the phone whenever she wished, since she would know it was not the father of the child calling." (para.6)

The "cannot reliably take a message" head would be satisfied if the claimant by reason of mental disablement is unable reliably to write down the message, since that is the normal way one would record a telephone message including the caller's telephone number. "Reliably" relates to the *quality* of the message the claimant can take, rather than to the act of picking up the telephone and answering it (*CSIB/491/00*; *CSIB/53/03*, para.21). The test is satisfied if the claimant cannot *normally* carry out the activity as and when called upon to do so (*CSIB/53/03*, para.20).

Since, however, the impediment to take an accurate message having answered the telephone can arise in different ways, Commissioner Parker in *CSIB/53/03* saw no reason in principle why the test should not be satisfied where apathy prevents the claimant from picking up the telephone when it rings, so long as the apathy results from some specific mental disease or disablement (paras 22, 23). Evidence that the claimant can use the telephone to make a call is not conclusive since the descriptor looks to ability to answer the telephone and reliably take a message (*CIB/748/2002*, para.4).

In *CIB/5536/2002*, Commissioner Jacobs emphasised that this can be satisfied where the claimant (a) cannot answer the telephone, and (b) where he can answer it, but cannot reliably take a message. If the evidence shows that he can never do either (a) or (b), the descriptor is satisfied. But where he can sometimes do one, or the other, but not always,

> "the tribunal must decide whether on an overall view it is proper to say that the claimant 'cannot' perform the descriptor. In applying the test, it is relevant to consider how often the claimant can and cannot perform the descriptor. However, the test does not depend on a purely arithmetical approach so that the descriptor is only satisfied if (for example) the claimant cannot perform the descriptor more often than not. The issue turns the proper use of the word 'cannot'." (para.9)

Here the evidence showed that difficulties occurred sometimes, but not with a frequency enabling one to say "cannot".

8.212 *Activity 15: completion of tasks; descriptor 15(c): "cannot concentrate to read a magazine article or follow a radio [or television] programme"* The words "or television" were added by the 1996 amending regulations which, following the *Howker* decision on the changes effected by them to reg.27, have raised questions as to their validity, an issue complicated by the disagreements on the scope of *Howker* and on approach between Commissioner May and Commissioner Jacobs. See further: *An Important Note on Amendments and Possible Invalidity* at the start of the commentary to this schedule; and the commentary to Activity 14. In *CSIB/279/2005*, Commissioner Parker held that the addition of the words 'or television' was valid "because it has added an extra hurdle for the decision maker (DM) rather than being adverse to the claimant" (para.4). She thus disagreed with a decision to contrary effect by Deputy Commissioner Gamble in *CIB/2821/2004* (para.9). He regarded the change as adverse since, in his view, less concentration was need to follow a television programme than to read or follow a radio programme. Commissioner Parker was not confident that his view on that was correct. She also noted that a "claimant may well have no interest in carrying out all these activities, even if mentally well, so that inferences will have to be drawn from analogous capabilities using concentration" (para.4).

8.213 *Activity 15: completion of tasks: descriptor (d) "cannot use a telephone book or other directory to find a number":* In *CIB/0215/2002*, the tribunal had found that the claimant could use a telephone book, since she only had a problem with long words and numbers beyond 98. Commissioner Turnbull held that they had erred in law by not exploring in more detail in its evidence and reasons, exactly what was the problem with numbers beyond 98: mathematical or something else which might prevent her using a telephone book (para.8).

8.214 *Activity 15: completion of tasks: descriptor (e): "mental condition prevents him from undertaking leisure activities previously enjoyed":* In *C29/01–02(IB)*, Commissioner Brown stated:

> "It appears to me that as regards descriptor 15(e), where an issue arises as to the applicability of this descriptor, a Tribunal should ascertain what leisure activities were enjoyed prior to the onset of the relevant mental condition and whether or not the claimant was, at the time of the decision under appeal, prevented by

that mental condition from undertaking those leisure activities. 'Undertaking' in this context does not appear to me to necessitate enjoyment but the taking on of the leisure activity. I consider that certain peripheral matters, if necessary to the undertaking of the activity, may, depending on the circumstances, also be embraced in the word 'undertaking'. However, the statutory phrase does not indicate that it is necessary to have the ability to undertake the leisure activities alone or at a particular venue or in a particular manner. Whether or not a person is prevented from undertaking a leisure activity by a mental disablement, must I think, be left to the common sense of the Tribunal as far as possible." (para.14)

Activity 15: completion of tasks: descriptor (h) "concentration can only be sustained by prompting": In *CIB/2008/1997*, Commissioner Howell was not persuaded that there was ground to impugn the tribunal decision to give no score on this descriptor. He noted that   **8.215**

"the majority record that apart from panic attacks of 5 to 10 minutes duration two or three times a week the claimant's condition did not fall within this descriptor because he was able to watch television a great deal and could concentrate to watch a full length film, or read. This it seems to me is plainly inconsistent with a condition where a person requires to be prompted in order to concentrate or pay attention at all, so that the tribunal's reasons for their conclusion are obvious."

Activity 16: daily living: descriptor (b) "needs alcohol before midday": The meaning of "needs" was considered by Northern Ireland Commissioner Brown in *R1/00(IB)*. Having examined the definitions in the New Collins Concise English Dictionary, and the ordinary person's understanding of the term, she saw it as imparting an element of "necessity or compulsion" and rejected the view that "needs" could be equated with "desires", stating: **8.216**

"While many people may like a drink before midday this is not per se indicative of any functional limitation nor any disablement or illness. Obviously what the descriptor is aimed at are persons who are alcoholic and who do not have their alcoholic desires under any sort of reasonable control so that they are compelled or obliged to drink before midday. I therefore share the views of the Great Britain Commissioner in CIB/17254/1996 when he states—'The fact that a person wishes for something does not mean he has a need for it. A person may wish to own a Rolls Royce, but it does not follow from this that he has a need for a Rolls Royce. Although the claimant might well like a drink before midday, it is clear that he is able to resist the temptation to have one, and in so doing he shows that there is no need for him to have a drink.' " (*R1/00(IB)*, para.10).

The mental stress associated with resisting temptation might be something considered under Activity 18(d), (e) and Activity 16(e), but not under Activity 16(b) (para.17). Nor could one award points because not doing so might encourage the claimant to abuse alcohol so as to get benefit; deliberate actions to qualify for benefit are not functional limitations arising from a specific disease or disablement which qualify for benefit (para.18).

Activity 16: daily living: descriptor (c): "is frequently distressed at some time of the day due to fluctuation of mood": In *CSIB/2/96*, Commissioner Walker considered that "frequent" connotes a substantial or significant number of times during the day. The descriptor looks to the frequency of the mood change rather than its significance or quality. A change once a day did not suffice. This issue has received further elucidation by Commissioners on both sides of the Irish Sea. Unfortunately, while they all disagree with the limitation set by Commissioner Walker in *CSIB 2/96*, they are not otherwise entirely in agreement on dealing with the descriptor.   **8.217**

In *CIB/1745/2002*, Commissioner Bano applied the Northern Ireland decision *R4/02(IB)*, and endorsed its disagreement with *CSIB/2/96*. Like the Northern Ireland Commissioner, he considered that this descriptor "does not require episodes of distress due to fluctuation of mood to take place more frequently than once each day" (para.5). In *C25/01–02*, Commissioner Brown stated that she thought that

> "distress once per day could or could not be frequent depending on other circumstances e.g. duration. The word 'frequently' is an ordinary English word and is for the Tribunal to apply. It would be reasonable to conclude depending on the context and the surrounding circumstances that distress once per day either was or was not frequent. I do not think it can be said as a matter of law that distress taking place at least once a day either can or cannot be said to be frequent. Had the legislature wished to say that distress had to take place more than once a day it could quite easily have done so by some phrase such as 'frequently and more than once per day'. It did not do so" (para.24).

A Northern Ireland Tribunal of Commissioners was of the same view in *R001/02(IB) (T)*, stating:

> "to be frequent in this particular context, it appears to us that, during the period under consideration, there must be habitual recurrence of distress at short intervals. The new Tribunal should bear this in mind in deciding whether or not descriptor DLc is applicable. Provided a Tribunal's conclusion on whether or not such distress occurs 'frequently' is within reasonable bounds, it should not be disturbed" (para.24).

Commissioner Bano, however, approached the matter in a somewhat different way. He said:

> "I share the view of the Commissioner that the words 'at some time of the day' do not indicate the unit of time by reference to which the frequency of episodes of distress must be assessed. However, I consider that the purpose of those words is to indicate that it is episodes of distress which occur during day-time hours which are to be taken into account in deciding if the descriptor is satisfied. In the context of mental disability, distress which occurs at night has a different significance from distress which occurs during the day, and I consider that the words 'at some time of the day' in descriptor 16(c) indicate that it is only diurnal episodes of distress due to fluctuation of mood which are to be taken into account. In my view, the descriptor is satisfied if day-time episodes of distress occur frequently over a period of days, irrespective of if they take place more than once per day. However, whilst the duration or severity of any particular incident may be relevant in deciding whether it is sufficiently significant to be taken into account, I respectfully question whether such matters are relevant is deciding whether distress is frequent" (para.5).

8.218 *Activity 16: daily living: descriptor (e) "sleeping problems interfere with daytime activities":* In *CIB/5336/2002*, Commissioner Jacobs held that

> "interference is not limited to preventing the claimant undertaking daytime activities. . . . Daytime activities may be prevented completely, or only be possible at certain times of the day, or be possible but only very intermittently or very slowly. All of these are potentially ways of interfering with the activities. Any of them is sufficient to satisfy the descriptor. This is subject to two qualifications. First, they must result from sleeping problems. Second, as with the word 'cannot' in descriptor 15(a), the issue depends on the proper use of language. When is a change in the activities undertaken or the pattern that would otherwise be followed an interference? A minimal change may not be sufficient to amount to an interference. So, for example, the fact that the claimant cannot start her daytime activities until a little later than normal or needs a rest at some time during the day, is not necessarily sufficient to satisfy the descriptor. Nor would it be necessarily be an interference just because the claimant has to change the time or order

in which she performs the activities. This is a question of fact and degree, turning on the proper use of language" (para.14).

In a Northern Ireland decision *C4/05–06 (IB)*, Commissioner Brown stressed the requirement that sleep problems must interfere with day to day activities (para.7) as well as the ability of the tribunal, deciding the case on all the evidence, to state that they rejected the claimant's evidence on a point because they disbelieved that evidence.

While a tribunal should be cautious in awarding points about sleep patterns without corroborative evidence about mental disorder, where there is such evidence which clearly points to an interconnection between the mental health problem and the daytime sleepiness a point should be awarded under the descriptor (*CIB/1374/2006*, para.10, *per* Commissioner Williams).

Activity 17: coping with pressure: descriptor (a): "mental stress was a factor in making him stop work": In *CIB/2008/1997*, Commissioner Howell found unjustified the criticism of 8.219

"the tribunal's acceptance of the examining doctor's award of no points on the ground that the claimant had stopped work because his factory closed. The reference to mental stress being a factor in *making* a claimant stop work indicates in my view that the descriptor is appropriate only to claimants who can demonstrate that stress played a causative role in their having to give up working. It does not include a person who happens to lose a job from other causes and afterwards suffers mental stress when he finds it difficult to get back into work. There is no real evidence that the claimant fell into the first category rather than the second" (para.10).

In *CIB/213/1999*, a tribunal considered the situation of someone, still employed, but on unpaid sick leave whilst a case of racial harassment was being pursued. It had concluded that mental stress was a factor in him stopping work thereby giving him points under descriptor 17(a). Commissioner Jacobs upheld that as a correct interpretation of the descriptor. Stress need only be *a* factor; it need not be the *sole* factor. "Stopping work" relates to the performance of duties under the contract of employment rather than requiring that contract to have been terminated (paras 7, 8).

In *CIB/3764/2001*, Commissioner Fellner saw no reason why "work" here should not be interpreted to include voluntary work by analogy with regs 16 and 17 (para.9). In obiter comments in *CIB/1361/2008*, however, Deputy Commissioner Wikeley doubted that leaving a college course in consequence of mental stress could properly be equated with stopping work for the purpose of this descriptor.

Note that stress need only be *a* factor. Moreover the emphasis in the personal capability assessment must be on the *impact* of the mental condition on the claimant's capacity for work. Hence in *CIB/4192/2004*, Commissioner Jacobs was able to decide that the claimant could still satisfy this descriptor where the immediate cause of him stopping work is that he was dismissed. Because, read as a whole, the descriptor does not require the initiative to come from the claimant. The immediate cause of the claimant may have been dismissal, so that, in that sense, the dismissal was what made him stop work. But where the stress was a cause of the dismissal, it was also a factor in making him stop work. The precise mechanism by which a particular effect is produced seems irrelevant. Any other interpretation would produce anomalous outcomes turning on the chance of who took the initiative in terminating the employment.

Activity 17: coping with pressure: descriptor (b): "frequently feels scared or panicky for no obvious reason": On "frequently" see *CSIB 2/96*; noted above under Activity 16, descriptor (c). In that case, Commissioner Walker further held that the claimant, who felt scared or panicky when he reflected on an assault and mugging he had 8.220

suffered, did not meet this descriptor because the assault or mugging constituted an "obvious reason" for the feelings. In a decision which may give those suffering from post-traumatic stress disorder some problems, Commissioner Walker rejected the adjudication officer's argument, in support of the appeal, that the rubric "obvious reason" referred to feeling scared or panicky as a result of some identifiable physical event occurring at the time.

A trend to a more generous approach is discernible from a number of decisions of other Commissioners. In *CSIB/451/01*, Commissioner Parker draws on *CIB/4251/97* and *CIB/7510/99*, to depart from *CSIB/2/96* in a way that may prove helpful to sufferers of post-traumatic stress disorder. She held that in applying the descriptor the emphasis is on what is normal, and that the test is objective. "Obvious" bears a dictionary meaning of "easily seen, recognised or understood". A tribunal must decide for itself on the facts of its case what is and is not an obvious reason. So that a tribunal must consider the normal responses of someone in straightforward circumstances and not in the unusual ones of having been previously mugged or assaulted or stabbed. In deciding whether there is an obvious reason for the claimant's frequent feelings of panic or being scared, stress on normality as a comparison applies as much to the person's past or present circumstances as to their reactions.

In *C47/97(IB)*, Commissioner Martin noted that:

"the descriptor requires frequency; in other words occasional fear or panic is not enough. It also requires a substantial amount of fear as a scared person is a person who is 'filled with fear or alarm' (see the New Collins Dictionary). When considering whether a reason is 'obvious' or not it seems to me that it must be considered in light of the self-evident reality that there will always be a considerable range of normal or ordinary reactions to situations where pressure is causing problems to individuals. For a Tribunal to conclude that an individual, in a pressure situation, 'frequently feels scared or panicky for no obvious reason', it would have to decide, on the facts, that the fear or panic was outside the normal range of reaction that a human being would have. A Tribunal in effect would be considering whether or not the reaction to the pressure is tantamount to being irrational." (para.15)

In *CIB/7510/99*, faced with a conflict between *CSIB/2/96* and *CIB/4251/97*, Commissioner Pacey preferred the approach in the latter, and like Commissioner Parker endorsed the view expressed by the Commissioner in *CIB/4251/97* that

"the argument that the descriptor does not apply if it is possible to identify an explanation for the claimant feeling scared and panicky overlooks the word 'obvious'. This is an ordinary English word which has to be applied rather than interpreted. I do not consider that it covers a claimant who experiences feelings in circumstances that would not normally give rise to those feelings. It is not to me obvious that a person should be scared of being in a crowd".

For Commissioner Pacey in *CIB/7510/99*, this meant that one looks for the "obvious reason" not to the origin of the claimant's condition which shows itself in the particular circumstances, but rather in the light of the identifiable physical event (the crowd or the closed space) which prompts the panic. This was endorsed by Commissioner Rowland in *CIB/4404/2002* who was of the opinion that

"a cause of fear and panic may be said to be an obvious reason for the fear and panic only if the reaction is proportionate to the cause. Thus a history of domestic violence may be an obvious reason for a woman to fear her partner. On the other hand, dealing with local government officers or civil servants may be thought not to be an obvious reason for panic giving rise to palpitations, so that, in a case such as the present, the panic may reasonably be attributed to mental disablement" (para.5).

Activity 17: coping with pressure; descriptor (c) "avoids carrying out routine activities because he is convinced they will prove too tiring or stressful": In *CIB/1374/2006*, Commissioner Williams commented

8.221

"This descriptor clearly requires (a) a finding whether the claimant "avoids carrying out routine activities", and (b) a finding whether "this is because he is convinced that they will prove too tiring or stressful". It does not require that the claimant *cannot* do these things. That would be in part a physical descriptor. It requires the claimant's approach to be as stated. As with problems with sleep, the general requirement is that this arises because of the mental health problems. There is evidence of (a) in this case from the past medical assessments, the approved doctor's IB85 (where there is also evidence of the opposite) and the claimant. As to (b), the tribunal found that the inactivity was of his own choosing. That misses the point. Why did he choose that? Was he convinced that they would prove too tiring or stressful? The secretary of state's representative submits that the evidence indicates that the claimant was so convinced. I accept that, and award 1 point" (para.12).

Activity 17: coping with pressure; descriptor (d): "is unable to cope with changes in daily routine": In *CIB/16/2007*, deputy Commissioner Ovey was of the opinion that

8.222

"a daily routine may have some variable elements if there is overall a broadly settled and regular pattern. In particular, it does not seem to me that a regular trip, such as the claimant's trip to Newcastle, which is not made every day necessarily amounts to a change in daily routine for this purpose if it is nevertheless something done regularly. The descriptor is not, in my view, directed to day-to-day variations determined by the claimant in a pattern which she has herself established" (para.31).

Activity 17: coping with pressure: descriptor (e): "frequently finds there are so many things to do that he gives up because of fatigue, apathy or disinterest": In *CIB/2008/1997*, Commissioner Howell considered that this

8.223

"refers . . . to a particular mental condition caused by 'overload' of actual or perceived tasks pressing to be done, and is not satisfied by a person who is simply lethargic and not feeling pressed or motivated to do anything. That would not give practical effect to the opening words of the descriptor, or to its place in a group of descriptors dealing with the ability to cope with pressure. For that reason the majority of the tribunal were . . . right to follow the examining doctor's view that no point should be awarded under this head, and the dissenting member wrong in taking the view that he was entitled to a point under this descriptor merely because there was evidence indicating that he had given up many activities because of fatigue, apathy or disinterest" (para.11).

In the Northern Ireland decision *C55/99–00*, Commissioner Martin stated:

"the context of the word 'disinterest' in descriptor 17(e), where it is put in a similar category to 'fatigue' and 'apathy', suggests to me that the adjudicating authorities must interpret the word 'disinterest' as meaning 'indifference' or 'lack of interest'. Perhaps this requires a purposive and strained construction (see Francis Bennion's article in Justice of the Peace, Volume 162(1998) 'Threading the Legislative Maze') but, in the circumstances, I find that this is the only possible construction)" (para.14).

Activity 18: interaction with other people: descriptor (a) "cannot look after himself without help from others": In *CIB/5536/2002*, Commissioner Jacobs accepted as correct this passage from Commissioner May in *CIB/4916/1997* (para.25):

8.224

"The question as to whether or not a person cannot look after himself without help from others is essentially in my view a question as to whether without such help the claimant would self neglect. It is not in my view meant to encompass asserted assistance with family finance that goes beyond the scope of looking after oneself. It would subvert the whole scheme for incapacity benefit if the meaning of descriptors was to be ingeniously stretched far beyond the scope that the plain English of the descriptors intended."

In Commissioner Jacob's opinion

"the natural meaning of the language of this descriptor relates to the immediate aspects of self care, like eating and maintaining an appropriate level of personal hygiene. It does not apply to the more remote aspects, like shopping (this case) and handling finances and paying bills (Mr May's case). The language and its context in the personal capability assessment combine to emphasise the claimant rather than the claimant's household, its provisioning or its finances." (para.19)

In *MF v SSWP* [2008] UKUT 29 (AAC), Judge Gamble considered what assistance provided to the claimant by other people constitutes "help from others". He rejected the claimant's argument that this covered counselling for the long-term psychological effects of childhood sexual abuse and prescriptions of anti-depressants. He held that these were too remote, not sufficiently "direct", and lacked immediacy and intimacy envisaged and required by the descriptor. He thought that "help from others" could take two forms: (1) physical attention in respect of things like feeding, washing, bathing or taking medication; (2) psychological prompting or encouragement to ensure that the claimant performs those tasks himself. The counselling and prescription of medication did not rank as such prompting or encouragement (see paras 8-10).

8.225   *Activity 18: interaction with other people: descriptor (b): "gets upset by ordinary events and it results in disruptive behavioural problems":* In *CSIB/1521/01*, Commissioner Parker held that the descriptor is not limited to physical violence by the claimant. Moreover, since there is no preclusion of double-counting (applying *CSIB/13/96*, now reported as *R(IB) 3/98*), the same circumstances could also bring into play descriptors 16(c) ("frequently distressed at some time of the day due to fluctuation of mood") and 18(d) ("gets irritated by things that would not have bothered him before he became ill"). On 18(b), Commissioner Parker stated that "the claimant's conduct has to be extreme enough to affect the fabric of life around him, whether at home or in the wider community" since one gets two points for 18(b) but only one for "irritated" in 18(d). Although there was substantial overlap with 18(d), there were differences: someone can satisfy 18(d) where the events which irritate him are not ordinary ones, as required by 18(b), so long as they would not have bothered him prior to becoming ill; while irritation shown in terms of sulking or becoming peevish would suffice for 18(d) but not for 18(b) which requires more extreme active conduct. Similarly sobbing and emotional displays could constitute "disruptive behavioural problems" meeting the requisites of 18(b), but not meet 18(d) because they do not demonstrate annoyance. If the displays of disruptive behaviour were ones of shouting and verbal abuse, both descriptors might be satisfied.

In *CIB/1374/2006*, Commissioner Williams agreed with Commissioner Parker's view in *CSIB/1521/2001* that these two descriptors overlap and that "disruptive behaviour" is not limited to aggressive behaviour. Applying this to the case before him, he considered that these.

"two descriptors are in ordinary English that do not warrant further definitions. 'Upset' and 'irritated' are widely drawn and overlapping terms. The phrase used by the claimant in his appeal notice was 'I get stressed'. That overlaps with both. The focus is on any upset or irritation arising from the mental health problems, in this case the claimant's anxiety problems. I agree with both parties that the two descriptors should be looked at together, with any relevant evidence assessed under both descriptors. On that basis, I am unable to accept the tribunal's 'no evidence approach'. Given the evidence before it, I fail to see how it reached the conclusion it did. My view might have been different had it taken a 'balance of evidence' approach, but its decision as it stands is either wrong or inadequate. Again on the evidence, and applying the test from CSIB/1521/2001, I accept the Secretary of State's representative's submission that both descriptors are met. That scores three points" (para.12).

Activity 18: interaction with other people: descriptor (c): "mental problems impair ability to communicate with other people": In *CIB/2008/1997*, Commissioner Howell considered that

8.226

"the view of the [tribunal] majority and that of the examining doctor was correct and that there was no real evidence to suggest that the claimant's mental problems impaired his ability to communicate with other people. The fact that as noted by the dissenting member the claimant spends a lot of his time reading and watching television, and as shown by the evidence of his daughter . . . worries a lot and wanders from room to room trying to hide the way he is feeling, does not . . . amount to evidence of a lack of *ability* to communicate within the terms of this descriptor" (para.12).

This last seems somewhat ill-focused since the word used is "impair" and one might have thought some comparison between the claimant's present state and his pre-illness state relevant. One might hazard that depression, as a recognised mental illness or disability, might well in some cases force a claimant in on himself: is that not "impairing" his ability to communicate? Or is the Commissioner perhaps implying that the descriptor is confined to conditions whose effect is akin to physically impairing ability to communicate?

In a Northern Ireland decision, *C79/98(IB)*, Commissioner Brown, dealing with the argument that depression may make someone reluctant to speak, commented:

"In my view mere reluctance does not satisfy descriptor OP(c). That descriptor reads as follows:—

'Mental problems impair ability to communicate with other people.'

It is the claimant's ability to communicate which must be impaired not his desire to do so."

The Social Security Contributions and Benefits Act 1992 (Modifications for Her Majesty's Forces and Incapacity Benefit) Regulations 2003

(SI 2003/737)

ARRANGEMENT OF REGULATIONS

8.227

The Treasury, with the concurrence of the Secretary of State, in exercise of the powers conferred on them by sections 116(2) and 175(3) and (5) of the Social Security Contributions and Benefits Act 1992, and of all other powers enabling them in that behalf, hereby make the following Regulations:

Citation and commencement

8.228   **1.**—These Regulations may be cited as the Social Security Contributions and Benefits Act 1992 (Modifications for Her Majesty's Forces and Incapacity Benefit) Regulations 2003 and shall come into force for the purposes of this regulation and regulation 3 on 6th April 2003 and for all other purposes on 5th May 2003.

Modification of section 30A of the Social Security Contributions and Benefits Act 1992

8.229   **2.**—Section 30A of the Social Security Contributions and Benefits Act 1992 (entitlement to incapacity benefit) shall be modified, in respect of persons who have been members of Her Majesty's forces, as if—

(a) at the beginning of subsection (3), there were inserted "Subject to subsection (3A)", and

(b) after subsection (3), there were inserted—

"(3A) Subsection (3) does not apply to a person—

(a) who is discharged from Her Majesty's forces, and

(b) for whom days of sickness absence from duty, which are recorded by the Secretary of State for Defence, are included in calculating the number of days for which the person has been entitled to short-term incapacity benefit.".

Modification of section 30D of the Social Security Contributions and Benefits Act 1992

8.230   **3.**—Section 30D of the Social Security Contributions and Benefits Act 1992 (calculating days of entitlement to incapacity benefit) shall be modified, in respect of persons who have been members of Her Majesty's forces, as if, after subsection (3), there were inserted—

"(3A) In respect of a person who is discharged from Her Majesty's forces after 3rd May 2003, there shall also be included such days as may be prescribed.".

Modification of paragraph 2(6) of Schedule 3 to the Social Security Contributions and Benefits Act 1992

8.231   **4.**—Paragraph 2(6) of Schedule 3 to the Social Security Contributions and Benefits Act 1992 (contribution conditions for entitlement to incapacity benefit) shall be modified, in respect of persons who have been members of Her Majesty's forces, as if—

(a) after "is" in paragraph (b) (meaning of "the relevant benefit year"), there were inserted, "subject to paragraph (c),", and

(b) at the end, there were added—

"(c) in the case of a person who is discharged from Her Majesty's forces, and for whom days of sickness absence from duty recorded by the Secretary of State for Defence are included in calculating the number of days for which the person has been entitled to short-term incapacity benefit, 'the relevant benefit year' is the benefit year in which there falls the beginning of the period to which the claim for incapacity benefit relates.".

Social Security (Incapacity Benefit) (Transitional) Regulations 1995

(SI 1995/310) (*as amended*)

ARRANGEMENT OF REGULATIONS

PART I

INTRODUCTION

8.232

PART II

PROVISIONS COMMON TO THE TRANSITION TO INCAPACITY BENEFIT FROM SICKNESS BENEFIT AND INVALIDITY BENEFIT

PART III

PROVISIONS FOR THE TRANSITION TO INCAPACITY BENEFIT FROM SICKNESS BENEFIT

PART IV

PROVISIONS FOR THE TRANSITION TO INCAPACITY BENEFIT FROM INVALIDITY BENEFIT

PART V

MISCELLANEOUS TRANSITIONAL PROVISIONS

PART VI

PROVISIONS FOR THE TRANSITION TO THE NEW TESTS OF INCAPACITY FOR WORK

Whereas a draft of these Regulations was laid before Parliament in accordance with the provisions of sections 4(12) and 7(5) of the Social Security (Incapacity for Work) Act 1994 and approved by resolution of each House of Parliament;

Now, therefore, the Secretary of State for Social Security, in exercise of the powers conferred by sections 4, 7 and 12(1) of the Social Security (Incapacity for Work) Act 1994 and of all other powers enabling him in that behalf, by this instrument, which is made before the end of the period of 6 months beginning with the coming into force of those enactments, hereby makes the following Regulations:

PART I

INTRODUCTION

Citation, commencement and interpretation

1.—(1) These Regulations may be cited as the Social Security (Incapacity Benefit) (Transitional) Regulations 1995 and shall come into force on 13th April 1995.

(2) In these Regulations—

"the 1992 Act" means the Social Security Contributions and Benefits Act 1992;

"the 1994 Act" means the Social Security (Incapacity for Work) Act 1994;

"the Administration Act" means the Social Security Administration Act 1992;

"the appointed day" means 13th April 1995;

"the increases for Dependants Regulations" means the Social Security (Incapacity Benefit—Increases for Dependants) Regulations 1994;

"pensionable age" means—

(a) the age of 65, in the case of a man; and

(b) the age of 60, in the case of a woman;

"the Unemployment, Sickness and Invalidity Benefit Regulations" means the Social Security (Unemployment, Sickness and Invalidity Benefit) Regulations 1983.

(3) In these Regulations, unless the context otherwise requires, a reference—

(a) to a numbered regulation is to the regulation bearing that number in these Regulations;

(b) in a regulation to a numbered paragraph is to the paragraph bearing that number in that regulation;

(c) in a regulation to a numbered Part is to the Part bearing that number in these Regulations.

PART II

PROVISIONS COMMON TO THE TRANSITION TO INCAPACITY BENEFIT FROM SICKNESS BENEFIT AND INVALIDITY BENEFIT

Days to be treated as days of incapacity for work

2.—(1) For the purposes of a transitional award of incapacity benefit under regulations 11 and 17 and for the purposes of enabling a claim for

8.233

8.234

incapacity benefit to be made on or after the appointed day on the basis that a day of incapacity for work on or after the appointed day forms part of a period of incapacity for work beginning before the appointed day—

(a) days before the appointed day which were days of incapacity for work for the purposes of sickness benefit or invalidity benefit and days specified in paragraph (2) shall be treated as having been days of incapacity for work; and

(b) days of entitlement to sickness benefit or invalidity benefit and days specified in paragraph (3) shall be treated as having been days of entitlement to incapacity benefit.

(2) The specified days referred to in paragraph (1)(a) are—

(a) any Sunday before the appointed day which—

    (i) immediately follows a day of incapacity for work; and

    (ii) immediately precedes a day of incapacity for work; and

    (iii) does not fall within a period of disqualification by virtue of section 32 of the 1992 Act and the provisions in regulation 17 of the Unemployment, Sickness and Invalidity Benefit Regulations in force immediately before the appointed day; and

    (iv) falls within a period of interruption of employment running at the appointed day;

(b) any Sunday which immediately follows a day of incapacity for work in a period of interruption of employment which comes to an end on a Saturday.

(3) The specified days referred to in paragraph (1)(b) are—

(a) any Sunday which falls within the description specified in paragraph(2)(a) and (b);

(b) days which are deemed to be days of entitlement to sickness benefit under regulation 7A of the Unemployment, Sickness and Invalidity Benefit Regulations;

(c) the seventh day in any week in which an employer was liable to pay a person statutory sick pay at the weekly rate specified in section 157(1) of the 1992 Act; and

(d) any additional days which would have been taken into account for sickness benefit and invalidity benefit purposes had the days referred to in the provisions in regulation 7A(4)(b) of the Unemployment, Sickness and Invalidity Benefit Regulations in force immediately before the appointed day been days in the week beginning with a Sunday which would be comprised in a fraction of a seven-day week.

DEFINITIONS

    "the appointed day"—see reg.1(2).
    "day of incapacity for work"—see SSCBA 1992, s.30C(1), above.
    "period of interruption of employment"—see SSCBA 1992, s.25A(1)(d), above.
    "period of incapacity for work"—see SSCBA 1992, s.30C(1), above.
    "the Unemployment, Sickness and Invalidity Benefit Regulations"—see reg.1(2).

GENERAL NOTE

8.235   This regulation applies for the purposes of a transitional award of incapacity benefit under regs 11 and 17 below. The former in effect deals with those transferees from sickness benefit, the latter with those transferring from invalidity benefit. This regulation also operates for the purposes of enabling a claim for incapacity benefit to be made on or after April 13, 1995 (the appointed day) on the basis that a day of incapacity for work after that day forms part of a period of incapacity for work beginning before April 13, 1995. Essentially, for both those purposes, days of incapacity for work for purposes of sickness and invalidity benefits are treated as days of incapacity for work for purposes of incapacity benefit, and days of entitlement to any of them are treated as having been ones of entitlement to incapacity benefit. In addition the days specified in para.(2) are to be treated as days of incapacity for work, and those listed in para.(3) are to be regarded as days of entitlement to incapacity benefit. Para.(2) was necessary because under the sickness and invalidity benefits regime, Sundays did not count, whereas incapacity benefit works on a seven day week in which Sundays can rank as days of incapacity. Note that the reference in para.(3)(b), (d) to USI Regs, reg.7A, must be a reference to that provision as in force immediately prior to April 13, 1995 (see pp.716–17 of Bonner, Hooker and White, *Non Means Tested Benefits: The Legislation* (1994)) since it was revoked from that date.

The provisions of this regulation form part of a chain, along with regs 3 and 9, whereby one determines the point at which transferees move from one rate of short-term incapacity benefit to another (after 196 days of entitlement), from short-term to long-term incapacity benefit (after 364 days of entitlement), and the point of time at which (at the latest) the all work test [personal capability assessment] applies (after 196 days of incapacity) (SSCBA 1992, ss.30A, 30C, 30C, 30D, 171B, above; regs 4, 32).

Linking periods of interruption of employment and periods of incapacity for work

3.—Where the last day of incapacity for work in a period of interruption of employment and the first day of incapacity for work in a period of incapacity for work are not separated by a period of more than 56 days, both these periods shall be treated as one period of incapacity for work.   8.236

DEFINITIONS

"period of incapacity for work"—see SSCBA 1992, s.30C(1), above.
"period of interruption of employment"—see SSCBA 1992, s.25A(1)(d), above.

GENERAL NOTE

This provides that two apparently separate days of incapacity (one part of a period of interruption of employment before April 13, 1995 and the other part of a period of incapacity for work after that date) "link" if not more than eight weeks (56 days) apart. This is another link in the chain, along with regs 2 and 9, whereby one determines the point at which transferees move from one rate of short-term incapacity benefit to another (after 196 days of entitlement), from short-term to long-term incapacity benefit (after 364 days of entitlement), and the point of time at which (at the latest) the all work test [personal capability assessment] applies (after 196 days of incapacity) (SSCBA 1992, ss.30A, 30B, 30C, 30D, 171B, above; regs 4, 32).   8.237

Calculation of days in a period of incapacity for work

4.—The days referred to in regulation 2 shall be taken into account for the purposes of sections 30A(4) (length of entitlement to short-term incapacity benefit), 30B(2) (period after which short-term incapacity benefit is payable at higher rate) and 30B(4)(period after which incapacity benefit is payable at long-term rate) of the 1992 Act.   8.238

GENERAL NOTE

This stipulates that the days set out in reg.2 count in determining the point at which transferees move from one rate of short-term incapacity benefit to another   8.239

(after 196 days of entitlement) and from short-term to long-term incapacity benefit (after 364 days of entitlement).

Claims for sickness benefit or invalidity benefit made on or after the appointed day

8.240   **5.**—Where a claim for sickness benefit or invalidity benefit is made on or after the appointed day in respect of a period of incapacity before the appointed day, the provisions in regulation 19 of, and paragraph 2 of Schedule 4 to, the Social Security (Claims and Payments) Regulations 1987 (time for claiming benefit) in force on the appointed day shall be read as if the reference to incapacity benefit were a reference to sickness benefit or invalidity benefit.

Interchange of sickness benefit and invalidity benefit with claims for other benefits

8.241   **6.**—Where a claim for sickness benefit, invalidity benefit, severe disablement allowance or maternity allowance is made in respect of a period before the appointed day, the provisions in regulation 9 of, and Part I of Schedule 1 to, the Social Security (Claims and Payments) Regulations 1987 (benefit claimed and other benefit which may be treated as if claimed in addition or in the alternative) in force on the appointed day shall be read as if regulation 10(1), (2), (4) and (6) to (9) of the Social Security (Claims and Payments) Amendment (No.2) Regulations 1994 had not come into force.

Persons deemed to be incapable of work

8.242   **7.**— [¹ . . .].

REVOCATION

1. Social Security (Incapacity) (Miscellaneous Amendments) Regulations 2002 (SI 2002/491), reg.5 (April 8, 2002).

GENERAL NOTE

8.243   This regulation had protected those transferees to incapacity benefit from sickness and invalidity benefits who had been subject to more generous rules on treating someone as incapable of work whilst working, which had been contained in reg. 3(3) of the Unemployment, Sickness and Invalidity Benefit Regs (on which see pp. 690–691 of Bonner, Hooker and White, *Non Means Tested Benefits: The Legislation* (1994)). The revocation of reg.7, effected from April 8, 2002, is, however, subject to a transitional provision in reg.6(2)–(4) of the revoking regulations, preserving the revoked reg.7 until the day specified in reg.6(3) of the revoking regulations. The transitional provisions read:

> "(2) Where, at any time during the pre-commencement period, a person was, by virtue of regulation 7(1) of the Social Security (Incapacity Benefit) (Transitional) Regulations 1995, deemed to be incapable of work notwithstanding that he was undertaking work for more than 16 hours in any week, that regulation 7 shall, until the end of the day specified in paragraph (3) below, continue to apply in his case as if regulation 5 of these Regulations had not come into force.
>
> (3) The day referred to in paragraphs (1) and (2) above is—
>   (a) 6th April 2003;
>   (b) where no work of a kind referred to in paragraph (1) or (2) above is undertaken by that person at any time during a period of 57 continuous days, the day which is the last day of that period; or

(c) the day on which the period of incapacity for work which, on the day on which these Regulations come into force, has effect in relation to that person comes to an end,

whichever first occurs.

(4) In this regulation—

'period of incapacity for work' is to be construed in accordance with section 30C(1)(b) and (c) of the Social Security Contributions and Benefits Act 1992; and

'pre-commencement period' means the period which began 56 days before the day on which these Regulations come into force and ended on the day preceding that day."

Direct credit transfer

8.—Where a person had an award of sickness benefit or invalidity benefit which was payable by automated credit transfer in accordance with regulation 21 of the Social Security (Claims and Payments) Regulations 1987, and that award has effect as an award of incapacity benefit under regulations 11 or 17, the award of incapacity benefit shall continue to be paid by automated credit transfer into the same bank or other account as the award of sickness benefit or invalidity benefit; and for this purpose, any application made and any consent given in relation to the award of sickness benefit or invalidity benefit shall be treated as made or given in relation to the transitional award of incapacity benefit. **8.244**

Disqualification

9.—Where immediately before the appointed day a person is disqualified by virtue of regulations made under section 32 or section 59 of the 1992 Act (disqualifications for sickness benefit and invalidity benefit), the period of disqualification in respect of sickness benefit or invalidity benefit shall continue to have effect and that person shall likewise be disqualified for receiving incapacity benefit for the period of disqualification which remains outstanding at the appointed day. **8.245**

DEFINITIONS

"the 1992 Act"—see reg. 1(2).
"the appointed day"—see reg. 1(2).

GENERAL NOTE

This means that disqualifications for sickness or invalidity benefit under USI Regs, reg. 17 (as in force immediately before April 13, 1995—see pp. 736–40 of Bonner, Hooker and White, *Non-Means Tested Benefits: The Legislation* (1994)), not completed by that date, continue to have effect as disqualifications for incapacity benefit for the period of original disqualification which remains outstanding at April 13, 1995. So, if of a six-week disqualification, only one week was "spent" before April 13, 1995, the period of disqualification will continue to run for five weeks after that date. **8.246**

Since days of disqualification are not ones of entitlement to incapacity benefit (SSCBA 1992, s.30D(4)), this provision forms part of a chain, along with regs 2 and 4, whereby one determines the point at which transferees move from one rate of short-term incapacity benefit to another (after 196 days of entitlement) and from short-term to long-term incapacity benefit (after 364 days of entitlement).

Suspension of payment of transitional awards

8.247   **10.**—Where the Secretary of State has made a direction to suspend payment of an award of sickness benefit or invalidity benefit in whole or in part, by virtue of regulations made under section 5(1)(n) of the Administration Act, that direction shall have effect as if it were made in respect of a transitional award of incapacity benefit and the payment of the transitional award of incapacity benefit shall likewise be suspended as if it were an award of sickness benefit or invalidity benefit.

PART III

PROVISIONS FOR THE TRANSITION TO INCAPACITY BENEFIT FROM SICKNESS BENEFIT

Transitional awards of short-term incapacity benefit

8.248   **11.**—(1) Where a person is entitled to sickness benefit immediately before the appointed day, that award of sickness benefit shall have effect on or after the appointed day as if it were an award of short-term incapacity benefit; and such an award shall be referred to in these Regulations as a transitional award of short-term incapacity benefit.

(2) A person shall cease to be entitled to a transitional award of shortterm incapacity benefit under paragraph(1)—

(a) when the period of incapacity for work comes to an end; or

(b) after 364 days of entitlement to short-term incapacity benefit in a period of incapacity for work; or

(c) if he was entitled to sickness benefit under section 102 of the 1992 Act (sickness benefit in respect of an industrial injury) immediately before the appointed day, when the incapacity for work is no longer a result of a personal injury of the kind mentioned in section 94(1) of the 1992 Act,

whichever first occurs.

(3) Subject to the provisions in Part VI, a person's entitlement to a transitional award of short-term incapacity benefit shall be subject to him being incapable of work as determined in accordance with Part XIIA of the 1992 Act (incapacity for work).

(4) [¹ Subject to paragraph (5) where] a person ceases by virtue of paragraph (2)(b) to be entitled to a transitional award of short-term incapacity benefit he is, subject to him being incapable of work as determined in accordance with Part XIIA of the 1992 Act (incapacity for work), entitled to long-term incapacity benefit in the same period of incapacity for work in which he is not over pensionable age.

[² (5) Where paragraph (4) applies to a person whose transitional award of short-term incapacity benefit was in respect of a personal injury of a kind mentioned in section 94(1) of the 1992 Act, he shall be entitled to the long-term incapacity benefit only if his incapacity for work continues to result from that personal injury.]

[³(6) The transitional award under paragraph (1) is treated as a decision of the Secretary of State under section 8(1) of the Social Security Act

1998 (decisions by Secretary of State) and as an incapacity decision for the purposes of the Social Security and Child Support (Decisions and Appeals) Regulations 1999.]

AMENDMENTS

1. Social Security (Incapacity for Work and Miscellaneous Amendments) Regulations 1996 (SI 1996/3207), reg.3(2)(a) (January 6, 1997).
2. Social Security (Incapacity for Work and Miscellaneous Amendments) Regulations 1996 (SI 1996/3207), reg.3(2)(b) (January 6, 1997).
3. Social Security Act 1998 (Commencement Nos 9 and 11) (Amendment) Order 2006 (SI 2006/2540), art.2(3)(b) inserting paras (15) and (16) into Social Security Act 1998 (Commencement No.9, and Savings and Consequential and Transitional Provisions) Order 1999 (SI 1999/2422) (as amended), art.3 (October 16, 2006).

DEFINITIONS

"the 1992 Act"—see reg.1(2).
"the appointed day"—see reg.1(2).
"pensionable age"—see reg.1(2).
"period of incapacity for work"—see SSCBA 1992, s.30C(1), above.

GENERAL NOTE

The central principle underlying the transitional provisions is that there should be no cash losers at the point of transfer. There was also concern not to subject certain existing benefit recipients to the rigours of the "all work" test.

8.249

Persons who transfer from sickness or invalidity benefit into incapacity benefit receive a transitional award of that benefit, distinguishing in certain respects the incapacity benefit they receive from the "standard" award of that benefit. This Part of these regulations deals with transferees from sickness benefit. Pt IV deals with transferees from invalidity benefit.

This regulation provides that those entitled to sickness benefit immediately before April 13, 1995 ("the appointed day": see reg.1(2)), including those without a valid contribution record whose incapacity is due to an industrial accident or prescribed industrial disease (hereinafter "industrially based"), transfer onto a transitional award of short-term incapacity benefit at the standard rate of short-term incapacity benefit, moving onto the higher rate in due course (after 196 days of entitlement including those pre-April 13, 1995: see regs 2–4 and 9) and eventually onto long-term incapacity benefit (after 364 days of entitlement including those pre-April 13, 1995: see regs 2–4 and 9).

All this depends, of course, on the transferee satisfying on or after April 13, 1995 the appropriate test of incapacity for work in SSCBA 1992, Pt XIIA, but this is "subject to the provisions in Part VI" of these regulations, whereby some people are exempt from the operation of the all work test (regs 29, 31).

Those to whom increases of sickness benefit for adult dependants were payable have their rate of incapacity benefit increased by that amount, subject to rules on residence, maintenance and earnings (regs 15, 16).

There are special rules preserving (if still higher than the standard rate) the transitional award rate for those who transferred in from sickness benefit and eventually received a transitional award of short-term incapacity benefit at the higher rate, before ceasing to be entitled to that transitional award because of a move into Disability Working Allowance or into relevant training, who later become entitled to the higher rate of standard short-term incapacity benefit, taking advantage of the up-to-two years linking rule under SSCBA 1992, s.30C(5) and (6), above (regs 12, 13).

Title to a transitional award of short-term incapacity benefit ceases if at any point the period of incapacity ends and is not restarted within eight weeks (para.2(a)), or (for those whose title is industrially based) if they cease to be incapacitated from

that cause and do not become so incapacitated again within eight weeks (para.(2)
(c) read with reg.14), or when the person has been entitled to it for 364 days in a
period of incapacity for work (para.2(b)). But in this last situation, if incapacity
continues, either immediately or within eight weeks, the person will be entitled to
long-term incapacity benefit so long as he is not over pensionable age (para.(4)).
Where, however, in such a case his title to benefit was industrially based, he can only
be entitled to long-term incapacity benefit if his incapacity continues to be due to an
industrial accident or prescribed industrial injury/disease (para.(5)).

Special provision for persons entitled to short-term incapacity benefit on termination of employment after a period of entitlement to disability working allowance

8.250   **12.**—(1) Where a person who was entitled to a transitional award of
short-term incapacity benefit becomes entitled to the higher rate of short-
term incapacity benefit by virtue of section 30C(5) of the 1992 Act and the
rate of that benefit is less than the rate at which the transitional award of
incapacity benefit would have been payable had he not ceased to be entitled
to that award, incapacity benefit shall be payable at the latter rate until—

(a) in the case where the transitional award included an increase under
regulation 15(1), the conditions in regulation 15(3) are no longer
satisfied;

(b) in any other case, the rate of short-term incapacity benefit under
section 30B of the 1992 Act together with any increase under section
86A of that Act (increase for adult dependants) equals or exceeds
that rate.

Special provisions for persons entitled to short-term incapacity benefit on termination of a period engaged in training for work

8.251   **13.**—(1) Where a person who was entitled to a transitional award of
short-term incapacity benefit becomes entitled to the higher rate of short-
term incapacity benefit by virtue of section 30C(6) of the 1992 Act and the
rate of that benefit is less than the rate at which the transitional award of
incapacity benefit would have been payable had he not ceased to be entitled
to that award, incapacity benefit shall be payable at the latter rate until—

(a) in the case where the transitional award included an increase under
regulation 15(1), the conditions in regulation 15(3) are no longer
satisfied;

(b) in any other case, the rate of short-term incapacity benefit under
section 30B of the 1992 Act together with any increase under section
86A of that Act (increase for adult dependants) equals or exceeds
that rate.

(2) Where a person—

(a) at any time in a period of not more than 57 days immediately before
the appointed day or at any time in a period of not more than 57 days
immediately after the appointed day attends a training course of the
type specified in regulation 7(1)(f) of the Unemployment, Sickness
and Invalidity Benefit Regulations (days when a person is attending
a training course not to be treated as days of incapacity for work);
and

(b) had been entitled to sickness benefit in a period of interruption
of employment [¹ occurring in whole or in part in a period] not

exceeding 57 days prior to the first day of attendance on the training course; and

(c) within a period not exceeding 57 days beginning on the day after the last day of attendance on the training course he becomes entitled to incapacity benefit by virtue of sections 30A, 40 or 41 of the 1992 Act; and

(d) the rate of short-term incapacity benefit is less than the rate at which a transitional award of short-term incapacity benefit would have been payable had the period of entitlement to sickness benefit referred to in sub-paragraph (b) been running at the appointed day,

incapacity benefit shall be payable at the latter rate until, in the case where the transitional award would have included an increase under regulation 15(1), the conditions in regulation 15(3) are no longer satisfied, and in any other case, the rate of short-term incapacity benefit under section 30B of the 1992 Act together with any increase under section 86A of that Act equals or exceeds that rate.

(3) For the purpose of paragraph (2), days of attendance on a training course referred to in that paragraph shall be treated as days of incapacity for work.

AMENDMENT

1. Social Security (Incapacity for Work) Miscellaneous Amendments Regulations 1995 (SI 1995/987), reg.3(2) (April 13, 1995).

Contribution conditions of short-term incapacity benefit in respect of an industrial injury

14.—(1) Where a person was entitled to sickness benefit under section 102 of the 1992 Act (sickness benefit in respect of industrial injury) immediately before the appointed day, the contribution conditions as specified in Schedule 3, Part I, paragraph 2 of the 1992 Act shall be taken to be satisfied—

8.252

(a) for the purposes of entitlement to a transitional award of the higher rate of short-term incapacity benefit in respect of that industrial injury;

(b) for the purposes of entitlement to the lower or higher rate of short-term incapacity benefit where—

(i) he ceased to be entitled to a transitional award as a consequence of regulation 11(2)(c); and

(ii) no more than 57 days after he ceased to be so entitled, he became incapable of work as a result of the personal injury in respect of which the transitional award referred to in head (i) above was payable;

(c) for the purposes of entitlement to short-term incapacity benefit by virtue of section 30C(5) or 30C(6) of the 1992 Act in a case where he becomes incapable for work as a result of the personal injury in respect of which a transitional award of incapacity benefit was made.

(2) Where a person is entitled to incapacity benefit by virtue of paragraph (1)(b), the rate at which incapacity benefit is payable shall be the rate at which a transitional award of short-term incapacity benefit would have been payable had he been entitled to a transitional award of shortterm

incapacity benefit; and these Regulations shall apply as if the award of incapacity benefit were a transitional award of short-term incapacity benefit.

DEFINITIONS

"the 1992 Act"—see reg.1(2).
"the appointed day"—see reg.1(2).

GENERAL NOTE

8.253   Incapacity benefit is a contributory benefit. Normally, only those who actually satisfy the relevant contribution conditions can have access to it. This is in contradistinction to sickness and invalidity benefits, where non-satisfaction of the contribution conditions for those benefits was not fatal to a claim if the person's incapacity was due to an industrial accident or a prescribed industrial disease (hereinafter referred to as "industrially based incapacity"). This regulation accordingly provides that for those so entitled to sickness benefit on April 12, 1995 ("immediately before the appointed day"), the contribution conditions for incapacity benefit are to be taken as satisfied for the purposes set out in para.(1):—

(a) those of entitlement to a transitional award of short-term incapacity benefit (higher rate) in respect of industrially based incapacity;

(b) those of entitlement to the lower or higher rate of short-term incapacity benefit where he ceased to be entitled to a transitional award of short-term incapacity benefit because his incapacity was no longer industrially based but before eight weeks had elapsed he again became so incapacitated (in which case under para.(2) the award, apparently one of "standard" benefit, is treated and paid as a transitional award of short-term incapacity benefit);

(c) those of entitlement to short-term incapacity benefit for those using the longer (up-to-two years) linking rule for those who moved from a transitional award of short-term incapacity benefit onto DWA (SSCBA 1992, s.30C(5)) or into training for work (SSCBA 1992, s.30C(6)) who, within the linking period, seek short-term incapacity benefit on the basis of the industrial injury or prescribed industrial disease which had been the basis of their entitlement to that transitional award.

Increase of rate of a transitional award of short-term incapacity benefit for adult dependants

8.254   **15.**—(1) Subject to paragraph (7), where at any time during a period of 56 days immediately before the appointed day—

(a) an increase of sickness benefit under Part IV of the 1992 Act was payable to a person for a spouse who was an adult dependant; and

(b) on the appointed day he becomes entitled to a transitional award of short-term incapacity benefit under regulation 11,

an amount equal to that increase shall be payable.

(2) Where, as a consequence of a review under section 150 of the Administration Act in the tax year, 1994–1995, the amounts specified in column (3) of paragraph 1A of Part IV of Schedule 4 to the 1992 Act are increased the increase payable under paragraph (1) shall likewise be increased by an equal amount; and thereafter an increase payable under paragraph (1) shall be an amount equal to the appropriate amount specified in column (3) of paragraph 1A of Part IV of Schedule 4 to the 1992 Act.

(3) Subject to the following provisions, an increase under paragraph (1) shall continue to be payable provided that—

(a) the spouse is residing with the beneficiary; or

(b) the beneficiary is contributing to the maintenance of his spouse at the weekly rate equal to or greater than the rate of the increase.

(4) The provisions in Part I (general) and Part III (adults), save for regulation 9(1)(a) and (b) of that Part, of the Increases for Dependants Regulations shall apply to an increase under paragraph (1) as they apply to an increase made by virtue of section 86A of that Act.

(5) A person shall cease to be entitled to an increase under paragraph (1) when no increase of sickness benefit or short-term incapacity benefit has been paid or payable for a period of at least 57 continuous days.

(6) In calculating the period referred to in paragraph (5) the days of entitlement to disability working allowance or the days of attendance on a training course of a type referred to in section 30C(6) of the 1992 Act or regulation 13(2) shall not be taken into account.

(7) Where a person is entitled to an increase under paragraph (1) and section 30B(4) of the 1992 Act applies to him the amount of the increase shall be equal to the rate specified in Schedule 4, Part IV, paragraph 2, column (3) of the 1992 Act.

(8) In a case where paragraph (7) applied, the increase shall continue to be payable if, when the transitional award of short-term incapacity benefit is terminated, he immediately becomes entitled to long-term incapacity benefit under section 30A(5) of that Act and he continues to satisfy the conditions in section 30B(4)(a) and (b); and this regulation shall continue to apply to that increase.

(9) Where a person becomes entitled to an increase under paragraph (1), he shall not be entitled to an adult dependency increase to which he would, but for this provision, be entitled under the Increases for Dependants Regulations.

DEFINITIONS

"the 1992 Act"—see reg.1(2).
"the Administration Act"—see reg.1(2).
"the appointed day"—see reg.1(2).
"the Increases for Dependants Regulations"—see reg.1(2).

GENERAL NOTE

This provision assists the achievement of the aim that there should be no cash losers at the point of changeover among transferees from the sickness and invalidity benefits regime to the incapacity benefit regime.

8.255

It stipulates that those transferees from sickness benefit who become entitled to a transitional award of short-term incapacity benefit on April 13, 1995 ("the appointed day"), to whom was payable at any time in the eight weeks prior to that date an increase of sickness benefit for a spouse who was an adult dependant, shall have their transitional award of incapacity benefit increased by an equivalent amount (para.(1)) up-rated in accordance with para.(2). That increase can only be payable, however, if the spouse is residing with the beneficiary of the transitional award or that beneficiary is contributing to the maintenance of the spouse at a weekly rate equal to or greater than the rate of this adult dependant increase (para.(3)). Note that under para.(4) the provisions of Pts I and III of the Incapacity Benefit (Increases for Dependants) Regulations, above, other than reg.9(1)(a) and (b) thereof, apply here just as they do to increases of "standard" incapacity benefit under SSCBA 1992, s.86A, above.

Entitlement to a para.(1) increase ceases when no increase of sickness benefit or short-term incapacity benefit has been paid or payable for a period of at least 57

911

continuous days (not including days of entitlement to DWA or training for work under SSCBA 1992, s.30C(6) or reg.13(2), above) (paras (5), (6)).

If a person entitled to such an increase becomes entitled to short-term incapacity benefit at the rate equivalent to that of long-term incapacity benefit because terminally ill or in receipt of the highest rate care component of disability living allowance (SSCBA 1992, s.30B(4)), then instead of the para.(1) increase, he becomes entitled to the adult dependant rate which attaches to long-term incapacity benefit (para. (7)). Entitlement to that higher rate continues to be payable if, immediately after reaching the exhaustion point for short-term incapacity benefit (364 days of entitlement including pre-commencement days: see regs 2 and 4), he becomes entitled to long-term incapacity benefit in the normal way but remains terminally ill or entitled to that highest rate care component, and this regulation shall continue to apply to that increase (para.(8)).

Paragraph (9) prevents duplication of payments; no one entitled to an increase under para.(1) can get any other adult dependency increase to which he would be entitled were it not for this provision.

Transitional provision for the treatment of earnings in respect of increases of short-term incapacity benefit for dependants

8.256   **16.**—Where—
  (a) on or after the appointed day no increase of short-term incapacity benefit is payable for—
    (i) an adult dependant as a consequence of regulation 5 (attribution of earnings) or regulation 10 (earnings rules for increases for adult dependants) of the Increases for Dependants Regulations; or
    (ii) a child dependant as a consequence of section 80(3) and (4) of the 1992 Act and regulation 5 of the Increases for Dependants Regulations; and
  (b) the earnings which caused there to be no payment of an increase in paragraph (a) had already resulted in no payment of an increase before the appointed day, a payment of an increase shall be made as if the provisions in the 1992 Act in force immediately before the appointed date continued to have effect in respect of those earnings and the 1994 Act had not been enacted and regulations 5 and 10 of the Increases for Dependants Regulations had not come into force.

DEFINITIONS

   "the 1992 Act"—see reg.1(2).
   "the 1994 Act"—see reg.1(2).
   "the appointed day"—see reg.1(2).
   "the Increases for Dependants Regulations"—see reg.1(2).

GENERAL NOTE

8.257   This provides that if after April 13, 1995 ("the appointed day") the effect of the specified provisions of the SSCBA 1992 (as amended by the IWA 1994) and of the Incapacity Benefit (Increases for Dependants) Regulations results in no increase of short-term incapacity benefit being payable for an adult dependant or a child dependant in consequence of earnings which had already caused there to be no payment of an increase of sickness benefit prior to April 13, 1995, then an increase of short-term incapacity benefit in respect of an adult or child dependant shall be made as if the unamended provisions of the SSCBA 1992 still applied and regs 5 and 10 of the Incapacity Benefit (Increases for Dependants) Regulations had never come into force.

PART IV

PROVISIONS FOR THE TRANSITION TO INCAPACITY BENEFIT FROM INVALIDITY BENEFIT

Transitional awards of long-term incapacity benefit

17.—(1) Where a person is entitled to invalidity benefit immediately before the appointed day, that award of invalidity benefit shall have effect on or after the appointed day as if it were an award of long-term incapacity benefit; and such an award shall be referred to in these Regulations as a transitional award of long-term incapacity benefit.

(2) Subject to the provisions in Part VI, a person's entitlement to a transitional award of long-term incapacity benefit shall be subject to him being incapable of work as determined in accordance with Part XIIA of the 1992 Act (Incapacity for Work).

(3) A person who reaches pensionable age before the appointed day and who is entitled to a transitional award of long-term incapacity benefit under paragraph (1) shall continue to be entitled to that award on any day that he is incapable of work as determined in accordance with Part XIIA of the 1992 Act for as long as he is not more than 5 years over pensionable age [¹ or until the first day on which he is entitled to retirement pension, whichever date is the earlier].

(4) Where a person reaches pensionable age on or after the appointed day, entitlement to a transitional award of long-term incapacity benefit shall terminate on his attaining pensionable age.

[²(5) The transitional award under paragraph (1) is treated as a decision of the Secretary of State under section 8(1) of the Social Security Act 1998 (decision by Secretary of State) and as an incapacity decision for the purposes of the Social Security and Child Support (Decisions and Appeals) Regulations 1999.]

8.258

AMENDMENTS

1. Social Security (Incapacity for Work and Miscellaneous Amendments) Regulations 1996 (SI 1996/3207), reg.3(3) (January 6, 1997).

2. Social Security Act 1998 (Commencement Nos 9 and 11) (Amendment) Order 2006 (SI 2006/2540), art.2(3)(b) inserting paras (15) and (16) into Social Security Act 1998 (Commencement No.9, and Savings and Consequential and Transitional Provisions) Order 1999 (SI 1999/2422) (as amended), art.3 (October 16, 2006).

DEFINITIONS

"the 1992 Act"—see reg.1(2).
"the appointed day"—see reg.1(2).
"pensionable age"—see reg.1(2).

GENERAL NOTE

The central principle underlying the transitional provisions is that there should be no cash losers at the point of transfer. There was also concern not to subject certain existing benefit recipients to the rigours of the "all work" test.

8.259

Persons who transfer from sickness or invalidity benefit into incapacity benefit receive a transitional award of that benefit, distinguishing in certain respects the incapacity benefit they receive from the "standard" award of that benefit. This Part of these regulations deals with transferees from invalidity benefit. Pt III deals with transferees from sickness benefit.

Those entitled to invalidity benefit immediately before April 13, 1995 ("the appointed day"), including those with a deficient contribution record whose incapacity is due to an industrial accident or a prescribed industrial disease (hereinafter "industrially based"), have that award treated as if it were one of long-term incapacity benefit, and transfer to a transitional award of that benefit. Those over pensionable age before commencement remain eligible for such an award for so long as they are not more than five years over that age or until the first day of entitlement to retirement pension, whichever date is the earlier. Those who attain pensionable age on or after April, 13, 1995 cease to be eligible and will have to rely on retirement pension. In *CIB/13368/1996*, Commissioner Levenson allowed the appeal of a female claimant whose entitlement to incapacity benefit was ended because of para.(4) of this regulation. He decided that she did not lose title at 60 (pensionable age for a woman) but could retain title until 65 (pensionable age for a man) because the provision discriminated on grounds of sex contrary to the prohibition in Art.4 of Council Directive 79/7 (the equal treatment directive) (see further *Vol. III: Administration, Appeals and the European Dimension*). Applying *Thomas* ([1991] 3 All E.R. 315) and *Graham* ([1995] All E.R. (EC) 736), such discrimination was not saved by Art.7(1) of the directive since it was not objectively necessary to avoid disrupting the complex financial equilibrium of the social security system, being very like the SDA scheme considered in *Thomas*. Commissioner Levenson's decision in *CIB/13368/96* was, by concession, reversed by the Court of Appeal in *CAO v Rowlands* on June 27, 2000, following the ECJ's decision in *Hepple*. Title to benefit ceases if at any point the period of incapacity ends and is not restarted within eight weeks or (for those whose title is industrially based) if they cease to be incapacitated from that cause and do not become so incapacitated again within eight weeks (this regulation read with reg.21).

All this depends, of course, on the transferee satisfying on or after April 13, 1995 the appropriate test of incapacity for work in SSCBA 1992, Pt XIIA, but this is "subject to the provisions in Pt VI" of these regulations, whereby some people are exempt from the operation of the all work test (regs 29, 31).

Special provision is made for those who moved from invalidity benefit to Disability Working Allowance or into relevant training, who become entitled to long-term incapacity benefit; and for those who move from a transitional award of long-term incapacity benefit onto DWA or into training for work, who become entitled to "standard" long-term incapacity benefit within the longer (up-to-two years) linking period set by SSCBA 1992, s.30C(5), (6) (regs 19, 20).

For those under pensionable age, the basic rate of a transitional award of long-term incapacity benefit is the same as the standard rate. For those over pensionable age, the basic rate is the appropriate rate of retirement pension for that claimant. Those receiving an earnings related additional pension with their invalidity benefit, continue to do so (known as the "additional rate") (reg.18(1)(b)), but the rate is frozen at commencement. Recipients of invalidity allowance (any of three rates) will continue to receive an equivalent up-rated amount (reg.18). Note carefully, however, the effect of reg.22 where someone is entitled to one or more guaranteed minimum pensions: the effect is to reduce the transitional award of incapacity benefit payable.

Old style additions for adult dependants, if payable at or within the eight-week period before commencement, continue to be payable, subject to rules on residence, maintenance and earnings, but will cease after an eight-week break in entitlement to them, to invalidity benefit or to incapacity benefit (regs 24–26). If the former rules on earnings produce a more favourable result than the operation of the new ones in the Increases for Dependants Regulations in respect of an adult or child dependant increase, then in certain cases (where the earnings in question had already resulted in no payment of or a reduced payment of an increase prior to April 13, 1995), the former rules continue to operate (reg.26).

Although this regulation means that an award of invalidity benefit has effect as, and is to be treated as, an award of long-term incapacity benefit, it does not become incapacity benefit, and so, for the purposes of reg.6 of the Decisions and Appeals Regulations 1999 it does not rank as an incapacity benefit decision because it could not have been a determination under Pt XIIA of the Social Security Contributions and Benefits Act 1992 since that did not come into force until April 1995. A decision in 1990 is not converted by reg.17 into an incapacity benefit decision "because it relates only to the continuing effect and not to a change into the new benefit" (*CSIB/510/2003*, para.10; *Hooper v Secretary of State for Work and Pensions* [2007] EWCA Civ 495, to be reported as *R(IB) 4/07*).

[¹ Awards of incapacity benefit in cases where periods of interruption of employment and periods of incapacity for work link

17A.—Where a person had been entitled to invalidity benefit in a period of interruption of employment occurring in whole or in part in a period not exceeding 57 days immediately before the appointed day and becomes entitled to an award of incapacity benefit on the basis that a day of incapacity for work on or after the appointed day forms part of a period of incapacity for work beginning before the appointed day, that award shall have effect as if it were an award of long-term incapacity benefit.]

8.260

AMENDMENT

1. Social Security (Incapacity for Work) Miscellaneous Amendments Regulations 1995 (SI 1995/987), reg.3(3) (April 13, 1995).

GENERAL NOTE

Anyone entitled to incapacity benefit on the basis that a day of incapacity on or after the appointed day links back with one of incapacity for invalidity benefit entitlement in a pre-commencement period of interruption of employment not more than eight weeks back, has his award of incapacity benefit treated as if it were an award of long-term incapacity benefit.

8.261

[¹ Calculating periods of incapacity for work for welfare to work beneficiaries in long-term incapacity benefit transitional cases

17B.—For the purposes of transitional cases, where a person, to whom regulation 17(1) (transitional awards of long-term incapacity benefit) or regulation 17A (awards of incapacity benefit in cases where periods of interruption of employment and periods of incapacity for work link) applies, has been determined in accordance with regulation 13A of the Social Security (Incapacity for Work) (General) Regulations 1995 to have become a welfare to work beneficiary, section 30C(1)(c) of the 1992 Act (any two periods of incapacity for work not separated by a period of more than 8 weeks shall be treated as one period of incapacity for work) shall have effect as if for the reference to 8 weeks there were substituted a reference to [² 104] weeks.]

8.262

AMENDMENT

1. Social Security (Welfare to Work) Regulations 1998 (SI 1998/2231), reg.3(2) (October 5, 1998).

2. Social Security (Miscellaneous Amendments) (No.4) Regulations 2006 (SI 2006/2378), reg.11(2) (October 1, 2006).

8.263   This is part of a package of "welfare to work" measures. It modifies SSCBA 1992, s.30C(1)(c) so as to introduce a 52-week linking rule, rather than the standard eight-week one, for those incapable of work for 28 weeks who go into remunerative work, or into training followed by remunerative work, and then seek to return to their previous incapacity benefit and rate. On "welfare to work beneficiary", see further IW (General) Regs, reg.13A. Note that the rule cannot apply to those who left incapacity benefit because of being found capable of work or treated as such. It is there to assist those who, while qualifying for benefit, wish to try out work or training for work, without prejudicing a return to their previous rate of benefit should things not work out.

Rate of long-term incapacity benefit in transitional cases

8.264   **18.**—(1) Subject to paragraph (7) in transitional cases, the weekly rate of long-term incapacity benefit shall consist of—

  (a) a basic rate of an amount equal to the rate of long-term incapacity benefit specified in Schedule 4, Part I, paragraph 2A, of the 1992 Act;

  (b) where an additional pension was paid or payable with invalidity benefit immediately before the appointed day, an additional rate of an amount equal to the rate paid or payable as an additional pension with invalidity benefit immediately before the appointed day; and that amount shall be referred to as the additional rate;

  (c) where an invalidity allowance was payable [1 pursuant to subsection (3) of section 34] of the 1992 Act immediately before the appointed day, an amount equal to the appropriate rate specified in paragraph (2); and that amount shall be referred to as a transitional invalidity allowance.

(2) The appropriate rate referred to in paragraph (1)(c) is—

  (a) where the higher rate of invalidity allowance was payable immediately before the appointed day, [2 £18.65];

  (b) where the middle rate of invalidity allowance was payable immediately before the appointed day, [2 £12.00];

  (c) where the lower rate of invalidity allowance was payable immediately before the appointed day, [2 £6.00].

(3) The transitional invalidity allowance shall be up-rated in accordance with the provisions of Part X of the Administration Act (review and alteration) as if that allowance were a sum specified in section 150(1)(a)(i), (2)(a) and (3)(a) of that Act.

(4) In a transitional case, where for any period a person is entitled to an award of long-term incapacity benefit which includes the additional rate and a transitional invalidity allowance, for that period the relevant amount shall be deducted from the appropriate weekly rate of the transitional invalidity allowance [3 . . .].

(5) In paragraph (4) "the relevant amount" means an amount equal to the additional rate reduced by the amount of any reduction in the weekly rate of incapacity benefit made by virtue of regulation 22.

(6) Where the rate of long-term incapacity benefit includes a transitional invalidity allowance no increase shall become payable by virtue of regulations made under section 30B(7) of the 1992 Act.

(7) In a transitional case where a person attained pensionable age before the appointed day and is not more than 5 years over that age, he shall continue to be entitled to long-term incapacity benefit until he reaches 5 years over pensionable age [⁴ or until the first day on which he is entitled to retirement pension, whichever date is the earlier,] payable at the rate at which the basic pension referred to in section 44(4) of the 1992 Act is payable.

(8) In determining the rate of long-term incapacity benefit in a transitional case where paragraph (7) applies, any increase of the following descriptions shall be disregarded—

(a) if he is also entitled to a transitional invalidity allowance under paragraph(1)(c), any increase under section 47(1) or 50(2) of the 1992 Act;

(b) any increase (for married women) under section 53(2) of, or (for deferred retirement) under Schedule 5 to, the 1992 Act;

(c) any increase (for dependants) under section 80, 83 or 85 of the 1992 Act; and

(d) any increase (for Category A or Category B pensions) under section 150 of the Administration Act (annual up-rating) of the sums mentioned in subsection (1)(e) of that section.

[⁵ (9) For the purposes of Part IV a "transitional case" means a case where a person is entitled to an award of long-term incapacity benefit by virtue of regulation 17 or 17A.]

AMENDMENTS

1. Social Security (Incapacity for Work and Miscellaneous Amendments) Regulations 1996 (SI 1996/3207), reg.3(4)(a) (January 6, 1997).
2. Social Security Benefits Up-rating Order 2009 (SI 2009/497), art.15 (April 9, 2009).
3. Social Security (Incapacity for Work and Miscellaneous Amendments) Regulations 1996 (SI 1996/3207), reg.3(4)(b) (January 6, 1997).
4. Social Security (Incapacity for Work and Miscellaneous Amendments) Regulations 1996 (SI 1996/3207), reg.3(4)(c) (January 6, 1997).
5. Social Security (Incapacity for Work) Miscellaneous Amendments Regulations 1995 (SI 1995/987), reg.3(4)(c) (April 13, 1995).

GENERAL NOTE

Note that, as part of moves towards transferring existing incapacity benefits claimants to ESA, since January 20, 2009 the Secretary of State has an ability to use the annual up-rating order to reduce the amounts of transitional invalidity allowance in respect of each of the tax years beginning with 2009/10 and ending with 2013/14 (see Employment and Support Allowance (Up-rating Modification) (Transitional) Regulations 2008 (SI 2008/3270, reg.2)).

8.265

Special provisions for persons entitled to long-term incapacity benefit on termination of a period of entitlement to disability working allowance

19.—(1) Where a person who was entitled to a transitional award of long-term incapacity benefit becomes entitled to incapacity benefit by virtue of section 30C(5) of the 1992 Act and the rate of that benefit is less than the rate at which the transitional award of long-term incapacity benefit would have been payable had he not ceased to be entitled to that award, incapacity benefit shall be payable at the latter rate until—

8.266

(a) in the case where the transitional award included an increase under regulation 24(1), the conditions in regulation 24(3) or any of the provisions referred to in regulation 25(2) are no longer satisfied;

(b) in any other case, the rate of long-term incapacity benefit under section 30B of the 1992 Act together with any increase under section 86A of that Act (increase for adult dependants) equals or exceeds that rate.

(2) Where a person—

(a) who was entitled to disability working allowance by virtue of section 129 of the 1992 Act before the appointed day or to disability working allowance at any time in a period of not more than 56 days beginning on or after the appointed day, becomes entitled to incapacity benefit; and

(b) would have become entitled to invalidity benefit by virtue of section 33(7) or section 42 of the 1992 Act had the 1994 Act not come into force; and

(c) the rate of incapacity benefit is less than the rate at which a transitional award of long-term incapacity benefit would have been payable had the days of entitlement to invalidity benefit in the period of interruption of employment which arose immediately before the period of entitlement to disability working allowance been days of entitlement to invalidity benefit in a period of interruption of employment running at the appointed day,

incapacity benefit shall be payable at the latter rate until, in the case where the transitional award would have included an increase under regulation 24(1), the conditions in regulation 24(3) or in any of the provisions referred to in regulation 25(2) are no longer satisfied, and in any other case, the rate of long-term incapacity benefit under section 30B of the 1992 Act together with any increase under section 86A of that Act equals or exceeds that rate.

(3) For the purposes of paragraph (2), the days of entitlement to disability working allowance referred to in that paragraph shall be treated as days of incapacity for work.

Special provisions for persons entitled to long-term incapacity benefit on termination of a period engaged in training for work

8.267

20.—(1) Where a person who was entitled to a transitional award of long-term incapacity benefit becomes entitled to long-term incapacity benefit by virtue of section 30C(6) of the 1992 Act and the rate of that benefit is less than the rate at which the transitional award of long-term incapacity benefit would have been payable had he not ceased to be entitled to that award, incapacity benefit shall be payable at the latter rate until—

(a) in the case where the transitional award included an increase under regulation 24(1), the conditions in regulation 24(3) or any of the provisions referred to in regulation 25(2) are no longer satisfied;

(b) in any other case, the rate of long-term incapacity benefit under section 30B of the 1992 Act together with any increase under section 86A of that Act (increase for adult dependants) equals or exceeds that rate.

(2) Where a person—

(a) at any time in a period of not more than 57 days immediately before the appointed day or at any time in a period of not more than 57 days immediately after the appointed day attends a training course of the type specified in regulation 7(1)(f) of the Unemployment, Sickness and Invalidity Benefit Regulations (days when a person is attending a training course not to be treated as days of incapacity for work); and

(b) had been entitled to invalidity benefit in a period of interruption of employment [¹ occurring in whole or in part in a period] not exceeding 57 days prior to the first day of attendance on the training course; and

(c) within a period not exceeding 57 days beginning on the day after the last day of attendance on the training course becomes entitled to incapacity benefit by virtue of sections 30A, 40 or 41 of the 1992 Act; and

(d) the rate of incapacity benefit is less than the rate at which a transitional award of long-term incapacity benefit would have been payable had the period of entitlement to invalidity benefit referred to in sub-paragraph (b) been running at the appointed day,

incapacity benefit shall be payable at the latter rate until, in the case where the transitional award would have included an increase under regulation 24(1), the conditions in regulation 24(3) or in any of the provisions referred to in regulation 25(2) are no longer satisfied, and in any other case, the rate of incapacity benefit under section 30B of the 1992 Act together with any increase under section 86A of that Act equals or exceeds that rate.

(3) For the purpose of paragraph (2), the days referred to as days of attendance on a training course in that paragraph shall be treated as days of incapacity for work.

AMENDMENT

1. Social Security (Incapacity for Work) Miscellaneous Amendments Regulations 1995 (SI 1995/987), reg.3(5) (April 13, 1995).

Special provisions for persons entitled to long-term incapacity benefit in respect of an industrial injury

21.—(1) Subject to paragraph(2), a person entitled to a transitional award of long-term incapacity benefit in respect of a personal injury of a kind mentioned in section 94(1) of the 1992 Act shall cease to be so entitled when the incapacity for work is no longer as a result of that injury.

8.268

(2) Where a person's entitlement to a transitional award of long-term incapacity benefit ceases as a consequence of paragraph (1) and no more than 57 days after entitlement to that award ceases he becomes incapable for work as a result of the same personal injury in respect of which the transitional award of long-term incapacity benefit was payable, he shall be entitled to benefit at the rate at which the transitional award of long-term incapacity benefit would have been payable had he not ceased to be so entitled, and these Regulations shall apply as if the award of incapacity benefit were a transitional award of long-term incapacity benefit.

Effect of entitlement to guaranteed minimum pensions on payment of the additional rate element in a transitional case of long-term incapacity benefit

22.—(1) Where a person who is a transitional case is entitled to both—

8.269

(a) an award of long-term incapacity benefit which includes the additional rate; and

   (b) to one or more guaranteed minimum pensions, and had been entitled to an invalidity pension under section 41 of the 1992 Act immediately before the appointed day, the weekly rate of the award of
long-term incapacity benefit shall be reduced by an amount equal—
      (i) to the additional rate; or
     (ii) to the weekly rate of the pension mentioned in paragraph (b) or
if there is more than one such [¹ guaranteed minimum pension],
their aggregate weekly rates,
whichever is less.

(2) Where a person is entitled to an award of long-term incapacity benefit
which includes the additional rate and the transitional invalidity allowance,
the weekly rate of that award shall be reduced by the relevant amount being
deducted from the weekly rate of the transitional invalidity allowance and
he shall be entitled to that allowance only if there is a balance after the
deduction and, if there is such a balance, at a weekly rate equal to it.

(3) Where for any period a person is entitled to—
   (a) an award of long-term incapacity benefit which does not include the
additional rate; and
   (b) one or more guaranteed minimum pensions, the weekly rate of the
award of long-term incapacity benefit shall be reduced by deducting
the weekly rate or aggregate weekly rates of the guaranteed minimum
pension or pensions from the weekly rate of the transitional invalidity allowance and a person shall be entitled to that allowance only
if there is a balance after deduction and, if there is a balance, at a
weekly rate equal to it.

(4) Where for any period a person is entitled to—
   (a) an award of long-term incapacity benefit which includes the additional rate but does not include the transitional invalidity allowance;
and
   (b) one or more guaranteed minimum pensions; and
   (c) an increase of unemployability supplement under section 106 and
paragraph 3 of Schedule 7 to the 1992 Act,
the relevant amount shall be deducted from the amount of the increase of
unemployability supplement specified in Schedule 4, Part V, paragraph 6
to the 1992 Act, and a person shall be entitled to an increase only if there is a
balance after that deduction and, if there is a balance, only an amount equal
to it.

(5) Where for any period a person who is a transitional case is entitled
to—
   (a) an award of long-term incapacity benefit which does not include the
additional rate; and
   (b) one or more guaranteed minimum pensions; and
   (c) an increase of unemployability supplement under section 106 and
paragraph 3 of Schedule 7 to the 1992 Act,
the increase of the unemployability supplement shall be reduced by the
weekly rate or aggregate weekly rates of the guaranteed minimum pension or
pensions and a person shall be entitled to an increase only if there is a balance
after that deduction and, if there is a balance, only an amount equal to it.

(6) In this regulation "the relevant amount" means an amount equal
to the weekly rate or aggregate weekly rates of the guaranteed minimum
pension or pensions and the additional rate reduced by—
   (a) the additional rate; or

(b) the weekly rate or aggregate weekly rates of the guaranteed minimum pension whichever is the less.

AMENDMENT

1. Social Security (Incapacity for Work) Miscellaneous Amendments Regulations 1995 (SI 1995/987), reg.3(6) (April 13, 1995).

[¹ Increase of Category A retirement pension for incapacity

23.—(1) Where a person has been entitled to invalidity allowance or tran-   8.270
sitional invalidity allowance at any time during a period of 57 days before
attaining pensionable age, sections 47 and 61 of the 1992 Act shall continue to have effect as though section 11 of, and paragraph 13 of Schedule
1 to, the 1994 Act had not come into force and as though any reference to
invalidity allowance in section 47 were a reference to transitional invalidity
allowance or invalidity allowance.

(2) In the case of a person who is a welfare to work beneficiary in accordance with regulation 13A of the Social Security (Incapacity for Work)
(General) Regulations 1995, the reference in paragraph (1) to a period of
57 days shall be treated as a reference to a period of [² 104]weeks.]

AMENDMENTS

1. Social Security (Welfare to Work) Regulations 1998 (SI 1998/2231), reg.3(3) (October 5, 1998).
2. Social Security (Miscellaneous Amendments) (No.4) Regulations 2006 (SI 2006/2378), reg.11(3) (October 1, 2006).

Increase of rate of long-term incapacity benefit for dependants in transitional cases

24.—(1) Subject to paragraphs (3), (4) and (5) and regulation 25, in a   8.271
transitional case where at any time during a period of 56 days immediately
before the appointed day—
  (a) an increase in the rate of invalidity benefit was paid by way of a con-
       cessionary payment to compensate for non-payment of an increase
       for a spouse who was an adult dependant under Part IV of the 1992
       Act; or
  (b) an increase in the rate of invalidity benefit was payable for a spouse
       who was an adult dependant under Part IV of the 1992 Act,
an amount equal to that increase shall be payable.

(2) Where, as a consequence of a review under section 150 of the
Administration Act in the tax year 1994–1995, the amounts specified
in column (3) of paragraph 2 of Part IV of Schedule 4 to the 1992 Act
are increased, the increase payable under paragraph (1) shall likewise be
increased by an equal amount; and thereafter an increase payable under
paragraph (1) shall be an amount equal to the appropriate amount specified
in column (3) of paragraph 2 of Part IV of Schedule 4 to the 1992 Act.

(3) Except as provided for in regulation 25, an increase under paragraph
(1) shall continue to be payable where—
  (a) the spouse is residing with the beneficiary; or
  (b) the beneficiary is contributing to the maintenance of his spouse at the
       weekly rate equal to or greater than the rate of the increase.

(4) Subject to regulations 25 and 26 and paragraph (5), the provisions in Part I (general) and Part III (adults), save for regulation 9(1)(a) and (b) of that Part, of the Increases for Dependants Regulations shall apply to the increase as if it were an increase under section 86A of the 1992 Act.

(5) Where an increase under paragraph (1) is paid or payable to a person over pensionable age, the provisions in regulation 13 of the Increases for Dependants Regulations (increase of short-term incapacity benefit for persons over pension age) shall apply to the increase of long-term incapacity benefit as if that increase were an increase of short-term incapacity benefit.

(6) Where a person becomes entitled to an increase under paragraph (1), he shall not be entitled to an adult dependency increase to which he would, but for this provision, be entitled under the Increases for Dependants Regulations.

(7) [¹ Except in a case where paragraph (7A) applies,] a person shall cease to be entitled to an increase under paragraph (1) when either—

(a) no invalidity benefit or long-term incapacity benefit has been paid for at least 57 continuous days;

(b) no increase of invalidity benefit or long-term incapacity benefit is paid or payable for at least 57 continuous days in a period of incapacity for work.

[¹ (7A) The exception referred to in paragraph (7) applies only if the person—

(a) has been determined to be a welfare to work beneficiary in accordance with regulation 13A of the Social Security (Incapacity for Work) (General) Regulations 1995; and

(b) is not entitled to incapacity benefit on any day in a period falling within a linking term within the meaning of regulation 13A of the Social Security (Incapacity for Work) (General) Regulations 1995.]

(8) In calculating the period referred to in paragraph (7), the days of entitlement to disability working allowance or the days of attendance on a training course of a type referred to in section 30C(6) of the 1992 Act and regulation 19(2) shall not be taken into account.

AMENDMENT

1. Social Security (Welfare to Work) Regulations 1998 (SI 1998/2231), reg.3 (October 5, 1998).

GENERAL NOTE

Paras (1), (7): "payable", "paid or payable"

8.272   In *CIB/3522/1997*, Commissioner Goodman held that the claimant transferee from invalidity benefit to long-term incapacity benefit could not ground entitlement to an increase in his incapacity benefit for his wife under these provisions because neither at the relevant date (April 13, 1995, the ending of invalidity benefit followed immediately by the introduction of incapacity benefit) nor at any point in the 56 days prior to that was any increase of invalidity benefit in respect of his wife paid or payable. No increase was being paid because her earnings were too high (para.10). The effect of SSCBA 1992, s.92 was simply that an award of increased invalidity benefit for a spouse continued in force even though the effect of earnings provisions in regulations meant that it was not payable (so as to obviate the need for review or revision each time the earnings fluctuated across the applicable "line"). Hence at April 13, 1995 and throughout the 56-day period preceding it the increase was

not payable so that the key condition in para.1(b) of this regulation was not fulfilled (para.11). The Commissioner rejected the argument that s.92 was somehow
"freestanding" and continued in force an award of increased invalidity benefit until
the section was amended or repealed. It referred to a benefit under "this Part of the
Act" and could not continue in force an award of a benefit which had as such ceased
to exist when the Incapacity for Work Act 1994 repealed ss.33 and 34 (invalidity
pension and invalidity allowance) of the SSCBA 1992. Thus the only provisions
which could assist the claimant were IWA, s.4 and this regulation, and, as explained
above, neither did (para.12). Nor could the claimant rely on IW (Dependants)
Regs, reg.9: his wife was not 60 at the relevant date, nor did the claimant have the
care of a child. The Commissioner in *CIB/27/1997* reached a similar result, but a
different conclusion was arrived at in *CIB/1483/1996*. This conflict has now been
resolved in favour of the approach in *CIB/3522/1997* and *CIB/27/1997* by a Tribunal
of Commissioners in *CIB/2836/2002*.

Further provisions for dependants in respect of the application of old saving provisions

25.—(1) In relation to transitional cases where the rate of incapacity
benefit falls to be calculated by reference to the rate of dependency allowance paid or payable before the appointed day, the old saving provisions
referred to in paragraph (2) shall continue to have effect subject to the following provisions of this regulation.

8.273

(2) The old saving provisions referred to in paragraph (1) are—
  (a) regulation 15 of the Social Security Benefit (Dependency) Regulations
    1997;
  (b) regulation 2 of the Social Security (Savings for Existing Beneficiaries)
    Regulations 1984;
  (c) regulation 3 of the Social Security Benefit (Dependency) Amendment
    Regulations 1984;
  (d) regulation 3 of the Social Security Benefit (Dependency) Amendment
    Regulations 1985;
  (e) regulation 4 of the Social Security Benefit (Dependency and
    Computation of Earnings) Amendment Regulations 1989;
  (f) regulation 4 of the Social Security Benefit (Dependency) Amendment
    Regulations 1992; and
  (g) any administrative provision which before the appointed day enabled
    a concessionary payment to be made to compensate for non-payment
    of an increase under Part IV of the 1992 Act as a consequence of any
    one of the regulations referred to in subparagraphs (a) to (f) ceasing
    to apply to an increase due to attendance on a training course.

(3) Except in a case where paragraph (3A) applies the old saving provisions referred to in paragraph (2) shall cease to have effect when—
  (a) no invalidity benefit or long-term incapacity benefit has been paid
    for at least 57 continuous days; or
  (b) no increase is paid for a dependant for a continuous period of at least
    57 days in a period of incapacity for work; or
  (c) in a case where regulation 4 of the Social Security Benefit
    (Dependency) Amendment Regulations 1992 applies, when the
    increase is not adjusted as a result of earnings for a continuous
    period of at least 57 days; or
  (d) in a case where a concessionary payment was made to compen-
    sate for non-payment of an increase under Part IV of the 1992

Act as a consequence of regulation 4 of the Social Security Benefit (Dependency) Amendment Regulations 1992 ceasing to apply due to attendance on a training course, when the increase is not adjusted as a result of earnings for a continuous period of at least 57 days.

[¹ (3A) The exception referred to in paragraph (3) applies only if the person—

(a) has been determined to be a welfare to work beneficiary in accordance with regulation 13A of the Social Security (Incapacity for Work) (General) Regulations 1995; and

(b) is not entitled to incapacity benefit on any day in a period falling within a linking term within the meaning of regulation 13A of the Social Security (Incapacity for Work) (General) Regulations 1995.]

(4) Regulation 4 of the Social Security Benefit (Dependency) Amendment Regulations 1992 shall not apply in any week to a case where a dependant has earnings which exceed £81.50 per week.

(5) Where an increase is payable as a consequence of a concessionary payment made to compensate for non-payment of an increase under Part IV of the 1992 Act as a consequence of regulation 4 of the Social Security Benefit (Dependency) Amendment Regulations 1992 ceasing to apply due to attendance on a training course, no payment shall be made in any week where a dependant has earnings which exceed £81.50 per week.

AMENDMENT

1. Social Security (Welfare to Work) Regulations 1998 (SI 1998/2231), reg.3(5) (October 5, 1998).

Transitional provision for the treatment of earnings in respect of increases of long-term incapacity benefit for dependants

8.274

26.—Where—

(a) on or after the appointed day—

    (i) no increase or a reduced amount of the rate of increase of long-term incapacity benefit is payable for an adult dependant as a consequence of regulation 5 (attribution of earnings) or regulation 10 (earnings rules for increases for adult dependants) of the Increases for Dependants Regulations; or

    (ii) no increase of long-term incapacity benefit is payable for a child dependant as a consequence of section 80(3) and (4) of the 1992 Act and regulation 5 (attribution of earnings) of the Increases for Dependants Regulations; and

(b) in a case where the increase for an adult dependant is reduced, the amount of reduction would have been less had the 1994 Act and regulations 5 and 10 of the Increases for Dependants Regulations not come into force; and

(c) the earnings which caused there to be no payment of an increase or a reduction of an increase in paragraph (a) had already resulted in no payment of or a reduced payment of an increase before the appointed day,

a payment of an increase shall be made as if the provisions in the 1992 Act in force immediately before the appointed day continued to have effect in respect of those earnings and the 1994 Act had not been enacted and regulations 5 and 10 of the Increases for Dependants Regulations had not come into force.

PART V

MISCELLANEOUS TRANSITIONAL PROVISIONS

Transition from a six day benefit to a seven day benefit

27.—Where a payment of an award of sickness benefit, invalidity benefit or severe disablement allowance would have been made in respect of a six day period ending on—

   (i) 13 April 1995, had the 1994 Act not come into force, the rate of the transitional award of short-term or long-term incapacity benefit or severe disablement allowance in respect of that day shall be 1/6th of the appropriate weekly rate of that benefit or allowance in force on the appointed day;

  (ii) 14 April 1995, had the 1994 Act not come into force, the rate of the transitional award of short-term or long-term incapacity benefit or severe disablement allowance in respect of 13 April and 14 April 1995 shall, in respect of each such day, be 1/6th of the appropriate weekly rate of that benefit or allowance in force on the appointed day.

8.275

DEFINITIONS

  "the 1994 Act"—see reg.1(2).
  "the appointed day"—see reg.1(2).

GENERAL NOTE

  Like its predecessors and severe disablement allowance (SDA), incapacity benefit is a daily benefit, but is now based on a seven-day week so that the daily rate is one-seventh of the weekly rate whereas the daily rate for those other benefits, based on a six-day week, was one-sixth of the weekly rate. This regulation provides that where a "six day award" of sickness benefit, invalidity benefit or SDA would have ended on either April 13 or 14, then the appropriate daily rate of a transitional award of short-term or long-term incapacity benefit or of SDA shall be one-sixth of the weekly rate for that or those days.

8.276

Transitional provisions for an increase of severe disablement allowance for adult dependants

28.—(1) Subject to paragraph (2), where an increase of severe disablement allowance is payable for an adult dependant at any time during a period of 56 days immediately before the appointed day by virtue of section 90 of the 1992 Act, that increase shall continue to be payable and the provisions in regulation [¹ 24(2) to (7A)] shall apply to that increase as if that increase were an increase of long-term incapacity benefit in a transitional case.

  (2) Where a person becomes entitled to severe disablement allowance by virtue of—

   (a) section 68(10) of the 1992 Act (treating days of entitlement to

8.277

disability working allowance as having been days on which a person was both incapable for work and disabled); or

(b)   section 68(10A) of the 1992 Act (treating days engaged in training as having been days on which a person was both incapable for work and disabled),

and an increase had been payable under section 90 of the 1992 Act or paragraph (1) when he was last entitled to that allowance, he shall be entitled to an amount equal to the amount of an increase payable under paragraph (1) if, by reason only of the fact that there is no child for whom he is entitled to an increase under section 80 of the 1992 Act, he would not be entitled to an increase for an adult dependant under the Increases for Dependants Regulations; and the amount payable shall be treated as if it were an increase under paragraph (1).

AMENDMENT

1. Social Security (Welfare to Work) Regulations 1998 (SI 1998/2231), reg.3(6) (October 5, 1998).

[¹ Transitional provision for entitlement to severe disablement allowance where a person has been engaged in training for work

8.278   **28A.**—For the purposes of entitlement to severe disablement allowance where a person—

(a)   at any time in a period of not more than 57 days immediately before the appointed day attends a training course of the type specified in regulation 7(1)(f) of the Social Security (Unemployment, Sickness and Invalidity Benefit) Regulations 1983; and

(b)   was entitled to severe disablement allowance in a period of interruption of employment within a period not exceeding 57 days prior to the first day of attendance on the training course; and

(c)   becomes incapable of work within a period of 57 days after the last day of attendance on a training course,

he shall be treated as incapable of work and disabled for the days falling within the periods referred to in paragraphs (a),(b) and (c) notwithstanding that he may have been capable of work on any of those days.]

AMENDMENT

1. Social Security (Incapacity for Work) Miscellaneous Amendments Regulations 1995 (SI 1995/987), reg.3(8) (April 13, 1995).

PART VI

PROVISIONS FOR THE TRANSITION TO THE NEW TESTS OF INCAPACITY FOR WORK

DEFINITIONS

"the 1992 Act"—see reg.1(2).
"the appointed day"—see reg.1(2).

General Note (to regulations 29–32)

Entitlement to transitional awards of incapacity benefit on or after April 13, 1995 ("the appointed day") is subject, for those not exempt by being treated as incapable, to the new tests for incapacity in Pt XIIA of the SSCBA 1992 (reg.29). Furthermore, issues of incapacity for work for purposes of the social security system other than SSP or industrial injuries benefits, are determined, other than in exempt cases, in accordance with those tests (reg.30). But which test applies and when in transitional cases?

8.279

In principle, for those transferring from invalidity benefit the "all work" test is applicable from that date (regs 17(2), 29(1)). The same in principle is true, given its qualifying period, for those on SDA, but reg.31(5)(c) exempts those receiving SDA on April 12, 1995 ("immediately before the appointed day"). Unless also exempt under the "severe condition" head (reg.31(5)(d)–(h)), existing recipients of SDA will have to continue to supply certificates from their doctor in order to be treated as having satisfied the all work test (reg.31(4)).

It is envisaged that existing recipients of sickness or invalidity benefit will, unless exempt, be assessed in accordance with it at some time in the two or three years after commencement (Mr W. Hague, Minister, *Hansard*, HC Vol.253, cols 1233, 1240). They will remain entitled until assessed or found exempt on provision of the appropriate medical certificate from their G.P. (reg.31(1), (2)). The categories of persons exempt are the same as those under the standard regime (basically those suffering from a severe condition) (reg.31(3), (5)(d)–(h); *cf.* IW (General) Regs, reg.10, above), with one important addition: someone 58 or over on April 13, 1995, entitled to invalidity benefit for an unbroken period of incapacity (breaks of less than eight weeks' capacity being ignored) between December 1, 1993 and April 12, 1995 inclusive, is to be treated as having satisfied the all work test, provided (if he does not also fall within the severe condition exemption) he supplies the appropriate medical certificate from his doctor (reg.31(3)–(5)). In this way, it is anticipated that some 850,000 existing recipients will not be required to satisfy the all work test (Viscount Astor, *Hansard*, HL Vol.553, col.504). Similar protection is afforded in respect of the disability premium element of income support, housing benefit and council tax benefit (reg.31(5)(b), (3), (4)).

What, however, is the position of those transferring from sickness benefit? Clearly, unless exempt because of a severe condition (reg.31(5)(d)–(h)) or otherwise treated as incapable of work (on which see IW (General) Regs, regs 11–14), they are subject to the all work test once they transfer to the higher rate of short-term incapacity benefit. That occurs after 196 days of incapacity (including those pre-commencement for sickness benefit purposes which may be reached quite soon for those unfortunates who had almost exhausted title to sickness benefit before commencement and not quite reached invalidity benefit) and represents the maximum period of application in any case of the "own occupation" test. But might they be subject to the all work test earlier, and, if so, when? Regrettably, the matter does not appear crystal clear, at least not to this writer. In principle, the all work test applies earlier to any non-exempt case to which the own occupation test is inapplicable (ss.171C, 171B(3)). The latter test applies, of course, where in the 21 weeks *prior to the day in respect of which it falls to be determined whether the claimant is incapable of work*, he has been engaged in remunerative work for more than eight weeks (s.171B(1)). For a wholly new claimant, of course, one looks back from the first day of incapacity, and once applicable, it remains applicable until transfer to the higher rate or, if earlier, the end of the period of incapacity (s.171B(3)). But what, in the transfer case before us, is the day in respect of which incapacity is being determined? S.171B(3) provides:

"Where for any purpose of this Act it is determined in relation to a person—
  (a) that the test applicable with respect to any day is the own occupation test, and
  (b) that he is on that test incapable of work,

that test remains applicable in his case until the end of the spell of incapacity beginning with that day, or, as the case may be, in which that day falls, or until the 197th day of incapacity for work in that spell, whichever is the earlier.

For this purpose a 'spell of incapacity' means a series of 4 or more consecutive days of incapacity for work; and any two such spells not separated by a period of more than 8 weeks shall be treated as one spell of incapacity."

Since, for these purposes, one includes the pre-commencement days of incapacity for sickness benefit purposes (s.171B(4), regs 2, 32), it is submitted that the most equitable interpretation is that in a transfer from sickness benefit case one looks back to the first day of incapacity in the spell of incapacity in which he transferred into a transitional award of short-term incapacity benefit, and asks whether the own occupation test would have applied then had it been in existence. If so, then that test applies until the point of transfer to the higher rate or (if earlier) the end of the spell of incapacity. In support of this approach is the fact that the own occupation test is said, after all, to represent the test in practice applied in the past to most sickness benefit recipients. And the interpretation means that transferees (for whom days of incapacity pre-commencement count towards the point of movement onto higher rate) are then treated in exactly the same way as wholly new claimants; if the test applies, it applies for 28 weeks of continuous incapacity for both groups. The other interpretation—that one looks to the day of transfer from sickness benefit to incapacity benefit (April 13, 1995 for most) as the day at issue and asks whether the own occupation test then applied—results in differential treatment. A transferee, in work continuously for several years immediately before falling sick and receiving sickness benefit, and transferring onto incapacity benefit after 14 weeks' continuous receipt of sickness benefit, would, unless exempt, be subject to the all work test immediately upon transfer. Whereas a wholly new claimant with the same work record would be subject to the own occupation test for a full 28 weeks. Perhaps this writer has missed something in the mass of legislation and the proper interpretation is obvious.

Transitional awards of incapacity benefit

8.280

29.—A person's entitlement to a transitional award of incapacity benefit shall, except as provided in regulation 31, be subject to him satisfying the tests of incapacity for work under Part XIIA of the 1992 Act.

Transitional provision in respect of other benefits

8.281

30.—A person's continued enjoyment on or after the appointed day of severe disablement allowance or any other advantage under any provision for the purposes of which Part XIIA of the 1992 Act applies shall, except as provided in regulation 31, be subject to satisfying the tests of incapacity for work under that Part of the 1992 Act.

Application of the new tests of incapacity for work.

8.282

31.—(1) Where it has been determined that a person is incapable of work for any purpose of the 1992 Act immediately before the appointed day and he continues to be incapable of work on or after the appointed day, [¹ the question of whether he is capable or incapable of work shall fall to be determined in accordance with the personal capability assessment], but he shall not be required to satisfy or be treated as having satisfied the condition of entitlement that he is incapable of work in accordance with [¹ that assessment] until he has been assessed as to incapacity for work in accordance with regulations made under section 171C of the 1992 Act [¹ (the personal capability assessment)] or until it is determined that he falls within one of the cases mentioned in paragraph (5), so long as he satisfies the condition in paragraph (2).

(2) The condition referred to in paragraph (1) is that, in respect of each day, a person shall be required to provide evidence of his incapacity for work in accordance with the Social Security (Medical Evidence) Regulations 1976 (which prescribe the form of doctor's statement or other evidence in each case).

(3) Subject to paragraph (4), a person who falls within one of the cases mentioned in paragraph (5) [² shall be treated as being incapable of work in accordance with regulations made under section 171C of the 1992 Act (the personal capability assessment)].

(4) Where it is determined that a person falls within one of the cases mentioned in paragraph (5)(a) to (c) and paragraphs (d) to (k) do not apply, that person shall continue to provide evidence of his incapacity for work in accordance with the Social Security (Medical Evidence) Regulations 1976; and provided that such evidence is furnished he shall be treated as [³ incapable of work in accordance with the personal capability assessment] in accordance with regulations made under section 171C of the 1992 Act.

(5) The cases referred to in paragraph (3) are—

(a) a person—
   (i) entitled to invalidity benefit on 1 December 1993 and on 12 April 1995; and
   (ii) between a period beginning on 1 December 1993 and ending on 13 April 1995, was incapable of work for that period or for two or more periods not separated by a period of more than 56 continuous days; and
   (iii) is aged 58 or over on the appointed day;

(b) a person—
   (i) entitled to income support, housing benefit or council tax benefit on 1 December 1993; and
   (ii) was incapable of work for a period of not less than 28 weeks immediately before 1 December 1993; and
   (iii) whose applicable amount included the disability premium on account of his own incapacity on 12 April 1995; and
   (iv) between the period beginning on 1 December 1993 and ending on 13 April 1995, was incapable of work for that period or for two or more periods not separated by a period of more than 56 continuous days; and
   (v) is aged 58 or over on the appointed day;

(c) a person in receipt of a payment of an award of severe disablement allowance under section 68 of the 1992 Act immediately before the appointed day and the spell or period of incapacity for work which is running at the appointed day continues;

(d) a person who was in receipt of a payment of an award of the highest rate of the care component of disability living allowance immediately before the appointed day and continues to be in receipt of such payment;

(e) a person who is suffering from a progressive disease and his death in consequence of that disease can reasonably be expected within 6 months;

(f) a blind person whose name is on a register compiled and maintained by a local authority in accordance with section 29 of the National Assistance Act 1948 (welfare services) or, in Scotland, has been certified as blind and in consequence he is registered as blind in a register maintained by or on behalf of a regional or islands council;

(g) a person suffering from one of the following conditions—
    (i) tetraplegia;
    (ii) persistent vegetative state;
    (iii) dementia;
    (iv) paraplegia or uncontrollable involuntary movements or attaxia which effectively renders the sufferer functionally paraplegic;

(h) [4 a person is suffering from any of the following conditions, and there exists medical evidence that he is suffering from any of them]—
    (i) a severe learning disability (which, for the purposes of this regulation, means a condition which results from the arrested or incomplete physical development of the brain, or severe damage to the brain, and which involves severe impairment of intelligence and social functioning);
    (ii) a severe and progressive neurological or muscle wasting disease;
    (iii) an active and progressive form of inflammatory polyarthritis;
    (iv) a progressive impairment of cardio-respiratory function which severely and persistently limits effort tolerance;
    (v) dense paralysis of the upper limb, trunk and lower limb on one side of the body;
    (vi) multiple effects of impairment of function of the brain or nervous system causing severe and irreversible motor, sensory and intellectual deficits;
    [5 (vii) manifestations of severe and progressive immune deficiency states characterised by the occurrence of severe constitutional disease or opportunistic infections or tumour formation];
    [6 (viii) a severe mental illness, involving the presence of mental disease, which severely and adversely affects a person's mood or behaviour, and which severely restricts his social functioning, or his awareness of his immediate environment.]
    [7 (i) a person who was in receipt of a payment of an increase of disablement pension by virtue of section 104 of the 1992 Act and regulation 19 of the Social Security (General Benefit) Regulations 1982 (increase of disablement pension for constant attendance) at a rate greater than that specified in paragraph 2(a) or at the rate specified in paragraph 2(b) of Part V of Schedule 4 to the 1992 Act immediately before the appointed day and continues to be in receipt of such payment;

(j) a person who was in receipt of a payment of constant attendance allowance by virtue of article 14(1)(b) of the Naval, Military and Air Forces Etc. (Disablement and Death) Service Pensions Order 1983 immediately before the appointed day and continues to be in receipt of such payment;

(k) a person who was in receipt of a payment of an increase of constant attendance allowance at a rate payable by virtue of article 14 of, and paragraph 3(a) of Schedule 3 to, the Personal Injuries (Civilians) Scheme 1983 immediately before the appointed day and continues to be in receipt of such payment.]

[⁸ (6) In sub-paragraph (h) of paragraph (5), "medical evidence" means—

(a) evidence from a doctor approved by the Secretary of State; and
(b) evidence (if any) from any other doctor, or a hospital or similar institution, or such part of such evidence as constitutes the most reliable evidence available in the circumstances.]

AMENDMENTS

1. Social Security (Incapacity for Work) Miscellaneous Amendments Regulations 1999 (SI 1999/3109), reg.7(a) (April 3, 2000).
2. Social Security (Incapacity for Work) Miscellaneous Amendments Regulations 1999 (SI 1999/3109), reg.7(b) (April 3, 2000).
3. Social Security (Incapacity) Miscellaneous Amendments Regulations 2000 (SI 2000/590), reg.2 (April 3, 2000).
4. Social Security (Incapacity for Work and Miscellaneous Amendments) Regulations 1996 (SI 1996/3207), reg.3(5)(b) (January 6, 1997).
5. Social Security (Incapacity for Work) Miscellaneous Amendments Regulations 1995 (SI 1995/987), reg.3(9)(b)(iii) (April 13, 1995).
6. Social Security (Incapacity for Work and Miscellaneous Amendments) Regulations 1996 (SI 1996/3207) reg.3(5)(b)(ii) (January 6, 1997).
7. Social Security (Incapacity for Work) Miscellaneous Amendments Regulations 1995 (SI 1995/987), reg.3(9)(b)(iv) (April 13, 1995).
8. Social Security (Incapacity for Work and Miscellaneous Amendments) Regulations 1996 (SI 1996/3207), reg.3(5)(c) (January 6, 1997).

GENERAL NOTE

Para. (1)

Note that *CSIB 611/1998* holds that deemed capacity for work under IW (General) Regs, regs 7 and 8 for failure respectively to return the all work test/personal capability assessment questionnaire or to attend a medical examination, will apply so as to override transitional protection afforded by para.(1). In other words, persons with transitional protection can be deemed capable of work for the defaults covered by those regulations, resulting in loss of benefit.

8.283

Para. (5) (h) (viii)

Note the meaning given to severe mental illness or disease by Deputy Commissioner White in *CIB/3328/1998* (see annotation to IW (General) Regs, reg.10, above).

8.284

Treatment of days of incapacity arising before the appointed day

32.—The days of incapacity for work before the appointed day and the days which are treated as days of incapacity for work in accordance with regulation 2 shall be taken into account for the purposes of calculating the days of incapacity referred to in section 171B(3) and (4) of the 1992 Act [¹ . . .].

8.285

AMENDMENT

1. Social Security (Incapacity for Work) Miscellaneous Amendments Regulations 1999 (SI 1999/3109), reg.7(c) (April 3, 2000).

PART IX

EMPLOYMENT AND SUPPORT ALLOWANCE

The Employment and Support Allowance Regulations 2008

(SI 2008/794) (AS AMENDED)

PART 1

GENERAL

9.1

PART 2

THE ASSESSMENT PHASE

PART 3

CONDITIONS OF ENTITLEMENT—CONTRIBUTORY ALLOWANCE

PART 4

CONDITIONS OF ENTITLEMENT—INCOME-RELATED ALLOWANCE

PART 5

LIMITED CAPABILITY FOR WORK

PART 6

LIMITED CAPABILITY FOR WORK-RELATED ACTIVITY

PART 7

EFFECT OF WORK ON ENTITLEMENT TO AN EMPLOYMENT AND SUPPORT ALLOWANCE

PART 8

CONDITIONALITY

CHAPTER 1

WORK-FOCUSED HEALTH-RELATED ASSESSMENT

CHAPTER 2

WORK-FOCUSED INTERVIEWS

CHAPTER 3

REDUCTION OF EMPLOYMENT AND SUPPORT ALLOWANCE

CHAPTER 4

NOTIFICATION

CHAPTER 5

MODIFICATION OF THE ACT IN RELATION TO CLAIMS TO WHICH SECTION 5(1)(C)
OF THE ADMINISTRATION ACT APPLIES

PART 9

AMOUNTS OF ALLOWANCE

CHAPTER 1

PRESCRIBED AMOUNTS

CHAPTER 2

DEDUCTIONS FROM THE CONTRIBUTORY ALLOWANCE

CHAPTER 3

STATUTORY PAYMENTS

PART 10

INCOME AND CAPITAL

CHAPTER 1

GENERAL

CHAPTER 2

INCOME

CHAPTER 3

EMPLOYED EARNERS

CHAPTER 4

SELF-EMPLOYED EARNERS

CHAPTER 2

WORK OR TRAINING BENEFICIARIES

CHAPTER 3

TEMPORARY ABSENCE FROM GREAT BRITAIN

CHAPTER 4

MEMBERSHIP OF HOUSEHOLD

PART 12

DISQUALIFICATION

PART 13

URGENT CASES

PART 14

PERIODS OF LESS THAN A WEEK

SCHEDULE 1

9.2

HER MAJESTY'S FORCES

PART 1

PRESCRIBED ESTABLISHMENTS AND ORGANISATIONS

PART 2

ESTABLISHMENTS AND ORGANISATIONS OF WHICH HER MAJESTY'S FORCES DO NOT CONSIST

SCHEDULE 2

ASSESSMENT OF WHETHER A CLAIMANT HAS LIMITED CAPABILITY FOR WORK

PART 1

PHYSICAL DISABILITIES

PART 2

MENTAL, COGNITIVE AND INTELLECTUAL FUNCTION ASSESSMENT

SCHEDULE 3

ASSESSMENT OF WHETHER A CLAIMANT HAS LIMITED CAPABILITY FOR WORK-RELATED ACTIVITY

SCHEDULE 4

AMOUNTS

PART 1

PRESCRIBED AMOUNTS

PART 2

PREMIUMS

PART 3

WEEKLY AMOUNT OF PREMIUMS SPECIFIED IN PART 2

PART 4

THE COMPONENTS

SCHEDULE 5

SPECIAL CASES

PART 1

AMOUNTS PRESCRIBED FOR THE PURPOSES OF SECTION 4(2) OF THE ACT

PART 2

AMOUNTS PRESCRIBED FOR THE PURPOSES OF SECTIONS 2(1) AND 4(2) OF THE ACT

SCHEDULE 6

HOUSING COSTS

SCHEDULE 7

SUMS TO BE DISREGARDED IN THE CALCULATION OF EARNINGS

(SI 2008/794) (as amended)

SCHEDULE 8

SUMS TO BE DISREGARDED IN THE CALCULATION OF INCOME OTHER THAN
EARNINGS

SCHEDULE 9

CAPITAL TO BE DISREGARDED

The Secretary of State for Work and Pensions, in exercise of the powers conferred by sections 2(1)(a) and (c), (4)(a) and (c), 3(1)(c), (2)(b) and (d) and (3)(1), 4(2)(a), (3), (6)(a) and (c), 5(2) and (3), 8(1) to (3), (4)(a) and (b), (5) and (6), 9(1) to (3) and (4)(a) and (b), 11(1), (2) (a) to (g), (3) to (5), (6)(a) and (7)(c), 12(1), (2)(a) to (h), (3) to (7), 14(1) and (2)(a) and (b), 16(2)(a) and (4), 17, 18(1), (2) and (4), 20(2) to (7), 22(2), 23(1) and (3), 24(1)(3), (2) (b) and (3), 25(1) to (5) and 26(2) of, and paragraphs 1(4), 3(2), 4(1)(a) and (c), (3) and (4) and 6(1)(b), (2) to (5)(4), (7) and (8) of Schedule 1 to, and paragraphs 1 to 7, 8(1), 9, 10, 12 and 14 of Schedule 2 to, the Welfare Reform Act 2007, section 5(1) of the Social Security Administration Act 1992 and section 21(1)(a) of the Social Security Act 1998(7) makes the following Regulations, which are made by virtue of, or consequential on, the provisions of the Welfare Reform Act 2007 and which are made before the end of a period of 6 months beginning with the coming into force of those provisions:

PART 1

GENERAL

Citation and commencement

1. These Regulations may be cited as the Employment and Support   9.3
Allowance Regulations 2008 and shall come into force—
(a) subject to paragraphs (b) and (c), on 27th October 2008;
(b) in relation to regulation 128(6)(a) and paragraph 15(2) of Schedule 6, so far as it applies to a maintenance calculation, in relation to a particular case, on the day on which paragraph 11(20)(d) of Schedule 3 to the 2000 Act comes into force for the purposes of that type of case;
(c) in relation to regulation 82 and paragraph 4 of Schedule 8, so far as it applies to additional statutory paternity pay, on the day on which regulations made under or by virtue of sections 171ZEA to 171ZEE of the Contributions and Benefits Act come into force.

Interpretation

2.—(1) In these Regulations—   9.4
"Abbeyfield Home" means an establishment run by the Abbeyfield Society including any body corporate or incorporate which is affiliated to that Society;
"the Act" means the Welfare Reform Act 2007;
"action plan" has the meaning given by regulation 58;
"adoption leave" means a period of absence from work on ordinary or additional adoption leave under section 75A or 75B of the Employment Rights Act 1996;

945

"aircraft worker" means a person who is, or has been, employed under a contract of service either as a pilot, commander, navigator or other member of the crew of any aircraft, or in any other capacity on board any aircraft where—

    (a) the employment in that other capacity is for the purposes of the aircraft or its crew or of any passengers or cargo or mail carried on that aircraft; and

    (b) the contract is entered into in the United Kingdom with a view to its performance (in whole or in part) while the aircraft is in flight, but does not include a person who is in employment as a member of Her Majesty's forces;

"Armed Forces and Reserve Forces Compensation Scheme" means the scheme established under section 1(2) of the Armed Forces (Pensions and Compensation) Act 2004;

"attendance allowance" means—

    (a) an attendance allowance under section 64 of the Contributions and Benefits Act;

    (b) an increase of disablement pension under section 104 or 105 of that Act;

    (c) a payment under regulations made under section 111 of, and paragraph 7(2)(b) of Schedule 8 to, that Act;

    (d) an increase in allowance which is payable in respect of constant attendance under section 111 of, and paragraph 4 of Schedule 8 to, that Act;

    (e) a payment by virtue of article 14, 15, 16, 43 or 44 of the Personal Injuries (Civilians) Scheme 1983 or any analogous payment;

    (f) any payment based on the need for attendance which is paid as an addition to a war disablement pension;

[[1] "basic rate" has the same meaning as in the Income Tax Act 2007 (see section 989 of that Act);]

"benefit Acts" means the Contributions and Benefits Act, Jobseekers Act and Part 1 of the Act;

"benefit week" means a period of 7 days ending on such day as the Secretary of State may direct but for the purposes of calculating any payment of income "benefit week" means the period of 7 days ending on the day before the first day of the first benefit week following the date of claim or the last day on which an employment and support allowance is paid if it is in payment for less than a week;

"board and lodging" means—

    (a) accommodation provided to a person or, if the person is a member of a family, to that person or any other member of that person's family, for a charge which is inclusive of the provision of that accommodation and at least some cooked or prepared meals which both are cooked or prepared (by a person other than the person to whom the accommodation is provided or a member of that person's family) and are consumed in that accommodation or associated premises; or

    (b) accommodation provided to a person in a hotel, guest house, lodging house or some similar establishment, except accommodation provided by a close relative of the person or any other member of the person's family, or other than on a commercial basis;

"care home" in England and Wales has the meaning assigned to it by section 3 of the Care Standards Act 2000, and in Scotland means a care home service within the meaning assigned to it by section 2(3) of the Regulation of Care (Scotland) Act 2001;

"carer's allowance" means an allowance under section 70 of the Contributions and Benefits Act;

"child" means a person under the age of 16;

"child tax credit" means a child tax credit under section 8 of the Tax Credits Act;

"close relative" means a parent, parent-in-law, son, son-in-law, daughter, daughter-in-law, step-parent, step-son, step-daughter, brother, sister, or if any of the preceding persons is one member of a couple, the other member of that couple;

"college of further education" means a college of further education within the meaning of Part 1 of the Further and Higher Education (Scotland) Act 1992;

"concessionary payment" means a payment made under arrangements made by the Secretary of State with the consent of the Treasury which is charged [³ . . .] to a Departmental Expenditure Vote to which payments of benefit or tax credits under the benefit Acts or the Tax Credits Act are charged;

"confinement" has the meaning given to it by section 171(1) of the Contributions and Benefits Act;

"co-ownership scheme" means a scheme under which a dwelling is let by a housing association and the tenant, or the tenant's personal representative, will, under the terms of the tenancy agreement or of the agreement under which the tenant became a member of the association, be entitled, on that tenant ceasing to be a member and subject to any condition stated in either agreement, to a sum calculated by reference directly or indirectly to the value of the dwelling and "co-ownership agreement" will be construed accordingly;

"councillor" means—

    (a) in relation to England and Wales, a member of a London borough council, a county council, a district council, a parish or community council, the Common Council of the City of London or the Council of the Isles of Scilly; and

    (b) in relation to Scotland, a member of a council constituted under section 2 of the Local Government etc. (Scotland) Act 1994;

"councillor's allowance" means—

    (a) in England or Wales, an allowance under or by virtue of—

        (i) section 173 or 177 of the Local Government Act 1972; or

        (ii) a scheme made by virtue of section 18 of the Local Government and Housing Act 1989, other than such an allowance as is mentioned in section 173(4) of the Local Government Act 1972; or

    (b) in Scotland, an allowance or remuneration under or by virtue of—

        (i) a scheme made by virtue of section 18 of the Local Government and Housing Act 1989; or

        (ii) sections 11 and 16 of the Local Governance (Scotland) Act 2004;

"couple" means—

    (a) a man and woman who are married to each other and are members of the same household;

    (b) a man and woman who are not married to each other but are living together as husband and wife;

    (c) two people of the same sex who are civil partners of each other and are members of the same household; or

    (d) two people of the same sex who are not civil partners of each other but are living together as if they were civil partners, and for the purposes of paragraph (d), two people of the same sex are to be regarded as living together as if they were civil partners if, but only if, they would be regarded as living together as husband and wife were they instead two people of the opposite sex;

"Crown tenant" means a person who occupies a dwelling under a tenancy or licence where the interest of the landlord belongs to Her Majesty in right of the Crown or to a government department or is held in trust for Her Majesty for the purposes of a government department, except (in the case of an interest belonging to Her Majesty in right of the Crown) where the interest is under the management of the Crown Estate Commissioners;

"dependent child" means any child or qualifying young person who is treated as the responsibility of the claimant or the claimant's partner, where that child or young person is a member of the claimant's household;

"descriptor" means, in relation to an activity specified in column (1) of Schedule 2, a descriptor in column (2) of that Schedule which describes a person's ability to perform that activity;

"disability living allowance" means a disability living allowance under section 71 of the Contributions and Benefits Act;

"doctor" means a registered medical practitioner, or in the case of a medical practitioner practising outside the United Kingdom of whom the Secretary of State may request a medical opinion, a person registered or recognised as such in the country in which the person undertakes medical practice;

"dwelling" means any residential accommodation, whether or not consisting of the whole or part of a building and whether or not comprising separate and self-contained premises;

"dwelling occupied as the home" means the dwelling together with any garage, garden and outbuildings, normally occupied by the claimant as the claimant's home including any premises not so occupied which it is impracticable or unreasonable to sell separately, in particular, in Scotland, any croft land on which the dwelling is situated;

"Eileen Trust" means the charitable trust of that name established on 29th March 1993 out of funds provided by the Secretary of State for the benefit of persons eligible for payment in accordance with its provisions;

"employed earner" is to be construed in accordance with section 2(1)(a) of the Contributions and Benefits Act;

"employment" includes any trade, business, profession, office or vocation and "employed" has a corresponding meaning;

"employment zone" means an area within Great Britain designated for the purposes of section 60 of the Welfare Reform and Pensions Act

1999 and an "employment zone programme" means a programme established for such an area or areas designed to assist claimants for a jobseeker's allowance to obtain sustainable employment;

"enactment" includes an enactment comprised in, or in an instrument made under—

(a) an Act; or

(b) an Act of the Scottish Parliament;

"failure determination" has the meaning given by regulation 63(1);

"family" means—

(a) a couple;

(b) a couple and a member of the same household for whom one of them is or both are responsible and who is a child or a young person;

(c) a person who is not a member of a couple and a member of the same household for whom that person is responsible and who is a child or a young person;

"first contribution condition" means the condition set out in paragraph 1(1) of Schedule 1 to the Act;

"full-time student" has the meaning prescribed in regulation 131 (students: interpretation);

"the Fund" means monies made available from time to time by the Secretary of State for the benefit of persons eligible for payment in accordance with the provisions of a scheme established by the Secretary of State on 24th April 1992 or, in Scotland, on 10th April 1992;

"guaranteed income payment" means a payment made under article 14(1)(b) or 21(1)(a) of the Armed Forces and Reserve Forces (Compensation Scheme) Order 2005;

"health care professional" means—

(a) a registered medical practitioner;

(b) a registered nurse; or

(c) an occupational therapist or physiotherapist registered with a regulatory body established by an Order in Council under section 60 of the Health Act 1999;

"Health Service Act" means the National Health Service Act 2006;

"Health Service (Wales) Act" means the National Health Service (Wales) Act 2006;

"housing association" has the meaning given to it by section 1(1) of the Housing Associations Act 1985;

"housing benefit expenditure" means expenditure in respect of which housing benefit is payable as specified in regulation 12(1) of the Housing Benefit Regulations 2006 but does not include any such expenditure in respect of which an additional amount is applicable under regulation 67(1)(c) or 68(1)(d)(housing costs);

"Immigration and Asylum Act" means the Immigration and Asylum Act 1999;

"income-related benefits" means the benefits listed in section 123(1) of the Contributions and Benefits Act;

"Income Support Regulations" means the Income Support (General) Regulations 1987;

"independent hospital" in England and Wales has the meaning assigned to it by section 2 of the Care Standards Act 2000, and in Scotland means an independent healthcare service as defined in section 2(5)(a) and (b) of the Regulation of Care (Scotland) Act 2001;

[¹ . . .]

"the Independent Living Fund (2006)" means the Trust of that name established by a deed dated 10th April 2006 and made between the Secretary of State for Work and Pensions of the one part and Margaret Rosemary Cooper, Michael Beresford Boyall and Marie Theresa Martin of the other part;

[¹ . . .]

"Jobseekers Act" means the Jobseekers Act 1995;

"Jobseeker's Allowance Regulations" means the Jobseeker's Allowance Regulations 1996;

"last day of the course" means the last day of the final academic term of the course in which the student is enrolled;

"limited capability for work assessment" means the assessment of whether a person has limited capability for work as set out in regulation 19(2) and in Schedule 2;

"London Bombings Relief Charitable Fund" means the company limited by guarantee (number 5505072) and registered charity of that name established on 11th July 2005 for the purpose of (amongst other things) relieving sickness, disability or financial need of victims (including families or dependants of victims) of the terrorist attacks carried out in London on 7th July 2005;

"lone parent" means a person who has no partner and who is responsible for, and a member of the same household as, a child or young person;

"long tenancy" means a tenancy granted for a term of years certain exceeding twenty one years, whether or not the tenancy is, or may become, terminable before the end of that term by notice given by or to the tenant or by re-entry, forfeiture (or, in Scotland, irritancy) or otherwise and includes a lease for a term fixed by law under a grant with a covenant or obligation for perpetual renewal unless it is a lease by sub-demise from one which is not a long tenancy;

"Macfarlane (Special Payments) Trust" means the trust of that name, established on 29th January 1990 partly out of funds provided by the Secretary of State, for the benefit of certain persons suffering from haemophilia;

"Macfarlane (Special Payments) (No. 2) Trust" means the trust of that name, established on 3rd May 1991 partly out of funds provided by the Secretary of State, for the benefit of certain persons suffering from haemophilia and other beneficiaries;

"Macfarlane Trust" means the charitable trust, established partly out of funds provided by the Secretary of State to the Haemophilia Society, for the relief of poverty or distress among those suffering from haemophilia;

"main phase employment and support allowance" means an employment and support allowance where the calculation of the amount payable in respect of the claimant includes a component under section 2(1)(b) or 4(2)(b) of the Act;

"mariner" means a person who is or has been in employment under a contract of service either as a master or member of the crew of any ship or vessel, or in any other capacity on board any ship or vessel where—

(a) the employment in that other capacity is for the purposes of that ship or vessel or her crew or any passengers or cargo or mails carried by the ship or vessel; and

(b) the contract is entered into in the United Kingdom with a view to its performance (in whole or in part) while the ship or vessel is on her voyage; but does not include a person who is in employment as a member of Her Majesty's forces;

"maternity allowance period" has the meaning it has in section 35(2) of the Contributions and Benefits Act;

"medical evidence" means—

(a) evidence from a health care professional approved by the Secretary of State; and

(b) evidence (if any) from any health care professional or a hospital or similar institution, or such part of such evidence as constitutes the most reliable evidence available in the circumstances;

"Medical Evidence Regulations" means the Social Security (Medical Evidence) Regulations 1976;

"medical examination centre" means premises which are equipped and suitable for conducting a medical examination;

"medical treatment" means medical, surgical or rehabilitative treatment (including any course or diet or other regimen), and references to a person receiving or submitting to medical treatment are to be construed accordingly;

"member of Her Majesty's forces" means a person, other than one mentioned in Part 2 of Schedule 1 who is—

(a) over 16 years of age; and

(b) a member of an establishment or organisation specified in Part 1 of that Schedule who gives full pay service, but does not include any such person while absent on desertion;

"mobility supplement" means any supplement under article 20 of the Naval, Military and Air Forces Etc. (Disablement and Death) Service Pensions Order 2006 including such a supplement by virtue of any other scheme or order or under article 25A of the Personal Injuries (Civilians) Scheme 1983;

"net earnings" means such earnings as are calculated in accordance with regulation 96;

"net profit" means such profit as is calculated in accordance with regulation 98;

"New Deal options" means the employment programmes specified in regulation 75(1)(a)(ii) of the Jobseeker's Allowance Regulations and the training scheme specified in regulation 75(1)(b)(ii) of those Regulations;

"non-dependant" has the meaning prescribed in regulation 71;

"non-dependant deduction" means a deduction that is to be made under regulation 67(1)(c) (prescribed amounts) and paragraph 19 of Schedule 6 (housing costs);

"occupational pension" means any pension or other periodical payment under an occupational pension scheme but does not include any discretionary payment out of a fund established for relieving hardship in particular cases;

"occupational pension scheme" has the meaning given by section 1 of the Pension Schemes Act 1993;

"ordinary clothing or footwear" means clothing or footwear for normal daily use, but does not include school uniforms, or clothing or footwear used solely for sporting activities;

"partner" means where a claimant—

    (a) is a member of a couple, the other member of that couple;

    (b) is a husband or wife by virtue of a polygamous marriage, the other party to the marriage or any spouse additional to either party to the marriage;

"passenger" means any person carried on a ship except—

    (a) a person employed or engaged in any capacity on board the ship on the business of the ship; or

    (b) a person on board the ship either in pursuance of the obligation to carry shipwrecked, distressed or other persons, or by reason of any circumstance that neither the master nor the owner nor the charterer (if any) could have prevented or forestalled;

"payment" includes a part of a payment;

"pay period" means the period in respect of which a claimant is, or expects to be, normally paid by the claimant's employer, being a week, a fortnight, four weeks, a month or other shorter or longer period as the case may be;

"pension fund holder" means in relation to a personal pension scheme or an occupational pension scheme, the trustees, managers or scheme administrators, as the case may be, of the scheme concerned;

"pensionable age" has the meaning given by the rules in paragraph 1 of Schedule 4 to the Pensions Act 1995;

"period of limited capability for work" means a period throughout which a person has, or is treated as having, limited capability for work;

"period of study" means the period beginning with the date on which a person starts attending or undertaking a course of study and ending with the last day of the course or such earlier date (if any) as that person finally abandons it or is dismissed from it;

"personal pension scheme" means—

    (a) a personal pension scheme as defined by section 1 of the Pension Schemes Act 1993;

    (b) an annuity contract or trust scheme approved under section 620 or 621 of the Income and Corporation Taxes Act 1988 or a substituted contract within the meaning of section 622(3) of that Act which is treated as having become a registered pension scheme by virtue of paragraph 1(1)(f) of Schedule 36 to the Finance Act 2004;

    (c) a personal pension scheme approved under Chapter 4 of Part 14 of the Income and Corporation Taxes Act 1988 which is treated as having become a registered pension scheme by virtue of paragraph 1(1)(g) of Schedule 36 to the Finance Act 2004;

"policy of life insurance" means any instrument by which the payment of money is assured on death (except death by accident only) or the happening of any contingency dependent on human life, or any instrument evidencing a contract which is subject to payment of premiums for a term dependent on human life;

"polygamous marriage" means any marriage entered into under a law which permits polygamy where—

    (a) either party has for the time being any spouse additional to the other party; and

   (b) the claimant, the other party to the marriage and the additional spouse are members of the same household;

"qualifying person" means a person in respect of whom payment has been made from the Fund, the Eileen Trust, the Skipton Fund or the London Bombings Relief Charitable Fund;

"qualifying remunerative work" has the meaning given by Part 1 of the Tax Credits Act;

"qualifying young person" has the meaning given by section 142 of the Contributions and Benefits Act (child and qualifying young person);

"relative" means close relative, grand-parent, grand-child, uncle, aunt, nephew or niece;

"relevant disease" means—

     (a) in England and Wales, any disease, food poisoning, infection, infectious disease or notifiable disease—

        (i) to which section 20(1) of the Public Health (Control of Disease) Act 1984 (stopping of work to prevent spread of disease) applies;

       (ii) to which—

           (aa) regulation 3 (public health enactments applied to certain diseases) of, and Schedule 1 to,

           (bb) regulation 9(1) (provisions for preventing the spread of typhus and relapsing fever) of, and Schedule 3 to, or

           (cc) regulation 9(2) (provisions for preventing the spread of food poisoning and food borne infections) of, and Schedule 4 to, the Public Health (Infectious Diseases) Regulations 1988 apply;

       (iii) to which regulation 9 (powers in respect of persons leaving aircraft) of the Public Health (Aircraft) Regulations 1979 applies; or

       (iv) to which regulation 10 (powers in respect of certain persons on ships) of the Public Health (Ships) Regulations 1979 applies; and

   (b) in Scotland, any food poisoning or infectious disease—

        (i) to which section 71(1) of the Health Services and Public Health Act 1968 (compensation for stopping employment to prevent spread of disease in Scotland) applies; or

       (ii) to which—

           (aa) regulations 8 and 9 (examination, etc. of persons on aircraft and powers in respect of persons leaving aircraft) of the Public Health (Aircraft) (Scotland) Regulations 1971; or

           (bb) regulations 9 and 10 (examination, etc. of persons on ships and powers in respect of certain persons on ships) of the Public Health (Ships) (Scotland) Regulations 1971, apply;

"relevant enactment" means the Army Act 1955, the Air Force Act 1955, the Naval Discipline Act 1957, the Matrimonial Proceedings Children Act 1958, the Social Work (Scotland) Act 1968, the Family Law Reform Act 1969, the Children and Young Persons Act 1969, the Matrimonial Causes Act 1973, the Domestic Proceedings and Magistrates' Courts Act 1978, the Adoption (Scotland) Act 1978, the

Family Law Act 1986, the Children Act 1989 and the Adoption and Children Act 2002;

"remunerative work" has the meaning prescribed in regulations 41 and 42 except in relation to Schedules 6 and 7;

"second contribution condition" means the condition set out in paragraph 2(1) of Schedule 1 to the Act;

"self-employed earner" is to be construed in accordance with section 2(1)(b) of the Contributions and Benefits Act;

"self-employment route" means assistance in pursuing self-employed earner's employment whilst participating in—

    (a) an employment zone programme; or

    (b) a programme provided or other arrangements made under section 2 of the Employment and Training Act 1973 (functions of the Secretary of State) or section 2 of the Enterprise and New Towns (Scotland) Act 1990 (functions in relation to training for employment etc.);

"single claimant" means a claimant who neither has a partner nor is a lone parent;

"Skipton Fund" means the ex-gratia payment scheme administered by the Skipton Fund Limited, incorporated on 25th March 2004, for the benefit of certain persons suffering from hepatitis C and other persons eligible for payment in accordance with the scheme's provisions;

"sports award" means an award made by one of the Sports Councils named in section 23(2) of the National Lottery etc. Act 1993 out of sums allocated to it for distribution under that section;

[1 . . .]

[1 "state pension credit" means a state pension credit under the State Pension Credit Act 2002;]

"subsistence allowance" means an allowance which an employment zone contractor has agreed to pay to a person who is participating in an employment zone programme;

"the Tax Credits Act" means the Tax Credits Act 2002;

"terminally ill", in relation to a claimant, means the claimant is suffering from a progressive disease and death in consequence of that disease can reasonably be expected within 6 months;

"training" means—

    (a) training in pursuance of arrangements made under section 2(1) of the Employment and Training Act 1973 or section 2(3) of the Enterprise and New Towns (Scotland) Act 1990; or

    (b) any training received on a course which a person attends for 16 hours or more a week, the primary purpose of which is the teaching of occupational or vocational skills;

"training allowance" means an allowance (whether by way of periodical grants or otherwise) payable—

    (a) out of public funds by a Government department or by or on behalf of the Secretary of State for Work and Pensions, [4 Skills Development Scotland] or Highlands and Islands Enterprise, the Learning and Skills Council for England or the Welsh Ministers;

    (b) to a person for that person's maintenance or in respect of a member of that person's family; and

    (c) for the period, or part of the period, during which the person is following a course of training or instruction provided by, or in pursuance of arrangements made with, that department or approved by that department in relation to that person or so provided or approved by or on behalf of the Secretary of State for Work and Pensions, [⁴ Skills Development Scotland] or Highlands and Islands Enterprise, or the Welsh Ministers, but does not include an allowance paid by any Government department to or in respect of a person by reason of the fact that that person is following a course of full-time education, other than under arrangements made under section 2 of the Employment and Training Act 1973 or section 2 of the Enterprise and New Towns (Scotland) Act 1990, or is training as a teacher;

"voluntary organisation" means a body, other than a public or local authority, the activities of which are carried on otherwise than for profit;

"war disablement pension" means [³ retired pay or pension or allowance payable] in respect of disablement under an instrument specified in section 639(2) of the Income Tax (Earnings and Pensions) Act 2003;

"war widow's pension" [³ means any pension or allowance] payable to a woman as a widow under an instrument specified in section 639(2) of the Income Tax (Earnings and Pensions) Act 2003 in respect of the death or disablement of any person;

"war widower's pension" [³ means any pension or allowance] payable to a man as a widower or to a surviving civil partner under an instrument specified in section 639(2) of the Income Tax (Earnings and Pensions) Act 2003 in respect of the death or disablement of any person;

"water charges" means—

    (a) as respects England and Wales, any water and sewerage charges under Chapter 1 of Part 5 of the Water Industry Act 1991;

    (b) as respects Scotland, any water and sewerage charges under Part 2 of the Local Government etc. (Scotland) Act 1994, in so far as such charges are in respect of the dwelling which a person occupies as the home;

"week" means a period of 7 days except in relation to regulation 26;

"work or training beneficiary" has the meaning prescribed in regulation 148;

"working day" means any day except for a Saturday, Sunday, Christmas Day, Good Friday or bank holiday under the Banking and Financial Dealings Act 1971 in England, Wales or Scotland;

"working tax credit" means a working tax credit under section 10 of the Tax Credits Act;

"young person" is a person who, except where section 6 of the Children (Leaving Care) Act 2000 (exclusion from benefits) applies, falls within the definition of qualifying young person in section 142 of the Contributions and Benefits Act (child and qualifying young person).

(2) In [² . . .] paragraph 15(2) of Schedule 6 (housing costs—linking rule)—

"child support maintenance" means such periodical payments as are referred to in section 3(6) of the Child Support Act 1991 and includes any payments made by the Secretary of State in lieu of such payments;

"the 1991 Act" means the Child Support Act 1991;

"the 2000 Act" means the Child Support, Pensions and Social Security Act 2000;

"maintenance assessment" has the same meaning as in the 1991 Act by virtue of section 54 of that Act as it has effect apart from the 2000 Act;

"maintenance calculation" has the same meaning as in the 1991 Act by virtue of section 54 of that Act as amended by the 2000 Act.

(3) Any reference to the claimant's family is to be construed as if it included in relation to a polygamous marriage a reference to any partner and any child or young person who is a member of the claimant's household.

(4) For the purposes of paragraph 5 of Schedule 1 to the Act, "week" means a period of 7 days.

AMENDMENT

1. Employment and Support Allowance (Miscellaneous Amendments) Regulations 2008 (SI 2008/2428), reg.3 (October 27, 2008).
2. Employment and Support Allowance (Miscellaneous Amendments) Regulations 2008 (SI 2008/2428), reg.20(1) (October 27, 2008).
3. Social Security (Miscellaneous Amendments) (No. 7) Regulations 2008 (SI 2008/3157), reg.11(2) (January 5, 2009).
4. Social Security (Miscellaneous Amendments) Regulations 2009 (SI 2009/583), reg.10(2) (April 6, 2009).

GENERAL NOTE

9.5   Most of these definitions are either self-explanatory, or references to definitions in other regulations or are similar to those in reg.2(1) of the IS Regs and reg.1(2) of the JSA Regs. The following merit comment

"*aircraft worker*": The definition is used in reg.11 (Condition relating to youth—residence or presence). By para.4 of Sch.1 to the Welfare Reform Act, those under 20 (or in prescribed cases 25) may, if they satisfy certain conditions (set out in reg.11), be entitled to contributory ESA even though they do not satisfy the second contribution condition. For the purposes of reg.11, the claimant is treated as being resident and present in Great Britain while absent "abroad in the capacity of being an aircraft worker or mariner". The definition covers all those employed on an aircraft while in flight under a contract that was entered into in the UK, other than members of the armed forces.

"*confinement*": The definition in s.171 of the Contributions and Benefits Act reads as follows:

"confinement" means—

(a) labour resulting in the issue of a living child, or
(b) labour after 24 weeks of pregnancy resulting in the issue of a child whether alive or dead,

and "confined" shall be construed accordingly; and where a woman's labour begun on one day results in the issue of a child on another day she shall be taken to be confined on the day of the issue of the child or, if labour results in the issue of twins or a greater number of children, she shall be taken to be confined on the day of the issue of the last of them;"

"*dependent child*": This definition (which does not appear in the IS Regulations or the JSA Regs) refers to any child or qualifying young person who a member of the claimant's household and is treated as the responsibility of the claimant or the claimant's partner (i.e., under reg.156(10)).

"*mariner*": See the commentary on "aircraft worker" above. The definition is similar except that the reference to "aircraft" is to "ship or vessel".

"member of Her Majesty's forces": Members of the armed forces and their families are, in certain circumstances, treated as being in Great Britain while abroad. The definition is supplemented by Sch.1 below.

[¹ Disapplication of section 1(1A) of the Social Security Administration Act 1992

2A. Section 1(1A) of the Social Security Administration Act 1992 (requirement to state a national insurance number) shall not apply to a person who—

(a) is a person in respect of whom a claim for employment and support allowance is made;

(b) is subject to immigration control within the meaning of section 115(9)(a) of the Immigration and Asylum Act;

(c) does not satisfy the basic conditions of entitlement to employment and support allowance for the purposes of section 1(3) of the Act; and

(d) has not previously been allocated a national insurance number.]

9.6

AMENDMENT

1. Social Security (National Insurance Number Information: Exemption) Regulations 2009 (SI 2009/471), reg.13 (April 6, 2009).

GENERAL NOTE

See the commentary to reg.2A(c) of the Income Support Regulations.

9.7

Rounding of fractions

3. For the purposes of these Regulations—

(a) where any calculation under these Regulations results in a fraction of a penny that fraction is, if it would be to the claimant's advantage, to be treated as a penny, otherwise it must be disregarded;

(b) where an employment and support allowance is awarded for a period which is not a complete benefit week and the applicable amount in respect of the period results in an amount which includes a fraction of a penny that fraction is to be treated as a penny.

9.8

GENERAL NOTE

Fractions are always rounded in the claimant's favour.

9.9

PART 2

THE ASSESSMENT PHASE

The end of the assessment phase

4.—(1) Subject to paragraph (2) and regulations 5 and 6, the assessment phase in relation to a claimant ends on the last day of a period of 13 weeks beginning on the first day of the assessment phase as determined under section 24(2)(a) of the Act.

9.10

(2) If at the end of the period of 13 weeks referred to in paragraph (1), it has not yet been determined whether the claimant has limited capability for work—

(a) the claimant having been assessed in accordance with a limited capability for work assessment; or

(b) as a result of the claimant being treated as having limited capability for work in accordance with regulation 20, 25, 26, 29 or regulation 33(2) (persons to be treated as having limited capability for work),

the assessment phase will end when the limited capability for work determination is made.

DEFINITIONS

"the assessment phase"—see WRA 2007, s.24(2).
"claimant"—see WRA 2007, s.24(1).
"limited capability for work"—see WRA 2007, s.1(4).
"limited capability for work assessment"—see reg.2(1).
"week"—see reg.2(1).

GENERAL NOTE

9.11   During an initial "assessment phase", generally (reg.7, below, affords exceptions) a claimant can only be entitled to "basic allowance" ESA; entitlement to the appropriate additional component (support or work-related) only arises after the end of that phase (WRA 2007, s.2(2), (3)). Section 24(2)(a) of the WRA 2007 stipulates that the "assessment phase" begins on the first day of entitlement to ESA, i.e. the first day of limited capability for work after service of the "waiting days" (these are days of non-entitlement: see WRA 2007, Sch.2, para.2 and reg.144). This regulation in contrast sets out when the "assessment phase" ends. It ends after 13 weeks, unless at that time it still has not been determined whether the claimant has, or is to be treated under the regulations enumerated in para.(2) as having, limited capability for work. In that case the "assessment phase" lasts longer than the 13-week period and ends when the limited capability for work determination is made, that is, when it is decided whether or not the person has, or is to be treated as having, limited capability for work.

In short, the assessment phase ends after the later of 13 weeks or the decision on whether the claimant has (or is to be treated as having) limited capability for work. Where, however, the claimant appeals a decision embodying an adverse determination on limited capability for work, the assessment phase ends only when the appeal is determined by an appeal tribunal (see reg.6).

The assessment phase—previous claimants

9.12   **5.**—(1) Where the circumstances in paragraph (2) apply in relation to a claimant the assessment phase —

(a) begins on the first day of the period for which the claimant was previously entitled to an employment and support allowance; and

(b) subject to paragraph (3) and regulation 6, ends on the day when the sum of the period for which the claimant was previously entitled to an employment and support allowance and the period for which the claimant is currently entitled to such an allowance is 13 weeks.

(2) The circumstances are that—

(a) (i) the claimant's current period of limited capability for work is to be treated as a continuation of an earlier period of limited capability for work under regulation 145(1) or (2);

(ii) the claimant was entitled to an employment and support allowance in the earlier period of limited capability for work; and

  (iii) the assessment phase had not ended in the previous period for which the claimant was entitled to an employment and support allowance; or
(b) (i) paragraph (3) or (5) of regulation 145 applies to the claimant; and
  (ii) the assessment phase had not ended in the previous period for which the claimant was entitled to an employment and support allowance.
(3) If, on the day referred to in paragraph (1)(b), it has not yet been determined whether the claimant has limited capability for work—
(a) the claimant having been assessed in accordance with a limited capability for work assessment; or
(b) as a result of the claimant being treated as having limited capability for work in accordance with regulation 20, 25, 26, 29 or regulation 33(2) (persons to be treated as having limited capability for work),
the assessment phase will end when the limited capability for work determination is made.

DEFINITIONS

"the assessment phase"—see WRA 2007, s.24(2).
"claimant"—see WRA 2007, s.24(1).
"entitled"—see WRA 2007, s.24(1).
"limited capability for work"—see WRA 2007, s.1(4).
"limited capability for work assessment"—see reg.2(1).
"week"—see reg.2(1).

GENERAL NOTE

This regulation deals with determining the end of the "assessment phase" in cases **9.13** of intermittent limited capability for work (where spells of limited capability for work are interspersed with spells in which capability for work is not limited), where the ostensibly separate spells of limited capability are fused into one by the operation of the "linking rule" in reg.145. As noted in the commentary to that regulation, this will happen generally where the two spells are not separated by more than 12 weeks, but in some cases the permissible separation period can be as long as 104 weeks. The effect of reg.5 is that the weeks of entitlement to ESA in each period thus linked are added together and the assessment phase ends when their sum reaches 13, unless no limited capability for work determination (see commentary to reg.4) has by then been made, in which case, as with continuous periods of limited capability for work under reg.4, it ends when that determination has been made. In short, the assessment phase ends after the later of 13 weeks (in two or more linked spells of limited capability) or the decision on whether the claimant has (or is to be treated as having) limited capability for work. Where, however, the claimant appeals a decision embodying an adverse determination on limited capability for work, the assessment phase ends only when the appeal is determined by an appeal tribunal (see reg.6).

The assessment phase—claimants appealing against a decision

6. Where the period for which the claimant is entitled to an employ- **9.14** ment and support allowance commences and the claimant has made and is pursuing an appeal against a decision which embodies a determination that that claimant does not have limited capability for work, the assessment phase in relation to that claimant ends when the appeal is determined by an appeal tribunal constituted under Chapter 1 of Part 1 of the Social Security Act 1998.

DEFINITIONS

"the assessment phase"—see WRA 2007, s.24(2).
"claimant"—see WRA 2007, s.24(1).
"limited capability for work"—see reg.2(1).

GENERAL NOTE

9.15 Where the claimant appeals a decision embodying an adverse determination on limited capability for work, the assessment phase ends only when the appeal is determined by an appeal tribunal under the SSA 1998.

Circumstances where the condition that the assessment phase has ended before entitlement to the support component or the work-related activity component arises does not apply

9.16 7.—(1) Subject to paragraph (2), sections 2(2)(a), 2(3)(a), 4(4)(a) and 4(5)(a) of the Act do not apply where—
(a) a claimant is terminally ill and has either—
(i) made a claim expressly on the ground of being terminally ill; or
(ii) made an application for supersession or revision in accordance with the Social Security and Child Support (Decisions and Appeals) Regulations 1999 which contains an express statement that the claimant is terminally ill; [¹ . . .]
(b) (i) a period of limited capability for work is to be treated as a continuation of an earlier period of limited capability for work under regulation 145(1) or (2);
(ii) the claimant was entitled to an employment and support allowance in the earlier period of limited capability for work; and
(iii) the assessment phase had ended in the previous period for which the claimant was entitled to an employment and support allowance. ; [¹ or
(c) (i) the claimant's entitlement to an employment and support allowance commences within 12 weeks of the claimant's entitlement to income support coming to an end;
(ii) in relation to that entitlement to income support, immediately before it ended the claimant's applicable amount included the disability premium by virtue of satisfying the conditions in paragraphs 11 and 12 of Schedule 2 to the Income Support Regulations; and
(iii) that entitlement to income support ended solely by virtue of the coming into force, in relation to the claimant, of the Social Security (Lone Parents and Miscellaneous Amendments) Regulations 2008.]
(2) Paragraph (1)(b) does not apply where the claimant is appealing a decision which embodies a determination that the claimant does not have limited capability for work.

DEFINITIONS

"claimant"—see WRA 2007, s.24(1).
"entitled"—see WRA 2007, s.24(1).
"limited capability for work"—see WRA 2007, s.1(4).
"period of limited capability for work"—see reg.2(1).

"terminally ill"—see reg.2(1).
"the assessment phase"—see WRA 2007, s.24(2).

GENERAL NOTE

WRA 2007, s.2 stipulates that generally until the "assessment phase" ends there   9.17
can be no entitlement other than to basic allowance ESA; entitlement to the appropriate additional component (support or work related) normally cannot arise until
the assessment phase has ended (on which see WRA 2007, s.24(2) and ESA Regs,
regs 4–6). This regulation provides that the general rule precluding entitlement does
not apply in three situations. First of all it does not apply to someone terminally ill
who has claimed ESA expressly on that basis or has sought supersession or revision
expressly stating that he is terminally ill (para.(1)(a)). Note that someone is terminally ill where he is suffering from a progressive disease and death as a consequence
of it can reasonably be expected within six months (reg.2(1)). The second situation where the general preclusive rule is disapplied is where the assessment phase
had ended in an earlier spell of limited capability for work which is forged into one
("linked") by the operation of the linking rule in reg.145(1) (the 12 week rule) or
that in reg.145(2) (the 104 week rule in respect of a work or training beneficiary
under reg.148). The third situation where the general preclusive rule is disapplied
is where the claimant's entitlement to ESA arises within 12 weeks of his entitlement to IS, which had included the disability premium, ending solely because of
the entry into force in relation to him of the Social Security (Lone Parents and
Miscellaneous Amendments) Regulations 2008. Note that the preclusion is *not*
disapplied where the two spells "link" because of the other 104 week rule which is
afforded by reg.145(3), (4) (person who has immediately before claiming ESA again
ceased qualifying remunerative work supported or (but for income) supportable by
tax credits).

AMENDMENT

1. Social Security (Lone Parents and Miscellaneous Amendments) Regulations
2008, reg.12(2) (November 24, 2008).

PART 3

CONDITIONS OF ENTITLEMENT—CONTRIBUTORY ALLOWANCE

Relaxation of the first contribution condition

8.—(1) A claimant who satisfies any of the conditions in paragraph (2) is   9.18
to be taken to satisfy the first contribution condition if—
  (a) the claimant paid Class 1 or Class 2 contributions before the relevant
      benefit week in respect of any one tax year; and
  (b) the earnings factor is derived—
      (i) from earnings, on which primary Class 1 contributions have
          been paid or treated as paid, which are not less than that year's
          lower earnings limit multiplied by 25; or
      (ii) from Class 2 contributions multiplied by 25.
  (2) The conditions referred to in paragraph (1) are that the claimant—
  (a) was entitled to a carer's allowance in the last complete tax year
      immediately preceding the relevant benefit year;
  (b) had been engaged in qualifying remunerative work for a period of
      more than 2 years immediately before the first day of the period

961

of limited capability for work and who was entitled to working tax credit where the disability element or the severe disability element of working tax credit specified in regulation 20(1) (b) or (f) of the Working Tax Credit (Entitlement and Maximum Rate) Regulations 2002 was included in the award;

(c) in respect of any week in any tax year preceding the relevant benefit year—

    (i) is entitled to be credited with earnings or contributions in accordance with regulation 9D of the Social Security (Credits) Regulations 1975 (credits for certain periods of imprisonment or detention in legal custody); or

    (ii) would have been so entitled had an application to the Secretary of State been made for the purpose of that regulation; or

(d) on the first day of the period of limited capability for work, had received a contributory allowance in the last complete tax year immediately preceding the relevant benefit year in which entitlement to a contributory allowance is now being decided.

DEFINITIONS

"benefit week"—see reg.2(1).
"carer's allowance"—see reg.2(1).
"claimant"—see WRA 2007, s.24(1).
"Class 1 contributions"—see WRA 2007, s.1, Sch.1, Pt 1, para.3(1)(b).
"Class 2 contributions"—see WRA 2007, s.1, Sch.1, Pt 1, para.3(1)(b).
"contributory allowance"—see WRA 2007, s.1(7).
"earnings"—see WRA 2007, s.1, Sch.1, Pt 1, para.3(1)(c).
"earnings factor"—see WRA 2007, s.1, Sch.1, Pt 1, para.3(1)(d).
"first contribution condition"—see reg.2(1); WRA 2007, Sch.1, para.1(1).
"lower earnings limit"—see WRA 2007, s.1, Sch.1, Pt 1, para.3(1)(e).
"period of limited capability for work,"—see reg.2(1).
"primary Class 1 contributions"—see WRA 2007, s.1, Sch.1, Pt 1, para.3(1) (b).
"qualifying remunerative work"—see reg.2(1).
"relevant benefit year"—see WRA 2007, s.1, Sch.1, Pt 1, para.3(1)(f).
"tax year"—see WRA 2007, s.1, Sch.1, Pt 1, para.3(1)(g).
"week"—see reg.2(1).

GENERAL NOTE

9.19   The national insurance contribution conditions, affording the sole route into CESA for anyone not incapacitated in youth, are found in WRA 2007, s.1(2)(a) and Sch.1, Pt 1, paras 1–3. They are the same as those governing access to IB from April 6, 2001 (SSCBA 1992, s.30A and Sch.3, para.2). The conditions were tightened from then so as to require a recent connection with the world of paid employment. Prior to that date the first contribution condition (then, as now, only able to be met by paid contributions) governing access to IB could be met by a sufficient record of paid contributions in any tax year prior to the claim. As now, IB contribution condition one had from April 6 2001 to be met in one of the last three tax years (April 6–April 5) complete before the start of the benefit year (early January–early January) in which falls the first day of the period of incapacity for work (now limited capability for work) of which the claim is part. This reg. affords some relief for some of the people disadvantaged by that rule. It is comparable to (but not wholly coterminous with) the relaxation in IB Regs, Pt 1A, reg.2B.

The rules are relaxed in the sense that if one of the conditions in reg.8(2) is met, such a claimant is treated as satisfying the first contribution condition if he has paid, in respect of any one tax/contribution year (complete or not) before the day of claim, Class 1 contributions to a level of 25 times that year's lower earnings limit or 25 Class 2 contributions (para.2B(1)). In short, such claimants are in effect subject to the first contribution condition as it stood before the April 6, 2001 changes. The rules are "relaxed" in the following situations:

(a) where the claimant was, in the last complete tax year immediately preceding the relevant benefit year in which occurred the first day of limited capability for work, entitled to carer's allowance (para.2(a)) (in express terms (but not effect) this is narrower than IB reg.2B(2)(a) which also explicitly covered someone who would have been entitled to one but for the provisions of reg.4 of the Overlapping Benefit Regs (he was receiving another higher value benefit), but this is because that regulation merely precluding benefit being payable, rather than affecting entitlement, the explicit reference was in law otiose);

(b) where the claimant was engaged in qualifying remunerative work for a period of more than two years immediately before the first day of limited capability for work and throughout that period was in receipt of working tax credit which included in the award the disability or severe disability element (para.(2)(b));

(c) certain convicted prisoners whose conviction is overturned whose contribution record is credited in respect of their period of imprisonment under Social Security (Credits) Regulations 1975, reg.9D or would be if they applied to the Secretary of State (para.(2)(c));

(d) where the claimant is on the first day of his limited capability for work someone who had received CESA in the last complete tax year before the relevant benefit year in which he again becomes entitled to it (para.(2)(d)).

Condition relating to youth—claimants aged 20 or over but under 25

9.—(1) For the purposes of paragraph 4(1)(a) of Schedule 1 to the Act, a claimant who satisfies the conditions specified in paragraph (2) falls within a prescribed case.

(2) The conditions are that the claimant—

(a) registered on a course of—
   (i) full-time advanced or secondary education; or
   (ii) training,
at least 3 months before attaining the age of 20; and

(b) not more than one academic term immediately after registration attended one or more such courses in respect of a period referred to in paragraph (3).

(3) The period mentioned in sub-paragraph (2)(b) is a period which—

(a) began on or before a day at least 3 months before the day the claimant attained the age of 20; and

(b) ended no earlier than the beginning of the last two complete tax years before the relevant benefit year which would have applied if the claimant was entitled to an employment and support allowance having satisfied the first contribution condition and the second contribution condition.

(4) For the purposes of this regulation a claimant is to be treated as attending a course on any day on which the course is interrupted by an illness or domestic emergency.

9.20

(5) In this regulation—

"advanced education" means education for the purposes of—

    (a) a course in preparation for a degree, a diploma of higher education, a higher national diploma, a higher national diploma of the Business and Technician Education Council or the Scottish Qualifications Authority, or a teaching qualification; or

    (b) any other course which is of a standard above ordinary national diploma, a diploma of the Business and Technical Education Council or a higher or advanced higher national certificate of the Scottish Qualifications Authority or a general certificate of education (advanced level);

"full-time" includes part-time where the person's disability prevents attendance at a full-time course;

"secondary education" means a course of education below a course of advanced education—

    (a) by attendance at an establishment recognised by the Secretary of State as being, or as comparable to, a university, college or school; or

    (b) elsewhere where the Secretary of State is satisfied that the education is equivalent to that given in an establishment recognised as being, or as comparable to, a university, college or school.

[[1](6) A claimant is to be treated as not having limited capability for work on a day which is not, for the purposes of paragraph 4(1)(d)(ii) of Schedule 1 to the Act (period of 196 consecutive days preceding the relevant period of limited capability for work), part of any consecutive days of limited capability for work.]

AMENDMENTS

1. Employment and Support Allowance (Miscellaneous Amendments) Regulations 2008 (SI 2008/2428), reg.4 (October 27, 2008).

DEFINITIONS

"advanced education"—see para.(5).
"claimant"—see WRA 2007, s.24(1).
"first contribution condition"—see reg.2(1); WRA 2007, Sch.1, para.1(1).
"full-time"—see para.(5).
"relevant benefit year"—see WRA 2007, s.1, Sch.1, Pt 1, para.3(1)(f).
"secondary education"—see para.(5).
"second contribution condition"—see reg.2(1); WRA 2007, Sch.1, para.2(1).
"tax year"—see WRA 2007, s.1, Sch.1, Pt 1, para.3(1)(g).
"training"—see reg.2(1).

GENERAL NOTE

9.21   Meeting the national insurance contributions conditions affords only one route to CESA (WRA 2007, s.1(2)(a) and Sch.1, Pt 1, paras 1–3; reg.8). The second route (condition relating to youth) is covered by WRA 2007, s.1(2)(a), Sch.1, Pt 1, para.4 (the key provision), this regulation and regs 10–12. This regulation stipulates when there can be access to CESA through the "youth" route for those 20 or over but under 25; it sets out the conditions in which their case is a "prescribed" one for purposes of WRA 2007, Sch.1, Pt 1, para.4(1)(a) (para.(1)). The comparable IB provision is IB Regs, reg.15. It is here assumed that case law on that almost identically worded provision will carry over into interpretation of this ESA provision.

Someone over 20 but under 25 can qualify for the "youth" route where, at least three months before reaching 20, he registered on a course of full time education or of training (see below), provided that not more than one academic term immediately after his registration, he attended one or more such courses in respect of a specified period (para.(2)). Note that he is treated as attending on any day on which the course or training is interrupted by an illness or domestic emergency (para.4). The specified period is set out in para.(3): a period beginning on or before a day three months before his twentieth birthday (para.(3)(a)) and ending on a day not earlier than the beginning of the last two complete tax years before the benefit year which would have governed a claim for CESA by the national insurance route. The terms "advanced education" and "secondary education" are defined in para.(5) in an interlocking way, so that "secondary education" is a level below that of "advanced education" and it requires attendance at a educational establishment recognised by the Secretary of State as, or as comparable, to a university, college or school, or elsewhere so long as the Secretary of State is satisfied that the education afforded there is equivalent to that in such an establishment. Note that while both "advanced education" and "secondary education" require a "full-time" course, para.(5) stipulates that "full-time" covers also "part-time" where the claimant's disability is such as to preclude him attending a full-time course.

The reference in the IB provision was to "vocational or work-based training". This regulation refers to "training", defined in reg.2(1) as (a) training in pursuance of arrangements made under s.2(1) of the Employment and Training Act 1973 or s.2(3) of the Enterprise and New Towns (Scotland) Act 1990; or (b) any training received on a course which a person attends for 16 hours or more a week, the primary purpose of which is the teaching of occupational or vocational skills. In respect of the IB provision, whether the claimant was registered on a "full-time" course or on a course of "vocational or work-based training" was considered by Commissioner Jacobs in *CIB/1410/2005*. Her course was described as part-time by the College in question (not conclusive in itself) and she was required to attend College one day a week and undertake eight to ten hours of private study. She had also to arrange and undertake 60 hours of work experience over the period of the course. Commissioner Jacobs held that the tribunal was entitled to disregard the work experience, since it was essential to, but not part of, the course, and to regard the course as part-time. Moreover, she could not in such circumstances be regarded as registered on a course of vocational or work-based training.

Condition relating to youth—previous claimants

10.—(1) Paragraph 4(1)(a) of Schedule 1 to the Act does not apply to a claimant—   **9.22**

- (a) who has previously ceased to be entitled to an employment and support allowance, entitlement for which was as a result of satisfying the condition set out in sub-paragraph (1) of that paragraph;
- (b) whose previous entitlement had not been ended by a decision which embodied a determination (other than a determination in the circumstances applicable to a claimant under paragraph (2)(a)) that the claimant did not have limited capability for work;
- (c) in relation to whom regulation 145 (linking rules) does not apply;
- (d) aged 20 or over, or, where regulation 9 would otherwise apply to the person, aged 25 or over; and
- (e) to whom paragraph (2) applies.

(2) This paragraph applies to a claimant—

- (a) whose previous entitlement to an employment and support allowance ended solely with a view to that person taking up employment or training;

    (b) whose earnings factor from an employment or series of employments pursued in the period from the end of the previous entitlement to the beginning of the period of limited capability for work, was below the lower earnings limit multiplied by 25 in any of the last three complete tax years before the beginning of the relevant benefit year; and

    (c) who—

        (i) in respect of the last two complete tax years before the beginning of the relevant benefit year has either paid or been credited with earnings equivalent in each of those years to the year's lower earnings limit multiplied by 50, of which at least one, in the last tax year, was in respect of the disability element or severe disability element of working tax credit; or

       (ii) makes a claim for an employment and support allowance within a period of 12 weeks after the day on which the last such employment pursued in accordance with sub-paragraph (b) ceased.

DEFINITIONS

"claimant"—see WRA 2007, s.24(1).
"earnings factor"—see WRA 2007, s.1, Sch.1, Pt 1, para.3(1)(d).
"employment"—see reg.2(1).
"limited capability for work"—see WRA 2007, s.1(4).
"lower earnings limit"—see WRA 2007, s.1, Sch.1, Pt 1, para.3(1)(e).
"period of limited capability for work"—see reg.2(1).
"relevant benefit year"—see WRA 2007, s.1, Sch.1, Pt 1, para.3(1)(f).
"tax year"—see WRA 2007, s.1, Sch.1, Pt 1, para.3(1)(g).
"training"—see reg.2(1).
"week"—see reg.2(1).
"working tax credit"—see reg.2(1).

GENERAL NOTE

9.23   Made pursuant to WRA 2007, Sch.1, Pt 1, para.4(3), this regulation, comparable to IB Regulations, reg.18, prescribes circumstances in which someone previously entitled to CESA under the youth route, can again be entitled even though the age condition in WRA 2007, Sch.1, Pt 1, para.4(1)(a) is not met. It deals with the situation where someone has been entitled to incapacity benefit as a person incapacitated in youth, ceases to be entitled to it other than on the basis of being found not to have limited capability for work, and claims again in a new period of limited capability for work (not being helped by the variety of linking rules in the ESA scheme (reg.145), but is over age (20 or 25 as the case may be) when he makes that new claim. He can again become entitled in certain cases where his previous entitlement was terminated solely with a view to him taking up employment or training which proved to be very low paid or very intermittent. The rule will not operate where entitlement ended because of a determination that he did not have limited capability for work (para.(1)(c)). The regulation covers the person whose entitlement terminated solely with a view to him taking up an employment or training (see definition of "training" in reg.2(1)) (para.(2)(a)). He can qualify by way of the "youth" route (albeit over-age) if his earnings factor from the employment or series of employments pursued since the termination of his previous entitlement was below a specified level in *any* of the three complete tax years relevant for qualification by way of the national insurance contributions route (see WRA 2007, s.1(2)(a), Sch.1, paras (1)–(3)). The specified level is less than 25 times the lower earnings level set for Class 1 contributions purposes in the tax year in question. However, he can only be eligible if in addition, he is either: (a) claiming by way of the youth route within 12 weeks of his last such employment (para.(2)(c)(ii)); or (b) in each of the last two complete tax years (identified as above) he has paid or been credited with earnings to the level of 50 times the year's lower earnings limit for Class 1 contributions purposes, and at least one of those contributions or creditings was, in the last such year, in respect of the disability or severe disability element of working tax credit (para.(2)(c)(i)).

Condition relating to youth—residence or presence

11.—(1) The prescribed conditions for the purposes of paragraph 4(1) (c) of Schedule 1 to the Act as to residence or presence in Great Britain are that the claimant—

    (a) is ordinarily resident in Great Britain;

    (b) is not a person subject to immigration control within the meaning of section 115(9) of the Immigration and Asylum Act or is a person to whom paragraph (3) applies;

    (c) is present in Great Britain; and

    (d) has been present in Great Britain for a period of, or for periods amounting in aggregate to, not less than 26 weeks in the 52 weeks immediately preceding the relevant benefit week.

9.24

(2) For the purposes of paragraph (1), a claimant is to be treated as being resident and present in Great Britain where the claimant is absent from Great Britain by reason only of being—

    (a) the spouse, civil partner, son, daughter, father, father-in-law, mother or mother-in-law of, and living with, a member of Her Majesty's forces who is abroad in that capacity;

    (b) in employment prescribed for the purposes of paragraph 7(1)(c) of Schedule 2 to the Act in connection with continental shelf operations; or

    (c) abroad in the capacity of being an aircraft worker or mariner.

(3) This paragraph applies where a person is—

    (a) a member of a family of a national of an European Economic Area state;

    (b) a person who is lawfully working in Great Britain and is a national of a State with which the Community has concluded an agreement under Article 310 of the Treaty of Amsterdam amending the Treaty on European Union, the Treaties establishing the European Communities and certain related Acts providing, in the field of social security, for the equal treatment of workers who are nationals of the signatory State and their families;

    (c) a person who is a member of a family of, and living with, a person specified in sub-paragraph (b); or

    (d) a person who has been given leave to enter, or remain in, the United Kingdom by the Secretary of State upon an undertaking by another person or persons pursuant to the immigration rules within the meaning of the Immigration Act 1971 to be responsible for that person's maintenance and accommodation.

(4) A person is to be treated as having satisfied the residence or presence conditions in paragraph (1) throughout a period of limited capability for work where those conditions are satisfied on the first day of that period of limited capability for work.

DEFINITIONS

    "aircraft worker"—see reg.2(1).
    "benefit week"—see reg.2(1).

"claimant"—see WRA 2007, s.24(1).
"continental shelf operations"—see WRA 2007, s.22, Sch.2, para.7(3).
"employment"—see reg.2(1).
"family"—see reg.2(1).
"Immigration and Asylum Act"—see reg.2(1).
"member of Her Majesty's forces"—see reg.2(1).
"mariner"—see reg.2(1).
"period of limited capability for work"—see reg.2(1).
"prescribed"—see WRA 2007, s.24(1).
"week"—see reg.2(1).

GENERAL NOTE

9.25   WRA 2007, Sch.1, para.4(1)(c) requires that to gain non-contributory access to incapacity benefit as a person incapacitated in youth, a claimant must on the relevant day satisfy the prescribed conditions as to residence or presence in Great Britain. This regulation sets out those prescribed conditions. They are such as to require both residence and presence. Residence is "ordinary residence" rather than simple residence (para.(1)(a)). There is no requirement of "habitual residence". "Presence" (para.(1)(c)) means "physically present". The requirements are that the claimant must on the first day of claim in the period of incapacity for work (see para. (4)) be both ordinarily resident and present in Great Britain. (On "ordinarily resident", see further the commentary to Persons Abroad Regs, reg.5.) He must also have been present in Great Britain for a period or aggregate periods of at least 26 weeks in the immediately preceding 52 weeks (para.(1)(d)). In addition he must not be subject to immigration control within the meaning of Immigration and Asylum Act 1999, s.115(9) (set out in *Vol.II: Income Support, Jobseeker's Allowance, Tax Credits and the Social Fund* and see the provisions noted in the commentary thereto) or (if prima facie he is) he must be someone protected by para.(3). That paragraph protects the same groups as are covered in Pt II of the Schedule to the Social Security (Immigration and Asylum) Consequential Amendments Regulations 2000, set out in *Vol.II: Income Support, Jobseeker's Allowance, Tax Credits and the Social Fund*.

Absence from Great Britain would negate presence. Paragraph (2) enables certain actual absences to be treated, legally speaking, as if the person was present or resident in Great Britain. It protects aircraft workers and mariners within the meaning of reg.2(1). It protects also those in employment prescribed for the purposes of SSCBA 1992, s.120 in connection with continental shelf operations. It also protects someone abroad as the spouse, son, daughter, father, mother, father-in-law, mother-in-law of and living with a member of the forces abroad.

Condition relating to youth—full-time education

9.26   **12.**—(1) For the purposes of paragraph 4(4) of Schedule 1 to the Act, a claimant is to be treated as receiving full-time education for any period during which the claimant—

(a) is at least 16 years old but under the age of 19; and

(b) attends a course of education for 21 hours or more a week.

(2) For the purposes of paragraph (1)(b), in calculating the number of hours a week during which a claimant attends a course, no account is to be taken of any instruction or tuition which is not suitable for persons of the same age who do not have a disability.

(3) In determining the duration of a period of full-time education under paragraph (1) any temporary interruption of that education may be disregarded.

(4) A claimant who is 19 years of age or over is not to be treated for the purposes of paragraph 4(1)(b) of Schedule 1 to the Act as receiving full-time education.

DEFINITIONS

"claimant"—see WRA 2007, s.24(1).
"week"—see reg.2(1).

GENERAL NOTE

WRA 2007, Sch.1, para.4(41)(b) precludes someone from ranking as a person   9.27
incapacitated in youth (thus denying non-contributory access to incapacity benefit)
where on the day of claimed incapacity he is receiving full-time education. This
regulation, pursuant to para.4(4) of that Schedule, sets out what is, and what is
not, to be regarded as full-time education. Someone who is 19 or over cannot be
so precluded even though he is in fact undergoing a full-time education (para.(4)).
Preclusive "full-time education" covers a person aged 16–18 inclusive for any period
in which he attends a course of education for 21 or more hours a week (para.(1)). In
determining the length of any such preclusive period, a decision-maker may disregard any temporary interruption of that education (para.(3)). This, it is submitted,
is ambiguous, leaving it unclear whether such periods are to be counted as part of
the preclusive period or ones that are to be left out. The DMG offers no assistance
in resolving the ambiguity. As regards the 21 hours aspect, no account is to be taken
in calculating those hours of any instruction or tuition unsuitable for a person of the
same age as the claimant but who is not suffering from a physical or mental disability (para.(2)). In other words, one ignores special classes for the disabled.

Modification of the relevant benefit year

13.—(1) Where paragraph (2) applies, sub-paragraph (1)(f) of paragraph   9.28
3 of Schedule 1 to the Act has effect as if "relevant benefit year" is the
benefit year which includes the day which would be the beginning of the
period of limited capability for work if regulation 145 did not apply.
(2) This paragraph applies where a claimant does not satisfy—
  (a) the first contribution condition;
  (b) the second contribution condition; or
  (c) both contribution conditions,
but would satisfy those conditions if the modified definition of "relevant
benefit year" provided in paragraph (1) applied.

DEFINITIONS

"claimant"—see WRA 2007, s.24(1).
"first contribution condition"—see reg.2(1); WRA 2007, s.1, Sch.1, para.1(1).
"period of limited capability for work"—see reg.2(1).
"relevant benefit year"—see para.(1).
"second contribution condition"—see reg.2(1); WRA 2007, s.1, Sch.1,
  para.2(1).

GENERAL NOTE

This operates where a claimant fails to satisfy one or both of the standard contri-   9.29
bution conditions for ESA. As noted in the commentary to WRA 2007, Sch.1, paras
1–3, the key to determining the tax years to which to have regard is determined by
identifying the benefit year in which there falls the first day of the period of limited
capability for work. The effect of the linking rules (where one period is fused with
an earlier one) may mean that the benefit year in question is not the current one
in which the most recent claim falls. If, ignoring the effect of the linking rules in
reg.145 (so that period of limited capability for work is not joined to an earlier
one) would mean that the relevant benefit year would be later so that the relevant
tax years to which to have regard would change to ones in which the contribution

condition(s) in question was (were) met, then the relevant benefit year for the purposes of the contribution conditions is to be the later one determined by ignoring the linking rules.

PART 4

CONDITIONS OF ENTITLEMENT—INCOME-RELATED ALLOWANCE

Meaning of education

9.30   **14.**—(1) Subject to regulations 15 and 16, for the purposes of paragraph 6 of Schedule 1 to the Act, "education" means a course of study to which paragraph (2) applies which is being undertaken at an educational establishment.

(2) This paragraph applies to a course of study which is—

(a) a full-time course which is not funded in whole or in part by—
   (i) the Learning and Skills Council for England;
   (ii) the Welsh Ministers; or
   (iii) the Scottish Ministers at a college of further education;

(b) a full-time course of higher education which is funded in whole or in part by the Scottish Ministers;

(c) funded in whole or in part by the Learning and Skills Council for England or by the Welsh Ministers if it involves more than 16 guided learning hours per week for the student in question, according to the number of guided learning hours per week for that student set out—
   (i) in the case of a course funded by the Learning and Skills Council for England, in the student's learning agreement signed on behalf of the establishment which is funded by that Council for the delivery of that course; or
   (ii) in the case of a course funded by the Welsh Ministers, in a document signed on behalf of the establishment which is funded by those Ministers for the delivery of that course;

(d) not a course of higher education and which is funded in whole or in part by the Scottish Ministers at a college of further education and involves—
   (i) more than 16 hours per week of classroom-based or workshop-based programmed learning under the direct guidance of teaching staff according to the number of hours set out in a document signed on behalf of the college; or
   (ii) 16 hours or less per week of classroom-based or workshop-based programmed learning under the direct guidance of teaching staff and it involves additional hours using structured learning packages supported by the teaching staff where the combined total of hours exceeds 21 per week according to the number of hours set out in a document signed on behalf of the college; or

(e) a sandwich course within the meaning prescribed in regulation 2(9) of the Education (Student Support) Regulations 2007, regulation 4(2) of the Education (Student Loans) (Scotland) Regulations 2007 or regulation 2(8) of the Education (Student Support) Regulations (Northern Ireland) 2007.

(3) In this regulation "higher education" means higher education within the meaning of Part 2 of the Further and Higher Education (Scotland) Act 1992.

GENERAL NOTE

It is a condition of entitlement to income-related ESA that a claimant is not receiving education (see para.6(1)(g) of Sch.1 to the Welfare Reform Act 2007). But see reg.18 below which exempts claimants who are entitled to disability living allowance from this requirement.   **9.31**

"Education" for these purposes means a course of study that comes within para. (2) that is being undertaken at an educational establishment. Paragraph (2) is in the same terms as the definitions of "full-time course of study" and "sandwich course" in reg.131(1) (which in turn reproduces the definitions of these terms in reg.61(1) of the Income Support Regulations; see also the definitions of "full-time student" and "sandwich course" in reg.1(3) of the JSA Regulations). Regulation 17 provides when a person will count as undertaking a course of study. It is in the same terms as reg.131(2)–(4) (which in turn reproduces the provisions in reg.61(2)–(4) of the Income Support Regulations and reg.1(3A)–(3C) of the JSA Regulations). The combined effect of regs 14 and 17 is to exclude full-time students from income-related ESA (except those who are entitled to disability living allowance: see reg.18 and the note to that regulation). But note that in the case of a person aged under 19 this will only apply if he is attending a course of advanced education (reg.16).

In addition, a "qualifying young person", unless he is entitled to disability living allowance, is to be treated as receiving education (see reg.15).

Claimants to be treated as receiving education

15. Subject to regulation 18, a qualifying young person is to be treated as receiving education for the purposes of paragraph 6(1)(g) of Schedule 1 to the Act.   **9.32**

DEFINITION

"qualifying young person"—reg.2(1), s.142 SSCBA.

GENERAL NOTE

A qualifying young person (other than one who is entitled to disability living allowance: see reg.18) is to be treated as receiving education and so is excluded from income-related ESA. A "qualifying young person" (as defined in s.142 of the Contributions and Benefits Act) is a person who is 16 or over but who has not attained a prescribed age and who satisfies prescribed conditions.   **9.33**

The substance of the definition of "qualifying young person" is in reg.3 of the Child Benefit Regulations 2006 (see Vol.IV in this series). It applies to a person who is (i) under 20; *and* (ii) undertaking a course of full-time, non-advanced education, which is not provided by virtue of his employment or any office held by him, but which is provided at a school or college, or elsewhere as approved by the Revenue (in the latter case he must have been receiving the approved education before he was 16); *or* (iii) undertaking approved training that is not provided by means of a contract of employment. "Approved training" covers various training programmes under "arrangements made by the Government" (see the definition of both these terms in reg.1(2) of the 2006 Regulations). "Full-time education" (also defined in reg.1(2)) requires contact hours of at least 12 a week during term-time. Note that a person aged 19 can only be a qualifying young person if he began, or was enrolled on, or had been accepted to undertake, the full-time, non-advanced education or approved training before he was 19 (although a person who was on such a course/ training and has been accepted or enrolled to undertake another such course/train- ing is also included).

Claimants not to be treated as receiving education

9.34   **16.** Where a claimant is under 19 but not a qualifying young person, that claimant is not to be treated as receiving education where the course of study is not—

(a) a course leading to a postgraduate degree or comparable qualifica- tion, a first degree or comparable qualification, a diploma of higher education or a higher national diploma; or

(b) any other course which is of a standard above advanced GNVQ or equivalent, including a course which is of a standard above a general certificate of education (advanced level) or above a Scottish national qualification (higher or advanced higher).

DEFINITION

"qualifying young person"—see reg.2(1), s.142 SSCBA.

GENERAL NOTE

9.35   The effect of this regulation is that if the claimant is aged less than 19 and is not a qualifying young person (see the note to reg.15), he will not count as receiving edu- cation unless he is undertaking a course of advanced education (see the definition of "course of advanced education" in reg.131(1) which is in the same terms as paras (a) and (b), and which in turn reproduces the definition of "course of advanced education" in reg.61(1) of the Income Support Regulations and reg.1(3) of the JSA Regulations). See further the note to reg.14.

Courses of study

9.36   **17.**—(1) For the purposes of the definition of "education" in regulation 14, a person is to be regarded as undertaking a course of study—

(a) subject to paragraph (2), in the case of a person undertaking a part of a modular course that would be a course of study for the purposes of these Regulations, for the period beginning on the day on which that part of the course starts and ending—

(i) on the last day on which the person is registered with the edu- cational establishment as attending or undertaking that part as a full-time course of study; or

(ii) on such earlier date (if any) as the person finally abandons the course or is dismissed from it;

(b) in any other case, throughout the period beginning on the date on which the person starts undertaking the course and ending on the last day of the course or on such earlier date (if any) as the person finally abandons it or is dismissed from it.

(2) For the purpose of sub-paragraph (a) of paragraph (1), the period referred to in that sub-paragraph includes—

(a) where a person has failed examinations or has failed to successfully complete a module relating to a period when the person was attend- ing or undertaking a part of the course as a course of study, any period in respect of which the person attends or undertakes the course for the purpose of retaking those examinations or that module;

(b) any period of vacation within the period specified in that paragraph or immediately following that period except where the person has registered with the educational establishment to attend or undertake the final module in the course and the vacation immediately follows the last day on which the person is required to attend or undertake the course.

(3) In paragraph (1), "modular course" means a course of study which consists of two or more modules, the successful completion of a specified number of which is required before a person is considered by the educational establishment to have completed the course.

GENERAL NOTE

See the note to reg.14.

9.37

Circumstances in which the condition that the claimant is not receiving education does not apply

18. Paragraph 6(1)(g) of Schedule 1 to the Act does not apply where the claimant is entitled to a disability living allowance.

9.38

GENERAL NOTE

Paragraph 6(1)(g) of Sch.1 to the Welfare Reform Act 2007 provides that it is a condition of entitlement to income-related ESA that the claimant is not receiving education—this effectively excludes full-time students and qualifying young persons from income-related ESA: see regs 14–17. However the effect of reg.18 is that such claimants will not be excluded if they are entitled to disability living allowance (either component at any rate). Note that this exemption only applies if the claimant is entitled to disability living allowance. Previously a full-time student could claim income support if he had been incapable of work for at least 28 weeks, qualified for the disability or severe disability premium, or was receiving a disabled student's allowance on the grounds of deafness (see paras 10 and 12 of Sch.1B to the Income Support Regulations in Vol.II of this series). Similarly, a qualifying young person who had been incapable of work for at least 28 weeks or met the conditions for the disability premium or severe disability premium was eligible for income support (see reg.13(2)(b) and (bb) of, and para.15 of Sch.1B to, the Income Support Regulations). However from October 27, 2008 *new* claims for income support on these grounds are no longer possible as they are treated as claims for ESA (see reg.2(1) of the Employment and Support Allowance (Transitional Provisions) Regulations 2008 (SI 2008/795)), unless they link with (i.e. are made not more than eight weeks after) a previous income support entitlement for at least four days on the grounds of disability: see reg.2(2)(c) of the Transitional Provisions Regulations, or the claimant is entitled to incapacity benefit or severe disablement allowance: see reg.2(2)(d) of those Regulations, as amended by the Employment and Support Allowance (Transitional Provisions) (Amendment) Regulations 2008 (SI 2008/2783), or they are in respect of a period before October 27, 2008. Income support on the grounds of disability means "income support awarded to a person to whom regulation 13(2)(b) or (bb) of, or paragraph 7(a) or (b), 10, 12 or 13 of Schedule 1B to, the Income Support (General) Regulations 1987 (prescribed categories of person) applies" (reg.1(4) of the Transitional Provisions Regulations, as amended by reg.42 of the Employment and Support Allowance (Miscellaneous Amendments) Regulations 2008 (SI 2008/2428)).

Thus from October 27, 2008 disabled full-time students or qualifying young persons making a new claim have to claim ESA but the basic rule is that such a person will not qualify for income-related ESA unless he is entitled to disability living allowance. Note also that such claimants, if they were eligible for income

9.39

support on grounds other than incapacity for work, would previously have been subject to the income support remunerative work (i.e. 16 hours a week) rule, whereas the "incapacity" remunerative work rules will now apply to them (see regs 41, 44 and 45).

See also reg.33(2) which treats a claimant who is receiving education but who is entitled to disability living allowance as having limited capability for work for the purposes of income-related ESA. But this does not apply in the case of a qualifying young person (reg.33(2)(a)). A qualifying young person who is entitled to disability living allowance and who claims income-related ESA will have to satisfy the limited capability for work test (as will any claimant who counts as receiving education who claims contributory ESA, even though he is entitled to disability living allowance).

PART 5

LIMITED CAPABILITY FOR WORK

Determination of limited capability for work

9.40   **19.**—(1) For the purposes of Part 1 of the Act, whether a claimant's capability for work is limited by the claimant's physical or mental condition and, if it is, whether the limitation is such that it is not reasonable to require the claimant to work is to be determined on the basis of a limited capability for work assessment of the claimant in accordance with this Part.

(2) The limited capability for work assessment is an assessment of the extent to which a claimant who has some specific disease or bodily or mental disableme nt is capable of performing the activities prescribed in Schedule 2 or is incapable by reason of such disease or bodily or mental disablement of performing those activities.

(3) Subject to paragraph (6), for the purposes of Part 1 of the Act a claimant has limited capability for work if, by adding the points listed in column (3) of Schedule 2 against any descriptor listed in that Schedule, the claimant obtains a total score of at least—

    (a) 15 points whether singly or by a combination of descriptors specified in Part 1 of that Schedule;

    (b) 15 points whether singly or by a combination of descriptors specified in Part 2 of that Schedule; or

    (c) 15 points by a combination of descriptors specified in Parts 1 and 2 of that Schedule.

(4) In assessing the extent of a claimant's capability to perform any activity listed in Part 1 of Schedule 2, the claimant is to be assessed as if wearing any prosthesis with which the claimant is fitted or, as the case may be, wearing or using any aid or appliance which is normally worn or used.

(5) In assessing the extent of a claimant's capability to perform any activity listed in Schedule 2, it is a condition that the claimant's incapability to perform the activity arises from—

    (a) a specific bodily disease or disablement;

    (b) a specific mental illness or disablement; or

    (c) as a direct result of treatment provided by a registered medical practitioner, for such a disease, illness or disablement.

(6) Where more than one descriptor specified for an activity apply to a claimant, only the descriptor with the highest score in respect of each activity which applies is to be counted.

(7) Where a claimant—

(a) has been determined to have limited capability for work; or

(b) is to be treated as having limited capability for work under regulations 20, 25, 26, 29 or 33(2),

the Secretary of State may, if paragraph (8) applies, determine afresh whether the claimant has or is to be treated as having limited capability for work.

(8) This paragraph applies where—

(a) the Secretary of State wishes to determine whether there has been a relevant change of circumstances in relation to the claimant's physical or mental condition;

(b) the Secretary of State wishes to determine whether the previous determination of limited capability for work or that the claimant is to be treated as having limited capability for work, was made in ignorance of , or was based on a mistake as to, some material fact; or

(c) at least 3 months have passed since the date on which the claimant was determined to have limited capability for work or to be treated as having limited capability for work.

DEFINITIONS

"claimant"—see WRA 2007, s.24(1).
"descriptor"—see reg.2(1).
"limited capability for work"—see WRA 2007, s.1(4).
"limited capability for work assessment"—see para.(2).

GENERAL NOTE

Entitlement to ESA requires that the claimant has limited capability for work (WRA 2007, s.1(3)(a)). Whether his capability for work is limited by his physical or mental condition such that it is not reasonable to require him to work is to be determined in accordance with regulations (WRA 2007, s.8(1)). This regulation, setting out how "actual" limited capability to work is to be determined through the limited capability for work assessment is the product. The remainder of this Part (regs 20–33), deal with situations in which someone, whatever the reality, is to be treated as having limited capability for work, and also with aspects of the decision-making process. **9.41**

Para.(1)

ESA is a benefit designed to help people with a limiting health condition overcome barriers, and where appropriate move into work and improve their lives. The Work Capability Assessment (WCA) seeks more accurately to relate to modern context than the 12-year-old IB/IS system, and to focus more on what people can do, rather on what they are unable to do. The matter of whether the claimant's capability for work is limited by his physical or mental condition, and, if so, whether the limitation is to such an extent that it is not reasonable to require him to work, is to be decided on the basis of the "limited capability for work assessment" (WCAt or LCWA). This is the first element in a new three-part "work capability assessment" (WCA), developed out of the review of the IB "personal capability assessment" (PCA), which governs entitlement to the basic allowance and the additional components of ESA. The new WCA underpinning ESA was devised by the DWP's Health Work and Wellbeing Directorate with input from two technical working groups, one focusing on mental health and learning difficulties, the other on physical function and conditions (hereinafter "review group"). The review group consisted of medical and other relevant experts. It examined how the IB Personal Capability Assessment (PCA) (characterized by them as "the best assessment of its type in the world" **9.42** could nonetheless be improved and updated so as to reflect the many changes since its inception:

> "in the prevalence of disabling conditions; in advances in medical science resulting in the availability of new and more effective medical interventions; and in the workplace environment. The Disability Discrimination Act, introduced after the PCA had been developed, has influenced the ability of employers to make reasonable adjustments to accommodate people with long term disabilities. It has also raised the expectations of disabled people that adjustments should be made to enable them to work."

Government anticipates that the WCA will "fail" some 60,000 claimants a year who would have "passed" the PCA. (DWP, *Impact Assessment of the Employment and Support Allowance Regulations 2008—Public sector Impact Only* in *Explanatory Memorandum to Employment and Support Allowance Regulations 2008 (SI 2008/794) and the Employment and Support Allowance (Transitional Provisions) Regulations 2008 (SI 2008/795)*, p.9). But the three-element WCA is not merely an incapacity-based tool for determining entitlement to ESA. That remains true of its first element the subject of this regulation. However, its second element is rather a more positive assessment considering ability to benefit from work-related activity with a view to promoting capacity for work. The assessment has two aspects: an assessment of limited capability to work (WCAt) and an assessment of limited capacity to engage in work-related activity (WRAAt). Both assessments will generally be conducted at the same time. The WCAt is a more rigorous test than the PCA and far fewer groups are exempted from it. Those found not to have limited capacity for work-related activity (expected to be some 90% of new claimants) will in addition have to undergo the third element of the WCA: a work-focused health related assessment (WFHRAt).

Paras (2) and (5)

9.43   This defines the "limited capability for work assessment" (WCAt). Like the IB "personal capability assessment" (PCA) and its predecessor, the "all work" test, the ESA WCAt is an assessment of the extent to which someone with a specific disease or bodily or mental disablement is (despite that) capable of performing the activities set out in Sch.2 or is because of it incapable of performing them. Since the test is thus so similar to that in IB (see Incapacity for Work Regs, reg.24 and Sch.), the position taken here is that case authorities (whether Commissioner or court) on the PCA will also apply to the WCAt. As with the IB PCA, the tasks involved in applying the WCAt are twofold:

1. ascertaining from all the evidence in the case which descriptors apply (paras (2), (5) and Sch.2);
2. computing the scores (paras (3), (6)).

The terms of para.(2) require the incapacity to perform the Sch.2 activities to arise by reason of "some specific disease or bodily or mental disablement". This is further stressed in paras (5)(a) and (b), the latter of which specifically also brings in "mental illness", while para.(5)(c) in effect adds that the rubric will also cover incapability as a direct result of treatment provided by a registered medical practitioner for such a disease, illness or disablement: This "specific disease or bodily or mental disablement" phraseology was found in the sickness/invalidity benefits statutory test and in both the "own occupation" test and the IB PCA, so decisions on this phraseology from those regimes will still be authoritative here.

"Specific" means "of a kind identified by medical science" (*CS/57/82*, noted in [1983] J.S.W.L. 306). "Disease" has been described as "a departure from health capable of identification by its signs and symptoms, an abnormality of some sort", and sickness falls within the definition (*CS/221/49*, para.3; *CS/7/82*, noted in [1983] J.S.W.L. 306). "Disablement"—which may be bodily or mental—constitutes a state of deprivation or incapacitation of ability measured against the abilities of a normal person (*CS/7/82, ibid.*). "Illness" is surely comparable to concepts of "disease" or "sickness".

In most cases there will be little problem, given the medical evidence, as to whether the claimant's condition amounts to disease or disablement; disagreement will generally centre on whether it prevents him carrying out the activities in Sch.2. However, a number of areas can be identified where difficult lines may have to be drawn on whether or not the condition comes within the rubric "disease or . . . disablement" at all. Pregnancy alone does not, but a disease or disablement associated with, but going beyond the normal incidents of, pregnancy does, as in *CS/221/49* where the certified incapacity, "sickness of pregnancy", was suffered throughout the day. See also *R(S) 4/93*. But note now that certain pregnant women are to be treated as incapable of work (see reg.20(e)). Alcoholism can come within the rubric, but in some circumstances might bring about a period of disqualification from benefit (see reg.157). Whether certain conditions constitute a disease of the mind or a mental disablement can be problematical in that the line between a recognisable mental illness or disablement, on the one hand, and states of malingering or being workshy on the other, can be fine and uncertain. The difficulty is to decide from the available evidence whether the claimant is genuinely ill or disabled and thereby incapacitated for work in the sense understood above, or whether his is a voluntary attitude of work shyness where he could but will not work. The problem will be compounded where the outward symptoms of these alternative states are the same. What will be crucial will be the terms in which the medical (psychiatric) evidence is cast, and the inevitable value judgments about whether a particular claimant's attitudes to doing work are voluntary or involuntary. Perhaps here the appellate authorities' jurisdiction to seek further medical (in this case psychiatric) reports at public expense could prove valuable. In *R(S) 6/59*, the Commissioner considered a particular case of Munchausen's syndrome, under which condition a person repeatedly presents himself for treatment to a hospital or series of hospitals recounting symptoms of a particular disease or disability from which he is not in fact suffering, which the Commissioner there described as a strange condition in the nature of malingering. The Commissioner in that case was not satisfied on the evidence that the claimant believed the symptoms actually to exist, and felt unable to regard the condition as a psychosis, which would have come within the statutory rubric. The claim for benefit failed, the Commissioner stating as an additional ground for the decision his view that the syndrome in any event did not affect that particular claimant's capacity to work since he had driven from hospital to hospital in his lorry. In effect, the condition was treated as a defect of character. In *CS/1/81* (noted in [1982] J.S.W.L. 48), the dispute initially centred on whether the claimant, suffering from what the RMO (now a DWP MS doctor) and his own doctor described as an anxiety state, was as a result incapable of work. The consultant psychiatrist to whom the claimant was referred considered him an inadequate personality by reason of his total self-indulgence and extreme degree of sheltering behind psychiatric symptoms to avoid responsibility. His condition resulted from a dismal personality structure rather than illness. Accordingly the Commissioner held that he was incapable of work but not by reason of disease or disablement, so the claim failed. Mesher (now Commissioner Mesher) suggests in [1982] J.S.W.L. 48 that the Commissioner there gave inadequate consideration to whether the defect (clearly on the evidence not an illness) could nevertheless be a mental disablement. In contrast, *CS 7/82* (noted in [1983] J.S.W.L. 306) dealt with a situation in which the claimant was said to have a severe personality disorder but not to be mentally ill. "Personality disorder" is a term sometimes used as a euphemism for workshy. The Commissioner held that its use in the particular case conveyed a notion of disability of mind sufficient to bring the claimant within the statutory rubric. It is submitted that one should avoid using euphemisms which may confuse; the loser in the case is entitled to know why he has lost. If he is thought workshy, that should be stated and reasons given for that conclusion. Sheltering behind euphemisms may also cloud the steps in reasoning which go towards good adjudication and decision-making.

What has to be established, to what standard of proof, and by what evidence, is analysed well by Commissioner Jacobs in *CIB/26/2004*. There must be established, on the civil standard of balance of probabilities, that the claimant has a recognised medical condition (paras 18, 25, citing *R2/99 (IB)*, para.8; *CSDLA/552/2001*, para.27; and *CDLA/944/2001*, paras 9 and 10). A medical diagnosis is useful evidence, but is not decisive in that an appeal tribunal, giving appropriate reasons, can refuse to accept it. The cogency of a diagnosis varies according to a number of factors: the nature of the condition (some being easier to diagnose than others); how well qualified in the relevant area of medicine the doctor is who makes the diagnosis; the range of information and material on which the diagnosis is based; and the degree of certainty with which it is made (e.g. is the diagnosis "firm", or qualified as "working", "presumptive" or "provisional") (para.22). If there is general consensus among medical authorities as to the existence of a particular condition, a tribunal (even one containing a medical member) will normally err in law if, being sceptical, it denies its existence (para.21, citing a Northern Ireland Tribunal of Commissioners in *C38/03–04 (DLA)*, para.20(3)). If a medical diagnosis is not necessarily decisive, nor is the lack of one necessarily fatal; in appropriate circumstances a tribunal can make a diagnosis without medical evidence (para.19). While agreeing to some extent with Commissioner Brown's view (*R 2/99 (IB)*, para.11) that a tribunal should be cautious of making a diagnosis of mental disease or disablement in the absence of supportive medical evidence, Commissioner Jacobs qualified that by noting that at the time of that decision there was no medical member on the tribunal—it merely then had advice from an assessor—that change in composition rendering it easier now for a tribunal to make a diagnosis on the evidence available (para.20).

Paras (3) and (6)

9.44   *Computing the scores:* Like the IB PCA, and its predecessor "all work" test (see Incapacity for Work Regs, reg.25), achievement of a particular score is required before the claimant can be found to have limited capability for work. Under ESA, the scoring system is simpler. The score attained must be at least 15 points whether from Sch.2, Pt 1 alone (physical disabilities), Pt 2 alone (mental, cognitive and intellectual function assessment), or from a combination of the descriptors in both parts. In each case, where more than one descriptor for an activity applies, only the highest scoring one counts (para.(6)). Following the approach to the IB PCA (see commentary to Incapacity for Work Regs, reg.25), it is submitted that there are no implied limits on simply adding together the highest scores from each activity (*R(IB) 3/98*).

Paras (7), (8)

9.45   These make clear that the matters of whether someone actually has limited capability for work, or whether he is to be treated as having it under regs 20, 25, 26, 29 or 33(2), are ones that can be revisited where one or more of the situations in para. (8) arise:

- a desire to determine whether there has been a relevant change of circumstances in relation to the claimant's health condition (is he getting better or worse?) (sub-para.(a);

- a wish to determine whether the prior determination of actual or deemed limited capability was made in ignorance of, or was based on a mistake as to, a material fact (sub-para.(b);

- at least three months have elapsed since the previous decision on actual or deemed limited capability (sub-para.(c)).

Certain claimants to be treated as having limited capability for work

9.46   **20.** A claimant is to be treated as having limited capability for work if—
    (a) the claimant is terminally ill;

(b) the claimant is—
  (i) receiving treatment by way of intravenous, intraperitoneal or intrathecal chemotherapy; or
  (ii) recovering from that treatment and the Secretary of State is satisfied the claimant should be treated as having limited capability for work;
(c) the claimant is—
  (i) excluded or abstains from work, or from work of such a kind, pursuant to a request or notice in writing lawfully made under an enactment; or
  (ii) otherwise prevented from working pursuant to an enactment,
  by reason of the claimant being a carrier, or having been in contact with a case, of a relevant disease;
(d) in the case of a pregnant woman, there is a serious risk of damage to her health or to the health of her unborn child if she does not refrain from work;
(e) in the case of a pregnant woman, she—
  (i) is within the maternity allowance period; and
  (ii) is entitled to a maternity allowance under section 35(1) of the Contributions and Benefits Act;
(f) in the case of a pregnant woman whose expected or actual date of confinement has been certified in accordance with the Medical Evidence Regulations, on any day in the period—
  (i) beginning with the first date of the 6th week before the expected week of her confinement or the actual date of her confinement, whichever is earlier; and
  (ii) ending on the 14th day after the actual date of her confinement,
  if she would have no entitlement to a maternity allowance or statutory maternity pay were she to make a claim in respect of that period.

DEFINITIONS

"claimant"—see WRA 2007, s.24(1).
"confinement"—see reg.2(1).
"Contributions and Benefits Act"—see WRA 2007, s.65.
"limited capability for work"—see WRA 2007, s.1(4).
"maternity allowance period"—see reg.2(1).
"Medical Evidence Regulations"—see reg.2(1).
"terminally ill"—see reg.2(1).
"week"—see reg.2(1).

GENERAL NOTE

This regulation—the parent power for which is WRA 2007, s.22 and Sch.2, para.9—sets out the situations in which a claimant is to be treated as having limited capability for work. This is important because such claimants will be exempt from the WCA and its information gathering processes (see reg.21). In conception, its IB comparator is Incapacity for Work Regs, reg.10. But in terms of detail the provisions are rather different. The IB reg. exempted a much longer group of claimants. In contrast the list in reg.20 is much more curtailed. This is because the ESA tests are designed to assess which claimants can benefit from the help towards work afforded by work-related activity, to "write off" from the chance of work as few people as possible. Those exempt are: **9.47**

- the terminally ill (para.(a))—"suffering from a progressive disease and death in consequence of that disease can reasonably be expected within 6 months" (reg.2(1));

- those receiving treatment by way of intravenous, intraperitoneal or intrathecal chemotherapy (para.(b)(i)); such of those recovering from such treatment as the Secretary of State is satisfied (note the discretion) should be treated as having limited capability for work (para.(b)(ii));

- those excluded or prevented from working as a carrier, or having been in contact with a case of relevant disease (food poisoning, infectious or notifiable diseases covered by a variety of public health enactments) (para. (c));

- pregnant women where there is a serious risk of damage to their or their unborn child's health if they do not refrain from work (para.(d));

- pregnant women at a certain stage in pregnancy (paras (e), (f)). Paragraph (e) covers the pregnant woman during the maternity allowance period (see reg.2(1) and SSCBA 1992, s.35(2)) entitled to a maternity allowance under SSCBA 1992, s.35. Para.(f) in contrast deals with the pregnant woman whose expected or actual date of confinement has been duly certified in accordance with the Medical Evidence Regulations. It covers her during a period beginning with the earlier of the actual date of confinement or the first day of the sixth week before the expected week of confinement and ending on the 14th day after the actual date of confinement. But it does so only where she would not be entitled to maternity allowance or SMP if she were to claim in respect of that period.

Information required for determining capability for work

9.48   **21.**—(1) Subject to paragraphs (2) and (3), the information or evidence required to determine whether a claimant has limited capability for work is—

(a) evidence of limited capability for work in accordance with the Medical Evidence Regulations (which prescribe the form of doctor's statement or other evidence required in each case);

(b) any information relating to a claimant's capability to perform the activities referred to in Schedule 2 as may be requested in the form of a questionnaire; and

(c) any such additional information as may be requested.

(2) Where the Secretary of State is satisfied that there is sufficient information to determine whether a claimant has limited capability for work without the information specified in paragraph (1)(b), that information will not be required for the purposes of making the determination.

(3) Paragraph (1) does not apply in relation to a determination whether a claimant is to be treated as having limited capability for work under any of regulations 20 (certain claimants to be treated as having limited capability for work), 25 (hospital in-patients), 26 (claimants receiving certain regular treatment) and 33(2) (additional circumstances in which a claimant is to be treated as having limited capability for work).

DEFINITIONS

"claimant"—see WRA 2007, s.24(1).
"doctor"—see reg.2(1).
"limited capability for work"—see WRA 2007, s.1(4).
"Medical Evidence Regulations"—see reg.2(1).

GENERAL NOTE

This regulation deals with the information required for determining whether   **9.49**
someone has limited capability for work. It is designed to give the decision-maker
sufficient information to decide that matter for himself (the minority of cases), or
whether to seek advice from a health care professional on the basis of the papers in
respect of that decision, or to refer the claimant for a face to face WCAt, including
a medical examination (see reg.23).

Unless para.(3) operates, the claimant will have to supply: (i) evidence of his incapacity for work in accordance with the Medical Evidence Regs (para.(1)(a)); and
(ii) such additional information relating to the relevant test as the Secretary of State
asks for (para.(1)(c)). Furthermore, he must generally complete and return the
appropriate questionnaire (para.(1)(b)), unless para.(3) operates or the Secretary
of State decides that completion of the questionnaire is not necessary because
without it he has sufficient information to determine whether the claimant does or
does not have limited capability for work (para.(2)). Note that where the claimant is
requested by the Secretary of State to complete and return the questionnaire, failure
to do so can result in his being treated as capable of work (and thus not entitled to
ESA) (reg.22).

Failure to provide information in relation to limited capability for work

22.—(1) Where a claimant fails without good cause to comply with the   **9.50**
request referred to in regulation 21(1)(b), that claimant is, subject to paragraph (2), to be treated as not having limited capability for work.

(2) Paragraph (1) does not apply unless—

(a) at least 6 weeks have passed since the claimant was sent the first
request for the information; and

(b) the claimant was sent a further request at least 4 weeks after the date
of the first request, and at least 2 weeks have passed since the further
request was sent.

DEFINITIONS

"claimant"—see WRA 2007, s.24(1).
"limited capability for work"—see WRA 2007, s.1(4).
"week"—see reg.2(1)

GENERAL NOTE

If a claimant fails without good cause (on which more, below) to comply with   **9.51**
the requirement to complete and return a limited capability for work questionnaire,
he must be treated as not having limited capability for work, that is, as having no
entitlement to ESA. This can only happen, however, if at least six weeks have passed
since the claimant was first sent the request for information, a further request for
information was sent at least four weeks after the first and at least two weeks have
gone by since the second request was sent. The comparably worded IB provision
is Incapacity for Work Regs, reg.7. Commissioners' decisions on that establish that
as regards calculating a period before the end of which something cannot be done
(e.g. "at least six weeks have passed"—para.(2)(a)), one must ignore the day from
which the period runs as well as the day on which it expires (per Commissioner
Jacobs in *R(IB) 1/00*). "Week" here means any period of seven days (reg.2(1)). But
note that the para refers, like the IB provision, to a request being "sent" rather than
"received" (as stressed by Commissioner Rowland in *CIB/3512/1998*). Non-receipt
has, however, an important bearing on "good cause". "Good cause" is not exhaustively defined in legislation, although reg.24 non-exhaustively prescribes certain
matters which must be taken into account in determining the issue. Some guidance

may be found in authorities on the corresponding area in unemployment benefit (see USI Regs, regs 7(1)(i), (j)—see pp.720–21 of Bonner, Hooker and White, *Non Means Tested Benefits: The Legislation* (1996)), the matter of relief from disqualification from sickness and invalidity benefit under the now revoked USI Regs, reg.17 (see pp.737–740 of the 1994 edition of *Non- Means Tested Benefits, The Legislation*), and that from disqualification/being treated as incapable under Incapacity for Work Regs, reg.18 or, in time, reg.157 of these ESA Regs. Some assistance may be derived from disqualification from unemployment benefit under the now repealed SSCBA 1992, s.28, but caution must be exercised because both that section itself and the now revoked USI Regs 12E set statutory limits to the concept applicable only for the purposes of that section, since use was made there of a power to circumscribe and define good cause (see pp.133–34, 143–44, 150, and 752–56 of *Non Means Tested Benefits: The Legislation* 1996). A similar power exists in this context (WRA 2007, s.8(4)) but has not yet been exercised other than as set out in reg.24.

Claimant may be called for a medical examination to determine whether the claimant has limited capability for work

9.52 **23.**—(1) Where it falls to be determined whether a claimant has limited capability for work, that claimant may be called by or on behalf of a health care professional approved by the Secretary of State to attend for a medical examination.

(2) Subject to paragraph (3), where a claimant fails without good cause to attend for or to submit to an examination listed in paragraph (1), the claimant is to be treated as not having limited capability for work.

(3) Paragraph (2) does not apply unless written notice of the time and place for the examination was sent to the claimant at least 7 days in advance, or unless that claimant agreed to accept a shorter period of notice whether given in writing or otherwise.

DEFINITIONS

"claimant"—see WRA 2007, s.24(1).
"health care professional"—see reg.2(1).
"limited capability for work"—see WRA 2007, s.1(4).

GENERAL NOTE

9.53 This regulation enables the DWP to have a claimant medically examined by a DWP Medical Service (DWPMS) health service professional (technically any health service professional approved by the Secretary of State) when a question arises as to the claimant's capability for work. Failure without good cause to attend for or submit to such an examination, of which he was given proper written notice (see para.(3)), will result in the claimant being treated as not having limited capability for work and not entitled to ESA.

This reg. is directly comparable to Incapacity for Work Regs, reg.8 and the approach taken here is that authorities on that and analogous regulations are applicable here.

Note that proper written notice means written notice of the time and place of the examination, sent to him at least seven days beforehand, unless the person agreed to accept a shorter period of notice, whether given in writing or otherwise. Interpreted by analogy with the approach to another time period issue in *R(IB)2/00*, para.(3) requires at least seven days' clear notice so that neither the day of sending nor that of receipt count in determining that period (*CIB/2576/2007*, para.6). The notice may be given by or on behalf of the approved (generally DWPMS) health care professional concerned (para.(1)). The notice must, however, be written. So, where an appointment had been made over the telephone by leaving a message with the claimant's sister, which the claimant asserted was not passed on, he could not properly be treated as capable of work for not having attended without good cause, since the regulation's clear requisite of written notice had not been satisfied (see *CIB/969/97*). In *R(IB) 1/01*, Commissioner Rowland considered that where, when a claimant stated that he would not be able to attend a medical examination, the Department in consequence said they would cancel it, the claimant cannot be held not to have attended it. If, however, a claimant makes it clear that he or she will not be medically examined, then that arguably constitutes failure to "submit to" an examination. Going to the medical examination but refusing to be examined, constitutes attendance but also a failure to submit. In *CIB/849/2001*, Commissioner Turnbull stated:

"The purpose of the medical examination was of course to enable the adjudica-tion officer, with the benefit of the doctor's report, to determine whether the Claimant passed the all work test. The condition which the Claimant wished to impose on his submitting to an examination—i.e. that the doctor's report should not be passed to any layman, including an adjudication officer—rendered an examination useless for the purpose for which it was required. I have no doubt that, by imposing such a condition, the Claimant was failing to submit himself to a medical examination within the meaning of reg.8(2) [by analogy ESA Regs, reg.23(2)]. A person 'fails' to submit himself to an examination not only if he absolutely refuses to be examined, but also if he seeks to impose as a condition of being examined a term which would render the examination useless for the purpose for which it is required" (para.11).

The nature and extent of the medical examination to which the claimant must submit is a matter for the examining health care professional rather than the claim-ant, tribunal or Commissioner, "fundamentally a medical matter and for the judg-ment of the clinician in each individual case" (*C1/07–08(IB)*, para.12). The health care professional's demands of the claimant must, however, fall within the bounds of a "medical examination" and there remains the issue of whether a claimant has good cause for refusing to submit to the examination (*C1/07–08(IB)*, para.15).

A health care professional can insist on the presence of a suitable chaperone (e.g. a DWP employee bound by confidentiality not to broadcast details to the world at large), and unreasonable refusal to allow such a chaperone to be present constitutes refusing to submit to the examination (*CIB/2645/99*; *CIB/2011/2001*, para.15). Claimants cannot expect their medical details to be kept from those who must determine their claims; those who insist on strict medical confidentiality can do so, but only at the cost of foregoing their rights to benefit or credits (*CIB/2011/2001*, para.15). In *CIB/1381/2003*, Deputy Commissioner Wikeley declined, after review-ing a range of authority on analogous provisions in child support and jobseeker's allowance, to determine whether "sent" meant "despatched" or "delivered", since a failure to attend because of not receiving the notice could in any event constitute "good cause" as the tribunal had held. In *CSIB/721/2004*, however, Commissioner Parker was of the view that where the claimant proved that the notification duly despatched (a matter for the Secretary of State to establish) had not in fact been received by him, in the ordinary course of post or at all, then it had not been "sent" within the meaning of para.(3), thus precluding treating the claimant as capable of work for "failure to attend or submit to examination" so that the issue of "good cause" never arose. She there took account of a Secretary of State concession on the point noted in *CIB/4512/2002* (not on the Commissioners' website), to which the Secretary of State's representative referred her. But in contrast note that Commissioner Rowland in *CIB/3512/1998*,dealing with an analogous Incapacity for Work Reg., stressed that it said "sent" rather than "received", albeit that non-receipt would be a matter as regards "good cause".

The Northern Ireland decision *C11/03–04(IB)* is a useful reminder of the need to ascertain the precise facts and be careful in applying to them the concept of "good cause". The case concerned a common "defence", where the claimant alleged he had never received a particular letter sent by the Department, a typical case of conflict of evidence. Deputy Commissioner Powell thought that sometimes it is right to reject such allegations in a robust manner, for example, where the excuse extends to a number of letters, or is coupled with suspicious circumstances, or if the non-receipt of mail is selective so that only certain letters are not received. The case before him, however, concerned a rather different situation—the uncontradicted evidence of the claimant, who did not attend the appeal hearing, of the non-receipt of a single letter in plausible circumstances, namely, a communal delivery of mail to particular premises and the possibility that another went through it before the claimant had a chance to do so. The Commissioner could not see how an effective challenge could be mounted to the claim and that, in these circumstances, the claimant had established good cause. The Secretary of State bears the burden of proof in establishing that the requirements of para.(3) have been met, a precondition for being able to find the claimant capable of work for non-attendance etc. In *CIB/4012/2004*, deputy Commissioner Mark, considering the cases noted above, found that the burden had not been discharged. Computer records showing that a letter had been issued were not sufficient evidence of it being "sent". He said helpfully:

"I can see no reason why, in establishing whether the requirements of regulation 8(3) have been met, the secretary of state cannot provide a simple short written statement from the appropriate person giving the date on which the written notice was posted, the time at least to an extent sufficient to show whether or not it would have been collected that day by Royal Mail from the post box, and the address to which it was posted, and also stating whether it was sent by first or second class post. The statement should also confirm that the letter has not been returned undelivered. It appears to me that in future there should be evidence available from the secretary of state dealing with those issues before a decision-maker comes to a decision. If it is not stated whether first or second class post was used, the decision-maker should either seek further evidence or assume that second class post was used. If there is a further issue as to whether it was posted to the correct address, as in this case where there has been a change of address, the secretary of state will normally need better evidence of the address to which it was posted than a later computer generated print out showing the address on the file at that later date" (paras 21–22).

The effect of a finding of lack of good cause precludes benefit until a new claim is submitted and a new period of incapacity for work begins (para.6 of the decision). It may also prevent the claimant being treated under reg.30 as incapable of work pending a limited capability for work assessment. However, if the claimant is found to have limited capability for work in that assessment, benefit can be backdated to the beginning of the period covered by the new claim or application. See also on this aspect *R(IB)2/01* and para.8 of *CIB/3512/1998*. On "good cause", see the commentary to reg.22 and note the non-exhaustive prescription in reg.24 of matters which must be taken into account in determining good cause. If it was unreasonable of the Secretary of State to arrange a medical examination, the claimant can argue that he had good cause for refusing to submit to it (*CIB/2645/99*; *CIB/2011/2001*, para.16). But since, as Commissioner Rowland stressed, "the integrity of the system depends upon their being appropriate tests in place" (*CIB/2011/2001*, para.16), establishing unreasonableness is unlikely to be easy.

Matters to be taken into account in determining good cause in relation to regulations 22 or 23

9.54   **24.** The matters to be taken into account in determining whether a claimant has good cause under regulations 22 (failure to provide information in relation to limited capability for work) or 23 (failure to attend a medical examination to determine limited capability for work) include—

    (a) whether the claimant was outside Great Britain at the relevant time;

(b) the claimant's state of health at the relevant time; and
(c) the nature of any disability the claimant has.

DEFINITION

"claimant"—see WRA 2007, s.24(1).

GENERAL NOTE

This regulation, made pursuant to WRA 2007, s.8(4), stipulates that in deter-   9.55
mining whether someone had good cause for failing to provide information (under
reg.22) or for failing to attend for or submit to a medical examination (under
reg.23) decision-makers and appellate bodies must take into account (i) whether
the person was outside Great Britain at the relevant time, (ii) his state of health
at the relevant time, and (iii) the nature of his disability. This list is not, however,
exhaustive (the regulation says "shall include"). On "good cause", see further the
commentary to regs 22 and 23.

Hospital in-patients

25.—(1) A claimant is to be treated as having limited capability for work   9.56
on any day on which that claimant is undergoing medical or other treatment as an in-patient in a hospital or similar institution, or which is a day of
recovery from that treatment.

(2) For the purposes of this regulation, "day of recovery" means a day on
which a claimant is recovering from treatment as an in-patient in a hospital or
equivalent under paragraph (1) and the Secretary of State is satisfied that the
claimant should be treated as having limited capability for work on that day.

DEFINITIONS

"claimant"—see WRA 2007, s.24(1).
"day of recovery"—see para.(2).
"limited capability for work"—see WRA 2007, s.1(4).
"medical treatment"—see reg.2(1).

GENERAL NOTE

This regulation is comparable to, but goes a little further than, Incapacity for Work   9.57
Regs, reg.12. Like that regulation, it stipulates that those undergoing medical or other
treatment as an in-patient of a hospital or other institution, must be treated as having
limited capability for work on any day on which they are undergoing that treatment.
The notion of "undergoing . . . treatment" is not defined. Note, however, that a
prolonged stay in hospital (more than 52 weeks) results in benefit being reduced: see
Hospital In-patients Regulations. Where this regulation goes further is that it also
treats the person as having limited capability for work on any day of recovery from
that treatment. "Day of recovery" is defined in para.(2). Note the discretion given
to the Secretary of State—the day on which the former in-patient is recovering from
that treatment will only count if the Secretary of State is satisfied that it the claimant
should on that day be treated as having limited capability for work.

Regulation 21(1) (information gathering requirements) does not apply to a determination under this regulation (see reg.21(3)).

Claimants receiving certain regular treatment

26.—(1) Subject to paragraph (2), a claimant receiving—   9.58
(a) regular weekly treatment by way of haemodialysis for chronic renal
failure;

(b) treatment by way of plasmapheresis or by way of radiotherapy; or
(c) regular weekly treatment by way of total parenteral nutrition for gross impairment of enteric function,
is to be treated as having limited capability for work during any week in which that claimant is engaged in that treatment or has a day of recovery from that treatment.

[¹(2) A claimant who receives the treatment referred to in paragraph (1) is only to be treated as having limited capability for work from the first week of treatment in which the claimant undergoes no fewer than—
(a) two days of treatment;
(b) two days of recovery from any of the forms of treatment listed in paragraph 1(a) to (c); or
(c) one day of treatment and one day of recovery from that treatment,
but the days of treatment or recovery from that treatment or both need not be consecutive.]

(3) For the purpose of this regulation "day of recovery" means a day on which a claimant is recovering from any of the forms of treatment listed in paragraph (1)(a) to (c) and the Secretary of State is satisfied that the claimant should be treated as having limited capability for work on that day.

AMENDMENTS

1. Employment and Support Allowance (Miscellaneous Amendments) Regulations 2008 (SI 2008/2428), reg.5(1) (October 27, 2008).

DEFINITIONS

"claimant"—see WRA 2007, s.24(1).
"day of recovery"—see para.(3).
"limited capability for work"—see WRA 2007, s.1(4).
"week"—see WRA 2007, s.24(1); reg.2(1).

GENERAL NOTE

9.59   This regulation has similarities with Incapacity for Work Regs, reg.13, but is narrower in the range of treatments covered and its wording reflects that ESA is a weekly rather than, as with IB, a daily benefit.

Someone undergoing certain treatments is treated as having limited capability for work on during any week in which he is engaged in that treatment or has a day of recovery from that treatment (para.(1)). The treatments concerned are: regular weekly treatment by way of haemodialysis for chronic renal failure (para.(1)(a)); treatment by way of plasmapheresis or by way of radiotherapy (para.(1)(b); or regular weekly treatment by way of total parenteral nutrition for gross impairment of enteric function (para.(1)(c)). "Day of recovery" is defined in para.(3) as one on which the claimant is recovering from any of the forms of treatment so long as the Secretary of State (note the discretion) is satisfied that the claimant should be treated as having limited capability for work on that day. Paragraph (2) deals with the first week of any such treatment. During that week, the claimant can only be treated as having limited capability for work if in that week he undergoes no fewer than two days of treatment, or two days of recovery from such treatment or one day of treatment and one day of recovery. The days of treatment or recovery from it need not be consecutive.

Regulation 21(1) (information gathering requirements) does not apply to a determination under this regulation (see reg.21(3)).

Claimant to be treated as having limited capability for work throughout a day

27. A claimant who at the commencement of any day has, or thereafter develops, limited capability for work as determined in accordance with the limited capability for work assessment is to be treated as having limited capability for work throughout that day.

9.60

DEFINITIONS

"claimant"—see WRA 2007, s.24(1).
"limited capability for work"—see WRA 2007, s.1(4).
"limited capability for work assessment"—see reg.2(1).

GENERAL NOTE

The situation encompassed here in which someone is to be treated as having limited capability for work, confers no exemption from the information gathering processes for the limited capability for work assessment (reg.21(3)).

9.61

This regulation is analogous to Incapacity for Work Regs, reg.15 and its predecessor (USI Regs, reg.3(2); see pp.688, 690 of Bonner, Hooker and White, *Non Means Tested Benefits: The Legislation* 1994). It is submitted that authorities on those provisions are also applicable to its interpretation and application.

The effect of this regulation is that those with limited capability for work at the start of a day or who thereafter develop it on that day are to be treated as having limited capability for work throughout that day. In *CIB/6244/1997*, Commissioner Jacobs considered the application of the IB regulation to intermittent and variable conditions. He considered that the provision must be read in the light that, under the all work test/PCA and its descriptors, one cannot confine consideration merely to a particular time on a particular day—otherwise a claimant could always satisfy the "cannot" descriptors and the "sometimes" ones (not in any event in the ESA limited capability for work assessment activities and descriptors) would never apply. The "cannot" and "sometimes" descriptors inevitably require a focus over a period and not at a specific moment in time. Thus he thought that Incapacity for Work Regs, reg.15 "does not operate to ensure that a claimant with a variable condition that incapacitates him for a part of each day must be considered as incapable throughout the whole of every day" (para.23).However, it will "apply where there is a sudden onset of or recovery from an incapacitating condition, including an intermittent incapacitating condition or the incapacitating intermittent features of a condition" (*ibid.* and see also *CIB/15482/1996*, paras 7–9). In *CIB/243/1998*. Deputy Commissioner Mark considered that a claimant who suffered an asthma attack for part of a day had to be treated as incapable of work throughout that day under this regulation, provided that the effect of the attack when ongoing was such that he would score at least 15 points for more than a minimal period on that day. In *CIB/399/2003*, Commissioner Mesher very firmly rejected that approach of Deputy Commissioner Mark in *CIB/243/1998* and preferred the approach taken by Commissioner Jacobs in *CIB/6244/1997* and by Deputy Commissioner Ramsay in *CIB/15482/1996*, thus establishing a strong line of authority against Deputy Commissioner Mark's view of the application of Incapacity for Work Regs, reg.15. Commissioner Mesher thought the rejected approach to be inconsistent with the concept of "reasonable regularity" applicable to the "cannot" descriptors and out of tune with the tenor of *R(IB)2/99(T)* (on which see further the commentary to Sch.2).

Night workers

28.—(1) Where a claimant works for a continuous period which extends over midnight into the following day, that claimant is to be treated as having limited capability for work on the day on which the lesser part of that

9.62

period falls if that claimant had limited capability for work for the remainder of that day.

(2) Where, in relation to a period referred to in paragraph (1), the number of hours worked before and after midnight is equal—

(a) if the days in question fall at the beginning of a period of limited capability for work, the claimant is to be treated as having limited capability on the second day; and

(b) if the days in question fall at the end of a period of limited capability for work, the claimant is to be treated as having limited capability for work on the first day.

DEFINITIONS

"claimant"—see WRA 2007, s.24(1).
"limited capability for work"—see WRA 2007, s.1(4).
"period of limited capability for work"—see reg.2(1).

GENERAL NOTE

9.63   This is analogous to IB Regulations, reg.5 and its predecessors in the sickness and invalidity benefits regime. Although unlike IB and those benefits, ESA is a weekly rather than a daily benefit, there is still need to be able to attribute limited capability for work to a particular day, where the person doing nightwork has a shift spanning midnight and thus covering two days. The ESA scheme in some circumstances permits awards for periods of less than a week (the amount payable being determined under regs 165–169) (e.g. the period at the start or end of a claim; persons receiving certain regular treatments). Although the ESA scheme neither in Act or Regs defines "day", the general rule for benefit purposes has been that a day is the period midnight to midnight, and performance of work on a day will generally preclude the week in which it is done ranking as one of entitlement to ESA (see reg.40(1)). But there are exceptions to that preclusive rule (regs 40(4), 46) where the preclusion is only to affect the day(s) actually worked. There is thus a need to attribute a nightshift spanning two days to one day or the other. Otherwise, the application of the rules to nightworkers whose shifts span midnight could cause hardship since they would, without this regulation, be regarded as working on two days and thus be treated less favourably than their day worker counterparts whose shift of exactly the same length (period of work) would be attributed to one day. Equally, even though the nightworker suffered the same degree of limited capability for work on one of those days, the day could not count as one of limited capability for work This regulation attempts some easing of the position of nightworkers in this regard.

Paragraph (1) provides that where someone works for a continuous period beginning one day and spanning midnight into the following day, the day on which there falls the lesser part of the period worked will be treated as one of limited capability for work if the claimant has limited capability for work for the rest of that day. To put it another way, the day with the longer period worked is to be treated for the purpose of the exceptions to the preclusive rules noted above as the day of work. Paragraph (2) deals with the situation in which the hours worked each side of midnight are equal. If the two days in question fall at the beginning of a period of limited capability for work, the second day is to be treated as one of incapacity and the first as the one of work. If the two days fall at the end of a period of incapacity for work, the first day is the one to be regarded as a day of limited capability for work and the second as the one of work.

Exceptional circumstances

9.64   **29.**—(1) A claimant who does not have limited capability for work as determined in accordance with the limited capability for work assessment is to be treated as having limited capability for work if paragraph (2) applies to the claimant.

(2) This paragraph applies if—

(a) the claimant is suffering from a life threatening disease in relation to which—

   (i) there is medical evidence that the disease is uncontrollable, or uncontrolled, by a recognised therapeutic procedure; and

   (ii) in the case of a disease that is uncontrolled, there is a reasonable cause for it not to be controlled by a recognised therapeutic procedure; or

(b) the claimant suffers from some specific disease or bodily or mental disablement and, by reasons of such disease or disablement, there would be a substantial risk to the mental or physical health of any person if the claimant were found not to have limited capability for work.

DEFINITIONS

"claimant"—see WRA 2007, s.24(1).
"limited capability for work"—see WRA 2007, s.1(4).
"limited capability for work assessment"—see reg.2(1).
"medical evidence"—see reg.2(1).

GENERAL NOTE

This has affinities with Incapacity for Work Regs, reg.27, and insofar as that is so, case authorities on equivalent terms in that reg. are applicable to the interpretation and application of this one. Of no relevance at all, however, to those questions are the authorities on the matter of whether changes sought to be made in 1997 to reg.27 were invalid as procedurally ultra vires. The precise terms of reg.27 have, of course, caused problems of interpretation and application since its inception, and issues about some of its provisions are still before the Court of Appeal and will be relevant to the interpretation and application of the comparable terms in this ESA regulation.   **9.65**

Like reg.27 in the IB scheme, this regulation reflects the fact that functional assessment systems like the IB PCA or the ESA WCAt would not properly measure the incapacitating effect of certain conditions, and so would "fail" some people who properly ought to be regarded as being incapable of work (IB) or having limited capability for work (ESA). Headed "exceptional circumstances", the regulation envisages two classes of case in which someone not assessed as having limited capability for work can nonetheless be treated as having it.

The first situation is where the claimant suffers from a life threatening disease (the IB requirement that it be "severe" is not continued into ESA) which medical evidence establishes is uncontrollable by a recognized therapeutic procedure or (but only with reasonable cause) is uncontrolled by such a procedure (para.(2)(a)). Dealing with the substantially similarly worded IB provision in *CIB/4506/01*, Commissioner Howell stated that here:

> "the question is only whether the nature of [the claimant's] condition is such that it is capable of being controlled by medical science, or not. Consequently the tribunal were right in taking account not only of the inhalers and adrenaline injector she is able to use for herself, but also the hospital treatment which unhappily she finds also has to be used on occasions as a means of bringing the condition under control. On the tribunal's findings the claimant's condition is thus controllable in the relevant sense, and their reasons are clearly and adequately given" (para.10).

The tribunal had not erred in law.

In *CIB/155/2004*, Commissioner Jacobs thought it inappropriate to deploy as a test whether the level of control would suffice to allow the claimant to work; since that test would always be satisfied. Rather, he thought that IB reg.27 [ESA reg.29] comes into play where a claimant is capable of work but has a condition that makes it inappropriate that he be expected to work. Since, as regards para.(2)(a) what makes that inappropriate is the fact that the condition is a threat to the claimant's life, the threshold for control should be whether the control is sufficient to remove the threat to the claimant's life. In the case at hand, while the evidence disclosed that the claimant's diabetes was poorly controlled, it was nonetheless sufficiently controlled that para.(2)(a) was inapplicable. While there were longer-term complications to which the Consultant referred, they were not yet present, and not currently threatening the claimant's life.

The term "medical evidence" embraces (i) evidence from a health care professional approved by the Secretary of State, (ii) evidence (if any) from any other health care professional, hospital or similar institution, or such part of evidence in (i) or (ii) as constitutes the most reliable evidence available in the circumstances (reg.2(1)). "Health care professional" covers a registered medical practitioner, a registered nurse or an occupational therapist or physiotherapist registered with a regulatory body established by an Order in Council under section 60 of the Health Act 1999 (reg.2(1). In a Northern Ireland decision *C5/00–01(IB)* Commissioner Brown stressed that the evidence "must relate to the claimant himself, it is not constituted by extracts from medical textbooks unless the doctor relates them to the claimant" (para.16).

The second class of case in which someone not assessed as having limited capability for work can nonetheless be treated as having it, concerns a claimant, suffering from some specific disease or bodily or mental disablement, and by reason of such there would be substantial risk to the mental or physical health of any person if the claimant were found not to have limited capability for work (para.(2)(b)). The scheme thus carries into ESA something the Department had tried unsuccessfully to remove as regards IB in 1997.

On "specific disease or bodily or mental disablement", see the commentary to reg.19.

The meaning of "substantial risk to the mental or physical health of any person if the claimant were found not to have limited capability for work" has produced a number of Commissioners' decisions, some of which conflict. "Substantial" does not only refer to the likelihood of the risk occurring: "a risk may be 'substantial' if the harm would be serious, even though it was unlikely to occur and, conversely, may not be 'substantial' if the harm would be insignificant, even though the likelihood of some such harm is great. Paragraph (b) must be viewed in the light of the other paragraphs of regulation 27 and the general scheme of the Regulations" (para.7).

Commissioner Fellner accepted this as "probably right" in *CIB/2767/2004*, but added that:

> "his invocation of the other paragraphs of regulation 27 as guides to interpretation suggests that the interpretation should be rather narrow. Under the original as well as the amended form, the other paragraphs refer to more or less factual medical questions—presence of life-threatening or severe uncontrolled or uncontrollable disease, need for an identified major medical procedure within a short time" (para.6).

Whether "substantial risk to health" had to be evaluated against specific employments or in the abstract generated a number of conflicting Commissioners' decisions on IFW Regs, reg.27(b), but its meaning and the approach to take to its application has now been resolved by the Court of Appeal in *Charlton v Secretary of State for Work and Pensions* [2009] EWCA Civ 42 (the appeal from the decision of Commissioner Williams in *CIB/143/2007*) in judgments that make it clear that they apply also to the same terms in the relevant ESA Regulations.

Regulation 29(2)((b) requires a decision firstly that a person suffers as a consequence of some specific disease or bodily or mental disablement which does not of itself cause such functional limitation as to justify a total score warranting a finding of limited capability for work; it can only come into play where it has been found that the claimant does not have limited capability for work under the LCWA. It requires, secondly, a decision on whether because of the disease or disablement there would be a substantial risk to the mental or physical health of any person if the claimant were found capable of work (*Charlton*, para.30). The risk to be assessed must arise as a consequence of work the claimant would be found capable of undertaking, but for reg.29 (*Charlton*, para.33). Paragraph 2(b) might be satisfied

> "where the very finding of capability might create a substantial risk to a claimant's health or that of others, for example when a claimant suffering from anxiety or depression might suffer a significant deterioration on being told that the benefit claimed was being refused. Apart from that, probably rare, situation, the determination must be made in the context of the journey to or from work or in the workplace itself" (*Charlton*, para.34).

The Court held that the correct approach to identifying the nature of the relevant work and workplace for the claimant was that identified with respect to IFW Regs, reg.27(b) in paras 17-18 of Deputy Commissioner Paines' decision in *CIB/360/2007*. It rejected the view that decision-makers and tribunals had to speculate as to the type of job which would have been set out for purposes of a JSA claim in a hypothetical Jobseeker's Agreement. Rather (reading Personal Capability Assessment as LCWA):

> "The decision-maker must assess the range or type of work which a claimant is capable of performing sufficiently to assess the risk to health either to himself or to others.
>
> Sufficient information may be elicited by reference to the claimant's completion of the initial questionnaire, questioning during his medical examination, or by any evidence he may choose to give on an appeal to the Tribunal. The process to be adopted by the decision-maker or Tribunal is to be regarded as inquisitorial and not adversarial. It is a process described by Diplock J in *R v Medical Appeal Tribunal (North Midland Region ex-parte Hubble)* 1958 2 QB 228 at 240 as a fact-gathering exercise in which there is no formal burden of proof on either side. There should be no difficulty provided the decision-maker or Tribunal recall that the essential question is whether there is an adequate range of work which the claimant could undertake without creating a substantial risk to himself or to others.
>
> This conclusion is consistent with the practical application of these regulations. Any interpretation must bear in mind that the regulations are designed to provide a fair and effective system for assessing entitlement to incapacity benefit and to allied benefits when a claimant has passed the Personal Capability Assessment. It would not be possible to achieve the aim of those regulations were the decision-maker to be required to make findings of the particularity for which the claimant contends. The decision-maker, it must be recalled, will be provided only with the report of the doctor based upon the doctor's interview with the claimant and the claimant's completion of the questionnaire. It is quite impossible for the decision-maker to identify actual positions of employment or the nature of the duties and location of any job which the claimant might undertake, not least because the decision-maker may often be based in Belfast, or elsewhere, and can have no possible means of discovering employment circumstances throughout the country. The conclusion which requires no more than that the decision-maker or Tribunal assess the range of work of which the claimant is capable for the purposes of assessing risk to health has the merit of achieving the objective of the regulations" (*Charlton*, paras 45-47).

The Court upheld Commissioner Williams' finding that Mr Charlton was capable of performing the kind of work:-

". . . to which a person with no physical limitations, no qualifications, no skills and no experience might be directed ([section] 48) and that he could undertake straightforward and unstructured, unskilled work."

Conditions for treating a claimant as having limited capability for work until a determination about limited capability for work has been made

9.66   **30.**—(1) A claimant is, if the conditions set out in paragraph (2) are met, to be treated as having limited capability for work until such time as it is determined—
  (a) whether or not the claimant has limited capability for work;
  (b) whether or not the claimant is to be treated as having limited capability for work otherwise than in accordance with this regulation; or
  (c) whether the claimant falls to be treated as not having limited capability for work in accordance with regulation 22 (failure to provide information in relation to limited capability for work) or 23 (failure to attend a medical examination to determine limited capability for work).
  (2) The conditions are—
  (a) that the claimant provides evidence of limited capability for work in accordance with the Medical Evidence Regulations; and
  (b) that it has not, within the 6 months preceding the date of claim, been determined, in relation to the claimant's entitlement to any benefit, allowance or advantage which is dependent on the claimant having limited capability for work, that the claimant does not have limited capability for work or is to be treated as not having limited capability for work under regulation 22 or 23 unless—
    (i) the claimant is suffering from some specific disease or bodily or mental disablement from which the claimant was not suffering at the time of that determination;
    (ii) a disease or bodily or mental disablement from which the claimant was suffering at the time of that determination has significantly worsened; or
    (iii) in the case of a claimant who was treated as not having limited capability for work under regulation 22 (failure to provide information), the claimant has since provided the information requested under that regulation.
  (3) Paragraph (2)(b) does not apply where a claimant has made and is pursuing an appeal against a decision that embodies a determination that the claimant does not have limited capability for work and that appeal has not yet been determined by an appeal tribunal constituted under Chapter 1 of Part 1 of the Social Security Act 1998.

DEFINITIONS

"claimant"—see WRA 2007, s.24(1).
"limited capability for work"—see WRA 2007, s.1(4).
"Medical Evidence Regulations"—see reg.2(1).

GENERAL NOTE

This has affinities with Incapacity for Work Regs, reg.28, and it is submitted that   9.67
case authorities on that are applicable to the interpretation and application of this
regulation.

Like that IB provision, this regulation, in the circumstances set out in para.(2),
treats the claimant as having limited capability for work (thus grounding eligibility for ESA) until: (a) the matter of actual capability is determined in accordance with the work capability assessment (WCAt) under reg.19 and Sch.2); (b)
it is decided whether some other "treated as having limited capability for work"
regulation applies (e.g. person receiving certain regular treatment); or (c) a decision is made that, as a sanction for non-compliance with information gathering
or medical examination aspects of the assessment process under regs 22 and 23,
he is to be treated as not having limited capability for work and thus disentitled
to ESA.

In short, if, but only if, para.(2) applies will the claimant be treated as having
limited capability for work. So it will be treated as satisfied only while the person
continues to provide a doctor's statement in accordance with the Medical Evidence
Regs (see further those regulations and the commentary to them), and, save in
appeal cases covered by para.(3), only if there has been no determination in the last
six months that he is capable of work or that he is to be treated as capable of work
for such failures to comply with those aspects of the process. Determination here
covers one in relation to any benefit, allowance or advantage (e.g. contributions
credits) dependent on the claimant having limited capability for work. If there has
been such a determination, however, benefit can still be paid pending assessment
if the specific disease or bodily or mental disablement from which he suffered at
the time of that earlier determination has significantly worsened or the one(s) he
is now suffering from is (are) different; or, if treated as capable because of failure
to supply claims information (reg.22), he has since complied with the Secretary of
State's requests. The supply of medical certificates will thus continue to be required
to support a claim.

Useful clarification of the operation of the comparable IB regulation has
been given by Commissioner Rowland in *CIB/3106/2003* and by Commissioner
Howells in *R(IB) 8/04*. Where the six-month period mentioned has expired, there
is no need to make a new claim to take advantage of the protection of the regulation. It should be considered by the decision-maker as a change of circumstances
(*CIB/3106/2003*, para.5). Moreover, where, on a claim for limited capability for
work, the decision-maker decides that the claimant cannot be treated as having
limited capability under the regulation pending assessment, the decision-maker
must still arrange a limited capability for work assessment (WCAt) to determine
the *actual* capability. If the result of that assessment was limited capability for work
arrears of benefit will be payable from the date of claim. As explained in *R(IB)
1/01* and *R(IB) 2/01*, the purpose of the regulation is simply to enable payment of
benefit pending assessment and irrespective of the results of that assessment (*ibid.*,
para.6). In contrast, where the period of six months since a previous determination has not expired, the regulation can only come into play where one of the conditions in para.(2)(b)(i)–(iii) are met, for example, that the claimant is suffering
from some fresh disease or disablement, or a significant worsening of an existing
disease or disablement, since the date of that determination (the determination by
the Secretary of State, not the date of a tribunal decision confirming it on appeal)
(*R(IB) 8/04*).

Since the regulation only applies until the claimant has been "assessed", it
cannot apply where the claimant is immediately assessed (*CIB/1959/1997 and
CIB/2198/1997*, paras 28, 29).

The words "significantly worsened", as regards the claimant's condition, must be
related to the limited capability for work assessment (WCAt), so that it will only have
significantly worsened if it has done so to an extent that the claimant would satisfy

that test of limited capability for work if he were subjected to it. If there is actual evidence that he would fail to satisfy that test, the Secretary of State can proceed on the basis that the condition has not significantly worsened (*CIB/1959/1977 and CIB/2198/1997*, para.30).

On "specific disease or bodily or mental disablement", see commentary to reg.19.

Paragraph (3) deals with the situation where a claimant is appealing a determination that he does not have limited capability for work. In this situation, supplying medical certificates evidencing limited capability for work will preserve the claimant's position. He is to be treated under para.(1) as having limited capability for work until the appeal has been determined—the "last six months" provisions in para.(2)(b) do not apply (para.(3)).

Claimant who claims jobseeker's allowance to be treated as not having limited capability for work

9.68

31.—(1) A claimant who—

(a) claims a jobseeker's allowance; and

(b) is able to show a reasonable prospect of obtaining employment,
    is, throughout the period of that claim, to be treated as not having limited capability for work.

(2) Paragraph (1) applies even though it has been determined that the claimant—

(a) has limited capability for work; or

(b) is to be treated as having limited capability for work under any of regulations 20 (certain claimants to be treated as having limited capability for work), 25 (hospital in-patients), 26 (claimants undergoing certain regular treatment) or 29 (exceptional circumstances).

DEFINITIONS

"claimant"—see WRA 2007, s.24(1).
"employment"—see reg.2(1).
"limited capability for work"—see WRA 2007, s.1(4).

GENERAL NOTE

9.69

This maintains a boundary between ESA and JSA; one can have one or the other but not both (WRA 2007, s.1(1)(f)). This regulation makes clear that days when one claims JSA and has a reasonable prospect of employment do not rank as ones of limited capability for work (para.(1)). The preclusion applies even where someone has been found to have limited capability for work in accordance with the limited capability for work assessment (WCAt)) (para.(2)(a)), or is treated as having limited capability for work under the regulations specified in para.(2)(b).

Certain claimants to be treated as not having limited capability for work

9.70

32. [¹(1)] A claimant [²who is or has been a member of Her Majesty's Forces] is to be treated as not having limited capability for work on any day which is recorded by the Secretary of State for Defence as a day of sickness absence from duty.

[³(2) A claimant is to be treated as not having limited capability for work on any day on which the claimant attends a training course in respect of which the claimant is paid a training allowance or premium pursuant to arrangements made under section 2 of the Employment and Training Act 1973 or section 2(3) of the Enterprise and New Towns (Scotland) Act 1990.

(3) Paragraph (2) is not to apply—

(a) for the purposes of any claim to employment and support allowance for a period commencing after the claimant ceased attending the training course in question; or

(b) where any training allowance or premium paid to the claimant is paid for the sole purpose of travelling or meal expenses incurred or to be incurred under the arrangement made under section 2 of the Employment and Training Act 1973 or section 2(3) of the Enterprise and New Towns (Scotland) Act 1990.]

AMENDMENTS

1. Employment and Support Allowance (Miscellaneous Amendments) Regulations 2008 (SI 2008/2428), reg.5(2)(a) (October 27, 2008).
2. Employment and Support Allowance (Miscellaneous Amendments) Regulations 2008 (SI 2008/2428), reg.5(2)(b) (October 27, 2008).
3. Employment and Support Allowance (Miscellaneous Amendments) Regulations 2008 (SI 2008/2428), reg.5(2)(c) (October 27, 2008).

DEFINITIONS

"claimant"—see WRA 2007, s.24(1).
"limited capability for work"—see WRA 2007, s.1(4).

GENERAL NOTE

Para. (1)

This draws a boundary between ESA and the sickness payment scheme operated by the Ministry of Defence. Days recorded by the Secretary of State for Defence as ones of sickness absence from duty are to be treated for ESA purposes as ones on which the person concerned does not have limited capability for work.

9.71

Additional circumstances where claimants are to be treated as having limited capability for work

33.—(1) For the purposes of paragraph 4(1)(d)(ii) of Schedule 1 to the Act, a claimant is to be treated as having limited capability for work on any day in respect of which that claimant is entitled to statutory sick pay.

9.72

(2) For the purposes of an income-related allowance, a claimant is to be treated as having limited capability for work where—

(a) that claimant is not a qualifying young person;
(b) that claimant is receiving education; and
(c) paragraph 6(1)(g) of Schedule 1 to the Act does not apply in accordance with regulation 18.

DEFINITIONS

"claimant"—see WRA 2007, s.24(1).
"income-related allowance"—see WRA 2007, s.1(7).
"limited capability for work"—see WRA 2007, s.1(4).
"qualifying young person"—see reg.2(1).

GENERAL NOTE

Para. (1)

9.73   Like WRA 2007, s.20(1), this regulation deals with the relationship between ESA and employer paid statutory sick pay (SSP). Days of entitlement to SSP cannot rank as ones of entitlement to ESA. However, para.(1) of this regulation stipulates that such days are to be treated as ones of limited capability for work for the purposes of computing the 196 consecutive days of limited capability for work essential if someone is to qualify through the "condition relating to youth route" to CESA (WRA 2007, Sch.1, para.4(1)(d)(ii)). Being so treated confers no exemption from the information gathering requirements in reg.21 (see para.(3) of that regulation).

Para. (2)

9.74   This deals only with IRESA. It treats certain disabled students as having limited capability for work. It covers someone receiving education (sub-para.(b)) but not debarred from IRESA on account of that because he is receiving DLA (sub-para. (c) [WRA 2007, Sch.1, para.6(1)(g) disapplied by reg.18]). If this person is not a qualifying young person, he is to be treated as having limited capability for work. A qualifying young person bears the same meaning as in SSCBA 1992, s.142 (see reg.2(1)): someone aged 16–19 inclusive undergoing a full-time course of non-advanced education or approved training which commenced before he attained 19 (see Child Benefit Regs, reg.3).

Being treated as having limited capability for work in this way confers exemption from the information gathering requirements in reg.21 (see para.(3) of that regulation).

PART 6

LIMITED CAPABILITY FOR WORK-RELATED ACTIVITY

Determination of limited capability for work-related activity

9.75   **34.**—(1) For the purposes of Part 1 of the Act, where, by reason of a claimant's physical or mental condition, at least one of the descriptors set out in Schedule 3 applies to the claimant, the claimant's capability for work-related activity will be limited and the limitation will be such that it is not reasonable to require that claimant to undertake such activity.

(2) A descriptor applies to a claimant if that descriptor applies to the claimant for the majority of the time or, as the case may be, on the majority of the occasions on which the claimant undertakes or attempts to undertake the activity described by that descriptor.

(3) In determining whether a descriptor applies to a claimant, the claimant is to be assessed as if the claimant were wearing any prosthesis with which the claimant is fitted or, as the case may be, wearing or using any aid or appliance which the claimant normally wears or uses.

(4) Where a determination has been made about whether a claimant—

(a) has limited capability for work-related activity;

(b) is to be treated as having limited capability for work-related activity; or

(c) is to be treated as not having limited capability for work-related activity, the Secretary of State may, if paragraph (5) applies, determine afresh whether the claimant has or is to be treated as having limited capability for work-related activity.

(5) This paragraph applies where—

(a) the Secretary of State wishes to determine whether there has been a relevant change of circumstances in relation to the claimant's physical or mental condition;

(b) the Secretary of State wishes to determine whether the previous determination about limited capability for work-related activity or about treating the claimant as having or as not having limited capability for work-related activity, was made in ignorance of, or was based on a mistake as to, some material fact; or

(c) at least 3 months have passed since the date of the previous determination about limited capability for work-related activity or about treating the claimant as having or as not having limited capability for work-related activity.

DEFINITIONS

"the Act"—see reg.2(1).
"claimant"—see WRA 2007, s.24(1).
"descriptor"—see reg.2(1).
"limited capability for work-related activity"—see WRA 2007, s.2(5).
"work-related activity"—see WRA 2007, ss.24(1), 13(7).

GENERAL NOTE

Establishing limited capability for work is the central condition governing entitlement to ESA. Establishing limited capacity for work related activity is, in contrast, the core condition of entitlement to support component, the more generous of the two components (support or work-related activity) only one of which can be added to ESA basic allowance. This regulation, read with WRA 2007, s.9 and Sch.3 to these Regs, sets out how limited capacity for work related activity is assessed and determined. **9.76**

The assumption behind ESA is that the vast majority of claimants, if given the right support, are in fact capable of some work. Government anticipates that only some 10% of claimants (those with more severe health conditions) will be entitled to the support allowance and so not be subject to work-related activity conditionality requirements (DWP, *Employment and Support Allowance Regulations 2008: Equality Impact Assessment* in *Explanatory Memorandum to Employment and Support Allowance Regulations 2008 (SI 2008/794)* and the *Employment and Support Allowance (Transitional Provisions) Regulations 2008 (SI 2008/795)*, p.19) Entry to this protected support group depends on it being established—generally through a work-related activity assessment (WRAAt) of a more stringent nature than the WCAt—that the claimant has limited capacity for work related activity. The WRAAt is the second element in the new Work Capability Assessment (WCA) which will eventually replace the IB PCA. Establishing limited capability for work related activity is based on someone demonstrating that they have a severe level of functional limitation. This is established when by reason of the claimant's physical or mental condition, at least one of the ranges of descriptors in Sch.3 applies to the claimant (WRA 2007, s.9; para.(1)).

There is no scoring system (it is a matter of the descriptor being applicable that counts) and the criteria are deliberately more stringent than in the WCAt:

"The levels of functional limitation used in the descriptors for determining limited capability for work-related activity are greater because we intend to place in the support group only the minority of customers who are so severely impaired that it would not be reasonable to require them to undertake work-related activity . . . People with less severe functional limitations across a range of descriptors might score highly and be inappropriately included in the support group when they might benefit from work-related activity. . . . A number of case studies were provided in the background information, which hon. Members will find helpful [see DWP, *Welfare Reform Bill: Draft Regulations and Supporting Material* (January 2007), pp.13–17]. Under the revised PCA, someone with a moderate learning disability would score 50 points. They would be significantly above the 15-point threshold, but we clearly would not wish to put even someone with 50 points into the support group automatically, because we are determined to ensure that the new system does not write off people with learning disabilities. The technical groups considered all the options. A crude points-based system would have unintended consequences." (*Hansard*, Standing Committee A, October 19, 2006 (afternoon), col.120 (Mr Jim Murphy MP, Minister for Employment and Welfare Reform)).

Paragraph (2) makes clear (as indeed does the expected transposition to the WRAAt of central elements in existing case law on approaching the PCA) that a descriptor applies to a claimant if it applies to him for the majority of the time or, as the case may be, on the majority of the occasions on which he undertakes or attempts to undertake the relevant activity. Moreover, as is the case with the IB PCA and the ESA WCAt, in matching claimant to descriptor, the claimant is to be assessed as if the claimant were wearing any prosthesis with which the claimant is fitted or, as the case may be, wearing or using any aid or appliance which the claimant normally wears or uses (para.(3) and see commentary to reg.19(4)).

There are only 11 activities in Sch.3: walking or moving on level ground; rising from sitting and transferring from one seated position to another; picking up and moving or transferring by means of the upper body and arms; reaching; manual dexterity; continence; maintaining personal hygiene; eating and drinking (conveying food or drink to the mouth and chewing or swallowing it); learning or comprehension in the completion of tasks; personal action (planning, organisation, problem solving, prioritising or switching tasks); and communication. The terms of the descriptors are also more stringent than in the WCAt, to avoid removing too many people from the group which affords incentive to engage in work-related activity and thus denying them the opportunity to take steps to make real their fundamental right to work. Thus, as regards walking, the single descriptor can only be met where a claimant cannot "walk" more than 30 metres without repeatedly stopping, experiencing breathlessness or severe discomfort. Here "walk" covers walking with a walking stick, other aid or crunches, each if normally used; and embraces the claimant moving by manually propelling a wheelchair (Sch.3, para.1). That on rising from sitting etc, requires in effect that the claimant fulfil two of the 15 point descriptors in the WCAt. Most, with counterparts in the WCAt, are couched in terms equivalent to the more difficult of their 15 point descriptors.

Those meeting the WRAAt test will be placed in the support group and receive support component without having to satisfy work-related activity conditions, although they can voluntarily participate in those programmes. Their position can be reviewed periodically or where there has been a change of circumstances in the claimant's physical or mental condition or it is thought that a previous determination was made in ignorance of or a mistake as to some material fact (paras (4), (5)) The threshold for membership of the support group is high; CPAG consider that "many claimants in receipt of the middle and higher rates of Disability Living Allowance (DLA) may not meet the eligibility criteria". Those who fail to establish limited capability for work-related activity will instead receive the work-related activity component, receipt of which has stringent conditions attached in terms of appropriate behaviour (participation in work focussed health related assessments, work focused interviews and, eventually, specified work-related activity (see regs.47–60), involving the private and voluntary sector as well as JobCentre Plus).

Certain claimants to be treated as having limited capability for work-related activity

35.—(1) A claimant is to be treated as having limited capability for work-related activity if—

   (a) the claimant is terminally ill;

   (b) the claimant is—

      (i) receiving treatment by way of intravenous, intraperitoneal or intrathecal chemotherapy; or

      (ii) recovering from that treatment and the Secretary of State is satisfied that the claimant should be treated as having limited capability for work-related activity; or

   (c) in the case of a woman, she is pregnant and there is a serious risk of damage to her health or to the health of her unborn child if she does not refrain from work-related activity.

(2) A claimant who does not have limited capability for work-related activity as determined in accordance with regulation 34(1) is to be treated as having limited capability for work-related activity if—

   (a) the claimant suffers from some specific disease or bodily or mental disablement; and

   (b) by reasons of such disease or disablement, there would be a substantial risk to the mental or physical health of any person if the claimant were found not to have limited capability for work-related activity.

9.77

DEFINITIONS

"claimant"—see WRA 2007, s.24(1).
"limited capability for work-related activity"—see WRA 2007, s.2(5).
"terminally ill"—see reg.2(1).
"work-related activity"—see WRA 2007, ss.24(1), 13(7).

GENERAL NOTE

This has affinities with reg.20 (treating someone as having limited capability for work). Regulation 35 treats someone as having limited capability for work-related activity but the range of groups so treated is much narrower. The terminally ill (para.(1)(a)) and those undergoing or recovering from chemotherapy (para.(1)(b)) are so treated, as is a pregnant woman where there is a serious risk of damage to her health or that of her unborn child if she does not refrain from work-related activity (para.(1)(c). Unlike reg.20 there is no protection for other pregnant women or for those receiving hospital treatment or certain regular treatments such as dialysis. However, in para.(2) there is a partial equivalent of the "exceptional circumstances" provision (reg.29) applicable to the limited capacity for work question, considered above. A claimant who does not pass the WRAAt can nonetheless be treated as having the requisite limited capability for work-related activity grounding membership of the support group where, by reason of the specific disease or bodily or mental disablement from which s/he suffers, "there would be a substantial risk to the mental or physical health of any person if the claimant were found not to have limited capability for work-related activity".

On "specific disease or bodily or mental disablement", see commentary to reg.19(2).

On "substantial risk to the mental or physical health of any person if the claimant were found not to have limited capability for work-related activity", see the commentary to reg.29.

9.78

Information required for determining capability for work-related activity

9.79 **36.**—(1) Subject to paragraph (2), the information or evidence required to determine whether a claimant has limited capability for work-related activity is—

(a) any information relating to the descriptors set out in Schedule 3 as may be requested in the form of a questionnaire; and

(b) any such additional information as may be requested.

(2) Where the Secretary of State is satisfied that there is sufficient information to determine whether a claimant has limited capability for work-related activity without the information specified in paragraph (1)(a), that information will not be required for the purposes of making the determination.

DEFINITIONS

"claimant"—see WRA 2007, s.24(1).
"limited capability for work-related activity"—see WRA 2007, s.2(5).
"work-related activity"—see WRA 2007, ss.24(1), 13(7).

GENERAL NOTE

9.80 This regulation deals with the information required for determining whether someone has limited capability for work-related activity. It is designed to give the decision-maker sufficient information to decide that matter for himself (the minority of cases), or whether to seek advice from a health care professional on the basis of the papers in respect of that decision, or to refer the claimant for a face to face WRAAt, including a medical examination (see reg.38).

Unless para.(2) operates, the claimant will have to supply (i) any information relating to the descriptors set out in Sch.3 as may be requested in the form of a questionnaire (para.(1)(a)), and (ii) such additional information relating to the relevant test as the Secretary of State asks for (para.(1)(b)). He must generally complete and return the appropriate questionnaire (para.(1)(a)), unless the Secretary of State decides that completion of the questionnaire is not necessary because without it he has sufficient information to determine whether the claimant does or does not have limited capability for work-related activity (para.(2)). Note that where the claimant is requested by the Secretary of State to complete and return the questionnaire, failure to do so can result in his being treated as not having limited capability for work-related activity (and thus not entitled to support component) (reg.37).

Failure to provide information in relation to work-related activity

9.81 **37.**—(1) Where a claimant fails without good cause to comply with the request referred to in regulation 36(1)(a), the claimant is, subject to paragraph (2), to be treated as not having limited capability for work-related activity.

(2) Paragraph (1) does not apply unless—

(a) at least 6 weeks have passed since the claimant was sent the first request for the information; and

(b) the claimant was sent a further request at least 4 weeks after the date of the first request, and at least 2 weeks have passed since the further request was sent.

DEFINITIONS

"claimant"—see WRA 2007, s.24(1).
"limited capability for work-related activity"—see WRA 2007, s.2(5).
"week"—see reg.2(1).
"work-related activity"—see WRA 2007, ss.24(1), 13(7).

GENERAL NOTE

If a claimant fails without good cause (on which more, below) to comply with the 9.82
requirement in reg.36(1)(a) to complete and return a limited capability for work-
related activity questionnaire, he must be treated as not having limited capability for
work-related activity, that is, as having no entitlement to support component. This
can only happen, however, if at least six weeks have passed since the claimant was
first sent the request for information, a further request for information was sent at
least four weeks after the first and at least two weeks have gone by since the second
request was sent.

On applicable IB case law on calculating periods and on the matter of good cause,
see further the commentary to the analogous reg.22, applicable in respect of similar
processes with respect to determination of limited capability for work questions.

Claimant may be called for a medical examination to determine whether the claimant has limited capability for work-related activity

38.—(1) Where it falls to be determined whether a claimant has limited 9.83
capability for work-related activity, that claimant may be called by or on
behalf of a health care professional approved by the Secretary of State to
attend for a medical examination.

(2) Subject to paragraph (3), where a claimant fails without good cause
to attend for or to submit to an examination listed in paragraph (1), the
claimant is to be treated as not having limited capability for work-related
activity.

(3) Paragraph (2) does not apply unless written notice of the time and
place for the examination was sent to the claimant at least 7 days in advance,
or unless the claimant agreed to accept a shorter period of notice whether
given in writing or otherwise.

DEFINITIONS

"claimant"—see WRA 2007, s.24(1).
"health care professional"—see reg.2(1).
"limited capability for work-related activity"—see WRA 2007, s.2(5).
"work-related activity"—see WRA 2007, ss.24(1), 13(7).

GENERAL NOTE

This regulation enables the DWP to have a claimant medically examined by 9.84
a DWP Medical Service (DWPMS) health service professional (technically any
health service professional approved by the Secretary of State) when a question
arises as to the claimant's capability for work-related activity. Failure without good
cause to attend for or submit to such an examination, of which he was given proper
written notice (see para.(3)), will result in the claimant being treated as not having
limited capability for work and not entitled to ESA.

This regulation is a direct analogue of reg.23 with respect to medical examination as regards the matter of limited capability for work. The points, including the
application of relevant IB case law, made in the commentary to reg.23 are equally
applicable here.

Matters to be taken into account in determining good cause in relation to regulations 37 or 38

39. The matters to be taken into account in determining whether a claim- 9.85
ant has good cause under regulations 37 (failure to provide information in

relation to work-related activity) or 38 (failure to attend a medical examination to determine limited capability for work-related activity) include—

(a) whether the claimant was outside Great Britain at the relevant time;
(b) the claimant's state of health at the relevant time; and
(c) the nature of any disability the claimant has.

DEFINITION

"claimant"—see WRA 2007, s.24(1).

GENERAL NOTE

9.86 This regulation, made pursuant to WRA 2007, s.9(4), stipulates that in determining whether someone had good cause for failing to provide information (under reg.37) or for failing to attend for or submit to a medical examination (under reg.38) decision-makers and appellate bodies must take into account: (i) whether the person was outside Great Britain at the relevant time; (ii) his state of health at the relevant time; and (iii) the nature of his disability. This list is not, however, exhaustive (the regulation says "shall include"). On "good cause", see further the commentary to regs 22 and 23.

PART 7

EFFECT OF WORK ON ENTITLEMENT TO AN EMPLOYMENT AND SUPPORT ALLOWANCE

A claimant who works to be treated as not entitled to an employment and support allowance

9.87 **40.**—(1) Subject to the following paragraphs, a claimant is to be treated as not entitled to an employment and support allowance in any week in which that claimant does work.

(2) Paragraph (1) does not apply to—

(a) work as a councillor;
(b) duties undertaken on either one full day or two half-days a week as—
  (i) a member of the Disability Living Allowance Advisory Board; or
  [²(ii) a member of the First-tier Tribunal where the member is eligible for appointment to be such a member in accordance with article 2(3) of the Qualifications for Appointment of Members to the First-tier Tribunal and Upper Tribunal Order 2008.]
(c) domestic tasks carried out in the claimant's own home or the care of a relative;
(d) duties undertaken in caring for another person who is accommodated with the claimant by virtue of arrangements made under any of the provisions referred to in paragraphs 28 or 29 of Schedule 8 (sums to be disregarded in the calculation of income other than earnings) where the claimant is in receipt of any payment specified in those paragraphs;
(e) any activity the claimant undertakes during an emergency to protect another person or to prevent serious damage to property or livestock; or

(f) any of the categories of work set out in regulation 45 (exempt work).

(3) This regulation is subject to regulation 46 (effect of work on entitlement to contributory allowance where claimant is receiving certain regular treatment).

(4) A claimant who does work to which this regulation applies in a week which is—

(a) the week in which the claimant first becomes entitled to a benefit, allowance or advantage on account of the claimant's limited capability for work in any period; or

(b) the last week in any period in which the claimant has limited capability for work or is treated as having limited capability for work,

is to be treated as not entitled to an employment and support allowance by virtue of paragraph (1) only on the actual day or days in that week on which the claimant does that work.

(5) Regulation 145 (linking rules) does not apply for the purposes of calculating the beginning or end of any period of limited capability for work under paragraph (4).

(6) The day or days in a week on which a night worker works, for the purposes of [¹paragraph (4)] above, are to be calculated by reference to regulation 28 (night workers).

(7) In this regulation—

"week" means a week in respect of which a claimant is entitled to an employment and support allowance;

"work" means any work which a claimant does, whether or not that claimant undertakes it in expectation of payment;

"work as a councillor" is to be taken to include any work which a claimant undertakes as a member of any of the bodies referred to in section 177(1) of the Local Government Act 1972 or sub-sections 49(1) or 49(1A) of the Local Government (Scotland) Act 1973, of which the claimant is a member by reason of being a councillor.

AMENDMENTS

1. Employment and Support Allowance (Miscellaneous Amendments) Regulations 2008 (SI 2008/2428), reg.6(1) (October 27, 2008).

2. Tribunals, Courts and Enforcement Act 2007 (Transitional and Consequential Provisions) Order 2008 (SI 2008/2683), art.6(1), Sch1, para.342 (November 3, 2008).

DEFINITIONS

"claimant"—see WRA 2007, s.24(1).
"entitled"—see WRA 2007, s.24(1).
"relative"—see reg.2(1).
"week"—see para.(7) and reg.2(1).
"work"—see para.(7).
"work as a councillor"—see para.(7).

GENERAL NOTE

This regulation needs to be read in conjunction with regs 44–46. 9.88

To find in any incapacity regime a general rule that working (whether or not for payment) negatives incapacity for work is unsurprising since, in principle, it is a strong indication of ability to work. This regulation contains just such a rule, precluding entitlement to ESA in any week in which a claimant does work. Moreover, in that period of non-entitlement, he or she will be treated as not having limited capability for work, unless the work done only negatives entitlement to IRESA (reg.44). That can happen in that work done in a week when someone, entitled to CESA, is receiving or recovering from certain regular treatments, does not negative title to CESA, but can to IRESA (regs 46 (to which para.(3) makes this regulation subject) and 44(3)). But like the incapacity benefit regime, the general preclusive rule is modified to permit engagement in a range of work without loss of benefit ("subject to the following paragraphs", one of which para.(2)(f) links this regulation to reg.45 and the concept of "exempt work"). These modifications recognize that work can assist recovery or help the claimant into thinking about work and a possibility to return to work, or merely not wanting to exclude the sick and disabled from participation in civic office or a range of voluntary or charitable work.

Although, unlike its IB comparator (Incapacity for Work Regs, reg.16) the point is no longer explicit, it is submitted that the regulation can operate despite the fact that, applying the limited capability for work assessment (WCAt) , the person in fact has limited capability for work, or is someone treated as having such limited capability by virtue of other regs.

Paragraph (1) sets out the general preclusive rule: a person must be treated as capable of work on each day of any week during which he does work. "Work" for the purposes of the regulation is defined in para.(7) as any work done whether or not undertaken in expectation of payment. "Week" is a period of seven days beginning with Sunday (para.(7)).

Note, however, that this ostensibly very wide general preclusive rule is subject to the partial relief afforded by para.(4) and by reg.46 (see para.(3)) and the complete relief afforded by para.(2). Execution of some *de minimis* tasks can also be ignored as not constituting "work". Discussion is divided accordingly.

Partial relief

9.89   *Paras (4), (5):* Together these afford some relief from the general preclusive rule set out in para.(1). Paragraph (4) contains an obviously necessary one, it covers the worker who initially falls sick part way through his working week and/or the period in which he is incapable of work finishes part way through a week in the course of which he returns to work. Here, the preclusive effect of the regulation is confined to ruling out only the days actually worked in that or those weeks.

Note that the linking rules in reg.145 do not apply for determining when, for the purposes of this relieving rule, a period of limited capability for work begins and ends (para.(5)). In effect, each "spell" of limited capability for work" is treated separately, thus helping those whose limited capability for work is intermittent and removing a disincentive to trying work for a while.

Para.(3): This regulation is "subject to regulation 46". That provides that those treated under reg.26 as having limited capability for work on days when receiving or recovering from certain regular treatments (e.g. chemotherapy), who work on other days of the week in which they receive or are recovering from such treatment such treatment, will not have their entitlement to CESA affected by doing that work. For the impact of such work on entitlement to IRESA, see the exclusionary "remunerative work" rules (WRA 2007, Sch.1, para.6(1)(e); reg.41) and, in terms of the IRESA "balance sheet", the impact of earnings on entitlement.

Complete relief

9.90   *Para.(2)* prevents the general preclusive rule in para.(1) applying to:
(i)   any of the categories of work in reg.45 (para.(2)(f));
(ii)   work as a councillor (see para.(7) for its breadth and see reg.88 for the abating effect on CESA of amounts of councillor's allowance over a specified weekly amount) (para.(2)(a);
The scheme, as before, seeks to encourage sick and disabled people to participate in civic office by enabling them to receive CESA reduced or abated

by the amount by which their councillor's allowance applicable to that week exceeds a specified amount.

(iii) care of a relative or domestic tasks carried out in his own home (para.(2)(c));

(iv) work as a foster parent or other specified carer in respect of someone accommodated in one's home in respect of which specified payments are made (para.(2)(d), Sch.8, paras 28, 29);

(v) limited duties (one full day or two half days per week) as a member of a the DLA Advisory Board or as First-tier Tribunal member with a disability qualification (para.(2)(b)) (i.e. someone other than a registered medical practitioner, who is experienced in dealing with the physical or mental needs of disabled persons because they work with disabled persons in a professional or voluntary capacity, or are themselves disabled (see art.2(3) of the Qualifications for Appointment of Members to the First-tier Tribunal and Upper Tribunal Order 2008 (SI 2008/2692));

(vi) any activity undertaken during an emergency solely to protect another person or to prevent serious damage to property or livestock (para.(2)(e)).

This exemption is essential to protect the benefit position of the rescuer; of the good neighbour who looks after his/her neighbour's children when she is rushed to hospital; of the person who helps round up livestock which have strayed into a busy road; or of the good neighbour who helps fight a fire until the emergency services arrive; or the husband on ESA who is compelled to drive to rush his pregnant wife in labour to hospital because the ambulance has not arrived. These can be but speculative examples.

"Emergency" is not defined. However, note it is not qualified by terms such as "severe" or "serious" or "great", so it ought not to be construed too narrowly. By way of comparison, in the industrial injuries context, case law dealing with "in the course of employment" has brought within that phrase persons responding to emergency. There "emergency" was construed broadly to encompass a wide range of unexpected occurrences (see commentary to SSCBA 1992, s.100). A broad approach ought to be taken, similarly, to the notion of "any activity to protect another person".

Applying the de minimis principle to ignore trivial or negligible amounts of work

It is submitted that this long-standing principle, which has applied to previous   **9.91**
inpacity for work regimes, is equally applicable to ESA and that previous case law applies here.

CIB/5298/1997 supports the view (then found in AOG, paras 18782 and 18783) that the de minimis principle applies to enable trivial or negligible amounts of work to be ignored (paras 5–12), recognising as a practical proposition something seen as a theoretical one in *CIB/14656/96*. Deputy Commissioner Wikeley's decision in *CIB/6777/1999* contains a thorough review of the authorities on this matter. He notes that the rule here can apply irrespective of whether the work might in any event be treated as exempt under Incapacity for Work Regs, reg.17 (and thus ESA Regs, regs 40, 45). Whether work done is trivial or negligible is a matter of fact and degree. Like Commissioner Williams in *CIB/5298/1997*, who had approved guidance in the AOG, the Deputy Commissioner supported as illustrative but not exhaustive, relevant factors, those set out in DMG para.13867:

"whether work on a day is negligible depends on its proportion to the normal working hours, the type of work and the effort required in relation to normal working duties."

Stressing the role of incapacity benefit as "an earnings replacement . . . benefit for those with the appropriate contributions record who cannot work in the labour market" he (rightly in the opinion of this commentator) disagreed with Commissioner Williams in *CIB/5298/1997* who took the view that the amount of remuneration earned was always wholly irrelevant since para.(6) states that work is "work" whether or not undertaken in expectation of payment. That means, of course, that the lack of remuneration or of the expectation of it is irrelevant. The key question is really what the tasks performed tell one about the person's capacity for work. But, in contrast to the irrelevance of lack of remuneration, this author, like the Deputy Commissioner, believes that the amount of remuneration received for a relatively small degree of work-like activity, when contrasted with the weekly rate of incapacity benefit (and now ESA), surely *is* a relevant factor in deciding whether work done should be disregarded as trivial or negligible—it brings into play the "anti-abuse" element of the rules here, which arguably takes one into the realm of when the public (including other recipients of benefit) might view as inappropriate receipt of incapacity benefit or ESA by someone with what looks like a source of income from "employment", albeit only in that one week. Is that not one purpose behind the earnings limits on exempt work in Incapacity for Work Regs, reg.17 (ESA Regs, reg.45)? However, that Incapacity for Work Regs, reg.16 (ESA Regs, reg.40) stipulates particular worthy tasks as ones to be disregarded seems to cast doubt on the Deputy Commissioner's view that the identity of the person for whom the task is performed may be a material factor in applying the de minimis rule.

CIB/3507/2003 affords another illustration of work being disregarded as de minimis. The work in question was described by the Commissioner as follows:

"On 28th November 2001, DW Windows wrote a letter in which they said: 'In July of this year we approached [the claimant] to see if he would like to do a couple of hours each week at [DW Windows] doing various light duties. i.e. Making coffees, emptying bins etc and occasionally driving a vehicle to transport [Mr S. E.] the Manager who holds no driving license. There is no dispute about what DW Windows say. Nor is there any dispute about the fact that the claimant was paid £3.85 per hour and that he worked between one and three hours per week. A schedule of his weekly hours and earnings between the beginning of July and the first week of October 2001 has been produced by DW Windows. He never worked for more than three hours and consequently never earned more than £11.55, in any one week. The period covered is one of 14 weeks. During three of those weeks he worked for 1 hour only. He worked for two hours for five of those weeks and for three hours for the remaining six weeks. The average is a little above two hours per week'" (paras 6, 7).

In marked contrast, in *CIB/4684/2003*, Commissioner Jacobs found the work done by the claimant was not so minimal that it could be disregarded. He did so, however, for a different reason to the tribunal which had so found on the basis that the claimant's contribution to the earnings from the post office was significant when compared to his wife's. Instead Commissioner Jacobs approached the matter thus:

"For 8 hours a week, spread over 2 mornings, the claimant manned the post office. He was not there merely to summon his wife if a customer arrived. He was there to serve any customer who wanted any of the services offered by the office. Covering the office in those circumstances amounted to work, even if there were no customers at all. He was in exactly the same position as a stallholder on a market who had no customers. Surely that stallholder would be working, even if no one bought from, or even visited, the stall? How the claimant spent his time when he was not actually serving customers is irrelevant. It would be just as irrelevant whether a market stallholder at a market spent the time trying to entice customers to the stall or merely sat reading a book" (paras 10, 11).

PART 7

EFFECT OF WORK ON ENTITLEMENT TO AN EMPLOYMENT AND SUPPORT
ALLOWANCE

Meaning of "remunerative work" for the purposes of paragraph 6(1)(e) of Schedule 1 to the Act

41.—(1) For the purposes of paragraph 6(1)(e) of Schedule 1 to the Act   9.92
(conditions of entitlement to an income-related allowance), "remunerative
work" means any work which a claimant does for which payment is made
or which is done in expectation of payment, other than work listed in paragraph (2) of regulation 40.

(2) Subject to paragraph (3), a claimant who was, or who was being
treated as—

(a) engaged in remunerative work; and

(b) in respect of that work earnings to which regulation 95(1)(b) and (d)
applies are paid, is to be treated as being engaged in remunerative
work for the period for which those earnings are taken into account
in accordance with Part 10 of these Regulations.

(3) Paragraph (2) does not apply to earnings disregarded under paragraph
1 of Schedule 7 (sums to be disregarded in the calculation of earnings).

DEFINITIONS

"claimant"—Welfare Reform Act 2007, s.24(1).
"earnings"—regs 95 and 97.

GENERAL NOTE

Under para.6 of Sch.1 to the Welfare Reform Act, it is a condition of entitle-   9.93
ment to income-related ESA that (among other things) the claimant is not engaged
in remunerative work (para.6(1)(e)) and that, where the claimant is a member of
a couple, neither is the other member of the couple (para.6(1)(f)). The meaning
of the phrase "remunerative work" differs according to whether it is the claimant
or her/his partner that is being considered. Regulation 41 sets out the test for the
claimant and reg.42 (below), the test for the partner.

ESA is a benefit for those with limited capability for work and the general principle is that a claimant who does any work will normally not be entitled to ESA for
that week (see reg.40 above). That is subject to the exceptions set out in reg.40(2).
Paragraph (1) defines remunerative work as any work other than that specified in
reg.40(2) with the additional requirement that it should be work "for which payment
is made or which is done in expectation of payment". It is difficult to see what purpose
this serves. The reg.41(1) definition is narrower than the reg.40 definition and therefore anyone falling within reg.41(1) will already have been disentitled by reg.40.

Perhaps more importantly, some claimants who are not actually working (and are
not therefore disentitled by reg.40) are nevertheless *treated as* being in remunerative
work (and therefore not entitled to income-related ESA) under powers conferred
by para.6(3) of Sch.1 to the Act. Paragraphs (2) and (3) provide that where a claimant's employment is interrupted or comes to an end and he or she receives payment
in lieu of remuneration (other than a redundancy payment) or holiday pay (unless
it is payable more than four weeks after the termination or interruption of employment) then, except where those earnings are disregarded under para.1 of Sch.7, s/
he is treated as engaged in remunerative work for the period during which those
earnings are taken into account under Pt 10.

Meaning of "remunerative work" for the purposes of paragraph 6(1)(f) of Schedule 1 to the Act

9.94
42.—(1) For the purposes of paragraph 6(1)(f) of Schedule 1 to the Act, (conditions of entitlement to an income-related allowance where a claimant must not be a member of a couple the other member of which is engaged in remunerative work), "remunerative work" means work in which the claimant's partner is engaged or, where the partner's hours of work fluctuate, the partner is engaged on average, for not less than 24 hours a week, being work for which payment is made or which is done in expectation of payment.

(2) In calculating the number of hours for which a claimant's partner is engaged in work so as to determine whether that partner is engaged in remunerative work, the number of hours are to be determined in accordance with paragraphs (8) and (9) of regulation 45 and those paragraphs are to be read as though they referred to the claimant's partner.

(3) The claimant's partner is to be treated as engaged in remunerative work during any period for which that partner is absent from work referred to in paragraph (1) if the absence is either without good cause or by reason of a recognised, customary or other holiday.

(4) Subject to paragraph (5), a claimant's partner who was, or who was being treated as—

(a) engaged in remunerative work; and

(b) in respect of that work earnings to which regulation 95(1)(b) and (d) applies are paid, is to be treated as being engaged in remunerative work for the period for which those earnings are taken into account in accordance with Part 10 of these Regulations.

(5) Paragraph (4) does not apply to earnings disregarded under paragraph 1 of Schedule 7 (sums to be disregarded in the calculation of earnings).

(6) For the purposes of this regulation, in determining the number of hours in which a claimant's partner is engaged or treated as engaged in remunerative work, no account is to be taken of any hours in which the claimant's partner is engaged in an employment or a scheme to which regulation 43(1) or (2) (claimants' partners not treated as engaged in remunerative work) applies.

DEFINITIONS

"claimant"—Welfare Reform Act 2007, s.24(1).
"couple"—reg.2(1).
"earnings"—regs 95 and 97.
"partner"—reg.2(1).

GENERAL NOTE

9.95
In contrast to the position for ESA claimants, it is not a condition of entitlement that their partners should also have limited capability for work. Regulation 42 therefore defines "remunerative work" for the claimant's partner in terms that are similar to reg.5 of the IS Regulations and reg.51 of the JSA Regulations.

Circumstances under which partners of claimants entitled to an income-related allowance are not to be treated as engaged in remunerative work

9.96
43.—(1) A claimant's partner is not to be treated as engaged in remunerative work in so far as—

(a) the partner is engaged in child minding in the partner's home;
(b) the partner is engaged by a charity or voluntary organisation, or is a volunteer, where the only payment received by the partner or due to be paid to the partner, is a payment which is to be disregarded under regulation 104(2) (calculation of income other than earnings) and paragraph 2 of Schedule 8 (sums to be disregarded in the calculation of income other than earnings);
(c) the partner is engaged on a scheme for which a training allowance is being paid;
(d) the partner is receiving assistance under the self-employment route;
(e) the partner is engaged in employment as any one of the following—
  (i) a part-time fireman in a fire brigade maintained in pursuance of the Fire and Rescue Services Act 2004;
  (ii) a part-time fire-fighter employed by a fire and rescue authority;
  (iii) a part-time fire-fighter employed by a fire and rescue authority (as defined in section 1 of the Fire (Scotland) Act 2005 or a joint fire and rescue board constituted by an amalgamation scheme made under section 2(1) of that Act;
  (iv) an auxiliary coastguard in respect of coast rescue activities;
  (v) a person engaged part-time in the manning or launching of a life boat;
  (vi) a member of any territorial or reserve force prescribed in Part 1 of Schedule 6 to the Social Security (Contributions) Regulations 2001; or
(f) the partner is undertaking work as a councillor;
(g) the partner is engaged in caring for a person who is accommodated with the partner by virtue of arrangements made under any of the provisions referred to in paragraphs 28 or 29 of Schedule 8 (sums to be disregarded in the calculation of income other than earnings) and the partner is in receipt of any payment specified in those paragraphs;
(h) the partner is engaged in an activity in respect of which—
  (i) a sports award has been made, or is to be made, to the partner; and
  (ii) no other payment is made or is expected to be made to the partner.

(2) A claimant's partner is not to be treated as engaged in remunerative work, where the partner is—
(a) a person who is mentally or physically disabled and by reason of that disability—
  (i) the person's earnings are reduced to 75% or less of what a person without that disability and working the same number of hours would reasonably be expected to earn in that employment or in comparable employment in the area; or
  (ii) the person's number of hours are 75% or less of what a person without that disability would reasonably be expected to undertake in that employment or in comparable employment in the area;
(b) subject to regulation 42(4) (partners treated as engaged in remunerative work), a person who would otherwise have satisfied section 126(1) of the Contributions and Benefits Act (trade disputes) or in

respect of whom section 124(1) of that Act (conditions of entitlement to income support) would otherwise have had effect as modified by section 127(b) of that Act (effect of return to work);
(c) a person who would otherwise satisfy the conditions set out in paragraph 4 of Schedule 1B to the Income Support Regulations;
(d) a person who—
    (i) is in employment;
    (ii) lives in, or is temporarily absent from, a care home, an
    Abbeyfield Home or an independent hospital; and
    (iii) requires personal care by reason of old age, disablement, past or
    present dependence on alcohol or drugs, past or present mental
    disorder or a terminal illness.

(3) The claimant's partner is not to be treated as engaged in remunerative work on any day on which that partner is on maternity leave, paternity
leave or adoption leave or is absent from work because the partner is ill.

(4) In this regulation—

"work as a councillor" has the same meaning as in regulation 40;

"volunteer" means a person who is engaged in voluntary work otherwise
than for a relative, where the only payment received or due to be paid
to the person by virtue of being so engaged is in respect of any expenses
reasonably incurred by the person in connection with that work.

DEFINITIONS

"Abbeyfield Home"—reg.2(1).
"adoption leave"—*ibid.*
"claimant"—Welfare Reform Act 2007, s.24(1).
"Contributions and Benefits Act"—Welfare Reform Act 2007, s.65.
"councillor"—reg.2(1).
"employment"—*ibid.*
"Income Support Regulations"—*ibid.*
"independent hospital"—*ibid.*
"maternity leave" "—*ibid.*
"partner"—*ibid.*
"remunerative work"—regs 2(1), 41 and 42.
"self-employment route"—reg.2(1).
"sports award"—*ibid.*
"training allowance"—*ibid.*
"work as a councillor"—reg.40.

GENERAL NOTE

9.97   This regulation is similar to reg.6 of the IS Regs and reg.52 of the JSA Regs.

**Claimants who are treated as not entitled to any allowance at all by
reason of regulation 40(1) are to be treated as not having limited
capability for work**

9.98   **44.**—(1) Where a claimant is treated as not entitled to an employment
and support allowance by reason of regulation 40(1), subject to paragraph
(2), the claimant is to be treated as not having limited capability for work.

(2) Paragraph (1) does not apply where the claimant remains entitled to
a contributory allowance, but is not entitled to an income-related allowance
by reason of regulation 40(1).

(3) Paragraph (1) applies even if—

(a) it has been determined that the claimant has or is to be treated as having, under any of regulations 20 (certain claimants to be treated as having limited capability for work), 25 (hospital in-patients), 26 (claimants undergoing certain regular treatment) or 29 (exceptional circumstances), limited capability for work; or

(b) the claimant meets the conditions set out in regulation 30(2) for being treated as having limited capability for work until a determination is made in accordance with the limited capability for work assessment.

DEFINITION

"claimant"

GENERAL NOTE

Regulation 40(1) precludes entitlement to ESA in any week in which a claimant does work. In the light of that, this regulation provides, moreover, that in that period of non-entitlement, he or she will be treated as not having limited capability for work (para.(1), unless the work done only negatives entitlement to IRESA (para.(2)). Such a situation can arise where reg.46 applies in that work done in a week when someone, entitled to CESA, is receiving or recovering from certain regular treatments, does not negative title to CESA, but can to IRESA. Paragraph (3) makes clear that the regulation can operate despite the fact that, applying the limited capability for work assessment (WCAt), the person in fact has limited capability for work incapable of work, or is someone treated as having such limited capability by virtue of certain other regs: 20 (certain claimants to be treated as having limited capability for work); 25 (hospital in-patients); 26 (claimants undergoing certain regular treatment); or 29 (exceptional circumstances). This suggests that this rule on treating the person as not having limited capability for work will not operate in other cases where regs treat someone (whatever the reality) as having limited capability for work: regs 30 (treated as having limited capability pending assessment) and 33(2) (certain disabled students). In those cases there will be no entitlement to ESA where the person is caught by reg.40, but the days might still rank as ones of limited capability for work.

9.99

Exempt work

45.—(1) The categories of work referred to in regulation 40(2)(f) are set out in the following paragraphs.

9.100

(2) Work for which the earnings in any week do not exceed £20.00.

(3) Work for which the earnings in any week do not exceed [¹£92.00] and which—

(a) is part of the claimant's treatment programme and is done under medical supervision while the claimant is an in-patient, or is regularly attending as an out-patient, of a hospital or similar institution; or

(b) is supervised by a person employed by a public or local authority or voluntary organisation engaged in the provision or procurement of work for persons who have disabilities.

(4) Work which is done for less than 16 hours a week, for which earnings in any week do not exceed [¹£92.00] and which—

(a) is done during a 52 week period beginning on the first day on which the work is done, provided that—

  (i) the claimant has not previously done specified work;

    (ii) since the beginning of the last period of specified work, the claimant has ceased to be entitled to a relevant benefit for a continuous period exceeding 12 weeks;

    (iii) not less than 52 weeks have elapsed since the claimant previously did the specified work; or

(b) done by a claimant who has or is treated as having limited capability for work-related activity.

(5) Work done in the course of receiving assistance in pursuing self-employed earner's employment whilst participating in a programme provided or other arrangements made under section 2 of the Employment and Training Act 1973(functions of the Secretary of State) or section 2 of the Enterprise and New Towns (Scotland) Act 1990(functions in relation to training for employment etc.).

(6) Work done where the claimant receives no payment of earnings and where the claimant—

(a) is engaged by a charity or voluntary organisation; or

(b) is a volunteer,

where the Secretary of State is satisfied in any of those cases that it is reasonable for the claimant to provide the service free of charge.

(7) Work done in the course of participating in a work placement approved in writing by the Secretary of State before the placement starts.

(8) The number of hours for which a claimant is engaged in work is to be determined—

(a) where no recognisable cycle has been established in respect of a claimant's work, by reference to the number of hours or, where those hours are likely to fluctuate, the average of the hours, which the claimant is expected to work in a week;

(b) where the number of hours for which the claimant is engaged fluctuate, by reference to the average of hours worked over—

    (i) if there is a recognisable cycle of work, the period of one complete cycle (including, where the cycle involves periods in which the claimant does no work, those periods but disregarding any other absences);

    (ii) in any other case, the period of five weeks immediately before the date of claim or the date on which a superseding decision is made under section 10 (decisions superseding earlier decisions) of the Social Security Act 1998, or such other length of time as may, in the particular case, enable the claimant's average hours of work to be determined more accurately.

(9) For the purposes of determining the number of hours for which a claimant is engaged in work, that number is to include any time allowed to that claimant by the claimant's employer for a meal or for refreshment, but only where that claimant is, or expects to be, paid earnings in respect of that time.

(10) In this regulation—

"relevant benefit" means—

(a) an employment and support allowance; or

(b) credits under regulations made under section 22(5) of the Contributions and Benefits Act,

in respect of which the question of the claimant's limited capability for work arises under the Act;

"specified work" means work done in accordance with paragraph (4);

"supervised work" means work done in accordance with paragraph (3) (a) or (b);

"volunteer" has the same meaning it has in regulation 43;

"work placement" means practical work experience with an employer, which is neither paid nor undertaken in expectation of payment.

AMENDMENTS

1. Employment and Support Allowance (Miscellaneous Amendments) Regulations 2008 (SI 2008/2428), reg.6(2) (October 27, 2008).

DEFINITIONS

"the Act"—see reg.2(1).
"claimant"—see WRA 2007, s.24(1).
"Contributions and Benefits Act"—see WRA 2007, s.65.
"employment"—see reg.2(1).
"relevant benefit"—see para.(10).
"self-employed earner"—see reg.2(1).
"specified work"—see paras (10), (4).
"supervised work"—see paras (10), (3) (a) or (b).
"voluntary organisation"—see reg.2(1).
"volunteer"—see para.(10) and reg.43(4).
"week"—see reg.2(1).
"work placement"—see para.(10).

GENERAL NOTE

This regulation needs to be read in conjunction with reg.40(1) which precludes entitlement to ESA in any week in which a claimant does work. "Work" for the purposes of that regulation is defined in reg.40(7) as any work done whether or not undertaken in expectation of payment. "Week" is a period of seven days beginning with Sunday (reg.40(7)). This regulation in contrast defines a variety of work which ranking as "exempt work" does not pursuant to reg.40(2)(f) preclude entitlement to ESA under the general preclusive rule in reg.40(1).

9.101

The regulation is part of the welfare to work strategy, of encouraging people to try out work, the better to enable a return to work.

The current categories of exempt work

Some embody an earnings limit, others both an earnings and hours limit. The matters of determining the hours of engagement and assessing earnings are examined further below, after considering the seven categories of exempt work:

9.102

(1) *Work for which the earnings in any week do not exceed £20 (para.(2)):* there is no hours limit as such here, but it is anticipated that in practice the effect of the minimum wage laws will mean that DWP staff will expect a claimant in this category to be working less than 5 hours a week. Its prime role is the encouragement of social contact.

(2) *Unpaid work for a charity or voluntary organization (para.(6)(a)):* Work done where the claimant is engaged by a charity or voluntary organization is exempt where he receives no payment of earnings and the Secretary of State is satisfied that it is reasonable for him to provide the service free of charge. "Charity" is not defined in the ESA Regs, so must bear the meaning it does in charity law. "Voluntary organization" means a body, other than a public or local authority, the activities of which are carried on otherwise than for profit (reg.2(1)).

(3) *Work done as a volunteer (paras (6)(b), (10)):* Voluntary work other than that covered by para.(6)(1)(a) is thus also protected where the claimant receives no payment of earnings and the Secretary of State is satisfied that

it is reasonable for him to provide the service free of charge. "Volunteer" is defined in para.(10) by reference to reg.43(4) to embrace a person who is engaged in voluntary work otherwise than for a relative, where the only payment received by him or due to be paid to him by virtue of being so engaged is in respect of any expenses reasonably incurred by him in connection with that work. "Relative" is widely defined: it means a close relative, grand-parent, grand-child, uncle, aunt, nephew or niece (reg.2(1)). "Close relative" covers a parent, parent-in-law, son, son-in-law, daughter, daughter-in-law, step-parent, step-son, step-daughter, brother, sister, or the spouse of any of these persons, or if that person is one of an unmarried couple, the other member of that couple (reg.2(1)). There are no hours or earnings limits.

(3) *Supervised work (paras (3, (10)):* there are two categories here. First, work done with the supervision of bodies providing or finding work for disabled people (para.(3)(a)). The bodies in question are a public or local authority or a voluntary organisation (that is, a body, other than a public or local authority, whose activities are carried on otherwise than for profit (reg.2(1)). The second category covers work while a patient of a hospital or similar institution under medical supervision as part of a treatment programme. The patient must be an in-patient or a regularly attending out-patient (para.(3) (b)). Whichever of the two categories, the earnings from the work must not exceed £92.00 a week (see further below). On "hospital or similar institution", some guidance is given in DMG, paras 18031–18033, 24018–24023. But this is not binding on tribunals or courts.

(4) *Work done in the course of receiving assistance in pursuing self-employed earner's employment whilst participating in certain programmes or arrangements (para. (5)):* this makes it easier for people receiving ESA to attempt self employment. Test Trading allows people to try out 'self employment' for a period of up to 26 weeks. Its introduction prevents participants being regarded as in work with the possibility of a loss of benefit should earnings exceed the permitted work limits.

(5) *Work done by those having, or treated as having, limited capability for work-related activity (para. (4) (b)):* those in the support group (receiving or eligible for support component) can work for an unlimited period providing it is for less than 16 hours a week (see further, below) and the earnings do not exceed £92.00 a week (see further below). This provides a new category of permitted work for people who face the greatest barriers to full-time employment.

(6) *Permitted ("specified") work for an initial period of up to 52 weeks (paras (4) (a), (10)):* this simplifies matters considerably compared to the previous reg.17(4) (A) (see 2005 edition of this book). The work done must be for less than 16 hours a week (see further, below) and the earnings in any week must not exceed £92.00 (see further, below). To qualify for this permitted work period, the person must (i) have not previously done specified work (i.e. work protected by this particular head (para.(10)); (ii) since the beginning of the last period of specified work, he must have ceased to be entitled to a "relevant" benefit (see para.(10)) for a continuous period of more than twelve weeks; and (iii) at least 52 weeks have elapsed since he last did specified work.

(7) *approved, unpaid work placements (paras (7), (10)):* "Work placement" is practical work experience with an employer, which is neither paid nor taken on in expectation of payment (para.(10)). The work placement must have been approved by the Secretary of State in writing prior to its commencement.

In determining the number of hours of engagement in work (paras (8), (9)) an averaging approach applies, varying according to whether there is or is not a recognizable cycle and whether the claimant's hours fluctuate (para.(8)). The hours of engagement include time the employer allows for meals or refreshment where the claimant is, or expects to be, paid earnings in respect of that time (para.(9)).

The earnings limit—Computation of Earnings Regs not applicable here

Unlike the position with IB, ESA is not within the sphere of the SSCBA 1992 and so the Computation of Earnings Regs cannot apply. Calculation of earnings is to be done under the rules in the ESA Regs.

9.103

Effect of work on entitlement to contributory allowance where claimant is receiving certain regular treatment

46. Where a claimant who is entitled to a contributory allowance and is treated as having limited capability for work by virtue of regulation 26 works on any day during a week when the claimant is, in accordance with regulation 26, receiving certain regular treatment or recovering from that treatment, that work is to have no effect on the claimant's entitlement to the contributory allowance.

9.104

DEFINITIONS

"claimant"—see WRA 2007, s.24(1).
"contributory allowance"—see WRA 2007, s.1(7).
"entitled"—see WRA 2007, s.24(1).
"limited capability for work"—see WRA 2007, s.24(1).
"week"—see reg.2(1), WRA 2007, s.24(1).

GENERAL NOTE

This (affording an exception to the preclusive rule on work in reg.40(1)) provides that those treated under reg.26 as having limited capability for work on days when receiving or recovering from certain regular treatments (e.g. chemotherapy), who work on other days of the week in which they receive or are recovering from such treatment such treatment, will not have their entitlement to CESA affected by doing that work. For the impact of such work on entitlement to IRESA, see the exclusionary "remunerative work" rules (WRA 2007, Sch.1, para.6(1)(e); reg.41) and, in terms of the IRESA "balance sheet", the impact of earnings on entitlement.

9.105

PART 8

CONDITIONALITY

CHAPTER 1

WORK-FOCUSED HEALTH-RELATED ASSESSMENT

Requirement to take part in a work-focused health-related assessment

47.—(1) The Secretary of State may require a claimant who satisfies the requirements in paragraph (2) to take part in one or more work-focused health-related assessments as a condition of continuing to be entitled to the full amount of employment and support allowance payable to the claimant.

(2) The requirements referred to in paragraph (1) are that the claimant—

(a) is either—

9.106

(i) entitled to an employment and support allowance; or

(ii) a person who has made a claim for an employment and support allowance to which regulations under section 5(1)(c) of the Administration Act apply;

(b) is not a member of the support group; and

(c) has not reached the age at which a woman of the same age as the claimant would attain pensionable age.

(3) Any requirement to take part in a work-focused health-related assessment ceases to have effect if the claimant ceases to satisfy the requirements in paragraph (2).

DEFINITIONS

"Administration Act"—see WRA 2007, s.65.
"claimant"—see WRA 2007, s.24(1).
"member of the support group"—see WRA 2007, s.24(4).
"pensionable age"—see reg.2(1).
"work-focused health-related assessments"—see WRA 2007, s.11(7).

GENERAL NOTE

9.107   This regulation, read with WRA 2007, s.11 and regs 48–53, deals with the first aspect of "conditionality", the requirements imposed on most of those who fall outside the support group as not having limited capability for work-related activity. These will constitute some 90% of ESA claimants. The policy is that ESA brings rights, responsibilities and opportunities to people with health conditions and disabilities by asking them to engage with Jobcentre Plus (and contracted providers in the private and voluntary sectors [PVS]) to work towards fulfilling their ambitions. The key to this is seen in the incorporation in entitlement to the work-related activity component of ESA of an element of conditionality modelled on those applied in the Pathways to Work programme. This has a number of elements: (i) participation in a work-focused health related assessment (WFHRAt); (ii) participation in a work-focused interview; and (iii) as resources permit (and not before 2011), undertaking work-related activity that increases the likelihood of getting a job (e.g. work trials). This regulation stipulates that as a condition of receiving in full the support component of ESA, a claimant may be required to participate in the third element of the new work capability assessment (WCA): a work-focused health related assessment (WFHRAt) (see WRA 2007, s.11 and reg.48), the first element of taking part in work-related activity (para.(1)). This requirement may, however, only be imposed on a claimant not in the support group, entitled to ESA or who makes a claim for it, who, whether male or female, has not reached the female pensionable age by reference to his/her date of birth (para.(2), reg.2(1) and link to Pensions Act 1995, Sch.4, para.1). Should such a requirement have been imposed when those conditions were met, it will cease to have effect when the claimant no longer satisfies one or more of them (e.g. ceases claiming, becomes a member of the support group because the health condition and its limiting effects have worsened, or has reached the exempting age).

    The exception for those in the support group (para.(2)(b)) may cause some practical problems, since it is envisaged that, despite its different outlook (looking to what people can do, rather than what they cannot), the WFHRAt will usually be conducted by the relevant health care professional immediately after the combined WCAt (governing eligibility for basic allowance ESA) and WRAAt (governing eligibility for support component), that is before it has been determined whether or not the claimant falls into the support group The review group which helped revise the PCA thought that conducting this assessment at the same time as the others had advantages, not least the convenience for the claimant of only having to attend a single appointment. Others expressed concerns that combining the two assessments risked confusing assessor and claimant, and creating a cause of anxiety to the latter. As is apparent from the wording of the regulations, the two assessments look at rather different things; both claimant and assessor at the same time have to consider what the claimant can and cannot do. A claimant might be fearful that elements from the WRHFAt might feed back and impact negatively on those other aspects of the WCA which determine title to benefit. Recent information from CPAG suggests that initially ATOS, the contractor responsible for medical examinations, conducted all three tests at one appointment, thus applying the second and third elements to persons who might not even be entitled to ESA at all, as well as applying the third element to those who might be in the support group. But ATOS is now understood to be trialling a system whereby the WRHFAt is applied only to those found to have limited capability for work and who are not in the support group.

Note that failure, without good cause, to participate in a WRHFAt (regs 51, 53) is sanctioned initially by halving the amount of work-related activity component and eventually by reducing it to nil (reg.63), the reduction to cease after compliance has been induced or the requirement to participate has ceased to have effect under para.(3) (reg.64).

Work-focused health-related assessment

48. For the purposes of section 11(7)(c) of the Act, matters to be assessed in the work-focused health-related assessment include—   **9.108**
- (a) difficulties which are likely to be experienced as a result of the claimant's physical or mental condition in relation to obtaining or remaining in work and how these might be managed or alleviated; and
- (b) the claimant's views on the impact of the claimant's physical or mental condition in relation to obtaining or remaining in work and any aspirations in relation to work in the light of that condition.

DEFINITIONS

"the Act"—see reg.2(1).
"claimant"—see WRA 2007, s.24(1).
"work-focused health-related assessment"—see WRA 2007, s.11(7).

GENERAL NOTE

"Work-focused health-related assessment" is defined in WRA 2007, s.11(7) as   **9.109**
an assessment by an approved health care professional for the purpose of assessing the extent to which a person still has capability for work; the extent to that may be improved by the taking of steps in relation to his physical or mental condition; and such other matters relating to his physical or mental condition and the likelihood of his obtaining or remaining in work or being able to do so, as may be prescribed. This regulation prescribes those matters so as to include (the list is thus not exhaustive) the matters set out in paras (a) and (b).

Notification of assessment

49.—(1) The health care professional who is to carry out the work-   **9.110**
focused health-related assessment, or a person acting on the health care professional's behalf, must notify the claimant of the requirement to attend the work-focused health-related assessment including details of the date, time and place of the assessment.

(2) Notification under paragraph (1) must be given in writing at least 7 days before the claimant is required to attend the work-focused health-related assessment unless the claimant agrees to accept a shorter period of notice whether given in writing or otherwise.

DEFINITIONS

"claimant"—see WRA 2007, s.24(1).
"health care professional"—see reg.2(1).
"work-focused health-related assessment"—see WRA 2007, s.11(7).

GENERAL NOTE

9.111   This requires proper notification to the claimant of the requirement to attend the work-focused health-related assessment. It must include details of that assessment's date, time and place (para.(1)). Notification must be given by, or on behalf of, the health care professional who is to carry it out (para.(1)). It must be in writing and be given at least seven days before the claimant is being required to attend, unless the claimant agrees to accept a shorter period of notice whether that shorter period be notified in writing or otherwise (para.(2)). On calculating periods of notice, see the commentary to reg.23 (requirement to attend medical examination for the limited capability for work assessment).

Determination of the place of the work-focused health-related assessment

9.112   **50.**—(1) Subject to paragraph (2), the work-focused health-related assessment must be carried out in a medical examination centre.

(2) A work-focused health-related assessment may take place at the claimant's home if the Secretary of State is of the opinion that requiring the claimant to attend elsewhere would cause the claimant undue inconvenience or endanger the claimant's health.

DEFINITIONS

"claimant"—see WRA 2007, s.24(1).
"medical examination centre"—see reg.2(1).
"work-focused health-related assessment"—see WRA 2007, s.11(7).

GENERAL NOTE

9.113   This stipulates that generally the work-focused health-related assessment must be carried out in a medical examination centre (para.(1)). This means premises equipped and suitable for carrying out a medical examination (reg.2(1)). But there is a discretion to carry out the assessment in the claimant's home if the Secretary of State considers that a requirement to attend a medical examination centre would endanger the claimant's health or simply cause undue inconvenience (para.(2)).

Taking part in a work-focused health-related assessment

9.114   **51.** A claimant is to be regarded as having taken part in a work-focused health-related assessment if the claimant—
(a) attends for the assessment at the date, time and place notified in accordance with regulation 49;
(b) provides all information which the Secretary of State requests as being necessary for the work-focused health-related assessment; and
(c) participates in discussions to the extent the Secretary of State considers necessary for the work-focused health-related assessment.

DEFINITIONS

"claimant"—see WRA 2007, s.24(1).
"work-focused health-related assessment"—see WRA 2007, s.11(7).

GENERAL NOTE

To receive the full amount of work-related activity component, a claimant may **9.115** be required to take part in a work-focused health-related assessment (WFHRAt) (WRA 2007, s.11; reg.48). Not taking part (without showing good cause) will be sanctioned by progressive reduction of the component, first by 50% and then by 100% (reg.63). This regulation stipulates when a claimant is to be regarded as having taken part. It requires not merely attendance at the proper date, time and place (para.(a)) and the provision of the information the Secretary of State considers necessary for the WFHRAt (para.(b)), but, also crucially, participation in the discussions to the extent the Secretary of State considers necessary (para.(c)).

Deferral of requirement to take part in a work-focused health-related assessment

52.—(1) Where— **9.116**
(a) a health care professional has conducted an assessment in relation to the claimant for the purpose of enabling the Secretary of State to determine whether the claimant has limited capability for work-related activity;
(b) it appears to the health care professional that—
  (i) at least one of the descriptors set out in Schedule 3 applies to the claimant; or
  (ii) regulation 35 applies to the claimant; and
(c) the Secretary of State has not made a determination about whether the claimant has limited capability for work-related activity,
the requirement to take part in the work-focused health-related assessment does not apply until such time after the Secretary of State has made a determination in relation to the claimant's limited capability for work-related activity as the Secretary of State may decide.

(2) Where paragraph (1) applies, the health care professional must notify the claimant that the requirement to take part in the work-focused health-related assessment has been deferred, pending determination by the Secretary of State of the claimant's capability for work-related activity.

DEFINITIONS

"claimant"—see WRA 2007, s.24(1).
"health care professional"—see reg.2(1).
"limited capability for work-related activity"—see WRA 2007, s.2(5).
"work-focused health-related assessment"—see WRA 2007, s.11(7).
"work-related activity"—see WRA 2007, ss.24(1), 13(7).

GENERAL NOTE

Those who are in the support group are exempt from the requirement to partici- **9.117** pate in a work-focused health-related assessment (WFHRAt) (reg.47(2)(b)). This may cause some practical problems, since it is envisaged that, despite its different outlook (looking to what people can do, rather than what they cannot), the WFHRAt will usually be conducted by the relevant health care professional immediately after the combined WCAt (governing eligibility for basic allowance ESA) and WRAAt (governing eligibility for support component), that is before it has been determined whether or not the claimant falls into the support group.

This regulation sensibly provides that the health care professional carrying out the WRAAt in relation to someone whose capability for work-related activity has not been determined, must defer the WFHRAt until after that matter has been determined if that professional considers that the claimant falls within the support group (para.(1)(b)(i)) or is otherwise treated as having limited capability for work-related activity under reg.35 as terminally ill, undergoing or recovering from chemotherapy, or pregnant where there is a serious risk of damage to the woman's health or that of her unborn child if she does not refrain from work-related activity (para.(1)(b)(ii)). The health care professional must notify the claimant of the deferral pending the decision on capability for work-related activity.

Failure to take part in a work-focused health-related assessment

9.118

53.—(1) A claimant who is required to take part in a work-focused health-related assessment but fails to do so must show good cause for that failure within 5 working days of the date on which the Secretary of State gives notification of that failure.

(2) The Secretary of State must determine whether a claimant who is required to take part in a work-focused health-related assessment has failed to do so and, if so, whether the claimant has shown good cause for that failure in accordance with paragraph (1).

(3) In determining whether a claimant has shown good cause for the failure to participate in a work-focused health-related assessment, the Secretary of State must take the following matters into account—

(a) whether the claimant was outside Great Britain at the time of the notification;

(b) the claimant's state of health at the time of the work-focused health-related assessment;

(c) the nature of any disability which the claimant has; and

(d) any other matter which the Secretary of State considers appropriate.

DEFINITIONS

"claimant"—see WRA 2007, s.24(1).
"work-focused health-related assessment"—see WRA 2007, s.11(7).

GENERAL NOTE

9.119

Failure, without good cause, to take part (see reg.51) in a work-focused health related assessment is sanctioned by progressive reduction of work-related activity component (initially 50%, then 100%) (reg.63). This regulation deals with showing good cause when the Secretary of State has notified the claimant of his failure to take part. It requires the claimant to show good cause for such failure within five working days of the date on which the notification was given (para.(1)). It must then be determined whether there was a failure and, if so, whether the requisite good case has been shown within the stipulated time frame (para.(2)). "Good cause" is not defined, although WRA 2007, s.11(2)(h) provides power to prescribe what ranks or does not rank as "good cause. Paragraph (3) merely provides, pursuant to subs.(2) (g) of that section, four matters which must be taken into account.

CHAPTER 2

WORK-FOCUSED INTERVIEWS

Requirement to take part in a work-focused interview

9.120

54.—(1) The Secretary of State may require a claimant who satisfies the requirements in paragraph (2) to take part in one or more work-focused interviews as a condition of continuing to be entitled to the full amount of employment and support allowance payable to the claimant.

(2) The requirements referred to in paragraph (1) are that the claimant—

    (a) is either—

        (i) entitled to an employment and support allowance; or

        (ii) a person in respect of whom the Secretary of State has made an award under regulation 146(1);

    (b) is not a member of the support group;

    (c) has not reached the age at which a woman of the same age as the claimant would attain pensionable age; and

    (d) is not only entitled to a contributory allowance payable at a nil rate.

(3) Any requirement to take part in a work-focused interview ceases to have effect if the claimant ceases to satisfy the requirements in paragraph (2).

DEFINITIONS

    "claimant"—see WRA 2007, s.24(1).
    "contributory allowance"—see WRA 2007, ss.24(1), 1(7).
    "member of the support group"—see WRA 2007, s.24(4).
    "pensionable age"—see reg.2(1).
    "work-focused interview"—see WRA 2007, s.12(7).

GENERAL NOTE

9.121

This regulation, read with WRA 2007, s.11 and regs 48–53, deals with the second aspect of "conditionality", the requirements imposed on most of those who fall outside the support group as not having limited capability for work-related activity. These will constitute some 90% of ESA claimants. The policy is that ESA brings rights, responsibilities and opportunities to people with health conditions and disabilities by asking them to engage with Jobcentre Plus (and contracted providers in the private and voluntary sectors [PVS]) to work towards fulfilling their ambitions. The key to this is seen in the incorporation in entitlement to the work-related activity component of ESA of an element of conditionality modelled on those applied in the Pathways to Work programme. This has a number of elements: (i) participation in a work-focused health related assessment (WFHRAt) (WRA 2007, s.11; regs 47–53); (ii) participation in a work-focused interview; and (iii) as resources permit (and not before 2011), undertaking work-related activity that increases the likelihood of getting a job (e.g. work trials). This regulation stipulates that as a condition of receiving the full amount of ESA, a claimant may be required to participate in one or more work-focused interviews, the second element of taking part in work-related activity (para.(1)). This requirement may, however, only be imposed on a claimant not in the support group, awarded ESA or an advance award of it under reg.146, who, whether male or female, has not reached the female pensionable age by reference to his/her date of birth, and who is not merely entitled to CESA at a nil rate (e.g. because of abatement under WRA 2007, ss.2, 3) (para.(2), reg.2(1) and link to Pensions Act 1995, Sch.4, para.1). Should such a requirement have been imposed when those conditions were met, it will cease to have effect when the claimant no longer satisfies one or more of them (e.g. becomes a member of the support group because the health condition and it limiting effects have worsened, or has reached the exempting age, or whose ESA entitlement drops to CESA at a nil rate) (para. (3)).

Although WRA 2007, s.16 and reg.63 enable contracting out so as to bring expertise from the private and voluntary sectors (PVS) into the process of assisting claimants to prepare for and enhance their prospects of starting or returning to work, it is envisaged, however, that the first work-focused interview will always be with someone from Jobcentre Plus and will be held around the eighth week of the assessment period.

Note that failure, without good cause, to participate in a work-focused interview (regs 55, 57, 58, 61) is sanctioned initially by halving the amount of work-related activity component and eventually by reducing it to nil (reg.63), the reduction to cease after compliance has been induced or the requirement to participate has ceased to have effect under para.(3) (reg.64).

Work-focused interview

9.122 **55.** The purposes of a work-focused interview are any or all of the following—

  (a) assessing the claimant's prospects for remaining in or obtaining work;

  (b) assisting or encouraging the claimant to remain in or obtain work;

  (c) identifying activities that the claimant may undertake that will make remaining in or obtaining work more likely;

  (d) identifying training, educational or rehabilitation opportunities for the claimant which may make it more likely that the claimant will remain in or obtain work or be able to do so;

  (e) identifying current or future work opportunities, including self-employment opportunities, for the claimant, that are relevant to the claimant's needs and abilities.

DEFINITIONS

  "claimant"—see WRA 2007, s.24(1).
  "training"—see reg.2(1).
  "work-focused interview"—see WRA 2007, s.12(7).

GENERAL NOTE

9.123 Pursuant to WRA 2007, s.12(7) this regulation prescribes the purposes of a work-focused interview as any or all of those listed in paras (a)–(e).

Notification of interview

9.124 **56.**—(1) The Secretary of State must notify the claimant of the requirement to attend the work-focused interview including details of the date, time and place of the interview.

  (2) A work-focused interview may take place at a claimant's home if it is determined that requiring the claimant to attend elsewhere would cause undue inconvenience to, or endanger the health of, the claimant.

  (3) The notification referred to in paragraph (1) may be in writing or otherwise.

DEFINITIONS

  "claimant"—see WRA 2007, s.24(1).
  "work-focused interview"—see WRA 2007, s.12(7).

GENERAL NOTE

9.125 The Secretary of State must give proper notification to the claimant that he is required to attend the work-focused interview. This must include details of its date, time and place (para.(1)). The notification need not be in writing (para.(2)). This is in marked contrast to other provisions imposing requirements with respect to the three elements of the work capability assessment (WCA) (see regs 22–24, 36–38, 49). So is the absence of any stipulation as to due period of notice. As to place, none is specified (a consequence of ability to contract-out the interviews—reg.62). But the interview can take place at the claimant's home if it is decided that requirement to attend elsewhere would endanger his health or simply cause undue convenience.

Taking part in a work-focused interview

57.—(1) A claimant is regarded as having taken part in a work-focused   **9.126**
interview if the claimant—
- (a) attends for the interview at the place and at the date and time notified in accordance with regulation 56;
- (b) provides information, if requested by the Secretary of State, about any or all of the matters set out in paragraph (2);
- (c) participates in discussions to the extent the Secretary of State considers necessary, about any or all of the matters set out in paragraph (3);
- (d) assists the Secretary of State in the completion of an action plan.

(2) The matters referred to in paragraph (1)(b) are—
- (a) the claimant's educational qualifications and vocational training;
- (b) the claimant's work history;
- (c) the claimant's aspirations for future work;
- (d) the claimant's skills that are relevant to work;
- (e) the claimant's work-related abilities;
- (f) the claimant's caring or childcare responsibilities; and
- (g) any paid or unpaid work that the claimant is undertaking.

(3) The matters referred to in paragraph (1)(c) are—
- (a) any activity the claimant is willing to undertake which may make obtaining or remaining in work more likely;
- (b) any such activity that the claimant may have previously undertaken;
- (c) any progress the claimant may have made towards remaining in or obtaining work;
- (d) any work-focused health-related assessment the claimant may have taken part in; and
- (e) the claimant's opinion as to the extent to which the ability to remain in or obtain work is restricted by the claimant's physical or mental condition.

DEFINITIONS

    "claimant"—see WRA 2007, s.24(1).
    "work-focused health-related assessment"—see WRA 2007, s.11(7).
    "work-focused interview"—see WRA 2007, s.12(7).

GENERAL NOTE

    Failure, without good cause, to take part in a work-focused interview (regs 55,   **9.127**
57, 58, 61) is sanctioned initially by halving the amount of work-related activity component and eventually by reducing it to nil (reg.63), the reduction to cease after compliance has been induced or the requirement to participate has ceased to have effect under para.(3) (reg.64).
    This regulation sets out when a claimant is to be regarded as having taken part: attendance at the proper place, date and time (para.(1)(a)); provision of the requisite information required by the Secretary of State (paras (1)(b), (2)); participation to such an extent as the Secretary of State considers necessary in discussion about

the key matters stipulated in para.(3); and assisting the Secretary of State (in reality someone in Jobcentre Plus or a contractor or employee of a contractor) in drawing up an "action plan" as defined in reg.58.

Action plan

9.128   **58.**—(1) An action plan is a document that is completed by the Secretary of State and contains—
(a) a record of a work-focused interview;
(b) a record of any activity that the claimant is willing to take which may make obtaining or remaining in work more likely or which may make it more likely that the claimant will be able to do so;
(c) any other information that the Secretary of State considers to be appropriate.
(2) An action plan must be in writing.
(3) The Secretary of State must provide a claimant who attends a work-focused interview with an action plan.

DEFINITIONS

"action plan"—see para.(1).
"claimant"—see WRA 2007, s.24(1).
"work-focused interview"—see WRA 2007, s.12(7).

GENERAL NOTE

9.129   In order to be regarded under reg.57 as having taken part in a work-focused interview, the claimant must assist the Secretary of State (in reality someone in Jobcentre Plus or a contractor or employee of a contractor) in drawing up an "action plan". This regulation defines "action plan" (para.(1)), requires it to be in writing (para.(2)), and that the Secretary of State provides a claimant who attends a work-focused interview with such a plan (para.(3)).

Deferral of requirement to take part in a work-focused interview

9.130   **59.**—(1) A requirement to take part in a work-focused interview may be deferred or treated as having been deferred if at the time the work-focused interview is to take place, or was due to take place, such an interview would not at that time be or have been—
(a) of assistance to the claimant; or
(b) appropriate in the circumstances.
(2) A decision under paragraph (1) may be made at any time after the requirement to take part in the work-focused interview is imposed, including after the time that the work-focused interview was due to take place or took place.
(3) Where a requirement to take part in a work-focused interview is deferred, or treated as having been deferred, then the time that the work-focused interview is to take place must be re-determined.

DEFINITIONS

"claimant"—see WRA 2007, s.24(1).
"work-focused interview"—see WRA 2007, s.12(7).

GENERAL NOTE

9.131   This regulation enables deferral of a work-focused interview (or treating it as deferred) if holding it would not assist the claimant or otherwise be inappropriate (para.(1)). The decision on deferral can be made at any time after the requirement to take part was imposed on the claimant, whether before or after it was due to take place (para.(2)). If deferred, the matter of when such an interview is to take place has to be re-determined (para.(3)).

Requirement to take part in a work-focused interview not to apply

60. The Secretary of State may determine that a requirement on a claimant to take part in a work-focused interview is not to apply, or is to be treated as not having applied, if that interview would not be, or would not have been, of assistance because the claimant is or was likely to be starting or returning to work.

9.132

DEFINITIONS

"claimant"—see WRA 2007, s.24(1).
"work-focused interview"—see WRA 2007, s.12(7).

GENERAL NOTE

This enables lifting of the requirement to take part in a work-focused interview, whether before or after it was due to take place, where it would not be (or be likely to have been of assistance) because the claimant is or was likely to be starting or returning to work.

9.133

Failure to take part in a work-focused interview

61.—(1) A claimant who is required to take part in a work-focused interview but fails to do so must show good cause for that failure within 5 working days of the date on which the Secretary of State gives notification of that failure.

9.134

(2) The Secretary of State must determine whether a claimant who is required to take part in a work-focused interview has failed to do so and, if so, whether the claimant has shown good cause for that failure in accordance with paragraph (1).

(3) In determining whether a claimant has shown good cause for the failure to take part in a work-focused interview, the Secretary of State may take the following matters into account—

(a) that the claimant misunderstood the requirement to take part in the work-focused interview due to learning, language or literacy difficulties or any misleading information given or sent by the Secretary of State;

(b) that the claimant had transport difficulties and that no reasonable alternative was available;

(c) that the claimant was attending an interview with an employer with a view to remaining in or obtaining work;

(d) that the claimant was pursuing employment opportunities as a self-employed earner;

(e) that the claimant was attending a medical or dental appointment and that it would have been unreasonable in the circumstances to re-arrange the appointment;

(f) that the claimant was accompanying another person for whom the claimant has caring responsibilities to a medical or dental appointment and that it would have been unreasonable for that other person to re-arrange the appointment;

    (g) that the claimant, a dependant or another person for whom the claimant provides care suffered an accident, sudden illness or relapse of a physical or mental condition;

    (h) that the claimant was attending the funeral of a relative or close friend on the day of the work-focused interview;

    (i) that the physical or mental condition of the claimant made it impossible to attend at the time and place fixed for the interview;

    (j) that the established customs and practices of the religion to which the claimant belongs prevented attendance on that day or at that time;

    (k) any other matter which the Secretary of State considers appropriate.

DEFINITIONS

> "claimant"—see WRA 2007, s.24(1).
> "relative"—see reg.2(1).
> "work-focused interview"—see WRA 2007, s.12(7).

GENERAL NOTE

9.135   Failure, without good cause, to participate in a work-focused interview (regs 55, 57, 58) is sanctioned initially by halving the amount of work-related activity component and eventually by reducing it to nil (reg.63), the reduction to cease after compliance has been induced or the requirement to participate has ceased to have effect under para.(3) (reg.64).

This regulation deals with showing good cause when the Secretary of State has notified the claimant of his failure to take part. It requires the claimant to show good cause for such failure within five working days of the date on which the notification was given (para.(1)). It must then be determined whether there was a failure and, if so, whether the requisite good case has been shown within the stipulated time frame (para.(2)). "Good cause" is not defined, although WRA 2007, s.12(2)(i) provides power to prescribe what ranks or does not rank as "good cause. Paragraph (3) merely provides, pursuant to subs.(2)(h) of that section, eleven matters which may be taken into account.

Contracting out certain functions relating to work-focused interviews

9.136   **62.**—(1) Any function of the Secretary of State specified in paragraph (2) may be exercised by, or by employees of, such person (if any) as may be authorised by the Secretary of State.

(2) The functions are any function under—

    (a) regulation 54(1) (requirement to take part in a work-focused interview);

    (b) regulation 56(1) and (2) (notification requirement);

    (c) regulation 57(1)(b) and (c) (taking part in a work-focused interview);

    (d) regulation 58(1) and (3) (action plan);

    (e) regulation 59(1) and (3) (deferral of requirement to take part in a work-focused interview);

    (f) regulation 60 (requirement to take part in a work-focused interview not to apply).

GENERAL NOTE

9.137   Pursuant to WRA 2007, s.16, which enables contracting-out, this regulation sets out in para.(2) functions of the Secretary of State under these regulations which can be exercise by an authorised contractor or the employees of such a contractor. The idea is to bring expertise from the private and voluntary sectors (PVS) into the process of assisting claimants to prepare for and enhance their prospects of starting or returning to work. It is envisaged, however, that the first work-focused interview will always be with someone from Jobcentre Plus and will be held around the eighth week of the assessment period. Note that sanctioning decisions (regs 63, 64) are not-contracted out, although clearly information provided by contractors will inform those decisions.

CHAPTER 3

REDUCTION OF EMPLOYMENT AND SUPPORT ALLOWANCE

Reduction of employment and support allowance

63.—(1) Where the Secretary of State has determined that a claimant who was required to take part in—   9.138

(a) a work-focused health-related assessment; or

(b) a work-focused interview,

has failed to do so and has failed to show good cause for that failure in accordance with regulation 53 or 61, as the case may be ("a failure determination"), the amount of the employment and support allowance payable to the claimant is to be reduced in accordance with this regulation.

(2) Subject to paragraph (3), the amount of the reduction in relation to each failure determination is—

(a) 50% of the amount of the work-related activity component as set out in Part 4 of Schedule 4 for the first 4 benefit weeks to which, by virtue of section 10(5) of the Social Security Act 1998 or regulations made under section 10(6) of that Act, the reduction applies; and

(b) 100% of the amount of that component for each subsequent benefit week.

(3) In any benefit week, the amount of an employment and support allowance payable to a claimant is not, by virtue of this regulation, to be reduced—

(a) below 10 pence;

(b) in relation to more than—

(i) one failure determination relating to a work-focused health-related assessment; and

(ii) one failure determination relating to a work-focused interview; and

(c) by more than 100% of the amount of the work-related activity component as set out in Part 4 of Schedule 4 in any circumstances.

(4) Where a claimant is entitled to both a contributory allowance and an income-related allowance, any reduction in the claimant's allowance must first be applied to the part of that allowance treated as attributable to the claimant's contributory allowance and only if there is any amount outstanding is it to be applied to the part of that allowance treated as attributable to the claimant's income-related allowance.

(5) For the purposes of determining the amount of any income-related allowance payable, a claimant is to be treated as receiving the amount of any contributory allowance which would have been payable but for any reduction made in accordance with this regulation.

DEFINITIONS

"claimant"—see WRA 2007, s.24(1).
"contributory allowance"—see WRA 2007, ss.24(1), 1(7).
"failure determination"—see para.(1).
"income-related allowance"—see WRA 2007, ss.24(1), 1(7).
"work-focused health-related assessment"—see WRA 2007, s.11(7).
"work-focused interview"—see WRA 2007, s.12(7).

GENERAL NOTE

9.139 In accordance with WRA 2007, ss.12(3), 13(3), this regulation provides the sanction for failure without god cause to take part in a work focused health-related assessment and/or a work-focused interview. The sanction, put simply, is a reduction in the amount of ESA to which the person would otherwise be entitled (para.(1)). On the face of the Act and the first para of this regulation, that could be a reduction of ESA as a whole, even to nil. The legal reality—effected by the words "in accordance with the provisions of this regulation" in para.(1) and by para.(3)(c)—is that the reduction is to be effected only against the work-related activity component and not basic allowance ESA. It would have been better to have included that "promise" in the Act itself, rather than in a regulation whose terms, legislatively speaking, are more easily changeable than a "promise" or restriction in primary legislation (see JHRC, *Second Report of Session 2006–07*, HL 34/HC 263 (2006–07), para.3.18), especially as it would seem that this limitation has always been the policy intention.

The reduction is to be 50% of the work-related activity component for the first four weeks after the decision on non-participation and increases to 100% of the amount for each benefit week thereafter (para.(2)). However, the amount cannot be reduced below 10 pence (para.(3)(a)). Nor does the amount of reduction increase because there is more than one failure determination (e.g. non-participation in both assessment and interview (para.(3)(b))).

Paragraphs (4) and (5) deal with the situation where the claimant's ESA is composed both of CESA and IRESA (a common situation). Reduction is to be effected first against the amount attributable to CESA and only if after that there is a balance of reduction still to be applied, against IRESA (para.(4)). However, even where CESA is thus reduced, for the purposes of deciding on the amount of IRESA when drawing up the IRESA "balance sheet" of "needs" and "resources", the claimant is to be treated as if he were receiving the full amount of CESA to which he would otherwise be entitled but for reduction in accordance with this regulation, and not the reduced amount of CESA left after the reduction demanded by this regulation has been effected (para.(5))

Cessation of reduction

9.140 **64.**—(1) Any reduction imposed as a result of a failure determination which resulted from a failure to take part in a work-focused health-related assessment ceases to have effect if—

(a) the claimant complies with a requirement to attend a work-focused health-related assessment; or
(b) the claimant subsequently ceases to meet the requirements set out in regulation 47(2).

(2) Any reduction imposed as a result of a failure determination which resulted from a failure to take part in a work-focused interview ceases to have effect if—

(a) the claimant complies with a requirement to attend a work-focused interview; or
(b) the claimant subsequently ceases to meet the requirements set out in regulation 54(2).

DEFINITIONS

"claimant"—see WRA2007, s.24(1).
"failure determination"—see reg.63(1).
"work-focused health-related assessment"—see WRA 2007, s.11(7).
"work-focused interview"—see WRA 2007, s.12(7).

GENERAL NOTE

Reduction in the amount of work-related activity component cease when the 9.141
failure to participate in respect of which the reduction was imposed has been rectified, whether by taking part in a work-focused health related assessment or a work-
focused interview, as the case may be. Reductions imposed must also cease to have
effect if the claimant ceases to be a proper subject of the relevant requirements to
participate (one or more of the conditions set out in regs 47(2) [work-focused health
related assessment] or 54(2) [work-focused interview), applies as the case may be).

CHAPTER 4

NOTIFICATION

Notification under this Part

65.—(1) Where written notification is to be given in accordance with this 9.142
Part, such notification may be sent by post.

(2) Any notification sent by post is to be taken to have been received on
the second working day after posting.

GENERAL NOTE

This deals with notifications in respect of the conditionality elements in Pt 8 of 9.143
these regulations. It stipulates that where written notifications are thereby required
or envisaged (see regs 49(2),56(3)) they may be sent by post (para.(1)). If so the
rule is that such notification is to be taken to have been received on the second
working day after posting. (para.(2)).

CHAPTER 5

MODIFICATION OF THE ACT IN RELATION TO CLAIMS TO WHICH
SECTION 5(1)(C) OF THE ADMINISTRATION ACT APPLIES

Modifications of the Act

66.—(1) Where a person has made a claim for an employment and 9.144
support allowance to which section 5(1)(c) of the Administration Act
applies, the Act applies with the following modifications.

(2) Section 11(1) of the Act applies—

(a) as if for sub-paragraph (a) there were substituted—

"(a) either—

    (i) entitled to an employment and support allowance; or

    (ii) a person who has made a claim for an employment and support
allowance to which regulations under section 5(1)(c) of the
Administration Act apply; and"; and

(b) as if for "continuing to be" there were substituted "being".

(3) Section 12(1) of the Act applies—
    (a) as if for sub-paragraph (a) there were substituted—
        "(a) either—
                (i) entitled to an employment and support allowance; or
                (ii) a person who has made a claim to which section 5 applies; and"; and
    (b) as if for "continuing to be" there were substituted "being".

DEFINITIONS

"the Act"—see reg.2(1).
"Administration Act"—see WRA 2007, s.65.

GENERAL NOTE

9.145   This regulation alters the terms of WRA 2007, ss.11(1) ("work-focused health-related assessment") and 12(1) ("work-focused interview") where a person has made a claim for ESA which falls to be governed by the AA 1992, s.5(1)(c) (a claim made, or treated as made, for a period wholly or partly after the date on which it is made). In such cases, s.11(1) is to read (modifications in square brackets):

"(1) Regulations may make provision for or in connection with imposing on a person who is—
    [(a) either—
        (i) entitled to an employment and support allowance; or
        (ii) a person who has made a claim for an employment and support allowance to which regulations under section 5(1)(c) of the Administration Act apply; and]
    (b) not a member of the support group,
a requirement to take part in one or more work-focused health-related assessments as a condition of [being] entitled to the full amount payable to him in respect of the allowance apart from the regulations."

Similarly, s.12(1) is to read (modifications in square brackets):

"(1) Regulations may make provision for or in connection with imposing on a person who is—
    [(a) either—
        (i) entitled to an employment and support allowance; or
        (ii) a person who has made a claim to which section 5 applies; and]
    (b) not a member of the support group,
a requirement to take part in one or more work-focused interviews as a condition of [being] entitled to the full amount payable to him in respect of the allowance apart from the regulations."

PART 9

AMOUNTS OF ALLOWANCE

CHAPTER 1

PRESCRIBED AMOUNTS

Prescribed amounts

9.146   **67.**—(1) Subject to regulations 68, 69 and 163 (amounts in other cases, special cases and urgent cases), the amounts prescribed for the purposes of the calculation of the amount of an income related allowance under section 4(2)(a) of the Act in relation to a claimant are such of the following amounts as may apply in the claimant's case—

(a) an amount in respect of the claimant or, if the claimant is a member of a couple, an amount in respect of both of them determined in accordance with paragraph 1(1), (2) or (3) of Schedule 4 (amounts) as the case may be;

(b) the amount of any premiums which may be applicable to the claimant determined in accordance with Parts 2 and 3 of that Schedule (premiums);

(c) any amounts determined in accordance with Schedule 6 (housing costs) which may be applicable to the claimant in respect of mortgage interest repayments or such other housing costs as are prescribed in that Schedule.

(2) Subject to regulation 69 (special cases) the amount prescribed for the purposes of the calculation of the amount of a claimant's contributory allowance under section 2(1)(a) of the Act is the amount determined in accordance with paragraph 1(1) of Schedule 4 as may apply in the claimant's case.

(3) Subject to regulation 69, the amount of the work-related activity component and the support component are prescribed in Part 4 of Schedule 4.

DEFINITIONS

"claimant"—see WRA 2007, s.24(1).
"contributory allowance"—see WRA 2007, s.1(7).
"couple"—see reg.2(1).
"income related allowance"—see WRA 2007, s.1(7).

GENERAL NOTE

Para. (1)

This regulation is similar to reg.17 of the IS Regulations and reg.83 of the JSA Regulations. The applicable amounts are set out in Sch.4 below.   9.147

In the same manner as IS and JSA, this read with Sch.4, paras 1(1) (single claimant, age related), (2) (lone parent, age-related) or (3) (couple, age related) as appropriate, specifies the amounts applicable in respect of a claimant as regards IRESA: an amount for him and any partner (para.(1)(a)); applicable premiums (para.(1)(b), Sch.4, Pts 2 and 3); and applicable housing costs (para.(1)(c), Sch.6). This is, however, subject to regs 68 (amounts in other cases [polygamous marriages]), 69 (special cases) and 163 (urgent cases).

Para. (2)

This sets the prescribed amount (basic allowance) of CESA (WRA 2007, s.2(1)   9.148
(a)) by reference to Sch.4, para.1(1). During the assessment phase (before entitlement to support component or work related activity component arises under WRA 2007, ss.2(2) or (3) or 4(4) or (5)), there are two rates, a lower rate for those under 25, a higher one for those 25 or over (Sch.4, para.1(1)). After the assessment phase is over and title to one or other component has been satisfied, the higher rate is applicable whatever the age of the claimant. For those terminally ill covered by reg.7(1)(a) the higher rate component is available from the start of the claim on the basis of terminal illness or the date of an application for revision or supersession on that basis. The prescription of the amount is, however, subject to reg.69 (special cases). Note also that, whatever the amount of CESA thus set, it is, under WRA 2007, ss.2(1)(c) and 3, subject to reduction in respect of a variety of payments: pension payments (including permanent health insurance payments)(s.3(1)

(a), (3); regs 72, 74 and 75); PPF periodic payments (s.3(1)(b), (3); reg.74); and prescribed payments to members of prescribed bodies carrying out public or local functions (currently limited to councillor's allowance and the bodies in the definition of councillor in reg.2(1)) (s.2(1)(c); regs 73, 76). The amount of CESA is also to be reduced by the amount of statutory maternity pay (s.2(2), (3); reg.80), statutory adoption pay (s.2(4), (5); reg.81) or additional statutory paternity pay (s.2(6), (7)); reg.82) to which the claimant is entitled during his period of limited capability for work.

Para. (3)

9.149   Subject to reg.69 (special cases), read with Sch.4, para.4, this specifies the amounts of the support and work-related activity components, the former being the more generous. Note further that, whatever the amount of work-related activity component thus determined, it is subject to reduction for failure to comply with the conditionality requirements set by WRA 2007, ss.11–13 and Pt 8 of these Regs.

Polygamous marriages

9.150   **68.**—(1) Subject to regulation 69 and 163 (special cases and urgent cases), where a claimant is a husband or wife by virtue of a polygamous marriage the amounts prescribed for the purposes of the calculation of the amount of an income-related allowance under section 4(2)(a) of the Act are such of the following amounts as may apply in the claimant's case—

(a)   an amount in respect of the claimant and the other party to the marriage determined in accordance with paragraph 1(3) of Schedule 4;

(b)   an amount equal to the difference between the amounts specified in paragraph 1(3)(a) (couple where both aged 18 and over) and 1(1)(b) (single claimant aged 25 and over) of Schedule 4 in respect of each spouse additional to the marriage;

(c)   the amount of any premiums which are applicable to the claimant determined in accordance with Parts 2 and 3 of that Schedule (premiums);

(d)   any amounts determined in accordance with Schedule 6 (housing costs) which may be applicable to the claimant in respect of mortgage interest payments or such other housing costs as are prescribed in that Schedule.

(2) In the case of a partner who is aged less than 18, the amount which applies in respect of that partner is nil unless—

(a)   that partner is treated as responsible for a child; or

(b)   that partner is a person who—

(i)   had that partner not been a member of a polygamous marriage would have qualified for an income-related allowance; or

(ii)   satisfies the requirements of section 3(1)(f)(iii) of the Jobseekers Act (prescribed circumstances for persons aged 16 but less than 18); or

(iii)   is the subject of a direction under section 16 of that Act (persons under 18: severe hardship).

DEFINITIONS

"the Act"—reg.2(1).
"claimant"—Welfare Reform Act 2007, s.24(1).
"couple"—reg.2(1).
"income-related allowance"—Welfare Reform Act 2007, s.24(1) and 1(7).
"Jobseekers Act"—reg.2(1).

"partner"—*ibid.*
"polygamous marriage"—*ibid.*
"single claimant"—*ibid.*

GENERAL NOTE

This regulation is similar to reg.18 of the IS Regulations and reg.84 of the JSA   **9.151**
Regulations.

Special cases

69.—(1) In the case of a claimant to whom any paragraph in column (1)   **9.152**
of Schedule 5 applies (amounts in special cases), the amount in respect of
the claimant is to be the amount in the corresponding paragraph in column
(2) of that Schedule.

(2) In Schedule 5—

"partner of a person subject to immigration control" means a person—

(a) who is not subject to immigration control within the meaning of
section 115(9) of the Immigration and Asylum Act; or

(b) to whom section 115 of that Act does not apply by virtue of regulation
2 of the Social Security (Immigration and Asylum) Consequential
Amendments Regulations 2000; and

(c) who is a member of a couple and the member's partner is subject to
immigration control within the meaning of section 115(9) of that Act
and section 115 of that Act applies to the partner for the purposes of
exclusion from entitlement to an income-related allowance;

"patient" means a person (other than a prisoner) who is regarded as
receiving free in-patient treatment within the meaning of regulation
2(4) and (5) of the Social Security (Hospital In- Patients) Regulations
2005;

"person from abroad" has the meaning given in regulation 70;

"person in hardship" means a person who satisfies regulation 158 but
only for a period not exceeding 6 weeks;

"prisoner" means a person who—

(a) is detained in custody pending trial or sentence on conviction or
under a sentence imposed by a court; or

(b) is on temporary release in accordance with the provisions of the
Prison Act 1952 or the Prisons (Scotland) Act 1989, other than
a person who is detained in hospital under the provisions of the
Mental Health Act 1983 or, in Scotland, under the provisions of the
Mental Health (Care and Treatment) (Scotland) Act 2003 or the
Criminal Procedure (Scotland) Act 1995.

DEFINITIONS

"claimant"—Welfare Reform Act 2007, s.24(1).
"couple"—reg.2(1).
"Immigration and Asylum Act"—*ibid.*
"income-related allowance"—Welfare Reform Act 2007, s.24(1) and 1(7).
"partner"—reg.2(1).

GENERAL NOTE

This regulation is similar to reg.21 of the IS Regulations and reg.85 of the   **9.153**
JSA Regulations. Applicable amounts in special cases are prescribed by Sch.5
below.

Special cases: supplemental—persons from abroad

9.154   **70.**—(1) "Person from abroad" means, subject to the following provisions of this regulation, a claimant who is not habitually resident in the United Kingdom, the Channel Islands, the Isle of Man or the Republic of Ireland.

(2) A claimant must not be treated as habitually resident in the United Kingdom, the Channel Islands, the Isle of Man or the Republic of Ireland unless the claimant has a right to reside in (as the case may be) the United Kingdom, the Channel Islands, the Isle of Man or the Republic of Ireland other than a right to reside which falls within paragraph (3).

(3) A right to reside falls within this paragraph if it is one which exists by virtue of, or in accordance with, one or more of the following—

(a) regulation 13 of the Immigration (European Economic Area) Regulations 2006;

(b) regulation 14 of those Regulations, but only in a case where the right exists under that regulation because the claimant is—

    (i) a jobseeker for the purpose of the definition of "qualified person" in regulation 6(1) of those Regulations; or

    (ii) a family member (within the meaning of regulation 7 of those Regulations) of such a jobseeker;

(c) Article 6 of Council Directive No. 2004/38/EC; or

(d) Article 39 of the Treaty establishing the European Community (in a case where the claimant is a person seeking work in the United Kingdom, the Channel Islands, the Isle of Man or the Republic of Ireland).

(4) A claimant is not a person from abroad if the claimant is—

(a) a worker for the purposes of Council Directive No. 2004/38/EC;

(b) a self-employed person for the purposes of that Directive;

(c) a person who retains a status referred to in sub-paragraph (a) or (b) pursuant to Article 7(3) of that Directive;

(d) a person who is a family member of a person referred to in sub-paragraph (a), (b) or (c) within the meaning of Article 2 of that Directive;

(e) a person who has a right to reside permanently in the United Kingdom by virtue of Article 17 of that Directive;

(f) a person who is treated as a worker for the purpose of the definition of "qualified person" in regulation 6(1) of the Immigration (European Economic Area) Regulations 2006 pursuant to—

    (i) regulation 5 of the Accession (Immigration and Worker Registration) Regulations 2004 (application of the 2006 Regulations in relation to a national of the Czech Republic, Estonia, Latvia, Lithuania, Hungary, Poland, Slovenia or the Slovak Republic who is an "accession State worker requiring registration"); or

    (ii) regulation 6 of the Accession (Immigration and Worker Authorisation) Regulations 2006 (right of residence of a Bulgarian or Romanian who is an "accession State national subject to worker authorisation");

(g) a refugee within the definition in Article 1 of the Convention relating to the Status of Refugees done at Geneva on 28th July 1951, as extended by Article 1(2) of the Protocol relating to the Status of Refugees done at New York on 31st January 1967;

(h) a person who has exceptional leave to enter or remain in the United Kingdom granted outside the rules made under section 3(2) of the Immigration Act 1971;

(i) a person who has humanitarian protection granted under those rules;

(j) a person who is not a person subject to immigration control within the meaning of section 115(9) of the Immigration and Asylum Act and who is in the United Kingdom as a result of deportation, expulsion or other removal by compulsion of law from another country to the United Kingdom; [¹ . . .]

(k) a person in Great Britain who left the territory of Montserrat after 1st November 1995 because of the effect on that territory of a volcanic eruption [¹ ; or

(jj) a person who—

    (i) arrived in Great Britain on or after 28th February 2009 but before 18th March 2011;

    (ii) immediately before arriving there had been resident in Zimbabwe; and

    (iii) before leaving Zimbabwe, had accepted an offer, made by Her Majesty's Government, to assist that person to move to and settle in the United Kingdom.]

AMENDMENT

1. Social Security (Habitual Residence) (Amendment) Regulations 2009 (SI 2009/362), reg.9 (March 18, 2009).

DEFINITION

"Immigration and Asylum Act"—reg.2(1).

GENERAL NOTE

See the commentary to reg.21AA of the IS Regs.   **9.155**

Definition of non-dependant

71.—(1) In these Regulations, "non-dependant" means any person,   **9.156** except someone to whom paragraph (2), (3) or (4) applies, who normally resides with a claimant or with whom a claimant normally resides.

(2) This paragraph applies to—

(a) any member of the claimant's family;

(b) a child or young person who is living with the claimant but who is not a member of the claimant's household;

(c) a person who lives with the claimant in order to care for the claimant or for the claimant's partner and who is engaged for that purpose by a charitable or voluntary organisation which makes a charge to the claimant or the claimant's partner for the care provided by that person;

(d) the partner of a person to whom sub-paragraph (c) applies.

(3) This paragraph applies to a person, other than a close relative of the claimant or the claimant's partner—

(a) who is liable to make payments on a commercial basis to the claimant or the claimant's partner in respect of the person's occupation of the claimant's dwelling;

(b) to whom the claimant or the claimant's partner is liable to make payments on a commercial basis in respect of the claimant's occupation of that person's dwelling;

(c) who is a member of the household of a person to whom sub-paragraph (a) or (b) applies.

(4) Subject to paragraph (5), this paragraph applies to—

(a) a person who jointly occupies the claimant's dwelling and who is either—

    (i) a co-owner of that dwelling with the claimant or the claimant's partner (whether or not there are other co-owners); or

    (ii) jointly liable with the claimant or the claimant's partner to make payments to a landlord in respect of the person's occupation of that dwelling;

(b) a partner of a person to whom sub-paragraph (a) applies.

(5) Where a person is a close relative of the claimant or the claimant's partner, paragraph (4) applies to that person only if the claimant's, or the claimant's partner's, co-ownership, or joint liability to make payments to a landlord in respect of occupation of the dwelling arose either before 11th April 1988 or, if later, on or before the date on which the claimant or the claimant's partner first occupied the dwelling in question.

(6) For the purposes of this regulation a person resides with another only if they share any accommodation except a bathroom, a lavatory or a communal area but not if each person is separately liable to make payments in respect of occupation of the dwelling to the landlord.

(7) In this regulation "communal area" means any area (other than rooms) of common access (including halls and passageways) and rooms of common use in sheltered accommodation.

DEFINITIONS

"child"—reg.2(1).
"claimant"—Welfare Reform Act 2007, s.24(1).
"close relative"—*ibid*.
"family"—reg.2(1) and (3).
"partner"—reg.2(1).
"voluntary organisation"—*ibid*.
"young person"—*ibid*.

GENERAL NOTE

9.157   See the notes to reg.3 of the IS Regs.

CHAPTER 2

DEDUCTIONS FROM THE CONTRIBUTORY ALLOWANCE

Permanent health insurance

9.158   **72.**—(1) For the purposes of sections 2(1)(c) and 3 of the Act (deductions from contributory allowance) pension payment is to include a permanent health insurance payment.

(2) In this regulation "permanent health insurance payment" means any periodical payment arranged by an employer under an insurance policy providing benefits in connection with physical or mental illness or disability, in relation to a former employee on the termination of that person's employment.

bodies carrying out public or local functions. This regulation defines councillor's allowance as a prescribed payment and stipulates that "prescribed bodies carrying out public or local functions" are those bodies in the definition of councillor in reg.2(1). On the reductive effect of councillor's allowance see reg.76.

Deductions for pension payment and PPF payment

9.164 **74.**—(1) Where—
(a) [¹a claimant] is entitled to a contributory allowance in respect of any period of a week or part of a week;
(b) there is—
(i) a pension payment;
(ii) a PPF periodic payment; or
(iii) any combination of the payments specified in paragraphs (i) and (ii),
payable to that person in respect of that period (or a period which forms part of that period or includes that period or part of it); and
(c) the amount of the payment, or payments when taken together, exceeds—
(i) if the period in question is a week, £85.00; or
(ii) if that period is not a week, such proportion of the amount mentioned in paragraph (i) as falls to be calculated in accordance with regulation 94(1) or (6) (calculation of weekly amount of income),
the amount of that allowance is to be reduced by an amount equal to 50% of the excess.

(2) For the purposes of this Chapter "payment" means a payment or payments, as the case may be, referred to in paragraph (1)(b).

AMENDMENTS

1. Employment and Support Allowance (Miscellaneous Amendments) Regulations 2008 (SI 2008/2428), reg.7(2) (October 27, 2008).

DEFINITIONS

"claimant"—see WRA 2007, s.24(1).
"payment"—see para.(2).
"pension payment"—see WRA 2007, s.3(3); regs 73, 73A.
"PPF periodic payment"—see WRA 2007, s.3(3).

GENERAL NOTE

9.165 WRA 2007, ss.2(1)(c) and 3(1)(a) stipulate that deductions are to be made from CESA in respect of "pension payments" and "PPF periodic payments". This regulation provides that where one or more of these is payable to a claimant in respect of a week in respect of which he is entitled to CESA, then where the amount (or combined amount) of that payment (those payments) exceeds £85, the amount of CESA otherwise due is to be reduced by half of the excess over £85. Where the period of CESA entitlement is less than a week, 50% of the excess over an appropriate proportion of the amount of £85 as determined under regs 94(1) or (6) (calculation of amount of income) is instead to be deducted.

Payments treated as not being payments to which section 3 applies

9.166 **75.** The following payments are to be treated as not being payments to which section 3 applies—
(a) any pension payment made to a claimant as a beneficiary on the death of a member of any pension scheme;

1038

(b) any PPF periodic payment made to a claimant as a beneficiary on the death of a person entitled to such a payment;

(c) where a pension scheme is in deficit or has insufficient resources to meet the full pension payment, the extent of the shortfall;

(d) any pension payment made under an instrument specified in section 639(2) of the Income Tax (Earnings and Pensions) Act 2003;

(e) any guaranteed income payment;

(f) any permanent health insurance payment in respect of which the employee had contributed to the premium to the extent of more than 50%.

DEFINITIONS

"claimant"—see WRA 2007, s.24(1).
"guaranteed income payment"—see reg.2(1).
"pension payment"—see WRA 2007, s.3(3); regs 73, 73A.
"permanent health insurance payment"—see reg.72(2).
"PPF periodic payment"—see WRA 2007, s.3(3).

GENERAL NOTE

WRA 2007, ss.2(1)(c) and 3(1)(a) stipulate that deductions are to be made from CESA in respect of "pension payments" and "PPF periodic payments". This regulation provides that the payments listed in it which would otherwise so rank are not to be treated as payments to which s.3 applies, and so are not to be deducted from CESA.   9.167

Deductions for councillor's allowance

76.—(1) Where the net amount of councillor's allowance to which a claimant is entitled in respect of any week exceeds [¹£92.00], an amount equal to the excess is to be deducted from the amount of a contributory allowance to which that person is entitled in respect of that week, and only the balance remaining (if any) is to be payable.   9.168

(2) In paragraph (1) "net amount", in relation to any councillor's allowance to which a claimant is entitled, means the aggregate amount of the councillor's allowance or allowances, or remuneration to which that claimant is entitled for the week in question, reduced by the amount of any payment in respect of expenses wholly, exclusively and necessarily incurred by that claimant, in that week, in the performance of the duties of a councillor.

AMENDMENTS

1. Employment and Support Allowance (Miscellaneous Amendments) Regulations 2008 (SI 2008/2428), reg.7(3) (October 27, 2008).

DEFINITIONS

"contributory allowance"—see WRA 2007, s.1(7).
"councillor's allowance"—see reg.2(1).
"net amount"—see para.(2).

GENERAL NOTE

This regulation provides that where the net amount of councillor's allowance or remuneration to which the claimant is entitled in any week exceed £92, the amount of the excess must be deducted from the amount of CESA to which he would   9.169

otherwise be entitled in respect of that week. The reduction can be to nil. Only the balance of CESA remaining (if any) is to be payable. On para.(3) (determination of net amount), compare SSCBA 1992, s.30E(3). That is in similar terms apart from not specifying as para.(3) of this regulation does that the expenses must be "*wholly, exclusively and necessarily* incurred by that claimant, in that week, in *the performance of the duties* of a councillor". The IB provision specified that the expenses must have been incurred in that week in connection with his membership of the [relevant council(s)]. Subject to that, however, existing IVB and IB case law on "net amount" is relevant.

Unlike the position with computation of earnings under the Computation of Earnings Regs, no concept of averaging across the year is to be applied. In *CS 7934/95*, Commissioner Rice decided:

> "that the expenses incurred in any week by the claimant for the performance of her duties as a local authority councillor (whether for clothes, telephone rental, telephone calls, subscriptions, travel, or whatever it might be) shall for the purposes of calculating her entitlement to invalidity benefit [pursuant to SSCBA 1992, s.58(4), the similarly worded precursor of para.(3) of this section, defining 'net amount'], be deducted from the allowance or allowances to which she is entitled in respect of that week" (para.1).

It is immaterial that the benefits of expenses incurred in that week (e.g. the purchase of a dress to be worn more than once for official functions) are enjoyed in future weeks (para.9). In *CIB 2858, 2859* and *2864/2001*, Commissioner Jacobs supported as correct the approach taken by Commissioner Rice in *CS 7934/95*. He disagreed with Commissioner Williams in *R(IB) 3/01*. He accepted that s.30E should be interpreted as a whole. The phrase "in connection with" membership of the council set a limit of reasonableness on the expenditure. An expense is incurred when the liability to discharge it arises (a matter on which he agreed with Commissioner Williams), but it is not incurred in the week in which the item is used (a matter of disagreement with Commissioner Williams). In Commissioner Jacob's view the result is that s.30E has to be applied week by week, either in each week or retrospectively over a past period. The change of wording to the stricter "in the performance of the duties of a councillor" (the stricter tax approach noted by Commissioner Williams in R(IB) 3/01, para.22) may well affirm that approach. An expense is incurred in the week in which the liability arises and can only be used to reduce the reduction in incapacity benefit for that week. Income tax and national insurance deductions do not rank as "expenses in connection with a claimant's membership of a council" and cannot be deducted from the gross councillor's allowances for purposes of incapacity benefit (*R(IB) 3/01*). It is difficult to see that the alteration to "in the performance of his duties as a councillor" alters the status of income tax and NI deductions in this respect.

Date from which payments are to be taken into account

9.170   **77.** Where regulations 74(1) and 76(1) apply, deductions must have effect, calculated where appropriate in accordance with regulation 94(1) or (6), from the first day of the benefit week in which the payment or councillor's allowance is paid to a claimant who is entitled to a contributory allowance in that week.

DEFINITIONS

"benefit week"—see reg.2(1).
"claimant"—see WRA 2007, s.24(1).
"contributory allowance"—see WRA 2007, s.1(7).
"councillor's allowance"—see reg.2(1).
"payment—see reg.74(2).

GENERAL NOTE

Deductions for pension payments, PPF periodic payments and councillor's allowance, calculated where appropriate under reg.94(1) or (6) (calculation of weekly amount of income) are to have effect from the first day of the benefit week in which they are paid to a claimant entitled to CESA in that week. **9.171**

Date from which a change in the rate of the payment takes effect

78. Where a payment or councillor's allowance is already being made to a claimant and the rate of that payment or that allowance changes, the deduction at the new rate must take effect, calculated where appropriate in accordance with regulation 94(1) or (6), from the first day of the benefit week in which the new rate of the payment or councillor's allowance is paid. **9.172**

DEFINITIONS

"benefit week"—see reg.2(1).
"claimant"—see WRA 2007, s.24(1).
"contributory allowance"—see WRA 2007, s.1(7).
"councillor's allowance"—see reg.2(1).
"payment—see reg.74(2).

GENERAL NOTE

Changes in the rate of pension payments, PPF periodic payments and councillor's allowance affect the amount to be deducted from CESA. The deduction at the new rate, calculated where appropriate under reg.94(1) or (6) (calculation of weekly amount of income), is to have effect from the first day of the benefit week in which the new rate of payment or councillor's allowance is paid to a claimant entitled to CESA in that week. **9.173**

Calculation of payment made other than weekly

79.—(1) Where the period in respect of which a payment or councillor's allowance is paid is otherwise than weekly, an amount calculated or estimated in accordance with regulation 94(1) or (6) is to be regarded as the weekly amount of that payment or allowance. **9.174**

(2) In determining the weekly payment, where two or more payments are payable to a claimant, each payment is to be calculated separately in accordance with regulation 94(1) or (6) before aggregating the sum of those payments for the purposes of the reduction of a contributory allowance in accordance with regulation 74.

DEFINITIONS

"benefit week"—see reg.2(1).
"claimant"—see WRA 2007, s.24(1).
"contributory allowance"—see WRA 2007, s.1(7).
"councillor's allowance"—see reg.2(1).
"payment—see reg.74(2).

GENERAL NOTE

This provides for the case where pension payments, PPF periodic payments and councillor's allowance are paid otherwise than weekly. The amount to be deducted is to be calculated or estimated, taking each payment or allowance separately, in accordance with reg.94(1) or (6) to ascertain an appropriate weekly equivalent for the pension payment, the PPF periodic payment and the councillor's allowance **9.175** (para.(1)) For the purposes of the deduction rule in reg.74, the weekly equivalents for each pension payment or PPF payment are then to be aggregated (para.(2)).

CHAPTER 3

STATUTORY PAYMENTS

Effect of statutory maternity pay on a contributory allowance

9.176
    80.—(1) This regulation applies where—
    (a) a woman is entitled to statutory maternity pay and, on the day immediately preceding the first day in the maternity pay period—
        (i) is in a period of limited capability for work; and
        (ii) satisfies the conditions of entitlement to a contributory allowance in accordance with section 1(2)(a) of the Act; and
    (b) on any day during the maternity pay period—
        (i) she is in a period of limited capability for work; and
        (ii) that day is not a day where she is treated as not having limited capability for work.
    (2) Where this regulation applies, notwithstanding section 20(2) of the Act, a woman who is entitled to statutory maternity pay is to be entitled to a contributory allowance in respect of any day that falls within the maternity pay period.
    (3) Where by virtue of paragraph (2) a woman is entitled to a contributory allowance for any week (including part of a week), the total amount of such benefit payable to her for that week is to be reduced by an amount equivalent to any statutory maternity pay to which she is entitled in accordance with Part 12 of the Contributions and Benefits Act for the same week (or equivalent part of a week where entitlement to a contributory allowance is for part of a week) and only the balance, if any, of the contributory allowance is to be payable to her.

DEFINITIONS

    "the Act"—see reg.2(1).
    "contributory allowance"—see WRA 2007, s.1(7).
    "Contributions and Benefits Act"—see WRA 2007, s.65.
    "maternity pay period"—see WRA 2007, s.20(8); SSCBA 1992, s.165(1).
    "week"—see reg.2(1).

GENERAL NOTE

9.177
    In essence this provides that, where a woman's entitlement to CESA and statutory maternity pay (SMP) overlap, then during the period they coincide, despite WRA 2007, s.20(2), entitlement to CESA is preserved, but the amount payable in respect of the week or part week, as appropriate, is to be reduced (even to nil) by the amount of SMP for that week or part week—only the balance (if any) of CESA is payable.

Effect of statutory adoption pay on a contributory allowance

9.178
    81.—(1) This regulation applies where—
    (a) a claimant is entitled to statutory adoption pay and, on the day immediately preceding the first day in the adoption pay period—

      (i) is in a period of limited capability for work; and

      (ii) satisfies the conditions of entitlement to a contributory allowance in accordance with section 1(2)(a) of the Act; and

  (b) on any day during the adoption pay period—

      (i) that claimant is in a period of limited capability for work; and

      (ii) that day is not a day where that claimant is treated as not having limited capability for work.

(2) Where this regulation applies, notwithstanding section 20(4) of the Act, a claimant who is entitled to statutory adoption pay is to be entitled to a contributory allowance in respect of any day that falls within the adoption pay period.

(3) Where by virtue of paragraph (2) a claimant is entitled to a contributory allowance for any week (including part of a week), the total amount of such benefit payable to that claimant for that week is to be reduced by an amount equivalent to any statutory adoption pay to which that claimant is entitled in accordance with Part 12ZB of the Contributions and Benefits Act for the same week (or equivalent part of a week where entitlement to a contributory allowance is for part of a week) and only the balance, if any, of the contributory allowance is to be payable to that claimant.

DEFINITIONS

    "the Act"—see reg.2(1).
    "adoption pay period"—see WRA 2007, s.20(8).
    "claimant"—see WRA 2007, s.24(1).
    "Contributions and Benefits Act"—see WRA 2007, s.65.
    "contributory allowance"—see WRA 2007, s.1(7).
    "week"—see reg.2(1).

GENERAL NOTE

In essence this provides that, where a claimant's entitlement to CESA and statutory adoption pay (SAP) overlap, then during the period they coincide, despite WRA 2007, s.20(2), entitlement to CESA is preserved, but the amount payable in respect of the week or part week, as appropriate, is to be reduced (even to nil) by the amount of SAP for that week or part week—only the balance (if any) of CESA is payable.   **9.179**

Effect of additional statutory paternity pay on a contributory allowance

82.—(1) This regulation applies where—   **9.180**

  (a) a claimant is entitled to additional statutory paternity pay and, on the day immediately preceding the first day in the additional paternity pay period—

      (i) is in a period of limited capability for work; and

      (ii) satisfies the conditions of entitlement to a contributory allowance in accordance with section 1(2)(a) of the Act; and

  (b) on any day during the additional statutory paternity pay period—

      (i) that claimant is in a period of limited capability for work; and

      (ii) that day is not a day where that claimant is treated as not having limited capability for work.

(2) Where this regulation applies, notwithstanding section 20(6) of the Act, a claimant who is entitled to additional statutory paternity pay is to be entitled to a contributory allowance in respect of any day that falls within the additional paternity pay period.

(3) Where by virtue of paragraph (2) a person is entitled to a contributory allowance for any week (including part of a week), the total amount of such benefit payable to that claimant for that week is to be reduced by an amount equivalent to any additional statutory paternity pay to which that claimant is entitled in accordance with Part 12ZA of the Contributions and Benefits Act for the same week (or equivalent part of a week where entitlement to a contributory allowance is for part of a week) and only the balance, if any, of the contributory allowance is to be payable to that claimant.

DEFINITIONS

"the Act"—see reg.2(1).
"additional paternity pay period"—see WRA 2007, s.20(8).
"claimant"—see WRA 2007, s.24(1).
"contributory allowance"—see WRA 2007, s.1(7).
"Contributions and Benefits Act"—see WRA 2007, s.65.
"week"—see reg.2(1).

GENERAL NOTE

9.181   In essence this provides that, where a claimant's entitlement to CESA and additional statutory paternity pay (ASPP) (yet to be introduced) overlap, then during the period they coincide, despite WRA 2007, s.20(2), entitlement to CESA is preserved, but the amount payable in respect of the week or part week, as appropriate, is to be reduced (even to nil) by the amount of ASPP for that week or part week—only the balance (if any) of CESA is payable.

PART 10

INCOME AND CAPITAL

CHAPTER 1

GENERAL

Calculation of income and capital of members of claimant's family and of a polygamous marriage

9.182   **83.**—(1) Subject to paragraph (4), the income and capital of a claimant's partner which by virtue of paragraph 6(2) of Schedule 1 to the Act is to be treated as income and capital of the claimant, is to be calculated in accordance with the following provisions of this Part in like manner as for the claimant; and any reference to the "claimant" is, except where the context otherwise requires, to be construed, for the purposes of this Part, as if it were a reference to the claimant's partner.

(2) Subject to the following provisions of this Part, the income paid to, or in respect of, and capital of, a child or young person who is a member of the claimant's family is not to be treated as the income or capital of the claimant.

(3) Subject to paragraph (5), where a claimant or the partner of a claimant is married polygamously to two or more members of the claimant's household—

   (a) the claimant is to be treated as possessing capital and income belonging to each such member; and

   (b) the income and capital of that member is to be calculated in accordance with the following provisions of this Part in like manner as for the claimant.

(4) Where at least one member of a couple is aged less than 18 and the applicable amount of the couple falls to be determined under paragraph 1(3) (e), (f), (g), (h) or (i) of Schedule 4 (amounts), the income of the claimant's partner is not to be treated as the income of the claimant to the extent that—

   (a) in the case of a couple where both members are aged less than 18, the amount specified in paragraph 1(3)(c) of that Schedule exceeds the amount specified in paragraph 1(3)(i) of that Schedule; and

   (b) in the case of a couple where only one member is aged less than 18, the amount specified in paragraph 1(3)(a) of that Schedule exceeds the amount which is specified in paragraph 1(3)(h) of that Schedule.

(5) Where a member of a polygamous marriage is a partner aged less than 18 and the amount which applies in respect of that partner under regulation 68(2) (polygamous marriages) is nil, the claimant is not to be treated as possessing the income of that partner to the extent that an amount in respect of that partner would have been included in the applicable amount if the partner had fallen within the circumstances set out in regulation 68(2) (a) or (b).

DEFINITIONS

   "child"—see reg.2(1).
   "family"—*ibid.*
   "partner"—*ibid.*
   "polygamous marriage"—*ibid.*
   "young person"—*ibid.*, s.142 SSCBA.

GENERAL NOTE

   This regulation contains the basic rule on aggregation of resources of the claimant   **9.183** and any partner for the purposes of income-related ESA. It is similar to reg.23 of the Income Support Regulations/reg.88 of the JSA Regulations.

   The rules governing income and capital for the purposes of income-related ESA are very similar to those applying to income support and income-based JSA. Where there are differences between the income support and the income-based JSA provisions ESA generally follows the income support model. The reader should therefore refer to the notes to the corresponding income support provision in Vol.II of this series for further explanation of the provisions in this Part.

Income of participants in the self-employment route

   84. Chapters 2, 3, 4, 6, 8 and 9 of this Part and regulations 132 to 137, 142   **9.184** and 143 do not apply to any income which is to be calculated in accordance with Chapter 5 of this Part (participants in the self-employment route).

DEFINITION

   "self-employment route"—see reg.2(1).

GENERAL NOTE

   This is similar to reg.23A of the Income Support Regulations/reg.88A of the JSA   **9.185** Regulations.

[¹Child maintenance or] liable relative payments

9.186   **85.** Regulations 91 to 109, 111 to 117 and Chapter 10 of this Part do not apply to any payment which is to be calculated in accordance with Chapter 8 of this Part ([²child maintenance and liable relative payments]).

AMENDMENTS

1. Employment and Support Allowance (Miscellaneous Amendments) Regulations 2008 (SI 2008/2428), reg.20(2)(a) (October 27, 2008).
2. Employment and Support Allowance (Miscellaneous Amendments) Regulations 2008 (SI 2008/2428), reg.20(3) (October 27, 2008).

DEFINITION

"child maintenance"—see reg.119.

GENERAL NOTE

9.187   This is similar to reg.25 of the Income Support Regulations/reg.89 of the JSA Regulations.

Child support

9.188   **86.** [¹ . . .]

AMENDMENT

1. Employment and Support Allowance (Miscellaneous Amendments) Regulations 2008 (SI 2008/2428), reg.20(4)(a) (October 27, 2008).

Calculation of income and capital of students

9.189   **87.** The provisions of Chapters 2 to 7 of this Part (income and capital) are to have effect in relation to students and their partners subject to the modifications set out in Chapter 10 of this Part (students).

DEFINITION

"partner"—see reg.2(1).

GENERAL NOTE

9.190   This is similar to reg.26 of the Income Support Regulations/reg.91 of the JSA Regulations.

Calculation of income which consists of earnings of participants in exempt work

9.191   **88.** Notwithstanding the other provisions of this Part, regulations 91(2), 92 to 99 and 108(3) and (4) and Schedule 7 (sums to be disregarded in the calculation of earnings) are to apply to any income which consists of earnings which is to be calculated for the purposes of regulations 45(2) to (4) (exempt work—earnings limits).

GENERAL NOTE

9.192   The general rule is that if a claimant does any work in a week he will not normally be entitled to ESA for that week (see reg.40(1)), but this does not apply to exempt work (see reg.40(2)(f)). See reg.45 for the rules for exempt work; in the case of work referred to in reg.45(2)-(4) this is subject to earnings limits. Regulation 88 is necessary because the exempt work provisions are relevant to both contributory and income-related ESA.

It provides that the following regulations apply for the purposes of calculating a claimant's earnings under the exempt work provisions in reg.45(2)-(4): reg.91(2) (period over which a payment is taken into account); reg.92 (calculation of earnings of self-employed earners); reg.93 (date on which income is treated as paid); reg.94 (calculation of weekly amount of income); reg.95 (earnings of employed earners); reg.96 (calculation of net earnings of employed earners); reg.97 (earnings of self-employed earners); reg.98 (calculation of net profit of self-employed earners); reg.99 (deduction of tax and contributions for self-employed earners); reg.108(3) and (4) (notional earnings) and Sch.7 (sums to be disregarded in the calculation of earnings). The broad effect is that earnings from exempt work (for both contributory and income-related ESA) will be assessed in the same way as earnings generally are for income-related ESA

Note that if the claimant is doing exempt work, any earnings that do not exceed the relevant weekly limit under reg.45(2), (3) or (4) are disregarded (see para.5 of Sch.7). In addition, if the claimant's earnings from the exempt work are less than the relevant limit, the remainder of the £20 or £92 disregard can be applied (up to a maximum of £20) to his partner's earnings (see para.6 of Sch.7). If the claimant is undertaking exempt work and also has earnings from work as a member of the Disability Living Allowance Advisory Board or as a disability member of a tribunal, the £20 disregard of such earnings under para.7 of Sch.7 only applies to the extent that the claimant's earnings from his exempt work are less than the relevant limit.

Calculation of income where pension payments, PPF periodic payments or councillor's allowance payable

89. Notwithstanding the other provisions of this Part, regulation 94(1) and (6) is to apply for the purposes of calculating the amount of any pension payments, PPF periodic payments or councillor's allowance to which Chapter 2 of Part 9 (deductions from the contributory allowance) applies.

9.193

DEFINITIONS

    "councillor"—see reg.2(1).
    "councillor's allowance"—*ibid*.

GENERAL NOTE

Contributory JSA may be reduced if a claimant receives certain pension payments, PPF periodic payments or councillor's allowances (see regs 72 to 79). This regulation provides that paras (1) and (6) of reg.94 (calculation of weekly amount of income) are to apply for the purposes of calculating such payments.

9.194

CHAPTER 2

INCOME

Calculation of income

90.—(1) For the purposes of paragraph 6(1) of Schedule 1 to the Act (conditions of entitlement to an income-related allowance), the income of a claimant is to be calculated on a weekly basis—

9.195

   (a) by determining in accordance with this Part, other than Chapter 7, the weekly amount of the claimant's income; and

   (b) by adding to that amount the weekly income calculated under regulation 118 (calculation of tariff income from capital).

(2) For the purposes of paragraph (1) "income" includes capital treated as income under regulation 105 (capital treated as income) and income which a claimant is treated as possessing under regulations 106 to 109 (notional income).

(3) For the purposes of paragraph 10 of Schedule 2 to the Act (effect of work), the income which consists of earnings of a claimant is to be calculated on a weekly basis by determining the weekly amount of those earnings in accordance with regulations 91(2), 92 to 99 and 108(3) and (4) and Schedule 7.

(4) For the purposes of paragraph (3), "income which consists of earnings" includes income which a claimant is treated as possessing under regulation 108(3) and (4).

(5) For the purposes of pension payments, PPF periodic payments and a councillor's allowance to which section 3 of the Act applies, the income other than earnings of a claimant is to be calculated on a weekly basis by determining in accordance with regulation 94(1), (2), (5) and (6) the weekly amount of the pension payments, PPF periodic payment or a councillor's allowance paid to the claimant.

DEFINITIONS

   "claimant"—see reg.83(1).
   "councillor"—see reg.2(1).
   "councillor's allowance"—*ibid.*

GENERAL NOTE

9.196   Paragraphs (1) and (2) are similar to reg.28 of the Income Support Regulations/reg.93 of the JSA Regulations. They confirm that all income resources, including resources specifically treated as earnings or income, are to be taken into account for the purposes of calculating entitlement to income-related ESA.

Paras (3) to (4)

9.197   Paragraph 10 of Sch.2 to the Welfare Reform Act 2007 provides for regulations to treat a person as not entitled to ESA because of undertaking work. See regs 40–46 which implement this. Under reg.45 certain categories of work are exempt; in the case of work referred to in reg.45(2)–(4) this is subject to earnings limits. Paragraph (3) provides that for the purpose of calculating a claimant's weekly earnings in these circumstances the following regulations apply: reg.91(2) (period over which a payment is taken into account); reg.92 (calculation of earnings of self-employed earners); reg.93 (date on which income is treated as paid); reg.94 (calculation of weekly amount of income); reg.95 (earnings of employed earners); reg.96 (calculation of net earnings of employed earners); reg.97 (earnings of self-employed earners); reg.98 (calculation of net profit of self-employed earners); reg.99 (deduction of tax and contributions for self-employed earners); reg.108(3) and (4) (notional earnings) and Sch.7 (sums to be disregarded in the calculation of earnings). See also reg.88 which makes similar provision. Paragraph (4) specifically provides that such earnings include notional earnings.

Para. (5)

Section 3 of the 2007 Act (together with s.2(1)(c)) provides for deductions to be made from a claimant's contributory JSA if he receives certain pension payments, PPF periodic payments or councillor's allowances. See regs 72 to 79. Paragraph (5) provides that paras (1), (2), (5) and (6) of reg.94 (calculation of weekly amount of income) apply for the purposes of calculating the weekly amount of such payments. See also reg.89 which makes similar, but not identical, provision, since it only brings reg.94(1) and (6) into play for the purpose of calculating the amount of such payments (the reason for this difference is not clear).

9.198

Calculation of earnings derived from employed earner's employment and income other than earnings

91.—(1) Earnings derived from employment as an employed earner and income which does not consist of earnings are to be taken into account over a period determined in accordance with the following provisions of this regulation and at a weekly amount determined in accordance with regulation 94 (calculation of weekly amount of income).

9.199

(2) Subject to the following provisions of this regulation, the period over which a payment is to be taken into account is to be—

(a) where the payment is monthly, a period equal to the number of weeks from the date on which the payment is treated as paid to the date immediately before the date on which the next monthly payment would have been so treated as paid whether or not the next monthly payment is actually paid;

(b) where the payment is in respect of a period which is not monthly, a period equal to the length of the period for which payment is made;

(c) in any other case, a period equal to such number of weeks as is equal to the number obtained (and any fraction is to be treated as a corresponding fraction of a week) by dividing—

    (i) the net earnings; or

    (ii) in the case of income which does not consist of earnings, the amount of that income less any amount paid by way of tax on that income which is disregarded under paragraph 1 of Schedule 8 (income other than earnings to be disregarded),

by the amount of an [1 employment and support] allowance which would be payable had the payment not been made plus an amount equal to the total of the sums which would fall to be disregarded from that payment under Schedule 7 (earnings to be disregarded) or, as the case may be, any paragraph of Schedule 8 other than paragraph 1 of that Schedule, as is appropriate in the claimant's case,

and that period is to begin on the date on which the payment is treated as paid under regulation 93 (date on which income is treated as paid).

(3) The period over which a Career Development Loan, which is paid pursuant to section 2 of the Employment and Training Act 1973, is to be taken into account is the period of education and training intended to be supported by that loan.

(4) Where grant income as defined in Chapter 10 of this Part has been paid to a claimant who ceases to be a full-time student before the end of the period in respect of which that income is payable and, as a consequence, the whole or part of that income falls to be repaid by that claimant, that income

is to be taken into account over the period beginning on the date on which
that income is treated as paid under regulation 93 (date on which income is
treated as paid) and ending—

    (a) on the date on which repayment is made in full;

    (b) where the grant is paid in instalments, on the day before the next
        instalment would have been paid had the claimant remained a full-
        time student; or

    (c) on the last date of the academic term or vacation during which that
        claimant ceased to be a full-time student,

whichever is the earlier.

(5) Where, but for this paragraph—

    (a) earnings not of the same kind are derived from the same source;
        and

    (b) the periods in respect of which those earnings would fall to be taken
        into account overlap, wholly or partly,

those earnings are to be taken into account over a period equal to the aggregate length of those periods and that period is to begin with the earliest date
on which any part of those earnings would otherwise be treated as paid
under regulation 93.

(6) In a case to which paragraph (5) applies, earnings under regulation 95
(earnings of employed earners) are to be taken into account in the following
order of priority—

    (a) earnings normally derived from the employment;

    (b) any payment to which paragraph (1)(b) or (c) of that regulation
        applies;

    (c) any payment to which paragraph (1)(j) of that regulation applies;

    (d) any payment to which paragraph (1)(d) of that regulation applies.

(7) Where earnings to which regulation 95(1)(b) to (d) applies are paid
in respect of part of a day, those earnings are to be taken into account over
a period equal to a day.

(8) Any earnings to which regulation 95(1)(j) applies which are paid in
respect of, or on the termination of, part-time employment, are to be taken
into account over a period equal to one week.

(9) In this regulation "part-time employment" means, if the claimant
were entitled to income support, employment in which the claimant is not
to be treated as engaged in remunerative work under regulation 5 or 6(1)
and (4) of the Income Support Regulations (persons treated, or not treated,
as engaged in remunerative work);

(10) For the purposes of this regulation the claimant's earnings and
income which does not consist of earnings are to be calculated in accordance with Chapters 3 and 6 respectively of this Part.

AMENDMENT

    1. Social Security (Miscellaneous Amendments) Regulations 2009 (SI 2009/583),
reg.10(3) (April 6, 2009).

DEFINITIONS

    "claimant"—see reg.83(1).
    "employed earner"—see reg.2(1).
    "full-time student"—*ibid.*

GENERAL NOTE

This is similar to reg.29 of the Income Support Regulations/reg.94(1) to (5) and **9.200** (10) of the JSA Regulations. Paragraphs (6) to (9) of reg.94 of the JSA Regulations contain different provisions defining the length of the period for which a "compensation payment" is to be taken into account.

Calculation of earnings of self-employed earners

92.—(1) Except where paragraph (2) applies, where a claimant's income **9.201** consists of earnings from employment as a self-employed earner the weekly amount of the claimant's earnings is to be determined by reference to the claimant's average weekly earnings from that employment—

(a) over a period of one year; or

(b) where the claimant has recently become engaged in that employment or there has been a change which is likely to affect the normal pattern of business, over such other period as may, in any particular case, enable the weekly amount of the claimant's earnings to be determined more accurately.

[¹ (2)(a) Where the claimant's earnings consist of any items to which this paragraph applies those earnings shall be taken into account over a period equal to such number of weeks as is equal to the number obtained (and any fraction shall be treated as a corresponding fraction of a week) by dividing the earnings by the amount of employment and support allowance which would be payable had the payment not been made plus an amount equal to the total of the sums which would fall to be disregarded from the payment under Schedule 7 (earnings to be disregarded) as is appropriate in the claimant's case;

(b) This paragraph applies to-

(i) royalties or other sums paid as a consideration for the use of, or the right to use, any copyright, design, patent or trade mark; or

(ii) any payment in respect of any book registered under the Public Lending Right Scheme 1982 or work made under any international public lending right scheme that is analogous to the Public Lending Right Scheme 1982,

where the claimant is the first owner of the copyright, design, patent or trademark, or an original contributor to the book or work concerned.]

(3) For the purposes of this regulation the claimant's earnings are to be calculated in accordance with Chapter 4 of this Part.

AMENDMENT

1. Social Security (Miscellaneous Amendments) Regulations 2009 (SI 2009/583), reg.10(3) (April 6, 2009).

DEFINITIONS

"claimant"—see reg.83(1).
"self-employed earner"—see reg.2(1).

GENERAL NOTE

This is similar to reg.30 of the Income Support Regulations/reg.95 of the JSA **9.202** Regulations.

Date on which income is treated as paid

9.203   **93.**—(1) Except where paragraph (2) or (3) applies, a payment of income to which regulation 91 (calculation of earnings derived from employed earner's employment and income other than earnings) applies is to be treated as paid—

(a) in the case of a payment which is due to be paid before the first benefit week pursuant to the claim, on the date on which it is due to be paid;

(b) in any other case, on the first day of the benefit week in which it is due to be paid or the first succeeding benefit week in which it is practicable to take it into account.

(2) Employment and support allowance, income support, jobseeker's allowance, maternity allowance, short-term or long-term incapacity benefit, or severe disablement allowance is to be treated as paid on the day of the benefit week in respect of which it is payable.

(3) [¹ Subject to paragraph (4),] Working tax credit [¹ . . .] is to be treated as paid—

(a) where the award of that tax credit begins on the first day of a benefit week, on that day;[¹ or]

(b) on the first day of the benefit week that follows the date the award begins; [¹ . . .]

(c) [¹ . . .],

until the last day of the last benefit week that coincides with or immediately follows the last day for which the award of that tax credit is made.

[¹ (4) Where working tax credit is paid under regulation 7D (ceasing to undertake work or working less than 16 hours a week) of the Working Tax Credit (Entitlement and Maximum Rate) Regulations 2002, it shall be treated as paid on the first day of the benefit week in which that award of tax credit begins; but this paragraph shall only apply until the last day of the last benefit week that coincides with or precedes the last day for which tax credit is awarded under that regulation.]

AMENDMENT

1. Social Security (Miscellaneous Amendments) Regulations 2009 (SI 2009/583), reg.10(5) (April 6, 2009).

DEFINITION

"benefit week"—see reg.2(1).

GENERAL NOTE

9.204   This is similar to reg.31 of the Income Support Regulations/reg.96 of the JSA Regulations.

Calculation of weekly amount of income

9.205   **94.**—(1) For the purposes of regulation 91 (calculation of earnings derived from employed earner's employment and income other than earnings) and Chapter 2 of Part 9 (deductions from contributory allowance), subject to paragraphs (2) to (8), where the period in respect of which a payment is made—

(a) does not exceed a week, the weekly amount is to be the amount of that payment;

(b) exceeds a week, the weekly amount is to be determined—

  (i) in a case where that period is a month, by multiplying the amount of the payment by 12 and dividing the product by 52;

  (ii) in a case where that period is 3 months, by multiplying the amount of the payment by 4 and dividing the product by 52;

  [² (iii) in a case where that period is a year and the payment is an award of working tax credit, by dividing the payment by the number of days in the year and multiplying the result by 7;

  (iiia) in a case where that period is a year and the payment is income other than an award of working tax credit, by dividing the amount of the payment by 52;]

  (iv) in any other case by multiplying the amount of the payment by 7 and dividing the product by the number equal to the number of days in the period in respect of which it is made.

(2) Where a payment for a period not exceeding a week is treated under regulation 93(1)(a) (date on which income is treated as paid) as paid before the first benefit week and a part is to be taken into account for some days only in that week (the relevant days), the amount to be taken into account for the relevant days is to be calculated by multiplying the amount of the payment by the number equal to the number of relevant days and dividing the product by the number of days in the period in respect of which it is made.

(3) Where a payment is in respect of a period equal to or in excess of a week and a part thereof is to be taken into account for some days only in a benefit week (the relevant days), the amount to be taken into account for the relevant days is, except where paragraph (4) applies, to be calculated by multiplying the amount of the payment by the number equal to the number of relevant days and dividing the product by the number of days in the period in respect of which it is made.

(4) In the case of a payment of—

(a) maternity allowance, short-term or long-term incapacity benefit or severe disablement allowance, the amount to be taken into account for the relevant days is to be the amount of benefit payable in respect of those days;

(b) an employment and support allowance, income support or a job-seeker's allowance, the amount to be taken into account for the relevant days is to be calculated by multiplying the weekly amount of the benefit by the number of relevant days and dividing the product by 7.

(5) Except in the case of a payment which it has not been practicable to treat under regulation 93(1)(b) (date on which income is treated as paid) as paid on the first day of the benefit week in which it is due to be paid, where a payment of income from a particular source is or has been paid regularly and that payment falls to be taken into account in the same benefit week as a payment of the same kind and from the same source, the amount of that income to be taken into account in any one benefit week is not to exceed the weekly amount determined under paragraph (1)(a) or (b) of the payment which under regulation 93(1)(b) is treated as paid first.

(6) Where the amount of the claimant's income fluctuates and has changed more than once, or a claimant's regular pattern of work is such

that the claimant does not work every week, the foregoing paragraphs may be modified so that the weekly amount of the claimant's income is determined by reference to the claimant's average weekly income—

    (a) if there is a recognisable cycle of work, over the period of one complete cycle (including, where the cycle involves periods in which the claimant does no work, those periods but disregarding any other absences);

    (b) in any other case, over a period of 5 weeks or such other period as may, in the particular case, enable the claimant's average weekly income to be determined more accurately.

(7) Where income is taken into account under paragraph (4) of regulation 91 over the period specified in that paragraph, the amount of that income to be taken into account in respect of any week in that period is to be an amount equal to the amount of that income which would have been taken into account under regulation 132 (calculation of grant income) had the person to whom that income was paid not ceased to be a full-time student.

(8) Where any payment of earnings is taken into account under [¹paragraph (8)] of regulation 91 (calculation of earnings derived from employed earner's employment and income other than earnings), over the period specified in that paragraph, the amount to be taken into account is to be equal to the amount of the payment.

AMENDMENTS

1. Employment and Support Allowance (Miscellaneous Amendments) Regulations 2008 (SI 2008/2428), reg.8(1) (October 27, 2008).

2. Social Security (Miscellaneous Amendments) Regulations 2009 (SI 2009/583), reg.10(6) (April 6, 2009).

DEFINITIONS

    "benefit week"—see reg.2(1).
    "claimant"—see reg.83(1).
    "full-time student"—see reg.2(1).

GENERAL NOTE

9.206   This is similar to reg.32 of the Income Support Regulations/reg.97 of the JSA Regulations (except that there is no equivalent of para.(8) in reg.97 as the JSA rules for the treatment of compensation payments made on the termination of part-time employment are different (see the note to reg.94(6)–(9) of the JSA Regs in Vol.II of this series)).

CHAPTER 3

EMPLOYED EARNERS

Earnings of employed earners

9.207   **95.**—(1) Subject to [¹paragraphs (2) and (3)], "earnings" means, in the case of employment as an employed earner, any remuneration or profit derived from that employment and includes—

(a) any bonus or commission;

(b) any payment in lieu of remuneration except any periodic sum paid to a claimant on account of the termination of the claimant's employment by reason of redundancy;

(c) any payment in lieu of notice;

(d) any holiday pay except any payable more than 4 weeks after the termination or interruption of employment;

(e) any payment by way of a retainer;

(f) any payment made by the claimant's employer in respect of expenses not wholly, exclusively and necessarily incurred in the performance of the duties of the employment, including any payment made by the claimant's employer in respect of—

   (i) travelling expenses incurred by the claimant between the claimant's home and place of employment;

   (ii) expenses incurred by the claimant under arrangements made for the care of a member of the claimant's family owing to the claimant's absence from home;

(g) any award of compensation made under section 112(4) or 117(3) (a) of the Employment Rights Act 1996 (the remedies: orders and compensation, enforcement of order and compensation);

(h) any payment or remuneration made under sections 28, 34, 64, 68 and 70 of the Employment Rights Act 1996 (right to guarantee payments, remuneration on suspension on medical or maternity grounds, complaints to employment tribunals);

(i) any such sum as is referred to in section 112(3) of the Contributions and Benefits Act (certain sums to be earnings for social security purposes);

(j) where a payment of compensation is made in respect of employment which is part-time employment, the amount of the compensation;

(k) the amount of any payment by way of a non-cash voucher which has been taken into account in the computation of a person's earnings in accordance with Part 5 of Schedule 3 to the Social Security (Contributions) Regulations 2001.

(2) "Earnings" are not to include—

(a) subject to paragraph (3), any payment in kind;

(b) any remuneration paid by or on behalf of an employer to the claimant in respect of a period throughout which the claimant is on maternity leave, paternity leave or adoption leave or is absent from work because the claimant is ill;

(c) any payment in respect of expenses wholly, exclusively and necessarily incurred in the performance of the duties of the employment;

(d) any occupational pension;

(e) any lump sum payment made under the Iron and Steel Re-adaptation Benefits Scheme.

(3) Paragraph (2)(a) is not to apply in respect of any non-cash voucher referred to in paragraph (1)(k).

(4) In this regulation—

"compensation" means any payment made in respect of, or on the termination of, employment in a case where a claimant has not received or received only part of a payment in lieu of notice due or which would have been due to the claimant had that claimant not waived the right to receive it, other than—

(a) any payment specified in paragraph (1)(a) to (i);

(b) any payment specified in paragraph (2)(a) to (e);

(c) any redundancy payment within the meaning of section 135(1) of the Employment Rights Act 1996;

(d) any refund of contributions to which that person was entitled under an occupational pension scheme; and

(e) any compensation payable by virtue of section 173 of the Education Reform Act 1988;

"part-time employment" means, if the claimant were entitled to income support, employment in which the claimant is not to be treated as engaged in remunerative work under regulation 5 or 6(1) and (4) of the Income Support Regulations (persons treated, or not treated, as engaged in remunerative work).

AMENDMENT

1. Employment and Support Allowance (Miscellaneous Amendments) Regulations 2008 (SI 2008/2428), reg.8(2) (October 27, 2008).

DEFINITIONS

"adoption leave"—see reg.2(1).
"claimant"—see reg.83(1).
"employed earner"—see reg.2(1).
"family"—*ibid*.
"occupational pension"—*ibid*.

GENERAL NOTE

9.208   The equivalent income support and JSA Regulations are regs 35 and 98 respectively. This regulation adopts the model of reg.35 of the Income Support Regulations rather than reg.98 of the JSA Regulations. For the differences between reg.98 and this regulation (and reg.35 of the Income Support Regulations), see the notes to reg.98 of the JSA Regulations in Vol.II of this series. Note also that unlike the equivalent provisions in reg.35 and reg.98, para.(1)(d) (which relates to holiday pay) does not contain any special rule relating to trade disputes.

Calculation of net earnings of employed earners

9.209   **96.**—(1) For the purposes of regulation 91 (calculation of earnings derived from employed earner's employment and income other than earnings) the earnings of a claimant derived from employment as an employed earner to be taken into account, subject to paragraph (2), are the claimant's net earnings.

(2) There is to be disregarded from a claimant's net earnings, any sum, where applicable, specified in paragraphs 1 to 12 of Schedule 7 (sums to be disregarded in the calculation of earnings).

(3) For the purposes of paragraph (1) net earnings are to be calculated by taking into account the gross earnings of the claimant from that employment less—

(a) any amount deducted from those earnings by way of—
    (i) income tax;
    (ii) primary Class 1 contributions under section 6(1)(a) of the Contributions and Benefits Act;

(b) one-half of any sum paid by the claimant in respect of a pay period by way of a contribution towards an occupational or personal pension scheme.

DEFINITIONS

"claimant"—see reg.83(1).
"employed earner"—see reg.2(1).
"occupational pension scheme"—*ibid.*
"pay period"—*ibid.*
"personal pension scheme"—*ibid.*

GENERAL NOTE

This is similar to reg.36 of the Income Support Regulations/reg.99 of the JSA Regulations.

9.210

CHAPTER 4

SELF-EMPLOYED EARNERS

Earnings of self-employed earners

97.—(1) Subject to paragraph (2), "earnings", in the case of employment as a self-employed earner, means the gross receipts of the employment and include any allowance paid under section 2 of the Employment and Training Act 1973 or section 2 of the Enterprise and New Towns (Scotland) Act 1990 to the claimant for the purpose of assisting the claimant in carrying on the claimant's business.

9.211

(2) "Earnings" do not include—

(a) where a claimant is involved in providing board and lodging accommodation for which a charge is payable, any payment by way of such a charge;

(b) any payment to which paragraph 28 or 29 of Schedule 8 refers (payments in respect of a person accommodated with the claimant under an arrangement made by a local authority or voluntary organisation and payments made to the claimant by a health authority, local authority or voluntary organisation in respect of persons temporarily in the claimant's care);

(c) any sports award.

DEFINITIONS

"board and lodging"—see reg.2(1).
"claimant"—see reg.83(1).
"self-employed earner"—see reg.2(1).
"sports award"—*ibid.*
"voluntary organisation"—*ibid.*

GENERAL NOTE

This is similar to reg.37 of the Income Support Regulations/reg.100 of the JSA Regulations.

9.212

Calculation of net profit of self-employed earners

98.—(1) For the purposes of regulation 92 (calculation of earnings of self-employed earners), the earnings of a claimant to be taken into account are to be—

9.213

(a) in the case of a self-employed earner who is engaged in employment on that self-employed earner's own account, the net profit derived from that employment;

(b) in the case of a self-employed earner whose employment is carried on in partnership or is that of a share fisherman within the meaning of the Social Security (Mariners' Benefits) Regulations 1975, that self-employed earner's share of the net profit derived from that employment less—

   (i) an amount in respect of income tax and of National Insurance contributions payable under the Contributions and Benefits Act calculated in accordance with regulation 99 (deduction of tax and contributions for self-employed earners); and

   (ii) one half of any premium paid in the period that is relevant under regulation 92 (calculation of earnings of self-employed earners) in respect of a personal pension scheme.

(2) There is to be disregarded from a claimant's net profit any sum, where applicable, specified in paragraphs 1 to 11 of Schedule 7.

(3) For the purposes of paragraph (1)(a) the net profit of the employment, except where paragraph (9) applies, is to be calculated by taking into account the earnings of the employment over the period determined under regulation 92 less—

(a) subject to paragraphs (5) to (7), any expenses wholly and exclusively defrayed in that period for the purposes of that employment;

(b) an amount in respect of—

   (i) income tax; and

   (ii) National Insurance contributions payable under the Contributions and Benefits Act,

   calculated in accordance with regulation 99 (deduction of tax and contributions for self-employed earners); and

(c) one half of any premium paid in the period that is relevant under regulation 92 in respect of a personal pension scheme.

(4) For the purposes of paragraph (1)(b), the net profit of the employment is to be calculated by taking into account the earnings of the employment over the period determined under regulation 92 less, subject to paragraphs (5) to (7), any expenses wholly and exclusively defrayed in that period for the purpose of that employment.

(5) Subject to paragraph (6), a deduction is not to be made under paragraph (3)(a) or (4) in respect of—

(a) any capital expenditure;

(b) the depreciation of any capital asset;

(c) any sum employed or intended to be employed in the setting up or expansion of the employment;

(d) any loss incurred before the beginning of the period determined under regulation 92 (calculation of earnings of self-employed earners);

(e) the repayment of capital on any loan taken out for the purposes of the employment;

(f) any expenses incurred in providing business entertainment.

(6) A deduction is to be made under paragraph (3)(a) or (4) in respect of the repayment of capital on any loan used for—

(a) the replacement in the course of business of equipment or machinery; and

(b) the repair of an existing business asset except to the extent that any sum is payable under an insurance policy for its repair.

(7) The Secretary of State will refuse to make a deduction in respect of any expenses under paragraph (3)(a) or (4) where the Secretary of State is not satisfied that the expense has been defrayed or, having regard to the nature of the expense and its amount, that it has been reasonably incurred.

(8) For the avoidance of doubt—

(a) a deduction is not to be made under paragraph (3)(a) or (4) in respect of any sum unless it has been expended for the purposes of the business;

(b) a deduction is to be made thereunder in respect of—

    (i) the excess of any VAT paid over VAT received in the period determined under regulation 92;

    (ii) any income expended in the repair of an existing asset except to the extent that any sum is payable under an insurance policy for its repair;

    (iii) any payment of interest on a loan taken out for the purposes of the employment.

(9) Where a claimant is engaged in employment as a child minder the net profit of the employment is to be one-third of the earnings of that employment, less—

(a) an amount in respect of—

    (i) income tax; and

    (ii) National Insurance contributions payable under the Contributions and Benefits Act,

    calculated in accordance with regulation 99 (deduction of tax and contributions for self-employed earners); and

(b) one half of any premium paid in respect of a personal pension scheme.

(10) Notwithstanding regulation 92 (calculation of earnings of self-employed earners) and the foregoing paragraphs, the Secretary of State may assess any item of a claimant's income or expenditure over a period other than that determined under regulation 92 as may, in the particular case, enable the weekly amount of that item of income or expenditure to be determined more accurately.

(11) For the avoidance of doubt where a claimant is engaged in employment as a self-employed earner and that claimant is also engaged in one or more other employments as a self-employed or employed earner any loss incurred in any one of the claimant's employments is not to be offset against the claimant's earnings in any other of the claimant's employments.

DEFINITIONS

"claimant"—see reg.83(1).
"employment"—see reg.2(1).
"personal pension scheme"—*ibid*.
"self-employed earner"—*ibid*.

GENERAL NOTE

This is similar to reg.38 of the Income Support Regulations/reg.101 of the JSA Regulations (except that there is no equivalent of reg.101(3) of the JSA Regulations which is concerned with calculating the amount of any earnings to be deducted from contribution-based JSA). **9.214**

Deduction of tax and contributions for self-employed earners

9.215   **99.**—(1) Subject to paragraph (2), the amount to be deducted in respect of income tax under regulation 98(1)(b)(i), (3)(b)(i) or (9)(a)(i) (calculation of net profit of self-employed earners) is to be calculated on the basis of the amount of chargeable income and as if that income were assessable to income tax at the [¹ . . .] basic rate of tax less only the personal allowance to which the claimant is entitled under sections 35 and 38 to 40 of the Income Tax Act 2007 (personal reliefs) as is appropriate to the claimant's circumstances.

(2) If the period determined under regulation 92 is less than a year the earnings to which the [¹basic rate] of tax is to be applied and the amount of the personal reliefs deductible under paragraph (1) is to be calculated on a pro rata basis.

(3) The amount to be deducted in respect of National Insurance contributions under regulation 98(1)(b)(i), (3)(b)(ii) or (9)(a)(ii) is to be the total of—

    (a) the amount of Class 2 contributions payable under section 11(1) or, as the case may be, 11(3) of the Contributions and Benefits Act at the rate applicable at the date of claim except where the claimant's chargeable income is less than the amount specified in section 11(4) of that Act (small earnings exception) for the tax year in which the date of claim falls; but if the assessment period is less than a year, the amount specified for that tax year is to be reduced pro rata; and

    (b) the amount of Class 4 contributions (if any) which would be payable under section 15 of that Act (Class 4 contributions recoverable under the Income Tax Acts) at the percentage rate applicable at the date of claim on so much of the chargeable income as exceeds the lower limit but does not exceed the upper limit of profits and gains applicable for the tax year in which the date of claim falls; but if the assessment period is less than a year, those limits are to be reduced pro rata.

(4) In this regulation "chargeable income" means—

    (a) except where sub-paragraph (b) applies, the earnings derived from the employment less any expenses deducted under paragraph (3)(a) or, as the case may be, (4) of regulation 98;

    (b) in the case of employment as a child minder, one-third of the earnings of that employment.

AMENDMENT

1. Employment and Support Allowance (Miscellaneous Amendments) Regulations 2008 (SI 2008/2428), reg.8(3) (October 27, 2008).

DEFINITION

"claimant"—see reg.83(1).

GENERAL NOTE

9.216   This is similar to reg.39 of the Income Support Regulations/reg.102 of the JSA Regulations.

CHAPTER 5

PARTICIPANTS IN THE SELF-EMPLOYMENT ROUTE

Interpretation

9.217   **100.** In this Chapter "special account" means, where a claimant was carrying on a commercial activity in respect of which assistance is received under the self-employment route, the account into which the gross receipts from that activity were payable during the period in respect of which such assistance was received.

DEFINITION

"self-employment route"—see reg.2(1).

GENERAL NOTE

This is similar to reg.39A of the Income Support Regulations/reg.102A of the JSA Regulations.

9.218

Treatment of gross receipts of participants in the self-employment route

101. The gross receipts of a commercial activity carried on by a claimant in respect of which assistance is received under the self-employment route, are to be taken into account in accordance with the following provisions of this Chapter.

9.219

DEFINITION

"self-employment route"—see reg.2(1).

GENERAL NOTE

This is similar to reg.39B of the Income Support Regulations/reg.102B of the JSA Regulations.

9.220

Calculation of income of participants in the self-employment route

102.—(1) The income of a claimant who has received assistance under the self-employment route is to be calculated by taking into account the whole of the monies in the special account at the end of the last day on which such assistance was received and deducting from those monies—

9.221

  (a) an amount in respect of income tax calculated in accordance with regulation 103 (deduction in respect of tax for participants in the self-employment route); and

  (b) any sum to which paragraph (4) refers.

(2) Income calculated pursuant to paragraph (1) is to be apportioned equally over a period which starts on the date the income is treated as paid under paragraph (3) and is equal in length to the period beginning with the day on which assistance was first received under the self-employment route and ending on the last day on which such assistance was received.

(3) Income calculated pursuant to paragraph (1) is to be treated as paid —

  (a) in the case where it is due to be paid before the first benefit week in respect of which the participant or the participant's partner first claims an income-related allowance following the last day on which assistance was received under the self-employment route, on the day in the week in which it is due to be paid which corresponds to the first day of the benefit week;

  (b) in any other case, on the first day of the benefit week in which it is due to be paid.

(4) This paragraph refers, where applicable in each benefit week in respect of which income calculated pursuant to paragraph (1) is taken into account

pursuant to paragraphs (2) and (3), to the sums which would have been disregarded under paragraph 7(1) of Schedule 7 had the income been earnings.

DEFINITIONS

"benefit week"—see reg.2(1).
"self-employment route"—*ibid.*

GENERAL NOTE

9.222   This is similar to reg.39C of the Income Support Regulations/reg.102C of the JSA Regulations.

Deduction in respect of tax for participants in the self-employment route

9.223   **103.**—(1) The amount to be deducted in respect of income tax under regulation 102(1)(a) (calculation of income of participants in the self-employment route) in respect of the period determined under regulation 102(2) is to be calculated as if—

(a) the chargeable income is the only income chargeable to tax;
(b) the personal allowance applicable to the person receiving assistance under the self-employment route by virtue of sections 35 and 45 to 55 of the Income Tax Act 2007 is allowable against that income; and
(c) the rate at which the chargeable income less the personal allowance is assessable to income tax is the [1 . . .] basic rate of tax.

(2) For the purpose of paragraph (1), the [1basic rate] of tax to be applied and the amount of the personal allowance deductible is, where the period determined under regulation 102(2) is less than a year, to be calculated on a pro rata basis.

(3) In this regulation, "chargeable income" means the monies in the special account at the end of the last day upon which assistance was received under the self-employment route.

AMENDMENT

1. Employment and Support Allowance (Miscellaneous Amendments) Regulations 2008 (SI 2008/2428), reg.8(4) (October 27, 2008).

DEFINITION

"self-employment route"—see reg.2(1).

GENERAL NOTE

9.224   This is similar to reg.39D of the Income Support Regulations/reg.102D of the JSA Regulations.

CHAPTER 6

OTHER INCOME

Calculation of income other than earnings

9.225   **104.**—(1) For the purposes of regulation 91 (calculation of earnings derived from employed earner's employment and income other than earnings) the income of a claimant which does not consist of earnings to be taken into account will, subject to paragraphs (2) to (7), be the claimant's gross income and any capital treated as income under regulation 105 (capital treated as income).

(2) There is to be disregarded from the calculation of a claimant's gross income under paragraph (1), any sum, where applicable, specified in Schedule 8.

(3) Where the payment of any benefit under the benefit Acts is subject to any deduction by way of recovery the amount to be taken into account under paragraph (1) is to be the gross amount payable.

(4) [¹Paragraphs (5) and (5A) apply] where—

   (a) a relevant payment has been made to a claimant in an academic year; and

   (b) that claimant abandons, or is dismissed from, that claimant's course of study before the payment to the claimant of the final instalment of the relevant payment.

(5) [¹Where a relevant payment is made quarterly, the] amount of a relevant payment to be taken into account for the assessment period for the purposes of paragraph (1) in respect of a claimant to whom paragraph (4) applies, is to be calculated by applying the formula—

$$\frac{A - (B \times C)}{D}$$

where—

A = the total amount of the relevant payment which that claimant would have received had that claimant remained a student until the last day of the academic term in which the person abandoned, or was dismissed from, the course, less any deduction under regulation 137(6) (treatment of student loans);

B = the number of benefit weeks from the benefit week immediately following that which includes the first day of that academic year to the benefit week immediately before that which includes the day on which the claimant abandoned, or was dismissed from, that claimant's course;

C = the weekly amount of the relevant payment, before the application of the £10 disregard, which would have been taken into account as income under regulation 137(3) had the claimant not abandoned or been dismissed from, the course and, in the case of a claimant who was not entitled to an income-related allowance immediately before that claimant abandoned or was dismissed from the course, had that claimant, at that time, been entitled to an income-related allowance;

D = the number of benefit weeks in the assessment period.

[¹(5A) Where a relevant payment is made by two or more instalments in a quarter, the amount of a relevant payment to be taken into account for the assessment period for the purposes of paragraph (1) in respect of a person to whom paragraph (4) applies, shall be calculated by applying the formula in paragraph (5) but as if—

A = the total amount of relevant payments which that person received, or would have received, from the first day of the academic year to the day the person abandoned the course, or was dismissed from it, less any deduction under regulation 137(6).]

(6) [¹In this regulation]—

"academic year" and "student loan" have the same meanings as for the purposes of Chapter 10 of this Part;

[¹"assessment period" means—

(a) in a case where a relevant payment is made quarterly, the period beginning with the benefit week which includes the day on which the claimant abandoned, or was dismissed from, the course and ending with the benefit week which includes the last day of the last quarter for which an instalment of the relevant payment was payable to that claimant;

(b) in a case where the relevant payment is made by two or more instalments in a quarter, the period beginning with the benefit week which includes the day on which the claimant abandoned, or was dismissed from, the course and ending with the benefit week which includes—

   (i) the day immediately before the day on which the next instalment of the relevant payment would have been due had the payments continued; or

   (ii) the last day of the last quarter for which an instalment of the relevant payment was payable to that claimant,

   whichever of those dates is earlier;]

"assessment period" means the period beginning with the benefit week which includes the day on which the claimant abandoned, or was dismissed from, the course and ending with the benefit week which includes the last day of the last quarter for which an instalment of the relevant payment was payable to that claimant;

"quarter" for the purposes of the definition of "assessment period" in relation to an academic year means a period in that year—

(a) beginning on 1st January and ending on 31st March;

(b) beginning on 1st April and ending on 30th June;

(c) beginning on 1st July and ending on 31st August; or

(d) beginning on 1st September and ending on 31st December;

"relevant payment" means either a student loan or an amount intended for the maintenance of dependants referred to in regulation 132(6) (calculation of grant income) or both.

(7) In the case of income to which regulation 91(4) (calculation of income of former students) applies, the amount of income to be taken into account for the purposes of paragraph (1) is to be the amount of that income calculated in accordance with regulation 94(7) (calculation of weekly amount of income) and on the basis that none of that income has been repaid.

(8) Subject to paragraph (9), for the avoidance of doubt there is to be included as income to be taken into account under paragraph (1)—

(a) any payment to which regulation 95(2) or 97(2) (payments not earnings) applies; or

(b) in the case of a claimant who is receiving support provided under section 95 or 98 of the Immigration and Asylum Act including support provided by virtue of regulations made under Schedule 9 to that Act, the amount of such support provided in respect of essential living needs of the claimant and the claimant's partner (if any) as is specified in regulations made under paragraph 3 of Schedule 8 to that Act.

(9) In the case of a claimant who is the partner of a person subject to immigration control and whose partner is receiving support provided under section 95 or 98 of the Immigration and Asylum Act including support provided by

virtue of regulations made under Schedule 9 to that Act, there is not to be included as income to be taken into account under paragraph (1) the amount of support provided in respect of essential living needs of the partner of the claimant and the claimant's dependants (if any) as is specified in regulations made under paragraph 3 of Schedule 8 to the Immigration and Asylum Act.

AMENDMENT

1. Social Security (Students and Miscellaneous Amendments) Regulations 2008 (SI 2008/1599), reg.7(2) (October 27, 2008).

DEFINITIONS

"academic year"—see reg.131(1).
"benefit week"—see reg.2(1).
"claimant"— see reg.83(1).
"full-time student"—see reg.2(1).
"student loan"—see reg.131(1).

GENERAL NOTE

This is similar to reg.40 of the Income Support Regulations/reg.103 of the JSA Regulations (except that there is no equivalent to para.(9) in reg.103 of the JSA Regulations). **9.226**

Capital treated as income

105.—(1) Capital which is payable by instalments which are outstanding on— **9.227**

(a) the first day in respect of which an income-related allowance is payable or the date of the determination of the claim, whichever is earlier; or

(b) in the case of a supersession, the date of that supersession,

is to be treated as income if the aggregate of the instalments outstanding and the amount of the claimant's capital otherwise calculated in accordance with Chapter 7 of this Part exceeds £16,000.

(2) Any payment received under an annuity is to be treated as income.

(3) Any earnings to the extent that they are not a payment of income are to be treated as income.

(4) Any Career Development Loan paid pursuant to section 2 of the Employment and Training Act 1973 is to be treated as income.

(5) Where an agreement or court order provides that payments are to be made to the claimant in consequence of any personal injury to the claimant and that such payments are to be made, wholly or in part, by way of periodical payments, any such periodical payments received by the claimant (but not a payment which is treated as capital by virtue of this Part), are to be treated as income.

DEFINITION

"claimant"—see reg.83(1).

GENERAL NOTE

This is similar to reg.104 of the JSA Regulations/reg.41 of the Income Support Regulations (except that there is no equivalent to reg.41(4) (repayment of PAYE tax in trade dispute cases)). **9.228**

Notional income—deprivation and income on application

9.229   **106.**—(1) A claimant is to be treated as possessing income of which the claimant has deprived himself or herself for the purpose of securing entitlement to an employment and support allowance or increasing the amount of that allowance, or for the purpose of securing entitlement to, or increasing the amount of, income support or a jobseeker's allowance.

(2) Except in the case of—

(a) a discretionary trust;

(b) a trust derived from a payment made in consequence of a personal injury;

(c) an employment and support allowance;

(d) a jobseeker's allowance;

(e) working tax credit;

(f) child tax credit;

(g) a personal pension scheme, occupational pension scheme or a payment made by the Board of the Pension Protection Fund where the claimant is aged under 60;

(h) any sum to which paragraph 43(2)(a) of Schedule 9 (capital to be disregarded) applies which is administered in the way referred to in paragraph 43(1)(a) of that Schedule;

(i) any sum to which paragraph 44(a) of Schedule 9 refers; or

(j) rehabilitation allowance made under section 2 of the Employment and Training Act 1973,

income which would become available to the claimant upon application being made but which has not been acquired by the claimant is to be treated as possessed by the claimant but only from the date on which it could be expected to be acquired were an application made.

(3) A claimant who has attained the age of 60 is to be treated as possessing—

(a) the amount of any income from an occupational pension scheme, a personal pension scheme or the Board of the Pension Protection Fund—

(i) for which no claim has been made; and

(ii) to which the claimant might expect to be entitled if a claim for it were made;

(b) income from an occupational pension scheme which the claimant elected to defer,

but only from the date on which it could be expected to be acquired were an application for it to be made.

(4) This paragraph applies where a claimant aged not less than 60—

(a) is entitled to money purchase benefits under an occupational pension scheme or a personal pension scheme;

(b) fails to purchase an annuity with the funds available in that scheme; and

(c) either—

(i) defers in whole or in part the payment of any income which would have been payable to the claimant by that claimant's pension fund holder; or

(ii) fails to take any necessary action to secure that the whole of any income which would be payable to the person by that claimant's pension fund holder upon the person applying for it, is so paid; or

(iii) income withdrawal is not available to the claimant under that scheme.

(5) Where paragraph (4) applies, the amount of any income foregone is to be treated as possessed by that claimant, but only from the date on which it could be expected to be acquired were an application for it to be made.

(6) The amount of any income foregone in a case where paragraph (4) (c)(i) or (ii) applies is to be the maximum amount of income which may be withdrawn from the fund and is to be determined by the Secretary of State who will take account of information provided by the pension fund holder in accordance with regulation 7(5) of the Social Security (Claims and Payments) Regulations 1987.

(7) The amount of any income foregone in a case where paragraph (4) (c)(iii) applies is to be the income that the claimant could have received without purchasing an annuity had the funds held under the relevant occupational or personal pension scheme been held under a scheme where income withdrawal was available and is to be determined in the manner specified in paragraph (6).

(8) In paragraph (4), "money purchase benefits" has the meaning it has in section 181 of the Pension Schemes Act 1993.

DEFINITIONS

"claimant"—see reg.83(1).
"occupational pension scheme"—see reg.2(1).
"payment"—*ibid.*
"pension fund holder"—*ibid.*
"personal pension scheme"—*ibid.*

GENERAL NOTE

This is similar to reg.42(1)–(2CA) of the Income Support Regulations/reg.105(1)–(5A) of the JSA Regulations. 9.230

Note that under para.(1) if a person has deprived himself of income he will be caught by this rule if the purpose of the deprivation was to secure entitlement to or increase the amount of ESA *or income support or JSA*. This avoids the question that might otherwise have arisen on a claimant transferring from income support (or JSA) to ESA whether a deprivation which had only been for the purposes of income support (or JSA) could be caught by para.(1).

Notional income—income due to be paid or income paid to or in respect of a third party

107.—(1) Except in the case of a discretionary trust, or a trust derived from a payment made in consequence of a personal injury, any income which is due to be paid to the claimant but— 9.231

(a) has not been paid to the claimant;

(b) is not a payment prescribed in regulation 8 or 9 of the Social Security (Payments on Account, Overpayment and Recovery) Regulations 1988 (duplication and prescribed payments or maintenance payments) and not made on or before the date prescribed in relation to it,

is, except for any amount to which paragraph (2) applies, to be treated as possessed by the claimant.

(2) This paragraph applies to—

(a) an amount which is due to be paid to the claimant under an occupational pension scheme but which is not paid because the trustees or managers of the scheme have suspended or ceased payments due to an insufficiency of resources;

(b) any amount by which a payment made to the claimant from an occupational pension scheme falls short of the payment to which the claimant was due under the scheme where the shortfall arises because the trustees or managers of the scheme have insufficient resources available to them to meet in full the scheme's liabilities; or

(c) any earnings which are due to an employed earner on the termination of that employed earner's employment by reason of redundancy but which have not been paid to that employed earner.

(3) Any payment of income, other than a payment of income specified in paragraph (5), made to a third party in respect of a single claimant or the claimant's partner (but not a member of the third party's family) is to be treated—

(a) in a case where that payment is derived from—
   (i) a payment of any benefit under the benefit Acts;
   (ii) a payment from the Armed Forces and Reserve Forces Compensation Scheme;
   (iii) a war disablement pension, war widow's pension or war widower's pension; or
   (iv) a pension payable to a person as a widow, widower or surviving civil partner under any power of Her Majesty otherwise than under an enactment to make provision about pensions for or in respect of persons who have been disabled or have died in consequence of service as members of the armed forces of the Crown,

   as possessed by that single claimant, if it is paid to the claimant or by the claimant's partner, if it is paid to the claimant's partner;

(b) in a case where that payment is a payment of an occupational pension, a pension or other periodical payment made under a personal pension scheme or a payment made by the Board of the Pension Protection Fund, as possessed by that single claimant or, as the case may be, by the claimant's partner;

(c) in any other case, as possessed by that single claimant or the claimant's partner to the extent that it is used for the food, ordinary clothing or footwear, household fuel, rent for which housing benefit is payable, or any housing costs to the extent that they are met under regulations 67(1)(c) or 68(1)(d) (housing costs), of that single claimant or, as the case may be, of the claimant's partner, or is used for any council tax or water charges for which that claimant or that partner is liable,

but, except where sub-paragraph (a) applies, this paragraph does not apply to any payment in kind to the third party.

(4) Any payment of income, other than a payment of income specified in paragraph (5), made to a single claimant or the claimant's partner in respect of a third party (but not in respect of another member of the claimant's family) is to be treated as possessed by that single claimant or, as the case may be, the claimant's partner, to the extent that it is kept or used by that claimant or used by or on behalf of the claimant's partner but, except where paragraph (3)(a) applies, this paragraph does not apply to any payment in kind to the third party.

(5) Paragraphs (3) and (4) do not apply in respect of a payment of income made—

(a) under the Macfarlane Trust, the Macfarlane (Special Payments) Trust, the Macfarlane (Special Payments) (No. 2) Trust, the Fund, the Eileen Trust or [¹the Independent Living Fund (2006)];

(b) pursuant to section 19(1)(a) of the Coal Industry Act 1994 (concessionary coal); or

(c) pursuant to section 2 of the Employment and Training Act 1973 in respect of a person's participation—

    (i) in an employment programme specified in regulation 75(1)(a)(ii) of the Jobseeker's Allowance Regulations;

    (ii) in a training scheme specified in regulation 75(1)(b)(ii) of those Regulations;

    (iii) in the Intensive Activity Period specified in regulation 75(1)(a)(iv) of those Regulations;

    (iv) in a qualifying course within the meaning specified in regulation 17A(7) of those Regulations; or

(d) under an occupational pension scheme, in respect of a pension or other periodical payment made under a personal pension scheme or a payment made by the Board of the Pension Protection Fund where—

    (i) a bankruptcy order has been made in respect of the person in respect of whom the payment has been made or, in Scotland, the estate of that person is subject to sequestration or a judicial factor has been appointed on that person's estate under section 41 of the Solicitors (Scotland) Act 1980;

    (ii) the payment is made to the trustee in bankruptcy or any other person acting on behalf of the creditors; and

    (iii) the person referred to in paragraph (i) and that person's partner (if any) does not possess, or is not treated as possessing, any other income apart from that payment.

(6) Where the claimant resides in a care home, an Abbeyfield Home or an independent hospital, or is temporarily absent from such a home or hospital, any payment made by a person other than the claimant or a member of the claimant's family in respect of some or all of the cost of maintaining the claimant or the claimant's partner in that home or hospital is to be treated as possessed by the claimant or the claimant's partner.

(7) In paragraph (2)(a) and (b) "resources" has the same meaning as in section 181(1) of the Pension Schemes Act 1993.

AMENDMENT

1. Employment and Support Allowance (Miscellaneous Amendments) Regulations 2008 (SI 2008/2428), reg.8(5) (October 27, 2008).

DEFINITIONS

"Abbeyfield Home"—see reg.2(1).
"Armed Forces and Reserve Forces Compensation Scheme"—*ibid.*
"benefit Acts"—*ibid.*
"care home"—*ibid.*
"claimant"—see reg.83(1).
"Eileen Trust"—see reg.2(1).
"family"—*ibid.*

"the Fund"—*ibid.*
"independent hospital"—*ibid.*
"the Independent Living Fund (2006)"—*ibid.*
"Macfarlane (Special Payments) Trust"—*ibid.*
"Macfarlane (Special Payments) (No. 2) Trust"—*ibid.*
"Macfarlane Trust"—*ibid.*
"occupational pension"—*ibid.*
"occupational pension scheme"—*ibid.*
"ordinary clothing and footwear"—*ibid.*
"partner"—*ibid.*
"payment"—*ibid.*
"personal pension"—*ibid.*
"personal pension scheme"—*ibid.*
"single claimant"—*ibid.*
"war disablement pension"—*ibid.*
"war widow's pension"—*ibid.*
"war widower's pension"—*ibid.*
"water charges"—*ibid.*

GENERAL NOTE

9.232   This is similar to reg.42(3)–(4A) and (8A) of the Income Support Regulations/ reg.105(6)–(11), together with the definition of "resources" in reg.105(16), of the JSA Regulations (except that paras (3) and (4) do not contain any special provisions relating to trade disputes).

Notional income—other income

9.233   **108.**—(1) Where a claimant's earnings are not ascertainable at the time of the determination of the claim or of any revision or supersession the Secretary of State will treat the claimant as possessing such earnings as is reasonable in the circumstances of the case having regard to the number of hours worked and the earnings paid for comparable employment in the area.

(2) Where the amount of a subsistence allowance paid to a claimant in a benefit week is less than the amount of income-based jobseeker's allowance that claimant would have received in that benefit week had it been payable to the claimant, less 50p, the claimant is to be treated as possessing the amount which is equal to the amount of income-based jobseeker's allowance which the claimant would have received in that week, less 50p.

(3) Subject to paragraph (4), where—
(a) a claimant performs a service for another person; and
(b) that person makes no payment of earnings or pays less than that paid for a comparable employment in the area,
the Secretary of State is to treat the claimant as possessing such earnings (if any) as is reasonable for that employment unless the claimant satisfies the Secretary of State that the means of that person are insufficient for the person to pay, or to pay more, for the service.

(4) Paragraph (3) will not apply—
(a) to a claimant who is engaged by a charitable or voluntary organisa- tion or who is a volunteer if the Secretary of State is satisfied in any of those cases that it is reasonable for the claimant to provide the service free of charge;
(b) in a case where the service is performed in connection with—
(i) the claimant's participation in an employment or training

programme in accordance with regulation 19(1)(q) of the Jobseeker's Allowance Regulations, other than where the service is performed in connection with the claimant's participation in the Intensive Activity Period specified in regulation 75(1)(a)(iv) of those Regulations; or

(ii) the claimant's or the claimant's partner's participation in an employment or training programme as defined in regulation 19(3) of those Regulations for which a training allowance is not payable or, where such an allowance is payable, it is payable for the sole purpose of reimbursement of travelling or meal expenses to the claimant or the claimant's partner participating in that programme;

(c) to a claimant who is engaged in work experience whilst participating in—

(i) the New Deal for Lone Parents; or

(ii) a scheme which has been approved by the Secretary of State as supporting the objectives of the New Deal for Lone Parents; or

(d) to a claimant who is participating in a work placement approved in writing by the Secretary of State before the placement starts;

(e) in sub-paragraph (d) "work placement" means practical work experience with an employer, which is neither paid nor undertaken in expectation of payment.

DEFINITIONS

"benefit week"—see reg.2(1).
"claimant"—see reg.83(1).
"partner"—see reg.2(1).
"payment"—*ibid.*
"subsistence allowance"—*ibid.*
"voluntary organisation"—*ibid.*

GENERAL NOTE

This is similar to reg.42(5)–(6AA) of the Income Support Regulations/ reg.105(11A)–(13A), together with the definition of "work placement" in reg.105(16), of the JSA Regulations. There are some differences in reg.105 of the JSA Regulations (e.g. there is no equivalent to para.(4)(c) which relates to lone parents).   **9.234**

Notional income—calculation and interpretation

109.—(1) Where a claimant is treated as possessing any income under   **9.235** regulation 106 or 107 the foregoing provisions of this Part are to apply for the purposes of calculating the amount of that income as if a payment had actually been made and as if it were actual income which the claimant does possess.

(2) Where a claimant is treated as possessing any earnings under regulation 108(1) or (3) the foregoing provisions of this Part are to apply for the purposes of calculating the amount of those earnings as if a payment had actually been made and as if they were actual earnings which the claimant does possess except that paragraph (3) of regulation 96 (calculation of net earnings of employed earners) does not apply and the claimant's net earnings are to be calculated by taking into account the earnings which the claimant is treated as possessing, less—

(a) where the period over which those earnings are to be taken into account is a year or more, an amount in respect of income tax equivalent to an amount calculated by applying to those earnings the [¹ . . .] basic rate of tax in the year of assessment less only the personal allowance to which the claimant is entitled under section 257(1) of the Income and Corporation Taxes Act 1988 (personal allowance) as is appropriate to the claimant's circumstances;

(b) where if the period over which those earnings are to be taken into account is less than a year, the earnings to which the [¹basic rate] of tax is to be applied and the amount of the personal allowance deductible under this paragraph is to be calculated on a pro rata basis;

(c) where the weekly amount of those earnings equals or exceeds the lower earnings limit, an amount representing primary Class 1 contributions under section 6(1)(a) of the Contributions and Benefits Act, calculated by applying to those earnings the initial and main primary percentages in accordance with section 8(1)(a) and (b) of that Act; and

(d) one-half of any sum payable by the claimant in respect of a pay period by way of a contribution towards an occupational or personal pension scheme.

AMENDMENT

1. Employment and Support Allowance (Miscellaneous Amendments) Regulations 2008 (SI 2008/2428), reg.8(6) (October 27, 2008).

DEFINITIONS

"claimant"—see reg.83(1).
"employed earner"—see reg.2(1).
"pay period"—*ibid.*
"payment"—*ibid.*

GENERAL NOTE

9.236   This is similar to reg.42(7)–(8) of the Income Support Regulations/reg.105(14)–(15) of the JSA Regulations.

CHAPTER 7

CAPITAL

Capital limit

9.237   **110.** For the purposes of paragraph 6(1)(b) of Schedule 1 to the Act as it applies to an income-related allowance (no entitlement to benefit if capital exceeds prescribed amount), the prescribed amount is £16,000.

GENERAL NOTE

9.238   This contains a similar provision to that in reg.45 of the Income Support Regulations/reg.107 of the JSA Regulations.

Calculation of capital

9.239   **111.**—(1) For the purposes of [¹sections 1(2)] and 4 of, and Part 2 of Schedule 1 to, the Act as it applies to an income-related allowance, the capital of a claimant to be taken into account is, subject to paragraph (2), to be the whole of the claimant's capital calculated in accordance with this Part and any income treated as capital under regulation 112 (income treated as capital).

(2) There is to be disregarded from the calculation of a claimant's capital under paragraph (1) any capital, where applicable, specified in Schedule 9.

AMENDMENT

1. Employment and Support Allowance (Miscellaneous Amendments) Regulations 2008 (SI 2008/2428), reg.8(7) (October 27, 2008).

DEFINITION

"claimant"—see reg.83(1).

GENERAL NOTE

This is similar to reg.46 of the Income Support Regulations/reg.108 of the JSA Regulations.

9.240

Income treated as capital

112.—(1) Any bounty derived from employment to which regulation 43(1)(e) and paragraph 12 of Schedule 7 apply and paid at intervals of at least one year is to be treated as capital.

9.241

(2) Any amount by way of a refund of income tax paid in respect of, or deducted from, profits or income chargeable to tax under the provisions in Part 2 of the Income Tax (Trading and Other Income) Act 2005 or Part 2 of the Income Tax (Earnings and Pensions) Act 2003 is to be treated as capital.

(3) Any holiday pay which is not earnings under regulation 95(1)(d) (earnings of employed earners) is to be treated as capital.

(4) Except any income derived from capital disregarded under paragraph 1, 2, 4 to 8, 10, 16, 43 or 44 of Schedule 9, any income derived from capital is to be treated as capital but only from the date it is normally due to be credited to the claimant's account.

(5) In the case of employment as an employed earner, any advance of earnings or any loan made by the claimant's employer is to be treated as capital.

(6) Any payment under section 30 of the Prison Act 1952 (payments for discharged prisoners) or allowance under section 17 of the Prisons (Scotland) Act 1989 (allowances to prisoners on discharge) is to be treated as capital.

(7) Any charitable or voluntary payment which is not made or not due to be made at regular intervals, other than one to which paragraph (8) applies, is to be treated as capital.

(8) This paragraph applies to a payment which is made under the Macfarlane Trust, the Macfarlane (Special Payments) Trust, the Macfarlane (Special Payments) (No. 2) Trust, the Fund, the Eileen Trust or [¹the Independent Living Fund (2006)].

(9) Any arrears of subsistence allowance which are paid to a claimant as a lump sum are to be treated as capital.

AMENDMENT

1. Employment and Support Allowance (Miscellaneous Amendments) Regulations 2008 (SI 2008/2428), reg.8(5) (October 27, 2008).

DEFINITIONS

"claimant"—see reg.83(1).
"Eileen Trust"—see reg.2(1).
"employed earner"—*ibid.*
"the Fund"—*ibid.*
"the Independent Living Fund (2006)"—*ibid.*
"Macfarlane (Special Payments) Trust"—*ibid.*
"Macfarlane (Special Payments) (No. 2) Trust"—*ibid.*
"Macfarlane Trust"—*ibid.*
"subsistence allowance"—*ibid.*

GENERAL NOTE

9.242   This is similar to reg.48 of the Income Support Regulations/reg.110 of the JSA Regulations (except that it does not contain any special provisions relating to trade disputes).

Calculation of capital in the United Kingdom

9.243   **113.** Capital which a claimant possesses in the United Kingdom is to be calculated at its current market or surrender value less—
(a) where there would be expenses attributable to sale, 10%; and
(b) the amount of any incumbrance secured on it.

DEFINITION

"claimant"—see reg.83(1).

GENERAL NOTE

9.244   This is similar to reg.49 of the Income Support Regulations/reg.111 of the JSA Regulations.

Calculation of capital outside the United Kingdom

9.245   **114.** Capital which a claimant possesses in a country outside the United Kingdom is to be calculated—
(a) in a case in which there is no prohibition in that country against the transfer to the United Kingdom of an amount equal to its current market or surrender value in that country, at that value;
(b) in a case where there is such a prohibition, at the price which it would realise if sold in the United Kingdom to a willing buyer,
less, where there would be expenses attributable to sale, 10% and the amount of any incumbrance secured on it.

DEFINITION

"claimant"—see reg.83(1).

GENERAL NOTE

9.246   This is similar to reg.50 of the Income Support Regulations/reg.112 of the JSA Regulations.

Notional capital

9.247   **115.**—(1) A claimant is to be treated as possessing capital of which the claimant has deprived himself or herself for the purpose of securing entitlement to an employment and support allowance or increasing the amount of that allowance, or for the purpose of securing entitlement to, or increasing the amount of, income support or a jobseeker's allowance except—

 (a) where that capital is derived from a payment made in consequence of any personal injury and is placed on trust for the benefit of the claimant;

 (b) to the extent that the capital which the claimant is treated as possessing is reduced in accordance with regulation 116 (diminishing notional capital rule);

 (c) any sum to which paragraph 43(2)(a) of Schedule 9 (capital to be disregarded) applies which is administered in the way referred to in paragraph 43(1)(a); or

 (d) any sum to which paragraph 44(a) of Schedule 9 refers.

(2) Except in the case of—

 (a) a discretionary trust;

 (b) a trust derived from a payment made in consequence of a personal injury;

 (c) any loan which would be obtainable only if secured against capital disregarded under Schedule 9;

 (d) a personal pension scheme;

 (e) an occupational pension scheme or a payment made by the Board of the Pension Protection Fund where the claimant is aged under 60; or

 (f) any sum to which paragraph 43(2)(a) of Schedule 9 (capital to be disregarded) applies which is administered in a way referred to in paragraph 43(1)(a); or

 (g) any sum to which paragraph 44(a) of Schedule 9 refers,

any capital which would become available to the claimant upon application being made but which has not been acquired by the claimant is to be treated as possessed by the claimant but only from the date on which it could be expected to be acquired were an application made.

(3) Any payment of capital, other than a payment of capital specified in paragraph (5), made to a third party in respect of a single claimant or the claimant's partner (but not a member of the third party's family) is to be treated—

 (a) in a case where that payment is derived from—

  (i) a payment of any benefit under the benefit Acts;

  (ii) a payment from the Armed Forces and Reserve Forces Compensation Scheme;

  (iii) a war disablement pension, war widow's pension or war widower's pension; or

  (iv) a pension payable to a person as a widow, widower or surviving civil partner under any power of Her Majesty otherwise than under an enactment to make provision about pensions for or in respect of persons who have been disabled or who have died in consequence of service as members of the armed forces of the Crown,

  as possessed by that single claimant, if it is paid to that claimant, or by the claimant's partner, if it is paid to that partner;

 (b) in a case where that payment is a payment of an occupational pension, a pension or other periodical payment made under a personal pension scheme or a payment made by the Board of the Pension Protection Fund, as possessed by that single claimant or, as the case may be, by the claimant's partner;

 (c) in any other case, as possessed by that single claimant or the claimant's partner to the extent that it is used for the food, ordinary clothing or footwear, household fuel, rent for which housing benefit is payable or any housing costs to the extent that they are met under regulation 67(1)(c) and 68(1)(d) (housing costs) of that single claimant or, as the case may be, of the claimant's partner, or is used for any council tax or water charges for which that claimant or partner is liable.

(4) Any payment of capital, other than a payment of capital specified in paragraph (5) made to a single claimant or the claimant's partner in respect of a third party (but not in respect of another member of the claimant's family) is to be treated as possessed by that single claimant or, as the case may be, the claimant's partner, to the extent that it is kept or used by that claimant or used by or on behalf of the claimant's partner.

(5) Paragraphs (3) and (4) will not apply in respect of a payment of capital made—

(a) under the Macfarlane Trust, the Macfarlane (Special Payments) Trust, the Macfarlane (Special Payments) (No. 2) Trust, the Fund, the Eileen Trust [¹, the Independent Living Fund (2006)], the Skipton Fund or the London Bombings Relief Charitable Fund;

(b) pursuant to section 2 of the Employment and Training Act 1973 in respect of a claimant's participation—

  (i) in an employment programme specified in regulation 75(1)(a)(ii) of the Jobseeker's Allowance Regulations;

  (ii) in a training scheme specified in regulation 75(1)(b)(ii) of those Regulations; or

  (iii) in the Intensive Activity Period specified in regulation 75(1)(a)(iv) of those Regulations; or

  (iv) in a qualifying course within the meaning specified in regulation 17A(7) of those Regulations;

(c) under an occupational pension scheme, in respect of a pension or other periodical payment made under a personal pension scheme or a payment made by the Board of the Pension Protection Fund where—

  (i) a bankruptcy order has been made in respect of the person in respect of whom the payment has been made or, in Scotland, the estate of that person is subject to sequestration or a judicial factor has been appointed on that person's estate under section 41 of the Solicitors (Scotland) Act 1980;

  (ii) the payment is made to the trustee in bankruptcy or any other person acting on behalf of the creditors; and

  (iii) the person referred to in paragraph (i) and that person's partner (if any) does not possess, or is not treated as possessing, any other income apart from that payment.

(6) Where a claimant stands in relation to a company in a position analogous to that of a sole owner or partner in the business of that company, the claimant is to be treated as if that claimant were such sole owner or partner and in such a case—

(a) the value of the claimant's holding in that company, notwithstanding regulation 111 (calculation of capital), is to be disregarded; and

(b) the claimant will, subject to paragraph (7), be treated as possessing an amount of capital equal to the value or, as the case may be, the claimant's share of the value of the capital of that company and the foregoing provisions of this Chapter are to apply for the purposes of calculating that amount as if it were actual capital which the claimant does possess.

(7) For so long as the claimant undertakes activities in the course of the business of the company, the amount which the claimant is treated as possessing under paragraph (6) is to be disregarded.

(8) Where a claimant is treated as possessing capital under any of paragraphs (1) to (6), the foregoing provisions of this Chapter are to apply for the purposes of calculating its amount as if it were actual capital which the claimant does possess.

(9) For the avoidance of doubt a claimant is to be treated as possessing capital under paragraph (1) only if the capital of which the claimant has deprived himself or herself is actual capital.

AMENDMENT

1. Employment and Support Allowance (Miscellaneous Amendments) Regulations 2008 (SI 2008/2428), reg.8(8) (October 27, 2008).

DEFINITIONS

"Armed Forces and Reserve Forces Compensation Scheme"—see reg.2(1).
"benefit Acts"—*ibid.*
"claimant"—see reg.83(1).
"Eileen Trust"—see reg.2(1).
"family"—*ibid.*
"the Fund"—*ibid.*
"the Independent Living Fund (2006)"—*ibid.*
"London Bombings Relief Charitable Fund"—*ibid.*
"Macfarlane (Special Payments) Trust"—*ibid.*
"Macfarlane (Special Payments) (No. 2) Trust"—*ibid.*
"Macfarlane Trust"—*ibid.*
"occupational pension"—*ibid.*
"occupational pension scheme"—*ibid.*
"ordinary clothing and footwear"—*ibid.*
"partner"—*ibid.*
"payment"—*ibid.*
"personal pension scheme"—*ibid.*
"single claimant"—*ibid.*
"Skipton Fund"—*ibid.*
"war disablement pension"—*ibid.*
"war widow's pension"—*ibid.*
"war widower's pension"—*ibid.*
"water charges"—*ibid.*

GENERAL NOTE

This is similar to reg.51 of the Income Support Regulations /reg.113 of the JSA Regulations.   9.248

Note that under para.(1) if a person has deprived himself of capital he will be caught by this rule if the purpose of the deprivation was to secure entitlement to or increase the amount of ESA *or income support or JSA*. This avoids the question that might otherwise have arisen on a claimant transferring from income support (or JSA) to ESA whether a deprivation which had only been for the purposes of income support (or JSA) could be caught by para.(1).

Diminishing notional capital rule

116.—(1) Where a claimant is treated as possessing capital under regulation 115(1) (notional capital), the amount which the claimant is treated as possessing—   9.249

    (a) in the case of a week that is subsequent to—
- (i) the relevant week in respect of which the conditions set out in paragraph (2) are satisfied; or
- (ii) a week which follows that relevant week and which satisfies those conditions,

is to be reduced by an amount determined under paragraph (2);

    (b) in the case of a week in respect of which paragraph (1)(a) does not apply but where—
- (i) that week is a week subsequent to the relevant week; and
- (ii) that relevant week is a week in which the condition in paragraph (3) is satisfied,

is to be reduced by the amount determined under paragraph (3).

(2) This paragraph applies to a benefit week or part-week where the claimant satisfies the conditions that—

    (a) the claimant is in receipt of an income-related allowance; and

    (b) but for regulation 115(1), the claimant would have received an additional amount of an income-related allowance in that benefit week or, as the case may be, that part-week,

and in such a case, the amount of the reduction for the purposes of paragraph (1)(a) is to be equal to that additional amount.

(3) Subject to paragraph (4), for the purposes of paragraph (1)(b) the condition is that the claimant would have been entitled to an income-related allowance in the relevant week, but for regulation 115(1), and in such a case the amount of the reduction is to be equal to the aggregate of—

    (a) the amount of an income-related allowance to which the claimant would have been entitled in the relevant week but for regulation 115(1); and for the purposes of this sub-paragraph if the relevant week is a part-week that amount is to be determined by dividing the amount of an income-related allowance to which the claimant would have been so entitled by the number equal to the number of days in the part-week and multiplying the quotient by 7;

    (b) the amount of housing benefit (if any) equal to the difference between the claimant's maximum housing benefit and the amount (if any) of housing benefit which the claimant is awarded in respect of the benefit week, within the meaning of regulation 2(1) of the Housing Benefit Regulations 2006 (interpretation), which includes the last day of the relevant week;

    (c) the amount of council tax benefit (if any) equal to the difference between the claimant's maximum council tax benefit and the amount (if any) of council tax benefit which the claimant is awarded in respect of the benefit week which includes the last day of the relevant week, and for this purpose "benefit week" has the same meaning as in regulation 2(1) of the Council Tax Benefit Regulations 2006 (interpretation).

(4) The amount determined under paragraph (3) is to be re-determined under that paragraph if the claimant makes a further claim for an income-related allowance and the conditions in paragraph (5) are satisfied, and in such a case—

    (a) sub-paragraphs (a) to (c) of paragraph (3) will apply as if for the words "relevant week" there were substituted the words "relevant subsequent week"; and

    (b) subject to paragraph (6), the amount as re-determined is to have effect from the first week following the relevant subsequent week in question.

(5) The conditions are that—

(a) a further claim is made 26 or more weeks after—

    (i) the date on which the claimant made a claim for an income-related allowance in respect of which the claimant was first treated as possessing the capital in question under regulation 115(1);

    (ii) in a case where there has been at least one re-determination in accordance with paragraph (4), the date on which the claim-ant last made a claim for an income-related allowance which resulted in the weekly amount being re-determined; or

    (iii) the date on which the claimant last ceased to be in receipt of an income-related allowance;

whichever last occurred; and

(b) the claimant would have been entitled to an income-related allow-ance but for regulation 115(1).

(6) The amount as re-determined pursuant to paragraph (4) is not to have effect if it is less than the amount which applied in that case immedi-ately before the re-determination and in such a case the higher amount is to continue to have effect.

(7) For the purposes of this regulation—

"part-week" means a period to which Part 14 (periods of less than a week) applies;

"relevant week" means the benefit week or part-week in which the capital in question of which the claimant has deprived himself or herself within the meaning of regulation 115(1)—

(a) was first taken into account for the purpose of determining the claimant's entitlement to an income-related allowance, a job-seeker's allowance or income support; or

(b) was taken into account on a subsequent occasion for the purpose of determining or re-determining the claimant's enti-tlement to an income-related allowance, a jobseeker's allow-ance or income support on that subsequent occasion and that determination or re-determination resulted in the claimant's beginning to receive, or ceasing to receive, an income-related allowance, a jobseeker's allowance or income support;

and where more than one benefit week or part-week is identified by ref-erence to paragraphs (a) and (b) of this definition the later or latest such benefit week or, as the case may be, the later or latest such part-week;

"relevant subsequent week" means the benefit week or part-week which includes the day on which the further claim or, if more than one further claim has been made, the last such claim was made.

DEFINITIONS

"benefit week"—see reg.2(1).
"claimant"—see reg.83(1).
"week"—see reg.2(1).

GENERAL NOTE

This is similar to reg.51A of the Income Support Regulations/reg.114 of the JSA Regulations.

9.250

is not a complete £250 that part is to be treated as equivalent to a weekly income of £1.

(6) For the purposes of paragraphs (1) and (2), capital includes any income treated as capital under [¹regulation 112 (income treated as capital)].

AMENDMENT

1. Employment and Support Allowance (Miscellaneous Amendments) Regulations 2008 (SI 2008/2428), reg.20(6) (October 27, 2008).

DEFINITIONS

"Abbeyfield Home"—see reg.2(1).
"care home"—*ibid.*
"claimant"—see reg.83(1).
"independent hospital"—see reg.2(1).

GENERAL NOTE

This is similar to reg.53 of the Income Support Regulations/reg.116 of the JSA   9.254
Regulations. It is not entirely clear why para.(4)(a) contains a separate rule for a claimant over pensionable age (reg.53(1C)(a) of the Income Support Regulations does the same but not reg.116 of the JSA Regulations), since claimants over pensionable age are not entitled to ESA (or income support or indeed JSA).

CHAPTER 8

[¹CHILD MAINTENANCE AND LIABLE RELATIVE PAYMENTS]

AMENDMENT

1. Employment and Support Allowance (Miscellaneous Amendments) Regulations 2008 (SI 2008/2428), reg.20(5) (October 27, 2008).

Interpretation

119. In this Chapter—   9.255
[¹"child maintenance" means any payment towards the maintenance of a child or young person, including any payment made voluntarily and payments made under—
(a) the Child Support Act 1991;
(b) the Child Support (Northern Ireland) Order 1991;
(c) a court order;
(d) a consent order;
(e) a maintenance agreement registered for execution in the Books of Council and Session or the sheriff court books;]
"claimant" includes a young claimant;
[¹"claimant's family" shall be construed in accordance with section 137 of the Contributions and Benefits Act (interpretation of part 7 and supplementary provisions);
"housing costs" means those costs which may be met under paragraph 1(2) of Schedule 6;]
"liable relative" means—
(a) a spouse, former spouse, civil partner or former civil partner of a claimant or of a member of the claimant's family;

(b) a parent of a child or young person who is a member of the claimant's family or of a young claimant;

(c) a person who has not been adjudged to be the father of a child or young person who is a member of the claimant's family or of a young claimant where that person is contributing towards the maintenance of that child, young person or young claimant and by reason of that contribution the claimant may reasonably be treated as the father of that child, young person or young claimant;

(d) a person liable to maintain another person by virtue of section 78(6)(c) of the Administration Act (liability to maintain) where the latter is the claimant or a member of the claimant's family,

and, in this definition, a reference to a child's, young person's or young claimant's parent includes any person in relation to whom the child, young person or young claimant was treated as a child or a member of the family;

[¹"ordinary clothing and footwear" means clothing and footwear for normal daily use but does not include school uniforms;]

"payment" means a periodical payment or any other payment made by or derived from a liable relative [¹ . . .] but it does not include any payment—

(a) arising from a disposition of property made in contemplation of, or as a consequence of—
    (i) an agreement to separate;
    (ii) any proceedings for judicial separation, divorce or nullity of marriage; or
    (iii) any proceedings for separation, dissolution or nullity in relation to a civil partnership;

(b) made after the death of the liable relative;

(c) made by way of a gift but not in aggregate or otherwise exceeding £250 in the period of 52 weeks beginning with the date on which the payment, or if there is more than one such payment the first payment, is made; and, in the case of a claimant who continues to be in receipt of an income-related allowance at the end of the period of 52 weeks, this provision is to continue to apply thereafter with the modification that any subsequent period of 52 weeks is to begin with the first day of the benefit week in which the first payment is made after the end of the previous period of 52 weeks;

[¹(d) made to a third party, or in respect of a third party, unless the payment is—
    (i) in relation to the claimant or the claimant's family; and
    (ii) the payment is in respect of food, ordinary clothing or footwear, fuel, rent, housing costs, council tax or water charges;]

(e) in kind;

(f) to, or in respect of, a child or young person who is to be treated as not being a member of the claimant's household under regulation 156 (circumstances in which a person is to be treated as being or not being a member of the same household);

(g) which is not a periodical payment, to the extent that any amount of that payment—
    (i) has already been taken into account under this Part by virtue of a previous claim or determination;
    (ii) has been recovered under section 74 of the Administration

Act (income support and other payments) or is currently being recovered; or

(iii) at the time the determination is made, has been used by the claimant except where the claimant has deprived himself or herself of that amount for the purpose of securing entitlement to an income-related allowance or increasing the amount of that allowance;

"periodical payment" means—

(a) a payment which is made or is due to be made at regular intervals [¹ . . .];

(b) in a case where the liable relative has established a pattern of making payments at regular intervals, any such payment;

(c) any payment [¹, after the appropriate disregard under paragraph 60 of Schedule 8 (sums to be disregarded in the calculation of income other than earnings) has been applied to it, that does not exceed] the amount of an income-related allowance payable had that payment not been made;

(d) any payment representing a commutation of payments to which paragraph (a) or (b) of this definition applies whether made in arrears or in advance,

but does not include a payment due to be made before the first benefit week pursuant to the claim which is not so made;

"young claimant" means a person aged 16 or over but under 20 who makes a claim for an income-related allowance.

AMENDMENT

1. Employment and Support Allowance (Miscellaneous Amendments) Regulations 2008 (SI 2008/2428), reg.20(7) (October 27, 2008).

DEFINITIONS

"benefit week"—see reg.2(1).
"child"—*ibid*.
"claimant"—see reg.83(1).
"family"—see reg.2(1).
"young person"—*ibid*.

GENERAL NOTE

This is similar to reg.54 of the Income Support Regulations/reg.117 of the JSA Regulations.

9.256

Treatment of [¹ child maintenance or] liable relative payments

120. Subject to regulation 121 (disregard of payments treated as not relevant income) and [²paragraph 60 of Schedule 8 (sums to be disregarded in the calculation of income other than earnings)] a payment—

9.257

(a) to the extent that it is not a payment of income, is to be treated as income;

(b) is to be taken into account in accordance with the following provisions of this Chapter.

AMENDMENTS

1. Employment and Support Allowance (Miscellaneous Amendments) Regulations 2008 (SI 2008/2428), reg.20(2)(b) (October 27, 2008).

2. Employment and Support Allowance (Miscellaneous Amendments) Regulations 2008 (SI 2008/2428), reg.20(8) (October 27, 2008).

DEFINITIONS

"child maintenance"—see reg.119.
"payment"—*ibid.*

GENERAL NOTE

9.258   This is similar to reg.55 of the Income Support Regulations/reg.118 of the JSA Regulations.

Disregard of payments treated as not relevant income

9.259   **121.** Where the Secretary of State treats any payment as not being relevant income for the purposes of section 74A of the Administration Act (payment of benefit where maintenance payments collected by Secretary of State), that payment is to be disregarded in calculating a claimant's income.

DEFINITIONS

"payment"—see reg.119.
"relevant income"—see reg.2(c), Social Security Benefits (Maintenance Payments and Consequential Amendments) Regulations 1996 (SI 1996/940).

GENERAL NOTE

9.260   This is similar to reg.55A of the Income Support Regulations/reg.119 of the JSA Regulations.
        For reg.2(c) of the Social Security Benefits (Maintenance Payments and Consequential Amendments) Regulations 1996 see Vol.II of this series.

Period over which periodical payments are to be taken into account

9.261   **122.**—(1) The period over which a periodical payment is to be taken into account is to be—
(a) in a case where the payment is made at regular intervals, a period equal to the length of that interval;
(b) in a case where the payment is due to be made at regular intervals but is not so made, such number of weeks as is equal to the number (and any fraction is to be treated as a corresponding fraction of a week) obtained by dividing the amount of that payment by the weekly amount of that periodical payment as calculated in accordance with regulation 124(4) (calculation of the weekly amount of a liable relative payment);
(c) in any other case, a period equal to a week.
(2) The period under paragraph (1) is to begin on the date on which the payment is treated as paid under regulation 125 (date on which a liable relative payment is to be treated as paid).

DEFINITION

"periodical payment"—see reg.119.

GENERAL NOTE

9.262   This is similar to reg.56 of the Income Support Regulations/reg.120 of the JSA Regulations.

[¹ Period over which payments other than periodical payments are to be taken into account

123.—(1) The period over which a payment other than a periodical payment (a "non-periodical payment") is to be taken into account shall be determined as follows.

9.263

(2) Except in a case where paragraph (4) applies, the number of weeks over which a non-periodical payment is to be taken into account shall be equal to the number obtained by dividing that payment by the amount referred to in paragraph (3).

(3) The amount is the aggregate of £2 and—

(a) the amount of employment and support allowance that would be payable had no payment been made, and

(b) where applicable, the maximum amount of disregard that would apply to the payment under paragraph 60 of Schedule 8.

(4) This paragraph applies in a case where a liable relative makes a periodical payment and a non-periodical payment concurrently and the weekly amount of the periodical payment (as calculated in accordance with regulation 124) is less than B.

(5) In a case where paragraph (4) applies, the non-periodical payment shall, subject to paragraphs (6) and (7), be taken into account over a period of the number of weeks equal to the number obtained by applying the formula—

$$\frac{A}{B-C}$$

(6) If the liable relative ceases to make periodical payments, the balance (if any) of the non-periodical payment shall be taken into account over the number of weeks equal to the number obtained by dividing that balance by the amount referred to in paragraph (3).

(7) If the amount of any subsequent periodical payment varies, the balance (if any) of the non-periodical payment shall be taken into account over a period of the number of weeks equal to the number obtained by applying the formula—

$$\frac{D}{B-E}$$

(8) The period under paragraph (2) or (4) shall begin on the date on which the payment is treated as paid under regulation 125 (date on which a liable relative payment is to be treated as paid) and the period under paragraph (6) or (7) shall begin on the first day of the benefit week in which the cessation or variation of the periodical payment occurred.

(9) Any fraction which arises by applying a calculation or formula referred to in this regulation shall be treated as a corresponding fraction of a week.

(10) In paragraphs (4) to (7)—

A = the amount of the non-periodical payment;

B = the aggregate of £2 and the amount of employment and support allowance that would be payable had the periodical payment not been made and, where applicable, the maximum disregard under paragraph 60 of Schedule 8;

C = the weekly amount of the periodical payment;

D = the balance (if any) of the non-periodical payment.

E = the weekly amount of any subsequent periodical payment.]

AMENDMENT

1. Employment and Support Allowance (Miscellaneous Amendments) Regulations 2008 (SI 2008/2428), reg.20(9) (October 27, 2008).

DEFINITIONS

"liable relative"—see reg.119.
"payment"—*ibid.*
"periodical payment"—*ibid.*

GENERAL NOTE

9.264   This is similar to reg.57 of the Income Support Regulations/reg.121 of the JSA Regulations.

Calculation of the weekly amount of a [¹child maintenance or] liable relative payment

9.265   **124.**—(1) Where a periodical payment is made or is due to be made at intervals of one week, the weekly amount is to be the amount of that payment.

(2) Where a periodical payment is made or is due to be made at intervals greater than one week and those intervals are monthly, the weekly amount is to be determined by multiplying the amount of the payment by 12 and dividing the product by 52.

(3) Where a periodical payment is made or is due to be made at intervals and those intervals are neither weekly nor monthly, the weekly amount is to be determined by dividing that payment by the number equal to the number of weeks (including any part of a week) in that interval.

(4) Where a payment is made and that payment represents a commutation of periodical payments whether in arrears or in advance, the weekly amount is to be the weekly amount of the individual periodical payments so commuted as calculated under paragraphs (1) to (3) as is appropriate.

(5) The weekly amount of a payment to which regulation 123 (period over which payments other than periodical payments are to be taken into account) applies, is to be equal to the amount of the divisor used in calculating the period over which the payment or, as the case may be, the balance is to be taken into account.

AMENDMENT

1. Employment and Support Allowance (Miscellaneous Amendments) Regulations 2008 (SI 2008/2428), reg.20(2)(c) (October 27, 2008).

DEFINITIONS

"child maintenance"—see reg.119.
"payment"—*ibid.*
"periodical payment"—*ibid.*

GENERAL NOTE

9.266   This is similar to reg.58 of the Income Support Regulations/reg.122 of the JSA Regulations.

Date on which a [¹child maintenance or] liable relative payment is to be treated as paid

9.267   **125.**—(1) A periodical payment is to be treated as paid—

(a) in the case of a payment which is due to be made before the first benefit week pursuant to the claim, on the day in the week in which it is due to be paid which corresponds to the first day of the benefit week;

(b) in any other case, on the first day of the benefit week in which it is due to be paid unless, having regard to the manner in which an income-related allowance is due to be paid in the particular case, it would be more practicable to treat it as paid on the first day of a subsequent benefit week.

(2) Subject to paragraph (3), any other payment is to be treated as paid—

(a) in the case of a payment which is made before the first benefit week pursuant to the claim, on the day in the week in which it is paid which corresponds to the first day of the benefit week;

(b) in any other case, on the first day of the benefit week in which it is paid unless, having regard to the manner in which an income-related allowance is due to be paid in the particular case, it would be more practicable to treat it as paid on the first day of a subsequent benefit week.

(3) Any other payment paid on a date which falls within the period in respect of which a previous payment is taken into account, not being a periodical payment, is to be treated as paid on the first day following the end of that period.

AMENDMENT

1. Employment and Support Allowance (Miscellaneous Amendments) Regulations 2008 (SI 2008/2428), reg.20(2)(d) (October 27, 2008).

DEFINITIONS

"benefit week"—see reg.2(1).
"child maintenance"—see reg.119.
"payment"—*ibid.*
"periodical payment"—*ibid.*

GENERAL NOTE

This is similar to reg.59 of the Income Support Regulations/reg.123 of the JSA Regulations.

9.268

Liable relative payments to be treated as capital

126. [¹ . . .]

9.269

AMENDMENT

1. Employment and Support Allowance (Miscellaneous Amendments) Regulations 2008 (SI 2008/2428), reg.20(4)(b) (October 27, 2008).

CHAPTER 9

CHILD SUPPORT

Treatment of child support maintenance

127. [¹ . . .]

9.270

AMENDMENT

1. Employment and Support Allowance (Miscellaneous Amendments) Regulations 2008 (SI 2008/2428), reg.20(4)(c) (October 27, 2008).

Calculation of the weekly amount of payments of child support maintenance

9.271   **128.** [¹ . . .]

AMENDMENT

1. Employment and Support Allowance (Miscellaneous Amendments) Regulations 2008 (SI 2008/2428), reg.20(4)(c) (October 27, 2008).

Date on which child support maintenance is to be treated as paid

9.272   **129.** [¹ . . .]

AMENDMENT

1. Employment and Support Allowance (Miscellaneous Amendments) Regulations 2008 (SI 2008/2428), reg.20(4)(c) (October 27, 2008).

Disregard of payments treated as not relevant income

9.273   **130.** [¹ . . .]

AMENDMENT

1. Employment and Support Allowance (Miscellaneous Amendments) Regulations 2008 (SI 2008/2428), reg.20(4)(c) (October 27, 2008).

CHAPTER 10

STUDENTS

Interpretation

9.274   **131.**—(1) In this Chapter—
"academic year" means the period of twelve months beginning on 1st January, 1st April, 1st July or 1st September according to whether the course in question begins in the winter, the spring, the summer or the autumn respectively but if students are required to begin attending the course during August or September and to continue attending through the autumn, the academic year of the course is to be considered to begin in the autumn rather than the summer;
"access funds" means—
(a) grants made under section 7 of the Further and Higher Education Act 1992 and described as "learner support funds" or grants made under section 68 of that Act for the purpose of providing funds on a discretionary basis to be paid to students;
(b) grants made under sections 73(a) and (c) and 74(1) of the Education (Scotland) Act 1980;
(c) grants made under Article 30 of the Education and Libraries

(Northern Ireland) Order 1993, or grants, loans or other payments made under Article 5 of the Further Education (Northern Ireland) Order 1997 in each case being grants, or grants, loans or other payments as the case may be, made for the purpose of assisting students in financial difficulties;

(d) discretionary payments, known as "learner support funds", which are made available to students in further education by institutions out of funds provided by the Learning and Skills Council for England under sections 5, 6 and 9 of the Learning and Skills Act 2000; or

(e) Financial Contingency Funds made available by the Welsh Ministers;

"college of further education" means, in Scotland, an educational establishment by which further education is provided;

[2 "contribution" means—

(a) any contribution in respect of the income of a student or any person which the Secretary of State, the Scottish Ministers or an education authority takes into account in ascertaining the amount of a student's grant or student loan; or

(b) any sums, which in determining the amount of a student's allowance or bursary in Scotland under the Education (Scotland) Act 1980, the Scottish Ministers or education authority takes into account being sums which the Scottish Ministers or education authority consider that it is reasonable for the following persons to contribute towards the holder's expenses-

(i) the holder of the allowance or bursary;

(ii) the holder's parents;

(iii) the holder's parent's spouse, civil partner or a person ordinarily living with the holder's parent as if he or she were the spouse or civil partner of that parent; or

(iv) the holder's spouse or civil partner;]

"course of advanced education" means—

(a) a course leading to a postgraduate degree or comparable qualification, a first degree or comparable qualification, a diploma of higher education or a higher national diploma; or

(b) any other course which is of a standard above advanced GNVQ, or equivalent, including a course which is of a standard above a general certificate of education (advanced level), a Scottish national qualification (higher or advanced higher);

"covenant income" means the income payable to a student under a Deed of Covenant by a person whose income is, or is likely to be, taken into account in assessing the student's grant or award;

"education authority" means a government department, a local education authority as defined in section 212 of the Education Act 2002 (interpretation), an education authority as defined in section 123 of the Local Government (Scotland) Act 1973, an education and library board established under Article 3 of the Education and Libraries (Northern Ireland) Order 1986, any body which is a research council for the purposes of the Science and Technology Act 1965 or any analogous government department, authority, board or body, of the Channel Islands, Isle of Man or any other country outside Great Britain;

"full-time course of advanced education" means a course of advanced education which is—

(a) a full-time course of study which is not funded in whole or in part by the Learning and Skills Council for England or by the Welsh Ministers or a full-time course of study which is not funded in whole or in part by the Scottish Ministers at a college of further education or a full-time course of study which is a course of higher education and is funded in whole or in part by the Scottish Ministers;

(b) a course of study which is funded in whole or in part by the Learning and Skills Council for England or by the Welsh Ministers if it involves more than 16 guided learning hours per week for the student in question, according to the number of guided learning hours per week for that student set out—

    (i) in the case of a course funded by the Learning and Skills Council for England, in the student's learning agreement signed on behalf of the establishment which is funded by that Council for the delivery of that course; or

    (ii) in the case of a course funded by the Welsh Ministers, in a document signed on behalf of the establishment which is funded by that Council for the delivery of that course; or

(c) a course of study (not being higher education) which is funded in whole or in part by the Scottish Ministers at a college of further education if it involves—

    (i) more than 16 hours per week of classroom-based or workshop-based programmed learning under the direct guidance of teaching staff according to the number of hours set out in a document signed on behalf of the college; or

    (ii) 16 hours or less per week of classroom-based or workshop-based programmed learning under the direct guidance of teaching staff and it involves additional hours using structured learning packages supported by the teaching staff where the combined total of hours exceeds 21 per week, according to the number of hours set out in a document signed on behalf of the college;

"full-time course of study" means a full-time course of study which—

(a) is not funded in whole or in part by the Learning and Skills Council for England or by the Welsh Ministers or a full-time course of study which is not funded in whole or in part by the Scottish Ministers at a college of further education or a full-time course of study which is a course of higher education and is funded in whole or in part by the Scottish Ministers;

(b) a course of study which is funded in whole or in part by the Learning and Skills Council for England or by the Welsh Ministers if it involves more than 16 guided learning hours per week for the student in question, according to the number of guided learning hours per week for that student set out—

    (i) in the case of a course funded by the Learning and Skills Council for England, in the student's learning agreement signed on behalf of the establishment which is funded by that Council for the delivery of that course; or

    (ii) in the case of a course funded by the Welsh Ministers, in a document signed on behalf of the establishment which is funded by that Council for the delivery of that course; or

(c) is not higher education and is funded in whole or in part by the Scottish Ministers at a college of further education if it involves—

    (i) more than 16 hours per week of classroom-based or workshop-based programmed learning under the direct guidance of teaching staff according to the number of hours set out in a document signed on behalf of the college; or

    (ii) 16 hours or less per week of classroom-based or workshop-based programmed learning under the direct guidance of teaching staff and it involves additional hours using structured learning packages supported by the teaching staff where the combined total of hours exceeds 21 per week, according to the number of hours set out in a document signed on behalf of the college;

"full-time student" means a person who is not a qualifying young person or child within the meaning of section 142 of the Contributions and Benefits Act (child and qualifying young person) and who is—

(a) aged less than 19 and is attending or undertaking a full-time course of advanced education;

(b) aged 19 or over but under pensionable age and is attending or undertaking a full-time course of study at an educational establishment; or

(c) on a sandwich course;

"grant" (except in the definition of "access funds") means any kind of educational grant or award and includes any scholarship, studentship, exhibition, allowance or bursary but does not include a payment from access funds or any payment to which paragraph 13 of Schedule 8 or paragraph 52 of Schedule 9 applies;

"grant income" means—

(a) any income by way of a grant;

(b) in the case of a student other than one to whom paragraph (c) refers, any contribution which has been assessed whether or not it has been paid;

(c) in the case of a student who is a lone parent or is a person to whom Part 4 applies, any contribution which has been assessed and which has been paid,

and any such contribution which is paid by way of a covenant is to be treated as part of the student's grant income;

"higher education" means higher education within the meaning of Part 2 of the Further and Higher Education (Scotland) Act 1992;

"last day of the course" means the date on which the last day of the final academic term falls in respect of the course in which the student is enrolled;

"period of study" means—

(a) in the case of a course of study for one year or less, the period beginning with the start of the course and ending with the last day of the course;

(b) in the case of a course of study for more than one year, in the first or, as the case may be, any subsequent year of the course, other than the final year of the course, the period beginning with the start of the course or, as the case may be, that year's start and ending with either—

    (i) the day before the start of the next year of the course in a case where the student's grant or loan is assessed at a rate appropriate to the student's studying throughout the year or, if the claimant does not have a grant or loan, where a loan would have been assessed at such a rate had the claimant had one; or

(ii) in any other case the day before the start of the normal summer vacation appropriate to the student's course;

(c) in the final year of a course of study of more than one year, the period beginning with that year's start and ending with the last day of the course;

"periods of experience" means periods of work experience which form part of a sandwich course;

"sandwich course" has the meaning prescribed in regulation 2(9) of the Education (Student Support) Regulations 2007, regulation 4(2) of the Education (Student Loans) (Scotland) Regulations 2007 or regulation 2(8) of the Education (Student Support) Regulations (Northern Ireland) 2007;

"standard maintenance grant" means—

(a) except where paragraph (b) or (c) applies, in the case of a student attending or undertaking a course of study at the University of London or an establishment within the area comprising the City of London and the Metropolitan Police District, the amount specified for the time being in paragraph 2(2)(a) of Schedule 2 to the Education (Mandatory Awards) Regulations 2003 ("the 2003 Regulations") for such a student;

(b) except where paragraph (c) applies, in the case of a student residing at the student's parent's home, the amount specified in paragraph 3(2) of Schedule 2 to the 2003 Regulations;

(c) in the case of a student receiving an allowance or bursary under the Education (Scotland) Act 1980, the amount of money specified for the relevant year appropriate for the student set out in the Student Support in Scotland Guide issued by the Student Awards Agency for Scotland, or its nearest equivalent in the case of a bursary provided by a college of further education or a local education authority;

(d) in any other case, the amount specified in paragraph 2(2) of Schedule 2 to the 2003 Regulations other than in paragraph (a) or (b) of that paragraph;

"student" means a person, other than a person in receipt of a training allowance, who is attending or undertaking a course of study at an educational establishment;

"student loan" means a loan towards a student's maintenance pursuant to any regulations made under section 22 of the Teaching and Higher Education Act 1998, sections [¹73(f)], 73B and 74 of the Education (Scotland) Act 1980 or article 3 of the Education (Student Support) (Northern Ireland) Order 1998 and is to include, in Scotland, amounts paid under regulation 4(1)(c) of the Students' Allowances (Scotland) Regulations 2007.

(2) For the purposes of the definition of "full-time student" in paragraph (1), a person is to be regarded as attending or, as the case may be, undertaking a full-time course of study, a full-time course of advanced education or as being on a sandwich course—

(a) subject to paragraph (3), in the case of a person attending or undertaking a part of a modular course which would be a full-time course of study for the purposes of this Part, for the period beginning on the day on which that part of the course starts and ending—

  (i) on the last day on which the claimant is registered with the educational establishment as attending or undertaking that part as a full-time course of study; or

  (ii) on such earlier date (if any) as the claimant finally abandons the course or is dismissed from it;

(b) in any other case, throughout the period beginning on the date on which the claimant starts attending or undertaking the course and ending on the last day of the course or on such earlier date (if any) as the claimant finally abandons it or is dismissed from it.

(3) For the purpose of sub-paragraph (a) of paragraph (2), the period referred to in that sub-paragraph is to include—

  (a) where a person has failed examinations or has failed to successfully complete a module relating to a period when the claimant was attending or undertaking a part of the course as a full-time course of study, any period in respect of which the claimant attends or undertakes the course for the purpose of retaking those examinations or that module;

  (b) any period of vacation within the period specified in that paragraph or immediately following that period except where the person has registered with the educational establishment to attend or undertake the final module in the course and the vacation immediately follows the last day on which the claimant is required to attend or undertake the course.

(4) In paragraph (2), "modular course" means a course of study which consists of two or more modules, the successful completion of a specified number of which is required before a person is considered by the educational establishment to have completed the course.

AMENDMENTS

1. Employment and Support Allowance (Miscellaneous Amendments) Regulations 2008 (SI 2008/2428), reg.8(9) (October 27, 2008).

2. Social Security (Miscellaneous Amendments) Regulations 2009 (SI 2009/583), reg.10(7) (April 6, 2009).

DEFINITION

"training allowance"—see reg.2(1).

GENERAL NOTE

This is similar to reg.61 of the Income Support Regulations. Under JSA the definitions applying to full-time students are in a slightly different form. See reg.130 of the JSA Regulations for some of the definitions but the main ones are to be found in reg.1(3) and (3A)–(3E) of those Regulations (see further the note to reg.130 of the JSA Regulations in Vol.II of this series).

Note that in the definition of "grant income" the cases where a contribution will only be included if it is actually paid are a lone parent or a person "to whom Part 4 applies". Since Part 4 concerns who or who is not to be treated as receiving education for the purposes of para.6(1)(g) of Sch.1 to the Welfare Reform Act 2007 it is not clear what this reference means. If the aim is to mirror the income support definition of "grant income", the reference is presumably only intended to be to reg.18 in Part 4 (which provides that students who are entitled to a disability living allowance are not to be treated as receiving education for the purposes of para.6(1)

9.275

(g) and so can qualify for income-related ESA). In this connection note that the equivalent provision for the treatment of student loans (see reg.137(5)(a)(ii)) only includes a student who is entitled to income-related ESA by virtue of reg.18.

Calculation of grant income

9.276   **132.**—(1) The amount of student's grant income to be taken into account, subject to paragraphs (2) and (3), is to be the whole of the student's grant income.

(2) There is to be disregarded from the amount of a student's grant income any payment—

  (a) intended to meet tuition fees or examination fees;
  (b) intended to meet additional expenditure incurred by a disabled student in respect of that student's attendance on a course;
  (c) intended to meet additional expenditure connected with term time residential study away from the student's educational establishment;
  (d) on account of the student maintaining a home at a place other than that at which the student resides while attending the course but only to the extent that the student's rent is not met by housing benefit;
  (e) on account of any other person but only if that person is residing outside of the United Kingdom and there is no applicable amount in respect of that person;
  (f) intended to meet the cost of books and equipment;
  (g) intended to meet travel expenses incurred as a result of the student's attendance on the course;
  (h) intended for the maintenance of a child dependant;
  (i) intended for the child care costs of a child dependant;
  [³(j) of higher education bursary for care leavers made under Part III of the Children Act 1989.]

(3) Where a student does not have a student loan and is not treated as possessing such a loan, there is to be excluded from the student's grant income—

  (a) the sum of [¹£295] per academic year in respect of travel costs; and
  (b) the sum of [²£380] per academic year towards the costs of books and equipment,

whether or not any such costs are incurred.

(4) Subject to paragraph (6), a student's grant income except any amount intended for the maintenance of adult dependants under Part 3 of Schedule 2 to the Education (Mandatory Awards) Regulations 2003 is to be apportioned—

  (a) subject to paragraph (7), in a case where it is attributable to the period of study, equally between the weeks in the period beginning with the benefit week, the first day of which coincides with, or immediately follows, the first day of the period of study and ending with the benefit week, the last day of which coincides with, or immediately precedes, the last day of the period of study;
  (b) in any other case, equally between the weeks in the period beginning with the benefit week, the first day of which coincides with, or immediately follows, the first day of the period for which it is payable and ending with the benefit week, the last day of which coincides with, or immediately precedes, the last day of the period for which it is payable.

(5) Any grant in respect of an adult dependant paid under section 63(6) of the Health Services and Public Health Act 1968 (grants in respect of the provision of instruction to officers of hospital authorities) and any amount intended for the maintenance of an adult dependant under the provisions referred to in paragraph (4) is to be apportioned equally over a period of 52 weeks or, if there are 53 benefit weeks (including part-weeks) in the year, 53 weeks.

(6) In a case where a student is in receipt of a student loan or where that student could have acquired a student loan by taking reasonable steps but had not done so, any amount intended for the maintenance of an adult dependant under provisions other than those referred to in paragraph (4) is to be apportioned over the same period as the student's loan is apportioned or, as the case may be, would have been apportioned.

(7) In the case of a student on a sandwich course, any periods of experience within the period of study is to be excluded and the student's grant income is to be apportioned equally between the weeks in the period beginning with the benefit week, the first day of which immediately follows the last day of the period of experience and ending with the benefit week, the last day of which coincides with, or immediately precedes, the last day of the period of study.

AMENDMENTS

1. Social Security (Students and Miscellaneous Amendments) Regulations 2008 (SI 2008/1599), reg.7(3)(a) (October 27, 2008).
2. Social Security (Students and Miscellaneous Amendments) Regulations 2008 (SI 2008/1599), reg.7(3)(b) (October 27, 2008).
3. Social Security (Miscellaneous Amendments) Regulations 2009 (SI 2009/583), reg.10(8) (April 6, 2009).

DEFINITIONS

"benefit week"—see reg.2(1).
"grant"—see reg.131(1).
"grant income"—*ibid.*
"period of study"—*ibid.*
"periods of experience"—*ibid.*
"sandwich course"—*ibid.*
"student"—*ibid.*
"student loan"—*ibid.*

GENERAL NOTE

This is similar to reg.62 of the Income Support Regulations/reg.131 of the JSA Regulations. 9.277

Calculation of covenant income where a contribution is assessed

133.—(1) Where a student is in receipt of income by way of a grant 9.278 during a period of study and a contribution has been assessed, the amount of the student's covenant income to be taken into account for that period and any summer vacation immediately following is to be the whole amount of the student's covenant income less, subject to paragraph (3), the amount of the contribution.

(2) The weekly amount of the student's covenant income is to be determined—

(a) by dividing the amount of income which falls to be taken into account under paragraph (1) by 52 or, if there are 53 benefit weeks (including part-weeks) in the year, 53; and
(b) by disregarding from the resulting amount, £5.

(3) For the purposes of paragraph (1), the contribution is to be treated as increased by the amount, if any, by which the amount excluded under regulation 132(2)(g) (calculation of grant income) falls short of the amount for the time being specified in paragraph 7(2) of Schedule 2 to the Education (Mandatory Awards) Regulations 2003 (travel expenditure).

DEFINITIONS

"benefit week"—see reg.2(1).
"contribution"—see reg.131(1).
"covenant income"—*ibid.*
"grant"—*ibid.*
"grant income"—*ibid.*
"period of study"—*ibid.*
"student"—*ibid.*

GENERAL NOTE

9.279   This is similar to reg.63 of the Income Support Regulations/reg.132 of the JSA Regulations.

Calculation of covenant income where no grant income or no contribution is assessed

9.280   **134.**—(1) Where a student is not in receipt of income by way of a grant the amount of the student's covenant income is to be calculated as follows—
(a) any sums intended for any expenditure specified in regulation 132(2)(a) to (e), necessary as a result of the student's attendance on the course, are to be disregarded;
(b) any covenant income, up to the amount of the standard maintenance grant, which is not so disregarded is to be apportioned equally between the weeks of the period of study and there is to be disregarded from the covenant income to be so apportioned the amount which would have been disregarded under regulation 132(2)(f) and (g) and (3) had the student been in receipt of the standard maintenance grant;
(c) the balance, if any, is to be divided by 52 or, if there are 53 benefit weeks (including part-weeks) in the year, 53 and treated as weekly income of which £5 is to be disregarded.

(2) Where a student is in receipt of income by way of a grant and no contribution has been assessed, the amount of the student's covenant income is to be calculated in accordance with paragraph (1), except that—
(a) the value of the standard maintenance grant is to be abated by the amount of the student's grant income less an amount equal to the amount of any sums disregarded under regulation 132(2)(a) to (e); and
(b) the amount to be disregarded under paragraph (1)(b) is to be abated by an amount equal to the amount of any sums disregarded under regulation 132(2)(f) and (g) and (3).

DEFINITIONS

"benefit week"—see reg.2(1).
"contribution"—see reg.131(1).

"covenant income"—*ibid.*
"grant"—*ibid.*
"grant income"—*ibid.*
"period of study"—*ibid.*
"student"—*ibid.*

GENERAL NOTE

This is similar to reg.64 of the Income Support Regulations/reg.133 of the JSA Regulations. 9.281

Relationships with amounts to be disregarded under Schedule 8

135. No part of a student's covenant income or grant income is to be disregarded under paragraph 16 of Schedule 8 (charitable and voluntary payments). 9.282

DEFINITIONS

"covenant income"—see reg.131(1).
"grant income"—*ibid.*
"student"—*ibid.*

GENERAL NOTE

This is similar to reg.65 of the Income Support Regulations/reg.134 of the JSA Regulations. 9.283

Other amounts to be disregarded

136.—(1) For the purposes of ascertaining income other than grant income, covenant income and loans treated as income in accordance with regulation 137 (treatment of student loans), any amounts intended for any expenditure specified in regulation 132(2) (calculation of grant income) necessary as a result of the student's attendance on the course is to be disregarded but only if, and to the extent that, the necessary expenditure exceeds or is likely to exceed the amount of the sums disregarded under regulation 132(2) and (3), 133(3) (calculation of covenant income where a contribution is assessed), 134(1)(a) or (b) (calculation of covenant income where no grant income or no contribution is assessed) and 137(6) on like expenditure. 9.284

(2) Where a claim is made in respect of any period in the normal summer vacation and any income is payable under a Deed of Covenant which commences or takes effect after the first day of that vacation, that income is to be disregarded.

DEFINITIONS

"covenant income"—see reg.131(1).
"grant income"—*ibid.*

GENERAL NOTE

This is similar to reg.66 of the Income Support Regulations/reg.135 of the JSA Regulations. 9.285

Treatment of student loans

137.—(1) A student loan is to be treated as income unless it is a specified loan or award in which case it is to be disregarded. 9.286

(2) For the purposes of paragraph (1), a "specified loan or award" means—

(a) in relation to England, a loan made by the Higher Education Funding Council for England under section 65 of the Further and Higher Education Act 1992;

(b) in relation to Wales, a loan made by the Higher Education Funding Council for Wales under section 65 of the Further and Higher Education Act 1992;

(c) in relation to Scotland, a loan made by an educational institution from funds it has received under the Education (Access Funds) (Scotland) Regulations 1990;

(d) in relation to Northern Ireland, an award made by the Department for Employment and Learning under article 51 of the Education and Libraries (Northern Ireland) Order 1986.

(3) In calculating the weekly amount of the loan to be taken in account as income—

(a) in respect of a course that is of a single academic year's duration or less, a loan which is payable in respect of that period is to be apportioned equally between the weeks in the period beginning with—

(i) except in a case where paragraph (ii) applies, the benefit week, the first day of which coincides with, or immediately follows, the first day of the single academic year;

(ii) where the student is required to start attending the course in August or where the course is less than an academic year's duration, the benefit week, the first day of which coincides with, or immediately follows, the first day of the course,

and ending with the benefit week, the last day of which coincides with, or immediately precedes, the last day of the course;

(b) in respect of an academic year of a course which starts other than on 1st September, a loan which is payable in respect of that academic year is to be apportioned equally between the weeks in the period beginning with the benefit week, the first day of which coincides with, or immediately follows, the first day of that academic year and ending with the benefit week, the last day of which coincides with, or immediately precedes, the last day of that academic year but excluding any benefit weeks falling entirely within the quarter during which, in the opinion of the Secretary of State, the longest of any vacation is taken;

(c) for the purposes of sub-paragraph (b), "quarter" is to have the same meaning as for the purposes of regulation 104(6) (calculation of income other than earnings);

(d) in respect of the final academic year of a course (not being a course of a single year's duration), a loan which is payable in respect of that final academic year is to be apportioned equally between the weeks in the period beginning with—

(i) except in a case where paragraph (ii) applies, the benefit week, the first day of which coincides with, or immediately follows, the first day of that academic year;

(ii) where the final academic year starts on 1st September, the benefit week, the first day of which coincides with, or immediately follows, the earlier of 1st September or the first day of the autumn term, and ending with the benefit week, the last day of which coincides with, or immediately precedes, the last day of the course;

(e) in any other case, the loan is to be apportioned equally between the weeks in the period beginning with the earlier of—

(i) the first day of the first benefit week in September; or

(ii) the benefit week, the first day of which coincides with, or immediately follows, the first day of the autumn term,

and ending with the benefit week, the last day of which coincides with, or immediately precedes, the last day of June,

and, in all cases, from the weekly amount so apportioned there is to be disregarded £10.

(4) A student is to be treated as possessing a student loan in respect of an academic year where—

(a) a student loan has been made to that student in respect of that year; or

(b) the student could acquire such a loan in respect of that year by taking reasonable steps to do so.

(5) Where a student is treated as possessing a student loan under paragraph (4), the amount of the student loan to be taken into account as income is to be, subject to paragraph (6)—

(a) in the case of a student to whom a student loan is made in respect of an academic year, a sum equal to the maximum student loan the student is able to acquire in respect of that year by taking reasonable steps to do so and either—

(i) in the case of a student other than one to whom paragraph (ii) refers, any contribution whether or not it has been paid to that student; or

(ii) in the case of a student who is entitled to an income-related allowance by virtue of being a student to whom regulation 18 (circumstances in which the condition that the claimant is not receiving education does not apply) applies;

(b) in the case of a student to whom a student loan is not made in respect of an academic year, the maximum student loan that would be made to the student if—

(i) the student took all reasonable steps to obtain the maximum student loan that student is able to acquire in respect of that year; and

(ii) no deduction in that loan was made by virtue of the application of a means test.

(6) There is to be deducted from the amount of income taken into account under paragraph (5)—

(a) the sum of [¹£295] per academic year in respect of travel costs; and

(b) the sum of [²£380] per academic year towards the costs of books and equipment,

whether or not any such costs are incurred.

AMENDMENTS

1. Social Security (Students and Miscellaneous Amendments) Regulations 2008 (SI 2008/1599), reg.7(4)(a) (October 27, 2008).

2. Social Security (Students and Miscellaneous Amendments) Regulations 2008 (SI 2008/1599), reg.7(4)(b) (October 27, 2008).

DEFINITIONS

"academic year"—see reg.131(1).
"benefit week"—see reg.2(1).
"last day of the course"—see reg.131(1).
"student"—*ibid*.
"student loan"—*ibid*.

GENERAL NOTE

9.287   Except in relation to the disregard of a "specified loan or award" (see paras (1) and (2)), this is similar to reg.136 of the JSA Regulations/reg.66A of the Income Support Regulations. Note however that the rules as to when the amount of the student loan will not include an assessed contribution if it has not been paid differ for each benefit: in the case of income-related ESA it applies if the student is entitled to disability living allowance; for income-based JSA it applies if the claimant qualifies for the disability premium; and in the case of income support it applies to disabled students and lone parents/lone foster parents.

Under para.(1) a "specified loan or award" (defined in para.(2)) is disregarded. Regulation 66A(1) of the Income Support Regulations and reg.136(1) of the JSA Regulations used to provide that a "hardship loan" (defined in para.(1A) of both sets of Regulations) was disregarded. However the words "unless it is a hardship loan in which case it shall be disregarded" were omitted from reg.66A(1)/reg.136(1), and regs 66A(1A) and 136(1A) were also omitted, with effect from November 17, 2008 by regs 2(10) and 4(9) respectively of the Social Security (Miscellaneous Amendments) (No. 6) Regulations 2008 (SI 2008/2767). According to the Explanatory Memorandum which accompanied these amending regulations these amendments were being made because hardship loans had not been payable since May 2004. It is not known why similar provision for a disregard of a "specified loan or award" has not been made in the Income Support/JSA Regulations.

Treatment of payments from access funds

9.288   **138.**—(1) This regulation applies to payments from access funds that are not payments to which regulation 142(2) or (3) (income treated as capital) applies.

(2) A payment from access funds, other than a payment to which paragraph (3) applies, is to be disregarded as income.

(3) Subject to paragraph (4) and paragraph 39 of Schedule 8, any payments from access funds which are intended and used for food, ordinary clothing or footwear, household fuel, rent for which housing benefit is payable or any housing costs to the extent that they are met under regulation 67(1)(c) or 68(1)(d) (housing costs), of a single claimant or, as the case may be, of the claimant's partner, and any payments from access funds which are used for any council tax or water charges for which that claimant or partner is liable is to be disregarded as income to the extent of £20 per week.

(4) Where a payment from access funds is made—
(a) on or after 1st September or the first day of the course, whichever first occurs, but before receipt of any student loan in respect of that year and that payment is intended for the purpose of bridging the period until receipt of the student loan; or
(b) before the first day of the course to a person in anticipation of that person becoming a student,
that payment is to be disregarded as income.

DEFINITIONS

"access funds"—see reg.131(1).
"claimant"—see reg.83(1).

"ordinary clothing or footwear"—see reg.2(1).
"payment"—*ibid.*
"single claimant"—*ibid.*
"student"—see reg.131(1).
"student loan"—*ibid.*

GENERAL NOTE

This is similar to reg.66B of the Income Support Regulations/reg.136A of the JSA   9.289
Regulations.

Treatment of fee loans

139. A loan for fees, known as a fee loan or a fee contribution loan, made   9.290
pursuant to regulations made under Article 3 of the Education (Student
Support) (Northern Ireland) Order 1998, section 22 of the Teaching and
Higher Education Act 1998 or section 73(f) of the Education (Scotland)
Act 1980, is to be disregarded as income.

GENERAL NOTE

This is similar to reg.66C of the Income Support Regulations/reg.136B of the JSA   9.291
Regulations.

Disregard of contribution

140. Where the claimant or the claimant's partner is a student and, for   9.292
the purposes of assessing a contribution to the student's grant or student
loan, the other partner's income has been taken into account, an amount
equal to that contribution is to be disregarded for the purposes of assessing
that other partner's income.

DEFINITIONS

"claimant"—see reg.83(1).
"contribution"—see reg.131(1).
"grant"—*ibid.*
"partner"—see reg.2(1).
"student"—see reg.131(1).
"student loan"—*ibid.*

GENERAL NOTE

This is similar to reg.67 of the Income Support Regulations/reg.137 of the JSA   9.293
Regulations.

Further disregard of student's income

141. Where any part of a student's income has already been taken into   9.294
account for the purposes of assessing that student's entitlement to a grant
or student loan, the amount taken into account is to be disregarded in
assessing that student's income.

DEFINITIONS

"grant"—see reg.131(1).
"student"—*ibid.*
"student loan"—*ibid.*

GENERAL NOTE

This is similar to reg.67A of the Income Support Regulations/reg.137A of the JSA   9.295
Regulations.

Income treated as capital

9.296   **142.**—(1) Any amount by way of a refund of tax deducted from a student's income is to be treated as capital.

(2) An amount paid from access funds as a single lump sum is to be treated as capital.

(3) An amount paid from access funds as a single lump sum which is intended and used for an item other than food, ordinary clothing or footwear, household fuel, rent for which housing benefit is payable or any housing costs to the extent that they are met under regulation 67(1)(c) or 68(1)(d), of a single claimant or, as the case may be, of the claimant's partner, or which is used for an item other than any council tax or water charges for which that claimant or partner is liable is to be disregarded as capital but only for a period of 52 weeks from the date of the payment.

DEFINITIONS

"access funds"—see reg.131(1).
"claimant"—see reg.83(1).
"ordinary clothing or footwear"—see reg.2(1).
"payment"—*ibid.*
"single claimant"—*ibid.*
"student"—see reg.131(1).

GENERAL NOTE

9.297   This is similar to reg.68 of the Income Support Regulations/reg.138 of the JSA Regulations.

Disregard of changes occurring during summer vacation

9.298   **143.** In calculating a student's income there is to be disregarded any change in the standard maintenance grant occurring in the recognised summer vacation appropriate to the student's course, if that vacation does not form part of the student's period of study, from the date on which the change occurred up to the end of that vacation.

DEFINITIONS

"period of study"—see reg.131(1).
"standard maintenance grant"—*ibid.*
"student"—*ibid.*

GENERAL NOTE

9.299   This is similar to reg.69 of the Income Support Regulations/reg.139 of the JSA Regulations.

PART 11

SUPPLEMENTARY PROVISIONS

CHAPTER 1

MISCELLANEOUS

Waiting days

9.300   **144.**—(1) A claimant is not entitled to an employment and support allowance in respect of 3 days at the beginning of a period of limited capability for work.

(2) Paragraph (1) does not apply where—

(a) the claimant's entitlement to an employment and support allowance commences within 12 weeks of the claimant's entitlement to income support, state pension credit, a jobseeker's allowance, a carer's allowance [¹, statutory sick pay or a maternity allowance] coming to an end;

(b) the claimant is terminally ill and has—

    (i) made a claim expressly on the ground of being terminally ill; or

    (ii) made an application for supersession or revision in accordance with the Social Security and Child Support (Decisions and Appeals) Regulations 1999 which contains an express statement of being terminally ill; or

(c) the claimant has been discharged from being a member of Her Majesty's forces and 3 or more days immediately before that discharge were days of sickness absence from duty, which are recorded by the Secretary of State for Defence [¹, or

(d) the claimant is the other member of a couple to whom regulation 4I(2) of the Social Security (Claims and Payments) Regulations 1987 applies and the former claimant was not entitled to an employment and support allowance in respect of 3 days at the beginning of the period of limited capability for work which relates to the former claimant's entitlement.

AMENDMENT

1. Employment and Support Allowance (Miscellaneous Amendments) Regulations 2008 (SI 2008/2428), reg.9(1) (October 27, 2008).

DEFINITIONS

"claimant"—see WRA 2007, s.24(1).
"a member of Her Majesty's forces"—see reg.2(1).
"terminally ill"—see reg.2(1).

GENERAL NOTE

WRA 2007, s.22 and Sch.2, para.2 provide that "except in prescribed circumstances" a claimant cannot be entitled to ESA for a prescribed number of days at the beginning of a period of limited capability for work. This regulation sets the number of these days of non-entitlement ("waiting days") at three (para.(1)) and provides in para.(2) for the exceptions to that general rule: terminally ill claimants (including those seeking revision or supersession on the basis of being terminally ill) (sub-para.(b)); discharge from Her Majesty's forces where three or more days of recorded sickness absence from duty preceded it (sub-para.(c); and where entitlement to ESA begins within 12 weeks of entitlement to IS, SPC, JSA, carer's allowance or SSP coming to an end (sub-para.(a)). In addition, the general rule is, of course, affected by the "linking rules" (on which see reg.145) in a case of intermittent incapacity where those rules fuse into one ostensibly separate spells of limited capability for work: the "waiting days" only have to be served once in a period of limited capability for work. **9.301**

Linking rules

145.—(1) Any period of limited capability for work which is separated from another such period by not more than 12 weeks is to be treated as a continuation of the earlier period. **9.302**

(2) Where the claimant is a work or training beneficiary in accordance with regulation 148, any period of limited capability for work which is separated from another such period by not more than 104 weeks is to be treated as a continuation of the earlier period.

(3) Where the claimant claims an employment and support allowance after ceasing to be in qualifying remunerative work and—

  (a) the period of limited capability for work began on the day immediately after the day on which the claimant so ceased;

  (b) the claimant has been entitled to an employment and support allowance within the period of 104 weeks before the beginning of that period of limited capability for work; and

  (c) the claimant satisfied the relevant tax credit conditions set out in paragraph (4) on the day before so ceasing,

the claimant is to be treated for the purposes of the claim as having had limited capability for work throughout the period during which those conditions were satisfied.

(4) A claimant satisfies the relevant tax credit conditions on a day if—

  (a) the claimant is entitled for the day to the disability element of working tax credit (on a claim made by the claimant or by the claimant jointly with another) or would be so entitled but for the fact that the relevant income (within the meaning of Part 1 of the Tax Credits Act) in the case of the claimant or the claimant and another is such that that person is not so entitled; and

  (b) either working tax credit or any element of child tax credit other than the family element is paid in respect of the day on such a claim.

(5) Where a claim for an employment and support allowance is made after the claimant ceases to be engaged in training and—

  (a) that claimant was entitled to an employment and support allowance within the period of 8 weeks immediately before becoming so engaged;

  (b) that claimant has limited capability for work on the day after ceasing to be so engaged; and

  (c) that day falls not later than the end of the period of 104 weeks beginning with the end of the last week for which the claimant was entitled to an employment and support allowance, the claimant is to be treated, for the purposes of the claim, as having had limited capability for work for the period when so engaged in training.

DEFINITIONS

"child tax credit"—see reg.2(1).
"claimant"—see WRA 2007, s.24(1).
"qualifying remunerative work"—see reg.2(1).
"relevant tax credit conditions"—see para.(4).
"training"—see reg.2(1).
"week"—see reg.2(1).
"work or training beneficiary"—see reg.148.
"working tax credit"—see reg.2(1).

GENERAL NOTE

9.303   The linking rules are crucial for those suffering from intermittent incapacity. They impact, to the claimant's benefit, as regards "waiting days"; those days of non-entitlement (see para.(2) and ESA Regs, reg.144) only have to be served once in any period of limited capability for work. They are also relevant to determining the relevant benefit year and hence the appropriate tax years to which to have regard with respect to the application of the national insurance contribution conditions (see further the commentary to Sch.1, Pt 1, paras 1–3).

Generally, the linking rule works on the basis that two ostensibly separate spells of limited capability for work will be fused into one where the separation period between the spells is not more than 12 weeks (para.(1)). This fusing does not, however, mean that days in the separation period thereby become ones of limited capability for work (*Chief Adjudication Officer v Astle* (Court of Appeal, judgment of March 17, 1999, available on LEXIS and noted in [1999] 6 J.S.S.L. 203). See further for more detail the commentary to SSCBA 1992, s.30C(1)(c) (the "linking" rule)). A period of limited capability for work can only be formed of days of actual limited capability for work and/or ones which the legislative scheme treats as ones of limited capability for work.

However, where a claimant is a "work or training beneficiary" (see reg.148), the "linking period" is 104 weeks (para.(2)). It is also 104 weeks between spells of limited capability for work where a claimant, entitled to ESA, then went into qualifying remunerative work supported or (but for income) supportable by tax credits ("satisfies the relevant tax credit conditions"), and the period of limited capability for work in respect of which the claimant is now seeking ESA began on the day after he ceased that work (paras (3), (4)).

Advance awards

146.—(1) Where section 5 of the Act (advance award of income-related allowance) applies to a claim and the claimant satisfies the conditions in paragraph (3)—

    (a) the claim is to be treated as if made for a period from the relevant day; and

    (b) the Secretary of State may award an employment and support allowance from the relevant day.

(2) In this regulation the "relevant day" is the day after the end of a period of 13 weeks beginning on the first day on which the claimant would be entitled to an income-related allowance if the claimant satisfied the condition in paragraph 6(1)(a) of Schedule 1 to the Act. (3) The conditions are that—

    (a) the Secretary of State is of the opinion that unless there is a change of circumstances the claimant will satisfy the conditions set out in section 1(3)(b) to (f) of, and Part 2 of Schedule 1 to, the Act when an income-related allowance becomes payable under the award; and

    (b) the claimant is treated as having limited capability for work under regulation 20, 25, 26, [¹ 30] or 33(2) (conditions for treating a person as having limited capability for work) for the period before an income-related allowance becomes payable under the award.

(4) Where an award is made under paragraph (1)—

    (a) the award for an employment and support allowance will become payable on the date on which the claimant would have been entitled to a main phase employment and support allowance if the claimant had satisfied the condition in paragraph 6(1)(a) of Schedule 1 to the Act before the relevant day;

    (b) sections 4(4)(a) and 4(5)(a) of the Act do not apply to that award.

9.304

AMENDMENT

1. Employment and Support Allowance (Miscellaneous Amendments) Regulations 2008 (SI 2008/2428), reg.9(2) (October 27, 2008).

DEFINITION

"claimant"—Welfare Reform Act 2007, s.24(1).
"income-related allowance"—Welfare Reform Act 2007, s.24(1) and 1(7).
"main phase employment and support allowance"—reg.2(1).

GENERAL NOTE

9.305   See the General Note to s.5 of the Welfare Reform Act 2007.

Recovery orders

9.306   **147.**—(1) Where an award of income-related allowance has been made to a claimant, the Secretary of State may apply to the court for a recovery order against the claimant's partner.

(2) On making a recovery order the court may order the partner to pay such amount at such intervals as it considers appropriate, having regard to all the circumstances of the partner and, in particular, the partner's income.

(3) Except in Scotland, a recovery order is to be treated for all purposes as if it were a maintenance order within the meaning of section 150(1) of the Magistrates Courts Act 1980.

(4) Where a recovery order requires the partner to make payments to the Secretary of State, the Secretary of State may, by giving notice in writing to the court which made the order, the liable person and the claimant, transfer to the claimant the right to receive payments under the order and to exercise the relevant rights in relation to the order.

(5) In paragraph 4, "the relevant rights" means, in relation to a recovery order, the right to bring any proceedings, take any steps or do any other thing under or in relation to the order.

DEFINITIONS

"partner"—see reg.2(1).
"payment"—*ibid.*

GENERAL NOTE

9.307   See s.23 of the Welfare Reform Act 2007 and the note to that section.
This regulation is similar to reg.169 of the JSA Regulations.

CHAPTER 2

WORK OR TRAINING BENEFICIARIES

Work or training beneficiaries

9.308   **148.**—(1) Subject to paragraph (2), a claimant is a "work or training beneficiary" on any day in a linking term where the claimant—

  (a) had limited capability for work for more than 13 weeks in the most recent past period of limited capability for work;
  (b) ceased to be entitled to an allowance or advantage at the end of that most recent past period of limited capability for work; and
  (c) became engaged in work or training within one month of so ceasing to be entitled to that benefit at the end of that most recent past period of limited capability for work.

(2) A claimant is not a work or training beneficiary if—

(a) the most recent past period of limited capability for work was ended by a determination that the claimant did not have limited capability for work; and

(b) that determination was on the basis of a limited capability for work assessment.

(3) For the purposes of this Part—

"allowance or advantage" means any allowance or advantage under the Act or the Contributions and Benefits Act for which entitlement is dependent on limited capability for work;

"linking term" means a period of 104 weeks from the first day immediately following the last day in a period of limited capability for work;

"work" means work, other than work under regulation 45 (exempt work), for which payment is made or which is done in expectation of payment.

DEFINITIONS

"the Act"—see reg.2(1).
"allowance or advantage"—see para.(3).
"claimant"—see WRA 2007, s.24(1).
"Contributions and Benefits Act"—see WRA 2007, s.65.
"limited capability for work assessment"—see regs 2(1), 19(2), Sch.2.
"linking term"—see para.(3).
"training"—see reg.2(1).
"week"—see reg.2(1).
"work"—see para.(3).

GENERAL NOTE

This regulation, important for understanding regs 145, 149 and 150, defines who is (para.(1)), and who is not (para.(2)), a "work or training beneficiary".   **9.309**

Linking rules—limited capability for work

149.—(1) Where the circumstances in paragraph (2) apply, a work or training beneficiary is to be treated as having limited capability for work for a period of 13 weeks beginning on the day within the linking term on which the work or training beneficiary claims an employment and support allowance.   **9.310**

(2) The circumstances are that—

(a) the work or training beneficiary provides evidence of limited capability for work in accordance with the Medical Evidence Regulations (which prescribe the form of the doctor's statement or other evidence required in each case); and

(b) in the most recent past period of limited capability for work, it had been determined that the work or training beneficiary had limited capability for work—

  (i) the claimant having been assessed in accordance with a limited capability for work assessment; or

  (ii) as a result of the claimant being treated as having limited capability for work in accordance with regulation 20, 25, 26, 29 or 33(2) (persons to be treated as having limited capability for work).

DEFINITIONS

"claimant"—see WRA 2007, s.24(1).
"Medical Evidence Regulations"—see re. 2(1).
"period of limited capability for work"—see reg.2(1).
"week"—see reg.2(1).
"work or training beneficiary"—see reg.148.

GENERAL NOTE

9.311   This allows a work and training beneficiary who reclaims ESA within the 104-week linking term to be treated as having limited capability for work for the first 13 weeks of that "reclaim", so long as he had in his most recent past period of limited capability for work either been assessed as having it or treated as having it under the terms of the regulations specified in para.(2)(b)(ii). This seems to mean that the assessment period will be treated as having ended and the (re)claimant can immediately be entitled not just to basic allowance ESA but also to the appropriate component. If reg.150 applies, entitlement will be to the support component.

Linking rules—limited capability for work-related activity

9.312   **150.** Where a work or training beneficiary was a member of the support group when the most recent past period of limited capability for work came to an end, that work or training beneficiary is to be treated as having limited capability for work-related activity for a period of 13 weeks beginning on the day within the linking term on which a claim for an employment and support allowance is made.

DEFINITIONS

"linking term"—see reg.148(3).
"member of the support group"—see WRA 2007, s.24(4).
"period of limited capability for work"—see reg.2(1).
"work or training beneficiary"—see reg.148.

GENERAL NOTE

9.313   This means that if a work or training beneficiary reclaims ESA within the 104-week linking term, he will be treated as having limited capability for work-related activity for 13 weeks if he was a member of the support group when his most recent past period of incapacity for work, before the linking term, came to an end. In other words, he can return on day one of his reclaim to his previous level of benefit (basic allowance plus support component).

CHAPTER 3

TEMPORARY ABSENCE FROM GREAT BRITAIN

Absence from Great Britain

9.314   **151.**—(1) A claimant who is entitled to an employment and support allowance is to continue to be so entitled during a period of temporary absence from Great Britain only in accordance with this Chapter.

(2) A claimant who continues to be entitled to a contributory allowance during a period of temporary absence will not be disqualified for receiving that allowance during that period under section 18(4) of the Act.

DEFINITIONS

"claimant"—Welfare Reform Act 2007, s.24(1).
"contributory allowance"—Welfare Reform Act 2007, s.24(1) and 1(7).

GENERAL NOTE

Under s.1(3) of the Welfare Reform Act, it is a condition of entitlement to ESA **9.315**
that the claimant should be "in Great Britain". However, para.5 of Sch.2 to that Act
empowers the Secretary of State to "make provision . . . as to the circumstances in
which a person is to be treated as being, or not being, in Great Britain".

In addition, those entitled to a contributory allowance are disqualified under
s.18(4)(a) while they are absent from Great Britain "except where regulations otherwise provide". Paragraph 6 of Sch.2 to the Act provides that "regulations may
provide that in prescribed circumstances a claimant who is not in Great Britain may
nevertheless be entitled to a contributory allowance".

The regulations in this Chapter are made under those powers

Short absence

152. A claimant is to continue to be entitled to an employment and **9.316**
support allowance during the first 4 weeks of a temporary absence from
Great Britain if—
  (a) the period of absence is unlikely to exceed 52 weeks; and
  (b) while absent from Great Britain, the claimant continues to satisfy
       the other conditions of entitlement to that employment and support
       allowance.

GENERAL NOTE

See the commentary to reg.4(1) and (2) of the IS Regs. **9.317**

Absence to receive medical treatment

153.—(1) A claimant is to continue to be entitled to an employment and **9.318**
support allowance during the first 26 weeks of a temporary absence from
Great Britain if—
  (a) the period of absence is unlikely to exceed 52 weeks;
  (b) while absent from Great Britain, the claimant continues to satisfy
       the other conditions of entitlement to that employment and support
       allowance;
  (c) the claimant is absent from Great Britain solely—
       (i) in connection with arrangements made for the treatment of the
            claimant for a disease or bodily or mental disablement directly
            related to the claimant's limited capability for work which com-
            menced before leaving Great Britain; or
       (ii) because the claimant is accompanying a dependent child in
            connection with arrangements made for the treatment of that
            child for a disease or bodily or mental disablement;
  (d) those arrangements relate to treatment—
       (i) outside Great Britain;
       (ii) during the period whilst the claimant is temporarily absent from
            Great Britain; and
       (iii) by, or under the supervision of, a person appropriately qualified
            to carry out that treatment; and
  (e) before leaving Great Britain the claimant sought and received the
       permission of the Secretary of State to do so.

(2) In paragraph (1)(d)(iii), "appropriately qualified" means qualified to provide medical treatment, physiotherapy or a form of treatment which is similar to, or related to, either of those forms of treatment.

GENERAL NOTE

9.319   Where the temporary absence is in connection with receiving medical treatment for a condition related to the claimant's limited capacity for work, or because the claimant is accompanying a dependent child who is receiving medical treatment, ESA remains payable for the first 26 weeks of absence, as long as the total length of the absence is unlikely to exceed 52 weeks. Note the requirement to obtain the Secretary of State's permission before departure. Where the medical treatment abroad is paid for by the NHS, see reg.154 below.

Absence in order to receive NHS treatment

9.320   **154.** A claimant is to continue to be entitled to an employment and support allowance during any period of temporary absence from Great Britain if—
   (a) while absent from Great Britain, the claimant continues to satisfy the other conditions of entitlement to that employment and support allowance;
   (b) that period of temporary absence is for the purpose of the claimant receiving treatment at a hospital or other institution outside Great Britain where the treatment is being provided—
      (i) under section 6(2) of the Health Service Act (Performance of functions outside England) or section 6(2) of the Health Service (Wales) Act (Performance of functions outside Wales);
      (ii) pursuant to arrangements made under section 12(1) of the Health Service Act (Secretary of State's arrangements with other bodies), section 10(1) of the Health Service (Wales) Act (Welsh Ministers' arrangements with other bodies), paragraph 18 of Schedule 4 to the Health Service Act (Joint exercise of functions) or paragraph 18 of Schedule 3 to the Health Service (Wales) Act (Joint exercise of functions); or
      (iii) under any equivalent provision in Scotland or pursuant to arrangements made under such provision; and
   (c) before leaving Great Britain the claimant sought and received the permission of the Secretary of State to do so.

GENERAL NOTE

9.321   See the commentary to reg.4(3A) of the IS Regs.

Absence of member of family of member of Her Majesty's forces

9.322   **155.**—(1) A claimant is to continue to be entitled to an employment and support allowance during any period of temporary absence from Great Britain if—
   (a) the claimant is a member of the family of a member of Her Majesty's forces and temporarily absent from Great Britain by reason only of the fact that the claimant is living with that member; and
   (b) before leaving Great Britain the claimant sought and received the permission of the Secretary of State to do so.
   (2) In this regulation "member of the family of a member of Her Majesty's forces" means the spouse, civil partner, son, daughter, step-son,

step-daughter, father, father-in-law, step-father, mother, mother-in-law or step-mother of such a member.

CHAPTER 4

MEMBERSHIP OF HOUSEHOLD

Circumstances in which a person is to be treated as being or not being a member of the household

156.—(1) Subject to the following provisions of this regulation— 9.323
(a) the claimant and the claimant's partner; and
(b) where the claimant or the claimant's partner is responsible for a child or young person, that child or young person and any child of that child or young person,
are to be treated as being members of the same household.

(2) Paragraph (1) applies even where any of them is temporarily living away from the other members of the family.

(3) Paragraph (1) does not apply to a person who is living away from the other members of the family where—
(a) that person does not intend to resume living with the other members of the family; or
(b) that person's absence from the other members of the family is likely to exceed 52 weeks, unless there are exceptional circumstances (for example where the person is in hospital or otherwise has no control over the length of absence), and the absence is unlikely to be substantially more than 52 weeks.

(4) Paragraph (1) does not apply in respect of any member of a couple or of a polygamous marriage where—
(a) one, both or all of them are patients detained in a hospital provided under section 4 of the Health Service Act (high security psychiatric services), section 4 of the Health Service (Wales) Act (high security psychiatric services) or section 102 of the National Health Service (Scotland) Act 1978 (state hospitals);
(b) one, both or all of them are—
  (i) detained in custody pending trial or sentence upon conviction or under a sentence imposed by a court; or
  (ii) on temporary release in accordance with the provisions of the Prison Act 1952 or the Prisons (Scotland) Act 1989;
(c) the claimant is abroad and does not satisfy the conditions of Chapter 4 of this Part (temporary absence from Great Britain); or
(d) any one of them is permanently residing in a care home, an Abbeyfield Home or an independent hospital.

(5) A child or young person is not to be treated as a member of the claimant's household where that child or young person is—
(a) placed with the claimant or the claimant's partner by a local authority under section 23(2)(a) of the Children Act 1989 or by a voluntary organisation under section 59(1)(a) of that Act;
(b) placed with the claimant or the claimant's partner prior to adoption;
(c) in accordance with a relevant enactment, boarded out with the claimant or the claimant's partner, whether or not with a view to adoption; or

(d) placed for adoption with the claimant or the claimant's partner pursuant to a decision under the [¹ Adoption and Children Act 2002] or the Adoption Agencies (Scotland) Regulations 1996.

(6) Subject to paragraphs (7) and (8), paragraph (1) does not apply to a child or young person who is not living with the claimant and who—

(a) in a case which does not fall within sub-paragraph (b), has been continuously absent from Great Britain for a period of more than four weeks commencing—

    (i) where that child or young person went abroad before the date of the claim for an employment and support allowance, on the date of that claim;

    (ii) in any other case, on the day which immediately follows the day on which that child or young person went abroad;

(b) where regulation 153 (absence to receive medical treatment) applies, has been continuously absent from Great Britain for a period of more than 26 weeks, that period commencing—

    (i) where that child or young person went abroad before the date of the claim for an employment and support allowance, on the date of that claim;

    (ii) in any other case, on the day which immediately follows the day on which that child or young person went abroad;

(c) has been an in-patient or in accommodation for a continuous period of more than 12 weeks commencing—

    (i) where that child or young person became an in-patient or, as the case may be, entered that accommodation, before the date of the claim for an employment and support allowance, with that date; or

    (ii) in any other case, with the date on which that child or young person became an inpatient or entered that accommodation, and, in either case, has not been in regular contact with either the claimant or any member of the claimant's household;

(d) is being looked after by, or in the care of, a local authority under a relevant enactment;

(e) has been placed with a person other than the claimant prior to adoption;

(f) has been boarded out under a relevant enactment with a person other than the claimant prior to adoption;

(g) has been placed for adoption pursuant to a decision under the [¹ Adoption and Children Act 2002] or the Adoption Agencies (Scotland) Regulations 1996; or

(h) is detained in custody pending trial or sentence upon conviction or under a sentence imposed by a court.

(7) Sub-paragraphs (a)(i), (b)(i) and (c)(i) of paragraph (6) do not apply in a case where immediately before the date of claim for an employment and support allowance the claimant was entitled to an income-based jobseeker's allowance or income support.

(8) A child or young person to whom any of the circumstances mentioned in sub-paragraphs (d) or (h) of paragraph (6) applies is to be treated as being a member of the claimant's household only for that part of any benefit week where that child or young person lives with the claimant.

(9) In this regulation—

"accommodation" means accommodation provided by a local authority in a home owned or managed by that local authority—

(a) under sections 21 to 24 of the National Assistance Act 1948 (provision of accommodation);

(b) in Scotland, under section 13B or 59 of the Social Work (Scotland) Act 1968 (provision of residential or other establishment); or

(c) under section 25 of the Mental Health (Care and Treatment) (Scotland) Act 2003 (care and support services etc.), where the accommodation is provided for a person whose stay in that accommodation has become other than temporary; and

"voluntary organisation" has the meaning assigned to it in the Children Act 1989, or in Scotland, by section 94 of the Social Work (Scotland) Act 1968.

(10) For the purposes of these Regulations a person is responsible for a child or young person if that child or young person usually lives with that person.

AMENDMENT

1. Employment and Support Allowance (Miscellaneous Amendments) Regulations 2008 (SI 2008/2428), reg.9(3) (October 27, 2008).

DEFINITIONS

"Abbeyfield Home"—reg.2(1).
"child"—*ibid.*
"claimant"—Welfare Reform Act 2007, s.24(1).
"family"—reg.2(1) and (3).
"income-based jobseeker's allowance"—*ibid.*
"income support"—*ibid.*
"independent hospital"—*ibid.*
"partner"—*ibid.*
"polygamous marriage"—*ibid.*
"relevant enactment"—*ibid.*
"young person"—*ibid.*

GENERAL NOTE

See the commentary to reg.16 of the IS Regs. Note however that the ESA has no equivalent of reg.15 of the IS Regs. Under para.(10) whether or not a person is responsible for a child or young person for the purpose of ESA depends upon whether the "child or young person usually lives with that person" rather than, for IS, who receives child benefit.   9.324

PART 12

DISQUALIFICATION

Disqualification for misconduct etc.

157.—(1) Subject to paragraph (3), paragraph (2) applies where a claimant—   9.325

(a) has limited capability for work through the claimant's own misconduct, except in a case where the limited capability is due to pregnancy or a sexually transmitted disease; or

(b) fails without good cause to attend for or submit to medical or other treatment (excluding vaccination, inoculation or major surgery) recommended by a doctor with whom, or a hospital or similar institution with which, the claimant is undergoing medical treatment, which would be likely to remove the limitation on the claimant's capability for work;

(c) fails without good cause to refrain from behaviour calculated to retard the claimant's recovery; or

(d) is, without good cause, absent from the claimant's place of residence without leaving word with the Secretary of State where the claimant may be found.

(2) A claimant referred to in paragraph (1) is to be disqualified for receiving an employment and support allowance for such period not exceeding 6 weeks as the Secretary of State may determine.

(3) Paragraph (1) does not apply where the claimant—

(a) is disqualified for receiving an employment and support allowance by virtue of regulations made under section 7 of the Social Security Fraud Act 2001; or

(b) is a person in hardship.

DEFINITIONS

"claimant"—see WRA 2007, s.24(1).
"doctor"—see reg.2(1).
"medical treatment"—see reg.2(1).
"person in hardship"—see reg.158.
"week"—see reg.2(1).

GENERAL NOTE

9.326   Disqualification here represents an attempt to deny ESA to those whose behaviour has in some way brought about their limited capability for work, or has worsened it, or where the claimant has behaved inappropriately in some other way.

This regulation provides that (subject to the two exceptions in para.(3)), someone who falls within one of the several "heads" of disqualification examined below must be disqualified for receiving ESA. As under the sickness and invalidity benefits regime (on which see USI Regs, reg.17, revoked from April 13, 1993—pp.737–40 of Bonner, Hooker and White, *Non-Means Tested Benefit: The Legislation* (1994)), and the incapacity benefit system, the maximum period imposable is six weeks. No minimum is specified (unlike disqualification in JSA where one week is specified—Jobseekers Act 1995, s.19(3)). Although, like JSA, ESA is in principle a weekly benefit, payment for less than a week is possible, so arguably the minimum should still be one day (the minimum unit for benefit purposes). While there have been some changes of wording from that in USI Regs, reg.17, governing sickness and invalidity benefits disqualifications and from Incapacity for Work (General) Regulations 1995, reg.18, in so far as the wording remains the same as that incapacity benefit provision, case authorities on that regime and its predecessors remain authoritative. Some of the "heads" are subject to a "good cause" saving. The rule-making power to further define or restrict "good cause" has not been exercised in this context (WRA 2007, s.18(3)).

If one or more of the "heads" apply, there must be some disqualification: the discretion afforded by the regulation goes only to the length of the period (maximum six weeks). As with exercising the equivalent discretion for jobseeker's allowance purposes, the determining authorities must act judicially and consider each case in the light of its circumstances and give reasons for their choice of period (see *R(U) 8/74(T)*; *R(S) 1/87*; *CS/002/1990*, para.6). The same rules on considering and recording decisions on the matter would apply (*R(U) 4/87*). Some of the factors relevant in exercising the discretion in that context may equally be relevant here. The burden lies on the decision maker to show that the claimant falls clearly and squarely within the head of disqualification (*R(S) 7/83*). Where "good cause" is the issue, it falls to the claimant to establish that he had it (*R(S) 9/51*). *R(S) 1/87* made it abundantly clear that in the same case the same facts could put in issue more than one of the heads of disqualification in USI Regs, reg.17(1). There the heads at issue were paras 17(1)(b) and (1)(d)(ii). The poorly completed record of the SSAT's decision did not make clear on which head they rested disqualification. This was an error of law, a breach of the duty to record reasons for the decision and the material facts on which it is based. Presumably as well as complying with this duty, a tribunal should also comply with *R(U) 2/71* where the case involves the Secretary of State relying on a head of disqualification not set out in the appeal papers or the tribunal relying on a different ground to that relied on by the Secretary of State.

Para. (1) (a)

This penalises certain behaviour by the claimant. Disqualification must be imposed if his incapacity is due to his own misconduct, but two instances where incapacity may have arisen in consequence of what might otherwise be treated as sexual misconduct are expressly stated not to ground disqualification: (a) where the incapacity is due to a sexually transmitted disease; and (b) the case of pregnancy.

9.327

Misconduct has not been exhaustively defined. Presumably, by analogy with its use in the unemployment benefit and jobseeker's allowance contexts, it denotes conduct which is blameworthy, reprehensible and wrong. It is unclear in this context, whether merely reckless or negligent conduct will suffice. *R(S)2/53* has been thought to import a requirement of wilfulness, but this may be to read too much into a particular example of misconduct. In that case the Commissioner considered alcoholism, and upheld disqualification. Drinking to such an extent to endanger health raises a prima facie inference of misconduct which can only be rebutted if the claimant proves that the alcoholism was involuntary, the result of disease or disablement which destroyed his willpower, so that he was *unable* to refrain from excessive drinking. The particular evidence in that case of an anxiety state was insufficient to rebut the presumption. Whether in the current medical and social climate the provision could apply to incapacity through heavy smoking remains to be seen. The paragraph could have unfortunate implications for some AIDS victims such as intravenous drug users who become infected nonsexually.

Para. (1) (b)

This seems designed to deal with a specific aspect of behaviour which may contribute to further limited capability for work or hinder recovery. Disqualification must be imposed where the claimant fails to attend for or submit to medical or other treatment. The medical or other treatment must be recommended by a doctor with whom, or a hospital or similar institution with which, he is undergoing medical treatment and be such as would be likely to render him capable of work. This formulation may reverse *R(S) 3/57*, depending on the scope of "other treatment". There the blind claimant gave up a vocational training course when she became pregnant and refused to resume it thereafter; under USI Regs, reg.17(1)(c) she had not refused treatment for her disablement since the course could have no effect on her blindness (para.6; *cf. R2/60SB*). Failure to attend for or submit to certain medical or other treatment is explicitly exempt from the sanction, namely failure to attend for or submit to vaccination or inoculation of any kind or to major surgery.

9.328

Establishing "good cause" for non-compliance precludes disqualification. In *R(S) 9/51* the claimant did so. Her non-attendance was founded on her own firm conviction that her religious beliefs (Christian Scientist) required her not to. It would not have been enough merely to establish membership of a sect whose religious rules forbade submission to treatment or examination.

Para. (1) (c)

9.329   Disqualification here penalises a claimant who fails to refrain from behaviour cal-culated to retard his recovery. "Calculated to retard his recovery" does not import an intention on his part to do so; the test is an objective one: was his behaviour likely to do so. Thus in *R(S) 21/52* the Commissioner upheld disqualification of the claimant, suffering from influenza bronchitis who was taken ill after undertaking a 60-mile drive when so suffering. However in *R(S) 3/57* (above para.(1)(b)) the course was irrelevant to recovery from blindness, so leaving and refusing to resume the course could not ground disqualification. Establishing good cause for the failure precludes disqualification. Mere ignorance of the rules is not good cause *(R(S) 21/52)*.

Para. (1) (d)

9.330   This requires the claimant not to be absent from his place of residence without leaving word as to where he can be found. It is designed to penalise those who delib-erately seek to avoid the Department's visiting officers who may call as part of the Department's claims control mechanisms. It will only be invoked where visits have already proved ineffective, and as a matter of law the absence must have occurred during the currency of a claim. The rule cannot apply unless the claimant has a residence; it is not to be interpreted as imposing a requirement to have one *(R(S) 7/83)*, so claimants of no fixed abode cannot be caught by it. *R(S) 1/87* requires findings be made as to place of residence, any absence in the relevant period, and on whether the claimant had failed to leave word where he could be found. If those findings showed the claimant's absence from his residence without leaving word as to his whereabouts, it would then fall to the claimant to establish good cause for so acting (see para.12). A claimant's genuine difficulty in leaving word where he might be found was held to constitute good cause in *R(S) 6/55*. There the claimant lived with relatives who were out at work on the three occasions that the visiting officer called. The claimant was out in the park or at the cinema on those occasions, and there was no one with whom he could leave a message. His doctor had advised him to get out as much as possible. Mere ignorance of the rules is not good cause *(R(S) 21/52)*.

Exceptions (para. (3))

9.331   Someone disqualified under the specified fraud provision cannot be disqualified under this regulation (sub-para.(b)). Nor can someone who qualifies as a "person in hardship" as defined in reg.158 (sub-para.(b)).

Meaning of "person in hardship"

9.332   **158.**—(1) A claimant is a "person in hardship" if the claimant—
    (a) has informed the Secretary of State of the circumstances on which the claimant relies to establish that fact; and
    (b) falls within paragraph (2), (3) or (5).
    (2) A claimant falls within this paragraph if—
    (a) she is pregnant;
    (b) a member of the claimant's family is pregnant;
    (c) the claimant is a single claimant aged less than 18; or
    (d) the claimant is a member of a couple and both members are aged less than 18.
    (3) Subject to paragraph (4), the claimant falls within this paragraph if the claimant or the claimant's partner—
    (a) is responsible for a child or young person who is a member of the claimant's household;
    (b) has been awarded an attendance allowance or the care component;

    (c) has claimed either attendance allowance or disability living allowance and the claim has not been determined;

    (d) devotes a considerable portion of each week to caring for another person who—

        (i) has been awarded an attendance allowance or the care component; or

       (ii) has claimed either attendance allowance or disability living allowance and the claim has not been determined; or

    (e) is aged 60 or more.

(4) A claimant to whom paragraph (3)(c) or (3)(d)(ii) applies is a person in hardship only for 26 weeks from the date of the claim unless the claimant is a person in hardship under another provision of this regulation.

(5) The claimant falls within this paragraph where the Secretary of State is satisfied, having regard to all the circumstances and, in particular, the matters set out in paragraph (6), that unless an employment and support allowance is paid, the claimant, or a member of the claimant's family, will suffer hardship.

(6) The matters referred to in paragraph (5) are—

    (a) the resources which are likely to be available to the claimant and the claimant's family and the length of time for which they might be available; and

    (b) whether there is a substantial risk that essential items, including food, clothing and heating, will cease to be available to the claimant or a member of the claimant's family, or will be available at considerably reduced levels and the length of time for which this might be so.

(7) In this regulation "care component" means the care component of disability living allowance at the highest or middle rate prescribed under section 72(3) of the Contributions and Benefits Act.

DEFINITIONS

    "attendance allowance"—see reg.2(1).
    "care component"—see para.(7).
    "claimant"—see WRA 2007, s.24(1).
    "Contributions and Benefits Act"—see WRA 2006, s.65.
    "disability living allowance"—see reg.2(1).
    "family"—see reg.2(1).
    "person in hardship"—see para.(1).

GENERAL NOTE

The effect of this regulation is similar to reg.140 of the JSA Regulations.   **9.333**

Para.(1)

A person in hardship cannot be disqualified from receiving ESA under   **9.334**
reg.157 (see para.(3)(b) of that regulation). This paragraph defines someone as a "person in hardship" who notifies the Secretary of State of the circumstances relied on to establish this, so long as he satisfies the conditions set in paras (2), (3) or (5).

Para.(2)

This covers a claimant who is pregnant; a claimant where a family member is   **9.335**
pregnant; the claimant is single and under 18; and the claimant who is a member of a couple and both the claimant and partner are under 18.

Paras (3), (4)

9.336   This covers someone aged 60 or over; someone responsible for a child or young person who is a member of his household someone who has been awarded attendance allowance (note the wider coverage of that term in reg.2(1)) or the care component (middle or higher rate) of disability living allowance (see para.(7)); and a carer who devotes a considerable portion of a week to caring for another who has been awarded attendance allowance (again note the wider coverage of that term in reg.2(1)) or the care component of DLA at middle of higher rate (see para.(7)). The paragraph also brings in, but only for 26 weeks unless the claimant also qualifies under another head, someone who has claimed attendance allowance (again note the wider coverage of that term in reg.2(1)) or middle or higher rate care component of DLA (see para. (7)), but the claim remains undetermined, or the carer devoting a substantial portion of the week to caring for someone in that position (paras (3)(c), (d)(ii), (4)).

Paras (5), (6)

9.337   These cover the claimant where the Secretary of State is satisfied that unless ESA is paid, the claimant or a member of his family will suffer hardship. In considering whether that is the case, he must have regard to all the circumstances, particularly those set out in para.(6).

Treating a claimant as not having limited capability for work

9.338   **159.**—(1) Subject to paragraph (2), the claimant is to be treated as not having limited capability for work if the claimant is disqualified for receiving a contributory allowance during a period of imprisonment or detention in legal custody if that disqualification is for more than 6 weeks.

(2) Where the claimant is entitled to an amount under paragraph 3 of Schedule 5 (special cases: prisoners) during a period of imprisonment or detention in legal custody, the claimant is to be treated as not having limited capability for work from the day after the day on which entitlement ended.

DEFINITIONS

"claimant"—see WRA 2007, s.24(1).
"contributory allowance"—see WRA 2007, s.1(7).

GENERAL NOTE

9.339   Those disqualified for contributory ESA under s.18(4) of the Welfare Reform Act for more than six weeks because they are imprisoned or detained in custody are treated by para.(1) as not having limited capability for work.

Under reg.69 and para.3(b) of Sch.5, a person may be entitled to income-related ESA at a reduced rate while detained in custody pending trial or pending sentence following conviction. In those circumstances, the person is treated by para.(2) as not having limited capability for work from the day after that entitlement ends.

Exceptions from disqualification for imprisonment

9.340   **160.**—(1) Notwithstanding section 18(4)(b) of the Act, a claimant is not disqualified for receiving a contributory allowance for any period during which that claimant is undergoing imprisonment or detention in legal custody—

(a) in connection with a charge brought or intended to be brought against the claimant in criminal proceedings;

(b) pursuant to any sentence; or

(c) pursuant to any order for detention,

made by a court in such proceedings, unless paragraph (2) applies.

(2) This paragraph applies where—

(a) a penalty is imposed on the claimant at the conclusion of the proceedings referred to in paragraph (1); or

(b) in the case of default of payment of a sum adjudged to be paid on
conviction a penalty is imposed in respect of such default.

(3) Notwithstanding section 18(4)(b) of the Act, a claimant is not to be
disqualified for receiving a contributory allowance, for any period during
which the claimant is undergoing detention in legal custody after the conclusion of criminal proceedings if it is a period during which the claimant is
liable to be detained in a hospital or similar institution in Great Britain as a
person suffering from mental disorder unless—

(a) the claimant is detained or liable to be detained under section 45A of
the Mental Health Act 1983 (hospital and limitation directions) or
section 59A of the Criminal Procedure (Scotland) Act 1995 (hospital direction); or

(b) the claimant is detained or liable to be detained under section 47 of
the Mental Health Act (removal to hospital of persons serving sentences of imprisonment, etc.) [' . . .], or

(c) section 136 of the Mental Health (Care and Treatment) (Scotland)
Act 2003 (transfer of prisoners for treatment for mental disorder).

(4) Where—

(a) paragraph (3)(a) or (b) applies, in relation to a claimant; and

(b) a certificate given by or on behalf of the Secretary of State or Scottish
Ministers shows the earliest date on which that claimant would have
been expected to be discharged from detention under the sentence
or order if the claimant had not been transferred to a hospital or
similar institution, those paragraphs are to be treated as not satisfied
in relation to that claimant from the day following that date.

(5) For the purposes of this regulation—

(a) "court" means any court in the United Kingdom, the Channel Islands
or the Isle of Man or in any place to which the Colonial Prisoners
Removal Act 1884 applies or any naval court-martial, army court-
martial or air force court-martial within the meaning of the Courts-
Martial (Appeals) Act 1968 or the Courts-Martial Appeal Court;

(b) "hospital or similar institution" means any place (not being a prison,
a young offender institution, a secure training centre, secure accommodation in a children's home or a remand centre, and not being at
or in any such place) in which persons suffering from mental disorder are or may be received for care or treatment;

(c) "penalty" means a sentence of imprisonment or detention under
section 90 or 91 of the Powers of Criminal Courts (Sentencing) Act
2000, a detention and training order under section 100 of that Act, a
sentence of detention for public protection under section 226 of the
Criminal Justice Act 2003 or an extended sentence under section
228 of that Act or, in Scotland, under section 205, 207 or 208 of the
Criminal Procedure (Scotland) Act1995;

(d) in relation to a person who is liable to be detained in Great Britain
as a result of any order made under the Colonial Prisoners Removal
Act 1884, references to a prison must be construed as including references to a prison within the meaning of that Act;

(e) criminal proceedings against any person must be deemed to be concluded upon that person being found insane in those proceedings so that the person cannot be tried or that person's trial cannot proceed.

(6) Where a claimant outside Great Britain is undergoing imprisonment or detention in legal custody and, in similar circumstances in Great Britain, the claimant would, by virtue of this regulation, not have been disqualified for receiving a contributory allowance, the claimant is not disqualified for receiving that allowance by reason only of the imprisonment or detention.

AMENDMENT

1. Employment and Support Allowance (Miscellaneous Amendments) Regulations 2008 (SI 2008/2428), reg.10 (October 27, 2008).

DEFINITIONS

"claimant"—see WRA 2007, s.24(1).
"court"—see para.(5)(a).
"hospital or similar institution"—see para.(5)(b).
"penalty"—see para.(5)(c).
"prison"—see para.(5)(d).

GENERAL NOTE

9.341   Under s.18(4) of the WRA 2007, a claimant is disqualified for contributory ESA while "undergoing imprisonment or detention in legal custody". This regulation establishes exceptions to that rule. Under paras (1) and (2), there is no disqualification while the claimant is in custody pending trial or sentence unless a penalty is imposed. Payment of contributory ESA is suspended under reg.161 below during the period when it is not known whether a penalty will eventually be imposed. By para.(6), the same rules is applied to claimants imprisoned outside Great Britain. Under para.(3), there is no disqualification where the claimant is compulsorily detained in hospital following the conclusion of criminal proceedings unless a prison sentence is imposed and the claimant is subsequently transferred to hospital under the specified legislation.

Suspension of payment of a contributory allowance during imprisonment

9.342   **161.**—(1) Subject to the following provisions of this regulation, the payment of a contributory allowance to any claimant—

(a) which is excepted from the operation of section 18(4)(b) of the Act by virtue of the provisions of regulation 160(2), (3) or (6); or

(b) which is payable otherwise than in respect of a period during which the claimant is undergoing imprisonment or detention in legal custody,

is suspended while that claimant is undergoing imprisonment or detention in legal custody.

(2) A contributory allowance is not to be suspended while the claimant is liable to be detained in a hospital or similar institution, as defined in regulation 160(5), during a period for which in the claimant's case, the allowance is or would be excepted from the operation of section 18(4)(b) by virtue of the provisions of regulation 160(3).

(3) Where, by virtue of this regulation, payment of a contributory allowance is suspended for any period, the period of suspension is not to be taken into account in calculating any period under the provisions of regulation 38 of the Social Security (Claims and Payments) Regulations 1987 (extinguishment of right to sums payable by way of benefit which are not obtained within the prescribed time).

DEFINITIONS

"claimant"—see WRA 2007, s.24(1).
"contributory allowance"—see WRA 2007, s.1(7).
"hospital or similar institution"—see reg.160(5).

GENERAL NOTE

See the commentary to reg.160.   9.343

PART 13

URGENT CASES

Urgent cases

162.—(1) In a case to which this regulation applies a claimant's weekly   9.344
applicable amount and that claimant's income and capital are to be calculated in accordance with the following provisions of this Part.

(2) Subject to paragraph (3), this regulation applies to a claimant who is
treated as possessing income under regulation 107(1) (notional income).

(3) This regulation is only to apply to a claimant to whom paragraph (2)
applies, where the income that claimant is treated as possessing by virtue of
regulation 107(1) is not readily available to that claimant; and—

(a) the amount of an income-related allowance which would be payable
    but for this Part is less than the amount of an income-related allow-
    ance payable by virtue of the provisions of this Part; and

(b) the Secretary of State is satisfied that, unless the provisions of this
    Part are applied to the claimant, the claimant or the claimant's
    family will suffer hardship.

GENERAL NOTE

This regulation is similar to reg.70 of the IS Regs and reg.147 of the JSA Regs.   9.345

Applicable amounts in urgent cases

163. For the purposes of calculating any entitlement to an income-related   9.346
allowance under this
Part—

(a) except in a case to which sub-paragraph (b) or (c) applies, a claim-
    ant's weekly applicable amount is to be the aggregate of—
    (i) 90% of the amount applicable in respect of himself or herself or,
         if the claimant is a member of a couple or of a polygamous mar-
         riage, of the amount applicable in respect of both of them under
         paragraph 1(1), (2) or (3) of Schedule 4 or, as the case may be,
         the amount applicable in respect of them under regulation 68
         (polygamous marriages);
    (ii) the amount, if applicable, specified in Part 2 of Schedule 4 (pre-
         miums);
    (iii) the amount, if applicable, specified in Part 4 of Schedule 4
         (components); and
    (iv) any amounts applicable under regulation 67(1)(c) or, as the
         case may be, 68(1)(d (housing costs);

1121

(b) in the case of a claimant to whom any paragraph of Schedule 5 (special cases) applies, the applicable amount is to be the aggregate of—

    (i) 90% of the amount applicable in column 2 of that Schedule in respect of the claimant and partner (if any);

    (ii) the amount, if applicable, specified in Part 2 of Schedule 4;

    (iii) the amount, if applicable, specified in Part 4 of Schedule 4; and

    (iv) any amounts applicable under regulation 67(1)(c) or, as the case may be, 68(1)(d); or

(c) in the case of a claimant to whom regulation 162(2) applies, where that claimant is appealing to an appeal tribunal constituted under Chapter 1 of Part 1 of the Social Security Act 1998, against a decision which embodies a determination that the claimant does not have limited capability for work, the applicable amount is to be the aggregate of—

    (i) 90% of the amount applicable in respect of himself or herself or, if the claimant is a member of a couple or of a polygamous marriage, of the amount applicable in respect of both of them under paragraph 1(1), (2) or (3) of Schedule 4 or, as the case may be, the amount applicable in respect of them under regulation 68 (polygamous marriages);

    (ii) the amount, if applicable, specified in Part 2 of Schedule 4 (premiums); and

    (iii) any amounts applicable under regulation 67(1)(c) or, as the case may be, 68(1)(d).

GENERAL NOTE

9.347   This regulation is similar to reg.71 of the IS Regs and reg.148 of the JSA Regs.

Assessment of income and capital in urgent cases

9.348   **164.**—(1) The claimant's income is to be calculated in accordance with Part 10 subject to the following modifications—

(a) any income other than—

    (i) a payment of income or income in kind made under the Macfarlane Trust, the Macfarlane (Special Payments) Trust, the Macfarlane (Special Payments) (No. 2) Trust, the Fund, the Eileen Trust or [¹ the Independent Living Fund (2006)]; or

    (ii) income to which paragraph 9 (but only to the extent that a concessionary payment would be due under that paragraph for any non-payment of an income-related allowance under regulation 162 (urgent cases) or of jobseeker's allowance under regulation 147 of the Jobseeker's Allowance Regulations (urgent cases)), 35, 41(2), (3) or (4), 42, 64 or 65 of Schedule 8 (disregard of income other than earnings) applies, possessed or treated as possessed by the claimant, is to be taken into account in full notwithstanding any provision in that Part disregarding the whole or any part of that income;

(b) any income to which regulation 118 (calculation of tariff income from capital) applies is to be disregarded;

(c) income treated as capital by virtue of regulation 112(1), (2), (3) and (7) (income treated as capital) is to be taken into account as income;

(d) in a case to which regulation 162(2) (urgent cases) applies, any income to which regulation 107(1) applies is to be disregarded.

(2) The claimant's capital calculated in accordance with Part 10, but including any capital referred to in—

(a) paragraph 3;

(b) to the extent that such assets as are referred to in paragraph 10 consist of liquid assets, paragraph 10;

(c) except to the extent that the arrears referred to in paragraph 11 consist of arrears of housing benefit payable under [¹ . . .] Part 7 of the Contributions and Benefits Act or any arrears of benefit due under regulation 162, or regulation 147 of the Jobseeker's Allowance Regulations (urgent cases), paragraph 11; and

(d) paragraphs 13(b), 24 and 32, of Schedule 9 (capital to be disregarded), are to be taken into account in full and the amount of an income-related allowance which would, but for this paragraph be payable under this regulation, is to be payable only to the extent that it exceeds the amount of that capital.

AMENDMENT

1. Employment and Support Allowance (Miscellaneous Amendments) Regulations 2008 (SI 2008/2428), reg.11 (October 27, 2008).

GENERAL NOTE

This regulation is similar to reg.72 of the IS Regs and reg.149 of the JSA Regs.   9.349

PART 14

PERIODS OF LESS THAN A WEEK

Entitlement for less than a week—amount of an employment and support allowance payable

165.—(1) This regulation applies where the claimant is entitled to an   9.350 employment and support allowance for a part-week and is subject to the following provisions of this Part.

(2) The amount payable by way of an income-related allowance in respect of that part-week is to be calculated by applying the formula—

(a) where the claimant has no income—

$$\frac{(N \times A)}{7}$$

or

(b) where the claimant has an income—

$$\frac{N \times (A - 1) - B}{7}$$

where—

A is the claimant's weekly applicable amount in the relevant week;

B is the amount of any employment and support allowance, jobseeker's allowance, income support, maternity allowance, incapacity benefit or severe disablement allowance payable to the claimant or the claimant's partner in respect of any day in the part-week;

I is the claimant's weekly income in the relevant week; and

N is the number of days in the part week.

(3) The amount payable by way of a contributory allowance in respect of a part-week is to be calculated by applying the formula—

$$\frac{(N \times X) - Y}{7}$$

where—

X is the amount calculated in accordance with section 2(1) of the Act;

Y is the amount of any widow's benefit, widowed parent's allowance, bereavement allowance, training allowance, carer's allowance and any increase in disablement pension payable in accordance with Part 1 of Schedule 7 to the Contributions and Benefits Act (Unemployability Supplement) payable in respect of any day in the part-week;

N is the number of days in the part-week.

(4) In this Part—

"part-week" means an entitlement to an employment and support allowance in respect of any period of less than a week;

"relevant week" means the period of 7 days determined in accordance with regulation 166.

GENERAL NOTE

9.351   This regulation is similar to reg.150 of the JSA Regs.

Relevant week

9.352   **166.**—(1) Where a part-week—

(a) is the whole period for which an employment and support allowance is payable, or occurs at the beginning of an award, the relevant week is the period of 7 days ending on the last day of that part-week; or

(b) occurs at the end of an award, the relevant week is the period of 7 days beginning on the first day of the part-week.

(2) Where a claimant has an award of an employment and support allowance and that claimant's benefit week changes, for the purpose of calculating the amounts of an employment and support allowance payable for the part-week beginning on the day after the last complete benefit week before the change and ending immediately before the change, the relevant week is the period of 7 days beginning on the day after the last complete benefit week.

DEFINITIONS

"benefit week"—reg.2(1).
"claimant"—Welfare Reform Act 2007, s.24(1).
"part-week"—reg.165(4).
"relevant week"—*ibid.*

GENERAL NOTE

9.353   This regulation is similar to reg.152 of the JSA Regs.

Modification in the calculation of income

9.354   **167.** For the purposes of regulation 165 (entitlement for less than a week—amount of an employment and support allowance payable), a claimant's income and, in determining the amount payable by way of an income-related allowance, the income of any person which the claimant is treated as possessing under regulations made under section 17(3) of the Act, regulation 68 (polygamous marriages) or regulation 83 (calculation of income and capital of members of claimant's family and of a polygamous marriage), is to be calculated in accordance with Parts 10 (income and capital) and 13 (urgent cases) subject to the following changes—

(a) any income which is due to be paid in the relevant week is to be treated as paid on the first day of that week;

(b) in determining the amount payable by way of an income-related allowance, any jobseeker's allowance, employment and support allowance, income support, maternity allowance, incapacity benefit or severe disablement allowance payable in the relevant week but not in respect of any day in the part-week is to be disregarded;

(c) the amount referred to as B in regulation 165(2) is to be disregarded;

(d) in determining the amount payable by way of a contributory allowance, any widow's benefit, training allowance, widowed parent's allowance, bereavement allowance, carer's allowance and any increase in disablement pension payable in accordance with Part 1 of Schedule 7 to the Contributions and Benefits Act (unemployability supplement) which is payable in the relevant week but not in respect of any day in the part-week is to be disregarded;

(e) where the part-week occurs at the end of the claim—
  (i) any income; or
  (ii) any change in the amount of income of the same kind, which is first payable within the relevant week but not on any day in the part-week is to be disregarded;

(f) where only part of the weekly balance of income is taken into account in the relevant week, the balance is to be disregarded.

GENERAL NOTE

This regulation is similar to reg.153 of the JSA Regs.   9.355

Reduction in certain cases

168. The reduction to be made in accordance with regulations 157 and   9.356
158 is an amount equal to one seventh of the reduction which would be made under those regulations for a week, multiplied by the number of days in a part-week.

GENERAL NOTE

This regulation is similar to reg.154 of the JSA Regs.   9.357

SCHEDULE 1   Regulation 2(2)

HER MAJESTY'S FORCES

PART 1

PRESCRIBED ESTABLISHMENTS AND ORGANISATIONS

1. Any of the regular naval, military or air forces of the Crown.   9.358
2. Royal Fleet Reserve.

3. Royal Navy Reserve.
4. Royal Marines Reserve.
5. Army Reserve.
6. Territorial Army.
7. Royal Air Force Reserve.
8. Royal Auxiliary Air Force.
9. The Royal Irish Regiment, to the extent that its members are not members of any force falling within paragraph 1.

PART 2

ESTABLISHMENTS AND ORGANISATIONS OF WHICH HER MAJESTY'S FORCES DO NOT CONSIST

10. Her Majesty's forces are not to be taken to consist of any of the establishments or organisations specified in Part 1 of this Schedule by virtue only of the employment in such establishment or organisation of the following persons—

(a) any person who is serving as a member of any naval force of Her Majesty's forces and who (not having been an insured person under the National Insurance Act 1965 and not having been a contributor under the Social Security Act 1975 or not being a contributor under the Contributions and Benefits Act) locally entered that force at an overseas base;

(b) any person who is serving as a member of any military force of Her Majesty's forces and who entered that force, or was recruited for that force outside the United Kingdom, and the depot of whose unit is situated outside the United Kingdom;

(c) any person who is serving as a member of any air force of Her Majesty's forces and who entered that force, or was recruited for that force, outside the United Kingdom, and is liable under the terms of engagement to serve only in a specified part of the world outside the United Kingdom.

GENERAL NOTE

9.359 See the commentary to the definition of "member of Her Majesty's forces" in reg.2(1).

9.360 SCHEDULE 2

ASSESSMENT OF WHETHER A CLAIMANT HAS LIMITED CAPABILITY FOR WORK

PART 1

PHYSICAL DISABILITIES

(1) Activity	(2) Descriptors		(3) Points
1. Walking with a walking stick or other aid if such aid is normally used.	1	(a) Cannot walk at all.	15
		(b) Cannot walk more than 50 metres on level ground without repeatedly stopping or severe discomfort.	15
		(c) Cannot walk up or down two steps even with the support of a handrail.	15
		(d) Cannot walk more than 100 metres on level ground without stopping or severe discomfort.	9
		(e) Cannot walk more than 200 metres on level ground without stopping or severe discomfort.	6
		(f) None of the above apply.	0

(1) Activity	(2) Descriptors	(3) Points
2. Standing and sitting.	2 (a) Cannot stand for more than 10 minutes, unassisted by another person, even if free to move around, before needing to sit down.	15
	(b) Cannot sit in a chair with a high back and no arms for more than 10 minutes before needing to move from the chair because the degree of discomfort experienced makes it impossible to continue sitting.	15
	(c) Cannot rise to standing from sitting in an upright chair without physical assistance from another person.	15
	(d) Cannot move between one seated position and another seated position located next to one another without receiving physical assistance from another person.	15
	(e) Cannot stand for more than 30 minutes, even if free to move around, before needing to sit down.	6
	(f) Cannot sit in a chair with a high back and no arms for more than 30 minutes without needing to move from the chair because the degree of discomfort experienced makes it impossible to continue sitting.	6
	(g) None of the above apply.	0
3. Bending or kneeling.	3 (a) Cannot bend to touch knees and straighten up again.	15
	(b) Cannot bend, kneel or squat, as if to [¹ pick up a light object], such as a piece of paper, situated 15cm from the floor on a low shelf, and to move it and straighten up again without the help of another person.	9
	(c) Cannot bend, kneel or squat, as if to [¹ pick up a light object] off the floor and straighten up again without the help of another person.	6
	(d) None of the above apply.	0
4. Reaching.	4 (a) Cannot raise either arm as if to put something in the top pocket of a coat or jacket.	15
	(b) Cannot put either arm behind back as if to put on a coat or jacket.	15
	(c) Cannot raise either arm to top of head as if to put on a hat.	9

(1) Activity	(2) Descriptors	(3) Points
	(d) Cannot raise either arm above head height as if to reach for something.	6
	(e) None of the above apply.	0
5. Picking up and moving or transferring by the use of the upper body and arms (excluding all other activities specified in Part 1 of this Schedule).	5 (a) Cannot pick up and move a 0.5 litre carton full of liquid with either hand.	15
	(b) Cannot pick up and move a one litre carton full of liquid with either hand.	9
	(c) Cannot pick up and move a light but bulky object such as an empty cardboard box, requiring the use of both hands together.	6
	(d) None of the above apply.	0
6. Manual dexterity.	6 (a) Cannot turn a "star-headed" sink tap with either hand.	15
	(b) Cannot pick up a £1 coin or equivalent with either hand.	15
	(c) Cannot turn the pages of a book with either hand.	15
	(d) Cannot physically use a pen or pencil.	9
	(e) Cannot physically use a conventional keyboard or mouse.	9
	(f) Cannot do up/undo small buttons, such as shirt or blouse buttons.	9
	(g) Cannot turn a "star-headed" sink tap with one hand but can with the other.	6
	(h) Cannot pick up a £1 coin or equivalent with one hand but can with the other.	6
	(i) Cannot pour from an open 0.5 litre carton full of liquid.	6
	(j) None of the above apply.	0
7. Speech.	7 (a) Cannot speak at all.	15
	(b) Speech cannot be understood by strangers.	15
	(c) Strangers have great difficulty understanding speech.	9
	(d) Strangers have some difficulty understanding speech.	6
	(e) None of the above apply.	0
8. Hearing with a hearing aid or other aid if normally worn.	8 (a) Cannot hear at all.	15
	(b) Cannot hear well enough to be able to hear someone talking in a loud voice in a quiet room, sufficiently clearly to distinguish the words being spoken.	15

(1) Activity	(2) Descriptors	(3) Points
	(c) Cannot hear someone talking in a normal voice in a quiet room, sufficiently clearly to distinguish the words being spoken.	9
	(d) Cannot hear someone talking in a loud voice in a busy street, sufficiently clearly to distinguish the words being spoken.	6
	(e) None of the above apply.	0
9. Vision including visual acuity and visual fields, in normal daylight or bright electric light, with glasses or other aid to vision if such aid is normally worn.	9 (a) Cannot see at all.	15
	(b) Cannot see well enough to read 16 point print at a distance of greater than 20cm.	15
	(c) Has 50% or greater reduction of visual fields.	15
	(d) Cannot see well enough to recognise a friend at a distance of a least 5 metres.	9
	(e) Has 25% or more but less than 50% reduction of visual fields.	6
	(f) Cannot see well enough to recognise a friend at a distance of at least 15 metres.	6
	(g) None of the above apply.	0
10. (a) Continence other than enuresis (bed wetting) where the claimant does not have an artificial stoma or urinary collecting device.	10 (a) (i) Has no voluntary control over the evacuation of the bowel.	15
	10 (a) (ii) Has no voluntary control over the voiding of the bladder.	15
	10 (a) (iii) At least once a month loses control of bowels so that the claimant cannot control the full evacuation of the bowel.	15
	10 (a) (iv) At least once a week, loses control of bladder so that the claimant cannot control the full voiding of the bladder.	15
	10 (a) (v) Occasionally loses control of bowels so that the claimant cannot control the full evacuation of the bowel.	9
	10 (a) (vi) At least once a month loses control of bladder so that the claimant cannot control the full voiding of the bladder.	6

(1) Activity	(2) Descriptors	(3) Points
	10 (a) (vii) Risks losing control of bowels or bladder so that the claimant cannot control the full evacuation of the bowel or the full voiding of the bladder if not able to reach a toilet quickly.	6
	10 (a) (viii) None of the above apply.	0
10. (b) Continence where the claimant uses a urinary collecting device, worn for the majority of the time including an indwelling urethral or suprapubic catheter.	10 (b) (i) Is unable to affix, remove or empty the catheter bag or other collecting device without receiving physical assistance from another person.	15
	10 (b) (ii) Is unable to affix, remove or empty the catheter bag or other collecting device without causing leakage of contents.	15
	10 (b) (iii) Has no voluntary control over the evacuation of the bowel.	15
	10 (b) (iv) At least once a month, loses control of bowels so that the claimant cannot control the full evacuation of the bowel.	15
	10 (b) (v) Occasionally loses control of bowels so that the claimant cannot control the full evacuation of the bowel.	9
	10 (b) (vi) Risks losing control of bowels so that the claimant cannot control the full evacuation of the bowel if not able to reach a toilet quickly.	6
	10 (b) (vii) None of the above apply.	0
10 (c) Continence other than enuresis (bed wetting) where the claimant has an artificial stoma.	10 (c) (i) Is unable to affix, remove or empty stoma appliance without receiving physical assistance from another person.	15
	10 (c) (ii) Is unable to affix remove or empty stoma appliance without causing leakage of contents.	15
	[¹10 (c) (iii) Where the claimant's artificial stoma relates solely to the evacuation of the bowel, has no voluntary control over voiding of the bladder]	15
	10 (c) [¹ iv] Where the claimant's artificial stoma relates solely to the evacuation of the bowel, at least once a week, loses control of bladder so	15

(1) Activity	(2) Descriptors	(3) Points
	that the claimant cannot control the full voiding of the bladder.	
	10 (c) [¹ v] Where the claimant's artificial stoma relates solely to the evacuation of the bowel, [¹at least once a month], loses control of bladder so that the claimant cannot control the full voiding of the bladder.	9
	10 (c) [¹ vi] Where the claimant's artificial stoma relates solely to the evacuation of the bowel, risks losing control of the bladder so that the claimant cannot control the full voiding of the bladder if not able to reach a toilet quickly.	6
	10 (c) [¹ vii] None of the above apply.	0
11. Remaining conscious during waking moments.	11(a) At least once a week, has an involuntary episode of lost or altered consciousness, resulting in significantly disrupted awareness or concentration.	15
	(b) At least once a month, has an involuntary episode of lost or altered consciousness, resulting in significantly disrupted awareness or concentration.	9
	(c) At least twice in the six months immediately preceding the assessment, has had an involuntary episode of lost or altered consciousness, resulting in significantly disrupted awareness or concentration.	6
	(d) None of the above apply.	0

PART 2

MENTAL, COGNITIVE AND INTELLECTUAL FUNCTION ASSESSMENT **9.361**

(1) Activity	(2) Descriptors	(3) Points
12. Learning or comprehension in the completion of tasks.	12 (a) Cannot learn or understand how to successfully complete a simple task, such as setting an alarm clock, at all.	15
	(b) Needs to witness a demonstration, given more than once on the same occasion, of how to carry out a simple task before the claimant is able to learn or understand how to complete the task successfully,	15

(1) Activity	(2) Descriptors	(3) Points
	but would be unable to successfully complete the task the following day without receiving a further demonstration of how to complete it.	
	(c) Needs to witness a demonstration of how to carry out a simple task, before the claimant is able to learn or understand how to complete the task successfully, but would be unable to successfully complete the task the following day without receiving a verbal prompt from another person.	9
	(d) Needs to witness a demonstration of how to carry out a moderately complex task, such as the steps involved in operating a washing machine to correctly clean clothes, before the claimant is able to learn or understand how to complete the task successfully, but would be unable to successfully complete the task the following day without receiving a verbal prompt from another person.	9
	(e) Needs verbal instructions as to how to carry out a simple task before the claimant is able to learn or understand how to complete the task successfully, but would be unable, within a period of less than one week, to successfully complete the task [¹ . . .] without receiving a verbal prompt from another person.	6
	(f) None of the above apply.	0
13. Awareness of hazard.	13 (a) Reduced awareness of the risks of everyday hazards (such as boiling water or sharp objects) would lead to daily instances of or to near-avoidance of: (i) injury to self or others; or (ii) significant damage to property or possessions, to such an extent that overall day to day life cannot successfully be managed.	15
	(b) Reduced awareness of the risks of everyday hazards would lead for the majority of the time to instances of or to near-avoidance of: (i) injury to self or others; or (ii) significant damage to property or possessions,	9

(1) Activity	(2) Descriptors	(3) Points
	to such an extent that overall day to day life cannot successfully be managed without supervision from another person.	
	(c) Reduced awareness of the risks of everyday hazards has led or would lead to frequent instances of or to near-avoidance of: (i) injury to self or others; or (ii) significant damage to property or possessions, but not to such an extent that overall day to day life cannot be managed when such incidents occur.	6
	(d) None of the above apply.	0
14. Memory and concentration.	14 (a) On a daily basis, forgets or loses concentration to such an extent that overall day to day life cannot be successfully managed without receiving verbal prompting, given by someone else in the claimant's presence.	15
	(b) For the majority of the time, forgets or loses concentration to such an extent that overall day to day life cannot be successfully managed without receiving verbal prompting, given by someone else in the claimant's presence.	9
	(c) Frequently forgets or loses concentration to such an extent that overall day to day life can only be successfully managed with pre-planning, such as making a daily written list of all tasks forming part of daily life that are to be completed.	6
	(d) None of the above apply.	0
15. Execution of tasks.	15 (a) Is unable to successfully complete any everyday task.	15
	(b) Takes more than twice the length of time it would take a person without any form of mental disablement, to successfully complete an everyday task with which the claimant is familiar.	15
	(c) Takes more than one and a half times but no more than twice the length of time it would take a person without any form of mental disablement to successfully complete an everyday task with which the claimant is familiar.	9

(1) Activity	(2) Descriptors	(3) Points
	(d) Takes one and a half times the length of time it would take a person without any form of mental disablement to successfully complete an everyday task with which the claimant is familiar.	6
	(e) None of the above apply.	0
16. Initiating and sustaining personal action.	16 (a) Cannot, due to cognitive impairment or a severe disorder of mood or behaviour, initiate or sustain any personal action (which means planning, organisation, problem solving, prioritising or switching tasks).	15
	(b) Cannot, due to cognitive impairment or a severe disorder of mood or behaviour, initiate or sustain personal action without requiring [1 daily] verbal prompting given by another person in the claimant's presence [1 . . .].	15
	(c) Cannot, due to cognitive impairment or a severe disorder of mood or behaviour, initiate or sustain personal action without requiring verbal prompting given by another person in the claimant's presence for the majority of the time.	9
	(d) Cannot, due to cognitive impairment or a severe disorder of mood or behaviour, initiate or sustain personal action without requiring frequent verbal prompting given by another person in the claimant's presence.	6
	(e) None of the above apply.	0
17. Coping with change.	17 (a) Cannot cope with very minor, expected changes in routine, to the extent that overall day to day life cannot be managed.	15
	(b) Cannot cope with expected changes in routine (such as a pre-arranged permanent change to the routine time scheduled for a lunch break), to the extent that overall day to day life is made significantly more difficult.	9

(1) Activity	(2) Descriptors	(3) Points
	(c) Cannot cope with minor, unforeseen changes in routine (such as an unexpected change of the timing of an appointment on the day it is due to occur), to the extent that overall, day to day life is made significantly more difficult.	6
	(d) None of the above apply.	0
18. Getting about.	18(a) Cannot get to any specified place with which the claimant is, or would be, familiar.	15
	(b) Is unable to get to a specified place with which the claimant is familiar, without being accompanied by another person on each occasion.	15
	(c) For the majority of the time is unable to get to a specified place with which the claimant is familiar without being accompanied by another person.	9
	(d) Is frequently unable to get to a specified place with which the claimant is familiar without being accompanied by another person.	6
	(e) None of the above apply.	0
19. Coping with social situations.	19 (a) Normal activities, for example, visiting new places or engaging in social contact, are precluded because of overwhelming fear or anxiety.	15
	(b) Normal activities, for example, visiting new places or engaging in social contact, are precluded for the majority of the time due to overwhelming fear or anxiety.	[¹ 9]
	(c) Normal activities, for example, visiting new places or engaging in social contact, are frequently precluded, due to overwhelming fear or anxiety.	6
	(d) None of the above apply.	0
20. Propriety of behaviour with other people.	20 (a) Has unpredictable outbursts of aggressive, disinhibited, or bizarre behaviour, being either: (i) sufficient to cause disruption to others on a daily basis; or (ii) of such severity that although occurring less frequently than on a daily basis, no reasonable person would be expected to tolerate them.	15

(1) Activity	(2) Descriptors	(3) Points
	(b) Has a completely disproportionate reaction to minor events or to criticism to the extent that the claimant has an extreme violent outburst leading to threatening behaviour or actual physical violence.	15
	(c) Has unpredictable outbursts of aggressive, disinhibited or bizarre behaviour, sufficient in severity and frequency to cause disruption for the majority of the time.	9
	(d) Has a strongly disproportionate reaction to minor events or to criticism, to the extent that the claimant cannot manage overall day to day life when such events or criticism occur.	9
	(e) Has unpredictable outbursts of aggressive, disinhibited or bizarre behaviour, sufficient to cause frequent disruption.	6
	(f) Frequently demonstrates a moderately disproportionate reaction to minor events or to criticism but not to such an extent that the claimant cannot manage overall day to day life when such events or criticism occur.	6
	(g) None of the above apply.	0
21. Dealing with other people.	21 (a) Is unaware of impact of own behaviour to the extent that: (i) has difficulty relating to others even for brief periods, such as a few hours; or (ii) causes distress to others on a daily basis.	15
	(b) The claimant misinterprets verbal or non-verbal communication to the extent of causing himself or herself significant distress on a daily basis.	15
	(c) Is unaware of impact of own behaviour to the extent that: (i) has difficulty relating to others for longer periods, such as a day or two; or (ii) causes distress to others for the majority of the time.	9
	(d) The claimant misinterprets verbal or non-verbal communication to the extent of causing himself or herself significant distress [¹ . . .] for the majority of the time.	9

(1) Activity	(2) Descriptors	(3) Points
	(e) Is unaware of impact of own behaviour to the extent that: (i) has difficulty relating to others for prolonged periods, such as a week; or (ii) frequently causes distress to others.	6
	(f) The claimant misinterprets verbal or non-verbal communication to the extent of causing himself or herself significant distress on a frequent basis.	6
	(g) None of the above apply.	0

AMENDMENT

1. Employment and Support Allowance (Miscellaneous Amendments) Regulations 2008 (SI 2008/2428), reg.12 (October 27, 2008).

DEFINITION

"claimant"—see WRA 2007, s.24(1).

GENERAL NOTE

I. A note on the Work Capability Assessment (WCA), decision-making, medical examination and process

The new Work Capability Assessment (WCA) underpinning ESA was devised by   9.362
the DWP's Health Work and Wellbeing Directorate with input from two technical
working groups, one focusing on mental health and learning difficulties, the other
on physical function and conditions (hereinafter "review group"). The review group
consisted of medical and other relevant experts. It examined how the incapacity
benefits' regime's Personal Capability Assessment (PCA) could be improved and
updated so as to reflect the many changes since its inception:

"in the prevalence of disabling conditions; in advances in medical science resulting in the availability of new and more effective medical interventions; and in the
workplace environment. The Disability Discrimination Act, introduced after the
PCA had been developed, has influenced the ability of employers to make reasonable adjustments to accommodate people with long term disabilities. It has also
raised the expectations of disabled people that adjustments should be made to
enable them to work."

The work of the review group fed into the drafting of the regulations on the WCA.
After that first element had been developed work continued on the second and third
elements of the WCA, although nothing has been published on this. Government
anticipates that the WCA will "fail" some 60,000 claimants a year who would
have "passed" the PCA (DWP, *Impact Assessment of the Employment and support
Allowance Regulations 2008—Public sector Impact Only* in *Explanatory Memorandum
to Employment and Support Allowance Regulations 2008 (SI 2008/794) and the
Employment and Support Allowance (Transitional Provisions) Regulations 2008 (SI
2008/795)*, p.9). But the three-element WCA is not merely an incapacity-based tool
for determining entitlement to ESA. That remains true of its first element, but its
second element is rather a more positive assessment considering ability to benefit
from work-related activity with a view to promoting capacity for work. The first
element is an assessment of limited capability to work (hereinafter the WCAt) (the
subject of this Schedule). The second element is an assessment of limited capacity

to engage in work-related activity (hereinafter WRAAt)(the subject of Sch.3). Both assessments will generally be conducted at the same time by the same health care professional. Those found not to have limited capacity for work related activity (expected to be some 90% of new claimants) will in addition have to undergo the third element of the WCA: a work-focused health related assessment (WFHRAt). In many cases, all three elements of the new WCA will be covered in a single appointment with a health care professional working for Medical Services (MS), the company which contracts with the DWP to deliver these assessments.

This schedule deals with the WCAt (what the DWP call the LCWA) and establishing limited capability for work: the core element of entitlement to ESA. The vast majority of claimants for ESA will be subject to this first element of the new WCA through a face to face assessment with a trained healthcare professional testing the claimant against the activities and descriptors in the Schedule, in the light of the material in the claimant's questionnaire, any evidence from the GP and the professional's examination. Assessment will take place much earlier than in an equivalent claim for IB.

The Government's view is that the overwhelming majority of customers are capable of some work, given the right support. The approach is designed to treat people in line with their capabilities, instead of making assumptions based on their condition. Hence, because the ESA tests are designed to assess which claimants can benefit from the help towards work afforded by work-related activity, to "write off" from the chance of work as few people as possible, very few groups are exempt from the WCAt: the terminally ill; those receiving treatment by way of intravenous, intraperitoneal or intrathecal chemotherapy; such of those recovering from such treatment as the Secretary of State is satisfied should be treated as having limited capability for work; those excluded or prevented from working as a carrier, or having been in contact with a case of relevant disease (food poisoning, infectious or notifiable diseases covered by a variety of public health enactments); and pregnant women at a certain stage in pregnancy or where there is a serious risk of damage to their or their unborn child's health if they do not refrain from work (reg.20) Hospital in patients (reg.25) and persons undergoing or recovering from certain regular treatments (e.g. plasmapheresis, radio therapy, dialysis, parenteral nutrition) for at least two days a week, (reg.26) are also treated as having limited capability for work. All such persons are exempt from the information gathering requirements with respect to the WCAt (reg.21(3) Decision-makers have discretion in respect of all claimants on whether it is necessary in their case to complete the questionnaire or require more information than is provided by the claimant's doctor under the Medical Evidence Regs (reg.21(2)). Whether someone is required to undergo a medical examination is also a matter of decision-maker discretion (reg.23) Typically, most claimants will have both to complete the questionnaire (form ESA50) and undergo medical examination, usually at a medical examination centre, but sometimes in the claimant's home. Failure to do so, without good cause, is as usual sanctioned by treating the person as not having limited capability for work, thus denying benefit (regs 22–24) The Work Capability Assessment is a face to face meeting, lasting between 75 and 90 minutes, depending on whether just two or all three elements of the WCA are carried out. It explores how the claimant's illness or disability affects their ability to work and carry out day-to-day activity Each part of the assessment will be carried out by specially trained healthcare professionals (whether doctor or nurse) approved by the Secretary of State to assess these matters and report to the decision-maker, generally in the form of a computer-generated report.

What, then, are the terms of the new WCAt (LCWA)? And in what key respects does it differ from the PCA with which readers will be familiar? The WRA 2007 stipulates merely that whether a person's capability for work is limited by his physical or mental condition and, if so, whether the limitation is such that it is not reasonable to require him to work is to be determined in accordance with regulations. ESA Regulations, reg.19(1) elaborates that this is to be determined on the basis of a limited capability for work assessment (hereinafter WCAt), that is by:

"an assessment of the extent to which a claimant who has some specific disease or bodily or mental disablement is capable of performing the activities prescribed in Schedule 2 or is incapable by reason of such disease or bodily or mental disablement of performing those activities" (reg.19(2)).

This is familiar stuff for those who have worked with the all work test or its successor, personal capability assessment. The claimant is to be matched, in the light of all the evidence, by the decision-maker or tribunal against a reformulated range of activities and descriptors, and an appropriate "score" awarded. The threshold "score" for entitlement remains 15 points, but as regards its computation, there are both "old" and "new" elements".

It is stressed that incapability to perform an activity must arise from a specific bodily disease or disablement, a specific mental illness or disablement, or as a direct result of treatment provided by a registered medical practitioner, for such a disease, illness or disablement (reg.19(5)). The extent of capability to perform a physical activity has, as with IB, to be assessed as if the claimant is wearing any prosthesis with which he is fitted or wearing or using any aid or appliance which is normally worn or used. In computing the score, where more than one descriptor in respect of a particular activity applies, only the highest is counted towards the total "score" (reg.19(4)). Otherwise one simply adds up the total of the particular scores in respect of each activity, whether physical or mental, to see if the threshold of 15 points is reached. If it is, or is exceeded, the claimant has established limited capability for work, grounding entitlement to the basic allowance in ESA. The matter may be determined afresh where the Secretary of State wishes to ascertain (i) whether there has been a relevant change of circumstances in relation to the claimant's physical or mental condition; (ii) whether the previous decision was made in ignorance of, or was based on a mistake as to, some material fact; or at least three months have passed since the last decision (reg.19(7), (8)).

If the threshold score is not attained, limited capability for work has not been established, there can be no entitlement to ESA and the unsuccessful claimant (subject to retention of ESA pending appeal) will have to look for income maintenance to JSA or IS.

Schedule 2 contains 21 activities. Eleven deal with physical disabilities. Some of these are familiar from the PCA. Others (vision, continence, remaining conscious during waking moments) have been elaborated or broadened (e.g. there is now no requirement as regards remaining conscious that this be "without having epileptic or similar seizures during waking moments"). Sitting (PCA activity 3), standing (PCA activity 4) and rising from sitting (PCA activity 5) have in the WCA been compressed into one activity (activity 2: standing and sitting). The review of the physical function aspect of the PCA that led to Sch.2 aimed to ensure that descriptors and scores remain relevant to today's pattern of disabling conditions and their relationship to the working environment; to ensure that "the activities assessed and the scores allocated accurately reflect the level of functional limitation at which it is unreasonable to require a person to engage in work". An aim was to refocus the physical functional areas "to better reflect the activities felt to be most relevant to capacity for work—those activities that an employer might reasonably expect of his workforce" (DWP, *Transformation of the Personal Capability Assessment: Report of the Physical Function and mental Health Technical Working Groups*). The "physical disability" activities are: walking with a walking stick or other normally used aid; standing and sitting; bending or kneeling; reaching; picking up and moving or transferring by the use of the upper body and arms (excluding all the other "physical disability" activities); manual dexterity; speech; hearing with a hearing aid or other normally worn aid; vision (including visual acuity [central vision and focus] and visual fields [peripheral vision], in normal daylight or bright electric light, with glasses or other aid to vision if such aid is normally worn); continence other than enuresis (bed wetting) where the claimant does not have an artificial stoma or urinary collecting device; continence where the claimant uses a urinary collecting device, worn for the majority of the time including an indwelling urethral or suprapubic catheter; conti-nence other than enuresis (bed wetting) where the claimant has an artificial stoma; remaining conscious during waking moments. As regards descriptors attached to these activities, as compared to the PCA, the number is not dissimilar, but those that attracted three points have gone, six now being the lowest "score" (nought not being a score at all). This was a matter which concerned several pressure groups. The review group stated that the "three point" descriptors were removed because a person could reach the threshold of 15 by satisfying five of them. It did not consider that, even in aggregate, such minimal levels of disability really amounted to "an overall level of functional limitation at which it is unreasonable to expect a person to work" (*ibid.*, p.10). But it did not explain exactly what had changed since 1995 to warrant that judgment. Some descriptors are more restrictive. The "sometimes" descriptors have gone. A score of 15 for those who cannot walk more than 50 metres without stopping applies for the PCA, but for the WCAt requires "repeat-edly stopping", greater distances and lesser scores remain tied merely to "without stopping or severe discomfort". It is now specified that the chair against which one assesses sitting is one with a "high" back. Bending or kneeling remains the activ-ity, but several of its descriptors (reflective of IB case law) specifically permit the task (picking up a light object such as a piece of paper) to be done by squatting. On "lifting and carrying" the "paperback book", of no specified size, has gone, the descriptors instead referring variously to half or full litre cartons of liquid or "a light but bulky object such as an empty cardboard box". For manual dexterity a "star-headed" sink tap is specified and the cooker control knob is no more. Advancing technology takes the activity beyond the pen and pencil to cover "a conventional keyboard or mouse" and sensibly embodies a descriptor related very much to real life problems: "cannot do up/undo small buttons, such as shirt or blouse buttons". The coin to pick up is now specified as a £1 coin or equivalent.

As regards mental functions, the review group sought to ascertain those relevant to ability to engage in work, taking into consideration the abilities and disabilities of persons with learning difficulties or other conditions which affect cognitive and intellectual function. It recognised that the level of support or prompting someone needs is an indication of how severe is their functional limitation. It considered that the mental health provisions of the PCA were not the most relevant to activities req-uisite for remaining in or returning to work. The exemption from the PCA for those with severe learning difficulties or autism too readily removed them from being considered in relation to ability to work without undertaking a more detailed and reliable assessment of their mental function. There are ten activities with respect to mental, cognitive and intellectual function, as opposed to the four with the PCA. This reflects a desire to deal better with the problems of this client group making up 41% of the IB caseload: This

> "extensively revised mental function assessment [aims to] address a current gap in the assessment of cognitive and intellectual function, in conditions such as learning disability, autistic spectrum disorder, and acquired brain injury. It also [embodies] a new scoring system for mental function, which addresses a bias in the current PCA against people with a mental health problem, as opposed to limitation of physical function" (*ibid*, p.3).

The ten activities are: learning or comprehension in the completion of (simple) tasks; awareness of hazard; memory and concentration; executing of (everyday) tasks; initiating and sustaining personal action (planning, organisation, problem solving, prioritising or switching tasks); coping with changes in routine; getting about; coping with social situations; propriety of behaviour with other people; and dealing with other people.

II. Order of treatment in this commentary

9.363   In the nature of things, this is a lengthy annotation to a Schedule which lies at the heart of determining the key question whether a claimant for ESA has limited capability for work. It aims to identify and highlight key issues and concerns and to indicate which features of a burgeoning case law on the IB personal capability assessment and its predecessor, the all work test, remain of significance and assistance: (a) in approaching what is in essence a similar task to the IB PCA (matching a claimant's health condition to a range of activities and descriptors and assigning a score); and (b) more specifically in interpreting and applying the often similarly worded terms of the activities and descriptors in the WCAt.

The case law on the IB tests is voluminous and will continue to burgeon as IB and ESA will co-exist for several years yet. That case law is fully treated in the commentary to the Schedule to the Incapacity for Work (General) Regs 1995 in Vol.I. The commentary here does not attempt to reproduce that, but instead to draw from it the crucial principles. The commentary is sub-divided as follows:

[A] Approaching the interpretation of the Schedule as a whole
[B] Case law on specific activities and descriptors: Pt I: physical disabilities
[C] Approaching Pt II: mental, cognitive and intellectual function assessment.

[A] Approaching the interpretation of the Schedule as a whole

Evidence and attention to detail: Decision-makers must pay very close attention to the precise wording of the activities and descriptors and to the matter of appropriate evidence to ground their findings (*CSIB/12/96*). Cases must be decided in the light of the totality of the evidence, medical or otherwise, including that from the claimant (*CIB/15663/1996*). His evidence does not require corroboration unless self-contradictory or improbable (*R (I) 2/51*). Differing medical opinions and reports must carefully be appraised, without rigid preconceptions on whether the report of the examining health professional is always to be preferred as more disinterested and informed than that of the claimant's GP or consultant, or vice versa (contrast *CIB/13039/1996* and *CIB/3968/1996* with *CIB/17257/1996*). Both types of evidence can, from different perspectives, prove valuable (*CIB/17257/1996; CIB/21/2002*). A tribunal is not *bound to* decide in the same way as any particular doctor certifies; when faced with a conflict of medical opinion, they are at liberty to prefer, giving reasons, one view rather than another (*R(S) 1/53; CSIB/684/1997; CSIB/848/1997; CIB/309/1997; R. v Social Security Commissioner Ex p. Dobie* (QBD, October 26, 1999)—but *cf. CIB/17257/1996*). But that does not warrant underestimating a DWPMS personal capability assessment report which is based on a more intensive and detailed clinical examination and history-taking than the invalidity benefit system (*CIB/15663/1996*). To prefer a DWPMS doctor's report on the grounds that it is more detailed is not, as such, irrational (*R. v Social Security Commissioner Ex p. Dobie*, QBD (October 26, 1999). A tribunal should not reject a claimant's appeal on the basis that he was "not a reliable or credible witness" without giving reasons for that finding (*CSIB/459/1997*). It should be made clear that the claimant's evidence has been considered, what account has been taken of it, and, if rejected, why it has been rejected (*CIB/309/1997*). Nor should a tribunal simply record acceptance of the DWPMS doctor's findings; rather it should make and record its own findings on the descriptors (*CSIB/459/1997; CIB/4232/2007*). The correct approach is to weigh all the evidence in the context of the case (*CIB/3620/1998*). In *CIB/3074/2003* Commissioner Bano allowed the claimant's appeal because the tribunal had dismissed the appeal "on the basis of a formulaic endorsement of the examining medical practitioner's report", rather than looking at it in the light of its nature and the evidence as a whole. Although a tribunal cannot conduct a physical examination of the claimant, it can use all its senses, including ocular observation of the claimant during the hearing when considering whether the WCAt is satisfied (*R1/01(IB) (T); R4/99 (IB)*) and a tribunal medical member can properly look at X-Rays put in evidence (*R (IB) 2/06*). Tribunals should also consider carefully evidence that the medical examination was perfunctory. Equally, where the health practitioner's report disputes the claimant's account of his disabilities in his questionnaire, natural justice requires that tribunals hear the claimant's oral evidence about his condition, before deciding which account to prefer (*CIB/5586/1999*). Tribunals should be wary

9.364

of adviser/representative revision of the picture painted by the claimant's question-naire answers and the health professional's report, and should look for supporting evidence where such statements differ significantly from the claimant's original own assessment of his or her condition (*CIB/2913/2001*).

The computerised medical examination report is the end product of the system. In that report statements or phrases can be produced mechanically by the software, which produces relevant phrases from its memory bank, and, unless the examining health professional using it is very careful, the statements in the report may not necessarily represent actual wording chosen and typed in by him. This generates an increased risk of accidental mistakes or discrepancies being left undetected in the final product of the process. The need for careful appraisal of the computerised report has been stressed by Commissioners Howell and Williams (*CIB/511/2005; CIB/476/2005; CIB/1522/2005; CIB/0664/2005; CIB/3950/2007; CIB/1006/2008*). Section 7 of the Electronic Communications Act 2000 has no application to the computerised report form (*R(IB) 7/05*).

To reiterate: the first task is to decide from all the evidence in the case which descriptors apply, the second to calculate the scores. Decision-makers and tribu-nals must in the light of all relevant evidence identify the relevant health condi-tion and consider carefully the full range of activities which may be impaired by it (*CIB/5797/1997; CIB/3589/2004*). Scoring should proceed from top to bottom, so as properly to identify the highest ranking descriptor in the range attached to the par-ticular activity which can properly be said to apply to the claimant (*CIB/5361/1997*; reg.19(6)).

9.365   *The WCAt is not a snapshot—the need for an approach characterized by "reasonable-ness"*: The "sometimes" descriptors in the PCA have not been carried over into ESA. However, the Government emphasised that, like the PCA, the WCAt was not intended to be a simple snapshot. The review group rightly emphasised that guid-ance to decision-makers and to the healthcare professionals involved in the assess-ments of capacity would indicate the factors to be taken into account in ascertaining whether a claimant can perform a particular function: ability to do it just once is not enough (the person must reliably be able to sustain or repeat the activity); distress, pain, and fatigue involved in carrying out the activity; and the detrimental effects of medication. But these are not just matters of guidance; they are legal rules estab-lished by the extensive jurisprudence on approaching the very similar exercise in the PCA. The requirement is for ability to perform the specified activities with "reason-able regularity"; there must be an element of reasonableness in the approach to the question of what someone is or is not capable of doing, including consideration of his ability to perform the activities most of the time (*C1/95(IB)*; *CSIB/17/96*), so that the question becomes whether the claimant would normally be able to perform the stated activity if and when called upon to do so (*CIB/13161/96*; *CIB/13508/96*)). The working environment and the matter of employability are both irrelevant (*C1/95*; *CIB/13161/96*; *CIB/13508/96*).

Where variable, intermittent and sporadic conditions and their impact on earning capacity are involved, difficult questions of judgment in assessing incapacity for work arise where the claimant can sometimes do things but at other times not. Neither the PCA nor the WCAt were designed to be a simple "snapshot". The system aims to assess the claimant's condition over a particular period, taking account of pain and fatigue (*CIB/14587/1996*; *CIB/13161/96*; *CIB/13508/96*), fears for health and the medical advice received by the claimant (*CSIB/12/96*). The questionnaire asks about variability—the claimant's own doctor can include mate-rial on this in the MED 4, and examining health care professionals with Medical Services have been trained to conduct examinations with these issues in mind. The structure of the legislative scheme, however, produces a problem. It embodies a test based on an examination on a particular day designed to provide information on, and assessment of, a claimant over a period of time. The "normality" approach as part of "reasonable regularity" deals with one aspect of the problem: the reference in *C1/95(IB)* to a claimant being able to accomplish a task most of the time is to be read as meaning "as and when called upon to do so". On this basis, one looks at the position which normally prevails in the period (see *CSIB/459/1997*, para.13; *CIB/911/1997*, paras 12, 13). The more difficult situation is where it is accepted that the claimant's condition is such that for certain periods he is able to cope satisfactorily with normal activities; the problem of the sporadic or intermittent condition. The problem generated significant disagreement among Commissioners on approach. The authoritative Tribunal of Commissioners' decision is *R(IB) 2/99(T)*, endorsed by a tribunal of Commissioners in Northern Ireland in *R1/02 (IB) (T)*. *R (IB) 2/99* concerned the situation where a claimant suffered from a condition causing greater disability on some days than on others. The key question was whether the claimant was incapable of work under the PCA on days on which, if the days were viewed in isolation, he or she might not satisfy that test (para.2). While the Tribunal decision does not prescribe any one approach as *universally* applicable, the central thrust of the decision is to see as justified for the majority of cases, the "broad approach" typified by *CIB/6244/97* rather than the stricter "daily approach" exemplified by *CIB/13161/96* and *CIB/13508/96*. The Tribunal did not, however, find helpful the distinction drawn between "variable" and "intermittent" conditions in *CIB/6244/97*. Moreover, the Tribunal recognised that in some cases at least—generally when looking backwards over a prolonged period in the course of which the claimant has only had "short episodes of disablement" (for example, in the dwindling number of cases where the First tier Tribunal has to consider matters "down to the date of the hearing", or in "review or overpayment cases")— something akin to the meticulous approach in *CIB/13161/96* and *CIB/13508/96* along the lines of Commissioner Jacobs' approach to intermittent conditions in *CIB/6244/1997* would be appropriate (para.17).

The practical reality is that most cases which fall to be decided by the decision-maker in the Department do not concern entitlement to benefit for a past period. Generally, a decision on the award of benefit is "forward looking" and usually made for an indefinite period. Although the decision-maker must of course consider the period from the medical examination up to the date of his decision, that decision will rarely be concerned with entitlement to benefit for a substantial period in the past. While both the "broad" and the "daily basis" approaches are each consistent with the wording of the legislation, the "broad approach" is "the only approach that can sensibly be applied by a decision-maker, making what is in effect a prospective determination for an extended period" (para.11). The Tribunal considered the broader-based approach adopted in *R(A) 2/74* to the attendance allowance issue— was there a period *throughout* which the claimant could be said to be so severely disabled as to require at night prolonged or repeated attention in connection with bodily functions? The Tribunal decided that such an approach applies equally to incapacity benefit despite its daily basis. It noted (without using those statements to support its construction of the legislation) that such an approach accorded with ministerial statements in Parliament on the introduction of the all work test (for example, that the "all work test" [now the "personal capability assessment"] is not a "snapshot"). Nonetheless, the Tribunal stressed that:

"the words of the legislation cannot be ignored . . . [I]n those cases where relevant descriptors are expressed in terms that the claimant 'cannot', rather than 'sometimes cannot', perform the activity, one should not stray too far from an arithmetical approach that considers what the claimant's abilities are 'most of the time'—the phrase used in *C1/95(IB)*. Nevertheless, we agree that all the factors mentioned by counsel [neither of whom argued for a 'daily basis' approach]—the frequency of 'bad' days, the lengths of periods of 'bad' days and of intervening periods, the severity of the claimant's disablement on both 'good' and 'bad' days and the unpredictability of 'bad' days—are relevant when applying the broad approach. Thus a person whose condition varies from day to day and who would easily satisfy the 'all work test' on three days a week and would nearly satisfy it on the other four days might well be considered to be incapable of work for the whole week. But a person who has long periods of illness separated by periods of remission lasting some weeks during which he or she suffers no significant disablement, might well be considered to be incapable of work during the periods of illness but not to be incapable of work during the periods of remission, even if the periods of illness are longer than the periods of remission. Each case must be judged on its merits and . . . there are some cases where a claimant can properly be regarded as incapable of work both on days when the 'all work test' is clearly satisfied and on other days in between those days and that there are other cases where the claimant can be regarded as incapable of work only on 'bad days' . . . " (para.15).

That ESA is a weekly benefit, coupled with the demise of the "sometimes" descriptors, emphasises the continued authority and propriety of this approach to the WCAt tasks. Hence, as regards forward-looking decisions, claimants whose condition is such as only to satisfy the test on four or five days a month (albeit days of severe disablement) cannot, however unpredictable those days may be, properly be regarded as satisfying the test for the whole month. It thus may be that some claimants who are unemployable nonetheless are seen as "capable of work" under the PCA or the WCAt.

In *R1/02(IB)(T)*, a Northern Ireland tribunal of Commissioners endorsed the "broad brush" approach to variable conditions in *R(IB)2/99(T)*, but also laid emphasis on para.15 of it, set out above, with one reservation. They were unhappy with the phrase "the unpredictability of 'bad' days", commenting that those who decide cases "will simply have to try to determine the likely patterns of functional limitation. Uncertainty as to the possibility of a future recurrence would not of itself usually be enough to satisfy the test which must be satisfied on the balance of probability at the time of the decision maker's decision" (para.26). Applying para.15 of *R(IB)2/99* in *CIB/2620/2000*, Commissioner Bano held that the case before him (a sufferer from dysmenorrhoea) was one of the minority of cases in which the broad approach could not be applied, one where the claimant could only be considered incapable of work on "bad days".

9.366   *Making and recording decisions*: Setting rigorous standards for tribunals (*cf.* his approach to activity 3 in *CSIB/12/96*), Commissioner Walker in *CSIB 324/97* stipulated the following approach to making and recording decisions under the "all work" test [the predecessor of the IB PCA]:

> "the best and safest practice is for a tribunal to consider and make findings of fact about, first, the disability or disabilities, be they disease or bodily or mental problems, from which an individual has been proved on the evidence to suffer. Second, they should consider and make findings of fact about which, if any of the activities set out in the Sch., are established to be adversely affected by any of those disabilities. Thirdly, and based upon appropriate findings of fact, in the case of each and every activity the tribunal should determine which descriptor best fits the case having regard to the evidence, in their view. Finally, in the reasons, they should explain why a particular activity has been held not to be adversely affected where there was a contention that it was so affected, and why a particular descriptor has been preferred to any other contended for" (para.11).

But that best and safest practice need not necessarily always be followed. For example where the issue is whether or not the tribunal believes the claimant on a matter fundamental and relevant, if on reasonable grounds the tribunal did not believe the claimant when he alleged that his responses in the questionnaire were not accurate, then the finding that the tribunal did not believe that he had been mistaken when providing those responses covered in reality all the disputed areas raised at the hearing, and it was not necessary to record specific findings of fact on each of the activity questions brought up by the claimant (per Northern Ireland

Chief Commissioner Martin in *C46/97(IB)*, drawing with approval on Deputy Commissioner Ramsay's decision in *CIB/16572/96*). In para.5 of *CIB/4497/1998*, Commissioner Rowland sets out useful guidance on the minimum requirements of giving reasons. He noted that:

> "a statement of reasons may be adequate even though it could be improved on and, in particular, a failure to observe the 'best and safest practice' recommended in *CSIB 324/97* . . . is not necessarily an error of law . . . What is required by way of reasoning depends very much on the circumstances of the case before the tribunal. Those challenging reasoning must explain its inadequacy and show the significance of the inadequacy."

When applying the principles to a particular case, it should be remembered that a First Tier Tribunal has an inquisitorial role (*CIB/14442/96*). It should be cautious about exercising that role when considering mental disablement (*CIB/14202/1996*, see head [C] below). Where the claimant is represented by a competent adviser (e.g. a Welfare Rights officer employed by a "responsible" local authority), a tribunal is entitled to proceed on the basis that the representative will put forward all relevant points on his client's behalf and to know the case that is being made for the client. The tribunal in such a case should not be expected to inquire further into the claimant's case; to require that would be to place an impossible administrative burden on tribunals (*CSIB/389/1998*). Overall, the tribunal's task is rendered easier now in that because of the SSA 1998, the focus is on matters as at the date of the Secretary of State's decision rather than covering matters in the often lengthy period down to the date of the hearing (see further *Vol. III: Administration, Appeals and the European Dimension*).

[B] Case law on specific activities and descriptors: Part I: physical disabilities
Activity 1 walking on level ground: Tribunals should not here have regard to the case law on the same words in the context of the statutory definition of virtually unable to walk as respects the mobility component of disability living allowance. This is not merely because of the different statutory context but because the tribunal issue is essentially one of degree (*CSIB/60/96*). A tribunal must not only consider the point in distance when a claimant stops walking because of severe discomfort but also the point of onset of that discomfort (descriptors 1(b)–(e) read "without stopping *or* severe discomfort") (*CIB/3013/97*).   **9.367**

The activity refers to walking with a walking stick or other aid "if such aid is normally used". This means if it is normally used by people acting reasonably (by analogy with the interpretation given "if such aid is normally worn" in *CIB/14499/1996* with respect to PCA activity 12 (vision), now Activity 9 in this Schedule).

Activity 2: standing and sitting: this combines in one activity things which in the PCA are spread across three: sitting in an upright chair with a back but no arms (activity 3); standing without the support of another person or the use of an aid except a walking stick (activity 4); and rising from sitting in an upright chair with a back but no arms without the help of another person (activity 5). Caution must therefore be exercised in extrapolating from IB case law on those PCA activities. But there still remains a need for exactitude in comparing evidence about ability to sit (e.g. at home watching Television or in the tribunal room) to ability to sit in the chair prescribed in the wording of the activity (upright, high back, no arms) (*CSIB/12/96*; *CSIB/324/97*; *CSIB/457/02*; *CIB/15663/1996*; *CIB/2404/2001*). "Standing" does not mean standing stock-still. The normal person (the yardstick for applying the descriptors) does not do so for any length of time. As Commissioner Lloyd-Davies stated in *R(IB) 6/04*:   **9.368**

> "The quasi-involuntary movements that most people make in standing for prolonged periods do not . . . count. Instead the tribunal should concentrate on how long a claimant can stand before needing or having to move around or sit down (usually because of pain in the back or legs)" (para.5).

Descriptor (d) now looks to "without physical assistance from another person", rather than (as in the PCA) "without the help of another person", so ability to do so with encouragement from another person would preclude a score under this head. The descriptor also no longer refers to "without holding on to something", so ability to rise only by using the seat or back of the chair to deliver the force necessary to rise, or provide stability while rising, no longer scores (compare *(R(IB) 2/03)*. Nor does holding onto one's knees to assist rising (*CIB/5083/2001*). Coupled with the general provision in reg.19(4) on taking account of aids normally used, ability to rise from sitting using crutches similarly precludes scoring (compare *CIB/614/98*).

9.369   *Activity 3: bending and kneeling:* this includes squatting, thus making explicit in descriptors (b) and (c) what *R(IB) 1/02* and *Purdy v Secretary of State for Social Services* reported with it, had read into the comparable PCA provisions. The references in descriptors (b) and (c) to "straighten up again *without help of another person*" weakens the basis the argument accepted in *CSIB/12/96* that this was implicit in descriptor (a) that was decided when the qualification was not used in PCA descriptors (b) and (c).

9.370   *Activity 4 reaching:* the comparator IB provision is activity (9). Descriptor (c) now scores only 9, as opposed to 15 under the IB regime. It does not involve raising the upper arm above head level (*CIB 2811/1995*). In contrast, descriptor (d) ("cannot raise either arm above head height as if to reach for something") requires that more than a minimal amount of the arm must be above head level. Reaching involves a degree of stretching, and involves being able to raise the upper arm above shoulder level and to go at least some way towards straightening the arm in moving it towards a notional object" (*CIB 2811/1995*, para.7) So that a claimant with full elbow flexion could probably achieve the task in (c) but not (d).

9.371   *Activity 5: picking up and moving or transferring by the use of the upper arms and body:* The comparator IB provision is activity 8 (lifting and carrying). The new descriptor formulations avoid previous ambiguity over the meaning of "carry", and make it clear that what is covered is picking up and moving, using the upper body and arms (compare *R(IB) 5/03*).

9.372   *Activity 6: manual dexterity:* The comparator IB provision is Activity 7. Whether one reads into the descriptors the words "safely or in safety" remains an unresolved disagreement between Commissioners (contrast *CSIB/20/1996* and *CIB/4315/1997*). A "star headed" sink tap is now specified in descriptors (a) and (g). The sink tap contemplated is "a tap requiring an ordinary amount of force to turn it, when it is closed so as to prevent water dripping through it" (*CIB/2404/2001*, para.10). So a tribunal there did not err by finding that the claimant could turn a tap "if it is not too tight", since anyone can have difficulty with a tap that is jammed or over tightened (*ibid.*).

Descriptor (d) ("cannot physically use a pen or pencil") probably means physically "with either hand" so as to write in a normal manner, rather than a total inability to use a pen or pencil for any purpose at all, for example, punching a hole in a sheet of paper (*R(IB)1/98; CIB/13161/96; CIB/13508/96*). The same approach would seem applicable to the more modern technology in descriptor (e).

9.373   *Activity 7: speech:* The comparator IB provision is Activity 10. In *CSIB/413/1998*, Commissioner May appeared to cast doubt on the proposition that the factor "pain" was relevant to the activity of speaking. In contrast, in *CIB/4306/1999* Deputy Commissioner White thought:

"descriptor (a) covers someone who has no power of speech, and could also cover someone whose condition was such that either they had been advised not to speak or whom speaking caused such pain that they could not reasonably be said to be able to speak. I can conceive of situations in which the act of talking causes such pain that it would be right to conclude that a claimant was unable to speak. . . . What the threshold of pain is in any particular case is an issue of fact for the tribunal in the light of all the evidence." (para.17)

Whether a claimant cannot be understood or cannot easily be understood so as to satisfy descriptors (b) to (d) is similarly a matter of fact for the tribunal to resolve in the light of all the evidence in the case.

Activity 8: hearing: The comparator IB provision is Activity 10, identically worded. The phrase "if normally worn" means if the aid in question is normally worn by people in the claimant's situation acting reasonably in all the circumstances (*CIB/14499/1996*). As regards descriptor (d), the wording has changed from "normal voice" to "loud voice", making the descriptor harder to satisfy than its comparator provision. But it is submitted that it still has to be considered in the light of what is reasonable. It is not reasonable (and a score could be awarded under the descriptor) if the understanding of someone talking in a loud voice can only be gained through frequent requests for repetition of what has been said (*CIB/590/1998*). Agreeing with this in *CIB/3123/2002*, Commissioner Bano added that the descriptor should be considered by reference to a claimant's ability to understand someone with whom s/he is not familiar, so that the tribunal erred in law in considering the claimant's ability to understand his wife (who always accompanied him outdoors) when on busy streets (para.8). 9.374

Ability to understand what is being said by lip-reading is irrelevant to assessment under the descriptors attached to this activity; understanding through hearing is what is being tested (*SM v SSWP* [2008] UKUT 39 (AAC), paras 5, 6).

Activity 9: vision: the comparator IB provision is Activity 12, but the ESA activity now includes visual fields [central vision and focus] and visual acuity [peripheral vision]. The phrase "if normally worn" means if the aid in question is normally worn by people in the claimant's situation acting reasonably in all the circum- stances (*CIB/14499/1996*). So if someone would be able to see perfectly well if wearing prescription sunglasses, but unreasonably refused to wear them and could not see without them, that person cannot score points under this activity. "Bright electric light" includes fluorescent light (*CIB/2952/2004*). The rubric is "daylight *or* bright electric light". In *CIB/2584/2002* Commissioner Williams saw this as meaning that an inability to meet the visual descriptors in one of those contexts, while being able to meet them in the other, would suffice to score (para.8). Dealing with a claimant adversely affected in the proximity of intense bright light, and taking account of concepts of reasonable regularity and the relevance of pain and discomfort, he was of the view (endorsing the interpretation in *C12/00–01 (IB,* below) that the 9.375

"claimant does not need a sustained ability to read in bright artificial light to have adequate vision for these purposes, but if the exposure to bright artificial light for any significant time causes pain and/or stops her focussing and/or makes her shut her eyes to avoid the effects of the light at some point, then from that point she presumably cannot meet that descriptor even for the shortest period. The ques- tion is whether, taking those limits into account, she does or does not have the relevant level of vision" (para.18).

Descriptor (b) ("cannot see well enough to read 16 point print at a distance of greater than 20 cm") covers the ability to distinguish 16 point characters so as to be able to decipher and distinguish individual words, rather than importing sustained reading ability (is the vision good enough to read 16-point characters at the requi- site distance?) (*C12/00–01 (IB); CIB/4998/1998; CIB/333/1998; CIB/2354/2001; CIB/2952/2004*).

Descriptors (d) and (f) both refer to "see well enough to recognize a friend" at the specified distances, five metres and 15 metres, respectively. This test only requires the claimant to be able to identify a friend who is alone at the requisite distance. It does not stipulate ability to pick the friend out from a number of people. The time it may take to "recognise" the friend is material in that it may take so long a time that it is proper to regard that time lapse as amounting to "cannot" recognise the friend (*CIB/1323/2007*).

9.376 *Activities 10(a)–(c): continence:* Applying the descriptors involves intrusive scrutiny of the lives of claimants, those in respect of Activities 10 (a)–(c) particularly so, embracing intimate and embarrassing areas affecting a claimant's dignity. It is necessary to appreciate the nature of the problems of sufferers, the varied nature and disabling effects of irritable bowel syndrome (IBS) (see *CIB/14332/96*) the role of diet (*CSIB/889/1999*), various urinary collecting devices (including an indwelling uretheral or suprapubic catheter), and the effect of medication (does it negate "voluntary control"—this remains a matter of Commissioner disagreement: contrast *CSIB/38/96* [ignore its effect] with *R2/00(IB)* [take account of its effect]. It is also necessary to define carefully the terms used in the descriptors and apply them carefully.

9.377 *Activity 10(a): Continence other than enuresis (bed wetting): the meaning of continence:* In *R(IB) 4/04*, a Tribunal of Commissioners rejected as too broad the definition advanced on behalf of the Secretary of State that "continence" relates to whether a person is able, by his actions, simply to contain his emissions of urine and excrement (para.34). Instead it made use of the relevant definition in *Blakiston's Gould Medical Dictionary* (4th edition):

> "The proper functioning of any sphincter or other structure of the gastro intestinal tract so as to prevent regurgitation or premature emptying".

9.378 *Activity 10(a): continence other than enuresis (bed wetting) where the claimant does not have an artificial stoma or urinary collecting device: descriptors (a)(i)–(vii):* These refer variously, in the context of "no voluntary control" or "loses control", to the "voiding of the bladder", the "full voiding of the bladder", or the "full evacuation of the bowel". This would suggest that IB case authorities bringing dribbling and leaking within the sphere of "loses control" are not applicable here (see, e.g., *CSIB/880/2003*). Thus stress incontinence sufferers will find it difficult to score. Incontinence pads were held irrelevant to the issue of "voluntary control" under the IB scheme (*CSIB/880/2003*). But it is not clear whether they constitute a "urinary collecting device"; the references in 10(b) to emptying such a device would suggest they might not, but references to affix or remove, if they are properly to be read disjunctively, might suggest that they do.

9.379 *Activity 10(b): continence where the claimant uses a urinary collecting device, worn for the majority of the time, including an indwelling uretheral or suprapubic catheter:* This has no counterpart in the IB PCA. The descriptors cover varying types of inability to use these artificial control devices to deal with urinary (bladder) incontinence. It is not wholly clear from the wording used whether incontinence pads constitute a "urinary collecting device"; the references in 10(b) to emptying such a device would suggest they might not, but references to affix or remove, if they are properly to be read disjunctively, might suggest that they do. Insofar as they may enable ability to cope outside the home without undue embarrassment, it is arguable that they should be covered.

9.380 *Activity 10(c): continence other than enuresis (bed wetting) where the claimant has an artificial stoma:* This has no counterpart in the IB PCA. Activity 10(c) covers both urinary (bladder) and faecal (bowel) incontinence. The descriptors cover varying types of inability to use the artificial stoma.

Activity 11 remaining conscious during waking moments: The comparator IB PCA or "all work test" activity was Activity 14, the wording of which changed from that used when IB first came into operation. The changes in wording need to be borne in mind the better to ascertain the relevance and continued import of case authorities on that activity. Initially, the activity read: "remaining conscious other than for normal periods of sleep". From January 6, 1997, it changed to: "remaining conscious without having epileptic or similar seizures during waking moments". Post-*Howker*, the change in wording was held valid by a Tribunal of Commissioners in *R(IB) 2/07(T)*.

In terms of the activity, the wording of Activity 11 more closely resembles that initial IB formulation. As regards the wording of the descriptors, the IB regime throughout has referred to an "involuntary episode of lost or altered consciousness", the level of points scored varying according to the frequency, with 15 points (the threshold test for incapacity for work) being attained where an episode occurred at least daily, weekly or monthly. Lower scores were attained where (for 12 points) there had been at least two such episodes in the preceding six months or where (for eight points) there had in that period been one such episode. The descriptors attached to ESA Activity 14 still centre on "involuntary episode of lost or altered consciousness", but to attract 15 points must occur at least weekly (descriptor 11(b)). A monthly occurrence now scores nine points (descriptor 11(b)) and a score of six points attaches to the "at least twice in the last six months" descriptor (11(c)). More importantly, however, the descriptors all require that the episode result in "significantly disrupted awareness or concentration".

Clearly, *R(IB) 2/07(T)* is the leading authority on the construction of the amended IB Activity 14 and the impact of the words "epileptic or similar seizures", importing an element of "suddenness". Its criticisms of a number of earlier cases on the pre-1997 wording needs now to be considered in the light of the changed wording of Activity 11 and its descriptors set out above. The Tribunal of Commissioners held in para.47 that *CSIB/14/1996*, giving hope to those who suffered severe headaches with its broad approach to "altered consciousness", was wrongly decided. In that case Commissioner Walker considered the meaning of "altered consciousness". He saw it as different from "lost consciousness" and as not coloured by that term:

"The discussion satisfied me that it is not possible to lay down guidelines as to what, in law, is meant by 'altered consciousness'. It is, I am equally satisfied, essentially a practical matter for a tribunal to determine in the light of medical guidance from their assessor [now medical member] and the application of commonsense. But where, as here, episodes of pain are the disabling condition it will be necessary for the tribunal to explore, and for the claimant to present appropriate evidence to allow such exploration, in some detail how the pain affects the individual during an episode. It is not, in my view, sufficient to find as a fact that during the period 'the appellant is disabled'. Nor that 'he is unable to conduct his normal daily activities'. *It is for determination first how pain forecloses these and the way in which and the extent to which it does so. Thus . . . if an individual is so distracted by the pain that he requires to lie down and otherwise retire from what he is doing then it may be possible to conclude that his consciousness has become altered by the degree of pain and he is incapable of doing anything effective other than coping with it.* But that would be a secondary finding which would require proper primary findings to justify it. Above all, I am persuaded that the concept of 'altered consciousness', which may have some medical significance, is impossible of legal definition and is a concept of difficulty for application by lay tribunals. For these reasons I do not think that it is appropriate that I should give any further guidance to the new tribunal in this case" (para.9, emphasis supplied by commentator).

The Tribunal of Commissioners instead preferred the approach taken by Chief Commissioner Chambers in Northern Ireland in *C13/96(IB)*, which he saw as embracing epilepsy, diabetes and possibly severe vertigo:

"a person has an involuntary episode of altered consciousness when he has reached a state of mental confusion such that he is no longer properly aware of his surroundings or his condition".

What was there envisaged was alteration of consciousness such that the sufferer was not capable of any deliberate act; merely losing *some* control of one's actions due to vertigo would not suffice. The Tribunal of Commissioners in para.47 approved that strict approach to the pre-1997 wording. It is, however, arguable that the link to "significantly disrupted awareness or concentration" (especially the latter) in descriptors 11(a)-(c) warrants some move away from that narrow approach, the more so given that episodes occurring less frequently than weekly now attract scores below the qualifying threshold for a finding of limited capability for work. That, and the removal of the requirement of "epileptic or similar seizures", thus opens up possibilities under Activity 11 for example, for those suffering frequent disabling migraines (a point supported by *C7/96(IB)* if severe) or very severe back pain. It might cover some effects of severe pain produced by endometriosis (*CIB/12668/1996*) or the effects of severe vertigo (*C8/96(IB); C13/96(IB); CIB/15231/1996*). The removal of the requirement of "epileptic or similar seizures" also reduces the relevance of the factor of "suddenness" seen as so significant in *R(IB) 2/07(T)* (para.46). Use of the wording "during waking moments" rather than during "normal periods of sleep" suggests that "lost consciousness" may now arguably embrace the person who due to medication falls asleep during the day. "Altered consciousness, resulting in significantly disrupted awareness or concentration" might also cover that person for periods of doziness or sleepiness, something rejected, on the stricter approach in *R(IB) 2/07(T)*, para.69, now, it is submitted, called into question by the wording "significantly disrupted awareness or concentration".

The matter of giving substance to the concepts "lost or altered consciousness resulting in significantly disrupted awareness or concentration" and applying them to the facts of disputed cases is very directly the task of the tribunal in the light of all the evidence and what they consider to be the impact on case authorities of the changed wording of the activity and descriptors.

9.382   *[C] Case law on specific activities and descriptors: Pt II: mental, cognitive and intellectual function assessment*

The terms of the activities and descriptors in Pt II are so different from those in the PCA that no specific IB case law on the PCA descriptors and activities can readily be made relevant. Not so, however, IB case law on the general approach to be taken, namely that, while a tribunal has an inquisitorial function, it should be cautious about exercising it when considering mental disablement (*CIB/14202/1996*), unless the matter has been raised beforehand and there is in addition some medical or other evidence on the point (*R (IB) 2/98*). It cannot be stressed too much that there must be link between inability to perform and activity or task and the specific disease or bodily or mental disablement from which the claimant suffers (reg.19(2)).

SCHEDULE 3

9.383   ASSESSMENT OF WHETHER A CLAIMANT HAS LIMITED CAPABILITY FOR WORK-RELATED ACTIVITY

Column 1 Activity	Column 2 Descriptors
1. Walking or moving on level ground.	Cannot— (a) walk (with a walking stick or other aid if such aid is normally used); (b) move (with the aid of crutches if crutches are normally used); or

Column 1 Activity	Column 2 Descriptors
	(c) manually propel the claimant's wheelchair; more than 30 metres without repeatedly stopping, experiencing breathlessness or severe discomfort.
2. Rising from sitting and transferring from one seated position to another.	Cannot complete both of the following— (a) rise to standing from sitting in an upright chair without receiving physical assistance from someone else; and (b) move between one seated position and another seated position located next to one another without receiving physical assistance from someone else.
3. Picking up and moving or transferring by the use of the upper body and arms (excluding standing, sitting, bending or kneeling and all other activities specified in this Schedule).	Cannot pick up and move 0.5 litre carton full of liquid with either hand.
4. Reaching.	Cannot raise either arm as if to put something in the top pocket of a coat or jacket.
5. Manual dexterity.	Cannot— (a) turn a "star-headed" sink tap with either hand; or (b) pick up a £1 coin or equivalent with either hand.
6. Continence. (a) Continence other than enuresis (bed wetting) where the claimant does not have an artificial stoma or urinary collecting device.	(a) Has no voluntary control over the evacuation of the bowel; (b) Has no voluntary control over the voiding of the bladder; (c) At least once a week, loses control of bowels so that the claimant cannot control the full evacuation of the bowel; (d) At least once a week, loses control of bladder so that the claimant cannot control the full voiding of the bladder; (e) At least once a week, fails to control full evacuation of the bowel, owing to a severe disorder of mood or behaviour; or (f) At least once a week, fails to control full-voiding of the bladder, owing to a severe disorder of mood or behaviour.
(b) Continence where the claimant uses a urinary collecting device, worn for the majority of the time including an indwelling urethral or suprapubic catheter.	(a) Is unable to affix, remove or empty the catheter bag or other collecting device without receiving physical assistance from another person; (b) Is unable to affix, remove or empty the catheter bag or other collecting device without causing leakage of contents; (c) Has no voluntary control over the evacuation of the bowel; (d) At least once a week loses control of bowels so that the claimant cannot control the full evacuation of the bowel; or

Column 1 *Activity*	Column 2 *Descriptors*
	(e) At least once a week, fails to control full evacuation of the bowel, owing to a severe disorder of mood or behaviour.
(c) Continence other than enuresis (bed wetting) where the claimant has an artificial stoma appliance.	(a) Is unable to affix, remove or empty stoma appliance without receiving physical assistance from another person;
	(b) Is unable to affix, remove or empty stoma without causing leakage of contents;
	(c) Where the claimant's artificial stoma relates solely to the evacuation of the bowel, has no voluntary control over voiding of bladder;
	(d) Where the claimant's artificial stoma relates solely to the evacuation of the bowel, at least once a week, loses control of the bladder so that the claimant cannot control the full voiding of the bladder; or
	(e) Where the claimant's artificial stoma relates solely to the evacuation of the bowel, at least once a week, fails to control the full voiding of the bladder, owing to a severe disorder of mood or behaviour.
7. Maintaining personal hygiene.	(a) Cannot clean own torso (excluding own back) without receiving physical assistance from someone else;
	(b) Cannot clean own torso (excluding [¹ own] back) without repeatedly stopping, experiencing breathlessness or severe discomfort;
	(c) Cannot clean own torso (excluding [¹ own] back) without receiving regular prompting given by someone else in the claimant's presence; or
	(d) Owing to a severe disorder of mood or behaviour, fails to clean own torso (excluding own back) without receiving—
	(i) physical assistance from someone else; or
	(ii) regular prompting given by someone else in the claimant's presence.
8. Eating and drinking. (a) Conveying food or drink to the mouth.	(a) Cannot convey food or drink to the claimant's own mouth without receiving physical assistance from someone else;
	(b) Cannot convey food or drink to the claimant's own mouth without repeatedly stopping, experiencing breathlessness or severe discomfort;
	(c) Cannot convey food or drink to the claimant's own mouth without receiving regular prompting given by someone else in the claimant's physical presence; or
	(d) Owing to a severe disorder of mood or behaviour, fails to convey food or drink to the claimant's own mouth without receiving—

Column 1 *Activity*	Column 2 *Descriptors*
	(i) physical assistance from someone else; or
	(ii) regular prompting given by someone else in the claimant's presence.
(b) Chewing or swallowing food or drink.	(a) Cannot chew or swallow food or drink;
	(b) Cannot chew or swallow food or drink without repeatedly stopping, experiencing breathlessness or severe discomfort;
	(c) Cannot chew or swallow food or drink without repeatedly receiving regular prompting given by someone else in the claimant's presence; or
	(d) Owing to a severe disorder of mood or behaviour, fails to—
	(i) chew or swallow food or drink; or
	(ii) chew or swallow food or drink without regular prompting given by someone else in the claimant's presence.
9. Learning or comprehension in the completion of tasks.	(a) Cannot learn or understand how to successfully complete a simple task, such as the preparation of a hot drink, at all;
	(b) Needs to witness a demonstration, given more than once on the same occasion of how to carry out a simple task before the claimant is able to learn or understand how to complete the task successfully, but would be unable to successfully complete the task the following day without receiving a further demonstration of how to complete it; or
	(c) Fails to do any of the matters referred to in (a) or (b) owing to a severe disorder of mood or behaviour.
10. Personal action.	(a) Cannot initiate or sustain any personal action (which means planning, organisation, problem solving, prioritising or switching tasks);
	(b) Cannot initiate or sustain personal action without requiring daily verbal prompting given by someone else in the claimant's presence; or
	(c) Fails to initiate or sustain basic personal action without requiring daily verbal prompting given by some else in the claimant's presence, owing to a severe disorder of mood or behaviour.
11. Communication.	(a) None of the following forms of communication can be achieved by the claimant—
	(i) speaking (to a standard that may be understood by strangers);
	(ii) writing (to a standard that may be understood by strangers);
	(iii) typing (to a standard that may be understood by strangers);

Column 1 Activity	Column 2 Descriptors
	(iv) sign language to a standard equivalent to Level 3 British Sign Language;
	(b) None of the forms of communication referred to in (a) are achieved by the claimant, owing to a severe disorder of mood or behaviour;
	(c) Misinterprets verbal or non-verbal communication to the extent of causing distress to himself or herself on a daily basis; or
	(d) Effectively cannot make himself or herself understood to others because of the claimant's disassociation from reality owing to a severe disorder of mood or behaviour.

AMENDMENT

1. Employment and Support Allowance (Miscellaneous Amendments) Regulations 2008 (SI 2008/2428), reg.13 (October 27, 2008).

DEFINITIONS

"claimant"—see WRA 2007, s.24(1).

GENERAL NOTE

9.384   Establishing limited capacity for work related activity might be said to be the central condition of entitlement to support component. The assumption behind ESA is that the vast majority of claimants, if given the right support, are in fact capable of some work. Government anticipates that only some 10% of claimants (those with more severe health conditions) will be entitled to the support allowance and so not be subject to work-related activity conditionality requirements. Entry to this protected support group depends on it being established—generally through a work-related activity assessment (WRAAt) of a more stringent nature than the WCAt covered by reg.19 and Sch.2—that the claimant has limited capacity for work related activity: the WRAAt is thus the second element in the revised Work Capability Assessment.

Entry to the support group is based on someone demonstrating that they have a severe level of functional limitation. This is established when by reason of the claimant's physical or mental condition, at least one of the range of descriptors in this Schedule to the ESA Regulations applies to the claimant. It is submitted here that the key elements of IB case law which carry across into interpreting and applying the provisions in Sch.2 on the WCAt will also apply here: decide in the light of the totality of the evidence, making a careful appraisal of differing medical reports; the need for careful attention to detail; the concept of reasonable regularity (the test is not a snapshot); relevant factors of pain, discomfort and of fears for the claimants health; and the need carefully to approach conditions which vary and fluctuate. But here reg.34(2) makes clear that a:

"descriptor applies to a claimant if that descriptor applies to the claimant for the majority of the time or, as the case may be, on the majority of the occasions on which the claimant undertakes or attempts to undertake the activity described by that descriptor."

There is no scoring system and the criteria are deliberately more stringent than in the WCAt. In Committee, the Minister for Employment and Welfare Reform explained both characteristics:

"The levels of functional limitation used in the descriptors for determining limited capability for work-related activity are greater because we intend to place in the support group only the minority of customers who are so severely impaired that it would not be reasonable to require them to undertake work-related activity . . . People with less severe functional limitations across a range of descriptors might score highly and be inappropriately included in the support group when they might benefit from work-related activity . . . A number of case studies were provided in the background information, which hon. Members will find helpful. [See DWP, *Welfare Reform Bill: Draft Regulations and Supporting Material* (January 2007), pp. 13–17.] Under the revised PCA, someone with a moderate learning disability would score 50 points. They would be significantly above the 15-point threshold, but we clearly would not wish to put even someone with 50 points into the support group automatically, because we are determined to ensure that the new system does not write off people with learning disabilities. The technical groups considered all the options. A crude points-based system would have unintended consequences." (*Hansard*, Standing Committee A, October 19, 2006 (afternoon), col.120 (Mr Jim Murphy MP).

However, there is an equivalent of the "exceptional circumstances" provision applicable to the limited capacity for work question, considered above. A claimant who does not pass the WRAAt can nonetheless be treated as having the requisite limited capability for work-related activity grounding membership of the support group where, by reason of the specific disease or bodily or mental disablement from which s/he suffers, "there would be a substantial risk to the mental or physical health of any person if the claimant were found not to have limited capability for work-related activity" (reg.35(2)).

There are only 11 activities in Sch.3: walking or moving on level ground; rising from sitting and transferring from one seated position to another; picking up and moving or transferring by means of the upper body and arms; reaching; manual dexterity; continence; maintaining personal hygiene; eating and drinking (conveying food or drink to the mouth and chewing or swallowing it); learning or comprehension in the completion of tasks; personal action (planning, organisation, problem solving, prioritising or switching tasks); and communication. The terms of the descriptors are also more stringent than in the WCAt, to avoid removing too many people from the group which affords incentive to engage in work-related activity and thus denying them the opportunity to take steps to make real their fundamental right to work. Thus, as regards walking, the single descriptor can only be met where a claimant cannot "walk" more than 30 metres without repeatedly stopping, experiencing breathlessness or severe discomfort. "Walk" covers walking with a walking stick, other aid or crunches, each if normally used; and embraces the claimant moving by manually propelling a wheelchair. That on rising from sitting etc, requires in effect that the claimant fulfil two of the 15 point descriptors in the WCAt. Most, with counterparts in the WCAt, are couched in terms equivalent to the more difficult of their 15-point descriptors.

Those meeting the WRAAt test (or satisfying the "exceptional circumstances" provision) will be placed in the support group and receive support component without having to satisfy work-related activity conditions, although they can voluntarily participate in those programmes. Their position can be reviewed periodically or where there has been a change of circumstances in the claimant's physical or mental condition or it is thought that a previous determination was made in ignorance of or a mistake as to some material fact (reg.34(4), (5)). The threshold for membership of the support group is high; many claimants in receipt of the middle and higher rates of Disability Living Allowance (DLA) may not meet it. Those who fail to establish limited capability for work-related activity will instead receive the work-related activity component.

Regulations 67(1)(a) and (2) and 68(1)(a) and (b)

SCHEDULE 4

AMOUNTS

PART 1

PRESCRIBED AMOUNTS

9.385   1. The weekly amounts specified in column (2) in respect of each person or couple specified in column (1) are the weekly amounts specified for the purposes of regulations 67(1) and 68 (prescribed amounts and polygamous marriages).

(1) Person or Couple			(2) Amount	
(1)		Single claimant—	(1)	
	(a)	who satisfies the conditions set out in section 2(2) or (3) or 4(4) or (5) of the Act;	(a)	[³£64.30];
	(b)	aged not less than 25;	(b)	[³£64.30];
	(c)	aged less than 25.	(c)	[³£50.95];
(2)		Lone parent—	(2)	
	(a)	who satisfies the conditions set out in section 4(4) or (5) of the Act;	(a)	[³£64.30];
	(b)	aged not less than 18;	(b)	[³£64.30];
	(c)	aged less than 18.	(c)	[³£50.95];
(3)		Couple—	(3)	
	(a)	where both members are aged not less than 18;	(a)	[³£100.95];
	(b)	where one member is aged not less than 18 and the other member is a person under 18 who—	(b)	[³£100.95];
	(i)	had they not been members of a couple, would (1) (2) Person or Couple Amount satisfy the requirements for entitlement to income support other than the requirement to make a claim for it; or		
	(ii)	had they not been members of a couple, would satisfy the requirements for entitlement to an income-related allowance; or		
	(iii)	satisfies the requirements of section 3(1)(f)(iii) of the Jobseekers Act (prescribed circumstances for persons aged 16 but less than 18); or		
	(iv)	is the subject of a direction under section 16 of that Act (persons under 18: severe hardship);		
	(c)	where the claimant satisfies the conditions set out in section 4(4) or (5) of the Act and both members are aged less than 18 and—	(c)	[³£100.95];
	(i)	at least one of them is treated as responsible for a child; or		
	(ii)	had they not been members of a couple, each would have qualified for an income-related allowance; or		
	(iii)	had they not been members of a couple the claimant's partner would satisfy the requirements for entitlement to income support other than the requirement to make a claim for it; or		

(1) Person or Couple	(2) Amount
(iv) the claimant's partner satisfies the requirements of section 3(1)(f)(iii) of the Jobseekers Act (prescribed circumstances for persons aged 16 but less than 18); or	
(v) there is in force in respect of the claimant's partner a direction under section 16 of that Act (persons under 18: severe hardship);	
(d) where both members are aged less than 18 and—	(d) [³£76.90];
(i) at least one of them is treated as responsible for a child; or	
(ii) had they not been members of a couple, each would have qualified for an income-related allowance; or	
(iii) had they not been members of a couple the claimant's partner satisfies the requirements for entitlement to income support other than a requirement to make a claim for it; or	
(iv) the claimant's partner satisfies the requirements of section 3(1)(f)(iii) of the Jobseekers Act (prescribed circumstances for persons aged 16 but less than 18); or	
(v) there is in force in respect of the claimant's partner a direction under section 16 of that Act (persons under 18: severe hardship);	
(e) where the claimant is aged not less than 25 and the claimant's partner is a person under 18 who—	(e) [³£64.30];
(i) would not qualify for an income-related allowance if the person were not a member of a couple;	
(ii) would not qualify for income support if the person were not a member of a couple;	
(iii) does not satisfy the requirements of section 3(1)(f)(iii) of the Jobseekers Act (prescribed circumstances for persons aged 16 but less than 18); and	
(iv) is not the subject of a direction under section 16 of that Act (persons under 18: severe hardship);	
(f) where the claimant satisfies the conditions set out in section 4(4) or (5) of the Act and the claimant's partner is a person under 18 who—	(f) [³£64.30];
(i) would not qualify for an income-related allowance if the person were not a member of a couple;	
(ii) would not qualify for income support if the person [¹ were] not a member of a couple;	
(iii) does not satisfy the requirements of section 3(1)(f)(iii) of the Jobseekers Act (prescribed circumstances for persons aged 16 but less than 18); and	
(iv) is not the subject of a direction under section 16 of that Act (persons under 18: severe hardship);	

(1) Person or Couple		(2) Amount
(g)	where the claimant satisfies the conditions set out in section 4(4) or (5) of the Act and both members are aged less than 18 and paragraph (c) does not apply;	(g) [³£64.30];
[¹ (h)	where the claimant is aged not less than 18 but less than 25 and the claimant's partner is a person under 18 who—	(h) [³£50.95];
	(i) would not qualify for an income-related allowance if the person were not a member of a couple;	
	(ii) would not qualify for income support if the person were not a member of a couple;	
	(iii) does not satisfy the requirements of section 3(1)(f)(iii) of the Jobseekers Act (prescribed circumstances for persons aged 16 but less than 18); and	
	(iv) is not the subject of a direction under section 16 of that Act (persons under 18: severe hardship);]	
(i)	where both members are aged less than 18 and paragraph (d) does not apply.	(i) [³£50.95].

Regulations 67(1)(b) and 68(1)(c)

PART 2

PREMIUMS

9.386   2. Except as provided in paragraph 4, the weekly premiums specified in Part 3 of this Schedule are, for the purposes of regulation 67(1)(b) and 68(1)(c), to be applicable to a claimant who satisfies the condition specified in paragraphs 5 to 8 in respect of that premium.

3. An enhanced disability premium in respect of a person is not applicable in addition to a pensioner premium.

4.—(1) For the purposes of this Part of this Schedule, once a premium is applicable to a claimant under this Part, a person is to be treated as being in receipt of any benefit—
   (a) in the case of a benefit to which the Social Security (Overlapping Benefits) Regulations 1979 applies, for any period during which, apart from the provisions of those Regulations, the person would be in receipt of that benefit; and
   (b) for any period spent by a person in undertaking a course of training or instruction provided or approved by the Secretary of State under section 2 of the Employment and Training Act 1973, or by [³ Skills Development Scotland] or Highlands and Islands Enterprise under section 2 of the Enterprise and New Towns (Scotland) Act 1990, or for any period during which the person is in receipt of a training allowance.

(2) For the purposes of the carer premium under paragraph 8, a claimant is to be treated as being in receipt of a carer's allowance by virtue of sub-paragraph (1)(a) only if and for so long as the person in respect of whose care the allowance has been claimed remains in receipt of attendance allowance, or the care component of disability living allowance at the highest or middle rate prescribed in accordance with section 72(3) of the Contributions and Benefits Act.

Pensioner premium

9.387   5. The condition is that the claimant or the claimant's partner has attained the qualifying age for state pension credit.

Severe disability premium

9.388   6.—(1) The condition is that the claimant is a severely disabled person.

(2) For the purposes of sub-paragraph (1), a claimant is to be treated as being a severely disabled person if, and only if—

    (a) in the case of a single claimant, a lone parent or a claimant who is treated as having no partner in consequence of sub-paragraph (3)—

        (i) the claimant is in receipt of the care component;

        (ii) subject to sub-paragraph (4), the claimant has no non-dependants aged 18 or over normally residing with the claimant or with whom the claimant is normally residing; and

        (iii) no person is entitled to, and in receipt of, a carer's allowance under section 70 of the Contributions and Benefits Act in respect of caring for the claimant;

    (b) in the case of a claimant who has a partner—

        (i) the claimant is in receipt of the care component;

        (ii) the claimant's partner is also in receipt of the care component or attendance allowance or, if the claimant is a member of a polygamous marriage, all the partners of that marriage are in receipt of the care component or attendance allowance; and

        (iii) subject to sub-paragraph (4), the claimant has no non-dependants aged 18 or over normally residing with the claimant or with whom the claimant is normally residing, and, either a person is entitled to, and in receipt of, a carer's allowance in respect of caring for only one of the couple or, in the case of a polygamous marriage, for one or more but not all the partners of the marriage or, as the case may be, no person is entitled to, and in receipt of, such an allowance in respect of caring for either member of the couple or any partner of the polygamous marriage.

(3) Where a claimant has a partner who does not satisfy the condition in sub-paragraph (2)(b)(ii) and that partner is blind or severely sight impaired or is treated as blind or severely sight impaired that partner is to be treated for the purposes of sub-paragraph (2) as if the partner were not a partner of the claimant.

(4) For the purposes of sub-paragraph (2)(a)(ii) and (b)(iii) no account is to be taken of—

    (a) a person receiving attendance allowance, or the care component;

    (b) subject to sub-paragraph (7), a person who joins the claimant's household for the first time in order to care for the claimant or the claimant's partner and immediately before so joining the claimant or the claimant's partner was treated as a severely disabled person; or

    (c) a person who is blind or severely sight impaired or is treated as blind or severely sight impaired.

(5) For the purposes of sub-paragraph (2)(b) a person is to be treated—

    (a) as being in receipt of attendance allowance or the care component if the person would, but for the person being a patient for a period exceeding 28 days, be so in receipt;

    (b) as being entitled to, and in receipt of, a carer's allowance if the person would, but for the person for whom the person was caring being a patient in hospital for a period exceeding 28 days, be so entitled and in receipt.

(6) For the purposes of sub-paragraph (2)(a)(iii) and (b), no account is to be taken of an award of carer's allowance to the extent that payment of such an award is backdated for a period before the date on which the award is first paid.

(7) Sub-paragraph (4)(b) is to apply only for the first 12 weeks following the date on which the person to whom that provision applies first joins the claimant's household.

(8) In sub-paragraph (2)(a)(iii) and (b), references to a person being in receipt of a carer's allowance are to include references to a person who would have been in receipt of that allowance but for the application of a restriction under section 7 of the Social Security Fraud Act 2001 (loss of benefit provisions).

(9) In this paragraph—

"blind or severely sight impaired" means registered as blind or severely sight impaired in a register compiled by a local authority under section 29 of the National Assistance Act 1948 (welfare services) or, in Scotland, has been certified as blind and in consequence the person is registered as blind in a register maintained by or on behalf of a regional or island council and a person who has ceased to be registered as blind or severely sight impaired where that person's eyesight has been regained is, nevertheless, to be treated as blind or severely sight impaired for a period of 28 weeks following the date on which the person ceased to be so registered;

"the care component" means the care component of disability living allowance at the highest or middle rate prescribed in accordance with section 72(3) of the Contributions and Benefits Act.

Enhanced disability premium

9.389   **7.**—(1) Subject to sub-paragraph (2), the condition is that—

(a) the claimant's applicable amount includes the support component; or

(b) the care component of disability living allowance is, or would, but for a suspension of benefit in accordance with regulations under section 113(2) of the Contributions and Benefits Act or, but for an abatement as a consequence of hospitalisation, be payable at the highest rate prescribed under section 72(3) of that Act in respect of—

  (i) the claimant; or

  (ii) the claimant's partner (if any) who is aged less than the qualifying age for state pension credit.

(2) An enhanced disability premium is not applicable in respect of—

(a) a claimant who—

  (i) is not a member of a couple or a polygamous marriage; and

  (ii) is a patient within the meaning of regulation 69(2) and has been for a period of more than 52 weeks; or

(b) a member of a couple or a polygamous marriage where each member is a patient within the meaning of regulation 69(2) and has been for a period of more than 52 weeks.

Carer premium

9.390   **8.**—(1) Subject to sub-paragraphs (2) and (4), the condition is that the claimant or the claimant's partner is, or both of them are, entitled to a carer's allowance under section 70 of the Contributions and Benefits Act.

(2) Where a carer premium is awarded but—

(a) the person in respect of whose care the carer's allowance has been awarded dies; or

(b) in any other case the person in respect of whom a carer premium has been awarded ceases to be entitled to a carer's allowance, the condition for the award of the premium is to be treated as satisfied for a period of 8 weeks from the relevant date specified in sub-paragraph (3).

(3) The relevant date for the purposes of sub-paragraph (2) is—

(a) where sub-paragraph (2)(a) applies, the Sunday following the death of the person in respect of whose care a carer's allowance has been awarded or the date of death if the death occurred on a Sunday; or

(b) in any other case, the date on which the person who has been entitled to a carer's allowance ceases to be entitled to that allowance.

(4) Where a person who has been entitled to a carer's allowance ceases to be entitled to that allowance and makes a claim for an income-related allowance, the condition for the award of the carer premium is to be treated as satisfied for a period of 8 weeks from the date on which—

(a) the person in respect of whose care the carer's allowance has been awarded dies; or

(b) in any other case, the person who has been entitled to a carer's allowance ceased to be entitled to that allowance.

Persons in receipt of concessionary payments

9.391   **9.** For the purpose of determining whether a premium is applicable to a person under paragraphs 6, 7 and 8, any concessionary payment made to compensate that person for the non-payment of any benefit mentioned in those paragraphs is to be treated as if it were a payment of that benefit.

Persons in receipt of benefit

9.392   **10.** For the purposes of this Part of this Schedule, a person is to be regarded as being in receipt of any benefit if, and only if, it is paid in respect of the person and is to be so regarded only for any period in respect of which that benefit is paid.

PART 3

WEEKLY AMOUNT OF PREMIUMS SPECIFIED IN PART 2

11.—   **9.393**

Premium		Amount	
(1) Pensioner premium for a person to whom paragraph 5 applies who—	(1)		
(a) is a single claimant and—		(a)	
(i) is entitled to the work-related activity component;			(i) [⁴£40.20];
(ii) is entitled to the support component; or			(ii) [⁴£34.85];
(iii) is not entitled to either of those components;			(iii) [⁴£65.70];
(b) is a member of a couple and—		(b)	
(i) is entitled to the work-related activity component;			(i) [⁴£72.00];
(ii) is entitled to the support component; or			(ii) [⁴£66.65];
(iii) is not entitled to either of those components.			(iii) [⁴£97.50];
(2) Severe disability premium—	(2)		
(a) where the claimant satisfies the condition in paragraph 6(2)(a);		(a)	[⁴£52.85];
(b) where the claimant satisfies the condition in paragraph 6(2)(b)—		(b)	
(i) if there is someone in receipt of a carer's allowance or if the person or any partner satisfies that condition only by virtue of paragraph 6(5);			(i) [⁴£52.85];
(ii) if no-one is in receipt of such an allowance.			(ii) [⁴£105.70].
(3) Carer premium.	(3)		[⁴£29.50] in respect of each person who satisfies the condition specified in [¹ paragraph 8(1)].
(4) Enhanced disability premium where the conditions in paragraph 7 are satisfied.	(4)(a)		[⁴£13.40] in respect of each person who is neither—
			(i) a child or young person; nor
			(ii) a member of a couple or a polygamous marriage, in respect of whom the conditions specified in paragraph 7 are satisfied;
	(b)		[⁴£19.30] where the claimant is a member of a couple or a polygamous marriage and the conditions specified in [¹ paragraph 7] are satisfied in respect of a member of that couple or polygamous marriage.

Regulation 67(3)

PART 4

THE COMPONENTS

12. The amount of the work-related activity component is £24.00.   **9.394**

13. The amount of the support component is £29.00.

AMENDMENTS

1. Employment and Support Allowance (Miscellaneous Amendments) Regulations 2008 (SI 2008/2428), reg.14 (October 27, 2008).

2. Social Security (Miscellaneous Amendments) Regulations 2009 (SI 2009/583), reg.10(2) (April 6, 2009).

3. Social Security Benefits Up-rating Order 2009 (SI 2009/497), art.27(2) and Sch.18 (April 6, 2009).

4. Social Security Benefits Up-rating Order 2009 (SI 2009/497), art.27(3) and Sch.19 (April 6, 2009).

GENERAL NOTE

9.395 See the commentary to reg.67 and to Sch.2 to the IS Regs. The work-related activity component and the support component are specific to income-related ESA. The amounts of those components are prescribed in paras 12 and 13 respectively.

Regulation 69

SCHEDULE 5

SPECIAL CASES

PART 1

AMOUNTS PRESCRIBED FOR THE PURPOSES OF SECTION 4(2) OF THE ACT

Claimants without accommodation

9.396 1. A claimant who is without accommodation.

1. The amount applicable to the claimant under regulation 67(1)(a).

Members of religious orders

9.397 2. A claimant who is a member of, and fully maintained by, a religious order.

2. Nil.

Prisoners

9.398 3. A claimant
(a) except where sub-paragraph (b) applies, who is a prisoner;
(b) who is detained in custody pending trial or sentence following conviction by a court.

3.
(a) Nil;
(b) only such amount, if any, as may be applicable under regulation 67(1)(c) and the amount of nil under regulation 67(3).

Specified cases of temporarily separated couples

9.399 4. A claimant who is a member of a couple and who is temporarily separated from the claimant's partner where—
(a) one member of the couple is—
(i) not a patient but is residing in a care home, an Abbeyfield Home or an independent hospital; or

4. Either—
(a) the amount applicable to the claimant as a member of a couple under regulation 67(1); or

    (ii) resident in premises used for the rehabilitation of alcoholics or drug addicts; or

   (iii) resident in accommodation provided under section 3 of and Part 2 of the Schedule to, the Polish Resettlement Act 1947 (provision of accommodation in camps); or

   (iv) participating in arrangements for training made under section 2 of the Employment and Training Act 1973 or section 2 of the Enterprise and New Towns (Scotland) Act 1990 or attending a course at an employment rehabilitation centre established under that section of the 1973 Act, where the course requires the person to live away from the dwelling occupied as the home; or

    (v) in a probation or bail hostel approved for the purpose by the Secretary of State; and

(b)   the other member of the couple is—

    (i) living in the dwelling occupied as the home; or

   (ii) a patient; or

  (iii) residing in a care home, an Abbeyfield Home or an independent hospital.

(b)   the aggregate of the claimant's applicable amount and that of the claimant's partner assessed under the provisions of these Regulations as if each of them were a single claimant or a lone parent, whichever is the greater.

Polygamous marriages where one or more partners are temporarily separated

5. A claimant who is a member of a polygamous marriage and who is temporarily separated from a partner, where one of them is living in the home where the other member is—

  (a) not a patient but is residing in a care home, an Abbeyfield Home or an independent hospital; or

  (b) resident in premises used for the rehabilitation of alcoholics or drug addicts; or

  (c) attending a course of training or instruction provided or approved by the Secretary of State where the course requires the person to live away from home; or

  (d) in a probation or bail hostel approved for the purpose by the Secretary of State.

5. Either—

  (a) the amount applicable to the members of the polygamous marriage under regulation 68; or

  (b) the aggregate of the amount applicable for the members of the polygamous marriage who remain in the home under regulation 68 and the amount applicable in respect of those members not in the home calculated as if each of them were a single claimant or a lone parent, whichever is the greater.

9.400

Couple where one member is abroad

9.401   6. Subject to paragraph 7, a claimant who is a member of a couple where one member of the couple is temporarily absent from the United Kingdom.

6. For the first 4 weeks of that absence, the amount applicable to them as a couple under regulation 67(1) or 69, as the case may be, and thereafter, the amount applicable to the claimant in Great Britain under regulation 67(1) or 69, as the case may be, as if the claimant were a single claimant or, as the case may be, lone parent.

Couple or member of couple taking child or young person abroad for treatment

9.402   7.— (1) A claimant who is a member of a couple where either—
     (a) the claimant or the claimant's partner is; or
     (b) both the claimant and the claimant's partner are, absent from the United Kingdom in the circumstances specified in
   (2) sub-paragraph (2).
     For the purposes of sub-paragraph (1) the
     (a) specified circumstances are—
in respect of a claimant, those in regulation 153(1)(a), (b), (c)(ii), (d) and (e);
     (b) in respect of a claimant's partner, as if regulation 153(1)(a), (b), (c)(ii), (d) and (e) applied to that partner.

7. For the first 26 weeks of that absence, the amount applicable to the claimant under regulation 67(1) or 69, as the case may be and, thereafter, if the claimant is in Great Britain the amount applicable to the claimant under regulation 67(1) or 69, as the case may be, as if the claimant were a single claimant or, as the case may be, a lone parent.

Polygamous marriages where any member is abroad

9.403   8. Subject to paragraph 9, a claimant who is a member of a polygamous marriage where one or more members of the marriage are temporarily absent from the United Kingdom.

8. For the first 4 weeks of that absence, the amount applicable to the claimant under regulation 68 and 69, as the case may be, and thereafter, if the claimant is in Great Britain the amount applicable to the claimant under regulations 68 and 69, as the case may be, as if any members of the polygamous marriage not in the United Kingdom were not a member of the marriage.

Polygamous marriage: taking child or young person abroad for treatment

9.404   9.—(1) A claimant who is a member of a polygamous marriage where one or more members of the marriage is absent from the United Kingdom in the circumstances specified in sub- paragraph (2).
   (2) For the purposes of sub-paragraph (1) the specified circumstances are—
     (a) in respect of a claimant, those in regulation 153(1)(a), (b), (c)(ii), (d) and (e);
     (b) in respect of a claimant's partner or part-ners, as the case may be, as if regulation 153(1)(a), (b), (c)(ii), (d) and (e) applied to that partner or those [¹ partners].

9. For the first 26 weeks of that absence, the amount applicable to the claimant under regulations 68 and 69, as the case may be, and thereafter, if the claimant is in Great Britain the amount applicable to the claimant under regulations 68 and 69, as the case may be, as if any member of the polygamous marriage not in the United Kingdom were not a member of the marriage.

Partner of a person subject to immigration control

10.

   (a) A claimant who is the partner of a person subject to immigration control.

   (b) Where regulation 68 (polygamous marriages) applies and the claimant is a person—

   (i) who is not subject to immigration control within the meaning of section 115(9) of the Immigration and Asylum Act; or

   (ii) to whom section 115 of that Act does not apply by virtue of regulation 2 of the Social Security (Immigration and Asylum) Consequential Amendments Regulations 2000; and

   (iii) who is a member of a couple and one or more of the person's partners is subject to immigration control within the meaning of section 115(9) of that Act and section 115 of that Act applies to that partner or those partners for the purposes of exclusion from entitlement to income-related allowance.

10.

   (a) The amount applicable in respect of the claimant only under regulation 67(1)(a) any amount which may be applicable to
the claimant under regulation 67(1)(b) plus the amount applicable to the claimant under regulation 67(1)(c) or, as the case may be, regulation 69.

   (b) the amount determined in accordance with that regulation or regulation 69 in respect of the claimant and any partners of the claimant who are not subject to immigration control within the meaning of section 115(9) of the Immigration and Asylum Act and to whom section 115 of that Act does not apply for the purposes of exclusion from entitlement to an income-related allowance.

9.405

Person from abroad

11. Person from abroad.

11.

Nil.

9.406

PART 2

AMOUNTS PRESCRIBED FOR THE PURPOSES OF SECTIONS 2(1) AND 4(2) OF THE ACT

Patients

12. A claimant who is detained, or liable to be detained under—

(a) section 45A of the Mental Health Act 1983 (hospital and limitation directions) or section 59A of the Criminal Procedure (Scotland) Act 1995 (hospital directions); or

(b) section 47 of the Mental Health Act 1983 (removal to hospital of persons serving sentences of imprisonment, etc.) or section

12. The amount applicable under regulation 67(2) and the amount of nil under regulation 67(3).

9.407

136 of the Mental Health (Care and Treatment) (Scotland) Act 2003 (transfer of prisoners for treatment for mental disorder),

but not if the detention continues after the date which the Secretary of State certifies or Scottish Ministers certify would have been the earliest date on which the claimant could have been released in respect of, or from, the prison sentence if the claimant had not been detained in hospital.

9.408

13. Subject to paragraph 12, a single claimant who has been a patient for a continuous period of more than 52 weeks or, where the claimant is one of a couple, the other member of the couple has been a patient for a continuous period of more than 52 weeks.

13. The amounts applicable under regulation 67(1)(a), (c) and (2) and the amount of nil under regulation 67(3).

Person in hardship

9.409

14. A claimant who is a person in hardship.

14. The amount to which the claimant is entitled under regulation 67(1)(a) and (2) or 68(1)(a) is to be reduced by 20%.

AMENDMENT

1. Employment and Support Allowance (Miscellaneous Amendments) Regulations 2008 (SI 2008/2428), reg.15 (October 27, 2008).

GENERAL NOTE

9.410

See the commentary to reg.67 and to Sch.7 to the IS Regs.

Regulations 67(1)(c) , 68[[1]](1)](d)

SCHEDULE 6

HOUSING COSTS

Housing costs

9.411

1.—(1) Subject to the following provisions of this Schedule, the housing costs applicable to a claimant are those costs—
  (a) which the claimant or, where the claimant has a partner, that partner is, in accordance with paragraph 4, liable to meet in respect of the dwelling occupied as the home which the claimant or that claimant's partner is treated as occupying; and
  (b) which qualify under paragraphs 16 to 18.
(2) In this Schedule—
"existing housing costs" means housing costs arising under an agreement entered into before 2nd October 1995, or under an agreement entered into after 1st October 1995 ("the new agreement")—
  (a) which replaces an existing agreement, provided that the person liable to meet the housing costs—
    (i) remains the same in both agreements; or
    (ii) where in either agreement more than one person is liable to meet the housing costs, the person is liable to meet the housing costs in both the existing agreement and the new agreement;

(b) where the existing agreement was entered into before 2nd October 1995; and
(c) which is for a loan of the same amount as, or less than the amount of, the loan under the agreement it replaces, and for this purpose any amount payable to arrange the new agreement and included in the loan must be disregarded;

"housing costs" means those costs to which sub-paragraph (1) refers;

"new housing costs" means housing costs arising under an agreement entered into after 1st October 1995 other than an agreement referred to in the definition of "existing housing costs";

"standard rate" means the rate for the time being determined in accordance with paragraph 13.

(3) For the purposes of this Schedule a disabled person is a person—
(a) in respect of whom the main phase employment and support allowance is payable to the claimant or to a person living with the claimant;
(b) who, had that person in fact been entitled to income support, would have satisfied the requirements of paragraph 12 of Schedule 2 to the Income Support Regulations (additional condition for the disability premium);
(c) aged 75 or over; or
(d) who is disabled or severely disabled for the purposes of section 9(6) of the Tax Credits Act (maximum rate).

(4) For the purposes of sub-paragraph (3), a person will not cease to be a disabled person on account of that person being disqualified for receiving benefit or treated as not having limited capability for work by virtue of the operation of section 18(1) to (3) of the Act.

Remunerative work

2.—(1) Subject to [¹sub-paragraphs (2) to (8)], a [¹non-dependant (referred to in this paragraph as "person")] is to be treated for the purposes of this Schedule as engaged in remunerative work if that person is engaged, or, where the person's hours of work fluctuate, is engaged on average, for not less than 16 hours a week, being work for which payment is made or which is done in expectation of payment.   **9.412**

(2) Subject to sub-paragraph (3), in determining the number of hours for which a person is engaged in work where that person's hours of work fluctuate, regard is to be had to the average of hours worked over—
(a) if there is a recognisable cycle of work, the period of one complete cycle (including, where the cycle involves periods in which the person does no work, those periods but disregarding any other absences);
(b) in any other case, the period of 5 weeks immediately prior to the date of claim, or such other length of time as may, in the particular case, enable the person's weekly average hours of work to be determined more accurately.

(3) Where no recognisable cycle has been established in respect of a person's work, regard is to be had to the number of hours or, where those hours will fluctuate, the average of the hours, which that person is expected to work in a week.

(4) A person is to be treated as engaged in remunerative work during any period for which that person is absent from work referred to in sub-paragraph (1) if the absence is either without good cause or by reason of a recognised, customary or other holiday.

(5) A person is not to be treated as engaged in remunerative work on any day on which the person is on maternity leave, paternity leave or adoption leave or is absent from work because the person is ill.

(6) For the purposes of this paragraph, in determining the number of hours in which a person is engaged or treated as engaged in remunerative work, no account is to be taken of any hours in which the person is engaged in an employment or a scheme to which regulation 43(1) (circumstances under which partners of persons entitled to an income-related allowance are not to be treated as engaged in remunerative work) applies.

(7) For the purposes of sub-paragraphs (1) and (2), in determining the number of hours for which a person is engaged in work, that number is to include any time allowed to that person by that person's employer for a meal or for refreshment, but only where that person is, or expects to be, paid earnings in respect of that time.

[¹(8) A person is to be treated as not being engaged in remunerative work on any day in which that person falls within the circumstances prescribed in regulation 43(2) (circumstances in which partners of claimants entitled to an income-related allowance are not to be treated as engaged in remunerative work).

(9) Whether a claimant or the claimant's partner is engaged in, or to be treated as being engaged in, remunerative work is to be determined in accordance with regulations 41 or 42

(meaning of "remunerative work" for the purposes of paragraph 6(1)(e) and (f) of Schedule 1 to the Act) as the case may be.]

Previous entitlement to other income-related benefits

9.413   **3.**—(1) Where the claimant or the claimant's partner was in receipt of, or was treated as being in receipt of, an income-based jobseeker's allowance or income support not more than 12 weeks before one of them becomes entitled to an income-related allowance or, where the claimant or the claimant's partner is a person to whom paragraph 15(2) or (13) (linking rules) refers, not more than 26 weeks before becoming so entitled and—

(a) the applicable amount for that income-based jobseeker's allowance or income support included an amount in respect of housing costs under paragraphs 14 to 16 of Schedule 2 to the Jobseeker's Allowance Regulations or, as the case may be, paragraphs 15 to 17 of Schedule 3 to the Income Support Regulations; and

(b) the circumstances affecting the calculation of those housing costs remain unchanged since the last calculation of those costs,

the applicable amount in respect of housing costs for an income-related allowance is to be the applicable amount in respect of those costs current when entitlement to an income-based jobseeker's allowance or income support was last determined.

(2) Where a claimant or the claimant's partner was in receipt of state pension credit not more than 12 weeks before one of them becomes entitled to [¹an income-related allowance] or, where the claimant or the claimant's partner is a person to whom paragraph 15(2) or (13) (linking rules) refers, not more than 26 weeks before becoming so entitled, and—

(a) the appropriate minimum guarantee included an amount in respect of housing costs under paragraphs 11 to 13 of Schedule 2 to the State Pension Credit Regulations 2002; and

(b) the circumstances affecting the calculation of those housing costs remain unchanged since the last calculation of those costs,

the applicable amount in respect of housing costs for an income-related allowance is to be the applicable amount in respect of those costs current when entitlement to state pension credit was last determined.

(3) Where, in the period since housing costs were last calculated for an income-based jobseeker's allowance, income support or, as the case may be, state pension credit, there has been a change of circumstances, other than a reduction in the amount of an outstanding loan, which increases or reduces those costs, the amount to be met under this Schedule must, for the purposes of the claim for an income-related allowance, be recalculated so as to take account of that change.

Circumstances in which a person is liable to meet housing costs

9.414   **4.** A person is liable to meet housing costs where—

(a) the liability falls upon that person or that person's partner but not where the liability is to a member of the same household as the person on whom the liability falls;

(b) because the person liable to meet the housing costs is not meeting them, the claimant has to meet those costs in order to continue to live in the dwelling occupied as the home and it is reasonable in all the circumstances to treat the claimant as liable to meet those costs;

(c) in practice the claimant shares the housing costs with other members of the household none of whom are close relatives either of the claimant or the claimant's partner, and—

(i) one or more of those members is liable to meet those costs; and

(ii) it is reasonable in the circumstances to treat the claimant as sharing responsibility.

Circumstances in which a person is to be treated as occupying a dwelling as the home

9.415   **5.**—(1) Subject to the following provisions of this paragraph, a person is to be treated as occupying as the home the dwelling normally occupied as the home by that person or, if that person is a member of a family, by that person and that person's family and that person is not to be treated as occupying any other dwelling as the home.

(2) In determining whether a dwelling is the dwelling normally occupied as the claimant's home for the purposes of sub-paragraph (1) regard must be had to any other dwelling occu-

pied by the claimant or by the claimant and that claimant's family whether or not that other dwelling is in Great Britain.

(3) Subject to sub-paragraph (4), where a claimant who has no partner is a full-time student or is on a training course and is liable to make payments (including payments of mortgage interest or, in Scotland, payments under heritable securities or, in either case, analogous payments) in respect of either (but not both) the dwelling which that claimant occupies for the purpose of attending the course of study or the training course or, as the case may be, the dwelling which that claimant occupies when not attending that course, that claimant is to be treated as occupying as the home the dwelling in respect of which that claimant is liable to make payments.

(4) A full-time student is not to be treated as occupying a dwelling as that student's home for any week of absence from it, other than an absence occasioned by the need to enter hospital for treatment, outside the period of study, if the main purposes of that student's occupation during the period of study would be to facilitate attendance on that student's course.

(5) Where a claimant has been required to move into temporary accommodation by reason of essential repairs being carried out to the dwelling normally occupied as the home and that claimant is liable to make payments (including payments of mortgage interest or, in Scotland, payments under heritable securities or, in either case, analogous payments) in respect of either (but not both) the dwelling normally occupied or the temporary accommodation, that claimant must be treated as occupying as the home the dwelling in respect of which that claimant is liable to make those payments.

(6) Where a claimant is liable to make payments in respect of two (but not more than two) dwellings, that claimant must be treated as occupying both dwellings as the home only—

(a) where that claimant has left and remains absent from the former dwelling occupied as the home through fear of violence in that dwelling or of violence by a former member of the claimant's family and it is reasonable that housing costs should be met in respect of both that claimant's former dwelling and that claimant's present dwelling occupied as the home;

(b) in the case of a couple or a member of a polygamous marriage where a partner is a fulltime student or is on a training course and it is unavoidable that that student, or they, should occupy two separate dwellings and reasonable that housing costs should be met in respect of both dwellings; or

(c) in the case where a claimant has moved into a new dwelling occupied as the home, except where sub-paragraph (5) applies, for a period not exceeding four benefit weeks from the first day of the benefit week in which the move occurs if that claimant's liability to make payments in respect of two dwellings is unavoidable.

(7) Where—

(a) a claimant has moved into a dwelling and was liable to make payments in respect of that dwelling before moving in;

(b) that claimant had claimed an income-related allowance before moving in and either that claim has not yet been determined or it has been determined but an amount has not been included under this Schedule and if the claim has been refused a further claim has been made within four weeks of the date on which the claimant moved into the new dwelling occupied as the home; and

(c) the delay in moving into the dwelling in respect of which there was liability to make payments before moving in was reasonable and—

    (i) that delay was necessary in order to adapt the dwelling to meet the disablement needs of the claimant or any member of the claimant's family;

    (ii) the move was delayed pending the outcome of an application for a social fund payment under Part 8 of the Contributions and Benefits Act to meet a need arising out of the move or in connection with setting up the home in the dwelling, and—

        (aa) a member of the claimant's family is aged five or under;

        (bb) the claimant is a person in respect of whom the main phase employment and support allowance is payable;

        (cc) the claimant's applicable amount includes a pensioner premium;

        (dd) the claimant's applicable amount includes a severe disability premium; or

        (ee) a child tax credit is paid for a member of the claimant's family who is disabled or severely disabled for the purposes of section 9(6) of the Tax Credits Act; or

    (iii) the claimant became liable to make payments in respect of the dwelling while that claimant was a patient or was in residential accommodation, that claimant is to be treated as occupying the dwelling as the home for any period not exceeding four weeks immediately prior to the date on which that claimant moved into the dwelling and in respect of which that claimant was liable to make payments.

(8) This sub-paragraph applies to a claimant who enters residential accommodation—

(a) for the purpose of ascertaining whether the accommodation suits that claimant's needs; and

(b) with the intention of returning to the dwelling which that claimant normally occupies as the home should, in the event, the residential accommodation prove not to suit that claimant's needs,

and while in the accommodation, the part of the dwelling which that claimant normally occupies as the home is not let or sub-let to another person.

(9) A claimant to whom sub-paragraph (8) applies is to be treated as occupying the dwelling that the claimant normally occupies as the home during any period (commencing on the day that claimant enters the accommodation) not exceeding 13 weeks in which the claimant is resident in the accommodation, but only in so far as the total absence from the dwelling does not exceed 52 weeks.

(10) A claimant, other than a claimant to whom sub-paragraph (11) applies, is to be treated as occupying a dwelling as the home throughout any period of absence not exceeding 13 weeks, if, and only if—

(a) that claimant intends to return to occupy the dwelling as the home;

(b) the part of the dwelling normally occupied by that claimant has not been let or sub-let to another person; and

(c) the period of absence is unlikely to exceed 13 weeks.

(11) This sub-paragraph applies to a claimant whose absence from the dwelling that that claimant normally occupies as the home is temporary and—

(a) that claimant intends to return to occupy the dwelling as the home;

(b) the part of the dwelling normally occupied by that claimant has not been let or sub-let; and

(c) that claimant is—

    (i) detained in custody on remand pending trial or, as a condition of bail, required to reside—

        (aa) in a dwelling other than the dwelling that claimant occupies as the home; or

        (bb) in premises approved under section 13 of the Offender Management Act 2007,

    or, detained pending sentence upon conviction;

    (ii) resident in a hospital or similar institution as a patient;

    (iii) undergoing or, as the case may be, that claimant's partner or dependant child is undergoing, in the United Kingdom or elsewhere, medical treatment or medically approved convalescence, in accommodation other than residential accommodation;

    (iv) following, in the United Kingdom or elsewhere, a training course;

    (v) undertaking medically approved care of a person residing in the United Kingdom or elsewhere;

    (vi) undertaking the care of a child whose parent or guardian is temporarily absent from the dwelling normally occupied by that parent or guardian for the purpose of receiving medically approved care or medical treatment;

    (vii) a claimant who is, whether in the United Kingdom or elsewhere, receiving medically approved care provided in accommodation other than residential accommodation;

    (viii) a full-time student to whom sub-paragraph (3) or (6)(b) does not apply;

    (ix) a claimant other than a claimant to whom sub-paragraph (8) applies, who is receiving care provided in residential accommodation; or

    (x) a claimant to whom sub-paragraph (6)(a) does not apply and who has left the dwelling that claimant occupies as the home through fear of violence in that dwelling, or by a person who was formerly a member of that claimant's family; and

(d) the period of that claimant's absence is unlikely to exceed a period of 52 weeks, or in exceptional circumstances, is unlikely substantially to exceed that period.

(12) A claimant to whom sub-paragraph (11) applies is to be treated as occupying the dwelling that claimant normally occupies as the home during any period of absence not exceeding 52 weeks beginning with the first day of that absence.

(13) In this paragraph—

"medically approved" means certified by a medical practitioner;

"patient" means a person who is undergoing medical or other treatment as an in-patient in a hospital or similar institution;

"residential accommodation" means accommodation which is a care home, an Abbeyfield Home or an independent hospital;

"training course" means such a course of training or instruction provided wholly or partly by or on behalf of or in pursuance of arrangements made with, or approved by or on behalf of, Scottish Enterprise, Highlands and Islands Enterprise, a government department or the Secretary of State.

Housing costs not met

6.—(1) No amount may be met under the provisions of this Schedule— **9.416**
  (a) in respect of housing benefit expenditure; or
  (b) where the claimant is living in a care home, an Abbeyfield Home or an independent hospital except where the claimant is living in such a home or hospital during a temporary absence from the dwelling the claimant occupies as the home and in so far as they relate to temporary absences, the provisions of paragraph 5(8) to (12) apply to that claimant during that absence.

(2) Subject to the following provisions of this paragraph, loans which, apart from this paragraph, qualify under paragraph 16 (loans on residential property) must not so qualify where the loan was incurred during the relevant period and was incurred—
  (a) after 27th October 2008; or
  [¹(b) after 2nd May 1994 and the housing costs applicable to that loan were not met by virtue of the former paragraph 5A of Schedule 3 to the Income Support Regulations, or paragraph 4(2)(a) of Schedule 3 to the Income Support Regulations, paragraph 4(2)(a) of Schedule 2 to the Jobseeker's Allowance Regulations or paragraph 5(2)(a) of Schedule 2 to the State Pension Credit Regulations]; or
  (c) subject to sub-paragraph (3), in the 26 weeks preceding 27th October 2008 by a person—
     (i) who was not at that time entitled to income support, income-based jobseeker's allowance or state pension credit; and
    (ii) who becomes, or whose partner becomes entitled to an income-related allowance after 27th October 2008 and that entitlement is within 26 weeks of an earlier entitlement to income support, an income-based jobseeker's allowance or state pension credit of the claimant or the claimant's partner.

(3) Sub-paragraph (2)(c) will not apply in respect of a loan where the claimant has interest payments on that loan met without restrictions under an award of income support in respect of a period commencing before 27th October 2008.

(4) The "relevant period" for the purposes of this paragraph is any period during which the person to whom the loan was made—
  (a) is entitled to an income-related allowance, an income-based jobseeker's allowance, income support or state pension credit; or
  (b) has a partner and the partner is entitled to an income-related allowance, an income-based jobseeker's allowance, income support or state pension credit,
together with any linked period, that is to say a period falling between two periods separated by not more than 26 weeks in which one of the paragraphs (a) or (b) is satisfied.

(5) For the purposes of sub-paragraph (4), a person is to be treated as entitled to an income-related allowance during any period when that person or that person's partner was not so entitled because—
  (a) that person or that person's partner was participating in an employment programme specified in regulation 75(1)(a)(ii) of the Jobseeker's Allowance Regulations or in the Intensive Activity Period specified in regulation 75(1)(a)(iv) of those Regulations; and
  (b) in consequence of such participation that person or that person's partner was engaged in remunerative work or had an income in excess of the claimant's applicable amount as prescribed in Part 9.

(6) A person treated by virtue of paragraph 15 as being in receipt of an income-related allowance for the purposes of this Schedule is not to be treated as entitled to an income-related allowance for the purposes of sub-paragraph (4).

(7) For the purposes of sub-paragraph (4)—
  (a) any week in the period of 26 weeks ending on 1st October 1995 on which there arose an entitlement to income support such as is mentioned in that sub-paragraph must be taken into account in determining when the relevant period commences; and

(b) two or more periods of entitlement and any intervening linked periods must together form a single relevant period.

(8) Where the loan to which sub-paragraph (2) refers has been applied—

(a) for paying off an earlier loan, and that earlier loan qualified under paragraph 16 during the relevant period; or

(b) to finance the purchase of a property where an earlier loan, which qualified under paragraph 16 or 17 during the relevant period in respect of another property, is paid off (in whole or in part) with monies received from the sale of that property,

then the amount of the loan to which sub-paragraph (2) applies is the amount (if any) by which the new loan exceeds the earlier loan.

(9) Notwithstanding the preceding provisions of this paragraph, housing costs must be met in any case where a claimant satisfies any of the conditions specified in sub-paragraphs (10) to (13), but—

(a) those costs must be subject to any additional limitations imposed by the sub-paragraph; and

(b) where the claimant satisfies the conditions in more than one of these sub-paragraphs, only one of them will apply in that claimant's case and the one that applies will be the one most favourable to the claimant.

(10) The conditions specified in this sub-paragraph are that—

(a) during the relevant period the claimant or a member of the claimant's family acquires an interest ("the relevant interest") in a dwelling which that claimant then occupies or continues to occupy, as the home; and

(b) in the week preceding the week in which the relevant interest was acquired, housing benefit was payable to the claimant or a member of the claimant's family,

so however that the amount to be met by way of housing costs will initially not exceed the aggregate of—

(i) the housing benefit payable in the week mentioned at sub-paragraph (10)(b); and

(ii) any amount included in the applicable amount of the claimant or a member of the claimant's family in accordance with regulation 67(1)(c) or 68(1)(d) in that week,

and is to be increased subsequently only to the extent that it is necessary to take account of any increase, arising after the date of the acquisition, in the standard rate or in any housing costs which qualify under paragraph 18 (other housing costs).

(11) The condition specified in this sub-paragraph is that the loan was taken out, or an existing loan increased, to acquire alternative accommodation more suited to the special needs of a disabled person than the accommodation which was occupied before the acquisition by the claimant.

(12) The conditions specified in this sub-paragraph are that—

(a) the loan commitment increased in consequence of the disposal of the dwelling occupied as the home and the acquisition of an alternative such dwelling; and

(b) the change of dwelling was made solely by reason of the need to provide separate sleeping accommodation for [¹persons of different sexes aged 10 or over but aged under 20] who belong to the same family as the claimant.

(13) The conditions specified in this sub-paragraph are that—

(a) during the relevant period the claimant or a member of the claimant's family acquires an interest ("the relevant interest") in a dwelling which that claimant then occupies as the home; and

(b) in the week preceding the week in which the relevant interest was acquired, the applicable amount of the claimant or a member of the claimant's family included an amount determined by reference to paragraph 18 and did not include any amount specified in paragraph 16 or paragraph 17,

so however that the amount to be met by way of housing costs will initially not exceed the amount so determined, and will be increased subsequently only to the extent that it is necessary to take account of any increase, arising after the date of acquisition, in the standard rate or in any housing costs which qualify under paragraph 18.

(14) The following provisions of this Schedule will have effect subject to the provisions of this paragraph.

Apportionment of housing costs

9.417   7.—(1) Where the dwelling occupied as the home is a composite hereditament and—

(a) before 1st April 1990 for the purposes of section 48(5) of the General Rate Act 1967 (reduction of rates on dwellings), it appeared to a rating authority or it was deter-

mined in pursuance of subsection (6) of section 48 of that Act that the hereditament, including the dwelling occupied as the home, was a mixed hereditament and that only a proportion of the rateable value of the hereditament was attributable to use for the purpose of a private dwelling; or
  (b) in Scotland, before 1st April 1989 an assessor acting pursuant to section 45(1) of the Water (Scotland) Act 1980 (provision as to valuation roll) has apportioned the net annual value of the premises including the dwelling occupied as the home between the part occupied as a dwelling and the remainder,
the amounts applicable under this Schedule are to be such proportion of the amounts applicable in respect of the hereditament or premises as a whole as is equal to the proportion of the rateable value of the hereditament attributable to the part of the hereditament used for the purposes of a private tenancy or, in Scotland, the proportion of the net annual value of the premises apportioned to the part occupied as a dwelling house.

(2) Subject to sub-paragraph (1) and the following provisions of this paragraph, where the dwelling occupied as the home is a composite hereditament, the amount applicable under this Schedule is to be the relevant fraction of the amount which would otherwise be applicable under this Schedule in respect of the dwelling occupied as the home.

(3) For the purposes of sub-paragraph (2), the relevant fraction is to be obtained in accordance with the formula—

$$\frac{A}{A+B}$$

where—
A is the current market value of the claimant's interest in that part of the composite hereditament which is domestic property within the meaning of section 66 of the Act of 1988;
B is the current market value of the claimant's interest in that part of the composite hereditament which is not domestic property within that section.

(4) In this paragraph—
"composite hereditament" means—
  (a) as respects England and Wales, any hereditament which is shown as a composite hereditament in a local non-domestic rating list;
  (b) as respects Scotland, any lands and heritages entered in the valuation roll which are part residential subjects within the meaning of section 26(1) of the Act of 1987;
"local non-domestic rating list" means a list compiled and maintained under section 41(1) of the Act of 1988;
"the Act of 1987" means the Abolition of Domestic Rates Etc. (Scotland) Act 1987;
"the Act of 1988" means the Local Government Finance Act 1988.

(5) Where responsibility for expenditure which relates to housing costs met under this Schedule is shared, the amounts applicable are to be calculated by reference to the appropriate proportion of that expenditure for which the claimant is responsible.

Existing housing costs

8.—(1) Subject to the provisions of this Schedule, the existing housing costs to be met in any particular case are—   **9.418**
  (a) where the claimant has been entitled to an employment and support allowance for a continuous period of 26 weeks or more, the aggregate of—
    (i) an amount determined in the manner set out in paragraph 11 by applying the standard rate to the eligible capital for the time being owing in connection with a loan which qualifies under paragraph 16 or 17; and
    (ii) an amount equal to any payments which qualify under paragraph 18(1)(a) to (c);
  (b) where the claimant has been entitled to an employment and support allowance for a continuous period of not less than 8 weeks but less than 26 weeks, an amount which is half the amount which would fall to be met by applying the provisions of sub-paragraph(a);
  (c) in any other case, nil.

(2) For the purposes of sub-paragraph (1) and subject to sub-paragraph (3), the eligible capital for the time being owing is to be determined on the date the existing housing costs are first met and thereafter on each anniversary of that date.

(3) Where a claimant or that claimant's partner ceases to be in receipt of or treated as being in receipt of income support, income-based jobseeker's allowance or state pension credit and one of them becomes entitled to an income-related allowance in a case to which paragraph 3

applies, the eligible capital for the time being owing is to be recalculated on each anniversary of the date on which the housing costs were first met for whichever of the benefits concerned the claimant or the claimant's partner was first entitled.

New housing costs

9.419

9.—(1) Subject to the provisions of this Schedule, the new housing costs to be met in any particular case are—

(a) where the claimant has been entitled to an employment and support allowance for a continuous period of 39 weeks or more, an amount—

(i) determined in the manner set out in paragraph 11 by applying the standard rate to the eligible capital for the time being owing in connection with a loan which qualifies under paragraph 16 or 17; and

(ii) equal to any payments which qualify under paragraph 18(1)(a) to (c);

(b) in any other case, nil.

(2) For the purposes of sub-paragraph (1) and subject to sub-paragraph (3), the eligible capital for the time being owing is to be determined on the date the new housing costs are first met and thereafter on each anniversary of that date.

(3) Where a claimant or that claimant's partner ceases to be in receipt of or treated as being in receipt of income support, income-based jobseeker's allowance or state pension credit and one of them becomes entitled to an income-related allowance in a case to which [¹paragraph 3] applies, the eligible capital for the time being owing is to be recalculated on each anniversary of the date on which the housing costs were first met for whichever of the benefits concerned the claimant or that claimant's partner was first entitled.

(4) This sub-paragraph applies to a claimant who at the time the claim is made—

(a) is a person who is described in paragraph 4 or 5 of Schedule 1B of the Income Support Regulations (person caring for another person);

(b) is detained in custody pending trial or sentence upon conviction; or

(c) has been refused payments under a policy of insurance on the ground that—

(i) the claim under the policy is the outcome of a pre-existing medical condition which, under the terms of the policy, does not give rise to any payment by the insurer; or

(ii) that claimant was infected by the Human Immunodeficiency Virus;

(iii) and the policy was taken out to insure against the risk of being unable to maintain repayments on a loan which is secured by a mortgage or a charge over land, or (in Scotland) by a heritable security.

(5) This sub-paragraph applies subject to sub-paragraph (7) where a person claims an income-related allowance because of—

(a) the death of a partner; or

(b) being abandoned by that claimant's partner,

and where that claimant's family includes a child.

(6) In the case of a claimant to whom sub-paragraph (4) or (5) applies, any new housing costs are to be met as though they were existing housing costs and paragraph 8 (existing housing costs) applied to them.

(7) Sub-paragraph (5) must cease to apply to a claimant who subsequently becomes one of a couple.

General exclusions from paragraphs 8 and 9

9.420

10.—(1) Paragraphs 8 and 9 will not apply where—

(a) the claimant's partner has attained the qualifying age for state pension credit;

(b) the housing costs are payments—

(i) under a co-ownership agreement;

(ii) under or relating to a tenancy or licence of a Crown tenant; or

(iii) where the dwelling occupied as the home is a tent, in respect of the tent and the site on which it stands.

(2) In a case falling within sub-paragraph (1), the housing costs to be met are—

(a) where paragraph (a) of sub-paragraph (1) applies, an amount—

(i) determined in the manner set out in paragraph 11 by applying the standard rate to the eligible capital for the time being owing in connection with a loan which qualifies under paragraph 16 or 17; and

(ii) equal to the payments which qualify under paragraph 18;

(b) where paragraph (b) of sub-paragraph (1) applies, an amount equal to the payments which qualify under paragraph 18(1)(d) to (f).

The calculation for loans

11. The weekly amount of existing housing costs or, as the case may be, new housing costs to be met under this Schedule in respect of a loan which qualifies under paragraph 16 or 17 are to be calculated by applying the formula— **9.421**

$$\frac{A \times B}{52}$$

where—

A = the amount of the loan which qualifies under paragraph 16 or 17; and

B = the standard rate for the time being applicable in respect of that loan.

General provisions applying to new and existing housing costs

12.—(1) Where on or after 2nd October 1995 a person enters into a new agreement in respect of a dwelling and an agreement entered into before 2nd October 1995 ("the earlier agreement") continues in force independently of the new agreement, then— **9.422**
  - (a) the housing costs applicable to the new agreement are to be calculated by reference to the provisions of paragraph 9 (new housing costs);
  - (b) the housing costs applicable to the earlier agreement are to be calculated by reference to the provisions of paragraph 8 (existing housing costs);
and the resulting amounts are to be aggregated.

(2) Sub-paragraph (1) does not apply in the case of a claimant to whom paragraph 10 applies.

(3) Where for the time being a loan exceeds, or in a case where more than one loan is to be taken into account, the aggregate of those loans exceeds the appropriate amount specified in sub-paragraph (4), then the amount of the loan or, as the case may be, the aggregate amount of those loans, will for the purposes of this Schedule, be the appropriate amount.

(4) Subject to the following provisions of this paragraph, the appropriate amount is £100,000.

(5) Where a claimant is treated under paragraph 5(6) (payments in respect of two dwellings) as occupying two dwellings as the home, then the restrictions imposed by sub-paragraph (3) are to be applied separately to the loans for each dwelling.

(6) In a case to which paragraph 7 (apportionment of housing costs) applies, the appropriate amount for the purposes of sub-paragraph (3) is to be the lower of—
  - (a) a sum determined by applying the formula—

$$P \times Q$$

where—

P = the relevant fraction for the purposes of paragraph 7; and

Q = the amount or, as the case may be, the aggregate amount for the time being of any loan or loans which qualify under this Schedule; or
  - (b) the sum for the time being specified in sub-paragraph (4).

(7) In a case to which paragraph 16(3) or 17(3) (loans which qualify in part only) applies, the appropriate amount for the purposes of sub-paragraph (3) is to be the lower of—
  - (a) a sum representing for the time being the part of the loan applied for the purposes specified in paragraph 16(1) or (as the case may be) paragraph 17(1); or
  - (b) the sum for the time being specified in sub-paragraph (4).

(8) In the case of any loan to which paragraph 17(2)(k) (loan taken out and used for the purpose of adapting a dwelling for the special needs of a disabled person) applies the whole of the loan, to the extent that it remains unpaid, is to be disregarded in determining whether the amount for the time being specified in sub-paragraph (4) is exceeded.

(9) Where in any case the amount for the time being specified for the purposes of sub-paragraph (4) is exceeded and there are two or more loans to be taken into account under either or both paragraphs 16 and 17, then the amount of eligible interest in respect of each of those loans to the extent that the loans remain outstanding is to be determined as if each loan had been reduced to a sum equal to the qualifying portion of that loan.

(10) For the purposes of sub-paragraph (9), the qualifying portion of a loan is to be determined by applying the following formula—

$$\frac{R \times S}{T}$$

where—

R = the amount for the time being specified for the purposes of sub-paragraph (3);

S = the amount of the outstanding loan to be taken into account; and

T = the aggregate of all outstanding loans to be taken into account under paragraphs 16 and 17.

[¹ (11) Sub-paragraph (12) applies to a person who, had the person been entitled to income support and not an employment and support allowance, would have been a person to whom any of the following transitional or savings provisions would have applied—

    (a) regulation 4 of the Income Support (General) Amendment No. 3 Regulations 1993 ("the 1993 Regulations");

    (b) regulation 28 of the Income-related Benefits Schemes (Miscellaneous Amendments) Regulations 1995 ("the 1995 Regulations").

(12) Where this sub-paragraph applies, the amount of housing costs applicable in the particular case shall be determined as if—

    (a) in a case to which regulation 4(1) of the 1993 Regulations would have applied, sub-paragraphs 12(4) to (9) do not apply;

    (b) in a case to which regulation 4(4) of the 1993 Regulation would have applied, the appropriate amount is £150,000; and

    (c) in a case to which the 1995 Regulations would have applied, the appropriate amount is £125,000.]

The standard rate

9.423   **13.**—(1) The standard rate is the rate of interest applicable per annum to a loan which qualifies under this Schedule.

[²(2) The standard rate is to be 6.08%.]

(3) [². . .].

Excessive Housing Costs

9.424   **14.**—(1) Housing costs which, apart from this paragraph, fall to be met under this Schedule are to be met only to the extent specified in sub-paragraph (3) where—

    (a) the dwelling occupied as the home, excluding any part which is let, is larger than is required by the claimant, that claimant's partner (if the claimant has a partner), any person under the age of 20 and any other non-dependants having regard, in particular, to suitable alternative accommodation occupied by a household of the same size; or

    (b) the immediate area in which the dwelling occupied as the home is located is more expensive than other areas in which suitable alternative accommodation exists; or

    (c) the outgoings of the dwelling occupied as the home which are met under paragraphs 16 to 18 are higher than the outgoings of suitable alternative accommodation in the area.

(2) For the purposes of paragraphs (a) to (c) of sub-paragraph (1), no regard is to be had to the capital value of the dwelling occupied as the home.

(3) Subject to the following provisions of this paragraph, the amount of the loan which falls to be met is to be restricted and the excess over the amounts which the claimant would need to obtain suitable alternative accommodation will not be allowed.

(4) Where, having regard to the relevant factors, it is not reasonable to expect the claimant and the claimant's partner to seek alternative cheaper accommodation, no restriction is to be made under sub-paragraph (3).

(5) In sub-paragraph (4) "the relevant factors" are—

    (a) the availability of suitable accommodation and the level of housing costs in the area; and

    (b) the circumstances of the claimant and those who live with the claimant, including, in particular, the age and state of health of any of those persons, the employment prospects of the claimant and, where a change in accommodation is likely to result in a change of school, the effect on the education of any person below the age of 20 who lives with the claimant.

(6) Where sub-paragraph (4) does not apply and the claimant or the claimant's partner was able to meet the financial commitments for the dwelling occupied as the home when these were entered into, no restriction is to be made under this paragraph during the 26 weeks immediately following the date on which—

    (a) the claimant became entitled to an income-related allowance where the claimant's housing costs fell within one of the cases in sub-paragraph (1) on that date; or

    (b) a decision took effect which was made under section 10 of the Social Security Act 1998 on the ground that the claimant's housing costs fell within one of the cases in sub-paragraph (1),

nor during the next 26 weeks if and so long as the best endeavours of the claimant are used to obtain cheaper accommodation.

(7) For the purposes of calculating any period of 26 weeks referred to in sub-paragraph (6), and for those purposes only, a person is to be treated as entitled to an income-related allowance for any period of 12 weeks or less in respect of which that person was not in receipt of an income-related allowance and which fell immediately between periods in respect of which that person was in receipt of that allowance.

(8) Any period in respect of which—

(a) an income-related allowance was paid to a claimant; and

(b) it was subsequently determined that such a claimant was not entitled to an income-related allowance for that period,

will be treated for the purposes of sub-paragraph (7) as a period in respect of which that claimant was not in receipt of an income-related allowance.

(9) Paragraphs (c) to (f) of sub-paragraph (1) of paragraph 15 will apply to sub-paragraph (7) as they apply to paragraphs 8 and 9 but with the modification that the words "Subject to sub-paragraph (2)" were omitted and references to "the claimant" were references to the person mentioned in sub-paragraph (7).

(10) References to an income-related allowance in sub-paragraphs (6) and (7) must be treated as including references to income support, income-based jobseeker's allowance and state pension credit in respect of any period which falls immediately before the appointed day.

Linking rule

15.—(1) Subject to sub-paragraph (2), for the purposes of this Schedule—   9.425

(a) a claimant is to be treated as being in receipt of an income-related allowance during the following periods—

(i) any period in respect of which it was subsequently determined that that claimant was entitled to an income-related allowance; and

(ii) any period of 12 weeks or less or, as the case may be, 52 weeks or less, in respect of which that claimant was not in receipt of an income-related allowance and which fell immediately between periods in respect of which—

(aa) that claimant was, or was treated as being, in receipt of an income-related allowance;

(bb) that claimant was treated as entitled to an income-related allowance for the purpose of sub-paragraph (9) or (10); or

(cc) (i) above applies;

(b) a claimant is to be treated as not being in receipt of an income-related allowance during any period other than a period to which (a)(ii) above applies in respect of which it is subsequently determined that that claimant was not so entitled;

(c) where—

(i) the claimant was a member of a couple or a polygamous marriage; and

(ii) the claimant's partner was, in respect of a past period, in receipt of an income-related allowance for that claimant's partner and the claimant; and

(iii) the claimant is no longer a member of that couple or polygamous marriage; and

(iv) the claimant made a claim for an income-related allowance within 12 weeks or, as the case may be, 52 weeks, of ceasing to be a member of that couple or polygamous marriage,

the claimant must be treated as having been in receipt of an income-related allowance for the same period as the claimant's former partner had been or had been treated, for the purposes of this Schedule, as having been;

(d) where the claimant's partner's applicable amount was determined in accordance with paragraph 1(1) (single claimant) or paragraph 1(2) (lone parents) of Part 1 of Schedule 4 (prescribed amounts) in respect of a past period, provided that the claim was made within 12 weeks or, as the case may be, 52 weeks, of the claimant and that claimant's partner becoming one of a couple or polygamous marriage, the claimant is to be treated as having been in receipt of an income-related allowance for the same period as the claimant's partner had been or had been treated, for the purposes of this Schedule, as having been;

(e) where the claimant is a member of a couple or a polygamous marriage and the claimant's partner was, in respect of a past period, in receipt of an income-related allowance for that claimant's partner and the claimant, and the claimant has begun to receive an income-related allowance as a result of an election by the members of the couple or polygamous marriage, that claimant is to be treated as having been in receipt of an income-related allowance for the same period as that claimant's partner had been or had been treated, for the purposes of this Schedule, as having been;

(f) where the claimant—

    (i) is a member of a couple or a polygamous marriage and the claimant's partner was, immediately before the participation by any member of that couple or polygamous marriage in an employment programme specified in regulation 75(1)(a)(ii) of the Jobseeker's Allowance Regulations, in the Intensive Activity Period specified in regulation 75(1)(a)(iv) of those Regulations, in receipt of an income-related allowance and the claimant's applicable amount included an amount for the couple or for the partners of the polygamous marriage; and

    (ii) has, immediately after that participation in that programme, begun to receive an income-related allowance as a result of an election under regulation 4(3) of the Social Security (Claims and Payments) Regulations 1987 by the members of the couple or polygamous marriage,

the claimant is to be treated as having been in receipt of an income-related allowance for the same period as that claimant's partner had been or had been treated, for the purposes of this Schedule, as having been;

(g) where—

    (i) the claimant was a member of a family of a person (not being a former partner) entitled to an income-related allowance and at least one other member of that family was a child or young person;

    (ii) the claimant becomes a member of another family which includes that child or young person; and

    (iii) the claimant made a claim for an income-related allowance within 12 weeks or, as the case may be, 52 weeks, of the date on which the person entitled to an income-related allowance mentioned in paragraph (i) above ceased to be so entitled,

the claimant is to be treated as being in receipt of an income-related allowance for the same period as that person had been or had been treated, for the purposes of this Schedule, as having been.

(2) Where a claimant, with the care of a child, has ceased to be in receipt of an income-related allowance in consequence of the payment of child support maintenance under the Child Support Act and immediately before ceasing to be so in receipt an amount determined in accordance with paragraph 8(1)(a)(i) or paragraph 9(1)(a)(i) was applicable to that claimant, then—

(a) if the child support maintenance assessment or, as the case may be, maintenance calculation concerned is terminated or replaced by a lower assessment or, as the case may be, calculation in consequence of the coming into force on or after 18th April 1995 of regulations made under the Child Support Act; or

(b) where the child support maintenance assessment or, as the case may be, maintenance calculation concerned is an interim maintenance assessment or, as the case may be, interim maintenance decision or default maintenance decision and, in circumstances other than those referred to in paragraph (a), it is terminated or replaced after termination by another interim maintenance assessment or, as the case may be, interim maintenance decision or default maintenance decision or by a maintenance assessment or, as the case may be, calculation made in accordance with Part 1 of Schedule 1 to the Child Support Act, in either case of a lower amount than the assessment or, as the case may be, calculation concerned,

sub-paragraph (1)(a)(ii) will apply to that claimant as if for the words "any period of 12 weeks or less" there were substituted the words "any period of 26 weeks or less".

(3) For the purposes of this Schedule, where a claimant has ceased to be entitled to an income-related allowance because that claimant or that claimant's partner is—

(a) participating in arrangements for training made under section 2 of the Employment and Training Act 1973 or section 2 of the Enterprise and New Towns (Scotland) Act 1990; or

(b) attending a course at an employment rehabilitation centre established under that section,

the claimant is to be treated as if that claimant had been in receipt of an income-related allowance for the period during which that claimant or that claimant's partner was participating in such arrangements or attending such a course.

(4) For the purposes of this Schedule, a claimant who has ceased to be entitled to an income-related allowance because—

(a) that claimant or that claimant's partner was participating in an employment programme specified in regulation 75(1)(a)(ii) of the Jobseeker's Allowance Regulations, in the Intensive Activity Period specified in regulation 75(1)(a)(iv) of those Regulations or in an employment zone scheme; and

  (b) in consequence of such participation the claimant or the claimant's partner was engaged in remunerative work or had an income in excess of the claimant's applicable amount as prescribed in Part 9,

will be treated as if the claimant had been in receipt of an income-related allowance for the period during which that claimant or that claimant's partner was participating in that programme or activity.

(5) Where, for the purposes of sub-paragraphs (1), (3) and (4), a claimant is treated as being in receipt of an income-related allowance, for a certain period, that claimant will, subject to sub-paragraph (6), be treated as being entitled to an income-related allowance for the same period.

(6) Where the appropriate amount of a loan exceeds the amount specified in paragraph 12(4), sub-paragraph (5) will not apply except—

  (a) for the purposes of paragraph 8(1) or 9(1); or

  (b) where a claimant has ceased to be in receipt of an income-related allowance for a period of 104 weeks or less because that claimant or that claimant's partner is a work or training beneficiary within the meaning of regulation 148 (work or training beneficiaries).

(7) For the purposes of this Schedule, in determining whether a claimant is entitled to or to be treated as entitled to an income-related allowance, entitlement to a contribution-based jobseeker's allowance immediately before a period during which that claimant or that claimant's partner is participating in an employment programme specified in regulation 75(1)(a)(ii) of the Jobseeker's Allowance Regulations, in the Intensive Activity Period specified in regulation 75(1)(a)(iv) of those Regulations is to be treated as entitlement to an income-related allowance for the purposes of any requirement that a claimant is, or has been, entitled to an income-related allowance for any period of time.

(8) For the purposes of this Schedule, sub-paragraph (9) applies where a claimant is not entitled to an income-related allowance by reason only that the claimant has—

  (a) capital exceeding £16,000; or

  (b) income exceeding the applicable amount which applies in that claimant's case; or

  (c) both capital exceeding £16,000 and income exceeding the applicable amount which applies in that claimant's case.

(9) A claimant to whom sub-paragraph (8) applies is to be treated as entitled to an income-related allowance throughout any period of not more than 39 weeks which comprises only days—

  (a) on which that claimant is entitled to a contributory allowance, a contribution-based jobseeker's allowance, statutory sick pay or incapacity benefit; or

  (b) on which that claimant is, although not entitled to any of the benefits mentioned in paragraph (a) above, entitled to be credited with earnings equal to the lower earnings limit for the time being in force in accordance with regulation 8A or 8B of the Social Security (Credits) Regulations 1975.

(10) Subject to sub-paragraph (11), a claimant to whom sub-paragraph (8) applies and who is either a lone parent or a person who is described in paragraph 4 or 5 of Schedule 1B of the Income Support Regulations (persons caring for another person) is, for the purposes of this Schedule, to be treated as entitled to an income-related allowance throughout any period of not more than 39 weeks following the refusal of a claim for an income-related allowance made by or on behalf of that claimant.

(11) Sub-paragraph (10) will not apply in relation to a claimant mentioned in that sub-paragraph who, during the period referred to in that sub-paragraph—

  (a) is engaged in, or is treated as engaged in, remunerative work or whose partner is engaged in, or is treated as engaged in, remunerative work;

  [¹(b) is in full-time education and in receipt of disability living allowance;]

  (c) is temporarily absent from Great Britain, other than in the circumstances specified in regulation 152 or 153(1)(c)(ii) (temporary absence from Great Britain).

(12) In a case where—

  (a) sub-paragraphs (9) and (10) apply solely by virtue of sub-paragraph (8)(b); and

  (b) the claimant's income includes payments under a policy taken out to insure against the risk that the policy holder is unable to meet any loan or payment which qualifies under paragraphs 16 to 18,

sub-paragraphs (9) and (10) will have effect as if for the words "throughout any period of not more than 39 weeks" there will be substituted the words "throughout any period that payments are made in accordance with the terms of the policy".

(13) This sub-paragraph applies—

(a) to a person who claims an income-related allowance, or in respect of whom an income-related allowance is claimed and who—

    (i) received payments under a policy of insurance taken out to insure against loss of employment, and those payments are exhausted; and

    (ii) had a previous award of an income-related allowance where the applicable amount included an amount by way of housing costs; and

(b) where the period in respect of which the previous award of an income-related allowance was payable ended not more than 26 weeks before the date the claim was made.

(14) Where sub-paragraph (13) applies, in determining—

(a) for the purposes of paragraph 8(1) whether a claimant has been entitled to an income-related allowance for a continuous period of 26 weeks or more; or

(b) for the purposes of paragraph 9(1) whether a claimant has been entitled to an income-related allowance for a continuous period of 39 weeks or more,

any week falling between the date of the termination of the previous award and the date of the new claim is to be ignored.

(15) In the case of a claimant who is a work or training beneficiary, the references in sub-paragraphs (1)(a)(ii), (1)(c)(iv), (1)(d) and (1)(g)(iii) to a period of 12 weeks is to be treated as references to a period of 104 weeks.

(16) For the purposes of sub-paragraph (1)(a)(ii), (1)(c)(iv), (1)(d) and (1)(g)(iii), the relevant period will be—

(a) 52 weeks in the case of a person to whom sub-paragraph (17) applies;

(b) subject to sub-paragraph (15), 12 weeks in any other case.

(17) This sub-paragraph applies, subject to sub-paragraph (18), in the case of a claimant who, on or after 27th October 2008, has ceased to be entitled to an income-related allowance because that claimant or that claimant's partner—

(a) has commenced employment as an employed earner or as a self-employed earner or has increased the hours in which that claimant or that claimant's partner is engaged in such employment;

(b) is taking active steps to establish that claimant or that claimant's partner in employment as an employed earner or as a self-employed earner under any scheme for assisting persons to become so employed which is mentioned in regulation 19(1)(r)(i) to (iii) of the Jobseeker's Allowance Regulations; or

(c) is participating in—

    (i) a New Deal option;

    (ii) an employment zone programme; or

    (iii) the self-employment route; or

    (iv) the Intensive Activity Period specified in regulation 75(1)(a)(iv) of the Jobseeker's Allowance Regulations,

and, as a consequence, that claimant or that claimant's partner was engaged in remunerative work or had income in excess of the applicable amount as prescribed in Part 9.

(18) Sub-paragraph (17) is only to apply to the extent that immediately before the day on which the claimant ceased to be entitled to an income-related allowance, that claimant's housing costs were being met in accordance with paragraph 8(1)(a), 8(1)(b) or 9(1)(a) or would have been so met but for any non-dependant deduction under paragraph 19.

(19) For the purpose of determining whether the linking rules set out in this paragraph apply in a case where a claimant's former partner was entitled to state pension credit, any reference to an income-related allowance in this Schedule is to be taken to include also a reference to state pension credit.

(20) Where a person is one to whom regulation 6(5) of the Income Support Regulations (persons not treated as engaged in remunerative work) applies, the period prescribed in paragraph (6) of that regulation is not to be included for the purposes of any linking rule or for determining whether any qualifying or other period is satisfied.

Loans on residential property

9.426   **16.**—(1) A loan qualifies under this paragraph where the loan was taken out to defray monies applied for any of the following purposes—

(a) acquiring an interest in the dwelling occupied as the home; or

(b) paying off another loan to the extent that the other loan would have qualified under paragraph (a) above had the loan not been paid off.

(2) For the purposes of this paragraph, references to a loan include also a reference to

money borrowed under a hire purchase agreement for any purpose specified in paragraphs (a) and (b) of sub-paragraph (1).

(3) Where a loan is applied only in part for the purposes specified in paragraphs (a) and (b) of sub-paragraph (1), only that portion of the loan which is applied for that purpose will qualify under this paragraph.

Loans for repairs and improvements to the dwelling occupied as the home

17.—(1) A loan qualifies under this paragraph where the loan was taken out, with or without security, for the purpose of—   9.427

- (a) carrying out repairs and improvements to the dwelling occupied as the home;
- (b) paying any service charge imposed to meet the cost of repairs and improvements to the dwelling occupied as the home;
- (c) paying off another loan to the extent that the other loan would have qualified under paragraph (a) or (b) of this sub-paragraph had the loan not been paid off,

and the loan was used for that purpose, or is used for that purpose within 6 months of the date of receipt or such further period as may be reasonable in the particular circumstances of the case.

(2) In sub-paragraph (1) "repairs and improvements" means any of the following measures undertaken with a view to maintaining the fitness of the dwelling for human habitation or, where the dwelling forms part of a building, any part of the building containing that dwelling—

- (a) provision of a fixed bath, shower, wash basin, sink or lavatory, and necessary associated plumbing, including the provision of hot water not connected to a central heating system;
- (b) repairs to existing heating systems;
- (c) damp proof measures;
- (d) provision of ventilation and natural lighting;
- (e) provision of drainage facilities;
- (f) provision of facilities for preparing and cooking food;
- (g) provision of insulation of the dwelling occupied as the home;
- (h) provision of electric lighting and sockets;
- (i) provision of storage facilities for fuel or refuse;
- (j) repairs of unsafe structural defects;
- (k) adapting a dwelling for the special needs of a disabled person; or
- (l) provision of separate sleeping accommodation for persons of different sexes aged 10 or over but under age 20 who live with the claimant and for whom the claimant or partner is responsible.

(3) Where a loan is applied only in part for the purposes specified in sub-paragraph (1), only that portion of the loan which is applied for that purpose will qualify under this paragraph.

Other housing costs

18.—(1) Subject to the deduction specified in sub-paragraph (2) and the reductions applicable in sub-paragraph (5), there are to be met under this paragraph the amounts, calculated on a weekly basis, in respect of the following housing costs—   9.428

- (a) payments by way of rent or ground rent relating to a long tenancy;
- (b) service charges;
- (c) payments by way of rentcharge within the meaning of section 1 of the Rentcharges Act 1977;
- (d) payments under a co-ownership scheme;
- (e) payments under or relating to a tenancy or licence of a Crown tenant;
- (f) where the dwelling occupied as the home is a tent, payments in respect of the tent and the site on which it stands.

(2) Subject to sub-paragraph (3), the deductions to be made from the weekly amounts to be met under this paragraph are—

- (a) where the costs are inclusive of any of the items mentioned in paragraph 6(2) of Schedule 1 to the Housing Benefit Regulations 2006 (payment in respect of fuel charges), the deductions prescribed in that paragraph unless the claimant provides evidence on which the actual or approximate amount of the service charge for fuel may be estimated, in which case the estimated amount;
- (b) where the costs are inclusive of ineligible service charges within the meaning of paragraph 1 of Schedule 1 to the Housing Benefit Regulations 2006 (ineligible service charges) the amounts attributable to those ineligible service charges or where that

amount is not separated from or separately identified within the housing costs to be met under this paragraph, such part of the payments made in respect of those housing costs which are fairly attributable to the provision of those ineligible services having regard to the costs of comparable services;

(c) any amount for repairs and improvements, and for this purpose the expression "repairs and improvements" has the same meaning it has in paragraph 17(2).

(3) Where arrangements are made for the housing costs, which are met under this paragraph and which are normally paid for a period of 52 weeks, to be paid instead for a period of 53 weeks, or to be paid irregularly, or so that no such costs are payable or collected in certain periods, or so that the costs for different periods in the year are of different amounts, the weekly amount will be the amount payable for the year divided by 52.

(4) Where the claimant or a member of the claimant's family—

(a) pays for reasonable repairs or redecorations to be carried out to the dwelling they occupy; and

(b) that work was not the responsibility of the claimant or any member of the claimant's family; and

(c) in consequence of that work being done, the costs which are normally met under this paragraph are waived,

then those costs will, for a period not exceeding 8 weeks, be treated as payable.

(5) Where in England and Wales an amount calculated on a weekly basis in respect of housing costs specified in sub-paragraph (1)(e) includes water charges, that amount is to be reduced—

(a) where the amount payable in respect of water charges is known, by that amount;

(b) in any other case, by the amount which would be the likely weekly water charge had the property not been occupied by a Crown tenant.

Non-dependant deductions

9.429   **19.**—(1) Subject to the following provisions of this paragraph, the following deductions from the amount to be met under the preceding paragraphs of this Schedule in respect of housing costs are to be made—

(a) in respect of a non-dependant aged 18 or over who is engaged in any remunerative work, [³£47.75];

(b) in respect of a non-dependant aged 18 or over to whom paragraph (a) does not apply, [³£7.40].

(2) In the case of a non-dependant aged 18 or over to whom sub-paragraph (1)(a) applies because that non-dependant is in remunerative work, where the claimant satisfies the Secretary of State that the non-dependant's gross weekly income is—

(a) less than [³£120.00], the deduction to be made under this paragraph will be the deduction specified in sub-paragraph (1)(b);

(b) not less than [³£120.00] but less than [³£178.00], the deduction to be made under this paragraph will be [³£17.00];

(c) not less than [³£178.00] but less than [³£231.00], the deduction to be made under this paragraph will be [³£23.35];

(d) not less than [³£231.00] but less than [³£306.00], the deduction to be made under this paragraph will be [³£38.20];

(e) not less than [³£306.00] but less than [³£382.00], the deduction to be made under this paragraph will be [³£43.50].

(3) Only one deduction is to be made under this paragraph in respect of a couple or, as the case may be, the members of a polygamous marriage, and where, but for this sub-paragraph, the amount that would fall to be deducted in respect of one member of a couple or polygamous marriage is higher than the amount (if any) that would fall to be deducted in respect of the other, or any other, member, the higher amount is to be deducted.

(4) In applying the provisions of sub-paragraph (2) in the case of a couple or, as the case may be, a polygamous marriage, regard will be had, for the purpose of sub-paragraph (2), to the couple's or, as the case may be, all the members of the polygamous marriage's, joint weekly income.

(5) Where a person is a non-dependant in respect of more than one joint occupier of a dwelling (except where the joint occupiers are a couple or members of a polygamous marriage), the deduction in respect of that non-dependant is to be apportioned between the joint occupiers (the amount so apportioned being rounded to the nearest penny) having regard to the number of joint occupiers and the proportion of the housing costs in respect of the dwelling occupied as the home payable by each of them.

(6) No deduction is to be made in respect of any non-dependants occupying the dwelling occupied as the home of the claimant, if the claimant or any partner of the claimant is—

(a)   registered as blind in a register compiled under section 29 of the National Assistance Act 1948 (welfare services) or, in Scotland, has been certified as blind and in consequence he is registered as blind in a register maintained by or on behalf of a regional or islands council, or who is within 28 weeks of ceasing to be so registered;

(b)   receiving in respect of that claimant or that claimant's partner either—
    (i)   an attendance allowance; or
    (ii)   the care component of the disability living allowance.

(7) No deduction is to be made in respect of a non-dependant—

(a)   if, although the [¹non-dependant] resides with the claimant, it appears to the Secretary of State that the dwelling occupied as the non-dependant's home is normally elsewhere;

(b)   if the non-dependant is in receipt of a training allowance paid in connection with youth training;

(c)   if the non-dependant is a full-time student during a period of study or, if the non-dependant is not in remunerative work, during a recognised summer vacation appropriate to the non-dependant's course;

(d)   if the non-dependant is aged under 25 and in receipt of income support, an income-based jobseeker's allowance or an income-related allowance which does not include an amount under section 4(2)(b) of the Act;

(e)   in respect of whom a deduction in the calculation of a rent rebate or allowance falls to be made under regulation 74 of the Housing Benefit Regulations 2006 (non-dependant deductions);

[¹(f)   to whom, but for paragraph (5) of regulation 71 (definition of non-dependant) paragraph (4) of that regulation would apply;]

(g)   if the non-dependant is not residing with the claimant because the non-dependant has been a patient for a period in excess of 52 weeks, or is a prisoner, and for these purposes—
    (i)   "patient" has the meaning given in paragraph 5(13) and "prisoner" has the meaning given in regulation 69(2) (special cases); and
    (ii)   in calculating a period of 52 weeks as a patient, any two or more distinct periods separated by one or more intervals each not exceeding 28 days is to be treated as a single period; or

(h)   if the non-dependant is in receipt of state pension credit;

(i)   in sub-paragraph (b)—
    "youth training" means—
    (i)   arrangements made under section 2 of the Employment and Training Act 1973 or section 2 of the Enterprise and New Towns (Scotland) Act 1990; or
    (ii)   arrangements made by the Secretary of State for persons enlisted in Her Majesty's forces for any special term of service specified in regulations made under section 2 of the Armed Forces Act 1966 (power of Defence Council to make regulations as to engagement of persons in regular forces),

for purposes which include the training of persons who, at the beginning of their training, are under the age of 18.

9.430

(8) In the case of a non-dependant to whom sub-paragraph (2) applies because that nondependent is in remunerative work, there is to be disregarded from that non-dependant's gross income—

(a)   any attendance allowance or disability living allowance received by that non-dependant;

(b)   any payment made under the Macfarlane Trust, the Macfarlane (Special Payments) Trust, the Macfarlane (Special Payments) (No. 2) Trust, the Fund, the Eileen Trust or [¹the Independent Living Fund (2006)] which, had that non-dependant's income fallen to be calculated under regulation 104 (calculation of income other than earnings), would have been disregarded under paragraph 22 of Schedule 8 (income in kind); and

(c)   any payment which, had that non-dependant's income fallen to be calculated under regulation 104 would have been disregarded under paragraph 41 of Schedule 8 (payments made under certain trusts and certain other payments).

Continuity with income support, an income-based jobseeker's allowance or state pension credit

20.—(1) For the purpose of providing continuity between income support, an income-based jobseeker's allowance or state pension credit and an employment and support allowance—

(a)   any housing costs which would, had the claimant been entitled to income support,

9.431

an income-based jobseeker's allowance or state pension credit, have been existing housing costs and not new housing costs will, despite the preceding provisions of this Schedule, be treated as existing housing costs, and any qualifications or limitations which would have applied to those costs had the award been an award of income support, an income-based jobseeker's allowance or state pension credit will likewise apply to the costs in so far as they are met in an employment and support allowance;

(b) had the award of an employment and support allowance been an award of income support or an income-based jobseeker's allowance and the housing costs which would then have been met would have included an additional amount met in accordance with paragraph 7 of Schedule 3 to the Income Support Regulations or, as the case may be, paragraph 18(1)(b) of Schedule 2 to the Jobseeker's Allowance Regulations (add back), an amount equal to that additional amount must be added to the housing costs to be met under this Schedule, but that amount must be subject to the same qualifications and limitations as it would have been had the award been of income support or an income-based jobseeker's allowance; and

(c) subject to paragraph 15(20), for the purposes of any linking rule or for determining whether any qualifying or other period is satisfied, any reference to an employment and support allowance in this Schedule must be taken also to include a reference to income support, an income-based jobseeker's allowance or state pension credit.

(2) Any loan which, had the claimant been entitled to income support and not an employment and support allowance, would have been a qualifying loan for the purposes of Schedule 3 to the Income Support Regulations by virtue of regulation 3 of the Income Support (General) Amendment and Transitional Regulations 1995 (transitional protection) must be treated also as a qualifying loan for the purposes of paragraph 16 or 17, (loans on residential property and loans for repairs and improvements to the dwelling occupied as the home) and for the purpose of determining whether a claimant would satisfy the provision of regulation 3(2) of those Regulations, a claimant in receipt of an income-related allowance must be treated as being in receipt of income support.

AMENDMENTS

1. Employment and Support Allowance (Miscellaneous Amendments) Regulations 2008 (SI 2008/2428), reg.16 (October 27, 2008).

2. Social Security (Housing Costs Special Arrangements) (Amendment and Modification) Regulations 2008 (SI 2008/3195), reg.2(1)(a) and (2) (January 5, 2009).

3. Social Security Benefits Up-rating Order 2009 (SI 2009/497), art.27(5) (April 6, 2009).

DEFINITIONS

"Abbeyfield Home"—see reg.2(1).
"attendance allowance"—*ibid.*
"care home"—*ibid.*
"child"—*ibid.*
"child support maintenance"—see reg.2(2).
"claimant"—see reg.83(1).
"couple"—see reg.2(1).
"Crown tenant"—*ibid.*
"dwelling occupied as the home"—*ibid.*
"Eileen Trust"—*ibid.*
"family"—*ibid.*
"full-time student"—*ibid.*
"the Fund"—*ibid.*
"housing benefit expenditure"—*ibid.*
"independent hospital"—*ibid.*
"the Independent Living Fund (2006)"—*ibid.*
"Macfarlane (Special Payments) Trust"—*ibid.*
"Macfarlane (Special Payments) (No. 2) Trust"—*ibid.*
"Macfarlane Trust"—*ibid.*
"maintenance assessment"—see reg.2(2).

"maintenance calculation"—*ibid.*
"non-dependant"—see reg.71.
"partner"—see reg.2(1).
"period of study"—*ibid.*
"polygamous marriage"—*ibid.*
"training allowance"—*ibid.*
"water charges"—*ibid.*

GENERAL NOTE

This is similar to Sch.3 to the IS Regulations/Sch.2 to the JSA Regulations (where there are differences between those Schedules Sch.6 generally adopts the income support model).

The following are the main differences from Sch.3:

- Paragraph 2 defines when a non-dependant will be treated as in remunerative work for the purposes of Sch.6. This paragraph is necessary because the definition of remunerative work in regs 41 and 42 only applies to the claimant and the claimant's partner and does not apply for the purposes of Sch.6 (see the definition of "remunerative work" in reg.2(1)). See also para.2(9) which specifically provides that whether a claimant or a claimant's partner is engaged in, or is to be treated as engaged in, remunerative work is to be determined in accordance with regs 41 or 42.

- There is no equivalent to para.2(2) of Sch.3 (which relates to trade disputes).

- Note also para.15(20) of this Schedule which provides that any period during which a claimant qualifies for a "housing costs run-on" under reg.6(5) of the Income Support Regulations does not count for the purpose of any linking rules or determining whether any qualifying or other period is satisfied under this Schedule.

- In relation to the excessive housing costs rules, note para.14(10).

- The transitional protection provisions in Sch.3 (see para.6(2)–(4) and para.7 of Sch.3) have been omitted, although note para.12(11)-(12) which preserves the transitional protection from the ceiling on loans that is contained in reg.4 of the Income Support (General) Amendment No. 3 Regulations 1993 (SI 1993/1679) and reg.28 of the Income-related Benefits Schemes (Miscellaneous Amendments) Regulations 1995 (SI 1995/516) (see Vol.II of this series for these Regulations) for a person to whom any of those provisions would have applied had he been entitled to income support.

Continuity with income support, income-based JSA and state pension credit

In addition to the transitional protection in para.12(11)–(12), note the provisions in para.20 (which are very similar to those in para.18 of Sch.2 to the JSA Regulations). Paragraph 20 is important for claimants transferring from income support or income-based JSA, or from state pension credit where their partner has been entitled to state pension credit, to income-related ESA. For the equivalent of para.20(1)(c) where the transfer is the other way round, see para.18(1)(c) of Sch.2 to the JSA Regulations for income-based JSA and para.14(15) of Sch.3 to the Income Support Regulations for income support.

There are no waiting periods for housing costs for state pension credit claimants. However, note para.15(19) which provides that for the purposes of the linking rules in para.15, if a claimant's former partner was entitled to state pension credit, any reference to an income-related allowance in Sch.6 also includes a reference to state pension credit.

With effect from January 5, 2009 the rules relating to waiting periods and the capital limit on loans have been modified by the Social Security (Housing Costs Special Arrangements) (Amendment and Modification) Regulations 2008 (SI

9.432

9.433

2008/3195) (see p.1213 in this Volume for these Regulations). However note that the changes made by these Regulations only apply to certain claimants. The same modifications have been made to Sch.3 to the Income Support Regulations and Sch.2 to the JSA Regulations. See the notes to Sch.3 to the Income Support Regulations for the effect of these modifications and the claimants to whom they apply.

Regulations 96(2), 98(2)

SCHEDULE 7

Sums to be Disregarded in the Calculation of Earnings

9.434
1.—(1) In the case of a claimant who has been engaged in remunerative work as an employed earner or, had the employment been in Great Britain, would have been so engaged—
  (a) any earnings, other than items to which sub-paragraph (2) applies, paid or due to be paid from that employment which terminated before the first day of entitlement to an income-related allowance;
  (b) any earnings, other than a payment of the nature described in regulation 95(1)(e) (earnings of employed earners), paid or due to be paid from that employment which has not been terminated where the claimant is not—
    (i) engaged in remunerative work; or
    (ii) suspended from employment.
(2) This sub-paragraph applies to—
  (a) any payment of the nature described in regulation 95(1)(e); and
  (b) any award, sum or payment of the nature described in—
    (i) regulation 95(1)(g) or (i); or
    (ii) section 34 or 70 of the Employment Rights Act 1996 (guarantee payments and suspension from work: complaints to employment tribunals),
including any payment made following the settlement of a complaint to an employment tribunal or of court proceedings.

2.—(1) In the case of a claimant to whom this paragraph applies, any earnings (other than a payment of the nature described in regulation 95(1)(e)) which relate to employment which ceased before the first day of entitlement to an income-related allowance whether or not that employment has terminated.
(2) This paragraph applies to a claimant who has been engaged in part-time employment as an employed earner or, had the employment been in Great Britain, would have been so engaged; but it does not apply to a claimant who has been suspended from employment.

3. If the claimant's partner has been engaged in remunerative work as an employed earner or, had the employment been in Great Britain, would have been so engaged, any earnings paid or due to be paid on termination of that employment by way of retirement but only if—
  (a) on retirement the partner is entitled to a retirement pension under the Contributions and Benefits Act; or
  (b) the only reason the partner is not entitled to a retirement pension under the Contribution and Benefits Act is because the contribution conditions are not satisfied.

4. In the case of a claimant who has been engaged in remunerative work or part-time employment as a self-employed earner or, had the employment been in Great Britain, would have been so engaged and who has ceased to be so employed, from the date of the cessation of the claimant's employment any earnings derived from that employment except earnings to which regulation 92(2) (royalties etc.) applies.

5. In the case of a claimant who is undertaking work which falls within one of the categories in regulation 45(2) to (4) any earnings derived from that work which do not exceed the limits specified for that work of £20 in regulation 45(2) or, as the case may be, [¹£92.00] in regulation 45(3) or (4).

6. Where regulation 45(2) to (4) applies to the claimant and that claimant's earnings are less than—

(a) in a case to which regulation 45(2) applies, £20;

(b) in a case to which regulation 45(3) and (4) applies, [¹£92.00],

the earnings of the claimant's partner are to be disregarded to the extent that the claimant's earnings are less than £20 or, as the case may be, [¹£92.00], but only up to a maximum of £20.

7.—(1) In a case to which this paragraph applies, £20; but notwithstanding regulation 83 (calculation of income and capital of members of claimant's family and of a polygamous marriage), if this paragraph applies to a claimant it will not apply to the claimant's partner except where, and to the extent that, the earnings of the claimant which are to be disregarded under this paragraph are less than £20.

(2) Subject to sub-paragraph (3), this paragraph applies in the case of a claimant to whom regulation 40(2)(a), (b) or (e), 43(1)(a), (d), (e) or (f), or (2) or 45(5) applies.

(3) Where a claimant is doing the work set out in regulation 40(2)(b) and is also undertaking any of the categories of work set out in regulation 45(2) to (4), this paragraph applies only to the extent that the claimant's earnings are less than the limit of—

(a) £20 set out in regulation 45(2); or

(b) [¹£92.00] set out in regulation 45(3) and (4),

as the case may be.

(4) This paragraph applies, in a case where the claimant's partner is in part-time employment and paragraph 6 does not apply.

8. Notwithstanding the foregoing provisions of this Schedule, where two or more payments of earnings of the same kind and from the same source are to be taken into account in the same benefit week, because it has not been practicable to treat the payments under regulation 93(1)(b) (date on which income treated as paid) as paid on the first day of the benefit week in which they were due to be paid, there is to be disregarded from each payment the sum that would have been disregarded if the payment had been taken into account on the date on which it was due to be paid.

9. Any earnings derived from employment which are payable in a country outside the United Kingdom for such period during which there is a prohibition against the transfer to the United Kingdom of those earnings.

10. Where a payment of earnings is made in a currency other than sterling, any banking charge or commission payable in converting that payment into sterling.

11. Any earnings which are due to be paid before the date of claim and which would otherwise fall to be taken into account in the same benefit week as a payment of the same kind and from the same source.

12. In the case of a claimant who—

(a) has been engaged in employment as a member of any territorial or reserve force prescribed in Part 1 of Schedule 6 to the Social Security (Contributions) Regulations 2001; and

(b) by reason of that employment has failed to satisfy any of the conditions for entitlement to an income-related allowance other than paragraph 6(1)(a) of Schedule 1 to the Act (income not in excess of the applicable amount),

any earnings from that employment paid in respect of the period in which the claimant was not entitled to an income-related allowance.

13. In the case of a person to whom paragraph (5) of regulation 6 of the Income Support Regulations applies, any earnings.

14. In this Schedule—

"part-time employment" means, if the person were entitled to income support, employment in which the person is not to be treated as engaged in remunerative work under regulation 5 or 6(1) and (4) of the Income Support Regulations (persons treated, or not treated, as engaged in remunerative work);

"remunerative work", for the purposes of this paragraph and paragraphs 1, 3 and 4, has the meaning prescribed in regulation 5, except for paragraphs (3B) and (4) of that regulation, of the Income Support Regulations.

AMENDMENT

1. Employment and Support Allowance (Miscellaneous Amendments) Regulations 2008 (SI 2008/2428), reg.17 (October 27, 2008).

DEFINITIONS

"benefit week"—see reg.2(1).
"couple"—*ibid.*
"employed earner"—*ibid.*
"family"—*ibid.*
"partner"—*ibid.*
"polygamous marriage"—*ibid.*

GENERAL NOTE

Paras 1–4

9.435   Paragraphs 1 to 4 are similar to paras 1 to 3 of Sch.8 to the Income Support Regulations/paras 1 to 4 of Sch.6 to the JSA Regulations (where there are differences between Sch.8 and Sch.6 this Schedule adopts the income support model). They contain the earnings disregards on the termination of "remunerative work" (defined in para.14) and on the stopping of "part-time employment" (also defined in para.14) before the claim, as well as on the cessation of self-employment. Note that the definitions of "remunerative work" and "part-time employment" largely (but not entirely) import the income support tests.

Paras 5–7

9.436   The disregards in these paragraphs are different from those in Sch.8 to the Income Support Regulations/Sch.6 to the JSA Regulations because of the different rules for the effect of work on entitlement to ESA (see regs 40–46 for these rules).

The earnings limit for "exempt work" under reg.45(2) is £20 and under reg.45(3) or (4) is £92. Paragraph 5 disregards earnings from such work up to the relevant limit. In addition, if the claimant's earnings from such work are less than the relevant limit, his partner's earnings are ignored to the extent of the spare amount below the relevant limit, subject to a maximum of £20 (para.6).

Under para.7 earnings from the following attract a £20 disregard:
  (i) work undertaken by the claimant as a councillor, as a member of the Disability Living Allowance Advisory Board or as a tribunal member with a disability qualification, during an emergency to protect another person, property or livestock, or while receiving assistance in pursuing self-employment under a government scheme;
 (ii) work undertaken by the claimant's partner as a childminder, as a councillor, as a part-time fire-fighter, auxiliary coastguard, part-time member of a lifeboat crew or member of the Territorial army, or where the partner is receiving assistance under the "self-employment route" (defined in reg.2(1)), or is not to be treated as in remunerative work under one of the categories in reg.43(2);
(iii) part-time employment (defined in para.14) undertaken by the claimant's partner where the disregard under para.6 does not apply.

But note that a couple cannot have a total disregard of more than £20.

Note also that if a claimant who is working as a member of the Disability Living Allowance Advisory Board or as a tribunal member with a disability qualification is also doing work that counts as exempt work under reg.45(2) to (4), the disregard under para.7 only applies to the extent that his earnings are less than the relevant limit for that exempt work.

Paras 8–13

9.437   These paragraphs are similar to paras 10 to 13, 15A and 15C of Sch.8 to the Income Support Regulations/paras 13–16 and 19 of Sch.6 to the JSA Regulations (there is no equivalent to para.13 in Sch.6 to the JSA Regulations as this is concerned with the disregard of earnings during any "housing costs run-on" under reg.6(5) of the Income Support Regulations).

Regulation 104(2)

SCHEDULE 8

SUMS TO BE DISREGARDED IN THE CALCULATION OF INCOME OTHER THAN EARNINGS

1. Any amount paid by way of tax on income which is taken into account under regulation 104 (calculation of income other than earnings).

9.438

2. Any payment in respect of any expenses incurred, or to be incurred, by a claimant who is—
  (a) engaged by a charitable or voluntary organisation; or
  (b) a volunteer,
if the claimant otherwise derives no remuneration or profit from the employment and is not to be treated as possessing any earnings under regulation 108(3) (notional income).

3. In the case of employment as an employed earner, any payment in respect of expenses wholly, exclusively and necessarily incurred in the performance of the duties of the employment.

4. In the case of a payment under Parts 11 to 12ZB of the Contributions and Benefits Act or any remuneration paid by or on behalf of an employer to the claimant who for the time being is unable to work due to illness or maternity or who is taking paternity leave or adoption leave—
  (a) any amount deducted by way of primary Class 1 contributions under the Contributions and Benefits Act;
  (b) one-half of any sum paid by the claimant by way of a contribution towards an occupational or personal pension scheme.

5. In Northern Ireland, in the case of a payment under Parts 11 to 12ZB of the Social Security Contributions and Benefits (Northern Ireland) Act 1992, or any remuneration paid by or on behalf of an employer to the claimant who for the time being is unable to work due to illness or maternity or who is taking paternity leave or adoption leave—
  (a) any amount deducted by way of primary Class 1 contributions under that Act;
  (b) one-half of any sum paid by way of a contribution towards an occupational or personal pension scheme.

6. Any guardian's allowance.

7.—(1) Any child tax credit.
(2) Any child benefit.

8. Any mobility component of disability living allowance.

9. Any concessionary payment made to compensate for the non-payment of—
  (a) any payment specified in paragraph 8 or 11;
  (b) an [¹income-related] employment and support allowance, income support or [¹ an income-based jobseeker's allowance].

10. Any mobility supplement or any payment intended to compensate for the non-payment of such a supplement.

11. Any attendance allowance or the care component of disability living allowance.

12. Any payment to the claimant as holder of the Victoria Cross or George Cross or any analogous payment.

13.—(1) Any payment—
 (a) by way of an education maintenance allowance made pursuant to—
  (i) regulations made under section 518 of the Education Act 1996;
  (ii) regulations made under section 49 or 73(f) of the Education (Scotland) Act 1980; or
  (iii) directions made under section 73ZA of the Education (Scotland) Act 1980 and paid under section 12(2)(c) of the Further and Higher Education (Scotland) Act 1992; or
 (b) corresponding to such an education maintenance allowance, made pursuant to—
  (i) section 14 or section 181 of the Education Act 2002; or
  (ii) regulations made under section 181 of that Act.
 (2) Any payment, other than a payment to which sub-paragraph (1) applies, made pursuant to—
 (a) regulations made under section 518 of the Education Act 1996;
 (b) regulations made under section 49 of the Education (Scotland) Act 1980; or
 (c) directions made under section 73ZA of the Education (Scotland) Act 1980 and paid under section 12(2)(c) of the Further and Higher Education (Scotland) Act 1992;
in respect of a course of study attended by a child or a young person or a person who is in receipt of an education maintenance allowance made pursuant to any provision specified in sub-paragraph (1).

14. Any payment made to the claimant by way of a repayment under regulation 11(2) of the Education (Teacher Student Loans) (Repayment etc.) Regulations 2002.

15.—(1) Any payment made pursuant to section 2 of the Employment and Training Act 1973 (functions of the Secretary of State) or section 2 of the Enterprise and New Towns (Scotland) Act 1990 (functions in relation to training for employment etc.) except a payment—
 (a) made as a substitute for an employment and support allowance;
 (b) of an allowance referred to in section 2(3) of the Employment and Training Act 1973 or section 2(5) of the Enterprise and New Towns (Scotland) Act 1990;
 (c) intended to meet the cost of living expenses which relate to any one or more of the items specified in sub-paragraph (2) whilst a claimant is participating in an education, training or other scheme to help the claimant enhance that claimant's employment prospects unless the payment is a Career Development Loan paid pursuant to section 2 of the Employment and Training Act 1973 and the period of education or training or the scheme, which is supported by that loan, has been completed; or
 (d) made in respect of the cost of living away from home to the extent that the payment relates to rent for which housing benefit is payable in respect of accommodation which is not normally occupied by the claimant as that claimant's home.
 (2) The items specified in this sub-paragraph for the purposes of sub-paragraph (1)(c) are food, ordinary clothing or footwear, household fuel, rent for which housing benefit is payable, or any housing costs to the extent that they are met under regulation 67(1)(c) or 68(1)(d) (housing costs), of the claimant or, where the claimant is a member of a family, any other member of the claimant's family, or any council tax or water charges for which that claimant or member is liable.

16.—(1) Subject to sub-paragraph (2) and paragraph 41, any relevant payment made or due to be made at regular intervals.
 (2) Sub-paragraph (1) is not to apply to a payment which is made by a person for the maintenance of any member of that person's family or of that person's former partner or of that person's children.
 (3) In this paragraph, "relevant payment" means—
 (a) a charitable payment;
 (b) a voluntary payment;
 (c) a payment (not falling within sub-paragraph (a) or (b) above) from a trust whose funds are derived from a payment made in consequence of any personal injury to the claimant;
 (d) a payment under an annuity purchased—
  (i) pursuant to any agreement or court order to make payments to the claimant; or
  (ii) from funds derived from a payment made,
  in consequence of any personal injury to the claimant; or
 (e) a payment (not falling within sub-paragraph (a) to (d) above) received by virtue of any

agreement or court order to make payments to the claimant in consequence of any
personal injury to the claimant.

17. Subject to paragraphs 39 and 40, £10 of any of the following, namely—

(a) a war disablement pension (except insofar as such a pension falls to be disregarded
under paragraph 10 or 11);

(b) a war widow's pension or war widower's pension;

(c) a pension payable to a person as a widow, widower or surviving civil partner under any
power of Her Majesty otherwise than under an enactment to make provision about
pensions for or in respect of persons who have been disabled or have died in consequence of service as members of the armed forces of the Crown;

(d) a guaranteed income payment [³ and, if the amount of that payment has been abated
to less than £10 by a payment under the Armed Forces Pension Scheme 1975 or the
Armed Forces Pension Scheme 2005, so much of the pension payable under either of
those schemes as would not, in aggregate with the amount of the guaranteed income
payment disregarded, exceed £10];

(e) a payment made to compensate for the non-payment of such a pension or payment as
is mentioned in any of the preceding sub-paragraphs;

(f) a pension paid by the government of a country outside Great Britain which is analogous to any of the pensions or payments mentioned in sub-paragraphs (a) to (d)
above;

(g) a pension paid to victims of National Socialist persecution under any special provision made by the law of the Federal Republic of Germany, or any part of it, or of the
Republic of Austria;

(h) any widowed mother's allowance paid pursuant to section 37 of the Contributions
and Benefits Act;

(i) any widowed parent's allowance paid pursuant to section 39A of the Contributions
and Benefits Act.

18. Where a claimant receives income under an annuity purchased with a loan which satisfies the following conditions—

(a) that the loan was made as part of a scheme under which not less than 90% of the proceeds of the loan were applied to the purchase by the person to whom it was made of
an annuity ending with that person's life or with the life of the survivor of two or more
persons (in this paragraph referred to as "the annuitants") who include the person to
whom the loan was made;

(b) that the interest on the loan is payable by the person to whom it was made or by one
of the annuitants;

(c) that at the time the loan was made the person to whom it was made or each of the
annuitants had attained the age of 65;

(d) that the loan was secured on a dwelling in Great Britain and the person to whom the
loan was made or one of the annuitants owns an estate or interest in that dwelling;
and

(e) that the person to whom the loan was made or one of the annuitants occupies the
accommodation on which it was secured as that person's home at the time the interest
is paid,

the amount, calculated on a weekly basis equal to—

(i) where, or insofar as, section 369 of the Income and Corporation Taxes Act
1988 (mortgage interest payable under deduction of tax) applies to the payments of interest on the loan, the interest which is payable after deduction of
a sum equal to income tax on such payments at the applicable percentage of
income tax within the meaning of section 369(1A) of that Act;

(ii) in any other case the interest which is payable on the loan without deduction of
such a sum.

19. Any payment made to the claimant by a person who normally resides with the claimant, which is a contribution towards that person's living and accommodation costs, except
where that person is residing with the claimant in circumstances to which paragraph 20 or
21 refers.

20. Where the claimant occupies a dwelling as the claimant's home and the dwelling is also
occupied by another person and there is a contractual liability to make payments to the claimant in respect of the occupation of the dwelling by that person or a member of that person's
family—

9.439

(a) where the aggregate of any payments made in respect of any one week in respect of the occupation of the dwelling by that person or a member of that person's family, or by that person and a member of that person's family, is less than £20, the whole of that amount; or
(b) where the aggregate of such payments is £20 or more per week, £20.

21. Where the claimant occupies a dwelling as the claimant's home and the claimant provides in that dwelling board and lodging accommodation, an amount, in respect of each person for whom such accommodation is provided for the whole or any part of a week, equal to—
(a) where the aggregate of any payments made in respect of any one week in respect of such accommodation provided to such person does not exceed £20, 100% of such payments; or
(b) where the aggregate of any such payments exceeds £20, £20 and 50% of the excess over £20.

22.—(1) Subject to sub-paragraphs (2) and (3), except where regulation 104(8)(b) (provision of support under section 95 or 98 of the Immigration and Asylum Act including support provided by virtue of regulations made under Schedule 9 to that Act in the calculation of income other than earnings) or regulation 107(3)(a) (notional income) applies, any income in kind;
(2) The exception under sub-paragraph (1) will not apply where the income in kind is received from the Macfarlane Trust, the Macfarlane (Special Payments) Trust, the Macfarlane (Special Payments) (No.2) Trust, the Fund, the Eileen Trust or [¹the Independent Living Fund (2006)].
(3) The first exception under sub-paragraph (1) will not apply where the claimant is the partner of a person subject to immigration control and whose partner is receiving support provided under section 95 or 98 of the Immigration and Asylum Act including support provided by virtue of regulations made under Schedule 9 to that Act and the income in kind is support provided in respect of essential living needs of the partner of the claimant and the claimant's dependants (if any) as is specified in regulations made under paragraph 3 of Schedule 8 to the Immigration and Asylum Act.
(4) The reference in sub-paragraph (1) to "income in kind" does not include a payment to a third party made in respect of the claimant which is used by the third party to provide benefits in kind to the claimant.

23.—(1) Any income derived from capital to which the claimant is or is treated under regulation 117 (capital jointly held) as beneficially entitled but, subject to sub-paragraph (2), not income derived from capital disregarded under paragraph 1, 2, 4 to 8, 10 or 16 of Schedule 9.
(2) Income derived from capital disregarded under paragraph 2 or 4 to 8 of Schedule 9 but only to the extent of—
(a) any mortgage repayments made in respect of the dwelling or premises in the period during which that income accrued; or
(b) any council tax or water charges which the claimant is liable to pay in respect of the dwelling or premises and which are paid in the period during which that income accrued.
(3) The definition of "water charges" in regulation 2(1) is to apply to sub-paragraph (2) with the omission of the words "in so far as such charges are in respect of the dwelling which a person occupies as the home".

24. Any income which is payable in a country outside the United Kingdom for such period during which there is prohibition against the transfer to the United Kingdom of that income.

25. Where a payment of income is made in a currency other than sterling, any banking charge or commission payable in converting that payment into sterling.

26.—(1) Any payment made to the claimant in respect of a child or young person who is a member of the claimant's family—
(a) pursuant to regulations under section 2(6)(b), 3 or 4 of the Adoption and Children Act 2002 or in accordance with a scheme approved by the Scottish Ministers under section 51A of the Adoption (Scotland) Act 1978 (schemes for payment of allowances to adopters);
(b) which is a payment made by a local authority in pursuance of section 15(1) of, and para-

graph 15 of Schedule 1 to, the Children Act 1989 (local authority contribution to a child's maintenance where the child is living with a person as a result of a residence order);

(c) which is a payment made by an authority, as defined in Article 2 of the Children (Northern Ireland) Order 1995, in pursuance of Article 15 of, and paragraph 17 of Schedule 1 to, that Order (contributions by an authority to child's maintenance);

(d) in accordance with regulations made pursuant to section 14F of the Children Act 1989 (special guardianship support services).

(2) Any payment, other than a payment to which sub-paragraph (1)(a) applies, made to the claimant pursuant to regulations under section 2(6)(b), 3 or 4 of the Adoption and Children Act 2002.

27. In the case of a claimant who has a child or young person—

(a) who is a member of the claimant's family; and

(b) who is residing at an educational establishment at which that child or young person is receiving relevant education,

any payment made to that educational establishment, in respect of that child or young person's maintenance by or on behalf of a person who is not a member of the family or by a member of the family out of funds contributed for that purpose by a person who is not a member of the family.

28. Any payment made by a local authority to the claimant with whom a person is accommodated by virtue of arrangements made under section 23(2)(a) of the Children Act 1989 (provision of accommodation and maintenance for a child whom they are looking after) or, as the case may be, section 26 of the Children (Scotland) Act 1995 or by a voluntary organisation under section 59(1)(a) of the 1989 Act (provision of accommodation by voluntary organisations) or by a local authority under regulation 9 of the Fostering of Children (Scotland) Regulations 1996 (payment of allowances).

29. Any payment made to the claimant or the claimant's partner for a person ("the person concerned"), who is not normally a member of the claimant's household but is temporarily in the claimant's care, by—

(a) a health authority;

(b) a local authority but excluding payments of housing benefit made in respect of the person concerned;

(c) a voluntary organisation;

(d) the person concerned pursuant to section 26(3A) of the National Assistance Act 1948;

(e) a Primary Care Trust established under section 16A of the National Health Service Act 1977 or by an order made under section 18(2)(c) of the Health Service Act; or

(f) a Local Health Board established under section 16BA of the National Health Service Act 1977 or by an order made under section 11 of the Health Service (Wales) Act.

30.—(1) Any payment made by a local authority in accordance with—

(a) section 17, 23B, 23C or 24A of the Children Act 1989;

(b) section 12 of the Social Work (Scotland) Act 1968; or

(c) section 29 or 30 of the Children (Scotland) Act 1995 (local authorities' duty to promote welfare of children and powers to grant financial assistance to persons in, or formerly in, their care).

(2) Subject to paragraph (3), any payment (or part of a payment) made by a local authority in accordance with section 23C of the Children Act 1989 or section 29 of the Children (Scotland) Act 1995 (local authorities' duty to promote welfare of children and powers to grant financial assistance to persons in, or formerly in, their care) to a person ("A") which A passes on to the claimant.

(3) Sub-paragraph (2) applies only where A—

(a) was formerly in the claimant's care; and

(b) is aged 18 or over; and

(c) continues to live with the claimant.

31.—(1) Subject to sub-paragraph (2) any payment received under an insurance policy, taken out to insure against the risk of being unable to maintain repayments on a loan which qualifies under paragraph 16 or 17 of Schedule 6 (housing costs—loans to acquire an interest in a dwelling, or for repairs and improvements to the dwelling, occupied as the home) and used to meet such repayments, to the extent that it does not exceed the aggregate of—

    (a) the amount, calculated on a weekly basis, of any interest on that loan which is in excess of the amount met in accordance with Schedule 6;

    (b) the amount of any payment, calculated on a weekly basis, due on the loan attributable to the repayment of capital; and

    (c) any amount due by way of premiums on—

        (i) that policy; or

        (ii) a policy of insurance taken out to insure against loss or damage to any building or part of a building which is occupied by the claimant as the claimant's home.

(2) This paragraph does not apply to any payment which is treated as possessed by the claimant by virtue of regulation 107(3)(c) (notional income—income due to be paid or income paid to or in respect of a third party).

32.—(1) Except where paragraph 31 (or 33) applies, and subject to sub-paragraph (2), any payment made to the claimant which is intended to be used and is used as a contribution towards—

    (a) any payment due on a loan if secured on the dwelling occupied as the home which does not qualify under Schedule 6;

    (b) any interest payment or charge which qualifies in accordance with paragraphs 16 to 18 of Schedule 6 to the extent that the payment or charge is not met;

    (c) any payment due on a loan which qualifies under paragraph 16 or 17 of Schedule 6 attributable to the payment of capital;

    (d) any amount due by way of premiums on—

        (i) an insurance policy taken out to insure against the risk of being unable to make the payments referred to in (a) to (c) above; or

        (ii) a policy of insurance taken out to insure against loss or damage to any building or part of a building which is occupied by the claimant as the claimant's home;

    (e) the claimant's rent in respect of the dwelling occupied by the claimant as the home but only to the extent that it is not met by housing benefit; or the claimant's accommodation charge but only to the extent that the actual charge exceeds the amount payable by a local authority in accordance with Part 3 of the National Assistance Act 1948.

(2) This paragraph does not apply to any payment which is treated as possessed by the claimant by virtue of regulation 107(3)(c).

33.—(1) Subject to sub-paragraph (2), any payment received under an insurance policy, other than an insurance policy referred to in paragraph 31, taken out to insure against the risk of being unable to maintain repayments under a regulated agreement as defined for the purposes of the Consumer Credit Act 1974 or under a hire-purchase agreement or a conditional sale agreement as defined for the purposes of Part 3 of the Hire-Purchase Act 1964.

(2) A payment referred to in sub-paragraph (1) is to only be disregarded to the extent that the payment received under that policy does not exceed the amounts, calculated on a weekly basis which are used to—

    (a) maintain the repayments referred to in sub-paragraph (1); and

    (b) meet any amount due by way of premiums on that policy.

9.440   **34.**—(1) Subject to sub-paragraphs (2) and (3), in the case of a claimant residing in a care home, an Abbeyfield Home or an independent hospital, any payment, except a charitable or voluntary payment disregarded under paragraph 16 made to the claimant which is intended to be used and is used to meet the cost of maintaining the claimant in that home or hospital.

(2) This paragraph does not apply to a claimant for whom accommodation in a care home, an Abbeyfield Home or an independent hospital is provided by a local authority under section 26 of the National Assistance Act 1948.

(3) The amount to be disregarded under this paragraph is not to exceed the difference between—

    (a) the claimant's applicable amount; and

    (b) the weekly charge for the accommodation.

35. Any social fund payment made pursuant to Part 8 of the Contributions and Benefits Act.

36. Any payment of income which under regulation 112 (income treated as capital) is to be treated as capital.

37. Any payment under Part 10 of the Contributions and Benefits Act (pensioner's Christmas bonus).

38. Any payment which is due to be paid before the date of claim which would otherwise fall to be taken into account in the same benefit week as a payment of the same kind and from the same source.

39. The total of a claimant's income or, if the claimant is a member of a family, the family's income and the income of any person which the claimant is treated as possessing under regulation 83(3) (calculation of income and capital of members of claimant's family and of a polygamous marriage) to be disregarded under regulation 133(2)(b) and 134(1)(c) (calculation of covenant income), regulation 137(1) and (2) (treatment of student loans), regulation 138(3) (treatment of payments from access funds) and paragraph 17 is in no case to exceed £20 per week.

40. Notwithstanding paragraph 39 where two or more payments of the same kind and from the same source are to be taken into account in the same benefit week, there is to be disregarded from each payment the sum which would otherwise fall to be disregarded under this Schedule; but this paragraph is to apply only in the case of a payment which it has not been practicable to treat under regulation 93(1)(b) (date on which income is treated as paid) as paid on the first day of the benefit week in which it is due to be paid.

41.—(1) Any payment made under the Macfarlane Trust, the Macfarlane (Special Payments) Trust, the Macfarlane (Special Payments) (No. 2) Trust ("the Trusts"), the Fund, the Eileen Trust or [¹the Independent Living Fund (2006)].

(2) Any payment by or on behalf of a person who is suffering or who suffered from haemophilia, or who is or was a qualifying person which derives from a payment made under any of the Trusts to which sub-paragraph (1) refers and which is made to or for the benefit of—

    (a) that person's partner or former partner from whom that person is not, or where that person has died was not, estranged or divorced or with whom that person has formed a civil partnership that has not been dissolved or, where that person has died, had not been dissolved at the time of that person's death;

    (b) any child who is a member of that person's family or who was such a member and who is a member of the claimant's family; or

    (c) any young person who is a member of that person's family or who was such a member and who is a member of the claimant's family.

(3) Any payment by or on behalf of the partner or former partner of a person who is suffering or who suffered from haemophilia or who is or was a qualifying person provided that the partner or former partner and that person are not, or if either of them has died were not, estranged or divorced or, where the partner or former partner and that person have formed a civil partnership, the civil partnership has not been dissolved or, if either of them has died, had not been dissolved at the time of the death, which derives from a payment made under any of the Trusts to which sub-paragraph (1) refers and which is made to or for the benefit of—

    (a) the person who is suffering from haemophilia or who is a qualifying person;

    (b) any child who is a member of that person's family or who was such a member and who is a member of the claimant's family; or

    (c) any young person who is a member of that person's family or who was such a member and who is a member of the claimant's family.

(4) Any payment by a person who is suffering from haemophilia or who is a qualifying person, which derives from a payment under any of the Trusts to which sub-paragraph (1) refers, where—

    (a) that person has no partner or former partner from whom that person is not estranged or divorced or with whom that person has formed a civil partnership that has not been dissolved, nor any child or young person who is or had been a member of that person's family; and

    (b) the payment is made either—

        (i) to that person's parent or step-parent; or

        (ii) where that person at the date of the payment is a child, a young person or a full-time student who has not completed full-time education and had no parent or step-parent, to that person's guardian,

but only for a period from the date of the payment until the end of two years from that person's death.

(5) Any payment out of the estate of a person who suffered from haemophilia or who was a qualifying person, which derives from a payment under any of the Trusts to which sub-

paragraph (1) refers, where—

   (a) that person at the date of that person's death (the relevant date) had no partner or former partner from whom that person was not estranged or divorced or with whom that person had formed a civil partnership that had not been dissolved, nor any child or young person who was or had been a member of that person's family; and

   (b) the payment is made either—

      (i) to that person's parent or step-parent; or

      (ii) where that person at the relevant date was a child, a young person or a full-time student who had not completed full-time education and had no parent or step-parent, to that person's guardian,

but only for a period of two years from the relevant date.

(6) In the case of a person to whom or for whose benefit a payment referred to in this paragraph is made, any income which derives from any payment of income or capital made under or deriving from any of the Trusts.

(7) For the purposes of sub-paragraphs (2) to (6), any reference to the Trusts is to be construed as including a reference to the Fund, the Eileen Trust, the Skipton Fund and the London Bombings Relief Charitable Fund.

42. Any payment made by the Secretary of State to compensate for the loss (in whole or in part) of entitlement to housing benefit.

43. Any payment made to a juror or a witness in respect of attendance at a court other than compensation for loss of earnings or for the loss of a benefit payable under the benefit Acts.

44. Any payment in consequence of a reduction of council tax under section 13 or section 80 of the Local Government Finance Act 1992 (reduction of liability for council tax).

45.—(1) Any payment or repayment made—

   (a) as respects England, under regulation 5, 6 or 12 of the National Health Service (Travel Expenses and Remission of Charges) Regulations 2003 (travelling expenses and health service supplies);

   (b) as respects Wales, under regulation 5, 6 or 11 of the National Health Service (Travelling Expenses and Remission of Charges) (Wales) Regulations 2007;

   (c) as respects Scotland, under regulation 3, 5 or 11 of the National Health Service (Travelling Expenses and Remission of Charges) (Scotland) (No. 2) Regulations 2003 (travelling expenses and health service supplies).

(2) Any payment or repayment made by the Secretary of State for Health, the Scottish Ministers or the Welsh Ministers which is analogous to a payment or repayment mentioned in sub-paragraph (1).

46. Any payment made to such persons entitled to receive benefits as may be determined by or under a scheme made pursuant to section 13 of the Social Security Act 1988 in lieu of vouchers or similar arrangements in connection with the provision of those benefits (including payments made in place of healthy start vouchers, milk tokens or the supply of vitamins).

47. Any payment made either by the Secretary of State for Justice or by the Scottish Ministers under a scheme established to assist relatives and other persons to visit persons in custody.

48. Any payment (other than a training allowance) made, whether by the Secretary of State or by any other person, under the Disabled Persons (Employment) Act 1944 to assist disabled persons to obtain or retain employment despite their disability.

49. Any supplementary pension under article 23(2) of the Naval, Military and Air Forces Etc. (Disablement and Death) Service Pensions Order 2006 (pensions to widows, widowers or surviving civil partners) and any analogous payment made by the Secretary of State for Defence to any person who is not a person entitled under that Order.

[³ **50.**–(1) If the claimant is in receipt of any benefit under Part 2, 3 or 5 of the Contributions and Benefits Act, any increase in the rate of that benefit arising under Part 4 (increases for dependants) or section 106(a) (unemployability supplement) of that Act, where the dependant in respect of whom the increase is paid is not a member of the claimant's family.

(2) If the claimant is in receipt of any pension or allowance under Part 2 or 3 of the Naval,

Military and Air Forces Etc. (Disablement and Death) Service Pensions Order 2006, any increase in the rate of that pension or allowance under that Order, where the dependant in respect of whom the increase is paid is not a member of the claimant's family.]

51. In the case of a pension awarded at the supplementary rate under article 27(3) of the Personal Injuries (Civilians) Scheme 1983 (pensions to widows, widowers or surviving civil partners), the sum specified in paragraph 1(c) of Schedule 4 to that scheme.

52.—(1) Any payment which is— **9.441**
    (a) made under any of the Dispensing Instruments to a widow, [¹widower or surviving civil partner] of a person—
        (i) whose death was attributable to service in a capacity analogous to service as a member of the armed forces of the Crown; and
        (ii) whose service in such capacity terminated before 31st March 1973; and
    (b) equal to the amount specified in article 23(2) of the Naval, Military and Air Forces Etc. (Disablement and Death) Service Pensions Order 2006.
(2) In this paragraph "the Dispensing Instruments" means the Order in Council of 19th December 1881, the Royal Warrant of 27th October 1884 and the Order by His Majesty of 14th January 1922 (exceptional grants of pay, non-effective pay and allowances).

53. Any payment made [⁴. . .] under section 12B of the Social Work (Scotland) Act 1968 or under regulations made under section 57 of the Health and Social Care Act 2001 (direct payments).

54.—(1) Any payment specified in sub-paragraph (2) to a claimant who was formerly a student and who has completed the course in respect of which those payments were made.
(2) The payments specified for the purposes of sub-paragraph (1) are—
    (a) any grant income and covenant income as defined for the purposes of Chapter 10 of Part 10;
    (b) any student loan as defined in Chapter 10 of Part 10;
    (c) any contribution as defined in Chapter 10 of Part 10 which—
        (i) is taken into account in ascertaining the amount of a student loan referred to in paragraph (b); and
        (ii) has been paid.

55.—(1) Subject to sub-paragraph (2), in the case of a person who is receiving, or who has received, assistance under the self-employment route, any payment to the person—
    (a) to meet expenses wholly and necessarily incurred whilst carrying on the commercial activity;
    (b) which is used or intended to be used to maintain repayments on a loan taken out by that person for the purposes of establishing or carrying on the commercial activity, in respect of which such assistance is or was received.
(2) Sub-paragraph (1) is to apply only in respect of payments which are paid to that person from the special account as defined for the purposes of Chapter 5 of Part 10.

56. Any payment made with respect to a person on account of the provision of after-care under section 117 of the Mental Health Act 1983 or section 25 of the Mental Health (Care and Treatment) (Scotland) Act 2003 or the provision of accommodation or welfare services to which Part 3 of the National Assistance Act 1948 refers or to which the Social Work (Scotland) Act 1968 refers, which falls to be treated as notional income under paragraph (6) of regulation 107 (payments made in respect of a person living in a care home, an Abbeyfield Home or an independent hospital).

57.—(1) Any payment of a sports award except to the extent that it has been made in respect of any one or more of the items specified in sub-paragraph (2).
(2) The items specified for the purposes of sub-paragraph (1) are food, ordinary clothing or footwear, household fuel, rent for which housing benefit is payable or any housing costs to the extent that they are met under regulation 67(1)(c) or 68(1)(d) (housing costs), of the claimant or, where the claimant is a member of a family, any other member of the claimant's family, or any council tax or water charges for which that claimant or member is liable.
(3) For the purposes of sub-paragraph (2) "food" does not include vitamins, minerals or other special dietary supplements intended to enhance the performance of the person in the sport in respect of which the award was made;

58. Where the amount of a subsistence allowance paid to a person in a benefit week exceeds the amount of income-based jobseeker's allowance that person would have received in that benefit week had it been payable to that person, less 50p, that excess amount.

59. In the case of a claimant participating in an employment zone programme, any discretionary payment made by an employment zone contractor to the claimant, being a fee, grant, loan or otherwise.

60.—(1) Subject to sub-paragraph (3), any payment of child maintenance where the child or young person in respect of whom the payment is made is a member of the claimant's family except where the person making the payment is the claimant or the claimant's partner.

(2) For the purposes of sub-paragraph (1), where more than one payment of child maintenance—

    (a) in respect of more than one child or young person; or

    (b) made by more than one person in respect of a child or young person,

falls to be taken into account in any week, all such payments are to be aggregated and treated as if they were a single payment.

[² (3) No more than £20 shall be disregarded in respect of each week to which any payment of child maintenance is attributed in accordance with regulations 120 to 125 (child maintenance and liable relatives).

(4) In this paragraph, "child maintenance" shall have the same meaning as in regulation 119.]

61. In the case of a person to whom paragraph (5) of regulation 6 of the Income Support Regulations (persons not treated as in remunerative work) applies, the whole of that person's income.

62. Any discretionary housing payment paid pursuant to regulation 2(1) of the Discretionary Financial Assistance Regulations 2001.

63.—(1) Any payment made by a local authority or by the Welsh Ministers, to or on behalf of the claimant or the claimant's partner relating to a service which is provided to develop or sustain the capacity of the claimant or the claimant's partner to live independently in the claimant's or the claimant's partner's accommodation.

(2) For the purposes of sub-paragraph (1) "local authority" includes, in England, a county council.

64. Any housing benefit to which the claimant is entitled.

65. Any council tax benefit to which the claimant is entitled.

AMENDMENTS

1. Employment and Support Allowance (Miscellaneous Amendments) Regulations 2008 (SI 2008/2428), reg.18 (October 27, 2008).

2. Employment and Support Allowance (Miscellaneous Amendments) Regulations 2008 (SI 2008/2428), reg.20(10) (October 27, 2008).

3. Social Security (Miscellaneous Amendments) (No. 7) Regulations 2008 (SI 2008/3157), reg.11(3) (January 5, 2009).

4. Social Security (Miscellaneous Amendments) Regulations 2009 (SI 2009/583), reg.10(9) (April 6, 2009).

DEFINITIONS

    "Abbeyfield Home"—see reg.2(1).

    "adoption leave"—*ibid.*

    "benefit week"—*ibid.*

    "board and lodging"—*ibid.*

    "care home"—*ibid.*

    "child"—*ibid.*

    "claimant"—see reg.83(1).

    "dwelling occupied as the home"—see reg.2(1).

"Eileen Trust"—*ibid.*
"employed earner"—*ibid.*
"employment zone"—*ibid.*
"family"—*ibid.*
"the Fund"—*ibid.*
"guaranteed income payment"—*ibid.*
"Immigration and Asylum Act"—*ibid.*
"independent hospital"—*ibid.*
"the Independent Living Fund (2006)"—*ibid.*
"the London Bombings Relief Charitable Fund"—*ibid.*
"Macfarlane (Special Payments) Trust"—*ibid.*
"Macfarlane (Special Payments) (No. 2) Trust"—*ibid.*
"Macfarlane Trust"—*ibid.*
"occupational pension scheme"—*ibid.*
"ordinary clothing or footwear"—*ibid.*
"partner"—*ibid.*
"payment"—*ibid.*
"personal pension scheme"—*ibid.*
"qualifying person"—*ibid.*
"self-employment route"—*ibid.*
"Skipton Fund" *ibid.*
"sports award"—*ibid.*
"subsistence allowance"—*ibid.*
"training allowance"—*ibid.*
"voluntary organisation"—*ibid.*
"week"—*ibid.*
"young person"—*ibid.*

GENERAL NOTE

This is similar to Sch.9 to the Income Support Regulations/Sch.7 to the JSA Regulations (subject to some reordering and minor adjustments in the wording). **9.442**

Regulation 111(2)

SCHEDULE 9

CAPITAL TO BE DISREGARDED

1. The dwelling occupied as the home but, notwithstanding regulation 83 (calculation of income and capital of members of claimant's family and of a polygamous marriage), only one dwelling is to be disregarded under this paragraph. **9.443**

2. Any premises acquired for occupation by the claimant which that claimant intends to occupy as the home within 26 weeks of the date of acquisition or such longer period as is reasonable in the circumstances to enable the claimant to obtain possession and commence occupation of the premises.

3. Any sum directly attributable to the proceeds of sale of any premises formerly occupied by the claimant as the home which is to be used for the purchase of other premises intended for such occupation within 26 weeks of the date of sale or such longer period as is reasonable in the circumstances to enable the claimant to complete the purchase.

4. Any premises occupied in whole or in part by—
(a) a partner or relative of a single claimant or any member of the family as the home where that person is aged 60 or over or is incapacitated;
(b) the former partner of a claimant as the home; but this provision is not to apply where the former partner is a person from whom the claimant is estranged or divorced or with whom the person formed a civil partnership that has been dissolved.

5. Where a claimant has ceased to occupy what was formerly the dwelling occupied as the home following the claimant's estrangement or divorce from, or dissolution of the claimant's civil partnership with, the claimant's former partner, that dwelling for a period of 26 weeks from the date on which the claimant ceased to occupy that dwelling or, where that dwelling is occupied as the home by the former partner who is a lone parent, for as long as it is so occupied.

6. Any premises where the claimant is taking reasonable steps to dispose of those premises, for a period of 26 weeks from the date on which the claimant first took such steps, or such longer period as is reasonable in the circumstances to enable the claimant to dispose of those premises.

7. Any premises which the claimant intends to occupy as the home, and in respect of which that claimant is taking steps to obtain possession and has sought legal advice or has commenced legal proceedings, with a view to obtaining possession, for a period of 26 weeks from the date on which the claimant first sought such advice or first commenced such proceedings whichever is earlier, or such longer period as is reasonable in the circumstances to enable the claimant to obtain possession and commence occupation of those premises.

8. Any premises which the claimant intends to occupy as the home to which essential repairs or alterations are required in order to render them fit for such occupation, for a period of 26 weeks from the date on which the claimant first takes steps to effect those repairs or alterations, or such longer period as is reasonable in the circumstances to enable those repairs or alterations to be carried out and the claimant to commence occupation of the premises.

9. Any future interest in property of any kind, other than land or premises in respect of which the claimant has granted a subsisting lease or tenancy, including sub-leases or sub-tenancies.

10.—(1) The assets of any business owned in whole or in part by the claimant and for the purposes of which that claimant is engaged as a self-employed earner or, if the claimant has ceased to be so engaged, for such period as may be reasonable in the circumstances to allow for disposal of any such asset.

(2) The assets of any business owned in whole or in part by the claimant where that claimant—

    (a) is not engaged as self-employed earner in that business by reason of some disease or bodily or mental disablement; but

    (b) intends to become engaged (or, as the case may be, re-engaged) as a self-employed earner in that business as soon as the claimant recovers or is able to become engaged, or reengaged, in that business,

for a period of 26 weeks from the date on which the claim for an income-related allowance is made, or is treated as made, or, if it is unreasonable to expect the claimant to become engaged or re-engaged in that business within that period, for such longer period as is reasonable in the circumstances to enable the claimant to become so engaged or re-engaged.

(3) In the case of a person who is receiving assistance under the self-employment route, the assets acquired by that person for the purpose of establishing or carrying on the commercial activity in respect of which such assistance is being received.

(4) In the case of a person who has ceased carrying on the commercial activity in respect of which assistance was received as specified in sub-paragraph (3), the assets relating to that activity for such period as may be reasonable in the circumstances to allow for disposal of any such asset.

11.—(1) Subject to sub-paragraph (2), any arrears of, or any concessionary payment made to compensate for arrears due to the non-payment of—

    (a) any payment specified in paragraph 8, 10 or 11 of Schedule 8 (other income to be disregarded);

    (b) an income-related allowance, an income-related benefit or an income-based job-seeker's allowance, child tax credit or working tax credit;

    (c) any discretionary housing payment paid pursuant to regulation 2(1) of the Discretionary Financial Assistance Regulations 2001,

but only for a period of 52 weeks from the date of the receipt of the arrears or of the concessionary payment.

(2) In a case where the total of any arrears and, if appropriate, any concessionary payment

referred to in sub-paragraph (1) relating to any one of the specified payments, benefits or allowances, amounts to £5,000 or more (referred to in this sub-paragraph and in sub-paragraph (3) as the "relevant sum") and is—

   (a) paid in order to rectify, or to compensate for, an official error as defined in regulation 1(3) of the Social Security and Child Support (Decisions and Appeals) Regulations 1999; and

   (b) received by the claimant in full on or after 14th October 2001,

sub-paragraph (1) is to have effect in relation to such arrears or concessionary payment either for a period of 52 weeks from the date of receipt, or, if the relevant sum is received in its entirety during the award of an income-related allowance, for the remainder of that award if that is a longer period.

(3) For the purposes of sub-paragraph (2), "the award of an income-related allowance" means—

   (a) the award either of an income-related allowance, income support or of an income-based jobseeker's allowance in which the relevant sum (or first part thereof where it is paid in more than one instalment) is received; and

   (b) where that award is followed by one or more further awards which in each case may be either of an income-related allowance, income support or of an income-based job-seeker's allowance and which, or each of which, begins immediately after the end of the previous award, such further awards until the end of the last such award, provided that for any such further awards the claimant—

      (i) is the person who received the relevant sum;

      (ii) is the partner of the person who received the relevant sum, or was that person's partner at the date of that person's death; or

      (iii) in the case of a joint-claim jobseeker's allowance, is a joint-claim couple either member or both members of which received the relevant sum.

12. Any sum—

   (a) paid to the claimant in consequence of damage to, or loss of, the home or any personal possession and intended for its repair or replacement; or

   (b) acquired by the claimant (whether as a loan or otherwise) on the express condition that it is to be used for effecting essential repairs or improvements to the home,

and which is to be used for the intended purpose, for a period of 26 weeks from the date on which it was so paid or acquired or such longer period as is reasonable in the circumstances to enable the claimant to effect the repairs, replacement or improvements.

13. Any sum—

   (a) deposited with a housing association as defined in section 1(1) of the Housing Associations Act 1985 or section 338(1) of the Housing (Scotland) Act 1987 as a condition of occupying the home;

   (b) which was so deposited and which is to be used for the purchase of another home, for the period of 26 weeks or such longer period as is reasonable in the circumstances to complete the purchase.

14. Any personal possessions except those which had or have been acquired by the claimant with the intention of reducing that claimant's capital in order to secure entitlement to an employment and support allowance, a jobseeker's allowance or to income support or to increase the amount of those benefits.

15. The value of the right to receive any income under an annuity and the surrender value (if any) of such an annuity.   **9.444**

16. Where the funds of a trust are derived from a payment made in consequence of any personal injury to the claimant or the claimant's partner, the value of the trust fund and the value of the right to receive any payment under that trust.

17.—(1) Any payment made to the claimant or the claimant's partner in consequence of any personal injury to the claimant or, as the case may be, the claimant's partner.

(2) But sub-paragraph (1)—

   (a) applies only for the period of 52 weeks beginning with the day on which the claimant first receives any payment [²in consequence of that personal injury];

   (b) does not apply to any subsequent payment made to the claimant in consequence of that injury (whether it is made by the same person or another);

    (c) ceases to apply to the payment or any part of the payment from the day on which the claimant no longer possesses it;

    (d) does not apply to any payment from a trust where the funds of the trust are derived from a payment made in consequence of any personal injury to the claimant.

(3) For the purpose of sub-paragraph (2)(c), the circumstances in which a claimant no longer possesses a payment or a part of it include where the claimant has used a payment or part of it to purchase an asset.

18. The value of the right to receive any income under a life interest or from a life rent.

19. The value of the right to receive any income which is disregarded under paragraph 9 of Schedule 7 or paragraph 24 of Schedule 8 (earnings or other income to be disregarded).

20. The surrender value of any policy of life insurance.

21. Where any payment of capital falls to be made by instalments, the value of the right to receive any outstanding instalments.

22.—(1) Any payment made by a local authority in accordance with—

    (a) section 17, 23B, 23C or 24A of the Children Act 1989;

    (b) section 12 of the Social Work (Scotland) Act 1968; or

    (c) section 29 or 30 of the Children (Scotland) Act 1995 (local authorities' duty to promote welfare of children and powers to grant financial assistance to persons in, or formerly in, their care).

(2) Subject to paragraph (3), any payment (or part of a payment) made by a local authority in accordance with section 23C of the Children Act 1989 or section 29 of the Children (Scotland) Act 1995 (local authorities' duty to promote welfare of children and powers to grant financial assistance to persons in, or formerly in, their care) to a person ("A") which A passes on to the claimant.

(3) Sub-paragraph (2) applies only where A—

    (a) was formerly in the claimant's care; and

    (b) is aged 18 or over; and

    (c) continues to live with the claimant.

23. Any social fund payment made pursuant to Part 8 of the Contributions and Benefits Act.

24. Any refund of tax which falls to be deducted under section 369 of the Income and Corporation Taxes Act 1988 (mortgage interest payable under deduction of tax) on a payment of relevant loan interest for the purpose of acquiring an interest in the home or carrying out repairs or improvements in the home.

25. Any capital which under regulation 105 or 137 (capital treated as income or treatment of student loans) is to be treated as income.

26. Where a payment of capital is made in a currency other than sterling, any banking charge or commission payable in converting that payment into sterling.

27.—(1) Any payment made under the Macfarlane Trust, the Macfarlane (Special Payments) Trust, the Macfarlane (Special Payments) (No. 2) Trust ("the Trusts"), the Fund, the Eileen Trust [[1], the Independent Living Fund (2006)], the Skipton Fund or the London Bombings Relief Charitable Fund.

(2) Any payment by or on behalf of a person who is suffering or who suffered from haemophilia or who is or was a qualifying person, which derives from a payment made under any of the Trusts to which sub-paragraph (1) refers and which is made to or for the benefit of—

    (a) that person's partner or former partner from whom the person is not, or where that person has died was not, estranged or divorced or with whom the person has formed a civil partnership that has not been dissolved or, where that person has died, had not been dissolved at the time of that person's death;

    (b) any child who is a member of that person's family or who was such a member and who is a member of the claimant's family; or

    (c) any young person who is a member of that person's family or who was such a member and who is a member of the claimant's family.

(3) Any payment by or on behalf of the partner or former partner of a person who is suffering or who suffered from haemophilia or who is or was a qualifying person provided that the partner or former partner and that person are not, or if either of them has died were not, estranged or divorced or, where the partner or former partner and that person have formed a civil partnership, the civil partnership has not been dissolved or, if either of them has died, had not been dissolved at the time of the death, which derives from a payment made under any of the Trusts to which sub-paragraph (1) refers and which is made to or for the benefit of—

(a) the person who is suffering from haemophilia or who is a qualifying person;

(b) any child who is a member of that person's family or who was such a member and who is a member of the claimant's family; or

(c) any young person who is a member of that person's family or who was such a member and who is a member of the claimant's family.

(4) Any payment by a person who is suffering from haemophilia or who is a qualifying person, which derives from a payment under any of the Trusts to which sub-paragraph (1) refers, where—

(a) that person has no partner or former partner from whom the person is not estranged or divorced or with whom the person has formed a civil partnership that has not been dissolved, nor any child or young person who is or had been a member of that person's family; and

(b) the payment is made either—

(i) to that person's parent or step-parent; or

(ii) where that person at the date of the payment is a child, a young person or a full-time student who has not completed full-time education and had no parent or step-parent, to that person's guardian,

but only for a period from the date of the payment until the end of two years from that person's death.

(5) Any payment out of the estate of a person who suffered from haemophilia or who was a qualifying person, which derives from a payment under any of the Trusts to which sub-paragraph (1) refers, where—

(a) that person at the date of that person's death (the relevant date) had no partner or former partner from whom the person was not estranged or divorced or with whom the person had formed a civil partnership that had not been dissolved, nor any child or young person who was or had been a member of that person's family; and

(b) the payment is made either—

(i) to that person's parent or step-parent; or

(ii) where that person at the relevant date was a child, a young person or a full-time student who had not completed full-time education and had no parent or step-parent, to that person's guardian,

but only for a period of two years from the relevant date.

(6) In the case of a person to whom or for whose benefit a payment referred to in this paragraph is made, any capital resource which derives from any payment of income or capital made under or deriving from any of the Trusts.

(7) For the purposes of sub-paragraphs (2) to (6), any reference to the Trusts is to be construed as including a reference to the Fund, the Eileen Trust, the Skipton Fund or the London Bombings Relief Charitable Fund.

28. The value of the right to receive an occupational or personal pension. **9.445**

29. The value of any funds held under a personal pension scheme.

30. The value of the right to receive any rent except where the claimant has a reversionary interest in the property in respect of which rent is due.

31. Any payment in kind made by a charity or under the Macfarlane Trust, Macfarlane (Special Payments) Trust, the Macfarlane (Special Payments) (No. 2) Trust, the Fund, the Eileen Trust or [²the Independent Living Fund (2006)].

32. Any payment made pursuant to section 2 of the Employment and Training Act 1973 or section 2 of the Enterprise and New Towns (Scotland) Act 1990, but only for the period of 52 weeks beginning on the date of receipt of the payment.

33. Any payment made by the Secretary of State to compensate for the loss (in whole or in part) of entitlement to housing benefit.

34. Any payment made to a juror or a witness in respect of attendance at a court other than compensation for loss of earnings or for the loss of a benefit payable under the benefit Acts.

35. Any payment [²in consequence of a reduction] of council tax under section 13 or, as the case may be, section 80 of the Local Government Finance Act 1992 (reduction of liability for council tax), but only for a period of 52 weeks from the date of the receipt of the payment.

36. Any grant made to the claimant in accordance with a scheme under section 129 of the Housing Act 1988 or section 66 of the Housing (Scotland) Act 1988 (schemes for payments to assist local housing authorities and local authority tenants to obtain other accommodation) which is to be used—
   (a) to purchase premises intended for occupation as the claimant's home; or
   (b) to carry out repairs or alterations which are required to render premises fit for occupation as the claimant's home,

for a period of 26 weeks from the date on which the claimant received such a grant or such longer period as is reasonable in the circumstances to enable the purchase, repairs or alterations to be completed and the claimant to commence occupation of those premises as the claimant's home.

37.—(1) Any payment or repayment made—
   (a) as respects England, under regulation 5, 6 or 12 of the National Health Service (Travel Expenses and Remission of Charges) Regulations 2003 (travelling expenses and health service supplies);
   (b) as respects Wales, under regulation 5, 6 or 11 of the National Health Service (Travelling Expenses and Remission of Charges) (Wales) Regulations 2007;
   (c) as respects Scotland, under regulation 3, 5 or 11 of the National Health Service (Travelling Expenses and Remission of Charges) (Scotland) (No. 2) Regulations 2003 (travelling expenses and health service supplies);
but only for a period of 52 weeks from the date of receipt of the payment or repayment.

(2) Any payment or repayment made by the Secretary of State for Health, the Scottish Ministers or the Welsh Ministers which is analogous to a payment or repayment mentioned in sub-paragraph (1); but only for a period of 52 weeks from the date of receipt of the payment or repayment.

38. Any payment made to such persons entitled to receive benefits as may be determined by or under a scheme made pursuant to section 13 of the Social Security Act 1988 in lieu of vouchers or similar arrangements in connection with the provision of those benefits (including payments made in place of healthy start vouchers, milk tokens or the supply of vitamins) but only for a period of 52 weeks from the date of receipt of the payment.

[⁴ **38A.** Any payment made under Part 8A of the Social Security Contributions and Benefits Act 1992 (entitlement to health in pregnancy grant).]

39. Any payment made either by the Secretary of State for Justice or by the Scottish Ministers under a scheme established to assist relatives and other persons to visit persons in custody, but only for a period of 52 weeks from the date of receipt of the payment.

40. Any arrears of supplementary pension which is disregarded under paragraph 49 of Schedule 8 (sums to be disregarded in the calculation of income other than earnings) or of any amount which is disregarded under paragraphs 51 or 52 of that Schedule, but only for a period of 52 weeks from the date of receipt of the arrears.

41. Any payment (other than a training allowance) made, whether by the Secretary of State or by any other person, under the Disabled Persons (Employment) Act 1944 to assist disabled persons to obtain or retain employment despite their disability.

42. Any payment made by a local authority under section 3 of the Disabled Persons (Employment) Act 1958 to homeworkers assisted under the Blind Homeworkers' Scheme.

9.446 **43.**—(1) Any sum to which sub-paragraph (2) applies and—
   (a) which is administered on behalf of a person by the High Court or the County Court under Rule 21.11(1) of the Civil Procedure Rules 1998 or by the Court of Protection;

(b) which can only be disposed of by order or direction of any such court; or
(c) where the person concerned is under the age of 18, which can only be disposed of by order or direction prior to that person attaining age 18.
(2) This sub-paragraph applies to a sum which is derived from—
(a) an award of damages for a personal injury to that person; or
(b) compensation for the death of one or both parents where the person concerned is under the age of 18.

44. Any sum administered on behalf of a person in accordance with an order made under section 13 of the Children (Scotland) Act 1995, or under Rule 36.14 of the Ordinary Cause Rules 1993 or under Rule 128 of the Ordinary Cause Rules, where such sum derives from—
(a) an award of damages for a personal injury to that person; or
(b) compensation for the death of one or both parents where the person concerned is under the age of 18.

45. Any payment to the claimant as holder of the Victoria Cross or George Cross.

46. In the case of a person who is receiving, or who has received, assistance under the self-employment route, any sum which is acquired by that person for the purpose of establishing or carrying on the commercial activity in respect of which such assistance is or was received but only for a period of 52 weeks from the date on which that sum was acquired.

47. (1) [²Any payment of a sports award] for a period of 26 weeks from the date of receipt of that payment except to the extent that it has been made in respect of any one or more of the items specified in sub-paragraph (2).
(2) The items specified for the purposes of sub-paragraph (1) are food, ordinary clothing or footwear, household fuel, rent for which housing benefit is payable or any housing costs to the extent that they are met under regulation 67(1)(c) or 68(1)(d) (housing costs), of the claimant or, where the claimant is a member of a family, any other member of the claimant's family, or any council tax or water charges for which that claimant or member is liable.
(3) For the purposes of sub-paragraph (2) "food" does not include vitamins, minerals or other special dietary supplements intended to enhance the performance of the person in the sport in respect of which the award was made.

48. In the case of a claimant participating in an employment zone programme, any discretionary payment made by an employment zone contractor to the claimant, being a fee, grant, loan or otherwise, but only for the period of 52 weeks from the date of receipt of the payment.

49. Any arrears of subsistence allowance paid as a lump sum but only for the period of 52 weeks from the date of receipt of the payment.

50. Where an ex-gratia payment of £10,000 has been made by the Secretary of State on or after 1st February 2001 in consequence of the imprisonment or internment of—
(a) the claimant;
(b) the claimant's partner;
(c) the claimant's deceased spouse or deceased civil partner; or
(d) the claimant's partner's deceased spouse or deceased civil partner,
by the Japanese during the Second World War, £10,000.

51. In the case of a person to whom paragraph (5) of regulation 6 of the Income Support Regulations (persons not treated as in remunerative work) applies, the whole of the claimant's capital.

52.—(1) Any payment—
(a) by way of an education maintenance allowance made pursuant to—
(i) regulations made under section 518 of the Education Act 1996;
(ii) regulations made under section 49 or 73(f) of the Education (Scotland) Act 1980;
(iii) directions made under section 73ZA of the Education (Scotland) Act 1980 and paid under section 12(2)(c) of the Further and Higher Education (Scotland) Act 1992; or
(b) corresponding to such an education maintenance allowance, made pursuant to—

(i) section 14 or section 181 of the Education Act 2002; or
(ii) regulations made under section 181 of that Act.

(2) Any payment, other than a payment to which sub-paragraph (1) applies, made pursuant to—

(a) regulations made under section 518 of the Education Act 1996;
(b) regulations made under section 49 of the Education (Scotland) Act 1980; or
(c) directions made under section 73ZA of the Education (Scotland) Act 1980 and paid under section 12(2)(c) of the Further and Higher Education (Scotland) Act 1992,

in respect of a course of study attended by a child or a young person or a person who is in receipt of an education maintenance allowance made pursuant to any provision specified in sub-paragraph (1).

53.—(1) Subject to sub-paragraph (2), the amount of any trust payment made to a claimant or a member of a claimant's family who is—

(a) a diagnosed person;
(b) the diagnosed person's partner or the person who was the diagnosed person's partner at the date of the diagnosed person's death;
(c) a parent of a diagnosed person, a person acting in the place of the diagnosed person's parents or a person who was so acting at the date of the diagnosed person's death; or
(d) a member of the diagnosed person's family (other than that person's partner) or a person who was a member of the diagnosed person's family (other than that person's partner) at the date of the diagnosed person's death.

(2) Where a trust payment is made to—

(a) a person referred to in sub-paragraph (1)(a) or (b), that sub-paragraph will apply for the period beginning on the date on which the trust payment is made and ending on the date on which that person dies;
(b) a person referred to in sub-paragraph (1)(c), that sub-paragraph will apply for the period beginning on the date on which the trust payment is made and ending two years after that date;
(c) a person referred to in sub-paragraph (1)(d), that sub-paragraph will apply for the period beginning on the date on which the trust payment is made and ending—
(i) two years after that date; or
(ii) on the day before the day on which that person—
(aa) ceases receiving full-time education; or
(bb) attains the age of 20,

whichever is the latest.

(3) Subject to sub-paragraph (4), the amount of any payment by a person to whom a trust payment has been made, or of any payment out of the estate of a person to whom a trust payment has been made, which is made to a claimant or a member of a claimant's family who is—

(a) the diagnosed person's partner or the person who was the diagnosed person's partner at the date of the diagnosed person's death;
(b) a parent of a diagnosed person, a person acting in the place of the diagnosed person's parents or a person who was so acting at the date of the diagnosed person's death; or
(c) a member of the diagnosed person's family (other than that person's partner) or a person who was a member of the diagnosed person's family (other than that person's partner) at the date of the diagnosed person's death,

but only to the extent that such payments do not exceed the total amount of any trust payments made to that person.

(4) Where a payment as referred to in sub-paragraph (3) is made to—

(a) a person referred to in sub-paragraph (3)(a), that sub-paragraph will apply for the period beginning on the date on which that payment is made and ending on the date on which that person dies;
(b) a person referred to in sub-paragraph (3)(b), that sub-paragraph will apply for the period beginning on the date on which that payment is made and ending two years after that date;
(c) a person referred to in sub-paragraph (3)(c), that sub-paragraph will apply for the period beginning on the date on which that payment is made and ending—
(i) two years after that date; or
(ii) on the day before the day on which that person—
(aa) ceases receiving full-time education; or
(bb) attains the age of 20,

whichever is the latest.

(5) In this paragraph, a reference to a person—

(a) being the diagnosed person's partner;

(b) being a member of the diagnosed person's family; or

(c) acting in the place of the diagnosed person's parents,

at the date of the diagnosed person's death will include a person who would have been such a person or a person who would have been so acting, but for the diagnosed person residing in a care home, an Abbeyfield Home or an independent hospital on that date.

(6) In this paragraph—

"diagnosed person" means a person who has been diagnosed as suffering from, or who, after that person's death, has been diagnosed as having suffered from, variant Creutzfeldt-Jakob disease;

"relevant trust" means a trust established out of funds provided by the Secretary of State in respect of persons who suffered, or who are suffering, from variant Creutzfeldt-Jakob disease for the benefit of persons eligible for payments in accordance with its provisions;

"trust payment" means a payment under a relevant trust.

54. The amount of a payment, other than a [³ war disablement pension, war widow's pension or war widower's pension], to compensate for the fact that the claimant, the claimant's partner, the claimant's deceased spouse or deceased civil partner or the claimant's partner's deceased spouse or deceased civil partner—

(a) was a slave labourer or a forced labourer;

(b) had suffered property loss or had suffered personal injury; or

(c) was a parent of a child who had died,

during the Second World War.

55.—(1) Any payment made by a local authority or by the Welsh Ministers, to or on behalf of the claimant or the claimant's partner relating to a service which is provided to develop or sustain the capacity of the claimant or the claimant's partner to live independently in the claimant's or the claimant's partner's accommodation.

(2) For the purposes of sub-paragraph (1) "local authority" includes, in England, a county council.

56. Any payment made under [⁴ . . .] regulations made under section 57 of the Health and Social Care Act 2001 or under section 12B of the Social Work (Scotland) Act 1968.

57. Any payment made to the claimant pursuant to regulations under section 2(6)(b), 3 or 4 of the Adoption and Children Act 2002.

58. Any payment made to the claimant in accordance with regulations made pursuant to section 14F of the Children Act 1989 (special guardianship support services).

AMENDMENTS

1. Employment and Support Allowance (Miscellaneous Amendments) Regulations 2008 (SI 2008/2428), reg.8(8) (October 27, 2008).

2. Employment and Support Allowance (Miscellaneous Amendments) Regulations 2008 (SI 2008/2428), reg.19 (October 27, 2008).

3. Social Security (Miscellaneous Amendments) (No. 7) Regulations 2008 (SI 2008/3157), reg.11(4) (January 5, 2009).

4. Social Security (Miscellaneous Amendments) Regulations 2009 (SI 2009/583), reg.10(10) (April 6, 2009).

DEFINITIONS

"Abbeyfield Home"—see reg.2(1).

"care home"—*ibid.*

"child"—*ibid.*

"claimant"—see reg.83(1).

"dwelling occupied as the home"—see reg.2(1).

"Eileen Trust"—*ibid.*
"employment zone"—*ibid.*
"family"—*ibid.*
"the Fund"—*ibid.*
"independent hospital"—*ibid.*
"the Independent Living Fund (2006)"—*ibid.*
"the London Bombings Relief Charitable Fund"—*ibid.*
"lone parent"—*ibid.*
"Macfarlane (Special Payments) Trust"—*ibid.*
"Macfarlane (Special Payments) (No. 2) Trust"—*ibid.*
"Macfarlane Trust"—*ibid.*
"occupational pension"—*ibid.*
"ordinary clothing or footwear"—*ibid.*
"partner"—*ibid.*
"payment"—*ibid.*
"personal pension scheme"—*ibid.*
"policy of life insurance"—*ibid.*
"qualifying person"—*ibid.*
"relative"—*ibid.*
"self-employed earner"—*ibid.*
"self-employment route"—*ibid.*
"single claimant"—*ibid.*
"Skipton Fund"—*ibid.*
"sports award"—*ibid.*
"subsistence allowance"—*ibid.*
"training allowance"—*ibid.*
"young person"—*ibid.*

GENERAL NOTE

9.447   This is similar to Sch.10 to the Income Support Regulations/Sch.8 to the JSA Regulations (subject to some reordering and minor adjustments in the wording).

Paragraphs 47 to 49 of Sch.10 to the Income Support Regulations have not been reproduced in this Schedule as they are no longer relevant.

Note that in para.14 the disregard of the value of personal possessions does not apply if they have been acquired in order to reduce capital so as to gain entitlement to, or increase the amount of, ESA, *JSA or income support*. This avoids the question that might otherwise have arisen on a claimant transferring from income support (or JSA) to ESA whether, if the acquisition had only been for the purposes of income support (or JSA), the disregard in para.14 applies.

The Employment and Support Allowance (Transitional Provisions) Regulations 2008

(SI 2008/795) (*AS AMENDED*)

ARRANGEMENT OF REGULATIONS

9.448   1. Citation, commencement and interpretation.
2. Claim for existing award.
3. Claim by person entitled or potentially entitled to existing award.
4. Claim for period before appointed day.
5. Transitional protection in relation to the Jobseekers Act 1995.

The Secretary of State for Work and Pensions in exercise of the powers conferred by section 25(2)(b) and (c) and 29 of, and paragraphs 1(1), 2 and 3(b), (c) and (d) of Schedule 4 to, the Welfare Reform Act 2007, makes the following Regulations which are made by virtue of, or consequential on, the provisions of the Welfare Reform Act 2007 and which are made before the end of a period of 6 months beginning with the coming into force of those provisions.

Citation, commencement and interpretation

1.—(1) These Regulations may be cited as the Employment and Support Allowance (Transitional Provisions) Regulations 2008.

(2) This regulation and regulations 2, 3 and 4 shall come into force on 27th July 2008.

(3) Regulation 5 shall come into force on 27th October 2008.

(4) In these Regulations "income support on the grounds of disability" means income support awarded to a person to whom regulation [¹ . . .] 13(2)(b) or (bb) of, or paragraph 7(a) or (b), 10, 12 or 13 of Schedule 1B to, the Income Support (General) Regulations 1987 (prescribed categories of person) applies.

9.449

AMENDMENT

1. Employment and Support Allowance (Miscellaneous Amendments) Regulations 2008 (SI 2008/2428), reg.42 (October 27, 2008).

DEFINITION

"income support on the grounds of disability"—see para.(4).

GENERAL NOTE

This regulation entered into force on July 27, 2008, three months before the main ESA scheme became operative.

9.450

Claim for existing award

2.—(1) A claim for incapacity benefit, severe disablement allowance or income support on the grounds of disability, whenever made, in respect of a period which begins on or after the appointed day, is to be treated as a claim for an employment and support allowance.

9.451

(2) Paragraph (1) does not apply to—

(a) a claim for incapacity benefit or severe disablement allowance relating to a period of incapacity for work which is one of two periods treated as one period of incapacity for work under section 30C(1)(c) of the Contributions and Benefits Act (linking rules);

(b) a claim made by a welfare to work beneficiary in accordance with regulation 13A of the Social Security (Incapacity for Work) (General) Regulations 1995 (welfare to work beneficiary); [¹ . . .]

(c) a claim for income support on the grounds of disability where—

(i) the claimant was previously entitled to income support on the grounds of disability, for a period of 4 or more consecutive days, and

(ii) the claimant ceased to be entitled to income support on the grounds of disability not more than 8 weeks before the commencement of the period in respect of which the current claim is made;

[¹(d) a claim for income support on the grounds of disability made by a claimant who is entitled to incapacity benefit or severe disablement allowance; or

(e) a claim for incapacity benefit made by a claimant who is entitled to income support on the grounds of disability.]

(3) Paragraph (1) does not apply insofar as a claim is treated as a claim for severe disablement allowance, maternity allowance or carer's allowance under regulation 9(1) of and Part 1 of Schedule 1 to, the Social Security (Claims and Payments) Regulations 1987 (claims treated as claimed in addition or in the alternative).

AMENDMENT

1. Employment and Support Allowance (Transitional Provisions) (Amendment) Regulations 2008 (SI 2008/2783), reg.2 (October 26, 2008).

DEFINITIONS

"appointed day"—see WRA 2007, s.29, Sch.4, para.11.
"claimant"—see WRA 2007, s.24(1).
"incapacity benefit"—see WRA 2007, s.29, Sch.4, para.11.
"income support on the grounds of disability"—see reg.1(4).
"severe disablement allowance"—see WRA 2007, s.29, Sch.4, para.11.

GENERAL NOTE

9.452   This regulation entered into force on July 27, 2008, three months before October 27, 2008, the "appointed day" when WRA 2007, s.1 and the main ESA provisions became operative (see WRA 2007, s.29, Sch.4, para.11, and the Welfare Reform Act 2007 (Commencement No.6 and Consequential Provisions) Order 2008 (SI 2008/787), art.2(4).

It deals with claims for one or more of the benefits in the already existing incapacity benefits' regime: incapacity benefit; severe disablement allowance (limited, of course, only to those entitled to it immediately before April 6, 2001) and "income support on the grounds of disability". This last covers claims for income support by someone to whom regulation 13(2)(b) or (bb) of, or para.7(a) or (b), 10, 12 or 13 of Sch.1B to, the Income Support (General) Regs 1987 (prescribed categories of person) applies (that is someone claiming IS as a person incapable of work; as a disabled or deaf student; or as a blind person).

Paragraph (1) provides that a claim for any such benefit made on or after October 27, 2008 (the "appointed day") is to be treated as one for ESA. To this there are within reg.2 three classes of exception:

(1) Where a claim for one of those benefits which is "linked" to a previous entitlement (para. (2)(a)–(c)).

9.453   This covers claims for IB or SDA linked to a previous period of incapacity for work by the standard eight week "linking rule" in SSCCBA 1992, s.30C(1)(c) (a period extendible by regs under s.30C(3)) (sub-para.(a)). It also embraces an IB claim by a "welfare to work beneficiary" under the Incapacity for Work Regs, reg.13A (the "104 week" rule) (sub-para.(b). It also covers an incapacity/disability-based claim for IS satisfying the four consecutive days "continuity rule" which ended not more than eight weeks prior to the claim now at issue (sub-para.(c)).

(2) Where a person entitled to incapacity benefit or severe disablement allowance claims income support on the grounds of disability and a person who is entitled to income support on the grounds of disability claims incapacity benefit (para. (2)(d), (e)).

Memo DMG 40/08 gives an example (IB entitlement enabling IS claim):   9.454

"Sue has been in receipt of IB for several years. She is not entitled to IS because her partner Mark is in remunerative work. Mark is made redundant in November 2008, and Sue claims IS on the grounds of disability. The DM makes a determination that Sue's claim is not treated as a claim for ESA, and decides the claim for IS accordingly."

(3) Where a claim is treated as a claim for severe disablement allowance, maternity allowance or carer's allowance under reg.9(1) of and Pt 1 of Sch.1 to, the Social Security (Claims and Payments) Regs 1987 (claims treated as claimed in addition or in the alternative).

See further the commentary to that regulation in Vol.III.   9.455

Claim by person entitled or potentially entitled to existing award

3.—(1) A person who is entitled to an existing award is excluded from   9.456
making a claim for an employment and support allowance.

(2) A claim for an employment and support allowance made by a person who would be entitled to an existing award if that person made a claim described in regulation 2(2), is to be treated as a claim for that award.

DEFINITION

"existing award"—see WRA 2007, s.29, Sch.4, para.11.

GENERAL NOTE

This regulation entered into force on July 27, 2008, three months before October   9.457
27, 2008, the "appointed day" when WRA 2007, s.1 and the main ESA provisions became operative (see WRA 2007, s.29, Sch.4, para.11, and the Welfare Reform Act 2007 (Commencement No.6 and Consequential Provisions) Order 2008 (SI 2008/787), art.2(4).

Paragraph (1) deals with claims for ESA by someone entitled to an "existing award", that is, one or more of the benefits in the already existing incapacity benefits' regime: incapacity benefit; severe disablement allowance (limited, of course, only to those entitled to it immediately before April 6, 2001) and "income support on the grounds of disability" (2007, s.29, Sch.4, para.11). This last covers claims for income support under by someone to whom 13(2)(b) or (bb) of, or para.7(a) or (b), 10, 12 or 13 of Sch.1B to, the Income Support (General) Regs 1987 (prescribed categories of person) applies (that is someone claiming IS as a person incapable of work; as a disabled or deaf student; or as a blind person).

Paragraph (1) provides that someone so entitled cannot be entitled to ESA. That and an existing award are mutually exclusive.

Paragraph (2) extends that preclusion to those who claim ESA but would be entitled to an "existing award" (IB, SDA or incapacity/disability-based IS, as the case may be) if they made a "linked" claim for it as envisaged by reg.2(2).

Claim for period before appointed day

4. Where—   9.458
  (a) (i) before the appointed day a person purports to make a claim, or
       (ii) on or after the appointed day a person makes a claim,
       for an employment and support allowance for a period beginning before the appointed day; and
  (b) it appears to the Secretary of State that the person would be entitled to incapacity benefit or income support on the grounds of disability if

that person made a claim for it in accordance with section 1(1)(a) of the Administration Act, the purported claim or claim may be treated by the Secretary of State as a claim in the alternative for incapacity benefit or income support on the grounds of disability.

DEFINITIONS

"appointed day"—see WRA 2007, s.29, Sch.4, para.11.
"incapacity benefit"—see WRA 2007, s.29, Sch.4, para.11.
"income support on the grounds of disability"—see reg.1(4).

GENERAL NOTE

9.459   This regulation entered into force on July 27, 2008, three months before October 27, 2008, the "appointed day" when WRA 2007, s.1 and the main ESA provisions became operative (see WRA 2007, s.29, Sch.4, para.11, and the Welfare Reform Act 2007 (Commencement No. 6 and Consequential Provisions) Order 2008 (SI 2008/787), art.2(4).

It deals with a claim for ESA made before October 27, 2008 (the "appointed day) or after that but for a period prior to the appointed day. No entitlement to ESA can arise until October 27, 2008. So such a claim can either be rejected or, under this regulation, instead treated by the Secretary of State as a claim in the alternative for incapacity benefit or income support on the grounds of disability (IS as a person incapable of work; as a disabled or deaf student; or as a blind person). But it can only be so treated if the Secretary of State is satisfied that he would have been entitled to one of those benefits has a claim been made for it.

Transitional protection in relation to the Jobseekers Act 1995

9.460   **5.** In relation to a person who—
    (a) is entitled to an existing award; or
    (b) would be entitled to an existing award if that person made a claim described in regulation 2(2),
the Jobseekers Act 1995 shall continue to have effect as if paragraphs 12(2), (5)(b) and (6) of Schedule 3 to the Welfare Reform Act 2007 had not come into effect.

DEFINITIONS

"existing award"—see WRA 2007, s.29, Sch.4, para.11.

GENERAL NOTE

9.461   An "existing award" is an award of one or more of the benefits in the already existing incapacity benefits' regime: incapacity benefit; severe disablement allowance (limited, of course, only to those entitled to it immediately before April 6, 2001) and "income support on the grounds of disability" (2007, s.29, Sch.4, para.11). This last covers claims for income support under by someone to whom reg.6(4)(a) or 13(2)(b) or (bb) of, or para.7(a) or (b), 10, 12 or 13 of Sch.1B to, the Income Support (General) Regs 1987 (prescribed categories of person) applies (that is someone claiming IS as a person incapable of work; as a disabled worker; as a disabled or deaf student; or as a blind person). This regulation deals with those entitled to an existing award or who would be if they claimed it in respect of a "linked" period under reg.2(2). It provides that in respect of them the Jobseekers Act 1995 continues to have effect as if the changes effected by the specified provisions in WRA 2007, Sch.3 had never taken effect. In short, read the relevant Jobseekers Act provisions as laid out in the 2008/09 edition of Vol. II.

Social Security (Housing Costs Special Arrangements) (Amendment and Modification) Regulations 2008

(SI 2008/3195)

Made by the Secretary of State for Work and Pensions under ss.123(1) (a), 135(1), 137(1) and 175(1) and (3) and (4) of the Social Security Contributions and Benefits Act 1992, ss.4(5), 35(1) and 36(2) and (4) of the Jobseekers Act 1995, ss.2(3)(b), 17(1) and 19(1) of the State Pension Credit Act 2002, and ss.4(2)(a) and (3), 24(1) and 25(2), (3) and (5) of the Welfare Reform Act 2007.

REGULATIONS REPRODUCED

GENERAL NOTE

The modifications to the rules for housing costs for income-related ESA made by   9.463
these Regulations only apply to certain claimants. See the note to Sch.6 to the ESA
Regulations.

Citation, commencement and interpretation

1.— (1) These Regulations may be cited as the Social Security (Housing   9.464
Costs Special Arrangements) (Amendment and Modification) Regulations
2008.

(2) Regulations 4 to 6, in so far as they relate to a particular person, come into force on the first day of the first benefit week to commence for that person on or after 5th January 2009.

(3) The remaining provisions of these Regulations come into force on 5th January 2009.

(4) In these Regulations-

"benefit week" has the same meaning as in-

(a) regulation 2(1) of the Employment and Support Allowance Regulations, where the relevant benefit is an employment and support allowance;

[(b) and (c)omitted as not relating to ESA]

"housing costs" has the same meaning as in paragraph 1(1) (housing costs) of-

(a) Schedule 6 to the Employment and Support Allowance Regulations, where the relevant benefit is an employment and support allowance;

[(b) and (c) omitted as not relating to ESA]

"relevant benefit" means-

(a) an employment and support allowance;

(b) income support;

(c) a jobseeker's allowance;

"the Employment and Support Allowance Regulations" means the Employment and Support Allowance Regulations 2008;

[Remaining definitions omitted as not relating to ESA]

PART 2

MODIFICATIONS RELATING TO CERTAIN CLAIMANTS WHO ARE ENTITLED TO A RELEVANT BENEFIT ON 4TH JANUARY 2009

Application

9.465   **3.**- (1) This Part applies in relation to a person who—

(a) is entitled to a relevant benefit on 4th January 2009; and

(b) on or after that date falls within paragraph (3) or (4).

(2) This Part ceases to apply in relation to a person who makes a further claim to the same, or claims another, relevant benefit after 4th January 2009.

(3) A person falls within this paragraph if, apart from these Regulations, the housing costs to be met in the benefit week that includes 4th January 2009 would be nil in that person's case because he or she has not been entitled to the relevant benefit concerned for the period mentioned in sub-paragraph (1)(a) in any of the following provisions—

(a) paragraph 8 (existing housing costs) or paragraph 9 (new housing costs) of Schedule 6 to the Employment and Support Allowance Regulations;

[(b) and (c) omitted as not relating to ESA]

(4) A person falls within this paragraph if he or she has been entitled to a relevant benefit for a continuous period, which includes 4th January 2009,

for at least 8 weeks but less than 26 weeks under any of the provisions mentioned in paragraph (5) as in force apart from these Regulations.

(5) The provisions are—

(a) paragraph 8(1)(b) (existing housing costs) or paragraph 9(6) (new housing costs) of Schedule 6 to the Employment and Support Allowance Regulations;

[(b) and (c) omitted as not relating to ESA]

Modification of the Employment and Support Allowance Regulations

4. Schedule 6 (housing costs) to the Employment and Support Allowance Regulations applies in relation to a person to whom this Part applies as if—

    9.466

(a) in paragraph 8(1) (existing housing costs) the reference to "26" were to "13" in each place it appears;

(b) in paragraph 9(1) (new housing costs) the reference to "39" were to "13";

(c) in paragraph 12(4) (general provisions applying to new and existing housing costs) the reference to "£100,000" were to "£200,000";

(d) in paragraph 15(14) (linking rule)—

  (i) in head (a) the reference to "26" were to "13";

  (ii) in head (b) the reference to "39" were to "13".

Saving

7. Nothing in this Part is to affect the applicable amount of a person to whom this Part applies in respect of—

    9.467

(a) any period ending before the date on which these Regulations come into force, or

(b) any period ending after that date throughout which he or she is entitled to the relevant benefit concerned for a continuous period that does not exceed 12 weeks.

PART 3

MODIFICATIONS RELTING TO CERTAIN PERSONS WHO CLAIM
A RELEVANT BENEFIT AFTER 4TH JANUARY 2009

Application and interpretation

8. — (1) This Part applies in relation to a person who-

    9.468

(a) claims a relevant benefit after 4th January 2009; and

(b) falls within any of paragraphs (2) to (4).

(2) A claimant falls within this paragraph if Part 2 applied to him at any time.

(3) A claimant falls within this paragraph if he or she—

(a) is entitled to a relevant benefit; or

(b) was previously entitled to a relevant benefit at any time after 4th January 2009; and

(c) in either case the entitlement is not or was not immediately preceded by a linked period.

(4) A claimant falls within this paragraph if—

(a) the claimant or his or her partner or, if the claimant is a member of a joint-claim couple, the other member of the couple, was in receipt of state pension credit;

(b) the claimant-
  (i) is entitled to a relevant benefit; or
  (ii) was previously entitled to a relevant benefit at any time after 4th January 2009; and

(c) none of the following provisions apply or applied in relation to the entitlement referred to in sub-paragraph (b)(i) or (ii).

(5) The provisions are—

(a) paragraph 3(2) (previous entitlement to other income-related benefits) of Schedule 6 to the Employment and Support Allowance Regulations;

(b) paragraph 1A(1A) (previous entitlement to income-based jobseeker's allowance, income-related employment and support allowance or state pension credit) of Schedule 3 to the Income Support Regulations;

(c) paragraph 1A(1ZA) or (1B) (previous entitlement to income support, income-related employment and support allowance or state pension credit) of Schedule 2 to the Jobseeker's Allowance Regulations.

(6) In this Part—

"joint-claim couple" has the meaning given in section 1(4) of the Jobseekers Act 1995;

"linked period" means a period in respect of which the claimant was required to be treated as being in receipt of a relevant benefit under the provisions of-

(a) paragraph 15 (linking rule) of Schedule 6 to the Employment and Support Allowance Regulations;

(b) paragraph 14 (linking rule) of Schedule 3 to the Income Support Regulations; or (as the case may be)

(c) paragraph 13 (linking rule) of Schedule 2 to the Jobseeker's Allowance Regulations.

Modification of the Employment and Support Allowance Regulations

9.469   **9.** Schedule 6 (housing costs) to the Employment and Support Allowance Regulations applies in relation to a person to whom this Part applies as if-

(a) in paragraph 1(2) (housing costs) the definitions of "existing housing costs" and "new housing costs" were omitted;

(b) paragraph 8 (existing housing costs) were omitted;

(c) in paragraph 9 (new housing costs)-
  (i) the reference to "new" were omitted-
    (aa) in the heading, and
    (bb) in sub-paragraphs (1) and (2),
  (ii) in sub-paragraph (1) the reference to "39" were to "13",
  (iii) sub-paragraphs (4) to (7) were omitted;

(d) in paragraph 10 (general exclusions from paragraphs 8 and 9)-
  (i) in the heading "paragraph 9" were substituted for "paragraphs 8 and 9",

    (ii) in sub-paragraph (1) "Paragraph 9" were substituted for "Paragraphs 8 and 9";

(e) in paragraph 11 (the calculation for loans) the reference to "existing housing costs, or as the case may be, new housing costs" were to "housing costs";

(f) in paragraph 12 (general provisions applying to new and existing housing costs)-

    (i) for the heading there were substituted "General provisions applying to housing costs";

    (ii) sub-paragraphs (1) and (2) were omitted;

    (iii) in sub-paragraph (4), the reference to "£100,000" were to "£200,000";

(g) in paragraph 14(9) (excessive housing costs) "paragraph 9" were substituted for "paragraphs 8 and 9";

(h) in paragraph 15 (linking rule)-

    (i) in sub-paragraph (2) the reference to "paragraph 8(1)(a)(i) or" were omitted;

    (ii) in sub-paragraph (6)(a) the reference to "8(1) or" were omitted;

    (iii) for sub-paragraph (14) there were substituted—

    "(14) Where sub-paragraph (13) applies, in determining for the purposes of paragraph 9(1) whether a person has been entitled to an income-related allowance for a continuous period of 13 weeks or more, any week falling between the date of the termination of the previous award and the date of the new claim is to be ignored.";

    (iv) in sub-paragraph (18) the reference to "8(1)(a), 8(1)(b) or" were omitted;

(i) in paragraph 20 (continuity with income support, an income-based jobseeker's allowance or state pension credit) sub-paragraph (1)(a) were omitted.

PART X

INDUSTRIAL INJURIES AND PRESCRIBED DISEASES

The Social Security (Claims and Payments) Regulations 1979

(SI 1979/628) (*as amended*)

ARRANGEMENT OF REGULATIONS

PART I

GENERAL

PART IV

SPECIAL PROVISIONS RELATING TO INDUSTRIAL INJURIES BENEFIT ONLY

SCHEDULES

The Secretary of State for Social Services, in exercise of powers conferred upon him by sections 45(3), 79 to 81, 88 to 90, 146(5) and 115(1) of, and Schedule 13 to, the Social Security Act 1975 and paragraphs 9(1)(a) and (c) of Schedule 13 to, the Social Security (Consequential Provisions) Act 1975 and of all other powers enabling him in that behalf, hereby makes the following regulations, which consolidate the regulations hereby revoked and which accordingly by virtue of sections 139(1) and 141(2) of the Social Security Act 1975—and paragraphs 20 of Schedule 15 and 12 of Schedule 16—are not subject to the requirements of section 139(1) and 141(2) of that Act for prior reference to the National Insurance Advisory Committee and the Industrial Injuries Advisory Council respectively:—

PART I

GENERAL

Citation and commencement

10.2 1. These regulations may be cited as the Social Security (Claims and Payments) Regulations 1979 and shall come into operation on 9th July 1979.

Interpretation

10.3 2.—(1) In these regulations, unless the context otherwise requires—
"the Act" means the Social Security Act 1975;
"approved place" means a place approved by the Secretary of State for the purpose of obtaining payment of benefit;
"benefit order" means an order for the payment of a weekly sum on account of benefit to which regulation 16 applies or of a weekly instalment of a gratuity;
"claim for benefit" includes an application for a declaration that an accident was an industrial accident and an application for the review of an award or a decision for the purpose of obtaining any increase of benefit mentioned in Schedule 1 to these regulations but does not include any other application for the review of an award or a decision and the expression "claim benefit" and every reference to a claim shall be construed accordingly;
[3 "health care professional" means—
(a) a registered medical practitioner,
(b) a registered nurse,
(c) an occupational therapist or physiotherapist registered with a regulatory body established by an Order in Council under section 60 of the Health Care Act 1999, or
(d) a member of such other profession, regulated by a body mentioned in section 25(3) of the National Health Service Reform and Health Care Professions Act 2002, prescribed by the Secretary of State in accordance with powers under section 39(1) of the Social Security Act 1998.]
[1 . . .]
"instrument of payment" means a serial order, benefit order, or any other instrument whatsoever which is intended to enable a person to obtain payment of benefit;
"serial order" means one of a series of orders, including benefit orders, for the payment of a sum on account of benefit which is or has been contained in a book of such orders;
"unemployment benefit office" means any office or place appointed by the Secretary of State for the purpose of claiming unemployment benefit;
and other expressions have the same meaning as in the Act.
[2(1A) The provision in paragraph (1) for the interpretation of the words "claim for benefit" shall not be taken to preclude the application of the regulations to a claim for attendance allowance expressed as

an application for review of an earlier determination but which discloses no grounds on which such a determination could be reviewed.]

(2) Unless the context otherwise requires, any reference in these regulations to—

(a) a numbered section is a reference to the section of the Social Security Act 1975 bearing that number;

(b) a numbered regulation is a reference to the regulation bearing that number in these regulations and any reference in a regulation to a numbered paragraph is a reference to the paragraph of that regulation bearing that number;

(c) any provision made by or contained in an enactment or instrument shall be construed as a reference to that provision as amended or extended by any enactment or instrument and as including a reference to any provision which it re-enacts or replaces, or which may re-enact or replace it, with or without modification.

(3) For the purposes of the provisions of these regulations relating to the making of claims every increase of benefit mentioned in Schedule 1 to these regulations shall be treated as a separate benefit.

(4) The provisions of Schedule 1 and 2 to these regulations shall have effect; and the following provisions of these regulations shall, in relation to any particular benefit, have effect subject to any provisions in those Schedules affecting that benefit.

AMENDMENTS

1. Social Security Act 1998 (Commencement No. 8, and Savings and Consequential and Transitional Provisions) Order 1999 (SI 1999/1958), Sch.4, para.1 (July 4, 1999)

2. Social Security (Attendance Allowance) Amendment Regulations 1980 (SI 1980/1136), reg.6(1) (August 25, 1980).

3. The Social Security (Miscellaneous Amendments) (No. 2) Regulations 2007, (SI 2007/1626) (July 3, 2007).

GENERAL NOTE

Most of the rules relating to claims and payments can now be found in the Claims and Payments Regulations 1987. The only surviving part of these regulations relates to specific aspects of claims and payments in industrial injuries cases.   10.4

Regulations 3–23 revoked.   10.5

PART IV

SPECIAL PROVISIONS RELATING TO INDUSTRIAL INJURIES BENEFIT ONLY

Notice of accidents

24.—(1) Every employed earner who suffers personal injury by accident in respect of which benefit may be payable shall give notice of such accident either in writing or orally as soon as is practicable after the happening thereof.   10.6

Provided that any such notice required to be given by an employed earner may be given by some other person acting on his behalf.

(2) Every such notice shall be given to the employer, or (if there is more than one employer) to one of such employers, or to any foreman or other official under whose supervision the employed earner is employed at the time of the accident, or to any person designated for the purpose by the employer, and shall give the appropriate particulars.

(3) Any entry of the appropriate particulars of an accident made in a book kept for that purpose in accordance with the provisions of regulation 25 shall, if made as soon as practicable after the happening of an accident by the employed earner or by some other person acting on his behalf, be sufficient notice of the accident for the purposes of this regulation.

(4) In this regulation—

"employer" means, in relation to any person, the employer of that person at the time of the accident and "employers" shall be construed accordingly; and

"employed earner" means a person who is or is treated as an employed earner for the purposes of industrial injuries benefit.

(5) In this regulation and regulation 25, "appropriate particulars" mean the particulars indicated in Schedule 4 to these regulations.

Obligations of employers

10.7   **25.**—(1) Every employer shall take reasonable steps to investigate the circumstances of every accident of which notice is given to him or to his servant or agent in accordance with the provisions of regulation 24 and, if there appear to him to be any discrepancies between the circumstances found by him as a result of his investigation and the circumstances appearing from the notice so given, he shall record the circumstances so found.

(2) Every employer who is required to do so by the Secretary of State shall furnish to an officer of the Department within such reasonable period as may be required, such information and particulars as shall be required—

(a) of any accident or alleged accident in respect of which benefit may be payable to, or in respect of the death of, a person employed by him at the time of the accident or alleged accident; or

(b) of the nature of and other relevant circumstances relating to any occupation prescribed for the purposes of Chapter V of Part II of the Act in which any person to whom or in respect of whose death benefit may be payable under that Chapter was or is alleged to have been employed by him.

(3) Every owner or occupier (being an employer) of any mine or quarry or of any premises to which any of the provisions of the Factories Act 1961 applies and every employer by whom 10 or more persons are normally employed at the same time on or about the same premises in connection with a trade or business carried on by the employer shall, subject to the following provisions of this paragraph—

(a) [¹ keep readily accessible a means (whether in a book or books or by electronic means), in a form approved by the Secretary of State, by which a person employed by the employer or some other person acting on his behalf may record the appropriate particulars (as defined in regulation 24) of any accident causing personal injury to that person; and

(b) preserve every such record for the period of at least 3 years from the date of its entry.]

AMENDMENT

1. Social Security (Claims and Payments) Amendment (No. 3) Regulations 1993 (SI 1993/2113), reg.2 (September 27, 1993)

Obligations of claimants for, and beneficiaries in receipt of [¹. . .] disablement benefit

26.—(1) Subject to the following provisions of this regulation, every claimant for, and every beneficiary in receipt of [¹. . .] disablement benefit shall comply with every notice given to him by the Secretary of State which requires him either—

    (a) to submit himself to a medical examination by a medical [²[⁶ health care professional approved by the Secretary of State] who has experience in the issues specified in regulation 12(1) of the Social Security and Child Support (Decisions and Appeals) Regulations 1999] for the purpose of determining the effects of the relevant accident or the treatment appropriate to the relevant injury or loss of faculty; or

    (b) to submit himself to such medical treatment for the said injury or loss of faculty as is considered appropriate in his case by the medical practitioner in charge of the case [³. . .]

(2) Every notice given to a claimant or beneficiary requiring him to submit himself to medical examination shall be given in writing and shall specify the time and place for examination and shall not require the claimant or beneficiary to submit himself [⁴ to examination before the expiration of the period of 6 days beginning with the date of the notice or such shorter period as may be reasonable in the circumstances]

(3) Every claimant and every beneficiary who, in accordance with the foregoing provisions of this regulation, is required to submit himself to a medical examination or to medical treatment—

    (a) shall attend at every such place and at every such time as may be required; and

    (b) may, in the discretion of the Secretary of State, be paid such travelling and other allowances (including compensation for loss of remunerative time) as the Secretary of State may with the consent of the Minister for the Civil Service determine.

(4) [⁵. . .]

10.8

AMENDMENTS

1. Social Security (Abolition of Injury Benefit) (Consequential) Regulations 1983 (SI 1983/186), reg.11 (April 6, 1983).
2. Social Security Act 1998 (Commencement No. 8, and Savings and Consequential and Transitional Provisions) Order 1999 (SI 1999/1958), Sch.4, para.2(a)(i) (July 4, 1999).
3. Social Security Act 1998 (Commencement No. 8, and Savings and Consequential and Transitional Provisions) Order 1999 (SI 1999/1958), Sch.4, para.2(a)(ii) (July 4, 1999).
4. Social Security Act 1998 (Commencement No. 8, and Savings and Consequential and Transitional Provisions) Order 1999 (SI 1999/1958), Sch.4, para.2(b) (July 4, 1999).
5. Social Security Act 1998 (Commencement No.8, and Savings and Consequential and Transitional Provisions) Order 1999 (SI 1999/1958), Sch.4, para.2(c) (July 4, 1999).
6. The Social Security (Miscellaneous Amendments) (No. 2) Regulations 2007, (SI 2007/1626) (July 3, 2007)

10.9   *Regulations 27–30 revoked.*

10.10   *Regulation 31 omitted*

10.11   *Regulation 32 revoked*

10.12   *Schedules 1–3 revoked.*

SCHEDULE 4   **Regulations 24 and 25**

PARTICULARS TO BE GIVEN OF ACCIDENTS

10.13   (1) Full name, address and occupation of injured person;
(2) Date and time of accident;
(3) Place where accident happened;
(4) Cause and nature of injury;
(5) Name, address and occupation of person giving the notice, if other than
the injured person.

10.14   *Schedule 5 revoked.*

Social Security (General Benefit) Regulations 1982

(SI 1982/1408) (*as amended*)

ARRANGEMENT OF REGULATIONS

PART II

PROVISIONS RELATING TO BENEFIT OTHER THAN INDUSTRIAL
INJURIES BENEFIT

PART III

PROVISIONS RELATING TO INDUSTRIAL INJURIES BENEFIT ONLY

Principles of assessment

Disablement benefit

16.   Earnings level for the purposes of unemployability supplement under section 58 of the Act.

Increase of disablement benefit

17.   Circumstances in which, for the purposes of section 60, a beneficiary may be treated as being incapable of following an occupation or employment notwithstanding that he has worked thereat.
18.   Payments in respect of special hardship where beneficiary is entitled to a gratuity.
19.   Increase of disablement pension for constant attendance.
20.   Determination of degree of disablement for constant attendance allowance.
21.   Condition for receipt of increase of disablement pension for constant attendance under section 61 while receiving medical treatment as an inpatient.
22.   Treatment of distinct periods of hospital in-patient treatment as continuous for the purposes of section 62 of the Act.

Industrial death benefit

Regulations 23–37 omitted.

Adjustment of benefit for successive accidents

38.   Adjustment of benefit for successive accidents where a disablement gratuity is payable.
39.   Adjustment of increase of benefit in respect of successive accidents.

Disqualification for receipt of benefit, suspension of proceedings
on claims and suspension of benefit

40.   Disqualification for receipt of benefit, suspension of proceedings on claims and suspension of payment of benefit.

Payments under the act to certain persons who contracted diseases or who were injured
before 5 July 1948

Regulations 42–45 omitted.

Miscellaneous provisions

46.   Conditions relating to payment of additional benefit under awards made before the day appointed for any increase of benefit under any Act amending the Act or under any up-rating order.

PART IV

47.   Revocation and transitional provisions.

SCHEDULES

Schedule 1—Provisions for the purpose of which disqualifications under the Act are to be disregarded.

Schedule 2—Prescribed degrees of disablement.
Schedule 3—Scale of disablement gratuities.
Schedule 4—Rate of disablement pension payable in lieu of disablement gratuity in accordance with regulation 18.

Schedules 5–9 Omitted.

SCHEDULES

Schedule 2—Prescribed degrees of disablement.

The Secretary of State for Social Services, in exercise of the powers conferred upon him by sections 50(4), 56(7), 57(5), 58(3), 60(4) and (7), 61(1), 62(2), 67(1), 68(2), 70(2), 72(1) and (8), 74(1), 81(6), 82(5) and (6), 83(1), 85(1), 86(2) and (5), 90(2), 91(1), 119(3) and (4) and 159(3) of and paragraphs 2, 3 and 6 of Schedule 8, paragraphs 1 and 8 of Schedule 9 and Schedule 14 of the Social Security Act 1975 and all other powers enabling him in the behalf, hereby makes the following regulations, which only consolidate the regulations hereby revoked, and which accordingly, by virtue of paragraph 20 of Schedule 3 to the Social Security Act 1980, are not subject to the requirements of section 10 of that Act for prior references to the Social Security Advisory Committee and by virtue of section 141(2) and paragraph 12 of the Schedule 16 of the Social Security Act 1975, do not require prior reference to the Industrial Injuries Advisory Council.

PART I

GENERAL

10.16   *For regs 1-4 see Vol. III: Administration, Appeals and the European Dimension.*

PART II

PROVISIONS RELATING TO BENEFIT OTHER THAN INDUSTRIAL INJURIES BENEFIT

Payment of benefit and suspension of payments pending a decision on appeals or references, arrears and repayments

10.17   **9.** *Omitted.*

Disqualifications to be disregarded for certain purposes

10.18   **10.**—(1) Subject to paragraph (2), where a person of any class mentioned in column (1) of Schedule 1 to these regulations would be entitled to the benefit set opposite that class in column (2) of that Schedule but for the operation of any provision of the Act disqualifying him for the receipt of that benefit, that person shall be treated as if entitled to that benefit for the purpose of the provisions of the Act set opposite thereto in column (3) of the said Schedule and of any regulations made thereunder. (2) For the purposes of determining whether the condition contained in section 79(1) of the Act (which makes a claim a condition of any person's right to any benefit) is satisfied, a person who would be entitled to any benefit but for the operation of any provision of the Act disqualifying him for the receipt of it, and who ceases to be so disqualified within a period of 3 months from the commencement of the disqualification, shall be treated as if entitled to it.

PART III

PROVISIONS RELATING TO INDUSTRIAL INJURIES BENEFIT ONLY

Principles of assessment

Further definition of the principles of assessment of disablement and prescribed degrees of disablement

11.—(1) Schedule [6] to the [SSCBA 1992] (general principles relating to the assessment of the extent of disablement) shall have effect subject to the provisions of this regulation.

10.19

(2) When the extent of disablement is being assessed for the purposes of section [103], any disabilities which, though resulting from the relevant loss of faculty, also result, or without the relevant accident might have been expected to result, from a cause other than the relevant accident (hereafter in this regulation referred to as "the other effective cause") shall only be taken into account subject to and in accordance with the following provisions of this regulation.

(3) [¹ Subject to paragraphs (5A) and (5B)] an assessment of the extent of disablement made by reference to any disability to which paragraph (2) applies, in a case where the other effective cause is a congenital defect or is an injury or disease received or contracted before the relevant accident, shall take account of all such disablement except to the extent to which the claimant would have been subject thereto during the period taken into account by the assessment if the relevant accident had not occurred.

(4) [¹ Subject to paragraphs (5A) and (5B)] any assessment of the extent of disablement made by reference to any disability to which paragraph (2) applies, in a case where the other effective cause is an injury or disease received or contracted after and not directly attributable to the relevant accident, shall take account of all such disablement to the extent to which the claimant would have been subject thereto during the period taken into account by the assessment if that other effective cause had not arisen and where, in any such case, the extent of a disablement would be assessed at not less than 11 per cent. if that other effective cause had not arisen, the assessment shall also take account of any disablement to which the claimant may be subject as a result of that other effective cause except to the extent to which he would have been subject thereto if the relevant accident had not occurred.

(5) [¹ Subject to paragraphs (5A) and (5B)] any disablement to the extent to which the claimant is subject thereto as a result both of an accident and a disease or two or more accidents or diseases (as the case may be), being accidents arising out and in the course of, or diseases due to the nature of,

employed earners' employment, shall only be taken into account in assessing the extent of disablement resulting from one such accident or disease being the one which occurred or developed last in point of time.

[¹ (5A) Where—

(a) a person has an award of industrial injuries disablement benefit in respect of the disease specified in paragraph D1 of Part I of Schedule 1 to the Social Security (Industrial Injuries) (Prescribed Diseases) Regulations 1985 (in this paragraph and in paragraph (5B) referred to as "disease D1"); and

(b) by virtue of either paragraph (3) or (4) that award takes account of disablement resulting from the effects of chronic bronchitis or emphysema, not being chronic bronchitis or emphysema prescribed in paragraph D12 of Part I of Schedule 1 to the Social Security (Industrial Injuries) (Prescribed Diseases) Regulations 1985 (in this paragraph and paragraph (5B) referred to as "disease D12"); and

(c) after the date on which the award referred to in sub-paragraph (a) of this paragraph was made the person becomes entitled to industrial injuries disablement benefit in respect of disease D12,

then, during any period when such disablement benefit is payable in respect of disease D12, paragraphs (3), (4) and (5) shall not apply to the assessment in respect of disease D1 for the purpose of assessing the extent of disablement resulting from disease D12.

(5B) Where—

(a) a person has an award of industrial injuries disablement benefit in respect of the disease D12; and

(b) by virtue of either paragraph (3) or (4) that award takes account of disablement resulting from the effects of pneumoconiosis, not being disease D1; and

(c) after the date on which the award referred to in sub-paragraph (a) of this paragraph was made the person becomes entitled to industrial injuries disablement benefit in respect of disease D1,

then, during any period when such disablement benefit is payable in respect of disease D1, paragraphs (3), (4) and (5) shall not apply to the assessment in respect of disease D12 for the purpose of assessing the extent of disablement resulting from disease D1.]

(6) Where the sole injury which a claimant suffers as a result of the relevant accident is one specified in column 1 of Schedule 2 to these regulations, whether or not such injury incorporates one or more other injuries so specified, the loss of faculty suffered by the claimant as a result of that injury shall be treated for the purposes of section [103] of, and Schedule [6] to, the Act as resulting in the degree of disablement set against injury in column 2 of the said Schedule 2 subject to such increase or reduction of that degree of disablement as may be reasonable in the circumstances of the case where, having regard to the provisions of the said Schedule [6] to the Act and to the foregoing paragraphs of this regulation, that degree of disablement does not provide a reasonable assessment of the extent of disablement resulting from the relevant loss of faculty.

(7) For the purposes of paragraph (6) where the relevant injury is one so specified in the said column 1 against which there is set in the said column 2 the degree of disablement of 100 per cent. and the claimant suffers some disablement to which he would have been subject whether or not the relevant

accident had occurred, no reduction of that degree of disablement shall be required if [² the Secretary of State or, as the case may be,] [³ the First-tier Tribunal] is satisfied that, in the circumstances of the case, 100 per cent is a reasonable assessment of the extent of disablement from the relevant loss of faculty.

(8) For the purposes of assessing, in accordance with the provisions of Schedule [6] to the [SSCBA 1992], the extent of disablement resulting from the relevant injury in any case which does not fall to be determined under paragraph (6) or (7), [² the Secretary of State or, as the case may be,] [³ the First-tier Tribunal] may have such regard as may be appropriate to the prescribed degrees of disablement set against the injuries specified in the said Schedule 2.

AMENDMENTS

1. Social Security (Industrial Injuries) (Prescribed Diseases) Amendment (No. 2) Regulations 1993 (SI 1993/1985), reg.7 (September 13, 1993).
2. Social Security Act 1998 (Commencment No.8, and Savings and Consequential and Transitional Provisions) Order 1999 (SI 1999/1958 (July 5, 1999).
3. Tribunals, Courts and Enforcement Act 2007 (Transitional and Consequential Provisions) Order 2008 (SI 2008/2683), art.6(1) and Sch.1, para.25 (November 3, 2008).

GENERAL NOTE

This regulation provides for the assessment of the extent of disablement in cases where a disability is due both to the relevant accident and another cause; and it also introduces Sch.2 to the Regs which sets out the prescribed degrees of disablement. S.57 of, and Sch.8 to, the SSA 1975 have been replaced by s.103 of, and Sch.6 to the SSCBA 1992.   **10.20**

For an illustration of the operation of these rules and a framework of questions for approaching these matters, see the decision of Commissioner Williams in *CI/2930/2005*, noted in the commentary to SSCBA 1992, s. 103 (disablement pension).

For an illustration of the complexities of applying the "multiple effective cause" provisions of this reg., see *CI/3745/2006*. The Schedule to the decision also contains useful evidence from the medical adviser to the DWP (Dr Reed) on PD A8 (tenosynovitis) and PD A12 (carpal tunnel syndrome).

For consideration of the current form BI 118A and the need to consider the connection factor arising out of two injuries both due to the same relevant accident, something not considered in *R(I) 1/95*, see *CI/3384/2006*.

Para.(2)

Adjudicating medical authorities used to distinguish between conditions that were regarded as "partly relevant" ("O pre" or "O post") and those that were regarded as merely "connected" ("C"). The former were those conditions considered to have more than one cause and the latter were those conditions considered to be quite separate from the one arising from the relevant accident but which were nonetheless thought to have some effect on the disability arising from the condition caused by the relevant accident. That approach (and Form BI 113 Accident) which reflected it has been criticised in *R(I) 4/94* and *R(I) 1/95*. Any contributory factor is either to be included in the relevant loss of faculty or else is an "other effective cause" within para.(2), in which case it is taken into account under paras (3), (4) or (5).   **10.21**

Para.(3)

This makes provision for a case where the "other effective cause" is either a congenital defect or is an injury or disease received or contracted *before* the relevant accident. In *R(I) 13/75*, the Commissioner said: **10.22**

"In the context of regulation [11(3)] I do not think that 'congenital' should receive its primary meaning, which is 'begotten' or 'born with'; see Shorter Oxford English Dictionary. In my view, the word is used in this regulation in a rather wider sense. I think that it must be taken to mean 'inherent' or 'constitutional,' this is to say that it refers to a defect which is a natural constituent of the person's make-up whether physical or mental. Since Dr. Wright [a principal medical officer of the Department of Health and Social Security] stated that a functional overlay is 'a manifestation of constitutional mental make-up,' I cannot hold that it is not covered by the phrase 'congenital defect' in regulation [11(3)]."

Disablement due to the "other effective cause" must be taken into account except to the extent to which the claimant would have been disabled if the relevant accident had not occurred. Usually this is done by making an assessment of the full extent of disablement resulting from the condition and then applying an "offset" in respect of disablement which would have been present even if the relevant accident had not occurred (*CI/2746/2002*, para. 5). There should be no offset in respect of a mere *predisposition* to hysteria (*R(I) 2/74*), functional overlay (*R(I) 13/75*), detachment of retina (*R(I) 3/76*) or development of multiple sclerosis (*R(I) 1/81*). In *R(I) 1/81*, it was held that

"constitutional liability to develop the disease cannot have been a 'disability' because it was wholly symptomless. Such liability corresponds with the statutory concept of 'loss of faculty,' that is to say it is a potential cause of disability but not itself a disability."

The Commissioner emphasised that the assessment was an assessment of disablement and not an assessment of loss of faculty. However, it does not follow that there can never be an offset in respect of a condition which was symptomless before the relevant accident. An adjudicating authority might legitimately apply an offset if a pre-existing, and previously symptomless, condition could have been expected to produced disability at some time even if the accident had not occurred. Nevertheless, such reasoning must be clear, and a tribunal which fails to record good reasons for applying an offset in a case where a claimant has asserted that he or she had no symptoms before the relevant accident is liable to find its decision set aside on appeal (*CI/34/93*). On the other hand, there are some conditions, such as arthritis, from which many older people suffer. That is not a ground for an offset. Rather, it is a ground for not including the effects of the arthritis, to the extent to which other people of the same age would suffer from them, in the assessment of total disability at all. That is because that assessment should be made by comparing the claimant "with a person of the same age and sex whose physical and mental condition is normal" (SSCBA 1992, Sch.6, para.1(a)). There is no reason why an adjudicating authority should not make an assessment which is tapered to take account of the fact that the claimant would have become increasingly disabled even if the accident had not occurred. Whether that is done by increasing an offset over the period of assessment or by simply reducing the total assessment of disablement depends on whether or not the increasing disability is something from which the "normal" person would suffer. In a case where the assessment of total disablement is 100 per cent, see para. (7).

Where the "other effective cause" is a different type of condition or an injury to a different part of the body, it is conventional to talk of a "connection factor" which is expressed as an increase of the disablement resulting from the relevant accident. Like an "offset", a "connection factor" is not a statutory concept, but both concepts are useful ways of explaining decisions. Use of the concepts enables a claimant to be told the proportion of his or her total disablement that is attributable to the relevant accident (*R(I) 2/74, R(I) 1/95*). A claimant ought to know the assessment of the total disablement to which he or she is thought to be subject, as well as the assessment of the disablement attributed to the relevant accident. In *R(I) 1/95*, it was observed that "[a]n inability to lift moderate weights with one hand may not be particularly significant when the claimant can use the other hand instead, but it is obviously a substantial handicap if the claimant has only the one hand and cannot be provided with a functional artificial limb".

The "connection factor" represented that additional degree of disablement from which the claimant would not have suffered but for the relevant accident, over and above the degree of disablement suffered by a person who had a fully functional second hand. The same result is reached if the claimant's total disablement is assessed and there is an "offset" in respect of the disablement from which he would have suffered had the relevant accident not occurred. Ideally, both the "connection factor" and the "offset" should be assessed so that it is quite clear that reg.11(3) has been applied correctly *(R(I) 1/95)*. In *R(I) 23/61*, the claimant had a pre-existing disability arising from a defective forefinger and then lost a thumb in the relevant accident. The Commissioner said that:

"where the medical authorities are dealing with an injury to a hand, the possibility of a connection factor is so obvious, or at any rate will seem so obvious to the claimant, that it is essential that they should satisfy themselves specifically whether or not there is any other defect in the hand which might bring the case within regulation [11(3)] and should give a clear decision on it one way or the other."

In *Murrell v Secretary of State for Social Services* (reported as an appendix to *R(I) 3/84*), a blind man who suffered an injury to his elbow, which resulted in a loss of sensation in his hand rendering him unable to read braille, had the 15 per cent assessment in respect of the elbow injury increased by a further 15 per cent to take account of the extra disability arising from that injury because of his pre-existing blindness. The Court of Appeal thought that the increase was rather on the low side.

The fact that the claimant is entitled to a disablement pension under the war pensions scheme in respect of the previous injury is not a ground for reducing the assessment in respect of the later one *(R(I) 1/79)*.

Para.(4)

This applies where the "other effective cause" arises *after* the relevant accident. The paragraph is in two parts. First, account must be taken of all disablement "to the extent to which the claimant would have been subject thereto . . . if *that other effective cause* had not arisen". Thus, a claimant who has lost his right forefinger in an industrial accident and then loses his right hand in a non-industrial accident continues to be entitled to an assessment based on the loss of the forefinger, notwithstanding that he or she would have lost it in the second accident even if the first had not occurred. Secondly, effect is given to the "connection factor", but only in a case where the disablement from which the claimant would have suffered would have been at least 11 per cent without the "other effective cause" arising. In such a case, account must be taken of all disablement to which the claimant is subject "*except* to the extent to which he would have been subject thereto if *the relevant accident* had not occurred". In the example given above concerning the loss of a forefinger followed by the loss of the rest of the hand, no increase would be awarded under the second part of the paragraph because the claimant would have been just as disabled after the second accident even if the first had never occurred. However, an assessment may be increased where a subsequent injury results in greater disablement than it normally would because of the effects of the relevant accident. In *R. v Medical Appeal Tribunal Ex p. Cable* (reported as an appendix to *R(I) 11/66* and decided under earlier legislation), a man who had lost the sight of one eye in an industrial accident was held by the Court of Appeal to be entitled to the benefit of the "connection factor" when he lost the sight of the other as the result of a non-industrial disease. If the assessment of total disablement is 100 per cent, adjudicating medical authorities must bear in mind paras (7) and (8) when considering the "connection factor" under this para.

10.23

Para. (5)

10.24   Where a person suffers disablement as a result of two or more industrial accidents or prescribed diseases, it may be appropriate simply for the adjudication officer to aggregate the resulting disablements under s.103(2) of the SSCBA 1992 (if all the causes were accidents) or reg.15A of the Prescribed Diseases Regs 1985. However, the total disablement resulting from the two accidents may be greater than the aggregate of the individual disablements; the loss of two eyes is more than twice as disabling as the loss of one eye. Effect must be given to that "connection factor" in assessing the extent of disablement resulting from the latest accident or disease for which it is relevant (*R(I) 3/91*).

Para. (6)

10.25   This introduces Sch.2 which sets out the prescribed degrees of disablement. The degree of disablement may be increased or reduced "as may be reasonable in the circumstances of the case" if the prescribed degree of disablement "does not provide a reasonable assessment of the extent of disablement". Thus a righthanded person who loses his or her right hand might be assessed as more disabled than a left-handed person would be, at least at the beginning of the period of assessment. It would also seem appropriate to make a higher assessment in a case where a person has had a limb amputated and has not yet been fitted with an artificial limb. The disabling effect of any unusual amount of pain must also be taken into account, a statement approved by Commissioner Williams in *CI/2553/2001*, para.17.

In *R(I) 4/04*, Commissioner Jacobs considered entries 26–28 dealing with amputations in lower limbs and, in particular, the need for a tribunal to specify where the measurement of the stump began and ended. What is assessed is the loss of function consequent upon anatomical loss, rather than the latter itself. The legislation does not specify the start and end points for measurement, but the length of the stump must be related to the likely disablement that will result. Given the possibility of fitting a prosthesis, the length of the stump is likely to relate to the effectiveness of that prosthesis. He concluded that

> "In a perfect world, the precise measurement would not matter. The tribunal would take account of the Scheduled assessments as a whole. It would realise that the length of the stump would affect the effectiveness of the prosthesis, which would affect the claimant's disablement. It would take account of the Scheduled assessment only as a starting point. It would adjust this as authorised by regulation 11(6). This process of adjustment, with a focus on disablement, would counteract any variation between adjudicating authorities on the precise way in which the measurement was taken.

> But life, in my experience, is not always perfect. This analysis presupposes an impossible degree of precision on a matter that is imprecise and impressionistic. In practice, tribunals begin their assessment of disablement with the Scheduled assessment, if there is one. That is the proper approach under regulation 11(6). Despite the infinite flexibility that regulation 11(6) allows in theory, the reality is that the starting point of the Scheduled assessment will affect the outcome.

> Disablement depends on the effectiveness of the prosthesis. That depends on the length of bone rather than soft tissue. So, it is obvious that it is only the supporting bone that should be measured. The key bone is the tibia, not the fibula. As the tibia is the inner of the two bones in the lower limb, the measurement should be made on the inner surface of the remaining stump, not the outer. So far, the Secretary of State's guidance does no more than put those conclusions into medical language. All that remains is the position of the leg when the measurement is taken. The Secretary of State recommends that the knee be flexed, which obviously is the best way to obtain the precise measurement required. In conclusion, therefore, the Secretary of State's guidance agrees with the measurement that can be deduced by normal interpretive principles from the legislation" (paras 23–25).

Para. (7)

In a case where the assessment of total disablement is 100 per cent, "not because   **10.26**
that in fact is the proper figure, but because the law permits no greater figure" a
smaller offset or even no offset at all in respect of a pre-existing injury might be reasonable *(R(I) 34/61)*. That reflects the fact that an assessment of 100 per cent does
not imply total disability.

Para. (8)

In a case where there is no prescribed degree of disablement, the adjudicating   **10.27**
authority "may have such regard as may be appropriate" to the Schedule (see *R(I)*
1/04 and *R(I) 5/95*). This is necessary in the interests of consistency and fairness
as between claimants. Both the unified tribunal and the Commissioners now have
jurisdiction over medical and non-medical matters. A Commissioner, allowing an
appeal on a point of law, can now take his or her own decision on the facts rather
than remitting it to another tribunal. Commissioner Williams did so in *CI/1307/1999*
giving a staged assessment of disablement in respect of post-traumatic stress disorder. The decision considers the medical aspects of the claimant's case found to be
an industrial accident in *CI/15589/1996*, noted in the annotation to "accident" to
SSCBA 1992, s.94. In paras 15–17, Commissioner Williams distinguished "diagnosis" and "disablement" decisions. The former is essentially "a question of medical
expertise". A "disablement" decision in contrast is not dissimilar to the tasks performed by judges in assessing common law damages or in applying the tariff of the
Criminal Injuries Compensation Authority. In assessing disablement for industrial
injuries benefits, however, that Criminal Injuries tariff is not an appropriate yardstick. Instead, supplementing SSCBA 1992, s.103 and Sch.6, regard should be had
also to this regulation and Sch.2 to these Regulations. Nonetheless, the import of
para. 37 of the decision is that exercise of the Commissioner's power to decide on the
facts, rather than remitting to another tribunal, may well be rare. Even so, the decision contrasts markedly with the traditional view of such matters as ones for medical
rather than legal judgment (see, for example, Commissioner Howell in *CI/636/93*).
That assessment of disablement is ultimately a matter of judgment for the tribunal
which hears and sees the evidence was stressed by a Tribunal of Commissioners in
R(I)2/06. That decision also elaborates on the nature of an error of law, and on the
difference between that and a disputed judgment of degree on a question of fact. It
also proffers guidance on reference to Sch.2 in non-prescribed cases, on consideration of the judicial guidelines on the assessment of damages in civil personal injury
cases, on cross-reference to other schemes such as that for criminal injuries, and
on the status of official departmental guidance such as the Medical Assessment
Framework (MAF). See further the annotation to SSCBA 1992, Sch.6.

[¹. . .] Disablement benefit

Regulations 12 and 13 revoked by SI 1983/186, reg. 13 (April 6, 1983)   **10.28**

Amount of disablement gratuities

14.—(1) Where the extent of a claimant's disablement is assessed at any   **10.29**
of the degrees of disablement severally specified in column 1 of Schedule
3 to these regulations, the amount of any disablement gratuity payable
shall—

    (a) if the period taken into account by that assessment is limited by ref-
         erence to the claimant's life or is not less than 7 years, be the amount
         calculated as the percentage of the maximum disablement gratuity

(specified in paragraph 2 of Part V of Schedule 4 to the Act) which is shown in column 2 of Schedule 3 to these regulations as being appropriate to that degree of disablement;

(b) in any other case, be the amount calculated as such a percentage of the maximum disablement gratuity as bears the same proportion to the percentage shown in column 2 of Schedule 3 to these regulations as being appropriate to that degree of disablement as the period taken into account by the assessment bears to a period of 7 years, a fraction of 5 pence being, for this purpose, treated as 5 pence.

[¹ (1A) Paragraph (1) applies in relation to cases where the claim for benefit was made before 1st October 1986.]

(2) For the purposes of this regulation, whenever such maximum disablement gratuity is altered by virtue of the passing of an Act or the making of an up-rating order, corresponding variations in the scale of gratuities payable under this regulation shall be payable only where the period taken into account by the assessment of the extent of disablement in respect of which the gratuity is awarded begins on or after the date of coming into operation of the provision altering the amount of the maximum disablement gratuity.

AMENDMENT

1. Social Security (Industrial Injuries and Diseases) Miscellaneous Provisions Regulations 1986 (SI 1986/1561), reg.7 (October 1, 1986).

Weekly value of gratuity for purposes of reduction of increase of disablement benefit during hospital treatment

10.30   15. For the purpose of reducing the weekly rate of disablement pension payable by virtue of section 62 to a person awarded a disablement gratuity wholly or partly in respect of the same period, the weekly value of the gratuity shall be the weekly rate of disablement pension which would be payable to that person in lieu thereof in accordance with regulation 18(2) if that regulation applied to his case.

Earnings level for the purpose of unemployability supplement under section 58 of the Act

10.31   16. For the purpose of section 58(3) (earnings level that does not disqualify for unemployability supplement) the prescribed amount of earnings in a year shall be [¹ £4,784]

AMENDMENT

1. Social Security (Miscellaneous Amendments) (No. 3) Regulations 2008 (SI 2008/2635), reg.2 (October 1, 2008).

Increase of [¹. . .] Disablement Benefit

Circumstances in which, for the purposes of section 59A, a beneficiary may be treated as being incapable of following an occupation or employment notwithstanding that he has worked thereat

10.32   17.—(1) For the purposes of [² section 59A (reduced earnings allowance)], when it is being determined whether a beneficiary has at all times since the end of [² the period of 90 days referred to in section 57(4) been incapable of following his regular occupation or employment of an equivalent standard which is suitable in his case, and in determining that question only, the fact that since the end of that period of 90 days] such beneficiary had worked at that occupation or any such employment (as the case may be)—

(a) for the purpose of rehabilitation or training or of ascertaining whether he had recovered from the effects of the relevant injury; or

(b) before obtaining surgical treatment for the effects of the said injury;

shall be disregarded in respect of the periods specified in the next following paragraph.

(2) The periods during which the beneficiary worked at his regular occupation or at employment of equivalent standard, which shall be disregarded in accordance with the provision of the preceding paragraph, shall be—

(a) in any case to which sub-paragraph (a) of that paragraph applies—
  (i) any period during which he worked thereat for any of the said purposes with the approval of the Secretary of State or on the advice of a medical practitioner, and
  (ii) any other period or periods during which he worked thereat for any of the said purposes and which did not exceed six months in the aggregate, and

(b) in any case to which sub-paragraph (b) of that paragraph applies—
  (i) any period during which he worked thereat and throughout which it is shown that having obtained the advice of a medical practitioner to submit himself to such surgical treatment he was waiting to undergo the said treatment in accordance therewith, and
  (ii) any other period during which he worked thereat and throughout which is shown that he was in process of obtaining such advice.

AMENDMENTS

1. Social Security (Abolition of Injury Benefits) (Consequential) Regulations 1983 (SI 1983/186), reg.13 (April 6, 1983).

2. Social Security (Industrial Injuries and Diseases) Miscellaneous Provisions Regulations 1986 (SI 1986/1561), reg.7 (October 1, 1986).

GENERAL NOTE

The regulation permits both the fact of work and the period for which it has been undertaken to be disregarded where the claimant seeks to establish entitlement to reduced earnings allowance under the "continuous condition", so long as the work is undertaken for either of the purposes specified in the regulation. (See generally, *R(I)1/51, R(I)35/55, R(I)35/58.*)

10.33

If the claimant relies upon the purpose in para. (1)(a), the extent of the qualifying period depends upon whether the return to work is upon the advice of a medical practitioner or with the approval of the Secretary of State—without such authorisation the period (or aggregate periods) may not exceed six months. "Rehabilitation", means getting better *(R(I)69/53)*, but "ascertaining the results of the relevant injury" has been more widely interpreted to mean discovering whether the claimant can still do the job *(R(I)1/69)*. The "advice" of the doctor referred to in the paragraph does not have to be specifically directed to value of a resumption of work, but there must be something which the claimant can point to in the general advice he receives which is relevant to one of the specified purposes—the "general approval and consent of his doctor" *(R(I)93/53)*, or "in allowing the claimant to continue at work while in receipt of treatment the doctor must be taken to have advised him to remain at work" (*R(I)69/53*).

If the claimant relies upon the purpose in para.(1)(b), the periods he may use depend upon whether he has actually received advice on surgical treatment, or is in the process of obtaining it. Note that, in this paragraph, the advice must be much more clear and the doctor must have given a specific opinion that surgical treatment should be carried out—further, the claimant must intend to give up work and undergo the treatment as soon as it can be arranged (*R(I)81/53*). The claimant can only avail himself of this paragraph if he has been seeking advice "throughout" the period he has been working, or he has been waiting for the treatment "throughout" the period, and he is not entitled to delay unduly in seeking treatment. He must use "reasonable zeal and expedition" to secure the treatment (*R(I)35/57*).

Payments in respect of special hardship where beneficiary is entitled to a gratuity

10.34 **18.**—(1) Where in any case a beneficiary is entitled to or has received a disablement gratuity, such beneficiary shall as respects that gratuity have the like rights to payments in respect of special hardship as he would have had by way of increase of disablement pension under section 60 if the disablement gratuity had been a disablement pension payable during the period taken into account by the assessment.

(2) A beneficiary who is entitled as respects a disablement gratuity to payments in respect of special hardship by virtue of the preceding paragraph shall, if he makes an application in that behalf at any time before that gratuity or any part thereof has been paid to him, be entitled, subject to the proviso to section 57(6), to a disablement pension in lieu of such gratuity for any part of the period taken into account by the assessment during which he may be entitled to an increase of such pension in respect of special hardship under section 60, and the weekly rate of such pension shall be determined in accordance with Schedule 4 of these regulations.

(3) For the purposes of paragraph (2) and notwithstanding the provisions of regulation 14(2) whenever the weekly rate of such pension is altered consequent upon the passing of an Act or the making of an uprating order, such variation shall have effect as from the date on which the provision varying the amount of the disablement pension specified in paragraph 3 of Part V of Schedule 4 to the Act comes into force, whether the period taken into account by the assessment began before or after that date.

(4) Where a pension has been payable under paragraph (2) in lieu of a gratuity for any period and the beneficiary ceases to be entitled to an increase of such pension under the provisions of section 60, the amount of that gratuity shall be treated as reduced by the amounts which have been paid to the beneficiary by way of such pension, other than an increase thereof under the said section 60 and, subject to the provisions of these regulations, the balance (if any) shall then be payable accordingly.

GENERAL NOTE

10.35 This regulation will only continue in force to cover those claimants who were in receipt of special hardship allowance under this regulation as at October 1, 1986. A claimant in that group became entitled to reduced earnings allowance on that day and will remain so entitled under this regulation until either the period of assessment has expired or the assessment is reviewed, or until reduced earnings allowance has ceased to be payable (whichever is the earlier). See the Social Security (Industrial Injuries and Diseases) Miscellaneous Provisions Regulations 1986 (SI 1986/1561), reg.7(5), (6).

Increase of disablement pension for constant attendance

19. The amount by which the weekly rate of disablement pension may be increased under [section 104 of the Social Security Contributions and Benefits Act 1992] where constant attendance is required by a beneficiary as a result of the relevant loss of faculty shall—

10.36

(a) where the beneficiary (not being a case to which paragraph (b) of this regulation relates) is to a substantial extent dependent on such attendance for the necessities of life and is likely to remain so dependent for a prolonged period, be the amount specified in paragraph [2](a) of Part V of Schedule 4 to the Act (unless the attendance so required is part-time only, in which case the amount shall be such sum as may be reasonable in the circumstances) or, where the extent of such attendance is greater by reason of the beneficiary's exceptionally severe disablement, a sum not exceeding one and a half times the amount specified in paragraph [2](a) of Part V of the said Schedule, a fraction of five pence being for this purpose treated as five pence;

(b) where the beneficiary is so exceptionally severely disabled as to be entirely, or almost entirely, dependent on such attendance for the necessities of life, and is likely to remain so dependent for a prolonged period and the attendance so required is whole-time, be the amount specified in paragraph [2](b) of Part V of Schedule 4 to the Act.

Determination of degree of disablement for constant attendance allowance

20.—(1) For the purpose of determining whether a person is entitled to an increase by way of constant attendance allowance under section 61 or to a corresponding increase by virtue of section 159(3)(b) of the Act or section 7(3)(b) of the Industrial Injuries and Diseases (Old Cases) Act 1975 of any other benefit, the Secretary of State shall, in a case where that person is subject to disabilities in respect of which payments of two or more of the descriptions set out in the next following paragraph of this regulation fall to be made, determine the extent of that person's disablement by taking into account all such disabilities to which that person is subject.

10.37

(2) The payments which may be taken into account are those of the following descriptions:—

(a) payments by way of disablement pensions under the Act;

(b) weekly payments to which that person is or has been at any time after 4 July 1948 entitled in respect of injury or disease being payments by way of compensation under the Workmen's Compensation Acts or under any contracting-out scheme duly certified thereunder;

(c) payments to which that person is or has been at any time after 4 July 1948 entitled as a former constable or fireman on account of an injury pension under or by virtue of any enactment in respect of an injury received or disease contracted by that person before 5 July 1948 or in respect of his retirement in consequence of such an injury or disease;

(d) payments by way of benefit under the Industrial Injuries and Diseases (Old Cases) Act 1975; and

(e) payments of personal benefit by way of disablement pension or gratuity under any Personal Injuries Scheme or Service Pensions Instrument or 1914–18 War Injuries Scheme.

(3) In sub-paragraph (2)(e) the expressions "personal benefit", "disablement

pension", "Personal Injuries Scheme" and "Service Pensions Instrument" have the meanings which are assigned to them by the Social Security (Overlapping Benefits) Regulations 1979 for the purposes of those regulations.

Condition for receipt of increase of disablement pension for constant attendance under section 61 while receiving medical treatment as an in-patient

10.38   21.—(1) For the purposes of section 61 (increase of disablement pension in respect of the need of constant attendance), subject to paragraph (2) it shall be a condition for the receipt of an increase of disablement pension under the said section 61 for any period in respect of any person that during that period he is not receiving, or has not received, free in-patient treatment, and for this purpose a person shall be regarded as receiving or having received free in-patient treatment if he would be so regarded for the purposes of the Social Security (Hospital In-Patients) Regulations 1975.

(2) Where a person was entitled to an increase of disablement pension under the said section 61 in respect of the period immediately before he commenced to undergo any treatment mentioned in paragraph (1), that paragraph shall not apply in respect of the first 4 weeks of any continuous period during which he is undergoing such treatment.

(3) For the purposes of paragraph (2), 2 or more distinct periods separated by an interval not exceeding 28 days, or by 2 or more such intervals, shall be treated as a continuous period equal in duration to the total of such distinct periods and ending on the last day of the later or last such period.

Treatment of distinct periods of hospital in-patient treatment as continuous for the purposes of section 62 of the Act

10.39   22. For the purposes of section 62 (increase of disablement benefit during hospital treatment) a person who receives medical treatment as an in-patient for 2 or more distinct periods separated by an interval of less than a week in each case shall be treated as receiving such treatment continuously from the beginning of the first period until the end of the last.

GENERAL NOTE

10.40   Section 62 of the Social Security Act 1975 has been replaced by para.10 of Sch.7 to the Social Security Contributions and Benefits Act 1992.

10.41   *Regulations 23–37 omitted.*

Adjustment of Benefit for Successive Accidents

Adjustment of benefit for successive accidents where a disablement gratuity is payable

10.42   38.—(1) In a case where—

(a) a person who is entitled, as a result of an accident, to a disablement pension (hereafter in this paragraph referred to as an "existing pension") which is payable in respect of an assessment for a period which is limited by reference to that person's life, becomes as a result of any other accident, entitled to an award as a result of an assessment of disablement in respect of which a disablement gratuity would, but for this regulation, be payable; and

(b) the aggregate amount of the assessment in respect of the existing pension and of the assessment in respect of which such disablement gratuity would be payable would, if it were the amount of the assessment of the extent of the disablement resulting from any one accident suffered by that person, have entitled him to receive a disablement pension at a higher rate than the rate of such existing pension;

then, if at any time before his claim for disablement benefit is determined, he so elects, that person shall be entitled to a disablement pension in lieu of the said disablement gratuity at a rate equal to the difference between the said higher rate and the rate of the existing pension.

(2) In a case in which a person who is entitled as a result of any accident to a disablement pension would but for the provisions of this paragraph become entitled in respect of any other accident to a disablement gratuity (not being a case in which he is entitled to a disablement pension in lieu of such gratuity)—

(a) if the assessment in respect of which such pension is payable to him amounts to not less than 100 per cent, such person shall not be entitled to receive any disablement gratuity in respect of such other accident;

(b) in any other case, such person shall not be entitled to receive, by way of disablement gratuity in respect of such other accident, an amount exceeding that which would be payable in respect of an assessment equal to the difference between 100 per cent. and the percentage of the assessment in respect of which such pension is payable to him.

(3) For the respective purposes of the two preceding paragraphs of this regulation—

(a) references to an existing pension within the meaning of paragraph (1) and to any disablement pension in paragraph (2) respectively shall include references to all such pensions which may be payable to the person concerned, and references to the amount of the assessment in respect of which, and the rate at which, any such pension is payable shall include references to the aggregate amount of the assessments in respect of which or the aggregate of the rates at which all such pensions are payable as aforesaid;

(b) the extent by which an assessment is increased by virtue of the provisions of section 62 of the Act (increase of disablement benefit during hospital treatment) shall be disregarded;

(c) for the purposes of paragraph (1)(a) a person shall be deemed to be entitled to a disablement pension and to an award as described in the said sub-paragraph from the respective dates of commencement of the periods taken into account by the assessments relating to such pension and to such award.

Adjustment of increase of benefit of successive accidents

39.—(1) Where a person who is entitled to a disablement pension in respect of any accident suffered by him—   10.43

(a) has received, or is entitled to, a disablement gratuity in respect of any other accident; and

(b) as a result of the loss of faculty in respect of which he has received, or is entitled to that gratuity, is incapable of work and is likely to remain permanently so incapable;

the provisions of section 58 (increase of disablement pension by way of unemployability supplement) shall apply as if that loss of faculty resulted from the accident in respect of which such disablement pension is payable.

(2) Where a person—

(a) would be entitled to a disablement pension in respect of any accident but for the provisions of section 91(1)(a) (limitations on the aggregate weekly rates of benefit payable for the same period in respect of successive accidents); and

(b) by reason only of those provisions, is unable to satisfy the conditions for the receipt of an increase of that pension by way of unemployability supplement under section 58;

the provisions of the said section 58 shall apply as if such disablement pension were payable to that beneficiary.

(3) At any time at which the sum total of the several assessments in respect of two or more accidents suffered by any person amounts to not less than 100 per cent during the continuance of the periods respectively taken into account thereby, the weekly rate of any disablement pension which is payable to him may be increased in accordance with the provisions of section 61 if he requires constant attendance as a result of the loss of faculty resulting from any one or more of such accidents, whether or not that pension is payable in respect of an assessment of 100 per cent or in respect of that loss of faculty.

(4) A beneficiary who has suffered two or more accidents shall not be entitled at any time to more than one of each of the following increases of benefit, that is to say—

(a) by way of unemployability supplement under section 58;

(b) in respect of the need of constant attendance under section 61;

(c) in respect of a child, under section 64;

(d) in respect of an adult dependant, under section 66.

Disqualification for Receipt of Benefit and Suspension of Benefit Pending Appeals etc.

Disqualification for receipt of benefit, suspension of proceedings on claims and suspension of payment of benefit

10.44   **40.**—(1)[¹. . .]

(2) If, without good cause—

(a) a claimant fails to furnish to the prescribed person any information required for the determination of the claim or of any question arising in connection therewith; or

(b) a beneficiary fails to give notice to the prescribed person of any change of circumstances affecting the continuance of the right to benefit or to the receipt thereof, or to furnish as aforesaid any information required for the determination of any question arising in connection with the award; or

(c) a claimant for, or a beneficiary in receipt of, disablement benefit fails to comply with any requirement of regulation 26 of the Social Security (Claims and Payments) Regulations 1979 (obligations of claimants for, and beneficiaries in receipt of [¹. . .] disablement benefit);

he shall, subject to the following provisions of this regulation, if the [² the Secretary of State, an appeal tribunal] or the Commissioner so decide, be disqualified for receiving any benefit claimed in respect of the period of such failure.

(3) If a claimant or beneficiary wilfully obstructs, or is guilty of other misconduct in connection with any examination or treatment to which he is required under regulation 26 of the Social Security(Claims and Payments) Regulation 1979 to submit himself, or any proceedings under the Act for the determination of his right to benefit or to the receipt thereof, he shall, subject to the provisions of this regulation, be disqualified for receiving any benefit claimed for such period as the insurance officer, a local tribunal or the Commissioner shall determine.

(4) In any case to which any of the foregoing paragraphs of this regulation relates, proceedings on the claim or payment of benefit, as the case may be, may be suspended for such period as the insurance officer, a local tribunal or the Commissioner may determine.

(5) Nothing in this Regulation providing for the disqualification for the receipt of benefit for any of the following matters, that is to say—

(a) [1. . .]
(b) for failure to comply with the requirements of regulation 26 of the Social Security (Claims and Payments) Regulation 1979;
(c) for obstruction of, or misconduct in connection with, medical examination or treatment;

shall authorise the disentitlement of a claimant or beneficiary to benefit for a period exceeding six weeks on any disqualification.

(6) No person shall be disqualified for receiving any benefit for refusal to undergo a surgical operation not being one of minor character.

(7) A person who would be entitled to any benefit but for the operation of any of the foregoing provisions of this regulation shall be treated as if he were entitled thereto for the purpose of any rights or obligations under the Act (whether of himself or any other person) which depend on his being so entitled other than the right to payment of that benefit.

AMENDMENTS

1. Social Security (Abolition of Injury Benefit) (Consequential) Regulations 1983 (SI 1983/186), reg.13 (April 6, 1983).

2. Social Security Act 1998 (Commencement No.8, and Savings and Consequential and Transitional Provisions) Order 1999 (SI 1999/1958), Sch.5 (July 4, 1999).

Regulation 41 revoked by the Social Security (Claims and Payments)   **10.45**

Regulations 1987 (SI1987/1968), reg.48 (April 11, 1988).   **10.46**

Regulations 42–45 omitted.   **10.47**

Miscellaneous Provisions

Conditions relating to payment of additional benefit under awards made before the day appointed for an increase of benefit under any Act amending the Act or under any uprating order

46. Where an award of any benefit under Chapter IV or V Part II of the   **10.48**
Act has been made before the day appointed for the payment of benefit of

the description to which the award relates at a higher rate by virtue of an Act or up-rating order which increases benefit payable under the Act, paragraph 2(1) of Schedule 14 to the Act (which relates to the effect of any such award) shall, if the period to which the award relates has not ended before that day, have effect subject to the condition that if the award has not been made in accordance with the provisions of sub-paragraph (2) of that paragraph which authorise the making of such an award providing for the payment of the benefit at the higher rate as from that day and a question as to—

    (a) the weekly rate at which the benefit is payable by virtue of the Act or up-rating order which so increases benefit or of these regulations, or

    (b) whether the conditions for the receipt of the benefit at the higher rate are satisfied;

the benefit shall be or continue to be payable at the weekly rate specified in the award until the said question shall have been determined in accordance with the provisions of the Act.

10.49   *Regulation 47 omitted.*

SCHEDULE 1   **Regulation 10**

PROVISIONS FOR THE PURPOSE OF WHICH DISQUALIFICATION UNDER THE ACT ARE TO BE DISREGARDED

10.50

Class of person (1)	Class of Benefit for which person is disqualified (2)	Section of the Act for the purposes of which disqualification is to be disregarded (3)	Subject matter (4)
	Widow's allowance	25(3)	Period for which a widowed mothers allowance is payable (being a period for which she is not entitled to widow's allowance
A widow	Widow's allowance or widowed mother's allowance	26(3)	Period for which a widow's pension is payable (Being a period for which she is not entitled to a widow's allowance or a widowed mother's allowance
	Widowed mother's allowance	26(1)(b)	Widow's pension for certain widows ceasing to be entitled to widowed mother's allowance
The husband of a widow	Category A retirement pension	24(1)(a)	Widow's allowance for the widow of a husband who at the date of his death was not entitled to a Category A retirement pension

In this Schedule "widowed mother's allowance" and "widow's pension" include benefit under section 39(4) corresponding to a widowed mother's allowance and a widow's pension respectively

SCHEDULE 2   **Regulation 11**

PRESCRIBED DEGREES OF DISABLEMENT

Description of injury	*Degree of disablement per cent*	**10.51**
1. Loss of both hands or amputation at higher sites	100	
2. Loss of a hand and a foot	100	
3. Double amputation through leg or thigh, or amputation through leg or thigh on one side and loss of other foot	100	
4. Loss of sight to such an extent as to render the claimant unable to perform any work for which eyesight is essential	100	
5. Very severe facial disfiguration	100	
6. Absolute deafness	100	
7. Forequarter or hindquarter amputation	100	

Amputation cases—upper limbs (either arm)

8. Amputation through shoulder joint	90	
9. Amputation below shoulder with stump less than 20.5 centimetres from tip of acromion	80	
10. Amputation from 20.5 centimetres from tip of acromion to less than 11.5 centimetres below tip of olecranon	70	
11. Loss of a hand or of the thumb and four fingers of one hand or amputation from 11.5 centimetres below tip of olecranon	60	
12. Loss of thumb	30	
13. Loss of thumb and its metacarpal bone	40	
14. Loss of four fingers of one hand	50	
15. Loss of three fingers of one hand	30	
16. Loss of two fingers of one hand	20	
17. Loss of terminal phalanx of thumb	20	

Amputation cases—lower limbs

18. Amputation of both feet resulting in end-bearing stumps	90	
19. Amputation through both feet proximal to the metatarso-phalangeal joint	80	
20. Loss of all toes of both feet through the metatarso-phalangeal joint	40	
21. Loss of all toes of both feet proximal to the proximal inter-phalangeal joint	30	
22. Loss of all toes of both feet distal to the proximal inter-phalangeal joint	20	
23. Amputation at hip	90	
24. Amputation below hip with stump not exceeding 13 centimetres in length measured from tip of great trochanter	80	
25. Amputation below hip and above knee with stump exceeding 13 centimetres in length measured from tip of great trochanter, or at knee not resulting in end-bearing stump	70	
26. Amputation at knee resulting in end-bearing stump or below knee with stump not exceeding 9 centimetres	60	
27. Amputation below knee with stump exceeding 9 centimetres but not exceeding 13 centimetres	50	
28. Amputation below knee with stump exceeding 13 centimetres	40	
29. Amputation of one foot resulting in end-bearing stump	30	
30. Amputation through one foot proximal to the metatarso-phalangeal joint	30	
31. Loss of all toes of one foot through the metatarso-phalangeal joint	20	

Other injuries	*Degree of disablement per cent*	
32. Loss of one eye, without complications, the other being normal	40	
33. Loss of vision of one eye, without complications or disfigurement of the eyeball, the other being normal	30	

Loss of:
A Fingers of right or left hand

Index finger—
34. Whole   14
35. Two phalanges   11
36. One phalanx   9
37. Guillotine amputation of tip without loss of bone   5

Middle finger—
38. Whole   12
39. Two phalanges   9
40. One phalanx   7
41. Guillotine amputation of tip without loss of bone   4

Ring or little finger—
42. Whole   7
43. Two phalanges   6
44. One phalanx   5
45. Guillotine amputation of tip without loss of bone   2

B Toes of right or left foot

Great toe—
46. Through metatarso-phalangeal joint   14
47. Part, with some loss of bone   3

Any other toe—
48. Through metatarso-phalangeal joint   3
49. Part, with some loss of bone   1

Two toes of one foot, excluding great toe—
50. Through metatarso-phalangeal joint   5
51. Part, with some loss of bone   2

Three toes of one foot, excluding great toe—
52. Through metatarso-phalangeal joint   6
53. Part, with some loss of bone   3

Four toes of one foot, excluding great toe—
54. Through metatarso-phalangeal joint   9
55. Part, with some loss of bone   3

GENERAL NOTE

10.52   See the notes to reg.11.

SCHEDULE 3   **Regulation 14**

SCALE OF DISABLEMENT GRATUITIES

10.53	*Degree of disablement* *(1)*	*(1) Appropriate proportion of maximum disablement gratuity (as specified in paragraph 2 of PartV of Schedule 4 to the Act (2)*
		per cent
	1 per cent	10
	2 per cent	15
	3 per cent	20
	4 per cent	25
	5 per cent	30
	6 per cent	35
	7 per cent	40
	8 per cent	45
	9 per cent	50

Degree of disablement (1)	(1) Appropriate proportion of maximum disablement gratuity (as specified in paragraph 2 of Part V of Schedule 4 to the Act (2)
10 per cent	55
11 per cent	60
12 per cent	65
13 per cent	70
14 per cent	75
15 per cent	80
16 per cent	85
17 per cent	90
18 per cent	95
19 per cent	100

SCHEDULE 4 **Regulation 18**

[*Schedule 4 saved for certain purposes by regulation 7(5) and (6) of The Social Security (Industrial Injuries and Diseases) Miscellaneous Provisions Regulations 1986, SI 1986/1561.*]

RATE OF DISABLEMENT PAYABLE IN LIEU OF DISABLEMENT GRATUITY IN ACCORDANCE WITH REGULATION 18

Where the degree of disablement is as specified in column (1) of the following table, the weekly rate of the pension shall be determined in accordance with column (2) of that table: **10.54**

Degree of disablement (1)	Rate of pension (2)
less than 20 per cent but not less than 16 per cent	the appropriate weekly amount of disablement pension payable in respect of a degree of disablement of 20 per cent as specified in paragraph 3 of Part V of Schedule 4 to the Act;
less than 16 per cent but not less than 11 per cent	75 per cent of the appropriate weekly amount of disablement pension payable in respect of a degree of disablement of 20 per cent as specified in the said paragraph 3:
less than 11 per cent but not less than 6 per cent	50 per cent of the appropriate weekly amount of disablement pension payable in respect of a degree of disablement of 20 per cent as specified in the said paragraph 3:
less than 6 per cent	25 per cent of the appropriate weekly amount of disablement pension payable in respect of a degree of disablement of 20 per cent as specified in the said paragraph 3: a fraction of a penny, being for this purpose treated as a penny.

10.55   *Schedules 5–9 omitted*

Social Security (Industrial Injuries) (Prescribed Diseases) Regulations 1985

(SI 1985/967) (*as amended*)

ARRANGEMENT OF REGULATIONS

PART I

GENERAL

PART II

PRESCRIPTION OF DISEASES AND PRESUMPTION AS TO THEIR ORIGIN

PART III

DATE OF ONSET AND RECRUDESCENCE

PART IV

APPLICATION OF SECTIONS 94 TO 107 OF THE SOCIAL SECURITY CONTRIBUTIONS AND BENEFITS ACT 1992 AND SECTIONS 8 TO 10 OF THE SOCIAL SECURITY ADMINISTRATION ACT 1992 AND OF REGULATIONS MADE THEREUNDER

PART V

SPECIAL PROVISIONS AS TO PNEUMOCONIOSIS,
BYSSINOSIS, OCCUPATIONAL DEAFNESS AND CERTAIN
OTHER DISEASES

Section A—Benefit

PART VI

TRANSITIONAL PROVISIONS AND REVOCATION

43.   Transitional provisions regarding relevant dates.
44.   Transitional provisions regarding dates of development and dates of onset.
45.   *Omitted.*

SCHEDULES

Schedule 1.—Part I: List of prescribed diseases and the occupations for which they are prescribed.
Part II: Occupations for which pneumoconiosis is prescribed.
Schedule 2.—Modifications of sections 94 to 107 of the Social Security Contributions and Benefits Act 1992 and sections 8 to 10 of the Social Security Administration Act 1992 in their application to benefit and claims to which these regulations apply.
Schedule 3.—Assessment of the extent of occupational deafness.
Part I.—Claims to which regulation 34(1) applies.
Part II.—Claims to which regulation 34(2) applies.
Part III.—Formula for calculating binaural disablement.
Schedule 4.—Prescribed diseases and relevant dates for the purposes of regulation 43.
Schedule 5.—Transitional provisions regarding dates of development and dates of onset.
Schedule 6.—*Omitted.*

The Secretary of State for Social Services, in exercise of powers conferred by sections 76, 77, 78, 113 and 155 of and Schedule 20 to the Social Security Act 1975, and of all other powers enabling him in that behalf, and for the purpose only of consolidating regulations hereinafter revoked, after consultation with the Council of Tribunals in so far as is required by section 10 of the Tribunals and Inquiries Act 1971, hereby makes the following regulations:

PART I

GENERAL

Citation, commencement and interpretation

10.57   **1.**—(1) These regulations may be cited as the Social Security (Industrial Injuries) (Prescribed Diseases) Regulations 1985 and shall come into operation on 31st July 1985.
(2) In these regulations, unless the context otherwise requires—
"the Act" means the [Social Security Contributions and Benefits Act 1992];
[¹ "the 1998 Act" means the Social Security Act 1998;]
"the Workmen's Compensation Acts" means the Workmen's Compensation Acts 1925 to 1945, or the enactments repealed by the Workmen's Compensation Act 1925, or the enactments repealed by the Workmen's Compensation Act 1906;

"the Adjudication Regulations" means the Social Security (Adjudication) Regulations 1984;

"the Benefit Regulations" means the Social Security (General Benefit) Regulations 1982;

"the Claims and Payments Regulations" means the Social Security (Claims and Payments) Regulations 1979;

[¹ . . .]

"asbestosis" means fibrosis of the parenchyma of the lungs due to the inhalation of asbestos dust;

"asbestos textiles" means yarn or cloth composed of asbestos or of asbestos mixed with any other material;

"coal mine" means any mine where one of the objects of the mining operations is the getting of coal (including bituminous coal, cannel coal, anthracite, lignite, and brown coal);

"diffuse mesothelioma" means the disease numbered D3 in Part I of Schedule 1 to these regulations;

"employed earner" means employed earner for the purposes of industrial injuries benefit and the term "employed earner's employment" shall be construed accordingly;

"foundry" means those parts of industrial premises where the production of metal articles (other than pig iron or steel ingots) is carried on by casting (not being diecasting or other casting in metal moulds), together with any part of the same premises where any of the following processes are carried on incidentally to such production, namely, the drying and subsequent preparation of sand for moulding (including the reclamation of used moulding sand), the preparation of moulds and cores, knock-out operations and dressing or fettling operations;

"grindstone" means a grindstone composed of natural or manufactured sandstone and includes a metal wheel or cylinder into which blocks of natural or manufactured sandstone are fitted;

[² "knock out and shake out grid" means a grid used for mechanically separating moulding sand from mouldings and castings;]

"a local office" means any office appointed by the Secretary of State as a local office for the purposes of the Act or of these regulations;

[³ . . .]

"medical board" has the same meaning as in regulation 30 of the Adjudication Regulations;

[¹ "medical practitioner" means a medical practitioner who has experience in the issues specified in regulation 12(1) of the Social Security and Child Support (Decisions and Appeals) Regulations 1999;]

[⁴ "metal" for the purposes of the disease number A10 in Part I of Schedule 1 to these Regulations, does not include stone, concrete, aggregate or similar substances for use in road or railway construction;]

"mine" includes every shaft in the course of being sunk, and every level and inclined plane in the course of being driven, and all the shafts, levels, planes, works, tramways and sidings, both below ground and above ground, in and adjacent to and belonging to the mine, but does not include any part of such premises on which any manufacturing process is carried on other than a process ancillary to the getting or dressing of minerals or the preparation of minerals for sale;

"occupational asthma" means the disease numbered D7 in Part I of Schedule 1 to these regulations;

"occupational deafness" means the disease numbered A10 in Part I of Schedule 1 to these regulations;

"the old regulations" means the Social Security (Industrial Injuries) (Prescribed Diseases) Regulations 1980, as amended by the Social Security (Industrial Injuries) (Prescribed Diseases) Amendment Regulations 1980, the Social Security (Industrial Injuries) (Prescribed Diseases) Amendment Regulations 1982 and the Social Security (Industrial Injuries) (Prescribed Diseases) Amendment (No. 2) Regulations 1982;

"prescribed disease" means a disease or injury prescribed under Part II of these regulations, and references to a prescribed disease being contracted shall be deemed to include references to a prescribed injury being received;

[3 "primary carcinoma of the lung" means the diseases numbered D8, [7 D8A,] D10 and D11 in Schedule 1 to these Regulations;]

"the Secretary of State" means the Secretary of State for Social Services;

"silica rock" means quartz, quartzite, ganister, sandstone, gritstone and chert, but not natural sand or rotten rock;

[2 "skid transfer bank" means the area of a steel mill where the steel product is moved from the area of its formation to the finishing area;]

"special medical board" has the same meaning as in regulation 30 of the Adjudication Regulations;

[5 "specially qualified adjudicating medical practitioner" means a specially qualified adjudicating medical practitioner appointed by virtue of section 62 of the Social Security Administration Act 1992;]

"tuberculosis" in the description of the disease numbered B5 in Part I of Schedule 1 to these regulations means disease due to tuberculosis infection, but when used elsewhere in these regulations in connection with pneumoconiosis means tuberculosis of the respiratory system only;

and other expressions have the same meanings as in the Act.

(3) Unless the context otherwise requires, any reference in these regulations—

(a) to a numbered section or Schedule is to the section of or, as the case may be, the Schedule to the Act bearing that number; and

(b) to a numbered regulation is a reference to the regulations bearing that number in these regulations, and any reference in a regulation to a numbered paragraph is a reference to the paragraph of that regulation bearing that number; and

(c) to any provision made by or contained in any enactment or instrument shall be construed as including a reference to any provision which it re-enacts or replaces, with or without modification.

[6 (4) In these Regulations, any reference to death benefit shall be taken as including also a reference to any benefit in respect of which contribution conditions are taken as having been satisfied in accordance with paragraph 10 of Schedule 3 to the Social Security Act 1986.]

AMENDMENTS

1. Social Security Act 1998 (Commencement No.8, and Savings and Consequential and Transitional Provisions) Order 1999 (SI 1999/1958), Sch.8, para.1 (July 5, 1999).

2. Social Security (Industrial Injuries) (Prescribed Diseases) Amendment Regulations 1994 (SI 1994/2343), reg.2 (October 10, 1994).

3. Social Security (Industrial Injuries) (Prescribed Diseases) Amendment Regulations 1993 (SI 1993/862), reg.2 (April 19, 1993).

4. Social Security (Industrial Injuries) (Prescribed Diseases) Amendment Regulations 1990 (SI 1990/2269), reg.2 (December 13, 1990).

5. Social security (Industrial Injuries and Adjudication) Regulations 1993 (SI 1993/861), reg.17 (April 19, 1993).

6. Social Security (Industrial Injuries) (Miscellaneous Amendment) Regulations 1988 (SI 1988/553), reg.5 (April 11, 1988).

7. Social Security (Industrial Injuries) (Prescribed Diseases) Amendment Regulations 2006 (SI 2006/586), reg.2(1) (April 6, 2006).

PART II

PRESCRIPTION OF DISEASES AND PRESUMPTION AS TO THEIR ORIGIN

Prescription of diseases and injuries and occupations for which they are prescribed

2.—For the purposes of [sections 108–110] of the Act—   10.58
  (a) subject to [¹ the following paragraphs] of this regulation and to reg-
      ulation 43(3), (5) and (6), each disease or injury set out in the first
      column of Part I of Schedule 1 hereto is prescribed in relation to
      all persons who have been employed on or after 5th July 1948 in
      employed earner's employment in any occupation set against such
      disease or injury in the second column of the said Part;
  (b) pneumoconiosis is prescribed—
      (i) in relation to all persons who have been employed on or after
          5th July 1948 in employed earner's employment in any occupa-
          tion set out in Part II of the said Schedule; and
     (ii) in relation to all other persons who have been so employed in any
          occupation involving exposure to dust and who have not worked
          at any time (whether in employed earner's employment or not) in
          any occupation in relation to which pneumoconiosis is prescribed
          by virtue of regulations (apart from this sub-paragraph) in force—
          (i) in the case of any claim for disablement benefit or a claim
              for death benefit in respect of the death of a person to
              whom disablement benefit has been awarded in respect of
              pneumoconiosis, on the date of the claim for disablement
              benefit;
         (ii) in the case of a claim for death benefit in respect of the
              death of any other person, on the date of the death of that
              person;
  (c) occupational deafness is prescribed in relation to all persons who
      have been employed in employed earner's employment—
      (i) at any time on or after 5th July 1948; and
     (ii) for a period or periods (whether before or after 5th July 1948)
          amounting in the aggregate to not less than 10 years in one or
          more of the occupations set out in the second column of para-
          graph A10 of Part I of Schedule 1 to these regulations [⁴ . . .]

[² (d) the disease specified in paragraph D12 of Part I of Schedule 1 is not prescribed in relation to persons to whom regulation 22 applies.]

[³ (e) cataract is not prescribed unless the person was employed in employed earner's employment in an occupation set out in the second column of paragraph A2 of Part I of Schedule 1 to these regulations for a period or periods amounting in aggregate to not less than 5 years.]

AMENDMENTS

1. Social Security (Industrial Injuries) (Prescribed Diseases) Amendment Regulations 2000 (SI 2000/1588), reg.2(2) (July 10, 2000).

2. Social Security (Industrial Injuries) (Prescribed Diseases) Amendment (No.2) Regulations 1993 (SI 1993/1985), reg.2 (September 13, 1993).

3. Social Security (Industrial Injuries) (Prescribed Diseases) Amendment Regulations 2000 (SI 2000/1588), reg.2(3) (July 10, 2000).

4. Social Security (Industrial Injuries) (Prescribed Diseases) Amendment Regulations 2005 (SI 2005/324), reg.2(1) (March 14, 2005).

DEFINITIONS

"employed earner's employment"—see SSCBA 1992, s.95, and note.
"pneumoconiosis"—see SSCBA 1992, s.122(1), above.

GENERAL NOTE

10.59   This regulation links with Sch.1 to the Regulations (below) to establish a list of diseases, and a list of the occupations in respect of which they are prescribed. It is not enough to suffer from a disease which happens to be in the list, it must have been linked to the occupation. Each disease is prescribed only in relation to claimants who have been employed in the occupations described in the Schedule. That is a significant limitation. It is also necessary for the occupation to have caused the disease but that is usually presumed under reg.4.

On July 5, 1999, AOs' functions with respect to industrial injuries benefits and the making of an industrial accident declaration were transferred to the Secretary of State (SSA 1998, ss.1, 8 and Commencement Order No. 8). He may, however, refer certain issues for report to a medical practitioner who has experience of the issues. The issues so referable are.

(a) the extent of a personal injury for the purposes of s.94

(b) whether the claimant has a prescribed industrial disease and the extent of resulting disablement; and

(c) whether, for disablement benefit purposes, the claimant has a disablement and its extent (Decisions and Appeals Regulations 1999, reg.12).

Decisions on industrial injuries benefits and on the matter of an industrial accident declaration, are appealable to a "unified" appeal tribunal composed of a legally qualified member and up to two medically qualified members (SSA 1998, ss.4, 12, Schs 2 and 3; Decisions and Appeals Regulations 1999, reg.36(2)). Like the Secretary of State, that tribunal is competent to deal with both the medical and non-medical aspect of industrial injuries matters. Note, however, that whether a claimant is an employed or self-employed earner, and whether a specific employment is, or is not, employed earner's employment is to be decided not by the Secretary of State, but by officers of the Board of Revenue and Customs (Social Security Contributions (Transfer of Functions, etc.) Act 1999, s.8(1)). Accordingly, such decisions are not matters of appeal for the "unified" appeal tribunal but rather for appeal to the tax appeal Commissioners (*ibid.*, s.11). Such decisions and appeals are regulated by the Social Security Contributions (Decisions and Appeals) Regulations 1999 (SI 1999/1027).

The key point from all this for industrial injuries matters, is that the distinction between medical issues (the disablement questions) and non-medical issues—previously crucial as demarcating the respective jurisdictions of MATs and SSATs—is no longer relevant.

Regulation 2 requires persons to have been "employed in" an occupation prescribed as relevant for the disease in question in Sch.1 to the regulations. Para.(c) (occupational deafness) further requires the employment in the relevant occupation to have been for a period or periods amounting in the aggregate to not less than 10 years. *R(I) 2/79(T)*, an occupational deafness case, makes it clear that

> "the focus of the regulations is directed to the work done rather than to the contractual obligation to do it. The benefit is for disablement incurred whilst working in any of the prescribed occupations and undergoing exposure to noise whilst so working." (para.15).

At the time that case was considered, an otherwise very similar regulation required 20 years' employment. The Tribunal of Commissioners said that to compute the relevant period, one should use this actual work test. However, one cannot look to whether the person worked on every available day. Normal breaks (weekends, holidays, short-term absences for sickness or absenteeism, short-term interruptions for industrial trouble) should be ignored in the sense of not breaking the period of employment. In contrast, abnormal interruptions would break the period of employment and not count towards the 20-year requirement. What, then, was an abnormal interruption? The Commissioners thought it undesirable to lay down an inflexible rule as to what constituted an abnormal interruption, considering the matter to be one of fact and degree in each case. But they considered that an abnormal interruption "should be a substantial or prolonged period of absence from work" and thought "that it would be a most exceptional case where it could be said that a man had been working during a continuous break in actual work of three calendar months or more for whatever reason" and opined that "such periods of absence should normally be excluded from the computation of the period of 20 years." (see especially paras 19, 20). The same approach had to be taken to determining when a person was last employed in a relevant occupation for the purposes of time limits on claims (see further annotation to reg.25, below).

Where an employed earner works for less than half the time in a prescribed occupation, he or she cannot be said to be working "wholly or mainly" in that occupation during the whole period of employment. However, there may have been parts of the period of employment during which the claimant was working for most of the time in a prescribed occupation and other parts when he or she was not. It is therefore wrong, on a claim in respect of occupational deafness, to look at the whole period of employment and consider whether the claimant was working "wholly or mainly" in a prescribed occupation throughout that period. The question is whether the parts of the period (or periods) of employment during which the claimant was working in a prescribed occupation total in the aggregate to not less than 10 years (*CI/1446/98*).

Special provision is made for pneumoconiosis and occupational deafness. In respect of pneumoconiosis, para.(b)(ii) gives potential entitlement to a group of people who do not work in the specific occupations for which the disease is prescribed in Pt II of the Schedule. Note that this group do not have the benefit of the presumption that the prescribed disease resulted from employment in the specified occupation (see reg.4, below), and the claimant bears the burden of proving that the disease results from being employed, "in any occupation involving exposure to dust". This means that the exposure to dust must be in excess of that met with in ordinary life (*R(I) 40/57*). The requirement was most recently considered in *R(I) 1/85*, which dealt with the same phrase in relation to the prescribed disease D4 (Inflammation of the mucous membrane etc.).

The amendment inserting para.(e) (cataract) is subject to a transitional provision in reg.7(2) and (3) of the amending instrument such that it "shall not apply in the case of a person—

    (a) who had an assessment of disablement in respect of the relevant disease for a period up to the date 3 months after the commencement date; or

    (b) in respect of whom a decision in relation to a relevant disease on a claim for disablement benefit made before or within 3 months after the commencement date is revised or superseded after that date under section 9 or 10 of the Social Security Act 1998 resulting in an assessment;

during any period when there is in respect of him a continuous assessment of disablement in respect of that disease, and for this purpose two or more assessments, one of which begins on the day following the end of a preceding assessment, shall be treated as continuous." (reg.7(2)).

Nor will it apply

"in the case of a person—

    (a) who had an assessment of disablement in respect of the relevant disease for a period which ended before or within 3 months after the commencement date;

    (b) who suffers a further attack of that relevant disease before or within 3 months after the commencement date;

    (c) who makes a claim for disablement benefit in respect of that disease after the commencement date; and

    (d) in respect of whom it is decided under regulation 7 of the principal Regulations (recrudescence) that the further attack is a recrudescence of that disease." (reg.7(3))

The commencement date is July 10, 2000 and "relevant disease" means the disease referred to in the amendment, or the regulation amended by the amendment (reg.7(4)).

Sequelae or resulting conditions

10.60   **3.**—Where a person—
    (a) is or was in employed earner's employment and a disease is or was prescribed under the Act and these regulations in relation to him in such employment; and
    (b) is suffering from a condition which, in his case, has resulted from that disease;
the provisions of [sections 108–110] of the Act and of these regulations shall apply to him as if he was suffering from that disease, whether or not the condition from which he is suffering is itself a prescribed disease.

GENERAL NOTE

10.61   Disablement resulting from a condition which is not prescribed but which has resulted from a prescribed disease is to be included in any assessment.

     In *CI/5972/99*, Commissioner Howell held that a tribunal erred in law when, in respect of someone who was a carrier of viral hepatitis (having had an attack of it in the past) they merely recorded that he was not suffering from the disease. They ought to have considered (as the AMA had) whether he suffered from a sequela of the disease.

Presumption that a disease is due to the nature of employment

10.62   **4.**—(1) Where a person has developed a disease which is prescribed in relation to him in Part I of Schedule 1 hereto, other than the diseases numbered A10, [¹A12], B5, [²C1, C2, C4, C5A, C5B, C6, C7, C12, C13, C16, C19, C20, C21, C22, C23, C25, C26, C27, C29, C30], D1, D2, [³. . .] [⁴ D5 and D12] in that Schedule, that disease shall, unless the contrary is proved, be presumed to be due to the nature of his employed earner's employment if that employment was in any occupation set against that disease in the second column of the said Part and he was so employed on, or at any time within one month immediately preceding, the date on which, under the subsequent provisions of these regulations, he is treated as having developed the disease.

(2) Where a person in relation to whom tuberculosis is prescribed in paragraph B5 of Part I of Schedule 1 hereto develops that disease, the disease shall, unless the contrary is proved, be presumed to be due to the nature of his employed earner's employment if the date on which, under the subsequent provisions of these regulations, he is treated as having developed the disease is not less than six weeks after the date on which he was first employed in any occupation set against the disease in the second column of the said Part and not more than two years after the date on which he was last so employed in employed earner's employment.

(3) Where a person in relation to whom pneumoconiosis is prescribed in regulation 2(b)(i) develops pneumoconiosis, the disease shall, unless the contrary is proved, be presumed to be due to the nature of his employed earner's employment if he has been employed in one or other of the occupations set out in Part II of the said Schedule 1 for a period or periods amounting in the aggregate to not less than two years in employment which either—

(a) was employed earner's employment; or

(b) would have been employed earner's employment if it has taken place on or after 5th July 1948.

(4) Where a person in relation to whom byssinosis is prescribed in paragraph D2 of Part I of Schedule 1 hereto develops byssinosis, the disease shall, unless the contrary is proved, be presumed to be due to the nature of his employed earner's employment.

(5) Where a person in relation to whom occupational deafness is prescribed in regulation 2(c) develops occupational deafness the disease shall, unless the contrary is proved, be presumed to be due to the nature of his employed earner's employment.

[4 (6) Where a person in relation to whom chronic bronchitis or emphysema is prescribed in paragraph D12 of Schedule 1 develops chronic bronchitis or emphysema, the disease shall, unless the contrary is proved, be presumed to be due to the nature of his employed earner's employment.]

[2 (7) Where a person in relation to whom primary neoplasm of the epithelial lining of the urinary tract is prescribed in paragraph C23 of Part I of Schedule 1 in respect of the occupation set out in sub-paragraph (a), (b) or (e) in the second column of the entry relating to the disease numbered C23, develops that disease, it shall, unless the contrary is proved, be presumed to be due to the nature of his employed earner's employment if he was employed in one of those occupations on, or at any time within one month immediately preceding, the date on which, under the subsequent provisions of these Regulations, he is treated as having developed the disease.]

AMENDMENTS

1. Social Security (Industrial Injuries) (Prescribed Diseases) Amendment Regulations 1993 (SI 1993/862), reg.3 (April 19, 1993).

2. Social Security (Industrial Injuries) (Prescribed Diseases) Amendment Regulations 2003 (SI 2003/270), reg.2 (March 17, 2003).

3. Social Security (Industrial Injuries and Diseases) (Miscellaneous Amendments) Regulations 1996 (SI 1996/425), reg.5(2) (March 24, 1996).

4. Social Security (Industrial Injuries) (Prescribed Diseases) Amendment (No. 2) Regulations 1993 (SI 1993/1985), reg.3 (September 13, 1993).

GENERAL NOTE

Para.(1)

10.63   This important regulation establishes a presumption that a prescribed disease is due to the nature of a scheduled occupation, provided that the claimant was employed in the scheduled occupation on the date of onset of the disease (see regs 5–7, below), or at any time within the preceding month. The decision-maker should only treat the contrary as proved if, on a balance of probabilities, the disease was not due to the nature of the scheduled occupation (*R(I) 38/52*). The following diseases do not attract the operation of the presumption on those terms:

A10   Occupational deafness;

A12   Carpal tunnel syndrome;

B5   Tuberculosis;

C1   Anaemia, peripheral neuropathy, central nervous system toxicity;

C2   Central nervous system toxicity characterised by parkinsonism;

C4   Primary carcinoma of the bronchus or lung;

C5A   Central nervous system toxicity characterised by tremor and neuropsychiatric disease;

C5B   Central nervous system toxicity characterised by combined cerebellar and cortical degeneration;

C6   Peripheral neuropathy;

C7   Acute non-lymphatic leukemia;

C12   Peripheral neuropathy, central nervous system toxicity;

C13   Cirrhosis of the liver;

C16   Neurotoxicity, cardiotoxicity;

C19   Peripheral neuropathy, central nervous system toxicity;

C20   Dystrophy of the cornea;

C21   Primary carcinoma of the skin;

C22   Primary carcinoma of the mucous membranes of the nose or paranasal sinuses, or primary carcinoma of the bronchus or lung;

C23   Primary neoplasm of the epilethial lining of the urinary tract (but see reg.4(7));

C25   Vitiligo;

C26   Liver or kidney toxicity;

C27   Liver toxicity;

C29   Peripheral neuropathy;

C30   (a) dermatitis; (b) ulceration of the mucous membrane or the epidermis;

D1   Pneumoconiosis;

D2   Byssinosis;

D5   Non-infective dermatitis;

D12   Chronic bronchitis, emphysema or both.

D4 was also in this list until its deletion from it by reg.5 of the Social Security (Industrial Injuries and Diseases) (Miscellaneous Amendments) Regulations 1996 (SI 1996/425). The deletion was effected from March 24, 1996, subject to a transitional provision in reg.7 of those amending regulations, reproduced later in this volume.

The "C" diseases were added with effect from March 17, 2003, subject to a transitional provision in reg.6 of the Social Security (Industrial Injuries) (Prescribed Diseases) Amendment Regulations 2003 (SI 2003/270), reproduced later in this volume.

Until March 24, 1996, PD D4 (allergic rhinitis) did not attract the presumption that a prescribed disease is due to the nature of a scheduled operation, provided that the claimant was employed in that occupation at the date of onset of the disease, or at any time within a month preceding the date of onset. From March 24, 1996, it does attract that presumption. So, once a tribunal had found the claimant to be suffering from allergic rhinitis, it erred in law by not considering whether the occupations in question were/were not prescribed. It could not simply say that the disease was constitutional rather than occupational. Commissioner Williams so held in *R(I) 7/02*. *R(I) 1/97* was decided before the change to reg.4.

Paras (2)–(7)

Claimants in respect of occupational deafness (para.(5)); chronic bronchitis, emphysema or both (para.6); tuberculosis (para.(2)); pneumoconiosis resulting from an occupation specified in the Schedule (but not from general exposure to dust) (para. (3)); and byssinosis (para.(4)) all have the benefit of the presumption but with differing or no time conditions. So do those suffering from C23 (primary neoplasm of the epilethial lining of the urinary tract) as regards the occupations set out in sub-paras (a), (b) or (e) of the prescription (para.(7)). Disease D5 does not attract the operation of the presumption at all, although disease D5 is very common. Nor does disease A12.

10.64

PART III

DATE OF ONSET AND RECRUDESCENCE

Development of disease

5.—[¹(1)] If on a claim for benefit under [sections 108 to 110] in respect of a prescribed disease a person is found to be or to have been suffering from the disease, or to have died as the result thereof, the disease shall, for the purposes of such claim, be treated as having developed on a date (hereafter in these regulations referred to as "the date of onset") determined in accordance with the provisions of the next two following regulations.

[² (2) Where a person claims benefit under Part V of the Contributions and Benefits Act and it is decided that he is not entitled on the basis of a finding that he was not suffering from a prescribed disease, the finding shall be conclusive for the purpose of a decision on a subsequent claim of that kind in respect of the same disease and the same person.]

10.65

AMENDMENT

1. Social Security, Child Support and Tax Credits (Miscellaneous Amendments) Regulations 2005 (SI 2005/337), reg.5 (March 18, 2005).

GENERAL NOTE

See regs 6 and 7, below.

10.66

Date of onset

10.67   **6.**—(1) For the purposes of the first claim in respect of a prescribed disease suffered by a person, the date of onset shall be determined in accordance with the following provisions of this regulation, and, save as provided in regulation 7, that date shall be treated as the date of onset for the purposes of any subsequent claim in respect of the same disease suffered by the same person, so however that—

   (a) [1 . . .] any date of onset determined for the purposes of that claim shall not preclude fresh consideration of the question whether the same person is suffering from the same disease on any subsequent claim for or award of benefit; and

   (b) if, on the consideration of a claim, [2 the degree of disablement is assessed at less than one per cent.], any date of onset determined for the purposes of that claim shall be disregarded for the purposes of any subsequent claim.

   (2) Where the claim for the purposes of which the date of onset is to be determined is—

   (a) a claim for sickness benefit made by virtue of section [102] of the Act by a person to whom regulation 8(1) applies (except in respect of pneumoconiosis, byssinosis, diffuse mesothelioma, occupational deafness, occupational asthma, [3 primary carcinoma of the lung] [4, bilateral diffuse pleural thickening or chronic bronchitis or emphysema]) the date of onset shall be the first day on which the claimant was incapable of work as the result of the disease on or after 5th July 1948;

   (b) a claim for disablement benefit (except in respect of occupational deafness), the date of onset shall be the day on which the claimant first suffered from the relevant loss of faculty on or after 5th July 1948; and the date of onset so determined shall be the date of onset for the purposes of a claim for sickness benefit made by virtue of section [102] of the Act in respect of pneumoconiosis, byssinosis, diffuse mesothelioma, occupational asthma, [3 primary carcinoma of the lung] [3, bilateral diffuse pleural thickening or chronic bronchitis or emphysema];

   (c) a claim for disablement benefit in respect of occupational deafness, the date of onset shall be the day on which the claimant first suffered from the relevant loss of faculty on or after 3rd February 1975; or, if later—

      (i) 3rd September 1979 in the case of a claim made before that date which results in the payment of benefit commencing on that date, and

      (ii) in any other case, the date on which such claim is made as results in the payment of benefit; or

   (d) a claim for death benefit, the date of onset shall be the date of death.

AMENDMENTS

   1. Social Security Act 1998 (Commencement No.8, and Savings and Consequential and Transitional Provisions) Order 1999 (SI 1999/1958), Sch.8, para.2 (July 5, 1999).
   2. Social Security (Industrial Injuries) (Prescribed Diseases) Amendment Regulations 1989 (SI 1989/1207), reg.2 (August 9, 1989).
   3. Social Security (Industrial Injuries) (Prescribed Diseases) Amendment Regulations 1993 (SI 1993/862). reg.4 (April 19, 1993).
   4. Social Security (Industrial Injuries) (Prescribed Diseases) Amendment (No.2) Regulations 1993 (SI 1993/1985), reg.4 (September 13, 1993).

GENERAL NOTE

This is an important provision because, under Sch.2, references in the Act to the   **10.68**
date of the relevant accident must, in disease cases, be construed as references to the
date of onset. It is also important when reduced earnings allowance is being claimed
because the claimant's "regular employment" is the employment he had at that date
(*CI/285/49*). Under para.(1), once there has been a claim for benefit, the date of onset
established for the purposes of that claim applies for any future claim in respect of the
same disease unless disablement is assessed at less than 1 per cent. Reg.7 deals with the
distinction between fresh attacks of a disease and recrudescence of an earlier attack.

In *R(I) 4/96*, Commissioner Goodman makes the important point that the date of
onset of a prescribed disease for a particular claimant and the date from which payment
of disablement benefit can be paid on or after the disease has been prescribed (added
to the Schedule) are not necessarily coincidental. So where prescribed disease D12
(miners' bronchitis etc.) was added from September 13, 1993, disablement benefit was
only payable from that date, despite the fact that the date of onset (the date from which
the claimant suffered from it) was much earlier. Unless the contrary is clearly indicated
in the particular prescription (and it was not here), the insertion into the Schedule of a
new prescribed disease is not retrospective so as to enable the payment of disablement
benefit (subject to showing good cause for delay in claiming) from the date of onset.

Para.(2)(b)

In *CI/17220/1996*, as regards a case where the claimant first began to suffer from a   **10.69**
disease in 1945, Commissioner Levenson held that the "obvious way" to read para.
(2)(b) of reg.6

"is that the date of onset is the 5 July 1948 or any later date on which the claimant
first suffers from the relevant loss of faculty if the claimant is not suffering from
the relevant loss of faculty on 5 July 1948. In other words, if a claimant begins to
suffer from the relevant loss of faculty before 5 July 1948, this provision deems
the date of onset to be 5 July 1948. In the present case, this interpretation avoids
a potentially unfair result and is also in keeping with the notion in regulation 5 of
the disease being treated as having developed on the date of onset. In the present
case the date of onset is 5 July 1948. The disease is treated as having developed
on that date. This is also the date on which, for the purposes of section 108(1) of
the Social Security Contributions and Benefits Act 1992 the disease developed.
Accordingly since it developed after 4 July 1948, industrial injuries benefit is
payable in an appropriate case. The adjudication officer and the tribunal, without
spelling it out, assumed in effect that regulation 6(2)(b) meant that the claimant
had to have first suffered from the disease on a date later than 4 July 1948. That
was the principal error of law by the tribunal" (para.12).

The matter of the date of onset in respect of PD A11 (vibration white finger) was
considered by Commissioner Williams in *CI/6027/1999*. On a first claim, the relevant provision is reg.6(2)(b), so that the date of onset is the date when there first is a
"relevant loss of faculty". Citing *CSI/382/2000* in support, as well as the agreement of
the parties on the point, he agreed that the date of onset is the date when the disease
reached the extent necessary to meet the prescribed amount of disablement set down
in the schedule of prescription. That prescription contains an "annual test"—it reads
"episodic blanching, occurring throughout the year". Commissioner Williams asked:

"How is that test to be applied? In cases of doubt, the question is from what date
it is more probable than not that the disease has reached the necessary extent,
applying the 'annual test' prospectively (that is, it will from that date meet the
test), not retrospectively. There may be doubt at a particular date whether
there is blanching *episodically throughout the year,* as there appears to have been
in this case in 1991. It might be argued that it cannot be finally decided that
someone has the prescribed disease until at least a year of episodic blanching
to the minimum physical extent has occurred, so that in one sense you can only

prescribe the disease some months after the date of onset. In my view, the law does not require this because it is looking to certainty rather than probability. PD A11 is well known to be a disease that does not improve. Onset should be judged on the balance of probabilities without waiting a year. The 'date of onset' is the date that the disease probably first reaches the relevant levels and causes disablement. This part of the test for PD A11 is to be stated as 'this probably will be episodic throughout the year'. It is not a test that 'this definitely has been episodic throughout the past year'. But once it is clear that the proper test is applied, determining the date of onset is a question of fact, not of law, and is not for appeal to a Commissioner. It is of the nature of probability decisions that some will be shown by later events to be wrong. There are mechanisms for dealing with that elsewhere in social security legislation." (para.13).

The Secretary of State appealed against this decision. In *Whalley v Secretary of State for Work and Pensions* [2003] EWCA Civ 166 (reported as *R(I) 2/03*), the Court of Appeal allowed the appeal, but on grounds that do not concern the principles stated above. The appeal was successful on other grounds: that one cannot claim REA without claiming disablement benefit; and that a decision by a tribunal determining the date of onset for a PD, whether given in respect of disablement benefit or REA, as the case may be, binds a later tribunal considering the issue for either benefit. Where there was a refusal by a tribunal of a claim for disablement benefit on the ground that the claimant did not have PD A11 at the date of the decision, a later decision maker, faced with a new claim for that benefit or for REA, cannot specify a date of onset for the disease which is prior to the refusal of the first claim. See also *CI/2531/2001*, para.15:

> "if a person makes a claim or successive claims for disablement benefit (and, by the same token, reduced earnings allowance, which depend on establishing the same loss of faculty) in respect of occupational deafness, the 'date of onset' can never be earlier than that of the *first* such claim which results in the actual payment of benefit; and the date so determined is also, by regulation 6(1), to be treated as the date of onset for the purposes of each subsequent claim" (*per* Commissioner Howell).

Whalley has also been applied in *R(I) 2/04* (Commissioner Rowland), *CI/226/ 2001*, *R(I) 5/04*). With the support of the Secretary of State's representative, Commissioner Howell applied in *CI/3463/2003*, his decision in *CI/5270 & 5271/2002* (now reported as *R(I) 5/04*) that *Whalley* reasoning does not apply to decisions made under the Social Security Act 1998 processes. He could not better the summary of the position as stated in his submission by that representative:

> "The effects of finality for the purposes of section 17 of the SS Act 1998 was considered by the Commissioner in *CI/5270/02*. In that case it was held that following the introduction of DMA, decisions on diagnosis were not freestanding but were a question of fact embodied in a decision of the Secretary of State under section 8(1) of the Act on entitlement to benefit. In paragraph 17 the Commissioner stated *'In the absence of such express provision, an earlier finding made under the 1998 Act machinery on such a question cannot fall within the modified statutory form of the principle of* res judicata *which now applies to social security decisions under section 17'*.
> The Secretary of State accepts the reasoning in decision *CI 5270/02* and submits that provided no claim had been made under the previous legislation where section 60 of the SS Admin Act [*1992*] did provide for finality on the question of the date of onset, then that question [*sc. the previous negative diagnosis*] is a matter of fact and not final for the purposes of section 17 of the SS Act 1998."

Commissioner Rowland in *R(I) 2/04* considered the remarks in *Whalley* to have been obiter. Moreover, the reasoning applied on the basis of the decision-making processes prior to the SSA 1998, so that the demise of the earlier provisions on finality of an MAT's decision, means that the binding nature of a decision on a date of onset of a PD for disablement benefit purposes flows from the terms of reg.6, now under consideration (para.14), a view endorsed by Commissioner Howell in *CI/5270 & 5271/2002* (paras16–18). On that basis the proper way to seek to challenge the earlier decision on date of onset, where the earlier decision found that the claimant was suffering from the prescribed disease, would be by way of seeking a supersession of that decision under SSA 1998, s.10, and appealing against the supersession decision or a refusal to supersede (*R(I) 2/04*, para.19). However, where the earlier decision on a first claim for disablement benefit was a negative one – the claimant was found not to be suffering from the claimed PD, there is nothing in the new decision-making and adjudication scheme or in reg.6 to make a diagnosis decision binding for any subsequent claim (*R(I) 5/04*, paras 18–22), so that the appeals tribunal had erred, having found that the claimant was, contrary to an earlier decision of the Secretary of State, suffering from carpal tunnel syndrome (PDA12), in setting the date of onset as the limited by the date of that earlier decision.

In the Northern Ireland decision *C1/04–05 (REA)*, applying *Whalley*, Commissioner Brown held that where a tribunal had in 2002 determined the date of onset for a prescribed disease, that decision bound a later tribunal in respect of any subsequent claim in respect of the same disease.

Para. (2) (c)

It was clear from *McKiernon v Secretary of State for Social Services* (*The Times*, **10.70** November 1, 1989), that reg.6(2)(c) was originally *ultra vires*. As a result, s.77(2) of the SSA 1975 (now s.109 of the SSCBA 1992) was amended by para.4(2) of Sch.6 to the SSA 1990. Para.4(3) of Sch.6 to the 1990 Act provided that reg.6(2)(c) should be taken always to have been validly made. An argument that the 1990 Act failed to have the desired effect was rejected in *Chatterton v Chief Adjudication Officer* CA, *R(I) 1/94*).

Recrudescence

7.—(1) [¹ Where in respect of a prescribed disease other than pneumo- **10.71** coniosis, byssinosis, diffuse mesothelioma, occupational deafness, occupational asthma, [² primary carcinoma of the lung][³, bilateral diffuse pleural thickening or chronic bronchitis or emphysema], a person's disablement has been assessed at not less than one per cent. and he] suffers from another attack of the same disease, or dies as a result thereof, then—

(a) if the further attack commences or the death occurs during a period taken into account by [¹ that assessment] (which period is in this regulation referred to as a "relevant period") the disease shall be treated as a recrudescence of the attack to which the relevant period relates, unless it is otherwise determined in the manner referred to in the following sub-paragraph;

(b) if the further attack commences or the death occurs otherwise than during a relevant period, or if it is determined [⁴...] that the disease was in fact contracted afresh, it shall be treated as having been so contracted.

(2) For the purposes of paragraph (1), a further attack of a prescribed disease shall be deemed to have commenced on the date on which the person concerned was first incapable of work or first suffered from the relevant loss of faculty, whichever is earlier, as a result of that further attack.

(3) Where, under the foregoing provisions of this regulation, a disease is treated as having been contracted afresh, the date of onset of the disease in relation to the fresh contraction shall be the date on which the person concerned was first incapable of work or first suffered from the relevant loss of faculty, whichever is earlier as a result of the further attack, or in the event of his death, the date of death.

(4) Where, under the provisions aforesaid, a disease is treated as a recrudescence, any assessment of disablement in respect of the recrudescence during a period taken into account by a previous assessment of disablement shall be by way of [⁵ a supersession of the assessment relating to the relevant period].

(5) This regulation shall not apply in relation to a claim for sickness benefit made by virtue of section [102] of the Act except where such a claim is made by a person to whom regulation 8(1) applies.

AMENDMENTS

1. Social Security (Industrial Injuries) (Prescribed Diseases) Amendment Regulations 1989 (SI 1989/1207), reg.3 (August 9, 1989).
2. Social Security (Industrial Injuries) (Prescribed Diseases) Amendment Regulations 1993 (SI 1993/862), reg.5 (April 19, 1993).
3. Social Security (Industrial Injuries) (Prescribed Diseases) Amendment (No. 2) Regulations 1993 (SI 1993/1985), reg.4 (September 13, 1993).
4. Social Security (Industrial Injuries) (Prescribed Diseases) Amendment Regulations 2003 (SI 2003/270), reg.3 (March 17, 2003).
5. Social Security and Child Support (Miscellaneous Amendments) Regulations 2000 (SI 2000/1596), reg.2 (June 19, 2000).

Workmen's compensation cases

10.72
8.—(1) If under the foregoing provisions of this Part of these regulations a date of onset has to be determined for the purposes of a claim for benefit in respect of a prescribed disease, other than pneumoconiosis or byssinosis, suffered by a person to whom compensation under the Workmen's Compensation Acts has been awarded or paid in respect of the same disease and, at the date of such claim for benefit, or, if it is a claim for death benefit, at the date of death—

(a) that person was in receipt of weekly payments in respect of such compensation; or

(b) any liability or alleged liability for such compensation had been redeemed by the payment of a lump sum, or had been the subject of a composition agreement under the provisions of the said Acts;

the disease in respect of which the claim is made shall be treated for the purposes of these regulations as a recrudescence of the disease in respect of which such compensation was awarded or paid and not as having developed on or after 5th July 1948 unless it is determined [1 . . .] that the disease was in fact contracted afresh.

(2) If it is determined as provided in the foregoing paragraph that the disease was contracted afresh, or if compensation is not being or has not been paid as provided in sub-paragraph (a) or (b) thereof, the date of onset shall be determined in accordance with regulations 5 to 7 as if no compensation under the Workmen's Compensation Acts has been paid in respect of that disease.

(3) If the date of onset has to be determined as aforesaid in respect of pneumoconiosis or byssinosis suffered by a person to whom compensation has been awarded or paid in respect of the same disease or in respect of whose death compensation has been awarded or paid under the provisions of any scheme made under the provisions of the Workmen's Compensation Acts relating to compensation for silicosis, asbestosis, pneumoconiosis or byssinosis, the disease in respect of which the claim is made shall (subject to the provisions of regulation 9(2)(b)) be treated for the purposes of these regulations as not having developed on or after 5th July 1948.

(4) If, after the date of a claim for benefit in respect of a prescribed disease, the claimant receives a weekly payment of compensation in respect of that disease under the Workmen's Compensation Acts which he was not receiving at the date of such claim, or if the amount of any such weekly payment which he was receiving at that date is increased, then any decision on any [2 issue]

arising in connection with that claim, if given before the date of, or in ignorance of the fact of, the receipt of such weekly payment or increased weekly payment, may be [² revised or superseded] as if it had been given in ignorance of a material fact, and on such [² revision or supercession] the [² issue] may be decided as if the claimant had been in receipt of such weekly payment or increased weekly payment at the date of the claim, and the foregoing provisions of this regulation shall apply accordingly.

(5) For the purposes of this regulation, a person shall be deemed to be, or to have been, in receipt of a weekly payment of compensation if—

(a) he is or was in fact receiving such payment; or
(b) he is or was entitled thereto under an award or agreement made under the Workmen's Compensation Acts.

(6) This regulation shall apply to compensation under any contracting out scheme duly certified under the Workmen's Compensation Acts as it applies to compensation under those Acts.

AMENDMENTS

1. Social Security (Industrial Injuries) (Prescribed Diseases) Amendment Regulations 2003 (SI 2003/270), reg 4 (March 17, 2003).
2. Social Security Act 1998 (Commencement No. 8, and Savings and Consequential and Transitional Provisions) Order 1999 (SI 1999/1958), Sch.8, para.3 (July 5, 1999).

Re-employment of pneumoconiotics and special provisions for benefit (workmen's compensation cases)

9.—(1) Where a person—   10.73

(a) has been certified by a medical board under the provisions of any scheme made under the provisions of the Workmen's Compensation Acts to be suffering from silicosis or pneumoconiosis not accompanied in either case by tuberculosis and has been awarded or paid compensation under the provisions of any such scheme, and by reason of such certification has been suspended from employment in any industry or process or in any particular operation or work in any industry, and
(b) wishes to start work in employed earner's employment in any occupation involving work underground in any coal mine, or the working or handling above ground at any coal mine of any minerals extracted therefrom, or any operation incidental thereto, being an occupation in which he is allowed by certificate of the medical board under the provisions of the scheme to engage,

he shall, before starting any such work, submit himself under arrangements made or approved by the Secretary of State for medical examination by a [¹ medical practitioner].

(2) Where a person submits himself for medical examination in accordance with the provisions of the foregoing paragraph, the provisions of the Act and the regulations made thereunder shall apply to him subject to the following modifications:—

[¹ (a) A medical practitioner shall provide a report to the Secretary of State to enable him to determine at what degree the extent of disablement resulting from pneumoconiosis should be assessed in his case.]
(b) Where the extent of disablement has been determined in his case in accordance with the provisions of the foregoing sub-paragraph by [¹ the Secretory of State or an appeal tribunal], and he starts any such work

as is mentioned in the foregoing paragraph, the provisions of regulation 38(a) (periodical examinations) shall apply to him as if he were making a claim for benefit in respect of pneumoconiosis, and the provisions of regulation 8(3) (pneumoconiosis shall in certain cases be treated as not having developed on or after 5th July 1948) shall cease to apply to him as from the date of starting such work.

(c) If, after having started work as aforesaid, he makes a claim at any time for disablement benefit in respect of pneumoconiosis, the extent of disablement in his case shall be assessed as if, [¹ to the extent decided by the Secretary of State or an appeal tribunal] given under sub-paragraph (a) of this paragraph, his disabilities resulting from pneumoconiosis were contracted before the date of onset and were not incurred as the result of the relevant loss of faculty.

(d) A person to whom a disablement pension is payable in respect of an assessment made in accordance with the provisions of the last foregoing sub-paragraph and who requires constant attendance shall, if the sum of that assessment and the assessment made in his case in accordance with the provisions of sub-paragraph (a) of this paragraph is not less than 100 per cent., have the like right to payments in respect of the need of such constant attendance as if the disablement pension were payable in respect of an assessment of 100 per cent.

(3) Where a person to whom sub-paragraph (a) of paragraph (1) applies has started any such work as is mentioned in sub-paragraph (b) thereof without having submitted himself for medical examination in accordance with the provisions of that paragraph, he may nevertheless, at any time whilst he is engaged in any such work, so submit himself for medical examination, and the provisions of the foregoing paragraph shall, if he continues thereafter to be engaged in any such work, apply to him as if he had started that work immediately after the medical examination.

(4) The Secretary of State, in making or approving any such arrangements for medical examination of any person as are mentioned in paragraph (1) shall, as far as possible, co-ordinate those arrangements with any arrangements for medical examination of that person made or approved under Part V of these regulations or under the Workmen's Compensation Acts.

AMENDMENT

1. Social Security Act 1988 (Commencement No. 8, and Savings and Consequential and Transitional Provisions Order 1999 (SI 1999/1958), Sch.8, para.4 (July 5, 1999).

PART IV

APPLICATION OF [SECTIONS 94 TO 107 OF THE SOCIAL SECURITY CONTRIBUTIONS AND BENEFITS ACT 1992 AND SECTIONS 8 TO 10 OF THE SOCIAL SECURITY ADMINISTRATION ACT 1992] AND OF REGULATIONS MADE THEREUNDER

Definition of "relevant disease"

10.74 **10.**—In this Part of these regulations, unless the context otherwise requires, the expression "relevant disease" means, in relation to any claim for benefit in respect of a prescribed disease, the prescribed disease in respect of which benefit is claimed, but does not include any previous or subsequent attack of that disease, suffered by the same person, which, under the provisions of Part III of these regulations, is or has been treated—

(a) as having developed on a date other than the date which, under the said provisions, is treated as the date of onset for the purposes of the claim under consideration;

(b) as a recrudescence of a disease for which compensation has been paid or awarded under the Workmen's Compensation Acts.

Application of [sections 94 to 107 of the Social Security Contributions and Benefits Act 1992 and sections 8 to 10 of the Social Security Administration Act 1992]

11.—The provisions of [sections 94 to 107 of the Social Security Contributions and Benefits Act 1992 and sections 8 to 10 of the Social Security Administration Act 1992] which relates to industrial injuries benefit and sickness benefit made by virtue of section 50A of the Act shall, in relation to prescribed diseases, be subject to the following provisions of this Part of these regulations, and, subject as aforesaid, to the additions and modifications set out in Schedule 2 hereto.

10.75

GENERAL NOTE

Section 50A of the Social Security Act 1975 has been replaced by s.102 of the Social Security Contributions and Benefits Act 1992.

10.76

Application of Claims and Payments Regulations and Benefit Regulations

12.—(1) Save in so far as they are expressly varied or excluded by, or are inconsistent with, the provisions of this Part of these regulations or of regulation 25 or 36, the Claims and Payments Regulations and the Benefit Regulations shall apply in relation to prescribed diseases as they apply in relation to accidents.

10.77

(2) Save as provided in this Part of these regulations or where the context otherwise requires, references in the aforesaid regulations to accidents shall be construed as references to prescribed diseases, references to the relevant accident shall be construed as references to the relevant disease, references to the date of the relevant accident shall be construed as references to the date of onset of the relevant disease, and in regulation 17 of the Benefit Regulations (increase of disablement pension in cases of special hardship), the reference to the effects of the relevant injury shall be construed as a reference to the effects of the relevant disease.

Benefit not payable in cases covered by the Industrial Injuries and Diseases (Old Cases) Act 1975

13.—Benefit shall not be payable by virtue of the provisions of these regulations in respect of the incapacity, disablement or death of any person as a result of any disease, if an award of benefit under the provisions of any Scheme made under the Industrial Injuries and Diseases (Old Cases) Act 1975 (not being an award which is subsequently [¹ revised or superseded so

10.78

as to terminate entitlement]) has at any time been made in respect of any attack of the disease suffered by him, or in respect of his death.

AMENDMENT

1. Social Security Act 1998 (Commencement No. 8 and Savings and Consequential and Transitional Provisions) Order 1999 (SI 1999/1958), Sch.8, para.5 (July 5, 1999).

Diseases contracted outside Great Britain

10.79   **14.**—For section 50(5) (accidents happening outside Great Britain) there shall be substituted the provision that, subject to the provisions of sections 129, 131 and 132, for the purpose of determining whether a prescribed disease is, or, under the provisions of Part II of these regulations is to be presumed to be, due to the nature of the person's employed earner's employment, that person shall be regarded as not being or as not having been in employed earner's employment during any period for which he is or was outside Great Britain, and accordingly benefit shall not be payable in respect of a prescribed disease which is due to the nature of employment in an occupation in which the person has only been engaged outside Great Britain.

GENERAL NOTE

10.80   Sections 50(5), 129, 131 and 132 of the Social Security Act 1975 have been replaced by ss.94(5), 117, 119 and 120 of the Social Security Contributions Act 1992.

[¹ Modification of paragraph 11(1) of Schedule 7 to the Social Security Contributions and Benefits Act 1992

10.81   **14A.**—The provisions of paragraph 11(1) of Schedule 7 to the Social Security Contributions and Benefits Act 1992 shall be modified by adding after the words "(the day on which section 3 of the Social Security Act 1990 came into force)" the words

"and a person shall not be entitled to reduced earnings allowance—

(i) in relation to a disease prescribed on or after 10th October 1994 under section 108(2) above; or
(ii) in relation to a disease prescribed before 10th October 1994 whose prescription is extended on or after that date under section 108(2) above but only in so far as the prescription has been so extended".]

AMENDMENT

1. Social Security (Industrial Injuries) (Prescribed Diseases) Amendment Regulations 1994 (SI 1994/2343), reg.3 (October 10, 1994).

Assessment of extent of disablement

10.82   **15.**—For the purposes of paragraph 1(b) of Schedule 8 (disabilities to be taken into account in assessing the extent of the claimant's disablement) and of regulation 11 of the Benefit Regulations (which further defines the principles of assessment of disablement), an injury or disease other than the relevant disease shall be treated as having been received or contracted before the relevant disease if it was received or contracted on or before the date of onset, and as having been received or contracted after the relevant disease if it was received or contracted after that date.

GENERAL NOTE

Sch.8 to the Social Security Act 1975 has been replaced by Sch.6 to the Social Security Contributions and Benefits Act 1992.

10.83

Aggregation of percentages of disablement

[¹ 15A.—(1) After the extent of an employed earner's disablement result- ing from the relevant disease has been determined, the [² Secretary of State] shall add to the percentage of that disablement the assessed percentage of any present disablement of his resulting from—

10.84

(a) any accident after 4th July 1948 arising out of and in the course of his employment, being employed earner's employment, or

(b) any other relevant disease due to the nature of that employment and developed after 4th July 1948,

and in respect of which a disablement gratuity was not paid to him under the Act after a final assessment of disablement.

(2) In determining the extent of an employed earner's disablement for the purposes of section 57 of the Act there shall be added to the percentage of disablement resulting from any relevant accident the assessed percentage of any present disablement of his resulting from any disease or injury pre- scribed for the purposes of Chapter V of Part II of the Act, which was both due to the nature of the employment and developed after 4th July 1948, and in respect of which a disablement gratuity was not paid to him under the Act after a final assessment of his disablement.

(3) This regulation is subject to the provisions of regulation 15B(3).]

AMENDMENTS

1. This whole regulation was inserted by the Social Security (Industrial Injuries and Diseases) Miscellaneous Provisions Regulations 1986 (SI 1986/1561), reg.3(2) (October 1, 1986).

2. Social Security Act 1998 (Commencement No. 8, and Savings and Consequential and Transitional Provisions) Order 1999 (SI 1999/1958), Sch.8, para.6 (July 5, 1999).

GENERAL NOTE

Section 57 of the SSA 1975 has been replaced by s.103 of the SSCBA 1992.

10.85

Rounding

[¹ 15B.—(1) Subject to the provisions of this regulation, where the assessment of disablement is a percentage between 20 and 100 which is not a multiple of 10, it shall be treated—

10.86

(a) if it is a multiple of 5, as being the next higher percentage which is a multiple of 10; and

(b) if it is not a multiple of 5 as being the nearest percentage which is a multiple of 10,

and where it is 14 per cent, or more but less than 20 per cent. it shall be treated as 20 per cent.

(2) In a case to which regulation 15A (aggregation of percentages of disablement) applies, paragraph (1) shall have effect in relation to the

aggregate percentage and not in relation to any percentage forming part of the aggregate.

(3) [² Where an assessment or a reassessment] states the degree of disablement due to occupational deafness as less than 20 per cent. that percentage shall be disregarded for the purposes of regulation 15A and this regulation.]

AMENDMENTS

1. This whole regulation was inserted by the Social Security (Industrial Injuries and Diseases) Miscellaneous Provisions Regulations 1986 (SI 1986/1561), reg.3(2) (October 1, 1986).
2. Social Security Act 1998 (Commencement No. 8, and Savings and Consequential and Transitional Provisions) Order 1999 (SI 1999/1958), Sch.8, para.6 (July 5, 1999).

10.87 *Regulation 16 omitted.*

Special provisions as to determination of regular occupation in relation to persons claiming reduced earnings allowance

10.88   17.—Where a person who has been assessed as at least one per cent. disabled in respect of a prescribed disease establishes that he has abandoned any occupation as a result of the relevant disease at any time after having been employed in employed earner's employment in any occupation prescribed for that disease but before the first day in respect of which he was so assessed, then for the purpose of determining his right to, or the rate of, reduced earnings allowance under [paragraph 11 of Schedule 7], any occupation he has so abandoned may be treated as his regular occupation for the purposes of that section.

GENERAL NOTE

10.89   This regulation simply permits the claimant's regular occupation (see SSCBA 1992, Sch.7, para.11 (formerly SSA 1975, s.59A), above, and note thereto) to include a job he may have been forced to give up because of the effects of the relevant prescribed disease. In other circumstances, an occupation abandoned by the claimant may be disregarded for the purposes of determining his regular occupation *(R(I) 5/52)*.

Exception from requirements as to notice

10.90   18.—Regulation 24 of the Claims and Payments Regulations (giving of notice of accidents in respect of which benefit may be payable) shall not apply in relation to prescribed diseases.

Provisions as to medical examination

10.91   19.—Those provisions of section [9(1) and (2) of the Social Security Administration Act 1992] which relate to the obligation of claimants to submit themselves to medical examination for the purpose of determining the effect of the relevant accident shall apply also to medical examinations for the purpose of determining whether a claimant or beneficiary is suffering or has suffered from a prescribed disease, and regulation 26 of the Claims and Payments Regulations shall be construed accordingly.

PART V

SPECIAL PROVISIONS AS TO PNEUMOCONIOSIS, BYSSINOSIS, OCCUPATIONAL DEAFNESS AND CERTAIN OTHER DISEASES

Section A—Benefit

Special conditions for disablement benefit for pneumoconiosis, byssinosis and diffuse mesothelioma

20.—[¹ (1) On a claim for disablement pension in respect of pneumo-coniosis, [² or] byssinosis [² . . .], section 57(1) shall apply as if for "14 per cent." there was substituted "1 per cent.".

(1A) Where on a claim for disablement pension in respect of pneumo-coniosis [² or] byssinosis [² . . .] the extent of the disablement is assessed at one per cent. or more, but less than 20 per cent., disablement pension shall be payable at the 20 per cent. rate if the resulting degree of disable-ment is greater than 10 per cent. and if it is not at one-tenth of the 100 per cent. rate, with any fraction of a penny being for this purpose treated as a penny.

(1B) Where immediately before 1st October 1986 a person is entitled to a disablement pension on account of pneumoconiosis [² or] byssinosis [² . . .] and in determining the extent of his disablement other disabilities were taken into account in accordance with regulation 11 of the Social Security (General Benefit) Regulations 1982, disablement pension shall continue to be payable on or after 1st October 1986 at the weekly rate applicable to the degree of disablement determined on the last assessment made before 14th October 1986 until—

(a) [³ on a reassessment of the extent of disablement or in consequence of an application for revision or supersession the degree of disable-ment is assessed either as less than 1 per cent. or as equal to or more than that determined on that last assessment, or

(b) the other disability ceases to exist.]

(2) Section 78(4)(b), in so far as it provides that disablement benefit shall not be payable in respect of byssinosis unless the claimant is found to be suffering from loss of faculty which is likely to be permanent, shall not apply.

(3) Notwithstanding paragraph 4(a) of Schedule 8 (period to be taken into account by an assessment of the extent of the claimant's disablement), the period to be taken into account by an assessment of the extent of the claimant's disablement in respect of byssinosis, if not limited by reference to the claimant's life, shall not be less than one year.

[⁴ (4) On a claim for disablement pension in respect of diffuse mesothelioma—

(a) section 103(6) of the Social Security Contributions and Benefits Act 1992 shall apply as if for the words "after the expiry of the period of 90 days (disregarding Sundays) beginning with the day of the rele-vant accident" there were substituted the words, "the day on which he first suffers from a loss of faculty due to diffuse mesothelioma";

10.92

(b) paragraph 6(1) of Schedule 6 to the Social Security Contributions and Benefits Act 1992 shall apply as if the words "beginning not earlier than the end of the period of 90 days referred to in section 103(6) above and in paragraph 9(3) of that Schedule and" were omitted.]

AMENDMENTS

1. Social Security (Industrial Injuries and Diseases) Miscellaneous Provisions Regulations 1986 (SI 1986/1561), reg.3(3) (October 1, 1986).
2. Social Security (Industrial Injuries) (Prescribed Diseases) Amendment Regulations 2002 (SI 2002/1717), reg.2(2) (July 29, 2002).
3. Social Security Act 1998 (Commencement No.8, and Savings and Consequential and Transitional Provisions) Order 1999 (SI 1999/1958), Sch.8, para.7 (July 5, 1999).
4. Social Security (Industrial Injuries) (Miscellaneous Amendments) Regulations 1997 (SI 1997/810, reg.5 (April 9, 1997).

GENERAL NOTE

10.93   Sections 57(1) and 78(4)(b) of the SSA 1975 have been replaced by ss.103(1) and 110(4) of the SSCBA 1992. Sch.8, para.4(a) has been replaced by Sch.6, para.6(2)(a).

Disablement benefit is still payable in respect of pneumoconiosis or byssinosis even if the extent of disablement is less than 1 per cent. The amount of disablement benefit payable is calculated under para.(1A) or (1B). An assessment of disablement in respect of byssinosis must be for at least one year. Para.(4) removes the usual 90-day waiting period for disablement benefit in cases where the claim is in respect of diffuse mesothelioma but makes it clear that there can be no entitlement until the disease results in a loss of faculty. Repeated assessments are seldom to be expected once the condition produces symptoms and so assessments should take into account anticipated deterioration in the claimant's condition. Thirty per cent of sufferers die within six months of the onset of symptoms. With effect from July 29, 2002, impaired function of the pleura, pericardium or peritoneum function caused by diffuse mesothelioma constitutes a loss of faculty for which the resultant degree of disablement is to be taken as 100 per cent (reg.20A, below).

[¹ Diffuse mesothelioma—prescribed loss of faculty

10.94   **20A.**—(1) For the purposes of paragraph 1 of Schedule 6 to the Social Security Contributions and Benefits Act 1992 (which provides for the assessment of the extent of disablement for the purposes of industrial injuries disablement benefit), the loss of faculty set out in paragraph (2) below is prescribed under sub-paragraph (d) of that paragraph 1 (loss of faculty from which the resulting disabilities are to be taken as amounting to 100 per cent. disablement).

(2) The loss of faculty referred to in paragraph (1) above is impaired function of the pleura, pericardium or peritoneum function caused by diffuse mesothelioma.]

AMENDMENT

1. This reg. was inserted by Social Security (Industrial Injuries) (Prescribed Diseases) Amendment Regulations 2002 (SI 2002/1717), reg.2(3) (July 29, 2002).

GENERAL NOTE

10.95   The effect of this new regulation is that impaired function of the pleura, pericardium or peritoneum caused by diffuse mesothelioma is a loss of faculty from which the resulting disabilities are to be taken as amounting to 100 per cent disablement for purposes of assessment of disablement under SSCBA 1992, Sch.6.

[¹Asbestos-related primary carcinoma of the lung—special conditions and prescribed loss of faculty

20B.—(1) This regulation shall apply to a claim for disablement pension   10.96
made in respect of the diseases prescribed in paragraphs D8 and D8A of Part I of Schedule 1.

(2) On a claim to which this regulation applies—

(a) section 103(6) of the Social Security Contributions and Benefits Act 1992 (entitlement after expiry of 90 days) shall apply as if for the words "after the expiry of the period of 90 days (disregarding Sundays) beginning with the day of the relevant accident" there were substituted the words "the day on which he first suffers from a loss of faculty due to primary carcinoma of the lung"; and

(b) paragraph 6(1) of Schedule 6 to the Social Security Contributions and Benefits Act 1992 (period to be taken into account by an assessment) shall apply as if the words "beginning not earlier than the end of the period of 90 days referred to in section 103(6) above and in paragraph 9(3) of that Schedule and" were omitted.

(3) On a claim to which this regulation applies, the loss of faculty prescribed for the purposes of sub-paragraph (d) of paragraph 1 of Schedule 6 to the Social Security Contributions and Benefits Act 1992 (assessment of extent of disablement) is lung impairment caused by primary carcinoma of the lung.]

AMENDMENT

1. This reg. was inserted by Social Security (Industrial Injuries) (Prescribed Diseases) Amendment Regulations 2006 (SI 2006/586), reg.2(1) (April 6, 2006).

GENERAL NOTE

The effect of this new regulation, on a claim for disablement pension in respect   10.97
of prescribed diseases D8 and D8A, is that entitlement may arise from the first day a person suffers from a loss of faculty due to that disease and that lung impairment caused by primary carcinoma of the lung is a loss of faculty from which the resulting disabilities are to be taken as amounting to 100 per cent disablement.

Pneumoconiosis—effects of tuberculosis

21.—Where any person is found to be suffering from pneumoconiosis   10.98
accompanied by tuberculosis, the effects of the tuberculosis shall be treated for the purposes of [sections 108–110] of the Act and of these regulations as if they were effects of the pneumoconiosis.

Pneumoconiosis—effects of emphysema and chronic bronchitis

22.—(1) [¹ Except] in the circumstances specified in paragraph (1A),]   10.99
where any person is disabled by pneumoconiosis or pneumoconiosis accompanied by tuberculosis to an extent which would, if his physical condition were otherwise normal, be assessed at not less than 50 per cent., the effects of any emphysema and of any chronic bronchitis from which that person is found to be suffering shall be treated for the purposes of [sections 108–110] of the Act and of these regulations as if they were effects of the pneumoconiosis.

[¹ (1A) The circumstances referred to in paragraph (1) are that the person is entitled to industrial injuries disablement benefit on account of the disease set out in paragraph D12 of Part I of Schedule 1.]

(2) Where, on a claim for death benefit, the question arises whether the extent of a person's disablement resulting from pneumoconiosis or from pneumoconiosis accompanied by tuberculosis would, if his physical condition were otherwise normal, have been assessed at not less than 50 per cent.—

   (a) if there has been no assessment of disablement resulting from pneumoconiosis or from pneumoconiosis accompanied by tuberculosis made during the person's life, or if there is no such assessment current at the time of death, [² that issue shall be determined by the Secretary of State];

   (b) if there is an assessment of disablement resulting from pneumoconiosis or from pneumoconiosis accompanied by tuberculosis current at the time of the person's death, that [² issue] shall be treated as having been determined by the decision of the [² Secretary of State or, as the case may be, appeal tribunal] as the case may be, which made such assessment.

AMENDMENTS

1. Social Security (Industrial Injuries) (Prescribed Diseases) Amendment (No. 2) Regulations 1993 (SI 1993/1985), reg.5 (September 13, 1993).
2. Social Security Act 1998 (Commencement No. 8, and Savings and Consequential and Transitional Provisions) Order 1999 (SI 1999/1958), Sch.8, para.8 (July 5, 1999).

Reduced earnings allowance—special provision for pneumoconiosis cases

10.100   [¹ **23.**—Where a beneficiary in receipt of a disablement pension in respect of pneumoconiosis receives advice from [² the Secretary of State] that in consequence of the disease he should not follow his regular occupation unless he complies with certain special restrictions as to the place, duration or circumstances of his work, or otherwise, then for the purpose of determining whether he fulfils the conditions laid down in [Schedule 7 of the 1992 Act] (reduced earnings allowance) and for that purpose only—

   (a) the beneficiary shall be deemed, unless the contrary is proved by evidence other than the aforesaid advice—

     (i) to be incapable of following his regular occupation and likely to remain permanently so incapable, and

     (ii) to be incapable of following employment of an equivalent standard which is suitable in his case;

   (b) where the beneficiary has ceased to follow any occupation to which the aforesaid special restrictions were applicable, the fact that he had followed such an occupation in the period between the date of onset of the disease and the date of the current assessment of his disablement, or for a reasonable period of trial thereafter, shall be disregarded.]

AMENDMENTS

1. Social Security (Industrial Injuries and Diseases) Miscellaneous Provisions Regulations 1986 (SI 1986/1561), reg.6 (October 1, 1986).

2. Social Security Act 1998 (Commencement No. 8, and Savings and Consequential and Transitional Provisions) Order 1999 (SI 1999/1958), Sch.8, para.9 (July 5, 1999).

[¹ Special requirement for pneumoconiosis claimants in unscheduled occupation cases

24.—(1) A claim for disablement benefit in respect of pneumoconiosis by a person in relation to whom the disease is prescribed by virtue of regulation 2(b)(ii) shall be referred by the Secretary of State to a medical practitioner for a report, unless the Secretary of State is satisfied on reasonable grounds that the claimant is not suffering or has not suffered from pneumoconiosis, in which case he may decide the claim without such a report.

(2) The provisions of paragraph (1) of this regulation shall apply to an appeal tribunal and a Commissioner as they apply to the Secretary of State.]

10.101

AMENDMENT

1. Social Security Act 1998 (Commencement No. 8, and Savings and Consequential and Transitional Provisions) Order 1999 (SI 1999/1958), Sch.8, para.10 (July 5, 1999).

Time for claiming benefit in respect of occupational deafness

25.—(1) Regulation 14 of the Claims and Payments Regulations (time for claiming benefit) shall not apply in relation to occupational deafness except in relation to a claim for sickness benefit payable by virtue of section [102].

(2) Subject to regulation 27(1)(c), disablement benefit, or sickness benefit payable by virtue of section [102] of the Act, shall not be paid in pursuance of a claim in respect of occupational deafness which is made later than 5 years after the latest date, before the date of the claim, on which the claimant worked [¹ in employed earner's employment] in an occupation prescribed in relation to occupational deafness [³. . .]

10.102

AMENDMENTS

1. Social Security (Industrial Injuries) (Prescribed Diseases) Amendment Regulations 2000 (SI 2000/1588), reg.3 (July 10, 2000).
2. Social Security Act 1998 (Commencement No.8, and Savings and Consequential and Transitional Provisions) Order 1999 (SI 1999/1958), Sch.8, para.11 (July 5, 1999).
3. Social Security (Industrial Injuries) (Prescribed Diseases) Amendment Regulations 2005 (SI 2005/324), reg.2(2) (March 14, 2005).

GENERAL NOTE

Note that para.4(3) of Sch.6 of the SSA 1990 (effective from July 13, 1990) provides that reg.25, and any former regulations which it directly or indirectly re-enacts with or without amendment, shall be taken to be, and always to have been, validly made. *R(I) 1/92* applied in *CI/276/1988* and *CSI/22/91*, and *CSI/84/89* and *R(I) 1/94* (affirmed by the Court of Appeal in *Chatterton v Chief Adjudication Officer*, July 8, 1993) (reported as *R(I) 1/94*), all hold that the validation effected by para.4(3) of Sch.6 of the SSA 1990 (which entered into force on July 13, 1990) operates retrospectively, thus transforming initially invalid decisions (the Court of Appeal had held reg.25 *ultra vires* in *McKiernon v Secretary of State for Social Security*) into valid determinations. Furthermore, in *Chief Adjudication Officer v McKiernon*, also decided on July 8, 1993, the Court of Appeal upheld the CAO's appeal against Commisioner Goodman's decision in *R(I) 2/94*. The

10.103

entry into force of para.4(3), notwithstanding its retrospective operation, was a change of circumstances enabling the AO to review an SSAT's decision that Mr McKiernon had good cause for his late claim so that his claim was timeous.

The regulation prevents disablement benefit or sickness benefit (payable only because of industrial disease) being paid in pursuance of a claim in respect of occupational deafness which is made later than five years after the latest date on which the claimant *worked in* a prescribed occupation, unless further conditions are met including a condition of *employment in* the occupation for a period or aggregate of periods amounting to not less than 10 years. The exemption afforded by those further conditions was revoked with effect from March 14, 2005 by reg.2 of the Social Security (Industrial Injuries) (Prescribed Diseases) Amendment Regulations 2005 (SI 2005/324). *CI/16/91* follows *R(I) 2/79* (see above, notes to reg.2) in holding that in dealing with both time periods one looks to "the work actually done rather than the contractual obligation to do it, so that, for example, time off work through ill-health was not time spent working in the occupation for the purposes of the relevant legislation" (*CI/16/91*, para.5). So, in *CI/16/91*, although the claimant's employment had been terminated on May 11, 1985, he had been on the sick from April 25, 1984. His claim was made in June 1989. Because the focus for the five-year period had to be on when he last *worked*, the Commissioner held that he ceased work in the prescribed occupation on April 25, 1984, and his claim was time-barred by reg.25.

In *CI/286/95*, Commissioner Howell held that "worked in an occupation" in lines four and five of reg.25(2) was *not* to be construed as if it read "worked *in employment earner's employment* in an occupation". He saw no absurdity in a claimant

> "being able to claim more than 5 years after ceasing to be an employed earner but within 5 years of stopping his actual work [albeit in self-employment] in a listed occupation which gives rise to exposure to noise. Before he can get the benefit, the question whether his disease is due to the nature of his employment as an employee still has to be determined."

He therefore saw nothing inconsistent with the purpose of the legislation or rendering reg.25(2) *ultra vires*, in reading it in the way he and the SSAT had done (*ibid.*) Commissioner Howell's approach was followed by Commissioner Walker in *CSI/89/96*. The amendments numbered 2 to para.(2), requiring work in employed earner's employment, reverse the effect of *CI/286/95* and *CSI/89/96*, noted immediately above. The amendment is the subject of a transitional provision in reg.7(1) of the amending instrument such that it "shall not apply in relation to a claim made within 3 months after the commencement date and the amendments made by regulations 2(3), 5 and 6 shall not apply where the date of onset of the relevant disease is prior to the commencement date and the claim is made within 3 months after that date".

Claims in respect of occupational deafness

10.104   **26.**—Where it appears that a person who has made a claim for sickness benefit by virtue of section [102] of the Act in respect of occupational deafness—

(a) may be entitled to disablement benefit, and

(b) has not previously made a claim for disablement benefit in respect of occupational deafness or such a previous claim has been disallowed,

such a claim for sickness benefit may also be treated as a claim for disablement benefit.

GENERAL NOTE

10.105   A claim for sickness benefit on the ground of occupational deafness may be treated as a claim for disablement benefit if the claimant has not already made an unsuccessful claim. This paragraph would seem to apply even if the claimant would have satisfied the contribution conditions.

Further claims in respect of occupational deafness

27.—(1) In the event of disallowance of a claim for disablement benefit or
sickness benefit made by virtue of section [102] of the Act in respect of occupational deafness because the claimant has failed to satisfy the minimum hearing
loss requirement prescribed in column 1 of paragraph A10 of Part I of Schedule
1 hereto, disablement benefit or sickness benefit made by virtue of section
[102] of the Act shall not be paid in pursuance of a further claim in respect of
occupational deafness made by or on behalf of that claimant unless—

    (a) it is a claim made after the expiration of three years from the date of
a claim which was disallowed because the claimant was not suffering
from occupational deafness; or

    (b) it is a claim made after the expiration of three years from the date of
a reassessment by [¹ the Secretary of State or an appeal tribunal] of
the extent of the claimant's disablement at less than 20 per cent; or

    (c) if the claimant would otherwise be precluded by regulation 25(2)
from making a further claim after the expiration of three years from
the date of the disallowed claim or from the date of a reassessment
by the Secretary of State or an appeal tribunal of the extent of his
disablement at less than 20 per cent., as the case may be, it is the first
claim made since that date and within five years from the latest date,
before the date of the claim, on which he worked [² in employed
earner's employment] in any occupation specified in column 2 of
paragraph A10 of Part I of Schedule I hereto.

[¹ (2) A claim to be paid benefit by virtue of paragraph (1)(c) may be
disallowed by the Secretary of State, an appeal tribunal or a Commissioner
("the determining authority") without reference to a medical practitioner
where the determining authority is satisfied by medical evidence that the
claimant is not suffering from occupational deafness.]

10.106

AMENDMENTS

1. Social Security Act 1998 (Commencement No.8, and Savings and Consequential
and Transitional Provisions) Order 1999 (SI 1999/1958), Sch.8, para.12 (July 5,
1999).

2. Social Security (Industrial Injuries) (Prescribed Diseases) Amendment
Regulations 2000 (SI 2000/1588), reg.4 (July 10, 2000).

GENERAL NOTE

The amendment, numbered 2 in the list above, requiring work in employed earner's
employment, reverses the effect of *CI 286/95* and *CSI 89/96*, noted in the annotation to
reg.25, above. The amendment is the subject of a transitional provision in regulation
7(1) of the amending instrument, reproduced later in this volume.

10.107

Availability of disablement benefit in respect of occupational deafness

28.—Where a person is awarded disablement benefit in respect of occupational deafness, section [103(6)] (period for which disablement benefit is
not available) shall not apply.

10.108

GENERAL NOTE

In occupational deafness cases, the date of onset of the disease is deemed to be
no earlier than the date of claim (see reg.6(2)(c)) and so the usual 90-day qualifying
period does not apply.

10.109

1277

Period to be covered by assessment of disablement in respect of occupational deafness

10.110   [¹29.—Paragraph 6(1) and (2) of Schedule 6 to the Social Security Contributions and Benefits Act 1992 shall be modified so that in respect of occupational deafness, the period to be taken into account by an assessment of the extent of a claimant's disablement shall be the remainder of the claimant's life.]

AMENDMENT

1. Social Security (Industrial Injuries) (Prescribed Diseases) Amendment (No.2) Regulations 2003 (SI 2003/2190), reg.2(2) (September 22, 2003).

Supersession of a decision in respect of occupational deafness

10.111   30.—[¹ . . .].

REVOCATION

1. Social Security (Industrial Injuries) (Prescribed Diseases) Amendment (No.2) Regulations 2003 (SI 2003/2190), reg.2(3) (September 22, 2003).

Requirement for leave of appeal tribunal

10.112   31.—[¹ . . .].

REVOCATION

1. Social Security (Industrial Injuries) (Prescribed Diseases) Amendment (No.2) Regulations 2003 (SI 2003/2190), reg.2(3) (September 22, 2003).

No appeal against a decision of disablement in respect of occupational Deafness

10.113   32.—[¹ . . .].

REVOCATION

1. Social Security (Industrial Injuries) (Prescribed Diseases) Amendment (No.2) Regulations 2003 (SI 2003/2190), reg.2(3) (September 22, 2003).

Cases in which reassessment of disablement in respect of occupational deafness is final

10.114   33.—[¹ . . .].

REVOCATION

1. Social Security (Industrial Injuries) (Prescribed Diseases) Amendment (No.2) Regulations 2003 (SI 2003/2190), reg.2(3) (September 22, 2003).

Assessment of extent of disablement and rate of disablement benefit payable in respect of occupational deafness

10.115   34.—(1) Subject to the provisions of Schedule [6] and regulations made thereunder and the following provisions of this regulation, the first assessment of the extent of disablement in respect of occupational deafness made in pursuance of a claim made before 3rd September 1979 by a person to whom disablement benefit in respect of occupational deafness is payable for a period before 3rd September 1979 [¹ shall be the percentage calculated by—

   (a) determining the average total hearing loss due to all causes for each ear at 1, 2 and 3 kHz frequencies; and then by

   (b) determining the percentage degree of disablement for each ear in accordance with Part I of Schedule 3; and then by

   (c) determining the average percentage degree of binaural disablement in accordance with the formula set out in Part III of Schedule 3.]

(2) Except in any case to which paragraph (1) applies and subject to the provisions of Schedule [6] and regulations made thereunder and the following provisions of this regulation, the extent of disablement in respect of occupational deafness [¹ shall be the percentage calculated by—

   (a) determining the average total hearing loss due to all causes for each ear at 1, 2 and 3 kHz frequencies; and then by

   (b) determining the percentage degree of disablement for each ear in accordance with Part II of Schedule 3; and then by

   (c) determining the average percentage degree of binaural disablement in accordance with the formula set out in Part III of Schedule 3.]

(3) In [¹ . . .] Schedule 3 hereto "better ear" means that ear in which the claimant's hearing loss due to all causes is the less and "worse ear" means that ear in which the claimant's hearing loss due to all causes is the more.

[¹ (3A) For the purposes of determining the percentage degree of disablement in Parts I and II of Schedule 3 to these Regulations, any fraction of an average hearing loss shall, where the average hearing loss is over 50 dB, be rounded down to the next whole figure.]

(4) The extent of disablement in respect of occupational deafness may be subject to such increase or reduction of the degree of disablement as may be reasonable in the circumstances of the case where, having regard to the provisions of Schedule 8 and to regulations made thereunder, that degree of disablement does not provide a reasonable assessment of the extent of disability resulting from the relevant loss of faculty.

[² (5) Where on re-assessment of the extent of disability in respect of occupational deafness the average sensorineural hearing loss over 1, 2 and 3 kHz frequencies is not 50 dB or more in each ear, or where there is such a loss but the loss in one or each ear is not 50 dB or more due to occupational noise, the extent of disablement shall be assessed at less than 20 per cent.]

(6) Where the extent of disablement is reassessed at less than 20 per cent. disablement benefit [³ or reduced earnings allowance] shall not be payable.

(7) In the case of a person to whom disablement benefit by reason of occupational deafness was payable in respect of a period before 3rd September 1979—

   (a) if no assessment of the extent of his disability has been made, [⁴ revised or superseded] on or after that date, the rate of any disablement benefit payable to him shall be the rate payable for the degree of disablement assessed in accordance with paragraph (1), but

   (b) if such an assessment has been made, [⁴ revised or superseded] in respect of a period commencing on or after that date and before 3rd October 1983, the rate of any disablement benefit payable to him shall be either—

      (i) the rate which would be payable if an assessment were made in accordance with paragraph (2), or

      (ii) the rate which was payable immediately before the first occa-
sion on which such [⁴ revision or supercession] took place,
whichever is the more favourable to him.

(8) Where in the case of a person to whom disablement benefit by
reason of occupational deafness was payable in respect of a period before 3rd
September 1979 the extent of his disability is reassessed and the period taken
into account on reassessment begins on or after 3rd October 1983 and—

    (a) immediately before that date, by virtue of paragraph (7) the rate at
which disablement benefit was payable to him was higher than the
rate which would otherwise have been payable, or,

    (b) the reassessment is the first reassessment for a period commencing
after 3rd September 1979,

the rate of disablement benefit payable to him shall be whichever of the
rates specified in paragraph (9) is applicable.

(9) The rate of disablement benefit payable in the case of a person to
whom paragraph (8) applies shall be—

    (a) if the current rate appropriate to the extent of his disability as reas-
sessed is the same as or more than the rate at which disablement
benefit was payable immediately before the beginning of the period
taken into account on reassessment, the current rate, or

    (b) if the current rate is less than the rate at which disablement benefit
was payable immediately before the beginning of the period taken
into account on reassessment, the lower of the following rates—

      (i) the rate at which benefit would have been payable if the reas-
sessment of the extent of his disability had been made in accordance with paragraph (1), or

      (ii) the rate at which benefit was payable immediately before the
beginning of the period taken into account on reassessment.

AMENDMENTS

1. Social Security (Industrial Injuries) (Prescribed Diseases) Amendment
Regulations 1989 (SI 1989/1207), reg.4 (October 16, 1989).

2. Social Security (Industrial Injuries and Adjudication) Miscellaneous
Amendment Regulations 1986 (SI 1986/1374), reg.3 (September 1, 1986).

3. Social Security (Industrial Injuries and Diseases) Miscellaneous Provisions
1986 (SI 1986/1561), reg.6 (October 1, 1986).

4. Social Security Act 1998 (Commencement No.8, and Savings and Consequential
and Transitional Provisions) Order 1999 (SI 1999/1958), Sch.8, para.16 (July 5,
1999).

GENERAL NOTE

10.116   This regulation and Sch.3 govern the assessment of disablement in occupational
deafness cases. Note, however, that paras (1) and (2) are expressed to be subject
to Sch.6 to the Social Security Contributions and Benefits Act 1992 and regulations made thereunder, including reg.11 of the Social Security (General Benefit)
Regulations 1982.

Paragraph (1) of this regulation and Pt 1 of Sch.3 only apply to the first
assessment of disablement in respect of claims made before September 3, 1979.
Therefore, virtually all assessments are now made under para.(2) of this regulation and Pt 2 of Sch.3 which is less generous. The percentage degree of disablement for each ear is calculated separately and the formula in Pt 3 of Sch.3 is then
applied to give an overall percentage of disablement. However, note that para.(4)
of this regulation enables an adjudicating medical authority to depart from the

Schedule if the result of applying the Schedule is to give an unreasonable assessment. A tribunal should first assess according to the Schedule and then give a reason for departing from that assessment *(R(I) 1/89)*. Para.(5) applies only on a reassessment.

Paras (7)–(9) are transitional and apply to a person who was in receipt of disablement benefit before September 3, 1979. If there has been no assessment since that date, entitlement to disablement benefit is calculated under the more favourable provisions of para.(1). If there was an assessment between that date and October 3,1983, disablement benefit is payable either at the rate which would be payable on an assessment calculated under para.(2) or at the rate payable immediately before the review or variation took place, whichever is the more favourable. In view of inflation, the latter option is unlikely to be more favourable. If there has been an assessment on or after October 3, 1983, it will be usual for the claimant to receive the rate appropriate to an assessment under para.(2). However, if that rate is lower than the rate payable immediately before the beginning of the period taken into account on the reassessment, the lower of the two rates mentioned in para.(9)(b) is payable instead. The greater the lapse of time since the review or variation, the less favourable will be the latter option.

The 1989 amendments removed the requirement that hearing loss should be measured by pure tone audiometry as opposed to evoked response audiometry or any other test. In *R(I) 2/98*, it was held that those amendments (in particular, the introduction of para.(3A)) are procedural and so operate retrospectively in respect of periods before October 16, 1989.

Commencement date of period of assessment in respect of occupational deafness

35.—Notwithstanding Schedule [¹ . . .] [6], the period to be taken into account by an assessment of the extent of disablement in respect of occupational deafness shall not commence before 3rd February 1975.   10.117

AMENDMENT

1. Social Security Act 1998 (Commencement No.8, and Savings and Consequential and Transitional Provisions) Order 1999 (SI 1999/1958), Sch.8, para.17 (July 5, 1999).

Time for claiming benefit in respect of occupational asthma

36.—(1) Subject to paragraphs (2) and (3), disablement benefit and sickness benefit payable by virtue of section [102] shall not be paid in pursuance of a claim in respect of occupational asthma which is made later than 10 years after the latest date, before the date of the claim, on which the claimant or, as the case may be, the person in respect of whom the claim is made worked [¹ in employed earner's employment] in an occupation prescribed in relation to occupational asthma.   10.118

(2) Paragraph (1) shall not apply to any claim made before 29th March 1983 by or in respect of a person who ceased on or after 29th March 1972 to [¹ work in employed earner's] employment in an occupation prescribed in relation to occupational asthma.

(3) Paragraph (1) shall not apply to any claim made by or in respect of a person who has at any time been found to be suffering from asthma as a result of an industrial accident and by virtue of that finding has been awarded disablement benefit either for life or for a period which includes the date on which the aforesaid claim is made.

(4) Subject to paragraphs (5) and (6), industrial death benefit shall not be paid in pursuance of a claim in respect of occupational asthma where the person in respect of whose death the benefit is being claimed died more than 10 years after the latest day on which he worked [¹ in employed earner's employment] in an occupation prescribed in relation to occupational asthma.

(5) Paragraph (4) shall not apply to any claim made in respect of the death of a person who died before 29th March 1983 and who on or after 29th March 1972 had not worked [¹ in employed earner's employment] in an occupation in relation to occupational asthma.

(6) Paragraph (4) shall not apply to any claim made in respect of the death of a person who had at any time been found to be suffering either from asthma as a result of an industrial accident or from occupational asthma and by virtue of that finding had been awarded disablement benefit either for life or for a period which included the date of his death.

(7) Regulation 14 of the Claims and Payments Regulations (time for claiming benefit) shall not apply to a claim in respect of occupational asthma made before 29th March 1983.

AMENDMENT

1. Social Security (Industrial Injuries) (Prescribed Diseases) Amendment Regulations 2000 (SI 2000/1588), reg.5 (July 10, 2000).

GENERAL NOTE

10.119   It was clear from *McKiernon v Secretary of State for Social Services* (*The Times*, November 1, 1989), that reg.36 was originally *ultra vires*. As a result, s.77(2) of the Social Security Act 1975 (now s.109(2) of the Social Security Contributions and Benefits Act 1992) was amended by para.4(2) of Sch.6 to the Social Security Act 1990. Para.4(3) of Sch.6 to the 1990 Act provided that reg.36 should be taken always to have been validly made. See the note to reg.25.

In *CSI/89/96* Commissioner Walker followed the approach of Commissioner Howell in *CI/286/95* (see annotations to reg.25, above) in holding that "worked in an occupation" in para.(1) is not limited to employed earner's employment but can embrace self-employment so that "so long as within 10 years of the date of claim the claimant has been exposed to a sensitizing agent by his self-employment his claim may be sound in law" (para.7). The amendments, requiring work in employed earner's employment in a prescribed occupation, reverse the effect of *CI/286/95* and *CSI/89/96*. The amendment is the subject of a transitional provision in reg.7(1) of the amending instrument reproduced later in this volume.

Initial examinations

10.120   37.—[¹ . . .].

REVOCATION

1. Social Security (Industrial Injuries) (Prescribed Diseases) Amendment Regulations 1994 (SI 1994/2343), reg.5 (October 10, 1994).

Periodical examinations

10.121   38.—[¹ . . .]

REVOCATION

1. Social Security (Industrial Injuries) (Prescribed Diseases) Amendment Regulations 1994 (SI 1994/2343), reg.5 (October 10, 1994).

Suspension from employment

39.—A certificate of suspension issued under the provisions of either reg-   **10.122**
ulation 43 or regulation 44 of the National Insurance (Industrial Injuries) (Prescribed Diseases) Regulations 1959 (regulations revoked with effect from 27th November 1974 by regulation 7(1) of the National Insurance (Industrial Injuries) (Prescribed Diseases) Amendment (No. 2) Regulations 1974) and in force immediately before 27th November 1974 shall continue in force subject to and in accordance with the provisions of regulation 40 of these regulations.

Conditions of suspension

40.—(1) A certificate of suspension issued under the provisions of   **10.123**
either regulation 43 or regulation 44 of the National Insurance (Industrial Injuries) (Prescribed Diseases) Regulations 1959, and remaining in force by virtue of the last preceding regulation, shall suspend the person to whom it relates from further employment in any occupation in relation to which pneumoconiosis is prescribed, with such exceptions and subject to such conditions (if any) as may be specified in the certificate.

(2) [¹ The Secretary of State] may at any time revoke or vary a certificate of suspension on the application of the person to whom it relates, but unless so revoked or varied such certificate shall remain in force throughout the life of such person.

(3) No person who has been suspended from employment may engage or continue in employment, and no employer may employ or continue to employ any such person, in any occupation in relation to which pneumoconiosis is prescribed, except in accordance with the terms of the certificate of suspension in his case.

AMENDMENT

1. Social Security Act 1998 (Commencement No. 8, and Savings and Consequential and Transitional Provisions) Order 1999 (SI 1999/1958), Sch.8, para.18 (July 5, 1999).

Duties of employers

41.—[¹ . . .].   **10.124**

REVOCATION

1. Social Security (Industrial Injuries) (Prescribed Diseases) Amendment Regulations 1994 (SI 1994/2343), reg.5 (October 10, 1994).

Fees for initial and periodical examination

42.—[¹ . . .].   **10.125**

REVOCATION

1. Social Security (Industrial Injuries) (Prescribed Diseases) Amendment Regulations 1994 (SI 1994/2343), reg.5 (October 10, 1994).

PART VI

TRANSITIONAL PROVISIONS AND REVOCATION

Transitional provisions regarding relevant dates

10.126   **43.**—(1) Subject to paragraph (2) the "relevant date", in relation to each disease set out in the first column of Schedule 4 hereto, is the date set against the disease in the second column of that Schedule.

(2) Where a disease set out in the first column of Schedule 4 hereto was prescribed in relation to any person by regulations which came into operation on a date earlier than the date set against that disease in the second column of that Sch., the "relevant date" in relation to such disease is such earlier date on which the disease was prescribed in relation to the person in question.

(3) It shall be a condition of a person's right to benefit in respect of any disease set out in Schedule 4 that he was—

(a) incapable of work, or

(b) suffering from a loss of faculty,

as a result of that disease on or after the relevant date.

(4) The "relevant date" in relation to byssinosis—

(a) in the case of a person employed in an occupation involving work in any room in which the weaving of cotton or flax or any other process which takes place between, or at the same time as, the winding or beaming and weaving of cotton or flax is carried on in a factory in which any or all of those processes are carried on is 3rd October 1983;

(b) in any other case, is 6th April 1979 except that where the disease was prescribed in relation to any person by regulations which came into operation on a date earlier that 6th April 1979 the relevant date is that earlier date.

(5) Byssinosis is not prescribed in relation to any person if neither of the following conditions is satisfied, namely:—

(a) that he was suffering from a loss of faculty as a result of bysinnosis on or after the relevant date;

(b) that he has been employed in employed earner's employment in any occupation mentioned in regulation 2(c) of the old regulation for a period or periods (whether before or after 5th July 1948) amounting in the aggregate to five years.

(6) Notwithstanding that a person does not satisfy paragraph (3) infection by leptospira is prescribed in relation to any person if he is or has been either incapable of work or suffering from a loss of faculty as a result of infection by—

(a) leptospira icterohaemorrhagiae in the case of a person employed in employed earner's employment before 7th January 1980 in any occupation involving work in places which are or are liable to be, infested by rats, or

(b) leptospira canicola in the case of a person so employed in any occupation involving work at dog kennels or the care or handling of dogs.

(7) A person who, immediately before 3rd October 1983, was in receipt of benefit in respect of a disease or injury which was prescribed by virtue of the old regulations, or who makes a claim for benefit in respect of a prescribed

disease after 2nd October 1983 where the date of onset of the disease or injury was before 3rd October 1983, shall be treated for the purpose only of determining whether the disease or injury is in relation to him a prescribed disease by virtue of the occupation in which he is or was engaged as if the old regulations were still in force and these regulations had not come into operation, if that would be more favourable to him.

Transitional provisions regarding dates of development and dates of onset

44.—Where a claim for benefit has been made before 6th April 1983 or a date of onset is determined which is before 6th April 1983 or a claim for injury benefit is made after 5th April 1983 for a day falling or a period beginning before 6th April 1983, these regulations shall take effect subject to the provisions of Schedule 5.

Regulation 45 omitted.

10.127

10.128

SCHEDULES

SCHEDULE 1   **Regulations 2 and 4**

PART I

LIST OF PRESCRIBED DISEASES AND THE OCCUPATIONS FOR WHICH THEY ARE PRESCRIBED

10.129

Prescribed disease or injury	Occupation
	Any occupation involving:
A. Conditions due to physical agents
[¹ A1. Leukaemia (other than chronic lymphatic leukaemia) or cancer of the bone, female breast, testis or thyroid.	Exposure to electro-magnetic radiations (other than radiant heat) or to ionising particles where the dose is sufficient to double the risk of the occurrence of the condition.]
	Any occupation involving:
A2. [² . . .] cataract.	[² Frequent or prolonged exposure to radiation from red-hot or white-hot material.].]
A3. Dysbarism, including decompression sickness, barotrauma and osteonecrosis.	Subjection to compressed or rarefied air or other respirable gases or gaseous mixtures.
[¹⁹ A4. Task-specific focal dystonia]	Prolonged periods of handwriting, typing or other repetitive movements of the fingers, hand or arm.
A5. Subcutaneous cellulitis of the hand [¹⁹ . . .]	Manual labour causing severe or prolonged friction or pressure on the hand.
A6. Bursitis or subcutaneous cellulitis arising at or about the knee due to severe or prolonged external friction or pressure at or about the knee [¹⁹ . . .]	Manual labour causing severe or prolonged external friction or pressure at or about the knee.
A7. Bursitis or subcutaneous cellulitis arising at or about the elbow due to severe or prolonged external friction or pressure at or about the elbow [¹⁹ . . .]	Manual labour causing severe or prolonged external friction or pressure at or about the elbow.

Prescribed disease or injury	*Occupation*
	Any occupation involving:
A8. Traumatic inflammation of the tendons of the hand or forearm, or of the associated tendon sheaths.	Manual labour, or frequent or repeated movements of the hand or wrist.
[¹⁹ A9. *Omitted.*]	*Omitted.*]
[³ A10. Sensorineural hearing loss amounting to at least 50 dB in each ear, being the average of hearing losses at 1, 2 and 3 kHz frequencies, and being due in the case of at least one ear to occupational noise (occupational deafness).]	[¹⁶ The use of, or work wholly or mainly in the immediate vicinity of the use of, a—

(a) band saw, circular saw or cutting disc to cut metal in the metal founding or forging industries, circular saw to cut products in the manufacture of steel, powered (other than hand powered) grinding tool on metal (other than sheet metal or plate metal), pneumatic percussive tool on metal, pressurised air arc tool to gouge metal, burner or torch to cut or dress steel based products, skid transfer bank, knock out and shake out grid in a foundry, machine (other than a power press machine) to forge metal including a machine used to drop stamp metal by means of closed or open dies or drop hammers, machine to cut or shape or clean metal nails, or plasma spray gun to spray molten metal;

(b) pneumatic percussive tool:—to drill rock in a quarry, on stone in a quarry works, underground, for mining coal, for sinking a shaft, or for tunnelling in civil engineering works;

(c) vibrating metal moulding box in the concrete products industry, or circular saw to cut concrete masonry blocks;

(d) machine in the manufacture of textiles for:—weaving man-made or natural fibres (including mineral fibres), high speed false twisting of fibres, or the mechanical cleaning of bobbins;

(e) multi-cutter moulding machine on wood, planing machine on wood, automatic or semi-automatic lathe on wood, multiple cross-cut machine on wood, automatic shaping machine on wood, double-end tenoning machine on wood, vertical spindle moulding machine (including a high speed routing machine) on wood, edge banding machine on wood, bandsawing machine (with a blade width of not less than 75 millimetres) on wood, circular sawing machine on wood including one operated by moving the blade towards the material being cut, or chain saw on wood;

(f) jet of water (or a mixture of water and abrasive material) at a pressure above 680 bar, or jet channelling process to burn stone in a quarry;

(g) machine in a ship's engine room, or gas turbine for:—performance testing on a test bed, installation testing of a

Prescribed disease or injury	Occupation
	Any occupation involving:
	replacement engine in an aircraft, or acceptance testing of an Armed Service fixed wing combat aircraft;
	(h) machine in the manufacture of glass containers or hollow ware for:— automatic moulding, automatic blow moulding, or automatic glass pressing and forming;
	(i) spinning machine using compressed air to produce glass wool or mineral wool;
	(j) continuous glass toughening furnace;
	(k) firearm by a police firearms training officer; or
	(l) shot-blaster to carry abrasives in air for cleaning.]
A11.	(a) the use of hand-held chain saws [21 on wood]
[20(a) Intense blanching of the skin, with a sharp demarcation line between affected and non-affected skin, where the blanching is cold-induced, episodic, occurs throughout the year and affects the skin of the distal with the middle and proximal phalanges, or distal with the middle phalanx (or in the case of a thumb the distal with the proximal phalanx), of—	(b) the use of hand-held rotary tools in grinding or in the sanding or polishing of metal, or the holding of material being ground, or metal being sanded or polished, by rotary tools; or
(i) in the case of a person with 5 fingers (including thumb) on one hand, any 3 of those fingers, or	(c) the use of hand-held percussive metal-working tools, or the holding of metal being worked upon by percussive tools, in riveting, caulking, chipping, hammering, fettling, or swaging; or
(ii) in the case of a person with only 4 such fingers, any 2 of those fingers, or	(d) the use of hand-held powered percussive drills or hand-held powered percussive hammers in mining, quarrying, demolition, or on roads or footpaths, including road construction; or
(iii) in the case of a person with less than 4 such fingers, any one of them or, as the case may be, the one remaining finger,	(e) the holding of material being worked upon by pounding machines in shoe manufacture.
where none of the person's fingers was subject to any degree of cold-induced, episodic blanching of the skin prior to the person's employment in an occupation described in the second column in relation to this paragraph, or	
(b) significant, demonstrable reduction in both sensory perception and manipulative dexterity with continuous numbness or continuous tingling all present at the same time in the distal phalanx of any finger (including thumb) where none of the person's fingers was subject to any degree of reduction in sensory perception, manipulative dexterity, numbness or tingling prior to the person's employment in an occupation described in the second column in relation to this paragraph, where the symptoms in paragraph (a) or paragraph (b) were caused by vibration.]	

Prescribed disease or injury	Occupation
[⁷A12. Carpal tunnel syndrome.]	[¹⁹ (a) The use, at the time the symptoms first develop, of hand-held powered tools whose internal parts vibrate so as to transmit that vibration to the hand, but excluding those tools which are solely powered by hand; or (b) repeated palmar flexion and dorsiflexion of the wrist for at least 20 hours per week for a period or periods amounting in aggregate to least 12 months in the 24 months prior to the onset of symptoms, where "repeated" means once or more often in every 30 seconds.]
[¹⁷ A13. Osteoarthritis of the hip.	Work in agriculture as a farmer or farm worker for a period of, or periods which amount in aggregate to, 10 years or more.]

B. Conditions due to biological agents

[¹⁷ B1. Anthrax.	(a) Contact with anthrax spores, including contact with animals infected by anthrax; or (b) handling, loading, unloading or transport of animals of a type susceptible to infection with anthrax or of the products or residues of such animals.]
B2. Glanders.	Contact with equine animals or their carcases.
B3. Infection by leptospira.	(a) Work in places which are, or are liable to be, infested by rats, field mice or voles, or other small mammals; or (b) work at dog kennels or the care or handling of dogs; or (c) contact with bovine animals or their meat products or pigs or their meat products.
[¹⁷ B4. Ankylostomiasis.	Contact with a source of ankylostomiasis.]
B5. Tuberculosis.	Contact with a source of tuberculous infection.
B6. Extrinsicallergicalveolitis (including farmer's lung).	Exposure to moulds or fungal spores or heterologous proteins by reason of employment in: (a) agriculture, horticulture, forestry, cultivation of edible fungi or malt-working; or (b) loading or unloading or handling in storage mouldy vegetable matter or edible fungi; or (c) caring for or handling birds; or (d) handling bagasse. [¹⁹ or (e) work involving exposure to metalworking fluid mists.]
B7. Infection by organisms of the genus brucella.	Contact with— (a) animals infected by brucella, or their carcases or parts thereof, or their untreated products; or (b) laboratory specimens or vaccines of, or containing brucella.
[¹⁷ B8A. Infection by hepatitis A virus.	Contact with raw sewage.
B8B. Infection by hepatitis B or C virus.	Contact with— (a) human blood or human blood products; or (b) any other source of hepatitis B or C virus.]
B9. Infection by Streptococcus suis.	Contact with pigs infected by Streptococcus suis, or with the carcases, products or residues of pigs so infected.

Prescribed disease or injury	Occupation
	Any occupation involving:
[⁸ B10. (a) Avian chlamydiosis.	Contact with birds infected with chlamydia psittaci, or with the remains or untreated products of such birds.
B10. (b) Ovine chlamydiosis.	Contact with sheep infected with chlamydia psittaci, or with the remains or untreated products of such sheep.
B11. Q fever.	Contact with animals, their remains or their untreated products.]
[⁹ 12. Orf.	Contact with sheep, goats or with the carcasses of sheep or goats.
B13. Hydatidosis.	Contact with dogs.]
[¹⁷ B14. Lyme disease.	Exposure to deer or other mammals of a type liable to harbour ticks harbouring Borrelia bacteria.
B15. Anaphylaxis.	Employment as a healthcare worker having contact with products made with natural rubber latex.]

C. Conditions due to chemical agents

[¹⁰ C1. (a) Anaemia with a haemoglobin concentration of 9g/dL or less, and a blood film showing punctate basophilia; (b) peripheral neuropathy; (c) central nervous system toxicity.]	The use or handling of, or exposure to the fumes, dust or vapour of, lead or a compound of lead, or a substance containing lead.
[¹⁰ C2. Central nervous system toxicity characterised by parkinsonism.]	The use or handling of, or exposure to the fumes, dust or vapour of, manganese or a compound of manganese, or a substance containing manganese.
C3. Poisoning by phosphorus or an inorganic compound of phosphorus or poisoning due to the anti-cholinesterase or pseudo anti-cholinesterase action of organic phosphorus compounds.	The use or handling of, or exposure to the fumes, dust or vapour of, phosphorus or a compound of phosphorus, or a substance containing phosphorus.
[¹⁰C4. Primary carcinoma of the bronchus or lung.	Exposure to the fumes, dust or vapour of arsenic, a compound of arsenic or a substance containing arsenic.
C5A. Central nervous system toxicity characterised by tremor and neuropsychiatric disease.	Exposure to mercury or inorganic compounds of mercury for a period of, or periods which amount in aggregate to, 10 years or more.
C5B. Central nervous system toxicity characterised by combined cerebellar and cortical degeneration.	Exposure to methylmercury.
C6. Peripheral neuropathy.	The use or handling of, or exposure to, carbon disulphide (also called carbon disulfide).
C7. Acute non-lymphatic leukaemia.	Exposure to benzene.]
C8. [¹⁰ . . .]	[¹⁰ . . .]
C9. [¹⁰ . . .]	[¹⁰ . . .]
C10. [¹⁰ . . .]	[¹⁰ . . .]
C11. [¹⁰ . . .]	[¹⁰ . . .]
[¹⁰ C12. (a) Peripheral neuropathy; (b) central nervous system toxicity.	Exposure to methyl bromide (also called bromomethane).]
[¹⁰ C13. Cirrhosis of the liver.	Exposure to chlorinated naphthalenes.]

Prescribed disease or injury	Occupation
	Any occupation involving:
C14. [¹⁰ . . .]	[¹⁰ . . .]
C15. [¹⁰ . . .]	[¹⁰ . . .]
[¹⁰ C16. (a) Neurotoxicity; (b) cardiotoxicity.	Exposure to the dust of gonioma kamassi.
C17. Chronic beryllium disease.	Inhalation of beryllium or a beryllium compound.
C18. Emphysema.	Inhalation of cadmium fumes for a period of, or periods which amount in aggregate to, 20 years or more.
C19. (a) Peripheral neuropathy; (b) central nervous system toxicity.	Exposure to acrylamide.
C20. Dystrophy of the cornea (including ulceration of the corneal surface) of the. eye.	Exposure to quinone or hydroquinone.
C21. Primary carcinoma of the skin.	Exposure to arsenic or arsenic compounds, tar, pitch, bitumen, mineral oil (including paraffin) or soot.
C22. (a) Primary carcinoma of the mucous membrane of the nose or paranasal sinuses; (b) primary carcinoma of the bronchus or lung.	Work before 1950 in the refining of nickel involving exposure to oxides, sulphides or water-soluble compounds of nickel.
C23. Primary neoplasm of the epithelial lining of the urinary tract.	(a) The manufacture of 1-naphthylamine, 2-naphthylamine, benzidine, auramine, magenta or 4-aminobiphenyl (also called biphenyl-4-ylamine); (b) work in the process of manufacturing methylene-bis-orthochloroaniline (also called MbOCA) for a period of, or periods which amount in aggregate to, 12 months or more; (c) exposure to 2-naphthylamine, benzidine, 4-aminobiphenyl (also called biphenyl-4-ylamine) or salts of those compounds otherwise than in the manufacture of those compounds; (d) exposure to orthotoluidine, 4-chloro-2-methylaniline or salts of those compounds; or (e) exposure for a period of, or periods which amount in aggregate to, 5 years or more, to coal tar pitch volatiles produced in aluminium smelting involving the Soderberg process (that is to say, the method of producing aluminium by electrolysis in which the anode consists of a paste of petroleum coke and mineral oil which is baked in situ).]
[¹⁸C24. (a) Angiosarcoma of the liver; or (b) osteolysis of the terminal phalanges of the fingers; or (c) sclerodermatous thickening of the skin of the hand; or (d) liver fibrosis, due to exposure to vinyl chloride monomer.	Exposure to vinyl chloride monomer in the manufacture of polyvinyl chloride.

Prescribed disease or injury	Occupation
	Any occupation involving:
C24A. Raynaud's phenomenon due to exposure to vinyl chloride monomer.	Exposure to vinyl chloride monomer in the manufacture of polyvinyl chloride before 1st January 1984.]
[¹⁰C25. Vitiligo.	The use or handling of, or exposure to, paratertiary-butylphenol (also called 4-tert-butylphenol), paratertiary-butylcatechol (also called 4-tert-butylcatechol), para-amylphenol (also called p-pentyl phenol isomers), hydroquinone, monobenzyl ether of hydroquinone (also called 4-benzyloxyphenol) or mono-butyl ether of hydroquinone (also called 4-butoxyphenol).
C26. (a) Liver toxicity; (b) kidney toxicity.	The use or handling of, or exposure to, carbon tetrachloride (also called tetrachloromethane).
C27. Liver toxicity.	The use or handling of, or exposure to, trichloromethane (also called chloroform).]
C28. [¹⁰. . .]	[¹⁰. . .]
[¹⁰ C29. Peripheral neuropathy.	The use or handling of, or exposure to, n-hexane or n-butyl methyl ketone.
C30. (a) Dermatitis; (b) ulceration of the mucous membrane or the epidermis.	The use or handling of, or exposure to, chromic acid, chromates or dichromates.]

D. Miscellaneous Conditions

D1. Pneumoconiosis.	*Any occupation—* (a) set out in Part II of this Schedule; (b) specified in regulation 2(b)(ii).
D2. Byssinosis.	*Any occupation involving:* Work in any room where any process up to and including the weaving process is performed in a factory in which the spinning or manipulation of raw or waste cotton or of flax, or the weaving of cotton or flax, is carried on.
D3. Diffuse mesothelioma (primary neoplasm of the mesothelium of the pleura or of the pericardium or of the peritoneum).	[¹¹ Exposure to asbestos, asbestos dust or any admixture of asbestos at a level above that commonly found in the environment at large.]
[⁷ D4. Allergic rhinitis which is due to exposure to any of the following agents— (a) isocyanates; (b) platinum salts; (c) fumes or dusts arising from the manufacture, transport or use of hardening agents (including epoxy resin curing agents) based on phthalic anhydride, tetrachlorophthalic anhydride, trimelliticanhydride or triethylene-tetramine; (d) fumes arising from the use of rosin as a soldering flux; (e) proteolyticenzymes;	Exposure to any of the agents set out in column 1 of this paragraph.]

Prescribed disease or injury	Occupation
	Any occupation involving:

(f) animals including insects and other arthropods used for the purposes of research or education or in laboratories;

(g) dusts arising from the sowing, cultivation, harvesting, drying, handling, milling, transport or storage of barley, oats, rye, wheat or maize, or the handling, milling, transport or storage of meal or flour made therefrom;

(h) antibiotics;

(i) cimetidine;

(j) wood dust;

(k) ispaghula;

(l) castor bean dust;

(m) ipecacuanha;

(n) azodicarbonamide;

(o) animals including insects and other arthropods or their larval forms, used for the purposes of pest control or fruit cultivation, or the larval forms of animals used for the purposes of research, education or in laboratories;

(p) glutaraldehyde;

(q) persulphate slats or henna;

(r) crustaceans or fish or products arising from these in the food processing industry;

(s) reactive dyes;

(t) soya bean;

(u) tea dust;

(v) green coffee bean dust;

(w) fumes from stainless steel welding.]

[¹⁷ (x) products made with natural rubber latex.]

D5. Non-infective dermatitis of external origin [⁷. . .] (excluding dermatitis due to ionising particles or electro-magnetic radiations other than radiant heat).	Exposure to dust, liquid or vapour or any other external agent capable of irritating the skin (including friction or heat but excluding ionising particles or electro-magnetic radiations other than radiant heat).
D6. Carcinoma of the nasal cavity or associated air sinuses (nasal carcinoma).	(a) Attendance for work in or about a building where wooden goods are manufactured or repaired; or
	(b) attendance for work in a building used for the manufacture of footwear or components of footwear made wholly or partly of leather or fibre board; or
	(c) attendance for work at a place used wholly or mainly for the repair of footwear made wholly or partly of leather or fibre board.
D7. Asthma which is due to exposure to any of the following agents: (a) isocyanates;	Exposure to any of the agents set out in column 1 of this paragraph.

Prescribed disease or injury	Occupation
	Any occupation involving:

(b) platinum salts;
(c) fumes or dusts arising from the manufacture, transport or use of hardening agents (including epoxy resin curing agents) based on phthalic anhydride, tetrachlorophthalic anhydride, trimelliticanhydride or triethylenetetramine;
(d) fumes arising from the use of rosin as a soldering flux;
(e) proteolyticenzymes;
[¹²(f) animals including insects and other arthropods used for the purposes of research or education or in laboratories];
(g) dusts arising from the sowing, cultivation, harvesting, drying, handling, milling, transport or storage or barley, oats, rye, wheat or maize, or the handling, milling, transport or storage of meal or flour made therefrom;
[¹²(h) antibiotics;
(i) cimetidine;
(j) wood dust;
(k) ispaghula;
(l) castor bean dust;
(m) ipecacuanha;
(n) azodicarbonamide];
[⁹(o) animals including insects and other arthropods or their larval forms, used for the purposes of pest control or fruit cultivation, or the larval forms of animals used for the purposes of research, education or in laboratories;
(p) glutaraldehyde;
(q) persulphate slats or henna;
(r) crustaceans or fish or products arising from these in the food processing industry;
(s) reactive dyes;
(t) soya bean;
(u) tea dust;
(v) green coffee bean dust;
(w) fumes from stainless steel welding;
[¹⁷ (wa) products made with natural rubber latex;]
(x) any other sensitising agent] (occupational asthma).

[¹⁸D8. Primary carcinoma of the lung where there is accompanying evidence of asbestosis.	(a) The working or handling of asbestos or any admixture of asbestos; or (b) the manufacture or repair of asbestos textiles or other articles containing or composed of asbestos; or (c) the cleaning of any machinery or plant used in any of the foregoing operations and

Prescribed disease or injury	*Occupation*
	Any occupation involving:
	of any chambers, fixtures and appliances for the collection of asbestos dust; or
	(d) substantial exposure to the dust arising from any of the foregoing operations.
D8A. Primary carcinoma of the lung.	Exposure to asbestos in the course of—
	(a) the manufacture of asbestos textiles; or
	(b) spraying asbestos; or
	(c) asbestos insulation work; or
	(d) applying or removing materials containing asbestos in the course of shipbuilding,
	where all or any of the exposure occurs before 1st January 1975, for a period of, or periods which amount in aggregate to, five years or more, or otherwise, for a period of, or periods which amount in aggregate to, ten years or more.]
[[18]D9. Unilateral or bilateral diffuse pleural thickening with obliteration of the costophrenic angle.]	(a) The working or handling of asbestos or any admixture of asbestos; or
	(b) the manufacture or repair of asbestos textiles or other articles containing or composed of asbestos; or
	(c) the cleaning of any machinery or plant used in any of the foregoing operations and of any chambers, fixtures and appliances for the collection of asbestos dust; or
	(d) substantial exposure to the dust arising from any of the foregoing operations.
[[15]D10. [[13] Primary carcinoma of the lung.]	(a) Work underground in a tin mine; or
	(b) exposure to bis (chloromethyl) ether produced during the manufacture of chloromethyl methyl ether; or
	(c) exposure to zinc chromate, calcium chromate or strontium chromate in their pure forms.]
[[13] D11. Primary carcinoma of the lung where there is accompanying evidence of silicosis.	Exposure to silica dust in the course of—
	(a) the manufacture of glass or pottery; tunnelling in or quarrying
	(b) sandstone or granite;
	(c) mining metal ores;
	(d) slate quarrying or the manufacture of artefacts from slate;
	(e) mining clay;
	(f) using siliceous materials as abrasives;
	(g) cutting stone;
	(h) stonemasonry; or
	(i) work in a foundry.]
[[11]D12. Except in the circumstances specified in regulation 2(d)—	[[23] Exposure to coal dust (whether before or after 5th July 1948) by reason of working—
(a) chronic bronchitis; or	(a) underground in a coal mine for a period or periods amounting in aggregate to at least 20 years;
(b) emphysema; or	
(c) both,	(b) on the surface of a coal mine as a screen worker for a period or periods amounting
where there is [[23] . . .] evidence of a forced expiratory volume in one second (measured from the position of maximum inspiration	

Prescribed disease or injury	Occupation
with the claimant making maximum effort) which is—	in aggregate to at least 40 years before 1st January 1983; or
[¹⁴(i) at least one litre below the Appropriate mean value predicted, obtained from the following prediction formulae which give the mean values predicted in litres—	(c) both underground in a coal mine, and on the surface as a screen worker before 1st January 1983, where 2 years working as a surface screen worker is equivalent to 1 year working underground, amounting
ii. For a man, where the measurement is made without back-extrapolation, $(3.62 \times$ Height in metres)$- (0.031 \times$ Age in years) $- 1.41$; or, where the measurement is made with back-extrapolation,$(3.71 \times$ Height in metres) $- (0.032 \times$ Age in years) $- 1.44$;	in aggregate to at least the equivalent of 20 years underground. Any such period or periods shall include a period or periods of incapacity while engaged in such an occupation.]
ii. For a woman, where the measurement is made without back-extrapolation, $(3.29 \times$ Height in metres)$-(0.029 \times$ Age in years)-1.42; or, where the measurement is made with back-extrapolation, $(3.37 \times$ Height in metres)$- (0.030 \times$ Age in years)$- 1.46$; or]]	
(ii) less than one litre.	
[²² D13. Primary carcinoma of the nasopharynx.	Exposure to wood dust in the course of the processing of wood or the manufacture or repair of wood products, for a period or periods which amount in aggregate to at least 10 years.]

PART II   **Regulations 2, 4, 38 and 40**

OCCUPATIONS FOR WHICH PNEUMOCONIOSIS IS PRESCRIBED

1.—Any occupation involving—

    (a) the mining, quarrying or working of silica rock or the working of dried quartzose sand or any dry deposit or dry residue of silica or any dry admixture containing such materials (including any occupation in which any of the aforesaid operations are carried out incidentally to the mining or quarrying of other minerals or to the manufacture of articles containing crushed or ground silica rock);

    (b) the handling of any of the materials specified in the foregoing sub-paragraph in or incidental to any of the operations mentioned therein, or substantial exposure to the dust arising from such operations.

2.—Any occupation involving the breaking, crushing or grinding of flint or the working or handling of broken, crushed or ground flint or materials containing such flint, or substantial exposure to the dust arising from any such operations.

3.—Any occupation involving sand blasting by means of compressed air with the use of quartzose sand or crushed silica rock or flint, or substantial exposure to the dust arising from sand and blasting.

4.—Any occupation involving work in a foundry or the performance of, or substantial exposure to the dust arising from, any of the following operations:—

    (a) the freeing of steel castings from adherent siliceous substance;

    (b) the freeing of metal castings from adherent siliceous substance—

        (i) by blasting with an abrasive propelled by compressed air, by steam or by a wheel; or

        (ii) by the use of power-driven tools.

10.130

5.—Any occupation in or incidental to the manufacture of china or earthenware (including sanitary earthenware, electrical earthenware and earthenware tiles), and any occupation involving substantial exposure to the dust arising therefrom.

6.—Any occupation involving the grinding of mineral graphite, or substantial exposure to the dust arising from such grinding.

7.—Any occupation involving the dressing of granite or any igneous rock by masons or the crushing of such materials, or substantial exposure to the dust arising from such operations.

8.—Any occupation involving the use, or preparation for use, of a grindstone, or substantial exposure to the dust arising therefrom.

9.—Any occupation involving—

    (a) the working or handling of asbestos or any admixture of asbestos;

    (b) the manufacture or repair of asbestos textiles or other articles containing or composed of asbestos;

    (c) the cleaning of any machinery or plant used in any foregoing operations and of any chambers, fixtures and appliances for the collection of asbestos dust;

    (d) substantial exposure to the dust arising from any of the foregoing operations.

10.—Any occupation involving—

    (a) work underground in any mine in which one of the objects of the mining operations is the getting of any mineral;

    (b) the working or handling above ground at any coal or tin mine of any minerals extracted therefrom, or any operation incidental thereto;

    (c) the trimming of coal in any ship, barge, or lighter, or in any dock or harbour or at any wharf or quay;

    (d) the sawing, splitting or dressing of slate, or any operation incidental thereto.

11.—Any occupation in or incidental to the manufacture of carbon electrodes by an industrial undertaking for use in the electrolytic extraction of aluminium from aluminium oxide, and any occupation involving substantial exposure to the dust arising therefrom.

12.—Any occupation involving boiler scaling or substantial exposure to the dust arising therefrom.

AMENDMENTS

1. Social Security (Industrial Injuries) (Prescribed Diseases) Amendment Regulations 2000 (SI 2000/1588), reg.6(1) and (2) (July 10, 2000).

2. Social Security (Industrial Injuries) (Prescribed Diseases) Amendment Regulations 2000 (SI 2000/1588), reg.6(1) and (3) (July 10, 2000).

3. Social Security (Industrial Injuries) (Prescribed Diseases) Amendment Regulations 1989 (SI 1989/1207), reg.4 (October 16, 1989).

4. Social Security (Industrial Injuries) (Prescribed Diseases) Amendment (No.2) Regulations 1987 (SI 1987/2112), reg.2 (January 4, 1988).

5. Social Security (Industrial Injuries) (Prescribed Diseases) Amendment Regulations 1994 (SI 1994/2343), reg.4 (October 10, 1994).

6. Social Security (Industrial Injuries and Diseases) (Miscellaneous Amendments) Regulations 1996 (SI 1996/425), reg.5(4) (March 24, 1996).

7. Social Security (Industrial Injuries and Diseases) (Miscellaneous Amendments) Regulations 1996 (SI 1996/425), reg.5 (March 24, 1996 with savings, see reg.7 below).

8. Social Security (Industrial Injuries) (Prescribed Diseases) Amendment Regulations 1989 (SI 1989/1207), reg.6 (August 9, 1989).

9. Social Security (Industrial Injuries) (Prescribed Diseases) Amendment Regulations 1991 (SI 1991/1938), reg.2 (September 26, 1991).

10. Social Security (Industrial Injuries) (Prescribed Diseases) Amendment Regulations 2003 (SI 2003/270), reg.5 (March 17, 2003).

11. Social Security (Industrial Injuries) (Miscellaneous Amendments) Regulations 1997 (SI 1997/810), reg.6 (April 6, 1997).

12. Social Security (Industrial Injuries and Adjudication) Miscellaneous Amendment Regulations 1986 (SI 1986/1374), reg.3 (September 1, 1986).

13. Social Security (Industrial Injuries) (Prescribed Diseases) Amendment Regulations 1993 (SI 1993/862), reg.6 (April 19, 1993).

14. Social Security (Industrial Injuries) (Prescribed Diseases) Amendment Regulations 2000 (SI 2000/1588), reg.6(1) and (4) (July 10, 2000).
15. Social Security (Industrial Injuries) (Prescribed Diseases) Amendment Regulations 1987 (SI 1987/335), reg.2 (April 1, 1987).
16. Social Security (Industrial Injuries) (Prescribed Diseases) Amendment (No.2) Regulations 2003 (SI 2003/2190), reg.3 (September 22, 2003).
17. Social Security (Industrial Injuries) (Prescribed Diseases) Amendment Regulations 2005 (SI 2005/324), reg.3 (March 14, 2005).
18. Social Security (Industrial Injuries) (Prescribed Diseases) Amendment Regulations 2006 (SI 2006/586), reg.3 (April 6, 2006).
19. Social Security (Industrial Injuries) (Prescribed Diseases) Amendment Regulations 2007 (SI 2007/811), reg.2 (April 6, 2007).
20. Social Security (Industrial Injuries) (Prescribed Diseases) Amendment (No. 2) Regulations 2007 (SI 2007/1753), reg.2(1), (2) (October 1, 2007).
21. Social Security (Industrial Injuries) (Prescribed Diseases) Amendment (No. 2) Regulations 2007 (SI 2007/1753), reg.2(1), (3) (October 1, 2007).
22. Social Security (Industrial Injuries) (Prescribed Diseases) Amendment Regulations 2008 (SI 2008/14), reg.2 (April 7, 2008).

GENERAL NOTE

I. The structure of this annotation 10.131
This annotation examines first some general matters pertaining to the whole of this Sch., dealing with prescribed industrial diseases. It then examines the prescribed diseases by category. The diseases in the Schedule are divided into four categories according to cause and are given letters and numbers for identification:

A1–12 Conditions due to physical agents;

B1–13 Conditions due to biological agents;

C1–30 Conditions due to chemical agents;

D1–12 Miscellaneous conditions.

Within each category, particular diseases will be treated in a depth consistent with the case law on that disease.

II. General matters
The diseases listed in the Schedule are there because there is some discernible 10.132
link between the disease and the occupation for which it is prescribed. The power to prescribe diseases is exercised by the Secretary of State, normally upon the advice of the Industrial Injuries Advisory Council which investigates occupational diseases and reports upon them, as well as keeping the Industrial Injuries scheme generally under review. The Secretary of State exercises his power under the SSCBA 1992, s.108(2) (formerly SSA 1975, s.76(2)) and must be satisfied that the disease is a risk of the occupation and not a common risk, and also that the attribution of particular cases to the nature of the employment can be established or presumed with reasonable certainty.
As regards decision-making and appeals, on July 5, 1999, the functions of adjudication officers with respect to industrial injuries benefits and the making of an industrial accident declaration were transferred to the Secretary of State (SSA 1998, ss.1, 8 and Commencement Order No. 8). He may, however, refer certain issues for report to a medical practitioner who has experience of the issues. The issues so referable are:

(a) the extent of a personal injury for the purposes of s.94;

(b) whether the claimant has a prescribed industrial disease and the extent of the resulting disablement; and

(c) whether, for disablement benefit purposes, the claimant has a disablement and its extent (Decisions and Appeals Regs 1999, reg.12).

Decisions on industrial injuries benefits, including those on prescribed industrial diseases, and on the matter of an industrial accident declaration, are appealable to a "unified" appeal tribunal composed of a legally qualified member and up to two medically qualified members (SSA 1998, ss.4, 12, Schs 2 and 3; Decisions and Appeals Regulations 1999, reg.36(2)). Like the Secretary of State, that tribunal is competent to deal with the both the medical and non-medical aspect of industrial injuries matters. Note, however, that whether a claimant is an employed or self-employed earner, and whether a specific employment is, or is not, employed earner's employment is to be decided not by the Secretary of State, but by officers of the Board of Inland Revenue (Social Security Contributions (Transfer of Functions, etc.) Act 1999, s.8(1)). Accordingly, such decisions are not matters of appeal for the "unified" appeal tribunal but rather for appeal to the tax appeal Commissioners (*ibid.*, s.11). Such decisions and appeals are regulated by the Social Security Contributions (Decisions and Appeals) Regs 1999 (SI 1999/1027).

The key point from all this for industrial injuries matters, is that the distinction between medical issues (the disablement questions) and non-medical issues—previously crucial as demarcating the respective jurisdictions of MATs (col.1 of the Schedule) and SSATs (col.2 of the Schedule)—is no longer relevant. Consequently, issues relating to the interpretation and application of any of the words in the Sch., whether in col.1 or 2, are now within the remit of the "unified" appeal tribunal.

Both the unified tribunal and the Commissioners now have jurisdiction over medical and non-medical matters. A Commissioner, allowing an appeal on a point of law, can now take his or her own decision on the facts rather than remitting it to another tribunal. Commissioner Williams did so in *CI/1307/1999* giving a staged assessment of disablement in respect of post traumatic stress disorder. The decision considers the medical aspects of the claimant's case found to be an industrial accident in *CI/15589/1996*, noted in the annotation to "accident" to SSCBA 1992, s.94(1). In paras 15–17, Commissioner Williams distinguished "diagnosis" and "disablement" decisions. The former is essentially "a question of medical expertise". A "disablement" decision in contrast is not dissimilar to the tasks performed by judges in assessing common law damages or in applying the tariff of the Criminal Injuries Compensation Authority. In assessing disablement for industrial injuries benefits, however, that Criminal Injuries tariff is not an appropriate yardstick. Instead, supplementing SSCBA 1992, s.103 and Sch.6, regard should be had also to reg.11 and Sch.2 to the General Benefit Regulations, above. Nonetheless, the import of para.37 of the decision is that exercise of the Commissioner's power to decide on the facts, rather than remitting to another tribunal, may well be rare. Even so, the decision contrasts markedly with the traditional view of such matters as ones for medical rather than legal judgment (see, for example, Commissioner Howell in *CI/636/93*). Note that the suitability of cross-reference to Sch.2 was also advocated in *R(I) 5/95*, where Commissioner Rowland stated that "assessment of disablement should be brought into line with those prescribed in the Schedule", with assessment also reflecting any intermittent or episodic character of the disablement (para.16).

In *R(I) 4/96*, Commissioner Goodman makes the important point that the date of onset of a prescribed disease for a particular claimant and the date from which payment of disablement benefit can be paid on or after the disease has been prescribed (added to the Schedule), are not necessarily coincidental. So where prescribed disease D12 (miner's bronchitis etc.) was added from September 13, 1993, disablement benefit was only payable from that date, despite the fact that the date of onset (the date from which the claimant suffered from it) was much earlier. Unless the contrary is clearly indicated in the particular prescription (and it was not here), the insertion into the Schedule of a new prescribed disease is not retrospective so as to enable the payment of disablement benefit (subject to showing good cause for delay in claiming) from the date of onset.

It is worth noting that the significance of some of the less serious prescribed diseases has been diminished by the abolition of injury benefit and the subsequent restrictions placed upon disablement benefit by the raising of the qualifying level to 14 per cent. Now, unless the disease is serious enough to bring an assessment of 14 per cent or more or, if the assessment is 1 per cent or more, lasts more than the ninety days which is the waiting period for reduced earnings allowance (see SSCBA 1992, Sch.7, para.11, above), the claimant will rely on incapacity benefits rather than an industrial benefit. (Different provision is made for claimants suffering from pneumoconiosis, byssinosis, or diffuse mesothelioma, where title to disablement benefit is established on an assessment of 1 per cent or more, Prescribed Diseases Regulations, reg.20, above.)

The occupations in respect of which the diseases are prescribed are commonly defined by prefacing the cause of the disease with the words "Any occupation involving". The occupations in the Schedule will be considered separately, as appropriate, but the general phrase is applicable to most of the diseases and occupations and is dealt with first.

Any occupation involving: The word "occupation" is not a term of art, it merely connotes the activities of an employed earner under his contract of employment (*R(I) 3/78*). Once some involvement with the prescribed cause of the disease, as a result of employment, has been established, the employment is likely to be accepted as giving rise to entitlement (*R(I) 4/53*) unless the involvement is so trivial or negligible that it can be discounted (*R(I) 8/57*). It is still important for the decision-maker or tribunal to consider carefully whether the occupation is prescribed for the disease—the fact that there is an outbreak of a prescribed disease in one factory is irrelevant to the question of whether the disease is prescribed for a particular employee or group of employees in the factory (*R(I) 2/77*). It is not the frequency of the disease which is significant, but the description of the occupation for which it is prescribed. 10.133

Although a claim for disablement benefit may be described as being in respect of a particular disease, there is nothing in the legislation to suggest that a separate claim has to be made in respect of each disease. Accordingly, if a tribunal find that a claimant is not suffering from the prescribed disease in respect of which he claimed but may be suffering from another prescribed disease, they should make a finding in respect of that other disease (*R(I) 6/94*). That may require an adjournment unless the parties are content for the new issue to be considered straightaway. It does not matter whether the diagnosis question is determined before or after the Secretary of State has decided whether the disease is prescribed in relation to the claimant (*CI/13664/96*). The more convenient course should be followed.

The proper approach to interpretation of the definitions of the prescribed occupations: In *Secretary of State for Social Security v Davies* (reported as part of *R(I) 2/01*, and noted further in the commentary on PD A11 [vibration white finger]), the Court of Appeal thought that, given the purpose of this compensation scheme, it would be wrong to give the words too narrow a definition (*per* Rix L.J. [para.23], Mummery L.J. expressly concurring [para. 36]). In para.35 of that case, Mummery L.J. quoted with approval from Commissioner Levenson in the decision under appeal: 10.134

"The Industrial Injuries Disablement Benefits Scheme was designed to compensate workers for industrial injuries and for contracting prescribed diseases, and the definitions of prescribed occupation should not be artificially narrowed. I do not see why a person doing essentially the same job in a city as is being done by a person in a forest should be denied that compensation" (*CI/729/1998*, para.15).

This approach is not to be confined to its specific context (*CI/2668/2002*, per Commissioner Williams).

Many cases make it clear that one can look for guidance to the relevant report of the IIAC recommending prescription (*Davies; R(I) 2/01; R(I) 4/99; R(I) 3/97; R(I) 3/95; R(I) 2/85; R(I) 5/83; R(I) 11/81(T); R(I) 15/75(T); CI/1884/2004; CI/2668/ 2002; CI/3261/2000; CI/808/95; CI/22/91*). The reports can be used to help resolve ambiguity or problems with the drafting of regulations, but, naturally, what each decision takes from the exercise varies.

The focus should be on the work the claimant does (did) rather than on the contractual obligation to do it (*R(I) 2/79(T)*); on the activity of the employee, rather than the generic description of the employer's activity(ies) (*CI/2668/2002*, para.16); on what the claimant does rather than on how the job is labelled (*CI/2668/2002*, para.18).

III. Prescribed Diseases: Category A: Conditions due to physical agents

A1 (Leukaemia (other than chronic lymphatic leukaemia) or cancer of the bone, female breast, testis or thyroid)

10.135   The insertion of a new formulation of PD A1 is subject to transitional provisions in reg.7(2) and (3) of the Social Security (Industrial Injuries) (Prescribed Diseases) Amendment Regulations 2000 (SI 2000/1588), reproduced later in this volume.

A2 (Cataract)

10.136   The revision of PD A2 is subject to the same transitional provision noted under PD A1, above.

A4 (Task-specific focal dystonia)

10.137   Until April 6, 2007, the terms of prescription referred to "Hand or forearm cramp—writer's cramp". From that date, it refers to "Task-specific focal dystonia". This was recommended as valuable updating and clarification by the IIAC in its report *Completion of the review of the scheduled list of prescribed diseases*, Cm 7003 (January 2007), para.28, referring back to its 2006 report on *Work Related Upper Limb Disorders*, Cm. 6868 (July 2006), para.78.

The occupation must involve *prolonged* periods of handwriting, etc. What amounts to prolonged periods must be a matter of fact for the Secretary of State/ tribunal, but remember to look at the nature of the job in assessing whether it displays the requisite characteristics. In *R(I) 3/97*, Commissioner Rice held that the words "other repetitive movements of the hand or arm" in A4 are to be read *ejusdem generis* (as of the same kind or nature) with "handwriting" and "typing", not at large to include repetitive movements of whatever kind and not so as to "be available at large to all those engaged in repetitive work" (para.10). So that in that case the tribunal did not err in law in finding that it did not cover the appellant analytical chemist whose laboratory bench work primarily involved the filtration and titration of chemicals. The tribunal had found that while the finger, hand and wrist movements were repetitive and carried out over a prolonged period they did not have the intensity or frequency comparable to handwriting or typing.

In *CI/349/2001*, Commissioner Angus considered the case of a cleaner who spent

> "a significant part of her working day in prolonged periods of handling the large Swiffer and the floor buffer, each involving repetitive movements of her wrists, and in prolonged periods of cleaning tables involving repetitive movements of the wrists and hands. There is also other cleaning and maintenance work such as cleaning glue off the sinks and repairs to the fabric of the school buildings which involve her in repetitive movements of the arm, wrist or hand. The A4 prescription does not mention movements of the wrist but, as the wrist is the joint between the arm and the hand, movement of the wrist involves the movement of either the hand or the arm in relation to the other. The question is whether the movements of her fingers, hands or arms which the claimant makes in the course

of those prolonged periods of activity amount to 'other repetitive movements of the fingers, hand or arm' within the meaning of the prescription in the Schedule to the Regulations" (para.24).

The Commissioner decided that her occupation was not one prescribed under A4, but reached his conclusion

"for slightly different reasons from those given by the tribunal and by the author of *R(I) 3/97*. I respectfully agree with the Commissioner who decided that the *ejusdem generis* rule is an aid to the interpretation of the Schedule 1 prescription of the occupation relevant to A4. However, apart from their involving repetitive movements of the fingers, hand or arm, there is little in common between the activities of handwriting and typing which is apparent from the face of the prescription. Because they are interpreting a regulation based code of law Commissioners and, I think tribunals, have always been entitled to go behind the text of the regulations and examine the background papers to ascertain what is the purpose of any particular provision which is under consideration. The Commissioner who decided *R(I) 3/97* looked at the report by the Industrial Injuries Advisory Council which considered the need to replace the prescriptions of telegraphist's cramp, writer's cramp and twister's cramp, which were prescribed in paragraphs 28, 29 and 30 of Schedule 1 to the 1947 Industrial Injuries and Prescribed Diseases Regulations, and the relevant occupations with one prescribed disease and relevant occupation which would cover all those who suffered from hand and arm cramps as a result of working in employments involving the use of the fingers, hands or arms. The Commissioner quoted most of paragraph 32 and all of paragraph 33 of the Committee's report in which two paragraphs the need for a new prescription which would embrace the three cramps and relevant occupations which were then prescribed as well as the cramps experienced by those engaged in the occupations involving the use of keyboards which were then proliferating. He did not quote the first sentence of paragraph 32 which identifies the characteristic which is common to all the occupations which the Committee had in mind. That sentence is as follows:—

'These diseases are characterised by spasm or other disordered action of muscles used in the performance of duties involving rapid and finely controlled movements of the hand of a repetitive nature.'

Therefore, the activity which the Committee had in mind when it devised the current prescription of the occupation relevant to A4 is movement of the hands and arms which are approximately as rapid, as finely controlled and as repetitive as the movements employed by somebody operating a typewriter or writing by hand. I do not think that there is any likelihood of the hand and wrist movements described by the claimant having the degree of rapidity, fineness of control and repetitiveness of the hand movements of a typist or somebody writing with a pen or a pencil. I take Mr Crawford's point that the twister in the textile industry would not be repairing broken yarns with the degree of repetitiveness with which a typist would be striking the keys of a typewriter but on a machine which could have as many as 70 pairs of bobbins the breaks in the yarn would be fairly frequent and I have no doubt that as the twister would be constrained to keep the pauses in the winding to a minimum the hand movements employed to repair the breaks, in particular the movements of the thumb and forefinger, would be very rapid and, to make effective joins, would be very finely controlled". (para.25).

A5 (subcutaneous cellulitis of the hand), A6 (bursitis or subcutaneous cellulitis(elbow)),
A7 (bursitis or subcutaneous cellulitis (knee))

Until April 6, 2007, the terms of prescription for these referred in brackets respectively to "Beat hand", "Beat knee" and "Beat elbow". From that date, those terms were deleted on the recommendation of the IIAC as "outdated"; the term "used

10.138

to denote repeated trauma at work, is not widely used or understood in modern clinical practice, being a historical description confined to the field of occupational medicine" (see *Completion of the review of the scheduled list of prescribed diseases*, Cm 7003 (January 2007), para.28, referring back to its 2006 report on *Work Related Upper Limb Disorders*, Cm. 6868 (July 2006), para.78).

Refer back to the definition of "an occupation involving" and note that manual labour of the type described need only be one of the incidents of the prescribed occupation. Hence, the category of jobs in which manual labour is incidental includes not only those which require "muscle", but also those where some physical or bodily work is required. Note also that the pressure on the hand, knee or elbow need only be prolonged *or* severe. These three diseases are good examples of the scheme taking account of the development of an injury by process over a period which would prevent the claimant from showing that it had been caused by accident, but compare *R(I) 11/74*. See also *R(I) 78/54* and *R(I) 60/51*. In *R(I) 5/98*, dealing with A6 (Beat knee), Commissioner Rice held that the prescribed occupation is to be interpreted in the context of the disease covered. Thus it covers not any kind of friction or pressure, but only the type of friction or pressure that causes beat knee. A medical report before him identified the key feature of beat knee as

"direct pressure and/or friction to the knee and immediate vicinity, for example just above or below the knee. This pressure or friction must be applied directly to the skin to cause cellulitis, or directly to the skin overlying the bursa" (para.7).

The anatomical parts affected are superficial, not within the knee joint itself (para.8). In this case, the damage to the claimant's knee through the consistent use of the brake pedal when operating his crane did not result in that sort of friction or pressure; the process involved repeated flexing and extending of the knee, with most of the action taking place at the ankle joint (*ibid*). Similarly in *CI/268/95* (noted in (1997) 4 J.S.S.L. D88). Commissioner Hoolahan held the tribunal decision erroneous in law: in looking at whether the claimant had been involved in any occupation within the A7 prescription (Beat elbow), it had failed to consider whether her work (as a cleaner in a social club) involved severe or prolonged "external" friction or pressure (para.6).

PD A8 (tenosynovitis)

10.139   For useful evidence from the medical adviser to the DWP (Dr Reed) on PD A8 (tenosynovitis), see the Schedule to *CI/3745/2006*.

A10 (Occupational deafness)

10.140   The revision from September 22, 2003 of the occupations in respect of which occupational deafness is prescribed, based largely on the IIAC Report on the prescription of occupational deafness (Cm 5672, November 2002), means that this commentary is now relevant only to those whose claim for disablement based on occupational deafness was made, or treated as made, on or after that date.

For claims made, or treated as made, before September 22, 2003, please see the commentary in the 2003 edition of this volume, as updated by the relevant pages of the Supplement 2003/2004.

In PD A10 occupational deafness is defined as

"Sensorineural hearing loss amounting to at least 50dB in each ear, being the average of hearing losses at 1, 2 and 3 kHz frequencies, and being due in the case of at least one ear to occupational noise."

CI/4567/1999 (now reported as *R(I)6/02*) contains useful material on a variety of tests measuring hearing loss.

In *CI/2012/2000*, Commissioner Jacobs said, rightly, that *CI/4567/1999* (now reported as *R(I)6/02*) neither is, nor purports to be, authority that ERA (evoked response audiometry), a form of assessment of hearing loss, is always to be preferred to PTA (pure tone audiometry), another form of assessment of hearing loss (para.16).

ERA "is a record of a person's brain activity in response to sound" (para.12), which is not dependent on the claimant to acknowledge that sound has been heard (and therefore not contingent on his honesty). However, the claimant's behaviour can affect other brain activity and render it more difficult to interpret the results (para.14). Adults are usually tested by cortical or slow vertex ERA. Young children are usually tested by another type, brainstem ERA so that the results are not affected by the anaesthetic or sedative administered to keep the child quiet and still during the test process (para.15).

PTA is cheap and fairly easy to administer. It is the starting point for all assessments by tribunals and the Secretary of State, but depends upon the claimant acknowledging when a sound (produced at different levels by the PTA equipment) has been heard (para.10).

The Commissioner advances the following approach for tribunals:

"a tribunal . . . has to weigh the evidence as a whole in order to determine the level of the claimant's sensorineural hearing loss. There is no rule that one type of evidence is always to be preferred to another. The evidence must be considered as a whole. The tribunal may conclude that one type of evidence is preferable to another, but that must be a judgment reached after considering the merits of all the evidence" (para.16).

There was in this case no error of law in the tribunal refusing to order, at public expense, brainstem ERA.

In *CI/1/2002*, without citing Commissioner Jacob's decision in *CI/2012/2000*, like him Commissioner Williams also concludes that *CI/4567/1999* (now reported as *R(I)6/02*) is not authority that CERA (cortical evoked response audiogram) is always to be preferred to PTA (pure tone audiometry). Noting that Prescribed Diseases Regulations, reg.34 gives precise details about testing and assessment but not the method of testing, Commissioner Williams stated that the matter is one for the experts on the tribunal using their expertise to decide. In the decision under appeal before him, the tribunal had relied on that expertise to conclude that in that case CERA would not be more reliable than PTA. However, the Commissioner noted that declining to order a CERA test on the basis of cost might be a denial of a fair hearing under the HRA 1998/ECHR.

Useful information and guidance—which cannot be binding on decision makers, tribunals or Commissioners—on both PTA and CERA can be found in the IIAC Report on the prescription of occupational deafness (Cm 5672, November 2002). See para.117 (audiometric testing) and App.6 (guidance on obtaining cortical evoked response audiometry). The IIAC recommended that PTA should be retained as the most appropriate routine assessment method for use in the benefit scheme. Where testing is not repeatable, or response to conversational voice seems better or worse than the audiogram would suggest, use of CERA should be considered. In any event, the IIAC recommended that methods of testing should be kept under review.

Tribunals can have regard to the Department's guidelines and its rather rough and ready conversational voice testing in its *Industrial Injuries Handbook for Adjudicating Medical Authorities*, so long as it was remembered that this was guidance and not statutorily prescribed. The Tables in the Handbook could be taken on board but only as part of a proper disablement assessment (*CI/5029/2002*, per Commissioner Fellner).

The wide range of occupations for which this disease is prescribed led to a significant number of Commissioners' decisions on the interpretation of the various parts of the Schedule relating to the disease. All, however, can only be authoritative today insofar as they deal with equivalent wording.

The expression which prefaces the reformulated occupations in column (2), "*wholly or mainly in the immediate vicinity of,*" was considered in *R(I)2/85*. That decision held that it was not necessary that the claimant should spend the majority of his time near the specified tools whilst they are in use, and that it was sufficient that the tools were in use more than a negligible amount whilst he was in the vicinity. But the formulation now requires work wholly or mainly in the immediate vicinity *of the use of* a specified tool or piece of equipment, removing the authority of that statement. Note also *CI/226/91* (para.7), citing *Fawcett Properties v Buckingham CC* [1961] A.C. 636 at 669 where Lord Morton said that mainly "probably means more than half". In *R(I) 7/76* it was held that whether the claimant was in the vicinity should be determined by the distance from him to the specified tools, taking into account walls, screens etc., but not measuring the level of residual noise at the claimant's workplace. An employee working in an exceptionally noisy factory may, therefore, be exposed to far greater noise than is acceptable but not entitled to benefit because he is not working near enough to the machines making the noise—

> "Whether an occupation involves work in the immediate vicinity of the designated plant is a question of fact in each case. I think it is to be answered first by ascertaining the locations, that is to say the area within which the designated plants (which from their nature cover considerable areas) are situated, and the area of the claimant's activities. The question whether the area of work is in the immediate vicinity of the plant then depends in my opinion on the weight to be given to the particular circumstances. The distance at which one area lies from the other may itself be decisive of the question. A second factor may be the physical separation of one area from the other because of intervening buildings . . . A further factor, as here . . . may be the presence of walls and screening, substantially dividing, enclosing or demarking the two areas lying at a distance apart, though under the same factory roof."

See also *R(I) 8/85* where the distance factor was held to be significant. In *CI/245/1991*, Commissioner Goodman stated that the notion of "working in the immediate vicinity" of percussive tools involved consideration of the physical proximity to the use of such tools and not just the noise level, so that the claimant's non-use of ear muffs or protectors supplied by his employer was legally irrelevant to the issue. The Commissioner concluded that the percussive tools were in constant and daily use and that the claimant worked in the immediate vicinity in his job as storeman, his store being separated from that work area only by a wire mesh (paras 10–13).

The original (see above) specified occupations were, broadly speaking, foundries, shipyards and mines and quarries. Whilst the occupations have been changed and widened, the Schedule still refers in paras A10(a) and (b) to the use of, or work wholly or mainly in the immediate vicinity of the use of, a pneumatic percussive tool. The nature of such a tool has been considered in *R(I) 5/76* (an "impact wrench" or "screwing up machine"); *R(I) 8/76* (a computer-controlled burning and marking machine); *R(I) 1/80* (a rivet gun); *R(I) 3/80* (upright pedestal grinder); *R(I)/13/80* (machine mounted vertical spindle surface grinder); *R(I) 6/83* (press set into the ground and operating on compressed air). Whether a particular tool is pneumatic is a question of fact, and it is necessary to look at the essential nature of the tool and determine its driving force (*R(I) 6/83*). But what constitutes a "tool"? The general trend of decisions has been to give the word "tool" a more technical meaning and, as a result, include some machines in the category of tools. A printing press, though pneumatic and percussive was held not to be a "tool" in *CI/17/93*. The test for "tool" was there said to be whether the machine now alleged to be a "tool" is now used to carry out a task traditionally carried out by what everyone would recognise as a hand-held tool. If there is no "recognisable previous identity as a hand-held tool" it is a machine and not a "tool" (*CI/17/93*, para.3. citing *R(I) 6/83*, para.6). In *Appleby v CAO* (reported as *R(I) 5/99*, judgment of June 29, 1999), the Court of Appeal stated that while the test propounded by Commissioner Sanders in *CI/17/93* was "useful", it was not "an exclusive test", particularly as regards new processes where the existence of a sufficiently manual input may enable the alleged tool to qualify. A useful starting point is whether the implement in question is classified in the trade or industry as a machine tool. In *Appleby*, the Court held the electrodes on the spot welding machine qualified as pneumatic, percussive tools; they banged the metal to be welded to ensure a tight fit before emitting the necessary electrical charge, and were, therefore, the mechanical equivalent of the hand held hammer used in the past when welding was effected by hammering together two pieces of preheated metal. The Court, obiter, was provisionally of the opinion that the spot welding machine had sufficient manual input to qualify as a "tool".

The number of paras has been reduced from 23 to 11, and occupations once in separate paras have been regrouped and reworded to simplify matters to aid under-standing and administration (IIAC Report, para.105, and App.4). The revision, however, has added occupations but not removed any previously prescribed, since the IIAC "had no evidence that any of the occupations and processes already pre-scribed have disappeared, ceased to be a hazard to hearing, or fundamentally altered to the extent that their removal from the list would be appropriate" (para.95).

Para.(a): "metal founding or forging industries": the IIAC saw no need to clarify   **10.141** "forging", considering it an understandable term with a definite meaning in indus-try (para. 101). The prescription covers the use of powered grinding tools on metal, but not hand-powered ones. On "tool" and "pneumatic percussive tool", see the discussion preceding coverage of this particular para. As regards "metal", note that despite common parlance referring to a metalled road, reg.1(2) provides that "metal" for the purposes of disease A10, does not include stone, concrete, aggregate or similar substances for use in road or railway construction. However in *CI/37/1988* the Commissioner accepted that "on metal" could include the use of pneumatic drills to break up reinforced concrete where the drill would from time to time strike the metal reinforcing rods. But in *CI/540/1994*, where the momentary or occasional contact with a metal reinforcing rod was minimal, the claim was unsuccessful. The ruling in *CI/540/1994* was held in *CI/13238/1996* to apply in respect of noise from drills striking metal reinforcing rods in concrete road structures in a claim by a foreman asphalter.

Note that the terms "foundry", "skid transfer bank" and "knock out and shake out grid" are each specifically defined in reg.1(2), above.

The term "metal nails" has a wider meaning than ordinary nails driven with a hammer; it can include any piece of wire or metal used for holding things together (*R(I)5/83*). In *CI/808/95*, Commissioner Mesher agreed

> "with the view expressed by the Commissioner in para.9 of *R(I)5/83*, supported by reference in that case to the report of the Industrial Injuries Advisory Council, that the prescription in paragraph A10(f) [the equivalent of A10(a) formulation 'machine to cut or shape or clean metal nails'] relates to the process of making nails. Thus the crucial question is whether what results from the operation of the claimant's machine can be called a nail in the extended sense described by the Commissioner in *R(I)5/83* [a piece of wire or metal used for holding things together]. One must ask what the product is used for. I conclude that its use in the manufacture of tyres is such that it cannot be called a nail. It does not hold things together in the way in which a nail or rivet holds things together. It does not hold one part of the tyre to another part of the tyre by connecting the two together." (para.9, words in square brackets added.)

The rubber-coated wire cut by the claimant's machine was used to reinforce the rubber moulding of the tyre.

There was brief consideration in *CI/246/1988* of the features of plasma spray gun to spray molten metal, but unfortunately the matter was not pursued very far since the materials deposited by the gun in the case were silica and quartz, neither of which is a metal.

Para.(b): On "pneumatic percussive tool", see the discussion preceding commen-   **10.142** tary on para (a).

"Underground" means properly underground, with an earth ceiling, and does not include a deep trench which is open to the air, even though the drilling operation is going on below ground level (*R(I)4/84*). It means "underneath the natural surface of the earth". It did not therefore embrace the claimant who was not but may have been working on the floor or below floor level in a prepared building, not under a natural roof (*CI/550/89*, para.6). A tunnel like the Mersey Tunnel is properly encompassed by the term "underground", although the inclusion in para. (b) of "for tunnelling in civil engineering works" in any event provides protection (*CI/13238/1996*).

In *CI/550/89*, Commissioner Heald decided, referring indirectly to *CI/308/1989* (now reported as *R(I)2/92*, noted below) on the meaning of "wood", that "rock" in sub-para. (c) means "rock in its natural state . . . and not in the form of a cement aggregate, at which stage the material which was originally rock, no doubt, had changed its nature and formed part of the cement mix." (para.5). Whether the same is true of "stone", so as to not to cover solid products (e.g. paving slabs, bricks or blocks) made from reconstituted crushed or powdered stone is unclear. The inclusion of new para.(c) will help some of those who work cutting concrete masonry blocks (e.g. builders).

10.143   *Para.(c)*: none of the terms in this prescription is defined. Nor does there appear to be any case law on its previous partial manifestation as PD A10(q). Its expansion will help some of those who work cutting concrete masonry blocks (e.g. builders).

10.144   *Para.(d)*: This covers the use of machines in the manufacture of textiles. This includes "weaving", but the para is not confined to "weaving".

On "weaving", *CSI/65/94* applying *R(I)13/81* was authority that deafness from working with noisy knitting machines does not come within A10(d) because "knitting" is not "weaving". Commissioner Mitchell reached his decision "with regret" and like the Commissioner in *R(I)13/81* expressed the hope that an anomaly might be rectified by amending the paragraph, since the evidence in the case showed that the knitting machines at the claimant's place of work were just as noisy as weaving machines. This has now been done as regards the process of "high speed false twisting of fibres" after the IIAC recommending it in its 2002 Report which largely formed the basis for these revised prescriptions. The IIAC accepted that there was enough evidence that high speed false twisting is a process that can take place prior to both knitting and weaving, and one which produces yarn for both of these areas of fabric manufacture.

In *CI/2879/1995*, Commissioner Goodman gave some consideration to the phrase "the high speed false twisting of fibres". He set aside the tribunal decision as erroneous in law on the basis that they had failed to consider whether the claimant's occupation from May 6, 1987 to August 12, 1988 (one bringing her within a five-year period prior to the 1994 claim) met the description. But, approving an argument founded on para.12 of *R(I)13/81*, he held that the tribunal was entitled to rely on a definition from a research fellow in a University Department of Textile Industries in conjunction with factual information supplied by the employer on the basis that where words are used in legislation with reference to particular trades or businesses and have a particular meaning within that trade or business, the words in the legislation should be construed in the light of that meaning (para.17). The material before the tribunal and letters before the Commissioner from an officer in the Health and Safety Executive and from another expert in the same University Department all confirmed that "false twisting", a technique rather than a process, involved machines operating at speeds in revolutions per minute varying according to whether dealing with staple yarns (a few tens of thousands per minute) or filament yarns (850,000 per minute in 1968, up to 7 million per minute today). Some suggested "false twisting" was limited to synthetic yarns. But, in setting out that material and in remitting the matter back to the tribunal because factual "loose ends" precluded him giving the decision, Commissioner Goodman stressed that the prescription "high speed" is not expressed as being a minimum of revolutions a minute, nor is the word "fibres in any way qualified to limit it to artificial fibres" (para.18). The prescription now explicitly covers man-made and natural fibres, and includes mineral fibres.

The prescription also covers the "mechanical cleaning of bobbins". It was reworded from the former prescription in the old PD A10(e), "mechanical bobbin cleaning" to clarify that what is prescribed is the mechanical cleaning of bobbins, rather than the cleaning of mechanical bobbins (IIAC, Cm 5672, 2002, para. 103)

Para.(e): This covers various machines and saws used to work with wood—In **10.145** *R(I)2/92* Commissioner Rice considered the meaning of "wood" in a previous occupational prescription in respect of occupational deafness. The claimant had worked in the newspaper print industry near machines cutting newsprint. The Commissioner supported the view of the dissenting chairman in the tribunal that this particular prescribed occupation "refers to wood in [the] accepted sense of the word, not to a material of which wood may be a constituent part. The prescribed occupation . . . clearly refers to working of wood or similar material such as chip-board, and not to the newsprint industry." Commissioner Rice stated that although "newsprint is derived from wood, it is not the same as wood. It has undergone a metamorphosis, and in its changed form as newsprint it has become an entirely different material. It follows that the claimant cannot satisfy the relevant statutory requirements," (para.7). *R(I)2/92* (then *CI/309/1989*) was approved and applied in *CI/175/90* (noted below, notes to D7). It was also followed in *CI/43/92*, where Commissioner Rice held that "logs of toilet paper and kitchen paper" had, like newsprint, undergone a metamorphosis and could not be regarded as "wood," (para.6).

The rewording of the prescription to cover the use of specific machines or saws on wood removes the need to argue over issues such as the meaning of "forestry", which the IIAC Report saw as in need of clarification (paras.99, 100). It recommended that prescription cover the *regular* use of chainsaws. Note that this was not carried into the prescription.

The prescription has been reworded on HSE advice to cover all circular sawing machines, including those operated by moving the blade towards the material to be cut (para.104).

Para.(f): Removal of references to "water-jetting industry" (see *CI/2286/2002* and **10.146** *CI/5331/2002*) helps clarify the scope of the prescription which is now confined (i) to the use of a jet of water (or a mixture of water and abrasive) above a specified pressure of 680 bar (10,000 psi)(much higher than the "at least 3000 psi" formulation used by the Secretary of State to denote "high pressure" in the previous prescription (see *CI/5331/2002*, paras 2 and 18), and (ii) to jet channelling process to burn stone in a quarry. The IIAC was concerned in its proposed revision to clarify that it intended to include only those water-jetting processes in which high pressure was used on a commercial basis, and where an employee would be put at regular and frequent risk of exposure to high levels of noise likely to damage hearing (para.97). In setting the 10,000 psi level evidence was taken from HSE experts on the level of pressure likely to be hazardous to hearing and produce disablement (para.98).

Para.(g): this covers a machine in a ship's engine room or gas turbine, provided that **10.147** it use covers the specified testing. The meaning of "ship's engine room" was considered in *R(I)2/97* where the Commissioner saw it as "clearly limited to engine rooms on ships, and does not extend to engine rooms on land, regardless of the nature of the engines located there". So, in that case, the fact that the claimant worked in an engine room providing power to a building and the engines in the room were of a type that could be used to power ships, was immaterial. So was the fact that had he been on a ship and rendered deaf by working with the self-same engines, his claim would have succeeded; the occupation has to be a prescribed one (*ibid.*, para.11).

The Commissioner in so deciding on the appropriate interpretation, made use of a report on Occupational Deafness by the Industrial Injuries Advisory Council. In *CSI/248/2003*, Commissioner Parker considered the meaning of "ship". After reviewing a number of statutory definitions and case law from a variety of legal subject areas, she accepted:

> "for the present purpose the value of generally applying the Merchant Shipping Act [1995] definition of a ship (' "ship" includes every description of vessel used in navigation') and how that definition was interpreted in *Perks* [a tax case, a decision of the Court of Appeal found at [2001] EWCA Civ 1228]

> The fact finding tribunal must therefore ask itself what is the design and capability of any particular structure and whether 'navigation' in the sense of 'movement across water' (and not requiring 'conveying persons and cargo from place to place') *is a significant part of the function of the structure in question.* The significance of the navigation is an issue of degree on the facts of a particular case and can be overturned by an appellate court only if the conclusions are perverse.

> As Carnwath J. noted in *Perks*, the test has enabled the courts to include structures of very specialised kinds within the scope of the definition of 'ship', and to exclude cases where it was considered that the function of 'moving across the seas' was minimal or non-existent" (paras 57—59).

The tribunal to which the case was remitted

> "having first found on what type of structures, and when, the claimant worked during the relevant period, must then consider with respect to each whether 'movement across water' was a significant part of its particular function. If the claimant worked only on the North Alwyn, and it is, as the Secretary of State suggests, a huge, fixed platform once set up in its location, it must be doubtful if this would constitute a ship. However, as always, everything depends on the facts found having regard to the evidence" (para.65).

See also *CSI/524/1999*, where the rig had propellers to enable it to move and to turn in bad weather. But, even if the rig at issue in *CSI/248/2003* were a "ship", the question remained whether the claimant, who drove a crane on the rig, worked in the ship's engine room. The Commissioner thought that:

> "as a ship is not inevitably self-propelled, then, having regard to the underlying purpose for prescribing the occupation set out in paragraph A(10), it seems inevitable that to constitute a ship's engine room rather than *any* engine room, the engine room in question must provide power *for the ship*. It is insufficient that a claimant works in an engine room, even if integrated with the ship, where the engine of the structure on which he works provides power to that particular structure only, rather than to the ship.

> So the question here is whether the claimant works in an engine room of a crane, such a crane being located on a ship, which in no substantial way differs from the engine room of a land crane; alternatively, does his engine room on the crane provide power beyond the crane and for the ship?" (paras 74, 75).

The remainder of the prescription gives aid and comfort to others who work with gas turbines for various specified forms of engine testing.

10.148   *Para. (h)*: This applies to machines used for certain specified matters in the manufacure of glass containers and hollow war. *R(I)4/99* remains authority for the proposition that the whole of the prescription is confined to glass manufacture. In that case, considering similar wording in para.(w) of the then prescription, the claimant was a clay worker in the pottery industry. He operated a "forming machine, used in the manufacture of ceramic (pottery) hollow ware, but not glass hollow ware" (para.4). The Commissioner rejected the argument of the claimant's representative that "hollow ware" was not confined to glass, but included metal and ceramics. Taking account of the Industrial Injuries Advisory Council Report [Cm. 817 (1994)], which had led to the introduction of para.(w)) in order to interpret ambiguous wording in the legislative prescription, Commissioner Goodman came to the conclusion that the:

> "prescription is . . . confined to glass manufacture. The words, '. . . forming machines used in the manufacture of glass containers or hollow ware' do in my view read in such a way that the adjective 'glass' applies not only to 'containers' but also to 'hollow ware'. That is the natural meaning of the sentence and it also coincides with the fact that the rest of sub-paragraphs (i) and (ii) and (iii) of paragraph (w) are all clearly confined to the manufacture of various kinds of glass (save 'mineral wool' in sub-paragraph (ii)). The report of the Advisory Council leads to the same conclusion and I am entitled to look at its contents in view of the ambiguity introduced in [sub-] paragraph (i) of paragraph (w) by the use of the word 'or' between 'glass containers' and 'hollow ware'. Overall, therefore, I am satisfied that the tribunal arrived at the correct decision and that the prescribed occupation in paragraph (w) of Paragraph A10 is not intended to apply to any kind of hollow ware except that made of glass. I must therefore dismiss the claimant's appeal accordingly" (para.13).

Para.(k): this was recommended for prescription since evidence from the HSE supported the view that the level of exposure to noise in this situation was at least as high as in the occupations already prescribed (IIAC Report, Cm 5672, 2002, para. 94) Note that cases might also fit (as single incidents or small series of incidents producing deafness) as accidents within SSCBA 1992, s. 94(1). See further *CI/5029/2002* on assessment of disablement in respect of deafness arising from accident in connection with police firearms training.   10.149

Para.(l): this was recommended for prescription since evidence from the HSE supported the view that the level of exposure to noise in this situation was at least as high as in the occupations already prescribed (IIAC Report, Cm 5672, 2002, para.94)   10.150

A11 (Vibration white finger)
In *R(I) 2/95*, the form of prescription of prescribed disease A11 was upheld as *intra vires*.   10.151

In *R(I) 3/02*, Commissioner Jacobs noted that the legal definition of vibration white finger in referring only to "blanching" is narrower than the medical one, which also takes on board sensory effects. He held that the legal definition only restricted those cases of vibration white finger that are to be subject to an assessment of disablement for purposes of disablement benefit. However, once a case thus comes within that definition because of blanching, when it comes to the loss of faculty causing the claimant's disabilities it is proper then to look to the broader medical concept and include the sensory effects (see paras 17, 22).

Despite suggestions from the Industrial Injuries Advisory Council in Cm.2844 (May 1995) that this should be represcribed as hand-arm vibration syndrome, vibration white finger remains prescribed only in respect of its vascular effect (blanching) and not its neurological effect. But in stressing that in *R(I) 1/02*, Commissioner Williams endorsed the approach in *R(I) 3/02* that

> "once there is episodic blanching of the relevant extent, the neurological effect of the disease will be relevant to compensation as well as the vascular effects" (para.10).

The Tribunal of Commissioners in *R(I) 2/06* approved the principle in *R(I) 3/02* as "correct, and now well-settled" (para.53). It also stressed that assessment of disablement is ultimately a matter of judgment for the tribunal which hears and sees the evidence. That Tribunal decision also elaborates on the nature of an error of law, and on the difference between that and a disputed judgment of degree on a question of fact. It also proffers guidance on reference to Sch.2 in non-prescribed cases, on consideration of the judicial guidelines on the assessment of damages in civil personal injury cases, on cross-reference to other schemes such as that for criminal injuries, and on the status of official departmental guidance such as the Medical Assessment Framework (MAF). See further the annotation to SSCBA 1992, Sch.6.

The terms of prescription of the prescribed disease or injury PD A11 were altered, subject to a transitional provision (Social Security (Industrial Injuries) (Prescribed Diseases) Amendment (No. 2) Regulations 2007 (SI 2007/1753), reg.3), with effect from October 1, 2007 so as to add sensorineural symptoms to the description of the disease and a proviso that both sets of symptoms are caused by vibration. It also provides that the prescription shall not cover blanching of the skin or sensorineural symptoms prior to employment in a prescribed occupation. Without renaming PD A11 as "hand-arm vibration syndrome" as there recommended, the changes in some degree reflect ones put forward by the Industrial Injuries Advisory Council in reports in Cm. 2844 (May 1995) and Cm. 6098 (July 2004), and reiterated in its review of the list of prescribed diseases in Cm. 7003 (January 2007) (see paras 38, 39), although the Explanatory Note to the amending regulations makes no mention of any of these reports. The change may also reflect the impact of *R(I) 3/02* as regards taking on board sensory effects in ascertaining loss of faculty, and *R(I) 1/02* in seeing them as relevant to compensation as well as the vascular effects. On limitations on the scope of the preclusive transitional provision, see *DG v SSWP* [2009] UKUT 41 (AAC), noted further in the commentary to the provision. On the need carefully to consider whether the tribunal is applying the "old" or the "new" blanching provision, see *Reid* [2009] UKUT 39 (AAC).

In *CI/4874/2001*, Deputy Commissioner McLachlan stressed the need to keep separate the issues, on the one hand, whether the claimant has the disease [the col.1 matter] (and the consequent degree of disablement) and, on the other, the question of causation [the col.2 matter]. He stated

> "It is misleading to say that 'the question of blanching . . . has to be considered in the context of vibration induced damage . . .'. The blanching must be considered first, and if the required degree of blanching is established attention should then be turned to causation" (para.10).

In *R(I) 3/04*, Commissioner Mesher ruled the matter of occupational cause to be irrelevant to the diagnosis question. He accepted that "blanching" means more than the normal paleness in the extremities experience on exposure to cold, where there is a reduction of the blood supply to the peripheral arteries in order to protect the system as a whole. He was not, however, prepared to limit "blanching" to intense whiteness, the profound deathly white referred to in the medical paper by Dr Reed, The Blood and Nerve Supply to the Hand, which the Commissioner embodied in an appendix to his decision. That was characteristic but the meaning of "blanching" was not restricted to that, and was rather a matter to be decided in particular cases by tribunals and medical decision makers. Nor was circumferential blanching a requisite, preferring here Commissioner Rowland in *CI/3596/2001* to Commissioner Henty in *CI/1807/2002*. Indeed Commissioner Mesher rejected Commissioner Henty's view that Commissioner Rowland's decision had been given *per incuriam*. He noted that the matter of the Cold Water Provocation Test in the Department's Notes on the Diagnosis of Prescribed Diseases (NDPD) had successfully been challenged in *R. (on the application of the National Association of Colliery Overmen, Deputies and Shotfirers) v Secretary of State for Work and Pensions* [2003] EWHC 607 (Admin). There Pitchford J. found irrational the Secretary of State's refusal to revise the NDPD guidance and required him to amend it to reflect the correct intention behind the words used, namely that a positive result could have diagnostic value but a negative one should be treated as having none (paras 107–109).

In *CI/1720/2001*, Commissioner Rowland gives some guidance to tribunals on the manner of questioning those who claim to suffer from vibration white finger, suggesting that they avoid closed questioning and too technical language (paras 12–14).

In *CI/1763/2002*, having consulted Commissioner Jacobs who gave the decision in *CI/14532/1996* (now *R(I) 3/02*), Commissioner Mesher stressed that they were both agreed that

> "there cannot be an automatic and mechanical rule, without examination of the particular circumstances of each case, that Stage 2 on the Taylor Pelmear Scale means that PD A11 cannot be diagnosed. Stage 2 covers blanching during winter. But it is possible for someone to in addition experience blanching during the summer (thus going towards throughout the year as the prescription requires) without quite reaching Stage 3 on the Scale which requires 'extensive blanching with frequent episodes in summer as well as in winter' " (see paras 11–13 of *CI/1763/2002*).

Although not mentioned in the Tribunal of Commissioners' decision *CI/535/2005*, that approach is consistent with the tenor of that Tribunal decision and in particular its rejection of the view that there can be produced a ready template for decisions on the assessment of disablement. See further commentary to SSCBA 1992, Sch.6.

In *CI/421/2006*, Commissioner Turnbull held that a claimant refused permission to stand outside the tribunal for a short while in cold weather the better to support his claim that he suffered from vibration white finger was denied natural justice. The Commissioner also suggested that since this claimant had also requested that the last tribunal conduct a Cold Water Provocation Test, it might be wise to offer one at the new hearing. Although a negative result from such a test did not disprove vibration white finger, a positive result could assist a claimant whose history or symptoms were inconclusive (citing *R. (on the application of NACODS) v. Secretary of State for Work and Pensions* [2003] EWHC 607, paras 41, 43). The result of any diagnostic test, however, had to be considered in the light of the history and clinical findings in the case.

In *CI/3596/2001*, Commissioner Rowland accepted that the prescription of PD A11 does not require circumferential blanching. While blanching only of the palmar side of the fingers might be atypical, it suffices to meet the terms of the prescription, the relevant question when determining whether the claimant is suffering from a prescribed disease (para.4). Its atypical nature might, however, in some cases be a basis for doubting the history given by the claimant or for deciding that it was not due to the nature of his/her employment, and might give some indication as to the degree of disablement (para.5).

The words "in forestry" in **sub-para.(a)** were replaced with the broader term "on wood" with effect (subject to a transitional provision) from October 1, 2007, thus giving effect to recommendations of the Industrial Injuries Advisory Council on the confusion generated by "in forestry" (see Cm. 6098 (July 2004), paras. 67, 78 and Cm. 7003 (January 2007), para.38). Happily, the case law on the meaning and scope of "in forestry", which had itself effected a broadening of the term (see below), is thus now only relevant to claims in respect of a period of assessment which relates to a claim made, or having effect, before the date these 2007 Regulations came into force or to a renewed break-out of a condition for which a claim was made before their entry into force. The change brings PD A11 into line with PD A10 where the broader term "on wood" has been applied since September 22, 2003. For the meaning of "wood", see the annotation to PD A10 (e). For the text of the transitional provision see the Social Security (Industrial Injuries) (Prescribed Diseases) Amendment (No. 2) Regulations 2007 (SI 2007/1753).

As indicated above, the meaning of "forestry" (now relevant to claims linked to periods prior to October 1, 2007), has been the subject of dispute, but case law gradually broadened the concept. In *CI/3924/1997*, Commissioner Rice considered it. The term "forestry" is also used in prescribed disease A10(i) and decisions *R(I) 5/96* (formerly *CI/362/94*) and *CI/319/94* on it in that context were cited in argument. Commissioner Rice used the same Shorter Oxford English Dictionary definition as in those cases: "the science and art of forming and cultivating forests, management of growing timber", the latter part of the definition being applicable to the case before Commissioner Rice. Here the claimant was employed by an urban local authority as an "arborist–tree surgeon". The Commissioner, deploying dictionary definitions, took "arborist" as someone who studies trees and, in the absence of a dictionary definition, took "tree-surgeon" as someone who cuts, trims or otherwise prunes trees. But an "arborist–tree surgeon" is not necessarily a forester and a restrictive meaning was given to the prescription:

> "He may be concerned . . . with trees which form no part of a forest and do not qualify as growing timber. They may, for example, simply be ornamental trees designed to improve the appearance of a city such as Liverpool. Where they are grown merely to enhance the scenery e.g. along the roadways or in strategic parts of the city or in parks, they clearly do not form part of a forest, nor are they normally 'growing timber' cultivated as a crop for eventual sale for commercial use. Of course when an ornamental tree reaches maturity, it may well be sold off for such a use, but that is not the primary purpose for which it was cultivated. It was merely an incidental consequence of the decorative purpose for which it was initially planted and nurtured" (para.6).

The matter was remitted to a new tribunal to consider the matter again in line with that interpretation in the light of the evidence, old and new, before them. The label attached to the claimant's department "Forestry Department" was not conclusive of its activities nor, if an accurate description of them, would it necessarily apply to all employees in the Department (para.7). Recently in *R(I) 2/01*, Commissioner Levenson took the view that "forestry" should be given a broader, ordinary non-technical meaning. He doubted that the approach in the decisions above, which followed those noted in respect of prescribed disease A10(i), accorded with the approach of the IIAC in its report on the prescription of vibration white finger (Cmnd.8350 (1981)). He declined to follow *R(I) 5/96* and the other cases (see paras 8–15). He considered that prescribed occupations should not be "artificially narrowed" (para.15). Accordingly, he held that the tribunal did not err in law in holding that the claimant who had pruned and felled trees in parks, schools and on highways for a city council had used chain saws in "forestry".

Commissioner Levenson's comments and broader approach were endorsed by the Court of Appeal in *Davis v Secretary of State for Social Security* (January 12, 2001) reported as *R(I) 2/01*. Rix L.J. stated:

> "It seems to me that while the words 'in forestry' in the statutory phrase are plainly intended as some form of limitation, it would be wrong to give to those words too narrow a definition when one considers the purpose of the statute, which was to provide compensation for those who suffered the prescribed disease as result of their occupation. There is great danger that, if too narrow a definition is adopted, then the very persons who fall within the purpose of the statutory protection would fall outside the definition. If, for instance, the requirement was that the work had to be done within a forest properly so-called, which was one part of Miss Lieven's definition of forestry, then someone who spent all his time in the use of chain saws, pruning or cutting down trees in large ornamental estates, or other amenity areas of the countryside which contained extensive woods, but which perhaps may not have been 'forest', would find themselves outside the statutory protection. Again, if the requirement was that the trees concerned, whether in a forest or not, had to be grown for some commercial or industrial purpose, as distinct from some amenity or leisure purpose, or simply the beauty or health of the environment, a similar result would follow.

In the present case, Miss Lieven was ultimately prepared to adopt the dictionary definition, including the words 'management of growing timber', but nevertheless she submitted that to fall within the words 'in forestry' a claimant would either have to work in a forest, or in the commercial production of growing timber.

In my judgment, that is to narrow the meaning of 'in forestry' both by going beyond the dictionary definition which has been adopted in all the previous decisions as well as in the current one, and by doing so in a way which is neither justified by that definition nor justified by the purpose of the statute. Various examples were canvassed in the course of argument. It is not necessary to make a decision in respect of any of them. Decisions of this kind are ultimately always for the tribunal, provided it founds itself on a proper understanding of the statute. But, for instance, the case of an employee of Railtrack who was involved constantly in the management of growing timber beside the railway, by means of pruning or felling it, is an example where, speaking for myself, I could well understand a tribunal deciding, on the particular facts before it, that his work fell within the phrase 'in forestry'.

In my judgment the words 'in forestry' are perfectly adequately defined by the expression 'the management of growing timber', and there is no need to cut down those words any further by requiring that growing timber should be in any particular kind of area, whether described as a forest or parkland or whatever, or should be grown for any particular purpose. Moreover, I would accept that the work of clearing away growing timber is part of its management.

The fact that the statutory phrase has to be taken as a whole, namely 'any occupation involving . . . the use of hand-held chain saws in forestry' suggests that the words 'in forestry' mean no more than 'in or in connection with forestry', and are intended to express a sense of scale about the occupation involved. The words 'occupation involving' are very wide words indeed and raise, of course, the possibility that the occupation may involve the use of hand-held chain saws in only an incidental way. By putting in the words 'in forestry', in my judgment the legislators intended to exclude the use of handheld chain saws in only an incidental way, as might occur in occupations which had nothing to do with forestry (as for instance, might very frequently occur in the case of those who are in occupation merely as gardeners and make some occasional use of a hand-held chain saw)."

The clear implication is disapproval of the approach and result in *CI/3284/97* and *R(I) 5/96*.

In *CI/373/89* Commissioner Mitchell stated with respect to **sub-para.(b)**:

"The most obvious application of the words of prescription in issue in this case is to occupations involving the holding of material in the form of a work-piece which is being ground by rotary tools. Transmission of vibration to the operator in such a process is as direct and obvious as the immediate application of the words used. The question is whether those words also cover the operation spoken to by the claimant and Mr. Alford [a consulting engineer familiar with the Churchill type machine at issue] and carried out several times daily between operations on workpieces. On the evidence before me I have no doubt that the dressing or resurfacing of the side of the grinding wheel by the manual use of the carborundum stone against it involves appreciable grinding away of the carborundum stone itself progressively from the corners at the end until it becomes too small and is discarded after about one to two weeks. That process of course also involves the transmission of substantial vibration as found by the tribunal. The stone therefore imparts a measure of grinding but also suffers grinding in its own turn and that to a marked extent. I have come to the conclusion that this operation comes within the prescription of an occupation involving 'the holding of material being ground . . . by rotary tools.' (para.14 words in square brackets added by annotator)

'Grinding' in para.(b) is not limited to grinding of 'metal'. In *CSI 987/00*, Deputy Commissioner Sir Crispin Agnew of Lochnaw Bt Q.C. considered the case of a claimant who had worked as a labourer to electricians. His work had involved cutting raggles in concrete walls with a grinder and then hammering and chiselling them out so that the electricians could insert conduits. Occasionally this would involve him striking the metal reinforcing rods in the concrete walls. The Deputy Commissioner rejected "the Secretary of State's submission that grinding relates to metal and that the only metal ground was the occasional action of cutting metal rods with a grinder" (para.15). Instead the Deputy Commissioner considered

"that 'grinding' can be on any 'material', whereas 'sanding or polishing' can only be on 'metal'. I reach this construction of the provision having regard to (i) the use of the word 'in' before 'grinding' and again before 'the sanding or polishing of metal' which suggests that the task of grinding is separate from the task of sanding or polishing of metal and (ii) the fact that the later part of the provision refers to the 'holding of material being ground' and 'the metal being sanded or polished'. Had the intention been that prescription (b) should only apply to the grinding, sanding or polishing of metal, I would have expected the word 'metal' to be used rather than 'material'. 'Material' is a word that can be applied to any substance and not just to metal" (para.16).

Grinding concrete was the grinding of material and was therefore within PD A11(b).

In *CI/22/91* Commissioner Johnson considered whether the claimant's employment fell within the description in **sub-para.(c)**:

"the use of hand-held percussive metal-working tools, or the holding of metal being worked on by percussive tools in riveting, caulking, chipping, hammering, fettling or swaging".

He considered that the 57lb hammer used by the claimant was a hand-held percussive tool used to hammer metal, and continued:

"However, I have to consider whether the words 'metal-working' have any special significance, and also whether 'hammering' should be given its ordinary or has some special meaning in the context of paragraph (c). Certainly the [Industrial Injuries] Advisory Committee recommended that 'prescription should be in terms of the use of certain specified tools in certain specified occupations' . . .; broadly speaking that would appear to be the scheme of Schedule 1, although a number of occupations are very widely defined, for example A5–A8 inclusive, which specify 'manual labour' involving certain movements, and the conditions prescribed under B, C and to a great extent D, depend more on contact with biological or chemical agents than work in any particular industry.

10. So far as prescribed disease A11 is concerned, (a) is restricted to forestry and (e) to shoe manufacture, (d) covers mining, quarrying, demolition and road construction, which is a much wider category, as is (b), specifying the grinding, sanding or polishing of metal, which must take place in a variety of different trades. Looking at it as a whole it cannot be said that any very clear pattern emerges. In my view the 57Lb hammers used by Mr D were 'metal-working tools' as they were used for the purpose of working upon metal objects, whether ships' propellers, crane buckets or friction bands, or on the superstructure of the crane itself. I have also considered whether the word 'hammering' (in the description 'riveting, caulking, chipping, hammering, fettling or swaging') should be given some specialised meaning such as, for example, in the sense of producing a 'hammered' finish to a piece of metal, but I can see no justification for giving 'hammering' anything other than its normal everyday meaning. In my judgment, although the words denote particular processes, the one thing they have in common is not some particular trade or industry, but the fact that they all involve striking metal with metal, with consequent vibration." (paras 9, 10).

"Fettling" means "to remove excess moulding material and casting irregularites from a cast component" (a dictionary definition adopted in *CI/141/93*).

In *CI/207/2004*, Commissioner Williams considered the particular tasks involved in a bedding industry process involving using an automatic staple gun (what the claimant knew as a "rammer") to fix the metal of the bed springs to the bounding metal strip that holds the bed springs together and thus to the wooden base of the bed (known as a Bonnell base). He held that the rammer was a metal-working tool. In *Secretary of State v Westgate* [2006] EWCA Civ 725 (reported as *R(I) 1/06*) the Court of Appeal rejected this view and allowed the Secretary of State's appeal. The Court held that his interpretation was not within the range of reasonable interpretations of that statutorily undefined term. For the Court of Appeal, a metal-working tool is one that "works metal" (para.5). The process involved in the rammer for fixing the metal of the bed springs to the wooden frame was no more working metal than was the act of banging a nail into a wal or driving a bolt through a hole—such processes involve "working with metal" rather than "working metal" (para.6).

A12 (Carpal tunnel syndrome)

For useful evidence from the medical adviser to the DWP (Dr Reed) on PD A12 (carpal tunnel syndrome), see the Schedule to *CI/3745/2006*.   **10.152**

In *R(I) 3/95* Commissioner Heggs considered the meaning of "hand-held vibrating tool" for the purposes of the prescription of occupation in respect of prescribed disease A12 (carpal tunnel syndrome) as worded prior to March 24, 1996 "the use of hand-held vibrating tools"). The Commissioner said:

> "There is no statutory definition of the expression and the words can be given an extremely wide or narrow interpretation. Mrs Cleave [the claimant's representative] submitted that any vibrating tool falls within the terms of prescribed disease A12 if it can be shown that any part of it is supported or held by the hand of the operator. That is an attractive argument which would afford benefit to a wide category of claimants who could establish that they had sustained carpal tunnel syndrome from the use of vibrating equipment. The expression is however susceptible to the narrower interpretation that the expression 'hand-held' is descriptive of the actual tool in function and not the use made of the tool by the claimant. On this construction as submitted by Mr Jones [the AO's representative] it therefore applies only to the particular kind of vibrating tool which is portable and held manually. It does not extend to the use of tools of any kind in which some part of the operation may involve hand steadying or control. I am entitled to have regard to the Report of the Industrial Injuries Advisory Council (see paragraph 15 of the Tribunal of Commissioners decision *R(I) 11/81* where *Black–Clawson International Ltd. v Papierweke–Walhof–Ascheffenburg AG* [1975] A.C. 591 was applied). In my view the Report supports the narrower interpretation because it refers to 'grip required to use such tools—many of which are cumbersome' and that 'other forceful and repetitive movement of the wrist is not sufficient to prescribe carpal tunnel syndrome in any other occupational category'. Accordingly I conclude that the narrower interpretation is that which must apply." (para.14).

That approach was followed by Commissioner May in *CSI/82/94*. This concept of "hand-held" as denoting portability does not necessarily mean that it covers only lightweight tools; as *R(I) 2/96* makes clear, provided the element of portability is there it can cover heavier tools. In *R(I) 2/96*, the claimant worked for a bus company and had to clean the garage floor and inspection pit with a heavy rotary scrubbing or buffing machine which had to be gripped tightly to steer it and to hold in the clutch. Pressure also had to be applied to it in order to remove stubborn patches of oil from the garage floor. As Commissioner Goodman noted:

> "There is no doubt that these machines vibrate considerably, that they have to [be] tightly held, gripped and steered about and that the kind of machine that the

claimant was using was heavy in nature, though it could be lifted about by two people and to that extent was portable" (para.6).

In a decision supplementing rather than dissenting from the emphasis in *R(I) 3/95*, he held that the machine came within the prescription as a "hand-held vibrating tool", but cautioned that "there being a substantial factural element in [his] decision, that it is not necessarily a precedent for other types of machine or tool" (para.11). In the original *CI/15408/1995*, in March 1996, Commissioner Rice followed *CI/160/94*, and decided the appeal against the claimant, holding that the buffing machine operated by her was not a hand-held vibrating tool within the meaning of the legislative prescription. But his decision was given in ignorance of two of Commissioner Goodman's decisions on ostensibly similar machines: *R(I) 2/96* (a concrete floor scrubber) and *CI/514/94* (a floor buffer). When he became aware of those decisions, Commissioner Rice set aside his decision and the appeal was reheard before Commissioner Henty. The product is a new decision *R(I) 6/98*. Commissioner Henty's decision reviews all the pertinent authorities. The decision is in favour of the claimant and follows the *ratio* of Commissioner Goodman's decisions. Its effect is that the approach to "hand-held" in the quotation from *CI/160/94* is seen as correct in so far as it prevents static, fixed machines of the type at issue in that case (on which hands merely rested) being within the prescription. The requirement of "portability" in that approach was seen as *obiter* (not necessary for that decision). Having reviewed the relevant cases and the relevant report of the Industrial Injuries Advisory Council on the prescription of carpal tunnel syndrome (March 1992). Commissioner Henty gave his reasoned opinion on what he found a very difficult question:

"All the previous decisions I have referred to are in agreement that a fixed machine, which requires the application of the hand to operate it, is not 'a hand-held tool'. However, it does not seem to me that there is much difference in fact between (i) a tool which vibrates and requires, during its operation, to be carried by hand either continuously or intermittently; and (ii) a tool which vibrates and, in its operation, requires to be moved either continuously or intermittently and that motion is provided by the energy of the operator. I exclude self-propelled machines. As I have pointed out, a buffing machine is self-supporting and is not mounted on some support. It is therefore clearly different from the fixed tools in *CI/160/94* and *CI/156/94* [both of which concerned fixed sewing machines]. For instance, a portable electric drill vibrates and, when in use, it has to be moved and firmly grasped by hand, and the operator, when drilling, is required to exert considerable pressure. In the same way, an industrial buffing machines vibrates, and, when in use, it has to be moved by the operator backwards and forwards, manoeuvred and guided, requiring a firm grasp, and the firmer the grasp, the more keenly will any vibration be transmitted. I have, therefore, come to the conclusion that an industrial buffing machine is within the definition of a hand-held vibrating tool . . ." (para.14).

He was assisted in so concluding by the fact that when the opportunity was taken to effect a legislative modification to the prescription to vitiate the effect of *CI/227/94* (below), no step was taken to remedy any dissatisfaction with Commissioner Goodman's decisions on hand-held, thus indicating acceptance of the effect of those decisions (*ibid.*). The previous form of prescription was wider covering use of "hand-held vibrating tools". "Vibrating tool" was held to mean nothing more than a tool which vibrates, so that any hand-held tool (powered or not) fell within the description (*CI/227/94*, para.4). So in *CI/227/94*, it covered a hammer and punch used for making marks on metal. There was no need for an independent vibration source within the tool (*CI/227/94; CI/136/95*). On the prescription as then worded, as the Court of Appeal put it in *Janicki v Secretary of State for Social Security* [2001] I.C.R.1220 (reported in *R(I) 1/01*), if the tool vibrates because of necessary contact with something else (in that case the sewing machine on which the heavy cutters held by the claimant had to rest to be used), the source of the vibration was immaterial. The occupational description was, however, altered to its current wording—"hand-held powered tools whose internal parts vibrate so as to transmit that vibration to the hand, but excluding those that are solely powered by hand—with effect from March 24, 1996. That new wording does not affect the cases on "hand-held". But it precludes the application of *CI/227/94*, *CI/136/95* and *Janicki* if the period under consideration falls after that date, unless the claimant's case is covered by the transitional provision noted at the end of this note, preserving for certain cases the old wording of the prescription. Similarly precluded by the new wording is the approach taken by Commissioner Howell in *CI/474/95* that the requirements are satisfied even when the source of the vibration is the force applied by the operator rather than the mechanism of the tool. Under the former wording, Commissioner Hoolahan held in *R(I) 8/98* that a bus steering wheel, which transmitted vibrations to the driver was not within the prescription: the wheel did not contain within itself "a source of vibration—it merely transmits vibration from something else" (para.16). The change in wording (from merely "hand-held vibrating tools" to "hand-held powered tools whose internal parts vibrate so as to transmit that vibration to the hand") further prevents such a claim succeeding.

A challenge to the validity of the prescription of disease A12 (carpal tunnel syndrome), because it is prescribed only for those whose occupations involved the use of certain tools, was rejected in *CI/5009/97*.

Paragraph (b) was added to the list of occupations with effect from April 6, 2007 on the recommendation of the IIAC, because its review found evidence "that flexing and extending of the wrist, when repeated over much of the work time, was associated with a more than doubling of risk of CTS" (see *Work Related Upper Limb Disorders*, Cm. 6868 (July 2006), para.46). Appendix 2 to that report contains a useful diagram of the action involved. That Appendix is reproduced in *FR v SSWP* [2008] UKUT 12 (AAC). In that decision, Judge Jacobs stressed that it is the nature and direction of the movement involved in dorsiflexion and palmar flexion, rather than the degree of movement, which are important. In that case and in *CI/1961/2008*, it was stressed that the IIAC Report is an appropriate aid to applying C23(b), even though the terms of prescription in it are not exactly the same as that recommended by the IIAC.

A13 (Osteoarthritis of the hip)

The prescription of osteoarthritis of the hip in relation to work in agriculture as a farmer or farm worker for a period of, or periods which amount in aggregate to, 10 years or more, was added to the Schedule with effect from March 14, 2005. Its prescription is subject to a transitional provision in reg.3 of the inserting regulations— Social Security (Industrial Injuries) (Prescribed Diseases) Amendment Regulations 2005 (SI 2005/324)—set out at the end of this section of the book: the prescription does not apply to a period of assessment relating to a claim made before March 14, 2005. The prescription implements the recommendations of IIAC as set out in their report on Osteoarthritis of the Hip (Cm 5977). The disease is common in the population at large, but the IIAC considered that the evidence now made it clear that in farmers and farmworkers there is a raised incidence of the disease sufficiently high that a clear association can be made between that occupation and the condition, even though there is still some uncertainty about exactly what aspect of farming is responsible. The Council thought that it would be most appropriate to prescribe for farmers whose work can be classified according to the Office of National Statistics Standard Occupational Classification 2000, "5111 farmers", "9111 farm workers" or "1211 farm managers", and who have been employed as employed earners in this capacity for 10 years or longer in aggregate. This definition was more restrictive than ones used in the field research, but the Council believed that it provided a workable definition of a level exposure for which the epidemiological evidence of a doubling (or greater) of risk is robust.

10.153

On accepted authority in prescribed diseases requiring work for particular periods, the focus should be on the work done rather than the contractual obligation to do it (*R(I) 2/79* and *CI/16/91*—see commentary to regs. 2 and 25, above).

On "agriculture", see *CI/56/95*, noted in the commentary to B6, below.

IV. Prescribed Diseases Category: B. Conditions due to biological agents

10.154   The IIAC in their report on Conditions due to Biological Agents (Cm 5997) in November 1993 updated the references for each prescribed disease, and reviewed the prescribed occupations in each case.

B1 (Anthrax)

10.155   These new terms of prescription were added to the Schedule with effect from March 14, 2005, subject to a transitional provision in reg.3 of the inserting regulations— Social Security (Industrial Injuries) (Prescribed Diseases) Amendment Regulations 2005 (SI 2005/324)—set out at the end of this section of the book: the prescription does not apply to a period of assessment relating to a claim made before March 14, 2005. The prescription implements the recommendations of IIAC as set out in their report on Conditions due to Biological Agents (Cm 5997). The IIAC stated

"Anthrax is a zoonotic disease (i.e. a disease passed from animals to humans) caused by the bacterium *Bacillus anthracis*. Generally, humans contract anthrax by exposure to infected herbivorous animals or their products. Bacterial spores enter the human body via the skin (cutaneous anthrax), the lungs (pulmonary anthrax) or the gut (intestinal anthrax). Cutaneous anthrax is the most common type of infection in humans, accounting for approximately 95% of all cases. It is characterised by an itchy skin lesion (or papule) which becomes a vesicle. This vesicle bursts forming a characteristic eschar (sloughed off dead tissue), with surrounding oedema and lymphangitis. This form of anthrax is readily treatable with antibiotics, but if left untreated can lead to death in a small proportion of cases. Pulmonary anthrax accounts for around 5% of human infections and has a high fatality rate. It is characterised by flu-like symptoms, which may lead to respiratory failure and death in a few days. Intestinal anthrax is rare, and is usually found outside the UK where infected meat may be eaten. Septicaemia and meningitis are possible complications of all forms of anthrax infection. Anthrax is common in livestock from parts of Turkey, Sudan and Pakistan" (para.44).

The IIAC recommended clarification of the prescription to go beyond exposure to infected herbivorous animals or their products (the previous prescription). The report acknowledged the potential for infection in other circumstances therefore the prescription has been widened to include any work involving contact with anthrax spores (see paras 45–48).

B3 (infection by leptospira)

10.156   This is prescribed in respect of rather wider occupations than may at first appear, with successful claims both by a building site labourer (*R(I) 20/52*) and by a surface worker at a mine (*R(I)531/92*) based on the fact that their work environment was "infested" with rats.

B4 (Ankylostomiasis)

10.157   These wider terms of prescription were added to the Schedule with effect from March 14, 2005, subject to a transitional provision in reg.3 of the inserting regulations—Social Security (Industrial Injuries) (Prescribed Diseases) Amendment Regulations 2005 (SI 2005/324)—set out at the end of this section of the book: the prescription does not apply to a period of assessment relating to a claim made before March 14, 2005. The prescription implements the recommendations of IIAC as set out in their report on Conditions due to Biological Agents (Cm 5997). The IIAC recommended alteration of the prescription to reflect the fact that contact with sources of ankylostomiasis is not restricted to work in mines (paras 62–67).

B5 (tuberculosis)

10.158

This is prescribed for a very wide range of occupations in which contact with a source of infection is involved. It was considered recently by Commissioner Williams in *CI/3625/2003*. There would seem to have been no other cases since 1960 and the pre-1960 cases were of limited assistance given changes in the terms of prescription. In *CI/3625/2003*, Commissioner Williams found that

> "Mr W fails to make out the case that his employment is prescribed in relation to bovine tuberculosis, prescribed disease B5. I do so without looking too closely at the details of the school and its catchment area, or his job as a senior teacher at that school. I do so because he puts the risk down to contact not with infected children or their families or home settings, but with a professional colleague who was not known to be infected, and not to contact with infected cows or badgers or individuals but with a tick on that colleague's clothing. The tribunal found that Mr W had not satisfied it that the infection from which he was suffering was tick-borne. In other words, he failed to establish a source of infection. There is sound evidence for that and I accept that finding. That answers the question. But even if—hypothetically—I found that Mr W was right and X did carry an infectious tick, and that tick had bitten Mr W and caused bovine tuberculosis, what was it about his *employment* that put him at this risk? Why was he at risk as a teacher from that tick, in a different way to any member of X's family, friends or any other contacts or, in the words of section 108, otherwise than 'as a risk common to all persons'. I find no such additional risk. On either analysis, Mr W fails to establish that his occupation was prescribed for prescribed disease B5 in the bovine form." (para.22).

B6 (extrinsic allergic alveolitis, including farmer's lung)

10.159

This was considered by Commissioner Angus in *CI/56/95*. There the claimant was an electrician by trade, whose work was said to have brought him into contact with the agents which cause the disease (e.g. he had had to clean mouldy material out of machinery in the food processing industry before repairing it and had spent some considerable time working on the wiring and cabling of a chicken farm among feathers and chicken muck and had had to handle the birds). The Commissioner, remitting the matter to another SSAT, stated that the new tribunal should first find as a fact whether the claimant had been exposed to "moulds or fungal spores or heterologous proteins". If he had, the SSAT should consider whether such exposure was by reason of his employed earner's employment in any of the activities set out in heads (a)–(d) of the prescription. These are not a list of particular trades. Rather the decision on whether the claimant's occupation (here electrician) comes within those specified is decided by reference to the work done bringing him into contact with the relevant agents. One looks to

> "whether he has been exposed to the specified agents by reason of his participation in one of the specified activities . . . in so far as that activity or those activities fell within the scope of his employed earner's employment as indicated for him by his employer" (para.12).

As to the meaning of "agriculture" in head (a), the Commissioner deployed a dictionary definition: "the science or occupation of cultivating land and rearing crops and livestock; farming" (Collins English Dictionary, cited in para.15). Where the claimant's employer was not a farmer then:

> "in order to establish whether or not the [claimant] is employed in agriculture it would be necessary to enquire into the nature and organisation of the employer's

business and the nature and pattern of the duties assigned to the claimant. Just as an electrician could be regarded as employed in agriculture because he was employed full-time by a farmer, a company of electrical engineers who specialised in servicing agricultural customers might be said to be engaged in agriculture. Alternatively a firm which had no particular tendency to specialise in agricultural customers might have assigned an employee to duties so involved with farming that the employee could be said to be engaged in agriculture" (para.15).

As to (b), the tribunal would have to be satisfied that as regards any handling of mouldy vegetable matter when cleaning out machines, the matter in question was "in storage". As to (c), the question would be did his employers expect him to "handle" birds (paras 18, 19).

Paragraph (e) was added with effect from April 6, 2007, subject to a transitional provision set out in the amending regulations at the end of this part of the book. The IIAC recommended this. It considered there was little doubt that exposure to aerosolised mists of metal working fluid has been the cause of occupational occurrences of EAA (see *Extrinsic Allergic Alveolitis*, Cm 6867 (July 2006), para.39).

B8A and B8B (viral hepatitis)

10.160   Prescription of viral hepatitis was originally rather restricted but, after modifications to the Schedule in 1983, is now prescribed for occupations involving any contact with human blood or a source of the disease. The current terms of prescription were substituted with effect from March 14, 2005, subject to a transitional provision in reg.3 of the inserting regulations—Social Security (Industrial Injuries) (Prescribed Diseases) Amendment Regulations 2005 (SI 2005/324)—set out at the end of this section of the book: the prescription does not apply to a period of assessment relating to a claim made before March 14, 2005. The prescription implements the recommendations of IIAC as set out in their report on Conditions due to Biological Agents (Cm 5997) (see paras 88–120). In particular, the Council reviewed hepatitis A infection in sewage workers and found evidence that the risk is more than doubled in those working with raw sewage, although overall sewage workers do not have a significantly increased risk of disease. In relation to hepatitis C, the Council thought some subgroups of health workers to be at elevated risk. Furthermore, HCV infection is the most commonly reported occupationally acquired blood-borne disease in England and Wales. In view of the uncertainty about the risk in some subgroups of health workers and the similar mode of transmission to hepatitis B, the Council thought that prescription of both hepatitis B and C should continue, with wording similar to the present prescription, for all those in contact with blood or body fluids.

B14 (Lyme disease)

10.161   This was prescribed from March 14, 2005, subject to a transitional provision in reg.3 of the inserting regulations—Social Security (Industrial Injuries) (Prescribed Diseases) Amendment Regulations 2005 (SI 2005/324)—set out at the end of this section of the book: the prescription does not apply to a period of assessment relating to a claim made before March 14, 2005. The prescription implements the recommendations of IIAC as set out in their report on Conditions due to Biological Agents (Cm 5997) (see paras 195–201). Since Lyme disease (a tick borne disease with musculo-skeletal, cardiac and neurological effects) was first considered by IIAC in 1990, enough evidence of occupational risk had accumulated to warrant prescription. The high incidence of the disease in deer hunters and forestry workers suggested a clear occupational risk in respect of exposure to *Borrelia*.

B15 (Anaphylaxis)

10.162   This was prescribed from March 14, 2005, subject to a transitional provision in reg.3 of the inserting regulations—Social Security (Industrial Injuries) (Prescribed Diseases) Amendment Regulations 2005 (SI 2005/324)—set out at the end of this section of the book: the prescription does not apply to a period of assessment relating to a claim made before March 14, 2005. The prescription implements the recommendations of IIAC as set out in their report on Conditions due to Biological Agents (Cm 5997) (see paras 261–271). "Anaphylaxis is a life-threatening IgE-mediated allergic Type I hypersensitivity reaction due to contact of a sensitised individual with an allergenic protein. Common allergens which can provoke anaphylactic shock include drugs, insect stings, latex and certain food ingredients, such as nuts. Initial exposure to the allergen induces specific IgE anti-body. Subsequent contact can provoke an anaphylactic reaction. An anaphylactic-like (anaphylactoid) reaction can occur during first exposure to certain drugs; but these are a manifestation of a toxic, rather than an allergic, reaction to the drug. Anaphylactic shock is due to a sudden massive release of histamine and other mediators from basophils into the bloodstream. These trigger constriction of the airways and swelling of tissue (angioedema), resulting indifficulty breathing, and dilatation of blood vessels, leading to shock and pulmonary oedema. Other symptoms of anaphylaxis include urticarial skin rash and gastrointestinal reactions, such as vomiting, abdominal cramps and diarrhoea. The onset of anaphylaxis can be very rapid, with symptoms occurring within minutes of contact with the allergen" (*ibid.*, para.261). A precipitating exposure at work could ground a claim through the accident route where loss of faculty lasting beyond 90 days, rather than death, ensued. The Committee recommended prescription of anaphylaxis and its sequelae that result from allergy to natural rubber latex in healthcare workers.

V. Prescribed Diseases: Category C: Conditions due to chemical agents

The prescriptions underwent very substantial revision from March 17, 2003, subject to a transitional provision in reg.6 of the amending regulations: the Social Security (Industrial injuries) (Prescribed Diseases) Amendment Regulations 2003 (SI 2003/270). The text of the transitional provision is reproduced later in this volume. For the text of the prescriptions prior to March 17, 2003, and annotations thereto, see the 2002 edition of this volume.

10.163

Prescribed Diseases C8, C9, C10, C11, C14, C15 and C28 were removed. New formulations were substituted for all or part of Diseases C1, C2, C4, C5A and 5B, C6, C7, C12, C13, C16–27, C29 and C30. The changes largely follow the recommendations of the IIAC in its report reviewing the prescription of conditions due to chemical agents (*Cm. 5395 (February 2002)*). These changes were recommended reflecting the fact that many of the "C" diseases were prescribed in the early days of the scheme and there was need to reflect advances in scientific knowledge as well as to bring the wording and terminology used up to date. The removals from the list were based on the view that the very few claims that have been made for these diseases in the past could have been dealt with more appropriately under the accident provisions of the industrial injuries scheme.

Although the chemical agents in C23(c) are primarily encountered in the manufacture of dyes, that does not mean that they cannot be encountered elsewhere. In *SSWP v JS* [2008] UKUT 35 (AAC), Judge Williams upheld a tribunal decision that a claimant who had worked in a coke works was entitled on the evidence to conclude that he had probably suffered relevant exposure.

A new C24 was substituted, and C24A added, with effect from April 6, 2006 (see Social Security (Industrial Injuries) (Prescribed Diseases) Amendment Regulations 2006 (SI 2006/586), reg.3). They cannot, however be applied to a period of assessment prior to that date (*ibid.*, reg.4)). These changes implement the recommendations of the IIAC as set out in their report *Vinyl Chloride Monomer-Related Diseases* (Cm 6645). As regards C24A, the totality of the evidence led the IIAC to "conclude that an association exists between VCM exposure and Raynaud's phenomenon in the absence of osteolysis in the digits, and also between VCM exposure and scleroderma in the absence of osteolysis in the digits". That evidence indicated that the increased frequency of these conditions enabled attribution to exposure to VCM in the individual case. Consistent evidence showed that the inhalation of VCM in PVC production workers causes a characteristic clinical triad of osteolysis of the terminal phalanges, scleroderma and Raynaud's phenomenon, but that not all three are invariably present together (see para.16). As regards reformulating C24, the IIAC considered the term acro-osteolysis too confusing in that it refers both to a specific condition and to a syndrome the features of which may vary from one person to another. The term should be dropped. Osteolysis of the finger-tips, Raynaud's phenomenon and scleroderma should each be prescribed independently. The IIAC were not prepared to extend coverage to liver tumours other than angiosarcoma. Nor could exposure to PVC itself warrant prescription (para.17).

Prior to April 6, 2006, C 24 prescribed separately: angiosarcoma of the liver; liver fibrosis; and acro-osteolysis. The prescription of acrosteloysis, however, required that it be characterised by (i) lytic destruction of the terminal phalanges, (ii) in Raynaud's phenomenon, the exaggerated vasomotor response to cold causing intense blanching of the digits, and (iii) sclerodermatous thickening of the skin. It was thus open to a strict, literal interpretation that all three aspects (i)–(iii) had to be present. In *CI/1884/2004*, taking on board the IIAC report that had led to that 2003 prescription, Commissioner Williams specifically rejected this interpretation, holding instead that it "must be read disjunctively. The test is met if an individual can show that he (or she) has worked in a prescribed occupation and has thereafter evidenced any one of the three physical conditions listed" (para.38).

VI. Prescribed Diseases: Category D: Miscellaneous conditions

10.164   D1 (pneumoconiosis) has already been considered in the note to reg.2, above, in respect of its prescription for all occupations involving exposure to dust. There is also a separate section of the Schedule which lists specific occupations for which the disease is prescribed. The diagnosis of pneumoconiosis (prescribed disease D1) was considered in *R(I) 1/96* where the Commissioner held that to say that minimal coalworker's pneumoconiosis "is insufficient radiologically for him to be eligible for industrial injuries benefit" is wrong in law. Pneumoconiosis is defined in s.122(1) of the SSCBA 1992 as "fibrosis of the lungs due to silica dust, asbestos dust or other dust, and includes the condition of the lungs known as dust-reticulation". Either the claimant has fibrosis due to dust or he does not. The International Labour Organisation's "International Classification of Radiographs of Pneumoconiosis" is a diagnostic aid but the radiological category does not determine the diagnosis.

In *R(I) 7/98*, the Commissioner held that the definition of pneumoconiosis in s.122 of the SSCBA 1992, "fibrosis of the lungs due to silica dust, asbestos dust, or other dust, and includes the condition of the lungs known as dust-reticulation", carried the implication that dust-reticulation was to be regarded as a form of fibrosis of the lungs whether or not it would otherwise always be medically described as constituting such fibrosis. The statutory definition dates back to 1943. In *R(I)3/03*, a Tribunal of Commissioners considered its interpretation and application in the light of developments in medical understanding and terminology, especially as they affect post mortem evidence of the effects of coal dust. Those changes meant that the medical evidence often does not reflect this statutory language. The key issue, however, was not changes in terminology, but whether the evidence showed that the statutory definition was met. As regards coal dust, tribunals cannot simply rely on "coal workers pneumoconiosis" in post mortem reports or death certificates as conclusive of the question: is the statutory definition met? This is because experts differ in their use of the term and whether it necessarily includes fibrosis. Moreover, such a statement represents only one doctor's opinion, which has to be assessed in the light of the evidence as a whole. In particular, where the phrase is found in a post mortem report, it represents only a provisional conclusion that might well be changed if microscopic examination reveals contrary findings.

D2 (byssinosis) is prescribed for cotton and flax workers. It is neither necessary that the claimant should be employed exclusively in the room within the scheduled description *(R(I) 17/56)*, nor that fine distinctions should be drawn in determining the meaning of "room" *(R(I) 26/58)*.

D3 (diffuse mesothelioma) and D4 (inflammation or ulceration of nose etc.) are both prescribed, in part, in respect of occupations involving exposure to dust. The meaning of "dust" was considered by the Commissioner in *R(I) 1/85* where he defined it as earth or other solid matter in minute particles so as to be easily raised and carried by the wind. The occupational prescription in D3 was altered to its present wording with effect from April 9, 1997. In *CI/13232/1996*, Commissioner Rowland considered the meaning of the earlier wording (see p. 938 of Bonner, Hooker and White, *Non-Means Tested Benefits: The Legislation* (1996)) and in particular the prescription "any occupation involving . . . (d) substantial exposure to the dust arising from any of the foregoing operations". The case concerned a claimant employed as a cooper on premises adjacent to those of another firm which handled asbestos whose extraction/ventilation equipment spewed out asbestos dust over his workplace. The Commissioner held that the Prescribed Diseases Regulations focus on the nature of the claimant's employment rather than on the nature of the employer's business, so that here the claimant had only to show that he was employed in an occupation involving something listed in col.2 of the Schedule. Commissioner Rowland stated:

> "It is true that paragraph (a), (b) and (c) are unlikely to be satisfied in the case of any claimant who is not working for an employer whose business necessarily involves work with asbestos and the overwhelming majority of cases to which paragraph (d) applies will also arise where the nature of the employer's business involves working with asbestos. However there is nothing in the language of the Regulations so to restrict it. I can see no reason for distinguishing between the present claimant and, say, a clerical worker employed in the neighbouring firm of asbestos processors. Neither was engaged in a type of work which could normally involve exposure to asbestos dust but in both cases the particular location of their employment caused them to be exposed to dust. It is difficult to see any practical reason or any reason of principle why the clerical worker should be entitled to disablement benefit and the present claimant should not." (para.8)

The revision of the prescription's wording to the broader formulation in the current text essentially endorses the validity of that approach, but clearly a claimant whose employment exposes him to asbestos, asbestos dust or any admixture of asbestos must show that such exposure was at a level above that commonly found in the environment at large.

D4 (allergic rhinitis), has, since March 24, 1996, attracted the presumption that a prescribed disease is due to the nature of a scheduled occupation, provided that the claimant was employed in that occupation at the date of onset of the disease, or at any time within one month preceding the date of onset. See, on the consequences of this, *R(I) 7/02*, noted in the commentary to reg.3, above.

D4(x)—allergic rhinitis due to exposure to products made with natural rubber latex- was added from March 14, 2005, subject to a transitional provision in reg.3 of the inserting regulations—Social Security (Industrial Injuries) (Prescribed Diseases) Amendment Regulations 2005 (SI 2005/324)—set out at the end of this section of the book: the prescription does not apply to a period of assessment relating to a claim made before March 14, 2005. The prescription implements the recommendations of IIAC as set out in their report on Conditions due to Biological Agents (Cm 5997) (see paras 252–260 on latex allergy). It is prevalent in healthcare workers, especially laboratory workers, nurses and physicians, but it should be noted that the terms of the prescription are in no way confined to those groups. Indeed the IIAC noted that individuals may encounter latex in many circumstances, including as part of their work: medical and surgical procedures; dentistry; laboratory work; latex processing and product manufacture; food preparation; dishwashing and cleaning; use and manufacture of condoms; use and manufacture of actors' masks; use and manufacture of sports equipment; use and manufacture of balloons and rubber bands, such as during teaching and nursery school work; and scene of the crime work (para.253).

D5 (non-infective dermatitis) was a very common source of claims for injury benefit but it is, perhaps, less likely to give rise to claims for disablement benefit. No presumption is made in favour of the claimant. It is for him to prove that the disease was due to the nature of his employment, and that his occupation falls within the terms of the Schedule (see note to reg.4, above).

D6(a) was considered by Commissioner Goodman in *R(I) 4/98*. He concluded that

"it is not legitimate to extend to the claimant (who in the course of his work as a painter came into contact for many years with quantities of respirable dust) the protection of sub-paragraph (a) of paragraph D6 because the wording of it does not justify it. I accept as correct in law Miss Lieven's submission that subparagraph (a) covers only buildings where, as part of the nature of the building, the manufacture or repair [of wooden goods] is carried out e.g. a factory or warehouse. It could not be said that the dwelling-houses and Royal Ordnance Factory buildings in or near which the claimant worked came within such a description . . . The intention of sub-paragraph (a), as is evidenced by the above cited Industrial Injuries Advisory Council's Report, was merely to extend the existing prescription for work on the manufacture or repair of wooden furniture to wooden goods generally. No further extension to all those who have in their work inhaled wood dust was intended nor is, in my view, shown by sub-paragraph (a)." (para.13).

D7 prescribes asthma in relation to a number of occupations. In D7(f) the words "used for the purpose of research or education or in laboratories" set the environment for the whole of the sub-para., so the claimant's appeal in *CI/383/92* (which is not to be reported) was disallowed because he had only worked with prawns (regarded as animals, being anthropods) in the food processing industry (see para.7).

Sub-paragraphs (o)–(x) of D7 (occupational asthma) were added with effect from September 26, 1991 (see SI 1991/1938). In *CI/175/90*. Commissioner Hallett considered whether the claimant could bring himself within sub-para.(j) because of his exposure to paper dust in the printing industry. Applying *CI/308/1989* (reported as *R(I) 2/92*), he concluded that the term "wood dust" had to be construed as an ordinary expression in the English language, that paper, while derived from wood was a different substance, so that the majority of the SSAT had been correct in regarding paper dust as different from wood dust. Nor did the claimant's exposure to printing mist help him, since the evidence showed that the inks forming the mist did not contain isocyanates, so that he did not fall within sub-para.(a) either. His claim failed. Cigarette smoke, while an irritant for those with asthma, appears not to be regarded by medical opinion as a sensitising agent within para.(x), any other "sensitising agent" (*CI/73/94*). One view is that sensitising agent has to read *ejusdem generis* (of a kind or nature) with the agents listed in paras (a)–(w) (*CI/73/94*). Another is that there is no such restriction on the term: para.(x) catches any agent so long as it is sensitising (*CI/4987/1995*). In any case the first question should be whether the identified agent relied on by the claimant is a "sensitising agent" (*CI/2543/2002*). He set out a "triage" approach to help cope with the difficulties of deciding whether something is a "sensitising agent", an approach agreed with and adopted by Commissioner Williams in *CI/564/2005*: there are agents known to be sensitising agents, agents known not to be sensitising agents, and cases where it is not known whether the agent is a sensitising agent. In *CI/3729/2005* Deputy Commissioner White found this a helpful approach. He decided that cardboard dust was not a sensitising agent. He also held (applying *R(I)2/92*) that it was not the same as wood dust and could not fall within D7(j).

In *R(I) 8/02*, Commissioner Howell considered the case of a bus driver claiming that the diesel fumes, dust and particulates he had inhaled during his work constituted "any other sensitising agent". The Commissioner stated:

"Taking into account the terms of the report of the Industrial Injuries Advisory Council dated August 28, 1990 which led to these extra provisions being introduced (Cm 1244, October 1990) from which it is quite clear that the expression 'sensitising agent' when used medically in this context means a chemical agent which actually *causes* a person to develop an asthmatic condition when inhaled at work, the tribunal were in my judgment quite correct in directing themselves that the question they had to consider on the evidence in the claimant's case was whether it had been shown that the diesel fumes, particulates, dust and so forth he inhaled while driving his bus had been the actual cause of his asthmatic condition, rather than merely irritating his chest and making it worse.

As the tribunal correctly recorded, the evidence before them on this issue consisted first of medical advice obtained by the department that diesel exhaust and other vehicle fumes and dust of the kind to which a person is exposed in heavy traffic, while they would certainly act as irritants, would not operate as 'sensitisors' or causative agents for occupational asthma in the way required by the regulations making this a prescribed disease. In addition there were medical reports by three separate doctors on behalf of the claimant himself at pages 35 to 41 which as the tribunal correctly recorded in their statement of reasons at page 46 did not at any point report or state that his asthma had actually been *caused* by exposure to diesel fumes, though they all agreed that it was made much worse by his continuing to work as a bus driver and that it would be a great deal better for him to move to another job" (paras 4, 5).

It would appear that asbestos is not a sensitising agent for purposes of D7 (*CI/2393/02*, paras 7, 8).

There is expert evidence that the chromium element in cement is a sensitising agent (*CI/564/2005*).

Latex constitutes "any other sensitising agent" and falls within D7(x) (*CI/3565/2004*). This is important as regards cases occurring before the specific prescription of occupational asthma due to exposure to products made with natural rubber latex in D7(wa).

D7(wa)—occupational asthma due to exposure to products made with natural rubber latex—was added from March 14, 2005, subject to a transitional provision in reg.3 of the inserting regulations—Social Security (Industrial Injuries) (Prescribed Diseases) Amendment Regulations 2005 (SI 2005/324)—set out at the end of this section of the book: the prescription does not apply to a period of assessment relating to a claim made before March 14, 2005. The prescription implements the recommendations of IIAC as set out in their report on Conditions due to Biological Agents (Cm 5997) (see paras 252–260 on latex allergy). It is prevalent in healthcare workers, especially laboratory workers, nurses and physicians, but it should be noted that the terms of the prescription are in no way confined to those groups. Indeed the IIAC noted that Individuals may encounter latex in many circumstances, including as part of their work: medical and surgical procedures; dentistry; laboratory work; latex processing and product manufacture; food preparation; dishwashing and cleaning; use and manufacture of condoms; use and manufacture of actors' masks; use and manufacture of sports equipment; use and manufacture of balloons and rubber bands, such as during teaching and nursery school work; and scene of the crime work (para.253).

A new D8 was substituted, and D8A added, with effect from April 6, 2006 (see Social Security (Industrial Injuries) (Prescribed Diseases) Amendment Regulations 2006 (SI 2006/586), reg.3). This implements IIAC recommendations in their report *Asbestos-Related Diseases* (Cm 6553). The Council recommended removing from D8 the requirement for the presence of diffuse pleural thickening because recent evidence indicates its unreliability as a marker of asbestos exposure (para.65). D8A (Primary carcinoma of the lung—with no requisite element of asbestosis) was added because the IIAC's literature review found evidence of a greater than doubled risk for lung cancer in the following groups of workers who have experienced substantial occupational asbestos exposure: workers in asbestos textile manufacture; asbestos sprayers; asbestos insulation workers, including those applying and removing asbestos-containing materials in shipbuilding and gas mask manufacturers (para.62). The requirement of exposure for the requisite number of years prior to 1975 reflects the IIAC view that the risk fell after the introduction of the 1969 Asbestos Regulations (para.63). The reformulation cannot apply to any period of assessment prior to April 6, 2006 (reg.4 of the Amendment Regs as further amended by SI 2006/769, reg.2).

The reformulation of disease D9 from the same date implements the IIAC recommendation that the requirement for measurements of pleural thickening be replaced by one involving costophrenic angle on plain chest radiographs (paras 70, 72(a)). The reformulation cannot apply to any period of assessment prior to April 6, 2006 (reg.4 of the Amendment Regs).

As regards Disease D12 (chronic bronchitis, emphysema or both), Commissioner Angus notes in *CI/126/2002* that in some circumstances a spirometric test can be inaccurate. He stated:

"In assessing the evidential value of the subsequent spirometry it would have been necessary to take into account whether or not the claimant's lung function might have been enhanced by medication. In assessing disablement it is legitimate to base the assessment on what the claimant can do when he has taken medication but for the purposes of diagnosis it is the unassisted function which is relevant" (para.16).

Commissioner Williams followed this in *CI/2683/2004*. He stressed that the regulations did not require a spirometry test—the diagnosis question must be considered in the light of all relevant evidence, including any such test—and that the focus must be on the claimant's condition as at the date of the original decision. He considered that

"tribunals should have in mind that individuals may or may not have been given guidance and may or may not have acted on it. They should therefore, to ensure fairness, directly check any necessary facts about pre-test medication if they conduct a test. They may also need to check that the medical adviser took appropriate note and account of any relevant medicaments when performing the original test. They should, at least in marginal cases, consider the possible effects of medication when forming a view about the conclusions to be drawn from the "accompanying evidence" (para.29).

Disease D12 is subject to a transitional provision in reg.9 of the Social Security (Industrial Injuries) (Prescribed Diseases) Amendment (No. 2) Regulations (SI 1993/1985) below. Furthermore, the amendment numbered "15" on the appropriate mean value and the prediction formula is subject to a transitional provision in reg.7(2) of the Social Security (Industrial Injuries) (Prescribed Diseases) Amendment Regulations 2000 (SI 2000/1588), reproduced later in this volume.

The prescription of D12 with effect from September 13, 1993 is not retrospective so as to enable payment of disablement benefit, for a period prior to prescription, to a claimant whose date of onset of the disease precedes that date and continues to suffer from it (see *R(I) 4/96*, noted in the notes to reg.6, above).

In *CI/1160/2004*, Commissioner Angus held

"that paragraph D12 of Schedule 1 to the Regulations is not irrational. On the matter of its application to smokers, as Mr Heath said, the fact that smokers who suffer from coal dust retention might be compensated for having contracted a coal dust related disease which they might have contracted in any case does not exclude any non-smoker with coal dust related emphysema or bronchitis from compensation under the legislation. As regards the use of the 1 litre drop in lung function as the prescribed decisive indicator of PD D12, Dr. A's opinion that it can result in the disease not being diagnosed in short men who have a disabling reduction in lung function due to the retention of coal dust has to be respected. It is an opinion which may well be shared by other chest physicians: but the D12 prescription is based on the equally respectable opinions of the members of the Industrial Injuries Advisory Council and the Secretary of State cannot be accused of irrationality in relying upon their opinion to devise the prescription" (para.26).

He also rejected the view that it was legally challengeable as discriminatory against short men.

The amendments effected from March 24, 1996 to prescribed diseases A12 (an alteration of terms), D4 (ability to benefit from the reg.4 presumption) and D5 (an alteration of its terms to reflect the newly prescribed disease C30) are subject to a transitional provision in reg.7 of the Social Security (Industrial Injuries and Diseases) (Miscellaneous Amendments) Regulations 1996 (SI 1996/425), below.

A new prescribed disease D13 (primary carcinoma of the nasopharynx) (nasopharyngeal cancer) was added with effect from April 7, 2008 by reg.2 of the Social Security (Industrial Injuries) (Prescribed Diseases) Amendment Regulations 2008 (SI 2008/14). The prescription, in respect of a number of occupations involving working with wood or wood products, reflects the recommendations of the Industrial Injuries Advisory Council in its report *Nasopharyngeal cancer due to exposure to wood dust* Cm 7162 (July 2007). Those suffering from this rare disease must have worked in the relevant occupations for a period or periods of at least 10 years in the aggregate. A list (not necessarily exhaustive) of the occupations at risk can be found in App.2 of the report.

SCHEDULE 2   **Regulation 11**

MODIFICATIONS OF [SECTIONS 94 TO 107 OF THE SOCIAL SECURITY
CONTRIBUTIONS AND BENEFITS ACT 1992 AND SECTIONS 8 TO 10 OF THE
SOCIAL SECURITY ADMINISTRATION ACT 1992] IN THEIR APPLICATION TO BENEFIT
AND CLAIMS TO WHICH THESE REGULATIONS APPLY

In [sections 94 to 107 of the Social Security Contributions and Benefits Act 1992 and sections 8 to 10 of the Social Security Administration Act 1992] references to accidents shall be construed as references to prescribed diseases and references to the relevant accident shall be construed as references to the relevant disease and references to the date of the relevant accident shall be construed as references to the date of onset of the relevant disease.   **10.165**

SCHEDULE 3   **Regulation 34**

ASSESSMENT OF THE EXTENT OF OCCUPATIONAL DEAFNESS

PART I

CLAIMS TO WHICH REGULATION 34(1) APPLIES

[¹*Average of hearing losses (dB) due to all causes at 1, 2 and 3 kHz frequencies*]	*Degree of disablement per cent.*
50–52 dB	20
53–57 dB	30
58–62 dB	40
63–67 dB	50
68–72 dB	60
73–77 dB	70
78–82 dB	80
83–87 dB	90
88 dB or more	100

10.166

PART II

CLAIMS TO WHICH REGULATION 34(2) APPLIES

10.167

[¹*Average of hearing losses (dB) due to all causes at 1, 2 and 3 kHz frequencies*]	*Degree of disablement per cent.*
50–53 dB	20
54–60 dB	30
61–66 dB	40
67–72 dB	50
73–79 dB	60
80–86 dB	70
87–95 dB	80
96–105 dB	90
106 dB or more	100

PART III

FORMULA FOR CALCULATING BINAURAL DISABLEMENT

10.168

$$\frac{(\text{Degree of disablement of better ear} \times 4) + \text{degree of disablement of worse ear}}{5}$$

AMENDMENT

1. Social Security (Industrial Injuries) (Prescribed Diseases) Amendment Regulations 1989 (SI 1989/1207), reg.4 (October 16, 1989).

SCHEDULE 4   **Regulation 43**

PRESCRIBED DISEASES AND RELEVANT DATES FOR THE PURPOSES OF REGULATION 43

Description of disease or injury	Relevant date
10.169 A3. Dysbarism, including decompression sickness, barotrauma and osteonecrosis.	Except in the case of a person suffering from decompression sickness employed in any occupation involving subjection to compressed or rarefied air, 3rd October 1983.
A11. Episodic blanching, occurring throughout the year, affecting the middle or proximal phalanges or in the case of a thumb the proximal phalanx, of— (a) in the case of a person with 5 fingers (including thumb) on one hand, any 3 of those fingers, or (b) in the case of person with only 4 such fingers, any 2 of those fingers, or (c) in the case of a person with less than 4 such fingers, any one of those fingers or, as the case may be, the one remaining finger (vibration white finger).	1st April 1985.
B1. Anthrax	In the case of a person employed in an occupation involving the loading and unloading or transport of animal products or residues, 3rd October 1983.

Description of disease or injury	Relevant date
B3. Infection by leptospira.	(a) In the case of a person employed in an occupation in places which are or are liable to be infested by small mammals other than rats, field mice or voles, 3rd October 1983; (b) in the case of a person employed in an occupation in any other place mentioned in the second column of paragraph B3 of Part I of Schedule 1 above, 7th January 1980.
B5. Tuberculosis.	In the case of a person employed in an occupation involving contact with a source of tuberculosis infection, not being an employment set out in the second column of paragraph 38 of Part I of Schedule 1 to the old regulations, 3rd October 1983.
B6. Extrinsic allergic alveolitis (including farmer's lung).	In the case of a person suffering from extrinsic allergic alveolitis, not being farmer's lung, employed in any occupation set out in the second column of paragraph B6 of Part I of Schedule 1 above, or in the case of a person suffering from farmer's lung, employed in any occupation involving exposure to moulds or fungal spores or heterologous proteins by reason of employment in cultivation of edible fungi or maltworking, or loading or unloading or handling in storage edible fungi or caring for or handling birds, 3rd October 1983.
B7. Infection by organisms of the genus brucella.	In the case of a person suffering from infection by organisms of the genus brucella, not being infection by Brucella abortus, or employed in an occupation set out in the second column of paragraph B7 of Part I of Schedule 1 above, not being an occupation set out in the second column of paragraph 46 of Part I of Schedule 1 to the old regulations, 3rd October 1983.
B8. Viral hepatitis.	In the case of a person employed in any occupation involving contact with human blood or human blood products, or contact with a source of viral hepatitis, 3rd December 1984.
B9. Infection by Streptococcus suis.	3rd October 1983.
[¹ B10. (a) Avian chlamydiosis.	9th August 1989.
B10. (b) Ovine chlamydiosis.	9th August 1989.
B11. Q fever.	9th August 1989.]
C3. Poisoning by phosphorus or an inorganic compound of phosphorus or poisoning due to the anti-cholinesterase or pseudo anti-cholinesterase action of organic phosphorus compounds.	In the case of a person suffering from poisoning by an inorganic compound of phosphorus or poisoning due to the pseudo anti-cholinesterase action or organic phosphorus compounds, 3rd October 1983.
C18. Poisoning by cadmium.	In the case of a person employed in an occupation involving exposure to cadmium dust, 3rd October 1983.

1329

Description of disease or injury	Relevant date
C23. Primary neoplasm (including papiloma, carcinoma-in-situ and invasive carcinoma) of the epithelial lining of the urinary tract (renal pelvis, ureter, bladder and urethra).	In the case of a person employed in an occupation involving work in a building in which methylene-bis-orthochloroaniline is produced for commercial purposes, 3rd October 1983.
C24. (a) Angiosarcoma of the liver; (b) osteolysis of the terminal phalanges of the finger; (c) non-cirrhotic portal fibrosis.	(a) In the case of a person suffering from angiosarcoma of the liver or osteolysis of the terminal phalanges of the fingers, 21st March 1977; (b) in the case of a person suffering from non-cirrhotic portal fibrosis, 3rd October 1983.
C25. Occupational vitiligo.	15th December 1980.
[²C26. Damage to the liver or kidneys due to exposure to Carbon Tetrachloride.	4th January 1988.
C27. Damage to the liver or kidneys due to exposure to Trichloromethane (Chloroform).	4th January 1988.
C28. Central nervous system dysfunction and associated gastro-intestinal disorders due to exposure to chloromethane (Methyl Chloride).	4th January 1988.
C29. Peripheral neuropathy due to exposure to n-hexane or methyl-p-butyl ketone.	4th January 1988.
D3. Diffuse mesothelioma.	In the case of a person suffering from primary neoplasm of the pericardium, 3rd October 1983.
D6. Carcinoma of the nasal cavity or associated air sinuses (nasal carcinoma).	In the case of a person employed in an occupation involving attendance for work in or about a building where wooden goods (other than wooden furniture) are manufactured or where wooden goods are repaired, 3rd October 1983.
D7. Occupational asthma.	[³ (a) In the case of a person suffering from asthma due to exposure to any of the following agents: (i) isocyanates; (ii) platinum salts; (iii) fumes or dusts arising from the manufacture, transport or use of hardening agents (including epoxy resin curing agents) based on phthalic anhydride, tetrachlorophthalic anhydride, trimellitic anhydride or triethylenetetramine; (iv) fumes arising from the use of rosin as a soldering flux; (v) proteolytic enzymes; (vi) animals or insects used for the purposes of research or education or in laboratories; (vii) dusts arising from the sowing, cultivation, harvesting, drying, handling, milling, transport or storage of barley, oats, rye,

Description of disease or injury	Relevant date
	wheat or maize, or the handling, milling, transport or storage of meal or flour made therefrom,
	29th March 1982;
	(b) In the case of a person suffering from asthma due to exposure to any of the following agents:
	(i) animals including insects and other anthropods used for the purposes of research or education or in laboratories;
	(ii) antibiotics;
	(iii) cimetidine;
	(iv) wood dust;
	(v) ispaghula;
	(vi) castor bean dust;
	(vii) ipecacuanha;
	(viii) azodicarbonamide,
	1st September 1986.]
D8. Primary carcinoma of the lung where there is accompanying evidence of one or both of the following— (a) asbestosis; (b) bilateral diffuse pleural thickening.	1st April 1985.
D9. Bilateral diffuse pleural thickening.	1st April 1985.
[⁴ D10. Lung cancer.	1st April 1987.]

AMENDMENTS

1. Social Security (Industrial Injuries) (Prescribed Diseases) Amendment Regulations 1989 (SI 1989/1207), reg.6 (August 9, 1989).

2. Social Security (Industrial Injuries) (Prescribed Diseases) Amendment (No. 2) Regulations 1987 (SI 1987/2112), reg.3 (January 4, 1988).

3. Social Security (Industrial Injuries and Adjudication) Miscellaneous Amendment Regulations 1986 (SI 1986/1374), reg.3 (September 1, 1986).

4. Social Security (Industrial Injuries) (Prescribed Diseases) Amendment Regulations 1987 (SI 1987/335), reg.2 (April 1, 1987).

SCHEDULE 5   **Regulation 44**

TRANSITIONAL PROVISIONS REGARDING DATES OF DEVELOPMENT AND DATES OF ONSET

1.—In this Schedule the "date of development" has the meaning attributed to it by regulations 5, 6, 7 and 56 of the old regulations.   **10.170**

2.—Where a claim for benefit has been made before 6th April 1983, a date of development shall be determined and regulation 16 of the old regulations shall apply as if the old regulations were still in force.

3.—Where a claim for benefit is made after 5th April 1983 and a date of onset is determined which is before 6th April 1983, regulation 16 of the old regulations shall apply as if the old regulations were still in force.

4.—Where in pursuance of a claim made before 6th April 1983 a date of development has been determined and an award of benefit has been made these regulations shall have effect in relation to that claim and any subsequent claim made by or on behalf of the same person in respect of the same disease (except where under regulation 7 the disease is treated as having been contracted afresh) as if references to the date of onset were references to that date of development.

5.—Subject to paragraph 6, where a claim for injury benefit for a day falling or a period beginning before 5th April 1983 is made after 6th April 1983 and no date of development or date of onset which can be treated as such for the purposes of that claim has already been determined, for the purposes only of determining the date on which the injury benefit period (if any) is to begin, a date of development shall be determined, so however that if it is later than 5th April 1983 no injury benefit period shall begin and injury benefit shall not be payable.

6.—There shall be no entitlement, in the following cases, to benefit for any day which is earlier than the date specified:—

(a) in the case of a person who is or has been suffering from

(i)	viral hepatitis	: 2nd February 1976
(ii)	angiosarcoma of the liver	: 21st March 1977
(iii)	osteolysis of the terminal phalanges of the fingers	: 21st March 1977
(iv)	carcinoma of the nasal cavity or associated air sinuses (nasal carcinoma)	: 8th August 1979
(v)	occupational vitiligo	: 15th December 1980
[¹ (vi)	occupational asthma arising otherwise than as described at (vii) below	: 29th March 1982;
(vii)	occupational asthma which is due to exposure to antibiotics, cimetidine, wood dust, ispaghula, castor bean dust, ipecacuanha or azodicarbonamide	: 1st September 1986;]

(b) in the case of a person who is or has been suffering from byssinosis but who has not been employed in employed earner's employment in any occupation mentioned in regulation 2(c) of the old regulations for a period or periods (whether before or after 5th July 1948) amounting in the aggregate to 5 years   : 6th April 1979;

(c) in the case of a person who is or has been suffering from infection by leptospira but neither is nor has been either incapable of work or suffering from a loss of faculty as a result of infection by—

(i) leptospira icterohaemorrhagiae in the case of a person employed in employed earner's employment in any occupation involving work in places which are, or are liable to be, infested byrats, or

(ii) leptospira canicola in the case of a person employed in employed earner's employment in any occupation involving work at dog kennels or the care or handling of dogs   : 7th January 1980.

AMENDMENT

1. Social Security (Industrial Injuries and Adjudication) Miscellaneous Amendment Regulations 1986 (SI 1986/1374), reg.2 (September 1, 1986).

10.171   *Schedule 6 omitted.*

Social Security (Industrial Injuries and Diseases) Miscellaneous Provisions Regulations 1986

(SI 1986/1561) (*as amended*)

ARRANGEMENT OF REGULATIONS

PART II

PART IV

11.   Unemployability Supplement and Reduced Earnings Allowance.
12.   *Omitted.*
13.   *Revoked.*
14.   Claims for disablement benefits made before 1st October 1986.

The Secretary of State for Social Services, in exercise of the powers set out in the Schedule below, and of all other powers enabling him in that behalf, by this instrument, which contains only provisions consequential upon section 39 of the Social Security Act 1986, makes the following regulations:

PART II

MISCELLANEOUS PROVISIONS RELATING TO INDUSTRIAL INJURIES AND DISEASES

Regular occupation for the purposes of Reduced Earnings Allowance

2.—(1) Employed earner's employment in which a claimant was engaged   **10.173**
when the relevant accident took place but which was not his regular occupation shall be treated for the purposes of [paragraph 11 of Schedule 7 of the Social Security Contributions and Benefits Act 1992] (reduced earnings allowance) as if it had been his regular occupation where the claimant, at the time the relevant accident took place, had no regular occupation but was pursuing a course of full-time education, either by attendance at a recognised educational establishment or, if the education is recognised by the Secretary of State in accordance with [section 142(2) of the Social Security Contributions and Benefits Act 1992], elsewhere.

(2) In determining for the purpose of paragraph (1) whether a person was pursuing a course of full-time education, any temporary interruption of that education not exceeding a period of 6 months, or such longer period as the Secretary of State may in any particular case determine, shall be disregarded.

GENERAL NOTE

This provision permits students and others in full-time education to establish a   **10.174**
regular occupation for the purposes of Reduced Earnings Allowance. Formerly, a vacation job would not have been regarded as a regular occupation. For commentary on SSCBA 1992, s.142(2), see above.

Regulations 3–7 omitted.   **10.175**

PART IV

TRANSITIONAL PROVISIONS

Regulations 8–10 omitted.   **10.176**

Unemployability Supplement and Reduced Earnings Allowance

10.177   **11.**—A reduced earnings allowance under [paragraph 11 of Schedule 7 of the Social Security Contributions and Benefits Act 1992] and an unemployability supplement shall not be payable for the same period.

10.178   *Regulation 12 omitted.*

10.179   *Regulation 13 revoked.*

Claims for disablement benefit made before 1st October 1986

10.180   **14.**—Where a claim for disablement benefit is made before 1st October 1986, that claim shall be determined as though—
   (a) paragraph 3(1) of Schedule 3 to the 1986 Act had not been enacted,
   (b) paragraph 3(2) had been enacted to the extent only of inserting subsection (1B) of section 57 of the 1975 Act but omitting the words "Subject to paragraph (1C)" and the words from "and where it is" to the end of the subsection.

GENERAL NOTE

10.181   This still has some effect because a claim is not finally determined until there is a final assessment of disablement. Where there has been a series of provisional assessments following a claim made before October 1, 1986, further awards of disablement benefit are made as though s.57 of the 1975 Act (now s.103 of the SSCBA 1992) had not been significantly amended. This means that a weekly disablement pension is awarded only if disablement is assessed as at least 20 per cent but that a disablement gratuity is payable if disablement is assessed at anything from 1 per cent to 19 per cent (see SSCBA 1992, Sch.7, para.9).

Social Security (Industrial Injuries) (Reduced Earnings Allowance and Transitional) Regulations 1987

(SI 1987/415) (*as amended*)

ARRANGEMENT OF REGULATIONS

PART I

GENERAL

10.182   1.   Citation, commencement and interpretation.

PART II

REDUCED EARNINGS ALLOWANCE

2.   Determination of the probable standard of remuneration.

3. Awards at the maximum rate.
4. Awards following relevant change of circumstances.

PART III

TRANSITIONAL

5. Claims before 6th April 1987.
6. Awards for special hardship made before 1st October 1986.
7. Abatement of Reduced Earnings Allowance.
8. *Omitted.*
9. Offsetting prior payment of gratuity against subsequent award.

The Secretary of State for Social Services, in exercise of the powers conferred by section 59A(10) of and Schedule 20 to the Social Security Act 1975 and sections 84(1) and 89(1) of the Social Security Act 1986, and of all other powers enabling him in that behalf, by this instrument, which is made before the end of the period of 12 months from the commencement of the enactments under which it is made, makes the following Regulations:

PART I

GENERAL

Citation, commencement and interpretation

1.—(1) These regulations may be cited as the Social Security (Industrial Injuries) (Reduced Earnings Allowance and Transitional) Regulations 1987 and shall come into force on 6th April 1987.   10.183

(2) In these regulations—

"the Act" means the [Social Security Contributions and Benefits Act 1992];

"the 1986 Act" means the Social Security Act 1986.

(3) Unless the context otherwise requires, any reference in these regulations to a numbered regulation is a reference to the regulation bearing that number in these regulations and any reference in a regulation to a numbered paragraph is a reference to the paragraph of that regulation bearing that number.

GENERAL NOTE

The reference in square brackets was added by the annotator to make the regulations more "user friendly" in the light of the consolidating legislation.   10.184

PART II

REDUCED EARNINGS ALLOWANCE

Determination of the probable standard of remuneration

2.—(1) On any award of reduced earnings allowance except the first award made in respect of a relevant accident or a disease prescribed in   10.185

accordance with [sections 108 to 110] of the Act, a person's probable standard of remuneration shall be determined in accordance with the following provisions of this regulation or, if applicable, of regulation 3.

(2) On the second award made in respect of an accident or disease, a person's probable standard of remuneration in any employment shall be determined in the same manner as on the first award.

(3) On a third or subsequent award made in respect of an accident or disease, a person's probable standard of remuneration in an employment shall be determined—

(a) if applicable, in accordance with paragraphs (4)–(8) of this regulation or with regulation 3, or

(b) otherwise in the same manner as on the first award.

(4) Where at the time of the award a person's regular occupation has ceased to exist, his probable standard of remuneration in the regular occupation shall be determined in accordance with paragraph (6).

(5) Where at the time of the award either—

(a) a person is not employed, or

(b) he is employed but the employment is not suitable in his case, and

(c) there has been no relevant change of circumstances since the last previous award,

the probable standard of remuneration in any employed earner's employment which is suitable in his case and which he is likely to be capable of following shall be determined in accordance with paragraph (6).

(6) For the purposes of paragraphs (4) and (5) a person's probable standard of remuneration shall be determined by reference to the standard determined for the purposes of the last previous award of reduced earnings allowance adjusted by a percentage equal to any percentage change in the level of relevant occupational groups.

(7) For the purposes of paragraph (6) and regulation 3(1)—

(a) the relevant occupational group is the number specified in data relating to earnings published from time to time by the Department of Employment which is the nearest to, respectively,

(i) the person's regular occupation,

(ii) any employed earner's employments which are suitable in his case and which he is likely to be capable of following; and

(b) the percentage change in the level of earnings shall be determined by reference to the movement in average gross weekly earnings of full-time employees on adult rates in the relevant occupational group where pay was not affected by absence; and

(c) a percentage change for any year shall be applied to a determination of the probable standard of remuneration on an award made for a period commencing on or after the first Wednesday in the February of the year following the year to which the change relates.

(8) For the purposes of paragraph (4), a person's regular occupation has ceased to exist where—

(a) his former employer has ceased to trade in the locality, or

(b) the work the person did at his former place of employment no longer exists or has changed to such a degree that the work amounts to a different occupation,

and there is in the person's locality no employer providing work similar to that in which he was engaged.

GENERAL NOTE

This regulation provides a mechanism for the determination of the probable standard of remuneration as required by SSCBA 1992, Sch.7, para.11(10) and (13), formerly SSA 1975, s.59A(8) and (10). Formerly, the tribunal would have to make a calculation based on information supplied to it on wage rates in individual jobs. This necessitated a great deal of research and information-gathering and this new provision provides a standard method of calculation by reference to published data relating to the earnings of relevant occupational groups.

10.186

The first award of reduced earnings allowance

The regulation does not apply to the first award when the calculation is made by reference to actual earnings in employments which would be suitable for the claimant and which he would be capable of following.

10.187

The second award

The same procedure is adopted as for the first award.

10.188

The third and subsequent awards

On the third and later awards the tribunal should first establish whether paras (4) to (8) of the regulation apply to the claimant. If not, the same procedure is adopted as for the first and second awards. Paras (4) and (5) apply the standardised calculation to the following claimants—

10.189

(a) those whose regular occupation has ceased to exist; or

(b) those who are unemployed at the time of the award, or employed in an unsuitable employment,

and in respect of whom there has been no relevant charge of circumstances since the last award.

The workings of the regulation have been briefly considered in unreported decision *CI/203/1989*. Take care to look also at regs 3 and 4, below, before applying the standard calculation set out in para.(6).

The standard calculation

Paragraph 6 requires that the standard of remuneration be determined by reference to the percentage change in the level of remuneration in relevant occupational groups, a phrase defined in para.7. That para. also directs the precise calculation of the percentage and fixes the date from which the annual standard change shall be applicable.

10.190

Awards at the maximum rate

3.—(1) Where on the second or subsequent award of reduced earnings allowance in respect of an accident or disease the award—

10.191

(a) is made at the maximum rate payable under [paragraph 11(10) of Schedule 7] of the Act, or

(b) would have been made at that rate but for paragraph 5(3) of Schedule 3 to the 1986 Act or regulation 8,

then, but subject to paragraph (2), on any award thereafter the probable standard of a person's remuneration in any employment shall be determined as being the same standard as that determined for the purpose of the last previous award of reduced earnings allowance increase by a percentage equal to any percentage increase in the level of earnings for the relevant occupational groups.

(2) This regulation does not apply where—

    (a) on an award, reduced earnings allowance would be payable at a rate below the maximum rate payable under [paragraph 11(10) of Schedule 7] of the Act otherwise than by virtue of paragraph 5(3) of Schedule 3 to the 1986 Act or regulation 8; or

    (b) there has been a relevant change in the person's circumstances since the last previous award.

Awards following relevant change of circumstances

10.192   **4.**—An award of reduced earnings allowance following a relevant change of circumstances shall be treated for the purpose of Part II of these regulations as the first such award.

GENERAL NOTE

10.193   What constitutes a relevant change of circumstances was discussed by Commissioner Walker in *CI/203/1989*. He was considering the case of a person who had been made redundant and concluded that redundancy did constitute a relevant change of circumstances. The Commissioner said,

> ". . . the phrase means no more than that if at the time of making an award there are circumstances different from those obtaining at the time of the making of the previous award, and which differences may have some bearing upon the calculation then there is a relevant change for the purposes of the regulation."

The significance of a change of circumstances is, of course, that it takes the calculation outside the ambit of reg.2 since the award will then be treated as the first award.

PART III

TRANSITIONAL

Claims before 6th April 1987

10.194   **5.**—Regulations 2 and 3 shall not apply to any award of reduced earnings allowance where the claim which resulted in that award was made before 6th April 1987.

Awards for special hardship made before 1st October 1986

10.195   **6.**—Any award made before 1st October 1986 of an increase in disablement pension under section 60 of the [Social Security Act 1975] (increase of disablement benefit for special hardship) shall be treated for the purposes of regulations 2 and 3 as an award of reduced earnings allowance.

Abatement of Reduced Earnings Allowance

10.196   **7.**—(1) For the purposes of paragraph 5(3) of Schedule 3 to the 1986 Act paragraph 5 of that Schedule shall be treated as having come into force on 6th April 1987.

(2) Paragraph 5(3) of Schedule 3 to the 1986 Act shall be modified by the substitution, in head (c), of the words "a reduced earnings allowance under section 59A" for the words "an increase under section 60" and by the substitution of the words "allowance was payable" for the words "increase was payable."

Regulation 8 omitted.   10.197

Offsetting prior payment of gratuity against subsequent award

9.—For the purpose of offsetting any amount paid by way of gratuity under   10.198
an award which is subsequently varied on appeal or revised on review, regulation 85 of the Social Security (Adjudication) Regulations 1984 shall have effect after 5th April 1987 as if made under section 53(5)(b) of the 1986 Act.

GENERAL NOTE

Amendments effected by the following regulations have been incorporated in the   10.199
text above.

Regulations
Social Security (Industrial Injuries) (Miscellaneous Amendments) Regulations 1988 (SI 1988/553).

Social Security (Industrial Injuries) (Regular Employment) Regulations 1990

(SI 1990/256) (*as amended*)

ARRANGEMENT OF REGULATIONS

1.   Citation, commencement and interpretation.
2.   Meaning of "regular employment".
3.   Circumstances in which a person over pensionable age is to be regarded as having given up regular employment.

Whereas a draft of this instrument was laid before Parliament in accordance with   10.200
the provisions of section 29(2)(e) of the Social Security Act 1989 and approved by a resolution of each House of Parliament:

Now, therefore, the Secretary of State for Social Security, in exercise of the power conferred by section 59B(7) and (8) of and Schedule 20 to the Social Security Act 1975, and of all other powers enabling him in that behalf, by this instrument, which is made before the end of the period of 6 months beginning with the coming into force of the aforesaid section 59B(7) and (8), makes the following Regulations:

Citation, commencement and interpretation

1.—(1) These Regulations may be cited as the Social Security (Industry   10.201
Injuries) (Regular Employment) Regulations 1990 and shall come into force on 1st April 1990.
(2) *Omitted.*

Meaning of "regular employment"

10.202   **2.**—For the purposes of paragraph 13 of Schedule 7 to the Social Security Contributions and Benefits Act 1992, "regular employment" means gainful employment—

(a) under a contract of service which requires a person to work for an average of 10 hours or more per week in any period of five consecutive weeks, there being disregarded for this purpose any week when the contract subsists during which he is absent from that employment in circumstances where such absence is permitted under the contract (for example in the case of sickness or taking leave); or

(b) which a person undertakes for an average of 10 hours or more per week in any period of five consecutive weeks.

GENERAL NOTE

10.203   In *R(I) 2/93*, Commissioner Hoolahan noted in passing that this provision does *not* require a person to return to regular employment within five weeks of leaving his previous employment; the five weeks can begin any time in the future (para.10).

As regards "average", see *CI/3225/2004*. There Commissioner Levenson, deploying para.(b), used "rolling five week averages" as a convenient way of assessing continuing entitlement and determined that this claimant had not given up regular employment. The Commissioner stated:

> "It has never been doubted that the word 'average' refers to the arithmetic mean. The use of the phrase 'any period of five consecutive weeks' means that weeks after a particular job comes to an end can be included, and that weeks in which no work is done or expected to be done can also be included. In so deciding, I agree with the conclusions of the Commissioner in paragraphs 20 to 22 of *CI/2517/2001*. Further, I see no reason why a five week period under consideration cannot include some weeks calculated with reference to regulation 2(a) and some calculated with reference to regulation 2(b). Although 2(b) can only be assessed or calculated retrospectively, because it must be established for those purposes whether gainful employment has in fact been undertaken, future weeks can be considered from any particular vantage point (para.12)."

Circumstances in which a person over pensionable age is to be regarded as having given up regular employment

10.204   **3.**—Unless he is entitled to reduced earnings allowance for life by virtue of paragraph 12(1) of Schedule 7 to the Social Security Contributions and Benefits Act 1992, a person who has attained pensionable age shall be regarded as having given up regular employment at the start of the first week in which he is not in regular employment after the later of—

(a) the week during which this regulation comes into force; or

(b) the week during which he attains pensionable age.

GENERAL NOTE

10.205   This regulation came into force on March 24, 1996, the date on which it was inserted by the Social Security (Industrial Injuries and Diseases) (Miscellaneous Amendment) Regulations 1996. In decisions reported as *R(I) 2/99* and affirmed in *Plummer v Hammond*, Commissioner Howell held that it removed entitlement to REA and replaced it with retirement allowance for life with effect from March 31, 1996 (the beginning of the week after March 24, 1996) even in the case of two ladies who had attained pensionable age prior to March 24 and had in normal parlance given up (but not retired from) regular employment because of incapacity long before either April 10, 1989 (the date in SSCBA 1992, Sch.7, para.13(1)) or

March 24, 1996 (the date reg.3 came into force). The two ladies would not otherwise have been deprived of REA by para.13(1) because of the fact that they had as at October 1, 1989 been long out of work so that they could not be said to have "given up" regular employment on any day on or after that date as para.13(10) (b) as supplemented by the original 1990 regulations required, "gives up" bearing its ordinary natural meaning *(R(I) 2/93, R(I) 3/93)*. Reg.3 did, however, deprive them of it and transfer them to retirement allowance by, albeit artificially, regarding them as having given it up. See in particular paras 37, 38 and 40–49.

The case is very useful in charting the bumpy and twisting path of attempts to make entitlements to REA cease on retirement, and makes clear that reg.3 is *intra vires* the rule making power in SSCBA 1992, Sch.7, 13(8).

Since both ladies had attained the age of 65 before the regulation deprived them of REA, "the condition linked to pensionable age in paragraph 13(1) has no discriminatory effect", rendering it unnecessary in their case to consider any possible application of Council Dir. 79/7: see *Vol.III: Administration Appeals and the European Dimension*.

Social Security (Industrial Injuries) (Prescribed Diseases) Amendment (No. 2) Regulations 1993

(SI 1993/1985) *(as amended)*

ARRANGEMENT OF REGULATIONS

1.   Citation, commencement and interpretation.   10.206
2.–8.   Omitted.
9.   Transitional provision with respect to claims for prescribed disease D12.

The Secretary of State for Social Security, in exercise of the powers conferred by sections 108(2) and (4), 109(2) and (3), 110(1) and (2), 122(1) and 175(1) and (3) of and paragraph 2 of Schedule 6 to the Social Security Contributions and Benefits Act 1992 and sections 5(1)(a) and (b), 58(1)(b) and 189(1) and (4) of the Social Security Administration Act 1992, and of all other powers enabling him in that behalf, after reference to the Industrial Injuries Advisory Council hereby makes the following Regulations:

Citation, commencement and interpretation

1.—(1) These Regulations may be cited as the Social Security (Industrial   10.207
Injuries) (Prescribed Diseases) Amendment (No. 2) Regulations 1993 and shall come into force on 13th September 1993.

(2) In these Regulations "the principal Regulations" means the Social Security (Industrial Injuries) (Prescribed Diseases) Regulations 1985.

Sections 2–8 omitted.   10.208

Transitional provision with respect to claims for prescribed disease D12

9.— (1) In this regulation—   10.209
"prescribed disease D12" means the disease bearing that number and listed in Part I of Schedule 1 to the principal Regulations (chronic bronchitis and emphysema);
"relevant claim" means a claim for benefit in respect of prescribed disease D12; and

"relevant date" means 13th September 1993 or the date upon which the claimant in question first satisfies the conditions specified in Schedule 1 to the principal Regulations in respect of prescribed disease D12, whichever is the later.

(2) The provisions of the Social Security (Claims and Payments) Regulations 1987 shall apply in relation to a relevant claim subject to the following provisions of this regulation.

(3) A person who is aged not less than 70 on 13th September 1993 may make a relevant claim at any time in the period beginning with 13th September 1993 and ending with 28th February 1994, and if so made the claim shall be treated as having been made on the relevant date.

(4) A person who is aged less than 70 on 13th September 1993 and who, on the date the claim is made, has an award of attendance allowance at the higher rate under section 65(3) of the Social Security Contributions and Benefits Act 1992 or of the care component of disability living allowance at the highest rate under section 72(4) of that Act, may make a relevant claim at any time in the period beginning with 13th September 1993 and ending with 28th February 1994, and if so made the claim shall be treated as having been made on the relevant date.

(5) A person who does not fall within either of paragraphs (3) and (4) above may not make a relevant claim before 1st March 1994, but if such a person, or a person falling within paragraph (4) above who has not previously made a relevant claim, makes a relevant claim in the period beginning with that day and ending with 31st August 1994 that claim shall be treated as having been made on the relevant date.

Social Security (Industrial Injuries and Diseases) (Miscellaneous Amendments) Regulations 1996

(SI 1996/425)

ARRANGEMENT OF REGULATIONS

The Secretary of State for Social Security, in exercise of the powers conferred by sections 108(2), 109(2) and (3), 113(1)(b), 122(1) and 175(1), (3) and (4) of, and sub-paragraphs (8) and (9) of paragraph 13 of Schedule 7 to, the Social Security Contributions and Benefits Act 1992 and sections 5(1)(k), 27(1)(b) and 189(1) and (4)(b) of the Social Security Administration Act 1992, and of all other powers enabling him in that behalf, after reference to the Industrial Injuries Advisory Council, hereby makes the following Regulations:

Citation and commencement

10.211   **1.** These Regulations may be cited as the Social Security (Industrial Injuries and Diseases) (Miscellaneous Amendments) Regulations 1996 and shall come into force on 24th March 1996.

10.212   *Sections 2–6. omitted.*

Transitional provisions

7.—(1) The amendments made by regulation 5 of these Regulations ("the relevant amendments") to the terms in which each of the prescribed diseases A12, D4 and D5 ("the relevant disease") is prescribed shall not apply in the cases specified in the following provisions of this regulation, and in this regulation "commencement date" means the date on which these Regulations come into force.

(2) The relevant amendments shall not apply in the case of a person—

(a) who had an assessment of disablement in respect of the relevant disease for period which includes commencement date; or

(b) in respect of whom a decision in relation to a relevant disease on a claim for disablement benefit made before commencement date is reviewed on or after that date under section 47 of the Social Security Administration Act 1992 (reviews of medical decisions) which results in an assessment for a period which includes commencement date;

during any period where there is in respect of him a continuous assessment of disablement in respect of that disease which began before commencement date, and for this purpose two or more assessments one of which begins on the day following the end of a preceding assessment shall be treated as continuous.

(3) The relevant amendments shall not apply in the case of a person who makes a claim for disablement benefit in respect of the relevant disease before commencement date which results in an assessment of disablement, where the date of onset of that disease is earlier than commencement date, during any period when there is in respect of him a continuous assessment of disablement in respect of that disease which began not later than 91 days (excluding Sundays) after commencement date, and for this purpose two or more assessments one of which begins on the day following the end of a preceding assessment shall be treated as continuous.

(4) The relevant amendments shall not apply in the case of a person—

(a) who had an assessment of disablement in respect of the relevant disease for a period which ended before commencement date;

(b) who suffers a further attack of that relevant disease before commencement date;

(c) who makes a claim for disablement benefit in respect of that disease after commencement date; and

(d) in respect of whom it is decided, under regulation 7 of the Social Security (Industrial Injuries) (Prescribed Diseases) Regulations 1985 (recrudescence) that the further attack is a recrudescence of that disease.

Social Security (Industrial Injuries) (Prescribed Diseases) Amendment Regulations 2000

(SI 2000/1588)

ARRANGEMENT OF REGULATIONS

10.213

10.214

3.   Amendment of regulation 25 of the principal Regulations.
4.   Amendment of regulation 27 of the principal Regulations.
5.   Amendment of regulation 36 of the principal Regulations.
6.   Amendment of Schedule 1 to the principal Regulations.
7.   Transitional provision.

The Secretary of State for Social Security, in exercise of the powers conferred by sections 108(2) and (4), 109(2) and (3), 122(1) and 175(1) to (4) of the Social Security Contributions and Benefits Act 1992 and of all other powers enabling him in that behalf, after reference to the Industrial Injuries Advisory Council, hereby makes the following Regulations:

Citation, commencement and interpretation

10.215   **1.**—(1) These Regulations may be cited as the Social Security (Industrial Injuries) (Prescribed Diseases) Amendment Regulations 2000 and shall come into force on 10th July 2000.

(2) In these Regulations, "the principal Regulations" means the Social Security (Industrial Injuries) (Prescribed Diseases) Regulations 1985.

Amendment of regulation 2 of the principal Regulations

10.216   **2.**—*Incorporated in text of principal Regulations.*

Amendment of regulation 25 of the principal Regulations

10.217   **3.**—*Incorporated in text of principal Regulations.*

Amendment of regulation 27 of the principal Regulations

10.218   **4.**—*Incorporated in text of principal Regulations.*

Amendment of regulation 36 of the principal Regulations

10.219   **5.**—*Incorporated in text of principal Regulations.*

Amendment of Schedule 1 to the principal Regulations

10.220   **6.**—*Incorporated in text of principal Regulations.*

Transitional provision

10.221   **7.**—(1) The amendments made by regulations 3 and 4 shall not apply in relation to a claim made within 3 months after the commencement date and the amendments made by regulations 2(3), 5 and 6 shall not apply where the date of onset of the relevant disease is prior to the commencement date and the claim is made within 3 months after that date.

(2) The amendments made by regulations 2(3) and 6 shall not apply in the case of a person—

(a) who had an assessment of disablement in respect of the relevant disease for a period up to the date 3 months after the commencement date; or

(b) in respect of whom a decision in relation to a relevant disease on a claim for disablement benefit made before or within 3 months after the commencement date is revised or superseded after that date under section 9 or 10 of the Social Security Act 1998 resulting in an assessment; during any period when there is in respect of him a continuous assessment of disablement in respect of that disease, and for this purpose two or more assessments, one of which begins on the day following the end of a preceding assessment, shall be treated as continuous.

(3) The amendments made by regulations 2(3) and 6(2) and (3) shall not apply in the case of a person—

(a) who had an assessment of disablement in respect of the relevant disease for a period which ended before or within 3 months after the commencement date;

(b) who suffers a further attack of that relevant disease before or within 3 months after the commencement date;

(c) who makes a claim for disablement benefit in respect of that disease after the commencement date; and

(d) in respect of whom it is decided under regulation 7 of the principal Regulations (recrudescence) that the further attack is a recrudescence of that disease.

(4) In this regulation—

"commencement date" means the date on which these Regulations come into force; and

"relevant disease" means the disease referred to in the amendment, or the regulation of the principal Regulations which is amended by the amendment.

Social Security (Industrial Injuries) (Prescribed Diseases) Amendment Regulations 2003

(SI 2003/270)

ARRANGEMENT OF REGULATIONS

10.222

The Secretary of State for Work and Pensions, in exercise of the powers conferred on him by sections 108(2) and (4), 109(2) and (3), 122(1) and 175(1) to (4) of the Social Security Contributions and Benefits Act 1992 and of all other powers enabling him in that behalf, after reference to the Industrial Injuries Advisory Council, hereby makes the following Regulations:

Citation, commencement and interpretation

1.—(1) These Regulations may be cited as the Social Security (Industrial Injuries) (Prescribed Diseases) Amendment Regulations 2003 and shall come into force on 17th March 2003.

10.223

(2) In these Regulations "the principal Regulations" means the Social Security (Industrial Injuries) (Prescribed Diseases) Regulations 1985.

Amendment of regulation 4 of the principal Regulations

10.224   2.—*Incorporated in text of principal Regulations.*

Amendment of regulation 7 of the principal Regulations

10.225   3.—*Incorporated in text of principal Regulations.*

Amendment of regulation 8 of the principal Regulations

10.226   4.—*Incorporated in text of principal Regulations.*

Amendment of Schedule 1 to the principal Regulations

10.227   5.—*Incorporated in text of principal Regulations.*

Transitional provision

10.228   6.—(1) Regulations 2 and 5 shall not apply—

(a) to a period of assessment which relates to a claim which is made before the commencement date;

(b) to a period of assessment which relates to a claim which is made within 3 months after the commencement date in respect of a period which began before the commencement date; or

(c) where a person suffers from an attack of a disease and under regulation 7 of the principal Regulations (recrudescence) the attack is a recrudescence of a disease for which a claim was made before the commencement date (or within 3 months after the commencement date in respect of a period which began before the commencement date).

(2) For the purposes of this regulation—

(a) "commencement date" means the date on which these Regulations come into force;

(b) the date on which a claim is made is the date on which the claim is made or treated as made in accordance with the Social Security (Claims and Payments) Regulations 1987; and

(c) a period of assessment which begins on the day following the end of a preceding period of assessment, shall be treated as a continuation of the preceding period of assessment.

Social Security (Industrial Injuries) (Prescribed Diseases) Amendment (No. 2) Regulations 2003

(SI 2003/2190)

ARRANGEMENT OF REGULATIONS

3.   Amendment of Schedule 1 to the principal Regulations.
4.   Transitional provision.

The Secretary of State for Work and Pensions, in exercise of the powers conferred on him by sections 108(2), 109(2), 122(1) and 175(1) to (4) of the Social Security Contributions and Benefits Act 1992 and sections 9(1), 10(3) and 79(1), (3) and (4) of the Social Security Act 1998 and of all other powers enabling him in that behalf, being satisfied of the matters referred to in section 108(2)(a) and (b) of that Act of 1992 and after reference to the Industrial Injuries Advisory Council, hereby makes the following Regulations:

Citation, commencement and interpretation

1.—(1) These Regulations may be cited as the Social Security (Industrial Injuries) (Prescribed Diseases) Amendment (No.2) Regulations 2003 and shall come into force on 22nd September 2003.

10.230

(2) In these Regulations "the principal Regulations" means the Social Security (Industrial Injuries) (Prescribed Diseases) Regulations 1985.

Amendment of the principal Regulations

2.—*Incorporated in text of principal Regulations.*

10.231

Amendment of Schedule 1 to the principal Regulations

3.—*Incorporated in text of Schedule 1 to the principal Regulations.*

10.232

Transitional provision

4.—(1) Regulation 3 shall not apply to a period of assessment which relates to a claim which is made before the commencement date.

10.233

(2) A provisional assessment of the extent of a claimant's disablement due to occupational deafness, which is in force immediately before the commencement date, shall, from the commencement date, have effect for the remainder of the claimant's life.

(3) For the purposes of this regulation—
(a) "commencement date" means the date on which these Regulations come into force;
(b) the date on which a claim is made is the date on which the claim is made or treated as made in accordance with the Social Security (Claims and Payments) Regulations 1987.

GENERAL NOTE

This principally protects those whose claims in respect of hearing loss were made, or treated as made, before the date of the change [September 22, 2003] (para.(1) read with (3)(b). But note also the provision in para.(2), which turns a provisional assessment of disablement due to occupational deafness, in force on September 21, 2003, into one for life as from September 22, 2003 ("commencement date"—see para.(3)(a)).

10.234

**The Social Security (Industrial Injuries) (Prescribed Diseases)
Amendment Regulations 2005**

(SI 2005/324)

10.235   The Secretary of State for Work and Pensions, in exercise of the powers conferred upon him by sections 108(2), 122(1) and 175(1) to (4) of the Social Security Contributions and Benefits Act 1992 and section 5(1)(a) of the Social Security Administration Act 1992 and of all other powers enabling him in that behalf, being satisfied of the matters referred to in section 108(2)(a) and (b) of the Social Security Contributions and Benefits Act and after reference to the Industrial Injuries Advisory Council, hereby makes the following Regulations:

Citation, commencement and interpretation

10.236   **1.**—(1) These Regulations may be cited as the Social Security (Industrial Injuries) (Prescribed Diseases) Amendment Regulations 2005 and shall come into force on 14th March 2005.

(2) In these Regulations "the principal Regulations" means the Social Security (Industrial Injuries) (Prescribed Diseases) Regulations 1985.

Amendment of regulations 2 and 25 of the principal Regulations

10.237   **2.**—*Incorporated in text of Schedule 1 to the principal Regulations.*

Transitional provision

10.238   **4.**—Regulation 3 shall not apply to a period of assessment which relates to a claim which is made before the date on which these Regulations come into force.

**The Social Security (Industrial Injuries) (Prescribed Diseases)
Amendment Regulations 2007**

(SI 2007/811)

10.239   The Secretary of State for Work and Pensions makes the following Regulations in exercise of the powers conferred by sections 108(2), 122(1) and 175(1) to (4) of the Social Security Contributions and Benefits Act 1992.

The Secretary of State is satisfied of the matters referred to in section 108(2)(a) and (b) of that Act.

In accordance with section 172(2) of the Social Security Administration Act 1992, reference has been made to the Industrial Injuries Advisory Council.

Citation and commencement

10.240   **1.** These Regulations may be cited as the Social Security (Industrial Injuries) (Prescribed Diseases) Amendment Regulations 2007 and shall come into force on the 6th April 2007.

Amendment of Schedule 1 to the Social Security (Industrial Injuries) (Prescribed Diseases) Regulations 1985

2. — *Incorporated in text of Schedule 1 to the principal Regulations.*   10.241

Transitional provision

3. Regulation 2 shall not apply to a period of assessment which relates to   10.242
a claim made before the date on which these Regulations come into force.

The Social Security (Industrial Injuries) (Prescribed Diseases) Amendment (No. 2) Regulations 2007

(2007 No. 1753)

ARRANGEMENT OF REGULATIONS

1.   Citation, commencement and interpretation
2.   Amendment of Schedule 1 to the principal Regulations
3.   Transitional provision

The Secretary of State for Work and Pensions makes the following Regulations in   10.243
exercise of the powers conferred by sections 108(2), 122(1) and 175(1), (3) and (4)
of the Social Security Contributions and Benefits Act 1992.
He is satisfied of the matters referred to in section 108(2)(a) and (b) of that Act.
In accordance with section 172(2) of the Social Security Administration Act
1992 he has referred proposals to make these Regulations to the Industrial Injuries
Advisory Council.

Citation, commencement and interpretation

1. —(1) These Regulations may be cited as the Social Security (Industrial   10.244
Injuries) (Prescribed Diseases) Amendment (No. 2) Regulations 2007 and
shall come into force on 1st October 2007.
(2) In these Regulations "the principal Regulations" means the Social
Security (Industrial Injuries) (Prescribed Diseases) Regulations 1985.

Amendment of Schedule 1 to the principal Regulations

2. *Incorporated into the text of Schedule 1 to the principal Regulations.*   10.245

Transitional provision

3. —(1) Regulation 2 shall not apply to a question relating to the blanch-   10.246
ing of a claimant's fingers where—
(a) the question arises in connection with a period of assessment which
    relates to a claim which is made—
    (i) before the commencement date, or
    (ii) within 3 months after the commencement date in respect of a
         period which began before the commencement date, or
(b) a person suffers from an attack of a disease and under regula-
    tion 7 of the principal Regulations (recrudescence) the attack is a
    recrudescence of a disease for which a claim was made before the

commencement date or within 3 months after the commencement date in respect of a period which began before the commencement date.

(2) For the purposes of this regulation—

(a) "commencement date" means the date on which these Regulations come into force; and

(b) a period of assessment which begins on the day following the end of a preceding period of assessment, shall be treated as a continuation of the preceding period of assessment.

GENERAL NOTE

10.247   Regulation 2 added sensorineural symptoms to the description of PD A11 with effect from October 1, 2007. There can clearly be no claim on the basis of such symptoms for any period prior to that date. This transitional provision, preventing claims within a three month period after that date, only prevents claims being made which raise a question of the blanching of a claimant's fingers, so that a claimant whose case is based on the new sensory condition does not have to wait until that three month period is over but can claim in respect of it for periods on or after October 1, 2007 (*DG v SSWP* [2009] UKUT 41 (AAC), paras 5-8).

PART XI

VACCINE DAMAGE PAYMENTS

Vaccine Damage Payments Regulations 1979

(SI 1979/432) (*as amended*)

ARRANGEMENT OF REGULATIONS

PART I

GENERAL

PART II

CLAIMS

PART III

REVIEW BY TRIBUNALS

PART IV

DECISIONS REVERSING EARLIER DECISIONS

The Secretary of State for Social Services in exercise of powers conferred on him by sections 2(5), 3(1)(b), 4(1), 5(2), 7(5) and 8(3) of the Vaccine Damage Payments Act 1979 and of all other powers enabling him in that behalf, hereby makes the following regulations:

PART I

GENERAL

11.2 **Citation, commencement and interpretation**

1.—(1) These regulations may be cited as the Vaccine Damage Payments Regulations 1979 and shall come into operation on 6th April 1979.

(2) In these regulations, unless the context otherwise requires—

"the Act" means the Vaccine Damage Payments Act 1979;

"hearing" means oral hearing;

"medical practitioner" means registered medical practitioner;

"payment" means a payment under section 1(1) of the Act;

[¹ . . .].

(3) Any notice required to be given to any person under the provisions of these regulations may be given by being sent by post to that person at his ordinary or last known address.

AMENDMENT

1. Social Security and Child Support (Decisions and Appeals), Vaccine Damage Payments and Jobseeker's Allowance (Amendment) Regulations 1999 (SI 1999/2677), reg.2 (October 18, 1999).

PART II

CLAIMS

Claims to be made to the Secretary of State in writing

11.3 **2.**—(1) Every claim for payment shall be made in writing to the Secretary of State on the form approved by him, or in such other manner, being in writing, as he may accept as sufficient in the circumstances of any particular case or class of cases.

(2) Any person who has made a claim in accordance with the provisions of this regulation may amend his claim, at any time before a decision has been given thereon, by notice in writing delivered or sent to the Secretary of State, and any claim so amended may be treated as if it had been so amended in the first instance.

Information to be given when making a claim

11.4 **3.**—Every person who makes a claim shall furnish such certificates, documents, information and evidence for the purpose of determining the claim as may be required by the Secretary of State.

Obligations of disabled person

11.5 **4.**—(1) Subject to the following provisions of this regulation, every disabled person in respect of whom a claim has been made under section 3 of the Act shall comply with every notice given to him or, where he is not the claimant, to the claimant by the Secretary of State which requires such disabled person to submit himself to a medical examination either by a medical practitioner appointed by the Secretary of State or by [¹ an appeal] tribunal for the purposes of determining whether he is severely disabled as a result of vaccination against any of the diseases to which the Act applies.

(2) Every notice given under the preceding paragraph shall be given in writing and shall specify the time and place of examination and shall not require the disabled person to submit himself to examination before the expiration of the period of fourteen days beginning with the date of the notice or such shorter period as may be reasonable in the circumstances.

AMENDMENT

1. Social Security and Child Support (Decisions and Appeals), Vaccine Damage Payments and Jobseeker's Allowance (Amendment) Regulations 1999 (SI 1999/2677), reg.3 (October 18, 1999).

Vaccinations to be treated as carried out in England

5.—(1) Vaccinations given outside the United Kingdom and the Isle of Man to serving members of Her Majesty's forces or members of their families shall be treated for the purposes of the Act as carried out in England where the vaccination in question has been given as part of medical facilities provided under arrangements made by or on behalf of the service authorities.

(2) For the purposes of section 2(5) of the Act—

(a) "serving members of Her Majesty's forces" means a member of the naval, military or air forces of the Crown or of any women's service administered by the Defence Council;

[¹ (b) a person is a member of the family of a serving member of Her Majesty's forces if—

(i) he is the spouse or civil partner of that serving member,

(ii) he and that serving member live together as husband and wife or as if they were civil partners, or

(iii) he is a child whose requirements are provided by that serving member.]

11.6

AMENDMENT

1. Vaccine Damage Payments (Amendment) Regulations 2005 (SI 2005/3070), reg.2 (December 5, 2005).

Circumstances prescribed in relation to cases of damage through contact

[¹ **5A.**—The circumstances prescribed for the purposes of section 1(3) of the Vaccine Damage Payments Act 1979 (Act to have effect with respect to a person severely disabled as a result of contracting a disease through contact with a third person who was vaccinated against it) are that:—

(1) the disabled person has been in close physical contact with a person who has been vaccinated against poliomyelitis with orally administered vaccine;

(2) that contact occurred within a period of sixty days beginning with the fourth day immediately following such vaccination; and

(3) the disabled person was, within the period referred to in paragraph (2) of this regulation, either—

(a) looking after the person who has been vaccinated, or

(b) himself being looked after together with the person who has been vaccinated.]

11.7

AMENDMENT

1. Vaccine Damage Payments (Amendment) Regulations 1979 (SI 1979/1441), reg.2 (December 13, 1979).

Claims made prior to the passing of the Act

11.8   **6.**—(1) A claim made before the passing of the Act in connection with the non-statutory scheme of payments for severe vaccine damage established by the Secretary of State for Social Services in anticipation of the passing of the Act and which has not been disposed of at the commencement of the Act shall be treated as a claim falling within section 3(1) of the Act.

(2) Any information and other evidence furnished and other things done before the commencement of the Act in connection with any such claim made before the passing of the Act shall be treated as furnished or done in connection with a claim falling within section 3(1) of the Act.

PART III

REVIEW BY TRIBUNALS

11.9   *Regulations 7–10 were revoked by the Social Security and Child Support (Decisions and Appeals) Regulations 1999 (SI 1999/991), reg.59 and Sch.4 (October 18, 1999). For previous text, see Rowland, Medical and Disability Appeals Tribunal: The Legislation 1998.*

[¹ PART IV

DECISIONS REVERSING EARLIER DECISIONS

Decisions reversing earlier decisions made by the Secretary of State or appeal tribunals

11.10   **11.**—(1) The Secretary of State may make a decision under 3A(1) of the Act which reverses a decision of his, made under section 3 of the Act, or of an appeal tribunal, made under section 4 of the Act—

(a) pursuant to an application in the circumstances described in paragraph (2) below; or

(b) except where paragraph (3) applies, on his own initiative.

(2) The circumstances referred to in paragraph (1)(a) above are—

(a) the application is made in writing and contains an explanation as to why the applicant believes the decision in respect of which the application is made to be wrong; and

(b) where the application is in respect of a decision of the Secretary of State, the application is made within six years of the date on which notification of that decision was given; or

(c) where the application is in respect of a decision of an appeal tribunal, the application is made before whichever is the later of—

(i) the date two years after the date on which notification of that decision was given; or

(ii) the date six years after the date on which notification of the decision of the Secretary of State which was appealed was given.

(3) This paragraph applies where—

(a) less than 21 days have elapsed since notice under regulation 12 below was given; or

(b) more than six years have elapsed since the date on which notification of that decision was given except where it appears to the Secretary of State that a payment was made in consequence of a misrepresentation or failure to disclose any material fact.

(4) Where the Secretary of State has made a decision under section 3A(1) of the Act, he shall notify—

(a) the disabled person (if he is alive) to whom the decision relates; and

(b) if the disabled person is not a claimant, the claimant who made the claim in respect of that disabled person,

of that decision and the reasons for it.

Procedure by which a decision may be made under section 3A of the Act on the Secretary of State's own initiative

12.—Where the Secretary of State on his own initiative proposes to make a decision under section 3A of the Act reversing a decision ("the original decision") of his or of an appeal tribunal he shall give notice in writing of his proposal to—   11.11

(a) the disabled person (if he is alive) to whom the original decision relates; and

(b) the claimant in relation to the original decision where he is not the disabled person.]

AMENDMENT

1. Social Security and Child Support (Decisions and Appeals), Vaccine Damage Payments and Jobseeker's Allowance (Amendment) Regulations 1999 (SI 1999/2677), reg.4 (October 18, 1999).

Vaccine Damage Payments (Specified Disease) Order 1990

(SI 1990/623)

ARRANGEMENT OF ORDER

1. Citation and commencement.   11.12
2. Addition to the diseases to which the Vaccine Damage Payments Act applies.

The Secretary of State for Social Security, in exercise of the powers conferred by section 1(2)(i) of the Vaccine Damage Payments Act 1979 and of all other powers enabling him in that behalf, hereby makes the following Order:

Citation and commencement

1.—This Order may be cited as the Vaccine Damage Payments (Specified Disease) Order 1990 and shall come into force on 9th April 1990.   11.13

Addition to the diseases to which the Vaccine Damage Payments Act applies

11.14   **2.**—Mumps is specified as a disease to which the Vaccine Damage Payments Act 1979 applies.

Vaccine Damage Payments (Specified Disease) Order 1995

(SI 1995/1164)

ARRANGEMENT OF ORDER

11.15   1.   Citation and commencement.
       2.   Addition to the diseases to which the Vaccine Damage Payments Act applies.

The Secretary of State for Social Security, in exercise of powers conferred by section 1(2)(i) of the Vaccine Damage Payments Act 1979(a) and of all other powers enabling him in that behalf, hereby makes the following Order:

Citation and commencement

11.16   **1.**—This Order may be cited as the Vaccine Damage Payments (Specified Disease) Order 1995 and shall come into force on 31st May 1995.

Addition to the diseases to which the Vaccine Damage Payments Act applies

11.17   **2.**—Haemophilus influenza type b infection is specified as a disease to which the Vaccine Damage Payments Act 1979 applies.

The Vaccine Damage Payments (Specified Disease) Order 2001

(SI 2001/1652)

ARRANGEMENT OF ORDER

11.18   1.   Citation and commencement.
       2.   Addition to the diseases to which the Act applies.
       3.   Modification of conditions of entitlement.

The Secretary of State for Social Security, in exercise of the powers conferred upon him by sections 1(2)(i) and 2(2) of the Vaccine Damage Payments Act 1979 and of all other powers enabling him in that behalf, hereby makes the following Order:

Citation, commencement and interpretation

11.19   **1.**—(1) This Order may be cited as the Vaccine Damage Payments (Specified Disease) Order 2001 and shall come into force on 30th May 2001.

     (2) In this Order, "the Act" means the Vaccine Damage Payments Act 1979.

Addition to the diseases to which the Act applies

2.—Meningococcal Group C is specified as a disease to which the Act applies.

11.20

Modification of conditions of entitlement

3.—The condition of entitlement in section 2(1)(b) of the Act (age or time at which vaccination was carried out) shall be omitted in relation to vaccination against Meningococcal Group C.

11.21

The Vaccine Damage Payments (Specified Disease) Order 2006

(SI 2006/2066)

ARRANGEMENT OF ORDER

11.22

The Secretary of State for Work and Pensions makes the following Order in exercise of the power conferred by section 1(2)(i) of the Vaccine Damage Payments Act 1979.

Citation and commencement

1. This Order may be cited as the Vaccine Damage Payments (Specified Disease) Order 2006 and shall come into force on 4th September 2006.

11.23

Addition to the diseases to which the Vaccine Damage Payments Act 1979 applies

2. Pneumococcal infection is specified as a disease to which the Vaccine Damage Payments Act 1979 applies.

11.24

The Vaccine Damage Payments (Specified Disease) Order 2008

(SI 2008/2103)

IN FORCE SEPTEMBER 1, 2008

ARRANGEMENT OF ORDER

11.25

The Secretary of State for Work and Pensions makes the following Order in exercise of the powers conferred by sections 1(2)(i) and 2(2) of the Vaccine Damage Payments Act 1979.

Citation, commencement and interpretation

11.26   1.—(1) This Order may be cited as the Vaccine Damage Payments (Specified Disease) Order 2008 and shall come into force on 1st September 2008.

(2) In this Order, "the Act" means the Vaccine Damage Payments Act 1979.

Addition to the diseases to which the Act applies

11.27   2. Human papillomavirus is specified as a disease to which the Act applies.

Modification of conditions of entitlement

11.28   3. The condition of entitlement in section 2(1)(b) of the Act (age or time at which vaccination was carried out) shall be omitted in relation to vaccination against human papillomavirus.

The Vaccine Damage Payments Act 1979 Statutory Sum Order 2007

(2007 No. 1931)

ARRANGEMENT OF ORDER

A draft of the following Order was laid before Parliament in accordance with section 1(4A) of the Vaccine Damage Payments Act 1979 and approved by resolution of each House of Parliament:

The Secretary of State for Work and Pensions with the consent of the Treasury, in exercise of the powers conferred by section 1(1A) of the Vaccine Damage Payments Act 1979, makes the following Order:

Citation and commencement

11.30   1. This Order may be cited as the Vaccine Damage Payments Act 1979 Statutory Sum Order 2007 and shall come into force on 12th July 2007.

Statutory sum for the purposes of the Vaccine Damage Payments Act 1979

11.31   2. For the purposes of the Vaccine Damage Payments Act 1979 the statutory sum is £120,000.

Revocation

3. The Vaccine Damage Payments Act 1979 Statutory Sum Order 2000   **11.32**
is hereby revoked.

GENERAL NOTE

This Order entered into force on July 12, 2007. The regulations raise the statu-   **11.33**
tory sum from £100,000 to £120,000.

PART XII

MESOTHELIOMA LUMP SUM PAYMENTS

Mesothelioma Lump Sum Payments (Claims and Reconsiderations) Regulations 2008

(SI 2008/1595)

The Secretary of State for Work and Pensions in exercise of the powers conferred by section 48(1) to (3), 49(2), 50(4) and 53(2) of the Child Maintenance and Other Payments Act 2008 makes the following Regulations.

Citation, commencement and interpretation

1.—(1) These Regulations may be cited as the Mesothelioma Lump Sum   12.2
Payments (Claims and Reconsiderations) Regulations 2008 and shall come into force on 1st October 2008.

(2) In these Regulations—

"claim" means a claim under section 46(1) of the Child Maintenance and Other Payments Act 2008;

"mesothelioma" means diffuse mesothelioma.

Making a claim

2.—(1) Subject to paragraph (2), a claim must be made in writing, signed   12.3
by or on behalf of the person making the claim, on a form approved by the Secretary of State and accompanied by the documents specified in the form.

(2) A claim may be made in such other manner, being in writing, as the Secretary of State may accept as sufficient in the circumstances of any particular case.

Time for making a claim

3.—(1) A claim by a person who has been diagnosed with mesothelioma   12.4
before the coming into force of these Regulations must be made within 12 months from the date on which these Regulations come into force.

(2) A claim by any other person with mesothelioma must be made within 12 months from the date on which that person was first diagnosed with mesothelioma.

(3) A claim by a dependant must be made within 12 months from the date of death of the person who, immediately before death, had mesothelioma.

(4) Where the Secretary of State considers there was good cause for the claim not being made within the 12 month time limit referred to in paragraphs (1) to (3), he may extend the time limit for such period as he considers appropriate in the circumstances, provided that the time limit is

not extended for a death or diagnosis which occurred more than 12 months before the date these Regulations come into force.

Reconsideration

12.5   **4.**—(1) An application made to the Secretary of State for reconsideration of a determination that a payment should or should not be made must—

(a) be made within one month of the date of notification of the determination, and

(b) specify the ground for the request and give such other relevant information as the Secretary of State may require in order to deal adequately with the reconsideration.

(2) The Secretary of State may, at any time, in writing, institute a reconsideration of a determination that a payment should or should not be made.

Appeal treated as reconsideration

12.6   **5.**—(1) Where a person appeals against a determination made by the Secretary of State on a claim, the Secretary of State may treat the appeal as an application for reconsideration under section 49 of the Child Maintenance and Other Payments Act 2008.

(2) Where—

(a) an appeal against a determination that a payment should not be made is treated as an application for reconsideration, and

(b) on the reconsideration the Secretary of State decides that a payment should be made,

the Secretary of State shall not refer the appeal to [¹ the First-tier Tribunal].

(3) Except where paragraph (2) applies, where an appeal is treated as an application for reconsideration, the Secretary of State shall delay referring the appeal to the [¹ the First-tier Tribunal] until after the reconsideration.

AMENDMENT

1. Mesothelioma Lump Sum Payments (Claims and Reconsiderations) (Amendment) Regulations 2008 (SI 2008/2706), reg.3 (November 3, 2008).

[¹ Appeals

12.7   **6.** Regulation 33 of the Social Security and Child Support (Decisions and Appeals) Regulations 1999 (notice of appeal) applies to an appeal against a determination made by the Secretary of State—

(a) on a claim; or

(b) on reconsideration under section 49 of the Child Maintenance and Other Payments Act 2008 of a determination made on a claim

as it applies to an appeal under section 12 of the Social Security Act 1998.]

AMENDMENT

1. Mesothelioma Lump Sum Payments (Claims and Reconsiderations) (Amendment) Regulations 2008 (SI 2008/2706), reg.4 (November 3, 2008).

GENERAL NOTE

See generally the annotations to ss.48-51 of the Child Maintenance and Other Payments Act 2008 above.

12.8

Mesothelioma Lump Sum Payments (Conditions and Amounts) Regulations 2008

(SI 2008/1963)

ARRANGEMENT OF REGULATIONS

12.9

The Secretary of State for Work and Pensions in exercise of the powers conferred by section 1(1) of the Pneumoconiosis etc. (Workers' Compensation) Act 1979 and sections 46(3) and 47 of the Child Maintenance and Other Payments Act 2008 makes the following Regulations.

Citation, commencement and interpretation

1.—(1) These Regulations may be cited as the Mesothelioma Lump Sum Payments (Conditions and Amounts) Regulations 2008.

12.10

(2) These Regulations shall come into force on 1st October 2008.

(3) In these Regulations—

"the Act" means the Child Maintenance and Other Payments Act 2008;

"claim" means a claim under section 46(1) of the Act;

"deceased" means a person who, immediately before death, had diffuse mesothelioma;

"mesothelioma" means diffuse mesothelioma;

"payment" includes a payment in money or money's worth or in kind.

Disqualifying payments

2.—(1) The following payments are prescribed for the purposes of section 47(1)(a), (2)(a) and (3)(e) of the Act (payments which, if made in consequence of diffuse mesothelioma, prevent the conditions provided for in section 47(1)(a) and (2)(a) from being fulfilled)—

(a) payment under the Naval, Military and Air Forces Etc. (Disablement and Death) Service Pensions Order 2006;

(b) payment under the Armed Forces and Reserve Forces (Compensation Scheme) Order 2005;

[1 (c) payment from any government department, authority, body corporate or employer exempted from insurance by or under section 3 of the Employers' Liability (Compulsory Insurance) Act 1969

12.11

or Article 7 of the Employers' Liability (Defective Equipment and Compulsory Insurance) (Northern Ireland) Order 1972];
  (d) payment under the UK Asbestos Trust established on 10th October 2006, for the benefit of certain persons suffering from asbestos-related diseases;
  (e) payment under the EL Scheme Trust established on 23rd November 2006, for the benefit of certain persons suffering from asbestos-related diseases.

(2) The following payments are prescribed for the purposes of section 47(1)(b) and (2)(b) of the Act (payments eligibility for which prevents the conditions provided for in section 47(1)(b) or (2)(b) from being fulfilled)—
  (a) payment under the Naval, Military and Air Forces Etc. (Disablement and Death) Service Pensions Order 2006;
  (b) payment under the Armed Forces and Reserve Forces (Compensation Scheme) Order 2005.

AMENDMENT

1. Social Security (Miscellaneous Amendments) (No. 3) Regulations 2008 (SI 2008/2365), reg.5 (October 1, 2008).

Disregarded payments

12.12   **3.** A payment made in error and which in consequence is liable to be repaid in accordance with a statutory provision or rule of law, is to be disregarded for the purpose of section 47(1)(a) or (2)(a) of the Act (conditions of entitlement).

Presence in the United Kingdom

12.13   **4.**—(1) In the case of a person with mesothelioma it is a condition of entitlement that the person was in the United Kingdom at a time when and place where that person was exposed to asbestos.

(2) In the case of a dependant it is a condition of entitlement that the deceased was in the United Kingdom at a time when and place where the deceased was exposed to asbestos.

GENERAL NOTE

12.14   See the commentary to s.47 of the Child Maintenance and Other Payments Act 2008 for discussion as to the potentially ultra vires nature of this provision.

Amount of lump sum payment

12.15   **5.**—(1) The amount of a payment made under section 46(2) of the Act to a person with mesothelioma shall be determined in accordance with Table 1 of the Schedule.

(2) In Table 1 of the Schedule, the reference to the age of the person is a reference to—
  (a) the age at which the person was first diagnosed with mesothelioma; or
  (b) where the age at which the person was first diagnosed with mesothelioma is unknown, the age at which the person made the claim.

(3) The amount of a payment made under section 46(2) of the Act to a dependant shall be determined in accordance with Table 2 of the Schedule.

(4) In Table 2 of the Schedule, the reference to the age of the person with mesothelioma is a reference to the age of that person at death.

Amendment of Pneumoconiosis etc. (Workers' Compensation) (Payment of Claims) Regulations 1988

6. At the end of regulation 3 of the Pneumoconiosis etc. (Workers' Compensation) (Payment of Claims) Regulations 1988(**6**) (payments to persons disabled by disease), add—

12.16

"(5) Where—

   (a) a payment is made to a person under section 46 of the Child Maintenance and Other Payments Act 2008 (the mesothelioma payment) in respect of diffuse mesothelioma,

   (b) subsequently it is determined that the same person is entitled to a payment under section 1(1) of the Act in respect of the same diffuse mesothelioma,

the amount payable under paragraph (1) shall be reduced by the amount of the mesothelioma payment.".

SCHEDULE

Regulation 5

Table 1
Amount of lump sum payment to person with mesothelioma

12.17

Age of person with mesothelioma at diagnosis, or, if unknown, at date of claim	Payment £
37 and under	52,772
38	51,747
39	50,722
40	49,698
41	48,673
42	47,648
43	47,137
44	46,621
45	46,112
46	45,599
47	45,086
48	43,653
49	42,219
50	40,781
51	39,349
52	37,911
53	36,888
54	35,864
55	34,841
56	33,812
57	32,789
58	30,125
59	27,460
60	24,799
61	22,133
62	19,469

Age of person with mesothelioma at diagnosis, or, if unknown, at date of claim	Payment £
63	17,829
64	16,189
65	14,551
66	12,911
67	11,272
68	10,939
69	10,604
70	10,273
71	9,941
72	9,608
73	9,325
74	9,037
75	8,759
76	8,480
77 and over	8,197

Table 2
Amount of lump sum payment to dependent

12.18

Age of person with mesothelioma at death	Payment £
37 and under	23,953
38	23,362
39	22,774
40	22,185
41	21,595
42	21,007
43	20,444
44	19,874
45	19,313
46	18,751
47	18,189
48	17,496
49	16,804
50	16,112
51	15,423
52	14,732
53	14,165
54	13,603
55	13,039
56	12,473
57	11,911
58	10,351
59	8,787
60	7,226
61	5,662
62	4,098
63	3,651
64	3,207
65	2,752
66	2,306
67 and over	1,859

INDEX

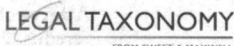

FROM SWEET & MAXWELL

This index has been prepared using Sweet and Maxwell's Legal Taxonomy. Main index entries conform to keywords provided by the Legal Taxonomy except where references to specific documents or non-standard terms (denoted by quotation marks) have been included. These keywords provide a means of identifying similar concepts in other Sweet & Maxwell publications and online services to which keywords from the Legal Taxonomy have been applied. Readers may find some minor differences between terms used in the text and those which appear in the index. Suggestions to *sweetandmaxwell.taxonomy@thomson.com*.

(All references are to paragraph number)

"Concrete masonry blocks"
occupational deafness, and, 10.143
"Conditionality"
And see **Employment and support
    allowance**
Administration Act modifications,
    9.144–9.145
contracting out, 1.779–1.780
notification, 9.142–9.143
reduction of allowance
    cessation, 9.140–9.141
    generally, 9.138–9.139
Regulations
    notification, 9.142–9.143
    reduction of allowance, 9.138–9.141
    work-focused health-related
        assessments, 9.106–9.119
    work-focused interviews, 9.120–9.137
statutory provisions
    action plans, 1.775–1.776
    contracting out, 1.779–1.780
    directions, 1.777–1.778
    work-focused health-related
        assessments, 1.769–1.770
    work-focused interviews, 1.771–1.772
    work-related activity, 1.773–1.774
work-focused health-related assessments
    deferral of requirement, 9.116–9.117
    determination of place, 9.112–9.113
    failure to take part, 9.118–9.119
    generally, 9.108–9.109
    notification, 9.110–9.111
    purposes, 9.108–9.109
    Regulations, 9.106–9.119
    requirement to take part, 9.106–9.107
    statutory provisions, 1.769–1.770
    taking part, 9.114–9.115
work-focused interviews
    action plans, 1.775–1.776,
        9.128–9.129
    contracting-out functions, and,
        9.136–9.137
    deferral of requirement, 9.130–9.131
    failure to take part, 9.134–9.135
    generally, 1.771–1.772
    notification, 9.124–9.125
    persons starting or returning to work,
        9.132–9.133
    purposes, 9.122–9.123
    Regulations, 9.120–9.137
    requirement to take part, 9.120–9.121
    statutory provisions, 1.771–1.772
    taking part, 9.126–9.127
work-related activity
    directions, 1.777–1.778
    generally, 1.773–1.774
Conditions (entitlement)
bereavement allowance
    general note, 1.488
    generally, 1.474
bereavement payment
    general note, 1.487
    generally, 1.473

satisfaction in early years, 1.490–1.492
child's special allowance
    general note, 1.526
    generally, 1.476
contribution-based employment and
        support allowance
    additional conditions, 1.820–1.826,
        9.20–9.29
    assessments, 1.761–1.766
    basic conditions, 1.734–1.741
definitions, 1.478
earnings factors, 1.40
employment and support allowance
    additional, 1.820–1.829
    assessments, 1.761–1.768
    conditionality, 1.769–1.780
    generally, 1.734–1.741
    Regulations, 9.18–9.39
general note
    coverage, 1.479–1.484
    division of responsibility, 1.480
    generally, 1.485–1.489
    satisfaction in early years, 1.490–1.492
generally, 1.39
income-based employment and support
        allowance
    additional conditions, 1.827–1.829,
        9.30–9.39
    assessments, 1.761–1.766
    basic conditions, 1.734–1.741
maternity allowance
    general note, 1.486
    generally, 1.472
miscellaneous provisions, 1.470–1.478
retirement pensions
    general note, 1.488
    generally, 1.474
satisfaction in early years
    general note, 1.490–1.492
    generally, 1.477
short-term incapacity benefit
    general note, 1.485
    generally, 1.471
    satisfaction in early years, 1.490–1.492
unemployment benefit, 1.470
vaccine damage payments, and, 1.6–1.7
widowed mother's allowance
    general note, 1.488
    generally, 1.474
widowed parent's allowance
    general note, 1.488
    generally, 1.474
widows' pension
    general note, 1.488
    generally, 1.474
"Confinement"
employment and support allowance, 9.5
"Connected conditions"
assessment of industrial injuries, and,
    10.21
"Connection factor"
assessment of industrial injuries, and,
    10.22

Index

Non-contributory benefits
adjustment
  hospital in-patients, 3.73–3.74
  persons abroad, and, 1.416–1.417
aged, for the
  See also **Elderly persons**
  age addition, 1.276–1.277
  category C pensions, 1.273–1.275
  category D pensions, 1.273–1.275
attendance allowance
  See also **Attendance allowance**
  entitlement, 1.182–1.186
  excluded persons, 1.196–1.199
  rate, 1.187–1.192
  terminal illness, 1.193–1.195
benefits for the aged
  See also **Elderly persons**
  age addition, 1.276–1.277
  category C pensions, 1.273–1.275
  category D pensions, 1.273–1.275
calculation of earnings
  See also **Calculation of earnings**
  generally, 3.5–3.13
carer's allowance
  See also **Carer's allowance**
  carers, 1.184
  entitlement, 1.204–1.214
  increases for dependants, 1.302–1.304
  rate, 1.495–1.496
disability living allowance
  See also **Disability living allowance**
  care component, 1.220–1.241
  generally, 1.215–1.219
  invalid carriages, 1.261–1.263
  mobility component, 1.242–1.260
  persons aged 65 or over, 1.264–1.266
  supplementary provisions, 1.267–1.271
disqualification
  See also **Disqualification (benefits)**
  generally, 1.398–1.403
  earnings, 1.396–1.397
guardian's allowance
  See also **Guardian's allowance**
  generally, 1.272
hospital in-patients, 3.73–3.74
invalid care allowance
  See also **Carer's allowance**
  generally, 1.206
meaning, 1.180–1.181
persons abroad, and, 1.416–1.417
rate, 1.495
severe disablement allowance
  See also **Severe disablement allowance**
  generally, 1.200–1.203
special cases
  airmen, 1.412–1.413
  continental shelf, employment on, 1.418–1.419
  Crown employment, 1.406–1.408
  Her Majesty's forces, 1.409–1.411
  mariners, 1.412–1.413
  married women, 1.414–1.415
  persons abroad, 1.416–1.417
  polygamous marriages, 1.420–1.421
  seafarers, 1.418–1.419
suspension
  See also **Suspension (benefits)**
  generally, 1.398–1.403
types, 1.180–1.181
"Non-dependant"
employment and support allowance, 9.156–9.157
Non-infective dermatitis
generally, 10.164
legal presumption, 10.63
Northern Ireland
employment and support allowance, 1.809–1.810
"Notices of accidents"
industrial injuries, and, 10.5
Notional capital
diminishing capital rule, 9.249–9.250
generally, 9.247–9.250
Notional income
determination methods, 3.12
employment and support allowance
  calculation, 9.235–9.236
  deprivation of income, 9.229–9.230
  due to be paid, 9.231–9.232
  other income, 9.233–9.234
  paid to third party, 9.231–9.232
generally, 3.8–3.9
low earnings, 3.11
no earnings, 3.11
unascertainable earnings, 3.10
Nursing homes
attendance allowance
  exemption, 4.20–4.21
  generally, 4.17–4.18
  relevant patients, 4.27
  terminally ill, 4.19
disability living allowance
  exemption, 4.50–4.51
  generally, 4.47–4.48
  relevant persons, 4.49, 4.96
Occupational asthma
prescribed occupations, 10.164
time limits for claims, 10.118–10.119
Occupational deafness
appeals, 10.112–10.113
assessment of extent
  binaural disablement, 10.168
  generally, 10.115–10.116
  relevant claims, 10.166–10.167
claims, 10.104–10.105
date of onset, 10.108–10.109
duration of assessment
  commencement date, 10.117
  generally, 10.110
further claims, 10.106–10.107
prescribed occupations
  cutting concrete masonry blocks, 10.143
  firearms training, 10.149
  glass container manufacturer, 10.148

generally, 1.119–1.121
post-employment or training,
   1.122–1.124
rate, 1.497
retirement pensions, 1.149–1.150,
   1.155–1.157
widowed parent's allowance
   generally, 1.104–1.105
   qualification criteria, 1.109–1.115
   rate, 1.108–1.109
Widows' benefits
See also **Contributory benefits**
adjustment of benefits
   hospital in-patients, 3.73–3.74
   overlapping benefits, 3.80–3.81
   persons abroad, 3.114–3.115
age addition, 6.96
bereavement allowance
   generally, 1.106–1.107
   qualification criteria, 1.109–1.115
   rate, 1.108–1.109
bereavement payment
   generally, 1.92–1.93
   rate, 1.494
conditions
   See also **Contribution conditions**
   earnings factors, 1.40
   general note, 1.479–1.492
   generally, 1.39
   miscellaneous provisions, 1.470–1.478
contribution credits
   widowed parent's allowance, 2.6–2.7
   widows' pension, 2.6–2.7
gender recognition, 1.711–1.712
hospital in-patients, 3.73–3.74
long-term incapacity benefit
   generally, 1.116–1.118
   post-employment or training,
      1.122–1.124
persons abroad, and, 3.114–3.115
types, 1.149–1.150
widow of man over 65 in 1948, for
   corresponding to widowed mother's
      allowance, 6.90
   corresponding to pension, 6.88–6.89
   restrictions, 6.91
widowed mother's allowance
   See also **Widowed mother's
      allowance**
   adjustment of, 3.80–3.81
   child benefit, 6.92–6.93
   generally, 1.96–1.98
   increases for dependants, 1.283–1.291
   national insurance numbers, 6.95
   rate, 1.102–1.103
widowed parent's allowance
   See also **Widowed parent's allowance**
   child benefit, 6.94
   generally, 1.104–1.105
   qualification criteria, 1.109–1.115
   rate, 1.108–1.109
widows' payment, 1.93
widows' pensions

See also **Widows' pensions**
days of increment, 6.71–6.74
election not to receive, 6.67–6.69
entitlement conditions, 6.76–6.83
generally, 1.99–1.101
incapacity for work, 6.70
national insurance numbers, 6.66
rate, 1.102–1.103
reduced rates, 6.75
Widows' payments
See **Bereavement payment**
Widows' pension
adjustment of benefits
   hospital in-patients, 3.73–3.74
Category A, under, 6.78–6.79
Category B, under, 6.76–6.77
Category C, under
   divorced woman of man over 65 in
      1948, for, 6.86–6.87
   entitlement conditions, 6.80–6.81
   widow of man over 65 in 1948, for,
      6.84–6.85
Category D, under, 6.82–6.83
Christmas bonus, and, 1.425–1.427
contribution conditions
   See also **Contribution conditions**
   earnings factors, 1.40
   general note, 1.488
   generally, 1.39
   miscellaneous provisions, 1.474
contribution credits, 2.6–2.7
days of increment
enhancement period, 6.74
generally, 6.71–6.73
election not to receive
   generally, 6.67–6.68
   post-election provisions, 6.69
entitlement conditions
   Category A, 6.78–6.79
   Category B, 6.76–6.77
   Category C, 6.80–6.81
   Category D, 6.82–6.83
gender recognition, 1.711–1.712
generally, 1.99–1.101
home responsibilities protection,
   2.41–2.42
hospital in-patients, 3.73–3.74
incapacity for work, 6.70
national insurance numbers, 6.66
rate
   generally, 1.102–1.103
   industrial injuries benefit, 1.497
   reduced rates, 6.75
"Wood working"
occupational deafness, and, 10.145
Work capability assessments
introduction, 1.762
limited capability for work, and
   additional circumstances, 9.72–9.74
   claimants receiving regular treatment,
      9.58–9.59
   claimants treated as having, 9.46–9.47
   definition, 1.737–1.738